𝔅𝔦𝔬𝔤𝔯𝔞𝔭𝔥𝔦𝔞 𝔍𝔲𝔯𝔦𝔡𝔦𝔠𝔞

A BIOGRAPHICAL DICTIONARY

OF THE

JUDGES OF ENGLAND

FROM THE CONQUEST TO THE PRESENT TIME

1066—1870

BY EDWARD FOSS, F.S.A.

OF THE INNER TEMPLE

SUÆ QUISQUE FORTUNÆ FABER
Sallust, de Republica ordinanda, I. 1.

(on the Serjeant's ring of Chief-Justice Fineux, 1485)

THE LAWBOOK EXCHANGE, LTD.
Clark, New Jersey

ISBN 9781886363861 (hardcover)
ISBN 9781616191771 (paperback)

Lawbook Exchange edition 2011

The quality of this reprint is equivalent to the quality of the original work.

THE LAWBOOK EXCHANGE, LTD.
33 Terminal Avenue
Clark, New Jersey 07066-1321

Please see our website for a selection of our other publications and fine facsimile reprints of classic works of legal history:
www.lawbookexchange.com

Library of Congress Cataloging-in-Publication Data

Foss, Edward, 1787-1870.
 Biographia juridica : a biographical dictionary of the judges of
  England from the conquest to the present time, 1066-1870 / by
  Edward Foss.
   p. cm.
 Originally published : London : J. Murray, 1870.
  1. Judges—Great Britain—Biography. I. Title. II. Title:
  Biographical dictionary of the judges of England from the conquest
  to the present time, 1066-1870.
KD620.F67   1999
347.42'014'0922—dc21   99-12577
 [B]   CIP

Printed in the United States of America on acid-free paper

𝕭iographia 𝕵uridica

A BIOGRAPHICAL DICTIONARY

OF THE

JUDGES OF ENGLAND

FROM THE CONQUEST TO THE PRESENT TIME

1066—1870

BY EDWARD FOSS, F.S.A.

OF THE INNER TEMPLE

SUÆ QUISQUE FORTUNÆ FABER
Sallust, de Republica ordinanda, I. 1.
(on the Serjeant's ring of Chief-Justice Fineux, 1485)

LONDON
JOHN MURRAY, ALBEMARLE STREET
1870

LONDON: PRINTED BY
SPOTTISWOODE AND CO., NEW-STREET SQUARE
AND PARLIAMENT STREET

PREFACE.

In my former work I endeavoured to trace, chronologically, the different incidents and changes in the Courts of Westminster that occurred from the reign of William the Conqueror to that of her present Majesty; and I gave an account under each reign of the judicial personages who then administered the law.

The arrangement then adopted, with its palpable historical advantages, had, biographically, one inconvenience, that when information was required for any individual judge, the time of whose existence was doubtful or uncertain, a search became necessary among several volumes or reigns in order to find the narrative.

To remedy this defect, and to facilitate the reference to every name in the judicial record, and also to reduce the bulk to one convenient volume, this publication has been undertaken. It is limited to the biographical portion of the larger work, and comprehends every name therein introduced, with slight abridgments and corrections, adding to them the judges who have been appointed since 1864: the whole number exceeding 1,600 lives.

I have not thought it necessary in the separate lives to refer specially to Dugdale's 'Chronica Series,' because, from the Conquest till the decapitation of Charles I., I have inserted every name that is included in his list. I have even done so when I have ventured to differ from him in regard to the individual filling the particular position, or flourishing at the precise period represented. In all these cases I have been careful to quote the authorities upon which I base the objections I have raised; and I have invariably, as well in the lives above alluded to as in those of the judges who flourished since Dugdale wrote, given such references as will, I trust, justify every fact I have introduced.

In the long period of eight hundred years over which the

history travels, there were many changes in the administration of justice and the arrangement of the courts, which when described under the different reigns in which they occurred would naturally account for the terms then used, and the titles then given to the persons commemorated; but some explanation of them seems necessary, or at all events desirable, when their biographies are collected in an alphabetical form, and names appear together which are sundered by centuries, as one in the reign of Henry II., and the next in that of Henry VIII. or William IV. I therefore add a short account of the various alterations in the respective reigns.

In the reign of William the Conqueror the highest court of judicature was the Curia Regis, in which the King himself frequently presided. Its members were the prelates and barons of the realm, and certain officers of the palace. Of these the principal was the Chief Justiciary, who in the King's absence was the ruling judge. This office continued till the reign of Henry III., a period of two hundred years, when its judicial duties were transferred to the Chief Justice of the King's Bench.

Many of the barons, as members of the Curia Regis, soon neglected the legal part of their duties, some from avocations that otherwise engaged them, some from unwillingness so to employ themselves, and some from incapacity to unravel the intricacies of the law. This naturally led to the association with those that remained, and eventually to the entire substitution for them, of persons whose lives had been devoted to judicial studies. These were called justiciaries, and seem to have been first introduced in the reign of Henry I., and their organisation to have been completed in that of Henry II. The justiciaries not only sat at Westminster, but went on circuits or *itinera* throughout the kingdom. To the commissions by which they were appointed some of the great men of the several counties, whether lay or clerical, were occasionally added, and all were designated as justiciers or justices itinerant; and from the reign of Edward I. to that of Richard II., justices of trailbaston for the trial of certain particular transgressions were appointed.

By the Charter of King John, confirmed and acted upon by Henry III., Common Pleas, being causes between private individuals, were directed to be held 'in some certain place.' This was to remedy the grievance felt by all litigants in being obliged to follow the Curia Regis to whatever distance the King might choose to travel. The Court of Common Pleas was thus originated; and in it the ancient advocates of the Curia Regis—the serjeants—had sole audience.

When the office of Chief Justiciary was abolished, the King's Pleas were left to be decided in a separate court, presided over by the Chief Justice of the King's Bench, the first of whom was appointed by Henry III.

The division of the courts, in nearly their present form, of King's Bench, Common Pleas, and Exchequer, was completed by Edward I., the English Justinian.

THE COURT OF KING'S BENCH at first took cognisance of no other suits than those in which the Crown was concerned; but from the increase of private suits, which were a source of great profit to the advocates, means were gradually employed to bring them within its jurisdiction, which was at last effected, so that now every description of cause may be tried there.

THE COURT OF COMMON PLEAS has now the same jurisdiction, and remains in nearly the same position, as when it was first established, with the exception that the serjeants, by a recent innovation, no longer monopolise the practice, which is now opened to all barristers.

THE COURT OF EXCHEQUER was, before the division of the courts, an integral department of the Curia Regis, under the name of Scaccarium, in which all cases touching the Revenue were decided, and now continue so to be. But by similar means to those before alluded to, the privileges of the Court of Common Pleas have been encroached upon, and private suits form a great part of its employment. The judges who sit in the court are called barons, the title being continued from the barons of the realm who originally sat in the Curia Regis. They were till the reign of James I. of a much lower degree than the other judges, and indeed were not considered men of the law, nor ever employed to go the circuits. The statute of Nisi Prius, 14 Edward III., enacts 'that if it happen that none of the justices of the one bench nor of the other come into the county, then the Nisi Prius shall be granted before the Chief Baron of the Exchequer, if he be a man of the law.' But the general increase of litigation occasioned by the extension of commerce, with the gradual combination of civil and revenue cases, by the cunning use of the Writ *Quo minus,* requiring the aid of learned lawyers for their decision, it was determined to place the barons on precisely the same footing as the other judges, and consequently those barons who were appointed after the twenty-first year of Queen Elizabeth were selected from the serjeants-at-law, and were distinguished from their predecessors by the term 'Barons of the Coif.' Robert Shute was the first of these. As soon as the court was filled with these legal barons, none of whom had been instructed in the business of the revenue, it became necessary to appoint a new officer, one who was acquainted with and could attend to the fiscal business of the Exchequer. He was called the puisne or cursitor baron, whose duty it was to inform the other barons of the course of the court in any matter that concerned the King's prerogative. The first of these cursitor barons was Nowell Sotherton, who was appointed in 1606; but the office, after existing 250 years, was abolished in 1856, its duties having gradually been removed to other departments of the State.[1] The Court of Exchequer had also an equitable jurisdiction, which in the year 1841 was abolished, and its suits were transferred to the Court of Chancery.

All the judges of these three courts must be selected from the serjeants-at-law, a practice originating from the advocates in the Curia Regis consisting only of serjeants, and they from their learning being raised to the bench. But as business accumulated, other efficient men, who practised only as barristers, had opportunities of distinguishing themselves, and were gradually advanced to the bench, on which occasions the old custom was still adhered to by investing them with the coif before they received their patent as judges. This change was commenced in the reign of Queen Elizabeth in the person of Robert Monson in the year 1572, and is now the general practice. The judges and serjeants always address one another as 'Brothers.'

The number of these judges from the time of the first division of the courts until the reign of Henry VII. varied considerably, according to the whim of the Monarch, the claims of the Government, or the necessity for additional or reduced assistance. By a reference to a little volume I published, called 'Tabulæ Curiales,' in which I have shown the state of each court under the different reigns, and the judges who sat in them in chronological order, it will be seen that there was no regular number, but that it varied in each court,

[1] See *Judges of England*, vi. 16–27, ix. 109.

sometimes extending to eight and even to nine on one of the benches. In the reign of Henry VIII., however, the number of four in each of the three courts seems to have been established, and by its continuance nearly without change till the reign of William IV., a period of 300 years, the *Twelve Judges of England* came to be regarded as a sacred institution. This number, however, was increased in the reign of William IV., by whom another judge was added to each court; and Queen Victoria has followed the example; so that instead of twelve there are now eighteen judges of England. It is to be hoped that litigation will not increase so much as to require another extension.

THE COURT OF CHANCERY originated from that department of the Curia Regis called the Cancellaria, in which were prepared and issued the various writs and precepts in reference to the Curia Regis. There also were all royal grants and charters, and other instruments requiring the King's seal, supervised. It was presided over by an officer called the King's Chancellor, who held at first a somewhat inferior rank in the Curia Regis, but who sat with the rest of the judges, and occasionally even went a circuit. He originally was the King's chief chaplain, and little more than his private secretary, being commonly rewarded at the end of his service with a bishopric. His intimate connection with the sovereign naturally led by degrees to a frequent reference to him upon the affairs of state; and gaining thus an ascendency in council, he at last became, on the extinction of the office of Chief Justiciary and the transfer of the legal duties of that functionary to a court of law, the recognised Prime Minister of the kingdom. This responsible position, after a lapse of several centuries, gradually devolved first upon favourites and next on party politicians; the Chancellor of subsequent times, though losing the lead, still held and now holds a most influential place in the Government and is recognised as the head of the law, but is removable, and always removed, with every change of Ministers. From his first title of the Chancellor of the King, he rose to that of Chancellor of England; soon after he was called Lord Chancellor, a title which has been since increased to that of Lord High Chancellor. A keeper of the Great Seal was sometimes appointed instead of a Chancellor, and it was somewhat difficult to distinguish the difference in dignity between the one and the other; but in the reign of Queen Elizabeth an Act of Parliament was passed declaring their identity in rank, power, and privileges. The Great Seal was also occasionally put into the hands of Commissioners, who held it for a temporary, and principally for a political purpose, till a Chancellor or keeper was appointed.

The duty of the Chancellor to supervise and issue the necessary writs and charters led of course to the discussion before him as to the propriety and expediency of them, but it was a long time before questions of legal wrong were referred to his decision. It was soon found however that there was much truth in the maxim 'Summum jus, summa injuria;' consequently questions involving private wrong were frequently submitted by petition to Parliament, where they were decided. These petitions multiplied to such an extent that it was found necessary to refer them to a separate court—naturally presided over by the Chancellor; and the rules which guided it were gradually moulded into a system of Equity Law. In its administration the necessity of additional assistance was soon apparent, and the clerks or masters in Chancery were resorted to. The principal one, who received the title of Master of the Rolls, from these records being specially entrusted to his care, was deputed to exercise the same jurisdiction. The first who was designated by that title was John de Langton, in the reign of Edward I. Commissions also were sometimes issued to some of the judges to ease the Chancellor in hearing causes. The Court of Exchequer also had a similar jurisdiction till 1841, when it was taken away, and its Equity cases were transferred to the Court of Chancery.

More permanent assistance had been previously required as litigation increased, and in the reign of George III. one Vice-Chancellor was appointed. To these three Equity Judges two others were added by our present Queen, on the Court of Exchequer losing its equitable jurisdiction; and the decisions of the Master of the Rolls and of the three Vice-Chancellors were made appealable to the Lord Chancellor, and two other new judges, called Lord Justices of Appeal. So that the Court of Chancery now consists of seven judges, instead of the two to which it was limited for more than 500 years, from the reign of Edward I. to that of George III.

These short particulars will be sufficient to explain the various designations given to the different judges included in this Dictionary. Those readers who are desirous of more ample details must be referred to my larger work, where I have given a full account, not only of the Division of the Courts, but also of the origin of the legal Terms and Vacations; the institution and formalities of Serjeants; and the perquisites of the Chancellors, and salaries and robes of the Judges. In it I have also traced the appointment of Attorney and Solicitor General, and the first designation *eo nomine* of King's Counsel; the various uses to which Westminster Hall has been applied; the origin of the various Inns of Court and Inns of Chancery, and of the different Serjeants' Inns, with other interesting details incidental to the History of the Law.

P.S.—In my eighty-third year I cannot expect to witness either the success or failure of the new scheme for the arrangement of the courts about to be introduced in pursuance of an Act of Parliament passed in the last Session. I own that I cannot predict that much material benefit will result from the intended change; and I am inclined to think that those who are conversant with the history of the past will consider the new HIGH COURT OF JUSTICE little more than a mere revival of the ancient CURIA REGIS, with all its varied powers and privileges, which were distributed into the present divisions so many centuries ago. Another remarkable restoration will be noted in the new statute—that by which the legal Terms are reduced from four to three, as they originally stood in the earlier times. But, be the innovation good or bad, I am sure it is well intended, and I sincerely hope that it may prove as beneficial to the administration of justice as its promoters anticipate.

NOTE.—Although the Bill referred to (which was brought into the Upper House of Parliament by Lord Chancellor Hatherley) did not pass during the Session of 1870, it has been thought well to preserve the author's remarks on it.

THE PRINTING of this volume was far advanced when the Author was attacked by illness, which ended fatally on the following day. In these circumstances it seems proper that the many Lives which are contained in the following pages should be accompanied by some notice of the Biographer.

Edward, the eldest son of Edward Smith Foss and Anne, daughter of Dr. William Rose, of Chiswick, and sister of Samuel Rose, the friend of Cowper, was born in Gough Square, Fleet Street, October 16, 1787. By his mother's side he was nearly related to the Rev. Hugh James Rose, one of the ablest and most eloquent among the English clergy of late times, and to his brother, the present learned Archdeacon of Bedford; and one of his maternal aunts was the wife of the eminent scholar Dr. Charles Burney. His younger brother, Henry, who died in January 1868, was for many years a partner in the firm of Payne and Foss, which stood at the head of the London trade in rare and valuable books, and was distinguished for his great bibliographical knowledge.

Edward Foss was educated under Dr. Burney, at Greenwich, and in 1804 was articled to his father, who was a solicitor in Essex Street, Strand. In 1811 he became a partner, and on his father's death in 1830 he succeeded to the whole business, which he carried on with a high reputation for ability and integrity. In 1827–8, when his friend Mr. Spottiswoode was one of the Sheriffs of London, he filled the office of Under-Sheriff. His professional work brought him into intercourse with most of the leading barristers of the day, so that, while he was able to turn to account his observation of the Judges who then occupied the Bench, he could speak from nearer personal knowledge of many who, by later promotion, came to be included among the subjects of his biographical labours. In 1822 he became a member of the Inner Temple, with the intention of being called to the Bar; but he afterwards relinquished this plan, and continued to practise in his original branch of the legal profession until 1840, when he retired from business.

In 1844 he removed from Streatham, where he had for some time lived, to Street End House, about three miles from Canterbury. The change was one which for most men would have involved no small risk; for in too many cases it has been found that a withdrawal from a life of busy engagements to one of competence and leisure does not bring the happiness which had been expected; and so it might have been with Mr. Foss. He had little taste for country occupations or amusements; and, although he took an active part in the public business of the neighbourhood—among other things, by acting as chairman of the Canterbury bench of magistrates, where his strong sense and his legal knowledge made his services very valuable—this was not enough to fill up his time. In his own words, he 'found that full employment was necessary to his existence and his happiness;'[1] and he was fortunately able to provide himself with the means of such employment. He had always felt a strong love of literature; he had already published some volumes, besides many contributions, both in prose and in verse, to periodicals and newspapers; and he had early formed a project of writing the lives of all the English Judges. Through many years of busy London life he had kept this project steadily in view, and had gradually accumulated large stores of materials for carrying it into effect. These he now set himself to arrange, to complete, and to employ in composition; and the first two volumes of 'The Judges of England' were published in 1848.[2]

Although these volumes were at once noticed with high praise by some of the most esteemed critics, the general reception of them was not very encouraging. Lord Campbell, in his 'Lives of the Chancellors,' had lately made the public familiar with a very different style of legal biography; and when readers came to take up Mr. Foss's account of the early judges with the expectation of finding it equally amusing with Lord Campbell's popular narratives, they could not but be disappointed. The Chancellors were commonly men who had played an important part in the history of their times: of the older Judges, the vast majority were utterly forgotten; as to many of them, it was necessary to enquire whether they ever existed at all, and, if so, whether they were judges or not; and perhaps nothing more could be ascertained, after all possible enquiry, than that their signatures were found attached to certain documents, and so prove them to have been in certain places at certain times. It was unfortunate for the author that the portion of his book which was first published should be that in which the names for the most part had nothing of attraction for the generality of readers, and were incapable of being invested with any other interest than that which arises from skilful investigation and scrupulous correctness.

The two volumes, therefore, could not be regarded as at first very successful. But Mr. Foss knew that he was doing a good and substantial work; he felt that in it he had found a source of continual interest, the chief occupation of his life; and he determined to persevere, even if the publication should involve (as at one time seemed not unlikely) a considerable pecuniary loss. The third and fourth volumes appeared in 1851; the fifth and sixth, in 1857; the last three, in 1864.

In the meantime the reputation of the book had been rising. The subject became more interesting as it advanced; the author's laborious research, his acuteness in enquiry, his sound and impartial judgment, were discerned, and were warmly acknowledged by the highest critical

---

[1] Introduction to 'Judges of England,' p. xiii.
[2] It may be well to mention that Mr. Foss's set (consisting of nearly 100 volumes) of the Record Commission's publications, for which, in the preface to the second instalment of his work, he acknowledges himself indebted to 'the liberality of Government,' was granted to him at the instance of Lord Langdale, then Master of the Rolls, to whom 'The Lives of the Judges' are dedicated, and who early showed his high estimation of them.

authorities;[1] and long before the concluding volumes were published, the work had taken its place as (what Lord Campbell's 'Lives' could never become) one of historical authority. How valuable it is in this character may be in some degree understood from the continual references to it in Dr. Pauli's learned 'Geschichte von England;' nor was this by any means the only testimony which the author received of the appreciation which his work has found among German men of letters. In America also its reputation is well established; and, resting as that reputation does on a foundation of solid merits, it is not likely to be disturbed.

From the lives of Judges, Mr. Foss was led on to the compilation of his 'Tabulæ Curiales;' and his last years were employed in the re-casting of his old materials with a view to the present publication.

While engaged on these labours, he removed in 1859 from Street End to Churchill House, near Dover; and in 1865 he finally settled at Frensham House, Addiscombe. The infirmities of age fell gently on him, and he retained to the last his powers of sight and hearing, with the full vigour of his mind. His death took place at Frensham House on July 27, 1870, and his remains are interred in the neighbouring church-yard of Shirley. By those who knew him he will be remembered as a man of strong understanding, of thorough uprightness, and of kind and generous heart.

He was twice married—first, in 1814, to Catherine, daughter of Peter Martineau, Esq.; and again, in 1844, to Maria Elizabeth, daughter of William Hutchins, Esq. By his second marriage he has left six sons and three daughters. The eldest son, Edward W. Foss, a barrister of the Inner Temple, assisted in the revision of this volume, and has completed the task since his father's death.

Mr. Foss was a Fellow of the Society of Antiquaries, to which he was elected in 1822; a member of several other antiquarian and literary societies; a member of the Incorporated Law Society, which elected him as its president in 1842 and 1843; a magistrate for Kent and Surrey; a Deputy-Lieutenant for Kent, &c.

His chief publications were—

I. 'The Beauties of Massinger,' 1817.

II. 'Abridgment of Blackstone's Commentaries,' published (1820) in the name of John Gifford, Esq., who had undertaken the work, but died before completing the first sheet. (This volume had a large sale, and was translated into German.)

III. 'The Grandeur of the Law; or, The Legal Peers of England,' 1843.

IV. 'The Judges of England,' 9 vols., 1848-64.

V. 'Tabulæ Curiales; or, Tables of the Superior Courts of Westminster Hall, showing the Judges who sat in them from 1066 to 1864.'—1865.

VI. 'Biographia Juridica: a Biographical Dictionary of the Judges,' 1870.

[1] 'Edinburgh Review,' vol. cvi.; 'Quarterly Review,' vol. cxix.; 'Saturday Review,' 'Times,' &c., including several legal periodicals.

VII. Contributions to the 'Archæologia :'—
(1) 'On the Lord Chancellors in the Reign of King John.'
(2) 'The Lineage of Sir Thomas More.'
(3) 'On the Relationship between Bishop Fitzjames and Lord Chief Justice Fitzjames.'
(4) 'On the Origin of the Title and Office of Cursitor Baron of the Exchequer.' (And other communications.)

VIII. 'On the Collar of SS' ('Archæologia Cantiana,' vol. i. 1858).

IX. 'Legal History of Westminster Hall' (in 'Old London—Papers read at the London Congress of the Archæological Institute, 1867').

Mr. Foss also contributed largely to the 'Monthly Review,' Aikin's 'Athenæum,' the 'London Magazine,' the 'Gentleman's Magazine,' the 'Legal Observer,' 'Notes and Queries,' &c. A small volume of his epigrams and other pieces in verse (most of which had appeared in newspapers) was privately printed in 1863, under the title of 'A Century of Inventions.'

J. C. ROBERTSON.

PRECINCTS, CANTERBURY:
September 1870.

BIOGRAPHIA JURIDICA.

1066—1870.

ABBINGWORTH, GILBERT DE, was one of the justices itinerant into the counties of Sussex, Surrey, Kent, and Middlesex, in 3 Henry III., 1218. His name also appears with that designation on fines levied at Westminster in that year; showing that the justices itinerant were accustomed to sit at Westminster. He was employed in the same manner in 1225, for Surrey; and in the next year was at the head of those appointed to collect the quinzime of that county. (*Rot. Claus.* i, 76, 146.)

ABBOTT, CHARLES, when created Lord Tenterden, far from following the example of many a new-made peer by endeavouring to trace his pedigree to an ancient race, gloried in his descent from parents in the lower ranks of life, as exemplifying the beauty of the British constitution, which excludes no one from its honours, and even opens the door of the peerage to the most humble individual, when merit claims an entrance. When he was at his highest elevation he attended the festival of the school in his native city, at which he imbibed the rudiments of his education, acknowledged the benefits he had received from its foundation, and perpetuated the memory of his connection with it, by founding two prizes for future aspirants. On his epitaph too, written by his own pen, he records himself as sprung 'humillimis sortis parentibus.'

He was born on October 7, 1762, in the precincts of Canterbury Cathedral, where his father, John Abbott, carried on a respectable business as a wigmaker and hairdresser. His mother was Alice, daughter of Daniel Bunce of the same city. Having entered the grammar-school there, called, from its foundation by Henry VIII., the King's school, by his industry and cleverness he gave such satisfaction to his master, Dr. Osmond Beauvoir, and to the reverend trustees of the cathedral, that he received one of the school exhibitions on his admission into Corpus Christi College, Oxford, in March 1781, where he immediately obtained a scholarship. At Oxford he distinguished himself by gaining the only two honours which the university then bestowed, the chancellor's medals for Latin and English compositions. The subject of the former (in 1784) was 'Globus Aërostaticus,' the novelty of Lunardi's balloon occasioning the thesis; and that of the latter (in 1786) 'The Use and Abuse of Satire,' an essay so much admired for its learning and reasoning that it was afterwards published. Having taken his degrees, he was rewarded with a fellowship in his college, and became sub-tutor under Dr. Burgess, afterwards Bishop of Salisbury. Soon after he was selected as the private tutor of Mr. Yarde, the son of Mr. Justice Buller; and that sagacious judge, seeing and appreciating his talents, recommended him to devote his attention to the legal instead of the clerical profession. He accordingly entered himself at the Middle Temple on November 16, 1787; but in May 1793 he removed to the Inner Temple, by which he was ultimately called to the bar. In the meantime, for the purpose of acquiring a practical knowledge of the working of the law, he attended for some months the office of Messrs. Sandys & Co., attorneys in considerable business, and then placed himself under Mr. (afterwards Baron) Wood, the leading pleader of that day. Subsequently Mr. Abbott selected the same department for his own commencement; and for several years devoted himself to this branch of the science, with so much success, that in July 1795 he was enabled to take the important step of marrying. His bride was Mary, daughter of John Lagier Lamotte, Esq., of Basilden in Kent. His call to the bar was in the following February; and he joined the Oxford circuit.

Such was his reputation as a special pleader, that no sooner did he assume the

B

barrister's gown than he was employed as junior counsel for the crown in all the numerous state prosecutions for the next ten years, under the attorney-generalships of Lord Eldon, Lord Redesdale, Lord Ellenborough, and the Hon. Spencer Perceval. In 1801 he was elected recorder of Oxford; and in 1802 he published a work on 'The Law Relating to Merchant Ships and Seamen,' a treatise which was praised by all jurists, and at once became the standard book and practical guide on the subject. It raised Mr. Abbott's reputation so high, and consequently brought him such an accession of employment in commercial and maritime cases, that when an income-tax was imposed in 1807 he returned his professional receipts during the previous year at 8,026l. 5s.

With such an income as this it is not surprising that he should have declined in 1808 to accept the offer then made him of a seat on the bench. Neither would he apply for the honour of a silk gown, conscious that his temperament and disposition disqualified him as a leader, and that his services as a junior would be more usefully employed and in greater requisition than if he aimed at the higher grade. But after eight years more of laborious but profitable application, he felt that his health would not bear the continued strain upon his faculties, and that he could with prudence accept the comparative relief of a judgeship. On the death therefore of Mr. Justice Heath, Mr. Abbott was raised to the vacant seat in the Common Pleas on January 24, 1816, receiving the customary honour of knighthood.

He remained in that court little more than three months, removing on May 3, very unwillingly, but at the urgent solicitation of Lord Ellenborough, to the court of King's Bench as the successor of Sir Simon Le Blanc. His excellence in a judicial character was so prominent that when Lord Ellenborough resigned two years and a half after, he was elevated to the chief justiceship on November 4, 1818. After having continued in the office for nine years, and established his fame by the exemplary manner in which he fulfilled its duties, the royal wish was intimated to him, that he should be created a peer; and he was accordingly ennobled, by the title of Baron Tenterden of Hendon in Middlesex, on April 30, 1827.

Soon after this elevation his health began to decline, and his infirmities were increased by his anxious exertions to contend with the growing business of his court. He betrayed no diminution of mental energy, and so far from shrinking from judicial duties he died almost in harness; being seized with his last illness while sitting on the third day's trial of the mayor of Bristol, for misconduct at the riots in that city. He immediately took to his bed, from which he never rose, but died on November 4, 1832, exactly fourteen years since he was constituted chief justice. He was buried in the Foundling Hospital, and on his monument is a modest inscription written by himself.

Various attempts have been made to analyse Lord Tenterden's mind and character, and a great deal of ingenuity and eloquence have been expended in the endeavour. All allow that both were peculiarly fitted for the judicial office. In his practice at the bar and in his opinions in answer to cases he exhibited less of the advocate than of the arbitrator. It was not till he was raised to the bench that his full powers were brought into play. There he soon proved himself one of the ablest judges that ever presided. He was peculiarly a common-sense judge. Complete master of every branch of law, strictly impartial and unprejudiced, and detesting anything that approached to quibbling, he applied himself to discover the justice of the case before him, and by his clear and perspicuous explanations most commonly led the jury to a right conclusion. Severe against everything that had the semblance of fraud or conspiracy, he was particularly so if an attorney was implicated; but to the respectable members of the profession he showed marked respect and urbanity. If he occasionally exhibited impatience at the long speeches and irrelevant arguments of counsel, it should be remembered that it was occasioned by his anxiety to clear away the accumulation of business, the extent of which may be estimated by the fact that while Lord Mansfield had to dispose of only 200 causes at a sitting, the number had increased in Lord Tenterden's time to above 800: but as a significant proof of the estimation and respect in which he was held by his bar, notwithstanding the rebukes sometimes administered, they paid him the unusual compliment of attending in a body his introduction as a peer into the House of Lords.

As a member of that house he carefully avoided all party politics, but with high Tory principles opposed any attempted innovation on the constitution. He spoke against the repeal of the Test and Corporation Acts, the Roman Catholic Relief Bill, and the several bills for reform in parliament, as dangerous speculations and not likely to produce the benefits which their advocates prophesied. In his own department he introduced and carried several useful measures, and to his care and diligence the legal profession is mainly indebted for the statutes 9 Geo. IV. c. 14 and 15, for the limitation of actions, and for the prevention of a failure of justice by reason of a variance between records and writings produced in evidence; and also for the statutes 2 and 3 Will. IV. c. 39, for uniformity of process.

It is pleasing to find that the relaxations of a mind so overburdened with the labours of a judicial life should be in botanical researches and in literary pursuits. The union of these in him produced some elegant Latin verses of great classical merit, in the composition of which he amused the little intervals of leisure during the latter portion of his life; as in his earlier years he had penned some graceful English trifles.

His was a truly domestic home. His wife survived him only six weeks. Of his four children, John Henry, the eldest son, is the present peer. (*Townsend's Twelve Judges*, ii. 234; *Jardine's Life, in Biog. Dict.*, Soc. Useful Knowl.)

ABEL, JOHN, was not improbably the son or grandson of a goldsmith named Richard Abel, who, in 27 Henry III., was appointed maker and cutter of the dies for the king's mint (*Madox*, ii. 88.), as the whole of John's property was situated in the neighbourhood of London. He was engaged in the king's service in 28 Edward I. (*Abb. Rot. Orig.* i. 112), and two years afterwards we find him seneschal of the queen and custos of her lands. (*Rot. Parl.* i. 146-205.) Both he and his wife were summoned to the coronation of Edward II. among those selected from the county of Kent.

On March 8, 1312, he was constituted one of the barons of the Exchequer, and in the next year he received the office of king's escheator, the duties of which he performed, principally on the south of Trent, for three years. (*Abb. Rot. Orig.* i. 195–216.) During that time he was employed to fix the tallage on the city of London and on the king's burghs, &c., in the home counties; and was also directed to attend the council, with instructions to be in readiness to proceed on the king's service beyond the seas.

It would appear that when he entered on the functions of escheator he resigned his seat in the Exchequer, for he was re-appointed a baron on May 4, 1315; and was probably again removed in 14 Edward II., as he was not summoned to parliament beyond that year, and because a new baron was then nominated. He died in 16 Edward II., possessed, among others, of large estates at Footscray and Lewisham in Kent, at Rochford in Essex, and at Camberwell in Surrey, besides the manor of Dadyngton in Oxfordshire, about which there was afterwards a suit in parliament between his three daughters by his wife Margery, and their husbands, and the Earl of Norfolk, who claimed it by a subsequent grant from Edward III. (*Parl. Writs*, ii. 421; *Cal. Inquis.* p. m. i. 303; *Rot. Parl.* ii. 391.)

ABINGER, LORD. See J. SCARLETT.

ABNEY, THOMAS. The Abneys were originally seated, almost from the time of the Conquest, at a village of that name in Derbyshire. They afterwards settled at Willesley in the same county; and the judge was the son of Sir Edward Abney, LL.D., of that place, an eminent civilian and M.P. for Leicester in 1690 and 1695, and the nephew of Sir Thomas Abney the famous lord mayor of London in 1701, whose virtues are celebrated in an elegy by Dr. Isaac Watts. (*Funeral Sermon, by Jer. Smith*, 1722.) His mother was Judith, daughter and co-heir of Peter Barr, a London merchant. He entered himself at the Inner Temple in 1697, put on his bar gown in 1713, and was made a bencher in 1733.

Being placed on the commission of the peace for Middlesex, he was chosen for the chairman of the quarter sessions at Hicks's Hall, in February 1731. In 1733 he was one of the commissioners to enquire into the fees, &c., of the officers of the Exchequer; and in the same year he was appointed attorney-general for the duchy of Lancaster, with the grade of king's counsel. From this he was advanced in December 1735 to be judge of the Palace Court and steward of the Marshalsea, and was then knighted. At the same time he was in full practice, and among the causes in which he distinguished himself was that of Moore v. The Corporation of Hastings, in which he established the right of the eldest son of a freeman to be admitted a freeman of the borough. (*Strange*, 1070; *State Trials*, xvii. 845.)

His elevation to the bench of Westminster was not long delayed, being made a baron of the Exchequer in November 1740. In little more than two years he was removed, in February 1743, to the Common Pleas. There he sat for the rest of his life, which was terminated by one of those afflicting visitations, too commonly occasioned by the infamous manner in which the common gaols were then conducted, and the confined construction of the criminal courts. The Black Sessions at the Old Bailey in May 1750 will be long remembered. An unusually large number of prisoners were arraigned, all most uncleanly, and some suffering from the gaol distemper; and a great concourse of spectators were crowded in the narrow court to hear the trial of Captain Clarke for killing Captain Innes in a duel. These, added to the filthy state of the rooms in connection with the court, so tainted the air that many of those assembled were struck with fever, of whom no less than forty died. Of the judges in the commission only the chief justice (Lee) and the recorder (Adams) escaped. Those who fell a sacrifice to the pestilence were Mr. Justice Abney, Mr. Baron Clarke, Sir

Samuel Pennant, lord mayor, and Alderman Sir Daniel Lambert; besides several of the counsel and jurymen.

Sir Michael Foster, who in his report of the Trial of the Rebels (p. 75), after designating Sir Thomas Abney as 'a very worthy man, learned in his profession, and of great integrity,' proceeds thus:—'He was through an openness of temper, or a pride of virtue habitual to him, incapable of recommending himself to that kind of low assiduous craft, by which we have known some unworthy men make their way to the favour of the great. . . . . In his judicial capacity he constantly paid a religious regard to the merits of the question in the light the case appeared to him; and his judgment very seldom misled him. In short, when he died the world lost a very valuable man, his majesty an excellent subject, and the public a faithful able servant.'

He married Frances, daughter of Joshua Burton, of Brackley in Northamptonshire, and left a son, Thomas, whose only daughter married General Sir Charles Hastings, Bart. Their descendants have assumed the name of Abney in addition to their own, and possess Willesley Hall, the judge's seat. Another branch of the Abney family is seated at Measham Hall in the same county.

ABRINCIS, or AVERENCHES, WILLIAM DE, is one of the twelve barons inserted in Dugdale's 'Chronica Series' as justices itinerant in 1170 for the counties of Kent, Surrey, Middlesex, Berks, Oxford, Buckingham, and Bedford. These barons, however, cannot be properly so considered; they seem, in fact, only commissioners appointed to enquire into the abuses of sheriffs, bailiffs, and other officers.

He was the grandson of a Norman noble of the same name; and the son of Roelandus de Abrincis, a valiant soldier under Henry I., by his wife Maud, the daughter and heir of Nigel de Monville, or Mundevil, who brought him the lordship of Folkestone in Kent, with all the lands and honours she inherited from her mother, Emma, the daughter of William de Arques.

According to the manner of the time, he devoted part of his property to religious purposes. In 1147 he ratified his mother's grant of the lordship of Siwelle in Northamptonshire, to the abbey of St. Andrew in Northampton: and he gave to the church of Our Lady of Merton two sheaves of his whole lordship, with the tithes of his mill, paunage, cheese, calves, colts, lambs, apples, and nuts, in pure almes. To the monks of Essay, in Normandy, he also gave the fourth part of the church of St. Saviour, with the tithe of the chapelry of his own house, and other benefactions.

He died before 2 Richard I., his son Simon being then in possession of the estates. The male branch of the family terminated a little before the year 1235, by the death of another William de Abrincis without issue. His sister became his heir, and married Hamon Crevequer, lord of Leeds Castle, in Kent. (*Dugdale's Baronage*, i. 467; *Monast.* v. 190.)

ABYNDON, RICHARD DE, held the important office of chamberlain of North Wales from the 12th to the 18th Edward I., his duty being the collection and disbursement of the royal revenues in that newly subjugated country. (*Archæol. Journ.* vii. 239.) He had no doubt been previously connected with the Exchequer in England, where, rising by degrees, he was, on October 17, 1299, 27 Edward I., constituted one of the barons of that court, and kept his place there during the rest of that king's life. In 37 Edward I. he and another were appointed custodes of the vacant bishopric of Ely. Though at the commencement of the next reign he was not immediately re-sworn a baron, his name being omitted in the patent of September, 1307 on January 30, 1308, he had a special patent constituting him a baron, 'ita quod in eodem Scaccario habuit eundem locum quem habuit tempore Domini Edwardi quondam regis Angliæ, patris regis nunc.' A salary of forty marks was attached to his office, in which he continued to act for the next ten years. (*Abbrev. Rot. Orig.* i. 120; *Madox*, ii. 57, 59, 325.) There is a complaint against William Randolf in 9 Edw. II. for insulting and imprisoning him and three others, justices who were assigned to hear and determine certain matters in the city of Bristol. (*Rot. Parl.* i. 130.) The next year his powers failed him; and John de Okham was appointed his successor by a patent of 10 Edw. II., dated June 18, 1317, in which his infirmity is thus described: 'quia dilectus clericus noster Ricardus de Abyndon, unus baronum nostrorum de Scaccario, adeo impotens sui existit, quod ea quæ ad officium illud pertinent non potest commode exercere.' He certified in 9 Edw. II. as lord of the township of Horton in Gloucestershire. (*Parl. Writs*, ii. div. ii. 114, 361.)

ACHARD, WILLIAM, possessed property in Berkshire, which was granted to his ancestor by King Henry I. Although he acted in 9 Richard I., 1197-8, as one of the justices itinerant in fixing the tallage for that county, he does not again appear in a judicial character, nor is he mentioned as an officer of the court. (*Madox*, i. 648-705.)

ACLE, REGINALD DE, having been constable of Marlborough Castle in 38 Henry III., became sheriff of Gloucester in the 50th, and so continued till the 56th year, when he was allowed to account by attorney. In 2 Edward I. he was directed to take that office into the king's hands, and commit it to a trusty person; and to go to the Exchequer to receive the king's commands thereon from the barons. (*Abbrev. Rot. Orig.* i. 12; *Madox,* ii. 68, 181.) It was no doubt as sheriff that he was added to the list of justices itinerant in 53 Henry III., 1268. In the same year he was custos of the bishopric of Hereford. (*Excerpt. e Rot. Fin.* ii. 484.)

ADAMS, RICHARD, was the son and heir of a gentleman of the same name residing at Shrewsbury. He was born in 1710, and was called to the bar of the Inner Temple in February 1735. He practised as a common pleader of the city of London, until elected its recorder on January 17, 1748. He obtained this honourable post after a severe contest, in which he was only successful by the casting vote of the lord mayor. During the time he held it he was knighted; and on February 3, 1753, he was promoted to the bench of the Exchequer. Miss Hawkins, in the second volume of her Memoirs, relates that he owed his elevation to the king's admiration of him in his character of recorder. The ministers not agreeing on the person who should succeed Mr. Baron Clive, George II. put an end to the discussion by calling out in his usual English, 'I vill have none of dese; give me de man wid de dying speech,' meaning the recorder, whose duty it was to make the report of the convicts under sentence of death.

After a judicial service of twenty years, he died on March 15, 1773, at Bedford, while on the circuit, of the gaol distemper, caught a fortnight before at the Old Bailey. In Lord Chief Justice Wilmot's Commonplace Book (*Life*, 199) his death is thus recorded:—'He was a very good lawyer and an excellent judge, having every quality necessary to dignify the character. I never saw him out of temper in my life, and I have known him intimately for forty years.'

ALAN was made abbot of Tewkesbury on June 16, 1187, having been previously a monk and then prior of the Benedictine Monastery of St. Saviour of Canterbury. In 1 John he fixed the tallage in Berkshire, and in the same year he is named as one of the justiciers before whom fines were levied. (*Madox,* i. 722.) He was a learned and a pious man, and greatly beloved by Archbishop Becket, to John of Salisbury's Life of whom he added a supplement. He wrote some other works, and died in 1202. (*B. Willis's Mitred Abbeys; Biog. Lit.* ii. 365.)

ALAND, JOHN FORTESCUE (LORD FORTESCUE), was the grandson of Hugh Fortescue, the seventh in lineal descent from the illustrious chief justice of Henry VI. His second son, Arthur, was the grandfather of the first Lord Fortescue, of Castle Hill, to which the earldom now enjoyed by his successors was added in 1789. Hugh's third son, Edmond, by his marriage with Sarah, daughter of Henry Aland, Esq., of Waterford, whose name he added to his own, was the judge's father.

He was born on March 7, 1670. Oxford has been supposed to be the place of his education, as he received from that university the honorary degree of doctor of civil law on May 4, 1733. But the language of that diploma leads to a different conclusion, and no trace is to be found of him in the register of matriculations. In 1688 he became a member of the Middle Temple, but afterwards removed to the Inner Temple; and having been called to the bar in 1712, arrived at the post of reader in 1716. In October 1714, immediately after the arrival of George I., he was appointed solicitor-general to the Prince of Wales (afterwards George II.), from which he was promoted in December of the following year to be solicitor-general to the king. He was chosen member for Midhurst in the first parliament of George I., but only sat during its first session, being raised to the bench of the Exchequer on January 24, 1717, when he was knighted. He occupied that seat for little more than a year; and one of his last duties as a baron was to give his opinion respecting the education and marriage of the royal family, his argument on which is fully reported by himself, and, though he had been one of the law officers of the Prince of Wales, was decidedly in favour of the prerogative of the crown. On May 15, 1718, he was removed to the King's Bench, and sat in that court till the death of George I. in June, 1727; but George II. about the middle of September, perhaps on account of the above opinion against his claim, superseded him. (*State Trials,* xv. 975, xvi. 1206; *Strange,* 86; *Lord Raymond,* 1510.)

After fifteen months' retirement, he was restored to favour, and placed in the Common Pleas on January 27, 1729. There he continued for above seventeen years, when, warned by his age and infirmities, he resigned in June 1746. So long before as 1741 he had petitioned for leave to retire with a pension, accompanied by the inconsistent request that a seat in the House of Commons might be obtained for him. When at last permitted to resign, after a service in all the three courts extending to twenty-eight years, his senatorial ambition was gratified by the grant of a barony in the Irish peerage in August 1746. His title was Lord Fortescue of Credan in the county of Waterford; but he enjoyed it for little more than four months, dying on December 19, 1746.

In addition to his legal reputation, he had the character of being well versed in Norman and Saxon literature. This he fully maintained in the introductory remarks to his edition of the treatise of his illustrious ancestor Sir John Fortescue, entitled 'The Difference between an Absolute and Limited Monarchy,' which he published in 1714, being then a Fellow of the Royal Society. His Law Reports of Select Cases were prepared for publication before his death, but not printed till 1748. Of his manner on the bench the following illustration in Bentley's case may serve as an example. 'The laws of God and man,' he said, 'both give the party an opportunity to make his defence if he has any. I remember to have heard it observed by a very learned man, that even God Himself did not pass sentence upon Adam, before he was called upon to make his defence. Adam (says God), where art thou? Hast thou not eaten of the tree whereof I commanded thee that thou shouldest not eat? And the same question was put to Eve also.' Of his appearance the 'Conveyancer's Guide' (p. 107) gives this description: 'The baron had one of the strangest noses ever seen: its shape resembled much the trunk of an elephant. "Brother, brother," said the baron to the counsel, "you are handling the cause in a very lame manner." "Oh! no, my lord," was the reply; "have patience with me, and I'll make it as plain as the nose in your lordship's face."'

Lord Fortescue's first wife was Grace, daughter of Chief Justice Pratt, by whom he had two sons, who died unmarried in their father's lifetime. His second wife was Elizabeth, daughter of Mr. Justice Dormer, by whom he left a son, his successor in his title and estates, one of which was Lamborn Hall in Essex; on whose death in 1781 without issue the peerage expired.

ALBEMARLE, EARL OF. See W. DE MANDEVIL.

ALBINI-BRITO, WILLIAM DE. Two persons named William de Albini lived at this time. One, called *Pincerna*, whose romantic adventures with Adelaide, Queen Dowager of France, are related by Dugdale in his 'Baronage,' married Adeliza, the widow of King Henry I. The other was surnamed *Brito*, probably in order to distinguish him from his celebrated contemporary.

He was the son of Robert de Todeni, the standard-bearer of William the Conqueror, who participated largely in the rich rewards distributed by his master, and founded Belvoir Castle, in Leicestershire, as his chief seat. He died in 1088, and by his wife Adela left four sons; the eldest of whom, this William, assumed the name of Albini, in consequence, it is believed, of his having been born in the parish of that name in Normandy.

In the town of Sawbridgeworth in Hertfordshire, which belonged to him, he exercised almost royal power, if we may judge from his charter or writ commanding his vassals there, that if any plaint or quarrel arose among the monks of that church, it should be stayed till it could be brought before him. (*Madox*, i. 120.)

He greatly distinguished himself, in 1106, at the battle of Tenchebrai, and afterwards appears to have been high in King Henry's favour. The county of Rutland was placed under his care as sheriff, or fermour; and the custody of the extensive lands of Otuer Fitz-Count was entrusted to him. He was also one of the council of the king, attended him in his movements, and was a witness, immediately after Hugh Bigot, and before Richard Basset, to the charter by which Henry, in 1134, granted the office of Great Chamberlain to Alberic de Vere and his heirs. (*Madox*, i. 56, 297, 327.)

When circuits were established by King Henry for the dispensation of justice throughout the kingdom, he was naturally selected to act in the county where his largest possessions were situate. The great roll of 31 Henry I. gives evidence of his holding pleas in Lincolnshire, and also as justice of the forest in Essex.

From this roll it appears that he was excused from the payment of Danegeld in seven counties in which he had property; an exemption he enjoyed in common with all those who were employed in the administration of justice.

Adhering, under the reign of Stephen, to the fortunes of the Empress Maude, he was for a time deprived of his extensive estates; but they were afterwards restored to him. His name appears as a witness to this king's charter granting the burgh of Hereford to Robert, Earl of Leicester. (*Madox*, ii. 139.)

He died about 1135, 2 Henry II., leaving by his wife Maud, daughter of Simon de Liz, Earl of Huntingdon, and widow of Robert, son of Richard de Tonbridge, two sons, William and Ralph.

1. William, who was surnamed Meschines, had a son, also William, subsequently mentioned as a justice itinerant.

2. Ralph, whose descendants called themselves Daubeney, by which name they were summoned to parliament. In 1538, Baron Daubeney was created Earl of Bridgewater, but both titles became extinct on his death, without issue, in 1548. (*Mag. Rot.* 31 Henry I.; *Dugdale's Baron.* i. 111; *Collins's Peerage*, i. 462, vi. 484, ix. 451.)

ALBINI, WILLIAM DE, was the third Earl of Arundel, being grandson of William de Albini, surnamed 'with the strong hand,' who obtained the earldom by his marriage with Queen Adeliza, the widow of Henry I., to whom the castle of Arundel had been assigned in dower. His father died in 1196, when he paid 100*l.* for the relief of his lands in Norfolk. With King John he was in high favour, receiving many grants from him; and his almost constant attendance at the court is shown by the fact, that in every year of the reign, except the last, he was a witness to charters or other royal documents. In the earlier contests with the barons, he adhered to the king, and was present, as one of his friends, at Runnymede. Disgusted at last with the tyranny and bad faith of his sovereign, he joined Prince Louis of France on his arrival in England. His lands were immediately ravaged by the royal army, and his whole possessions seized by the crown; but they were restored to him after the death of King John, on his returning to his allegiance in the following July. (*Rot. Claus.* i. 314.)

His entire restoration to the goodwill of the king, or rather of the protector of the kingdom, is shown by several entries on the rolls, and particularly by his acting as a justicier in 2 Henry III., in which year a fine was levied before him at Westminster. Roger de Wendover relates that in the same year, 1218, he proceeded to the Holy Land, and was at the siege of Damietta; and Matthew Paris adds that, in 1221, he died abroad, as he was returning from the crusade, and that his body was brought to England and buried at the abbey of Wimundham, of which he was a patron. His son William did homage for his lands on April 12, 1221, 5 Henry III. (*Rot. Claus.* i. 452.)

He is sometimes called Earl of Chichester; and on one occasion he signs himself William of Arundel, Earl of Sussex. (*Rot. Chart.* 14 John, 186.)

In December 1218, probably just previous to his embarkation for the Holy Land, the sheriff of Sussex was commanded to pay him twenty marks out of the issues of the county, which he ought and was accustomed every year to have by the name of the Earl of Sussex. (*Rot. Claus.* i. 383.)

He married Maude, daughter of James de St. Sidonio, and widow of Roger, Earl of Clare. By her he left two sons, William and Hugh, who successively held the earldom, and died without issue; and several daughters, one of whom, Isabel, married John Fitz-Alan, Lord of Clun (son of William Fitz-Alan, a justice itinerant under Richard I.), to whom the castle of Arundel, with its appendant title, was apportioned, which has come down in lineal descent to its present possessor, the Duke of Norfolk. (*Dugdale's Baron.* i. 118.)

ALBINI, WILLIAM DE, of Belvoir Castle, was the grandson of the before-named William de Albini, surnamed Brito, and the son and heir of William de Albini, surnamed Meschines, who died in 1167.

In 2 Richard I., 1190-1, he was entrusted with the sheriffalty of Rutland, which he held during the remainder of that reign; in the course of which he was also sheriff of the united counties of Warwick and Leicester, and of Bedford and Buckingham. In 1194 he was with the royal army in Normandy; and in 10 Richard I. he was one of the justiciers before whom a fine was levied at Norwich, but evidently only as a justice itinerant.

Under King John he was frequently employed. In the first year he was appointed one of the bailiffs of the Jews in England. (*Rot. Chart.* 61.) In 7 John he was sent on some embassy, the Close Roll (i. 56) containing an order for a ship to be provided for him on the king's service. In 10 John a fine was again levied before him as a justicier at Derby. In 14 John he was employed with four others on a commission of enquiry in Yorkshire and Lincolnshire (*Rot. Pat.* 97); and in the next year in collecting the assize of woad, in the latter county, and the duties on corn, salt, grease, honey, and salmon. (*Madox*, i. 773.) During the whole of this time he was frequently a witness to charters granted by the king; and on January 14, 1215, he was joined in a commission with the Archbishop of Canterbury and others to give safe conduct to those who came to supplicate the king's mercy for their great offences. (*Rot. Pat.* 126.) On the granting of Magna Charta, however, he was one of the twenty-five barons who were appointed to enforce its observance; and, though he afterwards neglected the invitation sent by the barons to be present at the tournament on Hounslow Heath, he subsequently joined them in London, and was entrusted with the command of Rochester Castle. There he bravely sustained a siege of three months, but being, in December 1215, compelled at last for want of provisions to submit, he narrowly escaped being hanged, a sentence which the angry monarch had pronounced against all the defenders. He owed his safety to the remonstrance of Savaricus de Malloleone, one of the king's Poictevin generals; and was, with his son Odenel, sent prisoner to Corff Castle. The loss of all his possessions was the consequence of his rebellion, to which was added the pope's excommunication. (*R. de Wendover*, iii. 329-355.) His wife, Agatha, however, succeeded in obtaining his pardon, with the restoration of his property, on the payment of a fine of six thousand marks. (*Rot. Claus.* i. 280, 287.)

According to Roger de Wendover, he was not released till November 25, 1216, about a month after the king's death; and it is certain that the whole of the fine was not paid before his liberation, or indeed up to the period of his own decease, nearly twenty years after; because his son was then permitted to pay what remained due by annual instalments of 20*l.* each. (*Excerpt. e Rot. Fin.* i. 306.) He was at once received into confidence, and had an early opportunity of proving his loyalty in the battle of Lincoln, fought on May 19, 1217, where he greatly distinguished himself. Entrusted with the castle of Muleton and the lands of Thomas of Muleton, which had been forfeited, and obtaining the valuable custody of the land and heir of Henry de Neville, he enjoyed the royal favour till his death. In 3 Henry III. he was placed high in the list of itinerant justices sent into the counties of Lincoln, Nottingham, and Derby; and again into Yorkshire in 9 Henry III. (*Rot. Claus.* ii. 77.) He died in May 1236. He was a great benefactor to the monks of Belvoir, and founded the hospital of Our Lady, called Newstead, at Wassebridge, between Stanford and Offington, in Lincolnshire, in which his body was interred, his heart being buried at Belvoir.

He married twice. His first wife was Margery, daughter of Odenel de Umfraville, by whom he had several children. With his eldest son, likewise William, the male branch of this family became extinct, but the possessions were carried by his daughter Isabel to her husband, Robert de Roos; and her male descendants continued to hold that barony till the year 1508, when, by the marriage of the heiress with Sir Robert Manners, it devolved on their son George, whose son, Thomas, was created Earl of Rutland in 1525. On the death of this earl's grandson without male issue the two titles became divided: but their present possessors—viz., the Duke of Rutland and Lord de Ros—plainly trace their descent from Isabel de Albini. His second wife was Agatha, daughter and coheir of the Baron William de Trusbot, for whom, with her inheritance, he accounted six hundred marks in 10 Richard I. It does not appear that she bore him any children.

ALCOCK, JOHN, the earliest chancellor of Henry VII., is described by Bale, who wrote about half a century after his death, as so devoted from his childhood to learning and piety, growing from grace to grace, that no one throughout England was more renowned for his sanctity. He was born at Beverley in Yorkshire, where his father, William Alcock, sometime burgess of Kingston-upon-Hull, was in circumstances sufficiently easy to be enabled to send him first to the grammar-school there and then to Cambridge, where he took the degree of Doctor of Laws in 1466. He was collated in 1461 to the church of St. Margaret's, New Fish Street, London, and subsequently received two prebends, one of Salisbury, and the other of St. Paul's. He was next advanced, on April 29, 1462, to the deanery of the Chapel of St. Stephen, in the Palace of Westminster.

It is not improbable, from the diplomatic services in which he was engaged, that he acted as an advocate in the ecclesiastical courts, the members of that branch of the law being then commonly selected for that duty. In March 1470, a few months before the restoration of Henry VI., he was one of the ambassadors to the King of Castile (*Rymer*, xi. 653), and having, on April 29 in the following year, immediately after the battle of Barnet, which replaced Edward IV. on the throne, superseded William Morland in the office of master of the Rolls (*Rot. Pat.* 11 Edw. IV. p. 1, m. 24; not 1 Edw. IV. as Dugdale has inadvertently called it), he was appointed, on August 26, a commissioner to treat with the Scotch ambassadors for a perpetual peace. (*Rymer*, xi. 717.)

He was made Bishop of Rochester on March 17, 1472, having on the previous day resigned the mastership of the Rolls to John Morton, and on September 20 the Great Seal was placed is his hands, when the lord chancellor, Bishop Stillington, gave up the duties on account of a temporary illness. (*Claus.* 12 Edw. IV. m. 16.) He opened the parliament as keeper on October 6; and the lord chancellor, having recovered, prorogued it on April 5, 1473. (*Rot. Parl.* vi. 3, 9, 41.)

King Edward entrusted to him the education of his infant son, and placed him on his privy council, and a curious instance of the royal favour occurred in the year 1475, when both Alcock and Bishop Rotheram held the title of lord chancellor for several months together, affording a solitary instance, in the history of this kingdom, of two chancellors acting at the same time. The fact is incontestably proved by the evidence of numerous Privy Seal bills addressed to both by the same title, from April 27 to September 28, 1475. This extraordinary circumstance may be thus explained. When the king planned his invasion of France, he intended to be accompanied by his lord chancellor, Bishop Rotheram, and feeling it necessary to provide for the business of the Chancery in England, he nominated Bishop Alcock to take the duty during the chancellor's absence. Instead, however, of pursuing the customary practice of making him merely keeper of the Seal, he, as a mark of special favour, invested him with the title of chancellor, intending that the regular chancellor should be with him during the whole period of his absence in France. It happened, however, that the armament was delayed from April till July, so that during those months Privy Seal bills were addressed to both officers in England, frequently on the same day and from the same place. The last writ of Privy Seal addressed to Bishop Alcock is dated on September 28, after which Bishop Rotheram, having returned from France, resumed his functions as sole chancellor.

The see of Worcester becoming vacant, the king was happy in the opportunity of appointing Alcock to fill it; and possession of the temporalities was granted to him on September 25, 1476. (*Rymer*, xii. 34.) He presided over the diocese for the rest of the reign, during which he enlarged the church of Westbury, and founded a school at Kingston-on-Hull, where he built a chapel over the remains of his parents at the south of the church, endowing a chantry there also. (*Cal. Rot. Parl.* 324.) In 1478 he was constituted President of Wales, but on the death of Edward he was removed from the preceptorship of his infant successor by the protector Richard, who, however, introduced a clause in the act of attainder passed when he became king, declaring it should not prejudice the bishop in reference to certain property in Kent. (*Rot. Parl.* vi. 201, 249.)

The battle of Bosworth, on August 22, 1485, placed Henry VII. on the throne; and Bishop Alcock was his first chancellor. The date of his appointment does not appear, though Dugdale erroneously states it to be on March 6, 1486, the date of Bishop Morton's appointment; but Alcock was present as chancellor at the coronation on October 30, 1485, and opened the first parliament on November 7, efficiently superintending the difficult questions it had to decide. (*Rutland Papers*, x. 10; *Rot. Parl.* vi. 267.) Bishop Morton succeeded him in the office on March 6, 1486, being then Bishop of Ely, to which see Alcock was translated on that prelate's advance to the primacy, and was admitted to the temporalities on December 7, having in the intervening July been employed in treating with the commissioners of the Scottish king. (*Rymer*, xii. 285, 318.)

The latter years of his life were occupied in building the beautiful hall at his palace of Ely, and in decorating all his manors with new edifices. On the site also of the old nunnery of St. Radegund, in Cambridge, he founded Jesus College, a lasting monument of his liberality and taste. Nor were the claims of literature forgotten. Various compositions connected with his profession issued from his pen, among which was one called 'Galli Cantus ad Confratres suos Curatos in Synodo apud Barnewell, September 25, 1498,' at the beginning of which is a print of himself preaching to his clergy, with a cock (his crest) at each side. In his sermons he must have fatigued his auditors, if they were all as long as one he preached at St. Mary's church, in Cambridge, which is said to have lasted two hours.

The bishop died at his castle at Wisbeach on October 1, 1500, and was buried in a magnificent chapel erected by himself in Ely cathedral. All writers concur in speaking highly of his erudition and his piety. The latter is said to have been carried to an extreme in mortifications and abstinence. He was greatly beloved and respected by his contemporaries, and was named by Judge Lyttelton as the supervisor of his will. Coke in relating this fact calls him 'a man of singular piety, devotion, chastity, temperance, and holiness of life.' (*Fuller's Worthies; Angl. Sac.* i. 381, 538, 675; *Godwin de Præsul.* 269; *Cooper's Ath. Cantab.* i. 3.)

ALDEBURGH, RICHARD DE, derived his name from Aldeburgh (Aldborough) in Yorkshire, where he had a grant of lands in 12 Edw. II., and seven years afterwards purchased the manor of Hundeburton and property in Mildeby. (*Abb. Rot. Orig.* i. 245, 293.) He is frequently mentioned as a counsel in the Year Books of Edward II., and the first five years of Edward III. In the third year of the latter reign he acted as the king's attorney in the pleas of quo warranto at Northampton; and in the same year he is noticed as one of the king's serjeants. In the fifth year he was a commissioner for preserving the peace between England and Scotland (*N. Fœdera*, ii. 809); and on February 3, 1332, 6 Edward III., he was constituted a judge of the Common Pleas, and knighted. Dugdale introduces two other patents, conferring on him the same office, dated November 19, 1333, and January 8, 1341; but I presume that, as on these days new chiefs of the court were appointed, these were merely formal renominations without any intervening retirement; especially as Dugdale does not record any break in the fines levied before him. These are stated to terminate at Michaelmas, 14 Edward III., 1340, in which year he had a licence to enclose one hundred acres of land in Rigton in Whernedale. (*Cal. Rot. Pat.* 114, 117, 119, 138.)

He is last mentioned as the head of a judicial commission in Yorkshire as late as May 20, 1343. (*N. Fœdera*, ii. 1225.)

ALDERSON, EDWARD HALL, was the additional judge in the Common Pleas under the new act passed at the commencement of the reign of William IV. His father, Robert Alderson, Esq., was an eminent member of the same profession, recorder of Norwich, Ipswich, and Yarmouth, and his mother was the daughter of Samuel Burry, Esq., of the latter place, where he was born on September 11, 1787. After-spending a short time at Scarning School, near Dereham, where Lord Thurlow commenced his education, he was removed to the Grammar School of Bury St. Edmunds, and subsequently had the advantage of the private tuition of Dr. Maltby, afterwards Bishop of Durham. His progress was so great and his intelligence so marked, that the highest expectations were formed of his college career; and so self-conscious was he of his own talents and acquirements that he afterwards acknowledged that if any one had offered him on entering the university the place of *second* wrangler, he would at once have refused it. Thus well prepared, he entered Caius College, Cambridge, in 1805, and by his indomitable perseverance and extraordinary genius he not only achieved the success his friends had prophesied, but exceeded his own prognostications, obtaining, besides the anticipated place of senior wrangler, the additional distinction of first Smith's prizeman and senior medallist, the highest honours which his university could give both in classics and mathematics, and a triple glory which few had previously obtained. During his progress through the university he also gained Sir Thomas Browne's medal for the best Greek and Latin epigrams, and the members' prize for the Latin essay. In 1809 he took his degree as bachelor, and in 1812 that of master of arts, when he was elected fellow of his college.

Having entered the Inner Temple, in 1811 he was called to the bar, and selected the Northern circuit and York sessions, in which he had no cause to complain of neglect at the outset of his career. In 1817, on the termination of the Reports of Maule and Selwyn, he joined with Mr. Barnewall in their continuation for the five succeeding years, when he felt obliged to relinquish the employment. In 1823 he married Georgina, daughter of the Rev. Edward Drewe, of Broadhembury, Devonshire.

He thence went on with such increase of employment and reputation that in 1828 he was appointed one of the commissioners for the amendment of the law. So much in demand were his services on the circuit that he himself described his position, 'Heir-apparent to the crown, upon the departure of the present holders.' At this time the act before referred to was passed, and, though he never had a silk gown, nor the advantage of a seat in parliament, he was at once selected from the outer bar for his acknowledged ability, as one of the three judges then added to the old number of twelve. He was first placed in the Common Pleas in November 1830, receiving the honour of knighthood. There he remained till February 1834, when he was removed to the Exchequer, where he performed the double duties on the equity and common law side till the former was transferred into Chancery by an enactment in 1841.

The only fault that has been found with him as a judge arose from the quickness of insight into the questions before him, which sometimes led him into too rapid a judgment of their real merits, producing a degree of impatience against those whose duty it was to argue against his preconceived opinions. Yet notwithstanding this failing he was in the main a popular judge, especially with juries; and while sitting in Banco he had much influence in the decisions of the court. His reasoning in the latter was deep, solid, and acute; and his relish of fun and his occasional witticisms on the bench no doubt made him a general favourite at nisi prius. Even in Banco he could not always refrain. Once a counsel on applying for a nolle prosequi, pronounced the penultimate syllable long; 'Stop, sir,' said the baron; 'consider that this is the last day of term, and don't make things unnecessarily long.' At an assize town a juryman said to the clerk who was administering the oath to him, 'Speak up, I cannot hear what you say.' The baron asked him if he was deaf, and on the juryman answering, 'Yes, with one ear,' replied 'Well then you may leave the box, for it is necessary that jurymen should *hear both sides.*'

With all this spirit of drollery, he was essentially of a serious and religious disposition; cordially loved in his private life, and highly esteemed and respected by the bar. He employed his leisure in the renewal of his early studies, and was himself a graceful poet. Several of his fugitive pieces, some of which are addressed to his literary cousin, Mrs. Opie, are introduced into an interesting memoir of his life, published by his son soon after his death. That event occurred on January 27, 1857, in his seventieth year, when he had been on the bench more than six and twenty years. His remains lie in the churchyard of Risby, near Bury, his brother's living.

ALENÇON, JOHN DE, was probably one of the clerks of the Chancery; and, obtaining ecclesiastical preferment according to the custom of these officers, was raised to the archdeaconry of Lisieux in 1185. He was selected by Richard I. to accompany him as his vice-chancellor to Normandy on his departure for the Holy Land. There are six charters 'data per manum Johannis de Alençoni, Archidiacono Lexoviensis, vice Cancellarii nostri,' granted by Richard in that country in the months of January, March, June, and July 1190. (*N. Fœdera*, i. 48, 51; *Dugdale's Monast.* i. 485; vi. 1115.) William de Longchamp, Bishop of Ely, was at that time chancellor and chief justiciary in

England, where, no doubt, according to the course duly recorded on the rolls of subsequent reigns, one great seal was left with him, while another was entrusted to a deputy in attendance on the king, to be used according to the royal pleasure. In the following March the duty was performed by Roger Malus Catulus. In February 1198 Alençon was one of the witnesses to a charter given under the hand of Warine, Prior of Loches, 'tunc agentis vicem Cancellarii nostri' (*Neustria Pia*, 897; *Monast.* vi. 1110); and he was appointed treasurer of Vaudreuil on September 6, 1199, 1 John. (*Rot. Chart.* i. 19.) The last time he is mentioned is when he accompanied Ralph de Furnellis to Rome, and letters of protection were granted to both while there. (*Rot. Pat.* 3 John, 5.)

ALENCUN, HERBERT DE, possessed property in Suffolk; and a suit previously instituted by him relative to the manor of Dinniveton, in that county, which was to have been heard before the justices itinerant in 9 Henry III., was directed to be removed before the judges at Westminster, in consequence of his being included in the commission for that Iter. (*Rot. Claus.* ii. 77, 79.) In 11 Henry III. he was employed to fix the tallage for Norfolk and Suffolk (*Ibid.* ii. 174, 208), and for the next five years he filled the office of sheriff of those counties. (*Fuller's Worthies.*)

ALEXANDER was the nephew of Roger, Bishop of Salisbury. He was born in Normandy, and, with such a connection, soon received advancement in England. Roger first appointed him archdeacon in his own diocese, and at Easter, 1123, he was advanced to the bishopric of Lincoln. His cathedral being soon after destroyed by fire, he rebuilt it with the greatest magnificence, increasing the number of prebends, and handsomely endowing them. He emulated his uncle in the erection of three castles—those of Banbury, Sleaford, and Newark—the last of which he was incautious enough to declare was designed as much for the security as the dignity of the Church. When King Stephen became jealous of the power of the clergy he shared in his uncle's disgrace, and was compelled to surrender his castles to the monarch. The defenders of that of Newark, however, resisted the royal power, and could not be prevailed upon to deliver it up until they found that the king had sworn that the bishop should not taste food so long as they held out. Even after their submission the bishop was kept in prison for some time; and when he at last was liberated, he quitted the strife of politics, and devoted himself and his property to his religious duties and the improvement of his see. He took two journeys to Rome, and so pleased both the king and the pope by his conduct that he was appointed legate from the latter in England, where he convened a synod, and passed some useful canons for repressing the enormities of the times. In 1147 he made a third visit to the pope, then in France, but, being seized with sickness, he had scarcely time to return ere he died, in the month of August.

Besides the above proofs of his munificence, the hospital of St. Leonard at Newark, the priory of Haverholm in Lincolnshire, and the abbeys of Dorchester and Thame in Oxfordshire, acknowledged him as their founder.

Henry of Huntingdon, who dedicated his History to him, paints him in glowing colours in some verses while living, and in his epistle 'De Mundi Contemptu' when dead.

His introduction into Thynne's and Dugdale's list of chancellors under King Stephen is founded on a passage in William of Newbury, in which, however, no name occurs, and the fact referred to evidently applies to the fate of his cousin Roger, the son, or, as he was often called, the nephew of the bishop, and an undoubted chancellor. No charter or other record mentions Alexander as chancellor. (*Godwin de Præsulibus*, 284; *William of Malmesbury*, 715, 716, 744; *Angl. Sac.* ii. 700; *Thoroton's Notts*, i. 389, 398, 406.)

ALEXANDER, WILLIAM, of Scottish birth and extraction, possessed property at Airdrie, in the county of Lanark. Born about the year 1761, at the age of twenty-one he was called to the bar of the Society of the Middle Temple; and, selecting the Court of Chancery, he practised there with a high reputation as an equity and real property lawyer for nearly twenty years, and was in 1800 rewarded with a silk gown. Lord Eldon appointed him on November 9, 1809, one of the masters in Chancery; and after filling this comparatively subordinate office for about fifteen years, he was, to the surprise, and somewhat to the dissatisfaction, of the profession, all at once by the same patronage raised to the head of the Court of Exchequer, being constituted lord chief baron on January 9, 1824, and thereupon made a privy counsellor and knighted. He himself hesitated to accept the appointment when offered, being aware of his limited acquaintance with criminal law and the practice of the common law courts. But, notwithstanding his own doubts, and those entertained by the legal world in general, he presided most ably for seven years, his experience in equity, which then formed a great part of the business of his court, being peculiarly valuable.

In January 1831 he was induced to resign, for the purpose of enabling Lord Lyndhurst, who had given up the Great Seal, to take his place as lord chief baron.

About the same time he had a large accession to his fortune from the discovery of iron ore on his estate at Airdrie. He survived his retirement more than twenty years, and dying on June 29, 1842, was buried in the chapel of Roslin Castle.

ALLERTHORPE, LAURENCE DE, derived his surname from the village in Yorkshire so called. There is no account of his family; but it is evident that his early life was spent as a clerk in the Exchequer. In 1370 he was an auditor of that department, receiving 10*l*. a year for his salary, together with sixty shillings for his expenses in going into the northern counties to affeer amercements. (*Issue Roll*, 44 Edward III. 143, 404.) An ecclesiastic, like his brethren, he obtained a canonry in St. Paul's.

On September 27, 1375, he was constituted a baron of the Exchequer. This office he retained during the remainder of Edward's reign, the whole of the next, and for nearly two years of that of Henry IV., during the last twelve years holding the higher position of second baron.

Having now sat upon the bench for above a quarter of a century, he was advanced, on May 31, 1401, 2 Henry IV., to the treasurership, which he held rather less than a year; and then accompanied the king's son, Thomas of Lancaster, to Ireland. (*Rymer*, viii. 227.) Dying on July 21, 1406, he was buried in St. Dunstan's chapel in St. Paul's Cathedral. Shortly before that event he is stated to have been the sole residentiary there, and to have had the whole revenue of the thirty canons at his own disposal, in consequence of all his brethren being excluded by the pope's bull from participating on account of their non-residence. (*Weever*, 366.)

ALLEYN, or ALEYN, JOHN, was entered at Lincoln's Inn on February 2, 1476, and was elected reader in autumn 1491, and again in Lent 1496. He is not mentioned as an advocate by any reporter, and probably held some office in the Exchequer. He was constituted fourth baron on February 18, 1504, 19 Henry VII., and was continued in the same position for the first two years of the reign of Henry VIII.

Phillips, in his 'Grandeur of the Law,' p. 69, says that Sir Thomas Allen, Bart., lord mayor of London, was one of the baron's descendants; but evidence is wanting in support of the statement. There is indeed the same difficulty as in former reigns in tracing the pedigrees of the barons of the Exchequer, who in general began their career as clerks in the department. He was appointed in 1509 supervisor of the will of John Perfay, draper, of Bury St. Edmunds, who bequeaths 'to hym for hys labor xx *s.* in mony, and a blak gowne' (*Bury Wills*, 113); and he was in the commission for the gaol delivery of that town in 1511, and in the commission of the peace for the county till 1514. (*Cal. St. Papers*, 1509-14.)

Blomefield (*Norfolk*, i. 758) is clearly in error when he states that John Wodehouse, of Kimberley in Norfolk, married the relict of 'John Aleyne, one of the barons of the Exchequer,' inasmuch as John Wodehouse himself died in 1465, and his lady lies buried with him.

ALLIBONE, RICHARD. The grandfather of this short-lived judge was an eminent divine, rector of Cheyneys in Buckinghamshire, whose third son, Job Allibond (for so Anthony Wood spells the name), turned Roman Catholic, got a comfortable place in the post office, died in 1672, and was buried at Dagenham in Essex. He was the father of Richard, who, born about 1621, rather late in life commenced his legal education at Gray's Inn on April 27, 1663. Though called to the bar on February 11, 1670, no mention is made of him till November 1686, when, being a papist, he was selected by King James to be one of his counsel, and knighted. On April 28, 1687, he was appointed a judge of the King's Bench. In the summer of that year he went the Northern Circuit, and Bishop Cartwright relates that at Lancaster, while his colleague Judge Powell, attended at the parish church, Allibone went to the school-house, and had mass. In his charge to the grand jury he took notice that only three of the gentry came out to meet the judges, and called it a great disrespect of the king's commission—a fact strongly indicative of the general feeling of dissatisfaction in the country.

At the trial of the seven bishops in Trinity Term 1688 Sir Richard laid down the most arbitrary doctrines, and exerted himself to the utmost to procure their conviction. On going the Home Circuit in July, immediately after the trial, he had the indecency in his charge to the Croydon jury to speak against the verdict of their acquittal, and to stigmatise their petition to the king as a libel that tended to sedition. His death on the 22nd of the following month at his house in Brownlow Street probably saved him from attainder at the revolution.

He was buried at Dagenham, where a pompous monument was erected over his remains. His wife was Barbara Blakiston, of the family of Sir Francis Blakiston, of Gibside, in Durham, Bart. (*Ath. Oxon.* ii. 440; *Bramston*, 275; *Diary of Bishop Cartwright*, 71; *Luttrell*, i. 287; *State Trials*, xii. 190.)

ALTHAM, JAMES, was of civic descent, both paternally and maternally. His grandfather, Edward, was sheriff of London in 1531; his father, James, of Mark's Hall, Latton, Essex, was sheriff of the same city in 1557, and of the county of Essex in 1570; and his mother was Elizabeth, daughter of Thomas Blanke, citizen and haberdasher, and the sister of Sir Thomas Blanke, lord mayor of London in 1582. (*Archæologia*, xxvi. 400–417.) After being called to the bar at Gray's Inn, he was chosen reader there in autumn 1600, and again in Lent 1603, on his being summoned by Queen Elizabeth to assume the degree of the coif in the following Easter Term. But her decease happening before that period, King James renewed the writ with the same return.

He represented Bramber in the parliament of 1589, and had acquired such a character in his profession that he was appointed a baron of the Exchequer on February 1, 1607, when he received the honour of knighthood.

Lord Chief Justice Coke seems to have been in the habit of treating the judges rather superciliously, since Justice Williams told Archbishop Abbot, who reported it to Lord Chancellor Ellesmere, 'of his utter dislike of all the Lord Coke his courses; and that himself and Baron Altham did once very roundly let the Lord Coke know their minde, that he was not such a maister of the lawes as he did take on him, to deliver what he list for lawe, and to despise all other.' (*Egerton Papers*, 448.)

He died on February 21, 1616–17; and Sir Francis Bacon (*Works*, vii. 267), in a speech to his successor, calls him 'one of the gravest and most reverend judges of this kingdom.' The numerous references to and reports by him in the State Paper Office prove the great respect that was entertained for his judgment by the government. He was interred in the chapel of Oxhey House, near Watford, which he had founded in 1612, under a monument on which he is represented in his robes.

He was thrice married. His first wife was Margaret, daughter and heir of Oliver Skinner, Esq., by whom he had one son; his second was Mary, daughter of Hugh Stapers, Esq., who brought him one son and three daughters; and his third was Helen, daughter of John Saunderson, merchant of London, and widow of John Hyde, citizen and mercer of London, by whom he had no children. His male issue soon failed, but all his daughters married into noble families. One of them was united to Arthur Annesley the first Earl of Anglesea; and her second son by him, christened Altham, was created Baron Altham in Ireland, his descendants eventually succeeding to the earldom. The sixth earl's son failed to make good his claim to the English peerage, which thus became extinct; but he succeeded in regard to the Irish titles, and was created Earl of Mountnorris in Ireland, which title also failed on the death of its second possessor. Another daughter of Sir James Altham married Richard Vaughan, second Earl of Carberry, a title which became extinct in the next generation. The third daughter had three husbands—Sir Francis Astley, of Hill Morton in Warwickshire, knight; Robert, Lord Digby in Ireland; and Sir Robert Bernard, baronet, serjeant-at-law. (*Morant's Essex*, 565; *Wotton's Baronet.* iii. 66, 364, iv. 402.)

ALVANLEY, LORD. *See* R. P. ARDEN.

AMBLY, WILLIAM DE, was one of the many who, having been in arms against King John, returned to their allegiance on the accession of Henry III. After the appointment, in 9 Henry III., of justices itinerant for Norfolk and Suffolk, in one of which his estates were situate, he was joined to those named, in the place of Bartholomew Glanville. (*Rot. Claus.* i. 340, ii. 77.)

ANDELEY, or AUNDELEY, MAURICE DE, was so called from a town in Normandy. In 17 John he was sent down to Northampton, with Simon de Pateshull and others, to hear a dispute relative to the presentation of the church of Oxenden (*Rot. Claus.* i. 270); and in Trinity Term 1219, 3 Henry III., he appears as one of the justices at Westminster before whom fines were levied, and as a justice itinerant in various counties, which duty he performed as late as 1230. (*Rot. Claus.* i. 516 ii. 77.)

ANDERSON, EDMUND. A younger son of the ancient family of Anderson of Northumberland having migrated into Lincolnshire, the first-named as resident in that county is Roger, who had an estate at Wrawbey, and was grandfather of Henry, whose son Edward, of Flixborough in the same county, married Joan Clayton, niece to the Abbot of Thornholme. They had three sons—Thomas, who married Ellinor, a daughter of Judge Dalison; Richard, of Roxby; and Edmund, the future chief justice.

Edmund was born about 1530, educated at Lincoln College, Oxford, and admitted to the Inner Temple in June 1550. He became reader in Lent 1567, and again in Lent 1574. He was one of seven who were called to the degree of the coif in Michaelmas 1577, and two years afterwards he was nominated queen's serjeant. In this character he went as assistant judge on the Western Circuit in that year, and in November 1581 conducted the trial of Edmond Campion and others for high treason. His introductory speech, which is described as having been 'very vehemently pronounced, with a grave and austere countenance,' is a fair example of the vicious rhetoric of the bar at that period. It seems to be directed more against the pope than the prisoner; and whatever may have been Campion's guilt, he certainly beats the crown lawyers both in eloquence and argument. (*State Trials*, i. 1051.)

Within six months, on the death of Sir James Dyer, the chief justice of the Common Pleas, Serjeant Anderson was appointed in his place, on May 2, 1582, and soon after knighted. The Recorder Fleetwood, in a letter to Lord Burleigh, relates that on the day of his investiture the Lord Chancellor (Hatton) 'made a short discourse what the dewtie and office of a good justice was;' and that after he was sworn, '*Father* Benloos, because he was auncient, did put a short case, and then myself put the next.' To both, he continues, the new chief 'argued very learnedlie and with great facilitie.' Anderson sat as president of that court not only during the remainder of Elizabeth's reign, but for more than two years under James I., a period in the whole exceeding twenty-three years. In the state trials which disgraced the earlier part of his judicial career there is certainly nothing that distinguishes the chief justice from his fellows; all were involved in the disgusting barbarity of the proceedings. He was one of the performers in the farce of Secretary Davison's trial, and was equally puzzled with the rest in drawing that distinction between the propriety of the act itself and the impropriety of its performance, which was necessary for the purpose of justifying the required condemnation. A strenuous supporter of the discipline of the Church of England, he showed himself too severe a condemner of all sectarians; and Browne, the founder of the Brownists, on his trial, and Udall, the Genevan minister, on his examination, felt that the chief justice was not an unprejudiced censor. (*State Trials*, i. 1229–1271.) He discouraged, however, the 'insolence of office;' and when the mayor of Leicester, who had caused a Maypole to be pulled down, had committed a poor shoemaker for saying that 'he hoped to see more morice dancing and Maypoles soon,' the chief justice, on coming to the assizes there in 1599, instantly ordered the lover of old customs to be discharged. (*Hist. of Leicester*, 305.)

As a judge in civil cases he was patient and impartial; his knowledge of law was extensive, and he was ready in its application; and the 'Reports' which he collected, and which were afterwards published, prove the industry and devotedness with which he pursued his profession. His successful resistance of an attempted encroachment on the rights of his place in the case of Cavendish, to whom Queen Elizabeth, at the instigation of Lord Leicester, had granted letters patent for making out writs of *supersedeas* upon exigents, on the ground that the queen had no power to grant the office, speaks highly for the judicial independence in those arbitrary times.

Sir Edmund died on August 1, 1605, and was buried at Eyworth in Bedfordshire, with a handsome monument, on which he is represented in his robes.

His first residence was at Flixborough, then at Arbury in Warwickshire, where he built a house out of the ruins of the monastery. This he exchanged with the Newdigates for Harefield in Middlesex, to be nearer the courts; and there he entertained the queen, who gave him a ring set with diamonds, which was long preserved in the family, till one of them had it reset, and afterwards gave away the jewels. Thus losing their identity, the present representatives will not probably be so fortunate as one of the Northumberland Andersons is said to have been, who, having dropped a ring into the sea, gave it up for lost, when some time after, having bought a cod in the market, on opening the fish the ring was found in his maw.

The judge married Magdalen, daughter of Christopher Smyth, Esq., of Annables in Hertfordshire, and Ackthorpe in Lincolnshire, and by her had nine children. His eldest son, Edmund, died without issue. His second son, Sir Francis, was the father of Sir John Anderson of St. Ives, who was created a baronet in 1628, and the grandfather, by another son, of Sir Stephen Anderson of Eyworth, who received a baronetcy in 1664; but both these titles have been long extinct. From this Sir Francis also, through another grandson, descended Charles Anderson of Manley, in the parish of Broughton in Lincolnshire, who, upon inheriting the estates of his maternal great-uncle, Charles Pelham of Brocklesby in the same county, assumed that name, and was raised to the peerage in 1794 as Baron Yarborough, a title which was erected into an earldom in 1837, the second possessor of which now represents the chief justice in the House of Lords. The third son of the judge was William, of Lea (a manor in Lincolnshire given to him by his father), whose son, Edmund Anderson of Broughton, was advanced in 1660 to a baronetcy, which is still enjoyed by his lineal representative. (*Ath. Oxon.* i. 753; *Wotton's Baronet.* iii. 191, 427; *Collins's Peerage*, viii. 393–398.)

ARCHER, JOHN. Morant, in his 'History of Essex' (i. 161), relates that the Archers derive themselves from Simon de Bois, who attended Henry V. at Agincourt, for which he received a pension of five marks a year for his life; and that he changed his name to Archer by command of the king for his excellence at a shooting-match before the monarch at Havering-at-Bower. John Archer, according to the same authority, was born in 1598, and was the son of Simon Archer, an alderman of London, of Coopersale in Theydon-Bois, Essex, by Anne his wife, but his admission to the society of Gray's Inn on January 15, 1617, more correctly described him as the son of Henry. Archer, of Haydon Clairon in that county. He was educated at Queen's College, Cambridge, and took his degrees of B.A. and M.A. in 1619 and 1622. His call to the bar was in March 1620, and his elevation to the bench of his inn in 1648.

In 1647 he was counsel for the corporation of Grantham, and was engaged in 1651 as one of the counsel for Christopher Love, tried for high treason against the Commonwealth before the High Court of Justice, though he was not allowed to plead for him because he had not taken the engagement. (*State Trials*, v. 211.) This sufficiently accounts for the fact that he was never employed by Cromwell; though, on his election for Essex in the parliament of 1656, he was one of the members approved by the council. (*Parl. Hist.* iii. 1480.) Soon after the Protector's death he was made a serjeant, on Nov. 27, 1658; and on the restoration of the Long Parliament was one of the judges appointed by that body on May 15, 1659. Whitelocke does not name the court to which he was then attached, but it may be presumed to have been the Common Pleas, as he is placed there on Jan. 17, 1660, when all the judges are designated with their particular courts. During the short time that elapsed before the return of the king he was assigned to go the Northern Circuit; and though on the Restoration he lost his seat on the bench, he was among the serjeants of the interregnum who were immediately confirmed in the degree by the restored government.

Two years afterwards he was made a judge of the Common Pleas, on Nov. 4, 1663. He sat there for nine years, when his services were interrupted in the Christmas vacation, 1672, by a royal prohibition; the reasons for which were unknown to Sir Thomas Raymond, who reports the fact, and adds that the judge, having been appointed 'quamdiu se bene gesserit,' refused to surrender his patent without a scire facias. As this would not have been a convenient proceeding, he retained his position, and received his share of the fees till his death, though forbidden to sit in the court. His place in the meantime was supplied by Sir William Ellis, who was in his turn removed before Archer's death, to make way for Sir William Scroggs. (*Siderfin*, i. 3, 163; *T. Raymond*, 217; *T. Jones*, 43.)

The only account of Archer as a judge is by Roger North (*Life*, 45–48), who says that he was one of those 'of whose abilities time hath kept no record, unless in a sinister way;' and he describes him as always desirous of staving off a long cause, relating the mode in which Sir Francis North (afterwards lord keeper) played upon this weakness. He survived his removal more than nine years, dying on Feb. 8, 1682. His burial-place is in the churchyard of Theydon, where there is a monument to him.

He had two wives: one was Mary, daughter of Sir George Saville, Bart.; and the other Eleanor, daughter of Sir John Curzon, Bart. His son John by the latter lived at Coopersale in Theydon Garnon, and was knighted. (*Wotton's Baronet.* i. 162, ii. 246, 347.)

ARDEN, or ARDERNE, RALPH DE, was son-in-law of Ranulph de Glanville, having married his second daughter, Amabilia. With this connection it is natural that he should have received employment in the king's service; and we accordingly find him sheriff of Hereford, where he had considerable property, from 1184 to 1189. (*Fuller's Worthies.*) In the latter year he was amerced in the large sum of 65*l*. for thirteen days' neglect in attending at the Exchequer according to his summons. (*Madox*, ii. 235.) In the same year, probably just before his father-in-law had retired from the place of chief justiciary, he acted as a justice itinerant in Shropshire, Herefordshire, Gloucestershire, and Staffordshire.

The Pipe Roll of 6 Richard I., 1195 (95, 144, 168, 248), charges him as a debtor in Essex and Hertfordshire for 362*l*. 16s. 8*d*. for his fine, and for having *benevolentiam regis*. But in 1198 he had recovered the king's favour, and accounts on the Norman Roll of that year as bailiff of Pont-Audemer, in which office he was succeeded, on the accession of King John, by Walter de Ely (*Rot. Norm.* ii. *observations*), and probably died soon after. His wife, however, had died before 6 Richard I., for in that year Thomas de Arden, their son and heir, was engaged in a lawsuit relative to the partition of the property of Ranulph de Glanville, who, previous to his departure to the Holy Land, had devised it among his three daughters. (*Rot. Cur. Regis*, 24.) This Thomas was alive in 14 John, when a compromise was effected between him and the Bohuns, with whom his father and he had been in litigation for some years.

ARDEN, or ARDERNE, RALPH DE, was, there is little doubt, the grandson of the justice itinerant last named, and the son of Thomas de Arden. (*Preface to Coke's 8th Report.*) He is mentioned by Dugdale as a justicier in 9 John, 1207, and by Mr. Hunter in the next year, when fines were levied before him at Derby.

He had previously incurred the king's

displeasure, and in 3 John fined 272*l*. 12*s*. 6*d*. for the royal favour (*Rot. Cancel.* 147), but in the following year he was employed in the king's service, being sent with Gerard de Rodes to Otho, King of the Romans, with an allowance of five marks for their passage. (*Madox,* ii. 340.) Two years afterwards he accompanied the abbot of Insula and Eustace de Fauconberg to Flanders, the sheriff of Kent being commanded to provide a good and secure ship to convey them. (*Rot. Claus.* i. 16.)

He endowed the priory of Butley, in Sussex, which was founded by Ranulph de Glanville, with half the town of Bawdesey, part of the inheritance which he had acquired through that great justiciary; and by his wife Agnes he left a son named Thomas. (*Monast.* vi. 381; *Rot. Cur. Regis,* i. 121.)

ARDEN, or **ARDERNE, JOHN.** To which particular branch of this ancient and numerous family he belonged no means of tracing are left. He was an officer of the Exchequer in the reign of Henry V., under whom and his successor he held the place of clerk and supervisor of the king's works. He received 23*l*. 6*s*. 8*d*. for making the tomb of Henry V. in Westminster Abbey; and various sums were advanced to him for the repair of the Tower of London and the palace of Westminster, and for building the prison in Wallingford Castle. In 7 Henry VI. he was appointed with William Fitz-Harry to enquire respecting certain jewels, gold, and silver which had been conveyed into the castles of Picardy without the king's licence; and so late as July 1443 he was a clerk of the works sent to York to superintend the repairs of 'all that was drowen down belongyng to the church of York,' being the property of the archbishop which had been destroyed in a popular commotion, and which the Earl of Northumberland had been awarded to restore. (*Devon's Issue Roll,* 376, 384, 385, 436; *Acts Privy Council,* iii. 54, 243, 329, v. 309, *and Introd.* cxxiii.)

On February 5, 1444, 22 Henry VI., he was constituted a baron of the Exchequer, an office which seems to have been granted to him as an honourable retirement from active life, as there is no later notice of his name.

His services were requited by the grant of the custody of the priory of Elyngham in Hants, and the manor of Totyngbek in Surrey, at small reserved rents, which were afterwards assigned by the king to the support of Eton College. (*Rot. Parl.* v. 48.)

ARDEN, or **ARDERNE, PETER,** was not improbably the son of the above John Arderne. In 18 Henry VI. he was deputy of William de la Pole, Earl of Suffolk, the chief seneschal of the king in his duchy of Lancaster. (*Plumpton Corresp.* liii.) He took the degree of the coif on February 14, 1443, 21 Henry VI., during the two years after which his name frequently occurs as an advocate in the cases recorded in the Year Books. He was afterwards made one of the king's serjeants, and was raised to the office of chief baron of the Exchequer on May 2, 1448, 26 Henry VI., and on June 7 following was constituted also a judge of the Common Pleas; thus, like three of his predecessors—Cokayne, Babington, and Juyn—holding both places at the same time. (*Rot. Pat.* p. 2, m. 9.)

On the accession of Edward IV., 1461, being then a knight, his patents for both offices were renewed, and he continued to act in the double capacity till September 10 in the following year, when a new chief baron being substituted for him, he retained the judgeship of the Court of Common Pleas, and fines were acknowledged before him so late as Easter 1467. From a case in the Year Book 3 Edw. IV., p. 6, in which he is called 'late chief baron of the Exchequer,' and now justice of the Common Bench *et secundar,'* it would seem that he also remained in the Exchequer as second baron; but the meaning of the title is not very clear. He had a grant of a tun of wine for his life, which was excepted from the act of resumption passed in 4 Edward IV. (*Rot. Parl.* v. 528.) He died on June 2, 1467.

He and his wife Catherine founded a chantry in the church of Nettleswell, in Essex; and another was endowed by him in the neighbouring parish of Latton, the manor of which belonged to him, where a monumental brass now lies over his grave. (*Morant's Essex,* ii. 439; *Inquis.* p. m. iv. 382; *Gough's Monum.* ii. 216.)

ARDEN, RICHARD PEPPER (LORD ALVANLEY), belonged to the same family, but the connection has not been precisely traced. His great-grandfather was Sir John Arderne of Harden; his grandfather was John Ardern, buried at Stockport in 1703; and his father was John Arden of Arden, who by his marriage with Mary, daughter of Cuthbert Pepper, Esq., of Pepper Hall in Yorkshire, had two sons, of whom he was the younger.

He was born at Bredbury in 1745, and, after attending the grammar-school in Manchester, was admitted a gentleman commoner of Trinity College, Cambridge, in October 1763, having in the preceding year been entered at the Middle Temple. He was named seventh wrangler in 1766, when he took his B.A. degree, and was elected in 1769 fellow of his college, when he proceeded M.A. His application did not prevent him from joining in society; and in the True Blue Club, as well as in his college, his gaiety and good-humour gained him the favour of his fellow-students. By the heads of the house he was no less respected, and was entrusted by them with the revision of their statutes. Called to the bar in 1769, he took his seat in the court of Chancery, and, according to the practice of the time, joined the Northern Circuit. At a very early period he was, by family interest, appointed recorder of Macclesfield, near his native place; and in 1776, when he had been scarcely seven years at the bar, he was constituted one of the judges on the South Wales Circuit, in conjunction with Daines Barrington. His chambers were in Stone Buildings, Lincoln's Inn, and it is said that those occupied by William Pitt were on the same staircase; but as he was fourteen years the senior of the great minister, the intimacy that existed between them must have commenced at a later period, and certainly could not have influenced his nomination to the Welsh judgeship, nor probably his advance to the honour of a silk gown, which he received in Michaelmas Term 1780, while Lord Thurlow was chancellor. This advance, especially considering that he was no favourite with his lordship, shows that he had gained a considerable standing at the bar. What was the origin of their mutual dislike is not very clear, since they were equally free of tongue and careless of observation. The chancellor was fond of snubbing Mr. Arden, and one day, the latter having in the excitement of his argument, in a cause in which the age of a woman was in dispute, said to the opposing counsel, 'I'll lay you a bottle of wine she is more than forty-five,' at once, seeing the indecency, apologised to the chancellor, declaring that he forgot where he was. Thurlow growled forth, 'I suppose you thought you were in your own court,' alluding to the free and easy manner in which the proceedings in the Welsh courts were then conducted.

When Lord Shelburne became prime minister on the death of the Marquis of Rockingham, in July 1782, Mr. Arden, no doubt by the instrumentality of his friend Mr. Pitt, then chancellor of the Exchequer, was, notwithstanding the disinclination of Lord Thurlow, appointed solicitor-general on November 7, and was elected M.P. for Newton in the Isle of Wight. On the dissolution of that ministry in the following April he of course retired; but in nine months, the Coalition Ministry being in their turn discarded, and Mr. Pitt entrusted with the conduct of affairs, Mr. Arden was restored to his place, in December 1783. He only held it for three months, when, on March 31, 1784, he succeeded Lord Kenyon, both as attorney-general and chief justice of Chester. During this time he strenuously opposed Mr. Fox's East India Bill, and was an unflinching supporter of Mr. Pitt in his memorable contest with the coalesced opposition immediately after his appointment. For the new parliament of May 1784, which confirmed the ministerial power, Mr. Arden was returned member for Aldborough in Yorkshire, and in those of 1790 and 1796 he represented Hastings and Bath respectively. In all the parliaments he was a frequent and effective, though not a brilliant, speaker. He exposed himself in 1784 to some just censure by proposing a loose enactment with reference to elections; and by indiscreet acknowledgments he laid himself open to the sarcastic taunts of his opponents. The shafts of the writers of the 'Rolliad' and of the 'Probationary Odes' were levelled against him, as well for his want of law as of personal beauty. But the good-humour with which he met these attacks disarmed them of their sting and silenced his assailants.

On the elevation of Lord Kenyon he succeeded as master of the Rolls, on June 4, 1788, notwithstanding Lord Thurlow's opposition, which was only silenced by a significant hint from the king. The animosity and disrespect of the defeated chancellor were unhandsomely shown against the new master on all occasions, and particularly by calling upon Mr. Justice Buller to sit for him when he was ill, or idle, which was frequently the case. The master of the Rolls was too good-natured and too wise to retaliate. He discreetly avoided the slightest appearance of any angry feelings existing between the judges; and the only revenge he took for the chancellor's dislike was by proving his antagonist mistaken in his estimate of him; and indeed at the same time surprising the legal profession by the excellent manner in which he decided the various cases in equity that came before him, his judgments being far the best that were pronounced in the court of Chancery during the period in which he sat. He was knighted at his promotion. After enduring philosophically the roughness of Thurlow for four years, he worked for nine more with complete harmony under Lord Loughborough, on whose retirement from the Seals, and the elevation of Lord Eldon to the chancellorship, Sir Richard was on May 30, 1801, constituted lord chief justice of the Common Pleas, which Lord Eldon had vacated. On the 22nd of that month he had been created a peer by the title of Lord Alvanley, a manor in the parish of Frodsham in Cheshire, which had been in the possession of his family ever since the reign of Henry III.

He performed the judicial functions of his new position with great efficiency and learning for nearly three years; when to the regret of all he was suddenly seized, while presiding in the House of Lords for Lord Eldon, with a violent attack of inflammation, which after three days of suffering terminated fatally, on March 19, 1804. He died at his house in Great George Street, Westminster, and was buried in the chapel of the Rolls.

As a judge he falsified the jokes of his early opponents by proving himself a good lawyer and a conscientious administrator of justice; and to the last he preserved the character he had borne from the commencement of his career, of a hearty, good-humoured, and entertaining companion, and of a simple, steady, and kind-hearted friend. His advance in dignity had not the common effect of rendering him either proud, formal, or reserved; neither did it have the better effect of sobering the quickness of his temper. His occasional irritabilities indeed made the French interpretation of his name, 'Mons. Poivre Ardent,' peculiarly applicable. These however were slight failings, and did not prevent his being universally esteemed, or being looked upon with affection and respect by 'troops of friends,' one of the earliest, most intimate, and steady of whom was the great minister William Pitt.

In 1784 he married Anne Dorothea, daughter of Richard Wilbraham Bootle, Esq., of Lathom Hall in Lancashire, the father of the first Lord Skelmersdale. This lady survived her husband till 1825. Of their children the two eldest sons held the title successively, which on the death of the latter in 1857 became extinct. (*Lives by Jardine, W. C. Townsend, &c.*)

ARESEY, or D'ARCY, NORMAN DE, was the fifth in descent from his namesake the founder of this noble family, whose chief seat was situate at Nocton in Lincolnshire, where he had thirty-three lordships from the immediate gift of the Conqueror. He was the son of Thomas de Aresey and Johanna, who afterwards married William de Lauda, and succeeded his father in 7 John, giving to the king a fine of six hundred marks, two palfreys, and a complete horse for livery of his lands. (*Rot. de Fin.* 340, 349.) He accompanied the king on his expedition to Ireland in 1210 (*Rot. de Præst.* 187-229); but, joining in the confederacy against him in 1215, his lands were seized into the king's hands for the remainder of that reign; nor were they restored under Henry III. till he had given hostages for his future fidelity. (*Rot. Claus.* i. 249, 311, 320.) That his subsequent conduct was quiet and loyal appears from his receiving in 3 Henry III. the confirmation of the grant of a market at his manor of Nocton, which had been made to him in 16 John (*Rot. Pat.* 201), presenting to his sovereign a goss hawk of Norway for the privilege, and from his being one of those employed in 9 Henry III. to conduct the quinzime, which had been collected for the county of Lincoln, to Northampton. (*Rot. Claus.* ii. 74.)

On the circuits which were appointed on August 1, 1234, he was placed as a justice itinerant for Lincolnshire; and in 1245, for the counties of Nottingham and Derby.

He died shortly before October 16, 1254, when livery of his lands was ordered to be made to Philip, his son and heir. (*Excerpt. e Rot. Fin.* ii. 196.)

This barony fell into abeyance among daughters about 1340. Another barony of Darcy was created in a younger son of one of Norman's successors, in 1332, which also fell into abeyance in 1418. A third barony was created in 1509 in another branch, one of whose descendants was advanced to the earldom of Holderness in 1682, which became extinct in 1778; but the barony of Conyers, which was also in the family, descended to the deceased earl's daughter, who married the Duke of Leeds. (*Dugdale's Baron.* i. 369.)

ARFASTUS, or HERFASTUS, by birth a Norman, was one of the chaplains of William the Conqueror before his invasion of England. He had previously been a monk in the Abbey of Bec in Normandy, where, from the greater ignorance of his brethren, his slender pretensions to learning made some show. It seems, however, that he was merely *luscus inter strabones*, a blinkard among the blind; and it is related that after Lanfranc had raised the character of the abbey, Arfastus, as one of the duke's chaplains, visited it in great pomp, when Lanfranc, soon discovering his deficiencies, somewhat rudely ridiculed and exposed them; an indignity which Arfastus revenged by procuring his temporary disgrace and banishment. (*Godwin de Præsul.* 60.)

After the Conquest, Arfastus continued in great favour with King William, and became his chancellor. The date of his appointment does not appear; but, as it is certain that he held the office at Whitsuntide §1068, his name with that addition being attached to the charter which William then granted to the church of St. Martin - le - Grand in London (*Monast.* vi. 1324), it is not unlikely that he was William's first chancellor. Dugdale and his followers, Oldmixon and Lord Campbell, give the date of 1073 to the same charter, an inspection of which will prove their error. Thynne, Philipot, and Spelman state it correctly.

He was chancellor in the following year, 1069, being an attesting witness to King William's charter to the church at Exeter (*Monast.* ii. 531); and probably retired about the middle of the year 1070, when he received the bishopric of Helmham in Norfolk—not Helmstadt in Germany, as

Oldmixon and Lord Campbell erroneously assert.

In 1075, in consequence of the mandate of the council of London that the episcopal sees should be transferred from villages to the most eminent towns in their dioceses, this see was removed to Thetford; and the bishop made a subsequent attempt to fix it at Bury. Alleging that a great part of the revenues then belonging to the monastery there had been alienated from the see by his predecessor, he took active measures against the Abbot Aylwin; but that dignitary, claiming to be exempt from the episcopal jurisdiction, strenuously defended the rights of his house; and the contest, notwithstanding the bishop's interest with the king, was decided against him in 1081. There are letters of Pope Gregory VII. to Lanfranc abusing Arfastus plentifully for his behaviour to the monks of Bury.

Thynne places Arfastus as chancellor again in 1077 (*Holinshed*, iv. 348), and Philipot (p. 4) mentions Maurice in the same year, but as they neither cite any authority, and as there is proof that Maurice was chancellor probably in 1078, and certainly in 1081, when the above decision was pronounced between the bishop and the abbot, no sufficient ground is offered for reliance on this statement.

That he was not deprived, however, of the royal favour is evidenced by the grant which he received of all the churches and various other possessions in Thetford; where, assisted by Roger Bigod, he rebuilt the church of St. Mary, and spared neither pains nor cost in augmenting and improving his see.

He died in 1084, and was buried in his cathedral. Weever (785, 827) has preserved his epitaph. He bequeathed his possessions among Richard and his other sons, who, no doubt, were born long before the promulgation of the decree of the synod of Winchester in 1076, enforcing the celibacy of the clergy. (*Blomefield's Norfolk*, i. 404; *Norwich*, i. 463.)

ARGENTINE, REGINALD DE, is named by Fuller in his 'Worthies of England' as sheriff of the counties of Cambridge and Huntingdon in 6 & 7 Richard I. An entry, however, on the roll of 5 John discharges him from the payment of ten marks 'de dono,' which he had promised for the sheriffalty of those counties, because he never had that office, but only accounted as sub-sheriff to the chancellor (*Madox*, i. 206), William de Longchamp, Bishop of Ely. He was no doubt, therefore, an officer of the court at that time, and appears to have held Wilmundele Magna, in Hertfordshire, 'per serjentiam pincerniæ.' (*Rot. Cur. Regis*, 162.)

His name stands at the end of a list of five justices itinerant who held pleas in Essex and Hertfordshire in 1193 (*Madox*, ii. 20), of which counties he was afterwards sheriff; and his presence as a justicier in the court at Westminster in the following reign is evidenced by fines in 3 & 4 John, 1201–2, being levied there before him. (*Hunter's Preface*.)

At the close of the reign he joined the barons and lost his lands; but restitution was made in 1 Henry III., on returning to his allegiance.

ARGENTINE, GILES DE, was the grandson of the above Reginald de Argentine, and the son of Richard, who was one of the justiciers in Normandy under King John, and steward of the household under Henry III. (*Madox*, i. 63, 156.) In 1247, on his father's death, Giles did homage for the lands held in capite, and paid 10*l*. for his relief. (*Excerpt. e Rot. Fin.* ii. 5.) He was a knight of great valour, and had been actively engaged in the wars with the Welsh, by whom he was taken prisoner in 16 Henry III.

He was made governor of Windsor Castle, and in 1253 he was at the head of the justices itinerant for Berkshire, Oxfordshire, and other counties, and was present in that year as judge at Alton, in Hampshire, when William de Insula took John le Falconer by the throat in open court. (*Abbrev. Plac.* 132.)

After the battle of Lewes, when the king fell into the hands of the barons, Giles de Argentine joined the latter, and was selected as one of the council to govern the realm. While in this office, the chancellor, Thomas de Cantelupe, during a temporary absence, delivered the Seal to Ralph de Sandwich, to be kept by him under the seals of Giles de Argentine and two others. The manor of Witherfield, which he had lately purchased, was seized from him as a rebel, and given back to Robert de Stuteville, its original proprietor. (*Cal. Rot. Pat.* 39.) He died in 1283, leaving a son, Reginald, who was summoned to parliament in 25 Edward I.; but neither he, nor any of his descendants, afterwards. (*Dugdale's Baron*. i. 615.)

ARMYN, WILLIAM. *See* W. ERMYN.
ARNULPH. *See* RANULPH.
ARUNDEL, EARL OF. *See* W. DE ALBINI.

ARUNDEL, ROGER, was of the clerical profession, and is generally mentioned with the addition of 'Magister.' He was one of the fermers of the see of York during its vacancy at the end of the reign of Henry II., and he and his colleagues account for it up to 1 Richard I. (*Madox*, i. 309, 655.) In that year he held pleas with Hugh Pusar, Bishop of Durham, and others, as a justice itinerant in Yorkshire, and in the ninth year of that reign performed the same duty in all the northern counties. (*Pipe Roll*, 9, 84.) In the following reign he acted as a

c 2

justicier, his name appearing on fines levied before him in 4 and 8 John. (*Hunter's Preface.*)

He died a few years afterwards, and his property must have been of considerable amount, as in 15 John his nephew, Thomas de Holm, paid a fine of 500 marks and five palfreys for having his land in Yorkshire and Leicestershire. (*Rot. de Fin.* 491.)

ARUNDEL, or FITZ-ALAN, THOMAS DE, the latter being his family name; but according to the common practice of the time, especially among the clergy, he adopted that of Arundel, from his birthplace or his father's title. He was the third son of Richard, Earl of Arundel, and Eleanor his second wife, who was the fifth daughter of Henry Plantagenet, third Earl of Lancaster, and the widow of John, Lord Beaumont. Born about 1352, and educated for the priesthood, he soon found the benefit of his noble connections, by being made Archdeacon of Taunton in 1373, and Bishop of Ely in 1374, before he was of canonical age for either preferment.

Attached to the party of the Duke of Gloucester, he assisted that prince in rectifying the misgovernment of King Richard, and opposing the unworthy favourites of that unfortunate monarch. On his application to the chancellor, Michael de la Pole, Earl of Suffolk, for the restoration of the temporalities to the Bishop of Norwich, the proud earl rebuked him, saying, 'What is it, my lord, that you now ask of the king? Seems it to you a small matter for him to part with the temporalities, when they yield to his coffers 1,000*l*. a year? Little need has the king of such counsellor to his loss.' Whereupon Bishop Arundel thus roundly retorted: 'What is it that you say, my lord Michael? Know that I desire not of the king that which is his own; but that which, by the counsel of you and such as you, he unjustly detains from other men, and which will never do him any good. If the king's loss weigh with you, why did you greedily accept 1,000 marks per annum when you were made an earl?' On the disgrace of that earl, Arundel was appointed chancellor, on October 24, 1386 (*Rot. Claus.* m. 35), and in the following month was passed the act which placed the royal authority in the hands of eleven commissioners. In the next parliament he presided, when his predecessor, and the Duke of Ireland, Alexander Neville, Archbishop of York, Chief Justice Tresilian, and Nicholas Brambre were charged with high treason. One of the immediate effects of their conviction was his own appointment to fill the vacant archbishopric of York, the pope's bull for his translation to which was dated April 3, 1388. (*Rymer,* vii. 574.)

Soon after the temporalities of the archbishopric were restored to him he retired from the chancellorship, being succeeded in that office on May 3, 1389, by William of Wykeham, Bishop of Winchester, on whose resignation, on September 27, 1391, the Great Seal was again entrusted to him. (*Rot. Claus.* ii. m. 5 and m. 34.) On each of his appointments as chancellor he received a patent from the king, stating that, as he has no domains or villas pertaining to his bishopric near London, where his people, family, and horses can be entertained while he is in the office of chancellor, the king assigns to him for his livery, by virtue of his office, the villas and parishes of Hakeney and Leyton on the first occasion, and Stebenhyth on the second, so that his people, &c., may be entertained therein liberally and without impediment. (*Rymer,* vii. 553–708.)

There is a curious instance of the application of the word 'uncle' in a letter to him from Henry of Lancaster, Earl of Derby (afterwards Henry IV.), who addresses him as 'his very dear and very entirely well-beloved uncle.' (*Proceedings in Chancery, temp. Eliz.* i. 7.) The actual relationship between them was this: Henry's mother, Blanch, the wife of John of Gaunt, was the granddaughter of the archbishop's grandfather, through his mother's elder brother, and was consequently the archbishop's first cousin. It thus appears that it was the custom in that age for children to designate the first cousins of their parents as uncles and aunts, a practice which is still prevalent in Wales.

On the death of Archbishop Courteneye he was translated, in 1396, to the province of Canterbury, being the first instance of a removal from one archbishopric to the other. He thereupon resigned the Great Seal, on September 27 (*Rot. Claus.* p. 1, m. 22), having held it on this second occasion for five years. With the attainment of the highest ecclesiastical position, his prosperity forsook him for a time; for shortly afterwards King Richard, having a subservient parliament, threw off the control of the party of the Duke of Gloucester, and determined to punish all who were implicated in the proceedings against his former favourites. One of the first victims was the archbishop's brother, Richard, Earl of Arundel; and immediately after his condemnation the Commons proceeded, on September 20, 1397, to impeach the archbishop of high treason. The principal charge against him was that, being the chief officer of the king, his chancellor, he aided and advised in making the commission in the tenth year of the king's reign, by which the royal authority was, in fact, placed in the hands of certain lords therein named; and that he put the said commission in execution. This fact, which the archbishop could not deny, being declared to be treason, he was thereupon convicted and sentenced to be banished the realm, and all his property to be confiscated. The king gave him six weeks to depart (*Rymer*, viii. 31), with a promise to recall him, which he treacherously broke.

Arundel joined Henry of Bolingbroke in his invasion of the realm, and, on King Richard's arrest, was placed for a third time in the chancellorship, in August 1399, holding it, however, for little more than ten days (*Hardy's Catal.* 46), when the Seal was placed in the hands of John de Scarle, the master of the Rolls.

The renunciation of the unfortunate king was made to the archbishop at Conway, and afterwards repeated at Westminster on September 30, when Henry was led by the primate to the vacant throne. He opened the parliament six days afterwards, and was in a short time replaced in full possession of the temporalities of his see.

The attempts hitherto made for the suppression of the opinions of Wickliffe having proved ineffectual, a statute was passed in 2 Henry IV. authorising the burning of heretics. Although probably the archbishop was no more guilty than the rest of his episcopal brethren in obtaining this detestable act, he cannot be acquitted of the disgrace of being the first who pressed its execution, and who sullied the English annals by bringing a man for his opinions to the stake. Within a month after the passing of the statute he delivered a priest named William Sautre over to the secular power to undergo the horrible sentence (*Rymer*, viii. 178), and ere his career was closed some others suffered under his condemnation.

His strenuous support of the rights of the Church was prominently shown in the bold resistance he made to the representation of the Commons to the king in 1405, that the royal necessities might be supplied by seizing on the revenues of the clergy. The king, fearful of offending that order, gave effect to the reprimand pronounced by the archbishop, and the Commons took nothing by their motion. He enjoyed King Henry's favour during the whole of his reign, and was for the fourth time constituted chancellor on January 30, 1407. His continuance in office on this occasion was only till December 21, 1409 (*Rot. Claus.* m. 35 and m. 3); but after an interval of about two years he was restored to it, on January 5, 1412, and retained it till the death of the king on March 20, 1413. (*Hardy*, 48.)

Thus did he hold the highest judicial office of the realm no less than five times, the aggregate extent of his tenure being eleven years and about eight months, out of twenty-six years and a half from his first appointment. We want little further evidence to show that he must have been a man of great vigour and capacity for business; and he left a high reputation as well for learning and intelligence as for personal courage.

That he was not re-appointed chancellor on the accession of Henry V. seems to have arisen from a dispute with the king while he was Prince of Wales. Of this we have no other notice than a reference which was made to it in the instructions given to certain lords in the following reign, with the view of accommodating the contention between the Duke of Gloucester, and Beaufort, Bishop of Winchester, the chancellor. It is apparent that the prince had then required Arundel's removal; and it looks as if he took the opportunity of his accession to effect his object.

His death took place at the rectory of Hackyngton on the 20th of the following February, at the age of sixty-two, and he was buried in Canterbury Cathedral. His disease was an inflammation of the throat, which increased so much as to prevent his taking any nutriment. The superstition of the time traced its commencement to the day on which he pronounced sentence against Sir John Oldcastle, Lord Cobham, for heresy, and asserted that it was a judgment of God that he, who had deprived the people of food for the soul, should himself suffer for want of food for the body. But, whatever may be our own opinions of these persecutions at the present time, we must not judge harshly of those who, brought up with strictness in their religious tenets, would naturally look with abhorrence on, and use every effort to exterminate, those ridiculers of their faith whose constant endeavour was to subvert the principles in which they had been educated, and to slight the authority they had been accustomed to reverence. His liberality to the three cathedrals over which he presided shows that a love of money was not one of his vices; and some Latin verses in 'his grace and commendation,' quoted by Weever (226), afford evidence of the estimation in which he was held by his contemporaries.

ASCWARDBY, ADAM DE, as Abbot of Bardney, was placed in the commission for justices itinerant for Lincolnshire, dated August 1, 1234, 18 Henry III. He was elected abbot in 1225, and resigned the office in 1237. (*B. Willis*, i. 30.)

ASHE, ALAN DE, is noted as an advocate in the Year Books of the early part of the reign of Edward III. He was made a baron of the Exchequer on July 2, 1346, and he had his robes in 21 Edward III. (*Abb. Rot. Orig.* ii. 192), but beyond that date all the published records are silent about him.

ASHHURST, WILLIAM HENRY, derived his name from Ashhurst, near Wigan, in

Lancashire, where his family was resident soon after the Conquest. It comprehended some famous knights, members of parliament, and merchants, one of whom was Sir William Ashhurst, lord mayor of London in 1693. Henry Ashhurst, one of the younger branches, settled at Waterstock in Oxfordshire, and was created a baronet by James II. in July 1688, but the title became extinct in 1732. The Waterstock property then devolved on Diana, the only child of Sir Richard Allin, Bart., of Somer-Leighton in Suffolk, by the daughter of Sir Henry Ashhurst; and by her marriage with Thomas Henry Ashhurst, vice-chancellor of the Duchy of Lancaster, and recorder of Liverpool and Wigan, the representative of the elder branch, the two estates became united. They were the parents of several children, the third son, and eventually the heir, being William Henry, the future judge.

He was born at Ashhurst on January 25, 1725, and was educated at the Charter House. After his admission to the Inner Temple in 1750 he practised as a special pleader under the bar, one of his pupils being his future colleague on the bench, Mr. Justice Buller. In 1754 he became a barrister, and in that character pursued an honourable career for twenty years, during which he was appointed to the office of auditor of the Duchy of Lancaster.

On June 25, 1770, he was appointed a judge of the King's Bench, and was then knighted. He sat in that court no less than twenty-nine years, preserving the character of an impartial administrator of justice, and a careful expounder of the law, united with a benevolent heart and polished manners. His countenance was expressive of the kindness and amiability of his disposition, but, being rather lank, was often made a subject for the barristers' jokes. Mr. (afterwards Lord) Erskine is said to have indited this complimentary couplet on him:

> Judge Ashhurst, with his *lantern* jaws,
> Throws *light* upon our English laws.

He was twice entrusted with the custody of the Great Seal as one of the commissioners—the first time from April 9 to December 23, 1783, during the interval between the two chancellorships of Lord Thurlow; and the second from June 15, 1792, to January 28, 1793, between that lord's retirement and the appointment of Lord Loughborough. While acting in that capacity he still performed his duties in the King's Bench, and during the latter period he delivered, in November 1792, a very able address to the grand jury of Middlesex on the subject of the seditious meetings and corresponding societies which were consequent on the French Revolution.

On June 9, 1799, being then in the seventy-fifth year of his age, he resigned his seat on the bench, and retired to his residence at Waterstock, where, eight years afterwards, he died, on November 5, 1807.

By his wife, Grace, daughter of John Whalley, of Oxford, M.D., and sister of Sir John Whalley Smythe Gardiner, Bart. (whom he married after he became a judge), he left several children, the descendants of whom now reside on the family estate and hold a distinguished position in the county. (*Croke Family*, 377, 559; *Blackstone's Rep*. 719.)

ASKE, RICHARD, belonged to a younger branch of an ancient Yorkshire family settled at Richmond. His grandfather Robert Aske of Aughton was high sheriff of the county in 1588; his father was John Aske of the same place; and his mother was Christiana, daughter of Sir Thomas Fairfax of Denton, knight. When admitted a member of the Inner Temple in 1606 he was described as of Rides Park in that county. He was called to the bar on January 29, 1614, but did not reach the post of reader till Lent 1636. His connection with the Fairfaxes probably introduced him to the notice of the parliamentary leaders. He was employed by Mr. Stroud, one of the imprisoned members in 1629, to argue against the return to the *habeas corpus*, and in several actions on that side of the question. (*Rushworth*, i. *App.* 18; *Cal. State Papers* [1625-6], 47.) On October 18, 1643, the Commons specially recommended him to the lord mayor and aldermen of London to be elected one of the four pleaders; and in June 1644 both houses presented him with the valuable office of coroner and attorney of the king in the King's Bench. (*Journ.* iii. 380, 521, 535.) He was next selected as junior counsel on the trial of King Charles; and on June 1, 1649, the parliament nominated him one of the justices of the Upper Bench, making him a serjeant for the purpose. (*State Trials*, iv. 1054; *Whitelocke*, 405.) For a short time, in June 1655, he was the only judge in the court (*Style's Rep.* 452), and on June 23, 1656, he died. (*Peck's Desid. Cur. B.* xiv. 29.)

ASKEBY, ROBERT DE, as early as 25 Edward I., 1297, held some office in the Chancery, all the writs of Privy Seal directed to the chancellor after the king's embarkation to Flanders being then delivered into his custody. (*Parl. Writs*, i. 56.) Like his fellows, he was an ecclesiastic; and as parson of Dokelington in Oxfordshire he was engaged in a suit with the abbot of Osney about tithes. (*Abb. Placit.* 246.) Again, in 35 Edw. I., he was rector of Hale in Lincolnshire, and in the parliament at Carlisle he was one of the proctors for the Bishop of

Lincoln. In 8 Edw. II. it was his business to make up the parliament roll; and in the following year, when he was appointed one of the receivers of the petitions for England, he is styled a clerk in the Chancery. (*Rot. Parl.* i. 189, 290, 350, 460.)

On August 16, 1316, the chancellor, John de Sandale, being about to proceed from York to London, on the business of his election to the bishopric of Winchester, was desired to leave the Great Seal in the custody of William de Ayremynne, the keeper of the Rolls, under the seals of two clerks of the Chancery, of whom Robert de Askeby was one. The same course was adopted on November 9, 1317, when the same chancellor went to his bishopric on business; and again, from February 13 to 19, 1318, on the bishop's taking a pilgrimage to St. Thomas of Canterbury; and on March 29, when he went to Leicester. (*Claus.* 10 & 11 Edw. II.)

In the following June, and subsequently under John de Hotham, Bishop of Ely, the new chancellor, the Seal was left in the same manner; with directions to do the business of the Chancery during his absence. Robert de Askeby, however, obtained leave to return home from Northampton on July 20, and his name does not appear later than the following year.

A Robert de Askby was appointed chancellor of Ireland in 15 Edward III., 1341. (*Cal. Rot. Pat.* 140.)

ASTON, RICHARD, belonged to the very ancient family of Aston of Aston in Cheshire, dating from the reign of Henry II., to the head of which Charles I., in 1628, granted a baronetcy. The judge was grandson of the second and brother of the fifth baronet, both named Sir Willoughby Aston. His father was Richard Aston of Wadley, the sixth son of the former; and his mother was Elizabeth, daughter of John Warren, Esq., of Oxfordshire.

As a barrister, he was so successful in his practice that he attained in 1759 the rank of king's counsel; from which he was advanced two years afterwards to the office of chief justice of the Common Pleas in Ireland. Here his career was unfortunate. He found that justice was very loosely administered, it being the common practice for grand juries to find the bills without examining witnesses, but upon the mere inspection of the depositions taken before the committing magistrate. Against this and other irregularities the chief justice naturally remonstrated; but his representations of the illegality of these proceedings produced no other effect than to create a prejudice against him, which was considerably heightened by the rude and overbearing manner in which he delivered his admonitions. These disputes frequently occurring, the judge's position became so disagreeable that he solicited a removal. Accordingly, on the death of Sir Thomas Denison, he bade adieu to his Irish antagonists, and was transferred to the English court of King's Bench on April 19, 1765, being at the same time knighted.

In this new arena his brusque demeanour nearly led to more serious consequences. On a motion relative to a libel, a barrister had the imprudence to make an affidavit that he believed it to be no libel. This being a mere matter of opinion, Lord Mansfield and the other judges good-naturedly overlooked the impropriety, as a foolish ebullition of the lawyer's zeal; but Sir Richard coarsely declared 'that he would not believe such a man's oath.' The barrister, naturally indignant, watched for an opportunity to be revenged, and, tracing the judge's movements, succeeded in detecting him 'in a sale of lottery tickets, presumed to be received as the wages of judicial prostitution in the memorable trials about Wilkes and Junius.' This evidence of guilt was proclaimed in a manly pamphlet and believed by every one, being unanswered and unnoticed by the subject of the charge.

Whether these charges were exaggerated, or wholly true, or partially false, they did not prevent Sir Richard Aston from being entrusted with a more responsible office. On the sudden death of Lord Chancellor Yorke he was appointed one of the commissioners of the Great Seal, on January 21, 1770. As neither of them had had much experience in equity, their rule was not a very distinguished one, and their decisions were supposed to be guided principally by Lord Mansfield's advice. Their trust terminated on January 23, 1771, when Sir Richard resumed his duties in the King's Bench, where he continued till his death, on March 1, 1778.

He married, first, a daughter of—Eldred; and secondly, Rebecca, daughter of Dr. Rowland, a physician of Aylesbury, and widow of Sir David Williams, Bart.; but he left no issue by either.

ASTY, HENRY DE, was connected with the county of Lincoln, in which he held the manor of Burwell, and the advowson of the priory there, paying to the king an annual rent of 100 marks. (*Abb. Rot. Orig.* ii. 348; *Cal. & Inv. Exch.* ii. 22.)

Of his official position there is no account until he was raised to the office of chief baron of the Exchequer, on November 12, 1375, 49 Edward III., in which he remained till December 6, 1380, 4 Richard II., when Robert de Plessington was appointed in his stead. He however was still retained on the bench, and acted as a judge of the Common Pleas until Hilary Term 1383.

ATKYNS, EDWARD. No less than four

generations of this family, which anciently came from Monmouthshire, attained legal honours. Thomas Atkyns was twice reader in Lincoln's Inn in the reigns of Henry VIII. and Edward VI., was judge of the Sheriff's Court in London, and argued the first case in Plowden's Reports. Richard, his son, was a reader in Lincoln's Inn in the time of Elizabeth, and chief justice of North Wales. Richard's third son by Eleanor, daughter of Thomas Marsh, Esq., of Waresby in Huntingdonshire, was Sir Edward, the subject of the present sketch, whose two sons, Sir Robert and Sir Edward the younger, followed him in the same career.

Edward Atkyns was born about 1587, and, having been admitted to Lincoln's Inn on February 5, 1600, he was called to the bar on January 25, 1613, became a governor of the society in 1630, and autumn reader in 1632. In the following year he was engaged as counsel for William Prynne, on his prosecution for writing the 'Histrio-Mastix,' and when Prynne was prosecuted a second time in 1637, in conjunction with Bastick and Burton; the two latter, on their sentences being called in question by the Long Parliament in 1640, prayed that he might be one of the counsel assigned for them. He was included in the last call of serjeants made by Charles I. on May 19, 1640, and there is a patent in Rymer, dated on October 7 following, appointing Serjeant Edward Atkyns a baron of the Exchequer. Dugdale, however, does not mention it, and it is evident that, if it really passed the Great Seal, it was never acted on, for when in February 1643 the parliament submitted their propositions to the king, they requested he would make 'Mr. *Serjeant* Atkyns' a justice of the King's Bench. (*State Trials*, iii. 564, 761, 763; *Rymer*, xx. 447; *Clarendon*, iii. 407.)

The Commons, though then disappointed, soon took upon them to fill the vacancies on the bench, and the serjeant, by their selection, was sworn a baron of the Exchequer on October 28, 1645. He continued till the death of the king, when, objecting to act under the usurping government, he courageously declined to accept a new commission. He was, however, induced afterwards to undertake the judicial office, and on October 19, 1649, he became a judge of the Common Pleas. In May 1654 he was one of the presiding judges on the trial of Don Pantaleon Sa, the Portuguese ambassador's brother, for murder. The subsequent mention of him by Whitelocke (178, 378, 590, 678) as having been made a judge with some others in May 1659 arose, probably, from his being re-appointed by the Long Parliament when they resumed their power. On their second return, after the committee of safety had been dissolved, Atkyns was omitted in the nominations; but on the return of the king, so satisfactory had been the proofs of his loyalty, he was at once placed in his old position as a baron of the Exchequer, and was thereupon knighted. One of his first duties was to sit on the trials of the regicides, and one of the last was to assist in the trial of the rioters in 1668, who were charged with high treason; but in neither did he take a prominent part; and on the subsequent discussion of the judges, whether the latter offence amounted to high treason, he took the merciful view, and several of them were in consequence saved. (*State Trials*, v. 986, vi. 912.)

He died in Michaelmas vacation 1669, at Albury Hall in Hertfordshire, being then above eighty years of age. By his first wife, Ursula, daughter of Sir Thomas Dacre, of St. Andrew le Mott in that county, he had several children, two of whom became judges. His second wife, Frances, daughter of John Berry, of Lydd in Kent, and widow of — Gulstone, of Hackney, whom he married in 1645, and who died in 1703, aged 104, brought him no issue. (*Atkyn's Gloucestersh.* 335; *Chauncy's Herts*, 149, 301; 1 *Siderfin*, 435.)

ATKYNS, EDWARD, second of that name, was the youngest son of the preceding judge. Born about 1630, he became, like the rest of his family, a member of Lincoln's Inn in 1648; and having been called to the bar in 1653, he attained the post of reader in autumn 1675, when he made a very learned reading, and kept a very bountiful table. (*Chauncy's Herts*, 149.) In Easter Term 1679 he was called serjeant, and on June 22 following was constituted a baron of the Exchequer, and knighted. On the trial at York, in July 1680, of Thomas Thwing and Mary Preswicks for high treason, both he and Justice Dolben conducted the proceedings and summed up the evidence with fairness and impartiality.

James II. promoted him to the office of lord chief baron on April 21, 1686, on the removal of Chief Baron Montagu for not agreeing with the royal claim to the dispensing power. It may therefore be presumed that Sir Edward gave in his adhesion to his majesty's opinion; which may very well account for his not being re-appointed at the revolution of 1688, while the omission of his name from the judges, who for that reason were excepted out of the act of indemnity, probably arose from the king's consideration for his brother, Sir Robert Atkyns, who was then appointed to fill his place.

He declined to take the oaths to King William, and retired to his seat at Pickenham in Norfolk, where he spent the remainder of his life in reconciling differences among his neighbours, who had so great a reliance on his integrity and judgment that they confided the most difficult causes to his decision. He died in London of the stone, in October 1698.

ATKYNS, ROBERT, was the eldest son of the first Sir Edward Atkyns, and the elder brother of the second Sir Edward. He was born in 1621. At which of the universities he was educated is disputed, Chalmers (*Oxford*, 60) claiming him as a member of Balliol College, Oxford, and Dyer (*Cambridge*, ii. 437) as of Sidney Sussex College, Cambridge. Admitted to Lincoln's Inn in 1638, he was called to the bar in 1645, became a bencher in 1661, and autumn reader in 1664. Long ere that date he commanded a good business as an advocate, his name appearing frequently throughout Hardres' Reports; and so great was his success in his profession that he was enabled to purchase several estates in Gloucestershire.

Though elected member for Evesham in Protector Richard's parliament of 1659, he was so well reputed for loyalty that on the Restoration he was selected as one of the persons of distinction who were created knights of the Bath at Charles's coronation. About the same time also he was chosen recorder of Bristol, and on the king's marriage was made solicitor-general to the queen. His royal mistress some time after rewarded him with a reversionary grant of the mastership of St. Catharine's, which however did not fall in till the year after his removal from the bench, when the grant was disputed, and the decision was pronounced in favour of his opponent. (*Luttrell*, i. 118, 145.)

He represented Penryn in the parliament that met in 1661, in which he paid assiduous attention to its business; and on the impeachment of the Earl of Clarendon he spoke against its proceeding. (*Parl. Hist.* iv. 381.) Little more than two years after his father's death, in 1669, he was himself called to the bench as a judge of the Common Pleas, on April 15, 1672. During the eight years he occupied that position he presided with fairness and moderation at many of the trials connected with the popish plot, in the existence of which he appears to have fully believed. He had the misfortune to go the Oxford Circuit with Chief Justice Scroggs, to whom his constitutional opinions were so obnoxious that Scroggs retailed them to the court. Whether Sir Robert was dismissed in consequence, or voluntarily resigned on finding that his colleagues and the government were discontented with him, does not precisely appear. But he received his quietus on February 6, 1680; and on his examination before the House of Commons in 1689 he attributed his removal principally to the two chief justices, besides enumerating other causes— viz., his expressed objections against pensions to parliament men; his assertion of the people's right to petition; and his denial of the king's power without parliament to forbid the publication of books. (*Luttrell*, i. 35; *Parl. Hist.* v. 308; *State Trials*, viii. 193.)

The presumed displeasure of the court stirred up the corporation of Bristol to oust Sir Robert from the recordership, first by prepared insults, and next by a prosecution for a pretended riot in an irregular civil election. They succeeded in procuring a conviction; but the judgment was arrested by the court, Sir Robert appearing in person to argue the case. He was however persuaded for the sake of peace to resign the place, which was the real bone of contention.

During the interval of Sir Robert's retirement he naturally took great interest in the political questions that agitated the country. He advised on the line of defence to be taken by Lord Russell, and after the revolution he issued two tracts in assertion of that nobleman's innocence. He resisted King James's attempt to dispense with the penal statutes, in the publication of a lucid argument proving its illegality. He also printed a discourse relative to the ecclesiastical commission issued by that monarch. These and some other of his tracts were collected in a volume, which was published in 1734. It does not appear that he took any further part in promoting the revolution than attending the Lords on their summons as one of their advisers after James's flight. His reputation as a lawyer was so high as to insure the admission of his name into the lists which King William desired the privy councillors to send in, and he was fixed upon to fill the office of lord chief baron. He is said to have declined it for some time, probably from a disinclination to supersede his brother in the place. But when he saw that his refusal would not secure his brother's re-appointment, he was induced to accept the office. In October 1689, the Great Seal being in commission, Sir Robert was appointed speaker of the House of Lords, over whom he presided till March 1693, when Lord Somers was constituted lord keeper. He resigned his judicial seat on October 22, 1694. He lived about fifteen years more, residing quietly at his manor of Saperton, near Cirencester, where, on February 18, 1710, he died, after half an hour's indisposition. (*Luttrell*, i. 490, 522, 593, iii. 386, iv. 547.) There is a monument to the memory of him and his father and brother in Westminster Abbey.

By his first wife, Mary, daughter of Sir George Clerk, of Watford in Northamptonshire, he had no issue. By his second wife,

Anne, daughter of Sir Thomas Dacre, and great niece of his father's wife, Ursula Dacre, he had a son, Robert, the author of the 'History of Gloucestershire,' and a daughter, who married into the Tracy family. (*Atkyns's Gloucestersh.; Jardine's Life.*)

ATKYNS, JOHN TRACY, was the third son of John Tracy, Esq., of Stanway in Gloucestershire (grandson of the third Viscount Tracy), by Anne, the daughter of the above Sir Robert Atkyns. He was called to the bar at Lincoln's Inn in 1732. It does not appear at what date he assumed the name of Atkyns, nor when he discarded it, resuming his father's name; but under the former he received the appointment of cursitor baron of the Exchequer on April 22, 1755, and under the latter he made a codicil to his will in 1768. He died on July 24, 1773; and left no issue by his wife, named Katherine.

He had earned the office to which he attained by the industry with which he devoted himself to taking notes in court. His Reports of cases in Chancery during the whole period that Lord Hardwicke presided there, which he had the boldness to publish without the judge's usual allocatur, in three folio volumes, are highly valued for their correctness, and have passed through several editions. Chief Justice Wilmot (*Life*, 199) describes him in his Diary as 'a cheerful, good-humoured, honest man; a good husband, master, and friend.'

AUBERVILLE, WILLIAM DE, was descended either from a baron of the same name, lord of Berlai in Hertfordshire, or from Roger de Auberville, or Otherville, who held divers lordships in Essex and Suffolk; both of whom flourished in the time of the Conqueror.

His father was Hugh de Auberville, on whose death, in 1130, he was a minor, and was placed under the care of Turgis de Abrincis, who gave three hundred marks of silver and one of gold, with a courser, for his wardship, and for the marriage of Wynanc, his mother, Hugh's widow.

He married Matilda, one of the three daughters of Ranulph de Glanville; and in 1182, 28 Henry II., he was present with that great justiciary at Westminster at the passing of two fines there, and evidently acting as a justicier. (*Hunter's Preface.*)

He was alive in 6 Richard I., 1194–5, being in that year a party to a suit relative to the partition of the inheritance of Ranulph de Glanville, his father-in-law. (*Rot. Cur. Regis*, 24.) In 1192 he founded an abbey of white canons of the Præmonstratensian order, removed from Leyston in Suffolk, at West Langdon in Kent, and endowed it with the whole of that manor and with other lands. In his charter of foundation he mentions a son, William,

and a daughter, Emma; besides whom he had another son, Hugh, who succeeded him. Hugh's son William left only a daughter, named Joan, who married Nicholas de Criol. (*Monast.* vi. 898; *Baron.* i. 499; *Hasted*, ix. 401.)

AUDLEY, or ALDITHLEY, JAMES DE, was the son of Henry de Aldithley, of Heleigh in Staffordshire, who adhered to King John in his troubles, and served the office of sheriff of that county under Henry III., besides being entrusted with the custody of various castles on the marches of Wales. Henry founded the abbey of Hilton in Staffordshire, and died about November 1246, having had by his wife, Bertred, daughter of Ralph de Meisnilwarin, of Cheshire, besides this son, a daughter named Emma, who married Griffin, son of Madoc, lord of Bromefield, a person of great power in Wales.

James, the son and heir, was constituted constable of Newcastle-under-Lyne, and did good service against the Welsh; and in 44 Henry III. was made sheriff of Shropshire and Staffordshire, acting as a justice itinerant into Huntingdon, and other counties. In 1263 he was appointed justice of Ireland, and in the reference made to the King of France relative to the dispute between Henry III. and the barons as to the provisions of Oxford, he was one of the peers who undertook for their sovereign's observance of the award. But in 1265 he joined Prince Edward when he escaped from his keepers at Hereford, and is designated as a rebel in the letters issued on that occasion. (*Cal. Rot. Pat.* 36.)

In 54 Henry III. he went on a pilgrimage to the Holy Land, and died two years afterwards, as it is stated, by breaking his neck, his eldest son James doing homage for his father's lands on July 29, 1272. (*Excerpt. e Rot. Fin.* ii. 574.) His descendants were regularly summoned to parliament; but the male line terminated on the death of Nicholas, the tenth baron, in 1392. The barony, however, survived in John Touchet, the grandson of his sister, in whose descendants it has remained till the present time. The earldom of Castlehaven, in Ireland, was added in 1617, but became extinct in 1777. (*Baron.* i. 747.)

AUDLEY, THOMAS (LORD AUDLEY), was born, according to Morant, of obscure parents at Earl's Colne in Essex, in 1488. It is believed that he went to one of the universities, and, if so, the claim of Cambridge may be preferred, from his afterwards becoming a great benefactor to, if not founder of, Magdalen College there. He studied the law at the Inner Temple, and became autumn reader in 1526. He had held the office of town clerk of Colchester, and had been of the council of the Princess Mary, when she held her court at Ludlow. (*Strickland's Queens*, v. 156.)

The step by which he raised himself to eminence seems to have been the obtaining a seat in the House of Commons in 1523, as member for Essex. He was elected speaker of the Black Parliament, that met in November 1529, which was signalised by the fall of Cardinal Wolsey, and by the first attack on the papal power. So zealous were the speaker's services that he was rewarded by being in 1530 appointed attorney for the duchy of Lancaster, and in 1531 king's serjeant.

It was then the practice for the king to communicate with the speaker and certain members of the house on subjects which he intended to come before them; and in all these matters he found Audley so willing an instrument that it was not long before he secured the speaker's services in a still more prominent position.

On May 30, 1532, he succeeded Sir Thomas More in the possession of the Great Seal, with the title of lord keeper, which on January 24, 1533, was changed to that of lord chancellor. (*Claus.* ii. 16, m. 24.) This office he held for the rest of his life; but during his last illness he sent the Seal to the king, who deposited it temporarily with Sir Thomas Wriothesley during Audley's infirmities, which in a few days terminated in his death. (*Claus.* p. 1, m. 3.)

Audley had the custody of the Seal for nearly twelve years, a period more disgraceful in the annals of England than any of a similar extent. Within it were comprehended the king's divorce from one queen, after a union of two and twenty years, under pretence of a scruple of conscience; the repudiation of another after a few days' intercourse, on the mere ground of personal antipathy; the execution of two others, one of them sacrificed to obtain a new partner; and innumerable judicial and remorseless murders, those of Sir Thomas More and Bishop Fisher leading the dreadful array. Even the Reformation, the foundations of which were laid during this period, though producing such glorious results to this country, brings nothing but disgrace on its active originators. Commenced by a despotic tyrant in defiance of the religious tenets which he had himself advocated and which he still professed, the power of the pope was abjured solely in revenge for the papal refusal to sanction his divorce; his own imposed supremacy was only used to introduce doctrines which it was equally difficult for Catholics or Protestants to adopt, each suffering in turn from the dilemma in which they were placed; and the monasteries were dissolved, not for the professed purposes of purification, but for the sake of the riches they produced to the king's treasury, and to supply the means of rewarding the subservient minions of his power.

Among these, Audley, who all along acted as a thorough tool to the king, and was a most zealous promoter of the suppression, secured no inconsiderable share of the confiscations, 'carving for himself in the feast of abbey lands,' as Fuller humorously remarks, 'the first cut, and that a dainty morsel.' This was the magnificent priory of the Holy Trinity, or Christchurch, in Aldgate, London, founded in the reign of Henry I. He pulled down the great church, and converted the priory into a mansion for himself, in which he resided during the remainder of his life. It was subsequently called Duke's Place, from his son-in-law the Duke of Norfolk. To this were next added many of the smaller priories in the neighbourhood of Colchester. But he was not satisfied with even these extensive spoils; for having fixed his eye on the rich monastery of Walden in the same county, in suing for it he not only lessened its value, but had the meanness to allege that he had in this world sustained great damage and infamy in his serving the king, which the grant of this abbey would recompense. He succeeded in his application, and took his title from the plunder, when the king, on November 29, 1538, raised him to the peerage as Baron Audley of Walden. The order of the Garter was soon after disgraced by his admission among its members.

The consciousness that the odious laws he had introduced might be turned against himself, and that his fate depended on the momentary whim of an inexorable tyrant, may most probably have brought on, only five years afterwards, that illness which terminated in his death on April 30, 1544. His remains were deposited under a magnificent tomb erected by himself in his chapel at Walden, with an epitaph in verse as contemptible as his career. (*Weever,* 624.)

Audley has acquired the character of undoubtedly equalling, if he did not exceed, all his contemporaries in servility. The only circumstance that rescues his name from entire opprobium is his appropriation of part of his ill-gotten wealth to the restoration of the college in Cambridge which Edward Stafford, Duke of Buckingham, had left incomplete, obtaining the King's licence to change its name of Buckingham College to that of St. Mary Magdalen. The only example recorded of his wit is in the application of two of 'Isope's fables' to the case of Sir Thomas More, then in the Tower for conscience' sake, which he related to Alice Allington, Sir Thomas's step-daughter, to show that the conscientious prisoner was only 'obstinate in his own conceite.' One of these was the story of the wise men who hid themselves in caves to avoid the rain which was to make all fools on whom it fell, hoping to rule the fools when the storm was over; but the fools were the more numerous, and would not then be ruled. The other was of the confessions of the lion, the ass, and the wolf, intimating that Sir Thomas's conscience was like that of the ass, who confessed that he had in his hunger taken one straw out of his master's shoe, by which he thought his master had taken cold. More, on receiving a report of the interview, showed that the first tale was a clumsy repetition of one often told to the council by Cardinal Wolsey as a reason for going to war, which fable, he adds, 'dydde in hys dayes help the king and the realme to spend manye a fayre penye.' The second tale he proved not to be Æsop's, and wittily turned the application of both from himself to the relater. (*Singer's Roper*, 127-138.)

His interference with the king to prevent the introduction of More's name into the bill of attainder with reference to Elizabeth Barton, the Holy Maid of Kent, seems to have been dictated rather by the dread of a defeat in the House of Lords than by any friendly interest in More's behalf. His spiteful reminder to Cromwell, to mark in his report to the king that More would not even swear to the succession 'but under some certaine maner;' his omission as president on the trial of the ex-chancellor, when about to pass the dreadful sentence of the law, to put the usual question to the prisoner, 'whether he could give any reason why judgment should not be pronounced against him;' and his ready adoption, after hearing More's argument, of the chief justice's equivocal reply, and hastily proceeding with the sentence, all manifest that he was imbued with the same spirit which prompted his vindictive master to seek for More's destruction.

Of his legal acquirements there is little evidence, beyond the reputation that he gained at the Inner Temple for his reading on the Statute of Privileges, which recommended him to the Duke of Suffolk, his first patron. The judicial decisions in which he was engaged during his period of office were too much mixed up with the political questions of the day, and too clearly controlled by the sovereign whose will he was so ready to obey, to have any weight attached to them. To this perhaps there is one exception; for the privilege that is now exercised by the Commons of punishing those who imprison their own members is said to have been first established under Audley's sanction, in 34 Henry VIII., in the case of George Ferrers, M.P. for Plymouth, for whose arrest the sheriff of London was sent to the Tower.

His interpretations of the law on the various criminal trials at which he presided are a disgrace, not only to him, but to every member of the bench associated with him, while both branches of the legislature are equally chargeable with the ignominy of passing the acts he introduced, perilling every man's life by the new treasons they invented, and every man's conscience by the contradictory oaths they imposed. It is a degradation to the pious and excellent Sir Thomas More to mention him even in contrast with such a man as Audley; and the name of More's less estimable predecessor, Cardinal Wolsey, acquires an added brightness when the moderation of his ministry, during the earlier years of the reign, is compared with the persecuting spirit which prevailed while Audley held the Seals at its close.

Lord Audley was married twice—first to a daughter of Sir Thomas Barnardiston, of Keddington, Suffolk, and secondly to Elizabeth, daughter of Thomas Grey, Marquis of Dorset. He left no son to inherit his title, but by his last wife he had two daughters—Mary, the elder, who died unmarried; and Margaret, thus his sole heir, who became the wife, first, of Lord Henry Dudley, a younger son of John, the first Duke of Northumberland, and secondly of Thomas, Duke of Norfolk, who had been previously married. By the latter she had a son Thomas, who erected on the ruins of the abbey of Walden, which he inherited from his mother, the stately mansion called, in memory of her father, Audley End. He was summoned to parliament by Queen Elizabeth as Baron Howard de Walden, and was created Earl of Suffolk by James I. Both titles still survive in different branches of the family, and were not divided till the death of James, the third possessor, in 1706. The barony then fell into abeyance between Essex and Elizabeth, his two daughters, and continued so for seventy-eight years, being terminated in 1784 in favour of the great grandson of the elder daughter. He was created Baron Braybroke in 1797, but dying in the same year without issue, and no other descendant of Essex, the elder daughter, remaining, the representative of Elizabeth, the younger daughter, was found to be Frederick Augustus Hervey, fourth Earl of Bristol and Bishop of Derry, on whom therefore devolved the barony of Howard de Walden.

The earldom of Suffolk was held till the death of the tenth earl in 1745, when it passed to the descendant of the second son of the first earl, and again in 1783 to the descendant of a younger grandson of the first earl. By this change in the descent, the titles of Baron Howard of Charleton,

Viscount Andover, and Earl of Berkshire, creations acquired by the second son of the first Earl of Suffolk, have been all united to the latter title. (*Baron.* ii. 382; *Morant's Essex*, i. 138; *Lingard; Nicolas's Synopsis.*)

AUMARI, ROBERT DE, was a regular justicier before whom fines were levied at Westminster from 10 to 13 John, and acting in the first of those years as a justice itinerant at Lincoln. In 2 Henry III. he was sent into Kent with Martin de Pateshull and Ralph Hareng to take an assize of novel disseisin. In 9 Henry III. he was one of the justices itinerant in Oxfordshire, and in the following year was appointed to collect the quinzime in that county, for his activity in performing which duty he was pardoned a fine of forty shillings, which he owed for permission to plough up part of his wood of Perye, in Oxfordshire, where his property lay. (*Rot. Claus.* i. 367, ii. 76, 147, 164.) He had been sub-sheriff there in 9 John (*Madox*, ij. 168); and one of his descendants was sheriff under Edward II.

AUNGERVILLE. See R. DE BURY.

AUNTRESEYE, ROGER DE, was one of the justices itinerant for the county of Wilts in 9 Henry III., 1225. (*Rot. Claus.* ii. 76.)

AURE, JOHN DE, who was a justice itinerant in 46 Henry III. and the following year in the counties of Cornwall, Devon, Dorset, and Somerset, had the custody of the two latter counties, with the castle of Shireburn, committed to him six years previously. (*Abb. Rot. Orig.* i. 15.) His family belonged to a place of his name in Gloucestershire, and he was probably the grandson of Walter de Aure, who died in 5 Henry III., and the son of Philip de Aure. (*Madox*, i. 118, ii. 27; *Excerpt. e Rot. Fin.* i. 70.)

AYLESTON, ROBERT DE, then Canon of Salisbury, in 1323, 17 Edward II., was keeper of the Privy Seal, and was employed in various counties to try the sheriffs and others accused of malversation and oppression. On May 21, 1323, he was nominated a baron of the Exchequer; and on July 18, 1326, was sworn in as chancellor of the Exchequer, by which he seems to have vacated his former seat on the bench, as he was not among the barons appointed on the accession of Edward III.

In the fourth year of that reign, however, he resumed his place as a baron, on December 20, 1330, having in the preceding August been collated to the archdeaconry of Berks. He again vacated his seat on the bench, on being constituted treasurer on March 29, 1332; and while he held that office the king made an unsuccessful application to the pope to procure his nomination to the vacant bishopric of St. Andrew's. He continued treasurer till February 3, 1334. There is no other trace of his death than is afforded by the appointment of his successor in the archdeaconry in September 1338, 12 Edward III. (*Parl. Writs*, ii. p. ii. 428; *Le Neve*, 279; *N. Fœdera*, ii. 847, 866.)

AYLOFF, WILLIAM. The town of Wye in Kent belonged in the reign of Henry III. to the ancient Saxon family of Ayloff, whose seat in its neighbourhood was called Bocton-Aloph. In the course of time the representative of the house removed into Essex, where he settled at Hornchurch, and possessed the manors of Brittons, Braxted Magna, &c. William seems to have been the favourite Christian name, and law the ordinary profession, of the family; for among the readers of Lincoln's Inn there are no less than three William Ayloffs from 16 Henry VII. to 10 James I. The first of these was this judge's grandfather. His father, also William, was sheriff of Essex and Hertfordshire; and his mother was Agnes, daughter of Sir Thomas Bernardiston, of Ketton in Suffolk. The judge himself was the second of these readers in Lent 1571. He was called to the bar in 1560; and the degree of the coif was conferred upon him in Michaelmas Term 1577, apparently for the purpose of his being raised to a seat in the Queen's Bench, his judgments in which are duly reported by Dyer, Coke, and Savile. Having been present at the trial of Edmund Campion and others for high treason in November 1581, he was made the subject of a fabricated miracle. In a book entitled 'An Epistle of Comfort to the Reverend Priestes, and to the Honorable, Worshipful, and other of the Laye Sort, restrayned in Durance for the Catholicke Fayth,' it is thus narrated: ' I omitt Judge Alephe,| who sitting to keepe the place when the other judges retyred, while the jurye consulted about the condemnation of Father Campian and his companye, pulling of his glove, founde all his hande and hys seale of armes bloodye without anye token of range pricking or hurte; and being dismayed therwith wipinge it went not away but still returned, he shewed it to the gentle men that sat before him, who can be witnesses of it till this daye, and haue some of them uppon theyr faythes and credites auouched it to be true.' He sat on the bench till his death, on November 8, 1585.

By his wife Jane, daughter of Eustace Sulyard, of Fleming in Suffolk, he had three sons—William, Thomas, and George. William was knighted by King James on his arrival in England; and in 1612 he was further honoured with a baronetcy, which continued in his line till 1781, when it became extinct for want of male issue. (*Wotton's Baronet.* i. 249; *Morant's Essex*, ii. 139.)

AYMER, or DANIEL. 'The Abbot of

'Chertsey' is the second of the 'barones errantes,' or 'inquisitores,' sent by Henry II. in 1170 to enquire into the conduct of the sheriffs, whom Dugdale erroneously designates 'justiciarii itinerantes.'

It is doubtful whether this abbot was Daniel or Aymer, but probably the latter. The date atached to the former in Manning and Bray's 'Surrey' is 1149. (Vol. iii. 217.) The 'Liber Niger Scaccarii' proves that the latter was abbot in 1175, if not earlier. (*Monast.* i. 423.)

AYREMYNNE, WILLIAM DE. Presuming that a patent of 2 Edward III. applies to this bishop, we have his pedigree for three generations. By it divers lands, tenements, and rents in the town of Ayrmyn and elsewhere are confirmed to 'William the son and heir of John the son of Adam the son of Sewall de Ayrmyn' in fee. (*Cal. Rot. Pat.* 102.) Another authority leaves out John, and makes him the son of Adam, and states that his mother's name was Matilda. The family was an ancient one, and was then settled at Osgodby in Lincolnshire. (*Angl. Sacra*, i. 802.) William was the eldest of three sons, his brothers being the under-mentioned Richard, and Adam, Archdeacon of Norfolk.

He is described as one of the clerks in the Chancery in 5 Edward II. (*Rot. Claus.* m. 27), when, from August 27 to September 28, 1311, the Great Seal was placed in the hands of the keeper of the Rolls during the absence of Bishop Reginald, the chancellor, under the seals of him and Robert de Bardelby. When sent by the chancellor to summon to parliament the Abbot of Oseney, who had used every evasion to avoid obeying the writs, he 'cunningly gained access to the abbot in the disguise of a penitent; but as soon as his errand was disclosed, he received such a salutary discipline from the knotted scourges provided by the monks for the benefit of the visitors to the shrine of St. Brithwold as induced him to decamp most speedily, adopting with entire sincerity the character which he had assumed.' (*Palgrave's Merchant and Friar*, 70.)

He was one of the three keepers of the Seal appointed on December 9, 1311, who held it till September 1314. He was clerk of the parliament which met at Lincoln in January 1316, and on the 19th of the following August was raised to the office of keeper or master of the Rolls. (*Rot. Claus.* 10 Edw. II. m. 28.) In this character the Great Seal was frequently placed in his custody, under the seals of three clerks, to perform the duties of the Chancery, when the chancellors, John de Sandale, John de Hotham, and John Salmon, were absent from court. About 1319, having joined the Archbishop of York, the Bishop of Ely, and others at the head of an irregular army of 8,000 men raised for suppressing the incursions of the Scots, they proceeded with so little caution that on being attacked they were quickly thrown into confusion and entirely routed. The two prelates escaped, but William de Ayremynne was taken prisoner (*Holinshed*, iv. 359), and probably remained in durance till the completion of the truce at the end of the year. From the number of priests and monks in the English ranks, the name of the White Battle was given to this encounter. (*Weever*, 792.)

He resigned the office of keeper of the Rolls on May 26, 1324, when his brother, Richard de Ayremynne, received the appointment (*Rot. Claus.* 17 Edw. II. m. 10.) He then became keeper of the king's Privy Seal, and in the following August had the Great Seal again committed to his custody during the temporary absence of Robert de Baldock, then chancellor. (*Ibid.* m. 38.)

His preferment in the Church proceeded no less rapidly than his civil advancement. He held the valuable rectory of the parish of Wearmouth, in addition to which he successively received canonries in the cathedrals of St. Paul, Lincoln, York, Salisbury, and Dublin. Not content with these rich benefices, he obtained through the influence of Queen Isabella, to whose cause he was devoted, the papal nomination to the vacant see of Norwich, to which he was consecrated in France, on September 15, 1325, but the temporalities were then refused by the king. He still remained in France till he accompanied Queen Isabella on her landing in England, in September 1326; and on November 30 the Great Seal, which the king had in the meantime sent to the queen and prince, was placed in the hands of Ayremynne, who, with Henry de Cliff, the keeper of the Rolls, retained it till the king's resignation of his crown, on January 20, 1327. (*Rot. Claus.* 20 Edw. II. m. 3.)

Under Edward III. he held no official position till April 1, 1331, when he was appointed treasurer (*Rot. Claus.* 5 Edw. III. p. 1, m. 13), and filled that office about a year. He presided over the bishopric of Norwich nearly eleven years, when he died at his house at Charing, near London, on March 27, 1336, and was buried in his cathedral.

AYREMYNNE, RICHARD DE, was a younger brother of the above William de Ayremynne. He probably was one of the clerks of the Chancery, as on December 2, 1319, 13 Edward II., he is recorded as being present at a delivery of the Great Seal, and as on May 26, 1324, he was constituted keeper of the Rolls in the place of his brother William. On November 16 following, the Great Seal was placed in his custody, under the seals of two other clerks, till December 12, the chancellor, Robert de Baldock, being then engaged on a mission to the Scots. He held the keepership of the Rolls little more than a year, Henry de Cliff being substituted for him on July 4, 1325. (*Rot. Claus.* 13, 17, 18 Edw. II.) No explanation is given of his removal, but it seems not improbable that it was connected with some suspicions then arising as to his brother's fidelity, as it occurred two days after the death of John Salmon, Bishop of Norwich, whose see was then the subject of contention. On his brother's consecration to that bishopric in the following September, Richard, who was then rector of Elvelay, was made chancellor or vicar-general of the diocese. (*Blomefield's Norwich*, i. 501.)

It seems probable that both he and his youngest brother Adam joined William de Ayremynne in France, inasmuch as the king, in a writ dated March 1326, complains of their refusal to appear before him, and commands the Archbishop of York to enforce their attendance. (*Rot. Claus.* 19 Edw. II. m. 9.)

On March 1, 1327, soon after the accession of Edward III., he is mentioned as clerk of the Privy Seal (*Rot. Parl.* ii. 440), and on the 8th of that month he was appointed custos of the House of Converts for life, an office which had been filled by his brother William. Richard resigned it on June 7, 1339. (*Rot. Pat.* p. 1, m. 13 & m. 10.)

The chancellorship of the church of Salisbury was added to his ecclesiastical preferments on July 16, 1329; and as his successor in this dignity was collated on April 19, 1340, the vacancy was probably occasioned by his death. (*Le Neve*, 215.)

AYSCOGHE, WILLIAM. The Ayscoghes were a very old Lincolnshire family, and the descendants of the judge for more than two centuries resided at Kelsey in that county, several of them filling the office of sheriff. William Ayscoghe's name appears among the advocates recorded in the Year Books from Michaelmas 1429. In about eight years he was called to the degree of the coif, and was raised to the bench as a justice of the Common Pleas two years afterwards, on April 17, 1440, 18 Henry VI. This rapid advance he represented in a petition to the king as a grievance, complaining that 'or he had ben fully two yere in that office at the barre [of serjeant] he was called by your heghnes unto the benche and made justice, by which makyng justice all his winnings that he sholde have hade in the said office of serjeant, and alle the fees that he had in England weere and be cessed and expired to his grete empovryssh-yng, for they weere the grete substance of his lyvelode.' He therefore prayed, as he was 'the porest of alle youre justices,' that the king would grant him for his life certain tenements he specified of the value of 25*l*. 12*s*. 10*d*. a year. He sat in the court for sixteen years, the last fine levied before him being dated at Midsummer 1454, 32 Henry VI. (*Dugdale's Orig.* 46.)

His son married Margaret, the daughter and heir of John Talboys, Esq., of Nuthall, Nottinghamshire.

AYSHTON, NICHOLAS, belonged to a branch of the ancient and knightly family of Ayshton, or Assheton, in Lancashire. He was created a serjeant-at-law in February 1443, 21 Henry VI., and a judge of the Common Pleas about Trinity Term 1444. His judicial career extended through the remainder of Henry's reign, and the first four years and a half of that of Edward IV., the last fine levied before him being on February 3, 1466. (*Dugdale's Orig.* 46.)

B

BAALUN, or BALUN, JOHN DE, was a baron, whose estates were in the counties of Gloucester, Hereford, and Wilts. He was descended from Hameline de Balun, who came into England with the Conqueror, and built the castle of Abergavenny. Reginald, the father of John, in the reign of Henry II. made a fine, with Geoffrey Fitz-Ace and Agnes his wife, of certain lands which had belonged to the said Hameline, for the performance of which the son paid a fine to the king of one hundred marks and a palfrey in 9 John. (*Rot. de Fin.* 382.). In 12 John he accompanied the king to Ireland (*Rot. de Præstito*, 189), but afterwards joined in the wars against his sovereign and forfeited all his lands. On the accession of Henry III. he returned to his duty, and was reinstated in his possessions. (*Rot. Claus.* i. 278, 280, 311.) In 9 Henry III. he was placed on the list of the justices itinerant for the county of Gloucester. (*Ibid.* ii. 76.) On his death, in 1235, his son John paid 100*l*. for his relief, and did homage for his inheritance. (*Excerpt. e Rot. Fin.* i. 276.) Another son, Walter, succeeded his brother in 3 Edward I. (*Abb. Rot. Orig.* i. 24.)

BAALUN, or BALUN, ROGER DE (who was probably of another branch of the same family), was also one of the justices itinerant in 9 Henry III., being appointed for Hampshire. In the next year he died, and was at that time coroner for the county. (*Rot. Claus.* ii. 76, 91.)

BABINGTON, WILLIAM, derived his name from a place so called in Northumberland, where his ancestors are said to have resided from the Conquest. His father was Sir John Babington, of East Bridgeford, Notts, and his mother was Benedicta, daughter and heir of Simon Ward, of Cambridgeshire. They had one daughter and five sons, the elder of whom, Thomas, obtained by marriage the rich manors of Dethick and Leachurch in Derbyshire, and several other rich possessions, which remained in the hands of his posterity until 1586, when Anthony Babington was attainted for high treason, and his enormous patrimony passed to a brother, who dissipated the whole. Another branch of this part of the family settled at Rothley Temple in Leicestershire.

William was the second son of Sir John; and by his marriage with Margery, daughter and heir of Sir Peter Martel, of Chilwell, Notts, acquired that and other considerable property. He pursued the study of the law, and on January 16, 1414, 1 Henry V., he was constituted the king's attorney, an office which in those times was inferior to that of a serjeant-at-law, as we find him summoned on July 11, 1415, to take upon himself the latter degree.

He and some others neglecting to obey the mandate, and there being then an insufficiency of serjeants to carry on the business of the courts, complaint was made in the parliament of November 1417, which issued an order that they should, under a great penalty, immediately take upon themselves the degree. Upon their promise of obedience they had a respite till the following Trinity Term. (*Rot. Parl.* iv. 107.) From that time his name frequently occurs in the Year Books till November 4, 1419, when he was appointed chief baron of the Exchequer. While he held this office he was placed on the bench of the Common Pleas also, on June 30, 1420, holding both places together till May 5, 1423, when he was advanced by Henry VI. to the chief justiceship of the Common Pleas, and held the presidency of that court for thirteen years, retiring on February 9, 1436. He survived his resignation for nineteen years; and dying in 1455, 33 Henry VI., he was buried at Lenton Priory in his native county.

The Reports show his active attention to his legal duties, and tradition speaks of his godly life and conversation. His piety is evidenced by his founding a chantry for two chaplains at the altar of St. Catherine, in the church at Thurgarton in Notts; and by endowing the chantry of Babington in Flaforth, in the same county, with several houses and rents. (*Cal. Inquis.* p. m. iv. 163, 298.)

He left two sons and a daughter, but his branch of the family, part of which was settled at Kiddington in Oxfordshire, has been long extinct.

BACON, JOHN, had almost always the title of Clericus Regis affixed to his name before he was raised to the bench. He held the office of 'custos rotulorum et brevium de banco' certainly from, if not before, May 1288, 16 Edward I.; for among the indentures in the treasury of the Exchequer is one of that date, the earliest existing instrument of the sort, acknowledging the delivery by him of certain 'pedes finium' to the treasurer and chamberlains. These are renewed at various intervals till 1 Edward II. (*Cal. Exch.* iii. 99–112.) In the third year he was directed to have a counter-roll of all pleas. The custody of Ledes Castle in Kent was committed to him in 19 Edward I. (*Abb. Rot. Orig.* i. 66); and two years before he is mentioned as one of the executors of Queen Eleanor, the record calling him 'attorney.' (*Devon's Issue Roll*, 98.) His name appears among the advocates in the Year Book in the earlier years of Edward II.; and in the sixth year, on February 19, 1313, he was advanced to the bench of that court, in which he had so long been an officer; and he continued a judge there till October 16, 1320, when John de Stonore was appointed in his place. (*Cal. Rot. Pat.* 79, 88.)

In 21 Edward I. he received permission to inclose a certain way in Reston in Suffolk (*Cal. Rot. Pat.* 56); and in 9 Edward II. he certified as having possessions in the townships of Shouldham in Norfolk, and of Hemingston, Cleydon, and Akenham, in Suffolk. (*Parl. Writs*, ii. p. ii. 464.)

BACON, THOMAS, there can be little doubt, was of the same family as that from which Sir Nicholas Bacon and Lord Verulam sprang. In 9 Edward II., 1316, he was certified as holding property in Stiffkey, Baconsthorpe, and other places in Norfolk, which formed part of the possessions of those eminent individuals. He was perhaps the Thomas Bacon, son of Sir Roger Bacon, of Baconsthorpe, on whom that knight settled lands in Isbenham, &c., on his marriage with Johanna, daughter of Roger de Antringham, in 8 Edward III.; but the Bacons were even then so numerous that the different branches can scarcely be distinguished.

Thomas is named in the Year Books of Edward III. both before and after he was a judge. He was raised to that dignity in the Common Pleas on September 30, 1329, and received the honour of knighthood. He was removed into the King's Bench on January 28, 1332, and he does not seem to have exercised his judicial functions after

10 Edward III., 1336; but if he were the son of Sir Roger, as above suggested, he was still alive in 1359. (*Parl. Writs*, ii. p. ii. 303; *Dugdale's Orig.* 102; *Rot. Parl.* ii. 68, 447; *Abb. Rot. Orig.* ii. 99, 109.)

BACON, NICHOLAS. The lineage of this family, so eminent in philosophy, literature, and law, has been traced up to one Grimbaldus, a landed proprietor in Normandy, who accompanied his relative William, Earl Warren, into England at the time of the Conquest, and settled at Letheringset in Norfolk. One of his great-grandsons in the reign of Richard I. first called himself Bacon, an Anglo-Saxon word signifying 'of the beechen tree,' in allusion to which he bore for his arms argent, a beech-tree proper. The family widely extended itself over Norfolk and Suffolk, holding considerable estates in the latter county, among which Monks Bradfield and Hesset belonged to the immediate ancestor of the lord keeper. The two last-named judges, John and Thomas Bacon, doubtless came from the same stock, both having property in these two counties.

Nicholas Bacon was the second son of Robert Bacon, of Drinkston in Suffolk, by Isabel, the daughter of John Cage, of Pakenham in the same county. His father, who held the office of sheep reeve to the neighbouring abbey of St. Edmund's Bury (*Masters's Corp. Christi Coll.* 220), had four other children, two sons and two daughters. Thomas, the elder of the two sons, died without issue; and James, the younger, was a salter in the city of London, of which he became an alderman, and served the office of sheriff in 1569. (*Machyn's Diary*, 280, 389.)

Fuller (*Worthies*, ii. 334) says that Nicholas was born not far from the abbey, meaning, no doubt, his father's residence at Drinkston; but most other writers fix the place of his birth at Chislehurst in Kent, and the date about 1509. He was sent very early to Corpus Christi (Benet) College, Cambridge, where he was one of the Bible clerks, and proceeded A.B. about 1527. At the university he formed that intimacy with Sir William Cecil which, afterwards riveted by their union with two sisters, lasted throughout their lives. On leaving college he pursued his studies at Paris, where he remained till 1532, in which year he was admitted a student at Gray's Inn. He was called to the bar in the following year, and was made an ancient in 1536, that office being distinct from the grade of a bencher, to which he did not arrive till 1550. In 1552 he held the office of its treasurer. That his name does not appear as an advocate in any of the reported cases may be accounted for by his holding the office of solicitor to the Court of Augmentations, to which he was appointed in 1537.

In 1540 he is mentioned as the first of the three commissioners to accept the surrender of the collegiate church of Southwell (*Rymer*, xiv. 674, 701); and in the same year he is styled solicitor for the university of Cambridge. His name appears as 'studiant of the lawe,' receiving one shilling a quarter in the accounts of the king's treasurer, during the first three years of Edward VI. (*Trevelyan Papers*), which seems to have been a customary fee to the dependents of the court.

One of the projects which the king had at heart on the dissolution of the monasteries in 1539 was the foundation of a house for the study of the civil law and the formation of young statesmen. A scheme was prepared by Bacon, but the lavish extravagance of Henry having exhausted the means which the monastic lands were to supply, this noble design died in its birth, not, however, without securing the royal favour to Bacon, whose abilities had been manifested in the composition. In 1545 he had a grant of the manors of Redgrave, Bottesdale, and Gillingham, in Suffolk, which had belonged to the monastery of St. Edmundsbury; and in the following year he was promoted to the office of attorney to the Court of Wards, his patent for which was renewed in 1547, on the accession of Edward VI.

During Edward's reign, Bacon purchased the estate of Gorham, which had belonged to St. Alban's abbey, where he fixed his residence, and seeing that all rule and authority in the town of St. Albans was overthrown with the fall of the abbot, he obtained a charter for its incorporation in 1553, being himself nominated high steward. (*Newcome's St. Albans*, 481.)

The accession of Queen Mary made no change in his official position; but he was so well known to be strongly affected to the reformed doctrines that Queen Elizabeth immediately selected him as her principal legal minister. On December 22, 1558, little more than a month after Queen Mary's death, he was knighted, and the Great Seal was placed in his hands as lord keeper. What was the precise difference between the two offices of lord keeper and lord chancellor few could explain, as the powers of both were apparently the same. Doubts, however, having been raised on the subject, it was deemed expedient to put an end to them in the second parliament of this reign, by passing an act declaring that the keeper of the Great Seal always had, and thenceforth should have, the same rights and powers as if he were lord chancellor. (*St. 5 Eliz.* ch. 18.)

In the first parliament, which met on January 25, 1559, Bacon contented himself with procuring an act for the recognition of Queen Elizabeth's title, without repealing

D

the statute by which she had been declared illegitimate, upon the maxim that the crown purged all defects, and 'chusing,' as David Lloyd observes, 'the closure of a festered wound more prudent than the opening of it.' Bills for the restoration of the queen's supremacy, and for the adoption of a reformed liturgy, having been then introduced, the queen commanded a conference to be held at Westminster, under the superintendence of the lord keeper as moderator, to settle some of the controverted points; at which a certain number of bishops and learned men were appointed to argue on each side. Those of the popish party, however, refusing to be bound by the regulations which had been made, no discussion took place, and the bills, after considerable debate in the two houses, were passed in both.

Through the influence of the Earl of Leicester, whose dislike to him is evident from some letters in the State Paper Office (*Cal.* [1547], 235, 237), he was charged with assisting John Hales in the composition of a book showing that the succession of the crown on the death of the queen would devolve on the house of Suffolk. Nothing could be more offensive to Elizabeth than any interference in a question upon which she was notoriously jealous, and the known prudence of Sir Nicholas Bacon might well raise a doubt whether he so far failed in his usual caution as to meddle in so dangerous a matter. It is said, however, that the queen believed the charge, and not only forbade him the court, but even offered the Seal to Justice Anthony Browne, and that Sir William Cecil had some difficulty in persuading her majesty to restore Sir Nicholas to her good graces. Some presumption of the truth of the story is afforded by the following facts. On October 25, 1566, the queen 'understanding the lord keeper's slow amendment' (which looks very like a politic excuse), appointed Sir Robert Catlin, lord chief justice of the Common Pleas, to execute the office of lord keeper in parliament. (*Parl. Hist.* i. 708.) In the same year Anthony Browne was knighted, an honour seldom bestowed by Queen Elizabeth on her puisne judges; and in that session there was much discussion about the succession and the queen's marriage.

The queen's confidence, with this slight interruption, was never withdrawn from him; and to the end of his life he enjoyed her favour so much that he even ventured sometimes to advise her in the form of a joke. When the queen asked him his opinion of one of the monopoly licences, which were then so obnoxiously obtained, he answered, 'Would you have me speak truth, madam? *Licentiâ omnes deteriores sumus.*' He knew also how to gratify her majesty by a happy repartee. When she remarked on one of her visits to his mansion, that it was too little for him, he answered, 'No, madam, it is you that have made me too big for it.' The queen took great delight in the early wit of Sir Nicholas's illustrious son Francis, whom she called 'her young lord keeper.' The great corpulency which oppressed him in his latter years was a subject with which, in good-humoured raillery, she would banter him, saying that 'his soul lodged well;' and he would not hesitate to make this infirmity an excuse for writing to her, instead of paying his personal respects, expressing himself thus: 'Oh! madam, not want of a willing hart and mynd, but an unhable and unweildy body is the onlie cause of this.' (*Cal. St. Papers* [1547], 555.) So burthensome was this increase of his size to him that he could not walk from one court to the other without suffering, and when he took his seat it was the custom for the lawyers to refrain from pleading till he gave the signal with his staff. It was to this infirmity he alluded when he said to a certain nimble-witted counsellor who interrupted him often, 'There is a great difference betwixt you and me; it is a pain to me to speak, and a pain to you to hold your peace.' In hearing the cases in Chancery and the Star Chamber he was remarkable for his patience, always saying; 'Let us stay a little, and we shall have done the sooner;' and his judgments were distinguished by soundness and moderation.

Sir Nicholas's death took place at York House, on February 20, 1579, after holding the Great Seal for above twenty years. His remains were deposited under a noble monument erected by himself in St. Paul's Cathedral, with an inscription penned by the famous George Buchanan.

All writers concur in their estimate of his character, which may be summed up by what Camden (in *Kennet*, ii. 472) says of him: 'He was a man of a gross body, but of great acuteness of wit, of singular wisdom, of great eloquence, of an excellent memory, and a pillar, as it were, of the privy council.' David Lloyd (*State Worthies*, 472) is equally eulogistic, but his conclusion, 'he was, in a word, a father of his country, and of Sir Francis Bacon,' savours something of a bathos. In his motto, 'Mediocria firma,' may be seen the modesty of his nature, to which no doubt may be attributed his long continuance in his position, unharmed, and almost untouched, by the assaults of envy or jealous rivalry.

His residence in London, before he became lord keeper, was at Bacon House in Noble Street, Foster Lane, which he built, and afterwards in York House, near Charing

Cross, which belonged to the Archbishops of York, and stood on the site of the streets now known by the name and title of George Villiers, Duke of Buckingham, to whom it was subsequently granted. The Cursitor's Office in Chancery Lane was erected by him, and he founded a free grammar school at Redgrave, allotting 30*l.* a year for its support, and settling 20*l.* a year for the maintenance of six scholarships in Corpus Christi College, to be chosen out of that school. Towards building the chapel to this college, the place of his education, he was so liberal a contributor that the society presented him with a silver mazer the year before his death. To the library also of his university he was a great benefactor, and his merits were so highly esteemed there that eulogistic verses were published to his memory.

Sir Nicholas married twice. His first wife was Jane, daughter of William Fernley, of West Creting in Suffolk, Esq., whose sister had married Sir Thomas Gresham. By her he had a family of three sons and three daughters. The eldest son, Sir Nicholas Bacon, of Redgrave, was the first person whom King James advanced to the dignity of baronet, on the institution of the order in 1611; and the title has continued uninterruptedly in his descendants to the present time. A second baronetcy, granted in 1627 to Sir Butts Bacon, of Mildenhall in Suffolk, the fifth son of the first baronet, became united to that of Redgrave in 1755; and a third baronetcy, granted in 1661 to Sir Nicholas Bacon, of Gillingham, a grandson of the first baronet, expired for want of issue in 1685.

The date of the death of the lord keeper's first wife does not appear, but his marriage with the second must have taken place some time before he received the Great Seal. She was Anne, daughter of Sir Anthony Cooke, of Giddy Hall, Essex, and sister of the wife of Sir William Cecil, afterwards the renowned Lord Burleigh. Her father, the learned and pious preceptor of Edward VI., had given to all his daughters a scholastic education; some of the fruits of which, in Lady Bacon, were her translations of twenty-five sermons from the Italian of Bernardine Achine, published in 1550, and of Bishop Jewell's Latin Apology for the Church of England, published in 1564. Her children by the lord keeper were Anthony and Francis, and to her early instructions may doubtless be attributed some of that eminence to which they both attained; the former in the short life to which he was limited, for he died early; the latter, not only in his own time and in his own country, but for all ages and throughout the civilised world.

BACON, FRANCIS (LORD VERULAM, VISCOUNT St. ALBANS). No uster interpretation of a man's transactions, no better explanation of his policy, can be found than that which his own letters furnish; and in the following sketch those of Bacon have been carefully used in order to form an impartial and unbiassed judgment of his real character. His letters have been collected in the edition of his works by Mr. Basil Montagu, and to that edition the references are made.

Francis Bacon was born at York House in the Strand on January 22, 1560–1, when his father, Sir Nicholas, had been lord keeper of the Great Seal for two years. His mother, Sir Nicholas's second wife, to whose early instructions the future philosopher owed much of his celebrity, was Anne, one of the five daughters of Sir Anthony Cooke, tutor of Edward VI., another of whom was Mildred, the second wife of Sir William Cecil, soon after ennobled by the title of Lord Burleigh. Anthony and Francis were the only issue of this union.

As no person has claimed the honour of being Francis Bacon's early instructor, it is to be presumed that he spent the first twelve years of his life at home, where, besides the tuition he received from his accomplished mother, he had all the advantage that could be derived from association with the great and learned men who frequented his father's house. In Queen Elizabeth's occasional visits to Gorhambury, she is said to have been so pleased with his readiness that she called him her young lord keeper; and his answer to her question how old he was, 'Two years younger than your majesty's happy reign,' is somewhat too easily accepted as a proof of his early wit.

When little more than twelve years old he was sent with his brother Anthony to Trinity College, Cambridge, then presided over by Dr. Whitgift, afterwards Archbishop of Canterbury. By the master's books, the account with him began on April 5, 1573, but he was not matriculated till June 10; and according to the same account he paid for sizings up to Christmas 1575. (*British Mag.* xxxiii. 444.) It is stated that he left the university from disgust at the system of education then adopted there, and which remained without much alteration to the days of Milton; but it seems unlikely that his father should have been induced to listen to such an objection from a boy not yet sixteen. His removal was probably caused by other plans being formed by him, which had diplomacy for their object; for in the course of the next year he went to France with Sir Amyas Paulet, our ambassador there. Sir Amyas having occasion to send to England, entrusted Bacon with the mission; and the queen is said to have expressed her approbation of the manner in which the youthful messenger performed the duty. After spending not quite two years and a half in France, during which his journeys into the interior seem to have been only those in which he accompanied Sir Amyas as his 'companion,' his father's death in February 1578-9 caused him to be suddenly summoned home from Paris.

At this period he was just turned eighteen; and, as the youngest of a large family, the provision that came to his share was not sufficient for his maintenance without some aid from his own exertions. He naturally selected the law for his profession, and entered himself at Gray's Inn, as his father had done before him. The date of his entry is uncertain, but in a questionable MS. of the society it is stated to be November 1576; and, although at that date he was either gone or going to Paris, it is possible that his father might have entered him previous to his departure; but he could not have kept his terms, or began his studies, till his return in March 1578.

Shortly afterwards he made some suit to his uncle Lord Burleigh, the precise nature of which, from the involved language in which he urged it in two letters addressed to his uncle and aunt (Sept. 16, 1580; *Works*, xii. 471), it is difficult to unravel. It was evidently connected with the law, and required the queen's approval; but his request being, as he acknowledges, 'rare and unaccustomed,' and one which might be deemed 'indiscreet and unadvised,' it will not excite much wonder if a youth not yet twenty should have failed in his application. It has been supposed that a letter without date, which Montagu extracts from the '*Cabala*' (*Works*, xii. 7), thanking Burleigh for his intercession with the queen on his behalf, was written in the next month after this application. But, adverting to the fact that he was then a minor, and to the contents of his subsequent letters to his uncle, it seems to belong to a much later date, speaking as it does of the queen having 'appropriated him to her service,' and of 'her princely liberality,' of which there are no signs at this time, nor were there for a long time after.

He was called to the bar on June 27, 1582, and on February 10, 1586, there is an order that he 'may have place with the readers at the readers' table, but not to have any voice in pension, nor to win ancienty of any that is his ancient, or shall read before him.' (*Lansdowne MSS.* 51, art. 6.) To a copy of this order some notes of Lord Burleigh are appended, being memoranda of the successive favours shown by the inn to Bacon. These are—1. That he had a 'special admittance to be out of commons, sending for beer, bread, and wine;' which, if he was entered in 1576, might be because he was going abroad. 2. 'Admitted to the Grad. Sop., whereby he hath won ancienty of 40, being bar. of 3 years continuance;' which is perhaps explained by the next. 3. 'Utter barrister upon three years study;' by which he would attain seniority over those who were not to be called till their full term of five or seven years' study had expired. 4. 'Admitted to the high table where none are but readers.' None of these memoranda have any date; but the last refers to the order of February 1586, which proves he was then made a bencher.

For this early call to the bench he was apparently indebted to Lord Burleigh, who was himself a member of the inn. He evidently refers to it in a letter to his lordship in the following May, when speaking of 'a late motion of mine own,' wherein 'I sought an ease in coming within bars,' meaning simply within the bar of his inn, which he calls in his letter 'not any extraordinary or singular note of favour.' He then alludes to some reports to his prejudice, upon which his lordship had admonished him. (*Works*, xii. 473.) He entered parliament for the first time in November 1584, as member for Melcombe Regis, but little record of the proceedings remains. In the next parliament, of October 1586, he sat for Taunton, and was 'vehement against the Queen of Scots,' joining in the general demand for her immediate execution; but he does not appear to have taken any other active part in the business of the session. (*Parl. Hist.* i. 837.)

In Lent 1588 he was elected reader, and double reader in Lent 1600, when his reading was on 'The Statute of Uses,' which was not published till seventeen years after his death. In the meantime, however, he had been actively employed in improving and ornamenting the premises of the society; and various sums were allowed to him for planting the gardens, &c. (*Dugdale's Orig.* 273.) He took also a prominent part in promoting those dramatic entertainments for which the society was famous, and with the performance of which the queen was so much gratified.

Soon after this his uncle procured for him a grant of the reversion of the registrarship of the Star Chamber, an office worth 1,600*l.* a year, which 'mended his prospect, but did not fill his barn,' as he truly said; for he had to wait nearly twenty years for the vacancy. (*Works*, xii. 142.) It is evident that during this time he was not getting on in his profession; for none of the reporters as yet mention his name. In a letter to his mother, dated February 18, 1591-2 (*Dixon*, 30), he applies to Lord Burleigh for the wardship of Alderman Hayward's son; and in another application to his lordship, later in the same year (*Works*, xii. 5), he says he was 'one and thirty years' old, and threatens 'if his lordship will not carry him on,' to sell his inheritance and purchase some office of gain that shall be executed by deputy, and so 'become a sorry bookmaker.' Though his views were afterwards altered, his petitions do not seem at this time to aim at any active legal place; for he says, 'I confess that I have as vast contemplative ends as I have moderate civil ends, for I have taken all knowledge to be my province.' His suit not receiving so much encouragement from his uncle as he hoped, he applied to his cousin, Sir Robert Cecil, to press it. At last Lord Burleigh, in September 1593, tells him that he had induced the lord keeper (Puckering), who had been required by the queen to give to her the names of divers lawyers to be preferred, to put him down as a meet man, but not equal to Brograve and Branthwait, two other barristers whom Puckering specially recommended. (*Works*, xii. 72.)

In the parliament of February 1589 he represented Liverpool, and busied himself in promoting the supply, being appointed to confer with the queen's learned counsel thereon. So in the next parliament, in February 1593, being then member for Middlesex, he supported the motion of his cousin Sir Robert Cecil to the same purport (*Parl. Hist.* i. 855, 881); but on a subsequent day he lost the credit he had gained, by objecting to the course proposed for its collection. Discovering his indiscretion, in the remaining debates, which continued for nearly three weeks, he had the prudence to be silent. For this interference he so deeply incurred the queen's displeasure that it had not subsided when he received Lord Burleigh's favourable note, nor till some time after. (*Works*, xii. 28, xiii. 275.)

In April 1593 Sir Gilbert Gerard, the master of the Rolls, died; and though this place was destined for Sir Thomas Egerton, it was kept vacant till his successor as attorney-general was determined on. The list of lawyers to be preferred, which the lord keeper had been required to give, had no doubt reference to this vacancy; for though Sir Edward Coke, as solicitor-general, had the first claim to the succession, it is evident that efforts were making to set aside his just pretensions. Bacon put himself forward as Coke's opponent (*Works*, xiii. 77), endeavouring to break through the accustomed routine; but, as he was then only a young man, and had not yet acquired any reputation either as a lawyer or as a writer, it is difficult to understand on what his claims to an office which had been lately increasing in importance were founded. He could not expect that his legal descent would alone avail him, and his parliamentary character had been lately damaged, so that his principal dependence must have been on the influence of his friends at court. There, in addition to Lord Burleigh and his son, he had enlisted the Earl of Essex in his cause.

The earl became his most strenuous advocate. His letters show that both he and the lord treasurer were zealous pleaders for him; for the queen was strongly prejudiced against him, telling them that none but they thought him fit for the place. It is grievous to be obliged to add that Bacon's letters betray an underhand endeavour to impede Coke's success by depreciating his abilities, and nicknaming him the 'Huddler.' (*Works*, xiii. 74, 75.) History may be searched in vain for an earlier example of such degrading solicitation for legal honours, and for such unworthy attempts to decry a rival; and it is to be lamented that almost all Bacon's future struggles for advancement were sullied by the same unprincipled accompaniments. Coke, however, could not with decency be passed over. He received the appointment on April 10, 1594; and in filling up the office of solicitor-general, which he vacated, a longer delay intervened, and a similar disappointment awaited Bacon.

This vacancy lasted from April 10, 1594, to November 6, 1595, a period of nineteen months. Bacon exerted every effort to get the place, in letters to Lord Burleigh and his son (*Works*, xii. 3, 475, xiii. 78, 85), to Lord Keeper Puckering (xiii. 51, 56), and to the Earl of Essex, to whom he says in one of them, 'The objections to my competitors your lordship knoweth partly; I pray spare them not, not over the queen, but to the great ones, to show your confidence and work their distrust.' (xiii. 77, 79, 82.) Notwithstanding the intercessions of the earl and some others of his friends, and his own petitions and new year's gifts to the queen, both of which she refused to receive, she was so disgusted by his pertinacity that she said if he 'continued in this manner she would seek all England rather than take him' (xii. 109, 166, xiii. 73, 81, 83); and in the end the office was given to Sir Thomas Fleming. Bacon was precluded from complaining of this appointment; for in a letter to the lord keeper, writen in the previous July, he had said, 'If her majesty settle her choice upon an able man, such a one as Mr. Serjeant Fleming, I will make no means to alter it.' (xiii. 56.)

During this contest the degree of Master of Arts was conferred upon him by the university of Cambridge, on July 27, 1594; and at the end of it, Essex, attributing to himself Bacon's want of success, gave him, as some compensation for his disappointment, an estate at Twickenham, which was afterwards sold for 1,800*l*. (vi. 249.) Lord Burleigh's 'constant and serious endeavours to have him solicitor' he gratefully acknowledges; but in the same letter complains that his lordship does not employ him in his profession in any services of his own. (*Works*, xii. 162.) The queen, probably through Lord Burleigh's interest, gave him, in July 1595, 60 acres in Zelwood Forest, and in November she granted him the reversion of Twickenham Park.

In May 1596 Egerton was made lord keeper, but as he still retained the mastership of the Rolls, no vacancy immediately occurred in that office. Bacon applied urgently and unsuccessfully for it (*Dixon*, 383); and Coke and Fleming probably did not aspire to it, as they were common lawyers. They remained in their respective posts during the rest of the reign, so that there was no opportunity for any further intrigue; and Bacon was obliged to content himself with receiving occasional employment in the service of the queen.

He has been represented as the first who held the office of queen's or king's counsel, distinct from the usual law officers; but that he had any special warrant for that purpose from Queen Elizabeth there is no evidence whatever from any existing record. Montagu and Macaulay say that he was so appointed in 1590; but the preceding facts sufficiently prove that it could not have been so early; and the precise time at which he began to be engaged in the queen's causes still remains in doubt. From his correspondence it seems probable that he was first employed shortly after Coke became attorney-general, in April 1594, during the vacancy in the office of solicitor. There is a mysterious expression in a letter to the queen, dated July 20, 1594, which may probably refer to the royal promise so to use him—'a gracious vail, it pleased your majesty to give me.' (*Works*, xiii. 81.) The undated letter to Lord Burleigh, already mentioned, apparently written about this time, seems also to allude to it. Bacon says in it that it is an exceeding comfort and encouragement to him, 'putting himself in the way of her majesty's service,' and 'seeing it had pleased her majesty. . . . to vouchsafe to appropriate me unto her service.' While engaged in his application for the solicitorship, he writes to Foulk Grevil, 'Her majesty had by set speech more than once assured me of her *intention* to call me to her service; which I could not understand but of the place I had been named to.' The queen, however, evidently had no such meaning; and it soon appears that she merely intended him to hold some of her briefs; for Bacon tells his brother Anthony, January 25, 1594-5, that the queen, complaining of his pertinacity, says 'she never deals so with any as with me, *she hath pulled me over the bar*, she hath used me in her greatest causes.' Yet any such regular employment does not seem to be consistent with his absenting himself during that term, as he tells Lord Burleigh he did, in a letter dated in the following March, in the latter part of which he adds, 'This last request I find it more necessary for me to make, because (though I am glad of her majesty's favour, that I may with more ease practise the law, which, percase, I may use now and then for my countenance); yet, to speak plainly, though perhaps vainly, I do not think that the ordinary practice of the law, not serving the queen in place, will be admitted for a good account of the poor talent that God hath given me.' (*Works*, xii. 160, 475, xiii. 83.) There is also a letter from Lord Burleigh to Sir Robert Cecil, dated February 14, 1594-5, which plainly proves that Bacon was not then recognised as a queen's counsel. His lordship is advising his son as to some rents to be reserved on the nomination of the new Bishops of Winchester and Durham, about which he had spoken to the attorney-general (Coke), who, he says, complained of the want of other counsellors, 'seeing ther is but one sargeant and no sollicitor; alledging that ther ar many weighty causes of her majesty to be ordered.' (*Peck's Desid. Cur.* b. v. 6.) Thus it is clear that the queen had not then bestowed on him any distinct appointment; and that the occasional employment he had for the government was not of such importance as to render his absence inconvenient.

Bacon was engaged in some crown causes during the vacancy of the solicitorship; but whether as having the independent management of them, or, as junior barristers are now employed, in assistance of the attorney-general, it is difficult to say. That he was desirous of producing the former impression is evident from two letters to Lord Keeper Puckering in 1594 and 1595, during the vacancy, in which he uses it for the purpose of being urged in furtherance of his suit. Both of them, curiously enough, are dated the same day in each year, September 25. In the first, he says, 'I was minded according to the place of employment, though *not of office*, wherein I serve, for my better direction, and the advancement of the service, to have acquainted your lordship, now before the term, with such of her majesty's causes as are in my hands; which cause . . . I find . . . your lordship of your favour is willing to use for my good, upon that satisfaction you may find in my travels.' In the second he says, 'I hope your lordship will not be the less sparing in using the argument of my being studied and prepared in the queen's causes.' (*Works*, xiii. 53, 58.) From a letter of his to King James, certainly written between July 1606 and June 1607, his own opinion as to the time when he was regularly employed may be collected; for in it he urges his 'nine years' service of the crown,' which would not make it earlier than 1597. (xii. 107.)

Whatever was the date, it is clear he was not a sworn adviser, nor had any patent conferring upon him the office of queen's counsel. That he was not so considered when, at the end of the reign, the names of all the existing officers were sent to King James for re-appointment, is manifest from the omission of his. His activiy and the interest of his friends, however, soon got this omission remedied, by procuring the introduction of his name in a warrant on a totally different subject, dated April 21, 1603, thus: 'Where[as] we have perceaved, by a lettre from our councell at Whitehall, that Francis Bacon, Esq., was one of the learned counsell to the late queen, our sister, by speciall commandment, and that in the warrant granted by us to them for the continewance of their places, he is not named, we have thought good to allow him *in such sort as she did*.' (*Egerton Papers*, 367.) He held this equivocal position for the sixteen following months, for it was not till August 25, 1604, that he obtained a patent formally appointing him 'consiliarium nostrum ad legem, sive unum de consilio nostro erudito in lege,' with such precedence as any other learned counsel, or as he had 'ratione *verbi regii* Elizabethæ, vel ratione warranti nostri;' and granting a fee of 40*l*. a year. (*Rymer*, xvi. 596.) He himself confirms this view of his position by stating in one of his letters to King James, 'You formed me of the learned council extraordinary, without warrant or fee, a kind of *individuum vagum*. You established me and brought me into ordinary; soon after you placed me solicitor.' (*Works*, xii. 402.)

This discussion is of more importance than it at first appears, because the judgment to be formed of Bacon's conduct in pleading against the Earl of Essex before the council, and on his trial in February 1601, mainly depends on the question whether the nature of his employment did or did not impose upon him the necessity for such appearance. So general was the disapprobation it caused that he wrote two letters in defence of himself to Sir Robert Cecil and Lord Henry Howard (nearly copies of each other); and so long did the stigma attach to him that he found it necessary, nearly three years afterwards, to address an elaborate apology for his conduct to the Earl of Devonshire, Lord Lieutenant of Ireland. (*Works*, xii. 168, 171, 245.) His justification is but a lame one, and can have satisfied few; and in pleading the necessity of his place as one of the queen's counsel, he forgets that, if his duty was absolute and compulsory, his position must have been so notorious that blame would not have been imputed, nor exculpation needed.

He was on the closest terms of friendship with Essex; the earl had been his most energetic advocate in his aspirations to the offices of attorney and solicitor general, and had even made his success a personal matter with the queen; and when Bacon had been disappointed of both the places, Essex generously presented him with an estate worth 1,800*l*. All this Bacon is forced to acknowledge, but with respect to the latter he asserts, in his apology, that he said to the earl, 'My lord, I see that I must be your homager, and hold land of your gift; but do you know the manner of doing homage in law? Always it is with a saving of his faith to the king and his other lords; and, therefore, my lord, I can be no more yours than I was, and it must be with the antient savings; and if I grow to be a rich man, you will give me leave to give it back again to some of your unrewarded followers.' The reliance that is to be placed on this minute report of a conversation occurring eight years previously may be estimated by the fact, mentioned in the same letter, that, notwithstanding this flourish about giving back the estate, he had already sold it for 1,800*l*. In such intimate relations as existed between the earl and him, both gratitude and common decency ought to have prevented him from taking any active part in the prosecution, unless absolute necessity compelled him. If there was no such necessity, some strong personal object must have prompted him 'officiously to intrude himself into the business.' To prove a necessity, it would be incumbent on him to show that there was a deficiency of the queen's ordinary legal counsel; but, besides the attorney and solicitor general and Serjeant Yelverton, all of whom assisted at the trial, there were two other queen's serjeants, Daniell and Drew, whose services would have fallen within the regular course of their duties. Even if additional aid was required, there was the whole bar to choose from, and the name of 'Nicholas Kempe, counsellor at law,' is actually recorded as taking some of the examinations. (*Works*, vi. 378, 380.) As to Bacon's services being indispensable, he, according to his own showing, held no office, but a new and extraordinary appointment; and it is a curious fact, that in a memorandum for the order of the arraignment, in Coke's handwriting, preserved in the State Paper Office, Bacon's name was not proposed in the list of counsel to be retained. There is, however, a note from the lords of the council, written the day before the trial, addressed to 'Mr. Francis Bacon, one of her majesty's counsel learned.' (*Jardine's Crim. Trials*, i. 385.) The non-introduction of his name in Coke's memorandum is a strong proof that his appearance was not a necessary part of his duty. No precedent could be urged against his refusal, if he had been earnest in his resistance; and if his aid was demanded by the council, with the knowledge of his connection with the earl, he ought to have felt that they sought rather to degrade than to advance or honour him. The truth, however, peeps out, even in the apology itself, in his avowal that one of his objects was 'to uphold himself in credit and strength with the queen;' and in another place, that as 'she was constant in her favours, and made an end where she began,' he was resolved to endure his condition 'in expectation of better.' The queen was offended at his friendship for Essex, which, he says, he 'saw would overthrow' him; and consequently he pursued a course by which he incurred the contempt of the world, without producing, as the event proved, any advantage for himself. Had he acted a more honourable part, he would have obtained the credit, without incurring the danger, of Sir Henry Yelverton, who refused to plead against his patron Somerset, and Sir John Walter, who indignantly rejected a brief against Sir Edward Coke.

This disposition to undertake anything with a view to his own advantage is still more manifest in the 'Declaration of the Treasons of the Earl of Essex,' published by him soon after the trial. (*Works*, vi. 299.) Though he says that he wrote it at the queen's command, 'her majesty taking a liking to my pen,' it is impossible to believe that he might not have avoided the task. In it he vilifies and blackens the earl's character to such an extent that it is surprising he should so long have associated with him without discovering or suspecting his criminal intentions; and it is curious to observe that in the 'Apology,' after the queen was dead, and when the enemies of the earl were in rather doubtful odour, all the criminal imputations against him are softened down to 'his misfortune,' and the designation of traitor converted into 'the unfortunate earl.'

Another remarkable circumstance connected with this conspiracy requires explanation. Catesby, afterwards known as a principal in the Gunpowder Plot, was also implicated in this, but succeeded in obtaining his pardon by the payment of a fine of 4,000*l*. to the queen. By a letter from the council to Mr. Attorney-General Coke, the queen's orders were conveyed to him to divide the said fine money among 'Mr. Francis Bacon, Sir Arthur Gorges, and Captain Carpenter;' and the share appropriated to Bacon was 1,200*l*. The date of this warrant is August 6, 1601, and it is signed by eight privy councillors. (*Counc. Reg.* xvii. 336.) Whatever may have been the motive with the royal donor inducing this extraordinary gift, it is difficult, under all the attendant circumstances, to draw an inference favourable to the courtly recipient.

To return. Within ten days after the appointment of Sir Thomas Egerton, Essex wrote to him to have a care of Bacon during his absence in Spain. (*Works*, xii. 91.) The new lord keeper had always been friendly to him, and when he was a candidate for the solicitorship had supplied him with observations for the exercise of the office. (*Egerton's Life*, 165.) Bacon's crown business no doubt would, with such patronage, be materially increased, and his personal access to the queen become more frequent. Her majesty even occasionally honoured him with her presence at his house in Twickenham Park.

This advance in favour had the natural effect of making him think more highly of his position than the actual nature of his employment warranted. That he was inclined to encroach beyond his province is apparently from the scene that occurred in the Court of Exchequer about 1601, when, Bacon having moved for the reseizure of certain lands, Coke, probably deeming it an interference with his duties, 'kindled at it,' and insulting and scornful words passed between them. Among the rest, Coke bade him 'not meddle with the queen's business,' and said he 'was unsworn.' (*Works*, vii. 338.)

He had in 1578 been an unsuccessful rival of Coke for the favours of Lady Hatton; and the Earl of Essex, with his wonted zeal, had been his advocate with both her parents. His disappointment in not obtaining the lady, whose violent temper had not yet been displayed, no doubt increased the feeling of jealousy and dislike which he already indulged against Coke, and which did not diminish as years rolled on.

Whatever reputation Bacon may have acquired among his friends and associates by his private studies, he was not yet known to the public in his literary character; nor was it till the year 1598 that he made his first appearance as an author. In it he published his 'Essays,' which, as it was the first, so it was, and still remains, the most popular of his works.

Notwithstanding all the professed advantages he enjoyed from his legal engagements, they did not keep him free from pecuniary pressure. His mother rebuked him for his extravagance in 1592 in setting up a coach, and in 1594 for keeping superfluous horses. (*Dixon*, 31, 58.) His involvements at length became so great, and his credit so small, that he was taken in execution and detained in a house in Coleman Street, in September 1598. He wrote to Lord Keeper Egerton, complaining that it was a breach of privilege, as he was coming from the Tower in 'a service of no mean importance', for the queen. The result of his complaint is not stated; but his letters to Mr. Michael Hickes and Lord Cecil show that his difficulties were still existing at least as late as 1603. (*Works*, xii. 275, 278, 478, 479.)

In the last two parliaments of Elizabeth in 1597 and 1601, he was a frequent speaker in support of the queen's measures; and in the interim he had been rewarded, in 1598, with the rectory of Cheltenham and the chapelry of Charlton-Kings.

No sooner was Queen Elizabeth's death announced than Bacon, instead of waiting with a decent and dignified patience for the king's arrival in London, exerted all his influence among persons high and low to get himself favourably mentioned to the new monarch. To Mr. Davis he writes, 'I commend myself to your love and the well-using my name, as well in repressing and answering for me, if there be any biting and nibbling at it in that place, as by imprinting a good conceit and opinion of me, chiefly in the king, as otherwise in that court.' To Mr. Foules he writes two letters, 'to further my being known by good note unto the king.' Dr. Morison, Sir Thomas Challenor, and Lord Kinloss were addressed in the same degrading style; and the Earl of Northumberland (to whom he volunteered a proclamation on the king's entry), the Earl of Northampton, and even the Earl of Southampton, were reminded of his services. (*Works*, xii. 26, 101, 113, 114, xiii. 24, 29, 48, 63, 102, 115.) It must have been a severe mortification to him to find that he had not been even named among the queen's servants to be re-appointed; but the efforts of his friends were, as already stated, successful in obtaining the warrant issued a month afterwards, allowing him as one of the learned counsel 'in such sort' as Queen Elizabeth did.

That at first he was not much encouraged, notwithstanding a most fulsome letter to the king (*Works*, xiii. 99), may be judged from a letter in July to Cecil, who was now raised to the peerage, wherein he says, 'I desire to meddle as little as I can in the king's causes, his majesty now abounding in council;' 'my ambition now I shall only put upon my pen, whereby I shall be able to maintain memory and merit of the times succeeding.' He, however, accepted the 'prostituted title of knighthood,' as he calls it, with three hundred others, at the coronation on July 23, 1603, and assigns as reasons for doing so, 'because of his late disgrace' (probably another arrest); 'and because I have three new knights in my mess at Gray's Inn commons; and because I have found out an alderman's daughter, a handsome maid to my liking.' (*Works*, xii. 278, 279.) This maid was Alice, one of the daughters and co-heirs of Benedict Barnham, an alderman of London, whose widow had married Sir John Pakington, of Hampton Lovet, Worcestershire. Bacon's marriage with Alice, however, did not take place till three years after, in May 1606, when it is stated that the stores of fine raiment drew deep into her portion. (*Cal. St. Papers* [1603], 317.) The alderman had left a large fortune, the lady's share in which much increased Bacon's means.

Bacon penned another voluntary proclamation touching the king's style, which had the same fate as the former; and in the session of parliament in that and the following year, being member for Ipswich, he made himself usefully prominent, delivering, however, a speech to the king himself, fulsomely flattering (*Works*, vi. 3, vii. 179), and another with reference to him still more so. (*Parl. Hist.* i. 1014.)

The only fact which is recorded of him in the second year of James's reign is his redeeming a jewel on August 21, on the security of which Lord Ellesmere had lent him 50*l.* (*Egerton Papers*, 395.) Four days afterwards he received the patent already mentioned, appointing him king's counsel, with a salary of 40*l.* per annum; and on the same day he had a grant in addition of a pension of 60*l.* for services performed by his deceased brother Anthony and himself. (*Rymer*, xvi. 597.)

He was not employed in the trial of Sir Walter Raleigh, in November 1603, though, besides the attorney-general, Serjeants Heale and Phillips were; nor in any of the crown prosecutions before he was made solicitor-general, the queen's serjeant being the only assistant to the attorney-general. From these omissions of his services some judgment may be formed as to the necessity of his appearing against the Earl of Essex, the remembrance of which was probably the cause of his being now so much in the shade. He occupied the interval in the composition of works, some addressed to the king himself, and others evidently intended for the king's eye, which, however excellent in their matter, contained more of flattery than became a great philosopher. Such were his letter to Lord Ellesmere, suggesting a History of England, and his letter to King James, 'On the True Greatness of the Kingdom of Britain.' To these may be added his tract on the union of the two kingdoms, and his speech on the subject. (*Works*, v. 16, 47, 311, xii. 69.) His leisure was not wholly devoted to politics, for he published his 'Advancement of Learning' in 1605.

In spite of his endeavours to force himself forward, Bacon did not obtain the object of his ambition till he had suffered two, or indeed three, more disappointments. He was passed over in October 1604, when Fleming was appointed chief baron, Sir John Doderidge being made solicitor-general. The death of Sir Edmund Anderson, in August 1605, created another vacancy; but, instead of Coke, Sir Thomas Gawdy was selected to supply it. On the elevation of Coke to the chief justiceship, in June 1606, Bacon was again set aside, Sir Henry Hobart being called upon to fill Coke's place, and Doderidge remaining solicitor-general. In a letter to Mr. Matthew, at the coming in of the king, he comforts himself that 'the canvassing world is gone, and the deserving world is come.' (xii. 230.) But he soon altered his opinion, for on this last occasion he renewed his application to Cecil (now Earl of Salisbury), somewhat depreciating the place, but professing to desire it chiefly to increase his practice. (14, 63.) An expedient was suggested by which Doderidge should vacate the solicitorship on being made king's serjeant. This plan he pressed in letters to the king, recapitulating all his deserts, parliamentary and literary; and also to the lord chancellor. (xii. 94, 105.) Chief Justice Popham died in the following year, and Chief Baron Fleming was put in his place; and instead of either the attorney or solicitor general succeeding, Judge Tanfield was placed at the head of the Exchequer. The opportunity was, however, taken to effect the plan of making Doderidge king's serjeant; and Bacon, after fourteen years' expectance, obtained at last his desire of entering the king's service by being created solicitor-general on June 25, 1607. His prosperous star was then in the ascendant, for in the next year his reversion in the Star Chamber fell in.

One of the first fruits of his leisure in his new office was 'Certain Considerations touching the Plantations in Ireland,' which he presented to the king as a new year's offering. (v. 169, xii. 73.) He was employed also in preparing his great work 'Instauratio Magna,' and in 1609 he published 'De Sapientia Veterum,' a collection of fables of the ancients moralised.

In 1611 he was appointed joint-judge of the Knight-Marshal's Court. His cousin, the Earl of Salisbury, died on May 24, 1612; and within a week Bacon wrote to the king, disparaging his abilities, saying 'that he was a fit man to keep things from growing worse, but no very fit man to reduce things to be much better;' and 'that he was more *in operatione* than *in opere.*' Comparing this with his letters to the earl himself, full of professions of gratitude and admiration, either they must be taken as mere flattery, or this must be regarded as false and ungrateful. In this and other letters to the king, depreciating the earl's powers, he recommends his own 'little skill' in the House of Commons, where he 'was never one hour out of credit,' and asks 'leave to meditate and propound some preparative remembrances touching the future parliament.' (*Works*, xii. 281, 285.) It was not till after the earl's death that he had the courage to publish his essay 'Of Deformity,' in which, under the semblance of a general description of the mental defects it produces, his cousin is ungenerously depicted. (*Dixon*, 165.)

Bacon held the office of solicitor-general rather more than six years, during which several puisne judgeships were filled up, for which it does not appear that he applied. He, however, was not idle. On a vacancy in the mastership of the Court of Wards and Liveries in 1612, he applied to the Earl of Rochester for the post, and felt so certain of success that he ordered new clothes for his servants. Sir Walter Cope, however, for a good sum, got the appointment. The wags laughed and said, 'Sir Walter has got the wards, and Sir Francis the liveries.' (*Dixon*, 176.) He sent one of his petitionary epistles to the king, begging his promise of the 'attorney's place whenever it should be void;' and another when the attorney was ill, indecently reminding his majesty of his promise. (*Works*, xii. 97, 121.) The attorney recovered; but upon the death of Fleming, the chief justice of the King's Bench, in August 1613, Bacon lost no time in urging upon the king that no one but the attorney and he should be thought of for the place, and that, if the attorney should refuse, he should not be passed over, intimating that the king would then have 'a chief justice which is sure to your prerogative.' (286.) But before the vacancy was supplied, Bacon, perhaps fearing that he should be overlooked, took another course, and in a paper presented to the king pointed out 'reasons why it should be exceeding much for his majesty's service to remove the Lord Coke from the place he now holdeth to be Chief Justice of England, and the attorney to succeed him, and the solicitor the attorney.' (vii. 340.) In it his ill-feeling towards Coke again shows itself. He says, 'It will strengthen the king's causes greatly amongst the judges; for my Lord Coke will think himself near a privy counsellor's place, and thereupon become obsequious;' and, 'the remove of my Lord Coke to a place of less profit, though it be with his will, yet will be thought abroad a kind of discipline to him for opposing himself to the king's causes; the example whereof will contain others in more awe.' After this shameless encouragement to destroy the independency of the bench, he proceeds in one breath to speak in terms of disparagement of his deceased relative and his present senior, thus: 'The attorney-general sorteth not well with his present place, being a man timid and scrupulous, both in parliament and other business, and one that in a word was made fit for the treasurer (Cecil)'s bent, which was to do little with much formality and protestation.' Not forgetting himself, however, he takes care to enhance his peculiar adaptation to the office, adding, 'Whereas the now solicitor, going more roundly to work, and being of a quicker and more earnest temper, and more effectual in that he dealeth in, is like to recover that strength to the king's prerogative which it had in times past, and which is due unto it.' This cunning plan was adopted. Coke, two months after, was removed to the King's Bench; Hobart, the attorney-general, went to the Common Pleas; and Bacon obtained, at last, his step of promotion, being made attorney-general on October 27, 1613.

In the two parliaments called by James in the first fourteen years of his reign, the one sitting from 1604 to 1610, and the other from April to June 1614, Bacon was of course an active member. So acceptable had he made himself to the House, and so highly were his qualities as an orator appreciated, that in the second parliament, though it was alleged that no attorney-general had ever been elected a member, he was allowed to sit; but this was not to be a precedent for the future.

Among the first cases in which Bacon exercised his office was his proceeding against James Whitelocke (afterwards the judge) for giving a verbal opinion, or perhaps for arguing as a barrister, on the legality of a commission from the crown. (*State Trials*, ii. 766.) The defendant probably owed his pardon as much to the bungling efforts of Bacon to justify the absurd charge as to the submission which he discreetly made. The attorney's speech in the following year against Oliver St. John, for writing a letter showing the unlawfulness of benevolences (for which he was fined 5,000*l.*), is loaded with flattery to the king, and futile arguments to prove that a benevolence is not a tax. In reference to the sentence on St. John, he adopted the unusual course of corresponding with the king, a novel practice which he introduced, and which he more particularly continued in the cases of Peacham and Owen. (*Works*, xii. 62, 123-136, 289, xiii. 64, 108.)

The charge against Peacham was founded on certain passages contained in a sermon which had never been preached, but which had been discovered in his study. The king was most desirous of proving that the mere writing constituted treason, and Bacon interested himself too much to procure a conviction. He wrote several letters to the king, with accounts of his examinations of the prisoner, to whom torture was applied in the course of them; and he describes his artful management in obtaining the separate opinions of the judges. Coke for some time resisted the 'auricular taking of opinions single and apart;' but eventually was forced to submit to this most unconstitutional mode of prejudging the case.

Then followed the trials connected with Overbury's murder, in the progress of which the letters of Bacon show his desire to assist the king in his determination to convict, and afterwards to save, the principal offenders. (vi. 219-241.)

When Sir Edward Coke resisted the jurisdiction of the Court of Chancery, though Bacon made to the king a fair exposition of the controversy, he could not refrain from aiming a blow at his rival, suggesting that, '*at this time*' he should not be disgraced, though 'this great and public affront' to the chancellor, ' thought to be dying, which was barbarous,' and to the High Court of Chancery, may not, he says, 'pass lightly, nor end only in some formal atonement.' His total disregard for the independence of the bench is further shown in this letter; for he proceeds to say that 'if any of the puisne judges did stir this business, I think that judge is worthy to lose his place: I do not think there is anything a greater *polychreston ad multa utile* to your affairs than upon a just and fit occasion to make some example against the presumption of a judge in cases that concern your majesty; whereby the whole body of those magistrates may be contained in better awe;' and he then recommends 'that the judges should answer it on their knees before your majesty and your council, and receive a sharp reprimand.' (xii. 36.) In the case of the *commendams*, or '*rege inconsulto*,' he not only took the part of the king, but was the principal instigator in calling the judges to account before the privy council (vii. 307-338); a course which has too much the appearance of being influenced by his inveteracy against Coke, especially when connected with a paper he drew up, enlarging on the various 'innovations into the laws' which Coke, as he alleged, had introduced. (vii. 401.)

The chancellor's illness occurring during the progress of these proceedings, Bacon set himself about his usual practice of begging for the reversion of the place. In a letter to the king, dated Feb. 12, 1615-16, he not only boasts of what he would do if he had the Seal, but depreciates those who might be competitors for it; particularly Coke, of whom he says, 'Your majesty shall put an overruling nature into an overruling place, which may breed an extreme: next you shall blunt his industries in matter of finances which seemeth to aim at another place: and, lastly, popular men are no sure mounters for your majesty's saddle.' (xii. 31.) He had taken care to secure the affections, or at least the interest, of Sir George Villiers, the new favourite, by a long paper of instructions how to govern himself in the station of prime minister (vi. 400), containing excellent advice, some points of which it would have been better if he himself had practised. One he evidently forgot: 'If any one sue to be a judge, for my own part, I should suspect him;' for after having sent a paper to Mr. Murray, of the king's bedchamber, 'concerning my honest and faithful services to his majesty,' he applied to Villiers, more than a year before the chancellor's resignation, to get it from him and go on 'with my first motion, my swearing privy councillor, not so much to make myself more sure of the other, and to put off competition.' Six days later he again urges the suit, and repeats it on May 30; and when in the following June the king gave him the choice either to be sworn privy councillor, or to have the assurance of succeeding Lord Ellesmere, he wisely accepted the former (xii. 143, 148, 149), and accordingly took his seat at the board on the 9th of that month.

In the nine months that followed, Bacon kept up a constant correspondence with Villiers, not only on public matters, but with reference also to the favourite's private concerns,—the peerage which was conferred on him in August, and the grants which were made to him to support his title, with the contrivances adopted for his benefit. Even in these, apparently for no other object than that of flattering Villiers, he speaks slightingly of 'the Cecils, father and son.' (xii. 59, 60, 152, 237.) During this time also the proceedings took place which expelled Coke from his seat in the King's Bench, in which Bacon, so far from attempting to moderate the king's groundless anger, took every means to justify and inflame it. The minute of council, and the 'remembrances,' prepared by him, are evidently composed in this spirit. (vii. 307–338, 349.) Nor did he show more generosity towards the chief justice, in reference to the absurd direction as to 'expurging of his Reports' (xii. 304); and if the long letter addressed to Coke, as soon as his disgrace had been rendered certain, was, as it has always been considered, the production of Bacon, it exhibits the mean spirit of triumphing over a fallen adversary, by dwelling, under the pretence of friendly admonition, on all his faults and infirmities, and painting them in colours which, however true to the life, reflect on the writer the imputation of their being dictated by cowardly and malicious feelings. (vii. 296.)

Lord Ellesmere's last days were approaching. During the two previous years he had petitioned to be relieved from his office, but could not prevail on the king till March 3, 1616–17. Four days afterwards Bacon attained the object of his late endeavours, by receiving the Great Seal from the king's hand, with the title of lord keeper. (*Claus.* 16 Jac. p. 15, n. 13.) In another week Lord Ellesmere died; and on May 7 Bacon took his seat in the Court of Chancery, delivering a long speech, stating his resolutions as to the practice. Even in this speech he could not refrain from giving a sly and contemptuous blow at Sir Edward Coke, by saying, in allusion to complaints against judgments at law, 'wherein your lordships may have heard a great rattle and a noise of præmunire, and I cannot tell what.' (*Works*, vii. 243.) He first removed from Gray's Inn to Dorset House in Fleet Street, and soon afterwards to York House in the Strand, where he was born.

On receiving the Seal he immediately wrote to Villiers (now created Earl of Buckingham), in strong terms of gratitude, stating that he 'shall count every day lost' wherein he shall not 'do your name honour in speech, or perform you service in deed.' (xii. 241.) The earl made good use of this promise, by writing numerous letters to Bacon in favour of suitors; and the success of his influence may be judged by the frequency of the applications. (*Passim*, from 314 to 411.) Herein both the earl and the lord keeper forgot the advice formerly given by the one to the other:—'By no means be you persuaded to interpose yourself, either by word or letter, in any cause depending in any court of justice.' (vi. 413.)

Within four months, however, his inveteracy against Coke, and his fear lest his old enemy should again triumph, induced him to interfere in a matter which the earl was likely to resent. He wrote letters to the king and the earl (then both in Scotland), advising against the projected marriage between the earl's brother, Sir John Villiers, and Coke's daughter by Lady Hatton, and representing the inconvenience to the state 'if there be but an opinion of his (Coke's) coming in.' (xii. 245.) From the former he received a severe letter of rebuke; when he not only made an abject submission, but reversed his policy by furthering the match, and altering his carriage towards Sir Edward Coke. (250, 324, 327.) Buckingham was not so easily appeased, but 'professed openly against' him, as reported in a letter from Sir Henry Yelverton, who gave him some sound advice how he should act. The earl was, however, soon afterwards apparently reconciled (331, 342); and not only was the correspondence between them resumed, but Bacon was so entirely restored to the king's favour that he received the title of lord chancellor on January 4, 1617–18.

The king had indeed much reason to be satisfied with Bacon's industry; for there was scarcely a single business touching the royal interests to which he did not devote himself. His correspondence with the king was incessant, comprehending all subjects—political, judicial, and, what seems out of his province, economical. It would be more satisfactory if it did not contain too many proofs of his endeavours to conciliate favour by occasional symptoms of his inclination to stretch, and even to overstep, the law for James's benefit (264, 374), and by perpetual flattery and allusions to the superiority of the king's judgment, which are repeated *ad nauseam*. In reward for his 'many faithful services,' the king, on July 11, 1618, created him Baron Verulam (*Rymer*, xvii. 17); and Bacon three months afterwards applied to Buckingham to obtain for him a grant of the farm of the Alienation, 'a little to warm the honour.' (*Works*, xii. 260.) In the following May he received a more substantial favour in the grant of 1,200*l*. a year (369); and in writing to Buckingham on Dec. 12, 1619, as to the appropriation of the fines imposed on the Dutch merchants for exporting gold and silver coin, he says, 'And if the king intend any gifts, let them stay for a second course (for all is not yet done), but nothing out of these, except the king should give me the 20,000*l*. I owe Peter Vanlore out of his fine, which is the chief debt I owe.' He adds, 'This I speak merrily.' Might he not have said 'advisedly' too? (380.)

His efforts in this case of the Dutch merchants, and in several other proceedings which resulted in fines, were dictated, to all appearance, too much by the desire of relieving the king's pecuniary difficulties, and avoiding the necessity of calling a parliament. To this, however, it became necessary at last to resort; and on November 6, 1620, a proclamation, in the preparation of which, both as to the business to be transacted and the members to be chosen, Bacon took an active part, was issued for one in January, being six years and a half since that assembly had met. Bacon was advanced in the peerage, with the title of Viscount St. Albans. (*Rymer*, xvii. 279.)

Before the parliament met, Yelverton, the attorney-general, who had incurred Buckingham's enmity, was prosecuted in the Star Chamber for introducing certain clauses in a charter to the city of London not authorised by the king's warrant. Bacon, who had been on friendly and familiar terms with him, seems to have pressed the case too hardly against him; and his letters bear the mark of his having been influenced in doing so by a desire to curry favour with Buckingham. (*Works*, vii. 446-9.)

In the preceding October he published his great work, 'Novum Organum,' which he dedicated to the king, who received it most graciously, promising 'to read it thorough with care and attention, though I steal some hours from my sleep, having otherwise as little spare time to read it as you had to write it.' (154.)

The parliament assembled on January 30; and Bacon, after the king had addressed it, made a short speech in the exaggerated style of flattery he was in the habit of using: 'I am struck with admiration in respect of your profound discourses, with reverence to your royal precepts, and contentment in a number of gracious passages, which have fallen from your majesty in your speech,' &c. The Commons were not so well satisfied with the king nor with his system; and, though they were liberal in their grants and respectful in their language, they resolved to investigate and repress the evils under which the people suffered, and to punish the oppressors. For this purpose they formed a committee of grievances, which proceeded to enquire into the various monopolies, patents, and grants of concealments, which had caused so much suffering and injustice. One of the first objects of their attack was Sir Giles Mompesson, a member of their house, the charge against whom was taken into the House of Lords; and while Bacon, as chancellor, was assisting in the examination, the committee of the Commons, on March 15, made a report, charging him with corruption in his high office, which was communicated on the 18th to the Lords.

Bacon seems to have been wholly taken by surprise at this accusation, which was at first confined to two cases. He immediately took to his bed, and addressed a letter to Sir James Ley, then acting as speaker in his stead, praying that the house would maintain him in their good opinion till his cause was heard, and for time to advise with his counsel, and to make his answer. On March 22nd four more charges were brought against him; and on the 26th the parliament adjourned till April 17, three committees of the Lords being authorised to examine witnesses during the recess. On the renewal of the session the lord chamberlain announced that Bacon had had an interview with his majesty, who had referred him to the Lords; and on the 24th Bacon sent them a general confession, stating that, though not communicated formally from the house, he found in the charges 'matter sufficient and full' to move him to desert his defence. This submission not being deemed satisfactory, the Lords resolved that he should be charged with the several briberies and corruptions, and that he should make a particular answer by the 30th. The charges had been greatly increased in number. They consisted of his having in no less than twenty-two instances received bribes and presents amounting to above 11,000*l*., from one or the other, or from both, of the parties in suits before him.

On April 30 he sent in his submission, confessing *seriatim* the receipt of the several sums charged. Some few he acknowledged were given while the suit was depending; but he asserted that others were not presented till after he had pronounced his decree. Some he said were new year's gifts, and some presents towards the furnishing of his house; and that there were 'few or none that are not almost two years old.' On the same day the Great Seal was sequestered, and three days later, Bacon being excused from attending on account of illness, the Lords pronounced sentence against him—of a fine of 40,000*l*.; imprisonment in the Tower during pleasure; incapacity to hold any office, &c., in the state; and prohibition against sitting in parliament, or coming within the verge of the court. They negatived the proposition that he should be suspended from all his titles of nobility during his life.

It has been suggested that Bacon was induced to 'desert his defence' at the instigation of the king and Buckingham. What passed at the interview between the former and Bacon cannot of course be known; but it is not improbable that the king, desirous as he must have been of putting a stop to the investigations of the Commons, lest other persons nearer to him should be implicated, advised him, if he had not a clear defence against all the charges, not to lengthen the proceedings. But it is impossible to read the evidence on which the charges were founded, or even the circumstances alleged by Bacon in extenuation of some of them, without feeling that it must have been more the consciousness of guilt than any tenderness towards other parties that dictated the submission that he offered. Indeed, his own letters, both previous and subsequent to this confession, contradict the idea that he sacrificed himself for the sake of others. In his first letter to the king after the charges were made, though he hopes he may not be found to have 'a depraved habit of taking bribes to pervert justice,' he adds, ' Howsoever I may be frail, and partake of the abuses of the times.' (xii. 66.) In another, petitioning his majesty to save him from the sentence, he ventures to say, ' But because he that hath taken bribes is apt to give bribes, I will go further, and present your majesty with a bribe.' And in a third letter pleading for pardon, he instances Demosthenes, Titus Livius, and Seneca, as having been restored after being condemned for bribery and corruption.

(xiii. 30, 32.) To Sir Thomas May also, in acknowledging and qualifying a present he had received from the Apothecaries, he says, 'As it may not be defended, so I would be glad it were not raked up more than needs. I doubt only the chair, because I hear he useth names sharply.' (xii. 406.) The language in these and other letters cannot by any interpretation be read as that of an innocent man.

After his sentence, he expresses in his letters no compunction for his offence, nor exhibits any shame at his exposure. How little he felt his disgrace appears in a letter to the Bishop of Winchester, in which he talks of his consolation being in the examples of Demosthenes, Cicero, and Seneca, —' all three ruined, not by war, or by any other disaster, but by justice and sentence as delinquent criminals; all three famous writers, insomuch as the remembrance of their calamity is now as to posterity but as a little picture of night-work, remaining amongst the fair and excellent tables of their acts and works.' (vii. 113.) In a letter also to Buckingham he says, ' I confess it is my fault, though it may be some happiness to me withal that I do most times forget my adversity.' (xii. 424.) Neither was it any impediment to his wit, for when Sir Henry Montagu, Earl of Manchester, who had been chief justice, and was lately removed from the office of lord treasurer to the less important one of lord president of the council, expressed to the fallen chancellor how sorry he was to see him made such an *example*, Bacon replied, ' It did not trouble him, since his lordship was made a *precedent*.' (*Aubrey*, 225.)

Camden says his imprisonment lasted but two days, and his letters prove that one of them was the 31st of May, and that the next day he was at Sir John Vaughan's, at Parson's Green. (*Works*, xii. 490, xiii. 31.) From this retirement he was allowed at the end of the month to remove to Gorhambury. (xii. 408.) In the following September he pressed his suit for some assistance in his fallen fortunes; and on October 8 he thanked the king for the remission of his fine, and offered his History of Henry VII. for correction. (410.) The fine was pardoned, and, at the same time, assigned to trustees to prevent the importunity of his creditors; to the passing of which Lord Keeper Williams at first made some objections, the proposed assignment being, as he said, ' full of knavery and a wicked precedent.' From a letter addressed to him by John Selden in February 1621-2, he seems to have at one time contemplated overturning the judgment against him, on account of a doubt he raised whether that meeting of parliament was a legal session; but he received no encouragement. (421.) He continued his importunities till his friends succeeded in March in obtaining a release from his confinement at Gorhambury, and a permission to go to Highgate. Subsequently he tells the Lord Treasurer Cranfield, who was negotiating with him for the purchase of York House, that he had taken a house at Chiswick (425, 428); and at the end of 1622 Buckingham obtained for him an interview with the king. (xiii. 37.) He continued, by means of friends and letters, his correspondence with Buckingham till the marquis, in February 1623, accompanied the prince on his romantic pilgrimage to Spain, when, as he says, 'the better to hold out,' he retired to his chambers in Gray's Inn. (439.) He never returned to York House, which became Buckingham's in 1624.

During the marquis's absence in Spain, Bacon appealed to the king himself in a long letter, which would have been pathetic but that it is over-laboured, praying his majesty to pity him so far as that he 'that hath borne a bag be not now in his age forced in effect to bear a wallet, nor he that desired to live by study may not be driven to study to live.' So reduced does he appear to be, by all his letters, that upon a vacancy in May 1623 he applied to the king, but unsuccessfully, for the provostship of Eton, 'a cell to retire unto.' (xii. 49, 440).

To Buckingham, while abroad (then created duke), his letters were frequent and flattering; and to Mr. Toby Matthew, who was also in Spain, his desires to keep him in the prince's and the duke's remembrance show his anxiety to be again received into favour. On their return in October he offered the duke counsel for his conduct, advising him to 'do some remarkable act to fix' his reputation, and reminding him of an old Spanish proverb, 'He that tieth not a knot upon his thread loseth the stitch.' In January 1624 he tells the duke that he is 'almost at last cast for means;' but it was not till November that he succeeded in getting 'three years advance,' to relieve him of his necessities. Shortly before this he had received a full pardon of his whole sentence. (445, xiii. 7, 70.)

King James died on March 27,. 1625, and King Charles immediately calling a parliament, Bacon had the firstfruits of his full pardon by receiving a writ of summons. Ill health, which had begun to make inroads upon him, prevented him from taking his seat, and for the whole of that year his correspondence was much curtailed. Such letters as remain show a continuance of straitened means. He writes to Sir Robert Pye 'to despatch that warrant of a petty sum, that it may help to bear my charge of coming up to London;' and at the end of the year he tells the Duke of Buckingham that 'his wants are great.' Even as late as January 18, 1626, he shows that his hopes of court favour are not exhausted, by requesting the French ambassador, the Marquis d'Effiat, to procure for him some mark of the queen's goodwill, and to take occasion to whisper something to his advantage in the Duke of Buckingham's ear. (xii. 460, 482, 483.) Indeed, a great part of the industry which he displayed during the five years that intervened between his disgrace and his death seems to have been employed in attempts to regain his lost consequence, and to forward his personal advantage. The rest of his time was consecrated to higher and better purposes. No moment seems to have been unoccupied; and his industry is manifested in the number of his original productions during that period, and in the publication of translations of his 'Advancement of Learning,' with great additions, and of some other of his works, into Latin.

His death was caused by the trial of an experiment whether flesh could not be preserved in snow as well as in salt. For this purpose, while taking an airing with Dr. Witherspoon, the king's physician, he went to a poor woman's cottage at the bottom of Highgate Hill, and bought a hen, the body of which he stuffed with snow. In doing this the chill seized him so suddenly and violently that he was unable to proceed, and was obliged to be carried to the Earl of Arundel's house in the neighbourhood, where the bed in which he was placed being damp, he caught so severe a cold that he died of suffocation. (*Aubrey*, 227.) His last letter, addressed to the earl on his deathbed, is preserved in his works (xii. 274); and his last breath was drawn in the arms of his benevolent relative, Sir Julius Cæsar. He expired on Easter Sunday, April 9, 1626, having exceeded the completion of his sixty-fifth year by nearly three months.

He was buried at St. Michael's Church, at St. Albans, where his faithful friend and servant Sir Thomas Meautys erected a monument, representing him seated in contemplation.

His wife, by whom he had no children, survived him till June 30, 1650, and was buried at Egworth in Bedfordshire, having had for her second husband Walter Doble, of Sussex. (xvi. note H H H; *Hasted's Kent*, v. 304.)

Authors differ in their accounts of Bacon's pecuniary means in the last years of his life. Howell says he died so poor that he scarce left money to bury him. Wilson, the historian, confirms this account, and adds that Lord Brook denied him beer to quench his thirst. Aubrey tells that Sir Julius Cæsar sent him 100*l*. in his necessities; and the perpetual appeals to the king and Buckingham for assistance seem to support the conclusion. But, on the other hand, it is related that the prince, on seeing him in a coach followed by a number of gentlemen on horseback, observed, 'Well, do what you can, this man scorns to go out like a snuff.' Indeed, his income after his pardon was apparently adequate, if prudently managed, to the demands of his station, consisting of his pension of 1,200*l.* and his grant of 600*l.* a year from the Alienation Office, besides the profits of his own estate. Both stories may, however, be true, and their discrepancy accounted for by remembering with what irregularity pensions were then paid, and the negligence and imprudence in money matters generally attributed to him.

As a lawyer Bacon's reputation does not, perhaps, stand so high as it ought. Queen Elizabeth said of him, 'Bacon had a great wit and much learning; but in law showeth to the uttermost of his knowledge, and is not deep;' and hers was probably the echo of the general opinion. But this was said when he was a candidate for the office of solicitor-general; and he had not then had the practical advantages which he afterwards enjoyed. With the knowledge of the principles of law which his writings evidence, it is not improbable that the experience he subsequently obtained made him as finished a lawyer as most of his contemporaries. His acquirements in this branch, whatever they were, were overshadowed by his eminence as a philosopher. He composed several legal treatises, but none of them were published during his life. His speeches which remain are fair specimens of forensic eloquence in his peculiar style, with sufficient mastery of legal learning, and with ample illustration from history.

In the performance of his judicial duties he boasts of extraordinary activity. He tells Buckingham, on June 6, 1617, a month after he took his seat in the court, that there is 'not one cause unheard; the lawyers drawn dry of all the motions they were to make; not one petition unanswered. And this, I think, could not be said in our age before.' (xii. 348.) His boasting might be passed over; but it becomes offensive when depreciating his predecessor, as he does in the following December:—'This very evening I have made even with the causes of Chancery, and comparing with the causes heard by my lord that dead is, of Michaelmas Term was twelve month, I find them to be double so many and one more; besides that the causes which I despatch do seldom turn upon me again, as his many times did.' (340.) Again, in May 1619, he writes, 'Yesterday was a day of motions in the Chancery. This day was a day of motions in the Star Chamber; and it was my hap to clear the bar that no man was left to move anything, which my lords were pleased to note they never saw before.' (xiii. 17.) To this account of his industry should be added his own view of his integrity. When imprisoned in the Tower, he says to the duke, 'I have been .... the justest chancellor that hath been in the five changes since my father's time.' When writing also to Buckingham of his poverty, he says, 'I never took penny for any benefice or ecclesiastical living; I never took penny for realising anything stopped at the Seal; I never took penny for any commission, or things of that nature.' (xii. 466, 490.) The conviction of Wraynham, prosecuted in the Star Chamber for slandering Bacon, who had pronounced a decree against him in favour of his opponent Sir Edward Fisher, would, on the statement of the case, appear to be just, but for the subsequent discovery that the chancellor had shortly afterwards received from Fisher a suit of hangings worth about 160*l.* (*State Trials,* ii. 1059, 1107.)

The biographers of Bacon have been puzzled how to give to his personal character the praise that he merited for his literary attainments and productions. By the former he must be judged of as the man, by the latter as the philosopher; and who but must regret that there is so much of contrast between them? who but must feel that the system of the one was in direct contradiction to the acts of the other? Bacon as a lawyer, a politician, and a man seems to be of a totally distinct nature from Bacon as a writer and propounder of everlasting truths. Considering him solely in the former view, taking by themselves the incidents of his life and the evidences of his character, as interpreted by his own letters, it seems impossible that any biographer can venture to pronounce a eulogy upon him. Are there grounds for it in his ardent desire for place, betrayed through every phase of his career? in his pertinacious and degrading applications for patronage? in his depreciation of his rivals? in his adulation of his sovereign? in his flattery of the favourite? in his double ingratitude to Essex, in pleading against his life and in blackening his memory? in his envy of Coke, and his underhand proceedings against him? in his attacks on the independence of the judges? in his encouragement of the despotic principles of James? in his acceptance, however extenuated, of the bribes which he acknowledged? in the indifference to shame which he exhibited in his disgrace? or in the unblushing attempts which he made to regain his ascendency? Would not these, if he had been a common man and undistinguished as a writer, have been visited with the contempt and indignation they merited? And how does his position as an author alter the feeling thus forcibly impressed? Must it not be more deeply imprinted by the conviction that he was acting contrary to his principles, that he had not the moral courage to withstand any temptation, and that in every act of his life he was pursuing a course which his conscience condemned? There is scarcely a fault of which he has been guilty against which he has not written strongly and truly; and he stigmatises the vices to which he is subject at the very time he is committing them. To himself may be applied the close of his twenty-third essay, 'On the Wisdom for a Man's self:'—'Wisdom for a man's self is, in many branches thereof, a depraved thing. It is the wisdom of rats, that will be sure to leave a house somewhat before it falls. It is the wisdom of the fox, that thrusts out the badger who digged and made room for him. It is the wisdom of crocodiles, that shed tears when they would devour. But that which is specially to be noted is, that those which (as Cicero says of Pompey) are "sui amantes, sine rivali," are many times unfortunate; and whereas they have all their times sacrificed to themselves, they become in the end themselves sacrifices to the inconstancy of fortune, whose wings they thought, by their self-wisdom, to have pinioned.'

BACON, FRANCIS, owed his origin to the same root from which the four preceding judges sprang, being of that branch of the family which settled at Hesset in Suffolk. His great grandparents are stated to be Thomas Bacon, of that place, and Anne Rowse, and his father was John Bacon, of King's Lynn in Norfolk, gentleman.

He was born about 1587, and commencing his legal studies at Barnard's Inn, he pursued them at Gray's Inn, where he was admitted a member in February 1607, called to the bar in 1615, and became reader in autumn 1634. His name does not appear in any of the contemporary reports; his practice probably being in Chancery or the provinces.

In 1636 he had a grant in reversion of the office of drawing licences and pardons of alienations to the Great Seal. (*Rymer*, xx. 123.) In May 1640 he was included in the batch of serjeants then called; and on October 14, 1642, he received the then dangerous promotion to a seat in the King's Bench, his patent being dated at Bridgenorth (*Ibid.* 541), on the king's march towards London, when he was knighted. That the new judge was not obnoxious to the parliament may be inferred from their request in the propositions made to the king, in February 1643, that he might be continued in his place. He does not appear to have joined the king at Oxford, but he attended his duty in his court at Westminster Hall, where, in Michaelmas Term 1643, he was the only judge sitting (*Clarendon*, iii. 407, iv. 342); and on the trial of Lord Macguire for high treason, as the fomenter of the great rebellion and horrible massacre in Ireland in 1641, before that court in Hilary Term 1645, he alone appears to have been present. (*State Trials*, iv. 666.) He is next mentioned in September 1647 as having, with Serjeant Creswell or Cresheld, committed James Symbal and others for speaking words against the king, with whom negotiations were proceeding. He continued to act till the king was beheaded, when he had the courage to refuse the new commission offered him by the Commons. (*Whitelocke*, 269, 378.)

He spent the remainder of his days in privacy, and died on August 22, 1657. By his wife Elizabeth, daughter of William Robinson, he had several children. His eldest son, Francis (who was a reader in Gray's Inn in autumn 1662), raised a handsome monument over his grave in St. Gregory's Church, Norwich.

BAINBRIDGE, CHRISTOPHER (ARCHBISHOP OF YORK), sprang from an ancient family seated at Hilton, near Appleby, in Westmoreland, where he was born. Educated at Queen's College, Oxford, he took his degree in laws, and having been admitted at the same time into holy orders, he obtained early preferment in the Church. This he probably owed to the patronage of Archbishop Morton, his intimate friend, with whom he had suffered under Richard III. He became almoner of Henry VII., and was rector of Aller, in the diocese of Bath and Wells. In 1485 he received a canonry, first in Salisbury and afterwards in York. In 1495 he was elected provost of his college, to which he was a liberal benefactor. In 1497 he was presented to the treasurership of St. Paul's; in 1500 to the archdeaconry of Surrey; and on December 9, 1503, to the deanery of York. He held the latter dignity when he succeeded William Barons as master of the Rolls, on November 13, 1504; and on February 18 in the following year he was made Dean of Windsor. (*Le Neve.*)

He resigned his judicial office on his being preferred to the bishopric of Durham, the temporalities of which were granted to him on November 17, 1507. Scarcely thirteen months had elapsed ere he was translated to the archbishopric of York, receiving the temporalities of that province, which had been in the king's hands for above a year, on December 12, 1508. It was probably in preparation for this removal that he obtained on November 11 a charter of general pardon (*Rymer*, xiii. 171, 233, 235); a caution rendered peculiarly

E

expedient in times when the extortions of informers were almost openly encouraged.

King Henry VIII., soon after his accession, deeming it politic to have a representative at the Roman court, Archbishop Bainbridge was selected for this honourable post; and his patent, with full powers as procurator of the king, was dated on September 24, 1509. (*Ibid.* 264.) How much of his future life he spent at Rome does not precisely appear; but while there he so negotiated in the war against the King of France as to please both his sovereign and the pope, from the latter of whom he received the reward of a cardinal's hat in March 1511, with the title of St. Praxedis. But, not exercising in his own family the prudence which he exhibited in diplomacy, he is said to have fallen a sacrifice to the violence of his temper. Having, in a fit of passion, given a blow to Rinaldo de Modena, a priest in his household, the malicious Italian, according to this account, avenged the insult by poisoning his master. The letters, however, of William Burbank and Richard Pace, the cardinal's secretaries, give a very different complexion to the transaction. They mention nothing about the blow, but state that the priest, in his first confession, acknowledged he was instigated by the Bishop of Worcester, Silvester de Giglis, the cardinal's known enemy, who gave him fifteen ducats of gold, and that, though he was afterwards induced to deny the bishop's complicity in the murder, the doctors and learned men to whom the case was referred would not admit the contradiction. Richard Pace (afterwards principal secretary of state) seems to have had some difficulty in saving the bishop, 'having respect unto him as your grace's orator,' from the execution of the judge's determination that he 'should not only be put in prison, but also suffer torments and be compelled to show the truth.' The poison was administered at Spoleto; and the cardinal's death took place on July 14, 1514. It was announced to the king in a letter, dated the same day, from the Cardinal de' Medici, afterwards Pope Clement VII.; and it is added in another letter that the priest 'smote himself with a small knyff,' and died twelve days afterwards. (*Rymer*, xiii. 404; *Ellis's Letters, First Series*, i. 100–108.)

The archbishop was buried in the cloister of the church of S. Tommaso degli Inglesi at Rome, under a fine monument, still to be seen, with a full-length recumbent figure of his handsome person. He bequeathed 20,000 golden ducats towards the building of St. Peter's. (*Four Years at the Court of Henry VIII.* ii. 146; *Surtees' Durham*, i. lxiv; *Gwinod*, 699, 753, 796; *Ath. Oxon*, ii. 702.)

BALDOCK, RALPH DE (BISHOP OF LONDON), was collated Archdeacon of Middlesex in 1276, 4 Edward I., from which he was raised, on October 18, 1294, to the deanery of St. Paul's, and was elected Bishop of London, February 24, 1304; but, owing to some dispute, his consecration was delayed till January 30, 1306. (*Le Neve*.)

He received the Great Seal as chancellor on April 21, 1307, from Edward I., who died on the 7th of the following July, at Burgh-on-the-Sands; and there is a curious entry on the Fine Roll, showing that Ralph de Baldock, being then in London, and ignorant of that event having occurred, continued to seal writs of course till July 25th. On the following Saturday he received the new king's commands to send him the Great Seal, which was accordingly delivered to the king at Carlisle on August 2. (*Rot. Fin.* 35 Edw. I. m. 1.)

In 3 Edward II. he was appointed one of the ordainers for the management of the affairs of government and the king's household.

He commenced the erection of the chapel of St. Mary in his cathedral, and bequeathed a sum sufficient for its completion. He died at Stepney, on July 24, 1313, and was buried in that chapel. He left some works which proved his devotion to literature; among which was one entitled 'Historia Anglia, or a History of British Affairs down to his own Time.' He also made 'A Collection of the Statutes and Constitutions of the Church of St. Paul's.'

BALDOCK, ROBERT DE, was probably in some way related to the last named, Ralph de Baldock. The earliest notice found of his history is a grant to him, in 15 Edward I., of all the king's right in the knights' fees, which Roger de Clifford held conjointly with John de Crombwell and Idonea his wife, and also of the manor of Shalford in Surrey, lately belonging to Roger, who was attainted. (*Cal. Rot. Pat.* 91.) The next entry, however, is of a different character, being a fine of twenty marks imposed upon him in Durham, in 1306, for some unadvised obedience to a papal precept without notice given to the king and his council, the Archdeacon of Cleveland being at the same time fined 100*l*. for the same offence. (*Abb. Placit.* 258.) It may be presumed, therefore, that Master Robert de Baldock (as he is always called) then held some ecclesiastical benefice in the north.

In 1314, 8 Edward II., he became Archdeacon of Middlesex (*Le Neve*), a dignity which Ralph de Baldock had held twenty years before. Probably at that time, and certainly two years afterwards, he filled some office about the court, as from February 1317 he was regularly summoned to the council and parliaments among the judges and other legal personages. In June 1320 he was keeper of the king's Privy Seal, and in the following year was sent by the king and council, with other solemn envoys, to treat for a peace with the Scots at Bamborough; for his expenses in which mission he was allowed the sum of 60*l.* in the wardrobe accounts. (*Archæologia*, xxvi. 334.) The Despencers, father and son, were then in the height of their ascendency; and, by his connection with their councils, he shared in the aversion with which they were regarded by the nobles and the people.

He was at last raised to the chancellorship on August 20, 1323, 17 Edward II., but had little cause to rejoice in his advancement. Though the defeat and execution of the Duke of Lancaster had produced a temporary quiet, within a few months after he had received the Seal a conspiracy by Roger Mortimer and others was discovered, or invented, the object of which was the murder of Baldock and the royal favourite. Though he escaped from this danger, he could not but experience many misgivings as to the results that were likely to follow from the arrogant indiscretions of Despencer.

He was elected to the bishopric of Norwich on July 28, 1325; but a rumour having reached him that the pope had reserved the presentation for himself, he renounced the election on September 3, an act which speaks well for his moderation, and his anxiety to prevent a collision between his sovereign and the papal court.

Baldock's concurrence in the advice which prompted Edward to fall into the trap laid by the French king, by which Queen Isabella was permitted to proceed to France, and the weak king was induced to give up Guienne and Ponthieu to his son, and to send the latter to do homage for them, is conclusive evidence that he cannot be considered a wise counsellor; for though perhaps the plan had not yet been formed that led to results so fatal to his sovereign and himself, there were sufficient indications of danger at home, and of treachery in the conduct of Charles le Bel, to have induced more cautious proceedings.

The invasion of Queen Isabella quickly followed. She landed on September 24, 1326; and the king, deserted by almost all parties, fled to Wales with the chancellor and the two Despencers. The elder of these was taken and executed at Bristol, and on November 10 the king and his two remaining companions fell into the hands of the queen's friends. The fate of the favourite was soon sealed, and that of the king was delayed till a resignation of his crown had been forced from him. Baldock had been specially denounced in the queen's first proclamation (*State Trials*, i. 35); but, being an ecclesiastic, was committed to the custody of Adam de Orleton, Bishop of Hereford. He remained at Hereford till February following, when he was removed to the bishop's house in London. His prison there was soon invaded by an outrageous mob, who treated him with violence, and thrust him into Newgate, where, after languishing about three months, he died, on May 28, 1327. All his possessions had been previously seized, and among them were the manors of Heibrigge and Tylingham in Essex. (*Abb. Rot. Orig.* i. 304.)

As he was never brought to trial, the precise charges against him do not appear; but in the mandates from the queen and prince, both before and after his capture and death, his name is always united with those of the Despencers, ascribing to them the guilt of estranging the king from his wife and real friends by false suggestions and evil procurement, and designating them as 'enemies of God, of the Church, and the whole kingdom.' Remembering, however, how great was the inveteracy between the contending parties, and how little there is to approve in the conduct of that which was successful, we must hesitate before we join in the popular cry against the chancellor without more substantial proof of his demerits. (*Parl. Writs*, ii. p. ii. 472; *Abb. Rot. Orig.* i. 303.)

BALDOCK, ROBERT, son and heir of Samuel Baldock, of Stanway in Essex, bore the same arms as those of the last-named, Robert de Baldock, Bishop of Norwich. He became a student at Gray's Inn on July 7, 1644, was called to the bar on February 11, 1651, and arrived at the degree of ancient in May 1667. By his first marriage, with Mary the daughter of Bacqueville Bacon (of the family of Redgrave), he became settled at Great Hocham in Norfolk. This lady died in 1662, after which he took a second wife, whose name has not been handed down. Of his early legal career there is no other record than that of Roger North (233), who says of him that he 'had wit and will enough' to contrive a fraudulent conveyance. In 1671 he was recorder of Great Yarmouth when Charles II. visited that place, on which occasion he was knighted. He took the degree of serjeant in Michaelmas Term 1677, and was included in the list of king's serjeants on the accession of James II.

He was one of the counsel employed by the crown in the prosecution of the seven bishops; and showed himself so thoroughpaced a stickler for prerogative that within a week after the trial he was appointed, on July 6, 1688, a justice of the King's Bench, in the place of Sir John Powell, who had declared his opinion in favour of the prelates (*Bramston's Autobiog.* 311); but he had very little opportunity of showing his judicial qualifications, for before the next term the Prince of Orange had embarked for England, and the king was on the point of flying from it.

In the new appointments he of course was not thought of. He died three years afterwards, on October 4, 1691, and his monument still remains in the church of Great Hocham.

BALDWIN, JOHN, was the son of William Baldwin, and Agnes the daughter of William Dormer, Esq., of Wycombe in Buckinghamshire, the ancestor of Lord Dormer. At the Inner Temple, where he studied the law, he attained so high a reputation that he received the uncommon distinction of being thrice appointed reader—in autumn 1516, in Lent 1524, and in autumn 1531. The last occasion was on account of his having been called upon to take the degree of the coif, which he accordingly assumed in the following November, when he was immediately constituted one of the king's serjeants. In 1530 he held the office of treasurer of his inn.

He probably practised in the Court of Chancery, as he was one of the persons assigned in June 1529 to aid Cardinal Wolsey in hearing causes there. He and Serjeant Willoughby were knighted in 1534, being the first serjeants, as is noticed in Spelman's MS. Reports, who ever submitted to receive that honour. In 1535 he was elevated to the chief justiceship of the Common Pleas. Within a few weeks he was called upon to act as a commissioner on the trials of Sir Thomas More and Bishop Fisher, in which, however, he does not appear to have taken any active part. He continued chief justice for ten years, resigning between Trinity Term 1545, the date of the last fine levied before him, and November 6. He died on December 22 following.

Notwithstanding his early promise, he does not seem to have been much esteemed as a judge. He differed frequently from his brethren, and was certainly thought little of by Chief Justice Dyer, who on one occasion says in his Reports, 'But Baldwin was of a contrary opinion, though neither I, nor any one else, I believe, understood his refutation.'

He possessed the manor of Aylesbury in Bucks, and in the last year of his life he obtained some valuable grants from the king. All his property, for want of male heirs, was divided among his daughters, one of whom, Catherine, was married to Robert Pakington, M.P. for London (assassinated in the streets in 1536), who was ancestor of the baronets of that name, of Aylesbury, whose title became extinct in 1830.

BANASTER, THOMAS, described as a 'clericus,' was constituted a baron of the Exchequer on November 4, 1423, 2 Henry VI. (*Acts Privy Council*, iii. 121); but his name nowhere else appears.

BANASTRE, ALARD, was sheriff of Oxfordshire in 20 & 21 Henry II., 1174-5; and in the former of those years his name is found as one of the justices itinerant fixing the assize for that county. But, in reference to the ordinary proceedings of the court, he is never mentioned; nor indeed is any other information given concerning him.

In the four previous years that sheriffalty was held by Adam Banastre, probably his father. (*Fuller's Worthies; Madox*, i. 124.)

BANISTER, WILLIAM, was of a family which resided at Turk Dean in the county of Gloucester, in possession of a very considerable estate. He received his legal education at the Middle Temple, and being honoured with the degree of the coif in 1706, was then appointed one of the judges of South Wales; from which position he was advanced, on the recommendation of Lord Harcourt, to be a baron of the Exchequer, on June 8, 1713, when he was knighted. He occupied this seat for little more than a year, being superseded on October 14, 1714, not three months after the accession of George I., having been reported by Lord Cowper as 'a man not at all qualified for the place.' (*Atkyns's Gloucestersh.* 413; *Lord Raymond*, 1261, 1318.)

BANKE, RICHARD. The barons of the Exchequer in the early reigns were of so little comparative importance, generally rising to the bench from being clerks in that department, and not engaged in the general judicial business of the country, that little information can be obtained regarding them either from records or tradition. Of the legal career of Richard Banke nothing is known, except that he was made a baron of the Exchequer on June 11, 1410, 11 Henry IV., and, continuing in his place to the end of that reign, was re-appointed in the next. He and his wife Margaret, the daughter of William de la Rivere, were buried in the Priory of St. Bartholomew, London. (*Stow*, 419.)

BANKE, THOMAS, who was perhaps the son of the preceding, is another instance of the paucity of materials respecting the barons of the Exchequer of this age. The sole mention of Thomas Banke is that he received that appointment on May 18, 1424, 2 Henry VI. (*Acts of Privy Council*, iii. 147.)

BANKS, JOHN, was of Keswick in Cumberland, where his father of the same name was a merchant, and his mother was Elizabeth, daughter of —Hassell. He was born in 1589, and in 1604 he entered Queen's College, Oxford. Without taking any degree there, he became a student at Gray's Inn in May 1607, and, after being called to the bar on November 30, 1614, and to the bench of the society in 1629, he was elected reader in Lent 1631, and treasurer in the following year. He had previous to arriving at these posts acquired a high reputation in his profession.

Returned to the parliament of 1628, he confined himself to legal questions (*Parl. Hist.* ii. 480), and was selected in July 1630 to be attorney-general to the newly born Prince Charles, Duke of Cornwall (*Rymer*, xix. 254), afterwards Charles II., whereupon he was knighted. On the death of William Noy, he was appointed attorney-general to the king, on September 27, 1634, and it is some proof of the estimation in which he was held, that a contemporary letter-writer says, with somewhat of exaggeration, that he was commended to his majesty as exceeding Bacon in eloquence, Ellesmere in judgment, and Noy in law. (*Corfe Castle*, 54.) He had then a residence at Hanwell, near Staines, but soon after his advance he purchased the manor of Corfe Castle in Dorsetshire, of Sir Edward Coke's widow, Lady Hatton.

Under his official direction the questionable proceedings in the Star Chamber were taken against Bastwick, Burton, and Prynne, against Bishop Williams, and against John Lilburn; and though he did not originate the plan for the imposition of ship money, he was employed in preparing and advising on the writs and to support them as the prosecutor against John Hampden. (*State Trials*, iii.) These duties he performed so satisfactorily to the court that upon the elevation of Sir Edward Lyttelton to the post of lord keeper, he received that of chief justice of the Common Pleas on January 29, 1641. (*Rymer*, xx. 447.)

Very soon after his appointment a commission was granted to him to sit as speaker in the House of Lords, in consequence of the illness of the lord keeper; and in that character he had the melancholy duty of presiding when the Earl of Strafford, who had been his client, and with whom he was in habits of friendly intimacy, was brought to the bar on his impeachment by the Commons. (*Corfe Castle*, 83.) Early in the next year, on the king retiring to York, Banks was among the first to join him, when he was admitted into the privy council, and subscribed the profession made by the lords of their belief that the king had no intention to make war upon the parliament, but that his anxious desire was to preserve the peace of the kingdom. (*Clarendon*, iii. 72.)

Notwithstanding the part which Sir John had formerly taken in the prosecution and in the case of ship money, and his present assistance to the royal counsels, he does not seem to have been an object of enmity to the parliament; for in the propositions they made to the king for peace in February 1643 they desired that he should keep his place in the Common Pleas. (*Parl. Hist.* iii. 70.) This recommendation he owed to his having friends in both houses, the Earls of Northumberland and Essex, the Lord Wharton, Denzil Holles, and Green, who were aware that Banks by his moderate counsels had hazarded the king's indignation. (*Corfe Castle*, 122-124.) Sir John's real devotion to the royal cause was proved by his liberal subscription to the king's necessities, and by his wife's noble defence of Corfe Castle in 1643, and after his death again in 1645.

The former good feeling of the parliament towards the chief justice was totally changed by his steady adherence to his royal master; and their inveteracy against him was excited by his charge to the grand jury at Salisbury in the summer assizes of 1643, denouncing the Earls of Northumberland, Pembroke, and Salisbury, and several members of the House of Commons, as guilty of high treason in taking up arms against the king. Though the bills were not found, he was ordered to be impeached for his charge, an order which was repeated in the following year on the occasion of his condemning Captain Turpin to be hanged at Exeter. (*Whitelocke*, 78, 96.) Though by his absence he escaped the consequences of these votes, he paid the price of his loyalty by the forfeiture of all his property. Even his books were seized and given by the parliament to Mr. Maynard.

Sir John did not live to see the destruction of his castle. He died at Oxford on December 28, 1644, and was buried in Christ Church Cathedral. Lord Clarendon describes him as 'a man of great abilities and unblemished integrity,' but at the same time intimates that he wanted courage to meet the exigencies of the time. All agree that he was thoroughly versed in the learning of his profession, and his whole conduct shows that, though cautious and moderate, he was steady in his attachment to the crown. He made a settlement of 30*l*. a year, and other emoluments, on the poor of Keswick, and chiefly to set up a manufacture there of coarse cottons. (*Fuller*, i. 237.)

His wife, who was Mary, the daughter of Ralph Hawtrey, Esq., of Ruislip, Middlesex, by compounding got rid of the sequestration. By her he had a numerous family, whose descendants represented Corfe Castle as long as that borough returned members to parliament.

BANKES, GEORGE, was the lineal descendant of the great chief justice, whose family introduced into the name the penultimate letter e. He was the third son of Henry Bankes, Esq., of Kingston Hall, Dorsetshire, who represented Corfe Castle from 1780 to 1826, and then was elected member for the county till 1831. His mother was Frances, daughter of William Woodley,

Esq., governor of the Leeward Islands. He was a member of Trinity Hall, in the University of Cambridge, and studied the law at first at Lincoln's Inn, and then at the Inner Temple, by which society he was called to the bar in April 1815, but had little opportunity to acquire any eminence in the profession. He succeeded Francis Maseres in the office of cursitor baron in July 1824, and continued to perform the duties of his office (which at last consisted of little more than joining in the Michaelmas solemnities of the sheriffalty of London) till his death, in 1856, having held the position of judge advocate general during the short administration of Lord Derby in 1852. No one was appointed to succeed him as cursitor baron, and the office was immediately abolished.

Succeeding eventually by the death of his brother to the family estates, he was chosen member for the county of Dorset, which he represented till his death; and was further honoured by being placed on the privy council. He died on July 6, 1856, leaving issue by his wife Georgina Charlotte, daughter and heir of Admiral Edmund Charles Nugent.

BANKWELL, or BAUKWELL, JOHN DE, whose name is variously spelled Bakwell, Bacwell, Bauquel, Bankwell, or Banquelle, was so called from a place formerly written Bankwell, but now Bankers, at Lee in Kent. Besides this, he had other property in the county, and in 31 Edward I. obtained for himself and his wife Cicily a grant of free warren over all their lands in Lee, Lewisham, Bromley, and Brokisham. (*Hasted*, i. 460, 493.)

In 1297 he was appointed to perambulate the forests of five counties, and was paid at the rate of six shillings a day; and in the next year he acted as one of the justices itinerant into Kent. (*Parl. Writs*, i. 396, 397.)

Shortly after the accession of Edward II., on November 10, 1307, he was nominated a baron of the Exchequer, but must have died within a few months, as his wife Cicily was assessed at four marks in the city of London for the quinzime imposed in 1308.

He left two sons, named Thomas and William, and perhaps others, to whom the property descended in gavelkind. (*Abb. Rot. Orig.* ii. 265.)

BANKWELL, or BAUKWELL, ROGER DE, was most probably of the family, and perhaps a younger son, of the above John. Roger is noticed as an advocate in the early part of the reign of Edward III. In the sixth year he was employed to tallage the counties of Nottingham and Derby (*Rot. Parl.* ii. 147); and from his being assigned in 14 Edward III. to enquire into a conflagration at Spondon, in the latter county (*N. Fœdera*, ii. 1133), it would seem probable that he was settled there; the more especially as Sir Godfrey Foljambe, one of his associates in that enquiry, many years afterwards gave a messuage and land to a clergyman named Roger de Bankwell (*Abb. Rot. Orig.* ii. 286), who, it may be presumed, was this Roger's son.

He was constituted a judge of the King's Bench before Easter in 1341, and is mentioned in the Year Books as late as 23 Edward III.

BARDELBY, ROBERT DE, is designated in various records, from 30 Edward I., 1302, to 15 Edward II., 1321, as a clerk of the Chancery, and acting under no less than eight chancellors. During that period he was one of those who were entrusted with the keeping of the Great Seal in the chancellor's absence, or in a temporary vacancy of the office. He is often styled one of the 'gardiens du Seal.' He is afterwards mentioned as a clerk of the Chancery as late as July 5, 1325.

In 9 Edward II. he was selected as an assessor of the fifteenth in the city of London; and in the previous year he was appointed keeper of the hospital of St. Thomas the Martyr of Acon in London, until his brother, Richard of Southampton, returned to England; and he held the ecclesiastical rank of canon of Chichester. (*Rot. Parl.* i. 287, 357; *Abb. Rot. Orig.* i. 227.)

BARDOLF, HUGH, was a younger son of Baron William Bardolf, of Stoke Bardolf, who was sheriff of Norfolk and Suffolk from 16 to 21 Henry II. The inclinations of his youth may be collected from the fact that in 22 Henry II. he was amerced for trespassing in the king's forests. In a very few years, however, his talents were discovered. In 30 Henry II., 1184, he was dapifer regis in conjunction with Hugh de Morewick, and afterwards with William Rufus. It is sometimes considered the same as seneschal or steward, and, indeed, he is occasionally designated by the latter title; and probably his appointment had reference to the Duchy of Normandy only, as in the Norman roll of that year he and Hugh de Morewick are allowed 100*l*. for money disbursed for the king's expenses while at Gisors. In the same year he received a gift of one hundred marks from the king. (*Madox*, i. 51, 168.)

From this time till the end of the reign he acted as a justicier, being present in the Curia Regis when fines were levied there, and assisting as a justice itinerant in assessing the tallage of Wiltshire, of which he was sheriff. (*Ibid.* 634.) He also held the sheriffalty of Cornwall, and was fermer of the honor of Gloucester (*Madox's Baron.* 63, 67), and was nominated one of the lieutenants of the kingdom during Henry's absence in Normandy.

Richard I., after his accession, although

he forced him as well as others to contribute to the expenses of the crusade under the name of a fine for not joining in it, treated him with equal distinction. He was appointed of the council to assist the two chief justiciaries in the rule of the kingdom and the administration of the laws; and his pleas on the itinera in several counties are recorded on the great rolls of 1 & 2 Richard I. When also the complaints against William de Longchamp became too loud to be disregarded, he was one of the persons whom the king nominated in the bishop's place. Although some historians question the authenticity of the letter containing this order, the insertion of the names in the forged document (if forged it were) shows the high position of the parties, and the estimation in which they were held at the period. There is no doubt that he joined Prince John and the barons in the removal of the unpopular bishop, and that the king (who never withdrew his confidence from the chancellor) punished him on his return by discharging him from the sheriffalty of York and Westmoreland. That he did not, however, remain long in disgrace is proved by his subsequent employments. His name frequently appears as a justicier in the Curia Regis on fines levied from the 5th to the 9th Richard I., and in the last four years of that reign he acted as a justice itinerant in various counties. (*Madox's Exch.* i. 35, 699, 704, 733.) He was one of those sent to York to determine the controversy between the archbishop and the monks there, and was also entrusted with the sheriffalty of the counties of Northumberland, Dorset and Somerset, Stafford, Wilts, and Leicester. In some of them he continued under King John, with the addition of Derby, Nottingham, Devon, and Cornwall. In the first year of King John's reign he was constituted custos of the castle of Tickhill, and had a grant of the manor of Brumegrave-cum-Norton, for which he procured the privilege of a market, together with a fair for it, and also for Carleton and Grimeston. (*Rot. Chart. John*, 55, 61, 91.)

In all the three reigns his scutage in the several counties of Warwick, Leicester, Kent, Oxford, Norfolk, and Suffolk, where his property lay, was excused 'pro libertate sedendi ad Scaccarium;' and in the reign of John the records show that he continued to act on the circuits as a justice itinerant, and in the Curia Regis as a justicier before whom fines were levied till the fifth year.

About that time he died, as in the next year Amabilis de Limesey, who was his wife, fined in two thousand marks and five palfreys that she should not be compelled to marry again; and that she should be quit of all aids to the sheriff, &c., as long as she should be a widow after the death of John de Braiosa, her late husband. (*Rot. de Fin.* 82.) This seems to show that soon after the death of Hugh Bardolf she had married a second husband, who had since died; and it appears that in the previous year William de Braiosa had given a fine to have her for the wife of one of his sons. (*Dugdale's Baron.* i. 415.)

BARKER, EDWARD, was born at Wandsworth in 1678, and was called to the bar at the Inner Temple, of which he was not admitted a member till 1724; but was one of the benchers of that society when he was appointed cursitor baron of the Exchequer on May 9, 1743. He resigned the place on April 19, 1755, and died in 1759. (*Lysons*, i. 507, 570.)

BARKING, RICHARD DE, was raised from the office of prior to that of abbot of Westminster in September 1223. (*Monast.* ii. 282.) He is first mentioned by Madox (ii. 318) among the barons of the Exchequer in 27 Henry III., 1242; and as he stands immediately after William de Haverhull, the treasurer, he no doubt occupied a high position there. In this, however, his ecclesiastical dignity would necessarily place him; and it by no means follows that he was, as Dugdale and Weever describe him, chief baron, according to the signification by which they evidently interpret the term. There is nothing to show that at that time there was an officer bearing that title; and if it had then existed, the rolls would not have been silent on the subject, nor would Madox have failed to notice it.

In the same year he alone tested the mandates issued to the sheriffs of the different counties, directing them to get in the scutage-money granted for the king's voyage into Gascony. This shows that he stood high in the royal confidence, and was in immediate attendance on the king; and about 1245 he was at the royal intercession excused from his attendance on a general council called by the pope, because he and the Bishop of Carlisle were the king's deputies or regents of England when he went abroad. (*Dart's Westm.* ii. xx.) He died on November 23, 1246 (*Weever*, 486), having, during his long presidency, greatly increased the revenues of his house. His character was that of a prudent, learned, and religious man.

BARNEWELL, THOMAS, was appointed second baron of the Exchequer on October 1, 1494, 10 Henry VII., and a successor was put in his place on May 2, 1496. Beyond this fact history is silent.

BARONS, WILLIAM, or, as he is sometimes called, William Barnes (Bishop of London), took the degree of Doctor of Laws at Oxford; but in which of the colleges or halls he studied has not been discovered. He became commissary of the Prerogative Court of Canterbury; and having entered into orders, he received in 1500 the livings of East Peckham in Kent, and of Beaconsfield in Buckinghamshire; in 1501, that of Gedney in Lincolnshire; in 1502, that of Bosworth in Leicestershire, and in 1503, that of Tharfield in the archdeaconry of Huntingdon.

He was appointed master of the Rolls on February 1, 1502. In June he was one of the negotiators of the treaty of marriage between Prince Henry and Catherine of Arragon; and on the 24th of the following January he assisted in laying the first stone of Henry VII.'s chapel at Westminster Abbey. He succeeded Bishop Warham as Bishop of London on August 2, 1504, but did not obtain the restitution of the temporalities till November 13. On the latter day he resigned his judicial office, and died in less than a year afterwards, on October 9 or 10, 1505. He was buried in St. Paul's. (*Godwin*, 190; *Athen. Ox.* ii. 694; *Rymer*, xiii. 78, 111.)

BAROWE, THOMAS, was appointed master of the Rolls on September 22, 1483, 1 Richard III. He was rector of Olney in Buckinghamshire; and three weeks after the accession of Richard had the grant of a prebend in St. Stephen's Chapel in the palace of Westminster. How he had ingratiated himself with that monarch does not appear; but perhaps by some services he had rendered in the Exchequer, of which he probably was a clerk. He was the first master of the Rolls who had a grant of the tun or two pipes of wine, which has been continued ever since, and nominally exists at present. His patent for it is dated December 6, 1483. (*Rot. Pat.* 1 Rich. III.) On August 1, 1485, he was appointed keeper of the Great Seal (*Rot. Claus.* n. 5), and it was in his custody at the time of Richard's death on the field of Bosworth, on the 22nd of that month, when it was of course given up to the conqueror.

His possession of the mastership of the Rolls seems to have been considered an intrusion; for his predecessor, Robert Morton, resumed his place without a new patent. Barowe's punishment for his adherence to the fallen party, however, extended no further; but on the contrary he appears very soon to have conciliated the goodwill of the new king; for on September 21 he obtained not only a general pardon, but a confirmation of his prebend in St. Stephen's Chapel, and his appointment as one of the masters in Chancery. (*Rot. Pat.* 1 Henry VII. p. i. m. ii.) In the latter character he attended parliament in the accustomed duty of receiving the petitions as late as 12 Henry VII., 1497, after which his name no more occurs.

BARRE, RICHARD, was a diligent and zealous servant of Henry II. After the peace concluded between that monarch and Louis of France in January 1169, he was sent with the Archdeacon of Salisbury to Beneventum to negotiate with Pope Alexander in relation to Archbishop Becket; and while there he succeeded in obtaining from the pontiff a new letter to the Archbishop of York, commanding him to crown Prince Henry at any time the king required him. After the murder of the archbishop, he was again appointed one of the ambassadors to the papal city; and when their passage through the mountains was impeded by the severity of the weather, he was selected to proceed without his companions and urge the king's innocence of the murder. Though on his arrival the pope refused to admit him to his presence, he at last contrived to mollify the indignant feelings of the pontiff, and by his representations, backed by the proofs he produced, his royal master escaped excommunication.

In recompense for these and other faithful services, the king appointed him chancellor to his son Henry when he crowned him; but on that prince rebelling against his father in 1173, Richard Barre proved his loyalty by restoring the Seal to the king. In 1184 he was raised to the dignity of Archdeacon of Ely.

In 7 Richard I., 1195-6, he was one of the justices itinerant holding pleas in Devonshire; and from that year till 1 John inclusive his name appears among the justices taking fines in the Curia Regis at Westminster. (*Madox*, i. 502.)

BARTON, JOHN DE, is the second of the two justices (Ralph Fitzwilliam being the first) to whom the commission of Trailbaston, confined to Yorkshire, and copied in Spelman (*Glossary*) is directed. The date is there omitted; but in Hemingford (p. 208) it is placed under the year 1304. Among the parliamentary writs (i. 407) is one dated November 23, 1304, addressed not only to these two, but to two others; so that it is probable there were two commissions, and that the first was issued before the great extent of the offence was known; especially as in April 1305 a still more formal appointment of judges for almost every county in England took place. (*N. Fœdera*, i. 970.)

In the above commission he is erroneously called 'de Ryton,' as he is afterwards designated 'de Fryton,' not only in the parliamentary writ, but also in subsequent commissions. He was summoned to perform military service against the Scots in 24 Edward I., and in the 28th and 31st years of that reign was named in commissions of array in Yorkshire (*Parl. Writs*, i, 277, 345, 370); and in 8 Edw. III.

he was assigned to collect and levy the scutage of the county of York. (*Abb. Rot. Orig.* i. 214.)

BASSET, RALPH, was baron of Welden in Northamptonshire, and had large possessions in several of the midland counties. He was a Norman by birth, but is stated to have been raised from an ignoble family by King Henry at the beginning of his reign.

Spelman places him as chief justiciary in the reign of William II., and states that he succeeded Ranulph Flambard, Bishop of Durham, in that office. But this is contradicted by the fact that the bishop had certainly all the power usually attributed to the chief justiciary at the time of William's death. Dugdale does not introduce him as chief justiciary till the reign of Henry I.; but it may be doubtful whether he was even then distinguished by that precise designation, notwithstanding the assertion of Henry of Huntingdon in his epistle 'De Mundi Contemptu,' as it is unquestionable that the principal power was exercised by Roger, Bishop of Salisbury, for the greater part of the reign, and especially during the king's frequent absences from England. The place he takes as last of fifteen subscribing witnesses to King Henry's charter to Westminster Abbey (*Monast.* i. 308), granted either in 1121 or 1122, demonstrates that he could not then have held the office.

He, however, certainly filled a very high position in the administration of justice, and seems to have been selected to carry into execution the just and severe laws enacted by Henry for the suppression of the system of rapine and robbery which the last reign had introduced. He is mentioned in 1124 as presiding over a court of the barons held at Huncote in Leicestershire for the trial of offenders, where he caused no less than forty-four men convicted of robbery to be hanged.

By the roll of 31 Henry I. it appears, not that he was chief justiciary, for that title never occurs in it, but that he had been justice of the forests in the counties of Norfolk, Suffolk, and Surrey; and that in the itinera which were appointed by King Henry for the purpose of relieving the Curia Regis, and of administering justice to the people almost at their own doors, no less than six counties, and probably more, were placed under his direction. He was manifestly dead before the date of that roll; and the entries in it, in which his name occurs, have reference to debts due to the crown from his pleas in previous years.

The precise date of his death is uncertain; but it took place at Northampton, where, falling sick, he called for a monk's habit of the order of those of Abingdon; and after disposing of his estate and sending no small sum to that abbey, with a grant of four hides of land in Chedelesworth, he died, and was honourably buried in the chapter-house there. He left several sons, some of which were justiciers; and from their issue various baronies sprang, the last of which lately became extinct. (*Dugdale's Baron.* i. 378; *Madox,* i. 12, 146, 541, ii. 224; *Thoroton's Notts,* i. 161; *Mag. Rot.* 31 Henry I., Hunter's ed., 31, 101, 124, 145.)

BASSET, RICHARD, was one of the sons of the above Ralph Basset, and succeeded him in the barony of Welden in Northamptonshire. From an early period of his life he was attached to the court, and assisted in the administration of justice in the Aula Regis. It is probable that during the life of his father he had advanced to a considerable position; for in the great roll of 31 Henry I. the same number of counties are mentioned as under the judicial superintendence of both; and the father could only have been recently deceased.

He is introduced as chief justiciary to Henry I. in Dugdale's list, on the authority of Henry of Huntingdon and Ordericus Vitalis; but some doubt may be entertained whether he can be correctly so described. If he had held the office in 31 Henry I., the roll of that year would have afforded some evidence of it; but it makes no distinction between him and the other justiciaries, whose pleas it records. In the grant, also, of the office of great chamberlain of England to Alberic de Vere, his name stands so low on a list of twelve witnesses as to preclude the possibility of his being invested with the title. That grant is dated 'apud Ferncham in Transfretatione Regis.' This must have been on occasion of the king's last visit to his Norman dominions in 1134; as is apparent from the fact that Geoffrey, Bishop of Durham, the chancellor, whose name stands as the second witness, was not elected to that see till 1133. The first witness is Roger, Bishop of Salisbury, which is strong presumptive evidence that he was then first minister or chief justiciary of the kingdom.

The expression of Ordericus Vitalis goes no further than that he had great power in this reign, 'utpote capitalis justitia.' Dugdale's opinion, also, that he held it jointly with Alberic de Vere is probably founded on the fact that they were joint sheriffs of no less than eleven counties. Although the latter author says in his 'Baronage' that he also held the office during the whole of King Stephen's reign, he does not so insert his name in his 'Chronica Series.'

He married Matilda, the daughter and heir of Geoffrey Ridel, the justiciary (whose land appears to have been in his custody), and increased his already large property by her possessions. Of these he devoted a great portion to pious uses. The priory of Laund, in Leicestershire, dedicated to St. John the Baptist, was founded by him and his wife, and munificently endowed by them with the town and manor of Lodington, in which it stands; with Friseby also; besides no less than fifteen churches in the neighbourhood, and one in Rutland. He died about 1154. His eldest son, Geoffrey, assumed his mother's name of Ridel. Another son, Ralph, who continued the surname of Basset, was lord of Drayton in Staffordshire; and a third son, William, subsequently mentioned, was lord of Sapcote in Leicestershire. (*Angl. Sac.* ii. 701; *Thoroton's Notts*, i. 161; *Monast.* vi. 189; *Mag. Rot.* 31 Hen. I.; *Madox*.)

BASSET, THOMAS, was the son and heir of Gilbert, a grandson, or, as Dugdale believes, a younger son of the above Ralph Basset. His military services in divers wars were rewarded by King Henry II. at an early period of his reign with the lordship of Hedendon in Oxfordshire, together with the hundred of Botendon, and that lying without the north gate of the city of Oxford. He was sheriff of that county in 10 Henry II., and in the 14th year of that reign, 1168, he was one of the justices itinerant for the counties of Essex and Hertford. (*Madox*, i. 587.)

From the year 1175 his name frequently appears among the barons acting judicially in the Curia Regis; and the superior character of his abilities is evident from his being employed as a justice itinerant for the six following years in no less than fifteen other counties; and in his having been one of those selected by the great council held at Windsor in 1179, when the kingdom was divided into four parts for the better administration of justice.

He married Alice, the daughter of — de Dunstanville, and died before 1183, in which year his elder son, Gilbert, had come into his possessions, and founded the priory of Burcester, or Bicester, in Oxfordshire.

Besides Gilbert he had two other sons, Thomas and Alan, the latter of whom is hereafter mentioned. (*Dugdale's Baron.* i. 383; *Madox*, i. 94, &c.; *Pipe Rolls*, Hen. II.)

BASSET, WILLIAM, lord of Sapcote in Leicestershire, was a younger son of the above Richard Basset and Matilda Ridel, his wife.

From 9 to 16 Henry II., 1163-1170, he executed the office of sheriff of the united counties of Warwick and Leicester, and was afterwards fined by the commissioners appointed in the latter year in the sum of one hundred marks for some transgressions he had committed in performance of his duties. He, however, afterwards held the sheriffalty of Lincolnshire in 24 Henry II., and the six following years.

His pleas as a justice itinerant commence in 14 Henry II., 1168, and extend till 26 Henry II., 1180, during which time he acted in twenty-four different counties. From 1175 he is frequently mentioned as assisting in the judicial business of the Curia Regis, in which he continued to sit till 1184. (*Madox*, i. 94, 103, 143, &c.)

He died about the latter date, and was succeeded in the barony by his son Simon, next mentioned.

BASSET, SIMON, is named among the justices itinerant who fixed the tallage for the counties of Nottingham and Derby in 9 Richard I., 1197-8. (*Madox*, i. 733.) He was the son of the last-named William Basset, lord of Sapcote. His connection with Derbyshire arose from his marriage with Elizabeth, one of the daughters and coheirs of William Avenel, of Haddon in the Peak in that county. In 7 John she fined eighty marks to the king to have her inheritance, which the king had seized on her husband's death, and that she should not be compelled to marry. (*Rot. de Fin.* 307.)

His male descendants failed in 1378, by the death of Ralph, the then baron, leaving two daughters only. (*Baronage*, i. 382.)

BASSET, ALAN, was the third son of the before-named Thomas Basset, of Hedendon. Under Richard I. and John he appears to have been a frequent partaker of the royal bounty. In the former reign he had a grant of the manors of Woking and Mapeldurewell (*Rot. Chart.* 37); and in the latter, of those of Wycumb and Berewick. Besides these, King John granted him the custody of the lands and heir of Hugo de Druvall, and excused him his scutage in Surrey, Oxfordshire, and Berkshire. An order to Stephen de Turnham and him, in 9 John, to deliver a sum of 2,250 marks from the treasury, shows that he was connected with the Exchequer; and in 15 John he was the bearer of 100*l*. from the treasury to the king at Oxford. That he was a personal favourite of the king may be inferred from a present he received from him of a dolium of the best wine. (*Rot. Claus.* 59, 99, 139.) He accompanied his sovereign in his visit to Ireland in 12 John (*Rot. de Præst.* 184, &c.), attended him at Runnymede, and was a faithful adherent to his fortunes till his death.

On the accession of Henry III. he was equally favoured and equally employed. In 2 Henry III. he acted as a justicier at Westminster, a fine being levied before him (*Dugdale's Orig.* 42); in 4 Henry III. he was sent on a mission to France, and in 7 Henry III. he and Emericus de Sacy were appointed to meet the King of Jerusalem on his landing in Kent. He was sheriff of Rutland from 2 to 12 Henry III., had the custody of the land and heir of William de Montacute given to him, obtained a grant of a market at Wutton in Wiltshire, and was allowed two bucks out of Windsor Forest. (*Rot. Claus.* i. 313, 385, 410, 460, 559.)

He died about October 1232, leaving several children by his wife Alice, the daughter and heir of Stephen de Gray. To judge from an entry on the Close Roll (i. 104), she was one of the ladies attached to the person of the queen.

Three of his sons were successively in possession of his honours and estate—viz., Gilbert, whose son died soon after him; Fulk, who was raised to the deanery of York and the bishopric of London; and Philip, who is the subject of the next notice. (*Chauncey's Herts*, 348; *Atkyns's Gloucestersh.* 420; *Brydges' Collins's Peerage*, iii. 2, vii. 335.)

BASSET, PHILIP, was the third son of the above Alan, and eventually succeeded to the barony of Wycombe.

In 1233, the year after his father's death, he joined the insurrection of Richard, Earl of Pembroke, but returned to his allegiance in the following year (*Baronage*, i. 384), and from that time seems to have been high in his sovereign's favour. In 1242 he was appointed one of the commanders of the knights who were sent to the king in Poitou (*Cal. Rot. Pat.* 20), and in 1243 he had a grant of the custody of the lands and heir of Matilda de Luci; in 1252, that of the lands and heir of Richard de Ripariis; and in 1257 the manor of Dimmock was granted to him and his wife, Ela, Countess of Warwick. (*Excerpt. e Rot. Fin.* i. 407, ii. 148, 248, 249.)

Besides being called upon to attend the king in his wars in France and in Wales, he was, in 29 Henry III., one of the ambassadors sent to the Council of Lyons to complain of the papal exactions in England; and in 44 & 45 Henry III. he was constituted governor of the castles of Oxford, Bristol, Corff, and Shireburn, with the sheriffalties of the counties in which they are situate, and of Berkshire. He is called bailiff of the King of the Romans in an entry of 43 Henry III. (*Abb. Placit.* 146).

When the king, in July 1261, openly resisted the control under which the barons had placed him since the parliament of Oxford of 1258, he appointed Philip Basset chief justiciary of England. The barons' chief justiciary was his son-in-law, Hugh le Despenser; and they both seem to have acted at the same time till the short accommodation that took place between the contending parties in the following April, when Philip Basset's appointment was fully established. Between July 15 and October 18, 1262, while the king was absent in France, all the mandates on the fine roll were signed by him, and he presided at a council, when the Earl of Leicester, taking advantage of the king's absence, is said to have produced a brief from the pope confirming the provisions of Oxford, and recalling the king's absolution. (*Rapin*, iii. 146.) His name appears on the plea roll of the Exchequer as justiciary of England at the end of June 1263. (*Madox*, i. 100.)

Another temporary reconciliation took place in the following year between the king and the earl, the effect of which was the reinstatement of Hugh le Despenser, whose name appears as justiciary of England to a mandate dated October 1, 1263; while Philip Basset is named without that addition in the reference of the Oxford provisions to the King of France, dated in December following. (*Excerpt. e Rot. Fin.* ii. 405; *Brady*, i. *App.* 283.)

Philip Basset, however, adhered firmly to the king, and in the outbreak of the London citizens, led by Hugh le Despenser, at the beginning of 1264, his house and possessions in London fell a sacrifice to their fury. (*Chron. Rishanger*, 22.) In the following March he greatly assisted the king in taking Northampton; and at the battle of Lewes, on May 14, valiantly fighting near the royal person, he continued the contest until he fell through loss of blood, when he shared the fate of his sovereign, and was taken prisoner. (*Lingard*, iii. 138.) He was placed in Dover Castle, under the custody of Simon de Montfort, younger son of the Earl of Leicester; but how long he remained in durance does not appear.

After the triumph of the royalists at the battle of Evesham, on August 4, 1265, there is nothing to show that Philip Basset was replaced in his office of chief justiciary, although there is ample evidence to prove that he continued to enjoy the king's favour and to hold a high place in his counsels. He was one of those who were appointed to carry into execution the Dictum of Kenilworth, in October 1266 (*Rapin*, iii. 171); and his name appears as one of the king's council in February 1270. (*Madox*, ii. 170.)

He died about the end of October 1271, 56 Henry III.

He married two wives: the first was Hawise, or Helewise, daughter of John Gray, of Eaton; and the second (who survived him) was Ela, daughter of William Longspee, Earl of Salisbury, and widow of Thomas, Earl of Warwick. By the former he left an only daughter, Alyna, or Aliva, who had first married Hugh le Despenser, the chief justiciary, but was then the wife of Roger Bigot, Earl of Norfolk, the son of Hugh Bigot (*Excerpt. e Rot. Fin.* ii. 551), being thus connected with three chief justiciaries, as the daughter of one, the wife of a second, and the daughter-in-law of a third.

BASSET, THOMAS, was probably the grandson of the before-mentioned Thomas Basset, lord of Hedendon, by his second son, Thomas; and the nephew of Alan Basset, above mentioned. Dugdale introduces him as a justice of the King's Bench, on the authority of a charter of 46 Henry II., 1262; but none of the customary proofs appear of his so acting, either by his going any iter, or having any writs of assize directed to him. He died, however, shortly after that date, as his widow Johanna is mentioned on the fine roll of 52 Henry III. (ii. 470.)

BASSET, WILLIAM, was the son of the above Simon Basset, lord of Sapcote, by his wife Elizabeth, daughter of William Avenel, of Haddon in the Peak in Derbyshire. In 10 Henry III. this lady died, and all the land which she held of the honour of Peverel, in the county of Buckingham, was ordered to be put into the possession of her son William, to whom she had given it 'as her heir.' (*Excerpt. e Rot. Fin.* i. 140.) From the terms of this entry, however, it may be inferred that he was not her eldest son. Long previous to this event he was possessed of property in the counties of Leicester, Derby, Lincoln, and Stafford; all which was forfeited for his adherence to the barons in 18 John, and restored in the following year, when he acknowledged his fealty to Henry III. In the tenth year of that reign, 1226, he was appointed one of the justices itinerant for Nottingham and Derby, and for various other counties up to 1232. (*Rot. Claus.* i., ii.) In July 1249 Robert Basset, his nephew and heir, did homage for his land in Buckinghamshire. (*Excerpt. e Rot. Fin.* ii. 57.)

BASSET, WILLIAM, was a native of Staffordshire, but of what branch of the family has not been traced. He was an advocate in the reign of Edward II., and in the first ten years of that of Edward III. In the latter of these, 1337, he was raised to the bench of the Common Pleas. When the king, in December 1340, dismissed some of his brethren for malpractices, he escaped, and was comprehended in the new patent issued on January 8, 1341. On October 28 he changed his court for that of the King's Bench, where he remained till 24 Edward III., his name occurring up to that date in the 'Year Book' and 'Book of Assizes' of that reign. (*Dugdale's Orig.* 45; *Rot. Parl.* ii. 164.)

BASSINGBORNE, HUMPHREY DE. Several fines were acknowledged at St. Edmunds, Cambridge, and Bedford in 8 John, 1206, before Humphrey, Archdeacon of Sarum, and Richard de Seing.

The Archdeacon of Sarum at that time was Humphrey de Bassingborne. (*Le Neve*, 276.) He suffered with the rest of the clergy on account of the interdict, his rents being seized into the king's hands; but they were restored to him in April 1208. At the end of the reign he again got into disgrace, and was obliged to pay a fine of one hundred marks and a palfrey for his restoration to the king's favour, and he then had a royal letter of protection. (*Rot. Claus.* i. 113, 251; *Rot. de Fin.* 582.)

BASTARD, WILLIAM, was the third of five justices itinerant, appointed in 20 Henry II., 1174, by writ of Richard de Luci, to set the assize of Hampshire (*Madox*, i. 125), but who he was cannot be traced with sufficient certainty.

BATESFORD, JOHN DE, was one of the eight justices appointed by Edward I., in 1293, to take assizes, jurats, and certificates throughout the kingdom in aid of the judges of each bench and the itinerant judges, who were often prevented from attending at the regular times and places. On February 18, 1307, he was the fourth of the justices of Trailbaston then nominated for ten of the midland counties (*Rot. Parl.* i. 99, 218); and as in 4 Edward II., 1310, he was sent as a justice of assize into Hampshire, Wiltshire, Somersetshire, Dorsetshire, Cornwall, and Devonshire, he may be presumed to have continued to act in the interim, the more especially as he was regularly summoned among the judges to parliament from the beginning to the eleventh year of that reign. He died soon after, his executors being commanded, in 13 Edward II., to bring all proceedings before him into the Exchequer. (*Parl. Writs*, ii. 499.)

BATHONIA, HENRY DE, according to Prince (55), was a native of Devon, and a younger brother of Walter de Bathonia, of Bathe House, in North Tawton, and of Colebrook, near Crediton. There does not appear any proof, nor indeed much probability, that this statement is well founded. The roll of fines shows that in 20 Henry III., 1236, the king directed the sheriff of Dorsetshire to appraise all the chattels which had belonged to Hugh de Bathonia, and to deliver them to Henry, taking security that he would answer for their value in discharge of the debts due from Hugh to the crown. (*Excerpt. e Rot. Fin.* i. 310.) In this record, as Hugh is frequently mentioned as 'clericus,' it must be charitably supposed that he was Henry's uncle, unless indeed the designation 'clericus' was attached to his name merely with an official instead of an ecclesiastical signification. Hugh de Bathonia was an officer of the king's wardrobe in the reign of John (*Rot. Pat.* 173, 174), sheriff of Buckingham in 7 Henry III., and of Berkshire in 11 Henry III.; and was afterwards one of the justices of the Jews. (*Rot. Claus.* i. 569, ii. 196; *Madox*, i. 134.) This official position which Hugh held in the court will account for Henry de Bathonia being brought up to the legal profession; and accordingly, so early as 10 Henry III., his name appears as the representative or attorney for Warin le Despenser in a suit against Nicholas de St. Bridget, for a debt of four marks and a half. (*Rot. Claus.* ii. 156.)

It was not till after Hugh's death that Henry de Bathonia was advanced to the bench. In 1238, 22 Henry III., his name first appears to the acknowledgment of a fine. Two years afterwards he was one of the justiciers on the circuit then sent through the southern counties. In that commission he stood second on the list; and from that time the fine roll teems with payments made for writs of assize to be taken before him. In November 1247 he stands in a higher place, an amerciament being mentioned as being made before him and his companion justices of the bench (*Excerpt. e Rot. Fin.* ii. 23; *Abb. Placit.* 125, 126); and in the circuits of that and the two following years his name is inserted at the head in every county which he is appointed to visit. In 1250 he had a grant of 100*l.* a year for his support 'in officio justiciarii,' an expression which would seem to show that the term 'capitalis,' or chief justice, as subsequently used, was not yet adopted, as it is quite manifest that he then sat as the senior of his fellows.

Not long after this grant he was accused by Philip Darcy of bribery and extortion, whereby he had raised a great estate on the ruin of others. Four-and-twenty knights became security for his appearance to answer the charge before the parliament summoned for February 17, 1251. On the day of hearing he was charged with incensing the barons against the king, and promoting a general rebellion; and among various complaints urged against him was one that he had received a bribe to allow a convicted criminal to escape. The vehemence of the king's anger may be estimated by his brutal exclamation, 'If any man will slay Henry de Bathonia, he shall not be impeached of his death; and I now pronounce his pardon.' This violence, however, was prevented by John Mansel's timely interference, and the threats of the Bishop of London, and the justicier's other friends, of ecclesiastical and temporal revenge.

The intercession of Richard, Earl of Cornwall, the king's brother, at last procured him a pardon, on a fine of two thousand marks, the whole of which was not paid at the time of his death. His disgrace continued more than two years—viz., from November 1250 till August 1253, after which date applications to him for writs of assize are frequent for the rest of his life.

A grant of land, also, in the latter year, addressed 'Henrico de Bathon. et sociis suis, justiciariis assignatis ad tenendum placita coram rege' (*Manning*, 298), proves that he had been restored to his former high position. Comparing the title here used with that in the amerciament in 32 Henry III. already referred to, 'coram Henrico de Bathon. et sociis suis, justiciariis de banco,' it would appear, according to the modern interpretation of the terms, that he had changed his court; but this seems to be contradicted by an entry in 20 Edward I., which refers to a proceeding in 41 Henry III., 'coram H. Bathon. et sociis suis, justiciariis regis de banco.' (*Abb. Placit.* 228.) In the preceding year he and his companions are mentioned without any designation to distinguish the court, the words used being 'et sociis suis, justiciariis regis.' These changes suggest the caution with which such appellations should be used in support of an hypothesis.

So late as 1260 he went the circuit through eight counties.

He died before the 22nd of the following February, as on that day the king, 'intuitu laudabilis obsequii quod Henricus de Bathon. R. impendit in vita sua,' grants to John de Bathon, his son and heir, that the arrears which remained due of the fine of two thousand marks which he made for having the king's favour, and of all other debts which he owed the king at his death, might be paid by instalments of twenty-five marks at each of the yearly Exchequer terms, Michaelmas and Easter. (*Excerpt. e Rot. Fin.* ii. 345.)

His widow, Aliva, afterwards married Nicholas de Yatingdon, and died in 1273. The above-mentioned John de Bathonia had a son, also named John, whose only child Joan was married to John de Bohun, and died in 1316. (*Blomefield's Norfolk*, i. 185.)

BATHURST, HENRY (LORD APSLEY, EARL BATHURST). The Bathursts were originally seated at Bathurst, near Battel, in Sussex, but afterwards removed into Kent. One member received a baronetcy (of Leachdale in Gloucestershire) in 1643, which is now supposed to be extinct; and several others were merchants and aldermen of London. The immediate ancestor of the chancellor resided at Staplehurst in the reign of Henry VIII., and one of his grandsons was the father of the celebrated Dr. Ralph Bathurst, president of Trinity College, Oxford, and dean of Wells. The dean's brother, Sir Benjamin, was the father of Allen, who, after serving in two parliaments for the borough of Cirencester, was one of the twelve peers created by Queen Anne in 1711, for the purpose of obtaining a majority in the House of Lords. To his title, Baron Bathurst of Battlesden in

Sussex, he received sixty-one years afterwards the additional rank of an earl, as an acknowledgment and reward for his services to the state, and his eminence in the social and literary world. He died, at the age of ninety-one, in 1775, having lived to see his son elevated to the peerage and to the dignity of lord high chancellor of Great Britain. That son was one of the nine children he had by his wife Catherine, daughter and heir of Sir Peter Apsley, of Apsley in Sussex.

Henry Bathurst, the second but eldest surviving son of the earl, was born on May 20, 1714. He took the degree of B.A. at Christ Church, Oxford, in 1733, and was called to the bar by the Society of Lincoln's Inn in Hilary Term 1736. He had already been returned to parliament in the previous year as member for Cirencester, which he continued to represent till 1754. Though his business in the courts was by no means commanding, he was in 1746 chosen solicitor-general, and shortly after attorney-general, to Frederick, Prince of Wales, after whose death, in 1751, he filled the same office to the princess till his elevation to the bench. He had on entering the prince's service been honoured with a patent of precedency; and in 1752 he was the leading counsel for the crown in the trial at the Oxford Assizes of Elizabeth Blandy for the murder of her father, his speech in which has been praised for its eloquence, but is too exaggerated an appeal to the feelings of the jury to be approved by modern ears. Soon after he was raised to the bench as a judge of the Common Pleas, on May 2, 1754, at the age of forty; and in the case of the sham patriot John Wilkes in 1763 he concurred in the constitutional decisions of his chief, Lord Camden. After occupying his seat for sixteen years, on the sudden death of the Hon. Charles Yorke, the Great Seal was, on January 21, 1770, placed in the hands of three commissioners, the second of whom was Mr. Justice Bathurst. They held it for a year, but their rule met with so little approbation that the minister found it necessary to appoint a lord chancellor. Though very limited in his choice, the profession was greatly surprised on finding Judge Bathurst, who was considered 'the most incapable of the three' commissioners, selected to fill that high and responsible post. The Seal was delivered to him on January 23, 1771, and he was on the same day created Lord Apsley. He naturally found himself in a wrong position, and it was said that he never entered his court with a firm and dauntless step. Overawed by Thurlow, Wedderburn, and other counsel practising at his bar, he was so little conversant with either the principles or practice of equity that his decisions have no value in the profession. But, being a staunch supporter of Lord North's measures, he was retained in his place for more than seven years; at the end of which, from a failure in his health, or perhaps a consciousness of his inefficiency, he resigned the Seal, on June 3, 1778, one of his last and most praiseworthy acts being the appointment of his nephew, Francis Buller, to a vacant judgeship. He declined any retiring pension, and was in the following year continued in the cabinet with the office of lord president of the council, which he held till Lord North's ministry terminated, in 1782. In the twelve years he survived he gradually retired from political life, and died from natural decay at his seat, Oakley Grove, near Cirencester, on August 6, 1794, in his eighty-first year.

In his public life he was honourable and sincere; as a judge, he was esteemed by the bar for his kindness of manner; and in private life he was thoroughly amiable. Though of a cheerful and good-humoured disposition, he was not quite so jovial as his father, who took his wine freely to the last day of his long life. On one occasion at a party at Oakley, the chancellor having retired somewhat early from the conviviality, the old earl chuckled and said to the rest of the company, 'Now, my good friends, since the *old* gentleman is off, I think we may venture to crack another bottle.' Neither was he so liberal a patron to literature as his father; but it should be remembered to his credit that he was the first to encourage Sir William Jones by substantial tokens of regard.

In 1775, while he was yet chancellor, he succeeded to his father's earldom. He married twice. By his first wife, Anne, daughter of — James, Esq., and widow of Charles Phillips, Esq., he had no issue; but by his second wife, Tryphena, daughter of Thomas Scawen, Esq., of Maidwell in Northamptonshire, he left six children. His successor held a distinguished place in the government, and the House of Lords is still graced by his descendants.

BAUKWELL. *See* J. and R. DE BANKWELL.

BAUMBURGH, THOMAS DE, is among the clerks or masters in Chancery mentioned from 1 to 14 Edward III., and was so named from the place now called Bamborough in Northumberland, where he had property. He seems to have been an especial favourite with the king, who presented him with the church of Emildon, and made him various beneficial grants of lands in that county. He acted as keeper of the Great Seal on several occasions, in 1332, 1334, 1336, and 1339. In the latter year, 14 Edward III., he was one of the receivers of the petitions to parliament, and probably died soon after, as he is not subsequently named. (*Rot. Parl.* ii. 22, 68, 112; *Cal. Inq.* p.m. ii. 53; *Cal. Rot. Pat.* 118; *Abb. Rot. Orig.* ii. 27, 75, 79.)

BAYEUX, JOHN DE (BAIOCIS), was the son of Hugh de Baiocis, a baron in Lincolnshire, by Alienora his wife. Before his father's decease he was outlawed for the death of a man, and his property in Bristol and in Dorsetshire, being forfeited, was given away in 16 and 17 John. He contrived, nevertheless, to make his peace; for in 3 Henry III. he was admitted to take possession of his paternal estates in Lincolnshire on payment of 100*l.* for his relief; and in the same year he was added to the list of justices itinerant for the counties of Cornwall, Devon, Somerset, and Dorset. (*Rot. Claus.* i. 237, 404; *Rot. Chart.* 201; *Excerpt. e Rot. Fin.* i. 32.) It would appear, however, that he was not even then entirely cleared of the charge, unless indeed he had subjected himself to a new accusation; for in 4 Henry III. he and his mother Alienora, his brother, and three others, fined for having an inquisition before the chief justiciary, whether the appeal against them by Robert de Tillebroc for the death of his father was malicious, or they were guilty. That the result of the enquiry was favourable may be presumed from his being again selected as a justice itinerant in Devonshire in 1225, and from his holding several responsible appointments about the same time, as justice of the forests, and constable of the castle of Plimpton. (*Excerpt. e Rot. Fin.* i. 45; *Rot. Claus.* i. 622, &c., ii. 76, &c.) In 18 Henry III. another charge of homicide was raised against him; and he paid a fine of no less than four hundred marks for permission to accommodate with the widow of Roger de Mubray for the death of her husband, in which he was someway concerned.

On his death, in 1249, his brother Stephen did homage for his lands as male heir. (*Excerpt. e Rot. Fin.* i. 264, ii. 51.)

BAYLEY, JOHN. No judge since the act was passed in 1799 granting a pension on retirement after fifteen years' service has declined to avail himself of the privilege for so long a period as Sir John Bayley. He occupied the bench for no less than twenty-six years, with the highest reputation as a lawyer, and undiminished respect and esteem from every one who acted either with or under him.

He was born on August 3, 1763, at Elton in Huntingdonshire, the residence of his father, John Bayley, Esq. His mother was Sarah, the daughter and heir of the Rev. White Kennett, prebendary of Peterborough, and granddaughter of Bishop Kennett, of that see. He was educated at Eton under the superintendence of his father's elder brother, Dr. Edward Bayley, fellow of St. John's College, Cambridge, and rector of Quinton and Courtcenhall; to whose cultivation of his taste and talents for classical composition the judge always ascribed his future success in life. The 'Musæ Etonenses' contain some favourable specimens of his proficiency. Though he was nominated in 1782 for King's College, Cambridge, it does not appear that he was ever matriculated.

He entered Gray's Inn in November 1783, but was not called to the bar till June 22, 1792. In the interim he probably practised as a special pleader, as in 1789 he published the 'Summary of the Law of Bills of Exchange,' &c., which has ever since been the standard work on the subject, and of which many editions have been issued. He also edited Lord Raymond's Reports, with valuable notes, in 1790. The fame he acquired by these publications naturally insured him, when he became a barrister, ample employment, which did not diminish when he was raised to the degree of the coif in 1799. About this time he was elected recorder of Maidstone. After successfully pursuing his profession as a serjeant both on the Home Circuit and in Westminster Hall, he was appointed in May 1808 a judge of the King's Bench, and was knighted.

There his peculiar adaptation for the judical office was at once seen, and his professional erudition soon placed him in the first rank. Though his quickness of apprehension enabled him to see the true bearings of a case, he was always open to conviction, and most patient in listening to the arguments raised by counsel in opposition to his opinion. No one who has attended the courts can forget the seven little red books which he always carried with him, to which he could instantaneously turn for every reported case. The ease and delight with which he got through his work at Nisi Prius caused M. Cotte, the French advocate, to exclaim, 'Il s'amuse à juger.' In this court he sat for more than twenty-two years, for seventeen of which he held the next place to the chief justice, pronouncing the judgments of the court upon delinquents with characteristic mildness. But at length he found the increasing labour too much for him, but still was willing to undertake a lighter duty. He therefore took advantage of the act authorising the appointment of a fifth judge in each court, and on November 14, 1830, was removed into the Court of Exchequer as the additional baron, taking his place however according to his seniority next to the chief baron.

On the new stage of the Exchequer he played the same prominent part for above three years more, when his advancing age prompted him to retire, before his mental powers decayed. He therefore resigned the position he had so long graced in February 1834, receiving in the next month the well-merited honour of a baronetcy, and an opportunity being given him of still serving the state in the character of a privy counsellor. He survived nearly twelve years, and died on October 10, 1841, at the Vine House, near Sevenoaks.

Few men in his prominent position ever passed through life with such unmingled respect. He had all the requisites of a good judge—clearness of intellect, integrity of purpose, urbanity of manner, strict impartiality, and a total absence of political bias. He was a favourite with all classes—his colleagues on the bench, the advocates over whom he ruled, and the litigants, whether he decided for or against them. Amiable and benevolent in his private life, he was deeply impressed with religious feelings, which were manifested in an edition of the Common Prayer Book published by him in 1816.

By his wife, Elizabeth, daughter of John Markett, Esq., of Meopham Court in Kent, he left, besides three daughters, three sons, the eldest of whom now enjoys the title; the second is a clergyman; and the third a barrister, who edited one of the editions of his father's work on Bills.

BAYNARD, FULCO, was of the noble family of that name, the ancestor of which, Ralph Baynard, possessed in the Conqueror's time various rich lordships in the counties of Essex, Suffolk, Norfolk, and Hertford. By the conspiracy of his grandson, William, the elder son of Geoffrey, against Henry I., the barony was lost; and its castle, called Baynard's Castle, near St. Paul's, in London, was granted to Robert, the son of Richard Fitz-Gilbert, from whom descended the Fitz-Walters. Fulco traced his lineage from a younger brother of Geoffrey. He held eight knights' fees and a half in Norfolk under Robert Fitz-Walter, and obtained a market in 1226 for his manor of Merton. (*Rot. Claus.* ii. 105.) In November of that year, 11 Henry III., 1226, he and three others were constituted justiciers to try some prisoners charged with murder in the custody of the Bishop of Ely. (*Ibid.* ii. 159.) In four previous instances he had been one of four appointed to take particular assizes of novel disseisin in the county of Norfolk; a practice then not uncommon, but which would not warrant the insertion of those so employed among the justices itinerant, from whom they were clearly distinct. Fulco's case is varied by his nomination to try the felonies above mentioned. Both in 2 and 11 Henry III. he was one of those selected to assess the tallage in Norfolk. (*Ibid.* i. 350, ii. 78, &c.)

In 1256 he fined for not being knighted, but was afterwards obliged to take that honour. In the reign of Edward I. he was nominated one of the conservators of the peace for his county, and died at a great age in 1306. By his wife, Alice, the daughter of John le Ditton, he left a son, the next-mentioned Robert. (*Blomefield's Norfolk*, i. 557.)

BAYNARD, ROBERT, the son of the above Fulco Baynard, so early as 18 Edward I. was returned as knight of the shire for Norfolk, and represented that county till 20 Edward II. In 5 Edward II. the custody of Norfolk was committed to him (*Abb. Rot. Orig.* i. 186), and in the two following years he was among the magnates who were specially summoned to parliament. Several of these were not barons, and were never afterwards summoned; and he, in all the subsequent entries, is merely called 'Miles.' He was one of the conservators of the peace for the county, and was employed as a commissioner of array, and in assessing the various grants made by the parliament. To him also was entrusted the custody of the bishopric of Durham, in 1311, on the death of Anthony Bek.

On the accession of Edward III. he was appointed, according to Dugdale, a judge of the King's Bench; and it is curious that the writ directing the payment of his expenses as knight of the shire, in the parliament of the preceding January, is dated on March 9, 1327, the same day on which he was raised to the judicial bench. He died in 4 Edward III., in possession of Hautboys, Whatacre, and five other manors in Norfolk, leaving a wife named Matilda, and a son named Fulk, among whose three daughters the inheritance was afterwards divided. (*Cal. Inq.* p. m. ii. 30, 148.)

BEALKNAP, ROBERT DE, had very considerable possessions in the county of Kent before he could have acquired them from the profits of his profession; yet there is no certainty who his parents were, except that their names were John and Alice. Probably his father was a lawyer, as an advocate of that name occurs in the Year Book of 20 Edward III. Robert's career in the courts commences in 36 Edward III.; and in 40 Edward III. he became a king's serjeant, for which he had a salary of 20*l.* a year, with another of the same amount as a justice of assize—a duty which he frequently performed till his elevation to the bench at Westminster. (*Liber Assisarum.*) This event occurred on October 10, 1374, 48 Edward III., when he was constituted chief justice of the court of Common Pleas. Three months before, he had been sent to treat with the pope's nuncios as to the reformer Wicliff. (*N. Fœdera*, iii. 1007, 1015.) He was knighted in 1385.

Retaining his place on the accession of Richard II., he continued in the steady performance of his duties in court and in parliament for thirteen years. Only one incident of importance varied the quietness of this period of his life. In May 1381 he was sent into Essex with a commission to bring to trial and punishment the insurgents who had risen against the poll-tax recently imposed. No sooner had the grand jury begun to find the indictments than they were broken in upon by the rioters, their heads chopped off and carried away on poles, and the chief justice was compelled to swear that he would hold no more such sessions. (*Turner's Engl.* ii. 245.) The circumstance that no personal injury was offered to him proves the respect with which he was regarded, and that the outrages of the people were not directed against lawyers as lawyers.

In October 1386 the parliament insisted on the removal of the king's favourites, impeached and convicted the chancellor, Michael de la Pole, and passed the ordinance by which the executive government of the country was substantially placed in the hands of eleven commissioners, with a complete control over the public revenue. The Archbishop of York afterwards charged Bealknap with having devised it; but this was evidently without foundation.

In the following year that prelate, with the Duke of Ireland, the Earl of Suffolk, and Chief Justice Tresilian, having stirred up the king to resist the encroachment on his authority, the judges were summoned to Shrewsbury to support this purpose by declaring the ordinance to be illegal. There a series of questions, with answers, as some allege, ready prepared, were submitted to them for signature. Bealknap refused for some time to sign the document, but the duke and earl threatening his life if he persisted, he at last submitted, exclaiming as he did so, 'Now here lacketh nothing but a rope, that I may receive a reward worthie for my desert; and I know if I had not doone this I might not have escaped your hands; so that for your pleasures and the king's I have doone it, and deserved thereby death at the hands of the lords.' (*Holinshed*, ii. 782.) The seals of all the judges present were accordingly attached to an act of council, dated at Nottingham, August 25, 1387, 11 Richard II., containing the questions and answers, by which they declared the whole proceedings to be contrary to the king's prerogative, and all the promoters of them to be guilty of high treason, thus in effect condemning the commissioners and all the lords of parliament to the death of traitors.

The lords were not idle in securing themselves from the danger to which they were thus exposed; and adding this charge to many others, they appealed the four favourites, together with Nicholas Brambre, of treason, of which they were all convicted in the next parliament. It is said that on February 3, the day of its meeting, Sir Robert Bealknap and the rest of the subscribing judges were arrested while sitting in court; but this could not be, as Bealknap was removed, and Robert de Charleton appointed his successor, three days before. He was, however, conveyed to close imprisonment in the Tower. At the trial, on March 2, Bealknap pleaded the compulsion under which he signed, and prayed mercy; but the temporal lords, not admitting that excuse, found him and the others guilty, and adjudged them to be drawn and hanged as traitors, their heirs to be disinherited, and their lands and goods to be forfeited to the king. The spiritual peers, who had previously retired from the house, the case being capital, now came forward and interceded for the lives of the unfortunate judges, whose sentence was ultimately commuted to that of banishment for life. The town of Drogheda, with three miles round it, was fixed as the retreat of Bealknap, and an allowance of 40*l.* was granted to him for his support. There he remained till January 1397, when the parliament remitted this part of his punishment, and he was allowed to return to England; and in the following year the whole of the judgment was reversed, and the restoration of such of the forfeited lands as had not been alienated was decreed. (*Rot. Parl.* iii. 233–244, 346, 358.) But all the acts of this parliament were annulled immediately on the accession of Henry IV., so that the forfeiture remained in full force.

The date of his death is not precisely known. His wife was next of kin and heir of Thomas Phelipp de Baldock, and is called sometimes Sybell, and sometimes Juliana. Their son Hamon did not obtain the complete removal of the attainder till 4 Henry VI., when he recovered possession of his estates, which descended eventually to his grandson Sir Edward Bealknap, who was a privy counsellor in the time of Henry VII. and VIII. Dying without issue, the property was divided among his three sisters, one of whom married Sir William Shelley, a judge in the latter reign.

BEAUCHAMP (BELLO-CAMPO), ROBERT DE, was the son of a baron of the same name, of Hache in Somersetshire, on whose death, about 7 John, he was left a minor, under the guardianship of Hubert de Burgh. In 17 John he was sheriff of Oxfordshire, and constable of the castle of Oxford. The manor and park of Woodstock were also committed to his charge, and in reward for his adherence to his sovereign in that time of revolt, he received various grants of land. (*Rot. Pat.* 62, 178; *Rot. Claus.* i. 220, 235, 251, 267.)

On July 6, 1234, 18 Henry III., he was constituted one of the king's justices of the Bench, and in 26 Henry III. he paid eighty

F

marks to be exempted from attending the king into Gascony.

He died in 36 Henry III., his son and heir, Robert, being admitted to do homage February 1, 1252, on paying 100*l*. for his relief. (*Excerpt. e Rot. Fin.* ii. 123.)

After a long succession of honours granted to his descendants, the judge is represented in the House of Lords by the Dukes of Norfolk and Somerset and the Marquis of Hertford.

BEAUCHAMP (BELLO-CAMPO), WALTER DE, the family of Walter de Bello-Campo was settled at Elmley Castle in Worcestershire, of which county his ancestors were hereditary sheriffs. His father, William, died before 13 John, leaving him as yet a minor. Roger de Mortuo Mari, and Isabella his wife, had a grant of his wardship and marriage on a fine of three thousand marks. He had attained his majority in February 1216, 17 John, for he was then entrusted with the sheriffalty of Worcestershire; but a few months afterwards he joined the barons' party for a short time. He soon, however, recovered the king's favour, but, having been excommunicated for his secession, he was obliged to apply to the pope's legate for absolution before his lands were restored to him; and from that time, with a short interval, till his death he retained the sheriffalty.

In 7 Henry III. he obtained the grant of a market for Kibworth in Leicestershire, and was allowed to have the scutage of his knights and tenants. He was twice selected to perform the duties of justice itinerant, in 1226 and in 1227. For some offence, which is not stated, he was disseised of his sheriffalty in 14 Henry III., in which year he was summoned to show cause why he had not accounted for the preceding year; but before the close of that year he was reinstated in his office on a fine of six palfreys. He died in 1236, when William, his son, on April 16, did homage for his father's lands, and paid the usual baronial relief of 100*l*. for the livery of them. The son of this William became Earl of Warwick, and one of his descendants was created Duke of Warwick, a title now extinct, as are several baronies derived from the same source. The only peers who can now claim a descent from this judge are the Earl of Abergavenny and Earl Beauchamp.

BEAUCHAMP (BELLO-CAMPO), WILLIAM DE, would seem to be the lord of the barony of Bedford, for livery of which, on the death of his father Simon, in 9 John, he gave five hundred marks and six palfreys. Although he was with the king's army in the expeditions to Scotland in 13 John, and to Poitou in 16 John, he afterwards deserted the royal cause, and entertained the rebellious barons at the castle of Bedford, which, in the following December, was captured by Faukes de Breaute. He was one of the barons who were excommunicated by name; and even on King John's death he did not return to his allegiance, but was taken in arms by the royal forces at the siege of Lincoln, in May 1217. Before October in that year, however, he made his peace and had restitution of his lands. When the castle of Bedford was destroyed, in 1224, in consequence of the resistance of Faukes de Breaute, William de Beauchamp had the site restored to him, with part of the materials to erect a mansion there. In the previous year, 7 Henry III., he was in the expedition to Wales, for his support in which he had a grant of the scutage of the tenants of his different possessions, which were situate in eight counties. (*Rot. Claus.* i. 325, 326, 571, 632, 654, ii. 23.) He was again engaged in that country in November 1233, and was present when Richard, earl marshal, surprised the king at the castle of Grosmunt, when he and many of his barons narrowly escaped with their lives.

In the following summer, on July 6, 1234, he was assigned to sit at the Exchequer 'tanquam baro;' and his attestation in that character appears three years after that date. (*Madox*, ii. 54, 317.) In 19 Henry III. he was constituted sheriff of the united counties of Bedford and Buckingham, which he held for the next two years. (*Fuller.*)

He lived to a good old age, the fine roll containing an entry of his lands being seized, as usual, into the king's hands on his death, on August 21, 1262. He had five years previously settled his estates on his son William, for the king's confirmation of which the latter paid a fine of five hundred marks. (*Excerpt. e Rot. Fin.* ii. 254, 381.)

He married three wives—Gunnora, the sister of William de Lamvallei, receiving with her the town of Bromley; Ida, with whom he had the manor of Newport in Buckinghamshire; and, thirdly, in the latter years of his life, Amicia, to whom, soon after his death, the manor of Belcham was committed in tenancy. (*Ibid.* ii. 383.)

Both his sons, William and John, dying without issue, the property was ultimately divided among his daughters. (*Dugdale's Baron.* i. 223; *R. de Wendover*, iii., iv.)

BEAUFORT, HENRY (BISHOP OF WINCHESTER). When the statute was passed, in January 1397, legitimating the children of John of Gaunt by his mistress Catherine Swinford, whom he had married in the preceding year, Henry Beaufort, the second son, was probably just of age, as he is called clericus on the roll, and his next brother, Thomas, is styled domicellus. (*Rot. Parl.* iii. 343.) He was educated in part at Aix-la-Chapelle, and in part at Queen's College, Oxford; and when he was little more than a boy he formed an amatory connection with Alicia, daughter of Richard, Earl of Arundel, sister to the Archbishop of Canterbury, and nearly related by marriage to John of Gaunt himself, and had by her an illegitimate daughter named Joan. The amour did not impede his future fortunes, nor prevent his brother, King Henry IV., from placing his own son, afterwards Henry V., under his tuition in the same college. This was about the year 1399, when Beaufort had been appointed chancellor of the university, an office which he held only one year. In the capacity of tutor he no doubt ingratiated himself with his pupil, and certainly was not a very severe preceptor, if we may judge from the money which he advanced to him while Prince of Wales; being no less a sum than 826*l*. 13*s*. 4*d*., the whole of which was repaid as soon as Henry came to the throne. (*Devon's Issue Roll*, 329.)

Bred up as an ecclesiastic, he received in the year of his legitimation the deanery of Wells, together with a prebend in the church of Lincoln, and was elected bishop of the latter see on July 14, 1398. He accompanied King Richard on his fatal expedition to Ireland, during which Henry of Lancaster came back from his exile; and he was one of three bishops who were with the king at Milford on his too long delayed return. His indifference to the event and the politic character which he then bore are shown by his appearing in the first parliament of the usurper, and consenting to the perpetual imprisonment of his late master. (*Rot. Parl.* iii. 426.) His presence at the earlier councils of Henry IV., and his being entrusted with the education of the young prince, prove that there was no interruption in the intercourse between him and his royal brother. In 1402 he was sent to escort the king's second wife, Joan of Navarre, Duchess of Brittany, to England. This marriage took place on the 7th and her coronation on the 25th of February 1403, within four days of which the young bishop received the Great Seal as chancellor of England. For his accommodation in attending the court the towns of 'Woltomstowe and Old Stratford' were assigned for his livery, and 'pro herbergiagio' of his servants and horses. (*Rymer*, viii. 324.)

The death of William of Wykeham occurring about this time, the king procured his election to the vacant bishopric of Winchester, the temporalities of which were restored to him on March 14, 1405. (*Ibid.* 392.) On his translation to this see he vacated the office of chancellor; but during the remainder of the reign he acted as one of the council; and on January 27, 1410, there being then no chancellor, he declared the causes for which the parliament was summoned. (*Rot. Parl.* iii. 622.)

On the accession of his pupil and nephew Henry V., March 13, 1413, the Great Seal was immediately replaced in his hands. He retained it during the whole of the first four years and part of the fifth year of the reign, opening all the parliaments that were held during that period, and having the satisfaction to announce to that of November 1415 the glorious victory of Agincourt, won little more than a week before. (*Ibid.* iv. 62.)

Just previous to the king's next expedition into France, for the support of which the bishop had advanced him the sum of 14,000*l*., secured on certain duties, and for the repayment of which a golden crown was deposited with him as a pledge on July 18, 1417 (*Ibid.* iv. 111), the Great Seal was resigned by Beaufort on the 23rd of that month, when he obtained a grant of pardon for all crimes and offences. (*Rymer*, ix. 471.) The apparent cause of this retirement was to undertake a pilgrimage to the Holy Land; but the probable one was to proceed to the Council of Constance, then sitting, for the purpose of settling the claims of three contending popes, and of arranging certain reformations in the Church. Though not originally appointed on the part of England to attend this council, he deemed his appearance there necessary in order to terminate a struggle which had already lasted too long. He reached Constance in the garb of a pilgrim, and his presence was deemed by some to be very prejudicial to the cause of the reform of the Church. The question then agitating was, whether that or the election of the pope should take precedence. By his suggestion, and on the promise of the cardinals not to delay the consideration of reform, the election was proceeded with; but on its falling on Martin V. every attempt to renew the question of reform was frustrated, and the council was dissolved without any sound improvement being effected. (*Tyler's Henry V.* ii. 61.) In November following, the new pope named the bishop cardinal and apostolic legate in England, Ireland, and Wales; but by the remonstrances of Archbishop Chichely, who considered this an encroachment on his authority, the king forbade him to accept the dignity. From Constance the bishop proceeded on his pilgrimage to Jerusalem, of his adventures in which, or of the precise date of his return, we have no certain information.

We find the bishop again in England in 1421, when he was one of the sponsors for the king's son, afterwards Henry VI.; and again lent his sovereign 14,000*l*. towards the prosecution of the war, for which and for the arrears of the former loan a golden crown was again given in pledge. (*Rot. Parl.* iv. 132.)

On the death of Henry V. the bishop

and his brother Thomas, Duke of Exeter, were appointed governors of the person of the infant king, their great-nephew; while John, Duke of Bedford, the king's uncle, was made protector of England when within the kingdom; but when absent his brother Humphrey, Duke of Gloucester, was to execute the same office. The Duke of Bedford being in France at the accession, the immediate government fell on the Duke of Gloucester; but jealousies arose, which soon resulted in a determined hostility between the duke and the bishop, to whom the former attributed the checks which were placed by the council on his exercise of the supreme authority. Historians differ as to which was in fault; but probably both were in some measure to blame in the commencement of their disputes, and certainly in the extent to which they were carried.

The bishop's ascendency in the council was naturally very great. The records prove that he never failed in his attendance there; and in February 1424 he assisted the government by advancing 4,000*l.*, afterwards increased to 11,302*l.* 16*s.* 1*d.*, for which he received certain crown jewels in pledge for repayment. On July 6 in the same year he was, by the advice of the council, invested for a third time with the office of chancellor; and his labours being greatly increased by the absence of both the dukes from the kingdom, the council assigned him 2,000 marks per annum beyond his accustomed salary. (*Acts Privy Council*, iii. 146, 165.) He opened the parliament of April 1425; but before that of the following year the disputes between him and the Duke of Gloucester ran so high as to require the presence of the Duke of Bedford, who came from France to endeavour to effect an accommodation. The immediate necessity for this interference arose from the refusal of the governor of the Tower to admit Gloucester on his return to England into that fortress, in consequence of an order of council to exclude every one more powerful than himself. Gloucester, attributing this order to the bishop, caused the gates of the city to be closed against him, whereupon the retainers of both prepared to attack each other, and were with difficulty prevented by the Archbishop of Canterbury and the Duke of Coimbra, a cousin of the king's. By their intercession the parties were induced to keep the peace till the Duke of Bedford was referred to.

The protector on his arrival seems to have acted most fairly, although his impressions were evidently in favour of the bishop. He issued instructions from St. Albans to the Archbishop of Canterbury and others to see the Duke of Gloucester, and endeavour to induce him to attend at Northampton, and be reconciled to the bishop previous to the parliament which had been summoned for the 18th of that month. But, the duke being inflexible, it became necessary, in order to prevent collision between the followers of the angry parties, to forbid any arms to be brought to the place of meeting. Evading this mandate, they attended with bats and clubs on their shoulders; from which circumstance the parliament was called the Parliament of Bats. The bishop opened the session as chancellor; and on the Commons praying that the differences might be settled, and the protector and the lords having taken an oath to judge with impartiality, the two contending parties thereupon agreed to submit to the arbitrament of certain lords then named. The rolls of parliament do not contain the charges made by the duke against the bishop as stated by the historians, but only the award made by the lords, by which they unanimously acquitted him; and he, by their award, made a public denial in parliament of their truth, and a public declaration of his having no ill-will to the duke; who in his turn was required by the award to say, 'Fair uncle, since you so declare you such a man as you say, I am right glad that it is so, and for such I take you.' The two then, according to the award, took each other by the hand. This occurred on March 12, 1426, and on the next day the bishop at his own request was exonerated from the office of chancellor. (*Rot. Parl.* iv. 296-299.) On May 14 he prayed for permission to undertake a pilgrimage which he had long deferred, and accompanied the Duke of Bedford to Calais. His mortification was in some measure diminished by the announcement of his nomination as a cardinal by Pope Martin V., with the title of Presbyter of St. Eusebius, Cardinal of England. He returned to England in September 1428, having been previously appointed legate of the pope, and captain-general of the crusaders against the Bohemian Hussites. Here the Duke of Gloucester, who still retained his enmity, took an opportunity of annoying him by inducing the council to refuse to allow him to officiate on St. George's Day as chancellor of the order of the Garter, on the pretence that it was unusual for a cardinal to retain the bishopric of Winchester. The cardinal submitted for the time, but had influence enough to obtain permission to raise 250 lances and 2,500 archers for that crusade. These forces, however, in less than a fortnight were, by reason of 'the great and grievous adversities and fortunes of war happened to the king's subjects in his realm of France,' directed to proceed to serve under the Duke of Bedford for half a year, for permitting which the cardinal was to receive a reward of 1,000 marks. (*Acts*

Privy Council, iii. 330-345; *Rymer,* x. 414.) The pope's displeasure at this equivocal transaction was well compensated by the popularity it procured for the prelate in England, where he was allowed to resume his seat at the council, notwithstanding his being a cardinal. He accompanied the young king to France, and performed the ceremony of his coronation at Paris on December 17, 1430.

The Duke of Gloucester died on February 28, 1447, previous to which the cardinal had for some years retired from court, and his own dissolution took place on April 11, within six weeks of the duke's. So powerful, however, has been the enchantment of Shakspeare's genius that his dramatic picture of the cardinal's character is too often accepted as historic truth, without reflecting that the simple object of the bard was to enliven scenes developing political events, and to create a powerful interest in his audience by exhibiting the great actors of the time in strong and exciting contrast. No doubt the cardinal was not exempt from the frailties which were then too common; he was evidently fond of money, ambitious of power, jealous of rivalry, and more attentive to his political than his episcopal duties. But looking at the public evidences that are still extant, not excluding the multiplied charges with which the duke perpetually assailed him, there is little that can affect his character as a man anxious at once to serve his sovereign and to promote his country's welfare. The popular voice had been strongly in his favour; and when it is recollected that during his ministerial career France was both won and lost to England, it is not surprising that the prejudice excited against him towards the close of his life should extinguish the memory of his former praises, and that, being the last popular impression of his character, it should alone survive him, and form a tradition sufficiently recognised to warrant its introduction into a dramatic representation.

Cardinal Beaufort was a bishop for forty-nine years—seven at Lincoln, and the rest at Winchester. No works of his are mentioned in the former diocese; but in the latter he expended vast sums in completing the cathedral, and particularly in his new endowment of the hospital of St. Cross, which owes many of its present buildings to his munificence, and to which he added the means of supporting an increased number of poor brethren. The charity which he dispensed among the poor during his life was continued under his will; and the pious dispositions which he made in his first codicil, dated only four days before his death, are a sufficient contradiction to the allegation that he died in despair. (*Godwin de Præsul.* 231, 296; *Testamenta Vetusta,* 249.)

BEAUFORT, THOMAS (DUKE OF EXETER), was the younger brother of Cardinal Henry Beaufort, being the third and youngest son of John of Gaunt, Duke of Lancaster, by his mistress Catherine Swinford, whom he afterwards married, and whose children by him were all legitimated by a statute passed in January 1397.

Thomas was then a minor, being called 'domicellus' in the record; but two years afterwards he received a grant from the king of the castle and town of Castle Acre in Norfolk. The first notice of his knightly career is in 1402, when he was custos of Ludlow Castle, and received 88*l.* 18*s* 6*d.*, for the wages of himself and his garrison, to resist the invasion of the rebels there. In the following year he was appointed admiral of the fleet towards the north, an office which he held for many years; and in 9 Henry IV. was made captain of Calais. That in these commands he exhibited considerable ability as a statesman may be inferred from his being selected as the successor of Thomas de Arundel, Archbishop of Canterbury, in the office of chancellor, being the only lay chancellor of that reign.

Sir Thomas received the Great Seal on January 31, 1410. From an entry in the following year it would seem that the duties were not agreeable to him, as he humbly prayed to be discharged. This, however, was refused by his royal brother (*Rot. Claus.* 11 & 12 Henry IV.); and he had completed nearly two years of service before he was allowed to retire, on January 5, 1412. During his tenure of office he had a grant of 800 marks per annum, besides the accustomed fee. (*Acts of Privy Council,* i. 338.) Little other record of his proceedings as chancellor remains than of his opening and adjourning the parliament of November 1411, and as an assistant of the Archbishop of Canterbury in trying John Badby for heresy. (*State Trials,* i. 219.)

On the 5th of July following his resignation of the Great Seal he was created Earl of Dorset; and during the remainder of his life he devoted himself to pursuits more congenial to his taste than the law, distinguishing himself to the last, in the wars of Henry V., as a brave knight and a wise commander. In the first year of that reign he was made lieutenant of Acquitaine. He next was appointed governor of Harfleur on its surrender to the English; and after the battle of Agincourt, October 25, 1415, in which he commanded the rear of the forces, he was constituted lieutenant of Normandy. On the 18th of November 1416 he was raised, in full parliament, to the title of the Duke of Exeter; and was also made a Knight of the Garter. Scarcely a year of Henry's reign was unmarked by his prowess, either in Scotland or in France. In all of these encounters he was victorious, except in the battle of Anjou, on April 3, 1421, when the Duke of Clarence was killed, and he was unfortunately taken prisoner.

He was an executor of the will of Henry V.; and on the death of that monarch, in 1422, he was one of the counsellors appointed by the parliament to assist the protectors of the kingdom during the minority of his successor.

The four remaining years of his life were employed in this duty, and in acting in the field in the foolish and unjust war which the English carried on against France; adding to his other honours the office of justice of North Wales.

He died at his manor of Greenwich on January 1, 1427; and, as he left no issue by his wife Margaret, the daughter of Sir Thomas Nevill, of Horneby, his titles became extinct. He was interred at the abbey of St. Edmund's Bury, where, 350 years after (see *Times*, Oct. 19, 1841), his coffin was discovered among the ruins, and his body was found to be 'as perfect and entire as at the time of his death.' (*Dugdale's Baron*. ii. 125.)

BEAUMONT, ROBERT DE (EARL OF LEICESTER), succeeded, as the elder of two twin sons, his father of the same name, who, as Earl of Mellent in Normandy, was one of the principal ministers of Henry I., and acquired the reputation of being the first statesman in Europe. He was allied to the family of the Conqueror; and, accompanying him as a young man in his expedition to England, he distinguished himself by making the first onset in the battle of Hastings. He reward was the grant of above ninety lordships in the counties of Warwick, Leicester, Wilts, Northampton, and Gloucester. Adhering to King Henry I. in his contests with his brother Robert, he was created Earl of Leicester; and, dying in 1118, Waleran, the younger of the twins, succeeded to the earldom of Mellent, and the lands in Normandy; while those in England, with the earldom of Leicester, devolved on this Robert, who was surnamed Bossu.

Although this earl was also in great favour with Henry I., and was with him at his death in 1135, he supported King Stephen in the early part of his reign, and obtained a grant of the town, castle, and county of Hereford. On the arrival, however, of Henry, Duke of Normandy, he declared for that prince, supplied him with necessaries, and assisted him with powerful military aid. He was a witness to the convention between the prince and King Stephen, which terminated this intestine warfare.

On Stephen's death, the earl was among the principal counsellors of his successor; and being as eminent for the qualifications of his mind and his knowledge of the law, as he had shown himself in state policy and civil affairs, he was immediately raised by Henry to the office of chief justiciary, or president of the Exchequer, which he retained during the remainder of his life. This appointment is said by some to have been held by him in conjunction with Richard de Luci; and there are some writs which seem to show that it was so.

Throughout the king's contest with Becket, he aided his royal master in maintaining the rights of the state against the encroachments of the clergy. His prudence was so great, and his piety so notorious, that even the violent archbishop did not venture to include him in the sentence of excommunication which he pronounced against several of the king's counsellors, although he had been one of the principal actors, and had joined in prevailing on Becket to sign the Constitutions of Clarendon.

Before that contest was terminated by the murder of Becket, the Earl of Leicester died, in 1167, at the abbey of Leicester, which he had founded in 1143. He is stated to have been a canon regular of that abbey for fifteen years before his death; but if so, his employments prove that he had a dispensation from the observance of the strict rules of the order. Besides this abbey, he founded three other religious houses, and was also a liberal benefactor to many more.

He married Amicia, daughter of Ralph de Waet, Earl of Norfolk, and had by her a son, Robert, surnamed Blanche-Maines, whose son and successor, Robert Fitz-Parnell, dying in 1206 without issue, the male branch of the family became extinct. (*Madox*, i. 34, ii. 138, 394; *Lord Lyttelton's Henry II.; Dugdale's Baron*. i. 84.)

BEAUMONT, JOHN, belonged to a very ancient family whose barony dates from the year 1309, but which in 1507 fell into an abeyance which was not terminated till the year 1840, when the father of the present baron (Miles Thomas Stapleton) was summoned to parliament as the representative of the eldest daughter of the last lord's sister.

The immediate ancestor of John Beaumont was Sir Thomas, the second son of the fourth baron, whose grandson, Thomas, was seated at Thringston, near Cole-Orton, and died in 1530, leaving, by his wife Anne Harcourt, two sons—this John, and Edward, whose representatives still flourish at Barrow-on-Trent in the county of Derby.

John Beaumont began his legal career at the Inner Temple, and, gradually rising to the bench of that society, filled the office of reader in autumn 1537, and a second time in Lent 1543, and was elected treasurer in 1547. As his name does not appear in any of the Reports, he probably did not practise in the common law courts, but confined himself to the Chancery and the Star Chamber, and to such duties as devolved upon him as surveyor of Leicestershire for the crown. In 1550 he was chosen recorder of Leicester; and his elevation to the mastership of the Rolls took place on December 13 of the same year.

On February 9, 1552, according to King Edward's journal, he 'was put in prison for forging a false deed from Charles Brandon, Duke of Suffolk, to the Lady Anne Powis, of certain lands and leases;' and it appeared by his subsequent confession that, in a cause before him in Chancery between the succeeding duke, Henry, and the lady, he had bought her title, and had forged the hand of the late duke to support it. In addition to this, he was charged with peculation to a large extent, an offence which was then too prevalent. In his submission, which is dated May 28, he designates this by the softer name of a debt charged upon him in the Court of Wards and Liveries, amounting to 20,871*l.* 18*s.* 8*d.*, in satisfaction of which he was 'pleased and contented' that the king should have all his manors and lands, and all his goods and chattels, with the issues and profits of the same, provided that all just allowances out of the said debt were made to him. To this submission the surrender of his office was added. The king records his subsequent denial of his guilt, and his ultimate confession of it in the Star Chamber on June 20. Sir Robert Bowes was designated as his successor as early as May 10; and the patent of his appointment on June 18 contains an entry of the disgraceful nature of Beaumont's dismissal. Hayward adds that 'he was a man of a dull and heavy spirit, and therefore the more senselessly devoted in his sensual avarice.' (*Burnet, Reform.* ii. pt. ii. 68, 80–3; *Kennett,* ii. [319].)

He was evidently treated with much leniency. The monastery of Grace-Dieu, with a considerable estate in Charnwood Forest in Leicestershire, given to him and his wife and their heirs by Sir Humphrey Foster in 1539, which he had given up at his disgrace, was in the following year granted by the king to Francis, Earl of Huntingdon, and his heirs. As the earl was uncle to John Beaumont's wife, it may be readily supposed that this was a merciful mode of restoring the estate to the family; and consequently, on Beaumont's death five years afterwards, the lady entered on the land, which was confirmed to her by the then Earl Henry (*Coke's* 9 *Rep.* 183), and was enjoyed by their son, to whose posterity it descended.

She was Elizabeth, the daughter and heir of Sir William Hastings, the younger son of William, Lord Hastings; and by her he had two sons—one of whom, Francis, is the subject of the next article. (*Wotton's Baronet.* iii. 235.)

BEAUMONT, FRANCIS, the eldest son of the last-named, John Beaumont, was a fellow-commoner of Peterhouse, Cambridge, in 1564, when Queen Elizabeth visited the University. He represented Aldborough in 1572, and in 1581 he was elected autumn reader in the Inner Temple, and though neither Dugdale nor Wynne include him among the serjeants, yet Nichols, in his 'History of Leicestershire' (iii. 655), quotes a letter from him to the Earl of Shrewsbury, which proves that he took that degree. It is dated at Normanton by Derby, one of his manors, on July 3, 1589, and in it, after apologising 'for omitting to pay 100*l.* on a certain day, he requests the earl's permission to name him as his chief patron in his introductory speech in the court of Common Pleas as a serjeant-at-law, such being the custom on those occasions.' He was evidently, therefore, included in the call of that year.

He was promoted to the bench as a judge of the Common Pleas on January 25, 1593; but sat there little more than five years, his death occurring at his paternal seat of Grace-Dieu on April 22, 1598. He was buried in the church of Belton, within which parish his seat is situated. (*Ath. Cantab.* ii. 246.) Burton, the historian of Leicestershire, who was three-and-twenty when Beaumont died, calls him a 'grave, learned, and reverend judge;' and it may well be believed that his legal attainments alone would not have procured his elevation to the judicial ermine, had not his character for integrity been such as to remove the stigma attached to his father's name. It would be curious to discover the origin of an absurd story told by Nichols from a manuscript note to Burton's work, which states that two men came before the judge at Grace-Dieu for justice, and one of them prayed that the ground might open and he might sink if what he attested was not true; that the ground immediately did open, but the judge, by pointing with his finger, ordered them to go off, and it closed again; and that, according to the affirmation of his great-granddaughter's son, the place sounded in his time, being struck on.

By his wife, Anne, daughter of Sir John Pierrepoint, of Holme-Pierrepoint in Nottinghamshire, and relict of Thomas Thorold, of Marston in Lincolnshire, he had three sons. His eldest son, Henry, was knighted, and died at an early age, leaving only a daughter. His second son, John, then succeeded to Grace-Dieu (*Beaumont's Case, Coke's 9 Rep.* 138) and obtained a baronetcy in 1626, which expired in 1686, after having been enjoyed by his two sons in succession. Sir John, however, has a better claim to memory than his title, in being the author of 'Bosworth Field' and other poems, which not only were admired by his contemporaries Jonson and Drayton, but have received high praise in our own time from Campbell and Wordsworth. The judge's third son, Francis, has given an immortality to the name of Beaumont which, it cannot be denied, the highest legal attainments fail to secure. Fletcher, the partner of his labours, was, curiously enough, the son of a bishop; and unbecoming as it might then have been deemed that the representatives of two respected members of the episcopal and judicial bench should devote themselves to the theatre, yet, such is the power of genius over learning, the twin stars of dramatic excellence have so entirely eclipsed the glories of their fathers, that little more is known of the bishop or the judge than that the poets were their sons.

BECKET, THOMAS (ARCHBISHOP OF CANTERBURY), was a native of London, having been born in the parish of St. Mary Colechurch, on the north side of Cheapside, in the year 1118. (*Monast.* vi. 646.)

His ancestors, according to his own account, were citizens there, somewhat above the lowest rank, 'non omnino infimi;' but the condition of the family had evidently improved in the time of his father, Gilbert, since he had filled the office of sheriff or portgrave of the city. His mother's name was Matilda, and the story of her union with Gilbert, of which neither Becket nor any of his contemporaries state anything extraordinary, was enlivened about two centuries after his death with a romantic addition, which soon after was popularly accepted as an undoubted truth. Gilbert was said to have become a captive in the Holy Land, and to have inspired with love his master's daughter, by whose assistance he escaped; that she followed him to England, and, with no other knowledge of the English vocabulary than the words 'London' and 'Gilbert,' was lucky enough to work her way to the metropolis, and to discover the object of her search; that Gilbert forthwith procured her baptism, at which six bishops assisted, and rewarded her devotedness by making her his wife.

Omitting the omens of future greatness by which Thomas's birth was said to be attended, and the miraculous incidents which were attributed to his youth, it will be enough to relate the simple course of his early years.

Intended for the Church, he was placed at the age of ten under Robert, the prior of Merton, and afterwards studied at the schools in London. He next proceeded to Paris to finish his education, and on his return is said to have been employed as a clerk to the sheriffs of London, an occupation not unlikely for him to obtain, considering that his father had held that dignity, and was now reduced in his circumstances.

The superiority of his parts and the captivating grace of his manners had already procured him the friendship of those who frequented his father's house. From one of them, a rich baron, he obtained little more than a zest for the amusements to which he was introduced; but to two Norman ecclesiastics he was indebted for more solid advantages, and in fact for the means by which he ultimately raised himself to his highest position. They procured his admittance about 1145 into the family of Archbishop Theobald, who, soon discerning his abilities, took him into his favour, and obtained for him canonries in St. Paul's and Lincoln, besides presenting him with the livings of St. Mary-le-Strand (or as some say St. Mary-at-Hill) in London, and of Otford in Kent. By the primate's kindness, also, Becket was sent to the schools of Bologna and Auxerre, to study the canon and civil law; and, returning to England no mean proficient in them, he was employed by his patron in several embassies to the court of Rome. Among these was one to obtain the restoration of the legatine power to the see of Canterbury, and another to procure a bull prohibiting the coronation of Eustace, the son of King Stephen. The abilities which he evinced in these negotiations, and his success in both of them, not only confirmed the archbishop's goodwill towards him, but formed the groundwork of the favour with which Henry, when he ascended the throne, immediately distinguished him.

In the meantime, however, he was rewarded with the archdeaconry of Canterbury, about 1153. Whether this dignity was followed or preceded by the provostship of Beverley is uncertain, but the date of 1139, as it stands in the lists, is obviously erroneous.

The death of Stephen, on October 25, 1154, enabled King Henry to show his appreciation of Becket's talents; and there seems very little doubt that immediately on his coronation he appointed him his chancellor, although Thynne, Philipot, Old mixon, and even Dugdale affix a later date to his nomination; inasmuch as a charter has been found, granted in the first year of Henry's reign, among the witnesses to which is 'Thomas the Chancellor.' (*Archæol. Journal*, xii. 235.)

Credit is taken on behalf of that monarch

for naming an Englishman to the office, and thus breaking through the practice, which had obtained from the time of the Conquest, of conferring all places of trust and confidence on Normans. It is, however, impossible not to see that the amalgamation of the two races, which one hundred years had produced, must have necessarily tended to destroy the exclusive system, and that the reason upon which it was founded no longer existed. Although the monarch might naturally regard his native land with affection, he would consider England as his dearest inheritance; and the disputed successions of William Rufus, Henry I., and Stephen must have shown how little ground there was for fearing opposition from an Anglo-Saxon claimant. Becket was undoubtedly an Englishman in reference to his own birth, and probably to that of his father also; but whether he was of Norman or Saxon descent is an undecided question. Though he speaks of his progenitors as citizens of London, it does not follow necessarily that they must therefore have been Saxons; and Fitz-Stephen, his chaplain and biographer, states that a Norman origin was the bond of connection between Gilbert and Archbishop Theobald. But even were he unquestionably a Saxon by lineage as well as birth, the mere desire to flatter that race by his appointment had probably little operation on the mind of Henry, who was much more likely to be influenced in his selection by the recommendation of Theobald, by his own observation of Becket's character, and by his conviction that his acknowledged abilities and popular manners best qualified him to meet the exigencies of the time.

During the eight years of Becket's chancellorship, Robert de Beaumont, Earl of Leicester, and Richard de Luci were chief justiciaries; and to the united efforts of these three, aided and encouraged by the wisdom of the king, is to be attributed that amelioration in the state of the country which became visible before many years of the reign had elapsed, in the removal of private oppression, the suppression of robbers, the restoration of property wrongfully withheld, the improvement of agriculture, and the encouragement of all peaceful arts.

His more laborious occupations were relieved by those diversions in which the court indulged, his apparent devotion to which could not but be gratifying to a youthful and joyous king, and is said by some to have been assumed for the purpose of riveting the influence he possessed over the royal mind. Nor are less innocent amusements omitted to be charged against him, which, on the other side, are met by an indignant denial. His intimate footing with Henry, however it may have been gained, is undoubted. The free and happy intercourse between them, which bore the appearance of fraternal concord, is enlarged upon by Fitz-Stephen, who relates their playful contest when the king transferred Becket's rich cloak to the shoulders of a beggar; and dwells upon the familiarity with which the king would appear without ceremony at his table, and either take a cup of wine in passing, or seat himself uninvited as a guest.

Henry in these visits could not be ignorant of the extent of Becket's liberality, nor of his general magnificence and profusion. He must have seen the extravagance in which he lived, the number of his attendants and the gorgeousness of their appointments, the splendour of his furniture and the richness of his apparel, the hospitality of his table and the luxurious delicacy of his wines and his viands. He must have been aware that the expenses of such an establishment could not be defrayed solely from the profits of the Chancery and the produce of his ecclesiastical and other preferments; and yet the knowledge produced no dissatisfaction, nor any alteration in Henry's behaviour. On the contrary, he loaded Becket with new benefits, granting him the prebend of Hastings and the wardenship of the castles of Eye and Berkhampstead, to the former of which one hundred and forty knights were attached. The custody also of various vacant bishoprics and abbeys was entrusted to him, from the proceeds of which much of his lavish expenditure was no doubt supplied.

The external dignity of the office of chancellor must have been considerably enhanced by the publicity of Henry's favour, and by the profuseness of the favourite. They formed in fact the first step towards that advanced position which the possessor of the Great Seal eventually obtained in the councils of the kingdom. It would almost seem that it was with some view of promoting such an advance that, in the embassy Becket undertook to the court of France in 1158, to ask the Princess Margaret in marriage for Henry's eldest son, he redoubled his habitual magnificence, and exhibited so pompous a cavalcade, the details of which are minutely described by Fitz-Stephen, that the inhabitants of the French towns through which he passed, on hearing that it accompanied the Chancellor of England, loudly speculated on the power of the master whose officers made such a display. At Paris he pursued the same course. He prevented Louis from paying him the customary compliment of providing for the ambassador's expenses, by contriving to anticipate the supply; he distributed his gold and silver, his jewels and plate, and even his rich apparel, in gifts around him; and the sumptuousness of his table surprised even the Parisians, by whom a dish of eels which cost a hundred shillings was not soon forgotten. But he attained his object, and brought back a favourable answer.

In the following year he appeared in a new character. The war of Toulouse broke out, occasioned by Henry's claim to that duchy in right of his wife Eleanor, whose former husband, Louis, King of France, insisted on his side of his power to dispose of it. It was on this occasion that, under the advice of Becket, a payment for every knight's fee, under the name of scutage, was first substituted for personal military service; and a new element was thus introduced into national warfare by the employment of mercenaries. Becket at his own expense led to the field no less than seven hundred knights, and a numerous and splendid retinue, heading them on every enterprise, and performing many acts of personal bravery. A French knight named Engelram de Trie was unhorsed by him in single combat, and left his steed as a trophy to the victor. After the retreat of King Henry, Becket remained behind, and with the aid of Henry de Essex took Cahors and other towns, and supported the king's name by his valour and conduct.

These acts, though somewhat inconsistent with his clerical character, and productive therefore of some remarks among his contemporaries, do not appear to have detracted from the general estimation in which he was held, nor to have raised any doubt as to his being elevated eventually to the highest ecclesiastical dignity. On the death of Archbishop Theobald, in April 1161, the king resolved to advance his favourite to the primacy; but the election did not take place till May in the following year. The delay is attributed by some to Becket's own repugnance to accept the appointment, and the conviction he felt that it would place the king and himself in collision. By others it is ascribed to the remonstrances of the English bishops and the Canterbury monks, together with the warnings of Matilda, the queen-mother, against the nomination of a man of so active and resolute a disposition. Nevertheless, the king, who considered that his own views would be forwarded by this promotion, persisted in his purpose; and Becket was consecrated on June 3, 1162, having been ordained priest on the day before.

Henry soon discovered his mistake. He at once lost a companion, a friend, and a counsellor; and obtained in their stead an opponent to his claims, a rival to his greatness, and a disturber of his peace. To which of the two the blame is to be principally attached will be decided according to the views of their several partisans, and as they may consider the claims of the state or of the Church should have the ascendency.

Whether the sudden change which Becket made in his mode of life on his attaining the archbishopric, from a free enjoyment of the luxuries of the world to a course bordering on asceticism, extending to the wearing of horsehair and the infliction of flagellation, which even his contemporaries attribute to him, is or is not to be entirely credited, there is no doubt that a considerable alteration in his conduct was soon apparent. The sacred nature of his office would demand an abstinence from all that would savour of irregularity, and a stricter attention to his external demeanour; and of these the king was not likely to complain. But it must be allowed that he had reason to consider himself deceived when, almost without notice, and certainly contrary to his expectation, Becket shortly afterwards sent in his resignation of the chancellorship, on the pretence of his incompetence to perform the duties of the two offices. As this doubt of his own powers could not have been the result of experience, inasmuch as sufficient time had not elapsed to try them, and as the two offices could not be considered incompatible, several bishops having already held the Great Seal, Henry might be justly indignant that Becket, far-sighted as he was, should not have anticipated the difficulty, and prepared him for such a determination. He could not, therefore, avoid suspecting that it was a foregone conclusion, and that some other cause had produced it. The stricter course of life which he had already adopted, and the resumption of some of the Church's ancient rights which he was then beginning to attempt, in conjunction with his resignation of the Great Seal, naturally led the king to fear that, instead of the able assistant in his plans of government which he had expected, the archbishop was about to become a declared antagonist in all those improvements connected with the clerical order which he contemplated.

The precise time of his retirement from the office of chancellor has not been mentioned; nor do any of the numerous charters that bear his name in that character afford any evidence by which the date can be ascertained. To none of these is his name attached as bearing the two offices of archbishop and chancellor; and it is generally believed that he resigned the latter before the close of the year 1162. The name of his successor has not been discovered; and there is an hiatus of about eleven years in the list of chancellors, which has still to be filled up.

The history of his after-years offers so many problems difficult to solve, even where both parties agree upon the facts, and so many discrepancies where they differ, that the pursuit of the enquiry is a thankless labour to one indifferent to the pretensions of either of the combatants, satisfied that such pretensions can never again come into controversy, and feeling that, with whatever justice each side was originally supported, the contest eventually became, as most contests do, an alternate exhibition of pride, temper, suspicion, and folly on both parts.

That Becket in the first instance claimed privileges for the Church to which no good government could submit few will attempt to deny; but it must also be admitted that Henry was aiming at a royal independence of papal authority, for which the time was not yet ripe. The first opposition of Becket no doubt led to an increased demand by the king, unaccustomed to be thwarted in his views; and thus those ultimate proceedings were caused which, by the violence of both parties, introduced the French king for his own political objects into the contest, and terminated in the catastrophe which not only obliged Henry to desist from his efforts, but made the crown for a time more than ever the slave of the papal power. Without entering into all the details of the conflict, it will be enough to notice the principal incidents in the order of their occurrence.

On Becket's resigning the chancellorship, the king required him to give up the archdeaconry of Canterbury, which he wished to retain; but at the same time he continued to entrust him with the education of Prince Henry, his eldest son, who for several years had been under his care; and the prince remained with him till the following May, when Becket proceeded to the Council of Tours.

The archbishop having resolved to resume all the possessions which had ever belonged to his see, claimed among others the custody of the castle of Rochester, because it had been bestowed on his predecessor; and required the Earl of Clare to do him homage for the castle of Tunbridge, though it had been held by that family of the crown for nearly a hundred years. He went further: on the pretence that he had a right to bestow all churches situated on the manors of his tenants, he presented one of his clerks, named Lawrence, to the church of Eynesford. William, the lord of that manor, however, who was also a tenant of the king, and possessed the advowson, immediately turned out the intruder, whereupon the archbishop incontinently excommunicated him; and it was not without some hard words between the prelate and the king that the sentence was taken off.

This kind of procedure, violent and intemperate as it was, would of course be displeasing to the king, and prompt him to dwell upon and endeavour to restrain other encroachments of the clergy. That body claimed the privilege of having every case in which any member of it was engaged tried before its own tribunals, however gross in its character or however obnoxious to the peace of the community. The sentence in the ecclesiastical courts was that of deprivation and loss of orders; operating, of course, as a very slight restraint. The consequence was, that murders and other atrocities by claimants of clerical exemption were sadly numerous. As a remedy for the evil, the king proposed that clerks should for such offences be subject to the same jurisdiction as lay offenders; and that, on conviction, they should be degraded by the Church before the secular sentence was executed. This the archbishop resisted as an innovation, contending for these immunities as an inherent right of the Church; but, a horrible case of the kind just then occurring, Henry determined to bring to issue a question in which all who were interested in preserving the public peace joined in wishing him success. Had he confined his endeavours to that object, he must have overcome all opposition.

At a meeting of the prelates at Westminster in October 1163 he stated his views; and on the bishops, at the instigation of Becket, hesitating to concur, the king asked them whether they would obey the customs of his ancestors. All of them, save one, Hilary, Bishop of Chichester, in answering that they were willing to do so, added the words 'saving their order.' On hearing this reservation, the king angrily broke up the council, and deprived the archbishop of the custody of the castles of Eye and Berkhampstead.

After some little time the bishops withdrew their opposition, and even Becket consented to retract the objectionable *salvo*. A council was accordingly held at Clarendon in January 1164 in order to record their assent. There the king required that the ancient customs of the kingdom should be reduced to writing; and they were forthwith drawn up in the form now known as the Constitutions of Clarendon. They not only made clerks accused of crimes amenable to the king's courts, and referred all questions of presentation to benefices to be decided there, but prohibited all ecclesiastics from leaving the kingdom without the king's licence, and forbad excommunication to be pronounced against his tenants in chief, and the members of his household. They brought also the patronage of the sees and abbeys more under the royal control, and gave the king power to compel the archbishop to do justice to the suitors in his court.

The barons gladly adopted them, and the bishops acquiesced. Becket alone resisted for some time; but eventually, on the pressing remonstrance of his brethren and others, went at their head to the king, and promised to keep the laws 'legitime et bonâ fide.' In doing this he can scarcely be excused from the charge of deliberate perjury, committed, as he himself previously said, 'to be repented hereafter as I may.' His successful solicitation for the pontiff's absolution from his oath would receive its natural interpretation from the king, and would at once show the insincerity with which he joined in the application for the pope's confirmation of the constitutions.

It is not to be wondered at that Henry should feel indignant at conduct which Becket's warmest admirers do not pretend to justify, or that the archbishop's request for an interview with the king at Woodstock should be refused. The royal displeasure was greatly increased by two attempts then made by Becket to proceed to Rome in defiance of the constitutions. On both occasions he was baffled by contrary winds; and in a subsequent conference with the king he was asked whether one kingdom had not room for both, and was advised to return to the duties of his province.

His friendly biographer, Herbert of Bosham, shows that his subsequent proceedings were far from temperate, and not conducted in a manner to soften the anger of the king. In a short time they came again into conflict. John the marshal, an officer of the Exchequer, having a suit in the archbishop's court relative to the manor of Pageham in Sussex, obtained a writ to remove it, requiring Becket to answer him in the king's court. Instead of appearing personally according to the law, he sent four knights with excuses, which the king deemed frivolous and insufficient. Another day was appointed, namely the 6th of October (1164), when a great council of the bishops and barons had been summoned to meet at Northampton. He was there charged with treason for his omission, and was condemned to be 'at the king's mercy,' or, in other words, to a forfeiture of all his effects, which was commuted for a fine of 500*l*.

Henry was not satisfied with this, but somewhat unfairly caused him to be arraigned on other charges, of which, as far as it appears, he had received no previous notice. He was called upon to refund 500*l*. which he had received as constable of the castles of Eye and Berkhampstead. He submitted, though he alleged that he had spent more in their repair, and gave security for the amount. It is curious that one of his bondsmen for this money was William de Eynesford (*Brady*, i. 385), the subject of his former excommunication. The next charge was for 500*l*. alleged to have been lent to him by the king during the war of Toulouse. For the payment of this also, though he declared it was a free gift, he was obliged to bind himself. And lastly, a demand was made upon him to account for the moneys he had received from the vacant sees and abbeys while under his charge, the amount of which is variously stated as 230,000, 30,000, and 44,000 marks. To answer a charge of such magnitude, he demanded, and obtained, a day for deliberation, during which his anxiety produced an illness which delayed the meeting till the following Tuesday. He then proceeded to the council, bearing his cross in his own hands; an unusual proceeding, caused by foolish reports that violence was intended him. The king, however, came not into the hall, but sent to him to know his answer. He declared that he had expended all he had received in the king's service; and that, on being raised to the primacy, he had been expressly discharged from all secular liabilities in the name of the king, by Prince Henry, and Richard de Luci, the chief justiciary. He refused, therefore, to account, and appealed to the pope. The bishops endeavoured to dissuade him, but he prohibited them from interfering in the cause. Others attempted to intimidate him, but without effect; and when the Earl of Leicester, at the head of the barons, came to pronounce judgment against him, Becket interrupted the earl, and, refusing to hear him, referred the cause to the pope, and slowly retired from the hall. Stigmatised by several of the courtiers as a perjurer and a traitor, he showed by his replies that he was by no means deficient in the grosser language of vituperation. Whether he really believed that the king would resort to personal violence may be doubted, but upon this pretence he contrived to escape in the middle of the night from St. Andrew's Monastery, where he lodged, and by a circuitous route to reach Sandwich about a fortnight after, where he embarked in a small boat, and safely landed near Gravelines.

Both Pope Alexander and King Louis of France attached themselves to Becket's interests—the one warmly, from political rivalry; the other with more caution, lest Henry should unite himself to the cause of the anti-pope. From both of them Becket had a most honourable reception—first at Soissons from Louis, who furnished him with a train of 300 knights to proceed to the pope at Sens. There he is said by some to have resigned the archbishopric into the hands of the pontiff, and to have been immediately reinstated. Alexander committed him to the care of the Abbot of Pontigny, a Cistercian monastery about twelve leagues from Sens.

King Henry, on Becket's flight, had sent ambassadors to Louis to demand that the archbishop should be given up, and to Pope Alexander to pray for his deprivation. No sooner had he heard a report of the failure of both missions, than he ordered all the archbishop's property and revenues to be seized, banished all his kindred and attendants, and deprived the clerks attached to him of the income of their preferments. These orders were rigorously executed, chiefly by Ranulph de Broc, an old enemy of Becket; and the unfortunate relations, without regard to age or sex, were transported beyond sea in the depth of winter, but were hospitably received and provided for in Flanders and France.

Becket remained at Pontigny nearly two years, habited as a Cistercian monk, but served as became his dignity. In this asylum he pursued a course of study ill-suited for one of his temperament and austere habit of life. Although his friend, John of Salisbury, remonstrated with him, and, pointing out his inflammatory tendency, recommended the perusal of the Psalms and St. Gregory's Books of Morals, wisely asking him, 'Who ever rises pricked in heart from reading laws or even canons?' the prelate still persisted; and the fruits were soon apparent.

The correspondence during this period was most voluminous. According to the opinion of one who has read much of it, it does not 'give a favourable idea of the time. There is abundance of violence, fraud, and insincerity; mean selfishness and artifice trying to veil themselves under fine professions and language; cant, too evidently known by those who used it to be nothing better than cant; strange tossing to and fro of Scripture perverted by allegory and misapplication; on the part of the pope there is temporising and much that must be called duplicity; the cardinals and other high dignitaries appear corrupt and crafty; Becket is arrogant, intemperate, and quarrelsome; Henry at once violent and slippery; Louis weakly hypocritical; and Foliot smooth, politic, and tricky.' (*Robertson's Becket*, 172.)

A negotiation opened between the king and archbishop had failed. It began in smoothness, proceeded in heat, and ended in threats and fury. Becket had been restrained by the pope from taking any steps against the king until after Easter 1166; and Henry, when that time arrived, thought it best to anticipate the sentence of excommunication which he expected Becket would pronounce by appealing to the pope. Envoys were sent to Pontigny to serve the notice of appeal, but were obliged to content themselves with reading it aloud, as Becket had gone on a pilgrimage to Soissons. There he remained a few days, and then proceeded to Vezelay, where, on the Sunday after Ascension-day, after preaching at high mass, he, in the presence of a vast concourse of people, without any previous communication to his clerks of his intention, pronounced sentence of excommunication against John of Oxford, Richard de Luci, and others; anathematised six of the Constitutions of Clarendon, and all who should act upon them; suspended the Bishop of Salisbury; and summoned King Henry to repent on pain of being anathematised if he should persist in his courses. The English bishops appealed to the pope, fixing the following Ascension-day as the term for hearing.

It was not to be supposed that Henry would permit such a provocation to pass unnoticed; and accordingly, in the following September, he caused an intimation to be given at a general chapter of Cistercians that if the archbishop were admitted into any of their monasteries, he would confiscate all the English possessions of their order. The consequence, of course, was his retirement from Pontigny; and the French king having desired him to choose a residence in his dominions, he selected a monastery near Sens.

The pope had by this time removed to Rome, whither Henry despatched a mission. At the head of it was John of Oxford, who contrived not only to procure a reversal of his excommunication, and a confirmation of his appointment to the deanery of Salisbury, but also to obtain the nomination of two cardinal legates, William of Pavia, and Otho, during the continuance of whose commission Becket's power was entirely inoperative; and the pope prohibited everybody but himself from excommunicating the king. Becket's indignation appears in violent and most offensive letters, in which the pope himself is not exempted from his vehemence. The cardinals made some efforts to procure a reconciliation, but through the obstinacy of both parties failed, and returned to Rome.

These proceedings occupied nearly a year, during which the term assigned for the appeal of the English bishops had expired. Becket refused a second appeal they wished to enter, and towards the close of 1167 extended his excommunications to the Bishop of London, Geoffrey Ridel, his own archdeacon (whom, as an instance of his choice of expressions, he called, in one of his letters, 'Archidiabolus noster'), and a long list of others, among whom were so many about the court of King Henry that 'there was hardly one that could offer him the kiss of peace at mass, but such as were excommunicated either by name or implicitly.'

The Roman pontiff was puzzled what to do between Henry's remonstrances adn Becket's representations, supported as the latter were by the French king. Irresolute to act firmly on either side, he took a middle course. He endeavoured to effect a reconciliation; and, despatching envoys for the purpose, he suspended the sentence Becket had pronounced till the following Lent; that is, Lent in 1169, for great part of the preceding year had been then exhausted in the diplomatic negotiations.

The world had now begun to be tired of the quarrel. To the pope, Becket's pertinacity could be productive of nothing but annoyance; Henry, feeling that his kingdom and his clergy were kept in a state of continual anxiety, was sincerely desirous of some accommodation; Louis was not unwilling to get rid of a troublesome guest; and Becket's own friends and dependents were sighing after a restoration to their former ease. Becket alone refused to make any concession. At an interview between Henry and Louis at Montmirail, in January 1169, Becket was admitted, when, after lamenting the differences which had arisen, and throwing himself upon the king's mercy, the inflexible archbishop qualified his submission by the words 'salvo honore Dei.' Henry was indignant, justly considering that the reservation was intended to, or at least would, warrant any future resistance; but, after reproaching him with his pride and ingratitude, declared that he would be satisfied if Becket would act towards him with the same submission which the greatest of former primates had shown to the least powerful of his predecessors. Becket, however, evaded the proposal. Even the King of France was disgusted, and the meeting terminated without further colloquy.

Becket accordingly prepared to retire from the French territory, when Louis, from a new quarrel with Henry, again changed his policy. On the termination of Lent, therefore, Becket resumed hostilities by renewing at Clairvaux the excommunications, and including among the denounced the Bishop of Salisbury and others. Notwithstanding the efforts made to prevent the admission into England of any letters from Becket, he contrived that the sentence against Foliot, Bishop of London, should be delivered at the altar of St. Paul's on the next Ascension-day.

The pope was annoyed, and directed that further proceedings should be stayed till he had tried the effect of another mission. This led to a second interview between Becket and the two kings, which took place at Montmartre, near Paris, on November 18, 1169, and had nearly led to a friendly result, when Becket demanded the kiss of peace, which Henry, in consequence of a foolish oath he had taken, having refused, the treaty was again broken off. Becket now threatened to place the kingdom under an interdict, and even to excommunicate the king; and the pope renewed his efforts to produce a reconciliation. Rotrou, Archbishop of Rouen, one of the new papal commissioners, absolved the Bishop of London; and Becket's letter of complaint shows that he was as little inclined to pay respect to the pope as to the king, when his own cause was not supported. He says, 'In the court of Rome the Lord's side is always sacrificed; Barabbas escapes, and Christ is put to death.'

Becket soon found a new grievance in the Archbishop of York having officiated at the coronation of the king's eldest son Henry, which was solemnised at Westminster on Sunday, June 14, 1170, that privilege rightfully belonging to him. This, however, did not prevent a meeting taking place near Freteval, on the 22nd of the following July, between him and Henry, when a formal reconciliation was concluded, the king promising to give him the kiss of peace in his own dominions. A full restoration of Becket's possessions, and those of his adherents, the advance of a sum of money to pay his debts, and amends for the injury he had sustained in the late coronation, were among the articles agreed on; and the archbishop was to return to the exercise of his functions, and to show all due obedience to his earthly sovereign.

The performance both of the king's promises and Becket's return was delayed; but, after two more interviews at Tours, the last of which was a friendly one, Becket resolved to set out; although Louis advised him first to insist on receiving the kiss of peace. Disappointed of meeting Henry at Rouen, as promised, and of receiving a supply for his expenses, he was obliged to submit to the escort of his warmest adversary, John of Oxford, and to borrow 300l. from the Archbishop of Rouen.

In the meantime he had received from Rome letters suspending the Archbishop of York and other prelates for assisting in the coronation, and renewing the excommunication which had been pronounced against the Bishops of London and Salisbury. Receiving these after the reconciliation, he might have suppressed them, and little doubt can exist that had he been acting with sincerity and good faith, he would have taken measures for the purpose. On the contrary, however, he forwarded them to England before he embarked; thus exhibiting the intolerance of his spirit, and exciting the greatest exasperation. He sailed from Witsand, near Calais, and landed on December 1, 1170, at Sandwich, where John of Oxford protected him from the threatened interruption of the sheriff of Kent and others.

His reception at Canterbury, after an absence of more than six years, was most enthusiastic; and his progress in the following week to see the young king was something in the nature of a triumph. His conduct, however, with reference to the bishops being known, he received orders to return to his diocese, without obtaining an interview. When there, he occupied himself till Christmas in exercising his archiepiscopal functions, Ranulph de Broc and his other enemies still offering him every species of annoyance.

On Christmas-day, at high mass, he preached to the people, and after affecting them by a reference to one martyr among their archbishops, and the possibility that there might be a second, he concluded with one of those furious denunciations by which he dealt 'damnation round the land;' uttering, in a tone 'fierce, indignant, fiery, and bold,' a vehement invective against his enemies, and pronouncing sentence of excommunication against Ranulph de Broc and his brother Robert, and also against Nigel de Sackville, a court chaplain.

The Archbishop of York and the excommunicated bishops had not been idle. They had sailed to Normandy, and meeting the king near Bayeux, had communicated to him the recent proceedings of Becket. Henry's anger knew no bounds, and in the heat of it he unguardedly dropped words reflecting on the cowardice of his courtiers for suffering him to be so long insulted by a turbulent priest. Four knights then present—Reginald Fitz-Urse, William de Tracy, Hugh de Moreville, and Richard Brito—interpreting these unhappy words too readily, at once embarked for England, and repaired to Saltwood, the castle of Ranulph de Broc, where they arrived on December 28. Henry, on their departure from the court, suspected their intention, and instantly despatched the Earl of Mandeville and two others, with orders to overtake them and to arrest the archbishop. But they did not arrive till the tragedy was completed.

On Tuesday, December 29, the knights arrived at Canterbury, and intruding into the chamber of the archbishop, they demanded of him the withdrawal of the bishops' excommunication. Becket's answer was proud and firm. He offered to absolve the Bishops of London and Salisbury if they would swear to submit to the determination of the Church; but he said the pope alone had jurisdiction over the archbishop. On reminding three of the knights that they had been his vassals, they broke into fury, and the discussion ended with most violent threats on their retirement from the room.

It was now the hour of vespers; and the monks and clergy, thinking he would be more safe in the church, hurried him through the cloisters. But the knights also, regardless of the sanctity of the place, had obtained an entrance, fully armed; and calling out, 'Where is the traitor?' and then, on receiving no answer, 'Where is the archbishop?' Becket replied, 'Here I am; no traitor, but a priest of God.' They repeated their demand for the bishops' absolution, which he met by a repetition of his denial, adding that he was ready to die, but commanding them not to touch his people. The knights then endeavoured to remove him from the church, but, finding their efforts to drag him away unavailing, Fitz-Urse struck him on the head with his sword, wounding at the same time Grim, his cross-bearer and biographer; and Tracy and Brito repeating the blows, the archbishop was soon a breathless corpse at their feet. Hugh de Moreville did not strike Becket, being employed in keeping off interference; and the four, rushing out of the church, repaired to Hugh de Moreville's castle in Yorkshire.

Though the above four knights only are recorded, other persons were apparently engaged in the atrocious project. Robert de Broc, who joined them, pointed out the private passage to the cloisters; and Robert Fitz-Ralph, or Fitz-Ranulph, is spoken of by Dugdale as having been concerned in it. William, the son of the latter, was a justicier in this reign, and will be mentioned in a subsequent page.

Thus terminated the life of one whose character, though distinguished by sterling qualities, was alloyed with many human imperfections: to which the preponderance is to be given is still, and seems likely to be, a question to be agitated by historians and biographers. Too frequently they become the advocates of the one or the other party, instead of being impartial judges between them; and the difficulty must be admitted of defining the precise line which divides firmness from obstinacy, energy from intemperance, and an honest zeal in claiming the privileges of one order from an insidious encroachment on the prerogatives of another. Whatever opinion may be formed of the claims made by Becket on behalf of the Church, few will praise him for temperance in his enforcement of them, or consider that he adopted the wisest course to obtain their recognition; and, while none will deny the extent of his acquirements or the brilliancy of his talents, many will attribute his canonisation more to the swords of his murderers than to the virtues of his life.

Two years after his assassination he was canonised; and his body, which the monks had hurriedly buried without ceremony in the crypt, from fear that it might otherwise be exposed to indignity, was removed in 1221 to a chapel prepared for its reception, where his shrine for many subsequent ages was visited by pilgrims from all parts, whom the successive popes, to keep alive the natural horror which his martyrdom had excited, and to connect it with religious zeal for papal supremacy, assiduously encouraged by granting them extraordinary indulgences. The riches which superstition lavished on this shrine were enormous, and continued to flow in, till Henry VIII., assuming the title of 'Defender of the Faith,' and deeming Becket's example a provocation to opposition, ordered the shrine to be destroyed, seized the accumulated treasures, and, directing his bones to be burned and his ashes to be scattered to the winds, stigmatised him as a rebel and traitor to his prince, and struck his name from the calendar of saints.

Becket had two sisters who survived him. One of them, Mary, was made Abbess of Barking in Essex, in 1173; and the other, Agnes, was married to Thomas Fitz-Theobald de Helles, by whom, about the end of Henry's reign, was founded a hospital in London, on the land which had belonged to Gilbert Becket, and where Thomas was born. It was called the Hospital of St. Thomas the Martyr, of Acon, and consisted of a master and several brethren of a particular order, professing the rule of St. Augustine, about that time instituted in the Holy Land. It of course did not escape the dissolution under Henry VIII., and now belongs to the Mercers' Company, part of it being called the Mercers' Chapel. (*Monast.* i. 437, vi. 645.)

BECKINGHAM, ELIAS DE, was one of the two judges who alone were found pure, when all the others were convicted of corrupt practices, and dismissed in disgrace from the seat of justice. Nothing is recorded of him beyond this fact and the dates of his judicial career. He is first mentioned at the bottom of the list of justices itinerant into Middlesex in 2 Edward I., 1274; but he clearly was not then a regular justicier, as he is mentioned in a liberate of the following year as a king's serjeant. In 4 Edward I. he was one of the justices of assize then appointed.

He afterwards filled the office of keeper of the records and writs of the Common Pleas; and an allowance of twenty shillings was made to him for the expenses of their carriage from Westminster to Shrewsbury, where the king, on his expedition to Wales in 11 Edward I., had ordered the court to be held. (*Madox,* ii. 7.)

It was not till Michaelmas, 13 Edward I., 1285, that he was raised to the bench as a judge of the Common Pleas; and when the judges were all apprehended by the king on charges of bribery and corruption, he and John de Metingham only were honourably acquitted. This occurred towards the end of 17 Edward I., 1289; and the Parliament Roll of 20 Edward I. contains an honourable record of his purity. (*Rot. Parl.* i. 84.)

He retired from the bench, or died, in 34 Edward I., 1305, the last fine levied before him being dated in fifteen days of St. Martin in that year. (*Orig. Jurid.* 44.)

He was buried at Bottisham Church in Cambridgeshire, and on his sepulchral memorial he is designated 'Justiciarius Domini Regis Angliæ.'

BEDINGFIELD, THOMAS, was the second son of Thomas Bedingfield, Esq., of Darsham Hall in Suffolk, which he afterwards purchased from his elder brother, Philip. He was born about 1593, and, having been admitted a student at Gray's Inn in 1608, was called to the bar on February 17, 1615, and was reader there in Lent 1636. He acquired such eminence in his profession that he was made attorney-general of the Duchy of Lancaster, and was thereupon knighted.

He was assigned by the House of Lords in 1642 to conduct the defence of Sir Edward Herbert, the attorney-general, against the impeachment of the Commons; but declining to plead, in consequence of the latter threatening any counsel who presumed to appear against them with their displeasure, he was committed to the Tower by the peers for his contempt of their commands. He did not, however, long suffer under this choice of predicaments, being released from his incarceration in three days. (*State Trials,* ii. 1126, 1129.) The Commons showed their estimation of him in 1646 and 1647 by several times inserting his name as one of the persons they proposed as commissioners of the Great Seal; but the appointment never was completed, in consequence of the disagreement of the Lords. But both houses concurred in October 1648 in a vote appointing him one of the judges of the Common Pleas. Not long, however, did he retain his new dignity, for on the decapitation of the king, in January 1649, Sir Thomas refused to act under the commission offered by the executioners. (*Whitelocke,* 224, 278.) Retiring into private life, he outlived the interregnum, and on the return of Charles II., in 1660, he received immediately and in legitimate manner the degree of the coif. He died at Darsham, on March 23, 1660-1, where his monument still remains. By his wife, Elizabeth, daughter of Charles Hoskins, of the county of Surrey, he left a son of the same name, and three daughters. (*Suckling's Suffolk,* ii. 222, 226.)

BEDINGFIELD, HENRY, was the fourth of five sons of John Bedingfield, of Halesworth in Suffolk, the younger brother of the above Thomas, and himself a bencher of Lincoln's Inn, by his wife, Joyce, daughter and coheir of Edmund Morgan, of Lambeth. He was born in 1633, and, having been called to the bar at Lincoln's Inn on May 7, 1657, was raised to the degree of the coif in 1663; being made king's serjeant some time after, and knighted. In 1684 he was elected sub-steward of Great Yarmouth.

Roger North calls him 'a grave but rather heavy lawyer; but a good churchman and loyal by principle.' He relates (p. 246) that Lord Guildford 'had cast his eye upon him,' and informed him of his intention to nominate him for a vacancy on the bench. The serjeant gratefully declared he would 'ever own his preferment as long as he lived to his lordship, and to no other person whatever.' But on hearing this, Chief Justice Jeffreys, jealous of the lord keeper's power, sent to the serjeant's brother, a woollen-draper in London, afterwards lord mayor, who was one of his creatures and boon companions, and told him that if his brother so much as went to the lord keeper, he would oppose him, and he should not be a judge at all. The poor serjeant, whose 'spirits were not formed for the heroics,' was obliged to conform, and accordingly was not raised to the bench during Lord Guildford's life. He however received the promotion soon after that nobleman's death, being appointed a judge of the Common Pleas on February 13, 1686. It is to be presumed that, either from his own conviction or the arguments of Jeffreys, he acknowledged the king's power to dispense with the penal laws, as two months after, upon the recommendation of the same arrogant patron, he was raised to the head of that court, on April 21, on the discharge of Chief Justice Jones. He did not enjoy this dignity much more than nine months, dying suddenly while receiving the sacrament in Lincoln's Inn Chapel, on Sunday, February 6, 1687. A mural monument of white marble was erected to his memory in Halesworth Church. (*Suckling's Suffolk*, ii. 337; *Bramston's Autobiog.* 221, 223, 268.)

BEK, THOMAS (BISHOP OF ST. DAVID'S), was second son of Walter Bek, or Becke, baron of Esseby in Lincolnshire; and Mr. Hardy (p. 12) places him in his 'Catalogue of Keepers of the Great Seal,' on the questionable ground that when John de Kirkeby, in whose possession it was left by Robert Burnel, the chancellor, was commanded to attend the king in May 1279, 7 Edward I., he was directed to leave the Seal, *sealed up with his own seal*, in the custody of Thomas Bek; and that in the same month they were both ordered to attend with it at Dover, and there to await the king's messenger. Bek was no doubt at that time, as he certainly was three years before (*Issue Roll*, iii. 91), keeper of the king's wardrobe, the usual place of the Seal's deposit. In the same year, also, he was constituted treasurer; but remained so a short time only, as Joseph de Cancy, prior of St. John of Jerusalem, held it very soon after.

Like most of the officers of the court in those days, he was an ecclesiastic, and in 3 Edward I. was in possession of the archdeaconry of Dorset, which he held till he was elected Bishop of St. David's, on June 3, 1280. He sat there for thirteen years, during which time he founded two colleges in Wales—one at Aberguilly, and the other at Landewy-brevy. He died on April 14, 1293. (*Godwin*, 580; *Le Neve*, 218, 512.)

His brother, Anthony Bek, was an officer in the Exchequer, and ultimately became Bishop of Durham.

BELER, ROGER, whose family was fixed at Kirkby, on the Wrethek, in Leicestershire, in which and in the neighbouring counties they held large possessions, was the son of William Beler and Avicia his wife, and the grandson of another Roger Beler, who was sheriff of Lincolnshire in 40 Henry III. (*Monast.* vi. 511; *Madox*, ii. 142.) In 12 Edward II. the king granted him the hundred of Framelond, and certain farms in Leicestershire, for his laudable services. (*Abb. Rot. Orig.* i. 230.) It is not stated in what capacity they were rendered; but in the same year he received a general pardon as an adherent of Thomas, Earl of Lancaster, and was confirmed in his office of bailiff and steward of Stapelford in Leicestershire. (*Cal. Rot. Pat.* 86.)

He was afterwards occasionally employed in judicial commissions till July 20, 1322, 16 Edward II., when he was raised to the Exchequer bench.

He came to a violent end, being attacked and murdered on January 29, 1326, on his journey from Kirkby to Leicester, by Sir Eustace de Folville, lord of the neighbouring manor of Ashby, who was himself mortally wounded with an arrow. A commission was issued to try the offenders; and the goods of Roger la Zousch, lord of Lubesthorp, and Robert de Helewell, charged as accessories and flying from justice, were thereupon ordered to be seized into the king's hands. Sir Roger was buried in the chantry chapel he had erected at Kirkby, where his tomb, with a fine alabaster effigies of him in complete armour, still remains. By his wife, Alicia, he left an infant son. (*Madox*, ii. 60; *Parl. Writs*, ii. 522; *Rot. Parl.* ii. 432; *Abb. Rot. Orig.* ii. 6-171; *Royal Progresses to Leicester*, by W. Kelly.)

BELET, MICHAEL, was the second son of Hervey Belet, and eventually succeeded to the lordship of Wrokeston in Oxfordfordshire, and to the manor of Shene or Richmond, which King Henry I. had granted to the family by the serjeanty of chief butler or cupbearer to the king.

The sheriffalty of various counties was entrusted to him—of Worcestershire, Wiltshire, Gloucestershire, Warwickshire, and Leicestershire—at various dates from 22 Henry II. to the end of the reign. (*Fuller's Worthies.*)

In 23 Henry II., 1177, and the two following years, he acted as a justice itinerant in various parts of England; and when the great council of Windsor, in the last of those years, divided the kingdom into four parts, and sent judges into each to administer justice, he was one of the five selected for the circuit comprehending ten counties of the home district. There are records of his acting in this character, not only in these but other counties, through many succeeding years, as late as 3 John, 1201–2. Many instances occur, also, of his partaking in the judicial duties of the Curia Regis at Westminster, fines being levied before him from 28 Henry II., 1182, through the reign of Richard, till the third of John.

About this period he died, leaving by his wife, Emma, daughter and coheir of John de Keynes, several sons, two of whom, Hervey and Michael, succeeded in turn to his honours. Hervey died without issue, and Michael is the subject of the next article.

BELET, MICHAEL. There were two Michael Belets in the reign of Henry III.— one, the son of Robert Belet, of Cumbe, who died in 3 Henry III.; and the other, the subject of this notice, who, from his profession, was always called Magister Michael Belet. He was the second son of the above Michael Belet. In 2 John the king granted to him, as his 'dilecto et familiari clerico,' the church of Hinclesham; and in 5 John that of Setburgham, in the diocese of Carlisle. (*Rot. Chart.* 75, 134.) In 3 John he paid forty marks for having the marriage of Robert de Candos 'ad opus sororis suæ;' and on the death of his brother, Hervey Belet, he fined 100*l.* for having the king's butlery, which he inherited as attached to his manor of Shene or Richmond in Surrey. (*Rot. de Oblatis*, 180, 358.)

He was some time afterwards disseised of his lordship of Wroxton in Oxfordshire, having incurred, as the record says, the king's 'malevolentiam' for some offence which is not named; but in 14 John he recovered his lands and the king's goodwill by a timely fine of five hundred marks. In the next year, however, the roll says that he is not to be summoned for sixty marks which he still owed for the butlery, 'because the king keeps that office in his own hands, and as yet holds it.' (*Madox*, i. 462, 474.) During King John's troubles he remained faithful to the royal cause, and in the last year of his reign had a grant of the land of Wischard Ledet, who was with the king's enemies. In 8 Henry III. he was custos of the rents of the bishopric of Coventry; and in the tenth year was appointed to audit the accounts of the justiciers of the quinzime, being himself one of those assigned to collect it in Northamptonshire. (*Rot. Claus.* i. 286, 583, 585, 599, ii. 95, 147.) These offices indicate that he was then in the Exchequer, and Madox (ii. 317) includes him among the barons of that court, on the authority of a writ attested by him in 22 Henry III., 1238.

He executed the office of chief butler at the marriage of King Henry in the twentieth year of his reign; and founded the priory of Wroxton, for canons of the order of St. Augustin. The date of his death is not stated.

BELL, ROBERT, a barrister of the Middle Temple, became reader there in autumn 1565. Though he is afterwards occasionally noticed in the Reports of Dyer and Plowden, he seems to have been more sedulously engaged in senatorial than in professional duties, having been a member for Lyme Regis in all Elizabeth's parliaments from 1562 till the period of his death. In October 1566 he was one of the committee appointed to petition the queen about her marriage, and expressed himself, as some other members did, with considerable boldness, on the unsatisfactory nature of her majesty's answer. This led to a dissolution in the following January, and no new parliament was called till April 1571, when Mr. Bell was named among those who were assigned to confer with the spiritual lords for the reformation of the abuses in religion. In a debate on the subsidy, having urged 'that the people were galled by two means, . . . namely, by licences and the abuse of promoters,' and having pressed 'for the calling in of certain licences granted to four courtiers to the utter undoing of 6,000 or 8,000 of the queen's subjects,' he was sent for by the council, 'and so hardly dealt with, that he came into the house with such an amazed countenance, that it daunted all the house in such sort, that for several days there was not one that durst deal in any matter of importance.' Another parliament was summoned in the following year, of which Mr. Bell was elected speaker on May 10. (*Parl. Hist.* i. 715–794.) By various prorogations this parliament was kept alive till February 8, 1576, when it again met, and the session was rendered remarkable by the committal of Mr. Peter Wentworth for the boldness of his speech on the first day. At the close of it the disagreeable duty was imposed on the speaker of moving the queen on the subject of marriage. This he seems to have done with a great deal of skill, artfully interlarding his address with graceful flattery, and concluding it with the welcome offering of a subsidy. It is evident, from the lord keeper's answer, that her majesty was not offended, for she gave a conditional assent to the prayer, and with gracious words prorogued the parliament on May 14. This prorogation lasted nearly five years, and the interval was an eventful one to the speaker.

Notwithstanding the freedom of his language in the earlier part of his parliamentary life, his conduct in the speaker's chair had been so satisfactory to the queen that she took the first opportunity to reward him. A vacancy occurring in the office of chief baron, he was invested with it on January 24, 1577, and was at the same time honoured with the order of knighthood. His judicial career, however, was brought to a fatal termination within a very few months. At the summer assizes at Oxford, on the trial of one Rowland Jenkes, 'a sawcy foul-mouthed bookseller,' for scandalous words uttered against the queen, every person in court was seized with such a malady, arising, it was believed, from the stench of the prisoners, that they all died within forty days, to the number of three hundred. Among the victims were Chief Baron Bell, the sheriff, and several knights and gentlemen of the county, Serjeant Barham, and other lawyers. (*Camden's Elizabeth, in Kennett*, ii. 459.) The chief baron was buried at Leominster.

Sir Robert's elevation to the bench rendered him incompetent to sit in parliament, and he consequently could no longer fill the speaker's chair; but, as the prorogation still continued, neither of the vacancies could be supplied till the next session, which did not occur till nearly four years after his death, when the first act of the House of Commons was to elect a speaker in his place. (*Parl. Hist.* i. 809.)

Camden describes him as 'a sage and grave man, and famous for his knowledge in the law.' He was of a respectable Norfolk family, and by his marriage with Dorothy, daughter of Edmund Beauprè, of Outwell in that county, he became possessed of Beauprè Hall. His male descendants long flourished in the county. (*Anecdotes and Traditions*, Camden Soc. 2, &c.; *Blomefield's Norfolk*, iv. 133.)

BELLA FAGO, ROGER DE, is proved by the Rolls of Parliament (i. 160, 218) to be one of the justices of assize for Warwickshire in 33 Edward I., 1305, and to have been afterwards appointed a justice of trailbaston for Cornwall and nine other counties. His harshness and cruelty in performing this duty are commemorated in a contemporary song. (*Wright's Pol. Songs*, 233.) He resided in Oxfordshire. It does not appear in what manner he was related to the opulent family of his name, which was settled in Norfolk, and which traced its lineage to Ralph de Bella Fago in the time of the Conquest.

BENDINGS, WILLIAM DE. When the great council which met at Windsor in 1179, 25 Henry II., divided the kingdom into four districts, and sent wise and learned men into each for the administration of justice, William de Bendings was selected as one of the six justiciers to whom the northern counties were appropriated, and who were also specially constituted to sit in the Curia Regis, to hear the plaints of the people. This seems to have been the first instance of the nomination of extra judges in the king's courts; the prelates and barons of the kingdom, with the great officers of state, having hitherto acted almost entirely in that capacity.

Previously to his elevation to the bench, he was one of four commissioners sent to Ireland in 1174 to settle the differences there, and to bring over Raymond, whom the king had recalled.

He was alive in the beginning of the reign of Richard I. (*Madox*, i. 94, 138, 285; *Brady's England*, 363; *Pipe Roll*, 1 Richard I.)

BENEFACTA, RICHARD. See R. FITZ-GILBERT.

BENET. The only notice recorded of Benet, 'Magister Benedictus,' is the sentence of excommunication pronounced against him by the chancellor, William de Longchamp, Bishop of Ely, because he presumed to hold the Great Seal against the statutes of the king and kingdom, as the denunciator asserts, and contrary to his prohibition. (*Madox*, i. 77.) This no doubt was when Prince John and the barons removed Longchamp from the government, and forced him to quit the kingdom, in 1192. The Seal was probably then placed in the hands of this Benet, to perform the necessary duties during the vacancy.

BENSTEDE, JOHN DE, was in frequent employment under Edward I. and Edward II. He was clerk, or secretary, to the former, whom he accompanied to Flanders on August 22, 1297, on which occasion the Great Seal, which the king took with him, was placed in his hands, and another seal left in England with the chancellor. On the king's return in the following March, John de Benstede was the messenger employed by him to carry this latter seal to the Exchequer, the Great Seal being then given back to the chancellor. (*Madox*, i. 72.) He afterwards held a place in the

G 2

king's wardrobe, when the Seal was several times deposited with him.

His closeness to the king's person in 33 Edward I. is shown by a letter addressed to him by Edward, Prince of Wales, requesting him to present to the king a petition which he enclosed from the Earl of Ulster and others, and to pray, on his part, that such justices should be assigned as would redress the grievances they complained of. He was advanced to the post of chancellor of the Exchequer in the same year (*Cal. Rot. Pat.* 65); but he resigned it in 1 Edward II., when he became keeper of the wardrobe. (*Madox*, ii. 29.)

In 2 Edward II. he was again in the Scottish wars, and was sent with Roger Savage to the King of France to arrange a meeting between him and the King of England. (*Baronage*, ii. 91.)

On October 6, 1309, in the third year, he was constituted one of the justices of the Common Pleas, and fines were levied before him from the next year till 1320; in which, on October 16, William de Herle was appointed a judge in his place. (*Orig.* 44; *Madox*, ii. 7, 31.) He probably resigned then, as, according to the inquisition (*Cal.* i. 319), his death did not occur till 1323 or 1324.

In 8 Edward II. he was sent on the king's service to Scotland, and in the tenth year had been selected as an envoy to Rome on the Scottish affairs; but the mission being stopped, he had a payment of 1*l*. per diem for the eleven days he was employed, together with an allowance of 12*s*. 5*d*. for a loss he had in the purchase and sale of 159 florins provided for his journey. (*Archæol.* xxvi. 322.) In the following year he was one of the commissioners to treat for peace with Robert de Brus; and in 12 Edward II. he was sent with the Bishop of Hereford and others to the papal court, to solicit his holiness for the canonisation of Thomas de Cantilupe, chancellor and Bishop of Hereford in the reign of Henry III.

He had large possessions in various counties, with a manor-house called Rosemont, at Eye, near Westminster, which he had licence to fortify with walls of lime and stone, and in 15 Edward II. he was returned by the sheriff of Hertford as a knight banneret. (*Parl. Writs*, ii. p. ii. 591.)

He was married twice: his first wife was named Isabella, and his second Petronilla, who survived him. His son Edward succeeded him, whose descendants were living in the county of Essex till the reign of Henry VII. (*Morant's Essex*, i. 34, ii. 495; *Chauncy's Herts*, 335; *Hasted's Kent*, v. 149.)

BEREFORD, RICHARD DE, was not improbably the brother of the undernamed chief justice, William de Bereford; and the only trace of the place of his residence while in England is in his being appointed assessor and collector in the county of Worcester for the thirtieth granted in 10 Edward I., 1283.

He was treasurer of the Exchequer of Dublin from the twenty-eighth to the last year of that reign, and probably at the beginning of that of Edward II.; but in the fourth year of the latter (1310) he was the last named of the three justices of assize assigned for six counties.

In 7 Edward II., 1314, he was raised to the chancellorship of Ireland, and retained that office till August 1317, after which date there is no mention of his name. (*Parl. Writs*, i. 404, ii. p. ii. 526; *Abb. Rot. Orig.* i. 112; *Abb. Placit.* 255; *Cal. Rot. Pat.* 61, 77.)

BEREFORD, WILLIAM DE. Mr. Nicholls, in his 'History of Leicestershire' (343), commences the pedigree of William de Bereford, or Barford, with his father, Osbert de Barford, whom, on the authority of a descent taken from Mr. H. Ferren's 'MSS. of Antiquities,' he calls chief gentleman of Ralph de Hengham, the chief justice. It seems, however, more probable, from two entries on the Plea Rolls, that this Osbert was his brother, and that both were the sons of Walter de Bereford. (*Abb. Placit.* 215, 280.)

He was a justice of the Common Pleas. Prynne (on 4th Inst. 20) gives two commissions to him, in conjunction with Robert de Hertford and Robert Malet, to enquire as to a murder in 20 Edward I.; and in the parliament that met after Easter in the following year Eustace de Parles and John his brother were convicted of insulting 'William de Bereford, a justice of our lord the king,' in the Aula Regis, by imputing to him corrupt and improper conduct during his iter into Staffordshire; and they were imprisoned in the Tower for their contempt. (*Rot. Parl.* i. 95.)

He continued to act during the remainder of the reign, and was one of those selected to treat with the Scots in 33 Edward I., and was placed in the commission of trailbaston for the northern counties in the last year of the reign. (*Rot. Parl.* i. 218, 267.) On the accession of Edward II. his patent in the Common Pleas was renewed, he holding the second place.

He was raised to the office of chief justice of that court, as the successor of Ralph de Hengham, on March 15, 1309, 2 Edward II.; and the last fine that was acknowledged before him in that character is dated in the first week of 20 Edward II., July 1326. (*Orig.* 44.) In the same month he died, leaving large possessions in eight counties, the principal of which were in Warwickshire and Oxfordshire. (*Cal. Inquis.* p. m. i. 333.)

By his wife Margaret he left two sons, named Simon and William.

BEREFORD, RALPH DE, was in all probability not very distantly connected with the above William de Bereford. According to the certificate in 9 Edward II., he possessed property in the townships of Bourton, Milcome, and Bereford, or Barford, in the county of Oxford. In the same year he was appointed one of the custodes of the vacant bishopric of Winchester; and on several occasions during the remainder of that reign was employed on commissions of Oyer and Terminer in various counties. In 1329, the third year of the reign of Edward III., he was the second of five justices itinerant into Nottinghamshire, and was named in a similar commission for five other counties. (*Parl. Writs*, ii. p. ii. 526; *Abb. Rot. Orig.* i. 227, 257, ii. 24; *N. Fœdera*, ii..537, 574.)

BEREWYK, JOHN DE, was an officer of the court, as appears from the nature of his various employments. In 7 Edward I. he was appointed custos of the vacant abbey of St. Edmund, and in the next year had a similar grant over the bishopric of Lincoln. (*Abb. Rot. Orig.* i. 33, 35.) In 11 Edward I. he was assessor in Dorsetshire of the thirtieth granted by the counties south of Trent. (*Parl. Writs*, i. 13.) In 13 Edward I. he was keeper of the queen's gold (*Madox*, i. 361); and in 18 Edward I. he delivered into the wardrobe the Roll of Peace and Concord between the chancellor and scholars of the university of Oxford and the mayor and burgesses of that city. (*Rot. Parl.* i. 33.) His high character is evidenced by his being one of the executors of Queen Eleanor. (*Abb. Rot. Orig.* i. 80.)

Although it does not appear that he was a judge at Westminster, he held a high place among the justices itinerant. In all the circuits in which he was named over various counties, extending from 20 Edward I., 1292, to nearly the end of the reign, he was invariably at their head. He was summoned also among the judges to parliament during the same interval, and on one occasion was appointed to receive and answer all petitions from Ireland and Guernsey which could be answered without reference to the king. (*Parl. Writs*, i. 468.)

That he acted as a justice itinerant under Edward II. there can be little doubt, as he is summoned among them to the parliaments of the first two years of that reign. (*Ibid.* ii. 536.)

He died in 6 Edward II., 1312, and was possessed of several manors and other lands in the counties of Essex, Hants, Wilts, Norfolk, and Suffolk. (*Cal. Inquis.* p. m. i. 250.) His heir in one entry is called 'Roger, his son,' and in another, 'Roger Huse, consanguineus.' (*Abb. Rot. Orig.* i. 194, 195.)

BERKELEY, MAURICE DE, was the son of Robert Fitz-Harding, who, having obtained a grant from Henry II., while Duke of Normandy, of the castle and lordship of Berkeley, of which Roger de Berkeley had been deprived for his adherence to King Stephen, assumed the surname; but Roger still urging his claim to the lordship, an agreement was entered into between them, with the consent of the duke and King Stephen, that Maurice, the son of Robert, should marry Alicia, the daughter of Roger. This taking effect, Maurice on his father's death, on February 5, 1170, succeeded to the barony, which he enjoyed till his own decease, on June 16, 1190, having just previous to that event added one thousand marks to the purse which King Richard was making for the support of his holy war, under the pretence of a fine for the confirmation of his title.

In the last year of his life he acted as a justice itinerant in Gloucestershire, his pleas appearing on the roll of that year. (*Pipe Roll*, 1 Ric. I. 168.)

He was buried in the church of Brentford, Middlesex, to the building of which he had greatly contributed. He was a liberal benefactor also to several religious houses, and founded two hospitals—one at Lorwing, between Berkeley and Dursley; and the other, that of the Holy Trinity, at Long-Brigge in Gloucestershire.

By his wife, the above-mentioned Alicia, he had six sons, the eldest of whom is the next-mentioned Robert. The present holder of the barony is his lineal descendant, with the title of earl.

BERKELEY, ROBERT DE, the eldest of the six sons of the above Maurice de Berkeley, on the death of his father, in 1190, succeeded to the large inheritance, paying a fine of 1000*l.* for livery thereof. In 10 John, 1208, he was one of the justiciers before whom fines were acknowledged at Derby.

He was among the principal movers in the contest between King John and his barons, and was accordingly included in the sentence of excommunication pronounced against them by Pope Innocent III. (*Wendover*, iii. 297, 356.) His castle of Berkeley and the whole of his lands were also seized, but by his submission at the commencement of the next reign they were all restored, except Berkeley and its castle, which were retained till his death. This event occurred on May 13, 1220, 4 Henry III., when he was buried in a monk's cowl, in the abbey of St. Augustin, near Bristol, to which he had been a munificent benefactor, as well as to many other religious houses. He also founded the hospital of St. Catherine at Bedminster, near Bristol, and two chantries.

He married twice. His first wife was

Julian, daughter of William de Pontearch, and niece to William Mareschall, Earl of Pembroke. The name of his second was Lucia, who after his death married Hugh de Gurney. Leaving no issue by either, he was succeeded by his brother, Thomas, to whom Berkeley and its castle were restored. (*Excerpt. e Rot. Fin.* 4 Hen. III. i. 52.)

BERKELEY, ARNALD DE, was a baron of the Exchequer, attesting a charter with that title in 48 Henry III., 1264 (*Madox*, ii. 1319); but nothing further has been discovered about him, except that he had manors in Merkele, Bradefeld, and Brokhampton, in Herefordshire, and that a process was issued to the sheriff in 51 Henry III., to enquire if Henry de Caldewell came and took his goods and chattels there. (*Abb. Placit.* 160.)

BERKELEY, ROBERT, traces his descent from the above Maurice and Robert de Berkeley, through a succession of a multitude of younger sons. His grandfather, William, was mayor of Hereford in 1545, whose eighth son was Rowland Berkeley, who, having little to begin the world with, by his industry became a very eminent and wealthy clothier at Worcester, and purchased, among others, a considerable estate in the neighbouring parish of Spetchley. By his wife, Catherine, daughter of Thomas Hayward, Esq., he had a family of seven sons and nine daughters.

Robert Berkeley, the second son, was born at Worcester in 1584. He was admitted at the Middle Temple in 1600, and called to the bar May 6, 1608. On the death of his father, in 1611, he became possessor of the Spetchley estate, and in 1613 he was sheriff of his native county, and thirteen years afterwards, in 1626, he became autumn reader of his inn of court. At the commencement of the next year he was called to the degree of the coif, and on April 12 was nominated one of the king's serjeants. From this time his name appears in the Reports; and it fell to his lot in 1629 to argue for the king that the return made to the Habeas Corpus obtained by William Stroud and the other members imprisoned for their conduct in the last parliament was good and sufficient in law, his argument showing great ability. (*State Trials*, iii. 844.)

On October 11, 1632, having been previously knighted, he was created a judge of the King's Bench. He had a deep feeling in favour of the king's prerogative; and, though he agreed that the king could not on all occasions impose charges on his subjects without consent of parliament, saying, 'The people of this kingdom are subjects not slaves, freemen not villains, to be taxed de alto et basso,' yet he contended that his majesty might do so when the good and safety of the kingdom in general are concerned, and that he is the sole judge of the danger. He therefore in the great case of ship money, after a most elaborate and learned argument, which, however wrong it may be thought in its foundation, at least showed his conscientious conviction of its truth, pronounced his opinion against Mr. Hampden. (*Ibid.* iii. 1087–1125.)

For this he was called to severe account by the Long Parliament. He was one of the six judges whom the Lords, on December 22, 1640, bound in 10,000*l.* apiece to answer the charges which the Commons were preparing against them. On February 13 he was singled out for the first example, and, being impeached for high treason, was arrested in open court while sitting on the bench, to 'the great terrour of the rest of his brethren, and of all his profession.' (*Whitelocke*, 40.) He was kept in custody of the sheriff of London till October 20, 1641, when he appeared at the bar of the House of Lords, and, pleading 'Not guilty,' obtained permission to go with a keeper to Serjeants' Inn to look out papers and advise with his counsel. The trial, which was fixed for November 2, was put off at the instance of the Commons for want of witnesses. In Michaelmas Term 1642, of the three judges of the King's Bench that were then left, Heath being with the king, Malet in the Tower, and Berkeley under impeachment, the two houses at a conference resolved 'That Judge Berkeley, having carried himself with modesty and humility, and inoffensively to both houses, be pitched upon for keeping the essoigns.' (*Parry's Parliament.*)

The Lords in the following September—that is, the ten that remained—sentenced the judge to pay a fine of 20,000*l.* and to be for ever disabled from holding any office in the commonwealth. But, the parliament being then pressed for money to pay an instalment of their subsidy to the Scots, he was let off on payment of half to their own officers. (*Clarendon*, iv. 286.) In the conflict that afterwards took place, Sir Robert Berkeley suffered much from the plundering and exactions of both the parties. Even Whitelocke represents him as 'moderate in his ways,' and acknowledges him to be 'a very learned man in our laws, and a good orator and judge.'

He outlived his sovereign above seven years, dying on August 5, 1656, at the age of 72. He was buried under a handsome monument, with an excellent marble figure of the judge upon it, in a chancel he had built to the church of Spetchley.

He married Elizabeth, daughter of Thomas Conyers, Esq., of East Barnet, Herts, by whom he had one son, Thomas, whose descendants still enjoy the family estate.

BERNINGHAM, RICHARD DE. There

were two families of this surname, and two individuals of both names flourishing in the reign of Edward II.; one connected with the county of York, and the other with that of Norfolk. The former was son of John de Berningham, or Barningham; and the latter not improbably was the son of Walter, who, in 1316, was lord of the manor of Hauteyns in Barnham, Norfolk.

Sir Francis Palgrave considers that the presumption is somewhat in favour of Richard de Berningham, of Yorkshire, being the person who was so often summoned to council among the justices and others, and the first entry among the Parliamentary Writs in which his name appears seems amply to justify this opinion. He is therein required to lay aside the caption of certain assizes in the *northern* counties, which had been fixed during the meeting of parliament, and to repair to Westminster instead. This was on September 6, 1313, 7 Edward II., and his summonses continue till the fourteenth year, during which period he is included in several commissions in the county of York, to which, perhaps, his judicial functions were confined. He is mentioned as a knight in that county in 17 Edward II., and his death is recorded in 3 Edward III., possessing property therein. (*Blomefield's Norfolk*, i. 636; *Parl. Writs*, ii. p. ii. 534; *Cal. Inquis.* p. m. ii. 19.)

BERSTEDE, WALTER DE, was sub-sheriff of Kent to Reginald de Cobbeham when he died, in December 1257, 42 Henry III., and was appointed to act as sheriff for the remainder of the year. In 1262 he was appointed constable of Dover Castle, and custos of the Cinque Ports (*Cal. Rot. Pat.* 33); and also went as one of the justices itinerant into Leicestershire, and the next year into Norfolk, Suffolk, and Lincolnshire. He is placed among the justices of the bench in 50 Henry III., on the authority of a fine levied in February 1266; and a writ of assize to be taken before him occurs in the following September. (*Excerpt. e Rot. Fin.* ii. 268, 446.)

BERTIE, VERE, was the fourth son of Montagu, second Earl of Lindsey, lord chamberlain, by his first wife, Martha, daughter of Sir William Cockayn, of Rushton in Northamptonshire, and widow of John Ramsay, Earl of Holderness. To the devoted loyalty of both his father and grandfather he probably owed his professional advancement, which was somewhat rapid. He was called to the bar of the Middle Temple on June 10, 1659, and, though chosen a bencher in January 1673, the law reports are silent as to his forensic merits. Though this may be accounted for by his employment by government as secretary of the treasury and treasurer of the ordnance, it may be presumed that he was not altogether deficient in legal acquirements, inasmuch as he was appointed a baron of the Exchequer on June 4, 1675.

From that court he was removed, on June 15, 1678, to the Common Pleas, where he sat for only ten months, being discharged from his place in April 29, 1679, with three other judges—viz., Sir William Wilde, Sir Edward Thurland, and Sir Francis Bramston. It is a remarkable circumstance that, five days previous, all these four judges were in the commission for the trial of Nathanael Reading, indicted, on the testimony of the infamous Bedloes, for endeavouring to stifle and lessen the king's evidence against the lords then in the Tower; and it may be a question how far their conduct or opinions on that trial caused their dismissal. Vere Bertie died unmarried ten months afterwards, on February 23, 1680, and was buried in the Temple Church. (*State Trials*, vii. 261.)

BERTRAM, ROGER. There were two noble families of this name in Northumberland—one Bertram of Mitford, and the other Bertram of Bothall—and the Christian name Roger was common to both. The subject of this notice belonged to the former family, and was the son of William de Bertram and Alice de Umfraville his wife. (*Baronage*, i. 543.) His father died about 1 John, for in that year the guardianship of Roger was granted to William Briwer, but was afterwards transferred to Peter de Brus, who fined thirteen hundred marks for the same. Towards the end of the reign, being found in the ranks of the insurgent barons, his lands and castle of Mitford were given into the custody of Philip de Ulecot, who seems to have resisted the royal order for their restoration when Roger returned to his obedience on the accession of Henry III. He was obliged, however, to submit, and Roger was reinstated on a fine of 100*l*. (*Rot. Chart.* 48; *Rot. Claus.* i. 70, 246, 316, 336, 342, 357.)

From this time he acted the part of a loyal subject, and was frequently employed as a justice itinerant in the northern counties, from 9 to 18 Henry III. He died before May 24, 1242, on which day his lands were delivered into the custody of Walter de Crepping on behalf of his son Roger, who did homage for them on June 28, 1246, on attaining his majority. (*Excerpt. e Rot. Fin.* i. 379, 456.) In the reign of Edward II. the barony terminated by the failure of male issue.

BEST, WILLIAM DRAPER, did not obtain his title of Lord Wynford till he had retired from the bench. He was born on December 13, 1767, at Hasselbury Plunknett in Somersetshire, and was the third son of Thomas Best, Esq., by a daughter of Sir William Draper, well known as the antagonist of 'Junius.' Left an orphan in infancy, he was sent to the school of the neighbouring town of Crewkerne, and at the age of fifteen was removed to Wadham College, Oxford, where he was educated with the view of entering the Church. This plan he relinquished in consequence of coming to the possession, by the death of a near relation, of a considerable estate: and, entering the Middle Temple, was called to the bar on November 6, 1789, and joined the Home Circuit.

Very early in his career he had the good fortune to extract a flattering eulogium from Lord Kenyon in a case which he argued in the court of King's Bench. This was so unwonted in the chief justice that it was sure to attract attention; and he consequently soon received ample employment. Though superficial in legal knowledge, his readiness of comprehension and fluency of speech enabled him to avail himself of his early success, and his increase of business warranted him in accepting the degree of the coif in 1800. His services were in great requisition, in all the courts of Westminster Hall; and he sometimes appeared on important criminal trials.

He entered parliament in 1802 as member for Petersfield, and took a prominent part in its proceedings, particularly in reference to naval affairs and public accounts. He was one of the acting managers on the impeachment of Lord Melville, and, with Sir Samuel Romilly, answered the legal objections taken by the counsel for the defence. In 1814 he represented Bridport; and from that time till his death, leaving the liberal party with whom he had hitherto acted, he was a zealous supporter of conservative principles.

In 1806 he had been appointed one of the king's serjeants, and recorder of Guildford; and in Michaelmas 1813 he was selected as solicitor-general to the Prince of Wales, then regent, succeeding in 1816 to the attorney-generalship to his royal highness. With that prince he was a great favourite; and by the royal patronage he became successively chief justice of Chester and a judge of the King's Bench, the latter promotion taking place in December 1818. He was knighted in the following June.

After sitting in that court rather more than five years, he was advanced in April 1824 to the head of the Court of Common Pleas, from which his increasing infirmities obliged him to retire in June 1829. By the continuance of royal favour he was at the same time raised to the peerage as Baron Wynford, the title being taken from an estate he had purchased in Dorsetshire; and he was then appointed a deputy speaker of the House of Lords. In that house and in the privy council he took his due proportion of labour in the judicial business, as often as his violent attacks of the gout enabled him to attend. In the debates he strenuously opposed the Reform Bill through all its stages, and was always found in opposition to the party who supported it. He lived for sixteen years after his retirement, and died at his seat called Leesons in Kent on March 3, 1845.

Lord Wynford's countenance, though not handsome, was very attractive. It indicated great cordiality and good humour, with much intelligence; but it also showed something of a hasty temperament. As an advocate, he was fluent if not eloquent, acute if not learned, and his zeal for his clients left no means untried for insuring their success. As a judge, he was apt to form hasty and questionable opinions, and when presiding at Nisi Prius to lean in his summing up so much to one side that he was nicknamed the 'judge advocate.' Though he was remarkable for the clearness and terseness of his decisions, he was considered by the profession as an indifferent judge, and brought himself into bad odour, as well by the political bias he often displayed as by his occasional irritability and intemperance on the bench. His disposition as a man was essentially kind, amiable, and charitable.

He married very early in life Mary Anne, the daughter of Jerome Knapp, Esq., of Haberdashers' Hall, London, and had by her ten children.

BETHELL, RICHARD (LORD WESTBURY), was born at Bradford in Wiltshire on June 30, 1800, and his father, Dr. Richard Bethell, who was a descendant from the old Welsh family of Ap-Ithell, practised as a physician at Bristol. From Bristol Grammar School he proceeded at the age of fourteen to Wadham College, Oxford, of which he was afterwards elected fellow, having distinguished himself by attaining a place in the first class in classics, and in the second class in mathematics. He took his B.A. degree when only eighteen, and then became for some time a favourite tutor in the university. Entering the Middle Temple, he was called to the bar on November 28, 1823.

For seventeen years he laboured as a junior counsel in the Court of Chancery, where his practice was very considerable; and in 1840 he attained the rank of queen's counsel, in which character he soon acquired a most prominent lead. His university employed him as their advocate; and he filled the office of vice-chancellor of the county palatine of Lancaster. While engaged in his vicarious duties as a barrister, he devoted himself to the improvement of the mode of legal education, his exertions in which are beyond all praise. A committee of the benchers of all the four inns was formed, of which he was the prime mover and selected chairman; and a body of rules was issued for the admission, regulation, and instruction of the students, which promise the most satisfactory results.

From 1851 till his elevation to the peerage he was a member of the House of Commons, at first for the borough of Aylesbury, and then for that of Wolverhampton. Throughout his senatorial career he supported the liberal party; and on the retirement of Lord Derby's ministry he was knighted on his appointment as solicitor-general, on December 28, 1852, and was nominated attorney-general in November 1856; but resigning in February 1858 on the change of ministry, he resumed it sixteen months after, in June 1859, on his party returning to power. On June 26, 1861, he succeeded to the office of lord high chancellor. During the existence of the ministry of which he formed a part he resigned his high position, under circumstances which, though he was acquitted of personal corruption by the two houses of parliament, his judges in those houses were of opinion exhibited so much laxity of principle, and so little consideration for the public welfare, that in those respects he was a fit object for their censure; and the general feeling of the people confirmed their decision. Without entering into the details of the cases of Edmunds and Wilde, upon which the charges were founded, or of the disclosures then made, Lord Westbury found it was impossible to contend against the resolution of parliament, and he accordingly resigned the Seal on July 7, 1865.

By his wife, the daughter of Robert Abraham, Esq., he has a numerous family.

BEYNVILL, RICHARD DE (or BAYVILL), was of a knightly family of the county of Huntingdon, where he held lands of the honor of the Earl of Chester. He was appointed one of the justices itinerant for that county and Cambridgeshire in 9 Henry III., and died in 1238, 23 Henry III. (*Rot. Claus.* i. 77, 209.)

BICKERSTETH, HENRY (LORD LANGDALE), was born on June 18, 1783, at Kirkby Lonsdale, and was the third of five sons of Mr. Henry Bickersteth, a medical practitioner of considerable repute in that town, and of Elizabeth, the daughter of Mr. John Batty, a farmer of the same place, and the sister of Dr. Batty, afterwards so eminent as a physician in London. To the moral and religious feelings impressed on his mind by his mother he always ascribed what was praiseworthy in his future career. After concluding his studies at the Free Grammar School of his native place, with the highest prize, he entered his father's business at Midsummer 1797, and in the autumn of the next year went to London to walk the hospitals under the guidance of his uncle Dr. Batty. To perfect himself in the science of his profession, he went to Edinburgh in October 1801, and had the advantage of attending the lectures of the eminent professors who then presided over the medical schools. He became a member of the Royal Medical Society, and distinguished himself in their debates by his eloquence, ingenuity, and energy. In the summer of the next year he was called home for the purpose of supplying the place of his father, whose health required a temporary absence from his professional duties. This experience confirmed his dislike to becoming a mere country practitioner, and induced him to decline his father's offer to give up the whole of his business to him.

With the intent, therefore, of preparing himself for the London practice of a physician, he entered Caius College, Cambridge, in October of that year, with a scholarship on Mr. Hewitt's foundation. The application to his studies there was so intense that he was seized with a serious illness when he went to London at the end of the term. His recovery was slow, and total relaxation became necessary to insure it. With this view his uncle Dr. Batty, fully satisfied as to his qualifications for the office, recommended him as medical attendant to the family of the Earl of Oxford, then on a tour in Italy, whom he started to join at the end of March 1803.

While at Florence the war with France broke out, and he and his noble friends had some difficulty in escaping the clutches of Bonaparte in his disgraceful seizure of all English travellers. After remaining some little time at Venice, Vienna, and Dresden, the continuance of the war induced Lord Oxford to return home, when his lordship experienced the benefit of the medical selection he had made, by being safely brought through a serious illness under the care and skill of his youthful adviser. Though proving himself a great proficient in the science, and taking great delight in the investigation of its mysteries, as is particularly apparent in his correspondence with Dr. Henderson, Mr. Bickersteth retained his dislike to the profession, and, determining to relinquish it, returned to Cambridge in 1805, where, after abandoning a passing desire to enter the army, he resolved to study for a degree in arts; though his long absence was much against him, and his want of practice in mathematics raised a temporary obstacle to his success. But his indefatigable industry and quick perception overcame all disadvantages, so that in January 1808 he graduated B.A. as senior wrangler and senior Smith's prizeman, in a year when he had no mean competitors to conquer, his principal opponents being Miles Bland, Bishop Blomfield, and Professor Sedgwick. He was of course immediately rewarded with a fellowship in his college; and, fixing upon the law as his new profession, he entered the Inner Temple as a student in 1808, and became a pupil of Mr. Bell, one of the most eminent counsel in the Court of Chancery.

The tendency of his mind was always to the liberal side of politics, and though his extreme opinions were much moderated by witnessing the tyrannical sequence of the French revolution, he still continued something more than a whig. Becoming also a friend and disciple of Jeremy Bentham, Mr. Bickersteth received from his conversation the first impressions of the necessity of amendment in the administration of the laws. He was thus enlisted into the band of law reformers, eventually producing those efforts to which his name is allied.

He was called to the bar on November 22, 1811; and for the next three or four years he had to contend against the usual slow progress of a barrister at the outset of his career, and even meditated giving up the profession rather than put his father to further expense. His circumstances were somewhat improved in 1814 by becoming a senior fellow of his college, and his business gradually increased. But his known connection with the philosopher Bentham and the politician Burdett, then deemed radicals, and particularly his support of the latter against Sir Samuel Romilly at the Westminster election of 1818, for a time proved an impediment to his success, which, however, by steady perseverance and moderation he was soon enabled to remove.

With his business his reputation advanced, and he was considered so conversant with the practice of his court, and so alive to its defects, that he was called upon to give evidence before the commissioners appointed in 1824 to investigate the subject. In his examination, which lasted four days, he boldly pointed out the evils that attached to the whole system, and suggested several remedies, some of which were eventually adopted. His evidence, though thought by some to be too comprehensive and visionary, was generally regarded with attention and respect, and was particularly lauded by the great oracle of legal reform, Bentham; and from that time all parties really desirous of amending the course of justice applied to him as an authority. Among others Sir John Copley, then attorney-general, requested his assistance in 1820, when preparing a bill for reforming the Court of Chancery, and in 1827, when appointed lord chancellor, recommended him to the king as one of his counsel, which he was appointed in May, and was then called to the bench of his inn.

In this character he was so fully employed that he was at length obliged to give up all practice in other courts, and to confine himself to the Rolls, and he actually refused to break his resolution, though tempted to go into the Exchequer in the great case of Small v. Attwood, by a fee of 3,000 guineas.

When the ministry of Lord Grey came in, and an act passed for erecting a Court of Bankruptcy in 1831, Mr. Bickersteth was offered the chief judgeship of it; but he at once declined it, as he disapproved its establishment, and thought it would be wholly inefficient; and in February 1834 he also refused to accept the vacant office of a baron of the Exchequer, which Lord Lyndhurst, then lord chief baron, was desirous that he should fill, from a conscientious feeling that as an equity judge of that court, for which he was intended, he could not efficiently perform the common-law duties which would in addition devolve upon him. In April of that year he created no slight sensation by a bitter rebuke he gave to Lord Chancellor Brougham in his answer to his lordship's question, *What was to prevent* the University of London conferring degrees, without the authority of an act of parliament? to which he replied, 'The utter scorn and contempt of the world.' This and the following year were remarkable in Mr. Bickersteth's history. In September he refused the offer of the solicitor-generalship made to him by Lord Brougham, though it was afterwards more regularly urged upon him by Lord Melbourne, the prime minister. On the dissolution of that ministry at the end of the year he was pressed by a large body of electors to stand for the borough of Marylebone, but, finding that he was expected to pledge himself to support certain measures, he not only refused to be nominated, but wrote a letter denouncing the demand of pledges and promises from any candidate as both improper and impolitic.

In April of the next year he drew up, at Lord Melbourne's request, a valuable and comprehensive paper containing excellent suggestions for the relief of the lord chancellor, which in a few years led, among other things, to the removal of the equity business of the Court of Exchequer, and the appointment of two additional vice-chancellors. In August Mr. Bickersteth married Lady Jane Harley, the daughter of his old friend and patron the Earl of Oxford. In the following December Lord Melbourne communicated to him the intention to appoint the master of the Rolls, Sir Charles C. Pepys, lord chancellor, offering Mr. Bickersteth Sir Charles's vacant seat at the Rolls, and urging him to accept a peerage in order that he might in parliament assist in carrying into effect his views for the reformation of the courts of equity. Mr. Bickersteth, though agreeing to accept the judicial office, hesitated to do so if united with a peerage. His objections however were ultimately removed, and he consented to enter the House of Lords upon the express terms, fully understood and agreed to by the minister, of perfect political independence. He was sworn of the Privy Council on January 16, 1835, and on the 19th and 23rd he received his two patents, the former constituting him master of the Rolls, and the latter creating him Baron Langdale of Langdale in the county of Westmoreland.

Acting on the understanding on which he had accepted the peerage, he abstained in parliament from interfering in party conflicts as inconsistent with his judicial office to do so; and devoted himself wholly to the consideration of the various schemes of legal reform, not hesitating, when they did not meet his approval, to state his objections, whether introduced by liberal or conservative legislators. To every bill that tended to render justice more easily accessible, and to diminish its expense, he gave a most hearty support, and urged with unanswerable arguments the injustice and impolicy of taxing the suitor with fees towards the establishment and support of the courts and their officers. He himself introduced several bills of great moment, some effecting substantial changes in the law and its administration, and others making important alterations in the mode of transacting Chancery business; but he never undertook the management of any of them without carefully considering whether the evil complained of would be effectually remedied by the supposed improvement, and without taking care that the holders of offices abolished were duly compensated for their loss. It was a pleasure to witness the extreme care he exercised in their preparation, and the great interest and anxiety he evinced in their progress and success. He lived to see the good effects of many of the measures he promoted.

As a judge he was remarkable for the strictness of proof he required on every point submitted to his decision, for the unwearied attention he paid to all the arguments urged on either side, and for the careful preparation and logical correctness of his judgments. By his own dignified example he made his court a model of propriety and respectful demeanour, and all attempts at professional fraud, or trickery, or any inexcusable neglect, were effectually suppressed by the dread of his stern denunciation. His judicial duties were not confined to his own court, but were greatly increased by his attendance on the judicial committee of the Privy Council, of which he was often the presiding member. The case which occasioned him most trouble and anxiety there was that of the Rev. Mr. Gorham v. the Bishop of Exeter (Dr. Phillpotts), relative to the bishop's refusal to institute Mr. Gorham to the vicarage of Brampton Speke, on account of a certain difference of opinion on a disputed point of doctrine with relation to baptism. The judgment pronounced by the committee, with the concurrence of the Archbishops of Canterbury and York, in favour of Mr. Gorham, was prepared by Lord Langdale, in a very learned and elaborate paper, and naturally occasioned a severe controversy between the parties interested on one side or the other.

Not contented with these labours, he devoted himself with indefatigable industry to cleanse the Augean stable of the public records, which justly gained for him the title of Father of Record Reform. His continued endeavours through the whole of his official life to induce the government to devote the proper attention to, and to provide the requisite funds for, this important and national object, are fully recorded in the memoir of Mr. Duffus Hardy, who was one of his most efficient assistants in the undertaking. The perseverance with which he pressed the necessity of providing an adequate repository for the preservation of the monuments of the kingdom, and the unwearied patience with which he met the difficulties and answered the repeated objections raised, were at last rewarded by the adoption of the plan he proposed. By the application of his discriminating judgment and patient perseverance he subjected the chaotic mass to an arrangement which, with the facility of reference afforded, must ever claim the gratitude of the statesman, the biographer, and the historian.

As a trustee and commissioner of the British Museum, and as the head of the Registration and Conveyancing Commission, he devoted himself with the same ardour to the several questions submitted to them respectively.

This continued exercise of the brain had such a detrimental effect on his health that when, on Lord Cottenham's retirement in May 1850, the office of lord chancellor was pressed upon him, he refused to accept it, convinced that he could not adequately perform the multifarious duties attached to the place, nor hope to effect the reforms which he contemplated. But during the chancellor's previous illness Lord Langdale undertook his duties as speaker of the House of Lords, and on his resignation consented to act as the head of the commission temporarily issued for the custody of the Great Seal till a lord chancellor was appointed. The Seal was delivered to him and to Sir Lancelot Shadwell and Baron Rolfe on June 19, 1850, and they held it till July 15, when Sir Thomas Wilde was appointed lord chancellor and created Lord

Truro. The great labour thrown on Lord Langdale by this addition to his ordinary duties, with the unfortunate illness by which his brother commissioner Sir Lancelot Shadwell was incapacitated, had a palpable effect on his health and strength, and brought on a serious illness. On his partial recovery he found that he must relieve himself from the burden of office, which, with the sincere regret of his bar, affectionately expressed by Mr. (afterwards Lord Justice) Turner, he resigned on March 28, 1851, after more than fifteen years of judicial life. No sooner was the sorrowful parting completed than his health wholly succumbed, and in three weeks he closed his mortal career. He died at Tunbridge Wells on April 18, 1851, and was buried in the Temple Church.

A man with higher principle, greater integrity, more fixed in his purpose to do right, more unwearied in his attempts to discover the truth, more regardless of self, and with a kinder nature, it would be difficult to find. Whether in the capacity of an advocate, a judge, a legislator, or in the sacred seclusion of private and domestic life, he secured the admiration, the respect, and the devoted affection of all.

He left no son to inherit his honours; but his lady and an only daughter still survive to venerate his memory.

BIDUN, WALTER DE, is inserted in Dugdale's list as chancellor to Henry II.; but, on looking to the authority to which he refers, it seems more likely that he was chancellor to the King of Scotland. All doubt, however, of Walter de Bidun being a Scottish chancellor will be removed by the fact that he is a witness, as chancellor, to a charter, dated Jedworth, of William the Lyon, King of Scotland, granted to William de Veteri Ponte. (*Robertson's Index to Scottish Royal Charters*, 179, No. 137.)

BIGOT, ROGER, second Earl of Norfolk, was the grandson of a Norman knight of the same name, whose lordships are recorded in Domesday Book as six in Essex and 117 in Suffolk, and the eldest son of Hugh, who was created Earl of Norfolk in 6 Stephen.

Richard I. appointed him one of the ambassadors to Philip, King of France, to make arrangements for the crusade; and during his sovereign's absence on that enterprise he supported his authority against the attempts of Prince John.

His name appears on the records as a justicier after the return of King Richard from the Holy Land, fines being levied before him from the fifth year of that reign till the third of John. (*Madox*, ii. 21.) That king sent him to summon William, King of Scotland, to do homage at Lincoln, and made various grants in his favour. But towards the end of the reign he was imprisoned on some account or other, as his wife Aelina fined in fifty marks for his release, the payment of part of which was excused, in 15 John. (*Rot. de Fin.* 465.). In that year he seems to have been restored to his sovereign's good graces, as he attended him into Poictou; and for a fine of two thousand marks obtained a respite for his whole life from the service of 120 knights, and from all arrears of scutages. (*Madox*, i. 190, 667.)

In 17 John he joined the barons, and was one of the twenty-five who were appointed to enforce the observance of Magna Charta. His name was accordingly included in the sentence of excommunication fulminated by Pope Innocent III., and his lands were cruelly ravaged among the last attempts of the tyrannic king. In the first year of the reign of Henry III. he returned to his allegiance; and, being again taken into favour, a disputed question between the king and him as to the stewardship of the household was finally settled on May 1, 1221. (*Rot. Claus.* i. 322, 455, 469.)

Before the following August he died, and was succeeded by his son Hugh, whose son Roger, the fourth earl, is the subject of the next article. (*Wendover*, iii. 297, 355, 381.)

BIGOT, ROGER, the fourth Earl of Norfolk, and the grandson of the preceding Roger, was at the head of the commission of justices itinerant into Essex and Hertford issued in 1234, 18 Henry III. He was the son of Hugh the third earl, and Matilda his wife, one of the daughters of William Mareschall, Earl of Pembroke. His father died in 1225, 9 Henry III., when he, being a minor, was placed under the wardship of William Longspee, Earl of Salisbury. In the following May he married Isabella, the sister of Alexander, King of Scotland, to whom, on the Earl of Salisbury's death in the following year, the guardianship of Roger was transferred. (*Excerpt. e Rot. Fin.* i. 125, 128, 168; *Rot. Claus.* ii. 58.)

He became eminent for his knightly skill, and was with the king in France in 1242. When the barons determined, in 1245, no longer to submit to the oppressive exactions made on the kingdom by the pope, he headed those who addressed a letter of remonstrance to the general council then sitting at Lyons, and joined in the dismissal of the papal nuncio from the shores of England.

By the death of the last of the four sons of William Mareschall, Earl of Pembroke, in 1245, their inheritance devolved on their five sisters, of whom his mother, Matilda, was the eldest. To her share the marshalship of England fell, which she transferred to Roger Bigot as her eldest son, the king soon after confirming him in the office.

He was one of the principal actors in the

great council held at Westminster in May 1258, when, on the barons appearing in complete armour, the king asked of them, 'Am I then your prisoner?' 'No, sir,' replied Roger Bigot, 'but by your partiality to foreigners, and your own prodigality, the realm is involved in misery. Wherefore we demand that the powers of government be delegated to a committee of barons and prelates, who may correct abuses and enact salutary laws.' The provisions of Oxford were the consequence of this procedure, under which his brother the undermentioned Hugh was nominated chief justiciary. After the battle of Lewes, Earl Roger was appointed by the barons governor of the castle of Oxford.

He died in 1270, leaving no issue.

BIGOT, HUGH, the younger brother of the above-mentioned Roger, fourth Earl of Norfolk, married two wives, the first of whom was Joanna the daughter of Robert Burnet, and the second Joanna the daughter of Nicholas de Stuteville and widow of Hugh Wake.

He received many marks of the king's favour, being made chief ranger of the forest of Farnedale in 39 Henry III., and governor of the castle of Pickering in the next year. He accompanied the king in 41 Henry III. in his expedition against the Welsh. On June 22, in the next year he was selected by the council nominated at the parliament of Oxford to fill the high station of chief justiciary, and at the same time the Tower of London was committed to his charge (*Brady, App.* 218), to which was afterwards added the command of Dover Castle, and the chamberlainship of Sandwich. (*Cal. Rot. Pat.* 31.)

In 1259 he selected Roger de Thurkelby and Gilbert de Preston, two of the principal judges, as his companions on a circuit from county to county to administer justice throughout the kingdom; and during the king's absence abroad, from November 1259 till April 1260, he attested all the mandates on the fine roll. (*Excerpt. e Rot. Fin.* ii. 319-324.) He is described by Matthew Paris as 'militem illustrem, et legum terræ peritum, qui officium justitiariæ strenue peragens, nullatenus permittat jus regni vacillare.'

Although no complaint was made against him, and he seems to have been zealous and active in the execution of the duties of his office, he resigned it about the end of 1260, possibly in order that the council of barons might carry into effect their desire to make it an annual appointment, but more probably because he was dissatisfied with their proceedings, as he afterwards joined the royal party. He was immediately succeeded by Hugh le Despenser, one of his coadjutors on the council.

He was engaged in the battle of Lewes on May 14, 1264, on the king's side; and when the rout began, he escaped with the Earl of Warren and others. Their flight is thus described by Peter Langtoft:—

The Erle of Warenne, I wote, he scaped over the se,
And Sir Hugh Bigote als with the erle fled he.

After the battle of Evesham, in the following year, he was replaced in the government of the castle of Pickering.

His death occurred about November 1266; his son Roger on the death of his uncle Roger became Earl of Norfolk, but dying childless in 1307, the title became extinct.

BILLING, THOMAS. Fuller (ii. 166) inserts Sir Thomas Billing among the worthies of Northamptonshire, where are two neighbouring villages of the name, adding that at Ashwell in that county the judge 'had his habitation in great state.' Unsupported by any authority yet discovered, Lord Campbell (*Ch. Justices,* i. 145) represents him as in every respect a contemptible and worthless person. In conformity with this view of his character, he remarks that Fuller 'is silent both as to his ancestors and descendants.' This omission, however, is not uncommon with Fuller; nor is there anything in his account of Billing to indicate, as Lord Campbell asserts, that he 'is evidently ashamed of introducing such a character among worthies.' Fuller was not a man to conceal a truth, though discreditable to the subject of his notice; and of this we have two instances immediately following the account of Billing, besides many others throughout his work.

The family was of great antiquity in the county. A Henry was certified to hold a sixth part of a knight's fee in Rushden in the time of Henry III.; a Robert Billing of Cuquenho was vicar of Brayfield in 1348; and a John Billing, probably the father of the judge, was one of the feoffees of Sir William Porter, knight, and presented to the rectory of Collyweston in 1430.

No certain memorial of Billing's ancestors or of the personal history of his early years has been found; but no authority exists for the supposition made by Lord Campbell that he had been 'the clerk of an attorney;' nor if he had been, would it justify the improbable conclusion, which his lordship invents, that he would thus necessarily become well acquainted with 'the less reputable parts of the law.'

He was a member of Gray's Inn, and if MS. preserved in that society is to be taken as authority in this instance, it appears not merely that 'he *contrived* to keep his terms and to be called to the bar,' as Lord Campbell insinuates, but that he was so well reputed as to be made a reader in that house.

That he distinguished himself in his early professional career appears certain, since he was returned in 1448 by the citizens of London as their representative in parliament, and was elected their recorder on September 21, 1450, an office which he resigned at the end of four years on account 'of his manifold labours, as well at Westminster as at the assizes in different counties.' The corporation voted him a present of 'cloth engreyned ... for his diligent services in the office of recorder,' and retained him as one of their counsel. (*City List of Recorders.*)

If this does not raise a sufficient doubt of Lord Campbell's assertion, that his business was 'not of the most creditable description,' further proof may be found in a letter in the 'Paston Correspondence' (i. 53), that he had already acquired a high reputation, that his advice was deemed valuable, and that his personal position was such as to warrant an intimate intercourse with the families of Paston and Lord Grey de Ruthyn. So high indeed was his reputation that Bishop Grey appointed him his chief justice in the Isle of Ely. (*Cole's MSS.* xxv. 47.)

Billing was summoned to assume the degree of the coif in 1453, and was appointed one of the king's serjeants in 1458, 36 Henry VI., a month after the hollow accommodation between the two contending parties in the state.

Lord Campbell quotes a treatise of Billing on the subject of the claims of the royal antagonists, without stating where it is to be found, and asserts that the Rolls of Parliament mention his name as appearing 'at the bar of the House of Lords as counsel for Henry VI., leading the attorney and solicitor-general,' and that on that occasion it was 'remarked that his fire had slackened much, and that he was very complimentary to the Duke of York, who since the battle of Northampton had been virtually master of the kingdom.' On referring to the Rolls of Parliament, however, no such entry is recorded, but, on the contrary, it appears that not only the judges, but the king's serjeants and attorney, none of whom are mentioned by name, excused themselves altogether from giving any opinion or advice on the question. (*Rot. Parl.* v. 376.)

Lord Campbell states, without giving his authority, that on the accession of Edward IV. 'instantly Sir Thomas Billing sent in his adhesion; and such zeal did he express in favour of the new dynasty that his patent of king's serjeant was renewed, and he became principal law adviser to Edward IV.' He then designates him as 'this unprincipled adventurer,' although Coke speaks of him among 'other excellent men' who flourished at the time. (*Preface to First Inst.*) Mr. Serjeant Billing did nothing more than exactly what not only the other serjeants, but every one of the judges except Fortescue, very naturally and very properly did on the change of dynasty,—he retained his legal position in the courts of law. In the very first parliament of Edward IV. we find that, besides Billing, the famous Lyttelton (who is named before him) and William Laken, serjeants in precisely the same position, were nominated by the parliament as referees in a case between the Bishop of Winchester and his tenants; but the Rolls do not supply any authority for the very improbable fact which Lord Campbell introduces, that *Serjeant* Billing 'assisted in framing the acts by which Sir John Fortescue and the principal Lancastrians, his patrons, were attainted;' or that he took an active part in the subsequent measures of hostility against King Henry and Queen Margaret.

No materials exist which would justify us in ascribing to Billing the private suggestions of which Lord Campbell makes him the author, or in judging of the correctness of the motives assigned for his elevation to the bench. Neither is any evidence to be found of his presumed dissatisfaction with the office of puisne justice, nor of his resolution that 'mere scruples of conscience should not hold him back' from the woolsack. The simple fact is that on August 9, 1464, 4 Edward IV., he was added to the three judges of which the Court of King's Bench then consisted.

Lord Campbell, quoting from Baker's 'Chronicle' and Hale's 'Pleas of the Crown,' mentions Billing as the judge who tried Walter Walker for saying he would make his son 'heir to the CROWN,' meaning his inn so called; and he gives the judge's ruling on the case, with the conviction and execution of the unfortunate prisoner. It is curious, however, that his lordship, when five pages before he cites Sir Nicholas Throgmorton's address to Chief Justice Bromley, omits there the chief justice's answer referring to this very 'Crown' case; by which it appears that Markham was the judge, and that an acquittal was the consequence of his honest ruling. (*State Trials*, i. 894.)

But if this omission is curious, it is more remarkable that neither Baker nor Hale states the case as occurring in Billing's time; and further, that Stow (p. 415) gives the precise date of Walker's trial—viz., March 12, 1460, more than four years before Billing was on the bench; adding that the charge against him was for words spoken of the title of King Edward when he was proclaimed; and Fabyan (p. 639) confirms him in the date.

On January 23, 1468-9, 8 Edward IV., Billing received his promotion as Chief Justice of the King's Bench. The trial and conviction of Sir Thomas Burdet, for wishing a favourite buck of his which the king had killed in hunting, horns and all, was in the king's belly, is said by Lord Campbell to have taken place before Chief Justice Billing in the very next term after his appointment, and that 'a rumour was propagated that the late virtuous chief justice (Markham) had been displaced because he had refused to concur in it.'

It has not been discovered whence Lord Campbell extracted the ruling of Billing in this or in Walker's case, which he has printed with inverted commas as quotations; but undoubtedly his lordship could not have been aware that Burdet's case had been lately referred to in Westminster Hall; that the record of his attainder was searched for,' and found in the 'Baga de Secretis;' and that this labour might have been spared by looking into Croke's 'Charles' (p. 120), where the proceedings against him are published. The result of all this would have proved that the whole story of the buck and the belly was a figment, and that the charge against Burdet was for conspiring to kill the king and the prince by casting their nativity, foretelling the speedy death of both, and scattering papers containing the prophecy among the people. By the record it appears also that, instead of the trial taking place in 'the very next term' after Billing became chief justice, no part of Burdet's crime was committed before 1474, and he was not tried till 1477.

Little more than two years after Billing had attained the chief judicial seat Henry VI. was restored to the crown, which he retained for about six months, when he was again expelled by his successful rival. It is a strong proof of the seat of justice being considered exempt from the consequences of the civil strife, that on both these occasions the judges, with a few exceptions, were all replaced in their seats by new patents issued immediately after each of these kings had gained the ascendency; so that all the conjectures as to Billing's deportment at either crisis in which Lord Campbell indulges must be deemed applicable, if at all, to his brethren as well as to himself. It seems more natural to infer, from Billing's double re-instalment, that he had not made himself obnoxious to either party by extreme partiality or 'outrageous loyalty.'

Sir Thomas Billing presided in his court up to the day of his death, which took place on May 5, 1481. He was buried in Bittlesden Abbey, under a large blue marble slab, on which are the figures of the chief justice in his official robes, and his lady. This slab, after the dissolution of the monasteries, was removed to the church of Wappenham, in Northamptonshire, where it now remains.

The name of the wife here represented with him is Katerina, the daughter of Roger Gifford, of Twyford in Bucks, a junior branch of the noble family of Gifford, Earls of Buckingham, whom he married so early as 1447. His second wife was equally well allied, being Mary, the daughter and heir of Robert Wesenham, of Conington in Huntingdonshire, whose first husband was Thomas Lacy, and her second, William Cotton, of Redware in Staffordshire.

By his first wife Sir Thomas had five sons and four daughters; and there is another slab recording the death of Thomas, his son and heir, in 1500, who left no male issue, but whose elder daughter, Joan, married John Haugh, the after-mentioned judge, and whose younger daughter married Richard Tresham, of Newton, the progenitor of the conspirator in the Gunpowder Plot. (*Baker's Northampton*, 730; and ex inf. of R. E. Waters, Esq., a connection of the family.)

BINGHAM, RICHARD. This family was established at Carcolston, in the hundred of Bingham, in the county of Nottingham. Richard was a younger son, and pursued the study of the law. He was called to the degree of serjeant-at-law on February 14, 1443, 21 Henry VI. His last appearance as an advocate in the Year Book is in Easter, 22 Henry VI.; and there is certain proof of his advance as a judge of the King's Bench before February 10, 1447, 25 Henry VI., he being among the judges who acted as triers of petitions in the parliament that met on that day. (*Rot. Parl.* i. 129.) On the deposition of Henry VI. in 1461 he was retained by Edward IV., and was continued in his place during the temporary restoration of Henry in 1470-1, being then described as a knight. On the return of Edward IV., however, he was not included in the new patent, being probably omitted by his own desire, as he must have then been considerably advanced in age.

He married Margaret, the daughter of Sir Baldwin Frevill, of Middleton in the county of Warwick, and widow of Sir Hugh Willoughby, of Wollaton in Nottinghamshire; and dying on May 22, 1476, he was buried at Middleton, where there is a monument representing him in his judicial robes. His son Richard married Margaret, daughter of Sir Thomas Rempston, uncle by the half blood to Sir William Plumpton. In the 'Plumpton Correspondence' is a letter from the judge to the latter knight, in which, 'be the advise of my master, Sir John Markham, chiefe justice,' he proposes that a variance between Sir William and Henry Pierpont should be submitted to their arbitration. (*Archæol. Journ.* ii. 250; *Thoroton's Notts*, i. 240; *Plumpton Corr.* 3, 259.)

BIRCH, JOHN, would at first sight appear to have been the earliest puisne baron of the Exchequer who was selected from among the serjeants-at-law; but a little closer enquiry makes it very doubtful whether he was the John Birch who took the degree of the coif. There were evidently at that time two members of Gray's Inn of that name. In autumn 1551 a John Birch was appointed reader, and was re-elected in Lent 1552; and there was also a John Birch who held the same office in autumn 1558, and again in Lent 1560, being on the latter occasion called 'duplex reader,' which could not have been his title if all the four readers had been the same man. One of these John Birches was made a serjeant on April 19, 1559 (*Machyn's Diary*, 373), and consequently then became a member of Serjeants' Inn; so that it could not have been he who was the reader in Gray's Inn in Lent 1560. It follows, therefore, that the reader of 1551 must have been the serjeant, and he may *possibly* have been, as Dugdale designates him, 'afterwards baron of the Exchequer.' But as, according to the baron's monumental inscription, he was born about the year 1515, it is far more probable that he should have been the reader of 1558, when he would have been in his forty-fourth year, than that he should have attained that rank in 1551, when he would have been only thirty-six. As it was not then the custom for the barons to be serjeants, and as there is no fact to show that any change took place on this occasion, there is little doubt that Dugdale applied the designation to the wrong man, and that John Birch the reader of 1558 and 1560, and not John Birch the serjeant, was the person who was promoted to the bench of the Exchequer on May 9, 1564, and who sat there for the next eighteen years; especially as in his patent of appointment he is described as 'Arm.,' and not as serjeant. (*Rot. Pat.* 6 Eliz. p. 8; *Cal. State Papers* [1547–80], 594.)

He died on May 30, 1581, at the age of sixty-six, and was buried in the old church of St. Giles-in-the-Fields, where this unique inscription (*Stow's London*, 867) was placed on his tomb:—

Interr'd the Corps of Baron Birch lies here,
Of Greyes Inn sometime, by Degree, Esquire.
In Chequer Eighteen Yeers a Judge he was,
Till Soule from aged Body, his did passe.
Alive his Wife, Eliza, doth remaine
Of Stydfolke stocke; one Sonne, and Daughters Twaine,
She bore to him: the eldest, in his Life,
He gave to Thomas Boyer, for his Wife.
His body sleepes till Angels Trumpe shall sound;
God grant we all may ready then be found.

BIRCH, JOHN, of the ancient family of Birch, of Ardwick, near Manchester, was the nephew of the famous Colonel John Birch, who in the Great Rebellion distinguished himself on the parliament side, and the son of the Rév. Thomas Birch, rector of Hampton Bishop in Herefordshire, and afterwards vicar of Preston in Lancashire, by his wife Mary. He commenced his legal career at Gray's Inn in 1680, but in 1686 he transferred himself to the Middle Temple, by which society he was called to the bar in 1687. He was elected for Weobly in the parliament of 1700, and in all the subsequent parliaments, except one, till his death. The only mention of his name in parliamentary history is connected with a disreputable transaction. He had been appointed one of the commissioners for the sale of the estates forfeited by the rebels of 1715, and in reference to those belonging to the Earl of Derwentwater had assisted in a most corrupt and illegal transfer. The transaction was declared void, and for the notorious breach of trust Birch was expelled the house in March 1732. He however had sufficient influence with his constituents to be re-elected in the new parliament that met in January 1735, but he died before the end of the year.

In the progress of his profession he had been included in the batch of serjeants called in 1706, and before the discovery of the above disgraceful transaction had been, on December 11, 1729, made cursitor baron of the Exchequer, in which office he remained till his death in October 1735.

After the death in 1701 of his first wife, Sarah, the daughter of his uncle Colonel John Birch, he married secondly Letitia Hampden, of St. Andrew's, Holborn; but had no children by either.

BIRCH, THOMAS, descended from the family of Birch, of Birchfield in the parish of Handworth, near Birmingham, which flourished in the early part of the reign of Queen Elizabeth. He was born at Harborne in the same neighbourhood in 1690, and was the eldest son of George Birch and Mary his wife, the daughter of Thomas Foster, Esq. Destined for the law, he took his barrister's degree at the Inner Temple, and, receiving the coif in June 1730, was made one of the king's serjeants before November 23, 1745. He is so named on going up with the judges' address to the king on occasion of the rebellion, when he received the honour of knighthood. In that year he served the office of high sheriff of Staffordshire, and in June following he was raised to the bench as a judge of the Common Pleas, and retained his seat for eleven years. He resided at Southgate, near London, and died on March 16, 1757, leaving by his wife Sarah, daughter and co-heir of J. Teshmaker, Esq., three sons and two daughters. (*Gent. Mag.*)

BLACKBURN, COLIN, is one of the present judges of the Queen's Bench. He was born at Levenside in Dumbartonshire in 1813, being the second son of John Blackburn, Esq., of Killearn in Stirlingshire. After passing through Eton College he matriculated at Trinity College, Cambridge, where he was eighth wrangler in 1835, and took his degree of M.A. in 1838. In Michaelmas Term of that year he was called to the bar by the society of the Inner Temple, and joined the Northern Circuit, attending the Liverpool Sessions. Though with no considerable business as a counsel, he was esteemed a sound lawyer, and after the bar by above twenty years' experience at the bar he was appointed a judge of the Queen's Bench in June 1859, and received the customary knighthood.

BLACKSTONE, WILLIAM. The name of Blackstone is inseparably connected with the law of England. What Lyttelton and his crabbed expositor were to our legal ancestors, Blackstone is to modern students; and though some of the more earnest or more ambitious of them may seek honours by endeavouring to fathom the mysteries of the 'Tenures,' the οἱ πολλοί of the profession are content to earn an easy degree by mastering the more attractive lessons conveyed in the 'Commentaries.' So popular have they become that, where the study was confined in former times to those who pursued it as an avocation, few men of rank or fortune now consider their education complete without gaining an insight into the constitution of the country through Blackstone's easy and perspicuous pages, and abridgments are even introduced into schools for the instruction of the young. Whether this facility is productive of better lawyers must be left as a question for our critical descendants.

William Blackstone was the fourth and posthumous son of Charles Blackstone, a respectable silkman in Cheapside, London, descended from a family originally settled in the neighbourhood of Salisbury. His mother, who was Mary, daughter of Lovelace Bigg, Esq., of Chilton Foliot in Wiltshire, also died before he was twelve years old. He was born on July 10, 1723, and from his birth his education was undertaken by the brother of his mother, Mr. Thomas Bigg, an eminent surgeon in Newgate Street. In 1730 he was put to school at the Charter-house, and in 1735 was admitted on the foundation there, becoming the head of the school at the age of fifteen, and distinguishing himself not only in the customary oration in commemoration of the founder, which he recited on December 12, 1738, but also by obtaining Mr. Benson's prize medal for verses on Milton. He had in the preceding month been entered at Pembroke College, Oxford, and elected to a Charter-house exhibition, to which in February following was added one of Lady Holford's exhibitions, unanimously given by the fellows of the college.

In the university he did not confine himself to the classics, but devoted himself to those sciences the investigation of which tended so much to the simplicity and clearness of his writings. Among these he was peculiarly fond of architecture, and before he was of age he composed a treatise on the subject, which, though never published, was much admired. His partiality for the Muses, already shown by his prize poem on Milton, and afterwards exhibited by several elegant fugitive pieces, he found too fascinating and engrossing for the profession to which he was destined; and, resolving upon 'total abstinence,' he wrote, on entering the Middle Temple, a 'Farewell to his Muse,' in strains which induced many to regret he should leave the flowery path of poetry for the more rugged and sterile ways of the law. Notwithstanding this formal adieu, he could not altogether refrain; and among other pieces he wrote some verses on the death of the Prince of Wales in 1751, which were published in the Oxford collection as the composition of his brother-in-law, James Clitherow. He amused himself also by annotating Shakspeare, and communicated his notes to Mr. Steevens, who inserted them in his last edition of the plays.

He was admitted a member of the Middle Temple on November 20, 1741, and was called to the bar on November 28, 1746. But in the intervals of his attendance on the courts he still continued his academical studies at the university, where he was elected in November 1743 into the Society of All Souls, of which he was afterwards admitted a fellow, and delivered the aniversary speech in commemoration of the founder. There also he took his degree of B.C.L. in June 1745. On being appointed bursar of his college he reduced the confusion in which he found the accounts into lucid order, and left a dissertation on the subject for the benefit of his successors. He not only arranged the muniments of their estates, but greatly assisted in the re-edification of the Codrington Library and in the classification of its contents; in gratitude for all which services the college appointed him in 1749 steward of their manors. In 1750 he commenced doctor of civil law, and in the same year published an 'Essay on Collateral Consanguinity,' with the view of removing the inconvenience felt by the college of electing any person who could prove himself of kin to the founder in preference to any other candidate. His arguments had so much weight that soon after a new regulation was introduced limiting the number of founder's kin.

His progress at the bar in the meantime was so slow and unproductive that, though he had been in 1749 elected recorder of Wallingford, he determined in 1753 to retire to his fellowship, and only practise as a provincial counsel. About this time the professorship of civil law in the university became vacant, and the solicitor-general, Mr. Murray (afterwards Lord Mansfield), with a just appreciation of Dr. Blackstone's abilities, strongly recommended him for the place. The Duke of Newcastle promised it, but it is believed was not satisfied with the devotion of the candidate to his grace's politics, for after a short interview with him it was given to another. Mr. Murray was naturally disgusted, and advised the doctor to read the lectures on law he had long been preparing to such students as were disposed to attend him. He at once adopted the plan and met with immediate success. These lectures form the basis of that work upon which is founded his imperishable fame; and, as a guide to those who listened to them, he published in the next year 'An Analysis of the Laws of England,' clearly methodising the intricate science.

One of the earliest fruits of the acknowledged excellence of his lectures was his unanimous election to the first professorship of law, on the foundation established under the recent will of Mr. Charles Viner, the laborious compiler of that 'Abridgment of Law and Equity,' the twenty-four volumes of which must necessarily occupy the shelves of a lawyer's library. The election took place in 1758, only two years after Mr. Viner's death; and the new professor in the same year published, not only his admired 'Introductory Lecture,' but also a treatise entitled 'Considerations on Copyholders,' which produced an act of parliament establishing their rights in the election of members of parliament. The fame of his lectures was so great that he was requested to read them to the Prince of Wales, an application which, though his engagements obliged him to decline it, he so far complied with as to transmit copies for his royal highness's perusal. Justly conscious that his legal character was now established, the professor resumed his attendance at the bar in Michaelmas 1759, but declined the honour of the coif that was offered to him, and afterwards that of chief justice of the Common Pleas in Ireland.

During the whole of this period he had exerted himself in various ways for the benefit of his alma mater in the different positions by which his efficiency was recognised. He was appointed the archbishop's assessor as visitor of All Souls' College; he was elected visitor of Michel's new foundation in Queen's College, and by his tact and management put an end to the disputes which had long frustrated the original intentions of the donor; and as one of the delegates of the 'Clarendon Press' he introduced new regulations, the good effect of which is seen at the present day. From that press one of the earliest and best specimens of its reformed typography was his publication in 1759 of a new edition of the Great Charter and Charter of the Forest, which led to a controversial correspondence on the authenticity of a particular copy between Dean (afterwards Bishop) Lyttleton and him, addressed to the Society of Antiquaries, of which he was a fellow.

By his marriage in 1761 with Sarah, daughter of James Clitherow, Esq., of Boston House, Middlesex, he vacated his fellowship of All Souls'; but in the same year the Earl of Westmoreland, then chancellor of the university, appointed him principal of New Inn Hall, by which he was enabled to continue his residence at Oxford for the delivery of his lectures. In the early part of that year he had been elected member for Hindon in the parliament then called; and also received a patent of precedence in the courts, to which he was well entitled, not only by the fame he had acquired, but by the increase of his business. The specimens preserved of his advocacy prove the excellence of his argumentative powers. In 1763 he was constituted solicitor-general to the queen, and became a bencher of his inn.

To repress the encroachments of piratical booksellers, who were selling imperfect copies of his lectures, he determined to issue them himself in the form of 'Commentaries on the Law of England.' He accordingly published his first volume in 1765, and the three succeeding volumes in the four following years; and from that time to the present the work has formed a textbook for all students, admired equally for its expositions and the eloquence and purity of its language. With the applause which it deservedly attained, it was not likely that it should escape some amount of critical detraction. Some political censors differed from his views of the principles of the constitution; Dr. Priestley animadverted on certain of his ecclesiastical positions, which were defended by the author; and to an attack upon him by a member of parliament for some observations he had made in the house, which were alleged to be contrary to the principles laid down in his work, he also published a reply justifying the position he had taken, which was severely commented on by Junius. But all, whether opponents or supporters of his doctrines, joined in a universal eulogy of the clearness and beauty of his style, the aptness of his classical allusions, and the allurements with which it enriched a science which had previously repelled the student by its rugged exterior. It has become, and will for ever remain, the student's manual; and the continued demand for it has found employment for a long succession of accomplished editors, who by introducing the subsequent changes in the law have made it as necessary and useful to its latest, as it was to its earliest, readers.

In the new parliament of 1768 he was returned for Westbury, but sat in it only two years; for, though from a disgust at political controversy he declined the place of solicitor-general in January 1770, he readily accepted a judgeship which was offered to him in the following month on the death of Mr. Justice Clive. He actually kissed hands as judge of the Common Pleas on February 9; but at the request of Mr. Justice Yates, who wished to escape collision with Lord Mansfield, he consented to take that judge's place in the King's Bench, and again kissed hands for that court on the 16th of the same month, when he received the honour of knighthood. Mr. Justice Yates died four months after, when Mr. Justice Blackstone removed into the Common Pleas, on June 22.

Whoever reads the reports of the period during which he sat upon the bench must acknowledge that he was equally distinguished as a judge as he had been as a commentator. Some of the judgments that he pronounced are remarkable for the learning they display, and for the clearness with which he supports his argument; and in the few instances in which he differed from his colleagues his opinion was in general found to be right.

He devoted his latter years to the improvement of prison discipline, and, in conjunction with Mr. Howard, obtained in 1779 an act of parliament for the establishment of penitentiary houses for criminals. The beneficial effects of the system, though not at first sufficiently perceived, are now universally acknowledged; and the amended condition of our gaols, in the cleanliness, classification, and employment of the prisoners, is the best proof of the wisdom and benevolence of the projectors. In the same year, having agitated the necessity of an augmentation of the judges' salaries, to meet the increased taxation and expenditure of the time, he obtained for them an addition of 400*l.* to their stipend.

Ere he had been long on the bench he experienced the bad effects of the studious habits in which he had injudiciously indulged in his early life, and of his neglect to take the necessary amount of exercise, to which he was specially averse. His corpulence increased, and his strength failed; and, after two or three attacks of distressing illness, he expired on February 14, 1780. He was buried in a vault at St. Peter's Church at Wallingford, where he possessed a seat called 'Priory Place.' A statue of the judge, by Bacon, was placed soon after his death in the hall of All Souls' College.

The Reports which he had taken and arranged for publication, commencing with the term in which he was called to the bar, and continuing with some intervals through the whole period of his life, were given to the world in the year following his death, under the editorship of his brother-in-law and executor, James Clitherow, Esq., with an introduction detailing all the incidents of his career, which from its fairness and impartiality has formed the groundwork of every future memoir. His investigation of the quarrel between Pope and Addison, which was published with the author's permission by Dr. Kippis in the 'Biographia Britannica,' is spoken of by Mr. Disraeli in high terms of praise.

He left behind him seven children, the second of whom held all the university preferments of his father, and eventually succeeded to the estate at Wallingford, which is still possessed by his representative.

Henry Blackstone, who reported cases from 1788 to 1796, was the judge's nephew, and his Reports were more popular than those of his uncle, three editions having been called for.

BLAGGE, ROBERT, was made king's remembrancer in the Exchequer for life on December 6, 1502. He was advanced to the bench of that court as third baron on June 26, 1511, 3 Henry VIII., with confirmation of the patent of remembrancer, the duties of which he still continued to perform by deputy. In 1515 he was one of the surveyors of crown lands and purveyor of the king's revenues, and received a grant of an annuity of eighty marks during pleasure. In that year he obtained a patent of the remembrancership for his son Barnaby for life, in reversion on his own death or other vacancy, which patent was the subject of discussion in Dyer's Reports (197), and the result was that it was annulled and revoked in 3 Elizabeth as insufficient and not good, because Robert Blagge had no legal estate at the time of its date, nor at any other time after he was constituted a baron. He is stated in the case to have been in possession of his place on the bench in 1523–4. He died in London, and was buried in St. Bartholomew's.

He was the son of Stephen Blagge, of an ancient family in Suffolk, and Alice his wife. He afterwards established himself at Broke Montagu in Somersetshire; and by his marriage with Katherine, sole daughter of Thomas Brune, or Brown, he became possessed of Horseman's Place in Dartford, and of considerable property in the county of Kent, which descended to his sons Robert and the above Barnaby. His second wife, Mary, daughter of John, Lord Cobham, survived him, leaving a son, Sir George, who was gentleman of the bedchamber to Henry VII. (*Cal. St. Papers* [1509], 263; *Hasted's Kent*, ii. 312, 375; *Gage's Suffolk*, 520.)

BLASTON, THOMAS DE, was probably of Leicestershire, where there is a hamlet of that name. The custody of the honor of Peverell, in that and two other counties, was committed to a Thomas de Blaston in the reign of Edward I.; and he may have been the father of the baron of the Exchequer. The latter is first mentioned in 3 Edward III., when, under the title of 'clericus regis,' he was constituted the king's chamberlain in Chester. He was raised to the Exchequer bench on November 2, 1332, 6 Edward III. A new patent was granted to him on January 20, 1341, when the king had weeded the court, on his return from Tournay, of those whom he considered to have failed in their duty. He held the rectory of Solihull, in Warwickshire. (*Abb. Rot. Orig.* i. 39, ii. 17; *Rot. Parl.* ii. 105; *Cal. Inquis.* p. m. ii. 85.)

BLENCOWE, JOHN, was born in 1642 on the manor of Marston St. Lawrence, on the Oxford border of Northamptonshire, which was granted in the reign of Henry VI. to Thomas Blencowe, whose family originally came from a place of that name in Cumberland. He was the eldest son of Thomas Blencowe, by his wife Anne, the daughter of the Rev. Dr. Francis Savage, of Ripple in Worcestershire. He was educated at Oriel College, Oxford, admitted a student at the Inner Temple in 1663, called to the bar in 1673, and elected a bencher in 1687. Raised to the degree of the coif in 1689, he was elected member for Brackley in 1690. Though not a prominent debater, he was a firm supporter of the government. To his marriage with Anne, the daughter of Dr. John Wallis, the celebrated Savilian professor of geometry and 'custos archivorum' of Oxford, and the great decipherer of his day, he probably owed in some measure his advancement to the bench. When the professor was offered the deanery of Hereford in 1692 he declined the advancement, but in his letter of refusal he intimated that a favour to his son-in-law would be more acceptable to him. 'I have,' he said, 'a son-in-law, Mr. Serjeant Blencowe, of the Inner Temple, a member of the House of Commons, an able lawyer and not inferior to many of those on the bench, of a good life and great integrity, cordial to the government and serviceable in it.' (*Baker's Northamptonshire*, 639–646.)

It was not, however, till four years afterwards that, in September 1696, the serjeant was constituted a baron of the Exchequer; but in Michaelmas Term of the following year he was further promoted to the Court of Common Pleas and knighted. He sat in that court for the next five-and-twenty years, though several memorialists of the judge, as Baker, Noble, and others, have represented him as having been removed to the Queen's Bench, for the whole of Queen Anne's reign, from 1702 to 1714. Luttrell (v. 183) records that in the beginning of her reign such removal was intended; but it is clear from Lord Raymond's Reports (769, 1317) that he was then re-appointed to the Common Pleas, and that he was still in that court at the end of it, and he is never mentioned as acting in the Queen's Bench. On the accession of George I. he was replaced in the same seat, and in 1718 he concurred with most of the other judges in favour of the king's prerogative over the marriage and education of the royal family. On June 22, 1722, being then eighty years of age, he obtained permission to resign, and a pension was granted to him for the remainder of his life, which terminated on May 6, 1726. He was buried at Brackley, where there is a monument to his memory.

Sir John is represented as an honest, plain, blunt man, with no brilliancy of genius nor any extraordinary attainments. He outlived his faculties, and conceived that he had discovered the longitude. A story is told of him that once he ordered his servant to lay him out, insisting that he was dead. Indulging his whim, the trusty fellow laid him on the carpet, and after some time came to him and observed that he thought his honour was coming to life again, to which the old judge, tired of his position, assented. A proof of his considerate kindness of heart appears in another anecdote. Lady Blencowe having suggested to him to pension off a hewer of stones who was so old that he spoiled the work he was employed on, he replied, 'No, no, let him spoil on; he enjoys a pleasure in thinking that he earns his bread at fourscore years and ten, but if you turn him off he will die of grief.'

He left a numerous family. His third son William was taught the mystery of deciphering by his maternal grandfather, Dr. Wallis, and was employed to give evidence of the letters written in cipher which were produced on the proceeding against Bishop Atterbury. He was the first person to whom a salary was granted as decipherer to the government, his allowance being 200*l.* a year. The judge's second daughter became the wife of Chief Baron Probyn. The estate of Marston St. Lawrence remains in the possession of Sir John's lineal descendant. (*Noble's Granger*, ii. 180; *Nichols's Lit. Anecdotes*, ix. 273.)

BLOCKLEY, JOHN DE. The parish of this name in Worcestershire was probably the native place of John de Blockley, who endowed the chantry of the church of St. Mary there with some of his lands in 30

Edward III. and subsequent years. He was an auditor of the Exchequer in 44 Edward III., with a salary of 10*l*. a year; and he at the same time received an annual pension of twenty marks for certain good services he had performed to the king and the late queen Philippa; besides which he had a grant of the custody of the manor of Exhulne in Warwickshire during the minority of the heir. Like most of the other officers, he was in holy orders. He was raised to the bench as a baron of the Exchequer in 47 Edward III., and so continued till the last year of the king's reign. (*Cal. Inquis.* p. m. ii. 194, 263, 352; *Issue Roll*, 49, 92; *Abb. Rot. Orig.* ii. 310; *Cal. Rot. Pat.* 189.)

BLOET, ROBERT (BISHOP OF LINCOLN), is stated by both Risdon (67) and Prince (84) to have belonged to a family of that name which held the lordship of Ragland, and which for many generations lived at Holcombe Rogus in the county of Devon, where it still flourishes. The name is often spelled Bluett. He is described by Prince as the second son of Sir Rowland Bloet, and great-grandson of William Bloet, Earl of Salisbury, of which earldom however, before the Conquest, Dugdale gives no account. But Godwin's editor, Richardson (283), calls him the brother of Odo, Bishop of Bayeux, quoting Claud. A. 8, f. 118, MSS. Hutton, and referring in corroboration to his grant of the manor of Charleton to the priory of Bermondsey, wherein he says, 'quod pro salute animæ Dom. mei Willelmi Regis, et *fratris mei* Bajocens. Episcopi, &c., confirmavi Monachis de Bermondsey Cherletonam,' &c. But this charter is of very doubtful authenticity; and with all these contradictory accounts, his birth, his lineage, and even his country, must remain in obscurity.

It seems very probable that he was the Bloet who is mentioned as accompanying William Rufus to England upon the death of the Conqueror. (*Lingard*, ii. 76.) The name of Robert Bloet, without any addition, appears as the witness to one of William's charters to the monastery of Durham, granted in 1088 or 1089; and the signature 'Rodberto Dispensatore' is attached to another to Chichester Cathedral, which was probably granted about the same time, and may perhaps be his.

He was appointed chancellor before July or August 1090, a charter to the cathedral of Lincoln of that date bearing his attestation; another to Salisbury, dated in 1191, and several without date (*Monast.* i. 174, 241, ii. 266, vi. 1167, 1177, 1271, 1295), but no doubt granted about the same time, record his name as chancellor; but no instance occurs of his signature as chancellor after he was raised to the bishopric of Lincoln. On his elevation to that see he was compelled to pay a large sum, varying, according to different authors, from 500*l*. to 5000*l*., as the price of his advancement, or, perhaps, for exempting the see from the jurisdiction of the Archbishop of York.

He was consecrated by Archbishop Lanfranc in 1093, and no doubt then resigned the Great Seal.

That he exercised considerable influence, not only over King William, but over his successor King Henry also, all writers agree; but it does not appear that he held any official character under William after he retired from the chancellorship.

Neither Spelman nor Dugdale introduces him in their list of chief justiciaries under Henry I., but Henry of Huntingdon, who was one of his archdeacons, and had lived long in his family, expressly states that he was 'justitiarius totius Angliæ.' Whatever doubt may be felt with regard to this author's attribution of the title to some others, it is impossible entirely to discard his authority here, considering the intimacy of his connection, and the consequent means of knowledge that he had. The period when he held the office is not mentioned, but he is further described as having been twice prosecuted in the last year of his life by the king's suggestion, and as having been fined so severely as to produce the lamentation that he was now compelled to dress those about him in woollen, who had formerly been clothed in rich garments. Even to the last, however, the king pretended kindness towards him; but when some royal flatteries were reported to him, he exclaimed with a sigh, 'He praises no one whom he does not mean to destroy.' He was in the king's company at Woodstock on the occasion of a royal hunt, when he was struck with apoplexy, and, falling off his horse, was carried to his bed, and died on January 10, 1123. His bowels were buried at Eynsham in Oxfordshire, a monastery which he had restored, and his body was deposited at Lincoln.

He had an illegitimate son named Simon, born to him when he was chancellor, whom he appointed, while yet in his nonage, dean of his church. Though this does not speak well for his morals, the character given him by his contemporaries in other respects is much in his favour. Henry of Huntingdon describes him as mild and humble, a raiser of many, a depressor of none, the orphan's father, and the delight of his family; and Matthew Paris testifies to the beauty of his person, and the sweetness and affability of his manners and conversation. (*Angl. Sac.* ii. 694; *Wendover*, ii. 41, &c.; *Turner's Engl.* i. 167; *Daniel's*, 58.)

BLUNDEVIL, RANULPH (EARL OF CHESTER), surnamed Blundevil (or, as Dugdale says, Blaudevil, from the town where he was born, then called Album Monasterium, now Oswestry), was the son of Hugh Cyvelioc, Earl of Chester, and Bertra, daughter of the Earl of Evreux. He succeeded to the title in 1181. While King Richard was in the Holy Land he resisted Prince John's attempts to obtain the government, and distinguished himself in the sieges of the castles of Marlborough and Nottingham, held by the prince's adherents.

In 1193 his name appears as one of the justiciers before whom a fine was levied; but there is no other trace of his having acted in a judicial capacity.

He loyally assisted King John throughout the troubles of his reign, and was equally conspicuous in securing the throne to his son Henry III. As soon as the rebels were defeated, and the kingdom was at rest, he departed for the Holy Land, and was present at the siege of Damietta. After his return in 1220 the activity of his disposition was frequently displayed, sometimes in opposition to the king, but more frequently in his support. He died in October 1231, having presided over the county of Chester above fifty years.

His first wife was Constance, daughter and heir of Conan, Earl of Brittany, and widow of Geoffrey, the son of King Henry II. Being divorced from her, 'by reason that King John haunted her company,' he then married Clemencia, daughter of Ralph de Feugers, and widow of Alan Dinant. He left no issue by either of them.

BLYTH, JOHN (BISHOP OF SALISBURY), was son of William Blyth, of Norton in Derbyshire, by a sister of Archbishop Rotheram. He and his brother Geoffrey were sent to the university of Cambridge, where each of them successively became master of King's Hall, each also being eventually raised to the episcopal bench—John as Bishop of Salisbury, on December 22, 1493; and Geoffrey as Bishop of Lichfield and Coventry, on December 26, 1503.

At the time of his elevation to the prelacy John Blyth was archdeacon of Richmond, to which he had been admitted on October 8, 1485. He was also master of the Rolls, having been appointed on May 5, 1492. This office he resigned on February 13, 1494, a few days before his consecration; and in the same year he was elected chancellor of the university in which he was educated. He enjoyed his honours only five years, dying about August 23, 1499. His remains were deposited in a handsome tomb behind the high altar in his cathedral. (*Rymer*, xii. 552; *Le Neve*, 326; *Godwin*, 323, 352.)

BOBI, HUGH DE, was sheriff of Yorkshire under Hugh Bardolph from 4 to 6 Richard I., and was one of the five justices itinerant who set the tallage in Lincolnshire in the eighth year of that reign, 1196–7.

(*Madox*, i. 704.) For the first four years of John's reign he acted as a justicier as well at Westminster as on the circuit.

In 2 John he was associated with Hugh de Wells in the custody of the bishopric of Lincoln during its vacancy (*Rot. Chart.* 99); and in the next year he accounted for the rents of Baldwin Wace's lands, then in the king's hands. (*Rot. Cancell.* 193.) The 'Rotulus de Oblatis' of 2 John (101, 212, 271) contains an entry of his gift of one hundred pounds and a palfrey to the king; and among the fines of 6 John is one of two hundred marks paid by him rather than trust his son as a hostage 'pro domino suo.'

BOCLAND, HUGH DE, was a canon of St. Paul's, and is mentioned by Dugdale and Spelman as chief justiciary at the commencement of the reign of Henry I., on the authority of that king's charter of liberties, as cited by Matthew Paris, being addressed to him in that character. Both Roger de Wendover and Matthew Paris give two copies of that charter—the first when it was promulgated by Henry in the first year of his reign; and the second when it was produced to the barons, 113 years afterwards, by Archbishop Langton. The first, therefore, would more probably be the correct copy, and that is addressed to him as sheriff of Hertfordshire, while the latter is addressed to him as Justiciarius Angliæ. The continuation of the address in both is 'et omnibus fidelibus suis, tam Anglis quam Francis, in Hertfordsyre,' words which show that similar copies were sent to each county, addressed no doubt to its particular sheriff, as this was—according to the royal direction at the time of its grant, recorded by both these historians, 'that as many copies of it were to be made as there were counties in England, to be deposited in the abbeys of each county as a public record.' A charter by which King Henry made a grant of land, in Essex to Otho 'aurifabro,' addressed to Maurice, Bishop of London, and Hugo de Bocland, 'et omnibus baronibus suis et fidelibus, Francis et Anglis, de Essexiâ' (*N. Fœdera*, i. 9), affords a corroboration that he was at this time sheriff of Hertfordshire, inasmuch as the two counties of Essex and Hertford were then, and for several centuries afterwards, united under one sheriff, and the sheriffalty was frequently held for many years together by the same individual. Many charters prove that he was also sheriff or portgrave of London, but his position in none of them affords the slightest evidence that he ever was chief justiciary. That he never held that high and responsible office is rendered more probable by the total silence of the historians with regard to him, a silence which is wholly unaccountable in reference to an officer whom they describe as the prime minister of the realm, and the next to the king in dignity.

BOCLAND, HUGH DE, may have been a descendant from the above-named Hugh de Bocland. The first mention of him is in 4 Henry II., 1158, when he was excused from the donum of Berkshire. In 1166 he certified that he held two knights' fees and a half in that county, and was sheriff of it from 1170 to 1176. He acted as one of the justices itinerant in 1173, to set the assize on the king's demesnes in Devonshire, and in the following year in his own county of Berks. (*Pipe Roll*, 124; *Madox*, i. 124, 701.)

His son William was sheriff of Cornwall.

BOCLAND, GEOFFREY DE, appears as a justicier from 7 Richard I., 1195, to 3 Henry III., 1218, during which years fines were levied before him at Westminster, and in 5 Henry III. he was one of the justices itinerant into Hertfordshire. There are also several entries on the rolls showing that he was connected with the Exchequer in the beginning of King John's reign. (*Rot. Claus.* i. 473; *Rot. Chart.* 99, &c.)

About the year 1200 he was appointed to the archdeaconry of Norfolk, which he held till he was advanced by the king to the deanery of St. Martin's-le-Grand, a benefice which he certainly enjoyed in 1216, having received grants in the interim of the churches of Tenham and Pageham. (*Le Neve*, 219; *Rot. Chart.* 156; *Rot. Pat.* 61.)

If he were the 'G. de Bocland' to whom a mandate was directed in 15 John, commanding him to let the king have, at the price any others would give for them, the corn, pigs, and other chattels at Berkhampsted which belonged to Geoffrey Fitz-Peter, his brother, recently deceased (*Rot. Claus.* i. 139), he was probably a younger brother of William de Bocland, who married the sister of Geoffrey Fitz-Peter's first wife, the daughter of Geoffrey de Say. As there was no other connection between Fitz-Peter and Bocland than this marriage, it would appear that in those times the title of brother was extended by courtesy to the brothers of the wife's sister's husband.

Geoffrey de Bocland seems to have committed himself with the barons in 17 John, as time and safe-conduct were granted to him to come before the king, which were twice afterwards renewed (*Rot. Pat.* 172, 174, 192); and in the same year his manor of Tacheworth in Hertfordshire was given by the king to Nicholas de Jelland. (*Rot. Claus.* i. 257.)

On the accession of King Henry, however, he soon returned to his duty, and was restored to his judicial position. He died before February 4, 1231, the date of a charter to Walter de Kirkham, then dean of St. Martin's. (*Maitland's London*, 767.)

BOHUN, HUMPHREY DE (EARL OF HEREFORD). Henry de Bohun, the father of Humphrey, was great-grandson of the afternamed Milo of Gloucester, the first Earl of Hereford, whose eldest daughter, Margery, married Humphrey de Bohun, the grandson of another Humphrey, who accompanied the Conqueror into England. After the death of Mahell, Earl of Hereford, her last surviving brother, her grandson Henry de Bohun, in 1199, was created Earl of Hereford, and was constable of England. He married Matilda, the daughter of Geoffrey Fitz-Peter, Earl of Essex, and died in 4 Henry III., 1220.

Humphrey de Bohun, then succeeding to the earldom of Hereford, was, on the death of William de Mandeville, his mother's brother, without issue, created in 1237 Earl of Essex.

His life was one career of activity, now boldly demanding from the king a redress of grievances, and now supporting his sovereign in resisting his enemies. He was sheriff of Kent in 23 Henry III. and the two following years; in 34 Henry III. he took the cross and went to the Holy Land; in 37 Henry III. he was present in Westminster Hall when the formal curse was pronounced, with bell, book, and candle, against the violators of Magna Charta. In 41 Henry III. he had the custody of the marches of Wales, and it was during the time that he held this office that his name appears, in 1260, as a justice itinerant for the counties of Gloucester, Worcester, and Hereford. In the troubles which shortly followed he joined Simon de Montfort, Earl of Leicester, and was taken prisoner at the battle of Evesham, August 4, 1265. His former services, however, availed him to obtain a restoration of his lands and honours, with additional marks of favour. He lived till September 24, 1275, 3 Edward I., and was buried in the abbey of Lanthony. He founded the church of Augustine Friars in Broad Street, in the city of London.

He married first, Maud, daughter of the Earl of Ewe, by whom he had a son Humphrey, who died during his lifetime, leaving a son, also Humphrey, who succeeded to the earldoms of Hereford and Essex. His second wife was called Maud de Avenebury, by whom he had a son, John de Bohun, lord of Haresfield.

BOLEBEC, HUGH DE, was the son of Walter de Bolebec, a great baron in Northumberland, by his wife Margaret, one of the sisters and co-heirs of Richard de Montfichet. He was a frequent attendant on the court, witnessing several charters, assisting his sovereign, King John, in his contentions with the barons, and receiving his reward from the lands of their adherents. In 4 Henry III. the county of Northumberland was placed under his charge (*Rot. Claus.* i. 421), and he was again sheriff of it in 20 Henry III., when he held it for ten years. Though placed at the head of the justices itinerant for the liberties of Durham in 1228, he does not seem to have had any subsequent judicial appointment till 1262, when he was named as one of the justices itinerant for pleas of the forest. He died in October in that year, leaving his wife Theophania surviving. By her he had a son Hugh, who died unmarried during his father's life, and four daughters, who succeeded to his property. (*Rot. Chart.* 179, 220; *Rot. Claus.* i. 246, 314; *Excerpt. e Rot. Fin.* ii. 385-393; *Baronage*, i. 452.)

BOLINGBROKE, EARL OF. *See* O. ST. JOHN.

BOLINGBROKE, NICHOLAS DE, judging from his name, belonged to the county of Lincoln. In 4 Edward II. he was the last of three judges of assize sent into that county and five others, and in the tenth year was named in a special commission to try some rioters in Lincoln. In 12 & 13 Edward II. he was commanded to cause all proceedings before him as a judge of assize to be estreated into the Exchequer.

He certified as one of the lords of the township of Gargrave in Yorkshire. (*Parl. Writs*, ii. p. ii. 561.)

BOLLAND, WILLIAM, was the eldest son of a London merchant of the same names, and was born in 1772. He was sent for his education to Dr. Valpy's school at Reading, then noted for producing scholars of high literary attainment. While there he was a great favourite with his master, and wrote several prologues and epilogues for the annual dramatic performances for which the school was renowned. He thence proceeded to Trinity College, Cambridge, where he formed a life-long intimacy with John Copley, afterwards Lord Lyndhurst, and took his degrees with him in 1794 and 1796. In the latter and two following years he gained the Seatonian prize for his poems on 'The Epiphany,' 'Miracles,' and 'St. Paul at Athens;' and subsequently evinced considerable poetic powers in several pieces of great elegance. But soon his devotion to Astræa compelled him to desert the Muses. He entered her (Inner) Temple, and placed himself under her priest George Holroyd, and, after some initiation into the mysteries, was permitted to join in the ministrations.

To descend from these altitudes, he was called to the bar on April 24, 1801, having previously acted for some time as a special pleader. He joined the Home Circuit, practising at the usual sessions attached to it, but principally at the Old Bailey, and in 1804 he became one of the four city pleaders. In all of these he commanded a large share of business, and acquired so good a reputation that in 1815 he was selected to join Mr. Holroyd in a commission to Jersey to enquire into the existence of certain 'doleances' complained of by the inhabitants. In 1817 he was made recorder of Reading, the place of his pupilage; and in 1822, when, from the respect he had obtained as senior city pleader, he would certainly in ordinary times have been elected common serjeant of London, he was, from the political excitement arising from the trial of Queen Caroline, defeated by a small majority in favour of Mr. (afterwards Lord Chief Justice) Denman, who had acted as one of her majesty's advocates.

After eight-and-twenty years' labour at the bar, he was called to the bench of the Exchequer on November 16, 1829. The nature of his business had not led him to that abstruse learning which is so necessary for a judge, except in regard to criminal law, with which he was intimately conversant. But, gifted with good sense and discriminative judgment, he fulfilled his duties with great discretion. He occupied the judicial seat for nearly ten years, when disorders and infirmities obliged him to resign in January 1839, after which he lived little more than a year, his death taking place on May 14, 1840.

He was one of the most popular men of his time. His eminently handsome and benevolent countenance made the first favourable impression, which his pleasantry, cordiality, and kind disposition more than confirmed. He had a mania for old English literature, and everything which was ancient and rare. The Roxburgh Club originated at a dinner party given by him, and he furnished the first book circulated among his associates, being a reprint of Lord Surrey's version of the second book of the Æneid, the first specimen of blank verse in our language. He figures as Hortensius in Dr. Dibdin's 'Bibliomania;' and his curious collection of books, pictures, and coins sold after his death for more than 3000*l*.

He married in 1810 his cousin Elizabeth, one of the daughters of John Bolland, Esq., of Clapham, and left several children.

BOLLING, WILLIAM, was appointed third baron of the Exchequer on October 11, 1501, 17 Henry VII., and was continued in his place for the first four years in the following reign. He was in the commission of the peace for Essex and Kent. (*Cal. St. Papers* [1509], 60, 101.) He was one of the ancients of the Middle Temple who were present when three members of that society were called serjeants in November 1503, thus plainly showing that barons at that time sat on the bench who, not being of the degree of the coif, still remained in the society in which they had been brought up. (*Dugdale's Orig.* 113.)

BONQUER, WILLIAM, or **BONCOUR,** was employed in 1255 and 1259 on missions to the pope relative to the election of Prince Edmund to the crown of Sicily, and upon the peace with the King of France. In the letter of credence on the latter occasion he is called 'milite et mariscallo regis.' (*Rymer*, i. 337, 386.) In 46 Henry III., 1262, a salary of 40*l*. was granted to four justices of the bench, of whom he is the last named; and in that and the next year he acted as a justice itinerant. The fines in which his name appears do not occur beyond Easter 1265.

BOOTH, LAURENCE (ARCHBISHOP OF YORK), to use the words of Dugdale (*Baronage*, ii. 481), was of 'a very antient and knightly family,' possessing property in Cheshire and Lancashire. From the reign of Edward I. there were five generations before John Booth, or Bouth, of Barton, who by two wives had twelve children—two of whom, William and this Laurence, became Archbishops of York; one, John, Bishop of Exeter; the son of another was raised to the peerage as Baron Delamere, and afterwards created Earl of Warrington; and the daughter of another of the twelve children married Ralph Nevill, the third Earl of Westmoreland.

Laurence was the youngest son, and the only child of the second wife, Maude, daughter of Sir John Savage, of Clifton, or Rock-Savage, in Cheshire. He pursued his studies at Cambridge, becoming master of Pembroke Hall in 1450, and afterwards chancellor of the university. Ecclesiastical preferments flowed quickly upon him. From the rectory of Cottenham in Cambridgeshire he was successively advanced to the provostship of Beverley in 1453; canonries in York and Lichfield; the archdeaconry of Richmond in 1454; the deanery of St. Paul's in 1456; and the bishopric of Durham, by papal bull, on September 15, 1457. (*Monast.* vi. 1307; *Le Neve.*)

Although Fuller describes him as 'neither for York or Lancaster, but England,' there is no doubt that until the Lancastrians were deprived of all hope he was zealously attached to their interest and employed in their service. In 1454 he was Queen Margaret's chancellor, and keeper of King Henry's privy seal. The battle of Towton in the following year sealed the fate of his party; but that he had not made himself obnoxious in his adherence to his royal master is apparent from the fact that he was not only not included in the act of attainder then passed by the conqueror in 1461, but that by the same statute his right to forfeitures within the palatinate was expressly excepted in his favour. Within a short period, however, he had incurred the king's displeasure for some offence which is not recorded. His temporalities were seized into the king's hands on December 28, 1462, and were not restored to him till April 17, 1464, when he had so far reinstated himself in the royal favour that all grants to him were excepted from the act of resumption passed in the parliament of that year. (*Rot. Parl.* v. 319.) From this time till the second imprisonment and death of Henry VI., in May 1471, he seems to have been convinced of the inutility of further resistance, as in the following July he united in the oath by which Edward, Prince of Wales, was accepted as heir to the crown, and he took his place as a trier of petitions in the next parliament. (*Ibid.* vi. 3, 234.)

He was so confirmed in King Edward's confidence as to be selected for his chancellor on July 27, 1473, and retained the office till February 1475. We may presume that his removal from it was occasioned by no dislike of the king, inasmuch as within ten days of the death of Archbishop Neville, in June 1476, the temporalities of the see of York were placed in his custody, and he was translated to that province on the 1st of the following September. He presided as primate less than four years, dying at Southwell on May 19, 1480. His remains were deposited in the collegiate church by the side of his brother, Archbishop William Booth, who had been interred there sixteen years before.' (*Godwin*, 697, 752; *Angl. Sac.* i. 777; *Surtee's Durham*, i. lix.)

BOREHAM, HARVEY DE, was of a family which took its name from the village so called in Essex. He was an officer of the Exchequer, and also belonged to the ecclesiastical profession, being a canon of St. Paul's. In 49 Henry III., 1264, fines were levied before him from November till the following Easter. Dugdale (*Orig.* 21, 42) accordingly introduces him at that time among the justices of the Common Pleas, but he does not appear to have acted afterwards in that character. He is, however, recorded as a baron of the Exchequer in 1 Edward I., and probably continued so till his death in the fifth year of that reign. (*Madox*, ii. 28, 320; *Cal. Inquis.* p. m. i. 62.)

BOSANQUET, JOHN BERNARD. The family of Bosanquet left France on the revocation of the Edict of Nantes in 1685, and settled in England, where several of its members flourished among the most eminent merchants of London. The judge's grandfather, Samuel Bosanquet, became lord of the manor of Low Hall in the county of Essex, and resided in Forest House, in Waltham Forest; and his father, also Samuel, who added to the property the estate of Dingestow Court in Monmouthshire, was sheriff of the former county in 1770, and governor of the Bank of England in 1792. The judge was the youngest of three sons, the issue of his marriage with

Eleanor, daughter of Henry Lannoy Hunter, Esq., of Beechill in the county of Berks. He was born at Forest House on May 2, 1773; and, after passing some years at Eton College, he completed his education at Christchurch, Oxford. Being called to the bar at Lincoln's Inn in 1800, he joined the Home Circuit, and attended the Essex sessions, of which his father was the chairman; but three years before his call he had commenced his legal career as a reporter of decisions in the Common Pleas, Exchequer Chamber, and House of Lords, in conjunction with Mr. (afterwards Sir Christopher) Puller. Of these reports there were two series, one from 1797 to 1804, and the other from 1804 to 1807. After a steady progress for seven years more, he was selected as counsel both for the East India Company and the Bank of England.

The extensive business in which he was thus engaged compelled him to quit the circuit; and taking the coif in Michaelmas Term 1814, he became from that time well known to the public in the numerous bank prosecutions which the then frequent forgeries of one-pound notes rendered necessary, and which he conducted with great discretion and effect for a period of thirteen years. In 1824 he was offered the chief justiceship of Bengal, but declined it; and in 1827 he became king's serjeant.

He was appointed a judge of the Court of Common Pleas on February 1, 1830, and was thereupon knighted. The ability and impartiality with which he exercised his important functions may be estimated by his being chosen one of the lords commissioners of the Great Seal, in conjunction with Sir C. C. Pepys and Sir Lancelot Shadwell, which they held from April 23, 1835, to January 16, 1836, after which date Sir John sat in the Common Pleas for six years more, when the failure of his health compelled him to resign in Hilary Term 1842.

His appointment as head of the Commission for the Improvement of the Practice and Proceedings of the Common Law Courts, and his selection as arbitrator between the Crown and the Duke of Athol, to fix the amount of the unsettled claims of the latter after he had resigned the sovereignty of the Isle of Man, are a sufficient proof of the high estimation in which he stood.

In other respects his reputation was equally established. He published without his name a 'Letter of a Layman' on the connection of the prophecies of Daniel and the Apocalypse, embodying in a small compass a great amount of research. He was a very considerable linguist, of accurate and various learning, and particularly fond of scientific enquiries. In these pursuits he occupied the six years which he lived after his retirement. He died on September 25, 1847, and was buried at Llantillio-Crossenny, Monmouthshire, in the vault of the family of his wife, Mary Anne, daughter of Richard Lewis, Esq., of that place. A monument to his memory is erected in the church of his own parish of Dingestow.

BOSCEHALL, WILLIAM DE. If Dugdale had not inserted his name among the justices itinerant, it would not have been introduced here; because he never appears to have acted in that capacity, except for pleas of the forest in the northern counties in 54 Henry III., 1270; the more especially as nothing has been ascertained relative to him.

BOSCO, JOHN DE, was an advocate who was employed in 18 Edward I. to plead on the part of the king. (*Abb. Plac.* 284.) On the appointment of the eight justices of assize in 21 Edward I., 1293, he was selected as one of them. In the same year he claimed, with his brothers-in-law, the manors of Toleshunt, Tregoz, and Blunteshale in Essex, as son of Lucy, one of the four sisters of Nicholas de Tregoz. (*Rot. Parl.* i. 92.) He was summoned among the judges to parliament in the 23rd and 25th years of that reign; but his career seems to have terminated disgracefully, as he was convicted in 6 Edward II. of abstracting a king's writ, and substituting a false one in its place. (*Parl. Writs.* i. 29, 52; *Abb. Plac.* 316.)

BOTELER, ALEXANDER LE, or PINCERNA. The history of the peerage shows several baronies which were held by individuals who were called by this name, from the office they filled in the families of royal and noble persons. The butler of the great Earl of Leicester, in the first Henry's reign, was the founder of the now extinct baronies of Oversley and Wemme, and the ancestor of the baron of Sudley; and from the butler of the Earl of Chester in the reign of Henry II. the barony of Warrington was derived. In the present Duke of Norfolk the blood of William de Albini, the pincerna or butler of King Henry I., continues to flow; and five titles in the English and Irish peerage, commencing with the Marquis of Ormond, owe their origin to Theobald le Boteler, the chief butler of Ireland under Henry II.

In what family Alexander le Boteler held that office does not appear, nor does Madox give any further information concerning him than that he, with Ralph Fitz-Stephen the sheriff, and Philip Fitz-Ernise, were the justices errant to make the assize of the king's demesnes in Gloucestershire in 20 Henry II., 1174, to which it appears by the record they were appointed by a writ of Richard de Luci, the chief justiciary. (*Madox*, i. 123.)

BOTELER, NICHOLAS LE, or PINCERNA,

held land in Filby in Norfolk, and claimed the right of presentation to the church there, which was decided against him in 2 John. (*Abb. Plac.* 31.) In 17 John he forfeited his possessions for his adherence to the barons, but they were restored to him on the accession of Henry III. In the ninth year of that reign he was added to the list of justices itinerant for the counties of Norfolk and Suffolk. (*Rot. Claus.* i. 334, ii. 77.)

BOTELER, JOHN. This judge may be presumed to derive his name from the office which he originally filled in Lincoln's Inn. In the Black Book of that society he is described as being admitted a member of it in 8 Edward IV., 1468, because 'bene et fideliter se gessit in officio pincernæ'—a practice of which another instance will be found in the life of Judge More. He became reader in autumn 1482, and read a second time in Lent 1488.

In 9 Henry VII., 1494, he was called to the degree of the coif with Humphrey Coningsby and several others, who held their feast at Ely House on November 16, 1494, which is the first recorded instance of this solemnity being honoured with the presence of the king and queen.

His elevation to the bench of the Common Pleas took place on April 26, 1508, just a year before the king's death; and receiving a new patent from Henry VIII., he continued in the exercise of his judicial duties for the next nine years.

BOTETOURT, JOHN DE, was appointed one of the justices of trailbaston in 33 Edward I., 1305, and in the same year received his first summons to parliament, and was sent to treat with the Scots on the affairs of that kingdom. Dugdale states nothing of his origin, but mentions his appointment as governor of St. Briavel's Castle in Gloucestershire, and as warden of the Forest of Dene in 19 Edward I. Two years afterwards he was a justice of gaol delivery in the counties of Warwick and Leicester; and in 22 Edward I., being then admiral of the king's fleet, he was summoned to serve in Gascony, and was in the expedition there in the twenty-fourth year, during which period various sums of money were paid to him on the king's account. (*Rot. Parl.* 95–478, ii. 432; *N. Fœdera*, i. 970.) In the following years he accompanied the king in his Scottish wars, and was present in June 1300 at the siege of Carlaverock, the metrical chronicler of which describes him as 'light of heart and doing good to all.' (*Nicolas's Siege*, 32, 202.) He was a party to the barons' letter to the pontiff in 29 Edward I., in which he is styled 'lord of Mendlesham' in Suffolk. Two years afterwards he was nominated the king's lieutenant in Cumberland, Westmoreland, &c., and in 33 Edward I. he was assigned with two others to hear and determine certain transgressions committed at Bristol. (*Parl. Writs*, i. 368; *Rot. Parl.* i. 168.)

Under Edward II. he was equally distinguished, being appointed one of the peers to regulate the royal household, and afterwards to treat with the Earl of Lancaster. He was again admiral of the king's fleet and governor of the castles of St. Briavel and Framlingham; he also served again against the Scots, besides being engaged in several commissions of a civil character. He died in 18 Edward II. (*Cal. Inquis.* p. m. i. 319), leaving, by his wife Matilda (the daughter of Beatrice de Beauchamp, widow of William de Beauchamp), several children. The barony, after many abeyances, is now held by the Duke of Beaufort.

BOUDON, WILLIAM DE, of a Northamptonshire family, was appointed second baron of the Exchequer on February 4, 1327, a few days after the commencement of the reign of Edward III.; but, as there is no subsequent entry whatever concerning him, he probably died within a few months, Robert de Nottingham succeeding him as second baron on October 15 following. (*Parl. Writs*, ii. p. ii. 527.)

BOURCHIER, or BOUSSER, JOHN DE, whose name underwent several variations, but at last settled down to Bourchier, is first mentioned as one of the attorneys of the Earl of Oxford, to appear in his place at the parliament held in May, 34 Edward I., 1306. (*Parl. Writs*, i. 166.) He was one of the justices of assize in the counties of Kent, Surrey, and Sussex in 8 Edward II. (*Rot. Parl.* i. 449), and was named in several other judicial commissions from that time till May 31, 1321, in the fourteenth year, when he was constituted a judge of the Common Pleas. In this court he continued to act for the remainder of that reign; but some short delay seems to have taken place in his re-appointment on the accession of Edward III., his patent not being dated till March 24, 1327, two months afterwards, while those to his brethren were immediately granted.

He was the son of Robert de Bousser and Emma, his wife; and by his own marriage with Helen, the daughter and heiress of Walter de Colchester, became possessed of Stansted in Halsted, and other manors in Essex. The last fine levied before him was dated on the morrow of the Ascension, 3 Edward III., 1329. Dying soon after, he left two sons, Robert and John, the former of whom is the under-mentioned chancellor.

He was the head of a curious commission in 19 Edward II. to hear and determine a charge made by the Bishop and Dean and Chapter of London against certain persons for taking and carrying away a great fish, 'qui[dicitur cete,' found on their manor of Walton, the prosecutors alleging that King Henry III. had, by his charter, granted them 'totum crassum piscem' which should be taken on their land, 'except the tongue, which the said king retained to himself.' (*N. Fœdera*, ii. 619.)

BOURCHIER, or BOUSSER, ROBERT DE, the eldest son of the above-mentioned John de Bousser, began his career in 17 Edward II. as a man-at-arms, and was returned in that character by the sheriff of Essex, as summoned to attend by general proclamation (*Parl. Writs*, ii. p. i. 652); and in 2 Edward III., before his father's death, he was one of the knights returned to parliament for that county, and received for his attendance at the rate of four shilling a day. (*Rot. Parl.* ii. 441.)

In July 1334, 8 Edward III., he was appointed chief justice of the King's Bench in Ireland. (*N. Fœdera*, ii. 890.) Whether he accepted the place, or how long he remained in it, does not appear; but at the commencement of Edward's claim to the crown of France he was engaged, in 1337, in the battle of Cadsant, where Guy, the brother of the Earl of Flanders, was taken prisoner; and we next meet with him attending at the Parliament held in Lent 1340. (*Rot. Parl.* ii. 113.)

When the king hurriedly returned from Tournay, at the end of November in that year, and dismissed Robert de Stratford, the chancellor, he resolved to appoint a lay chancellor; and accordingly selected Robert de Bourchier, who was sworn in on December 14, 1340, with a grant of 500*l.* a year beyond the accustomed fees. (*Cal. Rot. Pat.* 138.) That this appointment was very distasteful to all parties is evident from the petitions in the next parliament, praying that, in consequence of the evils arising from bad counsellors, the king should in future make the chancellor, chief justices, and other officers in full parliament, and that they should there be openly sworn to observe the laws. To this the king gave what appeared to be a consent, and his answer was confirmed as a statute. (*Rot. Pat.* ii. 128, 131.) Immediately after the parliament had closed its sittings he revoked the enactment as improperly forced upon him; but he soon found it expedient to part with his military chancellor, who gave up the Seal on October 29, 1341, and was succeeded by Sir Robert Parning. (*Rot. Claus.* 15 Edw. III.)

From this time Bourchier joined the king's army, with so large an array that his allowance amounted to 401*l.* 10*s.* He distinguished himself at the battle of Cressi, and was engaged as one of the ambassadors to treat for the subsequent peace. He was summoned to parliament as a peer from 16 Edward III.

Falling a sacrifice to the plague that raged in 1349, he was buried in Halsted Church, where his monument still remains. By his wife, Margaret, daughter and heir of Sir Thomas de Preyers, he had three sons—Robert, John, and William. Two of the grandsons of William are the next mentioned as entrusted with the Great Seal, in the reigns of Henry VI. and Edward IV.

BOURCHIER, THOMAS (ARCHBISHOP OF CANTERBURY), was great-grandson of the last-mentioned Sir Robert, through his younger son William, whose son, also named William, was created Earl of Ewe, in Normandy, by Henry V., and married Anne, the daughter of Thomas of Woodstock, Duke of Gloucester, sixth son of Edward III., and widow of Edmund, Earl of Stafford. Their eldest son Henry was created Earl of Essex in 1461; and their second son was this Thomas, the future archbishop.

Soon after his father's death in 1420 he became a student in Nevill's Inn, at Oxford; in which university he afterwards held the office of chancellor from 1434 to 1437. His relationship to the royal family had already procured him the valuable deanery of St. Martin's, London, to which he was admitted in 1433; and in November of the same year his 'neghnesse of blood,' as well as the desire of the Commons in parliament, is urged by the king to the prior and convent of Worcester as a recommendation for his election to fill the vacancy in that see. (*Rot. Parl.* v. 435.) The pope, however, appointed Dr. Thomas Brouns; and it was eighteen months before the king succeeded in placing Bourchier there, on March 9, 1435. Even at that time his profession was obliged to be delayed for a month on account of his not being of sufficient age. In the same year the monks of Ely, no doubt with the view of gratifying the king, chose him as their bishop, on the death of Philip Morgan, and the pope confirmed the election; but, for some cause the king refusing his assent, and the bishop having the fear of a præmunire before his eyes, a new election became necessary, which fell on Lewis of Luxemburgh. On the death of that prelate, however, in 1443, Bourchier was re-elected without royal or papal resistance, and was translated to Ely on December 20. The monkish historian of that diocese states that during his ten years' rule he never performed mass in the church but once, on the day of his installation; and that he heavily oppressed the prior and other of the brothers by fines, and the tenants by imprisonment. (*Angl. Sac.* i. 671.)

Eight days after the death of Archbishop Kempe, on March 22, 1454, the council, at the request of the Commons, 'for his grete merits, virtues, and grete blood that he is of,' joined in recommending Bishop Bourchier to the pope as successor to the primacy. (*Rot. Parl.* v. 450.) This is the second time that the Commons are stated to have interfered in his favour, which, if honestly recorded, evidences the popularity of his character, and tends to throw some discredit on the representation of the monk of Ely. He was elected on April 22, 1454; and having thus attained the highest ecclesiastical dignity in the kingdom, he was within a year entrusted also with the highest secular employment. On the king's recovery from his illness, the Earl of Salisbury, whom the Duke of York had appointed chancellor, was removed, and Archbishop Bourchier was put in possession of the Great Seal on March 7, 1455. (*Rot. Claus.* 33 Hen. VI.) He retained it not quite eighteen months, during which the Lancastrians and the Yorkists were alternately in power. He had not enjoyed his appointment by the former much above two months before the first battle of St. Albans, on May 22, gave the Yorkists again the ascendency. Still the chancellor was not removed, but opened the parliament that met in July. Even when their power was more firmly established by a renewal of the king's illness, and the reappointment of the Duke of York as protector in November following, the archbishop still continued in his place. And again when the king, resuming his authority, dismissed the protector on February 25, 1456, the chancellor was found to be as ready to act on that side as he had been on the other. (*Rot. Parl.* v. 278, 285, 321.) It is not therefore to be wondered at that Queen Margaret should be dissatisfied with so lukewarm a friend, and should seek a more steady adherent to her husband's cause. This will account for the removal, otherwise unexplained, of the archbishop, and the appointment of Bishop Waynflete as chancellor on October 11 in that year.

A temperament so easy could not be expected to make much resistance to the deposition of his royal patron. Accordingly we find him at once reconciling himself to the ruling power, and crowning Edward IV. on June 29, 1461, and four years afterwards entertaining the king and his new queen, Elizabeth Woodville, for several days at Canterbury, on their visit there to pay their devotions at Becket's shrine. By that time he had received the last honour he obtained in the Church, having been created cardinal-presbyter by the title of St. Cyriacus in Thermis on September 18, 1464. He was not, however, invested with the red hat till May 31, 1472; and he is first called cardinal in the Rolls of Parliament (vi. 3) of November in that year. In 1475 he was one of the arbitrators between Edward and the French king. (*Rymer*, xii. 15–19.)

On the death of Edward IV. he was induced by Richard, Duke of Gloucester, to urge the queen to give up her younger son into the protector's care, the elder being already in his charge; and there is no reason to doubt that the archbishop's endeavours were conscientiously made, without a suspicion of the tragic fate to which both were doomed. His coronation of the usurper Richard III., and of his successful rival Henry VII., offers a curious exhibition of the facility with which in those perilous times minds could accommodate themselves to political changes; but it savours too much of heartlessness and careless indifference, or perhaps too much of consideration of personal safety, not to create a degree of disgust, which, however, is somewhat tempered by the recollection that the archbishop had arrived at a period of life when feelings are not acute, and the desire of peace predominates. He did not survive the accession of Henry VII. above six months, his death occurring on March 30, 1486, at the manor of Knole, near Sevenoaks. He was buried in the choir of his cathedral.

He has the reputation of having been a learned man, and was certainly a most cautious one, guiding himself through the difficulties of a most troublesome period with infinite discretion. To judge from a letter in the 'Paston Correspondence' (i. 94), he did not dislike the diversion of the chase. We there find him going 'to hunt and sport at Hunsdon.' His two sees of Worcester and Canterbury benefited largely by his liberality, and to the poor he was a kind friend. But his memory is principally respected for having been an active instrument in introducing the art of printing into England. It is related that, having heard of its invention, he induced King Henry VI., towards the close of his reign, to send an officer of his wardrobe, Robert Turnour, to Haarlem, where John Guthenberg had set up a press, he himself supplying a considerable part of the expense. Turnour succeeded in bringing over Frederic Corsellis, one of the compositors, with a fount of types, which the archbishop caused to be taken to Oxford, where the first press was accordingly, through his means, established in, or soon after, the year 1464. (*Godwin*, 129, 268, 466; *Angl. Sac.* i. 63, 537; *Chalmer's Biog. Dict.*)

BOURCHIER, HENRY (EARL OF ESSEX), was the elder brother of the last-mentioned Thomas, the archbishop. The earl held the Great Seal after the retirement of the chancellor, Bishop Stillington, from June 23 to July 17, 1473, acting during the whole of Trinity Term, and bills in Chancery being addressed to him by the title of keeper of the Great Seal.

The father of the earl was William,

Earl of Ewe, in Normandy, son of Sir Robert Bourchier's youngest son, William. He married Anne of Woodstock, granddaughter of Edward III., and widow of Edmund, Earl of Stafford, and had by her several sons, one of whom was the archbishop.

On his father's death in 1420 he became Earl of Ewe, being then about twenty-one, and having served under the king in France for three years previously. He succeeded to the barony of Bourchier in 1435, and for his distinguished services in the French wars was created Viscount Bourchier in 1446. His marriage with Isabel, daughter of Richard, Duke of York, naturally made him a devoted adherent to that party; and after their success at the first battle of St. Albans, in May 1455, he was constituted treasurer of England, retaining the office about eighteen months. When his nephew, Edward IV., had assumed the throne, he was reinstated in it for one year, and in the following June was advanced to the earldom of Essex. He held the treasurership for the third time from 1472 till his death, and in 1473 he was temporarily employed, from June 23 to July 17, as keeper of the Great Seal till Edward had fixed upon his chancellor. He died on April 4, 1483, five days before the king, and was buried in the abbey of Bylegh, near Maldon, in Essex.

He had many children, the eldest of whom, William, died in his lifetime, leaving a son, Henry, who succeeded to the earldom, which on his death in 1539 became extinct. The barony, however, survived, and is now supposed to be merged in the Marquisate of Townshend.

BOURNE, or BURNE, WILLIAM DE, was appointed to superintend the collection of the fifteenth granted in 29 Edward I. in the county of Wilts. In the new commission assigning justices of the Common Pleas, issued on September 29, 1309, 3 Edward II., he was one of the two who were added to that bench. He seems to have been frequently engaged in assizes in the country, principally in the western counties. One of these occasions, in 10 Edward II., was for the trial of persons accused of conspiring to bring a false appeal of robbery against John de Treiagu, with whom it is somewhat curious to find that he was in the same year united in a commission to enquire into the transgressions alleged against the taxors in Devonshire. In 12 Edward II. he was appointed to perambulate the forests of Devon, and was commanded to cause all proceedings before him, as a justice of assize or otherwise, to be brought into the Exchequer to be estreated, and in 14 Edward II., when a commission into Guernsey, Jersey, &c., for the trial of certain offences, which had been directed to him and another, but which had been superseded, was, on the petition of the inhabitants, renewed. (*Parl. Writs*, i. 110, ii. p. ii. 578; *Rot. Parl.* i. 378; *Abb. Rot. Orig.* i. 239.)

BOUSSER. *See* BOUCHIER.

BOVILL, WILLIAM, the present lord chief justice of the Common Pleas, is the second son of B. Bovil, of Durnsford Lodge, Wimbledon. He was born at Allhallows, Barking, London, on May 26, 1816, and was called to the bar at the Middle Temple on January 15, 1841. Joining the Home Circuit, he soon acquired an extensive practice both there and at Westminster. On attaining a silk gown in 1855 he was elected a bencher of his inn, and ultimately its treasurer. He entered parliament in 1857 as representative of Guildford, for which he continued member till his elevation to the bench. He invariably advocated Conservative principles, and was selected by Lord Derby as solicitor-general on July 6, 1866, and was thereupon knighted. Within five months after this appointment he was called upon to resign it, and to fill his present high office, on November 29, as the successor of Chief Justice Sir William Erle, being about the same time made a member of the privy council.

By his wife Maria, the daughter of J. H. Bolton, Esq., of Lee Park, Blackheath, he has several children.

BOVINGTON, WALTER DE, is mentioned as a justicier before whom fines were levied in 8 John, 1206. He held property in Yorkshire, and was one of two 'intendentes' named by the king to Robert de Stuteville, sheriff of that county. (*Pref. to Fines of Rich. I. and John; Rot. de Oblatis*, 106, 107, 109.)

BOWES, ROBERT, belonged to a distinguished family seated at Streatlam Castle, Durham, for more than two centuries. He was the second son of Sir Ralph Bowes, by Margery, daughter of Richard Conyers, of South Cowton, but eventually succeeded to the paternal estate.

So experienced was he in all the peculiarities of border warfare that when negotiations were pending with the Scots, in December 1541, his presence was required by the council in London as one who could advise them on the subject. (*Acts Privy Council*, vii. 285.) In the following year he led a body of 3000 cavalry against the Scots, by whom, under the Earl of Huntley, he was defeated at Haddenrig and, as some say, made prisoner. (*Lingard*, ii. 333.) The war was terminated by the death of King James, and Sir Robert became warden of the East and Middle Marches. During the reign of

Edward he compiled his 'Informations' on the state of the marches and their laws and customs, addressed to Henry, Marquess of Dorset, the warden-general, and full of curious and interesting details. In June 1551 he was one of the commissioners to conclude the convention with Mary, Queen of Scots (*Rymer*, xv. 265, 272), and in the following September was sworn a member of the privy council.

The intelligence he had exhibited as a diplomatist and as an author probably pointed him out as the successor of John Beaumont in the office of master of the Rolls, for which he received his patent on June 18, 1552. In that character he was one of the witnesses to King Edward's will, fixing the succession of the crown on Lady Jane Grey, and he acted on her council during the short continuance of her nominal reign. On July 19, 1553, he signed the letter to Lord Rich on her behalf, but on the next day he signed another to the Duke of Northumberland, commanding him to disarm. (*Queens Jane and Mary*, 100, 109.) This probably saved him from the punishment with which several of Lady Jane's partisans were visited, and founded a claim on Queen Mary's favour. He was evidently continued in his office for two months of the new reign; and even then he seems to have retired voluntarily, the entry being that his patent was cancelled 'pure, sponte, et absolute,' on September 6. Resuming then his duties on the border, he was sent by the council to Berwick in the ensuing April, to assist Lord Conyers in taking the musters, with a warrant for 100*l.* as a reward from the queen.

By his wife Alice, the daughter of John Metcalfe, of Nappa, he had four sons; but these all dying in infancy, his property devolved on his younger brother Richard, the father of Sir George Bowes, the knight-marshal.

BOYLAND, RICHARD DE, probably the son of Roger de Boyland and Alice his wife, purchased in 1268 part of the manor of Brisingham in Norfolk, which was afterwards called by his name. In part payment he gave eighty acres which he had previously held in Pulham in the same county. He was then a successful lawyer, and in 7 Edward I., 1279, was appointed one of the justices itinerant into Dorsetshire, Somersetshire, and Wiltshire, an office which he continued to execute in various other counties, until, for his corruption in the administration of justice, he was disgraced in 1289, and was fined 4000 marks for his extortions.

After his discharge he retired to his manor of Boylands, and built a noble mansion there, famous for the moat that surrounded it, and for the magnificent conduit which he constructed. He lived for six years afterwards, dying in 24 Edward I. (*Cal. Inquis.* p. m. i. 129.)

The name of his first wife was Matilda, and his second was Ellen, the daughter of Philip de Colvile. The extent of his possessions, comprehending many manors and lands in Norfolk and Suffolk, over part of which he had a grant of free warren in 1285, may show either his success as a lawyer or his corruption as a judge; but it would be unjust to attribute his riches to the latter, considering that King Edward was not likely to be lenient, or to discourage complaints against him. (*Blomefield's Norfolk*, i. 38.)

BRABAZON, ROGER LE. Jaques le Brabazon, the first of this family who was established in England, was so called from the castle of Brabazon in Normandy. He came over with the Conqueror, and his name is inserted on the Roll of Battle Abbey. His great-grandson Thomas became possessed of Moseley in Leicestershire, by his marriage with Amicia, the heiress of John de Moseley. Their son, Sir Roger also described of Eastwell in the same county, married Beatrix, eldest of the three sisters and co-heirs of Mansel de Bisset, and by her had two sons, the elder of whom was Roger le Brabazon, the judge.

He is first mentioned in that character in 15 Edward I., 1287, when he acted as a justice itinerant for pleas of the forest in Lancashire; and two years afterwards, on the removal of the judges convicted of extortion and other corrupt practices, he was constituted a justice of the King's Bench in the place of one of them. That he held a high rank in the estimation of the king appears from his being employed to attend the meeting of the Scottish nobility and clergy at Norham on May 10, 1291, when Edward I. took upon himself the arbitration between the competitors for their crown. There, in a studied address in the French language, he required from the assembly an absolute recognition of King Edward's title as Lord Paramount of the kingdom of Scotland, which they were not in a condition to refuse. The prominent part taken by him in this transaction has led writers to speak of him as if he were then the chief justiciary. That office, however, no longer existed, and it was not till four years afterwards that he became chief justice of the King's Bench, to which he was advanced about 24 Edward I., 1295. He presided in the court till the end of the reign, when he was immediately re-appointed by the new king, and continued to perform the functions of this honourable post till February 23, 1316, 9 Edward II., when, pressed by age and infirmities, he applied for and obtained his discharge. The patent of that date is expressed in the most eulogistic terms, and records the king's commands that he should be retained 'de secreto consilio' during his life, and should be admitted to all the king's courts, councils, and parliaments as often as he might choose to be present. He died in the following year. Leaving no issue by his wife, Beatrix, the daughter of Sir John de Sproxton, his property devolved on his brother Matthew, whose descendant was created Lord Brabazon of Ardee in Ireland in 1616, to which, in 1627, was added the earldom of Meath, a title which is still borne by his lineal representative, whose father received an English peerage in 1831 with the title of Baron Chaworth. (*Thoroton's Notts*, i. 294; *Abb. Rot. Orig.* i. 238; *Hist. of the Family of Brabazon*, 1825.)

BRABOEF, WILLIAM DE, whose ancestor came into England with the Conqueror, and held lands in Surrey, Hampshire, and several other counties, acted as assessor for Hampshire for the fifteenth granted in 3 Edward I., and in the sixth year that county was committed to his charge as sheriff. He held the office for the next two years, in the latter of which he was the last named of the four justices itinerant in Hampshire, Devonshire, Cornwall, and Wiltshire; a duty which he again performed in Cornwall in 10 Edward I. Two years afterwards he died. (*Manning and Bray's Surrey*, i. 86; *Abb. Placit.* 48, 78, 164.)

BRACKLEY, LORD. *See* T. EGERTON.

BRACTON, or BRETTON, HENRY DE. In Dugdale's 'Chronica Series' the names of Henry de Bracton and of Henry de Bretton are separately introduced as justices itinerant, with an interval of fourteen years between them, and with nothing in either insertion leading to a supposition that the one or the other was a justicier at Westminster, or that they were the same person. There is no reasonable doubt, however, that both names belonged to one individual, and that he was for many years a judge of the superior court.

Dugdale makes Henry de Bracton a justice itinerant in 1245 and 1246, 29 Henry III., and Henry de Bretton a justice itinerant in 1260. In 1250 Henry de Bracton was evidently on the bench at Westminster, as he was present as one of the 'justiciarii' at a final concord made 'before the king himself' respecting common of pasture at Cheshunt. (*Harleian MS.* 371, p. 71.) In every year from 1250 also the entries on the fine roll prove beyond contradiction that there was a regular justicier, whose name is spelled indifferently Bratton and Bretton, and more frequently in the former mode. These are entries of payments made for assizes to be taken before him; and they continue, principally with the name of Bratton, till July 1267. (*Excerpt. e Rot. Fin.* ii. 92-458.) It is thus clear that Bratton and Bretton are synonymous; and there can be little question that Bracton is the same with both. Prince, in his 'Worthies of Devon,' designates the village in that county in which he supposes Bracton to have been born as 'Bracton, now Bratton-Clovelly,' a name it still retains. Collinson (*Somersetsh.* ii. 32) derives the name from Bratton, a hamlet of Minehead, where the family had property, and states that he lies buried in the church there, under an arch, with his effigy in long robes. Thus is Sir Edward Coke's assertion, in the Preface to the 8th Report, that Bracton was 'a justice of this realm,' corroborated, as he would hardly have given him that title had he been only a justice itinerant. He styles him, in the Preface to the 9th Report, 'Curiæ de Banco Judex;' but if the Common Pleas is to be understood by this expression, its correctness may be doubted, inasmuch as among the fines there levied none appear to have been acknowledged before him. It seems more probable, if the division of the courts had then been finally arranged, that he was a justice of the King's Bench.

According to Prince, he studied at Oxford, where he took the degree of doctor of both laws. He was certainly of the clerical profession: he is designated 'dilectus clericus noster' by the king, in a grant dated May 25, 1254, made to him of the use of a house in London belonging to William, late Earl of Derby, during the minority of the heir. (*Dugdale's Orig.* 56.) On January 21, 1263, he was collated to the archdeaconry of Barnstaple, but he resigned in the following year. (*Le Neve*, 98.) He died about 1267, as in that year his judicial duties evidently terminated.

Although Lord Ellesmere (*State Trials*, ii. 693), in his argument on the subject of the Postnati, calls him chief justice in the reign of King Henry III., and some other authorities so describe him (*Bale*, &c.), there does not appear a single proof that he ever attained that elevation. There is an interval, however, after the death of Hugh le Despenser, in 1265, during which he might possibly have held the office; and it may be remarked, as giving some weight to the suggestion, that the appointment of Robert de Brus as chief justice did not occur till March 1268, a few months after the supposed conclusion of Bracton's career.

Without enlarging, as Prince has done, on his personal reputation, he undoubtedly deserved the character he has obtained as a great lawyer and a learned and accurate writer. His work 'De Legibus et Consuetudinibus Angliæ' 'is a finished and systematic performance, giving a complete view of the law in all its titles, as it stood when it was written.' Reeve (*Hist. of Eng.*

Law, ii. 86), from whom this extract is taken, gives an analytical abstract of the several divisions of his chapters, and assists the student by an ample digest of their contents. He considers Bracton as far superior to Glanville; praises his style as clear, expressive, and nervous; and resists the attempt to throw discredit on his fidelity as a writer on the English law, which has been grounded on his reference to the Roman code, showing that it is rather alluded to for illustration and ornament than adduced as authority. His omission of the regulations made by the statute of Marlbridge affords internal evidence of his work having been written before the fifty-second year of Henry's reign, and greatly corroborates the preceding suggestion as to the period of his death.

Mr. Selden's opinion that the work called 'Britton' is only an abridgment of Bracton derives weight from the name of the latter being very frequently called Bretton. (*Ibid.* 281.)

BRADBURY, GEORGE, the eldest son of Henry Bradbury, of St. Martin's-in-the-Fields, Middlesex, was called to the bar of the Middle Temple on May 17, 1667. Acting as junior counsel in the famous trial in 1684, in which Lady Ivy attempted to establish her claim to lands at Shadwell by certain deeds of very doubtful authenticity, he alleged that their forgery was manifest, from the description of the year in Philip and Mary's reign, in which they professed to have been executed, being by a title which was not assumed by the king and queen till after the date they bore; and Chief Justice Jeffreys applauded him for the ingenuity of the discovery. Not content with this unaccustomed compliment from his rough chief, he by reiterating his remark later in the trial brought down upon himself this silencing castigation: 'Lord! sir,' exclaimed Jeffreys, 'you must be cackling too. We told you your objection was very ingenious; but that must not make you troublesome; you cannot lay an egg, but you must be cackling over it.'

That he must have been considerably distinguished as a lawyer may be inferred from his being summoned in December 1688, with the chiefs of his profession, to consult with the Lords as to what was to be done on the emergency that had then occurred. In July of the next year he was assigned by the House of Lords as counsel for Sir Adam Blair, Dr. Elliott, and others, the impeachment of whom for dispersing King James's declaration does not appear to have been afterwards prosecuted. On the 9th of the same month he was appointed cursitor baron of the Exchequer, and held the office till his death, which occurred on February 12, 1696. (*State Trials*, x. 616, 626; *Luttrell*, i. 490, 555, 557, iv. 17; *Parl. Hist.* v. 362.)

BRADSHAW, HENRY. Fuller fixes the nativity of Henry Bradshaw in Cheshire, judging from his surname, but evidently knows nothing of his family. He received his legal education at the Inner Temple, and was twice reader to that society—viz., in autumn 1536, and in Lent 1542. In 1540 he was appointed solicitor-general, and became attorney-general in 1545—a period so full of criminal prosecutions that it is remarkable so little is said of his conduct of them. Being created chief baron of the Exchequer on May 21, 1552, he witnessed King Edward's will, settling the crown on Lady Jane Grey, and would probably have been removed from his place by Queen Mary had not death overtaken him three weeks after her accession. He died on July 27, 1553. By his wife Johan, daughter of John Hurst of Kingston-upon-Thames, and widow of William Mainwayringe of Estham in Essex, he had four sons and four daughters. (*Dugdale's Orig.* 164, 170, 172; *Chron. of Queen Jane*, 100; *Gent. Mag.* lix. 1011).

BRADSHAW, JOHN, as it is now satisfactorily established, was a younger son of Henry Bradshaw, of Marple Hill, in the parish of Stockport in Cheshire, descended from a family of considerable respectability in Derbyshire, his mother being Catherine, daughter of Ralph Winnington, Esq., of Offerton.

Born at Marple in 1602, and baptised in the parish church of Stockport on December 10 in that year, he received his education first at the free school there, and then at Bunbury and Middleton, to all of which he bequeathed large sums for their endowment. Designed for the law, he was called to the bar at Gray's Inn on April 23, 1627, and to the bench of that society on June 23, 1645, when appointed judge of the Sheriffs' Court in London. He probably acted for some years as a provincial counsel, as he lived at Congleton, and served the office of mayor there in 1637, and was afterwards high steward; and at one time of his life he resided in Bradshaw Hall in Bolton, on a stone over the door of which his family arms remain. (*Gent. Mag.* lxxxviii., i. 328; *Baines's Lancashire*, i. 540.)

In the year 1643 he became a candidate for the office of one of the judges of the Sheriffs' Court of the city of London, then vacant, his antagonists being Richard Proctor and William Steele, afterwards chief baron. The right of election was claimed by both the Courts of Aldermen and Common Council, and Bradshaw was chosen by the latter on September 21. Immediately afterwards the Court of Aldermen elected Proctor, who thereupon brought an action in the King's (afterwards the Upper) Bench, which, however, did not come to a final hearing till February 1655, when the right was determined to be in the Common Council, with whom it has ever since continued. Bradshaw in the meantime had performed the duties of the office, for in February 1649 he was permitted to appoint a deputy at Guildhall 'in regard of his employment in the High Court.' (*Whitelocke*, 377.)

Clarendon says (vi. 217) he was 'not much known in Westminster Hall, though of good practice in his chamber and much employed by the factious.' In October 1644 he was assigned as one of the counsel against Lord Macguire for the rebellion in Ireland; and he probably assisted Prynne in his argument to prove that Irish peers were amenable to trial by an English jury. He next appears in the following year as leading Lilburn's appeal to the House of Lords for reparation against the iniquitous sentence of the Star Chamber in 1638; and in the discussions which arose in the two houses in 1646, as to placing the custody of the Great Seal in commissioners who were not members of parliament, he was among those voted by the Commons, but objected to by the Lords. The appointment of chief justice of Chester, however, was given to him in March 1647. In June he was retained as one of the counsel to assist in the prosecution of Judge Jenkins; and on October 12, 1648, he was included in the batch of serjeants then made by the parliament. (*Whitelocke*, 100, 224; *State Trials*, iii. 1347.)

When the Lords rejected the ordinance for the trial of the king, and the Commons determined to proceed without their concurrence, the names of the peers and judges who had been appointed were struck out of the commission, and those of Bradshaw, Nicholas, and Steele were substituted; and Bradshaw was dignified with the title of lord president of the so-called High Court of Justice. (*Whitelocke*, 366, 368.) The selection of a man of so little weight in his profession can only be accounted for by the supposition that the concocters of the tragedy could not prevail on any of the more eminent lawyers to undertake the obnoxious service. Whitelocke and Widdrington had refused the commission; neither Rolle nor St. John, the two chief justices, nor even Chief Baron Wilde, could be entrusted to obey their behest; and their own law-officer, Prideaux, either from objections on his part, or want of confidence on theirs, was displaced, while creatures of their own were appointed temporary attorney and solicitor general to conduct the charge. The trial began on January 20, 1649; and Bradshaw's conduct throughout its continuance fully answered the description of Clarendon (vi. 218), that he administered the office, 'with all the pride, impudence, and superciliousness imaginable.' Whatever may be the differences of opinion on the material point of the trial—and great will be the differences among men—no doubt can be entertained that it was ordained by usurped authority, that its end was determined before its commencement, that its proceedings were illegal and undignified, and that the conduct of the president was insolent and overbearing. During the sittings of the court lodgings were provided for him at Sir Abraham Williams's house in New Palace Yard, and all provisions and necessaries were ordered to be supplied. He was treated with all the forms of judicial state, decorated with a scarlet robe, a sword and mace were borne before him, and twenty gentlemen were appointed to attend him with partizans. When, after a long speech, he had pronounced the sentence, he was the first to sign the warrant for execution. But, however willing an instrument, he was not altogether a free agent; for all that he did, and almost all that he said, seems to have been directed and dictated by the majority of the commissioners, consisting of the king's most determined enemies. (*State Trials*, iv. 1008–1154.) In the subsequent trials of the Duke of Hamilton, the Earl of Holland, and others, he was continued lord president of the court; and the dean's house at Westminster was given to him for ever for his residence and habitation, with a donative of 5000*l*. He became one of the council of state, and, being elected its president, is noticed by Whitelocke for his lengthened arguments, and the inconvenience they occasioned. A vote to settle 2000*l*. a year in lands out of the Earl of St. Albans' and Lord Cottington's estates on him and his heirs was passed, and his appointment of chief justice of Chester was renewed, to which the chancellorship of the duchy of Lancaster was afterwards added. He does not seem to have acted as lord president of the High Court of Justice beyond 1650, Serjeant Keeble presiding in 1651, and Serjeant L'Isle in 1654. (*Whitelocke*, 390, 414, 420, 529; *State Trials*, v. 43, 518.)

Bradshaw was a staunch republican, and looked with a jealous eye on Cromwell's attempt to gain the sole authority. When the ambitious general ejected the Long Parliament on April 20, 1653, and came to the council of state to put an end to its sitting, Bradshaw, who still presided, rose and boldly addressed him in these words: —'Sir, we have heard what you did at the house in the morning, and before many hours all England will hear it; but, sir, you are mistaken to think the parliament is dissolved, for no power under heaven can dissolve them but themselves; therefore take you notice of that.' (*Ludlow*, 195.) He was not, of course, one of the members selected by the general to sit in what was called Barebone's Parliament; but in it an act was passed for continuing in him the jurisdiction of the county of Lancaster. (*Whitelocke*, 565.) Cromwell, when he became protector, summoned him to the council, and required him to take out a new commission for his office of chief justice of Chester; but he refused to do so, alleging that he held that place by a grant from the parliament of England, to continue *quamdiu se bene gesserit*; and whether he had carried himself with that integrity which his commission exacted of him he was ready to submit to a trial by twelve men to be chosen by Cromwell himself. Cromwell was silenced, and, though an order was actually signed dismissing him from the office, did not think it safe to prevent him from proceeding on his circuit. In Cromwell's parliament of 1654 Bradshaw was elected member for Cheshire, notwithstanding the protector's attempts to keep him out, and distinguished himself against the court party in the debate whether the government should be in one single person and a parliament. (*Parl. Hist.* iii. 1428, 1445.) That parliament was soon dissolved; and on summoning another, in September 1656, Cromwell was more successful in his efforts, and Bradshaw was not returned. The distaste between them continued to increase, and Bradshaw was omitted from the list of peers nominated by the protector.

On the death of Cromwell, Bradshaw was returned for Cheshire to Richard's parliament of January 1659. With its dissolution in April the protectorate terminated from mere imbecility, and the remnant of the Long Parliament, nicknamed the Rump, resumed its sittings. Bradshaw, a determined commonwealth's-man, was named on the council of state, and on June 3 was appointed one of the commissioners of the Great Seal, in conjunction with Tyrrell and Fountaine. He had been for eight months suffering from the ague, and was then in the country. His attendance, therefore, was dispensed with at that time, but on July 22 he took the oaths in the house. Ere four months had elapsed this Rump was again dismissed by the army, and Bradshaw, still sick and suffering, attended in the council of state, and almost with his last words expressed 'his abhorrence of that detestable action,' as he called it. (*Ludlow, Godwin, Whitelocke*.) He then withdrew, and survived the scene about a fortnight, dying on October 31, with the declaration that if the king were to be tried and condemned again, he would be the first man that should do it. His death occurred in the Deanery at Westminster, and he was buried with great pomp in the abbey, his funeral sermon being preached by John Rowe. (*Athen.*

Oxon. iii. 1129.) On the restoration of Charles II. his body, and those of Cromwell and Ireton, which had been deposited in the same place, were disinterred, and, with every mark of obloquy, were dragged on sledges to Tyburn, where they were hanged on the several angles of a triple gibbet, then beheaded, their trunks thrown into a hole under the gallows, and their heads exposed on poles on the top of Westminster Hall. (*Harris's Lives*, iii. 520.)

The partisans of the royal and the républican party of course differ essentially in their estimate of Bradshaw's character. The laudation of it during his life by Milton (whom he had patronised, and to whom he bequeathed 10*l.*) is too exaggerated, and Clarendon's description of him after his death is perhaps too severe. Whitelocke's (with whom he was evidently no favourite) is pithy, and nearer the mark: 'A stout man, and learned in his profession, no friend to monarchy.' The best part of his character is his consistency, for he showed as much resistance to the semblance of royalty as to the reality, opposing the usurpation first of Cromwell, and then of the army, as firmly as he had stood against the king.

BRAIOSA, WILLIAM DE, was one of the justices itinerant to impose the assize on the king's demesnes in Herefordshire in 20 Henry II., 1174, but seems to have only been so appointed as sheriff of the county, an office which he held in that and the following year. (*Madox*, i. 124.)

He was the grandson of a Norman baron of the same name, who, besides his honor of Braiose and other large possessions in Normandy, is recorded in Domesday Book as holding between fifty and sixty lordships in Sussex, Berks, Wilts, Surrey, and Dorset. His successor was Philip de Braiosa, who, by his wife Berta, the daughter of Milo, Earl of Gloucester, was father to this William.

In 3 Henry II. he fined one thousand marks for part of the honor of Barnstaple (*Pipe Rolls*, 183); and in 1164 he was one of the subscribers to the Constitutions of Clarendon. His favour with King Henry may be estimated by the grant, which he received in the twenty-fourth year of his reign, of the whole kingdom of Limerick. How far he deserved that favour depends on the truth or falsehood of an historian of Wales, who relates his horrible murder of Sitsylt ap Dynswald and a large company of Welshmen, whom he had treacherously invited to a feast in the castle of Bergavenny.

In 7 Richard I., 1195-6, he again acted as a justice itinerant in Staffordshire (*Madox*, i. 546); and for the last seven years of that reign he held the sheriffalty of the county of Hereford.

The preservation of his influence in the early part of King John's reign is shown, not only by his continuance in the office of sheriff of his county, but also by the special charter he received from the king in his second year, exempting the lands of the honor of Braiose from the interference of any of the king's sheriffs or other officers, and giving William de Braiosa sole jurisdiction there. (*Ibid.* 150.) About the ninth or tenth year of that reign he was the subject of royal persecution. One states the cause to have been that he refused to give the hostages which the king demanded to secure the obedience of his barons; another, that the king banished him for carrying war into Wales, and killing above three thousand men in the battle of Elvel; while the king's own narrative, as recorded in the Red Book of the Exchequer, attributes his outlawry to the nonpayment of five thousand marks, which he owed for the province of Munster, in Ireland, and of five years' arrears of the ferm of Limerick; to the repeated evasion of his promises to pay these moneys; to his resistance to the processes of distress sent against his castles; and to his rebellious conduct throughout the proceedings. The result was the capture of his wife and their eldest son, William, whom King John in 1210 barbarously commanded to be famished in their prison in Windsor Castle. The baron himself escaped, in the habit of a beggar, into France, where he died about 1212, and was buried in the abbey of St. Victor at Paris.

His wife was Maud de Haya, or St. Walerie, to whose instigation the murder of the guests at Bergavenny is attributed, and on whose violence is charged all the subsequent misfortunes of her family. Her husband, though a bold and active soldier, seems from some accounts to have been of a pious and kindly disposition, making grants to the monks with no niggardly hand, and remarkable for his charity and courtesy to the poor.

His issue consisted of three sons and four daughters. William, the eldest son, called Gam, perished by starvation with his mother, at Windsor; Giles was brought up to the Church, and became Bishop of Hereford; and Reginald succeeded in assuaging the wrath of the king, and regaining part of his father's possessions. (*Lord Lyttelton's Henry II.* iii. 389; *Wendover,* ii. 384, iii. 129, 225, 234, 237.)

BRAMSTON, JOHN, whose ancestor, William Bramston, was sheriff of London in 18 Richard II., 1394-95, was grandson of John, a mercer in the same city, and son of Roger Bramston, of Whitechapel, who first established himself in Essex. His mother was Priscilla, daughter of Francis Olovile, of West Haningfield Hall, and widow of Thomas Rushee, of Boreham, both in that county.

John Bramston, their eldest son, was born on May 18, 1577, at Maldon, and after receiving his early instruction in the free school there, he finished his education at Jesus College, Cambridge. Having entered the Middle Temple, he was duly called to the bar in 1602, and chosen in 1607 by his university as one of their counsel. In the preceding year he had married Bridget, daughter of Dr. Thomas Moundeford, an eminent physician of Milk Street, London. He was selected as Lent reader in 1623, when his reading was on the statute 32 Henry VIII. c. 2, concerning limitations; and again in the following autumn, when he took the statute 13 Eliz. c. 5, as his subject, treating on fraudulent conveyances. In Michaelmas Term he was one of the fifteen who took the degree of the coif; not, however, without contributing, as all the others did, 500*l.* to King James's purse. Obtaining great practice, as well in the courts of law as in Chancery, the Court of Wards, and the Star Chamber, he was selected in 1626 by the Earl of Bristol to defend him; in 1627 he pleaded for Sir John Heveningham, who was imprisoned for not contributing to the loan (*State Trials,* ii. 1380, iii. 6); in 1628 he was retained by the city of London as their counsel, with a fee *pro consilio impenso et impendendo*; and in 1630 he was constituted chief justice of Ely, on the nomination of the then bishop of that see, which was confirmed by his successor. He was made the queen's serjeant on March 26, 1632, and King Charles advanced him on July 8, 1634, to be one of his serjeants, and knighted him.

After the death of his first wife, leaving a numerous family, he married in 1631, for his second wife, Elizabeth, the daughter of Lord Brabazon, and the relict already of two husbands, the first being George Montgomerie, Bishop of Clogher, and the second Sir John Brereton, the king's serjeant in Ireland. He had no children by her, and she died in 1647, leaving him a second time a widower. Soon after his second marriage he purchased the estate of Skreenes, in Roxwell, Essex, for 8000*l.*, from Thomas Weston, afterwards Earl of Portland.

On the death of Sir Thomas Richardson he was called upon to fill the then not very enviable place of chief justice of the King's Bench, and received his patent on April 14, 1635. The people were discontented and seditiously inclined; King Charles was raising money by various means without the aid of parliament, which had not met for six years; the writs for ship money had just been issued and created general excitement. Bramston, who evidently was conscientious in considering that it was legally imposed, as chief justice headed the opinion in its favour that was given by all the judges, in answer to the case which the king had laid before them. In the prosecution of Hampden he supported that opinion upon the general principle that the defence of the realm must be at the subjects' charge; but, notwithstanding, gave his vote against the crown upon a technical point, that by the record it did not appear to whom the money assessed was due. (*State Trials*, iii. 1243.)

One of the earliest proceedings of the Long Parliament, which met in November 1640, was to impeach Chief Justice Bramston and five other of the judges who had given this answer to the king; and he was obliged to give security in 10,000*l.* to abide his trial. The principal charge against him was for signing the opinion, and did not touch his judgment in the case of Hampden. His answer, which his son thinks, though prepared and signed by counsel, was never called for, was that he, like Croke and Hutton, subscribed only for conformity, for he was overruled by the rest of the judges in his wish to insert that the charge could not be made except in case of necessity, and only during the time and continuance of that necessity. When the king went to York in July 1642 he commanded the attendance of the chief justice, and, though Bramston sent his sons to excuse him on account of the danger which those who had become bound for his appearance before the parliament would incur, the injunctions for his presence were reiterated. Bramston, however, from the same motives determined to stay away.

The consequence was, that on October 16, 1642, the king revoked his appointment (*Rymer*, xx. 536); but, as if to show that it was not from royal displeasure, sent him a patent as king's serjeant on the 10th of the following February. It is curious that this patent was granted a few days after the king had received the propositions of the Lords and Commons for an accommodation; one of which was a prayer that he would make Sir John Bramston chief justice of the King's Bench. By this it is evident that the parliament were not very inveterate against Sir John; and it seems probable that the king appointed him his serjeant as an earnest of his intention, if the negotiation had succeeded, to replace him in his office in compliance with the parliament's request. As a further proof that that body held him absolved, and esteemed him to be, as Lord Clarendon calls him, 'a man of great learning and integrity,' they made several attempts to induce him to resume his judicial duties, and when he refused, as another had superseded him, they ordered him to be advised with on some legal business before them. In January 1646-7 the Commons named him as one of the lords commissioners of the Great Seal; but by his interest with the peers he induced them to pass him over. In the following March the same attempt was made with the like result. In the interim the Lords had voted that he should sit in their house as an assistant; but without refusing the appointment he managed to avoid the attendance; and in April a vote was passed that he should be one of the judges of the Common Pleas (*Whitelocke*, 108-245), which he also declined. His son says that Cromwell, after he became protector, urged Sir John in 1654 to take the office of chief justice again, but that he excused himself, pleading his old age, then verging on seventy-seven. On September 22 of that year he died at Skreenes after a very short illness, and was buried in Roxwell Church.

Fuller (i. 349) gives him the character of being 'accomplished with all qualities requisite for a person of his place and profession, . . . deep learning, solid judgment, integrity of life, and gravity of behaviour;' adding that 'he deserved to live in better times.'

Six children survived him, three sons and three daughters. The present representative of his eldest son now resides at Skreenes, which took its name from Serjeant William Skrene, in the reign of Henry IV., and was afterwards possessed by Richard Weston, judge of the Common Pleas in the reign of Elizabeth, from one of whose family it was purchased by Chief Justice Bramston. (*Bramston's Autobiography*.)

BRAMSTON, FRANCIS, the third surviving son of the above-named Sir John Bramston, was removed from a considerable school in Goldsmith's Alley, Cripplegate, London, kept by Mr. Farnabie, to Queens' College, Cambridge, where he took his degree of M.A. in 1640. He was so feeble and unhealthy at this time that Dr. Martin, the master, wrote to his father that 'it was a great pitie so great a soul should have so weak a body;' and, to prove that this was no flattery, chose him in 1642 fellow of his college. He was admitted of the society of the Middle Temple in 1634, and was called to the bar on June 14, 1642. The troubles that followed putting a stop to his professional pursuits, 'the drumming trumpets,' as his brother expresses it, 'blowing his gown over his ears,' he travelled for four years into France and Italy, associating with Mr. Henshaw, Mr. Howard, and Mr. Evelyn. On his return he is not mentioned in the reports till the Restoration, when his steadiness to the royal cause secured him employment.

In August 1660 he was made steward of some of the king's courts in Essex, and of the liberty of Havering; and in 1665 his university chose him for their counsel, with a fee of 40s. a year. He was chosen reader of his inn in 1668. The extravagance of the feast on this occasion is noticed by Evelyn, who relates that there were present at it 'the Duke of Ormond, privy seal, Bedford, Belasys, Halifax, and a world more of earles and lords.' (*Evelyn*, ii. 303.)

In the following year he was one of the large batch of serjeants who were created, and he received the stewardship of the Court of Pleas at Whitchapel, with a salary of 100*l*. His next advance was to the bench of the Exchequer, being constituted a baron on June 17, 1678. Within a year, however, he was summarily discharged from this seat with three other judges—Wilde, Thurland, and Bertie—all of them being dismissed on April 29, 1679, for no express cause, but upon the king's forming a new council of thirty, and admitting Lord Shaftesbury into the ministry as its president. Though a pension of 500*l*. a year was assigned to him, he 'was never paid but only three terms,' so low was the Exchequer then; and so difficult was it to obtain any payment that the arrears were not received till above three years after his death; and of the various delays and excuses in obtaining it his brother gives a very amusing account in his interesting autobiography. The judge did not resume his practice at the bar, but, keeping his chamber at Serjeants' Inn, he died there four years afterwards, on March 27, 1683, and was buried in Roxwell Church. Never having been married, he left his brother, Sir John, his heir, who in his biography gives a very pleasing character of him.

BRAMWELL, GEORGE WILLIAM WILSHIRE, is the son of George Bramwell, a banker. He was born in London, and was called to the bar by the society of Lincoln's Inn in May 1838. He travelled the Home Circuit, and gained so good a reputation in his profession as to be appointed on the commission of enquiry into the process, practice, and system of pleadings in the superior courts. In 1851 he received a silk gown, and was raised to the bench in January 1856 as a baron of the Exchequer, and was thereupon knighted.

He married, according to Dod's Peerage, a daughter of Bruno Silva.

BRANCESTRE, JOHN DE, is introduced by Sir T. D. Hardy (*Cat.* 6) among the keepers of the Great Seal in 1203 and 1205 on the authority of charters of 5 and 7 John. Those charters are subscribed with the words 'Data per manum J. de Brancestre, Archid. Wigorn.' If this be sufficient to ground the title, he should have been so designated at an earlier date, as there are some charters given under his hand in September 1200, 2 John, as well as others so signed by him in conjunction with Hugh de Wells in August and September of that year.

He also subscribed several in the same manner in May, June, and July 1203, 5 John; but in 7 John there is *only one* charter so authenticated, which happens to be the first after the death of Archbishop Hubert, the chancellor, and is dated July 24, 1205.

On all these occasions the charters were authenticated by him in the form specified; but that he could not be a vice-chancellor or keeper is shown by the fact that *during the same period* he attested several charters as a *witness*, when the name of some other person was attached to the form of authentication. And this occurred not only then, but both at an earlier and a later period also, commencing from March 1200, 1 John, proceeding throughout the second year, and continuing at intervals up to May 5, 1208, 9 John.

There seems very little doubt that the persons whose names appear upon these authentications of the charters, when not otherwise described, were merely clerks of the Chancery, or officers in the treasury of the Exchequer. (See *Judges of England*, ii. 8 *et seq.*)

He received the reward usually accorded to these officers, by being advanced to the dignity of archdeacon of Worcester some time in 1200, and also grants of the church of Frotheham, in the diocese of Lincoln, in 3 John; of the perpetual vicarage of Brancestre in Norfolk, probably his native place, in 9 John; and of the prebend of Lidington in Lincoln Cathedral, in 10 John. In these grants the king calls him 'his clerk,' and in 6 John two sheaves of corn (garbas) out of the king's demesne of Wichton, in Norfolk, are conferred upon him, which are described as having been before granted by Henry II., 'cuidam clericorum suorum.' (*Rot. Claus.* i. 4.) Again, in 5 John the custody of the abbey of Malmesbury, and in 7 John that of the abbey of Ramsey were entrusted to him, charges in which the officers in question were frequently engaged. In 6 John he went into Flanders on the king's service, and had twenty marks allowed for his expenses (*Ibid.* i. 14); and there are entries on the Rotulus de Præstitis of 12 John (211, 237) showing that payments from the royal treasury were made through his hands. That he was of a joyous disposition, and that the king understood his character, may be presumed from the grant in 7 John of a dolium of good wine of price, and of two more in 9 John. He died in 1218. (*Le Neve*, 302.)

BRAYBROC, ROBERT DE, so called from the place of his residence in Northamptonshire, was the son of Ingebard, by his wife Albreda, one of the daughters and coheirs of Ivo Newmarch. In 9 Richard I. he accounted for the ferm of Bitebroc in Rutland (*Madox*, i. 235); and in the following year he was sheriff of the united counties of Bedford and Buckingham under William de Albini, an office which he continued to hold, with an interval of two or three years, till 15 John. His county of Northampton, also, he held as sheriff from 10 to 15 John, and that of Rutland from 12 to 15 John. (*Fuller's Worthies*.) That he filled some office in the court at Westminster appears by a notice on the great roll of 11 John that certain accounts were rendered 'in camera regis' before Richard de Marisco and Robert de Braybroc (*Madox*, ii. 252); and in the same year the Rotulus Misæ (148) records a payment to him of three hundred marks to be placed in the treasury at Northampton.

His name appears among the justiciers before whom fines were acknowledged in 1 and 8 John.

From some cause not explained, he got into disgrace with King Richard, in the tenth year of whose reign he fined 180 marks to be restored to his favour; but it is clear, from what has already been stated, that King John did not remove his confidence. He granted him in 7 John the manor of Coreby in Northamptonshire, and Dugdale (*Baronage*, i. 728) states that he made him master of his wardrobe and one of his council, distinguishing him with the special favour of allowing him to hunt in the royal forest. Roger de Wendover (iii. 237) names him as one of John's 'consiliarios iniquissimos' in the time of the interdict.

His death occurred during the last year of his sheriffalty, 15 John, when he was succeeded by his son Henry.

BRAYBROC, HENRY DE, was the eldest son of the last-named Robert de Braybroc, with whom he was united in the sheriffalties of Rutland, Northampton, and Buckingham and Bedford for the last two or three years of his father's life, but in 16 John he held them alone. Up to this period he had supported the king throughout his difficulties, but in that year (probably on his father's death) he united with the barons, and took so leading a part that he was excommunicated by name, and the whole of his possessions seized into the king's hands. At the death of John he still continued in rebellion, and successfully resisted the royal forces at the castle of Montsorel. (*Wendover*, iii. 237, 301, 356.) On the ultimate retirement of Prince Louis, however, he returned to his allegiance, and in September 1217 his lands were restored to him. (*Rot. Claus.* i. 321.)

Having been appointed, in 8 Henry III., one of the justices itinerant to take the assizes of novel disseisin for the counties of Buckingham and Bedford, at Dunstable, he and his associates fined Faukes de Breaute 100*l.* on each of more than thirty verdicts found against him for violent seizure of the property of his neighbours. Faukes, having hitherto acted with impunity, was too self-willed to submit tamely, but on the instant directed his brother William, with all the garrison of Bedford Castle, to seize the judges and put them into strict confinement. They all escaped, however, except Henry de Braybroc, who was taken and carried to the castle, where, though no injury was done to his person, he was treated with the greatest indignity. His wife Christiana, daughter of Wiscard Ledet, immediately appeared before the parliament then sitting at Northampton, and, loudly calling for justice, the indignant king took the most active measures to avenge the affront. Proceeding with a formidable force at once to Bedford, he demanded the release of the incarcerated judge, which was boldly refused. A regular siege then commenced on June 16, and so stoutly was the castle defended that it was not till August 15 that the garrison were forced to submit, when, so high was the king's indignation raised, that he ordered Faukes's brother William, who had been left in command, with several other knights, to be hanged on the spot. (*Wendover*, iv. 94.) Henry de Braybroc was thus released, and was afterwards employed to see the castle totally destroyed and the materials distributed according to the king's order. In the following year he was again appointed justice itinerant for the same counties, and in 10 Henry III. for the counties of Lincoln and York, in the former of which his wife had property. He is mentioned as 'Justiciarius de Banco' in a record of 11 Henry III., and Dugdale quotes a fine levied before him two years afterwards. (*Madox*, ii. 335.)

He died before June 1234, 18 Henry III., as in that year his widow paid a fine for permission to marry whom she pleased. They had two sons—Wischard, who afterwards took his mother's name of Ledet; and John, who retained the name of Braybroc. One of the descendants of the latter was Robert de Braybroke, Bishop of London, subsequently noticed; and another was Sir Reginald Braybroc, who in the reign of Henry IV. married the heiress of the Lord Cobham. (*Dugdale's Baron.* i. 728.)

BRAYBROKE, ROBERT DE (BISHOP OF LONDON), a lineal descendant from the above Henry de Braybroc, was a younger son of Sir Gerard Braybroke, who died in 1359, by Isabella his wife. Educated for the Church, he successively became a canon of Lichfield, archdeacon of Cornwall in 1376, dean of Salisbury in 1380, and ultimately Bishop of London on September 9 1381, as successor to William de Courteneye. (*Le Neve*.)

He was appointed Chancellor of England

on September 9, 1382, 6 Richard II., but did not receive the Seal till the 30th. Of his acts while in that office nothing is recorded beyond his opening the parliament in October, and his tenure of it was very short; for, in consequence of some disagreement between him and John of Gaunt, Duke of Lancaster, he was removed on March 10, 1383, the record delicately suggesting that he 'desired with great earnestness to be exonerated from the office.'

The remainder of his life, which extended till August 27, 1404, was devoted to his episcopal duties. He was buried in his own cathedral. Pepys records (iii. 9) the discovery of his body in a complete state of preservation after the fire of London in 1666; and in 'Notes and Queries' (2nd s. iii. 186) there is a curious account of its subsequent mutilation.

BRAYTON, or DRAYTON, THOMAS DE, had a grant of the prebend of Fynglas, in the church of Glasgow, in 13 Edward II. In 3 Edward III. he accompanied the king to France, and was engaged in various missions of trust for several of the following years. His appointment as a clerk in the Chancery, it would appear, occurred about 6 Edward III., as in the parliament of that year he was a receiver of the petitions. (*Rot. Parl.* ii. 68.) From 14 to 27 Edward III. he was frequently one of those entrusted with the custody of the Great Seal, either during the absence of the chancellors or in the intervals of vacancy in the office from 1340 to 1453. He continued to act as a clerk of the Chancery till 33 Edward III., 1359 (*New Fœdera*, iii. 452), after which his name is not mentioned.

He is frequently called Thomas de Drayton in the Rolls of Parliament. (ii. 146-264.) If this was his right name, he was probably connected with a Norfolk family having possessions at Great Yarmouth. (*Abb. Rot. Orig.* ii. 103, 242.)

BREAUTÉ, FAUKES DE, frequently acted as a justice itinerant, and Fuller says that he was a native of Middlesex, and that his family were named 'de Brent,' from the rivulet so called in that county. Matthew Paris, on the only occasion in which he gives him a surname, also calls him 'de Brent,' but he describes him as a bastard, born in Normandy. This seems to be supported by the fact that for eight years after 7 John (when he is first mentioned) he is never described except by his Christian name, Falcasius or Fulco. Neither does Roger de Wendover add any surname. Dugdale, both in his 'Baronage' and 'Chronica Series,' calls him 'de Breant;' but the rolls after 15 John invariably name him 'de Breauté,' or 'de Braute.' The probability is that this name was given him from a town so called in the department of the Lower Seine.

In 7 John he was sent with others to Poictou with one thousand marks (*Rot. Parl.* 59); in 10 John he was sheriff of Glamorganshire, and was actively employed in the Welsh marches until the fifteenth year of that reign. He then was sent with the Earl of Salisbury and others on a mission to Flanders, taking with them ten thousand marks. (*Rot. Claus.* i. 139, 145.) Zealously supporting King John in the wars with his barons during the last years of his reign, he was one of the generals left to check them in London when the king marched to the north in 1215. In the following November he took the castle of William Malduit, of Hamslape, and a few days afterwards that of Bedford. (*Wendover*, iii. 347, 349.)

In reward for his energetic proceedings the king granted to him the latter castle, and also gave him in marriage a rich but unwilling bride, Margaret, daughter of Warin Fitz-Gerold, and widow of Baldwin de Ripariis, or de Betun, Earl of Albemarle, the son of William, Earl of Devon, together with the wardship of her son Baldwin, and the custody of his lands. Part of these were in South Lambeth, where he built a hall or mansion-house, which was called by his name, and is termed Faukeshall, or 'La Sale Fawkes,' in 10 Edward I. It is mentioned in the charter of Isabella de Fortibus, Countess of Albemarle and Devon, and Lady of the Isle of Wight, dated in 1293, by which she sold her possessions to King Edward I. (*Archæol. Journ.* iv. 275.) Edward the Black Prince, by licence from his father, gave it in 1363 to the chapter of Canterbury for permission to found a chantry in the crypt of the cathedral, where two priests were to pray for his soul. (*Stanley's Hist. Mem. of Canterbury*, 112, 131.) It still belongs to the chapter; and, preserving its name ever since, it was long known as a favourite place of suburban entertainment, but has been lately converted into building land. Faukes was also appointed seneschal to the king, and obtained a mandate for all constables to treat him hospitably when he came to their castles. (*Rot. Claus.* i. 190; *Rot. Pat.* 135.) Other favours flowed in upon him; the castles and sheriffalties of Oxford, Northampton, Bedford and Buckingham, and Huntingdon and Cambridge, were entrusted to him; and he continued to hold them for the first eight years of King Henry's reign.

On the accession of Henry III. his bravery was instrumental in securing the throne to him. But, although valiant and courageous, he was brutal and oppressive. Not only during the war was he cruel in his exactions, but even after the peace with Louis had been completed, and the rebellious barons had returned to their allegiance, the desire of plunder would not allow him to desist from the most arbitrary claims. When the king was declared of full age, and was advised to resume the custody of his castles, Faukes was one of those who joined with the Earl of Albemarle in resisting the mandate; but he was at last compelled to submit. During the whole of this time, however, he received many proofs of royal favour, showing that his services were too valuable, and he too powerful, to permit his delinquencies to be examined with strictness. His reliance on this impunity increased his boldness, until his presumption betrayed him into excesses which were fatal to him. His tyranny and violence became so oppressive that his neighbours at last resisted, and, proceeding against him in the King's Court, three judges were sent down to try the cases at Dunstable, where no less than thirty verdicts were found against him, and fines of 100*l*. in each of them were imposed.

The haughty baron resolved to be revenged, and sent his brother William with a band of his followers to seize the judges. Two of them, Martin de Pateshull and Thomas de Muleton, escaped; the third, Henry de Braybroc, was unluckily captured and taken to Bedford Castle, where he was treated with every indignity. When this outrage was communicated to the council, then sitting at Northampton, they proceeded on the instant to his chastisement. His castle at Bedford was taken, though not till after two months' siege, and William, the brother of Faukes, with twenty-four other knights, was hanged. Faukes himself escaped into Wales, but, not succeeding in enlisting any powers in his cause, and hearing that the king had confiscated all his possessions (*Excerpt. e Rot. Fin.* i. 117), he prepared to return. The king issued an order to the sheriffs of Shropshire and Staffordshire to seize him and his followers. He however reached the court in safety, and, placing himself at the royal mercy, gave up into the king's hands all his property and possessions. (*Rymer*, i. 175.) Delivered into the custody of Eustace de Fauconberg, Bishop of London, his case was heard in the following March, 1225, whereupon the nobles, preserving his life in consideration of his former services, banished him the realm for ever. On landing in Normandy he was taken before the King of France, where he again narrowly escaped a disgraceful death; but, being signed with the cross, he was permitted to proceed on his journey to Rome. There he induced the pope to interfere with King Henry on his behalf; but that monarch was inexorable; and the life of Faukes, about 1228, was terminated by poison administered in a fish at St. Ciriac.

The manor of Whitchurch, in Berks, was assigned to his wife for her support, and she was allowed to answer to the king for all the debts owed to him at the rate of three hundred marks a year. The Close Rolls contain numerous entries of the restoration of lands to their possessors, from whom Faukes had unjustly seized them.

His daughter Eve married Lewellyn-ap-Jorwerth, Prince of North Wales. (*Dugdale's Baron.* i. 743; *Wendover*, iv. 10–137; *Rapin*, iii. 10–26.)

BRENCHESLEY, WILLIAM, by his marriage with Joane de Benenden, became lord of the manor of Benenden, near Cranbrook, in Kent. There is little account of his early career as a lawyer, except that he is mentioned in Richard Bellewe's Reports, and that he was one of the king's serjeants in 14 Richard II.

He attended the parliament of 21 Richard II., and was called upon to say what he thought of the answers which had been given by the judges to the questions proposed to them by Chief Justice Tresilian. He replied that they seemed to him to be good and loyal, and that he should have given the same. (*Rot. Parl.* iii. 358.) His fear of the consequences of expressing a different opinion, and still more his immediate prospect of advancement, probably prompted him upon the occasion; for in Trinity Term in the following year we find a fine acknowledged before him as a judge of the Common Pleas.

On the deposition of Richard II., King Henry made him a knight of the Bath on the day of his coronation, and continued him in his place in the Common Pleas, which he retained till Easter 1406.

He died on the 20th of May following at his house in Holborn, and was buried in Canterbury Cathedral, where his widow, who lived till 1453, built a small chapel or chantry. They left no children. (*Hasted*, xi. 347; *Weever*, 235.)

BREREWOOD, ROBERT. The family of Brerewood were flourishing citizens of Chester. The judge's grandfather is called a wet-glover there, and was thrice mayor. His uncle, Edward, was a famous scholar, and became the first Gresham professor of astronomy. His father, John, the mayor's eldest son, was sheriff of Chester; and the judge himself was born there about 1588. He was admitted into Brazenose College, Oxford, in 1605, and two years afterwards became a member of the Middle Temple, where he was called to the bar on November 13, 1615. After a lengthened practice of two-and-twenty years, during which he published several of his uncle's works, he was appointed a judge of North Wales in 1637, was chosen reader to his inn in the Lent following, and at Easter 1639 was elected recorder of his native city. The degree of the coif was conferred upon him in 1640, and in Hilary Term 1641 he was made king's serjeant. Receiving the honour of knighthood in December 1643, he was advanced to the bench at Oxford on the 31st of the next month. The exercise of Sir Robert's judicial functions was, however, of short continuance, and he never performed them in Westminster Hall.

Witnessing the extinction of regal authority, and lamenting his royal master's untimely death, he passed the remainder of his days in the retirement of his home, and dying there on September 8, 1654, he was buried in St. Mary's Church at Chester.

He married, first, Anna, daughter of Sir Randle Mainwaringe, of Over Pever in Cheshire, and, secondly, Katherine, daughter of Sir Richard Lea, of Lea and Dernhall, in the same county, and left several children by each of them. (*Ath. Oxon.* ii. 140.)

BRETON, JOHN LE (afterwards BISHOP OF HEREFORD), is stated to have been the son of a knight of that name, who, with his wife, was buried at Abbey Dore in Herefordshire. (*Archæol. Journ.* xix. 35.) Brought up to the double profession of the law and the church, he had the county and castle of Hereford committed to his custody in 38 Henry III. (*Abb. Rot. Orig.* i. 13), and was raised to the judicial bench at the latter end of 50 Henry III. (*Excerpt. e Rot. Fin.* ii. 430.) In the next year the keeper of the wardrobe was directed by the king to supply 'Johanni le Breton et Henrico de Monteforti, justiciariis suis,' with the full robes which the other judges were accustomed to be provided with. (*Selden's Hengham Magna*, 5.) The entries of assizes before him continue till the end of December 1268, or beginning of January 1269. On the 13th of the latter month the king consented to his election as Bishop of Hereford, when he no doubt retired from the bench. He was consecrated in the following July, and presided over the see about six years, dying in May 1275, 3 Edward I. (*Godwin*.)

The work called 'Britton,' which is a compendium of the English law, was at one time attributed to this judge and bishop. But from the contents it is manifest that it must have been written after 13 Edward I., inasmuch as the author cites a statute passed in that year, as well as another enacted in 6 Edward I., both of which periods were subsequent to the bishop's death. The work has been considered by others, and this seems the better opinion, to be little more than an abridgment of Bracton, with the addition of the subsequent alterations in the law; and the probability of this acquires greater weight when it is remembered that Bracton's name was sometimes written Britton or Bretton.

(*Hengham*, ut supra; *Reeves's Engl. Law*, ii. 280.)

BRETON, JOHN LE. The family of Breton held considerable possessions in Norfolk, but to what branch of it this John le Breton belonged is uncertain. He was probably the 'Dominus de Sporle' of that name who joined in the barons' letter to Pope Boniface VIII. in 29 Edward I. On January 9, 1305, 33 Edward I., he was one of the justices of trailbaston, then appointed for the counties of Norfolk and Suffolk, and again in 1307. In 3 Edward II. he was an assessor of the twenty-fifth granted in Norfolk, and he died in the next year. (*Parl. Writs*, i. 497, 592; *Rot. Parl.* i. 218.)

BRETON, WILLIAM LE, or BRITO, as he is frequently called in the earlier part of his life, was the brother of the after-mentioned Ranulph Brito, and was engaged in various ways in the service of Henry III. Fifty marks were paid out of the treasury to him and another in 6 Henry III. to purchase robes for the use of the king; and two years subsequently he held a judicial appointment in the court at Durham, he and his associates being commanded not to hold plea on any writ of the bishop which his predecessors had not been accustomed to issue. In 10 Henry III. he seems to have had some regulation of the ports, as he is directed to allow a person to send his corn in a ship to London, taking security that it is carried nowhere else. (*Rot. Claus.* i. 492, 631, ii. 118.)

From 11 to 16 Henry III. he held the sheriffalty of Kent in conjunction with Hubert de Burgh. (*Hasted*, i. 180.) His next advance was to the office of one of the justices or custodes of the Jews on July 6, 1234, 18 Henry III., which he held three years afterwards. (*Madox*, i. 234, ii. 317.)

He evidently became a regular justicier, and it is probable that he was appointed in the same year he acted as a justice itinerant in the county of Surrey, 32 Henry III., 1248. In the next year there are not only writs of assize to be taken before him, but he was also united with the same associates as in the last, in three several commissions. The writs of assize have his name inserted as late as August 1259.

He died in 45 Henry III., 1261, having considerable property in Northamptonshire and other counties, for which his son John le Breton did homage, paying 10*l.* for his relief. (*Excerpt. e Rot. Fin.* ii. 57-309, 349; *Cal. Inquis.* p. m. i. 20.)

BRETT, WILLIAM BALIOL, one of the present justices of the Common Pleas, was appointed as an additional judge under the statute 31 & 32 Vict. c. 125, s. 11, passed for amending the laws relating to election petitions.

He is the son of the Rev. Joseph George Brett, of Ranelagh, Chelsea, by Dorothy, daughter of George Best, Esq., of Chilston Park, Kent. He was born at Chelsea on August 13, 1815, and educated at Westminster School, and Caius College, Cambridge, where he took his degree of B.A. in 1840, and distinguished himself both as a mathematician and as a boating man. Entering Lincoln's Inn, he was called to the bar in January 1846, and joined the Northern Circuit. His success is evidenced by his soon becoming leader in the Passage Court of Liverpool, and by his being appointed a revising barrister in the districts adjacent. He was employed also on several government commissions and by the Court of Admiralty. His practice in London was very extensive, and continued so after he was raised to the rank of queen's counsel in March 1861. From July 1866 till his elevation to the bench he sat in parliament as member for Helston, for which he was re-elected on being appointed solicitor-general by the Derby ministry in February 1868. He was then knighted. The act above alluded to was passed on July 31 of that year, and Sir William was one of the three new judges appointed under it on August 24.

He married Eugenie, daughter of Louis Mayer, Esq.

BRETTON, HENRY DE. *See* BRACTON.

BRIDGEMAN, ORLANDO, belonged to the family of Bridgeman originally settled in Gloucestershire, a younger son of which, having removed to Exeter, became the father of Dr. John Bridgeman, who, after holding the living of Wigan in Lancashire, was made Bishop of Chester in 1619. By his wife Elizabeth, daughter of Dr. Helyar, canon of Exeter and archdeacon of Barnstaple, he was the father of several sons, the second of whom was the judge.

Orlando Bridgeman was born at Exeter on January 30, 1608. He entered Queen's College, Cambridge, in 1621, and he took his master's degree at Midsummer 1624, and was elected fellow of Magdalen College. In November of that year he was admitted a member of the Inner Temple, and, having been called to the bar on February 10, 1632, became a bencher a few weeks before the restoration of Charles II. He was made king's counsel in the duchy of Lancaster and judge of the county palatine of Chester in 1638; and was in 1640 appointed attorney of the Court of Wards, and solicitor-general to Charles, Prince of Wales, when he was knighted. He also had a grant in reversion of the office of keeper of the writs and rolls in the Common Pleas. (*Rymer*, xx. 447, 541; *Bp. Bridgeman's MS. Ledger*.)

In the Long Parliament of 1640 he was returned for Wigan, his father's former rectory, in which the family seems to have had some interest, as Anthony Wood relates that Sir Orlando about 1662 conferred the living upon John Hall, Bishop of Chester. He showed himself a strenuous supporter of monarchical government, voting against Lord Strafford's attainder, and opposing the ordinance by which the militia was taken out of the hands of the king. (*Parl. Hist.* ii. 611, 756; *Whitelocke*, 59.) When the civil war commenced he left the parliament and assisted his father the bishop in keeping the city of Chester firm in its adherence to the royal cause. In 1645 he was one of the king's commissioners in the fruitless endeavours to conclude a treaty of peace at Uxbridge, where Charles was somewhat dissatisfied at his carriage, expressing his surprise that the son of a bishop should have been willing to make any condescensions in matters of the Church. Clarendon (iii. 448) also joins in this censure, and, though giving him credit for excellent parts and honest inclinations, says, 'he was so much given to find out expedients to satisfy unreasonable men that he would at last be drawn to yield to anything he should be powerfully pressed to do.' On the ultimate success of the parliamentary party Sir Orlando discontinued his practice at the bar, but, as Ludlow relates (p. 401), 'upon his submission to Cromwell, was permitted to practise in a private manner.' He devoted his time to conveyancing, in which department he became, it is said, the great oracle, not only of his fellow-sufferers, but also of the whole nation in matters of law—his very enemies not thinking their estates secure without his advice. After his death his collections were published under the title of 'Bridgeman's Conveyancer,' which had so high a reputation that five editions were issued from the press.

His learning insured him immediate employment on the Restoration. Two days after the king's return he was invested with the serjeant's coif, followed on the next day by his promotion to the office of chief baron of the Exchequer. In the same week his loyalty was rewarded with a baronetcy, in which he is described of Great Lever in Lancashire, a property not far from Wigan. Pepys speaks of another seat in the county called Ashton Hall, near Lancaster, in which he caused four great places to be left in the great hall window for coats of arms. 'In one he hath put the Levers', with this motto, "Olim;" in another, the Ashton's, with this, "Heri;" in the next, his own, with this, "Hodie;" in the fourth, nothing but this motto, "Cras nescio cujus."' (*Pepys*, i. 349.)

The principal duty that he had to perform as lord chief baron was to preside at the trials of the regicides, which lasted from the 9th to the 19th of October 1660. Three days after their termination Sir Orlando was promoted to the chief seat in the Common Pleas. He sat in that court for nearly seven years, in high esteem as an able exponent of the law and an impartial administrator of justice.

That he was sometimes too precise in his legal interpretations is exemplified by a story told by Roger North (p. 97), that when it was proposed to move his court, which was placed near the door of Westminster Hall and exposed to the wind, into a back room called the treasury, the chief justice would not agree to it, declaring it was against Magna Charta, which enacts that the Common Pleas shall be held *in certo loco* (in a certain place), with which he asserted the distance of an inch from that place is inconsistent, and that all pleas would be *coram non judice*.

On the removal of Lord Clarendon the Great Seal was given to Sir Orlando on August 30, 1667, as lord keeper; but no successor was appointed to take his place in the Common Pleas till May 1668. He, therefore, during the interval filled both offices, which it was said were not incompatible; and though he did not sit in his old court, fines appear to have been levied before him during the whole of the time. (*Siderfin*, 2, 338; *Dugdale's Orig.* 49.) While he held the Seal, both Pepys (iv. 88) and Evelyn (ii. 376) state that he resided at Essex House in the Strand.

It is to Lord Clarendon's credit that he writes not a word in depreciation of his successor. Neither Burnet nor Roger North are so abstinent. The former says (i. 253, 307) that in his new office he did not long maintain the esteem he had previously acquired, and that his study and practice had lain so entirely in the common law that he never seemed to apprehend what equity was; nor had he a head made for business and for such a court. Roger North (*Lives*, 88; *Examen*, 38) is more particular in his animadversions. He described the lord keeper 'as timorous to an impotence, and that not mended by his great age. He laboured very much to please every body, a temper of ill consequence to a judge. It was observed of him that if a cause admitted of diverse doubts, which the lawyers call points, he would never give all on one side; but either party should have something to go away with. And in his time the Court of Chancery ran out of order into delays and endless motions in causes; so that it was like a fair field overgrown with briars.' After holding the Seal for about five years, he was made the victim of the strong parties which opposed him, and was removed on November 17, 1672. He died on June 25, 1674, at Teddington in Middlesex, where he lies buried. All parties unite in acknowledging his amiable disposition, his honest principles, his piety, his moderation, and his learning; to the last of which the late Lord Ellenborough (14 *East's Reports*, 134)—himself a great authority—bore honourable testimony, in calling him 'that most eminent judge,' and speaking of 'the profundity of his learning and the extent of his industry.'

He married, first, in 1627, Judith, daughter and heir of John Kynaston, Esq., of Morton in Shropshire, who died in 1644; and secondly, Dorothy, daughter of Dr. Saunders, provost of Oriel College, Oxford, and relict of George Cradock, Esq., of Carswell Castle in Staffordshire. By his first marriage he had a daughter and one son; by his second two sons and a daughter. The baronetcy, of course, devolved upon Sir John, his son by the first venter; but a second baronetcy was granted in 1673, the year following Sir Orlando's retirement from the Seal, to the eldest son by the second venter, Sir Orlando Bridgeman, of Ridley in Cheshire. The latter became extinct on the death of the third baronet in 1740; but the former still survives. The fifth baronet was ennobled by the title of Baron Bradford in 1794, his father having married Anne Newport, the sister and heir of the last Earl of Bradford of that name. The son of this baron was advanced to an earldom in 1815.

BRITO. *See* W. LE BRETON.

BRITO, RALPH, had the custody of the honor of Bologne and of the land of Henry of Essex for many years, and the rolls from 15 to 31 Henry II. contain entries of his accounting for them. In 1177, Robert Mantel and he, as justiciaries, fixed the aid to be paid in the counties of Norfolk, Suffolk, Essex, and Hertford; and in 1179 he was selected for the home counties to act as a justice itinerant in one of the four divisions into which the council of Windsor then apportioned the kingdom. (*Madox*, i. 130, 263, &c., ii. 200, &c.) By the roll of 1 Richard I. (he being then dead) it appears that Lageford and Chigwell in Essex belonged to him.

BRITO, RICHARD, was an officer of the Exchequer, to whom was committed the receipt of the rents of the vacant bishoprics of Lincoln and London while in the king's hands, the former in conjunction with Master Gregorius, and the latter with Ralph, archdeacon of Colchester. He is called archdeacon of Coventry in the roll of 31 Henry II., 1185.

In 1 Richard I. he was one of the justices itinerant in the counties of Devon, Dorset, Somerset, Wilts, Hants, and Oxford; and as he acted in so many counties, all probably in one circuit, without being recorded as a justicier at Westminster, it seems likely that officers of the court were sometimes sent on these itinera in addition to the regular justiciers. He no doubt continued to act in subsequent years, as the roll of 7 Richard I., 1195-6, contains an entry of the payment of sixty marks 'Ricardo Britoni et sociis suis.' (*Madox*, i. 309, 311, ii. 284.)

BRITO, RANULPH, or LE BRETON, the brother of the before-mentioned William le Breton, or Brito, was chaplain to Hubert de Burgh, the chief justiciary, in 1221, when a payment was made to him under that designation, besides many others up to 11 Henry III. He afterwards became a canon of St. Paul's. In 7 Henry III. he assessed the tallage in Wilton, and appears to have been about the king's person, as in the ninth year he had an order for the repayment of ten marks, with which he had accommodated the king to pay some messengers. A grant was made to him in 11 Henry III. of part of the wood of Engayne, in Blatherwick, and in Dudinton, Northamptonshire, to hold by the service of a pair of gilt spurs. (*Rot. Claus.* i. 457, ii. 47, 173, 184.)

Having, by the influence of his patron, Hubert de Burgh, been raised to the treasurership of the chamber of the Exchequer, he was, at the instigation of Peter de Rupibus, Bishop of Winchester, dismissed from the office in 1232 for fraud and corruption, and fined in no less a sum than 1000*l*. (*Wendover*, iv. 244.) Henry in his first anger had banished Ranulph Brito from the kingdom, but within two months, on payment of the fine, restored him to favour, though not to his place, with a condition, however, that he should not appeal to Rome. (*Cal. Rot. Pat.* 15.)

His death occurred in 1247, and the words 'cancellarius specialis,' used by Matthew Paris in recording that event, seem the only warrant for Dugdale and others introducing him into the list of chancellors, although, according to the construction of the sentence, the words appear rather to intimate that he was chancellor to the queen. None of the records describe him as the king's chancellor, and Sir T. D. Hardy has accordingly omitted the name in his catalogue. Lord Campbell, by mistake, calls him Bishop of Bath and Wells.

BRIWER, WILLIAM. This great man, who was in the confidence of four successive monarchs, is said by Camden to have been a foundling, and to have received his name from having been discovered by Henry II. on a heath (*bruyère*) while hunting in the New Forest. The king, he says, caused him to be taken up and placed under proper care, and when he arrived at man's estate employed him in his service. Unfortunately for this romantic tale, Dugdale's account of him, if correct, proves that it is not founded on truth. He says his father was Henry Briwer, and quotes a charter of Henry II. confirming to William Briwer and his heirs certain possessions and privileges, with the forestship of the forest of De la Bere, in as ample a manner as his father held them in the times of King William and King Henry I. However this may be, in 26 Henry II., 1180, he was entrusted with the sheriffalty of Devonshire, which he continued to hold till 1 Richard I.

His judicial career commenced in 33 Henry II., 1187, when he was associated with two others in fixing the tallage in Wiltshire. He acted in the same character in 1 Richard I. in Cornwall and Berkshire, and in 9 Richard I. in Nottingham and Derby. After the introduction of fines his name is found among the justiciers before whom they were levied at Westminster and other places, during the last four years of Richard's reign, and most of the years of that of John; and he is mentioned as a baron of the Exchequer as late as 5 Henry III., 1221. (*Madox*, i. 634, 733; *Pipe Roll*, 115, 185.)

That he attained an early character for wisdom and prudence may be inferred from the fact that King Richard, on his embarkation to the Holy Land, although he exacted from him a fine for not joining in the crusade, named him as one of the council to assist the Bishops of Durham and Ely in the government of the kingdom. Acting against the latter when the king's letter authorised the council to assume the government, he was included in the sentence of excommunication which the bishop induced the pope to pronounce against the supporters of the Earl John. All doubt of his loyalty, however, was removed by the hearty assistance he gave to release his sovereign from captivity; and the king's confidence in him is proved by his being selected as one of the ambassadors then sent to make a league with the King of France. In this and the subsequent reigns he was sheriff of several counties. The rolls also teem with grants of all kinds—of manors, lands, markets, custodies, wardships, licences for building castles, and of various other privileges, besides presents of wine, and on one occasion of a captured ship.

In frequent attendance on King John, he accompanied him to Ireland, dined with him at his table, eating flesh on certain prohibited days, for which indulgence money was given to the poor; and, adhering to him in all his troubles, he was a witness to his renunciation of the crown to the pope. In 15 John he was made seneschal to the king in conjunction with W. de Cantelupe (*Cal. Rot. Pat.* 4), and when the king marched northwards in 1215 he was one of those entrusted with the command of one of the forces left to check the barons remaining in London; and on several occasions till the end of the reign justified the royal confidence by the exertions which he made on behalf of his sovereign.

These exertions were continued on the accession of Henry III. till Prince Louis was forced to retire from the kingdom. Rewards still flowed upon him, and at various times he was appointed governor of the castles of Bolsover, Lidford, Devizes, and Newcastle-upon-Tyne.

He seems to have been an uncompromising supporter of the king's prerogative. Wendover relates (iv. 83) that when Archbishop Stephen and the nobles in 1223 urged the king to confirm the liberties and rights for which they had contended with his father, William Briwer exclaimed that 'those liberties, having been violently extorted, ought not to be observed.' The archbishop, however, mildly reprimanded him, and the king wisely promised to keep the oath he had taken to grant them.

His career of prosperity was only terminated by his death, which occurred in 1226, 11 Henry III. He was buried in the abbey of Dunkeswell in Devonshire, which he had founded for Cistercian monks.

His riches and his piety may be estimated by the following works. Besides the above abbey of Dunkeswell, he founded that of St. Saviour at Torre, in the same county, for Præmonstratensian canons; the priory of Motisfont, in Hampshire, for canons regular of St. Augustin; and a hospital for twelve poor people, besides religious and strangers, at Bridgewater in Somersetshire, where he also built a castle, constructed a haven, and began a handsome bridge.

He married Beatrix de Vallibus, by whom he had two sons and five daughters. On the death of the sons the inheritance was divided among the five daughters and their heirs. (*Dugdale's Baron.* i. 700.)

BRIWES, JOHN DE, is introduced as a justicier in Mr. Hunter's Preface to the Fines of Richard I. and John in the eleventh year of the latter reign, 1209. That he was in some office connected with the Exchequer appears from several entries on the Rot. de Finibus. (417, 442.) He died in 1229. (*Rot. de Oblatis*, i. 184.)

BROCLESBY, WILLIAM DE, of that place in Lincolnshire, was an ecclesiastic, who devoted much of his property both in that county and in Yorkshire to pious purposes. He held the office of remembrancer of the Exchequer in 1338 (*Hospitaller in Engl.* 203) till he was promoted to be a baron of that court on January 20, 1341, 14 Edward III. He is mentioned as being alive in 25 Edward III. (*Abb. Rot. Orig.* ii. 91, &c.; *Rot. Parl.* ii. 453.)

BROK, LAURENCE DEL, was an advocate in the reign of Henry III., evidently standing very high in his profession. As early as 1253 he was employed on the part of the crown, and there are no less than seventeen entries in that year in which he acted for the king in suits before the court. For an interval of seven years his name does not again occur, but in 1260 he seems to have resumed his position, and to have been regularly engaged on the king's behalf until Christmas 1267. He was raised to the bench before the following February, and continued there till the end of the reign, in the last year of which a judgment is mentioned. (*Rot. Parl.* i. 4.) He died in 3 Edward I., in possession of considerable property in the counties of Buckingham, Kent, Hertford, and Oxford. (*Cal. Inquis.* p. m. i. 54.)

BROME, ADAM DE, was a clerk or master in Chancery, and filled the office of a justice itinerant in the county of Nottingham in 3 Edward III., 1330. He probably was of the family settled at the manor of Brome-Hall in Norfolk, and is first mentioned in 6 Edward II., 1312, when he was assigned to talliate Warwickshire and other counties. From that time up to 3 Edward III., besides being frequently mentioned in connection with his duties in Chancery, he was several times employed in judicial commissions. (*Parl. Writs*, ii. p. ii. 602; *Abb. Placit.* 337.) Like his brethren in the Chancery, he received many ecclesiastical preferments. In 1315 he was rector of Hamworth in Middlesex; in 1316, chancellor of Durham; in 1319, archdeacon of Stow and rector of St. Mary, Oxford. In 17 Edward II. he had a licence to erect a school in that university, by the name of 'Rectoris Domus Scholarium Beatæ Mariæ, Oxon,' which, when founded, he presented to Edward II., who further endowed it, and appointed him the first provost. From a large messuage, called *la Oriole*, bestowed on it by Edward II., it received its present name, Oriel College. (*Cal. Rot. Pat.* 94; *Chalmers's Oxford*, 77; *Le Neve*, 171.)

BROMLEY, THOMAS. The ancient family of Bromley, established as early as the reign of King John at Bromleghe in Staffordshire, has supplied the ranks of the law with the three following judges. The first is Thomas Bromley, who was the son of Roger Bromley (a younger brother of the immediate ancestor of Queen Elizabeth's chancellor), by Jane, the daughter of Thomas Jennings. He was placed at the Inner Temple, and became reader there in autumn 1532. In June 1540 he was called to the degree of the coif, and was appointed one of the king's serjeants on the 2nd of the next month.

Succeeding Sir John Spelman, he was appointed a judge of the King's Bench on November 4, 1544. That he was highly esteemed by Henry VIII. is apparent from his having a legacy of 300*l.* under the king's will, and being appointed one of the executors of it. (*Testam. Vetust.* 43.) He thus became one of the council of regency under Edward VI., but seems to have avoided the political difficulties of that reign till its close, when he was most unwillingly involved in the project of the Duke of Northumberland to place Lady Jane Grey on the throne. His being sent for by the duke to prepare the king's will, and the conduct pursued to overcome his resistance, is subsequently detailed in the life of Chief Justice Montagu. Having submitted, under the compulsion to which he was subjected, to settle the instrument, it would seem that he was no further called upon to interfere; for his name does not appear among those who witnessed the will, and, instead of being committed to prison, as the two chief justices were, he was raised by Queen Mary to the head of his own court on October 4, 1553, in the place of Sir Roger Cholmley, from which it may be naturally inferred that he was, as Burnet says, 'a papist in his heart.'

He presided at the extraordinary trial of Sir Nicholas Throckmorton on April 17, 1554, when, though the prisoner had so much greater liberty of speech allowed to him than in any previous trial on record that the queen's attorney openly complained in court and threatened to retire from the bar, yet was he hardly pressed by the judges, who refused him the examination of a witness he produced, and denied him the inspection of a statute upon which he relied. The chief justice's summing up too was so defective, 'either for want of memory or good will,' that 'the prisoner craved indifferency, and did help the judge's old memory with his own recital.' (*Holinshed*, iv. 31–55.) Throckmorton's acquittal and the iniquitous punishment of the jury followed; and the impression which the whole proceedings leave upon the mind is anything but favourable to the lawyers who were concerned in them. Sir Thomas Bromley cannot escape from the charge of undue severity, though probably he was complained of at the time for giving too great licence to the prisoner. He was succeeded as chief justice on June 11, 1555, by Sir William Portman; but it does not appear whether the vacancy was occasioned by his death or by his being superseded. Wroxeter Church contains his remains, over which is a handsome altar tomb.

He left an only daughter, Margaret, who married Sir Richard Newport, the ancestor of the late Earls of Bradford, a title which became extinct in that family in 1762, but was revived in 1815 in the descendants of Sir Orlando Bridgeman, one of whom married the sister and heir of the last earl.

BROMLEY, THOMAS, descended from the same ancestor as his last-mentioned namesake. Established at Bromleghe in Staffordshire under King John, the family flourished in that and the neighbouring counties throughout the succeeding centuries. Roger Bromley, of Mitley in Shropshire, a lineal descendant, had, besides other children, two sons, William and Roger. The chief justice was son of the latter, and the lord chancellor was grandson of the former, his father being George Bromley, the only son of William, who was of Hodnet in Shropshire, and his mother, Elizabeth, daughter of Sir Thomas Lacon, of Willey in the same county. His father was himself distinguished in the law, being a reader at the Inner Temple in the reigns of Henry VII. and Henry VIII., and his brother, Sir George Bromley, attained in the same profession the rank of justice of Chester under Queen Elizabeth.

Sir Thomas was born about the year 1530, and, being destined for the law, was sent to the same inn at which his father had studied, where he was reader in autumn 1566, having been just previously elected recorder of the city of London. He held this honourable post till he became solicitor-general, to which office he was appointed on March 14, 1569, and filled it for ten years, during which, in 1574, he was elected treasurer of his inn.

He acted in 1571 on the trial of the Duke of Norfolk for high treason, and managed that part of the prosecution which had reference to Rodolph's message. (*State Trials*, i. 957, 1015.) As an advocate he arrived at great eminence, but was scrupulous in undertaking a suit till he was satisfied of its justice, 'not admitting all causes promiscuously,' says David Lloyd (*State Worthies*, 610), who adds that 'never failing in any cause for five years, . . . he was the only person that the people would employ.' An anecdote is told of him in 'Bacon's Apophthegms' which shows that he had a ready wit in escaping out of a dilemma. Having offered in evidence a deed which the counsel on the other side impeached as fraudulent, arguing that it had not been produced in two former suits on the same title, but some other conveyance relied upon, Justice Catlin, who inclined to that opinion, said to him, 'I pray thee, Mr. Solicitor, let me ask you a familiar question: I have two geldings in my stable, and I have divers times business of importance, and still I send forth one of my geldings and not the other; would you not say I set him aside as a jade?' 'No, my lord,' replied Bromley, 'I would think you spared him for your own saddle.'

Retained by Lord Hunsdon and patronised by Lord Burleigh, it is not surprising, with the professional character he had acquired, that Bromley, though not yet fifty years of age, should have been selected as the successor of Sir Nicholas Bacon. He received the Great Seal on April 26, 1579, with the rank of lord chancellor, a title which his predecessor had never enjoyed. It is not improbable, however, that there was some doubt which of the two titles should be given to him, for more than two months elapsed after Bacon's death during which, according to the entries on the Close Roll (24), the Great Seal remained in the queen's possession; and two speeches are preserved which, if both of them are rightly attributed to Bromley, would seem to have been prepared by him to deliver to the queen in the event of either determination. (*Egerton Papers*, 81.) Fuller says (*Worthies*, ii. 259), 'Although it was difficult to come after Sir Nicholas Bacon, and not *to come after him*, yet such was Bromley's learning and integrity that the court was not sensible of any considerable alteration.' He seems to have pursued a steady course in the performance of his official duties, without respect to persons. He presided as chancellor over the commission issued in October 1586 for the trial of Mary, Queen of Scots, in which he conducted himself with great decency and personal respect towards the unfortunate prisoner, though in the subsequent proceedings in parliament he was the organ of the house to represent to Elizabeth their unanimous request that the judgment might be executed. Before the next session, which was opened on February 15, 1587, he, was seized with an illness which necessitated the appointment of a temporary speaker of the House of Lords, and by which he no doubt escaped being a performer in the despicable proceedings against Secretary Davison on March 28. This illness terminated in his death on April 12, at the age of 57. He was buried in Westminster Abbey, where his son, Sir Henry, erected a splendid monument to his memory.

By his wife, Elizabeth, daughter of Sir Adrian Fortescue, K.B., he had four sons and four daughters. One of the latter married Sir Oliver Cromwell, the uncle of the Protector, and another married John Lyttelton of Frankley, whose eldest son was advanced to the peerage as Baron Lyttelton of Frankley.

Sir Thomas's eldest son, as well as several of his descendants, sat for the county of Worcester in parliament, and eventually, on May 9, 1741, the representative of the family was created Baron Montford of Horseheath, Cambridgeshire, a title which became extinct in 1851 by the death of the third lord without surviving issue.

BROMLEY, EDWARD, the third member of the same family who has been adorned with the judicial ermine, was the son of Sir George Bromley, justice of Chester, the elder brother of the chancellor.

He kept his terms at the Inner Temple, where he was a reader in Lent 1606. He was made a serjeant for the purpose of his being raised to the bench, his call taking place on February 5, and his patent as baron of the Exchequer being dated February 6, 1610. During the remaining sixteen years of James's reign, and for above two years in that of Charles I., he performed the functions of his office, and, according to Croke (*Car.* 85), he died in the summer vacation 1627.

BROMPTON, WILLIAM DE, whose name is sometimes spelled Burnton and Burton, was constituted a judge of the Common Pleas in 1278, 6 Edward I., and fines were levied before him from that year till Michaelmas, 17 Edward I., 1289. (*Parl. Writs*, i. 382; *Dugdale's Orig.* 44.) Soon after this he was disgraced and imprisoned in the Tower for corruption in his office. (*Stow's London*, 44.) One of the charges against him was that he impeded the prior of Huntingdon in an assize of darrein presentment to the church of Suho, whereby the bishop took it by lapse of time. (*Rot. Parl.* i. 48.) Another implicated the judge in cruel treatment towards Nicholas de Cerny, imprisoned in Newgate, by directing him to be put in irons and injured as much as possible. But his offences must have been of a far more heinous nature than either of these, as the fine of 6000 marks, which he was compelled to pay for his enlargement, was one of the highest that was imposed upon those who shared in his disgrace.

A William de Brompton is named as one of the king's councillors in the Statute de Escaetoribus, 29 Edward I., 1301, and as one of the justices of the Bishop of Durham in the same year (*Parl. Writs*, i. 108); and in the following a justice itinerant in Cornwall called William de Burnton occurs, but whether they were the same person is uncertain.

BROOK, DAVID, was a native of Glastonbury in Somersetshire, his father John, a serjeant-at-law, being principal seneschal of the famous monastery there. David was reader at the Inner Temple in 1534 and 1540, when he was also treasurer. In the first week of the reign of Edward VI., 1547, he was admitted to the degree of the coif, having been summoned thereto by Henry VIII., and in 1551 he was made one of the king's serjeants. Queen Mary soon after her accession advanced him, on September 1, 1553, to the office of chief baron of the Exchequer (*Dugdale's Orig.* 164, 170), and on October 2, the morrow of the coronation, he and a number of other persons were 'dobyd the knightes of the carpet.' (*Machyn's Diary*, 335.) His decisions are reported in Dyer till Hilary 1557, about a year after which he died.

David Lloyd, in his 'State Worthies' (386–390), gives the judge a highly encomiastic character, and concludes with an apophthegm which is worth remembering. 'A fat man in Rome riding always upon a very lean horse being asked the reason thereof, answered *that he fed himself, but he trusted others to feed his horse.* Our judge being asked what was the best way to thrive, said, *Never do anything by another that you can do by yourself.*'

Sir David left a widow, Margaret, daughter of Richard Butler, of London, who had previous to her marriage with him been already the wife of two husbands, Andrew Fraunces and Alderman Robert Chartsey, and who, after the death of the chief baron was married, for the fourth time, to Edward, Lord North, whom also she survived, and dying in 1575, was buried in St. Lawrence Jewry. (*Collins's Peerage,* iv. 458; *Fuller,* ii. 283.) This lady was the chief baron's second wife, his first being Katherine, daughter of John, Lord Chandos, who in a patent of 1553, granting to her and her husband the manor of Canonbury, is described as having been the suckling nurse of Queen Mary. (*Tomlins's Yseldon.*)

BROOKE, ROBERT, or BROKE, was the son of Thomas Broke, of Claverley in Shropshire, by Margaret, the daughter of Hugh Grosvenor, of Farmot in the same county; and he was buried in the church of that parish. (*Athen. Oxon.* i. 267.) He was reader at the Middle Temple in 1542 and 1551. His readings on these occasions were 'On the Statute of Limitations, 32 Henry VIII. c. 2,' and 'On Magna Charta, c. 16,' both of which were afterwards published. Between these dates— viz., in 1545—he was advanced from the office of common serjeant of the city of London to that of recorder in the room of Sir Roger Cholmley. In that character he is frequently mentioned in Dyer's Reports. In Michaelmas 1552 he was made a serjeant, and was several times returned to parliament as representative of the metropolis.

He was elected speaker in that which met on April 2, 1554, during which the marriage of the queen with Philip of Spain was solemnized. A new parliament was then called, and between the date of the summons and the day of meeting Brooke was put in the place of Sir Richard Morgan as chief justice of the Common Pleas on October 8. He was knighted by King Philip on January 27, 1555, but he enjoyed his judicial dignity little more than four years, dying on September 6, 1558, about two months before the death of the queen. On his tomb at Claverley he is represented in his official robes, with a wife on each side of him in splendid dresses. One of his wives was named Anne, and the other Dorothy; and between them they produced him seventeen children. (*Machyn's Diary,* 342.)

His name has a high reputation in Westminster Hall, not only on account of his great learning and his just administration of the law, but as the author of an 'Abridgment' or abstract of the Year Books till his own time, which Coke calls 'an excellent repertory,' and of 'Ascun's Novel Cases' in the three last reigns.

BROOKE, RICHARD, or BROKE, whose family was established at Leighton in Cheshire as early as in the twelfth century, was the fourth son of Thomas Brooke of that place, by the daughter and heir of John Parker of Copen Hall. He studied and practised at the Middle Temple so successfully that, dreading a summons to take upon him the degree of the coif, the usual reward of eminent advocates, he obtained a royal permission in July 1510, 2 Henry VIII., to decline the honour in case it should be offered to him. It would appear, however, that he soon altered his mind, and did not avail himself of the exemption; for he was one of the nine who were made serjeants in the following November. In the same autumn he was reader at his inn of court. In that year also he was raised from the office of under-sheriff to that of recorder of the city of London, and was elected its representative in parliament, a trust which was repeated in 1515.

In 1520 he was raised to the bench of the Common Pleas, receiving the customary knighthood on the occasion; and on resigning the recordership the corporation complimented him with a tun of wine at Christmas.

On January 24, 1526, he was constituted chief baron of the Exchequer, and performed the duties of that office in addition to those of the judgeship of the Common Pleas till April 1529, about which time he died.

He erected the mansion still called Broke Hall, at Nacton, near Ipswich, in Suffolk. From Sir Richard's son Robert descended another Robert, of Nacton, who was created a baronet in 1661, but dying in 1693 without male issue, the baronetcy expired, and the estates descended to a nephew, Robert, who had married one of his daughters. This Robert's great-grandson, Captain Philip Bowes Vere Broke, was raised to the same dignity in November 1813, for his victory as commander of the 'Shannon' over the American frigate the 'Chesapeake.'

BROUGHAM, HENRY, though born in Scotland, was the representative of one of the most ancient families in Westmoreland, in whose possession the manor of Burgham, now Brougham, can be traced uninterruptedly from the time of Edward the Confessor. By the intermarriage of one of his ancestors with the heiress of the family of Vaux of Catterlyn, he also represented that noble house. Before the death of his grandfather, John Brougham, his father resided at Edinburgh, where he married Eleanor, the only child of the Rev. James Syme, by Mary, the sister of Dr. Robertson the historian. Of that marriage the eldest son was the future chancellor, who was born in St. Andrew's Square, Edinburgh, on September 19, 1778.

In passing through both the High School and University of Edinburgh he distinguished himself by his rapidity and intelligence in receiving the instruction afforded, and in the latter he more particularly addressed himself to philosophical enquiries. The first fruit of his studies was a paper 'On the Inflection, Reflection, and Colours of Light,' written at the early age of seventeen, and forwarded by him to the Royal Society, and published in its 'Transactions' in 1796. To this he added in the next year some 'Further Experiments;' following these with 'General Theorems, chiefly Porisms of the higher Geometry,' which likewise appeared in successive years in the same publication. These successful exertions in physical science led him to an intimacy with Sir Joseph Banks, the president, and were rewarded in 1803 by his election as a fellow. In the meantime his pursuits introduced him into the best literary circles of Edinburgh, where he joined the 'Speculative Society,' and formed the more select association called 'the Academy of Physics.' He visited Norway and Sweden before he settled himself as an advocate in the Scottish law courts. In a letter to his friend, Sir Joseph Banks, dated December 10, 1800, he expresses his aversion to that profession, and his resolution to attempt an opening in the political world; but at the same time to cultivate its duties to secure a retreat, in case his plan should fail. He showed his capacity for the province he preferred by publishing in 1803 'An Enquiry into the Colonial Policy of the European Powers;' and in 1806 he exhibited his first acknowledged effort in behalf of the persecuted blacks, by issuing a pamphlet entitled 'A Concise Statement of the Question regarding the Abolition of the Slave Trade.' In 1802 he had joined with Lord Jeffrey, Sydney Smith, Horner, and other talented men then residing at Edinburgh, in founding the 'Edinburgh Review,' which up to the present time, after more than sixty years' existence, preserves the popularity it obtained on its first establishment. To this he was a most indefatigable contributor, advocating on all occasions the most liberal principles, in support of which it always took so prominent a part.

With an established reputation as a politician, a jurist, and an orator, he felt that Edinburgh was too confined a stage, and therefore, coming to London, he became for some time a pupil of Mr. (afterwards Chief Justice) Tindal, and, being called to the English bar in 1807 by the society of Lincoln's Inn, joined the Northern Circuit. His practice was less in the courts than in appeals to the House of Lords and the Privy Council, and before parliamentary committees. In 1808 he signalised himself at the bar of the House of Commons by his energetic advocacy of the application of the British merchants to obtain a repeal of the famous orders in council issued in opposition to the aggressions of Napoleon. His earnest exertions and his overpowering eloquence procured him a seat in parliament in 1810 for the borough of Camelford. He continued a member of that house till he was advanced to the other, twenty years later, except for four years from 1812, Mr. Canning having then defeated him in his attempt to be returned for Liverpool. In 1815 he was elected for Winchelsea, for which he sat till he succeeded in an arduous contest for the West Riding of Yorkshire in 1830, the year in which he was called to the House of Peers.

It is impossible in the present sketch to particularise all the incidents of his parliamentary career, so wide was the range of subjects which he discussed. No question found him unprepared, and whether the debate was upon African slavery, Catholic emancipation, or foreign politics, or upon the more domestic questions of charity abuses, distress in the agricultural districts, free trade and the laws that restrained it, the extravagance and corruption of our military and civil establishments, and the thousand other topics that agitated that assembly, he threw into them all that spirit and fervour for which his speeches were remarkable. He soon acquired the lead of the party to which he was attached, and was allowed to be a most brilliant debater, and to be an exception to the almost universal experience, that the eloquence of a lawyer did not succeed in the House of Commons. At the same time it was admitted that in the warmth of his addresses he was apt to exceed the limits of discretion, and sometimes to injure the cause he was advocating.

His reputation as a lawyer had so far advanced, aided, no doubt, by his political status, that he was occasionally consulted by the Princess Charlotte, and on her elopement from Warwick House in 1814 he was summoned by her to her mother's house at Connaught Terrace, to which she had fled, and it was by his advice that she returned home. But the great event on which his legal fame was to be established in the popular mind was now approaching. On the accession of George IV. in 1820, his queen, from whom he had been long separated, determined to return to England to assert her rights, and summoned Mr. Brougham, whom she appointed her attorney-general, as her adviser. A bill of pains and penalties was immediately brought into the House of Lords, charging her with adultery committed abroad. Mr. Brougham was the leading counsel for her defence against the bill, and by his extraordinary exertions and powerful advocacy produced such an effect, not only on the public mind, but on the noble jury who were to decide on her fate, that ministers were obliged to withdraw the bill. So severe had been his invectives against the king, not only in this defence, but in parliament also, on that and on other occasions, that, though his position at the bar had long entitled him to the usual precedence, his majesty refused to allow him the honour of a silk gown, the death of the queen depriving him in the next year of that which he wore as her attorney-general. Against Lord Eldon, to whom he attributed his exclusion, he took every opportunity of aiming the most pointed shafts of wit and sarcasm. His lordship refers to one of his direst attacks in 1825, in a letter to his daughter, Lady F. J. Banks, with cool indifference.

Of course the cause of Brougham's severity, and the assertion of Eldon's indifference, must be both taken with some allowance; but while his lordship remained chancellor, Brougham was obliged to content himself with a stuff gown. Under Lord Lyndhurst, who succeeded Lord Eldon, he received in 1827 a patent of precedence. At that time so conscious was he of his parliamentary powers that he refused the place of lord chief baron offered him by Mr. Canning, the new minister, objecting that it would exclude him from the house; and on Mr. Canning's suggestion that he would be only one stage from the woolsack, he replied, *'But the horses would be off.'*

Soon after the accession of William IV. the ministry of the Duke of Wellington was obliged to succumb, and that headed by Earl Grey took its place. So strong were Mr. Brougham's claims on the Whigs that no lower place than that of lord chancellor could be offered to him, and he accordingly received the Great Seal on November 22, 1830, and on the next day was created Lord Brougham and Vaux. During his chancellorship his utmost energies were applied in the House of Lords to the carrying of the Reform Bill, and to the support of all the measures suggested by the ministry; and in the Court of Chancery to the introducing many extensive reforms, some of doubtful value, but others of essential and permanent benefit. Among others, he swept away a host of sinecure places entailing great expense to the suitors, and, as a compensation for so great an annihilation of the patronage of the office, he procured for his successors an addition of 1000*l.* a year to their retiring allowance. He went out with his party, after exactly four years' enjoyment of the office, on November 22, 1834; but when in the next year its successors were obliged in their turn to give way to the whigs, for some cause or other, hitherto unexplained, Lord Brougham was not restored. Perhaps it was for the same reason which was adduced by Sir Robert Walpole just one hundred years before, that he would not 'make a man lord chancellor who was constantly complaining of the grievances of the law, and threatening to rectify the abuses of Westminster Hall.' (*Lord Hervey's Memoirs,* i. 434.)

Lord Brougham was now in his fifty-seventh year, a period of life at which many a man having filled the highest office in the state would have thought himself justified in resting upon his laurels. But he was of no such disposition; he did not approve of slothful inaction, but preferred exercising his talents, whether in or out of office, with a view to the benefit of the state, and to the improvement of his fellow-creatures. He continued regularly to attend the hearing of appeals in the House of Lords for many years; and for his indefatigable labours in that judicial capacity he was rewarded by Queen Victoria in 1860 with a new patent, entailing his title in default of male issue upon his brother, William Brougham, Esq., lately a master in Chancery. Time moderated his political feelings and tempered his party virulence, and he was charged by disappointed bigots with having joined the tory ranks. But the imputation arose from his not choosing to desert old friends of that party, with whom, amidst the most violent political contests, he had still kept up his intimacy. But no one could accuse him of any decay or discontinuance of his exertions for the extension of knowledge and instruction among the poor, or in the pursuit of the patriotic and benevolent objects it had been his life's endeavour to promote. Both before and after his exaltation these objects were numerous. Among the principal were the formation of the 'Society for the Diffusion of Useful Knowledge,' by which many valuable publications were issued; and the foundation of University College, London, extending the benefits of a superior education to a class of men who were incapable of incurring the customary expenses of Oxford or Cambridge, or who were unwilling to subject themselves to the tests or discipline required at those universities. To these may be added as a consequence the University College Hospital. He was also greatly instrumental in the establishment of the Social Science Association; and as its president, even so lately as 1863, in his eighty-fifth year, he delivered a lengthened address at Edinburgh, the scene of his earliest triumphs, which surprised all who heard it by its vigour and variety. His various contributions to the press have been collected in ten octavo volumes; and it is to be hoped that to these may be shortly added, as promised, 'His Life and Times.' He was elected lord rector of the University of Glasgow in 1825, and, retaining his popularity to the last, he was chosen chancellor of the University of Edinburgh in 1860. He purchased an estate at Cannes, in Provence, on which he built a mansion, to which he retired for several weeks of the last years of his life, and where he died on May 7, 1868.

By his wife, Mary Anne, daughter of Thomas Eden, Esq., and niece of Lords Auckland and Henley, the widow of John Spalding, Esq. (whom he married in 1819), he had two daughters, both since deceased, and no son; and his title has descended by the special limitation before mentioned to his brother, William Brougham, now Lord Brougham and Vaux.

BROWNE, ANTHONY, was the son of Wistan Browne, of Abbesroding and Langenhoo in Essex, and Elizabeth, the sister of Sir John Mordaunt, of Turvey in Bedfordshire, serjeant-at-law, who became chancellor of the duchy of Lancaster, and whose son was created Lord Mordaunt. (*Testam. Vetust.* 462.) Anthony was born about 1510, and studied at Oxford, where he did not take a degree, entered the Middle Temple, and became reader there in autumn 1553 and in Lent 1554.

Being a strict Roman Catholic, he made himself active in carrying into effect the new orders of religion promulgated under Queen Mary; and, being then a justice of the peace in his native county, a letter was sent by the council in August 1554 directing him and others to put those in ward who kept themselves from church and were not in other respects conformable. Among the persons brought before him was William Hunter, 'an apprentice of nineteen years,' who, according to the printed relation of his brother Robert, was 'pursued to death by Justice Brown for the gospel's sake.' Robert enlarges on the justice's 'fury' and 'rage,' and seems to lay more blame on him for sending the unfortunate youth to Bishop Bonner than on that brutal prelate for condemning him to be burnt. In the next year Justice Browne and his fellows sent up another prisoner, whom they called 'an arrogant heretic;' and in August 1557 a special letter was written to him by the council, 'geving hym thanks for his diligent proceeding against Trudgeover [whom he had taken and executed in Essex]; willing him to distribute his head and quarters according to his and his colleagues' former determinations.' (*Dr. Maitland on the Reformation*, 427, 468, 514, 559.)

These energetic exertions were not unrequited. He was called to the degree of the coif, and on the very day that he assumed it, October 16, 1555, he was appointed one of the queen's serjeants,[1] and on October 5, 1558, was made chief justice of the Common Pleas. Within six weeks Queen Mary died, and on the day succeeding that event he received a new patent from Elizabeth; but before Hilary Term it was deemed expedient to remove both the Catholic chief justices from their more prominent positions, still, however, retaining their legal services. Chief Justice Browne was accordingly removed into the seat of Mr. Justice Dyer, who was placed at the head of the court. This change having been completed on January 22, 1559, he continued to perform the duties of a puisne judge of the Common Pleas till the day of his death. Anthony Wood states that he was offered the Great Seal when the Lord Keeper Bacon was in temporary disgrace on the suspicion of having assisted John Hales in a pamphlet arguing that, in the event of Queen Elizabeth's death without issue, the crown would devolve on the house of Suffolk; but that Browne refused it, 'for that he was of a different religion from the state.' It was perhaps in connection with this offer that he received the honour of knighthood in 1566.

He died on May 16, 1567, at his estate of Weald Hall, or South Weald, in Essex, which he had purchased from Lord Chancellor Rich. He was buried in the church of that parish, and to his remains were added, within the same year, those of his wife Joan, daughter of William Farington, of Farington in Lancashire, and widow of Charles Booth, Esq. He left no issue.

His devotion to Queen Mary did not prevent him from resisting her encroachments on the rights of his chief justiceship. In the interval between Sir Robert Brooke's death and his own appointment the queen had filled up the vacant place of exigent of London, &c., the presentation to which belonged to his office. As soon as he was installed he at once admitted his nephew Skrogges, whose right was decided by the judges to be good against Coleshill, the queen's nominee. (*Dyer's Reports*, 175.)

Plowden, his contemporary (*Reports*, 356, 376), calls him a judge of profound learning and great eloquence, and gives some eulogistic verses composed on his death. He is said to have supplied Bishop Leslie with the legal arguments for his pamphlet in favour of the succession of Mary, Queen of Scotland, published under the name of Morgan Philipps, and answered by Sir Nicholas Bacon. (*Athen. Oxon.* i. 356, 405, 433; *Morant's Essex*, i. 118.)

BROWNE, HUMPHREY, of Ridley Hall, in Terling, Essex, was the uncle of the foregoing Anthony Browne, being the younger brother of Wistan Browne. Their father was Robert Browne, of Langenhoo in that county, and their mother Mary, daughter and heir of Sir Thomas Charlton. Humphrey was of the Middle Temple, where he was chosen reader in 1516, and again in 1521. He was not called to the degree of the coif till ten years afterwards, nor made a king's serjeant till Easter 1536. On November 20, 1542, he was elevated to the bench as a judge of the Common Pleas, a seat which he retained in four reigns. Although his name appears as a witness to King Edward's deed altering the succession, Queen Mary very properly considered the act as one more of compulsion than of choice, and Queen Elizabeth, on her accession, made no immediate change in the judges, whatever were their religious opinions. The quiet and unostentatious performance of his duties was undistinguished by any remarkable incident. Plowden relates that in a case in Hilary Term 1559 he 'did not argue at all, because he was so old that his senses were decayed and his voice could not be heard;' yet he acted for nearly four years after he had thus lost his judicial powers, the last fine levied before him being dated at the end of November 1562, and his death occurring on the 5th of the next month. (*Dugdale's Orig.* 47, 215; 1 *Plowden*, 190.)

His remains were removed from a house which he had built in Cow Lane, St. Sepulchre's, with great funeral pomp to the church of St. Mary Orgars in Cannon Street, where one of his wives had been buried, and to which parish he bequeathed several houses. (*Machyn's Diary*, 297, 393.)

His first wife was Anne, daughter of Sir Henry Vere, of Great Adlington; and his second wife was Anne, daughter of John, Lord Hussey. (*Morant*, i. 118.)

BROWN, ROBERT, does not appear to have been related to either of the preceding judges, nor has any certain trace been found of the family to which he belonged. All that is known of him is that he was promoted to the bench of the Exchequer as second baron on May 6, 1550, 4 Edward VI., and that he retained his seat during Mary's reign and for the first two months of that of Elizabeth, when he was replaced by George Freville.

BROWNE, SAMUEL, was the son of Nicholas Browne, Esq., of Polebrook in Northamptonshire, by Frances, daughter of Thomas St. John, Esq., of Cayshoe, Bedfordshire, the grandfather of Oliver St. John, the chief justice of the Common Pleas during the Protectorate. Samuel was admitted pensioner of Queen's College, Cambridge, in 1614, and was entered at Lincoln's Inn in 1616, where he was called to the bar in 1623, and elected reader in autumn 1642. He was returned member for the boroughs of Clifton, Dartmouth, and Hardness, in the Long Parliament of November 1640; and in February 1643, no doubt by the influence of his cousin St. John, who was then solicitor-general, he was recommended by the parliament to be a baron of the Exchequer, in the propositions made to the king for peace, which came to nothing. In the following November he and St. John were two of the four members of the House of Commons to whom, with two lords, the new Great Seal was entrusted. (*Parl. Hist.* ii. 606, iii. 70, 182.)

The commoners so appointed still continued to perform their parliamentary functions. Lord Commissioner Browne was most active in the proceedings against Archbishop Laud, summing up the case in the House of Lords and carrying up the ordinance for his attainder passed by the Commons in November 1644. (*State Trials*, iv. 576, 596.) His position did not exempt him from the inconveniences of the civil war. He had to complain to the parliament in December 1644 that his house at Arlesley in Bedfordshire was used for quartering troops, and he procured an order for their removal out of the county. (*Journals*, iii. 734.) After remaining in office for nearly three years, the lords commissioners were removed in October 1646, and the Great Seal transferred to the speakers of the two houses. Resuming then his practice at the bar, where by a vote of the house precedence was given him, he was included in the batch of twenty-two who were made serjeants by the parliament on October 12, 1648, when both he and his cousin were also elevated to the bench, he as judge of the King's Bench, and St. John as chief justice of the Common Pleas. Just previous to this he had been sent as one of the commissioners to treat with the king in the Isle of Wight, and what he witnessed there of his majesty's bearing, and the unseemly return with which it was met by the parliament's subsequent proceedings, tended no doubt to open his eyes to the violent objects of the party to which his cousin St. John was attached. He resolved, therefore, no longer to follow in his footsteps; but when the king, three months later, fell a victim to its machinations, he boldly refused to act as a judge under the usurped government, and, with five of his colleagues, resigned his seat on the bench. (*Whitelocke*, 154, 158, 226, 334, 342, 378.)

This conduct so effectually atoned in the eyes of the royalists for everything that might be deemed objectionable in his former acts, that on the Restoration he was not only immediately reinstated as a serjeant, but within six months was replaced on the bench, being constituted on November 3, 1660, a judge of the Common Pleas, where he retained his seat till his death in Easter Term 1668. (1 *Siderfin*, 3, 4, 365.) He was buried under a monument still existing in the church of Arlesley.

He married Elizabeth, daughter of John Meade, Esq., of Nortofts, Finchingfield, Essex.

BRUCE, EDWARD (LORD KINLOSS). The third son of Robert de Brus, the first chief justice of the Court of King's Bench as newly constituted under Henry III., and one of the competitors for the crown of Scotland in the following reign, was John de Brus, to whose grandson his cousin King David II. granted in 1359 the castle and manor of Clackmannan, with various other manors in the county of that name. In the middle of the sixteenth century Sir Edward Bruce, the second son of one of the lineal holders of this property, acquired the estate of Blair Hall, and by his marriage with Alison, daughter of William Reid, of Aikenhead in the same county, and sister of Robert Reid, Bishop of Orkney, had three sons, the second of whom, Edward, became master of the Rolls.

He was born about 1548, and was, according to the most probable accounts, brought up to the law, and practised at the Scottish bar. In 1597 he was preferred to be one of the senators of the College of Justice, and in 1600 was selected by King James as his ambassador to the English court, for the professed purpose of congratulating the queen on her escape from the Earl of Essex's insurrection, but with the secret mission to forward James's views on the succession, and to sound the disposition of the people in regard to it. He effected this object with so much judgment and address that he obtained the private assurance of most of the leading men of the country that they would support James's pretensions; and he opened a secret correspondence with Sir Robert Cecil (afterwards published by Lord Hailes), which insured the earliest communication of every detail that would aid the conjuncture. (*Robertson*, iii. 136; *Burnet*, i. 8.) Even before his royal master had reaped the fruits of his diplomacy he received, in reward for his services, a grant of the dissolved abbey of Kinloss in the shire of Elgin, and was created Lord Bruce of Kinloss by patent dated February 22, 1603.

On Queen Elizabeth's death, Lord Bruce of course accompanied his sovereign to witness that peaceful accession to the English throne which he had been so instrumental in securing. He was not long in being placed in a post which had some slight relation to his early studies, receiving in less than three weeks after King James's arrival in England the appointment of master of the Rolls on May 18, 1603.

Lord Bruce was at the same time admitted into the king's new council, and in the first parliament obtained an act of naturalisation for himself and his family. King James showed his continued favour to him, by making him large grants of money and lands, and by promoting the marriage of his daughter Christian with William, afterwards second Earl of Devonshire, giving her away with his own hand, and making up her fortune to 10,000*l*. In July 1604 the king also created him an English peer by his former title. He sat at the Rolls for nearly seven years, and his remains are deposited close to his court in the chapel there, where his effigy in his official dress is represented on a monument, the inscription on which states that he died on January 14, 1610–11, and concludes with these two lines:—

Conjuge, prole, nuro, genero, spe, reque beatus ;
Vivere nos docuit, nunc docet, ecce, mori.

By his wife, Magdalen, daughter of Alexander Clerk, of Balbirnie in Fife, Esq., he had, besides the daughter already mentioned, two sons, who successively possessed the title. Edward, the elder, was killed in a duel with Sir Edward Sackville, afterwards Duke of Dorset. Thomas, the younger, was created Earl of Elgin in Scotland in 1633, and Lord Bruce of Whorlton in England in 1641. To the last title his son received the addition of the earldom of Aylesbury in 1664. This title, though it failed in 1747, was re-granted to the last earl's nephew in 1776, to which a marquisate was added in 1821. The title of Earl of Elgin devolved, according to the Scotch patent, on the heir male, who was the Earl of Kincardine, a descendant from Sir George Bruce of Carnock, younger brother of Edward, the master of the Rolls, and the two titles of Elgin and Kincardine are now enjoyed by the present peer, who has also an English barony of the former name, granted in 1849.

BRUCE, JAMES LEWIS KNIGHT, descended from an old Shropshire family long settled near Ludlow. His father, John Knight, Esq., of Llanblethian in Glamorganshire, and Fairlinch in Devonshire, by his wife Margaret, the only married child of William Bruce, Esq., of the former place, a descendant from a junior branch of the ancient house of Bruce of Kennet, and granddaughter (by her mother) of Gabriel Lewis, Esq., of Lanishen in Glamorganshire, had a large family, of whom the lord justice was the youngest son. He was born at Barnstaple in 1791, and bore his father's name for the first forty-six years of his life; but in 1837 he added by licence that of his mother, upon the occasion of his eldest brother, John Bruce Bruce, Esq., assuming the surname of Pryce on succeeding to an estate.

He finished his education at Exeter College, Oxford, and, entering at Lincoln's Inn in 1812, he was called to the bar in 1817. In the first instance he attended the Welsh Circuit, where he is said to have had great success in handling the native juries. But in the Court of Chancery, to which he ultimately attached himself, his talents and industry were soon rewarded by so large a business that in 1829 he received a silk gown. From that time till he was raised to the bench he enjoyed the most extensive practice, through the labours of which he fought with unflinching energy and imperturbable good humour.

In 1831 he was elected member for Bishop's Castle, shortly before its disfranchisement by the Reform Act. In parliament he was a supporter of conservative principles. In 1834 the University of Oxford honoured him with the degree of D.C.L.

When the legislature decided that two additional judges were necessary for the assistance of the lord chancellor, Mr. Knight-Bruce, with the approbation of the whole bar, was selected for the first place. He became vice-chancellor on October 28, 1841, and was thereupon knighted, and soon afterwards was called to the privy council. Indefatigable in the performance of the duties that devolved upon him, no amount of labour seemed to distress or disconcert him. Before the long vacation of 1850, by the illness of the two other vice-chancellors, the whole business of the three courts at the most pressing period of the year having been thrown on his hands, he despatched it with so much discrimination, ability, and good temper that a public expression of respectful admiration was elicited from the whole bar, in an address from the attorney-general.

It seemed naturally to follow, when the Court of Appeal in Chancery was organised in October 1851, that Sir James should at once be selected for the senior lord justice; a position which he held for above fifteen years, when, suffering under a severe illness, he sent in his resignation in October 1866, which within a fortnight was followed by his death on November 7. The loss of few men on the judicial seat has been more regretted than that of Lord Justice Knight-Bruce, whose judgments, always well weighed and profound, were frequently enlivened with quiet humour and chastened wit.

He married Eliza, the only daughter of Thomas Newte, Esq., of Duvale in Devonshire, by whom he had several children.

BRUDENELL, ROBERT, lineal descendant of an ancient family established at Dodington in Oxfordshire as early as the reign of Henry III., and of which Edmund Brudenell, attorney-general to Richard II., was a member, was born in the year 1461. He was the second son of Edmund Brudenell, Esq., of Agmondesham, Buckinghamshire, where he had large possessions, by his second wife Philippa, daughter of Philip Englefield, Esq., of Finchingfield in Essex. After spending some time at the University of Cambridge, he studied the law at an inn of court which is not recorded; but his name occurs as an advocate in the Year Books in Hilary Term 1490, and he was called to the degree of the coif in Michaelmas Term 1504, receiving the appointment of king's serjeant in 1505. In eighteen months he was raised to a judicial seat in the King's Bench, on April 28, 1507, two years before the death of King Henry VII.

On the accession of Henry VIII. he was removed into the Court of Common Pleas, but afterwards returned to the King's Bench, where he sat as one of the puisne judges. At the end of twelve years he was appointed chief justice of the Common Pleas on April 13, 1521, and presided there till his death on January 30, 1531. He was buried in the church of Dean in Northamptonshire, under a beautiful alabaster monument, on which his effigy was placed between those of his two wives. The first of these was Margaret, the widow of William Wivil, Esq., of Stanton in Leicestershire, and daughter and co-heir of Thomas Entwissell, Esq., of Stanton-Wivil. The second was Philippa Power, of Beckampton. By the latter he had no issue; but by the former he had two sons—Thomas and Anthony. The descendants of the elder of these were elevated in the peerage to the highest from the lowest rank. Among those which have become extinct are the Duke of Montagu, Marquis of Monthermer, Earl of Cardigan, Baron Montagu of Boughton, and Baron Montagu of Dean; and the only one which still remains in the House of Peers is the Marquis of Aylesbury.

BRUNDISH, ROBERT, probably derived his name from a parish in Suffolk, which is also frequently called Burnedish. A John de Burndish acquired the manor of Morton, near Ongar in Essex, in the reign of Edward I. His son Nicholas was probably Robert's father or brother. Of Robert there is no other mention than that he was constituted a judge of the King's Bench on April 4, 1338, 12 Edward III. (*Abb. Rot. Orig.* i. 141, ii. 98, 129; *Cal. Inquis.* p. m. ii. 70, 159, 184.)

BRUS, PETER DE, or BRUIS, was descended from Robert de Brus, a valiant

Norman knight, who accompanied William the Conqueror on his invasion of England, and whose prowess was rewarded with no less than ninety-four lordships in Yorkshire, of which Skelton was his principal seat. The lordship of Annandale was afterwards added to the family by the marriage of Robert's son Robert to the heiress of that large property, which on his death devolved on William, the eldest son of that marriage, from whom descended Robert de Brus, or Briwes, afterwards noticed; while the English estates became the inheritance of Adam, the second Robert's eldest son by a first marriage. After two Adams, there were four Peters in succession, of whom the subject of the present notice is the third. His father was a strong adherent to Prince Louis of France when he was introduced by the barons in rebellion against King John, and gave him powerful aid in Yorkshire. His mother was Helewise, one of the sisters and coheirs of William de Lancaster, of Kendal, a justice itinerant. He did homage for his father's estates in February 1222, 6 Henry III., and married Hillaria, the eldest daughter of Peter de Mauley.

He was one of the justices itinerant appointed for the county of Northumberland on June 30, 1226, 10 Henry III., after which no further mention is made of him till November 15, 1240, 25 Henry III., when his son, the under-mentioned Peter, fined two hundred marks on having livery of the lands of which his father was seised on the day when he commenced his journey to the Holy Land, where, probably, he died. (*Rot. Claus.* ii. 151; *Excerpt. e Rot. Fin.* i. 80, 332.)

BRUS, PETER DE, the son of the preceding Peter, by Hillaria his wife, was joined in the commission issued to the justices itinerant for Yorkshire in 52 Henry III., 1268. In the next year he was appointed constable of the castle of Scarborough, and died on September 18, 1272. He left no issue, so that his four sisters divided his property.

BRUS, ROBERT DE, was the fifth lord of Annandale, to which he succeeded in 29 Henry III., 1245, on the death of his father, Robert the Noble, who, by his marriage with Isabel, the second daughter of Prince David, Earl of Huntingdon and Chester, grandson of David I., King of Scotland, became one of the greatest subjects in Europe. From June till October 1250 there are entries of payments made for assizes to be taken before him, and his name also appears upon fines, showing that he acted as a justicier at that time. There is then an interval of seven years; but from 1257 to 1263 he acted in the same manner, and on the circuits of the two last years he was placed at the head of the commissions.

In 1263, during the contest between the king and the barons, he stood firm to his royal master, with whom he was taken prisoner at the battle of Lewes, on May 14, 1264. (*Rapin*, iii. 154.)

In October 1266 the payments for assizes before him are resumed, and on March 8, 1268, he was appointed 'capitalis justiciarius ad placita coram rege tenenda,' being the first who was distinctly constituted chief justice of the King's Bench. He had a salary of one hundred marks assigned to him.

King Henry died in the following November, but Robert de Brus does not appear to have been replaced on the judicial bench on the accession of Edward I. Nothing is related of his career during the eighteen years which intervened before he became a competitor for the crown of Scotland on the death of Queen Margaret in 1290. The several claimants who then came forward were eventually reduced to two—John Balliol, the representative of the eldest daughter of David, Earl of Huntingdon; and Robert de Brus, the descendant of the second, but one degree nearer the common stock. The decision was referred to King Edward, who, in 1292, determined in favour of Balliol, who was accordingly declared king. Robert de Brus, however, would never acknowledge his title; but retiring in disgust, he died at his castle of Lochmaben in 1295, and was buried at the monastery of Gisburne in Cleveland, which had been founded by his ancestor, the first Robert.

By his wife Isabel, the daughter of Gilbert de Clare, Earl of Gloucester, he had three sons—Robert, Bernard, and John. Robert's son, Robert, eventually succeeded in securing the Scottish crown, by the signal victory obtained at Bannockburn over the forces of Edward II., on June 24, 1314.

The third son, John, was the progenitor of a long line of eminent knights, from whom descended the Earls of Elgin and Cardigan and the Marquis of Aylesbury.

BRYAN, THOMAS, studied the law in Gray's Inn, and is mentioned in the Year Books as an advocate so early as Hilary, 34 Henry VI., 1456. His call to the degree of the coif was in Michaelmas 1463; and his practice seems to have been considerable, both during the next seven years of Edward's reign and the short restoration of Henry VI. that followed. He was raised to the head of the Common Pleas on May 29, 1471, a few weeks after Edward's return. In 1475 he received the honour of knighthood on the same day as the Prince of Wales (*Holinshed*, iii. 344), and he continued to perform the duties of his office for the remainder of the reign.

There is evidence of his not being removed under Edward V. and Richard III.; and from the latter he received a grant, in tail male, of the manors of Wyllesford near

Uphaven in Wiltshire, of Over in Gloucestershire, and of Calverton in Buckinghamshire (9 *Report, Pub. Rec., App.* ii. 12, 122), properties forfeited to the king by persons attainted. These grants are stated to be for unnamed services against the rebels; but that they were judicial, and not political, may be presumed from his immediately receiving a new patent as chief justice on Henry VII.'s accession, and from his being appointed one of the commissioners to execute the office of steward at that king's coronation. (*Rymer*, xii. 277.)

He presided in his court till his death, about October 1500. His will was proved on December 11 in that year; and, inasmuch as both he and his son Thomas desired to be buried in the religious house of Ashruge, and the son of the latter was buried there, it may be presumed that he was seated in Buckinghamshire. The name of his wife does not appear; but he left a son named Thomas, whose son Francis was the intimate friend of Sir Thomas Wyatt, and was himself a scholar and a poet. His poetical powers are thus celebrated by Drayton in the 'Heroical Epistles':—

And sweet-tongu'd Bryan, whom the muses kept,
And in his cradle rock'd him while he slept.

BUBBEWITH, NICHOLAS (BISHOP OF BATH AND WELLS), was born at Menethorpe in Yorkshire, and was brought up in the neighbouring township of Bubbewith, from whence he acquired his name. The earliest notice of him is as a clerk or master in Chancery receiving petitions in parliament in 1397, 21 Richard II. (*Rot. Parl.* iii. 348.) He had been admitted prebendary of Hayes in the church of Exeter in 1396, and was collated to the archdeaconry of Dorset in 1400, to which was added in the following year that of Richmond, which he held, however, for only two days. (*Le Neve*, 281, 325.)

He succeeded Thomas de Stanley as master of the Rolls on September 24, 1402, but continued in that office less than two years and a half, resigning it on March 2, 1405.

It was not long before he was raised to the episcopal bench; and he affords a curious instance of one individual presiding over three sees in less than two years. He was elected Bishop of London on May 13, 1406; was translated to Salisbury on August 14, 1407, and to Bath and Wells on April 1, 1408. He was raised, during these changes, to the office of treasurer, which he held for about two years.

He presided over the diocese of Bath and Wells more than sixteen years; and his character for wisdom was so well established that he was one of the prelates sent to Rome in 1414 to assist the cardinals in deciding between the three candidates then contending for the papal chair, when the choice fell upon Martin V. While on that mission he joined in inducing Giovanni di Serravalli, Bishop of Fermo, to undertake the translation of Dante's 'Commedia.' (*Tiraboschi, Poes. Ital.* ii. 46.)

He is described as a man discreet, provident, and circumspect, both in temporal and spiritual affairs; and his charity and munificence were evidenced both in his life and the disposition of his will. He died on October 27, 1424, and was buried in his chapel at Wells. (*Godwin*, 379; *Rymer*, viii. 451, 496, 512; *Notes and Queries*, 3rd S. iii. 406).

BUKYNGHAM, JOHN DE, or BOKYNGHAM (BISHOP OF LINCOLN), was educated at Oxford, where he took the degree of Doctor in Divinity. He was collated archdeacon of Northampton in 1350. In 1351, 24 Edward III., he was appointed keeper of the king's great wardrobe. (*Abb. Rot. Orig.* ii. 211.) In 1357 he was a baron of the Exchequer, but it may be presumed that he resigned his seat on that bench on his becoming keeper of the privy seal two years afterwards, an office which he retained till the middle of the thirty-seventh year. In 1360 Robert de Herle and he were constituted the king's lieutenants and captains of the duchy of Brittany.

In the meantime he had been advanced successively to the deanery of Lichfield, about 1361, and to the bishopric of Lincoln on April 5, 1363. After ruling that diocese for thirty-four years, Pope Boniface IX., in revenge for certain contests between them, thought proper to remove him from it in 1397, offering him the see of Lichfield instead. The offended prelate, however, refused to accept what he considered as a degradation, but chose rather to retire to the cloisters of Canterbury, where in less than six months he died on March 10, 1398. (*Le Neve; Godwin*, 295.) His works are mentioned by Bale and Pits, and prove him to have been an able disputant and profound scholar.

BULLER, FRANCIS, is equally celebrated among both females and males, but not with equal admiration. While he is considered by the latter as one of the most learned of lawyers, he is stigmatised by the former as one of the most cruel of judges, since to him is attributed the obnoxious and ungentlemanly dictum that a husband may beat his wife, so that the stick with which he administers the castigation is not thicker than his thumb. It may perhaps restore him to the ladies' good graces to be told that, though the story was generally believed, and even made the subject of caricature, yet, after a searching investigation by the most able critics and antiquaries, no substantial evidence has been found that he ever expressed so ungallant an opinion.

Francis Buller was of an ancient and renowned Cornish family, the members of which were famous in the senate, in the Church, and in many distinguished posts in the service of the state. One of his uncles was father of Admiral Sir Edward Buller, of Trenant Park, who was honoured with a baronetcy, which expired in 1824. Another uncle became Bishop of Exeter; and the judge himself had legal blood in his veins, some of his ancestors being recorders of boroughs, and another the daughter of Chief Justice Pollexfen. His mother also was Lady Jane Bathurst, the sister of Lord Chancellor Bathurst, the second wife of his father, James Buller, Esq., of Shillingham, M.P. for Cornwall from 1747 till his death in 1765. Francis was born on March 17, 1746, and was entered at the Inner Temple on February 3, 1763. He became a pupil of Mr. (afterwards Judge) Ashhurst, and in 1765 felt competent to set up for himself. For seven years he was in full practice as a special pleader, and his reputation in that character was greatly enhanced by the publication in 1767 of a work (said to be founded on collections made by his uncle, Mr. Justice Bathurst) entitled 'An Introduction to the Law relative to Trials at Nisi Prius,' which was so much esteemed that it went through six editions before his death.

He was called to the bar in Easter Term 1772, and immediately took a high rank among his colleagues. His assistance and advice were in perpetual requisition, and there was scarcely any case of importance in which he was not engaged. The Reports of Henry Cowper and the State Trials amply show, not only the extent of his practice, but the excellence of his advocacy. Lord Mansfield soon recognised his genius and promoted his advancement, which was furthered by his uncle, Lord Chancellor Bathurst. In 1777 he was made a king's counsel and second judge on the Chester Circuit; and on May 6, 1778, he was appointed a judge of the King's Bench, being then only thirty-two years of age. Lord Mansfield's expectations were fully realised by the effectual assistance he received during the ten years he remained chief justice, in the last two of which, when his health began to decline, he found a most efficient and active substitute in Mr. Justice Buller, who not only conducted for him the sittings at Nisi Prius, but in the absence of the chief took the lead in Banco, though Judge Ashhurst was his senior. In those two years, in fact, he was little less than chief justice, and in the hope of inducing the minister to make him really so, it is understood that Lord Mansfield delayed his own resignation. Mr. Pitt, however, from political and other motives would not consent, but appointed Lord Kenyon as Lord Mansfield's successor, giving Mr. Justice Buller the very inadequate compensation of a baronetcy in January 1790. Under Lord Kenyon he remained for six years, and in Easter 1794 he removed into the Common Pleas, where he sat for six years more. Being then prostrated by physical infirmity, he arranged with the lord chancellor for the resignation of his seat; but on June 5, 1800, the very day after that arrangement, and before it could be effected, he died at his house in Bedford Square, at the age of fifty-four, and was buried in St. Andrew's, Holborn.

Thus terminated, at an age which had been the commencement of many a judicial life, the career of a judge who had sat on the bench with distinguished merit no less than twenty-two years. No one ever denied his extraordinary legal capacity, though the correctness of some of his decisions might be disputed. Not only was he the recognised substitute of his celebrated chief in his own court, but he won the admiration of that great grudger of praise, Lord Thurlow, who had so great a dependence on him that he frequently, when obliged or inclined to be absent, appointed him to preside in his place in the Court of Chancery, where his decrees excited the rough eulogy of his principal. Yet with all his 'industry, sagacity, quickness, and intelligence,' and notwithstanding his urbanity to the bar, he was not a popular judge. He was considered arrogant in his assumption of superiority, hasty in his decisions and decrees, and, which pressed harder upon him in public estimation, prejudiced, severe, and even cruel in criminal trials. But his character has outlived all detraction, and at the present day, due allowance being made for occasional mistakes and shortcomings, there are very few deceased judges whose decisions, whose opinions, or whose doubts are received with more respect. Even in his own day his penetration and impartiality were so far recognised that it was said of him that, though no person if guilty would choose to be tried by him, all persons if innocent would prefer him for their judge. Among the young and diffident members of the bar whom he encouraged and befriended were the eminent names of Fearne and Hargrave, and the future chief justices, Gibbs, Law, and Abbott, the latter of whom, when tutor to his son, he recommended to adopt the law. He married, at the early age of seventeen, Susannah, the only daughter of Francis Yarde, Esq., and by her had an only son, who, in compliance with the will of his mother's brother, assumed the additional surname of Yarde, and whose son, the third baronet, was raised to the peerage in 1858, by the title of Baron Churston in the county of Devon.

BURGH, HUBERT DE (EARL OF KENT). This distinguished man traced his ancestry as high as the Emperor Charlemagne, from whose fifth son, Charles, Duke of Ingeheim, descended Harluin de Burgh, who married Herleva or Arlotta, the mother of William the Conqueror, and had by her two sons, both to be hereafter noticed—viz., Odo, Bishop of Bayeux; and Robert, Earl of Moreton. Robert's son, William, who rebelled against Henry I., and, being defeated, was not only deprived of his eyes, but imprisoned for life, is stated to have left two sons, one of whom was John de Burgh, the father (or more probably the grandfather) of Hubert. (*Biog. Universelle.*)

From an early period of his life Hubert was in the service of Richard I., and in the first year of King John's reign he was sufficiently prominent at court to be one of the pledges on his sovereign's part that the convention with Reginald, Earl of Bologne, should be faithfully kept, and to be a witness to a royal charter. In the same year he was raised to the office of king's chamberlain, and is so designated, for the first time, in a charter dated April 28, 1200, confirming a convention made between him and William de Vernon, Earl of Devon, on his marriage with Johanna, the earl's younger daughter, by which the Isle of Wight and Christchurch were assigned as her portion. (*Rot. Chart.* 30, 36, 52.)

From this period he advanced rapidly in the royal favour. The castles of Dover and Windsor were committed to his charge, he was appointed sheriff of Dorset and Somerset, and he was entrusted with the custody of the county and castle of Hereford and the office of Warden of the Marches, for the defence of which the king gave him a hundred knights. In 3 John the sheriffalties of Cornwall and Berkshire were added to his employments; and he obtained a licence to fortify his castle of Dunestore in Somersetshire. (*Rot. Chart.* 100; *Rapin*, ii. 423; *Rot. Liberat.* 10; *Rot. Pat.* 6, 11.)

On the defeat of Arthur, Earl of Brittany, in August 1202, that prince was sent to Falaise under the charge, according to some relations (*Holinshed*, ii. 285), of Hubert de Burgh, whose refusal to obey the king's cruel behest against his royal prisoner is the subject of one of the most beautiful of Shakspeare's scenes. This disobedience and the concealment with which it was covered seem to have been forgiven when the murmurs of the barons on Arthur's supposed death were removed by Hubert's announcement that the prince was still alive. On King John's being summoned, after the completion of the real tragedy, to answer the charge before Philip of France and his peers, Hubert was sent with Eustace, Bishop of Ely, to that court, to demand a safe-conduct for his going and returning, the former of which was readily promised, but the latter, they were answered, would depend on the judgment to be pronounced. John, not venturing to expose himself to such a risk, was condemned for his non-appearance to the forfeiture of his French dominions. (*Rapin*, ii. 429.)

In 1214 he is mentioned as seneschal, and also as mayor of Niort, and shortly afterwards as seneschal of Poictou, in which character, after the battle at Bovines, he arranged a truce between the Kings of England and France for five years. (*Wendover*, iii. 193, 302.)

Having, on the death of his first wife, married Beatrice, the daughter of William de Warenne, and widow of Dodo Bardolf, in 1209, her death occurred before December 18, 1214; for on that day the sheriff of Lincoln was commanded to give Hubert's steward seisin of the land of Finigham, which was Beatrice's dower. (*Rot. Claus.* i. 181.)

As seneschal of Poictou, he was in attendance at Runnymede on July 15, 1215, 17 John, when Magna Charta was granted; but a few days afterwards he was raised to the high office of chief justiciary of England. To this office were added many grants, and the custody, among others, of Dover Castle.

He was in charge of this important fortress in May 1216, when, at the instigation of the barons, England was invaded by Prince Louis of France, who in the next month began to besiege it. Hubert by his skill and courage successfully resisted the enemy's attacks until the death of King John, when Louis, finding his warlike efforts unavailing, endeavoured to tempt him to deliver up the castle by promises of large rewards. The loyal governor's honour, however, being as impenetrable as his walls, the foiled prince raised the siege and hastened from the scene. (*Wendover*, iii. 368, 380, iv. 4.)

He next defeated the French armament sent under the command of Eustace le Moyne to aid Prince Louis, the consequence of which victory was the retirement of the French prince and the comparative restoration of peace to the kingdom, under the prudent management of William Mareschall, Earl of Pembroke, the young king's governor. (*Lingard*, iii. 79.)

That Hubert remained in the office of chief justiciary on the accession of the new king is proved by various mandates addressed to him under that character in 1216 and for many years after that date. A salary of 300*l*. per annum was assigned for his support in the office, and 1000*l*. for the custody of Dover Castle. (*Devon's Issue Roll*, 2.)

On the death of the earl marshal in 1219 the regency was conferred on Hubert, while the king's person was placed under the care of his rival, Peter de Rupibus, Bishop of Winchester. His government was marked by wisdom and firmness, not unaccompanied, however, with some degree of severity. He repressed a dangerous insurrection in London in 1222, and caused Constantine, the ringleader, to be executed; he compelled the barons to surrender their castles into the king's hands, and in 1224 he punished Faukes de Breaute, a ferocious magnate raised by the late king, for imprisoning Henry de Braybroc, one of the judges, by destroying his castle of Bedford, hanging those who had defended it, and banishing the principal offender.'

In 1222 Hubert's interest at court had been still further strengthened by his marriage with Margaret, the eldest sister of Alexander, King of Scotland, thus becoming allied to his sovereign, whose sister, the princess Johanna, had been recently united to the Scottish king.

When the king attained his majority he continued Hubert as his minister, and raised him, in 1227, to the earldom of Kent, a title which his ancestor, William, Earl of Moreton, had forfeited his freedom and his life in his endeavours to recover. In the following year his office of chief justiciary was confirmed to him for life; and the numerous grants with which he was enriched, and responsible offices entrusted to him about the same time, are proofs at once of the influence he possessed over the king's mind, and the manner in which he exercised it to his own aggrandisement.

His uncontrolled authority could not fail to excite some jealousy among the barons, nor could his enemies be slow to find instances of rapacity in the rewards which he accumulated. But the success of his ministry, and the favour of his sovereign silenced all loud complaints. The feeling of the time may, however, be judged from the derisive title of 'Hubert's Folly,' which was given to a castle, commenced but not completed by him, at Cridia, to overawe the Welsh. (*Wendover*, iv. 173.) His career was nearly arrested in September 1229 by the irritable temper of the king, who, having collected a vast army at Portsmouth with the object of making an attempt to recover his French dominions, found such scanty naval preparations to transport his armament that in his passionate disappointment he called Hubert an old traitor, charged him with receiving a bribe from France, and would have instantly despatched him with his own hand had he not been restrained by the Earl of Chester. The royal indignation did not long continue, and Hubert was restored for a time to his former power. Even in 1231 he obtained the privilege of appointing a substitute as Justiciary of England in case of illness or absence, and the grant of the office of chief justiciary of Ireland for life.

But the seed of suspicion had been sown, and there were many to encourage its growth. He was charged with conniving at certain depredations which had been made against the Italian clergy, under Robert de Tuinge; and the frequent disturbances on the Welsh frontier were attributed to his incapacity. The restoration of his ancient rival, Peter de Rupibus, Bishop of Winchester, to favour seemed to foretell the coming storm, and that prelate was not backward in insinuations which he knew would hasten it. He represented that the poverty of the treasury was occasioned by the rapacity of some, and the maladministration of others, of its officers, and used his interest to procure the dismissal of several functionaries who owed their places to the justiciary's protection.

Hubert's fall was not long delayed. He was removed from his office on July 29, 1232, 16 Henry III., and Stephen de Segrave was nominated in his stead. He was called upon to account, not only for the disposition of all the treasure he had received, but for the exercise of all the privileges entrusted to him, both in the reign of John and of the present king; and various criminal charges were brought against him by those who rejoiced in his disgrace.

So inveterate was the king against his former favourite that Hubert did not dare to appear at the time appointed, but took sanctuary on two occasions, the sanctity of the latter of which was harshly violated, and he was dragged to the Tower.

His imprisonment there did not last long, for the king, under the Bishop of London's threat of excommunication for violating the sanctity of the church, was compelled to replace his captive in the asylum he had chosen. The church was then encircled and besieged, so that, being deprived of food and the means of escape, Hubert was at last obliged to surrender himself and return to his prison in the Tower. The exertions of his friend Henry, Archbishop of Dublin, could only obtain authority to offer him the choice of abjuring the realm, or perpetual imprisonment, or confessing himself a traitor and putting himself at the king's mercy. He at once rejected all these conditions, but replied that, though he had done nothing deserving his present treatment, he would, for the satisfaction of the king, retire from the kingdom, although he would not abjure it.

The king being somewhat pacified by his submission, and by the remembrance of his former services to his father and himself, consented that he should retain his patrimonial inheritance and the lands he held of mesne lords, forfeiting those that he held in chief from the king, and that he should be kept in safe custody in the castle of Devizes under the charge of four earls. Thither he was accordingly transferred; but in the following year, hearing that his old enemy was about to obtain the custody of his person, he dropped from the wall into the moat, and took refuge in the church of St. John at Devizes. Here he was again violently dragged from the altar, but, the bishops interfering, was obliged to be restored to his sanctuary. On this, however, a precept, dated October 15, 1233, was issued 'to the good men of Wilts,' commanding them, if Hubert de Burgh would not give his abjuration of the realm to Ralph de Bray and Ralph de Norwich, justices whom the king had sent there, or submit himself to be judged by them, to surround the church and the cemetery thereof as they should be instructed. (*New Fœdera*, i. 211.)

He was, a few days afterwards, rescued from his intended starvation by a body of armed men, who, overpowering his guards, led him from the church, and conveyed him to the Earl of Pembroke, then in arms against the king in Wales. His outlawry immediately followed.

The disgrace of Peter de Rupibus occurred in April 1234, and was soon after followed by the restoration of peace between the king and the barons, with the restitution of their forfeited lands. In this reconciliation Hubert participated, but at the same time surrendered his title to the office of chief justiciary. (*Wendover*, iv. 204-310.)

Even after all these trials, his loyalty to the king was conspicuous. In the confederacy of the barons headed by Richard, the king's brother, in 1238, he alone remained faithful to his allegiance. But with a monarch so weak and fickle, so avaricious and extravagant, it was impossible to remain long in peace. In 22 Henry III. the king took offence at the marriage of Hubert's daughter Margaret with Richard, Earl of Gloucester; and, though it was proved that Hubert had no knowledge of the affair, the royal indignation could only be appeased by a considerable fine. In the following year, upon some frivolous pretence, a new quarrel was fixed upon him, and, many of the old charges against him having been revived, a day was appointed for the trial. His answers to all the eight articles alleged against him were full and satisfactory, but he felt compelled, in order to avoid an unjust sentence, to make a peace-offering to the king of four of his castles. (*State Trials*, i. 13.)

The few years that he lived afterwards he was suffered to pass in quiet, and his eventful life was closed on May 12, 1243, 27 Henry III., at Banstead in Surrey. He was buried within the church of the Friars Preachers, or Black Friars, in Holborn, to which he had been a large benefactor. His pious donations were too numerous to be recorded here, but among them may be mentioned his grant to that fraternity of his palace at Westminster, which was afterwards purchased by the Archbishop of York, and is now known by the name of Whitehall; and his foundation of the Hospital of Our Lady, and the church of the Maison Dieu, at Dover.

Whatever failings marked the character of Hubert, it cannot be doubted that he was a faithful servant and a wise counsellor to the monarchs whom he served. The distractions of the kingdom after he had ceased to be Henry's minister speak loudly of his power of guiding and controlling the passions of a foolish and capricious prince.

He left two sons and two daughters, but of which of his wives they were the issue is a debateable question.

The eldest son, John, did homage for his father's lands, but never bore the title of Earl of Kent. His branch of the family failed in 1279, by the death of John's son John, without male issue.

Hubert's second son was named Hubert, from whom descended Sir Thomas de Burgh, who in 1487 was created a peer, as Baron Borough of Gainsborough, a title which in 1598 fell into abeyance among the four sisters of Robert, the sixth baron. (*Nicolas's Synopsis.*)

One of his daughters, Margaret, was certainly by the Princess Margaret, as she is so described in a charter dated April 14, 1227. Her clandestine marriage with Richard de Clare, Earl of Gloucester, in 1237, already alluded to, was quickly followed by her death, as the earl took another wife in the following year. (*Archæol. Inst. at York*, 1816; *Holy Trinity*, 129.)

BURGH, HUGH DE. When John de Sandale, the chancellor, went from York to London on August 26, 1316, 10 Edward II., he, by the king's directions, left the Great Seal in the custody of William de Ayremynne, the keeper of the Rolls, under the seals of Robert de Bardelby and Hugh de Burgh, clerks of the Chancery. Hugh de Burgh, clericus, was paymaster of the forces raised in Cumberland and Westmoreland in 27 and 31 Edward I.; and was one of the procurators of the Bishop of Carlisle in the parliament of 16 Edward II., and for the abbot of St. Mary's, York, in that of the following year. (*Parl. Writs*, i. 506, ii. p. ii. 615.) He held the living of Patrick Brompton in Yorkshire, and died in 2 Edward III. (*Cal. Inquis.* p. m. ii. 21.)

BURGH, WILLIAM, was apparently of a Norfolk family, although he had property in the counties of Leicester, Rutland, and Lincoln. His first appearance as an advocate in the Year Books was in 43 Edward III., 1369; and he is mentioned as one of the king's serjeants in 3 Richard II., 1379 (*Rot. Parl.* iii. 79), receiving in the same year the appointment of seneschal of the domain of Okeham 'ad placitum regis.' (*Cal. Rot. Parl.* 203, 208, 231.) In Trinity 1383, 7 Richard II., we find him acting as a judge of the Common Pleas, to which he had probably been only just appointed, as in the following Christmas he was knighted at Eltham, having previously received the materials for his robes as a banneret. (*Dugdale's Orig.* 46, 103.)

He was one of the judges who, in August 1387, were induced, or, as he pleaded, compelled, to sign the opinions stigmatising as treason the ordinance of the previous parliament, appointing commissioners for the government of the kingdom; and, being impeached in consequence, was condemned with his colleagues to die. His sentence, like theirs, was commuted to banishment for life; and the city of Dublin, with two miles round it, was named as the place of his exile, with an allowance of 40 marks per annum to live on. His expatriation lasted till 1397, when he had liberty to return. The reversal of the original proceedings against him and the others, which passed in the next year, was in its turn annulled by the first parliament of Henry IV., two years afterwards. That king, however, in the fourth year of his reign, restored him wholly to the property which he had forfeited. (*Rot. Pat.* iii. 253-491; *Cal. Inquis.* p. m. iii. 107.)

BURGHERSH, HENRY DE (BISHOP OF LINCOLN). The family of Burghersh derived its name from a manor so called in the county of Sussex. Its possessor in the reign of Edward I. was Robert de Burghersh, who was constable of Dover Castle, and warden of the Cinque Ports. He died in 1306, and Henry, born about 1290, is described in the statutes of Oriel College, Oxford, as the son of Robert de Burghasse, knight, and Matilda, his wife.

He owed to his connection with Bartholomew de Badlesmere, of Ledes Castle, Kent, his uncle, that favour which produced the king's intercession with the pope to raise him to the vacant see of Lincoln. In one of the royal letters he is called canon of York. (*Parl. Writs*, ii. p. i. 405-418.) The necessary bull having been procured, he was consecrated bishop on July 20, 1320, 14 Edward II. In the next year his brother and his uncle were both in arms on the side of the Earl of Lancaster; and it is evident that he was suspected of adhering to the same party, as there is a memorandum on the Roll (*Ibid.* 550) that he is *not* to be requested to raise men-at-arms to march against the rebels and adherents of the earl. The strong terms of vituperation which the king uses in his letter to the pope on that occasion, praying for the bishop's expulsion, form a curious contrast with the laudatory expressions in his five letters of recommendation two years before. (*New Fœdera*, i. 464.) The temporalities of his bishopric were, however, seized into the king's hands; but were restored by the first parliament of Edward III. (*Ibid.* 697.)

Soon after the accession of Edward III. he was placed in the office of treasurer, which he filled till, in the next year, on May 12, 1328, he was appointed chancellor. In 1329 he accompanied the king to France, to do homage to King Philip for the lands held of that crown, and is said to have received some hint of an intention to surprise and seize the person of Edward, who thereupon lost no time in escaping. He retained the Great Seal till the downfall of Mortimer and Queen Isabella, when the king, on November 28, 1330, placed it in the hands of John de Stratford, Bishop of Winchester, but gave Burghersh a general pardon. (*Cal. Rot. Pat.* 109.)

We find him, however, in the royal confidence, as treasurer, from the eighth year of the reign till the end of his life, and engaged in various negotiations as to Edward's claim to the crown of France, accompanying the king in his expeditions, and becoming bound for him for a loan of 10,000*l*. (*New Fœdera*, i. 893-1134.)

The bishop died at Ghent in December 1340, and his body was removed to England for burial in his own cathedral.

He is reputed to have possessed great natural abilities and extensive learning. His political character must have been high, since for ten years after the king had released himself from his mother's domination he was employed, although one of her party, in embassies requiring skill and prudence as well as confidence and trust. He and his brother founded a grammar-school in Lincoln, to which he left maintenance for five poor priests and as many poor scholars for ever.

Bartholomew, his brother, was the ancestor of the present Earl of Westmoreland and the Baroness le Despencer and Burghersh. (*Godwin*, 294; *Barnes's Edward III.* 36-210.)

BURLAND, JOHN, belonged to a family which was for a long series of years settled at the manor of Steyning, in the parish of Stoke Courcy in the county of Somerset. His father was also named John Burland, and his mother was Elizabeth, the daughter of Claver Morris, of Wells, M.D. Their son was educated at Balliol College, Oxford, from 1740 to 1743, when he entered the Middle Temple, and was called to the bar in January 1746. The next year he married Letitia, daughter of William Berkeley Portman, Esq., of Orchard Portman, by

Anne, the daughter of the speaker, Sir Edward Seymour.

In 1762 he was honoured with the degree of the coif, and in 1764 was appointed king's serjeant. After he had held the recordership of Wells for some time with great reputation, the corporation thought fit to remove him, but on application to the Court of King's Bench in 1767 a peremptory mandamus was ordered to be made out for his restoration. He was constituted a baron of the Exchequer on April 8, 1774; but within two years he died by the bursting of a blood-vessel in his brain, on March 28, 1776, and was buried in Westminster Abbey. He left a son, who became member of parliament for Totnes. (*Collinson's Somerset*, i. 217; *Gent. Mag.* xxxvii. 91.)

BURNEL, ROBERT (BISHOP OF BATH AND WELLS), appears to have been (after consideration of the various descriptions) of his parentage) the son of another Robert Burnel, and to have been born at Acton-Burnell. In 1265, 50 Henry III., he is described as clerk or secretary to Edward, the king's eldest son (*Archæol. Journal*, ii. 326), and as being signed with the cross with the prince in 1269, whom he accompanied to the Holy Land. Having returned before him, he held in the first year of Edward's reign a high place in the council during the king's absence (*Madox*, ii. 207), and there are also several letters addressed by him to Walter de Merton, the chancellor. (6 *Report Pub. Rec.*, App. ii. 92, 93, 113.) He was at this time canon of Wells and archdeacon of York, and probably held some office in the Exchequer.

King Edward returned to England on August 2, 1274, and was crowned on the 19th. Within a month afterwards Burnel was raised to the chancellorship, the Great Seal being delivered to him on September 21, 1274. He filled this office all the remainder of his life, and never during the eighteen years that it lasted lost the confidence of his royal master; a distinction which he well merited from the wisdom of his counsels, and the zeal and assiduity with which he aided his sovereign's efforts in the improvement of the law.

In January 1275 he was elected Bishop of Bath and Wells, and was consecrated at Merton in the following April. On the abdication of the archbishopric of Canterbury by Robert Ascwardby in 1278, the monks elected Bishop Burnel as his successor, but the pope, not deeming him a man fitted for his purposes, annulled the appointment, and placed John Peckham in the vacant seat.

On his various expeditions into foreign parts he left the Great Seal in the custody of different officers of the Chancery, to transact the necessary business.

Acton-Burnell, the place of his birth and residence, has acquired an interest in historical recollections by having given its name to the Statutum de Mercatoribus, which was enacted there on October 12, 1283, 11 Edward I. The king was then paying a visit to his chancellor, while a parliament, which he had summoned to meet at Shrewsbury, were determining the fate of the Welsh Prince David. When that trial was over, the parliament joined the king at Acton-Burnell, and passed this statute, after which the king extended his royal visit till November 12. Some remains of the room in which the parliament sat still exist. They belong to the old mansion of the bishop's ancestors, which he replaced by a new building, still remaining, but with great alterations.

One of his last acts is his attendance at Norham as chancellor at the meeting of the Scottish peers on June 3, 1291, when King Edward acted as arbitrator between the competitors for that crown. (*Lingard*, iii. 206.)

On October 25, 1292, he died at Berwick-on-Tweed, when his body was removed to Wells and buried there.

Bishop Burnel was an active and a wise minister, serving the crown with zeal, energy, and prudence. No chancellor before him had ever held the Seal so long or retained so uninterruptedly his sovereign's confidence. The monk of Worcester gives his character in these words: 'Regi tam utilis, plebi tam affabilis, omnibus amabilis: vix nostris temporibus illi similis invenietur.' (*Angl. Sac.* i. 514.)

BURNET, THOMAS, was not the first of his family who obtained a seat on the judicial bench, his grandfather having acquired high legal eminence in the Scottish tribunal as Lord Cramond. His father was the celebrated whig prelate, Gilbert Burnet, Bishop of Salisbury, whose exertions at the Revolution, the piety of whose life, and the value of whose works have thrown around him a lustre which is rather brightened than diminished by the controversies which the latter occasioned. His mother was the bishop's second wife, Mrs. Mary Scott, a wealthy and accomplished Dutch lady of Scottish and noble extraction. Thomas Burnet was their third and youngest son, and was born about 1694. He was first sent to Merton College, Oxford, and afterwards in 1706 to the University of Leyden, where he studied for two years, and then visited Germany, Switzerland, and Italy. On his return he entered himself at the Middle Temple in 1709.

His student life was divided between law and politics, and he acquired equal notoriety for the wildness of his dissipations and for his genius and wit. Swift, in one of his letters to Stella of 1712, speaking of the Mohocks when they terrified the town by their lawless and mischievous exploits, reports that 'the Bishop of Salisbury's son is *said* to be of the gang.' This, however, may have been only a current calumny of the day, which the tory dean found pleasure in promulgating. The groundlessness of the report seems the more probable, inasmuch as at this period Burnet was issuing from the press no less than seven pamphlets against the administration, and in defence of the whigs; and was engaged in the composition of several poetical pieces, which were not given to the world till long after his death: occupations which would leave him little leisure for the imputed connection. One of the pamphlets, entitled 'A *certain* Information of a *certain* Discourse, that happened at a *certain* gentleman's house, in a *certain* county, written by a *certain* person then present, to a *certain* friend now in London; from whence you may collect the great *certainty* of the account,' so stung the ministers that they imprisoned the author. There is no doubt that his course of life at this time was dissolute and licentious. A story is told that his father one day, seeing him uncommonly grave, asked him the subjects of his thoughts. 'A greater work,' replied he, 'than your lordship's "History of the Reformation."' 'What is that, Tom?' 'My own reformation, my lord.' The bishop expressed his pleasure, but at the same time his despair of it.

On the accession of George I. he wrote some other political squibs, now forgotten, and at his father's death he published the 'character' of the bishop, with his last will. In 1715 he and Mr. Ducket wrote a travestie of the first book of the Iliad, under the title of 'Homerides,' which naturally procured them a place in Pope's 'Dunciad.' On the whig party regaining power he was sent as consul to Lisbon, where he got involved in some dispute with Lord Tyrawley, the ambassador, and adopted a curious mode of ridiculing his noble antagonist. Having learned what dress his lordship intended to wear on a birthday, he provided liveries for his servants of exactly the same pattern, and appeared himself in a plain suit. He continued at Lisbon several years, and on his recall to England he published his father's 'History of his own Time,' to the last volume of which he added a life of the bishop.

Resuming his original profession, he was called to the bar in 1729, twenty years after his admission to the Middle Temple. He showed so much ability and met with such success that in 1736 he received the degree of the coif, and in 1740 was appointed king's serjeant. In October of the next year he succeeded Mr. Justice Fortescue on the bench of the Common Pleas, where he administered justice with a great reputation for learning and uprightness for nearly twelve years. He was knighted in November 1745, on the occasion of all the judges, serjeants, and barristers presenting an address to the king expressive of their 'utter detestation of the present wicked and most ungrateful rebellion.' He died unmarried on January 5, 1753, of the gout in his stomach, and was buried near his father in St. James's Church, Clerkenwell.

Whatever were the frailties of his youth, he redeemed them by his after-life, commanding in the latter period the respect of the wise, as he had gained in the former the admiration of the wits who distinguished the reign of Queen Anne. He rejoiced in the esteem of many friends, and his merits and his worth were recorded after his death in several publications.

BURNHAM, THOMAS DE, was the last justice of four to whom the first commission of trailbaston into the counties of Lincoln, Nottingham, and Derby, dated November 23, 1304, 33 Edward I., was addressed. (*Rot. Parl.* i. 407.) On the renewal of the commissions in the following April, he was not reappointed; but he had in the meantime been returned as knight of the shire for Lincolnshire, which he had already represented in three parliaments, and was again elected to that of 2 Edward II.

BURNTON, WILLIAM DE, the last named of five justices itinerant appointed in 30 Edward I., 1302, for the county of Cornwall, may have been the same as William de Brompton, the justice of the Common Pleas in this reign, whose name was sometimes written Burnton; as thirteen years had elapsed since his disgrace.

BURROUGH, JAMES, was the third son of the Rev. John Burrough, of Abbotts-Ann in Hampshire, in which county and in Wiltshire he possessed considerable property. He was born in 1750, and, showing great ability as a youth, his father determined on bringing him up to the legal profession. He was called to the bar of the Inner Temple in 1773, having previously practised for a short time as a special pleader. Joining the Western Circuit, he gradually acquired a good share of business, and was particularly noticed for his profound knowledge as a sessional lawyer. In 1792 he was appointed a commissioner of bankrupts, and to Lord Eldon's estimation of his intelligence and worth he owed his ultimate elevation.

He was selected in 1794 by the Earl of Radnor as his deputy in the recordership of Salisbury, and afterwards became recorder of Portsmouth, both which appointments he held till he was advanced to the bench. That event did not occur till May 1816, when he was sixty-six years of age. He was then constituted a judge of the Common Pleas, and knighted.

As a judge he held a distinguished rank. To his legal knowledge he added patience and strict impartiality; and he was particularly esteemed for the kindness and simplicity of his demeanour. He was apt to deal in apophthegms, one of which was, 'Public policy is an unruly horse, which if a judge unwarily mounts, ten to one he is run away with.' His mode of illustration too was especially quaint. He once addressed a jury thus: 'Gentlemen, you have been told that the first is a *consequential issue*. Now, perhaps you do not know what a consequential issue means; but I dare say you understand nine-pins. Well, then, if you deliver your bowl so as to strike the front pin in a particular direction, down go the rest: just so it is with these counts; knock down the first, and all the rest will go to the ground; that's what we call a *consequential issue*.'

When he had attained the age of seventy-nine he was obliged by his infirmities to apply for his discharge, which he obtained at the end of 1829. His life was prolonged till March 25, 1839, and his remains were deposited in the Temple Church. His daughter Anne, his only surviving child, erected a monument to his memory in the church of Laverstock, near Salisbury. (*Lord Campbell's Chancellors*, iv. 666; *Law Mag.* iii. 299.)

BURSTALL, WILLIAM DE, is first mentioned as a clerk, or master, in Chancery in a document recording that the Great Seal was placed in the custody of four individuals, of whom he is the second named, on March 16, 1371, to hold during the absence of Sir Robert Thorpe, the chancellor. The next time his name appears is in an entry dated the 28th of the same month, stating the delivery by the Bishop of Winchester, the late chancellor, of certain seals which had been left in his possession. He is then called master of the Rolls, and Dugdale fixes that as the date of his appointment. In 49 Edward III. there was a contest in the court of Rome between him and a cardinal relative to the presentation to the parish church of Hoghton in the diocese of Durham, which the pope decided in his favour. (*New Fœdera*, iii. 1037.) Under Richard II. he continued master of the Rolls during the first four years of his reign, and died in 1381.

During his time the Domus Conversorum in Chancery Lane was permanently annexed by Edward III. to the office of master of the Rolls.

BURTON, JOHN DE, was appointed master of the Rolls on October 24, 1386, but whether he was the John de Burton who held benefices about this time in Cambridgeshire and Yorkshire, and was very liberal to the institutions of those counties, is uncertain. He held the office till July 22, 1394; and from March 26 to April 19, 1393, he was entrusted with the Great Seal during the absence of the chancellor. There is proof that he died in possession of the place by the mandate to give up the Rolls of the Chancery being directed, not to him, but his executors. (*Rot. Pat.* 18 Rich. II, p. i. m. 28.)

BURY, RICHARD DE, or DE AUNGERVILLE (BISHOP OF DURHAM). The real name of this learned and eminent prelate was Richard de Aungerville, a town in Normandy; but he assumed that of de Bury from the place where he was born, Bury St. Edmunds, in Suffolk. He was son of Sir Richard de Aungerville, and was born in 1281. Being of very tender years when he was left an orphan, the care of his education devolved on his uncle, John de Willoughby, a priest, by whom his youthful studies were well directed. In due time he was removed to Oxford, where he pursued them with so much diligence that he became distinguished for his learning, and at the same time acquired the higher character of a man pure in his life and manners.

On leaving Oxford he entered the convent of Durham as a monk. From this seclusion he was withdrawn by being selected as the tutor of the king's eldest son; but, as the prince was not born till 1312, this event could scarcely have occurred before the year 1319 or 1320, when our monk would have been nearly forty years old. His conduct in his new position was so exemplary that he was rewarded with the treasurership of Guienne, where he was established when Queen Isabella, and his pupil the prince, went to France in 1325. The asylum he gave them there, and the pecuniary aid he afforded out of the royal treasures in his keeping, had nearly proved fatal to him. Although the latter rightly belonged to the prince, as his father had transferred the duchy to him, he was pursued by the emissaries of the Despencers, and, escaping to Paris, was compelled to conceal himself for seven days in the belfry of the church of the Friars Minors in that city.

On the accession of his princely pupil to the throne his services were not forgotten. He was retained near the person of the king, then little more than fourteen years of age, and was rewarded successively with the offices of cofferer, treasurer of the wardrobe, and keeper of the privy seal. Nor was his clerical preferment overlooked. He held at first a small prebend in the church of Chichester; and the king, in a letter to the pope on de Bury's behalf, calls him 'his secretary,' and, speaking of his services, 'a pueritiâ nostrâ,' uses these strong expressions: 'Quod novimus ipsum

L

virum in consiliis providum, conversationis et vitæ munditiâ decorum, literarum scientiâ præditum, et in agendis quibuslibet circumspectum.' The object of this letter was to induce the pope to reserve for de Bury the prebends in the churches of Hereford, London, and Chichester, with the other benefices which Gilbert de Middleton, archdeacon of Northampton, lately deceased, had possessed. Before an answer could have been received to this application, de Bury was collated to the vacant archdeaconry on January 6, 1330-1; but the pope, according to the too common practice of the day, usurped the appointment, and, on the 1st of the following March, granted the dignity to Peter, one of his cardinals; but prebends in the cathedrals of Lincoln, Sarum, and Lichfield were among the grants soon after made to de Bury.

In October 1331 he went with Anthony de Pesaigne on a mission to the pope at Avignon, where he formed an intimacy with Petrarch, among his conversations with whom is one relative to the Island of Thule, on which, however, Petrarch complains that the learned ambassador was either unable or unwilling to offer any elucidation. On his return from this embassy he was sent, with two others, to Cambridge, with a commission to enquire into the conduct and claims of such scholars as were supported in that university by the king's bounty. It was probably during this visit that he became one of the guild of St. Mary's there, to the union of which with that of Corpus Christi the college of the latter name owed its foundation. (*Masters*, 9.)

In 1332 he was admitted dean of Wells, and in the next year was sent again as ambassador to the pope, by whom he was appointed one of his chaplains. While he was absent on this mission, Lewis Beaumont, Bishop of Durham, died; and the pope used the opportunity at once of exercising his own power, and of gratifying King Edward, by setting aside an election made by the monks of Durham, and placing Richard de Bury in the vacant seat. He was consecrated at Chertsey on December 19, 1333.

King Edward estimated his ability and his prudence so highly that he fixed on him to fill the most important offices in the state. He was accordingly constituted treasurer on February 3, 1334, and raised to the chancellorship on September 28 in the same year. Whether he found that he was unqualified for its cares and responsibilities, or that they withdrew him more than he wished from those of his diocese, he resigned the latter office, after holding it less than nine months, on June 6, 1335. He was employed in the following and several subsequent years in frequent embassies to France on the subject of the king's claims—an occupation to which his learning and talents were probably more peculiarly fitted. His allowance on these missions was at the rate of five marks a day. (*New Fœdera*, ii. 950.)

Though frequently absent, he neglected none of the requirements of his diocese. He had the habit of turning all his time to account, and neither his meals nor his travels were spent idly. During the former he was read to by his chaplains, among whom were numbered some of the most celebrated men of the day, and afterwards he discussed with them the various subjects suggested by the reading. During the latter he occupied himself in forming what became the largest library in Europe, the possession of which was one of his greatest glories, and its accumulation formed his chief delight. He spared no expense in securing the most curious and valuable manuscripts, and speaks with evident glee of the motives which influenced the donors of some, and of the difficulties he had to overcome in obtaining others. The stores he had thus collected he bequeathed to the students of Durham (since called Trinity) College, in Oxford, being the first public library that was founded at that university; and in his work called 'Philobiblon' he not only gives instructions for its management, but endeavours to excite a love of literature and a taste for the liberal arts.

His own devotion to books may be estimated by the language he uses regarding them:—'Hi sunt magistri qui nos instruunt sine virgis et ferulâ, sine verbis et colerâ, sine pane et pecuniâ. Si accedis non dormiunt, si inquiris non se abscondunt, non remurmurant si oberres, cachinos nesciunt si ignores.'

His ardour in their pursuit did not end with their attainment. He read and used them; and he relates that the first Greek and Hebrew grammars that ever appeared in England were derived from his labours. He encouraged the acquaintance and assisted the enquiries of all learned and intelligent men, and never enjoyed himself so fully as in the pleasures of their conversation; and his understanding was so cultivated, his wit so piercing, and his spirit of enquiry so eager, that few subjects were beyond his genius and penetration.

His virtues and his charities were equal to his talents and learning. He was beloved by his neighbours, with whom he lived on terms of reciprocal affection; to his clergy he was an indulgent superior; to his tenants and domestics a considerate master. He was most bountiful to the poor, distributing eight quarters of wheat every week for the relief of those around him, and never omitting in his journeys to appropriate large sums for the indigent in those places through which he passed.

He closed his useful life, in the 64th year

of his age, at his palace of Auckland, on April 24, 1345, and was interred in his cathedral.

BURY, THOMAS, the youngest son of Sir William Bury, knight, of Linwood in Lincolnshire, was born in 1655, and, entering Gray's Inn in 1668, was called to the bar in 1676. After twenty-four years' practice, he obtained the degree of serjeant in 1700, and on January 26 of the next year he was made a baron of the Exchequer. Speaker Onslow in his notes to Burnet states that it was said that it appeared by Bury's 'Book of Accounts' that Lord Keeper Wright had 1000*l*. for raising him to the bench. This discreditable story, however, depends on very slight testimony. The new baron was of course knighted, and sat in that court during the remainder of his life; for fifteen years as a puisne baron, and for six as chief baron, to which he was advanced on June 10, 1716. In the famous Aylesbury case in the House of Lords he supported the opinion of Chief Justice Holt, when the judgment which he had opposed was reversed.

He died on May 4, 1722, and was buried at Grantham, where there is a handsome monument to his memory.

BYLES, JOHN BARNARD, one of the present judges of the Common Pleas, was born at Stowmarket in Suffolk in 1801, and is the eldest son of John Byles, Esq., of that place, by the only daughter of William Barnard, Esq., of Holts in Essex.

Called to the bar by the Inner Temple in November 1831, he joined the Norfolk Circuit, and attended the sessions attached to it. In 1840 he was appointed recorder of Buckingham, and in 1843 received the degree of the coif, to which was added a patent of precedence in all the courts in 1846, the year in which the act was passed opening the Court of Common Pleas to all barristers. In 1857 he was promoted to the dignity of queen's serjeant. During the whole period of his career as an advocate his sagacity and sound judgment secured for him a considerable, and ultimately a leading, business.

His professional reputation must have been universally acknowledged to have induced a lord chancellor so much opposed to him in politics as was Lord Cranworth to select him for a judge's place. Mr. Serjeant Byles was not only a tory, or rather a conservative, in his opinions, but had advocated the principles of that section of his party which supported protection in an able pamphlet, called 'Sophisms of Free Trade.' Notwithstanding this apparent impediment to his advance, Lord Cranworth, deeming that a good judge was better than a political partisan, made choice of one who in the estimation of the legal world held the highest place. Mr. Byles was therefore appointed in June 1858 to fill the vacant seat on the bench of the Common Pleas.

He has been twice married. His first wife, a daughter of J. Foster, Esq., of Biggleswade, he lost very early; his second is a daughter of J. Weld, Esq., of Royston.

Besides the above-mentioned pamphlet, he published a work 'On the Usury Laws,' and some others.

BYNTEWORTH, RICHARD DE (BISHOP OF LONDON), had a grant of the manor of Bynteworth, now called Bentworth, in Hampshire, with the advowson of its church, from the Archbishop of Rouen, in 9 Edward III., and probably was a native of the place. He was employed in the previous year as one of the ambassadors to negotiate the marriage of the king's brother, John, Earl of Cornwall, with Maria, daughter of Ferdinand of Spain, and in several subsequent years on other missions, in all of which he is called 'juris civilis professor.' In 11 Edward III. he was keeper of the king's privy seal; and he appears to have been a canon of St. Paul's at the time of the decease of Stephen de Gravesend, Bishop of London. By his conduct in these employments his character had been so firmly established that he was immediately called upon to fill the vacant see, his election to which took place on May 4, 1338. On July 6 the king appointed him his chancellor. But his sudden death put an end to his tenure of both these offices on December 8, 1339, before he had illustrated either by any memorable act. (*Godwin*, 185.)

BYRLAY, WILLIAM DE (Birlaco), can hardly be considered entitled to the designation given to him by Sir T. D. Hardy as keeper of the Great Seal. He seems to have been merely a clerk in the Chancery, to whom, with two of his brethren, the Great Seal was on some occasions entrusted during the temporary absences of the chancellor, the first occurring in March 1298, 26 Edward I.; and the last in 1308.

BYRUN, JOHN DE, was named in a separate commission of trailbaston, issued on March 13, 1305, 33 Edward I., for the county of Lancaster, which in the following month was consolidated with the other northern counties in a new commission, in which his name was not included. (*Parl. Writs*, i. 407, 408.)

He was a lineal descendant from Ralph de Burun, who at the time of the Conqueror's survey had eight lordships in Nottinghamshire and five in Derbyshire, and whose family subsequently obtained considerable property in Lancashire. His father was also named John, and his mother was Joan, daughter of Sir Baldwin Thies, and widow of Sir Robert Holland.

Seated at Clayton, in Lancashire, his father was one of the conservators of the peace for that county in 15 Edward I., and

L 2

sheriff of Yorkshire for seven years from 21 Edward I., and actively engaged in raising the forces for the Scottish wars. In 28 Edward I. he held a high place in the commission to perambulate the forests of that and the neighbouring counties. (*Parl. Writs*, i. 299, 389, 398, ii. 8–17.)

John the son for the first nine years of the reign of Edward II. held an equally prominent position in Lancashire. Some little confusion, arising from the identity of name, renders it difficult to distinguish precisely the acts of the two. The date of neither of their deaths is given. The son married Alice, cousin and heir of Robert Banastre, of Hyndeley, Lancashire, and was succeeded by his son Richard de Byron. In regular descent from him came Sir John Byron, who for his faithful adherence to the fortunes of King Charles I., and his valiant support of his cause, was created Baron Byron of Rochdale on October 24, 1643. The present baron, the eighth lord, is his lineal descendant. The surpassing genius of George Gordon Byron, the sixth lord, has given to the title an immortality which it could have never derived either from the antiquity of the family or the devoted loyalty for which the peerage was granted: his works will remain a lasting monument of his glory, but a sad record of his unhappy disposition and of his unfortunate fate.

C

CAEN, JOHN DE (Cadomo), was one of the clerks in the Chancery. He is mentioned on many different occasions from 1292 to 1302 in connection with the Great Seal, as holding it with other clerks of the Chancery during the occasional absences of the chancellor, and in October 1298 he was acting in the Exchequer as *locum tenens* for the chancellor. (*Madox*, i. 421.) He also acted as a receiver of petitions to the parliaments 1305 and 1307, 33–35 Edward I., and as late as 1310, 3 Edward II.

CÆSAR, THOMAS. In the city of Treviso, near Venice, the noble family of Adelmare had long resided, when a member of it, named Peter Maria Adelmare, who was eminent as a civilian, married a daughter of the house of Cæsarini, and had three sons, the second of whom was christened, after his mother, Cæsar. This Cæsar Adelmare pursued his studies at Padua, and, having taken the degree of doctor in medicine, came to England to practise in 1550. Here he obtained such repute that he was employed by Queen Mary, and on one occasion received the enormous fee of 100*l*. for his attendance. (*Burgon's Gresham*, ii. 464.) Queen Elizabeth also placed him at the head of her medical department, and granted to him some beneficial leases under the crown. He fixed his residence in the close of the priory of Great St. Helen's, Bishopsgate, where he died in 1569. By his wife, Margaret, daughter of Martin Perin, or Perient, treasurer in Ireland, he left eight children, two of whom obtained judicial appointments—Julius Cæsar, the eldest son, after mentioned; and Thomas, the third son, the subject of this sketch.

Thomas Cæsar was born in 1561, and was educated at Merchant Taylors' School in London. In October 1580 he was entered of the Inner Temple, where he was not called to the bench until he was appointed a baron of the Exchequer, and never held the post of reader to the society. He seems to have used his father's name during the early part of his life, and to have afterwards partially adopted that of Cæsar, at first with an *alias*, and subsequently alone. His first wife, whose mother's name was Chapman, describes herself in her will, 'Susan, wife of Thomas Dalmare, alias Cæsar.' In this he no doubt followed the example of his brother, Sir Julius, who was then holding a prominent judicial situation, and was aiming at higher posts, for which he perhaps imagined his Italian surname might be deemed a disqualification.

Thomas's name does not appear in any of the Reports, and no account is given of his professional career, nor of any office which he held (except that of steward of St. Catherine's Hospital, of which his brother was master), before his appointment as a baron on May 26, 1610. On his receiving it, the Inner Temple ordered that 'he should not be attended to Westminster by any but the officers of the Exchequer, forasmuch as none but such as were of the coif ought to be attended by the fellows of the house.' He is there described as 'the puisne baron of the Exchequer (commonly called the baron cursitor).' Another order was made on June 10, that, though he had not read, but fined for not reading, he should have his place at the bench table notwithstanding a previous act, 'That none who should thenceforth be called to the bench that had not read should take place of any reader, or have a voice in parliament.' (*Dugdale's Orig.* 149.) It is thus manifest that the office of baron which he held was not of the same degree of dignity as the other barons; and that he had no judicial function is apparent from the absence of his name from all the Reports of the period.

But whatever was his position, he did not retain it quite two months, during which interval he was knighted. He died on July 18, 1610, and was buried in the church of Great St. Helen's, Bishopsgate.

His first wife died in 1590, leaving three children, who did not live to grow up. He married, secondly, Anne, the daughter of George Lynn, of Southwilk, Northampton, Esq., and widow of Nicholas Beaston, Esq. But she dying early, without children, he took for his third wife Susan, daughter and co-heir of Sir William Ryther, knight, an opulent alderman of London, and had by her three sons and five daughters. (*Lodge's Cæsars*, 39–41.)

CÆSAR, JULIUS, was the eldest son of Cæsar Adelmare, physician to Queens Mary and Elizabeth, by his wife Margaret Perin, or Perient. He was born at Tottenham in Middlesex in 1557, and enjoyed royal patronage from his infancy. He received the names of Julius Cæsar, the latter of which he seems very early to have substituted for that of his ancestors, though even so late as 1608 he was designated by both names with an *alias* in formal documents.

Having lost his father when he was twelve years old, and his mother having married again, he was sent to Magdalen Hall, Oxford, where he took the degree of B.A. in 1575, and that of M.A. in 1578. In 1580 he was admitted a member of the Inner Temple, and proceeding to Paris, he took the degree there of doctor in both laws in 1581, after which he returned to Oxford, and proceeded to the same degree in that university in 1583. (*Wood's Fasti*, i. 224.) In 1582 he married Dorcas, daughter of Sir Richard Martin, an alderman of London, afterwards master of the Mint, and widow of Richard Lusher. During the previous year he received two public appointments, and in 1583 he became commissary of Essex, Herts, and Middlesex, from which he was promoted in 1584 to be judge of the Admiralty Court. Although possessed of so important a post at the early age of 27, he was not contented, but made frequent applications for grants and promotion, in which he was only so far at that time successful that in October 1588 he was admitted one of the masters in Chancery, an office which was then frequently filled by doctors of the civil law. He still continued his importunities, alleging that he had spent 4000l. above his gains in the execution of his office of judge of the Admiralty, and in relieving the poor suitors of his court. This statement it would be scarcely possible to credit, if his unlimited charity were not evidenced by what Isaac Walton says of him, that when grown old 'he was kept alive beyond nature's course by the prayers of those many poor he daily relieved.'

At last his perseverance procured for him the appointment of a master extraordinary of the Court of Requests in 1591, but it was not till August 1595 that he was admitted one of the ordinary masters of that court, which gave him immediate access to the queen. During this time it is amusing to see how he paid his court to the influential ministers and favourites, and how ingeniously he contrived to remind them of his claims in his letters conveying new years' gifts, some curious specimens of which are preserved among the Lansdowne MSS. In 1593 he was elected treasurer of the Inner Temple, and on December 8 in the same year he was appointed governor of the mine and battery works throughout England and Wales. Having already procured (by a bribe of 500l. to Archibald Douglas, the Scottish ambassador, to use his influence with the queen) the reversion of the mastership of St. Catherine's, he succeeded to it on June 17, 1596.

His wife dying in June 1595, he entered in the following year into a second matrimonial connection with Alice, daughter of Christopher Green, and widow of John Dent, a rich merchant of London. In September 1598 her majesty inflicted on him the honour of a visit to his house at Mitcham, the expense of which, with the customary offering, amounted to 700l. sterling. No other incident occurred to him in Elizabeth's reign, except that he obtained a verdict of 200l. against a man for asserting that he had pronounced a corrupt sentence against him in the Admiralty. (*Croke, Eliz.* 305.)

King James knighted him on May 20, 1603, and in the same year reappointed him master of the Court of Requests and master of St. Catherine's. He was further favoured with grants of the manor of Linwood in Lincolnshire, and of the Forest of High Peak in Derbyshire, for life. On April 11, 1606, the important office of chancellor and under treasurer of the Exchequer was conferred upon him, and in the next year he was sworn of the privy council. During the eight years in which he performed the onerous duties of his place his main difficulty seems to have been the supplying means to meet the idle profuseness of his master. He obtained from the king, in January 16, 1611, a reversionary grant of the mastership of the Rolls; but he did not come into possession for nearly four years, when he was sworn in on September 13, 1614. In James's reign he sat in parliament for Westminster in 1604, for Middlesex in 1614, and for Malden in 1621.

Having lost his second wife, he married

Anne, the daughter of Henry Wodehouse, of Waxham in Norfolk, by Anne, daughter of Sir Nicholas Bacon, lord keeper, and widow of William Hungate, of East Brudenham in the same county.

Sir Julius continued master of the Rolls till his death, a period of more than twenty-one years; and during the interval between the disgrace of Lord Chancellor Bacon and the delivery of the Seal to Lord Keeper Williams—viz., between May 21 and July 10, 1621—he had a commission to hear causes in Chancery. To Bacon, with whom he was connected by marriage, he continued a kind friend, assisting him by his bounty, affording him an asylum in his misfortunes, and receiving his last breath in his arms. He had not any great reputation as a judge, and it is said that counsel would occasionally pass 'a slye jeste' upon him.

He died on April 18, 1636, at the age of seventy-nine, and was buried at Great St. Helen's, Bishopsgate, where his father lay. Over his remains was placed a monument with an inscription written by himself, in the form of a deed with a pendent seal, the connecting silk of which is broken.

He had no issue by his last wife, but his other two brought him eight children. Of the five by his first wife only one survived him—viz., the under-mentioned Charles. His second wife produced to him three sons —John, who was knighted at the age of ten; Thomas, who became a doctor in divinity; and Robert, who obtained the place of one of the six clerks in Chancery. (*Lodge's Cæsars.*)

CÆSAR, CHARLES, the eldest surviving son of the above Sir Julius, was born on January 27, 1589. Destined to pursue the profession by which his father had risen, he was sent to All Souls' College, Oxford, and was admitted to the degree of doctor of laws on December 7, 1612. (*Wood's Fasti*, i. 348.) Commencing practice in the ecclesiastical courts, he received the order of knighthood on October 6 in the following year, and was gradually promoted, first to the office of the master of the faculties, and then to that of judge of the audience. (*State Trials*, ii. 1452.) On May 19, 1615, he was made a master in Chancery, no doubt by the interest of his father, who had been sworn in as a judge of that court in the preceding year; and on the death of Sir Dudley Digges, in 1639, he was appointed master of the Rolls, on March 30; paying however, according to a memorandum made by his son, for that 'high and profitable place' no less than 15,000*l.*, 'broad pieces of gold,' with a loan of 2000*l.* more when the king went to meet his rebellious Scottish army. It is difficult to regret that he did not live long enough to profit by this iniquitous traffic of the judicial seat, as disgraceful to one party as the other. In November 1642 the smallpox seized the family, and proved fatal to one of his daughters on the 2nd of that month, to himself on the 6th of December, and to his eldest son five days after. They were buried at Bennington in Herts, where his estate was situate; and his monument there bears an inscription commemorative of his personal worth and his judicial integrity. It records besides that he had two wives— the first, Anne, daughter of Sir Peter Vanlore, knight, an eminent London merchant; and the second, Jane, daughter of Sir Edward Barkham, knight, lord mayor of London—and that he had six children by the first wife, and nine by the second, but of these fifteen no male descendant now preserves the name of the family. (*Lodge's Cæsars.*)

CAIRNS, HUGH M'CALMONT (LORD CAIRNS), within three years passed through three legal offices—attorney-general, lord justice of appeal, and lord chancellor—rising from a practising barrister to the highest seat in the law, from a simple member of the House of Commons to the speakership of the House of Lords, and, after less than ten months' enjoyment of that honourable office, has been entrusted with the still more responsible position of the leadership of the conservative party in the house of which he had been so short a time a member. Such a rapid advance as this has never been before witnessed, such proof of confidence is almost unparalleled.

He was born in 1819, and is the son of William Cairns, Esq., of Culha in the county of Down. At Trinity College, Dublin, where he was educated, besides other honours, he took the first place in classics. Called to the bar at Lincoln's Inn on January 26, 1844, he soon acquired so prominent a station in the Court of Chancery that he was made a queen's counsel in 1856, when he still maintained it with more than the usual success. Before this date he had commenced his parliamentary career, having been elected member for Belfast in 1852, and in every other parliament till he was raised to the bench. His eloquence and ability in that arena are the best proofs of the statesmanship which is generally attributed to him.

His official life began with the appointment, on February 26, 1858, of solicitor-general, which he held till the change of ministry on June 18, 1859, a little less than sixteen months. Seven years afterwards, on the conservative party resuming power, he was made attorney-general on July 6, 1866, and in less than four months was removed into the important office of lord justice of appeal in Chancery on October 29. On the following February 26 he was called up to the House of Peers by the title of Lord Cairns of Garmoyle in the county of Antrim; and on the 29th of the same month in 1868 he received the Great Seal as lord chancellor. This he retained only till December 9 in the same year, when the liberal party gained the ascendency, but was then immediately selected as the leader of the opposition in the House of Lords, with which office he has been again entrusted in the present session.

In 1867 his alma mater, the University of Dublin, elected him their chancellor.

He married Mary Harriet, daughter of John McNeile, Esq., of Parkmount in the county of Antrim.

CALETO, JOHN DE, or **DE CAUX.** A fine was acknowledged before John, abbot of Peterborough, in 1254, 39 Henry III., and in that and the following year his name appears at the head of the justices itinerant into several counties. From April till August 1258 also payments were made for assizes to be held before him. In October, 44 Henry III., he was constituted treasurer, and continued so till his death on March 1, 1262. This abbot was John de Caleto, or de Caux, who was elected to that dignity in 1249, being then prior of St. Swithin's at Winchester. He was a relative of Queen Eleanor. (*Bruce's Introd. to Chron. Petroburg.* x.) Browne Willis describes him as a pious and wise man.

CALOWE, WILLIAM, probably descended from a family seated at Holbeach in Lincolnshire in the reign of Richard II., was so short a time a judge that little is known about him. In the Year Books he is mentioned under the name of Collow in 1475, and as having been called serjeant from the Middle Temple in Trinity Term 18 Edward IV. In 2 Richard III., 1484, he was joined in the commission of assize for the county of Dorset, and on January 31, 1487, 2 Henry VII., he was raised to the judicial seat in the Common Pleas. The only fine levied before him is in the following Trinity Term, and from the absence of all notice of him from that time, it would seem that he then resigned or died.

CAMBHOU, WALTER DE, is mentioned in 14 Edward I. as a keeper of the tallies of the Exchequer. He was appointed a justice itinerant in Tindale in 21 Edward I. (*Rot. Parl.* i. 122), being at that time custos of the castle of Baumburgh; but he does not appear to have acted afterwards. In that year he and Isabella his wife levied a fine of considerable property in Colwell in Northumberland, for which county he was elected a member of parliament in 24 Edward I., and died in the same year. (*Parl. Writs*, i. 39; *Abb. Rot. Orig.* i. 94.)

CAMDEN, EARL. *See* C. PRATT.

CAMPBELL, JOHN (LORD CAMPBELL), born Sept. 5, 1781, at Springfield, near Cupar, in Fifeshire, was the younger son of Dr. George Campbell, minister of Cupar, and of Magdelene, daughter of John Haliburton, Esq., of Fodderance. He spent eight of his early years, from ten to eighteen, at the University of St. Andrews, studying for the ministry, and took the degree of A.M. there. Relinquishing, however, his clerical prospects, and aiming at legal distinction, he came to London, and in November 1800 entered the society of Lincoln's Inn, and placed himself under the guidance of Mr. Tidd. With that eminent special pleader he stayed three years, and to the tuition he received during that time he chiefly ascribed his success at the bar. He gratefully records the generosity of his instructor, who, he relates, on finding that it would not be convenient to him to pay a second fee of one hundred guineas, not only refused to take it, but insisted on returning him the first. (*Lord C.'s Chanc.* v. 484.) Before this, finding that the small allowance which his father could make him was inadequate for his support in the metropolis, he engaged himself for many years as a reporter to the 'Morning Chronicle,' then under the conduct of Mr. Perry, a countryman of his. To this he added occasionally a dramatic criticism, in which after some time he became an adept, though, from the strictness of his Presbyterian education, and consequent inexperience, this must at first have been a difficult task, and probably produced some strictures which in afteryears he would hesitate to indorse. The 'Morning Chronicle' was the organ of the whigs, to which party he attached himself at the outset of his career, and it is greatly to his credit that during the whole of his life, whether it was in opposition, or in power, he never deserted it. His occupation and his politics introduced him into various society, and among his relaxations were the enjoyments of the Cider Cellar in Maiden Lane, Covent Garden. There he had the advantage of associating with many men of celebrity, among whom was the learned and eccentric Professor Porson, who surprised him by reciting the whole of Anstey's 'Pleader's Guide' from memory. During the period of his novitiate, when Bonaparte threatened to invade the kingdom, he joined the 'Bloomsbury and Inns of Court Association' (*Lord C.'s Ch. Just.* ii. 604), a corps chiefly composed of members of the legal profession, and he looked back in after-years with so much pride to his position in the ranks that he left the musket he bore as an heirloom to his descendants.

Of Lord Kenyon, who was then chief justice, he relates that at the Nisi Prius sittings at Guildhall the chief used to hand the record to the students, who sat in a box close to him, and point out to them the important issues to be tried. During the latter part of Mr. Campbell's pupilage the chief justice was Lord Ellenborough, with whose 'very dignified, impressive, and awe-inspiring deportment,' especially at the trial of Colonel Despard in 1803 for high treason, he was much struck, and whose 'rough treatment' of him in his future career he regrettingly remembers. (*Ch. Just.* ii. 329, iii. 94, 177.)

He was called to the bar in Michaelmas Term 1806, and published in 1808 two volumes of 'Reports of Cases Argued and Tried at Nisi Prius, in the Courts of King's Bench and Common Pleas, in the Home Circuit, from Michaelmas Term 1807 to the sittings before Easter 1808,' which he afterwards continued in two additional volumes extending to the year 1816. This publication greatly aided his progress at the bar. Dr. Watt mentions also another publication under Mr. Campbell's name in 1808, 'A Letter to a Member of Parliament on the Articles of a Charge against Marquis Wellesley, which have been laid before the House of Commons;' probably an ephemeral pamphlet which died with the day. It would seem from the title of his reports that he at first attended the Home Circuit, though afterwards, about 1810, he joined the Oxford Circuit, on which, as well as in Westminster Hall, his success was so great that for three years before he obtained a silk gown he was the leader of it. (*Chanc.* iii 275.)

In 1821 he married Mary Elizabeth, the eldest daughter of Mr. Scarlett, then one of the most eminent advocates at the bar, who afterwards became lord chief baron of the Exchequer, and was created Lord Abinger. To the influence of his father-in-law, who was appointed attorney-general in 1827, he probably owed his promotion to the post of king's counsel in the same year, Lord Lyndhurst being chancellor.

In the next year he was named the chairman of a commission on the Registration of Deeds, and in 1830 he was placed at the head of the Real Property Commission. (*Ch. Just.* iii. 324.) In that year he began his senatorial career as member for Stafford, and soon showed himself active and useful in introducing and defending several important measures, among which were the Bill for the Registration of Deeds, and the Anatomy Bill. A friend to parliamentary reform, he gloried in having materially furthered the measure, attributing, not unnaturally, the one vote by which the second reading of Lord John Russell's first bill was carried to his leaving his circuit, 'at a considerable professional sacrifice,' and coming up to London to be present at the division. His speech on the second bill he afterwards published. (*Speeches*, 49.)

On November 26, 1832, he was rewarded with the solicitor-generalship, and consequent knighthood. In the new parliament then called he was elected member for Dudley, but only retained his seat till 1834, when, on his being made attorney-general, the fickle town would not re-elect him. For nearly a whole session he remained without a seat; but in the following June he succeeded with a more distinguished constituency, being elected member for Edinburgh in the place of Francis Jeffrey, made a lord of session. This city he continued to represent while he remained a commoner. His tenure of office was interrupted after little more than nine months by his party being turned out of the ministry in December 1834, but only to be restored with more confirmed power in April 1835, when Sir John was reinstated in his place.

Before his first period of office as attorney-general expired, Sir John Leach, the master of the Rolls, died. Though according to the usual practice he might have claimed the vacant place, he allowed himself to be passed over in favour of the solicitor-general, Sir Charles Christopher Pepys, who was appointed. On his resuming the office of attorney-general the Great Seal was put into commission, of which the new master of the Rolls was the head, and after so remaining about nine months, Sir Charles was constituted lord chancellor. Thus for a second time the office of master of the Rolls was vacant, and for a second time Sir John Campbell was passed over, Lord Langdale receiving the appointment. The avowed reason for thus overlooking his claims was that he was wholly inexperienced as an equity lawyer; but the real ground was supposed to be that he was so active and serviceable to the ministry in the House of Commons that he could not be spared without danger to its existence. Indignant at first with this usage, he resigned, but a peerage being given to his wife, with the title of Baroness Stratheden, he was appeased and resumed his post.

The whig party retained their ascendency for the next four years, and no vacancy occurred on the bench which Sir John Campbell was desirous to fill. During the whole period of his parliamentary career he devoted himself, both at this time and after his accession to the peerage, to the improvement of the laws, and several statutes owe their existence to his introduction. On the ministry beginning to totter in 1841, they were so determined before their exclusion to reward their attorney-general for his political and professional exertions, that they ventured on the bold and questionable step of removing their ancient colleague, Lord Plunkett, from the chancellorship of Ireland, for the purpose of raising Sir John to that dignity and decking him with a peerage. With reluctance Lord Plunkett submitted; and Sir John, on June 22, 1841, became Lord Campbell of St. Andrews and lord chancellor of Ireland. After sitting only one or two days in the Irish court he made a speech to the bar, in which he plainly intimates his expectation of soon being 'reduced to a private station.' (*Speeches*, 518.) The ministry succumbed in August, and Lord Campbell, retiring with them, finished his short tenure of office; but though entitled to a pension of 4000*l.*, the job was so gross and notorious that the ministry did not venture to offer nor he to claim it.

During the nine years that followed his retirement he applied himself to his senatorial duties, taking a leading part in the Lords' debates, and assisting greatly in the appellate jurisdiction of the house. But his active habits required further occupation, and in 1842 he found it by publishing his 'Speeches at the Bar and in the House of Commons.' But his ambition was not satisfied with this slight offering; aiming at literary fame, he next chose a subject from the execution of which he hoped to obtain it. This was 'The Lives of the Lord Chancellors,' the first three volumes of which he published at the close of 1845, continuing them in 1846 and 1847, till he had filled seven volumes, concluding with the Life of Lord Eldon. This work acquired an immediate popularity, and, though condemned by some critics for its looseness and occasional incorrectness, it should be remembered that the mere writing of seven volumes, each consisting of between six and seven hundred closely printed pages, in the course of little more than two years, was of itself an extraordinary effort of labour, and that it would be unreasonable to expect any strict investigation of records or authorities, or more than a compilation from previous writers. In 1849 he published two volumes of 'The Lives of the Chief Justices,' to which, in 1857, he added a third gossiping volume, including those of Lords Kenyon, Ellenborough, and Tenterden, in which a tendency to disparage his noble predecessors is too apparent. The only other literary production which he printed was 'Shakspeare's Legal Acquirements,' being an attempt to prove that the great dramatist spent his youth in an attorney's office. This was a mere enlargement of the idea that had been previously suggested by Malone, Chalmers, W. S. Landor, J. P. Collier, and, so lately as in 1838, by Charles Armitage Brown.

When his party came again into power in 1846, Lord John Russell, the prime minister, admitted him into the cabinet, and gave him the appointment of chancellor of the duchy of Lancaster. This office he filled till March 6, 1850, when, Lord Denman having retired from ill health and advanced age, Lord Campbell was raised to the chief justiceship of the Queen's Bench, although only two years younger than his predecessor. On assuming it he of course relinquished his seat in the cabinet council, as he had expressed his strong disapproval of the union of the two positions by Lord Mansfield in 1757, and Lord Ellenborough in 1806. (*Ch. Just.* ii. 451, iii. 185.)

Lord Campbell was specially fitted for the office to which he was thus appointed. During the nine years that he filled it he is acknowledged to have performed its important duties in a most exemplary manner, preserving the dignity of the place, and administering the law with apparent ease and strict impartiality. When Lord Palmerston assumed the premiership for a second time in 1859, he offered Lord Campbell the chancellorship; and it surprised the world that he should be tempted to leave a court where he was so much at home, for one in the practice of which he could not be expected to be so conversant, especially when its tenure was so uncertain. But ambition decided, and he received the Great Seal on June 18.

He presided over the Court of Chancery for two years, and the practisers in it were astonished at the readiness with which he mastered the forms of the court, and the discrimination he showed in the judgments he pronounced. In the midst of his duties, in the full tide of his triumph, he was suddenly cut off. On Saturday, June 23, 1861, he had attended a cabinet council, and, after having entertained a party of friends at his house at Knightsbridge, had retired to his chamber in his accustomed health and spirits, and applied himself to preparing a judgment which he had promised on Monday. On Sunday morning he was found dead in his chair with the blood oozing from his mouth, caused by the bursting of one of the great arteries near his heart.

Thus awfully terminated the life of one who, during its whole continuance, never relaxed from his labours, who never was satisfied unless he was doing something, and was indefatigable in all his pursuits. Commencing as a poor and dependent man, he worked his way by industry and perseverance, not only to wealth, but to the highest honours of his profession. In the temporary cessation of his legal life, his love of employment led him to aspire to the acquisition of a literary name. It is not, however, probable that his fame as a lawyer, a legislator, or a judge, will be superseded by his repute as an author. The transient popularity of his works has already in a great measure subsided, for, though they must ever be regarded as an extraordinary effort of laborious industry, and as composed in a pleasant and easy, though somewhat egotistic, style, they are not looked upon as authority by those who are best versed in the history of the various times of which they treat. It has been considered a material detraction from the merits of his works that from the beginning to the end of them he takes every opportunity of referring to the incidents of his own life, and the advice and opinions he gave in his professional capacity. It will be seen that this volunteer information has been serviceable in the preparation of the present sketch.

In the year before his own death he lost his wife, Lady Stratheden, to whose title their eldest son, William Frederick, succeeded, thus taking a place in the peerage which, but for his father's position as chancellor, would have given him precedence in the House of Lords. Lord Campbell left two other sons and four daughters.

CAMVILLE, GERARD DE (de Cana Villa), the ancestor of whose family came into England with William the Conqueror, was the eldest son of Richard de Camville, the founder of Combe Abbey in Warwickshire; and by his marriage with Nichola, the eldest of the three daughters of Richard de Haya, and the widow of William FitzErneis, had in her right the office of constable of the castle of Lincoln. A charter exists among the archives of the duchy of Lancaster (*Archæologia*, xxvii. 112) which is curious as having been granted by Richard I. between the demise of his father and his own coronation, and as showing that he did not then assume the style and title of 'King,' but only called himself 'Dominus Angliæ.' It confirms to Gerard de Camville and his wife Nichola all the right and heritage of Nichola in England and Normandy, together with the custody and constableship of Lincoln Castle. He was also made sheriff of the county of Lincoln.

On King Richard's departure to the Holy Land, Gerard de Camville having joined the party of Prince John, William de Longchamp, the chief justiciary, laid siege to Lincoln Castle, which Nichola resolutely defended (*Madox*, i. 22), and compelled Longchamp to withdraw his forces. On the king's return Gerard was not only deprived of the sheriffalty and constableship, but also of his own estate, and was reduced to the necessity of purchasing restitution of the latter, with the king's favour, by a fine of two thousand marks. On the accession of King John he recovered the sheriffalty, which he retained till the end of the seventh year of that reign, and received other proofs of the king's regard. When the kingdom was placed under interdict in 9 John, the king committed to him and to William de Cornhill all the lands and goods of the clergy in the diocese of Lincoln who refused to perform divine service. (*Cal. Rot. Pat.* 3.) He received the acknowledgment of fines at Cambridge in 10 and 11 John, 1208–9, and he and his associates are there specially called 'justicii itinerantes.'

He died in 16 John. (*Ibid.* 8, 10.) His wife, Nichola, survived him for some years, during which she held the sheriffalty of Lincolnshire, and was constituted governess of the castles of Frampton and Lincoln, the latter of which she gallantly defended against the confederated barons. She died about 15 Henry III., 1230–1.

CAMVILLE, THOMAS DE, was a nephew of the above Gerard de Camville, being the third son of his brother William by Albreda, the daughter and heir of Geoffrey Marmion. He held Westerham, in Kent, of the honor of Bologne, in 2 and 3 John, and paid fifteen marks for three knights' fees in that county, and two marks for one knight's fee in Essex. (*Rot. Cancell.* 161, 220.) His adherence to the rebellious barons at the close of that king's reign was punished with the loss of all his lands, which, however, were restored on his obedience to the government of Henry III. In 11 Henry III. he had the grant of a market for his manor of Fobbing, in Essex. (*Rot. Claus.* i. 243, 325, ii. 194.) He is only once named as a justicier, on the authority of a fine being levied before him in May 1229, 13 Henry III. (*Dugdale's Orig.* 42.) His death occurred in 1235, leaving Agnes, his widow, and a son Robert, who married a daughter of Hamo de Crevequer. (*Hasted*, iii. 162.)

CANTEBRIG, THOMAS DE (Cambridge), described as of the clerical profession, was an officer in the Exchequer in 29 Edward I., and his appointment as a baron of that court took place on September 16, 1307, two months after the accession of Edward II. In the following year, on October 24, he had a patent authorising him to take the place of William de Carleton, the senior baron, when he was absent, and to sit next to him when he was present—a clear proof of the royal favour, as there were then two barons in the court senior to him in standing. He remained in this place till July 17, 1310, when his removal doubtless arose from his services being more valuable in another character, as during the time he held the office, and for several years afterwards, extending to 1317, he was employed in foreign negotiations. (*New Fœdera*, i. 934, ii. 15, 175, 273, 333; *Madox*, ii. 58; *Parl. Writs*, ii. p. ii. 4, 630, 1408.)

CANTEBRIG, JOHN DE, could scarcely be the son of the above Thomas de Cantebrig, as Masters, in his 'Corpus Christi College' (p. 8), suggests, the latter being a clergyman, though he was probably nearly related to him. From 4 Edward II. he was continually employed in the judicial commissions in the county of Cambridge, and was returned member for it to several of the parliaments from the 14th to the 19th year. He is mentioned as a counsel in the Year Books of Edward II. and Edward III. In the third year of the latter he was one of the king's serjeants, and as such was joined in the commission into Northamptonshire, &c., and on October 22 in that year was made a knight, tanquam banerettus.

In 1331 he was seneschal of the abbot of St. Albans (*Newcome*, 223), and on January 18 he was raised to the bench of the Common Pleas, and, for some reason that does not appear, had a new patent on January 30, 1334. His death occurred in the next year.

His property was very extensive in the town and neighbourhood of Cambridge, and both during his life and by his will he devoted a great part of it to the guild of St. Mary, in that town (afterwards Corpus Christi College), of which he was a member, and twice alderman. (*Dugdale's Orig.* 45; *Abb. Rot. Orig.* 95; *Parl. Writs*, ii. p. ii. 630.)

CANTILUPE, SIMON DE. *See* S. NORMANNUS.

CANTILUPE, WILLIAM DE. The noble family of Cantilupe, so called from the original Champ de Loup, or Campus Lupi, followed the Norman Conqueror in his enterprise on the English monarchy. William, whose father was Walter de Cantilupe, in 2 John held the office of steward of the household. (*Rot. Liberat.* 1.) In the following year he was sheriff of Worcestershire, Warwick and Leicester, and Hereford; and over one or the other of these counties he presided for many years. From 5 to 10 John his name appears as one of the justiciers before whom fines were acknowledged. (*Hunter's Preface.*) During the remainder of that reign he was in frequent personal attendance on his sovereign, accompanying him to Ireland, and firmly supporting him both under the interdict and in his wars with the barons. It would be endless to recite the grants which were made to him by King John, even up to the last month of his reign (*Rot. Claus.* i. 290); and on the accession of Henry III. his loyalty was still conspicuous, both he and his son assisting in the siege of Montsorel in Leicestershire, and in raising that of Lincoln. In 2 Henry III. he was again made sheriff of Warwickshire and Leicestershire, with the custody of the castle of Kenilworth, where he fixed his chief residence; and in the next year he was appointed one of the justices itinerant into Bedfordshire and the neighbouring counties. He still enjoyed the office of seneschal, which his son also held after his death; and during the remainder of his life received repeated marks of the royal favour, the only interruption to which arose from his joining the barons who were dissatisfied with the ministry of Hubert de Burgh. He built a hospital at Studley, at the gates of a priory there, the advowson of which belonged to him.

His death occurred in April 1238, leaving four sons—William, the next-mentioned Walter, John, and Nicholas.

CANTILUPE, WALTER DE (BISHOP OF WORCESTER), the second son of the above William de Cantilupe, was educated for the Church, and in 10 John was presented to the living of Eyton. This was followed in the course of the next eight years by no less than seven benefices, besides a prebend in the church of Lichfield,— Wurefield, Burton, Long Huchendon, Rammcham, Preston, Herdewic, and half of Stokes. (*Rot. Pat.* 87, 106, &c.; *Rot. Chart.* 192.)

In 16 Henry III., 1231, he was one of the seven justices itinerant named for several counties, being the only occasion on which he appears to have acted in that capacity. In August 1236 he was elected to the bishopric of Worcester, and in his episcopal character he boldly resisted the papal exactions, influenced probably by the remembrance of his own pluralities; at the same time, however, exhibiting so much zeal 'that, to advance the heroic designs of Christian princes in the Holy Land, he went himself thither, accompanied by William Longspee, Earl of Salisbury.'

Towards the close of his life he sided with Simon de Montfort, Earl of Leicester, for which he was excommunicated by the pope's legate; but he lived long enough to repent of his disloyalty, and to obtain absolution. He died at his manor of Blockley on February 12, 1265. His character, according to the historian of his nephew, St. Thomas de Cantilupe, was that of 'a person of mind and courage equal to his birth.' He founded the nunnery of White Ladies, and was otherwise munificent to his see. (*Life and Gests of S. Thomas de Cantilupe, by R. S. S. I. Gant*, 1674.)

CANTILUPE, THOMAS DE (BISHOP OF HEREFORD), was the grandson of the above William de Cantilupe, whose heir of the same name was his father; his mother being Milicent, the daughter of Hugh de Gournay, and the widow of Almeric, Earl of Evreux in Normandy, and of Gloucester in England. He was born about the beginning of the reign of King Henry III., at his father's manor of Hameldone in Lincolnshire. Under the advice of his uncle, Walter, Bishop of Worcester, he was brought up with a view to the clerical profession, and studied at Oxford under Robert Kilwarby, who became Archbishop of Canterbury and a cardinal. He afterwards removed to Paris, and applied himself to the study of philosophy, in the College of Sorbonne, whence he proceeded to Orleans to read the civil law with an eminent professor there. Returning to Oxford, he applied himself to the canon law, and proceeded doctor. The nobility of his blood, as well as the eminence of his learning, pointed him out, in 1262, as worthy to fill the office of chancellor of the university, in performing the duties of which in the suppression of a riot between the southern and northern scholars, he is said to have greatly exerted himself, to the injury both of his person and habiliments.

The barons having assumed the ascendency, and the king being completely under their dictation, he was selected by them to fill the office of chancellor on February 21, 1265. Their power, however, being terminated by the battle of Evesham, and the death of De Montfort in the following August, his removal was the natural consequence.

Having retired to Oxford, he completed a course of divinity by taking the degree of doctor, his ancient friend and master, Robert Kilwarby, then Archbishop of Canterbury, honouring his act with his presence.

His connection with the insurgent barons did not blind King Henry to his merits, and accordingly, in 1266, he was appointed archdeacon of Stafford, to which were added 'many and fatt benefices,' as he held at the same time canonries in York, Lichfield, London, and Hereford. Neither was he in less favour with Edward I., being elected Bishop of Hereford on June 20, 1275.

The remainder of his life was devoted to the sacred duties of his office, on the performance of which his biographer is very eloquent, not forgetting 'his courage in defence of ecclesiasticall libertyes,' which engaged him in many controversies, and eventually led to his death. Archbishop Peckham having laid some injunctions on the sees within his jurisdiction which were prejudicial to their liberties, and considered to be beyond the verge of his power, our bishop volunteered a journey to Rome to obtain redress. There he was received with great distinction, and having prosecuted his suit to a successful issue, he commenced his journey homeward; but being seized with sickness, he could not proceed further than Monte Fiascone, where he died on August 25, 1282, in the sixty-third year of his age. His flesh was buried at the place of his death, and his bones were removed to England and interred in his cathedral. The miracles which were performed on both these events, and on other occasions during his life, and at his shrine, are stated to extend to the number of 425. The fame of them was so great that he was canonised about thirty-two years afterwards by Pope John XXII., on April 17, 1320, being the last Englishman so honoured.

The Bishops of Hereford in his honour assumed his family coat as the arms of their see—viz., Gules, three leopards' heads inverted, each with a flower de luce in his mouth, Or. (*Life and Gests of S. Thomas Cantilupe.*)

CARILEFO, WILLIAM DE (BISHOP OF DURHAM), a native of Bayeux, was so named from having been a monk of St. Carilefo, from which he was advanced to be abbot of St. Vincentius; both being monasteries in the province of Maine; the former being a cell at Covenham in Lincolnshire, and the latter one at Abergavenny in Montgomeryshire.

He was elected Bishop of Durham on November 10, 1080, in the place of Walcherus, who was slain about six months before. The church of Durham having been greatly neglected, the present edifice was commenced by him, and affords sufficient proof of the munificent expenditure, not only of this bishop, but of his successor, Ranulph Flambard, in its structure.

William of Malmesbury (*Gesta Regum*, 486, &c.), who describes him as a man of a ready tongue, and very powerful in his time, says that he was appointed by William Rufus to administer the public affairs in 1088, and Roger de Wendover (ii. 32, 34) distinctly mentions that he was made 'justiciarius.' His tenure of that office, however, must have been very short, for Odo, Bishop of Bayeux, is described as holding it at the previous Christmas, and Carilefo in the spring had joined that prelate in the confederacy to depose King William, and raise his brother Robert to the throne. The insurrection being quelled by the defeat of Odo, the king proceeded to Durham to chastise the bishop, whom he obliged to surrender and to quit the kingdom. After a banishment of two or three years he was permitted to return, when he endeavoured to ingratiate himself with the king by taking part against Archbishop Anselm. He was, however, soon after summoned to the court to meet certain charges made against himself. Compelled to obey, he reached the court of Windsor with difficulty, and, surviving only a few days, died there on January 2, 1095. His remains were removed to Durham, where they were deposited in his cathedral.

He is described as endowed with the highest mental gifts, with wit, erudition, eloquence, and subtlety, and as second to none in the conduct of business; but with unbridled ambition, and wanting faith and integrity. (*Dugdale's Monast.* i. 224, &c.; *Godwin*, 731; *Angl. Sac.* i. 704.)

CARLETON, WILLIAM DE, associated in 14 Edward I. with Henry de Bray in the custody of the vacant abbey of Ramsay, is inserted by Dugdale in his list of barons of the Exchequer in the same year, but he was only at that time one of the justices of the Jews. He is introduced in that character by Madox (i. 236) in the next and three following years, till which time the Jews were in the kingdom. The justices of the Jews seem always to have sat with the barons of the Exchequer; but their duties of course terminated after the expulsion of that people. William de Carleton and Peter de Leicester, who then held the office, were thereupon appointed regular barons, and the former continued to act from that time till the end of the reign. In 25 Edward I. he was employed by the king with two others to collect a sum of ten thousand pounds from the merchants at Antwerp. (*Rot. Parl.* i. 169, 194.)

Dugdale says that he was constituted chief baron on July 26, 1303, 31 Edward I.; but the liberate, on the authority of which this statement is made, contains no such designation. (*Madox,* ii. 62.) The title of chief baron indeed was not adopted till some years afterwards; but William de Carleton was at that time the senior baron, and was at the head of those reappointed on the accession of Edward II., 1307. On October 24, 1308, he had special licence from the king, on account of his long service, to retire to his own house as often and as long as his health or private affairs should require, and to attend at the Exchequer in his place when he should think fit (*Ibid.* ii. 57), and he does not appear among the justices who were summoned to parliament beyond the following March.

CARR, WILLIAM, in his admission to Gray's Inn in December 1655, is described of Newington, Middlesex. He was called to the bar in May 1663, and succeeded Sir Richard May as cursitor baron between 1685 and 1688, retaining his office at the Revolution. He died in 1689. (*Luttrell,* i. 557.)

CARTER, LAWRENCE, was born at Leicester about 1672, of a family which originally came from Hitchin in Hertfordshire. His father, who bore the same names, having projected the scheme of supplying Leicester with water, was chosen the representative of the borough in several parliaments of William III., of whom he was a firm supporter. His mother was Mary, the daughter of Thomas Wadland, Esq., of the Neworke at Leicester, an eminent solicitor, in whose office her husband had been articled. Their son, after being called to the bar by Lincoln's Inn, was elected recorder of his native town on September 1, 1697, and entering the House of Commons as its representative in the next year, sat there till the death of William III. In 1710, and in the two following parliaments of 1714 and 1715, he was returned for Beeralston, and at the dissolution of the latter in 1722 he was again elected for Leicester; but history has preserved no record of his senatorial eloquence. His professional career was distinguished by his being appointed in 1717 solicitor-general to the Prince of Wales, afterwards George II., by receiving in 1724 the degree of the coif, and by being made soon after one of the king's serjeants, when he was knighted.

On September 7, 1726, he succeeded Mr. Baron Price as a baron of the Exchequer, retaining his recordership for the next three years. He continued on the bench till his death on March 14, 1745, with the reputation of an upright judge. He was buried in the church of St. Mary de Castro, Leicester, where his monument is still to be seen. (*Nichol's Leicester,* i. 318.)

CARUS, THOMAS, was of a Lancashire family, and his descendants in 1684 were seated at Horton in that county. His legal school was the Middle Temple, where he became reader in Lent 1556. At the end of Mary's reign he was summoned to take the coif, which he received soon after the accession of Elizabeth, on April 19, 1559. From that time till Trinity 1565 his name occurs in Dyer's and Plowden's Reports. The date of his elevation as a judge of the Queen's Bench is not given, but from the latter author (*Plowden,* 376) it may be collected that he succeeded Mr. Justice Corbet, who sat in the court as late as Trinity Term 1566. Carus remained there till his death, the date of which has not been discovered; but no successor seems to have been appointed for him till May, 14 Elizabeth, 1572, although his name does not appear in the Reports after Easter in the twelfth year.

He married Catherine, daughter of Sir Thomas Preston of Furness Abbey, a lineal descendant of John de Preston, a judge of the Common Pleas in the reigns of Henry V. and VI.

CARY, JOHN, of an ancient and opulent family, seated in Devonshire, was the son of Sir John Cary, knight, bailiff of the forest of Selwood, and Jane, daughter of Sir Guy de Brien. He was appointed a captain of the Devonshire coast, and a commissioner of array in the same county, soon after his father's death in 1371. (*New Fœdera,* iii. 976, 1046.)

His name does not occur in the Year Books, and there is no proof of his ever having acted as an advocate. According to the practice of that period, neither the chief nor the puisne barons of the Exchequer were necessarily selected from the serjeants or pleaders, nor indeed otherwise connected with the law than as officers of that particular department. It is true that he was called by the king's writ to take upon himself the degree of a serjeant-at-law in 6

Richard II.; but it is equally true that he disobeyed the summons (*Manning*, 201), and it may not be unreasonably supposed that he refused the honour because he was not a regular pleader in the courts.

Whatever was his previous position, he was raised to the office of chief baron of the Exchequer on November 5, 1386, 10 Richard II.; but it turned out an unfortunate advancement for him. Within a fortnight after his appointment the parliament passed an ordinance placing the government of the kingdom under eleven commissioners, and in effect depriving, not only the king's favourites, but the king himself, of all power in the state. In the efforts made to regain the ascendency, the plan of obtaining the declaration of the judges that the ordinance was illegal was adopted. The chief baron was one of those who concurred in that declaration, being present with the others on the discussion at Shrewsbury. He, therefore, was included in the impeachment, and was condemned to death with his colleagues, but, like them, had his sentence commuted to banishment. The place of his exile was the city of Waterford and a circle of two miles round it; and for his support he had an allowance of 20*l*. per annum. As his name was not among those of his banished brethren who received permission to return to England in 20 Richard II., he probably died in Ireland, apparently in the previous year (*Cal. Inquis.* p. m. iii. 196); but his property, including Torrington and Cockington in Devonshire, was restored in 3 Henry IV., 1402. (*Rot. Parl.* iii. 484.)

He married Margaret, daughter and heir of Robert Holloway, by whom he had two sons, Robert and John.

The latter was Bishop of Exeter for a short space, and died in 1419. The former was a renowned knight, many of whose descendants were honoured with various titles in the peerage, all of which have become extinct, except that of Viscount Falkland and Baron Hunsdon.

CASSY, JOHN, was probably born at the manor of Wightfield, in the parish of Deerhurst in Gloucestershire, which had been held by the family from the time of Edward III., and continued in their possession certainly till the end of Elizabeth's reign. His name occurs among the counsel in Richard Bellewe's Reports of the time of Richard II.; and he was raised to the office of chief baron of the Exchequer on May 12, 1389, in the twelfth year of that reign.

He received a new patent on the accession of Henry IV., but died very shortly afterwards. His tomb affords an example of the practice of placing the royal arms on the monuments of persons holding office under the crown, the three lions of England occurring on the brass over his remains. (*Atkyns's Gloucestersh.* 202; *Gent. Mag.* Feb. 1840, p. 141.)

CATESBY, JOHN, of a family settled in Northamptonshire, was apparently the uncle of William Catesby, esquire of the household of Edward IV. and Richard III., who was attainted for his adherence to the latter in the field of Bosworth. (*Rot. Parl.* vi. 276, 278.)

He was a member of the Inner Temple, or the 'Inner Inne,' as it was then called, and first appears among the advocates in the Year Books in Michaelmas 1458. He was honoured with the coif in 1463, and made king's serjeant on April 18, 1469. He was promoted to the bench of the Common Pleas on November 20, 1481, 21 Edward IV., and was knighted in the following year. The three subsequent changes in the sovereignty of the kingdom made no alteration in his judicial position, though Henry VII. delayed his reappointment for nearly a month after his brethren, probably on account of doubts arising from his relationship to William Catesby, so closely connected with the late king.

The excellence of his character may be inferred from his being the first-named executor in the will of Bishop Waynflete (*Chandler*, 382), whom he survived but a short time, dying in 1486.

He married Elizabeth, the daughter of William Green, of Heese in Middlesex, Esq., and had by her seven sons and two daughters. He was buried in the abbey of St. James, in Northampton; and apparently was seated at his manor of Whiston in that county. (*Test. Vetust.* 277, 389.)

The conspirator in the gunpowder plot was one of his descendants.

CATLIN, ROBERT. There were two contemporary lawyers of the name of Catlin, Richard and Robert, of different branches of the same family. (*Fuller*, i. 568; *Blomefield's Norfolk*, i. 682.) Richard Catlin, of Lincoln's Inn, was made a serjeant in 1552, and queen's serjeant in 1556. He was connected with the county of Norfolk, and was steward of Norwich, which he also represented in parliament.

The branch from which Robert Catlin was descended was anciently seated at Raunds in Northamptonshire. He was born at Thrapstone in that county (*Plowden*, 342), and was elected reader of the Middle Temple in 1547. In 1555 he was admitted to the degree of the coif; and on November 4, in the following year, Philip and Mary appointed him one of their serjeants. He was raised to the bench as a judge of the Common Pleas on October 10, 1558, five weeks before the death of Queen Mary, and received a new patent the day after the accession of Queen Elizabeth. Previous to the following term, on the removal of the two Catholic chief justices, he was on January 22 promoted to the head of the Court of Queen's Bench, and knighted. He continued to preside as chief justice for the next sixteen years, with a high reputation for wisdom and gravity. That he was bold and independent also is apparent from a letter to Lord Burleigh, who had conveyed a message from the queen, complaining of his judgment in a suit in which the Earl of Leicester was a party, wherein he says he 'dares not alter the ancient forms of court.' (*Cal. State Papers* [1471], 416.)

However high the character of a judge may be, it is not to be expected that those against whom he decides will always join in his praises. In 1566 one Thomas Welsh of London was indicted in the Queen's Bench for saying, 'My Lord Chief Justice Catlin is incensed against me; I cannot have justice, nor can be heard; for that court now is made a court of conscience,' and was fined accordingly.

The chief justice died at his seat at Newenham in Bedfordshire in 1574. He married Ann, the daughter of John Boles, of Wallington in Hertfordshire, and relict of John Burgoyne. (*Chauncy*, 48.) By her he left an only daughter, Mary, who married first Sir John Spencer, and their son Robert was created Baron Spencer of Wormleighton in 1603, whose grandson was advanced to the earldom of Sunderland in 1643. The fifth earl succeeded under the act of parliament as Duke of Marlborough, his mother being second daughter of the great duke.

The earldom of Spencer of Althorp is derived from the same stock, the first earl having been a younger son of the third Earl of Sunderland. The barony of Churchill of Whichcote also was granted in 1815 to a younger son of the third Duke of Marlborough, and all these titles still grace the English peerage.

CAUX. See J. DE CALETO.

CAVE, JOHN DE, acted as a justicier from 1254 to 1261, 45 Henry III. (*Dugdale's Orig.* 43; *Excerpt. e Rot. Fin.* ii. 331–336.) If H. Phillipps (*Grandeur of the Law* [1684], 53) is right in stating that the baronets of that name of Stanford in Northamptonshire, a title still existing, are descended from him, his ancestor was Jordan de Cave, the brother of Wyamarus de Cave, who received lands in North and South Cave, in Yorkshire, from William the Conqueror, and transferred them to Jordan.

CAVE, HUGH DE, in 5 Edward I. was clerk to Ralph de Hengham, chief justice of the King's Bench. (*Dugdale's Orig.* 94.) In 21 Edward I., 1293, he was the last named of four justices itinerant assigned for the county of Surrey; and he was among the justices summoned to the parliament of August, 23 Edward I. (*Parl. Writs*, i. 29.) He and his brother, probably the undernamed John, in 15 Edward I., had a grant of land at Cokefrueddinge in Staffordshire, from Alwyn de Norton and his wife. (*Abb. Placit.* 213.)

CAVE, JOHN DE, is inserted by Dugdale as having been appointed a justice of the King's Bench in 1283, 11 Edward I. Although there is no absolute impossibility that he may have been the same person as the above John de Cave, the lapse of time from 1261 to 1283 renders it very improbable. There is, however, no subsequent record of his name in connection with the courts.

He appears to have been the brother of the last-mentioned Hugh de Cave, and to have had grants of land made to him till 2 Edward II. (*Abb. Placit.* 213, 215, 275, 305.)

CAVENDISH, JOHN DE. Notwithstanding the high legal rank which John de Cavendish attained, and the tragical termination of his life, and although his family was afterwards illustrated by two dukedoms, no account remains of his early career except that which may be collected from the Year Books. Nor can the want of any other memorials of him be wondered at, when we advert to the fact that nearly 250 years elapsed after the death of the chief justice before the family was ennobled. John de Cavendish was the son of Roger de Gernum, the grandson of Ralph de Gernum, an after-mentioned justice itinerant in the reign of Henry III. The name of Cavendish was first assumed by either his father or himself, each being said to have acquired it by marriage with the heiress of the lord of the manor so called in the county of Suffolk. John de Cavendish appears in the Year Books as an advocate as early as 21 Edward III., and as late as 45 Edward III., and was made a serjeant in 40 Edward III. Yet Dugdale introduces him in his 'Chronica Series' as chief justice of the King's Bench in 39 Edward III., 1365. This is evidently founded on mistake, for Dugdale, six years afterwards, gives a patent appointing him a puisne judge of the Common Pleas on November 27, 1371, besides showing that Sir Henry Green was chief justice till October 29, 1365, on which day he was succeeded by Sir John Knyvet, who kept the place till he was made chancellor, when Cavendish is again inserted in the list as raised to the chief justiceship of the King's Bench on July 15, 1372. From 40 to 44 Edward III. he was joined in the commissions as a judge of assize, his salary for which was 20*l.* a year (*Devon's Issue Roll*, 360); and fines were levied before him as a judge of the Common Pleas at the commencement of 46 Edward III., in the term next after his appointment to that court. (*Dugdale's Orig.* 45.) He was a trier of petitions in every parliament from 1372, and not before, which he undoubtedly would have been had he been then chief justice. He continued to fulfil his high duties with great credit till the end of the reign, when he was immediately reappointed, with the grant of 100 marks per annum, which had been for some years made to his predecessors.

He seems to have been a bit of a humourist. A case being heard before him in which a question arose upon a lady's age, her counsel pressed the court to have her before them, and judge by inspection whether she was within age or not. But 'Candish, Justice,' showing great knowledge of female character, says, 'Il n' ad nul home en Engleterre que puy adjudge a droit deins age ou de plein age; car ascun femes que sont de age de xxx ans voilent apperer d'age de xviii ans.' (*Year Book*, 50 Edw. III. fo. 6, pl. 12.)

The chief justice met with an untimely end. The insurrection of Wat Tyler in 1381 extended itself from Kent over various parts of England. In the county of Suffolk the rebels assembled to the number of 50,000, destroying the property and ill-treating the persons of all who would not join them. The principal objects of their vengeance seemed to be all those who had any sort of learning. They attacked Sir John Cavendish's house, and plundered and burned it; and having unfortunately got hold of the venerable man, they dragged him into the market-place of Bury St. Edmunds, and there, after a mock trial, ruthlessly beheaded him and insulted his remains.

Thus perished this amiable judge, after gracing the judicial bench for ten years, without an imputation of having perverted the course of justice, or of deviating from the path of rectitude and integrity, to justify or to palliate the brutal fate which overtook him. Shortly before his murder he was honoured by being elected chancellor of the University of Cambridge.

By his wife Alice, who died before him, he left two sons, the descendant of one of whom, William, became the biographer of Cardinal Wolsey, to whom he was gentleman usher. He was afterwards admitted into the service of the king, by whom his fortunes were greatly enriched by various profitable offices and valuable grants of lands belonging to the dissolved abbeys and priories. One of his sons, William, was ennobled by James I. with the title of Baron Cavendish of Hardwicke in 1604, to which that of Earl of Devonshire was added in 1618. The fourth earl was created Duke of Devonshire in 1694. A younger son of the fourth duke was created Earl of Burlington in 1831, a title which is now held by his grandson, the present Duke of Devonshire.

Another son of Wolsey's biographer, named Charles, was father of Sir William Cavendish, who was raised to the peerage by being created Viscount Mansfield in 1620, to which were successively added the earldom, marquisate, and dukedom of Newcastle, all of which titles became extinct in 1691.

CAXTON, JEREMIAH DE, although omitted in Dugdale's list, was undoubtedly a justicier, being expressly called so in 30 Henry III., as being present at the execution of a final concord 'before the king himself' at Westminster (*Harleian MSS.* 371, fo. 711a), and also payments being made for assizes to be taken before him in 28 and 31 Henry III. (*Excerpt. e Rot. Fin.* i. 424, ii. 9.) In the following year he is mentioned as one of the custodes of the archbishopric of Canterbury during its vacancy (*Madox*, i. 595), after which his name occurs in 37 Henry III., 1253, as holding pleas before the king with Henry de Bretton.

CECIL, WILLIAM (EARL OF SALISBURY), was one of the parliamentary commissioners of the Great Seal for less than four months. His grandfather was the renowned Lord Burleigh, and his father was Robert Cecil, the wise minister of Queen Elizabeth and James I., who, after serving both sovereigns, and after passing through the two lower grades of the peerage, was created Earl of Salisbury in 1605. On his death, in 1612, this William succeeded, but did not do much credit to his lineage. At first the obsequious servant of his sovereign, he concurred in every act proposed by the court, and attended King Charles when he retired in his troubles to York, joining the peers in signing the declaration that the king had no intention to take warlike measures. Soon after, without any apparent reason, he fled from court, deserting the king's party for that of the parliament, and forming one of the small knot of lords who legislated at Westminster. He had the effrontery to appear before the king at Oxford as a commissioner to treat for peace, and was named in the same capacity in the proposed treaty at Uxbridge. Though totally without credit with either party, he was appointed a commissioner of the Great Seal on July 3, 1646. The parliament, however, withdrew their confidence from him and the other commissioners on October 30, and placed the Seal in the custody of the speakers of the two houses.

On the decapitation of the king he allowed himself to be nominated one of the Council of State, and, as if this was not a sufficient degradation, he got himself, on the abolition of the House of Lords, returned as a member of the House of Commons for Lynn in Norfolk, in September 1649. After being expelled with the rest by Cromwell in 1653, he joined the Rump at its meeting in 1659, to be again expelled, and again restored. His insignificance probably saved him on the restoration of Charles II., who no doubt thought that the contempt which all men felt for the degraded earl was a sufficient punishment.

He died on December 3, 1668. His descendants have wiped out his disgrace, and, at the end of two centuries, flourish with the additional title of marquis, granted in 1789. (*Clarendon; Whitelocke; Parl. Hist.*)

CESTRETON, ADAM DE. King Henry III. before the seventeenth year of his reign founded a house for the maintenance of converted Jews, in the street, then called 'New Street,' but now known as Chancery Lane, endowing it with many houses and lands, and bestowing on it the church of St. Dunstan, in Fleet Street. Over this 'Domus Conversorum' a custos was appointed, sometimes during the king's pleasure and sometimes for life, who was generally an ecclesiastic, and connected with the legal profession. In the reign of Edward I. this office was first united with that of master of the Rolls; and when, by the banishment of the Jews from England, the object of its foundation gradually ceased, the house was eventually annexed to the office of master of the Rolls, and thenceforward received the name by which it is now distinguished.

Adam de Cestreton, both an ecclesiastic and an officer of the court, received in 50 Henry III. 1265, a grant of the custody of this house for his life; and during the whole of 52 Henry III. he was performing the functions of a justicier. (*Excerpt. e Rot. Fin.* ii. 465–478.) The short time that he remained on the bench may account for his non-appearance in Dugdale's 'Chronica Series,' inasmuch as his death occurred at the beginning of the following year.

CHACEPORC, PETER. A grant of 30 marks per annum was made in 31 Henry III. to Hugh de Chaceporc and his wife Guidonea, who in the patent is called 'cognatæ regis.' (*Cal. Rot. Pat.* 22.) Whatever was their relationship to Peter Chaceporc, it will account for his being constituted king's treasurer in 26 Henry III., and for his being keeper of the king's wardrobe from 29 to 37 Henry III. (*Ibid.* 19; *Madox*, i. 609, &c.) The wardrobe appears to have been used as one of the royal treasuries, and a certain class of fines was commonly paid into it. On May 15, 1253, William de Kilkenny being ill, the Great Seal was delivered to Peter Chaceporc and John de Lexinton, and there is little doubt that the former merely received it in one or other of the above characters, probably in the former, to be deposited in the wardrobe for safe custody. In that same year Peter Chaceporc received the archdeaconry of Wells, and in the following the treasurership of Lincoln, (*Le Neve*, 43, 151), after which no mention is made of his name, except that he is one of the executors named in King Henry's will. (*Rymer*, 496.) He is sometimes called Chaceport.

CHAMBERLAYNE, THOMAS, claims a descent from William, Count Tankerville, who was one of the Norman followers of William the Conqueror, and whose son John became lord chamberlain to Henry I.; the same office being held by several of his descendants, its name thus became attached to them. One of the branches of the family, William Chamberlayne, brother of Sir Thomas Chamberlayne, who was employed in diplomacy by Henry VIII. and his three successors, settled in Ireland, and was the father of the subject of the present article.

Thomas Chamberlayne was called to the bar by Gray's Inn in 1585, and became reader in 1607. He was raised to the degree of the coif in 1614, was made a Welsh judge in 1615, and in 1616 was advanced to the office of chief justice of Chester, and knighted. (*Cal. State Papers* [1611], 289, 363.) From this position he was selected to be one of the judges of the King's Bench on October 8, 1620. In that court he remained only four years; for, whether from feeling the duties too onerous, or from some other cause, he retired from it on October 18, 1624, and resumed his judicial seat at Chester, with a grant of the same precedency in the Court of Common Pleas, to be held without fee or charge, which was made to him within a week after the accession of Charles I. (*Croke, Jac.* 690; *Cal. State Papers* [1625–6], 5.) In a commission dated May 12, 1625, he is described not only as chief justice of Chester, but also as a judge of the Common Pleas. (*Rymer*, xviii. 673.) He is likewise mentioned by Sir William Jones (*Reports*, 70), under Easter Term, 1 Car., as one of the judges before whom the case of Lord Sheffield v. Ratcliffe was argued in the Exchequer Chamber, in which it appears that after various hearings, extending over two years, the judges were equally divided. Lord Bacon, in his address to Sir James Whitelock on succeeding to the chief justiceship of Chester, recommends him to follow the example of his predecessor Chamberlayne, who, he says, 'for religion, for lerning, for stoutnesse in course of justice, for watchfulnesse over the peace of the people, and for relation of matters of state to the counsell heer, I have not knowen (no disprayse to any) a better servant to the king in his place.' (*Liber Famelicus*, 80.)

He died on September 17 or 27, 1625, having married, first, Elizabeth, daughter of Sir George Fermor, knight, of Easton Nestor in Northamptonshire, and widow of Sir William Stafford, knight, of Blatherwick in the same county; and, secondly, Lady Elizabeth Berkeley, only daughter of Lord Chamberlain Hunsdon, and widow of Sir Thomas Berkeley. (*Cal. St. Papers* [1619], 346.) His eldest son, Thomas, of Wickham in Oxfordshire, was a loyal adherent to King Charles in his misfortunes, and was by him created a baronet in 1642, a title which lasted 134 years, and expired in 1776. (*Wotton*, ii. 374.)

CHAMBRÈ, ALAN. The family of De la Chambrè, De Camera, or Chaumperay was of Norman origin, and the name of one of its members occurs on the Roll of Battle Abbey. They settled in Westmoreland, where their descendants have flourished in an uninterrupted lineal succession till the present time. Alan Chambrè was the son of Walter Chambrè, of Halhead Hall in the parish of Kendal, and recorder of Kendal, by his marriage with Mary, daughter of Jacob Morland, of Capplethwaite Hall in the same county.

He was born in 1739, and, being destined to the law, he, reviving an ancient custom which had been long discontinued, first resorted to an inn of Chancery, and paid the customary dozen of claret on admission into the society of Staple Inn, and his arms are emblazoned on a window in the hall. From this inn he removed to the Middle Temple in February 1758, but transferred himself to Gray's Inn in November 1764, and was called to the bar in May 1767. The diligence with which he had devoted himself to his studies was proved by the success which he achieved, and his independent and upright conduct and amiable disposition may be estimated by his popularity among his colleagues. He selected the Northern Circuit, and soon became one of its leaders. In 1788 he was chosen treasurer of his inn, and in 1796 he was elected recorder of Lancaster. On the resignation of Mr. Baron Perryn in 1799 he was named as his successor, the announcement of which was received by the circuit bar with 'acclamations quite unprecedented.' A short act of parliament was passed on July 1, 1799, authorising, for the first time, a serjeant to receive his degree in the vacation, so that the vacant office might be immediately granted to him. In June of the following year he was removed from the Court of Exchequer to the Common Pleas, in which he remained till his resignation in Michaelmas vacation 1815.

In the exercise of his functions he merited and received universal praise both for his learning and urbanity. So extremely careful was he of doing anything that could by possibility be misinterpreted that on one occasion he declined the invitation to a house, at which the judges had been accustomed to be entertained during the circuit, because the proprietor was defendant in a cause at that assize.

Sir Alan lived seven years after his retirement, and, dying at Harrogate on September 20, 1823, was buried in the family vault at Kendal.

CHANNELL, WILLIAM FRY, is one of the present barons of the Exchequer. He is the son of Pike Channell, Esq., of Peckham in Surrey. He was called to the bar by the Inner Temple in May 1827, and was one of the five gentlemen who, in 1840, on the warrant for opening the Court of Common Pleas to all barristers being declared null and void, were the first who were called to the degree of serjeant-at-law with all its former privileges. On February 12, 1857, he was appointed to his present office, and knighted.

He married in 1834 a daughter of Richard Moseley, Esq., of Champion Hill, Camberwell.

CHANVILL, WILLIAM DE (ARCHDEACON OF RICHMOND), was one of the justiciers at Westminster before whom fines were levied. (*Hunter's Preface.*) That dignity he had enjoyed since 1189. He probably died in 1196, as his successor was then appointed. (*Le Neve*, 323.)

CHAPPLE, WILLIAM, belonging to a Dorsetshire family, and residing at Waybay House in the parish of Upway, was born in 1677. In 1722 he entered parliament as member for Dorchester, which he continued to represent till he was raised to the bench. History is silent as to his talents as a senator, but as a lawyer his reputation was high. Called serjeant in 1724, he was made a judge on the North Wales Circuit in 1728, and on his appointment as king's serjeant in 1729 he was knighted. On June 16, 1737, he was constituted a judge of the King's Bench, and occupied the seat for nearly eight years with credit and distinction. He died on March 15, 1745, leaving, by his wife Trehane Clifton, of Green Place, Wonersh, Surrey, four sons and two daughters, one of whom married Sir Fletcher Norton, afterwards Lord Grantley. (*Hutchins's Dorset*, i. 373, 596; *Strange*, 1075.)

CHARLETON, ROBERT DE (to which branch of the family of Charleton of Shropshire he belongs there is no account), was raised to the office of chief justice of the Court of Common Pleas on January 30, 1388, 11 Richard II., and the fines levied before him extend to Midsummer 1394. As his attendance in parliament is not noticed at a later period, he probably died soon after that date. He received the order of knighthood as a banneret in 1388. (*Dugdale's Orig.* 46, 103.) Some of his decisions are in Richard Bellewe's Reports.

CHARLETON, JOB, descended from the ancient Shropshire family of Charleton, and directly from Sir Alan Charleton, of Appley Castle near Wellington, the brother of John, the first Lord Powis. He was the eldest son of Robert Charleton, of Whitton, by his first wife, Emma, daughter of Thomas Harby, of Adston, Northamptonshire; from whose brother, Sir Job Harby (both eminent jewellers who had suffered much in the royal cause), he received his baptismal name. Born in London in 1614, and educated at Magdalen Hall, Oxford, he was called to the bar by Lincoln's Inn, but does not appear to have practised in the courts during the interregnum, but was elected to Protector Richard's only parliament in 1659, and also to the first two parliaments of Charles II. in 1660 and 1661, as member for Ludlow.

His reputation for loyalty may be inferred from his being included on the Restoration in the first batch of new serjeants, and being made one of his majesty's council at Ludlow for the Marches of Wales. In 1662 he had a grant of 370l. for the services rendered by his father to Charles I. (*Cal. St. Papers* [1662], 376), and also succeeded Sir Geoffrey Palmer as chief justice of Chester, being thereupon knighted. He became king's serjeant in 1668, but his name is very seldom mentioned by the law reporters of the day.

In the parliament of 1661 he was chairman of the committee for elections; and on February 4, 1673, he was unanimously elected speaker. His claim for the customary privileges was uttered in so neat and brief an address that Lord Chancellor Shaftesbury complimented him on having 'with so much advantage introduced a shorter way of speaking' on the occasion. His resignation of the chair, in a fortnight after, was not unlikely to have been the result of an intrigue of the Earl of Shaftesbury, who was then in the ascendant. By Sir Stephen Fox's confession to the parliament of 1679, Sir Job had a pension of 1000l. while he was speaker.

Sir Job retired to his chief justiceship of Chester, in which he desired to die; but after a few years he was disturbed in the enjoyment of it by the ambition of Sir George Jeffreys. That impudent aspirant pressed the king so hard for the place that, to make way for him, it was resolved that Sir Job should be removed to a seat in the Common Pleas. This Sir Job took heavily to heart, and, desiring to see the king to endeavour to divert him from the purpose, went to Whitehall and placed himself where the king must pass; but his majesty, seeing him at a distance and knowing his object, turned short off and went another way. The disappointed judge 'pitied his poor master, and never thought of troubling him more, but buckled to his business in the Common Pleas.' Roger North, who relates these particulars (p. 213), calls him 'an old cavalier, loyal, learned, grave, and wise,' and concludes his narration thus: 'May Westminster Hall never know a worse judge than he was.'

He sat as justice of the Common Pleas from April 26, 1680, till April 21, 1686, when he was one of the four judges who were removed by James II. for giving his opinion in opposition to the king's dispensing power. He was however restored to his chief justiceship of Chester (*Bramston's Autob.* 223; 2 *Shower*, 460), and was made a baronet on the 12th of May following. He died on May 27, 1697.

His seat was at Ludford in Herefordshire. By his first wife, Dorothy, daughter and heir of William Blundell, of Bishops Castle, Esq., he had four sons and three daughters; and by his second wife, Lettice, daughter of Walter Waring, of Oldbury, Esq., he had one son and one daughter. The baronetcy became extinct in 1784. (*Wotton*, v. 13; *Wood's Fasti*, i. 464.)

CHASTILLON, HENRY DE, or CASTILLION, was raised to the archdeaconry of Canterbury in 1195, 7 Richard I., and was then acting as a justicier in the Curia Regis, several fines being levied before him in that year. He probably had previously filled some office in the Exchequer, and may have been the Henry de Casteillun who accounted for the ministry of the chamberlainship ('chamberlengariæ') of London in 6 and 7 Richard I. (*Madox*, i. 775.)

During the controversy which arose in 1202 between King John and the monks of St. Augustine's, Canterbury, concerning the right of patronage to the church of Faversham, the archdeacon contrived to secure some advantage to himself by claiming the custody of the church during the vacancy. (*Hasted*, xii. 564.)

CHAUCOMB, HUGH DE, in the last three years of the reign of Richard I. was sheriff of Staffordshire, and from the 6th to the 9th John held the same office in Warwickshire and Leicestershire. In 2 John he was employed as a justicier in Normandy, and in 5 John he was one of the justiciers before whom fines were acknowledged in Hampshire and Nottinghamshire, and in the same year the king pardoned him a sum of money which he owed to certain Jews. He was also employed in making inquisition at all the ports as to those who brought corn from Normandy; and the castle of Kenilworth was committed to his custody. He held it for four years, and then for some unrelated cause he lost the royal favour; for in 9 John he was ordered to deliver the castle to Robert de Roppel, and was fined 800 marks to recover the goodwill of the king. His property lay in the counties of Lincoln and Oxford, and his wife's name was Hodierna. (*Rot. Pat.* 74; *Rot. de Finibus*, 382.)

CHAYNELL, JOHN, was summoned in 5 Edward II., 1312, among the legal assistants to parliament, in what precise character is not stated, and his attendance continued to be required in most of the parliaments till 1324. He is first mentioned as a justice of assize in 1314, and the last commission in which his name occurs is in 17 Edward II. (*Parl. Writs*, ii. p. ii. 654; *Rot. Parl.* i. 450.)

CHELMSFORD, LORD. *See* F. THESIGER.

CHESTER, EARL OF. *See* R. BLUNDEVIL.

CHESTER, PETER DE, was one of the justices itinerant in 54 Henry III., 1270, for pleas of the forest. He was appointed as a baron of the Exchequer in 12 Edward I., 1284, and continued to act till 1288. In 1282 he received the provostship of Beverley, and died about 1298. (*Madox*, ii. 322; *Monast.* vi. 1307.)

CHEYNE, WILLIAM, appears in an apocryphal List of Readers of Gray's Inn, but the Year Books prove that he was in practice as an advocate from 8 Henry IV. till 2 Henry V. In 12 Henry IV. he was called serjeant; and on June 16, 1415, 3 Henry V., he was constituted a justice of the King's Bench, and was reappointed on the accession of Henry VI. In 2 Henry VI., January 21, 1424, he was raised to the office of chief justice of the King's Bench (*Acts Privy Council*, iii. 132) and knighted. He presided in that court till 1439, when he resigned. His death occurred in 1442, and he was buried in the church of St. Benet, Paul's Wharf. (*Weever*, 686.)

By his wife Margaret he left a son and a daughter, to the former of whom he bequeathed 400*l.* and all his estates at Stoke and Trapeseles. (*Testam. Vetust.* 249.)

CHISHULL, JOHN DE (BISHOP OF LONDON), in 1264, 48 Henry III., was chancellor of the Exchequer, and records state that the king's signature was made to divers patents while the Seal was in his custody (*Cal. Rot. Pat.* 35), and that he gave it up in February 1265. He was archdeacon of London in 1262, and became dean in 1268. In the latter year, on October 30, the Great Seal was again committed to his custody, to be held at the king's pleasure, which he retained till the end of the following July, but whether with the title of chancellor does not appear.

In February 1270 he was constituted treasurer, in which office he continued about two years.

He was elected to the bishopric of London on December 7, 1273. He died on February 8, 1280, and was buried in St. Paul's. (*Godwin*, 183; *Le Neve*, 177, 183, 324.)

CHOKE, RICHARD, was of a Somerset-shire family, and the son of John Choke, of the manor of Long Ashton in that county. He is first mentioned as an advocate in 19 Henry VI., 1440, and was called to the degree of serjeant in July 1453. Six months after the accession of Edward IV. he was raised to the bench of the Common Pleas, not however as chief justice, as Dugdale erroneously states, but as 'one of the judges' of that court, according to his patent, which is dated September 5, 1461. That he was a useful judge, and did not unnecessarily interfere with the violent politics of the time, may be presumed from his successive reappointments on the temporary restoration of Henry VI. in 1470, on the return of Edward IV. in the following year, and on the accessions of Edward V. and Richard III. in 1483, in the first year of the latter of whom he died, and was buried at Long Ashton.

His first wife was Joan, daughter of William Pavey, of Bristol, by whom he had several children. His second wife was Margaretta Mones, who survived him a year. The family, after three generations, was settled at Avington in Berkshire. (*Ashmole's Berks*, iii. 318; *Collinson's Somerset*, ii. 291.)

CHOLMLEY, ROGER, was the natural son of Sir Richard Cholmley, descended from the ancient race of Cholmondeley in Cheshire, who was lieutenant governor of Berwick under Henry VII., and afterwards governor of Hull and lieutenant of the Tower of London. He died in 1522, leaving a handsome provision for Roger, whom he placed at Lincoln's Inn. The date of his first admission there cannot be found; but the fact of his being re-admitted in 1509, which the books of the inn record, gives some substance to the story that the embryo chief justice entered at first rather freely into the frolics of youth. It is evident that he soon reformed, and diligently pursued his legal studies, laying up stores for future use so assiduously that within two years after his father's death he was admitted to the bench of the society. He filled the office of reader there no less than three times—in Lent 1524, in Lent 1529, and in autumn 1531, on the occasion of his being called to the degree of the coif, which he assumed in the following Michaelmas Term.

Roger Ascham tells a story which Cholmley used to relate of himself, that when he was an ancient in Lincoln's Inn, certain students being brought before him to be corrected for their irregularities, one of them, remembering the old man's early career in the same house, said to him, 'Sir, we be yong gentlemen, and wise men before us have proved all fashions, and yet have done well.' 'Indeed,' answered Cholmley, 'in youthe I was as you are mow, and I had twelve felloes like unto myself; but not one of them came to a good end. And therefore foloe not my example in youth, but foloe my counsell in age, if ever ye think to come to this place, or to theis yeares that I am come unto, lesse ye meet either povertie or Tiburn in the way.' (*Seward's Anecdotes*, iv. 275.)

In 1530 he was appointed one of the commissioners to enquire into Cardinal Wolsey's possessions in Middlesex (*Rymer*, xiv. 402); and in October 1536 he was knighted, having in the preceding year been elected recorder of London. This office he held for ten years, during which he was twice returned as representative of that city in parliament—viz., in 1537 and 1542. He was named in 1540 as a commissioner in London to search for and burn all heretical books, and to enquire into transgressions against the acts of the Six Articles. His London residence was in the Old Bailey, and probably formed part of the property (now the London Coffee House) which he granted to his school at Highgate.

It was not till 1544 that he was made one of the king's serjeants. He then surrendered the recordership, on which occasion the corporation granted him yearly a new year's gift of twenty angels (nobles) in gold. In the following year, on November 11, he was appointed chief baron of the Exchequer—an office which he retained for the remainder of Henry's reign, and for above five years under Edward VI., when on March 21, 1552, he was promoted to the chief justiceship of the King's Bench.

He had been seated there little above a year before he was called upon to witness the will by which King Edward attempted to exclude his sister Mary from the throne. Although this was probably not a voluntary act, but under pressure of the powers that ruled, yet within a few days after the accession of that princess he was committed to the Tower, where he remained six weeks, at the end of which he was liberated on payment of a large fine. Though never replaced on the bench, he was soon restored to favour, and named in several commissions in the first year of Mary's reign. One of these was for the trial of Sir Nicholas Throckmorton, from whose remarks at the outset, as recorded by Holinshed (iv. 33), it may be inferred that his character for impartiality did not stand very high.

Queen Mary admitted him into her privy council, by the books of which it appears that he was on several occasions appointed to examine certain prisoners in the Tower, with the addition of the horrible discretion of putting them 'to such tortures as . . . shall be thought most convenient.' (*Jardine on Torture*, 75, 76.)

Sir Roger lived for seven years after Elizabeth's accession, and his name occurs as late as 1562 in a commission for the trial of persons charged with coining. The evening of his life he passed in the calm delights of literary retirement, closing it by establishing and amply endowing one of those useful foundations which then became the happy substitutes for chantries for priests, and which now remain as glorious memorials of the piety and forethought of their originators. This was a free grammar school at Highgate, incorporated on May 6, 1565. One of his last acts was an additional grant in its favour of various premises in the following month, at the close of which he died. He was interred on July 2 at St. Martin's, Ludgate, where his wife Christine had been buried in December 1558. (*Machyn's Diary*, 181, 290, 368.)

He left only two daughters, who inherited very extensive property, the books of the Augmentation Office showing that the judge had a considerable share in the lands distributed on the dissolution of the monasteries. (*Hasted*, i. 450, &c.; *Ormerod's Cheshire*, iii. 208.)

Sir Roger is confounded by Strype and others with his Cheshire kinsman Ranulph or Randle Cholmley, who, like him, was a reader of Lincoln's Inn, a serjeant-at-law, recorder of London, and M.P. for that city. He died two years before Sir Roger.

CHURCHILL, JOHN, and his namesake the first Duke of Marlborough were cousins, each being descended from Jasper Churchill, Esq., of Bradford in Somersetshire, who was the great-grandfather of the duke, and the grandfather of Sir John, whose father was also named Jasper. (*Collinson*, iii. 580.) He was called to the bar at Lincoln's Inn in 1647, and elected autumn reader in 1670, having then the title of knighthood. This dignity he had attained by his eminence at the bar, which enabled him to purchase in 1653 the manor of Churchill, near Banwell, in Somersetshire, probably attracted by its name, and caused his selection as one of the king's counsel, and attorney-general to the Duke of York. He practised in the Court of Chancery, and Roger North (p. 199) relates of him that on his walk from Lincoln's Inn to the Temple Hall, where the court sat out of term in Lord Keeper Bridgeman's time, he had taken no less than 28*l*. for motions and defences for hastening or retarding the hearings of causes only; a practice greatly amended by Lord Guilford.

He was the first counsel named by the House of Lords in 1675 to manage the famous case of Sir Nicholas Crispe against a member of the House of Commons, which occasioned the absurd contest about privilege between the two houses. In the course of the dispute Sir John and the other counsel, notwithstanding the protection of the Peers, were committed to the Tower by the Commons; and to such an extent was the quarrel carried that the king was obliged to prorogue the parliament, when Sir John and his imprisoned colleagues were of course released. He afterwards became a member of this parliament for Dorchester, and in the next for Newtown in Hampshire, and lastly for Bristol, which city chose him as its recorder in April 1683. On the death of Sir Harbottle Grimston he was invested with the office of master of the Rolls on January 12, 1685, less than a month before King Charles died; but an early end was put to his judicial career by his own decease in the summer vacation following. He left four daughters by his wife Susan, daughter of Edmund Prideaux, Esq. (*State Trials*, vi. 1144 *et seq.*; *Luttrell*, i. 254, 324; 2 *Shower*, 434.)

CLAHAUL, HUGH DE, held a judicial position in 9 Henry III. as one of the justices itinerant for Essex and Hertfordshire, in the latter of which counties his property was situate. He was among those who, having taken the barons' part in King John's reign, returned to his duty at the beginning of Henry's. (*Rot. Claus.* i. 323, 324, ii. 67, 147.)

CLARE, ROGER DE (EARL OF CLARE AND HERTFORD), was one among the twelve designated as itinerant judges in 1170 by Dugdale. There are good reasons, however, for considering that they did not really bear that character, but that they were rather inquisitors into the abuses attributed to the sheriffs and other officers of the king. This earl was great-grandson of Richard Fitz-Gilbert, called Richard de Benefacta, or Bienfait, afterwards noticed, and son of Richard who was created Earl of Hertford.

In 3 Henry II. Earl Roger obtained the king's grant of all lands he could win in Wales, and accordingly marched a great army there, and fortified divers castles in the neighbourhood of Cardigan.

One of the first acts of Becket, after he was raised to the archbishopric of Canterbury, was to summon the earl to do him homage for the castle of Tunbridge. He refused to appear, asserting that he held it by military service of the crown, and, as the king abetted him in his plea, the archbishop refrained from pursuing the claim. His grants to religious houses, which were numerous and munificent, are stated in detail by Dugdale. After his death in 1173, Matilda, his widow, the daughter of James de St. Hilaire, married William de Albini, Earl of Arundel, and the earldoms of Clare and Hertford descended to his son Richard, whose son Gilbert became Earl of Gloucester. All the earldoms became extinct in 1313 on the death of Gilbert, the tenth earl, without issue. (*Baronage*, i. 209; *Hasted*, v. 159, 203.)

CLAREMBALD (ABBOT OF ST. AUGUSTINE'S, CANTERBURY) is placed by Dugdale at the head of the twelve whom he calls 'justiciarii itinerantes' into certain counties in 1170, but who were rather inquisitors into the conduct of the sheriffs and other officers of the king.

The abbot was either a secular or, as some say, a fugitive and apostate monk in Normandy. Obtruded by King Henry in 1163 on the monks as their abbot, they refused to permit him to sit in their chapter or to celebrate any of the holy offices. Notwithstanding this opposition, he contrived to possess himself of the temporalities and to retain them for fifteen years, when, on the representation of the monks that he was a bad man and had wasted the revenues of the monastery, a papal mandate was directed to the Bishops of Exeter and Worcester and the Abbot of Faversham, under which he was deposed in 1176. During his time the greater part of the abbey was destroyed by a fire in 1168. (*Monast.* i. 122; *Weever*, 255; *Hasted*, xii. 190.)

CLARENDON, EARL OF. See E. HYDE.

CLARKE, ROBERT, was probably of the county of Essex, as he purchased and resided in the mansion house of Newarks, or Newlands-fee, in the parish of Good Estre, and he also possessed the manor of Gibbecrake in Purley, in that county. (*Morant*, i. 345, ii. 459.) He was called to the bar by Lincoln's Inn in 1568, and was reader in autumn 1582. He was constituted a baron of the Exchequer in June 1587, 29 Elizabeth. (*Coke's 3rd Report*, p. 16.) In the summer of 1590 he was the judge of assize at Croydon, before whom John Udall, the Puritan, was tried for the publication of the alleged libel called 'The Demonstration'—a trial which, notwithstanding the evident wish of the judge to be lenient with him if he would have submitted, is a curious instance of the shameful and absurd manner in which criminal proceedings were then conducted. (*State Trials*, i. 1277.) On the accession of King James his patent was renewed, and on July 23, 1603, he was knighted. He sat on the bench for nearly twenty years, and a few months before his death the information against Bates, raising the great constitutional question whether a duty could be imposed on the subject by the mere act of the king, was heard in the Exchequer. His feeble argument in favour of the crown is fully stated in 'Lane's Reports' (p. 22).

He died on January 1, 1606-7, and was buried at Good Estre. Though Morant says that he had only two wives, two more must be added, and all of them were widows. The parish register of Good Estre records that Mary Clarke, his wife, was buried 'the 26 daie of February 1585,' and she appears to have been the widow of — Hills. It further records the burial of Catheran, another wife of the baron, on January 16, 1590, and she appears to have been the widow of — Chapman. By each of these he had several children. The third wife was Margaret, the daughter of John Maynard, M.P. for St. Albans, and grandfather of the first Lord Maynard, and widow of Sir Edward Osborne, lord mayor of London in 1582, and ancestor of the first Duke of Leeds. This lady died in 1602, leaving two daughters by the baron. The fourth wife was Joyce, the widow of James Austen, who survived the baron for twenty years, and was buried in 1626 in the church of St. Saviour's, Southwark.

CLARKE, CHARLES, was the son of Alured Clarke, of Godmanchester in Huntingdonshire, by Ann, daughter of the Rev. Charles Trimnell, rector of Abbots Repton in Hampshire, and sister to the Bishop of Winchester of that name. In 1717 he entered Lincoln's Inn, and was in 1723 called to the bar, at which he was rewarded by so large a share of practice that he amassed a considerable fortune. The neighbouring borough of Huntingdon elected him recorder in 1731, and he was returned member for the county in 1739. In the new parliament of 1741 he was elected for Whitchurch in Hampshire; and in its second session he was raised to the bench, as baron of the Exchequer, in Hilary Term 1743.

His judicial career was terminated seven years afterwards by an infectious fever caught at the Black Sessions at the Old Bailey in May 1750, already described in the memoir of Sir Thomas Abney, another victim of the uncleanliness of the prisons. His death occurred on the 17th, and he was buried at Godmanchester. His first wife was Anne, a daughter of Dr. Thomas Green, Bishop of Ely; and his second was Jane, daughter of Major Mullins, of Winchester, and by both he left issue.

His brother, Dr. Alured Clarke, became dean of Exeter. (*Master's Corp. Christi Coll., Cambridge.*)

CLARKE, THOMAS, was, according to Mr. Nichols (*Literary Anecdotes*, viii. 507), 'generally supposed to be a natural son, and as having no relations.' Of his early life little is known, beyond his being educated at Westminster School. That he was intimate with the second Earl of Macclesfield, and was a fellow of the Royal Society, devoting himself to philosophical pursuits, appears from a letter of Lord Hardwicke's; and that he was reputed to be deep read in Roman law, is apparent from the description of him in the 'Causidicade' as a supposed candidate for the vacant solicitor-generalship in 1742 :—

Then Cl—ke, who sat snug all this while in his place,
Rose up and put forward his ebony face:
'I have reason,' quo' he, ' now to take it amiss,
That your lordship ha'n't call'd to me long before this.
If the old civil law, on which I would build,
Is in so much neglect and indifference held,
Let your common law dunces go on and apply,
Quoting chapter and sect. insipidly dry !
A student of moderate parts and discerning,
With intense application may master such learning:
But I, as a genius, the office demand,
That office my qualifications command!'

It is probable that his advance to the post of king's counsel took place before this date. In 1747 he was member for St. Michael's, and in 1754 for Lostwithiel, both Cornish boroughs, but had no seat in the house in 1761.

On the death of Sir John Strange in 1754 Mr. Clarke was immediately pointed out both by Lord Hardwicke and the Duke of Newcastle to succeed him as master of the Rolls; to which place he was appointed on May 29, 1754, and was thereupon knighted. The duke calls him a very deserving man, and intimates that he was greatly before his competitors in the Court of Chancery. He held the office with great credit a few months beyond ten years, dying on November 13, 1764. He was buried in the Rolls Chapel; and by his will he left, among other legacies, 30,000*l.* to St. Luke's Hospital, and appointed the Earl of Macclesfield his residuary legatee, his whole property being estimated at 200,000*l.* (*Harris's Lord Hardwicke.*)

CLAVER, JOHN, is introduced among the advocates under Edward II. and III. He was a native of Norfolk, and acted as custos of the see of Norwich during its vacancy in both reigns. He tallaged this county and Suffolk in 6 Edward III.; and in the following year he was added to the commission of justices itinerant into Kent. (*Parl. Writs*, ii. p. ii. 679; *Abb. Rot. Orig.* ii. 103, 106, 121.)

CLAY, STEPHEN DE, held under King John the manor of Tinden in Northamptonshire, at a rent of 26*l.* per annum. (*Rot. Chart.* 49.) He was one of the justiciers before whom fines were levied in 2 and 3 John.

CLEASBY, ANTHONY, the additional baron of the Exchequer appointed under the recent act relating to election petitions, is the son of Stephen Cleasby, Esq., of Cragg House, Westmoreland, by Mary, the daughter of George John, Esq., of Penzance.

He was educated at Eton, and at Trinity College, Cambridge, and came out when he took his degree in 1827 third wrangler and first class in classics, and in 1828 was elected fellow of his college. He studied law at the Inner Temple, and was called to the bar on June 10, 1831, choosing the Northern Circuit. In 1861 he became a queen's counsel; and on August 5, 1868, he was appointed to his present post.

He married Lucy Susan, daughter of Walter Fawkes, Esq., of Farnley Hall, Yorkshire, which county he formerly represented.

CLENCH, JOHN, the son of John Clench, of Wethersfield in Essex, and Joan, daughter of John Amias, of the same county, was called to the bar in Lincoln's Inn in 1568, and was elected reader in Lent 1574. In the same year he was elected the first recorder of Ipswich, and in Michaelmas 1580 he was raised to the degree of the coif, from which grade he was promoted to be third baron of the Exchequer on November 27, 1581, and acted in that capacity till May 29, 1584, when he was removed into the Court of Queen's Bench. He was one of the four judges who were assigned to hear causes in Chancery in November 1591, when the Great Seal was in commission after the death of Sir Christopher Hatton. Tradition says that Queen Elizabeth used to call him 'her good judge.'

He continued to sit till the beginning of 1602, but his death did not occur till August 19, 1607. He was buried in Holbrook Church, and upon his tomb are two full-length marble effigies of the judge and his wife in the costume of the day, with smaller figures on each side of his seven sons and eight daughters. The inscription describes him as the oldest judge of his time. He removed into Suffolk, and is described as of four different places there—Creeting, All Saints, Holesley, and Holbrook.

His wife was Katherine, daughter and heiress of Thomas Almot, of Creeting. Thomas, their eldest son, in 1620 was member for Suffolk. The family is now quite extinct. (*Shobert's Suffolk*, i. 150; *Davy's MSS.*)

CLERK, JOHN LE. In 20 Henry II., 1174, the assize or tallage of the united counties of Nottingham and Derby was set by the following itinerant justices—viz., William Basset, John Malduit, 'et Johannem Clericum.' Whether this John was a clerk of the Exchequer sent down to assist, or a clergyman resident in one of those counties, or a person who bore that designation as his surname, it would be useless to enquire.

CLERKE, JOHN. Ford, near Wrotham, in Kent, was the seat of the family of Clerke, or le Clerke, as the name was anciently called. John Clerke the father flourished there in the reigns of Henry V. and Henry VI.; and John Clerke the son was raised to the bench of the Exchequer as second baron on October 29, 1460, little more than four months before the deposition of the latter king. He evidently retained place during the first reign of Edward IV., as he is named as second baron, not only in the new patent of Henry VI., but in that of Edward IV. on his resumption of the crown six months afterwards. From the latter period till February 3, 1481, 20 Edward IV., no other second baron is mentioned. He married one of the daughters and co-heiresses of —— Tateshum, of Tateshum; and the estate at Ford continued in the possession of his descendants till 1644, when William Clerke, who had been knighted for his loyalty, was slain at Cropredy Bridge, commanding the regiment he had raised to aid the cause of his sovereign, Charles I. (*Hasted*, v. 19.)

CLERKE, JOHN (BISHOP OF BATH AND WELLS), was educated at Cambridge, where he took the degree of doctor in divinity. He probably was the John Clerke who, with Richard Pace, was in the service of Cardinal Bainbridge when he was poisoned at Rome in July 1514, and attributed the crime to Silvester de Giles, the Bishop of Worcester. Wolsey, however, took both into favour, making Pace secretary of state, and John Clerke dean of the Chapel Royal in 1516. (*Cal. State Papers* [1509], 868, 892, [1515], 875.) On October 22, 1519, he was collated to the archdeaconry of Colchester. He must have been recommended by extraordinary abilities to be selected in 1521 for a mission so important in the eyes of its royal author as that of laying at the feet of Leo X. King Henry's book against Luther. His oration on its delivery is not an inelegant composition, and is appended to the published work. His return to England as the bearer, not only of the pope's complimentary reply, but also of the bull conferring on the King of England the coveted title of 'Defender of the Faith,' was secure of a cordial welcome; and his services did not receive a less substantial reward from his having acted as Wolsey's private agent while at the Roman court.

On October 20, 1522, he was appointed master of the Rolls, but held the office not quite a year, vacating it on October 9, 1523, in consequence of his elevation to the bishopric of Bath and Wells, to which he was elected on March 26.

Despatched to the court of the Duke of Cleves with the lame explanation of his variable sovereign's repudiation of the Princess Anne, the unwelcome messenger is reported to have had poison administered to him in his food, as several of his suite died after partaking of it. The bishop, infected with the venom, survived till his return, when he died in London on January

3, 1540–1. He was buried in the nunnery of the Minories, whence his remains were removed to the church of St. Botolph, Aldgate, his epitaph in which is given in Weever.' (*Godwin*, 387; *Lingard*, vi. 104, 304; *Rymer*, xiii. 758, 792; *Weever*, 426.)

CLIDERHOU, ROBERT DE, held the manor of Bailey, a township in the neighbourhood of Cliderhou, or Clitherow, in Lancashire. In 35 Edward I. he recovered 200*l.* from three brothers who attacked him at that place, and beat him till they left him for dead.

He was a clerk in the Chancery under Edward I. and Edward II., and in the fourth year of the reign of the latter was appointed one of the three justices of assize for Kent, Sussex, and Surrey. During the eighth and ninth years of that reign he was the king's escheator beyond Trent, and afterwards became parson of the church of Wigan. He took so strong a part in behalf of the Earl of Lancaster that he not only sent his son Adam, and another man-at-arms, with four foot soldiers, to his assistance, but preached at Wigan in his favour, and promised absolution to those who aided him. The punishment he suffered for these offences was a fine of 200*l.* He was alive in 7 Edward III.

As he was a priest, it must be presumed that his son Adam was born before he took orders. (*Abb. Placit.* 300; *Abb. Rot. Orig.* i. 217–226; *Parl. Writs*, ii. p. ii. 686.)

CLIFF, HENRY DE. There were two clerks or masters in Chancery of the name of Cliff or Clyff in the reign of Edward II., who probably were brothers. Henry de Cliff accompanied the king abroad in May 1313 (*N. Fœdera*, ii. 215), and is first mentioned in connection with the Chancery in May 1317, when, during an absence of the chancellor, John de Sandale, Bishop of Winchester, the Great Seal was left in the bishop's house in Southwark, in the charge of Master Henry de Cliff. From this time till the year 1324 he was usually one of the clerks in Chancery under whose seals the Great Seal was secured during the occasional absences of the chancellors. On July 4, 1325 (being then a canon of York), he was raised to the office of keeper or master of the Rolls; and after the virtual abdication of Edward II., in the following year, he was commanded, on December 17, 1326, to add his seal to that of the Bishop of Norwich for the custody of the Great Seal, and they together transacted the business till the appointment of John de Hotham, Bishop of Ely, as chancellor, a few days after the accession of Edward III.

He continued in the office of master of the Rolls for the first seven years of this reign, during which the Great Seal was frequently entrusted to his custody, and died about the beginning of January 1334.

CLIFF, WILLIAM DE, probably the brother of the foregoing Henry de Cliff, was in 3 Edward II. commissioned to prepare certain ships in Yorkshire against the Scots. (*N. Fœdera*, ii. 109.) Two years afterwards he was appointed the king's steward in the forest of Galtres, in the neighbourhood of York. (*Abb. Rot. Orig.* i. 189.) In 12 Edward II. he was presented with the prebend of Kylbryde, in the church of Glasgow, and about the same time became one of the clerks of the Chancery, in which capacity he was, from 1319 to 1323, with others of his fellows, frequently entrusted with the Great Seal, in the absence of the chancellors, whose duties they accordingly performed.

It seems not improbable that he shared in the disgrace of the Despencers, inasmuch as a complaint was made, in the first parliament of the following reign, by Elizabeth de Burgh, that she had been arrested, in 16 Edward II., by the conspiracy and crafty plotting of Hugh le Despencer the younger, Robert de Baldock (afterwards chancellor), and William de Cliff; and in the parliament of the second year another complaint was made that Hugh le Despencer and he had disseised John de Larcheley of his manor. (*Rot. Parl.* ii. 23, 440.) If this were so, however, his offence appears to have been overlooked, as he was one of the commissioners appointed in 3 Edward III. to enquire into the chattels belonging to Hugh le Despencer, in his Lincolnshire manors. (*Abb. Rot. Orig.* ii. 24.)

CLIFFORD, WILLIAM DE, whose name is frequently abbreviated in the Rolls to Cliff, was the king's escheator on this side Trent from October 1265 till May 1268. Dugdale introduces him as a baron of the Exchequer in 55 Henry III., 1270, about which period he was appointed chancellor of the Exchequer, and had a liberate granting him a salary of 40*l.* a year. (*Madox*, ii. 320.)

CLIFFORD, ROGER DE, traced his descent from Richard, Duke of Normandy, grandfather of William the Conqueror. The duke's grandson became lord of Clifford Castle in Herefordshire, and left a son, Walter (the father of Fair Rosamond), who assumed that surname. Walter's grandson, Roger, married Sibilla, daughter and heir of Robert de Ewyas and widow of Lord Tregoz, and by her had the subject of the present notice, who at his father's death, in 16 Henry III., 1231, was a minor. He attended the king in his expedition into France in 43 Henry III. For a short time he joined the rebellious barons, but, returning to his duty, he gave effective assistance to his sovereign, both at the siege of Northampton and in Wales, and in the decisive victory at Evesham in 1265. In the next year he was made justice of the forests south of the Trent, the duties of which he performed till August 1, 1270, when he went to the Holy Land. Dugdale places him in the year previous to his retirement at the head of the justices itinerant visiting Rutland and five other counties, and he again held the same position in 8 Edward I., 1280.

His bravery and experience in military affairs obtained for him many important governments, among which were, at various times, the custody of the castles of Marlborough, Ludgershall, Gloucester (with the sheriffalty of that county), and Erdesley in Herefordshire. His last office of trust and responsibility was justice of North Wales, to which he was appointed in 8 Edward I.; and his severity in the execution of its duties is said to have induced David, the son of the Prince of Wales, to break out into open hostility. He was attacked by the Welsh in the castle of Hawardyn in 10 Edward I., and taken prisoner; and in a skirmish that followed in the next year his eldest son, Roger junior, was unfortunately slain on November 6, 1282. His own death occurred in 14 Edward I., 1286, when he was succeeded by his grandson Robert, the son of Roger junior.

The name of his first wife is not recorded, but his second, whom he married a few years before his death, was the Countess of Lauretania, who survived him.

Robert, his grandson, was summoned to parliament from 28 Edward I.; and his descendants enjoyed the title till 1525, when Henry Clifford, the then baron, was created Earl of Cumberland. By the death of the fourth earl in 1643 the earldom became extinct. The barony, however, fell to his daughter, and the future succession is remarkable for the frequency with which it fell into abeyance. The present Baroness de Clifford is the heir of the eldest daughter of the previous possessor. Another descendant of the family was created Baron Clifford of Chudleigh in 1672 by Charles II., a title which is enjoyed at the present time.

CLINTON, GEOFFREY DE. There are two accounts of the origin of Geoffrey de Clinton—one that he was of mean parentage and raised to high office by Henry I.; the other that he was the grandson of William de Tankervilla, chamberlain of Normandy, and Maud, the daughter of William de Arches.

How early he became in favour with King Henry I. there are no means of tracing. He is a witness, with no title attached to his name, to that king's charter to Westminster Abbey, granted either in 1121 or 1122; and he is also witness to a deed of King Henry, confirming a grant of the Soke of Knighten Guilde to the church of the Holy Trinity in Aldgate, London, executed between 1121 and 1128. In 1123 he calls himself chamberlain of the king; and in one of his grants, dated after 1125, treasurer; and in the charter of confirmation the king gives him both titles. (*Monast.* i. 308, vi. 153, 221.)

In 31 Henry I. he is mentioned as holding pleas in no less than eighteen counties in the roll appropriated to that year, and also as being justice of the forest for Huntingdonshire and sheriff of Warwickshire. No presumption, however, can be formed from this fact that he was chief justiciary, as there is very little doubt that Roger, Bishop of Salisbury, was then invested with the highest dignity in the kingdom.

It appears from that roll that his possessions were very large, and extended through no less than fourteen counties; and his exemptions from the Danegeld and other amerciaments to which they were liable amount to the large sum of 56*l*. 16*s*. 1*d*.

He built the castle at Kenilworth, and gave all the lands he held there, except those attached to the castle and park, to endow the priory of Augustin monks which he founded.

The male branch of his own family failed at the death of his great-grandson, Henry, in 1232; but from his nephew, Osbert de Clinton, descended a long line, which is now represented in the House of Lords by the Duke of Newcastle-under-Lyme and Baron Clinton.

CLIVE, GEORGE, of an ancient and honourable family, deriving their name from the village of Clive in Shropshire, was the son of George Clive, who became possessed of Wormbridge in Herefordshire, by his marriage with Mary, the daughter of Martin Husbands, Esq. They had three sons, of whom the eldest, Robert, was the grandfather of the great Lord Clive, whose son assumed the name of Herbert, and was created Earl of Powis; and the third son, Edward, was the father of Sir Edward Clive, the subject of the next article.

George was born about 1666, and became a bencher of Lincoln's Inn in 1719, though he obtained no eminence in the courts. He was appointed cursitor baron of the Exchequer on November 6, 1735, and filled the office for four years. He died unmarried on December 31, 1739, and was buried in Lincoln's Inn.

CLIVE, EDWARD, was the nephew of the last-mentioned George Clive, being the eldest son of his brother, Edward Olive, of Wormbridge in Herefordshire, by Sarah, daughter of — Key, of the city of Bristol, merchant, and was born in 1704. He was called to the bar by the society of Lincoln's Inn in 1725, and was returned to parliament in 1741 as member for St. Michael's in Cornwall, for which he sat till his elevation to the bench, as a baron of the Exchequer, in April 1745. He remained in that court nearly eight years without the honour of knighthood, which he did not receive till January 1753, when he was removed into the Common Pleas. He sat there for seventeen years more, thus extending his judicial service to twenty-five years, at the end of which he resigned in February 1770. The pension of 1200*l*. then granted to him he enjoyed for little more than a year, dying at Bath on April 16, 1771.

He married twice. His first wife was Elizabeth, daughter of Richard Symons, Esq., of Mynde Park in Herefordshire; and his second was Judith, the youngest daughter of his cousin the Rev. Benjamin Clive, a son of his uncle Robert Clive, of Styche in Shropshire, but he left no issue by either.

The judge's brother George was the husband of the eminent actress of that name, unrivalled in her particular walk.

CLOPTON, WALTER DE, descended from a knightly family, established originally at Newenham, in the parish of Ashdon, in Essex, but which afterwards removed into Suffolk, was the son of Sir William de Clopton, a commissioner of array in that county. (*Weever*, 695; *N. Fœdera*, iii. 449.) He is named as an advocate in the Year Books in 40 Edward III., 1360, and was one of the king's serjeants from 1 Richard II., 1377. (*Rot. Parl.* iii. 61, 169.)

On the eve of the parliament in which Sir Robert Tresilian was impeached he was raised to the office of chief justice of the King's Bench on January 31, 1388, and received the order of knighthood. Towards the end of the reign he was called upon to say what he thought of the answers given by the judges to the questions propounded to them in 11 Richard II. by Sir Robert Tresilian, by whose removal on that account he had himself been raised to the chief seat. It must be confessed that his answer, that 'had he been asked he should have made the same reply' (*Ibid.* 377), looks very like an evasion, to be justified, perhaps, by the consideration of the perilous consequences which might have resulted from his pronouncing a more decided opinion.

Notwithstanding this submission to the pliant parliament of Richard II., the chief justice, although all the acts of that assembly were repealed two years afterwards, escaped the censure of Henry IV.; for he was in the first parliament of that usurper appointed to investigate the case of Judge Rickhill, whose visit to the Duke of Gloucester while in prison at Calais was made the subject of enquiry, and no doubt felt a real pleasure in receiving the king's commands to acquit him of all criminality therein. (*Ibid.* 416, 430, 432.) In November 1400 he vacated his seat in the King's Bench; and it is stated that 'by the piety, mildness, and commendable example of Dr. Robert Coleman, chancellor of Oxford, he was induced to contemn all worldly vanity, and to become a friar of the Friars Minors.' (*Blomefield's Norwich*, ii. 115.) He died about 1410. (*Cal. Inquis.* p. m. iii. 335.)

COBBEHAM, HENRY DE, is the first named member of a noble family, holding large possessions in Kent, of which the lordship of that name near Rochester was the principal. Hasted (iii. 407) mentions him as being one of 'recognitores magnæ assisæ' in 1 John, and in 4 John for not obeying some precept of the king he was obliged to pay one hundred marks to recover the royal favour. (*Madox*, i. 473.) In 3 Henry III. he was appointed one of the justices itinerant into Sussex, Surrey, Middlesex, and Kent, and in the tenth year of that reign he was in the commission to collect the quinzime there. (*Rot. Claus.* ii. 147.) At his death, the date of which does not appear, he left three sons—John, Reginald, and William—each of whom occupied the judicial bench. Henry, the grandson of the first, was summoned to parliament by Edward II. The barony, after many changes, is now represented by the Duke of Buckingham.

COBBEHAM, JOHN DE, was the eldest son of the above, and succeeded to his father's manor on his death. In 20 Henry III. he was constable of Rochester Castle (*Cal. Rot. Pat.* 18), and from 26 to 32 Henry III. held the office of sheriff of Kent, with Bertram de Criol. He was raised to the bench about 28 Henry III., fines being levied before him from Easter in that year, 1244, till Michaelmas 1250 (*Dugdale's Orig.* 43), during which time also writs of assize were frequently directed to him. He married twice. His first wife was a daughter of Warine Fitz-Benedict, by whom he had two sons—John, afterwards noticed; and Henry, of Roundal, in Shorne, Kent. His second wife, Joane, daughter of Hugh de Nevill, produced to him Reginald, from whom the Cobhams of Sterborough Castle, in Surrey, sprung. (*Hasted*, iii. 231, 407.)

COBBEHAM, REGINALD DE, the second son of the above-mentioned Henry, was in 32 Henry III., 1248, one of the justices itinerant into Essex and Surrey, and in the next year into Kent, Middlesex, Hampshire, and Wiltshire. In 33 Henry III. he was appointed sheriff of Kent, and continued to hold that office during the remainder of his life, which terminated on December 14, 1257. Some time after, Maria, his widow, had permission to pay the debts he owed to the crown by instalments. (*Excerpt. e Rot. Fin.* ii. 268, 328.) While he held the sheriffalty he was appointed governor of Dover Castle and warden of the Cinque Ports. (*Baronage*, ii. 65.)

COBBEHAM, WILLIAM DE, the third son of the above Henry de Cobbeham, inherited the manor of East Shelve, or Shelve Cobham, in Lenham, in Kent. Entrusted, as well as his two brothers, John and Reginald, with judicial duties, he was in three successive years, 39, 40, and 41 Henry III., 1255-7, employed as a justice itinerant into a variety of counties. Hasted dates his death in 14 Edward II., 1320; but it seems scarcely possible that this was the same person. (*Hasted*, iii. 407, v. 435, 525.)

COBBEHAM, JOHN DE, the grandson of the above Henry de Cobbeham, and eldest son of the above John de Cobbeham, was made constable of Rochester Castle so early in life that he was called the young constable, and was entrusted with the sheriffalty of Kent for four years from 44 Henry III. His seat was at Monkton in the Isle of Thanet. In 52 Henry III., 1268, he acted as a justice itinerant for Surrey and Kent, and was advanced to the bench at Westminster in February 1270, 54 Henry III., but in which court is uncertain, as the mode of designating them was then scarcely fixed. In 4 Edward I. he was certainly constituted a baron of the Exchequer, the mandate for which is dated June 6, 1276, with a salary of forty marks per annum, and there are several records showing that he continued in that office during the remainder of his life. By an entry in the Year Book of Hilary, 28 Edward I., 1300, it appears that he was authorised to stay at home at his pleasure, and to come to the Exchequer and remain there when he would. This licence was no doubt granted to him in consequence of bodily infirmity, as he died in the same year. (*Cal. Inquis.* p. m. i. 156.)

He was twice married. His first wife was Joane, daughter and heir of Sir Robert de Septvans, by whom he left two sons— Henry and Reginald. His second wife was named Methania. (*Hasted*, iii. 408.)

COCKBURN, ALEXANDER JAMES EDMUND, the present lord chief justice of the Court of Queen's Bench, is the son of Alexander Cockburn, Esq., formerly envoy extraordinary and minister plenipotentiary to Columbia, by the daughter of the Viscomte de Vignier of St. Domingo, and the grandson of Sir James Cockburn, the seventh baronet, of Nova Scotia, created in 1627; whose next brothers, Admiral Sir George, and the Very Rev. Sir William, dean of York, the eighth and ninth baronets, died without male issue.

He became a member of Trinity Hall, Cambridge, in 1822, and in his second year gained prizes for the best exercises in English and Latin, and afterwards for the English essay. He graduated as B.C.L. in 1829, and was elected fellow of his college. He was called to the bar by the Middle Temple on February 6, 1829. Joining the Western Circuit, and attending the Devonshire sessions, he quickly established for himself a considerable business. Soon after the Reform Bill was passed, he and Mr. Rowe commenced the publication of reports of decisions which arose out of that measure, and the volume in which they were collected is of great and substantial merit. He was consequently engaged in several contests before election committees, in which he showed so much ability that in 1834 he was placed on the Municipal Corporation Commission. His parliamentary employments and the more regular business of the courts became of such magnitude that he felt warranted in 1841 in obtaining the precedence of a silk gown. 'Of his powers of advocacy,' one of his most distinguished contemporaries and professional competitors says, 'it is impossible to speak too highly. He was not perhaps so well fitted for the daily work of the profession, because he was always indisposed to bend his mind to it. But when any great occasion called for extraordinary exertion, he excelled all the eloquent advocates who were amongst my contemporaries. Although he soared to a high pitch, he never lost himself in the clouds, and he dealt with the facts of the case in a practical and at the same time in a masterly manner.' The same discriminating critic used to say to him in allusion to his powers, 'You fly better than you walk.'

In the year of his obtaining rank he ably defended his uncle, and assisted in overturning the attempt to deprive him of the deanery of York. Among other cases in which he distinguished himself as a leader was his eloquent and impressive defence in 1843 of M'Naughten, who had shot Mr. Drummond, in which he satisfied the jury that his client was not a responsible being. In the meantime he had been appointed recorder of Southampton, and in 1847 was elected member for that borough, which he continued to represent till he was elevated to the bench. His speeches in Parliament were less professional than those for which the members of the bar are generally noted, and he was of great assistance in supporting the liberal party, with whom he acted.

In July 1850 he was made solicitor-general and knighted, and in the following March he became attorney-general. He held this office till November 1856, with the exception of ten months between February 27 and December 28, 1852, during which the Earl of Derby conducted the government. His next promotion was that of recorder of Bristol in 1854, and on November 21, 1856, he was constituted chief justice of the Common Pleas. He presided in that court for nearly three years, during which, his uncle the dean of York dying, he succeeded to the baronetcy in 1858. On the elevation of Lord Campbell to the office of lord chancellor, Sir Alexander was raised to his present position of lord chief justice of the Queen's Bench on June 24, 1859.

The restriction under which I placed myself of not giving an opinion of my own on the judicial merits of the existing members of the bench ought not to prevent me from recording the estimation in which they are regarded by their eminent contemporaries. It is but justice therefore to quote a portion of the eloquent eulogy of Mr. Serjeant (afterwards Mr. Justice) Shee, in proposing the health of the chief justice, when presiding as chairman of the anniversary festival of the United Law Clerks' Society in 1863. After a few words introducing his name, he proceeded thus: 'He is the successor in, if not the highest, the second post in the law of England—of men than whom, as great magistrates, in no country of the world will men be found their equals, or at least their superiors. . . . . To say of him that he surpasses in the great and highest quality of a chief justice—the high legal attainments of some of his predecessors—would be flattery, of which I will not be guilty; but this I will venture to say, that he possesses qualities which have endeared him to us all, in which none of them have surpassed him. . . . We like him because we know that his distinction was achieved by no back-stairs influence, by no political intrigue, by no political subservience. We like him because we know that he did not arrive at the high position which he now occupies without having first obtained, solely by his own endowments and superior talents, the highest position at the bar. . . . . We like him because we know that not merely the honour of the profession, but the honour and character of every man who comes before him, are safe in his hands. We like and admire him because we observe every day that the command which he possesses of all the treasures and all the beauties of our noble language enables him, whenever there is occasion for it, to refute whatever fallacies and sophistries are put forward before him at the bar, and to vindicate at the close of every cause the innocence that belongs to those that are tried. But most of all we like him, we respect him, we love him, for this, because, whenever he has occasion to reprove or to rebuke—and no man in his position can be without having some occasion to reprove and to rebuke—he takes care always to temper authority with gentleness, and to rebuke without giving pain.'

COKAYNE, JOHN, was the second son of John Cokayne, of Ashbourn in Derbyshire, M.P. for that county in several parliaments of Edward III., by his wife Cecilia Vernon. His name is mentioned as an advocate in the Reports of the time of Richard II., collected by Richard Bellewe; and from 18 to 22 Richard II. he was recorder of London. In addition to the office of chief baron of the Exchequer, to which he was raised on November 15, 1400, 2 Henry IV., a puisne judgeship in the Common Pleas was granted to him on June 17, 1406, and he performed the duties of both offices during the remaining seven years of the reign.

On the accession of Henry V. his two offices were again divided, and a new patent was granted to him as a judge of the Common Pleas only. This was renewed by Henry VI., and he continued to perform his judicial functions during the first seven years of that reign. Having then sat on the bench nearly thirty years, he retired to private life, and died about nine years afterwards, in 1438. (*Cal. Inquis.* p. m. iv. 182.) He was buried in Ashbourn Church. (*Dugdale's Orig.* 100.)

By his wife Edith, sister of Lord Grey de Ruthyn, he had four sons and two daughters. A descendant from his elder brother Edmund, in 1642, was created Viscount Cullen, a title which became extinct in 1810. (*Lodge's Irish Peerage*, iv. 323.)

COKE, WILLIAM, was born at Chesterton in Cambridgeshire, and was educated at the university of Cambridge. From Barnard's Inn he removed to Gray's Inn in 1528, and was called to the bar in 1530. He became reader there in Lent 1544, and again in autumn 1546. On February 3, 1547, he was called serjeant, and was presented by Gray's Inn with eight pounds in gold on the occasion, *nomine regardi*. On October 22, 1550, he was made one of the king's serjeants, and on November 16, 1552, he was nominated a judge of the Common Pleas. He had previously been appointed steward of no less than four houses in his university, and in January 1546 had been elected recorder of Cambridge. (*Cooper's Ath. Cantab.* i. 114.)

The story told by Machyn (*Diary*, 26, 38), that he was, on July 27, 1553, sent to the Tower for signing King Edward's will settling the crown on Lady Jane Grey, is evidently a mistake, as Coke's name does not appear among the signatures to that document; and as his death occurred on the 24th of the following month, it is clear that Machyn mistook the name of (Sir Thomas) Wroth for Coke.

On Coke's monumental brass at Milton both he and his wife Alice, together with two sons and three daughters, are represented—he in his judicial robes, and they in the costume of the period. Above his head is a label, the inscription on which—'Plebs sine lege ruit'—was the motto on the rings of the serjeants who were called in the same term in which he was raised to the bench. (*Boutell*, 45; *Dyer*, 71.)

COKE, EDWARD. The ancestors of Sir Edward Coke are traced as far back as the twelfth century, Henry Coke, of Doddington in Norfolk, bearing arms and being mentioned in a deed dated 8 John. (*Hasted*, ii. 479.) In direct descent came Robert Coke, Sir Edward's father, of Mileham in the same county, who was a lawyer and a bencher of Lincoln's Inn. He married Winifred, daughter and coheiress of William Knightley, of Morgrave Knightley in Norfolk, and dying at his chambers in Lincoln's Inn on November 15, 1561, he was buried in St. Andrew's Church, Holborn. There Sir Edward erected a monument to his memory, as he did also in the church of Tittleshall to that of his mother, who, after marrying Robert Bosanne and having by him a son named John, died in January 1569.

Edward Coke, who was the only son out of eight children, was born at Mileham on February 1, 1551–2; so that he was ten years old when his father died, and near eighteen at the decease of his mother. He received the rudiments of his education at the grammar school at Norwich, and was thence removed in September 1567 to Trinity College, Cambridge, where he remained three years and a half. On the 21st of January 1571 he was admitted a student of Clifford's Inn, and was in the following year, on April 24, entered of the Inner Temple. On April 20, 1578, he was called to the bar; and in the very next term he held his first brief in the Court of King's Bench, and was successful in defending Mr. Denny, a clergyman of his native county, in an action brought against him by Lord Cromwell for *scandalum magnatum*. (4 *Reports*, 14.) His reputation for learning was already so great that within a year after his call the benchers of his house selected him as reader at Lyon's Inn—an honour usually conferred on an older barrister—where his lectures fully confirmed the character he had acquired.

On August 13, 1582, he married his first wife, Bridget, the daughter and heir of John Paston, Esq., deceased, of Huntingfield in Suffolk, a descendant of Judge Paston. At this time his name was pronounced Cooke, and is so spelled in the registry of his marriage, as also in a special commission ten years later, when solicitor-general. His acquisition of a fortune of 30,000*l.* with his wife, in addition to his paternal inheritance, did not diminish his industry; for from this date he seems to have been engaged in almost every prominent case noticed by the different reporters. About 1585 he was chosen recorder of Coventry; in the next year the same office was given to him by the citizens of Norwich; and in January 1591–2 the corporation of London called him to the distinguished post of recorder of the metropolis. The latter office he retained for six months only, resigning it on being selected by Lord Burleigh as solicitor-general on June 16, 1592. On his being nominated autumn reader of the Inner Temple in 1592, he composed seven lectures on the Statute of Uses, five of which he delivered to 160 auditors in August, when, on the appearance of the plague, he was compelled to withdraw from London. In his progress to his seat at Huntingfield, he says that 'nine of the benchers, forty of the bar, and other fellows of the Inner Temple,' accompanied him as far as Romford. In 1596 he was elected treasurer of his inn.

Hitherto he had confined himself to his legal avocations: he was now to enter on his political career. Before the parliament of 1593 was assembled, and even before Coke had been elected a member of it, the queen and council, on January 28, named him as the speaker. On the 5th of February he was returned as representative of his native county, 'nullo contradicente;' and he proudly adds that it was a free election, 'sine ambitu, seu aliqua requisitione, ex parte mea.' On the meeting of the house he was elected speaker, as had been previously arranged. The parliament lasted only seven weeks, and his speeches in it have the same ponderous verbosity for which they were ever remarkable, and too much of sycophantic subserviency, ill according with the boldness of his later years. But he was then a seeker after advancement, and he felt he had a mistress with whose power no one dared to trifle. Exactly one year after his speakership terminated, on April 10, 1594, he became attorney-general.

Coke had lived happily with his first wife for sixteen years, when he lost her on June 27, 1598. Within five months after this event he entered into another matrimonial speculation, which began inauspiciously, and was fatal to his future peace. His second wife was Elizabeth, relict of Sir William Hatton, and daughter of Thomas Cecil, who had just succeeded his father as Lord Burleigh, and the marriage took place at her house in Holborn on November 6, 1598, without either bans or licence, but is recorded in the register of that parish without remark. Even his friend Archbishop Whitgift could not overlook this irregularity, and it was only by a humble submission, and the extraordinary plea of ignorance of the law, that Coke and all the parties concerned escaped excommunication. The powerful connections and the large fortune of the lady had also attracted Bacon, who had previously become a suitor for her hand, and the success of his great rival did not tend to diminish the hostile feelings between the parties.

Coke continued attorney-general during the remainder of Elizabeth's reign, no vacancy having occurred in the chief seats of the common law courts during the nine years that it lasted. The only important state trial which is reported in the interval was that of the Earls of Essex and Southampton in February 1601. Here he gave the first specimen of that objurgatory and coarse style which makes his oratory so painfully remembered. He designates the prisoners as 'a Catiline, popish, dissolute, and desperate company;' he calls the Earl of Essex 'treason-bird,' and uses these harsh and indecent expressions:—'But now, in God's judgment, he of his earldom shall be Robert the last, that of the kingdom thought to be Robert the first.' (*Jardine's Crim. Trials*, i. 318–329.) His arrogance and ill-temper were displayed in 1601, when Bacon, in the Court of Exchequer, made some motion which Coke thought trenched upon his duties. Bacon was not backward in reply, and after many disgraceful words on both sides, the scene ended by Coke's threatening to 'clap a *cap. utlegatum*' on his back.

On the commencement of the new reign, Coke, who had cordially co-operated in the arrangements for the peaceable accession of James, was not only confirmed in his office, but received the honour of knighthood. He soon had ample opportunity of exhibiting his zeal in the prosecution of state offenders. On Sir Walter Raleigh's trial his heartless and unmanly behaviour forms an appropriate introduction to the shameful mode in which the proceedings were conducted, and the disgraceful verdict given by the jury; and his fulsome adulation of the king's wisdom and innocence has an awkward illustration in the absurd farce which the monarch caused to be performed at the intended execution of the lords implicated in the same treason, and in the cruel tragedy which, thirteen years after, he perpetrated in Raleigh's death on that condemnation. To Raleigh, a prisoner on trial for his life, he brutally says, 'Thou art a monster; thou hast an English face, but a Spanish heart;' 'Thou viper, for I *thou* thee, thou traitor!' 'Thou art thyself a spider of hell!' 'Oh, damnable atheist!' &c. Even Chief Justice Popham felt it necessary to apologise : 'Sir Walter,' said he, 'Mr. Attorney speaks out of the zeal of his duty for the service of the king, and you for your life; be patient on both sides.' And Secretary Cecil endeavoured to soften him: 'Be not so impatient, good Mr. Attorney, give him leave to speak.' On which Coke angrily exclaimed, 'I am the king's sworn servant, and must speak; if I may not be patiently heard, you discourage the king's counsel, and encourage traitors;' and sat down in a chafe. A more disgusting scene had never been witnessed in court.

During the trials of the conspirators in the gunpowder plot, Coke repeated his gross flattery of the king, and his cruel language to the prisoners. Soon after their termination he was elevated to the bench as chief justice of the Common Pleas, on June 30, 1606.

On ascending the judicial seat he discarded all appearance of subserviency, and boldly asserted the independence of the judge. He did not hesitate to oppose James in his attempts to extend his prerogative; and in the very next year after his appointment he told the king, in the case of prohibitions, that his majesty had not power to adjudge any case, either criminal or between party and party, but that it ought to be determined in some court of justice; and upon the king's saying that he thought the law was founded on reason, and that he and others had reason as well as the judges, Coke answered that 'true it was that God had endowed his majesty with excellent science and great endowments of nature, but his majesty was not learned in the laws of the realm of England;' with which the king was greatly offended. In another case, in 1608, when he and the other judges were summoned before the council to account for a judgment they had given, he said to the lords, 'We do hope that where[as] the judges of this realm have been more often called before your lordships than in former times they have been, which is much observed, and gives much emboldening to the vulgar, that after this day we shall not be so often, upon such complaints, your lordships being truly informed of our proceedings, hereafter called before you.' In 1610 he gave an opinion in opposition to the council, that the king could not, by his proclamation, create any offence which was not an offence before. In the next year he and the other judges of the Common Pleas discharged Sir William Chancey, brought before them by Habeas Corpus, who had been imprisoned by warrant from the High Commission in Causes Ecclesiastical, and afterwards justified their decision before the council. When a new commission was issued, in which he was named, he refused to sit upon it. (12 *Reports*, 51, 64, 74, 82, 84, 88.)

His old enemy, Bacon, did not fail to take advantage of Coke's resistance. On the death of Sir Thomas Fleming, he recommended the king to remove Coke from the Common Pleas to the King's Bench; and, among others, he gave the following reasons for this measure :—'It will strengthen the king's causes amongst the judges, for my Lord Coke will think himself near a privy counsellor's place, and thereupon turn obsequious.' 'The remove of my Lord Coke to a place of less profit . . . will be thought abroad a kind of discipline to him for opposing himself in the king's causes, the example whereof will contain others in more awe.' (*Bacon's Works* [*Montagu*], vii. 340.) His craft succeeded; Coke was *promoted* to the office of chief justice of the King's Bench on October 25, 1613, and was sworn of the privy council on November 4. He received a sincerer and more welcome compliment in the following June, by his unanimous and unsought election as steward of the University of Cambridge. At the beginning of the reign he had obtained for the university the privilege of sending two members to parliament. (*Seward's Anecdotes*, iii. 396.)

Coke was not more 'obsequious' in his new office than he had been in his old. Some portion of his uncomplying conduct may perhaps be attributable to his being brought frequently into collision with Bacon, now attorney-general, whom he despised, and whom he could not but consider as a watchful spy on his conduct, and a delighted talebearer of his supposed lapses. In Bacon's letters to the king his offences are carefully reported. The infamous case of Peacham was the first of these. The king having desired to have the private opinion of the judges whether Peacham could be convicted of treason, Bacon undertook to procure it. Coke, however, told him 'that this auricular taking of opinions, single and apart, was new and dangerous;' but on being pressed that the other judges had given theirs, he consented; and, to Bacon's disappointment, it was in writing, and was apparently against the prosecution. (*Johnson's Life*, i. 246.) Notwithstanding the infinite pains he took in regard to the murderers of Sir Thomas Overbury, he offended also on those trials by some mysterious and indiscreet expressions he used in the course of them. In their progress he not only repeated his flattery of the king, but resumed the coarse invectives in which he had formerly indulged, degrading the seat of justice by telling Mrs. Turner before the verdict was given that 'she had the seven deadly sins— viz., a whore, a bawd, a sorcerer, a witch, a papist, a felon, and a murderer.' Guilty as the parties undoubtedly were, Coke conducted the trials most unfairly, and the daily letters that passed between James and him on the subject of them are in strong contrast with his former protest against giving auricular opinions. (*Great Case of Poisoning*, 360-420.)

But the immediate causes that appeared to determine the court to remove him were his independent refusal to submit to its interference in the case of Commendams, and his more doubtful denial of the power of the Court of Chancery. In the first case, the legality of Commendams having been incidentally disputed by a counsel in his argument in a private cause, the king's pleasure was signified to the judges that they should not go on with the case till they had first consulted his majesty. But the judges thought it their duty, this being only a dispute between party and party, to proceed notwithstanding the king's mandate; and all the twelve signed a letter to the king, stating their reasons and justifying their conduct. They were immediately summoned before the council, and, being reprimanded by the king, they all fell down on their knees, and acknowledged their error, except Coke, who defended the letter; and upon further interrogation, whether they would stay their proceedings on a future command, Coke said, 'When the case should be, he would do that which should be fit for a judge to do.' (*Bacon's Works*, vii. 307-338.)

In the other case, Coke had not only resisted the power of the Court of Chancery to touch any cause which had been decided in the courts of common law, but had encouraged indictments being presented against all who had been concerned in a case where relief in equity had been applied for, including the counsel and solicitor to the parties, and even the master in Chancery to whom it had been referred. The question was taken up by the king, whose decision, confirming the Court of Chancery in all the powers which it claimed, is acted on to this day.

On both of these occasions Bacon's hand is visible. In the case of the Commendams he enlarges, in his letter to the king, on Coke's contempt; and in the Chancery question he dwells on the time chosen for pressing the indictments, 'that which all men condemn—the supposed last day of my lord chancellor's life,' as if that was in the power of the chief justice to select. The result of all this 'turbulent carriage,' as the king called it, was, that on June 30, 1616, he was sequestered from the council table, and ordered to 'forbear to ride the summer circuit.' This was soon followed by his removal from office, his discharge from which, on November 15, he is stated by one contemporary letter-writer to have 'received with dejection and tears,' while another describes him as bearing 'his misfortunes well,' and as retiring 'with general applause.'

On Coke's receiving a hint that his compliance with a private job of Buckingham's would prevent his dismissal, he refused the temptation, saying, 'A judge must not pay a bribe or take a bribe.' His successor, Sir Henry Montagu, sent him an offer to purchase the collar of SS; but Coke answered that 'he would not part with it, but leave it to his posterity, that they might one day know that they had a chief justice to their ancestor.'

Bacon, while this was in agitation, had the meanness to address a letter to Coke, in which, with an ungenerous and malicious pen, he describes the character of the chief justice. Whatever truth there is in this delineation, who must not wish it painted by another hand, and at another time?

An epigram, by Ben Jonson (*Gifford*, viii. 430), written about the same time, is a better proof of the estimation in which Coke was then held by his contemporaries as a lawyer and a judge, and affords some evidence that players were not inimical to him, nor he to them. And Milton (*Works*, ii. 218), years after, thus speaks of him, in a sonnet addressed to his grandson, Cyriac Skinner:—

Cyriac, whose grandsire on the royal bench
Of British Themis, with no mean applause,
Pronounc'd and in his volumes taught our laws,
Which others at their bar so often wrench.

Coke, at the time of his dismissal, was commanded to expunge and retract 'such novelties and errors and offensive conceits as were dispersed in his "Reports."' But he showed that there were no more errors in his 500 cases than in a few cases of Plowden, and delivered in a paper explaining other points. This frivolous enquiry, however, soon ceased, and, though he was not replaced in his judicial seat, he was received into a certain degree of favour. Bacon also, who had become lord keeper, was sharply rebuked by the king on Coke's account, and was nearly losing the friendship of Buckingham for opposing the marriage of Coke's daughter by Lady Hatton with the earl's brother, Sir John Villiers, afterwards Lord Purbeck. This marriage Coke had evidently negotiated for the purpose of securing the interest of Buckingham, and thus furthering his return to court. In this he was partially successful, being restored to the council table in September 1617, and appointed, on July 21, 1618, one of the commissioners for executing the office of lord high treasurer. (*Pell Records*, 211.) During three years he was employed in various commissions, and his assistance was required in the Star Chamber in all cases of difficulty; but he received no substantial proof of the renewal of the royal confidence.

He had not been in parliament since 1593, the office of attorney-general disqualifying him from sitting in the House of Commons in 1597, 1601, and 1604, and during the short parliament of 1614 he was chief justice. But when James summoned that of 1621 Coke was again eligible, and was accordingly returned for the borough of Liskeard in Cornwall. His parliamentary career may be truly said to have then commenced, his mouth being no longer stopped by the silence imposed upon him by his former office of speaker. He at once distinguished himself by taking a prominent part against monopolies, patents, and other grievances, and was one of the principal movers against Sir Giles Mompesson. In the impeachment of his old enemy Bacon, he did not, though one of the managers, actively interfere, nor in the other trials which then took place; but on the adjournment in June he is said to have stood up 'with tears in his eyes,' and to have 'recited the collect for the king and his issue, adding only to it, "and defend them from their cruel enemies."' When the house met again in November it immediately proceeded on the Spanish match and the supply for the palatinate, and Coke was made chairman of a committee to consider these and other subjects. A remonstrance and petition to the king being resolved on, Coke spoke strongly in their support. He made a bold stand also for the privileges of the house, and the protestation, which was then carried, so offended the king that with his own hand he tore it out of the journals. The parliament was again adjourned on December 18, and on January 6, 1621-2, was dissolved by a proclamation enlarging on the 'cunning diversions' of 'some ill-tempered spirits who sowed tares among the corn.' In the interim between the adjournment and the dissolution several of these 'ill-tempered spirits' were visited with the vengeance of the court. Coke had made himself a special mark for the royal indignation. The council debated on the means of excluding him from the general pardon at the end of the year; he was sent to the Tower on December 27; his papers were seized, and prosecutions were commenced against him on trumped-up and frivolous charges. His incarceration lasted seven months, at first without intercourse with his family or friends, and even when he obtained his discharge in August 1622, the king said 'he was the fittest instrument for a tyrant that ever was in the realm of England,' and ordered him to confine himself to his mansion at Stoke Pogis. Yonge, in his Diary (p. 62), records that 'the great cause concerning the Lord Coke, for 50,000*l*., followed in the king's behalf in the Court of Wards, is adjudged for my Lord Coke by the three chief judges and Justice Doderidge.'

In the new parliament which necessity compelled James to call in February 1623-4 Coke took his seat as member for Coventry. The questions on which he seemed mostly to interest himself were the Spanish match, the means of recovering the palatinate, and the impeachment of the Earl of Middlesex, on each of which he managed the conferences with the House of Lords. The session closed on May 29, and King James died on the 27th of the following March.

In the first parliament of Charles, Coke, who was chosen by his native county, at first dissuaded the house from renewing the committee for grievances, advising a petition for the king's answer to the former application; but afterwards he opposed the grant of a supply without a redress of grievances. This demand, and an evident preparation to bring charges against the Duke of Buckingham, led to a hasty dissolution on August 12, 1625, and to an endeavour to prevent the most unruly members from sitting in the next parliament, which Charles was necessitated to call in the month of February following, by nominating them sheriffs of the counties in which they resided. Coke was made sheriff of Buckinghamshire, but was elected member for Norfolk; and, notwithstanding a message from the king, no new writ was issued, though, in consequence of the parliament being dissolved before his sheriffalty expired, he did not take his seat. Two years elapsed before the third parliament was called, when Coke was returned for two counties, Buckingham and Suffolk, choosing the former because he resided there. It met on March 17, 1628, and in the first session, which ended on June 26, and was the last in which he took any part in public affairs, he advocated the liberty of the subject with an energy that was surprising in a man who had attained the age of seventy-eight. He suggested, and succeeded in carrying, the famous Petition of Right, in the conferences with the Lords being one of the principal managers, and overcoming, by his arguments and perseverance, all the objections and impediments raised against it. In the violent proceedings of the second session of this parliament he took no part; but, retiring to his seat at Stoke Pogis, he occupied the five remaining years of his life in publishing that celebrated work on which his fame is permanently established — 'The First Institute, or Commentary on Littleton,'—and in preparing for the press the three other volumes of the Institutes, treating respectively on Magna Charta, on Criminal Law, and on the Jurisdiction of the Courts. These, with his will and fifty-one other manuscripts, were seized while he was on his death-bed, by an order of the privy council, made by the peremptory direction of King Charles nearly three years before (*Cal. St. Papers* [1629], 490), under the pretence of searching for seditious papers, and were not published till seven years afterwards, when, by a vote of parliament, they were delivered up to his son. Four years before his decease, one Nicholas Jeoffes was indicted and fined in the King's Bench for writing a petition wherein he said that Lord Chief Justice Coke was a traitor. (*State Trials*, iii. 1375.)

He died on September 3, 1633, being then nearly eighty-two years of age, and was buried in the church of Tittleshall, in Norfolk, in which a marble monument, bearing his effigy at full length, is erected to his memory.

Besides the four books of Institutes, he published eleven volumes of Reports, to which two other volumes were added many years after his death, but not finished or prepared by him for publication. The first part came out in 1600, when he was in the height of his professional fame, and attorney-general to Queen Elizabeth. The others followed in quick succession till the eleventh, published in 1615, about a year before he was deprived of his office of chief justice of the King's Bench by James—an example of perseverance and indefatigable industry which no one occupied as he was with judicial and political duties, and harassed by domestic broils, could have exhibited, had not a cold-blooded temperament made him indifferent to the one, and a habit of early rising enabled him to overcome the other. They are distinguished in Westminster Hall by the name of 'The Reports,' and his jealous enemy, Bacon, is obliged to say of them, 'Had it not been for Sir Edward Coke's reports ... the law by this time had been almost like a ship without ballast, for that the cases of modern experience are fled from those that are adjudged and ruled in former time.' For some law tracts, also, of minor importance, but of great learning, the profession was indebted to him. They were not published till after his death, and are now, from the alterations in practice, become obsolete.

The early portion of Coke's life was not distinguished from that of any other advocate, except by his deeper studies and a more extensive and successful practice. The reputation he attained for legal knowledge pointed him out without a rival for the office of solicitor-general, which he filled at the age of forty. In less than two years he succeeded as attorney-general, and during the twelve years that he held that office he raised it to an importance it had never before acquired, and which it has ever since preserved. The coarseness and brutality of his language, both at the bar and on the bench, will ever leave a stigma on his memory; but it may be observed that no such ebullitions occurred till his rivalry with Bacon began, whose underhand endeavours to supplant and annoy him evidently tended to exacerbate his temper, which was not naturally good; and some of his violent and indecent exhibitions—towards Essex, for instance, who was supposed to be Bacon's friend—may, perhaps, be traced to that influence. His pride and arrogance, however, cannot be doubted, and to them it may be attributed, together with the coldness of his nature and his retired habits, that his biographers record no friendly intimacies, and that fewer sayings of his are repeated than of any person who held so prominent a position in public life. In his station as a judge, which he occupied for ten years, he shone with the brightest lustre; and, making some allowance for his equivocal conduct with regard to Overbury's murderers, he deserves great praise for his resistance of royal interference, and for upholding the independence of the bench. Judge Whitelocke (*Liber Famelicus*) gives testimony of his freedom from the prevailing vice of the time. 'Never was man,' he says, 'so just, so upright, so free from corrupt solicitations of great men and friends, as he was. Never put counsellors that practised before him to annual pensions of money or plate to have his favour. In all causes before him the counsel might assure his client from the danger of bribery.' By his subsequent career in parliament, and his energetic advocacy of liberal measures, he would have gained the admiration and applause of the world, were it not for the opinion, by some entertained, that his opposition to the court savoured too much of personal discontent and disappointed ambition. This mixed feeling has prevented him from being a popular character, and has led men to doubt his judgment and to deny his authority in matters unconnected with his profession; so that many, who allow his merit as a great lawyer and an incorrupt judge, refuse to acknowledge his claims as a disinterested patriot, or as an estimable man.

Against his private character even his enemies could bring no charge; but the contentions with his second wife, which did not terminate till his death, do not speak well for the temper of either. If his division of the hours of the day, 'Quatuor orabis,' was the rule of his life, he must be allowed to have been a pious man. Of his friendship to the Church he gave many proofs in his settlement of ecclesiastical property, and in his careful selection in the distribution of the patronage attached to his estates. With regard to the first, he threatened a nobleman, who was applying for some lands belonging to the see of Norwich, to put on his cap and gown again and plead in support of its rights; and as to the last he was wont to say that 'he would have Church livings pass by livery and seisin, not by bargain and sale.' He was liberal in his entertainments, but moderate in his household; and when a great man came to dinner without previously informing him, his common saying was, 'Sir, since you have sent me no notice of your coming, you must dine with me; but if I had known it in due time, I would have dined with you.'

Sir Edward, by his first wife, Bridget Paston, had seven sons and three daughters. The succession to the family estates fell finally on Robert, the grandson of Henry, his fifth son. Robert's grandson, Thomas, was created Baron Lovel in 1728, and Viscount Coke and Earl of Leicester in 1744; but, the earl leaving no surviving issue, the titles became extinct in 1759. The estates then devolving on Wenman Roberts, Esq., the son of the earl's sister, Anne, that gentleman assumed the name of Coke, and his son, Thomas William Coke, for many years the representative of Norfolk in parliament, was at last, in 1837, created Viscount Coke and Earl of Leicester, titles which are now borne by his eldest son.

Clement, the sixth son of the chief justice, was the father of Edward Coke of Longford, who obtained a baronetcy in 1641, which became extinct in 1727. (Many of these dates and facts are taken from Coke's 'Vade Mecum,' as he calls the interleaved copy of Littleton's 'Tenures,' written by himself, and extracted in the 'Collectanea Topographica et Genealogica,' by the late John Bruce, Esq.)

COKEFIELD, JOHN DE, so called from a place of that name in Suffolk, and probably connected with a powerful family seated there, is first recorded on a fine levied at Michaelmas 1256, 40 Henry III., and on others till the following Michaelmas, in which latter year he was added to the justices itinerant into the county of Suffolk. After that time payments were made for assizes to be taken before him, commencing in August 1258, 42 Henry III., and ending in June 1259. A long interval of eleven years then occurs, no payments being made for assizes before him till May 1270, 54 Henry III., after which they are frequent till May 1272. During this latter period he had a grant of 40*l.* a year for his support, according to Dugdale, as a justice of the King's Bench. His death is recorded on the Close Roll of 56 Henry III. (*Excerpt. e Rot. Fin.* ii. 286-573.)

COKEFIELD, ROBERT DE, or KOKEFIELD, holding a high position in Yorkshire, was selected in 9 Henry III. as one of the justices itinerant for that county. He was constable of the castles of Scarborough and Pickering, for the custody of which he had a salary of two hundred marks per annum. (*Rot. Claus.* ii. 77, 107, 117.) From 1226, 10 Henry III., to 1229, the sheriffalty of the county was entrusted to him, and he was excused 150*l.* which remained due from him for the profits of the county. He married Nichole, the daughter of Jordan de Sancta-Maria, by Alice, the daughter, or sister, of Geoffrey Haget. (*Archæol.* xxx. 485.)

COLEPEPER, JOHN. The Colepepers were of a very ancient Kentish family, which in the reign of Edward III. separated into two branches, one settled at Bay Hall, near Pepenbury, from which descended Baron Colepeper, master of the Rolls in the time of Charles I.; and the other seated at Preston Hall, near Aylesford, to which John Colepeper this judge belonged.

His grandfather was Sir Jeffrey Colepeper, who was sheriff of Kent in 40 Edward III., and his father's name was William. John is first reported in 4 Henry IV., as being appointed a king's serjeant, and as one of that degree who advanced 100*l.* each on loan to the king. (*Acts Privy Council*, i. 202.) On June 7, 1406, 7 Henry IV., he was made a judge of the Common Pleas, and received a new patent on the accession of Henry V. He died in 1414, and was buried in the church of West Peckham, which manor, together with those of Oxenhoath and of Swanton Court, he gave to the Knights Hospitallers of St. John of Jerusalem.

By his wife Catherine he left a son, William, to whose lineal descendant a baronetcy was granted in 1627, which became extinct in 1723.

COLEPEPER, JOHN (LORD COLEPEPER), was of the same family from one branch of which the preceding judge descended. He was the son of a knight of the same name, living at Wigsell in Sussex; and he spent some years in foreign parts, doing good service as a soldier, and reputed to be of great courage, but of a rough nature, his hot temper leading him too frequently into quarrels and duels. When he married he settled in the county of his ancestors, where he soon became popular among his neighbours, and, in consequence of the knowledge of business which he exhibited, and the ability with which he conducted it, he was frequently deputed by them to the council board, and at length was knighted, and elected member for Kent in the Long Parliament.

Within a week after its meeting he summed up in an eloquent speech the grievances of his country, concluding thus: 'One grievance more, which compriseth many; it is a nest of wasps, or swarm of vermin, which have overcrept the land: I mean the monopolies and polers of the people. These, like the frogs of Egypt, have gotten possession of our dwellings, and we scarce have a room free from them. They sup in our cup. They dip in our dish. They sit by our fire. We find them in the dye-vat, wash-bowl, and powdering-tub. They share with the butler in his box. They have marked and sealed us from head to foot. Mr. Speaker, they will not bate us a pin. We may not buy our own clothes without their brokage. These are the leeches that have sucked the commonwealth so hard that it is almost become hectical.' (*Rushworth*, ii. 917.)

The king, sensible of his value, admitted him of his privy council, and on January 6, 1642, made him chancellor of the Exchequer. (*Rymer*, xx. 516.) During that eventful year he, with the assistance of Lord Falkland and Edward Hyde, though sometimes disconcerted by the king's hasty measures, did what he could to serve his majesty. He acquired great influence, but his counsels were not always very wise or temperate. To his advice is attributed the king's consent to pass the bill for removing the bishops from the House of Peers, the transference of the court from Windsor to York, and the attempt to obtain possession of Hull. After the royal standard had been set up at Nottingham, Colepeper was one of the bearers of the king's message to the Commons, with an offer to treat, so as to prevent the effusion of blood and the miseries of civil war. He must have anticipated the answer, from the manner in which he was received by the house. They would not permit him to take his seat as a member, but obliged him to deliver his message at the bar, and then withdraw. (*Whitelocke*, 61.)

On January 28, 1643, he was promoted to the mastership of the Rolls, an office for which his previous education had in no degree prepared him. He took it as adding to his dignity and profit, without regard to its accustomed duties, for in those troubled times there was less need of lawyers than of counsellors and soldiers. As a counsellor, he was used on the most private occasions, and was added to the junto which, as a cabinet council, managed the king's affairs; as a soldier, he was ever by the king's side, and took part in all his battles with the most distinguished bravery.

In reward for these services, the king, on October 14, 1644, created him a peer, by the title of Lord Colepeper, of Thoresway in Lincolnshire, and named him of the council of the Duke of York. At the beginning of the next year he was one of the commissioners on the part of the king in the proposed treaty of Uxbridge. A very unpromising commencement was made by the parliament's refusing to recognise the peerage of Colepeper, or the titles of any of the others which had passed the Great Seal since Lord Lyttelton had sent it to the king. The commissioners wasted their time principally in religious discussions, and the treaty was ultimately broken off. In the calamitous events which followed, Lord Colepeper was zealously and actively engaged in serving the king and Prince Charles, the latter of whom, in 1646, he accompanied to Paris to join the queen. From this time he was the constant companion of the prince in his wanderings; and while at the Hague, in 1648, he had a serious quarrel with Prince Rupert, who was strongly prejudiced against him, which, but for Hyde's interference, might have led to a fatal result. When Prince Charles became king by the tragic death of his father, he sent Lord Colepeper to Russia, to obtain money to supply his necessities; and the mission resulted in the czar granting 50,000*l*. in rich commodities.

At the Restoration he accompanied the king to England, and resumed his place of master of the Rolls; but he was not destined long to enjoy it, for within little more than a month after his landing in England he was seized with an illness, of which he died on July 11, 1660. He was buried in the church of Hollingbourn in Kent, in which and the neighbouring parish the family property, including Leeds Castle, was situate.

Lord Clarendon, though evidently jealous of his ascendency over Charles I., and certainly not prepossessed in his favour, gives him full credit as well for his great parts, ready wit, and universal understanding, as for his sufficiency in council, his courage in the field, and his devoted fidelity. His letter to the chancellor, just after Cromwell's death, as to the counsels to be pursued, and the probable course of General Monk, confirms the opinion of his wisdom, and seems to be dictated by prophetic inspiration. (*Seward*, iv. 388.)

By his first wife, Philippa, daughter of — Snelling, Esq., he had one son, who died young. His second wife, who was his cousin, Judith, daughter of Sir Thomas Colepeper, of Hollingbourn, knight, brought him four sons, the three elder of whom enjoyed the title in succession, which then, for want of male issue, became extinct in 1725. (*Baronage*, ii. 472.)

COLERIDGE, JOHN TAYLOR (a lately retired judge), belongs to a family the name of which never occurs without associations of intellectual eminence—whether as poet, philosopher, biographer, scholar, ecclesiastic, or jurist. In the foremost rank of these, as a scholar and a lawyer, must be placed this retired judge.

John Taylor Coleridge was born at Tiverton on July 9, 1790. His grandfather was vicar of the parish of Ottery St. Mary in Devonshire, and master of the grammar school there. His father was Captain James Coleridge, who retired from the army soon after his marriage with Frances Duke Taylor, the daughter of one of the coheiresses of the family of Duke of Otterton and Power Hayes, one of the most ancient in the county of Devon. After receiving an excellent training from his uncle, the Rev. George Coleridge, then master of the school at Ottery St. Mary, young Coleridge, in June 1803, went to Eton, where he acquired a considerable reputation.

In April 1809 he was elected to a scholarship at Corpus Christi College, Oxford, where his career was most triumphant. In 1810 he won the chancellor's Latin verse prize, the subject being 'Pyramides Ægyptiacæ.' In 1812 he was placed alone in the first class for classics, and in the same year he was elected fellow of Exeter College and Vinerian law scholar. In 1813 he won the chancellor's prizes for prose composition, both in English and Latin, the former having for its subject 'Etymology,' and the latter 'The Moral Effects of the Censor's Office in Rome.' Since the foundation of these prizes it has only happened three times that they both have been gained by one man in the same year, the three conquerors being Mr. Coleridge, Mr. Keble, and Dr. Milman; and on each occasion the chancellor (Lord Grenville) testified his pleasure and approbation by adding to the prizes the gift of a costly and valuable classic. In 1852 the university presented to him the honorary degree of D.C.L.

In the same year in which he was elected Vinerian law scholar he entered the Middle Temple; and, after practising for a short time as a certificated special pleader, he was called to the bar on June 26, 1819, having in the preceding year married Mary, daughter of the Rev. Dr. Buchanan, rector of Woodmanstone in Surrey. For more than fifteen years he was a regular attendant on the Western Circuit, and, though he had for his competitors such eminent men as Serjeant Wilde (afterwards Lord Truro), Sir William Follett, Chief Justice Erle, Mr. Justice Erskine, and Mr. Justice Crowder, he obtained considerable success. As he expresses himself in one of his future lectures, 'The law was not a hard mistress to him, and did not allow him long to languish without business, nor suffer him to be without hope.' During this period he had been appointed, in 1827, a commissioner of bankruptcy; and in 1832 the corporation of Exeter elected him their recorder; the offer of a similar honour from both the boroughs of Southmolton and Barnstaple having been declined by him. In February 1832 he was raised to the dignity of the coif, and when, in April 1834, the attempt was made, under the warrant of King William IV., to open the Court of Common Pleas to all barristers, he, with the other serjeants-at-law, was supposed to be compensated by receiving a patent of precedence, giving him rank after the existing king's counsel.

Engaged as he was in his legal occupations, Mr. Coleridge never deserted his literary pursuits. He contributed occasionally to the 'Quarterly Review,' and on the retirement of its editor, William Gifford, he for one year (1824) undertook the post, but at the end of it, finding that its labours interfered too much with his professional practice, he resigned it into the able management of the late Mr. Lockhart. To professional literature he supplied an excellent edition of 'Blackstone's Commentaries' in 1825.

Mr. Coleridge was soon called upon to take the position which all allowed he was the most competent to fill. On January 27, 1835, he was appointed a judge of the King's Bench, by the recommendation of Lord Lyndhurst, and knighted. For more than three-and-twenty years he administered justice on that bench and on the different circuits in a manner which was most eloquently and truthfully described in the affectionate language of the bar, as expressed by their spokesman, the attorney-general (Sir Fitzroy Kelly, now chief baron of the Exchequer), on June 28, 1858, the day of his retirement. He was immediately admitted to a seat in the privy council, and to be a member of its judicial committee. On the sittings of that tribunal he has ever since regularly attended.

That his character and merits were appreciated most highly by those in power has been fully proved by the varied services that have been required of him. He was selected as a member of many important commissions. Among them was that in 1834, to enquire into the arrangements of the inns of court and Chancery for promoting the study of the law and jurisprudence; that in 1858, to enquire into the expediency of bringing into one neighbourhood the different courts of justice; besides the Oxford University Commission, which sat for four years, and the Education Commission, which sat for three.

In the devotion of his services to the public he has not been unmindful of private and local calls. On his resignation he retired to Heath's Court, Ottery St. Mary, the house in which his father resided, and devoted a good portion of his leisure to the charitable and educational establishments of the county, and by several interesting and amusing lectures (none of them more so than his 'Recollections of the Circuit') delivered to various literary societies, encouraged the efforts to promote rational enjoyment among all classes. The internal restoration of the beautiful priory church in his neighbourhood has been completely effected by his liberality and exertions.

Of Sir John Coleridge's six children, four still survive, the eldest of whom, Sir John Duke Coleridge, is following his father's footsteps in the law, and is now solicitor-general and M.P. for Exeter.

COLEVILL, GILBERT DE, appears on one occasion only in a fine of 28 Henry II. as being present in the King's Court at Westminster when it was acknowledged. (*Madox*, i. 113; *Hunter's Preface*, p. xxi.) As he is not again mentioned in a judicial character, it is possible that he merely held some official post there which required his attendance.

COLEVILLE, HENRY DE, was employed in 18 Henry III. to assess the tallage in Cambridge and Huntingdon, and was twice appointed sheriff for those counties—in 21 Henry III., when he held the office for six years; and again in 34 Henry III., when he held it for two. (*Madox*, i. 735, ii. 169.) In 1252 he acted as justice itinerant for Berkshire, Oxford, and Northampton, and in the following year for Cambridge, Huntingdon, Essex, and Hertford. (*Abb. Placit.* 141.) Whether either of the two belonged to the noble family of Coleville in Yorkshire is uncertain.

COLNEYE, WILLIAM DE, represented Robert de Tateshal in a suit the subject of a petition to the parliament in 18 Edward I., and on the accession of Edward II. he was summoned to the coronation, and to the next two parliaments, his place in the lists being low among those of the legal profession. He was returned as member for Norfolk, and when the justices of assize were appointed for that and the four neighbouring counties in 1310 he was the last of the three who were then nominated. His name does not appear after the next year, but that of his son Ralph is mentioned in 8 Edward II., in which he certified that he was one of the lords of Scottow and Lammas with Little Hautboys. (*Rot. Parl.* i. 37; *Parl. Writs*, ii. p. ii. 708; *Abb. Rot. Orig.* i. 212, 246.)

COLTMAN, THOMAS, was descended from an old and respectable family in the county of Lincoln, where they enjoyed considerable possessions. He was the youngest son of John Coltman, Esq., then resident at Beverley, and was born on July 9, 1781, but ultimately succeeded to the paternal estate. His education was commenced at the Charterhouse in London, from which he proceeded to Rugby, where he obtained an exhibition, and in 1798 was removed to Trinity College, Cambridge, where he took his degree of B.A. in January 1803, and in 1805 he gained the 'blue ribbon' of the university by being elected a fellow of his college.

Entering the Inner Temple, he acquired, under the tuition of that eminent special pleader Mr. Tidd, that mastery of the law which enabled so many of that gentleman's pupils to rise to high distinction. Called to the bar in 1808, he attended the sessions at Manchester, and joined the Northern Circuit, in which he secured so considerable a share of business that eventually in 1832 he was appointed a king's counsel.

On February 24, 1837, he was raised to the bench of the Common Pleas, receiving the customary honour of knighthood. In that court he remained for the last twelve years of his life, performing his duties in that quiet and calm manner which does not attract the 'million,' but which greatly assisted and was highly appreciated by his colleagues, who, in the language of a graceful tribute to his memory published by one of them (Lord Wensleydale) soon after his death, 'knew and admired his dispassionate, candid, and just mind; his clear, acute, and strong understanding; his sound and accurate knowledge of the law; his even temper, patience, and firmness; his care and skill in investigating cases; his excellent judgment in deciding them.' Though somewhat slow in forming his opinions, they were always to be relied on, and, though not brilliant or dashing, he was essentially a just and right-minded judge.

He fell a victim to the Asiatic cholera at his house in Hyde Park Gardens on July 11, 1849, leaving four children by his wife, Anna, sister of Samuel Duckworth, Esq., master in Chancery.

COLUMBIERS, GILBERT DE, or COLUMBARIIS, was of a Norman family. He is mentioned only once by Madox (i. 131) as a justice itinerant into Wiltshire on the roll of 23 Henry II., 1177. He held a fourth part of a knight's fee in England of William de Roumare; and Philip de Columbiers, probably his son, was fermor of the forest of Roumare, in Normandy, in 1180. (*Rot. Scacc. Normanniæ*, ii. clx.)

COLUMBIERS, MATTHEW DE, is confounded by Dugdale (*Baronage*, i. 633) with three others of the same name and family flourishing about the same time. It seems probable that he was the son of Michael, the brother of another Matthew, by his wife Avicia, daughter of Elias Croc.

In 44 Henry III. he was constituted governor of the castle of Salisbury, and soon after joined the rebellious barons, by whom, after the battle of Lewes, he was made governor of Rockingham Castle. He availed himself of the Dictum de Kenilworth to make his peace, and was appointed warden of the forests south of the Trent. Although Dugdale introduces him as an ordinary justice itinerant in 53 Henry III., 1268, it seems more probable that his duties on that occasion were confined to the trial of pleas of the forest, as well on account of his abovementioned appointment as because the commission was headed by Roger de Clifford, the chief justice of the forests. If Dugdale's statement, that this Matthew died in 1 Edward I., be correct, which is not improbable (*Cal. Inquis.* p. m. i. 53), there must have been still another Matthew, who was chief assessor in Hampshire of the fifteenth granted in 3 Edward I. (*Parl. Writs*, i. 3), and one of the king's butlers in the following year, to whom was committed in the sixth year the office of one of the king's chamberlains, and of gauger of the wines sold in England. (*Devon's Issues Exch.* iii. 92; *Abb. Rot. Orig.* i. 31.) He was a justice itinerant of the forests in 8 Edward I., 1280, and his death is recorded in 10 Edward I., when his brother Michael did homage for the lands he held in capite. (*Abb. Rot. Orig.* i. 41.) To make the difficulty still greater, there is among the records a roll entitled 'Compotus Mathæi de Columbariis Camerarii vinorum,' from Michaelmas at the end of the ninth year to the same feast in the thirteenth; and a Matthew is again mentioned as king's butler in 18 Edward I. (2 *Report, Public Records*, App. ii. 55; *Cal. Rot. Pat.* 54.)

COMYNS, JOHN, was born about the year 1667. His father, William Comyns, a barrister of Lincoln's Inn, was descended from a family of that name seated at Dagenham in Essex; and his mother was Elizabeth, daughter and coheir of Matthew Rudd, of Little Baddow in the same county. Their son was educated in Queens' College, Cambridge, and became a student in his father's inn in May 1683, where he took his degree of barrister in May 1690. Elected member of the House of Commons in the last parliament of William III. for Malden, he represented that borough (except from 1708 to 1710) till 1726, when he was promoted to the bench.

As a lawyer he early laid the foundation of that character for learning and industry which he ultimately attained. The first case in his Reports is dated so soon as Hilary Term 1695. His reputation was soon established, and in 1706 he was summoned to the degree of serjeant. He travelled the Home Circuit, and in 1719 he was counsel for the defence in the absurd prosecution for vagrancy instituted against a clergyman for preaching a charity sermon at Chislehurst in behalf of the poor children of a parish in London, four or five of them being present.

Notwithstanding his high repute as a lawyer, it was not till twenty years after he assumed the coif that he was promoted to the bench. On November 7, 1726, he was appointed a baron of the Exchequer, where he remained upwards of nine years, when he removed to the Common Pleas in January 1736. Two years and a half after this he was promoted, on July 7, 1738, to the head of the Court of Exchequer, where his presidency lasted little more than two years, his death occurring, at the age of seventy-three, on November 13, 1740. He was buried at Writtle, near Chelmsford, where is a monumental inscription to him, surmounted by his bust. (*State Trials*, xv. 1412; *Lord Raymond*, 1420; *Comyns' Reports*, 587.)

The two works, the labour of his life, on which his fame as one of the greatest lawyers of his time is permanently established, did not see the light till some years after his death. His Reports, which terminate in his last year, were first published in 1744, and his 'Digest of the Laws of England' was delayed till 1762. By the unanimous assent of the most eminent men in the profession, the latter is acknowledged to be the most accurate, methodical, and comprehensive abridgment of the law, profound in its learning and easy of reference to the authorities cited.

Sir John married three times. His first wife was Anne, daughter and coheir of Dr. Nathaniel Gurdon, rector of Chelmsford; his second was Elizabeth, daughter of — Courthope, of Kent; and his third was Anne, daughter of — Wilbraham. Neither brought him any issue. (*Morant's Essex*, ii. 60; *Gent. Mag.* x. 571, lx. 390.)

CONINGSBY, HUMPHREY, whose ancestor was lord of the manor of Coningsby in Lincolnshire as early as the reign of King John, was the son of Thomas Coningsby, of Nene Solers in Shropshire, by his wife, the daughter and heir of — Waldyffe.

After pursuing his legal studies at the Inner Temple, he is mentioned as an advocate in the Year Books in 1480, and as being called to the degree of the coif at the end of Trinity Term 1494, 9 Henry VII. During the whole of that reign he had a considerable share of practice, and on October 30, 1500, was made one of the king's serjeants.

Within a month after the accession of Henry VIII.—viz., on May 21, 1509—he was placed in the King's Bench as sole puisne judge and was knighted. The number of judges was afterwards increased, and Sir Humphrey retained his place among them for a very extended period, his seat not appearing to be supplied till the middle of 1532.

He resided, and according to Clutterbuck (i. 444) was buried, at Aldenham in Hertfordshire, but that author evidently errs in dating his death in 1551. By his wife, who was a daughter of — Ferebie, of Lincolnshire, he left three sons and four daughters. William, his second son, was the next-mentioned judge; and one of the descendants of Thomas, his eldest son, was raised to the earldom of Coningsby in 1719, which is now extinct. (*Chauncy*, 461; *Blomefield's Norfolk*, vii. 413.)

CONINGSBY, WILLIAM, the second son of the above-named Humphrey, was educated at Eton, and King's College, Cambridge, whither he went in 1497. He then became a member of the Inner Temple, where he was reader in Lent 1519, and again in Lent 1526. In 1516 he was in the commission for gaol delivery at King's Lynn, and was named in June 1529 a commissioner to assist Cardinal Wolsey in hearing causes in Chancery. He was recorder of Lynn, for which he sat in parliament in 1537, one of the prothonotaries of the Common Pleas, and attorney of the duchy of Lancaster, from the latter of which he was removed on February 1540 on being charged with counselling Sir John Shelton to make a fraudulent will of his lands, and committed to the Tower. That this charge was without foundation may be presumed from his being released in ten days, and being selected within five months to be a judge of the King's Bench, to which he was appointed on July 5, 1540. It would seem that he sat little more than four months, and that Edward Mervin succeeded him on November 20. (*Dugdale's Orig.* 163, 172; *Rymer*, xiv. 738.)

He resided in the Woollen Market in Lynn, and at Eston Hall, Wallington, Norfolk. By his wife, a daughter of — Thursby, of that county, he had an only son, Christopher, who was killed at Musselburgh in Scotland. (*Ath. Cantab.* 76.)

CONSTANTIIS, WALTER DE (ARCHBISHOP OF ROUEN), was a canon of Rouen, and held a responsible post in the Curia Regis under Henry II., but whether as chancellor or vice-chancellor it would be difficult to define.

In 1175 he was raised to the archdeaconry of Oxford; in 1176 he had an allowance of fifty marks for providing for the ambassadors of the King of Sicily, when they came to demand Henry's second daughter, Jane, in marriage; and in 1180 he accounted for the proceeds of the abbeys of Wilton and Ramsay, and of the honor of Arundel, then in the king's hands, of which he had been appointed custos. (*Madox*, i. 201, 367, ii. 252.) On none of these occasions is any official title affixed to his name.

He held the living of Woolpit, belonging to the abbey of St. Edmunds, until June 1183, when he was elected Bishop of Lincoln (*Chron. Josc. Brakelonda*, 35, 126), from which see he was promoted in the following year to the archbishopric of Rouen. In 1186 he was one of Henry's ambassadors to King Philip of France, and succeeded in obtaining a truce with that monarch; and in 1189 he and Baldwin, Archbishop of Canterbury, were appointed umpires to decide the disputes between them.

On Henry's death he invested Richard, in the cathedral of Rouen, with the sword of Normandy; and attending him into England, assisted at his coronation, and was present at the council held at the abbey of Pipewell. He accompanied that king on his progress to the Holy Land, but returned to England in February 1191, escorting Queen Eleanor on her departure from Sicily. He brought with him a letter from King Richard, appointing him the head of the council for the rule of the kingdom; but a doubt has been raised as to its authenticity, from its not having been produced till some months after his arrival in England. Longchamp, however, was dismissed in October 1191, and the Archbishop of Rouen, by virtue not only of this letter, but of the appointment of Prince John and the barons, was constituted chief justiciary.

Warned, perhaps, by the example of his predecessor, he was moderate in the exercise of his office, and cautious to avoid undertaking any important act without the advice of the barons and the consent of his associated council. (*Madox*, i. 220.)

When Richard's place of confinement was discovered, and the terms of his enlargement were settled, Walter de Constantiis was summoned to attend him in Germany, and his place of chief justiciary was, in September 1193, conferred on Hubert Walter, the new Archbishop of Canterbury. He accompanied Queen Eleanor with the king's ransom, paid it to the emperor at Mentz, and procured Richard's liberation.

In 1196 a contest arose between Walter and King Richard, in consequence of the latter interfering with some of the property of the church of Rouen. The archbishop thereupon placed Normandy under an interdict, which produced such horrible confusion in the country that Richard, unable to relieve the inhabitants by any other means, was compelled to appeal to Rome. By the pope's interposition the interdict was removed, and a convention was made between the king and the archbishop, exchanging the land in dispute for certain other property and privileges, no doubt greatly to the advantage of the Church. (*Nicolas's Chronology*, 303.)

On the accession of King John he performed the ceremony of investiture to the dukedom of Normandy in the church of Rouen, as he had previously done to his royal brother; and in the course of that reign his active life was terminated.

Richard of Devizes (27, 31, 45) wrote too near his time, and was too much of a partisan, to warrant his readers in placing entire credence on the hypocritical character which he ascribes to the archbishop. On the contrary, his conduct seems to have been guided by prudence and discretion, and not to have been deficient in firmness and courage. A strong proof of the latter would be shown by the admonition which, according to Brompton, he gave to King Richard against the indulgence of his three vices—pride, avarice, and lust; which produced the monarch's jesting reply, that he would give the first to the Templars, the second to the monks, and the third to the bishops. Other writers, however, attribute the rebuke to another divine. (*Godwin*, 286; *Wendover*, ii. 435, iii. 2–138; *Lord Lyttelton's Henry II.* iii. 441; *Lingard*, ii. 335.)

COOPER, ANTHONY ASHLEY (EARL OF SHAFTESBURY). The ancestors of this sagacious but versatile statesman were of a class of opulent gentry; but, from the frequent occurrence of the surname, his direct lineage cannot with certainty be traced beyond the reign of Henry VII. His great-great-grandfather, John Cooper, possessed estates in Sussex and Hants, and died in 1495. His great-grandfather Richard, designated Solutarius under Henry VIII., purchased Paulett in Somersetshire, and died in 1566. His grandfather John represented Whitchurch in parliament, and was knighted by Queen Elizabeth. On his death in 1610 he was succeeded by his son, also John, who was created a baronet in 1622, was member for Poole in 1628, and by his first marriage, with Anne, daughter and heir of Sir Anthony Ashley, of Wimborne St. Giles, Bart., became the father of two sons, the eldest of whom was the future lord chancellor.

Anthony Ashley Cooper was born at Wimborne St. Giles, on July 22, 1621, and, having lost his father in 1631, he inherited a large estate before he was ten years of age. From Puritan private tutors he received his early instruction, till, in Lent Term 1636, he was entered a fellow-commoner at Exeter College, Oxford. Under the tuition of Dr. Prideaux, the rector, afterwards Bishop of Worcester, he made such progress as to be accounted, according to the description of his eulogist, 'the most prodigious youth in the whole university.' By his own account he was more famous for putting an end to the 'ill custom of tucking freshmen,' and for preventing an alteration in 'the size of the beer.' (*Shaftesbury Papers*, 17.) Remaining at college about two years, he then, in consequence of lawsuits in which he was involved with some near relatives, caused himself to be admitted into the society of Lincoln's Inn, on February 18, 1638. His legal studies there were not interrupted till the commencement of the Great Rebellion, for though he was elected member for Tewkesbury in the parliament of April 1640, when he was not yet nineteen, his senatorial duties, during the short time it lasted, could not have been very onerous; and he was not admitted a member of the Long Parliament, which began its eventful sittings in the following November, although elected for Downton in Wiltshire by a double return, decided in his favour by the committee of privileges, that body having omitted, purposely, to report their decision to the house.

At the commencement of the contest between the king and the parliament Sir Anthony was a professed loyalist. In 1642 he acknowledges that he was with the king at Nottingham and Derby, adding evasively, 'but only as a spectator;' yet soon after he accepted a commission from the Marquis of Hertford, the king's general, to treat for the surrender of Dorchester and Weymouth. This he effected, and was thereupon made governor of the latter place, colonel of a regiment of foot, and captain of a troop of horse, both of which he raised at his own charge. And after Hertford's dismissal he received the king's confirmation in his government, and the appointments of high sheriff of Dorset and president of the council of war in those parts.

But the baronet's loyalty was not very deeply rooted. According to Clarendon, when it was thought necessary to substitute Colonel Ashburnham in his place as governor of Weymouth, he took such offence that he deserted his colours, and, immediately joining the other side, gave himself up 'body and soul to the service of the parliament, with an implacable animosity against the royal interest.' He himself says in his autobiography that, notwithstanding a flattering letter from the king, he resigned his government and came away to the parliament, 'resolving to cast himself on God, and to follow the dictates of a good conscience.' Mr. Locke gives a somewhat different account of the cause of his defection; but the uncontradicted fact remains that he went over to the malcontents and was hailed by them as a great acquisition. He was at once entrusted with a command as field-marshal-general of the army in Dorsetshire, and with his forces he besieged and took Wareham, and commanded in chief at the taking of Blandford and Abbotsbury, and in the relief of Taunton, besieged by the royalists. His military career seems to have terminated with the year 1645, in the September of which he was probably renewing his attempt to have his right to his seat for Downton acknowledged. Though he did not succeed in this, he was in such favour and trust with the parliament that in November he was made sheriff of Norfolk, and in January 1647 sheriff of Wiltshire, with the additional favour of permission to live out of the county. During the two months previous to the king's execution he was at his house in Dorsetshire, and that event is not even noticed in his diary, which merely records his arrival at Bagshot in his journey to London, where he arrived on the following day. He subscribed the engagement in 1650, and in January 1652 he was appointed one of the committee on the abuses and delays of the law, and the remedies to be adopted. For his former connection with the king he had been permitted in 1644 to compound by the payment of 500*l*., which was afterwards remitted by Cromwell; but he was not entirely cleared of his delinquency till March 1653, when the Commons passed the following resolution: 'That Sir A. A. Cooper, Bart., be and is hereby pardoned of all delinquency, and be and is hereby made capable of all other privileges as any other of the people of this nation are.'

On the forcible expulsion of that body, Sir Anthony was summoned to Barebone's Parliament in July 1650, as one of Cromwell's nominees for Wiltshire, and was elected for the same county, and also for Poole and Tewkesbury, in the subsequent parliament, which met in September 1654, and which was dissolved in the following January. In both these assemblies he was in Cromwell's confidence, acting in his interest in each, and being one of his council of state, both as general and protector. Dryden, in his 'Medal,' with much malice, but with some apparent truth, describes him at this time as

A vermin, wriggling in th' usurper's ear:
Bart'ring his venal wit for sums of gold,
He cast himself into the saint-like mould,
Groan'd, sigh'd, and pray'd, while godliness
    was gain,
The loudest bagpipe of the squeaking train.

But soon another change took place. From the supporter, he became the enemy of Cromwell, who, according to Anthony Wood and Ludlow, understanding his character, refused to receive him as his son-in-law. Whatever was the cause, it is certain that in the parliament of September 1656, to which he was returned again for Wiltshire, he did not receive the requisite certificate of approval from the council; and he was consequently, with above ninety other members in the same predicament, partly Presbyterians and partly Republicans, excluded from sitting, notwithstanding the bold remonstrance against this tyrannous proceeding addressed by them to the house. Those who remained, having confirmed Cromwell's power, and enabled him to appoint a certain number of peers, the excluded members, taking the oath of fidelity to the protector, were admitted to sit in the session that followed in January 1658, and by their number nearly overturned all that had preceded. A controversy was immediately raised, in which Sir Anthony actively joined, as to the title and privileges of the 'other house,' as it was called, which was carried on with so much violence that the protector hurriedly dissolved the parliament after a fortnight's sitting. He never called another during his life, which terminated seven months afterwards.

The short session of Protector Richard's parliament, to which Sir Anthony was returned both for his old county and for Poole, was wasted in tiresome and insidious debates, renewing the old question about the 'other house,' and discussing various points in the new form of government. In these Sir Anthony took a prominent part; and in a published speech of great satirical power he had the bad taste to blacken the character of the protector who had fostered him, and with whose administration he had been intimately connected. (*Burton's Diary*, iv. 286.) The dissolution of this parliament on April 22, 1659, was Richard's fall; and the Rump Parliament, which then resumed its sittings, appointed a council of state, of which Sir Anthony was elected as a member. His fidelity to the Commonwealth began, however, to be doubted. In May he was publicly charged with holding correspondence with the king, and so loud were his professions of innocence, and his imprecations on himself if he were guilty, that they only added weight to the suspicions against him. Whether he was imprisoned on this charge seems uncertain, but it was some months before he got rid of it. Though there can be little doubt that he was engaged in the plots that were then contriving in behalf of the king, he managed so artfully that he procured his acquittal by the parliament in the following September. On the second expulsion of the Rump by the army, in October, the government was carried on by a council of safety, whose powers lasted only two months, when the Rump was again restored. To this last event Sir Anthony mainly contributed, and was admitted upon his former election to take his seat for Downton on January 7, 1660. Besides resuming his position as a member of the council of state, he was made colonel of the regiment of horse lately commanded by Fleetwood, with which he joined Monk, and continued to act in conjunction with that general till the restoration of the king.

The Long Parliament dissolved itself in March 1660, and to the convention, or Healing Parliament, that met in the following month, Sir Anthony was returned by his old constituents. He was one of the deputation sent by the two houses to the Hague to invite the king to return, and was among the first who were sworn of the privy council; 'the rather,' says Clarendon, 'because, having lately married a niece of the Earl of Southampton, it was believed that his slippery humour would be easily restrained and fixed by the uncle.' When that earl was made lord high treasurer, in September 1660, Lord Clarendon states that Sir Anthony was appointed chancellor of the Exchequer. Other authorities delay his entrance into the office till May 1667; but Clarendon's account is confirmed, not only by several documents addressed to him in that character in the State Paper Office, but by Sir Anthony himself, in his speech in 1672 on Mr. Serjeant Thurland's being constituted a baron, in which he alludes to his 'eleven years' experience in that court.' He has been blamed, though without much reason, for allowing himself to be named on the commission for the trial of the regicides, in the proceedings of which, however, he does not appear to have taken any part. On April 20, 1661, he was called up to the House of Peers by the title of Baron Ashley of Wimborne St. Giles, the introduction to his patent, while it records his loyalty 'in many respects' to King Charles I., and his assistance in restoring King Charles II., carefully abstaining from all allusion to his conduct in the interval, in deserting the former king, in aiding his rebellious subjects, and in joining in the counsels of the usurper.

Till the death of his uncle Southampton in 1667 Lord Ashley took comparatively little ostensible interest in party politics, but showed himself an adept in the business of the state. At the same time he was preparing his way by making himself agreeable to the king, and by encouraging, or at least countenancing, the scandalous intrigues of the court. Ever ready in repartee, in which the king delighted, he once, when his majesty, in reference to his amours, said railingly to him, 'I believe thou art the wickedest fellow in my dominions,' replied with a low bow and grave face, 'Of a *subject*, may it please your majesty, I believe I am.'

On the dismissal of Lord Chancellor Clarendon in that year a new career was opened to Ashley's ambition. He had already been appointed lord lieutenant of Dorsetshire, and president of the new council of trade and plantations; and, gradually ingratiating himself with his easy sovereign, as well by his pliancy and wit as by his facility in the invention of expedients, he soon became one of a secret cabinet with Buckingham, Clifford, Arlington, and Lauderdale, by which every measure was determined before it was brought publicly forward, and which, from the initials of the names of its members, acquired the designation of the CABAL. Their ministry was rendered conspicuous by the shutting up of the Exchequer, the rupture of the triple alliance, and the mismanagement of the religious questions which then agitated the country; but though the discredit of these measures has been generally fathered upon Lord Ashley, Mr. Christie, in the 'Shaftesbury Papers' (ii. 77, 90), has shown satisfactorily that he objected to and opposed the two former. Whether he were the opponent or supporter of them, the king, regarding him with personal affection, and appreciating his abilities, raised him to the earldom of Shaftesbury on April 23, 1672. Not satisfied with this elevation, the new earl aspired to a still higher position, for the attainment of which the removal of Lord Keeper Bridgeman was necessary. His intrigue for that purpose was successful. An opportunity soon was taken, on the lord keeper's resistance to some of the ministerial measures, to represent him as weak and incapable, and the Great Seal, being consequently taken from him, was given to Shaftesbury on the 17th of the following November, with the title of lord chancellor. While he held that office he resided at Exeter House.

Though educated at Lincoln's Inn, he had never practised as a lawyer, his time during the rebellion having been employed in active service, and since the Restoration in court attendance. The consequence was that he had so little respect for the profession for which he had been intended that he despised the forms by which its proceedings were regulated, and even refused to assume the decent habit of a judge. 'He sat on the bench in an ash-coloured gown, silver-laced, and full-ribboned pantaloons displayed, without any black at all in his garb;' and at first, setting all rules at defiance, he was frequently obliged on rehearing to reverse his own orders, so that at last he became more reasonable, and submissive to the formulæ of the court. Without regarding the extravagant praises of his eulogists on the one side, or the adverse insinuations of his detractors on the other, his decrees in Chancery would appear to have met with general approbation; for in Dryden's severe description of him under the name of Achitophel he gives him full credit for judicial integrity. King Charles, too, is reported to have said of him, on deciding a very difficult case, that 'he had a chancellor that was master of more law than all his judges, and was possessed of more divinity than all his bishops.'

It was not in Shaftesbury's nature to be steady; even the high position which he enjoyed could not fix him. Finding the opposition more strong than he expected, and fearing the personal consequences which the leaders threatened, he determined to avert the danger by joining their ranks. Even while chancellor he showed his wavering disposition by gradually deserting the measures he had originated, and endeavouring to thwart the objects of the king. But his immediate hopes were disappointed: his plans being discovered, the parliament was prorogued, and the Seal taken from him on November 9, 1673, after a tenure of less than a year.

Immediately on his disgrace he was the chosen leader of the discontented party, and, without entering into the question as to the policy pursued on either side, for which this is not the place, we can only look to the repeated treachery of the man. From an arbitrary minister he was converted into the head of a popular faction, and from a royal favourite he became the king's enemy, ungratefully repaying the honours and favours he had received by continual attempts to injure and ruin the family of his benefactor. It bears too strong a resemblance to his former defections, and exhibits, if not the perfidy, at least the fickleness of his character.

The remainder of his life was spent in factious opposition, his chief object apparently being to exclude the Duke of York from the succession. For this purpose he entered into all sorts of intrigues and conspiracies, exciting the cry of 'No Popery,' and pretending first that his own life was in danger from the Roman Catholics, and next that the murder of the king was their object. Foremost in opposing all the measures proposed by the court, his manœuvres at one time subjected him to an imprisonment in the Tower for nearly a year, and at another they were so far successful that he forced himself again into the ministry as president of the new council of thirty. This event was effected in April 1679, on the fall of the Earl of Danby, and during the excitement produced by the pretended Popish Plot, which had been openly nurtured by Shaftesbury, and aided by him through all its ramifications, encouraging its inventor, the infamous Titus Oates, and explaining away his various contradictions, and those of his perjured coadjutors. Even during his presidency he continued to counteract the wishes of his royal master; and, opposing a bill offered by the king, limiting the powers of a Catholic successor to the throne, supported one to exclude the duke from the throne itself. On this the king, who had never trusted his mutable minister, designating him (from his stature and his falsehood) as 'Little Sincerity,' dismissed him from his councils in the following October. He then became more violent and less cautious in his endeavours to harass the court. He made an attempt to present the Duke of York as a recusant, which was defeated by the judges suddenly discharging the grand jury; he advocated, if he did not originate, another bill of exclusion, which, though it passed the House of Commons, was triumphantly rejected by the Lords; and he even proposed a bill divorcing the queen, that the king might marry again and have a Protestant heir.

The violence of his agitation at length caused its own defeat. The people began to open their eyes, and the court ultimately regained the ascendency. From the popular and patriotic leader, Shaftesbury became the suspected and trembling traitor. He was arrested and committed to the Tower in July 1681; and, though an indictment against him for compassing and imagining the death of the king was thrown out in the following November by a grand jury packed by sheriffs of his own party (a medal to commemorate this event is the subject of Dryden's bitter poem called 'The Medal'), the discovery of a treasonable association, in which he probably was engaged, and the fear lest his connection with other desperate projects should be betrayed, made it advisable for him to fly the country. By various disguises and concealments he eluded a warrant issued against him, and at last succeeded in escaping to Amsterdam, where, two months after, he died on January 21, 1683, of the gout in his stomach. His remains were conveyed to England, and buried at Wimborne St. Giles, where his great-grandson in 1732 erected a noble monument, with just such an encomiastic inscription as might be expected from an admiring descendant.

While on his mission to King Charles in Holland in 1660 he received an injury from the overturning of his carriage, which caused him great inconvenience in his after-life, and obliged him to have continued recourse to medical advice. Among those who attended him was the celebrated philosopher John Locke, then a young man, with whom his lordship was so much pleased that he took him into his household, entrusted to him the education of both his son and grandson, and, when in office, placed him in some responsible and profitable positions. Shaftesbury's publications are confined to speeches and political pamphlets at different periods of his life, and contain abundant evidence, were all else wanting, of his unprincipled mutability and his restless turbulence.

Shaftesbury is charged with participating in all the vices of the time except that of being tempted by pecuniary bribes; and, though all must acknowledge his talents, his eloquence, and his wit, his memory must be regarded with repugnance by all who remember the various desertions and intrigues of his career, and the factious fickleness of his character. His only claim for the respect and gratitude of posterity is the Habeas Corpus Act, which was passed by his instrumentality.

The earl married three times—first, so early as 1639, to Margaret, daughter of Thomas Lord Coventry, lord keeper, who died in July 1649; secondly, in April 1650, to Frances, daughter of David Cecil, Earl of Exeter, who died in 1654; and lastly, in 1656, to Margaret, daughter of William Lord Spencer of Wormleighton, and niece to the Earl of Southampton, who survived him. He had issue by his second wife only, two sons, of whom one survived him. Of his descendants the third earl was the celebrated author of the 'Characteristics;' and the present, the seventh earl, has already acquired a high reputation for his charitable exertions for the good of mankind.

COPLEY, JOHN SINGLETON (LORD LYNDHURST), was born at Boston in America on May 21, 1772, before the war of independence had commenced, and he lived to see the disseverance of those states, the union of which was the result of that war. His father, John Singleton Copley, of Irish extraction, was then practising in that city the art in which he became afterwards distinguished in England, whither he brought his family when his son was two years old. His fame was soon established as a painter, both in portraiture and history; and the high value at which his works are now estimated is proved by the large prices they produced in the recent sale of the late lord chancellor's collection. The artist died in 1815, aged seventy-four, when his son had already taken the first steps in his successful career; and his wife, who was a daughter of Richard Clarke, Esq., survived till 1836, happy in witnessing the highest honours by which her son was graced.

Young Copley was originally destined for his father's profession, in the elements of which he made some progress, but the plan was happily set aside in consequence of the mental powers he early exhibited. At the age of nineteen he was sent to Trinity College, Cambridge, where he pursued his studies so energetically that he took his degree of B.A. in 1794, with the honours of second wrangler and Smith's prizeman, and of M.A. in 1797, having in the interim been elected a fellow of his college. His delight in mathematical studies, and also in practical chemistry and mechanics, he retained throughout his long life, and his attainments in them were of infinite service to him in his professional career. This he commenced by entering himself as a member of Lincoln's Inn, and by becoming a pupil of Mr. Tidd, from whose instructions so many men have risen to eminence. He spent part of the following years in visiting the land of his birth.

On June 8, 1804, he was called to the bar, and selected the Midland Circuit. One of his earliest clients was Lord Palmerston, the late prime minister, then first entering into political life, for whom he appeared before a committee of the House of Commons on a double return for the borough of Horsham in 1806, but failed in securing the seat. The only book which Mr. Copley ever published with his name was a report of that case. Both on the circuit and in Westminster Hall he gradually acquired a sufficient practice to induce him to accept the degree of serjeant-at-law in 1813. Entering now in some measure into public life, he avowed tory, or what would now be called conservative, principles, to the surprise of some of his contemporaries, who charged him with having been notorious in the early part of his life for the ultra-liberality of his professions. Whatever were his youthful notions, and however unguardedly he may have expressed them among his private associates, it is hardly fair to refuse a man the exercise of more mature reflection, and to bind him down to the rash phrases of a juvenile imagination, especially when he had never joined any whig society, nor connected himself with any public measure of that party. But the subject of the charge ever denied its truth; and the best proof of the sincerity of his convictions is his steady adherence to them, through good report and bad report, for the long period of fifty subsequent years.

As a leading advocate, by the beautiful simplicity of his style, by the logical arrangement of his arguments, and by the aptness of his illustrations, his speeches were wonderfully effective both on juries and judges. The government were so struck with the talent which he exhibited that in October 1817 he was specially retained for the crown in the indictments against Brandreth and others for high treason tried at Derby. In the next year, besides being made king's serjeant and chief justice of Chester, he was introduced into parliament for the ministerial borough of Yarmouth in the Isle of Wight, which he soon after exchanged for Ashburton; and in 1826 he had the honour of being elected as representative of his own university.

In the senate his great capacity for debate was so efficiently displayed that in July 1819 he was appointed solicitor-general, and received the usual accolade of knighthood. During his tenure of this office the spirit of sedition was prevalent throughout England, and in the legislative remedies that were then introduced, as well as in the prosecution of Thistlewood and the other Cato Street conspirators, Sir John Copley exhibited his extraordinary talent. In the unfortunate trial also of Queen Caroline it was his duty to take an active part, in the performance of which he tempered the conviction he felt of the guilt of the accused lady with the decorum due to her exalted rank, satisfying his employers by his admirable performance, without incurring the obloquy to which they were subjected. At this time Lord Tenterden, in a letter to Sir Egerton Bridges, gives this opinion of him : ' The solicitor-general has less learning than the attorney-general (Gifford), but a much better person, countenance, and manner; a good head and a kind heart, and not deficient in learning. I suppose he will soon fill one of our high offices in the law.' (*Lord Campbell's Ch. Just.* iii. 296.) In January 1824 he was promoted to the attorney-generalship, and on September 14, 1826, he received the patent of master of the Rolls.

He held the latter office only eight months. On Mr. Canning becoming prime minister Lord Eldon resigned the Great Seal, which was delivered to Sir John Copley on April 30, 1827, as lord chancellor, he having been created Baron Lyndhurst a few days before. This his first chancellorship lasted three years and seven months, during the successive administrations of Mr. Canning, Lord Goderich, and the Duke of Wellington. On the accession of the whigs to power in 1 William IV., he resigned the Seal on November 22, 1830, but did not remain unemployed quite two months. He accepted the appointment of lord chief baron of the Exchequer on January 18, 1831, in the place of Sir William Alexander, with the perfect understanding that he retained his political opinions. His independence of ministerial influence was shown by his resistance, with all his energy and strength, of the bills for reform in parliament, and of various other measures proposed by the party while it remained in power.

When the conservatives regained the administration he was at once replaced at the head of the Court of Chancery, on November 21, 1834, retaining the office of lord chief baron for the next month. His presidency of the Exchequer had exhibited his high judicial capacity, and had been principally distinguished by the luminous judgment which he pronounced in the great case of Small v. Attwood, which, though it was reversed on appeal in the House of Lords by a close majority of a single vote, was by most people considered to be well founded, and by all, whether supporters or opposers, greatly admired.

After a short term of five months he again, on April 23, 1835, resigned the Seal to his political opponents, who retained power for the next six years. During that interval he maintained the ascendency he had gained in the House of Lords, by his powerful opposition to the various innovations introduced by the whig ministers, and by submitting to the house useful amendments of the law; and still more by the annual comprehensive exposure of the ineffective legislation at the end of each session, in which he visited the successive failures with alternate rebuke and sarcasm. These regular attacks increasing the general unpopularity of the party, the ministers were at length obliged to resign, and Lord Lyndhurst was installed in his third and last chancellorship on September 3, 1841. His merits had been recognised and rewarded in the previous year by his university electing him their lord high steward.

For nearly five years he devoted himself to his judicial duties, till the retirement of Sir Robert Peel, when he resigned the Seal on July 4, 1846. When the conservative party regained power for short periods in 1852 and 1858, Lord Lyndhurst felt himself too old to undertake the responsible labours of the chancellorship, or to accept the offered seat in the cabinet, being in his eightieth year at the first of these periods; but during nearly the whole time since his resignation to almost the last year of his life, when he had attained his ninetieth year, he entered with his accustomed spirit into most of the constitutional questions that arose, and surprised the house by his intellectual vigour.

No statesman maintained for so long a succession of years a name so unsullied as Lord Lyndhurst, and few have died in possession of more veneration and regard. His death occurred from natural decay on October 18, 1863, in the ninety-third year of his age, at his house in George Street, Hanover Square, where his father had lived and died.

He married, first, Sarah Geary, the daughter of Charles Brunsden, Esq., and widow of Colonel Charles Thomas, of the First Foot-guards, who fell at Waterloo. By her he had three daughters. His second wife was Georgiana, daughter of Lewis Goldsmith, Esq., by whom he had one daughter.

CORBET, REGINALD, was descended from an honourable family seated in Shropshire ever since the Conquest, some members of which were barons of the realm from the reign of Henry II. to that of Edward II., and others were ancestors of baronetcies, all of which are extinct except that of Corbet of Moreton Corbet, created in 1808. Reginald was the second son of Sir Robert Corbet of Moreton Corbet, by Elizabeth, the daughter of Sir Henry Vernon of Haddon. He pursued his legal studies at the Middle Temple, and was elected reader there in autumn 1551, but his reading was deferred till the following Lent. On October 27, 1558, he received a summons to take upon him the degree of the coif in the following Easter, but Queen Mary's death intervening, a new writ became necessary, and the solemnity of his inauguration took place on April 19, 1559. On the 16th of the next October he was constituted a judge of the Queen's Bench, where he sat till his death in 1566. (*Plowden's Reports*, 356.)

He married Alice, daughter of John Gratewood, Esq., and by her he had a son Richard, who was father of John Corbet, of Stoke in Shropshire, created a baronet in 1627. This title became extinct in 1750 by the death of its sixth possessor without issue; but his nephew, Corbet d'Avenant, succeeding to his estates and assuming his name, had a new creation in 1786, which also became extinct at his death in 1823. (*Wotton's Baronet*. ii. 74, 272, 274, 312.)

CORDELL, WILLIAM, the son of John Cordell, Esq., and Eva, daughter of Henry Webb, of Kimbolton, was born at Edmonton in Middlesex, and, having become possessed of the manor of Long Melford in Suffolk, he fixed his residence there, his family having been long seated in that county. From a branch of it descended Sir Robert Cordell, who received the dignity of baronet in 1660, which became extinct in 1704 by the death of his grandson without issue.

After being educated at Cambridge, he was admitted a member of Lincoln's Inn, and was called to the bar in 1543. He sat in the parliament of March 1553 as member for Steyning, and on September 30, two months after Queen Mary came to the crown, he was made her solicitor-general. On the 1st of the following November the benchers of the society of Lincoln's Inn appointed him their butler, and on February 2, 1554, he was fined in the sum of 'xxvjs. viij*d*.' 'for not exercysing the office.' (*Black Book*, iv. 270, 272.) This curious entry seems to show that the junior members of the bench had this duty imposed upon them, for in the Lent of that year he was nominated to the post of reader. As solicitor-general he took a part in the prosecution of Sir Thomas Wyat for his attempt against the queen; and on November 5, 1557, he was promoted to the office of master of the Rolls and knighted. In the last parliament of Queen Mary, being then member for Essex, he was chosen speaker; but her death at the close of it made no difference in his judicial position, which he retained for nearly twenty-four years. (*Dugdale's Orig.* 231.)

Troubling himself apparently very little with politics, though successively member for Middlesex and Westminster, he was regarded with favour by the court, and Queen Elizabeth paid him the compliment of commencing her progress in Suffolk, in 1578, by visiting him at Long Melford

Hall, where he gloriously feasted her. He died on May 17, 1581.

He married Mary, the daughter of Richard Clopton, Esq., but left no children.

CORNHILL, GERVASE DE, was so called from the ward of that name in London, where probably he resided, and was clearly a man of high note and authority there, holding in 2, 3, 6, and 7 Henry II. the post of sheriff (*Madox*, i. 204, 602), an officer in whom the temporal government of the city was then vested. After the latter year he is not noticed in connection with the metropolis; but his next residence being in Surrey, he was appointed sheriff of that county in 10 Henry II., 1164, and remained in that office, with the exception of one year, until 1183.

In 15 Henry II., and for the seven succeeding years, he held the same responsible office in Kent, where he had a seat at Lukedale, in the parish of Littlebourne; and in the contest with Becket he sided strongly with the king.

Among the justices itinerant in the 15, 16, 20, and 23 Henry II., 1169-1177, his name appears as acting in various counties. It does not clearly appear whether at that time he performed the same duties in the Curia Regis, but it is certain that he attended there in 28 Henry II., 1182, as his name is inserted as one of the barons and justiciers before whom fines of that year were taken. (*Madox*, i. 113, 123, 132, 143, 144.)

From the termination of his sheriffalty in Surrey, it may be presumed that his death occurred in 29 or 30 Henry II.

He left three sons, Henry, Reginald, and Ralph, the two former of whom held the office of sheriff of Kent for several years. Henry was bailiff of London, and also sheriff of Surrey. He was chancellor of St. Paul's, and had the management of the Mint (Cambium) of England in 3 Richard 1. Reginald was the next named justice itinerant. (*Hasted*, i. 178; *Lord Lyttelton's Henry II.* 583.)

CORNHILL, REGINALD DE, was the second son of the above Gervase de Cornhill, and after the death of his elder brother Henry, in 4 or 5 Richard I., he, or his son of the same name, held the sheriffalty of Kent, with some short interval, until 5 Henry III. His seat at Minster, in the Isle of Thanet, acquired the name of 'Sheriff's Court,' which it still retains; and he himself, discontinuing his own name, was styled Reginald le Viscount, even his widow being designated Vicecomitessa Cantii. (*Hasted*, i. 178-9.) He succeeded his brother also in the management of the Mint of England, and continued in connection with it and with the Treasury till late in the reign of John. (*Madox*, i. 459.)

That he acted in a judicial capacity in 1 John appears from the Rotulus de Oblatis (p. 47), where certain persons are summoned before him and John de Gestling and William de Wrotham, also justiciers. In the fines of that reign his name occurs as being present in court till 10 John.

Various other employments show that he was high in the king's confidence. In 5 John he was one of the custodes of the ports of England and the quinzime of merchants; and in the next year he and William de Wrotham were appointed 'superiores custodes,' when the king made an assize 'de moneta custodienda, et retonsoribus et falsonariis monete nostre destruendis.'

He was a staunch adherent of that king in all his earlier troubles, and received many substantial marks of his favour. The Reginald de Cornhill who, in the latter contests of his reign, joined the barons, and who was one of those taken prisoner in Rochester Castle in December 1215, was probably his son, to whom, and to William de Cornhill, the 'Cameraria' was granted in 14 John. His wife, Isabella, paid a fine of five thousand marks for his liberation. (*Rot. Claus.* i. 241; *Rot. Pat.* 189.)

CORNHILL, WILLIAM DE (BISHOP OF LICHFIELD AND COVENTRY), either the son or the nephew of the above Reginald de Cornhill, was an officer of the Exchequer, and connected with the Mint of England. (*Madox*, i. 338.)

Some houses in London were granted to him by the king in 5 John; and in that year Geoffrey Fitz-Peter was ordered to make a provision for him of twenty marks out of the first ecclesiastical benefice of the king's patronage that should drop. In 6 John he had a grant of twenty acres of the wood of Tilgholt in Kent; in 7 John he was made rector of Maidstone by the king's collation; in the same year he was appointed custos of the abbey of Malmesbury; in the next year he had the same office in the bishopric of Lincoln, and in 9 John he was raised to the archdeaconry of Huntingdon. (*Rot. de Liberate*, 69, 80; *Chart.* 137, 157; *Pat.* 57, 65, 73.)

His name occurs as a justicier in fines levied in 10 John, 1208, but not in any other year. In the two next years, and in 14 John, his personal attendance on the king is noticed on the rolls, and in the latter year he was presented to the churches of Somerton in Somersetshire, and of Fereby in Yorkshire, and, in conjunction with Reginald, the son of Reginald de Cornhill, received a grant of 'Cameraria nostra' from the king. (*Rot. Pat.* 95, 96.)

On January 25, 1215, 17 John, he was consecrated Bishop of Coventry and Lichfield, and dying on June 19, 1223, he was buried in Lichfield Cathedral. (*Godwin,* 315.)

CORNWALL, EARL OF. *See* ROBERT.

COSSALE, WILLIAM DE, so called from his manor of Cossale in Nottinghamshire, was a benefactor of Newstead Abbey in that county. He was appointed a baron of the Exchequer in 3 Edward III., but is not mentioned after the 14th year. (*Cal. Rot. Pat.* 106; *Rot. Orig.* ii. 78, 81; *Inquis.* p. m. ii. 97.)

COTESMORE, JOHN, resided at Baldwin Brightwell in Oxfordshire. He married Florence, the daughter of Sir Simon Harcourt, ancestor of Lord Chancellor Harcourt. He appears among the advocates in the Year Book till 8 Henry V., and was made a serjeant-at-law in 5 Henry V. In 9 Henry V. he was sent as a justice of assize to Norwich and other places with Justice William Babington. (*Cal. Exch.* iii. 380.) He afterwards became one of the king's serjeants, and was elevated to the bench as a judge of the Common Pleas on October 15, 1429, 8 Henry VI. After sitting in that court for nearly ten years, he succeeded as chief justice there on January 20, 1439, 17 Henry VI., but presided little more than eight months, the executors of his will being on October 14 following commanded to give up the records to his successor. He was buried at Brightwell, where there is a monumental brass to his memory. (*Notes and Queries,* 1st S. x. 520.)

COTTENHAM, EARL OF. *See* C. C. PEPYS.

COTYNGHAM, THOMAS DE, was one of the clerks in Chancery for nearly thirty years, from 14 to 43 Edward III., 1340-1369, but only on one occasion is mentioned as keeper of the Great Seal—viz., on the death of the chancellor, John de Offord, when it was placed in the custody of him and others from May 28 till June 16, 1349. (*Rot. Claus.* 23 Edw. III. p. 1, m. 8, 10.) During part of this period, however, he went to Ireland as master of the Rolls there, to which office he was appointed in 30 Edward III., 1356. (*Cal. Rot. Pat.* 166.) He was no doubt brought up in the Chancery, as he was presented by the king so early as 13 Edward II., 1319, with the church of Wygeton, and acted as the attorney of William de Herlaston, a clerk in the Chancery, in 1325. (*N. Fœdera,* ii. 401, 606.)

COVENTRY, THOMAS. With John Coventry, lord mayor of London in the reign of Henry VI., and one of the executors of the renowned Richard Whittington, began the prosperity of this family, which derived its surname from the city of Coventry, where it was originally established. One of his descendants, Richard Coventry, was settled at Cassington in Oxfordshire, and by his wife, a daughter of — Turner, had two sons, the younger of whom was Thomas the future judge. He was born in 1547, and educated at Oxford, where he took the degree of M.A. on June 2, 1565, and afterwards was elected fellow of Balliol College. He entered the Inner Temple, and became reader there in autumn 1593. He was one of those named on Sir Edward Coke's preferment to succeed him in the solicitor's place, and Bacon (*Works,* xii. 157) tells Sir Robert Cecil, though with a profession of disbelief, that it was asserted that Coventry had bought his interest for 2000 angels. Neither of them obtained the promotion, and it was not till two months before the queen's death that Coventry received a writ to take upon him the degree of the coif in the following Easter. On January 13, 1606, he was appointed a judge of the Common Pleas, and knighted. He enjoyed his place less than a year. Dying on December 12, 1606, he was buried at Croome d'Abitot in Worcestershire. His estate, called Earles Croome, he had acquired by his marriage with Margaret, the daughter and heir of — Jeffreys, of that place, and it still is the chief seat of his family.

The judge left three sons, of whom Thomas was the lord keeper.

COVENTRY, THOMAS (LORD COVENTRY), was the eldest son of the above-noticed judge. He was born in 1578, and, having passed the first fourteen years of his life under the tuition of his parents, he was placed as a gentleman commoner at Balliol College, Oxford, at Michaelmas 1592. At the end of three years he was admitted a member of the Inner Temple, and, having been called to the bar, he is mentioned in Coke's Reports as an advocate so early as 1611; he was elected reader in autumn 1616.

By the respect he showed to Sir Edward Coke he entailed upon himself the enmity of Bacon, who sought to impede his professional advance by prejudicing the king against him. When Coventry was a candidate for the recordership of London, Bacon suggested to the king that 'it is very material, as these times are, that your majesty have some care that the recorder succeeding be a temperate and discreet man. . . . The man upon whom the choice is like to fall, which is Coventry, I hold doubtful for your service; not but that he is well learned and an honest man, but he hath been, as it were, bred by Lord Coke and seasoned in his ways.' The shaft fell harmless, and Coventry was not only elected recorder on November 16, 1616, but on March 14, 1617, was taken into the king's own service as solicitor-general, and knighted. Four years after, also, when Sir Henry Yelverton, the attorney-general, was condemned by the Star Chamber, Coventry received the appointment, on January 11,

o

1621. One of the first duties he had to perform in his new office was to take a message from the Lords to Bacon, requiring him to send specific answers to the charges against him. Soon after he had to prosecute Edward Floyde for his presumption in calling the king's daughter and her husband 'Goodman Palsgrave and Goodwife Palsgrave;' but he was not answerable for the brutal sentence which the Lords pronounced upon the silly speaker. (*Parl. Hist.* i. 1239, 1260.)

On King James's death he was retained in his office by King Charles, and before the end of the year was called upon to supply the place of Bishop Williams, receiving the Great Seal as lord keeper on November 1, 1625. His letter to Buckingham forms a strong contrast with Bacon's on a similar occasion. It is a manly and modest doubt of his own capacity for the place, a dutiful submission, after full consideration, to the royal will, and a courtly acknowledgment of the duke's favour. But there is nothing in it that shows any previous application, nor any undue reliance on the interference of the favourite.

He had to open the second parliament of the reign, and soon after to deliver the king's reprimand to the Commons for their negligence in completing the supply, and their encouragement of seditious speeches. He had little to do in reference to the imprisonment of the Earl of Arundel and the demand of the Peers for his release, except as the messenger of the king and the organ of the house. The angry dissolution of this parliament, notwithstanding his earnest endeavours to prevent such a termination, soon after taking place, the king endeavoured to supply his necessities by forced loans; but, not succeeding to his wish, he called a third parliament in March 1628. Sir Thomas Coventry opened this in an eloquent speech, which would have been more effective had it not contained an intimation that, if there were not a readiness in voting supplies, the king might resort to other means by the use of his prerogatives. But before the end of the session he had to pray of the king a more explicit answer to the Petition of Right, which was accordingly given on June 7, 1628, in the well-known formula, 'Soit droit fait comme il est désiré.' (*Parl. Hist.* ii. 218, 409.)

On April 10 the lord keeper was created a baron by the title of Lord Coventry of Aylesborough in the county of Worcester. When Buckingham applied for the dormant office, and almost unlimited powers of lord high constable, Lord Coventry showed a patriotic spirit in opposing the grant, and thus incurring the hatred of the favourite. Peremptorily accosting him, the duke said, 'Who made you lord keeper?' 'The king,' said Coventry boldly. 'It's false,' said Buckingham; ''twas I did make you, and you shall find that I who made you can and will unmake you.' Coventry retorted, 'Did I conceive I held my place by your favour, I would presently unmake myself, by rendering the Seal to his majesty.' Buckingham would have put his threat into execution, and probably have obtained the Seal for Sir Henry Yelverton, had he not been assassinated in the following August. This parliament, after another session, was hastily dissolved like the former, the close of it being distinguished by the forcible detention of the speaker (Sir John Finch) in the chair while the protestation of the Commons against tonnage and poundage was passed.

No other parliament met for the eleven remaining years of Coventry's life—a circumstance which, however impolitic, could not be distasteful to his personal disposition. He was more of a lawyer than a politician, and would no doubt be glad to be relieved from defending measures which he could not honestly justify. The holder of the Great Seal was no longer, as in Wolsey's time, the director of the state; other and more active spirits acquired the ascendency, and their opinions prevailed. No one can read the history of the time without seeing that Coventry had but little influence in the councils of his sovereign, which were in a great measure directed personally by the king, under the guidance, first of a favourite, and then of unscrupulous and intemperate advisers. In times when all men's actions were open to censure, and none escaped who could be charged with too violent a support of the royal prerogative, or with too manifest a tendency to infringe on the liberty of the subject, the very absence of the name of one who held so high an official position tells strongly in his favour, as showing that his personal demeanour and his imputed principles were not to any great extent obnoxious to those who were assuming the rule and punishing their opponents. In Lilburn's case, though Coventry presided on the condemnation, his estate was not in the first instance attempted to be charged with the compensation awarded, and it was not till the estates upon which the reparation was voted were disposed of in another manner, nor till eight years after the lord keeper's death, that the pertinacious sufferer conceived the idea of coming on Lord Coventry's heir. The attempt was frustrated, even in the strong excitement of that period, by a large majority; and the vote, though perhaps influenced by some personal motives, was no doubt dictated principally by the conviction that the cruelty and illegality of the sentence against Lilburn could not be justly imputed to the lord keeper. At the same time it is difficult altogether to excuse his lordship from participation in the iniquitous punishments which were too often awarded in the Star Chamber, except on the presumption that, though presiding, he had but a single voice, and that, by the course of the court, he gave his opinion last, and was compelled to pronounce the censure of the majority. That his inclinations were on the side of mercy the judgment in Chambers's case proves. In Henry Sherfield's case, for breaking a painted glass window, he was, after giving a lenient sentence, actually outvoted; and in the case of Dr. Leighton, for publishing 'A Plea against Prelacy,' and in other similar accusations, it requires not much discrimination to decide to whom the severity of the punishment is to be attributed. (*State Trials*, iii. 374, 383, 519, 1315.) In April 1635 James Maxwell and Alice his wife were brought before the Star Chamber, for asserting in a petition to the king that the lord keeper disobeyed his majesty and oppressed the subject, and were fined 3000*l.* to the king and the same sum to the lord keeper, the female narrowly escaping a whipping moved for by one of the members. (*Cal..St. Papers* [1635], 31.)

At the introduction of the imposition of ship-money, in the speeches which he addressed to the judges previously to the commencement of the circuits both in June 1635 and Lent 1636, he enjoined them, in their charges to the grand jury, to urge the people to pay their contributions with alacrity and cheerfulness; but from his position as lord keeper he was precluded from giving any legal opinion on the case of Hampden, who resisted the levy, the judgment being pronounced by the twelve judges alone, and he was not a party to, nor a witness of, the consequences that resulted from these proceedings; for before the next parliament met his death occurred at Durham House in the Strand (where the Adelphi now stands), on January 14, 1640, and his remains were removed for interment in the family vault at Croome d'Abitot. His last message to the king was a request 'that his majesty would take all distastes from the parliament summoned against April with patience, and suffer it to sit without an unkind dissolution.' (*Hacket's Bp. Williams*, ii. 137.)

He had held the Seal for above fourteen years, and every writer of any authority has refrained from making any specific charge against him. Even Whitelocke, who had evidently no goodwill towards him, can say no more than he was 'of no transcendent parts or fame.' His other contemporaries differ from this judgment, and unite in praising him. Croke calls him 'a pious, prudent, and learned man, and strict in his practice, ... he died in great honour, and much lamented by all the people.' Clarendon says he discharged all his earlier offices 'with great ability and singular reputation for integrity,' and that in his place of lord keeper 'he enjoyed it with an universal reputation (and sure justice was never better administered).' Of his 'parts' the same author says, 'He was a man of wonderful gravity and wisdom, and understood not only the whole science and mystery of the law, at least equally with any man who had ever sate in that place, but had a clear conception of the whole policy of the government, both of Church and state, which by the unskilfulness of some well-meaning men justled each the other too much. He knew the temper, disposition, and genius of the kingdom most exactly; saw their spirits grow every day more sturdy, inquisitive, and impatient; and therefore naturally abhorred all innovations.' Anthony Wood, Fuller, and David Lloyd are equally encomiastic; and Lord Clarendon says, in recording his death, that he had 'the rare felicity in being looked upon generally throughout the kingdom with great affection, and a singular esteem, when very few men in any high trust were so.' A charge of bribery was got up against him by a disappointed suitor, but was so palpably unfounded and malignant that the Star Chamber visited the contriver and all his assistants with severe penalties of purse and person. (*Rushworth*, ii. App. 30.)

Lord Coventry was twice married. His first wife was Sarah, daughter of Edward Sebright, of Besford in Worcestershire; and his second was Elizabeth, daughter of John Aldersey, of Spurston in Cheshire, and widow of William Pitchford, Esq. By both of them he left issue. His grandson, Thomas, was advanced in 1697 to the titles of Viscount Deerhurst and Earl of Coventry, with a special limitation, under which they are now held, the original barony having become extinct in 1719, by the death of the fourth earl without male issue.

COURTENEYE, HUGH DE (EARL OF DEVON), was at the head of the commission of justices itinerant into Bedfordshire in 4 Edward III., 1330, but he seems to have been placed there more as one of the principal barons of that county than as in any other way connected with the law. He was also at the head of another commission, for the trial of offenders in the forests, in the same year. (*Abb. Rot. Orig.* ii. 24.)

He was the eldest son of Hugh de Courteneye, Baron of Oakhampton, and Eleanor, daughter of Hugh Despencer the elder, Earl of Winchester. His father died in 1291, when he was sixteen years of age.

o 2

He had no sooner attained his majority than he joined in various expeditions under Edward I., by whom he was knighted. He was summoned, also, to all the parliaments as a baron, both under that king and his two successors, until 8 Edward III., 1334; and on February 22, in the following year, he was created Earl of Devon, as the lineal descendant of Baldwin de Ripariis, the seventh earl. He died in 1340, 14 Edward III., and was buried at Cowick, near Exeter.

By his wife Agnes, daughter of John, Lord St. John, of Basing, he had six children. The title still remains in one of his descendants. The eighteenth earl was created Marquis of Exeter in 1553; but, dying without issue three years afterwards, this additional honour became extinct.

COURTENEYE, WILLIAM DE (ARCHBISHOP OF CANTERBURY), was the grandson of the last-mentioned Hugh de Courteneye, Earl of Devon, being the fourth son of Hugh, the second earl, by Margaret, daughter of Humphrey de Bohun, Earl of Hereford, and Elizabeth, a daughter of Edward I. He was born at Exminster about 1327, was educated at Oxford, where he took his degree of Doctor of Civil Law, and was afterwards chancellor of that university. With such connections he soon procured rich benefices, among which were prebends at Exeter, Wells, and York. He was elevated to the bishopric of Hereford in 1369, and thence translated in 1375 to London.

Among the followers of Wickliffe, whose opinions at this time gained so much ground as to alarm the Church, was John of Gaunt, Duke of Lancaster; and when, towards the end of Edward's reign, Bishop Courteneye, in obedience to the pope's mandate, summoned the reformer to be examined, the duke attended him to St. Paul's Church, where the meeting was held. There some violent words passed between the duke and the bishop, which ended in an unseemly threat on the part of the former. The assembled people, who as yet cared little for the religious question, fancying their bishop in danger, prepared to defend him, and by their clamours compelled the duke, who was no favourite with them, to retire. The populace, outside, excited by other reports to his disadvantage, joined in the outcry; and the ferment was not appeased till they had broken open the Marshalsea prison, ransacked the duke's house in the Savoy, and contemptuously dragged his arms through the streets.

On Edward's death, which occurred soon after, it was not likely that the council of the young king, the Duke of Lancaster being at its head, would allow the prosecution against Wickliffe to proceed. His doctrine, accordingly, spread widely through the kingdom; and though he died at his living of Lutterworth in 1384, his followers, under the name of Lollards, rapidly increased.

On the murder of Archbishop Sudbury, the king, on August 10, 1381, appointed Bishop Courteneye Chancellor of England, and assented to his election as Archbishop of Canterbury. Thus it would appear that the Duke of Lancaster no longer felt any animosity against him; yet it is difficult to account for Courteneye's resigning the Seal three months after, on November 30.

During the remainder of the archbishop's life, a period of nearly fifteen years, he was engaged in various contests with his bishops as to the right of visitation, in all of which he was triumphant; but the demand which he made on his clergy, of a sixtieth part of their revenues, being resisted by the Bishop of London, was carried by appeal to the court of Rome, where it was not decided while he lived.

He died at his palace at Maidstone, on July 31, 1396, and was buried in the church there. A monument was erected to his memory in his cathedral church, to which, besides contributing largely to the erection of the nave, he gave various rich presents.

Walsingham declares that he was dignified with a cardinal's hat; but the doubts of others seem to be supported by the absence of all notice of the fact in the epitaph inscribed on his gravestone in Maidstone Church. This edifice he had entirely rebuilt, and had restored the church of Mepham; besides many liberal donations, among others to the church of Exminster, his native town.

He is represented as having a noble presence and courtly manners, with the learning fit for his position, a clear and acute understanding, and a favourite with the monks of his cathedral. (*Godwin*, 120, 186; *Weever*, 225, 285.)

COWPER, WILLIAM (EARL COWPER), descended from that branch of the family which held a respectable position in Sussex in the reign of Edward IV., and then resided at Strode in the parish of Slingfield. His immediate ancestor became an alderman of London in Elizabeth's time, and had a son, Sir William, who was created a baronet by Charles I., and suffered imprisonment for his loyalty to that unfortunate king. His grandson the second baronet represented Hertford in several parliaments of Charles II. and William III., adopting the whig side in politics, and taking a prominent part in the proceedings against James II. when Duke of York. By his wife Sarah, daughter of Sir Samuel Hoiled, of London, he had two sons, William and Spencer.

William Cowper was born at Hertford

Castle about four or five years after the Restoration. He was some years at a school at St. Albans, and became a student at the Middle Temple on March 8, 1681-2. His years of probation were divided between his law-books and his pleasures, the latter it is reported claiming the greatest share, but the former evidently not neglected. Whatever were his excesses during that interval, it may be presumed that before the end of it he terminated them by his marriage about 1686 with Judith, daughter of Sir Robert Booth, a merchant of London living in Walbrook. He was called to the bar on May 25, 1688. Bred up in the principles of political liberty and with a deep hatred of popery, his youthful ardour prompted him a few months later to offer his personal aid in resisting the obtuse tyranny of James II. He and his brother Spencer, with a band of men, joined the Prince of Orange in his march to London: but on the peaceful establishment of William and Mary on the throne he returned to the stage of his profession, on which, whether on the Home Circuit or in the courts of Westminster, he soon became a favourite performer. He was chosen recorder of Colchester, and got into considerable practice within the first five years after his call. Before Easter 1694 he had been raised to the position of king's counsel, and by his assistance to the attorney and solicitor general in the prosecutions arising out of the assassination plot in 1696 he conspicuously demonstrated his superiority as an advocate. In the only other state trial in which he appears—that of Lord Mohun for the murder of Richard Coote—the peers paid him the compliment of naming him particularly to sum up the evidence instead of Sir John Hawles, the solicitor-general, whom from his dulness and lowness of voice they could not understand. But, as it was contrary to the etiquette of the bar, Sir John was allowed to proceed. (*State Trials*, xii. 1446, xiii. 123, 1055.)

In 1695 he was returned with his father to parliament for Hertford, and tradition reports that on the day of his entrance into the house he spoke three times, and with such effect as to establish his character as an orator. He represented the same constituency in the parliament of 1698, but in the following year the family interest in the borough was disturbed, and his own professional success materially endangered, by the unfounded charge brought against his brother Spencer of the murder of a young Quaker named Sarah Stout. Notwithstanding the acquittal that followed, the influence of the Cowpers in Hertford was so damaged that they did not venture to stand in the election of 1701; but William was returned for Beeralston in that and the last parliament of William III. and in the first of Queen Anne, at the end of which he ceased to be a commoner. The parliamentary history records only two important speeches delivered by him while in the House of Commons—one on the bill of attainder against Sir John Fenwick in 1696, and the other on the Aylesbury case in 1704, in support of the right of the subject to seek redress at law against a returning officer for corruptly refusing to receive his legal vote. He also defended Lord Somers when impeached, and in 1704 he was censured by the house for pleading for Lord Halifax. (*Parl. Hist.* v. 1007, 1141, vi. 279; *Burnet*, iv. 480; *Luttrell*, v. 488.)

When the tory ascendency began to be diminished, the removal of Lord Keeper Wright, the weakest and most inefficient man of the party, was determined on. Passing over the attorney and solicitor general, Cowper, at the urgent instigation of the Duchess of Marlborough, was selected from the whig ranks to hold the Seal. It was delivered to him as lord keeper on October 11, 1705. The commencement of his judicial career was illustrated by a noble reform. It had been a custom of long standing for the officers of the court and the members of the bar to present new years' gifts to the chancellor or keeper, a practice which, if not actual bribery, he considered looked very like it. These he at once refused to receive; and the extent of the sacrifice may be estimated, if not by his wife's calculation that they amounted to nearly 3000*l.*, by Burnet's more probable computation of 1500*l.* With such a proof of his moderation and delicacy, it is curious that he did not abolish the equally obnoxious custom of selling the offices in the chancellor's gift. By the evidence on the trial of the Earl of Macclesfield it appears that he received 500*l.* on the admission of a master in Chancery. Although it is difficult to perceive the distinction between the two customs, it is clear that he did not consider them as coming under the same category, and that he did not anticipate the evil consequences to which the latter might lead. At the same time he forbad the clerks to demand any extra fee for the performance of their duties. On the death of his father in November 1706 he succeeded to the baronetcy, and on the 9th of the same month he was ennobled with the title of Lord Cowper of Wingham. (*Evelyn*, iii. 407; *Burnet*, v. 243; *Luttrell*, vi. 111; *State Trials*, xvi. 1154.)

His first wife having died six months before his elevation, he married, secondly, Mary, daughter of John Clavering, Esq., of Chopwell in the bishopric of Durham. Lord Cowper was one of the commissioners for the Union with Scotland, and zealously assisted Lord Somers in the negotiations. Upon its being completed the queen invested him, on May 4, 1707, with the title of lord high chancellor of Great Britain; and from that time the designation of lord keeper fell into desuetude, only one other possessor of the Great Seal having been so distinguished up to the present day. For the next three years the whig party retained its influence; but at last, by its own folly in the impeachment of Dr. Sacheverell, the popularity it had acquired was transferred to its political opponents. The prosecution stirred up all the dormant feelings of the people, revived the cry of 'The Church in danger,' and so strengthened the efforts of the tory advisers of the queen that the whig members of the government were soon after dismissed. The Duke of Marlborough had during the contest ambitiously demanded to be made captain-general for life; but Lord Cowper, though united with him in politics, represented to the queen that such an appointment would be highly unconstitutional, and by his advice the application was rejected. His lordship, though strongly pressed by the queen to keep the Seal, was firm in his resolve to follow the fate of his colleagues, and resigned on September 23, 1710. He then entered at once into an avowed, and it must be acknowledged sometimes a factious, opposition to the new ministry; and, according to the fashion then prevalent, occasionally supported his views and answered the attacks of his opponents in the periodical publications of the day. He remained unemployed for the four remaining years of Queen Anne's reign; but on her death he was found to be one of the lords justices nominated by the Elector of Hanover, who showed the tendency of his opinions by selecting them principally from the whig party. The queen died on August 1, 1714, and King George, arriving in England on September 18, immediately formed his ministry and reinstated Lord Cowper in the office of lord chancellor on the 21st.

On his appointment he presented to the king a long paper which he called 'An Impartial History of Parties,' but which is anything but what its title imports. In professing to describe the two parties, whig and tory, into which the people were divided, he artfully depreciates all the acts and principles of the latter, and represents the former as the only one which it would be expedient or safe for his majesty to trust. The antipathy of one faction against the other was at its height, and was exhibited by the vindictive course which the new ministry pursued against the leaders of the party they had supplanted. Lord Cowper took too prominent a part in these proceedings, and it may not be improbable that the extremes to which their animosity was carried hurried on the rebellion of 1715. To his energetic representation to the king may perhaps be attributed the speedy suppression of that rebellion. His conduct on the trial of the rebel lords, when he acted as lord high steward, supported his previous reputation.

During his second chancellorship the Riot Act, the Septennial Bill, and the Mutiny Bill, after violent opposition, became law, and to the passing of them he gave his powerful aid. Intrigues were formed for his removal as early as October 1715, and continued in the two succeeding years, till at last, though his party remained in power, he resigned the Seal on April 15, 1718, having been on the 18th of the preceding month honoured, as a special mark of the royal approbation, with the additional title of Viscount Fordwich and Earl Cowper. He lived more than four years afterwards, and continued to the last days of his life to take a prominent lead in the debates, and a deep and impartial interest in the various measures proposed on the one side or the other. He died after a few days' illness at his seat at Colne Green on October 10, 1723, and was buried in the parish church of Hertingfordbury. His wife followed him four months afterwards, literally dying of a broken heart.

Of Lord Cowper's character as a statesman there will always be two opinions. The course of his conduct that would excite Burnet's or Wharton's applause would certainly be decried by Swift and the tory writers. But all would allow that he was a firm adherent to the principles he professed, and that those principles tended to civil and religious liberty, and that the motives which guided him were pure and straightforward, though occasionally tainted with a little too much of party prejudice. Of his extraordinary oratorical powers, of the singular gracefulness of his elocution, of the sweetness of his disposition, and of his integrity and impartiality as a judge there has never been any question. Of his urbanity and consideration for the feelings of others we have a striking instance in his repressing the harsh personal remarks made by a counsel against Richard Cromwell, in a cause to which he was a party, by immediately addressing the old protector, and kindly begging him to take a seat beside him on the bench.

Though not particularly eminent for classical learning, he was well versed in the literature of his country, and was a generous patron to its professors, among whom were John Hughes and Ambrose Philips, who devoted some graceful verses to his memory. Among his prose eulogists were Burnet, Steele, Lords Chesterfield and Wharton, and a host of other minor authors.

Even Swift himself, in his 'Four Last Years of Queen Anne,' is compelled to speak of him with as much praise as his crabbed nature and party prejudices would allow.

The earl's London residences were in Russell Street and Powis House, Lincoln's Inn Fields, and subsequently in Great George Street; and his country one was at a spot called Colne Green, in the parish of Hertingfordbury, the manor of which he had purchased. The house which he built there was pulled down in the beginning of this century, and replaced by the present stately mansion of Penshanger, where his successors flourish.

COWPER, SPENCER, was the younger brother of the above William Earl Cowper. Born in 1669, he received his education at Westminster School, and having been called to the bar by the society of Lincoln's Inn, he was immediately appointed by the corporation of London, in June 1690, comptroller of the Bridge House estates, a post of considerable responsibility, which entitled him to a residence at the Bridge House, in the parish of St. Olave, Southwark. There he lived for some years, and gained the respect of his neighbours by his exemplary conduct and social manners. There, too, he executed with great usefulness the duty of a magistrate, having been soon placed on the commission of the peace; and there he filled many offices of trust connected with the locality.

In the midst of these prosperous circumstances he was suddenly charged with a crime which threatened not only to blast the character he had acquired, but to consign him to an ignominious end. In the course of the Home Circuit which he travelled he was in the habit of visiting Hertford, of which both his father and his brother were representatives in parliament. Residing with her mother in that town was a young woman named Sarah Stout, the daughter of a respectable Quaker deceased, who had been a firm friend of the Cowpers; and both the brothers and their wives had shown a kind interest in her welfare. At the spring assizes of 1699 Spencer had dined with her on March 13, and after supper had gone home to his lodgings about eleven o'clock. On the next morning she was found in the river, and an inquest was immediately held on the body, at which Spencer Cowper was present and gave his evidence, which resulted in a verdict that the deceased drowned herself, being *non compos mentis*. About a month after this, with no further evidence than was submitted to the coroner's jury, the mother and brother commenced a prosecution, charging not only Spencer Cowper, but two attorneys and a scrivener, who had been heard making some loose remarks at their lodgings about the girl, with first strangling her and then throwing her into the water where she was found. The parties were summoned before Lord Chief Justice Holt, who at first dismissed them, but after two subsequent examinations was induced on May 19 to commit Mr. Cowper for trial to the King's Bench prison, where he remained till the next assizes. The prisoners were arraigned at Hertford on July 16, and after a long trial were acquitted, as Luttrell remarks, 'to the satisfaction of the auditors.' Every one who reads the trial must join in this satisfaction, for a more unfounded charge could not be made. Judge Hatsel presided, and by his querulousness at the trial and the stupidity of his summing up, the prisoners had certainly no cause to thank him for their acquittal.

But Cowper's persecution was not yet over. Whether from a conviction of his guilt and a thirst for revenge, which seems scarcely possible; or from a desire to clear the Society of Friends from the imputation that one of their body could be affected by worldly passions, which no doubt in some measure operated; or from the excitement of party spirit prompting the opponents of the Cowpers to endeavour to destroy the interest of the family in the borough, which is far more likely, as a new election was near at hand; for one or the other of these reasons the question was kept alive, at first by pamphlets, and subsequently by much more unjustifiable means. The law allowed an appeal for murder to be instituted within a year and a day after the death by the next heir of the deceased. Such an heir was immediately found, who was an infant; but, instead of at once obtaining the necessary writ, the prosecutors purposely delayed issuing it till three or four days before the expiration of the term; and this they did without the knowledge or consent of the infant heir, the nominal appellant, or of his mother, who were not even made acquainted with the proceeding for a month afterwards. Naturally disgusted at the prosecutors' conduct, they applied for and obtained from the sheriff the writ and return, which they forthwith put into the fire. This the prosecutors endeavoured to remedy by applying to the lord keeper for a new writ, which he, assisted by four learned judges, very properly refused, on the ground that the first writ had been clandestinely and fraudulently procured, that it was absolutely renounced by the pretended plaintiff, and the delay in its issue showed that the prosecutors did not design justice, but to spin out a scandal as long as they could, maliciously and vexatiously. Mr. Cowper during these discussions appeared in court, and declared his readiness to answer. Thus this affair terminated; but the principal object was answered, by the dissolution for the time of the Cowper interest in the town.

(*State Trials*, xii. 1105; *Luttrell*, iv. 518–650; *Lord Raymond*, 555.)

Every impartial man acquitted Cowper, whose professional success was only temporarily impeded. He steadily advanced at the bar, and in 1705, when he resigned the office of comptroller, he succeeded his brother as member for Berealston, which he continued to represent in the two following parliaments. During the last of them he was one of the managers in the impeachment of Dr. Sacheverell, and had to conduct the second article. (*Luttrell*, vi. 551, 555; *State Trials*, xv. 152.) This prosecution lost him his election for the next parliament; and he did not sit again till the accession of George I., when he was returned for Truro. He then became, on October 22, 1714, attorney-general to the Prince of Wales, and in 1717 chief justice of Chester.

On George II. coming to the crown he at once promoted his old servant, raising him first to the attorney-generalship of the duchy of Lancaster, and then to the bench at Westminster. He was constituted a judge of the Common Pleas on October 24, 1727, but died in the next year, on December 10, at his chambers in Lincoln's Inn. He was buried at Hertingfordbury, where there is a beautiful monument to his memory by Roubiliac, erected by order of his second wife, Theodora, widow of John Stepney, Esq. By her he had no issue, but by his first wife, Pennington, daughter of John Goodeve, Esq., he left three sons, the second of whom, the Rev. John Cowper, D.D., was the father of the delightful poet, William Cowper. (*Lord Raymond*, 1318, 1510.)

CRANWORTH, LORD. *See* R. M. ROLFE.

CRASSUS, RICHARD, had been prior of Henley in Buckinghamshire before he became abbot of Evesham. On the expulsion of Simon the Norman in 24 Henry III. 1239, the Great Seal is said to have been placed in his custody, and to have continued in his possession till his election as Bishop of Lichfield and Coventry (or Chester, as it was then sometimes called) in 1242, when he resigned it. This election took place about November, but before he had received the rite of consecration he died at Riola in Gascony, on December 8, 1242. (*Godwin*, 317; *Le Neve*, 124.)

CRAUCOMBE, JOHN DE, was probably the son of Godfrey de Craucombe, who served King Henry III. as seneschal. (*Madox*, i. 63.) He was evidently a clerk in the Chancery, and, like most of his fellows, an ecclesiastic, sharing in the dignities usually distributed among that class of officers, by being made archdeacon of the East Riding of Yorkshire.

The Great Seal was deposited in his hands and in those of Master John de Caen and William de Byrlay during the temporary absence of the chancellor, John de Langton, in March 1298, and again in December. He continued to be summoned to the parliament among the clerks of the Chancery till February 1305, 33 Edward I. (*Parl. Writs*, i. 138.)

CRAWLEY, FRANCIS, was of a Bedfordshire family, residing at Someris, near Luton. He received his legal education at Staple Inn and Gray's Inn, to the latter of which he was admitted on May 26, 1598, and, having been called to the bar in the usual time, was elected autumn reader in 1623, on the occasion of his being summoned to take the degree of the coif. In 1626 he was one of the counsel whom the Earl of Bristol desired to be assigned to him on his impeachment, and on October 11, 1632, he was appointed a judge of the Common Pleas, and knighted. In the great case of ship-money he not only joined the rest of the judges in their answer to the king's letter affirming its legality, but in an elaborate argument in the Exchequer Chamber, in February 1638, he gave a decided opinion in favour of the king against Hampden, which he repeated at the assizes, asserting in his charge to the grand jury 'that ship-money was so inherent a right in the crown that it would not be in the power of a parliament to take it away.' For these opinions, and particularly the last, he was impeached by the Long Parliament. In August 1641 the house resolved that the impeached judges should have no commissions to go the circuits; but it appears that they still continued to sit in Westminster Hall. Justice Crawley joined the king at Oxford in 1642, and in the following January was made doctor of civil law. (*Wood's Fasti*, ii. 44.) The state of the kingdom probably prevented his trial from taking place, notwithstanding his extreme unpopularity; but on November 24, 1645, the Commons passed an ordinance disabling him and four others 'from being judges, as though they were dead.' (*Whitelocke*, 181.)

He died on February 13, 1649, and was buried at Luton. His wife was Elizabeth, daughter of Sir John Rotherham, knight, of that place, by whom he left two sons, the younger of whom was the undermentioned Francis.

CRAWLEY, FRANCIS, second son of the above Sir Francis Crawley, was also of Gray's Inn, being admitted on August 7, 1623, and called to the bar in February 1638. His appointment to the office of cursitor baron of the Exchequer took place in 1679, when he must have been nearly seventy years of age, and he held it for four years, till his death in 1683.

He is described as having an estate of 1000*l*. a year in Bedfordshire in 1660, when named as one of the knights of the contemplated order of the Royal Oak; but he afterwards resided at Northaw in Hertfordshire. By his wife, Mary, daughter of Richard Clutterbuck, Esq., he had seven children, the descendants of whom now flourish at Stockwood Park in Hertfordshire.

CREPPING, WALTER DE, resided at Crepping, a manor in Essex which belonged to the Earls of Oxford, and was one of the justices itinerant who set the tallage on that county in 8 Richard I., 1186. He was soon after raised to the bench at Westminster, and his name appears on many fines levied during the first eleven years of the reign of King John, and he is named on a record of 13 John. (*Madox*, i. 704; *Abb. Placit*, 82.)

CREPPING, RICHARD DE, was of a Yorkshire family, and it seems probable was the son of Robert de Crepping, who for several years in the reign of Henry III. was one of the king's escheators beyond the Trent. (*Cal. Inquis.* p. m. i. 69.) Richard can scarcely be considered to have been a regular justice itinerant (as Dugdale calls him), as he only acted in reference to pleas of the forest in Lancashire and Nottinghamshire, in 14 Edward I., 1286. He was returned as knight of the shire for York in 18 Edward I. (*Parl. Writs*, i. 21.)

CRESHELD, RICHARD, is called three times by Whitelocke (269, 342, 378) 'Mr. Serjeant Creswell,' and in the propositions made by the parliament to the king in February 1643, of those whom they desire to be appointed justices of the Common Pleas, his name is so inserted. (*Clarendon*, iii. 407.)

But there was no serjeant of the name. The person intended is Richard Cresheld, who was summoned to take the coif in 1636 (*Rymer*, xx. 22), and who is recorded under that name in Dugdale's List of Serjeants. By an abbreviated mispronunciation of the name it became corrupted to Creswell, for even in Sir W. Jones's Reports (390) of the period he is called, when appointed, 'Creswell.'

He was admitted into the society of Lincoln's Inn on June 18, 1608, under the description of 'Richard Cresheld, son of Edward Cresheld, of Mattishall-Burgh in the county of Norfolk,' and was called to the bar on October 17, 1615, and became bencher in 1633. He sat for the borough of Evesham in Worcestershire in King James's last parliament, and was returned member for the same place (of which he was recorder) in all the parliaments in King Charles's reign. (*Notes and Queries*, 2nd S. i. 460.) In 1628 he led the van in the Committee of Grievances, in a speech sufficiently complimentary to the king, but arguing strongly against the legality of imprisonment without declaration of the cause (*Parl. Hist.* ii. 240); but he does not appear to have often taken part in the debates.

That he accommodated himself to the views of the popular party is apparent by his receiving the thanks of the Commons on November 2, 1642, for 'the good service done by Serjeant Cresweld in the country upon the matter of contributions and other services' (*Commons' Journals*, ii. 831), by their proposing him to be a judge in 1643, and by their appointing him one in 1648; but that he disapproved of their violent proceedings is equally apparent from his refusal to act under their usurped authority on the death of the king. He died in Serjeants' Inn in 1652, and was buried in St. Andrew's, Holborn, in the register of which his name is properly spelled.

CRESSI, HUGH DE, was for six successive years of the reign of Henry II., commencing in 1175, employed as one of the justices itinerant, and in 1177 his name appears among the king's regular justiciers at Westminster. (*Madox*, i. 94.)

He was a Norman by birth, and had been some time previously attached to the king's service; and that he added military to his judicial services is shown by his having the custody of the tower of Rouen in 1180, at a salary of 200*l.* a year, and by a grant which he received in 1184, 30 Henry II., of 100*l.* on the Norman Roll, for the soldiers whom he led in the war of Poictou. (*Rot. Scacc. Normanniæ*, i. 70, 115.)

He married Margaret, the daughter and heir of William de Cayneto, or Quesnay, who survived him, and afterwards became the wife of Robert Fitz-Roger, lord of Clavering in Essex. He left a son named Roger, who was in the wardship of this Robert Fitz-Roger till his majority in 1205, when he obtained possession of his father's lands in Suffolk, Sussex, and Lincoln.

The barony does not appear to have continued beyond the fifth generation, finishing with the after-named William de Cressi, justice of trailbaston under Edward I.

CRESSI, WILLIAM DE. His relationship with the above Hugh de Cressi is not known. Though he had a grant of forty librates of the Norman lands in Norfolk in 6 John (*Cal. Rot. Pat.* 8), he seems to have joined the barons in the last years of that reign, a safe-conduct having been given to him in December 1215 to go and speak to the king as to making his peace. (*Rot. Pat.* 162.) In this he was no doubt successful, being employed in the next year with others to take a recognition as to the last presentation of the church of Mareseye in Nottinghamshire. In that and the neighbouring counties he was one of the justices itinerant in 3 Henry III., 1219, and again in 1225.

CRESSI, WILLIAM DE, was the lineal

descendant of the above Hugh de Cressi, and the son of Stephen de Cressi, and Sibylla, the daughter and heir of John de Braytoft. He was summoned to attend the king on urgent affairs in 22 and 25 Edward I. He was returned as holding lands in Nottinghamshire, Derbyshire, and Lincolnshire, and when the commission of trailbaston was issued for those counties, on November 23, 1304, 33 Edward I., he was the second of the three justices then assigned. (*Parl. Writs*, i. 407–8; *Nicolas's Synopsis*.)

CRESSINGHAM, HUGH DE, son of William de Cressingham, was an officer of the Exchequer. In 18 Edward I. he is called seneschal of the queen (*Abb. Placit.* i. 30, 33), and in 1292 he was appointed with two others to investigate and audit the debts due to Henry III. (*Madox*, ii. 291.) In that and the three following years he was at the head of the justices itinerant for the northern counties. (*Year Book*, i. 33.) He was a canon of St. Paul's, and held at least nine parsonages. Prynne calls him 'an insatiable pluralist;' and Hemingford gives a similar character, and ascribes to him an immoderate passion for hoarding money. (*Archæologia*, xxv. 608.)

When the king defeated the Scotch, and Baliol renounced the throne, in 1296, Cressingham was appointed treasurer of that country, and on the disorders which followed Edward's departure was commanded not to scruple to spend the whole money in the exchequer to put them down. Proud, ignorant, and violent, he made himself hateful to the Scots by his oppressions; and on the rising of Wallace in the following year, preferring the cuirass to the cassock, he joined the Earl of Surrey in leading the royal army to Stirling. Wallace left the siege of Dundee, in which he was engaged, and by a rapid march drew up his army on the other bank of the river Forth before the arrival of the English forces. By Cressingham's rashness the latter were led over the bridge, and were terribly defeated, he being among the first who fell. 'So deep was the detestation in which his character was regarded that his body was mangled, the skin torn from his limbs, and in savage triumph cut to pieces.' It is said that Wallace ordered as much of his skin to be taken off as would make a sword-belt, a story which has been absurdly extended to its having been employed in making girths and saddles. (*Tytler's Scotland*, i. 123–143.) The Scots called him 'non thesaurarium sed trayturarium regis.' (*Triveti Annales*, 366, note.) He held the town of Hendon and land in Finchley in Middlesex, with the manor of Coulinge in Suffolk. (*Cal. Inquis.* p. m. i. 134.)

CRESSWELL, CRESSWELL. The family of Cresswell, of Cresswell, near Morpeth, in Northumberland, dates from the earliest age of English history, a regular succession of male heirs having possessed the estate from the days of Richard I. till the death of John Cresswell in 1781. That gentleman left two daughters, one of whom, Frances Dorothea, married Francis Easterby, Esq., of Blackheath, who, purchasing the other sister's moiety, became possessed of the whole estate, and assumed the name of Cresswell. Of that union Sir Cresswell Cresswell was the fourth son. He was born in 1793, and, passing through the Charterhouse from 1806 to 1810, he went in the latter year to Emmanuel College, Cambridge, where he had for his tutor the future Justice Maule. He took his degree of B.A. in 1814, and of M.A. in 1818, and then, pursuing his legal studies in the Inner Temple, was called to the bar in 1819, and naturally joined the Northern Circuit. Here he soon showed that ability and power that ever after distinguished him, and long before he became by seniority the leader of the circuit, scarcely any cause was tried in which he was not engaged on one side or the other. In 1830 he was appointed recorder of Hull, and in 1834 received a silk gown.

In 1841 he defeated Mr. William Ewart, the whig member, in a contest for Liverpool, and soon secured to himself that admiration in the house which it is not generally the fortune of lawyers to gain.

Sir Robert Peel, on the very first vacancy that occurred, selected him as a judge of the Common Pleas, whereupon he was knighted. In that court, from January 1842 to January 1858, he discharged the duties in the most admirable manner; and at the latter date he consented to undertake the organisation of the new court then created for deciding testamentary and divorce causes. The manner in which he overcame the difficulties attendant on the new judicature, and met the perpetually increasing demands on its decisions, which unexpectedly accumulated in overwhelming numbers, were eloquently and justly described by Sir Robert Phillimore, the queen's advocate, on the opening of the court after his lamented decease, which occurred on July 29, 1863, from the effects of a fall from his horse ten days before.

CREWE, RANULPHE, was a descendant from the younger branch of a family resident at Crew, or Crue, a manor in Cheshire, in the reign of Edward I. (*Cal. Inq.* p. m. i. 119.) His father, John Crewe, was settled at Nantwich, where he is said to have been a tanner. By his wife, Alice Mainwaring, he left two sons, both of whom were the ancestors of noble families. This Ranulphe (as he himself spelled it) was the elder. Thomas, the younger, was a serjeant-at-law, and speaker of the House of Commons in the reigns of both James I. and Charles I., and his son, John Crewe, in

1661 was created Baron Crewe, of Stene in Northamptonshire, which barony became extinct in 1721.

Ranulphe Crewe was born about 1558. He was called to the bar of Lincoln's Inn on November 8, 1584, and was elected reader in 1602. In 1597 he entered parliament as member for Brackley; and in 1598 he married Juliana, the daughter and heir of John Clipsby, of Clipsby in Norfolk, with whom he had a fair inheritance. (*Fuller*, i. 188.) He does not seem to have been much employed in the courts, yet it is evident that his reputation as a lawyer must have been considerable, as he was selected to defend the king's title to alnage in the House of Lords in 1606, for his 'travail and pains' in which he received 10*l*. (*Pell Records*, Jac. 64), and as his professional income was so considerable that he was enabled, two years afterwards, to gratify the great object of his ambition by the acquisition of the ancestral property from which he derived his name; and thus becoming repossessed of the estate which for nearly three hundred years had had no Crewe for its owner, he built the magnificent mansion there which has ever since been the seat of the family.

He was selected as speaker of that parliament which met on April 5, 1614, and was so hastily dissolved on the 7th of the following June, to which he was returned as representative of his native county, and was knighted the day after the dissolution. Called to the degree of the coif and made king's serjeant in the following month, he sat in 1615 as a commissioner on the trial of Weston for the murder of Sir Thomas Overbury, and was one of the counsel for the crown against the Earl and Countess of Somerset. (*State Trials*, ii. 911, 952, 989.) He was also concerned in the shameful trial of Edward Peacham for treason at Taunton. (*Walter Yonge's Diary*, 28.)

He was not in the next parliament of 1620, but conducted the proceedings in the House of Lords against Sir Francis Michell, the monopolist, Sir Henry Yelverton, late attorney-general, and Sir John Bennet, judge of the Prerogative Court. (*State Trials*, ii. 1136, 1143, 1146.) In the parliament of 1624 he opened some of the charges against Cranfield, Earl of Middlesex (*Parl. Hist.* i. 1447); and when Sir James Ley succeeded that nobleman as lord treasurer, Sir Ranulphe was selected to fill his place as chief justice of the King's Bench, to which he was promoted on January 26, 1625.

King James died in the following March. His successor, having angrily dissolved two parliaments in less than fifteen months, was compelled to resort to unconstitutional means to replenish his exhausted exchequer. One of these was by forced loans from his subjects according to the amount they would have paid towards a subsidy. The judges, who among the rest were applied to, paid the money demanded, but refusing to subscribe a paper recognising the legality of the collection, Chief Justice Crewe was selected as an example, and was discharged from his office on November 9, 1626. In 1628 he wrote a manly and modest letter to the Duke of Buckingham, pleading for his restoration to the king's favour. Whatever intentions the duke might have had of repairing the injury he had done to the chief justice, they were frustrated by his assassination by Felton, in the August of that year. After another application to the king himself, which produced no result, Sir Ranulphe retired from public life. He survived his dismissal more than nineteen years, witnessing the calamitous effects of those illegal measures to which he had refused his judicial sanction, and suffering much from the consequences of the civil war, his revenues being seized and his mansion ransacked by the soldiers of that parliament which had made those measures the ostensible motive of the rebellion. (*Hinchcliffe's Barthomley*, 238.)

He died at his house in Westminster on January 13, 1646, and his remains were interred in a chapel he had erected in the church of Barthomley, the parish in which Crewe Hall is situate.

As a lawyer he was learned and painstaking; as a judge he was assiduous and patient; of his honesty, independence, and integrity he gave the best proof that man can offer; and of his eloquence he has left a most favourable specimen, in his speech to the Lords on the titles of De Vere. After describing the 500 years of unbroken lineage in the family, he exclaimed: 'I have laboured to make a covenant with myself that affection may not press upon judgment; for I suppose there is no man that hath any apprehension of gentry or nobleness, but his affection stands to the continuance of so noble a name and house, and would take hold of a twig or a twine-thread to uphold it. And yet Time has his revolutions; there must be a period and an end of all temporal things—*finis rerum*,—an end of names and dignites, and whatsoever is terrene; and why not of De Vere? For where is Bohun? Where is Mowbray? Where is Mortimer? Nay, which is more and most of all, where is Plantagenet? They are entombed in the urns and sepulchres of mortality. And yet let the name and dignity of De Vere stand so long as it pleaseth God!' (*W. Jones's Reports*, 101.)

By his first wife he left a son, Clipsby Crewe, whose granddaughter (married to

John Offley, Esq., of Madeley in Staffordshire) ultimately succeeded to the inheritance. Their son took the name of Crewe, whose grandson was in 1806 created Lord Crewe of Crewe in Cheshire. Sir Ranulphe's second wife was another Juliana, daughter of Edward Fusey, of London, and relict of Sir Thomas Hesketh, Knt., by whom he had no children. (*Barthomley*, 239.)

CRIOL, NICHOLAS DE, was the son of Bertram de Criol, who was apparently an officer in the Exchequer and sheriff of Kent for many years, being then in such favour with Henry III. that part of the debt he owed to the crown was remitted.

That his son Nicholas retained the influence his father had possessed is shown by his receiving many favours from the king, and by his being entrusted with the sheriffalty of Kent in 48 Henry III. (*Excerpt. e Rot. Fin.* ii. 232), and by his being made governor of Rochester Castle and warden of the Cinque Ports. (*Cal. Rot. Pat.* 34.)

In 1265 he is mentioned as a baron of the Exchequer, and as such sued one of his debtors in that court. (*Madox*, ii. 13, 319.) He died in 1272. (*Abb. Rot. Orig.* i. 20.)

By his wife Joan, daughter and heir of William de Auberville, he left a son Nicholas, who was summoned to parliament by Edward I., but not afterwards.

CROKE, JOHN. The original name of the Croke family was Le Blount. Two brothers, Robert and William Le Blount, younger sons of the Count de Guisnes, held high military commands in the army of William of Normandy on his descent upon England. After the Conquest they were rewarded by extensive grants of lands. The elder branch failed by the death of the sixth baron at the battle of Lewes in 1264; and of the younger branch, Sir Robert Blount, who was deeply implicated in the conspiracy to restore Richard II., was beheaded in 1400. Nicholas, his kinsman, being engaged in the same conspiracy, was outlawed, and took service under the Duke of Milan; but four years afterwards he ventured into England, and escaped observation by changing his name to Croke. On the death of Henry IV. he came out of his retirement, and bought lands in Buckinghamshire, where he resided at Easington, in the parish of Chilton. His great-grandson, John Croke, a master in Chancery in the reigns of Henry VIII., Edward VI., and Mary, by his wife, Prudentia Cave, left a son, who succeeded to his ample inheritance. His name was also John, and he was knighted by Queen Elizabeth when he was sheriff of Buckinghamshire, which county he also represented in parliament. Marrying Elizabeth, daughter of Sir Alexander Unton, of Chequers in that county, he had by her a numerous family, of whom two, this John and the next-mentioned George, became judges. The fifth son, William, is the only one whose male representatives have continued to the present time. One of them, Sir Alexander Croke, judge of the Vice-Admiralty Court in America, has commemorated his family in an elaborate 'Genealogical History,' of which full advantage has here been taken.

John Croke, the eldest son, was born in 1553, and entered the Inner Temple on April 13, 1570, and, having been in due course called to the bar, was appointed Lent reader in 1596, and treasurer in 1598. At a very early period he had acquired so great a reputation for his professional attainments that he was consulted by Sir Christopher Hatton, who gave him as his fee, 'for his counsell in lawe, a silver gilt bole and cover.' In 1595 he was elected recorder of London, and his biographer gives a copy of one of his speeches on presenting the lord mayor to the Court of Exchequer, which, in its elaboration, puts to shame the curtailed addresses of the present day. The same city chose him for their representative in the parliaments of 1597 and 1601, he having before, in 1585, been returned for the borough of Windsor.

Of the parliament that met in October 1601 he was unanimously chosen speaker, and in his speech on presentation he offered up his solemn prayers to heaven to continue the prosperous estate and peace of the kingdom, which, he said, had been defended by the mighty arm of our dread and sacred queen. Elizabeth, interrupting him, cried out, 'No; but by the mighty hand of God, Mr. Speaker.' Early in the session Serjeant Heale, on the question of a subsidy, marvelled much that the house should stand upon granting it, or the time of payment, when all we had, he said, was her majesty's, and she may lawfully at her pleasure take it; 'yea,' added he, 'she hath as much right to all our lands and goods as to any revenue of the crown.' At which all the house laughing and hemming, the speaker was obliged to call them to order, saying that 'he that is speaking should be suffered to deliver his mind without interruption.' The grievance of monopolies occasioned great debates in this parliament, and the queen having politically anticipated the decision of the Commons, the speaker had the gratification of announcing to the house her resolution to revoke the patents that existed, and not to grant any other. On the division upon the bill for enforcing attendance at church, the ayes being 105, and the noes 106, it was contended that the speaker had a vote which would make the votes even, but Croke said 'he was foreclosed of his voice by taking that place which it had pleased them to impose upon him, and that he was to be indifferent to both parties.' At the close of the session, on December 19, the lord keeper concluded his speech by saying, 'For yourself, Mr. Speaker, her majesty commanded me to say that you have proceeded with such wisdom and discretion that it is much to your commendations, and that none before you have deserved more.'

About a year after this Croke received a summons to take upon him the degree of the coif on a day which occurred after the queen's death. The writ in consequence abated, but a new one was issued returnable the same day. He was called serjeant in Easter Term 1603, and knighted by King James, one of the king's serjeants on May 29, and a Welsh judge, whereupon he resigned the recordship. In 1604 he was appointed deputy to Sir George Hume, chancellor of the Exchequer. (*Cal. St. Papers* [1603], 79.)

On June 25, 1607, he was created a judge of the King's Bench, and fully sustained the character he had acquired as an advocate.

After performing his judicial duties for nearly thirteen years, he died at his house in Holborn on January 23, 1620, aged sixty-six, and was buried at Chilton.

His wife was Catherine, daughter of Sir Michael Blount, of Maple Durham in Oxfordshire, lieutenant of the Tower, by whom he had five sons, of whom no descendants remain.

CROKE, GEORGE, was seven years junior to his brother the above Sir John Croke. He was educated at the school at Thame, and at Christ Church College, Oxford. Having been entered of the Inner Temple, he was called to the bar in 1584, and appointed autumn reader in 1599, and again in Lent 1618. He commenced his parliamentary career in 1597 as member for Beeralston.

Though not mentioned in his own Reports as an advocate till Michaelmas 1588, he had commenced his collections for them seven years before, showing an early devotion to the practical part of his profession. He did not attain legal honours, however, till four years after his brother's death, in 1623, when he was made serjeant-at-law and king's serjeant nearly at the same time. King James knighted him on the occasion. Judge Whitelocke, in his Diary, says that he did not receive the coif sooner because he refused to give money, and offence was taken at his saying he thought 'it was not for the king'—so common it was in those days to pay for honours, and so large a part of these unholy payments were known to be appropriated by those about the court.

He was raised to the bench on February 11, 1625, as a justice of the Common Pleas, and in six weeks the death of James I. occurred, when his patent was renewed by King Charles, who, on October 9, 1628, removed him to the Court of King's Bench on the death of Sir John Doderidge. He had no successor in the Common Pleas, the opportunity being taken to reduce the judges from five, to which they had been increased by James I., to the original number of four. (*Croke, Car.* 127.)

The twelve years that he sat there were those that immediately preceded the Great Rebellion, which the courts of justice were greatly instrumental in hastening. They were used as tools to enforce the unconstitutional behests of the crown, which by the subservient decisions of the judges were declared to have the force of law. This servile spirit did not extend over the whole bench, and Sir George Croke was one of the minority whom neither the threats of power nor the hopes of favour could induce to swerve from the dictates of conscience. He was the only judge of the King's Bench excepted in the vote of the House of Commons from responsibility for delaying justice towards Selden, Holles, and the other members of parliament who were committed to the Tower for their speeches there; and in the great case of ship-money, though he had been induced in the first instance to join the rest of the judges, for the sake of conformity, in signing an abstract opinion declaring its legality, yet when it came judicially before him in Hampden's case he, in opposition to the majority, gave judgment against the crown; and in this courageous conduct he was imitated by Sir Richard Hutton, Sir Humphrey Davenport, and Sir John Denham. About 1640 Sir George, being then eighty years old, had petitioned to be relieved from his duties, and had received from the king a dispensation from his attendance in court or on the circuit, his judicial title, salary, and allowances being continued to him.

Sir George retired to his estate at Waterstock, where he spent the remainder of his life. He died on February 16, 1641-2, in the 82nd year of his age, and was buried at Waterstock in Oxfordshire, under a monument on which he is represented in his judicial robes, with an inscription commemorative of his private virtues and public patriotism, which, unlike the usual language of epitaphs, was acknowledged both by contemporaries and posterity to be a faithful picture of his character. His learning as a lawyer and his bearing as a judge are well described by his son-in-law, Sir Harbottle Grimston, in the preface to his Reports, which were not published till after his death. They were originally written by Sir George in the Norman-French language, but were translated by Sir Harbottle into English, and they consist of three volumes, one being appropriated to each of the reigns of Elizabeth, James, and Charles. The cases comprehend a period of sixty years, and afford an example of persevering industry not to be equalled. In the abbreviated language of the courts they are referred to as 'Cro. Eliz.,' 'Cro. Jac.,' and 'Cro. Car.,' and are always quoted with respect for their learning and accuracy.

He married Mary, the daughter of Sir Thomas Bennet, who was lord mayor of London in 1 James I., and whose brother Richard was ancestor to the noble houses of Arlington and Tankerville. This lady is said to have encouraged and confirmed her husband in his resolution not to be influenced by the persuasions of the king's friends to give a judgment in the case of ship-money contrary to conscience. She survived him fifteen years, and died on December 1, 1657. By her he had one son, who died early, and three daughters, one of whom married Sir Harbottle Grimston, the master of the Rolls.

CROKEDAYK, ADAM DE, was one of the two justices of assize appointed in 21 Edward I., 1293, for Lincoln and nine other counties, and was summoned among the justices to several parliaments. (*Parl. Writs,* i. 29–138.) He is mentioned in 25 Edward I. as assigned to assess and collect the ninth imposed for the king's confirmation of Magna Charta in the northern counties. (*Rot. Parl.* i. 239–241.) Three years afterwards he was appointed to perambulate the forests of the counties of York and Cumberland, and in 31 and 33 Edward I. there are writs in his name, showing he was still engaged in legal employments. In the latter year he died, possessed of very considerable property in Cumberland. (*Parl. Writs,* i. 398; *Abb. Placit.* 249, 254; *Cal. Inq.* p. m. i. 198.)

CROKESLEY, JOHN DE, was one of the king's escheators of the forest of Rockingham, and also custos of Skipton and other royal manors. (*Rot. Parl.* ii. 414; *Madox,* i. 721.) It was only for pleas of the forest that he was a justice itinerant in Essex, from 20 to 29 Edward I., 1292–1301, where he received six shillings a day for his expenses. (*Parl. Writs,* i. 88, 397.) He died in the following year.

CROKESLEY, RICHARD DE, succeeded the before-mentioned Richard de Barking as abbot of Westminster on March 25, 1247. (*Monasticon,* ii. 283.) He is twice named by Madox (ii. 318, 319) in his List of Barons of the Exchequer in 35 and 42 Henry III., taking precedence of the treasurer, instead of being placed, as his predecessor was, after him. In the interval between these two dates he had been despatched by the king as his ambassador to the court of Rome (*Rymer,* i. 344), and on two other occasions had been sent on missions to the Duke of Brabant, to negotiate a marriage between Prince Edward and the duke's daughter. Matthew Paris describes him as a learned and elegant man, with a handsome person and a pleasing voice. He died about July 21, 1258, as some say by poison (*Dart's Westminster,* ii. xxi.), leaving such extravagant bequests to the poor that a mandate was procured from the pope limiting the expense. (*Paddington, Past and Present,* by W. Robins, 1853.)

CROMPTON, CHARLES, was descended from an old family settled at Derby as eminent bankers, several of them having been members for the county, and one of them raised to a baronetcy in 1838, which died with him in 1849. The judge was the third son of Peter Crompton, Esq., M.D., of Eaton, near Liverpool, by his cousin Mary, the daughter of John Crompton, Esq., of Chorley in Lancashire.

It is somewhat remarkable that of the judges of the reign of Victoria there are at least eight who can boast of medical paternity—Lords Denman, Langdale, and Westbury, and Justices Maule, Park, Vaughan, Crompton, and Willes. To these may be added Lord Chancellor Lord Cottenham, who was the nephew of the eminent physician to George III., Sir Lucas Pepys, Bart.

Charles Crompton was born at Derby in 1797, and was educated at Trinity College, Dublin, where he graduated with great distinction, obtaining honours in 1814, 1815, and 1816. He then entered the Inner Temple, and was admitted as a barrister in November 1821. On the Northern and the Western Circuits he soon became known as a deeply read lawyer, and consequently acquired great experience in the practical part of the profession both there and in Westminster Hall. He successively filled the posts of tub-man and post-man in the Court of Exchequer, where he was counsel for the Board of Stamps and Taxes. Of the decisions in that court he was a reporter from 1830 to 1836, in conjunction at first with Mr. (afterwards Chief Justice) Jervis, and subsequently with Messrs. Meeson and Roscoe. In 1836 he was appointed assessor of the Court of Passage at Liverpool, and in 1851 he was selected as one of the commissioners of enquiry into the proceedings, practice, and jurisdiction of the Court of Chancery. On the retirement of Sir John Patteson from the Court of Queen's Bench, Mr. Crompton was appointed in February 1852, and received the customary knighthood. He was obliged from illness to resign his seat in October 1865, and on the 30th of that month he died.

He married a daughter of Thomas Fletcher, Esq., of Liverpool, by whom he left several children.

CROMWELL, THOMAS (EARL OF ESSEX), was born towards the latter end of the fifteenth century, at Putney, where his father Walter Cromwell carried on the business, first of a blacksmith, and then of a brewer. His mother, after Walter's death, was married to a cloth-sheerer in London. His education was that of his class, but his activity and intelligence were great, and early in life he had the advantage of going abroad, in what capacity is not known. During this period he so improved his opportunities that he mastered several foreign languages, and acquired that aptness in the conduct of affairs for which he was afterwards distinguished. He seems, from a letter addressed to him by Cecily, Marchioness of Dorset, commencing 'Cromwell, I woll that you send to me,' &c., to have been at one time in the household of that lady. (*Ellis's Letters*, 1st S. i. 218.)

While at Antwerp he was retained by the English merchants there to be their clerk or secretary, and during his employment in their affairs he became acquainted with Sir Richard Gresham, the father of the founder of the Royal Exchange. (*Burgon's Gresham*, i. 218.) Whether this took place before or after his admission to Gray's Inn in 1524 is uncertain; but there is no doubt that he afterwards went to Rome, since he was present as a soldier at the sacking of that city in May 1527 under the Duke of Bourbon. He is represented as having been engaged at Antwerp by two persons from Boston in Lincolnshire to accompany them and endeavour to obtain from the pope a renewal of the indulgences granted to the guild of Our Lady in their church of St. Botolph, and as having succeeded by gratifying his holiness's palate with some dainty jellies made after the English fashion. Drayton, in 'The Mirror for Magistrates,' intimates that the pope's favour was obtained by Cromwell's singing to him 'freemen's catches,' and further alludes to his playing there, with other of his countrymen, 'as a comedian.' (*Notes and Queries*, 3rd S. xi. 74.)

Returning to England, Cromwell was admitted into the family of Cardinal Wolsey, who had met him in France and at once appreciated his abilities. What office he held in that household does not clearly appear, but in the two years that he was retained in the family he made himself eminently useful, assisting Wolsey in many important matters, and particularly in the foundation of his colleges at Ipswich and Oxford. This short service was sufficient to create so great an affection as to prompt him to come boldly forward, apparently at the risk of the king's displeasure, in defence of his fallen master. Having procured a seat in the House of Commons, 'there was nothing,' to use Cavendish's words, 'at any time objected against my lord but he was ready to make answer thereunto; by means whereof he, being earnest in his master's behalf, was reputed the most faithful servant to his master of all other, and was generally of all men highly commended.' When the bill of impeachment was sent down to the Commons, 'against it Master Cromwel did inveigh so discreetly, and with such witty persuasions, that the same would take no effect.' It is impossible, however, considering the general subserviency of parliament, not to believe that he had received some encouragement from the king before he ventured on this opposition.

That he had then access to his [majesty is manifest from his being sent on various comforting messages to Wolsey, among which was the communication of the royal intention to give 10,000*l.* when the cardinal was going into the north. He was almost immediately taken into the king's service. Wolsey died on November 29, 1530; and in less than eighteen months Cromwell had made himself so serviceable to the king that he was rewarded with the post of master and treasurer of the king's jewels, on April 14, 1532. (*Auditor's Patent Book*, i. 130.)

Stow (*Thoms's*, 67) tells a story which charges Cromwell with making an oppressive use of the power he had thus attained, in the erection of his house and the enlargement of his garden in Throgmorton Street; but is is not unlikely that there is some exaggeration in the tale, since Cromwell on other occasions showed a grateful and a feeling heart, remembering in his prosperity the services he had received when he was poor. At the gate of this very house also, in Throgmorton Street, which is now the site of Drapers' Hall, two hundred persons were served with bread, meat, and drink twice a day when Cromwell had the means to be bountiful.

On July 16, 1532, he received the profitable office of clerk of the Hanaper, with an annual rent of 40*l.*; and on April 12, 1533, the still more important one of chancellor of the Exchequer. (*Rymer*, xiv. 456.) It was about this time that Sir Thomas More gave him that excellent advice, which it would have been well for him to have followed, and which was dictated probably by the great man's suspicions that Cromwell was the prompter of those ecclesiastical questions which were then being agitated. After communing together on a message Cromwell had delivered from the king, Sir Thomas, who had lately resigned the chancellorship, said to him, 'Mark, Cromwell, you are now entered into the service of a most noble, wise, and liberal prince; if you will follow my poor advice, you shall, in your council-giving to his grace, ever tell him what he *ought* to do, but never what he is *able* to do. ... For if a lion knew his own strength, hard were it for any man to rule him.' (*Singer's Roper*, 55.) On October 8, 1534, he was made master of the Rolls, having previously been appointed principal secretary to the king. In the next year he was nominated visitor-general of the monasteries, under the pretence of correcting the known abuses in them, but in fact to lay the foundation of their ultimate dissolution.

There can be no doubt that Cromwell was an early convert to the reformed opinions, and he is said even in his journey to Rome to have learned by heart Erasmus's translation of the New Testament. He had encouraged the writers and promoted the circulation of ballads and books ridiculing the pope and all popish idolatry. (*Maitland's Reformation*, 236.) His name therefore was naturally held in utter detestation by all those who adhered to the old religion, and every species of wickedness and cunning was charged upon him. We must consequently be cautious in adopting the terms of vituperation with which writers of that church assail his character, and hesitate to give full credit to all the stories they tell to his disadvantage. At the same time there is no doubt that his zeal in the king's service, strengthened possibly by his own convictions of the inutility, if not the evils, of the monastic establishments, betrayed him into measures which even now have the appearance of harshness, making no distinction between well-conducted houses and those which were a pest and a nuisance, nor discriminating between the virtuous and the guilty, but involving all in one common ruin. The personal grants also that he obtained out of the religious plunder of course occasioned, and perhaps justified, the imputation that avarice had a share in prompting his energetic proceedings. And yet, while doubting his motives in reference to these acts of severity, it would be unjust not to advert to that conduct which seems to result from the real feelings of his nature—his tenderness towards Sir Thomas More. He was one of those who urgently pressed the king to exclude the name of Sir Thomas from the bill of attainder in connection with the 'Holy Maid of Kent,' and he it was who sent the comforting message to the fallen chancellor, that he had succeeded. In the examinations which took place as to the oath of supremacy and matrimony, in which Cromwell was a necessary actor as the king's secretary, he exerted himself to save Sir Thomas, who in several letters speaks of him in terms of gratitude. (*Singer's Roper*, 114–158.)

After holding the office of master of the Rolls for somewhat less than two years, he resigned it on July 2, 1536, for the more elevated one of keeper of the privy seal (*Rymer*, xiv. 571), and on the 9th of the same month he was raised to the peerage by the title of Baron Cromwell of Okeham in the county of Rutland. This creation was no doubt made to give greater weight to a higher dignity which was reserved for him. The king having thrown off his obedience to the pope, and assumed the rule in all ecclesiastical matters, required a representative to conduct the business which thus devolved upon him. To this duty he appointed Cromwell on July 18, with the title of vicar-general and vicegerent, in which character he sat in synods and convocations above the whole prelacy of the kingdom—a position which a layman could scarcely be deemed competent to fill. Even in parliament precedence was allotted to him, not only above all peers, but above the great officers of the crown.

It is curious that, though Cromwell was never admitted into holy orders, the king in this very year, as if for the purpose of investing him with some ecclesiastical character, presented him with the prebend of Blewbury, in the church of Salisbury, and in the following with the deanery of Wells (*Rymer*, xiv. 569; *Le Neve*, 36)—preferments which he held till his death.

The proceedings which he took in the quality of vicar-general belong more to the history of the Church than to this biography. Suffice it to say that, steering wisely between the conflicting opinions of the king, who, while he repudiated the pope's authority, retained the principal points of the old religion, Cromwell discouraged the obnoxious practices of popery, as the worship of images, &c., and served the cause of the Reformation most effectually by directing the Lord's Prayer, the Creed, and the Commandments to be taught to children in their mother-tongue, and by ordering a Bible in English to be placed in all churches for the parishioners to read at their pleasure. To prevent the publication of corrupt copies of the Holy Scriptures, a patent was afterwards granted to him which prohibited all persons from printing an English edition except those who were deputed by him. To him also is to be attributed the useful introduction into each parish of a register of births, marriages, and deaths.

The rapid elevation of a man of so obscure an origin naturally disgusted the nobles; his efforts in suppressing the monasteries, and in promulgating the king's supremacy and the new tenets, created murmurs against him by a large portion of the clergy; and the extravagance with which the produce of the confiscated abbeys was wasted, together with the demands which he was in consequence compelled to make on both clergy and laity to supply the deficiency in the king's coffers, rendered him an object of odium in the eyes of all but the king, who, benefiting by his exertions, appreciated his zeal and capacity, and estimated them at a higher value from his resolute defiance of the unpopularity that followed him. He was accordingly rewarded with munificent grants of manors and lands which had belonged to the dissolved houses, a list of which is given in Dugdale; and additional dignities were conferred upon him, among which was the office of chief justice of the forests beyond the Trent.

With these continued proofs of the royal favour, he might still have disregarded the efforts of his enemies, had he not in his anxiety to support his position taken a step which alienated the affections of his only friend. The king's avowed adherence to the ancient doctrines of the Church had encouraged those who continued to be attached to them; they were gradually obtaining an ascendency in the royal councils, and the advocates of the reformed tenets were consequently placed in a difficult dilemma. Cromwell could not but see the danger that hung over him, and, deeming that his party would resume its power if it had the support of a Protestant queen, he recommended, in an evil hour to himself, the Princess Anne of Cleves as the new partner of the royal bed. The disgust taken by the king to this lady from his first introduction to her is well known, and Cromwell soon became the victim of his resentment. He did not, however, immediately betray his purpose, but, on the contrary, heaped upon the devoted statesman higher honours. The marriage with Anne of Cleves was celebrated on January 6, 1540, and on April 17 Cromwell was created Earl of Essex, which was immediately followed by his admission into the order of the Garter, and his appointment to the office of lord high chamberlain of England.

It would almost seem that Cromwell was raised to this high pinnacle of greatness for the mere purpose of gratifying the capricious malice of the tyrant, for within two months after his elevation to the earldom he was suddenly arrested at the council table on June 10, on charges which must have been for some time in preparation. The principal crime alleged against him was heresy and the encouragement of heretics, and this was embellished with accusations of having spoken heinous words against the king two years before. In order that he might not have an opportunity of answering, a bill of attainder was hurried through the parliament, in pursuance of which he was beheaded on Tower Hill on July 28.

Whatever were the faults attached to Cromwell's character, no one had less cause to complain of them than King Henry. Zealously devoted from his first introduction at court to the royal interests, disregarding public obloquy in his efforts to promote them, and evidencing by all his acts the most sincere affection for his master, his death by that master's hand adds a deeper shade to the aversion with which the whole of Henry's career after the death of Wolsey must ever be regarded.

Archbishop Cranmer, the only one of Cromwell's adherents who had the courage to come forward in his defence, wrote a letter to the king, which in its exposition of the claims the fallen favourite had on the royal mercy would have staggered a less obdurate heart; but both that and the humble and affecting letter of Cromwell himself, though it moved the king to tears, were unavailing.

It would seem, however, that when it was too late the capricious king regretted the haste with which he had sacrificed his active minister, and there is an evident proof of his 'compunctious visitings' in his patent, dated on the 18th of the following December, granting to Cromwell's son Gregory the barony which his father had held. This barony survived through seven generations. In 1687 it and the Irish earldom of Ardglass, which had been granted to the fourth baron, became extinct.

The Protector Oliver Cromwell was a descendant from Thomas Cromwell's sister, who married one Williams, and whose son Sir Richard Williams, one of King Henry's privy chamber, and afterwards constable of Berkeley Castle, assumed the surname of Cromwell, and was the great grandfather of Oliver. (*Herbert's Henry VIII.*; *Baronage*, ii. 370; *Weever*, 505.)

CROWDER, RICHARD BUDDEN, son of William Crowder, Esq., of Montague Place, was born in London about 1795, was educated at Eton, and Trinity College, Cambridge, and, entering the Middle Temple, was called to the bar in May 1821. On the Western Circuit he got into good practice as well as in London, and in both displayed great power and ability. He obtained a silk gown in 1837, and was appointed recorder of Bristol in 1846. For a short time he was in parliament, being elected member for Liskeard in 1849, but was not so eminent as a senator as he was as a barrister. In the latter character he was very effective with the jury and the court, by his sound common sense, and his forcible, if not eloquent, oratory. He

P

held the posts of counsel of the Admiralty and judge advocate of the fleet at the time of his promotion to the bench. That event occurred in March 1854, when he was selected to supply a vacancy in the Common Pleas. There he continued for nearly six years, distinguished by his honourable and manly bearing and his courtesy and urbanity. He died unmarried on December 5, 1859.

CULEWORTH, WILLIAM DE, in 11 Henry III. was engaged in fixing the tallage for the counties of Cambridge and Hertford. (*Rot. Claus.* ii. 176, 180.) This employment, in connection with his future position on the bench, makes it very probable that he was regularly engaged in forensic occupations. From Easter 1236, 20 Henry III., to Hilary 1242, he was one of the justiciers at Westminster, fines being regularly acknowledged before him; with a salary of 20*l.* per annum.

CUMIN, JOHN, or COMYN (ARCHBISHOP OF DUBLIN), a monk of Evesham, and then a canon of St. Paul's, was one of the chaplains of Henry II., who employed him in several important embassies. In 1164 he was sent to the emperor on the subject of the anti-pope, and by his long stay there caused considerable uneasiness to Pope Alexander and the adherents of Becket. Again, in 1166, he was one of the three ministers despatched to Rome, where they succeeded, not only in obtaining the appointment of two cardinals to hear and to determine the dispute with Becket, but also in bringing back to the king the letters which Becket had addressed to the pope, and which any other person had written in his favour.

In 1169 and the five following years his name appears as one of the itinerant justices into several counties, and it seems probable that he held a responsible office in the Exchequer, as in 1170 he had the custody of the bishoprics of Hereford and Bath, then vacant; and in 1180 William Malduit, the chamberlain, and he were employed to convey the treasury from Northampton to Nottingham. (*Madox*, i. 93, &c., 289.)

When the council of Windsor, in 1179, divided the kingdom into four parts for judicial purposes, he was one of the six justiciers who were not only appointed to act in the northern counties, but were also specially constituted to hear the complaints of the people in the Curia Regis. His services were not long unrewarded. In 1182 he was consecrated Archbishop of Dublin. Before this ceremony was performed he received priest's orders from the pope, which, it would seem, neither his canonry nor his chaplaincy required. There are, indeed, several instances of persons holding higher rank in the Church without being priests. He founded St. Patrick's Church in Dublin, and in 1186 he presided at a provincial synod, for the better regulation of the manners and discipline of the Irish clergy. He died about 1213. (*Brady's England*, 372; *Lord Lyttelton; Leland's Ireland*, i. 138, 195; *Holinshed*, vi. 43.)

CURSON, ROBERT, became a reader of Lincoln's Inn in autumn 1529, and a second time in Lent 1537. On the accession of King Edward VI. in 1547 he was promoted to the bench as second baron of the Exchequer, and his successor in that office was appointed on May 6, 1550.

CUSERUGGE, BALDWIN DE, had property in Berkshire, and was one of the justices itinerant employed in 9 Richard I., 1197–8, to fix the tallage in that county. (*Madox*, i. 705.)

D

DAIVILL, JOHN DE, or D'AYEVILL, was one of the justices itinerant appointed in 10 Henry III., 1226, for the county of Westmoreland. He was the son of Robert Daivill, a baron of Yorkshire and Nottingham, and had joined in the rebellion against King John, whereupon his lands were seized into the king's hands. Dugdale, in his 'Baronage' (i. 593), states that they were again forfeited for some offence in 38 Henry III., but being restored to favour, he was appointed justice of the forests beyond Trent in 41 Henry III., and was afterwards constituted governor of the castles of York and Scarborough. In the contest between the king and his barons he joined the latter, and was summoned to the parliament they held after the battle of Lewes. He even continued the contest after the royal victory at Evesham, and, suffering another defeat at Chesterfield, fled to the isle of Axholme in Lincolnshire. He, however, purchased his peace in 51 Henry III., and was again restored to his possessions.

He married Maude, the widow of James de Aldithley. (*Rot. Claus.* i. 243, 249, ii. 128, 151.)

DALISON, WILLIAM. William D'Alanzon, who came over with the Conqueror, was the founder of this family. The first who wrote himself Dalison, a direct descendant in the eighth generation, was of Laughton in Lincolnshire, which, near two centuries afterwards, gave the title to the baronetcy granted in 1611 to Sir Roger Dalison, but which failed in 1645. Sir Roger was the grandson of George, the elder brother of Judge William, and they were the children of William Dalison, sheriff and escheator of his native county, by a daughter of George Wastneys, Esq., of Haddon in Nottinghamshire.

William was educated at Cambridge, and, entering at Gray's Inn, was called to the bar in 1537, and was reader in 1548 and 1552. In the October of the latter year the society presented him with 5l. and a pair of gloves on his leaving them to assume the degree of the coif (*Dugdale's Orig.* 137, 293); and on November 2, 1555, he was made serjeant to King Philip and Queen Mary. In April 1554 he was elected representative of the county of Lincoln, and was appointed a justice of the Common Pleas in the county palatine of Lancaster.

He was constituted a judge of the Queen's Bench about Hilary Term 1556, being mentioned, not only in Dyer's Reports in that and subsequent terms, but also in a commission of the same and the succeeding year, among the proceedings preserved in the 'Baga de Secretis' (4 *Report Pub. Rec.*, App. ii. 255), and was then knighted.

On Queen Elizabeth's accession his patent was renewed, but he survived only till the 18th of January following. He was buried in Lincoln Cathedral under an altar tomb with his portrait thereon. By his wife Elizabeth, daughter of Robert Dighton, Esq., of Sturton Parva in Lincolnshire, he left four sons and five daughters.

His learning as a lawyer was in high estimation. His reading on the statute 3 Henry VIII, entitled 'That wrongful disseisin is no descent in law,' is quoted by Dyer (219); and his Reports in conjunction with Serjeant Bendlowes are a valuable record of the cases of the time.

DALLAS, ROBERT, was the son of a gentleman of the same name living at Kensington in Middlesex, and his mother was Elizabeth, daughter of the Rev. James Smith, minister of Kilberney in Ayrshire. He became a member of Lincoln's Inn, and trained himself to public speaking at the debating society held at Coachmakers' Hall, according to the common practice of the time. This was of considerable advantage to him when he was called to the bar, and enabled him to produce his arguments with much more ease to himself and with greater effect to the court, in which he soon acquired considerable practice. In January 1788 he was engaged in the defence of Lord George Gordon. He next appears as one of the counsel for Mr. Hastings, the trial of whose impeachment lasted seven years, from 1788 to 1795, and highly distinguished himself by his exertions, and by his polished addresses to the lords. Naturally disgusted with the inveteracy of Burke against his client, he gave the relentless prosecutor no credit for patriotic feelings, but, attributing his attacks to the innate malignity of his nature, composed this bitter epigram:—

Oft have we wonder'd that on Irish ground
No poisonous reptile has e'er yet been found:
Reveal'd the secret stands of Nature's work—
She sav'd her venom to produce her Burke.

In 1795 Mr. Dallas received a silk gown; and through all the succeeding years till he was raised to the bench the latter volumes of the State Trials record his efforts either for the defence or the prosecution. Among these his speech on the motion for a new trial in the case of General Picton was separately published. In the meantime he had obtained a seat in the House of Commons, where he represented St. Michael's, Cornwall, in 1802, and afterwards the Scotch boroughs of Kirkaldy, &c. In 1804 he was promoted to the chief justiceship of Chester, and presided there till 1813, when on May 4 he was appointed to the office of solicitor-general and knighted. Six months afterwards he was raised to the bench of the Common Pleas, on November 5, 1813, and on the same day in 1818 he was promoted to the headship of that court. There he presided for five years with acknowledged ability and universal respect.

A curious question having been raised in 1823, whether the Lord Lieutenant of Ireland had the same power to confer knighthood after the Union which he undoubtedly possessed before that measure had passed, a meeting of the judges was held in June at Chief Justice Dallas's to consider the point, when they were of opinion unanimously that the Act of Union did not deprive him of his former privilege. It was a matter of some speculation how the right should have remained undisputed for above twenty years, during which it had been frequently exercised, and only now be impugned; and it was suspected that the doubt was invented for the purpose of mortifying Lady Morgan, who had offended the ministers by the freedom of her writings, and whose husband had received an Irish knighthood. (*Lady Morgan's Memoirs*, ii. 172.)

At this time his health began to break, and he soon found he could no longer undergo the fatigues of his office. He therefore resigned his seat at the end of 1823, and lived little more than one year longer, dying on December 25, 1824. He left several children by his wife, Charlotte, daughter of Lieut.-Col. Alexander Jardine.

DAMMARTIN, MANASERIUS DE, was one of the justices itinerant named by Dugdale under the year 1170, but who were rather commissioners to enquire into the abuses of the sheriffs. Some of the family of Dammartins were settled in Surrey, and some in Norfolk.

DAMPIER, HENRY, descended from the Le Dampierres, anciently Counts of Flanders, was the son of the Rev. Thomas Dampier, a native of Somersetshire, who from being one of the masters at Eton College was raised to the deanery of Durham, and, having married twice, was most fortunate in his family. Thomas, the elder of his two sons by his first wife, Anne Hayes, became successively Bishop of Rochester (1802) and Ely (1808); and John, the younger, held a canonry in the latter cathedral. Henry, his only son by his second wife, Frances Walker, was born on December 21, 1758, at Eton, and, having received his early education there, was elected to King's College, Cambridge, in 1775. He took his degree of B.A. in 1781, and of M.A. in 1784; in the interim gaining the members' prizes both in 1782 and 1783. Preferring the legal to the clerical profession, for which he was at first intended, he entered the Middle Temple in 1781, and was called to the bar in the customary routine. During the next thirty years he pursued the rugged paths of the law, admired and esteemed for his intelligence as an acute counsel, and for his obliging disposition and his classical as well as legal learning, made more attractive by the brilliancy of his conversation and his wit. At last he was appointed a judge of the King's Bench on June 23, 1813, when he was knighted. His judicial career was doomed to be shorter than any who had lately preceded him. Ere he had graced the bench for two years and a half, he died on February 3, 1816. Few have left a name so universally respected.

He married in 1790 Martha, daughter of the venerable John Law, archdeacon of Rochester. She and five of their children survived him, one of whom, John Lucius Dampier, was recorder of Portsmouth, and became vice-warden of the Stannaries in Cornwall.

DANASTER, JOHN. In Dugdale's list of the governors of Lincoln's Inn the name of John Danaster occurs five times from 21 to 31 Henry VIII., 1529-39, and in the last year he is called 'Baro Scacc.' In the 'Chronica Series,' however, the name is not inserted among the barons; but in a list kindly supplied by Mr. Adlington, an officer of the Exchequer, John Banester appears in Michaelmas Term 1538 as third baron, who is also omitted in Dugdale's list. There can be no doubt that the same individual is intended in both cases; and the preference must be given to Dugdale's account, not only because the name of Danaster is so often repeated, for it appears that he was also a reader at Lincoln's Inn in 1530 and in 1535, but also because he is specially mentioned with the title as one of the commissioners for receiving the indictment against Henry Pole, Lord Montacute, on November 29, 1539, preserved in the 'Baga de Secretis.' He died before Easter 1540. (*Dugdale's Orig.* 251, 259; 3 *Report Pub. Rec.*, App. ii. 256, 258; *Manning and Bray's Surrey*, iii. 224.)

DANBY, ROBERT, of a Yorkshire family, in 1441 is mentioned as an advocate in a case before the privy council. The Year Books introduce his name as early as 1431, and he was called serjeant on February 14, 1443, 21 Henry VI., being appointed one of the king's serjeants soon afterwards. He was raised to the bench of the Common Pleas on June 28, 1452, 30 Henry VI., and held his place during the remainder of the reign.

If he be the Robert Danby mentioned in the 'Paston Letters' (i. 34), he was evidently an adherent to the Yorkist party. If so, we can well understand why on May 11, 1461, immediately after the accession of Edward IV., he was made chief justice of the Court of Common Pleas. Dugdale is in error when he introduces Sir Richard Choke as chief justice in 1 Edward IV., four months after the appointment of Danby. The Year Books plainly prove that throughout the next ten years both Danby and Choke were in the court together, the former described as chief justice, and the latter as justice only.

He was still chief justice on the restoration of Henry VI., who continued him at the head of the court during the six months of his renewed reign. On the return of Edward IV. in 1471 he was not re-appointed; but whether the change arose from his death or removal we are not informed.

In Holinshed's Chronicles (iii. 299) under this year is an account of the curious means adopted by Sir William Haukesford, knight (meaning Hankford), one of the chief justices, to rid himself of life, by directing his keeper to shoot any person whom he found in the park at night, and who would not stand when called upon, and then placing himself in the way of the fatal shot. That this could not apply to Sir William Hankford is evident from the fact that he had been dead for nearly fifty years. Whether it be true at all, or the mistake is only in the name, cannot now be determined; but the only chief justice who disappears at this time is Sir Robert Danby, and to him not only is the high character given by Holinshed in favour of the misguided man equally applicable, but the perplexities of the time afford a more probable reason for the tragic catastrophe.

That Sir Robert was an excellent judge is evidenced by the great deference with which he was treated by the other judges and by the counsel in the Year Books, and by the frequent reference made to his opinions.

DANIEL, WILLIAM, was a younger son of the ancient family of Daniels of Over-Tabley in Cheshire. The name was originally D'Anyers, and is to be found in the list of those who entered England with the Conqueror. He was entered at Gray's Inn in 1556, and became reader there in 1579, and treasurer in 1580 and 1587.

In 1584 he was admitted deputy recorder of London to Serjeant Fleetwoode, and his name appears in Coke's Reports in Hilary 1591. When about to be advanced to the degree of serjeant-at-law in 1594 his name was struck out of the list upon an information to his prejudice relative to one Hacket, but was restored at the request of Lord Burleigh, who contradicted the report, and testified to his being 'a vearie honest, learned, and discreat man.' On February 3, 1604, he was constituted a judge of the Common Pleas, as one of the two new judges King James had determined to add to the judicial staff. (*Egerton Papers*, 388.) There is no record of his argument in the great case of the post-nati, but he joined the majority in the affirmative view of the question. (*State Trials*, ii. 576.) He died in 1610.

DANVERS, ROBERT. The founder of this family in England was Roland D'Anvers, who accompanied the Conqueror on his invasion, and whose descendants, by grants and marriages, acquired considerable property in Berkshire and Oxfordshire. Robert was the eldest son of John Danvers, of Cothorp in the latter county, by his first wife Alice, daughter of William Verney, of Byfield. He became one of the governors at Lincoln's Inn in 1428, 6 Henry VI. In 1433 he was implicated in an erasure which had been made in an act of council (iv. 166), but was exonerated from all blame on that account by a special warrant under the privy seal. The record does not explain the particulars; but it seems probable that they were in some way connected with the city of London, of which he was about this time common serjeant. He was advanced to the recordership in 1442, and was called serjeant on February 14, 1443. In 1444 he was one of the king's serjeants, and in 1445 was member for the city of London.

In July 1450 Jack Cade, on taking up his head-quarters in London, forced Robert Danvers, the recorder, to be the head of a commission of oyer and terminer, at which several noblemen and gentlemen were tried for high treason, and some of them executed. That his conduct while acting in this capacity was not displeasing to the government appears by his being named on a commission into Kent, issued on August 1, to try the adherents of Cade, and by his being raised to the bench as a judge of the Common Pleas on August 14. He continued to sit there till the deposition of King Henry VI.; and, being re-appointed by Edward IV., he passed the remainder of his life in the quiet performance of his judicial functions. He died in 1467, being described as a knight in the inquisition then taken. (*Cal.* iv. 341.) He and his wife Agnes were buried in the church of St. Bartholomew, in Smithfield. By her, who was daughter of Richard Quatremains, of Rycot in Oxfordshire (or, according to Stow, of Sir Richard Delaber), he left no male heirs.

The baronetcy of Danvers and the earldom of Danby were granted to descendants from Sir Robert's brother Richard, but are both now extinct.

DANVERS, WILLIAM, was half-brother to the above Robert, being one of the sons of John Danvers, of Cothorp in Oxfordshire, by his second wife, Joan, daughter of William Bruly, of Waterstock in the same county. There must have been a considerable difference between the ages of the two, because William's career as an advocate, in the Year Books, does not commence till 1475, seven or eight years after his brother's death. He attained the degree of serjeant-at-law soon after the accession of Henry VII., and on February 5, 1488, he was raised to the bench of the Common Pleas. Fines appear to have been acknowledged before him as late as February 1504. (*Dugdale's Orig.* 47.)

He married Anne, daughter and heir of John Perry, Esq., of Chamberhouse in Berkshire; and his descendants were settled at Upton in Warwickshire.

DARNALL, JOHN, on February 26, 1544, was appointed ingrosser of the Great Roll of the Exchequer, otherwise called clerk of the Pipe; on May 5, 1548, he was constituted fourth baron of that court, and he retained his seat till his death, on November 28, 1549. Beyond this there is no account of him.

DAVENCESTER, PHILIP DE. In 11 Henry II., 1165, a charter between the abbots of St. Albans and Westminster was executed at the Exchequer, 'assidentibus justiciis regis,' the last of whom is 'Philippo de Davencestriæ' (Daventry), without any designation of the office he held. (*Madox*, i. 44.) He was sheriff of Cambridge and Huntingdon for three years, from 13 Henry II.

DAVENPORT, HUMPHREY, the second son of William Davenport, of an ancient and genteel family settled at Bromhall in

Cheshire, by Margaret, daughter of Sir Richard Ashton, of Middleton in Lancashire, was born at Chester about 1566, and after entering Balliol College went to Gray's Inn, where he was called to the bar on November 21, 1590, and in Lent 1613 became reader to this society. He was elected member for Brackley in 1588, and made an ineffectual effort to introduce a measure of Church reform. (*D'Ewes*, 438.) In June 1623 he took the degree of the coif; and, having been knighted by King James, he was created king's serjeant, shortly after King Charles's accession, on May 9, 1625. He was raised to the bench on February 2, 1630, as a judge of the Common Pleas, and had not sat there a year before he was called upon to fill the office of lord chief baron, to which he was nominated on January 10, 1631. (*Rymer*, xix. 133, 254; *W. Jones's Reports*, 230.)

In the case of ship-money he gave his opinion assuming the king's power to impose it, but acquitting Hampden on a technical point, that the writ was not good in law. The majority of the judges having decided against Hampden, it became the duty of the lord chief baron to deliver the judgment, which afterwards, in the Long Parliament, was declared to be void. His equivocal opinion in favour of Hampden did not avail to prevent that parliament from condemning the support he had given to the king's illegal impositions. Articles of impeachment against him were accordingly carried up to the House of Lords on July 6, 1641, and he was ordered to give 10,000*l.* bail for his appearance. It is probable that he then withdrew himself altogether from the duties of his office, for on January 25, 1644, the king appointed Sir Richard Lane his successor. It is curious, however, that Sir Humphrey's patent of revocation is not dated till January 11 in the following year.

The date of his death is not given. Fuller (i. 188) says he 'had the reputation of a studied lawyer and upright person;' and A. Wood (iii. 182) states that 'he was accounted one of the oracles of the law.'

DE GREY, WILLIAM (LORD WALSINGHAM). The root of this family can be traced to the twelfth century, and that branch of it to which the judge belonged possessed, with other large estates, the manor of Merton in Norfolk for about four hundred years before he came into the world. His father was Thomas De Grey, who represented that county in parliament; and his mother was Elizabeth, daughter of William Wyndham, of Felbrigge. William was their third son, and was born at Merton on July 7, 1719. After receiving his education at Christ's College, Cambridge, he entered the Middle Temple, and was called to the bar in 1742. He was made king's counsel to George II. in 1758, and in September 1761 solicitor-general to the queen of George III. In the latter year he was elected member of parliament for Newport in Cornwall, and in December 1763 was appointed solicitor to the king. In August 1766 he became attorney-general, and was knighted. He was also comptroller of the first-fruits and tenths.

He filled the office of attorney-general for nearly five years, and in the parliament following his appointment had the honour of being elected by three different constituencies—at first for Newport and Tamworth, selecting the former; and afterwards, in January 1770, for the university of Cambridge. In that parliament he contended against the legality of Mr. Wilkes's return for Middlesex; and on all other occasions strenuously supported the measures of Lord North's ministry. On a motion to abridge the power of the attorney-general in filing *ex officio* informations, he boldly defended himself, and proved that the power was not only constitutional, but, when discreetly exercised, essentially necessary. He conducted the proceedings against Wilkes, when he surrendered in 1768 after his conviction, on the question of his outlawry; in the various discussions previous to his sentence; and in the writ of error before the House of Lords, by whom the conviction and sentence were confirmed. Though sharing of course the unpopularity with which all the opponents of that demagogue were visited, Sir William De Grey does not seem to have excited any special animosity, but to have been regarded as merely doing his duty as an officer of the crown.

On January 25, 1771, he was appointed lord chief justice of the Common Pleas. After presiding over his court for nearly ten years, the failure of his health obliged him to resign in June 1780. In acknowledgment of his services, the king in the following October called him up to the House of Peers by the title of Lord Walsingham. He enjoyed his new honours for little more than six months, dying on May 9, 1781, when he was buried at Merton.

He was a most accomplished lawyer, and of the most extraordinary power of memory. 'I have seen him,' says Lord Eldon, 'come into court with both hands wrapped up in flannel (from gout). He could not take a note, and had no one to do so for him. I have known him try a cause which lasted nine or ten hours, and then, from memory, sum up all the evidence with the greatest correctness.' (*Twiss*, i. 113.)

He married Mary, daughter of William Cowper, Esq., M.P. for Hertford, and first cousin of the poet; and the title is still enjoyed by his descendants.

DELVES, JOHN DE, was the son of Richard

de Delves, of Delves Hall, near Uttoxeter, in Staffordshire, who was constable of Heleigh Hall, in that county. At the battle of Poictiers, in 1356, the Lord Audley, with his four esquires, of whom John de Delves was one, performed such acts of valour that Prince Edward granted to him, on the field, 'fyue hundred markes of yerely reuenewes,' which the generous lord immediately resigned to his four squires, saying that they had 'alwayes serued me truely, and specially this day; that honour that I haue is by their valyantnesse.' And each of them was allowed to add a part of their lord's arms to his own.

John de Delves was soon afterwards knighted, and retained in the service of the Black Prince. In 36 Edward III. he is called his 'valettus,' in an order to the sheriffs of London to supply him with as many bows and arrows as the prince should require; and he was entrusted with the wardship of the Duchess of Brittany.

However natural it was that the royal goodwill should be extended to him, it seems strange that a place on the judicial bench should be selected as a reward for his military services, since there is no evidence that he had been ever previously connected with the law. Yet so it was, and on February 3, 1364, 38 Edward III., he was constituted a judge of the Common Pleas. There is evidence, however, that he accompanied the Black Prince to Gascony two months afterwards, so that he did not devote himself much to his legal avocation. Fines, however, appear to have been levied before him till the middle of the following year. As his name was not afterwards inserted among the judges who received their salaries, he probably then retired from the bench. He was lucky enough, at this time, to announce to the king the birth of his grandson Edward, the son of the Prince of Wales, for which he had a grant of 40*l.* a year. (*Cal. Rot. Pat.* 180.)

He lived till 1369, and was buried at Audley in Staffordshire. By his wife Isabella, daughter of Philip de Malpas, he left a daughter, Joan, the widow of Henry de Kymes, and bequeathed to her most of his manors; but he was eventually succeeded in his estates by his brother Henry, one of whose descendants, Thomas Delves, of Dodington, obtained a baronetcy, which is now extinct. (*Froissart*, i. 197, 205; *Dugdale's Orig.* 45; *Cal. Inq.* p. m. ii. 296.)

DENE, HENRY (ARCHBISHOP OF CANTERBURY), although holding three sees successively, wore the episcopal mitre for little more than five years. His public career is equally short, and little is preserved of his private history. His origin is not recorded, except that he was a Welshman, which might perhaps operate as a recommendation to Henry VII. He was born about 1450, and the place of his education is claimed by both Oxford and Cambridge. He became in 1461 prior of Llanthony Secundus, near Gloucester, a cell to that in Monmouthshire, but afterwards, in 1481, made the principal house. In 1494 he was constituted Chancellor of Ireland, when his services in turning away the impostor Perkin Warbeck from the Irish shores secured the royal favour, and he was not only rewarded by being made deputy and justiciary of that kingdom in 1496, but also Bishop of Bangor. In this see he restored the rights of the church, and regained several valuable properties, and in March 1500 he was translated to the more important diocese of Salisbury. Six months afterwards, on October 13, he was invested with the custody of the Great Seal with the title of lord keeper, and in the following January he was consecrated Archbishop of Canterbury. The pope soon after appointed him his legate in England; and before the end of the year he solemnised the nuptials of Prince Arthur with Catherine of Arragon, and was engaged in negotiating the treaty of marriage between the King of Scots and the Princess Margaret. No reason being assigned for his early resignation of the custody of the Great Seal on July 27, 1502, it may probably be attributed to the failure of his health, as he survived his retirement only half a year. He died at Lambeth, on February 15, 1502–3; and his remains were deposited in Canterbury Cathedral. (*Godwin*, 132, 352, 625; *Rymer*, xii. 523, 642, 793; *Arch. Journal*, xviii. 256–267.)

DENE, RALPH DE, one of the twelve inquisitors against the sheriffs in 1170, who are called justices itinerant by Dugdale, was of a Sussex family, in which county he had considerable property. He settled some canons of the Præmonstratensian order at Ottham in Sussex. (*Madox*, i. 576, ii. 78; *Monast.* vi. 911.)

DENHAM, JOHN, in the memoir of his son Sir John Denham, the poet, is described as of Little Horsley in Essex. He was a member first of Furnival's Inn, and then of Lincoln's Inn, and, having been called to the bar in 1587, was chosen a reader of that society twenty years afterwards.

Eton College employed him as their counsel, and made him their steward. On June 5, 1609, having been first called serjeant, he was appointed lord chief baron of the Irish Exchequer, and knighted. From this office he was advanced within three years to that of lord chief justice of the King's Bench, in the same country. This he held for five years, and then exchanged it on May 2, 1617, for a seat in the English Court of Exchequer. How well he performed his duties in Ireland may be judged from the address of Lord Chancellor Bacon (*Works*, vii. 264) to his successor, Sir William Jones, who is recommended to imitate 'the care and affection to the commonwealth of Ireland, and the prudent and politic administration of Sir John Denham.' He was so good an 'administrator of the revenue' there, as Bacon calls him, that he set up the customs, which, bringing first only 500*l.*, were let before his death for 54,000*l.* per annum. (*Ibid.* 316, *note*.)

In the proceedings against his eminent eulogist, three years afterwards, he had the unpleasant duty of delivering the message of the lords to the fallen chancellor, requiring a special answer to the charges against him. (*Parl. Hist.* i. 1239.) In the case of ship-money he joined the other judges for the sake of conformity in the opinion they gave to the king in favour of its legality; but on the hearing of the case against Hampden he was absent during four days of the argument, and, being sick and weak, gave a short written judgment on May 28, 1638, in opposition to the king's claim. (*State Trials*, iii. 1201.) He lived only seven months after the unfortunate decision of the majority, and dying on January 6, 1639, was buried at Egham in Surrey, where there is a monument to him and his two wives. The first of these was Cicile, the widow of Richard Kellefet, Esq.; and the second Eleanor, the daughter of Sir Garrett Moore, first Viscount Drogheda.

The judge built the mansion called 'The Place' at Egham; but his estate was wasted in gambling by his only son, John Denham, equally celebrated as the author of 'Cooper's Hill' and other poems, and as a loyal adherent of King Charles through all his adversities. He was rewarded on the Restoration with the post of surveyor-general and the knighthood of the Bath, and died in 1668. (*Aubrey*, ii. 320; *Brit. Biography*, v. 453.)

DENISON, THOMAS, was the younger of two sons of Mr. Joseph Denison, an opulent merchant at Leeds, the elder of whom was the grandfather of the Right Honourable John Evelyn Denison, speaker of the House of Commons since 1857. He was born in 1699, and received his legal education at the Inner Temple, where he was called to the bar. His merits as a lawyer soon procured him a considerable practice, and, without having filled any of the minor offices of the profession, he was made a judge of the King's Bench in December 1741. He was knighted in November 1745, when he joined in the loyal address to the king on the rebellion. After administering justice in that court for more than twenty-three years, his health and his sight failing him, he resigned on February 14, 1765.

He sat under three successive chief justices—Sir William Lee, Sir Dudley Ryder, and Lord Mansfield; the latter of whom had so high an opinion of his learning, and so great an affection for him, that when he died on the 8th of the following September, he wrote the beautiful and characteristic epitaph on his monument in the church of Harewood in Yorkshire, where he lies near Lord Chief Justice Gascoigne.

He married Anne, daughter of Robert Smithson, Esq., but left no issue.

DENMAN, THOMAS (LORD DENMAN), than whom no chief justice of England since the death of the Earl of Mansfield has been regarded with more personal esteem and affection, and none since the days of Lord Chief Justice Holt have left a character of bolder independence or more fearless and uncompromising patriotism, was born on February 23, 1779, at his father's house in Queen Street, Golden Square, which in honour of the infant then brought into the world has lately assumed the name of Denman Street. He was the only son of Dr. Thomas Denman, the most eminent physician of his time in his particular branch of science, and of his wife Elizabeth, daughter of Alexander Brodie, Esq., a descendant from the ancient family of Brodie, of Brodie in Morayshire. The family from which he sprang was originally settled in Nottinghamshire, some time at East Retford, and more lately at Bevercotes, but Dr. Denman's father removed to Bakewell in Derbyshire, where for many years he practised as a surgeon. The judge therefore is another instance, of which there are so many in this reign, of the legal bench being supplied by men of medical lineage.

At three years he commenced his school education under that amiable and excellent woman Mrs. Barbauld, then resident at Palgrave in Norfolk, and to her system of instruction during the two years he was under her tuition the judge was accustomed to attribute the retentive memory and whatever grace and facility of diction he afterwards attained.

After leaving Mrs. Barbauld's, he was placed for a short time under the Rev. Dr. Thompson at Kensington, whence he proceeded when seven years old to Eton. His industry and application during the years that he remained there are evidenced by the stores of classical literature which remained in his memory, and by the delight which he took in them, and his readiness in quoting them; and his social character among his schoolfellows may be estimated by the many lasting friendships which he formed there. To the last period of his life he retained that affection for the noble establishment with which those who have been educated within its walls invariably regard it. Before proceeding to the university he spent one or two years as a pupil with his maternal uncle, the Rev. Peter Brodie (the father of Mr. Brodie the eminent conveyancer, and Sir Benjamin Brodie the great surgeon, his fellow pupils), under whom he added largely to the classical and historical knowledge which he had laid in at Eton.

From 1796 to 1800 he spent at St. John's College, Cambridge, and took his degree of B.A. in the latter year, and that of M.A. in 1803, without aiming at a place on the list of university honours, as he had a great distaste to mathematical studies, and devoted himself entirely to his favourite classics.

He then entered Lincoln's Inn, and placed himself as a pupil under the great conveyancer Charles Butler, and the eminent pleader Mr. Tidd, the initiator into legal mysteries of so many remarkable men. After due preparation, he practised for a short time as a special pleader until 1806, when he was called to the bar, and joined the Midland Circuit and Lincoln Sessions. He had two years before married Theodosia Ann, the eldest daughter of the Rev. Richard Vevers, rector of Saxby in Leicestershire.

While making the slow progress which is so much the fate of junior barristers, he employed some part of his leisure in writing critiques on the classical literature of the day for the 'Monthly Review,' then the leading whig journal, until it was superseded by the advances of its Edinburgh competitor. But he gradually got the ear of the court, and so early as 1809 by his lucid, elaborate, and successful argument on the right application of the rule in Shelley's case, in opposition to so able an opponent as Mr. Copley (afterwards Lord Lyndhurst), proved that he had not sat at the feet of the great conveyancing Gamaliel in vain. (11 *East*, 548.) But the event to which he attributed his ultimate success, and which recommended him to the first honours he received, was his employment on the trials of the Luddites in 1817, when he was engaged for the defence of the prisoners arraigned at Derby.

In 1818 Mr. Denman obtained his first seat in parliament as representative of Wareham in Dorsetshire. He soon embarked on the stormy sea of politics, and distinguished himself by the boldness with which he attacked abuses and pronounced opinions to which he adhered through life, and in particular by advocating the necessity of an amelioration of the criminal law. In this his first year he had obtained a position of considerable importance in the House of Commons, and had established a reputation which was soon to be extended throughout the country.

The old king George III. died on January 29, 1820, and the Prince of Wales, who had held the regency of the kingdom for the nine previous years, 'heavily in clouds' commenced his actual reign of George IV. A conspiracy, widely spread among the lower orders of the people, had been organised to overturn the government of the country just before his accession, and within a month after it a plan was concerted for the commencement of the outbreak by the murder of all the ministers at a cabinet dinner at Lord Harrowby's. The plot was discovered only just in time. On the very day of its intended execution the body of traitors were arrested in the midst of their preparations, and their conviction and execution soon followed. The agitation arising from what was called the Cato Street conspiracy had scarcely subsided before the public were excited by the prospect of an investigation of a very different nature, but threatening equally perilous consequences. In the meantime Mr. Denman had at the general election of that year been returned for Nottingham.

Queen Caroline, who was living apart from her husband in foreign lands, had intimated her intention of coming to England to claim the rights and privileges due to her new rank, which it was known that the king intended to resist, as he had already excluded her name from the usual prayers in the Liturgy. One of the first acts of her progress towards England was to appoint Mr. Brougham her attorney-general and Mr. Denman her solicitor-general. Numerous negotiations took place between the government and her law officers, in order to avert the inconveniences which threatened to follow her arrival. But all endeavours of accommodation failing, her majesty entered London on June 7, amidst the triumphant acclamations of the people, and the whole town, partly from sympathy and partly from force and fear, was illuminated in the evening.

The cause of this popular feeling was not so much a conviction of the queen's innocence, for of that the majority knew little and cared less, as a disgust at the indignities offered to a female, and an admiration of the spirit she exhibited in hastening to face her accusers, together with the growing unpopularity of the king, much increased by the knowledge of the grounds of recrimination which the queen, even if the charges against her were true, could justly bring against him. Meetings of arbitrators, motions in parliament, were alike ineffectual to produce an arrangement, the interesting protocols and debates in which will be found in Hansard and the 'Annual Register' for the year. In all these proceedings Mr. Denman of course took a prominent part, and in the new House of Commons he spoke with so much indignation, boldness, and force that he drew from the mouth of a member a question to which the spirit of prophecy might be attributed. Mr. R.

Martin asked her majesty's solicitor-general 'if by any train of fortuitous events he should at some future period find himself *elevated to the bench* of this country (and, as all things were in the hands of Providence, such an event was by no means unlikely), how he would like to have hurled against his judicial dignity any former opinion which he might have professed in that house or elsewhere?' Mr. Denman was certainly prophetic in the dignified answer that he gave to this impertinence. He said that 'he did not fear that any opinion he had delivered or should deliver in that house would ever rise up in judgment against him, nor should he desert those opinions in any situation in which he might be placed.'

The 'Green Bag' containing the dirty details was brought in and referred to a secret committee, upon whose report the Bill of Pains and Penalties was introduced into the House of Lords on July 5, the object of which was to deprive the queen of her title and to dissolve the marriage between her and the king. The second reading was put off till August 17. Nearly the whole talent of the bar was engaged, and of the eleven counsel who appeared, six on one side and five on the other, no less than ten were afterwards elevated to high legal distinction. Only one of the advocates for the queen—namely, Sir Nicolas Tindal—received his judicial promotion while George IV. remained on the throne, and though the two principal advocates received legal rank during the reign, it was not granted till near the end of it, and then with the greatest reluctance and difficulty. With so much displeasure did the king regard Mr. Denman for the bitter terms in which he had alluded to the grounds of recrimination which the king had afforded, that he was omitted from the batch of king's counsel created on the accession of the liberal-minded Lord Lyndhurst to the chancellorship, and it was only by his bold remonstrance that the Duke of Wellington was enabled to remove the injustice.

During the progress of the trial the excitement of the people was unbounded. They wholly discredited the evidence adduced against her majesty, declaring that the witnesses were suborned, and when the ministers were obliged to abandon the bill the delight of the populace almost amounted to frenzy. In the queen's popularity the advocates of her innocence, who had shown such fearless gallantry in her defence, of course largely participated.

The popular effervescence had not subsided when Sir John Sylvester, the recorder of London, died and Mr. Knowles was appointed his successor in 1822, leaving a vacancy in his former place of common serjeant. This was in the gift of the Common Council, and would naturally have fallen to their senior pleader, Mr. Bolland, who was a deserved favourite in the city. But the queen's party in the council determined to testify their admiration of the exertions made in her defence by Mr. Denman, on whom in the previous year they had conferred the freedom of the city, and elected him to the office by a majority of 131 over 119 for Mr. Bolland, who some years after was appointed a baron of the Exchequer.

In this new character Mr. Denman disappointed his opponents, who gave him credit for more eloquence than law, by exhibiting those judicial powers which are most admirable while presiding over a criminal court—patience, firmness, and humanity; and by the sweetness of his disposition, joined with the natural dignity of his character, he gained the affection and respect even of those who differed most from him in politics. These feelings found utterance in the various addresses they presented to him upon every occasion of his advancement.

He retired from parliament from 1826 to 1830, when on the general election consequent on the accession of William IV. he was again elected for Nottingham, which he continued to represent till his elevation to the bench.

On the death of the queen in 1821 he of course lost the precedence which his office of her solicitor-general gave him in the courts, and was obliged to retire behind the bar; and it was not till seven years afterwards, in 1828, that he received a silk gown. From that time his promotion was rapid. William IV. in 1830 succeeded to the crown, and on the accession of the whig ministry, scorning to remember the personal attack which Mr. Denman in his zeal had uttered against him on the queen's trial, sanctioned his appointment as attorney-general on November 26, and knighted him. He had not filled the office of attorney-general quite two years when Lord Tenterden died, and Sir Thomas was without a moment's hesitation appointed, on November 4, 1832, his successor as lord chief justice of the King's Bench.

For nearly eighteen years he graced that seat with the highest commendation from his brother judges, the bar, and the public. Without pretending to the deep black-letter learning of some of his colleagues, he had laid up a sufficient store of legal knowledge to meet every requirement, and being deeply imbued with the principles on which the law is founded, knew well how to apply them in the justice he administered. He maintained on the bench the same independence, and exhibited the same courage, as distinguished him at the bar, and in the famous case of Stockdale *v.* Hansard did not hesitate boldly to support the rights and liberties of the subject in opposition to the assumed privileges of parliament, and the threats of the House of Commons. No judge ever showed more unaffected dignity in his demeanour, more kindness and courtesy to all who were in communication with him, more patience and discrimination in investigating the rights of the parties before him, or more firmness and perspicuity in delivering his judgments.

In March 1834 he was created a peer by the title of Baron Denman of Dovedale in Derbyshire, and ventured to break through the custom of chief justices attending parliament in their judicial robes, by always sitting in his ordinary dress. Lord Denman was called upon, in consequence of the illness of Lord Cottenham the chancellor, to preside as lord high steward when the Earl of Cardigan was indicted for shooting Captain Tuckett in a duel, who was acquitted from the omission of the prosecution to prove the identity of the man wounded with the man named in the indictment.

At the age of seventy Lord Denman's health began to fail, and after several months' suffering he felt that he could no longer perform the duties of his office with satisfaction to himself or with benefit to the public. He therefore sent in his resignation at the end of Hilary Term 1850, and Lord Campbell, who was only two years his junior, was appointed in his place. In no instance of a judge's retirement was so much regret expressed. Not only from the citizens of London, who looked upon themselves as in some sort the founders of his fortune, and who had placed his portrait on the walls of their council chamber, but from the whole bar, and specially from the members of his own (the Midland) circuit, from the grand juries of Lincolnshire, Nottinghamshire, Derbyshire, Leicestershire, Warwickshire, Kent (conveying the sentiments of admiration and regret of the leading gentry of those counties), was he gratified by receiving the most affectionate addresses. The solicitors gave a permanent testimony of their participation in these feelings by placing his bust in their hall in Chancery Lane; and the poet-laureate of the Home Circuit, Sir Joseph Arnould, since a judge at Bombay, embodied them in a beautiful copy of verses describing in elegant and pathetic lines the various excellences by which he was distinguished, and their loss in being deprived of his example.

The sympathy thus shown in this country extended even to America, and was communicated in an elegant letter from Mr. Everett, who had been ambassador here. But the highest gratification experienced by Lord Denman was in receiving the unexampled compliment from his colleagues in the court in which he presided of a valuable inkstand, in a beautiful classical design, accompanied by a letter the language of which must have been even more precious than the gift. His four brethren say, 'We do desire to bear sincere and considerate testimony to the leading good sense and ability, the industry and uprightness, the candour, patience, dignity, and good temper with which you have adorned the bench on which we have had the happiness to sit as your assistants. But we are bound to add to this our gratitude for the uniform kindness which individually we have experienced at your hands, the hearty acceptance which you have ever given to such assistance as it was our duty and in our power to afford you, and the delightful friendliness, without change or diminution at any time, which has shed a peculiar charm on our private intercourse. By these we have been made, we trust, more useful servants to the public, as we are sure we have been enabled to enjoy our few leisure hours more perfectly.' The letter bears the subscription of the respected names of Sir John Patteson, Sir John Coleridge, Sir William Wightman, and Sir William Erle.

Throughout his life he preserved his enjoyment of every branch of literature and science; and, though he did not publish any work with his name, he contributed many elegant translations to Bland's 'Greek Anthology,' besides often relaxing himself in playful dalliance with the Muses.

He lived nearly five years after his resignation, spending most of his time at Stony Middleton, near Bakewell, which he had inherited from his father, in those acts of charity and kindness which endeared him to his fellow-creatures, and in contemplations which prepared him for his end. His death occurred on September 22, 1854, at Stoke Albany, near Rockingham. He left a large family.

DENNY, EDMUND, or EDWARD, from being a clerk of the Exchequer, was raised in 1504 to the office of king's remembrancer, and on May 6, 1513, 5 Henry VIII., to that of fourth baron, in which he continued till his death in 1520. He was buried in the church of St. Benet, Paul's Wharf, London. He is described as of Cheshunt in Hertfordshire, and was the son of Thomas Denny and Agnes his wife. He had three wives: the first was Margaret, daughter of Ralph Leigh, Esq., of Stockwell, Surrey, M.P. for the county; the second was Mary, daughter and heir of Robert Troutbeck, Esq., of Bridge-Trafford, Cheshire; and the third Jane, daughter of ——. By his second wife only he had issue. Besides several daughters, one of whom, Joyce, was the mother of the celebrated Sir Francis Walsingham, and the maternal ancestor of the Viscounts

Falkland, he had two sons, the younger of whom was Sir Anthony, the king's remembrancer, and gentleman of the king's privy chamber. His grandson was created Baron Denny and Earl of Norwich, both of which titles have become extinct. The family is now represented by a baronetcy, created in 1782.

DENTON, ALEXANDER, was the nephew of Sir Edmund Denton, a baronet, whose title is now extinct, and the son of another Alexander Denton, of Hillesden, near Buckingham. In 1704 he was called to the bar by the Middle Temple, and in February of the next year he was committed to the custody of the serjeant-at-arms by the House of Commons for pleading for the plaintiffs in the Aylesbury case. (*State Trials*, xiv. 809.) In 1708 and 1714 he was elected member of parliament for Buckingham. Taking a high rank in his profession, he was on June 25, 1722, appointed a judge of the Common Pleas, and after filling it with respectability for eighteen years, he died on March 22, 1740, holding at his death the office also of chancellor to the Prince of Wales.

He married a lady with a fortune of 20,000*l*., named Bond, but left no issue.

DENUM, WILLIAM DE, of a family established in Durham, was the son of Robert de Denum. Both he and his elder brother John were serjeants, and are probably the persons who are generally called J. and W. Devom in the Year Books of Edward II. and III. William, in the early part of the reign of the latter monarch, was frequently employed in conducting the negotiations with Scotland. In 1329 he was one of the itinerant judges into Nottinghamshire, and in 1331 was constituted king's serjeant. On September 24, 1332, he was made a baron of the Exchequer; and a little later in the same year Dugdale introduces him among the justices of the King's Bench, on the authority of a liberate. But it is most probable that this document was nothing more than the order for his salary as a baron, the titles not being always clearly distinguished. No entry occurs relative to him after this date, so that it is not unlikely that he retired from the bench when he succeeded to the manor of Herdwick-juxta-Hesilden, and other large family estates, on the death of his brother.

He died in 1350, leaving his wife, Isabella, and four daughters. (*Surtees's Durham*, i. 51, 192; *N. Fœdera*, ii. 704–849; *Abb. Rot. Orig.* ii. 91, 261.)

DERBY, WILLIAM, was a clergyman, and no doubt a clerk in the Exchequer. On February 8, 1435, 13 Henry VI., he was nominated third baron, and on June 16, 1436, was raised to the second seat in the court. He died in 1438. (*Acts Privy Council*, iv. 295.)

DESPENCER, HUGH LE, was, there is no doubt, the descendant of one who had been the steward of the king, and who was, in the language of the time, called Dispensator, or le Despencer, which title became a surname of the family. Dugdale calls Hugh a grandson of another Hugh, and the son of Thomas (*Baronage*, i. 389); while Collins makes him the son of Geoffrey, and grandson of Thurstan. (*Peerage*, iv. 496.) If the former, Dugdale leaves us in doubt as to his actual ancestors; but if the latter, his succession from the steward of Henry I. is clearly shown.

That Hugh le Despencer, however, was of the baronial family of that name is sufficiently proved by his accompanying Richard, King of the Romans, to Germany, in 1257 (*Rymer*, i. 355), and by his being selected as one of the twelve commissioners on the part of the barons at the parliament of Oxford in 1258, when Hugh Bigot was nominated chief justiciary by them. In 44 Henry III. he went as a justice itinerant into three counties, and on the retirement of Hugh Bigot at the latter end of that year he was appointed by the barons to succeed him. Although the king, in the following July, on resuming his authority, placed Philip Basset in the office of chief justiciary, Hugh le Despencer continued to act in the same capacity on the part of the barons till April 1262, when, an accommodation taking place, Philip Basset seems to have been established in the office, as he certainly performed its functions during the king's absence in Guienne in that year. (*Excerpt. e Rot. Fin.* ii. 385, &c.)

On a pretended reconciliation between the king and the barons in 1263 Hugh le Despencer was again appointed chief justiciary. Early in the next year the barons' war again broke out, and the Earl of Leicester having secured the citizens of London on his side, Hugh le Despencer, at the head of their associated bands, destroyed the houses of Philip Basset and the loyalist nobility, imprisoned the judges, and left the Jews, after enriching himself with the ransom of some of the most wealthy, to the tender mercies of the mob. (*Lingard*, iii. 135.)

In the battle of Lewes, fought on May 14, 1264, the chief justiciary distinguished himself on the barons' side, and after the king's defeat no less than six castles were placed under Hugh's government, with a grant of 1000 marks for his support in his office. (*Rymer*, ii. 445.)

In Leland's 'Collectanea' (ii. 378) there is a statement that he afterwards quarrelled with the Earl of Leicester; and it is somewhat curious that in three records quoted by Brady (i. 650–1), dated in May and June 1265, the title 'Justiciarius' is added to the earl's name. This bears the appearance of the retirement of Hugh; but as in the following August he was in arms with that nobleman, the difference could not have been of long continuance. The firmness of his friendship was shown at the battle of Evesham on August 4, 1265, when, refusing to quit the field before it began, though urged by the earl to do so, he and Leicester were slain together.

As a soldier he seems to have been valiant and bold; but the few facts that are recorded of him in his capacity of chief justice of the kingdom are marked with the violence and rapacity of the times.

He married Alyna, or Aliva, the daughter and heir of Philip Basset, of Wicombe, who, after his death, became the wife of Roger Bigot, Earl of Norfolk. By her he left a son and a daughter, the latter of whom married Hugh de Courtney, father of Hugh, first Earl of Devon. The son, Hugh, was created Earl of Winchester in 1322; but being beheaded in 1326, his honours became forfeited. His grandson, however, was summoned to parliament by Edward III.; but his successor (who had been created Earl of Gloucester in 1397) was beheaded in 1400, and the honours were again forfeited. This attainder being reversed in 1461, the barony was restored to his granddaughter Elizabeth, the wife of Edward Nevill, and, after falling several times into abeyance, still survives in the present Baroness le Despencer.

DEVON, EARL OF. *See* H. DE COURTENEYE.

D'EYNCOURT, EDMUND, the son and heir of John, who was lineally descended from Walter D'Eyncourt, who came over with the Conqueror, and was royally rewarded with many lordships in the counties of York, Northampton, Nottingham, Derby, and Lincoln, at his father's death, in 1257, was a minor, and when he attained his majority served the king in his wars in Wales, in Gascony, and in Scotland. He was summoned to parliament in 27 Edward I. (*Baronage*, i. 388), and subscribed the letter to the pope by the title of 'Dominus de Thurgerton.' In 1305 he was appointed one of the justices of trailbaston for Lincoln and nine other counties, and throughout the following reign he still continued to act as a judge. (*Parl. W.*, ii. 759.)

He died in 1327, 1 Edward III. His lands and title devolved by royal licence on his nephew William, the son of his brother John. On the death of the thirteenth baron, in 1422, the barony fell into abeyance, and ultimately became forfeited. (*Nicolas's Synopsis.*)

DIGGES, DUDLEY, whose pedigree, prepared by himself, commences in the reign of Henry III., was the grandson of Leonard Digges, 'insignem mathematicum,' and the son of Thomas, 'mathematicum insignissimum,' by Anne, the daughter of Sir Warham de Sentleger. Both of these progenitors, so eminent for their mathematical studies, were resident at Digges Court, Barham, in Kent, where Sir Dudley was born in 1583. He was entered a gentleman commoner of University College in Oxford, where he took the degree of B.A. in 1601, and, in the multitudinous distribution of honours by King James, he was knighted soon after the accession.

He was member for Tewkesbury from 1604 to 1611. Part of this time he spent abroad; and in 1611 he is mentioned as 'busy with the discovery of the north-west passage,' and in 1614 as 'moving every stone to obtain employment.' (*Cal. St. Papers* [1611], 96, 225.) He was subsequently employed on a mission to the Hague. Whether he then held any office at court is uncertain; but he probably did so in October 1615, when he deposed, on the trial of Weston for the murder of Sir Thomas Overbury, that the knight had imparted to him his readiness to be employed in an embassy to Russia, to which the king had appointed him. He was certainly a gentleman of the king's privy chamber in 1618, for he is so described in a commission of that date appointing him 'ambassador to the great duke and lord of all Russia, to treat concerning a loan from the king to the duke.' Of this voyage, in which John Tradescant accompanied him as a naturalist, there is a MS. account preserved in the Ashmolean Museum. (*Notes and Queries*, 1st S. iii. 392.)

In the parliament of 1621, so fatal to Lord Chancellor Bacon, Sir Dudley sat again for Tewkesbury, and was one of the committee that brought forward the charges against the noble delinquent. Though he seems to have taken altogether a moderate and conciliatory part, the king thought otherwise, for, though not included among the 'ill-tempered spirits' mentioned in his proclamation on the dissolution, whom he committed to the Tower, Sir Dudley and a few others were punished by being sent into Ireland on a frivolous commission. They were dismissed from their penal employment in February 1623, receiving each thirty shillings a day for 124 days from October 26, when they entered on their commission. (*Pell Records*, 266.)

Archbishop Abbot, in his narrative, says that Sir Dudley had been 'a great servant' of the Duke of Buckingham, who, he presumes, lost his friendship for some unworthy carriage offered to him; and also alludes to Sir Dudley being committed to the Fleet, and kept there for seven or eight weeks, without any known reason for his imprisonment. (*Rushworth*, i. 450.) It is apparent that these two persons bore great illwill towards each other, for Sir Dudley, in the second parliament of Charles I. (1626), was one of the most active managers of the impeachment against the duke. In the conference with the Lords, having made some allusion to the plaister administered to the late king, Buckingham endeavoured to fasten upon him expressions which were little less than treason to the present king, and thereupon obtained his committal to the Tower. There was evidently a wilful misrepresentation of the words used, and on the murmured resentment of the Commons, Sir Dudley was released, after three days' detention. (*Whitelocke*, 5.) In the next year he suffered another imprisonment in the Fleet, for some 'unfitting words' at the council table. (*Cal. St. Papers* [1627], 2, 64.)

In Charles's third parliament (1628) Sir Dudley was returned for the county of Kent, and took a prominent part in forwarding the Petition of Right, being appointed to open the conference with the Peers on the subject. The lord president in reporting to the house describes him as ' a man of volubility and elegance of speech.'

This parliament was angrily dissolved in March 1629, and the next was not called until eleven years afterwards. In the interim, Sir Julius Cæsar being a very old man, the reversion of his office of master of the Rolls had been granted to Sir Humphrey May, an old officer and constant supporter of the court, but he dying in fourteen months, the reversion in the following November (1630) was given to Sir Dudley Digges, who, though a strenuous advocate for the liberty of the subject, had, since the death of his enemy the duke, shown no disposition to oppose government measures, and had probably resumed his connection with the court. On obtaining this grant he entered himself as a member of the society of Gray's Inn, and, *honoris causâ*, was immediately made a bencher. He had to wait for nearly five years and a half before Sir Julius Cæsar died; but in the meantime he was admitted one of the masters in Chancery on January 22, 1631. He thus had a slight opportunity of acquiring some professional knowledge ; for neither he nor Sir Humphrey May, having never studied any branch of law, could from their legal experience found any claim to the judicial seat. On Sir Julius's death on April 18, 1636, Sir Dudley immediately acceded to the office; but of his proceedings in it, during the three years of his possession, there is no account.

He died on March 18, 1639, and was buried at Chilham, the manor and castle of which he acquired by his marriage with Mary, one of the daughters and co-heirs of Sir Thomas Kempe, of Ollantigh in the next parish. He was intelligent, eloquent, and ready as a public man, and pious, amiable, and generous in his private life. He published ' A Defence of Trade' during his life, and was the author of 'The Compleat Ambassador,' printed after his death. The family was famous for literature; his brother Leonard was an accomplished poet, and is connected with the memory of Shakspeare by his commendatory verses, which have been often reprinted; and his third son Dudley was also a good poet and linguist. His grandson, Sir Maurice Digges, received a baronetcy in 1666, which became extinct within the year. (*Ath. Oxon.* ii. 634; *Fasti*, i. 290; *Hasted*, vii. 265.)

DIGHTON, WILLIAM DE. In 48 Edward III., when he had letters of protection granted to him to accompany the Duke of Brittany abroad, he is called clericus, and is described as 'alias dictus Willielmus Marmoyn.' In the previous year his name, as canon of St. Paul's, London, is attached to the treaty with the King of Portugal. (*New Fœdera*, iii. 985, 1010.)

He was made keeper of the privy seal in the early part of the reign of Richard II.; and when the king dismissed Richard le Scrope from his second chancellorship, on July 11, 1382, Dighton was joined with Hugh de Segrave and John de Waltham in the custody of the Great Seal, until a new chancellor was appointed, and they held it for ten weeks. He is not mentioned later than the ninth year of the reign, when he is still called canon of St. Paul's. (*Rymer*, vii. 520.)

DIXON, NICHOLAS, was in holy orders, and held the church of Cheshunt in Hertfordshire for thirty years from 1418. He was then clerk of the Pipe, and soon after became sub-treasurer of the Exchequer. His next elevation was to the bench of that court on January 26, 1423, 1 Henry VI. (*Acts Privy Council*, iii. 22.) He is mentioned as late as 19 Henry VI. in a deed relating to property granted to Richard, Duke of York. (*Ibid.* v. 136.) His retirement from the court must have been previous to 22 Henry VI., as his name does not appear among those to whom the usual robes were then assigned (*Orig.* 99); but he lived till October 30, 1448, 27 Henry VI.

He was buried in the church at Cheshunt, which, together with a chancel dedicated to the Virgin, was erected by him; and his epitaph celebrates both his justice and his charity. (*Fuller's Herts*, i. 438; *Chauncy*, 302.)

DODD, SAMUEL, was descended from a Cheshire family, and was the son of Ralph Dod, who describes himself ' Civis et Pellio Londini.' He was born about 1652. The Inner Temple was his school of law, where he was called to the bar in 1679, and admitted to the bench in 1700. He was counsel for Dr. Sacheverell in the ill-judged impeachment against him in 1710, and pleaded so manfully and ably that he obtained a great amount of popularity among the high church party. (*State Trials,* xv. 213, &c.)

On the accession of George I. he was appointed the lord chief baron on November 22, 1714, and knighted. He occupied his seat barely seventeen months, dying on April 14, 1716, when he was buried in the Temple Church. He left a manuscript volume of Reports, which is preserved among the Hargrave Collection in the British Museum.

By his wife Elizabeth, sister and coheir of Sir Robert Croke, of Chequers, Bucks, he had two sons, who both died without issue.

DODERIDGE, JOHN, according to the more received opinion, was the son of Richard Doderidge, an eminent merchant at Barnstaple, and Joan Badcock, of South Moulton, and was born at Barnstaple in 1555. He entered Exeter College, Oxford, and, having taken the degree of B.A., became a member of the Middle Temple. At both his studies were so successful that Fuller says 'it was hard to say whether he was better artist, divine, civil or common lawyer.' Among his other pursuits, history was a favourite one, and he joined the learned men who formed the nucleus of the Society of Antiquaries, then meeting at the Heralds' College in Derby House. (*Reliq. Spelman,* 69.) In 1593 and 1602 he was selected by his inn to deliver lectures at New Inn. The subject of the last course was 'Advowsons and Church Livings,' published after his death under the title of 'A Compleat Parson.' In the following year he was appointed Lent reader to his own society; and on January 20, 1604, he was called to the degree of the coif, being at the same time nominated serjeant to Henry, Prince of Wales. Nine months after, on October 28, he was appointed solicitor-general, being at this time representative in parliament for Horsham in Sussex.

After filling the office of solicitor-general nearly three years, during which he argued the famous case of the post-nati (*State Trials,* ii. 566), he was induced on June 25, 1607, to resign it, and become principal serjeant to the king, in order that Bacon might be put into his place. For this accommodation he was knighted on July 5, with a promise of the first seat that should become vacant in the Court of King's Bench. This did not occur for the next five years, when, on November 25, 1612, he received his patent (*Croke, Jac.*); and in that court he continued during the remainder of his life.

When the practice of privately interrogating the judges was adopted, Bacon (*Works,* xii. 125) tells the king 'that he had found Judge Doderidge very ready to give opinion in secret,' a course in which it is lamentable to think that most of his colleagues concurred. When King James was negotiating for his son's marriage with the Spanish princess, and was desirous of showing some leniency to the Catholics, Walter Yonge (*Diary,* 69) reports that 'Judge Doderidge saith he thought they [the judges] should find out a way by law to dispense with the statute against recusancy.' This spirit of accommodating their opinions to the royal wishes was further shown when the judges refused to admit Hampden and others to bail for refusing to subscribe to the late loan. On their being called before the House of Lords in April 1628 to assign the reasons for their judgment, Judge Doderidge, though he attempted to justify the decision, seemed to acknowledge they had committed a mistake, by thus apologetically concluding: 'Omnia habere in memoria, et in nullo errare, divinum potius est quam humanum.' (*Parl. Hist.* ii. 291.) This speech exhibits somewhat of the drivelling of an old and failing man; but in it he says, 'God knoweth I have endeavoured always to keep a good conscience,' an assertion which is borne out by the general tenor of his life. He had the habit of shutting his eyes while sitting on the bench, for the purpose of concentrating his attention on the argument, without being distracted by surrounding objects, and was thence jocularly called the Sleeping Judge.

He survived his appearance in the House of Lords only five months, dying on September 13, 1628, at Forsters, near Egham, in Surrey, and was buried in the Lady chapel in Exeter Cathedral, where there is a stately monument erected to his and his wife's memory.

Croke, in recording his death, describes him as 'man of great knowledge, as well in common law as in other humane sciences, and divinity' (*Croke, Car.* 127), and Fuller (i. 282) says of him, 'His soul consisted of two essentials, ability and integrity, holding the scale of justice with so steady a hand that neither love nor lucre, fear or flattery, could bow him on either side.' But it must be acknowledged that in several instances he betrayed that subservience to the ruling powers for which the judicial bench was then remarkable. He composed a variety of works, legal and antiquarian, none of which were published in his lifetime, and some of which still remain in manuscript.

He married three wives, but outlived them all. His first wife was a daughter of — Germin; his second was a daughter of — Cullum, of Canon's Leigh in Devonshire; and the third was Dorothy, daughter of Sir Amias Bampfield, of North Molton, and widow of Edward Hancock, of Combe Martin, Esq. By the two former he had no issue, and by the latter only one son, who died before him. He was succeeded in his property by his brother, Pentecost Doderidge, of Barnstaple, whose son became recorder of that town, and edited one of his uncle's tracts concerning Parliament.' (*Athen. Oxon.* ii. 425.)

DOLBEN, WILLIAM, of an ancient and respectable Denbighshire family, was the son of John, Archbishop of York, and brother of Gilbert, the judge of the Common Pleas in Ireland from 1700 to 1719, who was created a baronet by Queen Anne.

He pursued his legal studies at the Inner Temple, was called to the bar in 1653, and was elected a bencher in 1672, and autumn reader in 1677. His legal merits probably procured him a royal recommendation for the recordership of the city of London, to which he was elected on February 8, 1676, and knighted. He held the place till he was advanced to the bench, when the corporation voted him a piece of plate 'as a loving remembrance.'

In 1677 he was the first-named serjeant, and was immediately made one of the king's serjeants. On October 23, 1678, he was constituted a judge of the King's Bench; and it was his misfortune to sit under Sir William Scroggs as chief, and to be present at all the trials arising out of the Popish Plot, in the existence of which, as far as it appears, he had a firm belief. But he saw and fairly pointed out the inconsistencies and improbabilities of the evidence against Sir Thomas Gascoigne, which resulted in an acquittal; and at the trial of Sir Thomas Stapleton at York for high treason he summed up favourably for the prisoner, who was thereupon acquitted. (*State Trials*, vi. 1321, vii. 964, viii. 326, 523.) Being found to be too independent, and suspected of not siding with the crown in its attempt against the charter of the city of London, he was, according to the vicious practice of the time, suddenly superseded on April 20, 1683, just before the judgment against the city was pronounced. Whether he returned to the bar is uncertain.

At the Revolution Sir William Dolben was replaced in his former seat on March 11, 1689. On the 29th of the following month, in delivering a charge to the grand jury in the King's Bench, Narcissus Luttrell says that 'he inveighed mightily against the corruption of juries the last seven years, and gave in charge the laws against Papists.' The same diarist records (i. 509, 527, ii. 253, 259, 262) that on a similar occasion in 1691 he directed the grand jury 'to enquire into malecontents to the government, such as disturbed the peace of the kingdom by dispersing seditious and false news.' He died on January 25, 1694, seized with an apoplectic fit while going into court, and was buried in the Temple Church.

DONCASTER, JOHN DE, in 28 Edward I. was a commissioner of array in Yorkshire. He was summoned to attend the ceremony of the coronation of Edward II., and also was included in the list of judges and others called to assist at the parliaments from the first year of that reign. In 1310 he was appointed a judge of assize for the northern counties, and he is named in various judicial commissions during the next seven years.

On June 5, 1319, he was raised to the bench of the Common Pleas; but the fines levied before him in that court do not extend beyond the next year, and he was not summoned to parliament after the early part of the fourteenth year. He was probably at that time removed from the court, although he was named in a special commission for trying some forest offences in his own county two years afterwards.

He was alive in 5 Edward III., when the king confirmed certain grants which had been made to him and his wife Alicia, and their heirs, by the Earl of Surrey. (*Parl. Writs*, i. 345, ii. p. ii. 781; *Abb. Rot. Orig.* ii. 52, 55.)

DORMER, ROBERT, a descendant of the Buckinghamshire family of that name, a branch of which was ennobled by James I., with the title of Lord Dormer of Wenge, which has flourished ever since, was the grandson of Sir Fleetwood Dormer, and the second son of John Dormer, of Ley Grange and Purston, a barrister, by Katherine, daughter of Thomas Woodward, of Ripple in Worcestershire. To his elder brother John, Charles II. in 1661 presented a baronetcy, which became extinct in 1726. Robert was born in 1649, and, having entered Lincoln's Inn, was called to the bar in 1675. He is mentioned as junior counsel for the crown in several trials in 1680, and was soon afterwards constituted chancellor of Durham.

In 1698 he represented Aylesbury, in 1701 the county of Bucks, and in 1702 Northallerton. In the great question of Ashby and White he opposed the assumed privilege of the House of Commons, which would have prevented an elector from proceeding at common law for the injury he sustained by the returning officer refusing his vote. On January 8, 1706, he was made a judge of the Common Pleas, and sat there nearly one-and-twenty years, till his death on September 18, 1726.

His seat was at Arle Court, near Cheltenham. His marriage with Mary, daughter of Sir Richard Blake, of London, produced him four daughters only, one of whom married Lord Fortescue of Credan, and another John Parkhurst, of Catesby in Northamptonshire, the father of the author of the Greek Lexicon to the New Testament. (*Atkyns's Gloucestersh.* 174; *St. Trials*,

vii. 967, 1188; *Parl. Hist.* vi. 267; *Lord Raymond*, 1260, 1420; *Luttrell*, vi. 15; *Gent. Mag.* lxx. 615.)

DORSET, EARL OF. See OSMUND.

DOUBRIDGE, or DOUNEBRIGGE, WILLIAM, was appointed a baron of the Exchequer on May 12, 1389, 12 Richard II., having previously held the office of auditor of the Exchequer, in which he was paid 6s. 8d. a day for going to Lostwithiel to audit the accounts of Cornwall and Devon. It seems probable that he died in 17 Richard II. (*Cal. Rot. Pat.* 115, 117; *Devon's Issues Exch.* 223, 235.)

DOVER, JOHN DE, and his companions, made the assize of the king's demesnes in Warwickshire and Leicestershire in 20 Henry II., 1174, as the justices errant for those counties. (*Madox*, i. 125.) He was the son of William de Dover, and nephew of Hugh de Dover, Lord of Chilham in Kent, to whom his son Fulbert de Dover eventually became heir. (*Madox*, i. 97, 125, 252, 630; *Arch. Cantiana*, iv. 214.) The family became extinct in the reign of Edward I.

DRAYTON, NICHOLAS DE, an ecclesiastic, was probably the son or nephew of the already mentioned Thomas de Brayton, who was sometimes called de Drayton, to whom the Great Seal of Edward III. was occasionally entrusted in the absence of the chancellor. On December 1, 1363, he was appointed custos of the scholars supported by the royal bounty at the Aula Regis in Cambridge (*N. Fœdera*, iii. 717); and a few years afterwards he was a disciple of John Wickliffe, and had the greater excommunication fulminated against him by Sudbury, Bishop of London, for promulgating among the people errors against the articles of the Catholic faith; and whom the king, on March 20, 1370, authorised that prelate to incarcerate until he renounced his heresies. (*Ibid.* 889.) How he purged himself does not appear; but it is by no means surprising that he should have been raised to the bench of the Exchequer on November 14, 1376, 50 Edward III., and been continued there in the following June, on the accession of Richard II., since the authority of John of Gaunt, Duke of Lancaster, who partook of the same opinions, was paramount at both these dates.

DRAYTON. See T. DE BRAYTON.

DROES, HUGH DE, was appointed one of the two coroners of Wiltshire in 7 Henry III., and it was no doubt in that character that two years afterwards his name was added to the list of justices itinerant for that county. In 10 Henry III., 1226, he was one of those appointed to take an assize at Devizes as to the last presentation of the church of Harrendon, and to collect the quinzime of the county. He was still alive in 20 Henry III., when he assessed the tallage there. (*Rot. Claus.* i. 560, ii. 76, 136, 140, 146.)

DROGO is the last witness in a charter of William II. granting the church of Andover to the monks of St. Florentius, and is there described with the words 'qui custodiebat sigillum.' Galdric was chancellor at the time, being the second witness to it; so that it is difficult to explain the nature of the office held by Drogo, unless, if the 'sigillum' mentioned was the royal seal, he was merely the officer attendant on the chancellor, whose duty it was to carry it. This is the less unlikely, from the fact that no previous evidence exists of any such appointment as keeper of the seal, either independent of or in connection with the chancellor, and from his position at the end of the list of witnesses. The charter has no date, but was probably granted in or soon after 1093. (*Monast.* vi. 992.)

DROKENESFORD, JOHN DE (BISHOP OF BATH AND WELLS), was keeper of the king's wardrobe, and on the chancellor's resignation on August 12, 1302, 30 Edward I., the Great Seal was placed, as was the usual custom, under his care in the wardrobe, but with no power to use it, and eleven days after it was given to Adam de Osgodby, the master of the Rolls.

He possessed the manor of Eston Crok, in the forest of Chute, and had a licence to impark his wood of Horsley there and eighty acres in addition. He had also grants from the king amounting to 260 acres in Wolnemere and Windsor forests. (*Cal. Rot. Pat.* 55, 62.)

He evidently had previously filled some office in the Treasury or the Exchequer, as he is mentioned in 1296 as the *locum tenens* of the treasurer, an office to which he was again appointed in 1305, in which year he is also described as pleading for the king in a suit relative to the manor of Woodhull in Bedfordshire. He retained the office of keeper of the wardrobe till the end of that reign, when it would appear that in 1 Edward II. he exchanged it with John de Benstede for the office of chancellor of the Exchequer. (*Madox*, i. 72, 325, ii. 71, 324; *Abb. Placit.* 256, 293.)

His ecclesiastical preferment consisted at this time of a canonry in the cathedral of Wells, and he was also a chaplain to the pope; but in the next year he was elected Bishop of Bath and Wells, and was consecrated on November 9, 1309. King Edward II. entrusted him with the care of the kingdom when he went into France in 1312, but he afterwards joined the partisans of the queen against her husband.

The nineteen years of his rule were continually disturbed by contests with the canons of his church. He died at Dogmersfield in 1329, and was interred in the chapel of St. Catherine in his own cathedral. (*Godwin*, 375.)

DUKET, RICHARD, was probably the son of Nicholas Duket, chamberlain of London in the reign of Richard I. (*Madox*, i. 776.) He held an office in the court, his name frequently appearing on grants in 5 to 8 John. (*Rot. Claus.* i. 4-73.) In the latter year, being then called 'clericus noster,' he received a grant of an annual pension of five marks out of the abbey of Whitby. (*Ibid.* 83.) In 6 and 7 Henry III. he was sheriff of the counties of Norfolk and Suffolk. In 1225 he was one of the justices itinerant commissioned to several counties, and while performing this duty in Norfolk and Suffolk he was summoned to the king to undertake an embassy to the court of Rome, whither he proceeded with Philip de Hadham. In the next year and till 17 Henry III. he was still employed as a justice itinerant, and from the numerous commissions in which his name thus occurs through so many years, and the position which he occupies in them, it is not improbable that he was at this time one of the regular justiciers at Westminster. His death occurred about 1245, when his son Hugh did homage for his lands in Lincolnshire. (*Ibid.* 77, ii. 68, 78, 103, 141, 151, 213; *Orig.* 104; *Excerpt. e Rot. Fin.* i. 446.)

DUREDENT, WALTER, is only known as a resident in Buckinghamshire, and as acting as one of the justices itinerant for that county in 9 Henry III. (*Rot. Claus.* i. 375, ii. 77.)

DUREM, JOHN, was appointed one of the barons of the Exchequer in 1449, 27 Henry VI., and remained in his seat till the restoration of that monarch in 1470, but does not appear to have been reappointed on the return of Edward in the following year. He died between that date and 1476, when his widow, Elizabeth, made her will, by which it appears that they left a son Thomas and two daughters, and that he possessed property at Wendover in Bucks, and also in the counties of Northampton, Bedford, and Huntingdon. He was buried in the church of St. Bartholomew in Smithfield. (*Test. Vetus.* 342.)

DYER, JAMES, was born at Roundhill in Somersetshire about the year 1512. His father, Richard Dyer, of Wincalton, was of an honourable family, which produced in a senior branch Sir Edward Dyer, the author of several poems, and an especial favourite of Queen Elizabeth, who conferred on him the chancellorship of the Garter. His mother's name was Walton. He is said to have been educated at Broadgate's Hall, Oxford, on the site of which Pembroke College was afterwards founded, and went from thence, first, to New Inn, and then to the Middle Temple. He must have been called to the bar before the year 1537, as he is then first mentioned as an advocate in his own Reports.

On May 19, 1552, he received his writ to take upon himself the degree of the coif in the following Michaelmas Term; and in the interval, according to a common custom of the time, he was appointed autumn reader to his society. The 'Statute of Wills' was the subject of his reading. He was admitted to the degree of the coif on October 17, 1552, and the ceremony was remarkable as the first *recorded* instance of a motto being inscribed on the rings presented, that adopted on this occasion being 'Plebs sine lege ruit.' (*Dyer*, 71.) But it appears, though not recorded, that it was an ancient practice, and instances occur in the reigns of Henry VII. and VIII. (*See* SIR JOHN FINEUX and SIR EDWARD MONTAGU.) Within a month he was nominated one of the king's serjeants, and in March 1553 he was returned member for Cambridgeshire, and elected speaker of the last parliament of Edward's reign. His next honour was the recordership of Cambridge, and he was soon after knighted. On May 8, 1557, he was constituted a judge of the Common Pleas. Another patent, dated April 23, 1558, appointed him a judge of the King's Bench during pleasure—a temporary appointment, without removing him from the Common Pleas, made for the sole purpose of his keeping the essoign of Easter Term, instead of Justice Francis Morgan, who was too ill to perform the duty. A question was mooted whether Dyer's first patent was not rendered void by this new patent; and, as this was decided in the affirmative (*Dyer*, 143, 158), it is more than probable that Judge Dyer was at once restored by a new patent to the Common Pleas. This view is strengthened by the facts that a fine was levied before him in Trinity Term following (*Orig.* 48), and that on the accession of Queen Elizabeth in November his patent was for that court.

Queen Mary's death took place in the middle of Michaelmas Term, and the new patents to all the then existing judges were issued on the following day. But before the commencement of the next term the two chief justices, who were Catholics, were removed to a lower grade, and Judge Dyer was promoted to the head of the Common Pleas on January 22, 1559. Here he presided till his death, on March 24, 1582, a period of more than twenty-three years, during which the law was administered in his court and on the circuit with such efficiency, firmness, and patience as not only to secure the confidence and admiration of his contemporaries, but also to fix a glory round his name which three centuries have failed to dim. His judicial manner is thus described by George Whetstone, who sung his praises in a long lament, which, written when flattery would be unprofitable, is more valuable than any epitaph:—

Settled to heare, but very slowe to speake,
Till either part, at large, his minde did breake.
And when he spake, he was in speeche repos'd;
  His eyes did search the simple sutor's harte;
To put by bribes his hands were ever closde,
  His processe just, he took the poore man's parte;
He rul'd by lawe and listned not to arte;
These foes to truth,—love, hate, and private gaine,
With most corrupt, his conscience would not staine.
The friendless wight, which did offend through need,
He evermore with mercy did respect;
The prowder thiefe, that did his trespasse feede,
  Through truste in friendes, with scourge of lawe he checkt;
For by the fault, not friendes he did direct.
Thus he, with grace, the poore man's love did drawe,
And by sharpe meanes did keepe the prowde in awe.

This last point of his character was perhaps suggested by the energy he displayed at the Warwick assizes in 1574 in supporting a poor widow against the oppression of a rich knight of that county, whose illegal proceedings were assisted by the bench of magistrates there; the particulars of which are related in the life of the judge prefixed to his Reports, edited by John Vaillant, Esq.; together with his reply to the articles exhibited against him to the privy council by the angry magistrates, whose punishment or dismissal of the complaint does not appear, but is alluded to by Lord Chief Justice Sir Edward Montagu in Wraynham's case in 1618. (*State Trials*, ii. 1080.) The judge continued to be an ornament to the bench for nearly eight years afterwards. He was buried in the parish church of Great Stoughton in Huntingdonshire, under a handsome monument still existing.

His Reports, which extend from 4 Henry VIII. to the period of his death, are remarkable for their conciseness and accuracy. They were first published in French three years after he died, and several editions have since issued from the press. That of 1688 was illustrated by marginal notes and references by Chief Justice Treby; and that of 1794, the edition now used, is an English translation by John Vaillant, Esq., with valuable additions of modern cases, and preceded by a life of the author.

He married Margaret, the daughter of Sir Maurice à Barrow, of Hampshire, and widow of Sir Thomas Elyot, the celebrated author of the 'Boke of the Governour,' but left no children; and on his death his mansion in Charterhouse churchyard and his estate at Great Stoughton descended to Sir Richard Dyer, his great-nephew, whose grandson Ludovick was created a baronet in 1627, but the title became extinct at his death. (*Whetstone's Poem; Vaillant's Life; Athen. Oxon.* i. 480.)

DYMOCK, ANDREW, descended from a branch of the family of Sir John Dymock, who acquired the manor of Scrivelsby in Lincolnshire in the reign of Edward III., and held it by the service of being the king's champion at the coronation, was constituted solicitor-general in 1485, 1 Henry VII.; but, as his name is never mentioned in the Year Books, his duties were probably confined to the advocacy of the king's interests in the Exchequer. To the second barony in that court he was preferred on May 2, 1496, 11 Henry VII., and filled the seat till the 16th year of that reign.

He married Elizabeth, daughter and one of the coheirs of Sir Peter Ardern. (*Cal. St. Papers* [1509], 190.)

DYVE, WILLIAM DE, sometimes called Dyne, is mentioned by Dugdale as a justice of the King's Bench in 1321-2, on the authority of a passage from Leland's 'Collectanea' (i. p. ii. 275); but, referring to it, we find that Geoffrey de Say and William de *Dyne*, 'justiciarii regis,' are stated by Gervas of Canterbury to have been sent into Kent to enquire 'de fautoribus Badelesmer.' Now the term 'justiciarius regis' was at that time applied, not only to the judges of the two benches and the justices of assize, but also to any others who were appointed on a special judicial commission; and it is not improbable that such a commission, although no record of it has yet appeared, may have been issued to those two gentlemen to try the adherents of Bartholomew de Badlesmere, who was executed for treason in that year. Though there is nothing whatever to show that William de Dyve, or Dyne, was connected with the courts at Westminster, it has been deemed right, on Dugdale's authority, to introduce his name.

There were two families of that name, one settled in Northampton, and the other lords of the manors of Docklington and Dadington in Oxfordshire.

E

EBROICIS, STEPHEN DE (Evreux), was appointed by a mandate of 4 Henry III. (*Rot. Claus.* i. 437), with three others, one of the justices to deliver the gaols of Hereford of all the prisoners therein detained. It is evident, however, that he was only included in this commission on account of his being a knight residing in that county, where his principal seat was the castle of Lenhall. (*Rot. Chart.* 156.) For his lands at Badelingham he was accustomed to pay annually thirty-two gallons of honey to the castle of Hereford, a charge from which he was for ever released in 17 John. (*Rot. Claus.* ii. 188.) He died in 12 Henry III. (*Excerpt. e Rot. Fin.* i. 168.)

EDENESTOWE, HENRY DE, so called from a place of that name in the county of Nottingham, now Edwinstowe, where he had possessions (*Cal. Inquis.* p. m. ii. 102), was a clerk in the Chancery in 18 Edward II., 1325, and in 4 and 6 Edward III. he acted as clerk of the parliament. (*Rot. Parl.* i. 420, ii. 52, 68.) In the latter year and on several occasions the Great Seal was placed in the custody of the master of the Rolls, in the absence of the chancellor, under the seals of two of the clerks, of whom Henry de Edenestowe was one (*Hardy's Catal.*); and in 20 Edward III., 1346, he is named for a loan to the king of 100*l.* (*N. Fœdera*, iii. 69.)

EDENHAM, GEOFFREY DE, had property in Lincolnshire, where there is a parish of that name. He was made a judge of the King's Bench on January 18, 1331, 4 Edward III., and is last mentioned, with Thomas de Longevillers, as possessing the manor of Aykle in Lincolnshire in 15 Edward III. (*Abb. Rot. Orig.* ii. 110, 138; *Rot. Parl.* ii. 446; *Cal. Inquis.* p. m. ii. 105.)

EDINGTON, WILLIAM DE (BISHOP OF WINCHESTER), was born at Edington, a parish in Wiltshire, where, when he became Bishop of Winchester, he built a church and founded a large chantry for a dean and twelve ministers. (*Monast.* vi. 535.)

He was educated at Oxford, and was presented in 1335 to the living of Cheriton in Hampshire, and also had a canonry in Salisbury Cathedral.

In 1341 he was receiver of the ninth granted by parliament (*N. Fœdera*, ii. 1154), and in 1343 he was keeper of the king's wardrobe. On April 10, 1344, he was appointed chancellor of the Exchequer, from which he was raised, at the end of two years, to the high and responsible office of treasurer. (*Cal. Rot. Pat.* 147, 154.) This he held for no less than ten years, and then only exchanged it for the higher post of chancellor.

On the death of Adam de Orlton he was placed in the vacant see of Winchester, by papal provision in his favour dated December 9, 1345; but he was wise enough to renounce the pope's nomination as prejudicial to the rights of the crown; and the king, 'of his special favour, and not by virtue of the said bulls,' accepted his fealty, and restored the temporalities to him on the 15th of the following February. (*Cal. Rot. Pat.* 153; *N. Fœdera*, iii. 39, 64, 69; *Devon's Issue Roll*, 150.)

His treasurership was illustrated by the unfortunate introduction of two new coins, called a groat and a half-groat, the real worth of which was so much less than their nominal value as to produce a corresponding increase in the price of all articles of consumption throughout the kingdom.

On the institution of the order of the Garter in 1349 Edward constituted him the prelate of it, perpetuating the dignity in his successors of the see of Winchester. In 1355 he was left one of the custodes of the kingdom in the absence of the king on his renewed invasion of France.

The Great Seal was placed in his hands, with the title of chancellor, on November 27, 1356, 30 Edward III., and he retained it for more than six years, during which he preserved the royal favour without losing the confidence of the people. He was, as the record says, 'gratefully absolved' from its duties on February 19, 1363.

He survived little more than three years, still continuing high in the confidence of his sovereign. Shortly before his death the monks of Canterbury elected him archbishop, on the decease of Simon Islip; but he refused the proffered dignity, humorously saying that, though Canterbury was the higher rack, Winchester was the better manger.

He died on October 7, 1366, and was buried at Edington. (*Godwin*, 225.)

EGERTON, THOMAS (BARON ELLESMERE, VISCOUNT BRACKLEY), whose surname was assumed from a manor in Cheshire so called, possessed by his father's ancestors when Domesday Book was compiled, was the natural son of Sir Richard Egerton, of Ridley in the same county, by a young woman named Alice Sparke.

He was born in 1540, and about 1556 was admitted a commoner at Brasenose

College, Oxford, where he remained for three years. He then entered Lincoln's Inn, and was called to the bar in 1572. He became governor in 1580, Lent reader in 1582, and treasurer in 1587. He practised principally in the Court of Chancery, and was raised to the office of solicitor-general on June 28, 1581. It is related that this appointment arose from the admiration of Queen Elizabeth on hearing him argue in a cause against the crown, when she is said to have exclaimed, 'In my troth, he shall never plead against me again.' (*Life of Egerton*, 8.)

During the intervals of his laborious avocations his chief relaxation was in the sports of the field, and several noble clients gave him licence to 'hunt and kill' in their parks and manors.

Egerton held the office of solicitor-general for the space of eleven years, till he became attorney-general on June 2, 1592, and so remained for nearly two years. During this long period of office he was of course engaged in all the prosecutions for high treason and offences against the state. His name appears in those against Campion and others in 1581, against Abingdon and others in 1586, against Secretary Davison in 1587, against Philip Earl of Arundel and against Sir Richard Knightly in 1589, and against Sir John Perrot in 1592. (*State Trials*, i. 1051-1322.) If these criminal proceedings were to be judged according to the present enlightened views with regard to the administration of the law, not one of the persons engaged in them would escape condemnation. But this would be palpably unjust. With whatever abhorrence the iniquitous principles on which these trials were conducted may be now regarded, the only fair enquiry which can be raised with respect to the advocates employed in them is whether they exceeded their duty according to the practice which then prevailed. Looking through the Reports from this point of view, Egerton must receive a full acquittal from all imputation of harshness towards the prisoners.

In 1593 the office of chamberlain of Chester was conferred upon him, and soon after he was knighted. By this title he was promoted to the mastership of the Rolls on April 10, 1594. So active and efficient did he prove himself in this office that the queen at once constituted him lord keeper on the death of Sir John Puckering, delivering the Great Seal to him on May 6, 1596.

His appointment arose entirely from the high reputation he had attained for his legal knowledge and integrity, and not only without the intervention of any courtly interest, but even, it is said, in opposition to the wishes and endeavours of Lord Burleigh, and his son Sir Robert Cecil. Fuller says (i. 186) that 'all Christendom afforded not a person which carried more gravity in his countenance and behaviour, ... so much that many have gone to the Chancery on purpose truly to see his venerable garb (happy they who had no other business), and were highly pleased with so acceptable a spectacle;' adding that 'his outward case was nothing in comparison with his inward abilities, quick wit, solid judgment, ready utterance.' He still retained the place of master of the Rolls, and executed during the rest of the reign the whole business of the Court of Chancery in his double capacity. The intrigues of the lawyers who aspired to the second place were counteracted by his influence with the queen, and her conviction that he needed no assistance.

In the foolish *émeute* raised by the Earl of Essex in February 1600, so fatal to himself, the grave lord keeper was placed in a position of some danger. On the queen's being informed of the earl's seditious meeting in Essex House, she sent the lord keeper there, accompanied by the lord chief justice and other lords of the council, 'to understand the cause of this their assembly, and to let them know that if they had any particular cause of grief against any persons whatever, it should be heard, and they should have justice.' On being admitted they found the courtyard crowded with armed men, who, after the lord keeper had delivered the queen's message, cried out, 'Kill them!' 'Cast the Great Seal out of the window!' &c. The earl, under pretence of conferring privately with them, took the lords into his back chamber, and, telling them that he was going to the lord mayor and sheriffs of London, and would be back in half an hour, left them under lock and key, 'guarded by Sir John Davis and others with musketshot.' There they were detained from ten o'clock in the morning till four in the afternoon, when Sir Ferdinando Gorges, who had joined Essex in his progress through the city, and found that he received no encouragement, hastened back and released them. Considering how much the earl was indebted to Egerton, who had always acted as a sincere and considerate friend, it is to be hoped that his allegation that he locked up the counsellors for their security against his irritated partisans was founded in truth; but the Earl of Rutland in his examination acknowledged that it was purposed to take the lord keeper with them to the court, which they intended to surprise. (*State Trials*, 1340-7.)

During Queen Elizabeth's life Egerton enjoyed her utmost confidence and favour. She employed him in various treaties with the Dutch and the Danes, in the management of which he showed himself a good diplomatist; and she entrusted him with great powers under several special commissions, which he exercised with mildness and moderation. Within eight months of her death she paid him the honourable but burdensome compliment of a three days' visit to his mansion at Harefield in Middlesex, the enormous expense attending which may well account for her majesty's subjects dreading such visitations. (*Egerton Papers*, 340-7.)

No sooner did King James hear of his peaceful accession to the throne than he issued a mandate from Holyrood House, dated April 5, 1603, appointing Egerton keeper of the Seal during pleasure, who met the king on his arrival at Broxbourne in Hertfordshire, on May 3, when his appointment was confirmed. He was also continued in the office of master of the Rolls till the 19th of the same month, Edward Bruce, Lord Kinloss, being then named as his successor. On delivering him the new Great Seal on July 19 his majesty created him Baron of Ellesmere in Shropshire, and on the 24th he was constituted lord chancellor. He held this high position for nearly fourteen years under King James, which, in addition to the seven years under Elizabeth, makes his term of service as the head of the law extend to the long period of twenty-one years. Few have filled so prominent a station with so much honour and so few enemies. Looking at the character of the two monarchs whom he served, he must have been endowed with more than ordinary wisdom, prudence, and learning, to suffer no alienation from the caprices of either, and to preserve such continued ascendency in their councils, without degrading himself by that abject and humiliating flattery to which they were both too much accustomed.

He was elected chancellor of Oxford in 1610, and his presidency lasted till within two months of his death, when he resigned it on January 24, 1617.

The best mode of judging of the character of an individual is to see the reputation which he held among his contemporaries of various grades. That of Egerton will stand the ordeal. Camden records an anagram on his name, 'GESTAT HONOREM,' which would not have been discovered if it had not been applicable; Ben Jonson wrote three epigrams in his praise, one of them the last time he sat as chancellor; and Bishop Hacket describes him as one 'qui nihil in vitâ nisi laudandum, aut fecit, aut dixit, aut sensit.' Among the writers of the next generation, Fuller gives the same testimony; and Anthony Wood says, 'His memory was much celebrated by epigrams while he was living, and after his death all of the long robe lamented his loss.'

Among the most eminent was Sir John Davies, the poet, statesman, and lawyer, who, after summing up the characteristics of a good chancellor, gracefully applies them to Lord Ellesmere. (*Preface to his Reports*.)

He is said to have been the first law chancellor since the Reformation who entertained a chaplain in his family. This was Dr. John Williams, who subsequently filled the same office as his patron, and became also Archbishop of York. Another eminent man, Dr. Donne, afterwards dean of St. Paul's, spent many years under Lord Ellesmere's roof, as his secretary, and there formed that secret connection with his wife Anne Moore, the niece of the chancellor's second marriage, which had so fatal an influence on his earlier fortunes.

Few of his judicial decisions are reported; but in the case of the post-nati, being the question whether persons born in Scotland after the accession of King James to the throne of England were aliens in the latter country, and therefore disabled from holding lands there, he delivered an elaborate judgment that they were entitled to all the rights of natural-born subjects, which by the king's command he published in 1609. Twelve out of the fourteen judges concurring in his opinion, his remarks on the doubts of the other two afford a curious specimen of the extraordinary manner in which Scripture allusions were introduced into the oratory of the period. He said, 'The apostle Thomas doubted of the resurrection of the Lord Jesus Christ, when all the rest of the apostles did firmly beleeve it; but this his doubting confirmed, in the whole Church, the faith of the resurrection. The two worthy and learned judges that have doubted in this case, as they beare his name, so I doubt not but their doubting hath given occasion to cleare the doubt in others, and so to confirme in both the kingdomes, both for the present and the future, the truth of the judgement in this case.' He does not name the two dissentients, and it is uncertain which they were, as three of the judges who pronounced their opinion were named Thomas —viz., Sir Thomas Fleming, Sir Thomas Walmesley, and Sir Thomas Foster, all of the Common Pleas. (*State Trials*, ii. 669.)

Besides the publication of this judgment, he printed no other work during his life; but he left several valuable manuscripts.

He objected strongly to the Statute of Wills, passed in the reign of Henry VIII., and he was wont to tell the following merry story as an illustration of its evils:—'A friar coming to visit a great man in his sickness, and finding him past memory, took opportunity, according to the custom of the times, to make provision for the monastery whereof he was, and, finding that the sick man could only speak some one syllable, which was for the most part "Yea" or "Nay," in an imperfect voice, forthwith took upon him to make his will; and demanding of him, "Will you give such a piece of land to our house to pray for your soul?" the dying man sounded "Yea." Then he asked him, "Will you give such land to the maintenance of lights to our Lady?" The sound was again "Yea." Whereupon he boldly asked him many such questions. The son and heir standing by, and hearing his land going away so fast by his father's word "Yea," thought fit to ask one question as well as the friar, which was, "Shall I take a cudgel, and beat this friar out of the chamber?" The sick man's answer was again "Yea," which the son quickly performed, and saved unto himself his father's lands.' (*Archæologia*, xxv. 384.)

In the latter part of his judicial career he was annoyed by Sir Edward Coke's attempt to restrain the jurisdiction of the Court of Chancery, and by the proceedings which were taken, not only against certain suitors there, but against the counsel who were engaged in the causes, and even the masters in Chancery to whom they were referred, to subject them to the penalties of præmunire, to which, under an old statute, all persons were subject who impeached the judgments of any of the king's courts. The enquiry resulted in the complete triumph of Lord Ellesmere, by the confirmation of the powers of his court, and it had no little effect in disgracing Coke, its instigator.

On November 7, 1616, the king rewarded his long services by advancing him in the peerage to the title of Viscount Brackley, which the wits of Westminster Hall, who objected to his interference with the judgments of the common law courts, converted into Viscount Break-law. He had in 1613, and several times since, requested the king to allow him to retire from his arduous post, the duties of which he felt were too heavy for his increasing age and infirmities. Sickness at last compelled him to press his resignation, and the Close Roll records that on March 3, 1617, being ill at his residence, York House, he was visited by the king himself, who then freed him from the custody of the Great Seal, but limited his retirement to two years. Within two weeks from this time, however, his earthly career was closed. He died on March 15, and his body being removed to Doddleston in Cheshire, was there buried.

The king, who appears to have regarded him with great affection, is said to have parted from him with tears of gratitude and respect, and to have signified his intention to raise him to an earldom. Though death prevented the chancellor from receiving this last mark of his sovereign's favour, little more than two months elapsed before his majesty proved his sincerity by creating the heir Earl of Bridgewater in Somersetshire on May 27, 1617. This title was changed into a dukedom in 1720, but both have since become extinct. The earldom, however, was revived in 1840 in the grand-nephew of the last duke.

The chancellor was thrice married, but had issue by his first wife only. She was Elizabeth, daughter of Thomas Ravenscroft, Esq., of Bretton in Flintshire. His second wife was Elizabeth, sister to Sir George More, knight, of Losely Farm, Surrey, lieutenant of the Tower, and widow, first of Richard Polstead, Esq., of Abury in the same county, and then of Sir John Wolley, knight, chancellor of the order of the Garter. His third wife was Alice, daughter of Sir John Spencer, of Althorpe, knight, and widow of Ferdinando, fifth Earl of Derby.

ELDON, EARL OF. *See* J. SCOTT.

ELERIUS was a monk in the priory of Cogges in Oxfordshire, of which he became prior in 1227. From that he was promoted to the abbacy of the monastery of Pershore in Worcestershire on March 19, 1251, 35 Henry III. In August of that year he was appointed the king's escheator on this side Trent, and continued in that office till 1255 (*Excerpt. e Rot. Fin.* ii. 112-220), in which year he was employed by the king on a financial commission into Wales, where he was most honourably received by Llewellyn and his nobles. (*Leland's Coll.* i. 243.)

In 1257-8 he is inserted in Madox's list of barons of the Exchequer (ii. 319), on the authority of the memoranda of that year; but he is not mentioned afterwards in that court. He retired from the abbacy of Pershore on October 24, 1262, having previously granted to it his manor 'de Hauekesburi.' (*Monast.* ii. 412, 418, vi. 1003.)

ELIOT, RICHARD, was allied to the ancient family of that name first seated in Devonshire and afterwards in Cornwall, a member of which was raised to the peerage in 1784 as Baron Eliot of St. Germains, whose son was created Earl of St. Germains in 1815. Richard was an advocate of the Middle Temple in 8 Henry VII. In 1503 he took the degree of the coif, and in 1506 he was appointed one of the king's serjeants. On April 26, 1513, he was raised to the bench of the Common Pleas, and exercised his judicial duties there till 1522. By his will he directed his body to be buried in the cathedral of Salisbury. (*Orig.* 47, 113, 215.)

ELIOT, WILLIAM, was named master of the Rolls, in conjunction with Robert Morton, on November 13, 1485, to hold for life and for the life of the survivor. There is no evidence of his exercising the duties of the office, nor of his retaining it, after his partner was consecrated Bishop of Worcester in February 1487. On the contrary, David William is mentioned in the office on the 22nd of that month, and William Eliot as acting as a simple master in Chancery, being named in that character as a receiver of petitions in parliament from the fourth to the eleventh year of the reign. (*Rot. Parl.* vi. 346, 409, 441, 458.)

ELLENBOROUGH, LORD. See E. LAW.

ELLESMERE, LORD. See T. EGERTON.

ELLESWORTH, SIMON DE, had a grant in 11 Edward I. from Simon de Torp of lands in Torveston, Bucks, with the advowson of the church there. (*Abb. Placit.* 206.) He was not a regular justice itinerant, but merely for pleas of the forest, in which he is mentioned as acting in 1292 for the county of Essex. In 23 Edward I. the custody of the religious houses belonging to France in the counties of Northampton, Rutland, Cambridge, and Huntingdon was committed to him, and in the next year he was joined with the chief justice of the forests in a commission to rent out the wastes of the forests beyond the Trent. (*Abb. Rot. Orig.* i. 91, 94.) In 21 Edward I. he was one of the sureties for the appearance of William de Luda, Bishop of Ely, on a complaint made against him by the Archbishop of Dublin (*Rot. Parl.* i. 112); and on Ellesworth's death, in 25 Edward I., the bishop returned the obligation by becoming security for the payment of his debts to the crown. (*Madox*, ii. 44.)

ELLIS, WILLIAM, son of Thomas, thrice mayor and once M. P. for Norwich, was a member of Lincoln's Inn, where he became a reader in Lent 1502. He was made a baron of the Exchequer in 1523, being so named in the list of the judges, &c., who were assessed to the subsidy in November of that year. He continued on the bench till 1536.

He was lord of the manor of Attlebridge in Norfolk, where his son William, whom he had by Elizabeth his wife, lies buried. (*Blomefield's Norwich*, ii. 199 ; *Orig.* 250.)

ELLIS, WILLIAM. Noble, in his 'House of Cromwell' (i. 437), states that the William Ellis who was solicitor-general to the protector became judge of the Common Pleas under Charles II.; and, notwithstanding the apparent improbability that one who had held so prominent a ministerial office under the Commonwealth should be selected to fill a judicial one under the monarchy, there seems little reason to doubt that the solicitor and the judge were one and the same individual. The appointment as solicitor is dated 1654, and the judge was chosen bencher of Gray's Inn in that year; he was a member of the parliaments of 1640 and 1654 for Boston, and in those of 1656 and 1659 for Grantham, the first being the place that the judge represented afterwards in 1679, and the last being the place of his father's residence : facts sufficient to support the identity.

The family of Ellis, or Ellys, is said to have been originally Welsh, but afterwards to have settled in Lincolnshire. Sir William Ellis, an ancestor of the judge, was an eminent lawyer in the reign of Queen Elizabeth, and from him descended Thomas Ellis of Grantham, who had two sons, Thomas and William. The former was made a baronet in 1660 for his loyalty during the rebellion, but the title became extinct in 1742; the latter sided with the opponents to the crown and was the future judge. (*Wotton's Baronet.* iii. 90.)

William Ellis was born about 1609, and was sent for his education to Caius College, Cambridge, where he took his degrees of B.A. and M.A. in 1632 and 1636. Admitted into Gray's Inn, he was called to the bar in 1634. The town of Boston returned him to the Long Parliament in 1640, where he subscribed the Solemn League and Covenant; but, in consequence of voting 'that the king's answers to the propositions of both houses were a ground for peace,' he was one of those excluded from the house by Pride's Purge, in December 1648. Whitelocke states (p. 405) that he was re-admitted in the following June, and accordingly he is found among the Rump who resumed their sittings on the dissolution of Protector Richard's government in 1659. (*Parl. Hist.* ii. 611, iii. 1248, 1547.)

In the meantime, however, he had accepted office under Cromwell, being appointed solicitor-general to his highness on May 24, 1654, the functions of which he continued to perform under Protector Richard. In the parliament of 1654 he was returned for Boston, and in those of 1656 and 1659 for Grantham, having in the interim received a baronetcy from the protector. In Richard's parliament he showed great activity, but all his speeches, as reported by Burton, were in a sober and accommodating spirit. Having from the beginning been an adherent to the supporters of the Commonwealth, he was opposed in his attempt to be re-elected at Grantham to the Healing Parliament of 1660. Probably his brother's loyalty, added to his own insignificance, preserved him from censure or even notice at the Restoration. (*Parl. Hist.* iii. 1430, 1480, 1533, iv. 4, 1081.)

Losing his title and his place on the king's arrival, he fell back into the legal ranks, and pursued his profession with so much success that, after having been chosen reader of his inn in 1663, he was called serjeant in 1669, and made one of the king's serjeants in 1671, when he was knighted.

He was appointed a judge of the Common Pleas on December 18, 1672, but in October 1676 he was removed from his place for some political reason not stated, but probably for the mere purpose of giving his seat to Scroggs, whom the minister Lord Danby favoured. His dismissal was evidently not caused by any reflection on his character, for he was replaced in less than three years, when Danby's influence had ceased. In the interval he again entered parliament, being chosen in 1679 by his old constituents at Boston, while his nephew, Sir William, was selected for Grantham. These elections may have been the cause of his being recalled to the bench on the 1st of the next May, when he was also allowed to resume his former precedency. He died at his chambers in Serjeants' Inn, Fleet Street, on December 3, 1680, leaving no issue. (*Sir T. Raymond,* 217, 251, 407.)

ELY, NICHOLAS DE (BISHOP OF WINCHESTER), was appointed archdeacon of Ely about 1249, 33 Henry III., and on October 18, 1260, the barons placed the Great Seal in his hands. He kept it only till the 5th of the following July, when King Henry transferred it into the hands of Walter de Merton, but by a separate patent specially recommended Nicholas for his good service.

In the following year the king appointed him his treasurer; and on July 12, 1263, the Great Seal was again entrusted to him, with the title of chancellor. On the king's going abroad soon afterwards, the Seal remained in his possession, with a prohibition, however, from affixing it to any instrument which was not attested by Hugh le Despencer, the chief justiciary. In the course of the next year he resigned the office of chancellor, and resumed that of treasurer. (*Madox,* ii. 319.)

In September 1266 he was elected Bishop of Worcester, from which see he was on February 24, 1267, translated to Winchester, over which diocese he presided about twelve years, and died on February 12, 1280, at Waverley in Surrey, where his body was buried, his heart being sent for interment at Winchester. (*Godwin,* 222, 261; *Le Neve,* 73, &c.; *Rapin,* iii. 142.)

ELY, RALPH DE, was according to Madox (ii. 318) a baron of the Exchequer in 24 and 27 Henry III., but there is no other notice of his name.

ELY, WILLIAM OF, a canon of the church of Lincoln, was the king's treasurer during the whole of the reign of John and part of that of Henry III. He is mentioned in that character as one of the justiciers before whom fines were acknowledged in 10 John, 1208, and Dugdale records his death in 8 Henry III., 1223, calling him then Angliæ Thesaurarius. (*Rot. Chart.* 49.)

ENGAINE, WARNER, is first mentioned in 19 Henry III., 1235, when, being then custos of the honor of Richmond, he was directed to deliver it up to Alexander Bacon. (*Madox,* i. 335.) In 1240 he was one of the justices itinerant for the northern counties, before whom a fine was levied at York. At this time he had the custody of the king's manors, and failing to account for the proceeds in 29 Henry III., his person was attached, and he was called upon to appear before the barons of the Exchequer. (*Madox,* ii. 243.) On his death, in 1253, he was still indebted to the crown, as the king then granted his brother, James Engaine, permission to pay the balance due into the Exchequer, by half-yearly instalments of 100 shillings each. (*Excerpt. e Rot. Fin.* ii. 166.)

ENGLEFIELD, ALAN DE, called so from the place of that name in Berkshire, of which he was the parson, was added to the commission of the justices itinerant for that county in 9 Henry III. He was at the same time coroner for Staffordshire, and possessed property, not only in both these counties, but also in Oxfordshire and Buckinghamshire, all of which were seized into King John's hands, but restored to him on returning to his allegiance in 1 Henry III. (*Rot. Claus.* i. 300; ii. 76, 124.)

ENGLEFIELD, WILLIAM DE, probably the nephew of the above, was sheriff of Devonshire in 36 Henry III., 1251, and the two following years. (*Madox,* i. 597, ii. 193.) In 1255 and the two following years he was one of the justices itinerant who visited several counties, and again in 1260. About that time it seems probable that he was made a justicier at Westminster, for the Rotulus de Finibus (*Excerpt.* ii. 335) contains an entry of an amercement imposed by him. From 46 to 50 Henry III. he was employed in a judicial character. (*Ibid.* ii. 422–445.)

He derived his name from the town of Englefield in Berkshire, where it is said his family had property above two hundred years before the Conquest. He was the son of John Englefield, of that place, and was succeeded by his own son John, one of whose descendants is the subject of the next article.

ENGLEFIELD, THOMAS. In regular descent from the above William came Sir Thomas Englefield, justice of Chester, and twice speaker of the House of Commons, who died about 1514, leaving by his wife Margery, daughter of Sir Richard Danvers, of Prescot, a large family. His second son was Thomas the judge, who on the death of his elder brother without issue succeeded to the inheritance, having previously entered the Middle Temple, where he was reader in 1520.

In 1519 he was sheriff of Berkshire and Oxfordshire. In 1521 he was called to the degree of the coif, and on December 3,

1523, he was advanced to be king's serjeant, at the same time receiving a grant of 100*l.* a year for life.

From the Year Books it appears that he sat as judge of the Common Pleas in Michaelmas 1526, 18 Henry VIII., being knighted at the same time. He performed the functions of his office till his death, which took place on September 28, 1537. To his judicial duties were added those of master of the king's wards, which he held in conjunction with Sir William Paulet. He was buried at Englefield, where there is a brass memorial of him in his robes, and of his wife Elizabeth, daughter of Sir Robert Throgmorton, of Coughton, Warwickshire.

His eldest son Francis lost the paternal estate by attainder for high treason in 35 Elizabeth. His second son John, seated at Wootton Basset, was the father of another Francis, created a baronet in 1612—a title which expired in 1822. (*Wotton's Baronet.* i. 254; *Dugdale's Orig.* 47, 215; *Kal. of Exch.* i. cxxxix.)

ERDINGTON, GILES DE, was the son of Thomas de Erdington, of an opulent family seated at Erdington, near Aston, in Warwickshire, who was honourably and frequently employed by King John, and died in 2 Henry III. His mother was Roesia, the widow of Adam de Cokefield. Giles was evidently a minor when his father died, and so continued for the twelve following years, for it was not till April 12, 1230, 14 Henry III., that he obtained permission from the king to pay his father's debts by instalments of 100 shillings a year. (*Excerpt. e Rot. Fin.* i. 195.) Though there are no reports of the period, it may be presumed that he practised in the courts of Westminster. He was made a judge before August 1251, 35 Henry III., the first date of a payment for an assize to be taken before him, and when he held pleas for the city of London. He retained his place on the bench till December 1267, soon after which he died. (*Ibid.* ii. 113–464; *Abb. Placit.* 137.)

Although Dugdale, in his 'Origines Juridiciales' (21), calls him a canon of St. Paul's, he makes him in the 'Baronage' (ii. 112) father of Henry, who succeeded to his estates, and whose son, also Henry, was summoned to parliament in 9 Edward III., but not afterwards.

ERLE, WILLIAM, is the lineal descendant of a very ancient family of that name, settled in Somersetshire, from the time of our earliest kings, several members of which have rendered themselves eminent for their services to the country. He is the son of the Rev. Christopher Erle, of Gillingham in Dorsetshire, and was born at Fifehead-Magdalen in its neighbourhood in 1793. After going through Winchester School he entered New College, Oxford, where he took his degree in civil law in 1818. In November of the next year he was called to the bar by the society of the Middle Temple, and joined the Western Circuit. He also purchased the situation of one of the counsel of the palace court, in which he acquired those habits of business which are of slow attainment in the superior courts. His erudition as a lawyer and his attainments as a scholar soon insured him such full employment on the circuit and in Westminster Hall that he was made king's counsel in 1834.

The city of Oxford returned him as their representative in parliament in 1837, and, though his support was given to the liberal party in the house, the conservative prime minister, Sir Robert Peel, regarding his merits only, did not hesitate to appoint him a judge of the Commons Pleas on November 6, 1844, whereupon he was knighted. He sat in that court nearly two years, and in October 1846 was transferred to the Queen's Bench. For little less than thirteen years he remained in this seat, when he was promoted on June 24, 1859, to take the vacant place of chief justice of the Common Pleas, in which high position the urbanity of his manner added force and effect to the unquestioned impartiality of his decisions.

These qualities were eloquently recognised by the attorney-general in his farewell address on the chief justice's retirement from the bench on November 26, 1866, after a judicial life of twenty-two years. He still gives his services at the privy council.

He married the daughter of the Rev. David Williams, warden of New College and prebendary of Winchester.

ERMYN, OR ARMYN, WILLIAM, possessed property at Osgodby in Lincolnshire. In 2 Richard II. he was treasurer of Calais, and in 3 Henry IV., 1402, he is mentioned as a baron of the Exchequer. Neither the date of his appointment nor of his death is recorded; but he was the ancestor of a knightly family which long flourished in the county. (*Devon's Issues Exch.* 211; *Cal. Inquis.* p. m. iii. 199.)

ERNLE, JOHN, whose name was derived from a family which had flourished at Ernle, a manor near Chichester in Sussex, before the reign of Edward I., was the second son of John Ernle, of Ernle, and Agnes, daughter and heir of Simon Best, who brought him her mother's inheritance of the manor of Etchilhampton in Wiltshire. He was made solicitor-general in 1507; and in 1509, a few days after the accession of Henry VIII., he was promoted to the attorney-generalship, which he occupied till he was raised to the chief seat of the Court of Common Pleas, on January

27, 1519, whereupon he received the honour of knighthood. He did not enjoy his presidency much above two years, his death occurring in 1521. He was buried at Ernle, where his remains lie under a monument still existing. He had two wives: the first was Anne, daughter of Constantine Darel, Esq., of Collinbourne, Wilts; and the second was Margaret, daughter of Edmund Dawtry, Esq.

From his second son, John, descended Sir John Ernle, knight, chancellor of the Exchequer to Charles II.; and also Walter Ernle, of Etchilhampton, who in 1660 was created a baronet—a title which became extinct in 1787.

ERSKINE, THOMAS (LORD ERSKINE). That only one short year of judicial life should have distinguished an advocate who retained for the long space of twenty-eight years the most prominent place at the British bar would naturally excite surprise, were it not for the recollection that the party to which he was attached was during that period wholly deprived of the power of selecting the law officers of the crown, except for an equally short interval at the beginning of his career, when he was too young and inexperienced to expect promotion. Such was the position of the Hon. Thomas Erskine in 1806, when he was raised *per saltum* to the highest office of judicial dignity; although without a single interruption from his very first entrance into the forensic arena in 1778, his progress had been one continued march of triumph.

This eminent advocate was the youngest of three sons of Henry David, Earl of Buchan, by Agnes, daughter of Sir James Steuart, Bart., the eldest of whom succeeded to his father's title, and the two others, Henry and Thomas, became equally distinguished for their extraordinary talents, the former being twice lord advocate of Scotland, in 1783 and 1806, and the latter earning honours in England which are now to be recorded.

Thomas Erskine was born at Edinburgh on January 21, 1750, and received his education at the High School of Edinburgh and the university of St. Andrews, the very restricted income of the earl his father forbidding any other advantage. In 1764 he left his native country as a midshipman in the 'Tartar,' and during the four years he remained at sea he visited America and the West Indies. He retired from the service in 1768, and entering the army as an ensign in the Royals or First Regiment of Foot, attained his lieutenancy in April 1773. While yet an ensign, in 1770, and when little more than twenty years of age, he married Frances, daughter of Daniel Moore, Esq., M.P. for Marlow, and spent the next two years with his regiment at Minorca, devoting his leisure hours to English literature with so much avidity that there was scarcely a passage in Shakspeare, Milton, Dryden, or Pope which he could not recite from memory. He used to relate that while in Minorca he not only read prayers to the regiment, but also composed and preached two sermons.

Returning to England in 1772, his agreeable manners and pleasant vivacity soon procured him access to the society of the metropolis, among the distinguished members of which are the names of Mrs. Montagu, Jeremy Bentham, Dr. Johnson, Boswell, Cradock, and Sheridan. He also commenced authorship in a pamphlet 'On the Prevailing Abuses in the British Army,' which had a considerable circulation. After serving in the army for seven years, he saw too palpably that without interest that profession would not secure a provision for his increasing family, and he could not but feel that his talents were more likely to be productive in a wider field for their exercise. Resolving, therefore, to enter the legal profession, he sold his lieutenancy, and was admitted a member of Lincoln's Inn in 1775. His next step was to be matriculated at one of the universities in order that by taking his degree his time of legal probation should be shortened from five to three years. With this object he entered Trinity College, Cambridge, on January 13, 1776, as a nobleman's son, which entitled him to a Master of Arts degree in two years without examination. This did not prevent him from striving for and obtaining the college prize for English declamation, the harbinger of his future fame. His degree was conferred in June 1778, and on July 3 he was called to the bar.

During the interval between his matriculation and his call he kept his terms both at Cambridge and Lincoln's Inn, dividing his time between literary and legal studies. For the latter purpose he placed himself under the instruction of Sir Francis Buller, and afterwards of Sir George Wood, both subsequently raised to the bench; and by steady application gained that knowledge of the principles of the law, and that mastery of the intricacies of special pleading, so necessary for his future success. He also attended a debating society in order to obtain fluency and confidence, and to accustom himself to the sound of his own voice. His circumstances were so straitened during this period that he himself acknowledged, and indeed vaunted, that his family were usually feed on cow-beef and tripe, and that when he was called to the bar he was almost reduced to his last shilling. But his sanguine disposition and his courageous self-reliance supported him through all his difficulties.

No sooner was he called to the bar than there was a propitious change in his circumstances. From being almost penniless he became suddenly affluent, and though a perfect novice in Westminster Hall, he was at once recognised as one of its brightest ornaments. One happy accident followed by another gave him the fortunate opportunity. Happening to dine in company with Captain Baillie, against whom a rule to show cause in the following Michaelmas Term why a criminal information should not be filed for a libel on the officers of Greenwich Hospital had been recently obtained, Erskine, in ignorance that the captain was present, expressed himself freely on the doomed pamphlet, which was then the general subject of conversation. He spoke with so much warmth and indignation against the tyranny and abuses imputed to Lord Sandwich, first lord of the Admiralty, and the officers of the hospital, that the captain, enquiring who he was, determined to employ him as his advocate. Erskine had not then taken his seat in court, and his first retainer and first brief was as counsel for the defence of Captain Baillie. But still, as he was the last of five barristers retained on that side, he could not expect to have any opportunity of distinguishing himself; but again fortune favoured him. His four seniors expended so much time in their arguments, and Mr. Hargrave was obliged by illness so often to interrupt his address, that at the close of it Lord Mansfield adjourned the court. Erskine therefore had to commence the proceedings on the next morning, and in a speech as powerful and effective as was ever heard in court he exposed and stigmatised the practices of Lord Sandwich and the officers of the hospital, with so much eloquent invective that the rule was dismissed, and Erskine was triumphant. The effect of this brilliant oration was so great that retainers flowed in upon him from all quarters, and from that time forward there was scarcely a cause or a trial of importance in which he was not engaged. This first appearance occurred on November 28, 1778, and as a consequence of his success he was employed in the following January to defend Lord Keppel, on the charges brought against him by Sir Hugh Pallisser. The trial lasted thirteen days, and, though from the restricted privileges of a counsel at a court-martial he was not allowed to examine witnesses nor to make a speech in defence, he suggested the questions to be put, and composed the address which Lord Keppel was to deliver. To the excellence of that address his noble client attributed his triumphant and unanimous acquittal, testifying his gratitude by the noble present of 1000*l*.

Though acquiring in less than a year the lead over many an elderly aspirant, his success was productive of no jealousy or illwill. His manners were so pleasing and his bearing so unpretending that he soon became a universal favourite, and his competitors willingly submitted to the superiority of his genius. His business became so extensive that he found it necessary to refuse to hold junior briefs, and he accordingly received a patent of precedence in May 1783, before he had been five years at the bar.

The coalition ministry, of which his whig friends formed a part, had in the previous March come into power, and, being naturally desirous of the assistance of one so much famed for his eloquence, procured his election for Portsmouth in the following November. He made his first speech on the introduction of Mr. Fox's India bill, and continued to support it in its progress through the house. When the rejection of that bill by the Lords caused the dismissal of his friends from the government, he took a prominent part in the vexatious attempts in the remainder of the session to oust Mr. Pitt, the new minister. The natural consequence was that, with the dissolution of that parliament in March 1784, Erskine was made one of 'Fox's Martyrs,' and his senatorial life suffered an interruption of more than six years. In truth, he had somewhat disappointed public expectation. His eloquence was less suited to the senate than to the forum; and, though he made some effective addresses, he was considered to have been cowed by the superior powers of Mr. Pitt, against whom he was indiscreetly put in collision.

During this interval he devoted himself to his profession, in the pursuit of which he increased his fame and fortune. Besides his command of business in Westminster Hall and on the Home Circuit, he was called by special retainer to prosecute or defend very many important causes in other parts of the kingdom. Among those of a more public nature was his defence of Dr. Shipley, the dean of St. Asaph, for publishing a tract by Sir William Jones, when, in a contest with his former master, Mr. Justice Buller, he boldly insisted on the verdict of the jury being taken in the very words they used, and afterwards, in a speech which Charles Fox declared to be the finest piece of reasoning in the English language, contended for the power and right of the jury to determine whether the publication complained of was or was not a libel. Though the judgment was afterwards arrested, the judges decided against him on this question; but his argument was the death-blow to their doctrine, and led to the enactment of Mr. Fox's libel bill in 1792, which fully established the right of juries to give a general verdict on the whole matter in issue. At this time Mr. Erskine had regained his seat in parliament for his old borough, and had the satisfaction of seconding Mr. Fox's motion on bringing in the bill. At this time also he was attorney-general to the Prince of Wales, who on the formation of his establishment had nominated him to that office. Another triumph in libel cases was in his inimitable defence of Stockdale, prosecuted for publishing Logan's pamphlet against the managers on Hastings' trial, when his forcible argument for free discussion, and his impressive introduction of the celebrated illustration of the Indian chief, produced so enthusiastic an effect on the auditory, and induced the jury, even before the libel bill was passed, to acquit the defendant.

When the French Revolution electrified the world, a schism arose among the whigs, many of whom, led by Burke, supported government in its efforts to counteract the spread of revolutionary principles in this country. The Prince of Wales took the alarm with this section, but Erskine, though his royal highness's attorney-general, and designed for the same office to the crown had the regency been established, had the spirit and independence to join the other section, led by Fox, to whom throughout his life he zealously adhered. Happening then to be retained for the defendant in the prosecution of Paine's 'Rights of Man,' attempts were made to induce him to refuse the brief; and on his firm refusal to do so, upon the principle that he was bound by professional etiquette to defend any man for whom he was retained, he received a message from the prince, unwillingly requesting him to resign his office, which he accordingly did in February 1793.

This episode of unpopularity was of short duration. In the next year he rose to the highest pitch of public admiration by the noble stand he made against the doctrine of constructive treason in his defence of Hardy, Horne Tooke, and Thelwall, severally indicted for high treason as members of societies professing parliamentary reform, but charged with conspiring to subvert the existing laws and constitution, and thus compassing the king's death. The trial of Hardy lasted eight days, that of Horne Tooke six days, and that of Thelwall four days, in all eighteen days, and each resulted in an acquittal, produced principally by the wondrous exertions, the powerful reasoning, the eloquence, and the tact of their advocate. This triumph was hailed by the general public as the preservation of the constitution from the perils that would have environed it if the subjects were liable to such proceedings. No further attempt has been since made to impute treason by construction or inference. The applause which Erskine received could scarcely be exceeded; honours flowed in to him from all quarters in the freedom of corporations, and the sale of his portrait and bust was excessive.

For the next twelve years he preserved his undisputed ascendency in the courts, and was engaged for the plaintiffs or defendants in almost every cause. In state trials the defence was generally entrusted to him as the advocate of liberty of speech, and resulted most frequently in verdicts of acquittal. In parliament he was always found on the liberal side, supporting Mr. Fox, and joining him in his temporary secession from the house. He published a pamphlet entitled 'A View of the Causes and Consequences of the present War with France,' of which no less than thirty-seven editions were called for. In it he made a violent attack on Mr. Pitt, against whom he had a strong animosity, arising, perhaps, from his consciousness of failure in competition with the minister in the senate. On Pitt's resignation in 1801, Mr. Addington offered Erskine the attorney-generalship, which from a doubt of the prince's approval he declined. He however supported that administration till it was superseded in 1804 by the return of Mr. Pitt, but he seldom addressed the house. In the following year the prince revived the office of chancellor to the duchy of Cornwall, and gave it to Mr. Erskine; and on the renewal of the war he for a time resumed his old profession by becoming colonel of the Law Association, a corps of volunteers which was familiarly called 'The Devil's Own.' It is curious that it should have fallen to his lot soon after to contend for the right of volunteers to resign, when the government wished to deprive them of that power; but, as usual, he was triumphant, the judges unanimously deciding that the service was entirely voluntary.

On Mr. Pitt's death in 1806 the whigs, after an exile from court of more than twenty years, were allowed a temporary taste of the sweets of office, and Erskine was certain to be a partaker. He would have preferred to preside over a common law court, conversant as he was with its rules and practice; but the existing chiefs, Lord Ellenborough and Sir James Mansfield, wisely resisting the temptation of the Great Seal, its possession was given to him on February 7, 1806, as lord high chancellor of Great Britain, and he was at the same time raised to the peerage by the title of Lord Erskine of Restormel Castle in Cornwall, a designation with which the Prince of Wales complimented him, as it had been the ancient residence of the Dukes of Cornwall. With whatever feelings of pride he went in state from his house in Lincoln's Inn Fields to take the oaths, or may have welcomed these rewards for his long public services in the cause of liberty, far greater must have been his gratification at the recognition of his private worth and personal character in the unprecedented address of congratulation which was unanimously voted to him by the whole bar of England. That body might well regret his retirement from its ranks, for never had they, and never could they expect to have, a leader whose hilarity of spirits, whose lively wit, and whose uniform kindness, added to such extraordinary powers, could secure at once their affection and respect.

Though little acquainted with the rules of equity or the practice of his new court, he had the wisdom to avail himself of the advice of more experienced men; and by his natural quickness of perception, his discretion and caution, he passed through his fourteen months of trial in so satisfactory a manner that only one of his decrees was appealed against, and that one, arising out of Mr. Thellusson's extraordinary will, was affirmed. In the trial of Lord Melville, Lord Erskine presided as chancellor, and acted with that dignity, firmness, and impartiality that excited universal admiration. As a peer of parliament he of course supported the measures introduced by his party, and had the satisfaction to announce the royal assent to the bill for the abolition of slavery. In the summer the death of his friend Mr. Fox was a source of sincere lamentation to him, which was followed in the following spring by the dissolution of the ministry, occasioned by the refusal of George III. to sanction a bill allowing Roman Catholics to hold commissions in the army. Though himself adverse to the measure, he shared in the dismissal, and gave up the Great Seal on April 7, 1807.

In the fifteen years during which he survived his loss of office he very rarely took a prominent part in the politics of the day; but on some occasions he exhibited the same command of argument and oratorical power which had formerly distinguished him. When the king's permanent illness necessitated a regency in 1810, Lord Erskine opposed the restrictions on his patron the Prince of Wales, who, in 1815, though he had deserted his old whig connections, complimented his former chancellor with the green ribbon of the order of the Thistle.

Lord Erskine now amused himself as a man of the world, mixing in all gay societies, and being acceptable to all by his liveliness and wit. His bon-mots and his vers de société at this time and while at the bar would fill a good-sized volume, and Mr. Townsend in his agreeable memoir has made a happy selection of them. He again ventured his fame by becoming an author on a more extended scale, and published a romance called 'Armata,' being a clever allegory, in the manner of Sir Thomas More's 'Utopia' and Dean Swift's 'Voyage to Laputa,' on the politics of England and the customs and manners of London life. It had a temporary popularity and passed through several editions, but from the want of interest in the story it is now almost forgotten.

When the popular tumults and discontent in 1817 led to the introduction of restrictive measures, Lord Erskine appeared again in the political world, and contended against them with all his ancient vigour. He stood boldly and prominently forward also in 1820 in defence of Queen Caroline, although by so doing he opposed his old patron and friend. But, deeming the queen an innocent and injured woman, he cast every personal consideration aside, and throughout the investigation battled on her part, and when the Bill of Pains and Penalties was withdrawn, he sounded its knell in the last speech he made in parliament. By this independent conduct his favour with the people, by whom he was almost forgotten, was revived, and was exhibited in every shape. His likeness was a treasure universally sought, addresses and municipal freedoms were showered upon him, and public dinners were given to do him honour. One, on which he most prided himself, was that at Edinburgh, which he had not visited since his departure from it as a midshipman in 1764, a period of fifty-seven years. In 1822 he published a 'Letter to Lord Liverpool' in support of the cause of the Greeks, proving that his love of freedom was unabated; and another pamphlet on agricultural distress, his advocacy of increased protection in which is strongly opposed to the principle of free trade that now prevails. His career was now drawing to its close. In the autumn of 1823, as he was proceeding by sea to pay a visit to his brother the Earl of Buchan at Dryburgh Abbey, he was suddenly attacked with inflammation in the chest. On landing he went direct to Ammondell, near Edinburgh, where the widow of his deceased brother Henry resided, and where the Earl of Buchan joined him. There he breathed his last on November 17, 1823, and his remains lie in the family burying-place at Uphall in the county of Linlithgow.

In the eloquent words of Lord Brougham, 'if there be yet among us the power of freely discussing the acts of our rulers; if there be yet the privilege of meeting for the promotion of needful reforms; if he who desires wholesome changes in our constitution be still recognised as a patriot, and not doomed to die the death of a traitor, let us acknowledge with gratitude that to this great man, under heaven, we owe this felicity of the times.' The courtesy of his manners, the cheerfulness of his disposition, the geniality of his wit, his 'generous impulses and honourable feelings,' and the wonderful power of his eloquence, live almost as vividly among the few who now survive as they impressed those who at his death erected a statute to his memory in Lincoln's Inn Hall. Against merits such as these the only failing that is suggested is a charge of egotism and vanity, with too great a tendency to introduce himself and the incidents of his life upon all occasions. Let those who laugh at him on that account ask themselves whether, if they had founded their fortunes in the same surprising manner, they could have altogether abstained from self-glorification.

Of the incidents of his private life there are few records. If they were mixed with some frailties, we may ask, What mortal is exempt from them? Whatever they were, they may be designated by the words of that rigorous moralist, Lord Kenyon, 'blots in the sun.' The great fortune which he must have acquired by his forensic success he lost by unfortunate speculations in Transatlantic funds, and by the purchase of an estate in Sussex, which produced nothing but brooms; so that at last he was obliged to part with his beautiful seat at Hampstead, and live upon the retiring allowance of chancellor.

He lost his first wife, after a union of thirty-five years, in December 1805, just before his attaining the peerage. His second wife was Miss Mary Buck. By both he left issue. Thomas, one of his sons by the first wife, having acquired judicial honours, is next to be noticed. (*Lives by Roscoe, Townsend, and Lord Campbell; Lord Brougham's Historical Sketches*; &c. &c.)

ERSKINE, THOMAS, the fourth son of the above celebrated advocate by his first wife, Frances, the daughter of Daniel Moore, Esq., was born on March 12, 1788, at No. 10 Serjeants' Inn, Fleet Street, then the abode of his father. He was educated at Harrow under Dr. Drury and Dr. Butler his successor. His career at school was interrupted by his father's elevation to the office of lord chancellor, whose inauguration he was summoned to attend, and who gave him the secretaryship of presentations, the duties of which did not require any great experience. At the same time he was entered at Trinity College, Cambridge, and in 1811 as a peer's son graduated as M.A., without residence or examination. In 1807 he became a member of Lincoln's Inn, commencing his study of the law as a pupil of the eminent special pleader Joseph Chitty, Esq., and acquired such a mastery of the science that in 1810 he began practice in the same branch on his own account. After a successful pursuit of it for three years, Mr. Erskine was called to the bar in 1813. He at first joined the Home Circuit, and afterwards availed himself of the privilege of changing it once, by attaching himself to the Western Circuit.

Taking no active part in political controversy, and more intent on the steady performance of his duties than in the pursuit of public distinction, he progressed slowly but surely, till he acquired such a position as to entitle him to claim the honour of a silk gown. He was appointed a king's counsel in 1827, and speedily acquired a place, if not among the first leaders of the common law bar, yet one of considerable distinction on his own circuit. His speeches as a leading advocate were not so much characterised by fluency or copiousness of language, or by strong appeals to the feelings, as by great clearness of statement, and, according to the subject of the case, placing it on a high moral ground, or treating it with dry humour and epigrammatic force. He possessed a power which in those days, when verdicts were more often won or lost on technical grounds than now, was of infinite importance,—he saw perfectly the points of attack and defence; and no one was more acute in detecting a latent non-suit in his opponent's pleadings. When Serjeant Wilde found on consultation that there was a weak point in his case, he would commonly ask, 'Whom have we against us?' and if the answer was 'Mr. Erskine,' would shake his head and say, 'Then we may be pretty sure this blot will be hit.'

When the new Court of Bankruptcy, established by stat. 1 and 2 Will. IV., c. 56, received the royal assent on October 20, 1831, Mr. Erskine was selected as the chief of the four judges who were thereby appointed as a Court of Review. Though the junior of his three colleagues, he soon by the unfeigned simplicity of his manner and attractive cordiality overcame any jealousy that might have existed among them; and by the clearness of his intellect, the soundness of his judgment, his great industry, impartiality, and care, amply justified the appointment. He presided over this court for eight years, assisting also in hearing appeals before the judicial committee of the privy council, and in the early period of its existence aiding greatly in shaping its proceedings into that course which has gradually raised it to so pre-eminent a rank among the judicial tribunals of the country. So effective were his services considered that he was appointed a judge of the Common Pleas on January 9, 1839; and for nearly four years he held both offices together, not resigning his chief justiceship of the Court of Review in Bankruptcy till November 1842.

He accompanied Mr. Justice Coleridge on the Northern Circuit in the spring of 1840, when the delinquents among the Chartists were to be tried; and it is to the credit of these two judges that the manner in which they disposed of these political trials contributed not a little to the settlement of disturbed minds, and to disabuse ill-informed persons of the prejudices they had entertained against the tribunals of the country. The effect was that the judges were not merely the objects of general admiration, but that their conduct was most highly applauded by those papers (especially the 'Northern Star,' of which Feargus O'Connor was the editor) which were supposed to guide and to express the feelings of the lower orders.

Mr. Justice Erskine's judicial career was short. Amid the performance of his duties he was seized with a sudden chill, which produced a severe attack of influenza and congestion of the lungs, which resulted in the rupture of a blood-vessel and tubercular disease in the lungs, producing such a state of bodily incapacity as to render him totally unfit to discharge the functions of his office, requiring as they did the active employment of the voice. Under this compulsion he reluctantly retired from the bench in November 1844, and many were the testimonials he received from his distinguished contemporaries of the value of those services they were about to lose.

The retired judge was long in a dangerous state, and it was nearly ten years before the bleeding from the lungs entirely ceased; and the continuance of his life for twenty years after his first seizure was little less than a miracle. He died at Bournemouth, on November 9, 1864. By his wife Henrietta Eliza, daughter of Henry Trail, of Dairsie in Fifeshire, he had a large family, of whom only four were living at his death.

ESCURIS, MATTHEW DE, was one of the five justices errant appointed by Richard de Luci to impose the assize in the county of Hants in 20 Henry II., 1174. (*Madox*, i. 125.) He is not otherwise noticed.

ESPEC, WALTER, was a powerful baron in the north, his principal estate being Helmsley, or Hamlake, in Yorkshire, and having also large possessions in Northumberland and several other counties. The loss of his only son Walter, by a fall from his horse, is said to have induced him to devote a great part of his estate to the service of God. He and his wife Adelina founded a priory of Augustin canons at Kirkham in Yorkshire, to the honour of the Holy Trinity, in 1121, endowing it with seven churches, and other lands to the amount of 1100 marks per annum. He also founded the abbey of Rievaulx in the same county, for Cistercian monks, in 1131, dedicating it to the Virgin Mary; and the abbey of Warden in Bedfordshire, in 1135, for the same order, with endowments of like munificence.

He was justice of the forest for Yorkshire in the reign of Henry I.; and he and Eustace Fitz-John, another northern baron, were justices itinerant in that county, and also in Northumberland, Cumberland, and the bishopric of Durham. The precise period of their appointment is uncertain, but they both fined to be relieved from being judges of Yorkshire in 31 Henry I. (*Mag. Rot.*) They had certainly acted as justiciers in the two preceding years, during which they were excused, as the judges then usually were, from the payment of Danegeld and other impositions.

In the early part of the reign of King Stephen, Walter Espec appears in the character of an experienced warrior, heading his countrymen against the ferocious invasions of the Scots. Animated by despair, under the barbarities which they witnessed, the northern barons summoned their neighbours and dependants, who put themselves under the command of Walter Espec and William of Albemarle, and marched to Northallerton. There they placed a silver pix containing the consecrated host on the top of a tall mast, with the banners of their patron saints, to serve as a rallying point; and from this sacred ensign the battle which followed, and which was fought on August 22, 1138, received the name of the Battle of the Standard. From the foot of this standard Walter Espec harangued his associates, and then, by giving his hand to William of Albemarle, and exclaiming with a loud voice, 'I pledge thee my troth either to conquer or to die,' he kindled such enthusiasm among his hearers that the oath was repeated by every chieftain around him. The result of the battle was the entire overthrow of the invaders, with the loss of 12,000 men.

He died in 1153, and was buried in his own monastery of Rievaulx. To his piety and bravery may be added that he was equally distinguished for wit, modesty, sincerity, and loyalty, and (not to omit what was a great recommendation in those days) was of high and commanding stature.

Leaving no issue by his wife Adelina, his property descended on his three sisters, from one of whom, Adeline, the wife of Peter de Roos, the Duke of Rutland and Lord de Roos are descended.

ESSEBY, JORDAN DE (Ashby), was the grandson of another Jordan, and had considerable possessions in the county of Lincoln. Others were subsequently conferred upon him by King John for his adherence to the royal cause. (*Rot. Claus.* i. 224, 290.) In 7 Henry III. he was appointed by the Archbishop of York to appear for him before the barons of the Exchequer relative to the debt due by his predecessor to the crown (*Ibid.* 335), from which it may be inferred that he was an advocate in the court. He was selected as one of the justices itinerant for Lincolnshire in 9

ESSEBY

Henry III., 1225, being at that time constable of Lincoln Castle. (*Ibid.* ii. 68, 77.)

ESSEBY, ROBERT DE, sometimes called Esseburne, appears in the acknowledgment of a fine in 27 Henry III., 1243. In 1221 a Robert de Esseby was appointed with William Basset to deliver the gaol at Roell in Leicestershire (*Nichols*, 579), and Robert and Thomas de Esseburn, in 10 Henry III., were attorned by William de Ferariis in a suit he had against Walter de Widevill. (*Rot. Claus.* ii. 153.) His property was situate in the counties of Leicester, Northampton, and Nottingham. (*Ibid.* i. 253, 258, ii. 25; *Abb. Placit.* 99.)

ESSEX, HENRY DE, whose grandfather, Swene, at the time of the general survey was lord of Rachley in Essex, and of no less than fifty-four other lordships in that county, besides others in Suffolk and Huntingdonshire, was the inheritor of this property after the death of Robert his father.

He was in great favour with Henry II., and held the high office of constable. His pleas as a justice itinerant in many counties are recorded on the rolls of that king from 1156 to 1158. (*Pipe Rolls*, 31, 78, &c.)

He was likewise sheriff or fermer of the counties of Bedford and Buckingham.

His prosperity, however, was not of long continuance. In the war which King Henry waged with the Welsh in 1157, his army, falling into an ambush at Coleshull in Flintshire, was thrown into confusion, and the king himself placed in great danger. Henry de Essex, who bore the king's standard, instead of hastening to his assistance, was seized with a sudden panic, and, exclaiming that the king was dead, threw away his banner and fled from the field. The king with much difficulty rallied the troops, and, though his army suffered severely, overlooked the dereliction of his officer, making allowance probably for the terror of the moment, and remembering his former services. The subsequent conduct and bravery of Henry de Essex in the war of Toulouse, in 1159, justified his sovereign's leniency, and tended to wipe out the stain from Essex's character. The disgrace would probably have been entirely forgotten but for a quarrel which he had six years afterwards with Robert de Montfort, who, publicly charging him with the fact, and offering to prove it in mortal combat, the king had no choice but to consent to the trial. The duel accordingly took place on April 18, 1163, at an island near Reading, and terminated in the defeat of Essex. The 'Chronicle of Bracelonda' (50, 136) says that, being believed to be dead, the king, on the petition of his relations, permitted his body to be taken to the neighbouring abbey for interment, and that there he recovered, and took the habit of the order. This account is stated to have been narrated by himself to the abbot of St. Edmunds, on his visit to the abbey of Reading about the year 1196; so that he had then been thirty-three years in the cloister, where, Fuller quaintly observes, 'between shame and sanctity he blushed out the remainder of his life.'

By his defeat the whole of his large possessions were confiscated, and several records show that they remained in the king's hands for many years afterwards. Before his disgrace he gave the church of Walde to the nuns of Clerkenwell, and his lordship of Little Fraincham to the Knights Templars. Dugdale states that he had two sons, Henry and Hugh, and that his widow, Alice, a sister of Alberic de Vere, afterwards married Roger Fitz-Richard, lord of Warkworth in Northumberland, and of Clavering in Essex. (*Baronage*, i. 463; *Brady*, 302; *Lord Lyttelton*, ii. 73, 76, 224; *Leland*, iii. 410.)

ESSEX, EARLS OF. See G. DE MANDEVIL; G. FITZ-PETER; H. BOURCHIER; T. CROMWELL.

EUSTACE (BISHOP OF ELY), of whose parentage and early life no memorial remains, was not improbably one of the clerks in Chancery. The appointment to accompany the king into Normandy, for the purpose of conducting such business of the Great Seal as might be required while he was abroad, would be the natural result of his official position; and the deanery of Salisbury, which he held in 1195, with the addition of the archdeaconry of Richmond, which was conferred upon him in the following year (*Le Neve*, 262, 324), would probably be the recompense to which he would be entitled from his standing in the court.

Hoveden calls him 'sigillifer' and 'vice-chancellor;' but in the charters which he authenticated, the first of which is dated April 7, 1195, 6 Richard I. (*New Fœdera*, i. 65), he simply uses the terms 'tunc gerentis,' or 'tunc agentis vices cancellarii.' He was raised to the bishopric of Ely on August 9, 1197, but was not consecrated till the 8th of March following. There is no positive evidence of the actual time when he received the Great Seal as chancellor, but he probably was appointed to office before his consecration as bishop.

Succeeding Longchamp thus both in his ecclesiastical and his civil honours, Eustace's name as chancellor appears in a charter dated August 22, 1198, 'apud Rupem Auree Vall.' (*Rymer*, i. 67), and he was officially present when a fine was levied at Westminster in the following year. (*Hunter's Preface*.) King Richard's death occurred on April 6, 1199, when Eustace's duties ceased, King John selecting his successor from among his own adherents.

R

That John, however, appreciated his abilities and judgment is proved by his being sent in 1202 with Hubert de Burgh to the court of France, to demand from King Philip a safe-conduct on his sovereign's appearance there to answer the charge made against him of having murdered his nephew, Prince Arthur. The ambassadors were told that their king might come in peace, but that his return would depend on the result of the trial, a decision which John was not so foolhardy as to risk.

In the subsequent troubles of that reign he was called upon to take a prominent and courageous part. Appointed in 1207, in conjunction with the Bishops of London and Worcester, to convey the papal remonstrance, they appeared before the king, and demanded of him the restoration of Stephen, the ejected Archbishop of Canterbury. The hardened monarch's angry and contemptuous refusal was followed by the bishops pronouncing the solemn interdict, which deprived the kingdom for so many years of the rites of religion. Warned by the king's threats, the bishops retired secretly from the kingdom, and in the following year, by the pope's directions, fulminated the sentence of excommunication against the royal person. They remained in voluntary exile till the year 1212, when, the king having found it necessary to obtain absolution from the pontiff, they ventured to return; and in the charter of submission afterwards executed a pecuniary compensation was made to them for their losses.

During the short remainder of his life Eustace was reconciled to his sovereign, and was one of his sureties to the barons for the redress of their grievances. He did not live to witness the grant of Magna Charta, but died at Reading on February 3, 1214, and was buried in his own cathedral.

He is described as well skilled in both sacred and profane learning, and as a pious and discreet prelate. To his church he was a considerable benefactor, and built the Galilee at the west end of it from its foundation. (*Godwin*, 254; *Angl. Sac.* i. 633; *Madox*, i. 29, 77; *Rapin*, ii. 429.)

EVERDON, SILVESTER DE (BISHOP OF CARLISLE), as one of the king's chaplains, appears as a witness to charters granted in 7 and 9 John. He had about that time presentations to the churches of Bulewell, Fremesfeld, and Tatham in succession. In all these he is called by his Christian name alone, and may possibly, therefore, not be the person who afterwards became bishop. In 8 Henry III., 1224, however, Silvester de Everdon is expressly mentioned as a demandant of a virgate of lands, which he claimed as belonging to his church of Everdon in Northamptonshire, and it was probably on acquiring this preferment that he assumed the name. In the following year he was evidently engaged in the king's service in the same way as the clerks of the Exchequer or Treasury frequently were, and is called 'clericus noster.' (*Rot. Claus.* i. 631, ii. 53, 63.)

It was no doubt in this character that he had the custody of the Great Seal when the king, on May 5, 1242, confided to the Archbishop of York the government of the kingdom during his absence in Gascony. Soon after the Bishop of Chichester's death (Sir T. Hardy says on November 14, 1244) he was appointed either chancellor or keeper, and is stated to have been one most cunning in the custom of the Chancery. In August 1246 he received the bishopric of Carlisle, and in November was succeeded in the Chancery by John Mansel. In 1251 and 1252 he acted as a justice itinerant in the counties of York, Nottingham, Derby, Warwick, and Leicester.

When the bishops and nobles in 1253 went to the king with the conditions upon which they granted the aid he demanded, and the former were sharply reminded that their elevation was effected by the very causes of which they complained, Matthew Paris relates that to Silvester de Everdon he addressed himself thus: 'And thou, Silvester of Carlisle, who, so long licking the Chancery, wast the little clerk of my clerks, it is well known to all how I advanced thee to be a bishop, before many reverend persons and able divines.'

He was killed by a fall from his horse on May 13, 1254.

EVERDON, JOHN DE, was an officer of the Exchequer, and, like his fellows, was of the clerical profession. He was appointed in 30 Edward I. to superintend the levying of the fifteenth in the counties of Oxford and Berks. In 1 Edward II. he was constituted a baron of the Exchequer on November 28, 1307. While he held a seat on that bench he frequently acted as an assessor of the taxes charged on the city of London, and as a justice of oyer and terminer in various counties for the trial of offences connected with the revenue and its collection. He continued in his place till 1322 or 1323. In 4 Edward II. he was dean of the free chapel of St. Peter in Wolverhampton, and was certified as lord of that township in the ninth year. He held the chancellorship of Exeter from May 1308 till August 1309, and was afterwards a prebendary of Sarum, which he exchanged for the deanery of St. Paul's, London, to which he was admitted on September 15, 1323. He died on January 15, 1336, and was buried in the church of St. Faith, under St. Paul's. (*Le Neve*, 89, 183.)

EVERDON, WILLIAM DE, probably the

brother or nephew of the above John de Everdon, in 5 Edward II., October 11, 1311, was appointed treasurer's remembrancer in the Exchequer, and had a fee of forty marks per annum for himself and his clerks; and in 10 Edward II. he had an additional grant of 20l. a year, *de dono*, for his good service, until the king should provide him with an ecclesiastical benefice suitable to his degree. From that time there is no entry relative to him till July 18, 1324, 17 Edward II., when he was raised to the bench as a baron, in which office he continued till the end of the reign, and was retained in it on the accession of Edward III. The date of his death is not recorded, but he was employed in 11 Edward III. to assist in levying money from the clergy of York for carrying on the French war, and is named as receiving a pension, or bribe, from the Knights Hospitallers so late as 1338. (*Madox*, ii. 267; *New Fœdera*, ii. 1005; *Hospitallers in England*, 203.)

EVESHAM, THOMAS DE, held some place in one of the departments of the court as early as 1313, 6 Edward II., when he accompanied the king abroad. In 1319 he was appointed one of the attorneys for Rigand de Asserio, the pope's nuncio (*N. Fœdera*, ii. 212, 399), and appeared as proxy for the abbot of Evesham in the parliaments of 16 and 18 Edward II. (*Parl. Writs*, ii. p. ii. 828.)

He is first mentioned as a clerk in the Chancery in July 1328, 2 Edward III., and on the appointment of Sir Robert Bourchier as chancellor the Great Seal was placed in his hands under the seals of two of the other clerks, and so remained from December 16, 1340, to the 1st of January following. On the 10th of that month he was raised to the office of master of the Rolls, but it would seem that this was a mere temporary appointment, for he was superseded by John de Thoresby on February 21, after only six weeks' enjoyment of the place. He immediately resumed his duties as a clerk in the Chancery (*N. Fœdera*, ii. 745, 1172), which he continued to perform during the remainder of his life. He died in 1343, possessed of land at Weston Underegge in Gloucestershire. His London residence was in 'Faytour Lane.' (*Cal. Inquis.* p. m. ii. 108.)

EVESK, HENRY LE, had property in Cambridgeshire, which was all seized into the king's hands during the troubles of King John. On the accession of his successor they were restored to him, and in 9 Henry III. he was one of the justices itinerant in that county and Huntingdonshire. (*Rot. Claus.* i. 324, ii. 76, 146.)

EWENS, MATTHEW, was reader in the Middle Temple in autumn 1591, and took the degree of serjeant in Hilary 1594, when he was raised to the bench of the Exchequer, and his judgments in that and the following years are reported by Savile and Coke. His death or resignation soon after occurred, as his successor, John Savile, was appointed in July 1598. (*Dugdale's Orig.* 218.)

EXETER, DUKE OF. *See* T. BEAUFORT.

EYNEFELD, HENRY DE, was appointed, in 21 Edward I., 1293, one of two justices to take assizes, &c., in Cornwall and nine other counties, and was summoned among the judges to parliament till the twenty-fifth. One of his name was returned knight of the shire for Middlesex in 26 and 28 Edward I. (*Parl. Writs*, i. 29, 52, 72-86.)

EYRE, GILES, was of an ancient and distinguished Wiltshire family, which supplied no less than three, and perhaps four, members to the judicial bench. Their common ancestor was Humphrey le Heyr, who accompanied Richard Cœur de Lion to the Holy Land. One of his lineal descendants, Giles Eyre, settled at Brickworth in Whiteparish, and had several children, one of the younger of whom emigrated with Ludlow to Ireland, and was the ancestor of Lord Eyre, of Eyre Court in the county of Galway, a title which died with the grantee in 1792. The eldest son, named also Giles, succeeded to Brickworth, and represented Downton in the parliament of 1660 and 1661. By his marriage with Anne, daughter of Sir Richard Norton, of Rotherfield, Hants, Bart., he became the father of Sir Giles Eyre, the judge, who was admitted a member of Lincoln's Inn in October 1654, and called to the bar in November 1661.

Of his early life we have no further account except that he lost his first wife, Dorothy, daughter of John Ryves, of Ranston in Dorsetshire, in 1677. To her monument in Whiteparish Church he attached an inscription in anticipation of his own death, leaving the date in blank, with eight lines expressing the warmest affection for her, and implying the impossibility of his ever being united to another. Notwithstanding this monogamistic resolution, we find that he afterwards married a second wife, who occupied the same grave with her predecessor.

In 1675 the corporation of Salisbury presented him with a tankard of 10l. value for his services in procuring their charter, being then their deputy recorder. He was afterwards elected recorder, but lost his place on the subsequent seizure of the charters. On the renewal of them in 1688 he was restored, and was elected representative of that city to the Convention Parliament. He took part in the conference with the Lords as to the vote of abdication, and in all the debates showed himself a hearty supporter of the new government.

He was immediately made a serjeant, and on the settlement of the Court of King's Bench was constituted one of the judges of it on May 4, 1689, receiving soon after the honour of knighthood. After filling this seat with great credit for six years, he died on June 2, 1695, and was buried in Whiteparish Church.

The Christian name of his second wife was Christabella; that of her family has not been discovered. She survived the judge, and took for her second husband Lord Glasford, a Scotch Papist, from whom she withdrew in 1699, leaving him a prisoner for debt in the Fleet, where he died in November 1703. The judge left issue by both his wives. Some of the male representatives of his family have had seats in parliament, and one of his female descendants married Thomas Bolton, the nephew of Admiral Lord Nelson, who succeeded to that earldom in 1835. (*Parl. Hist.* v. 107, &c.; *Luttrell*, i. 529, iv. 549.)

EYRE, SAMUEL, was the second cousin of the above Sir Giles Eyre, both having the same great-grandfather. He was the son of Robert Eyre, of Salisbury and Chilhampton, and Anne, daughter of Samuel Aldersey, of Aldersey in Cheshire, and was born in 1633. As his father had done before him, he took the degree of barrister at Lincoln's Inn in June 1661. He pursued his profession with considerable success, to which the patronage of the Earl of Shaftesbury, to whom he was reputed to be the confidential adviser, in some measure probably contributed, though the same cause in all likelihood prevented his promotion in Charles's and in James's reigns. After the revolution he was created a serjeant on April 21, 1692; and from that rank was advanced, on February 22, 1694, to take his place, by the side of his cousin Sir Giles, as a judge of the King's Bench.

Shortly after his appointment, Charles Knollys, claiming to be Earl of Banbury, who had been indicted for the murder of Captain Lawson, his brother-in-law, and had pleaded his peerage, brought the question into the Court of King's Bench, where judgment was given in the defendant's favour in Trinity Term 1694. On the discussion of the claim of peerage nearly four years afterwards, Chief Justice Holt and Sir Samuel Eyre were called before the House of Lords and required to give their reasons for that judgment. They resolutely and properly declined to do so, unless it came before the house on a writ of error, and their lordships, after threatening the two judges with the Tower for their refusal to answer, found it expedient to let the matter drop. Seven months after this incident Sir Samuel was seized with the colic, just upon finishing the circuit at Lancaster, where he died on September 12, 1698.

His body was removed to the family vault in St. Thomas's Church, Salisbury, a costly monument to his memory being erected at Lancaster.

His wife, Martha, daughter of Francis, fifth son of Sir Thomas Lucy, of Charlecote in Warwickshire, brought him a large family, the eldest of whom was Chief Justice Sir Robert Eyre. (*Luttrell*, ii. 427, iii. 273, iv. 343, 428, 436; 1 *Lord Raymond*, 10; *State Trials*, xii. 1179.)

EYRE, ROBERT, the son and heir of the above Sir Samuel Eyre, was born in 1666, and, having entered upon his legal studies at Lincoln's Inn in April 1683, was admitted to the bar in February 1689.

Before his father's death in 1698 he had succeeded his cousin Sir Giles in the recordership of Salisbury, and he represented that city in the last three parliaments of William III. and the first four of Queen Anne, from 1698 to 1710. He was sworn queen's counsel in May 1707, and in October of the following year he was made solicitor-general. In March 1710 he was one of the active managers of the unwise impeachment of Dr. Sacheverell, and was afterwards engaged in the trials of the parties connected with the Sacheverell riots. (*Luttrell*, vi. 166, 202, 263; *State Trials*, xv. 396, 522, &c.)

The whig ministry by which he was appointed fell a sacrifice to this prosecution, but fortunately for him, before their dismissal, the death of Mr. Justice Gould occasioned a vacancy in the Court of Queen's Bench, which he was appointed to supply. He was sworn in on March 13 and knighted, and sat in that court during the remainder of Queen Anne's reign. On the arrival of George I. he was appointed chancellor to the Prince of Wales. As in duty bound, on the great question agitated before the judges in 1718 as to the king's prerogative in regard to the education and marriage of the royal family, Sir Robert gave an opinion differing from the majority of his brethren, in favour of the prince his client. So satisfactory was his performance of his judicial functions, and so high his legal reputation, that, notwithstanding this opposition to the royal claim, the king on November 16, 1723, promoted him to the head of the Court of Exchequer as lord chief baron; and eighteen months after, on May 27, 1725, raised him to the still higher dignity of lord chief justice of the Common Pleas. (*Lord Raymond*, 1309, 1331; *State Trials*, xv. 1217.) He maintained the reputation he had earned for the ten years that he continued to preside in that court, his whole career on the three benches extending over one-and-twenty years.

Sir Robert, however, did not escape calumny. Some infamous and profligate persons brought a charge against him for visiting Bambridge, the brutal and corrupt keeper of the Fleet, when in prison, and of otherwise aiding and abetting him in his atrocities. On a strict investigation, however, the committee came to a resolution that it was a wicked conspiracy to vilify and asperse the chief justice, and that the informations against him were 'false, malicious, scandalous, and utterly groundless.' (*Parl. Hist.* viii. 707, &c.; *State Trials*, xvii. 619.)

That Sir Robert was somewhat haughty in his demeanour may be inferred from the Duke of Wharton's satire. He vows constancy to his mistress until the time

When Tracy's generous soul shall swell with pride,
And Eyre his haughtiness shall lay aside.

As a set-off against this, there is evidence of the general estimation of his character in the intimacy which existed between him and Godolphin, Marlborough, and Walpole; and of his kind and generous disposition a testimony is afforded by a legacy of 400*l*. bequeathed to his daughter by an old domestic, in grateful acknowledgment that he owed all his good fortune in life to his deceased master. The chief justice died on December 28, 1735, and was buried in St. Thomas's Church, Salisbury. By his wife, Elizabeth, daughter of Edward Rudge, Esq., of Warley Place, Essex, he left a large family. (*Sir R. C. Hoare's South Wiltshire; Frustfield; Salisbury.*)

EYRE, JAMES, was a descendant of the old Wiltshire family to which the three judges already noticed belonged, but it is uncertain of what branch of it. His great-grandfather was of the medical profession, and died mayor of Salisbury in 1685. His brother, Dr. Thomas Eyre, was a canon in the cathedral of that city. The judge was born in 1733, and his father is described in the Lincoln's Inn books as Mr. Chancellor Eyre. Having received his classical education first at Winchester and then at Oxford, he commenced his legal studies at Lincoln's Inn in November 1753, but two years after removed to Gray's Inn, by which society he was called to the bar in 1755. He purchased the place of one of the four city pleaders of London, and was for some time little known beyond the Lord Mayor's and Sheriffs' Courts. In them, however, his attendance was so regular, his manners so good, and his appearance so grave, that in February 1761 he was appointed deputy recorder, and in April 1763 recorder of the corporation, being then scarcely thirty years of age.

In the December of that year he was engaged as second counsel for John Wilkes in the action against Mr. Wood for entering into the plaintiff's house, and seizing his papers under a general warrant from the secretary of state. Though he acted in this case with great energy and spirit, as thinking that it affected the liberty of the subject, yet, when a few years after, in 1770, the corporation, joining in the political distractions excited by the cry of 'Wilkes and Liberty,' and the call for a new parliament, voted a remonstrance to the king, the recorder would not attend on its presentation; but on another address in harsher terms being voted, he boldly protested against it as a most abominable libel, and again refused to accompany the corporation to the palace. This was the occasion when Lord Mayor Beckford is supposed to have replied to his majesty in the speech that appears at the foot of his statue in Guildhall, but the language of which is said to have been subsequently composed by Horne Tooke. The common council of course resented their recorder's resistance, and voted that he should no more be advised with or employed in the city affairs, he 'being deemed unworthy of their future trust and confidence.' But the court of St. James's looked upon his conduct in a different light, and took an early opportunity of rewarding his loyalty, by raising him to the bench of the Exchequer in October 1772, when he was knighted. On resigning the recordership he received the thanks of the Court of Aldermen for the many eminent services he rendered the public, and was presented with a piece of plate with the city arms engraved thereon, as a grateful remembrance from the court for his faithful discharge of his duties.

After sitting in the Exchequer as a puisne baron for nearly fifteen years, he was raised to the head of it on January 26, 1787; and when Lord Chancellor Thurlow was removed in 1793, he was appointed chief commissioner of the Great Seal, an office which he held for seven months from June 15 to January 28, in the following year. On retiring from the Seal he was promoted to the chief justiceship of the Common Pleas, and at the end of the next year he was entrusted with the arduous duty of presiding at the memorable trials of Hardy, Horne Tooke, and Thelwall for constructive high treason. These trials lasted eighteen days, and throughout them he acted with the greatest patience and impartiality, but in the opinion of many with too great forbearance to the irregularities of Horne Tooke. In his summing up of the evidence in the different cases he carefully described the principles of the law, and in the most fair and unexceptionable manner explained the bearings of the evidence upon the charges. The result was the acquittal of all the prisoners; and the same verdict was given in 1796 in another trial before him of Crossfield and others for high treason in conspiring to make an instrument from which to shoot a poisoned arrow at the king. (*State Trials*, iv., v., vi.)

With an extensive knowledge of law he united the greatest judicial qualities; and to the unbiased integrity of the judge was joined a quickness of apprehension and a natural sagacity and candour that secured to him the respect and esteem as well of his brethren on the bench as of the members of the bar, whom he never interrupted in their arguments, and towards whom he preserved an invariable and unaffected courtesy. He presided over the Common Pleas six years and a half, and died on July 6, 1799, at his residence, Ruscombe in Berkshire.

F

FAIRFAX, GUY, the third son of Richard Fairfax, of an ancient family seated at Walton in Yorkshire, by Anastasia, daughter and co-heir of John Carthorpe, received from his father the manor of Steeton in that county, where he afterwards built a castle, which continued the chief residence of his posterity till the beginning of the last century, when the family removed to Newton Kyme, about six miles distant from the castle, which is now the principal farmhouse on the estate.

In 1435 he was a commissioner of array for the West Riding, and in 1460 he was joined with Sir William Plumpton and others to enquire concerning the lands of Richard, Duke of York, attainted in the preceding parliament. (*Plumpton Corr*. lii. lxvi.) It may be presumed that he participated in the mercy shown by the duke's son, King Edward, to his friend Sir William Plumpton, for in Michaelmas 1463 he was called serjeant from Gray's Inn (*Y. B. 3 Edw. IV*. fo. 10); and in April 1468 the king appointed him one of his own serjeants. In the following year he is noticed as being employed by Sir William Plumpton, and as receiving ten shillings for his fee, a sorry honorarium to be offered to a king's serjeant. A few years afterwards, in an appeal carried on, as the judges suspected, by the maintenance of Sir William, in which they expressed their opinion that the men charged were not guilty, Fairfax 'said openly att the barre that he knew so, verily they were not guilty; that he would labor their deliverance for almes, not takeing a penny;' whereupon Sir William's agent retained two other counsel. (*Corresp*. 23, 25.)

He was appointed recorder of York in 1476 (*Drake's York*, 363), which he held about a year. The date of his elevation to the bench is not preserved, but he is first mentioned in the character of a judge of the King's Bench in Trinity Term 1477. (*Y. B. 17 Edw. IV*. fo. 4, b.) On the death of Edward IV., and again on the usurpation of Richard III., he had a renewal of his patent, and a few days before Richard's assumption of the crown he was made chief justice of Lancaster (*Grants of Edw. V*. 6[1]); nor did the termination of the tyrant's career make any change in his judicial position. For the first ten years of the reign of Henry VII. he kept his seat, and died in possession in 1495, leaving behind him the character of an able lawyer and a conscientious judge.

By his marriage with Margaret, daughter of Sir William Ryther, he had six children, one of whom, Sir William, is the next-mentioned judge. The viscounty of Fairfax of Elmley in Ireland, granted in 1628 to a descendant of William, the elder brother of Sir Guy, became extinct in 1772. (*Biog. Peerage*, iii. 249.)

FAIRFAX, WILLIAM, the eldest son of the above Sir Guy Fairfax, pursued his father's profession, and probably in the same school, Gray's Inn. He was elected recorder of York in 1489 (*Drake*, 368), and was engaged as counsel for Sir Robert Plumpton in 1490 (*Corresp*. 101, 210), and in November 1504 he was called to the degree of the coif. Soon after the accession of Henry VIII. he was made a judge of the Common Pleas, the first fine levied before him being in Easter Term, 1 Henry VIII., April 1509. He died about the same season in 1514.

By his wife, Elizabeth, one of the three daughters of Sir Robert Manners, ancestor of the Duke of Rutland, he had an only son, William, whose grandson Thomas was created Baron Fairfax of Cameron in Scotland by Charles I. in 1627. The parliamentary general who defeated that unfortunate monarch at Naseby in 1645 was the third lord. Bryan, the eighth baron, resident in America, proved his title in the House of Lords, May 6, 1800; but his descendants have not claimed it. (*Biog. Peerage*, iii. 249; *Notes and Queries*, 1st S. ix. 156.)

FALEISE, WILLIAM DE, held a high and responsible office in the Treasury of England. The only year in which he is mentioned as acting as a justicier is 1 John, 1199, when a fine was levied before him. (*Liberat*. 37, 71, 76, 99, 107; *Hunter's Preface*.)

He was the custos of the honor of Gloucester for the first nine years of John's reign, and he and Maurice de Tureville at a later period had the custody of the castle of Winchester. (*Madox's Baron. Angl.* 59, 66, 76.)

He married Alice, the daughter of Philip de Linguire, and died in 1232, leaving a son, Elias. (*Excerpt. e Rot. Fin.* i. 220.)

FALLAN, WILLIAM, was appointed a baron of the Exchequer in 14 Henry VI., 1435-6. (*Cal. Rot. Pat.* 278.) There is a curious account of his removal from the court. Richard Forde, one of the remembrancers, in a petition to the parliament of 33 Henry VI., 1455 (*Rot. Parl.* v. 342), stated that Thomas Thorpe having superseded Forde in the office of remembrancer, would not restore it to him unless he was made third baron of the Exchequer, and that Forde thereupon arranged with Sir William Fallan, clerk, then third baron, to resign on receiving from Forde a bond to pay him 40 marks yearly for life, unless otherwise provided for to the same amount, with a remarkable condition, however, by Sir William Fallan, that such provision should not be 'any benefice havyng cure of soule.' The prayer of this petition, that this bond should be made void, was granted; so that the baron lost both his place and pension.

FASTOLF, NICHOLAS, was of Great Yarmouth in Norfolk, for which town he was returned to parliament in 2 and 7 Edward II. In 18 Edward II., 1324, he was appointed chief justice of the King's Bench in Ireland, and was still mentioned in that character in 1327, 1 Edward III. The patent of his successor in the office being dated in 1333, 7 Edward III., it may be presumed that Fastolf enjoyed it till that time. If so, he must have been on a visit to England when he was added to the commission of justices itinerant into Derbyshire in 4 Edward III., 1330. (*Parl. Writs*, ii. p. ii. 838; *N. Fœdera*, ii. 709; *Smyth's Law Officers of Ireland*, 97.)

FAUCONBRIDGE, EUSTACE DE (BISHOP OF LONDON), was born in Yorkshire, but his relationship to the noble family of that name is not distinctly traced. He appears in 1 John, 1199, among the justiciers before whom fines were levied at Westminster. In this capacity he regularly acted during the whole of that and for the first three years of the succeeding reign. (*Orig. Jurid.* 42; *Abb. Placit.* 39, 116.) In 2 Henry III. he was appointed treasurer of England, a station which he held for the remainder of his life, during the whole of which he was in the constant confidence of the sovereigns whom he served. Each of them employed him in embassies to the court of France, King John in 1204, and King Henry in 1223 and 1225, and from each of them he received various marks of favour. (*Rot.* *Claus.* i. 16, 32; 368, 447, 556, ii. 41, 47.)

To his judicial duties he added those of an ecclesiastic, and held a canonry in the cathedral of St. Paul's; and in 1221, 5 Henry III., he was elected Bishop of London. His high character may be estimated by the following distich, which was written on his being elevated in opposition to several other claimants:—

Omnes hic digni, tu dignior omnibus ; omnes
 Hic plene sapiunt, plenius ipse sapis.

He still continued actively to perform his duties at court, and was a frequent witness to charters and other royal documents until a fortnight before his decease. This occurred on October 31, 1228. He was buried in his cathedral, to which he had been a considerable benefactor. (*Godwin*, 179.)

FAUNT, WILLIAM, of whom neither in the Year Books nor in any other records is the name to be found, is inserted by Dugdale as a justice of the King's Bench on April 4, 1338, 12 Edward III., and H. Philipps mentions two persons as his descendants in 1684, one residing at Foston in Lincolnshire, and the other at Kingsthorpe in the county of Northampton. (*Grandeur of the Law* [1684], 220, 252.)

FENCOTES, THOMAS DE, of a Yorkshire family, was an adherent of Thomas, Earl of Lancaster, in the reign of Edward II., and obtained his release from prison by a payment of 20*l*. (*Parl. Writs*, ii. p. ii. 208.) When John de Britannia, Earl of Richmond, was taken by the Scots in 16 Edward II., Thomas de Fencotes was appointed one of his attorneys in England; and on the death of the earl in 8 Edward III. he still represented him, and acted as custos of the estate till the death of the earl's successor, John, Duke of Brittany, in the fifteenth year. (*N. Fœdera*, ii. 88, 524, 1159.) From the Year Books it appears that he acted as an advocate in Yorkshire as early as 2 Edward III., and as a justice of assize in the seventeenth year. He was appointed a judge of the Common Pleas on January 14, 1348, and seems to have resigned about 1354. (*Orig. Jurid.* 45.) He received the order of knighthood when or soon after he was raised to the bench. In 24 Edward III. he gave certain tenements to the priory of the order of Mary of Mount Carmel to enlarge their house in Fleet Street; and in 31 Edward III. he and his wife Beatrice endowed the convent of Egleston with the advowson of the church of Bentham in Yorkshire. (*Cal. Inquis.* p. m. ii. 168, 203.)

John de Fencotes, a serjeant-at-law in 40 Edward III., was probably his son.

FENNER, EDWARD, was the son of John Fenner, of Crawley in Surrey, by Ellen, the daughter of Sir William Goring, of Burton. Dallaway (i. 16) traces the family for five generations higher, the earliest of which he calls John atte Fenne. He took his legal degrees in the Middle Temple, where he became reader in autumn 1576. In Michaelmas 1577 he was made a serjeant-at-law, and on May 26, 1590, he was constituted one of the judges of the Court of King's Bench, in which he sat for one-and-twenty years, under Elizabeth and her successor. (*Orig. Jurid.* 218.) In the January before his appointment he, being a justice of the peace for Surrey, sat on the bench at the assizes when John Udall was brought up to receive sentence, and in kind and considerate language assisted the judges in urging the prisoner to submit himself to her majesty. (*State Trials*, i. 1297.) In 1595 an account was published of 'The arraignment, judgement, and execution of three wytches of Huntingdonshire, being recommended for matter of truthe by Mr. Judge Fenner;' and the Register of the Stationers' Company adds to the entry that the judge's note 'is layd up in the warden's cupbord.' (*Notes and Queries*, 3rd S. i. 402.)

He died on January 23, 1611–12, and was buried at Hayes in Middlesex. By a curious error, his name on his monument appears as 'Jenner' instead of 'Fenner.'

FERMBAUD, or **FERNYBAUD**, NICHOLAS, was constable of Bristol from 22 to 33 Edward I. (*Abb. Rot. Orig.* i. 82.) In 28 Edward I. he was appointed to perambulate the forests of Gloucestershire and the neighbouring counties (*Parl. Writs*, i. 398), and two years afterwards the custody of the bishopric of Bath and Wells was entrusted to him during its vacancy. (*Abb. Rot. Orig.* i. 121.)

He is mentioned with William Inge as a justice taking assizes in 1305, and was also appointed a justice of trailbaston for Essex and ten other counties. (*N. Fœdera*, i. 970.) He possessed considerable property at Wingrave and Rollesham in Buckinghamshire. (*Abb. Placit.* 222, 276.)

FERRIBY, THOMAS DE, was a clerk of Thomas Plantagenet, Earl of Buckingham (afterwards Duke of Gloucester), in 6 Richard II. (*Kal. Exch.* ii. 12.) It was not unnatural, therefore, that Henry IV., on ascending the throne, should advance him to be a baron of the Exchequer on October 14, 1399. But of the term of his continuance in the court there is no account.

FERTE, RALPH DE LA, so called from a town in Normandy, was a resident in Cumberland. In 17 John he was constable of Carlisle (*Rot. Pat.* 163); and in 3 Henry III., 1218, and several years afterwards, he was appointed a justice itinerant in that county and in Westmoreland. (*Rot. Claus.* ii. 77, 147, 151.)

FIENNES, NATHANIEL, was the second son of William, Lord Say and Sele, by Elizabeth, daughter of John Temple, Esq., of Stowe in Buckinghamshire. He was born about 1608 at Broughton in Oxfordshire, and was educated at Winchester and at Oxford, where he was admitted in 1624 fellow of New College, as founder's kin. (*Wood's Athen.* iii. 877.) He remained there about five years, and then spent some time abroad, 'in Geneva and amongst the cantons of Switzerland, where,' says Clarendon, ' he improved his disinclination to the Church, with which milk he had been nursed.' From his travels he returned through Scotland in 1639, at the time of the tumults there, which he assisted in fomenting. (*Clarendon*, i. 325, 510.)

In 1640 he was elected a member of the Long Parliament for Banbury, and soon became a leader of the party called 'root and branch.' He strongly supported the bill against the bishops, and so little had the consequences been considered that, in a conversation with Clarendon, in answer to the question what government they meant to introduce instead, he said 'there would be time enough to think of that.' He was appointed of the committee to attend the king on his journey to Scotland in 1641. (*Ibid.* 410, 494; *Life*, i. 90.) When the parliament took up arms in the following year, Fiennes not only undertook to find one horse and bring 100*l*. in money as his subscription towards the cause (*Notes and Queries*, 1st S. xii. 338), but accepted a commission of colonel of their forces. His first exploit, the defeated attempt to surprise Worcester (*Clarendon*, iii. 234, 625), did not speak much to the credit either of his courage or military skill, and his conduct at Bristol in 1643 confirmed the bad impression he had made. Professing great zeal for the parliament, he had removed the former governor on suspicion of disaffection, and had condemned and executed two principal citizens on the charge of plotting to give up the place to the king; and yet, after laying in stores of ammunition and provisions sufficient to sustain a siege of three months, no sooner had Prince Rupert invested the city than he surrendered it to the royalists, to the great advantage of their cause in the west, and the infinite discouragement of the parliamentarius.

On the colonel's return to parliament ' every one looked strangely on him with a discontented aspect,' so palpably showing their suspicion of either treachery or cowardice that he felt it necessary to make his apology openly in the house, concluding with a desire that his conduct might be examined by a council of war. This relation, being published by himself, was answered and exposed by Mr. Walker and

Mr. Prynne, in a book called 'Rome's Masterpiece,' for the publication of which the writers were summoned before the council to make good their accusation. The consequence was that Colonel Fiennes was called upon to defend himself, and after a solemn trial, conducted most ably by Mr. Prynne, which lasted no less than nine days, he was convicted by the council of war, and condemned to lose his head. The sentence, however, was not put in execution; by his family interest and connections, and perhaps by the consideration of his great civil ability and the eminent services and zeal he had previously shown in the cause, the general was induced to grant him a pardon. His military career, for which he was totally unfitted, thus ended in infamy, and he quitted the kingdom to cover his disgrace. (*Ibid.* iv. 141, 343, 611; *State Trials,* iv. 185–298.)

Returning after some years' retirement, he resumed his attendance in parliament and almost his former ascendency. He was one of the committee formed for the safety of the kingdom in January 1648; and on December 1 he made a speech in favour of receiving the king's answers from the Isle of Wight as satisfactory. In consequence he was one of the first victims of Pride's Purge, and, after being imprisoned for a short time, was secluded from the house. (*Whitelocke*, 286.)

In the parliament which Cromwell called after he was declared protector in September 1654, and which was dissolved in January 1655, he was elected one of the members for Oxfordshire. In the following May Fiennes was a commissioner of the protector's privy seal, and on June 15 he was appointed lord commissioner of the Great Seal, on the secession of Whitelocke and Widdrington, when they refused to carry into effect the ordinance concerning the Chancery.

Fiennes is said to have been the author of the declaration issued by Cromwell in the following October, vindicating the severity with which he had treated all the royalists, making them suffer in money or in person for the plots against him, whether they were implicated in them or not. (*Harris's Lives,* iii. 433–435.) In January 1656 he was united with Whitelocke and others in the negotiation of the treaty with the Swedish ambassador. In the next parliament he was returned for the university of Oxford, and confirmed as commissioner of the Great Seal. (*Whitelocke,* 632–649, 653.) In the endeavour to remove the scruples which Cromwell professed to assuming the title of king he was one of the principal speakers. This attempt being set aside, he bore the Seal at the solemn ceremony of the re-inauguration in June 1657. (*Parl. Hist.* iii. 1498, 1515.) Under the new constitution he was appointed one of Cromwell's lords, and on the protector's death in 1658 assisted in proclaiming Richard as his successor, and was reinstated in the custody of the Great Seal, with his former colleague and Bulstrode Whitelocke. (*Whitelocke,* 666, 675–6.) In the list of the members of the parliament called by Richard in January 1659 the name of Nathaniel Fiennes appears as member for Banbury (*Parl. Hist.* iii. 1533), which, as he was a member of the 'other house,' either must be a mistake, or some other person of the same name must be intended. He is not only mentioned as lord keeper in Richard's speech on the first day, as about to address the parliament on certain matters untouched by him (*Ibid.* 1540), but is named in April as going up to the bar of the 'other house' to receive a declaration from the Commons. (*Whitelocke,* 677.) Soon after the dissolution of the parliament on April 22 Richard's authority ceased, and with it Fiennes' office, the Long Parliament, which met again on May 7, appointing other commissioners. (*Ibid.* 678.)

On the king's return Fiennes retired to his country seat at Newton Tony in Wiltshire, where he died on December 16, 1669, and was buried in the church there, with a monument to his memory. However that memory might be cherished by his friends and family, the only claim to admiration by the public would be his undoubted talent and eloquence, of which his published speeches afford ample evidence; but in regard to his conduct either as a soldier or civilian, tainted in the former as it must ever remain with the suspicion of treachery and the imputation of cowardice, and exhibiting in the latter so many proofs of changeableness and timeserving, he cannot but be held in the lowest estimation.

He married twice. His first wife was Elizabeth, daughter of Sir John Eliot, of Port Eliot in Cornwall, by whom he had a son; and his second was Frances, daughter of Richard Whitehead, Esq., of Siderley, Hants, by whom he had three daughters. His son William, by the death of his first cousin without male issue, became third Viscount Saye and Sele, and the title remained in the family till 1781, when the viscounty became extinct, but the ancient barony survived in Thomas Twistleton, descended from the daughter of the eldest son of the first viscount.

FINCH, JOHN (LORD FINCH OF FORDWICH). This family originally bore the name of Herbert, and is said to have descended from Henry Fitz-Herbert, chamberlain to Henry I., and to have adopted the name of Finch in the reign of Edward I., being that of a manor in Kent, which came into their possession by a marriage with the daughter and heir of its lord. After a long train of succession, Sir Thomas Finch, in the reign of Queen Mary, married one of the coheirs of Sir Thomas Moyle, of Eastwell in Kent, and on his death by shipwreck, in 6 Elizabeth, he left three sons. Through two of them his connection with the law is worthy of remark, for he had one son, two grandsons, one great-grandson, and one great-great-grandson, all eminent in Westminster Hall, besides two female descendants connected by marriage with lawyers equally illustrious. Sir Thomas's second son, Sir Henry Finch, was an eminent advocate, and one of King James's serjeants, and by his wife Ursula, daughter and heir of John Thwaites, was the father of this John Finch, who was born on September 17, 1584, and was admitted of the society of Gray's Inn in February 1600. Nearly twelve years elapsed before he was called to the bar, on November 8, 1611; but in six years more, assisted by the patronage of Lord Bacon, he became a bencher, and was chosen autumn reader in 1618. In the meantime he had been elected member for Canterbury in 1614, and was chosen recorder of that city in 1617. The corporation rejected him in 1620, but being reinstated by the direction of the council (*Cal. St. Papers* [1619], 108–148), he held that office till 1621. Again representing that city in the first three of Charles's parliaments, he was chosen speaker of the last in 1628. Clarendon says (i. 130) that he had 'led a free life in a restrained fortune, and having set up upon the stock of a good wit and natural parts, without the superstructure of much knowledge in the profession by which he had to grow, he was willing to use those weapons in which he had most skill.' The first effect of his endeavours was his knighthood, the next his appointment as king's counsel, and then attorney-general to the queen in 1626. (*Rymer*, xviii. 633, 866.)

In his address to the king on his being elected speaker he showed some of the wit for which Clarendon gave him credit, and too much of the customary adulation. On the difficult subjects which agitated this parliament it was a difficult and delicate task to a man of Finch's disposition to avoid doing anything which might deprive him of the confidence of the Commons, or hazard the destruction of his hopes from the king. Through the first session he managed in his speeches to the throne to steer with tolerable safety; and though, towards the end of it, he ran some risk by interrupting, 'with tears in his eyes,' a speaker who was about, as he supposed, to fall upon the Duke of Buckingham, and requesting to withdraw, he redeemed himself by bringing back a conciliatory message from the king. At the termination, however, of the second session he lost all credit with the house, and incurred their censure by his conduct. After delivering a message from the king, ordering an adjournment, he refused to read a remonstrance against tonnage and poundage, proposed by Sir John Elliott, and left the chair. Upon being forced to resume it, he had again recourse to tears, saying, 'I am the servant of the house, but let not the reward of my service be my ruin . . . . I will not say I will not, but I dare not.' Sir Peter Hayman, a kinsman and a neighbour, called him 'the disgrace of his country, and a blot to a noble family.' The door of the house was locked, the usher of the black rod denied admittance, and the speaker was compelled to keep his seat while the resolutions were passed. Eight days after the king angrily prorogued the parliament. (*Parl. Hist.* ii. 222–492.)

But soon Sir John was to act a more prominent part. Noy, the attorney-general, who had invented or revived the tax called ship-money, died in the following August, before the writ for the imposition was issued; the removal of Sir Robert Heath from the chief justiceship of the Common Pleas, without any alleged cause, took place [in September; and on the 14th of October (1634) Finch, to the surprise of all, received the latter appointment. (*Croke, Car.* 375.) The writ for ship-money being issued six days after naturally induced the public to associate the removal, the substitution, and the writ as in some way connected together. Lord Clarendon (i. 127, 130) says that Finch 'took up ship-money where Noy left it, and, being a judge, carried it up to that pinnacle from whence he almost broke his own neck, having in his journey thither had too much influence on his brethren to induce them to concur in a judgment they had all cause to repent.' Though he denied having known of the writ at the time of his appointment, he acknowledged having collected his brethren's opinions on the subject, and when the case of Hampden came under discussion he gave so absolute an opinion in its favour, and contended so strenuously against the argument of his brother judges, Hutton and Croke, that he confirmed the general feeling that he was elevated to the bench for the purpose of carrying through the obnoxious impost, and, as Lord Clarendon says, by the judgment he delivered he made it 'much more abhorred and formidable' than before. (*State Trials*, iii. 1216.)

On his appointment in the place of Heath, and Sir John Banks succeeding Noy as attorney-general, the following specimen of bar wit was circulated (*Wood's Athen.* ii, 584):—

Noy's flood is gone,
The *Banks* appear;
Heath is shorn down,
And *Finch* sings here.

The prejudice against him was in no degree diminished by his heartless remark, when Mr. Prynne was brought up for sentence upon his second libel: 'I had thought Mr. Prynne had no ears, but methinks he hath ears.' Thus noticed, the hair was turned back, and the clipped members exposed, 'upon the sight whereof the lords were displeased they had been formerly no more cut off.' And the consequence was that the unfortunate gentleman was condemned to lose the remainder, which was done so cruelly and closely that a piece of his cheek was cut off with it. (*State Trials*, iii. 717, 749.)

Finch's unpopularity in the kingdom tended to advance his favour with the king, and on Lord Coventry's death he was appointed lord keeper on January 23, 1640. (*Rymer*, xx. 364.) Having been previously ennobled with the title of Baron Finch, of Fordwich in Kent, he opened the parliament that met in April (eleven years having elapsed since it had last assembled) with a fulsome speech, in which, alluding to the royal condescension in calling them together, he says that the king 'is now pleased to lay by the shining beams of majesty, as Phœbus did to Phaëton, that the distance between sovereignty and subjection should not barr you of that filial freedom of access to his person and counsels.' His majesty, however, felt it necessary to resume his beams in less than three weeks, and hastily dismissed the assembly on May 5. In the meantime the Commons had visited the lord keeper with a vote declaring that his conduct as speaker at the close of the last parliament was a breach of privilege (*Parl. Hist.* iii. 528, 552, 571), and the offence was not forgotten when the king was compelled to summon a new parliament in the following November. Lord Finch, finding by the resolution then passed by the Commons against ship-money and those who advised it, that preparations were making for proceeding against him personally, applied to the house, desiring to be heard in his own defence before it came to a vote; and, his request being granted, he delivered, on December 21, an artful and ingenious speech in his own vindication. But, notwithstanding his grace of elocution, the Commons were not to be diverted from their purpose, a vote being immediately passed for his accusation before the Lords, and a demand for his committal. On the following morning the message was delivered; but his lordship had taken advantage of the interval to escape, and,' first sending the Great Seal to the king, to sail for Holland. The articles against him charged him with endeavouring to subvert the fundamental laws of England, and to introduce an arbitrary tyrannical government against law; and comprehended, besides others, his refusal to put the question as speaker, his soliciting the judges' opinions on ship-money when chief justice, and his framing and advising the king's declaration after the dissolution of the last parliament. (*Ibid.* 626-698.)

From a passage in Lord Clarendon's work (i. 525), originally suppressed, it appears that many of the ascendant party were not desirous of urging the charges against Lord Finch to extremity; and their refraining from pressing for any further proceedings on the impeachment seems to warrant the assertion. His lordship remained quietly at the Hague, and the governing powers were content with receiving from him a composition of 7000*l*. (*State Trials*, iv. 18.) It does not appear when he returned to England, but he received two affectionate letters from Queen Henrietta Maria in 1640, and Elizabeth, Queen of Bohemia, in 1655, showing their continued interest in him. (*Archæologia*, xxi. 474.) On Charles II.'s return to his throne, Finch was named in the commission for the trial of the regicides in October 1660, and when Thomas Harrison in his defence asserted that the authority under which he acted was not usurped, but that it 'was done rather in the fear of the Lord,' Lord Finch interrupted him, and said, 'Though my lords here have been pleased to give you a great latitude, this must not be suffered, that you should run into these damnable excursions, to make God the author of this damnable treason committed.' In two or three of the other trials he also made some remarks. (*State Trials*, v. 986-1067.) He was then in his seventy-seventh year, which he did not live to complete, dying on November 20, 1660. He was buried in the ancient church of St. Martin, near Canterbury, in which parish his paternal seat, called The Moat, was situate; and a splendid monument to his memory was erected there by his widow.

However highly Lord Finch's talents and eloquence may have been spoken of, few have ventured to bear testimony to his independence as a judge or his wisdom as a statesman; and the general character that has with apparent truth been assigned to him is that of an unprincipled lawyer and a timeserving minister.

He was twice married, first to Eleanore, daughter of Sir George Wyat, of Boxley in Kent; and secondly to Mabella, daughter of Charles Fotherby, dean of Canterbury. As he left only a daughter (married to Sir George Radcliffe, of the privy council of Ireland), the title became extinct. (*Hasted*, xi. 162.)

FINCH, HENEAGE (LORD FINCH OF DAVENTRY, EARL OF NOTTINGHAM). Whatever discredit the family of Finch sustained from the equivocal character of the above John, Lord Finch of Fordwich, was amply redeemed in the person of his relative, the Earl of Nottingham, by the admiration and respect he commanded among his contemporaries, and the reverence with which his name is ever mentioned in the present day. He was great-grandson of Sir Thomas Finch, the ancestor of Lord Finch, and son of Sir Heneage Finch, recorder of London, by his first wife, Frances, daughter of Sir Edmund Bell, of Beaufré Hall, Norfolk (a descendant of the lord chief baron in the reign of Elizabeth). He was born on December 23, 1621, and, after passing through his curriculum at Westminster School, was admitted as a gentleman commoner at Christ Church, Oxford, in 1635, four years after his father's death. Anthony Wood records no degree that he took, although he remained at the university till he became a member of the Inner Temple in 1638. He was called to the bar in 1645, and must have soon obtained good practice in the courts, as his name frequently occurs in Siderfin's Reports during the Commonwealth as a leader in abstruse cases in the upper Bench. That he was no friend to the republican party may be inferred from his being selected for a prominent office immediately on the Restoration; and it was no doubt from the reputation of his loyalty that he was employed before the Protector Richard's parliament in February 1659 for Mr. Street, who had been returned for Worcester, and was petitioned against as having borne arms as a cavalier. On this occasion we have the first reference to the eloquence for which he has been so famed, the opposing counsel acknowledging that he had done the part 'not only of an advocate, but of an exquisite orator.' (*Burton*, iii. 423-434.) From his persuasive powers, he acquired the titles of 'the silver-tongued lawyer' and 'the English Cicero,' and from his graceful action that of 'the English Roscius.' Evelyn speaks (ii. 226) of his pleading 'most eloquently for the merchants trading to the Canaries;' and the gossiping Pepys (ii. 123, iv. 157) is in ecstasies when attending the court, exclaiming, 'So pleasant a thing is it to hear him plead.' Even the prejudiced Burnet (ii. 37) is obliged to concur, though he qualifies his praise by the depreciating remark that his eloquence was 'laboured and affected,' and that 'he saw it as much despised before he died.'

He was returned to the Convention Parliament of April 1660, by two constituencies, those of St. Michael's in Cornwall, and of the city of Canterbury, and, taking his seat for the latter, he was actively employed in all the steps adopted by the house to facilitate the king's return. A week after that event he was appointed solicitor-general and rewarded with a baronetcy. The trials of the regicides were conducted wholly by him, the attorney-general taking no part in them, and the whole proceedings were carried on with exemplary fairness and judgment. When the parliament met after the recess, he brought in the bill for keeping the fast of King Charles's martyrdom, which, after an observance of two centuries, has been lately discontinued; and in a debate with reference to the attempted exaction of 150*l.* by the serjeant-at-arms for fees against Milton, he is reported to have said 'Milton was Latin secretary to Cromwell, and deserved hanging;' a sentiment which shocks our modern ears, and which has been accordingly stigmatised by over-nice critics, without making due allowance for the frantic loyalty of the time, and without remembering that little was then known of the great bard beyond his republican writings; his 'Comus,' 'L'Allegro,' and 'Il Penseroso,' and other minor poems, having had a very limited circulation.

A new parliament met in May 1661, in which Sir Heneage represented the university of Cambridge. Later in the year he became treasurer of his inn of court, and, being selected as autumn reader, he had the expensive satisfaction of reviving the splendid festivities which had been so long discontinued, and on the last day of the feast had the honour of entertaining the king. Sir Heneage resided, at this time and till his death, at Kensington, in the mansion which afterwards became the palace, his son having sold it to King William.

At the trial of Lord Morley for murder, Sir Heneage summed up the evidence in an eloquent and impressive speech, which is fully reported in the 'State Trials.' (vi. 778.) Lord Clarendon then acted as high steward, and in the following year was himself the subject of prosecution. During its progress Sir Heneage, as far as can be judged from the published reports, showed his disapproval of the proceedings, and did what he legally could in behalf of the fallen statesman. (*Parl. Hist.* iv. 375, &c.) In 1670 he succeeded to the office of attorney-general, which he held for three years and a half; and on the removal of Lord Shaftesbury from the chancellorship, the Great Seal was on November 9, 1673, placed in his hands, where it remained till his death, a period of nine years. Two months after his advancement he was raised to the peerage as Baron Finch of Daventry. For two years he was distinguished by the title of lord keeper only, but at the end of that time, on December 19, 1675, he was constituted lord high chancellor, and in

1681 he was further honoured with the earldom of Nottingham. While he held the Seal he presided as lord steward on three occasions—in 1678, on the trials of the Earl of Pembroke and of Lord Cornwallis, both for murder; and in 1680, on that of Viscount Stafford, impeached for complicity in the Popish Plot. In pronouncing sentence on that unfortunate nobleman he shows his belief in the existence of the plot 'beyond all possibility of doubting,' and even carries it back so far as the Fire of London, exclaiming, 'Does any man now doubt how London came to be burnt?' He, however, according to Roger North, discredited the witnesses brought forward to support it, and pointed out the inconsistencies of their evidence. (*State Trials*, vi. 1310, vii. 143, 1294; *North's Examen*, 208.)

Towards the close of the chancellor's life he suffered greatly from the gout, and was in other respects so much afflicted that he often sat to hear causes when in great pain and more fit to keep his room. Frequently unable to perform his duties in the House of Lords, his place as speaker was supplied by Chief Justice North, with whom he preserved a cordial friendship. He died at the age of sixty-one at his house in Great Queen Street, Lincoln's Inn Fields, on December 18, 1682, and was buried in the church of Ravenstone in Bucks, where he had a seat, his son placing a splendid monument to his memory over his remains.

In the various steps of his career, while party animosities were most violent and the whole kingdom was divided into factions, he carried himself with so much wisdom and steadiness, modesty and forbearance, that he appeared to be of no faction himself, and not only retained the good opinion of his sovereign, but escaped even the assaults, if not the censures, from which few were exempt, of his political opponents.

As chancellor, Lord Nottingham is described by Blackstone (iii. 55) as 'a person of the greatest abilities and most uncorrupted integrity. ... The reason and necessities of mankind arising from the great change in property by the extension of trade and the abolition of military tenures enabled him in the course of nine years to build a system of jurisprudence and jurisdiction upon wide and rational foundations.' Burnet (ii. 67) calls him 'a man of probity, and well versed in the laws ... an incorrupt judge, and in his court he could resist the strongest applications even from the king himself, though he did it no where else;' forgetting his refusal to affix the Great Seal to Lord Danby's pardon, and the remark of the king on returning it after he had himself used it for the purpose, 'Take it back, my lord, I know not where to bestow it better.' In the disposal of his ecclesiastical patronage he was so particular that, not thinking himself a judge of the merits of the suitors for it, he charged it upon the conscience of his chaplain (Dr. Sharp, afterwards Archbishop of York) to make the closest enquiry and give the best advice, so that he might never bestow any preferment upon an undeserving man.

Tate, in the second part that he added to Dryden's 'Absalom and Achitophel,' describes him in encomiastic terms under the character of Amri; and the Duke of Wharton, in the 'North Briton' (No. 69), speaks of him in terms equally eulogistic. His character may be estimated by the reputation which has ever since been attached to his name, by the frequent references to his decisions as authority, and by the veneration with which he is still regarded by those who practise in Westminster Hall, where his common appellation is 'The Father of Equity.' As a law reformer too he must hold the highest place, since to him we owe the most important and most useful act of the reign—the Statute of Frauds.

He has been unfortunate in the contemporary reporters of his decisions, of whom there were three—namely, William Nelson, an anonymous author, and Sir Anthony Keck, the lord commissioner of the Great Seal under William III., none of whose publications are satisfactory or of much reputation. A few cases may be met with occasionally in other writers, and Lord Nottingham left a folio volume in manuscript of all the judgments he pronounced, some of the most important of which have been given to the world by Mr. Swanston, the learned editor of our own time. While attorney-general he superintended the edition of Sir Henry Hobart's Reports (1671). The other publications in his name are principally his speeches and legal arguments.

In his private life there is not one story told to his discredit, ready as that profligate age was to feed malice and deal in scandal. He kept up the dignity of his office with liberality and splendour, and was so far from being tainted with avarice that he gave up 4000*l.* a year out of his official allowances. He patronised largely learning and learned men. In the language of Bishop Warburton, 'he took into his notice and continued long in his protection every great name in letters and religion, from Cudworth to Prideaux.'

He married early in life Elizabeth, daughter of Mr. William Harvey, who died seven years before him, having produced him fourteen children. His eldest son, Daniel, succeeded to a second earldom, that of Winchilsea, a title given to his great-grandmother, the widow of Sir Moyle Finch; and in his descendants the double earldom of Winchilsea and Nottingham still survives.

The chancellor's second son, Heneage, also an eminent lawyer and solicitor-general before his father's death till he was removed by James II., greatly distinguished himself by his strenuous advocacy in the cause of the seven bishops. He received no office or other reward from King William, but when Queen Anne came to the throne he was raised to the peerage as Lord Guernsey, to which the earldom of Aylesford was added by George I., and has been enjoyed ever since by his descendants in regular succession. (*Collins's Peerage*, iii. 420; *Athen. Oxon.* iv. 66; *Welsby*, 51.)

FINEUX, JOHN, whose family was established at Swingfield in Kent, which Hasted says was bestowed on John Fineaux by Nicholas Criol, in 3 Richard II., in gratitude for saving his life at the battle of Poictiers, was one of three sons of William Fineux of that place, by a daughter of — Monyngs; and, taking Fuller's authority that he was eighty-four years of age when he died, he must have been born about 1441. Fuller states also that he was twenty-eight before he took to the study of the law, that he followed that profession twenty-eight years before he was made a judge, and that he continued a judge for twenty-eight years. His legal studies, therefore, must have commenced about the year 1469, 9 Edward IV. The inn of court to which he belonged is not ascertained, nor does his name appear in the Year Books till 1485, 1 Henry VII., when he was called serjeant-at-law; but David Lloyd states that he was steward of 129 manors at once, counsel to sixteen noblemen, and that he left behind him twenty-three folio volumes of notes, and 3502 cases he had managed himself. (*State Worthies*, 81–86.) The motto he selected for his serjeant's ring (the first recorded instance of its use) was, 'Suæ quisque fortunæ faber,' and one is in possession of a noble descendant of the judge.

He owed his elevation to the bench to his bold opposition to the imposition of the tenth penny. 'Let us see,' said he, 'before we pay anything, whether we have anything we can call our own to pay.' The king, when Archbishop Morton resisted his advancement as being an encouragement of the factious, more wisely suggested that 'so noble a patriot would be an useful courtier, and that one who could do so well at the bar might do more at the bench.' He was accordingly made a judge of the Common Pleas on February 11, 1494, and gave so much satisfaction in that court that in less than two years he was promoted to the office of chief justice of the King's Bench, on November 24, 1495. During the remainder of the reign, and for the first sixteen years of that of Henry VIII., he retained his high position with an unblemished reputation both as a lawyer and a man.

He died in 1525, residing then in the manor of Hawe in the parish of Herne, which he had purchased; and his remains were deposited in Canterbury Cathedral. He is represented as a person of great piety, though of a very cheerful temper and conversation. He was a considerable benefactor to the Augustin friars and the priory of Christchurch in Canterbury, and also to the abbey of Faversham; and it tells well of his character that Archbishop Morton, who had opposed him, made him his executor, and that he was nominated to the same duty under the will of Henry VII.

The inn of Chancery now called New Inn is said to have belonged to him, and to have been let by him to the students there when they first removed from St. George's Inn, at the rent of 6*l*. per annum. (*Orig. Jurid.* 230.)

He was twice married. His first wife was Elizabeth, daughter and heir of William Appulderfeld, Esq., and by her he had two daughters, the eldest of whom, Jane, married Attorney-General John Roper, whose grandson was created in 1616 Baron Teynham. His second wife was Elizabeth, widow of William Cleere, and daughter of Sir John Paston, grandson of William Paston, the judge in the reign of Henry VI. From his only son by her descended an only daughter, who married Sir John Smythe, of Ostenhanger in Kent, whose son Sir Thomas in 1628 was created Viscount Strangford in Ireland, to which was added the English title of Baron Penshurst in 1825, so that the chief justice was lately doubly represented in the House of Lords. (*Fuller*, i. 500; *Hasted*, vi. 141, vii. 122, ix. 87, 454.)

FISHEBURN, THOMAS DE, was probably the son of Ralph de Fisseburn, who in 42 Henry III. paid a fine of one hundred shillings in Northumberland for marrying Beatrice, the widow of William the Coroner. (*Excerpt. e Rot. Fin.* ii. 278.) He was appointed justice itinerant in 21 Edward I., and assizes taken before him in Cumberland in the same reign are referred to in 2 Edward II. (*Abb. Placit.* 307, 309.) He continued to act as a justice of assize until 10 Edward II.

FISHER, JOHN, is said to be descended from Osbernus Piscator, who held lands in Bedfordshire in the time of Edward the Confessor. The first time his name occurs is when he was made king's serjeant-at-law in 1486. From that period the Year Books frequently mention him as an advocate, till he was constituted a judge of the Common Pleas on November 3, 1501. In the summer preceding he acted as a judge on the circuit at Nottingham and Derby (*Plumpton Corr.* 159, 161), as serjeants then commonly did, and still frequently do. Fines continued to be levied before him till the end of the reign, and he received a new patent on the accession of Henry VII., but died in the next year.

FITZ-AILWYN, HENRY. Considerable difficulty frequently arises in tracing the families to which individuals who are solely designated in the records as 'filius Aluredi,' 'filius Bernardi,' 'filius Radulfi,' &c., belong; because, surnames not being at that period in general use, sons were often described by the Christian names of their fathers, their own Christian names being in turn assumed by their children. Thus the designation varied in the different generations, until one of the family, by acquiring possessions, or honours, or office, fixed his own name, or some other he had assumed, permanently for his descendants. The difficulty is materially increased where both the Christian names thus united were of common occurrence. In these cases two persons of different families not unfrequently bore the same appellation, so that much confusion often occurs in investigating the facts and records of the time, by the impossibility to distinguish the precise individual intended.

The frequent occurrence of names of this class (the prefix 'Fitz' being substituted for that of 'Filius') renders these observations necessary, in order to account for the doubt that is sometimes expressed as to their actual lineage. They will apply more forcibly to others than to the individual now to be noticed; but their introduction appeared more appropriate when the first example was to be considered.

Henry Fitz-Ailwyn, called of London Stone, was probably a lineal descendant of Ailwin Child, who founded the priory of Bermondsey in 1082, part of his family being buried there. In 1 Richard I., 1189, he was appointed mayor of London by the king, being the first who bore that title, and as such he is particularly mentioned to have officiated at the coronation as chief butler of the kingdom. It was not till 10 John, 1208, that the citizens obtained the power of annually electing a mayor for themselves. Their choice then fell upon Fitz-Ailwyn, who had presided over them from his first appointment, and whom they annually re-elected till his death in 14 John, 1212, so that he held the office for a period of twenty-four years.

His name is inserted in this list of justiciers because he was one of those present at Westminster in 8 John before whom a fine was acknowledged.

Sir Francis Palgrave, in p. cv. of the Introduction to the 'Rotuli Curiæ Regis,' gives a curious deed by which he grants a piece of land in Lim-Strete, in the city of London, to William Lafaite. The consideration is half a mark of silver 'in gersumiam,' and the annual rent reserved is twelve pence.

He died in 1212, 14 John (*Rot. Claus.* i. 124, 127), and was buried in the priory of the Holy Trinity, near Aldgate. By his wife Margaret, who survived him, he had four sons—Peter, Alan, Thomas, and Richard.

FITZ-ALAN, BRIAN, was the son of Alan Fitz-Brian, a grandson of Alan, Earl of Brittany and Richmond. (*Dugdale's Baron.* i. 23.) At the end of John's reign he took part with the insurgent barons; but his estates, which were thereupon seized, were restored soon after the accession of Henry III. (*Rot. Claus.* i. 165, 338.) From 9 to 15 Henry III. he performed the duty of justice itinerant in the northern counties. (*Ibid.* ii. 77, 151, 213.) From 13 to 19 Henry III. he was sheriff of Northumberland and from 21 to 23 Henry III. he held the same office in Yorkshire. (*Fuller's Worthies.*) The time of his death is not mentioned, but his son Brian succeeded him, and dying without male issue, the barony is in abeyance among the descendants of his two daughters—Agnes, the wife of Sir Gilbert Stapelton; and Katherine, the wife of John Lord Grey de Rotherfield. (*Nicolas's Synopsis.*)

FITZ-ALAN, THOMAS. See T. DE ARUNDEL.

FITZ-ALAN, WILLIAM, of Clun in Shropshire, was the grandson of Alan, the son of Flathald, who received from William the Conqueror the castle of Oswaldstre, and son of William of the same name.

In 1 Richard I., 1189, he was one of the justices itinerant into Shropshire, Hereford, Gloucester, and Stafford. (*Pipe Roll,* 95-248.) In the next year he became sheriff of Shropshire, and continued to hold that office through the remainder of the reign, and for the first three years of that of King John. (*Fuller.*) The manor of Chipping-Norton in Oxfordshire belonged to him, for a fair at which, and also at Clun, he obtained charters from King John. (*Rot. Chart.* 136.)

He died about 15 John, 1213-14, and left two sons, the younger of whom, John, by his marriage with Isabel, one of the sisters and coheirs of Hugh de Albini, Earl of Arundel, acquired, in the partition of the estates, the castle of Arundel, which, with its appendant earldom, has remained in the family ever since, and is now held by his lineal descendant, the Duke of Norfolk.

FITZ-ALDELM, WILLIAM, or ALDELIN, sometimes also called de Burgh, was descended from Robert, Earl of Moreton in Normandy, and Earl of Cornwall in Eng-

FITZ-ALDELM

land, the uterine brother of William the Conqueror. Earl Robert's son William succeeded him, and fighting against Henry I. was taken prisoner and confined for the rest of his life, and cruelly deprived of his eyes. He is said to have left two sons, the elder of whom was Aldelm, the father of the subject of the present notice. The younger was either the grandfather or father of the celebrated Hubert de Burgh.

In 11 Henry II. William Fitz-Aldelm is called one of the king's marshals, and in 1177, and probably before, he was one of the dapifers. (*Madox*, 44–50.)

It was no doubt in the latter character that he accompanied King Henry in his expedition to Ireland in October 1171. He was then sent with Hugh de Lacy to receive the allegiance of Roderick, King of Connaught, and on the king's return to England in the next year the city of Wexford was committed to his charge, with two lieutenants under him. In 1173 Pope Adrian's bull granting the kingdom of Ireland to Henry was entrusted to the prior of Wallingford and him to exhibit before the synod of bishops at Waterford, and on the death of Richard de Clare, Earl of Pembroke, in 1176, the king appointed him deputy over the whole of that kingdom, and granted him the wardship of Isabella, the earl's daughter and heir.

His government, which is represented as having been weak and negligent, did not last above a year, Prince John receiving a grant of the kingdom at the parliament held at Oxford in May 1177, Fitz-Aldelm himself being present there. The city of Wexford, however, was restored to his charge, together with the province of Leinster.

Luxurious, proud, and covetous, harsh, unkind, and tyrannical to his officers, his unpopularity was heightened by the disgust naturally felt by a brave people against one to whom was imputed a too careful avoidance of personal danger in the wars which he undertook. The complaints of the Irish deprived him for some time of Henry's favour, though they did not occasion his removal.

During his residence in Ireland he founded the priory of St. Thomas the Martyr at Dublin. Brady (i. 365) states that he was seneschal of Normandy, Poictou, and some other of the king's dominions in France.

After Henry's death he held the office of sheriff of Cumberland during the first nine years of Richard's reign, and in the first year he was one of the justices itinerant in that county and in Yorkshire, and in the former again in 8 Richard I. (*Madox*, i. 704, ii. 236.)

He afterwards returned to Ireland, obtained a great part of the province of Connaught, and while engaged in some cruel ravages was seized with an illness, of which he died in 1204.

He married Juliana, the daughter of Robert Doisnell, and by her he had Richard de Burgo, surnamed the Great, lord of Connaught and Trim, who left two sons, Walter and William. Walter, by marrying Maude, the heir of Hugh de Lacy, became Earl of Ulster in Ireland, and from him, by the marriage of the third earl's sole daughter and heir, Elizabeth, with Lionel, Duke of Clarence, third son of King Edward III., descended Richard, Duke of York, the father of King Edward IV. William was the ancestor of the present Marquis and Earl of Clanricarde in Ireland, who was created Baron Somerhill in England in 1826. The same title, with that of Viscount Tunbridge, was given to Richard, fourth Earl of Clanricarde, in 1624, to which was added the earldom of St. Albans in 1628; but these became extinct in 1659. The Irish earldom then devolved on a cousin, from whom the present marquis lineally proceeds. The Earl of Mayo also derives his lineage from the same root. (*Dugdale's Baron.* i. 693; *Leland's Ireland*, i. 113, &c.; *Lord Lyttelton's Henry II.* iii. 85, &c.; *Lingard*, ii. 261.)

FITZ-ALEXANDER, NIGEL, was one of the justiciers present in the Curia Regis in 31 Henry II., 1185, when a fine was levied there. (*Hunter's Preface*.) In the same year, and until 1 Richard I., he was sheriff of Lincolnshire (*Fuller*), in which county he had considerable property. He gave a carucate of land in Bolebi to the priory of Sempringham in that county in pure and perpetual alms; and it is a curious fact that in 29 Henry III. the prior was exempted from the scutage upon it, because the heirs of Nigel had then sufficient property in the county to discharge it. (*Madox*, i. 672.) In 1 Richard I., also, he was one of the justices itinerant in the counties of Buckingham, Bedford, and Lincoln; and by the roll of that year he appears to have been a justicier of the forest acting in Yorkshire. He died before 9 John, when his son Osbert was engaged in a suit relative to lands in Fulebec in Lincolnshire.

FITZ-ALURED, RICHARD, is only known by an entry on the Great Roll of 31 Henry I. In that record it is stated that he owed— i. e., that he fined—fifteen silver marks that he might sit with Ralph Basset to hold the king's pleas in Buckinghamshire. He is called pincerna, or butler, an office which he probably held under William de Albini, the king's chief butler. (*Madox*, i. 62. 457.)

FITZ-BERNARD, ROBERT, was among the eighteen justices itinerant appointed at the council of Northampton, held on

January 23, 1176, 22 Henry II., to distribute justice throughout the kingdom. Robert Fitz-Bernard was placed at the head of the three to whom the counties of Kent, Surrey, Sussex, Hants, Berks, and Oxford were entrusted, he being at that time, and until 29 Henry II., sheriff of the first-named county.

He had been sheriff of Devonshire also for six years from 1165. He died about 9 Richard II. (*Madox*, i. 120-138, 190; *Fuller; Lord Lyttelton*, iii. 93, 186.)

FITZ-BERNARD, THOMAS, was an officer of King Henry's household, and was twice subjected, in 1166 and 1169, to the sentence of excommunication pronounced against him by Becket, for the purpose of annoying the king. His pretence was that Fitz-Bernard had usurped the goods of the church of Canterbury; but the pope, on the king's representation that Fitz-Bernard and others were in attendance on his person, took off the ban.

In 1178, 24 Henry II., and the two following years, he acted as a justice itinerant in several counties; and in 1182 he is named as one of the justiciers and barons before whom fines were levied in the Curia Regis at Westminster. He was also justice of the forest, and from 1178 to 1184 he held the sheriffalty of Northamptonshire. (*Lord Lyttelton*, ii. 434, 506, iii. 404; *Madox*, i. 133-137; *Hunter's Preface*, xxi.; *Fuller*.)

FITZ-ERNISE, PHILIP, was one of the justices itinerant appointed by the writ of Richard de Luci to make the assize for the county of Gloucester in 20 Henry II., 1174. (*Madox*, i. 123.)

FITZ-GEROLD, HENRY, as one of the king's chamberlains, had a seat in the Curia Regis, and is one of the three 'justiciæ regis' directing an exchange of lands at Canterbury between the king and one Atheliza. In 16 and 17 Henry II., 1170-1, he was a justice itinerant into Kent.

There can be little doubt that he was either the son or brother (probably the former) of Warine Fitz-Gerold, the third lord mentioned by Dugdale, whom he succeeded in the office of chamberlain. (*Madox*, i. 145, 204.)

FITZ-GILBERT, RICHARD DE, had a variety of names. He was first called Richard Fitz-Gilbert from his father, and afterwards de Benefacta, from his estate of Benefield in Northamptonshire; de Tunbridge, from that castle in Kent; and de Clare, from the honor or earldom of that name in Suffolk, all of which were included in his possessions.

He was the son of Gilbert Crispin, Earl of Brion and Ou, whose father Geoffrey was a natural son of Richard I., Duke of Normandy, so that he was second cousin to the Conqueror on his father's side; and if his mother was, as one pedigree asserts (*Manning and Bray's Surrey*, i. xix.), Arlotta, who was also mother of the Conqueror, he was, on her side, that monarch's half-brother.

He was a participator in the dangers of the field of Hastings. His share in the lands distributed among the Norman adventurers was not a niggardly one. At the general survey he was found to be possessed (among others) of thirty-eight lordships in Surrey, thirty-five in Essex, three in Cambridgeshire, and ninety-five in Suffolk, of which Clare was the chief, the name of which his descendants adopted. He exchanged the strong castle of Brion in Normandy, which he inherited, for the town and castle of Tunbridge, with a circuit round them, the extent of which was fixed by the same rope by which his own domains at Brion had been measured, comprehending three miles from every part of the walls.

When King William went to Normandy in 1073 he was left as joint chief justiciary of the kingdom with William de Warenne, and during their rule they defeated Roger Fitz-Osberne, Earl of Hereford, and Ralph de Guader, Earl of Norfolk, who had headed a rebellion against the royal authority.

After the Conqueror's death he at first took the part of his son Robert, but afterwards adhered to William Rufus, and his successor Henry I. In the reign of the latter he was slain in an ambush, while marching to his property in Cardiganshire.

He married Rohais, the daughter of Walter Giffard, Earl of Buckingham, and by her he left five sons, the eldest of whom was Gilbert, who is generally spoken of as *de Tunbridge*, whose eldest son, Richard, was created Earl of Hertford, a title which was successively enjoyed (together with that of Clare) by his two sons Gilbert and Roger de Clare. Gilbert's second son, Gilbert, was created Earl of Pembroke by King Stephen, and this title devolved on the famous William Mareschall by his marriage with this earl's grand-daughter. (*Madox*, i. 32; *Dugdale's Baron.* i. 206; *Brady's England*, &c.)

FITZ-HELTON, WILLIAM, or FITZ-HELT, is named by Dugdale as one of the justices itinerant in 16 Henry II., 1170, but who have been shown to be commissioners of enquiry into the conduct of the sheriffs, &c. A family of that name is mentioned by Madox as paying seventy shillings for scutage in Kent; and by an entry on the Great Roll of 1 Richard I. (232) it appears that William Fitz-Helte and William de Enema attested the account of the sheriff of that county for money laid out in the works of Dover Castle. (*Madox*, i. 630.)

FITZ-HENRY, RANULPH, whose family

eventually adopted the name of Fitz-Hugh, and may be traced back to Bardolph, lord of Ravensworth in the time of William the Conqueror, was the son of Henry Fitz-Hervey, who died in 1201, 3 John. In 17 John, having shown symptoms of joining the discontented barons, he obtained a safe-conduct to go to the king to make his peace, which he effected on the payment of a fine of fifty marks. (*Rot. Pat.* 163.) He married Alicia, the daughter and heir of Adam de Staveley, and in 2 Henry III. fined forty marks for having livery of the lands held by his father-in-law in capite in Yorkshire. (*Excerpt. e Rot. Fin.* i. 14.)

In 18 Henry III., 1234, he was appointed one of the justices itinerant then sent into Cumberland.

He died, not as Dugdale states, in 1262, but before January 13, 1243; for on that day a writ was granted to Alicia, who '*was* the wife of Ranulph Fitz-Henry.' (*Ibid.* 393.) He was succeeded by his son, Henry Fitz-Ranulph, from whose son, Hugh Fitz-Henry, the name of Fitz-Hugh was permanently adopted. The barony continued in male heirs till 1512, since which time it has been in abeyance. (*Nicolas.*)

FITZ-HERBERT, MATHEW, a younger son of Herbert Fitz-Herbert, who was chamberlain to Henry I., was attached to King John's court, and is a frequent witness to his charters from the sixth year of his reign. (*Rot. Chart.* 140, &c.) From 12 to 17 John he was sheriff of Sussex, during part of which time he held the office of custos of the port of London (*Rot. Claus.* i. 145); and in 18 John the castle of Pontoise was delivered to his charge. His services and faithful adherence to his sovereign were not without reward: besides the lands of William Pont Arch in Gloucestershire, he received a grant of the manors of Wufrinton and Kinemesdon in Somersetshire; and he possessed the manor of Chedelinton in the same county, for which he obtained a market. (*Rot. Pat.* 184, 194; *Rot. Claus.* i. 17, 48, 363.) He married Joanna, daughter and heiress of William de Mandeville and Mabilia Patric, his wife, and by her right had the land of Ollonde in Normandy.

For the first thirteen years of the next reign he continued sheriff of Sussex, and acted twice as a justice itinerant, in 3 and 11 Henry III. (*Rot. Claus.* ii. 213.)

He died in 1231. His son Herbert (called Herbert Fitz-Mathew) died in 1245, when his possessions devolved on his next brother, Peter, who also dying in 1255 was succeeded by John, the son of the third brother, Mathew, after whom the descent is doubtful. (*Excerpt. e Rot. Fin.* i. 211, 430, 432, ii. 205.)

FITZ-HERBERT, ANTHONY, of Norbury, a manor in Derbyshire, granted in 1125 by William, prior of Tutbury, to William Fitz-Herbert, was the sixth and youngest son of Ralph Fitz-Herbert, the twelfth lord, by Elizabeth, daughter and sole heir of John Marshall, of Upton in Leicestershire; and by the death of all his brothers without male issue he eventually succeeded to the paternal estate, as fourteenth lord.

Anthony Wood claims him as a member of the university of Oxford, but is not able to say of what college; and the place of his legal education is equally uncertain, though, from the insertion of his arms in the window of Gray's Inn Hall, that society evidently adopts him. It is more surprising that there should be any difficulty in tracing the academical home of so eminent and learned a lawyer, than that any school should desire to be considered as having guided his studies. Although his name does not appear in the courts till some time after he was called to the degree of serjeant in 1510, it is evident that he had been long industriously employed in the composition of his laborious work, 'The Grand Abridgment,' containing an abstract of the Year Books till his time, the first edition of which was published in 1514. In 1516 he was made one of the king's serjeants, and about the same time he received the honour of knighthood. In less than six years his elevation to the bench as a judge of the Common Pleas took place, in Easter 1522. He sat in this court for the remainder of his life, a period of sixteen years.

Besides his judicial duties, he had frequent occupation on the king's affairs. He was one of the commissioners sent to Ireland, and a visitor of the monasteries; and during the latter period of his career his name appears more prominently in connection with the political events of the time. His signature is the last but one of the seventeen subscribers to the articles of impeachment against Cardinal Wolsey, and he was one of the commissioners appointed on the trials both of Sir Thomas More and Bishop Fisher. Notwithstanding the disgust which the conviction of these two excellent men universally excited, Fitz-Herbert's reputation sustained no blemish, the world knowing that his being joined in the commission was an act that he could not prevent, and that his interference with the will of the arbitrary despot would have been both useless and dangerous. His judicial character had been raised by his having allowed bills for extortion against Wolsey while in the height of his power to be found before him at York, for which he suffered the cardinal's rebuke (*State Trials*, i. 377-398; *Hall's Chron.* 685); and his legal reputation had continued to increase, not only from the sound judgments he pronounced, but from the seven useful and learned works with which he followed his early undertaking, showing that his labours were not confined to professional enquiries, but extended to subjects of general interest, and aimed at instructing all mankind.

Sir Anthony died, as appears by his epitaph in the church at Norbury, on May 27, 1538. In his last moments it is said that he enjoined his children, by a solemn promise, never to accept a grant or to make a purchase of any of the abbey lands. He was twice married. By his first wife, who was Dorothy, daughter of Sir Henry Willoughby, of Wollaton, Notts, he had no issue. By his second wife, Matilda, daughter and heir of Richard Cotton, of Hampstall-Ridware in Staffordshire, he left several children. Norbury, after a regular descent of more than seven hundred years, is still in possession of a lineal representative of the family.

The Fitz-Herberts of Tissington in Derbyshire are of a different but equally ancient family, which, however, became connected with the Fitz-Herberts of Norbury by marriage with one of the descendants of the judge.

FITZ-HERVEY, HENRY, was probably the father of Osbert, noticed in the next article; but the early history of the family is involved in some obscurity. If so, he attended King Richard in his expedition to the Holy Land, and was much esteemed by King John.

In 9 Richard I., 1197, he was one of the justices itinerant who fixed the tallage in Cumberland (*Madox*, i. 704); and in 10 John, 1208, he was present as a justicier when fines were acknowledged at Carlisle.

King John confirmed to him his lands at Hinton in Richmond, in Scorton, and other places; and the forest in Teisedale, as his ancestors held it, and authorised him to fortify his house at Cudereston.

He married Alice, the daughter of Henry Fitz-Yvo. When he died is uncertain, but he survived Osbert, his eldest son.

FITZ-HERVEY, OSBERT. Osbert Fitz-Hervey's name appears as one of the justiciers of the King's Court at Westminster for a period of twenty-five years—viz., from 28 Henry II., 1182, till 7 John, 1205–6—in almost every year of which he was present when fines were levied there (*Hunter's Preface*), and frequently he performed the duties of a justice itinerant. Joceline de Brakelonda (25) records that he was subsheriff of Norfolk and Suffolk.

He was a descendant of a younger son of Hervey, Duke of Orleans, named Robert, who accompanied William the Conqueror in his enterprise against England, and received part of the territorial spoil in reward for his services. The name of Osbert's father was Henry, probably the justicier last noticed, and his mother was Alice, daughter of Henry Fitz-Yvo. He married Dionysia, daughter of Geoffrey de Grey, and died in April 1206, leaving an only son Adam, who married Juliana, the daughter of the justicier John Fitz-Hugh, and their descendants through a long succession of years were conspicuous in the senate and the field. One of them, Sir William Hervey, was created by James I. baron of Ross in the county of Wexford, and by Charles I. Lord Hervey of Kidbroke in Kent, but on his death without male issue in 1642 his titles became extinct. Another representative of this distinguished family was raised by Queen Anne to the peerage, by the title of Lord Hervey of Ickworth in Suffolk, and by George I. he was advanced to the earldom of Bristol. The fifth earl was created Earl Jermyn and Marquis of Bristol by George IV. on June 30, 1826. (*Brydges' Collins's Peerage*, iv. 140, &c.)

FITZ-HUGH, JOHN, was among the justiciers before whom fines were acknowledged in 10 John, 1208. (*Hunter's Preface.*) He was of a Yorkshire family, and was high in the king's employment, being constable of Windsor Castle, in the custody of which he is noticed throughout the whole of the reign, and in that of Henry III.

In 10 and 12 John he held the sheriffalty of Sussex, and during the three following years that of Surrey, and in some of these years was concerned in the receipt of the tallage from the Jews, and in the collection of the customs of woad and wine. (*Madox*, i. 123, 774.) Among the mandates addressed to him, he is commanded on August 1212 to send the great crown, with all the regalia which he had in his custody, to the king at Nottingham. (*Rot. Claus.* i. 122.)

He was a firm adherent to King John, and was present with him on the expedition to Ireland (*Ibid.* 125), and during his subsequent contests with the barons. (*Wendover*, iii. 301.)

He died on March 7, 1222, 6 Henry III., leaving by his wife a son, who died young, and a daughter Juliana, who married Adam Fitz-Hervey, son of the last-noticed Osbert Fitz-Hervey.

FITZ-JAMES, JOHN, so far from Lord Campbell's assertion that he was 'of obscure birth' (*Chief Just.* i. 160), was of very good parentage and ancestry. The name, in connection with the county of Somerset, is as old as the reign of Edward III. (*Cal. Inquis.* p. m. ii. 163.) His grandfather is stated to have been James Fitz-James, who acquired the estate of Redlynch in that county, and considerable other property, by his marriage with Eleanor, the daughter and heir of Simon Draycott; and his father is described as John Fitz-James, whose wife was Alice, daughter of John Newburgh, of East Lullworth in Dorsetshire (*Godwin*, 190); and the Draycotts and Newburghs were second to none of the gentry of England in possessions and high blood. (*Athen. Oxon.* ii. 720; *Hutchins's Dorset*, ii. 337, &c.)

The last-named John was the father of three sons—1. John; 2. Richard, who was Bishop of Rochester, Chichester, and London in succession; and 3. Alored, the ancestor of the Lewesden branch of the family.

The eldest son, John, has by all writers been hitherto considered to have been the chief justice; but, on a full investigation of the family records, he is proved to be the father of the chief justice, who therefore, instead of being the elder brother, was the nephew of the bishop.

No evidence whatever exists of the place of Fitz-James's early education, and Lord Campbell is silent as to the authority on which he says that 'he made his fortune by his great good humour, and by being at college with Cardinal Wolsey.' If this were so, the cardinal was rather backward in his patronage; for Fitz-James's first promotion in the law was not till many years after Wolsey had attained supreme power. Lord Campbell adds, '*It is said* that Fitz-James, who was a Somersetshire man, kept up an intimacy with Wolsey when the latter had become a village parson in that county, and that he was actually in the brawl at the fair when his reverence, having got drunk, was set in the stocks by Sir Amyas Paulet.'

It would have been more satisfactory to his readers if his lordship had informed them where the facts he has thus announced are to be found. Though Anthony Wood did not know it, Fitz-James may possibly have been at Oxford; though Redlynch, Fitz-James's home, is at least sixteen miles from Lymington, Wolsey's parish, the intimacy between them may have existed; and though Fitz-James was very near the time of his solemn reading at the Temple, it is not impossible that he might have joined in the drunken brawl; yet all these circumstances, new and extraordinary as they appear, are of such interest in the lives both of the judge and the cardinal that a reference seems necessary, in order to decide whether their original relater is worthy of credit. The same enquiry will be made as to the authority on which his lordship states that Fitz-James at his inn of court 'chiefly distinguished himself on gaudy days by dancing before the judges, playing the part of the Abbot of Misrule, and swearing strange oaths;' that 'his agreeable manners made him popular . . . although very deficient in moots;' and that 'he was in deep despair' for want of clients till Wolsey, 'his former chum, . . . was able to throw some business in his way in the Court of Wards and Liveries.' Whatever may be the source from whence these curious particulars are extracted, the little dependence that should be placed on it may be estimated by the fact that the Court of Wards and Liveries was instituted, not only after the death of Wolsey, but even after that of Fitz-James, ten years later. (*Ellis's Letters*, 1st S. i. 176.)

He studied the law at the Middle Temple, where he sufficiently distinguished himself to be called to the bench of that society, to be made reader in 1505, and treasurer in 1509. He was recorder of Bristol in 1510 (*Cal. St. Papers* [1509], 157), and succeeded to the office of attorney-general on January 26, 1519, more than three years after Wolsey had become chancellor, and seven or eight years after he had acquired a complete ascendency over the king. In Trinity Term 1521 he was called to the degree of the coif, and on the 6th of the following February was constituted a puisne judge of the King's Bench, and two days afterwards chief baron of the Exchequer (*Dugdale's Orig.* 215, 221), a fact of which Lord Campbell does not seem to be aware. Judging from all appearances, he performed the duties of both offices at the same time, for which there were numerous precedents from the reign of Henry IV., with the slight variation that in former instances the judgeship was in the Common Pleas. He is named as chief baron in the will of Lord Zouche, dated October 1525. (*Test. Vetust.* 620.) When he had occupied this honourable position for four years he was promoted to the presidency of the Court of King's Bench on January 23, 1526, having been in the meantime serviceably employed to negotiate a marriage for Lord Percy, whose previous contract with Anne Boleyn stood in the way of the king's desires. (*Lingard*, vi. 112.)

He sat as chief justice for thirteen years, during a very trying period of the reign for one in his prominent position. There can be no doubt that he participated in the craven subserviency to the royal tyranny with which every one of his brethren was chargeable; but, in expressing disgust at the general failing, care must be taken not to visit on any one more than history justifies. Lord Campbell gives no authority for his assertion that Cardinal Wolsey incurred considerable obloquy by Fitz-James's appointment, or that the new chief justice was thought to be 'not only wanting in gravity of moral character, but that he had not sufficient professional knowledge for such a situation.' The prejudice also which his lordship displays against the chief justice renders it necessary to look with caution on his description of Fitz-James's conduct in the three great events in which he introduces his name—the disgrace of Wolsey, and the trials of Sir Thomas More and Bishop Fisher.

In reference to Wolsey, his lordship's endeavour to prove Fitz-James guilty of base ingratitude loses all its potency from the total want of evidence that the cardinal had been his benefactor. With this view, however, he makes the chief justice the active organ of the proceedings against the cardinal, charging him with having 'joined in the cry against him and assisted his enemies to the utmost,' and with having '*declared*' his readiness to concur in any proceedings by which the proud ecclesiastic . . . might be brought to condign punishment;' and he further represents Fitz-James as the *suggester* of Judge Shelley's argument to the cardinal with reference to the alienation to the king of the archiepiscopal palace of York House (now Whitehall). These are serious charges, and surely require more authentication than his lordship has afforded before they are admitted on the page of history. In addition to these, Lord Campbell describes the chief justice as the adviser and dictator of the articles adopted in the House of Lords against Wolsey, for no other apparent reason than that the name of 'John Fitz-James' appears as the last of the seventeen persons who subscribed them. The signature, even if his, is merely a formal one, and the articles no more 'indicate a pre-existing envy and jealousy' in Fitz-James than they do in Sir Thomas More, who signed at the head of all. There was, however, another John Fitz-James, of the Middle Temple, who might have held some office in the House of Lords.

Lord Campbell next introduces this 'recreant chief justice,' as he calls him, as one of the commissioners on the trial of Fisher, Bishop of Rochester, of which the lord chancellor was the head, and, though the chief justice is not personally mentioned in any one account of the proceedings, his lordship names him the spokesman on every occasion. Professing to quote verbatim from the 'State Trials' the answers of the court, which consisted of thirteen persons, nine of whom were lawyers, he includes *within* the marks of quotation with which he cites them the name of Chief Justice Fitz-James, instead of the words which are actually used—viz., 'some of the judges,' and 'the judges and lawyers;' the word 'judges' evidently applying to all members of the commission. Surely this mode of writing history cannot be defended. His lordship would have shown more charity, as there was clearly as much likelihood, if, in recording from the same report that 'some of the judges lamented so grievously' as to shed tears, he had suggested the possibility that Fitz-James was one of them.

At the trial of Sir Thomas More, Lord Campbell says that Fitz-James's conduct was 'not less atrocious,' adding that 'no one can deny that he was an accessory to this atrocious murder.' These are hard words, but the guilt must be divided among all those who sat in judgment. Fitz-James is mentioned once only in the report, and then an expression is put into his mouth which may well raise something more than a doubt whether he was satisfied of the justice of the proceedings. When Audley, the lord chancellor, who conducted the trial, 'loath to have the burden of the judgment to depend upon himself,' openly asked the advice of the Lord Fitz-James whether the indictment was sufficient or not, the chief justice answered, 'My lords all, by St. Gillian (that was ever his oath) I must needs confess that *if* the act of parliament be not unlawful, then is the indictment in my conscience not insufficient,' thus evading the very point raised by Sir Thomas More, which was that the act of parliament, being repugnant to the laws of God, was insufficient to charge any Christian man. (*Roper's More* [*Singer*], 88.) If he had not been previously overruled on that point, as the 'if' seems to infer, he was no doubt intimidated, as all his brethren were, by the fear of the consequences, of which they saw too many examples.

On the conviction of Queen Anne Boleyn Lord Campbell pursues the same course. He represents that 'the opinion of the judges was asked' whether the sentence upon her could be in the alternative, to be burnt or beheaded at the king's pleasure, and he puts a cruel speech into Fitz-James's mouth arguing against its being in the disjunctive, and consequently enforcing the former as the legal punishment of a woman attainted of treason. The sole words in the authority quoted, upon which this supposed speech is founded, are, '*The judges* complained of this way of proceeding, and said such a disjunctive in a judgment of treason had never been seen' (*State Trials*, i. 418; *Burnet's Reformation*, i. 407); and Lord Campbell not only translates 'the judges' into 'Fitz-James, C. J.,' but adds within inverted commas an argument as spoken by him on the occasion. It does not appear, however, that there was any opinion asked, or any public discussion on the subject, but, on the contrary, the above passage is merely a remark in Judge Spelman's Common-Place Book, and evidently shows nothing more than the judges' private doubts on the introduction of the precedent. Deeply as all Englishmen must feel the dreadful degradation of the law at this period, and disgusted as they must be at the despicable weakness of its professors, they would deem themselves guilty of injustice similar to that which was then administered if they convicted any individual on evidence concocted as this is. But the most curious part of the story remains to be told. The whole of the proceedings against the unfortunate queen are preserved in the 'Baga de Secretis,' and from them it is manifest that Fitz-James was not present at all. His name does not occur in any one of the writs, and Baldwin, the chief justice of the Common Pleas, was the principal judge in all of them. (3 *Report, Pub. Rec., App.* ii. 243.)

Is it not improbable that Fitz-James partook of those faults which pervaded the whole bench at the period in which he flourished; but they were faults arising more from that awful dread of majesty which the Tudors inculcated than from any personal cruelty or delinquency. Of Fitz-James nothing is told to distinguish him in this respect from the rest of the group, and certainly nothing to justify his being brought forward as a special object of vituperation. Indeed, if any credit is to be placed on David Lloyd (*State Worthies,* 114–118), who wrote little more than a century after the chief justice's death, he left a character behind him very different from that with which, two centuries later, Lord Campbell has depicted him. This author states that Sir John 'was so fearful of the very shadow and appearance of corruption that it cost his chief clerk his place but for taking a tankard after a signal cause of 1500*l.* a year, wherein he had been serviceable, though not as a bribe, but as a civility.' The following remarks in one of the additional MSS. (1523, f. 54) in the British Museum, which are either the foundation of or extracts from David Lloyd's sketch, convey also a pleasing picture:—

'Two maine principles y^t guide humane nature are conscience and law; by ye former we are obliged in reference to another world, by the latter in relation to this. What was law alwaye, was then a resolution, Neither to deny, nor defer, nor sell justice. When his cozen urged for a kindnesse, "Come to my house, (saith the judge,) I will deny you nothing; come to the king's court and I must do you justice."'

'He would attend each circumstance of an evidence, hearing what was impertinent, observing what was proper, saying, "We must have two soules as two sieves, one for the bran, and the other for the flowr; one for the grosse of a discourse, and the other for the quintessence."'

Fitz-James, however, did not escape those attacks from which even the best judges are not exempt. Sir R. Terres, the writer of a 'slanderous complaint against him, exhibited to the king in a written book,' was condemned to pay a fine, to stand in the pillory, and to lose his ears.

His retirement from his high office on January 21, 1539, arose probably from bodily infirmity; for in his will, which is dated in the previous October, he describes himself as 'weke and feble in bodye.' That he lived above two years afterwards may be presumed from the fact that the will was not proved till May 12, 1542. He was buried at Bruton, near to his manor of Redlynch, and a fine monument to his memory is in the parish church there.' His will contains a direction that his 'great book of Statutes in vellum or parchment . . . shall remayn to the howse [Redlynch] as an implement to the saide howse;' and his bequests in behalf of his poor neighbours and dependants are unmistakable proofs of his considerate benevolence.

FITZ-JOEL, WARIN, was one of the four justices itinerant sent in 8 Henry III., 1224, to Dunstable (*Rot. Claus.* i, 631), whose judgments against Faukes de Breauté led to such fatal consequences to that turbulent baron. In 1225 he went as justice itinerant into Cornwall; a fine was levied before him in Easter. In October he was sent with Thomas de Muleton on a special commission into Norfolk, to enquire into certain robberies committed on the merchants of Norway; and in the following January he acted as a justice itinerant in Hampshire and other counties.

FITZ-JOHN, THOMAS, was a justice itinerant in Cumberland in 18 Henry III., 1234. He had a grant in 17 John of the lands of Philip Fitz-John, in Yorkshire, during pleasure, and in 10 Henry III. was one of those appointed to assess the quinzime in Westmoreland. (*Rot. Claus.* i. 245, ii. 147.) He may possibly have been a second son of John Fitz-Geoffrey (the son of Geoffrey Fitz-Peter, Earl of Essex, by Aveline, his second wife), who in the same year was sheriff of Yorkshire. (*Dugdale's Baron.* i. 706.)

FITZ-JOHN, EUSTACE, appears on the Ancient Roll of 31 Henry I. as holding pleas on the northern circuits established by that king, in all of which he was united with Walter Espec. They seem to have taken some offence in Yorkshire, inasmuch as on the same roll it is recorded that they fined that they should not be any longer judges or jurors there. By the roll it is evident that he had held the office for at least two years.

He and Pain Fitz-John (next mentioned) were the sons of John de Burgo, called Monoculus, from having lost an eye, and the nephews of Serlo de Burgh, baron of Tonsburgh in Normandy, and founder of Knaresborough Castle, both of whom accompanied the Conqueror on his invasion of England. The latter dying without issue, Eustace succeeded as his heir, and thus became a powerful baron in the north, receiving very large additions to his inheritance from the bounty of King Henry, and being appointed governor of Bamburgh Castle in Northumberland. He held a high place in the confidence and favour of that king, and had the reputation of a wise and judicious counsellor.

On the death of Henry, the usurper Stephen took from him the custody of Bamburgh Castle, and on suspicion of a treasonable correspondence with David, King of Scotland, seized his person and kept him for a considerable time in confinement. On obtaining his release, he joined with Robert, Earl of Gloucester, in aiding the Empress Matilda; making good for her the castle of Malton, and raising a powerful force from his own vassals in support of the Scottish king's invasion. He held a command at the memorable battle of the Standard, fought at Northallerton on August 22, 1138, when the Scottish forces were entirely defeated. He must afterwards have made his peace with King Stephen, for in 1147 he founded the abbey of Alnwick in Northumberland, and in 1150 the priory of Walton in Yorkshire. In 3 Henry II., 1157, he was slain in battle with the Welsh, whom the king had attacked in a narrow and difficult pass in Flintshire.

He was twice married. His first wife was Beatrix, the daughter and sole heir of Yvo de Vesci, which name was afterwards assumed by Eustace's son William, who succeeded to the barony, which became extinct in 1297 by the death of William de Vescy, a justice itinerant in the reign of Edward I., without heirs.

His second wife was Agnes, daughter and heir of William Fitz-Nigel, baron of Halton, and constable of Chester, to both of which he succeeded. By her he had a son named Richard Fitz-Eustace, one of whose grandsons, Robert Fitz-Roger, was a justicier in the reigns of Richard I. and John, and another, Roger de Laci, was also a justicier in the latter reign. (*Madox*, i. 146, 457; *Monasticon*, vi. 867, 970; *Lord Lyttelton; Rapin; Nicolas's Synopsis*, 664.)

FITZ-JOHN, PAIN, brother of the abovementioned Eustace Fitz-John, was also a favourite baron and one of the chief counsellors of King Henry, in whose household he held the office of groom of the chamber (cubicularius). It was his duty to provide a measure of wine every night for the king, which, as it was seldom required by his majesty, Fitz-John and the pages generally drank. On one occasion the king, being thirsty, called for his wine, and it was gone; but, instead of being angry, he acknowledged that one measure was too little for both, and good-humouredly directed that the butler should supply two measures for the future, one for himself and one for Fitz-John. (*Mapes, De Nugis Curialium*, 210.)

In the roll of 31 Henry I. he is mentioned as a justice itinerant in the counties of Gloucester, Stafford, and Northampton. Besides his lands in Oxfordshire, Gloucestershire, and Norfolk, he likewise possessed the whole territory of Ewyas in Herefordshire. His castle of Caus, in 34 Henry I., was attacked in his absence by the Welsh, who burned it to the ground, and massacred all its inhabitants; and two years afterwards, in 1136, he himself was slain with 3000 of King Stephen's troops in a battle fought with the same enemy near Cardigan.

By his wife Sibyll he had a son and two daughters. Cecilia, the elder daughter, married Roger, the son of Milo of Gloucester (afterwards Earl of Hereford), his coadjutor as a justice itinerant; and Agnes, the younger daughter, married — de Montchensy. His son Robert took the name of Fitz-Payne, and his male descendants were summoned to Parliament until the reign of Edward III., when the title became in abeyance in the female line, and at last devolved on the Earls of Northumberland, but became extinct in 1670. (*Madox*, i. 146; *N. Fœdera*, i. 10; *Lord Lyttelton; Hasted; Baronage*, i. 90, 572; *Nicolas*.)

FITZ-JOHN, WILLIAM, in 9 Henry II., 1163, held pleas in the county of Hereford, and in 1168 he amerced Samuel, the priest of Pilton in Somersetshire. (*Madox*, i. 527, ii. 213.) He held some office about the court, and when Richard de Humet, the chief justiciary of Normandy, was sent to England by King Henry in 1170 to arrest Becket, with a view to save him from the mischief which he anticipated from the sudden absence of four of his knights, William Fitz-John and Hugh de Gundeville were despatched by Humet to Canterbury for the purpose; but before their arrival the archbishop's fate was accomplished. (*Lord Lyttelton*, iii. 2.)

FITZ-MARTIN, WILLIAM, who had land in Hampshire, was a justicier or baron acting in the Exchequer both in 4 and 16 Henry II., 1170. He is also one of the twelve commissioners, whom Dugdale calls justices itinerant, who in the same year were sent to enquire into the conduct of the sheriffs in the several counties of the kingdom. (*Madox*, ii. 253; *Pipe Roll*, 172.)

FITZ-NIGEL, or FITZ-NEALE, WILLIAM, is named among the commissioners appointed in 1170 to examine into abuses of the sheriffs, &c., whom Dugdale erroneously calls justices itinerant. He was sheriff of Kent in 1184, 30 Henry II., and in the certificate returned by the Bishop of Chichester for the aid on marrying the king's daughter in 12 Henry II., 1166, he mentions William Fitz-Neale as holding one knight's fee under that church.

It is not improbable that he was a son of Nigel, Bishop of Ely, and brother of the next-mentioned Richard Fitz-Nigel, Bishop of London. (*Madox*, i. 215, 576; *Fuller*.)

FITZ-NIGEL, or FITZ-NEALE, RICHARD (BISHOP OF LONDON), must have been born before the canon requiring the celibacy of the clergy was strictly enforced, because he seems to have been openly brought forward by his father Nigel, Bishop of Ely (who will be subsequently mentioned), and acknowledged as his son. He was educated in the monastery of Ely, and was then placed in the Exchequer, at the head of which his father held the office of treasurer.

Brought up to the Church, as most of the other clerks in those times were (whence indeed the derivation), his successive ecclesiastical preferments in Henry's reign were canon of St. Paul's; archdeacon of Ely, 1169; and dean of Lincoln, by which latter title he is described in 30 Henry II., 1184. (*Madox*, i. 215; *Le Neve*.)

In his early youth he was the author of a work called 'Tricolumnus,' from its being arranged throughout in three columns. It was a tripartite History of England under Henry II.—the first column treating of the transactions of the Church of England and the rescripts of the apostolical see; the second of the remarkable exploits of the king, which he says exceed all human credibility; and the third, of many affairs both public and domestic, and also of the court and its judgments. (*Madox*, ii. 345.)

His diligence and erudition, and the capacity he displayed for the conduct of the public revenue, soon justified his father in recommending him as his successor in the office of treasurer. He was accordingly appointed in 1165, but, as no royal favour was in those days conferred without an equivalent, Nigel was obliged to pay to the king four hundred marks for his son's nomination. (*Ibid.* i. 44, 113.) He continued in the office for the remainder of that reign, and managed the revenue with so much care and adroitness that, notwithstanding the continual wars in which the country was involved, King Richard found on his father's death no less a sum than one hundred thousand marks in the Exchequer.

That monarch's appreciation of his merits was evidenced, not only by retaining his valuable services, but by raising him, soon after his coronation, to the bishopric of London on December 31, 1189.

During Henry's reign he frequently shared in the duties of a justice itinerant, and from the time when fines were introduced into the court—namely, about 28 Henry II.—his regularity of attendance is particularly observable, for there is scarcely one until the end of that reign in which his name does not appear. So also after King Richard's return from the Holy Land till the year before his own death. (*Ibid.* 79–215.)

Under the regency of William de Longchamp, Bishop of Ely, he possessed considerable influence, and it was by his interference that Geoffrey Plantagenet, Archbishop of York, when seized and imprisoned by the orders of the chief justiciary, was liberated.

He left a most valuable legacy to his successors in the 'Dialogus de Scaccario,' copies of which are preserved both in the Black and the Red Books in the Exchequer. It is printed by Madox (ii. 331–452) at the end of his learned history of that court; and in a preliminary dissertation he has satisfactorily established the claim of the bishop to the authorship, in opposition to that of Gervas of Tilbury, to whom it was for many years attributed. It was composed in the 23rd or 24th Henry II., and describes the Exchequer, with all its officers and their duties, and the forms of proceeding and their origin; a treatise of inestimable value as well to historians and antiquaries as to lawyers.

He died on September 10, 1198. One of the monks of Winchester (*Angl. Sac.* i. 304), in describing this event, having designated his office of treasurer by the word 'apotecarius,' an author has been led to commit the somewhat absurd blunder of making him the king's medical adviser. (*Godwin*, 179; *Wendover*, iii. 39.)

FITZ-OGER, OGER, the son of Oger the Dapifer (afterwards noticed), was sheriff of the united counties of Buckingham and Bedford from 33 Henry II. to 1 Richard I. inclusive. In the next year he was made sheriff of Hampshire, and filled that office also in 5 Richard I. (*Fuller*.) From 7 Richard I., 1195–6, to the end of the reign, his name often appears as one of the justiciers before whom fines were acknowledged at Westminster, and in the first of those years he acted as a justice itinerant into Devonshire. (*Hunter's Preface; Madox*, i. 113, 502.)

He married Amy, one of the daughters and coheirs of William de Scheflega.

FITZ-OSBERNE, WILLIAM (EARL OF HEREFORD), was the son of Osberne de Crepon, and grandson of Herfastus, who was the brother of Gunnora, first concubine, and then wife, to Richard I., the third Duke of Normandy, and great-grandfather of William the Conqueror. He was consequently connected by distant relationship with the young prince, and was brought up with him from infancy. On his father's death he succeeded to the office of steward or dapifer in the ducal household, and was Count of

Bretteville in Normandy. He aided Duke William in quelling every civil commotion of his Norman subjects; and in the invasion of England he equipped forty of the ships at his own expense, and commanded one of the three divisions at the battle of Hastings.

Having contributed to the conquest of England, he assisted greatly in the maintenance of the acquisition by his valour and good counsels. To his vigilance was entrusted the erection of a castle at Winchester for the purpose of overawing the inhabitants, and when, in the year after the Conquest, the king returned to Normandy, to him and to Odo, Bishop of Bayeux, the government of the realm was committed as chief justiciaries. The southern division was appropriated to Odo, and the northern to Fitz-Osberne, on whom the earldom of Hereford and the office of constable or marshal (magister militum) were also conferred.

Besides presiding over the Curia Regis during the king's absence, they also managed the king's revenue; but their conduct was so arrogant and rapacious that the indignation of the English was roused. The efforts of the people, however, to relieve themselves were so ill-concerted that they were easily subdued, and the regents were rewarded, instead of being punished for their oppression.

In 1069 Fitz-Osberne assisted his sovereign in the suppression of various insurrections in England, and was employed by the king in aiding Queen Matilda in the defence of Normandy. In 1072 he proceeded to Flanders to assist Arnulph, the heir of Baldwin, its earl, in resisting the invasion of the disinherited Robert de Frison, by whom he was surprised, and perished through his careless security.

To his zeal, courage, and wisdom King William was greatly indebted for his success, and he was rewarded accordingly. Besides the grant of the county of Hereford, he received the Isle of Wight and various other possessions and advantages. But, notwithstanding the rich gifts which were lavished on him, his prodigality always left him in poverty, which King William, with whom he was a great favourite, at once chided and supplied. Quarrels, however, would now and then occur between his sovereign and him. On one occasion, being steward of the household, he had set upon the royal table the flesh of a crane scarcely half-roasted, when the king in his rage aimed a severe blow at him, which, though it was warded off by Eudo, another favourite, so offended Fitz-Osberne that he resigned his office.

Though brave and generous as a soldier, he was severe and oppressive in his government, and was looked upon as the pride of the Normans and the scourge of the English.

He was twice married. His first wife was Adeline, daughter of Roger de Toney, a great Norman baron, standard-bearer of King William; and the second was Richild, daughter and heir of Reginald, Earl of Hainault. By the former only he had children, three sons and two daughters; but the family and titles soon became extinct. (*Dugdale's Baron.* i. 67; *Will. Malmesbury,* 396, 431; *Madox,* i. 31-78; *Chauncy's Herts,* 121; *Turner,* &c.)

FITZ-PETER, SIMON, was one of the 'assidentes justiciæ regis,' before whom a charter or contract was executed at the Exchequer in 11 Henry II., 1165, and is the first of four after whom are the words 'marescallis regis.' Whether, as Madox (i. 44) seems to infer, these words apply to all the four may perhaps admit of question. If, however, he were not one of the marshals, it is clear he held some office in the court, since his property was exempted on that account from the Danegeld and other assessments so early as 2 Henry II. (*Pipe Roll,* 7.) From that year to the sixteenth he was sheriff of the latter county; and as Geoffrey Fitz-Peter, the great justiciary in the next reign (whose father is not mentioned in Dugdale's 'Baronage'), was entrusted with the same sheriffalty for many succeeding years, it does not seem an improbable conjecture that this Simon was his father.

Simon Fitz-Peter acted also for four years, commencing 2 Henry II., as deputy to Henry de Essex, the sheriff of the counties of Buckingham and Bedford. It was probably at a later period that he was a justice itinerant in the latter county, when his name is mentioned in connection with the case of a certain canon of Bedford, named Philip de Brois, who having been convicted of manslaughter before his bishop, was merely condemned to make pecuniary compensation to the relatives of the deceased. In the open court at Dunstable, the judge, alluding to the case, called him a murderer, whereupon a violent altercation ensued, and the priest's irritation drawing from him expressions of insult and contempt, the king ordered him to be indicted for this new offence. (*Lingard,* ii. 213; *Leland's Collect.* iii. 424.) This was one of the grounds for Henry's attack on clerical privileges.

FITZ-PETER, GEOFFREY (EARL OF ESSEX), was not improbably the son of the above Simon Fitz-Peter, for the reason suggested in his life. Dugdale commences his history without any mention of who his father was, and, independently of the sheriffalty of Northamptonshire, and also of the name, it is apparent that he had been brought up in the court where Simon had also filled some office.

In 31 Henry II. he was one of the justices of the forest, the duties of which he continued to perform till the death of King Henry (*Madox*, i. 547, ii. 132); and in 1 Richard I. he acted as a justice itinerant in various counties. (*Pipe Roll*, 35, &c.)

King Richard compelled him to pay a fine for not joining the crusade (*Ric. Divis.* 8), but at the same time showed the estimation in which he held him by appointing him one of the council to assist Hugh Pusar, Bishop of Durham, and William de Longchamp, Bishop of Ely, in the government of the kingdom, and in the subsequent disputes directing him, in conjunction with Walter de Constantiis, the Archbishop of Rouen, and others, to act independently of the chancellor. About this time he became sheriff of the united counties of Essex and Hertford, being probably so named on account of the property to which he had succeeded in right of his wife, Beatrice, one of the daughters and co-heirs of William de Say, by Beatrice, the sister of Geoffrey, father of the deceased Earl of Essex.

His continued employment as a justicier during Richard's reign is shown by his being present when fines were acknowledged at Westminster (*Hunter's Preface*); and in July 1198, 9 Richard I., he was placed in the high office of chief justiciary of the kingdom. His military talents were immediately called into exercise against the Welsh, whose king, Gwenwynwyn, he completely defeated.

On Richard's death in the following year, being continued in his office, he induced the nobles to take the oath of fealty to King John at Northampton. On the day of the coronation he was created Earl of Essex. His performance of the duties of his office was marked with exemplary activity, and he exerted himself with considerable energy in exacting the taxes which King John imposed. At the same time he appears to have joined in the king's amusements, as a payment of five shillings was made to him 'ad ludum suum,' and to have been not averse from the pleasures of the table, as he paid for eating flesh with the king on a fast-day. (*Cole's Documents*, 248, 272, 275.)

During the contest with Rome he supported his royal master, but was compelled to be a witness to the disgraceful document, dated May 15, 1213, 14 John, by which the crown was surrendered to the pope. In a few months after this event this great man terminated his career, dying on the second ide of the following October. He was buried at the priory of Shouldham in Norfolk, which he had founded.

For twenty-eight years he had filled a judicial position, fifteen of them as head of the law, and principal minister of the kingdom. Invested with extraordinary power, the absence of complaint in such difficult times is a proof that he used it without harshness; skilful in the laws, he seems to have administered them with firmness, and the lengths to which the king soon after resorted appear to show that the royal impetuosity had been previously checked by his prudence. Matthew Paris says that the king hated, but feared, him, and that upon his death he exclaimed, 'Per Pedes Domini, nunc primo sum rex et dominus Angliæ.' How the infatuated monarch used his freedom the history of the remainder of his reign affords a lamentable display.

So large were the various grants made to him that when his son did homage on succeeding him, the sheriffs of no less than seventeen counties were commanded to give possession of the lands he held in each of them. (*Rot. de Finibus*, 502.)

By Beatrice, his first wife, he left three sons, two of whom succeeded to his title, which continued in the family, through female channels, till the year 1646, when it became extinct.

Geoffrey Fitz-Peter's second wife was Aveline, by whom he had a son named John, lord of the manor of Berkhampstead in Hertfordshire, who was made justice of Ireland. (*Dugdale's Baron.* i. 703; *Wendover*, iii. 49, &c.; *Royal Tribes of Wales*, 71; *Turner's Engl.*)

FITZ-RALPH, GEROLD, whose lineage has not been traced, was one among the twelve inquisitores in 1170, 16 Henry II., whom Dugdale has mistakingly called justices itinerant.

FITZ-RALPH, WILLIAM, sometimes written Ranulph, and sometimes Randulph, for they are all three one and the same name, succeeded to the lordships of Alfreton, Norton, and Marnham, in Derbyshire, on the death of his father, Robert Fitz-Ranulph, who is supposed by some to have assisted in the assassination of Archbishop Becket in the year 1170, and to have founded the priory of Beauchief, in that county, in expiation of his crime. The fact that he retired about that time from the sheriffalty of the counties of Nottingham and Derby, which he had held for the four preceding years, in some degree gives weight to this opinion. His son, this William, was then placed in that office, and held it for the eight following years. (*Fuller.*)

Whether the father was guilty or not, the son was certainly not excluded from the court, but continued to be employed in places of trust up to the reign of King John. In 20 Henry II., 1174, he was, as sheriff of Nottingham and Derby, joined with Godfrey de Luci, one of the king's justices, in setting the assize of those counties; and in the six next years he sat in the King's Court, in which he seems to have held a high place, as his name often appears thus: 'Per Willielmum filium Radulfi et socios suos,' without noting who those companions were. During those years, also, he went as one of the justices itinerant into fourteen several counties. (*Madox*, i. 94, 123-138.)

In 1180 he was appointed dapifer or seneschal of Normandy, in right of which he had the custody of the castle of Caen, for which a livery of 300*l.* per annum was allowed him. (*Ibid.* 166.) This office, which comprehended that of justiciary, he continued to hold from that time till his death in 1200. When Richard I. went to the Holy Land he committed Alice, the King of France's sister, to the custody of William Fitz-Ralph, who resolutely refused to deliver her up to her brother, notwithstanding his repeated demands. In 2 John he is mentioned on the Norman Roll as being present in the King's Court at Caen with the other justices and barons there. (*Ibid.* 53-169.)

According to Dugdale's 'Baronage' (i. 678), he had, by his wife Agnes, one son, Thomas, who succeeded him and died without issue, and three daughters, who thus became his heirs.

FITZ-RANULPH, RALPH, was the son of the under-named Ranulph Fitz-Robert, and a descendant, therefore, from Ranulph de Glanville. (*Excerpt. e Rot. Fin.* ii. 147.) Dugdale introduces his name among the justices itinerant into the northern counties in 46 Henry III., 1262; but it is apparent that this iter was only for pleas of the forest. He died about April 1270. His wife's name was Anastasia, and he had by her three daughters.

FITZ-REGINALD, RALPH, was three times a justice itinerant—viz., in 14, 16, and 18 Henry III., 1229-1234. From these appointments, which are evidently not referable to any local property, it seems probable that he was connected with the courts of law. He had been a partisan of the barons against King John, but on the accession of Henry III. his forfeiture was reversed on returning to his allegiance.

FITZ-REINFRID, ROGER, is mentioned in 1176, 22 Henry II., as a justice itinerant, in which capacity he acted occasionally to the end of that reign. During this period he visited no less than thirteen counties, an extent of circuit sufficient of itself to show that he was a regular justicier in the King's Court, from whence these itinera emanated. But examples of pleas before him in the Exchequer at Westminster are mentioned from 25 Henry II., 1179 (*Madox*, 83-736), and fines were levied before him as late as 10 Richard I.

It was then a common custom for some of the judges to be in personal attendance on the king, and accordingly his name is attached to the charter, dated at Oxford in May 1177, by which the grant of the kingdom of Cork to Robert Fitz-Stephen and Milo de Cogan was confirmed, and he was also one of the witnesses to the will of King Henry, dated at Waltham, in 1182. (*Lord Lyttelton*, iv. [3], [14].) He was sheriff of Sussex for eleven years from 23 Henry II., and of Berkshire in 1 Richard I. (*Fuller.*)

The estimation in which he was held is evidenced by his being appointed one of the council to assist the two chief justiciaries who were left in the government of the kingdom during King Richard's absence in the Holy Land. (*Madox*, i. 34.)

He married Rohaise, niece of Ranulph, Earl of Chester, and widow of Gilbert de Gant, Earl of Lincoln, by whom he had a son Gilbert, who was a favourite of King John.

FITZ-RICHARD, WILLIAM, was sheriff of the counties of Buckingham and Bedford from 16 to 25 Henry II. He was preceded in this office by a *Richard* Fitz-Osbert, who probably was his father. According to the practice then adopted, he was appointed, as sheriff, one of the justices itinerant to fix the assize for those counties in 20 and 23 Henry II. (*Madox*, i. 124, 132.)

Nothing further occurs as to this William Fitz-Richard during Henry's reign, and it is difficult to ascertain whether facts subsequently related in connection with the same name refer to the same individual. The Christian names Richard and William were common in those times, and scarcely a roll occurs which does not mention several bearing the same designation in different and distant counties who are evidently not the same person.

FITZ-ROBERT, JOHN, was the son and heir of the after-noticed Robert Fitz-Roger, lord of Clavering in Essex, and Warkworth in Northumberland. Soon after his father's death, in 14 John, he was appointed to the sheriffalty of Norfolk and Suffolk, which he held for the next two years. He then joined the insurgent barons, and was one of the twenty-five to whom was entrusted the enforcement of Magna Charta. He obtained restitution of the possessions he then forfeited soon after the accession of Henry III., and in subsequent years received several marks of royal favour. He held the sheriffalty of Northumberland for four years, commencing in 9 Henry III., and in 10 Henry III. was nominated one of the justices itinerant for Yorkshire. There is a writ in the Exchequer in 1238 which bears the appearance of his then acting as a baron of the Exchequer.

His first wife was Joane, and his second Ada de Baillol, who, on his death in 25 Henry III., 1241, fined two thousand marks for the custody of his lands and heirs, Hugh and Roger. The former, of these, dying during minority, was succeeded by Roger, whose grandson assumed the name of Clavering. (*Dugdale's Baron.* i. 106; *Rot. Pat.*

136–180; *Rot. Claus.* i. 316–618, ii. 33–185; *Excerpt. e Rot. Fin.* i. 337, 342; *Madox*, ii. 317.)

FITZ-ROBERT, PHILIP, was among the justices itinerant who fixed the tallage in the county of Lincoln in 10 Richard I., 1198–9 (*Madox*, i. 705), being the only time he is noticed in that character. The roll of the following year, 1 John, contains a curious entry of his paying a fine of 200*l.* and one hundred bacons and one hundred cheeses, for the grant of the wardship and land of the heir of Ivo de Munby till he was of age. (*Rot. de Oblatis*, 24.)

FITZ-ROBERT, RANULPH, was the grandson of that Robert Fitz-Ralph who married the daughter of Ranulph de Glanville. He himself married Berta, the niece of Ranulph de Glanville, and succeeded to a third of his property with the representatives of that great man's two other daughters. (*Rot. de Finibus*, 337, 369.) In 12 John he accompanied the king to Ireland, but before the end of the reign took part against him in the contest with the barons. Returning, however, to his allegiance before the king's death, his manor of Saxtorp in Norfolk, of which he had been deprived, was restored to his possession. Little further is recounted of him, except that he twice filled the office of a justice itinerant—once in 10 Henry III., 1226, for Lancashire, and another time in 15 Henry III., 1230, for Yorkshire. His death occurred before December 25, 1252, 37 Henry III., when his son and heir, Ralph (who has been mentioned in a former page as Ralph Fitz-Ranulph), did homage for his lands in Norfolk, paying fifty shillings for his relief.

FITZ-ROBERT, or DE WELLS, SIMON (BISHOP OF CHICHESTER). Many of the charters of the early part of the reign of King John are concluded with the words ' Dat. per manus Simonis Archidiaconi Wellensis et J. de Gray,' both of whom some writers have therefore designated keepers of the Seal under the Chancellor Hubert, Archbishop of Canterbury. As in no instance have their names, or those of others who appear in the same manner, any addition designating that office, such as ' vice-cancellarius,' or ' tunc agens vices cancellarii,' as in the reign of King Richard, it admits of considerable doubt whether this character is properly assigned to them, especially as in every case the persons so introduced are known to have held some other office in the court. They were officers of the treasury of the Exchequer, where the Great Seal was usually kept.

The first date on which these two names appear is September 16, 1199, 1 John; and they continue to sign together till June in the following year, after which Simon the archdeacon's name alone is appended to numerous charters for a long period, ending in June 1204, 6 John. (*Rot. Chart.* 28, 74–135.) In March 1203 he was provost of Beverley, and in June 1204 he was consecrated Bishop of Chichester.

Le Neve, in his list of archdeacons of Wells, calls him Simon Fitz-Robert, and in that of the Bishops of Chichester introduces Simon de Wells (*Le Neve*, 43, 56), evidently not being aware that the two names belonged to one and the same person. Godwin also calls the bishop Simon de Wells. That his actual surname was Fitz-Robert is proved by two curious charters (*Rot. Chart.* 86, 88), by one of which King John, on February 7, 1201, confirms to him, by the name of ' Symoni filio Roberti,' archdeacon of Wells, a grant of certain lands in Stawell in Somersetshire, with the advowson of the church there, which had been estreated in consequence of the felony of Alice, the wife of *Robert* de Wattelai, in killing her husband, for which she was condemned and burnt; and by the other, dated the 22nd of the same month, the king grants to him the land of Burgelay in the manor of Meleburn, which the said *Robert* de Wattelai and Alice his wife had held as of her inheritance, but which had been forfeited by the same felony of which she had been convicted. No doubt, therefore, that the Robert of whom Simon was the son was the murdered man Robert de Wattelai, and that the grants were in fact a restoration of the property which he would have inherited but for the crime committed by Robert's wife. It was not uncommon in this age for an ecclesiastic to discard his family name, and adopt that of the place of his birth, education, or preferment. It is certain that this bishop is generally known as Simon de Wells; but, inasmuch as he had not discontinued the name of Fitz-Robert at the time when these grants were made, the assumption of the new name may possibly, in this instance, have been influenced by the tragical events recorded in them.

That Bishop Simon after his elevation continued to enjoy the royal favour is shown by the king in January 1207 giving him letters ' ad dominum S. de Malo Leon,' desiring all honour should be shown to him, with letters of protection during his absence. (*Rot. Pat.* 68.) In the course of that year he died. (*Godwin*, 504.)

FITZ-ROBERT, WALTER, was the grandson of the before-noticed Richard Fitz-Gilbert, called also Benefacta, and son of Robert, steward of King Henry I., by his wife Maud, the daughter of Simon de St. Liz, Earl of Huntingdon.

He was probably very young at his father's death, as no mention is made of him, beyond the usual assessments on his property, until 22 Henry II., 1176, when he is recorded as one of the three justices itinerant appointed by the council of Northampton to go into the eastern counties of England. In this employment he was engaged for several following years, during which time, and perhaps before it, he took his share in the judicial duties of the Curia Regis. Madox gives several instances from that time till 5 Richard I., 1193, in which he was present as one of the barons and justiciers there. (*Madox,*i. 94–137, ii. 20.)

His knightly pursuits were not forgotten in the performance of his civil duties. He supported William de Longchamp, Bishop of Ely, the governor of the realm, during King Richard's absence in the Holy Land, in his contest with John, the king's brother; and in 6 Richard I., 1194, he joined the expedition into Normandy.

He died in 1198, and was buried in the choir of the priory of Dunmow, which his father had founded, and to which he himself had given divers churches and lands.

His two wives were, first, Maud, daughter of Richard de Luci, the chief justiciary; and, secondly, Margaret de Bohun.

He left several sons, of whom Robert, the eldest, succeeded him, and was called Robert Fitz-Walter. His prowess as a warrior procured for him the addition of 'the Valiant;' and, as leader of the barons confederated against King John, they styled him 'Marshal of the Army of God and the Holy Church.' His grandson was regularly summoned to parliament in 23 Edward I. To the title of baron Fitz-Walter an earldom of Sussex was added in 1529, and other titles; but these becoming extinct in 1756, the barony fell into abeyance among the five daughters of Thomas Mildmay, Esq., whose wife Mary was sister to Benjamin, the fourteenth baron. (*Dugdale's Baron.* i. 209; *Nicolas.*)

FITZ-ROBERT, WALTER, was forester of the county of Huntingdon, and for some offence in the exercise of his office was imprisoned in 14 John, and did not obtain his liberty without a fine of two palfreys. He afterwards joined the barons against the king, but returned to his duty at the commencement of the next reign. His appointment as one of the justices itinerant in Huntingdonshire in 9 Henry III. no doubt arose from his continuing to hold the above office. (*Rot. Claus.* i. 120, &c., ii. 75, &c.)

FITZ-ROGER, ROBERT, was the son of Roger Fitz-Richard, a grandson of the before-noticed Eustace Fitz-John. He married Margaret, the daughter of William de Chesney, and widow of Hugh de Cressi, and obtaining with her considerable property in Norfolk, he became sheriff of that county and of Suffolk in 3 Richard I., and held the office at intervals till 14 John. (*Fuller.*)

In 3 Richard I., 1191, he was present in the Curia Regis as a witness to a final concord then made there; and in 1197 he was a justice itinerant in Norfolk, and was present in the following year on the acknowledgment of fines at Norwich. Other fines were levied before him in 3 John, 1201. (*Madox,* 704; *Hunter's Preface.*)

King John granted him a charter of confirmation of his inheritance of the castle and manor of Warkworth in Northumberland, of which county he held the sheriffalty from 3 to 14 John. He founded the priory of Langley in Norfolk about the end of Richard's reign (*Monast.* vi. 929), and dying in 14 John, left by his widow, Margaret, a son, the before-mentioned John Fitz-Robert. After three generations the family assumed the name of Clavering, from a manor so called in Essex, which belonged to this Robert. John de Clavering, who was summoned to parliament by the first three Edwards, died in 1332, leaving only female issue. (*Dugdale's Baron.* i. 106; *Nicolas.*)

FITZ-ROGER, WILLIAM, was one of the justices itinerant appointed for York and Northumberland in 3 Henry III., 1218. (*Rot. Claus.* i. 403.) If, as it seems probable, he were of Lincoln, he married Agnes de Scotney. (*Madox,* i. 488.)

FITZ-ROSCELIN, WILLIAM, is introduced by Dugdale as one of the justices itinerant for Norfolk and Suffolk in 9 Henry III., yet, being ill at the time, he did not act; but on several occasions he had been named with others to take assizes of novel disseisin in Norfolk; and in 11 Henry III. he was the first named in a commission into that county to try two prisoners of the Bishop of Ely, who were charged with murder, and for whom the bishop had not a gaol sufficiently secure. (*Rot. Claus.* i. 552, 633, 665, ii. 72, 77, &c.) In 15 John he was so far in the confidence of the court as to be employed as one of the commissioners appointed to enquire into the losses sustained by the clergy in the diocese of Norwich; and he obtained a licence not to be placed on any assize or jury in the county, except in cases in which the king was concerned. (*Rot. Claus.* i. 154–165.) Before the end of that reign he either fell off from his allegiance, or was suspected of intending to do so, as his son Andrew, and his granddaughter Alice, were placed as hostages for him in the custody of the constable of Orford Castle, and he fined two hundred marks. On the accession, however, of Henry III. he procured full restitution. (*Ibid.* i. 257, 332; *Rot. Fin.* 589.) His wife's name was Lecia or Alicia.

FITZ-SIMON, OSBERT, is inserted by Dugdale in his List of Fines as a justicier before whom one was levied in 7 Richard I., October 1195 (*Orig. Jurid.* 41), but Mr. Hunter omits his name.

FITZ-SIMON, RICHARD, in 1 Henry III. paid 100 shillings for having seisin of the lands which his father, Simon Fitz-Richard, forfeited in 17 John, situate in the counties of Leicester, York, Huntingdon, Norfolk, Suffolk, and Essex. He was one of the justices itinerant in 9 Henry III. for Essex and Hertfordshire, and in the two following years was a commissioner to collect the quinzime and to assess the tallage there, and in Cambridge and Huntingdon. He died in 17 Henry III. (*Rot. Claus.* i. 245-324, ii. 76-208; *Excerpt. e Rot. Fin.* i. 212, 234.)

FITZ-SIMON, TURSTIN, held some office in the Exchequer so early as 4 Henry II. (*Pipe Rolls*, 144, 150), and after the murder of Becket he was one of the custodes of the archbishopric of Canterbury. (*Madox*, i. 309, 631.)

. In 1173 he was a justice itinerant for setting the assize or tallage in Gloucestershire, and having been selected in 1176 as one of the eighteen justices appointed to administer justice throughout the kingdom, his pleas are recorded, in that and the two following years, on the rolls, not only of the four counties at first appropriated to him, but also of six others. In 1177 he is mentioned as holding pleas in the Exchequer. (*Ibid.* 127, &c.) In 1 Richard I. he had the custody of the castle of Ludlow. (*Pipe Roll.*)

FITZ-STEPHEN, RALPH, was an officer in the Chamber of the Exchequer from 3 to 19 Henry II., 1157-1173. He possessed lands in the counties of Warwick, Leicester, Northampton, and Gloucester, and the sheriffalty of the latter county was entrusted to him in conjunction with his brother William Fitz-Stephen in 18 Henry II., and from that time till 1 Richard I. either one or the other occupied the office. For that county also he acted as a justice itinerant in 1174, and having been appointed in 1176 at the head of one of the six divisions into which the circuits were then arranged, his pleas are recorded in the rolls of that and of the four following years in twenty-four different counties. (*Madox*, i. 123-137.)

. In 1182 he was one of the king's chamberlains, and his name appears as a witness to the king's will executed at Waltham in that year. (*Lord Lyttelton*, iv. [14].) In 1184 he was among the justiciers and barons before whom a fine was levied in the King's Court, and in 1187 he was appointed custos of the abbey of Glastonbury, and so remained till 3 John. (*Madox*, i. 635; *Rot. Cancell.* 195; *Abb. Plac.* 12.)

He died in or before 6 John, as Godfrey de Albini then paid a thousand marks, his fine for having his land. (*Rot. Claus.* 9.)

FITZ-STEPHEN, WILLIAM, the brother of the last-mentioned Ralph Fitz-Stephen, filled with him the office of sheriff of Gloucester from 18 Henry II., 1171, to 1 Richard I., 1190. He was (like Ralph Fitz-Stephen) placed at the head of one of the six circuits arranged by the council of Northampton in 1176, and his pleas are recorded in that and the four following years, not only in fourteen counties, but 'ad Scaccarium' also. (*Madox*, i. 127-139, 211.) His name likewise appears as a justice itinerant in Shropshire in 1 Richard I., 1190. (*Pipe Roll*, 95.)

There are many grounds for identifying the sheriff and justicier with a remarkable man of the same name who flourished at the same period; I mean William Fitz-Stephen, the author of 'The Life and Passion of Archbishop Becket,' in which is introduced the description of the city of London printed in Stow's 'Survey.'

Several circumstances in the career of the latter render it far from improbable that he should have been selected for judicial employment. He himself says that he was a fellow-citizen with Becket, one of his clerks, and an inmate of his family; that, being by express invitation called to his service when chancellor, he became 'in Cancellaria ejus dictator' [qu. remembrancer?], or, as another reads, 'scriba in Cancellaria Angliæ;' that when Becket sat to determine causes he was a reader of the instruments, and upon his request sometimes an advocate. (*Dr. Pegge's Dissertation*, 8.) All this must have occurred before 1162, when Becket resigned the chancellorship, and, from the expressions used, no doubt can exist that he was at that time established in some office in the Chancery, or in the Exchequer, where the business of the Chancery was usually transacted. There is nothing to show that he did not remain in his office after his patron's resignation of the Great Seal, and it is certain, from his own relation, that, though he was present with the archbishop on his trial at Northampton in 1164, he escaped being involved in the subsequent banishment of Becket's friends, in consequence of his having been the author of a rhyming Latin prayer, which he had once presented to the king in the chapel of Bruhull in Buckinghamshire. (*Biog. Brit. Lit.* 363.) The first two lines will be a sufficient specimen of its style:—

Rex cunctorum sæculorum, rex arcis ætheriæ;
Rector poli, rector soli, regum rex altissime.

That he was present at Canterbury, and was an eyewitness of Becket's murder, forms no objection to the presumption that he was a servant of the court, because it is to be recollected that the archbishop was then, at least nominally, reconciled to the king, and it could be considered no other than an act of decent respect for Fitz-Stephen to visit his former patron on his return from a long exile. After the murder had been accomplished King Henry would naturally be anxious to disconnect himself from its perpetration, by carefully avoiding any act which might be construed into a punishment of those who had adhered to the troublesome prelate, independently of his being too wise a prince to deprive himself of the services of a learned and useful man, who had never made himself personally obnoxious.

It would therefore be far from unlikely that a person so situated should not be interfered with in his office; indeed, the reasons adduced would rather operate to promote his further advancement, as tending to remove the suspicions which then certainly attached to the king. Accordingly, his nomination as sheriff of Gloucestershire in the following year can excite no surprise, especially as it was most usual in those times for officers of the Exchequer, or of other branches of the court, to be entrusted with such appointments, and the same reasons would account for the selection of such a man, palpably well experienced in the law, as one of the justiciers in 1176. That the termination of the sheriffalty and the last acts of the justicier both occur about 1190 or 1191, the period assigned for the death of the biographer, are curious circumstantial corroborations of the conjecture thus ventured. Fitz-Stephen's Life of Becket offers nothing to contradict the supposed identity; but, on the contrary, it is remarkable for being written in a calmer style than that of other partisans, and for not attempting to implicate the king in authorising the murder.

Fitz-Stephen had travelled to France to complete his education, and on his return, his erudition, which was conspicuous both as a scholar and a divine, recommended him to the notice of Becket, with whom he eventually became on terms of familiar intercourse. He is said to have been a monk of Canterbury, and is frequently called Stephanides.

FITZ-TOROLD, NICHOLAS, was one of those selected by the council held at Windsor in 25 Henry II., 1179, as a justice itinerant in one of the four divisions then established for the purpose of administering justice throughout the kingdom. (*Madox*, i. 79, 139.) His name occurs as a justice itinerant in the following year, and he probably acted subsequently, because, among the pleas of Godfrey de Luci and his companions in Berkshire, entered on the Roll of 1 Richard I. (181), there is an entry which seems to have reference to his misconduct in office—viz., 'Nicholas filius Turoldi redd. Comp. de 45*l*. 13*s*. 4*d*. pro falsa p'sent. plac. Corone et pro falso clam. de averiis detentis.'

FITZ-WARINE, FULCO, is introduced by Dugdale as a justicier of the bench, and in the chronicle of William de Rishanger (33) it is asserted that William de Wilton and Fulco Fitz-Warine, 'justiciarii regis,' were slain at the battle of Lewes, May 14, 1264. There is no doubt that both these persons met their death at that battle, nor that the former was a justiciary; but Fulco Fitz-Warine, who was a Shropshire baron, is never mentioned even as a justice itinerant. One of his descendants, John Bourchier, was created Earl of Bath, a title which became extinct in 1654. The barony then fell into abeyance among the daughters of the fourth earl. (*Dugdale's Baron.* i. 443; *Nicolas*.)

FITZ-WARINE, WILLIAM, a younger brother of the above-mentioned Fulco Fitz-Warine, was in the early part of John's reign greatly in the king's favour, receiving a grant of the manor of Dilun in Herefordshire in 6 John, and in 9 John obtaining royal 'literas deprecatorias' to Gila de Kilpec, urging her to marry him without delay. For this intercession on his behalf he presented the king with an entire horse and a palfrey. (*Rot. Claus.* i. 25, 28, 43; *Rot. de Finibus*, 375.) On this lady's death he was again indebted to royalty for a wife, paying a fine of fifty marks, in 2 Henry III., for permission to marry Agnes, one of the sisters and coheirs of John de Wahull, and widow of Robert de Bassingeham. He was at this time sheriff of Lincolnshire. (*Excerpt. e Rot. Fin.* i. 3, 7; *Rot. Claus.* i. 380.) In 9 Henry and several following years he was appointed one of the justices itinerant in many other counties, in most of which he had property; and in Easter, 12 Henry III., his name appears upon a fine levied before him, in consequence of which Dugdale has introduced him among the regular justiciers of this reign, but he is not subsequently noticed in a judicial capacity. (*Rot. Claus.* ii. 77–213.)

The castle of Rockingham was entrusted to him as constable in 10 Henry III., in which year he sent five hundred Welsh to Prince Richard, the king's brother, in Gascony. (*Ibid.* 110, 130.) In 13 Henry III. he was sheriff of Worcestershire, and executed the same office in Herefordshire in 16 Henry III. and the two following years. During the rest of his life he sustained the part of a loyal knight, assisting his sovereign as one of the lords of the Marches, and attending the king in 37 Henry III. in his expedition to Gascony.

He left an only daughter, Asselina, who married Thomas Lyttelton, ancestor of the eminent judge in the reign of Edward IV.

FITZ-WILLIAM, ADAM, forfeited his property in the county of Hertford in 17 John for his adherence to the barons; but on that king's decease he returned to his allegiance, and was restored to his lands. (*Rot. Claus.* i. 229, 245, 318.) He appears in a judicial character from 9 to 21 Henry III. as a justice itinerant and one of the regular justiciers at Westminster. (*Ibid.* ii. 76, 147; *Wendover*, iv. 469; *Orig. Jurid.* 42.) There are numerous mandates addressed to him from 18 to 20 Henry III. as one of the king's escheators. (*Excerpt. e Rot. Fin.* i. 260-303.)

FITZ-WILLIAM, HUGH. There are so many persons of the name of Hugh Fitz-William who lived about the same period that, without a better clue than has been obtained, it is impossible to decide which was the justice itinerant so called, who, in 30 Henry III., 1246, was appointed with five others to visit the northern counties. From 15 John to 43 Henry III. there are four persons so named on the rolls, all in different counties, and with different wives. (*Rot. de Oblatis*, 471; *Excerpt. e Rot. Fin.* i. 132, ii. 36, 293.)

FITZ-WILLIAM, ROBERT, was a knight of Nottinghamshire, who, having got into trouble in 17 John, when he was taken in arms against the king in the castle of Beauveer (Belvoir), was compelled to pay a fine of sixty marks for the restoration of the royal favour. (*Rot. Pat.* 162, 168; *Rot. de Finibus*, 591.) In 9 Henry III. his name appears among the justices itinerant in Nottingham and Derby. In the following year the sheriff of Cumberland is commanded to cause a successor to be elected in the place of Robert Fitz-William, one of the coroners of that county; and there is every probability that this was the same person, as in 11 Henry III. Ralph Fitz-Nichol paid 100*l.* for the custody of his lands and heirs, the sheriff of Nottingham and Derby being commanded to give him seisin of those which were in his bailiwick. (*Rot. Claus.* ii. 77, 119; *Excerpt. e Rot. Fin.* i. 157.)

FITZ-WILLIAM, OSBERT, in the last year of the reign of Richard I., 1198-9, was one of the justiciers before whom a fine was levied (*Hunter's Preface*), but his name does not appear in any fine of a subsequent date. He was, perhaps, therefore, merely an officer of the court, which is rendered more probable from his being sheriff or fermer of the county of Devon in 2 John, and of Hereford in 8 and 9 John.

FITZ-WILLIAM, OTHO, from 28 Henry II., 1183, to 2 Richard I., 1190, was sheriff of the united counties of Essex and Hertford. In 1194 he acted as justice itinerant in the same counties, and in that or the previous year he was one of the justiciers before whom a fine was levied at Westminster. (*Madox*, ii. 20; *Hunter's Preface.*)

FITZ-WILLIAM, RALPH. The first two justices of trailbaston whose names appear were Ralph Fitz-William and John de Barton. Their commission was dated 1304, and was for Yorkshire, where they both resided, and of which the former was the king's lieutenant. (*Hemingford, ed. Hearne*, 208.) In the next year new commissions, in which neither of them were named, were issued for all the counties of England, except those in the home district (*N. Fœdera*, i. 970), showing therefore that the offences which these commissions were intended to suppress were found to be of a more serious nature, and more universally extended, requiring larger powers and more experienced judges.

Ralph Fitz-William was a son of William Fitz-Ralph, of Grimsthorp in Yorkshire, by Joane, daughter of Thomas de Greystock. In 25 Edward I. he was one of the barons summoned to join the king's armies in Scotland. He served with so much zeal and valour in those wars that he was constituted capitaneus of the garrisons and fortresses in Northumberland, lieutenant of Yorkshire, and lord of the Marches, in which character, no doubt, the commission of trailbaston was directed to him. In 28 Edward I. he was present at the siege of Carlaverock, and was engaged in the Scottish wars to the end of the reign.

Under Edward II. he was employed in the same manner, and was made governor of Berwick-upon-Tweed and of Carlisle, was one of the ordainers to regulate the king's household and government, and was frequently appointed, in 8 Edward II., to take inquisitions as to wrecks and otherwise. He died about November 1316, and was buried in Nesham Abbey, Durham.

The barony of Greystock was settled upon him by his mother's nephew, John, the last lord of that name, upon whose death, in 1305, he succeeded to it.

By his wife Margery, the daughter and one of the coheirs of Hugh de Bolebec, and widow of Nicholas Corbet, he had two sons—William, who died in his father's lifetime, and Robert, who succeeded him, and died in 1317. His descendants assumed the name of Greystock, and held the barony till 1487, when, the then lord dying without issue male, it was, by the marriage of his granddaughter, united to that of Dacre of Gillesland till 1569, when it fell into abeyance among the sisters of George, the fifth Baron Dacre. (*Dugdale's Baron.* i. 740; *Nicolas.*)

FLAMBARD, RANULPH (BISHOP OF DURHAM). This extraordinary man was a Norman, whose father was an obscure priest, and whose mother had the reputation of being a witch. He followed the court of the Conqueror into England, and, having entered into holy orders, obtained from that prince the church of Godalming in Surrey, in which his name appears as Flambard. According to Domesday Book (fo. 30, 51), he had, besides one hide of the king's land in Bile in Hampshire, three tenements which William held in Guildford, belonging to the church of Godalming. After receiving many pluralities, he became chaplain to Maurice, Bishop of London, but left his service because that prelate refused him the deanery of the church of St. Paul.

He probably held an office in the Chancery under Maurice; and Malmesbury's description of him, as 'invictus causidicus,' shows he was connected with the courts. He is next found in 1088 and 1098 as one of the king's chaplains (*Monast.* i. 164, 174, 241); and it was not long before he contrived to ingratiate himself with Rufus, and soon discovered his sovereign's profuseness and extravagance. Unprincipled himself, he did not hesitate to suggest measures which, however oppressive to the people, or disreputable to the crown, would produce the desired object of filling the royal coffers. By his instigation, new offences were created for the sake of the fines which followed them; a price was set on crimes by substituting a pecuniary payment for the punishment; the forest laws were loaded with severe penalties; and the impost on the land, so lately established according to the entries in Domesday Book, was disturbed, and rendered more oppressive by a new survey of the kingdom. Not content with this, he drew down upon himself the deepest indignation of the clergy, by suggesting to the king that on the death of any dignitary of the Church, whether bishop or abbot, the temporalities devolved to the crown till the vacancy was supplied. The king was not slow in acting upon this advice; and the injurious effect on the ecclesiastical revenues may be easily conceived; since the parties to whom the Church lands were entrusted in the interim, having paid largely for their use, and knowing how precarious was their tenure, could not be expected to neglect any means, however detrimental to the property, of making the most of their bargain.

Flambard, as may be supposed, obtained the custody of several of these vacant benefices. In 1088 the abbey of Winchester, in 1089 the archbishopric of Canterbury, and in 1092 the bishopric of Lincoln and the abbey of Chertsey were severally entrusted to him; and by the spoil of their churches and the pressure of their tenants, both rich and poor, he did not fail to enrich himself. To these modes of imposition he added another device to supply the royal wants. When any of these vacancies were at last filled, he made a simoniacal contract for the king with the candidate for the clerical honour, compelling him to pay a large sum before he was instituted.

William looked more favourably upon his minister on account of the unpopularity which resulted from these proceedings, saying that he was the only man in his dominions who regarded not the hatred of others so that he pleased his master. His approval was manifested during the remainder of his reign by raising him to high office in the state.

What the precise nature or title of his office was it is difficult to determine. Dugdale introduces him into his list of chief justiciaries. The only historian who gives him that title is Ordericus Vitalis, whose words are 'Summus regiarum procurator opum et justitiarius factus est.' Henry of Huntingdon and Roger de Hoveden style him 'placitator et exactor totius Angliæ;' by the former of which titles, Madox says, may be meant chief justicier, and by the latter, intendant of the revenue, or treasurer. Roger de Wendover calls him by the names of 'placitator' and 'procurator regis.'

The only authority of any importance who describes him as chancellor is Spelman; but there is evidently no foundation for supposing that he held that office. He refers to Malmesbury, who says nothing like it; and to Godwin, whose language has been palpably misunderstood. That author, after saying, from Malmesbury, that Ranulph became 'totius regni procurator,' merely adds this explanation: 'Unde illam omnem authoritatem videtur consequutus, qua *hodie* potiuntur cancellarius, thesaurarius, et nescio quot alii.'

The office of chief justiciary seems scarcely yet to have been completely established; but, by whatever title Ranulph was distinguished, he was clearly the king's *chief* minister. The oppressive nature of his exactions naturally caused frequent complaints against him, which being unredressed, the instigator of them became the object of popular indignation, and narrowly escaped the fate that was prepared for him.

Being inveigled, by a pretended message from the Bishop of London, into a boat on the river, he was forced into a ship, and carried out to sea. A storm arising, and his intended murderers quarrelling among themselves, Ranulph took advantage of both, by working upon the fear and gratitude of Gerold, the principal of them, who had formerly been a mariner in his service, and they were prevailed upon to release him, and put him on shore. The terror and amazement of his enemies when, three days afterwards, he appeared in his usual place at court may well be imagined. His appointment to the bishopric of Durham immediately followed, in June 1099, three years and four months having elapsed since the death of William de Carilefo, its last incumbent. The king, however, benefiting by the lessons his minister had taught, made him feel the effect in his own person, by compelling him to pay one thousand pounds for his advancement.

T

On the death of William Rufus, one of the first acts of Henry was to satisfy the clamours of the people by imprisoning the hated Flambard in the Tower of London, to which he was committed on August 15, 1100. But even in this extremity his good fortune did not desert him. Out of the allowance of two shillings a day which he received for his subsistence (equal to thirty shillings now), with the additional help of his friends, he kept a sumptuous table, and by his affability and his wit captivated his keepers. Encouraging them in their habits of intemperance, he lulled their watchfulness; and on the 4th of the following February, taking advantage of their excess at a feast he had provided, he contrived to escape by means of a rope which his friends had concealed in the bottom of a pitcher of wine, not, however, without cutting his ungloved hands to the bone in the adventure.

He succeeded in obtaining shipping to Normandy, where he instigated the Duke Robert to pursue his claim to the English crown, and accompanied him on his invasion. By the settlement which the policy of Henry then effected, Ranulph, on the retirement of the duke, was permitted to return to his bishopric, and obtained a charter restoring all its immunities.

From this time it does not appear that he interfered further in politics, though Dugdale, on the authority of Matthew Paris, places him in the list of treasurers to Henry I.

The completion of his cathedral, the erection of Norham Castle, the fortification of the walls of Durham, and numerous other works, among which were the endowment of the college of Christchurch, where he had been dean, and the foundation of the priory of Mottisford, near Lincoln, not only are ample proofs of his munificence, but seem sufficient occupation for the remainder of his life. He filled the see rather more than twenty-nine years, and died on September 5, 1128.

The character of Flambard may be collected from the incidents of his life. There can be no doubt that he was an able, artful, and uncompromising minister; that he had considerable eloquence and ready wit; and that he was convivial in his habits and generous in his expenditure. It is evident also that he was ambitious, crafty, prodigal, and rapacious; but some abatement should be made from the unfavourable colouring with which he is painted by the historians, who, writing near his time, and being mostly ecclesiastics, would look with a jaundiced eye on one whom they considered to be the adviser of measures oppressive to the Church. (*Godwin*, 732; *Madox*, i. 32, 78; *Wendover; Malmesbury; Angl. Sac.; Turner; Lingard.*)

FLANDRENSIS, or LE FLEMING, RICHARD, was one of the justiciers before whom fines were levied at Westminster in the last year of Richard's reign, 1198-9, and the first three years of that of King John, 1199-1202. In 3 John and the two following years he held the sheriffalty of Cornwall, and was connected with the receipt of the king's revenue in Devonshire. His property was in the latter county; and he and William Fitz-Stephen in 7 John gave two palfreys for the grant of a market at Dartmouth. In the same year the king, in consideration of six hundred marks and six palfreys, granted to him, and his four sons after him, the custody of the lands in that county and eight others, and the wardship and marriage of the heir of Richard de Greinville. (*Rot. de Finibus*, 221, 295, 362.)

Either he or his son Richard, it would appear, was with the king in Ireland in 12 John, and the land of a Richard Flandrensis, in Gloucestershire, was given away by the king in 18 John, evidently having been forfeited in the rebellion. (*Rot. Claus.* i. 281, 283.) But the name being by no means uncommon at the time, it is impossible to say that either of these is of the same family.

FLEMING, THOMAS, was of a family long settled in Hampshire, and many of its members, from the early part of the thirteenth century, held high office in the town of Southampton. He was the son of John Fleming, established at Newport in the Isle of Wight, by his wife Dorothy Harris, and was born there in April 1544. In May 1567 he became a member of Lincoln's Inn, and, having been called to the bar in June 1574, he arrived at the bench of that society in 1587, and was elected reader in Lent 1590, and double reader in Lent 1594, on his receiving the degree of the coif. Before the end of the following year he was designated as the successor of Sir Edward Coke in the office of solicitor-general, and even Bacon, who was intriguing for it, acknowledged that he was an able man for the place. In order to hold it, however, it was then deemed necessary that he should vacate the degree of serjeant, when he was replaced as a governor of Lincoln's Inn. (*Dugdale's Orig.* 254-262; *Bacon*, xvi. App. LL.)

He attained sufficient eminence in his profession to be brought forward as a candidate for the recordership of London, a post to which, though he then missed it, he was elected in 1594, but resigned it in 1595 on being made solicitor-general. (*Maitland's London*, 1206.) In 1601 and in 1604 he was returned member for Southampton; and, having been knighted, was on October 27, 1604, raised to the office of chief baron of the Exchequer. Such was the reputation for integrity he had acquired in the House of Commons, that on the meeting after their adjournment it was resolved that, notwithstanding his elevation to the bench, he should still continue a member. (*Duthy's Hants*, 383.) When advanced on June 25, 1607, to the chief justiceship of the King's Bench, he vacated his seat, and his son was elected for Southampton in his place.

One of the first duties as chief baron was to sit on the trial of the gunpowder conspirators, but he appears to have been quite a silent commissioner. Not so, however, on the great case of impositions by royal authority, which, so important in its ultimate consequence, was tried in Michaelmas 1606. There, after expressing something like indignation that a subject should presume to plead that an act of the king was 'indebite, injuste, et contra leges Angliæ imposita,' he concluded a long argument which, though certainly most learned and ingenious, was anything but conclusive in favour of the crown. The only other important case in which he is recorded to have been engaged is that in which the refusal of the Countess of Shrewsbury to answer interrogatories relative to the marriage of Sir William Seymour with Lady Arabella Stuart, and her connivance in their subsequent escape, was considered before the privy council. It was a preliminary enquiry as to this being an offence in law, and whether it was cognisable in the Star Chamber, and the chief justice's speech, in favour of the affirmative, is curious as containing a recital of the privileges attached to the nobility, and the consequent duties which they are therefore peculiarly called upon to perform. (*State Trials*, ii. 159–770.)

After presiding over the Court of King's Bench for six years, he died suddenly at Stoneham Park, on August 7, 1613, and was buried in the church of that parish, under a stately monument, on which he is represented in his official costume, with an inscription that he had fifteen children, of whom eight were then living, by his wife, Dorothy, otherwise Mary, daughter of Sir Henry Cromwell, of Hitchinbroke, who was the aunt of the protector. (*Duthy's Hants*, 385.)

A prejudiced account of him is given by Lord Campbell (*Ch. Justices*, i. 237), who calls him a 'poor creature;' but Sir Edward Coke (10 *Reports*, 34), who knew him somewhat better, describes him as discharging all his places 'with great judgement, integrity, and discretion,' adding that 'he well deserved the good will of all that knew him, becaue he was of a sociable and placable nature and disposition.'

The male branch of the family failed in the early part of the last century, when the Hampshire property, including the Stoneham estate, devolved on the descendants of the great antiquary Browne Willis, who had married a daughter of the house. These assumed the name of Fleming, and the present possessor long represented the county in parliament.

FLOWERDEW, EDWARD, son of John Flowerdew, Esq., of Hetherset, Norfolk, after being educated at Cambridge was admitted a member of the Inner Temple in 1552, appointed reader in 1569 and 1577, and treasurer in 1579. (*Dugdale's Orig.* 165, 170.) He held a high character as a lawyer, and was the confidential adviser of the dean and chapter of Norwich, having also several annuities granted to him for his good and faithful counsel and advice, all charged on the estates of his clients. In 1580 he was called to the degree of the coif, and was appointed steward or recorder of Great Yarmouth. In 1564 he had purchased Stanfield Hall, at Windham in Norfolk, and taken up his residence there, so that probably his principal practice was in the country, which would account for the omission of his arguments from the Reports. On October 23, 1584, he was raised to the bench of the Exchequer as third baron, and in the following February he was one of the judges appointed to try Dr. Parry for high treason, being the first baron of the Exchequer whose name appears on a similar commission. (*Baga de Secretis; App.* 4 *Report Pub. Rec.* 273.) At the assizes held at Exeter on March 14, 1586, when a contagious and mortal disease broke out, which spread from the prisoners to many of the leading gentlemen of the county, Baron Flowerdew was one of those who were seized with the distemper, of which he died about April 11, and was buried in Hetherset Church. His wife was Elizabeth, daughter of William Foster, of Windham; and their daughter married Thomas, the son of Sir Robert Shelton, knight. (*Blomefield's Norfolk*, i. 721–732; *Ath. Cantab.* ii. 5; *Weever*, 864; *Holinshed*, iv. 868.)

FOLIOT, HUGH. Dugdale inserts among the justiciers before whom fines were acknowledged at Westminster in 3 Henry III., 1219, the name of H. Abbot of Ramsey, whom he also notices as a justice itinerant in the same year. This was Hugh Foliot, who, from being prior, was elected abbot of Ramsey in June 1216. (*Mitred Abbeys*, 154.) It seems probable that he is the same man who is called archdeacon of Salop in a record dated January 16, 1215, being a pressing application by the king to the Bishop of Hereford relative to the church of St. David's in his behalf, in which he is designated as a man 'magnæ honestatis et scientia et moribus bene ornatum.' (*Rot. Claus.* i. 203.) The archdeacon was raised to the bishopric of Hereford in November 1219, which would account for his no longer acting as a justicier; but the doubt whether

T 2

the abbot and the bishop were identical arises from the discrepancy between the dates given of their deaths, the abbot being stated by Browne Willis to have died in 1231, and the bishop by Godwin (484) on July 26, 1234.

FOLIOT, WALTER, was settled in Berkshire at the beginning of the reign of King John, whom he accompanied to Ireland in the twelfth and fourteenth years of his reign. (*Rot. Misæ*, 178, &c.) In 16 John he was summoned to attend with horses and arms at the castle of Wallingford, in which, by the king's order, the chamber appropriated for the royal wardrobe was assigned for the accommodation of him and his wife and family. Several other entries show that he was either the governor of that castle, or held some other high office in connection with it, and with the county of Berks. In 3 Henry III. he was a justice itinerant into Wiltshire, Hampshire, Berkshire, and Oxfordshire, and sheriff of the latter county in 9 and 10 Henry III. He died about June 1228, 12 Henry III., and was succeeded by his son Richard. (*Excerpt. e Rot. Fin.* i. 172, 426–443.)

FORD, WILLIAM (not Fulford, as Prince erroneously calls him, nor in any manner connected with the Devonshire family of that name), was, according to the only authentic information that exists about him, constituted a baron of the Exchequer in 8 Richard II., 1384, reappointed on the accession of Henry IV., and ceased to act, whether from death or removal, between 1403 and 1407, the entries of the intervening years not having been found.

FORTESCUE, JOHN, is one of the worthies of the county of Devon, of whom it may be justly proud. In Westminster Hall his name is still regarded with reverence, and his principal work, 'De Laudibus Legum Angliæ,' after more than three centuries, is referred to as the first treatise that entered minutely into the history of our legal institutions and described the professional education and habits of the period. The works of his three predecessors, Glanville, Bracton, and Hengham, were no doubt more useful to the legal student and forensic practitioner; but that of Fortescue offered greater attractions to general readers by its popular form and its historical details; and the consequence is that, while the former have become almost obsolete, the latter is still read with interest by the curious and philosophical enquirer.

The family traces its origin, without the loss of a single link, to the knight who bore the shield before William the Norman on his invasion of England, the assumed name commemorating the fact. His son Sir Adam, who was with him in the battle, received as the reward of their joint services, among other lands, the manor of Wimondeston or Winstone in the parish of Modberry, Devon. King John confirmed the grant, and it remained in possession of the family till the reign of Queen Elizabeth.

Two accounts are given of the judge's actual parentage; but, discarding that which makes him the son of Sir Henry Fortescue, the chief justice of the King's Bench in Ireland from June 1426 to February 1429, who was really his brother, the most probable seems to be that his father was Sir John Fortescue, knighted by Henry V. for his prowess in the French wars, and made governor of Meaux, which he had helped to reduce. This knight was a second son of William Fortescue of Winstone, and was himself seated at Shepham. He married Joan, the daughter and heir of Henry Norreis, of Norreis in the parish of North-Huish in Devonshire, by whom he had several children, the two elder being the above-mentioned Sir Henry, the Irish chief justice, and Sir John, who obtained the same rank in England.

John Fortescue is supposed to have been born at Norreis, the estate of his mother. The date of his birth must have been about the close of the fourteenth century. He received his education at Exeter College, Oxford, and pursued his legal studies at Lincoln's Inn, where he was a governor of the house from 1424 to 1429. (*Dugdale's Orig.* 257.) In Michaelmas Term of the latter year he took the degree of a serjeant-at-law, and from that time his arguments frequently occur in the Year Books. In 18 and 19 Henry VI. he acted as a judge of assize on the Norfolk Circuit (*Kal. Exch.* iii. 381), and at Easter in the latter year, 1441, he was named one of the king's serjeants.

So conspicuous were his merits that he was, without taking any intermediate step, raised to the office of chief justice of the King's Bench on January 25, 1442. In that court we have proof from the Year Books that he presided till Easter Term 1460, and no new chief justice is recorded until Edward IV. a few months afterwards seized the throne.

His salary on his appointment was 180 marks (120*l*.) a year, besides 5*l*. 16*s*. 11*d*. for a robe at Christmas, and 3*l*. 6*s*. 6*d*. for another at Midsummer. In addition to this he received in the following February a grant for life of one dolium of wine annually, to which a second was added in the next year. These two dolia (tunnes) of wine are expressly reserved to him by the act of resumption in 34 Henry VI. In March 1447, 40*l*. a year was granted to him beyond his former allowances. (*Rymer*, xi. 28; *Rot. Parl.* v. 317.)

It has been a question how far Sir John Fortescue was justified in calling himself, as he does in the title to his work 'De Laudibus,' Cancellarius Angliæ, a title which he reiterates in his retractation of what he had written against the house of York, by making the interlocutor in the dialogue say to him, 'Considering that ye were the chief chancellor to the said late king.' (*Selden's Preface.*)

Let us then follow him in his career, and see at what time he could have received the office after Easter 1460, up to which time he acted in the King's Bench. . The fatal battle of Northampton was fought on July 10, 1460, and three days before it the Chancellor Waynflete resigned the Seals in the king's tent on the field. Fortescue was clearly not appointed then, for the Seals were in the custody of Archbishop Bourchier on the 25th of that month, when the king delivered them to George Neville, Bishop of Exeter, the new chancellor. A parliament was held in the following October, which was opened by that prelate as Chancellor of England. Fortescue does not appear in that parliament in his usual place as a trier of petitions; but neither does Prisot, the chief justice of the other bench. Of the four judges who were among the triers of petitions, only one, John Markham, was of the Court of King's Bench (*Rot. Parl.* v. 461), of whom there is no evidence whatever to show that he became chief justice till the next reign. Neither is he named among the judges who were called upon, and refused, to give their opinion on the claim of the Duke of York. Henry continued under the control of his enemies till February 17, 1461, the second battle of St. Albans, and his reign practically expired on March 4, when Edward assumed the throne. At the battle of Towton on Palm Sunday, March 29, Fortescue was present, and when the field was lost fled with King Henry. That unfortunate monarch went first into Scotland, then into Wales, and afterwards lay concealed in the north of England until he was betrayed and taken to the Tower of London in June 1465. There he remained in durance till his temporary restoration in October 1470. During this period the Great Seal remained in the hands of Bishop Neville till June 1467, and then was transferred to those of Bishop Stillington; so that, without its possession, any appointment of Sir John Fortescue would have been merely illusory, and in fact could only have been legitimately recognised if made between February 17 and March 4, 1461. During the six months of Henry's renewed reign, from October 1470 to April 1471, it is certain that Fortescue did not hold the post, as Neville, then Archbishop of York, is expressly mentioned as chancellor. (*Rymer*, xi. 672.) It must therefore be concluded that his title was a nominal one, given during the exile of Henry, and that the dictum of Chief Justice Finch, rather oddly introduced into his argument upon ship-money in the reign of Charles I., is correct, that Fortescue was never actual Chancellor of England. (*State Trials*, iii. 1225.)

In the first parliament of Edward IV. Fortescue was attainted of high treason as one of those engaged in the battle of Towton, and all his possessions were forfeited to the king, who granted part of them to Lord Wenlock. (*Rot. Parl.* v. 477, 581.) He clearly was at some time in Scotland, going there probably with King Henry, for in his petition to King Edward some years afterwards he refers to the works he had written against his title to the crown 'in Scotland and elleswhere.' (*Ibid.* vi. 69.) About 1463 he was with the queen and prince, but without the king, 'at Seynte Mighel in Barroys' (in Lorraine), from which place he addressed a letter in December to the Earl of Ormond, then in Portugal, in which he describes himself, not as chancellor, but simply as one of the knights who were there with the queen. They must all have been much straitened for the means of living, for he says, 'We buth all in grete poverte, but yet the quene susteyneth us in mete and drinke, so as we, buth not in extreme necessite.' He remained in Lorraine for some time, and it was probably while there that he composed his learned work 'De Laudibus Legum Angliæ' for the instruction of the young prince.

During the whole of this time Sir John was energetically negotiating for the restoration of King Henry, and did not return with the queen to England till April 1471, after the battle of Barnet. His age did not prevent him, as we learn from Warkworth, from being present at the battle of Tewkesbury on May 4, 1471, where he was taken prisoner; but it no doubt exempted him from suffering under the subsequent execution of the Lancastrians. His royal master and his princely pupil being now both dead, no hope could remain for the party to which he had been devoted. Further opposition, therefore, to the ruling powers would have been fruitless, and the desire of peace for the short remainder of his life, and of obtaining a restoration of his property for his family was probably all that could now influence him. These feelings no doubt operated to produce the retractation, spoken of by Selden, of all he had previously written against Edward's title, and this it is apparent on the record was one of the causes of that monarch's reconciliation with him, and of the reversal of his attainder in October 1473, 13 Edward IV., when he was reappointed a privy councillor.

How long he lived afterwards is very uncertain. The only further recorded notice of him is in February 1476, when he delivered into the Exchequer an assize that had been taken before him while chief justice. (*Kal. Exch.* iii. 8.) Over his remains, at Ebrington in Gloucestershire, is a tomb on which he is represented at full length in his robes as chief justice. His seat there still belongs to the family.

He married Isabella, daughter of John Jamys, Esq., of Philips Norton in Somersetshire, not, as several biographers erroneously state, Elizabeth, daughter of Sir Miles Stapleton. From his grandson John descended Sir Hugh Fortescue, created in 1721 Lord Clinton, and in 1746 Lord Fortescue of Castle Hill, Devon, and Earl Clinton. In the latter barony he was succeeded, under a special limitation, by his half-brother Matthew, whose son Hugh was in 1789 advanced to the titles of Viscount Ebrington and Earl Fortescue, which still flourish. Besides Sir John Fortescue-Aland, already recorded as Lord Fortescue of Credan in Ireland, a third descendant was created in 1777 Earl Clermont in Ireland, who is represented by the present Lord Clermont, under a new creation, whose handsome edition of all Sir John's works has recently been printed—we are sorry to add, for private circulation only.

FORTESCUE, LEWIS, was the third son of John Fortescue, of Spurleston in Devonshire (descended from William of Winston, the elder brother of Sir John, the father of the eminent chief justice), and Alice, daughter of John Cookworthy, his wife. His legal studies were completed at the Middle Temple, where he became reader in autumn 1536. On August 6, 1542, he was constituted fourth baron of the Exchequer, but only sat there for about three years.

By his marriage with Elizabeth, the daughter and sole heir of John Fortescue, Esq., of Fallapit (lineally descended from Sir Henry Fortescue, the chief justice of Ireland), he acquired that property, which came in regular succession to Sir Edmund Fortescue, who received a baronetcy in 1664, which became extinct in 1682. (*Dugdale's Orig.* 216.)

FORTESCUE, LORD. See J. FORTESCUE-ALAND.

FORTESCUE, WILLIAM, lineally descended from the celebrated judge Sir John Fortescue, was the son of Hugh Fortescue, of Buckland Filleigh, and Agnes, daughter of Nicholas Dennis, of Barnstaple. He was admitted to the Middle Temple in September 1710, but removing to the Inner Temple in November 1714, he was called to the bar by the latter society in July 1715.

Sir Robert Walpole, when chancellor of the Exchequer, made him his secretary, and he was returned to parliament as member for Newport in Hampshire at the beginning of the reign of George II., and sat for that borough till 1736. He became attorney-general to the Prince of Wales, and king's counsel in 1730, and a baron of the Court of Exchequer on February 9, 1736. On July 7, 1738, he was removed to the Common Pleas, and after nearly six years' experience on both these benches he received the appointment of master of the Rolls on November 5, 1741, and sat there till his death on December 15, 1749, when he was buried in the Rolls Chapel.

Though considered a good lawyer, he is better known for his intimacy with the wits and literary men of the time. The friendship that existed between him and Pope appears in their correspondence, and he is reputed to have furnished the poet with the famous case of Stradling *versus* Stiles in Scriblerus's Reports. His mother after his father's death married Dr. Gilbert Budgell, who by his first wife was the father of the unfortunate poet Eustace Budgell. Mr. Fortescue married Mary, the daughter and co-heir of Edmund Fortescue, Esq., of Fallapit, and left an only daughter. (*Collins's Peerage*, v. 342; *Parl. Hist.* viii. 619; *Noble's Granger*, iii. 296.)

FOSTER, MICHAEL, was of legal descent, both his father and grandfather being attorneys in the town of Marlborough, with the reputation, eminently deserved, of being honest lawyers. He was born on December 16, 1689, and after attending the free school at Marlborough entered Exeter College, Oxford, in May 1705, and was called to the bar at the Middle Temple in May 1713. In 1720 he published 'A Letter of Advice to Protestant Dissenters,' to which class his family belonged. Little known in Westminster Hall, he pursued his profession principally as a provincial counsel, first in his native town, and then at Bristol, to which city he removed after his marriage in 1725 with Martha, daughter of James Lyde, of Stantonwick in its neighbourhood. In 1735 he issued a learned tract entitled 'An Examination of the Scheme of Church Power, laid down in the Codex Juris Ecclesiastici Anglicani,' which went through several editions, and of course led to a controversy on ecclesiastical law. In August of the same year he was appointed recorder of Bristol, and took the degree of serjeant in the following Easter Term.

In his character of recorder several very important questions came before him. Among others was the right of the city of Bristol to try capital offences committed within its jurisdiction, and the legality of pressing mariners for the public service. The former arose in 1741 in the case of the atrocious murder of Sir Dineley Goodere by his brother Captain Goodere, who was convicted, and the city authority fully established. The latter was the case of Alexander Broadfoot, indicted in 1743 for the murder of Cornelius Calahan, who was killed in an attempt to press the prisoner. On this occasion the recorder delivered a long opinion in support of the legality of impressment, but directed the jury to find Broadfoot guilty of manslaughter only, because Calahan had acted without any legal warrant. (*State Trials*, xvii. 1003, xviii. 1323.)

On April 22, 1745, he was sworn in as a judge of the King's Bench, and knighted, and for the long period of eighteen years he maintained the high judicial character he had established as recorder of Bristol. He was equally distinguished for his learning, his integrity, his firmness, and his independence. Three of his contemporaries who practised under him, and afterwards gained eminence as judges, have given testimony of his excellence. Lord Chief Justice De Grey says of him, 'He may truly be called the Magna Charta of liberty of persons as well as of fortune.' (3 *Wilson*, 203.) Sir William Blackstone (*Commentaries*, iv. 2) alludes to him as 'a very great master of the crown law;' and Lord Thurlow, in a letter written in 1758, describes his spirited conduct in the trial of an indictment for a nuisance in obstructing a common footway through Richmond Park. (*Life of Foster*, 85.) The general impression of his disposition may be collected from the passage in Churchill's 'Rosciad':—

Each judge was true and steady to his trust,
As Mansfield wise, and as old Foster just.

He died on November 7, 1763, and was buried in the church of Stanton Drew.

Besides the works mentioned above he published his 'Report of the Proceedings on the Commission for the Trials of the Rebels in 1746, and other Crown Cases,' in which the doctrines of the criminal law are very learnedly discussed. It is a work of very high authority, and two subsequent and enlarged editions have been issued under the superintending care of his nephew Michael Dodson, Esq., who was also author of a memoir of the judge's life, from which much has been extracted in the present sketch.

FOSTER, THOMAS, was born about 1549. He belonged to the family of Foster in Northumberland, one of whom was gentleman usher to Queen Mary, and another, Sir John Foster, his second cousin, was made a knight banneret at Musselburgh for his valour in defeating the Scots. (*Gent. Mag.* lxxxiv. pt. i. 341.)

He entered the Inner Temple in 1571, described as of Hunsdon, Herts, and became reader in autumn 1596. He being one of the persons designated by Queen Elizabeth to be serjeants two months before her death, the writ was renewed by King James, and he assumed the coif in Easter Term 1603, and was afterwards counsel to Queen Anne and Prince Henry.

On November 24, 1607, he was made a judge of the Common Pleas, and sat in that court for four years and a half, performing his duties in such a manner as to acquire the character of 'a grave and reverend judge, and of great judgment, constancy, and integrity.' (10 *Coke's Reports*, 235.) He was nominated by Thomas Sutton to be one of the first governors of his hospital—the Charterhouse.

He died on May 18, 1612, and was buried at Hunsdon in Hertfordshire, under a massive arched monument of variegated marble, with an effigy of the judge in his robes. His town residence was in St. John Street. The under-mentioned Robert was one of his sons.

FOSTER, ROBERT, the youngest son of the above Sir Thomas Foster, was born about 1589. Destined for his father's profession, he was called to the bar of the Inner Temple in January 1610, and in autumn 1631 attained the post of reader. In May 1636 he was created a serjeant, and on January 27, 1640, was promoted to the bench as a judge of the Common Pleas, and knighted. He joined the king on his retiring to Oxford, and that university conferred on him the degree of Doctor of Laws on January 31, 1643. Upon the execution of Captain Turpin in 1644, the House of Commons ordered the judges who had condemned him to be impeached of high treason, and proceedings were taken against Serjeant Glanville, who was in their power; but against the two chief justices and Justice Foster, who were also concerned in the trial, no further measures were adopted. The steady adherence of the latter to the royal cause, however, was not likely to go unpunished. An ordinance was accordingly passed on November 24, 1645, disabling him and four of his colleagues from being judges, 'as though they were dead,' and he was obliged to purchase his peace by compounding for his estate. (*Wood's Fasti*, ii. 44; *Rymer*, xx. 20, 380; *Whitelocke*, 96, 181.)

On the restoration of Charles II. he was immediately restored to his seat in the Common Pleas on May 31, 1660, and within five months, on October 21, was advanced to the chief justiceship of the King's Bench. During the three years that he presided in the court he was much engaged in the trials of the Fifth Monarchy men and other conspirators against the state, and also of the Quakers Crook, Grey, and Bolton, for refusing to take the oaths of allegiance and supremacy. It would have been well if he had confined himself to these judicial duties, but his memory is tarnished by his conduct in Sir Harry Vane's case. When the prisoner was convicted, and both houses of parliament had petitioned for his life, which the king had promised, the chief justice is reported to have urged his execution, saying 'God intended his mercy only for the penitent.'

Sir Robert's death occurred on October 4, 1663, while on circuit, and his remains were deposited under a handsome monument in the church of Egham, in which parish his family residence was situate, still called Great Foster House. (1 *Siderfin*, 2, 153; *State Trials*, vi. 188.)

FOUNTAINE, JOHN. Alternately a royalist and parliamentarian, this lawyer was commonly called Turncoat Fountaine. A monumental inscription in the church of Salle in Norfolk proves him to have been the eldest son of Arthur Fountaine, of Dalling in that county, one of the sons of another Arthur Fountaine, of Salle. His mother was Anne, the daughter and heir of John Stanhow. (*Pedigree in Heralds' Coll., Norfolk*, ii. 82.) The Lincoln's Inn books confirm this description, and record his admission to that house on October 30, 1622, and his call to the bar on June 21, 1629. A. Wood (*Fasti*, i. 473, 497) has evidently mistaken for him a member of another family of the same name settled in Bucks.

When the civil war broke out in 1642 John Fountaine showed his devotion to the crown by refusing to contribute to the subscription required by the parliament, whereupon the House of Commons committed him 'to the Gatehouse' on October 12, and Whitelocke in stating the facts adds, 'But, afterwards, he and many others refused, and again assisted on both sides, as they saw the wind to blow.' (*Com. Journ.* ii. 804; *Whitelocke*, 63.)

He was still in confinement on December 20, when his petition to be bailed was refused. (*Com. Journ.* ii. 896.) His discharge from custody was probably granted on condition of his leaving London, for Clarendon (86) mentions him in 1645 as assisting and counselling Sir John Stawel in forming the Association of the Four Western Counties, and calls him a 'lawyer of eminency, who had been imprisoned and banished London for his declared affection to the crown.' He is said to have joined Sir Anthony Astley Cooper in a project to raise a third army to force both parties to put an end to the civil war. (*Locke's Works* [1768], iv. 234.)

As long as the royal cause prospered Fountaine remained its staunch adherent, but as soon as he considered it was hopeless he deserted Oxford, and went over to the enemy under Colonel Rainsborough at Woodstock. The colonel announced his 'coming in,' and his being then at Aylesbury, to the Commons, who, evidently distrusting him, ordered that he 'should be sent prisoner to Bristol, and that Major-General Skippon should take care to keep him in safe custody.' (*Com. Journ.* April 25, 1646; *Whitelocke*, 202.) During the fortnight he was at Aylesbury he published a 'Letter to Dr. Samuel Turner concerning the Church and its Revenues,' urging him to advise the king, for the sake of peace, and to 'save what is left,' to concede all the parliament required, bishops and Church lands, and all. Dr. Richard Steuart wrote an answer (*Wood's Athen.* iii. 297), in which he calls the writer 'an Oxford Londoner,' and reminds him, in reference to his profession of 'reason and honesty,' of a sentence he was wont to utter, that 'when vessels do once make such noises as these, 'tis a shrewd sign they are empty.'

On his release he appears to have remained quiet for the next six years, and so far to have satisfied the parliament as to be appointed in January 1652 one of the committee of persons, not members, to take into consideration what inconveniences existed in the law, and to suggest remedies. He was fully cleared from his former delinquency in March 1653, compounding for his estate at 480*l*. (*Whitelocke*, 520; *Com. Journ.* vii. 69–268.) He must have acquired some reputation as a lawyer, as he was made a serjeant-at-law on November 27, 1658, in the short reign of the Protector Richard.

The Long Parliament, on its restoration, selected him on June 3, 1659, for one of the three commissioners of the Great Seal for five months, but before that term expired the Committee of Safety superseded the commission. He, however, was replaced on January 17, 1660, on the Long Parliament again resuming the government, and with his colleagues continued in possession of the Seal till its commonwealth emblems were defaced, and the Broad Seal of the monarchy restored. On the return of Charles II. he resumed his old political creed, and was immediately confirmed in his degree of the coif. (*Noble*, i. 438; *Whitelocke*, 680, 693; 1 *Siderfin*, 3.)

Pursuing his profession, he resided in Boswell Court, and survived the Restoration eleven years. He died on June 4, 1671, and was buried at Salle, the seat of his ancestors. His first wife died in 1642; his second was Theodosia, daughter of Sir Edward Harrington, Bart. By both he left a family, among the descendants of whom were several eminent churchmen.

Richard Baxter (*Reliquiæ*, pt. 3, 187) speaks highly of his piety, integrity, and liberality, and states that he received during the serjeant's life an annuity of 10*l*. from the time of his being silenced.

FOXLE, JOHN DE, had the custody of the temporalities of the vacant abbey of Westminster in 1 Edward II., 1307. On February 28, 1309, he was constituted a baron of the Exchequer. Besides performing the duties of that court, he was frequently named in commissions, and appointed to take inquests by the parliament, and called upon to act as a justice of assize and of oyer and terminer in the provinces as late as 17 Edward II.

He died in 18 Edward II., possessed of considerable property in the counties of Hants, Berks, and Buckingham, part of which was granted to him by the king. His wife's name was Constancia. (*Madox*, i. 314, ii. 60; *Parl. Writs*, ii. 891; *Rot. Parl.* i. 298–345; *Cal. Inquis.* p. m. i. 318; *Abb. Orig.* i. 199–283.)

FRAMPTON, ROBERT, is introduced by Dugdale as a baron of the Exchequer in 1444, with no other authority than a MS. volume belonging to the keeper of the wardrobe. He was the son of John Frampton, of Morton in the county of Dorset, by Edith, daughter of Sir Matthew Stawell, of Catherston, Somersetshire. By his wife Alicia he left a son Robert, but this branch is said to have failed for want of male issue. (*Cal. Inquis.* p. m. iv. 100, 271, 326.)

FRANCHEVILL, WILLIAM DE, was lord of the manor of Garboldesham in Norfolk, of which his father, also named William, had a grant from Hugh de Montfort. From 8 to 11 Henry III. several mandates are addressed to him and other gentlemen of the county to take assizes as to lands claimed by the Church, and as to the right of presentation. In 9 Henry III. he was one of the justices itinerant for Norfolk and Suffolk. (*Rot. Claus.* i. 592, ii. 77, 83, 157.) He left a son William.

FRANK, JOHN, was of a Norfolk family, and was probably the son of John Frank, of Norwich, and Alice his wife. (*Acts Privy Council*, ii. 149.) He was a clerk or master in Chancery in 2 Henry V., 1414, in which reign he was also clerk of the parliament, receiving 40*l.* a year as his salary for that duty. (*Ibid.* v. 106.) He was collated archdeacon of Suffolk on November 10, 1421 (*Le Neve*, 221); and on October 28, 1423, was constituted keeper of the Rolls in Chancery. During the absence at Calais of the chancellor John Stafford, then Bishop of Bath and Wells, the Great Seal was placed in his hands for a month, from April 22 to May 23, 1433. He held the office of master of the Rolls till May 13, 1438. By his will he bequeathed 1000*l.* to purchase lands for the maintenance of four fellows of Oriel College, Oxford, from Somerset, Dorset, Wilts, and Devon. (*Chalmers' Oxford*, 79.)

FRAUNCEYS, JOHN LE, or FRANCIGENA, as he is sometimes called, was the son of Hugh le Frauuceys. He was a servant of the crown, and acted as an escheator in the north of England. In 25 Henry III., 1241, he was assigned with the sheriff of Cumberland to extend the lands of John de Veteri Ponte, deceased. Some other similar entries occur in 29 and 31 Henry III. (*Excerpt. e Rot. Fin.* i. 349, 427, ii. 7.) In 27 Henry III. Robert de Veteri Ponte gave him the manor of Meburn in Cumberland, and he held the church of Caldebec in that county. (*Abb. Placit.* 120, 169.)

He is introduced by Madox (i. 615, ii. 318) among the barons of the Exchequer from 27 to 42 Henry III., 1243–57. It is probable that for some short time he was one of the regular justices, as assizes were ordered to be taken before him in Cumberland and Norfolk, in July 1254, and July 1255. (*Excerpt. e Rot. Fin.* ii. 192, 211.)

He died in 52 Henry III., when his property lay in the six counties of Lincoln, Bedford, York, Kent, Westmoreland, and Cumberland.

FRAUNCEYS, JOHN, was probably the nephew of the above John le Frauuceys, but the various and discordant circumstances mentioned in the entries connected with the name in the reign of Edward I. will give some idea of the difficulty in tracing any individual to whom it belonged. In the parliament of 18 Edward I., when Thomas de Weyland, the chief justice, was disgraced, there is a petition from one John Frauuceys, who had been imprisoned for a year and a half in the Fleet by that judge for a debt which Agnes de Valence claimed from him; and he was ordered to be bailed. In the same parliament there is a petition which charges John Frauucies with a murder, for which he had been acquitted, and a new trial is prayed for by reason of his kindred and his confederates having tried the appeal. In 35 Edward I. a John Frauuceys represents that he was taken in the battle of Rosslyn, had lost his horses, arms, and everything he had, and was detained in a Scotch prison for fifty-seven weeks, and only released on payment of a fine of forty marks; and he therefore prays for the grant of certain land in Staffordshire, the particulars of which are ordered to be reported to the king. And in the same parliament held at Carlisle, Master John Frauuceys, rector of Queldryk, is one of the proctors sent by the clergy of the diocese of York. (*Rot. Parl.* i. 47, 49, 191–193.)

The last of these was probably the subject of the present notice, as the duty to which he was appointed was commonly peformed by some officer in the court. Master John Frauuceys was a clerk in the Chancery, and on May 12, 1310, 3 Edward II., on the Great Seal being surrendered by the chancellor John de Langton, Bishop of Chichester, was one of the three persons under whose seals it was placed in the wardrobe, a proceeding which scarcely warrants his being included in the list of keepers. He was among the 'dilecti clerici' to whom, with others, the correction of the ordinances was submitted by the king in 5 Edward II. (*Ibid.* 447.)

FRAY, JOHN, so early as in the reign of Richard II. held the manor of Coldridge, or Codered, in Hertfordshire, for which county he was returned to parliament in 8 Henry V. (*Chauncy*, 67.) In 2 Henry VI., being then recorder of London, he was one of the commissioners appointed to enquire into the treasons of John Mortimer. He was raised to the bench as a baron of the Exchequer in 4 Henry VI., 1425 (*Cal. Rot. Pat.* 273), and is mentioned in that character on July 15, 1428. (*Rot. Parl.* iv. 202, 334.) Dugdale does not introduce him into that court till February 8, 1435, but that is the date of his advancement to be the *second* baron. (*Acts Privy Council*, iv. 295.) In every year after the seventh year he was sent as a justice of assize into Norfolk (*Ibid.* iii. 283; *Kal. Exch.* iii. 381), from which it may be inferred that he was a serjeant-at-law. He sat as second baron for twelve months only, being raised to the office of chief baron on February 9, 1436, and presided in the court for twelve years, till May 2, 1448. Two years afterwards we find him delivering a silver seal out of the treasury to the new chancellor, Cardinal Kempe, being described as 'deputatum Jacobi Fenys, militis,' the treasurer of England. In the same year an act was passed (*Rot. Parl.* v. 196) for the resumption of all the king's grants, from which was excepted 40*l.* yearly out of 100 marks given to him for life out of the ferm of London and Middlesex, with a yearly robe, vesture, and furrure.

Among his possessions in Hertfordshire was the manor of Munden, in right of which he had the patronage of Rowheiny or Roweney nunnery; which, by a licence in 37 Henry VI., he transferred to a chantry he had founded in the church of the nunnery, to be called the chantry of St. John the Baptist of Roweney, for a perpetual chaplain to pray for the souls of the founders and for the good estate of the king, &c., and of John Fray. (*Monast.* iv. 342.)

There is no other evidence of the part he took in the contest between the Roses, except that he made a loan (perhaps a compulsory one) of 200*l.* to King Edward IV. in his first year. (*Rot. Parl.* v. 471.) At the close of that year, 1461, he died, and was buried in the church of St. Bartholomew the Little in London. He left large estates in the counties of Bedford, Essex, and Hertford, which, as he had no sons, were divided among his five daughters. His wife Agnes, or Annes, one of the daughters of John Danvers, of Cothorp, Northamptonshire, and sister of the judges Sir Robert and Sir William Danvers, survived him till 1478, having since his death had two other husbands—viz., John, Lord Wenlock, who was killed in the field of Tewkesbury in 1471; and Sir John Say, knight, who also died before her. (*Cal. Inquis.* p. m. iv. 309, 390; *Morant,* ii. 592; *Test. Vetust.* 297, 347.)

FRENINGHAM, RALPH DE, held a canonry of St. Paul's, to which he was appointed in 1270. Fines were levied before him as a justice of the Common Pleas from 3 to 6 Edward I., 1275-8. (*Dugdale's Orig.* 21, 44.) He died in 15 Edward I., and one of his descendants, residing at East Farleigh, was sheriff of Kent in 17 Edward II. (*Parl. Writs,* i. 623; 3 *Report Pub. Rec. App.* ii. 209; *Abb. Rot. Orig.* i. 279.)

FREVILLE, GEORGE, was a descendant of a noble family of the fourteenth century. He was the second son of Robert Freville, of Little Shelford in Cambridgeshire, and Rose [Peyton], his wife.

Commencing his legal studies at Barnard's Inn, he completed them at the Middle Temple, where he was twice reader, in 1558 and 1559. On the first occasion his duties were performed by the celebrated Edmund Plowden, and the second occasion is remarkable from the fact that on the 31st of the previous January Queen Elizabeth had constituted him third baron of the Exchequer, thus affording an evidence that the degree of the coif was not yet a necessary qualification for those who sat on that bench. He became second baron on April 28, 1564, and remained in that place till June 1, 1579.

He was elected recorder of Cambridge in 1553, but was successfully opposed in 1559, when he was appointed a baron. (*Athen. Cantab.* i. 407, ii. 92.)

FRISKENEY, WALTER DE, whose name was derived from a parish so called in the county of Lincoln, is mentioned as a counsel in the Year Book of Edward II., and in the fourth year of that reign was summoned, with six others, as an assistant to the parliament then held. He was added to several judicial commissions in his own county in 7, 8, and 11 Edward II.

He was constituted a baron of the Exchequer on August 6, 1320, 14 Edward II., and, besides being frequently employed as a justice in the country, he was one of those who were empowered to pronounce the judgment upon the Mortimers in 16 Edward II. On July 9, 1323, he was removed from the Exchequer and appointed a judge of the Common Pleas. Remaining, as it seems evident, in that court till the end of the reign, he was reappointed to the same court six days after the accession of Edward III., viz., on January 31, 1327. On March 6 following, however, he was placed in the King's Bench, where he sat till Trinity Term in the second year, when the last notice of him occurs in the Year Book. (*Parl. Writs*, ii. p. ii. 897.)

FROWYK, THOMAS. From the time of Henry III. the records of the city of London afford evidence of the respectability and opulence of the family of Frowyk. In that reign the conduit in Newgate Street was built at the charge of Henry Frowyk and Sir Henry Basynges; under Edward I. and II. Thomas and Roger were successively goldsmiths to the king, and Simon was an alderman. Under Edward III. one of the assessors of the subsidy in Middlesex was Henry de Frowyk, and another of the same name gave lands for the support of four chaplains for the chantry in the chapel of 'St. Marie Gyhalle, London.' In that reign also John de Frowyk was prior of St. John of Jerusalem in Ireland, and chancellor of that kingdom, and Thomas de Frowyk was a justice of labourers and coroner and clerk of the King's House of Merchants. In the reign of Henry VI. Henry de Frowyk was an alderman and twice lord mayor of London, and justiciary of the German merchants in that city; and in the seventh year of Edward IV. Thomas Frowyk was a member of the parliament then assembled. (*Newcome's St. Albans*, 334; *Rot. Parl.* i. 474, ii. 426, 455, iv. 303, v. 634; *Palgrave's Merchant and Friar*, 140; *Cal. Rot. Pat.* 166, 174, 285; *Devon's Issue Roll*, 122, 128; *Abb. Rot. Orig.* i. 198, ii. 34, 229; *Maitland's London*, 1195.)

The latter was probably the father of the chief justice, who was born at the manor of Gunnersbury in the parish of Ealing, Middlesex. His mother was daughter and heir of Sir John Sturgeon, knight.

Fuller states that the judge died before he was full forty years old, so that he must have been born about the year 1466, and in Keilwey's Reports his death is recorded to have occurred 'in florida juventute sua.'

He was educated at Cambridge, and studied the law in the Inner Temple. From this society he was called to the degree of serjeant at the end of Trinity Term 1494 (*Y. B. 9 Henry VII.* fo. 23 b), and he attained such eminence in his practice as to be preferred, on September 30, 1502, to the high office of chief justice of the Court of Common Pleas, when he received the honour of knighthood. By a manifest error, an entry in the Year Books (15 *Henry VII.* fo. 13) would seem to fix his elevation three years earlier, as he is subsequently mentioned as counsel.

This 'oracle of the law,' as Fuller calls him, presided in his court only four years, and dying on October 17, 1506, was buried in the church of Finchley. His wife's name was Elizabeth; by her he left two daughters, between whom his estate was divided.

Elizabeth, the eldest, was married to the after-mentioned Sir John Spelman.

FRYSTON, RICHARD, had the custody from March 7 to May 12, 1470, of the Great Seal during the absence of the chancellor, Bishop Stillington. He was at that time a clerk or master in the Chancery, which office he had held since 1450, and continued to hold as late as 1472, 12 Edward IV. (*Rot. Parl.* v. 227-571, vi. 3.) During the above two months bills in Chancery were addressed to him as keeper, and not to the chancellor, although the latter still retained his office and received the Seal back from Fryston's hands on May 12. (*Introd. Proceedings in Chancery, temp. Eliz.* vol. i.)

FULBURN, WILLIAM DE, was no doubt a native of the place of that name in Cambridgeshire. He held an office in the court in the reign of Edward II., and was sent into that county and Huntingdonshire to instruct and assist the sheriffs in arresting the Knights Templars. Besides being employed in special commissions for the trial of offenders, he was on June 1, 1323, 16 Edward II., constituted a baron of the Exchequer, and having filled that office during the remainder of the reign, was reappointed on the accession of Edward III. The latest occurrence of his name is in a commission dated May 11, 1328, 2 Edward III. (*Parl. Writs*, ii. 900; *Rot. Parl.* ii. 25, 208.)

FULCON, ROBERT, before whom frequent assizes were holden from September 1267, is not introduced into Dugdale's list until May 15, 1271, 55 Henry III., when he was appointed a justice of the Common Pleas. As he was clearly raised to the bench at the former date, it is not improbable that he sat in the King's Bench for the intervening period.

That he was continued in his office on the accession of Edward I. appears from fines being levied before him till about Michaelmas in the second year of this reign (*Dugdale's Orig.* 42), and he is mentioned as a justice itinerant till 16 Edward I., probably retaining his position on the bench. (*Rot. Parl.* i. 4, 186; *Abb. Placit.* 202.)

FULTHORPE, ROGER DE, was the second son of Alan de Fulthorpe, of Fulthorpe, county Durham, where the family had been settled for several generations. He began his career as an advocate about 34 Edward III., 1366, and was made a king's serjeant in the thirty-ninth year. In 47 Edward III. he was one of the three commissioners assigned to hear and determine the dispute between Henry Lord Percy and William Douglas respecting the custody of the marches of the kingdom of England near Scotland. (*Issues Exch.* 195.) His elevation to the bench of the Common Pleas took place in the following year, on November 28, 1374, and, having been reappointed on the commencement of the new reign, he was knighted in 1385, and fines were continued to be levied before him till Midsummer 1387. (*Leland's Collect.* 185; *Dugdale's Orig.* 45.)

In the following August he was summoned to the council at Nottingham with the other judges, where, according to his own plea, he was compelled by the menaces of the Archbishop of York, the Duke of Ireland, the Earl of Suffolk, and Sir Robert Tresilian, to put his seal to the questions and answers already prepared by the latter, declaring the ordinance of the last parliament appointing eleven commissioners for the regulation of the kingdom to be illegal, and denouncing the promoters of it to be guilty of high treason. He and his colleagues were impeached for this act in the next parliament, and, notwithstanding the above excuse, were sentenced to death, which, however, was eventually commuted to banishment to Ireland for life, with forfeiture of all their property. Sir Robert was confined to the city of Dublin, and three miles round it, and he had an allowance of 40*l.* a year. (*Rot. Parl.* iii. 223–244.)

It is somewhat surprising that the same measure of severity should be meted to him as to his colleagues, since it appears by his plea that he immediately communicated the act he had done under fear of his life to the Earl of Kent, so that it was through his means that the lords, who were likely to be endangered by this extra-judicial opinion, had the earliest opportunity of securing themselves against the consequences. It was perhaps, however, on this account that in the same year an allowance of 40*l.* per annum was made to his son William out of the forfeited estates during his father's life, and that two years afterwards many of his father's manors and lands were granted to him on a fine of 1000 marks. (*Rot. Pat.* iii. 245; *Cal. Rot. Pat.* 219.)

It would seem that Fulthorpe died in his exile, probably in 16 Richard II., 1392 (*Cal. Inquis.* p. m. iii. 151), for his name was not included among those who in the twentieth year were recalled from Ireland; although he was mentioned in the proceedings of the next parliament, which reversed the judgment against the judges, and decreed the restoration of their lands to such as were living and to the heirs of those who were dead. Though the benefit of this reversal was lost by its repeal in the first year of Henry IV., the judge's forfeited lands were ultimately restored to his family, on the petition of his son William alleging all these facts in excuse for his father. (*Rot. Parl.* iii. 346, 358, 393.)

By his first wife, Sibella, Sir Roger had the above-mentioned William, who was the father of the next-noticed Thomas de Fulthorpe. His second wife, also named Sibella, was the daughter and heir of Sir Robert Salebury, and widow of Richard Radcliffe, of Ordsall, county Lancaster. (*Surtee's Durham*, iii. 126.)

FULTHORPE, THOMAS, was the grandson of the last-mentioned Sir Roger Fulthorpe, and the son of Sir William, who was the knight of the retinue of King Henry IV. who, on the refusal of Sir William Gascoigne, was assigned for the nonce to sit in judgment on Archbishop Scrope, the earl marshal, Ralph Hastings, and others in 1405. (*Rot. Parl.* iii. 633.) No evidence exists of Sir William having acted as a judge on any other occasion, and this was more a military execution than a judicial trial. His mother was Isabella, daughter of Ralph, Lord Lumley.

He was made a serjeant-at-law in 3 Henry VI., and often acted as a justice of assize, until he was raised to the bench of the Common Pleas, shortly before February 3, 1439, 17 Henry VI., when the first fine was acknowledged before him. The last fine was in November 1456, 35 Henry VI. (*Dugdale's Orig.* 46.) He died between that date and May 3 in the following year, when his will was proved. (*Surtees' Durham*, iii. 126.)

Among the patents of 27 Henry VI., 1448–9, is one declaring that 'pro salute sua' he shall not be compelled 'residere' in his office of judge, and that he may take cognitions wherever they may be brought to him (*Cal. Rot. Pat.* 293); but it does not appear whether this privilege was accorded on account of a failure in his health or of some personal danger which he apprehended.

FURNELLIS, or FURNAUS, ALAN DE, does not appear to have acted as a judge previous to 1179, 25 Henry II., when the kingdom was divided by the council held at Windsor into four parts, and certain wise men were selected to administer justice in each. He was one of the six who were specially appointed to hear the complaints of the people in the Curia Regis itself, and different counties were also appropriated to them for their circuit.

The roll of 1 Richard I., 1189, contains the entry of his death. He had been sheriff of Oxfordshire from 31 to 33 Henry II., and Cornwall also from 27 to 30 Henry II. The family, however, appears to have been more specially connected with Devonshire, as a Geoffrey de Furnellis was sheriff of that county at the end of the reign of Henry I. and the beginning of that of Henry II. Alan himself was joined in that sheriffalty in 21 Henry II., and Henry de Furnellis held it during the last nine years of the reign of Richard I. (*Madox's Exch.* i. 94, 139, 276, 328, ii. 220; *Fuller's Worthies; Pipe Roll*, 58, 105, 106, 107, 118, 131.)

FURNELLIS, or FURNAUS, HENRY DE,

a relative and probably the son of the last-named Alan, was according to Fuller sheriff of Devonshire during the last nine years of the reign of Richard I., though seemingly only under-sheriff. (*Madox*, i. 276.) In 3 John he accounts for Shropshire as the substitute of Geoffrey Fitz-Peter, then the sheriff of that county. (*Rot. Cancell.* 121.) There is little doubt, therefore, that he held an office in the Exchequer, and it was probably in that capacity that he was present in 1 John, when his name appears among the justiciers before whom a fine was acknowledged.

FURNELLIS, or FURNAUS, WILLIAM DE, as well as the two last members of this family, was connected with the court, and in 5 John was one of the fermers of the quinzime arising from merchandise in England. (*Madox*, i. 771.) According to the custom of the time, he was likewise of the clerical profession, and in the same year a royal mandate was directed to Geoffrey Fitz-Peter to give him ecclesiastical preferment to the extent of 40*l.* a year as soon as the other royal promises had been satisfied. (*Rot. de Liberat.* 69.) He was accordingly in possession of the living of Bromesgrove at the time of his death, in 1236, when the bishops gave it to the use of the monks of Worcester. (*Angl. Sacra*, i. 489.)

He was present at Cambridge in 10 and 11 John, 1208–1210, when fines were taken there before him, in which he is called a justice itinerant.

FURNELLIS, SIMON DE, was one of the justices itinerant for Essex and Hertford in 1234, 18 Henry III.; but his name does not again occur in the same character. He probably was a connection of the three above-named persons, and, like them, held some office connected with the courts.

FYNCHEDEN, WILLIAM DE, is mentioned as an advocate in the Year Books from 24 Edward III., and was made a king's serjeant in the thirty-sixth year, being also employed as a justice of assize two years after. On October 29, 1365, 39 Edward III., he was raised to the bench of the Common Pleas, and was advanced to its head on April 14, 1371. His successor was appointed on October 10, 1374, but whether the vacancy was occasioned by the death or retirement of Fyncheden does not appear. (*Cal. Rot. Pat.* 180, 186.)

G

GAERST, HUGH DE, was a justicier appointed by the great council held at Windsor in 1179, 25 Henry II., when England was arranged into four judicial divisions. He must have been held in some considerable estimation, as he was one of the six to whom not only the northern counties were appropriated, but who were also assigned to hear the complaints of the people in the Curia Regis. (*Madox*, i. 93, 138.)

GALDRIC. Dugdale erroneously calls this chancellor Baldricus, and places him in the reign of William I., on the authority of a charter granting the church of St. Mary of Andover to the abbey of St. Florence, at Salmur, in Anjou. This charter, however, was evidently granted by William II., though the gift of the church had been previously made by the Conqueror. That gift is recited in these words: 'Noscant qui sunt et futuri sunt, quod Willielmus rex, qui armis Anglicam terram *sibi subjugavit, dedit* Sancto Florentio ecclesiam de Andeura,' &c. (*Monast.* vi. 992)—language which the Conqueror himself never could have used, but which would be very natural in his son. But the date is placed beyond the possibility of doubt by the fact that the first witness to the charter is Robert, Bishop of Lincoln, who was Robert Bloet, not raised to the bishopric till some years after the accession of William II.

'Galdricus Cancellarius' is the second witness to this charter, and he probably was the immediate successor of Robert Bloet as chancellor, on his resigning the Seal when he was appointed bishop in 1093; because there is sufficient testimony that William Giffard was restored to the office soon afterwards, and retained it without interruption to the end of the reign.

In the reign of Henry I. there was a chancellor described by the name of Waldric, and, considering that the letters G and W were often indiscriminately used in spelling Christian names, as Gualterus, Walterus; Gulielmus, Willielmus; and also that there is only an interval of ten years between them, it does not appear improbable that Waldric was the same man. There is not, however, sufficient evidence to warrant a united notice.

Galdric was one of the royal chaplains, and accompanied King Henry in 1106 to Normandy, where he distinguished himself in the battle of Tenchebrai, fought on September 28, by taking Duke Robert prisoner. He was rewarded for his services with the bishopric of Laon, Laudunensis (*Notes and Queries*, 2nd S. v. 45), not, as elsewhere said, Llandaff, Landavensis (*Lingard*, ii. 115), being elected, notwithstanding the protest of Anselm, dean of the cathedral. Incurring the hatred of the citizens, he was murdered in a field with seven of his prebendaries. A curious account of his episcopate is in book iii. of Guibert of Nogent, 'De Vitâ Suâ.'

GANT, ROBERT DE. Philipot, following Thynne, names a Robert as chancellor to Stephen, without any surname. Spelman adds the surname, but neither Dugdale nor the author of the 'Lives of the Chancellors' (1708) mentions him. Madox (ii. 138), however, gives the copy of a charter of King Stephen, the first witness to which is Robert de Gant, chancellor. Another witness to this charter is William, Earl of Lincoln, who acquired that title in 1142, and died about 1152. 'Robert the Chancellor' is also the first witness to a grant of the church of Langeford made by that king to the Templars (*Monast.* vi. 320), which must have been dated between the years 1139 and 1151.

There were two Roberts de Gant who were alive about this time, uncle and nephew. The former was the second son of Gilbert, the first baron of that name (son of Baldwin, Earl of Flanders or Gant), by Alice de Montfort; the latter was the second son of Walter de Gant, the second baron, by Matilda, the daughter of Stephen, Earl of Brittany and Richmond. In the absence of any decisive authority, the presumption to be drawn from facts and dates seems to be that the uncle was the chancellor. He preceded Becket as provost of Beverley (*Ibid.* 1307), and was dean of York in 1148. He was succeeded in the deanery in 1153, which was doubtless the date of his death. The nephew lived till 1192, and was the ancestor of Maurice de Gant, the next-noticed justice itinerant. (*Arch. Inst. York; Holy Trinity*, 59, &c.; *Dugdale's Baron.* i. 402.)

GANT, MAURICE DE, was the son of Robert de Berkeley (son of Robert Fitz-Harding), by Alice, daughter of Robert de Gant (above named) and Alice Paganell, his wife. He attained his majority about 9 John, and soon afterwards assumed his mother's name, inheriting the large possessions she derived from her mother. In 15 John he married Matilda, the only child of Henry D'Oilly, baron of Hooknorton in Oxfordshire.

He was one of the principal instigators of the contest between the king and the discontented barons, and thereupon suffered excommunication and lost all his lands. (*Rot. Pat.* 162-198; *Rot. Claus.* i. 232, &c.) On the accession of Henry III. he continued to adhere to Prince Lewis of France, and was taken prisoner at the battle called the Fair of Lincoln, on May 20, 1217, by Ranulph, Earl of Chester, in whose custody he remained for a year, and ransomed himself by the cession of two of his capital manors, those of Leeds and Bingley in Yorkshire. After the treaty with Prince Lewis, he was allowed to make his peace, and in the latter part of the second year of Henry's reign his lands were restored to him. (*Rot. Claus.* i. 368, 376.)

His loyalty was thenceforward steadfast and active. In 9 Henry III. he assisted William, the earl marshal, in fortifying a castle in Wales; and although he had fortified his castle of Beverston in Gloucestershire without the necessary royal licence, he obtained the royal confirmation of his act. And in August of the same year, 1227, he was nominated one of the justices itinerant for five counties. (*Ibid.* ii. 180, 213.)

In April 1230 he embarked with King Henry on his expedition into France, during which, in the following August, he died. (*Excerpt. e Rot. Fin.* i. 201.)

After the death of his first wife, Matilda, he married Margaret, the widow of Ralph de Sumeri, who survived him; but he left no issue by either. (*Dugdale's Baron.* i. 402.)

GARDINER, STEPHEN (BISHOP OF WINCHESTER), is stated to have been an illegitimate son of a bishop, who concealed his incontinence by making one Gardiner, an under-servant in his household, marry his concubine, and thus become the apparent father of the child of which she was pregnant. The actual father is represented to have been Lionel Woodvill, brother of the queen of Edward IV., who was made Bishop of Salisbury in 1482, and died in 1485. He was born at St. Edmund's Bury in 1483. A will has been lately published (*Gent. Mag.* May, 1855, p. 495), made by one John Gardener, a cloth-maker of Bury St. Edmunds, dated January 18, 1506-7, which bequeaths some valuable legacies 'to Stevyn my sone,' one of which is to be paid to him 'when he comyth to the full age of xxj years,' and another 'when he shall take commensement in the scole at the universite;' and it is inferred with great probability that this John was the father of the lord chancellor.

He was sent to Trinity Hall, Cambridge, where his perseverance and attainments secured to him a reputation which he maintained through life. Proceeding doctor in both laws in 1520 and 1521, he entered into holy orders, and in 1525 he was elected master of his college, eventually, in 1540, becoming chancellor of the university. At an early period, however, he had been received first into the family of the Duke of Norfolk, and then into that of Cardinal Wolsey, who had made him his secretary. About the year 1525 the king, being on a visit to his minister, found Gardiner employed in drawing up the plan of an alliance projected by Wolsey with the king of France, which he did in a manner so satisfactory, supporting his views with so much ability, and suggesting expedients with so much ease, that he at once acquired the royal confidence, and was soon admitted into the council. In 1528, when he and Fox were sent to the pope, to negotiate the question as to the king's divorce from Catherine of Arragon, he gratified Henry by obtaining a new commission to Wolsey and to Cardinal Campeggio, and Wolsey also by reconciling the pope to the endowment of his two colleges at Oxford and Ipswich out of the revenues of some lesser monasteries which had been dissolved, as well as by his arduous exertions to secure the pontificate for the cardinal in the event of the pope's expected death.

On Gardiner's return he received his first preferment in the Church, that of the archdeaconry of Norfolk, on March 1, 1529. In the following October his name 'Stephen Gardyner' appears as 'counsellor to the king' in the record of the delivery up of the Great Seal by Cardinal Wolsey. (*Rymer*, xiv. 349.) Placed by the changes which took place on that event in the office of secretary of state, it has been a question how far he exerted the great influence which he certainly had with the king in behalf of his fallen master, and it is generally admitted that Cromwell's conduct was more generous, bold, and decided. A letter, however, from Wolsey to Gardiner, without entirely attributing to his interference the pardon which the king had consented to grant, seems to exhibit a firm reliance on his 'love and affection' in the preparation of the instrument. (*Archæologia*, xviii. 57.)

Gardiner was next employed in inducing the university of Cambridge to make a declaration affirming the prohibition by the divine and natural law for a brother to marry the relict of his deceased brother. This he and his coadjutor Fox, after some trouble, contrived by management to obtain (*Lingard*, vi. 386); and the king was not long in rewarding both. Gardiner received the archdeaconry of Leicester on March 31, 1531, and on the 27th of November in the same year he was consecrated Bishop of Winchester, the patent for the restitution of the temporalities, dated December 5, describing him as 'our principal secretary.' (*Rymer*, xiv. 429.)

Throughout the remainder of Henry's reign Gardiner devoted himself to the king's service, and until towards its close succeeded in preserving his ascendency in the royal councils. This he effected by accommodating himself to Henry's humours, whatever they might be. When the king's marriage was pronounced null and void, he went as ambassador to the French king. Bonner, who was joined in the embassy, complained loudly of his being obstinate and self-willed, and of his extreme jealousy of any interference in the management of the business, or of any supposed assumption of an equality of rank. This spirit he soon after exhibited toward his ecclesiastical superior, Archbishop Crammer, by raising every obstacle against the visitation which that prelate proposed to make in his diocese. Like all his brethren of the episcopal bench, he was compelled by the new statute to swear to the king's supremacy, which he not only appeared to do with the greatest readiness, but wrote strongly and ably in its support, although at the same time he was devotedly attached to the superstitious doctrines of the Romish Church. The king, though professing the same sentiments, was still desirous of introducing some reforms, and of permitting the Scriptures to be read in the vulgar tongue, but Gardiner vigorously opposed every step taken to promote the Reformation. He stirred up the king's zeal against those who denied the Real Presence, and seems to be justly chargeable with bringing Lambert and others to the stake for refusing to adopt the doctrine; he procured, or at least promoted, the enactment of the bloody statute of the Six Articles, under the cruel provisions of which so many suffered; and he plotted to get rid of Archbishop Cranmer, whom he hated as the great supporter of the Protestant party, by charges of an heretical nature. But in the latter he failed; the king saw through his malevolent design, and from that moment ceased to have confidence in him. He did not improve the impression on the royal mind by the servile submission and acknowledgment which he made in anticipation of a charge against himself of doubting the king's supremacy, although he obtained his pardon by an abject promise to reform his opinion. But he put a finishing stroke to the king's alienation from him by combining with Lord Wriothesley in the endeavour to implicate Queen Catherine Parr in reference to these religious questions. From that time Henry not only withdrew all show of favour to him, but his name was struck out of the king's will, of which he had before been appointed one of the executors. He was thus excluded from the council of regency.

Strongly opposing all the means then taken to advance the Reformation, he was committed to the Fleet in September 1547, resisting all the attempts of Archbishop Cranmer to bring him round to the new opinions. From this imprisonment he was released, in consequence of the general pardon granted at the close of the session, on December 24. In the following June, however, being commanded to preach before the king, his sermon was so little satisfactory that he was sent to the Tower on the next day. The removal of the lord protector, whom he looked on as his great enemy, made no change in his state, and at the end of two years he was subjected to a sort of examination, and offered his freedom if he would subscribe to certain articles submitted to him. This he declined to do until he was discharged from his imprisonment. A special commission was then appointed to try him, when, persisting in his refusal, his bishopric was sequestered, but three months were given him for consideration, at the end of which he was brought before a court of delegates, over which Archbishop Cranmer presided, and on February 14, 1551, he was deprived for disobedience and contempt of the king's authority. His contemptuous behaviour towards the court led to an increased rigour in his confinement, which continued till the end of the reign.

The accession of Queen Mary opened a brighter prospect to the determined prelate. On her public entry into the Tower on August 3, 1553, he made a congratulatory speech in the name of himself and his fellow-prisoners, among whom were the Duke of Norfolk, the Duchess of Somerset, the Lord Courtney, and Bishop Tunstall. The queen, in releasing them all, is said to have kissed them, and to have called them 'her prisoners.' Thus, after a confinement of more than five years, was he restored to liberty. He was immediately admitted to a seat in council, and within five days he exercised his episcopal functions, performing in the queen's presence the obsequies of the late king. On the 23rd of that month the Great Seal was delivered to him as chancellor, but it was not till September 21 that his patent was dated. He performed the ceremony of coronation on October 1, opened the first parliament of the reign four days afterwards, and from that time during the remainder of his life acted as Mary's chief adviser in all civil matters, and, until the arrival of Cardinal Pole in November 1554, in the affairs of the Church also.

The first difficulty which he had to encounter was the necessary confirmation of the marriage of Henry VIII. with Catherine of Arragon, in order to remove the illegitimation of Queen Mary. Here, though he had been one of the principal promoters of the divorce, by his contrivance the whole blame was thrown on Archbishop Cranmer. The repeal of the laws passed in the last reign with regard to religion, and the restoration of all the ancient Romish practices, were not delayed, but the measures adopted for this purpose, and the cruel consequences with which all opponents were visited, belong rather to the history of the period than to the biography of an individual. Suffice it to say that several Protestant bishops were deprived, others compelled to fly the country, the prisons were filled to overflowing, and after a short time innumerable victims suffered at the stake. With every desire to give an impartial consideration to the arguments of those writers who attempt to palliate his conduct, it is impossible to acquit Gardiner of originating the laws which authorised these cruel measures, and of carrying them into effect with their extremest severity, and conscientious as some may think him in his zeal for the ancient Church, none but the most bigoted can justify the means he adopted for its restoration. That his old enemy, Archbishop Cranmer, who had already been tried, did not suffer at the same time with Bishops Ridley and Latimer, has been ascribed to his desire to succeed to the archbishopric, with which he knew that Cardinal Pole would be immediately invested if his intrigues in the court of Rome against that powerful ecclesiastic were not successful. Whatever were his motives for delaying the execution, it is difficult to ascribe them to merciful considerations, since these did not operate to save the two other Oxford martyrs. During the interval, however, between the archbishop's trial and the execution of his sentence, Gardiner, after opening the parliament on October 21, 1555, was seized with a mortal disease, the nature of which has been variously represented, of which he died at Whitehall, on November 12, terminating a short ministry of two years and less than three months more disreputable than any other of similar extent recorded in the annals of the kingdom. He was buried in Winchester Cathedral.

Of Gardiner's learning there can be no doubt; but even in his contest with Sir John Cheke on the pronunciation of the Greek language he exhibited the obstinacy and tyranny of his disposition, visiting with punishment those who adopted the reformation proposed by his antagonist. With very quick parts and great acuteness of mind, his early initiation into business highly qualified him for a statesman, and the measures which he took on the marriage of Queen Mary to prevent foreign interference with the government of the kingdom are sufficient proofs of his abilities as a politician.

His work 'De Verâ Obedientiâ,' written against the Papal supremacy, he was afterwards obliged to retract by another called 'Palinodia Dicti Libri.' Besides these he published several other controversial pieces; and many of his sermons have been preserved. (*Godwin*, 236; *State Trials*, i. 551; *Brit. Biog.* ii. 202; *Robertson's Heylin; Lingard; Burnet*; &c.)

GARLAND, JOHN DE, was one of the custodes of the bishopric of Winchester during its vacancy in 1189. (*Pipe Roll, 5.*) There is no doubt, therefore, that he held some office in the court. In 8 Richard I., 1196, he acted as a justice itinerant, setting the tallage for the united counties of Essex and Hertford. (*Madox*, i. 704.)

GARROW, WILLIAM, one of the most successful advocates of his day, was born on April 13, 1760, at Monken-Hadley in Middlesex, where his father, the Rev. David Garrow, kept a school, in which his son received the whole of his education. At fifteen he was articled to Mr. Southouse, a respectable attorney residing in Milk Street, Cheapside, where he showed so much ability and quickness that he was strongly recommended by his master to aim at the higher branch of the law. His friends consenting, he was entered at Lincoln's Inn in 1778, and was called to the bar on November 26, 1783.

He attended the debating societies then established in the metropolis, and at Coachmakers' Hall and other similar schools he soon became a powerful debater, and his speeches were so admired for their eloquence and ingenuity that his presence at them was always welcomed. He assumed the gown, therefore, with a certain prestige, which immediately secured him some business at the Old Bailey, where, so early as the January after he was called, he was fortunate enough so to distinguish himself as to establish a sure foundation for his future success. A clever swindler, Henry Aickles, was indicted for stealing a bill of exchange, which he had obtained under the promise of getting it discounted; instead of doing which he had converted it to his own use. His counsel contended confidently that this was no felony, and it was considered a very doubtful point; but the acuteness of Mr. Garrow's reply, and the readiness and cogency of his arguments, so far satisfied the judge that he left the question of fact to the jury, who convicted the delinquent; and on a reference to the twelve judges, they coincided with Garrow's view of the law.

His reputation thus established, his business rapidly increased, not only in criminal but in civil cases. In the general election of the same year he was fully employed. First, he was chosen assessor to the sheriff of Hertford, in the county election; next, he was retained in the London scrutiny for Mr. Sawbridge; and then he acted as counsel for Mr. Fox in the famous Westminster scrutiny. In reference to the latter, when he was suddenly called upon to address the House of Commons, his unpremeditated speech was so forcible and luminous that it excited the applause, and he received the congratulations of even the opposing party. All this occurred in the first year after his call to the bar. He not only acquired the undisputed lead in the crown courts, but was also so much employed, both on the Home Circuit and in Westminster Hall, that in April 1793 he was appointed a king's counsel.

His services were perpetually engaged in honourable contest with the phalanx of eminent men who, during the twenty-four years that he remained at the bar with a silk gown, graced the courts in London and the country, the principal of whom were Erskine, Gibbs, and Best. He was employed by the government in most of the state trials occurring during that period; and in many of them the sole management was entrusted to him. (*State Trials*, xxii.–xxxi.) In June 1812 he was appointed solicitor-general, and knighted, having six years previously held the office of attorney-general to the Prince of Wales, before he was regent. In the next year he was raised to the same office as the king's attorney, and further promoted to the chief justiceship of Chester in March 1814.

He entered parliament in 1805, and represented successively Gatton, Collington, and Eye; but his senatorial harangues were not distinguished with more success than is usually attributed to members of the legal profession.

After performing the duties of attorney-general for four years with exemplary forbearance and general commendation, he relieved himself from its responsibility by accepting on May 6, 1817, a seat on the bench of the Exchequer. For nearly fifteen years he exercised the functions of a judge, when, prompted by the advance of age and infirmity, he retired in February 1832, receiving an honourable reward for his services by being made a privy counsellor. He lived nearly eight years afterwards, and died on September 24, 1840, at his house at Pegwell Bay, near Ramsgate, at the age of eighty.

The influx of business with which he had to cope from the very commencement of his career, although it made him an adept in the practice of the courts and in the superficial questions of law, deprived him of the opportunity of studying the abstruser points. So conscious was he of his deficiency in the knowledge of the law of real property that he always in cases which touched that branch relied on the intelligence of his junior.

As a judge his former experience gave him considerable advantages in the ordinary cases of Nisi Prius, by enabling him at once to pierce into the real merits of the question, and to detect any evasion or ambiguity, and in Banco he had the discretion not to go beyond the limits of his own learning. He maintained an intimate friendship with those who were his forensic antagonists and rivals, and he closed his long life without a single stain on his moral character, and with the respect and deep affection of all who were closely connected with him.

By his wife, whom he lost in 1808, he had two children—a son, Dr. David Garrow, who died rector of East Barnet; and a daughter, Eliza, who married the eldest son of the well-known Dr. Lettsom.

GARTON, THOMAS DE, was a member of the clerical profession, and appointed in 18 Edward II. to assist the bishops in removing foreign priests. Under Edward III. he held the offices of comptroller of the king's household and keeper of the wardrobe, and on October 10, 1331, 5 Edward III., he was placed on the bench of the Exchequer, as second baron. (*N. Fœdera*, ii. 574, 769, 785.)

GASCOIGNE, WILLIAM, is the first chief justice of whom we have any personal anecdotes, and the incidents related of him are not only creditable to himself as an individual, but afford also the first example of that honesty, independence, and courage which should characterise the judicial bench, and of which in our own days we have so much reason to be proud; but of him we know, and we can expect to know, but little, until he became chief justice of the King's Bench.

The family of Gascoigne, the derivation of which is sufficiently shown in the name, is very ancient, no less than seven successive Williams being recorded in the pedigree before the chief justice. The third of these is described as of Harewood, near Leeds, in Yorkshire, whose son acquired Gawthorp in the same parish by marrying the heiress of that manor. There the judge's father was settled, and there the judge was born, his mother being Agnes, daughter and coheir of Mr. Nicholas Franke.

In which of the legal seminaries he received his instruction it is impossible to determine, because the records of none of them extend to so ancient a date. Fuller says he was of the Inner Temple, but adduces no authority; and in the MS. account of Gray's Inn, written in the seventeenth century, his name stands among the undated and supposed readers of that society.

He was old enough in 48 Edward III., 1374, to be mentioned as an advocate in the Year Books, and in 21 Richard II., 1397, he was appointed one of the king's serjeants. In 1398 he was among the twenty attorneys assigned for different courts or jurisdictions by Henry of Lancaster, Duke of Hereford (*Rymer*, viii. 49), on his banishment from the kingdom in consequence of the quarrel with the Duke of Norfolk; but on the death of Henry's father, John of Gaunt, four months afterwards, the infatuated monarch seized the duke's lands, notwithstanding his declaration that Henry's succession to his inheritance should not be interrupted.

Henry IV. had not been fourteen months upon the throne before he rewarded Gascoigne for his services, by constituting him chief justice of the King's Bench on November 15, 1400. All writers acknowledge his legal merit in the ordinary execution of his office, and it was not long before he had occasion to exhibit the higher characteristics of his nature. In 1405 the army raised by Richard Scrope, Archbishop of York, and Thomas Mowbray, earl marshal, having been dispersed by the capture of the two leaders, they were taken to the royal presence at Bishop's Thorpe, the primate's palace, when the king commanded the chief justice to pronounce on them the sentence of death. Gascoigne resolutely refused to obey, saying, 'Neither you, my lord, nor any of your subjects, can, according to the law of the realm, sentence any prelate to death; and the earl has a right to be tried by his peers.' The king, however, was not to be stopped, and he found a willing instrument in a knight of Yorkshire, named Sir William Fulthorpe, in no way himself connected with the law. (*Scrope and Grosvenor Roll*, ii. 124.)

Henry on reflection could not help approving his judge's boldness, and, so far from withdrawing his confidence from him, seems to have been in the familiar habit of putting supposed cases for his opinion. The history of Gascoigne's committing Prince Henry to prison is told in various ways. The most authentic seems to be that the prince, on the arraignment of one of his servants for felony before the chief justice, imperiously demanded his release, and having been refused, with a rebuke for his interference, had angrily drawn his sword on the judge. His passion was instantly checked by the dignified demeanour of Gascoigne, who calmly called on him to remember himself, reminded him of the position in which he would one day stand, and committed him to prison for his contempt and disobedience. The prince submitted at once and went away in custody; and when the incident was related to the king, he exclaimed, 'How much am I bound to your infinite goodness, O merciful God, for having given me a judge who feareth not to administer justice, and a son who can thus nobly submit to it!'

Almost all of Gascoigne's biographers have fixed his death to have taken place on December 17, 1412, 14 Henry IV., and consequently have determined that Shakspeare's introduction of him, as chief justice to Henry V., is a poetic fiction invented for dramatic effect. Whatever enthusiasm we may indulge for the works of our immortal bard, it cannot extend to our accepting them as authority for historical facts, and unquestionably in a trial between him and the biographers we should feel bound in the absence of other evidence to give a verdict for the latter. But in this case there are materials which render it unnecessary to rely wholly on either, and which enable us to arrive with a clearer judgment at the truth. The result of the investigation proves that both are wrong—the biographers wholly, the poet partially.

The error of the biographers in fixing the death of Gascoigne in December 1412 is manifest in many ways.

In the first place, he is the judge in a case reported in February 1413. (*Y. B.* 14 *Henry IV.* fo. 19.) Secondly, he was summoned to the first parliament of Henry V. in Easter 1413. Thirdly, on the Issue Rolls of the same year the sum of 79*l.* 3*s.* 0½*d.* is stated to have been paid to him on July 7 for his salary and additional annuity. (*Devon's Issue Roll*, 322.) And lastly, his will has been found in the ecclesiastical court at York, the date being on December 15, 1419, and the probate being granted on the 23rd of the same month.

Thus therefore the poet correctly introduces Gascoigne as alive on the accession of Henry V.; but we fear we must convict him of falsifying history in his desire to enhance the character of his hero, when he makes Henry with a noble generosity reinvest the inflexible magistrate with 'the balance and the sword;' nor can we acquit Lord Campbell of a similar charge, when he asserts that he can 'prove to demonstration that Sir William Gascoigne * * * actually filled the office of chief justice of the King's Bench under Henry V.'

The only evidence that has the slightest tendency to support this view is the summons to parliament, which was dated March 22, 1413, the *day after* the accession, in which he is called 'chief justice of our lord the king.' This single fact, however, gives little assistance to the argument; because the title of chief justice would be properly applied to him until he was actually superseded, and because the king, having obviously had no more time than to order a parliament to be summoned, the writs of summons would be naturally addressed to those peers, judges, and others who were summoned to the preceding parliament, and consequently to the judicial officers existing at the demise of the late king. But the slight presumption founded upon the fact is invalidated by numerous contrary proofs.

Thus in the parliament held by virtue of that summons, which commenced on May 15, Gascoigne not only was not present, but his usual place among the triers of petitions was filled by Sir William Hankford, who, though previously only a puisne judge of the Common Pleas, is named in precedence of Sir William Thirning, the chief justice of that court. (*Rot. Parl.* iv. 4.)

Again, although Dugdale defers Hankford's elevation to the chief justiceship for more than ten months from the accession, and although he was not included in the new patents to the judges of the Common Pleas which were issued on May 2, a day or two before the opening of Easter Term 1413, yet in several cases reported in the Year Books, not only of that term but of Trinity also, we find him, not indeed acting in the Common Pleas, but presiding in the King's Bench.

Even if these two facts were not sufficient to remove any doubt upon the question, the two records to which reference has been already made contain such conclusive proof that Sir William Gascoigne was not reappointed to his place as chief justice that it seems impossible that any one can maintain the contrary.

In one of them, the payment on the Issue Roll of July 1413, Gascoigne is called '*late* chief justice of the Bench of Lord Henry, *father of the present king.*'

In the other, the inscription on his monument in Harewood Church in Yorkshire in 1419, he is described as '*nuper* capit. justic. de Banco Hen. *nuper* regis Angliæ *quarti*.'

Can it be for a moment supposed that in either of these records he would have been docked of his title had he ever been chief justice of the reigning king?

Still, however, the difficulty remained arising from Dugdale's date of Hankford's appointment as chief justice; but this has been removed by reference to the roll itself. It turns out, on inspection, that the date, instead of being January 29, 1414, as stated by Dugdale, is March 29, 1413, just eight days after King Henry's accession, and ten days previous to his coronation.

The peculiar period chosen for this act, and its precipitancy in contrast with the delay in issuing the new patents to the other judges, seem strongly to show that it resulted from the king's peremptory mandate rather than Gascoigne's personal choice, and consequently to raise a suspicion that the indignity he had laid upon the prince was not 'washed in Lethe, and forgotten' by the king.

A royal warrant dated November 28, 1414, twenty months after his dismissal, granting him four bucks and four does yearly during his life, out of the forest of Pontefract (*Tyler's Henry V.* i. 379), was a favour too long retarded to warrant a more lenient construction of the conduct of the king.

This great judge was buried in the parish church of Harewood, where the monument bears his effigy in judicial robes.

He married first Elizabeth, daughter and heir of Alexander Mowbray, of Kirthington, Esq.: and secondly, Joan, daughter of Sir William Pickering, and relict of Sir Henry Greystock, baron of the Exchequer. By both he had issue. The eldest son by his first was named William, and as there were seven successive Williams before the judge, so also were there seven after him.

The baronetcy of Gascoigne of Barnbow was granted by Charles I. to a descendant of Nicholas, a younger brother of the judge, and became extinct in 1810. (*Wotton's Baronet.* v. 334; *Testam. Ebor.* p. i. 410.)

GASELEE, STEPHEN, was the son of an eminent surgeon at Portsmouth, where he was born in 1762. He chose the legal profession and entered the society of Gray's Inn, became a pupil of Sir Vicary Gibbs, and was called to the bar in 1793. He joined the Western Circuit, and was so well respected as a careful and well-informed junior that when, after six-and-twenty years' practice, he was made a king's counsel in 1819, his professional income was probably diminished. But though not gifted with those oratorical powers which were likely to gain him employment as a leader, his deserved reputation for legal knowledge soon recommended him to a judge's place. Accordingly he was selected on July 1, 1824, to supply a vacancy in the Common Pleas, and was knighted. In that court he sat for nearly fourteen years, with the character of a painstaking and upright judge, and in his private capacity as a worthy and benevolent man. He resigned his place at the end of Hilary Term 1837, and died on March 26, 1839.

His widow survived him, and one of his sons is now a serjeant-at-law.

GATES, THOMAS, is described as of Churchill in the county of Oxford in his admission to the Inner Temple, on January 1, 1606-7. Having been called to the bar on January 29, 1614-15, he was elected reader to that society in autumn 1635. As his name is never mentioned in the Reports, there seems nothing but his politics to induce the Long Parliament (of which he was not a member) to recommend him to be called serjeant, and to be made a baron of the Exchequer. This however they did on October 12, 1648, and he accepted a renewal of his commission on the death of the king. His death on August 19, 1650, at the age of sixty-three, was occasioned by an infection taken at Croydon while engaged in his judicial duties, and he was buried in the Temple Church. (*Peck's Desid. Cur.* b. xiv. 23.)

GATESDEN, JOHN DE, is called by Dugdale (*Orig.* 21) a canon of St. Paul's; but if so, civilians must have held those appointments, inasmuch as he had a wife and children. He was possessed of property in Norton and Bradford in Somersetshire, and held the office of sheriff of Surrey and Sussex in 20 Henry III. and the three following years. (*Madox*, ii. 177.) In 25 Henry III. he had a liberate for 50*l*., to discharge the expenses of the queen. (*Pell Records*, iii. 17.)

He is inserted in Dugdale's list of justiciers of the Common Pleas in 34 Henry III., 1250, on account of a fine having been acknowledged before him in Hilary Term of that year, and also as a justice itinerant into Lincolnshire. He is again mentioned as a justicier in an entry of 38 Henry III. relative to certain 'heccagiis' in Sussex held by himself and some other persons. (*Abb. Placit.* 137.)

He and the Bishop of Ely were sent as ambassadors to Spain on the king's affairs in 40 Henry III. (*Rymer*, i. 343.) He died in April 1262, 46 Henry III., leaving large property both in Sussex and Somersetshire. By his wife Hawise he had a son named John, who died in his lifetime, leaving a widow; and at the date of his own death, Margaret, his daughter, or granddaughter, was a minor. She married John de Camoys. (*Excerpt. e Rot. Fin.* ii. 316-384; *Abb. Placit.* 187, 334.)

GAUNSTEDE, SIMON, was in holy orders, and connected with the court as early as 9 Richard II., 1386, when his name appears attached to the confederation with the King of Castile. Throughout the reign of Henry IV. he is mentioned as one of the clerks of the Chancery. (*Rymer*, vii. 515, 809.) On June 3, 1415, 3 Henry V., he was appointed master of the Rolls, and on the chancellor's going to France the Great Seal was left with him from September 5 to October 12, 1416. He held it again under Henry VI., from September 28, 1422, till November 16, when he was recognised as an independent keeper with all the usual powers, and received the accustomed salary. (*Rymer*, x. 262.) He probably died soon after, since John Frank was appointed his successor on October 28, 1423.

GAWDY, THOMAS, was the son of another Thomas Gawdy, of Harleston in Norfolk. Both were of the Inner Temple, and both serjeants-at-law. The father was reader there in Lent 1548 and 1553, and for refusing to read in the latter year he was amerced, although he had been promoted to be a serjeant in the previous October. (*Dugdale's Orig.* 164; *Machyn's Diary*, 26.) He represented Norwich in Queen Mary's first parliament. He died in August 1566, and his virtues, together with those of Serjeant Richard Catlin, are recorded in a joint Latin epitaph introduced into Plowden's Reports. (180.) By one of his wives, Anne, the daughter of John Bassingbourne, Esq., of Woodhall in Hertfordshire, he had two sons, Thomas and Bassingbourne, the latter of whom was the great-grandfather of two baronets—Gawdy of Crow's Hall in Suffolk, and Gawdy of West Herling in Norfolk; but both titles became extinct at the beginning of the last century.

Thomas Gawdy, the eldest son, who was born at Harleston, became in 1558 member for Norwich, as his father had been before him, and was among those who were summoned by Queen Mary in October of the same year to take the degree of the coif in the following Easter; but her death intervening, it became necessary to have a new writ, from which, probably at his own request, his name was excluded. In the following year he was reader at the Inner Temple, and treasurer in 1562. In 1563 he became recorder of Norwich, and on another summons he took the degree of the coif in 1567; and on November 16, 1574, he was constituted a judge of the Queen's Bench. Here he sat for fourteen years, and was one of the few puisne judges on whom Queen Elizabeth bestowed a knighthood. He was both in the commission for the trial of Dr. Parry in February 1585, preserved in the 'Baga de Secretis,' and in that of October 1586 for the trial of Mary Queen of Scots at Fotheringay. (*State Trials*, i. 1167.) His legal arguments are reported by Dyer, Plowden, and Coke; and the latter, in stating Rawlyn's case in Michaelmas 1587 (4 *Report*, 54), gives this character of him: 'This was the last case that Sir Thomas Gawdy argued, who was a most reverend judge and sage of the law, of ready and profound judgment, and venerable gravity, prudence, and integrity.' He died on November 4, 1588, and his place was supplied by the appointment of his half-brother, Francis Gawdy.

He was married twice: his first wife was named Helwise, and his second Frances, by both of whom he left issue.

GAWDY, FRANCIS, was the half-brother of his predecessor, Sir Thomas Gawdy, being the third son of Serjeant Thomas Gawdy, of Harleston in Norfolk, by his third wife, Elizabeth, daughter of Thomas or Oliver Shyres. He presents an instance as well of the same name being given to two sons as of a Christian name being altered at confirmation. At his baptism he was called Thomas, which at his confirmation was changed to Francis, and the latter name, 'by the advice of all the judges in anno 36 Henry VIII. (1544), he did beare, and after used in all his purchases and grants.' (*Coke Litt.* 3 a.)

He was admitted a member of the Inner Temple in 1549, and became Lent reader in 1566. In Lent 1571 he was appointed duplex reader, and also treasurer to the society. Being called to the degree of the coif in 1577, he was made one of the queen's serjeants on May 17, 1582, and was present at Fotheringay on the trial of Mary Queen of Scots, but no duty appears to have devolved upon him. On the arraignment of Secretary Davison in 1587, for forwarding the warrant for that unfortunate lady's execution, he joined in the solemn farce with as serious a face as any of the rest of the actors. (*State Trials*, i. 1173, 1233.)

On the death of his brother, Sir Thomas Gawdy, he was nominated his successor as a judge of the Queen's Bench on November 25, 1588. In none of the criminal trials on which he was a commissioner, either in the reign of Queen Elizabeth or of King James (by whom he was continued in his place and knighted), is he represented as taking any part except in that of Sir Walter Raleigh, when he is made to say, 'The statute you speak of concerning two witnesses in case of treason *is found to be inconvenient*; therefore by another law it was taken away.' (*Ibid.* ii. 18.) He was named as one of the commissioners to hear causes in Chancery on the death of Sir Christopher Hatton in 1591.

It seems not improbable that he owed his elevation to the bench to Elizabeth's favoured chancellor, whose nephew, Sir William Newport, alias Hatton, about six months after it took place, married the judge's only daughter Elizabeth. The judge perhaps was also indebted for his next promotion to the marriage of his granddaughter Frances, the only issue of the above union, to Robert Rich, second Earl of Warwick. These nuptials took place in February 1605 (*Nicolas's Hatton*, 478, 502), and on the 26th of the following August Sir Francis was raised to the post of chief justice of the Common Pleas. He enjoyed this high position, for which he is said to have paid at a dear rate, less than a year. He was stricken with apoplexy at his chambers in Serjeants' Inn about Whitsuntide 1606, and was taken to his mansion at Eston Hall, Wallington, in Norfolk; but, having converted the parish church into a hay-house or dog-kennel, his body was obliged to be buried in the neighbouring church of Rungton.

His wife was Elizabeth, the eldest daughter of Christopher Coningsby, the son of William Coningsby the judge.

GEDDING, RANULPH DE, is named among the justiciers and barons before whom fines were acknowledged in the Curia Regis in 28 Henry II., 1182, and the two following years (*Hunter's Preface*, xxi.; *Madox*, i. 82, 113, 213); but his attendance on these occasions probably arose from his holding an office connected with the Exchequer. In the last of those years he was paid out of the issues of the honor of the constabulary divers sums expended for cordage, instruments, and other necessaries for the ship of Henry de Schornis, when it sailed to Spain for the Infanta of Portugal. (*Madox's Baron. Angl.* 75.)

The Great Roll of 31 Henry II., 1185, contains a curious instance of the pretences made in those times for bringing money into the king's exchequer. William de Beaumont, it seems, had contracted to marry the daughter of Ranulph de Gedding, but, altering his mind, had taken to wife the daughter of Maurice de Barsham; whereupon the faithless William was fined fifty marks, while his manœuvring father-in-law was fined in double that amount for permitting the breach of the contract.

GENT, THOMAS, was the son of William Gent, Esq., of the manor of Moynes in the parish of Bumpstead-Steeple, Essex, who could trace his pedigree backwards more than two centuries, by his second wife Agnes, daughter and coheir of Thomas Carr, Esq., of Great Thurlow in Suffolk. Educated at Cambridge, he entered the Middle Temple, where he arrived at the post of reader in Lent 1571, and again filled it three years afterwards, having been elected member for Malden in 1572. He was called serjeant in June 1584, and in the meantime he enjoyed the lucrative appointment of steward of all the courts of Edward de Vere, Earl of Oxford. According to Dugdale he was not raised to the bench of the Exchequer till June 28, 1588, 30 Elizabeth; but this is clearly an error, for he is so designated in a special commission of oyer and terminer in Sussex on February 1, 28 Elizabeth, 1586, preserved in the 'Baga de Secretis.'

Coke reports his judgments, and he had the special privilege granted him of acting in his own county as a judge of assize, notwithstanding the prohibition in the statute 33 Henry VIII. c. 24. He died in 1593, and was buried at Bumpstead. His character may be estimated by the lines which Thomas Newton in his 'Encomia' addressed to him, commencing thus:

Religio, virtus, pietas, pudor, ac aletheia
Exulat e terris, mobile vulgus ait.
Fallitur: Eximias nam qui considerat in te
Dotes, &c.

He married first Elizabeth, only daughter and heir of Sir John Swallow, of Bocking; and secondly Elizabeth, the widow of Robert Hogeson, of London, and sister of Morgan Robyns, Esq. By the first he had a large family, and the estate has continued from that time to this in his descendants.

GEOFFREY was archdeacon of Berks from 1175 to 1200 (*Le Neve*, 278), and in 9 Richard I., 1197-8, was the first of four justices itinerant who set the tallages in that county. (*Madox*, i. 705.)

GEOFFREY THE TEMPLAR, to whom, with John de Lexinton, King Henry gave the custody of the Great Seal in August 1238, does not seem to have held it long, as it was soon after in the possession of Simon the Norman. There is very little information as to Geoffrey, and indeed of the persons so named at different dates the identification is doubtful. (*Mat. Paris*, 474.)

GEOFFREY (BISHOP OF COUTANCE) was a member of the noble Norman house of Mowbray, and was elected Bishop of Coutance (Constantia) in Lower Normandy in 1048. He was more of a soldier than a divine, and, accompanying William on his invasion of England, held a distinguished command in the battle of Hastings. He assisted at the coronation of the Conqueror, and harangued the Normans on the occasion. He afterwards exerted himself in suppressing the rebellions of the English and in resisting the incursions of the Danes. At the head of the men of Monmouth, London, and Salisbury, he checked the assault of the West Saxons of Dorset and Somerset on Montacute, and he joined in reducing to subjection the rebels under the Earls of Hereford and Norfolk. He was rewarded with no less than 280 manors.

He is said to have held the office of chief justiciary in conjunction with Lanfranc, Archbishop of Canterbury, and Robert, Earl of Moreton, during part of William's reign, several precepts having been directed to them by the king which bear that interpretation. There is no doubt that he presided *in loco regis* at the contest between Archbishop Lanfranc and Bishop Odo, relative to certain lands and rights of which the former alleged his church of Canterbury had been disseised by the latter. The trial took place on Penenden Heath, about 1076, lasting three days, and was decided in favour of Lanfranc.

After William's death he assisted Robert, the king's eldest son, in his attempt on the English crown, and with his nephew, Robert Mowbray, Earl of Northumberland, fortified themselves in Bristol. On the failure of Robert's enterprise the bishop was allowed to return to Normandy, where he died on February 4, 1093. (*Dugdale's Monast.* i. 546; *Will. Malmesb.* 487; *Madox*, i. 32; *Dugdale's Orig.* 20; *Baronage*, i. 56; *Hutchins's Dorsetsh.* i. 11; *Rapin; Turner; Lingard.*)

GERARD, GILBERT, a descendant from the family of Gerard of Bryn, which now enjoys a baronetcy granted in 1611, was the son of James Gerard and Margaret, daughter of John Holcroft of Holcroft. After receiving his education at Cambridge he entered Gray's Inn, and was called to the bar in 1539, became an ancient in 1547, reader in 1554, and in the next year he was joined with Sir Nicholas Bacon in the office of treasurer. (*Dugdale's Orig.* 293, 298.) He represented Wigan in the parliament of 1553, Steyning in 1554, and Lancashire in 1585. Dugdale says (*Baron.* ii. 417), 'In the time of Queen Mary (as by credible tradition I have heard), upon the Lady Elizabeth's being questioned at the council table, he was permitted to plead there on her behalf, and performed his part so well as that he suffered imprisonment for the same in the Tower of London during the remaining terme of Queen Marie's reign.' However true the former part of this story may be, the latter part is certainly incorrect, for Plowden records his appearance in court in Michaelmas 1557; and on October 27, 1558, he was summoned to take the degree of the coif in the ensuing Easter Term. Before that time arrived the death of Mary had taken place, and Queen Elizabeth had, on January 22, 1559, raised him to the office of attorney-general. He retained his important post for twenty-two years, during which time there are only two English state trials reported—those of the Duke of Norfolk and of his servant Hickford for high treason in 1571. At both of these Gerard assisted, and in the first took a prominent part. In the last Hickford pleaded guilty. (*State Trials,* i. 957-1030.)

He was knighted in 1579, and was promoted to the office of master of the Rolls on May 30, 1581. While occupying this post he seems to have been more engaged in criminal trials than when he was attorney-general, as the 'Baga de Secretis' contains the proceedings of five in which he is named as a commissioner. He was also one of the commissioners on the arraignment of Davison, and joined with his colleagues in the shameful sentence pronounced against the secretary, of whom he says that 'his great zeal made him forget his duty.' (*State Trials,* i. 1094, 1230, 1250, 1315.)

During the vacancy in the office of chancellor between November 20, 1591, and May 28, 1592, he was placed at the head of the commission for hearing causes in Chancery. This of itself would be a sufficient contradiction to the account of Dugdale, who says that he died shortly after January 8, 1592, 34 Elizabeth, the date of his will, which was proved in 'April next ensuing.' It turns out, however, that the probate is dated on April 6, 1593, and the entry in the parish register of Ashley in Staffordshire rather unusually records his death on February 4, 1592-3, and his burial on the 6th of March following. A noble monument was erected to his memory. (*Notes and Queries,* 1st S. vii. 609.)

By his wife Anne, daughter and heir of William Ratcliffe, he had, besides four daughters, two sons, Thomas and Ratcliffe, from both of whom peerages sprang, all of which have since become extinct. (*Dugdale's Baron.* ii. 417; *Wotton's Baronet.* i. 51, iv. 271, 279.)

GERNEMUE, ADAM DE (Yarmouth), was one of the justices itinerant who, in 19 and 20 Henry II., 1173-4, fixed the tallage for Essex and Hertford, and for Norfolk and Suffolk. (*Madox,* i. 124, 701.) He probably held some office in the king's court or household, for he was one of the four commissioners whom the king in 1174 sent over to Ireland to settle the affairs of that country, and to bring Raymond over to England. (*Brady's England,* 363.)

Camden (*Remains,* 247) relates a story of Adam de Gernemue, who, being clerk of the signet, was summoned before Henry I. by Thurstan le Despencer, or steward, for refusing to sign a bill he had without a fee, as was the custom among the officers of the court. Upon Adam's answering that he merely desired him to bestow two spice cakes made for the king's own mouth, the king compelled Thurstan to put off his cloak and to go and bring the two cakes on a white napkin, and with a low curtsey to present them to Adam. He then made them friends, observing that 'officers of the court must gratifie and shew cast of their office, not only one to another, but also to strangers, whenever need shall require.'

GERNUM, RALPH, was one of those before whom a fine was levied at Westminster in 3 Henry III., and described as justices itinerant.

He was descended from Robert de Gernon, a Norman who, for the assistance he gave to William the Conqueror, received various lordships in Hertfordshire. His father Ralph was great-grandson of this Robert, and his mother was a sister of William de Breuse. During John's reign he was one of his marshals (*Rot. Claus.* i. 77), and was a firm adherent to him in his troubles. Several valuable grants of land rewarded his loyalty, besides other marks of favour and confidence.

In 4 Henry III. he was twice sent over to Poictou, and the last time to accompany the king's sister Joanna to England. In 5 Henry III. he was appointed constable of the castle of Corfe, which he held for many years. In 7 and 8 Henry III. he was sheriff of the county of Dorset, and in the following year he was appointed one of the justices itinerant for that county. (*Ibid.* i. 418-586, ii. 76.) He lived to a good old age, and died in 1247. His son William had two sons, from one of whom, Geoffrey, descended Chief Justice Sir John Cavendish, a name assumed from a lordship so called in Suffolk.

GESTLING, JOHN DE, had property at Winchelsea, and is first named as a justicier in 9 Richard I., 1198, and acted regularly in that capacity during the first ten years of John's reign, and up to 4 Henry III. He died about 1223. (*Dugdale's Orig.* 41, &c.)

GIBBEWIN, GEOFFREY, is recorded by Madox (ii. 43), from the archives of Westminster Abbey, as taking a fine in the King's Court at Westminster in 3 Henry III., but he is not mentioned in any other record as occupying a place on the bench. He had land at Bixe in Oxfordshire, the corn of which he gave to the monks of Thame (*Rot. Claus.* ii. 62); and there is a hamlet near Henley in that county still called Bix Gibwen.

GIBBS, VICARY, was the son of George Abraham Gibbs, Esq., a member of the medical profession practising at Exeter till 1781, when he retired to a small estate he had inherited at Clyst St. George. He was born in October 1751, and was sent to Eton, and thence was elected scholar of King's College, Cambridge. At the former he contributed some elegant Latin compositions to the 'Musæ Etonenses,' and at the latter he was notorious for his scholarship in Greek. Taking his degree of B.A. in 1772, he was elected fellow of his college, and became a member of Lincoln's Inn in August 1769. When he commenced business for himself as a special pleader he soon acquired a high reputation for ability in the science. The most complicated cases were submitted to him, and they flowed in with such abundance that he was wont to complain of the absence of easy ones. Yet he enjoyed the usual pleasures of society, of which the theatre was one of his favourite relaxations, evidenced by an extensive familiarity with almost every line of Shakspeare, and with passages and scenes from the best comedies.

He was called to the bar in February 1783, and in the next year he married. Joining the Western Circuit, he soon obtained sufficient employment, leading naturally to equal success in Westminster Hall, and only ten years after his call Horne Tooke, disregarding Mr. Gibbs's known predilections on the side 'of public peace and public order,' and no doubt being aware of his energetic defence at Exeter of the Rev. Mr. Winterbottham, indicted for alleged sedition in two sermons (*State Trials*, xxii. 838, 884), strongly recommended him to be employed in aid of Erskine in the trials for high treason that were then about to take place. Discarding all political prepossessions, Mr. Gibbs threw himself into the cases with such zeal, and displayed so much constitutional learning, that by his exposition of the law and application of the facts, almost as much as by the wonderful eloquence of his leader, verdicts of acquittal were not only gained for all the defendants in those extraordinary trials, but also a release from apprehension for the numerous misguided men who might have been implicated in the transactions which formed the groundwork of the charge. Sir John Scott (Lord Eldon), the prosecutor on these trials, sent him across the table this written testimony at the termination of them: 'I say from my heart that you did yourself great credit as a good man, and great credit as an excellent citizen, not sacrificing any valuable public principle; I say from my judgment that no lawyer ever did himself more credit or his client more service; so help me, God!'

This masterly performance at once raised Mr. Gibbs to the front rank of his profession, and led to a rapid succession of forensic honours. The recordership of Bristol he had received in February 1794, before the treason trials, as a recognition of his legal merits. In the following years he was made king's counsel, and received the appointment of solicitor-general to the Prince of Wales, which was followed by that of his royal highness's attorney-general. In 1804 he was promoted to the chief justice-ship of Chester, and in February 1805 he became solicitor-general in Mr. Pitt's last administration, and was then knighted. He held this place for a year only, resigning on that statesman's death; but the whig administration that succeeded holding the reins of government little more than twelve months, Sir Vicary, on their exclusion, was restored to office, but in the higher grade of attorney-general.

In the parliament that followed the change of ministry he had the honour of being returned for his own university, defeating the late chancellor of the Exchequer, Lord Henry Petty, and also the late prime minister, Lord Palmerston, then first entering into political life. As a senator he undoubtedly did not shine, his style of eloquence not being adapted to the audience he was addressing. As a legislator, the only statute he introduced was one enacting that a person against whom an information had been filed might be arrested and held to bail (48 Geo. III. c. 58), the provisions of which were so obnoxious that neither he nor any subsequent attorney-general ever put them in force. In the exercise of his official functions he is considered to have been extremely severe, and there is no doubt that he filed many more ex-officio informations than any of his predecessors. The fact is that while Sir Vicary held office seditious libels were the order of the day, and there was so much licentiousness in certain publications of the daily and weekly press that it was deemed necessary to put some restraint on them. But it might well be a question whether the attorney-general's power was not too freely exercised, when by a return made to the House of Commons

It appears that from 1808 to 1810 no less than forty-two informations had been filed, while only fourteen had been filed during the preceding seven years. The wisdom of these proceedings becomes still more doubtful, when out of these forty-two informations no less than twenty-five were not prosecuted, but the subjects of them were left in a state of suspense and anxiety. The sentences passed on those who were convicted show, by their severity, how strongly the judges felt the necessity of stopping the seditious incitements, and how clearly they saw the danger that induced the attorney-general to prosecute them.

Among the acquitted were James Perry and John Lambert for an apparently innocent passage in the 'Morning Chronicle,' and John and Leigh Hunt for a much more questionable article in the 'Examiner.' These defeats seem to have put an end to any further proceedings on Sir Vicary's ex-officio informations, but not before a general outcry had been excited against the frequency of them; and the active mover no doubt incurred great unpopularity, which was aggravated by the personal character of severity and harshness which generally but undeservedly attached to him. Few men were really more sensitive, more kind-hearted, more anxious to atone for an unpremeditated wrong, and more desirous of the good opinion of good and moral men. But his manner was so caustic and bitter, and sometimes so rude and uncivil, that the prevalent feeling would be amply justified; and his assumption of superiority over his brother barristers, which on one occasion received a severe rebuke, did not tend to remove it.

At the same time his superior merits as a lawyer were universally acknowledged. After he had filled his office for five years he found its duties, together with his vast accumulation of business both in court and in chambers, so much more onerous than his strength or his health could bear that on May 28, 1812, he accepted a seat in the Common Pleas as puisne judge. He sat there only eighteen months, when he was promoted to be chief baron of the Exchequer in November 1813. In less than three months Sir James Mansfield's retirement enabled him to take the place which he most desired and was best fitted for. He was sworn lord chief justice of the Common Pleas in Hilary vacation 1814, and presided in that court for nearly five years. The attacks of ill-health from which he had long suffered, and to which it is charitable to attribute much of his ill temper, becoming more frequent, he felt himself compelled to resign his seat on November 5, 1818.

As a judge all competent authorities give him the highest praise. The prejudice which undoubtedly existed against him personally is altogether silenced when his judgments are the subject of observation. One of the most severe of his critics admits that 'there was but one opinion as to his fitness for the situation which he had been selected to fill, and that in point of learning and experience no one could be better qualified for it. . . . His decisions on the bench or at Nisi Prius furnished equal proofs of the extent of his learning and of the accuracy of his mind.'

On quitting the bench he retired altogether from public life. In his domestic society he had always shone, and they who partook of it are loud in their declaration of the charms he imparted to it. His familiar friends, and they were many from both sides of politics, bear witness to his virtues, his high religious feelings, his honourable principles, his goodness of heart, and the kindness of his disposition, notwithstanding occasional irritabilities of temper. After suffering for fifteen months, he died on February 8, 1820, and was buried in the family vault at Hayes, with a monumental inscription of great elegance and truth penned by his friend Sir William Scott, Lord Stowell.

He married, in June 1784, Frances Cerjoit Kenneth, sister of Francis Humberston Mackenzie, Lord Seaforth; and their only child, Maria Elizabeth, was married to Lieutenant-General Sir Andrew Pilkington, K.C.B.

GIFFARD, WILLIAM (BISHOP OF WINCHESTER), was a Norman of high birth, and probably a relative of Walter Giffard, who came over with King William at the time of the Conquest, and was rewarded with the earldom of Buckingham. In consequence of that connection he was in all likelihood received into the Conqueror's household as one of his chaplains; but the first certain notice of his name is as chancellor.

He is placed by all the authorities as the last chancellor to William I., succeeding William Welson, afterwards Bishop of Thetford; and is generally mentioned as the first chancellor under William II., and to have been succeeded by Robert Bloet in 1090. His restoration to the chancellorship between 1093 and 1098 is rendered certain by his witnessing in that character a charter granting the manor of Stone to Rochester Cathedral; for, though it is undated, one of its witnesses is Robert Bloet, Bishop of Lincoln, who was not raised to that see till 1093; while Walkeline, Bishop of Winchester, another witness, died in January 1098. (*Dugdale's Monast.* i. 164, 241, vi. 1271.) By a similar process of investigation his continuance in the office may be traced to the end of the reign, and that he so continued at the commencement of that of Henry I. appears by several charters granted by that king. (*Ibid.* i. 241, ii. 18, v. 14.) He was superseded in his office by Roger, afterwards Bishop of Salisbury, who is designated chancellor in two charters, dated September 3, 1101. (*Ibid.* iv. 16, 17.) After Roger's elevation to the episcopal bench, however, Giffard was reinstated, as appears from his being present as chancellor at the signing of the convention between King Henry and the Earl of Flanders, on March 10, 1103 (*Rymer*, i. 7, 12), shortly after which there is every probability that he was discharged from the office in consequence of the displeasure of the king.

At the coronation, or soon after the accession of Henry, Giffard had been nominated to the vacant bishopric of Winchester; but his consecration had been prevented at first by the absence of Archbishop Anselm, and then by that prelate's refusal to perform the ceremony upon him, and several others then appointed, unless the king would give up the right of investiture, which had been gradually assumed by the crown. This dispute lasted for the four following years, and was then terminated by mutual concessions, the king giving up the claim to invest with the crozier and ring, and being allowed to retain the more important right of receiving the fealty and homage of the bishops for their temporal possessions. This accommodation was arranged in 1107, and on August 11 Anselm solemnly consecrated seven bishops, William Giffard being among the number.

He presided over his see for nearly twenty-one years, during which period he performed many acts to make his rule remembered. He introduced monks of the Cistercian order into England, and in 1128 founded an abbey for them at Waverley in Surrey. He erected a priory for Augustin canons at Taunton in Somersetshire. He was either the founder of, or the principal contributor to, the priory of St. Mary Overy in Southwark, and he built the magnificent mansion there which was so long the residence of his successors when in London. His death occurred on January 25, 1129.

There is no act recorded of him that throws doubt on the praises awarded by Henry of Huntingdon, and Thomas Rudborne in his 'History of Winchester;' and, holding the office of chancellor five times under three kings, the last of whom was celebrated for his discrimination, he must have been endowed with no ordinary qualifications. (*Godwin*, 213; *Angl. Sac.* i. 279, 700; *Roger de Wendover*, ii. 164, &c.; *Rapin: Turner: Lingard.*)

GIFFARD, RICHARD, the great-grandson of Osbert, one of the Norman barons who accompanied the Conqueror, and a younger son of Elias Giffard, the third lord of Brinsfield in Gloucestershire, was one of the eighteen justices itinerant who were appointed to administer justice throughout the kingdom by the council of Northampton, 22 Henry II., 1176. (*Madox*, i. 126–135.) In 1180 he was bailiff of the Oximin in Normandy, receiving 200*l.* per annum as custos of the castle of Falaise. To the hospital of the latter town he was a benefactor. (*Rot. Scacc. Norm.* i. 41.) One of his descendants was summoned to parliament, but the title became extinct in 1322. (*Dugdale's Baron.* i. 499.)

GIFFARD, HUGH, if not, as not unlikely, the son of Osbert Giffard, who was a natural son of King John (*Dugdale's Baron.* i. 501), was undoubtedly of noble connection, as William, Earl of Salisbury, Hugh de Mortuo Mari, and Walter de Clifford became his pledges in 1 Henry III. that he would satisfy the king for a transgression which he had presumed to commit. From the rest of the record it may be collected that this offence was his marriage, without the royal licence, with Sibilla, the daughter of Walter de Cormaill, an heiress. (*Rot. Claus.* i. 301.) In 20 Henry III. Hugh Giffard was made constable of the Tower of London; and two years after a fine was levied before him as a justicier (*Dugdale's Baron.* i. 502), probably only sitting as constable, as his name does not afterwards occur in a judicial character. He was connected with the household of Edward the king's son, and several payments were made to him for the prince's expenses, and other payments up to 26 Henry III. (*Issue Roll*, iii. 15, 18, 29, 30.)

It appears that in 1256 King Henry gave his widow and her son, the next-mentioned Walter Giffard, permission to live in the castle of Oxford during pleasure (*Excerpt. e Rot. Fin.* ii. 243), and by a pedigree in Dugdale's 'Baronage' (i. 424), under the title 'Cormeilles,' it seems that she had another son, named Geoffrey, which is probably a misreading for Godfrey, Bishop of Worcester, also hereafter noticed, who, according to Richardson's notes on Godwin (461), was Walter's brother.

GIFFARD, WALTER (ARCHBISHOP OF YORK), was, as before stated, the son of the above Hugh Giffard, and of Sibilla de Cormaill. The first notice of his name occurs in the permission from King Henry III., on November 3, 1256, to 'Sibille Giffard, and her son, Master Walter Giffard,' to lodge in the castle of Oxford, and to use the mills below it. He afterwards became a canon of Wells and a chaplain to the pope, and on May 22, 1264, was elected Bishop of Bath and Wells.

After the battle of Evesham, which was fought on August 4, 1265, he was appointed chancellor, in the room of Thomas de

Cantilupe, who had been nominated by the barons. He was translated to the archbishopric of York on October 18, 1266; soon after which he is believed to have resigned the Great Seal, but the actual date of his retirement nowhere appears. He still continued a member of the king's council, and in 54 Henry III. was sheriff of the counties of Nottingham and Derby, an office which he filled from that time till 1 Edward I.

On the accession of Edward I. he was selected as one of the regents of the kingdom during the king's absence, and was made constable of the Tower of London, and according to Philipot was also treasurer. Various dates are assigned for his death, but the most probable seems to be April 25, 1278. He was buried in York Cathedral. (*Godwin*, 373, 682; *Le Neve*, 32, 308.)

GIFFARD, GODFREY (BISHOP OF WORCESTER), is said by Bishop Godwin (461) to have been near to the king in blood, and Richardson, his editor, adds that he was the brother of the above Walter Giffard, Archbishop of York.

On November 6, 1265, he was collated archdeacon of Barum (Barnstaple), (*Le Neve*, 98), and in the following May he occupied the post of chancellor of the Exchequer, and had permission to appoint a substitute to act during his absence. (*Madox*, i. 476, ii. 52.)

In 1266 he was appointed chancellor of England, in the room of his brother, Walter Giffard, probably soon after that prelate's promotion to the see of York. In June 1268 he was elected Bishop of Worcester, and continued chancellor till the 29th of October following. In 6 Edward I., 1278, he was at the head of the justices itinerant for the counties of Hereford, Hertford, and Kent.

He died on January 26, 1301. He was a man of high spirit, overbearing, and litigious, and made his visitations burthensome by the extent of his retinue, which amounted to near a hundred horse. (*Chambers's Illust. Worcestershire.*)

GIFFARD, GEORGE MARKHAM, one of the present lord justices of appeal in Chancery, is the son of Admiral Giffard, by Susannah, daughter of Sir John Carter. He was born at the Dockyard, Portsmouth, in the year 1813, and was educated at Winchester, and New College, Oxford, of which he eventually became a fellow. Entering the society of the Inner Temple, he was called to the bar on November 20, 1840, and practised in the Court of Chancery. He was raised to the rank of queen's counsel in 1858, and took a prominent lead without holding any official situation till 1868, when, on March 5, he was made a vice-chancellor and knighted, and in less than ten months was promoted, on January 1, 1869, to his present judicial seat, in each case succeeding Sir William Page Wood (Lord Hatherley). He was thereupon added to the privy council.

He is married to Maria, daughter of Charles Pilgrim, Esq., of Kingsfield, Southampton.

GIFFORD, ROBERT (LORD GIFFORD), was the son of Robert Gifford, carrying on the business of grocer and linendraper in the city of Exeter, where he was born on February 24, 1779. From his earliest youth he showed remarkable quickness and an ardent desire of improvement. His greatest delight was to attend the assizes and watch the proceedings of the courts, and he longed for an opportunity to emulate the talents he witnessed. Though his father could not afford to educate him for the bar, he so far encouraged his taste as to article him to Mr. Jones, a respectable attorney of his native city, with whom he served the whole of his time. Here he made himself so practically useful in the business of the office that during the illness of his master he was entrusted with its sole management. Before the end of his clerkship his father died, and at its termination he entered himself at the Middle Temple in 1800. After a year or two's study under Mr. Robert Bayley and Mr. Godfrey Sykes, eminent special pleaders, he commenced practice for himself in the same line. For five years he pursued this useful branch with considerable success, and was called to the bar on February 12, 1808.

He joined the Western Circuit, and the Exeter and Devon Sessions, where he soon acquired an extensive business. In London, too his abilities were soon recognised, and many opportunities occurred in which he distinguished himself by his intimate acquaintance with the law of real property, by the ready cogency of his arguments, and by his easy elocution.

He had been only nine years at the bar when he was appointed solicitor-general on May 9, 1817. So entirely did he owe it to his professional merit that many of those advocates who were opposed to the government acknowledged its propriety. He was then knighted and elected bencher of his inn, and took his place in the House of Commons as member for Eye in Suffolk. On that stage, though not acting a prominent part in politics, he assisted the government by the dexterity he displayed, and by the clearness with which he explained their legal measures. He was almost immediately called upon to take part in those state prosecutions rendered necessary by the treasonable practices of the time. The talent he displayed on these occasions at once dissipated all doubts upon the propriety of his promotion. In July 1819 he succeeded to the office of attorney-general, and, holding it at the commencement of the reign of George IV., it fell to his lot in April 1820 to conduct the prosecution of the conspirators who were implicated in the Cato Street plot for overturning the government, intended to be commenced by the assassination of all the ministers at a cabinet dinner. (*State Trials*, xxxii. 538, &c., xxxiii. 716, &c.) In the same year he had the more arduous duty imposed upon him of opening the charges against Queen Caroline in support of the preamble of the Bill of Pains and Penalties; his comparative failure in which was amply redeemed by his powerful reply, which in the most perspicuous manner collected all the facts and corroborative evidence into one focus, and to the satisfaction of most unprejudiced minds made clear and evident the guilt of that unfortunate lady. But few, though they could not shut their eyes to her misconduct, approved of the proceedings, and the outcry was so great at the harshness and impolicy of the measure that the ministers were obliged to withdraw the bill. The temporary popularity of the queen soon subsided, and her death, which was hastened by chagrin, occurred soon after the coronation in the next year.

Exercising his office with great moderation, he instituted very few prosecutions, and principally confined himself to his forensic duties in Chancery, to which court he had removed on being appointed solicitor-general. Here he obtained very considerable practice, which was greatly increased after the lamentable death of Sir Samuel Romilly. In the House of Lords also he had the principal lead, especially in the appeals from Scotland, having carefully made himself master of the laws of that country. As recorder of Bristol, to which he had been elected on the resignation of Sir Vicary Gibbs, he was such a favourite with the corporation that they placed his portrait, a whole-length by Sir Thomas Lawrence, in their town-hall.

After filling the office of attorney-general for four years and a half, he was raised to the bench on January 9, 1824, as lord chief justice of the Common Pleas, and was ennobled on the 31st of the same month by the title of Lord Gifford of St. Leonards in the county of Devon. This elevation to the peerage he owed to the alteration then adopted in the House of Lords in the hearing of appeals, and he was constituted at the same time deputy speaker for the special purpose of hearing those from Scotland. So satisfied were the Scottish lawyers with his decisions that on a visit to Edinburgh a short time after he was received and invested with extraordinary honours. In less than three months he changed his judicial post for the more appropriate one of master of the Rolls, to which he was removed on April 5. The increase of labour consequent on these appointments at length weighed upon his spirits, and so greatly affected his health and strength that he succumbed to a bilious attack on September 4, 1826, at Dover, where he was spending his vacation. His remains repose in the Rolls Chapel.

At the time of his premature death he was only in the forty-eighth year of his age. He was then the universally designated heir to the chancellorship upon the expected resignation of Lord Eldon. But he was not permitted thus to complete the parallel with Lord Chancellor King. Lord Tenterden wrote of him: 'The present attorney-general (Gifford) will probably be his (Lord Eldon's) successor; he is a sound lawyer and a sound-hearted man . . . . the fittest man living to succeed one for whom a successor must soon be found—though perhaps an equal will never be.' High as was his professional character, in private life he was equally to be admired. Unaffected, amiable, kind, and indulgent, he secured the affection of numerous friends, and totally disarmed whatever jealousy might at first have been entertained at his sudden advancement.

He married in 1816 the daughter of the Rev. Edward Drew, rector of Willand in Devonshire, and by her had seven children, the eldest of whom is the present peer.

GILBERT, JEFFREY, who, from his arms being somewhat similar to those of Sir Humphrey Gilbert, the noted seaman and discoverer in Queen Elizabeth's reign, is supposed to have belonged to a branch of that family, is said to have been born at Burr's Farm, a manor in the parish of Goudhurst in Kent, which he afterwards purchased, in 1674. He was the son of William Gilbert, Esq., and Elizabeth his wife. Admitted into the Inner Temple in 1692, he was called to the bar in 1698, and, judging from the numerous treatises of which he was the author, he must have been indefatigable in his early studies. He commenced taking notes of cases in 1706, when his Equity Reports begin. It is evident that he had established a good legal reputation before 1714, as on November 8 of that year he was appointed one of the judges of the King's Bench in Ireland, from which he was promoted on the 16th of the following June to be chief baron of the Exchequer there. In 1719 he and the other barons were committed by the Irish House of Lords to the custody of the usher of the black rod, for granting an injunction in pursuance of an order of the English House of Lords (*State Trials*, xv. 1301–16) in an appeal from the Irish courts (Annesley *v.* Sherlock). In the next year an act of parliament was passed putting an end to the dispute by excluding the Irish House of Lords from any jurisdiction, and, though this act was afterwards repealed, the whole question is since settled by the Act of Union. How long the barons remained in custody is not mentioned, but the conduct of the chief was evidently approved by the English government. His epitaph says that he was offered the Great Seal of Ireland, and that he refused the honour, and resigned his place upon being made a baron of the English Exchequer in May 1722. He received the honour of knighthood in January 1724. On the resignation of Lord Macclesfield he was nominated second commissioner of the Great Seal, and filled that position from January 7 to June 1, 1725, on which day he was promoted to the place of chief baron, which seat he only occupied for fifteen months, being snatched away by an early death on October 14, 1726. This event occurred at Bath, in the abbey church of which he was buried. A tablet to his memory is placed in the Temple Church, with an elegant eulogium in Latin of his legal and scientific attainments.

Of all the works that appear under his name, and which exhibit so much learning in almost every variety of legal investigation that they are still constantly referred to as authority, it is extraordinary that none were published in his lifetime. They comprehend Reports in Equity, histories of the Courts of Exchequer, Common Pleas, and Chancery, and treatises on Uses and Trusts, Tenures, Devises, Ejectments, Distresses, Executions, Rents, Remainders, and Evidence. This latter Blackstone describes as excellent, and calls it 'a work which it is impossible to abstract or abridge without losing some beauty and destroying the chain of the whole.' He was a fellow of the Royal Society, and was equally famous for his mathematical as for his legal studies, and for his refined taste in polite literature. The modesty he showed in not himself publishing any of his works distinguished him throughout his career; and he was held in as much esteem by his contemporaries as he is regarded with respect and admiration at the present day. (*Lord Raymond*, 1380-1420; *Hasted's Kent*, vii. 77, 195.)

GISELHAM, WILLIAM DE, probably took his name from the place so called in Suffolk. On several occasions from 7 to 14 Edward I. he is described as the king's attorney, and in the tenth year both he and Gilbert de Thornton are designated 'narratores pro rege.' In 9 Edward I. he was called to the degree of king's serjeant-at-law; but it should be observed that all who are noticed at this time as of the degree of the coif seem to have been so designated, and that it is doubtful whether the modern distinction then existed.

When Edward I. purified the bench in 1229 of those members who had disgraced it, William de Giselham was constituted one of the new judges of the Common Pleas. In January 1293 he came to an untimely end, but no other particulars of his death have been found than are contained in a letter from William de Wereminster to John de Langton, the chancellor, in which he simply communicates that William de Giselham had been killed. (7 *Report Pub. Rec. App.* ii. 249.)

GLANVILLE, RANULPH DE, was born at Stratford in Suffolk. He was a grandson of a baron of the same name, whose possessions were in the counties of Norfolk and Suffolk, and younger son of William de Glanville, and on the death of Bartholomew, his eldest brother, he succeeded to the barony.

Long previous to this event he had raised himself to a considerable position. It does not precisely appear in what capacity he began his career, but it seems most likely that he filled some office in the Exchequer. It was probably in this character that he held the office of sheriff of Warwick and Leicester in 10 Henry II., 1164, and that in the same year he was advanced to the sheriffalty of the more important county of York. The former he retained for only one year, but in the latter he continued during the whole remainder of the reign. These appointments took place twelve years before his name is recorded as a justicier; but after he was raised to the bench several other counties were placed under his care as sheriff.

According to Benedict Abbas, Queen Eleanor was consigned to his care during the sixteen years of her confinement in the castle at Winchester, of which, and also of the royal treasury there, he had the custody. That he treated her with the respect due to her station is shown by the confidence she reposed in him when placed in authority on her release.

During his northern sheriffalty his military talents were called into action by the incursion of the Scots, and his efficiency as an energetic and brave commander was soon proved. Having, with the assistance of King Henry's illegitimate son Geoffrey, then Bishop of Lincoln, forced the Scottish king to retire, that monarch a short time afterwards renewed his attack, and while his army was ravaging the neighbouring country he himself besieged Alnwick. There Ranulph de Glanville, at the head of the Yorkshire barons, surprised him on July 11, 1174, and, defeating his troops, took him prisoner. (*Lord Lyttelton*, iii. 135, 148.) This victory was of the highest importance to King Henry in the critical state of the kingdom, then distracted by the rebellious conduct of his sons. From this time, therefore, the valorous sheriff, brought more immediately under the king's notice, was employed in services for which he was not long in proving that he was equally fitted.

In the very next year he appears as a justice itinerant, his pleas being recorded not only in his own county of York, but in thirteen other counties, and in 1176 one of the six circuits into which the council of Northampton then divided the kingdom was appropriated to him and two others. When the council of Windsor in 1179 re-arranged the kingdom for judicial purposes into four divisions, although most of his brethren were removed, his capacity was so conspicuous and his integrity so unblemished that he was not only reappointed to act in one of them, but was among those specially selected to hear the complaints of the people in the Curia Regis at Westminster (*Madox*, i. 77, 125-137), and in 1180 he was appointed chief justiciary, and continued in the office during the whole remainder of the reign, as high in the royal favour and confidence at the close as at the commencement, being named one of the executors to the king's will. A dereliction from the path of judicial integrity is reported of him in having, in 1184, condemned Sir Gilbert de Plumpton to death on a charge of rape, for the purpose of giving the widow of the unfortunate knight, a rich inheritrix, to his friend Rainer, who performed his duties as sheriff of Yorkshire. The execution of the sentence was delayed by the interference of the Bishop of Worcester, and, the case being remitted to the king, Sir Gilbert's life was saved, but his person imprisoned for the rest of the reign. Presuming this story to be true, the chief justiciary's merit must have been great indeed to induce the king to pardon so monstrous a perversion of justice. Much doubt, however, cannot but be attached to the relation. It appears that in his account of the year as sheriff of York he charges 13s. for conveying Sir Gilbert from York to Worcester, and in the next year accounts for half a year's rent of his lands. Gilbert's brother afterwards pays a fine of 100 marks for his discharge, and Rainer pays a fine of 1000 marks for having the king's benevolence. These show no evidence that Ranulph de Glanville was cognisant of Gilbert's innocence, or a party to Rainer's intentions towards the lady. (*Plumpton Corresp.* x.) Indeed, it is scarcely possible to suppose that a king so just as Henry II. would have overlooked the guilt of the judge or have visited the innocence of the accused with imprisonment.

In the year after his appointment he headed a large army against the Welsh, and, though at first he made little progress, he succeeded at last, not only in bringing them back to their fealty, but in procuring from them a large body of infantry to serve in the subsequent wars against Philip of France. In those wars we find him successfully engaged in procuring a truce between the two kings. (*Lord Lyttelton*, iii. 369, 441.) So high an opinion had Henry of his wisdom and sagacity that he sent him with his son John to assist and direct in the government of Ireland. (*Leland's Ireland*, i. 143.)

In 1188, when the crusade was preached at Gedington, though his age and position would have been a sufficient excuse, he partook of the enthusiasm and engaged in the enterprise. The king's death, which happened the next year, only delayed, but did not prevent, the performance of his vow. His piety was further evidenced by the foundation and endowment of the priory of Butley and the abbey of Leystone, both in Suffolk, for canons of the order of St. Augustin. (*Dugdale's Monast.* vi. 379, 879.)

In his character of chief justiciary he assisted at the coronation of Richard I., on September 3, 1189, and was sent by the king to restrain the people from the massacre of the Jews which disgraced that solemnity. Two or three authors testify that he was deprived of his office at the beginning of this reign, and was obliged to purchase his release from imprisonment by an enormous fine, fixed by some at 5000*l*., and by others at 15,000*l*. The silence of other historians throws a discredit on the story, which is supported by his subsequent proceedings. His retirement from the office of chief justiciary would be a necessary result of his determination to proceed to Jerusalem, and his payment of a sum of money to assist the king in his holy war would be only what that monarch required from all who could afford it. The roll of that year, so far from giving any evidence of his disgrace, proves plainly that he continued to act in his judicial character after the death of King Henry. (*Pipe Roll*, 8, 15, &c.) There is also subsequent evidence of his being with the king in Normandy on his way to the Holy Land, as he is the first of the witnesses attesting a royal charter given under the hand of John de Alençon, the vice-chancellor, 'apud Moret.,' on April 11, 1190, 1 Richard I. (*Madox*, i. 77), and he afterwards travelled towards Jerusalem in company with Baldwin, Archbishop of Canterbury, and Hubert Walter, his nephew, Bishop of Salisbury, and landed at Tyre about Michaelmas 1190, all of them having been despatched by King Richard to assist at the siege of Acre, and having previously, according to some accounts, accompanied the king himself through France as far as Marseilles.

He and his companions reached Acre, before which Archbishop Baldwin first fell a victim, and then, before the end of the year, Ranulph de Glanville; not, as sometimes stated, in the heat of battle, but 'ex aëris nimia corruptione.' (*R. de Wendover*, iii. 30, 36.)

He married Berta, one of the daughters of Theobald de Valoins, lord of Parham. Leaving no male issue, he distributed his lands before he sailed on his last expedition among his three daughters—Matilda, the wife of William de Auberville, a beforenamed justicier; Amabilia, the wife of Ralph de Arden, a justicier also beforenamed; and Helewise, the wife of Robert Fitz-Robert.

Although some question has been raised whether the work generally attributed to this great man, entitled 'Tractatus de Legibus et Consuetudinibus Regni Angliæ,' was really composed by him, there are still stronger grounds for considering him as its author. If decisive evidence of the fact cannot be advanced, there is at all events no candidate who has superior claims to the honour of having produced it, nor is there any hypothesis of sufficient weight to counterbalance the presumptions in favour of the tradition. (*Dugdale's Baron.* i. 423; *Lord Lyttelton; Lingard.*)

GLANVILLE, WILLIAM DE, no otherwise appears in connection with his eminent namesake than that he was a witness, with the title of 'clericus,' to the charter of Hervey Walter, Ranulph de Glanville's brother-in-law, to the priory of Butley, which was founded by the chief justiciary. (*Monast.* v. 380.) He was one of the justiciers in 7, 8, and 9 Richard I., and was still alive in 3 John. (*Madox*, i. 705; *Hunter's Preface; Rot. Cancell.*)

Mr. Hunter, in his valuable preface to the 'Fines of Richard I. and John,' suggests the possibility of his having been the author of the treatise generally attributed to Ranulph de Glanville; but he offers no other grounds for the suggestion than the identity of the name.

GLANVILLE, OSBERT DE, was present as a justicier when fines were levied in the Curia Regis in 28 and 35 Henry II., 1182, 1189. (*Hunter's Preface.*) As the former of these years was soon after the appointment of Ranulph de Glanville to the office of chief justiciary, and the latter just before his retirement from it, it is probable that Osbert was in some way related to him, and had been brought into the court under his auspices. This is rendered still more likely by the fact that he was one of the witnesses to the justiciary's charter to the priory of Butley. (*Monast.* vi. 180.)

GLANVILLE, GILBERT DE (BISHOP OF ROCHESTER), was archdeacon of Lisieux when, on July 16, 1185, 31 Henry II., he was elected Bishop of Rochester, and was obliged to be ordained priest before he received consecration. He appears among the justiciers in 1 Richard I., 1189, and acted as a justice itinerant in several counties. He was present also in 5 and 7 Richard I., when fines were levied before him. (*Pipe Roll*, 27, &c.; *Hunter's Preface.*)

The whole of his episcopal life was engaged in a contest with the monks of his church relative to certain lands which he claimed as belonging to the see; and they are said by some to have carried their animosity so far as to refuse the ordinary funeral rites to the bishop's body when he died. This, however, according to others, was occasioned by the interdict then hanging over the kingdom. The bishop's death happened on June 24, 1214, and his tomb is within the rails of the altar of his cathedral. He founded, and amply endowed, the hospital at Stroud in Kent, an act which is a sufficient answer to the harsh character given to him by the monks in their doggerel rhymes written on his death.

GLANVILLE, BARTHOLOMEW DE, is inserted by Dugdale as one of the justices itinerant for Norfolk and Suffolk in 9 Henry III. It is found that the record in which his name was at first introduced is altered by substituting that of William de Ambly. (*Rot. Claus.* ii. 77.)

GLANVILLE, JOHN, is stated by Anthony Wood (*Fasti*, ii. 64) to have been bred an attorney. If so, he is the first judge who is recorded as having commenced his career in that branch of the profession. He was a younger son of another John Glanville, of Tavistock, and entered himself at Lincoln's Inn in 1567, and, having retired from his first occupation, he was called to the bar in 1574. He filled the office of reader both in Lent and autumn 1589, the latter occasion being in consequence of his having been called to the degree of the coif. Prince states that it was said of him, and of Thomas Harris and Edward Drew, who were called serjeants at the same time, that

One $\begin{Bmatrix} \text{gained} \\ \text{spent} \\ \text{gave} \end{Bmatrix}$ as much as the other two.

He does not specially appropriate these characters, but intimates that Drew was on the getting side.

He was promoted to the bench as a justice of the Common Pleas on June 30, 1598, a position which he occupied for little more than two years, his death occurring on July 27, 1600. His monument in Tavistock Church represents him as a corpulent man, in full judicial costume, in a recumbent posture, and is considered a superior work of art. It was erected by his wife, Alice, the daughter of — Skirret, who after his death married Sir Francis Godolphin. He left several children; his second son, Sir John Glanville, who became a serjeant, and was speaker of the House of Commons in

April 1640, gained a far higher eminence for his legal attainments than his father did, and his Reports on controverted elections are still in considerable estimation. (*Risdon*, 403.)

GLOUCESTER, MILO DE (EARL OF HEREFORD), sometimes called Milo Fitz-Walter, was son of Walter, 'constabularius princeps militiæ domus regiæ,' who built the castle of Gloucester on his own domain. His mother was Emma, sister of Hameline de Balun, also a powerful noble, and a companion of William the Conqueror on his invasion. By his marriage with Sibyl, the eldest daughter of Bernard de Newmarche, he acquired the honor of Brecknock.

In 31 Henry I. he was sheriff of Staffordshire and Gloucestershire; and one of the entries is an allowance to him as sheriff of thirty shillings for mead and beer provided for the king. By the same roll it appears that he was justice of the forest for the former county, and that he and Pain Fitz-John were justices itinerant in both counties.

On the death of Henry he concurred with the other barons in placing Stephen on the throne, he being then high constable as successor to his father, and received, as the first fruits of his acquiescence, a charter of confirmation of all his lands. The king, in this grant, covenants with him '*sicut baroni et justiciario meo*,' evidently using the expression as if the two titles were synonymous.

The royal favour, however, made no permanent impression; for soon after Milo forsook the king's party, and joined that of the Empress Matilda. To that unfortunate lady he proved himself a firm friend during the remainder of his life, receiving her as his guest in her difficulties, supporting her and her establishment at his own expense during a period of two years, guiding her by his counsels, and aiding her by his arms. The oldest patent on record shows the extent of her gratitude. It is dated on July 25, 1141. It confers upon him the title of Earl of Hereford, and gives him and his heirs the castle and moat of Hereford, and extensive privileges. In the following September he was one of those devoted warriors who covered Matilda's retreat from Winchester when closely pressed by the bishop.

He was renowned for his bravery and good conduct, and they were both strongly exemplified in his almost romantic rescue of the sister of the Earl of Chester, when she, after the murder of her husband, Richard de Clare, was besieged by the Welsh, and being without provisions, despaired of succour. He gained the castle on the side where it was considered inaccessible, and relieved her from her dreadful condition.

Unharmed amidst all the perils he had encountered, he was at last accidentally slain by an arrow in a hunting match, on December 24, 1146.

He translated the canons of the abbey of Lanthony in Monmouthshire, who were oppressed by the Welsh, to a place called the Hide, near Gloucester, where he established them in a new abbey called Lanthony Secunda.

He had five sons, all of whom died without issue, and three daughters, the descendants of the eldest of whom acquired, besides the earldom of Hereford, those of Essex and Northampton. These titles all became extinct in 1372. (*Dugdale's Monast.* vi. 131–136; *Madox*, i. 40, &c.; *Lord Lyttelton*; *Lingard*; *Magn. Rot.* 31 *Henry I.*)

GLOUCESTER, WALTER DE, one of the canons of Beverley, is called the son of Simon Lymereth. (*Abb. Placit.* 214.) He was an officer of the Exchequer, and in 22 Edward I. was entrusted with the sheriffalty of Dorset and Somerset, which he held for five years. He then was appointed to visit the seaports to enquire into the concealment of the king's customs on wool, &c. (*Madox*, i. 784, ii. 169.) In 28 Edward I. he was a perambulator of the forests in Hants and Wilts, and about the same time was selected as one of the king's escheators, acting in the north till the end of that reign, and in the south for the first four years of the following. In 35 Edward I. he was a commissioner of array in Glamorgan, and paymaster of the levies there. (*Ibid.* i. 740.)

During the early years of the reign of Edward II. he was summoned to parliament among the judges, and was regularly constituted one of the three justices of assize for Gloucestershire and four other counties in 1310. Dugdale does not notice him as a baron of the Exchequer, although there is no doubt that he was so, being designated by that title in two writs, directing him to confer with Nicholas de Segrave, and in the letters patent constituting Walter de Norwich a baron in his place. The patent of his own appointment has not been discovered, but it must have been between June 16 and July 5, 1311, the former being the date of his last summons to parliament, where he is evidently placed among the justices of assize, and the latter being that of the writ to Nicholas de Segrave.

He held his rank for little more than six weeks; for his death is recorded in Walter de Norwich's patent, which is dated on August 29. (*Parl. Writs*, ii. 929.) He died in possession of considerable property in Surrey, and the counties of Lincoln, Worcester, and Gloucester. By his wife Hawise he had a son Walter, who died in 16 Edward II. (*Cal. Inquis.* p.m. i. 247, 305.)

GLYNNE, JOHN, whose genealogy commences in the year 843 with Cilmin Droedtu, one of the fifteen tribes of North Wales, was the eldest son of Sir William Glynne, knight, of Glyn-Llivon in Carnarvonshire, by Jane, daughter of John Griffith, Esq., of Carnarvon (*Wotton's Baronet.* iii. 289), and was born in 1602 at the ancient seat of his ancestors. He was educated at Westminster School, and at Hart Hall, Oxford (now part of New College). At the same time he kept his terms at Lincoln's Inn, and having been called to the bar in 1628, he got quickly into practice, for he appears in Croke's Reports in Hilary Term 1633.

In August 1638 he received a grant of the office of keeper of the writs and rolls in the Common Pleas in reversion (*Rymer*, xx. 300), a place of considerable profit. Having been previously appointed high steward of Westminster, he was elected representative for that city in both the parliaments that met in 1640. In the last of these, the Long Parliament, he showed himself to be an active partisan of the discontented party. He took a prominent part in the prosecution of the Earl of Strafford; and one of the arguments he used to prove that the multitude of the earl's minor offences amounted to high treason, was 'Raine in dropps is not terrible, but a masse of it did overflow the whole world.' In all the proceedings his reasoning was inconsequential and his conduct harsh and inhuman. He was one of the committee to prepare the votes condemnatory of the canons, and to draw up a charge against Archbishop Laud, and was the messenger from the Commons with a charge of high treason against the bishops who had signed a protestation against the Lords proceeding in their absence. (*Whitelocke*, 53.) He supported the remonstrance on the state of the kingdom, the carrying of which had so great an effect in widening the breach with the king (*Verney's Notes*, 44–125); and he published a speech, delivered by him in January 1642, strenuously vindicating the privileges of the Commons on the occasion of the king's unadvised attendance at the house, and demanding the delivery of the five members whom he had caused to be accused of high treason. (*Parl. Hist.* ii. 1023.) He further showed his zeal in the cause by subscribing 100*l*. in money or plate, together with the maintenance of a horse, for the defence of the parliament. (*Notes and Queries*, 1st S. xii. 358.)

His active zeal will account for his being elected on May 30, 1643, recorder of London. In the next year he assisted at the Assembly of Divines, and had the thanks of the house for his speech on the Jus Divinum. In all the questions discussed he was a popular debater, but stoutly opposed the self-denying ordinance. (*Clarendon*, v. 89.) No unwilling sharer in the forfeited spoils of the loyalists, the small were as welcome as the great, and he did not disdain a grant of the books of Mr. Vaughan of Lincoln's Inn (*Whitelocke*, 177), at the time he was being gratified with the clerkship of the petty bag, worth 1000*l*. a year.

The Presbyterian party, with which he was connected, becoming jealous of the army, took measures in June 1647 for its being disbanded. Sir Thomas Fairfax counteracted this attempt by bringing a charge in the name of the army against eleven of the opposing leaders, including Glynne, and insisting on their being sequestered from their attendance on the house. Though the Commons at first resisted the interference, the accused members, upon the army's advance towards London, thought proper to withdraw. This was quickly followed by their impeachment, their expulsion from the house, and the attempt to place Mr. Steele as recorder instead of Glynne. After a year's byplay, resulting in the discharge of the accused, and their being restored to their seats, the farce concluded, having answered its purpose of getting rid for the time of the popular opponents of the army and their plans. (*Ibid.* 253–310.) Glynne was re-admitted on June 7, 1648, and was so entirely restored to confidence as to be appointed in the following September one of the commissioners to treat with the king in the Isle of Wight, and while engaged in that service to be named, on October 12, a serjeant-at-law. (*Ibid.* 334, 342.) In December, however, he was one of the victims of Pride's Purge, by the vote of the Rump repealing the previous revocation of the proceedings against the eleven impeached members, which, so far from being detrimental to him, turned out to his future advantage, by relieving him from all implication in the murder of the king.

Glynne's party having now lost all power, he soon after showed an inclination to side with that of Cromwell, who, willing enough to encourage his advances, made him, on becoming protector, his serjeant. In this character he appeared in the High Court of Justice, and went the Oxford Circuit as a judge in 1654. In the same year he received the appointment of chamberlain of Chester, and was returned member for Carnarvonshire in Cromwell's parliament of September, in which he seems to have been extraordinarily silent. In April 1655 he presided at the trial of Colonel Penruddock for the rising in the west, when the judges were seized at Salisbury (*State Trials*, v. 518, 604, 767; *Athen. Oxon.* i. xxiii., iii. 604); and on July 15, when Chief Justice Rolle, who had refused to be concerned in that trial, had retired, was put into his place as chief justice of the Upper Bench. (*Style's Reports*, 452.) This position, there being then no House of Lords, did not disqualify him from sitting for Flintshire in Cromwell's next parliament of September 1656. He supported Alderman's Pack's motion to offer Cromwell the title of king, and, being one of the committee to forward the application, in a roundabout inconclusive speech he endeavoured to remove the protector's scruples, by arguing that the kingly office is essential to our constitution. (*Harris's Lives,* iii. 472.) He cunningly published his speech as a pamphlet on the king's return, under the title of 'Monarchy asserted to be the best, most ancient, and legal form of Government.' In the new constitution which followed he accepted a seat in Cromwell's House of Peers. (*Whitelocke,* 666.)

The protector died on September 3, 1658, and Glynne was continued chief justice by Richard, on whose removal and the return of the Long Parliament, with a prophetic glance at the political horizon, he resigned his chief justiceship. In the new parliament, called the Convention Parliament, that met on April 25, 1660, he was returned for the county, and his son for the town, of Carnarvon, and played his cards so adroitly that, on the arrival of Charles II. in England, he was included in the first batch of serjeants, being those who had been appointed irregularly by the parliament. On November 8, in the same year, all bygones forgotten, he was made, according to Anthony Wood, 'by the corrupt dealing of the then lord chancellor' (Clarendon), the king's serjeant (*Siderfin,* 3), and was knighted. He and Maynard, who also attained the same rank, were both employed in the crown prosecutions that followed, and divided the shame of appearing against Sir Harry Vane, their old coadjutor and friend. (*Burton's Diary,* iii. 175, 182.)

Charles's coronation took place on April 23, 1661; and the account given by Pepys of an accident on the occasion shows the feeling that existed in regard to the two legal renegadoes: 'I have not heard of any mischance to anybody through it all, but only to Serjeant Glynne, whose horse fell upon him yesterday and is like to kill him, which people do please themselves to see how just God is to punish the rogue at such a time as this, he being now one of the king's serjeants, and rode in the cavalcade with Maynard, to whom people wish the same fortune.' That the hostile impression was not confined to the courtier is proved by Butler's immortalising their names in the following couplet:—

Did not the learned Glynne and Maynard
To make good subjects traitors strain hard?

He continued in the practice of his profession till his death, which occurred at his house in Portugal Row, Lincoln's Inn Fields, on November 15, 1666. He was buried in his own vault under the altar in St. Margaret's, Westminster.

The reputation of his wealth was no doubt founded in truth; for, besides his professional gains, the places which he enjoyed must have brought him considerable profit. He was undoubtedly an able lawyer, and in his judicial character, as between man and man, was just and impartial. Siderfin (159) states that his plainness and method in arguing the most intricate case were such that it was made clear to the comprehension of every student. But here his praise must end. As a politician, though the cunning with which he joined all the ruling powers in turn may be admired, who but must despise his various tergiversations?

Sir John was twice married. His first wife was Frances, daughter of Arthur Squib, Esq.; his second was Anne, daughter and coheir of John Manning, Esq., of Cralle in Sussex. By both he left children. His eldest son, William (by his first wife), was, during his father's life, created a baronet on May 20, 1661, and his descendants still enjoy the title.

GODBOLT, JOHN, was of Toddington in Suffolk, and after studying at Barnard's Inn was admitted into Gray's Inn, where he was called to the bar, and was elected reader in autumn 1627, and soon appears in Croke's Reports with considerable practice. He received the dignity of the coif at the great call in 1636; and it must have been from his professional reputation, for there is no account of his interfering in the political troubles of the time, that, when the parliament took upon them to appoint the judges, he was selected to fill a vacant seat in the Common Pleas. This occurred on April 30, 1647, and he was immediately added to the commission to hear causes in Chancery. (*Whitelocke,* 245; *Journals.*) He did not long retain his place, but died at his house in High Holborn on August 3, 1684. (*Register.*) His collection of Reports was published soon after his death. The family appears to be now extinct.

GODEREDE, WILLIAM, was a resident at Middleton in Norfolk. His name does not occur in the Year Books till he was called to the degree of a serjeant-at-law in 3 Henry VI. In 1431 he received the appointment of king's serjeant, and on July 3, 1433, he was constituted a judge of the King's Bench, his attendance in which court is noticed till Easter, 21 Henry VI., 1443.

His wife Catherine was a great promoter of the rebuilding of the church of Walpole St. Peter in Marshland, in the window of which her effigy is placed. (*Blomefield's Norfolk,* i. 715.)

GODFREY (BISHOP OF BATH) is placed erroneously by Thynne and Philipot and their followers in the list of the chancellors of Henry I. The sole authority they give is that of Matthew Parker, who in his life of Archbishop William Corbel says that he consecrated 'Godfridum, regni cancellarium, Bathoniensem Episcopum.' The word 'regni,' however, in this passage, was no doubt, by a mistake of the transcriber or the printer, substituted for 'reginæ,' as Godfrey certainly was chancellor to Queen Adeliza; and the term 'cancellarius regni,' or 'Angliæ,' was not introduced till long afterwards, that officer being invariably called at this period 'cancellarius regis.' This consecration occurred also in 1123, when Ranulph was chancellor.

Godfrey was a Belgian priest who came over to England with the queen on her marriage in 1121, as one of her chaplains. He was soon raised to the post of her chancellor; and, by her interest, shortly afterwards obtained the bishopric of Bath, to which he was consecrated on August 26, 1123. He presided over his see nearly twelve years, and, dying on August 16, 1135, was buried at Bath. (*Madox*, i. 60; *Godwin*, 368; *Angl. Sac.* i. 560.)

GOLDINGTON, WILLIAM DE, whose family was established in Essex, where he held the manors of Raurethe, Badewe Parva, and Ringgers in Terling, is mentioned in the Year Book as an advocate in the early part of the reign of Edward II., in the fourth year of which he was appointed one of the three justices of assize for Kent, Sussex, and Surrey. He continued to serve for several years in those and other counties, and was regularly summoned to parliament in virtue of his office till the eleventh year. He died in 12 Edward II., and left a son named John, who was an adherent of the Earl of Lancaster and the other barons in rebellion. (*Parl. Writs*, ii. p. ii. 934; *Cal. Inquis.* p. m. i. 292.)

GOLDSBOROUGH, EDWARD, of Goldsborough in Yorkshire, was of a very ancient and respectable family. He was probably an officer of the Exchequer, to the bench of which court he was raised, as third baron, on June 26, 1483, 1 Richard III. He was continued in his place by Henry VII., who made him second baron on December 5, 1488. After sitting there for about six years more, he was succeeded by Thomas Barnewell on October 1, 1494. His daughter Elizabeth married Sir John Gower, the ancestor of the Duke of Sutherland. (*Collins's Peerage*, ii. 444.)

GOODRICH, THOMAS (BISHOP OF ELY). This learned prelate was the second son of Edward Goodrich, of East Kirby in the county of Lincoln, by his third wife, Jane, sole daughter of Mr. Williamson, of Boston. The name was pronounced and often spelled Goodrick, notwithstanding that the epigram given by Granger (i. 136) suggests a different reading:—

Et bonus, et dives, bene junctus et optimus ordo;
Præcedit bonitas, pone sequuntur opes.

He was educated at Benett College, Cambridge, from which he was elected a fellow of Jesus College in 1510, and was proctor of the university in 1515. His proficiency in the canon and civil laws led to his appointment as one of the syndics in 1529, to prepare the university's answer on the question of the king's marriage with Queen Catherine. Thus introduced to the royal notice, he received the rectory of St. Peter's Cheap in London, and was nominated one of the king's chaplains, with a canonry in St. Stephen's, Westminster. On March 17, 1534, he was elected Bishop of Ely. (*Rymer*, xiv. 486.)

His zeal for the Reformation was soon manifested in his diocese by stringent orders to his clergy to erase the pope's name from all their books, and to demolish all images and relics in their churches. In 1537 he was one of the compilers of the work which was called the 'Bishops' Book;' and soon afterwards the Gospel of St. John was allotted to his share in the revision of the New Testament. In 1540 he seems to have been suspected of being concerned in the translation of Melancthon's Epistle, as his study was directed to be searched. (*Acts Privy Council*, vii. 98.) Under Edward VI. he assisted in the compilation of the Liturgy; and in 1549 and 1550 he was one of the commissioners assigned to enquire 'super hæretica pravitate.' (*Rymer*, xv. 181, 250.) On December 22, 1551, the Great Seal on the sudden retirement of Lord Chancellor Rich was given into the bishop's hands as keeper. This deposit, which seems in the first instance to have been only temporary till Rich's recovery from his pretended illness, was by the almost immediate discovery of the real cause of that minister's retirement converted into a permanent one, with the full title of lord chancellor, on January 19, 1552.

In the parliament which met on the next day the new Liturgy was made the law of the land. (*Robertson's Heylin*, 221, 252, 291.) Previously to the king's death he had settled the crown on Lady Jane Grey, by an instrument which the Duke of Northumberland had induced the bishop to authenticate with the Great Seal. He does not appear to have been consulted on the subject; but with the rest of the council he subscribed the undertaking to support the royal testament, and he acted on the council during the nine days of that unfortunate lady's reign, signing as chancellor several letters issued by them on her behalf, the last of which is dated on July 19. He was accordingly one of the prisoners named for trial on the accession of Queen Mary; and it was perhaps on account of his having joined in the order sent by the council on July 20, commanding the Duke of Northumberland to disarm, that her majesty struck his name out of the list. (*Chron. Qn. Jane,* 91, 109; *Lingard,* vii. 122.)

The Great Seal was of course taken from him, and his death within a year from his dismissal probably released him from those investigations which were so fatal to some of his brethren.

He died at his palace at Somersham on May 10, 1554, and on his brass in Ely Cathedral he is represented in his episcopal robes as he wore them after the Reformation, with a Bible in one hand, and the Great Seal in the other. Of his munificent expenditure on the buildings of his see the long gallery at Ely Palace is an existing memorial. (*Angl. Sac.* i. 676; *Godwin,* 272.)

GOULD, HENRY, was the son of Andrew Gould, of Winsham in Somersetshire. He was born about 1644, and was called to the bar of the Middle Temple in 1667, and elected a bencher in 1689. Included in the great call of serjeants in 1692, he was made one of the king's serjeants in the following year. In this character he conducted the case for the bill of attainder against Sir John Fenwick in 1696.

On January 26, 1699, he was promoted to be a judge of the King's Bench, and on his first circuit had the unpleasant necessity of inflicting a fine of 100*l.* on Sir John Bolls at Lincoln, for giving him the lie, kicking the sheriff, and other disorderly conduct. (*State Trials,* xiii. 546; *Luttrell,* iv. 545.)

On the death of King William his patent was renewed by Queen Anne, under whom he acted for the eight remaining years of his life, dying at his chambers in Serjeants' Inn, Chancery Lane, on March 26, 1710. His residence was at Sharpham Park, between Street and Walton, in Somersetshire, the future birthplace of the celebrated novelist and magistrate Henry Fielding, who was the son of Sarah, the judge's daughter, by her marriage with Lieutenant-General Fielding, nephew of the Earl of Denbigh.

He married Miss Davidge, of Worcester, and by her left a son, Davidge, the father of the next-named judge. (*Lord Raymond,* 414, 1309; *Collinson,* ii. 268.)

GOULD, HENRY, the grandson of the last-named, and the son of Davidge Gould, Esq., of Sharpham Park, a barrister of the Middle Temple, by his wife, Honora, daughter of — Hockmore, of Buckland Baron in Devonshire, was born about the year 1710.

The Middle Temple called him to the bar in June 1734; and at the end of twenty years he arrived at the dignity of a bencher on being made king's counsel. His business was considerable, but he was distinguished more by the soundness of his law than by the power of his oratory. In Michaelmas 1761 he was raised to the bench as a baron of the Exchequer, where he sat till the end of the next year, when he was removed into the Common Pleas on January 24, 1763.

With acknowledged ability he exercised his judicial duties till his death at the age of eighty-four on March 5, 1794, a period of thirty-three years from his first appointment.

In the riots of 1780, when the king, after Lord Mansfield's house had been burnt, offered to all the judges the protection of the military, Judge Gould is said to have declined the proffered aid, and to have declared that he would rather die than live under any other than the laws of England.

He was buried at Stapleford Abbotts in Essex, of which parish his brother, Dr. William Gould, was rector. He married Elizabeth, daughter of Dr. Walker, archdeacon of Wells. Their only son dying in the judge's life, his large fortune was divided between his two daughters, one the wife of the Hon. Temple Luttrell, and the other of the Earl of Cavan. (*Collinson,* ii. 268.)

GRAHAM, ROBERT, was the son and heir of James Graham, Esq., of Dalston in Middlesex, and was born at Hackney on October 14, 1744. He was educated at Trinity College, Cambridge, and entering the Inner Temple in 1766, he was called to the bar in due course. After many years' practice, he was in February 1793 made attorney-general to the Prince of Wales, and king's counsel in the April following. In June 1800 he was raised to the bench of the Exchequer, on which he sat for nearly twenty-seven years.

He was not considered a very efficient judge, and that his previous reputation as a lawyer was not very high appears from Sir Edward Law's remark when he was appointed, 'that he put Mr. Justice Rooke upon a pinnacle.' His principal distinction was his equanimity of temper. So great was his politeness and urbanity to every one that Jekyll said of him, 'No one but his sempstress could ruffle him.' His dignity must have been somewhat disturbed by an unlucky accident which befell him at Newcastle, while judge of assize there, and which was made the subject of a humorous song from the pen of Mr. John Shield, to be found by the curious in Dr. Bruce's interesting 'Handbook to Newcastle-upon-Tyne.' He resigned in February 1827, in his eighty-third year, but lived several years afterwards, and died at his sister's, at Long Ditton in Surrey, when he was beyond ninety.

GRANCURT, WILLIAM DE, is noticed both by Dugdale and Madox (i. 356, ii. 320) as a baron of the Exchequer in 52 Henry III., 1268, but no trace of his continuance in office or of his personal history has been ascertained, except that a Walter de Grancourt, perhaps his son, was sheriff of Norfolk and Suffolk in 5 Edward I. (*Abb. Rot. Orig.* i. 28.)

GRANDEN, WARIN DE, was one of the

four justiciers appointed in 4 Henry III. 1220, to deliver the gaols of Hereford (*Rot. Claus.* i. 437), but his name does not afterwards occur.

GRANT, WILLIAM. Among the judges that distinguished the reign of George III., Sir William Grant occupies one of the most prominent places, and of his seven countrymen who graced the judicial bench he stands next in reputation to Lord Mansfield. He was born at Elchies in Morayshire in 1755. His father, James Grant, was a humble member of that branch of the ancient clan of the Grants settled at Baldornie, having been at first a small farmer and afterwards collector of the customs in the Isle of Man. In consequence of the death of both his parents while he was in early youth, he was left to the care of his uncle, a wealthy merchant in London. After passing through the grammar school at Elgin, he was sent to the college of Aberdeen, and then spent two years at Leyden in studying the civil law. He is said to have resorted for a short time to an attorney's office as a useful introduction to practical knowledge. Entering Lincoln's Inn on January 30, 1769, he was called to the bar on February 3, 1774, and determined to try his fortune in Canada, where he went in the next year. Soon after his arrival he rendered military service by commanding a body of volunteers during the siege of Quebec by the Americans. The governor appointed him attorney-general of the colony, where for several subsequent years he had the principal lead as an advocate. Not satisfied with shining in so limited a sphere, he then resigned his office and returned to England. Here, however, his colonial fame had not extended, and his efforts in the common law courts and on the Home Circuit were attended with so little success that he contemplated returning to his former exile. But his good fortune introduced him to two patrons, who were capable both of appreciating and rewarding his superior talents. Mr. Pitt, requiring some information relative to Canada, was accidentally referred to him, and, having found his intelligence useful and abundant, and his views correct and statesmanlike, he at once saw his value and commenced that friendship which secured his future promotion. As one of its first fruits he was returned to parliament at the general election in November 1790 for the borough of Shaftesbury. He soon distinguished himself in the debates, giving an effective support to the minister in the political difficulties of that troublous time. In 1796 he was returned for the county of Banff, which he continued to represent while he remained in parliament.

His second patron was Lord Thurlow, who, after listening to his argument on a Scotch appeal in the House of Lords, expressed the highest opinion of his reasoning powers, and encouraged him to devote himself to the equity courts. There he consequently took his stand, and in April 1793 receiving a patent of precedence, he in a very short time acquired a leading business. In the same year he was appointed one of the judges of the Carmarthen Circuit, and in 1795 solicitor-general to the queen. In 1798 he became chief justice of Chester, and in July 1799 he was appointed solicitor-general, and knighted. He held this office nearly two years, and on May 27, 1801, was made master of the Rolls, and at once justified the great expectations formed of him. During the seventeen years in which he sat in the Rolls Court he was looked upon as a perfect model of judicial excellence. No judge ever gave more satisfaction. His judgments were not only convincing by their practical wisdom, but were remarkable for the clearness with which they explained the principles of equity on which they were founded. No one who has practised under him can forget the patient attention with which he listened to all the statements and arguments of counsel, or the discrimination he evinced in extracting from confused details all that was relevant, or the clearness and simplicity of his reasons when he pronounced his decisions.

To the regret of all, he retired from his court on December 23, 1817. The equity bar testified their respect and veneration for him by requesting him to sit for his picture, which, painted by Sir Thomas Lawrence, now graces the hall in which he sat. For a few subsequent years he assisted in hearing appeals at the cockpit, but afterwards altogether retired from public life, and lived to attain his eighty-third year. He died at Dawlish in Devonshire on May 25, 1832.

When England was threatened with invasion, Sir William, while master of the Rolls, for a second time assumed the military habit, and, joining the volunteers who embodied themselves for the safety of the country, he was called upon, no doubt from the tradition of his prowess and experience at Quebec, to take the command of the Lincoln's Inn corps, which he put into as good a state of efficiency as any in London. In 1809 he was elected lord rector of the university of Aberdeen.

The impression which he made in parliament was wonderful. Few men have gained a greater ascendency. Lord Brougham relates that even Mr. Fox felt it difficult to answer him, and that once, being annoyed by some members talking behind him while he was listening to one of Sir William's speeches, he turned round and asked them sharply, 'Do you think it so very pleasant a thing to have to answer a speech like that?' The effect of his addresses was thus described at a later period:—'There was one extraordinary oration that night—Sir William Grant's; quite a masterpiece of his peculiar and miraculous manner. Conceive an hour and a half of syllogisms strung together in the closest tissues, so artfully clear that you think every successive inference unavoidable; so rapid that you have no leisure to reflect where you have been brought from, or to see where you are to be carried; and so dry of ornament, or illustration, or reflection, that your attention is stretched—stretched—racked. All this is done without a single note.' (*Memoir of Francis Horner*, i. 285.) Though he opposed most of the beneficial alterations in the law suggested by Sir Samuel Romilly's intellectual and comprehensive mind, to Sir Samuel's amelioration of the criminal code he gave a hearty support.

GRAS, NICHOLAS LE, is the last named in a writ by which justices itinerant into Northamptonshire were appointed, dated August 3, 1285, 13 Edward I. (*Chron. Petroburg.* 102, 118.) He was appointed sheriff of Surrey and Sussex in 8 Edward I., and held the office for five years. The castle of Odyham in Hampshire was also committed to his charge in 10 Edward I. (*Abb. Rot. Orig.* i. 35, 41.)

He was possessed of the manors of Renger in Terling and of Little Badewe in Essex. (*Abb. Placit.* 190–305.)

GREEK, THOMAS, who was born and educated at Cambridge, held the office of baron of the Exchequer for one year and ten months, between January 20, 1576, and November 18, 1577, when he died; but all that is known of him is that he lived sixty-three years, and was buried in the church of St. Botolph, Aldersgate. He left a son and daughter. (*Stow's London*, 332–3.)

GREEN, HENRY. Queen Isabella having granted to Henry Green, probably for some services as an advocate, the manor of Briggestoke in Northamptonshire, her son Edward III. confirmed it to him for life. He was appointed one of the king's serjeants-at-law in 19 Edward III., and was called to the bench of the Common Pleas on February 6, 1354, 28 Edward III., when he was knighted.

In 1358, having been cited before the pope for pronouncing a judgment against the Bishop of Ely for harbouring one of his men who had burnt a manor of Lady Wake's, and slain one of her servants, he was excommunicated for his non-appearance. It is not related how he cleared himself from this sentence; but it did not prevent his being raised to the office of chief justice of the King's Bench on May 24, 1361. He retained his place four years and a half, and was removed on October 29, 1365.

Joshua Barnes says (624, 667) that he and Sir William Skipwith were then 'arrested and imprisoned for many enormities against law and justice, and were not redeemed without refunding large sums which by injustice they had got from others, and were for ever after excluded from their places and the king's favour.' It is somewhat curious, if this charge were made (of which no evidence, however, appears on the records), that in the warrant to Sir Henry Green, directing him to give over the rolls, &c., to his successor, the king should call him 'dilectus et fidelis.' He is referred to as the 'wise justice' in one of the cases in Richard Bellewe's Reports. (142.)

That he was not much damnified by any fine imposed upon him is apparent from the numerous manors and other lands in the counties of Northampton, Leicester, York, Hertford, Bedford, Buckingham, and Nottingham, together with a mansion in Silver Street, Cripplegate, London, which he possessed at the time of his death, which occurred in 1369. He married a daughter of Sir John de Drayton, and his son Thomas enjoyed the same property till his death in 1391–2. (*Abb. Rot. Orig.* ii. 195; *Bridge's Northampt.* ii. 247; *Cal. Inquis.* p.m. ii. 206, iii. 136.)

GREENFIELD, WILLIAM DE (ARCHBISHOP OF YORK), was born in Cornwall, and, from the practice that had been previously adopted by King Edward of raising the superior officers of the court to the chancellorship, it is not unlikely that he had passed his probation as a clerk of the Chancery or Exchequer. Like those officers, he was of the clerical profession, and had been rewarded with the dignities of the Church, the deanery of Chichester having, in 1299, been superadded to his canonry of York, and, like them, he had been summoned to the parliament from 1293, on one of which occasions he is called clerk of the council. (*Le Neve*, 60; *Parl. Writs*, i. 28–113.)

He was appointed chancellor on September 30, 1302, and on December 4, 1304, he was elected Archbishop of York. Soon after, on the 29th, he declared to the council that it behoved him to take a journey to Rome on the business of this election, and requested the king to declare his will as to the custody of the Great Seal. William de Hamilton was immediately invested with the office of chancellor, and the archbishop elect proceeded to the Roman court, where, notwithstanding the king's letters, the pontiff granted him consecration, only on the payment of 9500 marks. To relieve him from so extortionate an imposition, the clergy of his province raised the money among them.

The ten years of his rule were principally illustrated by his support of the Knights Templars in their fallen fortunes, and by his assisting at the general council held at Vienne in 1311, where one of the highest places was assigned to him.

He died at his palace at Cawood on December 6, 1315, and was buried in the chapel of St. Nicholas in his own cathedral. He had the character of an eloquent man and an able statesman, and his library was extensive enough to be worthy of a separate bequest to St. Alban's Abbey. (*Godwin*, 685.)

GREGORY, WILLIAM, son of the Rev. Robert Gregory, vicar of Fawnthorpe and rector of Sutton St. Nicholas in Herefordshire, and Anne, daughter of John Harvey, of Bradestone in Gloucestershire, was born on March 1, 1624, and educated at All Souls' College, Oxford, of which he was afterwards a fellow. Entering the society of Gray's Inn, he was called to the bar in 1650, made bencher in 1673, and elected autumn reader in 1675. He travelled the Oxford Circuit, and held several lucrative stewardships. He attained sufficient eminence in the law to be elected recorder of Gloucester in 1672, to be created a serjeant in 1677, and to be returned as member for Weobly in 1678, the last year of Charles's second parliament, and to the new one summoned for March 1679. When the latter met, the king rejected Mr. Seymour, who had been chosen speaker in opposition to the nominee of the court, to the great indignation of the house, which would not give up the privilege of choice. On a compromise, however, both candidates were excluded, and Mr. Serjeant Gregory, having been called to the chair, was immediately approved by the king. (*Pearce's Inns of Court*, 344; *Parl. Hist.* iv. 1112.)

In that parliament, which only lasted two months, but had the credit of passing the Habeas Corpus Act, parties ran so high that, though a supply was granted, and the bill read a third time, the opposition took every means to delay sending it up to the Lords, till their grievances were enquired into. Roger North (*Examen*, 460; *State Trials*, vii. 524) relates that the Speaker Gregory one day, by a concerted plan, immediately upon a member moving for the carrying up of the bill, rose from his chair without putting the question, and, followed by the court party, before the opposition could have time to say a word, carried up the bill to the Lords, where the king, being on his throne, at once gave it his fiat. At this time, the king having newly arranged the ministry, reducing the council to thirty members, and making the Earl of Shaftesbury the nominal president of it, four of the judges—Wilde, Thurland, Bertie, and Bramston—were summarily dismissed on April 29. In the place of the last Serjeant Gregory was appointed a baron of the Exchequer, and was knighted.

Though his patent is dated May 1, it is evident that he was not sworn in, nor his nomination announced, till some time after, for he still continued to sit as speaker till the prorogation of the parliament on the 26th of that month, which was followed by a dissolution in August. He retained his place till February 10, 1686, when he was discharged in consequence of giving his opinion against the king's dispensing power. (*Parl. Hist.* v. 312; *Bramston's Autobiog.* 221.) In the following year he was removed by royal mandate from the recordership of Gloucester.

To the Convention Parliament which met on January 22, 1689, Sir William was returned for the city of Hereford, but soon vacated his seat on being selected by King William as one of the judges of the King's Bench. In one of his circuits the mayor of Bristol thought proper to send him a message that he must not expect to have his charges borne by the city, to which he replied that they need not be frightened, for that he could bear his own expenses; but, receiving great insolences from the people on his entrance, he found that a purposed affront was intended. He therefore, on the sitting of the court, promptly fined the city 100*l*. and each sheriff 20*l*., and would not remit the fine till they had submitted and apologised. He maintained throughout his judicial life the character for integrity he had gained, and dying on May 28, 1696, at his manor of How Capel, Herefordshire, he was buried in the parish church there, which he had entirely rebuilt. By his wife, Catherine, daughter and heiress of James Smith, Esq., of Tillington, he had an only son, whose descendants in the male line failed in 1789. (*Manning's Speakers*, 374; *Kennett*, iii. 528; *Luttrell*, ii. 277.)

GREINVILL, ADAM DE, paid in 35 Henry III. a fine of forty marks for a grant of the bailiwick of the forest of Sellwood in Wiltshire. (*Cal. Rot. Pat.* 21; *Excerpt. e Rot. Fin.* ii. 106.) After this he was appointed justice of the Jews, and is mentioned in that character in 42 and 44 Henry III. (*Madox*, ii. 319.) In the three following years, 1261-3, he appears as a justice itinerant in several commissions. In 50 Henry III., 1266, Dugdale inserts him among the justices of the Common Pleas, on the authority of a liberate of that date, and till October 1272, a month before the king's death, there are continual entries of payments made for assizes to be taken before him.

GREVILL, WILLIAM, son of Richard Grevil, Esq., of Lemington in Gloucestershire, attained the serjeant's coif in November 1504. He was made a judge of the Common Pleas on May 21, 1509, 1 Henry VIII., and so remained till 1513, when he died, and was buried in Cheltenham Church, where there is a monument to his memory. (*Dugdale's Orig.* 47; *Atkyns's Gloucesters.* 173.)

GREY, JOHN DE, or GRAY (BISHOP OF NORWICH), was one of the descendants of Anchitel de Gray, a Norman who came over with the Conqueror, and received from that prince various large possessions. His grandfather was Richard de Gray, a great benefactor to the abbey of Ensham in Oxfordshire, and his father was Anchitel. John was a native of Norfolk, and filled some office in the Curia Regis: (*Rot. de Oblatis*, 12–73.) Being also brought up to the Church, he was, about 1200, preferred to the archdeaconry of Cleveland, which he exchanged for that of Gloucester. (*Le Neve*, 303, 308.) He was attached to prince John before he came to the crown, and his frequent attendance at the court after John's accession is shown by several royal charters given under his hand from September 1199 to June 1200. (*Dugdale's Monast.* ii. 168, 418, v. 112, vi. 956, 1090.) On this account Sir T. Hardy has inserted his name among the keepers of the Great Seal; but it may be doubted whether he is entitled to any other designation than that of a mere officer, who affixed the Seal for Archbishop Hubert, the chancellor at the time.

His erudition and his wit, for both of which he was remarkable, soon made him a favourite with King John, who procured his election to the bishopric of Norwich on September 24, 1200. Under that title his name frequently appears from this time till the eighth year of the reign as one of the justiciers in the Curia Regis at Westminster, and on the different itinera. (*Hunter's Preface*; *Rot. de Oblatis*, 211, 351.)

In 1205 he was, on the earnest recommendation of the king, elected Archbishop of Canterbury. Although he was actually enthroned, the pope set aside the election, pretending that he was too much employed by the king in secular affairs to have sufficient leisure to attend to the spiritual government of the Church. The appointment of Stephen de Langton followed; but the king, indignant at the pope's assumption, and at his favourite's election being annulled, refused to acknowledge him. This led to the kingdom being placed under interdict, and soon after to the excommunication of the monarch. The bishop was soon removed from the actual scene of contention, by being sent as lord deputy to Ireland, where, shortly after, in 1210, he aided King John, on his visit there, in the introduction of English laws.

On the invasion of England by Prince Louis of France in 1213, the bishop brought over from Ireland a powerful force to the king's assistance, but was soon after compelled to witness his royal patron's resignation of the crown to Pope Innocent, and to proceed to Rome to arrange the terms on which the clergy were to receive compensation for the losses they had sustained through the king's proceedings.

During his return from this embassy he fell sick at Poictiers, and died there on November 1, 1214. His remains were brought to England and honourably interred in his own cathedral. In February of that year he had been elected Bishop of Durham, but the pope's confirmation did not arrive till after his death. (*Surtees's Durham*, i. xxvii.)

He was a man of agreeable manners and sprightly conversation, well-informed and intelligent, ready in counsel and energetic in action. He was fond of antiquarian studies, and the author of some historical and other works. (*Godwin*, 429; *Weever*, 789; *Blomefield's Norfolk*, i. 274, 577; *R. de Wendover*, iii. 185, &c.; *Lingard*, ii. 17–25.)

GREY, WALTER DE (ARCHBISHOP OF YORK), was the nephew of the above-named John de Grey, being the second son of the bishop's elder brother John, by his wife Hawise.

The first fact recorded of him is his purchase of the Chancery for the sum of five thousand marks, to be paid by instalments of five hundred pounds at the feast of St. Andrew and at Pentecost in each year. The charter by which this grant is confirmed is dated October 2, 1205, 7 John, and his uncle makes himself responsible on the roll for the payment of the fine. (*Rot. de Fin.* 378; *Rot. Chart.* 158; *Rot. Claus.* i. 53.)

Various ecclesiastical preferments were now presented to him, and in May 1207 he was made archdeacon of Totnes, with the prebend in the church of Exeter. In 1210 or 1213 he was elected Bishop of Lichfield and Coventry, but it appears that it was only by the canons of Lichfield, the monks of Coventry choosing another person, and that both elections were made void. He was in October 1213 sent on a mission to Flanders, and previous to his departure he, of course, sent the Seal to the king, but still remained chancellor, and is so styled four days after. (*Rot. Claus.* i. 153; *Rot. Pat.* 105.) During his absence, however, which probably lasted longer than was expected, there is no doubt that the king appointed Peter de Rupibus his chancellor, who is so designated in two records dated November 21 and 24, 1213 (*Rot. de Fin.* 507–9), and the Seal was delivered to Ralph de Neville on December 22 to be held under him. The bishop did not, however, long continue in office, for Walter de Grey on his return resumed the title, and from January 12, 1214, till July 7, 1214 (although in the interval he had been again abroad), he is never mentioned without that designation. (*Rot. Pat.* 108–111; *Rot. Claus.* i. 160–8.)

During this second absence he was elected Bishop of Worcester, and was consecrated on October 5, 1214, when he probably resigned the office of chancellor, the 29th of that month being the date of the first record in which his successor, Richard de Marisco, is so denominated.

During the war with the barons, Walter de Grey adhered closely to the king; but, though he was chancellor at the time, he is not mentioned as having placed the Seal to the charter of May 15, 1213, 14 John, by which the king resigned the crown to the pope.

In the contest for the archbishopric of York, his faithful adherence to the king procured his election in opposition to Simon de Langton, brother to the primate. The immaculate chastity of his life was urged to the pope to procure his confirmation; and the plea was allowed on a promise to supply the papal treasury with a donative of no less than 10,000*l.*, and he accordingly received the pall on May 24, 1216. The straitened means to which he was reduced in order to meet the payment of a sum so enormous in those times obtained for him a character for sordid avarice, an imputation which no doubt induced his contemporaries to believe the absurd story that is related of his having, during a famine, hoarded a quantity of corn, which became the resort of innumerable snakes, serpents, and other reptiles, and from which a fearful voice proceeded, commanding the ricks to be avoided, as they and all the possessions of the bishop belonged to the devil.

That he was not truly charged with avarice, however, is proved by his generosity when he had cleared himself from his heavy debt. Not only did he restore part of his cathedral, and make many munificent additions to the see, and to his church, but he presented the manor of Thorpe as a residence for his successors, and purchased also for them the palace at Westminster, which had been built by Hubert de Burgh. The former is still, under the name of Bishopsthorpe, in the occupation of the archbishops; and the latter, with the name of York Place, continued to be so till Cardinal Wolsey alienated it to King Henry VIII., when it received the new designation of Whitehall. His character for wisdom, prudence, and integrity was so high that in 26 Henry III., 1242, though at a very advanced age, he was left by Queen Eleanor, then regent, in the government of the kingdom when she went to join her husband in France.

He presided over his see nearly forty years, and died at Fulham on May 1, 1255. His remains were removed to his cathedral, where a splendid monument was erected to his memory. (*Godwin*, 315, 459, 677; *Hasted*, i. 156; *Le Neve; Blomefield's Norwich*, i. 478.)

GREY, JOHN DE, was the nephew of the above Walter de Grey, being second son of his eldest brother, Henry, and of Isolda, the eldest of the five nieces and coheirs of Robert Bardolf. He was sheriff of Buckinghamshire and Bedfordshire in 23 Henry III., and had his seat at Eaton, near Fenny Stratford. In 30 Henry III. he was made constable of the castle of Gannoc in North Wales, and was also justice of Chester. He offended the king in 35 Henry III. by marrying without his licence Johanna, the widow of Pauline Peyvre, who had been devoted to another person, and he was fined five hundred marks for his transgression, but shortly afterwards he is stated to have greatly ingratiated himself with Henry by assuming the Cross. The Fine Roll of 1253 contains an evidence of the favour he thus obtained, in the grant of a pardon of 300*l.* of the above fine and other debts which he owed to the crown. (*Excerpt. e Rot. Fin.* i. 453, ii. 119, 167.)

He was made steward of Gascony, custos of the castles of Northampton, Shrewsbury, Dover, and Hereford, and sheriff of the latter county. In 1260 he was among the justices itinerant sent into the counties of Somerset, Dorset, and Devon. When Henry submitted the determination of the differences between him and his barons to the decision of Louis, King of France, he was one of the barons who undertook that he should abide by it; and during the war which followed he firmly adhered to his sovereign. After the battle of Evesham in 1265 he was made sheriff of the counties of Nottingham and Derby, and died in the following year.

Before his union with Johanna Peyvre, he had married Emma, daughter and heir of Geoffrey de Glanville, by whom he had a daughter and an only son, two of the descendants of whom now sit in the House of Peers as Earl Wilton and Earl De Grey and Ripon. (*Dugdale's Baron.* i. 712, 716; *Nicolas's Synopsis*; &c.)

GREY, HENRY (EARL OF KENT), a lineal descendant of the last-mentioned John de Grey, succeeded to the title of Earl of Kent on the death of his father Anthony in 1643, and had not long taken his seat among the peers before he was substituted for the Earl of Rutland in the commission from the parliament for the custody of their Great Seal. Clarendon (iv. 340, 403) calls him a man of far meaner parts than the Earl of Rutland, and says that the number of lords who attended the parliament was so small that their choice of the two who were to represent them was very limited.

The commissioners held the Seal from November 10, 1643, till October 30, 1646, when it was given to the speakers of the two houses. (*Journals*.)

In December 1647 the earl was one of the lords commissioners to take the four bills to the king at the Isle of Wight, and had to bring them back with the king's refusal to assent to the destruction of the royal authority which they involved. He was renominated on March 15, 1648, chief commissioner of the Seal, in conjunction with another lord and two commoners, who continued in office till the death of the king, not one of them approving or taking any part in the tragic event. With that the power of the lords who were commissioners virtually terminated, but they remained in office till the Commons, on February 6, 1649, voted the abolition of the House of Peers, and two days after put the Seal into other hands. (*Whitelocke*, 283–378.)

So ended the earl's political career. He died in 1651; and the title is now merged in that of Earl De Grey and Ripon.

GREY, WILLIAM (LORD GREY DE WERKE), was advanced to this peerage in 1624. From the commencement of the civil war he was an active partisan of the parliament, and one of the few peers that remained in the House of Lords while the rest joined the king. When Lord Fairfax suffered a defeat in the north, and the parliament were desirous to send to the Scots to assist them, Lord Grey on being named one of the deputation refused to go, and was committed to the Tower; but, making his peace, he was soon after selected by the Lords as their speaker, in the absence of the lord keeper. In 1648 he was added to the commissioners of the Great Seal, and performed the duties of the office for nearly eleven months, the last few days being after the king's death, in the planning or execution of which fearful event he is not charged with concurring. With the abolition of the House of Lords of course his office ceased, but he consented to be nominated on the Council of State. (*Whitelocke*, 295–488; *Clarendon*, iv. 153, 368, 415.)

He survived the restoration of Charles II. more than fourteen years, and died in July 1674. His title became extinct in 1706.

GREYSTOKE, HENRY DE, does not appear to have been a member of the baronial family of Greystoke in Cumberland. He may therefore have been so called from his being born in that place. He was connected with the king's household or Exchequer in 27 Edward I., as well as several times afterwards under Edward II. He acted as paymaster of the forces in Nottingham and Derby, and was appointed by the latter king to assist the sheriff of Cumberland in arresting the Knights Templars. From 16 Edward III. he held the office of custos of the lands and tenements which were reserved for the use of the king's chamber, and in this character various manors, &c., were placed under his charge; and in the parliaments of 25 and 28 Edward III. he was ordered to be present on the hearing of petitions touching these lands, to give information 'pur le roi et au le roi.' Dugdale introduces him in the twenty-seventh year as attorney-general; but it is probably in reference to these matters only, as he does not appear to have been otherwise connected with the law. Though he is described as a 'clericus,' he could not have taken that grade in holy orders which prevented him from marrying; for his widow Jane, the daughter of Sir William Pickering, is said to have married Chief Justice Gascoigne.

He had a grant of the French portion of the church of Mapeldurham, and of a messuage and lands in Resceby in Yorkshire for his good services, and he was made a baron of the Exchequer on October 6, 1356, 30 Edward III., beyond which no trace of him remains. (*Parl. Writs*, i. 956, ii. p. ii. 648, n.; *N. Fœdera*, ii. 1214; *Abb. Rot. Orig.* ii. 159–208; *Rot. Parl.* ii. 236, 254.)

GRIMBALD, ROBERT, is inserted by Dugdale as a justicier in the reign of Henry II. (*Orig.* 100; *Monast.* vi. 425); but in the multiplicity of names of justiciers in the rolls of this reign, quoted by Madox and others, that of Robert Grimbald never occurs, although it does forty years afterwards in that of Henry III. The document to which his seal is attached is a charter granting certain lands in Dunnington to the priory of Osulveston in Leicestershire, and there are four others of the same description, in none of which is there any addition to his name at all designating a judicial character. It appears, however, that he was united with Paganus from 2 to 8 Henry II., 1156–1162, in the sheriffalty of Cambridge and Huntingdon; and this, recollecting the judicial duties which appertained to that office, may have been the ground of naming him as a justicier. He married Matilda, daughter and heir of Paganus de Hocton, who was probably the sheriff with whom he was associated.

GRIMBALD, PETER, is introduced in Madox's List of the Barons of the Exchequer (ii. 318), with a reference to a writ tested in 25 Henry III., 1241. There is a mandate on the Close Roll (ii. 207) of 11 Henry III., 1226, addressed to Magister Philip de Ardern and P. Grimbald, relative to certain business entrusted to them to transact in the bishopric of Durham, a duty which was likely to devolve on one connected with the Exchequer.

GRIMBALD, ROBERT, was not improbably a descendant of his before-mentioned namesake. He, as well as the other, was certainly resident in Northamptonshire, and in 9 Henry III. was appointed to conduct the quinzime of that county to Oxford. (*Rot. Claus.* ii. 74.) In the commission for justices itinerant in 1234, 18 Henry III., he stood third of those nominated for Rutland.

GRIMSTON, HARBOTTLE, a descendant from Sylvester, the standard-bearer of the Conqueror, for whose services the parish of Grimston in Yorkshire, and various other manors in the East Riding, were the reward, was the son of Sir Harbottle Grimston, created a baronet in 1612, by Elizabeth, daughter of Ralph Coppinger, Esq., of Stoke in Kent.

He was born at Bradfield Hall in Essex, and was at first intended for the law and entered at Lincoln's Inn. But upon his brother's death he abandoned the study, till forming an attachment to the daughter of Sir George Croke, the judge refused to bestow her hand upon him unless he resumed his profession. He re-opened his law-books with all the ardour of a lover, and soon attained sufficient legal knowledge not only to satisfy Sir George, but also to obtain the post of recorder of Colchester, to which he was elected in 1638, being also returned member for that town to the two parliaments of 1640.

Between the two parliaments his father died, and he succeeded to the title. In both of them he was one of the most violent opposers to the encroachments of the court, and a powerful advocate for the liberties of the people, being no doubt instigated by the imprisonment suffered by his father for refusing to pay the loan-money. He was not very choice in his language, saying in his speech against the advisers of ship-money, that 'he was persuaded that they who gave their opinions for the legality of it did it against the dictamen of their own conscience,' and calling Secretary Windebank 'the very pander and broker to the whore of Babylon.' Contributing two horses and twenty pounds in 1642 for the defence of the privileges of parliament, he was looked upon as one of the most active among the popular party; yet in 1643 he refused to subscribe the Solemn League and Covenant, and discontinued sitting in the house till it was laid aside. He then joined with Holles and the Presbyterian party against the Independents, and Cromwell in particular. He was one of the commissioners selected to treat with the king in the Isle of Wight (*Notes and Queries*, 1st S. xii. 358; *Whitelocke*, 334), when, though the negotiation was unsuccessful, his majesty was well pleased with his conduct, and on his return he urged upon the house the acceptance of the king's concessions. He then began to see the real object of the dominant faction, and, not consenting to their determination to get rid of the monarchy, was with other members excluded the house. His influence with the army and the people was considered so great that he was put into confinement before the king's trial; but was discharged by an order from Lord Fairfax on the very day of the execution, first entering into an engagement not to act nor to do anything to the disservice of the parliament or the army.

Cromwell's subsequent forcible dissolution of the parliament made it a matter of prudence that Grimston should retire to the Continent. At the same time he resigned the recordership of Colchester.

Returning to England in a few years, he was elected in Cromwell's new modelled parliament in 1656 as one of the sixteen members for Essex; but, declining to sign the engagement recognising Cromwell's government, he was refused admittance to the house. He afterwards joined in the remonstrance of the secluded members, which protested against the assembly as not being the representative body of England; but no notice being taken of it, he quietly retired to the practice of his profession until more promising times. In December 1659 the Long Parliament was restored to its functions, and having dissolved itself in the following March, Sir Harbottle was appointed one of the council of state. Of the Convention Parliament, summoned on April 25, he was elected speaker, and distinguished himself by the peculiar style of his oratory. In the addresses which he made to the king after his return the fulsome style of his predecessors in the chair was revived, and even exceeded, with the addition of absurd reiterations. He called the actors in the rebellion 'the monsters who had been guilty of blood, precious blood, precious royal blood;' and in his speech, previous to the dissolution, he exclaimed, 'We must needs be a happy parliament, a healing parliament, a reconciling and peaceful parliament, a parliament *propter excellentiam*, that may truly be called *parliamentissimum parliamentum*.' (*Whitelocke*, 653; *Parl. Hist.* iv. 27, 113, 168.)

He had the honour of entertaining the king on June 25, 1660, at his house in Lincoln's Inn Fields, and soon received a more substantial proof of the royal gratitude in the appointment of master of the Rolls, which was given him on November 3, though it was said that he gave Lord Clarendon 8000*l.* for the place. (*Ch. Just. Lee's Memoir. in Law Mag.* xxxviii. 217.) He was then sixty-six years of age, and he held the office till his death, a period of twenty-three years. One of his decrees nearly cost him his life. Nathaniel Bacon, of Gray's Inn, against whom it was pronounced, offered a man 100*l.* to kill him;

and upon being convicted of the crime in 1664, was condemned to pay a fine of 1000 marks, to be imprisoned three months, and be of good behaviour for life, and to acknowledge his offence at the bar of the Chancery. Bacon was discharged as insolvent in 1667. (1 *Siderfin*, 230.)

Sir Harbottle was also made chief steward of St. Albans, where he had purchased the manor of Gorhambury and other property, and recorder of Harwich. His judicial position did not prevent his sitting in parliament, in which he continued to be one of the representatives of the borough of Colchester till his death. He at last grew out of favour with the court, from his known dislike to the Roman Catholic religion, which he made no attempt to conceal. When a bill was introduced in 1667 for changing the punishment of Romish priests and Jesuits from death to imprisonment for life, he indignantly asked, 'Is this the way to prevent Popery? We may as soon make a good fan out of a pig's tail as a good bill out of this.' He asserted the right of the House of Commons to choose their own speaker when the king rejected Mr. Seymour in 1679; and at the close of his life he was compelled to dismiss Burnet, the preacher at the Rolls, for a sermon on the 5th of November, which was interpreted as levelled against the king's conduct. (*Parl. Hist.* iv. 1096; *Burnet*, i. 596.)

He died on January 2, 1685 (*Luttrell*, i. 384; 1 *Vernon*, 284), of natural decay, being then above eighty years of age, and was buried in St. Michael's Church, St. Albans. Sir Henry Chauncy, his contemporary, thus describes him: 'He had a nimble fancy, a quick apprehension, a rare memory, an eloquent tongue, and a sound judgment. He was a person of free access, sociable in company, sincere to his friends, hospitable in his house, charitable to the poor, and an excellent master to his servants.' He published the Reports of his father-in-law Sir George Croke, having first translated them into English, and is said to have greatly assisted Burnet in his 'History of the Reformation.'

By his first wife, Mary, Sir G. Croke's daughter, he had six sons and two daughters; by his second, Annie, daughter of Sir Nathaniel Bacon, niece to Lord Bacon, and widow of Sir Thomas Meautys, he left no children. On the decease of his son Samuel in 1700 the title became extinct. The estate of Gorhambury, with large landed property, he left to his great-nephew William Lukyn, who assumed the name of Grimston, and in 1719 was created a peer of Ireland by the title of Baron of Dunboyne and Viscount Grimston. His grandson was created Baron Verulam in England in 1790, a title which was converted into an earldom in 1815. (*Croke Family*, 606–13; *Chauncy's Herts*, 465; *Collins's Peerage*, viii. 214.)

GROSE, NASH, was the son of Edward Grose, a resident of London, where he was born about the year 1740. He was called to the bar at Lincoln's Inn in November 1766, and took the degree of serjeant in 1774, soon commanding the leading business in the Common Pleas, which he retained till he was raised to the bench. He was appointed a judge of the King's Bench on February 9, 1787, and received the honour of knighthood. After occupying the same seat for twenty-six years, his infirmities obliged him to resign it in Easter vacation 1813. His death took place in the following year, on May 31, when his remains were interred in the Isle of Wight, where he had a beautiful seat called The Priory. (*Term Rep.* 551; *Gent. Mag.* 1814, 388, 629.)

Both in his private and judicial character he was highly respected; but contemporary critics, of course, differ as to his powers and efficiency. By some he was considered to have lost in credit what he gained in rank, and this couplet was perpetrated against him:

Qualis sit Grotius Judex uno accipe versu;
Exclamat, dubitat, balbutit, stridet et errat.

Lord Campbell (*Ch. Just.* iii. 155) says that his aspect was very foolish, and that he had the 'least reputation' among his colleagues; but he adds that 'this supposed weak brother, though much ridiculed, when he differed from his brethren, was voted by the profession to be right.'

Sir Nash married Miss Dennett, of the Isle of Wight.

GRYMESBY, EDMUND DE, was of the town of that name in Lincolnshire, where he had considerable property. (*Abb. Rot. Orig.* ii. 155, 176.) He was probably the son of Simon de Grymesby, escheator to the king, and is mentioned as one of the procurators to appear for the abbot of Thornton in the parliaments of 17 and 18 Edward II. (*Parl. Writs*, ii. p. ii. 938.) In the next year he was parson of the church of Preston. (*Rot. Parl.* i. 437.) In 7 Edward III., 1333, he received the appointment of keeper of the rolls in the Irish Chancery (*Cal. Rot. Pat.* 117), but two years afterwards he was sent to various parties in England to obtain loans for the king to carry on the war with Scotland. (*N. Fœdera*, ii. 912.) He was no doubt then a master or clerk in the English Chancery, in which office he continued to act till the 25th, and perhaps the 27th, year of the reign, being a receiver of petitions in all the parliaments assembled in that interval. (*Rot. Parl.* ii. 126–236.) During this period the Great Seal was twice placed under his seal, from December 16, 1340, to the end of the year, and from September 2 to October 8, 1351.

GUILFORD, LORD. *See* F. NORTH.

GULDEFORD, HENRY DE, settled at Hempsted in Kent, in 26 Edward I. was appointed to perambulate the forests of the northern counties, and two years afterwards to perform the same duties in the counties of Salop, Stafford, and Derby. In 32 Edward I. he appears at the head of the justices itinerant sent to visit the Isle of Jersey, and during the whole of this time he was summoned among the justices to parliament. (*Rot. Parl.* i. 130, 180, 421.) In November 1305 he was constituted one of the judges of the Court of Common Pleas; but he was not re-appointed under Edward II.; Hervey de Staunton was placed there in his stead.

He still continued to be employed to take assizes, and as a justice itinerant. He died in the early part of 6 Edward II., his last summons to parliament being dated on July 8, 1312, the first day of that regnal year. Several of his descendants were sheriffs of Kent, one of whom entertained Queen Elizabeth at his manor-house. Robert, the last of the name, was made a baronet in 1685 by King James II., but, leaving no issue, the title became extinct at his death.

GUNDEVILLE, HUGH DE, at the beginning of the reign of Henry II., filled some responsible office in the Exchequer or in the king's household. In 1170, 16 Henry II., he was despatched with William Fitz-John to arrest Becket, whose fate, however, was sealed before their arrival at Canterbury; and in 1172 he and Robert Fitz-Bernard were appointed lieutenants under Humphrey de Bohun in the government of the city of Waterford. He held the sheriffalty of Hampshire from 16 Henry II. for ten years, that of Northamptonshire from 21 Henry II. for three years, and that of Devonshire in the 24th and 25th years of that reign.

In 20 Henry II., 1174, he was appointed, by writ of Richard de Luci, the chief justiciary, one of the five justices itinerant to fix the tallage of Hampshire; and he was selected in 1176 by the council of Northampton as one of the eighteen justices itinerant who were sent round England. His pleas while so engaged extended over the four following years. (*Madox*, i. 125-138.) He died about the end of this reign, the Pipe Roll of 1 Richard I. (213) referring to property which had been his.

GUNDRY, NATHANIEL, of a Dorsetshire family, was born at Lyme Regis, and entered the Middle Temple as a member in 1720, but, after being called to the bar in 1725, removed to Lincoln's Inn, and was made a king's counsel in July 1742. He represented Dorchester in his native county from 1741 till his elevation to the bench. That he was considered stiff and pretentious by his brethren may be presumed from the following character given of him in the 'Causidicade,' as a supposed candidate for the office of solicitor-general vacant in 1742:—

In the front of the crowd then appear'd Mr. G—nd—y,
'To this office,' quo' he, ' my pretentions are sundry;
Imprimis my merit, e'en great as t' attract
His m—j—y's notice, so nice and exact,
As lately to call me inside of the bar,
From among the rear-guard—poor souls, how they stare!
Which is plain that he meant me some further preferment,
More worthy my learning, parts, and discernment.
More claims I might urge, but this I insist on
Is sufficient to merit the office in question.'
Then the president thus, ' You're too full of surmises';
The man who is stiff, like an oak, seldom rises.'

He waited eight years for his advancement, when in May 1750 he was appointed a judge of the Common Pleas. He enjoyed the post less than four years, dying on the circuit at Launceston on March 23, 1754. He was buried at Musbury in Devonshire. (*Hutchins's Dorset*, i. 249, 379; *Gent. Mag.* xxiv. 191, lxi. 1159.)

GUNTHORP, WILLIAM, described as 'clericus,' probably held some office in the Treasury or Exchequer before he received the responsible appointment of treasurer of Calais, on March 20, 1368, 42 Edward III. This place he held till October 26, 1373 (*N. Fœdera*, iii. 844, 992), and then was made a baron of the Exchequer.

The latest mention of him in that character it is 9 Richard II. (*Rot. Parl.* iii. 204), but up to 18 Richard II. he is recorded as granting lands to the chantry of the church of St. Wolstan, in Grantham, Lincolnshire, and to the chapter of St. Mary, Southwell, in Nottinghamshire. (*Cal. Inquis.* p. m. iii. 162, 187.)

GURDON, ADAM, son of Adam Gurdon, one of the bailiffs of Alton in Hampshire (*Madox*, ii. 304), married Custancia, the daughter and heir of John de Venuz, with whom he received extensive lands at Selborne in that county, together with the bailiwick of the king's forests of Wulvermar and Axiholt. He seems to have been of a litigious disposition, no less than six entries occurring in the 'Abbreviatio Placitorum' of causes decided against him. He joined the party of De Montford, and even after the battle of Evesham raised an array against his sovereign in Hampshire. Prince Edward advanced against the rebels, and coming up with them between Farnham and Alton, he inconsiderately leaped over the trench that surrounded their camp before his forces could follow him. Adam met him, and, after a severe fight hand to hand, was at last mastered and obliged to yield himself prisoner to the prince. Edward generously gave him his life, and eventually his liberty, and thus secured the services of a brave and grateful enemy. (*Rapin*, iii. 170.)

In 8 Edward I., 1280, Dugdale places him among the justices itinerant in Wiltshire; but the pleas of that iter were confined to the forest, and he was no doubt appointed in virtue of his bailiwick, as he is not mentioned upon any other circuit.

He was frequently summoned to perform military service, and in 23 Edward I. was nominated custos of the seashores of Hampshire, and a commissioner of array in that county and in Dorset and Wilts.

In 33 Edward I., 1305, he was elected a representative by the 'communitas' of Scotland, and constituted a justice there, and died in the same year. (*Rot. Parl.* i. 267; *Parl. Writs*, i. 161, &c.; *Cal. Inquis.* p. m. 12, 196, 212.)

Besides his first wife Custancia, he married two others—viz., Almeria, whom he divorced after having two sons; and Agnes, by whom he had a daughter, Johanna, to whom he left his property in Selborne, and who married Richard Achard. That estate, still called Gurdon Manor, now belongs to Magdalen College, Oxford.

GURNEY, JOHN. The family of Baron Gurney may boast of a legal pedigree extending over more than a century and a half, inasmuch as his grandfather, Thomas Gurney, flourishing from 1705 to 1770, and his father, Joseph Gurney, were the recognised shorthand writers, not only employed confidentially by the government and in parliamentary committees, but engaged by authority in reporting the proceedings on all the important trials occurring during the period. His mother was a daughter of William Brodie, Esq., of Mansfield, and he was born in London on February 14, 1768. His education was commenced at St. Paul's School, and completed under the Rev. Mr. Smith at Bottesdale in Suffolk. Accompanying his father on his professional occupations in the courts of law, he naturally imbibed a predilection for that profession, and for practice in the art of forensic eloquence he frequented those debating societies in which some of the greatest orators had made their first essays, adopting those political principles of freedom and reform which then made opposition popular. Having entered the Inner Temple, he was called to the bar by that society in May 1793. He had not long to wait for employment. In the very first term, and the sittings after, he was retained as junior counsel to defend Daniel Isaac Eaton for two libels; and in the following February, in consequence of the absence of his senior, he led the defence of the same individual for another libel. On that occasion he delivered an animated, humorous, and effective speech, which at once established him in his profession, and placed him on a height from which he never descended.

The first consequence was that he was engaged as assistant counsel to Messrs. Erskine and Gibbs in the memorable state trials of Hardy, Horne Tooke, and Thelwall for high treason, in all of which he proved himself a most efficient auxiliary. These occurred before he had been two years at the bar, and in all of them verdicts of acquittal were pronounced for his clients. The same success attended his efforts as counsel for Crossfield and others, arraigned in 1796 on what was nicknamed the Popgun Plot, and for John Binns when indicted with O'Coigley, Arthur O'Connor, and others for high treason in 1798, in both of which he most ably summed up the prisoners' defence. (*State Trials*, xxii.-xxvii.)

At the London and Middlesex Sessions, where he then practised, he soon got a decided lead, and gradually acquired such a footing in Westminster Hall and on the Home Circuit as warranted him in applying for a silk gown. But his supposed politics were against him, and it was not till he had been three-and-twenty years at the bar that he obtained it, and then only in consequence of the extraordinary ability he displayed in prosecuting Lord Cochrane, Cochrane Johnstone, and the other parties implicated in propagating a false story of Bonaparte's defeat and death, for the purpose of speculating in the funds. Here, in opposition to a whole phalanx of the most able counsel at the bar, he, almost unaided, gained a complete triumph in the conviction of all the defendants. His promotion could no longer be delayed, and in 1816 he took rank as king's counsel.

For sixteen years more he continued to labour as an advocate, during the whole of which period he shared the lead of the King's Bench with Sir James Scarlett, Sir John Copley, and one or two eminent members of the bar, and of the Home Circuit he soon became the acknowledged head. It fell to his lot to lead the prosecution of two of the Cato Street conspirators in 1820, who, with the remainder of those tried, were convicted on the clearest evidence. (*Ibid.* xxx. 711, 1341.)

He at length met his reward. After forty years of continued success, throughout the whole of which he was conspicuous for his respectful yet independent demeanour to the court, and his kindly and courteous manner to all, and particularly for the acknowledged virtues of his private life, he was promoted to the bench on February 13, 1832, as one of the barons of the Exchequer, when he was knighted.

For thirteen years Sir John Gurney held this judicial position; and then, from his advanced age and the failure of his health, he resigned his seat in January 1845, only to die on the 1st of the following March at his house in Lincoln's Inn Fields. Without taking a high rank as a deep-read and black-letter lawyer, he supported as a judge the reputation he had gained as an advocate for discrimination, acuteness, and discretion, and his former experience gave him a recognised superiority on criminal trials. He was brought up among Dissenters, but in his latter years he conformed to the Church of England. Whatever were his doctrinal opinions at different periods of his life, as a man he was universally respected, and his charities and practice during the whole of his lengthened existence were the best proofs of his having imbibed the spirit of the Master whom he ever professed to serve.

By his wife, Maria, daughter of Dr. Hawes, he left several children, one of whom, Russell Gurney, Esq., exhibits, as recorder of London, such high judicial powers and such deep legal knowledge that he has been frequently called upon by the government to preside at the assizes in the place of judges temporarily incapacitated by illness. He is member for Southampton, and has been called to the privy council of his sovereign.

H

HADFIELD, WALTER DE, was one of the justices itinerant who set the assize on the king's demesnes in Essex and Hertfordshire in 20 Henry II., 1174. (*Madox*, i. 124.) The manor of Writell in Essex was granted to him and John Fitz-William in 4 Richard I., 1192 (*Ibid.* ii. 167), between which date and 1201 he died. (*Chancellor's Roll, 3 John.*)

HADLOW, or HANDLO, NICHOLAS DE, of the manor of Court-at-Street in Kent, was raised to the bench about November 1254, and continued to act up to September 1266. In 42 Henry III. he was one of the three who were assigned 'ad tenendum Bancum Regis apud Westm.,' until the king arranged more fully for that court. (*Dugdale's Orig.* 43; *Excerpt. e Rot. Fin.* ii. 211–446.) He died in 1270.

HAGET, GEOFFREY, in 10 Richard I., 1198, was associated with two others as a justice itinerant over Yorkshire and the other northern counties, to hear pleas of the crown.

He was the eldest son of Bertram Haget, who possessed considerable property in Yorkshire, and who granted a hermitage and land in the park of Helagh in that county, upon which Geoffrey afterwards built a church. (*Monast.* vi. 437.)

HAGHMAN, or HAWMAN, NICHOLAS, was probably the son of Alan de Haghman, and Amicia his wife, as in 6 Edward II., 1313, he was parson of the parish of Eversley in Hampshire, of the manor and advowson of which Alan and Amicia became possessed in 5 Edward I.

He was constituted a baron of the Exchequer on October 3, 1336, 10 Edward III.; but his name was not included in the new patent on January 20, 1341. (*App. Rot. Orig.* i. 195]; *Abb. Placit.* 191.)

HALE, SIMON DE, whose principal estate was situate in Yorkshire, was sheriff of that county till 8 Henry III. In the next year he was at the head of the justices itinerant appointed to no less than ten counties, and in 11 Henry III. to three counties more. (*Rot. Claus.* i, 450, 630, ii. 45–213.) It is manifest, from his being placed at the head of the lists, that he was something more than an ordinary justice itinerant.

In 10 Henry III. he was appointed sheriff of Wiltshire, and his people in Yorkshire were exempted from the rates of the county and hundred during his absence. He is last mentioned in 1240, when he again appears as one of the justices itinerant before whom a fine was levied at York.

HALE, MATTHEW. This eminent judge, whom all look up to as one of the brightest luminaries of the law, as well for the soundness of his learning as for the excellence of his life, descended from an old and respectable family in Gloucestershire. His grandfather, Robert Hale, a wealthy clothier at Wootton-under-Edge, had five sons, the second of whom, also Robert, a barrister of Lincoln's Inn, had by his wife, Joan, daughter of Matthew Poyntz, Esq., of Alderley, an only son, the future judge, who was left an orphan five years after his birth. He was born at Alderley on November 1, 1609, and on his father's death he was placed under the guardianship of his kinsman, Anthony Kingscot, Esq., who first sent him to a puritanical grammar school at Wootton-under-Edge, and then to Magdalen Hall, Oxford, intending him for the clerical profession. He did not stay long enough to take a degree; but, like most young men, he was attracted by the pleasures incident to his age. He was expert in athletic exercises, and it is related of him that one of his masters, who was his tenant, having told him that he was better at his own trade than himself, Hale, proud of the praise, promised him the house he lived in if he could hit him a blow on the head. The master of course succeeded in doing so, and gained possession of the house, while Hale received an early lesson how to estimate a flattering tongue. He soon discarded the idea of becoming a divine, and determined on a soldier's life, an inclination which he would probably have followed had not a family lawsuit taken him up to London to consult Serjeant Glanville. That learned man soon observed his superior judgment and peculiar fitness for the study of the law, and advising him to adopt it as his profession, Hale entered himself at Lincoln's Inn, and was called to the bar on May 17, 1636.

During this interval he forsook all his former vanities, which had never been tainted with any vice or immorality, and devoted himself wholly to the improvement of his life and the study of his profession. He himself states that for the first two years his application extended to sixteen hours a day, which, nearly bringing him to his grave, he was obliged to reduce to eight hours, and acknowledged that he thought six hours, well used, were sufficient. (*Seward's Anecdotes*, iv. 416.) At the same time he paid strict attention to his religious duties, never once missing attendance at church on Sunday for six-and-thirty years. As a diversion from his abstruser studies he made himself a proficient in mathematics and various branches of philosophy, and acquired considerable skill in medical and anatomical knowledge, not neglecting history, both ancient and modern, nor, particularly, the varied forms of theological doctrines.

Besides introducing him into many desirable friendships, his deep learning and known industry soon insured him good practice at the bar. He was entirely a loyalist, though he religiously and upon principle avoided taking any part in the dissensions of the times. In 1643 he was engaged for Archbishop Laud, and is said to have composed the speech in defence which was spoken by Mr. Herne. In 1647 he was one of the counsel appointed to defend the eleven members, and he also appeared for Lord Macguire at his trial in the King's Bench for high treason. (*State Trials*, iv. 577, 702 ; *Whitelocke*, 258.) According to the statement of Burnet, he offered to plead for the king on his trial; and Serjeant Runnington (*Edit. of Hale's Common Law*) suggests that he furnished his royal client with the line of defence which he actually adopted, in denying the jurisdiction of the court, which of course precluded the appearance of any counsel. In the subsequent trials of the Duke of Hamilton, the Earl of Holland, Lord Capel, and others for high treason against the parliament, he was employed in their defence, and his arguments were urged with so much boldness and energy that the attorney-general threatened him for appearing against the government. Hale indignantly retorted that he was 'pleading in defence of the laws, which they professed they would maintain and preserve ; and that he was doing his duty to his client, and was not to be daunted with threatenings.'

Notwithstanding his monarchical principles, he deemed it his duty to acquiesce in the existing government, and not to engage in any faction. He therefore subscribed the engagement to be true and faithful to the Commonwealth, and was accordingly permitted to appear before the High Court of Justice in 1651 to take exceptions to the charge against the Presbyterian Christopher Love—a privilege refused to Mr. Archer and Mr. Waller, because they had not complied with that formality. (*State Trials*, v. 211.) Though thus acting against them, the parliament showed their estimation of his legal knowledge by placing Hale in the next year at the head of the committee for the prevention of the delays and expenses of law proceedings. (*Whitelocke*, 520.)

When Cromwell assumed absolute power Hale was one of the many who were disgusted at his usurpation. The protector, however, who was no doubt sincere in his wish to strengthen his government by having men of known ability and honesty on the bench, and seeing what influence Hale exercised by his learning and his courage, resolved to employ him as one of the judges. Hale naturally hesitated to accept the proffered office, but on the representation that he would not be required to acknowledge the usurper's authority, and at the urgent solicitation of Sir Orlando Bridgeman and other loyalists, backed by the opinion of his clerical friends, he determined to accept the appointment, upon the conviction that it was absolutely necessary that under all governments property should be secured, and justice impartially administered.

Accordingly, on January 25, 1654, he was made a judge of the Common Pleas. He altogether refused to try offenders against the state, not recognising the present authorities, and boldly and conscientiously administered justice between man and man, regardless of the party to which either was attached. He convicted and hung one of Cromwell's soldiers for a foul murder of a king's man, and he dismissed a jury because he discovered that it had been returned by Cromwell's order and not by the sheriff. The protector on his return from the circuit told him 'he was not fit to be a judge,' to which he simply answered 'that it was very true.' However angry and dissatisfied Cromwell might be, he could not afford to dismiss so popular a man, and was obliged, perhaps was glad, to pass over his refusal in 1655 to assist at the trial of Colonel Penruddock at Exeter. Hale therefore was continued on the bench, but upon the death of Cromwell in September 1658, not even the importunities of his friends and brother judges could induce him to accept a new commission from the Protector Richard.

In the July (1654) after he became a judge, which did not then disqualify him for a seat in parliament, Hale was returned for his native county. The first business of this parliament was the consideration of the system of government to be adopted. Violent discussions followed, till Mr. Justice Hale proposed an expedient that seemed reasonable to the majority. It was to the effect 'that the single person in possession should exercise the supreme magistracy, with such powers, limitations, and qualifications as the parliament should afterwards declare.' But the protector, fearing lest his power should thus be gradually taken from him, shut up the house, and would not re-admit the members till each had subscribed an unconditional recognition of his authority. Many refused to sign, and among them most probably was Hale, as his name does not subsequently appear either as a speaker or as a member of any of the committees. He was not elected to the only other parliament called by Cromwell, in 1656; but in that summoned by Protector Richard in January and dissolved in April 1659 he was chosen for the university of Oxford, but he seems to have been silent amid the dissensions of that short session. Upon the election of the Convention Parliament, in April 1660, Hale was again returned for Gloucestershire. In that he was most active, being selected as a manager of the conference with the Lords which led to the return of the king, and as one of the committee to examine the acts of government lately passed, and to report how the legal proceedings that had taken place might, notwithstanding all irregularities, be confirmed. (*Burton*, i. xxxii. iii. 142; *Parl. Hist.* iv. 24.) Burnet says (i. 88) that he attempted to bind Charles to certain conditions, by moving for a committee to look into the concessions that had been offered by the late king during the war, and to suggest such propositions as should be sent over to the king. This motion, leading to a settlement which might have prevented much future mischief, was dexterously counteracted by Monk.

On the arrival of Charles, though Hale was not immediately replaced in his judicial position, he was at once confirmed in his degree of serjeant, and in that character was included in the commission for the trial of the regicides. At the termination of those doleful proceedings he was, in spite of his declared reluctance, constituted chief baron of the Exchequer on November 7 (1 *Siderfin*, 3, 4), and so great was his desire to escape the honour of knighthood that he avoided the king's presence, until Lord Clarendon contrived an unexpected meeting with his majesty, who immediately conferred upon him the accustomed distinction.

In every stage of his career Hale was accustomed to put into writing his reflections on the incidents of the time, and to lay down regulations for his conduct. Among many excellent rules for his guidance as a judge was one 'to abhor all private solicitations.' Acting on this, he rebuked a noble duke who applied to him about a cause in which his grace was concerned, who, complaining of his rough reception, was told by the king to be 'content that he was no worse used, for he believed he himself should have been used no better if he had solicited him in any of his own causes.' Another of his rules was 'not to be biassed with compassion to the poor or favour to the rich;' and so strict was he in its application that he insisted on paying for a buck that was presented to him on the circuit before he tried a cause in which the donor was a party.

After presiding in the Exchequer for nearly eleven years, he was promoted to the chief justiceship of the King's Bench on May 18, 1671. He remained in that dignified post for almost five years, when his bad health and increasing infirmities induced him to resign it on February 21, 1676, in opposition to the wishes of the king and the solicitations of his friends and colleagues. But he felt that he could not conscientiously retain a position the duties of which he was not able fully to perform, and the near approach of death made him desirous of leisure for its contemplation. Sir Heneage Finch speaks of him as 'a chief justice of so indefatigable an industry, so invincible a patience, so exemplary an integrity, and so magnanimous a contempt of worldly things, without which no man can be truly great; and to all this a man that was so absolutely a master of the science of the law, and even of the most abstruse and hidden parts of it, that one may truly say of his knowledge in the law what St. Austin said of St. Hierome's knowledge in divinity—"Quod Hieronymus nescivit, nullus mortalium unquam scivit."' These and other contemporaneous eulogies have been echoed by almost every writer during the two centuries that have elapsed since he flourished, and the more fully have been laid open to the world the principles that guided him in his judicial career, and the daily practices and habits of his private life, the more confirmed has

Y

been the admiration of his character, so that he is scarcely ever named except in terms of respect and veneration.

Surving his resignation scarcely ten months, Sir Matthew died on Christmas Day 1676. By his special direction his remains were interred in the churchyard of Alderley.

A list of his numerous writings, few of which were published during his life, is given in most of the memoirs from which this sketch is compiled. Those which most will be remembered are his 'History of the Pleas of the Crown;' his 'Preface to Rolle's Abridgement,' containing excellent advice for the guidance of young students, in whom he ever took a special interest; and his 'Analysis of the Law,' which formed the basis of Blackstone's 'Commentaries.' His philosophical and religious works eminently show his varied learning and his contemplative piety, and the MSS. which he bequeathed to Lincoln's Inn library afford abundant testimony of his unwearied industry in collecting and transcribing the valuable records of the kingdom.

Of his two wives he had issue by the first only. She was Anne, daughter of Sir Henry Moore, of Fawley in Berkshire, and grandchild of Sir Francis Moore, the famous serjeant-at-law in the reign of James I. Two only of their ten children survived the judge. Late in life he married, secondly, Anne, daughter of Joseph Bishop, of Fawley, described by Baxter as 'a woman of no estate, but suitable to his disposition, to be to him as a nurse.' She survived him for many years, and is spoken of in his will in the most affectionate terms. The male line of his family has been long extinct.

HALE, BERNARD, was born in 1677 at King's Walden in Hertfordshire, an estate which had been in the possession of the family since the time of Queen Elizabeth. He was the eighth son of William Hale, who represented the county in 1661 and 1678, and of Mary, daughter of Jeremiah Elwes, Esq., of Roxby in Lincolnshire. Having entered the society of Gray's Inn, he took his degree of barrister in February 1704. He gained so considerable a reputation as an able lawyer that on June 28, 1722, he was constituted chief baron of the Irish Exchequer, where he remained for nearly three years. From this position he was removed on June 1, 1725, to the English Court of Exchequer as one of the puisne barons, when he was knighted. He sat there little more than four years, and died on November 7, 1729, at Abbots Langley, in the church of which his remains are interred.

He married Anne, daughter of J. Thoresby, Esq., of Northamptonshire, and left a large family.

HALES, CHRISTOPHER, derived his name from a place so called in Norfolk, where Roger de Hales possessed property in the reign of Henry II. Before the close of Edward III.'s reign the family had removed into Kent and was settled at Halden, near Tenterden. The unfortunate Robert de Hales, prior of St. John of Jerusalem and treasurer of England under Richard II., who was barbarously murdered by the rebels in 1381, was of this family, and from his brother Sir Nicholas descended no less than three eminent lawyers who graced the judicial bench—Christopher and John in the reign of Henry VIII., and James in that of Edward VI.

Christopher Hales was the son of Thomas, the younger brother of the father of John, so that the two judges were first cousins. His mother was Alicia, daughter of Humphrey Eveas. Receiving his legal education at Gray's Inn, he rose to be an ancient in 1516, and reader in 1524. On August 14, 1525, he became solicitor-general, and attorney-general on June 3, 1529. During the seven years that he filled this office he had to conduct the proceedings against several illustrious persons who had incurred the king's displeasure. He prosecuted Wolsey by an indictment to which the cardinal made no defence; he appeared for the king against Sir Thomas More and Bishop Fisher on their last arraignment; and the trials of Queen Anne Boleyn and those charged with being implicated with her occurred during the last few months of his official tenure (*State Trials*, i. 370, 389); but history charges him with no harshness in performing the delicate duties thus devolving upon him.

He succeeded Thomas Cromwell as master of the Rolls on July 10, 1536, and retained the place for the five remaining years of his life.

He died in June 1541, and was buried at Hackington, or St. Stephen's, near Canterbury. His large possessions, many of which were granted to him by the king on the dissolution of the monasteries, were divided among the three daughters he had by his wife Elizabeth, the daughter of John Caunton, an alderman of London. (*Weever*, 260; *Hasted*.)

HALES, JOHN, is described by Wotton (i. 219) to have been the first cousin of Christopher, but Hasted makes him the uncle of Christopher, representing him as the elder brother of Christopher's father, instead of the son of that elder brother. If Hasted is right, John's father was Henry Hales, and his mother Julian, daughter of Richard Capel, of Lenden, near Tenterden; if Wotton is right, Henry was his grandfather, and another John was his father.

There is a curious entry with regard to them in the books of Gray's Inn, of which they both were members, by which it appears that in July 1529 John Hales communicated to the society that Sir Thomas Nevill would accept Christopher Hales, then attorney-general, to be his bedfellow in his chamber there.

John Hales became a reader in that house in 1514, and again in 1520. Residing at the manor of the Dungeon, or Dane John, near Canterbury, he was the acting steward of the abbey of St. Augustine. As he does not appear as an advocate in the Reports, he probably held an office in the Exchequer, the barons of that court being at that time usually selected from among those who were conversant with that department. He attained the place of third baron on October 1, 1522, and was promoted to be second baron on May 14, 1528. He still held this position on August 1, 1539, as John Smith then received a grant of the office in reversion on his death or retirement. (*Orig.* 273, 292; *Rymer*, iii. 788.) He probably died shortly afterwards, John Smith taking his place in the next Michaelmas Term.

By his wife Isabel, daughter of Stephen Harris (Harvey, according to Hasted), he had four sons. His eldest, James, is the next-mentioned judge, and the descendants of two of the others respectively were raised to baronetcies in 1611 and 1660; but both have become extinct. (*Wotton*, i. 219, iii. 96, 162.)

HALES, JAMES. James Hales was the eldest son of the above John Hales, by his wife Isabel Harris, or Harvey. Like his father, he studied the law at Gray's Inn, where he was three times reader—in 1532, in 1537, and in 1540, when he assumed the decree of the coif. In 1544 he was made one of the king's serjeants, and soon after had a grant from Henry VIII. of the manor of Clavertigh, with lands called Monken Lands in Eleham, Kent. (*Hasted*, viii. 106.)

At the coronation of Edward VI. he was one of the forty who were made knights of the Bath. He was selected in 1549 as one of the commissioners 'super hæreticâ pravitate' (*Rymer*, xv. 181, 250); and having on the 10th of May following been advanced to the bench by Edward VI. as a justice of the Common Pleas, he sat there during the rest of the reign. He was one of the judges who pronounced the sentence of deprivation against Bishop Gardiner (*State Trials*, i. 630) in February 1551, and had reason to find that that prelate when he attained power did not forget those before whom he was arraigned.

Although firmly attached to the doctrines of the Reformation, and conscious as he must have been of the danger of a revulsion, should a princess who had even through persecution refused to renounce the ancient ritual succeed to the throne, Sir James Hales, when called upon by the Duke of Northumberland to join the other judges in authenticating the instrument by which the succession was to be changed and the crown was to be placed on a Protestant head, boldly refused to affix his signature, declaring the attempt to be both unlawful and unjust.

The same firmness he had thus shown in supporting the succession according to law, he exhibited immediately afterwards at the assizes in Kent in reference to the statutes relative to religion. Some indictments having been brought before him against certain persons for nonconformity, he in his charge to the grand jury, regardless of the changes which might be expected under the present government, courageously pointed out what the law then actually was, and what it devolved upon them in the exercise of their duty to do. Although this was certainly not the way to 'stand well in her grace's favour,' yet the queen appointed him one of the commission to try Sir Andrew Dudley and others for high treason in August, and on October 4 granted him his new patent in the Common Pleas, thus apparently overlooking his neglect of her known wishes, and doing justice to the honesty of his principles. But this would not satisfy the bigoted chancellor Bishop Gardiner, before whom two days afterwards he came with his fellows to take his oath of office. On that occasion the harsh prelate required him 'to make his purgation,' and a 'colloquy' took place, in which the judge justified his conduct, speaking plainly of his intentions to support the queen and the law, but at the same time to adhere to his religion, while the bishop taunted him with his 'lacking no conscience,' and, after threatening but not moving him, dismissed him without his oath.

Within a few days the bishop, in a true persecuting spirit, had him committed to prison, where his incarceration lasted several months, during which many attempts were made to induce him to embrace the Popish doctrine, not only by working on his fears of the torments prepared for those who persisted in their heresy, but by the earnest persuasions of Foster, a Hampshire gentleman sent for the purpose, of Bishop Day, and of his brother judge Sir William Portman. He was at last overcome, but his recantation had such an effect upon his mind that he attempted in the absence of his servant to kill himself with his penknife. The servant's return saved his life, and being discharged from confinement, he was 'brought to the queen's presence, who gave him words of great comfort.' His release took place about April 1554, but his mind was not at ease, and in the course of the next year, while staying at his nephew's house at Thanington, near Canterbury, he in a fit of despondency drowned himself in a river in the parish of St. Mildred.

There is another account, that Sir James's death was occasioned by his crossing the river over a narrow bridge, from which he accidentally fell and was drowned, at the age of eighty-five. (*Holinshed*, iv. 8; *State Trials*, i. 714; *Hasted*; *Burnet*.) Whichever of these stories is the true one, it is certain that a verdict of *felo de se* was pronounced by the coroner's inquest; for there are two cases reported—The Bishop of Chichester *v.* Webb (2 Dyer, 107), and Lady Margaret Hales *v.* Petit (Plowden, 253)—the arguments and judgments in which proceeded on that finding by the jury. The hair-splitting subtleties urged in these cases are supposed to have suggested the argument which Shakspeare puts into the gravedigger's mouth in Hamlet.

The name of Sir James's wife was Margaret; but whether she was the daughter and heir of Thomas Hales of Henley-upon-Thames, or one of the daughters and coheirs of Oliver Wood, called by Hasted a judge of the Common Pleas under Henry VIII. (there being no such judge), Hasted and Wotton differ; but both authors agree that the judge left an only son Humphrey, and that the line became extinct in 1665.

HALS, JOHN, had a seat at Kenedon, in the parish of Sherford, in Devonshire. His name appears in the Year Books from 11 Henry IV., 1409, and he was appointed one of the king's serjeants in 1413. On May 5, 1423, 1 Henry VI., he was made a judge of the Common Pleas, and on January 21, 1424, was removed to the King's Bench. But, notwithstanding the latter appointment, he seems to have continued to act in the Common Pleas also till Hilary 1425, a fine having been levied before him in that term. (*Orig.* 46; *Acts Privy Council*, iv. 71, 172.) His name occurs in the Year Books till Hilary 1434, in which year he probably died, as a new judge of the King's Bench was appointed in the following July.

He married the daughter of — Mewy, of Whitchurch, and his second son John afterwards became Bishop of Lichfield and Coventry.

HALTOFT, GILBERT, is stated by Dugdale to be dead on November 30, 1458, 37 Henry VI., but he gives no information when he entered on the office of baron of the Exchequer. The Exchequer list, however, dates his admission in Michaelmas 1447; and in the act of resumption of the crown grants, which passed in the parliament of November 1449, he is described as secondary baron, and 20 marks out of 40*l.* yearly, which had been granted to him by letters patent for life out of the ferms of London and Middlesex, were specially excepted. In 31 Henry VI. he received a further grant of 20*l.* yearly for life, which also was excepted from another act of resumption passed three years after. The last mention which is found of his name is in the latter year, when the Commons prayed that he might be appointed one of the administrators of the property of Humphrey, Duke of Gloucester. (*Rot. Parl.* v. 196, 317, 339.) In the four last years of his life Bishop Grey appointed him one of the judges of the Isle of Ely. (*Cole's MSS.* xxv. 47.)

HAMBURY, HENRY DE, was one of the sons of Geoffrey de Hambury, who resided at Hambury, or Hanbury, a parish in Worcestershire. (*Parl. Writs*, ii. p. ii. 364.) He was made one of the judges of the King's Bench in Ireland in 17 Edward II., and was raised to the office of chief justice of the Common Pleas there in the following year. (*Cal. Rot. Pat.* 94, 96.) He was soon afterwards removed from that country, being appointed a judge of the King's Bench in England in 2 Edward III., 1328. (*Abb. Rot. Orig.* ii. 24.) The cause of his elevation to the bench may have been his connection with Thomas, Earl of Lancaster, for his adherence to whom he had received a pardon in 12 Edward II. He is mentioned as being alive in 26 Edward III., in the herald's visitation of Worcestershire, but he must have long retired from the bench, as the Liberate Roll does not name him among the judges in 12 Edward III.

His lineal descendants are divided into several opulent branches, two of which have been recently ennobled—one having been created Baron Bateman, of Shobden in the county of Hereford; and the other, Baron Sudely, of Toddington in the county of Gloucester.

HAMILTON, WILLIAM DE, had property in Cambridge, and his name is first recorded as a justice itinerant, but for pleas of the forest only, in Hampshire and Wiltshire in 8 Edward I., 1280. In 10 Edward I. he was custos of the bishopric of Winchester, and of the abbey of Hide. (*Abb. Rot. Orig.* i. 401.) He seems afterwards to have become a clerk in the Chancery, as it was probably in that capacity that the Great Seal was occasionally placed under his care. There is one letter addressed to him as the king's vice-chancellor, dated November 12, 1286 (7 *Report Pub. Rec., App.* xii. 242, 251); and another from the regent Edmund, Earl of Cornwall, with directions relating to the Chancery. On Bishop Burnel's death, October 25, 1292, the Great Seal was delivered into the wardrobe under William de Hamilton's seal; and the record expressly states that he sealed the writs therewith for the few days that intervened before his accompanying the chancellor's remains to Wells as one of his executors. (*Rot. Parl.* i. 117.)

During the absences also of the next chancellor, John de Langton, from March 4 to 30, 1297, and from February 20 to June 16, 1299, he held the Seal and performed the necessary duties in the meantime.

He received the usual ecclesiastical preferments which were conferred on this class of officers, being in 1292 made archdeacon of the West Riding of York, and in December 1298 appointed dean of York. He was also dean of the church of St. Burian in Cornwall. (*Le Neve*, 313, 322; *Cole's Documents*, 421.) On December 29, 1304, the king named him chancellor; but, being then absent, the Seal was ordered to be deposited in the wardrobe till his arrival, and it was delivered to him on January 16, 1305. He held it till his death, on April 20, 1307. (*Madox*, i. 74.)

HANKFORD, WILLIAM, was born at a place of that name at Bulkworthy, in the parish of Buckland Brewer, in Devonshire, and was the second son of Richard Hankford, of an ancient and wealthy family, to whose large estates he eventually succeeded. The first mention of him is as one of the king's serjeants-at-law in 14 Richard II., 1390. In January 1398 he gave his opinion, by desire of the parliament, on the answers made by the judges to the questions propounded to them by Chief Justice Tresilian, which he declared to be good and loyal, and such as he himself would have given under the circumstances. (*Rot. Parl.* iii. 358.) It is to be hoped that this opinion was prompted rather by his fears of the danger that hung over him had he pronounced any other, than by the temptation of being raised to the seat on the bench of the Common Pleas then vacant. He was, however, appointed to fill it on the 6th of May following. Henry IV. renewed his patent on the very day he assumed the throne, feeling it a point of policy not to interfere so early in the judicial appointments; and Hankford was made a knight of the Bath at the coronation.

He continued in the Court of Common Pleas throughout that reign, and on the accession of Henry V. he was removed from the Common Pleas to the head of the Court of King's Bench, his patent being dated March 29, 1413, eight days after the death of Henry IV. He presided in the court during the whole of the reign, and was re-appointed at the commencement of that of Henry VI., being the fourth king under whom he had held a judicial seat. In a very few months, however, his career was closed, his death occurring on December 20, 1422, not four months after the accession. He was buried in the church of Monkleigh. He had a high reputation both in his moral and legal character.

A very improbable account of his death is given by his biographers. He is stated to have become weary of his life, and, with an intention of getting rid of it, to have given strict orders to his keeper to shoot any person found at night in his park who would not stand when challenged, and then to have thrown himself in his keeper's way, and to have been shot dead in pursuance of his own commands. The cause of this suicidal conduct is represented to have been his 'direful apprehensions of dangerous approaching evils,' which could only have arisen from a diseased imagination, as there was nothing at that time in the political horizon to portend the disasters of thirty years' distance. Holinshed introduces this event as happening in 1470, 10 Edward IV., very nearly fifty years after the death of the chief justice. The story, however, was long believed in the neighbourhood of his seat at Annery, in Monkleigh, and an old oak bearing his name was shown in the park, where it was said he had fallen. As Chief Justice Danby did actually disappear about that time, it is not improbable that the story applies to him, Holinshed having mistaken the name.

He left two sons, Richard and John, the first of whom had a daughter Anne, who married the Earl of Ormond; and their daughter Margaret, marrying Sir William Boleyn, was the grandmother of Anne Boleyn, the mother of Queen Elizabeth.

HANNEMERE, DAVID, was the grandson of Sir John Mackfel, constable of Carnarvon Castle in the reign of Edward I., who assumed the name of Hannemere from the town so called in Flintshire, which belonged to him. Philip, the youngest of his three sons, was ultimately his sole heir, and by his wife Agnes, daughter and heir of David ap Rice ap Evans ap Jones, had several children, of whom this David was the elder. His name appears as an advocate in the Year Books from 45 Edward III., and on the accession of Richard II. he was appointed one of the king's serjeants, and 'narrator' in all the courts. (*Cal. Rot. Pat.* 197.) On February 26, 1383, he was constituted a judge of the King's Bench, and from that time till the parliament of October 1386 he was among the triers of petitions. As his successor in the King's Bench was named in the following year, he probably died in the interval.

By his wife Angharad, daughter of Lhyvelin Dhu ap Griffith ap Jorworth Voell, he had, besides a daughter Margaret, who married the renowned Owen Glendower, two sons, Griffith and Jenkin, from the latter of whom sprang a long succession of knightly descendants. Two of these were created baronets, one of them in 1620, now extinct by the death in 1746 of Sir Thomas Hanmer, who was speaker of the House of Commons in the reign of Queen Anne, and distinguished by his elegant and correct edition of the works of Shakspeare; and the other granted in 1774, by whose descendant the title is now enjoyed. (*Wotton*, i. 411.)

HANNEN, JAMES, one of the present judges of the Queen's Bench, is the son of James Hannen, Esq., of London, and was born in 1821. After receiving the earlier part of his education at St. Paul's School, he finished it at the university of Heidelberg. Adopting the legal profession, he was called to the bar at the Middle Temple on January 14, 1848, and joined the Home Circuit. During the twenty years that he practised in the courts he distinguished himself by the solidity of his advice, and the readiness and ability of his advocacy. Though he never accepted the silk gown, which has become a common aspiration, nor was ever in parliament, yet, notwithstanding he was well known as a liberal in politics, he was selected solely for his legal acquirements by a conservative government to fill the vacancy in the Court of Queen's Bench occasioned by the death of Mr. Justice Shee. He was appointed on February 25, 1868, and was soon after knighted.

He married Mary Elizabeth, daughter of N. Winsland, Esq.

HANNIBAL, THOMAS, in 1504 entered the university of Cambridge, where he took the degree of Doctor of Laws in 1514. At the former date he received a prebend in the church of York, and at the latter became chancellor of the diocese of Worcester. In 1522 both he and Dr. John Clerke were engaged at the Roman court in the double capacity of King Henry's orators and private agents for Cardinal Wolsey. Both of them were rewarded in succession with the mastership of the Rolls, Hannibal following Clerke in that office on October 9, 1523, and retaining it till June 26, 1527, when he voluntarily surrendered it. In 1524 he presented to the king a rose of gold sent by the pope. (*Rymer*, xiv. 10; *Athen. Oxon.* ii. 735, 771; *Fasti*, i. 39.)

HARCOURT, SIMON (LORD HARCOURT), was directly descended from Bernard, of the royal blood of Saxony, who with other lordships received that of Harcourt, near Falaise, from Rollo on his settlement in Normandy. His descendant, Robert de Harcourt, accompanied William on his invasion of England, and his family had flourished during the succeeding period in knightly distinction, and had been resident during the twelfth century at Stanton, near Oxford, from that time called Stanton-Harcourt. The chancellor was the son of Sir Philip Harcourt, by his first wife, Anne, daughter of Sir William Waller, the parliamentary general. The family estate, by one side or the other in the previous troubles, had been seriously diminished at the time of the Restoration.

Simon Harcourt was born in 1660, and while receiving his education at Pembroke College, Oxford, was admitted in 1676 as a member of the Inner Temple. He was called to the bar in 1683, and in 1688 he was elected recorder of Abingdon. (*Athen. Oxon.* iv. 214.) That borough returned him to parliament in 1690, and in all the future parliaments of King William's reign. That he was strongly imbued with tory principles he evinced on his first entrance into the house, by the objections he then raised in the discussions on the bills for the settlement of the government, and afterwards in 1696 by powerful speeches in opposition to the bill of attainder against Sir John Fenwick, as a proceeding both unconstitutional and unjust. He carried his party feeling so far that he declined in the first instance to subscribe the Association of the Commons on the discovery of the assassination plot.

The tide of party turned, however, towards the latter end of King William's reign. The consequence of this was first the removal, and then the impeachment, of Lord Somers, the duty of carrying up the charge against whom to the House of Lords was entrusted to Harcourt, to whose management or mismanagement (as it may be variously considered) may probably be attributed the non-appearance of the prosecutors at the trial. (*State Trials*, v. 582–1314.) At this time he had acquired a complete ascendency, not only in the house, but in general estimation. His wit and eloquence, in addition to his legal ability, were so universally acknowledged that in after-years they were specially brought forward in the preamble to his patent of peerage as a principal reason for his advancement.

With the accession of Queen Anne the tories were established in power, and Harcourt was at once admitted to partake it, being made solicitor-general on June 1, 1702, and knighted. In the first parliament of that reign he was again returned for Abingdon, but in the second and third he sat for Bossiney in Cornwall. He supported the extraordinary claims of the Commons to decide on the rights of electors in the famous Aylesbury case, and has the credit of drawing the bill for the Union with Scotland in such a manner as to prevent a discussion of the articles upon which the commissioners had agreed. While solicitor-general he acted as chairman of the Buckinghamshire quarter sessions, and of his charges to the grand jury there are manuscript notes in the British Museum. In April 1707 he succeeded to the post of attorney-general, but before a year elapsed he resigned it, in February 1708, on the change of ministry and the admission of the whigs into the cabinet. In the new parliament called in November of that year he was returned again for Abingdon, but on a petition against him by his whig opponent, the house, notwithstanding the majority of legal votes at the close of the election were palpably in his favour, decided against him. He thus became the victim of an iniquitous system he had himself encouraged when in power in former parliaments, by which the faction in the ascendant decided on all petitions in favour of their own partisan. The Duke of Marlborough soon after removed him from the stewardship of the manor of Woodstock, which he had held for some time. (*Burnet*, v. 10, 48, 287, 345; *Parl. Hist.* vi. 264, 778; *Luttrell*, vi. 442.)

Before the close of that parliament he was elected member for Cardigan, but during his recess from the house the absurd impeachment of Dr. Sacheverell was resolved on, and Sir Simon was thus enabled to appear as his leading counsel at the bar of the House of Lords, and by a powerful argument to expose the folly of prosecuting his vain and silly client. This prosecution was the deathblow of the whigs. The tories were restored to power, and Sir Simon on September 19, 1710, resumed his office of attorney-general. He was returned to the new parliament for Abingdon, but before it met the Great Seal was delivered into his hands on October 19, with the title of lord keeper. He then took up his residence in Powis House, Lincoln's Inn Fields. (*State Trials*, xv. 196; *Luttrell*, vi. 620, 630, 644.)

Before he was solicitor-general his name only once occurs in the 'State Trials,' and after he obtained office there are only three cases in which he acted besides that of Dr. Sacheverell. (*State Trials*, xiii. 1084, xiv. 561, 989, 1100, xv. 196.)

The new lord keeper presided in the House of Lords for nearly a year without a title, but on September 3, 1711, he was raised to the peerage as Baron Harcourt of Stanton-Harcourt. On April 7, 1713, the queen changed his title of lord keeper to lord chancellor, which he retained till her death on August 1, 1714, steering cautiously amidst the dissensions in the cabinet and through the agitating scenes by which the last months of her reign were troubled. Although as chancellor he was forced to take the formal proceedings necessary for proclaiming the Hanoverian king, there was too much reason for believing that he had previously joined in the intrigue with Bolingbroke and Atterbury to restore the exiled family.

The lords justices however replaced him in his position as lord chancellor; and, notwithstanding the suspicion attaching to him, he escaped the consequences with which his colleagues were visited, and received no other punishment than an immediate discharge from his office on the arrival of George I. The king made his first entry into London on September 20, and on the next day he sent to Lord Harcourt for the Seal, which was delivered to Lord Cowper. Towards his old coadjutors he acted a friendly part, managing to defeat the impeachment of Oxford, and procuring a qualified pardon for Bolingbroke. (*Lord Raymond*, 1318; *Parl. Hist.* vii. 485.)

After some years, when the Hanoverian succession was recognised by the great majority of the people, he joined the whig party under Sir Robert Walpole, which procured him from his old allies the nickname of the Trimmer. His change of politics was accompanied, on July 24, 1721, by an advance in the peerage to the dignity of viscount, and an increase of his retiring pension from two to four thousand a year. To that administration he continued his support through the remainder of the reign, though he never held any other official position than that of one of the lords justices during the king's occasional visits to his German dominions. He survived George I. not quite two months, when, being seized with paralysis, he died at his house in Cavendish Square on July 28, 1727, and was buried at Stanton-Harcourt.

With undoubted abilities and a power of eloquence universally acknowledged, Lord Harcourt's reputation as a judge is not very great, nor are his decisions held in high estimation at the present day. That he was kind and amiable in his disposition, polished in his manners, and of social habits may be inferred from the number of friends that circled around him, from his being a frequenter of several literary and political clubs, and from his intimate association with Pope, Swift, Philips, Gay, and the other wits by which that age was distinguished.

Lord Harcourt was married three times —first, to Rebecca, daughter of Mr. Thomas Clark; secondly to Elizabeth, daughter of Richard Spencer, Esq., and widow of Richard Anderson, Esq.; and lastly, to Elizabeth, daughter of Sir Thomas Vernon, of Twickenham Park, and widow of Sir John Walter, of Saresden in Oxfordshire, Bart. He had issue by his first wife only, and, his son Simon having died before him, he was succeeded by his grandson, to whose other titles an earldom was added in 1749. These honours became extinct in 1830.

HARDRES, ROBERT DE, was in 1185 one of the custodes of the see of Coventry, then vacant, and possessed of property at Hadleigh in Suffolk. (*Madox*, i. 116, 309.) He was one of the justices itinerant in the county of Lincoln in 1 and 8 Richard I., 1189-96. (*Ibid.* 704; *Pipe Roll*, 69.)

He held the prebend of Lochton in the church of Lincoln, and died about 9 John. He derived his name from Hardres, a parish near Canterbury, and was no doubt a branch of the family who held the manor there under the Earls of Clare. They assumed the name about 1180, and several of them held a high position during the following reigns. One of their descendants was sheriff of the county in the reign of Elizabeth, and another was created a baronet by Charles I. in 1642. The title, however, became extinct in the early part of the reign of George III. (*Hasted*, iii. 732.)

HARDWICKE, EARL OF. *See* P. YORKE.

HARE, NICHOLAS, traces his descent in England to Jervis, Earl of Hare-court, or Harcourt, who accompanied William the Conqueror in his invasion of this island. He was the eldest son of John Hare, of Homersfield in Suffolk, and Elizabeth Fortescue his wife. Educated at Cambridge, he entered the Inner Temple, where he became reader in 1532. He received the honour of knighthood about the year 1539, and on April 28, 1540, he was elected speaker of the House of Commons, to which he was returned as member for Norfolk. He presided also in the following session, his speech at the close of which affords a curious specimen of the inflated oratory of the period. (*Parl. Hist.* i. 546.)

In September 1540 he was one in a commission into Wales to examine what jewels, plate, and ornaments were embezzled from the shrine of St. David's. (*Acts Privy Council*, vii. 46, 85.) At this time he was chief justice of Chester, and he was soon after made master of Requests, which he held during the remainder of Henry's and the whole of Edward's reign. Fortunately for himself, he was not called upon to witness the will of the latter, and was not implicated in the measures taken to place Lady Jane Grey on the throne. On September 18, 1553, he was appointed master of the Rolls; but it would appear that his judicial position did not prevent him from opposing the queen's marriage with Philip of Spain, since Sir Nicholas Throckmorton justifies his 'misliking' of that connection by the reasons for it which he had learned from 'Master Hare' and others in parliament. If he had offended by this, he amply redeemed himself in the eyes of the court by his harsh endeavours to procure Throckmorton's conviction. (*State Trials*, i. 875-896.) His severity however at the trial overstepped its object, since it is not improbable that his refusal to examine a witness called by Throckmorton and to refer to a statute cited by him tended materially to the acquittal of the prisoner.

Sir Nicholas died as master of the Rolls on October 31, 1557, and was buried in the Temple Church. By his wife, Catherine, daughter of Sir John Bassingbourn, of Woodhall in Hertfordshire, he had three sons, all of whom dying without issue, the estate went eventually to his younger brother John, one of whose sons was ancestor of Sir Ralph Hare, of Stow Bardolph, who was created a baronet in 1641, but the title became extinct in 1764. It was however revived in 1818, and the title is now enjoyed. Another son was the father of Hugh, who was created Lord Coleraine in Ireland in 1625, but this title is also now extinct. (*Oldfield and Dyson's Tottenham*, 30, 81; *Wotton's Baronet.* ii. 208.)

HARENG, RALPH, was a justicier as early as 10 John, and fines were levied before him as late as 8 Henry III. He is mentioned as seneschal or steward of Thomas de St. Valerico in 8 John, and that he was then advancing in the king's favour appears by the committal to his custody of the two churches of Cesteskton and Mixebir, of which his son, Jordan, had been deprived on account of the interdict (*Rot. Claus.* i. 82, 114); and in less than two years he was employed in a judicial capacity. In 17 John he was appointed sheriff of the united counties of Buckingham and Bedford, and in the following year he was specially employed by the king, and the constables of the castles of Wallingford, Oxford, and Windsor were commanded to give him safe conduct on his mission. (*Rot. Pat.* 146, 192.)

From the first year of the next reign there are frequent entries of his judicial employment, and of marks of royal bounty accorded to him. (*Rot. Claus.* i. 294-489.) He died about 1230.

HARPUR, RICHARD, was the son, or grandson, it is uncertain which, of Henry, the third son of Sir John Harpur, of Rushall in the county of Stafford, descended from a very ancient Warwickshire family, which had flourished from the time of Henry I. He was a student at Barnard's Inn, whence he removed to the Inner Temple, where he was elected reader in 1554. In 1558 he was nominated serjeant, and in May 1567 he succeeded as a judge of the Common Pleas. He died on January 29, 1577, and was buried in the church at Swarkestone in Derbyshire, under a monument finely representing him in full legal costume, to which the sculptor has added unaccountably a collar of SS. By his wife, Jane, daughter of George Findern, of Findern in the same county, he left several children, the eldest of whom, Sir John, was father of Henry Harpur, of Calke in Derbyshire, who was created a baronet in 1626. The seventh possessor of the title assumed the name of Crewe in addition to his own, and the present baronet bears both names. (*Wotton's Baronet.* ii. 3; *Fairholt's Costumes*, 278.)

HART, ANTHONY, a native of St. Kitt's in the West Indies, was born about 1754. He was educated at Tunbridge School, and, studying for the legal profession, was called to the bar in 1781, and practised throughout his life in the courts of equity. Sound as a lawyer, clear in his statements, fluent if not forcible in his language, and industrious and painstaking for his clients, he obtained, both before and after he received a silk gown, a very considerable share of business. He laboured before the equity judges with indomitable perseverance for forty-six years, before his extensive legal knowledge gained him promotion; but in May 1827 he was appointed vice-chancellor of England. His merits were then so much better appreciated that on the retirement of Lord Manners, in the following October, he was raised to the lord chancellorship of Ireland. One of Lord Norbury's innumerable jokes was made on this appointment: 'That the government had treated the Irish with their wonted injustice; deprived them of what they needed, and given them what they already possessed—taken away *Manners*, and given them *Heart*.'

His judgments were much admired, and his character was plain, unostentatious, and kind. He gave such universal satisfaction that his removal in December 1830 was a subject of sincere regret to the members of his court, which was shown in a most affecting scene at his departure. He survived his retirement only one year, and died in December 1831.

HARVEY, FRANCIS, commencing his legal studies at Barnard's Inn, completed them at the Middle Temple, where he was called to the bar, and became reader in 1611. In December 1612 (at which time he resided at Northampton) he was chosen recorder of Leicester; and in 1614 he attained the degree of the coif. On October 18, 1624, he was constituted a judge of the Common Pleas. On one of his circuits he fined a whole jury 10*l*. apiece for giving perverse and wrongful acquittals in four different criminal cases; and in another he showed some indignation on hearing an assize sermon at Norwich, in which the preacher alluded to the corruption of judges, saying in his charge to the grand jury, 'It seems by the sermon we are all corrupt; but know that we can use conscience in our places as well as the best clergyman of all.' (*Borough MSS. Leicester.*) He remained in that court till his death, which took place at Northampton in August 1632. (*Croke, Car.* 268.)

HARWEDON, ROBERT DE, who held land in the forest of Bernewood, was one of the four justices of trailbaston for Gloucestershire and ten other counties, dated on April 6, 1305, 33 Edward I. (*N. Fœdera*, i. 970; *Rot. Parl.* ii. 215.) He acted as deputy to Hugh le Despenser, the justice of the forests south of Trent in the next reign, in the fifth year of which the custody of the manor of Rokele in Wiltshire, belonging to the Templars, was committed to him at an annual rent of eleven pounds, ten shillings, and fourpence. (*Ibid.* i. 321; *Abb. Rot. Orig.* i. 184; *Cal. Rot. Pat.* 78.)

HATHERLEY, LORD. See W. P. WOOD.

HATSEL, HENRY, the son of Captain Henry Hatsel, of Saltram, near Plymouth (who took a strong part in the Great Rebellion), was born in March 1641, and, being admitted a member of the Middle Temple, was called to the bar in 1667, and in 1689 was summoned to take the degree of the coif. In another eight years he was constituted a baron of the Exchequer on November 23, 1697, and knighted. He filled the seat during the remainder of William's reign, and was re-appointed on the accession of Queen Anne, on March 2, 1702. But on the 4th of the following June he suddenly received a message from Lord Keeper Wright, informing him that he might forbear sitting the next morning, the first day of term, her majesty designing his quietus. His conduct at the Surrey Assizes on the extraordinary trial of Spencer Cowper, charged with the murder of Sarah Stout, and acquitted, does not tell much in favour of his judicial capacity. He lived twelve years after his discharge, and died in April 1714.

He married Judith, daughter of Josiah Bateman, merchant of London, and widow of Sir Richard Shirley, Bart. (*Lord Raymond*, 250, 768; *Luttrell*, iv. 309, v. 181; *State Trials*, xiii. 1105.)

HATTON, CHRISTOPHER. Something less than justice has been done to the character of Sir Christopher Hatton. He has been looked upon less as a grave counsellor than as an accomplished courtier, and the popular impression with regard to him is more connected with his youthful graces than with his mature services. The prevalence of this feeling is in a considerable degree to be attributed to the jocose stanzas of our poet Gray in his fanciful account of the mansion at Stoke-Pogeis, which he erroneously supposes to have been occupied by Sir Christopher:—

Full oft within the spacious walls,
 When he had fifty winters o'er him,
My grave lord-keeper led the brawls,
 The Seal and maces danc'd before him.

His bushy beard and shoe-strings green,
 His high-crown'd hat and satin doublet,
Mov'd the stout heart of England's queen,
 Tho' Pope and Spaniard could not trouble it.

It is difficult to reverse the sentence of a poetical judge, especially when the decree is pronounced in quotable phraseology; but truth in the end will triumph, and, whatever may have been the recommendations which introduced him at court, it will be acknowledged that he preserved his position there, and obtained his elevation, by qualities more solid and accomplishments more serviceable than an elegant address or a flattering tongue.

Although the son of a private country gentleman, his lineage, as is usual with the lineage of all men who become great, was satisfactorily traced to a Norman nobleman, whose descendants were long settled in Cheshire until a younger son of one of them married the heiress of Holdenby in Northamptonshire. William Hatton, the grandson of this gentleman, was, by his wife Alice, daughter of Robert Saunders, of Harringworth, father of three sons, the youngest of whom was Sir Christopher, who by the early death of his brothers succeeded to the paternal estate.

Born in 1540, at Holdenby, he became a gentleman commoner at St. Mary's Hall, Oxford, but took no degree (*Athen. Oxon.* i. 582); and on May 29, 1560, he was admitted a member of the Inner Temple. It is uncertain whether Hatton took the degree of a barrister, because the Inner Temple registry of calls to the bar does not commence till 1567, three or four years after he had entered into the service of the queen; but, as he was clearly a member of the Temple in the following year, the probability is that he would not have remained in the house for eight years merely in the character of a student. All that is known of his early residence in the inn is, that in the Christmas of his second year, 1561, the prominent office of 'master of the game' was assigned to him in that celebrated masque at which Lord Robert Dudley, afterwards Earl of Leicester, was the chief personage. (*Dugdale's Orig.* 150.)

The date of his introduction to court is established by Sir Harris Nicolas's discovery of a warrant, dated June 30, 1564, for 'one armour fit for the body of our well-beloved servant Christopher Hatton, one of our gentlemen-pensioners,' which, however, is only to be 'delivered to him on his paying the just value thereof.' (*Cal. State Papers* [1547-80], 242.) It may be presumed, therefore, that he had previously attracted the queen's notice.

In 1568 he and four other gentlemen of the Inner Temple composed a tragedy called 'Tancred and Gismund,' which was acted before the queen, each of them taking a part in the performance. Hatton contributed the fourth act. It is plain that by this time he had ingratiated himself with Elizabeth, as in that year he was appointed keeper of Eltham Park and the Park of Horne, and had effected an exchange of his manor of Holdenby for the site of the abbey and demesne lands of Sulby with her majesty, who at the same granted him a lease of his paternal manor for forty years. During the next three years he received continued marks of royal favour, among which were his nomination as one of the gentlemen of the privy chamber, and the reversion of the office of queen's remembrancer in the Exchequer.

Hitherto he had taken no apparent part in politics; but he was elected member for Higham Ferrers in the parliament of 1571, and for the county of Northampton in that of 1572. In the latter he was one of the committee appointed to confer with the Lords 'on the great matter touching the Queen of Scots;' but he does not appear to have spoken in the house till March 12, 1575, when he presented a message from the queen recommending the enlargement of Mr. Wentworth, who had been committed to the Tower for an offensive speech. At this time he is described as captain of the queen's guard, having succeeded Sir Francis Knollys in 1572. In 1573 he narrowly escaped assassination from the hands of Peter Byrchet, a fanatic who was hanged for the murder of another person, whom he believed to be Hatton. Her majesty gave him the affectionate nickname of 'Liddes,' and he addressed her in the warmest terms of love. Scandal indeed was busy as to the nature of his intercourse with the queen, and the reports were not limited to the common herd of calumniators, but were boldly repeated to Elizabeth herself by Queen Mary, and were believed by Catherine de Médicis and others. The letter written by Dyer to Hatton, advising him what conduct to pursue in consequence of a temporary loss of favour at the end of 1572, and his own letters to the queen in the following year, when he was sent to Spa for his health (preserved in Sir Harris Nicolas's valuable 'Life and Times of Sir Christopher Hatton'), all contain expressions which are very difficult to interpret under any other supposition than that an intimacy existed between him and the queen which would have been fatal to the character of any less elevated female. (*Ibid.* 453, 461-6.) To what extent that intimacy was carried it would be as unseemly as useless to attempt to penetrate; but seeing that the royal favour began when he was about five-and-twenty, and ended but with his life, extending over a period of twenty-six years, and that it was unbroken but by a few of those *amantium iræ* which rather proved its potency than caused any real interruption, it is impossible not to give him credit for a discretion most uncommon in that age, and for so extraordinary a degree of prudence and modest demeanour as to subdue the efforts of rival claimants, and to secure the esteem and confidence of the wisest counsellors of the crown.

During this period he frequently resided at the house in Eltham Park, apparently keeping up great hospitality. The churchwarden's accounts for 1576 contain an entry, 'Payd for brede and drynke when ye Quenes Grasse dyned at Eltham, for ringing, xx^d·;' her majesty's host being no doubt Sir Christopher. (*Archæologia*, xxxiv. 60.)

Between 1574 and 1577 Hatton obtained possession of the Bishop of Ely's house in Holborn, after an effort by the latter to fly from a contract made between them, which was speedily silenced by the interference of the queen in the following well-known letter:—

> Proud Prelate! I understand you are backward in complying with your agreement; but I would have you know that I who made you what you are can unmake you; and if you do not forthwith fulfil your engagement, by God I will immediately unfrock you. ELIZABETH.

In 1576 he obtained an act for the assurance of his lands, and was gratified with a pension of 400*l*. a year for life, with monopolies, and with special advances for the payment of his debts. After having been connected with the court for thirteen years with no higher position than that of gentleman of the queen's privy chamber and captain of her guard, he was raised on November 11, 1577, to the office of vice-chamberlain, and was sworn of the privy council, and as appears from the Diary of Dr. Dee the astrologer (p. 4), with whom he, like most of his contemporaries, conferred, he was knighted on December 1.

From this time his devotion to state affairs is apparent from the letters between him and the principal ministers, who advised with him on all important matters, both foreign and domestic, and evidently regarded his opinion with a deference which a mere favourite could not command. Still representing the county of Northampton, he appears to have been the queen's organ of communication with the parliament. In 1581 he conveyed her reprimand to the house for presuming to appoint a public fast without her authority; in 1585 he presented the queen's answer to the address of thanks, and communicated her desire that they should adjourn for the Christmas holidays. On this occasion he made the unusual motion that the house should join in prayer for her majesty's preservation, and accordingly every one knelt down while Mr. Vice-Chamberlain read a prayer 'devised and set down by an honest, godly, and learned man.' (*Parl. Hist.* i. 812, 827.)

In the trials of Babington and the other conspirators relative to Mary, Queen of Scots, which took place in September 1586, Sir Christopher took a prominent part, and, if a judgment is formed from modern prosecutions, not an impartial one. But, prejudiced as he could not but be by the confessions he had heard, there was more of indiscretion than unfairness in the remarks he interposed; and the kindness of his nature was manifested by his promise to pay the debts of one of the accused, of whose guilt there is no doubt. (*State Trials*, i. 1127-53.)

The trial of Queen Mary immediately followed, Hatton being one of the commissioners, and her consent to plead, which she at first refused, was at length yielded, 'persuaded,' as she declared, 'by Hatton's reasons,' which he had delivered with force and eloquence the day before. In the parliament which was called in the next month he took the lead in urging her execution, expressing, as plainly appears from the whole proceeding, the universal wish of all parties in both houses. The queen's answer to their joint petition was delivered on November 12; and the warrant, after an affected hesitation, was signed on February 1, 1587. Secretary Davison, to whom it was given, having resolved not to act on his own responsibility, the privy council was summoned, and, in consequence of their decision, the warrant was forwarded to Fotheringay. Notwithstanding this, all the counsellors escaped public censure, except the unfortunate secretary, who was no more guilty than the rest, if guilt there was. But the queen wanted a pretence to excuse herself, and Davison was sacrificed to her hypocrisy by a severe sentence of fine and imprisonment. Had there been any sincerity in the queen's complaint, the whole council would have felt the weight of her indignation, but there is nothing to show that any other member of it suffered from her frowns. On the contrary, Sir Christopher Hatton, whom she must have known to have been anxious to release her from all fears about the Scottish queen, and to have been present when the warrant was forwarded, was, within a month after the unjust proceedings against Davison, rewarded with the highest civil rank in the state, by being promoted to the office of lord chancellor on April 29.

That Hatton's elevation to this high and important office occasioned some surprise cannot be doubted, for the public would naturally consider him a mere courtier, and would have forgotten that he had received a legal education. But he had now been known to the ruling powers more than twenty years, during the last ten of which he had been one of the queen's most secret counsellors, advised with not only by her, but by her leading ministers on all occasions. They thus had a full opportunity of judging of his talents and abilities, and their high appreciation of them is sufficiently evidenced by the correspondence which Sir Harris Nicolas has published. Although his early call to a court life prevented him from pursuing the practice of the law, it is to be remembered that in his youth he spent some years in the study of it, and also that he had been long accustomed as a privy councillor to sit in the Star Chamber. That these advantages were not wholly unproductive of fruit is proved by the judicial character he acquired for care and industry in acquainting himself with the rules of his court, and for wisdom and impartiality in the judgments he pronounced. He had the caution to require the attendance of four masters in Chancery when he sat in court, and two when he heard causes in his own house. (*Egerton Papers*, 125.) One of these was Sir Richard Smale, whose advice he is reputed to have followed in all matters of moment. Fuller says 'that some sullen serjeants at the first refused to plead before him,' forgetting that his court was not their usual arena, but adding that, 'partly by his power, but more by his prudence, he convinced them of their errors and his abilities.' His supposed incompetency to his judicial duties does not seem to have weighed so heavily upon him as to prevent his enlivening the bench with a joke. In a cause relative to the boundaries of some land, the counsel for the plaintiff having said, 'We lie on this side, my lord,' and the counsel for the defendant. 'We lie on that side, my lord,' the chancellor stood up and said, 'If you lie on both sides, whom will you have me to believe?' (*Bacon's Apophthegms*, 97.)

During the remaining four years and a half of his life he continued to perform the duties of the chancellorship, in such a manner as to escape condemnation from his legal contemporaries and to retain the favour of his sovereign. In April 1588 he was honoured with the order of the Garter, and on the death of the Earl of Leicester he sought for, and attained on September 20, no doubt by the queen's encouragement and influence, the honourable position of chancellor of the university of Oxford, having been elected two days before high steward of the sister university. It is thus apparent that she did not even resent the courage he had recently displayed in remonstrating with her against affixing the Great Seal to letters patent granting to the earl the unconstitutional post of Lieutenant of England and Ireland. He only presided over one parliament, which met on February 4, 1589, and was dissolved on March 29. (*Parl. Hist.* i. 853-8.)

No further event of any importance in the chancellor's history is recorded before his death on November 20, 1591. Fuller (*Worthies*, i. 165) states that 'it broke his heart that the queen (which seldome gave boons, and never forgave due debts) rigorously demanded present payment of some arrears which he did not hope to have remitted, but did only desire to be forborn; failing herein in his expectation, it went to his heart, and cast him into a mortal disease. The queen afterwards did endeavour what she could to recover him, bringing, as some say, cordial broths unto him with her own hands.' On several occasions there are accounts of his suffering from sickness, and his last illness was probably a violent attack of his old disease, its termination being embellished with the story of the broken heart. But, whatever may have been the real cause of his illness, one fact is incontrovertibly proved, that to the last moment of his life the queen's regard for him was undiminished.

He was buried with great pomp in St. Paul's Cathedral, where a splendid monument was erected to his memory by his nephew, Sir William Hatton.

Surrounded as he was by statesmen of unrivalled talent, an acknowledged favourite among many rivals, honoured and rewarded above his compeers, and holding prominent positions in the council and the court during a long series of years, the absence of any weighty and the failure of every malicious charge against him, the respect and friendship of the great and good men of his day, and the amicable relations in which he lived with his competitors for the queen's personal favour, all prove that he was a man of no ordinary capacity, and that he was as amiable in his disposition as he was discreet in his conduct, neither exciting opposition by arrogance, nor using his known influence to the injury of others. His principal rival in the queen's affections, the Earl of Leicester, called him in his will his 'own dear friend,' and bequeathed to him, besides other valuable gifts, his George and Garter, 'not doubting that he shall shortly enjoy the wearing of it.' His love of literature has not been denied, and of his encouragement of the learned many evidences remain. In the religious contests of the time he always took the part of a moderator; and though suspected of being favourable to the Catholics, he endeavoured to intercept the rigour of the law against the Puritans, being of opinion that 'in the cause of religion neither searing nor cutting was to be used.'

Sir Christopher dying unmarried, his estates devolved on his nephew, Sir William Newport, the son of his sister. This gentleman, who took his uncle's name, married twice, and his second wife afterwards became the wife of Sir Edward Coke. The chancellor's estates descended on Sir Christopher Hatton, the grandson of a younger brother of the chancellor's father. His son was created Baron Hatton of Kerby in Northamptonshire in 1643, and the second baron was advanced to the viscounty of Hatton of Gretton in the same county in 1682; but both titles became extinct in 1762.

The name of Hatton still survives in the peerage, having been assumed by the present Earl of Winchilsea and Nottingham's grandfather, whose mother was only daughter, and eventually heiress, of the first Viscount Hatton. (*Nicolas's Life of Sir Christopher*.)

HAUGH, JOHN, whose portrait in a window of the church of Long Melford in Suffolk is the only remaining indication of the place in which he was born or resided, was a member of Lincoln's Inn, of which society he was reader in 1469, and again in 1473. He was raised to the bench of the Common Pleas in Hilary 1487, 2 Henry VII., and he ceased to act, whether by death or otherwise, after Trinity 1489. (*Dugdale's Orig.* 47–258.) He married Joan, daughter and coheir of Thomas, son of Chief Justice Sir Thomas Billing.

HAUNSARD, WILLIAM DE, was one of the justices itinerant appointed for Surrey in 9 Henry III., 1225 ; and in the two following years he assessed the quinzime and the tallage in that county. (*Rot. Claus.* ii. 76, 146, 208.)

HAUTEYN, HAMON, no doubt named from a manor called Hauteyn's in the parish of Bernham-Broom in Norfolk, held some office in the Exchequer, and was entrusted with the sheriffalty of Lincolnshire in 44 and 45 Henry III., during which he was either so negligent or corrupt as to incur an amercement of ten marks for delaying the execution of a writ till it was too late to act upon it. (*Abb. Placit.* 152.)

In 1 Edward I. he was one of the justices of the Jews, and acted as assessor in London and Middlesex of the fifteenth granted in 3 Edward I. (*Parl. Writs*, i. 4.) He also sat with Ralph de Hengham and others as a justice itinerant for the county of Suffolk in 1285, 13 Edward I. (*Abb. Placit.* 277.) In the next year, however, being called to account by the treasurer and barons of the Exchequer, and convicted of various misdemeanours, he was suspended from his office of justice of the Jews in Trinity Term 1286. (*Madox*, i. 254, ii. 321.)

HAYA, ROBERT DE, was of the same name and flourished at the same time as the noble Scotch family now represented by the Marquis of Tweeddale. In 7 John he commanded the king's galleys 'in insulis' (*Rot. Pat.* 63); and in 24 Henry III., 1240, he was one of the justices itinerant for York; and being then sheriff of Bedfordshire and Buckinghamshire, he had permission as long as he was on that iter to pass his accounts at the Exchequer by means of a substitute. (*Madox*, ii. 177.)

HAYES, GEORGE, was the last-appointed and the last-deceased judge of the Queen's Bench, receiving his patent on August 25, 1868, as one of the three added to the several courts in futherance of the recent act remitting the trial of election petitions to the judges, and within fifteen months dying almost in the exercise of his judicial duties.

He was born on June 19, 1805, and was the son of Sheedy Hayes, Esq., of Judd Place, a West India proprietor. Educated first at Highgate, and then at St. Edmund's Roman Catholic College at Ware, he entered the Middle Temple, where on January 29, 1830, he was called to the bar. He joined the Midland Circuit, of which he eventually became the leader. In 1856 he took the degree of serjeant-at-law, to which was added in 1860 a patent of precedence, and about the same time he was appointed recorder of Leicester. Whether as junior, or senior, or as recorder, he distinguished himself as a sound lawyer; and it was only his legal reputation, for he never entered into party politics nor ever sat in parliament, that pointed him out as an eligible recipient of the honour of the ermine. This selection was most acceptable to his brethren of the bar, for he was highly popular among them, being of the most amiable disposition, joined to a jovial power of enlivening his companions. He was, in fact, a man of 'infinite jests,' and if there had been an album kept in Westminster Hall, to record the witticisms of the bar, many would have been the pages devoted to his witty pleasantries and whimsical pieces. His judicial career was lamentably short. While unrobing at Westminster, after hearing a cause at Nisi Prius, he was seized with a severe attack of paralysis, which terminated in his death on November 25, 1869.

He married Sophia Anne, daughter of Dr. John Hill, of Leicester, and has left a large family.

HEATH, NICHOLAS (ARCHBISHOP OF YORK), was of a family seated at Apsley in the parish of Tamworth in Warwickshire, but was born in London. After attending St. Anthony's School, in which Sir Thomas More had been a pupil, he was entered of Corpus Christi College, Oxford; from whence he was transplanted to Christ's College, Cambridge, where he took his degree of M.A. in 1521, being soon after elected a fellow of Clare Hall there. He is said to have been maintained while at college by Queen Anne Boleyn and her father and brother, and to have been in the first instance a favourer of the new Protestant doctrines. (*Strype's Mem.* i. 279.) Though his assistance to Cranmer in his translation of the Bible seems to warrant this report, his opinions must have undergone great change. Taking holy orders, he was instituted into the church of Hever in Kent in 1531, and, having proceeded doctor in divinity in the meantime, into those of Bishopsbourn and Southmalling in 1537, and of Shoreham in 1538, to which was added the rectory of Cliff. In the following year he became archdeacon of Stafford, and was made almoner to the king (*Rymer*, xiv. 648), who promoted him to the bishopric of Rochester on March 26, 1540.

After remaining in this diocese for nearly four years, he was translated to Worcester, to which he was elected on December 22, 1543; and he sat there, quietly performing his episcopal functions, for the rest of

Henry's reign, and the first four years of that of Edward VI. The act for the adoption of the new Book of Common Prayer having been passed about that time, he, although he had voted against it, was appointed one of the commissioners for carrying it into effect. Refusing to sign the form prescribed for the ordination of bishops, &c., he was committed to the Fleet in December 1550 (*Chron. Grey Friars*, 68), and, being proceeded against for contempt, was deprived of his bishopric in the ensuing October. His imprisonment in Bishop Ridley's house, to which he was removed in July 1552, was alleviated by the kindness and liberal hospitality of that prelate, of whom Heath used always to speak as the most learned of the Protestant party.

On the accession of Queen Mary the sentence against him was reversed, and he recovered possession of his see. One of the first uses which Mary made of him was to attempt the conversion of the Duke of Northumberland, in which he showed so much dexterity as to induce the duke, either out of weakness or hope of life, to make a public profession of Romanism on the scaffold. (*Robertson's Heylin*, ii. 85.) The royal favour was further exhibited towards Heath by making him President of Wales, and, on the deprivation of Archbishop Holgate, by translating him to York. The *congé d'élire* is dated February 19, 1555; and the death of Bishop Gardiner in the same year leaving the office of chancellor vacant, the Great Seal was delivered to him with that title on January 1, 1556. Although the fires of Smithfield, begun by Gardiner, continued to rage during the chancellorship of Archbishop Heath, there is no evidence, and indeed no charge, that he assisted in feeding them.

On the day of Queen Mary's death, November 17, 1558, the parliament being then sitting, he communicated the event to the Lords and Commons, and declaring that the right and title of the Lady Elizabeth was free from all question and doubt, he directed her immediate proclamation. This prudent activity, which anticipated all pretenders and procured her a peaceful accession to the throne, could not but be gratefully felt by the new queen, who, though she did not again entrust him with the Great Seal, continued him in her privy council.

He joined with the other English prelates in refusing to assist at the coronation of Queen Elizabeth; but one of the number, Oglethorpe, Bishop of Carlisle, was at last prevailed upon to perform the ceremony on January 15, 1559, on her agreeing to take the accustomed oath. The parliament met on the 25th, and one of its earliest debates was with reference to an act for restoring the supremacy of the crown. To this bill Heath and eight other bishops were vigorous opponents, and the speech which he addressed to the house on the occasion has been published. It is firm and temperate and learned, but its arguments did not prevail. The bill passed into a law on March 22, and the archbishop and the opposing bishops refusing to take the oath, they were deprived of their sees, and the queen's licence to elect a new archbishop was issued on July 25, 1560. (*Rymer*, xv. 599.) In the preceding month Heath had been committed to the Tower, and in the following February sentence of excommunication was pronounced against him. (*Machyn's Diary*, 238, 249.)

The deprived archbishop was more fortunate than some of his colleagues, for his imprisonment was of short duration, he being allowed after two or three months' confinement to retire to his own property at Chobham in Surrey. For this comparative clemency he no doubt was indebted as much to the queen's gratitude for his early exertions in her behalf, as to her admiration of his learning and amiable character, and she showed her continued kindness by an occasional visit to him in his retirement. There he lived for many years, pursuing uninterruptedly and with patient devotion the studies which had first interested him, and there he died in the year 1579, and was buried in the chancel of the parish church. Such is the history of his last years which all his biographers have written; but a story is ventilated by Miss Strickland (*Elizabeth*, 155) as to a Nicholas Hethe's imprisonment in 1565, which she applies to the archbishop. The tale, however, is of itself highly improbable, the identification of the two wholly fails, while a letter from the archbishop to Lord Burleigh, dated at Chobham, September 22, 1573, wherein he expresses his gratitude 'for having lived many years in great quietness of mind,' confirms the original account. (*Cal. State Papers* [1547–80], 467.)

During his presidency over the province of York, Queen Mary gave to him and his successors as a residence in the metropolis, instead of York House, which had been appropriated by Henry VIII., Suffolk House, near St. George's Church in Southwark. This he was permitted to sell, and to purchase in its stead Norwich House, near Charing Cross, which, changing its name to York House, long continued in the possession of the archbishops, but was commonly let by them to the keepers of the Great Seal. After Lord Chancellor Bacon's disgrace, the Duke of Buckingham obtained it, giving other lands in exchange, and the site is now occupied by the streets which bear his name and title.

Writers of all parties describe Archbishop Heath as a man distinguished by his private virtues, of great abilities and integrity, of gentle temper and prudent conduct, firm in his principles and moderate amidst the bigots of both parties. (*Godwin*, 470, 537, 710; *Athen. Oxon.* ii. 817; *Lingard; Hayward; Burnet.*)

HEATH, ROBERT, son of Robert Heath, of Brasted in Kent, and Jane, his wife, daughter of Nicholas Poner, was born 'uppon the 20th day of May in the year 1575,' says the chief justice in a short memoir of his life written a few months before his death. He was educated at the free grammar school of Tunbridge, and at St. John's College, Cambridge, where he remained for three years. He was then admitted of Clifford's Inn, whence he removed to the Inner Temple, where he was called to the bar in 1603. In 1607 he was selected to be reader of Clifford's Inn, and became a bencher in 1617, filling the post of reader there in 1619, and that of treasurer in 1625. (*Dugdale's Orig.* 167, 171.) He had the fortune to be a favourite of the favourite Buckingham, for whose use he received by patent the profits of the King's Bench and Common Pleas offices, and thus ingratiated himself with the frequenters of the court. On November 10, 1618, he was elected recorder of London in opposition to James Whitelocke. On his nomination as solicitor-general on January 22, 1621, he resigned the recordership, but was elected by the citizens to represent them in the parliament of that year. In it he was a frequent debater, trying to accommodate matters for the king, who knighted him, and retained him in his office during the rest of his reign.

Soon after Charles's accession, Heath on October 31, 1625, was promoted to the attorney-generalship. In the following May he had to bring articles of impeachment against the Earl of Bristol (*Parl. Hist.* ii. 80), in the nature of a cross-bill to the charges which the earl had made against the Duke of Buckingham, who at the same time was also impeached by the House of Commons. All these proceedings were stopped by the sudden and intemperate dissolution of the parliament. In the next year he had the invidious task of opposing the release of the knights who, having refused to contribute to the loan, had been committed to prison, and in this difficult duty he displayed much learning, ingenuity, and eloquence. In 1628, when the judges' refusal to bail or discharge them was taken up by parliament, Sir Robert Heath had again almost singlehanded to maintain the argument against antagonists so powerful as Sir Edward Coke, Littelton, Selden, and Noy, and he did it with such ability and courage that, though defeated, he lost no credit by his exertions. (*State Trials*, iii. 30, 133.) The violent termination of this parliament in March 1629, and the imprisonment of the members who forcibly detained the speaker in the chair at its close, led to other proceedings in which Sir Robert Heath took a very prominent part. By the king's command, he obtained private opinions of the judges upon certain abstract questions, and upon the answers he obtained filed informations against the offending members, and, on their refusing to plead, judgment of fine and imprisonment was pronounced against them. When the conduct of the judges in this matter came to be canvassed by the Long Parliament, Sir Robert Heath seems almost to have escaped censure, as merely performing the duty which devolved upon him as the servant and advocate of the crown. In the exercise of his functions as attorney-general he was so zealous and active a partisan of the court that the king constituted him chief justice of the Common Pleas on October 26, 1631. (*Rymer*, xix. 346.)

On September 14, 1634, he was discharged from his place without any cause being assigned. His removal may perhaps owe its origin to his opposition to Laud, and his disinclination to the extreme views which that prelate adopted in ecclesiastical matters. It was generally believed, however, that the question of ship-money, the writs to collect which were issued four days after the appointment of Sir John Finch as Heath's successor, had some connection with the change. (*Rushworth*, ii. 253.) Anthony Wood, in his account of Noy, casually says that Sir Robert Heath was 'removed from the chief justiceship of the *King's Bench* for bribery;' but in his account of Heath himself he alludes in no way to his dismissal, and makes such mistakes in the courts to which he was appointed as to deprive his record of any value. (*Athen. Oxon.* ii. 584; *Fasti*, ii. 45.) Whitelocke, who was not his friend, would not have omitted all notice of his removal could he have alleged such an imputation as the cause. Upon the foundation of Wood's loose statement merely, for no other can be cited, Lord Campbell (*Ch. Just.* i. 415) makes this assertion: 'The truth seems to be that he [Heath] continued to enjoy the favour and confidence of the government, but that a charge had been brought against him of taking bribes, which was so strongly supported by evidence that it could not be overlooked, although no parliament was sitting, or ever likely to sit; and that the most discreet proceeding, even for himself, was to remove him quietly from his office.' Historians will be anxious for information of his lordship's authority for this statement; for they will be unwilling to suppose it to be gratuitous scandal, although it seems to be contradicted by the very act of the government that displaced him. In the next term after he was ousted from the bench he resumed his practice at the bar as junior serjeant (*Croke, Car.* 375), a privilege that the king would scarcely have granted, or that the fallen judge would have had the effrontery to ask, if his disgrace had been so notorious 'that it could not be overlooked.' That he was actually replaced on the bench, when the 'parliament was sitting'—a parliament, too, that was ready enough to find any blot in the king's appointments,—sufficiently shows the inconsistency of the charge. The chief justice himself says, in his memoir before cited, written when he was in sorrow, and just before his own death: 'At the end of three years I was on a sudden discharged of that place of chief justice, noe cause being then nor at any time since shewed for my removal.' In the next year (1635) the king required his presence at the council board to hear a certain cause (*Cal. State Papers* [1634–5], 87); and in the following year he was again taken into the actual service of the crown, his patent as king's serjeant being dated October 12, 1636. He continued at the bar for four years more, when he was replaced on the judicial seat on January 23, 1641, as a judge of the King's Bench; and was further favoured, on May 13, with the office of master of the Court of Wards and Liveries. (*Rymer*, xx. 448, 517.) When the king retired to York, Sir Robert joined him there, and on June 10, 1642, addressed a letter to the House of Lords, informing them that he had 'left the parliament to go to the king at York as by oath and duty bound;' whereupon they resolved to the contrary, and that his staying at the parliament, being sent for from them, was not against his oath. (*Parry's Parliaments.*) On February 7, 1643, he was created Doctor of Civil Law by the university of Oxford, and a few months later the king, being then in that city, appointed him chief justice of the King's Bench, and in a letter dated July 4, 1643, authorised him in the summer assizes 'to forbear those places whither you conceave you may not goe with convenient safety.' (*Notes and Queries*, 1st S. xii. 259.)

Several complaints were made to the parliament against Chief Justice Heath and other judges who acted with him on the circuit. On these charges, and for adhering to the king, then in arms against the parliament, the Commons impeached them on July 24, 1644; but as the chief justice never put himself in their power, he escaped trial. This, however, did not prevent them from venting their enmity. On November 25, 1645, they passed an ordinance disabling him and four others from being judges, 'as though they were dead;' and by another vote of October 24, 1648, they ordered that he should be excepted from pardon. (*Whitelocke*; *Parl. Hist.* iii. 285.) His estate was sequestered, but was recovered by his son Edward at the Restoration. According to his own relation, the parliament gave him liberty 'either to exile himself into a foreign country, or to run the hazard of further danger.' Of course he never took his seat as chief justice in Westminster Hall; and the prothonotaries of the King's Bench, Henley and Whitwick, took advantage of the distractions of the times to appropriate to themselves the fees received for his use. They were brought to account by the chief justice's son in 1663, when, notwithstanding they pleaded the Statute of Limitations, they were forced by a decree in Chancery to refund the whole amount. (*W. Nelson's Reports*, 75.)

Sir Robert fled into France in 1646, and survived his royal master just seven months, dying at Calais on August 30, 1649. His body was brought to England and entombed with that of his wife, under a stately monument, in Brasted Church.

Among his papers, now in the possession of his noble descendant, has been found a *jeu d'esprit* on the twenty-four links of the collar of SS., each link representing some judicial attribute commencing with the letter S. It is wholly in his handwriting, and was probably composed as an amusement of his exile. It not only shows great ingenuity, but exhibits in the strongest light with what solemn responsibility the writer regarded the qualifications, the virtues, and the duties of a judge. (*Notes and Queries*, 1st S. x. 357.) His short memoir also, written undoubtedly during his exile, gives pleasing evidence of an amiable and pious mind. He married, while yet a student, Margaret, daughter of John Miller, and by her he left several children.

HEATH, RICHARD, was called to the bar of the Inner Temple in November 1659, and was elected a bencher in October 1677. He was summoned to take the coif in 1683, and promoted to the bench of the Exchequer on April 21, 1686. Of his subserviency to the court there is manifest proof in his concurring with his colleagues in favour of the king's dispensing power, and in his conduct with regard to the seven bishops. Archbishop Sancroft thus relates it to King James, when called before him on November 6, 1688, after the invasion of the Prince of Orange: 'I will particularly acquaint your majesty with what one of your judges, Baron H. by name, said coming from the bench, where he had declared our petition to be a factious libel. A gentleman of quality asking him how he could have the conscience to say so, when the bishops had been legally discharged of it, he answered, "You need not trouble yourself with what I said on the bench: I have instructions for what I said; and I had lost my place if I had not said it."' He did lose his place shortly after, being superseded by James himself in the beginning of December. No wonder therefore that he was included among those who were excepted from the bill of indemnity at the revolution. He died in July 1702. His wife was Katherine, daughter of Henry Weston, of Ockham and Sende, Esq., sheriff of Surrey and Sussex. (2 *Shower*, 459; *State Trials*, xii. 503; *Parl. Hist.* v. 334; *Luttrell*, i. 482, v. 198.)

HEATH, JOHN, was the son of Thomas Heath, an alderman of Exeter, and the nephew of Benjamin Heath, town-clerk and a lawyer of eminence in that city, who was the father of Dr. Benjamin Heath, the head-master of Eton. He himself for a time filled the office of town-clerk of his native city.

A member of the Inner Temple, he was called to the bar in June 1762, and in 1775 he was graced with the dignity of the coif. On July 19, 1780, he was appointed a judge of the Common Pleas, and in that court he continued to sit for nearly thirty-six years. He died at the age of eighty on January 16, 1816, and was buried at Hayes in Middlesex.

That he was somewhat eccentric may be surmised from his refusal to accept the honour of knighthood, at that time and now almost invariably conferred on the occupiers of the judicial bench, declaring that he would die 'plain John Heath'—a resolution to which he firmly adhered. But his excellence in performing the functions of a judge is allowed by all who were witnesses of his career. Lord Eldon, who was part of the time chief justice of that court, took occasion to remark with admiration and surprise on the extent of his professional knowledge. Many also are the testimonies to his private worth, and to the universality and accuracy of his general knowledge. He was considered a severe judge, and, though capital punishments were then carried to an outrageous extent, the failure of the ticket-of-leave system which too frequently follows the penalties since substituted forcibly confirms the judge's opinion that 'the criminal is soon thrown upon you again, hardened in guilt.' Yet in his private intercourse he was kind, charitable, and good-natured. He died unmarried. (*Notes and Queries*, 3rd S. ii. 11, &c.)

HEGHAM, ROGER DE, was of a Kentish family, and probably the son of Robert de Hegham, whose widow, Matilda, paid for an assize in that county in 56 Henry III., 1272. (*Excerpt. e Rot. Fin.* ii. 571.) In 21 Edward I. he acted on the part of the king on a quo warranto at York. (*Arch. Inst. York*, 154.) In 25 and 26 Edward I, he assessed the tallage of London, and in the latter year he was appointed to perambulate the forests of five counties. At the end of the same year he is mentioned on the records as a baron of the Exchequer (*Madox*, i. 467, ii. 235; *Parl. Writs*, i. 397), although Dugdale does not introduce him into his list till two years afterwards. In 34 Edward I., having been grossly insulted by one William de Briwes, against whom he had pronounced a judgment, the delinquent was ordered to make an apology in full court, and to be committed to the Tower, there to remain at the will of the king. (*Abb. Placit.* 256.) In the last year of that reign he acted as a justice of assize in Durham, and was one of the justices of trailbaston for the home counties. (*Rot. Parl.* i. 198, 218, 267.)

On the accession of Edward II. he was re-appointed to his seat in the Exchequer, and died about the middle of the second year, in January or February 1309.

HEIGHAM, CLEMENT, whose family was so called from a village of that name in Suffolk, was the son of Clement Heigham, of Lavenham, and Matilda, daughter of Lawrence Cooke. Admitted into Lincoln's Inn in 1517, he became reader in 1538, and again in 1547. At an early period of his career the monastery of St. Edmunds Bury appointed him chief bailiff of the liberty of St. Edmund, but there is no appearance of his practising in the courts at Westminster, his name being nowhere mentioned in the Reports. This may have arisen in some measure from his being a Roman Catholic, a sufficient impediment to any professional advancement in the reign of Edward VI. He was soon engaged in Mary's service as a privy councillor, and sat in parliament successively for Rye, Ipswich, West Looe, and Lancaster. After the queen's marriage with King Philip he was selected as the speaker of the parliament that met on November 11, 1554, in which the attainder of Cardinal Pole was reversed, and the supremacy of the pope restored. The revival of the acts against heresy induced nearly forty members, whose names are preserved by Sir Edward Coke, to leave the house in disgust at the obsequiousness of the majority to the ruling powers. (*Parl. Hist.* i. 617–625.) The parliament was dissolved on January 16, and eleven days afterwards Heigham received the honour of knighthood from the hands of King Philip. (*Machyn's Diary*, 342.)

On March 2, 1558, he was promoted to the office of lord chief baron of the Exchequer; but, though on the accession of Queen Elizabeth he received a new patent, he was removed on January 22, 1559.

Sir Clement then retired to his seat, Barrow Hall in Suffolk, where he spent the remainder of his life, beloved for his piety and benevolence, and for the readiness he always evinced in accommodating the differences of his neighbours, showing himself in all respect a loyal subject, and making himself so little obnoxious by his religious opinions that the lord keeper, Sir Nicholas Bacon, was a visitor in his house. He died there on March 9, 1570, and was buried in Thurning Church in Norfolk.

He married twice. His first wife was Anne, daughter of John de Moonines, of Seamer Hall in Suffolk; and his second was Anne, daughter of Sir George Waldegrave of Smalbridge, and widow of Henry Bures of Acton in the same county. By each he had children, and his representatives have preserved the honour of the family from that time to this. (*Burgon's Gresham*, ii. 108; *Fuller's Worthies*, ii. 350.)

HELYNN, WALTER DE, is described in the Patent Roll of 52 Henry III. as 'justiciarius noster,' and there are continual entries of payments for assizes to be held before him to the end of the reign. (*Excerpt. e Rot. Fin.* ii. 460–574.) He is called 'one of the king's justices appointed to hold the pleas of the lord the king' in 1 Edward I.; and in the fourth year he was paid twenty pounds for his expenses in visiting 'eleven places to expedite the king's business.' (*Devon's Issue Roll*, 81, 96.) It would appear that he was removed to the Common Pleas in 6 Edward I., as from that year till Trinity, 9 Edward I., 1281, fines were levied before him. (*Dugdale's Orig.* 44.) There is no later mention of him after 1284, when a special commission was directed to him and Giles de Berkeley. (*Swinfield's Roll*, 182.) He was seated at Much-Marcle, near Ledbury, in Herefordshire.

HEMINGTON, RICHARD DE, was professionally engaged in the courts, and in 35 Henry III., 1251, appeared before the king at Windsor on the part of John de Bailiol, who afterwards, in 52 Henry III., proceeded against him for delivering up his castle of Fotheringay to Baldwin Wake, the king's enemy and his, without his assent. (*Abb. Placit.* 165.)

He performed the duties of a justice itinerant in 46 and 47 Henry III., 1262-3, and the Fine Roll proves that he was a regular justicier till near the end of the reign, the last entry of payments for writs of assize to be held before him being in October 1270. (*Ibid.* 178; *Excerpt. e Rot. Fin.* ii. 410–524.)

HENDEN, EDWARD, was descended from a branch of the old Kentish family of the Hendens, originally residing on an estate bearing its name in the parish of Woodchurch in Kent, but afterwards removed to Benenden in its neighbourhood, where they were clothiers in great repute.

Entering at Gray's Inn in 1586, he became reader there in 1614, and in the same year sat in parliament for Rye. Having been in 1616 called to the degree of the coif, for the next two-and-twenty years he had an extensive practice, and on January 22, 1639, he was constituted a baron of the Exchequer (*Rymer*, xx. 306) and knighted.

When the parliament entered the field against the king they passed an ordinance assessing all who had not voluntarily contributed to the army, in such sum as the committee meeting at Haberdashers' Hall should deem reasonable, not exceeding a twentieth part of their estate. In December 1643 the Commons applied to the Lords to rate Baron Henden, as an assistant to their lordships, who accordingly assessed him at 2000*l.* for the twentieth part of his estate, to be employed for the defence of Poole and Lyme. The baron not obeying this order, the house, on the 23rd of the same month, directed proceedings against him; but, as he was ill at the time, it seems that they were not then taken, and that he died in the following February. (*Lords' Journals*, vi. 324, 436.) He was buried in the chancel of Biddenham Church.

HENGHAM, WILLIAM DE, was a resident in Norfolk, and was probably a brother of Andrew, the father of Ralph de Hengham. He was one of four who, in 9 Henry III., 1124, were appointed to take an assize of novel disseisin in Norfolk; and in 1126 he was sent with three others to try certain prisoners in the custody of the Bishop of Ely, who were charged with murder. (*Rot. Claus.* ii. 78, 159.)

HENGHAM, RALPH DE, was the son of Sir Andrew de Hengham, of a knightly family seated at St. Andrew's Manor at Hengham in Norfolk. He was brought up to the then commonly united professions of the Church and the law, in the former of which he held a canonry in St. Paul's and the chancellorship of Exeter, to which he was collated in 1275, but resigned it within three years and a half. (*Le Neve*, 89.)

As a lawyer, the payment for assizes to be held before him commences in January 1270, 54 Henry III., which was probably the date of his appointment as a justice of the King's Bench. These entries of assizes before him are very numerous, and the rapidity with which he established his reputation in the court is evinced by his standing at the head of the circuits during the next two years till the end of the reign. (*Excerpt. e Rot. Fin.* ii. 504–584.)

That, on the accession of Edward I. he was immediately removed to the Common Pleas appears from a fine having been levied before him in November 1272; and that his elevation as chief justice of the

King's Bench must have been between November 1273 and September 1274 (though Dugdale does not name him in that character till 1278) is proved by an entry of pleas 'coram domino rege et R. de Hengham *et sociis suis,* justiciis de *Banco domini regis,* in Octabis S. Michaelis, anno regno &c. secundo, incipiente tercio, apud Westm.' (*Abb. Placit.* 263.)

In 18 Edward I. he was removed from his office and fined, but what was the precise charge against him is nowhere recorded, and the amount of the fine is variously stated. It has been generally fixed at 7000 marks; but the complaints against him in the next parliament were palpably too slight to warrant such a punishment, and probably were merely made by those mean spirits who are too ready to press a falling man. One was, that the chief justice had confirmed a false judgment pronounced by Solomon de Rochester, the justice itinerant; and another, that a man had been arbitrarily imprisoned by him. (*Rot. Parl.* i. 48, 52.) There is much more probability that the fine did not exceed 800 marks, according to the tradition in the reign of Richard III., which attributed its imposition to Hengham's pity for a poor man having induced him to erase from the roll a fine of 13*s*. 4*d.*, and substitute 6*s.* 8*d.* for it. The story went on to assert that with this fine the clockhouse at Westminster was erected, and a clock placed in it which could be heard in the hall. (4 *Inst.* 255.) This tradition has been frequently referred to by judges who have been urged to alter a record. That Hengham's offence could not have been a very grievous one is sufficiently proved by his restoration to the bench at a later date.

His retirement, however, was of ten years' continuance, and his return seems to have been gradual. His name is introduced nearly at the bottom of the list of judges and other officers who were summoned to the parliament of March 1300, 28 Edward I., as if among the justices itinerant. In the following April he was the first named of those appointed to perambulate the forests of Essex, Buckingham, and Oxford (*Parl. Writs,* i. 664); and it was not till eighteen months afterwards—viz., on September 14, 1301—that he was restored to the bench, and constituted chief justice of the Common Pleas. In this office he continued till the end of the reign, and was reappointed by Edward II. He served that king for a very short time, his death occuring in 1309. (*Ibid.* ii. 995.) He was buried in St. Paul's Cathedral, and Weever (p. 367) gives his epitaph, in which he is called 'flos Anglorum' and 'vir benedictus.'

Besides the 'Registrum Brevium,' which Coke calls 'the most ancient book of the law,' he left two works of note called 'Hengham Magna' and 'Hengham Parva,' which have been published with notes by Mr. Selden, and are printed at the end of his edition of 'Fortescue de Laudibus Angliæ' (1741).

HENLEY, ROBERT (EARL OF NORTHINGTON). The family from which he descended was originally established at Henley in Somersetshire, of which county some members of it were sheriffs. Its elder branch was honoured with a baronetcy in 1660, which expired in 1740. His great-grandfather, Sir Robert Henley, master of the Court of King's Bench in the reign of Charles I., having acquired the estate of the Grange in Hampshire, employed Inigo Jones to erect a considerable mansion on it. His third son, Sir Robert, and his grandson, Anthony, were both successively members of parliament for Andover, and the latter was afterwards representative for Weymouth till his death in 1711. This Anthony, who was one of the most accomplished wits of his day, by his marriage with Mary, the daughter and coheir of the Hon. Peregrine Bertie, second son of the Earl of Lindsey, became the father of three sons, of whom this Robert was the second. He was born about 1708, and was educated at Westminster, and St. John's College, Oxford, and was elected a fellow of All Souls' in 1727. Being then admitted to the Inner Temple, he was called to the bar in 1732.

As a young man he was jovial and hilarious, and indulged so much in the prevailing vice of drinking that he laid the foundation of that gouty habit from which he subsequently suffered. But he evidently acquired an early practice in the Court of Chancery, which increased so much that he was compelled in 1745 to take chambers in Lincoln's Inn, where equity lawyers 'most do congregate.' For this purpose he was also then admitted a member of that society. It was at that time the custom for Chancery barristers to attach themselves to a circuit, and thus to obtain some insight into the course of the common law and criminal courts (a practice which had not been altogether discontinued at the beginning of the present century), and Mr. Henley chose the Western Circuit, his connections being resident within it. Here his rough-and-ready advocacy soon procured him a lead; and a curious story is told of his being obliged to apologise to a Quaker of Bristol named Reeve for some indecent liberties he had taken with him in cross-examination. It speaks well for both that the Quaker was afterwards employed by the chancellor to pay the freight of some wine consigned to him, and that the chancellor invited his old antagonist to dine at his table, and good-humouredly related to the company the particulars of their early fracas.

He was elected recorder of Bath, where he resided during his vacations, and where he formed a romantic attachment to Jane, the beautiful daughter and one of the co-heiresses of Sir Hugh Huband, of Ipsley, baronet. She had at that time entirely lost the use of her limbs, but on her recovery they were united in 1743. Bath elected him its representative in the parliament of 1747, and he continued its member till his elevation to the equity bench. Attaching himself to the Leicester House party, he was an active debater in support of its line of politics. After the death of the Prince of Wales he continued his adherence to the princess, and on the establishment of the household of the young prince (afterwards George III.), in 1751, he was appointed his solicitor-general, and in 1754 his attorney-general, being on the former occasion admitted within the bar as one of the king's counsel, and elected a bencher of the Inner Temple. On November 6, 1756, he was appointed king's attorney-general, and knighted; and on the coalition ministry being formed in the following year, Sir Robert, after ineffectual offers of the Great Seal had been made to Lords Hardwicke and Mansfield, Sir Thomas Clarke, and Chief Justice Willes, was nominated lord keeper on June 30, 1757.

So unacceptable was he to George II., from his connection with Leicester House, that he was allowed to preside in the House of Lords for nearly three years without a title; but the necessity of appointing him lord high steward for the trial of the Earl of Ferrers for the murder of his steward, and the impropriety of a commoner holding that high office, obliged the king on March 27, 1760, to create him a peer as Baron Henley of the Grange. At that trial, judging from the printed account, his conduct was simple and unaffected, and the ill-natured and prejudiced assertion of Horace Walpole that it wanted dignity is fully refuted by the grave, appropriate, and affecting addresses delivered by his lordship to the noble prisoner, both on his arraignment and his condemnation.

George II. died six months afterwards, and soon after the accession of George III. Lord Henley's title of lord keeper was converted into that of lord chancellor. He was the last person who was designated by the former title, the single holder of the Great Seal being ever since that time, now more than a century, distinguished by the latter. It is difficult to account for the unmeaning imposition of the two titles since the time of Queen Elizabeth, when an act of parliament took away every essential difference that might have existed previously, and declared them to be equal in power, jurisdiction, and dignity.

On May 19, 1764, he was created Earl of Northington (the hamlet in which the Grange estate was situate), and in the following August he was made lord lieutenant of his county. Though Lord Northington owed his appointment of lord keeper to Mr. Pitt, he still retained the Great Seal when that minister was succeeded by Lord Bute, and also during the two subsequent administrations headed by the Duke of Bedford and the Marquis of Rockingham. From several points in the policy of the last he differed so materially that he induced his majesty to submit the guidance of the state to his old patron, Mr. Pitt, upon the formation of whose administration he retired from the post of lord chancellor on July 30, 1766, and took the less onerous position of lord president of the council. His principal inducement for making this sacrifice was the impossibility he found of performing the duties of the office of chancellor, enfeebled as he was by repeated attacks of the gout. The same cause obliged him eighteen months after to resign his new office; and from December 1767 he retired wholly from public life. He died on January 14, 1772, and was buried at Northington, where a handsome mural monument has been erected.

In the judgment of Lord Eldon, 'he was a great lawyer, and very firm in delivering his opinion,' an authority which few will dispute. Its justice will receive confirmation from a collection of his decisions, printed from his own manuscripts by his grandson, Robert Eden, second Lord Henley of that name, who afterwards published a memoir of his life. He retained to the end of his life his love of classical literature, and in his domestic circle he kept up the conviviality which distinguished him in his early years, tinctured rather too much with warmth and irritability, and with the common use of profane expressions, a vulgar and unmeaning habit which then unhappily prevailed, adopted more with the view of giving strength to expressions than with any thought or intention of being blasphemous. Though he was undoubtedly coarse and careless in his language, he has not been charged with being incorrect or immoral in his conduct, and the two beautiful prayers which Lord Henley informs us he composed for the use of his wife leave the impression that he was imbued with deeper religious feelings than he had the credit of entertaining.

His wife bore him several children. The only son who survived him, Robert, was the second and last earl, dying in 1786 unmarried. One of his daughters, Elizabeth, married Sir Morton Eden, K.B., who was created in 1799 Lord Henley of Chardstock in the peerage of Ireland, a title which still exists.

HENRY, DUKE OF NORMANDY, afterwards KING HENRY II., was the eldest son of Geoffrey, Earl of Anjou, by the Empress Matilda, daughter of King Henry I.

Being born in March 1133, he was but an infant during the contest between his mother and King Stephen. On the death of his father in 1150 he succeeded to the earldom of Anjou, and by consent of his mother assumed the title of Duke of Normandy. Having then attained the age of sixteen, he resolved to recover the English throne which his mother had lost. He accordingly received the honour of knighthood from his uncle David, King of Scotland, and strengthened himself by a politic marriage with Eleanor of Poictou, the divorced wife of Louis, King of France, acquiring with her the extensive duchy of Aquitaine. On his landing in England shortly after, his standard was joined by such of his mother's former adherents as survived, and by all those who were desirous of terminating the state of anarchy which prevailed throughout the kingdom. The contending armies met at Wallingford, but by the intervention of wise counsellors they parted without bloodshed, and an arrangement was effected between Stephen and Henry, by which it was agreed that the former should not be disturbed in his rule during his life, and that Henry should succeed him at his death. This treaty was concluded on November 7, 1153, when Stephen is said to have constituted Henry Chief Justiciary of England under him. He did not, however, long perform the duties of this office, as he returned to Normandy at the following Easter, and remained there till after Stephen's decease, which occurred on the 25th of the ensuing October. After a reign of more than thirty-four years, he died at Chinon on July 5, 1189.

HEPPECOTES, THOMAS DE, was one of those who were appointed to supply the place of the judges removed on the king's return from Tournay. His patent is dated January 8, 1341, 14 Edward III., but his death occurred before the end of the year. He was probably a native of Northumberland, where there is a hamlet called Hepscott in the parish of Morpeth. (*Dugdale's Orig.* 45; *Rot. Parl.* ii. 126.)

HERBERT, EDWARD, was the first cousin of the famous Lord Herbert of Cherbury, being the son of Charles Herbert of Aston in the county of Montgomery, third brother to the father of his lordship. Admitted to the society of the Inner Temple, he was called to the bar in 1618, and became reader in 1637. He had before this time acquired a seat in parliament, and in 1626 was one of the managers of the impeachment of the Duke of Buckingham. (*Whitelocke*, 6; *Parl. Hist.* iii. 719.) He was not in the next parliament of 1628, but after its dissolution he was one of the counsel employed by Selden in the prosecution against him. (*Cal. State Papers* [1628–9], 556.) His opposition to the court did not last long, for in 1633 he was selected by the Inner Temple as a manager of the famous masque designed by the four inns of court as a compliment to the king and queen in confutation of Prynne's tirade against players in his 'Histrio-Mastix.' (*Whitelocke*, 19.) In January 1635 his devotion to the court was confirmed by his appointment as attorney-general to the queen, and in 1637 he was employed on the part of the crown in the prosecution of Burton, Bastwick, and Prynne. (*State Trials*, iii. 719.) Having been soon after knighted, his next step was to the solicitor-generalship, which he obtained on January 25, 1640, and in that character he sat in the parliaments of the following April and November for New Sarum. He continued a member till January 29, 1641, when, on his being created attorney-general, and thereby becoming an assistant to the House of Lords, he was, according to the practice of the time, incapacitated from sitting in the Commons. (*Rymer*, xix. 606, xx. 380, 448; *Parl. Hist.* ii. 562, 623.) This removal from a scene of daily contention was peculiarly acceptable to him, for, according to Clarendon, he was 'awed and terrified' with the temper of the Commons, and glad to be 'out of the fire.'

On January 3, 1642, he, by the king's command, brought an accusation in the House of Lords against Lord Kimbolton and five members of the Commons for high treason, and the king on the next day committed the imprudence of going to the latter house and demanding their arrest. The Commons, highly resenting this proceeding, voted it a breach of privilege, and impeached Herbert for exhibiting the articles. Sir Edward put in his answer justifying himself as acting under his majesty's express personal commands, and without any advice from himself, and thereupon the trial commenced on March 8. Two of the counsel assigned for his defence were committed for contempt in refusing to plead, and the excuses of two others were allowed, all four being intimidated by the threats of the Commons. Mr. Hearne and Mr. Chute, however, boldly and ably exonerated the attorney-general. Yet the Lords, influenced in some measure by the same fear, found him guilty of the facts, but at the same time showed their estimate of the imputed crime by successively negativing motions that he should be punished by the loss of his office, by fine, by imprisonment in the Tower, or by mulcting him in damages to the accused members. More than a month after, their lordships, being compelled by the Commons to inflict some punishment, contented themselves with merely committing him to the Fleet during pleasure, and declaring him incapable of any other place than that of attorney-general, which he held. His incarceration lasted only eighteen days, from April 23 to May 11, when Sir Edward was permitted 'for his health' to go to any of his houses within a day's journey of London, but not to come to London without the order of the house. On July 4 the warden of the Fleet was ordered to bring him up, but, as was no doubt intended, he had taken the opportunity to escape and join the king at York. (*Parl. Hist.* ii. 1089, 1121–79; *Lords' Journals*, v. 177.) Venturing some time after to London, he seems narrowly to have escaped the clutches of the parliament, by whom an order was made on March 6, 1646, that he should be apprehended and brought to the bar. (*Whitelocke*, 196.)

Clarendon (*Life*, i. 212), who did not like him, states that his 'greatest faculty was, and in which he was a master, to make difficult things more intricate and perplexed, and very easy things to seem more hard than they were;' and gives an amusing account of certain conferences at Oxford in 1643, on the subject of the proposed proclamation for dissolving the parliament, which seems fully to justify his opinion.

The ground that he lost with the king on that occasion he did not regain. In a letter to Mr. Secretary Nicholas dated from Newark, October 16, 1645, his majesty says: 'For Mr. Atturny, tell him if the rebelles never did but justice, or what they had lawful power to do, then his answer good, otherwais it is not worth a button; wherefor if he confesse my power lett him accept my offer, otherwais I shall know what I have to do.' (*Evelyn's Memoirs*, v. 154.) The offer alluded to was probably that of the lord keepership, then vacant by the death of Lord Lyttelton. The result of this letter was that the Great Seal was entrusted to Sir Richard Lane on October 25, and that Sir Edward Herbert was discharged from his office on November 1. (*Docquets at Oxford*.)

Sir Edward seems to have been reinstated in his office by King Charles; for in 1648 Clarendon speaks of him in that character, as accompanying the Prince of Wales, and as a great favourite with Prince Rupert, describing him as always interfering with his advice, and as being 'of all men living most disposed to make discord and disagreement among men, all his faculties being resolved into a spirit of contradicting, disputing, and wrangling upon anything that was proposed.' If reliance is to be placed on the noble author's account of Sir Edward's subsequent conduct at the Hague, his intrigues and indiscretion well merit the censure; but the jealousy of a rival for court favour may account for some exaggeration of the facts. (*Clarendon*, vi. 63, 82, 127–30, 140.)

After the death of Charles I. Sir Edward is still mentioned with his official title. He attended the new king's court at the Hague, and afterwards was with the Duke of York at Paris, being one of this prince's private and confidential advisers, recommending and accompanying him on that inauspicious visit to Flanders and Holland in the following year. The regular councillors of the duke represented him 'as a man of that intolerable pride that it was not possible for any man to converse with him; . . . yet, by the knack of his talk, which was the most like reason without being it, he retained still too much credit with the duke, who, being amused and confounded with his positive discourse, thought him wiser than those who were more easily understood.' (*Ibid.* 321, 474, 483.)

Unless Sir Richard Lane was continued after the decapitation of the late king as nominal lord keeper till his death in 1650, of which there is no evidence except that on his widow's tomb, that office had not hitherto been filled by Charles II.; indeed, since the battle of Worcester there had been no Great Seal to keep. But in 1653 the king, having provided himself with a new Seal at Paris, entrusted it, against his own inclination, but at the urgent solicitation of the queen-mother (*Evelyn*, v. 284, 288), to Sir Edward Herbert in April of that year. The duties of the office, judicial or political, could not have been very onerous; and his time is described as being principally employed in endeavouring to effect the ruin of Sir Edward Hyde, of whose ascendency over the king he was inordinately jealous. He showed his enmity on every occasion, and was met with corresponding hatred on the part of Hyde, whose prejudice is so apparent in every sentence that the character he gives of Herbert would be altogether unworthy of credit, were it not that both Charles I. and his son appear to have concurred in his opinion. That the dislike of the latter was real is proved by his resolving that Herbert should not accompany him when he left France in June in the following year. Sir Edward was so indignant at this mark of disgrace that he immediately surrendered the Great Seal. He died at Paris in 1657; or, according to another authority, he survived till the Restoration, and died at Rouen.

He married Margaret, daughter of Sir Thomas Smith, master of the Requests, and widow of Thomas Carey, the second son of the Earl of Monmouth. His three sons all became distinguished in the succeeding reigns. The eldest, Charles, commanded a regiment of foot under King William, and was slain in the battle of Aghrim, in 1691. The second, Arthur, was the admiral who brought over that king in 1688, and was created Earl of Torrington, but, dying without issue, his title became extinct in 1716. The youngest, Edward, took the contrary side, and is the chief justice next noticed.

HERBERT, EDWARD, the third son of the above Sir Edward, was educated at Winchester, and at New College, Oxford, where he graduated as B.A. in 1669. He then went to the Middle Temple, and, becoming a barrister, migrated to Ireland, on his becoming attorney-general there. He was knighted in 1683, and was made chief justice of Chester. Subsequently appointed attorney to the Duke of York, he was soon after his royal highness's accession to the throne made attorney-general to the queen, and on October 23, 1685, was promoted to the vacant office of chief justice of the King's Bench. (*Athen. Oxon.* iv. 552; *Fasti*, ii. 304; *Bramston*, 207.) On his previous investiture with the necessary degree of serjeant he gave rings with the extraordinary motto 'Jacobus vincit, triumphat lex.'

Of his merits as a lawyer previous to his elevation we have no means of judging from the English Reports; but Burnet describes him (iii. 92) as 'a well-bred and virtuous man, generous, and good-natured,' but 'an indifferent lawyer. . . . He unhappily got into a set of very high notions with relation to the king's prerogative. His gravity and virtues gave him great advantages, chiefly his succeeding such a monster (Jeffreys) as had gone before him. So he, being found to be a fit tool, was, without any application of his own, raised up all at once to this high post.'

In the king's attempts for the establishment of Popery, one of his earliest steps was to appoint Roman Catholics to offices, and grant them a patent of dispensation from the oaths required by the Test Acts. Sir Edward Hales held the colonelcy of a regiment under these circumstances, and, for the purpose of trying the question whether the king had power to grant such dispensation, a sham action to recover the penalty was brought against Sir Edward by Godden, his coachman. On the case being argued on demurrer Chief Justice Herbert gave a decided opinion that there was no law whatsoever but what may be dispensed with by the king as supreme lawgiver; but, as it was a case of great importance, he promised to submit it to the twelve judges. On a subsequent day he gave judgment for Sir Edward Hales, stating that all his colleagues agreed with his opinion except Mr. Baron Street. There can be no doubt, however, that, unconstitutional as this doctrine is now allowed to be, the chief justice really and conscientiously held it; and afterwards, when his judgment was assailed by Sir Robert Atkyns and other writers, he published a vindication of it, with the authorities upon which it was founded. Almost immediately followed his appointment as one of the ecclesiastical commissioners, who had powers almost as extensive and quite as obnoxious as those of the old High Commission Court; but the chief justice formed one of the minority which subsequently voted against the tyrannical suspension of the fellows of Magdalen College. (*State Trials*, xi. 1195, 1251; *Evelyn*, iii. 212, 214; 2 *Shower*, 497.) In Easter Term 1687 he refused a rule for the execution at Plymouth of a soldier who had been tried for desertion at Reading, and so determined was the king to effect his purpose of introducing martial law that Sir Edward was at once removed, and within a day or two Sir Robert Wright, who was substituted for him, complied with the king's will as a matter of course.

Though discharged from the King's Bench, he was on the next day, April 22, made chief justice of the Common Pleas, in which court he continued till the flight of the king. Remaining true to his master, Sir Edward joined the self-exiled monarch, and was of course excepted from the bill of indemnity, notwithstanding the high character for honour and integrity universally accorded to him in the debates. In France King James created him Earl of Portland, and gave him the nominal office of lord chancellor, in which his principal duty was to draw up declarations, asserting his master's right to his deserted dominions. Some of the most violent ones were unjustly attributed to him; for he in truth had little or no influence over James, the Roman Catholic ministers monopolising all the sway. Though taking rank as chancellor, and possessing all the external marks of his office, he was not allowed, as a Protestant, to hold a seat in the council. A large majority of the Jacobites in England remonstrated; but to their prayer that he should be admitted James answered evasively, that he would be 'on all occasions ready to express the just value and esteem he has for the lord chancellor.' When James's Protestant servants were dismissed in October 1692 Sir Edward retired into Flanders, but afterwards returning to France, he died at St. Germains in November 1698. (*Burnet*, iii. 92, 149; *Evelyn*, iii. 235; *Luttrell*; *Lord Macaulay*, iv. 227, 386.)

HERBERT. *See* HERBERT LOSINGA.

HEREFORD, EARL OF. *See* W. FITZ-OSBERNE; M. DE GLOUCESTER; H. DE BOHUN.

HERIET, RICHARD DE, was sheriff of Essex and Hertfordshire in 4 Richard I., and was no doubt in some employment connected with the Exchequer. From 6 Richard I. to 6 John, 1194–1205, he acted as a justicier in the Curia Regis at Westminster, his name frequently appearing on the fines that were levied there. In 1 John, Robert Fitz-Torold granted him half the town of Bedefont; and in 3 John he paid

50*l.* for having the custody of his land in Surrey, and fifty-five marks for that in Wilts. He died in 1208. (*Madox*, i. 216; *Rot. Cancell.* 30, 225; *Rot. Claus.* i. 109.)

HERLASTON, WILLIAM DE, no doubt came from the place of that name in Staffordshire. In 6 Edward II. he accompanied the king abroad in the train of Ingelard de Warlee, keeper of the wardrobe. (*N. Fœdera*, ii. 213.) He soon afterwards became a clerk in the Chancery, and was parson of the church of 'Estwode near Reylegh;' and in July 1319 he had a grant of the prebend of Carnwyth in the church of Glasgow. (*N. Fœdera*, ii. 401.)

According to the practice of the time, the Great Seal was placed in the custody of some of the clerks of the Chancery during the occasional absence of the chancellor, and they transacted the business appertaining to it. William de Herlaston was frequently one of those entrusted with this duty from 1321 to 1324. (*Parl. Writs*, ii. p. ii. 1001.) He was also in the latter part of this reign keeper of the king's privy seal. (*Rot. Parl.* ii. 383.)

In 2 Edward III. he and Henry de Cliff, the master of the Rolls, were appointed keepers of the Great Seal during a vacancy in the office of chancellor, and he acted in the same character several times during that and the following year. He was a trier of petitions in the parliament as late as the twenty-first, and one of the justices itinerant in the twenty-second year.

HERLE, WILLIAM DE, was, according to Fuller (i. 281), born in Devonshire, because he was owner of Ilfracombe; but it is more likely that he was born in Leicestershire, both Robert de Herle, apparently his father, and he having been summoned by the sheriff of that county, the former in 1301, 29 Edward I., to perform military service, and the latter in 1324, 17 Edward II., to attend the great council at Westminster. (*Parl. Writs*, i. 355, ii. 639.) The principal part of his property was certainly in that county.

In 4 and 6 Edward II. he was summoned as an assistant to parliament, apparently in the character of a serjeant-at-law; and in the ninth year he was one of three 'qui sequuntur pro rege' in a suit against the men of Bristol. (*Rot. Parl.* i. 359.) The wardrobe account of 14 Edward II., 1320, contains the entry of a payment to him of the large sum of 133*l.* 6*s.* 8*d.* in these words: 'To William Herle, king's serjeant, who, by the king's order, will shortly receive the honour of knighthood, of the king's gift, in aid of his rank, 6th of August'. (*Archæologia*, xxvi. 345); and he was raised to the bench of the Common Pleas on the 16th of the following October.

On the accession of Edward III. he was immediately made chief justice of that court, his patent being dated February 4, 1327. Though he was displaced on September 3, 1329, by John de Stonore, it is evident he still continued to act as a judge, as he was at the head of the justices itinerant in Nottinghamshire in the following December, and also, in the succeeding year, in Derbyshire. Restored to his place as chief justice on March 2, 1331, he was again removed on November 18, 1333; but Henry le Scrope, who was then appointed, resumed his seat at the head of the Exchequer on the next day. The cause of these changes can only be inferred; but William de Herle, from that day, presided till July 3, 1337, when, at his own request, he was allowed to retire from his office, on account of his age and infirmities. The patent spoke in eulogistic terms of his approved fidelity, the solidity of his judgment, the gravity of his manners, and his laudable and unwearied services to the state; and required him to remain on the secret council, and to attend at his pleasure during the rest of his life. (*N. Fœdera*, ii. 913.) He lived nearly twelve years after his retirement, dying in 1347.

Through his wife Margaret, the daughter and heir of William Polglas, by Elizabeth, the heir of Sir William Champernon, the manor of Ilfracombe, and other large property in Devonshire, came into his possession. (*Cal. Inquis.* p. m. ii. 135, 265; *Nicholl's Leicestersh.* 622; *Prince*.)

HERMAN (BISHOP OF SHERBORNE AND SALISBURY) was of Flemish origin, and had been one of the chaplains of Edward the Confessor, by whom he was advanced in 1045 to the small bishopric of Wilton, which in the preceding century had been cut off from the diocese of Sherborne, and the seat of which was sometimes at Wilton, sometimes at Ramsbury, and sometimes at Sunning. In 1050 he visited Rome in company with Aldred, Bishop of Worcester, and on his return he used his utmost endeavours to remove his see to Malmsbury; but, though the king consented, he was defeated by the opposition of the monks there. Indignant and disgusted, he retired to Bertin, in France, in 1055, and remained in that monastery for three years. On the death, however, of Efwold, Bishop of Sherborne, in 1058, he returned and succeeded in procuring the reunion of the two sees of Sherborne and Wilton; and in 1075, taking advantage of the order of the Council of London, that the bishops' sees should be removed from obscure places to towns of greater note, he effected the transfer of his to Old Sarum, no doubt, however, under the influence of favour, as that place was then little better than a castle. He there commenced the erection of the cathedral, but did not live to witness its completion. His death is fixed by different writers in the years 1076, 1077, and 1078.

Thynne, in his Catalogue of Chancellors, introduces him with these words: 'He is that Hermanus which, I suppose, was chancellor to William the Conqueror.' With no other authority than this, the followers of Thynne have unhesitatingly admitted his name.

He wrote the 'Life and Miracles of St. Edmund,' King of the East Angles. (*Holinshed*, iv. 348; *Godwin*, 336; *Hutchins's Dorset*, ii. 373.)

HERON, EDWARD, was the grandson of John Heron, a physician at Barming in Kent, and the son of Richard Heron, settled at Harsted or Hastings Hall, in Birdbroke, Essex. Admitted at Lincoln's Inn, he was called to the bar in 1574, and elected reader in 1587. In 1594 he took the degree of serjeant-at-law, which he held for fourteen years before he was advanced to the bench of the Exchequer on November 25, 1607, having been previously knighted. He did not long enjoy his position, for he either resigned or died in 1610. (*Croke, Jac.* 197.)

He was twice married. His first wife was Anne, daughter of David Vincent, Esq., of Bernake in Northamptonshire, the ancestor of the present baronet of that name. His second wife was Dorothy, daughter of Anthony Maxey, Esq., of Bradwell, near Coggleshall. (*Morant's Essex*, ii. 345.)

HERTELPOLE, GEOFFREY DE, of the manor of Brereton in Northumberland, acted as a judge of assize at Newcastle in the reign of Edward I. In 34 Edward I. the king granted to him the manor of Kenweston in Durham for his services.

He was summoned to the coronation of Edward II., and held the office of recorder of London for about a year in 1320, and continued during that reign to act as a justice of assize, attending the parliament among his brethren as late as 1326. (*Abb. Placit.* 306–9; *Parl. Writs*, i. 379, ii. p. ii. 1003; *Rot. Parl.* i. 194, &c.; *Cal. Rot. Pat.* 65.)

HERTFORD, ROBERT DE, was one of the judges of the Common Pleas placed on the bench in the room of those who were superseded for corruption in 18 Edward I., 1290, and appears to have continued to act up to 1295, as he was summoned to the parliament of that year. (*Dugdale's Orig.* 44; *Parl. Writs*, i. 29.)

HESILL, or HESILT, WILLIAM, was auditor of the Exchequer (*Acts Privy Council*, ii. 290) at the time he was made a baron of that court on July 13, 1421, 9 Henry V. He was re-appointed on the accession of Henry VI., but on May 18, 1424, was exonerated from his office. (*Ibid.* iii. 147.) He died on April 9 in the following year, and was buried in the church of Northfleet in Kent. He married Agnes, the daughter of John Appleton. (*Hasted*, ii. 321, iii. 315.)

HEWITT, JAMES (LORD LIFFORD), the eldest son of William Hewitt, a mercer and draper at Coventry, who served the office of mayor in 1744, was born in 1709, commenced his life in an attorney's office, under articles to Mr. James Birch, but was subsequently induced to seek his fortune at the bar. Entering the Middle Temple, he became a barrister in 1742. His merits as a lawyer procured him in 1755 the dignity of the coif, and four years afterwards the position of king's serjeant. In 1761 being elected member for his native town, the style of his oratory in parliament may be surmised from the story that is told of Charles Townshend, who being met going out of the house, when Serjeant Hewitt was thundering away on some dull legal question, was asked whether the house was up. 'No,' said Townshend very gravely, 'but the serjeant is.' At this time he was in opposition, but in the next year, when the Earl of Chatham came in, and his friend Lord Camden was made lord chancellor, the latter offered him the vacant judgeship of the King's Bench, which he accepted on November 6, 1766, on a promise that if he held the Seal when the chancellorship of Ireland became vacant he should be promoted to that office. Within a year the Irish chancellor died, and, Lord Camden having succeeded in overcoming all obstacles, Mr. Justice Hewitt received his patent as Lord Chancellor of Ireland on January 9, 1768. In June following he was created Baron Lifford in the Irish peerage, to which a viscounty was added in 1781. He filled this high office till his death on April 28, 1789, a period of more than twenty-two years. With few advantages of education, and with no extraordinary powers of intellect, he was successful in the exercise of his functions as a judge by the accuracy of his technical knowledge and his general professional skill. Formal in his manner and old-fashioned in his ideas, he yet, by his patience and urbanity to all, acquired universal esteem and respect.

He married, first, a daughter of the Rev. Rhys Williams, D.D., rector of Stapleford-Abbotts in Essex, and secondly, Ambrosia, daughter of the Rev. Charles Bayley, of Knavestock in the same county. The viscounty is still held by the descendants of his eldest son. His third son Joseph became a judge of the King's Bench in Ireland; and his fourth son, John, was dean of Cloyne.

HEYDON, THOMAS DE, is described as 'clericus noster' in letters patent of 4 John, 1203, relative to lands in Heydon and in London, belonging to Robert Furree, the custody of whose daughter, Constance, had been previously granted to him. (*Rot. Pat.* 27.)

From 3 to 11 Henry III. he was one of the regular justiciers at Westminster, receiving the acknowledgment of fines during the whole of that period, and acting as a justice itinerant on several occasions. (*Dugdale's Orig.* 42; *Rot. Claus.* i. 473, 681, ii. 82, 209; *Madox*, ii. 335.)

HEYM, PETER, was appointed, in 20 Edward I., 1292, a justice to take assizes in divers counties, and his pleas are recorded in 23 Edward I. (*Abb. Rot. Orig.* i. 92.) He was perhaps the son of the undernamed Stephen Heym.

HEYM, STEPHEN, was one of the justices of the Common Pleas at Easter, 55 Henry III., 1271, and writs of assizes were taken in his name till the end of that reign. He was continued in the office under the succeeding king, as fines were levied before him from the former date till 3 Edward I., 1274, when he died. (*Excerpt. e Rot. Fin.* ii. 537-589; *Dugdale's Orig.* 44; *Abb. Rot. Orig.* i. 23.)

HEYRUN, JORDAN, was of a Northumberland family, and joined the barons in their contest with King John. He made his peace in the next reign, and in 9 Henry III., 1225, he was one of the justices itinerant for Northumberland and Westmoreland, and in 1228 he acted in the same character for the liberties of the bishopric of Durham. (*Rot. Claus.* i. 341, 631, ii. 77.)

HILDESLEY, JOHN DE, was parson of the church of Thynden, and canon of Chichester in the reign of Edward II., from the tenth year of which, till the seventh year of the next reign, he was continually employed in diplomatic missions to various courts. He was raised to the bench of the Exchequer on December 18, 1332, 6 Edward III., having evidently been previously an officer connected with that department. He was superseded on September 9, 1334, on his becoming chancellor of the Exchequer. He is so called in 12 Edward III., and is named two years afterwards as a trier of petitions in parliament. (*N. Fœdera*, ii. 329-875; *Rot. Parl.* ii. 99, 114; *Cal. Rot. Pat.* 120.)

HILL, HUGH, was born in 1802 at Craig in the county of Cork, the residence of his father, James Hill, Esq., a private gentleman, whose family originally settled in Ireland in Cromwell's time. Educated in Dublin University, he graduated there as A.B. in 1821, and, intending to pursue the profession of the law in Ireland, he then kept legal terms for two years in the inns of court there, and afterwards at the Middle Temple in London. He started as a special pleader under the bar in 1827, and for more than thirteen years devoted himself with unremitting energy to this department. Though his progress was at first not very rapid, at last his success exceeded his most sanguine expectations. So extensive and oppressive was his business that he felt it necessary to be called to the bar in January 1841, when he joined the Northern Circuit. Both there and in Westminster Hall his reputation as a deeply-read jurist and an ingenious and safe pleader secured to him an immense quantity of the heavy business, which required greater labour, but gave less profit, than the ordinary causes that occupy the courts.

From 1851, when he obtained the silk gown, till 1858, he was rewarded for his past labours by gaining a considerable lead, and on May 29 of the latter year he was constituted a judge of the Queen's Bench. But his labours had overtasked his strength; his constitution was completely undermined, and, becoming incapable of further exertion, he retired, after less than four years' service, in December 1861, to the regret of his colleagues and the loss of the legal world. He still survives, an example of patience in his sufferings, and of humble gratitude to a merciful God for the blessings he has received.

He married in 1831 a daughter of Richard Holden Webb, Esq., controller of the customs.

HILL, or HULL, JOHN (the name being as often spelled one way as the other), was born at Hill's Court, the seat of the family, near Exeter. The earliest mention of him as a lawyer is a writ of summons, dated November 26, 1382, to take upon himself the degree of a serjeant-at-law, being the first of that description which has hitherto been found, the previous entries only noticing those who were king's serjeants.

He was constituted a judge of the King's Bench on May 20, 1389, 11 Richard II., and on the accession of Henry IV. his patent was renewed, and his attendance in parliament as a trier of petitions is noted in every year from his first appointment till that of October 1407. (*Rot. Parl.* iii. 258-609.)

HILL, or HULL, ROBERT, was apparently of a Cornish family, and married two heiresses of that county, the first being Isabella, the sister of Thomas, the son of Sir Thomas Fychet, and the second being the daughter of Otto de Bodrugan, who or whose father had been sheriff of that county in 3 Richard II.

Robert Hill is mentioned among other lawyers in 16 Richard II. (*Rot. Parl.* iii. 302), and in the first year of Henry IV., 1399, he was appointed one of the king's serjeants, in which character he was required to contribute, or as it was called to lend, 100*l.* to enable the king to resist the Welsh and the Scotch. (*Acts Privy Council*, i. 202.) He was elevated to the bench of the Common Pleas on May 14, 1408, 9 Henry IV., and fines were levied before him as early as Midsummer in that year. (*Dugdale's Orig.* 46; *Cal. Rot. Pat.* 234.) He sat in the same court the whole remainder of his life.

In 3 Henry V. he was one of the judges by whom Richard Earl of Cambridge, Henry Lord Scrope, and Sir Thomas Grey were tried for treason at Southampton, and condemned to death, and in the first year of the next reign he is spoken of as having been chief justice of Ely. (*Y. B.* p. 8 b.)

He seems to have been rather a free-spoken judge on the bench. An action was brought against a dyer, who had bound himself not to use his craft for half a year, upon which Hill said that the bond was void because the condition was against the common law, adding, 'And, by God, if the plaintiff was here, he should go to prison till he paid a fine to the king.' (*Y. B.* 2 *Hen. V.* p. 5 b.) This is perhaps the only instance of an oath on the bench being *reported*.

The last fine acknowledged before him as a judge of the Common Pleas was in Hilary Term, 3 Henry VI., 1425, soon after which he died.

He settled himself at Shilston in Devonshire, and left a son named Robert, who was sheriff of that county in 7 Henry VI., and whose descendants flourished there for many generations. One of them was Abigail Hill, Lady Masham, the favourite of Queen Anne. (*Notes and Queries*, 2nd S. viii. 10.)

HILL, ROGER, belonged to a very ancient Somersetshire family, which had flourished at Hounston from the time of Edward III. In the reign of Henry VIII. it was seated at Poundsford, near Taunton, where William Hill, the father of the baron, lived and died in 1642. His mother was Margaret or Jane, daughter of John Young, of Devonshire, and he was born at Colliton in the latter county. He was called to the bar at the Inner Temple in 1632, and became a bencher in 1649.

In March 1644 he was the junior of the five counsel employed against Archbishop Laud, who, in allusion to the senior four being the only spokesmen, calls him 'Consul Bibulus.' (*Athen. Oxon.* iii. 130.) In the next year he was returned to the Long Parliament as member for Bridport, and one of the first fruits of his siding with the popular faction was the grant to him in 1646 of the chambers of Mr. Mostyn and Mr. Stampe in the Temple. (*Whitelocke*, 201.) Though named in the commission for the king's trial, he never sat on it.

Cromwell made him a serjeant-at-law on June 29, 1655, and in Easter Term 1657 he is mentioned in Hardres's Reports as a baron of the Exchequer. In that character he assisted at the ceremony of investiture of the protector in June 1657, and as one of the judges attendant on Cromwell's House of Peers he delivered a message from them to the Commons in the following January. (*Burton*, ii. 340, 512.) In the summer of 1658 he went the Oxford Circuit with Chief Justice Glynne, an account of the proceedings in which, 'writ in drolling verse,' was published soon after. (*Athen. Oxon.* iii. 754.) When the commonwealth was restored by the removal of Richard Cromwell and the return of the Long Parliament, Baron Hill resumed his place as a member, and on January 17, 1660, he was transferred from the Exchequer to the Upper Bench (*Whitelocke*, 693), where his name appears as a judge in Hilary Term in Siderfin's Reports.

The author of 'The Good Old Cause' says that the parliament granted him the Bishop of Winchester's manor of Taunton Dean, worth 12,000*l.* a year, on the determination of the estate for lives (*Parl. Hist.* iii. 1599), which he, of course, was not allowed to retain when the bishops were replaced at the Restoration. At that period he escaped the censure of the king, but, being one of the Rump Parliament, he had not the same favour shown to him as most of the other serjeants of the commonwealth experienced, in being confirmed in their degree. He survived Charles's return for seven years, during which he married his third wife, who brought him an estate at Alboro' Hatch in Essex, where he died on April 21, 1667, and was buried in the Temple Church.

He married three times—first, in 1635, Katherine, daughter of Giles Green, of Allington in the Isle of Purbeck; secondly, in 1641, Abigail, daughter of Brampton Gurdon, of Assington Hall in Suffolk; and thirdly, in 1662, Abigail, daughter and coheir of Thomas Barnes, of Alboro' Hatch, Essex, and twice a widow, first of John Lockey of Holms Hill, Herts, and secondly of Josias Berners of Clerkenwell Close, Middlesex. (*Family Memorials.*)

HILLARY, ROGER, of a very ancient family, which possessed large property in the counties of Lincoln, Warwick, and Stafford, was the son of William and Agnes Hillary, and is frequently mentioned as an advocate in the Year Books of Edward II. and Edward III. He was raised to the Irish bench as chief justice of the Common Pleas in 3 Edward III., where he remained for eight years. He was then constituted a judge of the same court in England on March 18, 1337, to the head of which he was advanced on January 8, 1341. Dugdale, in his 'Chronica Series,' makes William Scot supersede him in that office on April 27; but this is evidently an error, as the latter was then and for some years afterwards chief justice of the King's Bench. On May 9, 1342, however, Roger Hillary made way for John de Stonore, on his restoration to the chief justiceship, receiving himself, on June 4, a new patent as a judge on that bench. On the death of Stonore, Roger Hillary was, on February 20, 1354, again constituted in his place, and continued to preside in the court for the short remainder of his life.

His death occurred in June 1357, and he was buried in the church of All Saints in Staffordshire. By his wife Katherine he had, besides other children, a son Roger, who was probably the serjeant-at-law mentioned in the Year Books of 40 Edward III. (*Parl. Writs*, ii. p. i. 333; *Cal. Rot. Pat.* 106; *Rot. Parl.* ii. 119–254.)

HILTON, ADAM DE, was the last named of four justices itinerant who in 35 and 36 Henry III., 1251–2, were appointed to visit Yorkshire and several other counties. There is one instance, in December 1253, of a writ of assize being paid for to be taken before Alan de Watsand and him in Yorkshire (*Excerpt. e Rot. Fin.* ii. 177), which bears the appearance of his having been one of the regular justiciers.

HOBART, HENRY, belonged to a family of ancient descent in Suffolk and Norfolk, and was great-grandson of Henry VII.'s attorney-general, Sir James Hobart, and son of Thomas Hobart, of Plumsted in the latter county, by Audrey, daughter of William Hare, of Beeston in Norfolk, Esq.

Admitted a member of Lincoln's Inn, he was called to the bar in 1584. In 1595 he was steward of Norwich, and in 1597 was returned to parliament as the representative of Yarmouth, for which place and for Norwich he had a seat on several succeeding occasions. In 1601 he became reader of his inn, an honour which was repeated two years afterwards, on the occasion of his being called serjeant by Queen Elizabeth; but, in consequence of her death, he was included in a new writ by King James. (*Dugdale's Orig.* 254, 262.)

Having been knighted on the occasion, he was made attorney of the Court of Wards in 1605, and on July 4, 1606, he was created attorney-general. This office he held for above seven years, to the annoyance of Bacon, who served under him for six of them, and longed by his removal to take another step in promotion. Henry, Prince of Wales, made him his chancellor. In the case of the post-nati he of course took the part of the plaintiff (*State Trials*, ii. 609), and in the complaint raised by the Commons against Dr. Cowel's book, claiming the superiority of the civil to the common law, it is stated that Sir Henry 'did very modestly and discreetly lay open the offence of the party and the dangerous consequence of the book.' (*Parl. Hist.* ii. 1124.)

Modesty seems to have been his characteristic, and, though a very learned, he was not by any means a sparkling lawyer. On the death of Sir Thomas Fleming, the chief justice of the King's Bench, and Sir Edward Coke's succession to it, Hobart received the appointment of chief justice of the Common Pleas, from which Coke was removed, on November 26, 1613.

He presided in that court with great credit as a sound lawyer and upright judge for twelve years, and with so little imputation on his honesty and independence as to form one of the exceptions to the general subserviency of the bench. He was selected as chancellor to Prince Charles in 1617, and was obliged for the purpose of accepting the office to have his patent of chief justice revoked, and a new one granted, in order to enable him 'to take fee and livery' from any one besides the king. (*Croke, Car.* 1.) He was created a baronet in May 1611.

King Charles on his accession renewed his patent of chief justice, but he survived King James only nine months, dying at his house at Blickling in Norfolk on December 26, 1625. He was buried under a fair monument in Christ Church, Norwich.

Spelman says of him that he was 'a great loss to the public weal;' Croke (*Car.* 28) reports him as 'a most learned, prudent, grave, and religious judge;' and there is an excellent character of him in the preface to 5 Modern Reports. His own Reports were published after his death, and are so well reputed as to have passed through several editions.

By his wife Dorothy, a daughter of Sir Robert Bell, of Beaupré Hall, Norfolk, lord chief baron under Elizabeth, he had no less than sixteen children, of whom twelve were sons. From Sir Miles, his third son, who succeeded to the estates on the death of his brothers, descended Sir John, who in 1728 was created a peer by the title of Baron Hobart of Blickling, to which was added in 1746 the earldom of Buckinghamshire. (*Collins's Peerage*, iv. 362.)

HODY, JOHN, descended from a family of considerable antiquity, though of no great note, in the county of Devon, was the son of Thomas Hody, who was lord of the manor of Kington Magna, near Shaftesbury, in the adjoining county of Dorset, in 7 Henry V., and in the same year was king's escheator there. His mother was Margaret, daughter of John Cole, of Nitheway, near Torbay, in Devonshire. (*Rot. Parl.* iv. 285, v. 477.)

He is frequently mentioned in the Year Books from 3 Henry VI., and appears to have taken the degree of the coif about the fourteenth year. He was returned to parliament for Shaftesbury in 7 Henry V., and again in several parliaments of Henry VI., and subsequently for the county of Somerset. On April 13, 1440, 18 Henry VI., he was raised to the office of chief justice of the King's Bench, but held it not quite two years, dying in December 1441. He tried and condemned, a few days before, 'a gret and konnyng man in astronomye,'

Roger Boltingbroke, for labouring 'to consume the kinges persone by way of nygromancie,' stirred up, as he asserted, by Alienor Cobham, Duchess of Gloucester. He was executed declaring his innocence, and the chronicler concludes the narrative thus: 'And the justice that yaf of him iugement lived not long after.' (*English Chron.*, Camden Soc., 60.) The judge was buried at Wolavington in Somersetshire.

Notwithstanding the short period during which he presided in the court, he is stated by Prince to have won golden opinions by his integrity and firmness in the administration of justice. That author relates a tradition, that when his son Thomas was tried before him at the assizes, and found guilty of a capital crime, he with his own mouth pronounced sentence of death upon him. How this tradition originated it would be useless to enquire, but that it is untrue there can be no question, for his eldest son, John, could not have been more than six or seven years old at his father's death. Sir Edward Coke (*Pref. to First Inst.*) mentions him amongst the 'famous and expert sages of the law,' from whom Lyttelton had 'great furtherance in composing his Institutes of the Laws of England.'

The judge had an estate at Stowell in Somersetshire as early as 6 Henry VI.; but he was for some time seated at Pillesden in Dorsetshire, which came to him by his marriage with Elizabeth, daughter and heiress of John Jewe, son and heir of John Jewe, by Alice, daughter of John de Pillesden. By her he had a large family. His second son, William, is the subject of the next article.

HODY, WILLIAM, the second son of the above Sir John Hody, was quite an infant when his father died in 1441. Naturally pursuing his father's profession, his name is first mentioned in the Year Books in 1476. He must have attained some celebrity, as within a month after the accession of Henry VII., in 1485, he was appointed attorney-general. Before the close of that year he was made a serjeant-at-law, probably in preparation for his assumption of the office of chief baron of the Exchequer, to which he was promoted on October 29, 1486.

He presided in this court for the remaining twenty-three years of the reign, and for the first eight years of that of Henry VIII., being mentioned as receiving his salary in 1516. (*Cal. State Papers* [1515–18], 876.) On January 18, 1513, a grant of the place in reversion was obtained by John Scott (*Ibid.* [1509–14], 470); but there is no evidence of his ever having filled it. Sir William probably lived till 1522, when John Fitz-James was appointed lord chief baron.

By his wife Eleanor, daughter of Baldwyn Mallett, of Corypool in Somersetshire, he had issue two sons and two daughters. (*Prince's Worthies; Hutchins's Dorset,* i. 317.)

HOLDERNESS, ALEXANDER DE. At the head of the list of justices itinerant for the county of Lincoln in May 1226, 10 Henry III., appears the name of 'Abbas de Burgo.' He was Alexander de Holderness, who had been elected to that dignity in 1222. In consequence of this appointment, several causes between the abbot and other parties at those assizes were ordered to be heard in the ensuing Easter before the justices at Westminster. Before that period arrived, however, Alexander died, in November 1226. He was buried in the abbey, and in 1830 a grave that was opened in Peterborough Cathedral was identified to be his, by a piece of lead inscribed 'Abbas Alexan.' (*Browne Willis*, 147; *Rot. Claus.* ii. 151–160.)

HOLES, HUGH. See H. HULS.

HOLGRAVE, JOHN, was appointed fourth baron of the Exchequer on September 24, 1484, 2 Richard III., and his patent was renewed on the accession of Henry VII. He either resigned or died before Michaelmas 1487, as Nicholas Lathell was then fourth baron. He was buried in the abbey church of Bermondsey. (*Stow's London* [*Thoms*], 156.)

HOLLOWAY, RICHARD, the son of John Holloway, who is described by Anthony Wood as 'a covetous civilian and public notary' at Oxford, became a fellow of New College, and, though admitted a member of the Inner Temple on February 7, 1634, was not called to the bar till November 24, 1658, the interval being probably caused by the Great Rebellion, or perhaps by his pursuing his father's avocations at Oxford. His practice as a barrister seems to have been confined to that city, and the only record of his doings is that he was one of the first passengers in the 'flying coach . . . having a boot on each side,' that started from Oxford to London on May 3, 1669, and performed the journey in thirteen hours. He became reader of his inn in Lent 1675, and about this time the following descriptive hexameter was written on five of the family then resident in Oxford:—

Sarjeant, Barrester, Necessitie, Notarie, Mercer,
Gravely dull, ill-spoken, lawless, cum pergere, broken;

the first being Serjeant Charles Holloway, the uncle; the second being the future judge, 'living against the Blew-bore in St. Aldate's parish;' the third, Charles, the son of Serjeant Charles, so called from the old saw *Necessitas non habet legem*, as being a barrister but no lawyer; the fourth, the judge's father; and the fifth, another uncle, a broken tradesman. (*Athen. Oxon.; Life,* xliv., lxiii., lxxix.; *Fasti,* ii. 12.)

In July 1667 he was created a serjeant, and Luttrell (i. 260) calls him king's serjeant in June 1683, when he was knighted, and on September 25 of the same year he was constituted a judge of the King's Bench. In the following November he was engaged in the trial of Algernon Sidney, in that court, but took no active part in it, and in the other public trials of Charles's reign his conduct was irreproachable. (*State Trials*, viii. 591, ix. 867, x. 45, 151, 515.)

After the accession of James II. he concurred in the deserved but illegal sentence pronounced against the infamous Titus Oates, and in the excessive fine of 30,000*l.* imposed upon the Earl of Devonshire for an assault upon Colonel Culpepper in the king's palace, overruling his lordship's plea of privilege; and for both these judgments he and the other members of the court were called before parliament after the revolution, when the latter was declared a breach of privilege, and so much of the former as remained to be inflicted was remitted by the king. The judges were, however, permitted to depart unscathed. But having in the great case as to the king's power to dispense with the penal laws acquiesced in the judgment in favour of the crown, he and all who survived were excepted out of the bill of indemnity passed in 2 William III. (*Ibid.* x. 1315, xi. 1200, 1368.)

This was a severe measure towards Sir Richard, because he had already been made a victim to James's vengeance, and had amply atoned for his previous error by boldly resisting the king's attempt to impose martial law in time of peace without the consent of parliament, and by publicly declaring that the petition of the seven bishops was not a seditious libel. They were acquitted on June 30, 1688, and on July 4 the honest judge was dismissed.

He was still living at Oxford in November 1695, as at that time he drew up the will of Anthony Wood, the historian of the university. (*Bramston's Autob.* 272, 310; *Luttrell,* i. 449; *State Trials,* xii. 426; *Athen. Oxon.* i. *Life,* cxxiii.)

HOLME, JOHN, was constituted a baron of the Exchequer on February 3, 1446, 24 Henry VI.; and on May 28, 1449, he had a grant for life of his summer and winter robes, probably on his retirement, for his name does not again occur.

HOLROYD, GEORGE SOWLEY, owes his origin to the same stirps from which Lord Sheffield descended; the direct ancestors of both, George and Isaac, being the sons of Isaac Holroyd, of Crawcrofts in Rishworth, in the parish of Elland in the county of York. The judge was the great-grandson of George, and the eldest son of another George, by Eleanor, the daughter of Henry Sowley, of Appleby, Esq. He was born at York on October 31, 1758, and was sent to Harrow School, from which it was intended that he should proceed to the university; but, in consequence of his father suffering some severe losses from unfortunate speculations, he was removed from Harrow, and in April 1774 was articled to Mr. Borthwick, an attorney in London. At the end of three years he entered Gray's Inn, and commenced business as a special pleader in April 1779.

During the eight years that he pursued this branch of the profession he adopted, with Romilly, Christian, and Baynes, one of the most effective preparations for the contests into which they were about to enter. Meeting at each other's chambers, they discussed legal points previously arranged, one of them taking the affirmative side, another supporting the contrary part, and a third summing up the arguments and deciding the question as judge. On June 26, 1787, he was called to the bar, and about three months after married Sarah, the daughter of Amos Chaplin, Esq., who brought him fourteen children.

He joined the Northern Circuit, and the character he had acquired while under the bar for solidity of judgment and professional ability secured to him a fair proportion of business, both in the north and in Westminster Hall. Ere he had been called a year his name appears in two cases in the 'Term Reports.' (ii. 445, 480.) During the twenty-nine years that he remained at the bar his fee-book shows the rapid increase of his practice, proving also the advance of his reputation by the number and importance of the cases submitted to his direction. Of a retiring disposition, he persisted in declining the offer of a silk gown, and therefore his merits were comparatively unrecognised by the general public; but among the legal community his superiority was fully acknowledged, and it was said of him that 'he was absolutely born with a genius for law.' So highly were his instructions esteemed that, while at the bar, no less than forty-seven pupils availed themselves of them, among whom were Mr. Baron Hullock, Mr. Baron Bolland, and Mr. Justice Cresswell. In 1811 he greatly distinguished himself in the celebrated case of privilege, Burdett *v.* The Speaker of the House of Commons, by his luminous arguments on behalf of the plaintiff. (14 *East's Reports,* 11.) In the last year of his practice at the bar he was sent by the government to Guernsey, at the head of a commission to enquire into and determine certain 'doleances' complained of by persons resident in that island.

At length he was appointed a judge of the King's Bench. In that court he sat for more than twelve years, from February 14, 1816, to November 17, 1828, the date of his resignation, fully sustaining the reputation he had acquired, and largely contributing to the high character of the bench to which he belonged, when associated with such erudite and discriminating judges as Lord Tenterden, Sir John Bayley, and Sir Joseph Littledale. His patience never seemed to be wearied; his amiable temper was never ruffled; his decisions were always clear and well-founded, for his memory was the storehouse of all the arguments that had ever been advanced for or against the case he was to judge; and his taste, with no effort at display, was so exquisite that he made the driest subjects interesting. The infirmities which obliged him to retire, in three years terminated his life, on November 21, 1831, at his residence at Hare Hatch in Berkshire. A monument is erected to his memory in the parish church of Wargrave, with an inscription, written by Lord Brougham, faithfully and eloquently describing his merits and his virtues.

Of the judge's fourteen children six survived him, one of whom exercised as a commissioner of the Court of Bankruptcy till the recent alteration of that court the functions of his laborious office with the same legal learning, the same patience, and the same suavity of temper that distinguished his father.

HOLT, JOHN, was born in Northamptonshire, where he had considerable property. (*Abb. Rot. Orig.* ii. 240.) His name appears in the Year Books from 40 Edward III., in the last year of whose reign he was made a king's serjeant. His elevation to the bench as a judge of the Common Pleas took place in 7 Richard II., 1383. (*Cal. Rot. Pat.* 208.)

He obeyed the summons of the king to attend him at Nottingham, where, on August 25, 1387, he united with his colleagues in answering the questions placed before them by the king's confederated courtiers, pronouncing the proceedings of the last parliament, by which a permanent council was appointed, to be illegal, and its promoters punishable with death. For this act he was arrested, while sitting on the bench, on February 3 following, and on his trial, on March 2, alleged that he was compelled by the threats of the Archbishop of York, the Duke of Ireland, and the Earl of Suffolk to do so, and that he complied through fear of his life. The parliament, notwithstanding, found him guilty; and he only escaped the sentence of death that was pronounced by the intercession of the prelates, who succeeded in getting it commuted to banishment for life. To him was assigned the town of Drogheda and a circuit of two miles around it, with an allowance from the state of forty marks for his support. (*Rot. Parl.* iii. 233–44.)

Three years afterwards the king granted several of his manors to his son John; and in the parliament of January 1397, 20 Richard II., so much of the sentence as regarded his banishment was remitted, and he was allowed to return to England. In the following year the whole of the judgment was reversed, and his lands ordered to be restored. Richard's deposition unfortunately deprived the judge of the benefit of this reversal; but Henry IV., on his petition in the second year of the reign, directed that he should have again all his lands and tenements which were in the king's possession. This, however, turning out to be nearly a nullity, inasmuch as many of them had been alienated by King Richard, another ordinance was made in 4 Henry IV., by which he was allowed to resume possession on making such allowances to the purchasers as the council should deem reasonable. (*Ibid.* 346–461; *Cal. Rot. Pat.* 221.)

That he was successful in recovering them would appear from the extent of property in Northamptonshire and other counties contained in the inquisition taken on his death in 6 Henry V., 1418. (*Cal.* iv. 37, 52.) By his wife Alice he left another son named Hugh, who succeeded him.

HOLT, JOHN. After the succession of chief justices that disgraced the bench in the reigns of Charles and James since the death of Sir Matthew Hale, it is refreshing to record a name which excites universal admiration, as possessed by one who was erudite in law, independent in character, and just and firm in his decisions. In him may be fixed the commencement of a new era of judicial purity and freedom, marked with that perfect exemption from extraneous influences which has, with few exceptions, ever since distinguished the bench, and which is now the undisputed glory of our judicature.

The family of Holt had flourished for some centuries at Grislehurst in Lancashire, and in Queen Elizabeth's time had divided into several branches. The judge's father was Thomas Holt, a bencher of Gray's Inn and recorder of Abingdon, and afterwards a serjeant and knighted. His mother was Susan, daughter of John Peacock, of Chawley, near Abingdon; and this their eldest son was born at Thame in Oxfordshire, on December 30, 1642. (*Monumental Inscription; T. Jones,* 51.) If there is no error in this date, he had not completed his tenth year when he was admitted into the society of Gray's Inn on November 19, 1652; nor attained his majority when he was called to the bar on February 27, 1663, unless the latter entry means 1663-4. The early admission may perhaps be explained by his father being reader of the inn at the time. His previous education was at the free school in Abingdon, whence he was removed in 1658 to Oriel College, Oxford. There he is reputed to have been notorious for his idleness and for his association with dissolute companions, who led him into every kind of licence and extravagance. Some tales that were subsequently related of him give probability to the report of his juvenile delinquency; but he soon saw the error of his ways, deserted his old haunts and associates, left the university without taking a degree, and applied himself diligently, under the tuition of his father, to that profession of which he was destined to be one of the brightest ornaments.

So early did he exhibit his superiority that we find his name in Sir Thomas Raymond's Reports, with the addition of 'junior,' in the year 1668; and not long after it appears with great frequency, not only in those but in other Reports of the time. From 1679 till the beginning of James's reign he was engaged in almost all of the numerous state trials which occupied the courts of justice during that unhappy period. At first he was retained on the part of the prosecution, but, his distaste to the arbitrary proceedings of the government becoming apparent, he was soon employed by the unfortunate prisoners who were the victims. Whether on one side or the other, his advocacy was remarkable for so much lucidity of arrangement, and such fairness of statement, and his arguments displayed such profound knowledge of the principles of law, that his colleagues could not but augur his future promotion. But his nomination as counsel for three of the Popish lords impeached in 1679, and his appearance in the defence of Pilkington and others for a riot at a city election, of Sir Patience Ward for perjury, of Lord Russell for high treason, and of Sacheverell and others for a riot in the election of mayor of Nottingham—all political questions,—seemed to forbid any early fulfilment of the expectation of advancement. On the other hand, his arguments in favour of the monopoly of the East India Company, and in defence of Mr. Starkey against the Earl of Macclesfield, and his opinion in favour of the legality of the judgment upon the *quo warranto* against the city of London, in addition to the respect with which he was invariably treated by Chief Justices Scroggs, Pemberton, and Jeffreys, pointed him out as a fit object for royal favour. (*State Trials*, vii., ix., x.)

On February 18, 1686, he was induced rather unwillingly to take the recordership of London. He was thereupon knighted, and in the Easter Term following he received the degree of the coif, and was immediately made king's serjeant. But his independence and his sense of right would not allow him to act according to the king's unconstitutional desires. A soldier being found guilty of felony in running away from his colours, the recorder refused to pronounce sentence of death upon him, doubting, as the kingdom was at peace, whether the conviction was good in law. As the royal project of creating a standing army would have been frustrated if such a doubt was recognised, he was of course removed from his office. On James's desertion of the kingdom he was one of the lawyers called by the Lords to advise them on the course to be taken; and in the Convention Parliament that met in January 1689 he was returned for the borough of Beeralston.

In the early sittings of that parliament he took a leading part; but his senatorial duties were soon terminated by his removal to a judicial sphere. In order to insure a learned bench, King William required every privy councillor to furnish a list of twelve lawyers, and out of these lists he selected the twelve of most conspicuous merit. One of the most satisfactory appointments was that of Sir John Holt, whose patent as chief justice of the King's Bench was dated April 17, 1689. For twenty-one years did he grace that seat, his presidency extending over the whole of King William's reign and two-thirds of that of Queen Anne, during which period the administration of justice was distinguished by learning, sagacity, and integrity, and freed from the suspicion of private bias or courtly dictation, most effectually securing the confidence and commanding the applause of all parties, whether whigs or tories, from the contrast it presented to the experience of the preceding thirteen years. In all of the criminal trials at which he presided he acted with such honesty and impartiality that many of the accused, even when convicted, acknowledged the fairness with which they had been treated.

In February 1698 he and Justice Eyre had the courage to resist the House of Lords, when they were required to give their reasons for the judgment they had pronounced in 1694 in favour of Charles Knollys, claiming to be Earl of Banbury, who had pleaded his peerage to an indictment charging him as a commoner with the murder of Philip Lawson, his brother-in-law. The refusal of the two judges to do so, unless the case was brought before the lords by writ of error, gave such offence that there was some inclination to commit them both to the Tower; but, though the question was adjourned, it was never resumed, and the enquiry, as Lord Raymond (i. 18) says, 'vanished in smoak.' (*Luttrell*, ii. 231, 243.)

That this resistance did not arise from caprice, but from principle, is proved by his conduct in the Aylesbury case. The three puisne judges of the King's Bench having, in opposition to his opinion, reversed a verdict in which the constables of Aylesbury were cast in damages for refusing to permit a voter to exercise his franchise, the case was removed into the House of Lords on a writ of error. There, on the opinion of the judges being regularly required, he explained in a very learned argument the grounds of his judgment, and had the pleasure of being supported by Lord Somers and a great majority of peers, who set aside the order of his colleagues and confirmed the verdict given for the injured voter. (*Burnet*, v. 112, 191; *Vernon's Letters*, iii. 250; *State Trials*, xiv. 779.) In the iniquitous case of the bankers, also, where the Court of Exchequer had pronounced a judgment in their favour, which the Court of Exchequer Chamber had by a quibble reversed —such reversal having been strenuously opposed by Holt, and as strenuously supported by Lord Chancellor Somers and Chief Justice Treby,—the House of Lords confirmed Holt's opinion, and reversed the reversal. (*Ibid.* 29.) The correctness also of his judgment that a writ of error would not lie upon his denial of a prohibition prayed for by Dr. Watson, Bishop of St. David's, was acknowledged by the House of Lords in opposition to the dictum of Lord Chancellor Somers.

So highly were his services valued by King William that on the removal of Lord Somers he was urgently pressed to accept the Great Seal; but, wisely declining the responsible and unstable honour, he excused himself to his majesty by saying 'that he never had but one Chancery cause in his life, which he lost, and consequently could not think himself fitly qualified for so great a trust.' He however consented to act as chief commissioner till the vacancy was filled up, and, in conjunction with the two other chiefs, held the Seal from May 5 to 21, when Sir Nathan Wright was appointed lord keeper. On the death of King William he took out a new commission, notwithstanding that his office was held 'quamdiu se bene gesserit;' thus establishing the principle that the judges were removable at the demise of the crown, which continued to prevail till the accession of George III., who by one of his first acts secured them in their seats on the accession of a new king.

For eight years of the reign of Queen Anne he maintained the credit of the bench. He sat in court for the last time on February 9, 1709-10, and on March 5, during the progress of the unadvised trial of Dr. Sacheverell, he died at his house in Bedford Row. He was buried in the church of Redgrave in Suffolk, the manor of which, formerly possessed by Sir Nicholas Bacon, he had purchased; and a costly monument, representing him sitting in a chair in his robes and collar, was erected to his memory.

During the extended period of his judicial reign he retained the respect and the confidence of all. His appointment as executor of Chief Justice Treby is some proof of the estimation in which he was regarded by his contemporaries, which is still further displayed in the 'Tatler,' No. 14, written about a year before his death, and the character there eloquently given has been acknowledged to be a faithful description from that time to this. Thoroughly versed in the principles of the law, and perfect master of its practice, he was strict in its application, but humane, patient, and forbearing in its administration. Keeping himself entirely aloof from the political intrigues of the time, his decisions were free and unfettered, neither influenced by personal prejudice nor overawed by the threats of power. His spirited resistance of the latter has been already exemplified, and his personal courage is evidenced by the following tradition. A mob having assembled with the intention of pulling down a house in Holborn where persons were supposed to be kidnapped and then sent to the colonies, the Guards were called out. The chief justice, being applied to, asked the officer what he would do if the populace did not disperse. 'Fire on them,' said the officer, 'as we have orders.' 'Have you so?' replied the judge. 'Then take notice that if one man is killed, and you are tried before me, I will take care that every soldier of your party is hanged.' He then himself, accompanied by his tipstaves, went to the mob, and, boldly facing them, by explaining to them the impropriety of their conduct, with a promise that justice should be done against the crimps, induced them quietly to disperse.

Among the anecdotes that have reference to his early follies is the following, which shows that he did not hesitate to acknowledge them when the confession would serve the ends of justice. In a trial of an old woman for witchcraft, the witness against her declared that she used a 'spell.' 'Let me see it,' said the judge. A scrap of parchment being handed up to him, he asked the old woman how she came by it, and on her answering, 'A young gentleman, my lord, gave it me to cure my daughter's ague,' enquired whether it cured her. 'Oh! yes, my lord, and many others,' replied the old woman. He then turned to the jury and said, 'Gentlemen, when I was young and thoughtless, and out of money, I and some companions, as unthinking as myself, went to this woman's house, then a public one, and having no money to pay our reckoning, I hit upon a stratagem to get off scot-free. Seeing her daughter ill of an ague, I pretended I had a spell to cure her. I wrote the classic line you see, and gave it her, so that if any is punishable, it is I, and not the poor woman.' She was of course acquitted, and did not fail to receive from the judge a compensation for the trouble he had caused her. In none of the trials before him for this supposed crime was a conviction obtained, and 'prosecutions for it from his time fell into discredit, which was increased by his putting into the pillory one Hathaway, convicted of pretending to be bewitched by a poor woman whom he had recently indicted for the crime. Of the idle companions of his youthful frolics there is a melancholy tradition that it was his fate to have one of them tried before him and convicted of felony. The prisoner was afterwards visited by him in gaol, and to his enquiry after their college intimates, answered, 'Ah! my lord, they are all hanged but myself and your lordship.' (*Noble's Granger*, i. 165.) His only legal publication was an edition of Sir John Keyling's Reports, to which he subjoined three important cases which he had decided.

He married Anne, daughter of Sir John Cropley, Bart., who brought him no issue. (*Athen. Oxon.* iv. 505; *Life* [1764]; *Welsby's Lives*, 90.)

HOPTON, WALTER DE. To the ancestor of this family, whose property was situate in Herefordshire and Shropshire, King William is stated to have granted the celebrated rhyming charter, preserved in Blount's 'Tenures' (102). Whatever may be the authenticity of the record, there is little doubt that Walter de Hopton was a descendant of the alleged grantee. In 35 Henry III., 1251, Johanna, the widow of Walter de Hopton, paid for an assize in Herefordshire. (*Excerpt. e Rot. Fin.* ii. 119.) These probably were the father and mother of the judge. His own wife was Johanna, the daughter of William de Scalariis.

In 1272 he acted as a justice itinerant in Worcestershire, and on April 24, 1274, 2 Edward I., he was one of the barons of the Exchequer. At the end of that, or the beginning of the following year, he was removed into the King's Bench, and is mentioned as a justice itinerant in 6 Edward I. The name does not occur again till 13 Edward I., 1284, in which and in the two following years he was joined in various commissions as a justice itinerant (*Madox*, ii. 320), and was one of those who were fined for corruption by King Edward on his return to England in 1289. By his petition to the king in 1290, he represents that he was not guilty of a charge brought against Solomon de Rochester and his companion justices itinerant in Norfolk, inasmuch as he was not associated with them till after the time when the offence was committed, nor did he know of the presentment until he was taken before the council and committed to the Tower. If, as Weever says, he was fined in the sum of 2000 marks, there were probably further charges against him. It would seem, however, that his appeal to the royal favour was successful, for in the same year the king assigned to him the lands of which his wife had died seised. From the twenty-fifth to the thirtieth year of the reign also he was not only summoned to perform military service in respect of his lands, but was twice elected as assessor of the fifteenth and other charges on the county of Hereford. In 33 Edward I. he was returned as knight of that shire, and in the same year he died in possession of property in Shropshire of very considerable extent.

It seems to be more than probable that the above facts refer to two persons named Walter de Hopton; that they were father and son; and that the division should be made between the sixth and thirteenth years of the reign.

HORTON, ROGER, possessed the manors of Catton and Brysingcotes in Derbyshire, in which county he probably was born. His arguments as an advocate commence in 1 Henry IV., and continue till he was called to the judicial seat in the King's Bench on June 16, 1415, 3 Henry V. He was reappointed on the accession of Henry VI., but died before the termination of the first year —viz., on April 30, 1423. He was buried in St. Dunstan's Church, Fleet Street. (*Cal. Rot. Pat.* 264, 269.)

HOSE, GEOFFREY, or HOESE, was the son of Henry, and held a barony in the county of Wilts. He was sheriff of Oxfordshire in 26 Henry II. and two following years. In 1179 he was one of the persons selected by the council of Windsor to act as justices itinerant in certain counties forming one of the four divisions into which England was then arranged; and his pleas appear on the roll of the following year, but not subsequently. (*Madox*, i. 138.)

He gave the church of Little Fageham to the canons of St. Dionysius in Southampton, and some lands to the monks of Stanley in Wiltshire. (*Dugdale's Baronage*, i. 622.) He died in 1 John, 1199, when his wife, Gundred de Warenne, gave two hundred marks for the custody of Geoffrey, his heir, and all his lands until he was of age. (*Madox*, i. 202.)

HOSPITALI, RALPH DE, was another of the 'inquisitores' against the sheriffs in 1170, 16 Henry II. In the Great Roll of 31 Henry II. he and Hugh Cophin render an account of the proceeds of the abbey of Tavistock, then in the king's hands. (*Madox*, i. 311.) He held a prebend in Exeter Cathedral, and the chapel of Walingford, both of which he resigned in 9 John, 1207. (*Rot. Pat.* i. 75, 81.)

HOTHAM, JOHN DE (BISHOP OF ELY), was a descendant of John de Trehouse, who, for his assistance to the Conqueror at the battle of Hastings, obtained the grant of the manor of Hotham in Yorkshire, with others. In 27 Edward I. he was assessor of the tenth then granted, and in 2 Edward II. he was sent to Ireland as chancellor of the Exchequer (*Cal. Rot. Pat.* 69); but in the next two years he is found acting as the king's escheator on both sides of the Trent. (*Abb. Rot. Orig.* i. 168–174.) In 1311 he was 'custos domorum' of Peter de Gaveston in the city of London, the termination of whose career in June 1312 did not interrupt Hotham's advance. On December 13 he was made chancellor of the Exchequer in England, and in May 1313, being then called canon of York, was sent on a mission to the court of France. In August 1314, and again in September 1315 (*N. Fœdera*, ii. 147–276), he went with extraordinary powers to Ireland, then invaded by Edward Bruce, the King of Scotland's brother, to effect a reconciliation with the barons, and to treat with the natives. In this he was only partially successful; for though he induced the tenants of the crown to associate in binding themselves, under the penalties of forfeiture, to aid each other to the utmost in their efforts against the common enemy, he made little impression on the chiefs of the natives. (*Lingard*, iii. 306.) It does not appear that while thus employed he was removed from his office of chancellor of the Exchequer, which he certainly held in Easter 1316 (*Madox*, ii. 327), and probably did not retire from it till his election to the bishopric of Ely, which took place on July 20.

In 1317 he was raised to the treasurership of the Exchequer, and held that office till June 10, 1318. (*Madox*, ii. 39.) On the following day the Great Seal was delivered to him as chancellor; but for the next six or seven weeks he was obliged to leave the duties of his office to be performed by deputies, as he was engaged in frequent journeys on the king's affairs. He held the Great Seal for about nineteen months, during the latter part of which period he was engaged in negotiating a truce with the Scots. (*N. Fœdera*, iii. 409.) After his resignation on January 23, 1320, he still continued to be employed by the king on several confidential missions.

Three days after the accession of Edward III., viz. on January 28, 1327, he was again entrusted with the office of chancellor, and continued to perform its duties till March 1 in the following year. He then retired from its labours, and during the remainder of his life devoted himself to the administration of his diocese.

His expenditure for his cathedral was enormous for those times, and his confirmation to the see of the manor of Oldbourne in London was among the liberal acts which illustrated his presidency. During the last two years of his life he was entirely disabled by paralysis, which terminated in his death, at his palace of Somersham, on January 25, 1336, leaving behind him a high character for piety, prudence, and liberality. (*Godwin*, 260.)

His nephew was summoned to parliament as a baron in 8 Edward II., but not afterwards. It was the descendant of that nobleman who was created a baronet in 1621, and whose conduct as governor of Hull, in the civil wars, led to his own and his son's untimely execution. From his grandson descended Sir Beaumont Hotham, the subject of the next article.

HOTHAM, BEAUMONT (afterwards LORD HOTHAM), was of the same family as that of the above prelate. The seventh possessor of the baronetcy conferred in 1621 was Sir Beaumont Hotham, who by his wife Frances, daughter of the Rev. William Thomson, had five sons, on four of whom the title successively devolved. The third son, Admiral William Hotham, for his gallant achievements at the commencement of the French Revolution, was in 1797 created Baron Hotham in the Irish peerage, with a special remainder to the heirs of his father. On his death without issue in May 1813, his two elder brothers having left no representative, the heir to both titles was his next brother, the judge, now to be noticed.

Beaumont Hotham was the fourth son of Sir Beaumont, and was born in 1737. He was called to the bar at the Middle Temple in May 1758. He practised in the Chancery courts, but with little success and less distinction, and was member for Wigan in the two parliaments of 1768 and 1774. He was appointed on May 10, 1775, a baron of the Exchequer, and knighted. He sat in that court for the long space of thirty years, and the only variation in his judicial career was in 1783, when he was placed as third commissioner of the Great Seal in the interval between the two chancellorships of Lord Thurlow. This lasted for nearly nine months, from April 9 to December 23. Though he never had any business at the bar, by the effect of great natural sense and an excellent understanding he made a good judge, and was deservedly esteemed for his polished manners, marked by courtesy, kindness, and attention. So circumscribed was his knowledge of law that when any difficulty arose he was in the habit of recommending the case to be referred, thus acquiring among the wags of Westminster Hall the nickname of 'The Common Friend.' In criminal cases he was distinguished for his humanity, and for his impressive and pathetic addresses to prisoners.

Feeling the infirmities of age approaching, he resigned in Hilary Term 1805, but lived for nine years afterwards. On his brother's death on May 2, 1813, he succeeded to the title of Lord Hotham, but enjoyed it only ten months, his own death occurring on March 4, 1814. By his marriage with Susannah, daughter of Sir Thomas Hankey, an alderman of London, and widow of James Norman, Esq., he had three sons and three daughters. The title is now enjoyed by his grandson.

HOUBRUG, WILLIAM DE, is recorded on the Fine Roll of 8 Henry III., 1224 (i. 122), as taking some amerciaments of assizes of novel disseisin in Shropshire with Ralph, Bishop of Chichester; but this is the only entry which notices him in a judicial capacity.

William de Hobregge is mentioned by Roger de Wendover (iii. 297-356) as one of the confederates against King John in 1215, and as having incurred the sentence of excommunication in the following year. His lands in Kent and Essex were then seized and granted to Richard Fitz-Hugh. (*Rot. Claus.* i. 165, 239, 247.) Under the new reign he returned to his allegiance, and, with his wife, Agnes, and her sister Alicia, the wife of Richard le Buteiller, was admitted in 3 Henry III. to the lands of Richard Picot, whose heirs the ladies were. (*Excerpt. e Rot. Fin.* i. 23.)

HOUGHTON, JOHN DE, or HOUTON, was connected in early life with the Exchequer. In 19 Edward II. he accompanied the king to France in that character, and was then the parson of the church of Postwick, a parish in Norfolk. In that county he had the manor of Wormegay and considerable property. In 1 Edward III. he was clerk of the keeper of the wardrobe, and was advanced to be one of the chamberlains of the Exchequer in the twelfth year, in which office he continued till he was called to the bench of that court as a baron on March 8, 1347. We are not told the time of his death. (*N. Fœdera*, ii. 606, iii. 25, 53; *Devon's Issue Roll*, 139; *Cal. Exch.* iii. 166.) He was probably the father of the undermentioned Adam.

HOUGHTON, ADAM DE (BISHOP OF ST. DAVID'S), was probably the son of the above John de Houton. He was educated at Oxford, and adopted the clerical profession. His connection with the court is evidenced by his being appointed in 1360 one of the commissioners to receive possession of the counties and cities which the King of France had agreed to give up by treaty. (*N. Fœdera*, iii. 511, 679.)

In 1361 he was, by papal provision, placed in the see of St. David's, and was made chancellor on January 11, 1377, 50 Edward III. In the following April he was at the head of the commissioners to negotiate a peace with France, and for this purpose he proceeded to Calais, and was still there at the time of King Edward's death on June 21, 1377. On his immediate return to England he was re-sworn into his office. He then resided in Fleet Street.

His chancellorship, which lasted only till October 29, 1378, was remarkable for nothing but the resumption of Biblical texts into his addresses to the parliament, a practice which had been discontinued by William of Wykeham and his successors in the office. Among other somewhat ludicrous applications, he commenced one of his orations with the passage of St. Paul, 'Ye suffer fools gladly, seeing that ye yourselves are wise,' adding to the assembly, 'And as ye are wise and I am foolish, I presume you desire to hear me.' (*Rot. Parl.* ii. 361.) He died in April 1389. (*Godwin*, 581.)

HOUGHTON, ROBERT, born at Gunthorpe in Norfolk, in 1548, was called to the bar at Lincoln's Inn in 1577, and appointed reader in 1591, and again in 1600. He was one of several who were nominated by Queen Elizabeth to be serjeants; but in consequence of her death were re-summoned by James, and took the degree in Easter Term 1603. He represented the city of Norwich in the parliament of 1593, and was chosen its recorder in 1603, an office which he held till April 21, 1613, when he was made a judge of the King's Bench and knighted. In Peacham's case, who was tried in 1615 for divers treasonable passages contained in a sermon which was never preached nor intended to be preached, but only set down in writing and found in his study, King James, by the advice of Bacon, commenced the unconstitutional practice of obtaining the opinion of the judges before trial; and he joined with Sir Edward Coke in resisting 'this taking of auricular opinions single and apart,' as new and dangerous. The trial took place, and though the poor man was found guilty, yet, notwithstanding all Bacon's endeavours, he was not executed, many of the judges being of opinion, as every reasonable man must be, that the offence was not treason. (*State Trials*, ii. 869.)

Sir Robert Houghton died at his chambers in Serjeants' Inn, Chancery Lane, on February 6, 1623-4, and was buried at the church of St. Dunstan's-in-the-West. Croke calls him 'a most reverend, prudent, learned, and temperate judge, and inferior to none in his time.'

His wife was Mary, the daughter of Robert Rychers, Esq., of Wrotham in Kent, by whom he had three sons and three daughters. (*Blomefield's Norwich*, i. 359; *Norfolk*, i. 625.)

HOUTON, JOHN DE, frequently spelled Hocton, was archdeacon of Bedford when he was one of the justices itinerant appointed in 9 Henry III., 1225, for the counties of Bedford and Buckingham (*Rot. Claus.* ii. 77), and seems to have been much in the royal confidence. In January 1224 he was sent on a mission to the court of Rome; and on his return, the distribution of the stones of the castle of Bedford, then razed to the ground in consequence of Faukes de Breaute's rebellion, was entrusted to him, with Henry de Braybroc and the sheriff of the county. In the next year, besides his appointment as a justice itinerant, he was again employed in foreign parts, first in July, and then in October (*Rot. Claus.* i. 582-654, ii. 47-83); and in 1228 he took the principal part in the mission to Rome to oppose the election of Walter de Heynsham as Archbishop of Canterbury. In 1231 he changed his archdeaconry for that of Northampton, and died in 1246. (*Le Neve*, 161.)

HOWARD, WILLIAM, was the ancestor of the Dukes of Norfolk. Henry Howard, of Corby Castle, in his Memorials (*App.* xl.), makes him the grandson of Robert Howard, of Terrington and Wiggenhall, near Lynn in Norfolk, living in 12 Henry III., and son of John Howard, living in 45 Henry III., and Lucy Germund, his wife, adding that they were 'what we should call private gentlemen of small estate, probably of Saxon origin, living at home, intermarrying with their neighbours, and witnessing each other's deeds of conveyance and contracts.'

William Howard was selected as one of the eight special justices who were assigned in 21 Edward I., 1293, to take assizes throughout the realm, in aid of the judges of both benches, and of the justices itinerant. The district to which he was assigned comprehended the northern counties.

On October 11, 1297, he was constituted one of the judges of the Common Pleas. (*Madox*, ii. 91.) Both in 33 and 35 Edward I. he was one of the judges named in commissions of trailbaston. (*Rot. Parl.* i. 178, 218.)

On the accession of Edward II. he was re-appointed, and sat in the court during the whole of the first and part of the second year of that reign; the patent of his successor, Henry le Scrope, being dated November 20, 1308. Howard is described as chief justice of England on a window in the church of Long Melford in Suffolk, where he is portrayed in his judge's robes; but as this was not erected till about the reign of Edward IV. or of Henry VII. (*Dugdale's Orig.* 44, 99), and therefore nearly two hundred years after his death, it cannot be accepted as authority for a fact of which no other evidence appears.

He had two wives, both of whom were named Alice. The first was a daughter of Sir Robert Ufford, the ancestor of the family which acquired the earldom of Suffolk. The second was the daughter of Sir Edmund de Fitton, of Fitton in Wiggenhall, St. Germain's, which she afterwards inherited. She and her husband resided at East Winch, near Lynn, where he built a chapel, adjoining the church, in which he was probably buried.

The first marriage produced no issue; but by the second he left two sons, Sir John and Sir William. Sir Robert, the lineal descendant of this Sir John in the fifth generation, married Margaret, the daughter of Thomas Mowbray, Duke of Norfolk, who ultimately became coheir of John Mowbray, the fourth duke. Their son John Howard was summoned to Parliament as Baron Howard by Edward IV. in 1470, and was created earl marshal and Duke of Norfolk by Richard III. in 1485, and is Shakspeare's 'Jockey of Norfolk.'

Not only does this, the premier dukedom, remain in the family; but in the present House of Peers the earldoms of Suffolk and Berkshire, of Carlisle and of Effingham, and the barony of Howard of Walden are represented by descendants from the same parentage. Besides these, several other peerages which have now become extinct flourished during various periods: the viscounty of Bindon from 1559 to 1619; the earldom of Nottingham from 1597 to 1681; the earldom of Northampton from 1604 to 1614; the barony of Howard of Escrick from 1628 to 1714; the earldom of Norwich from 1672 to 1777; the earldom of Stafford from 1688 to 1762; the earldom of Bindon from 1706 to 1722.

HULL. *See* J. and R. HILL.

HULLOCK, JOHN, was a native of Durham, where his father, Timothy Hullock, was a master weaver, and proprietor of a timber yard at Barnard Castle. Born in 1764, he was articled to an attorney at Stokesley in Yorkshire, where he grounded himself so well in the principles of the legal science that the noted barrister Mr. Lee, whom he often met on his visits to an uncle, was so struck by his intelligence and application that he recommended him strongly to go to the bar. Acting on this advice, he was entered as a student at Gray's Inn, and, having become a barrister in May 1794, he joined the Northern Circuit. In 1792 he published a valuable work called 'The Law of Costs,' which became quite an authority, and went through several editions. This made his name known, and necessarily introduced him to extended employment; so that in 1816 he felt himself warranted in accepting the degree of the coif.

On the Northern Circuit his honourable feeling and his courageous conduct were on one occasion tried and exhibited. In a cause which he led he was particularly instructed not to produce a certain deed unless it should be absolutely required. Notwithstanding this injunction, he produced it before it was necessary, with the view of deciding the business at once. It proved to have been forged by his client's attorney; and Mr. Justice Bayley, who was trying the cause, ordered the deed to be impounded, that it might be made the subject of a prosecution. Before this could be done, Mr. Hullock requested leave to inspect it, and on its being handed to him, immediately returned it to his bag. The judge remonstrated, but in vain. 'No power on earth,' Mr. H. replied, 'should induce him to surrender it. He had incautiously put the life of a fellow-creature in peril; and, though he had acted to the best of his discretion, he should never be happy again were a fatal result to ensue.' The judge continued to insist on the redelivery of the deed, but declined taking decisive measures till he had consulted the associate judge. While retiring for that purpose the deed was of course destroyed, and the attorney escaped.

He signalised himself by the manner in which he conducted the prosecutions at Manchester against Hunt and his seditious associates. Just before he was raised to the bench, he was sent with Mr. (afterwards Sir Joseph) Littledale to Scotland, to arrange some criminal proceedings of the same nature on the part of the crown. He met his reward by being appointed on March 1, 1823, to fill a vacant seat in the Exchequer.

For little more than six years he discharged the duties of his office in a most exemplary manner. A perfect master of the law, he expounded it with a liberal spirit, clearing it from all useless technicalities, and acting upon its plain intention. Firmness and mildness were equally his characteristics, and to these were united integrity, sagacity, and knowledge. While on the circuit he was suddenly seized with a severe bowel complaint at Abingdon, which terminated his life on July 31, 1829. His estimation among his colleagues may be judged from the following energetic commendation with which a brother baron spoke of him to a grand jury: 'He circumscribed the ocean of law with firm and undeviating steps.'

HULS, or HOLES, HUGH, is stated by Ashmole to be the grandson of Sir William of the Hulse, in Cheshire, by that knight's second son, David. He is mentioned in Richard Bellewe's Reports, and on May 20, 1389, 12 Richard II., he was appointed a judge of the King's Bench. During the remainder of that reign, the whole of the reign of Henry IV., and the first two years of that of Henry V., he retained that position, and under King Richard he acted for several years as *locum tenens* for the justice of North Wales. (*First Rep. Pub. Rec.*, *App.* 91.)

He died in 1415, and was buried in the church of Watford in Hertfordshire. (*Weever*, 591.) On his tomb he is called Hugo de Holes, as he is also in the above-mentioned roll. His wife was Margaret, daughter of John Domville, of Moberley in Cheshire, and his descendants were settled at Sutton Courtney in Berkshire.

HUNT, ROGER, of Chalverston in Bedfordshire, was probably the son of Roger Hunt, who was attornatus regis in August 1406, 9 Henry IV. (*Cal. Rot. Pat.* 254.) Of this Roger the first mention occurs as speaker of the parliament of 8 Henry V., he being then member for Huntingdonshire. He next appears as counsel for John Mowbray, earl marshal, in his claim for precedence above the Earl of Warwick before the parliament in April 1425, 3 Henry VI. In July 1433 he was again presented as speaker of that parliament. (*Rot. Parl.* iv. 268, 296, 420.) On November 3, 1438, 17 Henry VI., he was appointed a baron of the Exchequer, and the last entry in which he is named is a grant to him, 'for divers considerations,' of 200*l.* out of the customs of London in 1443. (*Acts Privy Council*, iv. 327, v. 227.)

HUNTINGFIELD, ROGER DE, was the grandson of a baron of the same name, who in the reign of King Stephen gave the Isle of Mendham in Suffolk to the monks of Castle Acre in Norfolk, and the younger son of Roger de Huntingfield. In 8 John he was one of the justiciers before whom fines were levied, and in the following year his lands were seized on occasion of the interdict, and were placed by the king in the hands of his brother, the under-mentioned William. (*Rot. Claus.* i. 110; *Dugdale's Baronage*, ii. 7.)

HUNTINGFIELD, WILLIAM DE, the elder brother of the above-mentioned Roger, also acted as a justicier before whom fines were levied in 10 and 11 John, 1208–1210. In the fines themselves, which were taken at Cambridge and Lincoln, the justiciers are specially called justices itinerant.

During the greater part of John's reign he seems to have been a favourite with the king, being appointed constable of Dover Castle in 5 John, giving, however, his son and daughter as hostages for his safe holding thereof. (*Rot. Pat.* 34.) From 11 to 15 John he held the sheriffalty of the united counties of Norfolk and Suffolk. But on the barons forming their confederacy against the king he joined them, and was one of the twenty-five who were appointed to enforce the observance of Magna Charta. He made himself so prominent in the subquent wars that he was excommunicated by the pope, and his lands, being seized into the king's hands, were not restored to him till 1217, 1 Henry III., when he returned to his allegiance. In June 1219 he obtained licence to go to the Holy Land, constituting his brother Thomas his attorney to transact all business in his absence. (*Rot. Claus.* i. 215–393.)

His death occurred in or before 9 Henry III., as in that year his son Roger (by his wife Alice de St. Liz) instituted a suit against his bailiff for an account of rents. (*Ibid.* ii. 83.) Roger's grandson was summoned to parliament by Edward I., but in 1351 the barony became extinct. (*Dugdale's Baronage*, ii. 7.)

HUSCARL, ROGER, is frequently named in the fines levied at Westminster from 11 to 16 John. He continued to act as a justicier till 7 Henry III., when he was sent to Ireland, where it is evident he held the next place on the bench to the chief justice. (*Rot. Claus.* i. 526.)

The mode of remunerating the judges, both in England and Ireland, in that age seems to have been by appropriating to them certain lands during the king's pleasure. Thus, in 16 John, the land which was of Roger de Tanton, in Kent, was given to him 'ad se sustentandum in servicio domini regis quamdiu eidem domino regi placuit;' and in 10 Henry III. the town of Baliscadam in Ireland was devoted in the same manner to him and others. (*Ibid.* i. 204, ii. 125.) He seems to have been lord paramount of a manor in the vill of Stepney, which in 1290 was called 'Stebynhyth Huscarl.' (*Gent. Mag.* April 1855, p. 388.)

HUSE, JAMES, was not improbably a younger scion of the baronial family of that name. He was made a baron of the Exchequer on April 16, 1350, 24 Edward III. In 34 Edward III. he was employed as a commissioner to treat with the people of the counties of Somerset, Dorset, Wilts, Devon, and Cornwall, as to raising forces for the defence of the kingdom. (*N. Fœdera*, iii. 449.)

HUSE, WILLIAM, there is little doubt, belonged also to the noble family of Hoese or Huse, and in all probability was the son of Sir Henry Huse, knight, who had a grant of free warren in 8 Henry VI. within his manor of Herting in Sussex, a property which was held by the Baron Henry in the reign of Henry III. (*Cal. Rot. Pat.* 39, 276.) He was a member of Gray's Inn, and on June 16, 1471, 11 Edward IV., he received the appointment of attorney-general, with full power of deputing clerks and officers under him in any court of record (*Ibid.* 316)—a power which is still introduced into the modern patents. It was not till Trinity Term 1478 that he took the degree of the coif, probably resigning the attorney-generalship, as the degree of serjeant-at-law was at that time superior to the office of attorney-general, and no one had lately held the two together. Three years subsequently, on May 7, 1481, he was made chief justice of the King's Bench. (*Cal. Rot. Pat.* 326.)

On the accessions of Edward V., Richard III., and Henry VII., his patent of chief justice was renewed, showing how little the violent changes of the time interfered with the regular administration of the law, and how little connected with political movements the judges were deemed to be. He was named by Henry VII. as one of the commissioners to decide on the claims made to do service at his coronation. (*Rutland Papers*, 8.)

In the first year of this reign he supported the purity of his office by successfully remonstrating with the king against the judges being consulted beforehand in crown cases which were afterwards to come before them judicially. (*Coke's* 3 *Inst.* 29.)

In June 1492 he was one of those commissioned to treat with the ambassadors of the King of France (*Rymer*, xii. 481), and on November 24, 1495, Sir John Fineux was appointed his successor in the chief justiceship. Whether the vacancy was occasioned by the death or retirement of Sir William Huse there is no distinct information; but probably by the former.

The name was evidently then pronounced Husey or Husee, and was often so spelled, and also House and Howsy. It gradually was changed to Hussey, by which the representatives of the family have since called themselves.

Sir William married Elizabeth, the daughter of Thomas Berkeley, of Wymondham, Esq., by whom he had several children. The eldest, John, was summoned to parliament by Henry VIII. in 1534; but being attainted and beheaded two years afterwards, the barony was lost. From Sir William's son Robert descended Sir Edward Hussey, of Honnington in Lincolnshire, who was created a baronet in 1611, and whose third son, Charles Hussey, of Caythorpe in the same county, received the same honour in 1661. Both titles were united in 1706, and both became extinct in 1734. (*Dugdale's Baron.* ii. 309; *Burke's Ext. Baronet.* 275.)

HUSSEBURN, THOMAS DE, is almost always mentioned with the addition 'Magister,' which in the reign of Henry II. began to be adopted by the clergy. He appears to have been only a canon of St. Paul's (*Dugdale's Orig.* 22), but several of the bishoprics and abbeys which were vacant during the reigns of Henry II. and Richard I. were placed in his custody. (*Madox*, i. 310, 311; *Angl. Sacr.* i. 169.)

His judicial employment in those reigns, and in that of John, appears by his presence in the Curia Regis as one of the justiciers before whom fines were levied in 33 Henry II., 1187, from the fifth year of Richard I. to the end of the reign, and in the first year of King John; and also by his acting as a justice itinerant, holding pleas and assessing tallages, in 33 Henry II. and 3 Richard I. (*Madox*, i. 544, 634.)

HUTCHINS, GEORGE. Narcissus Luttrell relates in his Diary that on a motion in Chancery relative to the guardianship of a child, Parson Hickeringill the claimant said of Sir George Hutchins, who was counsel against him, that they were something akin to each other, not by consanguinity, but by affinity, for he was a clerk, and Sir George's father was a parish clerk. Whether this story had any foundation, or was only invented for the purpose which it effected, ' of setting the court a laughing,' has not been discovered. Sir George is described in the Gray's Inn books as son and heir of Edmund Hutchins, of Georgham in Devonshire, gentleman, and is stated to have been called to the bar in August 1667.

He was summoned by James II. in Easter 1686 to take the degree of the coif, and in May 1689 was appointed king's serjeant to William III., who knighted him. In May of the next year he was nominated third commissioner of the Great Seal, an office which he filled for nearly three years, till March 22, 1693. On his discharge Sir George claimed a right to retain his former position of king's serjeant, and on the question being referred to the judges they determined that, though his appointment of lord commissioner did not deprive him of his degree of the coif, it extinguished his post of king's serjeant, which was merely an office conferred by the crown. The king, however, re-appointed him his serjeant on May 6. He continued to practise at the bar till his death on July 6, 1705, and his success may be estimated by the fact that on the marriage in 1697 of his two daughters (afterwards his coheirs) he gave each of them a portion of 20,000*l*. The husband of Anne, the second daughter, was William Peere Williams, the eminent Chancery reporter of that time; and their eldest son, Sir Hutchins Williams, was in 1747 honoured with a baronetcy, which became extinct in 1784. (*Luttrell's Diary*, i. 529, 598, iii. 93, iv. 289, 651, v. 570; 3 *Levinz*, 351.)

HUTTON, RICHARD, is called by King Charles, although he declared the imposition of ship-money to be illegal, 'the honest judge.' He was the second son of Anthony Hutton, of a good Yorkshire family residing at Penrith in Cumberland, and was born there about 1560. He was sent to Jesus College, Cambridge, where he devoted himself to the study of divinity, but was induced to pursue the law as a profession. He became a member, first, of Staple Inn, in the hall of which his arms are emblazoned on the south window, and next of Gray's Inn, where he was called to the bar on June 16, 1586. When James came to the crown, he was added to the list of those whom Queen Elizabeth, just before her death, had summoned to take the degree of the coif at Easter 1603, and was then knighted. (*Fuller's Worthies*, i. 237; *Athen. Oxon.* iii. 27.) In this character he was the leading counsel for the defendant in the case of the post-nati. (*State Trials*, ii. 609.)

In 1608 he was made recorder of York, and on May 3, 1617, was appointed a judge of the Common Pleas. Lord Chancellor Bacon's address to him on his being sworn in is memorable for the character it gives of him, and the advice it offers. 'The king,' it begins, 'being duly informed of your learning, integrity, discretion, experience, means, and reputation in your country, hath thought fit not to leave you these talents to be employed upon yourself only, but to call you to serve himself and his people.' Among the counsels he gave were ' that you should draw your learning from your books, not out of your brain;' 'that you should be a light to jurors to open their eyes, but not a guide to lead them by the noses;' 'that your speech be with gravity as one of the sages of the law, and not talkative, nor with impertinent flying out to show learning;' and particularly 'that your hands, and the hands of your hands, I mean those about you, be clean and uncorrupt from gifts, from meddling with titles and from serving of turns, be they of great ones or small ones.' (*Works*, vii. 278.) Pity that his own precept was not followed by the lecturer as well as it was by his auditor.

On the accession of Charles I., Sir Richard Hutton was the eldest puisne judge of the court, and on the death of Chief Justice Hobart, so much confidence was placed in his learning and integrity that the vacancy was not supplied for nearly a year, during which he presided as prime judge. (*Croke, Car.* 56.) When Sir John Finch applied to each of the judges separately for their opinions with regard to ship-money, Justice Hutton refused to subscribe, and although he afterwards signed the united opinion which they gave in favour of its legality, he declared, when Hampden's case came judicially before him in 1637, that he had so subscribed only for conformity with the majority, but that his private opinion was ever against it; and he gave his reasons, as he said, ' with as much perspicuity as those imperfections which attend my age will give me leave,' why judgment ought not to be given for the king. (*State Trials*, iii. 844,

1191.) He repeated his interpretation of the law in his charge to the grand jury at Northampton when Thomas Harrison, a clergyman of that county, foolishly taking umbrage at this, came to the bar of the Common Pleas, and cried out in a loud voice, 'I do accuse Mr. Justice Hutton of high treason.' He soon suffered for his temerity. Being indicted for the offence, he was fined 5000*l.* and imprisoned, and required to make his submission in all the courts at Westminster. The only point of the story that does not tell to the judge's credit is that he also brought an action for damages against Harrison, and recovered 10,000*l.* (*Croke, Car.* 503.)

He died on February 25, 1638-9, leaving a large family and a fair estate at Goldsborough in Yorkshire, and was buried at St. Dunstan's-in-the-West. He compiled 'Reports of sundry Cases,' which were published after his death. (*Surtees*' *Durham*, i. clxvi.)

HYDE, NICHOLAS, to whose family Norbury, in the county of Chester, had belonged in regular descent from the time of the Conquest, was the youngest son of Lawrence Hyde, of West Hatch in Wiltshire, by Anne, daughter of Nicholas Sybill, Esq., of Chimbhams in Kent, and widow of Matthew Somerton, Esq., of Claverton in Somersetshire.

At his father's death he was left dependent on his mother, except an annuity of 30*l.* for life bequeathed to him by his father. Admitted to the Middle Temple, he was called to the bar by that society, who elected him their reader in Lent 1617, and their treasurer in 1626. He had previously entered parliament in 1603 as member for Christchurch, Hants, and he is first noticed in the Reports as an advocate in 1613. He had sufficiently distinguished himself to be employed by the Duke of Buckingham in preparing his defence to the articles of impeachment prepared against him by the House of Commons in 1626. (*Parl. Hist.* ii. 167; *Whitelocke*, 8.) The care and ingenuity evinced in that defence were so satisfactory to the duke that he was by the favourite's influence nominated chief justice of the King's Bench on February 5, 1627 (*Rymer*, xviii. 835), and knighted.

He presided in the court for four years and a half only, and had no easy time of it. He and the other judges had to justify themselves before the House of Lords for refusing to discharge the five gentlemen who were imprisoned for refusing to contribute to the loan. (*Parl. Hist.* ii. 291.) He had also, in 1629, to adjudge the case of Stroud, Sir John Eliot, and the other members, for their violence to the speaker on the last day of the session. They were at first refused bail, unless they gave sureties for their good behaviour, which they refusing, some of them were tried and sentence pronounced upon them. For these proceedings the judges in the commencement of the Long Parliament in 1640 were called to account, and their judgment reversed. (*State Trials*, iii. 235-335; *Whitelocke*, 38.) Long before this investigation took place Sir Nicholas was removed from the violence of the times. He was seized with a fever, which Lord Clarendon says he got from the infection of some gaol in the summer circuit, and died on August 25, 1631.

In the opinions given by him and his colleagues, in answer to the king's questions, they seem to have acted an independent part, and also on several other occasions, in refusing to stop the course of justice at the king's command. Sir Nicholas is said to have been mean in his person and bearing, and was so unostentatious that he rode his circuits on horseback, according to Sir Symonds D'Ewes, in a whitish-blue cloak, 'more like a clothier or a woolman than a lord chief justice.' But Croke and Whitelocke, his contemporaries and colleagues, and Lord Clarendon, his nephew, give evidence of the sterling points of his character. Croke (*Car.* 225) calls him 'a grave, religious, discreet man, and of great learning and piety.' Judge Whitelocke says that 'he lived in the place with great integrity and uprightness, and with great wisdom and temper, considering the ticklishness of the times. He would never undertake to the king, nor adventure to give him a resolute answer in any weighty business, when the question was of the law, but he would pray that he might confer with his brethren.' (*Rushworth*, ii. 111.) Lord Clarendon says of him (*Life*, i. 3-13), 'His justice and sincerity were so conspicuous throughout the kingdom that the death of no judge had in any time been more lamented.'

He married Margaret, daughter of Arthur Swayne, Esq., of Sarson, and left several children.

HYDE, EDWARD (EARL OF CLARENDON), will ever be regarded with admiration and reverence for his devoted adherence to Charles I. during his misfortunes, and to Charles II. for nearly twenty years after. His services to both monarchs, and the influence he exercised in the councils of that eventful period, must necessarily occupy a large and interesting portion of the annals of the kingdom; and though the principles by which he was guided, and the motives which prompted him, will no doubt be variously represented according to the political bias of the writers who record his actions— one party impugning what the other extols, and his conduct being painted now in deep shadow, and now in the brightest light,— the almost universal verdict, after two centuries of investigation, is an unreserved acknowledgment of his loyalty, his wisdom, and his integrity.

Henry Hyde, the father of the earl, was the third son of Lawrence Hyde of West Hatch, and the brother both of the above Sir Nicholas Hyde, and of Sir Lawrence, the father of the next mentioned Sir Robert Hyde. By his marriage with Mary, daughter and one of the coheirs of Edward Langford, Esq., of Trowbridge, he had a large family. Edward was the third of his four sons, and was born at Dinton in Wiltshire, the family residence, on February 18, 1608-9. He was sent to Oxford with a royal recommendation to be elected a demy at Magdalen College; on the refusal of which (*Cal. State Papers* [1623], 8, 120) he was admitted a student at Magdalen Hall in Lent Term 1623. On taking his degree of B.A. he began his legal curriculum at the Middle Temple on February 1, 1626, his uncle Sir Nicholas being then treasurer. Early in 1633 he and Whitelocke were chosen the representatives of that society to manage the famous masque given by all the four inns of court to the king and queen, for the purpose of showing their disapproval of the doctrines promulgated by Prynne against interludes in his 'Histrio-Mastix.' (*Whitelocke*, 19.) He acknowledges that at first he gave himself up to gay society and did not pursue his legal studies very industriously, but still enough to enable him to pass respectably through his uncle's nightly examinations.

Before his call to the bar he had been married twice—once in 1629 to Anne, daughter of Sir George Ayliffe, who died six months afterwards; and again in 1632 to Frances, daughter of Sir Thomas Aylesbury, Bart. He was called to the bar on November 22, 1633, and received in December 1634 a grant of the office of keeper of the writs and rolls of the Common Pleas. (*Rymer*, xix. 605.) His name does not appear as a barrister in the Reports of this period, but he was engaged in causes before the council, and, according to his own account, he got into good practice in the Court of Requests, and realised a good professional income. Dividing his time between forensic studies and polite literature, he formed intimacies with the most eminent men in both classes, and was happy in the enjoyment of their society, till the troubles that afterwards arose divided him from some of his early friends.

In the first parliament of 1640 he was returned by two constituencies, Wooton Basset and Shaftesbury, and sat for the former. During its short session he spoke against the grievous encroachments of the Earl Marshal's Court, of which, in the second (or 'Long') parliament of that year, representing then the borough of Saltash, he procured the suppression. Though exerting himself at first for the removal of this and other enormous grievances, as soon as he saw the intention to encroach upon the royal prerogatives he stood forward in their support. The dominant party in the house, he says, were inimical to him from the first, knowing his devotion to the Church and his loyalty to the king, and particularly for his endeavours to save Lord Strafford's life. Yet they appear to have used him for their purposes, by making him chairman of several of their committees, and sending obnoxious messages by him to the Lords. Cromwell, whom he had occasion to rebuke for intemperate conduct in a private committee where he presided, entertained against him a great enmity, to which may probably be traced the harsh votes against him that were afterwards adopted. In 1641 he had his first interview with the king, who was desirous to thank him for his exertions in parliament, and to induce him to delay the bill against episcopacy till his majesty returned from Scotland, which Hyde, who was chairman of the committee, managed to effect. He secretly penned the answer adopted by the king to the remonstrance of the Commons, and in reward for his services was offered the place of solicitor-general, which he declined to accept, advising the king that it would be dangerous to turn out St. John at that time. He continued privately to give information to the court, as well before as after its removal to York, of all that was transacting in the house, supplying answers to the various declarations of the parliament, which the king, to screen him from discovery, invariably copied with his own hand.

The republican leaders, though they suspected Hyde to be the author, had not sufficient evidence of the fact to visit him with the vengeance they contemplated. As soon however as he eluded their intentions by joining the king at York, they disabled him from sitting in the house and excepted him from the pardon they offered to all who would withdraw from the king. On March 3, 1643, the office of chancellor and sub-treasurer of the Exchequer was granted to him for life (4 *Report Pub. Rec., App.* ii. 187); and he was at the same time knighted and sworn a privy counsellor. He was consulted by the king in his most secret affairs, composing most of the important state papers issued, and was one of the conductors of the issueless negotiation at Uxbridge. When it was determined to send Prince Charles to the west, Sir Edward Hyde was one of those appointed to accompany him, and his interview with the king at his departure on March 4, 1645, was the last that he had with the unfortunate monarch. He attended the prince till July 1646, when, his highness leaving Jersey, to which he had retired, for France, Hyde remained at the former place for the two succeeding years, employing his leisure in preparing his great work on the History of the Rebellion, some of the materials for which were supplied by the king himself. He then joined the prince again, and was with him at the time of his father's murder, when he was immediately sworn of the new king's privy council. Soon after he and Lord Cottington were sent as ambassadors to Spain, where their mission was not successful, and then returning to his family at Antwerp, he stayed there till after the battle of Worcester, when, being summoned to the king at Paris, he continued in close attendance on his majesty in all the various places at which he resided during his exile. The king relying on him as his chief adviser, he not only performed such duties as attached to his office (which it may well be supposed, considering the straitness of the Exchequer, were difficult enough), but also acted for some time as the principal secretary of state, and carried on the most important part of the correspondence. The weight of these duties was greatly increased by the extremity of penury and want which he suffered, of which he gives a pitiable account in his letter to Sir Edward Nicholas. Yet even then his position excited envy, and, with a view to his removal from it, a ridiculous charge was invented against him that he was in intimate correspondence with Cromwell, into whose chamber it was alleged he had been seen to enter on a secret visit to England. Charles treated it as it deserved, by giving his personal testimony of its falsehood.

The Great Seal, ever since Sir Edward Herbert's resignation in June 1654, had remained in the hands of the king without any occasion for its use. But now, being pestered with perpetual applications by the companions of his exile for offices, titles, and reversions, and by the adherents of Cromwell for secret confirmations of grants and estates, the king put an end to the personal annoyance by entrusting it on January 29, 1658, to Sir Edward Hyde, with the title of lord chancellor, and in that character he accompanied the king to England on the Restoration in 1660, for which by his cautious counsels he materially cleared the way. As chancellor he resided at first at Dorset House in Fleet Street, and afterwards at Worcester House in the Strand, till he removed in 1667 to the palace which he built at the top of St. James's Street, the magnificence of which so greatly increased the popular prejudice against him.

To the heavy and multifarious duties of this office were added those of the chancellor of the Exchequer, which he executed for several months after Charles's return, besides the management of all the important business of the state, and the necessary changes consequent on the renewal of legitimate government. He was, in fact, prime minister, without the title, but with all the envy and discontent usually attendant upon one who is supposed to guide the councils of his sovereign. Notwithstanding the confidence placed in him both by the late and the present king, the queen-dowager had from the first shown a distaste and almost an aversion to him, and her jealousy of the ascendency of his counsels instead of her own was in no degree abated by the successful results which she could not but attribute principally to him. Charles's confidence however was not to be shaken, and he disappointed Hyde's enemies by calling the chancellor up to the House of Peers, as Baron Hyde of Hindon (November 3, 1660), and by presenting him with a royal gift of 20,000*l.* Soon afterwards his daughter Anne's marriage with the Duke of York was acknowledged, and her claims fully recognised. On April 20, 1661, three days before the coronation, the chancellor was advanced from a barony to a viscounty and an earldom, by the titles of Viscount Cornbury in Wiltshire (an estate presented to him by the king), and Earl of Clarendon.

This elevation for a time silenced his enemies, and for the next year or two his influence in the royal councils suffered no diminution. The king treated him with kindness and familiarity, applied to him for advice in all emergencies, and even patiently submitted to the remonstrances he sometimes ventured to offer against the immorality so openly practised and encouraged at court. But at length the panders to those practices obtained the mastery. By ridiculing and mimicking the chancellor's overstrict formality, they led the king gradually, first to suffer, then to laugh at their indecent reflections, till by degrees the fickle pupil was ashamed of appearing to be schooled. Clarendon's credit at court thus sensibly declining, his policy became the next subject of attack. To him were attributed every political oversight, every royal disappointment, and every national calamity, corruption was insinuated and bribery was hinted, till at last his enemies acquired such an ascendency over the king and the parliament that his downfall and his ruin became inevitable.

The king became more and more tired of his reproachful lectures, administered, as the chancellor acknowledges, with unadvised earnestness; his enemies at court were more and more jealous of the influence he still retained; he had been all along obnoxious both to Presbyterians and Roman Catholics; and the people, taught to attribute to his mismanagement the miscarriages of the state, were strongly prejudiced against him. The way was thus fully paved to the success of the intrigue for his removal, in which the chief actors were the Duke of Buckingham,

Lord Arlington, and Sir William Coventry, urged on and aided by the arts of the Duchess of Cleveland, the king's shameless mistress. Clarendon, conscious of innocence, refused to resign, and the Great Seal was taken from him on August 30, 1667. At the meeting of parliament in October, the malice of his opponents not being satisfied with the triumph they had obtained, an impeachment for high treason was voted against him by the Commons; but the Lords refused to commit him upon so general an accusation until some particular charge was exhibited. No one can read the articles without seeing the weakness and frivolity of the allegations, none of them, even if true, amounting to treason. To each and every of them Clarendon has left a satisfactory answer; but during the discussion on the subject of his committal, which continued for near a month, and nearly led to an open breach between the two houses, he withdrew to France. This he was induced to do, much against his own judgment and inclination, in consequence of an intimation from the king, who, though at first acknowledging his innocence, was worked upon ungratefully to desert him; and from the urgency of his friends, who, considering the temper of the parliament and the people, were fearful if he stayed that he would meet with Strafford's fate.

He left a justificatory letter to the House of Lords, which, from the reflections it contained against his persecutors, so excited the bile of the Commons that it was ordered to be burned by the common hangman; and they pursued their inveteracy so far as to pass an act banishing him from the kingdom, and prohibiting all correspondence with him, except by his own children and servants. Their malice followed him abroad, France by their influence at first refusing him an asylum; but soon altering her policy and withdrawing her prohibition, the banished earl retired first to Montpellier, then to Moulins, and eventually to Rouen, patiently employing the seven years of his exile in the completion of those works which have raised his character and extended his fame. He died at the latter city on December 9, 1674, in the sixty-sixth year of his age. It seems extraordinary, and looks as if the party prejudice against him had subsided, that his remains should have been allowed a resting-place in Westminster Abbey, his body having been buried in Henry the Seventh's Chapel.

The imputation of bribery to which he is sometimes subject is sufficiently refuted, as well by the absence of any specific charges being brought forward at a time when they would have been welcomed and encouraged, as by his leaving, after such opportunities of accumulation, his family so poorly provided for. The building of his great house in St. James's, which nourished the popular prejudice against him, greatly exceeded the cost he intended, and compelled him for want of funds to mortgage his estate; and the nicknames of Holland House, and Dunkirk House, and Tangier Hall, by which it was satirically called, have been long dismissed as unfounded misnomers by the prejudiced multitude.

His judicial career was that of a cautious and prudent man, conscious of his deficiencies and anxious to supply them with the experience of others. He selected the best men to fill the vacancies on the bench, and he is said never to have pronounced an important decree without the assistance of two of the judges. In the administration of justice he is acknowledged to have been strictly impartial; and his 'orders' for the regulation of the officers of his court, rendered necessary by the change in the government, are still considered admirably adapted for their purpose. His principal fame now rests upon his valuable 'History of the Rebellion,' and the interesting memoirs of his own life; works which, though evidently betraying a desire to justify his royal masters in the course they respectively pursued, and even to find excuses for their most equivocal acts, will always be valued as displaying a deep knowledge of mankind, and as ably picturing the scenes he describes. Admired as these works deservedly are, and beautiful as are some of the characters he draws, it must be acknowledged that the length of his sentences and turn of his periods give a certain turgidity and stiffness to his style. His other writings were chiefly theological, devotional, and political, and few of them are now regarded.

It may be doubted whether he was benefited by the union of his daughter with the Duke of York; in fact, he prophesied that it would sooner or later prove his ruin; and it certainly did not retard it. Two queens were the issue of that connection, both holding prominent and honourable place in our history, the reign of one of whom acquired, from the eminent men who flourished in it, the designation of the Augustan Age. The earl's eldest son Henry (the author of the Diary of his Time) succeeded to the title, which, with that of the Earl of Rochester, became extinct in 1753. The earldom of Clarendon was revived in 1776 in the person of Thomas Villiers, a scion of the house of Jersey, who had married the granddaughter and heir of the last earl. (*Clarendon; Wood; Whitelocke; Burnet; Macdiarmid's Lives*; &c.)

HYDE, ROBERT, was the first cousin of the Earl of Clarendon, both being nephews of the above Sir Nicholas Hyde. His father, Sir Lawrence Hyde, held the office of attorney-general to Queen Anne, the consort of James I. By his marriage with Barbara, daughter of — Castilion, of Benham, Berks, Esq., he had no less than eleven sons, most of whom distinguished themselves in their several vocations. Of the four in holy orders, one, Alexander, became Bishop of Salisbury; another, Edward, dean of Windsor; and a third, Thomas, fellow of New College and judge of the Admiralty. Another son, Sir Henry, bred to diplomacy, was beheaded by the parliament in 1651, for his adherence to the king; and the youngest son, James, a doctor in medicine, was elected principal of Magdalen Hall. Two only followed their father's profession: Sir Frederick, queen's serjeant, was promoted to a judgeship in South Wales; and Sir Robert, whose career is now to be traced, rose to the dignity which his uncle had previously attained.

Robert, who was the second son, was born at his father's house at Heale, near Salisbury, in 1595. He was called to the bar of the Middle Temple on February 7, 1617, and elected reader in Lent 1638. By this time he had got into considerable practice, and two years after, in May 1640, he was summoned to take the degree of the coif. Having been chosen recorder of Salisbury, he was returned as the representative of that city to the Long Parliament. A staunch loyalist, he joined the court party, and made himself obnoxious by voting against the bill for the attainder of Lord Strafford, for which his name was placarded in the list of the minority who opposed that unjust measure, under the title of 'betrayers of their country.' When the king retired to Oxford the serjeant joined him, and attended the meeting of parliament there, and also executed the commission of array; the consequence of which was that he was voted a malignant, and expelled from his seat at Westminster. After the fatal termination of that reign, his noble relative (vi. 340) relates that Charles II., in escaping from the disastrous battle of Worcester in 1657, was sheltered for many days in the mansion at Heale, which then belonged to the serjeant, and was occupied by the widow of his elder brother. (*Parl. Hist.* ii. 622, 756, iii. 219.)

During the Protectorate he resumed his practice at the bar, and his arguments are reported by Hardres and Siderfin. At the Restoration he was immediately knighted, and appointed a judge of the Common Pleas, his patent being dated May 31, 1660. He was one of the commissioners for the trial of the regicides, but, except on points of law, took no part in the proceedings. In the following spring the three Perrys, a mother and two sons, were tried before him, and condemned to be hanged for the murder of William Harrison at Campden in Gloucestershire, though the body had not been found, and though the judge at the preceding assize, Sir Christopher Turnor, had on that account refused to entertain the charge. Several years after their execution Harrison appeared again, and related that he had been kidnapped and sold to slavery, from which he had escaped. The judge was dead before this discovery was made. (*Siderfin*, 2; *State Trials*, v. 1030, xiv. 1312–24.)

He was indebted to his noble relative for his promotion on October 19, 1663, to the chief justiceship of the King's Bench, where he presided for about a year and a half, without any great reputation as a lawyer; but Sir Thomas Raymond (*Rep.* 130) says that he was expert in the pleas of the crown, and especially in those which concerned a justice of peace. The extreme horror that he felt at anything that tended to rebellion was strongly manifested in the next year on the trial of certain printers of seditious books. To one of them named Twyn, capitally convicted of printing a treasonable work, called 'A Treatise of the Execution of Justice,' &c., inciting the people against the king and the government, who prayed his lordship to intercede for him, he gave the extraordinary and unmerciful answer, that he 'would not intercede for his own father in this case, if he were alive.' He was as severe against any one who promulgated doctrines contrary to the Liturgy of the Church, and his conduct on the trial of Benjamin Keach at Aylesbury on an indictment for publishing an heretical book, called 'The Child's Instructor; or, A New and Easy Primmer,' does not redound to his credit or liberality. (*Ibid.* vi. 515, 702.)

He died on May 1, 1665 (*Siderfin*, 253), and was buried in Salisbury Cathedral. His wife, Mary, the sister of Francis Baber, M.D., of Chew Magna in Somersetshire, brought him no children.

HYDE, THOMAS DE LA, possessed considerable property in Cornwall, and was sheriff of that county as well as seneschal of the castles of Tintagel, Restormel, and Tremeton, and of the stannary and the coinage there. (*Madox*, i. 107, 132, 144, 291.) He was placed on the commission of trailbaston for the ten western and south-western counties in 1305, 33 Edward I. (*N. Fœdera*, i. 970.) He died in 8 Edward II. (*Cal. Inquis.* p. m. i. 256.)

HYNDE, JOHN, was of a family seated at Madingley in Cambridgeshire. He was educated at Cambridge, and called to the bar at Gray's Inn, where he was reader in 1517, 1527, and a third time in 1531, on his being called to the degree of the coif. On January 2, 1535, he was nominated a king's serjeant; and in December 1540 a letter was addressed to him by the council, directing him and three others to take a chaplain and a servant of Goodrich, Bishop of Ely, and to search their houses, and also the bishop's study, as to a 'sedycious epistle of Melancton's,' and if they found that he had assisted in the translation, to charge him to appear before the council. (*Acts Privy Council,* vii. 98.)

An act passed in 1542–3 in Hynde's favour (st. 34 and 35 Henry VIII. c. 24) affords a curious insight into the practice of those days as to the payments made to members of parliament. It recites that the manor of Burlewas, otherwise called the Shyre manor of the county of Cambridge, and certain lands in Madingley, were let to farm at 10*l.* a year, to the intent that the yearly profits should be applied to the payment of the fees and wages of the knights of that county sent to parliament; and that it might be perfectly known what person should be charged to pay the said rent of 10*l.*, all the gentlemen of the said county desired that it might be, and it was, enacted that John Hynde, one of the king's serjeants-at-law, and his heirs, should hold the same to him, his heirs and assigns for ever, upon condition to pay 10*l.* to the sheriff and members of the county, who were to divide the same between the two knights every year. Hynde's participation in the plunder of the monasteries is evidenced by various grants entered in the Augmentation Office.

On November 4, 1545, he was promoted to the bench of the Common Pleas, and knighted. He sat there during the remainder of Henry's reign, and for nearly four years in that of Edward, during part of which time he was one of the Council of the North. (*Burnet's Reform.* ii. pt. ii. 312.)

He died in October 1550, and was buried in St. Dunstan's, Fleet Street. Old Machyn's entry (p. 4) proves him to have been of good repute and character, for after saying, 'And my Lade Hinde dyd make anodur standard, and a cote armur, and a penon, and a elmet, and target, and sword, to be had at the moynthe's mynde in the contrey for him, and a grett dolle of money, and of mett and drynk, and gownes to the pore,' he adds, 'for ther was myche a doo ther for hym.' This is better than an epitaph.

I

IFELD, JOHN DE, was born at Ifeld in Kent, and was the third son of Thomas de Ifeld. During the reign of Edward II. he was actively employed in assessing the aids imposed by parliament, and arraying the men-at-arms. (*Parl. Writs,* ii. p. ii. 1037.) In 1 Edward III. he was one of the perambulators of the forests south of the Trent, and in 1329 was a justice itinerant into Nottinghamshire. He next represented his native county in parliament, and as late as 13 Edward III. was a commissioner of array for Surrey. (*Rot. Parl.* ii. 425; *Hasted,* i. 238; *N. Fœdera,* ii. 1071.)

ILLINGWORTH, RICHARD, was of a Nottinghamshire family, seated at Kirkby Wodhouse. He practised at the bar from 33 Henry VI.; and on September 10, 1462, 2 Edward IV. (*Rot. Parl.* v. 528), he was appointed chief baron of the Exchequer, and knighted. He continued in this place till the restoration of Henry VI., 1470, by whom he was not removed; but as soon as Edward IV. resumed the crown he was superseded. He had large grants of land in that county from Edward IV., all of which were excepted from the various acts of resumption passed in that reign.

His death occurred in 1476, and he and two of his sons, Ralph and Richard, were buried or had monuments in the church of St. Alban, Lad, or Ladle Lane, Cripplegate, in which ward, in the neighbouring parish of St. Giles, he possessed a house, where he died. (*Cal. Inquis.* p. m. iv. 305, 375; *Rot. Parl.* v. 472, 584; *Stow's London* [*Thoms*], 111.)

INGE, WILLIAM, was an advocate of great eminence in his profession, and the king's attorney as early as 15 Edward I., 1287, being then retained to prosecute and defend for the king at a salary of 20*l.* a year (*Issue Roll,* iii. 101), and in the twentieth year he is noticed as the king's serjeant-at-law. (*Rot. Parl.* i. 24–85.) In 1293 he was one of the eight who were assigned as justices to take assizes, &c., throughout the kingdom in aid of the regular judges, in which office he continued till the end of the reign. (*Rot. Pat.* i. 150–206.) On April 6, 1305, he was one of the five justices of trailbaston named for Norfolk and Suffolk, and again in February 1307. (*Rot. Parl.* i. 218; *N. Fœdera,* i. 970.)

The accession of Edward II. made no alteration in his position, and until his elevation to the bench his name appears among the advocates recorded in the Year Book, showing that, notwithstanding his employment as a justice of assize, he did not desert his practice at Westminster. The patent of his appointment as a judge of the Court of Common Pleas was dated September 28, 1314, 8 Edward II.; and in January 1315, while merely a justice of the Common Pleas, he opened, by the king's directions, the parliament then held at Lincoln. (*Rot. Parl.* i. 350.)

He succeeded as chief justice of the King's Bench in February 1316; but presided over this court for little more than a year, for on June 15, 1317, he was displaced by Henry le Scrope.

He died in 1321, leaving large possessions in ten counties. (*Cal. Inquis.* p. m. i. 299.) Part of his Kentish property, the manor of Stanstead, subordinate to Wrotham, he obtained by his marriage with Margery, one of the daughters of Henry Grapinell. (*Hasted*, v. 355.)

INGE, JOHN, though probably of the same family as the above William Inge, was of a different branch of it. He was settled in Somersetshire, and was employed from 10 Edward II. in various judicial commissions within that county, and also acted there as assessor of the aids granted by Parliament. In 15 Edward II. he was sheriff of Devonshire, and three years afterwards had the castles, towns, and honors of Roger de Mortimer in Wygeton and Ludlow committed to his custody.

On January 18, 1331, 4 Edward III., he was made a judge of the Common Pleas, and died about the twentieth year, leaving, by his wife Alicia, a son named John. (*Parl. Writs*, ii. p. ii. 1039; *Abb. Rot. Orig.* i. 25, 282, ii. 291.)

INGLEBY, THOMAS DE, settled at Ripley in Yorkshire, is mentioned in the Year Book of 21 Edward III., 1347, and as a judge of assize in the twenty-fifth year. His appointment as a judge of the King's Bench took place on September 30, 1361, 35 Edward III., and he retained his seat in that court for the sixteen remaining years of the reign, being, during most of them, the only judge there in addition to the chief justice. He received an extra grant of 40*l.* a year beyond his stated judicial salary of forty marks; and, besides this, he had a fee of 20*l.* annually for holding assizes in different counties. (*Issue Roll*, 353.)

On the accession of Richard II. he seems to have continued in the King's Bench, as no new judge was appointed there till towards the end of the first year. About that time he died, and was buried in Ripley Church, where his tomb still remains. By his wife, Catherine Ripley, he left several children, from whom descended the undermentioned Sir Charles Ingleby. Another of his descendants, Sir William Ingleby of Ripley, was created a baronet in 1642, and the title, becoming extinct in 1772, was renewed, and is now held by a kinsman of the family. (*Wotton's Baronet.* ii. 293; *Burke's Ext. Baronet.* 276.)

INGLEBY, CHARLES, whose father, John Ingleby, was a direct descendant from the above Sir Thomas Ingleby, was called to the bar at Gray's Inn in 1671. Being a Roman Catholic, he was involved, in February 1680, in a charge of being concerned with Sir Thomas Gascoigne in a plot against the king, and committed to the King's Bench prison; but on his trial at York in the following July he was acquitted, as Sir Thomas had been before. After the accession of James II. he was constituted on April 23, 1686, a baron of the Irish Exchequer; but, declining to go to that country, he was in May of the next year made a serjeant-at-law, and on July 6, 1688, was appointed a baron of the Exchequer in England, when he was knighted. One of the effects of James's apprehensions on the landing of the Prince of Orange was to supersede Sir Charles in the following November, before he had been four months in office. Returning to his practice at the bar, he was present at the York assizes in April 1693, and was fined forty shillings for refusing to take the oaths to King William. (*Luttrell*, i. 34–482, iii. 83; *Bramston*, 275; *Smyth's Law Off. Ireland*, 157; *State Trials*, xii. 263.)

INGLESHAM, ROBERT DE, in 31 Henry II. was one of the custodes of the bishopric of Worcester, and in the next year was appointed archdeacon of Gloucester. In 1187 he was one of the justiciers before whom a fine was levied, and his pleas as a justice itinerant in Hampshire and Devonshire occur in the roll of 1 Richard I., 1189. (*Pipe Roll*, 134, 203.)

He died about 1197. (*Le Neve*, 303.)

INGOLDESBY, JOHN, whose family was seated in the parish of that name in the county of Lincoln, probably held some inferior office in the Exchequer before he was raised to the bench of that court. His first patent as a baron is dated November 4, 1462, 2 Edward IV., but in September 1467 he was removed from his seat. In the following year, however, he received a new grant of the office for life in reversion on the next death or resignation, and this occurred on June 14, 1470. Henry VI. was restored in the following October, and Ingoldesby's name was omitted in the new patent; nor is there any appearance in the published records of his having resumed his seat on the return of Edward IV.

One of his descendants, though connected by marriage with the Protector Cromwell, deserted that side, and aided in the restoration of Charles II., who on August 30, 1660, created him a baronet; but the title became extinct in 1726.

INSULA, GODFREY DE, whose name appears among the justiciers before whom fines were levied from 10 Richard I. to 10 John, is also mentioned as a judge in the rolls of the Curia Regis in 13 John. (*Abb. Placit.* 82.)

INSULA, BRIAN DE, whether so called

from the Isle of Wight or the Isle of Ely is uncertain, held a high place in royal favour from 2 John, 1200. In 6 John the king gave him to wife Maud, the daughter and heir of Thomas, the son of William de Selebi, with her lands. In the next year the castle of Knaresborough was committed to his keeping, to which was afterwards added that of Bolsover. He was also appointed chief forester for the counties of Nottingham and Derby; one of the custodes of the archbishopric of York during its vacancy; and a warden of the seaports of Yorkshire and Lincolnshire. (*Rot. Claus*, i. 17–43; *Rot. Pat.* 72, 80, 88; *Madox*, i. 773.) The king frequently describes him as his beloved knight, and he was admitted to the intimacy of playing at tables with his sovereign. (*Rot. Misæ*, 14 John.) During the turbulent years of John's reign he was a devoted adherent to the king, and greatly benefited by grants of the forfeited estates. In 17 John he held the office of seneschal, or steward, and was appointed one of the governors of Yorkshire. (*Rot. Claus*. i. 219, 272; *Rot. Pat.* 164; *Wendover*, iii. 353.)

On the accession of Henry III. he had a renewal of the custody of the castle of Knaresborough and the forests of Nottingham, and aided the royal troops both at Montsorel and Lincoln. In 5 Henry III. he was constituted chief justice of the forests, but about three years afterwards was removed from his office, having got into disgrace by being one of the barons who refused to comply with the injunction to surrender the castles in their custody to the king. (*Rapin*, iii. 14, 21.) He was then disseised of various manors he held under the crown, and several of the amerciaments he had inflicted in his office were remitted. Soon, however, making his peace, he obtained the restoration of his lands, and received several marks of royal regard, as some deer for his park at Saleby in Lincolnshire, and the grant of a fair for that place. (*Rot. Claus*. i. 308–596, ii. 49–145.)

In 10 Henry III. he was nominated one of the justices itinerant for Yorkshire (*Ibid.* ii. 151), and continued to be entrusted with the guardianship of the castles of Knaresborough, Bolsover, and Peke. In the last year of his life, 1233, he was constituted sheriff of Yorkshire, and died before August 18, 1234. (*Excerpt. e Rot. Fin.* i. 263, 265; *Dugdale's Baron.* i. 737.)

INSULA, SIMON DE, or DE L'ISLE, was probably of the Isle of Ely, as he was one of the stewards of that bishopric in 9 and 15 John, and had property in Cambridgeshire. (*Rot. Pat.* 99, 140; *Rot. Claus.* i. 108.) In 12 John he accompanied the king to Ireland, but fell off from his allegiance in the troubles at the end of it. He soon, however, submitted to Henry III., in whose first year his lands were restored to him. (*Rot. de Præstit.* 117, 218; *Rot. Claus.* i. 318, &c.)

He was a justicier with fines levied before him at Westminster from 2 to 4 Henry III., and went as a justice itinerant into Essex and Hertford, Norfolk and Suffolk. (*Rot. Claus.* i. 350, 365, 383.)

INSULA, WILLIAM DE, was the son of a knight of that name who married Matilda, the daughter of William de Luddenham, of the manor of Luddenham in Kent. (*Hasted*, vi. 391.) He began his career in the service of Reginald de Cornhill, sheriff of Kent and comptroller of the Mint; and several instances occur from 6 John of his conveying money to the king. (*Rot. Claus.* i. 39–104.) In 16 John, in an order for some repairs at Brikestok in Northamptonshire, he is named as the king's bailiff, and as having the custody of the forests there, and in the next year as one of the justiciers appointed to take a recognition of the last presentation to the church of Oxeden in that county. (*Ibid.* 190, 196, 270.) About this time he was raised to the office of marshal of the Exchequer, and was sent in 17 John to the constable of Marlborough Castle to bring six hundred marks to the king at Windsor. He is so called in 2 Henry III. in a mandate to the barons of the Exchequer, who are directed to receive his clerk in his place till he returns from an embassy to Ireland. (*Ibid.* 214, 253.)

In 1222 he was appointed with others to hold pleas of the forest at Northampton, and became constable of Rockingham Castle. (*Ibid.* 497, 516, 573.) His first nomination as a justice itinerant was in 9 Henry III., for the counties of Northampton and Rutland; afterwards for Lincolnshire, and for several other counties. (*Ibid.* ii. 77, 151, 213.) The knowledge and experience he had acquired in his previous connection with the courts had become apparent; and as fines were levied before him from Easter 1228 till Easter 1231, it is manifest that he was then called to the higher position of a justicier in Banco at Westminster. During the whole of this period, and as late as 18 Henry III., 1233, his name appears as acting in numerous counties. (*Dugdale's Orig.* 42.)

INSULA, JOHN DE. Two of this name were summoned to the parliament at Carlisle in 35 Edward I., 1307 (*Rot. Parl.* i. 188)—one as a baron, and the other apparently as one of the judges or learned persons in the law.

It is certain that the latter was an advocate in the courts, and as early as 1290 was heard before the parliament on the part of the king in two suits there discussed. Two years afterwards he was amerced in 100 shillings for some contempt before the justices of assize (*Ibid.* 18–83), but in 21

Edward I. was himself appointed to act in that character in nine counties. On October 21, 1295 (*Ibid.*), he was admitted as one of the barons of the Exchequer. (*Y. B.* pt. i. 36; *Madox*, i. 320, ii. 44–324.) In 33 and 35 Edward I. he was one of the justices of trailbaston (*Rot. Parl.* i. 178, 218); but whether he preserved his seat in the Exchequer at the same time does not appear. He was not, however, numbered among those barons who received patents on the accession of Edward II., though he was still regularly summoned with the judges to parliament, and in 4 Edward II. was placed at the head of the justices of assize in the northern counties. He resumed his seat in the Exchequer, by a patent dated January 30, 1313, and is frequently noticed in that character till the twelfth year. He died in May or June 1320. (*Ibid.* 301–350; *Parl. Writs*, ii. 1104; *Abb. Rot. Orig.* 223.)

J

JAMES, WILLIAM MILBURNE, the recently appointed lord justice of appeal in Chancery, was born in 1807, his father being Christopher James, Esq., of Swansea, and his mother, Anne, daughter of — Williams, Esq., of Merthyr Tydvil. He was educated at the university of Glasgow, and was called to the bar by the society of Lincoln's Inn on June 10, 1831. He remained a junior in the equity courts for two-and-twenty years, when in 1853 he was made a queen's counsel, and obtained a distinguished practice for sixteen years as a leader, during which he held the office of vice-chancellor of the county palatine of Lancaster. After thirty-eight years' experience as a barrister, he was raised to the bench on January 1, 1869, as vice-chancellor, in the duties of which he was found so efficient that in July 1870 he was promoted to his present position, and to the Privy Council. He received the customary knighthood when made vice-chancellor.

He married Maria, daughter of Dr. William Otter, the late Bishop of Chichester.

JEFFREY, or **JEFFERAY, JOHN,** was of an old Sussex family. His father was Richard, the second son of John Jeffrey, of Chiddingly Manor, inherited from a long line of ancestors. His mother was Elizabeth, the daughter of Robert Whitfield, Esq., of Wadhurst, Sussex. He was called to the bar at Gray's Inn in 1546, and made reader in 1561. On his being summoned to the degree of serjeant in 1567 he was presented with a purse containing 10*l*. by the society. In 1571 he was returned member for East Grinstead, and in 1572 for Arundel. In the latter year he was nominated one of the queen's serjeants, and on May 15, 1576, he was promoted to a judicial seat in the Queen's Bench. Within a year and a half, on October 12, 1577, he was promoted to the chief barony of the Exchequer, but his seat was vacated by his death on May 23, 1578. He died in Coleman Street Ward, London, but was buried in Chiddingly Church, where, in a small chapel, a magnificent monument was erected to his memory, on which he is represented in his robes.

David Lloyd, in his 'State Worthies' (p. 221), gives a curious and eulogistic summary of his character in four pages of his sententious phrases. His first wife was Elizabeth, daughter and heir of John Ansley, Esq., of London, by whom he had an only daughter, who married the first Lord Montagu of Boughton. Sir John's second wife was Mary, daughter of George Goring, Esq. (*Horsfield's Lewes*, ii. 66; *Collins's Peerage*, ii. 14.)

JEFFREYS, GEORGE (LORD JEFFREYS OF WEM). The task of writing the life of 'this very worst judge that ever disgraced Westminster Hall,' as Mr. Justice Foster designated him, is most ungrateful, especially when the writer can find no ground for reversing the verdict that has been already pronounced.

George Jeffreys was the younger son of John Jeffreys, of Acton, near Wrexham, in Denbighshire, a gentleman of ancient stock, but of comparatively slender means, by Margaret, daughter of Sir Thomas Ireland, of Bewsey in Lancashire. Born in 1648, his education began at the free school of Shrewsbury, and was continued, first at St. Paul's School in London, and then at Westminster under Dr. Busby, to whose tuition he often referred in his after-life. He himself states in the Cambridge case that he was once a member of that university (*State Trials*, xi. 1329), but it is not known to what college he belonged, and he took no degree. 'His untractable disposition was early exhibited by his refusing to settle in some quiet course of trade, for which he was intended; and he was of so litigious a temper, and so fond of opposition and argument, that his father used to say to him, 'Ah! George, George, I fear thou wilt die with thy shoes and stockings on.' (*North's Lives*, 209.) Choosing the law as his profession, he commenced his legal studies, with the pecuniary aid of his grandmother, at the Middle Temple, and was called to the bar on November 22, 1669.

During his novitiate he had lightened the rigour of his studies by too great a devotion to the exciting pleasures of the times, which, as a natural reaction from the austerities of the Puritan rule, had become eminently hilarious and disgracefully profligate. Daring and impudence in that age were almost certain to insure success; and an apocryphal story of the proficiency of the young aspirant in these qualifications is related, of his appearing in a forensic gown at the Kingston assizes during the year of the plague, and pleading there as a barrister three years before he was called. A voluble tongue and a stentorian voice, joined with the interest of the disaffected party in the state, to which he at first attached himself, soon introduced him into considerable practice, principally confined to criminal business and the city courts. This led him into the society of the members of the corporation, to whom his jovial disposition was not a little recommendation. He found a firm friend in an alderman of the same name, through whose influence he was elected to the place of common serjeant on March 17, 1671, at the early age of twenty-three.

Seeing little prospect of advancement from his connection with the popular party, he gradually deserted it; and getting himself introduced to Chiffinch, the king's page, pimp, and factotum, he made himself so agreeable to that worthy, both by joining in his potations and by betraying the plans of the disaffected, that he soon was recommended to his majesty as a man likely to do good service. Through the same means, having also procured another powerful advocate in the Duchess of Portsmouth, he easily secured to himself the post of recorder of London on October 22, 1678, receiving, a year before, the first reward of his apostacy by being knighted and appointed solicitor to the Duke of York. He brazened out the disgrace of his desertion, and from this time forward he attached himself wholly to the court party, treating his former friends not only with contempt, but with the utmost violence of reprobation.

His first wife was Sarah, daughter of the Rev. Thomas Neesham, and the circumstances under which he married her (May 22, 1667) tell greatly to his credit. She was the kinswoman and humble friend of a merchant's daughter, a prize of 30,000l., to whose hand or fortune Jeffreys aspired, and had used the companion as his secret advocate. But the plot being discovered, the poor girl was dismissed, and, coming up to town to tell of her failure and disgrace, the discarded lover took pity on her and married her. She bore him several children during the eleven years of their union; and three months after her death, in May 1678, he contracted a second marriage with Mary, daughter of Sir Thomas Bludworth, lord mayor of London and M.P. for the city, and the widow of Sir John Jones, of Fonmon Castle, Glamorganshire. This lady, being supposed to be not remarkable for continence, formed the subject with her new husband of a lampoon called 'A Westminster Wedding.'

He held the recordership for two years, during which, though he did not betray all the violence and cruelty that afterwards distinguished him, he exhibited a sufficient inkling of his overbearing disposition. In his anxiety to follow the popular cry against Papists, he forgot the religious profession of his patron, the Duke of York, going out of his way to insult the prisoners of that persuasion, against whom he had to pronounce sentence as recorder, by ridiculing and inveighing against the doctrines they professed. But when the tide seemed to be turning, and the court party had managed to meet the petitions for a parliament by addresses of abhorrence, Sir George took so active a part in getting up the latter that he was visited with the censure of the House of Commons. On November 13, 1680, a vote was passed, declaring that by traducing and obstructing petitioning for the sitting of parliament he had betrayed the rights of the subject, and ordering that an address be made to his majesty to remove him out of all public offices, and that the members for London should communicate the said vote to the Court of Aldermen. On receiving this communication the aldermen resolved that Sir George be advised and desired to surrender the office, which he accordingly did on December 2, having in the interim obtained the reluctant permission of the king, who laughed and said that Sir George was not parliament-proof. With this concession and a reprimand on his knees at the bar, the house was satisfied, and Sir George kept his other places. (*Parl. Hist.* iv. 1216; *North's Examen*, 550.)

Since his election as recorder he had received the degree of the coif in February 1679, and had been made king's serjeant on May 12, 1680. In the preceding month he had also been constituted chief justice of Chester, an office which he retained till he became chief justice of the King's Bench. In almost all the numerous state trials during this period, connected with the Popish, the Meal-tub, and the Rye House Plots, he was engaged on the part of the crown, and after he became king's serjeant he took a prominent part in them. In few of these, as reported, is there much to complain of, except in that against Stephen

Colledge, whom he seemed to take a pleasure in ridiculing, and in which he came into collision with Titus Oates, who, being a witness for the prisoner, threatened the serjeant that he should 'hear of it in another place' (State Trials, viii. 601, 641, 664)—a threat that was not forgotten by Sir George when the brazen-faced plotter was sentenced four years afterwards for perjury. The serjeant's general character at the bar for insolence and browbeating his antagonists was so notorious that his brethren must have enjoyed the severe rebuke he received at Kingston assizes from Baron Weston.

In trials at Nisi Prius he sometimes was paid in his own coin, and, as chief justice of Chester, he soon behaved in such a manner as to draw down upon him general animadversion, being described by Mr. Booth (afterwards Lord Delamere and Earl of Warrington) in his place in parliament as acting 'more like a jack-pudding than with that gravity that becomes a judge.' (*Harris's Lives*, v. 331.) On November 17, 1681, he was created a baronet, of Bulstrode in Buckinghamshire, where he had bought an estate, and built a mansion, which was afterwards sold to William Earl of Portland.

During the last illness of Sir Edmund Saunders, the Earl of Sunderland recommended Jeffreys to the king for the chief seat in the King's Bench, but his majesty raised doubts of his capacity, and had too much knowledge of his character to expect that the appointment would be agreeable to the other judges. This hesitation was the cause of the place remaining vacant for three months after Saunders's death; but his majesty being at last overtalked, Jeffreys was installed chief justice on September 29, 1683. Evelyn (iii. 93, 140, 190), referring to his advancement, characterises him as being 'reputed to be most ignorant, but most daring,' and relates that between the sentence and execution of Algernon Sidney he attended a city wedding and was exceeding merry, dancing with the bride, drinking and smoking, and talking much beneath the gravity of a judge. On another occasion he calls him 'of nature cruel and a slave of the court.' And Burnet (ii. 389) says, 'All people were apprehensive of very black designs when they saw Jeffreys made lord chief justice, who was scandalously vicious and was drunk every day, besides a drunkenness of fury in his temper that looked like enthusiasm. He did not consider the decencies of his post, nor did he so much as affect to seem impartial, as became a judge; but run out upon all occasions into declamations that did not become the bar, much less the bench. He was not learned in his profession, and his eloquence, though viciously copious, was neither correct nor agreeable.'

Almost his earliest act as chief justice was to preside at Sidney's trial, when by his harsh and unfair treatment of the prisoner he gave the first sample of his brutal nature and his courtly subserviency. The same course he pursued in the subsequent trials, insulting and vilifying the accused, and acting rather as the advocate employed to procure a conviction, than as an impartial judge sworn to see fair play between the parties. Not only was he unfeeling and indecorous towards the prisoners, but he bullied and threatened the counsel practising in his court, instances of which are related in the lives of Sir Edward Ward, Mr. Wallop, and Mr. Bradbury.

Though King Charles had at first resisted the appointment of Jeffreys, he soon altered his opinion; and immediately after the condemnation of Sir Thomas Armstrong, who, having been brought to the bar on an outlawry had claimed to be tried, saying he demanded no more than the law, was brutally answered by Jeffreys that he should have it to the full, and thereupon ordered him for execution on the next Friday (*State Trials*, x. 114), his majesty took a valuable diamond ring from his finger, and gave it to the chief justice in acknowledgment of his services. This ring, Burnet (ii. 411) says, was thereupon called his blood-stone. He justified the king's approbation of him by his zeal and active aid to the court in obtaining the surrender of the charters of corporate boroughs. The lord mayor of London complained to Sir John Reresby (*Memoirs quoted in State Trials*, viii. 217) that the chief justice usurped all the power of his office, that the city had no intercourse with the king but through him, and that the court looked upon the aldermen as no better than his tools. In both London and York he treated the aldermen with contempt, and turned out many of them, without so much as allowing them to be heard as to the crimes they were accused of.

Soon after King James had succeeded his brother, Jeffreys had an opportunity of revenging himself on Titus Oates, who, being convicted on two indictments for perjury, received at his hands so pitiless a sentence that even those who most condemned the man pronounced it cruel and excessive. Though the House of Lords refused to reverse the judgment, King William at their request pardoned such part of the punishment as remained to be inflicted. (*State Trials*, x. 1315–29.) Within a week after these trials Jeffreys was created Baron Jeffreys of Wem in the county of Salop, on May 15, 1685; and that very day was signalised by another exhibition of his brutality against Richard Baxter, then applying for a delay of his trial. Alluding to Oates, then standing in the pillory, he called them 'two of the greatest rogues and rascals in the kingdom.' On this trial, his counsel, and particularly Mr. Wallop, were indecently silenced, and Baxter himself treated with the coarsest reproaches. The indictment against him was for reflecting against the bishops in his 'Paraphrase upon the New Testament;' and, notwithstanding the absurdity of the charge, the chief justice easily procured a conviction; but so repugnant to common sense and to truth was his punishment, that his fine of 500*l.* was remitted before the end of the year. (*Ibid.* xi. 497.) But his excesses soon reached their climax. After the defeat of Monmouth at Sedgmoor in July, a commission of five judges was sent into the western counties to try those who were concerned in the rebellion. This commission consisted of Chief Justice Jeffreys, Chief Baron Montagu, Sir Francis Wythens, Sir Creswell Levinz, and Sir Robert Wright; and in order to give greater importance to it, Jeffreys was invested with the temporary rank of lieutenant-general, and the command of a strong military escort that accompanied its progress. Commencing at Winchester and terminating at Wells, the unfortunate prisoners at each place that was visited met with the full rigour of the law, and, taking even the most favourable account, that of the historian Lingard, the willing apologist of all the acts of this reign, there were 330 executed as felons and traitors, above 800 given to different persons to be transported for ten years to the West Indies, besides many who were whipped and imprisoned. With indecent haste all those who were convicted after trial suffered in the course of twenty-four hours, while those who pleaded guilty were gratified with a short reprieve. Bad as this report is, it is not nearly so atrocious as the accounts of other writers, equthis deserving of credit. And in all ally 'western campaign,' as King James called it, no charge is brought against any of the judges but the chief: on him alone the harshness, the levity, the cruelty that attended the trials are fixed. His brutality in the examination of the witnesses in Lady Lisle's case, the blasphemy of his imprecations, his unjust insinuations against the unfortunate prisoner in his summing up, the ferocious anxiety he evinced for her conviction, and the threats to the jury by which he enforced it, are truly disgusting, and were equalled if not surpassed in what we hear of all the subsequent trials. Such dread was attached to his name that the memory of his fearful and sanguinary expedition is preserved to the present day in the district over which he exercised his terrific sway, by changing the name of the well-known children's game called 'Tom Tiddler's Ground' into 'Judge Jeffreys' Ground.' (*Lingard,* xiii. 53; *Notes and Queries,* 2nd S. vi. 432.) Even Lingard is compelled by irresistible evidence to acknowledge that Jeffreys converted his commission to his own advantage, by 'amassing a considerable sum of money, probably by the sale of his friendship and protection.' The journals of parliament prove, among other items, that he extorted above 14,000*l.* from Mr. Prideaux to save him from prosecution. (*State Trials,* xi. 297; *Parl. Hist.* v. 245.) When the atrocities of these proceedings came to be publicly discussed, the partisans of the king and the judge endeavoured each to acquit one by attributing the whole blame to the other, Jeffreys asserting 'that what he did he did by express commands, and that he was not half bloody enough for the prince who sent him thither;' and the advocates of the king asserting 'that he never forgave Jeffreys executing such multitudes, contrary to his express orders.' It seems scarcely necessary to enquire on which side the truth preponderates, for as it is allowed that 'the receiver is as bad as the thief,' so it will be acknowledged that 'the instigator is as bad as the actor;' and the world, in judging of the comparative innocence of either, will rather look at that which proves the complicity of both. It is certain that the king received daily accounts of the proceedings, and did nothing to check them; that he delivered up the convicted prisoners to his courtiers (including the judge himself) to make what profit they could extort from them for their pardon; and that he welcomed the commissioners on their return from the Bloody Assize, expressing his thanks, and rewarding Jeffreys immediately by raising him to the head of the law. The Great Seal was given to him with the title of lord chancellor on September 28, 1685, less than a week after his return. (*Burnet,* iii. 55; *Bramston,* 207.)

His elevation made no change in his manners. At a dinner he gave, at which Reresby was present, he not only drank deep, but made one of his gentlemen, named Mountfort, an excellent mimic, who had been an actor, plead before him in a feigned cause, during which he aped all the great lawyers of the age, in their tones, their actions, and their gestures, to the great diversion of the company. His intemperate habits were in no degree diminished, and the same author relates that, dining with one of the aldermen, he and Lord Treasurer Rochester got so furiously drunk that they stripped themselves to their shirts, and were with difficulty prevented from getting in that state on the signpost to drink the king's health.

In opposition to Burnet's opinion as to his legal knowledge, we have the better judgment of Sir Joseph Jekyll; and Speaker Onslow says he made a great chancellor in the business of that court, and that in more private matters he was thought an able and upright judge wherever he sat. Serjeant Davy in 1754 describes him as ever 'esteemed a great lawyer.' Even Roger North, who hated him, speaks thus favourably of him as a judge (p. 219): 'When he was in temper, and matters indifferent came before him, he became his seat of justice better than any other I ever saw in his place. He took a pleasure in mortifying fraudulent attorneys, and would deal forth his severities with a sort of majesty. He had extraordinary natural abilities, but little acquired, beyond what practice in affairs had supplied.'

In the January following his elevation he acted as high steward on the trial for high treason of Lord Delamere, who, when Mr. Booth, had formerly given too true a description of his proceedings at Chester, and was far from pleased with the acquittal. There is no doubt that soon after this Jeffreys was in some discredit at court, perhaps in consequence of the king's hearing of the extent of his pecuniary dealings with the prisoners in the west. To redeem his favour, and to aid the king's desire to introduce the Popish religion and to discover its opponents, he suggested and was made president of a new ecclesiastical commission, of which the first victim was the Bishop of London, who was suspended from his office, and under which the disgraceful proceedings against Magdalen College, Oxford, took place.

The prosecution of the seven bishops followed, for presenting a petition to the king praying that the clergy might be excused from reading the declaration which his majesty had issued proclaiming liberty of conscience. This being interpreted as seditious, a prosecution was determined on, and they were committed to the Tower. It is difficult to believe that this unwise measure could have been adopted without the concurrence and advice of the lord chancellor, the first legal functionary of the court; but he professed to Lord Clarendon that he was much troubled at the prosecution, and desired his lordship to let the bishops know his desire to be serviceable to them. This conversation, however, was after he saw the extreme unpopularity of their imprisonment, and when he wished to father it upon some other advisers, who, he said, 'would hurry the king to his destruction.' He gave a plain condemnation of his choice of the judges by asserting just before the trial that 'they were most of them rogues;' and soon after it was concluded he called them 'a thousand fools and knaves,' and Chief Justice Wright (to whose promotion to the bench he had been particularly instrumental) 'a beast.' (*Clarendon's Diary*, ii. 177-185.)

When King James was contemplating his departure after the arrival of the Prince of Orange, he required the chancellor to occupy Father Petre's apartments in the palace, in order, says Barillon, to have the Great Seal near him, that he might take it with him. Accordingly Jeffreys delivered it up eight days before the king's retreat (*Ibid.* 223-6; *Luttrell,* i. 481), and, conscious of the detestation in which he was held, and the danger he ran in remaining, took means for his own escape. He disguised himself in a seaman's habit, and proceeding to Wapping to embark, he went into a cellar to take a pot. While there a scrivener came in, who, Roger North relates (p. 220), had been concerned in a Chancery suit about a 'Bummery Bird;' and one of the counsel having called him a strange fellow, who sometimes went to church, sometimes to conventicles, and it was thought he was a *trimmer*, the chancellor immediately fired, and cried out, 'A trimmer! I have heard much of that monster, but never saw one: come forth, Mr. Trimmer, turn round, and let me see your shape,' and rated him so long that the poor fellow was ready to drop; and when on quitting the hall he was asked how he came off, 'Came off,' said he; 'I am escaped from the terrors of that man's face, and shall have the frightful impression of it as long as I live.' The scrivener never forgot that fearful countenance, and recognising the chancellor at once under his disguise, went out and gave the alarm. The mob poured in, and he was with difficulty rescued from their fury. He was hurried, with a shouting crowd at his heels, before the lord mayor, who was so shocked at his appearance that he could not do anything, and was seized with a fit from which he never recovered. By Jeffreys' own request he was taken, in a frenzy of terror, to the Tower, guarded by two regiments of militia, whose strongest efforts could scarcely keep off the thousands who pressed around the cavalcade with execrations and threats of vengeance. (*Lingard,* xiii. 201; *Bramston,* 339; *Luttrell,* i. 486.) There he remained for four months, suffering much from the injuries he received from the populace in his capture, and tormented with the stone, to which he had been for some years subject. There, too, from a complication of disorders, aggravated by his drunken habits, and most probably by his recollections and his fears, he died on April 18, 1689. There also he was at first interred; but on the petition of his friends his body was removed in 1692 by warrant from Queen Mary to the church of St. Mary, Aldermanbury, where in 1810 it was discovered in a vault near the communion table, enclosed in a leaden coffin, with a plate inscribed with his name. He had formerly lived in the parish, and several members of his family were buried there. He was without hesitation excepted out of the act of indemnity, and a bill was ordered to be brought in for the forfeiture of his estate and honours, but it dropped on the dissolution of the Parliament. (*Stat. Realm*, vi. 178; *Notes and Queries*, 1st S. vii. 46.)

However forbidding a portrait may be in its prominent features, there are often some rays of light that soften the general gloom of the resemblance. Even in Jeffreys' career the circumstances attending his first marriage evidence a generous disposition in his early years; and the latter part of his life is not without some redeeming proofs of a better disposition. An instance of his gratitude is recorded in saving Sir William Clayton, to whom he owed his first advance in city honours, from being hanged, when Charles's ministry had determined to sacrifice an alderman of London for the purpose of intimidating that corporation; and, even when in the midst of his bloodiest commission, he listened with calmness to the remonstrances of a clergyman of Taunton against his proceedings, and, though they had no immediate effect on his conduct, presented him on his return to London to a canonry in Bristol Cathedral.

His honours became extinct by his only son John's death in 1702 without male issue, having first dissipated his estates. One of his daughters married Sir Thomas Stringer, the after-named judge. (*Woolrych; H. Roscoe; The Western Martyrology*.)

JEKYLL, JOSEPH, held the office of master of the Rolls for one-and-twenty years, from 1717 to 1738. Pope describes him as an

Odd old whig,
Who never changed his principles or wig.

He was the fourth son of the Rev. Dr. Jekyll, a clergyman in Northamptonshire, and was born about 1663. In 1687 he was called to the bar by the Middle Temple, and was reader in 1699.

The talent which the youthful barrister exhibited, added to the identity of political feeling, gained him the honour of an intimacy with Lord Chancellor Somers, which led to his marriage with that nobleman's sister Elizabeth, a lady several years his senior. This connection no doubt procured him the post of chief justice of Chester in June 1697, followed soon after by the honour of knighthood, when his noble brother-in-law was in the height of his power. He was further promoted to the degree of the coif in 1770, and immediately made king's serjeant. From his Welsh judgeship the tory party on the accession of Queen Anne endeavoured to remove him; but on his withstanding the attempt, and insisting that his patent appointed him for life, the government did not think proper to try the question, but submitted to his continuing in the office, which he held till he changed it for the more honourable and lucrative post of master of the Rolls. (*Luttrell*, iv. 238, 319, 702–4; *Burnet*, v. 12.)

This decision was probably influenced in some measure by his position in parliament, of which he was an active member for forty years, from 1698 to the end of his life, representing successively the boroughs of Eye, Lymington, and Reigate. During that long period he steadily adhered to his party, and in the prosecution of its objects introduced and supported several useful measures. When Queen Anne in the session of 1704 proposed by a royal message to grant the first fruits and tenths for the augmentation of the livings of the poorer clergy, Sir Joseph moved that the clergy might be wholly relieved from the tax, and that another fund might be raised to augment the small benefices. The act however was passed (2 & 3 Anne, c. 11) carrying out the queen's suggestion; and a corporation thereupon formed for administering what is properly designated as Queen Anne's Bounty. In the debate on the famous Aylesbury case in the same year he ably maintained the right of injured electors to seek redress at law; and at the end of that year he risked the censure of the house by pleading in behalf of Lord Halifax. In the absurd impeachment of Dr. Sacheverell in 1710 he distinguished himself by his opening of the first article, and was so sore on the impotent result that he caused an indictment to be preferred against a clergyman in Wales, who in a sermon before him arraigned the proceedings and reflected on the managers. The grand jury, however, very sensibly threw out the bill. (*Parl. Hist.* vi. 271; *Luttrell*, v. 488, vi. 563; *St. Trials*, xv. 95.)

On the accession of George I., when the whigs regained power, Sir Joseph was chosen of the committee of secrecy to enquire into the conduct of the late ministry; and on their report being printed he stated, in opposition to it, that, though there was sufficient evidence to convict Lord Bolingbroke of high treason, there was not sufficient to implicate the Earl of Oxford in such a charge. The earl, notwithstanding, was committed to the Tower in July 1715, and remained a prisoner for two years without trial. So late as June 1717 Sir Joseph reiterated his objections; yet in less than a fortnight after he appeared as a manager, prepared to make good the first article of the impeachment. In the farce with which that trial terminated it looks as if Sir Joseph was induced to take a part in opposition to his openly avowed opinion, by the hope, and perhaps by the promise, of succeeding Sir John Trevor, who was lately dead, in the office of master of the Rolls, to which he was appointed in less than three weeks, on July 13. Indeed he had amply deserved this advance, not only for the constant support he gave to his party, but for his zealous assistance in the prosecution of those concerned in the rebellion of 1715, in conducting the impeachment of the Earl of Wintoun, and the indictment against Francis Francia. (*Parl. Hist.* vii. 67, 73, 478, 485; *State Trials*, xv. 830, 894.)

In addition to the judicial duties which now devolved upon him, he devoted himself to affairs of state, and took a prominent lead in the debates of the house. He energetically exposed the South Sea Bubble, and led the van of those who sought to punish the peculators. His age, his position, and the apparent impartiality with which he discussed the various questions that arose, gave his opinions much weight and influence; and, though a frequent speaker, he was always listened to with deference and respect. But with the people he risked his popularity by introducing a bill for increasing the tax on spirituous liquors and for licensing the retailers. This produced great disorders among the lower classes, who were thus deprived of their customary enjoyment; and Sir Joseph was obliged to have a guard at his house at the Rolls to resist their violence. As it was, he was hustled and knocked down in Lincoln's Inn Fields, then an open space and the common resort of the mob. Arising from this misadventure, which was nearly fatal to him, a great improvement was luckily effected, for, in order to prevent the recurrence of similar accidents, palisades were erected around the fields, and a pleasant garden laid out. Another useful measure which he originated was the Mortmain Act of 1736, by which the indiscriminate disposition of lands to charitable uses was restrained. (*Lord Hervey's Mem.* ii. 88, 139; *Lord Macaulay's Hist.* i. 359.)

His presidency at the Rolls was distinguished by legal ability, integrity, and despatch. On January 7, 1725, the Great Seal was put into his hands as the first of three commissioners; and they held it from January 7 to June 1. The work on 'The Judicial Authority of the Master of the Rolls,' published in 1727, and occasioned by a controversy with Lord Chancellor King, who maintained that that officer was only the first of the masters in Chancery, has been usually attributed to Sir Joseph; but, though he no doubt supplied some of the materials, it was really written by his nephew Sir Philip Yorke, at that time attorney-general, with whom he always lived on terms of the greatest intimacy, and to whom he left part of his estates. (*Harris's Lord Hardwicke*, i. 198, 416.)

He died of a mortification in the bowels on August 19, 1738, and was buried in the Rolls Chapel. Leaving no issue, he bequeathed 20,000*l.*, after his wife's death, to the sinking fund towards paying off the national debt, a bequest which Lord Mansfield said was a very foolish one, and that he might as well have attempted to stop the middle arch of Blackfriars Bridge with his full-bottomed wig. In consequence, however, of his munificent expenditure in the erection of the large and convenient mansion at the Rolls for himself and his successors, and the contiguous buildings in Chancery Lane, and of his being disappointed in having a long lease of them, the government, to make good the loss, restored the money to his relations. Lord Hervey, in his Memoirs (i. 473), though giving him a very prejudiced character, is obliged to allow that he was impracticable to the court, learned in his profession, and had 'more general weight in the House of Commons than any other single man in that assembly.'

JENNER, THOMAS, was the son of Thomas Jenner, Esq. He was born at Mayfield in Sussex in 1638, and was admitted a pensioner of Queen's College, Cambridge, in June 1655, but left the university without a degree. In 1660 he was fortunate enough to marry Anne, the daughter and heir of James Poe, the son of Dr. Leonard Poe, physician to Queen Elizabeth and her two successors. At the coronation of Charles II. in 1661 he figured as esquire to Sir John Bramston, then created a knight of the Bath; and in November 1663 he was called to the bar by the Inner Temple. On October 16, 1683, the king, having previously knighted him, appointed him recorder of London, immediately after the forfeiture of the charters of that corporation. Evelyn calls him (iii. 99) at this time 'an obscure lawyer.' He was raised to the degree of the coif on the 23rd of January following, and was at the same time made king's serjeant. (*Bramston*, 118; *Luttrell*, i. 296; *Wynne*, 85.)

In many of the state trials that followed he was employed to prosecute, and proved himself, if not a very efficient, a very zealous advocate for the crown. On King James's accession he was elected member for Rye, but had no opportunity of speaking during the month that the sittings lasted. The last occasion of his acting as king's serjeant was in January 1686, at the trial of Lord Delamere for high treason, who was acquitted by the Lords. A month after, on February 5, he was constituted a baron of the Exchequer, and no doubt had previously satisfied the king that he would support his majesty's claim of power to dispense with the penal laws, for disputing which his predecessor had been discharged. In October 1687 he was sent with Bishop Cartwright and Chief Justice Wright on the notorious visitation of Magdalen College, Oxford, when Dr. Hough was expelled from the presidency. He however voted in the minority against suspending the fellows of the college. (*State Trials*, xi. 528, xii. 36; 2 *Shower*, 453; *Burnet*, iii. 140.)

On July 6, 1688, Baron Jenner was removed to the Common Pleas, a seat which he retained during the short remainder of the reign. Previous to the king's flight he obtained a pardon, which was soon after stolen from his chamber in Serjeants' Inn, together with 400*l*. in money; and endeavouring to escape with the king, he was taken up by the Faversham men and carried to Canterbury, from whence he was removed to the Tower of London in January 1689. Here he remained till the suspension of the Habeas Corpus Act had ceased, when, on his being admitted to bail by the King's Bench, the House of Commons renewed their investigation of his case, and, having previously voted that he had a principal concern in the arbitrary proceedings of the late reign, committed him to the custody of the serjeant-at-arms on October 25. He was not released till the prorogation of the Convention Parliament in the ensuing January, which was immediately followed by its dissolution. In the first session of the next parliament the bill of indemnity was passed, from which he was of course excepted by name, but this led to no further penal consequence. In February 1693 he was obliged to plead King James's pardon in answer to a charge in the Exchequer of having levied 300*l*. on dissenters without returning the money into court. Resuming his practice as a serjeant, he is found employed as late as 1702 in the defence of Richard Holloway, charged at the Surrey assizes with being a cheat and impostor in pretending to have been bewitched. (*Luttrell*, i. 482, 486, 493, ii. 10, 612, iii. 37; *Parl. Hist.* v. 280, 405; *State Trials*, xiv. 668.) He died at his house at Petersham in Surrey on January 1, 1707, where is a monument to his memory. From one of his sons descended the late respected dean of the Arches, Sir Herbert Jenner Fust.

With very small pretensions to law, Sir Thomas Jenner was little more than a tool of the court; and that he was not only laughed at, but despised, by his contemporaries, is apparent from a laughable pasquinade in a supposed letter from the judge to his wife and children. (*Woolrych's Jeffreys*, 147.)

JENNEY, WILLIAM, whose name was sometimes spelled Gyney, and more frequently Genney, was the son of John Jenney, of Knodishall in Suffolk, and Maud, daughter and heir of John Bokill, of Friston. He became one of the governors of Lincoln's Inn in 1446. His practice at the bar began at least as early as Michaelmas 1439, 18 Henry VI., that being the date of his first appearance in the Year Books. The Paston Collection contains many proofs of the enmity which existed between him and the Paston family, and which led to those contests recorded in the Year Books in the next reign. (*Paston Letters*, i. 140, 196.)

He took the degree of the coif in November 1463, and in the next year are long arguments relative to the legality of an outlawry awarded against John Paston at the suit of Jenney. Another discussion arose in 1471, the principal question being whether Sir John Paston should proceed against the serjeant by bill or by original writ. (*Y. B.* 4 *and* 11 *Edward IV.*) In these cases he shows himself an acute lawyer, and his practice in the courts was consequently very extensive. Although it is clear that at one time (*Paston Letters*, i. 182) the king was favourable to the Pastons, this did not prevent the advance to which the serjeant's legal attainments evidently entitled him, and he was accordingly constituted a judge of the King's Bench. The date of his elevation, though Dugdale states it to have taken place in Trinity Term 1477, 17 Edward IV., could not, according to the Year Book and other evidences, have been before Easter Term 1481. He was re-appointed at the commencement of the reigns of Edward V. and Richard III., and sat in the court during the first six months of the latter reign, dying on December 23, 1483.

His first wife was Elizabeth, daughter of Thomas Cawse, Esq., and his second was Eleanor, daughter of John Sampson, Esq., and widow of Robert Ingleys, Esq. His eldest son, Sir Edmund, was the father of the undermentioned Sir Christopher Jenney.

JENNEY, CHRISTOPHER, was the grandson of the above William Jenney, and the third son of Sir Edmund Jenney, of Knodishall in Suffolk, by Catherine, the daughter and heir of Robert Boys, Esq. Pursuing the profession in which many of his family had become eminent, he became reader at Lincoln's Inn in 1521 and 1522. In 1520 there is an entry in the privy purse accounts of Sir Thomas Le Strange of Hunstanton, —' Itm. pd. to Cristofer Jenney for his half yers fee the xxi daye of Maye, x^s.,' which is afterwards several times repeated, showing that he had an annual retainer of 1*l*. for that family. This fee was increased in 1525 to 2*l*. 13*s*. 4*d*. per annum, but does not appear to have been paid beyond Easter 1531. (*Archæologia*, xx. 434–494.) He was one of those assigned to assist Cardinal Wolsey in hearing causes in Chancery in June 1529. Called to the degree of the coif in Michaelmas Term 1531, and having been made king's serjeant in 1535, he was raised to the judicial seat on June 30, 1538, as a judge of the Common Pleas. He remained there little more than four years, the last fine levied before him being dated in Michaelmas 1542. (*Dugdale's Orig.* 47, 251.) He married Elizabeth, daughter of William Eyre, Esq., of Bury St. Edmunds.

JERMYN, PHILIP, was called to the bar by the Middle Temple in 1612, and became reader in 1629, and before that date he had attained considerable practice in the courts. He attained the degree of the coif in January 1637, and was employed by the parliament in their prosecution of Judge Jenkins in 1647, and appointed by them on October 12 in the next year one of the judges of the King's Bench. The tragic destruction of the king made no change in his position, for he consented to act under the usurped power. (*Whitelocke*, 255, 342, 378.) In the extraordinary trial of Lieutenant-Colonel Lilburne in October 1649, at which the Lord Commissioner Keeble presided, Jermyn was one of the commissioners, and took a prominent and violent part against the prisoner, almost superseding the president. (*State Trials*, iv. 1269 et seq.)

Peck dates his death on March 18, 1655. (*Desid. Cur.* b. xiv. 26; *Morant*, i. 183.)

JERVIS, JOHN, a member of the family of the Earls of St. Vincent, was the younger son of Thomas Jervis, Esq., a king's counsel long leading the Oxford Circuit, and for many years a judge on the Chester Circuit. He was born on January 12, 1802, and was educated at Westminster School, and at Trinity College, Cambridge. Though destined for his father's profession, and being for that purpose entered of the Middle Temple, his love for a military life induced him to accept a commission in the Carabineers. Soon, however, leaving the army, he resumed his legal studies, and was called to the bar in Easter Term 1824.

At first he travelled the Oxford, and then the Chester Circuit, and in London he practised principally in the Exchequer. On each arena he soon attained great reputation, from his familiarity with legal practice, and from his quickness of apprehension and great discretion. In the Exchequer his opportunities were improved by holding the office of 'postman,' and by reporting its decisions in conjunction, first with Mr. Edward Younge, and then with Mr. (afterwards Justice) Crompton, from 1826 to 1832. He was the author also of some other useful practical works on criminal law, the law of coroners, &c.

In the first Reform Parliament he was returned for the city of Chester, which he continued to represent till his elevation to the bench, invariably supporting the liberal party, to whose principles he was zealously attached.

In 1837 he received a patent of precedence, and on July 4, 1846, on the restoration of the whig ministry, he was made solicitor-general, which he held only three days, being promoted to the attorney-generalship on the 7th by the elevation of Sir Thomas Wilde to the post of chief justice of the Common Pleas, when he was knighted. During the four years that he filled that office the manner in which he exercised its functions commanded universal approbation. His services as an adviser of the crown, in all the departments of the government, were so unremitting and laborious that they laid the seeds of that disease which shortened his life; and his conduct on the various prosecutions in those seditious times, especially in the Chartist trials, was so discreet and admirable that he well merited his promotion to the place of chief justice of the Common Pleas on July 15, 1850.

His judicial powers were of the highest order. His judgments were 'models at once of legal learning, accurate reasoning, masculine sense, and almost faultless language;' and the memory he displayed, as well in summing up the details of evidence as in reviewing the cases quoted before him, was quite surprising. The following curious case is a good exemplification of his qualities. 'A young man of large property had been fleeced by a gang of blacklegs on the turf and at cards. . . . A private note-book, with initials for names, and complicated gambling accounts, was found on one of the prisoners. No one seemed to be able to make head or tail of it. The chief justice looked it over and explained it all to the jury. Then there was a pack of cards which had been pronounced by the London detectives to be a perfectly fair pack. They were examined in court; every one thought them to be so. They were handed to the judge. . . When the charge began, he went over all the circumstances till he got to the objects found upon the prisoners. "Gentlemen," said he, "I will engage to tell you, without looking at the faces, the name of every card upon this pack." A strong exclamation of surprise went through the court. The prisoners looked aghast. He then pointed out that on the backs, which were figured with wreaths of flowers in dotted lines all over, there was a small flower, the number and arrangement of the dots on which designated each card.' (*His Life*, by *Brooke*, ii. 142.)

The disease under which he laboured sometimes made him impatient and irritable; but he was pronounced by the profession a judge of the highest rank, and in the relations of private life he was much esteemed for his amiable and cheerful disposition.

He died on November 1, 1856, leaving a family by his wife, Catherine, the daughter of Alexander Mundell, Esq. (*Law Mag. and Rev.* Feb. 1857, p. 302.)

JOHN is inserted as a chancellor under Henry II. by Philipot and Spelman, and their followers, Hardy and Lord Campbell, but without sufficient authority. Thynne, from whom Spelman avowedly forms his list, says nothing more than this:

'John, chancellor of England in the time of King Henrie the Second, but what he was or in what year of King Henrie he lived I doo not know.'

Dugdale does not notice him, nor is there any history which does; neither has any record been discovered in which his name occurs.

JONES, THOMAS, was the second son of Edward Jones, Esq., of Sandford in Shropshire, by Mary, daughter of Robert Powell, Esq., of The Park in the same county, and was descended from an ancient family, the nobility of which is traced by the Welsh heralds to a period earlier than the Conquest. His education was begun at the free school of Shrewsbury, and completed at Emmanuel College, Cambridge, where he took the degree of B.A. in 1632-3. He had previously been entered at Lincoln's Inn, and was called to the bar on May 17, 1634. The part which he took in the subsequent troubles has been variously represented. One writer says he was one of the loyal Shropshire gentlemen taken prisoner by the parliamentary forces on capturing Shrewsbury; while another remarks that 'his conduct spoke more of prudence than loyalty, or perhaps of timeserving than either,' adding, that though 'in 1662 he declared he was always for the king, yet he was never sequestered, though possessed of considerable property, but declared himself against the commission of array in the time of the wars, and refused to find a dragoon for the king's service, for which he was committed by Sir Francis Offley, then governor of Shrewsbury, which commitment he afterwards brought two men to testify before the parliament committee as an argument of his good affection to them;' that his brother was then recorder of Shrewsbury, and declared him from the bench well affected to the parliament; and that he was elected town-clerk of Shrewsbury by the parliamentary party, from which office he was accordingly dismissed at the Restoration. (*Gent. Mag.* 1840, pp. 2, 270.)

He was returned as one of the members for Shrewsbury to the parliament elected just previous to Charles's arrival, and again in 1661, but his name does not appear in any of the debates. He was dignified with the coif in 1669, and was promoted to be king's serjeant two years after. While holding that position he was knighted, and on April 13, 1676, he was constituted a judge of the King's Bench. During the ten years that he sat on the bench, seven in this court, and three as chief justice of the Common Pleas, he was engaged in most of the political trials that disgraced the latter part of Charles's reign, and the commencement of that of James II. In 1677 he properly refused to bail or discharge the Earl of Shaftesbury, imprisoned by the House of Lords. That he credited the testimony of Titus Oates and William Bedlow, and that of the other witnesses to the Popish Plot, notwithstanding all their contradictions, is manifest in the trials that took place before him in the two subsequent years, though he afterwards found reason to change his opinions.

In Trinity Term 1680, the Court of King's Bench having dismissed the grand jury suddenly, so as to prevent an information against the Duke of York for not going to church, the House of Commons directed Chief Justice Scroggs and Justice Jones to be impeached; but the parliament being soon after prorogued, the proceedings were not renewed. In the trials of Fitzharris, Dr. Plunket, and Colledge, in 1682, and of Lord Russell in 1683, there is nothing to distinguish Justice Jones favourably from the other judges who sat on them. In the absence of Chief Justice Saunders, he pronounced in June 1683 the judgment of the court in favour of the king taking the charter of the city of London into his hands; and on September 29 following he was rewarded by being promoted to the place of chief justice of the Common Pleas. On the subsequent trials of Fernley, Ring, Eliz. Gaunt, and Alderman Cornish, at which he presided, he showed great severity and harshness, and the attainder of the latter was reversed at the revolution. (*State Trials*, vols. vi. to xi.; *Parl. Hist.* iv. 1224, 1261, 1273.) But still he was too honest and plainspoken for King James. On being pressed by his majesty to declare himself in favour of the royal dispensing power, he said he could not do it; and on the king's answering that 'he would have twelve judges of his opinion,' he replied that possibly his majesty might find twelve *judges* of his opinion, but scarcely twelve *lawyers*. (*Kennett's Hist.* iii. 451.) He was accordingly dismissed from his place with three other judges, on April 21, 1686.

At the revolution he was called before the House of Commons to account for a judgment of the Court of King's Bench in the case of Jay v. Topham, the serjeant-at-arms, pronounced six years before, and was committed with Chief Justice Pemberton for the supposed breach of privilege on July 19, 1689, sharing the imprisonment with his chief till the prorogation of the parliament. (*State Trials*, xii. 822.) He died in May 1692, aged seventy-eight, and was buried in St. Alkmund's Church, Shrewsbury, where his monument still remains.

Roger North (*Examen*, 563) describes Sir Thomas as 'a very reverend and learned judge, a gentleman and impartial.' Looking, however, to his whole professional career, he appears to have exhibited too great a tendency to accommodate himself to the court or to the popular party, as the one or the other predominated; and his claim to the title of an upright judge is principally founded on his resistance to the king's dispensing power.

By his wife, Jane, daughter of Daniel Bernand, Esq., of Chester, he had three sons, William, Thomas, and Edward, from the latter of whom descended Catherine, who married Captain John Tyrwhitt, whose son Thomas, succeeding to the estates, assumed the name of Jones, and was created a baronet in 1808.

JONES, WILLIAM, belonging to an ancient family of North Wales, whose lineage is traced by the Welsh heralds from the princes and possessors of that country, was the eldest son of William Jones, Esq., of Castellmarch in Carnarvonshire, where the family had long been seated, and of Margaret, daughter of Humphrey Wynn ap Meredith, of Hyssoilfarch, Esq. He was sent from the free school of Beaumaris to the university of Oxford, where he pursued his studies at St. Edmund's Hall for five years, and then was entered of Furnival's Inn, from which he removed to Lincoln's Inn, where he was called to the bar in 1595, and became reader in Lent 1616. He had acquired sufficient eminence in his profession to be selected in 1617 for the chief justiceship of the King's Bench in Ireland. For this purpose he was called to the degree of serjeant on March 14, 1617, and knighted.

After staying in Ireland for about three years, during which he was one of the commissioners of the Great Seal of that kingdom, he resigned his seat in the King's Bench; and in the patent of his successor, June 1620, the services of Sir William are thus encomiastically alluded to. The king, while complying with his desire to be called from his charge, says 'he could wish, for the good of his service and his kingdom of Ireland, that a man so faithful, honest, and able would have affected to continue in that office longer.' (*Smyth*, 26, 88.) On returning to England, he resumed his practice at the bar, but in Michaelmas 1621 he was placed on the English bench as a judge of the Common Pleas. (*Dugdale's Orig.* 48.) He continued in that court for three years, during which he was also employed on a commission in Ireland, and was then, on October 17, 1624, transferred to the King's Bench, where he remained for the rest of his life.

In the great question, in 1628, as to the refusal of bail to the five gentlemen committed to prison for not contributing to the loan, Justice Jones, when called with his fellows before the House of Lords to assign his reasons for that judgment, adverted thus boldly, in his justification, to the antiquity of his house: 'I am myself,' said he, 'Liber Homo; my ancestors gave their voice for Magna Charta. I enjoy that house still which they did. I do not now mean to draw down God's wrath upon my posterity, and therefore I will neither advance the king's prerogative nor lessen the liberty of the subject, to the danger of either king or people.' (*Parl. Hist.* ii. 290.) What his view of the king's prerogative was may be judged by his joining in the opinion of the bench in favour of ship-money, and by the reasons he gave in support of that opinion in 1637, in Hampden's case (*State Trials*, iii. 844-1181); but, however erroneous his view of the case might be, there is no doubt that his decision was founded on a conscientious opinion of its correctness.

By his death before the Long Parliament took up the question, he escaped the impeachment instituted against his colleagues. That event occurred on December 9, 1640, in the seventy-fourth year of his age. He was buried under Lincoln's Inn Chapel. Hearne (*Cur. Discourses*, ii. 448) describes him as 'a person of admirable learning, particularly in the municipal laws and British antiquities.' His 'Reports of Special Cases,' from 18 Jac. I. to 15 Car. I., which were not published till after his death, have a good reputation in Westminster Hall; and, to distinguish them from those of Sir Thomas Jones, the judge in the reign of Charles II., they are cited as 'First Jones's Reports.'

He married, first, Margaret, eldest daughter of Griffith John Griffith, Esq., of Kevenamulch; and secondly, Catherine, daughter of Thomas Powys, of Abingdon, and widow of Dr. Hovenden, warden of All Souls' College, Oxford. (*Athen. Oxon.* ii. 673.)

JOSCELINE (ARCHDEACON OF CHICHESTER) was one of the custodes of the bishopric of Exeter in 31 Henry II., 1185, while it was in the king's hands. Two years afterwards his name occurs as a justice itinerant fixing the tallage of the counties of Lincoln and York (*Madox*, i. 310, 635, 713), and he was present in the Curia Regis as one of the justices before whom a fine was acknowledged. (*Hunter's Preface*.) The continuance of his judicial functions is shown by the roll of 1 Richard I., where his pleas as a justice itinerant in various counties, not only for that but the preceding years, appear. (*Pipe Roll*.) He probably died shortly afterwards, as the date of his successor in the archdeaconry is 1190. (*Le Neve*, 65.)

JUKEL, JOHN, is the last in the list of justices itinerant in 20 Henry II., 1174, appointed to take the assize of Hampshire (*Madox*, i. 123); but who he was has not been discovered.

JUYN, JOHN, is so called in the Rolls of Parliament and the Acts of the Privy

Council, but sometimes spelled Joyn, and on his monument Inyn, and so in Bishop Bubwith's will, of which he was one of the executors, which seems most probably correct, as his mansion is now called 'Inne Court.' He was of a Somersetshire family, his country seat being at Bishopsworth (now called Bishport) in that county, in which he possessed the manor of Long Ashton. (*Collinson's Somerset*, ii. 295.) He first appears in the Year Book of 11 Henry IV., after which his name is of frequent occurrence. In the next reign he was one of those who refused to obey two summonses to take upon them the degree of serjeant, but who were compelled by the parliament to do so in 1404. (*Rot. Parl.* iv. 107.) He held the office of recorder of Bristol, and about eight months after the accession of Henry VI. he was appointed, on May 5, 1423, to the double office of chief baron of the Exchequer and judge of the Common Pleas. (*Acts Privy Council*, iii. 71.) He was knighted in 4 Henry VI., and on February 9, 1436, he was raised to the principal seat of the latter court. There he remained for nearly three years, and then was made chief justice of the King's Bench on Jan. 20, 1439, and presided there till his death, on March 24, 1439-40. He was buried in St. Mary's Chapel, Redcliffe Church, Bristol. By his wife Alice he left a son. (*Barrett's Bristol*, 587.)

K

KARLEOL, WILLIAM DE, sometimes spelled Karlell, is erroneously placed by Dugdale as lord chief baron of the English Exchequer on June 27, 1383, 7 Richard II., having mistaken the patent which appoints him chief baron of Ireland. He had been second baron of the Irish Exchequer from 1371, 45 Edward III., and was succeeded as chief baron there in 1399. (*Smyth's Law Off. Ireland*, 146.)

KAUNE, RICHARD DE (Calne), is only mentioned as one of the justices itinerant into Wiltshire in 9 Henry III., 1225, and as being appointed about the same time to take assizes of last presentation, &c., in that county. (*Rot. Claus.* ii. 76, 136, 141.)

KEATING, HENRY SINGER, is one of the present judges of the Common Pleas. He was born at Dublin in 1804, and is the third son of the late Lieutenant-General Sir Henry Sheehy Keating, K.C.B., who highly distinguished himself in the West Indies and other parts of the world, and of the daughter of James Singer, Esq., of Annadale in the county of Dublin.

He was called to the bar by the Inner Temple on May 4, 1832, when he joined the Oxford Circuit, and attended the Oxford and Gloucester sessions, and after labouring as a junior for seventeen years he received a silk gown in 1849.

In 1852 he entered parliament as member for Reading, which he continued to represent till he was elevated to the bench. Supporting the liberal party in the house, he was appointed solicitor-general in May 1857, and knighted, during the first ministry of Lord Palmerston, on whose defeat in the following February he retired, but was replaced in June 1859, on that lord's return to power. Only half a year had elapsed before he was constituted a judge of the Common Pleas, in which court he has sat from December 14, 1859, till the present time.

He married a daughter of Major-General Evans, of the Artillery.

KECK, ANTHONY, the second commissioner of the Great Seal when King William and Queen Mary had settled themselves on the throne, was the son of Nicholas Kewk, of Oldcowcliffe in Oxfordshire. Admitted a barrister by the Inner Temple in 1660, he became a bencher in 1677. That as an advocate in Chancery he acquired a great reputation may be inferred from his being selected at such a crisis as one of the heads of the court on March 4, 1689. He was at the same time knighted. His tenure of office lasted only fourteen months, till May 14, 1690. After his retirement from the Seal he was returned to parliament for Tiverton in 1691, and died in December 1695. In 1697 was published a compilation from his papers under the title of 'Cases argued and decreed in the High Court of Chancery from the twelfth year of Charles the Second to the thirty-first.' One of his daughters married Richard Freeman, who became Lord Chancellor of Ireland, and another married into the Tracy family. (*Atkyns's Gloucester*, 133, 360; *Luttrell*, ii. 217, iii. 567; *Welsby*.)

KEEBLE, RICHARD, of Newton in Suffolk, traces his descent from Thomas Keeble, a native of that county, who, as a learned serjeant, fills a large space in the Year Books of Henry VII. (*Athen. Oxon.* iv. 575.) He was called to the bar at Gray's Inn in 1614, was elected an ancient in 1632, and reader in 1639. Though he was never in parliament, his political sentiments were sufficiently known to induce that body to elect him for one of the judges of Wales in March 1647, and to include him in the batch of serjeants appointed in October 1648. He was sent to Norwich in December to try the mutineers, and on the disposal of the Great Seal after the death of the king, he was the junior of the three commissioners to whose custody it was entrusted, an office which he held for above five years. (*Whitelocke*, 240, 342, 380.) Soon after his appointment he presided at the curious trial of Colonel Lilburne, and he seems to have acted with less severity and unfairness than some of the judges who were joined in commission with him. He was president also of the High Court of Justice on the trials of Christopher Love and John Gibbons in 1651 (*State Trials*, iv. 1269, v. 49, 268); but in April 1654, Cromwell having been proclaimed protector, he was displaced.

On the restoration of Charles II. the serjeant was excepted from the act of indemnity. (*Parl. Hist.* iv. 70.) How long he lived afterwards, or to what country he retired to avoid his trial, does not appear. His son, Joseph Keeble, published several law tracts, besides reports of cases in the King's Bench from 1660 to 1678.

KELLESAY, RICHARD DE, was the last named of the justices itinerant for the county of York in 1225, 9 Henry III. He was then abbot of Selby, having been elected thereto in 1223. He died in 1237, or at least was then succeeded by Abbot Alexander. (*Rot. Claus.* i. 533, 540, ii. 77; *Browne Willis.*)

KELLESHULL, RICHARD DE, was probably the son of Gilbert de Kelleshull, to whom a pardon was granted in 15 Edward II., for all felonies, &c., committed in the 'pursuit' of the Despencers. (*Parl. Writs*, ii. p. ii. 166.) The family no doubt came from Kelshull in Hertfordshire.

Richard was appointed to several judicial commissions from 9 Edward III., but was not raised to the bench of the Common Pleas till May 30, 1341. The date of the last fine levied before him is in 1354; but he was alive three years afterwards, when he enfeoffed the parson of the church of Heydon in Essex with that manor and advowson. (*Abb. Rot. Plac.* ii. 99-291; *Dugdale's Orig.* 45.)

KELLY, FITZ-ROY, has been chief baron of the Exchequer since July 16, 1866. This judge, according to Dod's Peerage, &c., was grandson of Colonel Robert Kelly, who distinguished himself in the East Indies, and the son of Captain Robert Hawke Kelly, by Isabel, daughter of Captain Fordyce, carver and cupbearer to George III. He was born in London in 1796. On being called to the bar at Lincoln's Inn on May 7, 1824, he first joined the Home Circuit, and then the Norfolk Circuit; and after practising with great success for ten years, he was appointed a king's counsel in 1834. He was unfortunate in several attempts to enter parliament, but at last in 1837 gained a seat for Ipswich. From 1843 to 1847 he sat for Cambridge. In April 1852 he was returned for Harwich, and in May for East Suffolk, which last seat he retained till he was called to the bench. During this period his professional advancement proceeded. He held the office of solicitor-general twice, with the customary knighthood, from June 29, 1845, to July 2, 1846, and from February 27 to December 28, 1852. On February 26, 1858, he was appointed attorney-general, but only held the place till June 18 in the following year. He remained out of office for the next eight years, when Lord Derby's administration placed him in his present position.

He has been married twice. His first wife was Agnes, daughter of Captain Mason, of Leith; and his second is the daughter of Mark Cunningham, of the county of Sligo.

KELYNG, JOHN, cannot be the same person described by Anthony Wood as 'John Keeling, a counsellor of the Inner Temple, and a person well read in the municipal laws of England, created M.A. in the House of Convocation in August 1621,' and noticed by him as being possibly the same person as the chief justice, because the admission of the latter into the Inner Temple, as a mere student of law, was more than two years after, on January 22, 1624. His father was of the same inn, and is described as a resident of Hertford. Croke in his Reports notices the name twice, once as Keeling in 1635, and next as Keeling *junior* in 1639. The former was probably the M.A. of Oxford. The son was called to the bar on February 10, 1632, and from this time to the Restoration no mention is made of him in the Reports. Lord Clarendon describes him to the king as 'a person of eminent learning, eminent suffering, never wore his gown after the Rebellion, but was always in gaol;' and he himself, on his being made a judge in 1663, speaks of his 'twenty years' silence.' (*Fasti Oxon.* i. 404; 1 *Keble*, 526.)

With such claims, it is not surprising that he was included in the first batch of new serjeants called by Charles II. in 1660, and was immediately engaged on the part of the crown to advise with the judges relative to the proceedings to be adopted against the regicides. He was counsel on the trials of Colonel Hacker and William Heveningham, and of John James, a Fifth Monarchy man. (1 *Siderfin*, 4; *Kelyng*, 7; *State Trials*, v. 1177, 1229, vi. 76.) Returned as member for Bedford in May 1661, he prepared the Act of Uniformity, passed in the next year. On November 8 he was made king's serjeant, and in that character was one of the counsel on the trial of Sir Harry Vane, towards whom his conduct was unfeelingly harsh and insulting. (*Ibid.* vi. 171; *Burnet*, i. 184.)

He was appointed a judge of the King's

Bench on June 18, 1663; and within two years afterwards he became chief justice of the King's Bench, on November 21, 1665. He retained the place during the remainder of his life, with little reputation as a lawyer, and frequently incurring censure by his want of temper and discretion. In 1667 complaints were made against him in parliament by gentlemen of the county for divers 'high proceedings' in the execution of his office, as fining of juries, &c., for which he was obliged to answer before the House of Commons. That body voted his proceedings to be illegal and tending to the introduction of arbitrary government, and at first seemed inclined to proceed with great severity, ordering that he should be brought to trial; but in the end, by the mediation of his friends, the matter was allowed to drop. (*State Trials*, vi. 697, 992; *Pepys*, iii. 278, 324–5.) Again in 1670 he was obliged to apologise publicly in the House of Lords for rudely affronting Lord Holles on a trial in the Court of King's Bench. (*Life of Holt, Pref.* vi.) Sir Thomas Raymond, however (p. 209), in recording his death, calls him 'a learned, faithful, and resolute judge.' He collected various crown cases in which he was the judge, which were published after his death by Chief Justice Holt.

He died at his house in Hatton Garden on May 9, 1671, leaving a son, who was named in 1660 as one of the intended knights of the Royal Oak, and who afterwards was knighted and became king's serjeant. The family name of the mother of that son has not been found, but the register of St. Andrew's, Holborn, records her burial under her Christian name Mary in September 1667, and the judge's marriage with Mrs. Elizabeth Bassett in the following March. Whether the William Kelynge who reported cases in the reign of George II. was of the judge's family does not appear.

KEMPE, *JOHN* (ARCHBISHOP OF YORK AND CANTERBURY), on whom his nephew Thomas, Bishop of London, is said to have penned this hexameter:—

Bis primus, ter præses, et bis cardine functus,

was descended from a good family, which had been long in possession of the estate of Ollantigh, in the parish of Wye, in Kent, where he was born in 1380. He was the younger son of Thomas Kempe and Beatrice, a daughter of Sir Thomas Lewknor.

He received his education at Merton College, Oxford, of which he became a fellow. Practising in the ecclesiastical courts, he was one of the counsellors called upon by Thomas Arundel, Archbishop of Canterbury, to assist in the proceedings against Sir John Oldcastle for heresy in 1413. (*State Trials*, i. 242, 262.) As these learned advocates were frequently joined to foreign missions, so we find him employed as an ambassador sent in July 1415 to negotiate a peace with the King of Arragon, and to treat for a marriage with his daughter. (*Rymer*, ix. 295.) In that year also he was appointed dean of the Arches, and vicar-general of the new archbishop Chicheley.

Unconnected as he was with any noble or influential family, these employments, and the rapidity of his subsequent preferments, both in the church and the state, speak strongly of his intellectual powers and the excellence of his character. By this time he had been already admitted archdeacon of Durham, and in 1418 he was elected Bishop of Rochester. In the following April Henry V. made him keeper of his privy seal, and within two years he was placed in the office of chancellor of the duchy of Normandy, which he retained till the end of that reign. After sitting at Rochester for about two years, he was removed to Chichester on February 28, 1421, and on November 17 in the same year he was translated to the bishopric of London.

On the accession of Henry VI. he delivered up the seal of the duchy of Normandy, and was appointed one of the young king's council. (*Rot. Parl.* iv. 171, 201.) He was sent to the Duke of Bedford in France, and was employed to treat for the release of the King of Scots. (*Acts Privy Council*, iii. 86, 137.) When Cardinal Beaufort retired from the chancellorship, on his temporary accommodation with the Duke of Gloucester, the bishop was raised to that office on March 16, 1426, and on the 8th of the following April was elected Archbishop of York. He retained the Great Seal for nearly six years, during which he was one of the peers who signed the answers to the Duke of Gloucester, resisting his claim to govern at his own will and pleasure, and explaining the limitation of his authority as protector. (*Rot. Parl.* iv. 327.) His resignation of the Great Seal on February 25, 1432, probably arose from the contests between the ruling powers; for it appears that the archbishop continued industriously to attend the council, and that in 1439 he was one of the ambassadors to treat for peace with France. In December of that year he was made cardinal priest by the title of St. Balbina. (*Rymer*, x. 758.)

Ten years after this he was called upon to resume the office of chancellor, and received the Great Seal on January 31, 1450, as the successor of John Stafford, Archbishop of Canterbury, on whose death in 1452 he was raised to the primacy, to which he was elected on July 21. On this translation the pope granted him the rank of cardinal bishop, by the title of St. Rufina; and he had the satisfaction of receiving the cross and the pall at the hands of his nephew Thomas Kempe, then Bishop of London.

The united labours which he thus undertook he continued to perform for nearly two years, when his career was closed by his death on March 22, 1453-4. He was buried in Canterbury Cathedral.

His name is still remembered in the university of Oxford, to the schools of which, as well as to his own college, he was a munificent benefactor, He beautified the collegiate church of Southwell, and rebuilt that of his native parish, Wye, where he erected a tomb to his parents, and in 1447 endowed a college of secular priests for the celebration of divine service and the instruction of youth, calling them the provost and fellows of St. Gregory and St. Martin. This establishment was dissolved with the other religious houses under Henry VIII.; but the buildings have been since devoted to the purposes of parish education with part of the original endowments. (*Godwin*, 127, &c.; *Hasted*, vols. iv. vii. xii.; *Gent. Mag.* Nov. 1845, p. 481.)

KENDAL, HUGH DE, had the Great Seal on July 25, 1284, 12 Edward I., during the temporary absence of the chancellor, left in his care and that of two others. (*Cal. Rot. Pat.* 51.) This was solely as clerks of the Chancery, many writs and directions being addressed to them on the business of the Chancery.

How long he had been one of the clerks of the Chancery does not appear, but he had been for several years engaged in official duties. In 1 Edward I. he received ten marks for his expenses in going to the king beyond the seas; two years afterwards he was assessor of the fifteenth imposed on the counties of Cambridge and Huntingdon; and in the ninth year he is styled the king's clerk. In 17 Edward I. he was paid 116s. 4½d. for erecting a house in the burial-ground of the abbot of Westminster, in which the statues of King Henry and Queen Eleanor, Edward's late consort, were being made; and in 20 Edward I. he received 20l. in reference to some latten metal provided for the tomb of the former. (*Devon's Issue Roll*, 87, 99, 105; *Parl. Writs*, i. 3, 9.)

KENT, EARL OF. *See* ODO; H. DE BURGH; H. GRAY.

KENYON, LLOYD (LORD KENYON), was the second but eldest surviving son of Lloyd Kenyon, of Bryn in Flintshire, a magistrate of that county, by Jane, daughter of Robert Eddowes, of Eagle Hall in the county of Chester. He was born at Gredington in Flintshire on October 5, 1732; and after passing through Ruthin grammar school in Denbighshire, then in high repute, and in which Lord Keeper Williams was formerly, and Chief Baron Richards more recently a pupil, was articled to Mr. Tomkinson, an attorney at Nantwich. There with extraordinary diligence and assiduity he mastered the elements of his profession, occasionally recreating himself by some boyish attempts at poetry. Luckily for his fame, he soon deserted the Muses, and acquired so much credit with his master for his proficiency in law and steadiness in conduct that negotiations were entered into to receive him into partnership. Some difference however arising as to terms, and his elder brother having lately died, it was determined that he should seek his fortune at the bar; and accordingly he was entered at the Middle Temple, and was called to the bar on February 7, 1756. During his years of pupilage and for the long interval after, in which his merits and even his name were unknown, he occupied every instant of his time in laying in that store of knowledge so essential for the man who aims at the character of a real lawyer. He lived in a small set of chambers in Brick Court in the Temple, and was constant in his attendance in Westminster Hall, where he began taking notes of the cases he heard there so early as 1753. The small means which his father could allow him obliged him to live with the greatest economy, by which he contracted a habit of parsimony which stuck to him to the last day of his life; and he was proud even in his prosperity of pointing out the eating-house near Chancery Lane in which he and Dunning and Horne Tooke used to dine together at the cost of 7½d. a head. With Dunning, who soon discovered his merits, he formed a close intimacy, attended with mutual benefit. When, by an unexampled success, Dunning was overwhelmed with cases and briefs, Kenyon was employed by him to answer many of the former and to look out the law and arrange the arguments arising from the latter. By this employment he not only improved in the exercise of his powers, but, when his assistance was discovered, the cases by degrees were sent direct to him, till at last he was well employed in that branch of business, and his opinions became much sought for and highly esteemed.

He was regular in his attendance on the different courts, particularly the Chancery, and travelled the Welsh and Oxford Circuits, which Chancery barristers had not then ceased to do. Interposing sometimes as *amicus curiæ* with some abstruse law or forgotten clause in an old act of parliament, he attracted the attention of Lord Thurlow, whose idle habits required the aid of a laborious helper; and he was soon joined with Mr. Hargrave in doing privately the work for which the great man received the credit. This assistance was well rewarded; for not long after Thurlow became lord chancellor he gratefully conferred on his 'devil' in 1780 the chief justiceship of Chester, an office most gratifying to Kenyon, as it not only gave him honour in his own country, but confirmed the standing he had attained at the bar. In the same year he was returned member for Hindon in Wiltshire. Soon after he made his first prominent appearance as leader in the defence of Lord George Gordon for high treason, in reference to the riots of 1780, in which his noble client was infinitely more indebted to the zeal and eloquence of Mr. Erskine, who acted as junior counsel, than to him. In fact, though a deeply learned lawyer and a forcible arguer, he was never, from his want of oratorical powers, an efficient leader in criminal or Nisi Prius cases.

Lord Thurlow advanced him, *per saltum,* to the attorney-generalship in March 1782, but he was not a very zealous assistant to the ministry. He continued in office till April 1783, when both he and Lord Thurlow were turned out by the Coalition. His exclusion lasted only till the following December, when he was re-appointed under Mr. Pitt, but did not hold the place above three months, receiving the office of master of the Rolls on March 30, 1784, and also the honour of a baronetcy on July 24. In the new parliament he was elected for Tregony, and fully ingratiated himself with the minister by his zealous opposition to Mr. Fox as a candidate for Westminster, actually having a bed put up in the loft of his stables to give him a vote, and supporting the scrutiny that followed that election with more energy than discretion. After presiding at the Rolls for four years, during which he was much commended both for efficiency and despatch, he was raised, on the resignation of Lord Mansfield, to the head of the Court of King's Bench on June 9, 1788, and on the same day was created a peer by the title of Lord Kenyon of Gredington.

In dignity, urbanity, and grace there was a sad falling off in the court; but in knowledge of law, application of principle, discrimination of character, intuitive readiness, and honesty of purpose, the new chief justice need not fear a comparison with his great predecessor. The disapprobation with which, from the offensiveness of his manner and his severity of expression, he was regarded by both branches of his profession was more than counterbalanced by the admiration which, from the inflexibility of his justice, was universally accorded to him by the suitors and the public. To his unpopularity with the former is to be attributed the multitude of anecdotes about his worn-out habiliments, shabby equipage, and bad Latin, circulated by the contemporary jesters of the bar. They have been minutely detailed by Mr. Townsend, and repeated by Lord Campbell; but, whether true or invented, they ought now to be forgotten, as the venial frailties of the man, in regard to his acknowledged merits as the judge. To make the most of them, they were, as he himself considerably declared of the errors of Erskine, merely 'blots in the sun.' He was truly honest and independent, and had an absolute abhorrence of anything that savoured of irreligion, immorality, or fraud. He was particularly sharp in punishing the misdeeds of unworthy practitioners; in actions for criminal conversation he urged the most exemplary damages; he made forcible war against the spirit of gambling, and neither high nor low escaped his invectives; and to the gross libels of the day, both political and personal, he was a stern opponent. Though his observations on these subjects might in some instances, no doubt, have been tempered with a little less warmth, they were dictated by the strictest moral principle, and tended, and were intended, to repress the evil practices upon which he was called to adjudicate. His addresses to juries were clear and distinct, and showed sound common sense and great discrimination; his arguments *in Banco* always exhibited soundness of law, both technical and material; and, notwithstanding all his minor failings, the decisions and rulings of no judge stand in higher estimation than those of Lord Kenyon. His presidency lasted nearly fourteen years, and his death, which was hastened by his grief for the loss of his eldest son, occurred at Bath on April 4, 1802. He was buried in the family vault at Hanmer, where there is a monument with his effigy by Bacon, jun., and an inscription recording his piety and worth. His notes of cases, which only extended from 1753 to 1759, were published some years after his death.

He married Mary, daughter of George Kenyon, of Peel in Lancashire, the elder branch of the family, and had by her three sons. The title is now enjoyed by the fourth baron.

KERDESTON, WILLIAM DE, was one of the justices of trailbaston appointed on April 6, 1305, 33 Edward I., for Norfolk and Suffolk (*N. Fœdera,* i. 970), of which he had been sheriff, and held considerable possessions in the former of them. When the new commissions were issued two years afterwards, his name was omitted, probably on account of his death, as the frequent entries about him in the parliamentary writs cease in the thirty-fourth year. They show him to have been summoned to perform military service, and to have been variously employed in those counties. He married Margaret, daughter of Gilbert de Gant, Baron of Folkingham. His son Roger was summoned to parliament in 6 Edward III., but the barony fell into abeyance in the next reign. (*Dugdale's Baron.* ii. 112; *Nicolas's Synopsis.*)

KILKENNY, WILLIAM DE (BISHOP OF ELY), was archdeacon of Coventry in 1248, and held some official position in the court from 1249, 33 Henry III., to 1252. (*Madox,* ii. 129, 202.) When John de Lexinton retired from court in 1250, the Great Seal was committed to Peter de Rivallis and William de Kilkenny, and it is not improbable, as they both were connected with the king's wardrobe, that it was merely deposited there under their safe custody during John de Lexinton's absence.

William de Kilkenny, however, was afterwards in the sole possession of the Seal, although the date of its delivery to him is not recorded. His signature appears to a patent dated July 2, 1253, relative to the government of the kingdom, during the king's absence in Gascony, by Queen Eleanor and Richard Earl of Cornwall, who had been appointed regents. They at the same time were directed to deliver to William de Kilkenny the seal of the Exchequer, to be kept by him in the place of the Great Seal, which the king had ordered to be locked up till his return.

About Michaelmas 1254 the monks of Ely elected him their bishop, and on the 5th of the ensuing January, the king having returned to England on the 1st, the bishop elect delivered up the Great Seal to him, and received a patent, 39 Henry III., m. 15, expressive of his diligent and acceptable service, with an entire quittance from all reckonings and demands in respect of the King's Court or otherwise, 'de tempore quo fuit *custos Sigilli nostri* in Anglia.' (*Madox*, i. 69, 71.)

Matthew Paris calls him 'cancellarius specialis;' and Sir T. Hardy, following him, has introduced him into his column of chancellors. There are only two recorded instances in which he is distinguished by that title, both in 37 Henry III. (*Rymer*, i. 288; *Abb. Placit.* 133.) It is observable, however, that in neither of the preceding entries of that year is he so designated, and the words above cited from his quietus seem conclusively to prove that his real office was that of keeper of the Seal.

He presided over his see for little more than one year, during which he gave to his monks the churches of Melburn and Swaffham. His decease occurred on September 22, 1256, while engaged on an embassy to Spain. His body was buried at Sugho, where he died, but his heart was brought to his own cathedral.

In times of violence and distraction, such as those he flourished in, it is pleasant to find all parties writing in his praise. He is represented as handsome in his person, modest in his demeanour, skilled in the municipal laws of the kingdom, wise, prudent, and eloquent; and he is mentioned among the benefactors of Cambridge. (*Godwin*, 256; *Angl. Sac.* i. 310, 636.)

KINDERSLEY, RICHARD TORIN, was born on October 5, 1792, at Madras, and is the eldest son of the late Nathaniel Edward Kindersley, Esq., of Sunning Hill, Berkshire, formerly in the civil service of the now defunct East India Company, and descended from a Lincolnshire family. Being brought to England for education, he proceeded from Haileybury to Trinity College, Cambridge, and graduated B.A. in January 1814, being fourth wrangler of his year, and gaining his election as fellow of his college in October 1815. He took his degree of M.A. in July 1817, and on the 10th of the following February was called to the bar by the society of Lincoln's Inn.

In January 1835 he was made one of the king's counsel, and occupied that position till 1848, having been advanced in the previous year to the honourable post of chancellor of the county palatine of Durham. During the whole of the thirty years that had elapsed since he assumed the barrister's gown he had practised in the Court of Chancery, and both as junior and senior, for juridical learning, patient industry, and solid judgment, had held so high a reputation that he was early ranked among those who would sooner or later be called to a judicial office.

Never having been in parliament, and not having any political interest, he had to wait till March 1848 for his advancement, and then only received a mastership in Chancery. In that position his judicial talent became so evident that on October 20, 1851, he was appointed vice-chancellor, and was knighted. This office he resigned in November 1866, and the fifteen years during which he held it confirmed the character he bore throughout his whole career.

He married the only daughter of the Rev. John Leigh Bennett, of Thorpe in Surrey.

KING, PETER (LORD KING). The career of this eminent judge affords another striking instance of how genius and industry may overcome the most unpromising beginnings, and, when united with modesty and good conduct, may raise the possessor from a subordinate position to the highest dignity in the state. Peter King's father, Jerome King, was a thriving and respectable grocer and salter in Exeter, and he himself was compelled reluctantly to pursue the same business for some years. His mother was Anne, daughter of Peter Locke, of a Somersetshire family, and first cousin of the great philosopher John Locke. He was born in 1669, and after receiving the ordinary education at the grammar school of his native city, he had no other apparent prospect than was opened to him by his father's trade. Though faithfully and diligently discharging the duties of this unattractive avocation, his mind, which was serious and contemplative, sought more congenial employment, and instead of occupying his leisure hours in the usual amusements of youth, he devoted them to literary pursuits. Encouraged by his celebrated relative, who saw with surprise and pleasure the progress in learning of one who could command so few opportunities for study, he published anonymously in 1691 a work suggested to him by the discussions in parliament on the scheme of Comprehension, which about that time agitated the religious world.

This was entitled an 'Enquiry into the Constitution, Discipline, Unity, and Worship of the Primitive Church that flourished within the first 300 years after Christ: faithfully collected out of the extant writings of those ages.' He soon afterwards produced a second part, leading to a correspondence between him and Mr. Ellis, which was published by the latter. In 1702 he issued another theological work, called 'The History of the Apostles' Creed,' which greatly increased his reputation. Bred up among Dissenters, he had in his first work naturally advocated the claims of the Presbyterians; but when Mr. Sclater's book called 'Original Draught of the Primitive Church' appeared, so late as 1717, he is said to have acknowledged that his principal arguments had been satisfactorily confuted. However this may have been, his early work attracted the notice of the learned world, and it displayed such an extent of reading and research that his relative induced his father to release him from his commercial engagements, and, by sending him to complete his education at the university of Leyden, prepare him for a position more suitable to his talents. He resided at Leyden for three years, and returned in 1694 and applied himself diligently to the study of the law at the Middle Temple, where he was called to the bar on June 8, 1698. To Chief Justice Treby and to his other whig connections he probably owed his early introduction into practice, in which he was soon successfully and extensively established, both in Westminster Hall and on the Western Circuit. By the same interest he was almost immediately provided with a seat in the senate, being, in both the parliaments of February and December 1701, elected for Beeralston, a close borough, for which he sat till he ascended the bench. During the whole of this time, although we know from his correspondence with Locke that he was an active partisan and an occasional speaker, the records of parliamentary oratory are so scanty that his name very seldom appears. The first occasion on which he is noticed is in January 1704, when he delivered an able and effective argument in support of the right of electors to appeal to the common law for redress against the returning officers of Aylesbury for refusing to receive their votes. (*Parl. Hist.* vi. 264.) This year was an eventful one to him, being marked by his marriage in September with Anne, daughter of Richard Seyes, Esq., of Boverton in Glamorganshire, and by the death in the next month of his cousin John Locke, who had been his affectionate guide and adviser, and who proved his confidence and love by making him his executor and leaving him his MSS., and a great part of his property.

In 1705 he received his first promotion, that of recorder of Glastonbury, which was succeeded by his election on July 27, 1708, to the recordership of London, and his knighthood in the following September. At this time his reputation was so high that he was designed for speaker of the new parliament; but his claims were withdrawn in favour of Sir Richard Onslow. He was one of the managers for the Commons in the impeachment of Dr. Sacheverell in 1710, and opened the second article in a most elaborate speech, replying also to the doctor's defence in one as able and as long. In these orations he displayed all his theological learning; but he could not effectively support a prosecution like this, which itself in some measure contravened the principles of that toleration which he had advocated. This however was a party affair, in which he probably was compelled to assist; but he soon after showed his adherence to his old opinions by his energetic defence of Whiston and of Fleetwood, Bishop of St. Asaph. (*State Trials*, xv. 134, 418, 703; *Parl. Hist.* vi. 1155.)

When George I. came to the throne the whigs regained their power, and Sir Peter was at once promoted. From the whig leader in the House of Commons and the acknowledged head of the bar, though undignified with office, he was raised on November 14, 1714, to the post of chief justice of the Common Pleas, in which he sat for more than ten years, with the approbation of lawyers for his learning, and of suitors for his impartiality. The 'State Trials' report only two criminal trials before him; and in both of them his summing up of the evidence and his statement of the law are most careful, clear, and distinct; and though his construction of the Coventry Act in that of Woodburn and Cope did not meet with universal acquiescence, it was agreed on all sides that the prisoners were most deservedly condemned. (*State Trials*, xv. 1386, xvi. 74.)

On the resignation of Lord Chancellor Macclesfield in January 1725, Sir Peter King was appointed speaker of the House of Lords; in which character he presided at the trial of that nobleman, and pronounced sentence against him on May 27. Five days after, on June 1, the Great Seal was placed in his hands as lord chancellor, he having three days before been raised to the peerage by the title of Baron King of Ockham in Surrey. His salary of 6000*l.* was increased by 1200*l.*, avowedly to compensate for the loss of the sale of certain offices in the Court of Chancery; thus in effect acknowledging that to have been theretofore a recognised privilege, for the exercise of which Lord Macclesfield had been punished. He had held the Seal for two years when George I. died; yet, though he had given his opinion on the subject of the marriage and education of the royal family in favour of that king's prerogative, and against the claim of the Prince of Wales, the latter when he came to the crown was so convinced of his unbiassed integrity that he was continued in his high trust for the first six years of the reign.

His earliest labours were devoted to the construction of a plan by which the frauds and misapplication of the suitors' money, as lately exposed, might be for the future prevented; and this was satisfactorily effected by the appointment of a new officer called the accountant-general, in whose name all the funds brought into court were immediately placed, to be dispensed under strict regulations to those found to be entitled to them. In the daily exercise of his judicial functions, though he exhibited the same learning, care, and impartiality, he did not sustain the same reputation he had won by his presidency of the Common Pleas. He had not had any experience in equity practice, and consequently was diffident, irresolute, and dilatory. So many of his decrees were appealed against, and so many of his decisions were reversed or controverted, that the admiration which he had earned as a judge cannot be extended to him as a chancellor. Lord Hervey (*Memoirs*, i. 281) relates that the queen once said of him that 'he was just in the law what he had been in the gospel—making creeds upon the one without any steady belief, and judgments in the other without any settled opinion.'

During the latter part of his career his health failed, and he became so lethargic 'that he often dozed over his causes when on the bench;' a circumstance which, according to Jeremy Bentham (an eyewitness), 'was no prejudice to the suitors,' owing to the good understanding between Sir Philip Yorke and Mr. Talbot, who, though opposed to each other as counsel, arranged the minutes of the decrees between them 'so as that strict justice might be done.' (*Cooksey*, 60.) No wonder then that this mode of settling their claims was unsatisfactory to the litigants. Lord King's infirmities increased so much that on November 29, 1733, he felt himself compelled to resign the Seal, after having held it for nearly nine years.

From this time he gradually sank till the close of his life. He died on July 29, 1734, and was buried at Ockham, where a handsome monument bears record of his many excellencies.

From the liberal principles in which he was educated he never swerved during the whole of his career, and against his private character no word has ever been whispered.

He left four sons, each of whom successively enjoyed the title. The great-grandson of the fourth brother was created by Queen Victoria, in 1838, Earl of Lovelace, and is now lord lieutenant of Surrey.

KINGESTON, HENRY DE, in 1197, 9 Richard I., was one of four justices itinerant who tallaged Kingeston, a small town in Berkshire (*Madox*, i. 705), and was no doubt of the same place. His name does not appear on any other occasion.

KINGSMILL, JOHN, was the son of John Kingsmill, of Barkham, Berks, and was himself afterwards seated at Sidmanton in Hampshire. He had his legal education at the Middle Temple, and, having been noticed in the Year Books from Michaelmas 1489, was called from that society to take the degree of the coif in 1494, and in 1497 he was made one of the king's serjeants. (*Y. B. 9 Henry VII.* fo. 23 b.) That he was held in high estimation at the bar is proved by the following letter from one of the correspondents of Sir Robert Plumpton (*Corresp.* 134), for whom the serjeant was professionally engaged:—'Sir, for Mr. Kingsmel, it were wel doon that he were with you, for his authority and worship; for he may speke more plainly in the matter than any counsel in this country will, for he knowes the crafty labour that hath been made in this matter, and also he will not let for no maugre. And yf the enquest passe against you, he may shew you summ comfortable remedy, for I suppose with good counsell you may have remedy; but, sir, his coming will be costly to you.'

On July 2, 1503, he was preferred to a judicial seat in the Common Pleas; and fines were levied before him as late as February 1509, two months before the king's death. His own death probably occurred about the same period, as his name does not appear in the reign of Henry VIII.

He married Joan, daughter of Sir John Gifford of Ishill, and had a son John, whose second son, George, is the next judge noticed.

KINGSMILL, GEORGE, the grandson of the above John Kingsmill, was the second son of Sir John Kingsmill, of Sidmanton in Hampshire, by Constance, the daughter of John Goring, of Burton in Sussex. He passed through the grades of legal study at Lincoln's Inn, where he was called to the bar in 1567, and became reader in autumn 1578. In 1594 he removed from the inn on being made a serjeant, and in the following year he received the additional honour of queen's serjeant. Lord Burleigh recommended him for advancement as a man 'well able to bear the burden of service' (*Peck's Desid. Cur.* b. v. 24), and soon after that minister's death he was elevated to the bench as a judge of the Common Pleas, on February 8, 1599. After the accession of King James, who knighted him, he retained his post till Hilary 1606, when he resigned, and in the April following he died.

He married Sarah, daughter of Sir James Harington, of Exton, and widow of Francis Lord Hastings. (*Collins's Peerage*, vi. 658.)

KINLOSS, LORD. See EDWARD BRUCE.

KIRKEBY, GILBERT DE, like many of his namesakes, was connected with the courts; and that his standing was a high one is shown by his being selected in 21 Edward I., 1293, as one of the eight justices of assize then appointed, when Kent and eight other counties were assigned to him and to John de Insula. He had property in Hinton and Brackley in Northampton, and was sheriff of that county for five years, commencing 2 Edward I. (*Abb. Placit.* 299; *Fuller.*)

KIRKEBY, JOHN DE. This name appears three times in the judicial list of the reign of Henry III.—viz., in 1227, 1236, and 1272. The presumption, therefore, is that they do not apply to the same individual, but that the party mentioned in the first of the two former years was probably the same person recorded in the second of them. Great difficulty, however, frequently arises in distinguishing individuals who are denominated from their native places, especially when towns of the same name occur, as in this case, in different counties. A John de Kirkeby, parson of the church of Kirkeby Lonsdale, in 11 Henry III., obtained the grant of a fair there; but there is nothing to prove, though it is very possible, that he was the same John de Kirkeby who, in August of the same year, 1227, was appointed one of the five justices itinerant selected for the counties of Northampton, Bedford, Buckingham, Cambridge, Huntingdon, and Rutland. (*Rot. Claus.* ii. 201, 213.) Again, the tallage of Yorkshire was assessed by a John de Kirkeby in 14 Henry III. (*Madox*, i. 708), and either a justice itinerant, or a clergyman in the neighbourhood, might have been so employed. In 19 Henry III. a John de Kirkeby paid seven hundred marks to the king for the wardship and marriage of the son and daughter of Philip, the brother of Thomas de Burgh (*Excerpt. e Rot. Fin.* i. 281); and in the next year again, in Easter 1236, the name appears as a justicier, taking the acknowledgment of fines. (*Dugdale's Orig.* 42.) As it may be easily presumed that the justice itinerant is the same as the justicier, and considering that it was not uncommon for the judges of that period to have ecclesiastical preferments, there is a reasonable ground for believing that he and the incumbent of the living of Kirkeby Lonsdale are one.

KIRKEBY, JOHN DE (BISHOP OF ELY), is, there is little doubt, the individual referred to in the last article under the date 1272. He was rector of the church of St. Berian in Cornwall, dean of Wymburn in Dorsetshire, a canon in the cathedrals of Wells and York, and in 1272, 56 Henry III., was appointed archdeacon of Coventry. (*Rot. Parl.* i. 14; *Le Neve*, 132.) When, on the death of Richard de Middelton on August 7 of the latter year, the Great Seal was delivered into the king's wardrobe under the seal of John de Kirkeby, there is no doubt that he was either an officer of the Exchequer or a clerk of the Chancery. On the king's death, on November 16 following, it was delivered up by him to the king's council. There is among the records in the Tower a letter addressed to him as the king's vice-chancellor about this time. (7 *Report Pub. Rec., App.* ii. 239.)

It was not till nearly six years after this that he had again possession of the Great Seal. When Robert Burnel, the chancellor, went abroad on February 11, 1278, 6 Edward I., John de Kirkeby was named as his substitute; and the same course was repeated on several other occasions during that chancellor's temporary absences—viz., on May 25, 1279; February 20, 1281; February 13, 1282; and March 1, 1283. As he was left to expedite the business of the Chancery in the meantime, it is manifest that he was cognisant of the duties of the office, and most probably that he was the senior clerk in the Chancery, then a place of high importance. From this he was promoted on January 6, 1284, to the office of treasurer. (*Madox*, ii. 36), which he filled until his death.

On July 26, 1286, he was elected Bishop of Ely, and, although he had previously held so many ecclesiastical dignities, was obliged to be ordained priest before his consecration. Within four years a violent fever terminated his career, on March 26, 1290. He was buried in his own cathedral, and was succeeded in his property by a brother named William. He is charged with neglecting the care of his diocese in his devotion to the affairs of the state, and to have borne himself with too much arrogance, sinking the bishop in the treasurer. His successors, however, would not fail to bless his memory for the munificent bequest he made to them of the manor of Holborn, where their London palace was built, near the site which is now called Ely Place. (*Godwin*, 257; *Angl. Sacr.* i. 637; *Chron. Petrob.* 150.)

KIRKEBY, THOMAS, was one of the masters in Chancery from 18 Henry VI., 1439, till March 29, 1447, when he received a grant of the office of master of the Rolls in reversion after the death of John Stopindon (*Rot. Parl.* v. 3-128, 317, 447); and probably came into possession before May

25 following, when Stopindon's successor in the archdeaconry of Dorset was collated. After his predecessor's death he took a new patent, dated January 26, 1448, when the grant was made to him for life; but his new grant on the accession of Edward IV. was only 'quamdiu se bene gesserit.' In little more than nine months he was directed to give up the Rolls to Robert Kirkham, who succeeded him on December 23, 1461. He died in 1476, being then treasurer of Exeter Cathedral. (*Le Neve*, 91, 281.)

KIRKETON, ROGER DE, although introduced by Dugdale among the justices of the Common Pleas in 39 Edward III., on the authority of a liberate for the payment, no doubt, of his salary, was then only made one of the king's serjeants, and was not raised to the bench till the early part of 46 Edward III., 1372. His arguments as an advocate extend from 28 to 45 Edward III., in the Year Books, in which he is named as serjeant in the fortieth year. It was not till 46 Edward III. that he was for the first time introduced as a regular judge. The fines acknowledged before him commence in February in that year.

He continued on the bench during the remainder of that reign, and was reappointed at the commencement of the following. His name on the fines does not occur beyond July 1380, 4 Richard II., but he lived till the ninth year of that reign.

He was of a Lincolnshire origin, and had property in the place from which he was called in that county; and there are some circumstances which raise a question whether he and Roger de Meres, aftermentioned, are not one and the same person.

KIRKHAM, ROBERT, was a master in Chancery in 1454, 32 Henry VI., till the end of that reign; and nine months after the accession of Edward IV. he superseded Thomas Kirkeby as master of the Rolls, on December 23, 1461. Twice during the absence of the lord chancellor, George Nevill, Bishop of Exeter, the Great Seal was placed in his custody, from August 23 to October 25, 1463, and from April 10 to May 14, 1464. From June 8 to 20, 1467, it was again put into his hands to transact the business of the Chancery. Although called keeper in the record, it was in a very restricted sense, for he was to act only in the presence of two lords and two knights, and to deliver the Seal to one or other of them every day when the sealing was finished. Kirkham certainly continued master of the Rolls till the restoration of Henry VI. on October 9, 1470; and it would seem that he was not removed during the four following months, for his successor, William Morland, was not appointed till February 12, 1471. It appears probable that he had been for some time ill, which perhaps was the cause of his not being disturbed in his office by Henry VI.; and, as he was not restored to it when Edward IV. resumed the throne, he probably died just before Morland's appointment.

KNOVILL, GILBERT DE, was sheriff of Devonshire from 21 to 28 Edward I., during which time he witnessed the charter by which Isabella de Fortibus, Countess of Albemarle and Devonshire, granted to the king the Isle of Wight, and the manors of Christchurch in Hants and Lambeth in Surrey, and was also one of her executors. (*Rot. Parl.* i. 335.) He was indebted to her for the manor of Batishorn in the parish of Honiton, which long remained in his family. (*Risdon*, 40.)

In 31 Edward I., 1303, he was sent as a justice itinerant into the isles of Jersey, Guernsey, Alderney, and Sark, and in 1305 and 1307 was appointed one of the justices of trailbaston into ten counties, of which Devonshire was one. (*Rot. Parl.* i. 218, 464.)

Judging from a contemporary song, he graced the seat of justice with mercy and a tender consideration for the poor. (*Wright's Pol. Songs*, 231.) In 2 Edward II. he petitioned the parliament for relief, in consequence of having received during his sheriffalty 108*l*. in a coin called pollards, which had been reduced to half their value by a royal proclamation; and the barons of the Exchequer were afterwards ordered to make him the allowance. (*Madox*, i. 294.) He died in 7 Edward II. (*Abb. Rot. Orig.* i. 203.)

KNYVET, JOHN, was a descendant of the very ancient family of Knyvets, which had been settled in England previous to the Conquest. He was the eldest son of Richard Knyvet, of Southwick in Northamptonshire, custos of the forest of Clyve, by Johanna, the daughter and heir of John Wurth, a Lincolnshire knight. In 21 Edward III. he was practising as an advocate in the courts (*Y. B.*); and in 31 Edward III. he was called to the degree of the coif; and there is Sir Edward Coke's authority (4 *Inst.* 79) that he was 'a man famous in his profession.'

On September 30, 1361, 35 Edward III., he was constituted a justice of the Common Pleas; and on October 29, 1365 (having been previously knighted), he was promoted to the office of chief justice of the King's Bench. (*N. Fœdera*, iii. 777.)

On June 30, 1372, he was constituted chancellor, and during the four years and a half that he retained the office he acted with great wisdom and discretion; but the king, being at the termination of that period under the influence of the Duke of Lancaster, was induced to revert to the old practice of having ecclesiastical chancellors; and Adam de Houghton, Bishop of St. David's, was substituted for Sir John on January 11, 1377. We have a proof in the Year Book of 48 Edward III. (fo. 32, pl. 21) that Knyvet, while chancellor, used to visit his old court.

It is there stated, 'Et puis Knivet le Chanc. vyent en le place, et le case luy fuit monstre par les justices, et il assenty,' &c. The king survived about five months, and Sir John Knyvet was one of the executors of his will, which was dated October 7, 1376. He lived several years after, dying in 4 Richard II. By his wife Alianora, the elder daughter of Ralph Lord Basset of Weldon, he left a son, whose descendants flourished till the end of the seventeenth century. The principal branch was established at the castle and manor of Buckenham in Norfolk in 1461, and Philip, its representative, was created a baronet at the first institution of that order in 1611. The title, however, became extinct in 1699. Other branches made themselves eminent in various ways; and one of them, Sir Thomas Knyvet, having been of the bedchamber of Queen Elizabeth and of the privy council of James I., was instrumental in the discovery of the Gunpowder Plot, and was raised to the peerage by the title of Lord Knyvet of Escrick in Yorkshire, on July 4, 1607; but dying without children in 1622, the barony became extinct. (*Dugdale's Baron.* ii. 424; *Blomefield's Norfolk*, i. 257.)

KUNILL, WILLIAM DE, is inserted by Mr. Hunter among the justiciers before whom fines were levied in 7 Richard I., 1195. The name does not again occur.

KYME, SIMON DE, held a lordship of that name in Kesteven, Lincolnshire, which he inherited from his father, Philip de Kyme. In 3 Richard I., 1191, he acted as a justice itinerant; and in 8 Richard I. he was one of those who set the tallage of Lincolnshire, of which county he was sheriff in the seventh and two following years of that reign. He seems to have been more fond of legal than of military contests, inasmuch as he paid one hundred marks to be exempted from attending King Richard on his Norman expedition, while there are several entries on the rolls of his fining for different processes, and for claiming lands to which he had no right. (*Madox*, i. 245–794.)

It is evident, however, that he was again employed as a justicier in the next reign, as in 1207, 8 John, he is so styled, with others who were sent to Lincoln to clear the gaol there, and to hear a certain appeal. (*Rot. Claus.* i. 83.)

By his wife Roese he had a son, also named Simon, who sided with the rebellious barons, and was excommunicated by the pope. His lands were restored after his death in 4 Henry III., 1219, to his brother Philip (*Excerpt. e Rot. Fin.* i. 44), whose successors were summoned to parliament in the reigns of the three Edwards; but the eighth baron dying in 1338 without issue, the male branch became extinct, and the barony is in abeyance among the representatives of Lucia, the sister of the last lord, who married Gilbert Earl of Angus.

KYNASTON, WILLIAM, was a member of a family long established at Ruyton-of-the-eleven-towns in Shropshire. He purchased in 1721 the office of master in Chancery from Mr. William Rogers, to whom, according to the vicious practice of the period, he paid 6000*l*. for the place, besides 1500 guineas to Lord Chancellor Macclesfield for his admission. When the investigation took place in 1725-6 into the malpractices of the court, among the deficiencies in the accounts of several of the masters, that of Mr. Kynaston was found to be above 26,000*l*. He suffered imprisonment in the Fleet for his debt, and was exposed in two acts of parliament, st. 12 Geo. I. c. 32 and 33. Afterwards making good his deficiency from his private estate, he was not excluded from his office, in which he still continued till his death. The 'Gentleman's Magazine' (x. 93) announces his appointment as cursitor baron of the Exchequer, in the room of George Olive, deceased, in February 1740; but as there is no patent nor other proof of his holding that office, and as Edward Barker had the grant of it in January 1744, it is probable that he only performed the duties temporarily during the vacancy. In 1733 he was elected recorder of Shrewsbury, and represented that borough in the parliaments of 1735, 1741, and 1747. He died in 1759, and was buried in the family vault at Ruyton. (*State Trials*, xvi. 858, 907; *Parl. Hist.* xiv. 76.)

L

LACY, ROGER DE, was descended from the before-mentioned Eustace Fitz-John, whose son Richard Fitz-Eustace, constable of Chester, married the daughter of Albreda, widow of Henry de Lacy, by her second husband Robert de Lizures, and had by her a son, John, who assumed the name and arms of Lacy, on becoming possessed of the property of the ancient family of De Lacy. Roger was the son of this John, by Alice de Vere, the sister of William de Mandeville, and on his father's death in 1179, inherited the constableship of Chester.

He accompanied King Richard to the Holy Land, and was present at the sieges of Acre and Damietta. In King John's confidence also he held a high place, and was sent by him with other eminent men to conduct the King of Scotland to Lincoln, to do homage and fealty to the English sovereign. A lively account is given by Roger de Wendover (173, 180, 236) of his bravery in defending for nearly a year the castle of Roche-Andeli in Normandy, when besieged by Philip, King of France, and of his ultimate capture in 1204, when famine compelled a surrender. King John advanced for him his ransom of one thousand marks, and afterwards exonerated him from its repayment (*Rot. Claus.* i. 4), conferring upon him, on his return to England, the sheriffalty of the counties of York and Cumberland, with the custody of their castles. (*Rot. Pat.* 48; *Fuller.*) His constant attendance on the king is shown by various records; and from two entries on the Rotulus de Præstito, of losses of forty shillings and twenty-five shillings, 'de ludo suo ad tabulas,' may be judged the familiarity which existed between him and the monarch, who, it may be observed, devoted part of Sunday to this amusement. (*Rot. Chart.* passim; *Rot. Misæ*, 139–164; *Rot. de Præstito*, 229, 238.)

Among other valorous acts of his life, it is related of him that, hearing, during Chester fair, that Ranulph, Earl of Chester, was besieged by the Welsh in the castle of Rothellan, he proceeded with a body of loose and unarmed people collected there, and delivered the earl from his danger. For this timely assistance the earl granted him 'magisterium omnium leccatorum et meretricum totius Cestreshire,' which he afterwards transferred to his steward, Hugh de Dutton, and his heirs.

That he acted as a justicier appears from fines which were levied before him in the tenth year of this reign. (*Hunter's Preface.*)

He married Maud de Clere, sister to the treasurer of York Cathedral, and, dying in January 1212, was buried in the abbey of Stanlaw in Cheshire. He was succeeded by his son, the next-mentioned John. (*Dugdale's Baron.* i. 100.)

LACY, JOHN DE (EARL OF LINCOLN), was the son of the above Roger de Lacy, by Maud de Clere. Though the king continued to him the favour which he had extended to his father, it is evident that some suspicion of his loyalty existed, inasmuch as, when his castle of Dunington was committed to his charge in July 1214, 16 John, he was called upon to provide four of his vassals, as well as his brother Roger, as hostages for his faithful services. (*Rot. Claus.* i. 151, 167, 169.) He nevertheless joined the insurgent barons, and was one of the twenty-five who were appointed to enforce the observance of Magna Charta.

Obtaining, however, the pardon of the king in January 1216, he not only had his lands restored, but several other favours were soon after conferred upon him; and in August he had letters of protection *sine termino.* (*Rot. Pat.* 162, 176, 179, 180.) Two subsequent records, however, afford proof of a second revolt—one in September 1216, by which the king committed his land of Navesby in Northamptonshire to Ernald de Ambleville; and another in August 1217, 1 Henry III., by which, on returning to his allegiance, his property was again replaced in his possession. He then made a pilgrimage to the Holy Land, but had returned to England before 5 Henry III., in which year he and his wife Margaret had a grant of the chase of Wynburneholt. (*Rot. Claus.* i. 289, 318, 339, 462.) She was the daughter of Robert de Quincy, by Hawise, daughter of Hugh Cyvelioc, Earl of Chester, and one of the coheirs of her brother, Ranulph Earl of Chester, who had been also created Earl of Lincoln. On Ranulph's death without issue the earldom of Lincoln was granted to this John de Lacy.

Although, at first, the new earl joined the party of Richard Mareschal, Earl of Pembroke, in his resistance to the king's authority, he was soon induced to return to his duty. He continued loyal for the remainder of his life, and was entrusted with the sheriffalty of Cheshire in 21 and 24 Henry III., and with other honours and privileges.

He twice filled the office of justice itinerant—in 10 and 18 Henry III., 1226–1233. (*Ibid.* ii. 151.)

He died on July 22, 1240, and was buried in the abbey of Stanlaw. By his wife Margaret, who survived him, and was afterwards married to Walter Mareschal, Earl of Pembroke, he had a son, Edmund, whose son Henry, the third earl of this name, died in 1312 without issue male. (*Excerpt. e Rot. Fin.* i. 255, 338, 390; *Wendover*, iii. 297, 355, iv. 44, 256, 270.)

LAKEN, WILLIAM, was of an opulent family seated at Willey in Shropshire. He was the son of Sir Richard Laken, knight, by Elizabeth, the daughter of Sir Hamond de Peshall, of the county of Stafford, knight, and widow of Henry Grendon. He is mentioned in the Year Book in Michaelmas, 31 Henry VI., 1452; and in the February following he was summoned to take upon him the degree of the coif. On June 4, 1465, 5 Edward IV., he was constituted the fifth judge of the Court of King's Bench, and sat there till the restoration of Henry VI. in 1470, when he was re-appointed; as he was also by Edward IV. on his return in the following year.

He died on October 6, 1475, and was buried at Bray in Berkshire, where his monumental brass still remains. He married twice: his first wife was named Matilda; his second was Sybella, one of the daughters of John Syterwalt, of Cleaver. They left issue, which was afterwards widely spread; and he is now represented by Sir Edmund Lacon, baronet, of Norfolk, the third of that title. (*Hasted*, ii. 397; *Ashmole's Berks*, iii. 4.)

LAMVALLEI, WILLIAM DE, was a baron holding lands in Essex; and his attendance on the court is shown by his being one of the witnesses to the king's charter in 10 Henry II. He was selected as a justice itinerant and associated with Thomas Basset, a man experienced in the laws, in 21 Henry II., 1175; and their pleas continue to be recorded for the five following years, though they probably are only the arrears of the pleas of the first year. (*Madox*, i. 125–139.)

Nothing further is related of him during the rest of Henry's reign; but in that of Richard he lost the royal favour and his lands, recovering both, however, by a timely fine of one hundred marks. Under John, although he never acted as a justicier, he is so described in the letters sent by Baldwin de Betun as security for the fine on the charter of liberties granted to the burgesses of Heddun. (*Rot. de Oblatis*, 89.) In the same year he was, for a fine of two hundred marks, entrusted with the custody of Colchester Castle and of the forest up to Chelmsford Bridge, as he formerly held them in Richard's reign. But he again forfeited the royal favour, for in 3 John he paid seventy marks for the king's 'benevolentiam;' and in 6 John, Geoffrey Fitz-Peter had the custody of his lands in Essex. (*Rot. de Finibus*, 279.)

Dying in 12 John, he left by his wife, Hawyse, a son William, whose daughter married John, son and heir of Hubert de Burgh, Earl of Kent. (*Dugdale's Baron*. i. 633; *Nicolas*.)

LANCASTER, WILLIAM DE, was the grandson to Roger Fitz-Reinfrid, a justicier. His father, Gilbert, had married Helewise, the only daughter of William de Lancaster, Baron of Kendal, who not only himself confederated with the barons in their wars with King John, but involved his son, William, who assumed the name of Lancaster from his mother, in the same troubles. He was one of the knights who were taken in Rochester Castle in 17 John, and it was only by a fine of twelve thousand marks that his father could obtain his release, and a remission of the royal anger; nor was it till 1 Henry III. that he was discharged from prison. (*Rot. Claus*. i. 241, 385; *Rot. de Finibus*, 570.) He afterwards conducted himself as a loyal subject, and in 10 Henry III. was named as one of the justices itinerant for the county of Cumberland.

He held, the sheriffalty of Lancashire from 18 to 30 Henry III., and the honor of Lancaster was committed to his trust. He died in December 1246, and was buried in Furness Abbey. He left no issue by his wife, Agnes de Brus. (*Dugdale's Baron*. i. 421.)

LANE, RICHARD, the lord keeper of the Great Seal of Charles I., was son of Richard Lane, of Courtenhall, near Northampton, by Elizabeth, daughter of Clement Vincent, of Harpole in the same county, where he was born in 1584. (*Baker's Northamptonsh*. i. 181.) He was called to the bar at the Middle Temple, and his early practice was in the Exchequer, the cases in which he reported from 1605 to 1612. He was reader to his inn in 1630, and treasurer in 1637, and had previously in 1615 been appointed counsel or deputy recorder of Northampton, and in 1634 attorney-general to the Prince of Wales. (*Clarendon's Life*, i. 67.) When the House of Commons impeached the Earl of Strafford, Mr. Lane was assigned to conduct the earl's defence, which he did so ably that the Commons, seeing the great probability of the earl's acquittal by the Lords, desisted from the trial, and effected their malicious purpose by a disgraceful bill of attainder, which by popular clamour was eventually passed. (*State Trials*, iii. 1472.) Officially connected with the court, he of course joined the king at Oxford, where, having been previously knighted, he was appointed lord chief baron on January 25, 1644.

The first duty that Sir Richard had to perform was to act as one of the commissioners on the part of the king in treating for an accommodation at Uxbridge, when he joined the other lawyers in resisting the demand of the parliament to have the militia entirely vested in them. There appearing no probability of satisfactorily settling this question, or that upon religion, which was violently debated, the treaty was broken off and the war proceeded. On Lord Lyttelton's death, the Great Seal was placed in the hands of Sir Richard as lord keeper, on August 30, 1645. The king, whose difficulties increased daily, was at last obliged to escape from Oxford, and that city was surrendered to the opposing army under General Fairfax on June 24, 1646, under articles in which the lord keeper was the principal party on the king's behalf. By one of them it was provided that the Great Seal and all the other official seals should be left for the victors. (*Whitelocke*, 210.) Thus deprived of the insignia of his office, nothing remained to him but its name, which he retained during the remainder of the king's life. The only evidence that his patent was renewed by Charles II. is in the epitaph on his wife's tomb at Kingsthorp. Like the king, he became an exile from his native land, and died in 1650 in France, as appears by the commission, dated April 22, 1651, to his relict the Lady Margaret, to administer to his personalty.

LANFRANC (ARCHBISHOP OF CANTERBURY) was born at Pavia about the year 1005, and belonged to an illustrious family which is said to have descended from the Emperors Carus and Numerian. After acquiring some celebrity in his native city, where he was for several years professor of laws, his anxiety to travel took him to Normandy, where he first opened a school at Avranches, and eventually, about 1042, retired to the poor and lonely abbey of Bec, then one of the most insignificant of the Norman monasteries. Herluin, the abbot, discovering his talents, induced him to resume his office of teacher; and the fame of his lectures became so widely extended that students flocked to them from all parts, Pope Alexander II. being one of his pupils.

He thus diffused a taste for knowledge among the clergy, and to him, in a great degree is to be attributed the revival of Latin literature and the liberal arts in France. His exposure of the ignorance of Arfastus has been already mentioned, and the enmity it occasioned. Its effect, however, was soon removed by the good humour of Duke William, and he became first a monk, and then prior, of the monastery. Among the students who came to receive his instructions there were some who had been pupils of Berengarius, archdeacon of Angers, who was master of a school at Tours. This desertion exciting the envy of Berengarius, who had propounded some doctrines relative to the Eucharist in opposition to those maintained by the Roman Church, he in revenge endeavoured to implicate Lanfranc in the same opinions. Lanfranc, however, had little difficulty, not merely in satisfying the pontiff of his orthodoxy, but in establishing such a reputation at Rome as to be called upon to refute the obnoxious heresy in the council then assembled.

Duke William, who highly appreciated his talents, took the advantage of his visit to Rome by employing him to obtain a repeal of the sentence of excommunication to which he had been subjected by Mauger, Archbishop of Rouen, on account of his marriage with Matilda, alleged to be related to him within the forbidden degrees of consanguinity. Lanfranc was successful in obtaining the papal dispensation, accompanied by a condition that William and his wife should each found an abbey at Caen. This injunction they immediately obeyed, dedicating one of them to St. Stephen, and the other to the Holy Trinity. Of the former, Lanfranc was appointed the first abbot in 1063, and pursued his lectures there with increased celebrity.

William entrusted to him the education of his children, and offered him the archbishopric of Rouen, which he was allowed to refuse: but after the Conquest, on the removal of Stigand from the archbishopric of Canterbury, the king, feeling the importance of supplying his place with a man of weight and prudence, faithful to his interests, and equal to the burden, selected Lanfranc as his successor, and overcame the scruples with which the modest abbot resisted his elevation. He was not only willingly accepted by the monks, and approved by the barons and people, but gladly confirmed by the pope. He was accordingly consecrated in August 1070, and on visiting Rome in the following year to receive the pall was welcomed with particular respect by his former pupil Alexander II., who rose to give him audience, kissed him instead of presenting his slipper for that obeisance, and, not satisfied with giving him the usual pall, invested him with that which he had himself used in celebrating mass. In this visit he defended the rights of the church of Canterbury against the claims of Thomas, Archbishop of York, and eventually succeeded in establishing them before the king, to whose decision the pontiff referred the question.

On his return from Rome he laboured successfully in reforming the irregularities and rudeness of the clergy. His severity in depriving many occasioned considerable complaints; but the introduction of foreign scholars in their places contributed effectually to the enlightenment of the nation. His efforts in support of his church were unremitting, nor were they repressed by the power of his opponents. Finding that the king's brother, Odo, Bishop of Bayeux, and Earl of Kent, while Stigand was in disgrace, had taken possession of many of the manors belonging to the archbishopric, Lanfranc instituted a suit against him, which was tried before Geoffrey, Bishop of Coutance, at a shiremote on Penenden Heath, when, after three days' hearing, the restoration of twenty-five manors was adjudged to him.

Enjoying the favour of the Conqueror and of his successor, he employed his power in the advancement of justice and the protection of the English. His private charities were widely diffused, and his munificence as a prelate is proved by his rebuilding the cathedral of Canterbury, recently destroyed by fire, together with all the buildings for the monks, whose numbers he increased from twenty to one hundred and forty. He founded also the two hospitals of St. Nicholas at Harbledown, and of St. John at Canterbury, for lepers and the infirm; he repaired many churches and monasteries in his diocese which had suffered in the wars; and he contributed largely to the restoration of Rochester Cathedral.

Dugdale (20) infers that Lanfranc, in conjunction with Geoffrey, Bishop of Coutance, and Robert, Earl of Moreton, held the office of chief justiciary during some part of the Conqueror's reign, from the existence of several precepts he had seen, directed to them by the king, which he can only thus interpret. That this inference is correctly drawn we have the evidence of some letters of Lanfranc addressed to the king while in Normandy. His influence with William was undoubted, and the arrest of Odo is ascribed to his overcoming the Conqueror's reluctance to touch an ecclesiastical person, by suggesting that he might take him, not as Bishop of Bayeux, but as Earl of Kent.

After a useful and active occupation of the primacy for nineteen years, he died on May 24, 1089, at the age of eighty-four, and was buried in his cathedral.

Although devoted to literature during the whole of his life, few proofs of his learning remain. His principal work was his treatise against Berengarius. The others were chiefly upon ecclesiastical matters, including a commentary on the Epistles of St. Paul. (*Biog. Brit. Literaria*, ii. 1; *Godwin*, 59; *Madox*, i. 8, 32; *Will. Malmesb.* 447–495; *R. de Wendover*, ii. 8–36; &c.)

LANGDALE, LORD. See H. BICKERSTETH.

LANGHAM, SIMON DE (ARCHBISHOP OF CANTERBURY), became a monk of Westminster in 1355, and till his death, forty years afterwards, he was a devoted friend to the house. Appointed prior in April, and abbot in May, 1349, he applied his early savings to the discharge of the engagements of the monastery; he suppressed its abuses, regulated its discipline, and gained the esteem of the brotherhood by his kind and equitable sway.

He was raised to the office of treasurer of the kingdom on November 21, 1360, 34 Edward III., and elected two years afterwards to two bishoprics, London and Ely, to the latter of which he was appointed, by his own selection, on January 10, 1362.

He continued treasurer till February 1363, when he succeeded William de Edington, Bishop of Winchester, as chancellor. On July 22, 1366, he was translated to Canterbury by papal provision, and about the same time resigned the Great Seal.

During his primacy he greatly exerted himself in the correction of the abuse of the privilege of pluralities; but he incurred some censure by the removal of John Wickliffe from the headship of Canterbury Hall in Oxford, which was in consequence of the appointment having been contrary to the statutes of Simon Islip, its founder. And if this Wickliffe be the same man as the reformer, of which some doubt has been lately raised, there is evidence in his writings to show that his attacks on the popish exactions were not occasioned by this quarrel, as he had commenced them some years earlier.

On September 27, 1368, Pope Urban V. promoted Langham to the dignity of a cardinal presbyter, by the title of St. Sixtus. The king taking umbrage at his acceptance of it, he resigned the archbishopric on November 27, and retired to Avignon. Pope Gregory XI. advanced him to the title of Cardinal Bishop of Preneste, having first employed him in several negotiations in 1372 to mediate peace between the Kings of England and France and the Earl of Flanders, during which he revisited his native country. In these treaties he is styled the Cardinal of Canterbury, and the king calls him his 'dear and faithful friend.' (*N. Fœdera*, iii. 932–970.) It is certain that he retained so much of the royal favour as to be permitted to hold various preferments at this time in England. Besides a prebend in the church of York, he was treasurer and archdeacon of Wells, and dean of Lincoln, his filling the latter place while a cardinal being the subject of a complaint to the parliament of April 1376. (*Rot. Parl.* ii. 339.)

It is stated that at this time he had applied for and procured permission to return to England, and that he projected the rebuilding of Westminster Abbey. But all his plans were frustrated by a paralytic stroke, which occasioned his death on July 22, 1376. He was first buried in the church of the Carthusian monastery which he had founded in Avignon, and was three years afterwards removed to St. Benet's Chapel in Westminster Abbey, where his tomb still remains.

He was a man of great capacity, wise, affable, temperate, and humble; and of his munificence we have evidence in his benefactions to Westminster, so that it is probable that the 'railing hexameters' on his translation from Ely to Canterbury—

Lætentur cœli, quia Simon transit ab Ely ;
Cujus in adventum flent in Kent millia centum,

were rather the malicious effusion of an individual enemy than the expression of popular feeling. (*Godwin*, 115, 261 ; *Weever*, 479 ; *Le Neve*, 6, 39, 44, 69 ; *Angl. Sac.* i. 46.)

LANGLEY, or **LONGLEY**, THOMAS (BISHOP OF DURHAM), was descended from an honourable family in Yorkshire. He studied at Cambridge, and in his youth was a retainer of the house of Lancaster. Educated as a priest, he was preferred in

1400 to a canonry, and in 1401 to the deanery of York.

His connection with the reigning family soon introduced him to the court, where he began his political career as keeper of the king's privy seal in 1403 (*Devon's Issue Roll*, 298), retaining it till March 1405, 6 Henry VI., when he received the Great Seal.

A vacancy in the archbishopric of York occurring soon after by the execution of Richard Scrope, Langley was elected his successor on August 8 (*Rymer*, viii. 407); but the pope resisting, and the death of Bishop Skirlawe opportunely happening soon afterwards, he took the wiser course of avoiding a contest with the papal power by accepting the bishopric of Durham, to which he was elected on May 17, 1406. He retained the Great Seal till January 30, 1407.

During the remainder of the reign of Henry IV. he was frequently employed in state affairs. In 1409 he had letters of protection on going into Tuscany on the king's business, and in 1411 he acted as a commissioner at Hauden-Stank, on the borders of Scotland. In the latter year, on June 11, he received a cardinal's hat from Pope John XXIII., an elevation which was not displeasing to his sovereign, whose continued confidence in him was shown by making him one of the executors of his will. (*Devon's Issue Roll*, 335.)

Henry V. soon after his accession sent him as one of the ambassadors to the King of France (*Ibid.* 336, 340), with whom a truce for one year was concluded. He was a second time raised to the office of chancellor on July 23, 1417, and retained it to the end of the reign, when, finding himself in the possession of the Great Seal with a new sovereign only a few months old, he had the precaution to obtain a formal entry of his delivering it up to the king's uncle, Humphrey Duke of Gloucester, and other lords, and to have the same recorded on the Rolls of Parliament. With the full assent of that parliament the bishop was re-appointed on November 16, 1422 (*Rot. Parl.* 170–1), but continued in office only about twenty months, being succeeded, on July 6, 1424, by Beaufort, Bishop of Winchester.

He was nominated one of the king's council in the parliament at Leicester in February 1426; but in the following June he prayed to be excused therefrom on account of his age and infirmities, so that he might attend to his episcopal duties. (*Acts Privy Council*, iii. 197.) Thus relieved from political attendance, he occupied the rest of his life in numerous magnificent and charitable works in his diocese, among which was his restoration of the Galilee in his cathedral built by Bishop Pusar, and the foundation of two schools for grammar and music. He did on November 30, 1437, having presided over his see for more than thirty-one years. (*Godwin*, 751; *Le Neve*, 314, 346; *Angl. Sac.* i. 775; *Surtees's Durham*, i. iv.)

LANGTON, JOHN DE (BISHOP OF CHICHESTER), of whose parentage nothing is known, was a clerk in the Chancery, and is the first person to whom the title of master or keeper of the Rolls can be distinctly traced. In a patent of 14 Edward I., 1286, quoted by Sir T. Hardy, he is called 'Custos Rotulorum Cancellariæ Domini Regis,' a duty which then, probably, devolved on the senior clerk of the Chancery, as even in the present reign that officer was still considered as the head of the masters of that court. Like his brethren in that department, he was an ecclesiastic, and held, among other preferments, canonries in the churches of Chichester, Lincoln, and York, and the treasurership of Wells.

He was appointed chancellor on December 17, 1292, and continued the prudent and sagacious course pursued by Bishop Burnel, his predecessor. He witnessed, during his ministry, the triumph of his sovereign's arms in Scotland, and the resignation of that kingdom by Baliol. An event much more important in its consequences also occurred while he held the Seal—viz., the enactment of the statute called 'Articuli super Cartas,' 28 Edward I., 1300, by which the Great Charter was fully confirmed, and regulations made to prevent any future encroachments on its provisions.

On the death of William de Luda, Bishop of Ely, in 1298, a contest arose between the monks of that abbey, one party electing their prior, and the other John de Langton, to fill the vacancy. The king gave his assent to the latter choice, but the pope, to whom the two candidates hastened to submit their pretensions, superseded both, and placed another in the seat. (*Godwin*, 259.) To conciliate all parties, however, the cunning pontiff raised the prior to the bishopric of Norwich, and gave the archdeaconry of Canterbury, then a very valuable preferment, to John de Langton. This appointment took place in 1299. (*Le Neve*, 12.)

He resigned the chancellorship on August 12, 1302, and in May 1305 he was raised to the bishopric of Chichester.

Soon after the accession of Edward II. he was again, about August 1307, appointed chancellor, and on January 21, 1308, he delivered up the Great Seal to the king, who was then proceeding to Boulogne to celebrate his nuptials with the French princess, Isabel, and received another to be used during the king's absence. He continued chancellor till May 11, 1310, when he retired from the office.

He presided over his diocese during the remainder of the troubled reign of Edward II., and for the first ten years of that of his successor, dying on June 17, or July 19, 1337. He was resolute in the performance of his ecclesiastical functions. Having excommunicated Earl Warren for adultery, that nobleman came with his retainers to lay violent hands on him; but the bishop, aided by his servants, succeeded in resisting their attempt, and threw the earl and all his party into prison. He was very bountiful to his see, and in the university of Oxford he founded a chest, still called by his name, out of which any poor graduate might, on proper security, borrow a small sum for his immediate necessities. (*Godwin*, 506; *Chapter Books, Chichester.*)

LANGTON, WALTER DE (BISHOP OF LICHFIELD AND COVENTRY), is introduced by Sir T. Hardy among the keepers of the Great Seal, because on the death of Bishop Burnel, the chancellor, on October 25, 1292, 20 Edward I., it was delivered to him as custos of the king's wardrobe, *under the seal of William de Hamilton.* If either of these is to be called keeper, however, the latter is the more entitled to the designation. They had no more than the temporary care of the Seal, while in its usual place of deposit, till the appointment of a new chancellor, the above John de Langton, which took place on December 12.

Walter de Langton was born at West Langton in the county of Leicester, and was nephew of William de Langton, dean of York. He was himself dean of the free chapel at Bruges, a canon of Lichfield, and one of the pope's chaplains. He held the office of keeper of the wardrobe until he was raised to the treasurership of England, on September 28, 1295; and in the following February he was elected Bishop of Coventry and Lichfield, still retaining the office of treasurer. (*Madox*, ii. 42.)

Although possessing the king's confidence and favour, his integrity and boldness in correcting the insolence of Peter de Gaveston and Prince Edward's other servants, and restraining their expenses, occasioned him much trouble and persecution. In 1301 he was charged with such heinous crimes by one Sir John Lovetot, as adultery, simony, and homicide, that the king was obliged to dismiss him till he had purged himself. For this he was compelled to take a journey to Rome, where, after great cost, he succeeded, and was not only reinstated in June 1303, but received the strongest proof of his sovereign's conviction of his innocence by being made principal executor of the king's will. On Edward's death, however, his persecution recommenced. He was turned out of his office, cast into prison, and a long list of charges brought against him for malversation, which were directed to be heard before William de Bereford, one of the judges. After a long imprisonment at London, Wallingford, and York, no proof could be brought against him, and he was absolved by the court in October 1308. In 1311 he was again imprisoned on a charge of homicide, but again succeeded in confounding his accusers.

His adherence to the king against the barons was followed by his restoration to his office in March 1312, 5 Edward II., from which he finally retired in September 1314, and spent the remainder of his days in the quiet exercise of his episcopal duties.

He died on November 16, 1321, and was buried in the chapel of St. Mary, which he had added to his cathedral at Lichfield. His benefactions to his see were numerous and munificent. (*Angl. Sac.* i. 441; *Godwin*, 318.)

LASINGBY, WILLIAM, derived, probably, from a manor of that name in Lincolnshire, is first mentioned in the Rolls of Parliament of 8 Henry IV., where there are copies of commissions to him and two others to treat on the part of the Earl of Northumberland with Robert, King of Scotland, and the ambassadors of France. For his connection with the earl's treasonable proceedings he was attainted, and all his lands forfeited. In the last year of Henry's reign, however, he obtained his pardon, and was restored to his possessions with the assent of the parliament. (*Rot. Parl.* iii. 605, 655.)

On the accession of Henry V. he was appointed chief baron of the Exchequer; but the only judicial transaction in which we find him engaged is on the commission to try Richard, Earl of Cambridge, Sir Thomas Grey, and Sir Henry Lescrop, of Marsham, who were condemned for conspiracy against the king's life. (*Ibid.* iv. 65.)

A new chief baron was appointed on November 4, 1419; but whether the vacancy was made by Lasingby's death or resignation does not appear.

LATHELL, NICHOLAS, who in 1 Edward IV., 1461, is described of the Exchequer, had a grant of 20*l.* a year out of the profits of Bedfordshire and Buckinghamshire. In 1473 he was clerk of the Pipe, and fourteen years afterwards, in Michaelmas 1487, 3 Henry VII., he was promoted, no doubt on account of his experience as an officer, to the bench of the Exchequer, as fourth baron. On December 5, 1488, he was advanced to the office of third baron, and retained his seat till the seventeenth year of that reign. (*Rot. Parl.* v. 472, 529, vi. 97.)

LAUNFARE, JOHN DE, is introduced by Madox (ii. 319) in his List of Barons of the Exchequer in 42 Henry III., 1258.

LAW, EDWARD (LORD ELLENBOROUGH), was of a family distinguished by clerical honours. His father was the learned Edmund Law, Bishop of Carlisle; his elder.

brother John became Bishop of Clonfert in 1782, of Killala in 1787, and of Elphin in 1795; and another brother, George Edward, was consecrated Bishop of Chester in 1812, and was translated to the diocese of Bath and Wells in 1824. His mother was Mary, the daughter of John Christian, Esq. of Unerigge in Cumberland; and, of the thirteen children she produced, he was the sixth child and fourth son.

Edward Law was born at Great Salkeld in Cumberland on November 16, 1750. In 1762 he was placed on the foundation of the Charterhouse, where he remained six years, and rose to the head of the school. Proceeding in 1768 to Cambridge, he entered Peterhouse College, of which his father had been master since the year 1754. Among his friends there was Archdeacon Coxe, by whom his picture at that time has been so faithfully drawn that it may be recognised in all his future career. His disposition is described as warm and generous, his thoughts as great and striking, his language as strong and nervous, and somewhat inclined to express his opinions with a little too much abruptness; active and enterprising, and preferring in his studies 'the glowing and animated conceptions of a Tacitus to the softer and more delicate graces of a Tully.' In 1771 he took his degree of B.A., coming out of the school as third wrangler, and gaining the gold medal for classical learning. In the next two years he obtained the members' prize for the second best dissertation in Latin prose, and honourably completed his university career by being elected fellow of his college.

He had been admitted at Lincoln's Inn in 1769, and when he left the university he attended at the chambers of Mr. (afterwards Baron) Wood, studying the mysteries of special pleading for two years, at the end of which he devoted himself for five years more to the practice of that science, the mastery of which is so essential to all who hope for future success and honour. He then was called to the bar in Hilary Term 1780, and joined the Northern Circuit, where he was not long before his merits were tested. His name, so familiar in the north, added to his already gained repute in London, insured him an immediate accession of business. In 1787 he had earned sufficient professional credit to be honoured with a silk gown, and in the same year held a crown brief on the trials of Lord George Gordon and others for libels. (22 *State Trials*, 183.) But the best proof of the estimation with which his forensic efforts were regarded was that before he had been eight years at the bar he was entrusted with the conduct of the defence of Warren Hastings, his juniors being Mr. Dallas and Mr. Plumer, both subsequently raised to the bench. In this arduous and deeply responsible undertaking, opposed to all the eloquence, inveteracy, and power of the greatest orators of the day, he manfully and successfully struggled during the seven years of that famous trial, from February 1788 to April 1795, when his exertions were rewarded by the acquittal of his persecuted client. During the continuance of that trial he was, in 1792, made attorney-general of Lancaster; and on February 14, 1801, he was selected by Mr. Addington as attorney-general, and knighted. In little more than a year he was, by the death of Lord Kenyon, called to the high position of lord chief justice of the King's Bench. His promotion took place on April 12, 1802, accompanied by his being called to the House of Peers with the title of Baron Ellenborough, a small village in Cumberland.

At the time when he was appointed attorney-general for Lancaster the political world was agitated by the excesses of the French Revolution, and he became necessarily engaged in all the trials that resulted from the seditious attempts of its admirers in this country. In conducting the extraordinary prosecution at Lancaster of Thomas Walker and others for a conspiracy, he at once consented to an acquittal, on finding that the evidence in support of it was in the highest degree suspicious, and prosecuted the perjured witness. He succeeded at York in convicting Henry Redhead Yorke of conspiracy, and he assisted in London on the trials of Thomas Hardy and John Horne Tooke for high treason, in which his duties were confined to the examination of the witnesses. During the few months in which he held the office of attorney-general to the king, besides prosecuting to conviction Joseph Wall on a charge of murder committed twenty years before, while governor of the island of Goree, he originated no prosecution for political offences. On commencing his official career a seat in parliament was provided for him, and during the short time that he held it he supported the ministerial measures with a nerve and vigour which at once fixed the attention of the house. These characteristics distinguished his oratory in the House of Lords. His arguments were enforced with extraordinary power, and seemed to be urged without preparation; but, his temper being too easily ruffled, he was apt to use expressions the violence of which rather astonished than convinced that august assembly, and their coarseness and intemperance frequently called down upon him deserved castigation.

On the death of Mr. Pitt in 1806, Lord Ellenborough, according to established custom, held the seal of chancellor of the Exchequer till the new ministry was appointed. By that ministry, composed of the whigs and a few of Lord Sidmouth's friends, he was offered and refused the Great Seal, but by unadvisedly accepting a seat in the cabinet, subjected himself, as Lord Mansfield had done before him, to the suspicions which must attach to one who at the same time holds a political and a judicial position. However honourably and independently the individual may act, there is so palpable an indecorum in the connection between the two that it is to be hoped no further example will revive the controversy. His adherence to the whigs lasted only till the ministry expired. Thenceforward he disconnected himself from party, though all his tendencies were strongly towards the support of government and the resistance of innovations. He opposed most of the excellent endeavours of Sir Samuel Romilly to amend the criminal law, but was himself the author of an act, which goes by his name, making more stringent the punishment for malicious injuries. So inimical was he to all changes that he resisted the attempt of the same enlightened lawyer to subject real estates to the payment of the debts of the proprietor.

Though the bigotry of his opinions as a legislator incurred grave censure, in his character as a judge he won the admiration of all. At least equal to his predecessor in legal learning, in personal deportment and in judicial eloquence he formed a complete contrast to him. His dignified bearing bespoke the chief justice, and his forcible language gave weight to his judgments, while the dread of his indignation against every attempt to impose upon the court tended greatly to improve the practice. His powers of sarcasm were very great, sometimes inconsiderately exercised; but prevarication by a witness, frivolous objections by a counsel, or any appearance of indecorum in the conduct of a case, never escaped the severity of his rebukes. In all questions between man and man he was inflexibly just, and in the trial of cases where the laws of morality were outraged by either party he exposed the delinquent with indignant austerity.

During his presidency the press teemed with libels both political and personal, and the chief justice partook most unjustly of the unpopularity which attended the numerous prosecutions for them, particularly in the time when Sir Vicary Gibbs was attorney-general. Unmindful that a judge has nothing to do with originating charges, the people forgot that he is not answerable for the cases brought before him for trial, and they were apt to tax his lordship with being the promoter of the obnoxious proceedings, as well as to blame him for the boldness with which he exposed the licentiousness of the press, and the severity with which the convicted were punished. His judgments, indeed, in all criminal cases were considered severe, and that pronounced against Lord Cochrane, found guilty of a charge of conspiracy (his complicity in which was never positively proved and is now more than doubted), was particularly condemned. The most degrading part of it was immediately remitted, and the sentence led to the abolition of the punishment of the pillory, except for perjury. Even Lord Cochrane's own counsel acknowledged the judge's strict impartiality on the trial, and fairly attributed the sentence to his abomination of all fraud, and to his determination to prove that in the eyes of the law there can be no distinction of persons.

Few judges have equalled him in learning, sagacity, and unsuspected integrity, and none have surpassed him. His rule was resolutely firm and inflexibly just, unswayed by the hope of popular applause or the fear of popular frenzy. Yet, though the admiration and respect which must necessarily attend those qualities could not be withheld from him, he failed in securing the affection of those over whom he presided. His severity of demeanour, his intolerant manner, and his frequent petulance, naturally produced more fear than love. In the exercise of his wit, of which he had a large share, there was too much sarcasm and ridicule; and in the numerous examples of it, which have been over and over again repeated, there is scarcely one of them which, however it may amuse the hearers by its humour, does not inflict a wound upon its victim.

At length overcome by his incessant labours, he felt the necessity of retiring. His resignation was received by the government with real regret, and the prince regent, in an elegant and eloquent letter, expressed his sorrow. This event occurred on November 6, 1818, and in little more than a month he ceased to live. He died on December 11, and was buried in the Charterhouse, where an excellent statue of him has been placed.

He married Ann, the daughter of George Phillips Towry, Esq., formerly in the royal navy, and by that union he was the father of five sons and five daughters. Edward, the eldest, for his services to the state, was in 1844 promoted to an earldom; and Charles Ewan, the second son, held the important office of recorder of London, and was M.P. for the university of Cambridge at the time of his early death. (*Lives by Townsend, Lord Campbell*, &c.)

LAWRENCE, SOULDEN, whose family is traced by the heralds as far back as a knight who was honoured with their present shield of arms by Richard Cœur de Lion, for his bravery at the siege of Acre, was great-grandson to a physician to five crowned heads, grandson to a captain in the royal navy, and son of Dr. Thomas Lawrence, of Essex Street in the Strand, president of the College of Physicians. He was born in 1751, and was educated at St. Paul's School, and St John's College, Cambridge, where he took his degree of B.A. in 1771, coming out seventh wrangler, and of M.A. in 1774, when he was elected fellow of his college. Called to the bar by the Inner Temple in June 1784, he was honoured with a serjeant's coif in 1787. Seven years afterwards he was raised to the bench of the Common Pleas, in March 1794, but in the course of a month exchanged his seat with Mr. Justice Buller, for one in the Court of King's Bench, receiving the honour of knighthood.

The Reports of the time will show how well he justified the selection, and the soundness of his law was not questioned when he differed in opinion, as sometimes he did, with Lord Kenyon. That chief was succeeded in 1801 by Lord Ellenborough, who had been Sir Soulden's college friend; but after a few years a difference arose between them, which induced the latter to take the opportunity that the resignation of Mr. Justice Rooke in 1808 gave him, of returning to his original position in the Common Pleas. There he sat for the four following years, when he resigned in Hilary vacation 1812. Surviving his retirement only two years and a half, he died on July 8, 1814, and was buried in St. Giles's-in-the-Fields, where there is a monument to his memory.

He was a great favourite with the bar, who respected him for his learning, and loved him for his courtesy, a habit to which there was no exception, unless it was a little roughness towards those who were connected with the newspaper press. He was so conscientious a judge that by a codicil to his will he directed the costs to be paid to a litigant who had been defeated in an action in which he considered that he had wrongly directed the jury. (*Hoare's Wilts; Freshfield*, 84; *Gent. Mag.* lxxxiv. p. ii. 92, lxxxv. p. ii. 12–17; *Notes and Queries*, 3rd S. iii. 18, 395.)

LEACH, JOHN, was born on August 28, 1760, at Bedford, where his father, Richard Leach, carried on the trade of a coppersmith. He was educated at the grammar school of that town, and, being intended for an architect, was placed in the office of Sir Robert Taylor, then eminent in that profession. One specimen of his constructive talents remains at the present day in a house called Howlett's, at Bekesbourne, near Canterbury, which he planned for the proprietor of the estate; and there is nothing in this example to indicate that he was unwise in leaving that calling for a more ambitious career. How the change occurred is variously related, but the result was that, by the recommendation of some of his friends who were struck with his energy and acuteness, he commenced the study of the law when he was about twenty-five years old, entering the Middle Temple in January 1785, and placing himself under the tuition of Mr. (afterwards Lord Chief Baron) Alexander, an equity counsel in considerable practice.

He was called to the bar in February 1790, and, as the custom in those days was for even Chancery barristers, selected the Home Circuit and Surrey sessions. During the next ten years he attended them, and in both he secured an extensive business by his neat and forcible speeches and his lucid statement of facts. He also was engaged as counsel at the Seaford election and on the subsequent petition, being his first connection with that borough, for which he was elected recorder in 1795, and over which, by his residence there and his purchases of property, he ultimately acquired such an influence as to be enabled to return both of its members. From 1800, when he left the sessions and the circuit, his business in the equity courts increased to such an extent that in Hilary Term 1807 he was called within the bar with a patent of precedence, and proved himself an able opponent to the counsel who then took the lead in those courts. His style was peculiarly precise and terse, and his language remarkably correct and perspicuous, so that his arguments were very effective. In the previous year he entered parliament for Seaford, for which he continued to sit till 1816, when he left the ranks of the whigs, which he had at first joined, and adopted the politics of the regent, who had set him the example of change. With that royal personage he had gradually obtained favour from the time he defended the Duke of York in 1809 against the attacks of Colonel Wardle, in one of the few speeches which he uttered in the house. Another of his speeches was in support of the Regency Bill in 1811, thus confirming the favourable impression he had made on the regent, by whom he was appointed chancellor of the duchy of Cornwall in February 1816. To this in the next year was added the chief justiceship of Chester.

The next proof of royal favour which he received was the appointment of vice-chancellor of England, the bill establishing which office he had four years before strenuously opposed. He succeeded to that seat on January 9, 1818, and was knighted; and in May 1827 he was nominated master of the Rolls, and was sworn a privy counsellor. In this office he remained till his death, on September 16, 1834, when he was buried at Edinburgh.

Though remarkable for the gentleness of his manner and the suavity of his address, Sir John Leach was the most unpopular judge of his time, and, though his legal experience was great, his judgments gave but scant satisfaction. His irritable temper frequently involved him as a barrister in unseemly altercations with those opposed to him, and as a judge in violent collisions with the leading members of the bar. His manner of treating those who differed from him, or against whom he had imbibed a prejudice, became so obnoxious that a deputation of the most distinguished counsel practising in his court waited upon him with a formal remonstrance upon his intemperate and dictatorial deportment towards the profession. The known intimacy between him and the prince regent, and the strong suspicion that he assisted in getting up the case against Queen Caroline, did not tend to diminish the dislike with which he was generally regarded.

Sir Samuel Romilly, writing in his Diary in 1816, while he speaks highly of his talents and his powers of argumentation, says that he is worse qualified for a judicial situation than almost any one he has known in the profession, as 'he is extremely deficient as a lawyer,' only knowing what he has acquired by daily practice, and being extremely wanting in judgment. And he prophesies that if he should be ever raised to a great situation, this deficiency, and 'his extraordinary confidence in himself, will involve him in some serious difficulty.' This prophecy was verified in the result. Both as vice-chancellor and master of the Rolls, though he despatched the causes before him with immense celerity, he relied so little upon authorities, and listened so indifferently to any arguments that conflicted with his own opinion, sometimes not even condescending to give any reasons for his judgments, that his decisions were frequently appealed against, and not unfrequently overturned. In comparing his summary judgments with Lord Eldon's proverbial delays, the chancellor's court was designated the court of *Oyer sans terminer*, and Sir John's that of *Terminer sans oyer*.

In private life his amenity and courteousness were as remarkable as his sharpness and want of temper on the bench. One of his failings tended to make him somewhat ridiculous. Not content with distinction as a lawyer, he had the absurd ambition of being considered a man of fashion. He prided himself on his aristocratic intimacies, and, seldom associating with his professional brethren, frequented the crowded parties of the great, even after the fatigue of sitting in his court to a late hour in the night. This perpetual round of fatigue and gaiety probably occasioned, or aggravated, the diseases under which he suffered towards the end of his life—diseases requiring painful operations, which he underwent with the greatest fortitude, and which he never allowed to interfere with the discharge of his duties. He was in his seventy-fifth year when he died, and was never married. (*Legal Observer*, Oct. 1834; *Law and Lawyers*, ii. 88; *Law Mag.* xii. 427.)

LE BLANC, SIMON. This amiable judge was the second son of Thomas Le Blanc, of Charterhouse Square, London, Esq., and was born about the year 1748. Admitted a pensioner of Trinity Hall, Cambridge, in January 1766, he became a scholar in November following, proceeded LL.B. in 1773, and was elected a fellow of his house in January 1779. He studied the law at the Inner Temple, and was called to the bar in February 1773, joining the Norfolk Circuit. He accepted the degree of the coif in Hilary Term 1787, obtaining in the Common Pleas a considerable lead, and in 1791 he was chosen as counsel for his alma mater.

He was promoted on June 6, 1799, to the post of justice of the King's Bench, and knighted. In that court he sat for nearly seventeen years, with the character of an excellent lawyer and a conscientious and impartial judge. The absence of incidents worthy of being related in so long a period —if we may except an atrocious libel on him in a newspaper called 'The Independent Whig,' in 1808, for which the editor was speedily punished by a long imprisonment (*State Trials*, xxx. 1131–1322)—is a proof that the whole of it was employed in the regular discharge of duty, uninfluenced by political bias or personal prejudice. There is not a more graceful testimony that this was the case with Sir Simon Le Blanc than the sentence 'Illo nemo neque integrior erat in civitate, neque sanctior,' with which his death on April 15, 1816, is recorded by the respected reporters of his court —Messrs. Maule and Selwyn (vol. v. p. i.).

LECHMERE, NICHOLAS, of a Worcestershire family, second to none in antiquity and reputation, was the third but eldest surviving son of Edmund Lechmere of Hanley Castle, by Margaret, the sister of the accomplished and ill-fated Sir Thomas Overbury. He was born in September 1613, the year in which his uncle was poisoned in the Tower, and was bred up in Gloucester School, whence he was removed to Wadham College, Oxford. After taking his degree of B.A. he became a student of the law at the Middle Temple, where he was called to the bar in 1641, and elected a bencher in 1655. Before that date he had taken a prominent part on the side of the parliament against Charles I. His name is appended, with several others, to a summons to the governor of

Worcester in June 1646; and he was one of the committee who came to that city on its surrender in the following month. (*Nash's Worcester*, ii. !*App.* c.-cvi.) In 1648 he was elected member for Bewdley, and sat during the remainder of the Long Parliament. When Charles II., accompanied by the Scotch army, possessed himself of Worcester in 1651, Hanley Castle was twice used by the Scottish horse as their quarters, while its master joined Cromwell's forces and shared in his triumph at the battle. In Cromwell's second and third parliament of 1654 Lechmere was one of the members for Worcestershire. In the latter he promoted the Petition and Advice, pressed that it should be published, called it a Magna Charta, and afterwards likened it to the Petition of Right. Before Cromwell's death he was appointed attorney of the duchy of Lancaster, and walked in that character at the protector's funeral. In this office he was continued under Richard, in whose parliament he was one of his staunchest supporters. On its dissolution he took his place as part of the Rump, both before and after its second expulsion. Two days previously to its dissolving itself in preparation for the king's return, a bill was passed for reviving the duchy of Lancaster, and Nicholas Lechmere was voted its attorney. (*Parl. Hist.* ii. 624, iii. 1583; *Burton's Diary*, ii. 136, 526, iii. 586.)

In the meantime Lechmere had made his peace with the king, who before he left Breda granted him a full pardon; but he could not expect to be elected for the Convention Parliament; and during the rest of his life he never resumed his senatorial dignity. In his legal capacity he bore a good reputation; and it is evident that he enjoyed an ample share of professional emoluments, from his being enabled not only to repurchase those portions of the patrimonial estates which had been alienated by the former necessities of the family, but to add other lands and manors to it. At the revolution his exemplary character, and, perhaps, his early opposition to the Stuart dynasty, recommended him to the new government. Though he had attained the age of seventy-six, he was raised to the bench of the Exchequer on May 4, 1689, and was thereupon knighted. He sat there for eleven years; but in the last year he was so infirm that he sent his opinion on the bankers' case in writing, and was obliged to be excused from going the circuit. He received his quietus at the end of June 1700; and on April 30, 1701, he died at his mansion at Hanley. (*Pepys*, i. 337; *Luttrell*.)

He married Penelope, daughter of Sir Edwin Sandys, of Northborne in Kent, and left several children. Among their descendants one was raised to the peerage as Baron Lechmere of Evesham, in 1721, which died with him in 1727; and another received the honour of a baronetcy in 1818, whose representative now enjoys the title.

LEDENHAM, EUSTACE DE, was one of the justices itinerant into Lincolnshire in 8 Richard I., 1196-7 (*Madox*, i. 704), of which county he had been sheriff two years before. His principal property was at Lange Ledenham.

LEE, WILLIAM, was the second son of Sir Thomas Lee, baronet, of Hartwell, Buckinghamshire, and of his wife Alice, daughter of Thomas Hopkins, a merchant of London. (*Wotton's Baronet.* iii. 149.) He was born in 1688, and was educated at the university of Oxford, where he took his bachelor's degree. He was entered in July 1703 at the Middle Temple, whence he removed in February 1717 to the Inner Temple, from which he proceeded as barrister.

His classical attainments may be inferred from his being appointed Latin secretary to the king in 1718 (6 *Report Pub. Records*, *App.* ii. 119); and his forensic talents from his success at the bar and his being made one of the king's counsel, an office in those times of far greater distinction than it holds at the present day, when the multiplicity of courts requires an almost infinite number of silken leaders. In the first parliament of George II., January 1728, he was elected member for Chipping Wycombe, and between its third and fourth sessions he was raised to the bench, being constituted a judge of the King's Bench in June 1730. During the seven years that he sat in that court as a puisne judge he refused the customary honour of knighthood, but on his elevation to the head of it on June 8, 1737, he was induced to accept the honorary distinction. He presided as lord chief justice of the King's Bench for seventeen years; and, though succeeding so eminent a judge as Lord Hardwicke, his impartial administration of justice and his perfect mastery of the science of law secured to him the respect and admiration of his contemporaries. It fell to his lot to try the persons implicated in the rebellion of 1745, and he performed the obnoxious duty with dignity and firmness. In March 1754, shortly before his death, the office of chancellor of the Exchequer having become vacant by the sudden death of Mr. Pelham, the seals were placed in his hands as chief justice of England till the office should be filled up. This was done in compliance with a custom which had been acted on from time immemorial, and originated in the fact that the chief justiciary in former ages was the president of the Exchequer. He died on April 8, 1754, and was buried at Hartwell. (*State Trials*, xvii. 401, xviii. 329; *Burrow's S. C.* 105, 364.)

Lord Campbell (*Ch. Just.* ii. 213), though

D D

with an ineffectual attempt to place his character in a ridiculous light, is obliged to speak highly of his legal and intellectual powers, and to acknowledge the purity of his intentions, the suavity of his manners, and the justice of his decisions. Sir James Burrow, who had sat under him during the whole period of his career, in his 'Settlement Cases' (p. 328) thus expresses himself:—'He was a gentleman of most unblemished and irreproachable character, both in public and in private life; amiable and gentle in his disposition; affable and courteous in his deportment; cheerful in his temper, though grave in his aspect; generous and polite in his manner of living; sincere and deservedly happy in his friendships and family connections; and to the highest degree upright and impartial in his distribution of justice. He had been a judge of the Court of King's Bench for nearly twenty-four years, and for nearly seventeen had presided in it. In this state the integrity of his heart and the caution of his determination were so eminent that they never will, perhaps never can, be excelled.'

His brother, Sir George, was at the same time the president of the highest court of civil law, as dean of the Arches and judge of the Prerogative Court of Canterbury; a coincidence of which there is another recent example in Lord Eldon and his brother Sir William Scott, Lord Stowell.

Sir William Lee married, first, Anne, daughter of John Goodwin, of Burley in Suffolk; and secondly, Margaret, daughter of Roger Drake, Esq., and widow of James Melmoth, Esq. The baronetcy, after being enjoyed for a hundred and sixty-seven years, failed in 1827.

LEEKE, THOMAS, was the eldest son of Ralph Leeke, of Wilsland in Shropshire, where the family had been established since 1334. He was educated at Shrewsbury School, and at St. John's College, Cambridge, where he took his degrees of B.A. and M.A. in 1622 and 1626. Beyond his being admitted as a student at Gray's Inn in 1615 no other fact is known of him in the law till he was appointed cursitor baron on November 25, 1642. As he was certainly not a serjeant, and is not named by any law reporter as a barrister, he probably held some office in the Exchequer before his promotion. His loyalty prompted him to join the king in the troubles, and, in consequence of the inconvenience occasioned by his leaving his post, Mr. Richard Tomlins was put in his place by the parliament on September 29, 1645, in order that he might on the next day receive the new sheriffs of London, and preserve the forms which, the entry says, had never been omitted for the space of three or four hundred years.

At the Restoration Mr. Baron Leeke reappeared and resumed his official position, which he enjoyed for the short remainder of his life. He died in 1662. (*Lords' Journals*, vii. 606.)

LEEKE, WILLIAM, though inserted in Dugdale's 'Chronica Series' as a baron of the Exchequer in 1679, and though in the reports of the kingdom there is a grant to him of the office on May 8 in that year, is found on investigation to have refused the honour thus bestowed upon him. Many instances are to be found of modesty declining an offer of advancement, but this is a unique example of an office actually conferred being immediately abdicated.

He was the eldest son of William Leeke, of Wimeswould in the county of Leicester, Esq. Born about 1630, he was admitted into the society of Gray's Inn, and called to the bar in 1661, becoming an ancient in 1676. His monument speaks of his knowledge of the science of the law, and his great pains to prevent litigation among his clients, which may account for his being nowhere mentioned by the reporters. On February 12, 1679, he was summoned to take the degree of serjeant-at-law in the following Easter Term, with the view, probably, to his further elevation. Accordingly on May 8 he received a patent as a baron of the coif. An entry in the Gray's Inn books shows that he had given up that title (if he ever took it) before May 28, for on that day liberty was given to him, under the description of Mr. Serjeant Leeke, to assign his chamber in the inn to any other gentleman of the society—an entry which did not necessarily show that he meant to retire from practice, as he had of course a chamber appropriated to him in Serjeants' Inn.

He died at the age of 57, on October 9, 1687; and in the encomiastic inscription on his monument in Wimeswould Church occurs this passage:—

> In alta enim Purpuratorum Judicum subsellia
> a Carolo II. evectus, munere se
> tam præclaro statim abdicavit;
> moderationis plane singularis
> rarum exemplum.

He married Catherine, daughter of William Bainbrigge, Esq., of Lockington in Leicestershire. (*Nichols's Leicestershire*, iii. 506.)

LEGGE, HENEAGE, was the second son of William, first Earl of Dartmouth, by Lady Anne Finch, third daughter of Heneage, first Earl of Aylesford, and great-grandson, through his mother, of the celebrated lord chancellor of Charles II., the Earl of Nottingham. Born in 1704, he was called to the bar at the Inner Temple in 1728. He was chosen high steward of the city of Lichfield in 1734, and in 1739 became one of the king's counsel. In 1743 he was appointed counsel to the Admiralty and auditor of Greenwich Hospital, and in the same year was engaged to defend William Chetwynd, indicted for the murder of his schoolfellow Thomas Ricketts by stabbing him with a knife for taking away a piece of cake. The jury found a special verdict; but the question whether it was murder or manslaughter was never decided, the king granting a free pardon, and the vindictive efforts of the deceased's friends to sue out an appeal not being successful.

In June 1747 he was raised to the bench as a baron of the Exchequer, and sat there for twelve years, respected as well for his learning as for his impartiality and moderation. The latter qualities were manifested in his able summing up on the trial in 1752 of Mary Blandy for the murder of her father.

He died on August 30, 1759, leaving issue by his wife Catherine, daughter of Mr. Jonathan Fogg, a merchant of London. (*Collins's Peerage*, i. 121; *State Trials*, xviii. 290, 1170.)

LEICESTER, EARL OF. *See* R. DE BEAUMONT.

LEICESTER, PETER DE, in 1290, 17 Edward I., was one of the justices of the Jews; but in 1291, the duties of his office having terminated with the expulsion of the Jews from England, he was appointed a regular baron of the Exchequer, in which office he continued to act till his death, in the thirty-first year of the reign. (*Madox*, i. 237-54, ii. 62-323.) He left a son named Thomas, and had property in Buckinghamshire, Warwickshire, and Northamptonshire. (*Abb. Placit.* 348; *Cal. Inquis.* p. m. i. 163, 187, 223; *Abb. Rot. Orig.* i. 163.)

LEICESTER, ROGER DE, was the son of Sir Nicholas de Leicester, who possessed large estates in Cheshire, by Margaret, the daughter of Geoffrey Dutton, and widow of Robert de Denbigh. He became a justice of the Common Pleas in 1276, 4 Edward I., from Trinity in which year till Michaelmas 1289 fines were levied before him. (*Dugdale's Orig.* 44.) Being then removed from his office with several of his brethren for extortion and other judicial crimes, he was compelled to pay for his release from imprisonment 1000 marks (*Weever*, 367), a sum so much less than that imposed upon some of the others that it is to be hoped his offence was not of so deep a dye. Dugdale introduces his name again on January 2, 1293, as being then appointed a baron of the Exchequer; but both on the above account, and because in Madox's list of those who attended in the court after that date he is never mentioned, it seems not unlikely that his name was by mistake substituted for that of Peter de Leicester, who certainly was appointed about the same time, and whose subsequent attendance is regularly noted.

Peter Leicester of Tabley, his lineal descendant, was created a baronet on August 10, 1660; but the title became extinct in 1742. A daughter, however, married Sir Peter Byrne, baronet, whose grandson, Sir John Fleming Leicester (the surname having been assumed), was created Baron de Tabley on July 16, 1826. His son George, who has taken the name of Warren, is the present baron.

LENTHALL, WILLIAM, of an ancient Herefordshire family, one member of which shared with Henry V. the glories of Agincourt, was the son of William Lenthall, of Latchford in Oxfordshire, and Frances, daughter of Sir Thomas Southwell, of St. Faith's in Norfolk, and was born in June 1591. After receiving the rudiments of his education at Thame School, he was sent to St. Alban's Hall, Oxford. Here he continued for three years, when, without taking a degree, he was removed to Lincoln's Inn (*Athen. Oxon.* iii. 608), where he was called to the bar in 1616, became a bencher in 1633, and elected reader in 1638. Long before this date he had got into considerable practice, since, writing to Secretary Nicholas in 1641, he speaks of his previous labours of twenty-five years, the profits of the last years of which he subsequently states to have amounted to 2500*l.* a year. (*Notes and Queries*, 1st S. xii. 358.) Clarendon (i. 240, 297) describes him, when elected speaker, as 'a lawyer of no eminent account,' but 'of competent practice.' He became recorder of Gloucester in 1637, and held the same office in the borough of Woodstock, of which he was elected representative in both the parliaments of 1640, over the latter of which he was chosen to preside as speaker. It is curious to contrast the fulsome compliments and humble professions of his opening and earlier addresses to the king, as the organ of the Commons, with the proceedings against that sovereign which he was soon to authenticate; and to watch the gradual diminution of courtly expressions as those proceedings became more violent, and the adulatory and submissive strain he adopted towards those who ultimately acquired the ascendency. Clarendon says, with truth, that he was a weak man, and unequal to the task; yet his answer to King Charles on January 4, 1642, on his coming to the house to demand the five members whom he had accused, bore some semblance both of spirit and ingenuity. When the king asked him 'whether any of these persons were in the house? whether he saw any of them? and where they were?' the speaker, falling on his knees, replied, 'May it please your majesty, I have neither eyes to see nor tongue to speak in this place, but as the house is pleased to direct me, whose servant I am here; and humbly beg your majesty's pardon that I cannot give any other answer than this to what your majesty is pleased to demand of me.' (*Whitelocke*, 52.)

When the parliament set on foot the subscription for their defence in June 1642, the speaker, as his contribution, promised to maintain a horse and to give 50*l*. in money or plate. So well pleased were the Commons with his conduct in the chair, that on their adopting a new Great Seal for themselves, one of the first uses they made of it was to constitute him master of the Rolls, taking no account of the king's previous appointment of Sir John Colepeper. He was accordingly sworn into that office on November 22, 1643, and was continued by special votes in 1645, notwithstanding the self-denying ordinance. (*Ibid.* 78, 146, 177.) In consequence of the difference of opinion in the two houses as to the persons to be named commissioners of the Great Seal in 1646, they placed it ad interim in the custody of the two speakers on October 30, to hold it for a week; but that period, by their continued irresolution, extended to March 15, 1648, when new commissioners were agreed to.

In July 1647 the London apprentices tumultuously presented petitions to parliament concerning the militia, and acted so insolently, threatening all manner of violence if their demands were not complied with, that both houses were from terror compelled to revoke the ordinances complained of. The speakers accordingly withdrew to the army, and put themselves under its protection; and though the Commons had in the meantime elected another speaker in Lenthall's place, he was, on his return with the army, after a week's absence, allowed to resume the chair. It was believed that the whole transaction was a plot to give power to the army, and that the speaker was compelled to join in it by a threat that he should be impeached for embezzlement if he did not comply. He was charged also, in the next year, with endeavouring to impede the treaty with the king in the Isle of Wight (*Clarendon*, v. 461–469; *Parl. Hist.* iii. 729–736, 1050); and in all the subsequent measures affecting the king's life he did not hesitate to preside. After the tragic scene of January 30, 1649, 'the parliament of England,' or rather the House of Commons, assumed the government, Lenthall, as speaker, being nominally the head. The same honours were ordered to be paid to him when visiting the city of London as had been used to the king, by delivering to him the sword on his reception, and by placing him above the lord mayor at the feast. (*Whitelocke*, 406.) But the real power was in a council of state, and that was constituted by the army, over which Cromwell, by his superior energy and his success in battle, soon acquired unlimited ascendency. In four years both the army and the nation got tired of the parliament, and on April 19, 1653, the speaker was compelled to vacate his chair by Cromwell's forcible expulsion of all the remaining members from the house.

Retiring to the Rolls, he seems to have kept aloof from any public interference in politics till Cromwell summoned his second parliament on September 3, 1654, when Lenthall, who sat for Oxfordshire, was again chosen speaker. It sat for nearly five months, and then, being too argumentative for the protector's purposes, was dissolved without passing a single act. (*Parl. Hist.* iii. 1444, 1460, 1481.) The protector and his council, in the April following, proposed to the commissioners of the Seal and the master of the Rolls a new ordinance for the better regulation of the Chancery, and for limiting its jurisdiction, which all those officers (except L'Isle) strongly opposed. Lenthall was most earnest against its adoption, protesting 'that he would be hanged before the Rolls gate before he would execute it;' but no sooner did he see that the two opposing commissioners were dismissed than he 'wheeled about,' and gave in his adhesion. (*Whitelocke*, 625–6.) The next parliament, called by Cromwell in September 1656, though Lenthall was again returned for Oxfordshire, was presided over by Sir Thomas Widdrington. In the farce that was enacted in it of offering to Cromwell the title of king the master of the Rolls performed a leading part, using the most specious arguments to induce him to accept it. Upon Cromwell's refusal and the establishment of a new constitution, Lenthall was not at first included in the number of lords which the protector was authorised to nominate; but on complaining of the omission he received a summons to take his seat. That parliament was dissolved within a fortnight after the new Lords met, principally from the hostility occasioned by their appointment, and Cromwell died seven months after its dissolution. In the parliament which his son, the Protector Richard, called in January 1659, Lenthall again appeared as one of the Lords; but on its dismissal three months after, the Long Parliament having resumed its sittings, he, after some hesitation, was induced to forget his short-lived nobility, and again take his seat as speaker. (*Parl. Hist.* iii. 1488, 1519, 1546; *Ludlow*, 252, 254.) On May 23 he was voted keeper of the Great Seal for eight days, at the end of which other commissioners were appointed, who, in turn, were superseded by the Committee of Safety. He again, for a third time, held the Seal for a fortnight in January 1660, by order of the Long or Rump Parliament, which had again met, but which in the following March was finally dissolved, having in the interval conferred on him the chamberlainship of Chester. (*Whitelocke*, 679, 698.)

This and his other places the Restoration obliged him to resign, though Ludlow says (p. 383) he offered 3000*l.* to be continued master of the Rolls. As he had been excepted by name, together with Cromwell and Bradshaw, from the pardon offered by Charles's proclamation, dated Paris, May 3, 1654, Lenthall no doubt trembled at his present position, till he found that the extreme penalty was to be confined to those actually concerned in the king's death. (*Harris's Lives*, iv. 129.) During the discussions on the Act of Indemnity he found it necessary to address a letter to the House of Commons, denying the reports of his 'great gains' as speaker. The Commons, notwithstanding, excepted him from the bill, to suffer such pains and penalties, not extending to life, as should be proper to inflict on him; but the Lords, probably through the influence of Monk, moderated the vote, by directing that the exception should only take place if he accepted any office or public employment. (*Parl. Hist.* iv. 68, 91.) Eventually he received the king's pardon.

Thus preserving the wealth he had acquired in his various offices, he retired to Burford Priory, his seat in Oxfordshire, but not before he had offered another proof of his timeserving pusillanimity, by forgetting his famous reply to the king, and giving evidence of words spoken in parliament by Thomas Scott the regicide. (*State Trials*, v. 1063.) He died on September 3, 1662, and was buried at Burford. His confession or apology in his last illness, made to Dr. Brideoak, afterwards Bishop of Chester (*Athen. Oxon.* iii. 608), confirms the impression universally formed of the weakness of his character, and the narrowness and timidity of his disposition.

By his wife Elizabeth, daughter of Ambrose Evans, of Lodington in Northamptonshire, he left several children. His eldest son, John, whom Anthony Wood calls 'the grand braggadocio and lyer of the age,' was a member of the Long Parliament, and held several offices under Cromwell, who created him a baronet. After the Restoration he was sheriff of Oxfordshire, and was knighted by Charles II.

LEONARD affords a remarkable instance to prove that those who were appointed justices itinerant to impose the tallages on the different counties were not always selected from the members or officers of the Curia Regis. One of the two who acted for Berkshire in 20 Henry II., 1174, was this Leonard, who is simply described as 'a knight of Thomas Basset.' (*Madox*, i. 124.) He thus probably was a resident in the county, and was well acquainted with the various properties.

LEUKNORE, GEOFFREY DE, was a son or brother of Nicholas de Leuknore, who was keeper of the king's wardrobe at the time of his death in 52 Henry III. In the year after his death Geoffrey had a royal grant of a field in Chiselhampton in Oxfordshire, with a mill late belonging to a Jew, and two years afterwards he had an additional grant of further property there. (*Cal. Rot. Pat.* 42, 44.) He appears with three others as a justice itinerant in 39 Henry III., 1255, for that and other counties, perhaps only for pleas of the forest; but he is next mentioned in the forty-fifth and two following years as a justice itinerant into various counties. Dugdale does not introduce him at all as a regular justicier in the reign of Henry III., but it would seem that he held that position, inasmuch as from March 1265 till September 1271 there are numerous entries on the Rotulus de Finibus (*Excerpt.* ii. 422–549) of payments made for assizes to be held before him. If he were then on the bench, he must have been removed on the death of Henry, for his name does not occur among those appointed to either court on the accession of Edward I. Dugdale, however, introduces him as a justice of the Common Pleas on November 2, 1276, in the fourth year; but the patent which he quotes as his authority can scarcely have been read by him, for it merely appoints Geoffrey de Leuknore and two others to be justices to hold assizes and pleas in the liberty of Dunstable. He is mentioned as a justice itinerant in 6 Edward I., but there is no record of his acting beyond the following year. (*Parl. Writs*, i. 382.)

LEVESHAM, THOMAS, is not introduced by Dugdale in his list of appointments to the office of baron of the Exchequer, but he notices that John Durem was constituted in his place on May 26, 1449, 27 Henry VI. He had been long in the service of the Exchequer, and is always distinguished by the clerical designation. At the end of Henry V.'s reign he was employed in the marches of Picardy, 'upon divers inquisitions taken for the kynges avayle' (*Acts Privy Council*, iii. 56); in 2 Henry VI. he is mentioned as delivering a certain commission to the lord treasurer in the presence of the barons of the Exchequer (*Kal. Exch.* ii. 122); in 14 Henry VI. his name stands next to that of Sir John Juyn, the chief baron, in the list of those called upon to contribute to the equipment of the king's army (*Acts Privy Council*, iv. 325); and in 16 Henry VI., being then called 'remembrancer on the king's remembrancer's side of the Exchequer,' he wa paid 1l. 'as an especial reward for writing out the statutes of Wales in two rolls for the king's use.' (*Devon's Issue Roll*, 434.)

His appointment as baron must therefore have taken place after the latter entry; but neither that date nor any other fact of his subsequent life has yet been discovered.

LEVINTON, RICHARD DE, was the son of Adam de Levinton, constable of Wallingford Castle, who held a barony in Cumberland, and died about 12 John. Richard was implicated in the barons' war with King John, for in 2 Henry III. his lands were restored to him on his returning to his allegiance. (*Baronage*, i. 708; *Rot. Claus.* i. 374.) His barony of Burgh-on-the-Sands not being held by military service, but by cornage, he was not liable to be summoned to join the king's armies; and in 8 Henry III. the sheriff of Cumberland was commanded not to summon him to the army of Bedford on that account. It seems doubtful whether he was not about this time constable of Carlisle, that title immediately following his name on the mandate of 9 Henry III., relative to the conveyance of the quinzime of Cumberland to York; but it may possibly be a distinct person. In the same year he was appointed a justice itinerant for the counties of Cumberland and Westmoreland, and in 18 Henry III. for Lancashire. (*Rot. Claus.* i. 614, ii. 73-77.)

He died about June 1250.

LEVINZ, CRESWELL, descended from an ancient and respectable family, seated at Levinz Hall in Westmoreland, was the son of William Levinz, and was born about 1627 at Evenle in Northamptonshire. Admitted a sizar of Trinity College, Cambridge, in 1648, he took no degree, and entering Gray's Inn, he was called to the bar in 1661, was made a bencher in 1678, and became treasurer in the following year. What part he took during Cromwell's sway is not known, but his name is found in the Reports from the earliest year of the Restoration. About 1678 he was appointed king's council and knighted, and was employed for the crown in the several prosecutions arising out of the Popish Plot. Though joining, as he apparently did, in the popular belief in the plot, and in reliance on the witnesses who supported it, he conducted them with great decency and fairness. He was appointed attorney-general in October 1679, and during the sixteen months that he held that office he took the lead in many other trials of persons implicated in the same charge, in all of which he showed as much lenity as was consistent with his position.

In December 1679 he was directed by the king in council to prepare the famous 'proclamation against tumultuous petitions,' for which he was called to account and required to state who assisted him in drawing up the proclamation, a demand which he at first resisted, stating that he alone was responsible; but on being strongly pressed he at last was compelled to give up the name of Chief Justice North. For this he is visited by Roger North (*Examen*, 546-54; *Life*, 176) with rather unnecessary blame. If he had persisted in his refusal, he would have certainly incurred great personal risk, without benefiting any one; and he knew that the proclamation was so cautiously worded that no harm could come to the chief justice, the threatened impeachment against whom soon dropped to the ground.

He was constituted a judge of the Common Pleas on February 12, 1681, and filled that seat for five years, respected for his legal knowledge and upright conduct. Soon after the accession of James II. he was joined with three other judges in the commission to Sir George Jeffreys on the 'Bloody Assizes' in the West; but little is related with reference to that horrible visitation implicating any other judge than the brutal chief justice. On February 6, 1686, he suddenly received a supersedeas to discharge him from his office, 'whereto,' he modestly says in his Reports, 'I humbly submit;' and when called upon by the House of Commons in 1689 to explain the cause of his dismissal, he said, 'I thought my discharge was because I would not give judgment upon the soldier who deserted his colours, and for being against the dispensing power.' (*Levinz's Reports*, iii. 257; *Parl. Hist.* v. 313.)

Sir Creswell immediately returned to the bar, and Bramston (p. 221) says he 'is not likely, 'tis thought, to loose by the change.' That this prophecy was well founded is evident from the contemporary Reports, in which his name frequently appears. On the trial of the seven bishops in 1688 he was one of the counsel employed in the defence. By Lord Macaulay's account (ii. 376), Sir Creswell 'was induced to take a brief against the crown, by a threat of the attorneys that if he refused it he should never hold another.' The authority his lordship cites for this extraordinary statement seems hardly sufficient to overthrow the contrary impression which Sir Creswell's conduct tends naturally to produce. He appears to have played a very active part in the trial, and to have taken the objection that there was no proof of publication in Middlesex, which very nearly put an early end to the case of the crown. This does not look as if his was a compulsory or unwilling appearance; and the fact that his brother, Baptist Levinz, was Bishop of Sodor and Man will more probably account both for his being engaged, and for the energy of his advocacy. (*State*

Trials, xii. 320, &c.) He continued to practise up to 1696, when his Reports terminate. They were published in three parts the year after his death, which occurred on January 29, 1701. He was buried at Evenle, where there is a monument to his memory. Lord Hardwicke says of him that, though a good lawyer, he was a very careless reporter.

By his wife, Mary, daughter of William Livesay, of Lancashire, he had three children. (*Noble's Granger*, i. 167; *Thoresby's Notts*, iii. 264; *Luttrell*, v. 12.)

LEXINTON, JOHN DE, was the eldest son of Richard de Lexinton, a baron so called from a manor of that name near Tuxford in Notts. (*Baronage*, i. 743.) He was evidently an officer connected with the court, and probably one of the clerks of the Chancery, the Great Seal having been several times placed in his hands apparently in that character—viz., in 1238, in 1242, in 1249, and in 1253. (*Hardy's Catalogue*.)

Within these years he went to Rome on the king's business, and performed other duties in connection with the court. In 1241 he had the custody of Griffin, Prince of Wales, in the Tower of London (*Rapin*, iii. 71); and in 1247 he is spoken of as the king's seneschal. (*Cal. Rot. Pat.* 22.)

It is apparent that, though he might be occasionally called to take possession of the Great Seal on a particular emergency after June 1248, 32 Henry III., he had then been elevated to the judicial bench; for on that date and afterwards, till December 1256, a few week before his death, there are numerous entries of payments made for assizes to be taken before him, precisely in the same manner as before the other judges. In 1251 also he was one of those appointed to hear the pleas in the city of London (*Excerpt. e Rot. Fin.* ii. 36-246); and in 1254 he is mentioned as having been sent by the king and council to pronounce a judgment 'ad Bancum domini regis.' *Abb. Placit.* 132.) In 37 Henry III. he was made chief justice of the forests north of the Trent, and governor of the castles of Bamburgh, Scarborough, and Pickering.

He married Margaret Merlay, but left no children. His property devolved, on his death in February 1257, on his youngest brother, Henry, Bishop of Lincoln. (*Thoroton's Notts*, iii. 220; *Excerpt. e Rot. Fin.* ii. 250, 287.)

LEXINTON, ROBERT DE, was a younger brother of the above-mentioned John. Brought up as an ecclesiastic, he followed the practice of those times by pursuing also the study of the law; but never appears to have been further advanced in the former profession than to a prebend in the church of Southwell, to which he was presented in 16 John. In the same year he acted as custos of the archbishopric of York during its vacancy. (*Rot. Pat.* 115; *Rot. Claus.* i. 208.)

As a lawyer he is first mentioned as taking the acknowledgment of a fine in Michaelmas, 4 Henry III., from which period until a short time before his death there are numerous evidences of his having acted as a justicier, both at Westminster and in the provinces.

In 1228 his name is at the head of four justiciers before whom a fine was levied at Westminster, and in July 1234 three justiciers appointed 'ad Bancum' were ordered to be admitted by Robert de Lexinton and William of York, he being at that time the oldest judge on the bench, and perhaps the chief of the court. When the king, in 1240, sent justices itinerant through all the counties, under pretence of redressing grievances, but with the real object of extorting money from the people, Robert de Lexinton was placed at the head of those assigned for the northern counties. (*Rot. Claus.* 461, 468, 631; *Madox*, ii. 355.) The subsequent entries of his acting as a judge do not extend beyond Hilary 1243, 27 Henry III. (*Excerpt. e Rot. Fin.* i. 348), in all of which he is placed at the head of his associates. He then probably retired, having been on the bench nearly twenty-four years; but his death did not occur till seven years afterwards.

He appears to have added military to his judicial duties, and to have received various proofs of the royal confidence and favour. In 8 Henry III. he was constituted custos of the honor of Pec (*Rot. Claus.* i. 594, &c.) and governor of its castle, and that of Bolsover in Derbyshire; and there is a letter from him to Hubert de Burgh, detailing the progress of William, Earl of Albemarle, through Nottingham, with his own preparations to oppose him, and stating his intention to proceed himself into Northumberland. (4 *Report Pub. Rec., App.* ii. 157.) He afterwards also had the charge of the castle of Orford. On his death, in June 1250, his brother, the last-mentioned John, succeeded as his heir to all his property. (*Rot. Claus.* i. 439, &c.; *Excerpt. e Rot. Fin.* i. 56.)

LEY, JAMES (EARL OF MARLBOROUGH), was born about 1552 in the parish of Teffont-Evias in Wiltshire, the residence of his father, Henry Ley, Esq. He became a commoner of Brazenose College, Oxford, and, having taken a degree in arts, he entered on his legal studies at Lincoln's Inn, where, having been called to the bar on October 11, 1584, he worked his way up to the bench of that society in 1600, and was chosen reader in 1602. He had previously held the post of one of the Welsh judges, and in 1603 he had a separate call to the degree of the coif, probably in preparation for holding the office of lord chief justice of the King's Bench in Ireland, to which he was appointed in the following year, when he was also knighted. While filling that position he was one of the commissioners of the Great Seal of that country from April 6 to November 8, 1605. He presided in the Irish King's Bench about four years, resigning in December 1608; and Bacon (*Works*, vii. 263) speaks of his 'gravity, temper, and discretion' in that office. Returning to England, he received the profitable place of attorney of the Court of Wards and Liveries, at the same time establishing the right of that officer to take precedence in court of the king's attorney-general, for which he had a privy seal dated May 15, 1609. He must then have resigned his rank as serjeant; for in that and the twelve succeeding years he is recorded as one of the governors of Lincoln's Inn. On the elevation of Sir Francis Bacon to the Great Seal in 1617, Sir James was a candidate for the attorney-generalship, and the Duke of Buckingham told Sir Henry Yelverton that he offered 10,000*l*. for the office. (*Liber Famelicus*, 56.) Not succeeding in this, he was created a baronet on July 15, 1619.

On January 29, 1621, he was constituted lord chief justice of the King's Bench. He was then about sixty-nine years of age, and in that year (*Yonge's Diary*, 40) married his third wife, Jane, daughter of John Lord Butler, by Elizabeth, the sister of the favourite, George Villiers, Duke of Buckingham, to whose patronage he probably owed his future advance. Within two months after his appointment he was called upon, in consequence of the proceedings against Bacon, to take the place of speaker of the House of Lords; and in that character he had to pronounce their judgment, first, in the cases of Sir Giles Mompesson and Sir Francis Michell, and then against the chancellor himself and Sir Henry Yelverton. (*Parl. Hist.* i. 1207-1258.)

After performing the duties of his judicial office for nearly four years, he imitated the example of his predecessor, Sir Henry Montagu, by retiring from it, and accepting the profitable place of lord treasurer on December 20, 1624. On the 31st he was created Lord Ley of Ley in the county of Devon, the ancient seat of his family. He was more fortunate, however, than Sir Henry Montagu; for he retained the royal purse for the remainder of James's reign, and for more than three years in that of Charles I., who in the May following his accession created him Earl of Marlborough. He was removed in July 1628, to make way for Sir Richard Weston, and retrograded to the almost empty title of president of the council, which he held for the few remaining months of his life.

He died on March 14, 1629, and was interred at Westbury, Wilts, in the parish church of which a magnificent monument is erected to his memory.

In the midst of corruption among lawyers and statesmen, and holding the highest offices on the bench and in the council, he is said by Milton to have

Liv'd in both unstained by gold or fee.

Sir James Whitelocke, however, says that he was a great dissembler, and was wont to be called 'Volpone,' and that having borrowed money from some of the judges, he would have favoured them, but Sir Robert Pye refused to execute the warrant. (*Liber Famelicus*, 108.) His character is undisputed for ability, temperance, and erudition; the latter not confined to his legal studies, but extending over subjects of general interest. His professional attainments and industry were exhibited by his Reports, and by his treatise on the king's right of wardship, &c.; and he contributed various papers to the Society of Antiquaries, of which he was an early member. He was three times married. His first wife was Mary, daughter of John Pettey, of Stoke Talmage in Oxfordshire; his second was Mary, the widow of Sir William Bower, knight; and the third was Jane, daughter of John Lord Butler. His honours expired on the death of his third son, William, in 1679. (*Baronage*, ii. 451; *Athen. Oxon.* ii. 441.)

LEYE, ROGER DE LA, was an experienced officer of the Exchequer, acquiring those royal favours and clerical dignities which were usually distributed among the high in place in that department. In 35 Henry III., 1251, he held the office of remembrancer of the Exchequer. (*Madox*, ii. 266.) During the contests with the barons in 1263, the affairs of the Exchequer having got into great disorder, the rents not being paid, and no baron being resident there, the king, on November 1, directed that he should fill the office of a baron there, and on the 30th of the same month commanded that he should execute the offices of treasurer and chancellor of the Exchequer until otherwise ordered. In the next year he was directed to continue to act as baron and treasurer. In 52 Henry III. he was again constituted chancellor of the Exchequer, and remained so for the three following years.

He continued one of the barons of the court during the first two years of Edward's reign, and then was a third time raised to the office of chancellor of the Exchequer. In the latter year, 1276, he was removed, as he is spoken of as 'nuper cancellarius,' and was about that time appointed archdeacon of Essex. (*Ibid.* ii. 28, 52, &c., 320.) From that dignity he was raised, on October 25, 1283, 11 Edward I., to the deanery of London, which he held for less than two years, his death occurring on August 18, 1285. (*Le Neve*, 183, 189.)

LIFFORD, Lord. See J. HEWITT.

LINCOLN, ALURED DE, is another instance of a sheriff being appointed a justice itinerant to fix the assize on the demesnes of the crown in the county under his jurisdiction. He was so employed in 20 Henry II., 1174, for Dorsetshire and Somersetshire, of which he held the sheriffalty for six years, commencing 16 Henry II. (*Madox*, i. 123.)

His grandfather of the same name, at the general survey possessed Wimentone in Bedfordshire, and fifty-one lordships in Lincolnshire. His father was Robert, who held the castle of Wareham for the Empress Maud, against Stephen.

Alured died in 10 Richard I., 1199, leaving by his wife, Albreda, the next-named Alured. (*Baronage*, i. 412.)

LINCOLN, ALURED DE, the son of the above, was in King John's service, and seems to have been connected with the treasury from various entries on the rolls recording payments of money by him. (*Rot. de Liberate*, 53; *Rot. Claus.* i. 1, 31, 46, 97.) In 12 John he accompanied the king to Ireland (*Rot. de Præstito*, 184, 204, 216); but in the barons' wars he deserted his sovereign, and his lands were consequently seized, but were restored to him in 1 Henry III. He thenceforward pursued so loyal a course that in 9 Henry III. he was selected as one of the justices itinerant for the county of Dorset, in which a principal part of his estates were situate. (*Rot. Claus.* i. 236, 302, ii. 76.) He died about 1240, leaving by Maud his wife a son, also named Alured, who died in 1264, without issue. (*Baronage*, i. 412.)

L'ISLE, JOHN, was born about 1606 at Wootton in the Isle of Wight, the residence of his father, Sir William L'Isle, who was descended from a branch of the noble family of that name. After being educated at Magdalen Hall, Oxford, where he took the degree of bachelor of arts in February 1625–6, he repaired, it is said, to one of the Temples as a student in law; but whether he was ever called to the bar is uncertain. He was chosen member for Winchester in both the parliaments of 1640, and in the latter he at once took the popular side, advocating the violent measures on the king's removal to the north, and obtaining some of the plunder arising from the sale of the crown property. In November 1644 he was made master of St. Cross, and retained that valuable preferment till it was given to Mr. Solicitor-General Cook in June 1649. (*Fasti Oxon.* i. 422, 437; *Whitelocke*, 441.) In December 1647, when the king was in duress at the Isle of Wight, L'Isle was selected as one of the commissioners to carry to him the four bills which were to divest him of all sovereignty, and to which they had to bring back the king's magnanimous refusal to consent. He showed his extreme inveteracy against his majesty by his speech on September 28, 1648, in support of the motion that the vote which the Commons had come to two days before, that no one proposition in regard to the personal treaty should be binding if the treaty broke off upon another, should be rescinded; and by his further speech, some days later, urging a discontinuance of the negotiation. (*Parl. Hist.* iii. 823, 828, 1025, 1038.)

He took a prominent part in the king's trial as one of the managers for conducting its details, being present during its whole continuance, and drawing up the form of the sentence. (*State Trials*, iv. 1053, et seq.) The result of this activity was his receiving the appointment on February 8, 1648–9, little more than a week after the king's death, of one of the commissioners of the Great Seal, and being placed in the council of state. He not only concurred in December 1653 in nominating Cromwell protector, but administered the oath to him; and, having been re-appointed lord commissioner, was elected member in the new parliament for Southampton, of which town he was the recorder. (*Parl. Hist.* 1287, 1290, 1426, 1431.) In June he was constituted president of the High Court of Justice, and in August he was appointed one of the commissioners of the Exchequer. When the ordinance for better regulating the Court of Chancery was submitted to the keepers of the Seal, L'Isle alone was for the execution of it, his colleagues pointing out the inconvenience of many of the clauses. The consequence of his subserviency to Cromwell's wishes was that he was continued in the office on the removal of his colleagues in June 1655, and was again confirmed in it in October 1656 by Cromwell's third parliament, to which he was again returned as member for Southampton. (*Whitelocke*, 571–653.) In December 1657 Cromwell, having revived the House of Lords, summoned L'Isle as one of his peers. (*Parl. Hist.* iii. 1518.) The death of Oliver in September 1658 made no difference in L'Isle's position, Protector Richard preserving him in his place; but when the Long Parliament met again in the following May he was compelled to retire, and other commissioners were appointed. (*Whitelocke*, 666, 676, 678.) The house, however, named him on January 28, 1660, a commissioner of the Admiralty. (*Mercurius Politicus*, No. 605.)

In the changes that soon occurred, L'Isle, conscious that he had taken such a part that he could not hope for pardon, thought it most prudent to leave the kingdom; and, escaping to Switzerland, he established himself first at Vevay, and afterwards at Lausanne. There he was shot dead on August 11, 1664, on his way to church, by an Irishman, who was indignant at the respect and ceremony with which a regicide was treated. The assassin escaped, and the murdered man was solemnly buried in the church of the city.

He married Alice, daughter and heiress of Sir White Beckenshaw, of Moyle's Court in Hampshire, who lived long after him, and perished at last by a violent death, being beheaded in 1685 on a conviction, forced by the brutal Judge Jeffreys' from a jury who had twice returned a verdict of not guilty, for harbouring John Hicks, a preacher, who had been out with the Duke of Monmouth. (*Athen. Oxon.* iii. 665; *State Trials*, xi. 297.)

LITTLEBERE, MARTIN DE, was evidently brought up to the profession of the law. In 31 Henry III., 1247, an assize was held before him in Kent (*Excerpt. e Rot. Fin.* ii. 9), but it was not till July 1261 that he was appointed a regular justicier. From that date assizes to be taken before him commence, and they continue without interruption till November 1272. (*Ibid.* ii. 355–589.) He is mentioned as a judge of the King's Bench in 1 Edward I. (*Devon's Issue Roll*, 87); and Dugdale quotes a liberate in his favour in the following year, after which his name does not occur.

LITTLEDALE, JOSEPH, descended from an ancient Cumberland family, was the eldest son of Henry Littledale, Esq., of Eton House, Lancashire, and of Mary, daughter of Isaac Wilkinson, Esq., of Whitehaven. Born in 1767, he completed his education at St. John's College, Cambridge, in 1787, with the honourable distinction of Senior Wrangler and First Smith's Prizeman. Entering Gray's Inn, he practised for some years as a special pleader under the bar till 1798. Being then called, from that time till 1824, a period of twenty-six years, his intimate knowledge of the law and patient industry insured the confidence of all who had the management of business, and gave him very extensive employment.

In 1822 he was sent into Scotland with Mr. (afterwards Baron) Hullock for the purpose of arranging some government prosecutions. He never accepted a silk gown, nor sought a seat in parliament, and was indeed so little of a party man, and so entirely a lawyer, that when he was asked by a friend what his politics were he is said to have answered, 'Those of a special pleader.'

His professional merits alone recommended him to a seat in the Court of King's Bench, to which he was appointed on April 30, 1824, with the usual honour of knighthood. With such colleagues as Chief Justice Abbott, Mr. Justice Bayley, and Mr. Justice Holroyd, the court presented for many years as perfect a phalanx of learned and efficient men as had ever been united in the administration of justice. For the remaining years of the reign of George IV., for the whole of that of William IV., and for nearly four years of the present reign, a period altogether of seventeen years, Sir Joseph Littledale performed the duties of his office to the admiration not only of lawyers, but of the public in general. There was scarcely a barrister who did not regard him as a judicial father, and none could recall an unkind word of his utterance, or an impatient expression of his countenance. He was so devotedly attached to his profession that he heartily enjoyed the discussion of the legal points before him. Once when the author of these pages ventured to express a hope that he was not fatigued with the labours of a heavy day, he answered, 'Oh! no, not at all; I *like it*.'

At the end of Hilary Term 1841, being then seventy-four, he resigned his seat, to the regret of his colleagues, and also of an admiring bar, who paid him the well-merited compliment of an affectionate address, expressive of their sorrow at parting, and of good wishes for his future welfare.

Though he was immediately called to the privy council, he had very little opportunity of aiding in the hearings before its judicial committee, for in less than a year and a half the infirmities that had warned him to retire made rapid way, and he died on June 26, 1842.

LLOYD, RICHARD, is described in the books of the Middle Temple as the son and heir of Talbot Lloyd, of Lichfield, deceased. He was sent for his early instruction to the grammar school of that city, where no less than four of his contemporary judges were educated—viz., Lord Chief Justice Willes, Chief Baron Parker, Mr. Justice Noel, and Sir John Eardley Wilmot. Called to the bar in 1723, he was elected a bencher of his inn in 1728, and reader in 1744. About that time he was made one of the king's counsel.

In 1746 he opened the indictment against Lord Balmerino in the House of Lords, and is on that occasion designated a knight. He was returned to parliament in 1745 for the borough of St. Michael's, in 1747 for Maldon, and in 1754 for Totnes; but only two of his speeches are recorded, one on the Westminster election in 1751, and the other on the repeal of the Jew bill in 1753. In 1754 he was advanced to the office of solicitor-general; but on the change of the ministry in November 1756 he was removed, to make way for the Hon. Charles Yorke. On November 14, 1759, his ambition was obliged to be satisfied by being placed on the bench of the Exchequer. His judicial career was very short, as he died on September 6, 1761, at Northallerton, on his return from the Northern Circuit. His wife was Elizabeth, daughter of William Field, Esq., of Crastwick in Essex. (*Henley's Lord Northington*, 11; *Harris's Lord Hardwicke*, iii. 12, 96; *Wright's Essex*, ii. 790.)

LODELOWE, THOMAS DE, belonged to one of the three families of the name of Lodelowe (Ludlow) which flourished in the reign of Edward II., two of which sent members to parliament respectively for Shropshire and Surrey, and the third held the manor of Campedene in Gloucestershire; but it is uncertain which. He himself appears to have been established in Kent, as in 33 Edward III. he was one of the commissioners for keeping the peace in that county, and in 46 Edward III. was among the custodes of the seashore there. (*N. Fœdera*, iii. 464, 952.)

He was elected recorder of London in 1353, being then an alderman of the city, and held that office till he was constituted chief baron of the Exchequer on October 29, 1365. He acted as a trier of petitions in all the subsequent parliaments till the 47th year (*Rot. Parl.* ii. 289–317), when probably his death occurred. During this period he is several times mentioned in the Year Books as a justice of assize. (*Issue Roll*, 83, 280.)

LODINGTON, WILLIAM, in 1 Henry IV. was constituted the king's attorney 'in Communi Banco et in aliis locis quibuscunque' (*Cal. Rot. Pat.* 237), and was called to the degree of serjeant-at-law in 12 Henry IV. It is possible, however, that the serjeant was son of the attorney-general. He was made one of the king's serjeants on the accession of Henry V.; and on June 16, 1415, in the third year of that reign, he was constituted a judge of the Common Pleas. He enjoyed the office only four years, as he died on January 9, 1419–20. He was buried in the church of St. Peter, at Gunby in Lincolnshire, where there is a monumental brass to his memory. (*Proceedings Archæol. Inst. Lincoln*, liv.)

LOKTON, JOHN DE, derived his name from the township of Lokton in Yorkshire, where he had property at Malton in its neighbourhood. He was probably the son of Thomas de Lokton and Beatrice, his wife, who purchased half of the manor of Canewyk in Lincolnshire in 24 Edward III., and sold it in the same year. (*Abb. Rot. Orig.* ii. 213, 215.) He is described as a king's serjeant in 7 Richard II., 1384, assisting at the trial of John Cavendish for defaming the chancellor, Michael de la Pole. (*Rot. Parl.* iii. 196.) In the same character he subscribed the questions and answers prepared by Chief Justice Tresilian at Nottingham, on August 25, 1387, for which he, with Sir Robert Bealknap and other judges, was afterwards impeached and condemned to death. As no other of the king's serjeants were then present, he was no doubt summoned to that council in consequence of his being designed as the successor of David Hannemere, the judge of the King's Bench, then recently deceased, since his appointment took place two months afterwards, on October 25.

On his trial on March 2, 1388, having pleaded, like the rest, that he acted under compulsion, his sentence was commuted into banishment for life, Waterford, with a circuit of two miles round it, being fixed for his residence, and 20*l.* per annum assigned for his support. It would appear that he died in exile, but his property was ultimately restored to the family. (*Ibid.* 233–244, 442; *Cal. Inquis.* p. m. iii. 107, 162.)

LONDON, HENRY OF (ARCHBISHOP OF DUBLIN), when archdeacon of Stafford is invariably described at the time by his Christian name, Henry, only; but he is called by Le Neve (133) Henry of London. He was probably the same person who, in 16 Henry II., is mentioned under the name of Magister Henricus de Lundonia, as having been sent to Chichester by Richard de Luci, the chief justiciary, to collect the rents of that bishopric, then vacant. The precise year of his being raised to the archdeaconry does not appear; but it is certain he held it in 1 John, as he is then stated to have paid under that title 50*l.* 6*s.* 8*d.*, which he owed for having the goodwill of King Richard, into the 'Scaccarium Redemptionis.' In the same year also he is so called as one of the justices itinerant who fixed the tallage in Berkshire, and as a justicier before whom fines were levied. (*Madox*, i. 190, 307, 722.)

In 3 John he went on an embassy to the King of Navarre (*Rot. Pat.* 3); and in 5 John on another to the King of Connaught, with Meiller Fitz-Henry, justiciary of Ireland. (*Rot. de Liberate*, 83.)

After his return to England he resumed his duties as one of the regular justiciers (*Rot. de Fin.* 306, 398, 401), and was gratified with various ecclesiastical preferments, terminating in March 1213 with the archbishopric of Dublin. (*Rot. Pat.* 11–97; *Rot. Chart.* 200; *Leland's Ireland*, i. 195.)

He witnessed the charter by which King John resigned the crown to the pope, and was present when he granted Magna Charta. (*R. de Wendover*, iii. 254–302.) Holinshed (vi. 43) relates that he obtained the name of Scorch-bill or Scorch-villein, in consequence of throwing into the fire the evidences of their titles which his tenants had brought for his inspection. His motive for this remains a mystery, as none of the tenants were turned out of their lands.

He assisted at the coronation of Henry III., under whom he was appointed justiciary of Ireland in October 1221, and administered the affairs of that kingdom till the middle of 1224, when he surrendered the office to William Mareschall, Earl of Pembroke. (*Rot. Claus.* i. 470–491.) During his presidency he built the castle of Dublin, and dying in the year after his retirement, was buried in Christ Church.

LONDON, WILLIAM DE, the nephew of the above Henry de London, was of the clerical profession, and in 12 John accompanied the king to Ireland. In 16 John he was presented to the prebend of Stokes in the chapel of Wallingford Castle, and two years afterwards to the church of Bretenham in the diocese of Ely. (*Rot. Pat.* 118, 186.) He is called 'our beloved clerk' by Henry III., and had some grants from him, proving the royal favour. (*Rot. Claus.* i. 354, ii. 88.) It is not improbable that he was appointed a regular justicier about 11 Henry III.; for in the list of justices itinerant nominated in August of that year, 1227, his name in the commission for several counties stands the next to Stephen de Segrave, and in 1230 he holds an equally prominent position. From 13 to 15 Henry III. fines were levied before him at Westminster (*Ibid.* ii. 213; *Dugdale's Orig.* 42) ; so that there is no doubt that he must have been elevated to the bench shortly after, if not before, his first selection as a justice itinerant.

LONGCHAMP, WILLIAM DE (de Longo Campo) (BISHOP OF ELY), was a Norman by birth and of the lowest extraction, his grandfather being little more than an agricultural labourer. The earliest notice of him is in the employment of Geoffrey, the natural son of King Henry; afterwards he was taken into that of Richard, while Earl of Poictiers.

In what capacity his earlier services were rendered is not related; but before Richard's coronation as King of England, and while he assumed the title of 'Dominus Angliæ' only, Longchamp had acquired such favour with his royal master as to be appointed his chancellor; and his name, with the addition of 'cancellarius meus,' appears on a charter granted to Gerard de Camville, while the king was at Barfleur, in his progress to this country to take possession of his crown. (*Archæologia*, xxvii. 112.)

He was confirmed in his office on Richard's coronation, and at the council of Pipewell, on September 15, he was nominated to the see of Ely. King Richard then appointed Hugh Pusar, Bishop of Durham, and William de Mandeville, Earl of Essex and Albemarle, to be chief justiciaries and regents of the kingdom during his absence; but, the earl dying in November, the king named Longchamp in his place, assigning the rule of the northern parts to the Bishop of Durham, and that of the southern to the Bishop of Ely, and at the same time associating with them as a council, Hugh Bardolf, William Marshall, Geoffrey Fitz-Peter, and William Briwer.

The power which Longchamp thus acquired by holding two such offices as chief justiciary and chancellor was still further increased in the following June by Pope Clement appointing him legate in England, Wales, and Ireland.

After the king's departure on his progress to the Holy Land, Longchamp, who had up to that period exhibited the greatest prudence and humility, began to display an arrogant and overbearing disposition. Without believing all the tales which are related of him by monkish historians, with whom he was no favourite, it is certain that he assumed to himself the whole authority, neglecting altogether the council appointed by the king, and superseding his coadjutor, the Bishop of Durham, and actually casting him into prison till he delivered up the castles in his portion of the kingdom. He engrossed all the ecclesiastical patronage, and accumulated vast sums by appropriating the rents of the vacant abbeys and bishoprics to himself. He affected a royal state, and the sons of nobles not only waited on him at table, but were happy to take his relations in marriage. He never travelled without such an enormous attendance that the churches and monasteries where he was entertained were nearly ruined by providing for him and his retinue; and if Benedictus Abbas tells truly, the bishop required rather expensive delicacies at his table. The people suffered severely from the taxes he imposed on them for the supply of the absent king; the clergy were equally oppressed; and the gentry and nobles, besides being obliged to contribute, were disgusted with his insolence and rapacity; so that it was not long before all classes were ready to welcome any opportunity to rid themselves of so tyrannous a ruler.

Earl John, the king's brother, was not backward in fomenting this dissatisfaction for the furtherance of his own ambitious views, and matters in a short time were brought to a crisis.

Longchamp, having ejected Gerard de Camville from the sheriffalty of Lincolnshire, besieged the castle of Lincoln, which the sheriff refused to surrender. Earl John, by surprising the castles of Nottingham and Tickhill, obliged the regent not only to raise the siege, but to enter into certain conditions before he was allowed to resume the royal authority. Not warned by this lesson, he persisted in his violent career, and in September 1191 seized the king's natural brother, Geoffrey, Archbishop of York, at the altar of St. Martin at Dover, where he had taken refuge on his arrival in England, contrary to the king's prohibition. The archbishop was dragged through the streets and imprisoned in the castle, whence he was not released until Longchamp, finding that the popular indignation could not be resisted, at the end of eight days allowed him to depart. An assembly of the bishops and barons, at which the archbishop and Earl John attended, was immediately afterwards held at Reading, where a letter from King Richard, which some writers consider to have been forged, was read, appointing the Archbishop of Rouen at the head of a council of regency. Longchamp, after an ineffectual attempt at resistance, was eventually, at a council held in St. Paul's Churchyard, on October 10, 1191, condemned to resign his offices to the Archbishop of Rouen, and, fearful of personal consequences, deemed it advisable to quit the kingdom. For this purpose he proceeded to Dover, and, disguising himself in female attire, waited on the beach for the arrival of the boat that was to convey him to Calais. His awkward gait, however, and his total inability to speak the English language, caused his discovery before his escape was effected, and he was obliged to be taken to the prison of the town to save him from the insults of the populace. After some time he was permitted to depart, when he proceeded to Normandy. Here he fulminated sentence of excommunication against his adversaries, and, among them, against 'Master Benet, who presumed to hold the Great Seal contrary to the ordinances of the king and the kingdom, and his own prohibition.' It would thus appear, therefore, that on his discharge the office of keeper of the Seal was entrusted to this Master Benet. He afterwards ventured over to Dover, and opened a negotiation with Earl John for the restoration of his powers, but without effect, and he was compelled again to depart.

Longchamp, on hearing of the detention of King Richard, was the first to discover his prison, and to assist in his restoration to liberty. The bearer of the royal order to the council of regency for raising the tax for his redemption, he rested in his journey at the abbey of St. Edmund's Bury, where Abbot Samson would not permit mass to be sung before him until the sentence of excommunication issued by the Bishop of London against him had been removed.

On Richard's release, although Longchamp was not restored to the chief justiciaryship, he was continued in the office of chancellor. He signed in that character the treaty of peace between England and France in July 1195 (*Rymer*, i. 66), and in the next year he was present at Winchester when a fine was levied before the king himself. (*Hunter's Preface*.) There is nothing to show that he did not continue chancellor till the day of his death.

He held the sheriffalty of Essex and Hertfordshire in 1196, and at the latter part of that year, he and Philip, Bishop of Durham, were sent to Rome to induce the supreme pontiff to remove the interdict which the Archbishop of Rouen had pronounced against all Normandy. He, however, never reached his destination, for, falling sick on the journey, he died at Poictiers on January 31, 1197, and was buried in the Cistercian monastery of Pina.

It is difficult, amid the conflicting opinions of historians, to form a just estimate of the character of this prelate. While some denounce him as a monster of impiety, and charge him with pride, lust, arrogance, and tyranny, others describe him as loved of God and of men, wise, amiable, generous, benign, and meek, and their relation of the incidents of his life are coloured accordingly. That he was too much elated with his prosperity, and exercised his office with too free a hand, cannot, however, be denied; but, recollecting the difficulties of his position, and the ambitious and treasonable designs of Earl John, it would be unjust entirely to condemn him, the more especially as the countenance he subsequently received from King Richard tends to show that the complaints against him were greatly exaggerated. (*Godwin*, 251; *Stow*, 41; *Madox*, i. 22, 34, &c; *Angl. Sac.* i. 478, 632; *Ric. Devizes*, 6–59; *Lingard*, iii. 333–340.)

LORD, JAMES, is known only, like many of the puisne barons of the Exchequer in these reigns, by his appointment to that position under Elizabeth on November 12, 1566. His death occurred about January 1576.

LOSINGA, HERBERT (BISHOP OF THETFORD AND NORWICH). Thynne, in his 'Collection of Chancellors,' has this passage: 'Herbertus, chancellor in the fourth year of Henry I., in the year of our salutation 1104 (as appeareth by an anonymall pamphlet in written hand), of whom I am not resolved whether this were Herbertus Losinga, Bishop of Norwich, or noe.' (*Holinshed*, iv. 349.)

This is the sole authority for inserting Herbert as a chancellor, for the 'anonymall pamphlet in a written hand' is not forthcoming, and no record of the time contains any fact which gives authenticity to the assertion. Besides this, there is sufficient evidence that Waldric was chancellor at the specified date.

Bishop Herbert was the son of Robert Losinga, but authorities differ whether he was a Norman or a Briton, and, if the latter, in what county he was born. One says, 'In pago Oxunensi in Normannia;' another, 'In pago Oxunensi in Sudovolgia Anglorum Comitatu,' which some interpret Orford in Suffolk; and again another, that he was born at Oxford. The first of these seems the most probable, as there is no doubt that he was prior of Fescamp in Normandy, previous to his coming over to England with William Rufus. Making himself useful in every way at court, he became a great favourite with that monarch. In 1087 he was preferred to the rich abbey of Ramsey, and four years afterwards, in 1091, was promoted to the bishopric of Thetford. For this advancement he is stated to have paid to the king the sum of 1900*l.*, and is charged with using the same simoniacal means for procuring the abbacy of Winchester for his father.

His conscience reproving him for these transgressions, he undertook a journey to Rome, where he succeeded in obtaining absolution from Pope Pascal II., on condition that he proved his penitence by devoting his riches to the Church. On his return, he, with the consent of the king and the pontiff, in April 1094, removed the see from Thetford to Norwich, where, in redemption of his pledge, he built the cathedral at his own expense, laying the first stone in the year 1096, and endowing it with lands sufficient for the support of sixty monks.

His munificence did not end here, for he erected the palace, and founded five parish churches in the county, and a monastery for Cluniac monks at Thetford.

He died on July 22, 1119, and was buried in his own cathedral. Weever gives the epitaph on his monument.

He was an excellent scholar for those times, and composed several learned treatises, mentioned by Pits, who calls him ' vir omnium virtutum, et bonarum literarum studiis impense redditus, mitis, affabilis, corpore venusto, vultu decoro, moribus candidus, vitâ integer.' (*Will. Malmesb.* 515–648; *Godwin*, 426; *Weever*, 786–7; *Angl. Sac.* ii. 700; *Blomefield's Norfolk*, i. 405, and *Norwich*, i. 465.)

LOUDHAM, WILLIAM DE, was the last of seven justices itinerant appointed in 15 Henry III. for the county of York; but no further information has been obtained of him.

LOUGHBOROUGH, LORD. *See* A. WEDDERBURN.

LOUTHER, HUGH DE, was descended from a long line of ancestors, settled at Louther in Westmoreland. His father was of the same name, and his mother was a daughter of Moriceby, of Moriceby in Cumberland. He practised as an advocate, and in 19 Edward I., 1291, was employed by the king. (*Devon's Issue Roll*, 102.) Dugdale on this account represents him as the king's attorney-general; but it is to be remarked that Richard de Breteville and William Inge in those years acted in the same manner in other counties, and there is no proof that the office then existed as a separate appointment.

In the second commission of justices of trailbaston, issued on February 18, 1307, 35 Edward I., Louther was named among five to act in Norfolk and Suffolk; and in the same year he was assigned with John de Insula to enquire into a case which was brought by petition before the parliament, according to the course then usually adopted, of referring these investigations to judges and learned men in the law. Some other instances occur in 2 and 8 Edward II., in the latter of which he acted as a justice itinerant in Yorkshire. (*Rot. Parl.* i. 209–341.)

He was returned a knight for the county of Westmoreland in 33 Edward I., and was one of the supervisors of the array for that county in 4 Edward II. (*Parl. Writs*, i. 714, ii. 1118.) He died in the tenth year of the latter reign; and by his wife, who was a daughter of Sir Peter de Filiol, of Scaleby Castle in Cumberland, he left two sons, Hugh and the next-mentioned Thomas. The lineal descendant of the eldest son Hugh was in 1696 raised to the peerage as Viscount Lonsdale and Baron Lowther, which titles became extinct in 1750. During the life of the last lord there were no less than four baronets of the family alive at the same time. The earldom of Lonsdale was subsequently granted to the representative of the family, and is now borne by his successor. (*Collins's Peerage*, v. 695–716; *Nicolas's Synopsis.*)

LOUTHER, THOMAS DE, second son of the above Hugh de Louther, was constituted a judge of the King's Bench on December 15, 1330, 4 Edward III., and remained in that court only till the following year, when he was appointed chief justice of the King's Bench in Ireland. (*Cal. Rot. Pat.* 113–120.) In 1334 he was superseded by Robert de Bourchier, being, however, at the same time directed to proceed to Dublin to take upon himself the office of chief justice, in case Robert de Bourchier declined to go, with a mandate to act as second judge if Bourchier went. (*N. Fœdera*, ii. 891.) It seems probable that he took the second place accordingly, for he was again raised to the chiefship in 1338. (*Cal. Rot. Pat.* 133.) How long he remained there afterwards, or when he died, does not appear; but in 33 Edward III. a commission was issued to enquire into a charge made against a Thomas de Louther, and John de Louther, the son of his brother, for a breach of the law of arms in forcing a Scottish knight, made prisoner, to pay a second ransom for his release. (*N. Fœdera*, iii. 418.)

LOVEDAY, ROGER, is introduced by Dugdale among those raised to the bench of the Common Pleas on November 2, 1276, 4 Edward I., but it turns out to be an error, the patent quoted only constituting him and two others justices to hold assizes and pleas in the liberties of the priory of Dunstable. He was appointed a justice itinerant in 6 Edward I., and continued to act in that character till the fourteenth year of the reign. (*Parl. Writs*, i. 8, 16, 382; *Chron. Petroburg.* 136.) He was one of the eight judges whom the king in the eighth year selected to enquire what were the services due from the tenants of the manor of Tavistock; and again in the twelfth year he was a commissioner of enquiry into the state of the walls, ditches, sewers, and bridges in Heyland in Lincolnshire, and the damage done by an inundation there. (*Abb. Placit.* 205, 270.)

His property was at Wytheresfield in Suffolk; and in 15 Edward I. he died, leaving a son named Richard. His widow, Sibilla, afterwards married William de Ormesby, the judge. (*Ibid.* 207-307; *Cal. Inquis.* p. m. i. 49.)

LOVEL, JOHN, had the living of Yling in the diocese of London in 18 Edward I., and complaints were made against him to the parliament by his parishioners for undue severity. (*Rot. Parl.* i. 60.) He was one of five justices itinerant sent into the northern counties in 20 Edward I., 1292, and two years afterwards is introduced into Dugdale's list as a judge of the King's Bench. He seems to have held that place in 23 and 28 Edward I.; but in the intervening years he is called clerk of the council, and appears among those known to be clerks in Chancery. In 26 and 28 Edward I. he was one of the justices appointed to perambulate the forests. (*Parl. Writs*, i. 29-83, 397.)

LOVELL, SALATHIEL, was the son of Bernard Lovell, of Lapworth in the county of Warwick, and was born about the year 1619. He was called to the bar at Gray's Inn in November 1656, and was made an ancient in 1671. In 1684 he appears as one of the counsel employed for Mr. Sacheverell and others on their trial for a riot at the election of mayor of Nottingham. He was called to the degree of the coif in 1688, and in June 1692 he stood for the recordership of London, and was elected by the casting vote of the lord mayor. In the following October he was knighted on carrying up the address of the corporation on King William's return from abroad. (*State Trials*, x. 61; *Luttrell*, i. 446, ii. 478, 598.)

He performed the duties of his office so much to the satisfaction of the court that he was promoted to be king's serjeant in May 1695, and a judge on the Chester Circuit in the following year.

He was on the verge of ninety years of age when he was at last appointed a fifth baron of the Court of Exchequer on June 17, 1708. He sat for the next five years, but from his extreme age could not be of much use to his colleagues. Distinguished principally by his want of memory, his title of recorder was converted into the nickname of the obliviscor of London. His great-grandson, Richard Lovell Edgeworth (*Life*, i. 118), relates that a young lawyer pleading before him was so rude as to say, 'Sir, you have forgotten the law;' on which he replied, 'Young man, I have forgotten more law than you will ever remember.' This story, however, is told, with a difference, of Serjeant Maynard and of other old lawyers. He died on May 3, 1713, leaving several children. One of them, Samuel Lovell, also became a Welsh judge, of whom a ludicrous anecdote is told, of his refusing, when overtaken by the tide near Beaumaris, to mount the coach-box to escape drowning, unless a precedent could be quoted for a judge's doing so. (*Luttrell*, vi. 316.)

LOVETOT, JOHN DE, of the noble family of that name, lords of Wirksop in Nottinghamshire, was the son of Oliver de Lovetot, of Carcolston in that county, and Alicia, his wife. (*Baronage*, i. 569; *Thoroton's Notts*, i. 235.) He was raised to the bench of the Common Pleas in 3 Edward I., 1275, and there are entries of fines levied before him from that year till 1289. (*Dugdale's Orig.* 44.) At this time he was charged with extortion and other crimes committed on the judicial seat, and he was accordingly removed and imprisoned in the Tower, for his redemption from which he paid a fine of 3000 marks. (*Stow's London*, 44; *Weever*, 367.) He died in 1294. (*Parl. Writs*, i. 717.)

LUCI, REGINALD DE, of whose parentage nothing is known, had the honor of Egremont, with land in the mountainous territory of Copland, in Cumberland, by his wife Annabel, one of the daughters of William Fitz-Duncan, Earl of Murray, in Scotland.

In 19 Henry II., 1173, and two following years, he was one of the justices itinerant to set the assize for the united counties of Nottingham and Derby, being at that time governor of Nottingham for the king, in the rebellion of the Earl of Leicester and others on behalf of Henry, the king's son.

He attended with the rest of the barons at the coronation of King Richard I., and died soon after. (*Madox*, i. 123, 125, 701; *Baronage*, i. 566, 612.)

LUCI, RICHARD DE. The ancestors of this eminent man held lands in Kent, Norfolk, and Suffolk, for which they performed the service of castle-guard at Dover. The first fact that history records of him is that Henry I. granted to him the lordship of Disce, now Diss, in Norfolk.

Under King Stephen he was entrusted with the government of Falaise in Normandy, which he resolutely defended against the attacks of Geoffrey Earl of Anjou, the husband of the Empress Matilda. In the contest between her and the king he distinguished himself on various occasions in support of the latter, and so high did he stand in the estimation of the contending parties, that on the solemn agreement made by King Stephen with Henry, the son of the empress, in 1153, the Tower of London and the castle of

Windsor were both put into his hands, by the desire of the whole clergy, he swearing to deliver them up to Henry on the death of Stephen, and giving his son as a hostage for his performance of the trust.

Madox (i. 33) quotes a writ, addressed 'Ricardo de Luci, *Justic.* et Vicecomiti de Essexâ,' to prove that he was chief justiciary in the reign of Stephen. But it affords no evidence to that extent. It would simply prove that he was a justicier, a term which in those days was almost synonymous with that of baron; as when the king covenanted with Milo of Gloucester, '*sicut justiciario et barone meo.*' In this instance the word is used as a mere designation, and the writ is addressed to him, not as justicier or baron, but simply as sheriff of Essex, to lands in which county it has reference.

Under Henry II. there is full evidence that he was placed in the high office of chief justiciary, though some doubt exists as to the precise period of his appointment. At a very early period Robert de Beaumont, Earl of Leicester, and he held the office jointly, and their separate precepts occurring in the rolls of the 2nd, 3rd, and 4th years of the reign, show that each had high power. He accompanied the king in 1161 into Normandy, the Earl of Leicester being left in England to direct the government. They appear to have acted together till the 13th year of the reign, when the Earl of Leicester died.

Richard de Luci then became, without any question, sole chief justiciary. From that year till 24 Henry II., 1178, numerous writs in his own name, some of them being grounded on a king's writ *de ultra mare*, and the confirmation in the Exchequer of a convention relative to certain land, made '*coram Ricardo de Luci et aliis baronibus*,' plainly prove that he then held the highest judicial place in the Curia Regis.

Of his judicial acts as chief justiciary little is recorded beyond the committal of some London rioters to prison; but there is sufficient evidence of his activity and diligence in the execution of the legal branch of his office (*Madox*, i. 146), at the same time that he showed no negligence in his ministerial and political duties.

The preparation of the celebrated Constitutions of Clarendon, in January 1164, was entrusted to him and to Josceline de Baliol, both of whom were accordingly subjected to the rancour of Becket, who two years afterwards pronounced sentence of excommunication against them, as the favourers of the king's tyranny, and the contrivers of those heretical pravities. This sentence was repeated by Becket in 1169 against him and others; but it does not appear to have produced much effect on the laymen included in it.

In 1167, on the threat of an invasion by the Earls of Boulogne and Flanders, Richard de Luci made such preparations of defence as effectually to deter them. His conduct and valour as a warrior were brought more actively forward in 1173, when the king's sons raised the standard of rebellion against their father. The Earl of Leicester, the son of his late coadjutor, having joined their party, Richard de Luci besieged the town and castle of Leicester, and soon reducing the former, and demolishing its fortifications, he granted a truce to the garrison of the latter, in order to march against William, King of Scotland, who had invaded Cumberland and was besieging Carlisle. Joined by Humphrey de Bohun, the king's constable, he not only forced the Scots and Galwegians to retire, but, in revenge for their horrible devastations, he set fire to Berwick and ravaged Lothian. The Earl of Leicester during this time had arrived in England with a large body of Flemings; but Richard de Luci and Humphrey de Bohun, concluding a truce with the Scottish king, marched immediately against them, and, giving them battle at Fernham in Suffolk, on November 1, 1173, not only defeated them with great slaughter, but took the Earl of Leicester and his countess prisoners. The justiciary's activity was not less prominent during the succeeding year, in opposing the Earls of Derby and Huntingdon; and the return of King Henry to England, and the capture of William, King of Scotland, occurring about the same time, the rebellion was effectually suppressed before the end of the year.

His services were not unrewarded by the king, who gave him the hundred of Ongar in Essex, with Stanford and Greensteed, and many broad lands in that county and in Kent.

After a life devoted to his country, he prepared himself a retirement at its close, by founding, in 1178, an abbey at Lesnes or Westwood, in the parish of Erith in Kent, for canons regular of the order of St. Augustin, endowing it nobly with half of his possessions there. Resisting the entreaties of his sovereign, who knew how to appreciate his abilities, he resigned his office at the commencement of the following year, and, assuming the habit of one of the canons of the house, withdrew from the turmoil of the world to devote the remainder of his days to piety. His seclusion, however, was not of long duration, for he died on July 14, 1179, and was buried in a sumptuous tomb in the choir of his church.

To the integrity of his character the best testimony is afforded by the conduct of his sovereign, who, though finding him in arms against himself, and highly in the confidence of his opponent, wisely showed his admiration of fidelity and worth even in an enemy, by admitting him into his own counsels, and entrusting him with the sole administration of the realm.

By his wife, Rohaise, he had, according to Dugdale (*Baronage*, i. 563), two sons and two daughters. Maude, the elder of his two daughters, was married to the before-noticed Walter Fitz-Robert; and Rohaise, the younger, was married to Fulbert, the son of John de Dover, lord of Chilham, also previously noticed. Other authors give a somewhat different account of the family. (*Weever*, 777; *Blomefield's Norfolk*, i. 2; *Morant's Essex*, i. 127, ii. 115; *Lord Lyttelton; Pipe Rolls*, 2, 3, and 4 Henry II.)

LUCI, ROBERT DE, was probably a relative of the great Richard de Luci, but in what manner does not appear. He was joined to Richard de Wilton, the sheriff of Wiltshire, as justice itinerant to set the assize or tallage for that county, in 20 Henry II., 1174. In the following year he was sheriff of the county of Worcester, beyond which no further information occurs. (*Madox*, i. 124–546.)

LUCI, GODFREY DE (BISHOP OF WINCHESTER), son of Richard de Luci, completed the abbey of Lesnes, in Erith, Kent, which his father had founded. He was appointed one of King Henry's chaplains, and from canonries in St. Paul's, Lincoln, and York, was advanced to the deanery of St. Martin's in London (*Angl. Sac.* i. 302), and afterwards to the archdeaconries of Derby and the East Riding of York. On September 15, 1189, 1 Richard I., he was elected Bishop of Winchester, and presided over that see for fifteen years. (*Le Neve*, 135, 283, 326.)

In 1179, 25 Henry II., he was named by the council held at Windsor, on the division of the kingdom into four parts for the administration of justice, at the head of the six justiciers to whom the northern counties were appropriated, and, who, besides, were specially appointed to sit in the Curia Regis to hear the complaints of the people. From this time to the end of that reign he regularly acted as a justiciary, not only in the King's Court at Westminster, but on the itinera in various counties. (*Madox*, i. 113–737, ii. 146.)

By a bribe or fine of 3000*l*. he is said to have obtained the restoration of certain manors which had been taken away from the diocese, and to have been made custos of the county of Hants, and of the castles of Winchester and Porchester. But the latter, on the king's departure, were seized by the chancellor, William de Longchamp, Bishop of Ely, nor were they restored till that prelate was removed from the regency of the kingdom.

During the last four years of Richard's reign, Bishop Godfrey was much engaged in his judicial duties, his name appearing frequently on the fines levied both at Westminster and on the circuits. His death occurred on September 4, 1204, and his character was that of an amiable, discreet, and kind-hearted man. (*Ric. Devizes*, 10, 39, 54; *Godwin*, 217.)

LUCI, STEPHEN DE, was one of the sons of Walter de Charlecote, upon whom Henry de Montford conferred the village of that name in Warwickshire, and he and his brother William were the first who assumed the surname of Luci. He held some office in the court in 7 and 8 John, several mandates being countersigned by him. Seventeen years afterwards he was sent, in 8 and 9 Henry III., on royal missions to Rome, in conjunction, on each occasion, with Godfrey de Craucombe. (*Rot. Claus.* i. 66, 578, ii. 42–57.) On his return he was appointed custos of the bishopric of Durham, which he held during the two years of its vacancy. It was no doubt on this account that in 1228 he was nominated one of the justices itinerant within the liberties of that bishopric, for his name does not otherwise appear in a judicial capacity. His brother, William de Luci, to whom the king granted the hundred of Kineton in Warwickshire to farm (*Excerpt. e Rot. Fin.* 130–156), and who was afterwards sheriff of that county, was the progenitor of Sir Thomas de Luci, the Justice Shallow of Shakspeare, and the property is still retained by one of his lineal representatives.

LUKE, WALTER, is said to have advanced himself in the world by marrying the nurse of Henry VIII., with whom he received an estate at Cople in Bedfordshire, and two annuities of 20*l*. during her life. Her name was Anne, and she is described in the visitation of Huntingdon of 1513 as the daughter and heir of Launcelin of Launcelinsbury in that county, and the widow of William Oxenbridge. (*Visit. Hunts*, 60; *Gent. Mag.* July 1823, 28.) In the Middle Temple he attained the post of reader in 1514 and 1520. He probably practised in the Court of Chancery, since his name as counsel does not occur in any of the Reports, and he was one of those assigned in June 1529 to hear causes in Chancery in aid of Cardinal Wolsey. He had previously been connected with the royal household, for when the king's illegitimate son, Henry Fitzroy, Duke of Richmond, was in 1525, at the age of about six years, made lord warden of the North, Walter Luke was appointed to attend him as attorney-general. (*Camden MSS.* iii.; *Mem. H. Fitzroy*, xxiii.) The degree of serjeant was conferred upon him in Michaelmas 1531, and in the following year, on August 23, he was promoted to the ermine as a judge of the King's Bench, and knighted. He sat a silent commissioner on the trials of Sir Thomas More and the Bishop of

E E

Rochester (*State Trials*, i. 387, 398), and dying in 1544, was buried in Cople Church, where there is an effigy of him and his wife on a brass plate. (*Gent. Mag.* lxxxvii. (2), 394.) His only son is the next-mentioned Nicholas.

LUKE, NICHOLAS, the only son of the above Sir Walter Luke, received his legal education also at the Middle Temple, and filled the office of reader in 1534. On April 14, 1540, 31 Henry VIII., he was constituted third baron of the Exchequer, and retained his seat there throughout the reigns of Edward VI. and Mary, receiving a renewal of his patent on the accession of Queen Elizabeth. He died in 1563, and was buried at Cople.

His wife was Cecily, daughter of Sir Thomas Walton, of Bassingmede. (*Dugdale's Orig.* 216; *Gent. Mag.* ut supra.)

LUSH, ROBERT, now one of the judges of the Court of Queen's Bench, was born on October 13, 1807, at Shaftesbury. His father was Robert Lush, Esq., of that place, and his mother was Lucy, daughter of — Foote, Esq., of Tollard in Wiltshire. After some creditable exertions in the lower branches of the profession, he was called to the bar by the society of Gray's Inn on November 18, 1840, and attended the Home Circuit. In 1857 he was appointed a queen's counsel, and though he never held any official station, nor ever had a seat in parliament, he was for his professional merits alone selected as the successor of Mr. Justice Crompton, and received his patent as a judge of the Queen's Bench on October 30, 1865, when he received the customary honour of knighthood.

He married Elizabeth Ann, daughter of Christopher Woolacott, Esq., of London.

LUTWYCHE, EDWARD, was the son and heir of William Lutwyche, of an old Shropshire family of respectability, and, being called to the bar at Gray's Inn in June 1661, was elected an ancient in 1671. Receiving the distinction of the coif in 1683, he was made king's serjeant on February 9, 1684, and knighted. In October 1685 James conferred upon him the chief justiceship of Chester, and raised him to the bench of the Common Pleas on April 21, 1686, where he continued to sit till the abdication. He fell with his sovereign, and, in consequence of his having concurred in the royal claim to dispense with the penal laws in Sir Edward Hale's case, he was excepted out of the act of indemnity passed in the next reign. Returning to the bar, he was fined at the York assizes in April 1693 for refusing to take the oaths, but he continued to practise till 1704, as his 'reports and entries' to that time show. He died in June 1709, and was buried at St. Bride's, London. (*Bramston*, 207; *Luttrell*, iii. 83; 2 *Shower*, 475; *Parl. Hist.* v, 334.)

LYDIARD, RALPH DE, was appointed a justice itinerant for the county of Somerset in 9 Henry III., 1225. He was either an advocate in the court, or in the service of Josceline de Wells, Bishop of Bath, as he was named by that prelate in the following year as his attorney in a suit against a man whom the bishop claimed as 'nativum suum.' (*Rot. Claus.* ii. 76, 154.)

LYMBERGH, ADAM DE, who was of a Lincolnshire family, was in constant employment in offices of trust and responsibility under both Edward II. and III. In 5 Edward II., 1311, he was appointed one of the remembrancers of the Exchequer; and in 1321 he was made constable of Bordeaux, where he remained three or four years, and afterwards, on the accession of Edward III., became keeper of the privy seal. From 5 to 8 Edward III. he was chancellor of Ireland, when from this office he was transferred to the English Court of Exchequer as a baron on November 9, 1334, and probably sat there till his death in 13 Edward III. (*Madox*, ii. 267; *Parl. Writs*, ii. p. ii. 1096; *N. Fœdera*, ii. 519-596, 812, 891; *Cal. Inquis.* p. m. ii. 89; *Abb. Rot. Orig.* 49, 139.)

LYNDE, JOHN DE LA, was of ancient descent and special note in the county of Dorset, where he was bailiff of the forest of Blakemore. One of his family, probably he himself, having killed a white hart which Henry III. while hunting had spared on account of its beauty, was not only imprisoned and fined, but his lands were subjected to an annual tax under the name of the 'White Hart Silver.' He resided at Hartley in Great Minton. (*Hutchins's Dorset*, ii. 272-476.) He was employed in Gascony by the king, one of his letters to whom shows that he acted as a justicier in Yorkshire, in which character his name appears in Trinity 1266 on a fine, in the next year on the pleas of the court, and in May 1270 in a payment made for an assize to be taken before him in Essex. (*Dugdale's Orig.* 43; *Excerpt. e Rot. Fin.* ii. 512.) In 1250 he was joint custos of the city and Tower of London. (*Cal. Rot. Pat.* 39.) On his death in 1272 he possessed manors and lands in six counties. (*Cal. Inquis.* p. m. i. 48.)

LYNDHURST, LORD. See J. S. COPLEY.

LYSTER, RICHARD, was the grandson of Thomas and the son of John, both of Wakefield in Yorkshire. His mother was a daughter of Beaumont of Whitley in the same county. He had his legal training in the Middle Temple, where he arrived at the dignity of reader in Lent 1516 and 1522, and was appointed treasurer in 1523. (*Dugdale's Orig.* 215, 221.)

He was placed in the office of solicitor-general on July 8, 1521; and was succeeded in this post by Christopher Hales on August 14, 1525; and, although he is not introduced into the list of attorney-generals in Dugdale's 'Chronica Series,' there is little doubt that he then followed Ralph Swillington in that office, as he is mentioned with the title in the will of Cicily Marchioness of Dorset, dated May 6, 1527. (*Testam. Vetust.* 634.) This office he held till May 12, 1529, when he was appointed chief baron of the Exchequer, and knighted. After presiding in that court above sixteen years, he was advanced to the office of chief justice of the King's Bench on November 9, 1545, 37 Henry VIII.; and in this character he attested the submission and confession of Thomas Duke of Norfolk on January 12, 1547, a fortnight before the king's death. (*State Trials*, i. 387, 398, 458.)

On the accession of Edward VI. he was re-appointed, but resigned at the end of the first five years of the reign, on March 21, 1552.

The remainder of his life he spent at his mansion in Southampton, and, dying on March 14, 1554, he was buried in the church of St. Michael there. His first wife was Jane, daughter of Sir Ralph Shirley, of Wistneston, Sussex, and widow of Sir John Dawtrey, of Petworth; and his second was a daughter of — Stoke.

LYTHEGRENES, JOHN DE, was either a native of or established as an advocate in one of the northern counties, his name being mentioned so early as 52 Henry III. as employed on the part of the king in a quo warranto against the mayor of Newcastle-upon-Tyne. (*Abb. Placit.* 170.) In 8 Edward I. he was appointed sheriff of Yorkshire, and retained that office for five years; and he is noticed in the parliament of 18 Edward I. as a commissioner to enquire into the liberties claimed by the priors of Tynemouth and Carlisle. (*Rot. Parl.* i. 29, 38.) In 1293 he acted as one of the justices itinerant for Surrey; two years afterwards he was king's escheator beyond the Trent, but in the next year exchanged the office for that on this side the Trent. In 28 Edward I., and two years afterwards, he was employed in the perambulation of the forests of the northern counties (*Parl. Writs*, i. 397-8), being also recorded in the intervening year as a justice itinerant in the county of Kent. He was still alive in January 1301, when his name appears in the Statute de Escaetoribus as one of the king's council. (*St. at Large*, i. 147.)

LYTTELTON, THOMAS, was descended from a family established at South Lyttelton in Worcestershire so early as the reign of Henry II. In that of Henry III. the successor of the family became possessed of the manor of Frankley, whose representative, Elizabeth, carried the estate to her husband, Thomas Westcote, of Westcote, near Barnstaple, with a provision that her issue inheritable should be called by the name of Lyttelton. This eminent judge was the son of that marriage, upon whom the name devolved.

He was born at the family seat, and we have Coke's authority that his legal studies were pursued at the Inner Temple, and that the subject of his public reading there was the statute of Westminster 2, De Donis Conditionalibus. In 1445 a suitor petitioned the lord chancellor to assign him as counsel in certain proceedings against the widow of Judge Paston, whom none of the 'men of court' were willing to oppose. (*Paston Letters*, i. 8.) From this it would seem that his practice was at that time principally in the Court of Chancery, which may perhaps account for the infrequent occurrence of his name in the Year Books, in which Chancery cases are seldom recorded. In 30 Henry VI. he had a grant from Sir William Trussel of the manor of Sheriff Hales in Staffordshire for his life, 'pro bono et notabili consilio;' affording an example of the manner in which advocates were sometimes rewarded by their opulent clients in those days, when current coin was scarce.

He was called to the degree of the coif on July 2, 1453, and was also appointed steward (or judge) of the Court of Marshalsea of the king's household. His services were soon afterwards further retained by the crown, by granting him a patent as king's serjeant on May 13, 1455.

In the first parliament of Edward IV. he was named as an arbitrator in a difference between the Bishop of Winchester and his tenants (*Rot. Parl.* v. 476); and two years afterwards he was in personal attendance on the king with the two chief justices on one of the royal progresses. (*Paston Letters*, i. 175.) On the next vacancy he was raised to the bench, being constituted a judge of the Common Pleas on April 17, 1466, and he added a dignity to the law by his learning and impartiality throughout the remainder of his life, uninfluenced by the passions of the contending parties, and unremoved by either of the royal disputants on the two temporary transfers of the crown which he witnessed. In 15 Edward IV. he was honoured with the knighthood of the Bath.

He died where he was born, at Frankley, on August 23, 1481, and was buried in Worcester Cathedral.

From his obtaining two general pardons under the Great Seal it has been inferred that he was alternately a partisan of the houses of York and Lancaster, and thus required a double protection. But seeing that the first was granted in 1454, before the civil war had commenced, and while he was in the king's service as judge of the Marshalsea, it seems more probable that the indemnity he then sued for was against any irregular acts he might have committed while he was high sheriff or escheator of

Worcestershire; and as to the second grant, dated 1461, when he was in favour with King Edward IV., his desire of a renewal of his pardon must be considered rather as an act of prudent caution at the end of a violent civil convulsion, and the introduction of a new dynasty, a conclusion to which we more readily arrive since we find that the latter was granted to him as 'late sheriff of Worcester, or under-sheriff' (*Chaufepie's Cont. of Bayle*, iii. 86), the Earl of Warwick being the hereditary high sheriff.

His name is still sacred in Westminster Hall, and his celebrated work, 'THE TREATISE ON TENURES,' which Coke describes as 'the most perfect and absolute work that ever was written in any human science,' and for which Camden asserts that 'the students of the common law are no less beholden than the civilians are to Justinian's Institutes,' will ever prevent its being forgotten. The treatise itself is, however, now seldom read without the valuable Commentary of Sir Edward Coke, a production which, as no one would dare to enter the legal arena without fully digesting, has been illustrated successively by the eminent names of Hale, Nottingham, Hargrave, and Butler.

Sir Thomas greatly enlarged his possessions by his marriage with Joan, one of the daughters and coheirs of Sir William Burley, of Bromscroft Castle, Shropshire, and widow of Sir Philip Chetwynd, of Ingestre in Staffordshire. By her he had three sons, each the progenitor of a noble house—viz., the present Lord Lyttelton of Frankley, from the eldest; the present Lord Hatherton, from the second son; and from the third, Lord Lyttelton of Mounslow, whose name will be next noticed.

LYTTELTON, EDWARD (LORD LYTTELTON), was the great-grandson of Thomas, the youngest of the three sons of the last-mentioned judge, and the son of Edward Lyttelton, seated at Henley in Shropshire, who became chief justice of North Wales, was knighted, and married Mary, the daughter of Edmund Walter, chief justice of South Wales, and sister to Sir John Walter, the distinguished lord chief baron of the Exchequer in the reign of James I.

Edward Lyttelton was born at Mounslow in 1589, and took his first degree in arts at Christ Church, Oxford, in 1609. At the Inner Temple he was called to the bar. Lord Clarendon (ii. 491) describes him as 'a handsome and proper man, of a very graceful presence, and notorious for courage, which in his youth he had manifested with his sword. He had taken great pains in the hardest and most knotty part of the law, as well as that which was more customary, and was not only very ready and expert in the books, but exceedingly versed in records, in studying and examining whereof he had kept Mr. Selden company, with whom he had great friendship, and who had much assisted him, so that he was looked upon as the best antiquary of the profession who gave himself up to practice.' His early reputation in his profession is proved by his being on his father's death, in 1621, appointed to succeed him as chief justice of North Wales.

Returned in 1626 to the second parliament of Charles I., he took an active part in the proceedings against the Duke of Buckingham, arguing that common fame was a sufficient ground for the house to act upon. In the midst of the enquiry the king, to save his favourite, dissolved the parliament. When it met again in March 1628 Lyttelton was placed in the chair of the committee of grievances, and on April 3 presented to the house their report, upon which was founded the famous Petition of Right. In the subsequent conferences with the Lords he ably enforced the resolutions, and replied to the objections of the crown officers with temper and point. He was designated by the lord president in reporting the arguments as 'a grave and learned lawyer,' and great must have been his elation when he heard the king's answer to the petition, 'Soit droit fait comme il est désiré.' On the dissolution of this parliament in the following March several members were imprisoned for their violence in holding the speaker in the chair while the protestation against tonnage and poundage was passed. On their application to the Court of King's Bench, Lyttelton appeared for John Selden, who was one of those arrested, and learnedly contended for his right to be discharged on bail. (*Parl. Hist.* ii. 58-323; *State Trials*, iii. 85, 252.)

Though a strenuous advocate for the liberty of the subject, he had never exhibited any asperity in his language, nor shown himself a violent partisan of those who opposed the measures of the court. The king could not fail to see the benefits which would result from his services, and accordingly earnestly recommended him as recorder of the city of London, to which he was elected on December 7, 1631. About the same time he was appointed counsel to the university of Oxford, and in autumn of the next year he arrived at the post of reader to the Inner Temple. In October 1634 he was made solicitor-general, and knighted. This office he held above five years, and principally distinguished himself by his elaborate argument against Hampden in the case of ship-money, in delivering which he occupied three days. (*State Trials*, iii. 923.)

An extraordinary compliment was paid by his inn of court to the name of his illustrious ancestor. The solicitor-general having applied for a chamber, then vacant, over his own, to be assigned to his kinsman, Mr. Thomas Lyttelton, 'the whole company of the bench with one voice' not only granted his request, but desired that the 'admittance should be freely without any fine, as a testimony of that great respect the whole society doth owe and acknowledge to the name and family of Lyttelton.' (*Inner Temple Books.*)

He was promoted to the office of chief justice of the Common Pleas on January 27, 1640. (*Rymer*, xx. 380.) In the April following a new parliament was called, and after sitting barely three weeks was dissolved. Another, the Long Parliament, met in November, and one of its first enquiries was into the conduct of Lord Keeper Finch, who, dreading the consequences, fled the country. The Seal, being thus deserted, was delivered to Lyttelton, with the title of lord keeper, on January 18, 1641 (*Croke, Car.* 565); and on the 18th of the following month he was created Lord Lyttelton of Mounslow. This advance did not add to his reputation or his peace. In the Common Pleas he had presided with great ability; in the Chancery he was only an indifferent judge. At the council and in parliament he felt himself out of his element, and was so disturbed with the unhappy state of the king's affairs that he fell into a serious illness, and was absent from his place for some months. On the impeachment and attainder of his friend the Earl of Strafford he was prevented from pleading on his behalf by his illness. Soon after, on May 18, the lord keeper was placed at the head of a commission to execute the office of lord high treasurer. On his resuming his seat he had the difficult duty of presiding during all the violent measures that occupied the house. His conduct, while it could not but be displeasing to the king, raising doubts of his fidelity, was so satisfactory to the Commons, and so apparently compliant with their wills, that on their nomination of lieutenants for the several counties they placed him at the head of his native shire. (*State Trials*, ii. 1085.) In March 1642 the king, offended by the parliamentary proceedings, retired to York. He had been for some time suspicious of the lord keeper's devotion to him, and was particularly disgusted with his vote in favour of the ordinance for the militia, and his arguments in support of its legality. (*Whitelocke*, 59.) Lord Lyttelton, however, took an opportunity of explaining to Mr. Hyde (afterwards Lord Clarendon), who was secretly in the confidence of the king, that he was in great perplexity how to act, that he had no person to confer with or to confide in, and that he had given this vote and others, which he knew would be obnoxious to the king, for the purpose of disarming the rising distrust of the Commons, and of preventing their proposed intention of taking the Seal from him. He thereupon planned with Mr. Hyde that he would take advantage of the customary recess of the house, between Saturday and Monday morning, to send the Great Seal to the king, and himself to follow after. This important service, as it was then deemed, was successfully effected, and on May 23 the lord keeper's escape was reported to the Lords, who immediately ordered him to be taken into custody; but at the end of the third day after his departure he kissed the king's hand at York. This statement would seem to be contradicted by his subsequent letter to the Lords, in which he says that Saturday was *the first time* that he ever heard of going to York, and that he did so by the king's absolute commands. He encloses an affidavit showing his inability from illness to travel to Westminster, as ordered, and at the same time proves the evasiveness of the excuse by 'taking the boldness' to inform the Lords that he has the king's express commands upon his allegiance not to depart from him. Such weakness of purpose, and such useless attempts to be well with both parties, sufficiently account for his not being respected by either.

It was not till a year afterwards that the parliament voted that if Lord Keeper Lyttelton did not return with the Great Seal within fourteen days he should lose his place, and whatever should be sealed with that Great Seal afterwards should be void (*Whitelocke*, 70); and the two houses passed an ordinance for a new Great Seal on November 10, 1643. The king was, at first, much dissatisfied with Lyttelton, whose hesitation and fears were rather annoying. But Hyde convinced his majesty of his lord keeper's fidelity, and prevented his being removed from his place, though he was not for some time entrusted with the actual custody of the Seal. Of Lyttelton's loyal devotion to the crown all suspicion was at last removed. In March he was again appointed first commissioner in the Treasury (*4 Report Pub. Rec., App.* ii. 187); and on May 21, 1644, he was actually entrusted with a military commission to raise a regiment of foot-soldiers, consisting of gentlemen of the inns of court and chancery, and others. Of this regiment, the ranks of which were soon filled, he acted as colonel. Two centuries had elapsed since a keeper of the Seal and a soldier were united in the same person; and in the two centuries that have since passed no other person has served the king in a like double capacity.

Notwithstanding this ebullition of zeal and spirit, Lyttelton was an altered man. The sad position of public affairs depressed him; he became melancholy, and the vigour of his mind and the strength of his body gradually decayed, so that he could not contend against an attack of illness, which carried him off on August 27, 1645. He was buried in the cathedral of Christ Church, Oxford.

That he was a learned lawyer, powerful advocate, and an excellent judge; that in his private character he was highly esteemed; that he was incorrupt amidst corruption, and moderate among the violent; and that he never used power for the gratification of private malignity, nor for the prosecution of party purposes, both friends and enemies readily acknowledge. Desertion of the popular party for place is somewhat harshly alleged against him. His subsequent career must rather be blamed as weak than stigmatised as treacherous; and his flight with the Great Seal from the parliament, so dangerous, and indeed so fatal to himself, if he had been stopped, showed a degree of personal courage that must dissipate all doubts as to the principles by which he was guided. He felt it to be his duty to resist the encroachments on the constitution, and he did resist them; he felt it equally to be his duty to support the sovereign when his power was threatened, and he flew to him for that purpose. But he was not a man for the times he lived in. He was not made for power; he could not cope with the spirits of the day; he was weak and wavering; and by endeavouring to be the friend of all parties he experienced the usual consequence of being confided in by none. But he had dear friends on both sides who did not doubt his integrity. Hyde, who knew him well, was his friend to the last. Whitelocke, of the parliament side, always speaks kindly of him, and even in relating his flight calls him 'a man of courage and of excellent parts and learning.'

A volume of Reports in the Common Pleas and Exchequer, from 2 to 7 Charles I., was published with his name in 1683; but doubts have been raised as to their being of his composition.

His peerage died with him. His first wife was Anne, daughter of John Lyttelton of Frankley; and his second wife was Elizabeth, one of the daughters of Sir William Jones, the judge of the King's Bench, and widow of Sir George Calverley, of Cheshire. (*Ath. Oxon.* iii. 175.)

LYTTELTON, TIMOTHY, the brother of the above lord keeper of Charles I., and the seventh son of Sir Edward Lyttelton, of Henley in Shropshire, chief justice of North Wales, was admitted into the Inner Temple in 1626, called to the bar in 1635, and elected a bencher in 1640. During the Rebellion his history is a blank; but at the Restoration he held the office of recorder of Bewdley, and was appointed one of the Welsh judges. The only subsequent notice of him is that he was constituted a baron of the Exchequer on February 1, 1670, and that he died early in 1679, and was buried in the Temple Church. (*Wood's Fasti*, ii. 231; *Nash's Worcestershire*, ii. 279; *Cal. St. Papers* [1660], 212; *Gent. Mag.* iii. 69.)

M

MACCLESFIELD, EARL OF. *See* T. PARKER.

MACDONALD, ARCHIBALD, was descended from the old Lords of the Isles, one of whom was created a baronet of Nova Scotia in 1625. The seventh baronet was Sir Alexander, who by his second wife, Margaret, daughter of Alexander, ninth Earl of Eglinton, was father of three sons, the two elder of whom succeeded in turn to the title, and the latter was in 1776 raised to the barony of Macdonald in the peerage of Ireland, which his representative still enjoys. Archibald, the youngest, was born in 1746, and received his education at Westminster School.

On being called to the bar in England his connection with Scotland insured him liberal employment in appeals from that country to the House of Lords; and in the courts of Westminster, though he had not great practice, he acquired such a character as a lawyer as to be engaged in the great Grenada case in 1775, for his argument in which he was highly praised by Lord Mansfield. (*State Trials*, xx. 287, 303, 306.) His union in 1777 with Louisa, the eldest daughter of Granville, second Earl Gower (afterwards Marquis of Stafford), was a certain precursor of promotion to one who possessed competent legal qualifications. In the same year he was made one of the king's counsel, and was returned to parliament for the borough of Hindon, and in 1780 for Newcastle-under-Lyne. He gave his support to Lord North while he remained prime minister; but when that nobleman afterwards joined Mr. Fox in the Coalition Ministry, he strenuously opposed the unholy alliance, and made an able speech against the famous East India Bill in answer to Mr. Erskine. From the very first entrance of Mr. Pitt into the senate in 1781 Mr. Macdonald attached himself to that remarkable man, anticipating his future greatness, and fought boldly by his side in the doubtful parliamentary conflict that raged after the dispersion and ejection of the Coalition in December 1783. (*Parl. Hist.* xix.–xxiv.) He was not long in receiving his reward, being appointed solicitor-general on April 8, 1784. To the parliaments of 1784 and 1790 he was returned by his old constituents, and while he continued in the House of Commons he was a steady and useful adherent to the minister, particularly in reference to the king's illness in 1789.

In 1780 he was appointed a Welsh judge on the Carmarthen Circuit, and succeeded Sir Pepper Arden as attorney-general on June 28, 1788, and was then knighted. It fell to his lot to prosecute Stockdale by order of the House of Commons, for publishing Mr. Logan's defence of Mr. Hastings; and also Thomas Paine as the author of 'The Rights of Man;' both of them affording Mr. Erskine opportunities of displaying his extraordinary oratorical powers, in the former case with a success which he could not expect in the latter. In the exercise of his office Sir Archibald was distinguished for his prudence and humanity, which Mr. Burke acknowledged was a striking feature in his character, though in the latter years of his official life the seditious spirit that then prevailed obliged him to institute several prosecutions. (*State Trials*, xxi. 61, xxii. 247, 285, 380; *Parl. Hist.* xxix. 512.)

His promotion to the place of lord chief baron of the Exchequer took place on February 12, 1793, a post for which his discriminating powers and judicial mind peculiarly fitted him. After a presidency of twenty years, esteemed by all for his careful and impartial administration of the law, for his patient attention to every argument, never interrupting the speaker, as well as for the kindness of his disposition and the courtesy of his manners, he retired into private life in November 1813, and in the same month was rewarded with a baronetcy. He survived his resignation nearly thirteen years, and died on May 18, 1826. His grandson is now the third baronet.

MADDINGLEY, ROBERT DE, of Maddingley, a parish in Cambridgeshire, was the son of Thomas de Maddingley, member for Cambridge in several parliaments of Edward I. He was one of the assessors of the tallage of that and three neighbouring counties in 6 Edward II., and was in several judicial commissions in that locality about the same period. In 1314 he was one of the justices of assize in Norfolk and Suffolk, and he continued to perform the same functions in these and other counties till 1321, in which year he died. (*Parl. Writs*, 720, p. ii. 1129; *Rot. Parl.* i. 374, 448, 450.)

MALBERTHORP, ROBERT DE, was so called from a manor of that name in Lincolnshire. In 6 and 8 Edward II. he is mentioned in connection with property in that county (*Abb. Rot. Orig.* i. 198, 216), and was occasionally employed in commissions there from 10 Edward II. till he was raised to the bench. This event occurred about August 1320, as a judge in the King's Bench. From that time till the end of the reign he was actively engaged in the performance of his judicial duties, principally in the country.

His re-appointment on the accession of Edward III. was delayed on account of Queen Isabella's indignation against him, in consequence of his being concerned in the judgment pronounced, five years before, upon Thomas Earl of Lancaster. But he obtained his pardon on March 7, 1327, on the testimony of the prelates and peers that he gave that judgment by command of the king, whom he did not dare to disobey, and to avoid danger to himself. Such is the disgraceful entry on the patent of pardon. (*N. Fœdera*, ii. 690.) It may be presumed, therefore, that he was then permitted to resume his judicial functions. We accordingly find him acting as a justice of assize in this first year, and sitting in court in Hilary Term of the second. (*Year Book*.)

On February 2, 1329, he was named in the commission to try certain malefactors in the city of London (*N. Fœdera*, ii. 755), and on May 1 following had so entirely recovered favour as to be promoted to the office of chief justice of the King's Bench during the temporary absence of Geoffrey le Scrope. This lasted till October 28 in the same year, when he remained in that court till January 18, 1331, and was then removed into the Common Pleas. The fines levied before him do not extend beyond Martinmas in the same year, and his death soon after occurred. (*Rot. Parl.* ii. 25, 208; *Parl. Writs*, ii. p. ii. 1131; *Abb. Rot. Orig.* i. 198, ii. 59.)

MALDUIT, JOHN, held a place in the Curia Regis or Exchequer in 16 Henry II., 1170. Two years afterwards he and Turstin Fitz-Simon accounted for the profits of the see of Canterbury, which had been committed to their care on the murder of Becket. (*Madox*, i. 309, 631, ii. 253.)

In 1174 he was one of the justices itinerant for setting the assize in the counties of Nottingham and Lincoln, in the latter of which he is also mentioned on the rolls of 22 and 23 Henry II. (*Ibid.* i. 123, 127, 129.)

MALDUIT, WILLIAM (Maledoctus), is mentioned in only two instances (*Madox*, i. 44, 215) as a baron acting judicially. These are in 11 and 30 Henry II., 1165 and 1184; and in both cases he is represented as being present among those sitting in the Exchequer when charters or agreements relative to land were executed or acknowledged there. On each of these occasions he is described as chamberlain, in which character he would have a seat in that court. He does not appear to have been employed as a justice itinerant. He succeeded to the office of chamberlain on the death of his elder brother, Robert, about 31 Henry I., 1130–1.

Robert and William were the sons of William Mauduit, who is mentioned in Domesday Book as possessing seven lordships in Hampshire, and who was afterwards appointed chamberlain to Henry I., from whom he received in marriage Maud, the daughter of Michael de Hanslape, with the lands of which he died possessed.

It is evident that there were several chamberlains in the King's Court, and that there was one at the head of all, called magistra cameraria, which was an hereditary office. Whatever were their duties in the king's household, it is certain that they were officially connected with the Exchequer, and had the care of the receipts and payments of the revenue. They also sat at this time as barons or justices in the Exchequer.

That there was some interval during the reign of Stephen in which William Mauduit did not enjoy the office, or that some doubt existed as to the right of possession, seems likely, from his obtaining from Henry II., while Duke of Normandy, a grant of the inheritance of the office of chamberlain of his Exchequer, with the castle of Porchester, and all the lands to the chamberlainship and the castle appertaining, both in England and Normandy. These were confirmed to him when Henry II. attained the crown. He held the sheriffalty of Rutland from 26 Henry II. till the end of the reign, and his name is recorded as chamberlain up to 7 Richard I., 1195, soon after which he probably died, having in the previous year joined an expedition into Normandy. He was succeeded by his son, the next-mentioned Robert. (*Dugdale's Baron.* i. 398; *Pipe Rolls, Henry II. and Richard I.*)

MALDUIT, ROBERT, who sat as a justicier in the Curia Regis in 10 John, 1208–9, when fines were acknowledged there, was the son of the above William Mauduit. During the last nine or ten years of the reign of Henry II. he held the sheriffalty of Wiltshire; and on his father's death he succeeded to the office of chamberlain of the Exchequer, which he exercised during the whole of the reign of John. (*Rot. de Liberate*, passim.) In 1 John, for a fine of 100*l.*, he obtained the custody of Rockingham Castle (*Rot. de Oblatis*, 9); and from 2 to 7 John he was sheriff of Rutland.

He accompanied the king in his Irish expedition in 1210 (*Rot. de Præstito*, 185, &c.), but afterwards joined the standard of the discontented barons in the contest for their liberties. The Close Roll of 17 John records his name among those who took up arms against the king, his son William acting a still more prominent part. The consequence of this revolt was the loss of the family estates, which were seized into the king's hands, and the excommunication and capture of William. Soon after the accession of King Henry III. both of them returned to their allegiance, their submission being accompanied by a restoration of their property. (*Rot. Claus.* i. 237–346.)

Robert died about June 1222, 6 Henry III. His widow, Isabella, daughter of Thurstan Basset, survived him; and William, their son, married Alice, the daughter of Waleran, Earl of Warwick, whose son, also William, succeeded to that earldom, which continued in the family till the year 1589, when it became extinct. One of the earls, Henry de Beauchamp, was created Duke of Warwick in 1444, but the title died with him. (*Baronage*, i. 398; *R. de Wendover*, iii. 297, 349, 356, iv. 24.)

MALEBYSSE, RICHARD, was the son of Hugh de Malebysse, who came over from Normandy, and was settled in 3 Stephen at Scawton in Yorkshire. His mother was Emma, daughter and heir of Henry de Percy. He was called Richard Malebysse of Acaster, and was one of the foresters of the county of York.

In the beginning of the reign of Richard I. he was in some manner implicated in the horrible massacre of the Jews at York, for which his lands were seized into the king's hands; and in 4 Richard I. he paid twenty marks to recover them till the king's return. He was afterwards implicated in some other disturbances, which drew upon him and his brother Hugh the excommunication of the pope; and in 6 Richard I. he paid a fine of three hundred marks to regain the king's favour, and for having the full restoration of his lands, wards, and forests.

His latter offence was evidently too close a connection with Earl John; for though, when that prince came to the throne, he had to pay another fine for some of his lands, he seems to have at once been admitted into the royal confidence. In 2 John he had the custody of the castle of Queldric; in the next year he was employed as a justice itinerant to fix the tallage in Yorkshire; and in 4 John he was present at Westminster when fines were acknowledged there. (*Madox*, i. 316, 722.) Besides these judicial duties, he was sent as one of the embassy to accompany William, King of Scotland, to England; and in 5 John was engaged in enforcing the payment of the aids required by the king. He was keeper of the forests of Galtres, Derwent, and Wernerdale, and had permission to stub and cultivate eighty acres of land of the king's forest, between Owse and Derwent, at Queldric. (*Rot. de Oblatis*, 41, 55; *Rot. Chart.* 42.) He incurred some disgrace by his negligence in keeping the forest of Galtres, and before he could recover the land and castles, which the king thereupon summarily seized, he was compelled, in 6 John, to pay a fine of five pounds into the royal treasury.

Although he seems to have been a little turbulent in character, he was apparently of a generous nature, and in the disposition of his property, which was very extensive, to have acted with great liberality. He made grants of lands to various abbeys, and founded that of Newbo, near Grantham in Lincolnshire, for monks of the Præmonstratensian order, endowing it with a third part of the church of Kniveton in Nottinghamshire, and with the church of Acaster. (*Monast.* vi. 887.)

He died in 11 John, 1209, and was succeeded by his son John. One of his descendants, Sir Hercules Malebysse, in compliance with stipulations entered into on his marriage with Lady Beckwith Bruce, assumed the name of Beckwith, which the family has since preserved, and within the last century has been highly distinguished in our military annals.

MALET, ROBERT, was amerced in 14 Edward I. for not appearing at the Exchequer with his accounts as sheriff of the counties of Bedford and Buckingham. (*Madox*, ii. 237.) But the offence was no doubt speedily removed, for in 18 Edward I., 1289, he was appointed a judge of the King's Bench. He is mentioned in that character as late as 1294, in which year he died. (*Abb. Rot. Orig.* i. 87, 88.)

MALET, THOMAS, was a great-grandson of Sir Baldwin Malet, of St. Audries, Somersetshire, solicitor-general of Henry VIII., a descendant from the Norman baron of that name, who fought on William's side at the battle of Hastings. His connection with the above Robert Malet cannot now be traced. He was born about 1582, and took his legal degrees in the Middle Temple, being called to the bar in 1606, and becoming reader in 1626.

In the first two parliaments of Charles I. he sided with the government, and in the case of the Duke of Buckingham he argued forcibly against common fame being received as a sufficient ground of accusation. After filling the office of solicitor-general to the queen he was honoured with the coif in 1635, and was appointed a judge of the King's Bench on July 1, 1641 (*Rymer*, xx. 517), a few days before the impeachment of six of his brethren, and was thereupon knighted. Not deterred by fear of the parliament, at the very next Lent assizes he threw no discouragement on the proposed petition of the grand jury of Kent against the ordinance for the militia without the king's assent, and in support of the Book of Common Prayer; and for having shown this petition to the Earl of Bristol without first revealing it to the house he was committed to the Tower by the Lords on March 28, 1642, but released on May 2 on entering into a recognisance of 1000*l.* to appear before the Lords when called upon. (*Parl. Hist.* ii. 1148; *Lords' Journals*.) In that summer he again went the Home Circuit, and on some members of the House of Commons coming to the bench at Maidstone, where he was sitting, and producing certain votes of parliament on behalf of the militia ordinance and against the king's commission of array, he boldly refused to permit them to be read, as not authorised by the commission under which he sat. For this courageous conduct King Charles sent him a letter of thanks, with a promise of protection. This however the parliament rendered inoperative, by promptly despatching a troop of horse and violently taking the judge from the bench at Kingston in Surrey. Carried prisoner to Westminster, the house immediately committed him to the Tower. There he remained a prisoner for above two years, till in October 1644 he was redeemed by the king in exchange for another, whose liberty the parliament desired. They still regarded him 'as the fomenter and protector of the malignant faction,' and by an ordinance in November 1645 they disabled him and four of his colleagues 'from being judges as though they were dead.' (*Clarendon*, iii. 153; *Whitelocke*, 107, 181.)

During the succeeding fifteen years he suffered severely for his loyalty, losing a son in the king's service, and his property being greatly reduced by sequestrations. Two days after the restoration of Charles II., though then seventy-eight years of age, he was replaced in his old seat in the King's Bench. From his speech on the trial of one of the regicides, showing much of the garrulity of old age, it is evident that he was then nearly superannuated; but he was, however, sufficiently alive to his interest to petition for and obtain grants of land in Somersetshire and Devonshire. Sitting in court for the three succeeding years, the king on his petition on June 18, 1663, dispensed with his further attendance, continuing to him the name and salary of a judge (*Cal. State Papers* [1663], 348, 435; *State Trials*, v. 1030; 1 *Siderfin*, 150), and granting him a pension of 1000*l.* a year. At the same time he was honoured with a baronetcy, the fiat for which, for some reason or other, he refrained from having completed during the two remaining years of his life.

He died on December 19, 1665, and was buried in Pointington Church, Somersetshire. Under the recent sufferings of the family, his descendants for the three next generations did not solicit the completion of the honour which King Charles had awarded to their ancestor. The judge's great-great-grandson, Charles Warre Malet, however, who filled some high offices in India, accepted in 1791 a new patent of baronetcy, but afterwards failed in his claim for precedence under the old patent, and his son now enjoys the new honour. (*Malet Papers; Collinson's Somerset*, ii. 377.)

MALINS, RICHARD, one of the present vice-chancellors, was born in 1805 at Evesham. He is the son of the late Richard Malins, Esq., of Alston in Warwickshire, by a daughter of Thomas Hunter, Esq., of Pershore. Educated at Gonville and Caius College, Cambridge, he took his degree of B.A. in 1827, with mathematical honours. Before this time he had entered the Inner Temple, and was called to the bar on May 14, 1830. With an extensive practice in Chancery, he obtained a silk gown in 1849. In 1852 he entered parliament as member for Wallingford, and retained the seat till July 1865, supporting the conservative side of politics. On December 1, 1866, he was appointed vice-chancellor as the successor of that estimable judge Sir R. T. Kindersley, and was then knighted.

He married Susannah, daughter of the Rev. Arthur Farwell, rector of St. Martin's, Cornwall.

MALLORE, PETER, was probably a descendant of Gislebert Mallore, one of the Conqueror's followers, and of Anchetil Mallore, employed in the reign of Henry II. He married Matilda, the widow of Elyas de Rabayne, and a daughter of Stephen de Bayeux. Holding the town of Melcombe, and certain lands at Dodemerton in Dorsetshire, in ferm under the king (*Madox*, i. 335), he was summoned to perform military service against the Scots in 28 Edward I.

Nothing is told of his legal life before he was raised to the bench of the Common Pleas, where he sat for above seventeen years, from 1292 to 1309. (*Serviens ad Legem*, 282; *Dugdale's Orig.* 44.) During this period he seems to have been very actively employed. Sir William Wallace was tried before him in 1304 (*Turner's England*, ii. 90, n.), and in 1307 he was selected as one of the justices of trailbaston for the home counties. He died about July 1310. (*Cal. Inquis.* p. m. i. 239.)

MALO LACU, or MAULEY, PETER DE, was great-grandson of Peter, a Poictevin, who, being esquire to King John, is said to have owed his fortunes to undertaking the murder of Prince Arthur; in reward for which act Isabel, the daughter of Robert de Turnham, was given to him in marriage, with all her rich possessions, principally in Yorkshire. He was the fourth baron in succession, and his father (also Peter) married Nichola, daughter of Gilbert de Gant, grandson of he Earl of Lincoln, and died about 7 Edward I., when he, then only three years of age, succeeded to his inheritance. (*Archæologia*, xxi. 209.)

He was engaged in the Welsh and Scottish wars under Edward I., and was summoned to parliament from the twenty-third year of that reign till his death. In 29 Edward I. he signed the barons' letter to the pope by the title of Dominus de Musgreve. In 1305 and 1307 he was placed at the head of the justices of trailbaston appointed for Lincolnshire, Yorkshire, and eight other counties. (*N. Fœdera*, i. 970; *Rot. Parl.* i. 188–218.)

He married Eleanor, daughter of Thomas Lord Furnival, and died in 3 Edward II., 1310, leaving his son Peter, who succeeded him. On the death of the seventh Peter in 1415 without issue, the barony fell into abeyance between his sisters. (*Baronage*, i. 733.)

MALTON, ROBERT, is only known as having been constituted a baron of the Exchequer on November 14, 1413, 1 Henry V., and re-appointed at the commencement of the following reign. (*Cal. Rot. Pat.* 262, 269.)

MALUS CATULUS, ROGER, was one of the chaplains of Richard I., and is mentioned by Hoveden as his vice-chancellor in 1191. He accompanied the king on his voyage to the Holy Land, and two charters given under his hand are extant, dated on March 27 and April 3 in that year, at Messina. (*Rymer*, i. 53; *Monast.* v. 565.) In the lamentable shipwreck which occurred in the following May off the island of Cyprus he was drowned; and the king's Seal, which is stated to have been suspended round his neck, was lost with him. Richard converted this accident into an expedient to raise money, by proclaiming that no grants under it should be deemed valid, and thus compelling the holders of them to pay the fines a second time, for a confirmation under the new Seal. (*Madox*, i. 77.)

Burke, in his 'Dictionary of Landed Gentry' (nom. Machell), makes him the great-grandson of Halthe Malus Catulus, son of 'Catulus de Castro Catulino,' in Westmoreland, and younger son of William Malchael, or Malus Catulus, of Crackenthorpe. The present family of Machell of Beverley trace their descent from his elder brother John.

MANCHESTER, EARL OF. *See* E. MONTAGU; H. MONTAGU.

MANDEVILLE, GEOFFREY DE (EARL OF ESSEX), whose name is corrupted from Magnaville, a town in Normandy belonging to his ancestors, was the second Earl of Essex after the Conquest. His great-grandfather, of the same name, was one of the companions of the Conqueror in his expedition against England, and was rewarded with many broad lands and lordships, of which no less than one hundred and nineteen are noted in Domesday Book. Besides these, the Conqueror granted him the custody of the Tower of London, with the hereditary sheriffalty of London and Middlesex and Hertfordshire. His son William succeeded him, and married Margaret, the sole daughter of Eudo the Dapifer, by whom he had a son, named Geoffrey, who was steward of Normandy by descent of his mother. King Stephen raised him to the dignity of Earl of Essex, but the Empress Maud won him over to her party by a still more ample charter, confirming to him all the rights and honours and lands which any of his ancestors had held, and making to him most extensive grants. His future prowess was disgraced by so many savage outrages that, although he had founded the abbey of Walden in Essex, and had made several gifts for pious uses, he was excommunicated; and being in 1144 mortally wounded in battle, the rights of sepulture were refused to his body until some years afterwards, when, his absolution being obtained, it was buried in the porch of the Temple Church, where his monumental effigy is still preserved. By his wife, Rohese, the daughter of Alberic de Vere, Earl of Oxford, he had Geoffrey, the subject of the present notice.

Henry II. created him Earl of Essex, restoring to him all the lands of his family, and employing him both in the council and the field.

He and Richard de Luci were sent in 1166-7 as justices itinerant to hear criminal and common pleas throughout England; and they were also entrusted with the expedition against the Welsh, during which the earl fell sick at Chester, and died there on October 21, 1167. He was buried in the abbey of Walden. Leaving no children, he was succeeded by his brother, the next-mentioned William. (*Madox*, i. 49, 28, ii. 138, 164; *Dugdale's Baron.* i. 201.)

MANDEVILLE, WILLIAM DE (EARL OF ALBEMARLE AND ESSEX), was the brother of the above Geoffrey Earl of Essex, on whose death he succeeded to that title. He had spent the chief part of his youth with Philip Earl of Flanders, whom he afterwards assisted in his wars with the French king. On his attaining the earldom he was welcomed with distinction by King Henry, whom he accompanied into France in 1173, as one of the generals of his army, and was not only marked for his military prowess, but was entrusted by his sovereign with many businesses of nicety and confidence.

In 1177 he joined his patron, the Earl of Flanders, in his expedition to the Holy Land, and, after spending two years there with no diminution of his fame, he returned to England in 1179. In the following year the king bestowed on him the hand of Hawise, the only daughter of William le Gros, Earl of Albemarle, recently deceased, together with the property and the earldom, by which title he was afterwards usually known. During the remainder of the reign, besides being sent on an embassy to the emperor, he was employed in the various wars in France, both for King Henry and the Earl of Flanders; and the French king had good cause to regret that the one had so powerful an ally, and the other so valiant a general.

On Henry's death, the merits of the earl were not overlooked by his successor. When Ranulph de Glanville retired shortly afterwards from the chief justiciaryship, King Richard appointed the earl to that important office, in conjunction with Hugh Pusar, the aged Bishop of Durham. This appointment was made at the council of Pipewell, on September 15, 1189; but he was not destined long to enjoy the dignity of his new office, for two months afterwards he died at Rouen in Normandy, before Richard had commenced his progress.

Dugdale gives an account of his works of devotional benevolence to various houses, and of his sole foundation of the monastery at Stoneley in Huntingdonshire. But he adds a blundering statement of his marriage with a second wife, Christian, daughter to Robert Lord Fitz-Walter, who, he says, survived him, and afterwards married Raymond de Burgh; having in a previous page stated that his wife Hawise, *after his death*, married William de Fortibus, who, as her first husband died childless, became Earl of Albemarle in her right. (*Dugdale's Baron.* i. 63, 204; *Lord Lyttelton*, iii. 399, 441, 449.)

MANNERS, LORD. See T. M. SUTTON.

MANSEL, JOHN, is said to have been the grandson of Philip de Mansel, who came in with the Conqueror, and the son of Henry, the eldest of Philip's five sons. (*Weever*, 273; *Burke*.) It would seem, from a letter written by the king in 1262 to the college of cardinals, that he was brought up at court, for the king says that he was 'sub alis nostris educatus, cujus ingenium, mores, et merita, ab adolescentiâ suâ probavimus.' (*Rymer*, i. 414.)

He is first noticed in a close writ, dated July 5, 1234, 18 Henry III., commanding Hugh de Pateshull, the treasurer, to admit his beloved clerk John Mansel to reside at the exchequer of receipt in his place, and to have one roll of the said receipt. (*Madox*, ii. 51.) As Mansel's office appears to have been a new one, it was probably that of chancellor of the Exchequer, which is first spoken of by name a few years afterwards.

He is noted for one of the greatest pluralists that were ever known. Being already one of the royal chaplains, he was in 1242 presented to a prebend in St. Paul's, and was advanced in the next year to the chancellorship of that church, to which stalls in the cathedrals of Wells and Chichester were in a short time added. These were grants by the king, to whom his activity of mind and capacity for business made him peculiarly useful in the straitened circumstances of the royal revenue. He was accordingly soon engaged in confidential and honourable employments, to which he was partly recommended by having received a dangerous wound in an attack on a besieged castle. (*Leland's Coll.* i. 266.)

He had the custody of the Great Seal from November 8, 1246, to August 28, 1247, on which day the king sent him on an embassy to foreign parts. On his return he received back the custody of the Seal on August 10, 1248, and held it till September 8, 1249. In none of these entries is he called chancellor.

During this second possession of the Great Seal he obtained the valuable appointment of provost of Beverley, which was the highest clerical dignity he ever enjoyed. The extent of his yearly income from the various benefices he held is probably greatly exaggerated. Some assert that the number amounted to 700, producing 18,000 marks per annum; while others limit the number to 300, and the annual produce to 4000 marks. The munificence of his expenditure may be judged from the stately dinner he gave in 1256 at his house in Tothill Fields, when he entertained the Kings and Queens of England and Scotland, Prince Edward, and the nobles and prelates of the kingdom. It is recorded that his guests were so numerous that he was compelled to erect tents for their reception, and that seven hundred dishes were scarcely sufficient for the first course. (*Stow's London*, 525.)

In 1253 he accompanied William Bitton, Bishop of Bath and Wells, on a special mission to Spain to negotiate a marriage between Eleanor, the sister of Alphonso, King of Castile, with Prince Edward, King Henry's eldest son; and the charter which they brought back is still preserved with its golden seal among the archives at Westminster. In his commission for this embassy he is called 'secretarius noster,' being the first occasion on which that title is used.

Fabyan (*Chron.* 340–343) says that in 1257 he was 'made knyte and chefe iustyce of Englande,' and that under that name, in the June following, he was one of the twelve peers appointed by the parliament at Oxford to correct the enormities that had crept into the government. He adds that he was thereupon discharged of his office, and Sir Hugh Bygot admitted in his place. There is, however, no reasonable ground for believing that he ever was appointed chief justiciary, and the title is never added to his signatures or his description at the period.

When the barons compelled the king at Oxford, in 1258, to consent to the appointment of twenty-four of their number to draw up articles for the government of the realm, John Mansel was one of the twelve selected on the king's part, and he is charged with having urged the king to disregard the provisions then made, and with having procured the pope's dispensation from the oath he had taken to keep them. During the conflict that followed he firmly adhered to his royal master, and was entrusted with the command of the Tower of London. About the same time he again held the Great Seal for a short period, accompanying the king abroad with it in July 1262, and resigning it on October 10 following. (*Hardy's Cat.*)

The period of his prosperity was now drawing to its close. When the Earl of Leicester, in 1263, took up arms, his first attacks were directed against the king's favourites, and the principal of these was John Mansel, whose estates were accordingly plundered and property wasted. He retired with the king to the Tower of London, and thence accompanied Prince Edmund, the king's younger son, to Dover; and about the end of June, finding himself unsafe in England, he hastily fled from the kingdom. Although he was present in the following January at Amiens, when the King of France decided in favour of Henry (*Chron. Rishanger*, 12, 17, 118), he did not venture to return to the English court, and his career is said to have terminated in poverty and wretchedness. The date of his death is stated by some to have been 1264, by others 1268, but it seems to have been even beyond the latter date, as he is named as one of the executors of King Henry's will, dated in June 1269. (*Rymer*, i. 496.) The place of his death has never been recorded.

Whatever may be considered of his clerical or political character, it is clear that upon an emergency he could act the part of a brave and resolute soldier. In 1253 he founded the priory of Bilsington, near Romney, and amply endowed it. (*Monast.* vi. 492.)

A wife, with issue, has been given to him, which as an ecclesiastic is not very probable. The confusion may have arisen from there having been another John Mansel at the period.

MANSFIELD, EARL OF. *See* W. MURRAY.

MANSFIELD, JAMES. Under the act for the regulation of attorneys (st. 2 Geo. II. c. 23), the father of Sir James Mansfield, who was an attorney practising at Ringwood in Hampshire, is entered on the roll in November 1730 as John James Manfield. It has been a question when the name was altered to Mansfield, and what was the motive. The Ringwood attorney was the son of a gentleman who came to England with one of the Georges, and held an appointment in Windsor Castle; and it was asserted that the attorney thought it more advantageous to him to Anglicise his name by calling himself Mansfield. But it is clear that he had not formed this determination in 1730, when he was in practice. Neither had he done so up to 1754, when his son was nominated a fellow of King's College, Cambridge, under the name of Manfield. But on the latter taking his degree of B.A. in 1755 he signed his name Mansfield. By this date the imputation, which has prevailed, that he made the alteration with the hope of being supposed to be connected with the great lord chief justice, entirely falls to the ground, inasmuch as Sir William Murray did not receive the title of Lord Mansfield till the end of the following year, November 1756.

He entered the society of the Middle Temple under that name in February 1755, and was called to the bar in November 1758. He began to practise in the common law courts, but ultimately removed into Chancery, where he was very successful. In 1768 he was one of the counsel for John Wilkes on his application to be admitted to bail; and four years after, in Michaelmas 1772, he was made king's counsel. His university appointed him their counsel, and returned him as their representative to the parliament of 1774. On the trial of the Duchess of Kingston for bigamy in 1776 he appeared for the defendant, when, though he failed in procuring her acquittal, he succeeded in obtaining her release without any punishment at all.

In September of 1780 he accepted the solicitor-generalship, and while in office was engaged in the prosecution of those concerned in the riots of 1780, and in that of Lord George Gordon he had the disadvantage of replying to the splendid speech of Mr. Erskine for the prisoner, resulting in an acquittal. The same duty devolved upon him on the trial of De la Motte for high treason, whose palpable guilt insured a conviction. On the defeat of Lord North's ministry in March 1782 Mr. Mansfield was necessarily superseded, and immediately placed himself in the ranks of the opposition. Soon after the constitution of the Coalition Ministry Mr. Mansfield was again appointed solicitor-general, in November 1783, but was fated to be again removed in less than a month, the Coalition having in its turn succumbed to the ministry of Mr. Pitt. (*Parl. Hist.* xxi. 193, xxiii. 9; *State Trials*, xxi. 621, 794.)

In the new parliament called in the following May, Mr. Mansfield had the mortification of surrendering his seat for the university of Cambridge to the popular minister, and never afterwards entered the house. He remained unemployed for nearly sixteen years, when in 1799 he was constituted chief justice of Chester. Five years afterwards, at the close of Mr. Addington's administration, he succeeded Lord Alvanley as chief justice of the Common Pleas, in April 1804, and was thereupon knighted. The motto on his rings on his necessarily taking the degree of a serjeant alludes humorously to his long exclusion: 'Serus in coelum redeas.'

Though a good average lawyer, his promotion occurred rather too late in life; and, though anxious to dispense justice in the cases that came before him, he was too apt to give way to the irritation of the moment. Of this deficiency of temper the serjeants were not backward in taking advantage; and towards the end of his career they worried him to such a degree that he could not always refrain from venting in audible whispers curses against his tormentors. So great was the annoyance that he resigned his post in Hilary vacation 1814.

He lived nearly eight years afterwards, and died on November 23, 1821.

MANTELL, ROBERT, was for twelve years from 16 Henry II., 1170, sheriff of the united counties of Essex and Hertford. In 1173 and the six following years he acted as a justice itinerant, not only in those counties, but also in eight others; and his name appears as one of the justiciers in the Curia Regis in 1177. Besides these duties, he seems likewise to have been employed as a justice of the forest in 17 and 18 Henry II., and again in 1 Richard I.

His parentage is not recorded, but in 1184 his son Matthew came before the Exchequer as his 'future heir,' and acknowledged that he had no claim to a certain field called Holm. (*Madox*, i. 94–701, ii. 134; *Pipe Roll*, 79.)

MANWOOD, ROGER, was the grandson of Roger Manwood, twice mayor of Sandwich, and its representative in parliament in 1523; one of whose sons, Thomas, was a draper in the town, and by his wife Catherine, the daughter of John Gallaway, of Clare in Norfolk, was the father of three sons, of whom this Roger was the second. He was born at Sandwich in 1525, and was educated in a grammar school there. No account is given of any further place of study till he was entered at the Inner Temple. He was called to the bar by that society before 1555, when he was appointed steward or recorder of his native town, and was elected its representative in that and the following parliament in Mary's reign, and in all those of Queen Elizabeth, till he was elevated to the judicial bench.

In his progress towards that advancement he seems to have owed much to the popularity of his manners and a happy choice of friends. He was evidently a favourite among his brethren of the Inner Temple, since he was selected at Christmas 1561 as one of the chief officers in the grand revel then held there, over which Lord Robert Dudley, afterwards Earl of Leicester, presided under the title of Palaphilos. Curiously enough, the *rôle* which Manwood then performed was that which, eighteen years later, he was called upon actually to fill—that of chief baron of the Exchequer. In Lent 1565 he attained the degree of reader. (*Dugdale's Orig.* 150, 165.)

At this period of his life he testified his gratitude for the favours he was receiving from the town of his birth by establishing and liberally endowing a free school there, which was incorporated in 1563, and still exists under his name. In 1566 he resigned his office of recorder, but still continued the principal adviser of the corporation, receiving an annual salary of 3*l.*, which, according to the corporation papers, would appear to have been paid to him even after he had attained his highest preferment. He held also the office of steward of the Chancery and Admiralty Court at Dover.

Among his friends was Sir Thomas Gresham, who took great interest in his success; through whose recommendation he probably received the grant of the house and park in the queen's manor of Hawe in the parish of Hackington, near Canterbury, where he then resided, and also in 1567 the degree of serjeant. The profits and privileges of the coif were so great that when an opening occurred for his elevation to the bench, in April 1572, he again employed Gresham's influence with the minister to avert it. (*Burgon's Gresham,* ii. 175, 478.)

The serjeant, however, saw reason to change his inclination, on another vacancy in the same court, which soon after occurred, for on October 14 he received his patent as justice of the Common Pleas. He does not seem the most merciful of judges, for in a letter to Sir Walter Mildmay, dated November 18, 1577, he recommends either imprisonment for life, or the cutting off part of his tongue, as the punishment to be awarded to a man who persisted in speaking ill of the queen, after having suffered the pillory and had his ears cut off. (*Cal. State Papers* [1547–80], 566.)

He was promoted to the chief seat in the Exchequer on November 17, 1578, and knighted. There is no doubt that he was a man of great activity and energy, both of which were shown in his exertions towards upholding Rochester Bridge, and regulating the estates which had been originally devoted to its repair. He built also a new House of Correction in Westgate Street, Canterbury, and erected seven almshouses in St. Stephen's or Hackington. All these works he had performed before he arrived at the post of chief baron; so that it is not surprising that he should have been looked upon with favour by the court as a man peculiarly fitted for his position. But, as a set-off to these good qualities, he was ambitious and arbitrary, and somewhat regardless of the means by which he obtained the objects on which he had set his heart.

On the death of Sir James Dyer, in March 1582, the chief baron was suspected of offering a large bribe to be appointed to the vacant office of chief justice of the Common Pleas; and this, being privately communicated by Recorder Fleetwood to Lord Burleigh, 'was the means of keeping him from that cushion,' and no doubt rendered the lord treasurer less inclined to doubt the charges that were subsequently brought against him. One of these was that on a barbarous murder being committed in the streets of Canterbury, the chief baron had expressed a solemn determination to pursue the murderer to justice, but, instead of this, he procured him a free pardon, after which the murderer paraded the streets in the chief baron's livery. It was imputed to the chief baron that this impunity was purchased by the payment of 240*l.* by the murderer's father, a rich brewer there. Numerous charges of oppression, of more or less weight, were made from time to time by various persons in Kent.

In the meantime, however, he was one of the commissioners for the trial of the Queen of Scots, but does not appear to have taken any active part in the proceedings. In those against Secretary Davison, which were consequent upon her execution, he made himself more conspicuous. After going through the whole history of Queen Mary, he came at last to the offence of the unfortunate secretary, which, making the same evasive distinction as the other commissioners, he termed ' a misprision because you prevented the time in doing it before you were commanded, although the thing were lawful; for you did *justum,* but not *juste.*' (*State Trials,* i. 1167, 1235.)

From various letters addressed by him to the lord treasurer, preserved among the Harleian MSS., it is evident that frequent complaints were made against him which he was called upon to justify; and by one, in May 1591, it appears that he was under the queen's displeasure for taking money for a place in his gift, and that he brought forward as his warranty the example of other judges, his contemporaries, who had pursued the same course. In addition to these public attacks, private suits had been commenced against him, and some of the complainants had succeeded in their causes. In a letter to Lord Burleigh on April 13,

1592, he speaks of the lord treasurer's bitterness against him in a recent interview, and, assuming a high hand, demands that upon any future complaints of his adversaries his goods may not be taken 'without due course of justice in some of her majesty's public courts,' meaning that he was not to be called upon to answer before the lords of the council. Burleigh, however, thought differently, probably considering that the conduct of a public officer was a fit subject of investigation. The chief baron was forthwith restricted to his own house in Great St. Bartholomew's, and within a month after his former letter he humbled himself in another, and two days afterwards, on May 14, he signed at Greenwich an abject submission to answer all complaints before their 'honourable lordships.'

What was the result of these proceedings does not appear, but his presence in court is not again mentioned by the reporters, and it is not improbable that the grief and anxiety he suffered from his disgrace hastened his decease, which occurred on the 14th of the following December.

Notwithstanding the blots in his escutcheon, it is clear (so curious is the mixture of which mortality is compounded) that he was pious and charitable according to the fashion of the times, and in many respects a kind-hearted man. The foundation during his life of a school for the young and a hospital for the aged speak strongly in his favour; and to these may be added his erection of the south aisle of the church of St. Stephen, and his liberal augmentation of the vicarage of the parish by a grant of the great tithes, subject only to a fixed payment of 10l. a year to the archdeacon of Canterbury. From his will (a tedious and somewhat vainglorious document) we learn that he erected during his life the superb monument still remaining in the church, which is ornamented with his bust in his robes as chief baron, and with small figures of his two wives and of his children.

His first wife was Dorothy, the daughter of John Theobald, Esq., of Shepey in Kent, and widow first of Dr. John Crooke, and next of Ralph Allen, alderman of London. By her he left a son Peter, whose family failed in 1653. His second wife was Elizabeth, daughter of Mr. John Copinger, of Allhallows, near Rochester, and widow of John Wilkins, of Stoke Parsonage. (*Holinshed*, iv. 550; *Hasted*, ix. 46, 52; *Boys's Sandwich*.)

MAP, WALTER, more commonly though erroneously called Mapes, the facetious poet and satirist, was one of the justices itinerant in 19 Henry II., 1173, joined with John Cumin and Turstin Fitz-Simon in setting the assize for the king's demesnes in Gloucestershire (*Madox*, i. 701), in which county he held the living of Westbury. He was probably omitted in future years, because he always insisted on adding to the accustomed oath required to be taken by his colleagues and himself, that they would administer right to every one, an exception against the Jews and white monks. His hostility against the latter originated, according to Giraldus, in the encroachments made by the Cistercians of Newenham on the rights and property of his church of Westbury, and was exhibited against the whole order in various Latin compositions, both in prose and verse, highly humorous and severe. None of them, however, remain, those which have been preserved being of a more general character.

He was born on the Marches of Wales, probably in the county of Pembroke; but of his parents he states nothing, except that they had rendered important services to King Henry both before and after his accession to the throne. He studied at Paris, and attended the school of Gerard la Pucelle, who lectured there about 1160. Distinguished as well by his wit and learning as by his courtly manners, he became on his return a favourite of the king, and he repeats conversations he had with Becket before he was made archbishop in 1162. He was employed by the king in missions to the courts of France and Rome, and at the latter he was selected by Pope Alexander III. to examine and argue with the deputies of the then rising sect of the Waldenses. With these proofs of the consideration in which he was held, he received substantial marks of the royal favour. Besides several smaller ecclesiastical preferments, he held at various periods canonries in the churches of Salisbury and St. Paul's, was precentor of Lincoln, and ultimately archdeacon of Oxford, to which he was advanced about the year 1196. He was alive in 9 John, 1207, as in that year the custodes of the abbey of Eynsham were ordered to pay him his accustomed rent of five marks per annum from that abbey (*Rot. Claus.* 106); but he certainly died before Giraldus Cambrensis wrote the preface to his 'Hibernia Expugnata,' which was dedicated to King John.

Some of his writings, which were composed in short rhyming verse, were so popular in his day that the copies of them were greatly multiplied, and any effusions which were remarkable for their wit and sprightliness were attributed to his pen. Among the numerous compositions which go under his name, it is difficult to ascertain with certainty how many he really wrote. In the introduction to the Collection of Poems attributed to him, published by the Camden Society, Mr. Wright gives satisfactory proof that several of those which appeared under the name of 'Golias Episcopus' were written by Map, and that Golias was no real person, but a mere fanciful appellation given to the burlesque representative of the ecclesiastical order, and the instrument of holding up to ridicule the vices of the Romish Church. The jovial character of some of these poems has caused him to be considered as a toper, but there is no other evidence to support such an imputation; and the drinking-song which is ascribed to him, commencing

Meum est propositum in taberna mori,

is a compilation of a much later period, from the 'Confessio Goliæ,' containing a mock confession of his three vices, of which one was his love of wine.

His prose works are a treatise 'De Nugis Curialium,' and a tract entitled 'Valerius ad Rufinum de non ducenda Uxore,' the former of which has been printed by the Camden Society. (*Biog. Brit. Liter. by Thomas Wright*, ii. 295.)

MARA, HENRY DE, or DE LA MARE, was raised to the judicial bench before June 1248, 32 Henry III., as in that month writs were paid for to have assizes held before him. These continued till 1256, but his name does not occur upon fines, except in Michaelmas 1251. (*Excerpt. e Rot. Fin.* ii. 36, &c.; *Dugdale's Orig.* 42.) In 38 Henry III. the castle and manor of Marlborough were committed to him. (*Abb. Rot. Orig.* i. 13.) He died in 1257. (*Excerpt. e Rot. Fin.* ii. 257.)

MARCHIA, WILLIAM DE (BISHOP OF BATH AND WELLS), though called keeper by Sir T. Hardy, because the Great Seal was delivered to him on February 24, 1290, 18 Edward I., by Bishop Burnel the chancellor, was then merely an officer of the wardrobe, the usual place for depositing the Seal, and had been a clerk there five years before. He was promoted to the office of treasurer at the end of the same year (*Madox*, ii. 323), and on the death of Burnel he was elected his successor in the bishopric of Bath and Wells on January 30, 1293, being a canon of the latter cathedral at the time. After sitting there for nearly ten years, during several of which he continued treasurer, he died on June 11, 1302, and was buried at Wells. So great were his virtues, and so many were the miracles reported to have been performed at his tomb, that the pope was vehemently urged to canonise him. His merits, however, were not deemed worthy of that honour. (*Godwin*, 374.)

MARESCHALL, WILLIAM (EARL OF PEMBROKE), holds a prominent place in history. He flourished in four reigns, during three of which he was high in the royal confidence, and acted with unshaken loyalty. He was the grandson of Gilbert, and the second son of John, who held the office of marshal of the court (magistratum marisc. curiæ nostræ), the former under Henry I., and the latter under Henry II. (*Dugdale's Baron.* i. 599.) By the death of his elder brother without issue, at the end of Richard's reign, William succeeded to the office of marshal, which was confirmed to him in 1 John. (*Rot. Chart.* 46, 47.)

He was surety for King Richard that he would meet the king of France at Easter to proceed to the Holy Land (*R. de Wendover*, iii. 1249), and was the first named of the council then appointed to assist the chief justiciary in governing the kingdom during the king's absence on that enterprise. (*Madox*, i. 34.) At that time he was one of the justiciers, and fines were levied before him in 5 and 10 Richard I. (*Hunter's Preface.*)

King Richard, however, showed him a greater mark of favour by giving him in marriage Isabella, daughter and heir of Richard Strongbow, Earl of Pembroke, or, as it was sometimes called, Strigul (Chepstow), where the chief residence was, by which he not only acquired the title, but became possessed of all the large inheritance of the late earl, both in England and Ireland. He held the sheriffalties of Lincoln and of Sussex during part of this reign.

On the death of Richard I., John, being then in Normandy, sent William Mareschall to England with Hubert, Archbishop of Canterbury, to pave the way for him; when they and Geoffrey Fitz-Peter, the chief justiciary, called together the nobles and others at Northampton, and induced them to promise him their oaths of fealty. During that turbulent reign he was a strenuous supporter of his sovereign, and, from his being witness to charters and other documents from the beginning to the end of it, seems to have been in constant attendance on the king, except when engaged in the active services confided to him. In 1201 he was with the king in Normandy, and in 1209 in Ireland, where he was left as lord deputy, and in 1214 he was one of those bound for the king to make compensation to the clergy, and acted for him in the council held at London, becoming surety, with the Archbishop of Canterbury and the Bishop of Ely, that the king would satisfy the barons. In the following April he was sent to the barons to know what were the laws and liberties they asked for, and was afterwards the messenger to announce the king's readiness to comply with their demands. He was accordingly present at the great day of Runnymede, when Magna Charta was signed. (*R. de Wendover*, iii. 137, 283–302.)

During John's reign he was entrusted with the sheriffalties of Gloucestershire, Sussex, and Surrey, and with the custody of the castles of Carmarthen, Cardigan, and Goher. The king was not deficient in generosity to him, rewarding him with grants of

Goderich Castle in Herefordshire, and of the whole province of Leinster, besides several others of minor importance. The Great Roll of 16 John contains a singular example of the mode in which royal influence was purchased and exercised: Roger Fitz-Nicholas fined in all the lampreys he could get to have the king's request to Earl William Mareschall that he would grant him the manor of Laugeford, at ferm. (*Madox*, i. 481.)

In 1212 Prince Henry had been specially committed to his care (*Rot. Pat.* 95), and on John's death he was at once appointed 'rector regis et regni,' and lost no time in procuring Henry's coronation at Gloucester. All the first mandates issued in the king's name were sealed with the earl's seal, because the king then had none.

Dugdale inserts his name as chief justiciary at the beginning of this reign, but this is a mistake. He held the higher rank of guardian of the royal person and regent of the kingdom; while the office of chief justiciary, which had gradually lost much of the power originally attached to it, was manifestly filled by Hubert de Burgh, Earl of Essex, as it had been during the last years of the reign of John.

No person could have been chosen more competent to contend with the critical position in which the affairs of the kingdom were then placed. By the skill of his arrangements and the activity of his movements he defeated the invading prince, intercepted and destroyed the French fleet sent to his aid, and compelled him to sue for peace and abandon his enterprise; by his moderation he induced most of the discontented barons to submit to the royal authority; and by his energy in punishing those few who still resisted he compelled the respect that was due to the sovereign power, and in less than two years restored to the kingdom, which had so long suffered from civil contentions, the blessing of internal peace.

One of his first acts was to confirm the Great Charter of John, introducing some improvements and omitting those clauses which trenched too deeply on the royal prerogative.

Unfortunately for his country and his sovereign, this great man did not long survive to enjoy the fruits of his exertions. He died in 1219, at his manor of Caversham, near Reading, and was buried on May 16, Ascension-day, in the church of the New Temple, in London, where his monumental effigy still remains.

His pious benefactions were numerous and munificent. He founded the priory of Cartmel in Lancashire; of Kilrush in Ireland, as a cell to Cartmel; of St. Augustine at Kilkenny; and for Knights Hospitallers at Logh-Garmon in Wexford; besides many rich donations to other houses.

Dugdale (*Baronage*, i. 63, 601) gives him a second wife in Alice, the daughter of Baldwin de Betun, Earl of Albemarle, in 5 John, an assertion which he also makes in his account of the latter earl. He, however, contradicts himself in a following page by stating that an abbey which he had commenced for Cistercian monks, in the land of Dowysken in Ireland, was completed by his wife Isabel, according to the appointment of his will. The roll which Dugdale quotes shows his carelessness, and proves that Alice de Betun's husband was not the earl, but William, his son. (*Rot. Chart.* 112.)

He left five sons, who successively held the earldom, but dying all without issue, the inheritance descended among the heirs of his five daughters. (*N. Triveti Annales*, 205.)

MARESCHALL, JOHN, was the great-grandson of Gilbert, marshal of Henry I., and nephew to the above William Earl of Pembroke. Early in the reign of King John he was connected with the court, several documents being countersigned with his name, and the castle of Falaise being committed to his keeping in 4 John. In the next year he proceeded to Ireland to take the stewardship of his uncle's lands and castles in Leinster; and in 9 John he obtained the grant of the office of Marshal of Ireland, the duties of which he was afterwards permitted to perform by deputy (*Rot. de Liberate*, 46; *Rot. Pat.* 24, 42, 155; *Rot. Chart.* 173; *Rot. Claus.* i. 407); and he was with the king in that country in 12 and 14 John. (*Rot. de Præstito*, 192, 233, 235; *Rot. Misæ*, 240.) In the latter year the custody of the castles of Whitchurch and Screward in Shropshire was entrusted to him, to which was added, in the next year, the guardianship of the Marches of Wales, and also the sheriffalty of the county of Lincoln. He held the latter office in Norfolk and Suffolk in 17 John for a short time, and also in Dorset, Somerset, and Worcester (*Rot. Pat.* 100–193), with the charge of the castles of all these counties.

In the next reign he was not less active under the protectorate of his uncle, the Earl of Pembroke. He not only joined the army for the relief of Lincoln, but was united with Philip de Albini in the command of the fleet which intercepted and destroyed the French armament in August 1217 (*R. de Wendover*, iv. 19, 28), and thus forced the retirement of Prince Louis from the kingdom. He was then made sheriff of Hampshire and constable of the castle of Devizes, and in 2 Henry III. was appointed chief justice of the forests (*Rot. Claus.* i. 407), which he held for several years. In 3 Henry III. he acted as a justice itinerant in Lincoln, Nottinghamshire, and Derby, and is mentioned as taking the acknowledgment of a fine in 12 Henry III.

During the remainder of his life he was employed in various embassies for the king, whose favour he retained till his death, which occurred about June 1235. (*Excerpt. e Rot. Fin.* i. 284.)

His wife was Alina, one of the daughters and heirs of Hubert de Rie, by whom he left a son John, in whose descendants the barony remained for four generations, when the last baron, John, died in 10 Edward II. without issue.

MARESCHALL, WILLIAM LE, was the second son of the above John Mareschall, and succeeded on the death of his brother in 1242 to the family property. (*Excerpt. e Rot. Fin.* i. 284, 387, 391.) During the troubles under Henry III. he was appointed by the council one of the barons of the Exchequer in 1264; but, adhering to the fortunes of Simon de Montfort, he forfeited his lands both at Haselberg and Norton in Northamptonshire, and died about that time. (*Madox*, ii. 56, 120.)

MARISCO, RICHARD DE (BISHOP OF DURHAM), of whose early history no trace remains, held a subordinate office in the Exchequer in 8 Richard I., 1197. (*Madox*, i. 714.) In 9 John, 1207, he is specially mentioned as a clerk in the Chamber of the Exchequer, and numerous entries on the Close, Patent, and other Rolls show also his frequent attendance on the person of the king. (*Rot. Pat.* 74, 81, &c.; *Rot. de Præstito*, 177, &c.)

He received the ecclesiastical preferments with which the clerks of the court were usually rewarded, among which were prebends in Ely and York, and the archdeaconries of Northumberland and Richmond, besides several livings. In 1212 he was appointed sheriff of Dorset and Somerset, and was gratified with a royal present of one of three ships which had been captured. (*Rot. Pat.* 95; *Rot. Claus.* i. 118.) In 14 John, 1212, he was one of the justiciers before whom fines were levied at Westminster, and is mentioned as 'residens ad Scaccarium.' (*Rot. Claus.* i. 132.) Dugdale introduces him as chancellor in the same year; but this is clearly an error, the Patent and Close Rolls of 15 John containing merely an entry that on October 9, 1213, he delivered the Seal to the king at Ospringe (*Rot. Pat.* 102; *Rot. Claus.* i. 153); but this entry proves nothing more than that he was the messenger by whom the Seal was delivered into the royal hands. The fact was that Walter de Grey, the chancellor, was then about to proceed on an embassy to Flanders; and Marisco, as an officer of the Chamber of the Exchequer, where the Seal was commonly deposited, was naturally employed to convey it to the king.

Prynne gives a charter dated October 3, 1213, subscribed 'Data per manum Ric. de Marisco;' but if this is to be taken as a proof that he was chancellor at that time, the same argument would be equally conclusive for the three preceding years, during which there are numerous charters authenticated by him in the same manner. Not only is it well known that Walter de Grey was then chancellor, but upon the same evidence there would be many competitors. Neither they, however, nor Richard de Marisco, can be regarded as anything more than the official persons who, under the chancellor, took their turns of adding the formal authentication to those instruments. It was not till the following year, on the ultimate resignation of Walter de Grey, that he became chancellor, and the day of his appointment may be collected from the Charter Rolls. On October 28, 1214, he subscribed a charter simply with his name, as he had invariably done before; but to a charter on the following day he added 'Cancellarii Domini Regis' (*Rot. Chart.* 202), and so signed himself on every future occasion. He was therefore installed in the office either on the 28th or 29th October 1214. From this time till the end of the reign he continued chancellor.

On the accession of Henry III. he was continued in the office, from which he was not removed during the remainder of his life. In the third year of the reign he was placed at the head of the justices itinerant in Yorkshire and Northumberland, and he is mentioned as chancellor on the Close Roll as late as June 15, 1225, 9 Henry III. (*Rot. Claus.* i. 313, 403, ii. 73.)

In 1 Henry III. he was raised to the bishopric of Durham, which had been vacant for nearly nine years. He is called 'our beloved chancellor, Master Richard de Marisco, elect of Durham,' on a record dated June 29, 1217 (*Rot. Claus.* i. 326), so that he was not consecrated till after that date.

During his rule of his great diocese he is said to have exhibited such profuse prodigality as to have excited the fear of the monks that he would waste their property as well as that of the church. Encroaching upon their privileges, they retaliated by charging him before the pope, not merely with the minor offences of extravagance and waste, but with the crimes of perjury, simony, sacrilege, adultery, and blood. He was obliged to proceed to Rome to meet the charges, and there is a record that shows he was absent from England in January 1221. (*Excerpt. e Rot. Fin.* i. 59.) It is alleged that he softened the pontiff by his presents, and induced him so to protract the contest that, in fact, no sentence was pronounced while he lived. Before his death, however, he restored to the monks the rights and liberties of which he had deprived them, and gave some churches for their benefit. (*Angl. Sac.* i. 732.)

The annoyance occasioned by these litigations was increased by the disrespect with which he was treated by Ralph de Neville, dean of Lichfield, who was employed as his deputy in the duties of the Chancery, and was evidently attempting to supersede him in his office. A letter is extant among the public records, in which Richard de Marisco reprimands the dean for suppressing his title of chancellor in some letters he had addressed to him. (5 *Report Pub. Rec.*, App. ii. 66.)

His death was very sudden. Travelling to London to attend a legantine council, he stopped for one night at the monastery of Peterborough, and was found dead in his bed on the following morning. This occurred on May 1, 1226. His body was removed to Durham, where it was buried in the cathedral. (*Godwin*, 739.)

MARKHAM, JOHN, of Sedgebrook in Lincolnshire, whose ancestors were settled at a village so called in Nottinghamshire, was the son of Robert Markham, a serjeant-at-law in the reign of Edward III., by a daughter of Sir John Caunton, knight. He is said to have received his legal education at Gray's Inn, and became a king's serjeant in 1390, 14 Richard II. On July 7, 1396, he was raised to the bench of the Common Pleas. From that time fines were levied before him till February 1408, 9 Henry IV. (*Dugdale's Orig.* 46.) He was united with Chief Justice Thirning in the commission to announce to Richard II. his deposition from the throne; but he left the distressing duty to be performed by Thirning alone, adding no words of his own to that judge's address. (*Rot. Parl.* iii. 338, 424, 609.)

It is almost useless to notice that Markham has been mentioned as the judge who committed Prince Henry to prison. (*Tyler's Henry V.* i. 370.) The tale is sufficiently confuted by the fact that he sat in the Common Pleas, and that he never was chief justice of either court.

He retired from the bench before his death, and by his monument in Markham Church it appears that he died on December 31, 1409.

He was twice married. His first wife was Elizabeth, the daughter of Sir John, and sister and coheir of Sir Hugh Cressy. From their son Robert descended Dr. William Markham, Archbishop of York. The judge's second wife was Milicent, widow of Sir Nicholas Burdon, and daughter and coheir of Sir John Bekeringe. She is stated by Thoroton (*Notts*, i. 341, iii. 230, 417), and other authorities to be the mother, by him, of the next-noticed Sir John Markham; but a case in the Year Book (12 *Henry IV.* fo. 2), which was a writ of dower brought by her in the year after Judge Markham's death, distinctly states the defendant John to be son and heir of the judge by Elizabeth, his former wife. (*Wotton's Baronet.* ii. 330; *Paine's Parish of Blyth*, 135.)

MARKHAM, JOHN, the son of the above-mentioned John Markham by either his first or his second wife, must have been very young at the time of his father's death in 1409. He probably studied the law at Gray's Inn, and first appears in the Year Books as an advocate in 1430, 9 Henry VI. In Easter 1440 he was called to the degree of the coif; and within four years, having been in the interim employed in the king's service as one of his serjeants, he was raised to the judicial seat in the King's Bench, on February 6, 1444. He steadily performed the duties of this place during the seventeen remaining years of the reign; and there is no appearance of his having taken any active part in the civil contest which then troubled the kingdom.

On May 13, 1461, the next term after the accession of Edward IV., he was appointed chief justice of his court, his long service and high legal attainments, rather than any political reason, pointing him out as a proper successor to the place. He presided in the court with the highest reputation for nearly eight years, when he was superseded on January 23, 1469. The cause of his removal is thus stated by Fuller (*Worthies*, ii. 207):—'It happened that Sir Thomas Cooke, late lord mayor of London, one of vast wealth, was cast beforehand at the court (where the Lord Rivers and the rest of the queen's kindred had pre-devoured his estate), and was only, for formality's sake, to be condemned in Guildhall by extraordinary commissioners in Oyer and Terminer, whereof Sir John Markham was not the meanest. The fact for which he was arraigned was for lending money to Margaret, the wife of Henry VI. This he denied, and the single testimony of one Hawkins, tortured on the rack, was produced against him. Judge Markham directed the jury (as it was his place, and no partiality in point of law to do) to find it only misprision of treason; whereby Sir Thomas saved his *lands*, though heavily fined, and *life*, though long imprisoned.' Fabian and Holinshed tell the story of the prosecution, but without naming the judge. Stow, however, in his 'Annals,' supplies the deficiency.

He popularly acquired the title of the 'upright judge,' naturally given to one who was supposed to have suffered for conscience' sake; but we have other evidence to show that his character continued to be esteemed and his authority quoted in after-ages. Sir Nicholas Throgmorton, on his trial in 1554, said to his judges, 'As to the said alledged four precedents against me, I have recited as many for me; and I would you, my lord chief justice, should incline your judgments rather after the example of your honourable predecessors, Justice Markham and others, which did eschew corrupt judgments, judging directly and sincerely after the law and the principles in the same, than after such men as, swerving from the truth, the maxim, and the law, did judge corruptly, maliciously, and affectionately.' (*State Trials*, i. 894.)

The discarded, but not disgraced, judge retired to his seat in Lincolnshire, called Sedgebrook Hall, and there in piety and devotion spent the remainder of his life, which terminated in 1479. (*Cal. Inquis.* p. m. iv. 395.) He was buried in the church there.

By his wife Margaret, daughter and co-heir of Sir Simon Leke, of Cotham in Nottinghamshire, he had a son Thomas, one of whose descendants was created a baronet in 1642, but the title became extinct in 1779. (*Wotton's Baronet.* ii. 330.)

MARLBOROUGH, EARL OF. *See* J. LEY.

MARMION, ROBERT, was son and grandson to two barons bearing the same names. The grandfather was a Norman, and received from William the Conqueror the castle of Tamworth in Warwickshire. The father succeeded to this and to other property, among which were the strong castle of Fontney in Normandy, and the manor of Scrivelsby in Lincolnshire, which was held by grand serjeanty to perform the office of champion at the king's coronation. This second Robert was killed at Coventry, by falling into one of the ditches he had made to entrap the Earl of Chester's forces in 8 Stephen, 1143, when this, the third Robert, his son by his wife Milicent, must have been quite an infant.

He is first mentioned on the Great Roll of 14 Henry II., 1169, with a charge for the aid on marrying the king's daughter (*Madox*, i. 574); but it is not till towards the latter end of the reign that he is mentioned in connection with the court. He was then entrusted with the sheriffalty of Worcestershire, an office which he continued to hold in the first year of Richard's reign.

In 1184 he was one of the justiciers present on the passing of a fine, and was a justice itinerant in the thirty-third year, and on several occasions during the reign of Richard. In 6 John, 1204, also he was one of the justiciers before whom fines were levied in the country. (*Madox*, i. 503, 591, 698.)

He accompanied King Richard into Normandy in the sixth year of his reign, and joined in the expedition into Poictou in 15 John. To the Knights Templars he was a benefactor, by giving them a mill at Barston in Warwickshire.

His death occurred before May 15, 1218,

2 Henry III. (*Excerpt. e Rot. Fin.* i. 9.) His first wife was Matilda, the daughter of William de Beauchamp; and his second wife was named Philippa; and by both he had issue. The male branch failed about the reign of Edward III.; but a daughter, to whom the manor of Scrivelsby fell, marrying Sir John Dymoke, the right of acting as champion at the royal coronation is still preserved to the representative of that family.

MARSH, RALPH DE, as abbot of Croyland, stands at the head of the justices itinerant who were commissioned in 56 Henry III., 1272, into the county of Leicester, but never appears afterwards in a judicial character. He had been a monk there, and was raised to the abbacy about October 1254. He died on Michaelmas-day 1281. (*Browne Willis.*)

MARTIN, SAMUEL, one of the present barons of the Exchequer, is of Irish extraction, being the second son of the late Samuel Martin, Esq., of Calmore in the county of Londonderry, and of Arabella his wife. Born on September 23, 1801, he received his education at Trinity College, Dublin, where he graduated as Bachelor of Arts in 1821, and was admitted to the degree of D.C.L. at a later period of his life.

He at first, in May 1821, entered as a student at Gray's Inn, but in December 1826 he transferred himself to the Middle Temple, by which society he was called to the bar on January 29, 1830. In the interim he had practised for two years as a special pleader—a plan wisely adopted as an excellent introduction to the abstruser parts of the science. With the experience thus obtained he joined the Northern Circuit with great advantage, and soon reaped the harvest which resulted from his previous reputation. In thirteen years he acquired such a lead on circuit and in London as to entitle him to a silk gown, which was given to him in 1843; and after seven years more, in which he enjoyed a large share of important business in the courts, he was promoted to the bench of the Exchequer in November 1850, when he was knighted. For the three previous years he had represented Pontefract in parliament.

In 1838 the baron married Frances, the eldest daughter of Sir Frederick Pollock, afterwards lord chief baron.

MARTIN, WILLIAM, was of a family commencing with a Norman knight named Martin de Tours, who acquired the lordship of Camoys in the county of Pembroke, and founded there the monastery of St. Dogmaels. He was the sixth baron, and aided Edward I. in his expeditions against Scotland. He signed the barons' letter to the pope, under the title of Dominus de Camesio. When the justices of trailbaston were appointed, on April 6, 1305, he was placed at the head of those sent into Cornwall and nine other counties, and so again in February 1307. His clemency and kindness to the poor during these commissions are commemorated in a Norman song of the age. Both before and after this time he is mentioned as acting in a judicial capacity, as well in civil as in criminal pleas. (*Rot. Parl.* i. 188, 196, 218; *Wright's Pol. Songs*, 231.) In 4 Edward II. a writ of enquiry was addressed to him, and in 9 Edward II. he was justice of South Wales. (*Abb. Placit.* 312; 1 *Report Pub. Rec.* 101.)

On his death, which occurred in 1325, he left, by his wife Eleanor, daughter of William de Mohun, a son William, who died childless, and two daughters, among the representatives of whom the barony is in abeyance. (*Baronage*, i. 729.)

MARTYN, JOHN, son of Richard Martyn, of Stonebridge in Kent, and Anna, daughter of John Boteler, of Graveney, Esq., is first mentioned in the Year Books of 8 Henry IV., from which time he seems to have been in considerable practice. He was summoned no less than three times to take upon himself the degree of serjeant-at-law, and on each occasion he disobeyed the summons. Several other apprentices of the law having been guilty of the same neglect, the parliament of November 1417 took the matter up, and commanded them under a heavy penalty to comply with the requisition, which they did in the following Trinity Term. (*Rot. Parl.* iv. 107.) He had not worn the coif long before he was raised to the bench of the Common Pleas. His patent is not recorded, but the first fine levied before him was in 8 Henry V., 1420, and the last was in 15 Henry VI., 1436. He died on October 24 in that year, and was buried in Graveney Church, where his gravestone is of a very large size, richly inlaid with brass, and having the figures of himself and his wife represented upon it. (*Hasted*, ii. vi. vii.; *Weever*, 282.)

MASERES, FRANCIS, held the office of cursitor baron of the Exchequer for above fifty years, a period longer than any other judge has retained his place. This venerable man died 'in harness' in the ninety-third year of his age, and to the last persevered in wearing the costume of the reign in which he was born. No part of his long life was wasted in idleness, and his numerous works, legal, political, scientific, and literary, prove that the whole of it was profitably employed.

He was of a French family, which settled here on the revocation of the Edict of Nantes. His grandfather was a colonel in the army of William III., and his father was a physician, resident in Rathbone Place, which the baron afterwards occupied. He was born on December 15, 1731, and after receiving the elements of his education at a school at Kingston-upon-Thames, he became a member of Clare Hall, Cambridge. He took his degree of B.A. in 1752 as fourth wrangler and senior chancellor's medallist, and proceeded M.A. in 1755, obtaining a fellowship of his college.

He was called to the bar by the Temple, and was then elected one of the common pleaders of the city of London, and joined the Western Circuit. Of the extent of his forensic practice there is little record, beyond the fact of his being present in 1764 at the trial of Mr. Webb, the solicitor of the Treasury, for perjury connected with the proceedings on the general warrants, a note of which he supplied to the editor of the 'State Trials' (xix. 1172). He was sent out as attorney-general of Quebec, where, during the American contest, he distinguished himself by his loyalty. On his return to England he was, in August 1773, appointed cursitor baron of the Exchequer, the duties of which were so slight that he added to them those attached to the deputy recordership of London in 1779, and of senior judge of the Sheriff's Court in 1780. The former of these two appointments he resigned in 1783, but the latter he retained till 1822.

By his scientific and antiquarian knowledge he was infinitely more conspicuous than in his legal attainments; though that in the latter he was by no means deficient is shown by his 'Treatise on the Power of Juries in Cases of Libel' (1792), his 'Essay on the British Constitution' (1772), and various other works. He was elected a fellow of the Royal Society in 1771, and was also a fellow of the Society of Antiquaries; contributing many learned papers to the 'Philosophical Transactions' of the former, and to the 'Archæologia' of the latter. In other branches—historical, political, and theological—his publications were numerous.

Better than all, his memory is without stain; and when he died at Reigate on May 19, 1824, his character for urbanity, integrity, and liberality was gracefully recorded in an elegant Latin inscription on a monument in the church, erected by his friend Dr. Fellows. He showed his attachment to the Church of England by endowing a Sunday afternoon sermon at Reigate. (*Gent. Mag.* xciv. (1), 569.)

MAUCLERK, WALTER (BISHOP OF CARLISLE), was one of King John's chaplains, and was rewarded with the presentation to various churches. (*Rot. Pat.* 14, 74, 93, 103.) He was employed in various ways by the king, being in 6 John one of the bailiffs of the county of Lincoln; in 14 John he acted in the Exchequer in Ireland (*Ibid.* 47, 95); and in 16 John he was sent as an ambassador to Rome to urge the royal complaints against the barons. A letter of his while engaged in this mission is extant in Rymer's 'Fœdera' (i. 120).

In 3 Henry III. he was one of the justices itinerant into the counties of Lincoln, Nottingham, and Derby, and in 5 Henry III. was a justice of the forest. He next was sheriff of Cumberland and constable of Carlisle, offices which he held for several years. In August 1223 he was elected Bishop of Carlisle, and was several times sent on special embassies abroad (*Rot. Claus.* i. 387–652, ii. 11–212), till in July 1232 he was raised to the office of treasurer. By the instigation, however, of Peter de Rupibus, Bishop of Winchester, he was in the next year ejected from his office, fined one hundred pounds of silver, and deprived of various possessions which had been previously granted to him. His intention to appeal to Rome was frustrated by his being stopped at Dover at the moment of embarkation, with such violence that Roger, Bishop of London, immediately excommunicated the officers who had impeded him, and boldly repeated the sentence before the king. (*R. de Wendover*, iv. 264, 272.) The bishop afterwards recovered the royal favour, and was not only appointed catechist to Prince Edward, but in 1246, when the king went into Gascony, he and William de Cantilupe were united with Walter de Grey, the Archbishop of York, in the government of the kingdom during the royal absence. He resigned his bishopric on June 29, 1246, and took the habit of a preaching friar at Oxford, where he remained till his death, on October 28, 1248. (*Godwin*, 763.)

MAULE, WILLIAM HENRY, was born on April 25, 1788, at Edmonton in Middlesex. His father was a medical practitioner there, and his mother was the daughter of one of the family of Rawson of Leeds. In October 1806 he entered Trinity College, Cambridge, where he pursued both his mathematical and classical studies with such avidity and success that on taking his degree of B.A. in 1810 he came out as senior wrangler, and in October 1811 was elected fellow. In the science of mathematics he was not only an extraordinary proficient, but an original inventor in some of its branches. His friend Mr. Babbage acknowledges the assistance he received from his suggestions, and speaks of his wonderful powers and acuteness. So high was his reputation in this respect that he was offered the professorship of mathematics at Haileybury College, but, having chosen the law as his profession, he declined it.

He entered Lincoln's Inn and was called to the bar in 1814, joining the Oxford and the Welsh Circuits. He had acquired the same mastery over law as he possessed over the other branches of learning; added to which he had fluency of language, fertility of illustration, and many of the powers by which barristers succeed, together with an infinite deal of humour and wit. Yet, notwithstanding these advantages, his advance in the profession was of slow growth, the principal cause of which was such a fear of appearing to conciliate clients that he drove them away by the brusqueness of his address. But his soundness as a lawyer and ingenuity as a disputant gradually made their way, and he by degrees obtained a considerable footing both in the provinces and the metropolis. In the city particularly, from his great excellence in commercial law and on questions of marine insurance, he had full and profitable employment.

With some reluctance and misgiving he accepted a silk gown in Easter 1833, and soon after he was appointed counsel to the Bank of England. Distinguishing himself greatly in the conduct of the Carlow county election in 1835, he was invited to represent the borough of Carlow in 1837, and after a severe contest and subsequent petition succeeded. He took his place in the House of Commons on the liberal side, and, short as his career in parliament was, he gave promise of being a most successful debater. But in March 1839 he was raised to the bench of the Exchequer, from which he was removed to the Common Pleas in the following November.

During the sixteen years that he sat in that court he displayed all the qualities of an excellent judge, his distinguishing characteristic being practical common sense and great ingenuity in defeating mere technicalities. His judgments were remarkable for their striking observation, their pithy power, and happy illustrations. At Nisi Prius he was strictly impartial, patient, and courteous, enlivening the court frequently with that peculiar irony which was natural to him. In trying prisoners the exercise of the latter faculty sometimes bewildered the jury, and led them by mistaking his intention to deliver a verdict just the reverse of what he recommended.

So frequent were his attacks of illness that he was obliged to resign in June 1855, but was immediately placed on the privy council and added to its judicial committee. He was an effective member of it for the remainder of his life, which terminated rather suddenly on January 16, 1858.

In his social circle he was remarkable for pleasantry and humour, for kindliness of disposition, and for cordiality of friendship. Like all men of intellect, he was an admirer of real genius, and his greatest aversion was against pert pretence and ignorant conceit. Some of his caustic but playful epigrams in Latin and French are directed against them. His powers of conversation were very great, and his memory retained all the facetiæ he had ever read, while the *mots* that he uttered were a never-failing source of mirth in Westminster Hall. He died unmarried.

MAULEY. See P. DE MALO LACU.

MAURICE (BISHOP OF LONDON) was at the time of the Conquest one of William's chaplains, and so continued until he was appointed Bishop of London in 1083 or 1085, according to different authorities.

He is generally named as the first chancellor of King William, and Dugdale (*Orig.* 34) quotes a charter of confirmation to Westminster Abbey, dated 1087, which he witnesses as 'Regis Cancellarius.' That document, however, on examination, is found to be a forgery; and no other record of that period, with his name as chancellor, having been found, his appointment must be removed to a later date. The earliest that occurs is William's charter confirming the deed by which William de Warenne and Gundreda his wife gave the priory of Lewes to the monastery of Cluny (*Archæologia*, xxxii. 123), and this was granted about 1078. His name is also attached to the king's decision of the controversy between Arfastus, Bishop of Thetford, and the Abbot of Bury, which was pronounced in the year 1081 (*Monast*. iii. 141), and to a charter granted to the abbey of Karilephus in 1082 (*Ibid*. vi. 993), in the latter of which he is styled 'Cenomanensis Ecclesiæ Archidiaconus.'

His retirement from the chancellorship took place shortly afterwards, possibly on his election to the bishopric of London, if it occurred in 1083, but certainly before 1085, as his successor, William Welson, was himself raised to the episcopal bench in that year.

The private character of Maurice does not seem to have stood very high, although the grounds on which it is slightingly mentioned are not named. But after his elevation to the bishopric of London he is universally praised for the liberality and zeal with which he devoted himself to the re-edification of the cathedral of St. Paul, when it was destroyed by the fire that consumed the greatest part of London in 1086. He laid foundations so vast in extent that his contemporaries would not believe that the pile could ever be completed, nor was it till some time after his death, although he applied himself diligently and energetically to the work during the remainder of his life.

That Maurice, on the death of the Conqueror, did not side with his eldest son Robert, appears from his attending the first court of William II. at Christmas 1087, and crowning Henry I. in 1100. He died on September 26, 1107. (*Stow's London*, 35, 61; *Godwin*, 175; *Madox*, i. 7, 8; *Ellis's Introd. to Domesday Book*.)

MAY, RICHARD, was the fourth son of John May, of Rawmere in Sussex, Esq. This John was brother to Sir Humphrey May, who held many valuable places under James I. and Charles I., from the latter of whom he had a grant of the office of master of the Rolls in reversion after the death of Sir Julius Cæsar, whom however he did not survive. Richard's mother was Eliza Hill, daughter of a merchant in London. He was admitted into the Middle Temple in January 1632, and was one of the performers in Davenant's masque of the 'Triumphs of Prince d'Amour,' represented before Charles, the Elector Palatine, in 1635. Though called to the bar in May 1639, we hear nothing further of him till the Restoration. Having then been elected recorder of Chichester, he was chosen member for that city in 1673, and was re-elected in 1679. The honour of knighthood was conferred upon him in May 1681, on presenting an address thanking the king for his declaration on the dissolution; and on March 17, 1683, he became cursitor baron of the Exchequer. He was again returned for Chichester in 1685, to the only parliament called by James II., before the termination of whose reign he died. (*Hay's Chichester; Athen. Oxon.* iii. 807; *Luttrell*, i. 91, 557.)

MAYNARD, JOHN. In the history of Sir John Maynard we have the remarkable instance of a man not only raised to the judicial bench, but placed on its highest seat as first commissioner of the Great Seal at the age of eighty-seven years; a sufficient explanation of which may be found by considering the political necessity of the time of his appointment in connection with the political status he held in the preceding reigns.

Born at Tavistock in 1602, he was the son of Alexander Maynard, a gentleman of that town, who was probably a barrister also, from his being described of the Middle Temple in his son's admission to that inn in 1619. In the next year he took the degree of B.A. at Oxford, and is stated by Anthony Wood in his 'Athenæ' (iv. 292) to have been of Exeter College, but in his 'Fasti' (i. 386) of Queen's College. He was returned for Chippenham to the first parliament of Charles I. in 1625, while yet a student of the law; and we find him speaking in opposition to the subsidies demanded. This parliament lasted but nine months, and he does not appear in those of 1626 or 1628. In November 1626 he was called to the bar, and got into such early practice as to be reported by Croke two years after, from which time his business rapidly increased, his intelligence and ability having attracted the attention and gained the friendship of Attorney-General Noy, which greatly assisted his advancement. (*Parl. Hist.* ii. 32.)

In the parliaments of April and November 1640 he was returned for Totnes. In both he had for his colleague the future chief justice Oliver St. John, with whom he was added to the committee to manage the impeachment of the Earl of Strafford, and opened one of the charges against him. He was one of the managers also in the prosecution of Archbishop Laud, and in exposing the real grievances of the country he took a very active part, in conjunction with his friend and companion Edward Hyde, the future Earl of Clarendon, who (*Life*, i. 67) gives him the credit of conducting his opposition with less rancour and malice than his enterprising colleagues, and characterises him as of eminent parts and great learning out of his profession, and in it of signal reputation. In the course of the revolutionary proceedings contentions naturally arose between the temperate and violent members of the party, and Whitelocke and Maynard were called upon by Lord General Essex and the Scotch Commissioners to give the perilous counsel whether Cromwell could not be proceeded against as an incendiary. They so managed however as to escape the danger, and, though of the Presbyterian party, to make Cromwell their friend. At this time he was so popular an advocate that he gained 700*l.* in one circuit, a sum, Whitelocke says, larger than any barrister ever got before. In 1648 he was elected a bencher of his inn. (*Whitelocke*, 32–273; *Bramston*, 75.)

Against the motion made in that year that the parliament should make no more addresses to Charles, Maynard spoke forcibly but unsuccessfully; and on the subsequent debate on the famous remonstrance from the army demanding justice upon the king, he is described as arguing as if he had taken fees on both sides, one while magnifying the gallant deeds of the army, and then 'firking' them for their remonstrance, as tending to the destruction of the kingdom and the dissolution of the government. (*Clarendon's Reb.* v. 516; *Parl. Hist.* iii. 1128.) From this time he seems voluntarily to have seceded from the house, and to have taken no part in the violent measures that followed. Lord Campbell (*Chanc.* iv. 12) and Townsend (345) have erroneously confounded him with Sir John Maynard, K.B., member for Lostwithiel, and brother of the first Lord Maynard. Maynard was not summoned by Cromwell to the Barebone's Parliament in 1653, nor was he a member of that of 1654; but in Cromwell's third parliament of 1656 he was returned for the borough of Plymouth.

In the interval he pursued his profession with credit and success, and in state prosecutions he was engaged now for and now against the Commonwealth. In the case of Cony, who brought an action against a collector for violently seizing certain customs, Maynard argued showing the illegality of the seizure, whereupon Cromwell committed him to the Tower, and Ludlow unjustly abuses him for the submission he was necessitated to make before he was released, as if a continuance of resistance to irresponsible power would have been beneficial to his client or the country. It is clear, however, that Cromwell, though he thought it expedient to support his own impositions, felt no animosity against Maynard, whom he called to the degree of the coif in 1654, and made serjeant to the Commonwealth in May 1658. (*State Trials*, v. 348, 432; *Ludlow*, 223; *Whitelocke*, 673.)

The parliament that met in September 1656 was dissolved on February 4, 1658. The serjeant does not appear to have taken any part in the proposal to give the title of king to Cromwell; and he himself subsequently declared that he 'was not at the making of the petition and advice,' under which the Commonwealth was resettled, and the lord protector reconstituted. The few instances of his addressing the house were confined to questions of form, abstaining entirely from political subjects, except on the day of the dissolution, when he made an able speech in favour of calling the 'other house' the House of Lords. This no doubt was the cause of the protector's advancing him two months after to be one of his serjeants, in which character he walked in Cromwell's funeral procession in the following November. In Protector Richard's parliament, which sat only from January 27 to April 22, 1659, and was principally occupied in disputes relative to the protector's title and to the 'other house,' he was returned for Beeralston, for Camelford, and for Newton in the Isle of Wight, and elected to sit for the latter place. His language in speaking in favour of the Recognition Bill was manifestly contrived with a view to a future change. (*Burton*, ii. 184, 189, 458, 526, iii. 183, 322, 594.) On the termination of Richard's power, Maynard was wise enough not to take his seat at the first meeting of the Rump; but on its second renewal, and the appearance of Monk on the scene, he not only became one of the thirty-one members of the council of state, but was appointed to carry into effect a vote discharging the declaration previously required from the members, that they would be faithful to the Commonwealth, without a king or House of Lords; thus removing one of the greatest obstacles to the return of the king. (*Parl. Hist.* iii. 1583; *Mercurius Pol.* No. 609, March 1.)

This accommodation to the spirit of the times naturally led to his being confirmed at the Restoration in his degree of serjeant. It is said that he had also a judgeship offered, but that he refused the temptation.

So perfectly, however, did he make his peace with the new government that he was appointed in November 1660 one of the king's serjeants, and at the same time accepted the honour of knighthood. From this time Maynard acted the politic part of siding with the government. In the Convention Parliament, and all the parliaments during Charles's reign, in which he sat for either Exeter, Beeralston, or Plymouth, he cautiously avoided attaching himself to any of the extreme parties in the state. In most of the state trials he took his natural precedence as king's serjeant, and was the principal manager for the Commons in the impeachment of Lord Stafford. He was throughout a firm believer in the Popish Plot, and in the testimony of Oates and his infamous coadjutors, but had a convenient forgetfulness when called upon at Oates's trial to speak in his favour. (*Parl. Hist.* iv. 149, 162; *State Trials*, vii. 1298, x. 1162.)

At the commencement of the reign of James II. Maynard was in his eighty-third year, but still preserved his activity and his faculties. He represented Beeralston in the only parliament called by that king, and forcibly opposed the encroachments of the court. He refused to be employed for the crown in the prosecution of the bishops, but was present as one of the king's serjeants at the council called in June 1688 to prove the genuineness of the birth of the heir to the throne, which in six months was declared to be vacant. (*Parl. Hist.* iv. 1374; *Burnet*, iii. 39; *State Trials*, xii. 125.)

On the Prince of Orange's arrival in London and being welcomed by the peers, the prelates, and the people, the lawyers of course were not backward in their congratulations. Maynard was at their head; and on his great age being noticed by the prince made that solitary speech which has handed him down to the present day with the undisputed title of a wit. To the prince's observation 'that he had outlived all the men of law of his time,' he answered 'he had like to have outlived the law itself if his highness had not come over.' He was one of the lawyers called by the Peers to consult on the necessary proceedings to be taken, and in the convention or parliament summoned by the prince which met on January 22, 1689, he took his seat as member for Plymouth. He ably conducted the conference with the Lords on the question of the 'abdication,' and was a frequent speaker in the debate as to voting the convention a parliament. A difficulty having arisen as to filling the office of lord chancellor, which was declined both by the Earl of Nottingham and the Marquis of Halifax, it was determined to put the Great Seal into commission, and Sir John Maynard was selected as first commissioner on March 4, with Sir Anthony Keck and Sir William Rawlinson for his colleagues. Sir John did not thereby vacate his seat in the House of Commons, but mixed in the debates till the dissolution in January 1690, and also in the first session of the new parliament that met in the following March. His speeches were short, pithy, and effective, and showed little of the garrulity of age. Soon after the adjournment he resigned his place, and on the 9th of the following October closed his long-extended life, in the eighty-ninth year of his age, at Gunnersbury in the parish of Ealing in Middlesex, in the church of which he was buried. (*Burnet*, iii. 341; *Luttrell*, i. 490–506; *Parl. Hist.* v. 36–623.)

Of the character of a man who passed through so many convulsions opinions must be expected to vary according to the conflicting views of the actors in them; but in Maynard's early career we have seen two antagonistic writers, Whitelocke and Clarendon, agree in their good report of him. To the estimation of the latter he probably owed the favours he received at the Restoration—favours which he endeavoured to repay by speaking against the great chancellor's impeachment. Burnet speaks of him only as eminent in his profession; but Burnet's annotator, Dean Swift, stigmatises him as an old rogue, and a knave and fool with all his law. With Roger North, who perforce acknowledges his legal ascendency, of course he was no favourite. He used to call the law 'ars bablativa,' and delighted so much in his profession that he always carried one of the Year Books in his coach for his diversion, saying that it was as good to him as a comedy. His passion for law ruled him to such a degree that he left a will purposely worded so as to cause litigation, in order that sundry questions, which had been 'moot points' in his lifetime, might be settled for the benefit of posterity. Judge Jeffreys is said to have availed himself of the serjeant's legal knowledge; but one day, when Maynard was arguing against some judicial dictum, the coarse judge told him that 'he had grown so old as to forget his law.' 'Tis true, Sir George,' he retorted, 'I have forgotten more law than ever you knew.' (*Woolrych's Jeffreys*, 99; *Forsyth's Hortensius*, 431.)

The editor of Burton's Diary, and after him Lord Campbell, holds Maynard up to public censure for joining in the prosecution of Sir Harry Vane, condemned for acting, as he himself had done, under the authority of the Commonwealth. But if we are to accept the account in the State Trials as the true one, the charge is entirely without foundation, since Maynard's name does not appear in it. Looking at the whole of his career, though he was not chargeable with any extraordinary faults, neither was he distinguished by any high-minded or spirited actions. After his youthful ebullition of patriotism he subsided into a plodding lawyer, taking as little part in politics as he could, accommodating himself to all governments, and devoting himself with energy and industry to his profession; never deviating from the principles he professed, and now and then venting them; but cautious not to offend those in power, and anxious only to increase the amount of his fees and to retain the honours he had earned. If it be true that he refused a former offer of advancement, it cannot be supposed that he sought his last elevation, which he more probably submitted to as a necessity arising from the emergency. In short, though all must acknowledge him to have been a great lawyer, none can regard him as a great man.

He married three wives. The name of the first is not recorded; the second was Jane, daughter of Cheney Selherst, Esq., of Tenterden, and widow of Edward Austen, Esq.; and the third was a daughter of the Rev. Ambrose Upton, canon of Christchurch, and widow of Sir Charles Bermuden. (*Noble's Granger*, i. 172; *Gent. Mag.* lix. 585.)

MEADE, THOMAS, was the son of Thomas Meade, or Mede, of Elmdon in Essex. He spent some time at the university of Cambridge before he was placed at the Middle Temple, where he arrived at the grade of reader in 1562, and again in 1567. In the Easter of the latter year he was raised to the degree of the coif, and the date of his elevation to the judgeship of the Court of Common Pleas was on November 30, 1577, the first fine levied before him being in Hilary Term 1578. (*Dugdale's Orig.* 48, 217.) Having filled the seat about seven years and a half, he died in May 1585, and was buried at Elmdon under a rich monument. He left by his wife, Joane, the widow of — Clamp, of Huntingdon, three sons, whose descendants long flourished at Wendon Lofts in Essex. The learned divine Joseph Mede was of the same family. (*Morant*, ii. 593.)

MELLOR, JOHN, one of the present judges of the Queen's Bench, was born on January 1, 1809, at Hollinwood House in the borough of Oldham, where his family had been settled for many generations. His father belonged to the old mercantile firm of Gee, Mellor, Kershaw, & Co., well known in Lancashire above fifty years ago. Soon after the judge's birth the calls of business required his father to reside at Leicester, where he served the office of mayor and acted for many years as a magistrate, and where he at first sent his son to the grammar school. From this he was removed to the care of the Rev. Charles Berry, a learned and accomplished Unitarian minister at Leicester. The doctrines of his master did not shake his pupil's orthodoxy, while the controversy then carried on between the supporters of conflicting opinions, of which the advocate on the other side was the celebrated Robert Hall, naturally led him to a deeper consideration of the distinctions of religious belief, and of the foundations on which the different sects are based, than is usual for one so young. This produced in his mind an inveterate repugnance to the subscription to all dogmatic articles of religion, his impressions on the subject being confirmed and intensified by the strongly expressed remarks attributed to Lord Brougham.

With these impressions, though it was originally arranged that he should go to Lincoln College, Oxford, yet, as subscription to the Thirty-nine Articles was then required as a condition of admission, he felt himself compelled to forego the advantage to be derived from a university education. He accordingly continued his studies under Mr. Berry, and at the same time, being intended for the bar, obtained some instruction in the law of real property by entering the office of a conveyancing attorney in the town. He then became a student in the Inner Temple, and at the same time a pupil of the younger Mr. Chitty, who in eminence as a special pleader equalled his father; here he remained for four years, during which he attended the lectures given at University College by that eminent jurist John Austin. He was called to the bar on June 7, 1833, and in the same year married Elizabeth, only daughter of the late William Moseley, Esq., of Peckham Rye. Joining the Midland Circuit, he became a member of the Leicester borough and Warwick sessions, and acquired a considerable practice both in criminal and civil business. His readiness, if not his eloquence of address, his clear statement of facts and prompt application of the law to them, and particularly his skill in the examination of witnesses, soon established him in the courts and marked him for early promotion. In 1849 he became recorder of Warwick, which he resigned in 1852. In 1851 he had attained the rank of queen's counsel, and found no reason to regret the change, often injurious to many. In 1855 he received the appointment of recorder of Leicester, which he retained till he was elevated to the bench at Westminster.

In the meantime, after one unsuccessful contest at Warwick in 1852, and another at Coventry in 1857, he was elected in the latter year member of parliament for Great Yarmouth, and sat for it till the dissolution in 1859, when he contested Nottingham with success. Throughout his senatorial career he was an unflinching advocate of the liberal opinions to which he had been all along attached, and a firm supporter of Lord Palmerston's administrations, gaining the regard of both parties by his honourable bearing and his amiable and attractive manners.

On December 3, 1861, he was constituted a judge of the Queen's Bench, which he has ever since filled with general approbation. He then received the honour of knighthood.

He is the author of two most interesting lectures—one 'The Christian Church before the Reformation,' delivered at Leicester in 1857; and the other 'The Life and Times of John Selden,' delivered at Nottingham in 1859; both showing great liberality of sentiment, and that disregard of party and of class which, while it marks the impartiality of the man, is the best promise of excellence in the judge.

MELTON, WILLIAM DE (ARCHBISHOP OF YORK), is supposed to have been a native of Melton in Holderness. In 28 Edward I., 1300, he was parson of the parish of Repham in Lincolnshire (*Cal. Inquis.* p. m. i. 165); and in the next year, under the title of 'our beloved clerk,' he was employed to pay the foot soldiers raised in Wales. (*Parl. Writs*, i. 359.) It appears probable, also, that he had been employed in the education of the king's son, who at this time was about sixteen years of age; for in the letter which that prince addressed to the pope on his behalf, in the third year of his reign, he uses these expressions: 'qui a nostræ ætatis primordiis nostris insistebat obsequiis.' (*N. Fœdera*, ii. 107.)

On the accession of the young king he was appointed comptroller of the royal wardrobe, and was afterwards advanced to be the keeper of that department. In the former character the Great Seal was delivered to him on January 21, 1308, to be carried abroad with the king, who was proceeding to France to marry Isabella, the daughter of Philip le Bel. Another seal was given to John de Langton, the chancellor, to be used in England, which, after the king's return, was in the following March carried to the Exchequer by William de Melton, then bearing the additional title of 'Secretarius Regis.' (*Madox*, i. 75.) Again, from May 11 to July 6, 1310, the Great Seal was placed in the wardrobe, under the seals of Melton and two of the clerks of the Chancery. The king's confidence in him is apparent, from numerous royal mandates, countersigned 'nunciante W. de Melton,' from his being employed on an embassy to France, and from his being raised to the office of keeper of the wardrobe.

During this time ecclesiastical honours flowed rapidly upon him. He was made a canon of York, dean of St. Martin's, London, archdeacon of Barnstaple, provost of Beverley, and was elected Archbishop of York on January 21, 1316, but was obliged to wait more than two years for his consecration, notwithstanding the king's numerous and urgent applications to the pope. (*Godwin*, 685.)

On July 3, 1325, 18 Edward II., he was constituted treasurer of the Exchequer; but, as the king's friend, was displaced on the transfer of the crown to his son in January 1327. During the troubles in the previous year his chapel was broken into, and his episcopal ornaments, including his pall, were stolen; and messengers were sent to the pope with the king's request for a new one. (*N. Fœdera*, ii. 624.)

The new government, however, showed no illwill to the archbishop. On the contrary, in 1 Edward III. they employed him also in treating for peace with the Scots. (*Ibid.* ii. 797.) In 4 Edward III. he was indicted as an adherent of the Earl of Kent, and, being fully acquitted, obtained a writ of conspiracy against his accusers. (*Rot. Parl.* ii. 31, 54.) That his accusation was not credited appears from his restoration to the treasurership in the same year. This office he held from November 28, 1330, to April 1, 1331; and on August 10, 1333, he was appointed sole keeper of the Great Seal during the temporary absence of John de Stratford, the chancellor. He acted in that character till January 13, when he delivered up the Seal by the king's direction. It would seem that his removal was occasioned by his having confirmed and consecrated Robert de Graystanes as Bishop of Durham, without first obtaining the king's approval, for on March 30 following there is an entry of a grant of the royal pardon to the archbishop for that offence. (*N. Fœdera*, ii. 882.)

He lived for five years more, and died at Cawood on April 22, 1340, after presiding over his province for about four-and-twenty years, and expending considerable sums on his cathedral, in which his remains were deposited. The character that is given to him speaks as highly of his private as of his public life, representing him as pious, charitable, lenient, and hospitable in the former, and zealous, faithful, and energetic in the latter.

MERES, ROGER DE, was of a Lincolnshire family, established at Kirketon in the district of Holland. He was appointed one of the king's serjeants in 40 Edward III. On November 27, 1371, he was raised to the bench of the Common Pleas; but there is no record of any fines being levied before a judge of that name, nor of his attending the parliament beyond November in the next year.

There are, however, some circumstances

which raise a suspicion that this Roger de Meres was the same with Roger de Kirketon, and that he used both names indifferently. We know that he had property at Kirketon, and it was quite a common practice for a man to call himself after his estate. The name of Meres does not at all occur in the Year Book, which is somewhat extraordinary for one who was clearly a serjeant; but that of Kirketon is continually introduced, and the period within which the latter is mentioned not only tallies with the career of Meres, but notices him as serjeant in the right year, and terminates at the precise date required—viz., Trinity Term, 45 Edward III., 1371. Meres was constituted a justice of the Common Pleas on November 27 following; and Dugdale, while he records no fines as levied before him, introduces Kirketon, without giving the date of his appointment, from a fine acknowledged before him in February 1372.

The name of Roger de Meres appears as a trier of petitions in the parliament of that year, and then stops; but in the next and following parliaments of the reign Roger de Kirketon is named instead of him. (*Rot. Parl.* ii. 309, 317.)

Roger de Kirketon is not mentioned as a serjeant or in any other way in the Issue Roll of 44 Edward III., while payments are made to Roger de Meres, both as a serjeant and a judge of assize. The death of Roger de Meres is not noticed among the inquisitions post mortem, while that of Roger de Kirketon is in 9 Richard II. And lastly, in 15 Richard II., John de Meres, apparently the son, in the inquisition on his death, has the addition of 'de Kirketon' to his name, while a subsequent page (iii. 75, 142, 165) notices a Robert de Meres de Soterton, affording positive proof that the name of Kirketon was sometimes used, and, by the fact of two families of the same name existing in Lincolnshire, sufficiently accounting for the assumption by one of them of the name of his estate. As the question, however, is disputable, they are treated separately as two individuals, leaving it to the curious to pursue the investigation.

MERLAY, ROGER DE, was the son and heir of a Northumberland baron of the same name, who died in 34 Henry II., by Alice de Stuteville his wife. The manor and castle of Morpeth formed part of his possessions, for which he procured a market and fair. In 12 John he accompanied the king to Ireland (*Rot. de Præstito*, 221), but afterwards joined the barons against him, whereupon his castle and lands were seized and given to Philip de Ulecot. On the accession of Henry III. he joined those who returned to their allegiance, and recovered his possessions. He acted as one of the lords of the Marches between England and Scotland, and assisted the king in the siege of the castle of Bedford in 8 Henry III. (*Rot. Claus.* i. 246–616.)

He twice was appointed a justice itinerant—first in 9 Henry III., 1225, for Northumberland, and in the next year for Cumberland. (*Ibid.* ii. 77, 151.)

He died in 1239, and was buried in the abbey of Newminster, founded by his grandfather. His son, also named Roger, died in 1266, without male issue. (*Baronage*, i. 570.)

MERSTON, HENRY, before he was a baron of the Exchequer was an officer in that department. In 5 Henry IV. an entry occurs of his paying certain moneys to John Earl of Somerset, captain of Calais. (*Devon's Issue Roll*, 298.) Three years afterwards he was raised to the bench of the Exchequer, where he continued during the rest of the reign, and was re-appointed by Henry V. (*Cal. Rot. Pat.* 252, 260.) How much longer he kept his place is uncertain; but he was not named as a baron on the accession of Henry VI. He belonged, like most of his brethren, to the clerical profession, and was one of the executors of the king's son Thomas Duke of Clarence. (*Test. Vetust.* 194.)

MERTON, WALTER DE (BISHOP OF ROCHESTER). This eminent benefactor to learning was born at Merton in Surrey. His father was William de Merton, archdeacon of Berks, and his mother, Christina, the daughter of Walter Fitz-Oliver, of Basingstoke. He was educated in the convent of Merton, and became one of the clerks in Chancery, with some other place in the court. As was usual with those officers, he received various ecclesiastical preferments, among which were prebends in St. Paul's, Exeter, and Salisbury.

Several records show that the Great Seal was temporarily placed in his hands, no doubt as one of the clerks in Chancery, on May 7, 1258, and on March 14 and July 6, 1259.

But on July 5, 1261, the king, without reference to the assumed authority of the barons, appointed him chancellor. In the two following years there are several letters among the public records addressed to him in that character, and one from the king, thanking him and Philip Basset for their attention to his affairs. (4 & 5 *Report Pub. Rec.*) He was superseded on July 12, 1263, by his predecessor, Nicholas de Ely.

That he was not reinstated in the following year, when the king triumphed at Evesham, arose, probably, from his being then actively engaged in the foundation of the college which has made his name familiar from that time to the present. It would appear, however, that he acted as a justicier, as there is an entry of a payment made for an assize to be held before him on December 10, 1271. (*Excerpt. e Rot. Fin.* ii. 555.)

On the death of Henry III., in November 1272, King Edward being then absent in the Holy Land, the council selected Merton to fill the office of chancellor. A document on the Close Roll, dated on the 29th, is attested by him in that character. (*Fœdera*, i. 498.) That King Edward approved of the choice is evidenced by a letter he addressed 'to his beloved clerk and chancellor, Walter de Merton,' on August 9 following, from Mellune-super-Skeneham, thanking him for his zeal, and exhorting him to continue to discharge the duties of the office. (6 *Report Pub. Rec., App.* ii. 89.)

About July 20, 1274, he was elected Bishop of Rochester, and resigned the chancellorship on September 21 following. After presiding over his see little more than three years, he was drowned in crossing the Medway on October 27, 1277, and was buried in Rochester Cathedral. The marble tomb under which he was placed was taken down in 1598, and an elegant monument erected in its place, by Sir Henry Savile, the warden, and the fellows of Merton College, with an appropriate inscription.

Previously to his founding the college which bears his name he had commenced one at Maldon, near Merton; but, altering his intention he began his erection at Oxford, and removed to it the warden and priests of the former. Merton College is the most ancient establishment of that nature, and was incorporated by three charters, all of which are preserved among its archives. The first is dated January 7, 1264, 48 Henry III.; the second in 1270; and the third in 1274, 2 Edward I. The regulations by which it was governed were esteemed so wise that its charters were consulted as precedents on the foundation of Peterhouse, the earliest college in the sister university. (*Godwin*, 530.)

MERVIN, EDMUND, the second son of Walter Mervin, Esq., of Fonthill in Wiltshire, by Mary, daughter of John Mountpenson, Esq., of Bathanton Welley in the same county, received his legal education in the Middle Temple, where he was elected reader in 1523, and again in 1530, and was raised to the degree of the coif in 1531. King Henry, in 1539, made him one of his serjeants, and on November 23, 1540, constituted him a judge of the King's Bench. Little is told of him by the reporters, either as an advocate or a judge, but he was continued in his seat on the accession of Edward VI., and is frequently named in that reign in the criminal proceedings which have been preserved in the 'Baga de Secretis.' Though Dugdale does not introduce him as a judge under Queen Mary, it is evident that she continued him in his place, as he is one of the special commissioners named for the trial of Sir Andrew Dudley and others for high treason on August 18, 1553. (4 *Report Pub. Rec., App.* ii. 218–235.)

It may be inferred, therefore, that he was in no way concerned in the attempt to change the succession of the crown. He was probably ill at the time, and died very shortly afterwards. (*Dyer's Reports*, 113.) He married Elizabeth, daughter of Sir Edmund Pakenham.

MESSENDEN, ROGER DE, was a chaplain of the king, and was presented by him to the church of Colchyrch in London. (*Abb. Placit.* 130, 139.) He was raised to the bench in or before 51 Henry III., 1267, at Midsummer, in which year fines were levied before him. Although none occur of a subsequent date, he is mentioned as one of the justices of the bench before whom Robert de Coleville apologised for an assault on Robert de Fulham, justice of the Jews, in Michaelmas Term in 1268. No writs were taken for assizes to be held before him after that date. (*Excerpt. e Rot. Fin.* ii. 463–479; *Madox*, i. 236.)

METINGHAM, JOHN DE, was born at a village so called in Suffolk. In 3 Edward I., 1275, he is mentioned as one of the king's serjeants, and in 1276 he was constituted a judge of the King's Bench, and his name frequently occurs as acting in the court and on the circuits.

In the sweeping exposure of the corruption of the bench made by King Edward in 1289, the only two who were found pure in the administration of justice were John de Metingham and Elias de Beckingham. Both the chief justices were disgraced, and Metingham in Hilary Term 1290 was raised to the head of the Common Pleas, where he presided till his death in 1301. Among the benefactors of the university of Cambridge, prayer is directed to be made ' pro animâ Lñi John de Metyngham.' He wrote a treatise called 'Judicium Essoniorum.' (*Dugdale's Oriy.* 44, 57; *Rot. Parl.* i. 6–99; *Madox*, ii. 25; *Suckling's Suffolk*, i. 172.)

MIDDLETON, ADAM DE, the possessor of the manor of that name in the county of York in 33 Edward I., 1305, was the last named of five justices of trailbaston appointed for the ten northern counties (*N. Fœdera*, i. 970), and again in 1307. In 5 Edward II. the custody of the castle of Kingston-upon-Hull and of the manor of Mitton was committed to him (*Abb. Rot. Orig.* i. 187); and by a mandate to attend the parliament in 1313, it appears that he was then employed as a justice of assize. He is last named in 9 Edward II., when he was certified as holding several lordships in the counties of Notts and York. (*Parl. Writs*, ii. 1172.) The next-mentioned Peter de Middleton was his son.

MIDDLETON, PETER DE, was son of the

above Adam de Middleton, and was appointed a justice itinerant in the county of Bedford in 4 Edward III., 1330, and in the eighth year was made a justice of the forests in Yorkshire. In 9 Edward III. the latter county was entrusted to his custody as sheriff; but in the following year he died, and his son Thomas succeeded to his possessions. (*Abb. Rot. Orig.* ii. 88, 94, 106; *Cal. Inquis.* p.m. ii. 70.)

MIDDLETON, RICHARD DE, was one of the justiciers in 46 Henry III., 1262, and there is evidence that he continued to act in that capacity from that time till 1269. (*Excerpt. e Rot. Fin.* ii. 383–492.)

At the end of July in that year he was appointed keeper of the Great Seal, but was afterwards raised to the dignity of chancellor, by which title he is designated in a document in Rymer (i. 492) dated February 20, 1272, and in the record mentioning his death, which took place, while in office, on the 7th of the following August.

MIDDLETON, WILLIAM DE, held the place of keeper of the Rolls and Writs of the Jews in 2 and 3 Edward I., together with the key of the Jewish tallage. In 1276 he was appointed Custos Brevium of the Court of Common Pleas, and in 11 Edward I. the lands of Isabella, the widow of Henry de Gaunt, were committed to his custody. In 1286 he was associated with the escheator in the custody of the bishopric of Ely on its becoming vacant, and was also appointed a baron of the Exchequer, where he continued for the four following years. (*Madox*, i. 234, 243, 313, ii. 322; *Abb. Rot. Orig.* i. 45.)

MILTON, CHRISTOPHER, was the brother of John Milton the poet. How wide the difference in their several careers! How great the contrast between the republican and the royalist, the Puritan and the Catholic, the Latin secretary of the usurper Cromwell and the subservient judge of the despotic James! The lustre that shines round the head of the poet, and which time has not dimmed, has thrown so much light on the lineage of the family that it is not necessary to trace it higher here than to his parents. John Milton, a scrivener of London, living in Bread Street, Cheapside, at the sign of the Spread Eagle (the family crest), by his marriage with Sarah Bradshaw (a kinswoman of the Lord President Bradshaw), was the father of three daughters and two sons, John born in 1608, and Christopher born in 1615.

Christopher after passing through St. Paul's School was admitted a pensioner of Christ's College, Cambridge, on February 15, 1631, but took no degree. Being destined for the law, he was entered at the Inner Temple, and having been called to the bar on January 26, 1639, he reached the grade of bencher in November 1660, and of reader in 1667. During the civil wars he took part against the parliament, acting as 'commissioner for the king for sequestering the parliament's friends of three counties, and afterwards went to Excester and lived there, and was there at the time of the surrender.' In an entry on the journals dated August 25, 1646, he is described 'of Reddinge in the county of Berks, counsellor at lawe,' and having then taken the national covenant, is allowed to compound for his 'delinquency' by a fine of 200*l*. on 'a certain messuage or tenement situate in St. Martin's parish Ludgate, called the signe of the Crosse Keyes, of the yearely value before theis troubles, 40*l*.' At this time his brother John, though he had published some controversial works, had not acquired any influence with the ruling powers; but when the commissioners for sequestrations, not content with Christopher's return of property in London, wrote in 1651–2 into Berks and Suffolk to enquire if he had any possessions in those counties, John Milton was Latin secretary to the protector. That he did not take any ostensible part on behalf of his brother may be attributed to a doubt whether his connection with a 'delinquent' might not endanger his political position; but that he exerted his private influence to mitigate the pressure seems very probable, for it does not appear that Christopher ever paid more than half of his fine, and it is manifest that no estrangement existed between the brothers. On the contrary, Christopher acted in 1653 as counsel before the commissioners of relief for Mrs. Powell, the mother of his brother's wife, and they continued on friendly and affectionate terms up to the time of his brother's death in 1674. He was also employed in other causes against the government during the Commonwealth.

Showing himself thus no friend to the republicans, it was natural that King Charles at the Restoration, on giving a charter to the town of Ipswich, should constitute Christopher Milton the first deputy recorder of it. Here he took up his residence, and it is probable confined himself to country practice, for he is not noticed in the Reports of the time. It is not precisely known when he turned Catholic, which was the faith of his grandfather; but it was probably that conversion and his high prerogative ideas that led to his selection by James, on April 26, 1686, as a baron of the Exchequer. He was thereupon knighted, and after sitting in that court for a year he was removed on April 17, 1687, to the Common Pleas, receiving a dispensation from subscribing the test. On July 6 in the following year he had a writ of ease, with a continuance of his salary, on account of his age, which one would think would have been a sufficient reason for not appointing him little more than two years before, when he was seventy-one years old. He retired to Rushmere in Suffolk, where he had a residence as well as in Ipswich, and dying five years afterwards, in March 1693, was buried in the church of St. Nicholas in the latter town. He was apparently of a quiet and easy disposition, but of no literary or legal eminence.

His wife, Thomasine, daughter of William Webber, of London, brought him several children, of whom his son Thomas was deputy clerk of the crown in Chancery. (*Milton Papers* [Camden Soc.]; *Dugdale's Orig.* 169; *Bramston*, 225, &c.)

MIRFIELD, WILLIAM DE, was of a Yorkshire family. He held the rectory of Bradford, and was a clerk or master in Chancery from 36 to 49 Edward III., 1362–1375, when he died. On March 18, 1371, he was one of those officers to whom the Great Seal was entrusted during the absence of the chancellor, but it is not stated how long they held it. His property, on his death, was divided among his sisters. (*Abb. Rot. Orig.* ii. 198, 342; *Cal. Inquis.* p. m. ii. 329, 346; *Rot. Parl.* ii. 268–317, 340.)

MOHUN, REGINALD DE, was a lineal descendant from William de Mohun, who for his assistance in the invasion of England received from William the Norman a large number of lordships in Devonshire, Wiltshire, Warwickshire, and particularly Somersetshire, with the castle of Dunster in the latter county. He was the son of another Reginald, and of Alicia, daughter of William Briwer. At his father's death he was very young, and was consigned to the wardship of Henry Fitz-Count, on whose decease, in 6 Henry III., he was removed to the guardianship of his grandfather, William Briwer; and he is still mentioned as a minor in 8 Henry III. (*Excerpt. e Rot. Fin.* i. 79, 169; *Rot. Claus.* i. 137, 518, 603.)

On July 6, 1234, 18 Henry III., the justiciers of the bench were commanded to admit him and Robert de Bello-Campo among them. In 1242 he was appointed chief justice of the forests south of the Trent, an office which he enjoyed for many years. In 1253 he was made governor of Sauveye Castle in Leicestershire, and died in 1261 or 1262. He founded the abbey of Newenham, near Axminster. He married first a sister of Humphrey de Bohun, Earl of Hereford and Essex, and had by her a son John, who succeeded him; but the barony failed in the reign of Edward III. His second wife was Isabella, daughter of William de Ferrers, Earl of Derby. (*Baronage*, i. 497.)

MOLYNEUX, EDMUND, was a member of a family which can trace their descent in uninterrupted knightly succession from a warrior who accompanied William of Normandy into England. Its present representative is the Earl of Sefton, whose immediate ancestor was made a baronet in 1611, to which was afterwards added an Irish viscounty in 1628, an Irish earldom in 1771, and an English barony in 1831.

The judge was the son of Sir Thomas Molyneux, of Haughton in Nottinghamshire, by his second wife, Catherine, daughter of John Cotton, of Ridware in Staffordshire, and widow of Thomas Poutrell, of Hallam in Derbyshire. He received his legal instruction at Gray's Inn, to which society he was twice reader, in 1532 and 1536. He was invested with the coif on November 20, 1542, and while he held that degree he was appointed one of the council in the North. On October 22, 1550, he was constituted a judge of the Common Pleas, and was knighted. His death occurred towards the end of 1562; and his character is very favourably depicted by Gregory King, Lancaster herald.

By his wife, Jane, daughter of John Cheney, of Chesham-boys in the county of Bucks, he left a large family, which flourished at Thorpe, near Newark, for many generations. (*Wotton's Baronet.* i. 149; *Thoroton's Notts*, i. 351; *Burnet*.)

MONACHUS, GEOFFREY, was among the 'assidentes justiciæ regis' present in the Exchequer in 11 Henry II., 1165, on the execution of a charter between the abbots of St. Alban's and Westminster. That he held an office in the Chamber of the Exchequer in 2, 3, and 4 Henry II. is evidenced by entries on the rolls of those years recording many payments made to and by him on the king's account.

It may be presumed that he was a monk no otherwise than in name, from the fact that he held lands in five counties, and that he was relieved from the Danegeld, &c., as an officer of the court. (*Madox*, i. 44; *Pipe Rolls*, 17-180.)

MONMOUTH, JOHN DE, was descended from William Fitz-Balderon, recorded in Domesday Book as the possessor of many lordships and other lands in Gloucestershire, Herefordshire, and Monmouth. The latter name was adopted by his successors, the fourth of whom was the subject of the present notice. He was the son of Gilbert de Monmouth, and in 3 John seems to have been a minor under the wardship of William de Braiosa. (*Rot. Cancell.* 108, 110.)

A few years afterwards he in some manner offended the king, and gave his two infant sons, John and Philip, as hostages for his good conduct (*Rot. Pat.* 87), paying a large fine for his restoration to the royal favour, which he ever afterwards preserved. In 16 John he was sent with others into several counties, on a confidential commission to explain the king's affairs, and was summoned to proceed to Cirencester with horse and arms. A royal present of a complete horse was the immediate reward of his readiness on that occasion; but others quickly followed, among which were the custody of the castles of St. Briavel and Bremble, with the forest of Dean, and grants of the lands of Hugh Malbisse, and of the castles of Grosmount, Skenefrict, and Lantelioc, in Wales. (*Ibid.* 128–194.) He was also keeper of the New Forest, together with the forests of Clarendon, Pancet, and Bocholte. (*Ibid.* 314–531.) His wife was Cicely, the daughter of Walter Walerond, to whom they had belonged.

Situated as he was on the Marches of Wales, he had to sustain the attack of the earl marshal; and when the king, in 1233, had been defeated at Grosmount, he was appointed one of the commanders of the Poictevins whom the king had introduced to resist the rebellious earl. That active general having discovered that the royal army intended to attack him, placed an ambush on the line of its march, surprised and totally defeated it, John of Monmouth only escaping by a hasty flight. (*R. de Wendover*, iv. 279, 287.) He died about September 1248.

There is little to record of his judicial career. In 4 Henry III. he was one of four justices itinerant who were sent to deliver the gaol at Hereford, and in the next year he, with other associates, visited that county and eight others in the same capacity. (*Rot. Claus.* i. 437, 476.)

MONSON, ROBERT, was a younger son of William Monson, of an ancient knightly family seated at South Carlton in Lincolnshire, by Elizabeth, daughter of Sir Robert Tirwhit, of Kettelby in the same county. His elder brother, John, was the ancestor of several persons who are remarkable in history, and of two noble families which still grace the peerage, Lord Monson and Lord Sondes.

Robert Monson was educated at Cambridge, was called to the bar at Lincoln's Inn on February 2, 1550, and elected reader in 1565 and in 1572. One of his readings was on 'The Act for the True Payment of Tithes,' the ten lectures of which it consisted being still preserved in the British Museum. (*Harl. MSS.* 2565, p. 29.)

He was elected member for Dunheved (Launceston) in the last parliament of Edward VI., 1553, and for that or other Cornish boroughs in four out of the five parliaments of Queen Mary; and in Elizabeth's first parliament, his father's recent death having put him into possession of much property near Lincoln, he was elected member for that city, which he continued to represent in the two next parliaments, 1563 and 1571. He finished his parliamentary career as member for Totnes in 1572. (*Willis's Parl. Not.*) Taking an active part in the debates, he was chosen on various important committees. Among them was that appointed in 1566, to petition the queen in relation to the succession and her marriage, her answer to which is expressed with her usual equivocation. He made some strong remarks on the evasive nature of the reply, and with Sir Robert Bell, 'grated hard on her royal prerogative;' but the parliament, in spite of their remonstrances, could obtain no satisfaction. (*Camden's Elizabeth; Parl. Hist.* i. 709, 715, 779.)

Monson's senatorial energy did not impede his professional career. In 1562 he was nominated a commissioner of the North, and in 1569 he was elected recorder of Lincoln. In Michaelmas Term 1574 he was created serjeant-at-law by special mandate, being the first barrister who was called to that degree for the purpose of being raised to the bench, to which he was elevated on October 31 of the same term as a judge of the Common Pleas.

One of the most repulsive duties imposed upon him was the necessity of obeying the order directed to him and others in 1575 to burn John Peters and Henry Turwest. (*Rymer*, xv. 740.) In 1576 he appears in some manner to have displeased the queen (*Cal. St. Papers* [1547], 530), and there is no doubt that three years after his judicial life came to an abrupt termination. John Stubbs, of Lincoln's Inn, having published a book called 'The Gulph wherein England will be swallowed by the French Marriage,' in which he slandered the Duke of Anjou in not very civil terms, was sentenced under a statute of Queen Mary to have his right hand cut off, which he suffered on November 3, 1579. Doubts were felt by many lawyers as to the force of that statute; and Dalton, who expressed too strongly that it was only temporary and died with Queen Mary, was punished for his indiscretion by being sent to the Tower. Camden adds that Judge Monson, who seems to have uttered the same sentiments, 'was so sharply reprehended that he resigned his place.' (*Camden in Kennett*, ii. 437.)

That this 'reprehension' extended to imprisonment appears by a letter from Mr. Secretary Wilson to Lord Burleigh, dated December 3, 1579. There is a letter also from the Archbishop of York to the Earl of Shrewsbury, dated the 5th of the following March, containing this passage: 'Mr. Monson hath gotten leave to be at his own house in Lincolnshire, but not restored to his place.' (*Harl. MSS.* 6992, art. 59; *Lodge's Illust.* i. 223.)

Though the judge was imprisoned, he was not then deprived, and his name was, according to the customary form, inserted in the fines as being still a member of the court; and on his release from incarceration, though he was 'not,' as the archbishop says, 'restored to his place,' yet he was not actually dismissed from it, or, according to Camden, did not 'resign' till after Easter Term had commenced.

He survived these events between two and three years, his death occurring on September 24, 1583. He was buried in Lincoln Cathedral, where, upon a brass plate, this curious inscription was engraved:

Quem tegit hoc marmor si forte requiris, Amice,
Lunam cum Phœbo jungite, nomen habes.
Luce Patrum clarus, proprio sed lumine major;
De gemina merito nomina luce capit.
Largus, doctus, amans, aluit, coluit, recreavit
Musas, jus, vinctos, sumptibus, arte, domo.
Tempora læta Deus, post tempora nubila misit;
Læta dedit sancte, nubila ferre pie,
'Et tulit, et vicit; superat sua lumina virtus;
Fulget apud superos, stella beata facit.

By his wife Elizabeth, daughter and heir of John Dyon, Esq., of Tathwere, he left no issue. (*Peck's Desid. Cur.* b. viii. 14.)

MONTAGU, EDWARD, was the second son of Thomas Montagu, of Hemington in Northamptonshire, by Agnes, daughter of William Dudley, of Clopton in the same county. He was born at Brigstock, and was educated at Cambridge. He kept his terms at the Middle Temple, and attained the office of reader there in 1524, and again in 1531, upon his being named as a serjeant-at-law.

A story is told that, being speaker of the House of Commons, when some hesitation was shown in passing a bill for subsidies, he was sent for by King Henry, who said to him, 'Ho! will they not let my bill pass? Get it to be passed by such a time to-morrow, or else,' laying his hand on the head of Montagu, kneeling before him, 'by such a time this head of yours shall be off.' There is very little authority for the tale, and if he ever had any such interview with the monarch, it must have been as a private member of the parliament, and not as speaker, for he never held the office.

On October 16, 1537, he was made one of the king's serjeants, and fifteen months afterwards was raised, without any intermediate step, to the office of chief justice of the King's Bench on January 21, 1539, receiving at the same time the honour of knighthood. He presided over that court for nearly seven years, when he was removed on November 6, 1545, to the more profitable but less exalted post of chief justice of the Common Pleas, a change which he is said to have sought, observing, 'I am now an old man, and love the kitchen before the hall, the warmest place best suiting with my age.' That it was not intended as any mark of disfavour by his sovereign is evidenced by his being selected as one of the sixteen executors of the king's will, in whom were deposited the management of the kingdom during the minority of his infant son.

In the earlier contests for power after Edward's accession, Montagu sided with the Duke of Somerset, but afterwards assisted Dudley, Earl of Warwick, in promoting that nobleman's fall. His adherence to the earl, who soon became Duke of Northumberland, eventually led him into a difficulty which was nearly fatal to him. Continuing in his judicial post during the whole of this reign, he had acquired so high a character, both for his legal knowledge and his honest principles, that his concurrence was deemed of infinite importance when Northumberland had formed the ambitious project of settling the crown on Lady Jane Grey. Accordingly, when the duke had worked up the king to his purpose, Montagu was summoned to court with Sir John Baker, Justice Bromley, and the attorney and solicitor general, and informed of his majesty's desire to make such a disposition. They at once pointed out the illegality of the proceeding, and begged time for consideration. The next day they repeated their objections, and added that it would be high treason, not only in those who prepared such an instrument, but in those who acted under it. The duke, on being informed of this resistance, burst into the council chamber and abused the chief justice most outrageously, calling him traitor and even putting him and Justice Bromley in bodily fear. Two days after a similar scene was acted; but the king commanding Montagu on his allegiance to make quick despatch, he, 'being a weak old man and without comfort,' at last consented, on receiving a commission under the Great Seal requiring it to be done, and a general pardon for obeying the injunction.

No sooner had Mary been proclaimed than Montagu was committed to the Tower, and placed on the list for trial. During his imprisonment, however, he drew up a narrative of all that had occurred, and declared that after he had compulsorily put his name to the articles so prepared he had 'never meddled with the council in anything, nor came amongst them until the queen's grace was proclaimed;' but that, at his no little cost, his son, by his command, had joined the Buckinghamshire men in defending her. The result was that after six weeks' confinement he was discharged, his pardon having been granted on payment of a fine of 1000*l*. and the surrender of King Edward's grant to him of lands called Eltyngton, of the yearly value of 50*l*. He also lost his office, which was given to Sir Richard Morgan. (*Fuller's Church Hist.* ii. 369; *Machyn's Diary*, 38, 43; *Lingard*, vii. 122.)

The short remainder of his life he spent at his mansion at Boughton, near Kettering, in hospitality and quiet. He died on February 10, 1557, and was buried at Kettering, under a tomb with an inscription which, if it may be depended on more than similar testimonials, must impress the reader with a very high opinion of his character both as a judge and a man. His will contains ample proof of his charitable disposition, and shows also a very large extent of property.

He was thrice married. His first wife was Elizabeth, daughter of William Lane, of Orlingbury, Northamptonshire; his second wife was daughter of George Kirkham, of Warmington in the same county; and his third wife, Helen, daughter of John Roper, the attorney-general, of Eltham in Kent. From Edward, his eldest son by this last marriage, five peerages trace their descent, two of which still flourish, the dukedom of Manchester and the earldom of Sandwich, and three are extinct.

MONTAGU, HENRY (BARON KIMBOLTON, VISCOUNT MANDEVIL, and EARL OF MANCHESTER), was grandson of the above Edward Montagu, being the third son of Edward his eldest son, who was seated at Boughton in Northamptonshire, and sheriff of that county, and its representative in parliament, by his wife Elizabeth, daughter of Sir James Harington, of Exton in the county of Rutland. He was born at Boughton about 1563, and showed so much intelligence that even at school it was prognosticated 'that he would raise himself above the rest of his family.' After well employing his time at Christ's College, Cambridge, he became a member of his grandfather's inn of court, the Middle Temple, where he attained the rank of reader in 1606. (*Dugdale's Orig.* 219.) He had been knighted previous to the coronation of King James, and had already acquired distinction as a lawyer by being elected recorder of London in the year of that king's accession.

He was returned for Higham Ferrers in 1601, and distinguished himself by his courageous answer to the absurd assertion made by Serjeant Heale, the aspirant for the office of master of the Rolls, 'that all we have is her majesty's, and she may lawfully at her pleasure take it from us,' which he 'could prove by precedent in the times of Henry III., King John, King Stephen, &c.,' declaring 'that there were no such precedents, and if all preambles of subsidies were looked upon, he should find they were of free gift.' In the first parliament of King James he was elected one of the representatives of the city of London, and took an active part in its important discussions, particularly in that relating to tenures. (*Parl. Hist.* i. 921, 1125.)

In September 1607 he was appointed king's counsel, and the degree of the coif was conferred upon him in February 1611, when he was immediately constituted king's serjeant. In this character he is only noticed as a commissioner to try the murderers of Sir Thomas Overbury, and as one of the counsel engaged in the prosecution of the great delinquents. (*State Trials*, ii. 911, 952.)

In his private practice he had an action brought against him by one Brook, for words charging the plaintiff with having been convicted of felony. He pleaded that they were spoken by him on a trial in which he was engaged as counsel against the plaintiff, and the court decided that the justification was good; for a counsel has a privilege to enforce anything pertinent to the issue that is informed him by his client, and not to examine whether it be true or false. (*Croke, Jac.* 90.)

On being selected on November 16, 1616, to succeed Sir Edward Coke as chief justice of the King's Bench, the speech of Lord Chancellor Lord Ellesmere, on swearing him in, gives him a significant hint of the tenure by which he holds his place, by reminding him of the 'amotion and disposing' of his predecessor 'in the peaceable and happy reign of great King James, the great king of Great Britain, wherein you see the prophet David's words true, "He putteth down one and setteth up another;" a lesson to be learned of all, and to be remembered and feared of all that sit in judicial places.' He recommends him to follow the example of his grandfather, Sir Edward Montagu, of whose name he takes advantage to introduce allusions to the imputed faults of Sir Edward Coke. (*Moore's Reports*, 826.) He is said to have procured the place by consenting to give to the Duke of Buckingham's nominee the clerkship of the Court of King's Bench, worth 4000*l*. a year, which Coke, in whose gift it was, refused to part with, although by doing so he might have retained his office.

It fell to Sir Henry's lot to be called on to award execution against Sir Walter Raleigh upon the sentence of death which had been pronounced fifteen years before. His address to the unfortunate prisoner evidently showed his regret in being compelled to the performance of this duty, and its terms do credit to his humanity. (*State Trials*, ii. 35, 1080.)

Montagu did not long rest satisfied with the place of chief justice. He aimed still higher, and after sitting in the judicial seat for four years he succeeded in obtaining the more elevated and lucrative post of lord treasurer on December 14, 1620. He was obliged to pay 20,000*l*. for the place, and one of the charges against Buckingham on his impeachment was the receipt of this money; but his answer alleged that it was a voluntary loan to the king, and that he had not a penny of it. The correspondence at the time seems to confirm this (*Tanner's MSS.*); but this view of the fact does not remove the venality of the transaction, nor account for Montagu being deprived of the office on October 13 following, when the unfortunate Lionel Cranfield, Earl of Middlesex, was by the duke's interest named as his successor. It was ever considered a place of great charge and profit, and when Montagu was asked what it might be worth per annum, he answered, 'Some thousands of pounds to him who after death would go instantly to heaven; twice as much to him who would go to purgatory; and a *nemo scit* to him who would venture to a worse place.' (*Lloyd's State Worthies*, 1028.) While treasurer he was one of the commissioners of the Great Seal from the abdication of the chancellorship by Bacon till July 10, 1621, when Dean Williams received the Seal.

On his appointment to the treasurership he was ennobled with the titles of Baron Montagu of Kimbolton and Viscount Mandevil, and on his removal he was but poorly compensated for his loss by being made lord president of the council. In this office he remained for the rest of James's reign and for the first three years of Charles's, when he exchanged it for that of lord privy seal, which he enjoyed for the rest of his life. King Charles also in the first year of his reign, on February 5, 1626, created him Earl of Manchester.

He was an active minister of the crown and a faithful adherent to King Charles, maintaining a good reputation and credit with the whole nation. He did not live to witness the fatal termination of Charles's career, but died on November 7, 1642, shortly after the commencement of the hostilities between the royalists and the parliamentary forces. He had nearly attained his eightieth year, and showed as much activity and sagacity in business as at any former period of his life. Fuller says, 'When lord privy seal, he brought the Court of Requests into such repute that what formerly was called the almsbasket of the Chancery had in his time well nigh as much meat in and guests about it (I mean suits and clients) as the Chancery itself.' In his last years he published a book entitled 'Manchester al Mondo, Contemplatio Mortis et Immortalitatis; or, Meditations on Life and Death,' which conveys a most favourable impression of the wisdom and piety of the writer. He was buried at Kimbolton under a noble monument.

Like his grandfather, Sir Edward, he married three wives. The first was Catherine, daughter to Sir William Spencer, of Yarnton in Oxfordshire; the second was Anne, daughter of William Wincott, of Langham in Suffolk, Esq., and widow of Sir Leonard Haliday, knight, lord mayor of London; and the third was Margaret, daughter of John Crouch, of Cornbury, Herts, Esq., and widow of John Hare, of Totteridge.

His eldest son and successor is the next-noticed Edward Earl of Manchester.

His son George, by his third wife, was father of Charles, who in 1694 was made chancellor of the Exchequer, in 1700 was created Baron Halifax, and in 1714 was advanced to the earldom of Halifax. These titles became extinct in 1772. (*Collins's Peerage*, ii. 51.)

MONTAGU, EDWARD (EARL OF MANCHESTER), was son of the above Henry, the first earl, and during his father's life was called up to the House of Peers by the title of Lord Kimbolton. At the meeting of the Long Parliament, Lord Kimbolton, having been for some time estranged from the court, took the popular side, and became a favourite organ of the party in the upper house, and the secret adviser of Pym, Hampden, and the other active spirits in the lower. In the attempt made by the king to draw off some of the leaders, Lord Kimbolton was designed to be keeper of the privy seal after his father's death, but the endeavour failing, the plans of the opposition were urged on with greater violence and rapidity. The hasty resolution of the king to impeach Lord Kimbolton and the five members, and his unadvised appearance in the House of Commons to seize the latter, led to the most fatal results, and were among the signal causes of the civil war. Lord Kimbolton, on the charge being made by the attorney-general, stood forward, and pressed for immediate enquiry; and on the king's withdrawing the prosecution, the Commons, not satisfied, passed a bill 'for clearing the Lord Kimbolton and the five members from the feigned charge,' and impeached Sir Edward Herbert, the attorney-general, for the part he had taken in the proceeding. When the parliament resorted to arms his lordship accepted a colonelcy in their forces, and was present on October 12, 1642, at the indecisive battle of Edgehill. His father dying on the 7th of the following month, he became Earl of Manchester, and was entrusted with the independent command of a considerable army. He proved his capacity as a soldier by investing the town of Lynn, so that it fell into his hands, and by defeating the Earl of Newcastle's forces in Lincolnshire with great slaughter. In May 1644 he took the city of Lincoln by storm, and in July, with Cromwell under him, was mainly instrumental in gaining the important victory of Marston Moor. The consequence of this battle was the fall of York. After several further successes he was in the second battle of Newbury on October 27, where each party claimed the victory; and the king having subsequently been able to relieve Donnington Castle, Cromwell, who was jealous of the earl and disobeyed his commands, took the opportunity of making a complaint to the parliament that he was lukewarm and unfaithful to their interests, and wished to promote a peace with the king. This led to recrimination on the earl's part, but the mutual charges fell to the ground without investigation. The self-denying ordinance soon followed, in consequence of which the earl resigned his command in the following April, and the feelings between the two were anything but friendly. That Cromwell's dislike was not partaken by either house is evident from the Lords passing a complimentary vote in favour of him and the Earls of Essex and Denbigh, acknowledging their faithfulness and industry, and recommending their services for the consideration of parliament. The Lords also chose the earl for their speaker, and at the end of 1645, in the propositions to the king for peace, the parliament named him to be made a marquis.

On October 30, 1646, the Lords and Commons, not being able to agree upon the persons to be named commissioners of the Great Seal, determined to put it into the custody of the Earl of Manchester and William Lenthall, the speakers of the two houses, till they had decided, and limited their power for a week after the end of the then Michaelmas Term. When that period came the same irresolution existed, and continued for near a year and a half, so that the earl and Lenthall remained keepers till March 15, 1648.

On the question of the king's death the opinion of the House of Lords was set aside, and a few days after the blow had fallen that body was entirely abolished. Considering the relations that existed between the earl and Cromwell, it seems surprising that the latter, when he became protector and instituted the 'other house,' should have named the earl as one of his peers, a nomination which was of course declined.

When Cromwell was dead, the dismissal of his son Richard and the restoration of the Long Parliament seeming to open a prospect of the king's return, the earl concerted with Monk and others the means to effect it. The House of Lords being restored in the Convention Parliament which met on April 25, 1660, he was replaced in his former position as speaker, and on May 5 was added to three other commissioners of the Great Seal, which they continued to hold till the same was defaced on May 28, and the Seal of the kingdom came again into operation under Sir Edward Hyde as lord chancellor. The duty of conveying the Lords' congratulations on his majesty's safe arrival devolved upon this earl, and his address was eloquent and dignified. He was rewarded with the Garter, and the office of lord chamberlain of the household, in which capacity he died at Whitehall on May 5, 1671.

Lord Clarendon's high character of him must be received with some allowance, influenced as he probably was by the latter phase of the earl's career. In many points, however, it is just. He was gentle and generous, and had a natural reverence and affection for the person of Charles I., upon whom he had attended in Spain when prince. When he saw the arbitrary acts of the government, he joined the popular party in resisting them, and by force of circumstances was led on to take part in the war, with a view of remedying what was wrong. But when he found that the object was likely to be attained without further bloodshed, he became a strenuous advocate for peace, and thus insured the hostility of Cromwell and his party, when he suspected of different views. The cruel fate awarded to the king convinced him he was right, and the efforts he made for the restoration of the legitimate monarch were dictated as much by abhorrence of the king's murder as by the conviction that the governments substituted were injurious to the happiness and liberties of the people.

George I. gave his grandson a dukedom in 1719, which has been enjoyed by his descendants till the present time. (*Clarendon; Whitelocke; Noble; Collins's Peerage*, ii. 57.)

MONTAGU, WILLIAM, was the son of Edward Montagu, the elder brother of the above Henry the first Earl of Manchester, who was himself ennobled in 1621 by the title of Baron Montagu of Boughton. By his second wife, Frances, sister of Sir Robert Cotton, Bart., he had three sons, the youngest of whom was this William. The third baron was created Duke of Montagu by Queen Anne, but on the death of the second duke in 1749 without male issue all the titles became extinct.

William Montagu was born about 1619, and was entered of Sidney Sussex College, Cambridge, in 1632, but took no degree. The Middle Temple called him to the bar in 1641, and made him a bencher in 1662, treasurer in 1663, and reader in 1664. He became attorney-general to the queen in June 1662, and so continued till he was raised to the bench on April 12, 1676, being then appointed lord chief baron of the Exchequer, where he presided for ten years. Very few incidents of his judicial career are recorded. At the trial in 1678 of Ireland and four others for high treason before him and Chief Justice Scroggs, the evidence not being sufficient against two of the prisoners, Whitebread and Fenwick, they were set aside after all the witnesses for the prosecution had been heard, which would in all fairness have entitled them to an acquittal. But the chief baron directed the gaoler to keep them strictly, saying they were 'in no way acquitted,' thus deciding, according to the cruel practice of the time, that, though their lives had been clearly in jeopardy, they might be tried again, which was done shortly afterwards, and they were both found guilty and executed. Though called as a witness by Titus Oates on his trial for perjury in 1685, he acknowledged that he 'never had any great faith in him.' In the same year he accompanied Chief Justice Jeffreys on the western assizes to try the prisoners concerned in Monmouth's rising; but it does not appear that he personally took any other part in those brutal proceedings than to urge a reluctant witness to speak the truth. Soon after, when King James, having madly resolved to do away with the Test Acts, found that the chief baron and some of the judges were opposed to his opinion, he determined to put others who were more pliant into their places. Accordingly on April 21, 1686, Chief Baron Montagu and three of his colleagues received their discharge. (*State Trials*, vii. 120, x. 1168, xi. 344; *Bramston*, 193.)

He survived his removal for eleven years, dying in 1707. His wife, Mary, daughter of Sir John Aubrey, Bart., brought him three children; but their issue, if they had any, had all failed in 1749, when his father's great-grandson, the second Duke of Montagu, died, and the barony of Boughton became extinct. (*Pepys*, i. 38; *Evelyn*, ii. 323.)

MONTAGU, JAMES, was another scion of this noble house, being the son of the Hon. George Montagu, of Horton in Northamptonshire, one of the above Earl Henry's children by his third marriage. His mother was Elizabeth, daughter of Sir Anthony Irby; and his brother Charles, the eminent statesman and poet, was created Baron Halifax in 1710, to which was added an earldom in 1714; but the latter title became extinct on the death of the third earl in 1771.

James entered the Middle Temple, and was called to the bar. On attaining the rank of solicitor-general he removed to Lincoln's Inn, of which he was elected a bencher on May 2, 1707. He sat in parliament as member for Tregony in 1695, and for Beeralston in 1698, in which year he was appointed chief justice of Ely. He did not obtain a seat in the two remaining parliaments of William, nor in the first parliament of Anne, devoting himself entirely to professional avocations. In Michaelmas Term 1704 he was one of the counsel who moved for a habeas corpus in favour of the Aylesbury men committed to Newgate by the House of Commons for bringing actions against the returning officer, and pleaded strongly against the absurd privilege claimed by the house. For the mere exercise of this duty as a barrister the Commons on February 26, 1705, committed him and his colleagues to the custody of the serjeant-at-arms, where he remained till March 14, when the queen felt compelled to prorogue, and afterwards to dissolve, the parliament, in order to prevent the collision between the two houses of which there was every appearance. In the following April the queen conferred the honour of knighthood upon him at Cambridge, and in November appointed him one of her majesty's counsel. (*State Trials*, xiv. 808, 850, 1119; *Luttrell*, v. 524, 542, 609.)

In the second parliament of Queen Anne he was elected member for the city of Carlisle, which he continued to represent till 1714; but of his speeches in the house little record remains, though he became solicitor-general on April 28, 1707, and attorney-general on October 6, 1708. From the latter office he was removed in September 1710, but the queen granted him a pension of 1000*l*. This pension, which was represented by Colonel Gledhill as intended to defray the expenses of Sir James's election at Carlisle, was in 1711 made the subject of a complaint to the house, which resulted in the complete disproval of the charge. Sir James, however, was not returned for Carlisle in the queen's last parliament of 1714, and before the first parliament of George I. he was raised to the judicial bench. In 1705 he was leading counsel in the prosecution of Robert Fielding for bigamy in marrying the Duchess of Cleveland; in 1710 he opened the charges against Dr. Sacheverell in the House of Lords; and when that trial was concluded he conducted the prosecutions of the parties who were found guilty of high treason for pulling down meeting-houses in the riots that followed. (*Parl. Hist.* vi. 1009; *State Trials*, xiv. 1329, xv. 53, 549-680.)

On the arrival of George I. in England, Sir James received the degree of the coif on October 26, 1714, and on November 22 was sworn a baron of the Exchequer. While holding that position he was nominated one of the lords commissioners of the Great Seal, on the resignation of Lord Cowper, and held it from April 18 till May 12, 1718, when Lord Parker was appointed lord chancellor. On May 4, 1722, Chief Baron Bury died, and before the end of the month Sir James was sworn as his successor. He presided in the Exchequer little more than a year, his death occurring on October 1, 1723.

His first wife was Tufton Wray, daughter of Sir William Wray, of Ashby, baronet;

and his second wife was Elizabeth, daughter of Robert, third Earl of Manchester. (*Lord Raymond*, 1319-1331; *Collins's Peerage*, ii. 83; *Gent. Mag.* v. 151.)

MONTEALTO, ROGER DE, was son of Robert de Montealto, whose father built a castle on a little hill in Flintshire, then called Montalt, but now Mould. His early life was engaged in opposing the aggressions of David, son of Llewellyn, Prince of Wales, in which he eminently distinguished himself. In 34 Henry III. he took the cross, and prepared, at great expense, for the expedition to the Holy Land; but it is not related that he went there. In 42 and 44 Henry III. he was called upon, with the other barons marchers, to quell new insurrections of the Welsh; and in the latter year he was placed at the head of the justices itinerant into Shropshire and Staffordshire and the neighbouring counties. Before June 27 in that year, 1260, he died, leaving his wife Cecilia, one of the sisters of Hugh de Albini, surviving, with two sons, John and Robert, both of whom successively inherited the title; but the barony became extinct in 1329. (*Baronage*, i. 527.)

MONTEFORTI, HENRY DE, with the addition of 'Clericus,' appears in 48 Henry III., 1263, as an escheator south of the Trent (*Excerpt. e Rot. Fin.* ii. 411), and also as one of the conservators of the peace in Kent. (*Hasted*, i. 218.)

There was probably no close relationship between him and Peter de Montfort, or Simon Earl of Leicester, who were both slain in 1265 at the battle of Evesham, in arms against their sovereign, since Henry's elevation to the bench took place about October 1266, from which date till the end of that reign the Fine Rolls contain frequent entries of writs for assizes to be held before him. (*Excerpt. e Rot. Fin.* ii. 446–586.)

He was continued in office on the accession of Edward I., and an entry on the Liberate Rolls of 3 Edward I. names him as a justice of the bench. He died at the end of the next or beginning of the following year. (*Abb. Rot. Orig.* i. 27.)

MONTFICHET, RICHARD DE, whose ancestor William came over to England with the Conqueror, and founded the abbey of Stratford-Langton in Essex, was the son of another Richard, who had the charge of the forests of Essex under Henry II., by his wife Milicent, and was a minor on the death of his parents. On attaining his majority, about 16 John, he was in attendance at the court, and in 1215 the forests of Essex were restored to his custody as his right. (*Rot. Chart.* 197–204.) He became so active an adherent to the rebellious barons that he was one of the twenty-five who were appointed to enforce the observance of Magna Charta. For this he was put under the ban of excommunication, and his lands were seized into the king's hands. Even after the death of King John he did not desert the standard of Louis, till he was taken prisoner at Lincoln in May 1217, when, the cause becoming desperate by the issue of that battle, and Prince Louis returning to France, he, with other barons, was allowed to make his peace. (*R. de Wendover*, iii. 297, 356, iv. 24; *Rot. Claus.* i. 259, 327.) Within a few years his impetuosity again led him into trouble. Contrary to the king's prohibition, he chose to attend the tournament given at Blythe in 7 Henry III., for which his lands were again seized; but, after a few months, and no doubt upon the payment of some penalty, they were restored to him. (*Rot. Claus.* i. 416–539.)

It is evident, however, that this affair was looked upon rather as the intemperance of youth than as an act of concerted disobedience; for in 9 Henry III. his name was inserted in the list of justices itinerant for the counties of Essex and Hertford (*Ibid.* ii. 76); and in 18 Henry III. the treasurer and barons of the Exchequer were commanded to admit him as their companion, 'ad residendum ad Scaccarium nostrum tanquam baro, pro negotiis nostris quæ ad idem Scaccarium pertinent.' (*Madox*, ii. 54.)

Three years afterwards he was constituted justice of the forests over nineteen counties, and from 26 to 30 Henry III. he held the office of sheriff of Essex and Hertford, in which his possessions were situate, the principal of which was the barony of Stanstead. (*Excerpt. e Rot. Fin.* ii. 471.)

Having lived to a good old age, he died in 52 Henry III., 1268, but left no issue. (*Baronage*, i. 438.)

MORE, JOHN, the judge who sat on the bench for twelve years in the reign of Henry VIII., was the father of the illustrious chancellor Sir Thomas More; but whose son John More was has never been mentioned by any of the chancellor's biographers. The inference from their silence, and more particularly from the expression used in the epitaph on the chancellor, written by himself, 'familiâ non celebri sed honestâ natus,' seems to lead to no other conclusion than that the family was an obscure one. The subject having been fully discussed in a paper in the 'Archæologia' (xxxv. 27–33), it is unnecessary to repeat the argument in this place, or to state more than the result of the investigation.

It appears then that John More was the son of another John More, who in 4 Edward IV., 1464, was raised from the office of butler to the society of Lincoln's Inn to that of seneschal or steward, an officer at the head of the servants of the house, and was in 1470, 49 Henry VI. (the year of that monarch's temporary restoration), admitted a member of the society, in reward for his long and faithful services as butler and seneschal.

He was then progressively called to the bar, and raised to the bench of the society, and appointed a reader in autumn 1489, and in Lent 1495, 5 and 10 Henry VII. His son, John More the judge, succeeded him as butler, and in like manner was admitted a member of the society, and called to the bar, and in November 1503, 19 Henry VII., received the degree of the coif. (*Dugdale's Orig.* 113.) This origin, so far from detracting in any degree from the merit either of the chancellor or the judge, must be considered as speaking loudly, not only to their credit, but to the credit of those to whom they owed their elevation; showing that, even in those days, virtue and learning met their due reward, and contradicting the general impression that none but rich men's sons were admitted members of the inns of court. It proves also that, at a time when the barriers between the different grades of society were far more difficult to be passed than in the present day, such a combination of talent with integrity and moral worth as distinguished the progenitors of Sir Thomas could overcome all the prejudices in favour of high descent which were the natural result of the feudal system.

It is related by the chancellor's son-in-law, Roper, that Sir John was imprisoned in the Tower until he had paid a fine of 100*l.* for some groundless quarrel devised against him by the king. This must have been in the year following that in which he was made a serjeant, as the real cause of the royal anger was that his son Thomas, the future chancellor, had successfully opposed a grant demanded of the parliament which met in January 1504. Of Sir John's practice at the bar there is little evidence.

Of the date of his elevation to the bench neither his biographers nor Dugdale give any precise information, and the only account afforded by the latter contradicts his biographers as to the court in which he sat. Their statement, however, that he was a judge of the Court of King's Bench is confirmed by his will, dated in February 1526, in which he so designates himself; and by Sir Thomas's epitaph, in which he describes his father as of that court, without any allusion to his having sat in any other. And yet Dugdale notices him solely as a judge of the Common Pleas, and proves that he was so from Hilary Term 1518 to Hilary Term 1520, by the occurrence of his name in fines acknowledged between those dates.

It is evident, therefore, that he was successively a member of both benches. No patent of his appointment either as a judge of this court or of the King's Bench has been found; but the period of his removal to the latter must be fixed between his last fine and November 28, 1523, when he is named as a judge of the King's Bench in a list of his brethren chargeable with the subsidy imposed in that year (*Ibid.* 47; 3 *Report Pub. Rec., App.* ii. 62); and it is not unlikely that he was placed on that bench in April 1520, when Richard Broke first occurs as a judge of the Common Pleas, without any other apparent vacancy.

Looking at the period of Sir John's advancement, and considering how little he distinguished himself as a lawyer either before or after his elevation to the bench (for in the Year Books he is mentioned only once as a judge, and that in a case in the Exchequer Chamber), it seems not improbable that he owed his appointment to the character his son had already attained, and that this was one of the temptations held out to secure Sir Thomas's services at court. The pleasing description which his son gives of him in his epitaph—'Homo civilis, suavis, innocens, mitis, misericors, æquus et integer'—presents a higher idea of his moral than of his intellectual qualities, and illustrates the attractive pictures which are drawn of the affectionate intercourse existing in the family. None who contemplate the character of both can fail to dwell with sympathy and pleasure, as the certain consequence of such a union of hearts, on the unaffected deference which the son continued to pay to the father after his own promotion, on his defying ridicule by publicly begging the parental blessing in his way to his court, and on the unrestrained expression of his love in the last moment of the judge's life.

Sir John died about November 1530, judging from his will, which was proved on the 5th of the following month, and, according to its directions, he was buried in the church of St. Lawrence in the Old Jewry.

His age at the period of his decease was not 90, as his great-grandson Cresacre More erroneously describes him, but 76, according to the inscriptions on the family pictures preserved at Burford Priory and at Nostell Priory, painted, one of them certainly by Holbein, in 1530, after Sir Thomas became chancellor, and just previous to Sir John's death. They represent all the members of the family then in existence, and their ages are inscribed on their respective portraits. Both of these pictures agree as to the then age of Sir John—viz., 76; and this evidence, which is manifestly the most trustworthy, would make the birth of Sir John take place about the year 1453, so that he would have been 29 when he is first mentioned as butler, about 50 on his assumption of the serjeant's coif, and his elevation to the bench would have happened at the more probable age of 64 or 65.

His union with three or four wives

seems to prove that his theory with regard to the ladies was less complimentary than his practice. It is reported of him, 'for proof of his pleasantness of wit, that he would compare the multitude of women which are chosen for wives unto a bag full of snakes having among them but one eel; now if a man should put his hand into this bag, he may chance to light on the eel, but it is a hundred to one he shall be stung with a snake.' But whether he made this remark before or after his last nuptials is not recorded.

His first wife, according to his great-grandson Cresacre More, was Johanna, daughter of — Hancombe, of Holywell, Bedfordshire; but whether he was ever married to this lady is very doubtful, and it has been clearly shown by entries in an old MS. in Trinity College Library (*Notes and Queries*, 4th S. ii. 365) that John More married, in 1474, when he was 21, Agnes, daughter of Thomas Graunger, at St. Giles's, Cripplegate. The second wife was Mrs. Bowes, a widow, whose maiden name was Barton; and his third was Alice Clarke, named in a commission as relict of William Huntyngdon of Exeter (*Cal. State Papers* [1509–14], 292), the daughter of John More of Loseley in Surrey. By his first wife only, whether Hancombe or Graunger, had he any issue, and she produced him, with three other children who probably died early, one son, Thomas More the chancellor, and two daughters. Jane, the elder, was married to Richard Stafforton, or Staidton. Elizabeth, the younger, became the wife of John Rastell the printer, and the mother of William Rastell the judge.

The manor of Gobyons in North Mimms in Hertfordshire, belonging to Sir John at his death, he left to his wife for life, and then to the chancellor, on whose attainder in 1534 his mother-in-law was illegally evicted. She died about ten years afterwards at Northall in that neighbourhood.

MORE, THOMAS, the only son of the above Sir John by his first wife, whether her maiden name was Graunger or Hancombe, was born on February 7, 1478, in his father's house in Milk Street, London. The rudiments of his education he received under Nicholas Holt, at St. Anthony's School in Threadneedle Street, which bore the highest reputation of any of the London establishments, and produced some other celebrated men, among whom were Heath, Archbishop of York; Whitgift, Archbishop of Canterbury; and Dean Colet. More's father, who was at that time merely an apprentice-at-law, not having been yet called to the degree of a serjeant, obtained an early introduction for him into the house of Cardinal Morton, who, like other ecclesiastics of the age, received young persons of name and character into his family, nominally as pages, but really to be instructed under his own eye in all the learning of the time. More's quickness and ready wit soon made him a favourite with his fellows. In the plays which it was then the custom, even in bishops' houses, to perform at Christmas, he would intermingle with the actors, and, adopting a character appropriate to the piece, would improvise the part to the sport and admiration of the audience. The worthy cardinal, of whom More always spoke with affectionate gratitude, was not the last to see his merit and to prophesy his future eminence; and, that no opportunity might be lost for improvement, he placed the promising youth at the university of Oxford. Both Canterbury College (now part of Christ Church) and St. Mary Hall are mentioned as his place of study, but the deficiency of the registers has left the question in doubt.

There is less uncertainty in fixing the date of his college career. His friendship with Erasmus commenced in 1497, when that eminent man first visited England, who in a letter to a friend in Italy dated on December 5, 1497, after eulogising the learning of Colet, Grocyn, and Linacre, who were all at Oxford at that period, adds, 'Nor did nature ever form anything more elegant, exquisite, and better accomplished than More.' This fascinating character is peculiarly appropriate to a youth between nineteen and twenty, and suggests the great probability of that year being the date of his entrance at Oxford. With all the three eminent men mentioned by Erasmus he formed an intimacy, and with their encouragement, and Thomas Linacre for his tutor, he enthusiastically pursued his Greek studies, and successfully resisted the faction in the university which, under the name of Trojans, attempted to prevent the introduction of that language into the system of education there. Here he also began those epigrams and translations that appear in his works, and devoted himself entirely to the allurements of literature. His allowance was scarcely sufficient to provide necessaries, and of his expenditure of it he was required to give a most exact account. Whether his father so closely curtailed him from frugal motives, or from the fear that his son's delight in these studies would create a distaste for the legal profession, for which he was designed, the son ever after spoke of it in terms of commendation, as preventing him from indulging in idle pleasures and extravagance. There is no record of his having taken any degree, and his stay at the university is stated not to have exceeded two years. The period of his return to London is uncertain, but the records of Lincoln's Inn show that his admission into that society must have taken place either during or before his residence at Oxford. The entry is under 11 Henry VII., 1496, when he was eighteen, and is as follows :—

Thomas More admissus est in Societat. xij die Februar. a° sup. dicto. et pardonat. est quatuor vacacões ad instanciam Johis More patris sui.

Although his name is not to be found on the books of New Inn, a society then recently established, there is no doubt that he was placed there for some time either before or after his leaving Oxford. He was in due time removed to Lincoln's Inn, and, having passed through the usual course of study, he was admitted as an utter barrister, but the early books of the society do not give the date of the calls to the bar. The character he acquired as a lawyer may be judged from his being soon afterwards selected to deliver lectures on the science at Furnival's Inn, which were so highly estimated that this annual appointment was renewed for three successive years.

At this period he seems to have been impressed with strong religious feelings, and not only to have employed his time in devotional exercises, but to have subjected his body to penitential austerities. For the purpose of pursuing these spiritual objects, he established himself near the Charterhouse, that he might daily attend the services of that foundation, and during the four years of his residence there his mind wavered between the choice of a monastic life and the adoption of the priesthood. It was perhaps while in this state of mental probation that he delivered lectures at St. Lawrence's Church in the Old Jewry on the work of St. Augustine, 'De Civitate Dei,' to a crowded audience comprehending the most learned men, both lay and clerical, in the city. That these lectures formed no part of his legal requirements may be presumed from the absence of any other similar example, and it is even doubtful, from a passage in one of Erasmus's letters, whether they were not in fact delivered at Oxford.

But time, or perhaps the attractions of female society, cured him of his disposition to a pious retirement. His son-in-law Roper thus simply relates his course of love: 'He resorted to the house of one Maister Colte, a gentleman of Essex, that had oft invited him thither, having three daughters, whose honest conversation and virtuous education provoked him there specially to set his affection. And albeit his mind most served him to the second daughter, for that he thought her the fairest and best favoured, yet when he considered that it would be both great grief and some shame also to the eldest to see her younger sister preferred before her in marriage, he then of a certain pity framed his fancy towards her, and soon after married her, never the more discontinuing his study of the law at Lincoln's Inn, but applying still the same until he was called to the bench, and had read there twice, which is as often as any judge of the law doth ordinarily read.'

This marriage, which took place in 1505, proved a very happy one, but was dissolved by the death of the lady in little more than six years, after giving birth to three daughters and one son, whom Roper quaintly says 'he would often exhort to take virtue and learning for their meat, and play for their sauce.' They lived in Bucklersbury.

It must have been about a year previous to this marriage that the incident related by Roper occurred which distinguishes More as the first public opponent to a parliamentary grant of money to the crown. The last parliament in the reign of Henry VII. met in January 1504, and in it a bill was introduced demanding an aid of three fifteenths for the recent marriage of the king's eldest daughter Margaret with the King of Scots. On the debate of this bill, More, who had been returned a burgess, used 'such arguments and reasons there against that the king's demands were thereby clean overthrown.' The statute itself shows that the king excused not only the aid, but 10,000l. also of the 40,000l. offered by the Commons. (*Stat. of Realm*, ii. 975.) But his majesty being informed 'that a beardless boy had disappointed all his purpose,' and 'conceiving great indignation against him, could not be satisfied until he had some way revenged it. And forasmuch as he, nothing having, nothing could lose, his grace devised a causeless quarrel against his father, keeping him in the Tower till he had made him pay to him a hundred pounds' fine.'

It was not till after the accession of Henry VIII. that More was appointed one of the governors of Lincoln's Inn. In the autumn of 1511 his first reading took place, and his second in Lent 1516, about two years before his father became a judge.

In the interval between these two dates More's legal reputation rose so high that there was scarcely any controversy in the courts in which he was not employed as counsel for one of the parties. On September 3, 1510, he had been made under-sheriff of London, on whom in those days not only devolved the duties which that officer has now to perform, but he acted also as the judicial representative of the sheriff in all those numerous cases which came under his jurisdiction, part of which have since been decided by a regularly constituted judge of the Sheriff's Court. An entry in the city records states that on May 8, 1514, it was agreed by the common council 'that Thomas More, gentleman, one of the under-sheriffs of London, should occupy his office and chamber by a sufficient deputy during his absence as the king's ambassador in Flanders.' As this shows that he still held the office, and as there is evidence of his continuing in it for several years beyond this licence, and that the nomination was then in the common council, there is no doubt that, though it might nominally receive an annual confirmation, it was the practice to select for the sheriff's assessor some eminent individual learned in the law, and not to remove him but for serious cause.

Although in the above entry he is called 'the king's ambassador in Flanders,' there is no record in Rymer of such an appointment. It may be presumed, however, that this was one of the two occasions mentioned by Roper, when he was sent, with the king's concurrence, to arrange certain questions between the English and foreign merchants established in the Steel Yard, who enjoyed great privileges in this country. The other embassy was probably that in 1515 (for which he received a similar licence from the city), for in a letter of 1516 he tells Erasmus, 'When I returned from my embassage of Flanders the king's majesty would have granted me a yearly pension; which, surely, if I should respect honour and profit, was not to be contemned by me; yet have I as yet refused it, and I think I shall refuse it, because either I should forsake my present means which I have in the city, which I esteem more than a better, or else I should keep it with some grudge of the citizens, between whom and his highness if there should happen any controversies (which may sometime chance), they may suspect me as not trusty and sincere with them because I am obliged to the king with an annual stipend.' He might indeed very reasonably hesitate to risk any change in his position, since he estimated the gains from his office and his private business at 400*l*. a year, which according to the then value of money would be considered a splendid income. It is not unlikely that the appointment of his father as a judge two years afterwards operated more effectually in securing his services to the court.

Hall's description of him (p. 588) as '*Syr* Thomas More *late* undershrife and then of the kinges counsaill,' in the account given by that chronicler of the London insurrection on Evil May-day 1517, is clearly erroneous in two parts of it, and probably so in the third. The city records, as quoted by Sir James Mackintosh, state his resignation of the undersheriffalty on July 23, 1519. His entrance into the privy council was not likely to precede that event, and probably occurred immediately afterwards. The earliest recorded notice of his connection with the court is in April 1520, when he was the last named of four commissioners to settle provisions in the treaty of commerce with Charles V. His name is there inserted without any addition, and he is only called 'Armiger' in another commission of June in the same year, by which he was one of those appointed to accommodate certain questions with the 'socios' of the Hanse Towns. Between this date and May 1522 he received his knighthood, being then named as one of the knights assigned to attend the king on the visit of the emperor. (*Rymer*, xiii. 714, 722, 768.) The immediate cause of his elevation is stated to have been his successful resistance in the Star Chamber to the king's claim for the forfeiture of a ship belonging to the pope, which had been seized at Southampton. The erudition which he then displayed, and his powerful arguments in the cause, so pleased the king that he would listen to no further excuses, but at once retained More in his service, by introducing him into the privy council. In May 1522 and January 1525 he was rewarded with divers manors and lands to the value of 60*l*. a year, the grants of which were annulled soon after his disgrace. (*Stat. Realm*, iii. 528.)

His intimate relation both with the king and Cardinal Wolsey at this period is manifest from a variety of letters, published in Sir Henry Ellis's first series, exhibiting the closest confidential communication on political affairs. The conferences to which they relate generally took place in the royal closet after supper. He became engaged in many other diplomatic missions besides those before referred to, and he appears from his correspondence with Erasmus to have been for a long time stationed at Calais for the convenience of continental negotiations, a position which was not only distateful to him, but unprofitable also. He accompanied Wolsey in his ostentatious embassy to France in 1527, and it was probably on this occasion that the cardinal, on asking him to point out anything that was objectionable in the treaty he had prepared, flew into a rage because More ventured to suggest some amendment, concluding his violence by saying, 'By the mass, thou art the veriest fool of all the council.' More, smiling, answered simply, 'God be thanked the king our master hath but one fool in his council.' His last mission was two years afterwards to Cambray, in conjunction with his old friend Bishop Tunstall, as ambassador to the emperor.

It was on one of these journeys that More silenced a bragging fellow who had posted a challenge in Bruges that he would answer whatever question could be propounded to him in any art whatsoever. Sir Thomas demanded an answer to the following: 'An Averia capta in Withernamia sunt irreplegibilia?' adding that there was one of the

English ambassador's retinue who would dispute with him thereof. The derision of the city was fairly excited by the arrogant presumer being obliged to acknowledge that he did not even understand the terms of the proposition.

Not long after the death of his first wife he contracted a second marriage with Mrs. Alice Middleton, a widow, who survived him without giving any addition to his family. As over his first choice, so over this, a little romance is thrown; for the lady is reported to have suggested to him while urging the suit of a friend that if he pleaded in his own behalf he might be more successful. 'Upon this hint he spake,' and, his friend wisely withdrawing, he soon after married her. From Bucklersbury he removed to Crosby Place (*Burgon's Gresham*, i. 420), and in 1523 to the house he built at Chelsea. The picture of his domestic life is most delightfully drawn by Erasmus. His family circle, increased as it was by the husbands of his daughters and the wife of his son, seems to have been the centre of happiness. The duties of religion were never omitted; every hour was employed in useful study, or intellectual intercourse, or sober mirth; gentleness was the spirit that guided, and love the bond that united them.

While employed in the study and practice of the law he had not deserted the literary path in which he had first delighted. He improved himself in all the learning then attainable; he associated with the most eminent and intellectual men of the time; he kept up a constant correspondence with Erasmus; and he even found leisure for literary composition. The 'History of Richard III.' is published among his works, but doubts have been raised whether he was really its author, some attributing the composition of the Latin original to Cardinal Morton, and only the English translation to More. His 'Utopia,' upon which his fame as an author principally rests, is the history of an imaginary commonwealth, in which he advances and advocates some doctrines in philosophy and religion greatly in advance of the age, with so much force and liberality that it seems surprising that the work escaped the censures of the government. It was written in Latin, and published about 1516.

Being now a member of the privy council, he was selected as speaker of the parliament which, after eight years' discontinuance of that assembly, met on April 15, 1523. His address on being presented to the king, containing the protestation of his own disability and the claim for freedom of debate so customary at the present day, will always serve as a model for future speakers.

Though the Commons did not make a grant equivalent to the extravagant demand of the court, they imposed a tax with which Cardinal Wolsey was obliged to appear content; and he not only requested the king to grant the usual reward of 200*l*. to the speaker, 'because no man could better deserve the same than he had done,' but added this complimentary expression to his letter: 'I am the rather moved to put your highness in remembrance thereof, because he is not the most ready to speak and solicit his own cause.'

But the cardinal could not entirely suppress his dissatisfaction. He said to the speaker, 'Would to God you had been at Rome, Master More, when I made you speaker.' 'Your grace not offended,' answered More, 'so would I too, my lord.' And Roper charges the cardinal with endeavouring to remove him from his path by counselling the king to send him ambassador to Spain. More, however, remonstrated with his majesty, who replied, 'It is not our pleasure, Master More, to do you hurt, but to do you good we would be glad; we therefore for this purpose will devise upon some other, and employ your service otherwise.'

The date of More's appointment as under-treasurer of the Exchequer is uncertain, but he is described in that character in August 1525 as one of the ambassadors to conclude a treaty with France. (*Rymer*, iv. 56, 69, 74.) From this office he was raised to that of chancellor of the duchy of Lancaster on December 25 following (*Mackintosh*, 48), which he held till he became chancellor of England.

The Great Seal was delivered to More by the king, 'at his manor of Plesaunce, alias Estgrenewiche,' on October 25, 1529, eight days after Cardinal Wolsey had been deprived of it. The next day he was inducted into his seat in the Court of Chancery, 'after a noble exhortation' by the Duke of Norfolk, 'as well to the chancellor as to the people, and an answer of the chancellor.' No previous example of any introductory address on such an occasion occurs, and the object of the duke's speech seems to have been to justify the king's selection of a layman instead of an ecclesiastic or a nobleman, by enlarging on the wisdom, integrity, and wit of Sir Thomas, and the extraordinary abilities he had already shown in the affairs that had been entrusted to him. More's answer was modest and becoming, with a graceful and feeling allusion to the fall of his predecessor.

The contrast between his modesty and the cardinal's arrogance could not fail to secure universal satisfaction at his appointment to this high office, and his whole conduct while he retained it justified the favourable opinion that had been formed of him. Although he presided in the court little more than two years and a half, his diligence in the performance of its duties was so great that he is said on one occasion to have risen from his seat because there was no other cause depending before him. It must not be forgotten, however, that the number of suits in that age will bear no comparison with those in the present day. At the time of his elevation his father was a judge of the King's Bench. The two courts were opposite to each other in Westminster Hall, and every day during the sittings a rare example of filial piety was exhibited to those around, of the head of the law kneeling before his aged parent to receive his blessing ere the business commenced. The old man died in the course of the following year; but his death added little to the fortune of his son, for the estate was settled on Sir John's widow during her life, which extended ten years beyond that of Sir Thomas.

Various anecdotes are told of him during his elevation, which, while they show his own integrity, raise a suspicion that corruption in the judgment-seat had not been previously uncommon. The poorest suitor obtained ready access to him and speedy trial, while the richest offered presents in vain, and the claims of kindred found no favour. Even his son-in-law Giles Heron, refusing, in his reliance on the chancellor's family affection, to fall into a reasonable arbitrament, was obliged to submit to 'a flat decree against him.' The custom of presenting new year's gifts often afforded a cover to suitors in his court for tendering bribes, which, when attempted, he would with sly humour evade. A rich widow named Croker, who had obtained a decree against Lord Arundel, presented him one new year's day with a pair of gloves and forty pounds in angels in them. Emptying the money into her lap, he told her that, as it was 'against good manners to forsake a gentlewoman's new year's gift, he would take her gloves, but refuse the lining.' Another suitor brought him a gilt cup, 'the fashion whereof he very well liking, caused one of his own, better in value, to be brought, which he willed the messenger in recompense to deliver to his master.' And on a complaint made to the council after his resignation, that he had accepted a great gilt cup which a party in whose favour he had pronounced a decree had sent to him by his wife, he acknowledged that he had done so, but 'further declared that albeit he had indeed received that cup, yet immediately thereupon caused he his butler to fill it with wine, and of that cup drank to her; and that when he had so done, and she pledged him, then as freely as her husband had given it to him, even so freely gave he the same again to her to give unto her husband for his new year's gift.'

Besides his regular attendance in the court, he encouraged those who had complaints to resort to him at his own house, where he would sit in his open hall, in many instances bringing the parties to a friendly reconcilement of their disputes. He forbade any subpœna to be granted until the matter in issue had been laid before him with the lawyer's name attached to it, when if he found it sufficient he would add his fiat, but if too trifling for discussion would refuse the writ. Even in the performance of this duty he could not restrain his humour; and it is related that a case having been laid before him by one 'Tubbe,' an attorney, which he found to be on a very frivolous matter, he returned the paper with the words, 'a tale of a' prefixed to the lawyer's signature, 'Tubbe.' The common law judges having complained then, as indeed they did for a long time afterwards, that their judgments were suspended by injunctions out of Chancery, Sir Thomas caused a list of those he had granted to be made out, and inviting the judges to dinner, discussed with them the grounds of his decision in each case. On their acknowledging these to be just and reasonable, he recommended them themselves in future to qualify the extreme rigour of the law by like equitable considerations, and thus prevent the necessity of the chancellor's interference.

More's retirement from the chancellorship arose from no diminution of the king's favour, but was the result of his own earnest application. During his whole tenure of it, the question of the king's marriage, which had been so fatal to Wolsey, continued to be agitated. The opinions of the foreign as well as the English universities had been taken, and the chancellor had been called upon to present these, and the answers of many theologians and canonists, to the House of Commons; but still his own conscience was not satisfied, and, not only dreading the evil consequences which he thought he foresaw from these proceedings, but looking no doubt with a suspicious eye on the interference in ecclesiastical matters which Cromwell was then anxiously urging, he sought to be relieved from the responsibility of measures which he could not conscientiously sanction. Still so prudent had been his bearing that when, under pretence of illness, he obtained permission to resign the Seal on May 16, 1532, the king granted his discharge with cordial acknowledgments of his services, and gracious promises of continued favour, causing the Duke of Norfolk, on introducing his successor, to say that he had been only allowed to retire at his own earnest entreaty, and obliging the new chancellor to repeat the expression in the royal presence at the opening of parliament.

It is much to the credit of King Henry's discrimination that from More's first entrance into his service he distinguished him with peculiar confidence. He not only recognised in Sir Thomas that solidity of understanding and that integrity of character so valuable in a counsellor, but appreciated those intellectual powers and that liveliness of humour which made him so attractive as a companion. Thus, while he was employed abroad in most important missions, he was honoured when at home with a large share of royal familiarity. So frequently was his presence required by the king, as well to enter into scientific and learned discussions as to enliven the royal table by his merry conversation, that, in order to relieve himself from a restraint which kept him from his own family, he was compelled to assume a more solemn deportment, and by gradually discontinuing his former mirth to secure himself from such frequent invitations. The king's continued enjoyment of his society would be often shown by his sudden visits to More's house at Chelsea, partaking of his dinner, and treating him with that sort of playful kindness of which there is no other example than the intercourse between Henry II. and Becket before the latter was invested with the archiepiscopal mitre. More, however, was not deceived as to the real character of his sovereign. On one occasion, when the king had been strolling for an hour in the garden at Chelsea with his arm round More's neck, his son-in-law Roper congratulated him on being 'so familiarly entertained,' saying he had never seen the king do so to any before except Cardinal Wolsey, with whom he had once seen ' his grace walk arm in arm.' 'I thank our Lord,' answered More, 'I find his grace my very good lord indeed, and I believe he doth as singularly favour me as any subject within this realm; howbeit, son Roper, I may tell thee I have no cause to be proud thereof, for if my head would win a castle in France it should not fail to go.'

In less than a year after More's resignation, the king's marriage with Anne Boleyn was acknowledged. Many were the attempts made by Henry to induce Sir Thomas, at first by flattering messages and large promises, and afterwards by menaces, to give his concurrence. His inflexible adherence to his opinion gradually irritated the king to such an extent that in his anger he forgot all the services More had rendered, and determined either to force his acquiescence or to punish his refusal. It was only by the strong representations made by the new chancellor (Audley) and his other ministers, of his imminent risk of being defeated in parliament, that the king consented to leave More's name out of the bill of attainder against parties supposed to be implicated in the treason of Elizabeth Barton, the Holy Maid of Kent. The desired opportunity, however, was not long wanting.

On the king's marriage an act had been passed, fixing the succession of the throne on his issue by Anne Boleyn; and by one of its clauses an oath was required from all the king's subjects to maintain that settlement. (*Stat. Realm*, iii. 471.) This oath More would not have hesitated to take, as he admitted the right of parliament to regulate the settlement. But the form submitted to him containing in addition assertions of the invalidity of the king's first marriage, and of the validity of the second and of the divorce, More felt himself obliged to refuse it. He was accordingly committed to the Tower on April 17, 1534, and was attainted for misprision of treason on this account, by a separate act passed in the following November, which rendered void the king's former grants to him, and deprived him of all his other property of every kind. (*Ibid.* 538.)

Not content with keeping his unfortunate victim in strict confinement for more than a year, the arbitrary monarch, urged on, it is feared, by the new queen, resolved to pursue him to extremities. Another statute of the same parliament enacted that the king should be reputed the only supreme head on earth of the Church of England, and should have the title and style thereof annexed to his imperial crown; and by this act it was declared high treason to attempt to deprive the king of his title. (*Ibid.* 492, 508.) More, in all the interrogatories to which he was artfully subjected with a view to entrap him, evaded the question either by total silence or by saying, 'I will not meddle with such matters, for I am fully determined to serve God, and to think upon his passion and my passage out of this world.' At last, on June 12, 1535, a deputation waiting on him to take away his books, Rich, the solicitor-general, who was one of the party, under pretence of friendly remonstrance, inveigled More into an argument, by putting the case whether he would not acknowledge Rich to be king if parliament had declared him so. To this More answered in the affirmative, because parliament could both make and depose kings; but in return asked Rich whether he could, in obedience to an act of parliament, say that God was not God. Rich agreed that he could not, because it was impossible, but, suggesting that this was too high a case, cunningly proposed one which he said was between the two, asking him why, if he would acknowledge a king made by act of parliament, he should not take King Henry as supreme head of the Church, since he was so constituted by act of parliament. The reply to this, as alleged by Rich, but denied by Moore, was, that a subject could not be thus bound, because it was not a thing to which he *could* give his consent in parliament.

Disgracefully interpreting these words into a malicious denial of his title, the sanguinary tyrant, glad to find any pretence to vent his animosity, caused an indictment to be immediately prepared. (*Mr. Bruce in Archæologia*, xvii. 361-374.) On the trial Rich made himself infamous by his perjured representation of this 'familiar secret talk,' an obsequious jury declared More to be guilty, and the traitor's sentence was pronounced against him by the court—the former no way regarding his unanswerable defence, and the latter disallowing all his exceptions to the indictment. With a solemn prayer that his judges might be pardoned for his condemnation, he retired from the bar. On leaving the court his son met him, and kneeling down begged his blessing; and as he entered the Tower, his favourite daughter Margaret rushed through the crowd, and throwing her arms round his neck covered him with kisses, but, overwhelmed by her grief, could utter nothing but 'Oh my father! oh my father!'

Little time was allowed to elapse ere the final scene was enacted. His conviction took place on July 1, 1535 (*Baga de Secretis*), and on the 6th his head was severed from his body in the front of the Tower. Even in his last moments, impressed as he showed himself to be with the awful solemnity of his position, he exhibited no fear, and, amidst the prayers that he piously uttered, could not repress the humour which had always characterised him. When he was informed that the horrible part of the sentence was changed into beheading, he answered merrily, 'God forbid the king should use any more such mercy unto my friends, and God bless all my posterity from such pardons.'

'Pray, master lieutenant,' said he to that officer as he was ascending the scaffold, which seemed to give way, 'pray see me safe up, and as to my coming down I will shift for myself.' And when he laid his head on the block, he desired the executioner to stop till he had put his beard aside; 'for that,' said he, 'has committed no treason.'

His body was buried in St. Peter's within the Tower, but was at last removed by his daughter Margaret to the tomb in Chelsea Church which he had prepared during his life. His head, after remaining for some time exposed on London Bridge, a disgusting evidence of the ingratitude of princes, came also into the possession of his affectionate child, on whose death it was buried in her arms in St. Dunstan's, Canterbury.

Two years after his execution an annuity of 20*l*. was granted to his widow, Lady Alice More, and subsequently a lease of one of his houses at Chelsea. (*Auditor's Patent Book*, i. 160; 26 *Report Pub. Rec., App. 2.*) His three daughters were all married during his life. The eldest, Margaret, was united to William Roper, whose memoir of his father-in-law forms the staple of all his subsequent biographies. He was son of John Roper, Esq., of St. Dunstan's, near Canterbury, at first prothonotary of the Court of King's Bench (in which office William succeeded him), and afterwards the king's attorney-general. The second daughter, Elizabeth, was married to William Dauncy, Esq.; and the husband of the third daughter was Giles Heron, Esq. John, the only son and last-born child of Sir Thomas, married Anne, daughter and heir of Edward Cresacre, of Barnburgh in Yorkshire; and his grandson Cresacre More has been proved by Mr. Hunter to be the author of the life of his ancestor, which had been previously attributed to his brother Thomas. Mr. Hunter conceives that the male progeny of the chancellor became extinct in 1795.

MORETON, EARL OF. *See* ROBERT.

MOREVILLE, HUGH DE, who had the barony of Burgh-on-the-Sands in Cumberland, and other possessions in that and the neighbouring counties, as successor to his father Roger, and his grandfather Simon, was forester of Cumberland, and added to his property that of his wife, Helewise de Stuteville, a relative, probably a sister, of the Baron Robert de Stuteville.

In conjunction with the latter, he was a justice itinerant for the counties of Northumberland and Cumberland in 16 Henry II., 1170 (*Madox*, i. 144); but although Robert de Stuteville acted in the same capacity in the following year, the name of Hugh de Moreville no longer appears as his associate. His discontinuance in this honourable office arose from the part he took in December 1170 in the murder of Becket, as before related. After the assassination, he and his colleagues retired without interruption, and repaired to a castle at Knaresborough, which belonged to Hugh de Moreville, where they stayed many months, not daring to return to Henry's court. It is added by William of Newbury, 'that, being stung with remorse, they willingly went to Rome, and were sent by the pope to Jerusalem, where, after they had for some years performed not remissly the penance enjoined them, they all ended their lives.' However this may be with regard to the others, it certainly is not true in reference to Hugh de Moreville's death.

During the remainder of the reign of Henry II., and the whole of that of Richard I., no mention is made of his name; but in the first year of King John he is recorded as paying fifteen marks and three good palfreys for holding his court with his liberties 'de Tol et Theam, et Infangenetheif, et Furto, et de Judicio Ferri et Aquæ,' as long as Helewise his wife should continue in a secular habit. (*Rot. de Oblatis*, 54.) He died shortly afterwards, leaving two daughters, one of whom, Ada, became the wife of the after-mentioned justicier, Thomas de Muleton. (*Dugdale's Baron.* i. 612; *Lord Lyttelton,* ii. 3, 101, 589; *Hasted,* xii. 331.)

MOREWIC, HUGH DE, the son of Ernulf de Morewic, held the manor of Chidington in Northumberland, by the service of one knight's fee. He was in attendance on the king at Waltham in 1182, whose will then made he witnessed. In 30 Henry II., 1184, he was one of the justiciers and barons before whom a fine was acknowledged in the King's Court at Westminster, and he afterwards acted as a justice itinerant in Lincolnshire and Yorkshire. (*Pipe Roll,* 60, 78.) He held the sheriffalty of Cumberland in 31 Henry II. and two following years.

On the fine he is styled 'dapifer regis,' an office which he held with Hugh Bardolf. It is not improbable that they were dapifers of Normandy, since an allowance was made to them in the Norman Roll of that year for 100*l.* disbursed for the king's expenses when he was at Gisors. (*Madox,* i. 168.) His death occurred about 1190. (*Baronage,* i. 678.)

MORGAN, HAMON, although one of the justices itinerant who actually fixed the assize of the county of Hants in 20 Henry II., 1174, by virtue of the writ of Richard de Luci, does not seem to have been originally appointed, the words 'qui fuit in loco constabularii' being added to his name. (*Madox,* i. 125.) The constable at that time was either Henry or Mabel, sons of Milo de Gloucester, Earl of Hereford.

MORGAN, FRANCIS, is frequently confounded with the under-mentioned Richard Morgan. They were not even of the same family. That of Francis was settled at Kingsthorpe in Northamptonshire, in which county he was born. His legal training took place in the Middle Temple, where he was reader in 1553. He was advanced by Queen Mary to the degree of the coif on October 16, 1555; and his elevation to the judgeship of the Queen's Bench did not occur till January 23, 1558 (*Dugdale's Orig.* 128, 217; *Dyer,* 158), more than eighteen months after the death of his namesake the chief justice. He survived his appointment for seven months only, during a great part of which he was prevented by illness from acting, and died on August 19 in the same year. His funeral monument is in the church of Nether Heyford in Northamptonshire.

He married Anne, the daughter of Christopher Pemberton, and both his sons died without male issue. (*Bridges' Northamptonshire,* i. 521; *Baker's,* i. 40, 183–189.)

MORGAN, RICHARD, of whose family no certain account is given, was admitted at Lincoln's Inn in 1523, and called to the bar in 1529. He became reader in 1542, and again in 1546, when he was summoned to take the degree of the coif. He was elected recorder of Gloucester in 1546, and was returned member for that city in both the parliaments of Edward VI. His name occurs occasionally in Plowden's Reports, but he does not appear to have acquired any eminence as an advocate, his religion, which was Roman Catholic, perhaps operating to the injury of his practice.

Attached no doubt by this tie to the family of the Princess Mary, he was committed to the Fleet in March 1551 for hearing mass in her chapel (*Strype's Cranmer,* ii. 233); and on King Edward's death, in July 1553, he was among the first of those who, disregarding the proclamation of Lady Jane Grey as queen, immediately joined the princess at Kenninghall Castle in Norfolk. He did not wait long for his reward for this early proof of his devotion. In the same month he acted as one of the commissioners to hear Bishop Tunstall's appeal against his conviction (*Rymer,* xv. 334), and on September 5 was raised to the office of chief justice of the Common Pleas and knighted.

One of the earliest commissions he was named upon was that for the trial of Lady Jane Grey on November 13, when she pleaded guilty, and was condemned by him to burned alive on Tower Hill, or beheaded, as the queen should please. (4 *Report Pub. Rec., App.* ii. 238.) Morgan remained chief justice for nearly two years after this, his successor, Sir Robert Brooke, being appointed on October 8, 1555. His death, however, did not take place till the following year, when he was buried on June 2, at St. Magnus's, London Bridge. (*Machyn's Diary,* 106.) His removal from the bench before his death gives some weight to the story that he became mad from the bitter remembrance of the dreadful sentence he had pronounced upon the Lady Jane, and that in his raving he cried continually to have her taken away from him. (*Holinshed,* iv. 23.)

MORIN, RALPH, was an officer of the Exchequer, and seems to have been a careless keeper of the treasure, as Adam de Sanford accounts for him on the roll of 1 Richard I. for five marks of the money from Winchester which were deposited in the castle at Northampton, and lost. (*Pipe Roll,* 34.) In 2 and 3 John he acted as a justicier in the country, when fines were levied before the court. In the first of these years he was appointed sheriff of Devonshire; but in 4 John he was ordered to deliver up the castle of Exeter to William Briwer, for whom, in 7 John, he accounts for that county. (*Rot. Chart.* 100; *Rot. Pat.* 12; *Madox,* i. 276.) Fuller says that he held the same office for Northamptonshire in 30 Henry II.

MORLAND, WILLIAM, held the office of master of the Rolls only during the last two months of the temporary restoration of Henry VI., between February 12 and April 29, 1471. He had previously been one of the masters in Chancery, and after Edward's re-conquest of the throne he fell back into his former place, acting like his brethren as a receiver of petitions in parliament until 4 Henry VII. (*Rot. Parl.* vi. 167–409.)

In February 1470 he was installed dean of Windsor, but was deprived in October 1471, a few months after Edward's return. (*Le Neve*, 375.)

MORTIMER, WILLIAM DE, probably one of the many collateral branches of the noble families of Mortuomari, was one of the justices itinerant appointed in 20 Edward I., 1292, for the northern counties, and in the thirty-second year acted as a justice of assize in ten of the inland counties. In the following year he was named a receiver of the petitions of Ireland and Guernsey, in the parliament held at Westminster in September. (*Rot. Parl.* i. 159.) During the reign of Edward II. he continued to act as a justice itinerant, and to be summoned as such to parliament till the ninth year. (*Parl. Writs*, ii. 1205.)

MORTON, JOHN (ARCHBISHOP OF CANTERBURY), was born either at Bere Regis, or at Milborne St. Andrew, in the county of Dorset, places not above three miles apart. He was the son of Richard Morton, of a very ancient Nottinghamshire family. One of the archbishop's brothers was ancestor of a baronet created in 1619, but whose male descendants failed in 1698.

John Morton was educated in Cerne Abbey, and he is even said to have been for some time a monk there. It is certain, however, that he was sent to Balliol College, Oxford, where he took the degree of doctor in both laws. His conduct and learning caused him to be appointed one of the commissaries of the university in 1446, and moderator of the civil law school. In 1453 he was made principal of Peckwater Inn, and in 1494 he was advanced to the head of the university as chancellor.

Commencing his public career as an advocate in the Court of Arches, he soon attracted the notice of Archbishop Bourchier, to whose friendship and estimation of his talents he owed several of his advancements in the Church and the state. In 1456, while that prelate still held the Great Seal, Morton was placed about the person of Edward Prince of Wales, son of Henry VI., as his chancellor (*Cal. Rot. Pat.* 297), and was also made clerk or master in Chancery.

His ecclesiastical preferments were numerous. Besides several prebends and livings, he was from 1474 to 1477 successively instituted into four archdeaconries—those of Winchester, Huntingdon, Berks, and Leicester (*Le Neve*)—some of which he retained till his elevation to the episcopal bench.

On the dethronement of Henry VI., neither his clerical nor official character prevented him from joining his unfortunate sovereign in the field of Towton, on Palm Sunday 1461. He escaped from the battle, and accompanied Queen Margaret to Flanders. Beyond his being among those who were attainted of high treason in the parliament of the following November, he is not mentioned during the first ten years of Edward's reign, nor in the short restoration of Henry VI. The tragical events which soon after occurred having left no immediate representative of the house of Lancaster, Morton sued for and obtained his pardon in July 1471, with the reversal of his attainder in October of the following year. (*Rot. Parl.* v. 477, 480, vi. 26.) It is not improbable that his restoration to royal favour was as much owing to King Edward's admiration of his constancy to the fallen fortunes of Henry, as to the intercession of his friend Archbishop Bourchier; for in less than a year after his pardon he was appointed master of the Rolls, his patent being dated March 16, 1472. In 1473 the Great Seal was several times deposited with him as keeper; and at the end of that year he was sent with Sir Thomas Montgomery on an embassy to Nuys in Germany, then under siege, to negotiate a treaty with the Duke of Burgundy. (*Paston Letters*, ii. 78, 90.)

There is a second patent to him as master of the Rolls, dated May 2, 1475, more than three years after his first appointment. On comparing the two, the cause of this renewal seems to be a doubt he entertained whether the grant in the first patent of the Domus Conversorum, 'pro habitatione suâ,' did not prevent him from residing in any other place, as the only variation in the second patent is in reference to that house, the custody of which was then granted to him 'per se vel per sufficientem deputatum suum, sive sufficientes deputatos suos.' Soon after this, King Edward revived his claim to the crown of France; and Dr. Morton was one of the negotiators of the treaty by which Louis XI. stopped the invasion by giving to the English king an annual pension, and distributing large sums among the most powerful in his court, of which Dr. Morton, with such examples before him, deemed it no disgrace to be a participator. (*Cal. Rot. Pat.* 321; *Rymer*, xii. 45, 48; *Turner*, iii. 355.)

If there was any previous doubt entertained by the king in reference to Morton's loyalty, it is manifest that it was now entirely dissipated. The earliest opportunity was taken to advance him in the Church. Bishop William Grey had not been dead above four days ere Morton was, by the king's request, elected as his successor in the see of Ely on August 8, 1478.

On January 9, 1479, he resigned the mastership of the Rolls to his nephew Robert Morton, for whom he had procured the grant in reversion nearly two years before. (*Rymer*, ii. 57.)

During the remaining four years of Edward's reign the new bishop quietly performed his episcopal duties; and the king's confidence in his prudence and attachment is said to have been further evidenced by his making him one of the executors of his will, of which, however, no record has been discovered. That this was so, and that he was therefore supposed to feel a devoted interest in Edward's infant family, is rendered probable by the violent conduct of the Protector Richard towards him, for which no other reason appears. The young king's council had been summoned on the 13th of June, to deliberate on the coronation; and the protector, attending it, had courteously requested the bishop to let him have some strawberries from his garden in Holborn for his dinner, and had then retired. Shortly afterwards he returned, and that furious scene which terminated in the hurried execution of Lord Hastings was performed, Bishop Morton and the Primate of York being immediately arrested, and imprisoned in the Tower. The petition, however, of the university of Oxford procured his release from that fortress, and he was sent to Brecon under the wardship of the Duke of Buckingham. On that nobleman's subsequent discontent and retirement to Brecon, the bishop contrived to glide into his confidence; and between them they concocted the plan of raising the Earl of Richmond to the throne, and uniting the two factions of York and Lancaster by the marriage of the earl with Elizabeth, the eldest daughter of the late King Edward. He urged his dismissal, under the pretence that by his presence in Ely he could assist the project; but the duke would not part with so wise and politic an adviser. The bishop therefore contrived his own escape, and, obtaining a supply of money in Ely, immediately joined the Earl of Richmond in Flanders. The duke's capture, and sudden execution on November 2, quickly followed; and the bishop, in the parliament of January, was deprived of all his possessions. (*Rot. Parl.* vi. 245, 250, 273.) The Earl of Richmond's fleet having been scattered by a storm, it was not till nearly two years afterwards that his hopes of acquiring the English crown were realised by the defeat of Richard at Bosworth, on August 22, 1485.

During the interval Bishop Morton had remained in Flanders, and had been of great service to Richmond in advising him of Richard's projects against him. The earl had not long assumed the crown, with the title of Henry VII., ere he summoned the bishop to England, and, admitting him into the council, loaded him with favours. His attainder being reversed in the first parliament, he was constituted lord chancellor on March 6, 1486; and in July, on the death of Cardinal Bourchier, the temporalities of the see of Canterbury were placed in his custody during the vacancy, in preparation for his own election to the primacy, which immediately followed, the papal bull of translation being dated on October 6. (*Rymer*, xii. 302, 317.) Thus placed in possession of the highest offices, both in Church and state, he retained them during the remainder of his life.

As a minister of the former, one of his first efforts was directed to the reformation of the priests, who, living in luxurious extravagance, were guilty of drunkenness and incontinence, and even worse crimes. The dissolute life led in the monasteries was the next object of his attention, and the laxity of morals and general profligacy of the monks are incontestably proved by his letter to the abbot of St. Alban's. His strenuous exertions in pursuing his ecclesiastical reforms naturally produced hostility on the part of those attacked, and were even opposed by some of the bishops. Conspiracies formed against his life were said to have occasioned the passing of the statute 3 Henry VII. c. 14, making such an offence against any of the king's servants felony. His energy, however, was supported by the king, and approved by the pope, by whom he was rewarded with the cardinal's hat, with the title of St. Athanasius, in 1493.

As a minister of the crown, historians differ as to his character, some asserting him to be the author of Henry's oppressive measures, and others vindicating him from the charge by showing that after his death the king did not diminish his severity. The former, in support of their views, cite the argument he used to the unwilling to enforce the 'benevolence'—a dilemma which received the name of the Bishop's Fork or Crutch, and which Fuller, with his usual quaintness, describes as 'perswading *prodigals* to part with their money because *they did spend it most*, and the *covetous* because *they might spare it best*; so making both *extreams* to meet in one *medium*, to supply the king's necessities.' The latter declare, on the contrary, that, so far from encouraging, he endeavoured to soften and restrain the king. The truth probably lies something between the two extremes. The haughtiness of his manners would make him unpopular; but his wisdom and eloquence, his zeal and discretion (which all allow him), must have secured the favour of his sovereign; while his loyal devotion to the family he had served (not leaving it till its total extinction), and his

H H

successful efforts to terminate the civil war which had so long distracted the kingdom, are claims on the admiration of posterity which cannot fail to be acknowledged.

After presiding over the province of Canterbury for fourteen years, he died on September 13, 1500, at his palace of Knoll in Kent, whence his remains were removed for interment in Canterbury Cathedral.

To both his dioceses he was a liberal benefactor, restoring their cathedrals and repairing their palaces, and executing in Ely a work of public utility in draining the fens, by a cut called the New Leame, or Morton's Leame, more than twelve miles long. The poor were not forgotten by him, either in his life or his testamentary remembrances, and both the universities were partakers of his bounty. (*Godwin*, 130, 269; *Athen. Oxon.* ii. 683; *Hutchins's Dorset*, i. 478; *Holinshed*, iii. 404, &c.; *Turner*, iv. 109, 135.)

MORTON, ROBERT (BISHOP OF WORCESTER), was the son of Sir Rowland Morton, of Thwining in Gloucestershire, who was a younger brother of the above Archbishop John Morton. To that celebrated prelate he was probably indebted for his advancement in the Church, and to the judicial position he filled; for there is nothing in his history which would give him a personal claim to either. His uncle, previous to his elevation to the episcopal bench, had procured for Robert, on May 30, 1477, a grant in reversion of the mastership of the Rolls on his death or resignation. The latter contingency occurred on his promotion to the bishopric of Ely, and Robert took possession of the office on January 9, 1479. He also succeeded his uncle in the archdeaconry of Winchester.

During the four remaining years of the reign of Edward IV., and the few weeks of which that of Edward V. consisted, Robert Morton preserved his place; but no sooner had his uncle, then Bishop of Ely, become suspected of implication in the Duke of Buckingham's conspiracy against Richard, than his supposed crime was visited upon Robert, who was at once superseded by Thomas Barowe, on September 22, 1483.

On the termination of the usurper's short career, Thomas Barowe retired from the mastership of the Rolls, as an intruder, and Robert Morton was of course reinstated. He was named as one of the commissioners to perform the office of steward at Henry's coronation (*Rymer*, xii. 277), and he seems to have been otherwise actively employed in the king's affairs, since that is stated to be the reason why his request to have a partner in his office of master of the Rolls was complied with. He and William Eliot accordingly received a joint appointment for their lives and that of the longest liver, by patent dated November 13, 1485. On October 16 in the following year he was advanced to the bishopric of Worcester. Having then resigned the mastership of the Rolls, for the next ten years he performed the duties of his prelacy in a quiet and unobtrusive manner. He died (between three and four years before his uncle) in the first week of May 1497, and was buried in St. Paul's Cathedral.

It is curious that about six weeks before his death he deemed it necessary to obtain a charter of general pardon for all offences he had in any way committed. (*Rymer*, xii. 648.) This was, no doubt, applied for by the cautious recommendation of the archbishop, for the purpose of securing the property of his dying nephew from those extortions to which too many in that reign were compelled to submit, under the pretence of breaches of unrepealed but obsolete laws, the power of enforcing which had been revived by a statute of the preceding year. (*Godwin*, 467; *Le Neve*, 290, 298; *Stat. Realm*, v. 475.)

MORTON, WILLIAM, was great-grandson of Sir Rowland Morton, one of the masters of requests in the reign of Henry VIII., and son of James Morton of Clifton, in the parish of Severne Stoke in Worcestershire, by Jane, daughter of William Cook, of Shillwood in the same county. (*Visitation Worcester*, 1634.) Educated at Sidney Sussex College, Cambridge, he took the degrees of B.A. and M.A. in 1622 and 1625, and was admitted into the Inner Temple. He was called to the bar in 1630, and is mentioned in Croke's Reports in 1639. The troubles immediately succeeded that date, when the young barrister exchanged his gown for the sword and joined the king, who conferred on him the honour of knighthood. He served as lieutenant-colonel in Lord Chandos's regiment of horse, and was entrusted with the government of his lordship's castle at Sudeley when it was attacked in 1644 by the parliamentary general Waller; and being betrayed by an officer of the garrison, he was made prisoner and sent to the Tower. Clarendon says (iv. 489) that 'he had given so frequent testimony of his signal courage in several actions, in which he had received many wounds both by the pistol and the sword, that his mettle was never suspected, and his fidelity as little questioned; and after many years of imprisonment, sustained with great firmness and constancy, he lived to receive the reward of his merit, after the return of the king.' Some years after the end of the war he was released, and resumed his profession, probably confining himself to chamber practice.

He was made a bencher of his inn in 1659, and within a few days after the Restoration was summoned to take the degree of the coif. In 1662 he was elected recorder of Gloucester, and was appointed 'consiliarius' to the dean and chapter of Worcester. In July 1663 he was created king's serjeant, and on November 23, 1665, he was nominated a judge of the King's Bench. This position he filled respectably for nearly seven years, and had the good fortune to avoid censure, but was the terror of highwaymen; and they had some reason so to regard him, for when Claude Duval, the French page of the Duke of Richmond, took the road, and was after many wonderful escapes at last captured and convicted, the judge prevented the mercy of the crown being extended to him by threatening to resign if so notorious an offender was allowed to escape. Duval was the most popular of his stamp, and an especial favourite with the ladies, to one of whom he returned 300*l.* out of 400*l.* he had taken from her, upon her dancing a coranto with him on the heath where he had stopped her coach. Dames of high rank visited him in prison and interceded for his life, and the good-natured king would probably have granted his pardon but for the interference of the judge. (*Lord Macaulay's England*, i. 383.)

Sir William married Annie, daughter and sole heir of John Smyth, of Kidlington in Oxfordshire, and died in the summer vacation of 1672.

MOTELOW, HENRY DE, appears among the advocates in the Year Books from 18 Edward III., and was raised to the bench of the Common Pleas on July 4, 1357. Fines were not acknowledged before him later than Easter 1361, 35 Edward III. (*Dugdale's Orig.* 45.)

MOUBRAY, JOHN DE, was lineally descended from Robert de Moubray, a younger brother of the ancestor of Moubray Duke of Norfolk. He is described as of Kirklington in Yorkshire, and had evidently very extensive practice as an advocate from 17 Edward III., attaining the rank of king's serjeant in the 28th year. He was raised to the bench of the Common Pleas on July 11, 1359, and was soon after made a knight of the Bath. The fines acknowledged before him extend to 1373. (*Dugdale's Orig.* 45, 103.)

He married Margaret, sister of Sir Alexander Percy, of Kildare. (*Testam. Ebor.* 158; *Notes and Queries,* 2nd S. xi. 293.)

MOYLE, WALTER, acquired the manor and large demesnes of Stevenstone in Devonshire by his marriage with Margaret, the heiress of that property. He probably was born in Cornwall, as his father, Henry, was the third son of Thomas Moyle, of Bodmin. He was afterwards established at Eastwell in Kent, and was named a commissioner in that county in 33 Henry VI., 1454, to raise money for the defence of Calais. (*Acts Privy Council,* vi. 239.)

He is said to have been a reader at Gray's Inn. In 1443 he was called to the degree of the coif, and is mentioned as one of the king's serjeants in 1454. (*Rot. Parl.* v. 240.)

On July 9, 1454, he was constituted a judge of the Common Pleas, where he acted for the next seventeen years, extending through the remaining portion of Henry's reign, the first ten years of that of Edward IV., and the six months in 1470-1 during which Henry reassumed his seat on the throne. (*Dugdale's Orig.* 46.)

Whether his non-appointment on the return of Edward IV. was occasioned by the act of the king or his own retirement does not appear; probably the latter, as he must have been then considerably advanced in age. He died before July 31, 1480, when his will was proved. In it he grants two acres of land in Eastwell, in trust for the use of the church there, 'in recompense of a certain annual rent of 2lbs. of wax, by me wrested and detained from the said church against my conscience.' The estate of Eastwell was carried by one of his female descendants in marriage to the noble family of the Earl of Winchilsea. (*Hasted,* vii. 392; *Collins's Peerage,* iii. 379, viii. 510; *Testam. Vetust.* 349.)

MOYNE, JOHN LE, is first mentioned when he was fined twenty marks in 26 Henry III., 1242, for marrying Isabella, one of the heirs of Eustace de Fercles, without the king's licence. (*Excerpt. e Rot. Fin.* ii. 471.) In 38 Henry III. he was sheriff of the counties of Cambridge and Huntingdon, and complaints were made against him that he took money at the sheriff's tourn contrary to the custom in those counties; and also that he received a conveyance of sixty acres of land, twenty-three acres of meadow, and two messuages, from a man charged with the murder of his father, of which he was convicted and hanged. (*Ibid.* ii. 213; *Madox,* i. 446.) The result of the investigation does not appear.

But on December 5, 1265, he and Robert de Fulham were constituted justices of the Jews (*Madox,* i. 234), in which office he did not long remain, for at the end of the following September there are entries of assizes directed to be held before him in conjunction with William de Poywick, which extend to August 1267, in the counties of Hereford, Gloucester, and Worcester; and on December 25, 1268, his name appears as the king's escheator south of Trent, and mandates are directed to him in that character till August 1, 1270. (*Excerpt. e Rot. Fin.* ii. 444, 457, 481-519.) He died about 1274. (*Cal. Inquis.* p.m. i. 54.)

MUCEGROS, MILO DE, is not otherwise mentioned than as one of the justices itinerant to settle the assize of Herefordshire in 20 Henry II., 1174 (*Madox,* i. 124), and as sheriff of the county with William Torell in 29 Henry II.

MUCEGROS, RICHARD DE, was the son of a gentleman of the same name who was sheriff of Gloucestershire in 2 and 3 Richard I., which the son afterwards held in 9 John, paying 250*l*. for holding it at the old rent, with 100*l*. of increase for every year. (*Rot. de Fin.* 385.) In that year he was allowed a payment of ten marks for the queen's expenses during her stay at Gloucester. (*Rot. Claus.* i. 96.) In the previous year the castle of Gloucester, with the prisoners and hostages there, was committed to his custody, and soon afterwards the castle of Chichester also. (*Rot. Pat.* 71, 74, 79.)

His employment as a justicier for six years, commencing 6 John, 1204, appears from various fines acknowledged before him. (*Hunter's Preface.*) During the intestine troubles at the end of the reign he adhered to the king, and was rewarded by a mandate to William the earl marshal to provide him with some escheats from the lands of 'the king's enemies,' and by a grant of the estate of John Fitz-Richard. He was still alive in 5 Henry III. (*Rot. Claus.* i. 237, 243, 470.)

MULETON, THOMAS DE, was the son of Lambert de Muleton, whose possessions were at a place of that name in Lincolnshire, where his ancestors for three generations had resided. (*Baronage*, i. 567.) He was in 7 John and the two following years sheriff of that county, for which appointment he paid a fine of five hundred marks and five palfreys. (*Rot. de Fin.* 338, &c.) At the termination of his office he seems to have offended the king, since Reginald de Cornhill was commanded to take his body and imprison him in Rochester Castle until he had paid what he owed to the crown to the last penny. (*Rot. Pat.* 85.) He was not long in disgrace, but in 12 John accompanied the king to Ireland, and was with him in 14 John, when he appears to have been responsibly employed. His attestation is appended to several charters during this and the two following years. (*Rot. Chart.*) On the rising of the barons he joined their party, and was unlucky enough to be taken prisoner with his son Alan in the castle of Rochester. He had been previously excommunicated, and was now imprisoned in the castle of Corff, and his own castle and other possessions were seized into the king's hands, but soon after the accession of Henry III. they were fully restored to him on his returning to his allegiance. (*Rot. Claus.* i. 241, 317; *Rot. Pat.* 164.)

Early in the reign of King John he was married to the daughter of Richard Delfliet (*Rot. Cancell.* 193), on whose death he contracted a second marriage, without applying for the king's licence, with Ada, the widow of Richard de Luci of Egremont, and daughter of the before-noticed Hugh de Moreville. This rashness met immediate punishment in the seizure of all his lands in Cumberland, which were only restored by the ultimate payment of a large fine for his transgression. (*Rot. Claus.* i. 354, 358, 366.) By virtue of this marriage he obtained the office of forester of Cumberland, which was confirmed to him by the king. (*Ibid.* 513, 532.)

Holding now large possessions in those parts, he was in 3 Henry III., 1219, appointed one of the justices itinerant in the counties of Cumberland, Westmoreland, and Lancaster. His legal abilities were probably brought under observation by this appointment, as within five years afterwards he was raised to the bench at Westminster, on which he continued to sit until nearly the close of his life. The fines acknowledged before him extend from Easter 1224 to Easter 1236. (*Dugdale's Orig.* 42.) In the earlier years he held a second or inferior station; but in January 1227 he was placed at the head of one of the commissions, and he retained this position in all his remaining circuits, except that in one instance, 1232, he was preceded by Stephen de Segrave, who then was Justiciarius Angliæ. In 1235 Dugdale inserts him among the justices of the Common Pleas, the expression in the record being 'Justiciarius de Banco;' and he adds, 'Capitalis ut videtur,' a suggestion difficult to be reconciled with the position ascribed to Robert de Lexinton about the same period, the more especially as there is no proof of Thomas de Muleton's acting in a judicial character after that year. He lived, however, till 1240.

He was evidently of an impetuous disposition, somewhat covetous and overbearing, and disinclined to allow any obstacle to stand in the way of his ambition. Of his learning in the laws nothing remains for us to judge; but the proofs of his charity appear in his pious benefactions. By his first wife he had three sons, one of whom obtained with his wife Anabel, a daughter of Richard de Luci, the barony of Egremont, which fell into abeyance in 1334.

By his second wife, Ada, he had two children—Julian, who married Robert le Vavasour; and Thomas, who succeeded him, and obtained the barony of Gillesland by his marriage with Maud, the daughter and heir of Hubert de Vaux. He is now represented in the House of Lords by two peerages—viz., Lord Dacre and the Earl of Carlisle.

MURDAC, HUGH, was a chaplain of Henry II., and doubtless of the same family as Henry Murdac, Archbishop of York. He was one of the justices itinerant selected by the king at the council of Windsor in 1179, and was appointed with four others to exercise judicial functions in the counties of the home district, in which he acted also in the following year. Madox quotes an entry in a book in the possession of the dean and chapter of London, showing that he was present in the Exchequer in 30 Henry II., when an acknowledgment as to certain lands was made there. In the next year he had the custody of the abbey of Selby, then in the king's hands. (*Madox*, i. 138, 215, 309.) The archdeaconry of Cleveland was given to him in 1200, and he held it till 1204. (*Le Neve*, 328; *Rot. Chart.* 103.)

MURDAC, RALPH, appears as one of those present in the Exchequer on an acknowledgment relative to some land being made there in 30 Henry II., 1184, immediately following that of the above Hugh Murdac (*Madox*, i. 215), and he acted as a justice itinerant in some of the subsequent years of that reign. The Pipe Roll of 1 Richard I. (35–194) contains proof that he held a high place among the justices itinerant of that year also, in no less than ten counties. He was sheriff of Derbyshire and Nottinghamshire from 27 Henry II. to 1 Richard I. In the latter reign he seems to have contributed some fine to the royal coffers 'pro habendo amore Regis Ricardi,' an arrear of 50*l*. 6*s*. 8*d*. being charged on that account at so late a date as the roll of 11 John, in the county of Oxford. (*Madox*, i. 474.) He, however, died about 1 John, and the custody of his land and heir was given to William Briwer. (*Rot. de Liberate*, 13.)

MURRAY, WILLIAM (EARL OF MANSFIELD), than whom there never has been a judge more venerated by his contemporaries, nor whose memory is regarded with greater respect and affection, even at this distance of time, as the great oracle of law, and the founder of commercial jurisprudence, was the fourth son of David the fifth Viscount Stormont and third Lord Balvaird, being one of fourteen children borne to him by Margery, daughter of David Scot of Scotstarvet, of the noble family of Buccleuch. He was born at his father's palace of Scone, near Perth, on March 2, 1704–5. Educated at the grammar school at Perth till he was fourteen years old, he was then sent to Westminster School in May 1718, and was elected king's scholar in the next year. Here his proficiency was so great, both in his exercises and declamations, that at the examination in 1723 he was placed at the head of the list selected for Christ Church, Oxford. In his admission there on June 18 his place of birth is mistakenly written 'Bath,' owing probably to the broad pronunciation of the word 'Perth' by the giver of his description. Though intended for the Church, he felt a natural vocation for the bar, in which he was conscious that his father with his fourteen children could not afford to indulge him. Fortunately for the world, he was enabled to gratify his inclination, by the assistance of the first Lord Foley, whose son had formed an intimacy with him at Westminster, and who had in his visits in the holidays been at once taken by his amiable disposition and promising abilities. He was accordingly entered at Lincoln's Inn on April 23, 1724. In both places he pursued his studies assiduously. In the former, besides industriously mastering the usual academic course, he especially devoted himself to the improvement of his natural powers of oratory, taking Demosthenes, and, above all, Cicero as his models. In the latter his sedulous application was successfully employed in acquiring that knowledge of practice and of law by which he was enabled so soon to prove himself an accomplished advocate, and to use his eloquence, not in mere ornamentation, but in unravelling the contradictory facts and the abstruse points of the cases which he might have to conduct. At Oxford he took his degree of B.A. in 1727, at the same time gaining the prize for a Latin poem on the death of George I.; and in June 1730 he became M.A., and was called to the bar at Lincoln's Inn on November 23.

In the interval between his two degrees he familiarised himself with the courts by frequenting Westminster Hall, and he practised his argumentative and rhetorical powers by discussing knotty questions of law at a debating society. As a relaxation from his severer studies he amused himself with the current works of literature, and by associating freely with that class to which his rank and his talents gave him an easy introduction. Though strictly temperate in his habits, Boswell tells us that he sometimes 'drank champagne with the wits,' introduced probably by Alexander Pope, with whom he had from boyhood contracted an intimacy, and who showed his affection for his young friend not only by devoting some lines at an early period of his career to a eulogistic allusion to his merits, and even by dedicating to him the 'Imitation of the First Book of Horace,' but also by teaching him to add grace of action to the charm of his voice. On one occasion an intimate friend, it is said, surprised him in the act of practising before a glass, with Pope sitting by as his instructor.

He commenced his career as a barrister in the Court of Chancery; and that for the first eighteen months he was entirely without adequate encouragement, as has been asserted, seems scarcely probable, since he is found at the end of that time to be engaged in no less than three appeals in the House of Lords, one of which was on the all-absorbing subject of the South Sea Bubble. He so distinguished himself by his arguments in them that, whatever may have been his former progress, no doubt of his advance could any longer exist. Not only was he immediately engaged in numerous cases before the same august tribunal, but he came into regular employment in Westminster Hall, where his rising fame was universally recognised. This was fully confirmed by his eloquent defence of Colonel Sloper in an action of *crim. con.* brought against him by Theophilus Cibber, and by his argument before parliament against the bill to disfranchise the city of Edinburgh on account of the Porteous riots, in gratitude for which that corporation presented him with the freedom of the city in a gold box. The dean and chapter of Christ Church also complimented him with the nomination of a student in their college, in acknowledgment of his successful efforts in the Court of Chancery on a question of much importance to them.

In November 1742, soon after the dissolution of Sir Robert Walpole's ministry, he was made solicitor-general, and entered parliament as member for Boroughbridge. He held the post of solicitor for twelve years, and in May 1754 succeeded to the place of attorney-general, which he held for two years more.

His success in the House of Commons was as brilliant as it was at the bar. During these fourteen years he continued to sit for Boroughbridge, and from his entrance into the senate till the hour of his removal from it he acquired by the force of his arguments, by the clearness of his expositions, and by the eloquence in language, manner, and action in which they were clothed, an undisputed ascendency, out-shining every other speaker, except his chief antagonist and rival Mr. Pitt, whom he equalled in everything but the power of invective. To him the Pelham administration were indebted for the most effective support of their measures; and in that of the Duke of Newcastle he was the trusted leader and almost the entire prop of the government. When the weakness of that government was nearly overcome by a powerful opposition, the death of Sir Dudley Ryder, chief justice of the King's Bench, occurred; and so essential to the existence of the ministry was the continuance of the attorney-general deemed in the House of Commons that, though Sir Dudley died in May 1756, the office was not filled up till November, the interval being occupied by the offer to Sir William of every species of inducement in the shape of tellerships, reversions, and a large pension, to induce him to forego his acknowledged right to the office. Murray however resisted all temptation, and at last was obliged to tell the duke that, if not immediately appointed chief justice and created a peer, he would no longer sit in the house as attorney-general. The duke was obliged to submit, but, with the loss of his able lieutenant, was soon forced to resign his command.

In the exercise of his official duties as solicitor and attorney general he had never outraged popular feeling by undue severity; and against the few prosecutions which he sanctioned, or his manner of conducting them, no possible objection could be raised. His success in those he instituted was to be attributed to his rule never to prosecute where there was any risk of failure. In the proceedings against those implicated in the rebellion of 1745 he was necessarily concerned for the crown, but was careful to avoid everything that could aggravate the crimes of the prisoners, or inflame the passions of those who were to try them. In all the trials, and more particularly in that of Lord Lovat, he exercised a degree of candour and humanity which drew forth the admiration of all his hearers. In reference to that rebellion an absurd charge was made against him, that he had in his youth joined some Jacobite friends in drinking the health of the pretender on his knees. Although the king treated the imputation with the contempt that it deserved, the folly of one of the parties implicated forced an enquiry before the privy council, in which Murray indignantly denied its truth. The result of course was a complete acquittal from every part of it. His last appearance as a barrister was one of the most graceful of his life. On the ceremony of taking leave of Lincoln's Inn for the purpose of being called to the degree of the coif, he delivered a farewell address, in which, after a well-merited and eloquent eulogy of Lork Hardwicke, the chancellor under whom he had practised, he paid an elegant compliment to the Hon. Charles Yorke, the treasurer, who had delivered to him, with warm congratulations, the customary offering of the society.

He received his appointment as lord chief justice of the King's Bench, and his patent of creation as Lord Mansfield of Mansfield in the county of Nottingham, on the same day, November 8, 1756. From that date for the long period of thirty-two years he presided over his court with such extraordinary power and efficiency that, by his learning, discrimination, and judgment, he not only gained the admiration of all who were competent to appreciate them, but by the fairness and impartiality of his decisions, and by the patient courtesy of his manners, his private virtues, and the firmness he displayed in trying circumstances, he lived down and nullified the charges and insinuations which jealousy and party spirit at one time raised against him. He introduced some reforms in his court, and removed some impediments in its practice, which had much delayed the decision of the causes and unnecessarily increased the expense of the suitors; and by his punctuality and despatch he kept down all accumulation of arrears, and thus was enabled to meet the vast increase of business which was caused by the advancing commerce of the country. In dealing with the numberless cases arising from this increasing commerce, he not only carefully weighed the justice of the particular claim, but laid down the principle upon which all similar questions should be in future decided, and in the end established such a system that, in the words of Mr. Justice Buller, he acquired the character of being 'the founder of the commercial law of the country.' Though his decisions both in this branch of law, and on other questions in reference to colonial and international principle, are most curious, satisfactory, and instructive, a detail of them would fail to be interesting. But some of those which will be ever connected with his name deserve to be commemorated. He first pronounced that a slave once brought into England became free; that Turks, Hindoos, and others of different faith from our own, may be sworn as witnesses according to the ceremonies of their own religion; that governors of English provinces are amenable in English courts for wrongful acts done while governors against individuals; and that the property of wrecks does not belong to the king or his grantee, where it can be identified by the real owner, although no living thing comes to shore with the wreck.

Though, besides the three judges whom he found on the bench of his court, there were no less than eight who took their places afterwards as his colleagues, it is a strong evidence of the soundness of his law that during the thirty-two years of his presidency there were only two cases in which the whole bench were not unanimous; and, what is still more extraordinary, two only of his judgments were reversed on appeal; but some of them were not entirely approved by the legal community. The system on which he acted was censured as introducing too much of the Roman law into our jurisprudence; and he was charged with overstepping the boundary between equity and law, and of allowing the principles of the former to operate too strongly in his legal decisions. How far these criticisms were justified still remains a question; but recent legislation proves how little his system deserved censure. Lord Thurlow used to say that Lord Mansfield was 'a surprising man; ninety-nine times out of a hundred he was right in his opinions and decisions; and when once in a hundred times he was wrong, ninety-nine men out of a hundred would not discover it. He was a wonderful man.'

He was particularly attentive to the students who attended his court, admitting them to sit on the bench with him, and explaining the points that happened to be raised. In his time the king's counsel used the same courtesy towards the young aspirants, but after the accession of Lord Kenyon the practice was discontinued both by the bench and the bar.

In the upper house of parliament he shone with as much brilliancy as he had done in the lower. During the greater part of his senatorial life the 'Parliamentary History' contains comparatively few of his speeches, because the prohibition against reporters was rigidly enforced. But those which have been by other means given to the world amply confirm the general opinion of their elegance and effectiveness, and justify the universal admiration which they elicited. His contests with his old antagonist in the House of Commons, the Earl of Chatham, were renewed with even more virulence than formerly, and when they were expected to occur were attended by crowds desirous of witnessing the gladiatorial exhibition. Though he was as often the victor as the vanquished in these trials of strength, it would have been better for his fame if he had more strictly confined himself to judicial questions. However transcendent his talents, political controversy should be avoided by a judge, whose decisions should never be subjected to the suspicion even of political bias. The last intended display between the two combatants was on the subject of the American war in 1778, but was prevented by the fatal seizure of the great statesman at the commencement of his address.

Though several times pressed to accept the office of lord chancellor, he persisted in his refusal to change his court, from his love of the position he held and his conscious aptitude for his duties, as well as from the uncertainty attendant on the possession of the Great Seal. Soon after he became chief justice he by virtue of that office received the seal of chancellor of the Exchequer during the three months' vacancy occasioned by the removal of Mr. Legge, but he performed no other than its formal duties, and ten years after he again temporarily held that office on the death of the Hon. Charles Townshend. On the establishment of the joint ministry of Mr. Pitt and the Duke of Newcastle in 1757, the coalition between whom he was the principal instrument in effecting, he consented to become, with questionable propriety, one of the cabinet council. He remained so for some years; and this was no doubt the cause of the unpopularity under which he laboured in the early part of the reign of George III.— an unpopularity which was not diminished by the suspicion that he was the secret adviser of his sovereign, by his continued defence of ministerial measures in the House of Lords, and by his acting subsequently for a long period as speaker of that assembly—an unpopularity which was kept alive and greatly increased by the virulent attacks made against him by Junius, which continued till that bold, powerful, and impudent writer was in 1772, by means yet unknown, effectually silenced. Yet during the whole period his fame as a great magistrate was spreading over the whole of Europe as well as in his own country; and there even the populace might have seen his disregard of political influence, in his affirmation of the verdict against those who had illegally acted under the general warrant against the 'North Briton,' and in his reversal of the outlawry of the demagogue Wilkes, its disreputable author. Though assailed with abuse, lampoons, and personal threats, the most uncharitable of his libellers could not but be impressed by the noble and dignified speech made by him on granting that reversal.

His liberal opinions on the subject of religion, and the principles of toleration which he advocated in all cases in which the question arose, whether relating to Dissenters or Roman Catholics, while they raised him in the estimation of the honest and well-disposed, had a contrary effect on the bigoted class of society, by whom the old story of his being a Jacobite was revived, with the additional stigma of his being a Jesuit in disguise. The sad effect of these mistaken notions appeared in the disgraceful No Popery riots of 1780, in which he was not only personally attacked and insulted, but his house in Bloomsbury Square, containing his valuable library, was burnt down to the ground by the mob. Nothing more tended than his conduct on that occasion to establish his character, and to dissipate and overcome the prejudices against him, which some men still continued to foster. The courage also which he displayed when the houses of parliament were threatened, the philosophic calmness with which he met his personal calamity, his generous justification of ministers in calling in the military to quell the riots, and particularly his impartiality and total absence of resentment in the trial of Lord George Gordon, whose violent harangues had first evoked the outbreak, excited universal admiration, and increased the respect with which he was regarded.

For six years after this event he continued to exercise, almost without a day's intermission, the functions of his high office, when, being then eighty-one years of age, his weakness and infirmity prevented him attending the court. He did not immediately resign, but, with the expectation of being enabled still to act, he delayed his retirement for nearly two years, leaving a most efficient substitute to perform his duties. This was Mr. Justice Buller, whom he hoped to see, and endeavoured to induce the minister to appoint, his successor. But when he found that Mr. Pitt had determined otherwise, and that his declining strength totally prevented him from again taking his seat, he closed, on June 4, 1788, a legal career which had extended over fifty-eight years, twenty-six as an advocate, and thirty-two as a judge, in both capacities achieving such a character as few can equal, and none will ever surpass. Both branches of the profession expressed in affecting addresses their respect, their veneration, their attachment to his person, and their regret at his retirement—sentiments in which the whole community united.

The aged lord survived for nearly five years, enjoying life at his beautiful seat at Caen Wood, near Highgate, in social and intellectual converse, and with unabated health and undecayed memory, but with increasing feebleness, till his exhausted frame at last gave way on March 20, 1793, having just entered the eighty-ninth year of his age. He was buried in Westminster Abbey, in the same grave as his wife, Lady Elizabeth Finch, daughter of the Earl of Winchilsea, whom he had married in 1738, and who, after a happy union of forty-six years, had preceded him by nine years. By the gratitude of one of those whom he had benefited by his advocacy a splendid monument was erected, the work of Flaxman.

When he had graced the seat of justice for twenty years, the king in 1776 rewarded his judicial and political services by creating him Earl of Mansfield in Nottinghamshire, a title which under a special remainder is now enjoyed by a descendant. (*Lives by Halliday, Burke, Welsby, Lord Campbell, and Roscoe.*)

MUSARD, RALPH, was the great-grandson of Hascoit Musard, a baron who is recorded in Domesday Book as having large possessions in various counties. These were afterwards held by his son Richard, his grandson Hascoit, and then by this Ralph, who succeeded to them on the death of the latter. In 17 John he was appointed sheriff of Gloucester, an office which he retained till the end of 9 Henry III. (*Rot. Pat.* 148; *Rot. Claus.* i. 276, &c.) He adhered to King John during all his troubles, as is evident from the grants which were made to him out of the forfeited lands. Under Henry III. he was several times from the fifth to the eleventh year appointed a justice itinerant for various counties. (*Rot. Claus.* i. 274, ii. 151, 203, 213.)

He married Isabella, the widow of John de Neville, without licence of the king, whose pardon he procured by a fine of one hundred marks. It would seem that she must have been his second wife, inasmuch as on his death, only ten years afterwards, in 14 Henry III., Robert, his son, was of full age, and entered on some of his father's lands. (*Excerpt. e Rot. Fin.* i. 43, 198, 203.) The male line of the family failed in 1300, 29 Edward I. (*Baronage*, i. 512.)

MUSCHAMPE, CHRISTOPHER, the third son of William Muschampe, of Camberwell, Surrey, by his second wife, Elizabeth, daughter of Richard Sandes and relict of Richard Mimes, is another of the barons of the Exchequer of whom little is told, except that his patent of appointment is dated November 8, 1577, and that he was buried at Carshalton in Surrey on June 4, 1579, thus making his tenure of office only about nineteen months. By his wife Dennys he had several sons. (*Manning and Bray's Surrey*, iii. 414.)

MUTFORD, JOHN DE, of a knightly family settled in the parish of that name in Suffolk, in pursuing the profession of the law, arrived at that eminence to be engaged in conducting the king's causes in 22 and 30 Edward I. Although it does not appear that the office of attorney-general was then established in a separate individual, an entry on the Rolls of Parliament (i. 197) in 35 Edward I., in which John de Mutford is directed to be called before the treasurer and barons of the Exchequer, to inform them of the king's right in the matter of a petition then presented, seems to show that his duties were very similar to those now performed by that officer. In that same year (the last of the king) he was appointed one of the justices of trailbaston to act in Cornwall and nine other counties. (*Rot. Parl.* i. 218.)

From the commencement of Edward II.'s reign he attended the parliament among the judges, and we find him on various occasions acting as a justice itinerant, and commanded to cause his proceedings to be estreated into the exchequer. In 5 Edward II. he was sent to Ireland as one of the commissioners to quiet the discontents and disturbances there, and two years afterwards was summoned to appear before the council ready to proceed on the king's service to parts beyond the seas.

After being in continual and active employment as a justice of assize, he was raised to the bench at Westminster, being constituted a judge of the Common Pleas by patent, dated April 20, 1316, 9 Edward II. In this court he continued to act during the remainder of the reign, and for the first three years of that of Edward III., the last fine acknowledged before him being dated in Hilary 1329, in which year he died and was buried in Norwich Cathedral. (*Ibid.* 341–350; *Parl. Writs*, ii. 1213; *Blomefield's Norwich*, ii. 39.)

N

NARES, GEORGE. This judge's father, who was for many years steward to the Earls of Abingdon, had two sons, both of whom became eminent in the professions they had selected. The elder was Dr. James Nares of musical celebrity, and the younger was Sir George Nares of legal fame. George was born at Hanwell in Middlesex in 1716, and having been first sent to the school of Magdalen College, Oxford, was afterwards admitted into New College. Becoming a student at the Inner Temple, he was called to the bar in 1741. His marriage in 1751 with Mary, daughter of Sir John Strange, master of the Rolls, is an indication of his early success in his profession. His practice seems to have been principally in the criminal courts, to judge from the speeches he made in defence of Timothy Murphy, convicted of forgery in 1753, and of Elizabeth Canning, convicted of perjury in 1754.

In 1759 he received the degree of the coif, and was made king's serjeant at the same time. From 1763 to 1770 he was engaged on the part of the crown in most of the cases arising out of the general warrant issued against the author, publisher, and printers of No. 45 of the 'North Briton;' and the unpopularity which he shared with all the opposers of Mr. Wilkes may perhaps account for Mr. Foote holding him up to ridicule under the character of Serjeant Circuit in his farcical comedy of the 'Lame Lover.' In May 1768 he was elected member for the city of Oxford, which soon after chose him its recorder. In the fourth session of that parliament he was appointed a judge of the Common Pleas on January 25, 1771, and was at the same time knighted. After filling that honourable post with great credit for more than fifteen years, he died at Ramsgate of a gradual decay, on July 20, 1786, and was buried at Eversley in Hampshire. His cheerfulness of disposition and pleasing manners endeared him to his contemporaries, enhanced as they were by the strict integrity of his life and his unaffected piety.

Sir George left several children, one of whom became regius professor of modern history in the university of Oxford. (*Gent. Mag.* lvi. 622; *State Trials*, xix. 451, 702, 1153; *Harris's Lord Hardwicke*, iii. 349; *Blackstone's Rep.* 734.)

NEEDHAM, JOHN, was the second son of Robert Needham, of Cravach, and Dorothy, daughter of Sir John Savage, K.G., of Clifton in Cheshire, from whose eldest son descended the present Earl of Kilmorey. John became common serjeant of London in 1449, and was elected member for that city in the parliament of the following year. He was called to the degree of the coif in 1453, and on July 13, 1454, was appointed one of the king's serjeants. From that time his name appears in the Year Books, till he was advanced to the bench as a judge of the Common Pleas on May 9, 1457, 35 Henry VI. On the deposition of that monarch, Edward IV. continued him in his place, and he was still there at the end of ten years, when Henry was restored in October 1470. It is a clear proof that at that time politics little influenced the legal appointments, since we find not only that he was included in Henry's new patent to the judges of the court, but that after Edward's return in the following April he was removed into the Court of King's Bench. His judgments are recorded as late as Hilary Term 1479. He was knighted by Henry VI., and Phillips (*Grandeur of the Law* [1684], 31) says that he had a seat at Shevington, or Sheinton, in Shropshire, and was chief justice of Chester. (*Dugdale's Orig.* 46; *Rot. Parl.* vi. 3, 167.)

NEELE, RICHARD, was a judge under five sovereigns, and was buried at Prestwould in Leicestershire, being described on his tomb as lord of that manor.

He was a member of Gray's Inn, whence he was called serjeant in Michaelmas 1463, 3 Edward IV., and was made king's serjeant in the next year. His first elevation to the judicial ermine was on the restoration of Henry VI., when he was added to the other judges of the King's Bench on October 9, 1470. Edward IV., on his return, did not degrade him, but removed him into the Court of Common Pleas on May 29, 1471, where he remained through the short reigns of Edward V. and Richard III., and for the first ten months of that of Henry VII.; when he died.

By his wife Isabella, daughter of — Butler, of Warrington in Lancashire, he left two sons. (*Y. B.*; *Gough's Munum.* ii. 294.)

NEVILLE, ALAN DE (Nova-villa), is mentioned as one of the 'assidentes justiciæ regis' in the Exchequer in 11 Henry II., 1165, before whom a charter was executed between the abbots of St. Alban's and Westminster; and from 12 Henry II. for many years he filled the office of justice of the forests throughout all England. (*Madox*, i. 44, 144, &c.)

According to Dugdale, he was the brother of Gilbert de Neville, of Lincolnshire, Rutland, and Oxfordshire, but with some confusion as to the latter. He held the forest of Savernac in Wiltshire, and was one of those lords of the council who, for the energy of their measures in support of the king against Becket, were excommunicated in 1166; but he afterwards received absolution from Gilbert Foliot, Bishop of London, on condition that he should go to Rome and submit himself to the pope. He died in 2 Richard I., leaving two sons, the under-mentioned Alan, and Geoffrey. (*Dugdale's Baron.* i. 287.)

NEVILLE, ALAN DE, Junior, was employed as a justice itinerant during his father's life, being so called in the Great Rolls, which mention his pleas in twelve counties from 16 to 25 Henry II., 1170-1179. He seems to have acted also as justice of the forest, perhaps as deputy to his father. This office was afterwards possessed by several members of the family; but the account which Dugdale gives is too indistinct to decide on the precise relationship they bore to this justicier. (*Madox*, i. 133, 144, &c.; *Baronage*, ut supra.)

NEVILLE, GEOFFREY DE, the younger brother of the under-mentioned Robert de Neville, of Raby, was in 54 Henry III., 1270, appointed governor of Scarborough Castle, and succeeded his brother as warden of the king's forests beyond Trent (*Cal. Rot. Pat.* 42), being in that year at the head of the justices itinerant for pleas of the forest in the northern counties. In 8 Edward I., 1280, also, he sat at Blithworth in Nottinghamshire, concerning forest matters. (*Thoroton*, i. 178.) He died in 1285, leaving by his wife, Margaret, the daughter and heir of Sir John Longvillers, of Hornby Castle in Lancashire, a son named John, the father of a long line settled at that place. (*Baronage*, i. 291.)

NEVILLE, JOLLAN DE, and his elder brother, John, are called by Dugdale (*Baronage*, i. 288) the grandsons of Ralph de Neville, the founder of the priory of Hoton in Yorkshire, and the sons of Hugh de Neville, whose prowess in slaying a lion in the Holy Land was recorded in this verse:

Viribus Hugonis vires periere leonis.

By the entries on the rolls, however, it is manifest that they were the sons of another Jollan, who perhaps was the son of that Hugh, as he had livery of his property in 1 John, which Dugdale fixes as the date of Hugh's death. This last-mentioned Jollan, the father, was connected with the Exchequer, the Rot. de Oblatis of 2 and 7 John containing entries that evidence his employment. He died in 9 John, leaving two sons, John and this Jollan, who on John's death without issue in 4 Henry III. succeeded to his property. (*Rot. Claus.* i. 409, 490, ii. 43.) He appears as a justice itinerant in 1234, and again in 1240. But from

Michaelmas 1241 to Hilary 1245 he was present when fines were levied (*Dugdale's Orig.* 43), and during the latter interval there are several instances of payments being made for writs of assize of novel disseisin to be taken before him (*Excerpt. e Rot. Fin.* i. 418–426), plainly proving that he was then one of the superior justices at Westminster. He died in the next year.

The ancient record in the Exchequer, called 'Testa de Neville,' containing an account of the king's fees throughout a great part of England, with inquisitions of lands escheated and lands held in grand or petit serjeanty, is traditionally reported to have received its name from, and to have owed its existence to, Jollan de Neville; and he is generally spoken of as the justice itinerant. A question, however, may be fairly raised, whether this celebrated MS. is the work of the father or of the son. Dugdale and other genealogists were evidently ignorant that there were two of the same name; and, adverting to the fact that the father was an officer in the Exchequer, it seems more likely that he should have made such a compilation than the son, of whom there is no proof that he ever was connected with that department, and who, neither in his capacity of justice itinerant, nor in that of justicier, which he held only for the last four years of his life, would be called upon to pay any peculiar attention to the king's revenue.

NEVILLE, RALPH DE (BISHOP OF CHICHESTER), in a MS. account of his life in the chapter-books of the cathedral of Chichester is stated to have been born at Raby Castle, the seat of the baronial family of De Neville, in the county of Durham.

He is entered on the Patent Roll of 15 John as having had 'the Great Seal delivered to him on the 22nd of December, 1213, to be held under the Bishop of Winchester,' Peter de Rupibus, then the chancellor, and certainly was not, as some state, chancellor during John's reign. Several churches were successively given to him about this time, and in April 1214 he was appointed dean of Lichfield. (*Rot. Pat.* 113.)

On the accession of Henry III., Sir T. D. Hardy has inserted Ralph de Neville's name as keeper of the Seal under Richard de Marisco, referring to several original letters written between the years 1218 and 1222, addressed to him as the king's vice-chancellor, and relating to his custody of the Seal. It is difficult to ascertain precisely what were the duties which he performed. Richard de Marisco was absent from England in 5 Henry III., 1221, and it is probable that his duties as chancellor were then performed by Ralph de Neville. There is a curious letter from the chancellor to him given in Lord Campbell's work (i. 127), which, remonstrating for his suppression of the title of chancellor in the letters he had addressed to him, shows that the old man was somewhat apprehensive of being superseded by his disrespectful deputy.

In 1222 he was appointed chancellor of Chichester, and on November 1 in the following year he was elected bishop of that see. In 1224 he sat as a justicier in Shropshire with William de Houbrug. (*Excerpt. e Rot. Fin.* i. 122.)

On the death of Richard de Marisco on May 1, 1226, the chancellorship became vacant. Although the date assigned by Dugdale and other writers to Ralph de Neville's appointment as chancellor is not till February 12, 1227, it is quite clear that his elevation occurred shortly after Richard de Marisco's death. In the grant to him of a market at Preston in Sussex, dated June 28, 1226 (*Rot. Claus.* ii. 113), he is expressly designated by that title; and there are charters under his hand in the following December. (*Rymer*, i. 183-4.) The date of February 12, 1227, was that of the charter which he subsequently received, granting to him the Chancery for his life, a charter which was renewed in 13, 16, and 17 Henry III. There is also another charter, dated June 14, 16 Henry III., granting to him the custody of the Great Seal during his life, and enabling him to appoint a deputy. No cause is apparent for these renewals, and it is difficult to account for them otherwise than by his apprehensions lest the disgrace of Hubert de Burgh, which occurred about that time, might operate to his disadvantage, as there is no doubt he was chancellor during the whole period, and no want of the royal confidence had as yet been exhibited. On the contrary, he had been further gratified with the chancellorship of Ireland for life, G. de Turville being appointed to act as his deputy there. (*Ibid.* i. 212.)

On the death of Richard Weathershed, Archbishop of Canterbury, in 1231, Ralph de Neville was elected by the monks as his successor, and, being approved by the king, was admitted into the temporalities. The pope, however, at the instigation of Simon de Langton that he was unlearned and hasty, and would endeavour to shake off the papal yoke, refused to confirm the election. It is on the other hand stated that the bishop himself objected to assume the primacy, and that when applied to by the monks for the expenses of their journey to Rome, he declared that he would not contribute 'obolum unum' for the purpose.

In 1233 he was with the king when he was surprised and defeated by the Earl of Pembroke before the castle of Grosmont in Monmouthshire, and was one of those who escaped 'nudi fugientes omnia quæ sua erant amiserunt.' (*R. de Wendover*, iv. 227, 279.)

Hitherto Ralph de Neville had continued

high in the king's confidence; but on the arrival of the queen's uncle, William of Provence, Bishop of Valence, all the royal favours were bestowed on the foreign prelate and his connections. No doubt the chancellor joined in the dissatisfaction expressed by the barons; and Matthew Paris relates that the king attempted, in 1236, to remove him from the chancellorship. Depending on the support of the barons, and conscious of their approval of his conduct in his office, he at once refused to resign, alleging that he had been entrusted with the office by the parliament, and could not quit it without their authority. But the royal indignation against him was greatly increased two years afterwards by his being elected Bishop of Winchester, where the king had earnestly desired to place his favoured relative. Henry not only induced the pope to annul the election, but took away the Great Seal from the bishop, and committed it to the custody of Geoffrey the Templar and John de Lexinton, reserving, however, to the bishop as chancellor the profits of the office. Matthew Paris adds that the king afterwards endeavoured to induce him to resume the Seal, and on his refusal placed it in the hands of Simon the Norman.

It was not till 1242 that Ralph de Neville was restored to the king's favour, from which year till his death there are several documents to which his name is attached with the title of chancellor. (*Rymer*, i. 244, 253.)

That event occurred on February 1, 1244, at the magnificent mansion he had erected for the residence of himself and his successors, Bishops of Chichester, while in London. This house was situate 'in vico novo ante Novum Templum' (*Rot. Claus.* i. 107), now called Chancery Lane, and, becoming afterwards the hospitium or inn of the Earls of Lincoln, was ultimately transferred to the students of the law, and is still designated by the name of its last possessor. The memory of the original founder is preserved in the name of the lane, corrupted from Chancellor's Lane, and in that part of the estate which alone remains to the see, and is now called Chichester Rents.

That Ralph de Neville was an ambitious man none can deny; that he accumulated vast riches is equally certain; but that he misused the one, or that the other led him into degrading courses, there is no evidence. On the contrary, the highest character is given him by contemporary historians, not only for his fidelity to his sovereign in times of severe trial, but for the able and irreproachable administration of his office. He was as accessible to the poor as to the rich, and dealt equal justice to all.

To his church he was a signal benefactor, defending its rights on many occasions, obtaining various grants for its benefit, devoting large sums to the repairs of the cathedral, increasing the endowments of the dean and chapter, and bequeathing to his successors the estate he had purchased and the palace he had erected in London. (*Godwin*, 504; *Angl. Sac.* i. 488; *Le Neve; Dugdale's Orig.* 231.)

NEVILLE, ROBERT DE, was a clerk in the Exchequer; and in 15 John he countersigned a mandate on the part of Richard de Marisco, to whom, in 18 John, he had a letter of safe conduct to go and return, no doubt on the business of his office. Another charter is also countersigned by him in 3 Henry III. Madox gives the copy of a fine taken before him in the King's Court at Westminster in the latter year, in which he is designated as a justicier. He was, as was then usual with the officers of the Exchequer, an ecclesiastic, and in 16 John had letters patent of presentation to the church of Wigborough in the diocese of London. He died about 1229. (*Rot. Claus.* i. 137, 383; *Rot. Pat.* 129, 198; *Madox*, ii. 43; *Excerpt. e Rot. Fin.* i. 190.)

NEVILLE, ROBERT DE, was of the noble house of Raby, being the son of Geoffrey de Neville, whose father, Robert Fitz-Maldred, lord of Raby, married Isabel, the daughter, and ultimately the heir of the first Geoffrey de Neville. Robert de Neville had livery of his grandfather's lands in 38 Henry III., paying, besides his fine to the king, a sum of 15*l.* 6*s.* 3*d.* to the queen, in the nature probably of aurum reginæ. (*Excerpt. e Rot. Fin.* ii. 185.) In 45 Henry III. he was made warden of the king's forests beyond Trent, and in the next year, 1262, was at the head of the justices itinerant for the northern counties, the pleas, however, being confined to the forests. He then was appointed captain-general of the king's forces in those parts, sheriff of Yorkshire, and governor of the castles of York and Devizes. Although he for a time joined the rebellious barons, he contrived to regain the royal favour, and was afterwards entrusted with the custody of the castles of Pickering and Bamburgh. He died in 1282, having had, by his wife Ida, the widow of Roger Bertram, a son, two of whose representatives now sit in the House of Lords as Earls of Abergavenny and Westmoreland. (*Baronage*, i. 291; *Nicolas's Synopsis.*)

NEVILL, RICHARD (EARL OF SALISBURY), the only lay chancellor in the reign of Henry VI., was one of the twenty-two children of Ralph Nevill, the first Earl of Westmoreland. That nobleman married two wives, by the first of whom he had two sons, the elder succeeding to his honours. The second wife was Joane, daughter of John of Gaunt, Duke of Lancaster, by Catherine Swinford. She produced him eight sons, of whom the eldest was this Richard Nevill, born about 1400.

He married Alice, the only daughter of

Thomas de Montacute, Earl of Salisbury, and upon the death of her father in 1428, had a grant of the title for his life. Engaged from his earliest youth in the profession of arms, he had served with considerable personal distinction in the French wars; so that the appointment of so inexperienced a person as chancellor, at a period when legal and statesmanlike attainments were required for the execution of its duties, could not fail to excite wonder. It was in fact a mere political proceeding, and arose thus:—When the late chancellor, Archbishop Kempe, died on March 22, 1454, the king was afflicted with one of those sicknesses to which he was subject, and which rendered him altogether incompetent to attend to the affairs of government. The parliament accordingly a few days afterwards named Richard Duke of York protector of he kingdom, one of whose first acts was to invest the earl with the office of chancellor, in which character he is named in an ordinance dated March 30 (*Rot. Parl.* v. 450), but the Great Seal was not delivered to him till April 2. It was a curious commencement of his judicial career, that on the next day he, with four other lords, was appointed to 'entende with all diligence to them possible, to the saufgarde and kepyng of the see,' for the resistance of the king's enemies. (*Ibid.* 144.)

His tenure of office was very short, and was undistinguished by any important incident. On the king's recovery no time was lost in removing the protector and his chancellor, the successor of the latter being sworn in on March 7, 1455.

Then commenced the civil war, and in less than three months the first battle of St. Albans was fought, in which the Duke of Somerset was killed; and the king, being defeated and left in the Duke of York's power, was compelled to pardon all the rebels, among whom was the Earl of Salisbury. At the end, however, of the miserable events of the succeeding years, the duke was defeated and killed in the battle of Wakefield on December 30, 1460, and the earl himself taken and beheaded the next day at Pontefract. His eldest son, Richard, the famous Earl of Warwick, succeeded in placing the duke's son on the throne by the name of Edward IV., and his youngest son George became the next-mentioned chancellor of England. (*Baronage*, i. 302.)

NEVILL, GEORGE (ARCHBISHOP OF YORK), was the youngest son of the above Richard Earl of Salisbury, and, being designed for the Church, was educated at Balliol College, Oxford, of which university he was afterwards chancellor. One of the first acts of the council, after his father's acceptance of the Seals, was to recommend him to the first vacant bishopric, although he was not yet twenty-two years of age. The bishopric of Exeter became void before the close of the following year, and though the earl had been removed from the chancellorship, he and his son Richard Earl of Warwick had such ascendency that George Nevill was elected (*Rymer*, xi. 376); but the pope would not permit him to be consecrated till he had attained the age of twenty-seven.

He presided over that diocese about nine years, during which there is nothing to show that he took any active part in the unhappy contests with the crown until the fatal battle of Northampton had placed the king in the hands of his enemies, who, taking care to have their friends about him, obliged him to nominate Bishop Nevill as his chancellor. Accordingly on July 25, 1460, fifteen days after the battle, he received the Seal, and took it home to his house in St. Clement Danes, being that which was afterwards called Essex House, on the site of which Essex Street and Devereux Court now stand. In the next parliament the Duke of York openly claimed the crown; an illusory compromise was arranged; the civil war again broke out, resulting in the death of the claimant, and the momentary triumph of the royalists in the fields of Wakefield and St. Albans; but succeeded within five days by the successful entry of the Earl of Warwick into London, and in less than a fortnight by the proclamation, on March 4, 1461, of Edward, the duke's son, as king.

Six days after this event the bishop took the oath as chancellor to Edward IV. (*Rymer*, xi. 473.) For the next six years he uninterruptedly retained the Great Seal, during which, in 1465, he was raised to the archbishopric of York. A coolness had already commenced between King Edward and the Nevills, arising from the precipitancy with which the relatives of the new queen were advanced, and the jealousy created by their sudden rise, and by the powerful influence they acquired. This feeling became more apparent by the Earl of Warwick's resistance to the marriage of Margaret, the king's sister, to Charles, the son of the Duke of Burgundy, which the Wydevilles had suggested; and the earl was further disgusted by being sent to negotiate a pretended treaty for a union with one of the French princes, which he soon found was never intended to be effected.

During the earl's absence in France a parliament was held, from which for the first time the chancellor absented himself. Five days afterwards, June 8, 1467, the king went to his house and demanded the Great Seal. The act of resumption, however, passed in this parliament, excepted all the grants which had been made to Nevill. (*Rot. Parl.* v. 571, 604, 607.) In the course of the next year he was instrumental in promoting a reconciliation between his brother the earl and the king, and for his good services therein he was rewarded with the manor of Penley and other lands in the counties of Hertford and Buckingham. (*Rymer*, xi. 640.)

This reconciliation could scarcely be expected to be permanent. In disobedience to the king, Warwick soon after gave his daughter in marriage to the Duke of Clarence, the king's brother, and the archbishop accompanied them to Calais to solemnise the nuptials. Thus united to the duke, the Warwick faction, taking advantage of a rising soon after under Robin of Redesdale in Yorkshire, vented its animosity against the Wydevilles by executing the queen's father and brother, and proceeded with such spirit that King Edward, in 1469, found himself a prisoner to the duke, the earl, and the archbishop at Olney (Oundle), and was therefore placed for security in the custody of the latter at Middleham. How the king obtained his release from confinement is somewhat doubtful; but the better opinion seems to be that it was with the consent of Warwick, who proved that he had not yet cast off his allegiance to Edward by attacking and defeating Sir Humphrey Nevill on his raising the standard for King Henry. The archbishop, who had treated the king with the greatest courtesy during his detention, accompanied him to London, where the king issued a general pardon to all concerned in the outbreak.

Apparently restored to favour, the archbishop had invited the king, in the following February, 1470, to meet Clarence and Warwick at an entertainment at the Moor in Hertfordshire; but a hint, whether true or false is uncertain, being whispered in the royal ear that treachery was intended, the king revived the dissensions by secretly departing from the house. Though peace for the moment was with difficulty restored, Clarence and Warwick soon flew to arms, and eventually restored King Henry to the throne, from which they had assisted in expelling him ten years before.

That Archbishop Nevill, as was natural under the ministry of his powerful brother, was restored to his former office of chancellor there is no doubt; for, though the record of his appointment does not exist, his name appears with that designation in three several documents, dated respectively December 20, 1470, and February 13 and 16, 1471. (*Rymer*, xi. 672, 681, 692.) He was also rewarded with the grant of the manors of Wodestoke, Hangburgh, Wotton, and Stonefield, and the hundred of Wotton for life. But even these favours could not make him more faithful to his brother Warwick than he had before shown himself first to King Henry and then to King Edward. The latter soon re-appeared on the scene to reclaim the kingdom; and the city of London and the person of Henry being entrusted to the archbishop, Edward found means, by tempting the prelate's avarice or exciting his fears, to secure his treacherous assistance. Edward marched to the capital, where the recorder Urswyke, by the archbishop's order, admitted him on April 11 through a postern in the walls; and Henry, who had been purposely kept out of sanctuary, became again the prisoner of his rival. Two days after, the archbishop, regardless of the ruin in which he involved his brother, took the oath of fidelity to Edward on the Sacrament at St. Paul's Cross, and immediately received a full pardon for all offences he had previously committed. (*Ibid.* 709, 710.) It would seem, however, from a passage in a letter of Sir John Paston (*Letters*, ii. 60), who fought for King Henry at Barnet on the next day, that the archbishop was then a prisoner in the Tower. This might perhaps have been done as a cover to his treason, the same letter mentioning that he was in possession of a pardon, or perhaps Edward could not trust him at large when leaving London on so momentous an expedition.

The successful battles of Barnet and Tewkesbury, and the murders of King Henry and his son, having secured the throne to Edward, that monarch took an early opportunity of getting rid of the archbishop, whose fidelity we cannot be surprised that he doubted. Under the mask of friendship he had agreed to hunt at the Moor with the prelate, who accordingly prepared a magnificent entertainment, embellished with all the plate he possessed, besides much that he had borrowed to do honour to the occasion. But on the day before he was summoned to the king's presence, and immediately imprisoned on a pretended charge; the riches which he had thus foolishly exposed were confiscated, and the revenues of his bishopric seized into the king's hand. In the list of the plunder a magnificent mitre is mentioned, the jewels of which were so large and precious that they were appropriated by the king to form a crown for himself. His confinement, which was sometimes in Calais and sometimes at Guisnes, lasted for about three years; but eventually, through the intercession of his friends, he procured his release, and returned to England in December 1475. He did not long survive his liberation. Although only in the prime of life, he sunk under his disgrace; and dying at Blithlaw on June 8, 1476, was buried in his own cathedral without tomb or gravestone.

He is spoken of as a patron of scientific men; but no literary character can counteract the unfavourable sentence which every honest man must pronounce against him, on the manifest proofs which his life offers of fickleness, deceit, and treachery. (*Godwin*, 413, 693; *Lingard*; *Drake's Eborac.*)

NEVIL, EDWARD, was the second son of Henry Nevil, of Bathwick in Somersetshire. Admitted a member of Gray's Inn in 1650, he was called to the bar in 1658, and became an ancient in 1676. He received the honour of knighthood in June 1681, when, as recorder of Bath, he presented the address of that corporation thanking Charles II. for his recent declaration. That king having raised him to the degree of the coif in January 1684, King James on his accession made him one of his serjeants, and on October 11, 1685, further promoted him to be a baron of the Exchequer. This seat he occupied only six months, being too honest to support the royal assumption of the dispensing power. He accordingly received his quietus on April 21, 1686, and remained unemployed during the rest of the reign. But on the settlement of the courts by King William he was immediately replaced in his former position, and sworn in on March 11, 1689. (2 *Shower*, 434; *Luttrell*, i. 97–509.)

When interrogated by the parliament of 1689 he gave a detailed account of what took place previous to his discharge. (*Parl. Hist.* v. 311.)

In October 1691 Sir Edward was removed from the Exchequer to the Court of Common Pleas, and on King William's death was re-appointed to the same place by Queen Anne, under whom he sat for a little more than three years. He died at Hammersmith on August 8, 1705. He assisted in several of the state trials, and seems to have acted an honest and independent part on the bench. (*State Trials*, xi. and xii; *Luttrell*, ii. 299, v. 580.)

NEWBALD, GEOFFREY DE. Dugdale, by a misreading of the patent he quotes, states that on November 2, 1276, 4 Edward I., Geoffrey de Newbald was appointed one of the judges of the Common Pleas, the record plainly proving that he was merely constituted a justice to hold pleas in the liberties of the priory of Dunstable. He was soon removed to a more important station, for on August 22, 1277, he was raised to the office of chancellor of the Exchequer. (*Madox*, ii. 52, 62, 321.) He is recorded as attending the Court of Exchequer as late as 9 Edward I.

NEWDIGATE, RICHARD, was of a family of extreme antiquity, which derived its name from, or perhaps gave its name to, the town of Newdigate in Surrey, where its property was situated as early as the reign of King John. The descendant of a younger branch was settled in the reign of Elizabeth at the manor of Arbury in Warwickshire, where Chief Justice Sir Edmund Anderson had erected a mansion, which thenceforward became the seat of the Newdigates. The judge was the second son of Sir John Newdigate, and Anne, the daughter of Sir Edward Fitton, of Gawsworth in Cheshire, Bart., and on the death of his elder brother became inheritor of the estate.

He was born on September 17, 1602, and after receiving his education at Trinity College, Oxford, was admitted a member of Gray's Inn. (*Athen. Oxon.* iv. 842.) He had considerable practice as an advocate in Chancery and on the circuits, and in 1644 was engaged by the state with Prynne and Bradshaw in the prosecution of Lord Macguire and others for being concerned in the Irish massacres. In 1647 he was one of the counsel assigned for the defence of the eleven members against the charges made by General Fairfax and the army (*Whitelocke*, 106, 259; *State Trials*, iv. 654, 858), which, however, having answered the purpose for which they were brought, were dropped without trial. These employments, at least the former of them, Mr. Newdigate probably owed in some measure to his relationship to John Hampden, who was his second cousin, and to his connection with Oliver Cromwell, whose aunt had married Hampden's father.

Seven years after, on January 25, 1554, soon after Cromwell became protector, he was made a serjeant and sent the Home spring circuit, and on May 30 he accepted a seat on the Upper Bench. He is said to have been one of those lawyers who, when summoned before Cromwell and offered judgeships, declined to act under his commission; but on being answered by the protector, 'If you gentlemen of the long robe will not execute the law, my redcoats shall,' they, dreading such an alternative, consented to serve. Newdigate soon showed that he would not be subservient to the ruling powers. On the trial of Colonel Halsey and others at York he directed the jury to acquit the prisoner, saying that though it was high treason to levy war against the king, no statute declared it to be so for levying war against the protector. This mode of interpreting the law was not likely to be satisfactory to Cromwell, and consequently Judge Newdigate was removed from the bench on May 1, 1655, 'for not observing the protector's pleasure in all his commands.' Godwin gives a somewhat different account. (*Godwin*, iv. 26, 179, 180; *Whitelocke*, 591, 625.)

By an entry in Burton's Diary (ii. 127) it appears that Newdigate resumed his practice at the bar, but the date of his restoration to the bench has been generally misrepresented. Because Whitelocke does not mention him again till May 15, 1659, it has been supposed that he was not re-appointed till that time, the fact being forgotten that Richard Cromwell had just then been removed from the protectorship, and that the Long Parliament had again seized the government. It thus became necessary to re-appoint the judges, whose commissions under Richard were of course void, and only one of the four then named by Whitelocke was a new judge, while the other three had probably nothing more than new patents. With respect to Newdigate, it is certain that he was re-appointed before Michaelmas Term 1657, for his decisions are recorded in Siderfin's Reports (ii. 11) from that date to the restoration of the king, and, as these Reports commence with that term, he might have been replaced in his seat a long time before. Indeed, when Cromwell's reinvestiture in the office of protector took place on the 26th of the previous June, Newdigate attended the ceremony as one of the judges of the Upper Bench. (*Whitelocke*, 678; *Burton*, ii. 512.) It seems probable, therefore, that Cromwell's displeasure did not last long, and that, either from his family connections, or from his anxiety to supply the bench with respectable and independent judges, he allowed but a short time to elapse after Newdigate's removal before he restored him to his place.

On the resignation of Chief Justice Glynne, the parliament advanced Newdigate to the presidency of the Upper Bench on January 17, 1660. (*Whitelocke*, 629.) Siderfin reports (ii. 179) some of the cases that were heard before him as chief justice, and among them is that of Sir Robert Pye and another, who applied for their Habeas Corpus, having been imprisoned some time on suspicion of treason without prosecution. The court said they could not be denied bail, if the counsel for the commonwealth would not proceed against them, 'for it is the birthright of every subject to be tryed according to the law of the land.' In direct contradiction to this apparently authentic report, Ludlow (356) relates that Newdigate demanded of the counsel of the commonwealth what they had to say against the Habeas Corpus being granted, and on being answered that they had nothing to say against it, the judge, 'though no enemy to monarchy, yet ashamed to see them so unfaithful to their trust, replied that if they had nothing to say, he had; for that Sir Robert Pye being committed by an order of parliament, an inferior court could not discharge him.' A curious instance of the manner in which party prejudice will misrepresent a true narrative!

The Long Parliament being at last dissolved by its own act, preparations were made for the restoration of the monarchy, and the Convention Parliament was summoned for April 25, 1660. Chief Justice Newdigate was returned for Tamworth—a plain proof of the sentiments he entertained, and that he felt that his judicial status no longer existed. Having only acted ministerially, and never having exhibited any political hostility, no sooner had Charles returned, than a writ was issued to the late chief justice to take upon him in a regular manner the degree of serjeant. (1 *Siderfin*, 3.)

Seventeen years after the Restoration, they who had known the serjeant's worth and experienced his lenity were anxious that he should receive some further honour from the king in recognition of his loyalty. With that view a baronetcy was conferred upon him on July 24, 1677, without fees; but the good old man did not long enjoy the dignity, dying on October 14, 1678. He was buried under a splendid monument at Harefield in Middlesex, an ancient patrimony of the family.

By his wife, Juliana, daughter of Sir Francis Leigh, of King's Newman, Warwickshire, and sister of the Earl of Chichester, he had a large family. The male line failed in 1806 by the death of the celebrated Sir Roger Newdigate, the fifth baronet, without issue; but the estates devolved on the representatives of a female descendant, who adopted the family name, and they are now possessed by Charles Newdegate Newdegate, Esq., M.P. for North Warwickshire. (*Wotton's Baronet.* iii. 618.)

NEWENHAM, THOMAS DE. There were two Newenhams who held office about the same time in the reign of Edward III., being probably brothers. The one was John de Newenham, who was chamberlain of the Exchequer (*Issue Roll*, i. 255), and the other Thomas de Newenham, who was one of the senior clerks in the Chancery. The latter is mentioned in this character from 45 Edward III., 1371, to 15 Richard II., 1391, during the whole of which period his name appears on the Parliament Rolls (ii. 303–iii. 284) as a receiver of petitions. On two occasions he was appointed with two others to hold the Great Seal during the absence of the chancellors in 1377 and 1386.

NEWMARKET, ADAM DE (Novo Mercato), held lands of the honor of Tickhill. He accompanied the king to Ireland in 12 John (*Rot. de Præstito*, 187, &c.), but in 15 John he was imprisoned in Corff Castle, probably for implication with the barons, and gave his two sons, John and Adam, as hostages, who were released on the undertaking of Saherus, Earl of Winchester. (*Rot. Pat.* 105.) That he succeeded in removing the suspicions against him may be presumed from his being in the next year appointed with three others and the sheriff of Yorkshire to take an assize of mort d'ancestor between two parties in that county. Under Henry III. he was employed as a principal landed proprietor in collecting the quinzime in Yorkshire, and acted as a justice itinerant in 3, 9, 16, and 18 Henry III. in various counties. (*Rot. Claus.* i. 203, 387, ii. 77, 147.)

NEWTON, RICHARD, the original name of whose family was Cradock, or Caradoc, is stated to have been the first to assume the name of Newton. His father was John Cradock, and his mother was Margaret, the daughter of Howell Moythe, of Castle Ordin and Fountain Gate; or, as another pedigree says, Christiana Ley. He adopted the name of Newton before 3 Henry VI., 1424, as he was then summoned by that name to take the degree of serjeant-at-law. After that date he was apparently very fully employed, and in 1426 he acted as a justice errant in Pembrokeshire. (*Rot. Parl.* iv. 474.) On October 5, 1429, he was appointed one of the king's serjeants, and having held that office, and filled the responsible position of recorder of Bristol, he was constituted a judge of the Common Pleas on November 8, 1438. He was raised to the head of that court on October 14, 1439, and he presided there for nearly nine years. The last fine acknowledged before him was in November 1448, and Sir John Prisot was appointed in his place on June 16, 1449. (*Dugdale's Orig.* 46.)

His death occurred between these two dates, and he was buried either in Bristol Cathedral or in the Wyke chapel of Yatton Church in Somersetshire. There are handsome monuments in each, but neither has any arms or inscriptions left. Although the former, which has no effigy, has been generally appropriated to the judge, the evidence in favour of the latter, which is adorned with an effigy, seems the more weighty. The canopied altar-tomb in the cathedral of Bristol is in the style of the sixteenth century; while that at Yatton, the figure on which undoubtedly represents a judge, and is peculiarly curious as exhibiting the first example of a collar of SS worn by a judge, is of the fifteenth, being the century in which Newton died. His wife is represented with him; and in the same church is a second monument of rather later date, with the figures of another couple; and the tradition of the place is, that one is the tomb of Sir Richard Newton and his wife, and the other that of his son Sir John and his wife. An entry in the churchwardens' books tends to confirm this tradition. It acknowledges, under the date 1451, the receipt of 20*s.* ' de Domina de Wyke per manum J. Newton filii sui de legato Domini Ricardi Newton ad . . . , campanæ;' and there is a further entry in the same year of the cost of re-casting and hanging the 'grete belle.' The Domina de Wyke is evidently the widow of Sir Richard, being so called from living at the manor-place of Wyke, which had been partly built by her husband, and was then and for some time afterwards in possession of the family.

His decisions have no great weight in Westminster Hall, as he is reputed to have been a most unconscientious prerogative lawyer, his bias towards the rights of the crown rendering, wherever they are concerned, a close examination of his judgments necessary.

Different accounts are given of his matrimonial connections. One says that he had two wives—the first being Emma, daughter of Sir Thomas Perrott, of Harleston and Yestlington; and the second being Emmota, daughter of John Harvey, of London. (*Nicholls's Leicestershire.*) Another states that he had only one wife, naming the first of the above two. Neither of these accounts can be quite relied on. A pedigree in the British Museum gives him only one wife, Emmota, the daughter of John Hervey, of London. From him descended Sir John Newton (the last of the family), of Barr's Court, Bitton, Gloucestershire, who was advanced to the dignity of a baronet on August 16, 1660, a title which expired in 1743. (*Wotton's Baronet.* iii. 145, and ex inf. of the Rev. H. T. Ellacombe.)

NICHOLAS, ROBERT, is said by Anthony Wood to be of the same family with Sir Edward Nicholas, secretary of state to Charles I., and Dr. Matthew Nicholas, dean of St. Paul's, who were both born at Winterbourn-Earles in Wiltshire. (*Athen. Oxon.* iii. 129.) He is described of Allcanning in that county in his admission to the Inner Temple in 1614. In 1640 he was elected member of the Long Parliament for the neighbouring borough of Devizes, and was an active manager of the impeachment against Archbishop Laud. He treated the archbishop with most unseemly virulence and insult, using such foul and gross language, and calling him, among other opprobrious names, 'pandar to the whore of Babylon,' that the archbishop desired the Lords, ' if his crimes were such as he might not be used like an archbishop, yet that he might be used like a Christian;' and they accordingly checked the member in his harangue. (*State Trials,* iv. 525, &c.) He gave another specimen of his harshness and intolerance in 1648 by starting up when a member objected to Lord Goring being included among the delinquents, and saying, 'What, Mr. Speaker, shall we spare the man who raised a second war more dangerous than the first, and cudgelled us into a treaty?' (*Parl. Hist.*

iv. 1068.) Although his motion was negatived, the Commons showed their liking to the man by making him a serjeant-at-law on October 30, 1648, and they very appropriately appointed him one of their assistants on the king's trial. (*Whitelocke,* 346, 366.) But, though his name is included in the act as one of the king's judges, he appears to have abstained from attending at the trial. (*State Trials,* iv. 1052.)

On June 1, 1649, he accepted the office of judge of the Upper Bench, and in April of the following year he and Chief Justice Rolle were much commended by the Commons for settling the people's minds to the government by their charges to the grand jury on the Western Circuit. When Oliver Cromwell assumed the protectorate, Nicholas was removed from the Upper Bench into the Exchequer, and was sworn a baron in Hilary Term 1653–4, an appointment which he still held on the succession of Protector Richard in September 1658, when he was resworn. His next change was made by the Rump Parliament, who restored him to his former place on the Upper Bench on January 17, 1659–60. (*Whitelocke,* 405, 448, 693; *Exchequer Books.*) Soon after the return of king Charles he obtained a pardon, but, being of the Rump Parliament, he was omitted from those serjeants who were confirmed in their degree. (*Cal. State Papers* [1660], 283.)

NICHOLS, AUGUSTINE, of an old and respectable Northamptonshire family, was the second son of Thomas Nichols, Esq., of Hardwick in that county, and Anne, the daughter of John Pell, Esq., of Eltington. Born at Ecton in 1559, he entered as a student of the Middle Temple, in which he became reader in 1602. In the following January he received a writ summoning him to take the degree of the coif, which in consequence of the death of Queen Elizabeth was renewed by King James, by whom he was knighted. He was elected recorder of Leicester in 1603, and his arguments in Westminster Hall are reported till, on November 26, 1612, he was elevated to the bench as a judge of the Common Pleas. On being appointed chancellor to Charles Prince of Wales it became necessary for him to have a renewal of his patent, in order that he might 'take fee and livery of the prince,' the usual oath prohibiting a judge from being paid by any but the king himself. (*Dugdale's Orig.* 219; *Croke, Jac. Prom.*) He died at Kendal in August 1616, while on the summer circuit: 'judex mortuus est, jura dans,' as Fuller describes him. He was buried there, and has fair monuments both in that church and in his own church at Foxton, both with the same epitaph.

King James commonly called him 'the judge that would give no money;' and Fuller (*Worthies,* ii. 163) speaks glowingly of his character.

He married Mary, the widow of Edward Bagshaw, Esq.; but, having no children by her, his estate at Foxton in Northamptonshire devolved on his brother's son Francis, who was created a baronet in 1641, but the title failed in 1717.

NIGEL (BISHOP OF ELY) was the nephew of Roger, Bishop of Salisbury, the great justiciary of Henry I. The influence of that prelate procured for him, first, the office of treasurer of England, and next, the bishopric of Ely, to which see he was elected in May 1133.

On the death of King Henry, historians differ as to the part he took in the usurpation of Stephen. There is little doubt, however, that the king suspected his fidelity, and that, though for a short time at the beginning of that reign he was continued in the office of treasurer, his detention was intended when his uncle Roger, and his cousin Alexander, Bishop of Lincoln, were seized at the council of Oxford in 1139. His escape to the castle of Devizes, and his refusal to deliver it into the king's hands until his uncle had been subjected to three days' fast, are related in the account of Roger, Bishop of Salisbury. Nigel's suspension or ejection from his bishopric for several years was the consequence of his resistance.

With the accession of Henry II. his prosperity returned. He probably resumed the office of treasurer until he purchased it for his son Richard, whom Alexander Swereford describes as his successor. That at an early period he held a high judicial position appears from a writ being directed in his name alone to the sheriff of Gloucester in which he is styled 'Baro de Scaccario.' (*Madox,* i. 209.) In 1165 his name stands the first of those before whom a charter or contract between the abbots of St. Alban's and Westminster was executed, in which they are described as 'assidentibus justiciis regis.' (*Ibid.* 44.) At this time Richard, his reputed son, was treasurer, and is so called in the charter. This Richard, who was afterwards Bishop of Lincoln, is supposed to have been the author of that valuable 'Dialogus de Scaccario' which Madox has printed at the end of his 'History of the Exchequer.' In that work a high character is given of Nigel, as most learned in his office, representing him as having an incomparable knowledge of the business of the Exchequer, and as restoring the science and renewing the forms which had been almost lost in the struggles of the preceding reign. It adds also that his suggestions for the raising of money were distinguished for their mildness. (*Ibid.* ii. 337, 388.)

Hardy introduces his name in his Catalogue of Chancellors immediately following that of Geoffrey Plantagenet. This, however, could not be the case, as Nigel was dead before Geoffrey was chancellor, and it would seem that his introduction at all as chancellor is founded on a mistake in transcribing the charter which is the only authority brought forward.

For three years before his death, which happened in May 1169, he was afflicted with paralysis. His public cares are stated to have rendered him inattentive to his pastoral duties; but that he did not altogether disregard them is proved by his foundation of a hospital for regular canons at Cambridge on the site where St. John's College now stands. (*Ibid.* i. 56, 78; *Angl. Sac.* i. 618; *Godwin*, 250, 340.)

NOEL, WILLIAM, was a descendant of the noble family of Noel, the ancestor of which came into England with the Conqueror, and was amply rewarded. One of his representatives became Earl of Gainsborough in 1682, a title which became extinct in 1792; another was made a baronet in 1660; and the judge was the second son of Sir John Noel the fourth baronet, by his wife Mary, daughter of Sir John Clobery, of Winchestead and Bridstope in Devonshire, knight.

He was born in 1695, and educated in the grammar school of Lichfield. Entering the Inner Temple, he took the degree of barrister in June 1721, and having been chosen recorder of Stamford, he was elected member for that borough in 1722. In 1747 and 1754 he was returned for the Cornish borough of West Looe. The 'Parliamentary History' gives no examples of his senatorial labours, and the Reports record very few of his forensic ones. He was nominated king's counsel in 1738, and on the trial of Lord Lovat in 1746 he was one of the managers for the House of Commons, and made a short speech in answer to some of the accused lord's objections. (*State Trials*, xviii. 817.) He received the post of chief justice of Chester in 1749, which he retained when he was appointed a judge in Westminster Hall. The latter elevation he owed to the patronage of Lord Hardwicke, who, even after he had resigned the Great Seal, applied to the king on his behalf. (*Harris's Life*, iii. 111.) Mr. Noel was accordingly constituted a judge of the Common Pleas in March 1757, and continued in that court till his death on December 8, 1762.

Horace Walpole calls him 'a pompous man of little solidity;' and the satirical author of the 'Causidicade' seems to regard him in the same light.

By his wife Elizabeth, daughter of Sir Thomas Trollope, Bart., he left only four daughters. (*Collins's Peerage*, vi. 211; *Wotton's Baronet.* iii. 91.)

NORFOLK, EARL OF. *See* ROGER BIGOT.
NORMANDY, DUKE OF. *See* HENRY.

NORMANNUS, or DE CANTILUPE, SIMON, was a great favourite of King Henry III., who gave him the archdeaconry of Norwich, and on the disgrace of Ralph de Neville, the chancellor, in 1238, placed the Great Seal in his hands. He did not, however, retain its custody very long, for in the next year he was dismissed from his office and expelled the court. He was also removed from all of his preferments, except the archdeaconry, and the corn of his church of Rossington was seized, but he was afterwards allowed to redeem it on finding security for fifty marks. (*Excerpt. e Rot. Fin.* i. 350; *Abb. Rot. Orig.* i. 8, 9.) The cause of his disgrace is represented to have been his refusal to seal a patent, granting to Thomas Earl of Flanders a tax of fourpence upon every sack of wool that was transported from England into his dominions. He died in 1249. (*Philipot's Catal.* 18.)

NORMANVILL, THOMAS DE, was of a Yorkshire family, of whom Gerard and Margery his wife, who were, perhaps, his parents, paid for an assize in that county in 53 Henry III., 1269. (*Excerpt. e Rot. Fin.* ii. 491.) He is called 'senescallus regis' in the king's grant to him, in 4 Edward I., of the custody of the castle of Bamburgh; and the title is continued in numerous instances till the tenth year, when he was appointed to the same duties under the designation of king's escheator beyond Trent. He retained the latter office till the twenty-third year, except that he exchanged it for a short time for the southern escheatorship. (*Abb. Rot. Orig.* i. 26-88.) It was probably in this official capacity that in 11 Edward I., 1283, he received the king's commands to remove the sheriff of Cumberland, his commission for which, and his letters to the barons of the Exchequer communicating his having obeyed the order, are mentioned in the Year Book of that reign (fo. 12). He was one of the justices itinerant for pleas of the forest only in 1286, but his name appears as a regular justice itinerant in 1292 and 1293. He died in 1295. (*Cal. Inquis.* p. m. i. 124.)

NORTH, FRANCIS (LORD GUILFORD), was of a family long connected with the law. Edward, the first Lord North of Kirtling, was king's serjeant under Henry VIII., and married the widow of Lord Chief Baron Sir David Brooke. His eldest son Roger married a daughter of Lord Chancellor Rich, and his second son Sir Thomas was of Lincoln's Inn in the time of Queen Mary. His grandson married the daughter of Sir Valentine Dale, master of the requests in Elizabeth's reign; and the lord keeper now to be noticed was the second son of the fourth Lord North, by Anne, daughter of Sir Charles Montagu.

He was born on October 22, 1637. Being

nearly thirty years old when his grandfather died, and his father having fourteen children to provide for, his introduction into the world was necessarily accompanied by a very limited provision. How he rose to the eminence he attained, and how he acted throughout his career, has been pleasantly told by Roger North, whose biography of his illustrious brother is the foundation of all succeeding memoirs.

The early politics of his father as a member of the Long Parliament, and his subsequent disgust at its proceedings (for he was secluded by Pride's Purge), sufficiently account for the changes in Francis's education. It was commenced under the tutelage of one Mr. Willis, a rigid Presbyterian, who kept a school at Isleworth; he next was sent to Bury School, where Dr. Stevens the master was a cavalier; and lastly he was matriculated at St. John's College, Cambridge, in June 1653. At each he was a diligent student, and his advances in all branches of learning are particularly recorded. On November 27, 1655, he was removed to the Middle Temple, occupying the moiety of a petit-chamber which his father bought for him. His uncle, Mr. Challoner Chute, who died shortly after as speaker of Protector Richard's parliament of 1659, was then treasurer of the inn, and swept the admission-fee into the new student's hat, saying, 'Let this be a beginning of your getting money here.' With his limited allowance he was obliged to avoid the expensive practices then prevalent among his fellows, his principal relaxation being music, in which he was a great proficient. He used to say that if he had not had his base or lyra viol to divert himself alone, he had never been a lawyer. Knowing that he should be dependent on his profession, he pursued his studies with unremitting assiduity, yet not neglecting those sciences without some knowledge of which no one can become great in the law. After acquiring some experience by keeping the courts of his grandfather and of other relations, he was called to the bar on June 28, 1661, and began his practice in a chamber in Elm Court, soon having a fair share of business, and being lucky enough to recover for his college an estate, for which it had long had an unsuccessful litigation.

Sir Geoffrey Palmer, the attorney-general, was his greatest patron and friend, not only directing his reading while a student, but encouraging his practice as a barrister, by giving him junior briefs in state prosecutions, and sometimes even employing him as his substitute. Among other duties, the attorney-general engaged him to argue for the crown before the House of Lords on the writ of error brought by the five members who had been convicted of a breach of the peace in holding the Speaker Finch down in his chair. Although unsuccessful, he so pleased by his manner and reasoning that he was immediately made king's counsel, and thereupon, after a little demur by the benchers on account of his youth, which subjected them to a rebuke by the court, he was called to the bench of the Middle Temple on June 5, 1668. On the Norfolk Circuit his success was greatly aided by his being placed as chairman on the commission for dividing the Fens, and being constituted by Bishop Lane judge of the Isle of Ely. He was a favourite with Chief Justice Hyde and many others of the judges; and Chief Justice Hale, though prejudiced against him, had so good an opinion of his talents that, seeing him pushing through the crowd to get into the court, he called out to the people to 'make way for the little gentleman,' adding, 'for he will soon make way for himself.'

In May 1671 he was selected to fill the office of solicitor-general, when he received the honour of knighthood. He soon after established himself in the Court of Chancery, having previously practised principally in the King's Bench. This change of court was probably influenced in a great measure by the appointment of Sir Matthew Hale as the head of the latter; for it appears plainly that each had such a violent dislike to the other as was likely to lead to frequent contentions. In the autumn following he became reader to his inn, when he took the Statute of Fines for his subject. His brother Roger records that the expense of his feasts was 1000*l*. at least, the extravagance of which and of some other recent ones deterred others from continuing the practice, and from that time public readings ceased.

In March 1672 he married Lady Frances Pope, a daughter of Thomas, third Earl of Down. Soon after he was returned to parliament for the borough of Lynn, and when he was made attorney-general on November 12, 1673, he was allowed to keep his seat, no notice being taken of the disqualification which the possession of that office was formerly deemed to impose.

On January 23, 1675, Sir Francis joyfully accepted the office of chief justice of the Common Pleas, being already tired of the bustle and turmoil of his former place, although the profits of it greatly exceeded those of the chief justice, his brother representing the former as amounting to 7000*l*. a year, while the latter did not exceed 4000*l*. One of the first attempts of the new chief justice was to restore the proper business of the Common Pleas, which had been almost entirely diverted from that court to the King's Bench, by means of the *ac etiam* inserted in the writ of Latitat. In this he succeeded by a similar introduction in the Common Pleas writ, thus equalising the business of the two courts, to the manifest benefit of the suitors in each. Soon after he was appointed the ridiculous scene called the Dumb-day was enacted, the result of which satisfied the rebellious serjeants that their new chief would not allow the court to be insulted with impunity. His brother enlarges on Sir Francis's labours to improve the rules and regulate the practice of his court, and there is no doubt that the chief deserved the praise of an able and honest administrator of justice, acting with exemplary prudence in party cases, neither showing any bias towards either side, nor affecting to conceal the loyal principles which guided him. The only exception that can be suggested is his conduct on the trial of Stephen Colledge, when he refused to restore the papers provided for the prisoner's defence which had been forcibly taken from him. The judge's friendly biographer attempts a justification, but in a lame and unsatisfactory manner; and Burnet (ii. 284) cautiously says that if the judge 'had lived to see an impeaching parliament he might have felt the ill effects of it.' (*State Trials*, vii. 551.)

For four years he enjoyed the quiet of a judicial life unbroken by the anxieties of politics. But in 1679 he was joined to the newly-formed council of thirty, by whom the government of the country was to be administered, being selected as one of the members to counterbalance those of the country or opposition party at the same time introduced. When that council was dissolved Sir Francis was admitted into the cabinet; and for advising and assisting the Attorney-General Levinz in the preparation of the proclamation against tumultuous petitions, by which the addresses of the so-called abhorrers were encouraged, the new parliament, without hearing him, ordered an impeachment against him on November 24, 1680. The committee appointed to prepare it, however, must have found it no easy task, as they failed to produce it before the dissolution on January 18. (*Parl. Hist.* iv. 1229.) Having acquired the entire confidence of the king, he became one of his majesty's chief advisers, and during the last years of the life of Lord Chancellor Nottingham, who entertained for him a sincere friendship, he was of great assistance to his lordship in his illnesses, and frequently acted for him as speaker of the House of Lords. On that nobleman's death there was no doubt as to his successor, and accordingly Sir Francis was made lord keeper on December 20, 1682, at the same time a pension of 2000*l.* a year being added, according to the practice which had previously been adopted. The king on presenting the Great Seal to him accompanied the gift with this prophetic warning: 'Here, take it, my lord, you will find it heavy,' the truth of which was afterwards acknowledged by the recipient, who declared that since he had had the Seal he had not enjoyed one easy or contented minute. He held it as long as King Charles lived, and under King James till his own death; and in less than a year after his appointment he was called to the peerage by the title of Baron Guilford, on September 27, 1683.

While lord keeper he devoted himself, as far as his leisure would permit him, to the correction of some of the abuses for which the Court of Chancery was even then notorious. But the period of his presidency was too short, for one so cautious in making innovations, to effect all the improvements he contemplated. He succeeded however in restraining unnecessary motions, too commonly made for the purpose of delay, and introduced many wholesome regulations that rendered the proceedings less expensive and oppressive to the suitors. To Roger North's encomium of the justice of his decisions no substantial objection is found by other writers, though party spirit vented some frivolous strictures at the time.

During the latter part of his career, as well under the reign of Charles II. as after the accession of James II., Sir George Jeffreys exerted the utmost art and cunning to supplant him, seizing every opportunity to insult and entrap him, and using language the most coarse and contemptuous. But the reliance which both kings placed on his wisdom and his honesty foiled all such underhand endeavours; and though it is probable that the lord keeper's disinclination to support James's encroachments on the constitution would have eventually occasioned his removal, such a consummation was prevented by his death seven months after the close of Charles's reign. For the greatest part of that short period he was afflicted by illness, which at last obliged him to retire to his seat at Wroxton, where, after several weeks of suffering, he died on September 5, 1685. Both Lord Guilford and his wife, who died some years before him, were buried in the vault of the Earls of Down in Wroxton Church. She brought him three sons and two daughters. His grandson, the third lord, was created in 1752 Earl of Guilford, having also, by the death of his cousin the sixth Lord North without children in 1734, succeeded to that barony. Both titles were held together till the death of the third earl in 1802 with only three daughters, between whom the barony of North remained in abeyance till 1841, when, two of them having died, it devolved upon the third, the present baroness. Two of the last earl's brothers enjoyed the earldom successively, and upon the death of the last of them it descended to his cousin Francis, the grandson of the first earl, and son of Brownlow North,

Bishop of Winchester, whose grandson, a minor, is its present possessor.

Of the life and character of the lord keeper there are two leading biographers, neither to be entirely depended on. The one is Roger North, his affectionate brother and constant companion, who, detailing every incident of his life and recording his inmost feelings and thoughts, cannot speak of his actions but in terms of praise. The other is Lord Campbell, who, writing nearly two centuries after his death, and using precisely the same materials, speaks of him with all the bitterness of party prejudice, ridiculing his respectability, sneering at his caution, disparaging his law, and in general giving a jaundiced colouring to his most worthy acts, evidently grudging the faint praise which he sometimes is obliged to bestow. A much fairer, and abler, summary of his character is given by Henry Roscoe in his 'Lives of Eminent British Lawyers' (p. 110).

NORTHAMPTON, HENRY DE, was the son of Peter de Northampton, and is sometimes called Henry Fitz-Peter. He held the church of St. Peter at Northampton (*Rot. Claus.* i. 520), and was a canon of St. Paul's (*Dugdale's Orig.* 21), preferments which he had probably received as an officer in the Exchequer.

He acted as a justice itinerant in 1 Richard I. (*Pipe Roll*, 69, 194), after which his name does not appear in a judicial character till 4 John, 1202, in which year, and 10 John, fines were levied before him as a justicier both at Westminster and in the country.

In 6, 7, and 8 John he was joined with Robert de la Saucey in the sheriffalty of Northamptonshire (*Rot. Pat.* 54); but in the troubles at the end of the reign he either sided with the barons, or was suspected of doing so, for in November 1215 his lands and houses in Northampton were given away by the king, and in the following March he had letters of protection. (*Ibid.* 169.)

He founded a hospital within the precincts of the cathedral church of St. Paul. (*Monast.* vi. 767.)

NORTHBURG, WILLIAM DE, is only mentioned as one of the justices appointed in 3 Edward I., 1275, to take assizes beyond the Trent, and in 6 and 7 Edward I. as a justice itinerant in several counties, and again in that character at Lancaster in 23 Edward I., but apparently in reference to a plea of earlier date. (*Abb. Rot. Orig.* i. 92.)

NORTHBURGH, ROGER DE (BISHOP OF LICHFIELD AND COVENTRY), was early employed in the service of Edward II., whom he accompanied to Scotland in 1314 as keeper of the royal signet (custos targiæ), and was taken prisoner with that in his possession at the bloody battle of Bannockburn. (*Cont. of Trivet's Annals*, ii. 14.) In April 1316 he was keeper of the wardrobe, and in 1320 he was employed on a mission to Carlisle, to treat for a truce with the Scots. (*Archæologia*, xxvi. 334.) On April 16, 1321, the king, in consequence of the chancellor's illness, delivered the Great Seal into his custody, as keeper of the wardrobe. It would appear that writs were then sealed in his presence and that of two of the clerks in Chancery, after which the Seal was replaced in the wardrobe, where it remained at that and a subsequent period. (*Parl. Writs*, ii. p. ii. 731, 1231.)

In 1317 the king presented him with the archdeaconry of Richmond, and subsequently procured his election to the bishopric of Lichfield and Coventry on April 12, 1322. Over that see he presided for nearly thirty-eight years, with nothing to distinguish the remainder of his life, except that he held the office of treasurer for two short periods in the second and fourteenth years of the reign of Edward III. He died in 1359, and is commemorated among the chancellors and benefactors of Cambridge. (*Godwin*, 320; *Le Neve*, 124, 324.)

NORTHINGTON, EARL OF. See R. HENLEY.

NORTHWELL, WILLIAM DE, was in holy orders, and held the office of clerk of the kitchen in the household of Edward II. (*Parl. Writs*, ii. p. ii. 82.) He was gradually advanced in his position, and in 11 Edward III. he was clerk or keeper of the wardrobe. He is so called as late as March 2, 1340 (*N. Fœdera*, ii. 1116), and doubtless still held the office when he was constituted a baron of the Exchequer on June 21 in the same year. He did not remain there long, as certain bills dated in August, September, and November 1340 are mentioned as being under his seal as treasurer of the king's household (*Kal. Exch.* i. 165), and there is no doubt that on receiving this last appointment he retired from his seat as baron.

NORTHWOLD, HUGH DE (BISHOP OF ELY), was a justicier in 12 Henry III., 1228. (*Dugdale's Orig.* 42.) He was elected abbot of St. Edmund's, having been previously a monk there, in 1214. (*Rot. Pat.* 124, 140, 142.)

In January 1229 he was nominated Bishop of Ely, being only a few months after he had acted as a judge. He held the see till his death, on August 9, 1254. His charity, his hospitality, his munificent expenditure in the erection of his church, and his splendid entertainment to the king and the nobles on its dedication in 1252, are the admiration of his contemporaries; and Matthew Paris, in speaking of his decease, says 'flos magistrorum obiit et monachorum, quia sicut abbas abbatum in Anglia extiterat, ita et episcopus episcoporum.

coruscavit.' (*Godwin*, 255; *B. Willis's Mitred Abbeys.*)

NORTHWOOD, ROGER DE, of Northwood-Chasteners, a manor near Milton in Kent, granted in the reign of King John to Stephen, the son of Jordan de Shepey, who built a mansion there and assumed its name, was the son of Roger de Northwood, who was with King Richard in the Holy Land, by Bona Fitzbernard his wife. In 42 Henry III. he accounted for the proceeds of the sheriffalty of Kent as one of the executors of Reginald de Cobbeham, and was possessed, besides the above manor, of a variety of other property in the same county. In 41 Henry III. he procured the tenure of his lands to be changed from gavelkind to knight's service. (*Hasted's Kent.*)

He was a baron of the Exchequer in 2 Edward I., and in 5 Edward I. he was excused from his service in the army against Wales on account of his residence in the Exchequer, and there is sufficient proof of his continuing in the office till his death, which occurred in the thirteenth year. (*Madox*, i. 726, ii. 20–320; *Cal. Inquis.* p. m. i. 86.) His son John was summoned to parliament, as were his successors, till 49 Edward III. The male line failing in 1416, the barony fell into abeyance among the representatives of his sisters. (*Baronage*, ii. 70.)

NORTON, RICHARD, was the son of Adam Conyers, seated in the bishopric of Durham, who adopted the name of Norton from his wife, the heiress of Norton in Yorkshire.

He appears as an advocate in the Year Book from 1 Henry IV., 1399, and his first public appointment was that of justice of assize for Durham in 1406, when it is most probable that he was a serjeant-at-law, although his writ of summons is not recorded, his name occurring in 1403 among several known to be of that degree, as lending the king 100*l*. to meet the emergencies of the state. (*Acts Privy Council*, i. 203.) He was made one of the king's serjeants in 1408. (*Dugdale's Orig.* 46.)

Within three months after the accession of Henry V. he was appointed chief justice of the Common Pleas, on June 26, 1413, and remained in his seat till his death on December 20, 1420. (*Rot. Parl.* iv. 35–123.) By his wife Elizabeth, daughter of Sir John Tempest of Studley, he left a family behind him, two of whose descendants were attainted for treason—Richard Norton, some time governor of Norham Castle, in 1569, who died in exile; and Thomas Norton, executed at Tyburn in 1570. (*Surtees' Durham*, i. lvii. clx.)

NORWICH, RALPH DE, is called 'clericum nostrum' in a safe-conduct granted to him in 18 John, when he was sent to Ireland. There he was employed in matters relating to the Exchequer, frequently going thither during the first six years of the following reign, and being united with the chief justice there and the Archbishop of Dublin in assessing the aid in 4 Henry III. While in England he had the management of the duty on wool; and the lands of Eustace de Vesci, of Robert de Berkeley, and of the Earl of Hereford were successively committed to his charge. In 8 Henry III. he had the church of Acle in Buckinghamshire, and in the next year was parson of that of Brehull in Oxfordshire.

After acting with Elyas de Sunning as justice of the Jews, he was constituted one of the 'king's justices of the Bench' on April 29, 1230, and fines were levied before him till Hilary 1234. (*Dugdale's Orig.* 43; *Rot. Pat.* 185; *Rot. Claus.* i. 187, &c., ii. 47, 62.)

NORWICH, WALTER DE, the son of Geoffrey de Norwich, was possessed of very large estates in Norfolk, Suffolk, Lincoln, and Hertford, over which he obtained a charter of free warren, together with a fair at Ling in Norfolk. No mention is made of the commencement of his career in the Exchequer; but he was remembrancer in 35 Edward I. In this office he acted in the first years of the next reign, and was raised to the bench as a baron of the Exchequer on August 29, 1311, 5 Edward II. On October 23 he was appointed *locum tenens* of the treasurer of the Exchequer, and on March 3, 1312, was again named baron.

As he still continued to act as treasurer's lieutenant, we can no otherwise account for these two nominations as baron than by supposing that Roger de Scotre his predecessor, though not so described in his patent, held the highest place in the court, and that Walter de Norwich's second patent advanced him to fill it. The suggestion derives support from the fact that only five days afterwards John Abel was made a baron in the place of Walter de Norwich, who is described in that patent as 'nunc capitalis baro,' which is the first occasion on which that title is used.

The interval between this and the eighth year of the reign was devoted to the performance of the double duties of baron and of treasurer's lieutenant; but in the latter year, on being raised to the office of treasurer on September 26, 1314, he vacated his seat on the bench.

He retained the treasurership till May 30, 1317, when he was relieved from the office on account of illness, and not only received the honourable appointment of chief baron, but was also commanded to assist at the privy councils of his sovereign whenever he was able. He is called by this title in 13 Edward II., as present on the delivery of the Great Seal. He was immediately re-appointed chief baron on the accession of Edward III., and kept his seat in the court till his death in the third year of that reign.

By his wife, Margaret, he had three sons, John, Roger, and Thomas; the elder of whom was summoned as a baron to parliament, but the title became extinct before the end of the reign by failure of his issue. (*Madox*, i. 75, ii. 49, 84; *Baronage*, ii. 90; *N. Fœdera*, ii. 428; *Blomefield's Norwich*, i. 76; *Norfolk*, i. 749.)

NORWICH, ROGER, was admitted a member of Lincoln's Inn on February 3, 1503, and attained the rank of reader in 1518; and again in 1521, on his being called to the degree of the coif, which he assumed in the following Trinity Term, and was appointed king's serjeant on July 11, 1523. On November 22, 1530, although there was then no vacancy in the court, he was raised to the bench as a puisne judge of the Common Pleas, but evidently as the designated successor of Chief Justice Sir Robert Brudenell, who was a very old man, and on whose death in the following January Robert Norwich was immediately promoted to his place. His presidency lasted till the beginning of 1535. (*Dugdale's Orig.* 47, 251.)

NOTTINGHAM, EARL OF. See H. FINCH.

NOTTINGHAM, ROBERT DE, had fines acknowledged before him from Hilary to Midsummer, 29 Henry III., 1245. (*Dugdale's Orig.* 43.) It is probable that he then died, as no further mention occurs relative to him, and no records have been discovered by which his personal history can be traced.

NOTTINGHAM, WILLIAM DE, is recorded twice as a justice itinerant into the northern counties, in 46 and 54 Henry III., 1262, 1270; but both confined to subjects relating to forest matters. He was sheriff or under-sheriff of Lincolnshire in 49 Henry III.

NOTTINGHAM, ROBERT DE, possibly the son of William de Nottingham, who acted for the king in the Exchequer in 5 Edward II. (*Madox*, i. 732), was appointed remembrancer of the Exchequer on June 21, 1322, 15 Edward II.; and on October 15, 1327, 1 Edward III., was raised to the office of second baron of that court; but on April 16, 1329, Robert de Wodehouse was made second baron. Whether this arose from the death or retirement of Robert de Nottingham does not appear. (*Parl. Writs*, ii. p. ii. 194.)

NOTTINGHAM, WILLIAM, was probably a native of Gloucestershire, as he possessed there, at the time of his death, several manors, besides many other lands in the county. (*Cal. Inquis.* p. m. iv. 417.) He was appointed the king's attorney on June 30, 1452, 30 Henry VI., which office he filled till the end of that reign. In 7 and 13 Edward IV. he is styled 'oone of our counseillours;' and on April 3, 1479, he was appointed lord chief baron. He enjoyed the place for little more than four years, surviving his royal master about two months, a new chief baron being named on June 15, 1483.

NOTTON, WILLIAM DE, was of a Yorkshire family, and probably a native of the place of that name. He became an advocate of considerable eminence, to judge from the frequent recurrence of his arguments in the Year Books. In 20 Edward III. he had a confirmation from the king of a messuage and above 200 acres of land, part of the manor of Fishlake in Yorkshire, by the service of one rose. In the same year he was one of the king's serjeants, and on October 12, 1355, he was constituted a judge of the King's Bench. He was subjected in 1358 to excommunication for neglecting to appear to the pope's citation to answer for the sentence he had pronounced against the Bishop of Ely, for harbouring the man who had slain one of Lady Wake's servants.

His period of service in the King's Bench was terminated in 35 Edward III., when he was constituted chief justice of the Common Pleas in Ireland; and two years afterwards he is noticed as one of the council of the king's son, Lionel Earl of Ulster, then lieutenant of that county.

He and his wife Isabella were benefactors to the priory of Bretton in Yorkshire, and of Royston in Hertfordshire. (*Cal. Rot. Pat.* 153, 174; *N. Fœdera*, iii. 101, 297, 622; *Abb. Rot. Orig.* 212; *Rot. Parl.* ii. 455; *Barnes's Edward III.* 551; *Cal. Inquis.* p. m. ii. 168, 190.)

O

ODO (BISHOP OF BAYEUX and EARL OF KENT) was a younger son of Arlotta, the mother of William the Conqueror, by Herluin de Conteville, whom she married after her connection with Robert Duke of Normandy. Herluin was in but moderate circumstances till William succeeded to the dukedom, after which the confiscated estates of the rebellious nobles enabled the duke to enrich his uterine brothers. The elder of them, Robert Earl of Moreton, is afterwards noticed. Odo, the younger, obtained the earldom of Eu on the banishment of William, its former earl, who had opposed the duke's succession: to which was added, in 1049, the valuable bishopric of Bayeux. His disposition, however, exhibiting more of the soldier than the priest, he was employed to lead part of his brother's forces against the King of France, to whose defeat he is said to have greatly contributed. In William's enterprise against England, also, he not only accompanied him, but contributed a supply of forty ships.

Forbidden by his clerical character from bearing offensive arms, he is represented in the tapestry of Bayeux on horseback and in complete armour, but without any sword. He bears a staff only; and the superscription, 'Hic Odo Eps baculum tenens confortat,' is meant to intimate that his peculiar duty was to encourage the soldiers. After the battle the castle of Dover and the whole county of Kent were committed to his care.

Early in 1067 King William, returning to his Norman dominions, left Odo and William Fitz-Osberne regents and justiciaries of England; Kent, of which he was then created earl, being particularly placed under Odo's care. The conduct of the viceroys was harsh and rapacious, occasioning many insurrections, which were quickly suppressed. After Fitz-Osberne's death Odo was still continued regent, or, as Malmesbury calls him, 'vice dominus,' on another visit of the king to Normandy, in 1073; and his energy and address were exhibited in assisting Richard de Benefacta and William de Warenne, the chief justiciaries, in crushing the conspiracy of Roger Fitz-Osberne, Earl of Hereford (the son of his former coadjutor in the government), and Ralph de Guader, Earl of Suffolk and Norfolk.

The king, with his accustomed munificence, not only rewarded Odo's services with the honours already mentioned, which raised him to the second rank in the kingdom, but by more substantial gifts enabled him splendidly to support it. His share in the distribution of crown lands amounted to 184 lordships in Kent alone, with above 250 in other counties. With the immense riches thus amassed, he aspired to a still higher dignity, and conceived the mad project of purchasing the papacy. He bought a magnificent palace at Rome, and engaging many of the English nobles in the enterprise, he prepared a number of ships for the conveyance of them and his treasures there, to await the death of the reigning pope, Gregory VII. Taking advantage of the king's absence in Normandy in 1079, he had collected his friends, and was ready to sail from the Isle of Wight, when, adverse winds delaying the expedition, the king received intelligence of his project, and, hastening to the scene, ordered the ambitious prelate to be arrested. The fear, however, of incurring ecclesiastical censure, by laying violent hands on a bishop, restrained his officers from obeying the royal commands, so that the king was reduced to the necessity of being his own officer, and made the arrest himself. Odo claimed the privilege of his order, and appealed to the pope; but William was too determined in his purpose to desist, and on the suggestion of Lanfranc, Archbishop of Canterbury, answered, 'I do not arrest the clergyman or the bishop, but my own earl, whom by my own will I made governor of my kingdom, and from whom I require an account of his stewardship.' Odo was accordingly committed to safe custody in the castle of Rouen, where he remained a prisoner till the end of his brother's reign, and all his property was confiscated to the king's use.

Even on his death-bed William could scarcely conquer his resentment against his ungrateful brother, and in the first instance excepted him from the general liberation which he then commanded of all persons in confinement. By the importunity of his nobles, however, he was at last induced, reluctantly, to consent to his enlargement; but not without expressing surprise at their intercession, and prophesying that new troubles would arise from the release of so restless a disturber.

On the Conqueror's death, in September 1087, Odo returned to England, and was restored to his earldom of Kent and the vast possessions which he had forfeited. He was present at the court which William Rufus held at the following Christmas, on which occasion he is described as 'justiciarius et princeps totius Angliæ.'

Whatever friendship the king might profess for him at this time, it is probable that it did not last long. Odo soon found that he no longer possessed the influence he had formerly exercised, and that the counsels of Lanfranc prevailed. Instigated by disappointment and jealousy, he excited the Norman barons to join in raising Robert, the king's elder brother, to the English throne. A conspiracy was formed, and by the following Easter the standard of rebellion was raised in various counties. William, however, wisely attacked Odo, the principal insurgent, at Pevensey, where he had retired to await the arrival of Robert, and after seven weeks' siege compelled him to surrender, granting him his life and liberty on condition that he would deliver up the castle of Rochester and leave England for ever. On being taken to Rochester for this purpose, Eustace Earl of Boulogne, to whom he had entrusted his command, pretended he was a traitor, and took him and his guard prisoners; whereupon William, justly indignant, made a vigorous attack on the castle, which, after an obstinate defence, he took; and, though the lives of the garrison were spared, Odo was compelled to evacuate the place amid the taunts of the conquerors. In the vexation of the moment he could not restrain his threats of revenge; but no opportunity was afforded him of carrying them into execution.

Retiring to Normandy, he assisted Robert in the management of his dukedom, and, according to some writers, accompanied him in his expedition to Jerusalem, and was killed at the siege of Antioch. According to others, he died and was buried at Palermo, in his way to Rome. If the event, as it is generally allowed, occurred in the year 1096, the latter account is most probable, as the siege of Antioch did not begin till October 1097.

His career affords the best evidence that the Church was not the profession he should have selected. His talents and his tendencies were of a military character, and he was formed to shine in the active duties of the field. Energetic in counsel, he was daring and prompt in the execution of his conceptions. Although ambitious and worldly, and making riches and power the principal objects of his pursuit, he was at the same time bountiful to the poor, and an encourager of learning. He expended his splendid revenue with a liberal hand; spent large sums in the erection of his cathedral, and in beautifying his episcopal city. Even in the contradictory accounts of the historians, some of whom were his contemporaries, enough is shown to prove that, if he had some vices, there were many virtues to counterbalance them. (*Dugdale's Orig.* 20; *Baronage*, i. 22; *Madox*, i. 8; *Hutchins's Dorsetsh.* i. 11; *Will. Malmesb.* 456, &c.; *Roger de Wendover*, ii. 20, &c.; *Rapin; Daniel; Turner; Lingard;* &c.)

ODYHAM, WALTER DE, was on July 25, 1284, entrusted with the Great Seal in conjunction with Hugh de Kendal, during the absence of Bishop Burnel, the chancellor. On this account they are placed in Sir T. D. Hardy's catalogue among the keepers of the Seal. Both of them, however, were simply clerks in Chancery. (*Madox*, ii. 257.)

OFFORD, ANDREW DE, was the brother of the undermentioned John de Offord, and, like him, was employed in diplomatic missions. From 17 to 29 Edward III. he is named on embassies to Rome, Castile, Portugal, Flanders, and France. (*N. Fœdera*, ii. 1224, iii. 308.) It was probably during the chancellorship of his brother that he was made a clerk or master of the Chancery, although he is not distinctly named among those officers till a later period. On August 4, 1353, when the chancellor, John de Thoresby, went to York, he left the Seal in the hands of David de Wollore, M.R., Thomas de Brayton, and Andrew de Offord, but how long he remained absent does not appear. Offord was a receiver of petitions in the parliaments of 28 and 29 Edward III. (*Rot. Parl.* ii. 254, 264), and died in 1358.

He was at first described as juris civilis professor, afterwards as canon of York, and lastly as archdeacon of Middlesex, to which he was admitted in 1349. (*Le Neve*, 193.)

OFFORD, JOHN DE (ARCHBISHOP OF CANTERBURY), is sometimes called Ufford, and it is the fashion to call him one of the sons of Robert de Ufford, the first Earl of Suffolk. It is doubtful, however, whether he was in any way connected with that family, as he is not mentioned in the earl's will. There was, however, a John de Ufford, who was contemporary with the chancellor. He was the son of Ralph de Ufford, the brother of Robert, the first earl, but he is in every way distinguished from the chancellor. He is always called a knight, and was summoned to parliament as a baron in 1360, eleven years after the death of the chancellor, and his own death occurred in the following year. The discrepancies in these dates appear to settle the question, but if any doubt remained it would seem to be extinguished by the following fact. The first earl's grandfather, whose name was Robert, assumed the name of Ufford, from a place in *Suffolk*. There is evidence to prove that the chancellor's family derived its name from the manor of Offord in *Huntingdonshire*, and that he is apparently the younger son of John de Offord, who had property at Offord-Dameys in that county, and that in 5 Edward III., 1331, he had the custody of that manor during the minority of his nephew, the infant heir. (*Baronage*, ii. 47; *Abb. Placit.* 266; *Abb. Rot. Orig.* ii. 50.)

In the early part of the reign of Edward III. John de Offord was dean of the Arches. (*Newcome's St. Albans*, 229), and from the eighth to the eighteenth years he was continually engaged in important foreign embassies to the courts of France, Scotland, and Avignon. At first he is described as juris civilis professor and as canon of St. Paul's, in 12 Edward III. as archdeacon of Ely, and on August 3, 1344, as dean of Lincoln. From October 4, 1342, he is mentioned as keeper of the privy seal, and on one occasion as the king's secretary. (*N. Fœdera*, ii. 880, 1239, iii. 18, 176.) In these negotiations he exhibited so much wisdom and tact as to point him out as a fit recipient of the honours with which he was afterwards invested.

On October 26, 1345, he was appointed chancellor, and held the Seal till his death, being the third chancellor during this reign who died in office. In September 1348 he was raised to the archbishopric of Canterbury, Pope Clement VI. and the English king uniting to set aside the monks' election of Thomas Bradwardin; but he was fated.

never to obtain full possession of his dignity. Before his installation he was seized with the mortal disease which for several months had devastated England, and was one of the last of its victims, dying at Tottenham on May 20, 1349. He was buried privately at Canterbury. (*Godwin*, 111; *Angl. Sac.* i. 42, 375, 794.)

OGER was one of the dapifers of the household, of whom so many are noticed among the justiciers of the reign of Henry II. The office is believed to be the same as seneschal or steward, and, as there were several at the same time, some perhaps were of England and others of Normandy. In 14 Henry II. the honor of Eye was committed to his charge. He was then sheriff of Norfolk and Suffolk, and held that office for several years.

His name appears in 1170-1 as one of the justices itinerant in those counties with Guy the dean; probably only as sheriff, as was common at that time, for the purpose of assisting in settling the assessments to the tallages and aids then imposed. (*Madox*, i. 144, 145, 573.)

He was the father of the before-mentioned Oger Fitz-Oger.

OKETON, JOHN DE, was a justice itinerant into various counties from 52 to 56 Henry III., and from the very numerous entries on the Fine Roll up to October 29, 1272, 57 Henry III., of payments made for assizes to be held before him, there can be little doubt that he was a regular justicier. (*Excerpt. e Rot. Fin.* ii. 490-588.) He held the office of sheriff of Yorkshire in 44 Henry III., and for several subsequent years; and there is an entry in 52 Henry III. that he could not levy the ferm for the county, 'propter turbationem regni.' (*Madox*, ii. 160.)

OKHAM, JOHN DE, was joined in the commission with the escheator ultra Trentam to take into the king's hands the property of Anthony, Patriarch of Jerusalem and Bishop of Durham, on his death in 4 Edward II. (*Abb. Rot. Orig.* i. 175.) During the four following years he was clerk to Ingelard de Warlee, keeper of the wardrobe (*Rot. Parl.* ii. 437), and held the office of cofferer of that department. (*Cal. Rot. Pat.* 74.) On June 18, 1317, he was constituted one of the barons of the Exchequer, and is not named in that character beyond 1322. He became custos of the deanery of the free chapel of St. Martin, London, in 19 Edward III. (*Abb. Rot. Orig.* i. 290.)

OLIVER, JORDAN, was one of the knights of Somersetshire and Dorsetshire who were summoned before the barons of the Exchequer in 14 John for not keeping the fine which they had made with the king for having the sheriffs of those counties from among themselves. (*Rot. Claus.* i. 131.) This fine was made with William Malet on the king's part, and, as he continued sheriff for four years, the knights probably thought that, as there were no symptoms of any of them obtaining the appointment, they were not called upon to perform their part. Certainly none of them enjoyed the office at that period, although Jordan Oliver, twenty-eight years afterwards, in 24 Henry III., held it for one year. In 5 Henry III. he was one of the king's escheators for the county of Devon. From the ninth year to the twenty-second he was appointed a justice itinerant in that and several other counties. (*Rot. Claus.* i. 473, ii. 76, 205, 206; *Excerpt. e Rot. Fin.* i. 239, 283.)

ORMESBY, WILLIAM DE, was appointed a judge of the King's Bench in 24 Edward I., 1296. He had, however, acted previously as a justice itinerant into the northern counties in 20 and 21 Edward I.

On the reduction of Scotland in 1296 he was constituted justiciary of that country, and by the rigour with which he extorted the penalties imposed by King Edward on those who refused to take the oath of fealty to him he naturally excited the deep and general odium of that people. Wallace, in the following year, surprised him while holding his court at Scone, and, his followers being dispersed, he himself barely escaped. (*Triveti Annales*, 356; *Tytler's Scotland*, i. 123, 128.)

On his return to England he resumed his duties in the King's Bench, in which he is mentioned till the end of the reign, and also as chief of the justices of trailbaston assigned for the counties of Norfolk and Suffolk in 1305. (*Abb. Placit.* 242, 259, 294; *Rot. Parl.* i. 166, 198; *Parl. Writs*, i. 407-8.)

Some doubt may arise as to his having been re-appointed to his seat in the King's Bench on the accession of Edward II., as no such writ was directed to him to take the oaths as was addressed to his fellows on September 6, 1307; and his name does not judicially appear in the Abbreviatio Placitorum after the death of Edward I. It is true that he was summoned to attend the first parliament, and stands in his proper place in the list, but this was by a previous writ, dated August 26; and though he is summoned to all the subsequent parliaments up to 11 Edward II., he is generally placed in that part of the list appropriated to the justices itinerant. That he acted in the latter capacity during the remainder of his life there can be no question; and it is not unlikely that he was allowed, at the commencement of the new reign, to retire from the heavier duties of the King's Bench to his estates in Norfolk and Suffolk, in which counties he was principally employed as a justice of assize during the whole period. (*Parl. Writs*, i. 766, ii. 1246.) He died about 1317, and was buried at the abbey of

St. Benet's, at Hulme in Norfolk, to which he was a benefactor. (*Taylor's Index Monast.* 2.)

In the pleas of 2 Edward II. he is spoken of as the husband of Sibilla, late the wife of Roger Loveday, a justice itinerant in the previous reign (*Abb. Placit.* 307); and among the escheats or inquisitions post mortem of 7 Edward II. (i. 254) occurs the name of Elena, the wife of William de Ormesby. This may perhaps be explained by supposing that there might be two Williams de Ormesby, both of Norfolk; a suspicion which receives some probability from the fact that while the judge was summoned with his fellows to the parliament at Carlisle in 35 Edward I., a burgess of the same name was returned to the same parliament for Yarmouth in Norfolk. They might, however, be still the same person, for there is no proof that judges, or at all events justices itinerant, were then precluded from sitting among the Commons.

OSBERT (? BISHOP OF EXETER) has not hitherto been introduced among the chancellors, and is now inserted on the authority of a charter granted by King William I. to the monastery of St. Augustine at Canterbury, among the signatures to which appears 'Signum Osberti Cancellarii.' Two other signatures are those of Scotland the Abbot, and William, Bishop of London; and as the former was appointed in 1070 and the latter died in 1075, the date of the charter must have been between those two years, or in one of them. (*Monast.* i. 144.)

If, as is most probable, he were the Osbert who was made Bishop of Exeter in 1074, the period within which he held the chancellorship is reduced even to a shorter compass. The bishop was a Norman by birth, son of Osbern de Crespon, and is described by Malmesbury as 'frater Gulielmi pre-excellentissimi comitis,' the Earl of Hereford, and brought up in the court of King Edward. He ruled the see for nearly thirty years, and died in 1103. He sometimes is called Osbern, under which name he attested the charter to St. Martin's in London, in 1068, as chaplain, and he used both names indiscriminately as bishop. (*Ibid.* iii. 141, iv. 16, 17, 20, vi. 1325; *Le Neve*, 80; *Godwin*, 401.)

OSGODBY, ADAM DE, was appointed keeper of the Rolls of Chancery on October 1, 1295, 23 Edward I. He no doubt had been previously one of the clerks of the Chancery, and from several entries relating to the deposit of the Seal during the temporary absence of the chancellor, it is plain that he was still considered as the chief of them. He remained uninterruptedly in the office till 10 Edward II., 1316, a period of nearly twenty-one years. In both reigns he frequently performed the functions of the chancellor when absent, sometimes alone, and sometimes in connection with two or three of the other clerks. In that of Edward I. he held it three times under the seals of three clerks, during the vacancy or absence of the chancellors, and from the third to the eighth year of Edward II. the Seal was frequently deposited with Osgodby in the same manner. At first it was merely in the absence of the chancellor, but between the resignation of Walter Reginald, Bishop of Worcester, as chancellor, and his appointment as keeper of the Seal—viz., between December 9, 1311, and October 6, 1312—Adam de Osgodby, Robert de Bardelby, and William de Ayremynne are distinctly described as keepers of the Seal (*Rot. Parl.* i. 337), and transacted all the business connected with it. While Reginald continued keeper the Great Seal was always secured by the seals of these three. (*Parl. Writs*, ii. p. ii. 1249.)

At the parliament held at Carlisle in January 1307, 35 Edward I., he acted as proctor for the dean and chapter of York, being then a canon of that cathedral. (*Rot. Parl.* i. 190.)

Like all his brethren in the Chancery, he was an ecclesiastic, and held the living of Gargrave in Yorkshire. On November 7, 1307, 1 Edward II., the king granted to him the office of custos of the House of Converts in Chancery Lane during pleasure, but by a patent in the seventh year secured it to him for life. It was not, however, till the year 1377 that this office was permanently annexed to that of keeper of the Rolls.

His death occurred in August 1316, leaving property in Yorkshire, to which Walter de Osgodby, probably his brother, succeeded. (*Cal. Inquis.* p. m. i. 194, 279.)

OSMUND (EARL OF DORSET, BISHOP OF SALISBURY) is described as the nephew of William the Conqueror, being son of his sister Isabella, the wife of Henry, Count of Seez in Normandy. To this title he succeeded, and came over as a layman in the retinue of his uncle, who is said to have created him Earl of Dorset, and to have selected him for his superior judgment as one of his principal advisers, and placed him in the office of chancellor.

The date of his appointment is uncertain, but it is evidently not so early as is usually assigned. Arfastus was chancellor in 1068, if not before, and Osbert somewhere between 1070 and 1074. William's charter of confirmation to the cathedral church of St. Paul (*Dugdale's St. Paul's*, 51), to which the name 'Osmund the Chancellor' is attached as one of the witnesses, must have been granted after 1070, inasmuch as Lanfranc the archbishop is another witness, and he was not consecrated till that year. Osmund probably succeeded on Osbert's elevation to the prelacy about 1075, one of the dates given by Thynne and Philipot; and there is every reason to presume that he retained the Seal till his own appointment as Bishop of Salisbury in 1078, as no other chancellor occurs in the intervening period.

There is another charter with his name as chancellor, confirming the land of Staning in Sussex to the abbey of Fescamp in Normandy (*Monast.* vi. 1082), but it affords no evidence of having been granted either at an earlier or a later date.

On the death of Herman, Bishop of Salisbury, Osmund, having become an ecclesiastic, was appointed his successor. His first efforts were devoted to the completion of the cathedral commenced by Herman, which he effected in the year 1092, founding a deanery and thirty-six canonries in it, and nobly endowing it with various churches and towns.

He died in December 1099, and was buried in the cathedral he erected, but his remains were removed in 1457 to the new cathedral.

The title of Osmund the Good, which he acquired in his life, is the best illustration of his character; he was a prelate of the severest manners and strictest moderation, filling his office with dignity and reputation, the patron of learned men, and an impartial assertor of the rights of his see. He was canonised by Pope Calixtus in 1457, above 350 years after his death.

To bring into some uniformity the services of the Church, he compiled the breviary, missal, and ritual which, under the name of 'The Use of Sarum,' was afterwards generally adopted, and continued to be employed till the Reformation. He is also stated to have written the life of St. Aldhelm, first Bishop of Sherborne. (*Godwin*, 336; *Hutchins's Dorset*, i. 10, &c.; *Le Neve*, 256; *Biog. Brit. Literaria*, ii. 23.)

OVERTON, THOMAS, is another of the barons of the Exchequer of whom there is no distinct information, except that, according to a list kept in the Exchequer, he was admitted to that office in Hilary 1402, 3 Henry IV., and that his place was vacant in the ninth year. (*Liber.* 9 *Henry IV.*)

OWEN, THOMAS, was born at Condover in Shropshire, the seat of his father, Richard Owen, a merchant of the neighbouring town of Shrewsbury, who, according to the pedigrees of the family, could trace his descent from the ancient Kings of Wales. His mother was Mary, one of the daughters of Thomas Ottley, Esq., of that town. He received his education at the university of Oxford, but Wood is uncertain whether at Broadgate's Hall (now Pembroke College) or Christ Church. After taking his degree he was removed to Lincoln's Inn, where he was called to the bar in 1570, and became reader in 1583. Six years afterwards he was raised to the degree of the coif, and on January 25, 1593, was made queen's serjeant. On January 21, 1594, he was promoted to the bench as a judge of the Common Pleas, where he sat till his death on December 21, 1598. (*Dugdale's Orig.* 45, 233.) Wood describes him as a learned man, and a great lover of those who professed learning; and the Reports which he collected in the King's Bench and Common Pleas, and which were printed with some additional cases in 1650, manifest his legal erudition and his industry both before and after he was raised to the bench. He was buried in Westminster Abbey under a noble monument.

His first wife was Sarah, daughter of Humphrey Baskerville, by whom he had five sons and five daughters. His second wife was Alice, the widow of William Elkins, mercer and alderman of London. She survived him, and erected and endowed a hospital at Islington for ten poor women, and a school for thirty boys, in grateful remembrance of her escape from death in her childhood, when an arrow, shot at random while she was sporting in the fields, pierced the hat that she wore. (*Stow's London*, 110.)

The judge's son was Sir Roger Owen, who distinguished himself among the literary men of the day, and was an active member of parliament. Both he and several of his successors filled the office of sheriff, and the estate of Condover still remains with the family. (*Athen. Oxon.* i. 672; *Dart's Westminster Abbey*, ii. 83.)

OXFORD, CONSTANTIUS DE, a justice itinerant appointed by the writ of Richard de Luci, in conjunction with Alard Banastre, the sheriff, to assess the tallage on the county of Oxford in 20 Henry II., 1174 (*Madox*, i. 124), was probably a priest, or other ecclesiastical person of Oxford; for the religious orders very commonly cast off their family names, and adopted either that of the monastery to which they belonged, or the locality in which their clerical duties were exercised.

OXFORD, EARL OF. See R. DE VERE.

OXFORD, JOHN OF (BISHOP OF NORWICH), was so called from the place of his birth, being son of a burgess of that city named Henry. Educated for the ecclesiastical profession, he was appointed one of the king's chaplains, in which office he must soon have distinguished himself, since, though holding no higher dignity, he presided at the famous council of Clarendon in January 1164, and was afterwards sent with Geoffrey Ridel to the pope to obtain his confirmation of the ancient customs of the realm as they were there propounded.

In this embassy they of course failed;

but in the following year he was again despatched with another associate, and in their way to Rome they attended a diet at Wurzburgh, which had been assembled for the acknowledgment of the opposition pope, Pascal III. They are charged with having undertaken that the king should support this pope, a charge which, though they denied it, was made the pretence by Becket, in 1166, for excommunicating John of Oxford, and for excluding him from the deanery of Salisbury, to which he had been just previously admitted. John, however, being again sent to Rome in the same year, succeeded so well in exculpating himself that the pope reinstated him in his deanery, and absolved him from Becket's sentence. The negotiation for his sovereign also he conducted with equal ability and success, obtaining from the pontiff the appointment of two cardinals as legates *a latere* to hear and determine the dispute with Becket, which was in fact a suspension of the legatine power previously granted to him; and bringing home, in addition, the pope's dispensation for Prince Geoffrey to marry his third cousin, the heiress of Bretagne. So high was his credit with Henry that in 1167 he was entrusted with a confidential embassy to the Empress Maud, the king's mother, to counteract the efforts which Becket was then making to induce her to interfere in his quarrel, efforts which were rendered of no avail by her death towards the end of the year. In 1170 he was again employed in another embassy to the papal court, then at Beneventum, in reference to Becket's affair; and when the agreement between the king and that prelate was at last effected, he was, to the great annoyance of the latter, appointed to accompany him to England. This duty he performed in good faith, and prevented the interruption to his landing at Sandwich threatened by Gervase de Cornhill, the sheriff of Kent.

On December 14, 1175, he received the reward of his services by being consecrated Bishop of Norwich, and in the next year was sent to accompany the king's daughter, Jane, to her intended husband, the King of Sicily.

In 1179 he with three other English bishops attended the Lateran council held against schismatics. On his return he was one of the three prelates to whom, on the retreat of Richard de Luci to the abbey of Lesnes, the execution of the office of chief justiciary was entrusted, the other two being Richard Tocliffe, Bishop of Winchester, and Geoffrey Ridel, Bishop of Ely. They were at the same time placed at the head of three of the four divisions (*Dugdale's Orig.* 20) in which England was then arranged for the administration of justice. It is curious that this appointment was in direct opposition to one of the canons of the Lateran council, from which John of Oxford had just returned, and naturally produced a remonstrance from the pope, which led to a justification by the Archbishop of Canterbury of their acceptance of the office. Whatever may have been the cause, however, it is certain that the bishops were soon removed from the presidency of the court, which, in the course of the following year was conferred on Ranulph de Glanville, one of their lay associates. That John of Oxford continued to perform judicial duties after this event is evident from the roll of Richard I., which proves that he acted either in that or the preceding year as a justice itinerant in several counties. (*Pipe Roll,* 27, 50, 211, 238.)

Seized with the mania of the age, he devoted himself to the crusade in 1189, but, being attacked by robbers on his way to the Holy Land, and despoiled of all his property, he turned his steps to Rome, where, representing the inadequacy of his means to support the expense of the undertaking, he procured an absolution from his vow.

The remainder of his life was devoted to his episcopal duties, and to the restoration of his church, which had been injured by a fire. Many houses also which had been destroyed at the same time he caused to be rebuilt, and to his other benefactions to the poor he added the erection of a hospital.

He died on June 2, 1200, and was buried in his own cathedral. The history of his life supports the character he acquired of being an able negotiator, a graceful orator, and a man of sound judgment and quick discernment. To his other occupations he added that of an author, having written a history of all the kings of Britain, besides some occasional works, among which were a book 'Pro Rege Henrico contra S. Thomam Cantuariensum,' an account of his journey into Sicily, and some orations and epistles to Richard, Archbishop of Canterbury. (*Godwin,* 428; *Weever,* 789; *Angl. Sac.* i. 409; *Lord Lyttelton,* ii. 362, 416, &c., iv. 100; *Ric. Devizes,* 12.)

P

PAGE, FRANCIS, was the son of the Rev. Nicholas Page, the vicar of Bloxham in Oxfordshire, and was born about 1661. Admitted at the Inner Temple, he was called to the bar in 1690, and was raised to the bench of that society in 1717. He varied his legal studies by entering into the political controversies of the time, taking the whig view of the subjects in discussion, and adding some pamphlets to those which then almost daily issued from the press. In 1705 he appeared as one of the counsel for the electors of Aylesbury who had been committed by the House of Commons for proceeding at law against the returning officers, who had illegally refused their votes. The Commons, having then resolved that the counsel had thereby been guilty of a breach of privilege, ordered their committal to the custody of the serjeant-at-arms. Page evaded the arrest, and Queen Anne was obliged to dissolve the parliament in order to prevent a collision between the two houses on the question.

He was member for Huntingdon in the two parliaments of 1708 and 1710, and soon after the accession of George I. he received the honour of knighthood, and was not only made a serjeant, but also king's serjeant, in 1715. An early opportunity was taken of promoting him to the bench, and on May 15, 1718, he took his seat as a baron of the Exchequer. He purchased an estate and built a mansion at Steeple Aston in Oxfordshire, not many miles from Banbury, with the elections of which borough he interfered so much that he was charged in the House of Commons, in February 1722, with corrupting the corporation by bribery, and the evidence was so nearly balanced that he was only acquitted by a close majority of four votes. On November 4, 1726, he was removed from the Exchequer to the Common Pleas, and in the middle of September 1727, three months after the accession of George II., he was again translated to the King's Bench. Though then sixty-six years of age, he remained on the bench fourteen years more, dying on October 31, 1741. He was buried at Steeple Aston under a monumental pile with full-length figures of himself and his second wife by the eminent sculptor Scheemacker. This he caused to be erected during his life, and in order to its construction he destroyed the ancient monuments in the church.

He has left behind him a most unenviable reputation. Without the abilities of Judge Jeffreys, he was deemed as cruel and as coarse. The few reported cases in the State Trials at which he presided do not indeed appear to warrant this character, nor does his learned judgment in Ratcliffe's case, reported in 1 Strange (269); but he could not have been known among his contemporaries by the sobriquet of the 'hanging judge,' nor have obtained the inglorious distinction of being stigmatised by some of the best writers of the age, unless there had been pregnant grounds for the imputation. Pope, in his Imitation of the First Satire of the Second Book of Horace, thus introduces him:—

Slander or poison dread from Delia's rage,
Hard words or hanging if your judge be Page.

Long before Page's death Pope had gibbeted him in the 'Dunciad' (book iv. lines 26-30):—

Morality, by her false guardians drawn,
Chicane in furs, and Casuistry in lawn,
Gasps, as they straighten at each end the cord,
And dies, when Dulness gives her [Page] the word,—

leaving blank the name in the last line. If it were not vouched by Dr. Johnson in his Life of Pope, it would be scarcely credible that the conscious judge had the folly to fit the cap on himself, and to send a complaint to the poet by his clerk, who told the poet that the judge said that no other word would make sense of the passage. The name is now inserted at full length.

Dr. Johnson also enlarges in his Life of Savage on the vulgar and exasperating language by which Judge Page obtained the conviction of the unfortunate poet for the murder of Mr. Sinclair. No wonder that Savage, after he was pardoned, revenged himself by penning a most bitter 'character' of the judge, who escapes no better under Fielding's lash, in 'Tom Jones' (book viii. c. xi.). When Crowle the punning barrister was on the circuit with Page, on some one asking him if the judge was *just behind*, he replied, 'I don't know, but I am sure he never was *just before.*'

When old and decrepit, the judge perpetrated an unconscious joke on himself. As he was coming out of court one day, shuffling along, an acquaintance enquired after his health. 'My dear sir,' he answered, 'you see I keep *hanging on, hanging on.*'

He was very desirous of founding a family, but though he was twice married he left no issue. The name of his first wife, who was buried at Bloxham, has not been preserved; that of his second was

Frances, daughter of Sir Thomas Wheate, of Glympton, Bart. He left his estates to Francis Bourne, on condition that he took the name of Francis Page only; but his object of perpetuating his name was frustrated by his devisee dying unmarried, and his property passing away to strangers. (*Noble's Granger*, iii. 203; *Notes and Queries*, 3rd S. i. 153.)

PAGE, JOHN or WILLIAM, is called by Dugdale William, and by Rymer John, but there is no account of him before he is inserted in the 'Chronica Series' as being appointed a baron of the Exchequer on October 29, 1638. That he was a cursitor baron there is no doubt, for he is never mentioned in the judicial proceedings of the court, and his name as baron appears in a commission at a distance of five from the regular barons. He only held his office for four years, dying suddenly on November 9, 1642. (*Rymer*, xx. 409, 433; *Peck's Desid. Cur.* b. xiv. 19.)

PAGITT, JAMES, belonged to the branch of the Pagitt family which was settled in Northamptonshire, where his great-grandfather, Thomas, is described of Barton-Segrave, and his grandfather, Richard, of Cranford. His father was Thomas Pagitt, an eminent lawyer, twice reader at the Middle Temple, and treasurer there in 1599. His mother, Barbara Bradbury, died in 1583, and was buried in St. Botolph's, Aldersgate. (*Maitland's London*, 1076.) He was born about 1581, and, receiving his legal education at the same inn of court as his father, was called to the bar in 1602. Apparently placed at an early age in the Exchequer, he is described as comptroller of the Pipe in 1618, and on October 24, 1631, he was raised to the office of a baron of the court. (*Rymer*, xix. 347.)

It is manifest, however, that this office was not that of one of the judicial barons. There was no vacancy among them at the time of his nomination; and during the whole of his career he neither took part in the business of the court, nor is ever mentioned in the conferences of the judges. Anthony Wood (iv. 354) calls him 'puisne baron of the Exchequer,' the precise title given to Sir Thomas Cæsar, with the addition, 'commonly called the baron cursitor.' (*Dugdale's Orig.* 149.) He died on September 3, 1638, at Tottenham, in the church of which parish is a monument to his memory.

He married three wives, but had issue only by the first. She was Katherine, daughter of Dr. William Lewin, dean of the Arches. The second was Bridget, daughter of Anthony Bowyer, of Coventry, draper, and widow of — Moyse, of London. The third was Mazaretta, daughter of Robert Harris, of Reading and Lincoln's Inn, who had previously had two husbands, as he had had two wives, viz., Richard Vaughan and Zephaniah Sayers, both of London. (*Oldfield's and Dyson's Tottenham*, 48; *Ashmole's Berks*, iii. 88; *Wotton's Baronet.* ii. 33.)

PANTULF, HUGH, was the second son of Hugh, the grandson of William Pantulf, a renowned Norman knight, who, besides large possessions in Normandy, is recorded in Domesday Book as holding twenty-nine lordships in Shropshire, of which Wemme was the chief. This Hugh held the sheriffalty of that county from 26 Henry II., 1180, to 1 Richard I., 1189-90; and in the latter year he travelled the counties of Salop, Gloucester, and Stafford as one of the justices itinerant. (*Pipe Roll*, 91, 95, 168, 248.)

He must have lived to a good old age, since it was not till 9 Henry III., 1224–5, that his son William, being charged with 100*l*. relief as a baron for the land which his father held of the king *in capite*, was excused, and his fine reduced to 25*l*. (*Madox*, i. 318.)

PARDISHOWE, THOMAS DE, had the custody of the Great Seal when Sir Robert Bourchier the chancellor left London on February 14, 1341, under the seals of Thomas de Evesham, the master of the Rolls, and Thomas de Brayton. It is clear from the terms of the record that the two latter only were appointed to execute the functions of the office, which they did till his return on March 3. Pardishowe is called a clerk in the Chancery, but there is no other entry of his name.

PARK, JAMES ALAN, was the son of James Park, Esq., a respectable surgeon in Edinburgh, and was born in that city on April 6, 1763. When very young he came to England, and was admitted into the society of the Middle Temple, by which he was called to the bar in June 1784. He was fortunate enough to gain the friendship and patronage of his noble countryman Lord Mansfield, under whose encouragement he published in 1787 a work on the 'Law of Marine Insurances,' comprehending the decisions and dicta of the chief justice, who had been almost the creator of the system. This work was found to be so useful to mercantile and legal men that it passed through many editions, with improvements by its author, and at once brought him into professional notice. Joining the Northern Circuit, he was successful in obtaining a considerable practice, which before long increased till he became one of the leaders of that bar. In Westminster Hall also he acquired much business, as well from that numerous body engaged in maritime affairs and insurance cases, as from other clients who were observant of the extreme interest he took in his causes, and the clearness and earnest simplicity of his advocacy. He gleaned much learning and experience from his intimacy with Lord Mansfield, to whom, after his lordship's retirement, he was in the habit of taking an account of the daily proceedings in court, and profiting by the observations made by the legal Nestor upon the different points decided.

In 1791, before the death of Lord Mansfield, Mr. Park was appointed vice-chancellor of the duchy of Lancaster, and in 1795 recorder of Preston. In 1799 he received a silk gown as king's counsel, and in 1802 he was elected recorder of Durham. On the retirement from the circuit of Mr. Law (afterwards Lord Ellenborough) when he became attorney-general, he succeeded to the undisputed lead, which he retained for more than a dozen years, dividing that in London with Sir Vicary Gibbs and Sir William Garrow; and in 1811 he was made attorney-general of Lancaster.

A sincere and zealous churchman, he was by the religious classes of the community looked up to with great esteem. Among his intimates was William Stevens, the modest and benevolent treasurer of Queen Anne's bounty, with whom he formed a committee in support of the Scotch episcopal clergy, and succeeded in obtaining the repeal of the penal statutes then in force against them. He was one of the original members of 'Nobody's Club,' so called from the *nom de plume* of Mr. Stevens, in whose honour it was founded, and which, lasting till the present day, has numbered among its members some of the most eminent men in the Church and in science, law, and literature. At Mr. Stevens's death Mr. Park published a memoir of him, which has been lately reprinted. He was also the author in 1804 of 'A Layman's Earnest Exhortation to a Frequent Reception of the Lord's Supper.'

Without any pretensions to eloquence, his advocacy was effective from the extreme anxiety he displayed for his client; and he gained his verdicts by the apparent confidence and sincerity with which he impressed the jury with the injustice of withholding them, as much as by the merits of the causes themselves.

After thirty years' successful practice at the bar, he succeeded Sir Alan Chambers as a judge of the Common Pleas on January 22, 1816, and was knighted. He sat in that court till his death on December 8, 1838, a period of nearly twenty-three years, during which he served under four sovereigns. With no particular eminence as a lawyer, he proved himself by his good sense and strict impartiality, as well as by the respectability of his character, a most useful administrator of justice; the only drawback from the general respect which he commanded was a certain irritability about trifles, which too frequently excited the jocularity of the bar.

PARKE, JAMES (LORD WENSLEYDALE). His elevation to the peerage on retiring from the Court of Exchequer gave rise to the important constitutional question whether the patent which created him Baron Wensleydale of Wensleydale for the 'term of his natural life' entitled him to sit and vote in parliament. After a long and able discussion, the committee of privileges decided it in the negative, and a new patent was accordingly issued in the usual form with the title of Baron Wensleydale of Walton.

He was the youngest son of Thomas Parke, Esq., a merchant at Liverpool, residing at Highfield, near that town, by the daughter of William Preston, Esq., and was born there in 1782. He was educated at the free grammar school at Macclesfield, and at Trinity College, Cambridge. Elected university scholar in his first term, 1799, and a scholar of his college in 1800, he took his degree of B.A. in 1803, with the honourable position of fifth wrangler and senior chancellor's medallist. He gained a fellowship in the following year, and proceeded M.A. in 1806. It was not till seven years after the latter date that he was called to the bar by the society of the Inner Temple (to which he had removed from Lincoln's Inn), in Easter Term 1813, having practised previously for some years as a special pleader, and shown that proficiency in legal science which led to his rapid success as an advocate, both on the Northern Circuit and in Westminster Hall. Within four years he was enabled to resign his fellowship, on his marriage in 1817 with Cecilia, daughter of Samuel F. Barlow, Esq., of Middlethorpe in Yorkshire.

Only seven years after his call to the bar he was selected to assist the crown officers in conducting the memorable case against Queen Caroline in the House of Lords; and so high was his reputation for legal knowledge that, without ever having had a silk gown, and without the suspicion of any parliamentary or political interest, he was chosen on November 28, 1828, to supply the place of that excellent judge Sir George Holroyd, and thus to continue the acknowledged efficiency of the Court of King's Bench. On that occasion he was, as usual, knighted. Here he remained for nearly six years, till on April 29, 1834, he and Mr. Justice Alderson, to strengthen the staff of the Exchequer bench, were removed into that court. For the additional two-and-twenty years that he remained on the bench he administered justice there and on the circuits with that weight and experience, and with that temper and consideration, which commanded the respect of the bar, and secured the acquiescence of litigants. He was a zealous labourer for the removal of all useless formalities in legal proceedings, and one of the principal

K K

amendment acts passed in the reign of William IV. was his work.

In 1833 he was called to the privy council, and became a most efficient member of its judicial committee, and in 1835 he received the degree of LL.D. at his university. After twenty-eight years of judicial service, during the whole of which he never flagged in his duties, his age (74) warned him to retire. He resigned his seat at the end of December 1855; but the government were so conscious of his judicial powers, and so desirous to secure his assistance in the hearing of appeals in the House of Lords, that he was raised to a peerage for life on the 10th of the following January as Lord Wensleydale. The subsequent change in his patent took place for the reason before given, and without any desire on his part, as he had no male heir to succeed to the title, his only surviving child being a daughter.

He survived till the age of eighty-five, with his intellects unimpaired, giving his valuable assistance in the last court of appeal till his death in February 1868.

PARKER, JAMES, held the office of vice-chancellor only for ten short months, but during that time he afforded such evidence of intellectual power, promising a most brilliant judicial career, that his sudden death was almost as great a grief to the legal world as it must necessarily have been to his family and private friends. He was only in his forty-ninth year when he died, having been born in Glasgow in 1803. He was the son of Charles Steuart Parker, Esq., of Blockairn, near that city, in the grammar school and college of which he received his early instruction. He then proceeded to Trinity College, Cambridge, where he graduated as B.A. in 1825, gaining the seventh wrangler's place, and as M.A. in 1829. On February 6 in the same year he was called to the bar by the society of Lincoln's Inn, and, practising in the equity courts, his merits were soon acknowledged. By his indefatigable industry and clearness of intellect the difficulties of the science were quickly mastered, and in advocating the cases entrusted to his care there was an exhibition of learning and shrewdness that secured to him numerous retainers.

He was made queen's counsel in July 1844, and his reputation was so high that he was named on the Chancery Commission, in the investigations of which he took a very prominent part. At the election in 1847 he stood for Leicester on the conservative side, but was defeated after a close contest. Notwithstanding his avowed political principles, his character as a lawyer was so well established, and the necessity of a reform in Chancery, of which he was a zealous advocate, was so urgent, that the whig ministry selected him, although their opponent, to fill the office of vice-chancellor on October 20, 1851, when he was knighted.

Short as was his presidency of his court, it was long enough to prove him a most excellent judge. Patient in hearing, careful in deciding, courteous to all, his judgments manifested his full comprehension of the facts, and satisfied the understanding by the acute and sagacious application of the law to them. He survived the last sittings before his first long vacation only a few days, dying of an attack of angina pectoris on August 13, 1852, at Rothley Temple in Leicestershire, where he was buried.

He married Mary, daughter of Thomas Babington, Esq., of Rothley Temple, M.P. for Leicester, by whom he left several children.

PARKER, JOHN, in his admission to Gray's Inn in 1611, is described of Weylond Underwood in Buckinghamshire. He was called to the bar on June 26, 1617, became an ancient in 1638, a bencher in 1640, and in 1642 arrived at the post of reader.

In March 1647 he was appointed a judge of one of the Welsh circuits, and in the next year was sent by the Commons with others to try the rioters in that country. The parliament included him in the serjeants they made on October 30, 1648, and on the death of the king confirmed him in his office of Welsh judge. He was sent on the summer circuit of 1653, either as a serjeant or a judge; for there is some doubt as to the precise date of his being placed on the bench of the Exchequer; Hardres' Reports, which record his judgments as a baron, not commencing till Trinity Term 1655. He kept his seat till the Restoration, through all the changes occasioned by the accession of the Protector Richard and the return of the Long Parliament. In the parliaments of 1654 and 1656 he represented Rochester; and when Cromwell composed an upper house, he with the other judges was summoned as an assistant. (*Godwin*, ii. 235, iii. 527; *Whitelocke*, 305–693; *Parl. Hist.* iii. 1430, 1480, 1519.)

Anthony Wood says that he was one of the assistant committee men in Northamptonshire; that he was of the High Court of Justice which tried Lord Capell, the Earl of Holland, and the Duke of Hamilton, in 1649; that in the next year he published a remarkable book, called 'The Government of the People of England, Precedent and Present,' &c.; and that on June 22, 1655, he was sworn serjeant-at-law, being a member of the Temple. (iv. 225.) The learned author seems, however, to have confounded two individuals; for, besides the difference of the inn of court, it appears manifest that the John Parker who, according to Whitelocke, was made a serjeant in 1648 was the same man who by Hardres' Reports is proved to have been a baron in 1655.

At the Restoration he of course was removed from his place; but, instead of being subjected to any enquiry into his previous conduct, he was summoned to take the degree of serjeant-at-law: Anthony Wood says, 'by the endeavours of Lord Chancellor Hyde.' The same author describes him as father of Dr. Samuel Parker, made Bishop of Oxford by James II., and placed by that king as president of Magdalen College in opposition to the lawful elevation of Dr. Hough. (1 *Siderfin*, 4.)

PARKER, THOMAS (EARL OF MACCLESFIELD), belonged to a branch of a respectable family long seated at Norton Lees in Derbyshire. His father, Thomas Parker, a younger son of George Parker, of Park Hall in Staffordshire, high sheriff of that county in the reign of Charles I., was an attorney practising in the neighbouring town of Leek; and his mother was Anne, daughter and coheir of Robert Venables, of Wincham in Derbyshire. He was born at Leek, and his birthday, July 23, 1666, was commemorated in a subsequent year by the poet John Hughes, to whom both he and Lord Cowper had been munificent benefactors, in the following eulogistic lines:—

Not fair July, tho' Plenty clothe his fields,
   Tho' golden suns make all his mornings smile,
Can boast of aught that such a triumph yields,
   As that he gave a Parker to our isle.

Hail, happy month! secure of lasting fame!
   Doubly distinguish'd thro' the circling year:—
In Rome a hero gave thee first thy name,
   A patriot's birth makes thee to Britain dear.

After receiving the rudiments of his education at Newport in Shropshire, and at Derby, he was sent to Trinity College, Cambridge, on October 9, 1685, having already been admitted a student at the Inner Temple in February 1683-4. It is not impossible, though very unlikely, that he might have been articled to his father at the time he became a member of the Inner Temple; but his subsequent entry at Cambridge, and still more his call to the bar on May 21, 1691, seem completely to negative the story mentioned by Lysons (*Derbysh.* 111), and asserted as a fact by Lord Campbell (iv. 503), that he was placed on the roll of the junior branch of the profession, or practised as an attorney at Derby 'at the foot of the bridge next the Three Crowns.' He attended the Midland Circuit, and probably acted as a provincial counsel in the town of Derby, of which he was soon elected recorder. The statement that he was designated the 'silver-tongued counsel' is merely a second edition of the title given forty years before to Heneage Finch, afterwards Earl of Nottingham.

The town of Derby returned him as one of its representatives in 1705, and again in the two following parliaments; but though he sat as a member for the five years he continued at the bar, there is no record of any speech he delivered in the house, nor of any part he took, except in the proceedings against Dr. Sacheverell. In June 1705 he was not only raised to the degree of the coif, but immediately made one of the queen's serjeants and knighted. Attached to the whig party, he was naturally appointed one of the managers in the unpopular impeachment of Dr. Sacheverell in 1710, when his speeches were so effective, and his denunciations against the vain and factious doctor were so strong, that in his return to his chambers he with difficulty escaped from the mob, which since the commencement of the trial had been furiously excited against the prosecution. His exertions were soon rewarded and his fright quickly compensated by the appointment of chief justice of the Queen's Bench on March 13.

Within a month he was called upon to preside at the trial of Dammaree, Willis, and Purchase, who had been engaged in the riots arising out of Sacheverell's trial, and were charged with pulling down dissenting meeting-houses; and, though he summed up for the conviction, and they were found guilty of high treason, he interceded for them and procured their pardon. During the eight years of his presidency he fully justified the wisdom of the choice; for though immediately following so renowned a lawyer as Sir John Holt, he escaped any injurious comparison, and conducted the business of his court with discrimination and learning.

Two years after the accession of George I., on March 10, 1716, he was raised to the peerage by the title of Baron Parker of Macclesfield, and at the same time received the grant of a pension for life of 1200*l.* a year. This is a sufficient proof of the estimation with which he was regarded by the king, whose favour was two years after firmly established by the opinion which the chief justice gave, that his majesty had the sole control over the education and marriages of his grandchildren (*State Trials*, xv. 1222); an opinion which, though subsequently confirmed, insured the enmity of the Prince of Wales. The fruits of the king's favour were immediate; the effect of the prince's animosity was for some time concealed.

The Great Seal was presented to Lord Parker on May 12, 1718, with the title of lord chancellor, accompanied by the extraordinary present of 14,000*l.* from the king. To his son also a yearly pension of 1200*l.* was at the same time granted till he obtained the place of teller of the Exchequer, to which he was appointed in the following year. Lord Parker held the Seal for nearly seven years, and proved himself as able in equity as he had shown himself in law, his decisions being regarded to this day with as much respect as those of any of his predecessors. On November 5, 1721, he was created Viscount Parker of Ewelme, and Earl of Macclesfield, with a remainder, failing his issue male, to his daughter Elizabeth, the wife of William Heathcote, Esq., and her issue male. This uncommon limitation may have been caused by his son's absence abroad and the uncertainty of the father as to his existence. The earl had been already made lord lieutenant of the counties of Warwick and Oxford, in the latter of which he had purchased Sherburn Castle, near Watlington. In September 1724 he was chosen lord high steward of the borough of Stafford. Yet with these and other proofs of the king's countenance and favour, with the reputation of an able dispenser of justice, in the full possession of his faculties, and without any change or any dissension in the ministry, he suddenly resigned the Great Seal on January 4, 1725.

His high position for the last four years in which he filled it had been anything but a bed of roses. In the latter end of 1720 Mr. Dormer, one of the masters in Chancery, had absconded in consequence of the failure of a Mr. Wilson, his goldsmith or banker, in whose hands he had deposited a large amount of the suitors' cash. The deficiency this occasioned, added to his own losses by speculating with the same cash in the South Sea bubble, which at that time burst, amounted to nearly 100,000*l.*, which it was impossible for him to meet from his own private means. Those means were applied as far as they would go, and various palliatives were adopted by the chancellor to satisfy the incoming claims, such as by applying for that purpose the price given by the successor for the mastership, by obtaining a contribution of 500*l.* from each of the other masters except one, and by some payments out of his own pocket. But these were not nearly sufficient, and the refusal of the masters to make any further contribution, with the urgency of unsatisfied applicants, determined the chancellor to put an end to his anxiety by resigning the Seal.

Then did he experience the effect of the prince's displeasure. He had not resigned three weeks before petitions were presented to the House of Commons by his royal highness's friends from parties complaining of non-payment of the moneys they were entitled to; addresses to the king were voted, commissions of enquiry granted, and reports made, which resulted in the earl's impeachment for corruption on February 12. The charges were not like those against Lord Chancellor Bacon for taking bribes of the suitors, but the twenty-one articles were confined to his selling offices contrary to law, and for taking extortionate sums for them, with the knowledge that the payment was defrayed out of the suitors' money. The trial lasted thirteen days, from the 5th to the 27th of May, and the report occupies no less than 632 columns of the 'State Trials' (vol. xvi. 767 et seq.). The proceedings were most tiresome, and the repetitions and the quibblings do no credit either to the managers for the Commons or to the accused earl. The Lords unanimously found him guilty and fined him 30,000*l*. This sum the king, though he was obliged to strike his name from the privy council, intimated to him that he would pay out of his privy purse as fast as he could spare the money, and actually gave him 1000*l*. towards it in the first year, and in the second directed 2000*l*. more to be given to him; but before the earl applied for it the king died, and Sir Robert Walpole evaded the payment, probably from his fear of offending the implacable successor.

This prosecution was attended with important results. Though many will consider that the earl was treated harshly and made to suffer for irregularities introduced by his predecessors, all must rejoice in the exposure and removal of them which the investigation produced. A vicious system had prevailed for a long series of years, not only in the Court of Chancery, but in the other courts also, of disposing of the various offices in the gift of the chiefs to any person who would offer what was called 'a present' to the bestower. In the Court of Chancery not only the executive and honorary officers who were entitled to fees were expected to contribute to the purse of the chancellor, but the system extended to the masters in Chancery, who were the chancellor's judicial assistants, and moreover were entrusted with the care of the moneys, the right to which was disputed, or the application of which was to be determined, in the various causes that came within the jurisdiction of the court. The practice had been notoriously acted upon for many years by the chancellor's predecessors, and, though the equally objectionable custom of receiving new year's gifts had been abrogated by those whom he immediately succeeded, Lords Cowper and Harcourt, yet even they had not hesitated to receive payment from those masters whom they had appointed. Bad as the system was, the blot would not have been removed but for the accident of Mr. Dormer's insolvency; and even with that discovery Lord Macclesfield would probably have escaped censure had he confined himself to the former practice, which had been in some sort recognised by the legislature—inasmuch as at the revolution a clause prohibiting the sale of the office of master of Chancery, which had been proposed to be inserted in a bill then before the house, had been negatived by the Lords. Either his acquittal or his condemnation would have equally resulted in the abolition of that practice, and in a more safe investment of the suitors' money. But, unfortunately for the accused earl, the investigation proved that he had not been content with the accustomed honorarium, but had increased the price so enormously that it became next to impossible for the appointees to refund themselves, or even to pay the amount, without either extorting unnecessary fees by delaying causes before them, or using the money deposited with them to defray the sum demanded. That he employed an agent to bargain for him and to higgle about the price there is no doubt, and that he was aware of the improper use that was made of the suitors' money, and took means to conceal the losses that occasionally occurred, there is too much evidence. Though therefore his friends might assert that he was made to suffer for a system of which he was not the author, and which had been knowingly practised by his predecessors with impunity, it is impossible to acquit him entirely of the charge of carrying that system to an exorbitant extent, and of corruptly recognising, if not encouraging, practices dangerous to the public credit, and destructive of that confidence which should always exist in the judicature of the country. The contradictions sometimes found in human nature are extraordinary, for while the disclosures of the trial tend to exhibit an avaricious disposition in the earl, the evidence he produced, with questionable delicacy, satisfactorily proves that he was at the same time extremely liberal, dispensing with an almost extravagant hand large sums in the promotion of learning and in aid and encouragement of poor scholars and distressed clergymen. That the price paid by the masters for their places was considered a legitimate part of the profit of the chancellor, received a curious confirmation in the grant to Lord Macclesfield's immediate successor, Lord King, of a considerable addition to his salary, as a compensation for the loss occasioned by the annihilation of the practice consequent upon this investigation.

Lord Macclesfield lived seven years afterwards, but mixed no more in public affairs. He spent his time between Sherburn Castle, his seat in Oxfordshire, and London, where at the time of his death he was building a house in St. James's Square, afterwards inhabited by his son. He died on April 28, 1732, and was buried at Sherburn.

His wife, Janet, daughter and coheir of Charles Carrier, of Wirksworth in Derbyshire, Esq., brought him two children only, a son and a daughter. The son, who succeeded to the earldom, was renowned as a philosopher, and had a principal share in preparing the act of parliament for the alteration of the style. The present earl is the sixth who has borne the title.

PARKER, THOMAS, was a near relation of his namesake, Lord Chancellor Macclesfield, George Parker, of Park Hall in Staffordshire, being the grandfather of the chancellor, and the great-grandfather of the judge, whose father, George, succeeded to the estate of Park Hall.

Thomas Parker was born about 1695, and received his education at the grammar school of Lichfield, from whence he was removed to the office of Mr. Salkeld, a solicitor in Brook Street, Holborn, where three other eminent lawyers and judges were at nearly the same time initiated into the mysteries of the science. These were Lord Jocelyn, lord chancellor of Ireland; Sir John Strange, master of the Rolls; and Lord Hardwicke, lord chancellor of England. With the latter he contracted a lasting intimacy, and when he was called to the bar at the Inner Temple in June 1724 Lord Hardwicke was attorney-general. This was less than a year before his noble relative's disgrace, of whose patronage though he was thus deprived, he found an ample compensation in the friendship of Lord Hardwicke, who never forgot what he owed to the early encouragement of the persecuted peer, in gratitude to whom he took every opportunity of promoting Parker's advancement. Thus in June 1736, when Parker had been a barrister only twelve years, he was raised to the dignity of the coif, and made king's serjeant at the same time; and in two years after, on July 7, 1738, he was raised to the bench as a baron of the Exchequer. From this court he was removed in April 1740 to the Common Pleas, where he remained till November 29, 1742, when, having been previously knighted, he was advanced to the head of the Court of Exchequer as lord chief baron. All these promotions he owed to Lord Hardwicke, who in a letter to the Duke of Somerset said that 'Parker was in every way deserving, and has gained a very high character for ability and integrity since his advancement to the bench.' (*Harris's Lord Hardwicke*, ii. 25.)

Lord Hardwicke, even when out of power, did not neglect him, but endeavoured on the death of Sir John Willes to procure for him the chief justiceship of the Common Pleas, and to the last showed his regard by naming him as a trustee under his will. (*Ibid.* iii. 269, 394.)

Sir Thomas presided in the Exchequer for thirty years, when, having arrived at the age of seventy-seven, he resigned in the summer vacation 1772, being gratified with a pension of 2400*l*., and being sworn a privy councillor, a post not then usually given to the chief barons while in office. He lived for twelve years after his retirement, during which he published a volume of Reports of Revenue Cases in the Exchequer from 1743 to 1767, which display considerable acuteness. A judgment may also be formed of the manner in which he had executed his judicial functions by the remark of Lord Mansfield, who, on the frequent absence of his successor Sir Sidney Stafford Smythe from infirmity, observed, 'The new chief baron should resign in favour of his predecessor.' (*Lord Campbell, Ch. Justices,* ii. 571.)

He died on December 29, 1784, and was buried in the family vault at Park Hall. He was twice married—first to Anne, daughter of James Whitehall, of Pipe-Ridware in Staffordshire; and secondly to Martha, daughter of Edward Strong, of Greenwich, by each of whom he left issue. The estate of Park Hall is still in possession of his descendants.

PARNING, ROBERT, was possessed of considerable property in Cumberland, and was returned to parliament in the last year of the reign of Edward II., as one of the representatives of that county. He took the degree of a serjeant-at-law in 3 Edward III. (*Coke,* 4*th Inst.* 79), and is mentioned as a king's serjeant in the eighth year. From this time till he was called to the bench he frequently acted as a judge of assize.

On May 23, 1340, he became a justice of the Common Pleas, but only remained in that court for two months, being raised on July 24 to the office of chief justice of the King's Bench. His presidency there, however, did not continue longer than the 15th of the following December, when he changed the office of chief justice for that of treasurer. Being distinguished, as Coke says, for his profound and excellent knowledge of the laws, his elevation to the bench can be well understood; but the cause of his early removal from a sphere in which he was so fitted to shine is not so readily apparent. It arose, probably, from the king having as high an opinion of his integrity as of his legal attainments.

He held his new position for little more than ten months; for on October 27, 1341, the Great Seal was placed in his hands. He continued chancellor till his death, and it is remarkable that, though there is no imputation against him for neglecting his duties, he was still in the habit of attending the Court of Common Pleas to hear arguments there, and sometimes to take part in them. Instances of this occur in Hilary, 17 Edward III., and in the two following terms.

He died on August 26, 1348, leaving by his wife, Isabella, a son named Adam, who succeeded to eight manors and other property in the counties of Cumberland and Northumberland. (*Abb. Rot. Orig.* ii. 202; *Cal. Inquis.* p. m. ii. 110.)

PASSELEWE, SIMON, of Norman origin, was probably brother of Robert, deputy treasurer to Henry III. He was a justice of the Jews in 1237, and in 52 Henry III. his name appears as a baron of the Exchequer. (*Madox,* ii. 319, 320, 727.) In 1258 he is mentioned as applying to the abbey of St. Albans for a loan to the king. (*Newcome's St. Albans,* 171.)

PASSELE, or PASSELEWE, EDMUND DE, as several members of his family did before him, held office in the Exchequer. He was probably the son of Robert de Passelewe, who was knight of the shire for Sussex in 24 and 28 Henry III., as he himself had considerable estates in that county, part of which he devoted to pious uses. In 16 Edward I. he was appointed one of the commissioners to enquire as to the damage done by the overflowing of the sea in the Isle of Thanet (*Lewis's Thanet,* 77); and in 3 Edward II. he was specially employed by the king and the council to attend to the king's pleas, and is designated by Dugdale a serjeant. From that till the sixteenth year he was frequently engaged as a justice of assize, or otherwise, and as such was commanded to bring his proceedings into the Exchequer to be estreated, and received the customary summons to attend the parliaments.

On September 20, 1323, 17 Edward II., he was constituted a baron of the Exchequer, the duties of which he continued to perform till the end of the reign. He died in 1 Edward III., leaving a widow and two sons. (*Abb. Rot. Orig.* i. 132, 207; *Parl. Writs,* ii. 1261; *Abb. Placit.* 325.)

PASTON, WILLIAM, was a descendant from Wolstan, a knight who came from France with Henry I., and receiving a grant of lands at Paston in Norfolk, adopted the name of that place. His parents were Clement Paston, and Beatrice, the daughter of John de Somerton.

He was born in 1378, and, being brought up to the law, was in 1413 made steward of all the courts and leets belonging to Richard Courtney, Bishop of Norwich. (*Blomefield's Norfolk,* vi. 479.) He was called to the degree of serjeant in Hilary, 8 Henry V., 1421, and soon after was selected as one of the king's serjeants. He was raised to the bench as a justice of the Common Pleas on October 15, 1429, 8 Henry VI., and retained his seat during the remainder of his life. (*Acts Privy Council,* iv. 4, 5; *Dugdale's Orig.* 46.)

Although his judicial character was so high as to acquire for him the title of the Good Judge, it did not prevent an accusation being brought against him in the parliament of 1434. This was contained in a petition from one William Dalling, in which he charged the judge that he 'taketh divers fees and rewards of divers persons within the shires of Norfolk and Suffolk, and is withhold with every matter in the said counties;' and then he names nine cases, two being towns, one an abbot, four priors, and two individuals, with sums varying from 1s. to 40s., except the last, which is evidently the origin of the complaint, and is thus stated:—

'And of Katherine Shelton X marks, against the king for to be of her counsel for to destroy the right of the king and of his ward, that is for to say, Ralph, son and heir of John Shelton.' (*Paston Letters* [Knight's ed.], *Introd.* xxiv.)

The petition was rejected, and is endorsed 'Falsa Billa;' but it exposes practices which, even if some of them were old annuities granted while he was an advocate for past or future services, and not withdrawn when he rose to the bench, might well make his impartiality suspected when these parties were engaged before him.

He was too ill to *ride* the Home Circuit in January 1444, as was then the practice; and it is curious to find, from a letter addressed to him, that no other conveyance was then thought of except that by water; and that so his colleague, Chief Justice Hody, arranged for them to go. (*Ibid.* 5.) On the 14th of the following August he died, and was buried in Norwich Cathedral, to which he had been a benefactor. (*Index Monast.* 6.)

He married Agnes, daughter of Sir Edmund Berrye, of Harlingbury Hall, Herts, who after her husband's death was proceeded against by one John Hauteyn to recover the manor of Oxnead; and it affords a strong proof of the respect paid to the memory of the judge that Hauteyn was obliged to petition the chancellor to assign certain persons to be of counsel for him in the process, because no men of court would act in his behalf. (*Paston Letters*, 8.)

From his eldest son, John, descended Sir William Paston, distinguished as an antiquary, who was made a baronet of Oxnead, Norfolk, in 1641; and whose son, Sir Robert, was created Baron Paston of Paston, and Viscount Yarmouth, by Charles II., to which an earldom of Yarmouth was added in 1679; but all these titles became extinct in 1732 on the death of his son William, the second earl. (*Morant's Essex*, ii. 316; *Genealogy of the Paston Family, by F. Worship, Esq.*)

The collection of letters written by or to the members of this family during the reigns of Henry VI., Edward IV., Richard III., and Henry VII., published originally by Sir John Fenn, and reprinted by Charles Knight in 1840 under the name of the 'Paston Letters,' contains a most interesting record of the domestic manners and habits of the fifteenth century.

PATESHULL, SIMON DE, is first mentioned when he appears on the judicial bench in 5 Richard I., 1193, from which time till the end of John's reign his name is frequently recorded on fines, and as performing the various duties of a justicier, besides acting as a justice of the Jews. (*Madox*, i. 235, ii. 315.) His position during the principal part of the latter reign was evidently very high, and from the fact that many of the mandates in causes before the court, from 7 John, are addressed 'Rex Sim. de Pateshull et sociis suis, justiciis suis,' an inference may perhaps be drawn that he was at the head of that division of the Curia Regis in which 'common pleas' were tried. In John he and James de Poterna appear to have been fined in one hundred marks each for granting a term in a cause before them without the king's licence, but they were afterwards excused. (*Rot. Claus.* i. 61, &c., 113, 114.)

Numerous entries show his continued attendance on King John, from whom he received many marks of favour. (*Rot. Chart.* 52, 131, 184.) He held the sheriffalties of Northampton from 6 Richard I. to 5 John, and of Essex and Hertford in 6 Richard I.

In the wars between King John and the barons he was more than suspected of a defection from his sovereign; but in May 1215 the king granted him a safe-conduct, with an intimation expressed in it that 'if it is so as the abbot of Woburn tells us on your part, we will relax all the anger and indignation we had against you.' (*Rot. Pat.* 94.) He succeeded in clearing himself with the king, and his lands, which had been seized, were restored to him in December. (*Rot. Claus.* i. 200, 244.)

The time of his death is uncertain; but as the rolls give only one other instance, in the following March, of his performance of judicial duties (*Ibid.* 270), and as his son Hugh's subsequent connection with the barons' party is shown by the restoration of his lands to him in 2 Henry III., it is more than probable that Simon died before that date.

Dugdale, however, in his 'Chronica Series,' inserts him as chief justiciary in 17 Henry III., from an apparent misapprehension of a parenthetical sentence in a passage in Matthew Paris, speaking of the next-mentioned Hugh de Pateshull, who, he says, was son of Simon the justiciary, 'qui *quandoque* habenas moderabatur totius regni.' Whether such an *obiter dictum* is a sufficient authority for describing him at all as chief justiciary or not, it clearly does not pretend to make him so at that time or in any part of that reign.

PATESHULL, HUGH DE (BISHOP OF LICHFIELD AND COVENTRY). Although Dugdale introduces him as chief justiciary in 18 Henry III., 1234, when Stephen de Segrave was disgraced, the authority of the passage in Matthew Paris which he quotes does not appear to authorise any such statement. That passage goes no further than to show that he was then nominated treasurer in the place of Peter de Rivallis, an appointment which is proved to have been made by a patent of the same date. (*Madox*, i. 35.)

He was the son of the last-mentioned Simon de Pateshull, and in his early life, probably just after his father's death, he joined the popular cry against King John, and lost his lands accordingly, which were, however, restored after the accession of Henry III., when he returned to his allegiance. (*Rot. Claus.* i. 340.) He obtained, no doubt from his father's connection with the court, a place in the Exchequer, and united, as was then common, the clerical profession with the performance of his official duties. In the former department he became a canon of St. Paul's (*Angl. Sac.* i. 439), and in the latter he was gradually advanced to that position in which he had the custody of the seal of the Exchequer, and the receipt of the revenue accounted for by the sheriffs, a post which, if not at that time, was shortly afterwards distinguished by the title of chancellor of the Exchequer.

The date of the patent appointing him treasurer is June 1, 1234, and there are entries to show that he still continued to perform the duties in 22 Henry III. (*Madox*, ii. 35, 255, 317); and there is no notice of any successor being appointed till 24 Henry III., 1240, on July 1 in which year he was consecrated Bishop of Lichfield and Coventry. His short presidency over this diocese was terminated by his death, while yet comparatively a young man, on December 7, 1241. (*Godwin*, 317; *Baronage*, ii. 143.)

PATESHULL, MARTIN DE, is stated by one authority to be a native of Northamptonshire (*Fuller*, ii. 166), and by another of Staffordshire (*Gent. Mag.* Aug. 1813), and there is a village of his name in both these counties.

During the reign of John he probably held some office in the court, with the title of 'clerk' added to his name (*Rot. Chart.* 180), and in 17 John he had letters of safe-conduct to come to the king (*Rot. Pat.* 142), then in the midst of his troubles.

Very soon after the accession of Henry III. he was raised to the bench, for his name appears in 1217, not only at Westminster, when a fine was levied there, but also as a justice itinerant in York and Northumberland, and in other counties.

From this time until the end of his life he was actively engaged in judicial duties, scarcely a year occurring in which he was not sent on various itinera. In 1224 he was one of the justices itinerant at Dunstable whom Faukes de Breaute endeavoured to capture; but he was fortunate enough to escape. (*R. de Wendover*, iv. 94.) From the next year, when he stands the first of those who were appointed, he is in every subsequent commission mentioned in the same prominent position. Even if the division of the courts had then taken place, which is very doubtful, there is no other evidence that he was at the head of either branch.

The Fourth Report of the Public Records (*App.* ii. 161) gives an amusing testimony to his activity in performing his legal functions. In a letter to the authorities, a brother justicier appointed to go the York Circuit with him prays to be excused from the duty, 'for,' says he, 'the said Martin is strong, and in his labour so sedulous and practised that all his fellows, especially W. de Ralegh and the writer' (whose name does not appear), 'are overpowered by the labour of Pateshull, who works every day from sunrise until night.' The writer therefore prays to be eased of his office, and allowed to go quietly to his church in the county of York, to which he had been lately presented.

Martin de Pateshull was appointed archdeacon of Norfolk in 1226, and two years after he was raised to the deanery of St. Paul's, London, of which he had previously been a canon, but did not long enjoy his dignity, as he died on November 14, 1229. (*Le Neve*, 182, 219.)

Fuller quotes (ii. 166) from Florilegus this character of him: 'Vir miræ prudentiæ, et legum regni peritissimus.'

PATESHULL, WALTER DE, resided in Bedfordshire, and the only notice that occurs of him in a judicial character is in 3 Henry III., when he was one of the justices itinerant for that and the neighbouring counties. On the disgrace of Faukes de Breaute he was appointed sheriff of Bedfordshire and Buckinghamshire, and under the direction of him and Henry de Braybroc, the captured judge, the castle of Bedford was demolished. He retained the sheriffalty for four years, and died in August 1232. (*Rot. Claus.* i. 581, 632; *Excerpt. e Rot. Fin.* i. 225.)

PATTESON, JOHN, was the son of the Rev. Henry Patteson, of Drinkstone in Suffolk, by Sophia, the daughter of Richard Ayton Lee, Esq., a banker in London. He was born on February 11, 1790, at Norwich, of which city his uncle, John Patteson, Esq., was the representative in parliament for some years.

Educated at Eton, he was elected on the

foundation, and succeeded to King's College, Cambridge, in 1809, as a scholar, where in 1812 he became a fellow, having in the meantime been the first to win the Davies University Scholarship.

Entering the Middle Temple, he placed himself successively under the instructions of two among the most eminent special pleaders of the day, Mr. Godfrey Sykes and Mr. (afterwards Justice) Littledale, and, having gained by their guidance sufficient knowledge of the then abstruse science, commenced the practice of it on his own account. Here great success attended him, and soon his reputation was so well established that many pupils resorted to his chambers to share in the benefit of his teaching.

When in 1821 he was called to the bar and joined the Northern Circuit, his name as an accurate and subtle pleader soon secured him a prominent place among his compeers; and Mr. Littledale, who then acted as counsel for the Treasury, showed his confidence in him by securing his assistance in the business of the crown. At the close of one of his arguments, 'Rennell v. The Bishop of Lincoln,' Mr. Justice Bayley is said to have thrown down to him from the bench a note with these words: 'Dear P. Lord Tenterden, C.J. An admirable argument; shows him fit to be an early judge.'

The implied prophecy was speedily accomplished. When three new judges were to be appointed, Lord Chancellor Lyndhurst selected Mr. Patteson as the most eligible person to take the additional place in the King's Bench. He received his promotion on November 12, 1830, without a murmur among his colleagues, though no other instance had ever occurred of one who after only nine years' practice at the bar had been raised to the bench; so unreservedly were his merits acknowledged. He of course then received the honour of knighthood.

The choice proved a most successful one. For rather more than one-and-twenty years, under three chiefs (Lord Tenterden, Lord Denman, and Lord Campbell), he contributed greatly, by his high judicial faculty, to the efficiency of the court, as was frequently and publicly acknowledged. No one was more soundly versed in the principles of the common law, or more firm in his enunciation of them; no one was more lucid in his reasonings, or less liable to be misled by the sophistries of counsel; and, what is of the greatest importance, no one was more courteous and kind to all applicants, whether in court or in chambers. As a criminal judge he was inflexibly just, and, where he could be, most merciful; and in every branch of his duties he established a character inspiring so much respect and confidence that there have been few judges whose retirement was more regretted.

But he was visited with an infirmity, that of deafness, which, though at first moderated by the use of ingenious instruments, at last increased to such an extent that he felt that he could not adequately fulfil the duties which devolved upon him, and, most unwillingly, he tendered his resignation. The scene on his last appearance in court, February 9, 1852, was a most affecting one; and no better evidence can be produced of the bar's appreciation of him than is afforded by the following passage in the address of the present chief justice of that court, Sir Alexander Cockburn, then attorney-general:—

'As we are now about to lose you, it may not be entirely unbecoming in me to offer, nor wholly unwelcome to you to receive, the assurance of the universal sense of the whole profession that the high and sacred duties of the judicial office were never more honestly or ably discharged than by you during your whole judicial life. Though we lose you, your memory will yet remain to us, assuming its proper position among those revered names which dignify this place and this hall, and will be cherished by us not more for that vast and varied learning by which all have profited and which all have admired, than for that untiring love of justice and truth, and that hatred of oppression and wrong, that unflinching integrity of purpose, that simplicity and singleness of heart, and that benevolent kindness of nature, which leave us in doubt whether we should more revere the judge or love the man. You will carry into your retirement the respect and veneration, and the enduring attachment, of every member of the profession. We rejoice to hope that, though the sense of one infirmity, and the apprehension lest that should interfere with the perfect discharge of your duty, have made you withdraw from your office in the vigour of your powers, you will long remain in unimpaired health, and long enjoy all the pleasures of life.'

He was immediately sworn of the privy council, and for five years assisted in the adjudication of the difficult cases that come before its judicial committee. His failing health then compelled him to desist from all mental labour, and for the short remainder of his life he devoted himself to the enjoyments of domestic society and to the friendly assistance of his neighbours. He expired on June 28, 1861, at Feniton Court, near Honiton, an estate he had purchased at a short distance from the residence of his brother-in-law and colleague Sir John Taylor Coleridge, with whom he kept up the most affectionate intimacy, and who has feelingly recorded his worth on the brass his admirers put up to his memory in Eton College chapel.

He was twice married—first to Elizabeth, daughter of George Lee, Esq., of Dickleborough, Norfolk; and secondly to Frances Duke, sister of Mr. Justice Coleridge, whom he survived. One of his two sons is the missionary bishop to the western isles of the South Pacific Ocean, and the other a revising barrister on the Northern Circuit.

PAULET, WILLIAM (MARQUIS OF WINCHESTER), was the son of Sir John Paulet, an eminent soldier, created a knight of the Bath at the marriage of Prince Arthur in 1501, and of Elizabeth, daughter of Sir William Paulet, of Hinton St. George. He was born about 1475, if it be true that he lived to his ninety-seventh year.

Though he appears to have been sheriff of Hampshire in 1518, the history of his early life is limited to the fact that he was a learned and accomplished man, and that he received the honour of knighthood before he was made comptroller of the household by Henry VIII., in 1532, when, according to the above account, he must have been fifty-seven years of age. Five years afterwards he became treasurer, and on March 9, 1539, was advanced to the baronage by the title of Lord St. John of Basing. On the establishment of the new Court of Wards, in 32 Henry VIII., he was the first master appointed, and in the thirty-fifth year he was installed a knight of the Garter. He next became great master of the king's household, and the last service he performed to Henry VIII. was in accompanying him on the expedition to France, when he was present at the taking of Boulogne. Of that king's will he was the third named of the sixteen executors, and under its provisions one of the privy council of his infant successor.

Of this council he was appointed president when Somerset became protector, and within a few weeks after the accession of Edward VI. the Great Seal was placed in his hands on March 6, 1547, with the title of lord keeper. It is evident that this was not meant to be a permanent appointment, from the time during which he was to hold it being limited in the first instance to fourteen days, and on two subsequent occasions to defined periods. The protector, however, was so uncertain as to the person with whom he should ultimately entrust it that Lord St. John retained the possession for more than seven months, when Richard Lord Rich was constituted lord chancellor on October 23.

As soon as the power of the protector seemed to be slipping away from his grasp, Lord St. John is found on the side of his opponents and assisting in his downfall. The reward of this suppleness was the earldom of Wiltshire and the office of lord treasurer, both of which were granted in the beginning of 1550. To the former title that of Marquis of Winchester was added in October of the following year, and in little more than a month he presided as lord steward at the trial of the late Protector Somerset. He was one of the twenty-four subscribers to the document prepared by the Duke of Northumberland, undertaking to support the succession of the kingdom on Lady Jane Grey; but on the death of King Edward, though, acting as lord treasurer, he presented the crown to that unfortunate lady, he had the wit very soon to see his dangerous position, and contrived to be one of those lords who met at Baynard's Castle, and caused Queen Mary to be proclaimed. This secured to him a continuance in his office of treasurer for the whole of that reign, during which he is said to have been active in the persecutions which disgraced it. His patent, however, was renewed when Queen Elizabeth succeeded. He lived for nearly thirteen years after that event, and died on March 10, 1572, and was buried at Basing in Hampshire.

It is not supposed that a man so old as he was could interfere much in politics in the last two reigns; but it is apparent that he must have possessed a wonderfully accommodating spirit to have remained unscathed in such perilous times under four sovereigns, professing alternately different systems of religion. His own solution of the difficulty seems to be the right one. When he was asked how he had attained so great an age, he pleasantly answered,—

> Late supping I forbear,
> Wine and women I forswear;
> My neck and feet I keep from cold;
> No marvel then that I am old.
> *I am a willow, not an oak;*
> I chide, but never hurt with stroke.

He married two wives. The first was Elizabeth, daughter of Sir William Capel; the second, Winifred, daughter of Sir John Bruges, and widow of Sir William Sackville, chancellor of the Exchequer. His titles descended in regular succession till the sixth marquis in 1689 was created Duke of Bolton. The sixth duke dying without male issue in 1794, the dukedom became extinct, but the marquisate devolved on the descendant of a younger son of the fourth marquis, whose grandson now enjoys the title. (*Baronage*, i. 376; *Collins's Peerage*, ii. 367; *Hayward; Rapin; Lingard*, &c.)

PAUNTON, JAMES DE, was settled in Lincolnshire, his father, William, being sheriff there in 50 and 51 Henry III., and he himself in the four following years. He was constituted a justice of the King's Bench in 1270, and died almost immediately after his appointment; for in 1 Edward I., Philip de Paunton, probably his son by Isabella his wife, obtained an extent in aid against those who owed

James money, to pay his debts to the crown. (*Madox*, 173, 194; *Abb. Placit.* 199, 233, 312.)

PAUPER, ROGER, was the son of Roger, Bishop of Salisbury, the great minister of Henry I., and of Matilda of Ramsbury, whom some authors call his wife, and some his concubine. The charitable presumption is, that he had been legally united to her, and that he had refused to obey the canons which were then attempted to be enforced, enjoining married priests to put away their wives.

There are three documents proving that Roger Pauper was chancellor in the first year of Stephen's reign—one dated in 1135 (*Monast.* ii. 482); another granted at the general council held at Westminster in the following Easter (*Madox*, i. 13); and a third, being the Charter of Liberties, dated near the same time at Oxford (*App. to Reports, Rec. Commis.*); to all of which the attestation of his father, the bishop, is also attached.

In July 1139 he was still chancellor, when he and his father were seized by Stephen at Oxford. The manner in which he was carried in fetters before the castle of Devizes, and threatened with instant death unless it was surrendered to the king, is more fully related in the subsequent life of Bishop Roger.

Although the bishop was released when the castle was taken, the king kept the chancellor in confinement, and for a long time refused to give him his liberty unless he would join the court party, an offer which he invariably rejected. At last, however, he procured his freedom, on condition that he retired from the kingdom. His exile continued during the remainder of his life, and history is silent as to its close. (*Madox*, i. 14; *Godwin*, 341; *Wendover*, ii. 226.)

PAUPER, HERBERT (BISHOP OF SALISBURY), enjoyed the archdeaconry of Canterbury in 1175, and in 1185 and the following years was one of the custodes of the see of Salisbury during its vacancy (*Madox*, i. 311, 634), which lasted till 1188. To this bishopric he was afterwards elected in May 1194, 5 Richard I. From that time he acted regularly as a justicier in the Curia Regis, his name appearing to several fines from the sixth to the ninth year of the reign inclusive. (*Hunter's Preface.*) He died on May 9, 1217, and was buried at Wilton. (*Godwin*, 342; *Le Neve*, 11, 257.)

PEC, RICHARD DE, was among the justices itinerant selected by the king when the council of Windsor, in 1179, 25 Henry II., divided the kingdom into four circuits. (*Madox*, i. 137.) In 27 Henry II. he was sent with the constable of Chester to Ireland, to take away the government from Hugh de Lacy, who had offended the king by marrying a daughter of Roderick, King of Connaught. (*Lord Lyttelton*, iii. 351.)

In 3 Richard I. he had the custody of the castle of Bolsover (*Madox*, ii. 220); and in 1195 he appears again as a justice itinerant, fixing the tallage in Gloucestershire.

He married Matilda, the widow of the before-mentioned Robert Grimbald. (*Ibid.* i. 704.)

PEMBERTON, FRANCIS. Chauncy, the historian of Hertfordshire, is the only author who speaks of his contemporary Sir Francis Pemberton with unmixed commendation. His other biographers, with whatever party they are connected, almost invariably qualify the encomiums they are compelled to utter with some expressions of depreciation. One says that he was a great lawyer, but that he had so towering an opinion of his own sense and wisdom that he made more law than he declared. Another, while acknowledging that he was an excellent judge, asserts that his passion for preferment led him sometimes to do wrong. The various incidents of his career are so tinted by the different prejudices of the writers, whether whig or tory, that, not receiving the entire approbation of either party, the natural inference to an unprejudiced mind is, that he acted independently of both. That he was 'damned with faint praise' receives its explanation in Burnet's admission that ' he was not wholly for the court.'

The family of Pemberton came originally from a town of that name in Lancashire; but a branch of it settled at St. Albans in Herts, and gave many sheriffs to that county. Ralph Pemberton, who was twice mayor of the borough in the reign of Charles I., was the father of the judge, who was born there in 1625, and, after receiving the rudiments of his education in one of its private seminaries, was removed in August 1640 to Emmanuel College, Cambridge, under the tuition of the learned Dr. Whichcote, whose niece he afterwards married. He remained at the university till February 1644, having taken the degree of B.A., and, entering the Inner Temple, was called to the bar in November 1654. Chauncy omits any mention of his youthful follies, probably considering that he redeemed them by his future life; but both Roger North and Burnet, the courtier and the whig, agree in describing his beginnings as very debauched, and leading him into such extravagance that he soon wasted his patrimony, and involved himself in such debt that he lay many years in gaol. While there he is represented by both to have made up for lost time, following his studies so closely that according to one he came out a sharper at the law, and according to the other he became one of the ablest men of his profession. He no doubt had plenty of exercise for legal subtleties in the cases of his fellow prisoners, to aid whom his necessities obliged him to apply himself. How or when he obtained his release is not related, except by Lord Campbell, who enters into minute details, for which he has not given any authority. His brother lawyer Serjeant Chauncy says that he was made one of the counsel of the Marshalsea Court, an arena in which his prison experience would stand him in good stead. But soon after the return of Charles II. he is mentioned in the courts at Westminster, and evidently got into considerable practice. Pepys (iii. 371) consulted him on prize business, and mentions the heaps of gold upon his table; and in 1668 he was employed by the crown in the prosecution of the apprentices tried for high treason in tumultuously assembling under colour of pulling down disorderly houses. (*State Trials*, vi. 880.) In 1671 he was called to the bench of his inn, and became Lent reader in 1674, on which occasion Chauncy says he kept a 'noble table' there. It is thus apparent that he soon outlived his early reputation; and that he was held in high estimation in his profession is proved by his being appointed king's serjeant in August 1675, not seven months after his being summoned to assume the coif. In the interval he became the innocent victim of an absurd quarrel about privilege between the two houses of Parliament. An appeal in a suit, wherein a member of the lower house was a defendant, having been made to the House of Lords in its judicial capacity, the Commons pertinaciously contended that their members were privileged from appearing before that assembly. The counsel appointed by the Lords to plead in the cause were ordered into custody by the Commons for their compliance, and on being released by the Lords were again seized, and committed to the Tower. The journals of the two houses (*Ibid.* vi. 1146) give a very amusing account of this ridiculous farce; and 'so high at last the contest rose' that the king was obliged to put an end to it by proroguing and afterwards dissolving the parliament. Serjeant Pemberton was one of these counsel, and after being released by the Lords was retaken by the speaker (Seymour) himself in the middle of Westminster Hall. His imprisonment of course ended with the session.

On being made king's serjeant he received the honour of knighthood; and in less than four years—viz., on May 1, 1679—he was constituted a judge of the King's Bench. At this time, as the trials arising out of the pretended Popish Plot were proceeding, he of necessity took part in several of them; and from the questions that he put it is very evident that, though he had some belief in the plot, he had not much confidence in the witnesses. Before he had sat a twelvemonth, Scroggs, who was then chief justice, intrigued for his removal, and he received his discharge on February 16, 1680, three weeks after the trial and acquittal of Sir Thomas Gascoigne. He immediately returned to his practice at the bar, and at the end of another year he was selected to displace Scroggs in the higher office of chief justice of the King's Bench, his patent being dated April 11, 1681. From this court he was removed to preside in the Common Pleas on January 22, 1683. Sir T. Raymond says in his Reports (p. 478) that this change was made by his own desire, for that the latter was a place, though not so honourable, yet of more ease and profit. And so no doubt it was given out; but both Burnet (vol. i. 535) and North (p. 233) agree that the proceedings against the city of London then coming on for argument, Pemberton, who was not considered sufficiently favourable to the views of the crown, was made to give way to Sir Edmund Saunders, who had advised on all the pleadings. Sir Francis was at the same time sworn a privy counsellor. He however kept neither honour very long, being dismissed from his office of judge on September 7 following, and removed from the privy counsel in the next month. This second dismissal is attributed by Burnet to the judge's showing 'so little eagerness against Lord Russell,' whose trial had taken place in the previous July. Whether that was the real cause or not, his removal from the privy council shows that he was turned out for political purposes. He is said to have boasted that 'while he was a judge'—a period of only three years and a half—'he had for his own share made more law than King, Lords, and Commons, since he was born.' (*Lord Campbell's Chanc.* iii. 394.)

He then a second time returned to the bar, and practised with great success as a serjeant for the next fourteen years, till his death in 9 William III. Though in 1688 he was the leading counsel who defended the seven bishops, and, by obtaining their acquittal, produced the revolution, yet in the very next year the Convention Parliament called him to account for a judgment by which six years before he had overruled a plea of Topham the serjeant-at-arms to the jurisdiction of the court. Both he and Sir Thomas Jones, who had joined in the judgment, were committed to prison, though they gave very sufficient reasons for their decision. They remained in durance from July 19 till August 20, when the parliament was adjourned, or October 21, when it was prorogued. (*State Trials*, xii. 822-834.)

He died at his house at Highgate on June 10, 1697, and was buried in the chapel there, upon the pulling down of which his monument was removed to the church of Trumpington, near Cambridge, in the neighbourhood of which some of his family have property. By his wife, Anne, daughter of Sir Jeremy Whichcote, Bart., he had eleven children, of whom seven survived him—three sons and four daughters.

Sir Francis Pemberton is reputed to have been a generous and charitable man, and to have been endowed with a ready wit and quick apprehension. At the same time his notions are described as curious, and his distinctions nice; and certainly his phraseology was peculiar, for he was in the habit of commencing his addresses to counsel, jury, and prisoner with Captain Fluellen's expression, 'Look you.' Roger North's account of him (p. 222–3) is a very prejudiced one, because he was in some sort a rival of the author's brother, Lord Guilford; and while he is obliged to acknowledge his excellence as a lawyer, he imputes to him, without the slightest evidence, misconduct both as counsel and as judge. Burnet describes him as one of the ablest men of his profession, and allows that he summed up against Lord Russell 'at first very fairly;' yet he evidently regards him with a somewhat jaundiced eye. Though he accounts for his removals by saying 'he was not wholly for the court,' he was not quite satisfied with him because he was not wholly a whig. The best proof that the family of Bedford did not impute to him any injustice or cruelty is that the old earl advised with him whether the attainder would prevent Lord Russell's son from succeeding to the earldom. The opinion that he gave remains among the archives of Woburn. Serjeant Chauncy also describes his general conduct while presiding in the most flattering terms, an opinion in which all must concur who read the trials of the period. His career was curiously marked by vicissitudes. After a youth of dissipation he became a profound lawyer; he was raised to the bench twice, and was twice dismissed by the king as being too lenient to those who opposed the court, and was twice imprisoned by the House of Commons—once at least, as acting arbitrarily and unjustly on the bench; after filling the highest judicial offices he twice resumed his place at the bar; and, notwithstanding all his reverses, and in spite of the condemnation of party writers on both sides, his memory is regarded with that respect which always accompanies moderation and independence. (*Lord Macaulay's England*, iii. 380.)

PEMBROKE, EARL OF. See W. MARESCHALL.

PENECESTRE, STEPHEN DE. Although Dugdale introduces him in his list of judges of the Common Pleas, quoting the 'Communia' of Trinity Term, 12 Edward I., there is considerable doubt whether he ever held that office or sat at all on the bench at Westminster. He certainly was often employed in a judicial character, but it seems to have been in his capacity of warden of the Cinque Ports.

The manor of Penshurst in Kent belonged to him, together with the manor of West Leigh and the castle of Allington in the same county. He was sheriff of Kent in 53 Henry III. and the two following years, and was then appointed constable of Dover Castle and warden of the Cinque Ports, posts which he retained as late as 33 Edward I. (*Excerpt. e Rot. Fin.* ii. 552; *Madox*, i. 613; *Abb. Rot. Orig.* i. 47.) There are several instances of his being assigned to try malefactors and to decide rights within his jurisdiction (*Rot. Parl.* i. 3, 18, 98, 126; *Abb. Placit.* 203), but none that show him to have been one of the regular judges.

His first wife was Roese de Beseville; and his second was Margaret, daughter of John de Burgh, the grandson of Hubert de Burgh, and widow of Robert de Orreby. He largely endowed the free chapel of his manor of Penshurst, and lies buried in the church there under an altar tomb, on which he is represented in armour, and not in judicial robes. (*Hasted*, i. 182, iii. 75, &c., iv. 450, vi. 84; *Abb. Rot. Orig.* i. 162, 164.)

PENGELLY, THOMAS, is said by tradition to owe his origin to an illicit amour of the Protector Richard Cromwell. This story seems principally to be founded on the fact that Pengelly showed uncommon zeal in a suit between Richard and his daughters, and that the protector died in Pengelly's house at Cheshunt. That this parentage was credited in his own times appears probable from the sly answer given by a witness to his question, how long a certain way through Windsor Park had been so used—'As far back as the time of Richard Cromwell.' The register states his birth to have taken place in Moorfields on May 16, 1675, and records him as the son of Thomas Pengelly, who in the son's admission to the Inner Temple is described of Finchley, Middlesex; but who this father was is nowhere explained. He was called to the bar in November 1700, and was dignified with the coif in 1710. Elected member for Cockermouth in both the parliaments of George I., he was in the latter one of the managers on the impeachment of the Earl of Macclesfield, and undertook the duty of replying to that nobleman's defence. In a long and laboured harangue he with great ability and force answered all the legal points raised by the earl, and with more harshness than was requisite aggravated the offences with which he was charged. At this time he was the king's prime serjeant, to which he had been appointed on June 24, 1719, having been knighted in the previous month, and in this character he, with the other law officers of the crown, had the conduct of the indictment of Christopher Layer for high treason in conspiring against the king in 1722, very ably and efficiently performing his duty on that important trial. On October 16, 1726, he was appointed chief baron of the Exchequer. (*Lord Raymond*, 1309, 1410; *State Trials*, xvi. 140, 1330.) He presided in that court for four years and a half, and during that time he exhibited that patience and firmness, as well as legal knowledge and discrimination, by which a good judge is distinguished. He fell a victim to the cruel and disgusting manner in which prisoners were treated in that age. Travelling the Western Circuit, some culprits were brought before him from Ilchester for trial at Taunton, the stench from whom was so bad that an infection was spread which caused the death of some hundreds of persons. Among them was the lord chief baron, who died at Blandford on April 14, 1730. (*State Trials*, xvii. 219-250; *Gent. Mag.* xx. 235.)

He was considered when at the bar a florid speaker and bold advocate, though perhaps at times too vehement. Steele's quibble on his name—'As *Pen* is the Welsh term for head, *guelt* is the Dutch for money, which with the English syllable *ly*, taken together, expresses one who turns his head to lye for money'—must be wholly disregarded, as it was prompted by anger at having the licence of his theatre taken away. As a judge he held a high reputation for his learning and his equal distribution of justice; and in his private character he was esteemed for his probity and cheerfulness. His charity was not confined to his life, for by his will he left a considerable sum for the discharge of prisoners confined for debt. (*Noble's Cromwell*, i. 175; *Cont. of Granger*, iii. 194.)

PENROS, JOHN, was of a Cornish family. He was raised to the office of a judge of the King's Bench in Ireland on February 27, 1385, 8 Richard II. (*Cal. Rot. Pat.* 211.) From this position he was removed to the English bench on January 15, 1391, in the fourteenth year; but to which of the two courts seems uncertain. Although Dugdale places him in the Common Pleas, the words in the patent seem rather to express the King's Bench (*Ibid.* 221); and no fines appear, from Dugdale's account, to have been levied before him. In the following year he was made justice of South Wales; and the last time we find him mentioned is as a trier of petitions in the parliament of 17 Richard II. (*Ibid.* 228; *Rot. Parl.* 310.)

PENZANCE, LORD. *See* J. P. WILDE.

PEPYS, RICHARD, was the second son of John Pepys, of Cottenham in Cambridgeshire, and the nephew of Talbot Pepys, who was a reader at the Middle Temple in 1623. His mother was Elizabeth, daughter of John Bendish, of Steeple Bumpstead in Essex. He studied at the Middle Temple, and, arriving at the post of reader in 1640, was elected treasurer of the society in 1643. In January 1654 he was called serjeant, immediately after which he was named on the commission for the spring circuit through the midland counties; and on May 30, 1655, he was made a baron of the Exchequer. (*Dugdale's Orig.* 220-222; *Whitelocke*, 591.)

Within a year he was removed to the chief justiceship of the Upper Bench in Ireland; and on June 14, 1655, he was placed in that character as chief commissioner of the Great Seal of that country, in which he continued till August 20, 1656. At the time of his death, in January 1658, he was the sole judge of his court; and it is much to his credit that in times like those in which he flourished no touch of calumny sullies his name. (*Smyth's Law Off. Ireland*, 31, 90.)

The grandson of Richard, the judge's eldest son, was the father of two baronets—Sir Lucas Pepys, physician to George III., created in 1784; and Sir William Weller Pepys, a master in Chancery, created in 1801. The latter title devolved in 1845 on the next-noticed Charles Christopher Pepys.

Notwithstanding all these honours attaching to the family, the name of Pepys will be longer remembered through the literary reputation of Samuel Pepys, the descendant of a younger branch, who was secretary of the Admiralty in the reigns of Charles II. and James II.

PEPYS, CHARLES CHRISTOPHER (EARL OF COTTENHAM), was directly descended from the above-noticed Richard Pepys, being the second son of Sir William Weller Pepys, who held the office of master in Chancery from 1775 till 1807, and obtained his baronetcy in 1801 by his wife, Elizabeth, eldest daughter of the Right Honourable William Dowdeswell, chancellor of the Exchequer in 1765. He was nephew also to Sir Lucas Pepys, Bart., physician to George III. Both the baronetcies centred in him by the decease of his brother in 1845, and his cousin in 1849, and are now merged in the earldom he afterwards attained. His younger brother Henry held the bishopric of Worcester from 1841 to 1861.

He was born on April 29, 1781, and was educated at Harrow, from whence he proceeded to Trinity College, Cambridge, where he took his degree of Bachelor of Laws in 1803. Having previously entered himself as a member of Lincoln's Inn, he availed himself of the instructions of the two most eminent men in common law and equity, Mr. Tidd and Sir Samuel Romilly, till he was called to the bar in November 1804. He attached himself to the Court of Chancery, but, though esteemed a skilful draftsman, his progress was not rapid. He did not obtain a silk gown till 1826; but afterwards he had no reason to complain.

Soon after the accession of William IV. he was appointed, in November 1830, solicitor-general to the queen; and in July 1831 he entered parliament, first as the representative of Earl Fitzwilliam's borough of Malton, and afterwards of Higham Ferrers. In the senate he supported the whig party, to which he was always attached; and was raised by that party in February 1834 to the post of solicitor-general to the king, on which occasion he was knighted.

He had filled that office for little more than six months when the mastership of the Rolls became vacant, to which post, passing over the Attorney-General Campbell, Sir Christopher was appointed on September 29, 1834. In the interval between that month and April 1835 there had been two changes of ministry; and on the second change, when the liberal party resumed power, the Great Seal was put into commission, at the head of which the new master of the Rolls was placed. At the end of nine months, on January 16, 1836, the Seal was delivered to Sir Christopher alone as lord chancellor, and four days afterwards he was created Baron Cottenham.

For nearly the six following years he performed the functions of his high office in a most satisfactory manner; but on September 3, 1841, on the restoration of the conservative party, he retired, and remained out of office while that ministry retained power, but assisted in hearing appeals to the House of Lords and the privy council. When the conservatives were in their turn obliged to quit the government he resumed his seat on the woolsack, on July 4, 1846, being the only whig chancellor, except Lord Cranworth, who during the present century has been restored to his place.

Towards the end of four years Lord Cottenham's health began to succumb under the labours of his position, and his sufferings at last interfered much with his duties. In the prospect of his retirement, her majesty, or rather perhaps the party to which he was attached, showed the value placed on his services by raising him two steps in the peerage. He was on June 1, 1850, created Viscount Crowhurst and Earl of Cottenham; and on the 19th of the same month, under the pressure of severe illness, he resigned the Seal, having held it as chancellor nearly ten years. With the hope of restoring his health, he travelled on the continent, but, as in the case of Lord Langdale, his relaxation came too late. Within nine months he died at Pietra Santa in the duchy of Lucca on April 19, 1851.

Lord Cottenham, though he attained no great eminence as an advocate, proved himself a most excellent judge. In the former capacity he was a sound and practical adviser, and an accurate and logical reasoner, but without that ready eloquence which is often the principal attraction. But these very qualities rendered his decisions in the latter character of the greater value, enabling him at once to see the real merits of the point in dispute, and to discard from his consideration useless technicalities and irrelevant arguments. As a senator, both in and out of office, he supported and sometimes originated several amendments of the law, and in his own court he introduced some regulations for the simplification and more satisfactory conduct of its proceedings. It speaks highly in his favour that his judicial merits were not praised by his own friends only, but fully acknowledged by the opposite party also. He was peculiarly cold and sedate in his manner, and extremely tenacious of his opinions, and though he was a staunch adherent to the whig party, he was not considered of any use to it as a politician.

In 1821 Lord Cottenham married Caroline, daughter of William Wingfield, Esq., the master in Chancery, by Lady Charlotte Maria, daughter of the first Earl of Digby. By her he had twelve children.

PERCEHAY, or PERCY, HENRY DE, may have been a younger branch of the noble house of Percy, but was probably the son of William and Isabella Percehay, the possessors of Lewesham and other manors in Yorkshire and Lincolnshire. From 39 Edward III. he received a fee as one of the king's serjeants, after which he was occasionally employed as a justice of assize. He was raised to the bench at Westminster on October 5, 1375, being then constituted a baron of the Exchequer, in which office he remained during the rest of that and the first five months of the following reign. He was then, on November 26, 1377, removed to the Court of Common Pleas, in which fines are recorded as levied before him till Midsummer 1380, 4 Richard II. (*Dugdale's Orig.* 45.)

PERCY, ROBERT DE, was one of the justiciers before whom fines were taken in 10 John. (*Hunter's Preface.*) They were acknowledged in the country, and he is mentioned in that character in no previous or subsequent year.

He was the third son of Josceline of Lovaine (son of Godfrey Duke of Brabant, and brother of Adelicia, the second wife of Henry I.), who assumed the name of Percy for himself and his descendants on his marriage with Agnes, one of the daughters and coheirs of Lord William de Percy, the third baron, on whose death the male branch became extinct. *

He accompanied the king to Ireland in 1210, and in the following year had various allowances for the expenses of the Spanish ambassadors and their knights, and for conducting them to Dover. (*Rot. de Præstito*, 180–236.) In 14 John the sheriffalty of Yorkshire was committed to him, but he subsequently appears to have joined with the barons, as his lands were given to Brian de Insula; but they were restored on his submission soon after the accession of Henry III. (*Rot. Claus.* i. 245, 324, 373.) In the tenth year of that reign he is mentioned as one of the justices assigned to hold a special assize of last presentation to a church in Yorkshire. (*Ibid.* ii. 138.) He is said to have assumed the name of Sutton, which was borne by his posterity. (*Baronage*, i. 271; *Collins's Peerage*, ii. 232.)

PERCY, WILLIAM DE, was also named in Mr. Hunter's list of justiciers before whom fines were acknowledged in 8 John, 1206, but none of the fines in which he is so introduced have yet been published.

He seems to have been nephew of the above-mentioned Robert de Percy, and the son of Henry de Percy, Robert's elder brother, by Isabel, daughter of Adam de Brus, lord of Skelton.

He was employed by King John, a mandate being recorded for a secure ship for him to pass over in the king's service into Poictou with horses and arms. (*Rot. de Fin.* 547.) Under Henry III. he received various grants of land, and obtained a weekly market for his manor of Spofforth in Yorkshire, and in 26 Henry III. he paid one hundred marks to be exempted from attendance on the king in Gascony.

He died in 1245, and was buried in the abbey of Sallay. His first wife was Joan, one of the daughters of the before-noticed William Briwer. His second wife was Ellen, daughter of Ingelram de Balliol. By both he had issue.

The thirteenth baron was in 1377 created Earl of Northumberland, a title which still exists, notwithstanding various forfeitures, in the present Duke of Northumberland, who is the lineal descendant, sometimes through female heirs, of this William de Percy. The dukedom was added by George III. on October 18, 1766. (*Baronage*, i. 271; *Collins*, ii. 233.)

PERCY, PETER DE, was probably a branch of the same noble family, and was certainly a native of the North. From the numerous entries in the Rotulus de Finibus (*Excerpt.* ii. 263–388) of payments made for assizes before him, it is apparent that he was a regular justicier. They extend from 41 to 47 Henry III., 1257–1263. After that date there is no further mention of him until 1267, when his son Robert does homage for the lands his father held in capite. (*Ibid.* 456.)

PERROT, GEORGE, was the son of the Rev. Thomas Perrot, rector of Welbury and Martin-cum-Gregory in York, and a prebendary of Ripon, by Anastasia, daughter of George Plaxton, Esq., of Berwick. He was born in 1710, and was initiated in the study of the law at the Inner Temple, obtaining his grade of barrister in 1732, and of bencher in May 1757. Two years after he was made a king's counsel, and in 1760 he opened the indictment against Lord Ferrers when he was tried for murder by the House of Lords. In January 1763 he obtained a seat on the bench as a baron of the Exchequer, but was never knighted. His power of discrimination may be estimated by his summing up on a trial at Exeter as to the right to a certain stream of water, which he concluded thus: 'Gentlemen, there are fifteen witnesses who swear that the watercourse used to flow in a ditch on the north side of the hedge. On the other hand, gentlemen, there are nine witnesses who swear that the watercourse used to flow on the south side of the hedge. Now, gentlemen, if you subtract nine from fifteen, there remain six witnesses wholly uncontradicted; and I recommend you to give your verdict accordingly for the party who called those six witnesses.'

His judicial life extended to twelve years, and was terminated by a fit of the palsy, with which he was seized at Maidstone during the Lent assizes in 1775, which induced him to resign in the following May, receiving a grant of 1200*l.* a year as a retiring pension. He was buried at Laleham.

He married Mary, the daughter of William Bower, of Bridlington in Yorkshire, and the widow of Peter Whitton, who in 1728 was lord mayor of York, but left no issue. (*State Trials*, xix. 894.)

PERRYN, RICHARD, the son of Benjamin Perryn, Esq., of Flint, commenced his study of the law at Lincoln's Inn, but was called to the bar in July 1747 by the society of the Inner Temple, to which he had transferred himself, and became a bencher in April 1771. Choosing the Court of Chancery for his legal arena, he soon acquired such a reputation there as to be employed in almost every cause. After a long apprenticeship, he obtained a silk gown in 1771, and received the appointment of vice-chamberlain of Chester. It is insinuated by a contemporary that he owed his success more to chance than to merit, and that his professional colleagues had no very high opinion of his legal acquirements. On April 5, 1776, he was promoted to a barony in the Court of Exchequer, and knighted. After a respectable career of three-and-twenty years as a judge, he resigned in the summer vacation of 1799. (8 *Term Reports*, 421; *Strictures on Lawyers*, 175.) He died in 1803.

PERYAM, WILLIAM, was the eldest of the two sons of John Peryam, an opulent citizen and twice mayor of Exeter; and of Margaret, one of the daughters and coheirs of Robert Hone, Esq., of Ottery St. Mary. The other son, John, was an alderman of Exeter and a knight, and was a considerable benefactor to Exeter College, Oxford (*Chalmers' Oxford*, 68), where William, who was born at Exeter in 1534, is said to have been educated. His arms are placed in one of the windows of Middle Temple Hall. Receiving the serjeant's coif in Michaelmas Term 1579, he was constituted a judge of the Common Pleas on February 13, 1581, 23 Eliz. (*Dugdale's Orig.* 225.)

For the twelve years during which he retained his seat the reputation he enjoyed may be estimated as well by his being named as one of the commissioners to hear causes in Chancery on the death of Sir Christopher Hatton, as by the number of commissions into which his name was introduced for the trial of state offenders. Among these were Mary Queen of Scots, the Earls of Arundel and Essex, Sir John Perrot, and others of less note. (*App.* 4 *Report Pub. Rec.* 272–296; *State Trials*, i. 1167, 1251, 1315, 1333.) In January 1593 he was promoted to the office of chief baron of the Exchequer, and was knighted. He continued to preside in that court during the ten remaining years of Elizabeth's reign, and for eighteen months under King James I. (*Dugdale's Orig.* 48.)

After a judicial life of nearly twenty-four years, he died on October 9, 1604, at his mansion at Little Fulford, near Crediton, in the church of which he was buried under a stately monument.

He married three wives. The first was Margery, daughter of John Holcot, of Berkshire, Esq.; the second was Anne, the daughter of John Parker, of North Molton, Devon, Esq.; and the third was Elizabeth, one of Sir Nicholas Bacon the lord keeper's daughters, to whom he was also the third husband, she having been previously married to Sir Robert d'Oyly and Sir Henry Nevill. He left four daughters. (*Prince's Worthies; Diary of Walter Yonge*, 8.)

PETER, as abbot of Tewkesbury (elected in 1216), is added to the list of justices itinerant for the county of Gloucester in 9 Henry III., 1225. His name does not again appear in a judicial character, and he died in 1232. (*Rot. Claus.* i. 271, ii. 76; *Rot. Pat.* 184; *Mitred Abbeys*, i. 185.)

PETIT, JOHN, was a member of Gray's Inn, and filled the post of reader there in 1518, and again in 1526. He was in the commission of the peace for Kent from 1514. He became a baron of the Exchequer in Michaelmas 1527, but Dugdale is somewhat confused in respect to whether he was second or third baron. (*Dugdale's Orig.* 292; *Cal. State Papers* [1509–14], 723.)

PEVERELL, HUGH, is named on a fine of 6 Richard I., 1194, as one of the justiciers before whom it was levied at Westminster, and in 8 Richard I. was at the head of the justices itinerant who fixed the tallage in the counties of Essex and Hertford. (*Madox*, i. 704.)

That he held a distinct official appointment in the Exchequer appears from several entries on the rolls. (*Ibid.* ii. 274–5.)

He was probably a scion of the noble house of Peverell, which commenced in the person of Ranulph Peverell, who married a concubine of William the Conqueror, and was perhaps that Hugh Peverell who in John's reign was seated at Sanford in Devonshire; or the Hugh Peverell, of Ermington in the same county, whose lands were forfeited for his adherence to the barons, but afterwards restored on his submission to King Henry III. (*Rot. Claus.* i. 200, 283, 307); or more probably the father of one of them.

PHELIPPS, or PHILLIPS, EDWARD, was descended from an ancient Welsh family, which migrated into the county of Somerset, where they long resided at Barrington, a few miles from Montacute. He was the fourth son of Thomas Phelipps, Esq., of that place, by Elizabeth, the daughter of — Smith, Esq., whose second son was father of Sir Thomas Phelipps, raised to a baronetcy in 1620, which became extinct in 1690.

It is not improbable that Edward studied at Broadgate's Hall (now Pembroke College), Oxford, as Wood notices one of his name taking the degree of B.A. in 1579, and of M.A. in 1582. He kept his legal terms at the Middle Temple, and attained to the rank of reader in autumn 1596. (*Dugdale's Orig.* 218.) He was called serjeant at the end of the reign of Queen Elizabeth, but did not assume the degree, on account of her death intervening, till the beginning of King James's. He was appointed king's serjeant on the 18th of May following, and was knighted. In November he assisted in the trial of Sir Walter Raleigh, but took no part in the brutal manner with which Sir Edward Coke conducted the prosecution. In July 1604 he was made justice of the Common Pleas in the county palatine of Lancaster. (*Cal. State Papers* [1603–10], 133.)

In January 1606 he opened the indictment against Guy Fawkes and the other conspirators in the Gunpowder Plot, and his speech on the occasion is a curious specimen of oratory. (*State Trials*, ii. 164.)

In the first parliament of King James, which met on March 19, 1604, he was returned for his native county, and elected speaker. His address to the king is in his usual ponderous style, and he apparently vied with his majesty which should most fatigue the audience by the length of their orations. The reporter, however, was out of patience and leaves his harangue un-

L L

finished. On the close of the session in July his speech is full of the most fulsome absurdities, beginning with solemn pomposity, 'History, most high and mighty sovereign, is truly approved to be the treasure of times past; the light of truth; the memory of life; the guide and image of man's present estate; pattern of things to come, and the true work-mistress of experience, the mother of knowledge,' &c. (*Parl. Hist.* i. 969, 1045.) This parliament continued till February 1611, during which period there were four more sessions, in all of which Sir Edward acted as speaker, having in the interim been rewarded for his flattery by the reversion of the office of master of the Rolls, granted to him on December 2, 1608, to which he succeeded on the death of Lord Bruce of Kinloss, on January 14, 1611. He was also made chancellor to Henry Prince of Wales.

Of Sir Edward's proceedings in Chancery little more is known than appears incidentally in the report of Wraynham's case, against whom proceedings were instituted for slandering Lord Bacon. A cause in which Wraynham was concerned had been referred to the master of the Rolls, who had made a report adverse to his interests, on which Lord Chancellor Bacon had afterwards founded his decree, and Wraynham had thereupon conveyed the slander in a petition to the king. On the hearing of the charge, the character of Sir Edward Phelipps (then dead) is given by three eminent lawyers his contemporaries. Yelverton, the attorney-general, calls him 'a man of great understanding, great pains, great experience, great dexterity, and great integrity.' Sir Edward Coke says, 'As for this master of the Rolls, never man in England was more excellent in Chancery than that man; and for aught I heard (that had reason to hear something of him) I never heard him taxed with corruption, being a man of excellent dexterity, diligent, early in the morning, ready to do justice.' Chief Justice Montagu, however, lets us into a little bit of his real character as a judge, for, after declaring that 'whoever knew that man knows him to be a true reporter and a judicious collector of proofs as ever was,' he adds, 'I will not dissemble what others thought a fault in him, to be over swift in judging, but this was the error of his greater experience and riper judgment than others had.' (*State Trials*, ii. 1062, 1073, 1079.)

He had left the scene long before this trial took place, having died on September 11, 1614. He built the large and noble mansion still standing at Montacute. He married first Margaret, daughter of — Newdigate, Esq.; and secondly Elizabeth, daughter of Thomas Pigott, Esq., of Bucks. His representatives still enjoy the paternal estate.

PHESANT, PETER, was of a family established at Tottenham in Middlesex, and the son of Peter Phesant, of Bletchworth in the county of Lincoln, an eminent lawyer and reader of Gray's Inn in 1582, and Queen Elizabeth's attorney 'in partibus borealibus.' A student at Gray's Inn, he became a barrister in 1608, and was chosen reader in 1624. In May 1640 he was honoured with the degree of the coif, and having been one of the common pleaders of the city of London, was elected recorder on May 2, 1643, but resigned the office on the 30th of the same month, on the plea of ill-health, but probably in order to make room for John Glynne, the favourite of the parliament. Under the same plea he had in the previous year excused himself from appearing in defence of Sir Edward Herbert, the attorney-general, on his impeachment. (*Parl. Hist.* ii. 1125, 1127.)

In February 1643 the parliament proposed him to the king as one of the judges of the Common Pleas (*Clarendon*, iii. 407), and, on their assumption of the government, voted him into that place on September 30, 1645. On the king's death, in January 1649, he consented to act in his judicial capacity under 'the keepers of the liberties of England;' but in the following June he was allowed to stay at home from the circuit, 'being sickly' (*Whitelocke*, 174, 378, 409); and dying three months after, on October 1, 1649, at Upwood in Huntingdonshire, he was buried in the church there. The inscription on his monument describes him as having been twice the only judge of his court. By his wife, Mary, of the family of Bruges, of Gloucestershire, he had several children. (*Hatfield's Hunts.*)

PHILIP is mentioned as the successor of Roger Pauper, who was removed from the office of chancellor in 1139; and a charter to the monastery of St. Frideswide (Christchurch), Oxford, one of the witnesses to which is 'P. the chancellor,' seems to corroborate this account, as it must have been dated before 1148, and perhaps before 1144. (*Monast.* ii. 146; *Philipot.*)

The author of the 'Lives of the Chancellors' (1708) is evidently mistaken in saying that he held it till Becket was appointed, in the next reign, as Robert de Gant was certainly chancellor during part of the interval.

PICHEFORD, GEOFFREY DE, the son of Ralph de Picheford, was constable of the castle and forest of Windsor in 1 Edward I. (*Abb. Rot. Orig.* i. 21), and was a justice itinerant of the forests from the sixth to the eighteenth year. He was afterwards Queen Eleanor's bailiff at Langley. (*Rot. Parl.* i. 4, 59, ii. 81.) The last time any record of his name appears is as constable of Windsor Castle, in 26 Edward I. (*Madox*, ii. 224.)

PIGOTT, GILLERY, is one of the present barons of the Exchequer. His family is traced from a knight who accompanied William the Conqueror on his invasion of England, and its members have held possessions in various counties ever since. He is the fourth son of Paynton Pigott, Esq., of Archer Lodge in Hampshire, and of Banbury in Oxfordshire (who assumed in 1836 the additional names of Stainsby Conant), and of Maria Lucy, daughter of Richard Drosse Gough, Esq., of Loudern in the latter county. He was born at Oxford in 1813, his Christian name being given him from his great-grandmother, the daughter of Colonel Gillery; and he received his education at a private school at Putney.

A member of the Middle Temple, he was called to the bar by that society in May 1839; and joining the Oxford Circuit, and attending the sessions of that and the neighbouring county of Gloucester, he gained a considerable practice. In a few years he was elected recorder of Hereford. His next promotion was to the degree of the coif in 1856, to which was added in the following year a patent of precedence. In October 1860 he was elected representative for Reading, and, professing liberal opinions, he supported Lord Palmerston's administration. But his senatorial career was soon interrupted by his elevation to the bench of the Exchequer on October 8, 1863, when he received the honour of knighthood.

He married Frances, only daughter of Thomas Duke, Esq., of Ashday Hall, near Halifax.

PIKENOT, ROBERT, is the last named of the eighteen justices itinerant to whose judicial superintendence the six divisions into which the kingdom was apportioned in 22 Henry II., 1176, was submitted, the northern counties being allotted to him and two others. (*Madox,* i. 128.)

PILBOROUGH, JOHN, was admitted a member of Lincoln's Inn in 1515, and became reader there in 1535, and again in 1543. He was appointed a baron of the Exchequer on November 28, 1545, 37 Henry VIII.; and within a week after the death of that monarch, being still a governor of Lincoln's Inn, he delivered 'an ornate oration' to two new-made serjeants of that society. His death occurred in the following year. (*Dugdale's Orig.* 119, 251, 252.)

He married Elizabeth, daughter of John Roper, attorney-general to Henry VIII., and Jane, daughter of Lord Chief Justice Fineux; and was thus the brother-in-law to Chief Justice Sir Edward Montagu, who married Eleanor, another daughter. (*Collins' Peerage,* vii. 80.)

PINCERNA, ALEXANDER. See BOTELER.

PINKENI, GILBERT DE, or **PINCHENI,** was a baron whose property lay in Northamptonshire and Berkshire. Having succeeded his father Ralph, he held the sheriffalty of Berkshire in 4 Henry II. and two following years.

His appearance in this catalogue arises solely from his being one of the twelve named by Dugdale as justices itinerant in 1170, but whose real office was to enquire into the abuses of the sheriffs, and had nothing to do with the ordinary legal proceedings.

He died about the end of that king's reign, leaving a son named Henry, who succeeded to his possessions. The ninth baron, Henry de Pinkney, was summoned to parliament by Edward I., as Dominus de Wedon, but the barony became extinct on his death without issue. (*Baronage,* i. 556; *Pipe Rolls,* 123; *Nicolas.*)

PIPARD, GILBERT, in 14 Henry II., and for the three following years, held the sheriffalty of Gloucestershire, succeeding William Pipard, probably his father, who had been sheriff for the four previous years. At the distribution of England, in 1176, among the eighteen justices itinerant appointed by the council of Northampton, he was the last of the three to whom the counties of Wilts, Dorset, Somerset, Devon, and Cornwall were appropriated. In the subsequent arrangement also, made by the council of Windsor in 1179, when England was divided into four parts, he was selected to administer justice in one of them. (*Madox,* i. 128–137.)

Three other counties, in addition to that of Gloucester, were entrusted to his superintendence as sheriff (*Ibid.* 205); and in 1180 he was employed in Normandy, being the custos of the castle of Exmes and fermor of the Vicomté, in which year he accounts for the issues of the forests of Moulin-la-Marche and Bonmoulins. (*Rot. Scacc. Norm.* i. 50, 103, 104.)

PLANTAGENET, GEOFFREY (ARCHBISHOP OF YORK), was the younger of the two sons of Henry II. by Fair Rosamond, one of the daughters of Walter de Clifford, a baron of Herefordshire. The date of his birth, like the whole of his mother's history, is involved in some doubt. If, when he was elected Bishop of Lincoln in 1173, he had, as is said by Giraldus Cambrensis, scarcely completed his fourth lustre, he must have been born about 1153. This might have been the case had he been the *elder* son, as his father was in England in this year. But as the other son, William Longsword, afterwards Earl of Salisbury, was his senior, the period of Geoffrey's birth must have been later, unless Henry's connection with Fair Rosamond had commenced in his first visit to England in 1149, when he was only sixteen years of age, which was not a very likely occurrence. The date of 1158 or 1159, which other writers give of his birth, seems more probable, especially as on his seal, attached, after his election as bishop, to a grant of certain churches to the priory of Burlington in Lincolnshire, an impression from which is published in the 'Archæologia' (vol. xxi. p. 31), he is represented as a boy, which he would scarcely have permitted had he attained his twentieth year.

Notwithstanding his youth and the irregularity of his birth, Henry easily obtained the confirmation of the English bishops, and contrived also to procure a dispensation from the pope from those impediments. Although, previously to his election to the bishopric, he had held an archdeaconry in the same cathedral, he was not of course admitted into priest's orders; so that he could not yet be consecrated nor enter on his pastoral duties. It is stated that his father sent him to Tours to prepare himself in the schools there for undertaking his episcopal charge.

This was probably at a somewhat later period, because he took an active part in 1174 in aiding his father, when his sons raised the standard of rebellion against him. With this view he had applied to, and obtained from, the gentry and people of his diocese, a considerable sum of money as a free contribution; but on being apprised that it was deemed an exaction, he at once returned the whole. By this popular act he found himself at the head of a large body of volunteers, with whom, throwing off his ecclesiastical character, he surprised and levelled to the ground the castle of Kinardsferry, a strong fortress in the Isle of Axholme, belonging to Roger de Mowbray. He then, at the request of Ranulph de Glanville, the sheriff of Yorkshire, raised another fine army, and, marching into that county, took and demolished the castle of Malepart, or Malesart, which Roger de Mowbray had built, about twenty miles from York. On joining his father shortly afterwards at Huntingdon, the king welcomed him with affection, and declared that his other children were bastards, and he alone had shown himself his true and legitimate son.

The tendency of his inclinations being thus exhibited towards a military rather than a clerical career, it is not surprising, when the pope, in 1181, insisted that he should either take priest's orders, and be consecrated, or renounce the see of Lincoln, the profits of which he had received without performing its duties, that he should voluntarily resign his bishopric. In his letter of resignation he calls himself chancellor, to which office the king had previously appointed him. This office he continued to hold during the remainder of his father's reign (*Dugdale's Monast.* v. 588, vi. 938), and he is said to have acted in it, notwithstanding his youth, with extraordinary equity and discretion. The affection of his father for him may be seen as well in the charters as in his will, in all of which he is called 'my son and chancellor.'

In 1187 his native talents as a military commander were again called into exercise by the king's placing him at the head of one of the divisions of the army he had raised in Normandy; and his affectionate adherence to his father in all his troubles was strongly evidenced in the last war in which the king was engaged. Philip Augustus of France had attacked Mans, the capital of Maine, into which Henry, with Geoffrey, had thrown himself. On the town taking fire, Geoffrey in vain aided the attempts to extinguish the flames; but was obliged to fly with the king, and taking refuge in the castle of Fresnelles, he offered to remain without, as a guard against the expected attacks of the pursuers. Henry, however, not willing that, exhausted with the fatigues he had undergone, he should expose himself further, insisted on his entering the castle and sharing his own bed. He distinguished himself greatly during the short remainder of the war; and when the peace was concluded on June 28, 1189, and the ingratitude of Prince John, which was then exposed, had so severely stung his father's heart as to produce the fever from which he never recovered, he continued with him in the last trying moments, and soothed him with that affection and respect which his other sons had never shown him. Among the last wishes expressed by the king was his desire that Geoffrey should resume his clerical character, and obtain either the bishopric of Winchester or the archbishopric of York, and, giving him two rings of great value as a mark of his love, he died at Chinon on July 6.

The roll of the first year of Richard's reign mentions Geoffrey as chancellor; but, as part of the accounts in that roll necessarily refer to the last year of Henry's life, it affords no proof that he continued in the office after his father's decease. Richard was at that time abroad, and there is evidence that both before and immediately after his coronation William de Longchamp was acting as his chancellor.

King Richard, however, treated Geoffrey with the kindness he deserved, and in compliance with Henry's wish nominated him to the vacant archbishopric of York, even before his arrival in England, requiring, however, from him at the same time a contribution of three thousand marks towards the expenses of the crusade.

Taking up his residence at the priory of St. Martin at Dover, the sheriff of the county, by order of the chancellor, William de Longchamp, now Bishop of Ely, to whom Richard had entrusted the government of the kingdom during his absence in the Holy

Land, kept him in siege for several days, and then obtaining entrance, on September 19, 1191, had him violently dragged from the altar itself, and on his refusal to return to Flanders, carried him to the castle prison, and detained him in custody there for eight days. On the Bishop of London's interference, and marks of public indignation appearing, the chancellor thought proper to order his liberation. The precise cause of this outrage is uncertain; but it possibly arose from a dispute which seems to have occurred between the king and the archbishop as to the appointment of certain officers of his church. Be this as it may, the king was soon after compelled, for this and other causes, to consent to the removal of the chancellor.

Geoffrey's reception by the clergy and people after his imprisonment was a triumph both in London and York; and for some years he appears to have quietly employed himself in the affairs of his province, and to have refrained from interfering in politics.

Soon after the death of Richard, Geoffrey fell under the displeasure of King John, the principal cause of which was his refusal to permit the carucage, which had been generally granted to the king throughout the rest of England, to be collected in his province. The immediate effect of this was the seizure of all his manors and other possessions; and though the archbishop did not hesitate to punish James de Poterna, the sheriff, and all others engaged in it, with those who had excited the king's anger against him, he succeeded in effecting a reconciliation with the monarch which lasted for several years. In 1207, however, he resisted the payment of the thirteenth penny which the king had imposed, and found it necessary to retire privately from England, in order to avoid the royal resentment. In this exile he continued nearly seven years, and at last died at Gromont in Normandy, on December 18, 1213.

The affectionate duty which he showed to his father, King Henry, must incline us to a favourable interpretation of his conduct in the two succeeding reigns, and induce us to attribute his misfortunes to the irritability of Richard and the overbearing tyranny of John, each of whom his independence of character and his strict sense of justice would, though in a different manner, excite. His military inclinations do not appear to have prevented him from being a good bishop; nor do some minor dissensions between him and the canons of his cathedral at all detract from the character he must ever hold in history as a valiant soldier, an able commander, a wise counsellor, and an excellent son. (*Godwin*, 286, 675; *Rich. Divis.* 15, 34; *Madox*, i. 35, 87, ii. 139; *Wendover*; *Lord Lyttelton.*)

PLATT, THOMAS JOSHUA, the son of Thomas Platt, Esq., an eminent solicitor in London, who lived to be the father of the profession with undiminished respect till the age of eighty-two, and held the office of principal clerk to three chief justices, Lords Mansfield, Kenyon, and Ellenborough, during a period of thirty years, was born about 1790, and was sent first to Harrow, and then to Trinity College, Cambridge, where he took his degrees of B.A. in 1810, with honours, and of M.A. in 1814. He had in the meantime been admitted to the Inner Temple, and in 1816 was called to the bar. Joining the Home Circuit, he gradually was entrusted with briefs, and by his ready address and confident bearing eventually acquired a considerable practice. In January 1835 he received a silk gown, and became in the end a favourite leader of his circuit. Before a common jury he was a formidable adversary to his opponent, but before a special jury he was not so successful. In January 1845 he was raised to the bench of the Exchequer, and sat there more than eleven years, when, in consequence of the failure of his health, he retired in November 1856.

As an advocate he was remarkable for the energy of his manner and the simplicity of his language; and as a judge, though not deeply read, his good sense led him to sound conclusions, while his blunt courtesy and amiable disposition made him a favourite with the bar. He died on February 10, 1862.

PLESSETIS, JOHN DE (EARL OF WARWICK), stands second among the six justices assigned in 35 Henry III., 1251, to hold the pleas of the city of London, which were usually tried before the justices itinerant, the others being regular justiciers. This is the only time in which he appears in a judicial position, and he held it then no doubt in his character of constable of the Tower, where the sittings were to take place.

He was Earl of Warwick for life only, in right of Margery, his second wife, the sister and heir of Thomas de Newburgh, the last earl. His marriage with her was obtained for him by the king, in addition to numerous other favours by which he had been raised from a comparatively low origin to a high position in the court.

He was a Norman by birth, and is first named in 1227, as the last of four whom the king often describes as his knights (*Rot. Claus.* ii. 202), and who are always introduced *together*, receiving various payments for their services. They were all evidently servants in the king's household, and each partook of the king's generosity. Hugo de Plessetis, another of the four, was probably the father of John.

John advanced rapidly in the king's good graces, and for his services in the Welsh wars received ample rewards. He was appointed governor of Devizes, warden of

Chippenham Forest, and sheriff of Oxford; had grants of the wardships of various minors, with the custody of their lands (*Excerpt. e Rot. Fin.* i. 319–409); and, to raise his fortune to the highest point, the king took such measures that Margery, the sister and heir of the Earl of Warwick, whose first husband, John Mareschall, had lately died, did not venture to refuse him as her second. He married her accordingly in 1243, but did not assume the title of Earl of Warwick until he had obtained the consent of William Malduit, the presumptive heir to the earldom in the event of the countess's death, that he should enjoy it for his life if he survived her.

He had been appointed constable of the Tower of London in 28 Henry III., and the remainder of his life is chiefly remarkable for the liberal proofs he received of the king's favour, and for his steady adherence to his royal master. After attending the king into Gascony, and the conclusion of the truce there, he was, in 38 Henry III., treacherously seized by the people of Pontes in Poictou, notwithstanding a safe-conduct from the King of France, and cast into prison, whence he was not released till the following year. In his last years he saw the commencement of the troubles between the king and the barons, during which he was entrusted with the sheriffalty of Warwick and Leicester. He died in the midst of them, on February 26, 1263. (*Baronage,* i. 772.)

PLESTE, ROBERT DE, is not mentioned in any of the published records, but, according to Dugdale's 'Chronica Series,' was a baron of the Exchequer in 1362, 36 Edward III. There was a William de Pleste, who, in the same year, is called 'attornatus regis.'

PLESYNGTON, ROBERT DE, evidently mixed much in the politics of his day. His name is that of a township in the parish of Blackburn in Lancashire, which was probably his native place. In 50 Edward III., 1376, he was appointed one of the custodes of certain property in the town of Lancaster, and of several manors in the neighbourhood. (*Abb. Rot. Orig.* ii. 341.) At this time he held an office in the Court of Exchequer, to the head of which he was advanced four years afterwards, being constituted chief baron on December 6, 1380, 4 Richard II.

Dugdale removes Plesyngton from his seat on the bench on June 27, 1383; but William de Karleol, whom the learned author names as his successor, was appointed chief baron, not of the English, but the Irish Exchequer; and the Liberate Rolls show that Robert de Plesyngton continued in office without interruption till the tenth year of the reign.

His actual retirement took place on November 5, 1386, 10 Richard II. This day was during the sitting of the parliament which impeached the chancellor Michael de la Pole, Earl of Suffolk, and which passed the ordinance constituting commissioners for regulating the government. This ordinance, however, was not dated till a fortnight after Plesyngton's removal, which therefore, there is little doubt, was the act of the king himself. It not improbably arose from a desire to thwart and counteract his uncle, Thomas Duke of Gloucester, to whose party Plesyngton was strongly attached. The reasons for his removal nowhere expressly appear; but if they are to be found in the articles against him which are referred to in Appendix II. to the Ninth Report of the Deputy Keeper of the Public Records, 1848 (p. 244), they are of the most frivolous character.

It is not likely that any proceedings were taken upon these articles, because, on the passing of the ordinance, the influence of Plesyngton's friend, the Duke of Gloucester, would be paramount; but they were perhaps considered sufficient to prevent his reinstatement in the court at the time. In the parliament of the following year we find Plesyngton acting as the spokesman of the duke and the four other lords appellant, when they exhibited their charges against the Archbishop of York, the Duke of Ireland, the Earl of Suffolk, Sir Robert Tresilian, and Nicholas Brambre, the conviction of whom was quickly followed by that of the judges who had answered the unconstitutional questions propounded to them, among whom was Sir John Cary, the new chief baron. But, even upon the attainder of the latter, Plesyngton was not replaced on the bench of the Exchequer, nor is any explanation to be found why he was then passed over.

He died in 17 Richard II., 1393–4, but the king was so inveterate against all those who were connected with the Duke of Gloucester's proceedings that, when he resumed his authority in the twenty-first year of his reign, he was not content with punishing the survivors, but he caused those who were dead, and among them Robert de Plesyngton, to be impeached for their share in the supposed treasons. The parliament, being then under his control, of course confirmed his law, and the chief baron's property was declared forfeited to the crown. These unjust sentences, however, were all overturned in the first parliament of Henry IV., and the possessions of Robert de Plesyngton in Rutland and Yorkshire seemed to have descended to the son of the same name, whom he had by his wife Agnes. (*Rot. Parl.* iii. 384, 425; *Cal. Inquis.* p. m. iii. 176, 305.)

PLUMER, THOMAS, descended from an old and respectable Yorkshire family, was the second son of Thomas Plumer, of Lilling Hall in that county. He was born on

October 10, 1753, and at eight years of age he was sent to Eton, where he gained that character for classical ability and suavity of disposition which afterwards distinguished him at University College, Oxford. While William Scott (afterwards Lord Stowell) was regarded as the best tutor in the university, Plumer was considered one of the best scholars. He was elected Vinerian Scholar in 1777, and, taking his degree of B.A. in 1778, became fellow of his college in the next year, and proceeded M.A. in 1783.

He had become a member of Lincoln's Inn so early as April 1769, but was not called to the bar till February 1778. Before that event took place he had the advantage of attending Sir James Eyre on his circuits, and frequently assisting the judge, whose eyes were weak, in taking down the evidence on the trials at which he presided. This employment was of great benefit to him in his future practice, which was principally in the Court of Exchequer. In 1781 he was made a commissioner of bankrupts, and attended the Oxford and also the Welsh Circuits, at the end of the latter of which he joined in the revelry of the Horseshoe Club, instituted by the members for their relaxation and indulgence in all sorts of fun and nonsense. (*Notes and Queries*, 2nd S. xii. 87, 214.) He soon acquired practice, and stood so high in estimation that he was employed in the defence of Sir Thomas Rumbold at the bar of the House of Commons, and there exhibited such powers that he was selected in 1787 as one of the three counsel to defend Warren Hastings, his coadjutors being Mr. Law and Mr. Dallas, each of whom, as well as he, eventually filled high offices in the law. In 1793 he was made a king's counsel, in which character he was often employed in the public trials that took place during the next ten or twelve years. He successfully defended John Reeves when absurdly prosecuted in 1797 for a libel. In the next year he defended Arthur O'Connor and others on a charge of high treason, one only of the defendants, James O'Coigley, being found guilty. In 1802 he was engaged in the prosecution of Governor Wall for a murder committed twenty years before, in the next year in the prosecution of Colonel Despard for high treason, both of whom were condemned and executed. He was leading counsel in the defence of Lord Viscount Melville in 1806, on his impeachment by the House of Commons, and contended with so much success against the case of the managers as to procure an acquittal for his noble client on all the ten charges in the articles. Just before this trial, on March 25, 1805, he was appointed a judge on the North Wales Circuit. He had a great reputation as a tithe lawyer, and had much employment before election committees. Of the suppressed volume called 'The Book,' arising out of the 'Delicate Investigation' into the conduct of Caroline, Princess of Wales, in 1806, he was supposed to be, if not the author, at least the corrector, joining with Lord Eldon and Mr. Perceval as her royal highness's friends.

In April of the next year, on the defeat of the whig ministry, Mr. Plumer was appointed solicitor-general, and was knighted. He then entered parliament for Lord Radnor's borough of Downton, which he continued to represent till he was raised to the bench. He remained solicitor-general for five years, Sir Vicary Gibbs being the attorney-general; but he does not appear to have taken part in any of the numerous prosecutions instituted by the latter, except in the case of the 'Independent Whig,' when he spoke for two hours in the House of Lords in support of the sentence pronounced against the libellers. On Sir Vicary's elevation to the bench Sir Thomas Plumer succeeded him on June 27, 1812, but filled the post for less than a year, being appointed on April 10, 1813, the first vice-chancellor under the statute 53 Geo. III. c. 24. After presiding in the new court for nearly five years, he received another and a last promotion as master of the Rolls on January 6, 1818. He filled this station till his death, which occurred six years after, on March 24, 1824, when he was buried in the Rolls Chapel.

Though a deep-read lawyer, and exhibiting great powers and ability in his pleadings, his style was so heavy and his speeches of such length and elaboration that he fatigued his hearers without interesting them. His estimation as a judge may be seen by the manner in which Sir Samuel Romilly, a sufficient authority, records in his Diary Sir Thomas's appointment to the mastership of the Rolls. While acknowledging his great anxiety to do the duties of his office to the satisfaction of every one, and most beneficially to the suitors, Sir Samuel pronounces him to be wholly incapable of discharging those duties, and accounts for the fact that Sir William Grant, his predecessor at the Rolls, notwithstanding his great dispatch, left an arrear of more than 500 causes, by stating that causes were set down at the Rolls for a two-fold object—that Sir William Grant might hear them, and that Sir Thomas Plumer might not hear them. His judgments were as prolix as his speeches used to be; and in allusion to them and to the delays attributed to Lord Eldon this epigram was perpetrated:

To cause delay in Lincoln's Inn
Two diff'rent methods tend:
His lordship's judgments ne'er begin,
His honour's never end.

Though unpopular in his court, his manners were most obliging, and his disposition most kind. His judgments too were so exceedingly learned and forcible, and in general correct, that he left a reputation of being an urbane and erudite, though a tedious, judge.

By his marriage with Marianne, the eldest daughter of John Turton, Esq., of Sagnal Hall in Staffordshire, he left several children. (*Gent. Mag.* xciv. 610; *State Trials,* xxvi. xxvii. xxix. xxx.; *Romilly's Diary.*)

POER, WALTER LE, was in some way engaged in the service of King John. In February 1215 he was sent with three others into Worcester to explain the king's affairs, and in the following August was employed to make an extent on the manor of Budiford in Warwickshire, and on that of Sukeleg in Worcestershire, for the use of Llewellyn. The county of Devon was committed to his charge as sheriff in 6 Henry III., 1222; and in 1226 he was one of those appointed to collect the quinzime in Worcestershire. In the same year he was nominated a justice itinerant into Gloucestershire, and in 1227 into the counties of Oxford, Hereford, Stafford, and Salop. (*Rot. Pat.* 128; *Rot. Claus.* i. 266, 499, ii. 146, 151, 205.)

POICTIERS, PHILIP OF (BISHOP OF DURHAM), was a confidential servant of Richard I., and was employed by him as his clerk or chaplain in the expedition to Palestine. After the truce with Saladin was made, he was one of the few whom the king selected as his companions on his return. Soon after Richard's redemption he was rewarded with the bishopric of Durham, in January 1196. He received priest's orders in the following June, but was not consecrated till May 12, 1197, when that ceremony was performed by Pope Celestine at Rome, whither he had been sent with William de Longchamp, Bishop of Ely (who died during the journey), in order to procure the pontiff's interference in removing the interdict which Walter de Constantiis, the Archbishop of Rouen, had laid on Normandy. His representations succeeded in inducing the pope to promote an agreement between the king and the archbishop, and in restoring the afflicted duchy to the rites of the Church.

On his return to England he took his place as a justicier in the Curia Regis, having probably been educated to the legal profession, and filled some office in the court before he was selected as clerk to the king. His name does not appear to fines levied at Westminster after 10 Richard I.

He undertook a pilgrimage to Compostella in 1200, and on his return home the next year he is stated to have been one of the chief advisers of that monarch in disregarding the pope's anathemas, which seems little to accord with the above act of devotion, or with his having been fined a thousand pounds the year before his death for having the king's goodwill. (*Madox,* i. 408.) The statement, however, whether true or false, drew the papal thunder on his own head, and the sentence of excommunication was pronounced against him. As this was not removed before his death, in 1208, his body was buried outside the church, without the performance of any funeral rites (*Godwin,* 738; *R. de Wendover,* iii. 66–237); an indignity which would not be very distressing to the monks, whom he had violently persecuted. (*Surtees' Durham,* i. xxvii.)

POLE, WILLIAM DE LA, was one of the two sons of William de la Pole, a rich merchant in the newly rising port of Kingston-upon-Hull. Both of them rendered valuable pecuniary assistance to Edward II. and Edward III., and were rewarded accordingly.

William was born at Ravenser, in the neighbourhood of Kingston-upon-Hull, to which he ultimately removed. In 1 Edward III. he had a grant of 4000*l.*, out of the first issues of the customs of that port, in payment of an advance he had made to meet the royal necessities, and in 1332 he sumptuously entertained the king when he visited Kingston on his way to Scotland. On this occasion he is said to have received the honour of knighthood, and to have procured the title of mayor for the principal officer of the town, being himself the first who bore it. The next year he was one of those employed in a mission to Flanders, and was several times engaged in similar duties during the six following years. In 9 Edward III. he was constituted custos of the exchanges of England, and receiver of the old and new customs of Hull and Boston. The immediate consideration of the last appointment was his undertaking to pay the expenses of the king's household at the rate of 10*l.* a day. He was the general agent for the crown with the trading interest, and was commonly denominated the king's merchant. In the twelfth year Edward III. gave him a royal acknowledgment for 10,000*l.* advanced, and for 7,500*l.* for which he had become bound; and in consideration of moneys paid by him in aid of the royal expenses, and for the defence of the kingdom, the king granted him various manors in Nottinghamshire and Yorkshire, and afterwards invested him with the order of knight banneret, adding other rents for the support of the honour, together with a reversionary assignment of 1000 marks of rent in France, when the king recovered his rights there. Besides this, houses in Lombard Street, London, which had belonged to the 'Societas Bardorum,' were appended to the royal donation. (*N. Fœdera*, ii. 862–908, 1065, 1085; *Abb. Rot. Orig.* ii. 11–142.)

He was constituted second baron of the Exchequer on September 26, 1339, and in the parliaments held in the following October and April he was present as one of the judges (*Rot. Parl.* ii. 103, 112); but he was removed, or retired, from his seat on the bench on June 21.

When Edward III. returned from Tournay, in November 1340, grievously disappointed by the ill-success of his ministers in the collection of funds, William de la Pole was among the sufferers from his indignation. (*Barnes*, 212.) He was imprisoned, and all his estates were taken into the king's hands. The particular charge against him arose from a commission which he had received as to the purchase and sale of wools for the king's use. (*N. Fœdera*, ii. 988.) A judgment was given against him in the Exchequer, but the whole process was annulled in the parliament of July 1344. (*Rot. Parl.* ii. 154.)

He lived for more than twenty years afterwards, highly in the king's favour. The remainder of his life is principally illustrated by his founding and liberally endowing an hospital at Kingston-upon-Hull, which in the last year of his life he obtained a licence to convert into a religious house of nuns, of the order of St. Clare. (*Abb. Rot. Orig.* ii. 286.) He died on April 21, 1366. (*Cal. Inquis.* p. m. ii. 274.) By his wife, Catherine, daughter of Sir John Norwich, he had several sons, one of whom was the next-mentioned Michael Earl of Suffolk. (*Baronage*, ii. 182; *Monast.* iv. 20; *Buryon's Gresham*, i. 56; *Allen's Yorkshire*, iii. 12.)

POLE, MICHAEL DE LA (EARL OF SUFFOLK), long before the death of his father, the above William de la Pole, devoted himself to arms, and was engaged in the French wars; in 1355 in the retinue of Henry Duke of Lancaster, and in 1359 accompanying Edward the Black Prince. (*N. Fœdera*, iii. 443.) His military character was sufficiently established in 50 Edward III. to warrant his appointment as admiral of the king's fleet in the northern seas, a commission which was renewed in 1 Richard II. (*Ibid.* 1065; *Rymer*, vii. 172.) In the following year his talents in diplomacy were tried in two missions, one to the court of Rome, and the other to treat for a marriage between his royal master and Catherine, the daughter of Barnabo, 'Lord of Millaine,' which came to no successful issue.

Having by this time completely ingratiated himself with the young king, he was appointed in the parliament of November 1381, 5 Richard II., one of the counsel to regulate the household (*Rot. Parl.* iii. 104); and in little more than a year he was raised to the highest office in the state, being constituted chancellor of England on March 13, 1383.

In January 1384 he received a payment of 933*l*. 6*s*. 8*d*. for his expenses in going to the court of Rome, to the King of the Romans and Bohemia, to treat for the marriage of King Richard with Queen Anne, and for the money paid for her release (*Devon's Issue Roll*, 224), she having been taken prisoner on her way to England.

Though he presided in the Chancery three years and a half, he soon had reason to regret that he had aimed at so high an elevation. He had been in office little more than a year when he was impeached by one John Cavendish, a fishmonger, for taking a bribe to favour him in a cause in which he was engaged. It turned out, however, and indeed was acknowledged by Cavendish, that the chancellor, as soon as he heard of the delivery of some fish, and of the bargain that had been made by Ottere, his clerk, insisted on paying the full price for the former, and on the obligation being destroyed. Notwithstanding this fact, Cavendish had been foolish enough to persist, and the consequence was that, a commission being appointed to try Cavendish for defamation, he was condemned to pay 1000 marks as damages to the chancellor, and such further fine to the king as should be imposed on him. (*Rot. Parl.* iii. 168–170.)

Although de la Pole escaped on this occasion, he was not so fortunate two years afterwards. In the meantime the king's weakness and extravagance had excited great discontent among all classes, and a general cry was raised against the favourites who surrounded him, to whose mismanagement and waste the distress of the people was, probably with some justice, attributed. The honours and more substantial favours which were extravagantly distributed did not tend to allay the public discontent. De la Pole was created Earl of Suffolk on August 6, 1385, and for the support of this title he had a munificent grant of the lands of the last earl, whose family had become extinct. (*Rot. Parl.* iii. 206.)

The jealousy with which these favours were regarded is evidenced by the bold retort given to the new-made earl by Thomas Arundel, Bishop of Ely, as related in the bishop's life.

The unpopularity of the earl increased so rapidly that, though he opened the next parliament on October 1, 1386, as chancellor, the king, under a threat of deposition in case he refused, was compelled by the complaints of both houses to remove him from the office on the 3rd of that month; and Bishop Arundel was appointed his successor.

The Commons immediately exhibited seven articles of impeachment against him, which certainly were of no great weight or importance. Notwithstanding an able defence by himself and his brother-in-law, Richard le Scrope, who referred to his thirty years' good services as a knight, the earl was convicted on most of the charges, and condemned to make restitution of all the purchases and grants acquired, except the title of earl and the 20*l*. a year out of the county. He was thereupon ordered to be committed to prison, there to remain at the king's will until he had paid such fine and ransom as should be imposed on him. (*Ibid.* 216–220.) At the close of these proceedings the king was compelled, before he could obtain a subsidy, to agree to a statute appointing eleven commissioners as a permanent council for the regulation and correction of all state matters, with a complete power over the royal revenue.

Although the king, on hearing the charges against de la Pole, is said to have exclaimed, 'Alas! alas! Michael, see what thou hast done!' it may be well doubted that he felt any real indignation, for as soon as the parliament was dissolved he not only released the earl from the castle of Windsor, where he had been confined, but gave a willing ear to his dangerous counsel at once to break the bonds which the parliament had thus imposed. To effect this object, the judges were summoned to Nottingham in the following August, and in a measure compelled to give answers to certain questions propounded to them, whereby they declared that the late statute was illegal and void, and that all those who procured it were traitors, and, further, that the judgment against the Earl of Suffolk was erroneous.

The plans of de la Pole and the other royal favourites were, however, so badly laid that they soon came to the knowledge of the members of the council, who took the promptest steps to counteract them, forcing the king to call a parliament in February 1388, and there appealing the Archbishop of York, the Duke of Ireland, de la Pole, Tresilian the chief justice, and Nicholas Brambre, an alderman of London, of high treason. The articles were thirty-nine in number, which, besides comprehending every act they had committed in their previous career, mainly pressed their last attempt to overturn the statute of the preceding parliament. The archbishop, the duke, the earl, and the chief justice, failing to appear, were found guilty, by default, of fourteen of the charges which were declared to be high treason, and were condemned to the punishment of traitors. (*Ibid.* 229–237.)

De la Pole, wisely escaping before the meeting of the parliament, avoided the fate of Tresilian and Brambre. On going to Calais, he is said to have been refused admission by his brother Edmund, who was then captain of the castle there; and, proceeding to Paris, he did not long survive his disgrace, but died on September 5 in the following year, 1389.

By his wife, Catherine, the daughter and heir of Sir John Wingfield, he left four sons. Michael, the eldest, was restored to his father's lands and honours, and his descendants were successively created Marquis of Suffolk, Earl of Pembroke, Duke of Suffolk, and Earl of Lincoln; but all these honours became extinct in 1513 by death or attainder. (*Baronage*, ii. 181; *Nicolas's Synopsis*.)

POLE, RALPH, appears to have belonged to a family the various branches of which have been honoured with three baronetcies, all of which are extinct, except that of Shute in Devonshire. It seems probable that he was the brother of Thomas, the direct ancestor of the baronet of Poole in Cheshire, whose title became extinct in 1821; and that he was one of the sons of Thomas Pole or Poole, of Barretspoole in Cheshire (descended from Gwenwinwyn de la Pole, lord of Powis), by Elizabeth, daughter of Sir William Stanley, of Hooton in the same county. (*Wotton's Baronet.* ii. 124, iv. 635.) He was called to the degree of a serjeant in Michaelmas, 21 Henry VI. 1442; and on July 3, 1452, he was constituted a judge of the King's Bench, and certainly continued to perform the duties of that office till Michaelmas 1459, after which his name does not occur. He was one of the commissioners for Derbyshire in the thirty-third year, to raise money for the defence of Calais (*Acts Privy Council*, vi. 243), and acted as a judge of assize in Yorkshire in 1457. (*Newcome's St. Albans*, 361.)

Another account makes him the son of Sir Peter de la Pole, of Newborough in Staffordshire, and of Radborne in Derbyshire, and states that he married Joan, daughter of Thomas Grosvenor, that several of his descendants served as sheriffs of the county of Derby, and that his representative still enjoys the family seat called Radborne Hall. (*Topog. and Geneal.* i. 176; *Burke's Landed Gentry*, 1050.)

POLLARD, LEWIS, was the son of Robert Pollard, whose father, John Pollard, of Way, settled on him lands at Roborow, near Great Torrington. He was born about 1465, and was called to the bar by the society of the Middle Temple, where he was reader in 1502. He received the degree of the coif in November of the following year, and was made one of the king's serjeants on July 9, 1507, his patent being renewed on the accession of Henry VIII. In the sixth year of that reign, on May 29, 1514, he was raised to the bench of the Common Pleas. Prince, who wrote about 150 years after him, says that 'the fragrant odour' of his faithfulness and reputation 'perfumes his memory unto this day.'

If he died, as Prince states, in 1540, he must have retired from the bench many years previously, for the last fine acknowledged before him was in Michaelmas 1525, and he is not mentioned in the Reports even so late as that date.

By his wife, Agnes, daughter of Thomas Hext, Esq., of Kingston, near Totnes, he had no less than eleven sons and eleven daughters, all of whom with his wife and himself were represented in a window of the church of King's Nympton, in which parish he had purchased an estate and erected a stately mansion. One of the descendants of his eldest son, Hugh, was created a baronet in 1627, but the title became extinct in 1693. (*Dugdale's Orig.* 47, 113, 215.)

POLLEXFEN, HENRY, derives his descent from one of the branches of an ancient Devonshire family. He was the eldest son of Andrew Pollexfen, of Shorforde in that county, and was born about 1632. In 1658 he was called to the bar by the Inner Temple, and arrived at the dignity of bencher in 1674. Long before that date he had made himself prominent in the courts, and soon acquired a lead in the state prosecutions, principally for the defence. In 1679 he advised Lord Derby to plead his pardon, and was assigned as counsel for Lord Arundel, one of the five Popish lords, who however was never brought to trial. He defended Sir Patience Ward, William Lord Russell, William Sacheverell, and others, and delivered an able argument in support of the charters of the city of London. All these occurred in the reign of Charles II., and show that his reputed tendencies were in opposition to the court. Roger North says he 'was deep in all the desperate designs against the crown,' and was 'a thoroughstitch enemy to the crown and monarchy.' It therefore excited considerable surprise that Chief Justice Jeffreys should select him to conduct the prosecutions in the bloody western assize against the victims of Monmouth's rebellion. From the reports of the trials he does not appear to have done more than his usual duty of stating the case for the prosecution. Before the end of James's reign he resumed his original position, and on the trial of the seven bishops in June 1688 he was offered a retainer on their behalf, which he refused to accept, unless Mr. Somers were associated with him. This being reluctantly conceded, as the bishops thought Somers too young and inexperienced, Pollexfen exerted himself zealously for his reverend clients, and Somers justified the recommendation of his discriminating patron by the effective assistance he afforded. (*State Trials*, vii.-xii.; *North's Lives*, 214.)

Pollexfen's strong opinion on King James's desertion of the government, and in favour of the establishment of the Prince of Orange, were so well known that he was one of the lawyers summoned by the Peers to advise them on the emergency, and was returned for the city of Exeter to the Convention Parliament. In February 1689 he received the appointment of attorney-general and the honour of knighthood, and when the nomination of judges took place he was made chief justice of the Common Pleas on May 4. In the following month he was called before the House of Lords for turning the Duke of Grafton out of the treasury office of the Common Pleas, which his grace held by a grant from the crown. After enjoying his promotion for little more than two years, he died at his house in Lincoln's Inn Fields, from the bursting of a blood-vessel, on June 15, 1691, and was buried in the chancel of Woodbury Church in Devonshire. (*Clarendon's Corresp. and Diary*, ii. 227, 231; *Luttrell*, i. 490-545, ii. 247; *Prince's Worthies*, 327.)

Roger North adds to the opinion already given that when Pollexfen was raised to the bench 'he proved the veriest butcher of a judge that hath been known;' but there does not appear any ground for so harsh a dictum. Burnet (ii. 209), more inclined to look favourably upon him, gives him but a qualified character in describing him as ' an honest and learned, but perplexed lawyer;' but his colleague Judge Rokeby in recording his death describes it as 'a great and publike loss, he being a very learned, upright, and usefull man.' His Reports, commencing in 1670, which were not published till after his death, are not held in any great repute.

POLLOCK, FREDERICK, was the third son of Mr. David Pollock, of Piccadilly, the highly respected saddler to King George III., and of Sarah, daughter of Richard Parsons, Esq., comptroller of a department in the Customs. The family was originally settled in the north, and his father was an eye-witness of the Pretender Charles Edward and his army triumphantly crossing the Tweed in November 1745; within a few months to retrace their steps and to be defeated and almost annihilated at Culloden. Good fortune attended him both in his business and his family, three of his five sons greatly distinguishing themselves in their respective professions—the eldest, Sir David, becoming chief justice of Bombay; the third, Sir Frederick, the subject of the present sketch; and the fifth, Sir George, who obtained imperishable fame in the Indian army, by his exploits in Afghanistan, and in numerous other well-fought fields in that part of the world.

Frederick Pollock was born on September 23, 1783. In his early years he lost much time at three metropolitan and suburban schools, in which he told his father that he learned nothing. On being taken away from the last he remained at home for sixteen months, employing them in very miscellaneous reading, principally devoted to English literature, chemistry, physiology, and other scientific subjects. He was then placed under Dr. Roberts at St. Paul's School. A story is related on good authority that young Pollock, fancying that he was wasting his time there, as he intended to go to the bar, intimated to the head-master that he should not stay; and that the doctor, who was desirous of keeping so promising a lad, thereupon became so cross and disagreeable that one day the youth wrote him a note, saying he should not return. The doctor, ignorant of the cordial terms on which the father and son lived together, sent the note to the father, who called on him to express his regret at his son's determination, adding that he had advised him not to send the note. Upon which the doctor broke out, 'Ah! sir, you'll live to see that boy *hanged*.' The doctor, on meeting Mrs. Pollock some years after his pupil had obtained university honours and professional success, congratulated her on her son's good fortune, adding, quite unconscious of the humorous contrast, 'Ah! madam, I always said he'd fill an *elevated* situation.'

At the end of a year and a half he accordingly left St. Paul's, and entered Trinity College, Cambridge, in October 1802. There, although prevented by a serious accident, which confined him to his bed, from attending any lectures during the whole of his third term, he went up for the college examination, and to his surprise was placed in the first class. Before he knew of his honourable position he had come up to town, with the intention of not revisiting Cambridge, considerately thinking that his father could not afford the expense. But with the announcement of his success, his tutor, the Rev. George Frederick Tavel, expressed a strong hope that he would return, and continue a career so auspiciously begun. His parents being equally anxious, the young man returned, fully resolved in his own mind to be senior wrangler, but also with a determination to relieve his father from part of the expenses by taking pupils. On applying for permission to do so his tutor generously, and with true college patriotism, said that the college could not afford to let him waste his time in teaching others, and that he should never send another bill to his father, but that whatever he wanted should be supplied, and he should not be expected to refund till after he had taken his degree.

Mr. Tavel felt himself more amply repaid for his munificence by his pupil's gratitude, and subsequent success, than by the ultimate discharge of the pecuniary debt. From that time Pollock was noted as a regular reading man, alternating his college studies with reading and reciting the best specimens of ancient and modern oratory, and with laying in an unusual stock of general literature. The effect of such studious habits was sure to be tested at the trial for his degree. After the examination, which took place in January 1806, a laughable incident occurred. He of course went to the senate-house, with a crowd of others, to see how he was placed. Another's name appeared to be at the top, bracketed alone with a line above and below. Then looking for his own, he got down to a name he felt certain could not be above his; and having gone carefully up the list, he found his name above the one he had supposed to be at the top, but pierced by the nail on which the paper hung, and that he had attained the honour to which he had aspired. In the next year he had an equal triumph in classics by being elected a fellow of Trinity; and his connection with the university was kept up long after his marriage had deprived him of his fellowship by receiving the appointment of its commissary.

Having been previously admitted a student at the Middle Temple in 1802, he was on November 27, 1807, called to the bar, where the reputation he brought from the university was one of the great elements of his future success. He joined the Northern Circuit, but did not attend any sessions, as his knowledge of bookkeeping and of commercial business in general was found so useful in cases of bankruptcy that it introduced him at once to considerable employment before the seventy lists of commissioners at that time existing. Many of the questions arising there requiring further investigation led consequently to his engagement in the actions that resulted in Westminster Hall, so that he almost immediately obtained full practice at Nisi Prius. On his circuit he was ultimately equally fortunate. Among the eminent advocates who attended it he soon acquired a prominent station, and at last had the undisputed lead. His business there was greatly increased before he had been three years at the bar by his very able and judicious management on the part of Captain (afterwards Admiral) Blake, in the famous trial of Colonel Arthur before a court-martial for his implication in a rebellion against the captain while governor of New South Wales. His success on that occasion attracted to his chambers many influential clients. A remarkable evidence of the rapid effect arising out of an occasional success happened to him. On the trial of a cause at the Guildhall sessions after Hilary Term in 1827, in which Mr. Brougham as his junior opened the pleadings, it was his fortune to gain a triumphant verdict against Sir James Scarlett, who led on the other side. At the ensuing spring assizes at Lancaster, where he had previously never had above four briefs, he found no less than sixty-one delivered to him. Mr. Pollock received his patent as king's counsel some weeks after.

In the forensic conflicts in which he was subsequently engaged he had the usual alternations of victory and defeat. In May 1831 he became member for Huntingdon, and in the autumn of 1834, when Sir Robert Peel became prime minister, he was at once promoted to the office of attorney-general, without having, as is usually the case, filled any minor post. His appointment, which was made on December 17, and was accompanied with the customary honour of knighthood, lasted only four months, Lord Melbourne's administration being restored to power, and retaining it for more than the five succeeding years. On the resumption of the government by Sir Robert Peel in 1841, Sir Frederick was replaced in his former office on September 6; and in April 1844 he was raised to the distinguished position he lately held, of lord chief baron of the Exchequer, and was immediately called to the privy council.

He continued to represent Huntingdon till his elevation to the bench. In the House of Commons, by his general deportment and unaffected eloquence, and particularly by the temperate manner in which he had on each occasion performed the duties of his responsible office of attorney-general, he occupied that most enviable position of being popular with both sides of the house, the evidence of which was specially shown in the cordial congratulations he received from opponents as well as friends on the brilliant victories at that time gained by his gallant brother, General Sir George Pollock, in the Indian campaign.

Of the chief baron's legal and judicial merits these pages profess not to speak. But at the end of two-and-twenty years from his appointment, and of near eighty-three from his birth, it may be allowed to record that he was to be found in his place exercising all the functions of his arduous office as efficiently as when he was at first appointed; frequently called upon to preside in most important cases, and never flinching from undertaking them; tempering his judgments so as not unnecessarily to hurt the feelings of those against whom he was obliged to decide; and ever acting towards his brethren on the bench, and the counsel at the bar of his court, so as to be a general favourite. On July 13, 1866, he retired from his position, having sat on the bench at a more advanced age than any common law judge before him; Lord Mans- field, though a little older when he actually resigned, having refrained from attending the court for two years before, when he was only eighty-one years old. To the last Sir Frederick never excused himself from his daily duties, but enjoyed the conflict of mind which arose in an important argument, and the exercise of his faculties called forth in addressing a jury. His merits were recognised by the immediate grant of a baronetcy. Having suffered little from attacks of illness, and retaining much of his former activity, he may be truly said to enjoy a green old age.

He has been long a fellow of the Royal Society, and among other essays contributed to that body he read in 1843, while he was attorney-general, a paper 'On a Method of Proving the Three Leading Properties of the Ellipse and Hyperbole,' and he still has delight in pursuing his mathematical studies.

Sir Frederick has been twice married. His first wife was the third daughter of H. Rivers, Esq., of Spring Gardens. His second wife was a daughter of Captain Richard Langslow, of Hatton near Hounslow, where Sir Frederick now resides. He had children by each of them, no less than twenty-five in all, of whom twenty survive, ten by the first union, and ten by the second. He can boast of a more numerous issue than is usually the lot of humanity. Besides his twenty children, he counts fifty-four grandchildren, and seven great-grandchildren; and he has had the gratification of seeing his eldest son's eldest son the first man of his year at his own alma mater.

PONTE, RICHARD DE, is inserted by Mr. Hunter among the numerous justiciers before whom fines were taken in 10 John (*Abb. Placit.* 83); but none of the fines hitherto published appear to have been acknowledged before him, nor do any of the contemporary rolls notice such a person.

PONTE AUDOMARE, HENRY DE, was a Norman, and in 1295 was custos of the escheats of the bailiwick of the Evrecin, and in 1298 bailiff of Caux. (*Rot. Scacc. Norm. Observations*, i. clxix., ii. cxxxiii.) He held one knight's fee in Perinton, of the honor of Gloucester, from the scutage of which he was excused in 7 John, and had a grant in 16 John of sixty shillings, the customs of the salt upon his land there. (*Rot. Claus.* i. 49, 206.)

His regular employment as a justicier for eight years is evidenced by his name appearing on fines acknowledged both at Westminster and in the country from 9 to 16 John inclusive. (*Rot. de Fin.* 484, 521.) It would seem that he soon afterwards got into disgrace, as his property fell into the king's hands, which is proved by an entry on the Close Roll of 2 Henry III., 1218, whereby it is ordered to be restored to him. (*Rot. Claus.* i. 339.)

He was entirely reinstated in the royal favour and entrusted in the same year with the custody of the lands of William Earl of Devon, and of Lucas Fitz-John; and there is a record in the next year of certain wool being seized in Northampton market by him and Ralph de Norwich, subsequently one of the justiciers. (*Rot. Claus.* i. 343–602.)

POORE, RICHARD (BISHOP OF CHICHESTER, SALISBURY, and DURHAM), appears once only in the character of a justice itinerant, being, as Bishop of Salisbury, at the head of those who in 3 Henry III., 1218, were appointed for Wiltshire, Hampshire, Berkshire, and Oxfordshire.

He was born at Tarent in Dorsetshire, and was made dean of Salisbury in 1197, 8 Richard I., from which he was raised to the bishopric of Chichester on January 7, 1215, 16 John. His translation to Salisbury occurred about June 1217, 1 Henry III.; and during the time that he held that see he undertook the removal of the cathedral church from Old Sarum, commencing the present magnificent building in 1219. The Close Rolls contain many royal grants of timber and other materials to aid this erection, to the progress of which he devoted the next nine years. Its completion, however, which occupied thirty years, he left to his successors, as he was advanced to the see of Durham in May 1228. There he presided for nine years, and died on April 15, 1237, with the character of a man of extraordinary sanctity and profound science. He founded a hospital for the poor at Salisbury, and greatly endowed a convent at the place of his birth, in the latter of which his heart was deposited, his body being interred in Salisbury Cathedral, or, according to Surtees (i. xxvii.), conveyed to Durham. (*Godwin*, 343, 504, 740; *Monast.* v. 619.)

POPHAM, JOHN, was descended from a family settled at Popham, a hamlet in Hampshire, early in the twelfth century. The estate of Huntworth in Somersetshire was acquired in marriage in the reign of Edward I.; and there John, the future chief justice, was born about the year 1531, being the second son of Alexander (or, as some say, Edward) Popham, of that place, by his wife Jane, the daughter of Sir Edward Stradling, of St. Donat's Castle, Glamorganshire.

He received his education at Balliol College, Oxford, whence he removed to the Middle Temple to pursue the study of the law. Instead of doing this, tradition charges him with entering into wild courses, and even with being wont to take a purse with his profligate companions. However this may be, he must have soon reformed, and, as Fuller says (ii. 284), 'applied himself to a more profitable fencing;' for he does not seem to have been delayed in obtaining the usual honours of his society. His nomination as reader took place in 1568, when he was thirty-seven years old; and he became treasurer twelve years afterwards. (*Dugdale's Orig.* 217, 221.) In the interval between these two dates he had obtained, as member for Bristol, a seat in parliament, where in 1571, when the subsidy was under discussion, he joined with Mr. Bell (the future chief baron) in calling for the correction of some abuses, and pointed out the evil of allowing the treasurers of the crown to retain in their hands 'great masses of money,' of which, becoming bankrupt, they only repaid an instalment. In the next year he was one of the committee appointed to confer with the Lords on the subject of the Queen of Scots. (*Parl. Hist.* i. 735, 779.)

He was called to the degree of the coif on January 28, 1578; and in the following year he was offered the place of solicitor-general. This office being inferior in rank to that of a serjeant-at-law, he obtained a patent exonerating him from the latter degree, and was thereupon appointed solicitor-general on June 26, 1579. (*Dugdale's Orig.* 127.) While holding that office he was elected speaker of the House of Commons in January 1581; and some idea may be formed of his wit, and also of the lightness of the parliamentary labours during that session, by his reply to Queen Elizabeth, when, on his attending her on some occasion, she said, 'Well, Mr. Speaker, what hath passed in the Lower House?' he answered, 'If it please your majesty, seven weeks.' His last and indeed principal duty in this capacity was the making the customary speech to the queen on presenting the subsidy voted at the end of the session. This was on March 18, after which that parliament never again met. (*Parl. Hist.* i. 311, 828.)

On June 1, 1581, he became attorney-general, and held that office for eleven years, during which he took part in all those criminal trials, the perusal of which, even where the guilt of the prisoners is most apparent, cannot but excite feelings of indignation at the gross injustice of the proceedings. His conduct in them, however, is not chargeable with any unnecessary harshness; and even in the opening of the unwarrantable charge against Secretary Davison he performed the difficult duty without any words of aggravation. (*State Trials*, i. 1051–1321.)

His elevation to the office of lord chief justice of the King's Bench took place on June 2, 1592, when he was immediately knighted. He presided in that court for the fifteen remaining years of his life—eleven under Queen Elizabeth, and four under King James.

He accompanied Lord Keeper Egerton in February 1600 to the Earl of Essex's house, as already related; and when Sir Ferdinando Gorges offered to deliver him from his forced detention there, he refused to depart without his companions in confinement, saying that 'as they came together, so would they go together, or die together.' This fact is not mentioned at the earl's trial, either in the chief justice's evidence or in Gorges' examination; but it is related by himself on the subsequent trial of Sir Christopher Blunt and others implicated in this insurrection, at which was exhibited the unbecoming spectacle of prisoners tried, and sentence pronounced, by a judge who had himself been a sufferer. (*Ibid.* i. 1340, 1344, 1428.)

One of his earliest duties after the accession of James was to preside at the trial of Sir Walter Raleigh—stained not only by a conviction founded on weak and unsatisfactory evidence, but also by that disgusting conduct towards the prisoner of Sir Edward Coke, which will ever disgrace his name, and for which the chief justice felt himself called upon to apologise, saying to Sir Walter, 'Mr. Attorney speaketh out of the zeal of his duty for the service of the king, and you for your life; be valiant on both sides.' (*Ibid.* ii. 10.) He would have done better to have silenced the brutal tongue.

The last state trials which he presided over were those against the conspirators in the Gunpowder Plot, finishing with that of Garnet the Jesuit, on March 28, 1606. (*Ibid.* ii. 159, 217.) He was then seventy-five years old; but he sat on the bench for another year, pronouncing a judgment in the Court of Wards as late as Easter Term 1607. On June 10, in the following term, he died, and was buried under a magnificent tomb in the church of Wellington in Somersetshire, where he had long resided in a stately house he had erected, and to which he left a testimony of his charity and goodwill by the foundation of a hospital for the maintenance of twelve poor and aged people.

Sir John died in possession of several valuable estates, one of which was that of Littlecott in Wiltshire. In connection with this a dark and improbable story is related of its having come into the chief justice's hands as the price of his corruptly allowing one Darell, the former proprietor, to escape on his trial for an atrocious murder. There is no doubt of the existence of such a tradition; it is told by Aubrey, who was certainly no admirer of the judge, and it is related by Sir Walter Scott in illustration of a ballad in Rokeby. Sir Walter does not give the judge's name, but that appears in full in other accounts both in prose and verse detailing the horrid particulars. It would be curious to trace the circumstances to which such a tradition owes its origin, especially in a case where every other incident in the career of the party implicated seems to render its occurrence impossible, and where contemporaries so eminent as Lord Ellesmere, Sir Edward Coke, and Sir George Croke give voluntary testimony to the purity of his character.

Lord Ellesmere, in the year after Popham's death, says of him, 'And here I may not omit the worthy memory of the late grave and reverend judge Sir John Popham, chief justice of the King's Bench, deceased, a man of great wisdom, and of singular learning and judgment in the law.' (*Ibid.* ii. 669.) Coke, not long afterwards, in reporting Sir Drew Drury's case (6 *Reports*, 75), says, 'And this was the last case that Sir John Popham, the venerable and honourable chief justice of England, &c., resolved, who was a most reverend judge, of a ready apprehension, profound judgment, most excellent understanding, and admirable experience and knowledge of all business which concerned the commonwealth; accompanied with a rare memory, with perpetual industry and labour for the maintenance of the tranquillity and public good of the realm, and in all things with great constancy, integrity, and patience;' and Croke, in noticing his death, calls him 'a person of great learning and integrity.' These are qualities which oppose the idea of the possessor of them being possibly guilty of such a dereliction of principle and duty as that with which the tradition charges him. If the petition which Sir Francis Bacon, in his argument against Hollis and others for traducing public justice, states was presented to Queen Elizabeth against Chief Justice Popham, and which after investigation by four privy councillors was dismissed as slanderous (*State Trials*, ii. 1029), could be found, it might possibly turn out that this story was the slander; and the chief justice's subsequent enjoyment of his high office would be a sufficient proof of its utter falsehood.

An able defender has at last been found. Mr. Long, in a recent article in the 'Wiltshire Archæological Magazine,' has not only refuted the story as it regards the chief justice, but raises reasonable doubt whether the charge against Darell himself is not altogether a myth. Aubrey's account, which is the first printed authority for the tradition, was written about eighty years after the judge's death; while Camden, the judge's contemporary, speaks of him as a man of 'distinguished virtue,' and, in writing of Littlecott, says nothing of the astounding crime of Darell, its late proprietor. Neither Symonds nor Evelyn, when mentioning the place, make any allusion to this mysterious tradition. Mr. Long confutes Aubrey's loose statement by proving that Darell was never a knight and was never married, as asserted, and that he died before Popham was advanced to the bench; so that he could not have been the judge who pronounced the supposed sentence. No record has been found of the trial, though every search has been made in the proper repositories. But a deposition has been found among some of Darell's papers in the Rolls Chapel, made before his relation and correspondent Anthony Bridges by the midwife concerned in the deed, whose story has evidently no reference to Darell or to Littlecott Hall, and was apparently taken in 1578, eleven years before Darell's death, and one year before Popham was even solicitor-general.

He is reputed to have been a severe judge, and, according to Fuller (*Worthies* ii. 284), to have recommended King James to be more sparing in his pardons to the malefactors who then infested the highways. This author adds, 'In a word, the deserved death of some scores preserved the lives and livelyhoods of more thousands, travellers owing their safety to this judge's severity many years after his death.' David Lloyd, in his 'State Worthies' (760), gives him credit for having 'first set up the discovery of New England to maintain and employ those that could not live honestly in the Old; being of opinion that banishment thither would be as well a more lawful as a more effectual remedy against these extravagancies.' And Aubrey (ii. 495) says that 'he stockt and planted Virginia out of all the gaoles of England.' Neither of these accounts is quite correct, the truth being that, having associated himself with Sir Ferdinando Gorges (the knight who released him from the Earl of Essex's house) in a speculation for the establishment of a colony in North America, and a patent having been granted to them and several others, their expedition sailed on December 19, 1606 (*Bancroft's America*, i. 123), about six months before the chief justice's death; so that whatever might have been his intentions as to transportation, he did not live to see them carried into effect.

After his death some Reports collected by him were published with his name; but the book is considered as of no authority.

The chief justice married Amy, daughter of Robert Gaines, of Glamorgan, Esq., and by her, besides several daughters, left a son, Sir Francis, whose descendants are still in possession of the Littlecott estate.

PORT, HENRY DE, was the son and heir of a great Norman baron named Hugh de Port, who held fifty-five lordships under William the Conqueror at the general survey, the principal of which was the barony of Basing in Hampshire.

By the roll of 31 Henry I. he appears to have been one of the justices itinerant acting in Kent, in which county part of his property was situated.

He founded the priory of West Shirburn in Hampshire, and endowed it with his manor of Shirburn. He also gave the tithes of his manor of Hageley, in Hawley, near Dartford, Kent, to the church of Rochester.

His wife's name was Hadewise, and by her he left two sons, John and William, the former of whom succeeded to his barony. John had a son Adam, generally supposed to be the under-mentioned justiciary. (*Dugdale's Baron.* i. 463; *Monast.* i. 170, vi. 1013; *Hasted*.)

PORT, ADAM DE, is stated by Dugdale (*Baronage*, i. 463) to be the grandson of the above Henry de Port, and the son of John de Port, and that he fled out of the kingdom and was outlawed in 1172, 18 Henry II., having become implicated in the treasonable machinations carried on against the king by his eldest son and Queen Eleanor. (*Lord Lyttelton's Henry II.* ii. 104.) But from the records and other documents of the period, the detail of which would be uninteresting, it is manifest that there were two individuals named Adam de Port, both probably descended from the same great-grandfather, and therefore second cousins, and that while one Adam was a fugitive, the other was in continued attendance on the king, and was the justice itinerant now to be noticed.

He was the son of Roger de Port by Sybilla de Albinero, and the grandson of another Adam, the brother of the above-noticed Henry. The Charter Rolls of King John contain numerous instances of his acting as a witness among the magnates of the land from the first to the fourteenth year. (*Rot. Chart.* 23–189.)

In 9 John he had the custody of the priory of Shireburn, then in the king's hands on account of the interdict (*Rot. Claus.* i. 108); and in 10 John he was one of the justiciers before whom fines were acknowledged at Carlisle; but he is not otherwise mentioned in a judicial character. On June 25, 1213, 15 John, the custody of the castle of Southampton was committed to him; but before the 25th of the following month he died. (*Rot. de Oblatis*, 477.) He married Mabil, the daughter of Reginald de Aurevalle, whose wife, Muriel, was the daughter of Roger de St. John, to whom Mabil ultimately became heir, and their son William assumed the name of St. John. The title of St. John of Basing, by which his descendants were summoned to parliament, eventually devolved, sometimes through female representatives, on William Paulet, Marquis of Winchester, which title still survives. (*Nicolas's Synopsis*.)

PORT, JOHN, was a native of Chester, where his ancestors were merchants for several generations. His father was Henry Port, a mercer in that city, who became mayor in 1486; and his mother was Anne, daughter of Robert Barrow, of Chester, who had also attained the same dignity.

Pursuing his legal studies at the Inner Temple, he reached the post of reader in 1507, and again in 1515, becoming treasurer in the latter year, and governor in 1520. (*Dugdale's Orig.* 163, 170.) In 1504 he was one of the commissioners for raising the subsidy in Derbyshire, and was attorney for the earldom of Chester. On May 31, 1509, he was constituted solicitor-general, the duties of which office he performed till Trinity Term 1521, when he was raised to the degree of the coif. (*Rot. Parl.* vi. 539; *Cal. State Papers* [1547–80], 132.)

Though Dugdale does not date his elevation to the bench till January 1533, it certainly took place several years before. He is called a judge of the King's Bench and a knight in the will of Lawrence Dutton of Dutton, proved on January 22, 1527–8 (*Lanc. and Cheshire Wills* [Chesham Soc.]), and he was summoned to parliament in that character in November 1529. He was again summoned in April 1536 (*Rymer*, xiv. 304, 565), and was one of the commissioners on the trials of Sir Thomas More and Bishop Fisher in 1535. His death occurred before November 1541.

He married twice. One of his wives was Margery, daughter of Sir Edward Trafford, of Trafford in Lancashire; and the other was Joan, widow of John Pole of Radburn, and daughter of John Fitz Herbert, remembrancer of the Exchequer, by whom he acquired the manor of Etwall in Derbyshire. (*Nicholls's Leicestershire*, 853.)

PORTESEYE, ADAM DE, is mentioned among the justices itinerant for the county of Hants in 9 Henry III., 1225, and there is no further reference to his name except that in the next year he assessed the quinzime for that county. (*Rot. Claus.* ii. 76, 147.)

PORTINGTON, JOHN, was of a Yorkshire family which was still flourishing at the end of the seventeenth century. Though we have not the date of his call to the degree of the coif, we find him appointed one of the king's serjeants on April 17, 1440, 18 Henry VI., and in the next year he acted as a justice of assize in Yorkshire. (*Kal. Exch.* iii. 283.) Three years afterwards he was made a judge of the Court of Common Pleas. (*Cal. Rot. Pat.* 285.) How long after Easter 1454, when the last fine was acknowledged before him (*Dugdale's Orig.* 46), he remained in the court we have no account, nor of the date of his death; but he was one of the executors of Ralph Lord Cromwell, treasurer of England, who died in January 1455. (*Testam. Vetust.* 276.)

PORTMAN, WILLIAM, belonged to a family which flourished in the county of Somerset from a period earlier than the reign of Edward I. His grandfather, William, was a reader at the Middle Temple, and by marriage with Christian, the daughter of William Orchard, acquired the estate of that name in the same county, to which he added his own; and it still remains with the double designation in the family. His father was John, also a member of the Middle Temple, where the judge himself became reader in 1532 and 1540. (*Dugdale's Orig.* 175, 215, 216.) He was called to the degree of the coif in the following Trinity Term, and was nominated one of the king's serjeants on November 23. In January 1541 he was sent to Plymouth on a commission to examine into an unlawful assembly of its inhabitants 'uppon a Portugalles ship.' (*Acts Privy Council*, vii. 115.)

His elevation as a judge of the King's Bench took place on May 15, 1546, and on the death of King Henry in the following year he was continued in his seat, which he retained during the whole of Edward's reign, and for the first two years of Mary's, when he was raised to the head of his court on June 11, 1555. His name frequently appears in the commissions for the trial of state prisoners, among whom was Sir Nicholas Throckmorton (*State Trials*, i. 894); but he presided over his court for little more than a year and a half, his death occurring on February 5, 1557. He was buried at St. Dunstan's-in-the-West, and his epitaph is given in Maitland's 'London' (p. 1095). Whatever religion he professed during the reign of Edward, he clearly belonged to the Roman Catholic body in the last years of his life, and was considered so earnest in that faith as to be sent to Sir James Hales, his brother judge, then in the Fleet, to persuade him to recant. (*Wotton's Baronet.* i. 221.)

Sir William's grandson was honoured with a baronetcy in 1612, which failed in 1695. The barony of Portman of Orchard-Portman was granted on January 27, 1837, to Edward Berkeley Portman, the present lord, a descendant of the eldest daughter of the first baronet, whose estates devolved upon him. (*Hutchins's Dorsetsh.* i. 87.)

POTERNA, JAMES DE, acted as a justicier from 9 Richard I., 1197, through the whole of the reign of John. (*Abb. Placit.* 83.) His name also appears on various itinera within the same time; and on one occasion he incurred a fine of one hundred marks for granting leave to settle a cause without the king's licence, which was, however, afterwards remitted. He was continued in his judicial position under Henry III., in the third year of whose reign he was one of the justices itinerant into Wiltshire, &c.

In 1200, 2 John, he was under-sheriff of York to Geoffrey Fitz-Peter, and was the principal instrument in despoiling the archbishop's lands and goods when he refused to pay the cornage imposed by the king. For his severity in the performance of this duty he was introduced by name into the sentence of excommunication fulminated by the irritated prelate. (*R. de Wendover*, iii. 154, n.) In 5 John the county of Wilts was committed to his charge, and in the next year the manor of Wellop in Hampshire was given to him for his support. This manor, in 17 John, the sheriff was ordered to deliver up to Roger Elys, 'si Jacobus de Poterna non sit ad servicium nostrum,' showing that in that troublesome period his fidelity was suspected. It would appear that he soon cleared himself, for the property was subsequently in his possession. He died in 5 or 6 Henry III. (*Rot. Claus.* i. 8, 114, 232, 475, 487.)

POWELL, THOMAS. There are three contemporaneous judges of the name of Powell, the Christian name of one being Thomas, and of two being John; of whom two sat on the bench in the reign of James II., two in that of William III., and for a short time in the same court, and one of them in the reign of Queen Anne. It is difficult always to distinguish them, and it is therefore not surprising that writers have frequently appropriated to one the character and the anecdotes and even the lineage which belong to another of his namesakes. Thomas, the subject of this memoir, is not so liable to this misapprehension as the two Johns. He was of Welsh extraction, tracing his lineage to the princes of North Wales. His father was John Powell, of Llechwedd Dyrys in the county of Cardigan; and his mother was Anne, daughter of Thomas Pryce, of Glanfread. On his admission to Gray's Inn in 1655 he is described as of Staple Inn, where probably he was initiated in legal studies. He was called to the bar in 1660, and after nearly four-and-twenty years' practice he was sworn a serjeant in 1684.

Three years after, on April 22, 1687, he was appointed a baron of the Exchequer, and was knighted; and on July 6 in the next year he was removed to the King's Bench in the place of Sir John Powell, turned out for the bold expression of his opinion in the case of the seven bishops. He had little opportunity of showing his legal ability, for his judicial career terminated a few months afterwards with the flight of the king. He survived his removal from the bench for sixteen years, and died in January 1705. He married Elizabeth, daughter and heir of David Lloyd of Aberbrwynen, by whom he left a son, whose descendant still occupies the family seat at Nanteos in Cardiganshire. (*Bramston*, 275, 311; *Luttrell*, 514.)

POWELL, JOHN, was the senior of the two John Powells who were contemporary judges, and was, like Sir Thomas Powell, descended from a very ancient Welsh family. He was the son of John Powell, of Kenward in Carmarthenshire, and was born about 1633. The inscription on his monument states that he received his first instructions from Jeremy Taylor, the renowned Bishop of Down, and subsequently at the university of Oxford, but Anthony Wood does not name him as taking any degree. His legal education commenced in 1650, at Gray's Inn, where he was called to the bar seven years after, and became an ancient in 1676. We have no detail of his professional experience till his nomination as a judge of the Common Pleas on April 26, 1686, when he was knighted. In the next Trinity Term he was called upon to give his opinion with the rest of the judges at Serjeants' Inn as to the king's dispensing power in Sir Edward Hale's case, when he required time for consideration; and, according to his own statement, the judgment was pronounced without his having had an opportunity to give his decision. The chief justice evidently considered that Powell coincided with the majority, and therefore he at that time escaped the dismission to which some of his fellows were subjected. He was removed to the King's Bench on April 16, 1687, and in the same month Thomas Powell was made a baron of the Exchequer, so that there were then two judges of the name. During the whole time he sat on the bench in James's reign he was always associated on the circuit with Sir Robert Wright, a junction which was probably dictated by the necessity of supplying Wright's deficiency with Sir John's profound knowledge of law. (*Bramston*, 225, 278; *State Trials*, xi. 1198; *Parl. Hist.* v. 333.)

Sir Robert Wright, a few days after Powell's appointment to the King's Bench, was restored to that court as its chief, and Powell was therefore an unfortunate and unwilling participator in the outrageous sentence on the Earl of Devonshire, fining him in the sum of 30,000*l.*, and committing him to prison till it was paid. It must be acknowledged that when called upon by the House of Lords after the revolution to account for this breach of privilege he made a very lame excuse. The Lords overlooked the offence, and contented themselves with voting the committal to be a breach of privilege, and the fine to be excessive. On June 29, 1688, came on the trial of the seven bishops, and the remarks made by Sir John Powell during its progress sufficiently indicated his opinion of the prosecution, and must have prepared his colleagues for the exposition of the law which he pronounced when his turn came. He declared that he could not see anything of sedition or any other crime fixed upon the reverend fathers, for they had with humility and decency submitted to the king not to insist on their reading his majesty's declaration, because they conceived that it was against the law of the land, it being founded on the dispensing power, which, he boldly said, if 'once allowed of, there will need no parliament.' The consequence of this honest demonstration, and of Justice Holloway's concurrence in it, was the bishops' acquittal, and the dismissal of both these judges, which took place on July 7, Sir Thomas Powell being substituted for Sir John in the King's Bench. (*State Trials*, xi. 1369, xii. 426; *Parl. Hist.* v. 311.)

On King William's government being established, Sir John Powell was immediately restored to his original seat in the Common Pleas, a place which he preferred to the more prominent one of keeper of the Great Seal, which, according to his epitaph, was offered to him. He was sworn in on March 11, 1689, and for the next seven years he administered justice in that court with undiminished reputation. He died of the stone at Exeter on September 7, 1696, and being removed to his mansion at Broadway, near Laugharne, in Carmarthenshire, he was buried in the church of that parish, where a tablet was erected to his memory. His son Thomas was created a baronet a short time afterwards, but the dignity became extinct in 1721. (*Luttrell*, i. 504, 509; *Gent. Mag.* July 1839, p. 22.)

POWELL, JOHN, Junior. As he and the last-mentioned judge sat at the same time in the same court, it almost unavoidably followed that frequent mistakes occurred as to their identity. Several biographers, as Chalmers, Noble, Britton, and others, have run in this error, confounding the two, and mixing up the history of the Carmarthenshire judge with that of the native of Gloucester, whose career is now to be related.

His family was originally resident in Herefordshire, but migrated to Gloucester, where his father held various municipal honours, and was mayor in 1663. The judge was born there in 1645, and became in 1664 a member of the Inner Temple, being called to the bar in 1671. In 1674 he was elected town clerk of his native city, and chosen representative of it to the sole parliament of James II. in 1685. In September of that year he was turned out of his office, but was restored in 1687, having first been obliged to make an application to the Court of King's Bench. (*Rudge's Gloucester,* 89; 2 *Shower*, 490.)

At the revolution he was included in the first batch of serjeants; and in May 1691, the king having ordered that the vacant seat in the Common Pleas should be filled by Mr. Powell, the serjeant named his officers and bespoke his robes; but by the interference of Sir John Trevor and others in behalf of Sir William Poulteney, the intended promotion was delayed till the king's return from Holland, when, Trevor's plot being counteracted, Powell was, on October 27, appointed a baron of the Exchequer instead. He was thereupon knighted, and remained in that court till October 29, 1695, when he was transferred to the Common Pleas, where he sat till the death of the king. Three months after the accession of Queen Anne he made another change, and on June 24, 1702, took his seat in the Court of Queen's Bench, which he graced with universal esteem and respect till the last year of her reign. He died at Gloucester, unmarried, on June 14, 1713, and was buried in the cathedral, where a monument, with an effigy of him in his robes, records his judicial excellencies. (*Luttrell*, ii. 220, 229; *Lord Raymond*, 769; *Rudder's Gloucester*, 119.)

During the two-and-twenty years he sat in one court or the other his conduct on the bench was without reproach; and in the last eleven he ably seconded the efficient rule of Chief Justice Holt. Distinguished as a profound lawyer, he was equally respected in his private life. Dean Swift represents him in his letter to Stella of July 5, 1711, as the merriest old gentleman he ever saw, speaking pleasant things and chuckling till he cried again. When Jane Wenham was tried for witchcraft before him, and charged with being able to fly, he asked her whether she could fly, and on her answering in the affirmative he said, 'Well, then, you may; there is no law against flying.' The poor woman was saved from the effects of her own faith, and received the queen's pardon. (*Fosbrooke's Gloucester.*)

POWER, WALTER, who was one of the commissioners of array for the counties of Bedford and Buckingham in 20 Edward III., held the manor of Brereby and other property in Yorkshire, part of which he gave to the prior of the convent of Monk Bretton. He was a clerk or master in Chancery from 25 to 47 Edward III., 1351–1373; and in that character was at the head of four in whose custody the Great Seal was left on March 18, 1371, during the temporary absence of the chancellor, Sir Robert de Thorpe.

He is noticed as holding the office of attorney-general to John of Gaunt, Duke of Lancaster, in 1336. (*N. Fœdera*, iii. 78, 483; *Abb. Rot. Orig.* ii. 220; *Cal. Inquis.* p. m. ii. 172; *Rot. Parl.* ii. 225–317.)

POWLE, HENRY, was rather a politician than a lawyer. His oratory was oftener heard in the chapel of St. Stephen's than in the courts of Westminster, and he owed his promotion to the office of master of the Rolls more to his being a whig leader than to his prominence at the bar. He was born about 1629, and was the younger son of Henry Powle, of Shottisbrooke in Berkshire, sheriff of that county in 1632, by Catherine, daughter of Matthew Herbert, of Monmouth.

From his being returned for Cirencester to the Convention Parliament of 1660, it may be presumed that he was known to be averse from a monarchical government, with a view to the resumption of which that parliament was summoned. In it he seems to have preserved a modest silence, and not to have spoken in the next till it had sat for nine sessions, occupying nearly twelve years. His first appearance, as reported, was in February 1673, when in a clear and convincing speech he exposed the tricks played by Lord Chancellor Shaftesbury in issuing writs for the election of members without the speaker's warrant, and procured a vote declaring all the returns under them void. He next by his strenuous opposition succeeded in obtaining the cancelment of the king's declaration of indulgence to dissenters; and from that time he took the lead in getting the Test Act through the house, and in all the other important proceedings of the session. In the remaining seven sessions he continued to be one of the most active heads of the country party in opposition to the court. That parliament, having lasted eighteen years, was brought to a close in January 1679; and to the next, summoned in the following March, he was returned by his old constituency. He distinguished himself in it by the bold stand he made against the king's rejection of the speaker (Seymour), thereby confirming to the Commons for the future their right to uncontrolled election; and also by his severe recapitulation of the crimes imputed to the Earl of Danby, thus securing the passing of the act of attainder which obliged the earl to surrender himself. In this session also some enquiries were made into the money distributed by ministers among the members who supported them for secret service. It is more than probable that neither party were free from contamination; for according to a late discovery several of the leading members of the opposition, and among them Powle himself is named, disgraced themselves by accepting large gratuities from the King of France.

Before the dissolution of this short parliament he was taken into the ministry as one of the thirty privy councillors, part whig and part tory, to whom by Sir W. Temple's advice the king confided the government. As might be expected from its heterogeneous materials, the structure fell to pieces in the following October; and Powle once more returned to the ranks of opposition. There he joined with Shaftesbury in his endeavours to exclude the Duke of York from the throne, and procured a strong declaration against the illegal and arbitrary discharge of the grand jury to avoid their presentment against the duke for recusancy. For this an impeachment was voted against Chief Justice Scroggs, who only avoided the consequence by a lucky dissolution of the parliament and a timely sacrifice of his place. Strongly prejudiced against the Roman Catholics, Powle gave his full belief to the existence of the Popish Plot; and as a manager for conducting the trial of Lord Stafford he summed up the evidence against him with peculiar severity. In the Oxford parliament of March 1681, which lasted only a week, Powle took very little part; and to the single parliament called by James II. he was not returned.

When that king fled to France, and the old parliamentary members were summoned, Mr. Powle was selected as their chairman, and presented the address to the Prince of Orange to take upon him the government till the meeting of the Convention on January 22, 1689. In that Convention, the second in which it was his fortune to have a place, he represented Windsor, and on its first sitting was unanimously chosen speaker. He had the satisfaction in that character of presenting the Declaration of Rights, and of hearing the prince and princess's acknowledgment of them in their acceptance of the crown. In the new arrangement of the judicial bench he received the post of master of the Rolls, and was admitted into the privy council. With the dissolution in January 1690 his senatorial life terminated.

He died on November 21, 1692, and was buried in Quenington Church, where there is a marble with a flattering inscription to his memory. He married, first, Elizabeth, daughter of the first Lord Newport, of High Ercall; and, secondly, Frances, daughter of Lionel Cranfield, first Earl of Middlesex, and widow of Richard Earl of Dorset. (*Atkyns's Gloucestersh.* 322; *Manning's Speakers*, 389; *Townsend's Commons*, i. 33; *Parl. Hist.* iv. v.)

Powle was a violent partisan in violent times; but he was evidently an honest one. Though his line of conduct cannot always be approved, it is difficult to credit the doubtful imputation of his receiving gratuities from the French king. His speeches bear the impress of sincerity; they were ready, effective, and often eloquent, particularly some of his addresses as speaker. For that office his historical knowledge and parliamentary learning peculiarly qualified him. How far they aided him in the distribution of justice as master of the Rolls we have but little means of knowing; but as no complaints have come down to us we may conclude that he performed his duties with efficiency. He was a member of the Royal Society, and an industrious collector of MSS., principally those relating to English history, a great part of which are now in the Lansdowne Collection in the British Museum.

POWYS, LITTLETON, was descended from the Princes of Powys in the twelfth century, according to his pedigree as authentically traced by veracious genealogists, who carry it down till the reign of Edward II., about which time the Welsh appendage was discarded, and the more pronounceable name of Powys adopted. The family subsequently divided into several branches, one of which settled in Shropshire. Thomas Powys, of Henley in that county, reader of Lincoln's Inn in 1667, and serjeant-at-law in 1669, by his first wife Mary, daughter of Sir Adam Littleton, Bart., was the father of four sons, the eldest of whom, who was baptized with his mother's maiden name, and the second, Thomas, both became judges. (*Collins's Peerage*, viii. 577.)

Littleton Powys was born about 1648, and was instructed in the mysteries of law at Lincoln's Inn, where he was called to the bar in May 1671. At the revolution he took arms in favour of William with three servants, and read aloud that prince's declaration at Shrewsbury. He was rewarded for his zeal by being made in May 1689 second judge on the Chester Circuit. In 1692 he was raised to the degree of the coif, and soon after knighted; and on October 29, 1695, he was promoted to the bench as a baron of the Exchequer. In that court, and afterwards in the King's Bench, to which he was removed on January 29, 1701, he sat during three reigns till October 26, 1726, when, being then seventy-eight years old, he was allowed to retire on a pension of 1500*l*. (9 *Reports Pub. Rec.*, App. ii. 252; *Lord Raymond*, 622, 1420.)

On the accession of George I. in 1714 Lord Cowper had represented to the king that as the judge and his brother frequently acted in opposition to their two colleagues in the court, it was expedient to remove one of them, and recommended that Sir Littleton should be retained, as a blameless man, though 'of less abilitys and consequence.' (*Lord Campbell's Chanc.* iv. 349, 364.)

He was a good plodding judge, though, according to Duke Wharton's satire, he could not 'sum a cause without a blunder,' and was somewhat too much inclined to take a political view in the trials before him. With moderate intellectual powers, he filled his office with average credit, but was commonly laughed at by the bar for commencing his judgments with 'I humbly conceive,' and enforcing his arguments with 'Look, do you see.' He is the reputed victim of Philip Yorke's badinage, who, dining with the judge, and being pressed to name the subject of the work which he had jokingly said he was about to publish, stated that it was a poetical version of Coke upon Lyttelton. As nothing would satisfy Sir Littleton but a specimen of the composition, Yorke gravely recited,—

> He that holdeth his lands in fee
> Need neither to shake nor to shiver,
> I humbly conceive; for look, do you see,
> They are his and his heirs' for ever.

That Sir Littleton was ridiculed by the bar appears in another metrical lampoon written by Philip Yorke, called 'Sir Littleton Powis's Charge in Rhyme, 1718,' humorously quizzing his insipid phraseology. (*State Trials*, xv. 1407–1422; *Cooksey's Lords Somers and Hardwicke*, 57, 66; *Harris's Lord Hardwicke*, i. 84.)

The judge lived nearly six years after his retirement, and died on March 16, 1732.

POWYS, THOMAS, was the brother of Sir Littleton, and only a year his junior. He filled a larger space in the history of his time, though he occupied a judicial position for the brief period of a year and a quarter. After being educated at Shrewsbury School, he became a student at Lincoln's Inn, and was called to the bar in 1673. Burnet calls him a young aspiring lawyer; and he certainly outstripped his elder brother in the race for legal honours, though neither of them had any eminence in legal attainments.

When James II. found that his law officers declined to comply with his arbitrary requirements, he selected Thomas Powys on April 23, 1686, to fill the post of solicitor-general, and thereupon knighted him. Offering no objection to the issue of warrants to avowed Papists to hold office, and arguing Sir Edward Hale's case in favour of the power assumed by the king to dispense with the test, he was advanced in December 1687 to the attorney-generalship. In that character he conducted the case against the seven bishops in June 1688, when the moderation, if not lukewarmness of his advocacy contrasted strongly with the indecent intemperance of Williams, the solicitor-general. It may readily be believed, as he expressed himself in a letter to the Archbishop of Canterbury in the following January, excusing his acting in that 'most unhappy persecution,' that 'it was the most uneasy thing to him that ever in his life he was concerned in.' (*Burnet*, iii. 91, 223; *State Trials*, xii. 280; *Clarendon's Corresp.* ii. 507.)

The abdication of James of course brought his official career to a close; and during William's reign, though he was a fair lawyer and fully employed, especially in the defences on state prosecutions, he remained on the proscribed list. From 1701 till 1713 he represented Ludlow; and at the beginning of Queen's Anne's reign he was made at one step serjeant and queen's serjeant; and before the end of it, on June 8, 1713, was promoted to a seat in the Queen's Bench, where his brother was then second judge. He did not long remain there, for, the queen dying in August 1714, King George on his coming to England superseded him on October 14, at the instigation of Lord Chancellor Cowper, who, though he allowed that he had 'better abilitys' than his brother, objected to him as zealously instrumental in the measures that ruined King James, and as still devoted to the pretender. He was, however, restored at the same time to his rank as king's serjeant. (*Lord Raymond,* 1318.) He survived his dismissal nearly five years, and dying on April 4, 1719, was buried under a splendid monument at Lilford in Northamptonshire, the manor of which he had purchased.

Though strongly opposed in politics, Burnet had evidently a high opinion of him; and Prior gives a graceful summary of his legal character in his epitaph.

He married twice. His first wife was Sarah, daughter of Ambrose Holbech, of Mollington in Warwickshire; his second was Elizabeth, daughter of Sir Philip Medows, knight; by both of whom he had a family. His great-grandson Thomas Powys was created Lord Lilford in 1797, and his descendants still enjoy the title. (*Collins's Peerage,* vii. 579.)

POYNTON, ALEXANDER DE, is named in 4 and 10 John as being present at Westminster when fines were levied before him; and he acted in the country also in those years; but his name does not again appear judicially. (*Hunter's Preface.*)

In 1 John he had a charter confirming a large grant of property in Lincolnshire, which had been made to him by Simon de Bret. This grant included the town of Wrengel in Hoyland, for which he obtained a market in 7 John. (*Rot. Chart.* 60, 156.) In 14 John he was entrusted with the sheriffalty of Lincolnshire, the duties of which he performed during the two following years. (*Rot. Pat.* 97.) But having then joined in the barons' war, he was taken prisoner in Rochester Castle in December 1215, and remained in confinement till the following July. His property was restored to him in 2 Henry III. (*Rot. Claus.* i. 241, 250, 308, 374; *Rot. Pat.* 190.)

POYWICK, WILLIAM DE, visited the counties of Huntingdon, Buckingham, and Northampton as justice itinerant in 46 and 47 Henry III., 1262–3. He was of the clerical as well as the legal profession. In 50 Henry III. he seems to have been raised to the bench, for from July 1266 till August in the following year there are entries of no less than eleven writs of assize to be held before him. (*Excerpt. e Rot. Fin.* ii. 440–459.) After the latter date his name does not appear.

PRATT, JOHN. The name of Pratt is highly distinguished in legal annals, having been borne both by a lord chief justice and by a lord chancellor, father and son. None of the biographers of the family state who the chief justice's father was; but they record that his grandfather, Richard Pratt, was ruined by the civil wars and obliged to sell his patrimonial estate at Carcwell Priory, near Collumpton, in Devonshire, which had been long in possession of his ancestors. The parents of John Pratt, however, had sufficient means to afford him a liberal education. He was sent to Oxford, and eventually became a fellow of Wadham College. He studied the law at the Inner Temple from November 18, 1675, till February 12, 1681, when he was called to the bar. He obtained sufficient prominence in his profession to be included in the batch of serjeants who were honoured with the coif in 1700, and to be employed in 1711 to defend the prerogative of the crown in granting an English peerage to the Scotch Duke of Hamilton, against which the Lords decided by a small majority. Speaker Onslow calls him a man of parts, spirits, learning, and eloquence, and one of the most able advocates of that time. (*Collins's Peerage,* v. 264; *Burnet,* vi. 80, n.) His success must have been very considerable to have enabled him to purchase in 1703 the manor and seat of Wilderness (formerly called Stidulfe's Place) in the parish of Seale in Kent. In the parliament of November 1710 he was returned for Midhurst, and again in February 1714, after the first session of which the queen died. In neither parliament did he take any prominent part in the debates, nor is there any appearance of his being specially connected with either of the political parties in the state; but on the accession of George I., by the recommendation of Lord Cowper he was appointed a judge of the King's Bench, on November 22, 1714, and knighted. In Hilary Term 1718 he gave a decided opinion in favour of the crown respecting the education and marriage of the royal family; and on the resignation of the Seals by Lord Cowper in the same year he was appointed one of the lords commissioners, holding that office from April 18 to May 12. Three days after he was elevated to the post of lord chief justice of the King's Bench.

He presided over the court for nearly seven years, and ably supported its dignity. In the only two reported criminal cases that came before him, those of Reason and Tranter for murder, and Christopher Layer for high treason, he acted with equal patience and fairness; and in the exercise of his civil jurisdiction his rulings are looked upon with respect and consideration. One of them, which has however been partially overruled, formed a subject for the wits of Westminster Hall. A woman who had a settlement in a certain parish had four children by her husband, who was a vagrant with no settlement. The chief justice decided that the wife's settlement was suspended during the husband's life, but that it was revived on his death, and that the children were then chargeable on the mother's parish. This judgment, though not regularly reported, is preserved and quoted in the following catch:—

> A woman having a settlement
> Married a man with none :
> The question was, he being dead,
> If that she had were gone.
>
> Quoth Sir John Pratt, 'Her settlement
> *Suspended* did remain
> Living the husband ; but he dead,
> It doth *revive* again.'
>
> Chorus of puisne judges :
> Living the husband; but he dead,
> It doth revive again.

Sir John died at his house in Ormond Street on February 14, 1725. He married twice. His first wife was Elizabeth, daughter of the Rev. Henry Gregory, rector of Middleton Stoney in Oxfordshire. His second wife was Elizabeth, daughter of the Rev. Hugh Wilson, canon of Bangor. She produced to him, besides four daughters, four sons, the third of whom, Charles, is the following chief justice of the Common Pleas and lord chancellor. (*Lord Raymond*, 1319, 1381.)

PRATT, CHARLES (EARL CAMDEN), was the third son of the above Sir John Pratt by his second wife Elizabeth, daughter of the Rev. Hugh Wilson, canon of Bangor. He was born in 1713, and was educated at Eton. Among his schoolfellows was William Pitt, afterwards Earl of Chatham, with whom he contracted a friendly intimacy, at first personal and eventually political, which was never interrupted till death closed the minister's career. From Eton Charles Pratt proceeded in 1731 to the university of Cambridge, honourably obtaining his election to King's College. Intending to pursue his father's profession, he had already, in June 1728, been entered at the Middle Temple ; and while waiting for his call and his degree he devoted himself diligently to the study of constitutional law. He took his degree of B.A. in 1735, and that of M.A. in 1740, having been called to the bar in June 1738, thirteen years after his father's death.

As the son of a chief justice he might fairly have expected early encouragement; but for some years his merits, though highly appreciated by his college associates and his brother barristers, failed to attract the dispensers of business, and his fee-book exhibited almost a total blank. On the eve of riding one of his western circuits he wrote to a friend, 'Alas! my horse is lamer than ever; no sooner cured of one shoulder than the other began to halt. My hopes in horseflesh ruin me, and keep me so poor that I have scarce money enough to bear me out in a summer's ramble; yet ramble I must, if I starve for it.' So disheartening were his prospects that he at last determined to retire on his fellowship at King's, and, entering the Church, to take his turn for one of the college livings. This resolution he communicated to his bar friend Sir Robert Henley (afterwards Lord Northington), who strongly dissuaded him from pursuing it, and induced him at least to try another circuit. Henley then contrived to get him retained as junior to himself in an important case, and, knowing that his talents only wanted an opportunity to be recognised, feigned illness at the hearing and left his young friend to defend the cause. This he did in so effective a manner as to secure him that full share of business which relieved him from any future anxiety.

He now had the opportunity of showing his soundness as a lawyer and his eloquence as an advocate, both on the circuit and in Westminster Hall, and the liberal principles which he enforced in those arenas and at the bar of the House of Commons soon marked him as a rising man. In the trial in 1752 of William Owen for publishing a libel he was engaged for the defence, and boldly insisted on the jury's right to judge both the law and the fact, which to the end of his life he so strenuously, and at last successfully, maintained. Owen's acquittal was one of the earliest instances of a jury adopting the same doctrine. He received a silk gown in 1755, and was appointed attorney-general to the Prince of Wales.

When his schoolfellow Pitt came into power, and the Great Seal was given to Sir Robert Henley, the attorney-general, on June 30, 1757, Pratt was immediately selected, with the consent of Lord Hardwicke, to fill the vacant post, and thus to be placed over the head of Charles Yorke, the solicitor-general. A seat in parliament was found for him as member for Downton in Wiltshire. Here he introduced a bill to extend the provisions of the Habeas Corpus Act to persons under impressment, which, though it was almost unanimously passed in the House of Commons, was thrown out by the Lords, being resisted by Lords Hardwicke and Mansfield. Though the judges were ordered to prepare another bill, it does not appear that they did so, and the remedy it sought to provide was delayed till the year 1803. The recordership of Bath was conferred upon him in 1759. In the parliament called after the accession of George III. he was elected by his former constituents, but within less than two months he vacated his seat for a more prominent position. While attorney-general he confined his practice to the Court of Chancery, except when engaged in state prosecutions. In them he exercised the utmost moderation and fairness, not seeking a conviction for the sake of a triumph, but satisfying all men's minds of the delinquency of the accused by the force of the testimony adduced against them.

The death of Sir John Willes in December 1761 created a vacancy in the office of chief justice of the Common Pleas, which was pressed upon Mr. Pratt, though his patron Mr. Pitt was no longer in power. With some reluctance he was obliged to accept it, and was accordingly knighted, and took his seat on the first day of Hilary Term 1762. In the following year commenced the important proceedings connected with the 'North Briton,' and its author, John Wilkes. The question of the legality of general warrants, and the actions for damages brought by the sufferers under them against those who executed them, were tried in the Common Pleas, where the known principles of the chief justice led the complaining parties to expect at least an unprejudiced hearing. His independent conduct throughout these investigations, his discharge of Wilkes from imprisonment, his boldness in pronouncing the general warrant of the secretary of state to be wholly illegal, with other similar proceedings in reference to the 'Monitor or British Freeholder,' raised him to the very height of popular favour. Numerous addresses of thanks were presented to him, with the freedom of the corporations of Dublin, Norwich, Exeter, and Bath in gold boxes. The city of London added to a similar honour the request that he would sit for his picture to Sir Joshua Reynolds. This portrait was hung up in the Guildhall, with a Latin inscription, written by Dr. Johnson, designating him the 'zealous supporter of English liberty by law.' Though these distinctions would seem to be a reflection on the general course of justice, as implying that in no other court would the same opinions have been expressed, it should be remembered, for the honour of the law, that the Court of King's Bench upon an appeal in one of the cases confirmed the ruling of Sir Charles Pratt.

A ludicrous story is told of his being on a visit to Lord Dacre in Essex, and accompanying a gentleman, notorious for his absence of mind, in a walk, during which they came to the parish stocks. Having a wish to know the nature of the punishment, the chief justice begged his companion to open them, so that he might try. This being done, his friend sauntered on and totally forgot him. The imprisoned chief tried in vain to release himself, and on asking a peasant who was passing by to let him out, was laughed at and told he 'wasn't set there for nothing.' He was soon set at liberty by the servants of his host, and afterwards on the trial of an action for false imprisonment against a magistrate by some fellow whom he had set in the stocks, on the counsel for the defendant ridiculing the charge and declaring it was no punishment at all, his lordship leaned over and whispered, 'Brother, were you ever in the stocks?' The counsel indignantly replied, 'Never, my lord.'. 'Then I have been,' said the chief justice, 'and I can assure you it is not the trifle you represent it.' (*Law and Lawyers*, i. 260.)

When Lord Rockingham's administration was formed in 1765, one of the first of its acts was to raise the chief justice to the peerage, and on July 17 he was created Lord Camden. He commenced his career in the House of Lords by exposing the injustice of taxing the unrepresented American colonies and by strenuously supporting the repeal of the Stamp Act. The Earl of Chatham the next year resumed power, and gratified himself and the public by giving on July 30, 1766, the Great Seal to his old friend Lord Camden, with the title of lord chancellor, who received at the same time the reversion of a tellership of the Exchequer for his son, with the usual pension for himself upon his retirement from the chancellorship. He then resided in Great Ormond Street. Ere long his position in the cabinet was anything but satisfactory to him, and after the secession of the Earl of Chatham he so strongly disapproved of many of its measures, especially in regard to the American import duties and the Middlesex election, that, publicly denouncing them as illegal and arbitrary, he was removed from his office on January 17, 1770. He was justly blamed for continuing so long in a cabinet whose counsels were opposed to the sentiments he entertained.

His bearing in the two courts of Common Pleas and Chancery supported the character he had acquired. To his profound legal knowledge and clearness of reasoning were added an attractive benignity and a graceful eloquence, which, according to Mr. Butler, was 'of colloquial kind—extremely simple—diffuse but not desultory. He introduced legal idioms frequently, and always with a pleasing and great effect. Sometimes, however, he rose to the sublime strains of eloquence; but the sublimity was altogether in the sentiment; the diction retained its simplicity, this increased the effect.' Many important questions were ventilated before him in both courts and in parliament, and though some of his decisions excited considerable controversy, none of them were overturned.

During the next eleven years he stood in the foremost rank of opposition to the ministry of Lord North, uniting with the Earl of Chatham in the arraignment of the American war, and as well in that question as in all others assailing Lord Mansfield with uniform and somewhat undignified acrimony. He evidently felt a deep personal animosity against his learned opponent, who undoubtedly quailed under the severe eloquence of his antagonist. In March 1782 Lord North was obliged to retire, and under the next two short administrations of Lord Rockingham and Lord Shelburne, Lord Camden filled the post of president of the council. During the Coalition Ministry, and the first year after Mr. Pitt's accession to power, he remained out of office, but resumed it in December 1784. In May 1786 he received the additional titles of Viscount Bayham and Earl Camden.

He continued to enjoy his office for the ten remaining years of his life, actively supporting the measures of his leader, without deserting the principles on which he had founded his fame. Though a zealous Pittite, he still continued essentially a whig—that party becoming every day less distinct from the tories, in consequence of its more moderate members not concurring in the factious extremes to which the spirit of party led the others. His last appearance in the House of Lords was as the strenuous assertor of the right of juries to decide on all questions of libel, a principle which he had always advocated, and which he lived to see triumphant.

From the commencement to the termination of his public life he was a universal favourite. His independence of character could not fail to secure the respect of his political antagonists, and his amiable disposition to engage the affection of all. Of social habits, yet of exemplary life, he retained the friendship of his youthful companions, and with true wisdom never failed to provide a succession of intimates to supply the place of those who were departed. His relaxation, like that of Lord Keeper Guilford, was a devotion to music and the drama; and he did not disdain to vary his graver studies with the light literature of the day. In his early years he was the author of a 'Treatise of the Process of Latitat in Wales,' published anonymously, but afterwards acknowledged.

He died on April 18, 1794, at the age of eighty, and was buried in Seale Church in Kent. His wife, Elizabeth, daughter of Nicholas Jeffreys, Esq., of The Priory in Breconshire, left him several children. His son succeeded to the earldom, and, having held with distinguished honour several responsible employments, was created a marquis on August 15, 1812, with the second title of Earl of Brecknock. To relieve the pecuniary pressure of the country, he with patriotic and magnanimous self-denial gave up to the state the large annual income derived from his office of teller of the Exchequer. He was elected a knight of the Garter, and his son, the late marquis, was decorated worthily with the same order. (*Collins's Peerage*, v. 265; *Lives by Welsby and Lord Campbell; Harris's Life of Lord Hardwicke.*)

PRESTON, GILBERT DE, was the son of Walter de Preston, who was in the service of King John, and on whose death in 1229 he paid 100 shillings for his relief on having his father's lands in Northamptonshire. (*Excerpt. e Rot. Fin.* i. 204.)

His name is first mentioned at the bottom of the list of the four justices itinerant who were assigned to take the Southern Circuit in 24 Henry III., 1240. He was probably not then one of the justiciers at Westminster, but was added to the commission in the same manner serjeants are at the present day. That he was raised to the bench before the Purification (February 2), 26 Henry III., there is no doubt, as fines were levied before him from that time, and in Easter of the same year his name appears on the pleas of the bench. (*Dugdale's Orig.* 43.) Till the end of this long reign no year occurs in which payments are not made for writs of assize to be taken before him.

Of his precise position on the bench these entries afford no certain evidence, the writs being principally addressed to him, as they were to other judges, alone. That he was eventually, however, raised to the highest place, 'capitalis justiciarius,' of the Court of Common Pleas, there can be no doubt, and as the transition from the old to the new forms occurred in this reign, it will be interesting to endeavour to trace the successive steps of his judicial career.

In 1242 he was at the bottom of the justiciarii de banco. From this time, judging from the lists of justices itinerant, he gradually advanced to a higher station, until in 1252 he stood at the head of one of the commissions, and retained the same position, with one or two slight exceptions, till 1257. It is not, however, to be presumed from this circumstance that he was then at the head of either of the courts, but simply that in the division of the circuits he was the senior in those he was appointed to take. Accordingly it appears that on October 3, 1258, he was the second of three, Roger de Thurkelby being the first, who were assigned to hold the King's Bench at Westminster until the king should arrange more fully. (*Cal. Rot. Pat.* 29.) In 1263 there are pleas before him and John de Wyvill at Westminster, and in 1267 pleas 'de banco' before him and John de la Lynde, which would seem to imply that he was no longer in the King's Bench, but that he acted in the Common Pleas. In the following year also he was called 'justiciarius de banco' (*Madox*, i. 236), and was at the head of the justices itinerant in various counties. His salary in 1255 was forty marks per annum, but in 1269 he had a grant of one hundred marks annually for his support 'in officio justiciariæ.' Although the term 'capitalis' is not used, the amount of this stipend shows that he was then chief justice, and it may be concluded that this was the date of his advance to that rank.

The actual title of chief justice does not seem to have been applied to him till the following reign, when, on his re-appointment by Edward I., he was so called in the liberate that grants him livery of his robes, and Dugdale remarks that he is the first whom he has observed to have the title of capitalis justiciarius of the Court of Common Pleas. He continued to preside there till his death, which occurred in 1274. (*Dugdale's Orig.* 39, 43; *Cal. Inquis.* p. m. i. 52.)

PRESTON, ROBERT DE, is erroneously introduced by Dugdale as receiving the appointment of chief justice of the Court of Common Pleas on October 5, 1377, 1 Richard II., but he never held that office in England.

He became a judge of the Irish Court of Common Pleas on October 17, 1342, 16 Edward III.; but it would seem that he was afterwards removed from the bench and returned to his practice at the bar, since there are records to show that in 1357 he acted as the king's serjeant-at-law in that country, and accompanied the lord justice in Leinster and Munster to plead and defend the pleas of the crown. On October 14, 1358, however, he was made chief justice of the Common Pleas in Ireland, and presided in that court during the remainder of Edward's reign, a period of nearly nineteen years.

The patent quoted by Dugdale is his reappointment, on the accession of Richard II., to the same seat, from which he was allowed to retire in the following April. In the eleventh year of that reign his services were again required, and he was constituted chancellor of Ireland, in which office he remained till October 25, 1389. Two years afterwards he received a patent as keeper of the Great Seal in Ireland, but was eventually relieved on May 29, 1393. (*Smith's Law Officers of Ireland*, 7, 114, 123, 132; *N. Fœdera*, iii. 833; *Cal. Rot. Pat.* 196, 216, 222, 226.)

PRESTON, JOHN, of a very ancient family settled at Preston-Richard and Preston-Patrick in Westmoreland, was the second son of Sir John Preston, who represented the county in 36, 39, and 46 Edward III.

He was employed in 18 Richard II., 1394, in the prosecution of one David Panell, adjudged to death for the murder of nine men and one woman; for his cost and labour in which the king gave him 2*l.* 6*s.* 8*d.* (*Devon's Issue Roll*, 261.) He was made recorder of London in 7 Henry IV., 1406, and was present in court in that character, declaring the custom of the city, in the thirteenth year of that reign. (*Y. B.* 16.) From this it may be inferred that his first practice was confined to criminal cases and the city courts. He was called to the degree of serjeant-at-law in 1411, and four years afterwards, on June 16, 1415, 3 Henry V., was raised to the bench of the Common Pleas, up to which time he continued to hold the recordership. He remained in that court throughout the reign of Henry V., and up to Hilary Term, 6 Henry VI., when, on January 28, 1428, being broken down with age, he was exonerated from his office and permitted to retire. The date of his death is not recorded, but he left a son, Richard, whose descendants continued to enjoy the property, and became at last possessed of the manor of Furness in Lancashire, by which title one of them, named John, was created a baronet in 1644—a dignity which became extinct in 1710.

PRICE, ROBERT, a descendant from the ancient stock of one of the noble tribes of Wales, was the son of Thomas Price, of Geeler in Denbighshire, and of Margaret, daughter of Thomas Wynne, of Bwlch-y-Beyde in the same county. He was born in the parish of Cerrig-y-Druidion on January 14, 1653, and, after receiving his education at Wrexham, and St. John's College, Cambridge, he entered Lincoln's Inn in 1673. In 1677 he took the grand tour, and spent two years in visiting all parts of France and Italy. Among the books which he took with him was Coke upon Lyttelton, which the scrutinising officers at Rome thought was an heretical English Bible, and seizing it carried off its possessor to the pope. Mr. Price soon satisfied his holiness that the laws it illustrated, though not divine, were orthodox; and presenting it to the holy father, it is to be hoped that it still graces the Vatican Library. On his return he was called to the bar in July 1679.

In September he married Lucy, daughter of Robert Rodd, Esq., of Foxley in Herefordshire. After being the mother of three children, it seems that her misconduct dissolved the connection. Under the date of November 21, 1690, Luttrell (ii. 231) records that 'Robert Price, Esq., got 1500*l.* damages in an action against Mr. Neal for *crim. con.*' He did not obtain a divorce, but, though she survived her husband, the 'Life' that was published of him immediately after his death omits all subsequent allusion to her; and the judge's will, which speaks with affection of, and provides with liberality for, all his other connections, only coldly mentions her in a legacy of 20*l.* 'for mourning,' and in a charge on his estates of an annuity of 120*l.* 'pursuant to a former agreement and settlement between us.'

He was made attorney-general of South Wales in 1682, and recorder of Radnor in the following year. He was complimented also by being elected alderman of Hereford, about five miles from his seat at Foxley. On the death of Charles II. King James appointed him steward to the queen dowager, and king's counsel at Ludlow. The corporation of Gloucester also elected him town clerk in 1687, in the place of Mr. (afterwards Justice) John Powell; but upon the latter appealing to the Court of King's Bench, Mr. Price consented to his restoration. (2 *Shower*, 490.) In James's short and only parliament he represented Weobly.

King William removed him from his Welsh attorney-generalship. Although of course he was not returned to the Convention Parliament, he was elected by his former constituents to that summoned in the next year, and also for the two following in 1695 and 1698, and that which met in December 1701. In 1695 he distinguished himself by strenuously opposing the exorbitant grant made by the king to the Earl of Portland of extensive lands and lordships in Wales, and enforced his objections with such power and effect that upon an address of the house the king was obliged to annul it. In the next year he took an active part in the proceedings in Sir John Fenwick's case. The only state trial in which he was engaged as counsel was that of Lord Mohun in the House of Lords for the dastardly murder of William Mountford the actor, which resulted in the acquittal of his client; and the only promotion he received was that of a Welsh judgeship in 1700, when the tories had regained power, which appointment he held to the end of the reign. (*Parl. Hist.* v. 979, 1016, 1041, 1045; *State Trials*, xii. 1020.)

On the accession of Queen Anne, Mr. Price was constituted a baron of the Exchequer on June 14, 1702. In this court he remained the whole of that reign and nearly to the end of the next, when he obtained a removal into the Common Pleas on October 16, 1726. The excellent manner in which he performed his judicial duties may be estimated by the following lines in some eulogistic verses written after his death:—

When Price reviv'd the crowding suitors' sight,
The Hall of Rufus was the seat of Right.
In all her arts was Fallacy beguil'd,
The orphan gladden'd, and the widow smil'd;
Sure to behold, in ev'ry just decree,
The friend, the sire, the consort, shine in thee.
Mild Equity resum'd her gentle reign,
And Bribery was prodigal in vain.

In 1718 he and Mr. Justice Eyre were the only two judges who gave an opinion adverse to the king's claim of prerogative with regard to the education of the royal grandchildren, and supported their view by an able argument delivered to his majesty. George II. was of course impressed in his favour, and on coming to the crown continued him in his place, which he filled during the remainder of his life. After a long judicial career of no less than thirty-one years, he died on February 2, 1733, and was buried in the church of Yazor in the county of Hereford.

The 'Life' of Mr. Justice Price, written by its publisher, the notorious Edmund Curll, within a year of his death, is the foundation of all the biographical notices that have since appeared. As it was compiled 'by the appointment of the family,' it cannot fail to be regarded as little more than an extended epitaph, and the eulogies of which it is full would naturally be received with considerable qualifications. Yet, making due allowance for its party exaggerations, and for some errors in facts and dates, which its copyists have carelessly repeated, from all that can be collected of his career, the character that it gives him is substantially true. Though a steady tory in politics, no whig pen writes a word in his dispraise; his courage in opposing the royal wishes receives no check, in consequence of the known honesty of his principles; his desire and pains to get at the truth of matters on which his opinion was required is evidenced by letters recently published by the Camden Society; and his charity is manifested by his erection and endowment of an almshouse for six poor people in the parish of his birth, and by the care that he took in his will not only for the perpetuation of that institution, but for the continuance also of his other benefactions.

As he never received the knighthood by which the judges were usually distinguished, it may be presumed that he declined the honour. The grandson of his son, Uvedale, who succeeded to his estates, received a baronetcy in 1828, which became extinct in 1857.

PRIDEAUX, EDMOND, who belonged to an ancient and honourable family, tracing its lineage as far back as the Norman Conquest, when it was seated in Prideaux-castle in Cornwall, was the second son of an eminent lawyer of the same name, by Catherine, daughter of Piers Edgecombe, Esq., of Mount Edgecombe in Devonshire. The father in 1622 received from King James the dignity of a baronet, which survives at the present day. (*Wotton's Baronet.* i. 517.)

Edmond was born at his father's residence at Netherton, near Honiton, and seems to have received his education in the university of Cambridge, and to have taken his master's degree there, since, some years after, in July 1625, he was admitted *ad eundem* at

Oxford. His legal course is traced with greater certainty, having been called to the bar at the Inner Temple on November 23, 1623. His name does not appear in the Reports of Charles's reign, his practice being chiefly in Chancery; but at one time he was recorder of Exeter. (*Fasti Oxon.* i. 424, ii. 66.) The electors of Lyme-Regis in Dorsetshire returned him in 1640 as a member of the Long Parliament, where he took the popular side, and subscribed in June 1642 100*l.* towards its defence. (*Notes and Queries,* 1st S. xii. 359.) He was an active partisan, and when the two houses adopted a Great Seal of their own he was one of the four members of the House of Commons, who with two peers were nominated commissioners on November 10, 1643. He filled the post for nearly three years, the parliament then changing the custody of the Seal and placing it in the hands of the speakers of the two houses on October 30, 1646. While holding this office he still kept his place in the House of Commons, and was named as one of the commissioners who assembled at Uxbridge in January 1645, to negotiate a treaty of accommodation with the king. On his removal from the Great Seal the Commons ordered that, as a mark of honour and of their acknowledgment of his services, he should practise within the bar, and have precedence next after the solicitor-general. (*Journals; Whitelocke,* 92, 125, 226.)

Prideaux then resumed his professional practice till 1648, when the parliament, on filling up the vacancies on the bench, named him solicitor-general on October 12. When he saw, however, what proceedings were adopted for taking the king's life, it is evident that he threw up the office; for on Charles's trial in the succeeding January William Steele acted as attorney, and John Cook as solicitor-general (*Ibid.* 342, 357, 368); and also on the subsequent trials of the Duke of Hamilton and others. (*State Trials,* iv. 1167, 1209.) That he lost no favour with the parliament by his conduct in avoiding these trials is apparent from his receiving the appointment of attorney-general on the 9th of the following April, and from his retaining it during the remainder of his life, through all the different changes that took place in the government. During the whole of this time he continued member for Lyme Regis. (*Whitelocke,* 394; *Parl. Hist.* iii. 1429, 1480, 1532.) The dignity of baronet was conferred upon him on May 31, 1658, 'in respect of his voluntary offer for the mainteyning of 30 foot-souldiers in his highnes army in Ireland.' (5 *Report Pub. Rec.,* App. 273.) He survived Cromwell about a year, dying on August 19, 1659.

Whitelocke describes him as 'a generous person, and faithful to the parliament's interest. A good Chancery lawyer.' This is not great praise; and it seems that he was equally faithful to his own interest. Besides his practice at the bar, which was worth about 5000*l.* a year, he was postmaster for all the inland letters, an office which, at sixpence a letter, is said to have netted him 15,000*l.* a year. (*Parl. Hist.* iii. 1606.) No wonder, therefore, that he made a large fortune, and that he was enabled to purchase Ford Abbey in the parish of Thorncombe, Devon, and to build on its ruins a noble mansion.

He married two wives: the first was a daughter of — Collins, Esq., of Ottery St. Mary in Devonshire; the second was the daughter of — Every, Esq., of Cottey in the county of Somerset, by whom he left an only son, also named Edmond. (*Wotton's Baronet.* i. 513; *Hasted,* xii. 27.)

PRISOT, JOHN, was a native either of Kent or Hertfordshire: in the former county his family possessed the manor of Westberies, in the parish of Rucking, in the reign of Henry IV., where his descendants continued till they sold it in that of Henry VIII. (*Hasted,* viii. 355); and in the latter the judge held the manor of Wallington, in which his widow, Margaret, resided after his death. (*Chauncy,* 48.) Though we have no account of the court of his practice previous to his being called to the degree of the coif in 21 Henry VI., 1443, it is evident that he must have already acquired some reputation as a lawyer, as six years afterwards, on June 16, 1449, he was advanced to the office of chief justice of the Common Pleas. 'Certen ordinances made in the tyme of Sir John P'sott, chef justice of the Commen Place, touchyng the officers there,' are to be found in p. 8 of the first volume of the 'Recovery Indexes' now in the Record Office. He continued to preside in the court till Edward IV. had seized the throne, when he was not re-appointed. As we do not find that he took any decided part in the contest between the royal rivals, it is not improbable that, if his death did not occur about that time, he took the opportunity of the commencement of a new reign voluntarily to retire to private life.

In one of the letters of the 'Paston Correspondence' (i. 29) he is represented as a partial judge, but this is merely the representation of a disappointed partisan in a particular case. There is no doubt that he was a considerable and expert lawyer; and he is said to have given 'great furtherance' to Judge Lyttelton in the composition of his 'Tenures.' (*Dugdale's Orig.* 58.)

PROBYN, EDMUND, whose ancestors were long known and esteemed among the gentry of the county of Gloucester, was the son of William Probyn, of Newland in the Forest of Dean, and of Elizabeth, daughter of Edmund Bond, of Walford in Herefordshire.

He was born about 1678, and went through the legal curriculum at the Middle Temple, where he took the degree of barrister in 1702.

After spending nearly twenty years in the usual forensic drudgery of the profession, he occupied the position of a Welsh judge in 1721. Called serjeant in 1724, he was employed in January of the next year by the Earl of Macclesfield to conduct the defence against his impeachment; but, notwithstanding the pains he took and the lucid argument he delivered, he failed to satisfy the peers of his client's innocence. (*State Trials*, xvi. 1080.) The ability he showed on that occasion no doubt pointed him out for promotion, and accordingly, on November 4, 1726, he was constituted a judge of the King's Bench, and knighted. He displayed so much learning and judgment in the exercise of this office for fourteen years that he was selected on November 28, 1740, to succeed Sir John Comyns as lord chief baron of the Exchequer, a dignity which he held less than eighteen months, his death occurring on May 17, 1742. He was buried in Newland Church.

He married Elizabeth, daughter of Mr. Justice Blencowe, but left no issue.

PUCKERING, JOHN, was the second son of William Puckering, of Flamborough in the county of York. He was born about 1544, and, entering at Lincoln's Inn, he was called to the bar on January 15, 1567. He became one of the governors in 1575, and was elected reader in 1577, at the age of thirty-three, a proof that he had made himself remarkable for his learning at a very early period. He was raised to the degree of the coif in 1580, and was made queen's serjeant in 1586, when he conducted the trial of Abington and others for high treason, and also took part in the proceedings against Secretary Davison in March 1587. (*State Trials*, i. 1143, 1233.)

In the parliament of 1585, Puckering, having been returned for Bedford, was elected speaker. During the session he had to reprimand Dr. William Parry (shortly afterwards executed for high treason) for the intemperate speech he uttered on the passing of the bill against Jesuits, and at the end of it to address the queen on presenting the subsidy granted—duties which he performed with so much discretion and propriety that he was re-elected speaker of the new parliament opened on October 15, 1586, by which the fate of the Scottish queen was decided.

In a few days after the execution of the unfortunate Mary the speaker was again called upon to check the rising demand for greater freedom of debate. The immediate question was quickly decided by the committal of Mr. Wentworth and four others to the Tower (*Parl. Hist.* i. 822–852); but the spirit was not subdued. The attempt to control it was afterwards attended with serious consequences, and its ultimate recognition, though leading occasionally to fiery discussions, has been happily found to be practically conducive to the real benefit of the realm.

In the following parliament, which sat from February 4 to March 29, 1589, Puckering was not called to the chair, probably because his services were required on the state trials which were then proceeding. In the arraignment of Sir Richard Knightley and others in the Star Chamber on February 13, he enlarged on the evil tendency of the different libels—'Have you any Work for the Cooper?' and others—with the publication of which they were charged. On April 18 he again appeared as the leader for the crown on the trial of Philip Earl of Arundel for high treason, conducting it without any unnecessary harshness.

The last trial of which he had the conduct as queen's serjeant was that of Sir John Perrot, lord-deputy of Ireland, after which, between the verdict and sentence, the Great Seal was placed in his hands as lord keeper, on May 28, 1592, the honour of knighthood being conferred upon him at the same time. During the four years that he sat in the Court of Chancery he preserved a 'good repute for his own carriage, but unhappy for that of his servants, who for disposing of his livings corruptly left themselves an ill name in the Church, and him but a dubious one in the state.' (*State Worthies*, 609.)

He presided over only one parliament as lord keeper, and in his opening speech, after declaring the queen's will that there should be no new statutes passed, he added, 'So many there be that, rather than to burthen the subjects with more, to their grievance, it were fitting an abridgment were made of those there are already.' (*Parl. Hist.* i. 859.) If subsequent legislators had acted on this principle, the cry for a digested code would not now be so loud, nor its execution so difficult.

He died on April 30, 1596, and was buried in Westminster Abbey. By his wife, Anne, daughter of Nicholas Chowne, Esq., of Kent, he left several children. His son and heir, Thomas, was created a baronet in 1612, but died without surviving issue in 1636. One of the lord keeper's daughters having married Adam Newton, tutor to King James's son Prince Henry, also created a baronet, her son Sir Henry became heir to the Puckering estates on the death of his uncle, and assumed the name, but that title also expired in 1700. (*Manning and Bray's Surrey*, i. 446; *Hasted*, i. 423; *Wotton's Baronet.* iv. 270.)

PULESTON, JOHN, of a very ancient

family settled at Emral in Flintshire as early as the reign of Edward I., was the son of Richard Puleston, by Alice, daughter of David Lewis, of Bulcot in Oxfordshire; and received his legal education at the Middle Temple, where he became reader in 1634. (*Dugdale's Orig.* 220.) In February 1643 he was recommended by the Commons as a baron of the Exchequer in the propositions they made to the king. (*Clarendon*, iii. 407.) Failing in this application, they invested him with the dignity of the coif in October 1648; and after the king was beheaded he was substituted for one of the judges who then refused to act, and took his place as justice of the Common Pleas on June 1, 1649. (*Whitelocke*, 342, 405.) His conduct in the following August at the assizes at York, when he and Baron Thorpe tried and condemned Lieut.-Colonel Morrice, the governor of Pomfret Castle, for high treason, speaks strongly against his justice and humanity. (*State Trials*, iv. 1249.)

It seems probable, though he did not die till September 5, 1659, that Cromwell, when he become protector in 1653, did not renew his patent; for then, by the appointment of Sir Matthew Hale, the court had its full complement.

By his marriage with Elizabeth, daughter of Sir John Woolrych, knight, he had a son, the last of whose male descendants died, leaving an only daughter, who carried the estate of Emral to her husband, Richard Price, Esq. Their son took the name of Puleston, and was created a baronet in 1813.

PUSAR, or PUDSEY, HUGH (BISHOP OF DURHAM), is said to have been the son of a sister of King Stephen, who in a charter to him 'De Mineraria in Werdale' calls him 'nepoti meo.' (*Surtees' Durham*, i. cxxvi.) In that reign he became treasurer of York, archdeacon of Winchester, and ultimately Bishop of Durham. (*Le Neve*, 289, 319, 347.) To this last dignity he was elected on January 22, 1153, but was refused consecration by the Archbishop of York, as well because of his age, which did not exceed twenty-five years, as on account of the irregularity of his life, evidenced by his having three illegitimate sons by as many mothers. The pope, to whom he applied, listened to the representations of the archbishop; but the death of both put an end to the objections, and the new bishop obtained consecration from the succeeding pontiff on December 20, 1153. His conduct in his see was correct and praiseworthy, and his memory will last while the beautiful building called the Galilee, which he added to the cathedral, exists. His munificence extended throughout his diocese in many useful and pious works. He caused a survey to be made of the possessions of the see, which is known as the 'Boldon Book,' and has been published by the Surtees Society.

He was present at the council of Tours in 1163, and at that of Lateran in 1179. In the early part of his career he mixed little in politics; but in 1170 he assisted at the coronation of Prince Henry, the son of Henry II., an act which, at the instigation of Becket, occasioned his temporary suspension by Pope Alexander from his episcopal duties. When this young prince and his brothers rebelled against their father in 1173, the bishop found himself suspected of adhering to their party, and deemed it prudent to deliver into the king's hands his castles of Durham, Norham, and Alverton. The latter was totally destroyed, but the two former were some time after restored to the prelate, on the payment of a fine of two thousand marks; while the king, as a proof of his recovered favour, granted to his son Henry the royal manor of Wickton. A few years afterwards he got into a new disgrace with King Henry by a somewhat pert answer he sent to him. Roger, Archbishop of York, had made a verbal will, which Henry declared to be invalid, and demanded of Pusar, who was one of the executors, the restoration of three hundred marks which he had received of the property. The bishop replied that he had distributed them, as directed by the deceased, among the poor, the blind, and the lame, from whom he could not collect them again. Henry resented this by depriving him of his palace at Durham till the money was returned. The bishop, however, was employed by the king in 1188 in collecting in Scotland the disme he had imposed for his purposed expedition to the Holy Land.

When Richard succeeded to the throne, and, for the purpose of raising funds to carry on the Holy War, exposed offices, honours, and estates to sale, the bishop, urged by ambitious promptings, was induced to give a large sum for the enjoyment, during the short remains of his life, of the earldom of Northumberland. Even the king, though benefiting by the infatuation, could not refrain from a sneer, remarking at his investiture upon his cleverness in thus being able to make a young earl out of an old bishop. At the same time, and for a further consideration, he appointed him, in conjunction with William Earl of Albemarle, chief justiciary of the kingdom, associating with them five others as a council for the government of the realm during his absence. (*Madox*, i. 21, 34.) The Earl of Albemarle, however, dying two months afterwards, and before the king's departure, the chancellor, William de Longchamp, Bishop of Ely, was named in his stead. The government of England north of the Trent was entrusted to the Bishop of Durham, while the Bishop of Ely's authority was limited to the south of that river. As might naturally be expected, however, the sole power was soon usurped by the latter, who, not content with this, deprived his weak coadjutor of his newly-acquired earldom, and seized his person till he gave hostages for the delivery of the king's castles committed to his charge. The king's commands for his reinstatement were disregarded, nor were the castles restored to him till the fall of the arrogant chancellor. Pusar was not, however, replaced in the office of chief justiciary, which was then given to Walter, Archbishop of Rouen.

He died on March 3, 1195, having presided over his see above forty-two years. (*Godwin*, 735; *Lord Lyttelton*, iii. 152, 290-363; *Ric. Devizes*, 8, 11, 39; *R. de Wendover*, ii. 298, iii. 9-15.)

PYMME, THOMAS, whom Dugdale calls in one place Pyne, was appointed a baron of the Exchequer on September 30, 1562; but nothing whatever is recorded of him, except that he died a short time before his successor, James Lord, received his patent, on November 12, 1566.

PYNCHEBEK, THOMAS, whose family received its name from a parish so called in Lincolnshire, was made chief baron of the Exchequer on April 24, 1388, 11 Richard II., and his successor, John Cassy, was appointed on May 12 of the following year. That this change was occasioned by his death appears probable, as part of the Lincolnshire property of Sir John de Bello Monte, who died in 20 Richard II., is stated to have come from 'the *heirs* of Thomas de Pynchbek.' (*Cal. Inquis.* p. m. iii. 199.)

Q

QUINCY, SAHERUS DE (EARL OF WINCHESTER), was the second son of another Saherus de Quincy, who was possessed of the lordship of Buchby in Northamptonshire, by royal grants from Henry II. and Richard I. His mother was Maud de St. Liz, daughter of Simon Earl of Huntingdon, and widow of Robert Fitz-Richard, of Tunbridge. He was early in the confidence of King John, and was present at Lincoln when William, King of Scotland, did homage. (*Madox*, i. 665.)

In 5 John, Robert Fitz-Walter and he, being besieged in the castle of Ruil in Normandy, of which they had the command, delivered it up without resistance to the French king, who, disgusted at their apparent treachery, placed them in strict confinement. He, however, succeeded in satisfying King John, for in the next year, on the death of Robert de Breteuil, Earl of Leicester, whose sister Margaret he had married, he had a grant, on a fine of one thousand marks, of all the earl's lands; to which was added in 7 John, on another fine of five thousand marks, the lands of the honor of Grentemesnil. (*Rot. de Liberate*, 38; *Rot. de Fin.* 268, 320.)

In the charter of 8 John, 1210, Saherus is for the first time called Earl of Winchester, to which dignity he had been just raised. (*Madox*, i. 51.) He was in personal attendance on the king in 11 and 12 John, accompanying him into Ireland, and partaking, according to the record, of his amusements at play. (*Rot. Misæ*, 152, 162; *Rot. de Præstito*, 183-240.)

For the three following years he acted as a justicier, fines being levied before him in 13 and 15 John, and his name being mentioned in Rot. Claus. 14 John, as one of those 'tunc ad Scaccarium residentes.' (*Rot. Claus.* i. 132; *Dugdale's Orig.* 50.)

Although he had hitherto continued loyal to the king, and had been one of the witnesses to the resignation of the crown to the pope on May 15, 1212, and afterwards one of the sureties for the restitution to the clergy, he eventually joined the insurgent barons; and being chosen of the twenty-five who were appointed to secure the fulfilment of Magna Charta, he underwent in consequence the pope's excommunication. He was one of the ambassadors from them sent to invite Louis of France to assume the throne, and, adhering to him even after the accession of Henry III., was defeated and taken prisoner at the battle of Lincoln, on May 19, 1217.

On his submission, however, to the king, his lands were restored, and he went the next year to the Holy Land, where he was present at the siege of Damietta. He died in 1220 on his journey to Jerusalem, and was succeeded by his son Roger, on whose death, in 1264, without male issue, the title became extinct. (*Baronage*, i. 686; *Roger de Wendover*; *Nic. Trivetus*, 206.)

R

RADECLYVE, THOMAS DE, a native of Radcliff on Sore in the county of Nottingham, was summoned among the judges to the great council at Westminster in 17 Edward II. He was the last named of six justices itinerant into Bedfordshire in 4 Edward III., 1330, and was sub-sheriff of the county of Nottingham in the same year, as appears by a complaint made against him in parliament, the result of which is not recorded. (*Issue Roll,* ii. 1319; *Rot. Parl.* ii. 411.)

RADENHALE, JOHN DE, derived his name from the parish of Radenhale, or Redenhale, in Norfolk, where, and in Suffolk, the family possessed property. A Henry Redenhale was in the king's household, and was paid 20*l.* to provide small pike, and ten marks to obtain lampreys from Gloucester for the coronation of Edward II. John, who was perhaps his son, was employed in judicial investigations in those counties in the latter years of that monarch, and his name occurs in the Year Books as an advocate in 3 Edward III. In 1329 he was appointed a justice itinerant into Northamptonshire, and he continued to act in other counties till 7 Edward III. (*Issue Roll,* 120–1; *Parl. Writs,* ii. p. ii. 1319.)

RADESWELL, or **REDESWELL,** JOHN DE, was probably the complainant in a suit in 18 Edward I., wherein he recovered a considerable estate in Bedfordshire from Henry, the son of Beatrice, the widow of Robert de Radeswell, by proving that Henry was born eleven days after the forty weeks which is the legitimate time of bearing by women, the more especially as it was further shown that Beatrice had no access to her husband for one month before his death. (*Abb. Placit.* 221, 234.)

In 18 Edward II. he is mentioned as 'senescallum regis,' and principal custos of the lands and tenements of Queen Isabella in England and Wales. Two years afterwards, on September 1, 1326, he was advanced to the office of a baron of the Exchequer, which he held only for the few remaining months of that reign.

Though not re-appointed by Edward III., he was still employed in Exchequer business, being assigned towards the end of the first year to supervise and appraise the goods and chattels of Walter Reginald, Archbishop of Canterbury, then lately deceased; and in the record he is called 'clericus regis.' (*Abb. Rot. Orig.* i. 262, ii. 11; *Parl. Writs,* ii. 1319.)

RAINSFORD, RICHARD, was born in 1605 at Staverton, near Daventry, the residence of his father, Robert Rainsford, who was descended from an old Lancashire family. His mother was Mary, daughter of Thomas Kirton, Esq., of Thorpe-Mandeville. Admitted to Lincoln's Inn, he was called to the bar on October 16, 1632, and for this society, as his legal mother, he showed his admiration and regard by presenting a silver cup when he was chief justice. He was appointed in 1630 recorder of Daventry, and in 1653 recorder of Northampton, and, known as a loyalist, he was elected member for the latter borough in the Convention Parliament that met before Charles's return, and was nominated after that event as one of the knights of the Royal Oak, had that order been instituted as at first intended. He sat also for the same borough in the parliament of 1661, but took no ostensible part in the debates.

On October 5, 1661, he was called serjeant, and soon after was knighted, for he is named with that title in his patent as baron of the Exchequer, dated November 26, 1663. After sitting in that court a little more than five years, he was removed into the King's Bench on February 6, 1669. Baker (i. 323) states that in 1667, while a baron, he officiated as recorder of Daventry; and Roger North (*Lives,* 130) relates a curious story about a witch brought to Salisbury to be tried before him. 'Sir James Long came to his chamber and made a heavy complaint of this witch, and said that if she escaped his estate would not be worth anything, for all the people would go away. It happened that the witch was acquitted, and the knight continued extremely concerned; therefore the judge, to save the poor gentleman's estate, ordered the woman to be kept in gaol, and that the town should allow her 2*s.* 6*d.* per week, for which he was very thankful. The very next assize he came to the judge to desire his lordship would let her come back to the town. And why? They could keep her for 1*s.* 6*d.* there, and in the gaol she cost them a shilling more.'

Sir Richard was promoted to the chief justiceship of his court on April 12, 1676. The only important state question which is reported as discussed before him was the Habeas Corpus applied for in June 1677 by the Earl of Shaftesbury, on his imprisonment by the House of Lords, when it was decided that the court had no jurisdiction, and the earl was remanded to prison. Ventris (p. 329) says that Sir Richard was removed from his office in Trinity Term 1678. It might be that his age and incapacity, which ought to have prevented his promotion to so prominent a position, had then become more apparent, or that the minister, Lord Danby, made them the excuse, in order to promote his favourite, Sir William Scroggs, to the place ; but it is far from improbable that Sir Richard's own feelings of decay prompted his retirement, for he did not survive it much above eight months. His death occurred on February 17, 1679, at Dallington, where there is a monument over his remains, and where he left a memorial of his charity in an almshouse for two old men and two old women, with a weekly allowance of two shillings each.

He was very estimable in his private life, and would have had a fair, though secondary, reputation as a lawyer, had he not been so unfortunate as to succeed such an eminent judge as Sir Matthew Hale, whom he was as much below in point of learning as he was above Sir William Scroggs his successor in point of integrity. He married Catherine, daughter of the Rev. Samuel Clarke, of Kingsthorpe, D.D.; his eldest son by whom, by his marriage with Anne, daughter of Richard Neville of Billingsbere, had a daughter from whom Lord Braybrooke is descended. (*Bridge's Northampt.* i. 436 ; *Baker's do.* i. 134, 323 ; *Collins's Peerage*, viii. 157.)

RALEIGH, WILLIAM DE (BISHOP OF NORWICH and WINCHESTER), sometimes called de Radley, was a native of Devonshire. He was brought up to the Church, and in 14 John was presented by the king to the living of Bratton in the archdeaconry of Barnstaple. (*Rot. Pat.* 93.) He pursued at the same time the study of the law, and it is as difficult to distinguish him from as to identify him with persons bearing the same name, and flourishing at the same period. There is, for instance, a William de Raleigh, who, being coroner, was raised in 9 Henry III. to the sheriffalty of the county of Devon. (*Rot. Claus.* ii. 67.) There is nothing to show distinctly that he was the same man; but either office might have been held by him, as a clergyman, or an officer of the court. In the next year he was one of those appointed to collect the quinzime in Lincolnshire, and in the following to assess the tallage in Cumberland and Northumberland. (*Ibid.* 146, 208.) His nomination as a justicier at Westminster took place soon after. Fines were levied before him in this character from 1228 till 1234, during which time he also performed the duties of a justice itinerant. There are instances likewise of parties paying fines for writs to take assizes of novel disseisin before him in 1235 (*Excerpt. e Rot. Fin.* 286), beyond which date there is no evidence of his acting as a judge. In 1237 he was employed to open the parliament, and by his eloquence to induce the barons to grant a subsidy to the king. (*Rapin,* iii. 55.)

His clerical preferment proceeded at the same time: he was appointed a canon of St. Paul's and of Lichfield, and treasurer of Exeter Cathedral. So high was his character both as an ecclesiastic and a lawyer that he was soon after elected to two bishoprics—those of Lichfield and Coventry, and of Norwich—the latter of which he accepted, and was consecrated on September 25, 1239. Almost immediately afterwards the chapter of Winchester, on the death of Peter de Rupibus, selected him as his successor, in opposition to the king, who wanted to force upon them William of Valence, his wife's uncle. The chapter were, however, forced to proceed to a new election; but their next choice, Ralph de Neville, being equally obnoxious to the sovereign, it was also made void, and the see remained vacant for three or four years longer. The monks then proceeded to a third election, when, persisting in the nomination of William de Raleigh, their choice was confirmed by the pope on September 13, 1243. Though the new bishop was compelled to avoid the indignation of the king by retiring into France, he succeeded at last, by the intercession of the pope and of Archbishop Boniface, in procuring the royal concurrence. For the interference of the pope he is reported to have paid no less a sum than six thousand marks, and is foolishly supposed to have expected the pontiff to return him a part of the bribe. In 1249 he retired to Tours, where he died in September of the following year, and was buried in the church of St. Martin in that city. Some letters addressed to him by Robert Grossetete, Bishop of Lincoln, are extant. (*Godwin,* 219, 316, 430 ; *Brown's Fascicul.* 316.)

RALPH (ARCHDEACON OF COLCHESTER) was one of the justiciers in the latter part of the reign of Henry II. He was present when fines were levied in the Curia Regis at Canterbury in the thirty-third year, 1187, and at Oxford in the thirty-fifth. (*Hunter's Preface.*) The Pipe Roll of 1 Richard I. (11–236) records his pleas in various counties. He died in 1190. (*Le Neve,* 195.)

RALPH (ARCHDEACON OF HEREFORD) is considered by Le Neve (118) to be surnamed Foliot, and to have held that dignity as early as 1163 and as late as 1197. He appears to have been a justicier for several of the latter years, as fines were acknowledged before him in 33 Henry II., 1188, and from the 7th to the 9th years of Richard I., 1195–7. (*Hunter's Preface.*)

RAMSEY, ABBOT OF. In Mr. Hunter's list of justiciers extracted from the fines he introduces 'Abbas Sancti Benedicti de Ramsey' in 10 and 15 John, 1208–1213, but in the fines hitherto published his name does not appear. When Robert de Redinges resigned the abbacy in 1207, the king issued a precept to the monks, commanding them to elect the prior of Frenton in his place, which they refused to obey. He thereupon kept the abbey vacant for seven years. (*Willis's Mitred Abbeys*, 154; *Monasticon*, ii. 554.) It would seem, however, that the prior of Frenton, whose name has not been discovered, assumed the title of abbot of Ramsey, notwithstanding the monks' resistance.

RANDOLPH was prior of Worcester at the time he was appointed abbot of Evesham in 1214, 15 John. The only occasion on which he acted as a justice itinerant was in 5 Henry III., 1221, when he and the abbot of Reading were placed at the head of the commission for nine counties. He died on January 16, 1229. (*Willis's Mitred Abbeys; Rot. Claus.* i. 162, 476.)

RANDOLPH, JOHN, belonged to a family settled in Hampshire, and is first mentioned in 13 Edward I., 1285, as one of the executors of William de Braboef, the justice itinerant. He was connected with the Exchequer, and in 26 Edward I. was appointed one of the commissioners to visit the seaports, and enquire into the concealment of the customs on wool, &c. (*Madox*, i. 231, 784.) The only time his name appears in Dugdale's 'Chronica Series' is as the third of five justices itinerant into Cornwall in 30 Edward I.; but a document contained in the Rolls of Parliament of 8 Edward II. proves not only that he acted for four years as a justice of assize, as well as a justice itinerant in the last circuit into Cornwall, but also that his salary for these services then remained unpaid. (*Rot. Parl.* i. 332.)

In the first two years of the reign of Edward II. he had been summoned to parliament among the judges, and was employed in a variety of ways in a judicial character as late as the thirteenth year, when he was commanded to cause his proceedings as a justice of assize, or otherwise, to be estreated into the Exchequer. (*Parl. Writs*, i. 799, ii. p. ii. 1323.)

Although he is not judicially mentioned for the next seven years, there are several entries relative to him in the interval; and in 2 Edward III. he was named on a commission to try certain malefactors of France charged with molesting the merchants of Southampton. In 1329 he was one of the justices itinerant into Northamptonshire; but after 4 Edward III., when he had the custody of the castle and manor of Porchester committed to him, he is not again noticed. (*Abb. Rot. Orig.* i. 284, ii. 41, 81; *N. Fœdera*, ii. 751.)

RANULPH, who succeeded to the treasurership of the church of Salisbury in 1192 (*Le Neve*, 270), acted as a justice itinerant in 10 Richard I., 1198, making amercements in Essex and Hertfordshire, and fixing the tallage in Surrey. (*Madox*, i. 565, 783.)

RANULPH, sometimes called Arnulph by the historians, but not in the records, was one of the chaplains of Henry I., who raised him to the office of his chancellor. In Thynne's Catalogue, from which all the subsequent writers copy, the first date attached to his holding the Seal is 1116, but from the following evidence it will be apparent that he was in possession of it at a much earlier period. He attested, as chancellor, a charter granted to the priory of St. Andrew at Northampton in 8 Henry I., 1107 (*Monast.* v. 191), and another at Whitsuntide 1109, granting the archbishopric of York to Thomas. (*Ibid.* vi. 1180.) His continuance in office until 1123 is proved by his name and title being appended to seven other charters in the 'Monasticon.' (i. 308, 483, 629, ii. 267, iii. 86, vi. 188, 1075.)

At Christmas 1123 the king held his court at Dunstable. It is related that, riding there with the monarch, the chancellor fell from his horse and was carelessly (*improvide*) ridden over by a monk of St. Albans, 'cujus possessiones,' Roger de Wendover slyly adds, 'male occupaverat.' In a few days his career was closed.

Although he did not live long enough to attain the episcopal honours usually awarded to chancellors, he had made some way in his ecclesiastical preferment, being described in one of the above charters as 'Abbas de Salesbia,' probably Selby.

He is described by Wendover (ii. 202) as suffering under heavy bodily infirmity during the last twenty years of his life, but as ready for all kinds of wickedness; and Henry of Huntingdon (*Angl. Sac.* ii. 698), in recording the characters of those great men whose lives he had witnessed, while he bears the strongest testimony to his learning, sagacity, and experience, speaks in terms of severe censure of his impiety, oppression, and avarice.

RASTALL, WILLIAM, was the son of John Rastall, who was educated at Oxford, and established himself in London as a printer, an occupation which, in those times, was deemed more as a profession than a trade, and was pursued by men of learning and education. That John Rastall deserved this character is manifest from various works, some connected with the law, which he wrote and which were published at his own press. His marriage with Elizabeth, the daughter of Sir John More the judge, and the sister of Sir Thomas More the chancellor, shows the grade in which he moved. He was a most zealous Catholic, and his known hatred of the innovations of Henry VIII. was not diminished by witnessing the sacrifice of his brother-in-law as one of the victims. (*Wood's Athen.* i. 100.) He died in 1536, leaving two sons, the elder of whom, William, afterwards the judge, was born in London in 1508.

He was sent to the university of Oxford, which he left without taking a degree. The increasing infirmities of his father probably drew him from his studies, and induced him to enter into the printing business, for books with his imprimatur appear from the year 1531. How long he continued to exercise this calling, or whether he did so after his becoming a student of Lincoln's Inn, where he was admitted on September 12, 1532, is not known; but it may be presumed that he had renewed his legal course before the end of the reign of Henry VIII., inasmuch as he was appointed reader in 1547 (*Dugdale's Orig.* 252), within a few months after Edward VI. came to the crown. Feeling that one of his religion was not then safe in England, he retired to Louvain, where he remained during Edward's life, and where he buried his wife Winifred, the daughter of the learned Dr. John Clement.

On the restoration of the Catholic worship, Rastall returned to England and resumed his professional practice. In October 1555 he was raised to the degree of serjeant-at-law, and in three years was promoted to the judicial seat, receiving his patent as a judge of the Queen's Bench on October 27, 1558, not a month before Queen Mary's death. All the judges were re-appointed the day after Elizabeth's accession, without regard to their religious persuasion; and three months after, Mr. Justice Rastall was appointed one of the justices of assize in Durham during the vacancy of that see. (*Cal. State Papers* [1547-80], 122.) He continued on the bench at Westminster, at least as late as Michaelmas 1562, his name appearing in that term in Plowden's Reports; but his resignation occurred shortly after, as the date of his successor Mr. Justice Southcote's patent is February 10, 1563.

He spent the remainder of his life in Louvain, where he died on August 27, 1565, and was buried there in the church of St. Peter.

He was the author of several works; but some confusion has arisen in distinguishing them from those written by his father. Among his undoubted compositions, are 'The Chartuary,' 'A Collection of Entries of Declarations, &c.,' 'Les Termes de la Ley,' and a 'Collection of Statutes to 4 & 5 Philip and Mary,' which is spoken highly of by Sir Edward Coke. (*Watt's Biblio. Brit.*)

RAVENSER, JOHN DE, and the next-mentioned Richard, apparently his brother, were natives of Ravenser, the place in the neighbourhood of Kingston-upon-Hull where William de la Pole was born. To the influence of this powerful merchant was probably owing the advance of these brothers. Both were ecclesiastics; and John in 48 Edward III. granted an endowment to a chantry at 'Hellewe,' in connection with the church of Waltham. (*Abb. Rot. Orig.* ii. 333.) He was keeper of the Hanaper in 1386, 10 Richard II., and it was in that character that he was appointed with the master of the Rolls on March 26, 1393, to hold the Great Seal till April 19, while Thomas de Arundel was chancellor. As William de Waltham was keeper of the Hanaper in the following year, Ravenser probably died in the interval. (*Rymer*, vii. 548.)

RAVENSER, RICHARD DE, apparently the elder brother of John, in 31 Edward III., 1357, had a grant of the office of keeper of the Hanaper. In the next year he was assigned to administer the goods of the late Queen Isabella (*Abb. Rot. Orig.* ii.), and was rewarded for his services in 36 Edward III. by being appointed one of the twelve clerks in the Chancery of the higher grade, still, however, retaining the Hanaper for some years afterwards. (*Cotton. Julius. F. X.* 15 fo. 103; *N. Fœdera*, iii. 703, 934.)

He continued a clerk of the Chancery during the remainder of his life, and was endowed with the usual ecclesiastical preferments, the last of which was that in 42 Edward III. he was made archdeacon of Lincoln. He was rich enough to lend the king 200*l.*, which was repaid in 44 Edward III. (*Pell Records*, i. 190.) He died at the end of May 1386, 9 Richard II., and was buried in Lincoln Cathedral. His will is printed in the 'Proceedings of the Archæological Institute at Lincoln' (1848), pp. 312-17. He was twice called upon, with two other clerks, to hold the Great Seal during the temporary absence of the chancellors—first, from May 4 to June 21, 1377, the day of King Edward's death; and secondly, from February 9 to March 28, 1386, 9 Richard II., but two months before his own death.

RAWLINSON, WILLIAM, of Graythwaite, near Newby Bridge, on the Lake of Windermere, a scion of a family of great eminence and antiquity in Westmoreland and Lancashire, descended from two brothers, Walter and Edward, who shared in the glory of the field of Agincourt, was born at Graythwaite about 1640, and was the son of Captain William Rawlinson, who for his services in the civil wars had a grant of arms in which three swords were introduced to commemorate the gallantry of himself and his two ancestors. Studying the law at Gray's Inn, he was called to the bar in 1667, and attained the dignity of the coif in 1686. With a fair practice and a good repute he was selected at the Revolution to be third commissioner of the Great Seal, to which he was appointed on March 4, 1689, in conjunction with Sir John Maynard and Sir Anthony Keck. He was at the same time knighted; and when both his colleagues retired in June 1690 he was retained, being then joined with Sir John Trevor and Sir George Hutchins. Luttrell (ii. 128) records that in November he was heard in the House of Lords against the bill for the regulation of the Court of Chancery. He sat under this commission for three years, when in March 1693 the Seal was delivered to Sir John Somers as sole keeper. King William wished on his removal to make him chief baron of the Exchequer, but the lord keeper objecting that it was necessary the chief judge of that court 'should be experienced in the course of the Exchequer and knowing in the common law,'—thus inferring his ignorance of both,—his appointment was not insisted on, and Sir William returned to the bar, where we find him pleading as a serjeant for the Duke of Devonshire in October 1697. He died on May 11, 1703, and was buried in Hendon Church, Middlesex. (*Lyson's London*, iii. 8.)

RAYMOND, THOMAS, is described in his admittance into Gray's Inn as the son of Robert Raymond of Bowers-Giffard in the county of Essex, which is near Downham, where the judge possessed an estate called Tremnals. He was called to the bar on February 11, 1650, and from the period of the Restoration he was a diligent reporter during the remainder of his life. In 1677 he was created a serjeant, and less than two years afterwards was raised to the bench and knighted, though, as he declares, he laboured, and not without reason, to prevent his promotion. He filled, in the course of one year, a seat in each of the three courts, receiving a patent as baron of the Exchequer on May 1, 1679, from which he was removed to the Common Pleas on February 7 following, and on April 29 was transferred to the King's Bench. In the latter court he sat for little more than three years, during which he assisted in the trials and acquittals of Mr. Cellier and the Earl of Castlemaine, luckily coming into office at the fag end of the pretended Popish Plot, when the tide was beginning to turn, and Chief Justice Scroggs thought it his interest to test the credibility of the witnesses whose evidence he had before received with undoubting faith.

Though Roger North (136) relates of Sir Thomas that two old women were tried before him at Exeter for witchcraft, and that, by his passive behaviour, and neglecting to point out to the jury the irrationality of their confessions, he suffered them to be convicted, and one of them to be hanged, by his general conduct on the bench he escaped the censure to which too many of his colleagues in this reign were liable, and probably by his early death avoided the dismissal which was the too common reward of straightforward independence and an honest administration of justice. As there is no evidence of the 'extraordinary servility' which Lord Campbell imputes to him, nor any other ground adduced for designating him as an 'unprincipled judge' except his concurrence with the rest of the court in the decision on the quo warranto against the City of London (a case turning on many difficult points of law), the prophetic future, which his lordship's prejudice would ascribe to him if he had lived may in fairness be disregarded and set aside, receiving only the noble author's reluctant admission that he was a judge of 'extraordinary learning'—a subject on which every lawyer is ready to allow his lordship to have been a sufficient authority.

He died in the fifty-seventh year of his age on July 14, 1683, while engaged on the circuit, and was buried in the parish church of Downham. By his wife, Ann, daughter of Sir Edward Fish, Bart., he had one only child, his more famous son, the next-mentioned Robert Lord Raymond. The Reports both of the father and son are in great repute in Westminster Hall. (*Morant's Essex*, i. 206.)

RAYMOND, ROBERT (LORD RAYMOND), the only son of the above Sir Thomas Raymond, was born in 1673, and his father nine months before his death induced the society of Gray's Inn to admit the boy on November 1, 1682, when only nine years old. No doubt the young student was excused attendance on the usual exercises until he had completed the rest of his education, but the devotion which he paid to his father's wishes is shown by his early adoption of the most efficient course of acquiring practical legal knowledge. He constantly attended the courts, and his successors at the bar benefit to the present day by the fruits of his industry. His Reports commence in Easter Term 1694, when he was but twenty years old, and more than three years before he was called to the bar. They finish in Trinity Term 1732, a year before his death, thus extending over thirty-eight years, during the reigns of four sovereigns. They were not published till ten years after his death, but are so highly valued, and still regarded as such high authority, that they have been several times reprinted under the editorial care of eminent lawyers.

His call to the bar did not take place till November 12, 1697, fifteen years after his admission; but he got into immediate practice, he himself reporting a case in which he was engaged in a learned argument in Michaelmas 1698. In 1702 we find him employed as junior counsel in the prosecution of Richard Hathaway as a cheat and impostor in pretending to be bewitched by Sarah Murdock, whom he brought to trial for her life. After the conviction in this case indictments for witchcraft almost entirely ceased. In 1704 he very ably and strenuously (and in the event effectually) defended David Lindsay on a charge of high treason in returning to England from France without leave, and in 1706 he was of counsel for the prosecution of Beau Fielding for bigamy, in marrying the Duchess of Cleveland, his first wife being alive.

In Queen Anne's parliaments of 1710 and 1714 he was returned for Bishop's Castle, having been knighted on May 13 in the former year on being made solicitor-general, an office from which he was removed on October 14 in the latter year by the advice of Lord Cowper on the arrival of George I. in England. In that king's first parliament of 1715 Sir Robert was elected for Ludlow, and in the second of 1722 for Helston. In the former he joined with the tories in opposing the Septennial Bill in 1716, which was however passed by a large majority. While still a member he was again taken into the king's service, and appointed attorney-general in May 1720, in which character he conducted the prosecution against Christopher Layer for high treason in November 1722. On January 31, 1724, he was appointed a judge of the King's Bench.

On the removal of Lord Chancellor Macclesfield, Sir Robert was appointed one of the three commissioners of the Great Seal, which they held from January 7 to June 4, 1725. On March 2 he succeeded Sir John Pratt as chief justice of the King's Bench, still continuing to act as commissioner till Lord King became chancellor. The judgments delivered by him during the eight years he presided in the King's Bench are most elaborate, and display a great fund of legal knowledge. In the state trials before him he was patient, impartial, careful, and discriminating. In one of them, that against Curll, the bookseller, he established the doctrine that to publish an obscene libel is a temporal offence; and the delinquent was punished on this confirmation of his conviction. George II. on his accession continued him in his place, and raised him to the peerage on January 15, 1731, by the title of Lord Raymond of Abbots Langley in Hertfordshire. In the House of Lords he distinguished himself by opposing the bill enacting that all proceedings in courts of justice should be in the English language, alleging that if the bill passed the law must likewise be translated into Welsh, as many in Wales understood not English. Though the alteration was unpopular among lawyers (even Lord Ellenborough thought it tended to make attorneys illiterate), it happily became law, to the great benefit and comfort of the community.

Lord Raymond died on March 19, 1733, and was buried at Abbots Langley, in which parish his country seat was situate, and where a handsome monument was erected to his memory. By his wife, Anne, daughter of Sir Edward Northey, the attorney-general, he left an only son, of his own name, upon whose death in 1753 the title became extinct. (*Lord Raymond*, passim; *State Trials*, xiv. 642, 989, 1329; *Parl. Hist.* vii. 335, 861; *Strange*, 948; *Collins's Peerage*, ix. 432.)

READ, or REDE, ROBERT, was of a family which originally came from Morpeth in Northumberland. His grandfather John was a serjeant-at-law in the reign of Henry IV., and was settled at Norwich; and his father's and mother's names were, according to his will, William and Joan, though Burke calls them Edward and Izod, daughter of Sir Humphrey Stanley. Robert was their third son, and was educated at Buckingham Hall, afterwards Magdalen College, in Cambridge, and became a fellow of King's Hall, on the site of which part of Trinity College was built. He was placed at Lincoln's Inn, where he became reader in 1480, and again in 1486, having in the previous November received his summons to take on himself the degree of the coif. On April 18, 1494, he was appointed king's serjeant; and was made a judge of the King's Bench on November 24, 1495, 11 Henry VII., when he was knighted.

In October 1506 he was raised to the chief justiceship of the Court of Common Pleas, for which advancement the judge was obliged to pay to the avaricious king the sum of 400 marks, as appears by an account rendered by the noted Edmond Dudley. (*Turner's England*, iv. 158.) King Henry named him as one of the executors of his will. (*Testam. Vetust.* 35.)

Henry VIII. continued him in his place, which he retained till his death on January 8, 1519. He was buried in the chapel of St. Catherine at the Charterhouse, where he founded a chantry of 8*l.* a year for thirty years. (*Supp. of the Monasteries*, 68.) He also left 100*l.* to Jesus College to found a fellowship and brewery there, and established three public lectures at the university of Cambridge, called 'Barnaby's Lectures,' on humanity, logic, and philosophy, which are now consolidated into one lecture every year, with the name of the founder. (*Dyer's Cambridge*, i. 82, ii. 69, 269.)

By his marriage with Margaret, one of the daughters of John Alphew, of Bore Place in Chiddingstone, Kent, he became possessed of considerable property in Kent. (*Hasted*, iii. 133, 219.)

REEVE, EDMUND, was of a Norfolk family, and is rightly claimed by the society of Barnard's Inn as having commenced his legal studies there. He completed them at Gray's Inn, where he attained the post of reader in 1632. In 1629 he was named as the first recorder of Great Yarmouth. (*Cal. State Papers* [1629-31], 131.) He was called serjeant on May 30, 1636, and was promoted to the bench of the Common Pleas on March 24, 1639. (*Rymer*, xx. 381.)

In the propositions made to the king in February 1643 he was one of the judges whom the parliament requested to be continued; and in Michaelmas Term of that year he sat alone in his court at Westminster, when the king's proclamation to adjourn it to Oxford was delivered to him. In subservience to the parliament, he caused the apprehension of the messenger, who was tried by a council of war, and condemned and executed as a spy. (*Clarendon*, iii. 407, iv. 342.) The judge retained his seat till his death, on March 27, 1647, when his remains were interred in the church of Estratuna (Stratton) in Norfolk. Lord Clarendon (iii. 145-9) speaks of him as 'a man of good reputation for learning, who in good times would have been a good judge,' and represents him as giving some prudent counsel to the king on his coming to Leicester during the assizes in July 1642.

Phillips states that Sir George Reeve of Thwaite in Suffolk (who obtained a baronetcy in 1663, which failed about 1688) was descended from him. (*Grandeur of the Law* [1684], 87; *Gent. Mag.* lxxxviii. 396.)

REEVE, THOMAS, frequently miscalled Reeves, was the son of Richard Reeve, Esq., of New Windsor, who erected four almshouses in the parish. Admitted first a member of the Inner Temple, he transferred himself to the Middle Temple, and was called to the bar by the latter society in 1713. He had such success that he was made king's counsel so early as 1718, and soon afterwards attorney-general for the duchy of Lancaster. He became a bencher of the Middle Temple in 1720, and reader in 1722. In the latter year he was counsel for the crown in support of the bill of attainder against Bishop Atterbury and the other parties implicated in the same conspiracy; and in 1730 he most ably advocated the cause of the widow of Robert Castell in the appeal of murder against Bambridge, the warden of the Fleet. In April 1733 he was constituted a judge of the Common Pleas, and knighted; and after sitting there for nearly three years he was advanced to the head of the court in January 1736. His enjoyment of this post was limited to a single year, as on January 13, 1737, he died. (*State Trials*, xvi. 469, 607, xvii. 398; *Gent. Mag.* iii. 215, vi. 56, vii. 60.)

Learned himself, he was an encourager of the aspirants to learning; and that he was a favourite among the literary men of the day is apparent from numerous printed and manuscript verses written in his laudation.

He resided at Eton, and at Gey's House, Maidenhead; and at his death his personal estate was estimated at 22,675*l.*, besides real estates of considerable rental, among which was a moiety of the playhouse in Lincoln's Inn Fields, let to Rich at 100*l.* per annum. His wife was Annabella, sister of Richard Topham, Esq., of New Windsor, keeper of the records in the Tower; but he left no issue. (*Ex inf. of John Payne Collier, Esq., F.S.A.*, who occupied the family residence, Gey's House.)

REGINALD (ABBOT OF WALDEN) is introduced among the chancellors of Stephen's reign on the sole authority of 'one anonymall brief-written chronicle,' in which Thynne and his copyist Philipot say that they have seen him so termed. How far this information is correct may be judged from the fact that Walden did not exist as an abbey till the year 1190, previously to which date it was only a priory. Although Reginald was the first abbot and the last prior, he did not attain even the latter dignity till 1164, ten years after Stephen's death. (*Philipot*, 11; *Browne Willis's Mitred Abbeys*.)

REGINALD is introduced as chancellor to Henry I. by Thynne, on no other foundation than the following words in Leland's 'Itinerary:' 'Then came one Reginaldus Cancellarius, so namyd, *by likelyhode*, of his office, a man of gret fame, about King Henry the First.' Upon such vague evidence as this the name has been continued in subsequent lists, when there is not a single document to support the supposition, and when it is notorious that queens, and barons, and bishops, and others had offices of this title, from which Reginald might have been named.

Leland goes on to say that 'he felle to religion, and was prior to Montegue, and enlarged yt with buildings and possessions.' Yet it is curious that his name is not in the list of priors contained in the Cottonian Manuscript copied by Willis in his 'Mitred Abbeys,' and that in the recapitulation of the grants to that priory set forth in its various charters his name does not appear as a benefactor.

REGINALD, or **RAYNALD**, WALTER (ARCHBISHOP OF CANTERBURY), whose career affords an early instance in English history of the advance of an individual from the lower ranks of life to the highest ecclesiastical honours, was the son of a baker at Windsor, and, being bred up to the Church, was brought under the notice of Edward I., a monarch whose powers of discrimination were seldom at fault. The king soon discovered merit in the youthful aspirant, whose appointment as tutor to the young prince is no small evidence in favour of his character and abilities. Judging both from the earlier and the more matured career of his pupil, he failed (as might be expected from the events of his own life) to check the weakness of the prince's judgment, or to instil into him steadiness of purpose. He, however, satisfied the father, from whom he received the living of Wimbledon in 1298, and ingratiated himself with the son, on whose accession he was rapidly advanced. He immediately obtained a canonry in St. Paul's, and was constituted treasurer of the Exchequer on August 22, 1307. To this was added the bishopric of Worcester in April 1308; and on July 6, 1310, resigning the treasurership, the Great Seal was placed in his hands. The terms used on the roll recording this event make it doubtful whether he was invested with the office of chancellor or with that of keeper. The oath he is described as taking is, ' de officio Sigilli illius fideliter exequendo,' which would seem to apply more directly to the latter. In subsequent records, however, he is certainly called chancellor. (*Madox*, ii. 38, 48.) Soon after his appointment he lent 1000*l.* to the king, to the advance of which has been attributed, without sufficient evidence, his attainment of the Seal; but, as the loan was made after his elevation, it may more charitably be ascribed to his desire to assist the king in the necessities which then pressed upon him, the ordainers being in fact at that time in possession of the government and the royal purse: an order, indeed, for the repayment of nearly one-half of it was made so early as May 1, 1311.

Between December 19, 1311, and October 6, 1312, the Seal never appears to have been under his control; but on the latter day it was again placed in his hands, only, however, as custos or keeper, remaining sealed up under the seals of the master of the Rolls and two other clerks in Chancery, in whose presence it would seem that all writs were sealed. In this manner the office was executed till April 5, 1314, which is the last date on which the bishop is mentioned in connection with the Seal.

His removal from this high office, which no doubt took place about that time, was not occasioned by any diminution of his sovereign's favour, but rather by his having attained a higher elevation. On the decease of Archbishop Winchelsey in May 1313, although the monks had elected Dr. Cobham, the sub-dean of Salisbury—a most learned and excellent man—in his place, the king contrived to get the election annulled by the pope, and his favourite, Walter, to be substituted for him. The bull by which this was effected is dated October 1, 1313;

and he was with great pomp enthroned on April 19, 1314. His rule over the archbishopric was illustrated by the acquisition of many important privileges from the papal see.

During the earlier troubles with the barons he remained faithful to the king; but on the queen's invasion of the kingdom he basely deserted his patron and master, adding strength to her party by the weight of his position, and, on the king's deposition, completing his infamy by crowning the son of his benefactor.

This event, which took place on February 1, 1327, was quickly followed by his own death. The adulterous queen is said to have so pressed the consecration of James de Berkley, elected Bishop of Exeter, that the pusillanimous archbishop, more fearful of the prevailing and present power than that of the pope at a distance, did not dare to resist. The Roman pontiff, enraged that his confirmation had not been first obtained, by his threats and reproaches against the offending prelate created such terror or such remorse in his mind that, within a few days after the announcement of the pope's anger, a mortal sickness fell upon him. His death occurred at Mortlake on November 16, 1327, and his remains were interred in Canterbury Cathedral. (*Godwin*, 103, 462; *Hasted*, xii. 379; *Angl. Sac.* i. 18, 59, 532.)

REINGER, or RENGER, JOHN, was the eldest son of the under-named Richard; and when his father was sheriff of London, in 6 Henry III., he and his brother Matthew were delivered as pledges for the peace of that city. (*Rot. Claus.* i. 517, 569.) Madox (ii. 319) introduces him as a baron of the Exchequer in 42 Henry III., but nothing further has been discovered concerning him in that character. In 52 Henry III. he proceeded against Stephen Bukerel for taking away his goods and chattels from his houses in 'Enefeud, Edelmeton, Mimmes et Stebeneth,' in Middlesex (*Abb. Placit.* 175), and died in the following year. (*Cal. Inquis.* p. m. i. 32.)

REINGER, or RENGER, RICHARD, was an alderman of London, serving the office of sheriff in 5, 6, and 7 Henry III., and that of mayor in the four following years. During part of this time the king committed the chamberlainship of the city to him and John Travers; and in 11 Henry III. he had a grant of the Queen's Hithe (Ripa Reginæ) to hold at 40*l.* a year. About the same time he and Alexander de Dorset had the custody of the Mint of London; but in 13 Henry III. it was transferred, together with that of Canterbury, to him alone, for four years, at an annual rent of seven hundred marks. It was while he held this office that he acted as a justicier, fines being levied before him from Hilary 1230 till Easter 1231. There is a record showing that he was still alderman in 19 Henry III. He died soon afterwards. (*Stow's Survey; Rot. Claus.* i. 517, &c., ii. 21, &c.; *Madox,* i. 709–781, ii. 134.)

REINY, JOHN DE, was the son of a knight of the same name to whom' the manor of Hemmeston in Devonshire belonged, and who bore arms against King John. His mother, in 6 Henry III., married Nicholas de Heaulton without the king's licence; and he was placed under the wardship of Warin Fitz-Joel. In 9 Henry III., 1225, he was appointed one of the justices itinerant for Somersetshire, in which county also he had property. No other mention is made of him till 1246, when his executors were allowed to have administration of his property. (*Rot. Claus.* i. 270, 577, ii. 4, 76; *Excerpt. e Rot. Fin.* i. 88, 89, 460.)

RETFORD, ROBERT DE, was the son of Richard, who was the son of Richard de Retford (*Abb. Placit.* 284), so called from a town in Nottinghamshire. He was first summoned to parliament among the judges in August 1295, 23 Edward I., and there are records of his pleas as a justice itinerant at Norwich and at Dunstable in the next year. (*Abb. Rot. Orig.* i. 96, 97.) His attendance in parliament in that character is noted till the end of the reign (*Parl. Writs,* i. 801); and in February 1307 he was placed among the justices of trailbaston for the home counties. (*Rot. Parl.* i. 218.)

From the commencement of the next reign there are regular writs summoning him to parliament in the same manner, which are continued till June 1318, 11 Edward II.; and there is evidence of his exercising his functions, not only in the home district, but in Durham and in Leicestershire, up to the ninth year of that reign. (*Ibid.* 346; *Parl. Writs,* ii. 1331.)

RETFORD, WILLIAM DE, was probably the son of the above Robert de Retford. The document by which he was appointed keeper of the great wardrobe is on the Roll of Nottinghamshire, the county to which that Robert belonged. This is dated in 23 Edward III.; and he is there called 'clericus.' He was raised to the Exchequer bench as a baron on November 27, 1354, and 'is mentioned as a justice of assize in 32 Edward III., in Serjeant Benloe's Reports. The period of his death or retirement has not been discovered. (*Abb. Rot. Orig.* ii. 205; *N. Fœdera,* iii. 114.)

REYGATE, JOHN DE, in 52 Henry III., 1268, was appointed king's escheator north of Trent, and during the time he held that office he performed the duties of a justicier, from May 1269 to August 1271, numerous payments being made for assizes before him in the northern counties. He held the escheatorship to the end of that reign. (*Excerpt. e Rot. Fin.* ii. 467–585.)

Under Edward I. there is no actual entry showing that he was a justicier at Westminster; but from his frequent employment as a justice itinerant, and the position he gradually attained in the commissions, it seems probable that he continued to hold the office. In 3 Edward I. he was the third of four justices itinerant into Worcestershire, and in the next year the head of four justices of assize. In 6 Edward I. his name in two commissions of itinera was preceded only by that of the Bishop of Worcester; in the following year he headed the circuit into Dorset, Somerset, and Wilts; and in 12 Edward I. a writ was addressed to him and another to hold an assize in Northumberland. (*Abb. Placit.* 276.)

REYNOLDS, JAMES (1). There were two judges of the name of James Reynolds in the reign of George II.—one lord chief baron, and the other baron of the Exchequer. They were not contemporaries in Westminster Hall, the former being dead before his namesake ascended the English bench, although he had been chief justice of the Common Pleas in Ireland for nearly thirteen years before. The chief baron's great-grandfather (who was also the baron's ancestor) was Sir James Reynolds, of Castle Camps in Cambridgeshire, who flourished in the reign of Queen Elizabeth. His grandfather and father were also named James, both residing at Bumstead Helions in Essex. The estate of the former, who married Dorothy, a daughter of Sir William De Grey, of Merton in Norfolk, was decimated during the Rebellion, on account of his loyalty and great zeal for King Charles. The latter in 1655, at the age of twenty-two, married Judith, the eldest daughter of Sir William Hervey, of Ickworth, near Bury St. Edmunds, ancestor of the Marquis of Bristol. By this lady, who was then forty years of age, he had three sons; and soon after her death, in 1679, he took for his second wife, in 1682, Bridget, daughter of — Parker, who survived her husband thirty-three years, and died in 1723. Both the ladies were buried at Castle Camps.

By the latter marriage he had an only son, James, the future chief baron, who was born on January 6, 1686, at the house of his mother's aunt Gibbs in Clerkenwell. His precise relationship to the other judge is not traced with certainty, but as by his will he bequeathed a large legacy to his niece, bearing the family name of Judith, and as the other judge (to whom the chief baron had before his second marriage devised his estates in Cambridgeshire) had a sister named Judith, it would seem, if she were the same Judith, that he was the nephew of the chief baron, and perhaps the son of the chief baron's half-brother, Robert. (*Collins's Peerage,* i. 149; *Gage's Suffolk,* 287; *Morant's Essex,* ii. 522, 532.)

The chief baron was initiated into the mysteries of the law at Lincoln's Inn, where he was called to the bar in 1712, and was included in the batch of serjeants created by George I. in the first year of his reign. Having been in 1712 elected recorder of Bury St. Edmunds, probably by the influence of the Hervey family, then ennobled, that borough returned him as its representative in 1717 and 1722. In 1718 he was selected by the Prince of Wales to argue in favour of his royal highness's claim to educate his own children; but the judges, with only two dissentients, decided that the care and education of the king's grandchildren belonged to his majesty by the royal prerogative. (*State Trials*, xvi. 1203.)

His argument did not prevent George I. from promoting him to a judgeship of the King's Bench in March 1725; nor did his old client George II. forget him, but in April 1730 raised him to the office of lord chief baron. After presiding in the Exchequer for eight years he resigned in July 1738; and dying on February 9, 1739, he was buried in St. James's Church, Bury St. Edmunds, where there is a splendid monument to his memory.

That the graceful account of his merits as a judge and as a man which his epitaph records is not exaggerated, may well be believed from the prayer (still in existence) which he was in the daily habit of using, petitioning for 'that measure of understanding and discernment, that spirit of justice, and that portion of courage, as may both enable and dispose me to judge and determine those weighty affairs which may this day fall unto my consideration, without error or perplexity, without fear or affection, without prejudice or passion, without vanity or ostentation, but in a manner agreeable to the obligation of the oath and dignity of that station to which Thou in Thy good providence hast been pleased to advance me.'

He was twice married. His first wife was Mary, daughter of Thomas Smith, Esq., of Thrandeston Hall, Suffolk; and his second was Alicia, daughter of — Rainbird. He left no issue by either. On his elevation to the bench he resigned the recordership of Bury, but showed his affection for that borough by leaving 200*l.* to its corporation. (*Ex inf. of Ven. Archdeacon Hale, Rev. J. C. Bode, Rev. A. Wratislaw, and Mr. Herbert Frere; Notes and Queries,* 3rd S. i. 235, iii. 54.)

REYNOLDS, JAMES (2), born in 1684, was, according to the inscription on his monument at Castle Camps, Cambridgeshire, 'the last male descendant of Sir James Reynolds, knight, who flourished in these parts in the reign of Queen Elizabeth.' Though it is difficult to ascertain the real connection by relationship between him and Chief Baron James Reynolds, it would appear, for the reasons already given in the life of the latter, that he was the nephew of the chief baron, although born two years before that judge. They both had property in the manor of Castle Camps, which lies on the borders of Essex in the neighbourhood of Bumstead-Helions. The baron is described in the books of Lincoln's Inn, to which he was admitted in February 1704, as the son and heir-apparent of Robert Reynolds, of Bumstead in Essex. This gentleman was, it seems probable, the half-brother of Chief Baron James Reynolds, and a son of James Reynolds of Bumstead by his first wife Judith, daughter of Sir William Hervey of Ickworth. Robert married Kesiah Tyrrell, the granddaughter of Sir William Hervey, another of whose daughters, Kesiah, married Thomas Tyrrell, of Gipping in Suffolk.

The baron was called to the bar in May 1710, but nothing is recorded of him till he was sent to Ireland on November 3, 1727, as chief justice of the Common Pleas. In that court he sat for thirteen years, and by his professional talents and accomplished manners endeared himself to all parties. On retiring from this honourable post he was appointed a baron of the English Exchequer, and took his seat there in May 1740. He was not knighted till May 23, 1745, on going up with the judges' address. He administered justice on the English bench for seven years, and dying on May 20, 1747, he was buried in the church of Castle Camps; and, as his monument there was erected by his sister Judith, it is probable that he never married. (*Smyth's Law Off. of Ireland,* 121, 309; *Gent. Mag.* at the dates.)

RICH, RICHARD (LORD RICH), was no doubt of a very ancient family. One of the earliest of the name is John de Rich, who flourished at Rich's Place in Hampshire in the reign of Edward II. His great-grandson was Richard Rich, the father of another Richard, mercer in London, who was sheriff of that city in 1441, died possessed of large estates in Middlesex and Hertfordshire, and was the founder of five almshouses at Broxbourne. His second son, Thomas, had a son Richard, who, by his wife Joan Dingley, was the father of the chancellor. (*Wotton's Baronet.* iv. 586; *Baronage,* ii. 387; *Testam. Vetust.* 299.)

Richard Rich resided in his youth in the same parish in London where Sir Thomas More dwelt, and, according to the authority of that eminent man, was of no commendable fame, very light of tongue and a great dicer—one with whom neither he nor any man else would ever in any matter of importance vouchsafe to communicate. 'And so,' More adds (*Roper,* 82), 'in your house at the Temple, where hath been your chief bringing up, were you likewise accounted.' Assured of the truth of More's representation, it would be curious to discover by what means a character of this stamp pushed himself up so as to become a reader at the Middle Temple in 1529. (*Dugdale's Orig.* 216.)

By what patronage he acquired the office of attorney-general of Wales in 1532 is not told. That of solicitor-general to the king followed on October 10, 1533. This he held till April 13, 1536, a period of two years and a half, during which, by his intrigues, his degrading subserviency, and his bold-faced perjury, though he paved the way to worldly honours, he at the same time secured to his name the everlasting infamy that attaches to it. Cunning much less than Rich's would soon discover that his interest lay in gratifying the humours of the king, but it required a hardened conscience to pursue the perfidious course which he adopted to secure the royal favour. The refusal of Sir Thomas More and Bishop Fisher to acknowledge the king's supremacy had irritated the monarch beyond even his usual ferocity, and every attempt that hitherto failed in bringing the two contumacious prisoners within the terms of the recent statute which made it high treason to deny it. Either Rich was sufficiently known to be considered a fitting instrument to make another trial, or he voluntarily undertook the degrading office. The manner in which he acted towards both these good and pious men was exposed on their trials. That of Bishop Fisher came on first, the sole evidence against whom was Mr. Solicitor-General Rich. It was there asserted by the bishop, and not denied, that Rich came to him with a message from the king desiring his real opinion on the disputed point, and that on the bishop's reminding him of the penalty in the new act in case anything was said contrary to that law, Rich assured him on the king's honour, and on the word of a king, that no advantage would be taken against him for declaring his secret mind, which he professed that the king was desirous to know for his own guidance in future. To this Rich added his own faithful promise that he would never utter the bishop's words but to the king alone. Compelled thus, as it were by the king's command, the bishop expressed his real sentiments on the statute; and upon these alone, so uttered and so perfidiously betrayed, was the aged bishop most unrighteously condemned. Without charging the witness with perjury (for there is too much reason to believe he was the bearer of such a message from the king), it is difficult to determine where the greater share of infamy rests—on the man who would suffer himself to be made an instrument in so vile a plot, or on the judges who could permit conviction on such evidence.

On the next trial Sir Thomas More directly charged him with perjury in his representation of what passed between them. There it appears that Rich, on going to the Tower to take away Sir Thomas's books, led him under pretence of friendship into an argument, in the course of which, as Rich alleged, Sir Thomas asserted that the parliament had no more power to make the king supreme head of the Church than it had to declare that God was not God. Who will doubt More's asseveration of the falsehood of Rich's evidence? For who can believe that More would be incautious enough, especially to a man of Rich's known character, to betray his sentiments so unreservedly on such an occasion, when he had guardedly concealed them in all the various attempts which persons of high position and ability had previously made to entrap him? Even Rich's impudence must have been daunted before Sir Thomas's exposure of his former life, and his dignified denial of the evidence now offered. The two witnesses called to support Rich's testimony failed to assist him, for though they acknowledged that they were present, they declared that they were too busy in packing the books to give ear to the conversation. (*State Trials*, i. 387-400.)

Rich, however, procured what he sought for—his own advancement. In the next year he obtained the valuable place of chirographer in the Court of Common Pleas, and resigned the solicitorship for the more dignified and profitable office of chancellor of the Court of Augmentations, then newly established. He did not neglect the opportunity thus obtained of securing to himself an enormous share of the plunder arising from the dissolution of the monasteries. The inquisition of his possessions, taken at his death, proves the immense extent of his acquisitions. One of the earliest and richest was Leeze Priory and manor in Essex, which he made his capital seat, and from which he subsequently took his title. (*Morant*, ii. 101.)

At the new parliament which met on June 8, 1536, he was chosen speaker, and made himself as remarkable for the grossness of his flattery as he had previously done for the baseness of his actions. (*Parl. Hist.* i. 529, 534.) In his introductory speech he compared the king 'for justice and prudence to Solomon, for strength and fortitude to Samson, and for beauty and comeliness to Absalom;' and on another occasion he likened him to the sun, which exhaled all noxious vapours hurtful to us, and cherished those seeds, plants, and fruits necessary for the support of human life: 'so,' said the obsequious flatterer, 'this our most excellent prince takes away by his prudence all those enormities which may hereafter be hurtful to us and our posterity, and enacts such laws as will be a defence to the good, and a great terror to evil doers.' He was soon after knighted.

He was a regular attendant at the council; and at one of the meetings in 1541 he was charged by one John Hillary with not doing what pertained to his duty with respect to a supposed concealment by the abbot of Keynsham of a part of his income, but the unfortunate informer got nothing for his pains but imprisonment in the Marshalsea. (*Acts Privy Council*, vii. 101.) He is charged also with having assisted Lord Chancellor Wriothesley in working the rack on which poor Anne Askew was stretched; but even prejudice must hesitate to believe this.

In 1544 he resigned the chancellorship of the Court of Augmentations; but in the expedition against Boulogne in that year he accompanied King Henry as treasurer of the army—an office which he held in Scotland as well as in France; and he assisted in negotiating the treaty of peace with the French king. Under Henry's will he had a legacy of 200*l.*, and was appointed one of the twelve assistants to the sixteen privy councillors.

On February 16, 1547, about a fortnight after the accession of Edward VI., in consequence of an asserted promise by the late king, he was created Baron Rich of Leeze in Essex. On Lord Wriothesley's dismissal from the chancellorship on March 6, Rich hoped to supply his place; but the lord protector hesitated for more than half a year as to the choice he should make, leaving the Seal in the meantime in the temporary keeping of Lord St. John. Rich, however, having at last managed to acquire the confidence of Somerset, was invested with the office on October 23. Within two years he turned against the protector, and, joining the Earl of Warwick, headed the subscribers to the proclamation against him. The last public duty he is mentioned as performing was on August 28, 1551, when he went with Sir Anthony Wingfield and Sir William Petre to the Princess Mary at Copped Hall in Essex, to announce to her the determination of the council that private mass should not be performed in her household. She returned a resolute answer, declaring that none of the new service should be used in her house. (*Archæologia*, xviii. 161.)

Very shortly after this there are two entries in King Edward's journal which, though subsequently erased by his own pen, show the commencement of doubt and uneasiness on the part of Rich. On October 1, the king mentions that the chancellor had sent back a letter for the execution of the commission against the Bishops of Chichester and Worcester, because but eight members of the council had signed it, though ten were present; whereupon his majesty wrote a letter to Rich marvelling at his refusal. (*Cal. St. Papers* [1547–80], 55.) In less than three months Lord Rich resigned his office on December 21, 1551. By an entry in the journal the king attributes his retirement to illness; and there is no doubt that in the previous year he had been so incapacited by sickness that a commission had been issued to the master of the Rolls and others to hear causes for him. (*Rymer*, xv. 246.) Hayward (*Kennet's Hist.* ii. 323), however, gives a different version. He suggests that a wish to keep the 'fair estate' he had got, and his desire to avoid the troubles he foresaw in the coming parliament, made him petition for his discharge on account of his infirmities. Heylin's explanation (i. 251) of the occurrence is more curious. 'It so happened,' he says, 'that the lord chancellor, commiserating the condition of the Duke of Somerset,' who had been committed to the Tower on his second disgrace in October, 'though formerly he had showed himself against him, despatched a letter to him, concerning some proceedings of the lords of the council which he thought fit for him to know. Which letter, being hastily superscribed "To the Duke," with no other title, he gave to one of his servants, to be carried to him. By whom, for the want of a more particular direction, it was delivered to the hands of the Duke of Norfolk. But, the mistake being presently found, the lord chancellor, knowing into what hands he was like to fall, makes his address unto the king the next morning betimes, and humbly prays that, in regard to his great age, he might be discharged of the Seal and office of chancellor.'

Lord Rich did not wholly retire from political life, nor could he refrain from joining in the closing plot of the reign. He protested in the parliament of 1553 against a bill for the regulation of the revenue (*Parl. Hist.* i. 600); and he not only witnessed the king's will and subscribed the undertaking to support its provisions, which altered the succession of the crown and settled it on Lady Jane Grey, but he also gave such prominent aid to the project as to induce the lords of the council to address a letter of thanks to him for his services. (*Lingard*, vii. 103, 120.)

By a timely desertion of the party he escaped the immediate consequences, and he probably obtained favour with Queen Mary by his profession of the Roman Catholic faith. In a month after she was proclaimed he was nominated as one of the council to attend at a sermon preached at St. Paul's Cross, when a tumult was apprehended, and was actually summoned among the twenty-five peers appointed to try the Duke of Northumberland for the crime in which he himself had participated. (4 *Report Pub. Rec.*, App. ii. 234.) He formed part of the commission for deciding on the claims to do service at the queen's coronation (*Rymer*, xv. 338), and his name was frequently placed at the head of the commissions in his county for trying heretics, at the cruel execution of some of whom he was directed to be present. (*Archæologia*, xviii. 181.)

During the ten years that he lived under the reign of Queen Elizabeth little is told of him, except that in the first year he voted against the new Book of Common Prayer, and that in 1566 he was one of the committee of Lords appointed to confer with the Commons on the subject of the queen's marriage. (*Parl. Hist.* 607, 703.)

He survived nearly seventeen years after his retirement from the chancellorship, and employed himself in several charitable works in the neighbourhood of his mansion. Dying about May 1568, he was buried in Felsted Church.

By his wife, Elizabeth, sister of William Jenks, of London, grocer, he had a very numerous family. He was succeeded in the title by his eldest son, Robert, whose son, also Robert, was created in 1618 Earl of Warwick. The earl's second son was advanced to the peerage in 1622 as Baron Kensington, to which was added the earldom of Holland in 1624, but both titles became extinct in 1759. (*Wotton's Baronet.* iv. 586; *Nicolas's Synopsis.*)

RICHARD (BISHOP OF HEREFORD) was one of King Henry's chaplains, and is mentioned by Thynne as keeper of the Seal when Ranulph was chancellor. In no document, however, is he so designated, and Malmesbury, with greater probability, calls him 'Clericus de Sigillo.' In 1120 he was preferred to the bishopric of Hereford, and dying at Ledbury on August 15, 1127, he was buried in his own cathedral. (*Godwin*, 482; *Le Neve*, 108.)

RICHARD was archdeacon of Wilts, and although his pleas and those of his companions are mentioned on the roll of 1 Richard I. for the county of Cornwall, they evidently refer to an iter in a previous year, as they are immediately followed on the same roll by two other series of pleas, the last of which are entitled 'nova placita,' and were taken before other justiciers in that year. (*Pipe Roll*, 112.) In 31 Henry III., 1185, he and two others were the custodes of the see of Exeter while it was in the king's hands (*Madox*, i. 310), and it was probably while he had that charge that he acted as a justice itinerant in the diocese.

His death occurred about 1203, 5 John. (*Le Neve*, 276.)

RICHARDS, RICHARD, son and heir of Thomas Richards of Coed in Merionethshire, and Catherine, sister of the Rev. William Parry, warden of Ruthyn, was born at Dolgelly on November 5, 1752, and commenced his education at Ruthyn grammar school. Entering the society of the Inner Temple, he was called to the bar in 1780. By his marriage in 1785 with Catherine, the daughter of Robert Vaughan Humphreys, he became possessed of the estate of Caerynwch in the same county, of which she was the heiress. Shortly after he was appointed counsel to Queen Anne's Bounty, of which William Stevens was then treasurer, and was one of the members, and ultimately president, of 'Nobody's Club,' instituted in honour of that amiable gentleman. His principal practice was in the Court of Chancery. He formed an early friendship with Lord Eldon, and when promoted often sat for him as speaker of the House of Lords. But a long time elapsed before that promotion arrived, for, though he became successively king's counsel and solicitor-general to the queen, he was above sixty years old before he was appointed chief justice of Chester, in May 1813. He went only one circuit in that character, being raised to the bench as a baron of the Exchequer in the following February, when he was knighted. From this position he was promoted to the head of the court in April 1817. He presided for the next five years and a half with the reputation, though not of a brilliant lawyer, yet of an excellent judge, learned in his arguments and sound in his decisions. Few men have been more respected and esteemed in private life, so amiable and benevolent was his disposition; yet so fearful was he that his temper might have the appearance of partiality that when in court he was apt to assume an asperity of manner that was wholly opposed to his real character.

He died on November 11, 1823, leaving a large family, several of whom gained considerable eminence in their father's profession. His eldest son became a master in Chancery, and was for many years the representative in parliament of his native county. (*Gent. Mag.* Jan. 1834; *Life of Stevens* [1859].)

RICHARDSON, JOHN, was the third son of Anthony Richardson, a merchant of London, and was born in Copthall Court, Lothbury, on March 3, 1771. He commenced his education at Harrow, and finished it at University College, Oxford, where he took his degree of M.A. in 1795, having been assisted in his progress through the university by the benevolent aid and steady patronage of Mr. Stevens, the worthy treasurer of Queen Anne's Bounty. He aided his patron in procuring the repeal of the penal statutes against the episcopal clergy of Scotland, and was highly instrumental in forming a club to Mr. Stevens's honour, called 'Nobody's Club,' from the pseudonym under which that gentleman's various writings were published. The club still exists, and has numbered among its members men the most famous in literature, theology, and law.

Having been entered at Lincoln's Inn in June 1793, he practised as a special pleader for several years, and was not called to the bar till June 1803. In the very next year he appeared as counsel for William Cobbett, who was defendant in an action brought by Mr. Plunkett, and again for him when indicted for publishing a libel against the lord lieutenant and lord chancellor of Ireland, which was written by Mr. Justice Johnson of that country. He also soon after argued ably, though unsuccessfully, in support of the plea filed by that judge against the jurisdiction of the Court of King's Bench, and afterwards on his trial in that court. (*State Trials*, xxix. 1, 53, 394, 423.)

Joining the Western Circuit, both there and in Westminster Hall he soon established such a character for industry and legal learning as secured to him competent encouragement. When to this was added experience and observation, he obtained the laborious and responsible office of adviser to the attorney and solicitor general, commonly denominated their 'devil.' So efficient did he prove himself in this capacity, and so universally acknowledged were his superior attainments, that in November 1818 he was selected with the approbation of all to supply the vacant seat in the Court of Common Pleas, and in June following he was knighted. After filling this post with the reputation of one of the soundest lawyers of the time, he was compelled by ill health to retire from its labours in May 1824. He lived nearly seventeen years after his resignation, several of which he spent in Malta, where he composed a code of laws for that island. He died on March 19, 1841.

That excellent judge Sir John Coleridge describes him in a lecture he delivered in 1859 as 'a thoroughly instructed lawyer, an accomplished scholar, and a man of the soundest judgment—a tender-hearted, God-fearing man.' (*Life of Stevens; Gent. Mag.* July 1841.)

RICHARDSON, THOMAS, the son of Dr. Thomas Richardson, a clergyman of Mulbarton, Norfolk, was born at Hardwick in the same county on July 3, 1569. Admitted a member of Lincoln's Inn, he was called to the bar in 1595, and was elected recorder, first of Bury, and afterwards of Norwich, having been previously under-steward of the dean and chapter of that cathedral. (*Blomefield's Norfolk*, i. 684.)

He was appointed reader of Lincoln's Inn in 1614, on occasion of his being called serjeant. His next advance was to be chancellor to the queen; and soon after her death, being elected member for St. Albans, he was chosen speaker of James's third parliament in January 1621, which was remarkable for the proceedings which resulted in the disgrace of Lord Chancellor Bacon, against whom Mr. Speaker Richardson had to demand the judgment of the Lords. During this parliament he received the honour of knighthood, and after two noisy sessions it was dissolved in December following. (*Parl. Hist.* i. 1191–1371.) He was not replaced in the speaker's chair in the next parliament; but on February 20, 1625, he received the appointment of king's serjeant.

On the place of lord chief justice of the Common Pleas becoming vacant at the end of that year, eleven months were allowed to pass before it was filled up. It was then given to Sir Thomas Richardson on November 22, 1626, not without suspicion that its acquisition cost him 17,000*l*. (*Yonge's Diary*, 97.) There is a letter in the State Paper Office (*Cal.* [1625–6] 482) from the king directing him as soon as he has the chief justiceship to admit one Edward Nicholas to a clerkship of the Treasury, anciently called the clerk of Hell, which the chief justice of the Common Pleas had been used to appoint. This perhaps was one of the conditions of his advance; but his marriage in the next month with his second wife, Elizabeth, daughter of Sir Thomas Beaumont, of Staughton in Leicestershire, and widow of Sir John Ashburnham, sister of the Duke of Buckingham's mother, more probably accounts for the elevation. When, two years afterwards, the duke was assassinated, Sir Thomas, on a question put to him by the king, whether the murderer might not be put to the rack, had the gratification to convey the judges' unanimous opinion that torture was not known or allowed by the law. On two or three other occasions he showed himself moderate in his sentences and independent in his principles (*State Trials*, iii. 359–374); but he was considered by the parliament to be a favourer of the Jesuits. (*Parl. Hist.* ii. 475.) After presiding for five years in the Common Pleas, he was removed on October 24, 1631, to the chief justiceship of the King's Bench, where he sat during the remainder of his life. He died on February 4, 1635, and was buried in Westminster Abbey, where his monument may still be seen.

Although esteemed a good lawyer, he was not respected on the bench. Evelyn (i. 10) calls him 'that jeering judge;' and no doubt he carried his inclination to humour and jocularity too much into court. The chief justice was inclined to the Puritans. His sentence against Sherfield for breaking a painted glass window was more lenient than that of other members of the court; and he made an order, while on the Somersetshire Circuit, to suppress wakes and other pastimes on Sundays. For this the bishops, who considered it an intrusion on their power, encouraged Archbishop Laud to complain; and the chief justice received a reprimand from the council. (*Whitelocke*, 47.) Even then he could not refrain from joking; as he passed out he declared that 'the lawn sleeves had almost choked him.' To remove, perhaps, all suspicion of his principles, he was as violent and absurd as any of his colleagues in the Star Chamber, in the unjustifiable sentence pronounced shortly after against William Prynne for writing his 'Histrio-mastix.' (*Rushworth*, ii. 234, 248.) And upon Prynne's being brought before the council on a subsequent occasion, and the question being, whether he might go to church and be allowed books, the chief justice, not being able to restrain his joke, said, 'Let him have the Book of Martyrs, for the Puritans do account him a martyr.'

While attending at the assizes at Salisbury, a prisoner, whom he had condemned to death for some felony, threw a brickbat at his head; but, stooping at the time, it only knocked off his hat. On his friends congratulating him on his escape he said, 'You see, now, if I had been an upright judge I had been slaine.' The additional punishment upon this offender is thus curiously recorded by Chief Justice Treby, in the margin of Dyer's Reports (p. 188, b):—

'Richardson, C. J. de C. B. at Assizes at Salisbury in Summer 1631, fuit assault per Prisoner la condemne pur Felony;—que puis son condemnation ject un Brickbat a le dit Justice, que narrowly mist. Et pur ceo immediately fuit Indictment drawn pur Noy envers le Prisoner, et son dexter manus ampute et fixe al Gibbet, sur que luy mesme immediatement hange in presence de Court.'

By his first wife, Ursula, daughter of John Southwell, Esq., of Barham Hall in Suffolk, he had a large family. His second wife, Lady Ashburnham, brought him no issue. She, in 1628, Sir Thomas being then chief justice of the Common Pleas, was created a baroness of Scotland, by the title of Lady Cramond, with remainder to his children, which became extinct in 1735. (*Collins's Peerage*, iv. 253.)

RICKHILL, WILLIAM, is described by Sir Edward Coke as a native of Ireland, and by Hasted as establishing himself in the county of Kent, and becoming possessed of the manor of Ridley there. He is first mentioned as one of the king's serjeants in 1384, 7 Richard II. Five years afterwards, on May 20, 1389, he was constituted a judge of the Common Pleas.

When the king's uncle, the Duke of Gloucester, was arrested and taken to Calais in July 1397, Sir William Rickhill was employed to take his deposition. He states that he was awakened in the middle of the night of September 7 at his house at Essingham in Kent, by a king's messenger with a writ requiring him to go to Calais with the Earl of Nottingham, the captain of that town, and there to do as the earl should order him; and he was directed immediately to proceed to Dover. On his arrival at Calais another writ was presented to him commanding him to hear all that the Duke of Gloucester had to communicate, and to report the same to the king. Sir William was wholly at a loss to understand the object of this commission, as there had been a report of the duke's death for some time previously both in England and Calais. The earl, however, satisfying him that the duke was still alive, Sir William had the precaution to insist on having two witnesses present during the interrogatory. At his first interview with the royal prisoner Sir William requested that the duke would put in writing what he had to say, and keep one copy for himself. To this the duke agreed, and afterwards gave to Sir William nine articles to be taken to the king, at the same time soliciting the judge to return the next day in case he should wish to add anything to his communication. On the following morning, being refused admittance, Rickhill returned to England, and made his report to the king. (*Rot. Parl.* iii. 340.) The duke was soon after privately murdered, and so much of the articles which he had delivered to the judge as were deemed necessary were brought as his confession before parliament. That assembly, notwithstanding his death, condemned him as a traitor, and adjudged all his lands, &c., to be forfeited.

On the accession of Henry IV., September 30, 1399, Sir William received a new patent for his place; but on November 18 he was called upon by the parliament to answer before Chief Justice Clopton for his conduct in obtaining the duke's confession. He gave the 'round unvarnished tale' related above, showing that he had merely executed the commission he had received, without any previous knowledge of its intent, and strictly in performance of his duty. The Lords could do no other than acquit him. (*Ibid.* 342.)

Resuming his seat on the bench, fines continued to be levied before him till Trinity Term 1407. (*Dugdale's Orig.* 46.) How soon after this he died does not appear; but William his eldest son was member of parliament for Kent in the following reign. (*Hasted*, i. 243, ii. 460.)

RIDEL, GEOFFREY, was a baron in the reign of Henry I., of whom very few particulars remain.

The authority on which he is called chief justiciary of England is that of Henry of Huntingdon, in his 'Epistle de Mundi Contemptu,' one copy of which, however, omits his name. This author gives the title to several parties who were acting as justiciaries at the same period, and may, perhaps, have considered all those who sat judicially in the Aula Regis as entitled to that designation. The assertion in this instance certainly requires some confirmation, especially as the chief authority was undoubtedly exercised by Roger, Bishop of Salisbury, during the greater part of the reign.

Dugdale mentions him as united with Robert Bloet, Bishop of Lincoln, Ralph Basset, and others, in a commission to hear and determine a case relating to the privilege of sanctuary in the church of Ripon, and then adds that he succeeded Ralph Basset as justice of England. This, however, is not very probable, as Ralph Basset lived several years after the death of Ridel.

That event occurred in 1119, when he shared the fate of Prince William, who was drowned on his return from Normandy. William of Malmesbury, who relates the disaster, mentions among the sufferers 'dapiferi, camerarii, pincernæ regis, ac multi proceres cum eis,' and would scarcely have omitted the name or the title of so important a personage as a chief justiciary.

He married Geva, the daughter of Hugh de Abrincis, Earl of Chester, by whom he left only a daughter, named Matilda, who married Richard Basset, the justiciary. Their eldest son assumed the name of Ridel, and the barony became extinct in the third generation. (*Angl. Sac.* ii. 701; *Dugdale's Baron.* i. 555.)

RIDEL, GEOFFREY (BISHOP OF ELY), was, according to the account of one writer (*Allen's Yorkshire,* vi. 154), a younger brother of the before-mentioned Eustace Fitz-John, but the authority is not sufficiently distinct to be entirely depended on. He was one of the chaplains of Henry II., and so much in the royal favour that, after Becket's elevation to the primacy, he was appointed his successor as archdeacon of Canterbury, about Christmas 1162. He probably continued to be employed at court, for his name stands second of the 'assidentes justiciæ regis' before whom, in 1165, a charter between the abbots of St. Alban's and Westminster was executed in the Exchequer. (*Madox,* i. 44.) He took a prominent part in the king's contest with the archbishop, and was sent with John of Oxford, in 1164, to the pope, to obtain his confirmation of the ancient customs and dignities of the realm; and again, in 1169, he was one of the ambassadors to the court of France, with the king's request that Becket, who had withdrawn there, might not be permitted to remain. Both embassies were unsuccessful. The irritated primate included him in the excommunication which he pronounced in 1169 against several of the bishops and chief men of the kingdom; and in announcing the sentence to the Bishop of Hereford, he designated the archdeacon 'archidiabolum et Antichristi membrum.' On Henry's remonstrance, however, the pope's nuncios found it necessary to absolve him before the end of the year, he being one of those who personally attended the king. Geoffrey's favour at court increased with Becket's oppression, and, accordingly, in the same year the custody of the see of Ely was placed in his hands, and so remained during its vacancy, which lasted about four years. In 1173 the bishopric itself was given to him; but he was not admitted to it until he had made his solemn protestation, in the chapel of St. Catherine in Westminster, that he had been in no ways knowingly accessory to the murder of the archbishop.

In 1179 Bishop Geoffrey was appointed, with the Bishops of Winchester and Norwich, to fill the office of chief justiciary; and on the division of the kingdom by the council of Windsor into four judicial circuits these prelates were respectively placed at the head of three of them. (*Dugdale's Orig.* 20.) They were superseded the next year by the appointment of Ranulph de Glanville as sole justiciary. Geoffrey appears, however, to have acted subsequently in court, as he was one of the justiciers before whom a fine was levied in 1182. (*Hunter's Preface.*)

In the roll of 1 Richard I. (67, &c.) his pleas are recorded as a justice itinerant in no less than five counties. As, however, he died on August 21, 1189, in the interval between the death of King Henry and the coronation of King Richard, this circuit probably took place during the last months of Henry's reign.

King Richard, finding that he had died intestate, appropriated to the expenses of the coronation the treasure he found in his coffers.

The cognomen 'superbus,' which he acquired, is stated to have been given from the arrogance of his disposition and his want of affability. The history of Ely relates that his tomb was violated, and that his successor, William de Longchamp, on the day of his enthronisation, ascended the pulpit, and, with the other bishops present, excommunicated all those who had committed or consented to the sacrilege. (*Godwin,* 251; *Angl. Sac.* i. 631; *Madox,* i. 307; *Lord Lyttelton; Hasted.*)

RIDEWARE, WILLIAM DE, only occurs

as one of the justices itinerant with William Briwer and Simon Basset, fixing the tallage for the counties of Nottingham and Derby in 9 Richard I., 1197–8 (*Madox*, i. 733); and in 1 John he is one of the pledges for the payment of a fine to the king in Northamptonshire. (*Rot. de Oblatis*, 3.)

RIGBY, ALEXANDER. 'That Colonel Rigby be a baron of the Exchequer' is the curious entry of June 1, 1649, in Whitelocke's 'Memorials' (405). It appears, however, that he was bred a lawyer, and took up arms on behalf of the parliament at the earliest stage of the troubles. He was of a Lancashire family, then and now seated at Middleton, and was probably the son of another Alexander Rigby, clerk of the peace in Lancashire in 1611. (*Cal. State Papers* [1611–18], 100.) Elected member for Wigan in that county in the Long Parliament of 1640, he distinguished himself by moving, in a violent speech, plentifully interspersed with scraps of Latin and Biblical quotations, that Lord Keeper Finch should be accused of high treason. Made a colonel by the parliament, and entrusted with the command of the Lancashire forces, his first exploit was routing a party of the king's near Thurland Castle in 1643, and taking 400 prisoners and their commander-in-chief; which, says Whitelocke, 'was the more discoursed of because Rigby was a lawyer.' His next service is in the lengthened siege of Latham House, just before the battle of Marston Moor; and immediately after he was appointed one of the commissioners for executing martial law. In the 'Mystery of the Good Old Cause' he is said to have been governor of Boston.

When the death of the king rendered the military assistance of Colonel Rigby no longer necessary the parliament raised him to the bench as a baron of the Exchequer. (*Parl. Hist.* ii. 611, 692, iii. 286, 1607; *Whitelocke*, 77, 93, 405.) He retained his judicial dignity little more than a year, dying on August 18, 1650, of an infection taken at Croydon on the circuit. (*Peck's Desid. C.* b. xiv. 23.)

He married twice. His first wife was Margaret, daughter of Sir Gilbert Hoghton, Bart.; his second was Anna, daughter of John Gobert, Esq., and widow of Thomas Legh, Esq. By both he had a large family. (*Wotton's Baronet.* i. 20, 152.)

RIPARIIS, ROBERT DE (Rivers), is recorded once as a justice itinerant in 36 Henry III., 1252, into Berkshire, Oxford, and Northampton; and as the under-noticed Walter lived in the first-named of these counties, it is not unlikely that Robert was his son, and that both in succession were placed in the commission on account of their residence within it.

RIPARIIS, WALTER DE, is no further noticed than that he was one of those appointed in 1 Henry III. to assess and receive the hidage of Berkshire. (*Rot. Claus.* i. 306.) His possessions in that county were no doubt the cause of his being selected to act as a justice itinerant in it in 3 Henry III.

RIVALLIS, PETER DE, who is sometimes called de Orivallis, was a Poictevin by birth, and Roger de Wendover plainly describes him as the son of Peter de Rupibus, Bishop of Winchester. Other writers more delicately describe him as the nephew of that powerful prelate; and of course he is so designated in any record where their connection is alluded to. Whatever was the real relationship, he soon experienced the benefit arising from such patronage. So early as 6 John, 1204, that king presented to him all the churches which Gilbert de Beseby, deceased, held in Lincolnshire of his donation. (*Rot. Pat.* 43.) He is not mentioned during the remainder of that reign; but in 3 Henry III., 1218, he was one of the king's chamberlains, and was a clerk in the wardrobe. (*Rot. Claus.* i. 383, &c.) In 1232 he is recorded as custos of the escheats and wards (*Excerpt. e Rot. Fin.* i. 225–252); and in the next year his patron, the Bishop of Winchester, procured for him the high appointment of treasurer. (*Madox*, ii. 34.) About the same time he signed himself 'Capicerio Pictaviæ.' (*Ibid.* i. 65.) He now so effectually ingratiated himself with the king that to this high office several others of great responsibility and emolument were added, among which were those of custos of the forests, and of most of the castles in England. But the dismissal of the old ministers, and the substitution of Poictevins for all the former officers, naturally disgusted the nobles and the people, and led to a reaction, which produced the disgrace of the bishop, his father, in April 1234, and his own expulsion from court, with a threat that, if he did not resume the tonsure, he should lose both his eyes. He fled with the bishop to Winchester; but, being summoned before the king to render an account of his ministry, he appeared 'in habitu clericali cum tonsura et lata corona.' His answers were so unsatisfactory that he was made to give up all his possessions, and was sent to the Tower, from which, however, he was shortly released by the Archbishop of Canterbury, and allowed to return to his sanctuary at Winchester. From this retirement he was suddenly recalled in 1236, and, notwithstanding all his former offences, was restored to the royal confidence.

He resumed his original duties in the wardrobe, of which he was appointed keeper, and in 1251 he had a quittance from all debts and accounts to be rendered to the king from the time he first had the custody of the wardrobe till that date. (*Ibid.* ii. 230.)

It was probably in this character that the Great Seal was committed to him in conjunction with William de Kilkenny in 1249, when John de Lexinton retired from court, the wardrobe being a usual place of depositing the Seal when the chancellorship was vacant. There is nothing to show that Peter de Rivallis was concerned in the Chancery, nor that he acted in the office.

In February 1249 he was one of the king's council sent to receive the tallage of the city of London, and on July 16, 1255, he was constituted a baron of the Exchequer, retaining his place at the wardrobe. (*Madox*, i. 712, ii. 17; *Pell Records*, iii. 39, 40.) Matthew Paris relates that about Michaelmas 1257 he was again appointed treasurer of the chamber on the death of Hurtaldus, but probably soon after died, as the last notice of his name occurs in a royal grant to him in May 1258 of a piece of land in Winchester. (*Holinshed*, iv. 289; *R. de Wendover*, iv. 244-313; *Excerpt. e Rot. Fin.* ii. 279.)

ROBERT (EARL OF MORETON or MORTAGNE, and EARL OF CORNWALL). Arlotta, the mistress of Robert Duke of Normandy, and mother of William the Conqueror, afterwards married Herluin de Conteville, the founder of the abbey of Crestein, and had by him two sons, the eldest of whom was this Robert, and the youngest was Odo, Bishop of Bayeux. Robert received from Duke William the barony of Bourgh and the earldom of Moreton or Mortagne in Normandy.

When the invasion of England was projected, Robert greatly promoted the expedition, and assisted in the triumph of his brother, bearing the banner of St. Michael before him in the battle. As a warrior, he would not have been overlooked by the generosity of William; but, considering even his relationship to the Conqueror, his share in the spoil seems enormous. He not only was created Earl of Cornwall, but received vast possessions in various counties, amounting, it is stated, to no less than 973 manors.

Although he is described as somewhat heavy in intellect, yet, with these proofs of the king's affection, it is not unlikely that he should have been appointed, in conjunction with Archbishop Lanfranc, and Geoffrey, Bishop of Coutance, to the office of chief justiciary during some part of this reign, as Dugdale supposes from several precepts having been discovered which appear to bear that interpretation.

It is believed that he outlived the Conqueror, and died about 1090. His remains were buried in the church of Bermondsey, where he had a mansion.

By his wife, Maud, the daughter of Roger de Montgomery, Earl of Shrewsbury, he left a son William, who succeeded to both his earldoms; but, having joined with Duke Robert against King Henry I., and been defeated at Tenchebrai in 1105, he died in prison, suffering in addition the cruel deprivation of his eyes. (*Will. Malm. Gesta*, 456; *Baronage*, i. 24; *Hutchins's Dorset*, i. 31.)

ROCELINE is mentioned in no former list as a vice-chancellor to Richard I., but there are three royal charters in the 'Monasticon' (v. 372, 456, 625), given under the hand of 'Magistri Rocelini, tunc agentis vices Cancellarii nostri,' all dated at Rupes Andeli, in 10 Richard I.—one on November 11, 1198; another on December 9, 1198; and the third on February 3, 1199.

ROCHE, THOMAS, is only known as being appointed fourth baron of the Exchequer in Michaelmas, 3 Henry VII. 1487. He probably retained his place till 1504, when John Alleyn became fourth baron. (*Exchequer Books.*)

ROCHESTER, SOLOMON DE, or, as his name is usually abbreviated, Solomon de Roff, was one of the canons of St. Paul's. He was first selected as a justice itinerant to assist the regular judges in 2 Edward I., 1274, when he acted in Middlesex, and in the following year in Worcestershire. In 1276 he is called by Dugdale one of the justices of assize, but there was not at that time any distinction between the two classes; and two years afterwards his name again appears among the justices itinerant, and so continues till 1287, on the last occasion being placed at the head of the list. (*Dugdale's Orig.* 21.) In this position he is named in various documents among the Rolls of Parliament as acting for the two following years. (*Rot. Parl.* i. 42, 48, &c.) These rolls contain several complaints against him by parties in the country, but they probably were the consequence, not the cause, of the disgrace which he shared with most of his judicial brethren in 1289. The corruption charged against him must have been of a far deeper dye than those complaints exhibit, for he was compelled to pay a fine of no less than 4000 marks before he was discharged from his imprisonment.

There is no evidence of his having been allowed to resume his duties as a judge, and the only other published record concerning him is a presentation made to the justices itinerant in Kent of his being poisoned at his house at Snodland in that county by Master Wynand, the parson of the parish, on August 14, 1293. (*Abb. Placit.* 200.) Sir Edward Coke, however, in pronouncing the sentence against Sir John Hollis and others, tried in the Star Chamber in 1615, for traducing the public justice, refers to this case, and states that the prayer of the monk (as he calls him) to be delivered to the censure of the Church was denied, 'because the same was a wrong to the state to poison a judge.' (*State Trials*, ii. 1031.) But the entry by no means supports Sir Edward either in his fact or his inference. Solomon de Rochester is not mentioned in it as a judge, nor is any reference made to his having filled that office; and though it appears that the king refused at first to deliver the delinquent to the Bishop of Rochester, it was because he had shown too great a desire to procure his liberation and to purge him from the charge. Wynand was therefore handed over to the church of Canterbury, the archbishopric being then vacant, but eventually was actually given up to the Bishop of Rochester. The result of the investigation does not appear.

RODBOROUGH, MILO DE, took his name from that town in Gloucestershire, but was apparently resident in Worcestershire in the early part of the reign of Edward II., as in the third year he was one of the assessors and collectors in that county of the twenty-fifth which was granted by parliament, and was also in a local judicial commission therein. In the next year, 1310, he was the last named of the three justices of assize appointed for both these counties and three neighbouring ones. In May 1311 a commission was issued into Gloucestershire to four justices to hear the complaints made against him in a petition from the men of that county, charging him with many acts of oppression, corruption, and malversation in the execution of his office. The result of this enquiry does not appear, but it may be presumed to have been favourable to him, inasmuch as in the two following years he was responsibly employed, and in the latter was one of three assigned to talliate the cities, &c., in the same five counties. He died in 7 Edward II. (*Parl. Writs*, ii. p. ii. 1344; *Abb. Rot. Orig.* i. 205.)

RODES, FRANCIS, was a descendant from Gerard de Rodes, of Horncastle in Lincolnshire, a powerful baron in the reign of Henry II., whose family eventually settled in Derbyshire. He was the son of John Rodes, Esq., of Staveley Woodthorpe, and of Attelina, daughter of Thomas Hewitt, of Walles in Yorkshire. Born about 1534, he was educated at St. John's College, Cambridge, and being admitted a member of Gray's Inn, he was called to the bar in 1552, arriving at the dignity of reader in 1566, and again in 1576. In Hilary Term 1578 he was advanced to the degree of the coif, and on August 21, 1582, was made queen's serjeant. His elevation to the bench as a judge of the Common Pleas is dated June 29, 1585, and the last fine which was acknowledged before him was in November 1588. (*Dugdale's Orig.* 48, 294.) In the following year he died at Staveley Woodthorpe, leaving issue by both of his marriages. His first wife was Elizabeth, daughter of Brian Sandford, Esq., of Thorpe Salvine in Yorkshire; and his second was Mary, daughter of Francis Charlton, Esq., of Appley in Shropshire.

His eldest son, John, who was knighted and served as sheriff of Derbyshire, was the father of Francis, whom Charles I. raised to the baronetcy in 1641, a title which became extinct in 1743. (*Wotton's Baronet.* ii. 255.)

ROGER (BISHOP OF SALISBURY) was curate of a small church in the neighbourhood of Caen, and is said to have ingratiated himself with Henry by the celerity with which he despatched the service when the prince and his followers chanced to be present. From that time he became attached to the fortunes of the prince, who, though the apparent motive for the selection was not very commendable, had no reason to regret in after years the confidence he reposed in him.

Roger became an active and zealous servant, and, by the dexterous management of whatever business he was engaged in, so endeared himself to Henry during his adversity that when he mounted the throne of England he not only enriched him with many preferments, but advanced him to the highest employments.

In the first or second year of Henry's reign he was appointed chancellor, succeeding William Giffard. Thynne, and after him Spelman and Philipot, place him in the same office in 1107, and again at the end of the reign. But, taking the charters as the best authority, it appears from them that he did not retain the Great Seal long after he was appointed Bishop of Salisbury, which was on April 13, 1102. In the 'Monasticon' there are six charters with his name as chancellor, four of which are before he was bishop, the earliest being dated in September 1101, and two only with the addition of his episcopal title. (*Monast.* i. 164, 521, ii. 145, iv. 16, 17, v. 1114.) In March 1103 William Giffard was again in office, and from that time to the end of the reign there is a regular succession of other chancellors.

Whatever was the position he held in the state, there is little doubt that from a very early period the whole of the business of the kingdom was submitted to his care, the treasures were in his keeping, and the expenses under his regulation. That he was well versed in the knowledge of the Exchequer is proved by the author of the ancient 'Dialogus de Scaccario,' Richard Fitz-Nigel, who, though his grand-nephew, yet, writing nearly forty years after his death, may be fairly trusted when describing his official character. He calls him 'vir prudens, consiliis providus, sermone discretus, et ad maxima quaeque negotia per Dei gratiam repente praecipuus;' and adds, 'Hic igitur, succrescenti in eum principis, ac cleri, populique favore, Sarisburiensis Episcopus factus, maximis in regno fungebatur honoribus, et de Scaccario plurimum habuit scientiam: adeo ut non sit ambiguum, sed ex ipsis Rotulis manifestum, plurimum sub eo floruisse.'

Part of his duty as chancellor was to attend to the business of the revenue, but it was peculiarly so in the offices of treasurer and chief justiciary or president of the Exchequer, in which he was afterwards placed. It is probable that he was not invested with the latter till the year 1107, because, having been offered that charge immediately after his appointment to the prelacy, he would not consent to accept it, deeming a judicial office incompatible with his episcopal functions, without the authority of the pope and the archbishop. Although, therefore, his election to the bishopric took place in April 1102, yet, being one of those whose consecrations were in abeyance pending the contest between the king and Anselm, his scruples could not be removed till that dispute was accommodated. This did not occur till 1107, on August 11 in which year his consecration took place.

From this period, therefore, we may consider him in full power, presiding over the administration of justice, and regulating the revenue of the realm and the affairs of the state. The suppression of those violations of the law which were prevalent in the last reign, the improvement in the purity of the coin, the punishment of the oppression of the royal purveyors, were the results of his wise and considerate counsels; and, though the whole government of the kingdom was entrusted to him in the frequent and long-continued absences of the king in Normandy, no contemporary historian hints a doubt of his integrity, and no fact is recorded which can raise a suspicion that his ministry was distasteful to the people.

His conduct was equally satisfactory to his sovereign, who never withdrew his confidence nor neglected to bestow upon him substantial marks of his favour. Among others, his two nephews, Alexander and Nigel, were invested with the bishoprics of Lincoln (in 1123) and Ely (in 1133); and to his own care was entrusted the safe custody of the king's brother Robert, the captive Duke of Normandy. When King Henry was anxious to insure the succession of the kingdom to his daughter the empress, Roger not only joined with the other nobles in taking the oath of fealty to Matilda on this occasion, but overcame the scruples of some who were unwilling to do so. Yet no sooner was King Henry dead than, setting aside his oath, from which he pretended the subsequent marriage of the empress with Geoffrey Earl of Anjou, without the consent of the peers, had absolved him, he aided Stephen in his assumption of the crown. Stephen, however, entertained doubts of his fidelity, which he at first endeavoured to secure by numerous favours, continuing him in some of his offices, either as chief justiciary or treasurer, presenting him with the borough of Malmesbury, and conferring on his son, Roger, the office of chancellor. Thynne and some others place the bishop himself as chancellor in the early part of Stephen's reign; but they evidently confound him with his son Roger, as both their names appear on three charters of the first year, the one being designated as bishop, and the other as chancellor.

The king's jealousy was at last excited by the representations made to him that the magnitude and strength of the castles built by the bishop at Devizes, Malmesbury, and Shirburn, and the additions he had made to that of Salisbury, were intended to support the cause of Matilda, whenever he should find an opportunity to declare for her. Whether the king really believed these suggestions, or whether, being now, as he imagined, firmly seated on the throne, he forgot the assistance he had received in his anxiety to obtain possession of the bishop's wealth, may well be doubted. He determined, however, to seize his castles and his property on the first opportunity. This was soon contrived. In June 1139 the reluctant bishop was compelled to attend a council at Oxford, where, on a pretended quarrel between his servants and those of the Earl of Brittany, the king required him, in satisfaction for the breach of the peace, to give up his castles as pledges of his fealty, and thereupon committed him and his son Roger, the chancellor, and his nephew Alexander, Bishop of Lincoln, to close custody until this should have been done. His other nephew, Nigel, Bishop of Ely, suspecting to what these proceedings tended, fled, and shut himself up in his uncle's castle of Devizes, which he refused to surrender. The king immediately marched thither, taking his prisoners with him, and, having erected a gibbet in front of the walls, pronounced in the presence of Bishop Roger sentence of death upon his son, which he declared should be forthwith executed unless the gates were opened to him. Nigel, regardless of the entreaties of his uncle, persisted notwithstanding in his refusal, and the king directed the sentence to be executed. The victim ascended the scaffold, and the rope was adjusted, when Bishop Roger, horrified that his son should be so murdered, threw himself at the king's feet, and bound himself by an oath, if his son were saved, to taste no food till the royal mandate was obeyed. Nigel at last unwillingly submitted, but not till his uncle had endured three days' fast.

The king, on taking possession of the castle, appropriated to his own use a treasure of 40,000 marks, besides an immense quantity of plate and jewels which he found there.

A council was held at Winchester to examine into this extraordinary affair, and others of a similar character affecting the bishops and clergy, at which Bishop Roger made his last appearance in public life. The king was represented at it by certain earls, and his claim was defended by Alberic de Vere, then renowned in the law. Nothing, however, could be done against the power of Stephen, who retained the possessions he had thus acquired.

The unfortunate bishop, either through grief at his loss, or from the effect of his long fasting, was soon after seized with a quartan ague, of which he died on December 4, 1139. As his death approached, he directed the small remainder of his wealth to be placed on the altar of his church, devoting it to the completion of the building; but even this he had the mortification of hearing was seized and taken away by the king's orders.

While in the conduct of public business, he is stated to have invariably devoted his mornings to the performance of his episcopal duties, and he grudged no expense in the renovation and ornament of his cathedral. He was seated at Salisbury more than thirty-two years; his remains were deposited there, and his memory was regarded with such high estimation that he is usually named with the addition of 'Magnus.' (*Madox,* i. 33, 78, ii. 381; *Godwin,* 337; *Angl. Sac.* ii. 700; *Wendover,* ii. 183, &c.; *Malmesbury,* 636, &c.; *Lord Lyttelton; Lingard,* &c.)

ROKEBY, THOMAS. As the knightly deeds of the house of Rokeby, illustrious both in council and in camp, have been fully recorded in ancient annals and modern verse, the legal honours by which the family was distinguished ought not to be forgotten. Sir Thomas Rokeby was lord justice of Ireland in the reign of Edward III.; William Rokeby, Archbishop of Dublin, was lord chancellor of that kingdom under Henry VII. and VIII.; Dr. John Rokeby, a famous civilian, became vicar-general of the province of York in the reign of the latter king; Ralph Rokeby, by his eminence as a lawyer, received the dignity of the coif from Edward VI.; and Thomas Rokeby, whose career is now to be traced, was elevated to the English bench in the reign of William and Mary.

The Rokebys were a very prolific race, and the family was multiplied into numerous branches, most of whom settled in various parts of Yorkshire. William Rokeby of Skiers was honoured in 1661 with a baronetcy, which became extinct in 1678; and his brother, Thomas Rokeby of Barnby, after having had eleven children by Elizabeth, sister of Sir William Bury of Grantham, was killed at the battle of Dunbar in 1650. Thomas, the future judge, was the second of his sons. Born about 1632, he was educated at Catherine College, Cambridge, and took his degree of B.A. in January 1650, becoming a fellow of the college at the following Christmas. Towards its new buildings in 1674 he contributed 20*l.*, and bound himself to pay 5*l.* a year during his life towards the discharge of certain annuities to persons who had advanced money for the completion of the works. He qualified himself for legal honours at Gray's Inn, was called to the bar in June 1657, and became an ancient in 1676.

When not engaged in term he took up his residence at York, and engrossed much of the practice of that and the neighbouring counties, being the chief adviser of the Puritans of the north, of whose religious opinions he was a zealous and consistent supporter. He seems to have been in some way connected with the court of Cromwell, for he himself relates (as Dr. Henry Sampson records in his Diary) that he was present when the Duke of Crequi was received by Cromwell at the Banqueting House as ambassador from the French king, and delivered a letter to him superscribed 'To his most Serene Highness Oliver, Lord Protector of England, France, and Ireland.' Cromwell, looking at the address, turned upon his heel, and put the letter in his pocket without reading it. The indignant ambassador, on enquiring the cause of this insult, found that the offence was that the letter was not directed 'To our dear Brother, Oliver,' on hearing which the great Louis felt it expedient to comply. (*Gent. Mag.* April 1851, p. 386.)

In the last months of the reign of James II. he took an important part in the great movement at York in favour of the Prince of Orange. His known principles, his high character, and probably a desire to conciliate the Presbyterian party, pointed him out for selection as one of the first judges at the revolution. He was accordingly placed in the Common Pleas on May 8, 1689, his serjeant's ring bearing the appropriate motto 'Veniundo restituit rem.' He soon after received the honour of knighthood. After sitting for six years and a half in the Common Pleas, he was removed on October 29, 1695, to the King's Bench, where he remained till his death, on November 26, 1699. He was buried at Sandal, near Doncaster, where a sumptuous monument was erected to his memory in the chapel of Archbishop Rokeby.

His excellence as a man, his piety as a Christian, and his uprightness as a judge are exemplified by his Diary and the correspondence which has come down to us. He married Ursula, daughter of James Danby, of New Building (formerly Kirby Knowle Castle), near Thirsk, who brought him no issue. (*Memoir of Judge Rokeby*, 38, 56, *in Surtees Soc. Public. for* 1860; *Luttrell*, i. 529, iii. 543, iv. 587.)

ROKELE, ROBERT DE, was of a family which, according to Hasted, originally came from Rochelle in France, and was settled in Kent, where they held the manor of Beckenham. In another place, however, he says that they received their name from the parish of Rokesle (now Ruxley) in that county. The latter seems the more probable account; for it appears that Robert de Rokele had land in Rokesle, which, in consequence of his joining the insurgent barons, and being taken prisoner in Rochester Castle in 17 John, was forfeited with his other possessions. His mother, Margaret de Modingden, negotiated his release, which she succeeded in procuring in the following May, on the payment of a fine of five hundred marks, his two sons, Henry and Richard, becoming hostages for his good behaviour. (*Rot. Pat.* 161-199; *Rot. de Finibus*, 596, 604; *Rot. Claus.* i. 267.)

In 18 Henry III., July 6, 1234, he was admitted as one of the king's justices of the bench; but he does not appear to have joined any of the circuits. He died about 1248. (*Excerpt. e Rot. Fin.* ii. 40; *Hasted*, i. 529, ii. 134.)

ROLFE, ROBERT MONSEY (LORD CRANWORTH), was of a family which has held a respectable position in the county of Norfolk for the last three centuries, and his ancestors for three generations have been beneficed clergymen in it. His grandfather, the Rev. Robert Rolfe, rector of Hilborough, by his marriage into the Nelson family became connected with the gallant admiral, who was first cousin of the lord chancellor's father, the Rev. Edmund Rolfe, rector of Cockley-Clay. His mother was Jemima, daughter of William Alexander, Esq., and granddaughter of the celebrated Dr. Monsey, physician to Chelsea Hospital. He was the elder of their two sons, and was born at Cranworth on December 18, 1790.

After spending some little time at the Bury school he was sent to Winchester, from whence he proceeded to Trinity College, Cambridge. He took his degree as seventeenth wrangler in 1812, and was then elected fellow of Downing College. Called to the bar by Lincoln's Inn in 1816, he received, after sixteen years' practice as a junior barrister in Chancery, the honour of a silk gown in 1832, and entered parliament in the same year as member for Penryn. Supporting there the liberal side of politics, he was appointed solicitor-general on November 6, 1834, but was obliged in little more than a month to give place to Sir William Webb Follett, on the accession to power of the conservative party. But at the end of six months more he was restored to his place with the return of the whigs to power, and was then knighted. He continued solicitor-general from May 4, 1835, to the end of November 1839, when he was raised to the bench of the Exchequer. Though he had only practised as a barrister in the Court of Chancery, he had acquired experience in cases at Nisi Prius and criminal law as recorder of Ipswich, an office which he had held for many years. To this is to be attributed the facility with which he entered on his new duties, and the excellent manner in which he discharged them.

During the eleven years that he sat in the Exchequer he acted, from June 19 to July 15, 1850, as one of the commissioners of the Great Seal, and on November 3 he was constituted the third vice-chancellor. In the following month he was created Lord Cranworth, being the first and only instance of a vice-chancellor receiving the dignity of the peerage. In the next year the act passed for constituting two lord justices of appeal in Chancery; and on October 8, 1851, Sir James Lewis Knight-Bruce and Lord Cranworth were the first two selected for the experiment.

Before fifteen months were passed he was called upon to take a still higher office. On the resumption of power by the liberal party, the Great Seal, on December 28, 1852, was placed in his hands, where it remained for the five years during which they conducted the administration. On the accession of Lord Derby in February 1858 he of course resigned his office, and was not replaced in it when Lord Palmerston, in June 1859, became prime minister, his increased age inducing him not to resist the claims of Sir Richard Bethell, afterwards Lord Westbury. In temporary retirement he devoted himself to hearing appeals both in the House of Lords and the privy council, till the end of the session of 1865, when, on the resignation of Lord Westbury, he accepted the Seal for the second time on July 7. The conservative ministry acceding to power in the following year, he of course again retired from office on July 6, 1867. Continuing his legislative and judicial duties till less that a week before his death, he succumbed to the tremendous heat of the weather on July 26, 1868, when from failure of issue the title became extinct.

He married Laura, daughter of William Carr, Esq., of Frognal, Middlesex.

ROLLE, HENRY. The founder of the opulent family of Rolle was a merchant in London, who acquired a large fortune in the reign of Henry VIII., and settled himself at Stevenstone in Devonshire. To a descendant of his second son, George, the barony of Rolle of Stevenstone was granted in 1748, but the title became extinct in 1842. The judge was the grandson of the merchant's fourth son, Henry, whose eldest son, Robert, married Joan, the daughter of Thomas Hele, of Fleet in the same county, and left four sons, the second of whom was the judge.

Henry Rolle was born at Heanton-Sachevil in Devonshire, about 1589, and was sent to Exeter College, Oxford. From thence he went to the Inner Temple, where he was called to the bar; and, practising in the King's Bench, his name is of frequent occurrence in the Reports after Michaelmas Term 1629, the arguments of the juniors being frequently omitted by the reporters. He had used his time well in reporting the cases of James's reign, which were published after his death, and are still in considerable repute. That he had acquired too some eminence at an earlier period is manifest from his being selected as member of the last parliament of James I., representing Kellington, and of the first three parliaments of Charles I., in which he represented Truro. He took the popular side from the commencement of his political career, in the first parliament of Charles urging a redress of grievances, and in the second arguing in the case of the Duke of Buckingham that common fame was a sufficient ground for accusation. (*Parl. Hist.* ii. 35, 55.)

He subsequently devoted himself wholly to his profession, and was fully engaged in the courts. Four times appointed reader of his inn, he was prevented by the prevailing plague from performing the duties of that office till the last occasion in Lent 1639; but during his leisure he employed himself in compiling that 'Abridgment of Cases and Resolutions of the Law,' which has been held up by some of the ablest lawyers as an example to be followed for its perspicuity and method. In May 1640 he was made a serjeant-at-law.

He contributed 100*l.* in 1642 for the defence of the parliament against the king, and, siding with the Puritans, he took the covenant, and was in such esteem that he was recommended as a judge of the King's Bench on the propositions for peace which the two houses made to the king on February 1, 1642-3. (*Clarendon*, iii. 407.) After they had assumed the government, one of their first legal appointments, on September 30, 1645, was of Mr. Serjeant Rolle to that office, which he filled for three years, when, on October 12, 1648, the Commons voted him to be chief justice of the same court. The king's decapitation soon followed, and Rolle was one of the six judges who accepted a renewal of their commission, on the condition that they should proceed according to the fundamental laws of the kingdom. He was also nominated a member of the council of state; and, in his charges to the grand jury on his different circuits, he endeavoured to settle the people's minds in regard to the existing government. When Cromwell was made protector, the chief justice was appointed in 1654 one of the commissioners of the Exchequer. (*Whitelocke*, 174-397; *Style's Reports*, 140.)

In that year, being surprised at Salisbury by the party of royalists who had seized the town, he narrowly escaped being hanged, but was permitted to depart with the loss of his commission of assize. His refusal to assist in trying the delinquents when taken, on the ground of his being a party concerned, offended Cromwell, who soon found further cause to be dissatisfied with his chief justice, as too honest a man to be relied upon in the impositions he attempted to raise without the consent of parliament. One Cony having refused to pay the customs charged on him, and being committed by Cromwell to prison, applied for his Habeas Corpus. His counsel were arbitrarily sent to the Tower for advocating his cause; and he was obliged to plead for himself. This he did so stoutly and with so much reason that the chief justice, afraid of resisting the ruling powers, yet too conscientious to give judgment against Cony, delayed his decision till the next term. In the meantime, fearing that this was only the beginning of similar illegal measures, he applied to the protector for his quietus, which was willingly granted on June 7, 1655, and Serjeant Glynne was put in his place. (*Clarendon*, vii. 144, 294.) Sir Matthew Hale, who edited his 'Abridgment,' in the preface to that work speaks in the highest terms of his character as a judge, enlarging on his great learning and experience, his profound judgment, his great moderation, justice, and integrity, his patience in hearing, and his readiness and despatch in deciding; and even royalists allowed his honesty on the judicial seat.

He survived his retirement little more than a year, and died on July 30, 1656, He was buried in the church of Shapwick, near Glastonbury, in Somersetshire, where he had a mansion.

His son, Sir Francis Rolle, of Tuderley in Hampshire, represented that county in the parliament summoned to meet at Oxford in 1681; but the family of the chief justice failed in two other generations, his great-grandsons dying without issue, and leaving the estates to the father of the first Lord Rolle. (*Wood's Athen. Oxon.* iii. 416; *Collins's Peerage*, viii. 519.)

ROLT, JOHN, of Ozleworth Park, Wotton-under-Edge, Gloucestershire, whose retirement from his recently acquired honours, occasioned by the sudden prostration of his powers, is still the subject of lamentation and regret to the bar and the public, is the son of John Rolt, an architect and merchant at Calcutta. He was born there on October 5, 1804. His mother was the widow of Mr. Brundson, one of the missionaries noticed in 'Masterman's Memoirs.' His parents died very soon after he was sent to England in 1810; and, as he was left almost without resources, he was educated at private schools with a view to trade, in which he was employed till 1826, when he became clerk to a proctor in Doctors' Commons. Remaining there for nearly seven years, he boldly entered the other branch of the profession, and was admitted to the Inner Temple in 1833. His call to the bar is dated June 9, 1837, having been in the interim a pupil of that eminent barrister Mr. Sutton Sharpe. Practising in the equity courts, his merits were so quickly acknowledged that he was made a queen's counsel in 1846. From that date for twenty years he was one of the most distinguished and most successful leaders at the Chancery bar. During its progress, after two failures to represent Stamford and Bridport, he obtained a seat in parliament as member for West Gloucestershire in 1857, which he retained till he was raised to the judicial bench.

On October 9, 1866, he was appointed attorney-general and knighted; and in less than ten months was promoted to the dignity of lord justice of appeal, on July 22, 1867. Soon after he was seized with an illness so severe that he felt himself compelled to resign his appointment, and his successor, Sir Charles Jasper Selwyn (whose death occurred shortly afterwards), received his patent on February 8, 1868.

Sir John's first wife was Sarah, daughter and coheir of Thomas Bosworth, Esq., of Bosworth in Leicestershire; and his second was Elizabeth, daughter of Stephen Godson, of Croydon.

ROMILLY, JOHN (LORD ROMILLY), is the present master of the Rolls. To him the literary world owes a deep debt of gratitude, not only for the energetic manner in which he has carried out and completed the great undertaking so worthily commenced by his predecessor, Lord Langdale, and rendered the public records, political, domestic, and legal, accessible to all; but also for the ready aid and increased facilities he has given to those who are pursuing historical enquiries. The useful calendars of state papers and the interesting early chronicles which have been, and which continue to be, published under his direction, the former affording an easy reference to a multitudinous and valuable collection, and the latter adding greatly to the authentic annals of the kingdom, will remain a lasting monument of his taste, judgment, and discrimination.

He is descended from a French Protestant family which took refuge in England on the revocation of the Edict of Nantes. His father was Sir Samuel Romilly, whose name will be less remembered for his official rank as solicitor-general during the short administration of the whigs in 1806-7, than for his commanding talents as an advocate, as a senator, as the unflinching assertor of the rights and liberties of the people, and as the first proposer of those amendments of the law, both civil and criminal, which, though their value or necessity was disparaged at the time, have since been fully recognised and adopted into our jurisprudence. The author cannot refer to his name without recalling the reverence and admiration with which for many years from his youth upwards he regarded him, nor without remembering, not only the valuable professional assistance, but the kindness which he invariably experienced in his intercourse with him. By his wife, Ann, daughter of Francis Garbett, Esq., of Knill Court in Herefordshire, he had a large family, of whom the master of the Rolls was the second son.

His lordship was born at the beginning of this century, and completed his education at Trinity College, Cambridge, taking his degree of M.A. in 1826. He had previously entered Gray's Inn, and was called to the bar in 1827. In 1832 he was returned to parliament by the borough of Bridport, a constituency he changed for Devonport from 1847 to 1852, since which, having in the meantime been constituted master of the Rolls, he has confined his attention to his double duties as a judge and as the official comptroller of the records of the state, in the performance of the latter of which (for of the former, as of all existing judges, I purposely avoid any remark) he has gained universal admiration.

His professional life in the interval did not much vary from the career of every successful barrister. After obtaining the honour of a silk gown he was appointed solicitor-general in March 1848, and in July 1850 he became attorney-general, from which in eight months he was raised to the office which he has since so usefully occupied, to which he was appointed on March 28, 1851. On December 19, 1865, he was raised to the peerage as Lord Romilly of Barry, Glamorganshire.

He married Caroline, daughter of the late Dr. William Otter, Bishop of Chichester.

ROMSEY, NICHOLAS DE, performed the functions of justice itinerant several times in 39 and 40 Henry III., 1255-6, probably on both occasions, but certainly on the last, taking pleas of the forest only in various counties; and also in 46 and 53 Henry III. In 52 Henry III. he and Walter de Burges were employed to collect the issues of the bishopric of Winchester. (*Madox*, i. 719.)

ROMSEY, WALTER DE, had the custody of the forests of Hampshire in 8 Henry III., 1224, and it was, no doubt, under this character that he was appointed one of the justices itinerant for that county in the next year. (*Rot. Claus.* i. 605–635, ii. 76.) He became sheriff of that county and of Wiltshire in 13 Henry III., and was afterwards fined one mark for receiving moneys in the latter by summons from the Exchequer which he did not account for at the time. (*Madox*, ii. 234.)

ROOKE, GILES, bore the same Christian name as his grandfather and father. The former was resident at Rumsey in Hampshire, and the latter a merchant in London, who became a director of the East India Company, was the associate of literary men, and indulged himself in some very creditable translations of the classic poets. By his marriage with Frances, daughter of Leonard Cropp, of Southampton, he had a numerous family. His third child, the future judge, was born on June 3, 1743, and from Harrow proceeded to St. John's College, Oxford. There he was an indefatigable student, and he used to relate his mortification at the only reward he received from the college tutor for the great pains he had bestowed on a copy of Latin verses being the cold remark, 'Sir, you have forgotten to put your tittles to your i's.' Having taken his degrees of A.B. in 1763 and of A.M. in 1765, he was in 1766 elected to a fellowship of Merton College, which he held till his marriage in 1785. Although intended for the legal, it was thought that he preferred the clerical profession, from his devotion to the study of divinity. But his motive for pursuing the latter was to get rid of early prejudices and a tendency to scepticism, and to satisfy himself of the truths of Christianity. The effects of this study and conscientious application were evident in all his future life, producing that character for genuine piety by which he was ever distinguished. The deep impression they made upon him is shown in a small pamphlet containing 'Thoughts on the Propriety of Fixing Easter Term,' which he published anonymously in 1792.

This did not prevent him from preparing for the profession he had chosen, and, having been called to the bar, he joined the Western Circuit, of which he eventually became the leader. He accepted the dignity of the coif in 1781, and had the honour of being made king's serjeant in April 1793. Soon after he succeeded in obtaining verdicts at the Exeter assizes against William Winterbotham for preaching two seditious sermons at Plymouth, which, as connected with the French Revolution, were considered especially dangerous, and for which the reverend defendant was sentenced to a large fine and a long imprisonment. At that troubled period it was Sir Giles's lot to be brought very prominently forward. Having been, on November 13 in the same year, appointed a judge of the Common Pleas, and knighted, he delivered in his first circuit a charge to the grand jury at Reading on the excited state of the country, and in July 1795 he presided at York on the trial and conviction of Henry Redhead Yorke for a conspiracy with others to inflame the people against the government, for which a severe punishment was inflicted. (*State Trials*, xxii. 826, xxv. 1049.)

Though not considered a deep lawyer, nor very highly reputed on the bench, he was a mild and merciful judge. A story is told of him that a poor girl, having from the pressure of extreme want committed a theft, was tried before him and reluctantly convicted; and that, while applauding the jury for giving the inevitable verdict, he declared that he so sympathised with them in their hesitation that he would sentence her to the smallest punishment allowed by the law. He accordingly fined her one shilling, adding, 'If she has not one in her possession, I will give her one for the purpose.' Towards the end of his life he suffered much from illness, which was greatly aggravated by his grief for the death of his two elder sons. After nearly fifteen years of judicial labours, he died suddenly on March 7, 1808, having gained during the whole of his life the respect of his contemporaries for his strict integrity, his amiable temper, and his love of literature.

His wife, Harriet Sophia, daughter of Colonel William Burrard, of Walhampton, Hants, and sister of Admiral Sir Harry Burrard-Neale, Bart., brought him a large family.

ROS, PETER DE, was not improbably a younger brother of Everard de Ros, the grandson of that Peter who assumed the surname of Ros from his lordship so called in Holderness in Yorkshire, and of whom the present Baroness de Roos is a lineal descendant.

He was one of the justices itinerant in the county of Cumberland in 1 Richard I., 1189; and in the ninth year of that reign he, with several associates, fixed the tallage in the same county. (*Pipe Roll*, 139; *Madox*, i. 704.)

ROS, ROBERT DE, was the second son of Robert de Ros, lord of Hamlake in Yorkshire, and of Isabel, the daughter of William the Lion, King of Scotland. His father, on his death in 11 Henry III., gave him the barony of Werke in Northumberland, with the castle which he had founded there, and a barony in Scotland.

By a writ dated July 6, 1234, he was

associated with the justices of the bench; and in August of that year he was appointed a justice on three iters.

Three years afterwards he was constituted chief justice of the forests in the northern counties, and so continued, at least till 28 Henry III. He then retired to Scotland, where, with John de Baliol, he had the guidance of that kingdom; and being charged with severely and improperly treating Queen Margaret, the wife of Alexander, King of Scotland, and sister of Henry III., the latter sent his forces there to restore her to her rights, and imposed a fine upon him of one hundred thousand marks; but its payment was eventually remitted. Dugdale goes on to relate that in 22 Edward I., 1293, he was summoned to give the king counsel, and that he went to Portsmouth with horse and arms to join the expedition to Gascony; and further, that, in 1295, being in love with a Scotch woman, he endeavoured to inveigle his kinsman William de Ros to the Scots party, which he joined himself, and was concerned in planning a surprise on the English power.

Recollecting, however, that he was of full age certainly in 12 Henry III., 1228, and that these last events are stated to have occurred about 1296 or 1297, when he would have been near ninety years of age, it is difficult to believe that Dugdale has not missed a generation, and that this lover of the Scottish girl was not his son.

Whichever the last-mentioned person was, he married Margaret, one of the four sisters and heirs of Peter de Brus, of Skelton, with whom he had the lordship of Kendall, which devolved on his son William, whose family ended in 1359 with a daughter. (*Baronage*, i. 546, 555.)

ROSSLYN, EARL OF. *See* A. WEDDERBURN.

ROTHERAM, JOHN, was admitted fellow of Lincoln College, Oxford, in 1648, as of kin to the next-mentioned Archbishop Rotheram, the second founder. The family afterwards settled at Luton in Bedfordshire, where the judge was born. His father was the Rev. John Rotheram, vicar of Boreham and rector of Springfield in Essex, in which county the judge afterwards purchased the manor of Waltham Abbey. He took his degree of B.A. in 1649 and of M.A. in 1652, and received his legal education at Gray's Inn, where he was called to the bar in 1655, and elected ancient in 1671. (*Fasti Oxon.* ii. 120, 170; *Morant*, ii. 88.)

Adopting the popular side in politics, he drew the plea which Algernon Sidney put in on his trial; and in the prosecution of Richard Baxter, when Mr. Wallop had been brutally put down by Chief Justice Jeffreys, Rotheram stood up for some time boldly in defence, but all to no purpose. Being applied to by order of King James to know 'whether he was for the dispensing power,' he answered 'No, he was against it; for it was both against law and reason.' He was therefore naturally surprised that he was selected for promotion, 'as he thought it was enough to have hindered any man from being a judge, so freely to declare his opinion as he had done.' So he expressed himself in his examination before the House of Lords in December 1689.

His promotion as a baron of the Exchequer took place on July 6, 1688, a week after the trial of the seven bishops. Notwithstanding their acquittal, King James directed the judges in the circuits that immediately followed to speak against them; and Archbishop Sancroft afterwards informed the king that the new baron attacked them, 'and endeavoured to expose them as ridiculous, alleging that they did not write English, and it was fit they should be corrected by Dr. Busby for false grammar.' This no doubt was the baron's cunning method of avoiding the political part of the question. (*State Trials*, ix. 988, xi. 499, xii. 504.) His judicial career was not of long duration, terminating a few months afterwards with James's flight from the kingdom, and leaving him with the title of knighthood and the grade of a serjeant, to resume his practice at the bar. Bramston calls him 'a phanatic;' but he seems to have been an honest and zealous advocate. James appointed him high steward of Maldon under the new charter, and his son became recorder of that place. (*Bramston*, 311.)

ROTHERAM, *alias* SCOT, THOMAS (ARCHBISHOP OF YORK), adopted the name of his native place. His family was named Scot, and resided at Rotheram in Yorkshire, where he was born on August 24, 1423. His parents, though not in an elevated rank, were sufficiently opulent to send him first to Eton and then to Cambridge, where, in 1444, he was one of the first scholars at King's College after its foundation. He then was elected a fellow of Pembroke Hall, of which he afterwards became master in 1480; and he presided over the university for some time as chancellor.

Having been selected as one of the chaplains of King Edward IV., he quickly acquired the royal favour, and in one year, 1468, was advanced to the post of keeper of the privy seal, with the profitable appointment of provost of Beverley, and a seat on the episcopal bench as Bishop of Rochester. That his talents were not inconsiderable may be presumed from his being sent in the following August as sole ambassador to treat for peace with the King of France. (*Rymer*, xi. 625.)

He remained at Rochester about four years, when he was translated to the diocese of Lincoln in 1472; and two more years had scarcely elapsed before he was raised to the high office of lord chancellor. Sir T. D. Hardy (*Catal.* 55) places his nomination shortly after February 25, 1475; but there seems to be evidence to warrant his introduction nearly a year earlier. The parliament that met on October 6, 1472, was continued by various prorogations till its dissolution on March 14, 1475; and during that short period of twenty-nine months no less than three chancellors presided in it. Stillington was chancellor at its opening; Laurence Booth prorogued it as chancellor on December 13, 1473, and again on the 1st of the following February; and Thomas Rotheram as chancellor prorogued it on May 28, 1474. The date of his patent must therefore have been between February 1 and May 28, 1474. He acted in the same character at another prorogation and at its ultimate dissolution. (*Rot. Parl.* vi. 104, 120, 153.)

Sir T. D. Hardy refers to some privy seal bills, from which he collects that John Alcock, Bishop of Rochester, held the Great Seal in the following year from April 27 to September 28, 1475. There are however in Rymer (xii. 6, 14) two documents in which Rotheram, Bishop of Lincoln, is designated as chancellor, dated on June 1 and August 13, both within that interval; and a letter from Sir John Paston (*Letters*, ii. 93) to his brother Edmund, dated at Calais on June 13, 1475, mentions the Bishop of Lincoln as then chancellor. Besides these evidences of his being still in possession of the office, there are a large number of privy seals addressed to him in that character during the whole of the time in which the same documents were also addressed to the Bishop of Rochester, some of them, addressed to both, bearing date on the same day. No doubt therefore exists that during the short period in question there were TWO CHANCELLORS. This unusual occurrence, of which no other instance can be found, arose from the Bishop of Rochester being appointed in contemplation of Edward's invasion of France, and of the king's intention that Bishop Rotheram should accompany him in the expedition as chancellor. The delay of the armament for more than two months accounts for this duplication of privy seals from various places in England during the months of May and June. On the king's return from the expedition Bishop Alcock's services were no longer required; and the last privy seal addressed to him is dated September 28, 1475. Bishop Rotheram then resumed the whole of his official functions, and continued to perform them during the remainder of Edward's reign.

On the peace of 1476 between England and France the chancellor is reported to have received from Louis an annual pension of 2000 crowns (*Lingard*, v. 225), a payment to which no disgrace seems to have been attached, as not only many of the English nobles, but even the monarch himself, condescended to be pensioners of the French king. Rotheram sat as chancellor in the two remaining parliaments of the reign, which met respectively on January 16, 1478, and January 20, 1483; and in the interim he received his highest ecclesiastical dignity, as Archbishop of York, on September 3, 1480.

On the death of his royal patron, to whom he was zealously attached, the archbishop continued in possession of the Great Seal as chancellor for about five or six weeks, that is to say, for nearly half the reign of his infant sovereign, Edward V. The coronation of the unfortunate child had been fixed to take place on May 4, but before that day arrived the Duke of Gloucester had obtained possession of his person. To dissipate any fears that might arise from this act, the wily duke sent a messenger to the archbishop assuring him that all would be well. 'I assure him,' was the answer of the chancellor, 'be it as well as it will, it will never be so well as we have seen it.' Arming his retainers, he forthwith went to the queen in the sanctuary at Westminster, taking the Great Seal with him. This, after giving her what comfort he could, he placed into her hands to the use and behoof of her son, declaring that if they crowned any other king than him, his brother, who was then with the queen, should the next day be crowned. Although he quickly repented of this unauthorised surrender of the Seal, and contrived to get it back on the same night, his devotion to the royal family was not likely to be overlooked by a man of the duke's character. The error he had committed was taken advantage of to remove him from the chancellorship some time in the month of May 1483.

A few days afterwards, pursuing his ambitious projects, and to get rid of one who was likely to impede them, the duke consigned the archbishop to the Tower as a prisoner. His confinement, however, was not of long duration, as he was released by the usurper about the time of his own coronation in the following month.

It is certain that Archbishop Rotheram was at liberty on January 23, 1484, when King Richard's first parliament met, as he was then appointed one of the triers of petitions. Whatever may have been the inducement for his appearance on that occasion, which it is not difficult to understand, we can conceive the pleasure he experienced in performing the same duty less than two years afterwards in the first parliament of Henry VII. (*Rot. Parl.* vi.

238, 268), and in witnessing the peaceful establishment of the government during the remainder of his life. This terminated, at the age of 76, on May 29, 1500, when he died at Cawood of the plague which then raged, and was buried in a marble tomb he had himself erected in York Cathedral.

The universities of Cambridge and Oxford and the see of York received munificent proofs of his bounty, and in his native town he founded a college for a provost, five priests, and six choristers, with three schoolmasters for grammar, singing, and writing. (*Drake's Eborac.* 446; *Godwin*, 299, 698.)

ROUBURY, GILBERT DE, before he became a judge, evidently held some place of consideration in the courts, several instances occurring of his name being added to those of the justices commissioned to take inquisitions, and of his carrying records into court. His appointment as a justice of the Court of King's Bench occurred in 23 Edward I., 1295, during the remainder of which reign he seems to have taken a prominent part in the administration of justice. Summoned among his brethren to parliament, he was frequently selected as one of the receivers of petitions, and in the Statute of Champerty, 33 Edward I., he is specially mentioned as clerk of the king's council, and as recommending the writ of conspiracy. (*Rot. Parl.* i. 29-189.)

On the accession of Edward II. he was re-appointed to his seat in the King's Bench, and on March 10, 1316, was removed into the Common Pleas. Fines were levied before him there from that year till the beginning of 14 Edward II. (*Dugdale's Orig.* 44); and the last summons to council addressed to him is dated November 29, 1320. He retired from the court, or died, before May 31, 1321.

ROUCLIFFE, BRYAN, possessed the manor of Colthorpe in Yorkshire. His name does not appear as an advocate in the Year Books; but there is a letter from him to Sir William Plumpton (*Corresp.* 2, 259), who had been sheriff of Yorkshire, which plainly shows that he was conversant with the practice of the Court of Exchequer, with reference to the passing of the accounts of those officers; and as he states that he has 'labored a felaw of mine to be your attorney in the court, *for I may nought be but of counsel*,' it may be presumed that at that time he either held an office in the Exchequer too high to appear for a sheriff, or that he practised as an advocate there.

He was constituted third baron of the Exchequer on November 2, 1458, 37 Henry VI., and was re-appointed when Edward IV. assumed the crown in 1461. In 1463 he entered into a contract with Sir William Plumpton, in which he is called 'Brian Roucliffe, of Colthorp, *gent.*, third baron, &c.,' by which Joan, Sir William's granddaughter, then only four years old, is placed under his government, to the intent that John his son and heir shall marry her. The union took place, and led to a long litigation after the death of the knight, who seems to have been an unprincipled character, between John Roucliffe and a son of Sir William by a subsequent marriage.

The restoration of Henry VI. in 1470, and the return of Edward IV. in the next year, made no difference in the place which Roucliffe occupied in the court, nor was he advanced till the accession of Richard III., when, on June 26, 1483, he was promoted to the office of second baron. In this he was continued by Henry VII., under whom he acted for nearly nine years.

He died on March 4, 1494, and was buried in the church of Colthorpe, or Cowthorp, which was built by him, and consecrated in 1458. (*Ibid.* 8 n.; *Cal. Rot. Pat.* 300, 316.)

RUFUS, GEOFFREY (BISHOP OF DURHAM), is called only Geoffrey in the remaining records of the time. The 'History of Durham' and Bishop Godwin say that he received the cognomen of Rufus, by which he is now generally distinguished, without stating on what account, and nothing is known of his family or himself until he became chancellor to Henry I.

He succeeded to this office about Christmas 1123, and his name appears to a charter to Exeter Cathedral (*Monast.* ii. 539), which, though without date, as is common in those times, must have been granted between August 1123, when Godfrey, Bishop of Bath, one of the witnesses, was raised to that see, and the death of Teoldus, Bishop of Worcester, another witness, which occurred some time in 1124.

That he was not removed from his office during the remainder of the reign may be concluded from his witnessing as chancellor numerous instruments, the last of which was dated 'apud Ferneham in transfretatione regis' (*Madox*, i. 36), and was apparently signed in the autumn of 1134, when the king went for the last time to Normandy, and died there.

Geoffrey was raised to the bishopric of Durham on August 6, 1133. Some authors fix his elevation in 1128; but the history of Durham in the 'Anglia Sacra' gives the former year, and the correctness of this is substantiated by the fact that his signature to the Lincoln charter in 1132 is only 'Geoffrey the Chancellor,' while that to the grant to Alberic de Vere in 1134 is 'Geoffrey the Chancellor, Bishop of Durham.'

In the Great Roll of 31 Henry I. there is an entry, from which it has been argued that he purchased the Chancery for 3006*l.* 13*s.* 4*d.* It is there stated that he *owed* that sum 'pro sigillo.' How far the words used warrant the presumption that this was a fine which he had undertaken to pay for an office of which he had been in possession for seven or eight years I have discussed in my other work (*Judges of England*, i. 82). It is now impossible to come at the real truth, but the probabilities seem to be in opposition to the inference drawn.

That roll shows that he then had the care of the temporalities of the bishoprics of Coventry and Hereford, and of the abbey of Chertsey, during their vacancies, and also the custody of various manors and lands then vested in the crown. From no less than twenty entries of his being excused the payment of Danegeld and other taxes, it appears that he had property in fifteen counties, and that the impositions from which he was thus exempted amounted to the then large sum of 46*l*. 3*s*. 2*d*.

He does not appear to have been continued in his office of chancellor by King Stephen, and he died at the castle of Durham on May 6, 1140. (*Godwin*, 734; *Le Neve*, 347; *Madox*, i. 56, &c., ii. 472.)

RUFUS, GUY (BISHOP OF BANGOR), was presented to the church of Swinestead by Robert de Gant, brother of Gilbert Earl of Lincoln, before the year 1152. Some time afterwards, but before 1165, he became dean of Waltham in Essex, and was the last who bore that title, King Henry, in 1177, altering King Harold's foundation, by substituting an abbot and twenty regular canons for a dean and eleven seculars.

So early as 11 Henry II., 1164, he was one of the justices sitting in the Exchequer; and from 14 to 23 Henry II. he was actively employed as a justice itinerant, his pleas being recorded in at least sixteen counties.

On July 1, 1177, he was consecrated Bishop of Bangor, to which see Henry no doubt raised him for the purpose of facilitating the above-mentioned change in the foundation of Waltham. He died about 1190, and does not appear to have acted in a judicial character after his elevation to the bishopric. (*Madox*, i. 44, 123, &c.; *Monast.* vi. 57; *Le Neve*, 25.)

RUFUS, RICHARD, or RUFFUS, was one of the king's chamberlains in 14 Henry II., 1168, and held the office till his death, about 5 John. His name appear as a justice itinerant on the roll of 1180, for Oxfordshire. (*Madox*, i. 137, 581.) But the pleas there accounted for evidently, from their position, are those of a former year; and there seems reason to doubt whether his name has not been erroneously substituted by the transcriber for that of Richard Giffard, who is inserted on the previous roll as justicier for that county, and is omitted on the corresponding entries of this. And this suspicion derives greater weight from the fact that this is the only occasion on which Richard Rufus's name is so introduced.

In 1 Richard I. he was custos of the honor of Berkhampstead, and also held the manors of the county of Oxford under the king. (*Pipe Roll*, 32, 106, 149.) The property which King Henry gave him to be held by the service of the chamber was in Wiltshire, and of considerable amount.

RUFUS, WILLIAM, often spelled Ruffus, was one of the sons of Ralph de Rufus, whose father, also Ralph, was a Norman knight in the train of the Conqueror, by the daughter of Asceline de Yvery. He acted as a justice itinerant from 19 to 26 Henry II., 1173-1180 (*Madox*, i. 128-701), and was one of the justiciers present at Westminster before whom fines were levied in 1182-1189, in the latter of which years he is styled dapifer regis. (*Hunter's Preface.*) This office is supposed to be the same as seneschal or steward; but if so, from the number mentioned in this reign, there must have been several at one time, probably holding different grades, with one above them all. He was one of the witnesses to the will which the king executed at Waltham in 1182. (*Lord Lyttelton*, iv. [14].) He also held the office of sheriff of Devonshire in 22 and 23 Henry II., and of the united counties of Bedford and Buckingham from 26 Henry II. (with an interruption of a year or two) to 6 Richard I.

His death would seem to have been a violent one, and to have occurred in 6 or 7 Richard I., for by the roll of the latter year the hundred of Redderbrugg in Sussex was fined forty shillings 'pro concelamento retatorum de morti Willelmi Ruffi.' (*Madox*, i. 544.)

His descendants flourished in a long succession under the name of Rous, and the family is now lineally represented by Thomas Bates Rous, Esq., of Courtyrala in Glamorganshire.

RUPIBUS, PETER DE (BISHOP OF WINCHESTER), was a Poictevin by birth. He was a clerk in the king's chamber in the reigns of Henry II. and Richard I.; and in that of the former he held the rectory of Dartford in Kent. (*Hasted*, ii. 327.) In 1 John he is called 'clericus noster,' and is mentioned as prior of Loches (*Rot. Chart.* 10, 34); and so early as 3 John he filled the office of treasurer of Poictiers, and was also archdeacon of the church there. (*Rot. Pat.* 1; *Godwin*, 217.) About the same time he was raised to the dignities of archdeacon of Stafford and precentor of Lincoln, and was soon after elevated to the episcopal bench, being consecrated Bishop of Winchester at Rome on September 5, 1205. Roger de Wendover (iii. 181), in announcing his election, calls him 'vir equestris ordinis et in rebus bellicosis eruditus.'

So high was he in the royal favour that the king on this occasion presented him with two thousand marks. (*Madox*, i. 388.) Both before and after this event he was in continual attendance on his sovereign in his frequent progresses throughout the kingdom, many of the most minute as well as the more important payments on the king's account being made by him. Throughout the king's difficulties he acted as one of his counsellors, and during his whole reign received many proofs of his bounty. In 1208 he is named as a justicier, fines being levied before him in the King's Court. (*Hunter's Preface.*)

When Walter de Grey, the chancellor, went on a special mission to Flanders, he sent the Great Seal to the king at Ospringe, on October 9, 1213, by Richard de Marisco; and there is an entry on the Patent Roll stating that, on December 22, the king delivered it to Ralph de Neville, 'sub Domino Wintoniensi Episcopo deferendum.' Although Sir T. D. Hardy, and after him Lord Campbell, explain these words as meaning that Ralph de Neville so held the Seal because the bishop was then custos of the kingdom, or chief justiciary, their interpretation cannot be accepted, because Peter de Rupibus was not placed in that high position till the following February, and because, indeed, there is no other instance of the Great Seal being held under any one but a chancellor. In no list hitherto published has the name of Peter de Rupibus been introduced as chancellor or keeper; but, independently of the presumption which is raised by the words above used that he held the former office, all doubt of the fact is removed by the entry of two records on the Fine Roll of the year, dated respectively November 21 and 24, 1213 (507, 509), in both of which the title of chancellor is distinctly added to his name. There are also no less than eight charters between October 31, 1213, and January 3, 1214, inclusive, given under his hand (*Rot. Chart.* 195–6); and though the title of chancellor does not appear in his subscription to these, the omission probably arose from his holding the office only temporarily. He retired from it on the return of Walter de Grey, who is again spoken of as chancellor in a record dated January 12, 1214. (*Rot. Claus.* i. 160.)

On February 1, while the king was at Portsmouth ready to embark for Poictou, he appointed Peter de Rupibus justiciary of England to act in his place and keep the peace during his absence. (*Rot. Pat.* 110.) In this character fines were levied before him at Westminster in 15 and 16 John; and there are mandates of his dated as late as October 20, 1214. (*Rot. Claus.* i. 213.) He was present at Runnymede on June 15, 1215, when Magna Charta was signed, but evidently not as chief justiciary, to which office Hubert de Burgh was a few days afterwards raised.

Ten days after the death of King John he assisted at the hasty coronation of Henry III. in the abbey church of Gloucester; and when, two years afterwards, William Mareschall, Earl of Pembroke, died, the custody of the royal infant was entrusted to his care. A rivalry had for some time existed between him and the chief justiciary, which now led them into mutual attempts to ruin each other. In this contest Hubert de Burgh obtained such an ascendency over the king's mind as to procure in 1227 the dismission of the bishop, who soon after undertook a journey to the Holy Land, where he remained for nearly three years. But Hubert then becoming unpopular, the bishop was recalled to court, where, using his influence with the king, he soon succeeded in producing the disgrace of his antagonist, and acquiring the chief conduct of the royal counsels.

His encouragement of the harsh treatment received by his rival reflects as little to the credit of his generosity, as his management of the finances and the introduction of his countrymen into places of trust did to his wisdom. The English barons soon became disgusted with both, and commenced the resistance which afterwards led to intestine war. He is charged with procuring the betrayal and death of Richard Earl of Pembroke, by issuing a charter in the king's name, but without his authority, promising the earl's confiscated lands in Ireland to those who should take him, dead or alive.

The king's eyes were at length opened by the remonstrances of Edmund, Archbishop of Canterbury, who, pointing out the certain consequences of following such counsels, procured the dismissal of the bishop in April 1234.

Being called to account for his administration of the Treasury, he took refuge with his nephew, or son, Peter de Rivallis, at the altar of his church, and eventually escaped to Rome, from which he returned in 1236. He died in his palace at Farnham on June 9, 1238, and was buried at Winchester.

Experienced from an early period of his life in the duties of office, he acquired a high character for wisdom and intelligence, which he seems to have deserved, except where he allowed his personal feelings to betray his judgment. However we may disapprove some of the acts of his life, we must allow him the merit of liberality and piety in founding monasteries, building churches, and endowing hospitals. (*Godwin*, 217; *Dugdale's Orig.* 12; *Angl. Sac.* ii. 305, 506; *R. de Wendover; Rapin.*)

RUSSELL, JOHN (BISHOP OF LINCOLN),

was born in the parish of St. Peter's in the suburbs of Winchester. He received his education at Oxford, being admitted a fellow of New College in 1449, and taking the degree of doctor of the canon law. In his after-life, probably about 1484, he was elected chancellor of that university, an office which in his time was converted from an annual to a permanent appointment. He held a prebend in the cathedral of St. Paul, and was collated to the archdeaconry of Berks on February 28, 1466. (*Rymer*, xi. 682, 738, 778, 793.)

Having attained considerable eminence at court, he was the only learned ecclesiastic among the four ambassadors who were sent in February 1470, 9 Edward IV., to invest the Duke of Burgundy with the order of the Garter, when he was entrusted with the duty of making the complimental address on the occasion. The publication of this address in that year is connected with the earliest history of English typography; for, although printed at Bruges or Rouen, it is the first specimen of the press of Caxton. In the following February, during the short restoration of Henry VI., he was one of those appointed to treat with the French ambassadors, and again in February 1472 he was sent by King Edward to the Duke of Burgundy to conclude a treaty of peace with him. (*Ibid.* xi. 651, 737.) In the latter commission he is styled secondary in the office of the privy seal, to the keepership of which he probably succeeded when Bishop Rotheram was made lord chancellor in May 1474, but he is not mentioned with the title till the following year. He retained the office certainly till the end of that reign (*Rot. Parl.* vi. 122, 202), and probably till he was appointed chancellor under that of Edward V.

In the meantime he was raised to the episcopal bench as Bishop of Rochester on September 20, 1476, and was soon after entrusted with the government of the king's infant son. From Rochester he was translated to Lincoln on September 9, 1480, and was one of the executors of King Edward's will.

In that character, and from his long connection with Edward IV., it is natural to suppose that he would feel an interest in the welfare of the new sovereign, and that he would not advisedly have taken any part in supplanting him. There is nothing to show that when he was fixed upon to succeed Bishop Rotheram in the chancellorship the Protector Richard, Duke of Gloucester, contemplated his subsequent usurpation. Indeed, the contrary would appear from the many acts done by him in the name of King Edward V. The patent of the bishop's appointment as lord chancellor has not come down to us, but it may be presumed that he received the Great Seal about the middle of May. A speech is extant among the Cottonian MSS. (Vitell. E. 10), which, if not delivered, was prepared for delivery by the bishop to the parliament, in which the young king is spoken of in terms of the highest eulogy. The first document which we find with his name as chancellor attached is dated June 2, 1 Edward V. (*Rymer*, xii. 185.) We have also an instance of his exercising his judicial functions in Chancery even in that short reign, a case heard before him about June 22 being reported in the Year Book (fo. 6 b), in which it appears that, besides the master of the Rolls, he called to his assistance two justices, Choke and Catesby.

Whether the bishop was satisfied with the representations made in support of Richard's title to the crown, or whether he deemed it expedient at that time to overlook the objections to them, certain it is that he received the Great Seal from King Richard on June 27, the day after he began his reign. That the king considered him a faithful servant appears from a letter dated at Lincoln on October 12, 1483, addressed to the chancellor, then ill in London, desiring the Great Seal to be sent to him, in which he states his intentions against the Duke of Buckingham, and his determination to 'subdue his malys.' While the Seal remained in the king's hands the duke was taken and beheaded, and it was returned to the chancellor on November 26. (*Turner's England*, iii. 511.) He opened the parliament in the following January with the customary speech preceded by a text (*Rot. Parl.* vi. 237), during which, as the king was present, he would of course avoid, whatever his private feelings might be, any but the most complimentary expressions. For two years he preserved his place; but when the Earl of Richmond was hovering about the English coast some suspicion of his loyalty evidently arose, for the king commanded him on July 24, 1485, to deliver up the Seal to the master of the Rolls, who was constituted keeper on August 1, the very day on which the earl reached Milford Haven. The real traitor in Richard's council was Morgan Kydwelly, the attorney-general, whose communications enabled Richmond to take those steps which led to his success. (*Turner*, iv. 30.) No doubt, however, Bishop Russell was, or was considered to be, favourable to Richmond; for not only was he named one of the triers of petitions in that prince's first parliament after he became king, in November 1485, but in the June and July following he was employed in negotiations with the King of Scots and the Duke of Brittany. (*Rot. Parl.* vi. 268, 386, 441; *Rymer*, xii. 285, 303.) He lived in quiet the remainder of his days, and dying in the beginning of January 1494, at his manor of Nettleham, he was buried in his cathedral.

Sir Thomas More describes him as 'a wise man, and a good, and of much experience, and one of the most learned men undoubtedly that England had in his time.' The only doubt upon his character arises from his continuing in the chancellorship after Richard had shown himself in his true colours. But we must remember that the usurper had so much art, and manners so insinuating, that we may readily believe that it would be long before those about him, whom he was desirous to retain, would credit the reports to his prejudice; and we cannot but give some weight to the peril and inutility of resistance in an age when most parties concurred so easily in a transfer of their allegiance. (*Godwin*, 299, 536.)

RYDER, DUDLEY, was the grandson of the Rev. Dudley Ryder, a nonconformist minister living at Bedworth in Warwickshire, and the son of Richard Ryder, a respectable mercer in the Cloisters, West Smithfield, London, where his elder brother carried on the same business. His mother was Elizabeth, daughter of — Marshall. He was born on November 4, 1691, and commenced his education at a dissenting school at Hackney, whence he was sent first to the university of Edinburgh, and then to that of Leyden. By two lines in the satirical poem the 'Causidicade,' he appears to have been designed for the ministry. The author makes a Puritan candidate for the solicitor-generalship say,—

The Cloak and the Band, it is very well known,
I've, like R—d—r, declin'd for the sake of this gown.

That this had some foundation seems probable from his not choosing the law as his profession till he was twenty-two years of age. He delayed his admission to the Middle Temple as a student till 1713, and was not called to the bar till 1719. Like Lord Talbot, he subsequently removed to Lincoln's Inn, where he was called to the bench in 1733, and made treasurer in the following year.

His success in prosecuting his forensic duties was secured by his abilities, his attention, and his punctuality, which met their reward in December 1733, when he was made solicitor-general. He had been in the early part of that year elected representative in parliament for St. Germains. In January 1737 he was appointed attorney-general, and in 1740 was knighted. For more than seventeen years he filled this important office, no vacancy in the headship of either of the principal common law courts occurring in the interval. One of the most unpleasant duties he had to perform was that of conducting the trials of the noblemen and others who were concerned in the rebellion of 1745. (*State Trials*, xviii. 529–864.) He represented Tiverton in the parliaments of 1735, 1741, and 1747, and was a frequent speaker, principally on subjects connected with his official position, and in defending bills introduced by the government. None of his speeches were particularly brilliant, but all showed extreme good sense and temperance in judgment.

The death of Sir William Lee at length gave the ministers the opportunity of rewarding the long services of Sir Dudley, who was accordingly inaugurated as lord chief justice of the King's Bench on May 2, 1754. He presided in that court for little more than two years, but long enough to prove himself so efficient and accomplished a judge that his elevation to the peerage was determined upon, the warrant signed, and a day appointed for him to kiss hands as Lord Ryder of Harrowby; but being taken ill on the same day, he could not attend, and dying on May 25, 1756, the day after, before the patent was completed, the creation of course fell to the ground. That his son's name was not immediately substituted was considered by some as a hardship; and the omission, which was probably occasioned by his minority, was not supplied till twenty years afterwards, when, being ennobled by the same title, he adopted the happy motto 'Servata 'fides cineri.' The chief justice was buried at Grantham, where there is a handsome monument erected to his memory.

By his wife, Anne, daughter of Nathaniel Newnham, of Streatham in Surrey, he left an only son, who, having been created Baron Harrowby in 1776, was succeeded by his son Dudley, who for his services to the crown in various important offices was promoted to an earldom in 1809, to which was added the viscounty of Sandon in Staffordshire. (*Collins's Peerage*, v. 717; *Walpole's Memoirs*, ii. 46; *Strange*, 1133; *Burrow's S.C.* 365, 368.)

S

SACKVILLE, JORDAN DE, or **DE SAUKE-VILLE**, so called from a town of that name in Normandy, was descended from Herbrand, who assisted in King William's invasion of England, and returning home left in this country Robert, his third son, who held various manors in Essex and Suffolk. He was the grandfather of Geoffrey, the father of this Jordan, by Constance, daughter of Sir Edmund Brooke. (*Baronage*, ii. 399; *Collins's Peerage*, iii. 90; *Hasted*, iii. 74.) Both father and son were involved in the proceedings of the barons against King John, but on the accession of Henry III. their forfeited lands were restored to them, and further favours conferred. (*Rot. Pat.* 172; *Rot. Claus.* i. 305, 313, 316.) Jordan de Saukeville's name appears on a fine acknowledged at Westminster in 3 Henry III., 1219, he being then, according to Dugdale, a justice itinerant, but on no other occasion is he mentioned as a justicier. Both he and his father were alive in 10 Henry III. (*Rot. Claus.* ii. 146), and the time of their deaths is uncertain.

Jordan married Maud de Normanvill, and by her he had three sons, from William, the eldest of whom, regularly descended Thomas Sackville, who in 1567 was created Lord Buckhurst, and in 1603 Earl of Dorset. This title was raised into a dukedom in 1720, but all became extinct in 1843.

SADINGTON, ROBERT DE. Although it has been suggested that the names of the two after-named judges Shottindon and Sodington may be only varieties of that of Sadington, there is nothing positive to prove that it is so, nor any evidence that they and the subject of the present notice are of the same family. Robert de Sadington was clearly so called from a place of that name in Leicestershire, and, we conceive, was the son of John de Sadington, in the household (valettus) of Queen Isabella, by whose request the custody of the hundred of Gertre in that county was committed to him. (*Abb. Rot. Orig.* i. 243.)

This connection may probably account for Robert's first employment about the court. In 3 Edward III. he was commissioned, with the sheriff of Leicester and another, to sell the corn in certain manors which had fallen into the king's hands; and his name occurs in the Year Books as an advocate from that to the tenth year, during which period he was placed on two or three commissions of enquiry. (*Ibid.* ii. 29, 107; *N. Fœdera*, ii. 829, 840.) It does not appear, however, that he held the degree of a serjeant-at-law.

He was appointed to the office of chief baron of the Exchequer on March 20, 1337, 11 Edward III.; and Prynne (*on 4th Inst.* 4) says that he was the first chief baron whom he finds summoned to parliament, meaning, we presume, by that specific title. On July 25, 1339, he acted as the *locum tenens* of William de Zouche, the treasurer, then abroad; and from May 2 to June 21, 1340, he held the office of treasurer. During this time he still continued chief baron. His removal from the treasurership was, perhaps, fortunate for him, as he otherwise would probably have been swept away with the rest on King Edward's angry return from Tournay in the following November.

On September 29, 1343, the Great Seal was delivered to him as chancellor. He held it for about two years. During his time there is a curious entry of the seizure, by the mayor and bailiffs of Sandwich, of nine bulls and numerous letters and processes from the Roman court, attempted to be surreptitiously introduced into the kingdom 'in quâdam lineâ celâ ceratâ inclusos;' and of their being delivered by the chancellor, in '*full* Chancery at Westminster,' to the chamberlain of the Exchequer to be kept in the treasury. (*N. Fœdera*, iii. 25.)

There is no trace of his being more deficient or less successful than his contemporaries; and though the cause of his resignation of the Seal on October 26, 1345, is not given, yet, from anything that appears, it is quite as likely to have arisen from political as from legal motives. His reinstatement as chief baron of the Exchequer on the 8th of the following December seems to exclude the idea suggested by Lord Campbell, that he was inefficient as a judge.

In the next year he was appointed one of the custodes of the principality of Wales, the duchy of Cornwall, and the earldom of Chester, during the minority of the king's son, Edward, Prince of Wales. (*Cal. Rot. Pat.* 154.) In 1347 he was the head of the commission assigned 'ad judicium ferendum,' that is to say, to sentence and to execute the Earls of Menteith and Fife, taken with King David in the battle of Nevil's Cross, in which they are described as traitors to Edward de Baliol, King of Scotland. Though there is no distinct entry of his death, it probably took place in the first quarter of 1350. In that year his successor as chief baron, Gervase de Wilford, was appointed on April 7.

He married Joyce, the sister and heir of Richard de Martival, Bishop of Salisbury; and John de Sadington, mentioned in 37 Edward III., was probably his son. (*Nicholls's Leicestershire*, 192.)

SADINGTON. *See* THOMAS DE SODINGTON.

SAHAM, RICHARD DE. Dugdale names Richard de Saham as having been constituted a baron of the Exchequer in 23 Edward I., 1295, in the place of Master Elias de Wynton. The Year Book (pt. i. 35), however, accounts for the mistake, for it there appears that Richard de Saham was sworn in as baron of the Exchequer *in Ireland* in Trinity Term of that year, before the chancellor and barons of the Exchequer in England. He was a son of Robert de Saham, of the manor of Saham-Toney in Norfolk, and brother of the under-mentioned William. (*Blomefield's Norfolk*, i. 598.)

SAHAM, WILLIAM DE, his brother, founded a chantry at Saham-Toney in Norfolk. He was raised to the bench on the accession of Edward I., and continued for many years to act as a judge of the King's Bench, and to be employed in various itinera till 18 Edward I. In that year, although he shared in the disgrace of many of his brethren, and was not only removed from his seat, but fined in the sum of 3000 marks (*Weever*, 367; *Rot. Parl.* i. 52, 63), he is described in a document (Bib. Cott. Claud. E. VIII, p. 206) as entirely innocent, 'in quo dolus seu fraus non est inventus,' and as paying the fine to conciliate the king. He was alive in 28 Edward I., when he was defendant in an action brought against him for damage done to property at Huningham in Norfolk. (*Abb. Placit.* 242.)

ST. ALBANS, VISCOUNT. *See* F. BACON.

ST. EDMUND, ROGER DE, is the last of the five justices itinerant who fixed the tallage for Norfolk and Suffolk in 9 Richard I., 1197-8 (*Madox*, i. 705), and being a clergyman named from that town in Suffolk, was, according to the common practice of the time, added to the ordinary justices for the performance of this duty in his own neighbourhood. He had been previously in the king's service, having been employed in 1194 to collect the aid for the wages of the army appointed to meet King Richard at Tubœuf in Normandy.

In 10 Richard I. he was appointed by the king archdeacon of Richmond, and was witness in that character to a charter dated December 19, 1198.

ST. EDMUND, WILLIAM DE, is no otherwise mentioned than as having fines acknowledged before him as a justicier for twelve years, commencing at Midsummer 1233, 17 Henry III., and ending at Midsummer 1245, during which period also various entries occur of payments made for writs before him. (*Dugdale's Orig.* 43; *Excerpt. e Rot. Fin.* i. 255, 399, 402.)

ST. HELENA, JOHN DE, held lands of the king at Abingdon in Berkshire, which he forfeited in 17 John. They were no doubt restored to him on the accession of Henry III., although no record thereof appears. In 9 Henry III., however, he was constituted a justice itinerant for that county, and in the following year assessed the quinzime there. (*Rot. Claus.* i. 236, 241, ii. 76, 247.)

ST. JACOBO, STEPHEN DE, is only mentioned as a justicier in a fine levied at Westminster, either in 4 or 5 Richard I. (*Hunter's Preface.*)

ST. JOHN, JOHN DE, held the barony of Stanton in Oxfordshire, and in 9 Henry III., 1225, was appointed one of the justices itinerant in his own county. He died in 14 Henry III., when Geoffrey le Despenser paid 100*l*. for the guardianship of Roger his heir, who fell at the battle of Evesham in 1265, after which none of his descendants were summoned to Parliament. (*Baronage*, i. 539; *Rot. Claus.* ii. 75, 76.)

ST. JOHN, OLIVER (EARL OF BOLINBROKE), who was descended from the same family to which the last-named John St. John belonged, is no otherwise famous than for being one of the very few peers (who, Wood says, were 'all of the Presbyterian dye') remaining with the parliament after Charles I. retired to York, and concurring with the House of Commons in the violent votes and ordinances then passed. It was from this contraction of choice, rather than from any special ability in him, that he was selected, in 1643, as one of the two members of the House of Lords, to be united with four Commoners, in whom the custody of the new Great Seal was to be placed. They were accordingly appointed commissioners on November 10. He occupied this position about two years and a half, and died in possession of it in June or July 1646. The earldom became extinct in 1711, but the barony of St. John of Bletsoe survived, and still flourishes. (*Baronage*, ii. 398; *Athen. Oxon.* iii. 134; *Journals.*)

ST. JOHN, OLIVER, connected by relationship with both the preceding, was the son of Oliver, settled at Cayshoe in Bedfordshire, a grandson of the first Lord St. John of Bletsoe, by his wife Sarah, daughter of Edward Buckley, Esq., of Odell in the same county. (*Wotton's Baronet.* iv. 178.) Clarendon calls him 'a natural son of the house of Bullingbroke,' and the writer of 'The Mystery of the Good Old Cause' says that his father 'was supposed to be a byeblow of one of the Earls of Bedford.' (*Parl. Hist.* iii. 1600.) The unpopularity of the man, and the circumstances of the times, will sufficiently account for these reports,

P P

but the above is the pedigree given by an unprejudiced genealogist, and confirmed by the description in his admission as a member of Lincoln's Inn.

He was born about the year 1598, and was sent to Queen's College, Cambridge, in August 1615. Lord Campbell (*Ch. Just.* i. 450) fathers upon him the 'Letter to the Mayor of Marlborough' against a benevolence then in collection, which was made the subject of prosecution in the Star Chamber in April 1615, when he was only seventeen. To have formed such decided opinions, with reasons so clearly stated, and statutes and authorities so precisely quoted, as are found in the letter in question, would be an instance of most remarkable precocity in any youth who had not even commenced his college studies. But the statement will not bear the slightest investigation. There is absolutely nothing in the whole proceeding to lead to a suspicion that the writer of the letter could have been ' a mere stripling;' but, on the contrary, it is manifest from the letter itself, and from Bacon's well-prepared speech, who would scarcely have wasted his eloquence on a boy, that he was 'a principal person, and a dweller in that town,' and 'a man likely to give both money and good example.' (*State Trials*, ii. 899.) Instead of the youth who was quietly preparing for his academical course, the person so described was Oliver, the son of St. John of Lydiard-Tregoze, a seat not far distant from Marlborough, whose relative and namesake afterwards became Viscount Grandison and Lieutenant of Ireland. (*Lord Carew's Letters* [Camd. Soc.], 143.)

From the university our student proceeded to Lincoln's Inn, where he was called to the bar on June 22, 1626. He received early employment in the law business of the Earl of Bedford, to whom he was distantly related. In consequence of this connection he was really brought before the Star Chamber in 1630; both he and the earl, with Selden, Sir Robert Cotton, and some others, being charged with publishing 'A Proposition for his Majesty's service to Bridle the Impertinence of Parliaments' — a piece of irony which was proved to be written by Sir Robert Dudley at Florence in the reign of James I. The government was glad to withdraw from this absurd prosecution, by availing itself of the birth of the king's son as a plea for extending mercy to the defendants. (*State Trials*, iii. 387.) They were consequently discharged; but Clarendon (i. 325) says that St. John never forgave the court this '*first* assault.' This feeling of bitterness was no doubt increased by his study being searched and his papers seized in 1637, in consequence of being suspected of having drawn the answer of Burton to the information filed against him in the Star Chamber for a libellous publication. (*Harris's Lives*, ii. 267.)

About 1629 he had married his first wife, Johanna, sole child of Sir James Altham of Mark's Hall, Latton, Essex, and of Elizabeth, daughter of Sir Francis Barrington, by Joan, one of the daughters of Sir Henry Cromwell of Hinchinbroke, and aunt both to Oliver Cromwell the protector, and John Hampden the patriot.

Bound thus more intimately to that party, who were dissatisfied with the unconstitutional measures of the court, this connection made St. John the natural adviser of Hampden in the celebrated resistance to the payment of ship-money. His argument against the legality of that imposition was so learned and so powerful that he acquired so much reputation that 'he was called into all courts and to all causes where the king's prerogative was most contested.' (*Clarendon*, i. 324.) His first wife having died in childbed, he in 1638 strengthened the tie with the Cromwells by marrying Elizabeth, the first cousin of Oliver, and daughter of Henry Cromwell of Upwood.

When the king, after a cessation of eleven years, was obliged to call a parliament in April 1640, St. John· was elected member for Totnes. (*Fasti Oxon.* 453.) In the short period of three weeks during which this parliament lasted, though he does not appear to have put himself forward as a speaker, the journals show that he was named on all the committees connected with popular grievances, and that he was charged to speak on one of them in the conferences with the Lords. Finding that redress was insisted on before supplies would be granted, the king dissolved the parliament, to the disappointment of the moderate, but to the joy of the extreme party. Clarendon relates (i. 246) that within an hour after the dissolution he met St. John, 'who had naturally a great cloud on his face, and very seldom was known to smile, but had then a most cheerful aspect;' and that after lamenting what had taken place, St. John answered him with a little warmth, 'That it was well; but that it must be worse before it could be better; and that this parliament could never have done what was necessary to be done.'

In the new parliament, which met in the following November, St. John again represented Totnes, and was immediately appointed on several committees, and chairman of that with regard to ship-money. On December 7 he brought up its reports, on which were founded the memorable resolutions that not only the impost itself, but all the proceedings to enforce it, and the decision of the judges, were against law. These resolutions were adopted by the House of Lords, after hearing a luminous address from St. John, which is also remarkable for vindictive sternness towards the judges. (*State Trials*, iii. 1262.) On January 29, 1640-1, within a fortnight after this speech was delivered, St. John was constituted solicitor-general. (*Rymer*, xx. 449.)

This promotion arose from a desire to gain over some of the popular party, among whom various places were to be distributed. The Earl of Bedford entered into the plan, and was to be treasurer, and Pym and others were to accept situations of trust. The king readily consented to St. John's appointment, 'hoping that he would have been very useful in the House of Commons, where his authority was then great; at least, that he would be ashamed ever to appear in anything that might prove prejudicial to the crown.' But the Earl of Bedford's death three months after, and other circumstances, stopping these negotiations, the king found himself with a solicitor-general neither abating nor dissembling his enmity to the court, and who still retained the confidence of his party.

The king soon had reason to see how much he had been mistaken in his expectations. The accusation of the Earl of Strafford by the Commons had been made in the previous November, but the trial did not begin till the 22nd of March; and St. John, though he was the king's officer, and well knew his royal master's anxiety to save the earl, used his utmost efforts to urge on the proceedings, and even dissuaded the Commons from hearing the argument of the earl's counsel on the matter of law. When the Commons found that the offences alleged against Strafford could not be touched by the existing laws, and that he was likely to be acquitted by the Lords, they brought in a bill of attainder, in the promotion of which unjustifiable course St. John was a prominent actor, and in its support addressed the Lords in a speech betraying so much sophistry, brutality, and malice as fully to justify Clarendon's condemnation of it, and the disgust of all unprejudiced men. (*Verney's Notes* [Camd. Soc.], 49, 55; *Rushworth*, iv. 675; *Clarendon*, i. 407.)

In all the violent measures that succeeded—the bill for the continuance of the parliament, the bill against the bishops, the militia bill, &c.—St. John took the same actively adverse part. The king, naturally desirous of releasing himself from his obnoxious officer, offered the place to Hyde; but he prudently declined it, and dissuaded the king from removing St. John at that time, though agreeing that he might have filled it with a better man when the place was actually void. But soon after, the breach with the Commons becoming complete, and no hope remaining of any alteration in St. John's conduct, the king revoked his appointment on October 30, 1643, and put Sir Thomas Gardner in his place. The parliament, however, refused to recognise the new solicitor; and on providing a Great Seal for themselves, in lieu of that which had been taken to the king by Lord Lyttelton, and appointing on November 10 two Lords and four of the Commons for its custody, they named St. John as the first of the latter, with the title of 'his majesty's solicitor-general;' and by this designation he was distinguished until he became chief justice. Whitelocke's statement (71, 88) that in May 1644 he was assigned to be attorney-general is evidently a mistaken account of an ordinance of the Commons, enabling him to do all acts as effectually as the attorney-general, if present, might have done. (*Journals*.)

St. John was one of the commissioners to treat for a peace at Uxbridge in January 1645, but, as neither party was sincere, the negotiation failed. In April of that year the self-denying ordinance, by which St. John and the other commissioners of the Great Seal would have been disqualified, was passed by both the houses; but before the forty days limited by it had expired the parliament voted their continuance in office till the end of the following term; and this vote was repeated from time to time till October 30, 1646, when they delivered up the Seal to the speakers of the two houses, who were nominated its keepers. (*Whitelocke*, 124, 226.) St. John had, in the previous February, joined in the vote abolishing the Court of Wards; and now, resuming his functions as solicitor-general, he was ordered to prosecute Judge Jenkins for exercising his judicial duties in defiance of the parliament. But before that sturdy royalist was brought to trial, the Commons had determined to fill up the vacancies on the bench. They accordingly appointed St. John chief justice of the Common Pleas on October 12, 1648, and, the Lords having concurred, he was sworn in on November 22. (*Ibid.* 194–356.)

It was not then the custom, any more than it is now, for the judges to sit in the House of Commons. St. John, therefore, on his elevation to the bench, though his seat for Totnes was not vacated, abstained from attending parliament, and took no part in the tragic debates of the next two months, which brought his sovereign to the block; and he asserts, in the case which he published in 1660, that, so far from being one of the advisers of the sanguinary proceedings, he was not even consulted, but 'upon all occasion manifested his dislike and dissatisfaction.' In this he is confirmed by Thurloe, who acted then as his secretary, and by the vote which the Commons passed when the Peers rejected the ordinance, that the Lords, and the chief judges of each court, whom they had named, should be left out of the commission for the trial. But his denial that he favoured the alteration of the government to a commonwealth, and his assertion that he was ever for King, Lords, and Commons, require more credit than can be easily given to a man who had accepted a high judicial office from the opponents of the monarchy, and who, within eight days after they had murdered their king, and after their vote that the office of king was 'unnecessary,' and the House of Peers was 'useless and dangerous,' and that both 'ought to be abolished,' consented not only to remain as a judge under the usurping government, but to be a member of its council of state. That he acted on that council, and was trusted by it, is apparent from his being one of the committee in 1650 to confer with General Fairfax as to the invasion of Scotland—a conference which led to the appointment of Cromwell to be lord-general of the army. (*Whitelocke*, 366–462.)

In March 1651 he and Mr. Strickland were sent ambassadors to the Dutch. It is curious that in speaking of this embassy Clarendon calls him 'the known confident of Cromwell,' and Whitelocke designates him 'Cromwell's creature'—an agreement between writers of opposite parties which goes far to show the general impression at the time, and to warrant the nickname he received of 'The Dark Lanthorn,' notwithstanding his denial of its justice. In June he returned without having concluded the treaty he went to negotiate. His residence at the Hague was not unattended with danger. He was treated with indignity by the people, and with something like indifference by the States; he received a gross insult from Prince Edward, the Palgrave's brother; he was engaged in a personal quarrel with the Duke of York, the details of which do not tell to his credit; and he narrowly escaped an attempt upon his life, similar to that lately practised by the Thugs in India. The parliament, indignant at the slight endeavours made to punish the delinquents, and at the trifling impediments that were every day thrown in the way of completing the treaty, recalled the ambassadors. On their return St. John took his seat in the House of Commons, and, after giving a detailed account of all their proceedings, they received thanks for their faithful services. (*Ibid.* 487–496; *Parl. Hist.* iii. 1367.)

A resolution that the several judges who were members should be discharged from their attendance in the house whilst they executed their offices, which was passed in October 1649, was rescinded on June 27, 1651, no doubt for the purpose of enabling St. John to resume his seat, and make his diplomatic report on July 2. From that time he continued his attendance, and to his indignation at the treatment he received in Holland, and the failure of the negotiation, is to be attributed the adoption in the next month of the ordinance upon which was founded the Navigation Act passed at the Restoration, prohibiting foreign ships from bringing any merchandise or commodities into England but such as were the proceeds and growth of their own country, an ordinance which was much more injurious to the Dutch, wholly suppressing their carrying trade, than to any other nation. (*Clarendon*, vi. 599.) In September he was one of the four who were sent to compliment Cromwell on his victory at Worcester, and in October he was appointed a commissioner for the affairs of Scotland. In November he was re-elected on the council of state, and was named by the committee for the reformation of the universities, chancellor of Cambridge.

At the meeting called by Cromwell on the 10th of December to consider what was fit to be done for the settlement of the nation, in which the general agreed with Whitelocke that the question was whether a republic or a mixed monarchical government were the best, and gave his opinion that the latter would be most effectual, St. John declared that 'the government, without something of monarchical power, would be very difficult to be so settled as not to shake the foundation of our laws and the liberties of the people.' (*Whitelocke*, 516.) Here is nothing to show that he was then opposed to Cromwell, who was feeling his way towards attaining that power which he afterwards assumed, and who, as soon as he found that some of the party suggested the selection of one of the late king's sons, put an end to the debate. On the 14th of the previous month St. John had been teller with Cromwell of the majority of two which voted that a time should be declared beyond which the parliament should not sit, which limit was on a subsequent day fixed for November 3, 1654. (*Parl. Hist.* iii. 1375.)

He then went to Scotland, where he was actively engaged with his colleagues in arranging the intended union with that country. After his return on May 6, 1652, he was ill for some time, but in April 1653, though it does not appear that he was a party to the violent mode adopted by Cromwell of dismissing the parliament, he strongly supported the general's determination to put an immediate period to its sittings. Cromwell, however, did not summon him to the convention (called Barebone's Parliament) which met on July 4, and dissolved itself on the 12th of the following December, resigning its power to the lord general, who four days after was declared lord protector of the commonwealth of the three kingdoms. St. John alleges that he had nothing to do with this elevation of Cromwell, falling dangerously ill in the previous October, and not recovering till the May after the event; and so far from approving it, Thurloe testifies that he expressed himself strongly against it. In further proof of his dislike, he says that, though Cromwell named him on his council, and appointed him a commissioner of the treasury (*Whitelocke*, 517–597), he never attended in either capacity, nor received any salary.

According to St. John's account, the cordiality between him and Cromwell had cooled since the latter had assumed arbitrary power, and their intercourse was limited to formal visits before or after the terms. But when the parliament of 1657 presented their 'Humble Petition and Advice' to the protector, pressing him to take the title of king, St. John is found as one of the committee that waited upon him, and as a speaker contending against his scruples. (*Parl. Hist.* iii. 1498.) Cromwell's refusal to comply with this request led to a new arrangement of the government, by which he was confirmed as lord protector, with the additional power of naming his successor, and of calling not more than seventy nor less than forty persons to sit in what was designated 'the other house.' In the exercise of this power St. John was one of the *quasi* peers whom he selected. They had not, however, a long enjoyment of their honours, for within a fortnight after the parliament met the Commons showed so much hesitation in acknowledging this upper chamber that Cromwell dissolved the parliament on February 4, 1658. Within seven months after this Cromwell died, and his son Richard, who was immediately proclaimed his successor, continued St. John as chief justice, and summoned another parliament on January 27, 1659. This parliament did not last three months, during which the Commons were principally occupied in debates as to their intercourse with the 'other house,' manifesting all their former jealousy. St. John states that he never would sit as a peer, but it would seem that he had no great opportunity of doing so, for in the very limited period that either parliament sat after the first nomination of the new peers little is recorded of their proceedings.

In the following month (May) the army recalled the remains of that parliament which Oliver Cromwell had expelled in 1653, and St. John not only took his place in it, but was named one of the council of state. The old government, 'without a single person, kingship, or House of Peers,' having been re-established, St. John and Sir John Pickering waited on Richard Cromwell, and obtained his written acquiescence in this arrangement, by which he was thus deprived of his short-lived dignity. The sittings of the Rump Parliament, as it was called, were violently interrupted in October by the same military power that had called them together, and a Committee of Safety formed. They were again, however, by the aid of Monk, reinstated on December 26. St. John attended a meeting on February 17, 1659-60, at Monk's quarters, with reference to the members who were secluded in 1648, and was instrumental in restoring them to their places a few days after. (*Mercurius Politicus*.) The house dissolved itself on March 16, first passing an act for a new parliament to meet on April 25. Among the qualifications proposed for the members was an oath abjuring the title of Charles II., which St. John declares that he came out of the country on purpose to oppose, adding that it was he that made the motion to put a period to the Long Parliament.

At the Restoration, which soon followed, St. John found himself in a difficult position. His harsh and active proceedings at the commencement of the troubles; the lead he took against the king while holding an office under the crown; the inhumanity of his speech against Strafford; his partisanship in all Cromwell's earlier, if not later, measures; his recent adherence to the principle of a government without a single person, kingship, or House of Peers; and even his relationship to the two protectors—setting aside his personal collision with the Duke of York at the Hague—could not but operate prejudicially against him. In the discussions, therefore, in the House of Commons upon the act of indemnity, he was included among those reserved for such pains, penalties, and forfeitures, not extending to life, as by a future act should be imposed. To counteract this vote, he published the case before referred to, which is drawn up with a great deal of art and plausibility, but must be received with an equal degree of caution both as to its statements and its omissions. With the strenuous aid of Thurloe, who had a grateful remembrance of his early patronage, it had its desired effect upon the Lords, who mitigated the clause against him by the substitution of another (to which the Commons afterwards assented), declaring that if he accepted or exercised any office after September 1 (two days subsequent to the royal assent), he should stand as if excepted by name from the benefit of the act. The king, on hearing of his narrow escape, is said to have expressed a wish that he had been added to those excepted. (*Parl. Hist.* iv. 70, 91, 114; *Ludlow*, 393.)

St. John, after residing for a few years in privacy on his estate at Longthorpe, a hamlet near Peterborough, where he had erected an elegant mansion, retired to the continent under the assumed name of Montagu. It is uncertain whether he ever returned to England, authorities differing as to the place of his death, though all agree that it occurred on December 31, 1673, at the age of 75.

St. John's powers as an advocate were certainly great; of his qualities as a judge there are few means of forming an opinion, for there are no reports of his court during the time that he presided in it. Of his private disposition all authorities concur in describing it as gloomy, reserved, and unamiable; but the charge which is made by some, that he was avaricious and died disgracefully rich, is not supported by sufficient evidence. The Bedford Level was completed principally by his exertions, and in commemoration of his services his name is still connected with its greatest work, called 'St. John's Eau.'

His third wife was Elizabeth, daughter of Daniel Oxenbridge, M.D., of Daventry, and widow of Caleb Cockcroft, of London, merchant, who after his death married Sir Humphrey Sydenham, of Chilworthy, Somersetshire. By her he had no issue, but by both his other wives he had several children. One of his grandsons was made a baronet in 1715, but the title became extinct at his death in 1756. (*Wotton's Baronet.* iv. 178.)

ST. LEONARD'S, LORD. See E. B. SUGDEN.

ST. MARIÆ ECCLESIA, WILLIAM DE (BISHOP OF LONDON), so called from a town of that name in Normandy, held some office in the Exchequer in 1 Richard I., 1189-90, he and Hugh Bardolf then attesting two accounts of Henry de Cornhill, the sheriff of London. (*Pipe Roll*, 11.) He is stated to have acted as secretary to King Richard, and appears to have been quickly advanced in ecclesiastical and civil preferment. He held the living of Harewood in Yorkshire, and successively became a canon of York and of St. Paul's, and dean of the College of St. Martin's-le-Grand in London. He was appointed sheriff of Surrey in 5 Richard I., and continued so for two years. In 6 Richard I. he paid five hundred marks for the custody of the heir of Robert, the younger son of Robert Fitz-Harding, with all his inheritance, and the power of marrying him to one of his kinswomen; and he had the charge of the abbey of Glastonbury, the honor of Wallingford, and various other lands in the king's hands. (*Rot. Cancell.* 6, &c.) By the Norman Roll of 1195 (i. clxxvi.), it appears that a pension of 35*l.* 12*s.* had been granted for his and his mother's lives out of the manor of St. Mère Église.

From the 5th to the 10th year of Richard I. his name frequently appears as one of the justiciers before whom fines were levied (*Hunter's Preface*), and in the latter year he was promoted to the bishopric of London, but was not consecrated till May 1199, about two months after King Richard's death.

He was one of the bishops who conveyed the pope's remonstrance to King John in 1208, and who, on his continued resistance, placed the kingdom under an interdict. Two years afterwards he pronounced the sentence of excommunication against the king, which was not removed till the year 1213. He was obliged to fly the kingdom and to remain an exile till King John had made his peace with the pope and received absolution. In the meantime his castle at Stortford, which William the Conqueror had given to the see, was entirely demolished. After his return to England he was present at the granting of Magna Charta, in 1215.

When he had presided over his see for twenty-two years, he retired from its duties, by a voluntary abdication, on January 26, 1221; and after living in seclusion for little moie than three years, he died at St. Osyth on March 27, 1224. (*Godwin*, 179; *Le Neve*, 177; *R. de Wendover*, iii. 220-302.)

ST. MARTIN, RALPH DE, is named in 10 Richard I., 1198-9, as one of the justices itinerant fixing the tallage for the county of Surrey; and in the same year they are recorded as making amercements in Essex and Hertfordshire. Ralph de Martin, who, in 31 Henry II., 1185, was one of the custodes of the see of Salisbury, then in the king's hands, was no doubt the same person, and was probably so entrusted in consequence of holding some office in the Exchequer. (*Madox*, i. 311, 565, 733.)

ST. OMERO, WILLIAM DE, had the custody of the castle of Hereford in 38 Henry III. (*Cal. Inquis.* p. m. i. 13); and the only entry on the rolls of that reign which proves that he sat on the judicial bench is a grant to him, in the fifty-third year, 1269, of an annual salary of 40*l.*, 'quamdiu placitis prædictis intenderit.' Although Dugdale thereupon inserts his name in the column of the justices of the King's Bench, it is doubtful whether he was more than a justice itinerant. He is not mentioned afterwards in the former character; and the only instance found of his acting in the latter is the taking of an inquisition by him and Sir Warine de Chaucomb at Lincoln in 3 Edward I., 1275. (*Proceed. Arch. Inst. York*, 132.) In the previous year he attended at the general council held at Lyons under Pope Gregory X. (*Devon's Pell Records, Int.* xxxiii.)

ST. PAUL, JOHN DE (ARCHBISHOP OF DUBLIN), whose family had property in the county of York, was not improbably the son of Robert de St. Paul, lord of the township of Byram, who was one of the adherents of the Earl of Lancaster in the reign of Edward II. (*Parl. Writs*, ii. p. ii. 1387.) John was a clerk in the Chancery, and is the last named of three of those officers to whom the custody of the Great Seal was entrusted at York, from January 13 to February 17, 1334, during the temporary absence of John de Stratford, the chancellor.

On April 28, 1337, he was constituted master of the Rolls; and in 1340 the House of Converts, in Chancery Lane, was granted to him for life. While master of the Rolls, the Great Seal was twice deposited with him and other clerks—viz., from July 6 to 19, 1338, and from December 8, 1339, to February 16, 1340; but on the latter day he was appointed sole custos till the restoration of Archbishop Stratford on April 28. He again held it for a short time on the resignation of the archbishop in the following June.

On the king's hurried return from the siege of Tournay, John de St. Paul was one of the victims of his indignation. He was charged with some malversation in his office, and cast into prison; but he obtained his release as a clergyman through the intervention of Archbishop Stratford. He however was deprived of the custody of the Rolls on December 2, two days after the king arrival in England. (*Barnes's Edward III.* 217; *Angl. Sac.* i. 20.) The royal anger did not long continue; for though St. Paul was not restored to the mastership of the Rolls, he after a little while was allowed to resume his old position among the masters in Chancery. On the death of the Chancellor Parning on August 26, 1343, he was again one of the three to whom the Seal was entrusted till the appointment of Robert de Sadington on September 29.

In 1346 he was made archdeacon of Cornwall (*Le Neve*, 94), and about the month of October 1349 was elected Archbishop of Dublin. He presided there for thirteen years, and died in 1362. (*N. Fœdera*, iii. 190, 433; *Holinshed*, vi. 44.)

ST. QUINTIN, WALTER DE, is only mentioned as one of the justices itinerant fixing the assize or tallage in Dorsetshire and Somersetshire in 20 Henry II., 1174, in conjunction with Alured de Lincoln, the sheriff. (*Madox*, i. 123.)

ST. VALERICO, or ST. WALERICO, JOHN DE (a town in Normandy), was the descendant of a noble family of that name, Ranulph the ancestor of which at the time of the general survey possessed several manors in Lincolnshire. The elder branch failed for want of male issue in 1219. (*Baronage*, i. 454.) John was probably an officer in the Exchequer; for in 55 Henry III. and 1 Edward I. he was appointed sheriff of the counties of Somerset and Dorset, with a special commission to enquire what debts several sheriffs of those counties and their bailiffs had received, and not accounted for. He became a baron of the Exchequer about 2 Edward I., 1274. He is not mentioned after 1276, during which a sum of 20*l*. was allowed for his expenses. (*Madox*, ii. 112, 195, 269, 320.)

ST. VIGORE, THOMAS DE, was appointed in 9 Edward I., 1281, to take assizes in different counties. He was summoned to the parliament at Shrewsbury in 11 Edward I., and died in the twenty-third year of the reign, leaving property in Wiltshire and Somersetshire. (*Cal. Inquis.* p. m. i. 123; *Parl. Writs*, i. 16, 824.)

SALCETO, ROBERT DE, or DE LA SAUCEY, was the son of Roger de la Saucey, and held the sheriffalty of Northamptonshire with Henry Fitz-Peter, or de Northampton, in 6 and 7 John. During the troubles in that reign he seems to have been a waverer, for in 15 John he gave hostages for his faith; in the next year he was employed to explain the king's affairs to his neighbours in Northampton and Rutland; and in the following his property was seized, it must be presumed on his open hostility. (*Rot. Pat.* 47, 104, 128, 168; *Rot. Claus.* i. 34, 77, 236.) Soon after the accession of Henry III., however, it was restored to him; and in the seventh year of the reign he was engaged in fixing the tallage, and again in 10 Henry III. in assessing the quinzime of his county. (*Rot. Claus.* i. 306, 540, ii. 147.) He was at the head of the justices itinerant for Rutland in 18 Henry III., 1234, beyond which date nothing is recorded of him.

SALISBURY, EARL OF. See R. NEVILL, W. CECIL.

SALMON, JOHN (BISHOP OF NORWICH), was the son of Salomon and Amicia, as appears from his appointing four priests to pray for their souls in a chapel he founded in the chancel of Norwich Cathedral; and it may be presumed that the family was not of any eminence, from the bishop's assuming for his arms a rebus of his name—three silver salmons hauriant on a sable field. He is sometimes called John of Ely, having been prior of the convent there. While holding this dignity he was elected Bishop of Norwich, on July 15, 1299. Salmon was not employed by Edward I., but he visited Rome in 1306; and on the accession of Edward II. he was sent to France as one of the ambassadors to demand Isabella, the daughter of King Philip, as the wife of his sovereign. In the third year of the reign he was chosen one of the lords ordainers; and in the ninth he was among the commissioners to open the parliament then held. He took the part of his sovereign throughout his troublesome reign.

On January 26, 1320, 13 Edward II., he was appointed chancellor in full parliament; but, though he retained the office for three years and a half, he seems to have been so severe a sufferer from ill health that the business of the Chancery was frequently performed by deputies. His delivery of the Seal to the custodes directed to act for him, on June 5, 1323, when he was confined to his bed, may be considered as the date of his ultimate retirement, although the new chancellor was not named till the 20th of August following.

He recovered from that sickness, for in the following year he went as ambassador to the court of France, and succeeded in negotiating a peace between the two kings. His health, however, again failing, he died at the priory of Folkestone on July 2, 1325, having presided over his diocese for nearly six-and-twenty years. (*Godwin*, 433; *Angl. Sac.* i. 412, 802; *Le Neve*, 210; *Rot. Parl.* i. 350, 443; *Blomefield's Norwich*, i. 497.)

SALVEYN, GERARD, had large possessions in Yorkshire, and was appointed one of the four justices of trailbaston for that county in the commission dated November 23, 1304. In the following April his name was omitted, but he had been returned knight of the shire in the interval, and was again elected in 35 Edward I. (*Parl. Writs*, i. 143, 190, 407-8.)

The family was founded by Josceus le Flemangh, who came in with the Conqueror, and was settled at Cukeney in Nottinghamshire. His grandson Ralph received the designation of Le Silvan from his manor of Woodhouse in that county; and this was afterwards corrupted to Salveyne. Gerard was the son of Ralph Salveyn of Duffield in Yorkshire, and Sibilla, daughter and coheir of Robert Beeston of Wilberfoss. He was one of the assessors of the fifteenth for that county, granted in 30 Edward I., and two years afterwards was sent on an embassy to the court of France. In 1 Edward II. he was appointed escheator north of Trent, and held it till the middle of the third year. He was then entrusted with the sheriffalty of York for four years, commencing in 4 Edward II. In the twelfth year he obtained a pardon as one of the adherents of Thomas Earl of Lancaster, and died in the following year. His grandson, Gerard Salveyn, succeeded him, and the two united names continued to designate every head of the family for more than four centuries, thirteen in number, and is still held by its representative, Gerard Salvin, Esq., of Croxdale in Durham. (*Inquis.* p.m. i. 292; *Abb. Rot. Orig.* i. 159.)

SAMFORD, THOMAS DE, is first mentioned in 5 John, 1203, when Mr. Hunter introduces him in his list of the justiciers before whom fines were levied. As this is the only year in which his name so occurs, he was probably present only as an officer of the treasury of the Exchequer, with which he was evidently then connected, and was for many years afterwards employed in a confidential manner by the king. Besides several entries of his delivering money and plate into the chamber, there is a mandate directed to him in 15 John to deliver forty thousand marks, fifteen golden cups, a golden crown, and various other valuable articles then in his custody to two persons therein named. Two years afterwards he is quitted of sixty-six sacks of money, which were in the treasury at Corfe, and which ought to contain nine thousand nine hundred marks. (*Rot. Pat.* 61, 110, 146.)

It appears from the Rotuli Misæ of 11 and 14 John (110, 113, 137) that he was at both periods in personal attendance on the king, when several payments were made through his hands, many of which relate to the royal sports. He had the custody of the abbey of Malmesbury, was governor of the castle of Devizes, and custos of the forests of Chippenham, Melkesham, and Braden. In 14 John he was sent on a mission to Flanders (*Rot. Claus.* i. 395, 478; *Rot. Misæ*, 244); and to the last day of the reign he preserved his loyalty to his sovereign.

Among the rewards which he received are the manors of Kening, Poterna, and Lavington; the lands of Saherus de Quincy, in Wiltshire, which were given to him in conjunction with Geoffrey de Neville; and, lastly, ten dolia of good wine. (*Rot. Claus.* i. 41, 123, 230, 263.)

He was one of the pledges for the payment of that curious fine of two hundred hens, which the wife of Hugh de Neville offered to King John for liberty to lie with her husband for one night. (*Madox*, i. 471.) He died about 6 Henry III. (*Rot. Claus.* i. 478, 490.)

SANDALE, JOHN DE (BISHOP OF WINCHESTER), held an office connected with the Treasury or Exchequer in 30 Edward I., 1302, when he is mentioned as receiving a crown for Queen Margaret (*Rot. Parl.* i. 474); in the following year he and John de Drokenesford are called treasurers (*Devon's Issue Roll*, 116); and he was likewise one of those appointed to assess the tallage in London and Middlesex, &c. In 33 Edward I. he became chamberlain of Scotland, an office which he held till the end of the reign, being at the same time commissioned to treat with the Scots on the affairs of that country. (*Abb. Rot. Orig.* i. 154.)

Called from Scotland at the accession of Edward II., he was constituted chancellor of the Exchequer on August 7, 1307, and at the end of the year was one of those directed to instruct the sheriffs of London and Middlesex in arresting the Knights Templars. On May 14, 1308, we find him acting as *locum tenens* for Walter Reginald, Bishop of Worcester, the treasurer, and continuing to do so till that prelate became chancellor, on July 6, 1310, when the office of treasurer was placed in Sandale's hands. There it remained until March 14, 1312, when he was succeeded by Walter de Langton, Bishop of Lichfield and Coventry, whose *locum tenens* he was named in the following October. He occupied this station till he was appointed chancellor, on September 26, 1314 (*Madox*, i. 75, ii. 8, &c.), an office which he held till June 9, 1318.

Sandale was an ecclesiastic, and one of the king's chaplains. On January 10, 1310, he had been made treasurer of Lichfield, was a canon of York, and is inserted in Le Neve's catalogue of the deans of London. It seems, however, doubtful whether he ever held the latter dignity. During his chancellorship the bishopric of Winchester became vacant, and he was elected to that see in August 1316, but presided over it for little more than three years. (*Le Neve*, 130, 183, 286.)

Soon after his resignation of the Great Seal he was restored to his office of treasurer, which was committed to him on November 16, 1318. (*Madox*, ii. 39.) He held it during the remainder of his life. He died on November 2, 1319, at Southwark, and was buried in St. Margaret's Church there. (*Godwin*, 223; *Angl. Sac.* i. 316.)

His life seems to have been employed in a routine of official duties, of which no further interruption is noticed than a pilgrimage he made to the shrine of St. Thomas of Canterbury a few months before he resigned the Seal. Previous to his elevation to the bishopric, his London residence, as chancellor, was in Aldgate. From Edward I. he received the manor of Berghby in Lincolnshire, and from Edward II. a house in the suburbs of Lincoln belonging to a religious society then dissolved. (*Abb. Rot. Orig.* i. 165, 195, 197.) It is probable, therefore, that his family was settled in that county, although from its name it no doubt had its origin in Yorkshire, in which, at his death, he had property in the manor of Whetlay, near Doncaster. (*Cal. Inquis.* p. m. i. 292.)

SANDWICH, RALPH DE, was of a knightly family in Kent, in which county he held the manors of Eynsford and Ham. In 49 Henry III. he was keeper of the wardrobe, and in that capacity, during the temporary absence of Thomas de Cantilupe the chancellor, the Great Seal was placed in his custody on May 7, 1265, under the seals of three clerks of Chancery. In 1 Edward I. the custody of the vacant bishopric of London was committed to him, and in 5 Edward I. the castle of Arundel. From that year to the ninth he acted as escheator south of the Trent under the title of 'seneschallus regis.' In 14 Edward I. he was appointed constable of the Tower of London, and, having held the office to the end of that reign, was confirmed in it on the accession of Edward II. (*Abb. Rot. Orig.* i. 21, 27–34, 155; *Madox*, i. 270, ii. 108–9.)

Dugdale introduces him as a judge of the Court of King's Bench in 17 Edward I., 1289, on the authority of a fine levied before him in Michaelmas Term of that year. This, however, would rather seem to place him in the Common Pleas, in confirmation of which there is a letter dated September 24, 1289, by which he was associated with John de Lovetot and the other judges of that court as chief justice in the place of Thomas de Weyland, then disgraced. As term was about to commence, King Edward no doubt commissioned him, in his character of constable of the Tower, an office then of great importance, to act *ad interim*, to prevent an interruption in the ordinary business till the charge was investigated. In this office he continued till February 1290. (*Gent. Mag.* March 1852, p. 267.) In 30 Edward I. he is called 'justice de Newgate.' (*Rot. Parl.* i. 154; *Hasted*, ii. 529, x. 178.)

He probably died in 1 Edward II., when John de Crumbwell was appointed constable of the Tower.

SANSETUN, BENEDICT DE (BISHOP OF ROCHESTER), was appointed on March 26, 1204, to the office of precentor of St. Paul's, London, when it was first erected and endowed with the church of Sording, and he enjoyed it till he was raised to the bishopric of Rochester, in December 1214, 16 John. (*Rot. Chart.* 124; *Le Neve*, 199, 248.) In 3 Henry III. he was at the head of the justices appointed for the four home counties (*Rot. Claus.* i. 396, 405), and fines were levied before them at Westminster in that character. In May, 8 Henry III., he had a donum of twenty marks as resident in the Exchequer, and in the following November ten marks for his support 'dum moram facit ad Scaccarium nostrum' (*Ibid.* i. 596, ii. 8), terms which seem to imply that he then acted as a regular justicier. In October 1225 he went on an embassy to France, and dying on December 21, 1226, was buried in his own cathedral. (*Ibid.* ii. 64, 163.)

SAUNDERS, EDMUND, commenced his career in the deepest poverty. His associates being selected from the lowest class, his habits in accordance with theirs, and his elevation being of so short continuance, no endeavours were made during his life to trace his real history. Yet one would think that these very circumstances would have given a peculiar interest to an account of the process by which he first extricated himself from his low condition, of the means which he used, and the energy which he exercised, to acquire that mastery over the intricacies of the law which his Reports exhibit, and of those powers by which he gradually acquired the ear of the court, and attained the high rank to which he was at last promoted.

Roger North (p. 223) is the only contemporary author who gives any description of his career, but the colouring with which he paints it requires perhaps some softening. He says that Saunders 'was at first no better than a poor beggar boy, if not a parish foundling, without known parents or relations.' By his will, however, it appears that he was born in the parish of Barnwood, about two miles from Gloucester, to the poor of which place he bequeathed 20*l*. It leaves legacies to his 'father and mother Gregory' also, from which fact Lord Campbell (*Ch. Just.* ii. 59) fills up the blank by saying, on what authority does not appear, that 'his father, who was above the lowest rank of life, died when he was an infant, and that his mother took for her second husband a man of the name of Gregory.' His lordship's suggestion that he ran away because he was 'hardly used by his father-in-law' seems to be ignored by the confidence placed in the discretion of his 'father Gregory' by his will.

Roger North's account proceeds thus: 'He had found a way to live by obsequiousness (in Clement's Inn, as I remember) and courting the attorney's clerks for scraps. The extraordinary observance and diligence of the boy made the society willing to do him good. He appeared very ambitious to learn to write; and one of the attorneys got a board knocked up at a window on the top of a staircase. . . . He made himself so expert a writer that he took in business, and earned a few pence by hackney-writing. And thus by degrees he pushed his faculties and fell to forms; and by books that were lent him became an exquisite entering clerk.' This course of education was pursued during the Commonwealth, for by the time of the Restoration he had so advanced in his means as to become a member of the Middle Temple, to which he was admitted on July 4, 1660, being described 'of the city of Gloucester, gentleman.' Called to the bar on November 25, 1664, he began to compile his Reports two years afterwards; and as he was himself in most of the cases in his work, and Sir T. Raymond mentions his name frequently from January 1668, it is clear that he got into early practice.

A curious and pictorial description of his person, habits, and general character is given by Roger North; representing him as corpulent and beastly in his person, and offensive to his neighbours, and as intemperate in his habits; but with wonderful wit and repartee, and a goodness of nature and disposition in so great a degree that he might be deservedly styled a philanthrope. A great favourite with the students of the law by his mirth and jests, he gained credit at the bar by his readiness and dexterity in special pleading, and his honesty and good nature were universally acknowledged. By degrees he was taken into the king's business, and had the part of drawing and perusal of almost all indictments and informations that were then to be prosecuted. Sometimes also he is to be found acting for the defence in government prosecutions—as for Mr. Price in 1680, when indicted for attempting to suborn one of the witnessess to the Popish Plot; and for the five Popish lords charged with high treason, of whom only Lord Stafford was tried. In 1681 he was counsel for the crown against Edward Fitzharris and against Lord Shaftesbury, and in 1682 for the Earl of Danby, on his application to be bailed. In that year he was elected a bencher of his inn; and on January 13, 1683, he was suddenly raised to the chief justiceship of the King's Bench and knighted. This elevation he owed, it is said, to the doubt which the court entertained whether Chief Justice Pemberton was sufficiently devoted to it to carry out the great object which the king then contemplated of obtaining a forfeiture of the charters of the city of London, and to the certainty felt that Saunders, who had advised the proceedings and settled all the pleadings, would, if placed in that office, decide against the corporation. The case was argued before him, and, though he was on his death-bed when judgment was pronounced, the other judges united in declaring that he agreed with them in decreeing the forfeiture. In the interval Saunders presided at the trial of the sheriffs of London and others for a riot at the election of new sheriffs, but he died between the conviction and the sentence. (*State Trials,* vols. vii. viii. ix.)

The habits of his life were necessarily changed by his promotion; his diet was altered, his labour incessant, and his anxiety greater. His constitution consequently, which had been much damaged by his former intemperance, soon utterly gave way. Before he had been six months on the bench he was seized with apoplexy and palsy, and died on June 19, 1683, at his house on Parson's Green, whither he had removed on becoming chief justice. By his will he makes Nathaniel Earle and Jane his wife (his host and hostess in Butcher Row) his residuary legatees, 'as some recompense for their care of him, and attendance upon him, for many years.'

'While he sat in the Court of King's Bench,' says Roger North, 'he gave the rule to the general satisfaction;' and it is universally allowed that he was abundantly versed in the mysteries and technicalities of law. His Reports, printed after his death, extend from 1666 to 1672, and are esteemed for their simplicity and precision. They are composed in so dramatic a form that Lord Mansfield called him the Terence of reporters.

SAUNDERS, EDWARD, was one of the sons of Thomas Saunders, Esq., of Harrington in Northamptonshire, by Margaret, daughter of Richard Cave, of Stanford in that county. Admitted at the Middle Temple, he was elected reader in 1525, and again in 1533 and 1539. His call to the degree of the coif was in Trinity Term 1540, and he was made one of King Edward's serjeants on February 11, 1547, within a fortnight after the accession. He was successively elected member for Coventry, Lostwithiel, and Saltash. The Reports of Dyer and Plowden show that he was in full practice, and before the end of the reign he had been appointed recorder of Coventry. At the king's death, in July 1553, he was in that city, and by his instigation the mayor refused to obey the orders sent by the Duke of Northumberland on the part of Lady Jane Grey, and immediately proclaimed Queen Mary. (*Chron. of Qu. Jane*, &c. 113.)

This prompt service was not overlooked, for on the 4th of the next October he was raised to the bench as a judge of the Common Pleas, and was knighted by King Philip in the following January. (*Machyn's Diary*, 342.) Among the trials on which he sat was that of Sir Nicholas Throckmorton, but he was little more than a silent commissioner, making only one slight remark. (*State Trials*, i. 894, 957.) Though these circumstances might raise a doubt as to his being, as Wotton says, the brother of Laurence Saunders, who was burnt for heresy at Coventry in May 1555, the more especially as on the death of Sir William Portman Sir Edward was promoted to the chief justiceship of the Queen's Bench on May 8, 1557, yet two letters remain from him to Lawrence which authenticate the relationship. Although a Roman Catholic, Sir Edward was re-appointed by Queen Elizabeth immediately after Mary's death, but the day before the next Hilary Term he was superseded by Sir Robert Catlin, and removed into the Court of Exchequer as chief baron, a change arising probably from the feeling that the former place was too important to be held by one of his religious persuasion, but that his services as a judge were too valuable to be altogether dispensed with. He was present at the trial of the Duke of Norfolk in 1571, but does not appear to have uttered a word. In the business of his court, however, this charge cannot be made against him, for his learning and his industry are amply exhibited by both Dyer and Plowden.

He died November 12, 1576, and was buried at Weston-under-Wethale, under a handsome monument. He married first Margaret, daughter of Sir Thomas Englefield, judge of the Common Pleas, and widow of George Carew, Esq.; and secondly Agnes Hussey. By the first he left a daughter, and by the second he had no child. (*Athenæ Cantabrigienses*, i. 359, 565.)

SAUNFORD, JOHN DE (ARCHBISHOP OF DUBLIN), was a justice itinerant in 3 Edward I. (7 *Report Pub. Rec., App.* ii. 248), but whether of England or Ireland is uncertain. The latter seems the more probable, as he was the king's escheator in Ireland from the eighth to the twelfth year. (*Abb. Rot. Orig.* i. 36, 42, 48.)

In 1285, 13 Edward I., he was made Archbishop of Dublin, and there is a letter from him to John de Langton, apparently before he was chancellor, and which therefore may have been written either before or after Saunford was elected to the archbishopric, requesting new writs relative to the process in the plea of Pencriz, to bear the same date as the former, as arranged when he attended at Knaresburgh before Langton and William de Hamilton. (7 *Report*, ut supra, 247.) As Pencriz is either the collegiate church in Staffordshire or the church in Derbyshire, it would appear that Saunford was then acting in a judicial capacity in England, but there is nothing positively to decide the question.

A contention arose between the archbishop and William de Luda, Bishop of Ely, in 21 Edward I., in consequence of a man of the former having been killed by a servant of the latter. (*Rot. Parl.* i. 111, 152.) The date of the archbishop's death was probably 30 Edward I., as his successor, William de Hotham, was then appointed.

SAUVAGE, GEOFFREY LE, held property in the counties of Warwick, Stafford, Derby, and Worcester, and on the death of his father, of the same name, in 1222, 6 Henry III., was excused his fine for admission, at the intercession of Hugh le Despencer, whose daughter, Matilda, he married. (*Rot. Claus.* i. 494, ii. 94; *Excerpt. e Rot. Fin.* i. 205.) In the following year he was custos of the forest of Savernake in Wiltshire, in which county he was also a justice itinerant in 9 Henry III. Dugdale (*Orig.* 42) notices fines levied before him at Westminster in 7 Henry III., and from that time till Easter, 10 Henry III. (*Rot. Claus.* i. 528, ii. 76.)

He died in 1230, when Hugh le Despencer paid fifty shillings for the custody of his lands and the wardship of his heir.

SAUVAGE, JAMES LE, was the rector of the church of St. Peter at Hotham, or Ocham, probably Woking in Surrey, and probably on that account was joined to the justices itinerant of the home counties in 3 Henry III., 1219. He was chaplain to Hubert Walter, Archbishop of Canterbury and chancellor, and was one of the executors of his will. (*Rot. Pat.* 26; *Rot. Claus.* i. 60–1.) On that prelate's death, in 1205, the king nominated him as custos of the archbishopric during the vacancy, and made him one of his own chaplains. (*Rot. Claus.* i. 46, 47, 71.)

SAVILE, JOHN, belonged to the ancient family of Savile, long settled in Yorkshire, which was represented in the reign of Edward I. by two brothers, John and Henry. From John descended the Marquis of Halifax, a title which became extinct in 1700. From Henry descended a baronet whose title expired in 1689, and Henry Savile of Bradley Hall in Stainland, in the parish of Halifax, who by his wife Elizabeth, daughter of Robert Ramsden, was the father of three sons, John, Henry, and Thomas, the two elder of whom became eminent in their respective vocations, John as a baron of the Exchequer, and Henry for his profound learning and his valuable publications—the memory of the latter being perpetuated in the university of Oxford by his endowment of two professorships in geometry and astronomy, which are distinguished by his name.

John Savile was born at Over Bradley in 1545, and after studying at Brazenose College, Oxford, entered the Middle Temple, where he advanced to the office of reader in 1586. That he was a regular attendant in the Common Pleas and Exchequer (in the latter of which he probably practised) is apparent from his reports of cases decided in those courts, which commence in Easter Term 1580. He was about this time steward of the lordship of Wakefield, and was called on November 29, 1592, to take the degree of a serjeant-at-law. In less then five years afterwards, on July 1, 1598, he was raised to the bench as a baron of the Exchequer, being recommended by Lord Burleigh, though described by him as a man of small living. (*Peck's Desid. Cur.* b. v. 24.) He sat in that court for the remainder of his life, King James renewing his patent in 1603 and knighting him, with the additional grant in 1604 of king's chief justice in the county palatine of Lancaster. (*Cal. State Papers* [1603–10], 133.) In 1599 he had been named as a commissioner 'de schismate supprimendo' (*Rymer*, xvi. 386); and in Michaelmas Term 1606 he joined with his colleagues in giving judgment for the crown in the great case of impositions. (*State Trials*, ii. 382.) This was one of the last legal duties he performed, his death occurring on February 2, 1607. His body was buried at St. Dunstan's-in-the-West, in Fleet Street, London, but his heart was deposited in the church of Methley in Yorkshire, where his ancestors were interred, and over it a magnificent monument was afterwards erected.

He was fond of historical studies, and was one of the first members of the Society of Antiquaries. An intimacy existed between him and Camden, his letter to whom pointing out a variety of mistakes in the 'Britannia' is extant. His benevolence was equal to his learning, and there was scarcely a manor of his in Yorkshire in which he did not leave some charities behind him.

He married four wives—1, Jane, daughter of Richard Garth, of Morden in Surrey, Esq.; 2, Elizabeth, daughter of Thomas Wentworth, of Elmshall in Yorkshire, Esq., and relict of Richard Tempest, of Bowling, Esq.; 3, Dorothy, daughter of Lord Wentworth of the South, and relict of Sir William Widmerpool and Sir Martin Forbisher; and, 4, Margery, daughter of Ambrose Peate, of London, and relict of Sir Jerom Weston. He had issue by the first two of these only.

Henry, his son by his first wife, was created a baronet in 1611, but the title died with him in 1632. From John, his son by his second wife, descended Sir John Savile, who was installed a knight of the Bath in 1749, and created Baron Pollington in 1753, and Earl of Mexborough in 1765, both in the Irish peerage, the third possessor of which titles still enjoys the family estates of Methley. (*Athen. Oxon.* i. 778; *Biog. Peerage*, iv. 81; *Wotton's Baronet.* i. 153.)

SAXBY, or SAXILBY, EDWARD, was placed on the bench of the Exchequer on November 28, 1549, 3 Edward VI., when the patent merely describes him as 'late clerk in the Remembrancer's Office.' His re-appointment at the commencement of the reigns of Queens Mary and Elizabeth is recorded, and on September 30, 1562, the date of the patent of Thomas Pymme, his successor, he is mentioned as lately deceased. No other event of his private life is known than his marriage with Elizabeth, daughter of—Fisher, of Longworth in Oxfordshire, and relict of William Woodcliffe, Esq., citizen and mercer of London, lord of the manor of Wormley in Hertfordshire. (*Gent. Mag.* Nov. 1839.)

SAY, GEOFFREY DE, is inserted by Dugdale among the judges of the King's Bench in 1321–2, 15 Edward II.; but, for the reasons previously given under the account of William de Dyve, great doubt exists as to the fact. This is almost confirmed by the additional circumstance that, though a distinguished member of an ancient and noble family, there is no proof that he was seated in that court.

Geoffrey de Say was descended from Picot de Say, a Shropshire baron in the reign of the Conqueror. His father, William, who had large possessions in Kent, besides some in other counties, died in 23 Edward I., 1295, leaving him an infant of fourteen years of age. He and his wife Idonea, the daughter of William de Leybourne, attended the coronation of Edward II., in 1308; and he was first summoned to parliament as a baron in 1313. He was frequently called upon to perform military services, but was never, as far as appears from the records, employed judicially. It is extremely probable, however, that among the numerous commissions issued for the trial of the adherents of Thomas de Badlesmere, there should have been one for his county of Kent; and that he, as a baron of that county, should have been named in it, and thus be entitled to the description of justiciarius regis, which Gervas of Canterbury gives to him, and by which every person so employed would be then designated during the continuance of the commission.

He died in 1321-2, the very year named by Dugdale as that of his judicial appointment, leaving a son, also Geoffrey, only seventeen years old, who succeeded him; but his male descendants failed in 1382, and the barony is said to be in abeyance among the representatives of Idonea and Joane, the two aunts of the last baron. In 1447, however, the grandson of Sir William Fiennes, who had married the said Joane, was summoned to parliament with the title of Lord Say and Sele, to which was added that of viscount in 1624. The viscounty became extinct in 1781; but the barony still survived, and was carried through females into the family of Twistleton. (*Leland's Collect.* i. p. ii. 275; *Baronage*, i. 511; *Parl. Writs*, ii. p. ii. 1402; *Nicolas's Synopsis.*)

SCARDEBURG, ROGER DE, as abbot of Whitby, headed the list of justices itinerant appointed for the county of Northumberland in 10 Henry III., 1226. He was born at Scarborough, and was elected to the abbacy in 1222, having previously acquired great veneration during a long residence in the cell at Middleburgh Church. He was a man of considerable abilities, and, during the twenty-two years that he presided over the monastery, much advanced its interests and increased its revenues. He died in 1244. (*Rot. Claus.* ii. 151; *Charlton's Whitby*, 169-203.)

SCARDEBURGH, ROBERT DE. It has been generally believed that Robert de Scardeburgh, the justice, and Robert de. Scorburgh, the baron of the Exchequer, were one and the same person, from the names Scord, Scorb, and Scarde frequently occurring among the advocates in the Year Books of Edward II. and Edward III., and disappearing after the sixth year of the latter reign. It is certain, however, that they were two persons, although the latter was sometimes called by the former name, and that the first derived his name from Scarborough, in the North Riding of Yorkshire, while the last obtained his from Scorbrough, in the East Riding. Their disappearance as advocates from the Year Books arises from their both receiving judicial appointments nearly at the same time—Scardeburgh in Ireland, in 1331-2; and Scorburgh in England, in 1332.

Robert de Scardeburgh stands at the head of a commission of assize into the islands of Guernsey, Jersey, Sark, and Alderney, in 5 Edward III. (*Abb. Rot. Orig.* ii. 57); and at the close of that year, 1331, he was made chief justice of the Common Pleas in Ireland, in which character he is mentioned two years afterwards. In 8 Edward III. his services were transferred to the Court of King's Bench in England, of which he was constituted a judge on September 14, 1334. (*Cal. Rot. Pat.* 113, 117, 120.)

He was in a commission of array for York in 13 Edward III. (*N. Fœdera*, ii. 105); and on September 6 in that year, 1339, he changed his seat in the King's Bench with John de Shardelowe, for the latter's place as a judge of the Common Pleas. In this court, however, he remained little more than a year, resuming his seat in the King's Bench on January 8, 1341, and retaining it for nearly four years. He was then, in 1344, restored to his former position of chief justice of the Common Pleas in Ireland (*Cal. Rot. Pat.* 135, 149); and in the same year two new seals were for the first time provided, by the advice of the council, for sealing the judicial writs of the two benches there, the custody of which was granted to him, with the fees appertaining to the duty. (*Abb. Rot. Orig.* ii. 166.) His history terminates here, for his name is not again mentioned.

SCARLE, JOHN DE, was so called from a place of that name in Lincolnshire, in which county some of his family were located in the reign of Edward III. (*Abb. Rot. Orig.* ii. 121, 155.) He was a clerk of the Chancery, of the higher grade, as early as 6 Richard II., 1382, from which year till 1397 he was always one of the receivers of petitions in parliament, of which he also acted as clerk for the eight years between 9 and 17 Richard II. (*Rot. Parl.* iii. 133-337.)

On July 22, 1394, he was raised to the office of keeper of the Rolls, and held it about three years and two months, during which he several times acted as keeper of the Great Seal, and it was in his possession when Archbishop Arundel was removed on November 23, 1396. On September 11 in the following year he resigned the mastership of the Rolls, and resumed his position as clerk in the Chancery, as appears from his witnessing under that title a charter to the city of Norwich, dated February 6, 1399. (*Blomefield's Norwich*, i. 118.) ₰After the arrest of King Richard he was appointed chancellor; and Sir T. D. Hardy gives September 5, 1399, as the date of the first privy seal bill addressed to him, so that he held the office for twenty-five days of this unfortunate king's reign, being the whole of its nominal remainder. He was of course not removed when Henry IV. was seated on the throne, but he occupied the post for little more than one year and five months under that king, delivering up the Seal in full parliament on March 9, 1401. He continued, however, one of the king's council for the rest of his life. (*Acts Privy Council*, i. 126–197.)

In the December following his retirement he received the archdeaconry of Lincoln, which he enjoyed about a year, his death occurring about April 1403. (*Le Neve*, 156.)

His residence in London was in Chancery Lane, on the site which is now known as Serjeants' Inn. It is sometimes called 'Tenementum' and sometimes 'Hospitium Domini Joh. Skarle,' and belonged to the Bishops of Ely.

SCARLETT, JAMES (LORD ABINGER), belonged to that branch of the family which in the seventeenth century was settled in Sussex. His immediate ancestor, Thomas Scarlett, of Eastbourne, migrated to Jamaica, where his brother Captain Francis Scarlett had established himself soon after Cromwell's conquest of that island in 1655, and sat in the first assembly. Thomas became possessed of large estates there, and his descendants were men of considerable wealth. Robert Scarlett, the fourth in lineal succession from Thomas, by his marriage with Elizabeth Anglin, a great-great-granddaughter of Henry Laurence, who was president of Cromwell's council, had several sons, two of whom attained high legal honours—one, the subject of the present sketch, as chief baron of the English Exchequer; and the other, the youngest son, Sir William Anglin Scarlett, as chief justice of Jamaica.

James Scarlett, who was the second son, was born in Jamaica in 1769, and was soon sent to England for the purpose of education. He was entered at a very early age as a fellow commoner of Trinity College, Cambridge, and took his degrees of B.A. in 1790, and of M.A. in 1794. In the meantime having entered the Inner Temple, he was called to the bar on July 28, 1791. His marriage in the next year with Louisa Henrietta, daughter of Peter Campbell, Esq., of Kilmory in Argyleshire, shows that he did not rely wholly on his success at the bar for the support of a family; but his early independence did not render him indolent, or prevent him from pursuing assiduously those studies which would prepare him for the contests into which he was about to enter. He joined the Northern Circuit and the Lancaster sessions, and for nearly a quarter of a century was doomed to remain as a junior counsel undecorated by a silk gown. But long before that period had elapsed his extraordinary merits and intellectual powers were appreciated both on the circuit and in the courts at Westminster. His extensive legal knowledge, his steady attention to the work before him, his quiet management and prudent judgment in the conduct of his case, soon inspired clients with entire confidence in his advice, and while yet in a stuff gown it was no uncommon thing to see him entrusted with a leading brief. In his arguments in banco he was remarkable for his ingenuity and acuteness, and for the peculiar power he had, by subtle distinctions, of extricating the point in dispute from the involvments that surrounded it. It was considered that he had too great an influence over the judges, and it was said of him that 'he had invented a machine, by a secret use of which in court he could always make the head of a judge nod assent to his proposition.'

This striking success rendered it impossible any longer to refuse him the accustomed distinction, and in 1816 he was called within the bar as king's counsel. From that time for the next eighteen years he enjoyed such an ascendency in the courts that it became an actual race between litigants which should secure his services in the impending contest, and the loser felt that one of his best chances of success was snatched from him. His influence over juries was wonderful—some called it magical; it was not obtained by any extraordinary eloquence, for he seemed carefully to avoid any rhetorical flourishes, but it was produced by laying before them in clear and simple language such a well-digested exposition of the case of his client as made it appear that he himself was satisfied of its justice, and that they had no choice but to endorse his opinion by their verdict. There was no apparent effort in his argument, no violent expression in his address, no attempt at brilliant periods; but the impression was effected by an easy, gentlemanly, and colloquial appeal to their understandings—perhaps in some degree heightened by his handsome person, his musical voice, and pleasing countenance. Yet, when the occasion demanded it, neither energy nor eloquence was wanting. Coleridge, in his 'Table Talk' (June 29, 1833), says, 'I think Sir James Scarlett's speech for the defendant, in the late action of Cobbett *v.* The Times for a libel, worthy of the best ages of

'Greece or Rome, though to be sure some of his remarks could not have been very palatable to his clients.' Whether the case was trifling or important, he took the same pains for his client, and seemed to be equally interested in the result. One of his greatest merits was that when he was engaged in a cause his services might always be relied upon. He disdained to adopt the vicious practice of some barristers, then far too common, of wandering about from court to court, and taking contemporaneous briefs in all, to the damage of those whose retainers and even whose briefs they had accepted, and many has been the time when Mr. Scarlett, deserted by those employed in the same cause, has borne the brunt of a long day's investigation sole and unaided. He occasionally expressed his indignation against what he deemed dishonesty in practice or conduct with great severity, and soon after he became a king's counsel an action was brought against him for a lashing animadversion he had administered to an attorney at the York assizes. A verdict was given in his favour, which was afterwards confirmed by the full court in London, on the ground that for words spoken by a counsel 'pertinent and relative to the matter in dispute' an action could not be maintained.

With the natural ambition to enter parliament, he contested the borough of Lewes twice, in 1812 and 1816, both times unsuccessfully. But in 1818 Lord Fitzwilliam provided him with a seat as the representative of Peterborough. In 1822 he stood a contest for the university of Cambridge, but was again defeated. He afterwards sat for Maldon, then for Cockermouth, and lastly, at the first election after the first Reform Act, for the city of Norwich. In the senate he was not so successful as in the forum. The easy style which commanded the attention of juries was not altogether suitable to a more enlightened and critical audience, and failed to produce any deep impression. In politics he ranked at first as a moderate whig, and supported Sir Samuel Romilly in his efforts towards the amelioration of the criminal law. He also introduced a proposition for the improvement of the Poor Laws, which, though not then encouraged, was the groundwork of future legislation. When something like an amalgamation of parties took place on Mr. Canning's becoming prime minister in April 1827, Mr. Scarlett, with the consent of the whig leaders and the approval of his patron Earl Fitzwilliam, accepted the office of attorney-general on the 27th of that month, and was as usual knighted. Before the end of the year the death of Mr. Canning, and the failure of Lord Goderich, his successor, brought that ministry to an end, and on the Duke of Wellington assuming the administration Sir James retired from his office in January 1828, to resume it, however, in June 1829, when Sir Charles Wetherell, his successor, resigned in disgust at the liberal measures proposed by the duke. With the accession of King William IV. came the triumph of the whigs, in November 1830, and the consequent removal of Sir James, who from his first entrance into office had been gradually approaching those conservative, but liberal, principles which for the whole remainder of his life he consistently maintained. His permanent change of opinion was no doubt confirmed by the coldness, and what he deemed the ingratitude, of the leaders of the whig party, who forgot that he accepted office at their request, or at least with their approbation.

During the time that he executed the functions of attorney-general he lost some of his popularity by his prosecutions of the 'Atlas' and 'Morning Post' for libels; but he amended the law relating to them by an act modifying the provisions of the six acts against public libels. To h m the profession is indebted for several improvements in the administration of justice. He got rid of the movable terms, and placed their commencement and their close upon fixed days in the year; and he prepared the bill for the abolition of the Welsh judicature and for enabling the judges of Westminster Hall to administer justice on circuit throughout the Principality; at the same time extending the number of the judges from twelve to fifteen.

Joining in a bold opposition to the various measures of radical reform that were then introduced, and largely increasing his fortune by his undisputed ascendency in the courts, he awaited a change in the administration with the certainty of then receiving the reward of his labours. That change was delayed till 1834, when Sir Robert Peel became minister. Sir James Scarlett was then, on December 24, constituted lord chief baron of the Exchequer. In the next month he was created Baron Abinger of Abinger in Surrey, an estate he had purchased, being the first chief baron who received while in that office the honour of the peerage.

His reputation as a judge did not equal his fame as an advocate. He had too much the habit of deciding which of the two parties in a cause was in the right, and arguing in his favour; while juries, who had been accustomed to be led by his pleadings as a counsel, refused to submit to his dictation as a judge. The consequence was that he frequently lost verdicts which, had he shown less bias, would have been conformable to his opinion. He presided in the Exchequer for nearly ten years, and attended the Norfolk Circuit in the spring of 1844, apparently in full health and vigour. But after sitting in court at Bury St. Edmunds, and going through the business of the day with his accustomed clearness and skill, till seven o'clock in the evening, he was two hours after struck with paralysis, which left him speechless, and in five days terminated his life, on April 7. His remains were removed for interment at Abinger.

His first wife, after producing to him three sons and two daughters, died in 1829, and left him a widower for fourteen years. In 1843, the last year of his life, he married, secondly, the daughter of Lee Steere Steere, Esq., of Jayes in Surrey, and the widow of the Rev. H. J. Ridley, of Ockley, by whom he left no children. His eldest daughter married Lord Campbell, and before he attained that title was honoured with a peerage in her own right as Baroness Stratheden. His eldest son enjoyed the title after him till 1861, and was succeeded by the present, the third, baron. The chief baron's second son, Sir James Yorke Scarlett, K.C.B., has acquired great fame as a soldier; and his youngest son, Peter Campbell Scarlett, has gained considerable distinction as a diplomatist.

SCORBURGH, ROBERT DE, took his name from Scorbrough in the East Riding of Yorkshire, and was sometimes called by the name of Robert de Scardeburgh. Under the name of Scorburgh he had a licence in 17 Edward II. to assign a lay fee in Beverley and Etton; and on his death, in 14 Edward III., he is described, under the name of Scardeburgh, as possessing the manor of Scorby, and also property in Stamford Bridge and Etton, both of which are in the East Riding, and in the neighbourhood of Beverley and Scorbrough. (*Abb. Rot. Orig.* i. 274, ii. 136.) No question, however, can be entertained that Robert de Scorburgh and his contemporary, Robert de Scardeburgh, were not, as has been asserted, the same individual. Robert de Scorburgh's connection with the law appears from his being employed on special commissions in Yorkshire in 16 and 20 Edward II. (*Parl. Writs*, ii. p. ii. 1406); in both of which he is called Scorburgh, and is evidently added to the regular judges, as a serjeant is in the present day. In 18 Edward II. he was appointed also on a commission of enquiry, his name being then spelled Scoreburgh. Again, in 2 Edward III. there is a petition to parliament by the people of 'Scartheburgh,' relative to a trial before Robert de Scoresburgh and his companions, justices of Oyer and Terminer in that town; and in the fourth year he was amongst the justices itinerant into Derbyshire, as Scorburgh. (*Rot. Parl.* i. 420, ii. 28.)

He was raised to the bench of the Exchequer on November 2, 1332, 6 Edward III., the record calling him Scorburgh, by which name he received knighthood in the same year. (*Dugdale's Orig.* 102.) He is also so named in the following year, in the record commissioning him to treat with the Earl of Flanders (*N. Fœdera*, ii. 875), while at this time his contemporary Robert de Scardeburg was chief justice of the Common Pleas in Ireland.

After this we hear nothing of him till his death in 14 Edward III., when it appears, by the document above referred to, that his property was committed to the custody of Wolfand de Clistere, because Thomas, his son and heir, was an idiot.

SCOTHOU, WILLIAM DE, to whom no reference whatever is made, except in Dugdale's list of justices itinerant for Kent in 22 Edward III., 1348, probably took his name from a parish so called in Norfolk. A Peter de Scothow was returned member for Norwich in 12 Edward II.

SCOTRE, ROGER DE, was possessed of Coringham and several other manors in Lincolnshire. In 1309, 3 Edward II., he and Edmund Passelegh, designated as serjeants, were appointed to transact the king's business of pleas, and were directed to appear at the Exchequer on Michaelmas-day to do as the king and his council should order. On July 17, 1310, 4 Edward II., he was constituted a baron of the Exchequer, and in the same year was the first named of three justices of assize for six counties, of which Lincoln was one. His tenure of office was very short, for he died before March 3, 1312, when his successor, Walter de Norwich, received his patent.

He left a wife, called both Agnes and Elizabeth, and an only daughter, named Elizabeth, who died a minor.

SCOTT, WILLIAM. The name of Scott was so common even at this early period that it is difficult to speak with certainty of the family of this William Scott. If H. Phillips, in his 'Grandeur of the Law,' (1684), is right in saying that Sir Thomas Scott, then of Scott's Hall in Kent, was descended from him, it would seem that the original name of the family was Baliol, and that William, the brother of John Baliol, King of Scotland, who frequently wrote his name as William de Baliol *le Scot*, after the contest for the crown in the reign of Edward I. had terminated in his brother's overthrow, politically dropped his patronymic, and retained only the national addition he had assumed. In the reign of Edward III. this family was seated in the parish of Braborne in Kent, and it was not till Henry VI.'s time that they removed to Scott's Hall, a manor in the neighbouring parish of Smeeth. (*Hasted*, viii. 5.)

William Scott was a pleader in the courts from 3 Edward III., and was made one of the king's serjeants in the eighth year. On

March 18, 1337, 11 Edward III., he was raised to the bench of the Common Pleas, but was removed into the King's Bench on May 2, 1339, and was promoted to the chief justiceship of that court on January 8, 1341. He still held that office at his death in 20 Edward III., 1346, though Dugdale by mistake transfers him to the Common Pleas as chief justice there in 1342. (*Abb. Rot. Orig.* ii. 179.)

One Humphrey Hunney, probably a discontented suitor, having complained that the chief justice had awarded an assize contrary to law, was imprisoned, judged, fined, and ransomed for the offence. (*State Trials,* ii. 1024.)

His descendants numbered among them many eminent in offices of trust, as well in the state as in the county; and the next-noticed John Scott, chief baron, is said to have been of the same family, which was not extinct at the end of the last century.

SCOTT, JOHN, is said by Phillips, in his 'Grandeur of the Law,' to have been a descendant from the above William Scott, but no means are supplied for tracing the pedigree.

An apprentice of his name is mentioned in the Year Books in 20 Henry VII., 1504, who probably was the same person who on January 8, 1513, 4 Henry VIII., had a grant in reversion to be chief baron of the Exchequer, then held by Sir William Hody. (*Cal. State Papers* [1509-14], 470.) His name does not occur as a judge in any of the reporters; and his accession to and continuance on the bench is only to be inferred from the fact that a new chief baron, John Fitz-James, was appointed in February 1521.

Dugdale mentions a John Scott who received a patent as third baron on May 15, 1528, being six years after the appointment of John Fitz-James as chief baron. If this be the same man as John Scott the chief baron in reversion, he must either have not taken the place under the patent, or have been removed to make way for Fitz-James, and replaced in an inferior seat on the bench at this time; but history is totally silent on the subject, and the name of Scott was so common as to defy the endeavours of the most industrious to determine whether this third baron was or was not the same individual. He is named two years afterwards as one of the commissioners to enquire into the possessions of Cardinal Wolsey in Surrey. (*Rymer,* xiv. 402.)

SCOTT, JOHN (EARL OF ELDON), was the grandson of William Scott of Sandgate in Newcastle-upon-Tyne, who exercised the trade of a 'fitter' of coals, and was the owner of several 'keels;' and the son of William Scott, who pursued the same occupation, was a freeman of Newcastle, and member of the Hoastman's Company there, which consisted of the first tradesmen in the place. He married Jane, the daughter of Henry Atkinson of Newcastle, by whom he had thirteen children, the fourth of whom, and eldest son, William, became judge of the High Court of Admiralty, and was created Lord Stowell in 1821; and the eighth of whom, and third and youngest son, was John Scott, the lord chancellor.

John Scott was born in Love Lane, Newcastle, on June 4, 1751. He was first sent to the Royal Grammar School there, where he made great progress under his excellent master, the Rev. Hugh Moises. The anecdote book, which he wrote late in life for the amusement of his grandchildren, contains many of his adventures while there, and the floggings inflicted upon him, which in this delicate and effeminate age would be called indecent and cruel. In May 1766, his father, who had intended to bring him up to his own business, was persuaded to send him to Oxford by his eldest son William, who had by this time become fellow and tutor of University College. There he was instructed under the tuition of his brother, and was elected to a fellowship in 1767. He took his degree of B.A. in 1770, and in 1771, being then under twenty, gained Lord Lichfield's prize for English prose, the subject being 'The Advantages and Disadvantages of Foreign Travel.' On November 19, 1772, he was guilty of the apparent indiscretion of running away with Elizabeth, daughter of Aubone Surtees, Esq., a banker at Newcastle; and though the couple were quickly forgiven by their parents, they felt for some years the effect of their imprudence. The husband was, of course, obliged to give up his fellowship, and, resigning his hope of a provision in the Church, to support himself and his wife on the very small provision made for them.

Adopting the law as his alternative, he entered the Middle Temple on January 28, 1773, and in the following month took his degree of M.A. During his three years of probation he spent no more time in London than was necessary for the keeping of his terms, but was employed in assisting his brother as tutor at University College, and in acting as deputy Vinerian professor to Sir Robert Chambers. While so engaged, he pursued his legal studies with so much perseverance and energy that his health was seriously endangered, rising every day at four in the morning, and reading at night with a wet towel round his head to prevent him from falling asleep. At the end of 1775 he removed to London with his family, now increased by an infant son, and took up his abode in Cursitor Street. He had the advantage of spending the interval before his call to the bar in the

Q Q

office of Mr. Duane, where he acquired a perfect knowledge of conveyancing. That of pleading he obtained with no other instruction than naturally resulted from his own industry in copying precedents. On February 9, 1776, he was called to the bar, and removed into Carey Street, and in November following his father died. Though by that event his circumstances were slightly improved, his business for some time gave him no addition. In the first year his whole receipt amounted to half a guinea, and though he went the Northern Circuit, few briefs were entrusted to him. But he made friends with the leaders, and gained some experience by observing how they managed their causes. He at first attended the common law courts, but soon fancying that Lord Mansfield did not encourage young lawyers who were not educated at Westminster and Christ Church, he left the King's Bench, and joined the Chancery bar, then not exceeding twelve or fifteen in number.

There his progress was so little encouraging that he had almost determined to retire to his native town as a provincial counsel, and had even taken a house there, not without hope of being elected recorder in the event of a vacancy. His prospects, however, were materially altered by a decision which Lord Thurlow pronounced in the case of Ackroyd v. Smithson, in accordance with an argument which he had made, against not only the opinion of Sir Thomas Sewell, the master of the Rolls (*Brown's Chanc. Cases*, i. 505; 2 *Jarman's Powell*, 77 et seq.), but even contrary to the expectations of his own client. He soon after had the good fortune, by one of those accidents which occasionally happen, to be very suddenly engaged as leading counsel in the Clitheroe election case, for which he had but four hours to prepare. He exhibited so much ability that Sir James Mansfield and Mr. Wilson, both afterwards judges, strongly encouraged him to remain in London, the latter offering to insure him 400*l*. the next year. From that time his success was no longer doubtful in Westminster Hall, and his practice on the circuit, which it was then the custom of Chancery men to attend, was equally increased, aided by some important causes in which he had the good luck to lead and to be triumphant. At Carlisle, however, he had no business till, by the absence of another counsel, he was engaged to defend an old woman for an assault, and succeeded by a joke in getting her off with only nominal damages. This immediately procured him briefs to the amount of seventy guineas, where he had not received one for seven years before. He had now taken up his residence in Powis Place, and afterwards removed to No. 42 Gower Street, where he lived about thirteen years before he went to Bedford Square.

He was a favourite with Lord Thurlow, who proved his friendship by purposely refusing him a commissionership of bankrupts, and thus forcing him to work. He received a patent of precedence on June 4, 1783, when he was elected a bencher of his inn. In the same month he was, through Lord Thurlow's recommendation, elected member for Lord Weymouth's borough of Weobly. In the succeeding session of parliament Mr. Fox brought forward his famous East India Bill, which Mr. Scott strenuously opposed, and the defeat of which was the dismissal of the Coalition Ministry. The storm that followed ended in a dissolution. Mr. Scott, in the new parliament, again represented Weobly, and soon acquired such an ascendency by his arguments in support of Mr. Pitt's ministry as even to compel Mr. Fox's admiration and respect.

In March 1787 he was appointed chancellor of Durham by Lord Thurlow's brother, the bishop; and in June of the next year he was selected by Mr. Pitt as solicitor-general, when he was knighted. One of his first duties on the reassembling of parliament was to support the measures consequent on the king's illness, in the performance of which he so greatly signalised himself that he received the king's personal thanks.

So high was his reputation at this time, and so extensive his practice, that he was enabled in 1792 to invest 22,000*l*. in the purchase of Eldon, an estate in the southern part of the county of Durham, and to devote the whole of its rents to its improvement. From this estate he afterwards took his first title of nobility. Early in the next year (February 13, 1793), in the midst of the anxieties consequent upon the French Revolution, he succeeded to the office of attorney-general, and upon him devolved the difficult duty of concerting and carrying into effect the measures necessary to counteract the seditious principles that were then too prevalent in this country. Revolutionary agitators formed themselves into associations, which, under the pretence of seeking a reform in parliament, had more serious objects in contemplation, tending to the deposition of the king. To repress these was the great object of the minister; and to this end it was determined to prosecute the leading instigators. The subsequent trials of Hardy, Horne Tooke, and Thelwall, who, by the eloquence of Erskine and the learning of Gibbs, narrowly escaped conviction for high treason, succeeded in satisfying the public of the danger of these societies, and eventually in putting a stop to the seditious agitation; and Sir John

Scott, though much abused by one party for his attempt to establish what they termed 'constructive treason,' was as much applauded by the other for the energy and learning, humanity and courage, with which he conducted the several prosecutions. Before, however, the agitation had subsided, it became necessary to introduce bills for further security in this and the succeeding parliament of 1796, to which he was returned for Boroughbridge instead of Weobly. The preparation and support of these measures devolved principally on the attorney-general, as well as several prosecutions for seditious writings and other political offences.

In July 1799 his official labours terminated by the death of Sir James Eyre, chief justice of the Common Pleas, to which office he claimed the right of succession. It was accorded to him on two conditions—one, by Mr. Pitt, that he should accept a peerage, so that his services in parliament might not be lost; and the other by the king, that he should not refuse the Great Seal when he should be called upon to accept it. He was sworn of the privy council on July 17; on the 18th he received his patent as Baron Eldon; and on the 19th he was appointed lord chief justice of the Common Pleas. Though he held that office less than two years, he more than fulfilled the expectations of those who could appreciate his powers. In the exercise of his judicial functions he exhibited none of the doubt and hesitation which were ascribed to him in his subsequent career; but both before and after the death of his colleague, Mr. Justice Buller, he sustained the high character of his court by his excellent decisions.

When Mr. Pitt resigned, on the subject of the Catholic question, Lord Eldon, in performance of his promise to the king, accepted the Great Seal on April 14, 1801, but, owing to the temporary illness of his majesty, did not resign the chief justiceship till May 21, discharging the duties of both offices during the interval. Before the close of the year he was appointed high steward of the university of Oxford, of which his brother, Sir William Scott, was at that time the representative in parliament. During the ministry of Mr. Addington and his successor, the chancellor was treated with the utmost confidence by the king, whose occasional attacks of illness gave great embarrassment to the government, which were not diminished by the differences which existed between the Prince of Wales and his father. On Mr. Pitt's resumption of power in 1804 Lord Eldon was continued in his office, and retained it till the death of that great minister, on January 23, 1806, which made way for Lord Granville's and Mr. Fox's ministry, called 'All the Talents.' He then, on February 7, resigned the Great Seal into the hands of Lord Erskine.

Ere fourteen months were expired that administration was dismissed on the Catholic question, and Lord Eldon resumed his seat as lord chancellor on April 1, 1807. He held it undisturbed for the next twenty years under the premierships of the Duke of Portland, Mr. Perceval, and Lord Liverpool—a period pregnant with the most important events in the political and domestic history of the country. The malicious attack upon the Duke of York; the duel between Lord Castlereagh and Canning, causing the break-up of the Duke of Portland's ministry; the negotiations following, and the pluck of Mr. Perceval in undertaking the premiership, all occurred during the first three years, and naturally occasioned him much anxiety, which was not diminished by Lord Granville's defeating him by about a dozen votes in the contest for the chancellorship of Oxford. But he found comfort in his disappointment in the conviction that had the Duke of Beaufort, who stood upon the same interest, retired as at first was intimated, he would have had a triumphant majority over his political rival.

In November 1810 the parliament opened without the usual commission, the king being visited by an attack which prevented him from affixing the sign-manual, and which unfortunately could not be subdued as the former one had been, but lasted for the ten remaining years of his life. This led to a renewal of the conflicts of 1788-9, relating to the restrictions to be put upon the regency, in the conduct of which Lord Eldon was treated with the bitterest acrimony by Lord Grey and the expectant ministers. The prince regent not only, to the surprise of the whigs, kept the tories in office during the year limited for the restrictions imposed upon him, but, to their infinite disgust and disappointment, still continued to repose his confidence in the old ministers when that year had expired. Lord Eldon was thus confirmed in his position, but had to submit to the attacks in the House of Commons of Michael Angelo Taylor on the alleged delays in the Court of Chancery, and in the appeals in the House of Lords. A more serious visitation soon followed in the assassination of Mr. Perceval, the prime minister, by Bellingham, on May 11, 1812. This had nearly broken up the ministry; but the negotiations with the whig party failing, the prince regent was compelled, not unwillingly, to go on with them; and the glorious successes of the British arms under the Duke of Wellington, which led to the restoration of the Bourbon king to France, established them firmly in the confidence of the country. In the corn-law riots of 1816 the mob broke into Lord Eldon's house in Bedford Square, and he himself narrowly escaped by retiring into the garden of the British Museum. Returning thence, not with 'a band of fifty chosen men,' but with a corporate guard of four, he drove back the mob, showing the greatest bravery and presence of mind, and capturing two of them with his own hands. In the same year Bonaparte's escape from Elba obliged the government to make extraordinary efforts, leading to the crowning victory of Waterloo, and resulting in Bonaparte's delivering himself up to England, and his final detention in the island of St. Helena.

On the death of George III., on January 29, 1820, the prince regent as king for the third time placed the Great Seal in the hands of Lord Eldon. In the following month he escaped assassination by the timely discovery of the Cato Street conspiracy to murder all the ministers at a cabinet dinner given by Lord Harrowby. Soon after followed the queen's trial, in which his conduct as speaker of the House of Lords was the subject of unmixed praise; and he was so fully convinced, from the evidence produced, that she was guilty of the crime charged in the preamble to the bill, that he moved the second reading in a powerful speech. Though the bill was prudently withdrawn, the queen's temporary popularity soon subsided, and was not restored by her unadvised and unsuccessful attempt to take part in the king's coronation. Previous to that solemnity the king insisted, much against Lord Eldon's inclination, on promoting him to a higher rank in the peerage; and he was accordingly created Viscount Encombe and Earl of Eldon on July 7, 1821, the viscounty being named from his estate in the Isle of Purbeck in Dorsetshire, purchased by him in the year 1807, where he spent all his vacations.

For the first seven years of the new reign Lord Eldon retained his place under the same prime minister, Lord Liverpool, no otherwise disturbed in his political feelings than by the pressure of the Catholic claims, and the gradual advance of radical opinions. He was, however, personally annoyed by the captious attacks that were annually made upon him and his court in the House of Commons, by those who, seeing the powerful influence he exercised in the state, were desirous of forcing him to resign. But these attacks produced the contrary effect, and prompted him boldly to repel them, and to refrain from insisting on a retirement which for several years he had repeatedly pressed upon the government, but which, at one time from the representations of his colleagues that his secession would break up the ministry, and at another from the personal solicitation of the king, he had been induced to withdraw. When, however, Lord Liverpool was seized with an affliction which terminated his political existence, and the government was re-organised under Mr. Canning, Lord Eldon felt that he could no longer continue as the colleague of a minister who adopted opinions with respect to the Catholic question in direct opposition to those he had himself all along advocated. He therefore, on April 30, 1827, resigned the Seal, which he had holden for the space of a quarter of a century, minus little more than a month. His successor was Lord Lyndhurst.

At the time of his retirement he was in the seventy-sixth year of his age, but he did not then wholly withdraw from the political world. During many of the eleven years that he survived he took an active but ineffectual part in opposing the numerous innovations that were introduced into the legislature. To his strictly conscientious, if mistaken, feelings, the repeal of the Test and Corporation Acts, the Emancipation of the Catholics, and the Reform Bill were peculiarly distressing. He saw nothing that would result from the two latter but the most calamitous effects upon the constitution, and during the time he lived after them he had not much reason to alter his opinion. The former of them only led to new demands from the Catholic agitators, and amidst the various mischiefs and partialities of the latter of them, the solitary benefit it conferred was the shortening the period of elections. He looked with scarcely less disgust at the various speculative alterations in the law that were from time to time propounded. He had removed from Bedford Square to Hamilton Place, and there and at his mansion at Encombe he continually resided, with occasional journeys to his property in Durham. His life terminated on January 13, 1838, in Hamilton Place, by a gradual decay of bodily strength, but in the preservation of his intellect and spirits to the last. His remains were removed to Encombe for interment in the family vault which he had built at Kingston for the reception of Lady Eldon, whom he lost in 1831, after a union of fifty-nine years.

Living in the reigns of five successive sovereigns, one the longest in the annals of England, enjoying high office in the state for the long period of fifty years, it would have been a miracle if, whatever were his deserts, he should wholly have escaped censure. But even the small party which delighted to attack him were obliged to acknowledge his superior merits. They admitted his eminent talents, his extensive learning, the wonderful readiness of its application, and the justice of his decisions. They could not deny his patience in listening to the arguments of counsel, his courteousness to the bar, and his conciliatory demeanour to all; but they charged him with a habit of doubting everything, and attributed to it all the delays of the Court of Chancery. This disposition to hesitate was a judicial defect with which he was undoubtedly chargeable; but the most candid and best informed of his adversaries in politics could not help allowing that it arose from an over-anxiety to do strict justice to the litigants. The epigrammatic turn of the following lines shows how his slowness was estimated in comparison with the 'quick injustice' of his vice-chancellor, Sir John Leach:—

In Equity's high court there are
Two sad extremes, 'tis clear;
Excessive slowness strikes us there,
Excessive quickness here.

Their source, 'twixt good and evil, brings
A difficulty nice;
The first from Eldon's *virtue* springs,
The latter from his *Vice*.

This habit of dubitation was grossly exaggerated solely for party purposes. A hope was entertained by his political antagonists that the personal annoyance he suffered would induce his resignation, and the consequent defeat of the ministry of which he was one of the main supports. Few indeed were the cases in which they could make their charge good; and he not only justified, but continued the practice, upon the principle that extreme care to give a right decision prevented not only the annoyance and expense of appeal in the case before him, but also future litigation on the same class of subjects. The consequences were such as he anticipated; and the judgments of Lord Eldon are not only treated with the greatest respect, but regarded as of the highest authority. There is little justice in attributing to him the delays of his court and the increase of arrears, since the complaints were mere repetitions of the same outcry which had been heard against the Court of Chancery for hundreds of years —aggravated by the increase of population and the spread of commerce, both necessarily leading to a multiplication of litigation to an immense degree. Even with the stupendous exertions of Lord Eldon (and they exceeded those of any former chancellor) he could not with the most extraordinary despatch keep pace with the perpetual advances made upon the list of causes set down for his hearing; and it was at length found necessary to give him assistance in clearing off some of the arrears by appointing a vice-chancellor. To this proposal the most violent opposition was raised by the adverse party; yet they themselves, when they came into power, added four more judges to the same court—namely, two additional vice-chancellors and two lord justices of appeal—thus proving the injustice of their attack upon Lord Eldon, and acknowledging that the business of the court could not be despatched by the efforts of a single individual.

Of his profound knowledge and superior excellence as a judge it is not surprising that the testimony of such men as Mr. Charles Butler, Lord St. Leonard's, Lord Lyndhurst, and a host of others, should be expressed in the strongest terms; but that his principal opponents, Lord Brougham, Sir Samuel Romilly, and more of the same party, at the very moment of their attack, should speak of him in the same eulogistic manner, proves the universal acknowledgment of his merits. Without being brilliant as an orator, his speeches were highly effective from his reasoning powers; and without being remarkable for wit, he had a great deal of quiet humour, and was peculiarly happy in his retorts and repartees. By the courtesy of his demeanour, by the solidity of his judgment, and by the straightforward consistency of his conduct he acquired the respect of the Peers, among whom, while he presided, he gained the utmost ascendency. By the bar and the officers of his court he was beloved beyond any other head; and in his private life he was the kindest and most amiable of men. None who had the happiness of being connected with him, or the privilege of practising under him, but must regard his memory with affection and veneration; and as he was to the last hour of his life, so he will be for the time to come, recognised as the unflinching supporter of the constitution.

Of his six children two daughters only survived him, one of whom married George Stanley Repton, Esq., and the other the Rev. Edward Bankes. His eldest son, John, left a son, who succeeded his grandfather as second earl, upon whose death his son, also John, became the third and present earl.

SCOTT, THOMAS. *See* T. ROTHERAM.

SCROGGS, WILLIAM. The last four of the chief justices of the King's Bench in the reign of Charles II.—Scroggs, Pemberton, Saunders, and Jeffreys—may be cited as remarkable proofs of the general profligacy of the period, each having been elevated to his high position notwithstanding the notorious looseness of his early life. The obloquy which is attached to the name of Scroggs may serve as a warning to every man to avoid obsequiousness to those from whom favour flows. An apostate, from party spirit, ambition, or personal interest, to principles he had once strongly advocated, will ever be repudiated by both parties and defended by neither. If there are any good points in his character they will be misconstrued or misrepresented; and if there is the least blot in his escutcheon he will be sure to have

<blockquote>
all his faults observed,
Set in a note-book, learn'd and conned by rote,
To cast into his teeth.
</blockquote>

Such was the fate of Sir William Scroggs, whose extravagant zeal for each of the contending parties, as he supposed one or the other to be in the ascendant, led to the usual consequence—his fall between both; his name being blackened so universally that scarcely any writer shows the slightest tenderness to his memory, except Anthony Wood in his 'Athenæ Oxonienses' (iv. 115). Even his lineage does not escape calumny, and his reputed low birth, which in the height of his popularity would be mentioned to his credit, is blazoned as an addition to his disgrace when the tables are turned.

How true Sir William Dugdale's assertion that his father was 'a one-eyed butcher near Smithfield Bars, and his mother a big fat woman with a red face like an ale-wife,' may be, can only be collected from the fact that the squibs written against the chief justice made perpetual allusion to his father's business, and from the failure of any account of his ancestors or family. A. Wood says that his father was of the same name, and that he was born at Deddington in Oxfordshire. But in whatever business his father had been engaged, it is clear that he was a man of some intelligence, and must have acquired a comfortable fortune, inasmuch as he showed his desire and his power to give his son a good education by sending him to the university of Oxford. Entered at first at Oriel College in 1639, when at the age of 16, he soon after removed to Pembroke College, where he took the degree of B.A. in 1640, and of M.A. in 1643. He entered Gray's Inn in February 1640, but was not called to the bar till June 1653, the delay perhaps arising from the disturbed state of the country. He was enabled about 1662, either by his practice or his patrimony, to purchase the estate of Southweald in Essex, which had formerly had Lord Chancellor Rich and Lord Chief Justice Anthony Browne for its owners. (*Morant*, i. 111.)

A bold front, a handsome person, an easy elocution, and a ready wit are strong recommendations for a young barrister. The possession of these introduced Scroggs to some connections at court, who would not be scandalised by the irregularity of his life. He is described as a great voluptuary and debauchee, and so noted for the coarseness of his language and the looseness of his habits as to be despised by all good and respectable men. About this time he became counsel for the city of London; and by the profession of excessive loyalty, together with his interest at court, he obtained the honour of knighthood. He is designated by his title in a petition which he preferred in April 1665, alleging that, it being his duty to walk before the lord mayor on certain days of solemnity, but being unable to do so from wounds sustained in the cause of the late king, he had been therefore suspended from his place, and praying redress. (*Cal. State Papers* [1664–5], 310.) In April 1668 he was assigned as counsel for Sir William Penn, and in June 1669 was summoned to take the degree of the coif, and in the very next term promoted to be king's serjeant. (*North's Lives*, 151; *State Trials*, vi. 876; 1 *Siderfin*, 435.) Roger North perhaps speaks too strongly when he says that Chief Justice Hale detested him; but that estimable judge could have little regard for a man of Scroggs's character. Being arrested on a King's Bench warrant for assault and battery, the chief justice and the whole court refused him the privilege of a serjeant, on the ground that the proceeding was not against him only, but against him and another. (2 *Levinz*, 129; 3 *Keble*, 424.)

Lord Danby was his principal patron, and to his influence Scroggs entirely owed his next advances, as he had no reputation in his profession. On October 23, 1676, a seat on the bench of the Common Pleas was given to him, and nineteen months afterwards Sir Richard Rainsford was discharged to make way for him as lord chief justice of the King's Bench, to which he was appointed on May 31, 1678. The Reports are so silent as to his previous professional career that the three years during which he presided in this court may be almost said to contain the whole history of his legal life. It presents such a combination of ignorance, arrogance, and brutality as fully to justify the censure almost universally pronounced upon the judicial appointments of the latter part of this reign.

The Popish Plot was first started soon after his advancement, and, from a mistaken idea of the inclinations of the court, he thought he should be doing an acceptable service to the king by taking a strong part against the supposed participators in it, at the same time that he was insuring for himself an immense popularity amongst its deluded believers. When the infamous promoters were detailing their narrative before the Commons he was sent for, and, in reply to the speaker, declared he would use his best endeavours, for he feared the face of no man where the king and country were concerned. (*Bramston's Autobiog.* 179.) Withdrawing into the speaker's chamber, he took the informations, issued his warrants, and threw himself at once into the ranks of its most zealous advocates.

On the trials he gave public credit to the testimony of the witnesses, explained away their palpable contradictions, browbeat and threatened those who came forward with opposing evidence, inflamed the juries, who were too ready to act on his suggestions, and barbarously insulted the unfortunate victims. Even in the first state trial before him, that of Stayley, he had the inhumanity to call out to the prisoner on the verdict of 'guilty being pronounced, 'Now you may die a Roman Catholic, and when you come to die I doubt you will be proved a priest too.' On another occasion he exclaimed to three convicted prisoners, 'And now much good may their thirty thousand masses do them.' The seventh volume of the 'State Trials' is almost wholly occupied with those arising out of the Popish Plot, in which Titus Oates, William Bedlow, and the chief justice so infamously distinguished themselves.

In the trials of Coleman, of Ireland and two others, of Reading, of Whitehead and four others, and of Langhorn (whom he afterwards acknowledged to be innocent), he pursued the same course; but in the next, that of Sir George Wakeman and three others, there was a sudden alteration. He there threw discredit on the witnesses he had before encouraged, pointing out their several contradictions, and, though the evidence was much the same as that by which the others had suffered, summed up in such a manner as to obtain an acquittal. The former trials had extended from November 20, 1678, to June 14, 1679; that of Wakeman occurred on July 18 following, and 'the occasion of the judge's conversion,' Roger North (*Examen*, 568) says, 'was this. The lord chief justice came once from Windsor with a lord of the council (Chief Justice North) in his coach, and, among other discourse, Scroggs asked that lord if the Lord Shaftesbury (who was then lord president of the council) had really that interest with the king as he seemed to have? No, replied that lord, no more than your footman hath with you. This sank into the man, and quite altered the ferment, so as that from that time he was a new man.' Luttrell (i. 17, 19, 74) tells us that gross bribery with Portugal gold was said to have influenced him on this trial, but the result was that he at once lost the popularity which he so eagerly sought, and, instead of the applause he had been accustomed to receive, he was on one side daily assailed with abuse and lampoons, in which he was commonly designated by the nickname of 'Mouth,'—

'their work is done,
Down must the patriots go, and Mouth must run,'—

while his gross partiality and brutal conduct in the former trials were exposed on the other. In addition, he had raised two inveterate enemies, the witnesses Oates and Bedlow, who, not having yet lost their power and being still believed by the multitude, were not so easily cowed. As the parliament which had supported all their inventions had been dissolved, they exhibited before the king and council 'articles of high misdemeanours' against the chief justice, charging him with browbeating them, depreciating their evidence, and misleading the jury; also with setting at liberty several persons charged with high treason, with imprisoning loyal subjects for printing books exposing the errors of Popery, and refusing to take bail, and with various other things tending to the disparagement of the witnesses, and the encouragement of Roman Catholics; to which they added charges against the chief justice of cursing and swearing, drunkenness, and corruption in the sale of licences to print the different trials. To all these charges Scroggs, not having the fear of parliament before him, answered with contemptuous impudence, and on the hearing before the king and council on January 1680 ran down his accusers with such severity and wit that the complaint was dismissed.

The chief justice's triumph was not of long duration. A new parliament met towards the end of the year, and the attack against him was renewed before a more willing audience. He and the other judges of the King's Bench had in the previous Trinity Term defeated an intended presentment against the Duke of York for not going to church, by suddenly discharging the grand jury. This the Commons made the principal ground of impeachment, adding similar charges to those before made, and another for issuing illegal warrants to a messenger of the press. On carrying the impeachment to the upper house in January 1681, the peers refused to commit the chief justice, or to address the king to suspend him from the execution of his office. This parliament being dissolved a few days after, on the meeting of the new parliament at Oxford in the following March Scroggs put in his answer, which was merely a plea of not guilty; but a dissolution also of this parliament, the last in Charles's reign, before the end of the month, put a stop to the proceedings. The king however felt that prudence required the removal of a judge so universally obnoxious, and accordingly Sir Francis Pemberton was appointed on April 11 to fill his place. His dismissal was made as easy to him as possible, being accompanied with a pension of 1500*l.* to himself, and a patent of king's counsel to his son, also Sir William.

After a retirement of two years and a half he died on October 25, 1683, of a polypus in his heart, and was buried in Southweald

Church. By his wife, a daughter of Matthew Black, Esq., he left a son, the above Sir William, and two daughters, one of whom was married to Sir Robert Wright, the notorious chief justice in the next reign, and the other to a son of Lord Hatton. (*State Trials*, vi. vii. viii.; *Parl. Hist.* iv. 1224, 1261, 1274; *North's Examen*, 80, 206, 567; *Burnet*, 448, 468.)

SCROPE, GEOFFREY LE, descended from a Norman family which in the reign of Henry II. had baronial possessions in Gloucestershire, and in that of Edward I. large estates in Yorkshire also, was the son of Sir William le Scrope, a knight distinguished both in tournaments and the field, by his wife Constance, daughter and heiress of Thomas, the son of Gillo de Newsom upon Tyne.

In the parliament held in January 1316, 9 Edward II., he is mentioned as suing for the king; and a grant was made to him of 20*l.* for his expenses, in the liberate of which, according to Dugdale, he is called serjeant. In that character he was evidently summoned to the councils and parliaments of the seven subsequent years, and was also occasionally added to some judicial commissions for the trial of offenders. Dugdale has inadvertently inserted his name in the list of judges of the King's Bench in 9 Edward II., though he has taken no notice of such a fact in his sketch of him in the 'Baronage.' There is no doubt, however, that this is an error, as he is described as one of the king's serjeants in 14 and 16 Edward II., and as attornatus regis in the former year (*Abb. Placit.* 351), in the wardrobe account of which, also, there is an entry of the payment of 13*l.* 6*s.* 8*d.* 'To Geoffry le Scrop, king's serjeant, staying near the person of the king by his order, when journeying through divers parts of England in the months of April, May, and June, in the present fourteenth year, of the king's gift, for his expenses in so staying.' (*Archæologia*, xxvi. 345.) In 14 and 16 Edward II. he was employed in negotiating with the Scots. (*N. Fœdera*, ii. 434–524.)

It was not till September 27, 1323, 17 Edward II., that he was raised to the bench, when he was constituted a judge of the Common Pleas, and fines were levied before him till the following Hilary Term. (*Dugdale's Orig.* 45.) On March 21, 1324, he was promoted to the chief justiceship of the King's Bench; and he presided in that court till the end of the reign.

He was certainly removed from the office on the accession of Edward III., which not improbably arose from a suspicion of his being a partisan of the Despencers and Baldock the chancellor. Whatever was the reason of his non-appointment, he soon succeeded in clearing himself by the testimony of the peers, and was reinstated on February 28, 1328, 2 Edward III. His services were so highly appreciated by his sovereign that they were frequently employed in diplomatic engagements, which obliged him for a time to resign his place in the court. Thus, when Edward went to France in May 1329, 3 Edward III., Robert de Malberthorpe and his brother, Henry le Scrope, were successively substituted for him till December 19, 1330, when he was re-appointed. Again, Richard de Wilughby held his place from March 28 till September 20, 1332, 6 Edward III.; and, on a third occasion, Richard de Wilughby took his seat on September 10, 1333, in consequence of Geoffrey le Scrope being about to go on a foreign embassy. But in February 1334 the King's Bench was ordered by the parliament at York to stay in Warwickshire after Easter next, 'for that Sir Geoffrey le Scroop, chief justice, is busie in the king's weighty affairs, whose place to supply Sir Richard Wilughby is appointed.' (*Rot. Parl.* ii. 377.)

Dugdale quotes a patent of July 16, 1334, 8 Edward III., by which Scrope was constituted second justice of the Common Pleas, in the place of John de Stonore, with an exemption annexed from being called upon to go out of the kingdom against the king's enemies against his will. (*Cal. Rot. Pat.* 118.) As no fines appear to have been levied before him, he probably did not long remain in that court, and certainly was not one of its eight judges enumerated by Dugdale (*Orig.* 39) in 11 Edward III. It was perhaps about this time that he resumed his place as chief justice of the King's Bench, which he certainly held on April 4, 1338, when the nomination of two new judges was directed to him in that character. He is mentioned in the Book of Assizes in the same year, and ultimately resigned his office before the following October, a payment being then made to him as 'nuper capitalis justiciarus.'

He was employed by both his sovereigns to treat with the Scots, and by Edward III. to assist in the negotiations relative to the marriages between his sister Eleanor and the French king's eldest son, and between John, the son of the Earl of Kent, and a daughter of one of the French nobles. After his retirement from the King's Bench he was engaged in many other diplomatic missions on behalf of the king, in one of which he is styled 'secretarius noster.'

But it was not only as a lawyer and negotiator that he was distinguished; he made himself equally prominent as a knight and a soldier. At the tournaments held at Northampton, Guildford, and Newmarket, at the first of which he was knighted, he gained great distinction. He accompanied the king in the invasion of Scotland, and displayed his banner and pennon at the affair of Stannow Park. He was one of the royal retinue several times in Flanders and France, with a train of two knights and forty men-at-arms; and he served at the siege of Tournay in July 1340, 14 Edward III.

An anecdote is related of a characteristic revenge which he took of Cardinal Bernard de Monte Faventio, during those wars, for some insulting remarks he had made to the king in reference to the strength of the French. He brought him one night into a high tower, and pointing to the frontiers of France, in flames for several leagues, he said, 'My lord, what thinketh your eminence now? Doth not this silken line wherewith you say France is encompassed seem in great danger of being cracked, if not broken?' The cardinal was struck speechless, and dropped down apparently lifeless with fear and sorrow.

Besides many valuable grants from both Edward II. and Edward III. in reward for his services, he was in 14 Edward III. created a banneret, and had a grant of 200 marks per annum for the support of that dignity. (*Report on Peerage*, i. 354.)

He did not long survive this last honour, but died in the same year at Ghent in Flanders. His body was removed to Coversham, where it was buried in the church of the abbey, under a tomb on which his effigy was placed.

He married first Ivetta, daughter of Sir William Roos, of Igmanthorp; and secondly, as it is believed, Lora, daughter and coheiress of Sir Gerard de Furnival, and widow of Sir John Uflete. By the latter he had no children, but by the former he had five sons and three daughters.

His second son, Sir Thomas, died during his father's life; his third and fourth sons, Sir William and Sir Stephen, distinguished soldiers, were both present at the battle of Cressy; and his youngest son, Geoffrey, became a priest, and held some dignities in the Church.

His eldest son, Sir Henry le Scrope, who was governor of Guisnes and Calais, was summoned to parliament as a baron in 1342, and was generally called Lord Scrope of Masham. His descendants held the title till 1517, when on the death of the ninth lord without issue it fell into abeyance among his three sisters. (*Baronage*, i. 657; *Parl. Writs*, ii. 1409; *Nicolas's Scrope and Grosvenor Controversy*.)

SCROPE, HENRY LE, was the eldest son and heir of Sir William le Scrope, and Constance his wife. Like his brother, the last-mentioned Geoffrey, he was distinguished both as a knight and a lawyer.

His name appears as an advocate in the Year Book of 1 Edward II., and in the next year, on November 27, 1308, he was raised to the bench of the Common Pleas. Fines were levied before him in that character till Trinity, 10 Edward II. (*Dugdale's Orig.* 44), and during the same interval he frequently acted as a judge of assize and on various criminal commissions.

He was promoted to the office of chief justice of the King's Bench on June 15, 1317, which he retained for above six years, and was then superseded, about September 1323, by Hervey de Staunton, who after a few months made way for Henry's brother, Geoffrey le Scrope. Some confusion often arises in the reports in the Year Books from the difficulty of distinguishing which brother is referred to.

The cause of his removal is nowhere related, nor whether it was at his own request. That it was occasioned by no dissatisfaction on the king's part may be inferred from his being constituted, in the same year, custos of the forests beyond Trent, an office which he still retained at the commencement of the next reign. (*Abb. Rot. Orig.* i. 271; *Rot. Parl.* ii. 10; *N. Fœdera*, ii. 578.)

Within a few days after the accession of Edward III.—viz., on February 5, 1327—Sir Henry le Scrope had a patent constituting him *second* justice of the Common Pleas, the first instance of such a designation being adopted, and the fines acknowledged before him extended to Hilary in the third year. It was not, however, till October 28 in that year, 1329, that he changed his position for that of chief justice of the King's Bench, to which he was then re-appointed during the temporary absence of his brother, Geoffrey le Scrope who, upon his return, superseded him on December 19 in the following year.

His judicial services, however, were too valuable to be lost, for on the same day he was made chief baron of the Exchequer, and he continued on that bench during the remainder of his life. There are, it is true, two patents bearing date respectively the 18th and 19th of November 1333, 7 Edward III., by the former of which he is constituted chief justice of the Common Pleas, and by the latter chief baron of the Exchequer. From this we can only infer that the removal into the Common Pleas was without his consent, and the restoration to the Exchequer at his solicitation, the more especially as William de Herle, whom he was to have superseded in the former court, was immediately replaced.

Besides the numerous royal rewards for his good services from both kings, he was also made a knight banneret.

His death occurred on September 7, 1336, leaving very considerable possessions in Middlesex, Leicestershire, Hertfordshire, Rutlandshire, and Bedfordshire, but chiefly in the county of York. He was buried in the abbey of St. Agatha, at Easby, near Richmond, in the latter county, of which he was esteemed the founder, having purchased the property of the family of the Earl of Richmond, and been a large contributor to the house.

His wife's name was Margaret, but there is a doubt whether she was the daughter of Lord Roos or of Lord Fitz-Walter. She afterwards married Sir Hugh Mortimer, of Chelmarsh in Shropshire, and of Luton in Bedfordshire, and lived till 1357.

They left three sons, all of whom were minors at the time of their father's death. William and Stephen, the two elder, died without issue before 19 Edward III., in which year the inheritance devolved on the third son, the next-mentioned Richard, the first Baron Scrope of Bolton. (*Baronage*, i. 654; *Monast.* vi. 921; *Nicolas's Scrope and Grosvenor Controversy*.)

SCROPE, RICHARD LE, was about eight years old at the death of his father, the last-mentioned Sir Henry le Scrope, in 1336, 10 Edward III. He was the youngest of three sons, and ultimate heir to his father's extensive property. From his earliest youth he devoted himself to arms, and was only eighteen when he accompanied the king on his invasion of France, and partook of the glory of the battle of Cressy on August 20, 1346. In the following October we find him so signalising himself at the battle of Nevil's Cross, where the Scots were completely vanquished, as to be knighted on the field; and during the remainder of that year and part of the following he assisted at the siege of Calais, which surrendered into the king's hands on August 4, 1347. In 1350 he was present in the sea-fight near Rye, when Don Carlos de la Cerda was signally defeated by King Edward and the Black Prince, and twenty of his ships taken; and during the succeeding years his name appears in the array of his sovereign both in the French and Scottish wars.

In 1359 he began the connection with John of Gaunt, Earl of Richmond, which lasted the remainder of the life of that celebrated man, serving under him in the army which then invaded France (*N. Fœdera*, iii. 412), and made its way almost to the walls of Paris. In 1366 he accompanied his patron, who had been created Duke of Lancaster, into Spain, and distinguished himself in April of the following year at the decisive victory of Najarre, which restored Don Pedro to the Spanish throne, and on the renewal of the war with France in 1369 he filled his usual place by the side of the duke.

During the progress of his military career in 1364 he had been selected by his own county of York as its representative in parliament; and on January 8, 1371, he was summoned to the upper house as a baron. On March 27 of that year he was invested with the responsible office of treasurer, the king selecting him when the Commons petitioned that the great offices should no longer be filled by the clergy. He retained this place for four years and a half, retiring in September 1375; but during the interval, in July 1373, he again formed part of the Duke of Lancaster's retinue into France, and in March 1375 was joined with Sir John Kynvet to act as attorney for the duke during his absence from England. (*Ibid.* 1026.) In the last year of Edward's reign he was one of the commissioners for the preservation of the truce with Scotland, and for the protection of the Marches.

On the accession of Richard II. he was appointed steward of the household, in which character he addressed the Commons in the first two parliaments of the reign. (*Rot. Parl.* iii. 5.) But a great honour was reserved for him; for on October 29, 1378, the Great Seal was delivered to him as chancellor of England. He remained in this office only eight months, during which we find him charging the judges and serjeants in parliament to give their opinion on certain points of law. Retiring from the chancellorship on July 2, 1379, and resuming his military duties in Scotland under the Duke of Lancaster, he received the appointment of warden of the Western Marches.

In the parliament of 1381 he is spoken of on November 18 as 'lors novellement crees en Chanceller d'Engleterre.' It is curious, however, that, according to the record on the Close Roll, Bishop Courteneye, the late chancellor, did not give up the Seal till November 30, and Richard le Scrope did not receive it till December 4. Thus was he a second time chancellor; but he did not keep his place above seven months, his straightforward honesty inducing him to remonstrate with his royal master against giving inconsiderately away the lands that fell to the crown. The king, incensed at the interference of his minister, is said by Walsingham to have sent messenger after messenger to demand the Great Seal, which the chancellor refused to give up to any other person than the king himself. The entry on the record seems to support this relation, and plainly evidences a hasty proceeding. It alleges that, the king being desirous that Scrope should be exonerated from the office, the Seal was delivered up to him, *ut debuit*, and though he was not as yet provided with a chancellor; but being unwilling that the affairs of the kingdom should be retarded for want of a Seal, he delivered it to certain commissioners to be kept at his will. This occurred on July 11, 1382.

The king's irritation, however, seems soon to have subsided, since Scrope was in the same year appointed to negotiate a truce with Scotland. Although between fifty and sixty years of age, he exhibited no diminution of his military ardour; but was present, with his old patron the duke, at the capture of Edinburgh in 1384, and joined King Richard's expedition against Scotland in the following year. It was then that he challenged the right of Sir Robert Grosvenor to bear the arms 'Azure, a bend or.' This was the third dispute of a similar nature in which Scrope had been engaged. At the siege of Calais in 1347 his right to the crest of a crab issuing from a ducal coronet was challenged; but without effect, as he ever afterwards continued to bear it. Again, in Paris in 1360, a Cornish squire, named Carminow, disputed his right to the arms on his shield, when both parties were adjudged to be entitled. The third controversy, with Sir Robert Grosvenor, which lasted four years in the Court of Chivalry, and terminated in Scrope's complete triumph over his opponent, is the subject of a most interesting work by the late Sir Harris Nicolas, to which we are indebted for most of the materials from which this account has been drawn up. (*See also* Rymer, vii. 620–1, 676, 686.)

During the remainder of Richard's reign Scrope was a regular attendant on his parliamentary duties. In 1386 he was appointed one of the king's permanent counsellors, and had the courage to defend Pole, Earl of Suffolk, his brother-in-law, when impeached by the Commons. In 1387 he was one of the commissioners on the trial of Nevill, Archbishop of York, Tresilian, and others; and conducted himself with such prudence and moderation during the following years, that when the parliament of 21 Richard II., 1397, reversed the proceedings of that of 1386, and impeached those who were implicated in them, Scrope, though one of the number, was declared innocent by the Commons, and a patent of pardon was granted to him.

The Duke of Lancaster died in February 1399; and none can contemplate without pity the feelings which must have embarrassed the aged knight, when he watched on the one hand the mad and foolish conduct of his sovereign, and saw on the other the insidious and treasonable proceedings of his patron's son. He took no active part in the contest; and on the deposition of Richard, although his eldest son, the Earl of Wiltshire, had lost his life for his adherence to the royal cause, he was summoned to Henry's first parliament, and was among those peers who assented to the late king being placed in imprisonment; a vote to which, under the circumstances, he could scarcely object, qualified as it was by the words 'sauvent sa vie.' The scene in the parliament a few days afterwards must have been most affecting, when, on the attainder of his son being confirmed, he rose in his place, his eyes streaming with tears, and 'implored the usurper that the proceedings might not affect the inheritance of himself or his other children; and after admitting the justice of the sentence, and deploring the conduct of his son, the unhappy father was consoled by Henry, who deigned to assure him that neither his interest nor those of his children then living should suffer from it; for that he had always considered and still deemed him a loyal knight.' The only other instance of his mixing in public affairs after this event was his presence in parliament in January 1401, when the Earls of Kent, Huntingdon, and Salisbury were attainted of high treason. (*Nicolas*, 30, 39; *Parl. Hist.* iii. 427, 453, 459.)

He lived little more than a year afterwards, his death occurring on May 30, 1403, at about the age of seventy-five. His remains were deposited in the abbey of St. Agatha, near Richmond, where those of his father rested. His will is in the 'Testamenta Vetusta' (i. 156.)

The union of such qualities as he possessed both as a soldier and a statesman are seldom to be found in one man. Throughout his long military career he was highly distinguished for his valour, and the talents and sagacity he exhibited in his civil employments were equally remarkable. Though connected with all the intricate proceedings of the unfortunate reign of Richard II., he steered clear of the shoals on which his contemporaries stranded, and, preserving the esteem of all classes to the close of his life, he well deserved the character which Walsingham gives him, that he was a man who had not his fellow in the whole realm for prudence and integrity.

Some authorities say that he was twice married, but others doubt whether he had more than one wife. She was Blanche, the daughter of Sir William de la Pole, and sister of Michael Earl of Suffolk. The name of his second wife is variously stated by those who assert that he had one—some calling her Margaret, daughter of Sir John Montford, and others describing her as a daughter of — Spencer. By Blanche he had four sons, the eldest of whom, William, after being created by Richard II. Earl of Wiltshire in 1397, and knight of the Garter in 1398, was for his attachment to his benefactor beheaded without trial in 1399, and his honours and estates were forfeited to the crown. (*Baronage*, i. 661.) The second son, Roger, succeeded his father; the third, Stephen, was an adherent of Richard II., but afterwards was received into Henry's confidence; and the fourth, Richard, Archbishop of York, was beheaded for conspiracy against Henry in 1405.

The barony of Scrope of Bolton continued through eleven generations. The last holder of it, Emanuel, was created Earl of Sunderland on June 19, 1627; but dying without issue in 1640, the earldom became extinct, and the barony devolved on the representatives of the daughter of his grandfather. It has been hitherto, however, unclaimed. The Bolton estate was bequeathed by the earl to Mary, one of his natural daughters, whose second husband, Charles Paulet, Marquis of Winchester, was created Duke of Bolton in 1689, a title which became extinct in 1794. The present barony of Bolton was granted in 1797 to Thomas Orde, who had married a natural daughter of the fifth duke, and who took the name of Paulet. (*Scrope and Grosvenor Controversy*, ii. 17–39.)

SCROPE, JOHN, had possession of the Great Seal for the limited period of three weeks, but, though short his career and trifling his services in this capacity, his merits were afterwards rendered highly conspicuous in another sphere. He was the son of Thomas Scrope of Wormsley in Oxfordshire, a mansion which had formerly been the seat of Colonel Adrian Scrope (a scion of the noble family of Scrope, barons of Bolton), who took a prominent part on the parliament side in the Great Rebellion, holding among other important offices that of governor of Bristol, and sitting in the High Court of Justice which condemned Charles I., for which he suffered death as a regicide at the Restoration.

John Scrope received his legal education at the Middle Temple, where he was called to the bar in 1692. After practising for sixteen years, he was in May 1708 appointed a baron of the Exchequer in Scotland, and while enjoying that office the removal of Lord Chancellor Cowper occurred, on which the Great Seal of England was placed in the hands of three commissioners, one of whom was Mr. Baron Scrope. They received it on September 26, 1710, and held it till October 19, when it was delivered to Sir Simon Harcourt as lord keeper. So ended Baron Scrope's judicial character in England; but in Scotland he continued to exercise the functions of a baron of the Exchequer till he was selected as joint secretary to the Treasury, when he entered parliament at the general election in 1722 as member for Ripon. In the new parliament on the accession of George II. in 1728 he was chosen for Bristol, his native city, and in those of 1735, 1741, and 1747 he represented Lyme Regis. His senatorial exertions were confined to matters connected with the revenue, and his term of office comprehended the whole period during which Sir Robert Walpole was first lord of the Treasury. With that minister he was closely allied, and when on Sir Robert's fall a secret committee sat to enquire into his conduct for the previous ten years, Mr. Scrope, who was called upon to give evidence as to the disposal of above a million of money which had been traced to his and Sir Robert's hands as secret service money, refused to take the oath offered to him, and declared that he was authorised by his majesty to state 'that the disposal of money issued for secret service, by the nature of it, requires the utmost secrecy, and is accounted for to his majesty only, and therefore his majesty could not permit him to disclose anything on that subject.' The Commons took no notice of his refusal, and he enjoyed his place for ten years after his patron's dismissal. Tindal says of him that he 'was perhaps the coolest, the most experienced, and most sagacious friend the minister ever had.'

He died on April 9, 1752, at a great age, leaving no issue. His estate of Wormsley is still in the possession of the descendants of Henry Fane, who married one of his sisters and coheirs, and whose eldest son became the eighth Earl of Westmoreland. (*Collins's Peerage*, iii. 302; *Luttrell*, vi. 304, 633; *Parl. Hist.* xii. 823; *Tindal*, xx. 138, 544.)

SECULER, ALEXANDER LE, of a family established in Herefordshire, was probably the son of Nicholas le Seculer, who assessed the tallage of that county in 19 Henry III. Alexander was constituted, as the king's 'beloved clerk,' one of the barons of the Exchequer in Easter 1265, 49 Henry III. (*Madox*, ii. 56), after which date no further mention of him occurs.

SEFRED (BISHOP OF CHICHESTER), who, from being a canon, was appointed archdeacon, of Chichester, was from 19 to 23 Henry II., 1173–1177, employed as a justice itinerant in several counties. (*Madox*, i. 43, 700.) He was then advanced to the deanery, and appears to have held both dignities in October 1180, when he was raised to the bishopric of that see. (*Le Neve*, 65.) The cathedral and episcopal palace having been, with great part of the city, destroyed by fire on October 19, 1187, he rebuilt and restored them to their former splendour.

He was present at the coronation of King John on May 27, 1199, and died on March 17, 1204. (*Godwin*, 502.)

SEGRAVE, GILBERT DE, was the second son of the under-named Stephen de Segrave, by Rohese, the daughter of Thomas le Despenser; but his elder brother, John, dying in his father's lifetime, he succeeded to the property on his father's decease in 1241. Dugdale (*Orig.* 21) states that he was a canon of St. Paul's; but if so, unless that dignity was held by civilians, he must have obtained a dispensation from his holy orders (which he perhaps did on his brother's death in 1231), as he married Amabilia, the daughter and heir of Robert de Chaucomb. (*Excerpt. e Rot. Fin.* i. 462.) In 15 Henry III. he had a grant from Simon de Montfort, lord of Leicester, of the town of Kegworth in Leicestershire, and a short time after he was constituted governor of Bolsover Castle. In 26 Henry III., the year following his father's death, he was made justice of the forests south of Trent, and governor of Kenilworth Castle.

He was raised to the bench at Westminster in 35 Henry III., 1251, and was one of the justiciers appointed to hear such pleas of the city of London as were wont to be determined by the justices itinerant. He is not noticed in a judicial character after January 1252. Two years afterwards he was sent on a mission into Gascony, on his return from which, in company with John de Plessetis, Earl of Warwick, and other nobles, they were, in spite of the King of France's letters of safe conduct which they bore, seized and imprisoned at Pontes, a city in Poictou. Although ultimately released, his sufferings there impaired his health and caused his death, which happened shortly before November 11, 1254, 39 Henry III., when his lands were taken into the king's hands, as usual on that event. (*Ibid.* ii. 198.)

He was succeeded by his son, Nicholas de Segrave. The barony failed in the male line in 1353, but survived in Elizabeth, daughter of Baron John, who married John Lord Mowbray. Their son Thomas was created Earl of Nottingham in 1383, and Duke of Norfolk in 1400, in which title this barony continued merged till the death of John, the fourth duke, in 1475, and on the death of his daughter Ann without issue it fell into abeyance between the representatives of Margaret and Isabel, sisters of John, the second Duke of Norfolk, the present Earl of Berkeley being heir of the former, and the Barons Petre and Stourton being heirs general of the latter. (*Nicolas's Synopsis; Baronage,* i. 671.)

SEGRAVE, STEPHEN DE, was the son of Gilbert, son of Hereward, who assumed the name of his lordship of Segrave in Leicestershire, of which county he acted as sheriff during several years in the reign of Richard I. In 6 John, Stephen was excused a part of his father's debt to the crown, for the love the king bore to Hugh le Despenser, whose sister Rohese he married. (*Rot. de Finibus,* 422.) In 8 John he was one of the two 'custodes placitorum coronæ' (*Abb. Placit.* 55), and in 16 John he was sent into the county of Worcester to forward the king's affairs. His loyalty during the barons' wars was rewarded by a grant of the lands of Stephen de Gant, and of the manor of Kinton in Warwickshire, for which he afterwards procured a weekly market. (*Rot. Pat.* 128; *Rot. Chart.* 223; *Rot. Claus.* i. 428.)

He had in his youth been brought up as an ecclesiastic, but had changed his clerical profession for that of arms. No doubt, however, he added to the former, as was then usual, the study of the law, and continued his attention to it, for though there is no account of his forensic progress, his interest or ability soon raised him to the bench. In 2 Henry III., 1218, fines were levied before him as a justicier at Westminster, and he had a grant of one hundred shillings as his fee at two several periods in the year. (*Dugdale's Orig.* 42; *Rot. Claus.* i. 350, 365.) There are records of fines in which his name occurs from this date till Michaelmas, 14 Henry III., and during the whole of that time and in the two following years he was frequently employed as a justice itinerant in the provinces, holding from the tenth year the highest place in the commissions to which he was attached. In a judgment of him and his companions pleaded in a cause of a subsequent year, they are called 'justiciarii de Banco,' but whether its date was before or after he was chief justiciary does not appear. (*Abb. Placit.* 128.)

During the former period he was entrusted with other important commissions. In 3 Henry III. he was sent on an embassy to the legate; in the next year he was appointed governor of Sauvey Castle in Leicestershire; and for the three following he acted as sheriff of the counties of Lincoln, and of Essex and Hertford, and as constable of the Tower of London, with an allowance of 50*l*. per annum. (*Rot. Claus.* i. 396, 459, &c.) He was made sheriff of Buckingham and Bedford in 12 Henry III., and then of Warwick and Leicester and Northampton for his life, and he was joined with the chancellor in the administration of affairs during the king's absence in Poictou in 1230. (4 *Report Pub. Rec., App.* ii. 152; 5 *Report, App.* ii. 63.)

He had united himself with the party of Peter de Rupibus, Bishop of Winchester, aiding his efforts against the justiciary Hubert de Burgh, and had taken every opportunity of ingratiating himself with King Henry. His immediate success was evidenced by the above appointments, and by other grants of great extent and value.

When the bishop had succeeded in procuring the discharge of Hubert de Burgh, his office of chief justiciary was, on July 29, 1232, given to Stephen de Segrave (*R. de Wendover,* iv. 245), together with the government of all the castles from which his predecessor had been removed. The acquisition of this post might be an object of honourable ambition, but his efforts to irritate the monarch against the fallen favourite, and to aggravate the charges against him, deserve another designation. His ministry was not a fortunate one, and in the next year he had the ill-luck to be present when the king was defeated before Grosmont, and to be one of those who were surprised in their beds and compelled to fly almost naked from the field.

His support of the pope's exactions, and his adherence to the Bishop of Winchester, were sufficient to cause his unpopularity, one effect of which was the burning of his mansion at Alcmundberry, while he was with the king in the neighbouring town of Huntingdon. (*Ibid.* 278, 297.) This occurred in the early part of February 1234, and it was probably in compensation for his loss that, on March 2, the king granted him an exemption from the forest laws in this manor. But within a very few weeks he shared in the fall of the disgraced bishop, and in the middle of the following April was ejected from the high position he had occupied for so brief a period. (*Ibid.* 299.)

Being shortly afterwards summoned with the rest of the discarded ministers to render an account of his stewardship, rather than meet his accusers he retired to the abbey of St. Mary at Leicester, where he resumed the clerical tonsure which he had formerly relinquished. He, however, eventually thought fit to appear on July 4, under the protection of Edmund, Archbishop of Canterbury, when, after the king had angrily attributed to his counsels the disgrace of Hubert de Burgh and the exile of the nobles of the kingdom, he was given till Michaelmas to prepare his defence. The times becoming more quiet, and milder counsels prevailing, he was, in the following February, allowed to make his peace with the king, on paying a fine of one thousand marks. (*Ibid.* 312, 314, 325.)

Although in one of his fits of fickleness the king recalled him to court after three years' absence, made him justice of Chester in 21 Henry III. (*Baronage,* i. 672), and for a time listened to his counsels, he was never restored to his former elevation. His death happened in the abbey of Leicester, in which he had become a canon regular, before October 13, 1241, on which day his lands were, as usual on such events, seized into the king's hands. (*Excerpt. e Rot. Fin.* i. 356.)

Evidently a man of energy and enterprise, his grasping and timeserving disposition threw suspicion over all he did; and the popular hatred that he incurred by his encouragement of the king's extravagance, and the expedients he used to supply it, blinded the people to such of his acts as were meritorious. But, excepting the harshness with which he urged the persecution of Hubert de Burgh, no imputation of cruelty or even severity can be made against his conduct as a judge either before or after he was raised to the highest post; while his grants to the abbeys of Stoneley, Combe, and Leicester, and his subsequent retirement to the latter, are evidences of his pious disposition.

After the death of his first wife, Rohese, daughter of Thomas le Despenser, he married Ida, the sister of Henry de Hastings, who, six years after his death, was fined 500*l.* for marrying Hugh Pecche. (*Ibid.* ii. 6, 17.)

By his first wife he had two sons, the elder of whom, John, dying ten years before him, he was succeeded by his second son, the last-mentioned Gilbert.

SEGRAVE, HUGH DE, was one of the branches of the illustrious house of Segrave, and is first noticed in the records by the confirmation, in 43 Edward III., of Queen Philippa's grant to him (styled a knight) for life of the offices of constable of the castle of Brustwyk, and of keeper of the forests of Kingswood and Filwood in Gloucestershire. (*Abb. Rot. Orig.* ii. 304.) In 46 Edward III. he was one of the commissioners to treat with the Flemings, and held the same diplomatic character in the last year of Edward's reign. (*N. Fœdera,* iii. 932, 1076.)

On the accession of Richard II. he was selected as one of the king's council, and in the third year was appointed steward of the household. (*Cal. Rot. Pat.* 203.) In that and the following year he was one of the ambassadors employed to treat with France, and to negotiate the king's marriage with Anne, the sister of the emperor. (*Rymer,* vii. 161, 229, 281.)

Two days after the brutal murder of Archbishop Sudbury the Great Seal was placed in Segrave's hands, on June 16, 1381, to be held as keeper until the king could more conveniently appoint a chancellor; and he performed all the duties pertaining to the office for eight weeks, till August 10. On the same day he was made treasurer in the room of Robert de Hales, another victim of the popular fury. In that year also he had a grant of the manor of Overhall in Essex, to hold by the service of making 'wafres,' and attending on the king at his coronation. (*Cal. Rot. Pat.* 205.) In the parliament that met in November he opened the business on the part of the king.

On July 11, 1382, when the king angrily took away the Seal from Richard le Scrope, Segrave again received it as the head of a commission of three, and they continued to hold it till September 20, a period of ten weeks.

Segrave continued treasurer till January 17, 1386, about which time his death occurred. (*Cal. Inquis.* p. m. iii. 84.)

SEINGES, RICHARD DE, was probably an officer in one of the departments of the Curia Regis, being united with Hubert de Burgh as his deputy in the sheriffalty of Hereford for three years, commencing 3 John. (*Rot. Cancel.* 106, 360.) He had the custody of the castle of Wilton, which, in 6 John, he was ordered to deliver to William de Cantilupe (*Rot. Pat.* 46); and in the same year he was fined one hundred shillings in respect of a false oath taken in an assize of novel disseisin between Cecil de Felsted and Hugh de Windsor, who was in his custody. (*Rot. de Finibus,* 237.) The offence, however, does not seem to have been very flagrant, as two years afterwards a great many fines were levied at St. Edmunds, Cambridge, and Bedford, before Humfrey, archdeacon of Sarum, and him. In 3 Henry III., 1219, he appears as one of the justiciers before whom fines were levied at Westminster, and in 1226 he was sent with other justiciers to try certain malefactors in Norfolk. (*Rot. Claus.* ii. 159.)

SELBY, RALPH DE, is described with the addition 'Magister,' showing that persons in orders were still appointed to the office of baron of the Exchequer, his patent to which is dated October 24, 1393, 17 Richard II. Little more is to be found concerning him, unless he were the Ralph Selby 'in utroque jure Doctor' who was made master of King's College, Cambridge, in the fourteenth year. (*Cal. Rot. Pat.* 221.) He is mentioned as of the council of the king in 21 Richard II. (*Proc. Privy Council,* i. 75), but evidently retired or died soon after, as his name does not occur on the Liberate Roll of the first day of the reign of Henry IV., directing the payment of the salaries of the barons for the previous half-year.

SELWYN, CHARLES JASPER, late Lord Justice of Appeal, whose recent death has been universally regretted, was born in Church Row, Hampstead, Middlesex, on October 13, 1813. His father, William Selwyn, of whom he was the youngest son, attained great eminence in the law as a reporter in the Court of King's Bench from 1814 to 1817, as recorder of Portsmouth and queen's counsel, as instructor of the Prince Consort in the laws and constitution of the kingdom, and as the author of an abridgment of the law of Nisi Prius, of such standard reputation that it passed through nine editions. His mother was Letitia, daughter of Thomas Kynaston, Esq., of Witham, Essex, the grandfather of the present head-master of St. Paul's School in London. His two brothers attained high positions in the Church, one as successively Bishop of New Zealand and of Lichfield, and the other as canon of Ely and Margaret Professor of Divinity.

Charles was educated first under Dr. Nicholson at Ealing, then at Eton, and next at Trinity College, Cambridge, where he took his degrees of B.A. and M.A. in 1836 and 1839. Following his father's profession, he entered Lincoln's Inn, and was called to the bar in January 1840. He practised with such success in the Court of Chancery that he was made queen's counsel in 1856, and having in the previous year been appointed commissary of his university, he was elected one of its representatives in parliament in 1859. In that assembly he took an active part in the debates upon the engrossing topics of the day, in speeches that were both intelligent and effective, as a churchman and conservative.

In July 1867, while yet member for the university, he received the appointment of solicitor-general and was knighted. Soon after, a vacancy happening in the Court of Appeal by the resignation of Sir John Rolt, he was selected to fill it on February 8, 1868. Before the end of that month, his able senior, Lord Cairns, being invested with the Great Seal as lord chancellor, the vacancy was filled up by Vice-Chancellor Sir William Page Wood (now Lord Hatherley), who would of course take the second seat in the court. But Sir Charles Selwyn, modestly feeling that it would be unbecoming in him, so recently placed on the judgment seat, to take precedence of a judge who had already presided over a court of equity for fifteen years, nobly insisted that Sir William Wood should take the senior place, a course of conduct which gave no surprise to those who knew his character, and which increased the respect and admiration with which he was generally regarded.

His judicial dignity was of short duration. Before eighteen months had elapsed he died at his house at Richmond in Surrey, on August 11, 1869, from the effects of a painful operation. He was buried at Nunhead Cemetery.

He married first Hester, daughter of J. G. Ravenshaw, Esq., chairman of the old East India Company, and widow of Thomas Dowler, Esq., M.D.; and secondly Catherine Rosalie, daughter of Colonel G. S. Green, C.B., and widow of the Rev. Henry Dupuis, vicar of Richmond.

SETONE, THOMAS DE, is named in the Year Books for ten years before he was raised to the bench. He was one of the king's serjeants in 19 Edward III., when he applied to the council, on behalf of the community of the bishopric of Durham, to forego the iter there for that year; and he obtained his prayer on their paying 600 marks for the favour. (*Abb. Rot. Orig.* ii.

177.) Dugdale places him as a judge of the King's Bench in 28 Edward III., and of the Common Pleas in 29 Edward III., without any date of appointment to either. He may, however, have been mistaken, as the authority he quotes is the Liberate Roll, in which the word 'bancum' sometimes applies to both courts. He was certainly a judge of one of them in April 1354, 28 Edward III., for he was one of the triers of petitions in the parliament then held (*Rot. Parl.* ii. 254); and he was a judge of the Common Pleas in Michaelmas 1355, 29 Edward III., for fines were then acknowledged before him; and it appears probable that he was appointed to this court between the previous Hilary and Trinity Terms, as the list in the Year Book omits his name in the former, and includes it in the latter term. In 30 Edward III. he recovered damages from a woman for calling him 'traitor, felon, and robber' in the public court. (*Lib. Assis.* 177.)

On July 5, 1357, he was made chief justice of the King's Bench; but it would seem, from the words 'ad tempus' in the mandate, that it was at that time a mere temporary appointment; and, from the fact that his name appears on fines up to Midsummer, 33 Edward III., we may infer that he acted up to that date as a judge of the Common Pleas also, especially as in the same year he is designated by the latter title, when he was admitted of the king's secret council. Thus it was not till afterwards that he was permanently fixed in the presidency of the King's Bench; but there is no doubt that he then held it till the thirty-eighth year, when, on May 24, 1360, Henry Green was appointed his successor. (*Dugdale's Orig.* 45; *Cal. Rot. Pat.* 171.)

SEWELL, THOMAS, was the son and heir of Thomas Sewell, of West Ham, Essex, Esq., and was called to the bar by the Middle Temple on May 24, 1734. It is told of him that in his youth he was 'bred up under an attorney, and afterwards engaged in the laborious business of a draughtsman in Chancery,' and that 'he was called to the bar, where he procured a considerable practice,' making at the time he was made master of the Rolls 'between 3000*l*. and 4000*l*. per annum.' In 1754 he was appointed one of the king's counsel.

He was a member of the two parliaments of 1754 and 1761, representing Harwich in the former, and Winchelsea in the latter. A story is told that on the debate relative to the illegality of general warrants he spoke in favour of an adjournment of the debate, because it would afford him opportunity to examine his books and authorities, and he should be prepared to give an opinion on the subject, 'which at present he was not.' Appearing on the adjournment in his great wig, as his custom was, he said that 'he had turned the matter over as he lay upon his pillow, and after ruminating and considering upon it a great deal, he could not help declaring that he was of the same opinion as before.' On which Mr. Charles Townshend started up and said 'he was very sorry that what the learned gentleman had found in his nightcap he had lost in his periwig.'

On the death of Sir Charles Clarke he was very unexpectedly offered the place of master of the Rolls, which he accepted on December 12, 1764, to the surprise of the bar, as his professional income greatly exceeded that attached to the office. He was thereupon knighted. He presided most efficiently in his court for twenty years, but in the latter part of his career he suffered much from those infirmities the anticipation of which no doubt influenced his determination to quit the laborious duties of a leading barrister. His offers of resignation were ineffectual, the terms he required being too high to be granted. He therefore died 'in harness,' on March 6, 1784, and was buried in the Rolls Chapel.

He married twice. His first wife was Catherine, daughter of Thomas Heath, of Stansted Mountfichet in Essex, M.P. for Harwich; and his second was Mary Elizabeth, daughter of Dr. Coningsby Sibthorp, of Canwick in Lincolnshire, professor of botany at Oxford. He had issue by both marriages. (*Corr. of Lord Chatham; Gent. Mag.* liv. 237, 257; *Notes and Queries*, 1st S. vii. 388, 521, 621, ix. 86, 2nd S. x. 396; *Manning and Bray's Surrey*, i. 498, iii. 196, 304.)

SEYTON, ROGER DE, who was of the clerical profession, is not mentioned till April 1268, 52 Henry III., from which date fines were acknowledged and payments made for assizes before him till the end of the reign. (*Dugdale's Orig.* 44.)

On the accession of Edward I. he was continued in the Common Pleas, and was constituted chief justice of that court in Michaelmas of the second year, in which he also stands at the head of the justices itinerant. As the last fine acknowledged before him is dated on the octaves of Trinity, 6 Edward I., 1278, the period of his death or retirement may be fixed about that time. In the same year he was succeeded by Thomas de Weyland.

SHADWELL, LANCELOT, was the eldest son of Lancelot Shadwell, Esq., of Lincoln's Inn, and Elizabeth, third daughter of Charles Whitmore, Esq., of Southampton. His father was a barrister of high reputation and immense practice as a real property lawyer, from whom he naturally inherited his great love of that branch, and the excellence in it which he afterwards exhibited. He was born on May 3, 1779, and was educated at Eton, from whence he removed to St. John's College, Cambridge, where he exercised that industry, without which no success is to be attained, to so good an effect that on his taking his degree of B.A. in 1800 he was honourably placed as seventh wrangler, and highly distinguished himself in classics by obtaining one of the chancellor's medals. With such results he was nearly sure to succeed in passing the very strict examination for a fellowship in the college, to which he was accordingly elected, and he proceeded M.A. in 1803, to which was added in 1842 the honorary degree of LL.D.

Following his father's footsteps, he entered the society of Lincoln's Inn, by which he was called to the bar in 1803, and in little more than a year lost his fellowship by marrying a sister of Sir John Richardson, the judge of the Common Pleas. After a very successful practice in the Court of Chancery as a junior barrister for eighteen years, he was honoured with a silk gown in 1821. He then acquired a considerable lead, but submitted to a serious loss in a pecuniary sense, by honourably confining himself to the lord chancellor's court, and not following the practice, which was then too commonly adopted, of taking briefs in the other equity courts; not being able, according to his own expression, 'to induce himself to think that it is consistent with justice, much less with honour, to undertake to lead a cause, and either to forsake it altogether or give it an imperfect, hasty, and divided attention—consequences that inevitably result from the attempt to conduct causes before two judges sitting at the same time in different places.'

In 1826 he entered parliament as member for Ripon, a borough in which he had the opportunity, of which he fully availed himself, of doing much good, as the manager of the large property of Miss Lawrence, the principal owner. In the year to which his senatorial career was confined he applied himself to remedy some of the evils attendant upon the existing laws of real property, by limiting the periods during which titles might be disputed. Time was not given him to bring his suggestions to a successful issue, but many of them have since been adopted.

He was appointed vice-chancellor of England on November 1, 1827, and presided in his court for twenty-three years, during which he twice filled the office of second commissioner of the Great Seal—the first time from April 23, 1835, to January 16, 1836, in conjunction with Sir Charles Pepys (afterwards Lord Cottenham), the master of the Rolls, and Mr. Justice Bosanquet; and the second time from June 19 to July 15, 1850, his colleagues being Lord Langdale, the master of the Rolls, and Mr. Baron Rolfe (afterwards Lord Cranworth). Whether as vice-chancellor or lord commissioner, he was a universal favourite both with the bar and the public for the courteousness of his demeanour and the kindness of his nature. No one who ever advised with him as a barrister or sat under him as a judge can remember a word of harshness coming from his lips, or can forget the patient way in which he listened to the arguments of counsel or the pleasant mode in which he delivered his judgments. Yet there was no want of decent gravity in his manner, nor of solidity in his decisions. They exhibited the legal learning he had early imbibed, and proved his eminent qualifications for the judicial chair.

His handsome person and sweet yet manly countenance impressed all in his favour, and his active habits, with the custom he had of bathing every day, whatever the weather, gave him a robust appearance that promised an extreme length of life. So fond was he of the water that it was said, with what truth we will not decide, that he once granted an injunction during the long vacation while immersed in that element. But he was not destined for the long life that his healthy aspect promised. Soon after the termination of the duties of his last commission he was seized with an illness which terminated fatally at his residence at Barn Elms in Surrey on August 10, 1850. The estimation in which he was regarded by his brother judges may be judged from the affecting language used by Vice-Chancellor Knight-Bruce on opening his court at the beginning of the next term. Addressing the attorney-general, Sir John Romilly, he said, 'It has been impossible for me to enter the court to-day without a renewal of sorrow for the loss of one so lately taken from us, by whom for so many years this chair was filled, and from which it is almost startling to hear another voice than his. In these feelings I am sure the bar participate. We have lost at once a friend dear to us all, and a judge distinguished for his great knowledge of the law that he administered — distinguished for various acquirements — distinguished for judicial patience—ever " swift to hear and slow to decide "—pure and blameless in life—an example of courtesy, gentleness, and amenity—who never said a word intended to give pain, nor ever harboured an unkind thought, or one acrimonious feeling—"*flere et meminisse relictum est.*"'

Sir Lancelot's first wife died after bringing to him six sons. His second wife was Frances, daughter and coheir of Captain Locke, and by her he had six more sons and five daughters, in all seventeen children, of whom he left eleven surviving.

SHAFTESBURY, EARL OF. *See* A. A. COOPER.

SHARDELOWE, ROBERT DE, or, as his name is sometimes spelled, **CHERDELAWE**, united the clerical and the legal professions. He was one of the justiciers at Westminster from Michaelmas, 13 Henry III., 1228, to Easter 1232. (*Dugdale's Orig.* 43.) During this period he is recorded to have been appointed to three circuits. He was of the same Norfolk family to which the next-mentioned John de Shardelowe belonged. (*Thoroton's Notts,* i. 375; *Gage's Suffolk,* 59.)

SHARDELOWE, JOHN DE, belonged to a family settled at Thompson in Norfolk, in the church of which his ancestors were interred, and both he and his wife reposed. Besides possessions in this county, he had manors in Suffolk and Cambridge, and considerable property in the latter.

His name appears as an advocate in the Year Books of Edward II. and III., and in the sixth year of the latter reign he was raised to the bench of the Common Pleas, and was created a knight of the Bath. Dugdale says that he exchanged his court with Robert de Scardeburgh for that of the King's Bench on September 6, 1339. Yet the same author states that fines continued to be levied before him till a month after Michaelmas 1340, and this being a duty solely devolving on judges of the Common Pleas, it would seem that his absence from the court was but temporary. It was about the latter period that Edward III. returned to England from Tournay, and visited upon his ministers his disappointment at the failure of supplies. Shardelowe, in whichever court he then acted, was one of the victims, being removed from his office and imprisoned. The charge against him does not appear, but in little more than a year he was restored to his place in the Common Pleas, his patent being dated May 16, 1342. He was a trier of petitions in the parliament of the next year, and died in 18 Edward III.

He left two sons, John and Thomas, the latter of whom we take to have been attorney-general in 40 Edward III. The family continued to flourish in Norfolk till 11 Henry VI., 1433, when it failed for want of male issue. (*Blomefield's Norfolk,* i. 476, 625–630; *Dugdale's Orig.* 39, 45, 102; *Rot. Parl.* ii. 135; *Cal. Inquis.* p. m. ii. 117; *Gage's Suffolk,* 60.)

SHARESHULL, WILLIAM DE, was born at the manor of Shareshull in the county of Stafford. He is mentioned among the advocates in the Year Book of Edward II. In 5 Edward III. he was a king's serjeant, and in the next year was one of the council whom the king selected to advise him (*Rot. Parl.* ii. 69), being about the same time invested with the knighthood of the Bath.

On March 20, 1333, he was constituted a judge of the King's Bench, but remained in that court for little more than two months, being removed into the Common Pleas on May 30 following. His continuance on the bench was interrupted in December 1340, by his dismissal and imprisonment on some charge of maladministration made by the king on his return from the siege of Tournay. (*Barnes's Edward III.* 212.) The particulars are not recorded; but in no very long time he recovered the royal favour, being reinstated on May 10, 1342; and on July 2, 1344, he was raised to the office of chief baron of the Exchequer. He sat in that court about sixteen months, when, on November 10, 1345, he was removed to the Common Pleas, with the title of second justice, which he retained for the next five years, and was appointed one of the custodes of the principality of Wales, &c., during the minority of the king's son. (*Cal. Rot. Pat.* 154.)

On October 26, 1350, he was advanced to the head of the Court of King's Bench, and presided in it till July 5, 1357. While holding that office he declared the causes of the meeting of five parliaments, from 25 to 29 Edward III. (*Rot. Parl.* ii. 226–264.) He seems, indeed, at this time to have been more a political and parliamentary judge than a man of law, for no chief justice is so seldom mentioned in the Year Books. Having pronounced a judgment against the Bishop of Ely, for harbouring one of his people who had slain a man of Lady Wake's, he was excommunicated by the pope, in the last year of his judicial career, for not appearing when summoned. (*Barnes's Edward III.* 551.)

In Clarke's 'Ipswich' (p. 14) it is related that at that town some sailors thinking he stayed too long at dinner, one of them mounted on the bench and fined the judge for not appearing. He took such offence at this joke that he induced the king not only to take away the assizes from the town, but also to seize the liberties of the corporation into his own hands, which he held for about a year.

After retiring from the bench, on which he had sat, with a slight interruption, for above twenty-four years, he still retained the royal favour; for we find him in confidential positions as late as the thirty-fourth year of the reign. (*N. Fœdera,* iii. 457, 469.)

He lived beyond 37 Edward III., in which year he granted his manor of Alurynton in Gloucestershire to the abbot and convent of Oseney, in addition to lands at Sandford in Oxfordshire which he had given six years before. He was a benefactor also to the convents of Bruera and Dudley.

SHEE, WILLIAM, was the first judge who was raised to the English bench under the Roman Catholic Relief Act, which was passed nearly forty years before, to take away the disabilities which attached to persons of that persuasion. In all other departments, civil, military, and legislative, it has been ever since acted upon; but the judicial office had been hitherto excepted.

William Shee was of an old Irish family. His father, Joseph Shee, Esq., of Thomastown in the county of Kilkenny, was a London merchant, and his mother was Teresa, daughter of John Darell, Esq., of Scotney Castle in Kent. He was born at Finchley in Middlesex in 1804, and, being brought up in the religion of his parents, was sent for instruction to the Roman Catholic College of St. Cuthbert, near Durham, from whence he proceeded to the university of Edinburgh. Having next been admitted a member of Lincoln's Inn, he was called to the bar by that society on June 19, 1828, and began his forensic labours by travelling the Home Circuit, and attending the Surrey sessions. Both there and in the London courts his advocacy received great encouragement, and in a few years he gained such a position as to justify him in accepting the serjeant's coif in 1840, when that honourable degree was for a short period restored to all its privileges. His reputation was greatly increased by his publication in the same year of an edition of Lord Tenterden's work on Shipping, and the extensive knowledge he displayed on that branch of law. In 1847 he received a patent of precedence, and ten years afterwards he was made queen's serjeant.

On the liberal side of politics, to which he had attached himself from the outset of his career, he was desirous of entering parliament; and after an unsuccessful attempt in 1847 to represent the borough of Marylebone, he obtained a seat in 1852 for his family county of Kilkenny, which, however did not return him at the next election in 1857. In the House of Commons he supported the principles which he had always professed, and naturally advocated the claims of the Roman Catholics.

In his professional course he had long been the head of his circuit, and in London he was one of the most popular leaders. It was not, however, till he had been more than thirty-five years at the bar that he was called to the bench, although on more than one occasion he had been employed on the circuit to preside in the place of an absent judge. He was at length selected as a judge of the Queen's Bench on December 18, 1863; but an attack of apoplexy terminated his career on February 19, 1868.

He married Mary, daughter of Sir James Gordon, the premier baronet of Scotland.

SHELLEY, WILLIAM, was of an ancient family of Norman extraction, one of whose members accompanied William the Conqueror in his expedition against England. Doubts exist as to the precise branch to which the judge belonged, but he is claimed, and apparently on valid grounds, as the ancestor of the baronet of Michelgrove. If this be so, his grandfather was John Shelley, member for Rye from 1415 to 1423; and his father, another John, married Elizabeth, daughter and heir of John Michelgrove, of Michelgrove in Sussex. (*Horsfield's Lewes*, ii. 176; *Wotton's Baronet.* i. 59.) He was the second son; and after studying the law at the Inner Temple, he was appointed reader there in autumn 1517. At that time he was one of the judges of the Sheriff's Court in London, from which office he was raised to the recordership of that city in 1520; and three years afterwards he was elected one of its representatives in parliament. He took the degree of the coif in 1521, and was promoted to be a judge of the Common Pleas about the beginning of 1527, the first fine levied before him being dated on the octave of Hilary in that year, 18 Henry VIII. (*Dugdale's Orig.* 47, 163.)

Soon after Wolsey's disgrace, Judge Shelley was selected to apply to him for York House, the London residence of the Archbishops of York, to which the king had taken a great fancy. The cardinal, objecting that it was not his to give, as he was only tenant for life, Shelley informed him that all the judges and learned counsel were resolved that his grace might make a recognisance thereof to the king, which would be a sufficient surrender. 'Tell his highness,' answered the cardinal, 'that I am his most faithful subject and obedient beadsman, whose command I will in nowise disobey, but will in all things fulfil his pleasure, as you the fathers of the law say I may. Therefore I charge your conscience to discharge me, and show his highness from me that I must desire his majesty to remember there is both heaven and hell.' (*Cavendish's Wolsey*, 155.) He then executed the instrument, and York House changed its name to Whitehall. It was probably soon after performing this service that Shelley had the honour of entertaining the king at Michelgrove. (*Gent. Mag.* iv. 713.)

The judge seems to have been somewhat of a humourist on the bench. In a case which he thought overlaboured beyond its merits he 'compared it to a Banbury cheese, which is worth little in substance when the parings are cut off; for so this case,' said he, 'is brief, if the superfluous trifling which is on the pleadings be taken away.' (*Dyer*, i. 42 b.) He was continued in his place on the accession of Edward VI., and his death occurred between November 3, 1548 (the date of his last fine), and May 10, 1549, when his successor was appointed.

His property was greatly increased by his marriage with Alice, the daughter of

Sir Henry Belknap, grandson of the chief justice in the reign of Richard II. They had several children, one of whom was Sir Richard Shelley, the last English prior of St. John of Jerusalem. From their eldest son descended John Shelley of Michelgrove, who was one of the first baronets created by James I. on May 22, 1611.

The baronetcy of Shelley of Castle Goring in Sussex was granted in 1806 to Bysshe Shelley, Esq., the descendant of a younger brother of the judge. He was grandfather of the eminent poet of that name, who was unfortunately drowned during his father's life, and whose son now enjoys the title. The second son of the first Bysshe Shelley inheriting the estates of his mother, the granddaughter of Robert, fourth Earl of Leicester, assumed her maiden name of Sidney, and was created a baronet (of Penshurst) in 1818; and his son, having married the Lady Sophia Fitz-Clarence, was raised to the peerage in 1835 as Baron De l'Isle and Dudley.

SHIRLAND, ALMARIC DE, had a conveyance to him of the manor of Mutford in Suffolk in 45 Edward III. He was placed on the bench of the Exchequer as second baron on October 29, 1365, 39 Edward III., when a considerable change was made in the judges of all the courts. Beyond that day his name does not appear in the published records, except in the forty-fourth year, when he was sent into Lincolnshire and three neighbouring counties to borrow money for the king's use. (*Cal. Inquis.* p.m. ii. 315; *Issue Roll*, 112, 346.)

SHORDICH, JOHN DE, whose name is unquestionably derived from the parish so called, formerly in the suburbs of London, and now forming part of it, was not improbably the son of Benedictus de Shordich, who in the reign of Edward I. had a grant from the king of some houses of a Jew in the Old Jewry, in the parish of St. Olave, in Colcherche-strete. (*Abb. Rot. Orig.* i. 74.)

John was an advocate in the Court of Arches, and in 18 Edward II. was employed as one of the nuncios to treat in Flanders, and in the following year accompanied the king to France as part of his retinue. (*N. Fœdera*, ii. 550, 606.) He is styled 'legum doctor,' and 'juris civilis professor.' The 'Magister' which is sometimes prefixed to his name applies, no doubt, to this degree, and not to any clerical order, as he was knighted in 17 Edward III., and is always afterwards described with that rank. For his services to Edward II. he was rewarded with the chief clerkship of the Common Bench, and with the manor of Passenham in the county of Northampton. But by a petition to parliament in 4 Edward III. (after the king had freed himself from the control of his mother) he complained that he had been ousted by the queen both of his office and a large part of the manor, whereupon compensation was awarded to him. (*Rot. Parl.* ii. 41.) From the previous year to the end of his life he was perpetually engaged in missions to different courts, both before and after he was appointed second baron of the Exchequer on November 10, 1336, 10 Edward III. (*Cal. Rot. Pat.* 126.) How long he remained in office does not appear; but when the court was reconstituted on January 20, 1342, his name was omitted. He continued, however, to be engaged in diplomatic employments till the eighteenth year, about which time his death probably occurred, as he is not mentioned subsequently. (*N. Fœdera*, ii. 772-1241, iii. 12.)

SHOTTINDON, ROBERT DE, was of a Kentish family, and farmed property at Ospringe under the crown. In 1235 the vacant bishopric of Norwich was committed to his charge, and in 1243 he had a grant of the custody of the land and heirs of Thomas de Acton, for a fine of thirty marks. Matthew Paris calls him 'domini regis clericus specialis.' He was raised to the bench about the beginning of 39 Henry III., 1254, and his name appears upon fines till 1257. He died in that year at Hertford, while on his circuit, and was buried in the priory there. Weever (543) calls him Sotington or Sadington; so that he may have been the ancestor of Thomas de Sodington, the justice itinerant under Edward I., and Robert de Sadington, chief baron and lord chancellor under Edward III. (*Excerpt. e Rot. Fin.* i. 398, 429; *Abb. Rot. Orig.* i. 2; *Dugdale's Orig.* 43.)

SHUTE, ROBERT, was of Hockington in Cambridgeshire, in which county and in Leicestershire his family was of some standing; but he was born in Yorkshire, as appears by a licence to him to hold assizes in that county, notwithstanding his birth. (*Rot. Pat.* 7.)

Having passed through his legal studies, first at Barnard's Inn and then at Gray's Inn, he was called to the bar by the latter in 1552, and became reader in 1568, and again in 1577, on his being summoned to take the degree of the coif. He must have acquired a considerable reputation in the law, as he is the first serjeant who was raised to the bench of the Exchequer as a puisne baron, and the terms of his patent show that a new system was then introduced into that court. Up to this time the puisne barons had been principally selected from the other officers of the department; they were not looked upon as lawyers, and did not go the circuits; various instances have been mentioned of their still continuing in their original inn of court after their becoming barons, and there is no doubt that till this period they held an inferior grade to the judges of the two other benches.

But cases connected with the revenue and crown debts becoming more numerous and intricate, it was deemed expedient that the court should be gradually filled with able lawyers; and accordingly, in Serjeant Shute's patent, dated June 1, 1579, constituting him second baron, it is for the first time ordered that 'he shall be reputed, and be of the same order, rank, estimation, dignity, and pre-eminence, to all intents and purposes, as any puisne judge of either of the two other courts.' After nearly nine years' occupation of this seat, during which he acted occasionally as a judge of assize, he was removed to the Queen's Bench on February 8, 1586, where he remained till his death, which occurred in 1590. (*Savile's Reports*, 59; *Dugdale's Orig.* 294.)

He left a son, Francis, who was settled at Upton in Leicestershire, and whose grandson, John Shute, having had a large estate bequeathed to him by Francis Barrington, Esq., of Tofts in Essex, assumed that gentleman's name, and was raised in 1720 to the Irish peerage as Baron and Viscount Barrington. (*Biog. Peerage*, iv. 224; *Nichol's Lit. Anecdotes*, vi. 444.)

SIGILLO, NICHOLAS DE. Among the justices itinerant of this reign the name of Nicholas occurs three times, and, though distinguished on each occasion by different appellations, it is probable they all belong to the same individual.

First, in 19 Henry II., 1173, 'Nicholas de Sigillo et Ricardus Thesaurarius' set the assize on the king's demesnes in Oxfordshire (*Madox*, i. 701); and, as his name is placed before the king's treasurer, it may be presumed he held a high rank.

Again, in the roll of 1174, the assizes set by Nicholas the archdeacon 'et socios suos' in Buckinghamshire and Bedfordshire appear (*Ibid.* 123); and they are clearly assizes made of a former year, as the new assize for that year is made by other justices. Le Neve (158) says that Nicholas de Sigillo was archdeacon of Huntingdon as early as 1155. It appears, therefore, by the first of these entries, that it was not always the custom to designate the clerical dignity.

And, thirdly, when the kingdom was divided by the council of Windsor, in 1179, into four districts for judicial purposes, and judges were sent into each, 'Nicholaus, Capellanus Regis,' was the second of five appointed to act in Cambridgeshire and eight other counties. It is not unlikely that the title of king's chaplain may have been considered equal, if not superior, to that of archdeacon; and we have already seen that the latter was not always used.

The official position of Nicholas de Sigillo was no doubt the same as that held under Henry I. by Robert de Sigillo, afterwards Bishop of London. It was called Clericus or Magister Scriptorii, and in the Red Book of the Exchequer is placed next in order to the chancellor, with considerable allowances, which that king increased for Robert de Sigillo to two shillings a day, with one sextary of household wine, one seasoned simnel, one taper, and twenty-four pieces of candle. (*Ibid.* 195.)

In 1156 Nicholas de Sigillo accounted for two hawks in Lincolnshire, being probably his fine for his archdeaconry, which was in that diocese; and other entries in the Pipe Rolls in that and the two following years plainly prove that he was connected with the Exchequer. In 1172 Nicholas, the king's chaplain, was sent to assist at the counsel of the clergy held at Cashel in Ireland. (*Brady's England*, 360.) He is mentioned in 1 Richard I., 1189 (*Pipe Roll*, 200), but the archdeaconry was held by another in 1191.

SIMON was the tenth abbot of Reading, succeeding Helias in 1212. He was frequently employed under both John and Henry III. In 16 John he was sent on a mission to France, and in 4 Henry III. he was in the commission of enquiry issued as to the forests, and also had the custody for a short time of the castle of Devizes. In 5 Henry III. he was placed at the head of the justices itinerant sent into nine counties; and in the next year he had a grant of twenty oaks from the New Forest to repair his houses at Wichebury. He died in February 1226. (*Willis's Mitred Abbeys*; *Rot. Claus.* i. 175, 434, 458, 476, 513, ii. 99.)

SIMPSON, WILLIAM, is described in his admission to the Inner Temple in November 1657 as of Bromsgrove in the county of Worcester. His call to the bar did not take place till November 1674, seventeen years after; and he was not elected a bencher of the society till he was constituted cursitor baron. To that office he was appointed on October 2, 1697, receiving the honour of knighthood, and filled it nearly nine-and-twenty years (under three sovereigns), when his great age obliged him to surrender it on May 23, 1726. (*Lord Raymond*, 748, 1317; *Luttrell*, iv. 287, 319.)

SKIPWITH, WILLIAM DE, the lineal descendant of Robert de Stuteville, whose younger son assumed the name in the reign of Henry III., from the lordship so called in Yorkshire, which he received as his portion from his father, was the second son of another William, by Margaret, the daughter of Ralph Fitz-Simon, lord of Ormsby in Lincolnshire. His father died in 10 Edward III., and his brother a few months afterwards, so that he then succeeded to the estates. He is stated (but upon somewhat questionable evidence) to have belonged to the society of Gray's Inn, and to have been the first reader there. His eminence as an advocate may be inferred from the frequent recurrence of his arguments in the Year Books from 17 Edward III. He was appointed one of the king's serjeants in 28 Edward III., and was raised to the bench, as a judge of the Common Pleas, on October 25, 1359, 33 Edward III., soon after which he was created a knight. From this bench he was advanced in less than three years to be chief baron of the Exchequer. (*Kal. Exch.* i. 195.)

His removal from this office took place on October 29, 1365, 39 Edward III., when both he and Sir Henry Green, the chief justice of the King's Bench, who was deprived of his place on the same day, were imprisoned on the charge of various enormities, which, according to the historian, the king *understood* they had committed against law and justice; and it is added that they did not get their discharge until they had refunded large sums of money which they had unjustly acquired. Barnes (p. 607) states that they were ever after secluded from their places and the king's favour. Whether this were so with regard to Skipwith remains to be considered.

Wotton and Collins, in their Baronetages, state that Skipwith continued in office till 40 Edward III., at which time he died, and that *his son William* was constituted a judge of the Common Pleas in 50 Edward III. In the first of these assertions they are manifestly wrong, as the records clearly prove that the new chief baron was appointed in 39 Edward III.

Barnes's relation proves that they must be equally wrong in their statement that Sir William was chief baron till his death; and, as no evidence exists of the date of this latter event, the question arises whether the William de Skipwith who became a judge of the Common Pleas in 50 Edward III. was not the chief baron himself; and we are inclined, for several reasons, to think that this was so.

In the first place, there is no second advocate of the name mentioned in the Year Books, nor any second serjeant among the writs; and it can hardly be supposed that a man would be raised to the bench who had not previously distinguished himself in some way in the courts.

Secondly, it is not probable, and indeed scarcely possible, as we shall presently show, that the chief baron could have had a son old enough to be made a judge in 50 Edward III., a period when lawyers are reputed to have passed through a lengthened ordeal before they were raised to the bench.

Thirdly, we find that on February 15, 1370, 44 Edward III., a Sir William de Skipwith was constituted chief justice of the King's Bench in Ireland (*N. Fœdera*, iii. 887); and that on the 21st the sum of 26*l.* 13*s.* 4*d.*, or 40 marks, was paid to him for his expenses and equipment in going there (*Issue Roll*, 458), showing, therefore, that he went from England. This is a fact which the genealogists have entirely omitted, and it would be difficult to accommodate it to their account. If the father was dead, as they state, then it must have been the son, which would thus take six more years from his age as a judge, and consequently create a greater improbability. But if it were the father, as we feel satisfied it was, it is easily reconciled to the supposition that King Edward, having satisfied himself that the charges against him were unfounded, restored the victim of his haste, as he did on several other occasions, to his judicial functions on the first opportunity.

Fourthly, in the pedigree of the family, to which we have had access through the kindness of the late Sir Gray Skipwith, Bart., and which appears to have been drawn up about the end of the seventeenth century, Sir William, the undoubted judge, is called 'capitalis *justiciarius*,' and his son William is not described as a judge at all. Now the former never was chief justice, unless he was the chief justice of Ireland; and if he were so, of which this entry seems a confirmation, then he could not have died at the period named by Wotton and Collins; while the fact of the latter having been a judge, if he had indeed been the man, could not have been overlooked by the herald, when there was exposed before him a painted window in the mansion at Newbold Hall, presenting a portrait in judge's robes, and inscribed in allusion to an incident of life which we shall presently relate,

Solus inter impios mansit integer Gulielmus Skipwith miles, clarus ideo apud posteros, anno decimo Ricardi 2^{di}.

It may be remarked, further, that if the son could not be old enough in 44 or in 50 Edward III., 1370–1376, to be made a judge, neither would the father have been too old in 10 Richard II., 1386, the alleged time of his final retirement, to sit on the bench. To obtain his probable age we must refer back a little to his ancestors. There was a Reginald, who was old enough to be a hostage in the barons' wars, 9 John, 1209. The chief baron's father died in 1336, 10 Edward III., leaving an interval of 127 years, during which there were four generations, thus giving to each little more than thirty years. It is clear, therefore, that the chief baron's father could not have been an old man when he died; and there is every 'appearance that all his children were minors at his death. The eldest, John, died in the same year with his father, childless; and the chief baron, who succeeded, is not mentioned as an advocate till seven years afterwards. Presuming, then, that he was eighteen years old when his father died, he would be twenty-five when he appeared in the courts, thirty-six when he became a serjeant, forty-one when made a judge, forty-four as chief baron, fifty-two as chief justice of Ireland, fifty-eight when he returned as a judge to England, and only sixty-eight or sixty-nine at the date of his retirement in 10 or 11 Richard II. Even if three or four years were added, his age would not exceed the bounds of reasonable probability.

It will be at once seen that, if this calculation approaches in any degree to correctness, it would be next to impossible that he should have a son old enough in 1370 to be placed in so high a judicial office as chief justice of the King's Bench in Ireland; and this becomes still less probable when we find that the chief baron's second son, John, ultimately succeeded to the estates by the death of the elder son, William, without male issue, and lived till 9 Henry V., 1422, in which reign he was returned to parliament as one of the members for Lincolnshire.

If the father died, as is alleged, in 1366, leaving one son of sufficient age, in 1370, to be made a judge, and another not too old, fifty years afterwards, to be member of parliament, the discrepancy between the two ages must have been somewhat extraordinary; while, if the father lived, as the evidence seems to justify us in supposing, till after 1387, all difficulty is removed, and everything appears natural and in common course.

We feel that we are warranted, therefore, in regarding the Sir William de Skipwith who was appointed chief justice of the King's Bench in Ireland in 1370 as the same person who was removed from the office of chief baron in 1365, and consequently as the same person who was restored to his old position as justice of the Common Pleas in England in 1376. It is evident that Dugdale so considered him, as in his list of the judges (*Orig.* 45) before whom fines were levied he mentions only one William Skipwith, and connects the two periods of his acting by the words 'et iterum;' and no one can observe the manner in which Skipwith is noticed, in the only case in which his name is mentioned, in Michaelmas, 50 Edward III., in the Year Books, without being satisfied that it is no new judge who speaks, but one who had experience and authority. 'Et adonques vient Mons. W. Skipwith en le place quant le matt. fuit pled, et did,' &c. The great case of the Bishop of 'Sancte Davy,' and John Wyton, clerk, was then in discussion, and his opinion having been given with dignity and distinctness, the other judges concurred, and the judgment was pronounced in accordance with it. (*Year Book,* 50 *Edward III.* fo. 27, pl. 8.) This probably took place on his first appearance in the court after his return from Ireland, his re-appointment being dated October 8, 1376.

On the accession of Richard II., in the following year, he was retained in his place as second justice of the Common Pleas, and continued in the active performance of his duties throughout the first ten years of that reign. He was summoned, with the rest of the judges, to the council of Nottingham in August 1387, 11 Richard II., when the king's favourites compelled his brethren to subscribe certain questions and answers condemnatory of the proceedings of the parliament in appointing a council for the government of the kingdom. Whether he did or did not suspect the object does not appear; but, by pleading illness, he fortunately escaped the consequences in which they involved themselves. He was the only one of those who had previously sat on the bench who acted as a trier of petitions in the parliament of the following February, in which all his brethren were impeached and attainted.

They were all of course removed from their seats, and he seems to have taken the same opportunity of retiring from the bench, as no fines were levied before him after that date. His death did not occur till some years afterwards, as he was alive in 15 Richard II.

He married Alice, sole daughter and heir of Sir William de Hiltoft, lord of Ingoldmells in Lincolnshire, by whom he had several children. On the death of his elder son, William, without issue male, the bulk of his estate descended to his second son, John, whose family was distinguished by no less than three baronetcies, two of which are now extinct—viz., 1. Sir Fulwar Skipwith, of Newbold Hall, Warwickshire, received the title on October 25, 1670, which failed in 1790; 2. Sir Thomas Skipwith, of Metheringham in Lincolnshire, a serjeant-at-law, was created a baronet on July 27, 1678, but his grandson dying without issue in 1756, the title expired. The third, however, which is the more ancient, being granted to Sir Henry Skipwith, of Prestwould in Leicestershire, on December 20, 1622, still survives.

SKIRLAWE, WALTER (BISHOP OF DURHAM), had the custody of the Great Seal with three others for the period of six weeks, from August 8 to September 20, 1382. It had been first committed to Hugh de Segrave, William de Dighton, and John de Waltham on July 11; but Skirlawe, having succeeded Dighton as keeper of the privy seal, was then added to them in the execution of this duty.

According to tradition, he was the son of a sieve-maker, and was born at Swine in Holderness, Yorkshire. Educated at Durham College, Oxford, he took the degree of Doctor in Laws, or, as he is frequently called 'Decretorum Doctor.' He seems to have been one of the clerks in Chancery, as he was named a receiver of petitions in the parliament of January 1377, this function being usually assigned to that class of officers. He held the same position also in the first four parliaments of Richard II. (*Rot. Parl.* ii. 363, iii. 4-89.) As was usual with the Chancery clerks, he soon received ecclesiastical dignities. He was first made dean of St. Martin's in London, and held that rich benefice on April 26, 1377, when he was sent by King Edward as one of the ambassadors to negotiate a treaty with France. (*N. Fœdera,* iii. 1076.) In the beginning of the next reign he was likewise engaged in other diplomatic missions. (*Rymer,* vii. 223, 229.) About 1381 he became treasurer of Lincoln and archdeacon of Northampton, and, soon after, archdeacon of the East Riding of York. (*Le Neve,* 152, 162, 327.)

His elevation to the office of keeper of the privy seal took place as we have seen in 1382, and he held it till he was elected Bishop of Lichfield and Coventry in 1385. During his possession of this post he was selected to announce to the parliament of October 1385 the creation of the king's uncles, Edmund and Thomas, to the dukedoms of York and Gloucester, and of Michael de la Pole to the earldom of Suffolk; and the Parliament Roll, in describing the ceremony, calls him 'doctor egregius, eloquens et discretus.' (*Rot. Parl.* iii. 205-9.)

He had held the bishopric of Lichfield and Coventry for a year only, when he was removed to that of Bath and Wells in August 1386, where he remained less than two years, being translated to the richer see of Durham in April 1388. He presided over this diocese for seventeen years, and, dying on March 24, 1405, was buried in his cathedral.

Surtees describes him as 'a pious and humble prelate, whose name is transmitted to posterity only by his works of charity and munificence,' and of these many are recorded. (*Godwin,* 321, 378, 751; *Surtees' Durham,* i. liv. lv.)

SKYNNER, JOHN, had not the advantage of a very opulent parentage, but owed his success in life to his own exertions. He was one of the sons of John and Elizabeth Skynner, living in the parish of Milton in Oxfordshire, on a property which the lady inherited, and was born about 1723. The date of his call to the bar has not been found, nor any incidents of his early career, but he must soon have acquired considerable practice and reputation in the courts to enable him to obtain a seat in the parliaments of 1768 and 1774, as the representative of Woodstock. There, though not a frequent speaker, he showed his superior qualifications in several debates. In 1771 he was made king's counsel, and attorney of the duchy of Lancaster; and in the next year he was constituted second judge on the Chester Circuit.

On November 17, 1777, he was promoted to the head of the Court of Exchequer, in which he presided with great learning and ability for nine years. His want of health obliged him to resign his seat in January 1787, when he was honoured with a seat in the privy council.

The chief baron lived nearly nine years after his retirement, and died on November 26, 1805, at Milton, where he was buried in the same vault with his wife, Martha, the daughter of Edward Burn and Martha Davie. They left a daughter, Frederica, who married Richard Ryder, brother of the first Earl of Harrowby, and afterwards secretary of state. (*Collins's Peerage,* v. 718; *Gent. Mag.* xc. 107; *Blackstone's Rep.* 1178; 1 *Term Rep.* 551.)

SMITH, JOHN. The original name of this family, tracing its lineage to the standard-bearer of Richard I., was Carrington, which was changed in the reign of Henry VI. to that of Smith, by John Carrington, who was obliged to fly the country. His son Hugh, of Cressing in Essex, who died in 1485, was father to this John Smith, who became a clerk in the office of treasurer's remembrancer in the Exchequer, and had a grant of that office in January 1513. On August 1, 1539, he received a grant of the office of second baron of that court, in reversion after the death or retirement of John Hales, whom it appears he succeeded in the following Michaelmas Term. He preserved his seat on the bench during the remainder of the reign, but was not re-appointed on the accession of Edward VI.

He married twice. By his first wife, Alice, daughter and coheir of Edward Wood, grocer, of London, he had six sons. By his second wife, Agnes, daughter and heir of John Harwell, of Wotton Waven in Warwickshire, he had two sons and six daughters. From one of his sons descended Sir Charles Smith, whom Charles I. created Lord Carrington of Wotton Waven on October 31, 1643, adding on November 4 the Irish viscounty of Carrington of Barrefore, but both titles became extinct in 1705. (*Baronage,* ii. 470; *Morant's Essex,* ii. 114; *Cal. St. Papers* [1509-14] 473, [1515-18] 877; *Collins's Peerage,* viii. 549.)

SMITH, JOHN, is distinguished by having held a judicial seat in each of the three kingdoms. He was the son of Roger Smith, Esq., of Frolesworth in Leicestershire, and went through his legal training at Gray's Inn, by which society he was called to the bar on May 2, 1684. He was sent as a judge of the Common Pleas to Ireland on December 24, 1700. In less than a couple of years he was recalled and made a baron of the English Exchequer, on June 24, 1702.

In the great case of Ashby and White on the Aylesbury election, he opposed the judgment of the three puisne judges of the Queen's Bench, concurring in the opinion of Chief Justice Holt in favour of the voter who had been deprived of his franchise by the returning officer. The reversal of that judgment and the confirmation of Holt's opinion by the House of Lords was then represented as a whig triumph, but must be considered, now that party spirit no longer is predominant, as a triumph of common sense over a fanciful claim of privilege by the House of Commons. In May 1708 he was selected to settle the Exchequer in Scotland, and was sent as lord chief baron for that purpose, being still allowed, though another baron was appointed here, to retain his place in the English court, and receiving 500*l.* a year in addition to his salary. He enjoyed both positions till the end of his life, being re-sworn on the accession of George I. in his office of baron of the English Exchequer, although he performed none of its duties. He died on June 24, 1726, and by his will he founded and endowed a hospital at his native village of Frolesworth for the maintenance of fourteen poor widows. (*Nichol's Leicestersh.* 185; *Lord Raymond*, 769, 1317; *Luttrell*, iv. 713, v. 184, vi. 299; *Gent. Mag.* lxiii. 1131.)

SMITH, MONTAGUE EDWARD, one of the present judges of the Common Pleas, was born at Bideford in Devonshire, where his father, Thomas Smith, Esq., resided. His mother was Margaret Colville, daughter of M. Jenkyn, Esq., commander in the navy. After an education in the grammar school of his native town, he entered the Middle Temple, by which society he was called to the bar on November 18, 1835. He joined the Western Circuit, and, after nearly seventeen years of successful practice, he was honoured with a silk gown in 1852. After two unsuccessful attempts, in 1849 and 1852, he entered parliament in 1859 for Truro, which he continued to represent till February 7, 1865, when he was appointed a judge of the Common Pleas and was knighted.

SMYTHE, SIDNEY STAFFORD, descended from Thomas Smythe, commonly called Customer Smythe, from his being farmer of the customs, who first settled himself in the reign of Queen Elizabeth at Westenhanger in Kent, was the son of Henry Smythe, of Bounds, and Elizabeth, daughter of Dr. John Lloyd, canon of Windsor.

He was an infant at his father's death, and was called to the bar by the Inner Temple in February 1728. He travelled the Home Circuit, and in 1740 was made steward and one of the judges of the Palace Court at Westminster. In June 1747 he received the honour of a silk gown, and as a king's counsel he was engaged for the crown in 1749 in the special commission in Sussex for the trial of a band of smugglers for the heinous murder of a tide-waiter and another man who was a witness in a transaction in which they were concerned. He was returned as member for East Grinstead to the parliament of 1747, and between its second and third sessions was promoted to the bench of the Exchequer in June 1750, being soon after knighted. (*Gent. Mag.* x. xvii. xx.; *State Trials*, xviii. 1086.)

He sat as a puisne baron for more than two-and-twenty years, during which period he was twice appointed a commissioner of the Great Seal. On the first occasion he held it from November 9, 1756, to June 30, 1757, and on the second, when he was principal commissioner, from January 21, 1770, to January 28, 1771. These appointments manifest that he held that high reputation as a judge that secured him an advance to the higher dignity of this court as soon as a vacancy occurred. This did not happen till October 28, 1772, when he was raised to the place of lord chief baron of the Exchequer, where he presided for the next five years. His infirmities then obliged him to resign in December 1777, when he received a pension of 2400*l.* a year, and was immediately sworn of the privy council.

He died in less than a year afterwards, on October 30, 1778, leaving no issue by his wife, Sarah, the daughter of Sir Charles Farnaby, Bart., of Kippington in Kent. (*Hasted*, iii. 58, 237, v. 274; *Blackstone's Rep.* 1178.)

SNIGGE, GEORGE, belonged to a family at Bristol, several of whom had filled the offices of sheriff and mayor of the city. His father, George Snigge, was sheriff in 1556 and mayor in 1574–5; and his mother was Margery, daughter of — Taylor. He was born about 1545, and was called to the bar of the Middle Temple on June 17, 1575, was nominated reader in 1560 and 1598, and in May 1602 was elected treasurer of the society. He became recorder of his native city, was raised in Easter Term 1604 to the degree of the coif, and on June 28 was placed in the Court of Exchequer as an additional or fifth baron. (*Rot. Pat. Jac.* p. 7.) It is curious that there are two grants to him of this office, one as 'baron of the Exchequer,' and the other as 'baron of the coif of the Exchequer' (*Cal. State Papers* [1603–10], 125, 156), an example of the change that was then taking place in the court, rendering it necessary to appoint a cursitor baron. In May 1608 he was appointed a Welsh judge in addition. (*Ibid.* 429.) In Bates's case, on the duty imposed on currants by the king's authority, he joined with his brethren in the decision in favour of the crown, and was one of the majority in affirming the rights of the *post nati*; but in neither case is his argument preserved. (*State Trials*, ii. 382, 576.) After sitting on the bench for nearly thirteen years, he died on November 11, 1617, and was buried in St. Stephen's Church, Bristol.

By his wife, Alice, daughter of William Young, of Ogborne, Wiltshire, he had nine children. (*Barrett's Bristol*, 514; *MSS. Coll. Arms*, G, 77.)

SNYTERTON, THOMAS DE, took his name from Snyterton, a village in Norfolk. In 29 Edward I. he was engaged in a suit in which he claimed the manor of Denham in Suffolk. (*Abb. Placit.* 243.) He is only mentioned once as employed in a judicial capacity, being one of the justices of trailbaston appointed in 35 Edward I., 1307, for Essex and ten other counties, but not including Norfolk (*Rot. Parl.* i. 218), from which omission it would seem that he was a lawyer by profession. In the same year he was returned as knight of the shire for Norfolk. (*Parl Writs*, i. 187.)

SODINGTON, or SADINGTON, THOMAS DE. Weever (543), in speaking of the death of Robert de Shottinden, the justice itinerant in the reign of Henry III., calls him Sotingdon or Sadington. If he is correct in this, probably he was the father or grandfather of this judge, whose name is written both ways, and in some instances Suddington. (*Abb. Placit.* 229.) He was a clergyman, and was probably, therefore, one of the officers of the court before he became a justice itinerant. His first appointment to that duty was in 4 Edward I., 1276, when he acted in the city and Tower of London; and from that time he was regularly employed in various parts of the kingdom till 17 Edward I. He was one of the ambassadors to the Earl of Holland in 12 Edward I., and was a party to the contract for the marriage of the earl's son John with the king's daughter Elizabeth. (*N. Fœdera*, i. 645, 658, 661.) Sharing the corruption which pervaded the whole bench, he did not escape the retribution which they were all called upon to make; he was dismissed with disgrace from his office in 1289, when he was sent a prisoner to the Tower, from which he was only discharged on the payment of a fine of 2000 marks. He died in 27 Edward I., in possession of the manor of Tidberst in Hertfordshire, and considerably in debt to the king, inasmuch as all his goods were sequestered in the dioceses of York, Lincoln, Chichester, and Sarum, and in the county of Northampton. (*Cal. Inquis.* p. m. i. 153; *Abb. Rot. Orig.* i. 104.)

SOMER, HENRY, was a clerk of the Exchequer by whom payments were made in the first years of the reign of Henry IV. (*Devon's Issue Roll*, 274–286.) In the seventh year the Commons, suspecting that their proceedings were not properly entered, selected him as one of those who were to overlook the engrossment of the Rolls of Parliament. (*Rot. Parl.* iii. 585.) He was made a baron of the Exchequer on November 8, 1407; and on January 23, 1413, he was advanced to the office of chancellor of the Exchequer. (*Kal. Exch.* ii. 85.)

He was also under-treasurer, as we find from a song written by Occleve (*Works*, Mason, 59–70) thus entitled : 'Cestes Balade et Chanceon Ensuyantz Feurent Faites à Mon Meistre H. Somer quant il Soustresorer.' Whether this office was then, as now, united with that of chancellor of the Exchequer is uncertain; but we should judge not, from the more respectful address which Occleve prefixed to another song, entitled, 'Cestes Balade Ensuyante Fust Par la Court de Bone Compagnie Envoiee a Lonure Sire Henri Somer Chancellor De Leschequer et un De la Dite Court.'

This 'court' was evidently a convivial association of good fellows, and forms an early example of the modern club. The first of these ballads was the congratulation of his brethren on his appointment as sub-treasurer, and the second appears to be an answer to a letter of remonstrance the 'court' had received from him for undue extravagance and a breach of some of their rules. In reply to which, with true English freedom, their poet says,—

To the which in this wyse we answere,
Excesse for to do be yee nat bounde
Ne noon of us, but do as we may bere,
Up on swich rule we nat us in grownde,
Yee been discreet, though yee in good habownde,
Dooth as yow thynkith for you honestee,
Yee and we all arn at our libertee.

It is not improbable that Geoffrey Chaucer was a fellow of this ' good company,' as we find that Henry Somer, on June 5, 1400, 1 Henry IV., received his pension for him; and no doubt Somer was a relation, perhaps a brother, of the 'Frere John Somere' whose Kalendar is mentioned in Chaucer's treatise on the Astrolabe. (*Nicolas's Chaucer*, 56.)

SOMERS, JOHN (LORD SOMERS). It has been too much the practice of party writers, in the absence of other objections, to endeavour to depreciate their antagonists by allusions to their low birth. When Dean Swift, following the vulgar example, said that Somers 'sprang from the dregs of the people,' he not only disregarded truth, but failed to reflect how nearly, if true as to Somers, the assertion might be applied to himself. Swift's grandfather was the vicar of a country parish ; Somers's grandfather was the possessor of considerable landed property which had belonged to his family for many generations. Swift's father was an Irish attorney of no eminence, and he himself almost a child of charity; Somers's father was a member of the same profession, in extensive practice, farming his own estate, and affording to his son the best of educations. The imputation therefore comes with peculiarly bad grace from Swift; but, be it true or false, it will have no influence on unprejudiced minds, or, if it operates at all, it will be to the advantage of the object of it, telling rather to his credit than to his dishonour. Few will deny that the man who has raised himself by his own merits has more true nobility than one who can only boast an unimpeachable pedigree.

No means exist of tracing whether the ancestors of the great lord chancellor were allied with the last-noticed Henry Somer, but this family originally spelling their name Somer would seem to give probability to the connection. Subsequently it was changed to Sommers, often written Somers, with a circumflex over the m, denoting the double letter. By degrees the circumflex was omitted, and the modern method of writing the name adopted.

The father of Lord Somers was John Somers, a respectable attorney practising at Worcester, who had taken arms during the civil war on the side of the parliament, and commanded a troop of horse in Cromwell's army. So zealous a partisan was he, that while attending divine service at Severnstoke, near which he was quartered, he is said to have once fired a pistol over the head of the clergyman, a furious loyalist, who was haranguing his congregation with violent invectives against the opposite party. The shot, which was meant to caution, not to injure, the indiscreet minister, whom he had frequently warned, lodged in the sounding-board of the pulpit, where its mark is still pointed out. When he performed this foolish feat he was still a young man, for his marriage with Catherine Ceavern, of a good Shropshire family, did not take place till November 1648, when his father settled the family estate of Severnstoke upon him. On the termination of the civil war with the battle of Worcester, fought on September 3, 1651, Mr. Somers returned to that city, and commenced or resumed his practice as an attorney, for it is uncertain whether he had actually entered the profession before he had adopted the military life. He soon established a very profitable business in settling the deranged affairs of those who had suffered in the late disturbances, and in superintending the estates of the Earls of Shrewsbury, at the same time engaging in the clothing trade, then a staple employment of his county, and also in brickmaking, a profitable speculation at a time when his city required extensive repairs and rebuilding. At the Restoration he followed the example of others who had been implicated in the Rebellion, by suing out a full pardon for all offences he had committed, and, with an excellent character for integrity and charity, he died in January 1681, nearly five years after his son was called to the bar.

The biographers of the chancellor all concur in stating that he was born in the mansion of White Ladies, the remains of an ancient nunnery in the parish of Cluines, contiguous to the city of Worcester, which had been held sacred and left uninjured by both parties in the convulsions of the times. It was then occupied by Mr. Blurton, the husband of the chancellor's aunt, on whom it had been settled by her father as a marriage portion; and Mrs. Somers is represented as retiring to this mansion as a safe retreat to await her accouchement of her second child, the future chancellor, with whom she was then pregnant. It turns out, however, that this account is totally incorrect. He was born in the city itself; the house is shown in which his father then resided; and the register of the parish of St. Michael's, which is close to the cathedral and nearly a mile from the White Ladies, records his birth there on March 4, 1650–1. As the battle of Worcester was not fought till September 1651, Mrs. Somers must have retired there after the birth of her child; and King Charles, whose last resort it was before his escape, must have found the boy six months old.

Young Somers was brought up under the care of his aunt at the house of White Ladies, which was his home till he went to the university. The rudiments of his education he received partly at the college school in Worcester, and partly at private schools at Walsall in Staffordshire, and at Sheriff-Hales in Shropshire. While at the school at Worcester he regularly dieted with his father, at whose country house at Clifton in Severnstoke he also spent his summer vacations. At this period of his life he showed little inclination for the amusements of boyhood, seldom joining in the games of his schoolfellows, and more often to be seen with a book in his hand. (*Seward's Anecdotes*, ii. 112.) His early biographers fix his entrance into Trinity College, Oxford, so late as the year 1674, when he was twenty-two or twenty-three years of age, and consequently find a difficulty in accounting for his time in the interval between this date and his leaving school. Subsequent enquiry has removed the difficulty, by showing that he was matriculated on March 23, 1667, at the age of 16, and the books of the Middle Temple record his admission into that society on May 24, 1669. The eminence to which he attained in his future career both in literature and in law sufficiently proves how industriously he must have employed the years he spent in each of these seminaries. In the former he continued occasionally to reside till 1682, though he did not aspire to any academical honour, nor even take a degree; and by the latter he was called to the bar on May 6, 1676.

While his father lived he retired in the vacations to White Ladies, where, in 1672, Charles, Earl (afterwards Duke) of Shrewsbury, then a boy of eleven or twelve years old, came to reside. Between him and Somers was then formed a close intimacy, which lasted throughout their lives, the young lawyer benefiting by the society to which his noble friend introduced him, and the young earl profiting by the wise and constitutional lessons which he insensibly imbibed from the conversation and conduct of his more staid companion. The total want of any authentic particulars of his occupations or course of study during these years some of his biographers, regardless of date or probability, have supplied by minute details that exhibit more of fancy than ingenuity. The story that he held a desk in his father's office, by which they attempt to fill up the supposed interval, is refuted by the fact that he was sent at sixteen to the university, and that he was entered two years after as a student in an inn of court, and is rendered still more mprobable by their making him at the same time clerk to Sir Francis Winnington. This honest lawyer and statesman was a native of Worcester and a friend of Somers's father. In his chambers young Somers was doubtless at one time a pupil; but, as Sir Francis was removed from his office of solicitor-general in 1679, and was not elected member for Worcester till that year, it seems likely that his then joining the party in opposition to the court was the commencement or the increase of the intimacy between the families. Young Somers at that time had been for three years called to the bar, and there can be no doubt that Sir Francis's countenance and advice greatly assisted him in his professional pursuits.

The political principles of Somers were already known, from his association with the leaders of the liberal party, and his talents were soon recognised by the use they made of his pen. Within the next two years several pamphlets, both legal and political, appeared, of which, though published without his name and never publicly acknowledged, he was then believed, and has since been proved, to have been the author. Their ability and power at once marked him as an opponent of the court, and no doubt, during the remainder of Charles's reign, and the whole of James's, prevented the promotion in his profession which his talents would have otherwise commanded. His reputation among his legal companions, as a staunch advocate of popular principles at this early period, is exemplified by a curious scene which Narcissus Luttrell, under the date of June 16, 1681, thus describes:—

'An address of thanks to the king for his late declaration [with his reasons for dissolving the last two parliaments] moved in the Middle Temple, where several Templars meeting began to debate it, but they were opposed till the hall began to fill, and then the addressers called out for Mr. Montague to take the chair; those against it called for Mr. Sommers; on which a poll was demanded, but the addressers refused it, and carried Mr. Montague and sett him in the chair, and the other party pulled him out; on which high words grew, and some blows were given; but the addressers, seeing they could do no good in the hall, adjourned to the Divill tavern, and there signed the addresse; the other party kept in the hall, and fell to protesting against such illegal and arbitrary proceedings, &c., and presented the same to the bench as a grievance.'

The tracts the reputation of which had raised Somers's fame among his brother Templars were 'A History of the Succession,' published during the discussion of the Exclusion Bill in 1679 and 1680; and 'A just and modest Vindication of the proceedings of the two last Parliaments,' written in answer to the king's declaration of April 8, 1681, on the dissolution of the Oxford parliament. To the latter Algernon Sidney and Sir William Jones contributed, but it was principally composed by Somers. Subsequently appeared 'The memorable case of Denzil Onslow,' tried at Kingston in July 1681, in which the rights of electors were supported; and 'The security of Englishmen's Lives, or the Trust, Power and Duty of Grand Juries in England,' in which the privileges of that important body were defended. The latter arose from the abuse vented against the grand jury which refused to find the bill of indictment against the Earl of Shaftesbury in November 1681, and passed at the time as written by the Earl of Essex, but was afterwards known to be the production of Somers. (*Burnet*, ii. 276, 290; *State Trials*, xiv. 707, n.). Classical subjects also employed his pen; and some translations from Ovid which he produced are elegant samples of his poetical powers. 'Dryden's Satire to his Muse,' occasioned by the 'Absalom and Achitophel' of that poet, though often given to Somers, could not have been wholly his. Mr. Cooksey considers it as the joint production of him and Lord Shrewsbury; and it may possibly have been so, parts of the poem being too coarse for the polished lawyer, and parts too well balanced for the free and easy earl. To their united genius also Mr. Cooksey attributes the original conception of 'The Tale of a Tub,' which Swift, with their permission, afterwards (in 1704) published as his own. The evidence adduced, however, will not be considered sufficient to disprove the dean's authorship; but the biographer, had he been aware of the following incident, would doubtless have pressed it into his service, as a remarkable coincidence confirmatory of his argument, and would have quoted it as suggesting to the young lawyer a title to the amusing tale he was then engaged in sketching. On the trial of Sheriff Pilkington and others in May 1683 for a riot, Somers, who was one of the counsel for the defendants, challenged the array, and Serjeant (afterwards Chief Justice) Jeffreys, upon the challenge being read, called out, 'Here's a Tale of a Tub indeed!' (*Cooksey's Life*, 18, 23; *State Trials*, ix. 226.)

It is manifest that Somers must have had some business in the courts long previous to that trial, if the anecdote be true of his being engaged in a case before Lord Nottingham. He is stated to have been the junior of several counsel employed in it, and that on rising after them he said that 'he would not take up his lordship's time by repeating what had been so well urged by the gentlemen who went before him;' to which the lord chancellor replied, 'Pray go on, sir; I sit in this place to hear everybody; you never repeat, nor will you take up my time, and therefore I shall listen to you with pleasure.' Lord Nottingham died in December 1682, having been for many months before confined by illness, and could not have made such a reply, unless he had had several previous opportunities of noticing Somers's talents as an advocate.

During the next few years he industriously pursued his profession, and with such success that his fees amounted to 700*l*. a year. With such a proof of business, added to his political associates and literary reputation, it seems unaccountable that Sir Henry Pollexfen should have found any difficulty in inducing the seven bishops to employ him for their defence, or that they should have objected that he was too young and obscure—he being then in his thirty-eighth year and one of the 'consiliarii·' of the dean and chapter of Worcester. Pollexfen's threat to withdraw unless Somers was engaged was effectual, and the bishops had every reason to be grateful for his pertinacity, as Somers's assistance contributed in a considerable degree to secure the triumphant result, which was hailed with so much delight by all ranks of people. So greatly was his popularity increased that when James, frightened at the threatened approach of the Prince of Orange, restored the charters to the city of London, the citizens elected Somers their recorder on October 23, 1688, an office which he respectfully declined, anticipating no doubt the prince's perseverance, notwithstanding the dispersion of his invading fleet a few days before. To the Convention Parliament, summoned by the prince for the following January, Somers was returned as the representative of his native city. In it he acted a most conspicuous part. Appointed one of the managers of the conference with the Lords upon the word 'abdicated,' he learnedly justified the vote of the Commons, and induced the Lords to agree with the resolution. As chairman of the committee to whom the Declaration of Rights was referred, that valuable charter of England's liberties owes much of its excellence to his judgment and care; and to his temperance, caution, and foresight the country is mainly indebted for the happy settlement that was then secured, and for the freedom it now enjoys.

In the re-establishment of the legal courts, and the appointment of the new officers, the claims of Somers were sure not to be overlooked. In May 1689 he was named solicitor-general, and was knighted in the following October, having been elected bencher of his inn on May 10. During the remainder of this parliament he entered actively into all the important debates, and by his effective services in this critical time he gained a great ascendancy in the counsels of the state. In 1690 he was elected recorder of Gloucester, and in the next parliament, meeting in March of that year, he sat again for Worcester, and pursued the same course, ably defending the principles of the Revolution, and carefully guarding the liberty of the subject. When this parliament had sat three sessions Somers received in May 1692 the office of attorney-general; and within a year he was removed to a more responsible station. Upon a change in the ministry the Great Seal was taken out of the hands of the commissioners, and offered to Sir John Somers, who, after attempting to decline it for some time, was at last induced to accept the charge as lord keeper on March 23, 1693, with a pension of 4000*l*. a year. On his elevation he took up his residence in Powis House, Lincoln's Inn Fields.

King William left England at the end of the month, and remained abroad till November, when, on the meeting of the parliament, the new lord keeper, not being yet a peer, sat (as in its future sessions) a silent speaker of the House of Lords. On its prorogation in May 1695, after the queen's death, the king proceeded to his customary campaign in Flanders, leaving Somers as lord keeper one of the lords justices for the administration of the government during his absence—a position which he occupied in all the future years in which he held the Great Seal. In the next session the ruinous depreciation of the coin by clipping and sweating was brought under consideration; and the remedy boldly proposed by Somers and Montagu, with the advice and assistance of Locke and Newton, was adopted, by which the currency was restored to a healthy state. On April 22, 1697, his title of lord keeper was changed to that of lord chancellor; and in December, though he had several times previously refused a peerage, he was created Baron Somers of Evesham; at the same time receiving from the king for the support of his honours some considerable grants, among which were the manors of Reigate and Hawleigh in Surrey. A new parliament was called at the end of the following year, which only sat till April 1700. In its last session the tories, having obtained a great ascendency, assailed the ministry, and directed their principal attack against Lord Somers, as having the greatest influence over the king, and forming the strongest barrier to their acquisition of power. So high ran party rage that a motion was made for an address to remove him from his majesty's presence and councils for ever. Though this, as were two other motions levelled against him, was negatived, by a large majority, the king, desirous of trying the effect of a complete change in his ministry, recommended Lord Somers to resign; but his lordship, disdaining to quail before his enemies, declined to take this course; and at length the king sent him an order to deliver up the Seal, which he immediately obeyed on the 17th of April.

Thus, though still possessing the confidence of the king, was Lord Somers by the malice of faction (for the term may be applicable to either party) dismissed from an office which he had held for seven years with the most unimpeachable integrity, preserving in the performance of its duties the high reputation he had previously gained, administering justice with inflexible impartiality, and establishing for himself a name, among lawyers for his capacity as a judge, and among statesmen for his ability as a legislator, which has lived in honour to the present day, and which even those who differ from him in politics do not venture to sully. So anxious was he to form correct opinions on the questions that came before him that he is said to have expended many hundred pounds in the purchase of books to prepare his famous judgment in the bankers' case; the reversal of which by the House of Lords, just before his dismissal, arose, it is believed, more from a sense of compassion for the individuals interested, joined with the spirit of party, than from a consideration of the legal points on which it turned. His decisions in Chancery are reported by Vernon and Peere Williams; and there are two state trials on which he presided as lord high steward while he held the Seal, one of Lord Warwick, and the other of Lord Mohun, both for murder, the former of whom was found guilty of manslaughter, and the latter was a second time acquitted. So deep was the admiration of his ability among the lawyers, and so great their hesitation to risk a comparison with him, that King William found a difficulty in procuring a successor, many eminent members of the legal body refusing to accept the offer of the Seal.

But Lord Somers had still another ordeal to undergo. The tories, now being admitted into power, renewed their attack upon him in the next parliament, which met in February 1701. On April 1 they carried a vote, by the small majority of ten, that 'by advising his majesty in the year 1698 to the Treaty of Partition of the Spanish monarchy, whereby large territories were to be delivered up to France,' he was 'guilty of a high crime and misdemeanour;' and thereupon they sent up to the House of Lords an impeachment against him, together with Lords Portland, Orford, and Halifax, against whom they had passed similar votes. The articles against Lord Somers, which were not presented till May 19, were fourteen in number, six of which had reference to the Partition Treaty; five were charges of obtaining extraordinary grants for his own benefit; another, that he granted a commission to the famous pirate William Kidd, of the Adventure galley, with a view of participating in the spoils to be obtained thereby; and, lastly, a general one imputing maladministration in his court, by delaying and making illegal orders in the causes before him. To these charges he gave full and satisfactory answers five days after they were delivered. A dispute then arose between the two houses as to the order and time of proceeding, which was aggravated by some bitter truths uttered by Lord Haversham at a free conference. The Commons took advantage of these to refuse to appear at the trial, which was fixed for June 17, on which day the Lords, in consequence of the absence of all evidence in support of the charges, acquitted Lord Somers and dismissed the impeachment. The same course was afterwards taken on the trial of Lord Orford; and the impeachments against the other lords were dismissed at the close of the session, no articles being exhibited against them. The whole of these proceedings were prompted by party animosity, and it seems evident that the accusers had no real intention of bringing the lords to trial, and got up the disagreement with the other house as a pretext for not proceeding in the business. To put an end to these heats the king first prorogued and then dissolved the parliament, calling another to meet in December 1701. In the interim a plan was formed by Sunderland to restore the Seal to Somers, who, though he held no ostensible place in the ministry, is supposed to have assisted in framing the king's speech on the opening of the new parliament. This speech, in consequence of the recent recognition by the King of France of the son of James II. as successor to the throne of England, was rapturously welcomed by the people as highly spirited and patriotic, and was the more valued as it was the last which William addressed to parliament, his death occurring on the 8th of the following March. To his last moments he continued his friendship for Lord Somers, and had so complete a confidence in him that he was privately engaged with him in reconstructing the whig ministry when his decease confirmed the tories in power.

During the first six years of the reign of Queen Anne, to whom Somers was personally obnoxious, he confined himself to his duties as a peer of parliament. He carried a bill for the amendment of the law; he laid the foundation of improvements in the introduction of private bills; he greatly assisted in passing the Regency Bill, which provided for the Hanoverian succession; he took an active part in promoting the union with Scotland, the scheme of which he had projected in the previous reign, and one of the managers of which he was now appointed; and from his pen proceeded most of the important papers of the time. The prejudices of the queen were in some measure softened in 1705, and on the death of her husband, Somers was, in November 1708, again taken into the ministry as lord president of the council, an office which he held for two years, when on another change it was given to the Earl of Rochester. Though the queen dismissed him with the rest of the whigs, she professed great regard for him, and declared that she could always trust him, for he had never deceived her. She died in August 1714, and for the two years that he survived in the reign of George I., though his friends were restored to power, and he had a place in the cabinet without office, he took no public share in business, being gradually incapacitated by a paralytic affection, which at last reduced him to a state of imbecility. He died on April 26, 1716, and was buried at Mimms in Hertfordshire, in which parish his country residence, called Brockman's, was situate.

As the leader of a great party, Lord Somers's character among his contemporaries was as much assailed by his opponents as it was lauded by his supporters, the estimate of each being possibly greatly exaggerated. But the same individual is very rarely to be found in the ranks both of extollers and detractors who is so indiscreet as to leave a public record of his contradictory judgments. Dean Swift was not ashamed to be guilty of this. In his 'Discourse of the contests and dissensions between the Nobles and Commons in Athens and Rome,' written while he was united with the whig party, he represents Lord Somers, under the character of Aristides, as a person of the strictest justice, and as having performed such mighty service to his country that to his recall to power the state would owe its preservation. His 'History of the last years of the Queen,' published when he was connected with the tories, is written in a directly contrary spirit, depreciating the services his lordship had performed, imputing selfish motives to all his actions, and disparaging all the good qualities attributed to him. Addison's noble character of Somers in the 'Freeholder,' written soon after his death, affords a picture which, though somewhat too strongly coloured to suit all opinions, is recognised in the present day, even by those of different politics, as forming a just and fair representation. The truest estimate of a man's character is made by those who come after him and are not influenced by personal partialities or prejudices; and Somers's learning and judgment, his honesty, his eloquence, his modesty, mildness, candour, and taste, together with his sweetness of temper, have been acknowledged by all modern authors of whose writings he has been the subject. He was elected president of the Royal Society in 1698, and resigned it in 1703 in favour of Sir Isaac Newton; and among the men of literature and science whom he honoured with his patronage were Newton, Locke, Addison, and Bayle. The encouragement he extended to the publication of that valuable collection of state papers called 'Rymer's Fœdera,' and also to that excellent history of the Exchequer by Madox, justifies the latter author in placing him in the upper ranks of the lovers of antiquity, and in celebrating in his 'Prefatory Epistle' the public benefit he conferred on the nation by the care of its repositories and the preservation of its records.

As he never married, his title became extinct, but was revived in 1784 in the person of Sir Charles Cocks, Bart., the grandson of his sister Mary. The name still graces the House of Lords, with the additional title of an earl, granted in 1821. He left a fine and well-assorted library, which was divided between Sir Joseph Jekyll, master of the Rolls, who married his sister Elizabeth, and his nephew Sir Philip

Yorke (afterwards Earl of Hardwicke), and contained a valuable collection of tracts and manuscripts. A selection of the former was published in 1795 under the name of the 'Somers Tracts' in sixteen volumes, and again in 1809 in twelve volumes, edited by Sir Walter Scott. The manuscripts, which originally filled sixty quarto volumes, were unfortunately destroyed in an accidental fire in Lincoln's Inn in 1752, which consumed the chambers of the Hon. Charles Yorke, where they were deposited. A few fragments were preserved from the flames, and were published by the Earl of Hardwicke in 1778. (*Life of Lord Somers*, 1716; also Lives by *Cooksey*, *Maddock*, *Roscoe*, *Lord Campbell*, in *Chalmers's Biog. Dict.*, and in *Townsend's House of Commons*.)

SOREWELL, WILLIAM DE, or SHOREWELL, was united with Peter de Rupibus, Bishop of Winchester, in the sheriffalty of Hampshire for seven years, commencing 2 Henry III.; and with Joscelin, Bishop of Bath, in the sheriffalty of the county of Somerset, in part of the ninth year of that reign. In 10 Henry III. he was one of those employed to collect the quinzime of the former county; and early in the next year, 1227, he was selected as a justice itinerant into the latter county, and also into Dorsetshire and Wiltshire. He did not long survive this appointment, for on August 7, 1228, his brother and heir, Robert, was permitted to pay a sum of 22*l*. due from him for the time he was sheriff of Hants, in three instalments. (*Rot. Claus.* ii. 23, 147, 205; *Excerpt. e Rot. Fin.* i. 175.)

SOTHERTON, JOHN, whose name was probably derived from a village so called in Suffolk, was of a family long settled at Norwich, to which city it had provided several sheriffs and representatives in parliament. He was born there about 1525, and, being placed in the Exchequer, was in 1558 admitted to the office of foreign apposer. (*Exch. Records*.) After performing the duties belonging to it for above twenty years, he was raised to the bench of that court as a puisne baron on June 16, 1579. During the remainder of Elizabeth's reign he continued to occupy the seat, and receiving a new patent on the accession of James I., he held it till his death on October 26, 1605. His remains were deposited in the church of St. Botolph, Little Britain, Aldersgate Street, in the same tomb with his two wives—Frances, daughter and heir of John Smith of Cromer in Norfolk; and Maria, daughter of Edward Woton, M.D. By the former he had a son, Christopher; and by the latter a son, John, and a daughter, Maria. (*Stow's London*, 332.)

Queen Elizabeth granted him the manor of Wadenhall in Waltham, Kent, and he possessed property in Norwich, on which the city Bridewell now stands. (*Hasted*, ix. 322; *Blomefield's Norwich*, i. 277, ii. 318.)

SOTHERTON, NOWELL, was probably of the same family as the above John Sotherton, by whom he was in all likelihood introduced into the Exchequer. He was the son of John Sotherton, sheriff of Norwich in 1565, and Mary, daughter of Augustin Stevens. He is called of Gray's Inn, but never was a reader there, nor does his name occur in any of the Reports either as an advocate or a judge. Nearly nine months after Baron John Sotherton's death he was made a baron of the Exchequer, his patent being dated July 8, 1606; but as there were at that time already four barons on that bench, who were all serjeants-at-law and entirely unaccustomed to the fiscal duties attached to the office, the probability is that he was the first extra baron appointed for that special service, under the title of cursitor baron, with minor privileges and holding a lower rank than the other barons, and in no way joining with them in their judicial functions. He became master of the Merchant Taylors' Company in London in 1597.

He died before October 27, 1610, as a certificate of the rest of the barons to the lord high treasurer, in favour of Thomas Cæsar, bears that date, and was buried at St. Botolph's, Aldersgate. His wife was a daughter of Anthony Williams, auditor of the Mint. (*Blomefield's Norwich*, ii. 317.)

SOTHERTON, JOHN, was probably the son of the above-named baron John Sotherton, by his second wife, Maria, daughter of Edward Woton, M.D. He was an officer of the Exchequer, and in July 1604 was appointed receiver-general for the counties of Bedford and Buckingham. On October 29, 1610, he was placed as a baron of the Exchequer (*Cal. St. Papers* [1603-10], 135, 639), and was allowed by an order of the Inner Temple (to which he had been admitted in 1588) to 'have his place at the bench table above all the readers in such sort as Sir Thomas Cæsar, knight, late puisne baron of the Exchequer, had.' (*Dugdale's Orig.* 149.) This proves that he had not been a reader to the society, and that he was not of the degree of the coif, because if he had been, he would no longer have been a member of that house, but of Serjeants' Inn. On December 5 he was one of the commissioners with the lord mayor who tried Mackalley's case at the Old Bailey (9 *Coke's Reports*, 62), and was so employed on other occasions; but, as he is never mentioned as sitting in the Exchequer Court, nor as joining in the conferences of the other judges during the remainder of James's reign, it would seem, in connection with the above facts, that he held the office which is now called cursitor baron. This impression derives greater weight from the fact that in a special commission to enquire into defective titles, issued in 1622, he is named after the attorney-general, though two other barons of the Exchequer, Denham and Bromley, are inserted previous to that officer. The same order of precedence is preserved in another commission in the following year on the same subject; and in a commission relative to nuisances in London, in 1624, several knights and the recorder of London intervene between the other barons and him. (*Rymer*, xvii. 388, 512, 540.)

The same remark applies also to the reign of Charles, in which he lived several years. The Reports never mention him but once, and then only as transacting business which was 'of course' (cursitor). In the year 1630, the plague raging in London, Michaelmas Term was adjourned from one return to another, and it is recorded that the essoigns of one of them was kept by Mr. Baron Sotherton (2 *Croke, Car.* 200), which was a mere formality. He died in the course of the next year, his successor, James Pagitt, being appointed on October 24, 1631.

He married Elizabeth, widow of Sir John Morgan, of Chilworth, Surrey. (*Manning and Bray's Surrey*, ii. 118.)

SOUTHAMPTON, EARL OF. See T. WRIOTHESLEY.

SOUTHCOTE, JOHN, of Southcote, belonged to an old Devonshire family, and was the eldest son of William, a younger son of Nicholas Southcote, of Chudleigh in that county. He was born in 1511, and being sent to the Middle Temple, he rose to be reader in autumn 1556, and again in 1559, on the occasion of his being called upon to take the degree of the coif. Previously to this, however, he is mentioned in Plowden as under-sheriff, and one of the judges of the Sheriff's Court in London, in 1553; and his arguments after he became serjeant are reported both by that author and Dyer. He was nominated as a judge of the Queen's Bench on February 10, 1563, and performed his judicial duties with high reputation for the space of twenty-one years, when he retired on May 29, 1584. He died on April 18, 1585, and was buried under a stately monument in the parish church of Witham in Essex, in which county he had purchased the manors of Bacons or Abbotts, and Petworths.

By his wife, Elizabeth, daughter and heir of William Robins of London, he had thirteen children. His son John succeeded him; and one of his descendants, then of Blighborough in Lincolnshire, was raised in January 1662 to a baronetcy, which became extinct in 1691. (*Dugdale's Orig.* 217; *Machyn's Diary*, 373; *Morant*, ii. 110.)

SOUTHWELL, ROBERT, was of a family which took its name from the town of Southwell in Nottinghamshire, records of which exist as ancient as the reign of Edward I. One of its branches was established at Felix Hall in Essex; and Robert was the second son of Francis, auditor of the Exchequer to Henry VIII., and his wife Dorothy, daughter and heir of William Tendring, Esq. Their eldest son was Sir Richard Southwell, privy councillor to Henry VIII., and ancestor of the present Baroness de Clifford.

Robert, after studying at the Middle Temple, became reader there in autumn 1540. (*Dugdale's Orig.* 216.) His connection with the court at this time is evidenced by several entries in the books of the privy council. In October he was employed to enquire into a riot in the county of Surrey; in January 1541 he is mentioned as one of the masters of the Court of Requests, and as directed to search the coffers of one Mason, apprehended for some offence, and to provide him with bedding, &c., in the Tower; and in April he was joined with the president and council of the North in a commission of Oyer and Terminer. On July 1 in that year he received the appointment of master of the Rolls, and was thereupon knighted. In the following November he was engaged as one of the king's commissioners at Calais; and his opinion on the subject of his mission was read to the council. (*Acts Privy Council*, vii. 74, &c.)

Beyond commissions granted to him and other masters in Chancery in aid of Lord Wriothesley in 1544 and 1547, and of Lord Rich in 1550, no account remains of the exercise of his judicial functions. It is known that he benefited largely in the distribution of the estates belonging to the suppressed monasteries, among which he had a grant of Bermondsey Abbey, and erected a capital mansion on its site. (*Phillips's Hist.* 6.)

In December 1550 he surrendered his patent of master of the Rolls, and retired to his estate at Jote's Place in the parish of Mereworth in Kent, which he acquired by his marriage with Margaret, daughter and heir of Thomas Nevill, a younger son of George Lord Bergavenny. He was sheriff of that county on the accession of Queen Mary, and signalised himself in the suppression of Wyat's rebellion. For his good services on this occasion he was rewarded with the manner of Aylesford, forfeited by this foolish adventurer. (*Hasted*, iv. 426, v. 83.) Burnet and Carte have confounded him with his brother Sir Richard.

His death occurred in November 1559, and the heraldic honours of his funeral in Kent are recorded in Henry Machyn's Diary (p. 217). His portrait, in the possession of Lord Clifford, is said to have been drawn by Hans Holbein at one sitting.

SPAIGNE, NICHOLAS DE, is first mentioned as one of the clerks in Chancery in 45 Edward III., when he was the last of four of them appointed to hold the Great Seal during the absence of Sir Robert de Thorpe, the chancellor, on March 18, 1371. In that and the two following years he was one of the receivers of petitions to the parliament, and died about 1374. He seems to have been connected with the county of York. (*Rot. Parl.* ii. 303, 309, 317; *Abb. Rot. Orig.* ii. 304.)

SPALDEWICK, WILLIAM DE (ABBOT OF COLCHESTER), was placed at the head of the justices itinerant who visited Essex and Hertfordshire in 38 Henry III., 1254, according to the not unusual practice of so honouring a dignified ecclesiastic of the neighbourhood. He was elected abbot on April 22, 1245, and died about July 8, 1272. (*Browne Willis,* i. 66.)

SPALDING, JOHN DE, prior of Spalding, was one of the justices itinerant into Essex in 56 Henry III., 1272. He was eminent for his knowledge of the laws, and had been summoned to council in 49 Henry III. (*Law and Lawyers,* ii. 331.)

SPELMAN, JOHN. The pedigree of the Spelmans, as drawn out by the learned antiquary Sir Henry Spelman, commences three generations before the reign of Henry III., with William Spileman, knight, lord of Brokenhurst in Hampshire. The family afterwards removed into Suffolk, and in the fifteenth century into Norfolk, where they possessed very large estates. Henry Spelman, the father of the judge, is described in this pedigree as holding no less than eight manors. He was himself a lawyer, and for many years recorder of Norwich, and once its representative in parliament. He died in 1496, leaving by his second wife, Ela, daughter and heir of William de Narburgh of Narburgh in Norfolk, seven children, of whom the judge was the youngest son.

John Spelman studied the law at Gray's Inn, where he was appointed reader in 1514, and again in 1519. He was called to the degree of the coif in Trinity Term 1521, and made king's serjeant in 1528, and he is introduced among the judges of the King's Bench in 24 Henry VIII., 1532; and Coke, in 3 Report (44), mentions a judgment of his in Trinity Term of that year. In 1535 he officiated as a commissioner on the trials of Sir Thomas More and Bishop Fisher; and in the following year he was no doubt present at that of Queen Anne Boleyn, since Burnet says that he had seen an account of it written in the judge's own hand. (*State Trials,* i. 387, 398, 412.) He died on February 26, 1544, according to the inscription on his tomb in Narburgh Church, his figure on which, in the robe and coif of a judge, is engraved in Cotman's 'Norfolk Brasses.'

He married Elizabeth, the daughter and heir of Sir Henry Frowyk, of Gunnersbury in Middlesex, the elder brother of Chief Justice Sir Thomas Frowyk. By her he had a family of twenty children, thirteen sons and seven daughters. His fifth son, Henry, was the father of the eminent antiquary Sir Henry, whose second son was the next-mentioned Clement Spelman. (*Gibson's Life of Sir H. Spelman;* Weever, 820; *Blomefield's Norwich,* i. 171.)

SPELMAN, CLEMENT, was the great-grandson of the last-named judge, and the son of Sir Henry Spelman, by his wife, Alienora, the eldest daughter and coheir of John Le Strange of Hunstanton in Norfolk. Sir Henry was knighted by King James I. for his public services, and devoted the last thirty years of his life to those studies, and the production of those works, which have established his reputation as one of the most learned antiquaries this country ever produced. He died in October 1641, leaving four sons and four daughters, and was buried in Westminster Abbey.

Clement, the youngest of these sons, was admitted a pensioner of Queens' College, Cambridge, on September 16, 1616. He had been previously entered at Gray's Inn, the school in which his great-grandfather had studied, so early as March 1613, but was not called to the bar till 1624. As his name never occurs in the Reports of the time, he probably devoted himself to literary pursuits, and assisted his father in his antiquarian enquiries; for to the Oxford edition (1646) of Sir Henry's treatise 'De non Temerandis Ecclesiis,' he wrote a large preface containing many things relating to impropriations and several instances of the judgments of God upon sacrilege. In 1647 he published anonymously 'Reasons for admitting the King to a personal treaty in Parliament and not by Commissioners;' and in the next year, 'A Letter to the Assembly of Divines concerning Sacrilege.' These works, and the active assistance he gave to the king in 1648, are evidences sufficient that he was a decided royalist.

In connection with the law, he is stated to have been one of the performers in 1635 in a masque called the 'Triumphs of Prince d'Amour,' by Sir William Davenant, provided for the entertainment of Charles, the Elector Palatine, at the Middle Temple; but it is not clear how this could be, unless the Middle Temple borrowed assistance from Gray's Inn. Of the latter inn Spelman was made an ancient in 1638 and a bencher at the Restoration. At that time, A. Wood says, on the authority of Dugdale, that Spelman published a 'Character of the Oliverians,' which he intimates is the same as 'The Mystery of the Good Old Cause briefly unfolded in a Catalogue of such Members of the late Long Parliament, who held offices both civil and military, &c.,' which will be found at the end of the third volume of Hansard's 'Parliamentary History.'

His loyal services were rewarded by the appointment of cursitor baron of the Exchequer on March 9, 1663, an office which he occupied till March 1679. He died in the ensuing June, and was buried in St. Dunstan's Church in Fleet Street. (*Athen. Oxon.* iii. 807, iv. 8; *Notes and Queries*, 3rd S. v. 152.)

SPIGURNEL, HENRY. Spigurnel was the name given to the officer who sealed the writs in Chancery, and was by degrees adopted as the surname of the family, by which the duty continued, probably during many successions, to be executed. The first who is mentioned is Godfrey Spigurnel, who, in a grant in 9 John of five bovates of land and a mill in Skeggeby in Nottinghamshire, is styled 'serviens noster de capellâ nostrâ. (*Rot. Chart.* 169.) He had a grant of three 'oboli' a day out of the ferm of the town of Hertford, and is last mentioned in 11 Henry III. (*Rot. Claus.* i. 356, ii. 182.)

In succession came Henry Spigurnel, who possessed lands in Northamptonshire above 20*l.* a year, and was summoned in respect thereof to perform military service in 25 Edward I., 1297. In the same year his name is among the justices and members of the council summoned to parliament, and he appears to have acted in a judicial character in the previous year. (*Parl. Writs*, i. 52, 289; *Abb. Rot. Orig.* i. 97.)

In Hilary 1301 he and William de Ormesby are recorded as holding 'locum regis' at Lincoln, 'in absencia R. de Brabanzon;' and in Easter of the same year, on the Roll of Pleas 'coram domino rege' at Worcester, these two and Gilbert de Roubury are mentioned as holding the court in the absence of the chief justice (*Abb. Placit.* 242, 245); and further, in the writ directing him to take the oaths on the accession of Edward II., his previous seat in the court is referred to. (*Parl. Writs*, ii. p. ii. 3.)

From his appointment till 19 Edward II., he seems to have been most active in the performance of his duties, and to have been employed as one entrusted with affairs of confidence. In 4 Edward II. he was one of the king's nuncios to the council, and was sent to Rome on a special mission; and in the seventh year he was summoned to undertake, with the Bishop of Worcester and three others, an embassy beyond the seas. Although returned by the sheriff of Bedford in 17 Edward II. as a knight beyond sixty years of age and unfit for service, we find him acting in the following year as a justice itinerant in the islands of Jersey and Guernsey. His last recorded appearance as a judge is in the parliament of November 1325, 19 Edward II., but his death did not occur till three years afterwards.

The only account of his character is in a political song, in which, when spoken of as a justice of trailbaston in 33 Edward I., he is described as 'gent de cruelté;' but too much reliance must not be placed on so suspicious an authority.

He lived at Kenilworth, and, according to his own return in 1316, was lord or joint-lord of various townships in the counties of Bedford, Buckingham, Oxford, and Northampton. He had also property in Essex and Leicestershire. By his wife, Sarah, he had issue, and his sons represented the county of Bedford in 1 and 14 Edward II. (*Rot. Parl.* i. 137–449; *Wright's Political Songs*, 233.)

STAFFORD, EDMUND DE (BISHOP OF EXETER), was the grandson of Sir Richard de Stafford, of Clifton in Staffordshire, who was the younger brother of Ralph, created Earl of Stafford in 1351, and the son of another Richard, who was summoned to parliament as a baron in 1371. He was born about the year 1345, and, being educated for the priesthood, he was appointed dean of York in August 1385. (*Le Neve*, 314.) He became keeper of the privy seal in 1391, 14 Richard II. (*Rot. Parl.* iii. 264), and was raised to the bishopric of Exeter on January 15, 1395.

The Great Seal was delivered to him on November 23, 1396, and he sat as chancellor in the parliament of the following January and September, and in the latter swore to observe the arbitrary statutes which, by the royal influence, were then passed, and which in a short time led to the king's ruin. (*Rot. Parl.* iii. 337, 347, 355.)

The precise date of his retirement from the office is not known, but he certainly held it when Henry of Bolingbroke landed at Ravensburn on July 4, 1399. So soon afterwards, however, as August 13, his predecessor, Archbishop Arundel, having returned with Henry from his banishment, was again in possession of the Great Seal, and exercising the duties of chancellor.

Although a friend of King Richard, it is evident that he succeeded in disarming the new monarch of any enmity he might indulge against him on that account. He attended in his place in the first parliament of Henry IV., and was one of the prelates who assented to the imprisonment of the deposed king. In little more than seventeen months after the commencement of the new reign he was reinstated in the office of chancellor. The Seal, which was delivered to him by the king on March 9, 1401,' remained in his hands about two years—viz., till the end of February 1403. History is silent as to the cause of his retirement; but that he retained the favour of the king is manifest, from his being selected as a trier of petitions in several subsequent parliaments, and also as one of the king's council. (*Rot. Parl.* 427, 545, 567, 572.)

He survived Henry IV. more than six years, and died on September 4, 1419, having presided over his diocese nearly a quarter of a century. His remains were deposited in his own cathedral, under an alabaster tomb, with a rhyming Latin inscription.

It may be presumed that he was educated at the university of Oxford, in the college then called Stapledon Hall, as he added two to its fellows, providing estates for their support, and as the name of Exeter College, which it now bears, is supposed to have been given from him. (*Godwin*, 412.)

STAFFORD, JOHN (ARCHBISHOP OF CANTERBURY), was the second son of Sir Humphrey Stafford, surnamed (whether from his generous disposition, or from having an artificial hand, does not appear) Sir Humphrey of the Silver Hand, and his wife Elizabeth, daughter and heir of — Dynham, and widow of Sir John Maltravers. His brother, Sir Humphrey Stafford, was the ancestor to another Humphrey, who was created Earl of Devon in 9 Edward IV., a title which he enjoyed only a few months, being beheaded in the same year. (*Baronage*, i. 172.)

Born at Houke in the parish of Abbotsbury, Dorsetshire, he was educated at Oxford, and, taking his degree in laws, afterwards practised as an advocate in the ecclesiastical courts. There he was advanced to be dean of the Arches; and in September 1419 he was collated archdeacon of Salisbury, and was made chancellor of that diocese in 1421. In May in the latter year he was in possession of the place of keeper of the privy seal, which he retained during the remainder of the reign of Henry V., and was re-appointed on the accession of Henry VI., his salary being twenty shillings a day. (*Rymer*, x. 117; *Rot. Parl.* iv. 171; *Acts Privy Council*, iii. 8.) In December 1422 he succeeded William Kynwelmersh both as dean of St. Martin's, London, and in the high office of treasurer of England. (*Monasticon*, vi. 1324.) The former he probably gave up on his becoming dean of Wells on September 9 in the following year; the latter he retained till March 13, 1426, when he resigned it. Elected Bishop of Bath and Wells on May 12, 1425, he was named as one of the lords of the council during the king's minority, and was most regular in his attendance at its meetings.

By a MS. letter in the British Museum, addressed by the king to him on July 11, 1428, it would appear that he had resumed his former office of keeper of the privy seal. In 1430 he accompanied the king to France, and had a salary as one of his counsellors there (*Acts Privy Council*, iii. 310, iv. 29); and in 1432, when Archbishop Kempe resigned the chancellorship, the Great Seal was transferred to his hands on March 4. He remained in this high office uninterruptedly for eighteen years wanting thirty-two days. He is the first possessor of the office who is known to have been called 'lord chancellor.' (*Rot. Parl.* v. 103.)

He was elected Archbishop of Canterbury on May 15, 1443; and about the same time he was appointed apostolic legate in England, by which title he is several times described. That of cardinal, which is frequently attached to his name in the list of the bishops, we do not find that he ever received; and the mistake has probably arisen from confounding him with Archbishop Kempe, who bore the same Christian name, and certainly was a cardinal.

The absurd practice of opening the parliament with a political speech introduced by a Scripture text was still continued; and he had numerous opportunities of displaying his eloquence, which occasionally was animated and impressive, but too often, according to the practice of the time, far-fetched, and tasteless in its application.

Throughout his lengthened possession of the Great Seal Archbishop Stafford was allowed to have exhibited that learning and caution and intelligence which were to be expected from his early character and his long experience. But it was his misfortune to witness during the same period the gradual loss of all those dominions in France for the acquisition of which Henry V. had been almost worshipped by the English; and thus to share in the unpopularity consequent on the reverses. Fuller, mistaking his parentage, quaintly says of him, 'No prelate (his peer in birth or preferment) hath either less good or less evil recorded of him.'

Whether induced by the consciousness of increasing infirmities, or dreading the storm then collecting against the Duke of Suffolk, or forced by the dissatisfaction of the people with the terms of the peace with France, for which he with the other ministers would be deemed responsible, he resigned the office of chancellor on January 31, 1450, or, in the terms of the record, 'exoneratus fuit.' The first use made by the king of the Great Seal was to attach it to a patent of pardon to the archbishop. He lived a little more than two years after his retirement, and dying at his palace at Maidstone on July 6, 1452, was interred in Canterbury Cathedral. (*Godwin*, 127, 379; *Le Neve*; *Hasted*, xii. 422.)

STANES, RICHARD DE, affords another example of a clerical judge, as the designation 'Magister,' always placed before his name, sufficiently proves. He seems to have acted as a justice itinerant before he became a justicier, visiting eleven counties in the former capacity in 52 Henry III., 1268, while his appointment as a justice of the King's Bench did not take place till the following year. From July 1269 till the end of the reign there are frequent entries of assizes to be held before him. In 55 Henry III. he is specially mentioned as a 'justiciarius ad placita tenenda coram rege;' and in the last month of the reign, 1272, he had a salary of 40l. a year assigned to him. (*Excerpt. e Rot. Fin.* ii. 493–586; *Madox*, ii. 203.)

There is no reason to suppose that he did not retain his place on the accession of Edward I.; but if he did so he must have been removed to the Court of Common Pleas in that or the following year, inasmuch as from Michaelmas in the latter till February 1276 (*Dugdale's Orig.* 44) fines were levied before him. He was present at the council held at the following Michaelmas. (*Parl. Writs*, i. 6.)

STANLEY, THOMAS DE, was one of the clerks of the Chancery from 11 Richard II., when he first appears as a receiver of petitions. (*Rot. Parl.* iii. 228–455.) He held this office for the ten following years, when he was constituted master of the Rolls, on September 11, 1397, 21 Richard II. On the banishment of Henry of Lancaster in the next year he was selected as one of his attorneys during his absence (*Rymer*, viii. 49), and, therefore, naturally retained his place when that prince usurped the government. He was superseded in September 1402 ; and it would seem that his offence was that he obtained the pope's bulls for certain benefices, a pardon being granted to him in the same year on that account. (*Cal. Rot. Pat.* 245.)

STAPLETON, MILO DE, was the son and heir of the undernamed Nicholas de Stapleton, and served Edward I. throughout his Scottish wars. When the first commission of trailbaston into Lancashire was issued, on March 12, 1305, he and John de Byrun were the two justices appointed under it; but in the following month they were superseded by the more comprehensive commissions which were then issued. (*Parl. Writs*, i. 407, ii. 67.)

He was seneschal of Knaresborough Castle in 33 Edward I. (*Abb. Rot. Orig.* i. 145), and was summoned to parliament as a baron in 6 and 7 Edward II., in the latter of which years he obtained a pardon, as an adherent of the Earl of Lancaster, for his participation in the murder of Gaveston. He died in the following year. (*Cal. Inquis.* p. m. i. 256.)

By his wife, Sibilla, a daughter of John de Bella Aqua, he left Nicholas, his son and heir; but the barony, by failure of male heirs in 47 Edward III., became vested in the representatives of Elizabeth, the wife of Thomas Metham, the sister of Thomas, the last lord. (*Baronage*, ii. 70.)

STAPLETON, NICHOLAS DE, was either son or grandson of a knight of the same name, who was governor of Middleham Castle in Yorkshire in the reign of John. (*Rot. Claus.* i. 248.) His residence was at Hachilsay (Weshacheslay) in that county. He is first mentioned in a Liberate Roll of 1 Edward I. as a judge of the King's Bench; and by another entry in 6 Edward I. it appears that a salary of fifty marks yearly was assigned to him in that character. Various judicial acts are recorded of him until Trinity, 17 Edward I., 1289; and he was summoned to parliament among the judges up to the previous year. (*Rot. Parl.* i. 349; *Parl. Writs*, i. 845; *Abb. Placit.* 205–279.)

He died in 1290 (*Cal. Inquis.* p. m. i. 103), leaving the above-named Milo his son and heir, and a daughter, Julian, who married Richard de Windsor. (*Collins's Peerage*, iii. 647.)

STARKEY, HUMPHREY, was descended from the Starkeys of Oulton and Wrenbury in Cheshire, a branch of the Starkeys of Nether Hall in Stretton in that county, a very ancient family. Sir Humphrey, having purchased the manor of Littlehall in the parish of Woldham in Kent, gave it his own name, and built there a good house, still standing, and a handsome chapel, very little of which remains.

The Inner Temple was the place of his legal studies, and the first instance of his forensic employment recorded in the Year Books is in Hilary Term, 32 Henry VI., 1454. In 11 Henry VII., 1471, he was elected recorder of London, and the Year Books notice his appearance in court in that character as late as 1483, when he resigned the office on being raised to the bench at Westminster. Before that event happened he was called serjeant in Trinity Term 1478. His appointment as chief baron of the Exchequer is dated June 15, 1483, only ten days before the dethronement of Edward V., so that he was obliged to have a new patent from the usurper, which he received on the 26th of the same month, having previously been knighted. Although Dugdale does not introduce him among the justices of the Common Pleas in the reign of Richard III., it is certain that he held both appointments, as several of his predecessors had done, and it is probable that his patent for the latter bore even date with that for the former. Two fines levied before the judges of the Common Pleas in the first and second years of the reign are referred to in the Rolls of Parliament, and his name appears in each of them. (*Rot. Parl.* vi. 332, 341.) On the accession of Henry VII. his patents for both places were renewed on the same day.

He died early in the second year of that reign; his last fine is at Midsummer 1486 (*Dugdale's Orig.* 47), and William Hody was appointed his successor as chief baron on October 29. He was buried in St. Leonard's, Shoreditch, with his wife, whose name was Isabella. They left no male issue, and their four daughters divided the inheritance. (*Hasted*, iv. 404; *Morant*, i. 161.)

STATHAM, NICHOLAS, was elected reader of Lincoln's Inn in Lent 1471, 11 Edward IV. (*Dugdale's Orig.* 249), and received on October 30, 1467, a patent for the grant of the office of second baron of the Exchequer in reversion on the death or surrender of John Clerke. As the date of John Clerke's death is not known, and as Statham's name is never mentioned afterwards, it is uncertain whether he ever filled the office. All we know is, that either on his or on Clerke's death Thomas Whitington was appointed second baron on February 3, 1481, 20 Edward IV.

Although he never once is mentioned in the Year Books, an 'abridgment of the cases reported in them to the end of the reign of Henry VI., being the first attempt at a work of that nature, goes under his name.

STAUNFORD, WILLIAM, was grandson of Robert Staunford of Rowley in Staffordshire, and son of William Staunford of London, mercer, by his wife Margaret, the daughter and heir of — Gedney of London. His birth took place in his father's house at Hadley in Middlesex on August 22, 1509. After receiving a classical education at Oxford, he pursued his legal studies at Gray's Inn, where he was called to the bar in 1536, and was appointed reader in 1544, and again in 1551. (*Dugdale's Orig.* 293.)

He designates himself as attorney-general on May 3, 1545, in his surrender to King Henry of all the title he had in the rectory of South Mymes in Middlesex. (*Rymer*, xv. 69.) The date of his nomination to that office does not appear, and it is certain that he did not hold it later than the 18th of the following month, when Henry Bradshaw received the appointment. Edward VI. called him to the degree of the coif on May 19, 1552; and on October 19, 1553, three months after the accession of Mary, whose religion he professed, he was made one of the queen's serjeants. He was named on the commission under Edward which deprived Bishop Tunstall, a sentence which in the first year of Queen Mary was set aside (*Ibid.* 346); and he conducted on the part of the crown the prosecution against Sir Nicholas Throckmorton, in which, making allowance for the difference of times, he does not seem to have pressed the prisoner with any unfair harshness. (*State Trials*, i. 869.)

A few months after this trial, which took place on April 17, 1554, Staunford was raised to the bench, and the first fine levied before him was in the month after Michaelmas 1554. (*Dugdale's Orig.* 48.) He was knighted by King Philip on January 27, 1555 (*Machyn's Diary*, 342), and retained his seat in the Common Pleas during the rest of his life, which terminated on August 28, 1558, three months before the demise of Queen Mary. He was buried in Hadley Church.

He was a great and learned lawyer, and distinguished himself not only by encouraging the first publication of Ranulph de Glanville's 'Tractatus de Legibus et Consuetudinibus Angliæ' (*Coke's* 4 *Inst.* 345), but also as the author of two highly esteemed works—viz., a Treatise on the Pleas of the Crown, and an Exposition of the King's Prerogative, the former of which is still of great authority. The antithetical David Lloyd (219) describes his character in his usual encomiastic manner, and sums it up thus: 'He had those lower virtues that draw praise from the vulgar, which he neglected (knowing that they were more taken with appearances than realities); he had middle, that they admired and good men observed; he had his highest virtues, which they received and great men honoured. In a word, a fragrant fame he had, that filled all round about, and would not easily away.'

His wife, Alice, the daughter of John Palmer, Esq., survived him, and took as her second husband Roger Carew, Esq., of Hadley. By her he had issue six sons and four daughters. The name is frequently spelled Stamford by Dyer, Coke, and other reporters, and also on the tomb of his wife in Hadley Church. (*Athen. Oxon.* i. 262; *Machyn*, 362.)

STAUNTON, WILLIAM DE (of what family is not known), was appointed, with three others, a justice itinerant to visit Cornwall, Devonshire, Dorset, and Somerset, in 46 and 47 Henry III., 1262–3.

STAUNTON, HERVEY DE (sometimes called Henry), was of a Nottinghamshire family of large possessions and ancient lineage, which is still flourishing at Staunton Hall in that county. He was the son of Sir William de Staunton, by Athelina, daughter and coheir of John de Musters, lord of Bosingham in Lincolnshire. (*Thoroton's Notts*, i. 305.)

He was an ecclesiastic as well as a lawyer; and on one occasion he is described as prebendary of Hustwhait, in the cathedral of York. (*Abb. Placit.* 259, 335.) As a lawyer he is first mentioned in 30 Edward I., 1302, among the justices itinerant into Cornwall, and in the next year as holding the same character in Durham. In the parliament held at Westminster in September 1305 he was one of those appointed to receive and answer the petitions from Ireland and the isle of Guernsey. (*Rot. Parl.* i. 159); and on April 20, 1306, he was called to the bench as a judge of the Common Pleas.

On the accession of Edward II. he was re-appointed in the same court, and continued to perform the duties of the office till September 28, 1314, 8 Edward II., when he exchanged his seat in the Common Pleas for that of a baron of the Exchequer. On June 22, 1316, he became chancellor of the Exchequer; but seems, however, to have been still employed in a judicial character on various commissions, and to have been regularly summoned to parliament with the other judges. (*Parl. Writs*, ii. 1457.)

In 1323 he was raised to the office of chief justice of the King's Bench. Dugdale (*Orig.* 38) quotes a Close Roll commanding him not to quit the office of chancellor of the Exchequer, but cause it to be executed by some other fit person at such times as he should be necessitated to attend the hearing of causes; and Madox (ii. 53, e) gives a writ, dated September 17 or 27 in that year, by which the seal of the Exchequer was temporarily committed to the custody of the treasurer. Staunton retained the chief justiceship of the King's Bench for a very few months, being superseded, on the 21st of March following, by Geoffrey le Scrope; but he was five days afterwards re-appointed chancellor of the Exchequer. On July 18, 1326, 20 Edward II., he was constituted chief justice of the Common Pleas, and gave up the seals of the Exchequer. (*Parl. Writs*, ii. p. ii. 1458.)

Dugdale cites the same patent as appointing him not only chief justice of the Common Pleas, but chief baron of the Exchequer also. This is a manifest blunder, as the patent is wholly silent on the subject.

Half a year after this the king was deposed, and Hervey de Staunton died about the same time, William de Herle being immediately made chief justice in his place. (*Abb. Rot. Orig.* ii. 10.) He was buried in St. Michael's Church, Cambridge, where he founded the house of that name (now incorporated into Trinity College, where his name is introduced into the grace after dinner), and endowed it with the manor of Barenton and the advowson of the church there. (*Holinshed*, ii. 574; *Cal. Rot. Pat.* 98.)

STAVERTON, JOHN, who was connected with the county of Suffolk, appears among the officers of the Exchequer in 15 Richard II. (*Kal. Exch.* ii. 108), and on the accession of Henry IV. he was constituted a baron of that court. He acted throughout the reign, and was re-appointed by Henry V.

STEELE, WILLIAM, was the son of Richard Steele, of Giddy Hall, a moated house at Sandbach in Cheshire (*Ormerod's Cheshire*, iii. 449), and of Finchley in Middlesex. He became a barrister at Gray's Inn on June 23, 1637, and was one of the candidates for the judgeship of the Sheriff's Court in London in 1643, but was unsupported either by the Common Council or the Court of Aldermen, between whom there was a contest as to the right of election, and John Bradshaw, afterwards president of the High Court of Justice, was chosen. In 1647 he had the conduct of the prosecution of the unfortunate Captain Burley for his loyal but fruitless attempt to rescue the king in the Isle of Wight; and the zeal and energy he displayed so ingratiated him with the parliament, that when they were seeking a successor for Mr. Glynne in the recordership of London in January 1648, they recommended him to the city for the post. The vacancy did not then take place, and at the end of the year the Commons found more active employment for him by appointing him attorney-general of the Commonwealth, for the purpose of conducting the charges against the king. (*Whitelocke*, 290, 368.) But when the court sat on January 18 to make arrangements for the trial, Steele was or pretended to be ill, and in sending a message announcing that he was 'not like as yet to attend the service of the court,' he signified that 'he no way declined the service out of any disaffection to it, but professed himself to be so clear in the business that if it should please God to restore him he should manifest his good affection to the cause.' He thus escaped the odious office which Solicitor-General Cook performed; but within ten days after the execution he was well enough to appear in the High Court of Justice on the prosecution of the Earl of Cambridge (Duke of Hamilton), against whom he delivered a long and laboured speech. So also against the Earls of Holland and Norwich, Lord Capel, and Sir John Owen, who were tried about the same time. (*State Trials*, iv. 1064, 1067, 1209.)

He was elected recorder of London on August 25, 1649. Having been in the previous April superseded in his temporary office of attorney-general by Mr. Prideaux, the Commons were glad of this opportunity of rewarding his services, their sense of which they still further marked by giving him the privilege of pleading within the bar, and ordering that he should be freed from his reading at his inn of court. (*Whitelocke*, 394, 420.)

He was one of the committee named in January 1652 to consider of the delays, the charges, and the irregularities in the proceedings of the law, and in May 1654 was a commissioner to try the Portuguese ambassador's brother for murder. In the last case he is called Serjeant Steele, to which degree he had been admitted on January 25. (*Ibid.* 520, 590; *Noble's Cromwell*, i. 436.)

Cromwell, when he became protector, in December 1653, left the office of chief baron vacant for more than a year, when he bestowed it on Mr. Serjeant Steele, who was sworn in, after a learned speech from Mr. Commissioner Whitelocke, on May 28, 1655. (*Athen. Oxon.* iii. 1045.) Three days after he resigned his recordership. On August 26, 1656, he was advanced to the lord chancellorship of Ireland (*Smyth's Law Off. Ireland*, 33, 34); and on December 10, 1657, he was nominated one of Cromwell's House of Lords. (*Parl. Hist.* iii. 1518.) He was continued in his office on the accession of the Protector Richard, on whose deposition and the second expulsion of the Long Parliament he was named by Fleetwood, in October 1659, as one of the committee of safety. With this body, however, he refused to act, declaring his opinion to be that the parliament were the only proper judges as to the future establishment. (*Ludlow*, 302, 313.)

At the restoration of Charles II. he of course lost his place, but is said to have secured his personal safety and made his peace with the government by betraying the secrets of Henry Cromwell to Clarendon and Ormond, and, what is worse, by giving up his former colleague in the prosecution of the king, Solicitor-General Cook.

He was a lawyer of ability and learning; but his character is described by the writers on one side as proud, crafty, insincere, and insolent (*Clarendon; Dubigge*), while on the other it is stated that he was generally esteemed to be a man of great prudence and uncorrupted integrity (*Ludlow*, 313); and nothing appears in his recorded history in contradiction to this, if confined to pecuniary transactions. He died in Dublin and was buried in St. Werburgh's. By his first wife, Elizabeth Godfrey, he had a son, Richard, who was the father of the distinguished essayist Sir Richard Steele. His second wife was the widow of Michael Harvey, younger brother to the celebrated Dr. William Harvey. (*Notes and Queries*, 2nd S. xii. 72; *Noble*, i. 396.)

STEYNGRAVE, ADAM DE, no doubt belonged to the knightly family settled at the manor of that name in the parish of Edenbridge in Kent. He was constituted a baron of the Exchequer on July 24, 1332, 6 Edward III., and remained there till January 20, 1341. He was not included in the new patent of that date; but on October 28 following he was made a judge of the Common Pleas; and on January 10, 1342, he became, by another change, a judge of the King's Bench. The time of his death or removal must have been before April 1347, as his name is not included in the order for the judges' robes then issued. In 14 Edward III. he was one of the commissioners appointed to enquire into the true value of the bishoprics north of Trent. (*Hasted*, iii. 182; *Rot. Parl.* ii. 119.)

STIKESWALD, ROGER DE, probably so called from belonging to a place of that name in Lincolnshire, where there was a Cistercian nunnery, was the last named of five justices itinerant who fixed the tallage for that county in 8 Richard I., 1196–7. (*Madox*, i. 704.) He was alive in 18 John, and had a grant during pleasure of the land of Osbert de Bobi, 'qui est cum inimicis nostris.' (*Rot. Claus.* i. 290.)

STILLINGTON, ROBERT (BISHOP OF BATH AND WELLS), was the son of John Stillington, Esq., probably of the place of that name in Yorkshire, who possessed property at Nether Acaster, a short distance from York, of which city one of his progenitors was bailiff in 1388. (*Drake*, 361.) He became a student of the college of All Souls in the university of Oxford, where he took the degree of doctor in both laws. His first ecclesiastical preferment was a canonry in the cathedral of Wells in 1445; which was quickly followed by the treasurership of the same church in 1447; the rectory of St. Michael, Ouse Bridge, in York, in 1448; and the archdeaconry of Taunton in 1450. He became a canon of York in 1451; dean of St. Martin's, London, in 1458; archdeacon of Berks in 1463, and of Wells in 1465; and, lastly, Bishop of Bath and Wells on January 11, 1466. Many, if not all, of these preferments he owed to the patronage of the house of York, to which he was strongly attached. On their attaining power at the end of the reign of Henry VI. he was appointed keeper of the privy seal (*Devon's Issue Roll*, 484); and in the acts of resumption passed in the early parliaments of Edward IV. the grants made to him in this character, and also as dean of St. Martin's, are all excepted in his favour. (*Rot. Parl.* v. 470, 578.)

He was appointed lord chancellor on June 20, 1467, and on May 17 in the following year he announced to the parliament the royal intention to recover the kingdom of France (*Ibid.* 618, 622), a project, however, which the dissensions at home prevented the king from attempting. The bishop was still chancellor when Warwick succeeded in replacing Henry on the throne, and during the few months of the restoration we have no precise account of his conduct, with the exception that the Great Seal was taken out of his hands and put into those of Archbishop Nevill. That it was not offensive to Edward IV. we may presume from his being still in the office of chancellor at the next parliament in October 1472, although absent on account of illness (*Ibid.* vi. 2); but that he had some suspicion that it might be questioned if too closely investigated may be collected from his obtaining in the previous February a general pardon for all crimes committed by him previous to the day of the grant. (*Rymer*, xi. 736.) His illness seems to have continued throughout the first half of the next year, during which temporary keepers were at first appointed; but at last, on July 27, 1475, Laurence Booth, Bishop of Durham, was invested with the office, which Stillington never again recovered. He was still, however, employed by the king; and when the Earl of Richmond (afterwards Henry VII.) escaped from England, and took refuge in the territories of the Duke of Bretagne, the bishop was sent to that prince to demand that the fugitive should be given up. He failed in his embassy, and we hear no more of him during the remainder of the reign than that he was a trier of petitions in the parliament of the seventeenth year, and that in the eighteenth, for some unexplained cause, he received a new patent of pardon. (*Ibid.* xii. 66.)

From the day of Edward's death Stillington became an adherent of his ambitious brother, Richard Duke of Gloucester; and, though we may charitably hope that he was not a party to or a believer in the usurper's grosser enormities, there is no doubt that he drew up the act by which the children of Edward IV. were bastardised, that he assisted at the coronation of Richard, and that he gave him every aid and countenance throughout his troublous reign. So devoted a partisan of the Yorkists was not likely to be looked upon with much favour by Henry VII. On the very day of the battle of Bosworth, August 22, 1485, the king issued a warrant for his apprehension; and on August 27 he was already in prison at York, 'sore crased by reason of his trouble and carying.' (*Drake*, 122.) He succeeded, however, before the end of the year in obtaining his full pardon from the king, who, when the act of bastardy was repealed, refused on that account to call him before the parliament to answer for its composition, although pressed by the Lords to do so. He was, however, deprived of the deanery of St. Martin's, and the act that ousted him, after a flourish about the impropriety of benefices being held in augmentation of bishoprics, speaks of 'the horrible and haneous offences ymagined and doune by' him against the king. (*Rot. Parl.* vi. 292.)

His escape on this occasion does not seem to have rendered him more cautious in his future conduct. He became implicated in the absurd attempt of Lambert Simnel in 1487, was discovered, and committed to the castle at Windsor, where he remained a prisoner for nearly four years, and died there in May 1491, without that pity which is usually afforded to a sufferer for political crimes. Whatever merit he might claim as a supporter of the house of York he forfeited by his abject desertion of the children of his patron.

In the reign of Edward IV. he founded the collegiate chapel of St. Andrew, at Acaster, or Nether Acaster, for a provost and fellows, building it on property which had belonged to his father, and in 1 Richard III. he procured a confirmation of the grant of land he had made to it. (*Godwin*, 382; *Angl. Sac.* i. 574; *Le Neve*.)

STIRCHELEYE, WALTER DE, was appointed sheriff of Gloucestershire in 9 Edward I., and in the next year sheriff of Lincolnshire, holding the former office for four, and the latter for three years. (*Abb. Rot.* i. 37, 43.) He is the last named of six justices itinerant sent into Hertfordshire in 15 Edward I., 1287. In Michaelmas Term of that year there was a suit between Walter the son and heir of Walter de Stircheleye, and Walter the son of Reginald de Stircheleye and others, relative to a considerable property in Stircheleye in Shropshire (*Abb. Placit.* 216); but which of the three Walters was the justice itinerant there is nothing to show.

STIVEKEL, JOSCELINE DE, so called probably from the place of his birth, now Stukeley, in Huntingdonshire, was sheriff of that county and of Cambridgeshire in 8 and 9 John, and in the latter year paid twenty marks to be released from the employment. (*Rot. de Fin.* 382, 401.) He was probably an officer connected with the Exchequer. Several fines were acknowledged at Westminster in 15 and 16 John, 1213–14, in which his name appears among the justiciers present, but in no other year.

He soon afterwards went over to the side of the barons, and his lands were given to Simon de Campo Remigii. He had at the same time letters of safe conduct to go to the king; but he does not appear to have used them, as his estates were not restored till eleven months after the accession of Henry III., when the sheriffs of Bedford, Hunts, and Lincoln were ordered to give him possession. (*Rot. Pat.* 170; *Rot. Claus.* i. 251, 323.)

STOKE, RALPH DE, was of the clerical profession. Dugdale, by mistake, calls him archdeacon of Stafford in 7 John, Henry of London, already noticed, then holding that dignity. From 2 to 8 John, 1200–1206, the fines levied at Westminster, and on the circuits, contain his name as a justicier present, without that designation. (*Madox*, i. 734.)

He had the church of Wodeford in

Northamptonshire in 4 John (*Abb. Placit.* 41), and in the next year he was presented to the church of Alrewas in Staffordshire (*Rot. Pat.* 40); and two years afterwards he seems to have got into some disgrace, as he was fined a palfrey for tampering with a jury in Yorkshire. (*Rot. de Fin.* 309.)

STOKE, RICHARD DE, seems to have been implicated in the barons' war against King John, as he returned to his allegiance in 2 Henry III., when his lands were restored to him. They were situate in Buckinghamshire, in which county, some years afterwards, he held the office of coroner. It was probably on that account that in 9 and 11 Henry III., 1225–7, he was selected to act there as one of the justices itinerant. (*Rot. Claus.* i. 340, ii. 77, 147, 215.)

STOKES, JOHN DE. There was in the reign of Edward II. a Ralph de Stokes who was a clerk of the great wardrobe, and in that of Richard II. an Alan de Stokes who held the same office; and it is not improbable that this John de Stokes may have been the son of one and the father of the other. He was raised to the bench of the Exchequer on November 3, 1365, 39 Edward III.; and in the forty-fourth year he was sent into Yorkshire and Northumberland, to obtain loans for the king from the wealthy of those counties, and to survey the alien priories. (*Devon's Issue Roll*, 133, 209; *N. Fœdera*, iii. 778; *Issue Roll*, 256.)

STOKES, RICHARD, was constituted a baron of the Exchequer on October 9, 1377, 1 Richard II., and appointed auditor of the accounts of the king's bailiwicks in Wales and in Cheshire. He retained his seat on the bench till the twenty-first year, but certainly did not occupy it at the end of the reign. (*Cal. Rot. Pat.* 196, 198, 217.)

STONORE, JOHN DE, probably was born at Stonore, not far from Sandwich in Kent, as we find him, so early as 10 Edward II., taking a release of all the lands of Robert de Dumbleton, in Lesnes in that county. (*Abb. Placit.* 326.) A manor, however, of the same name in Oxfordshire may be thought to have a better claim to his nativity, unless, as is not unlikely, he gave his name to the manor, following the example of those spoken of by the Psalmist, who 'call the lands after their own names.' An effigy in judges' robes, bearing his arms, is in the church of Dorchester, which is near to the manor.

He is frequently mentioned as an advocate in the Year Books; and he was so far advanced among the serjeants as to be summoned to assist at the parliament of 6 Edward II. In the ninth year he had a grant of 20*l.* per annum for his expenses in prosecuting and defending suits for the king; and on several occasions he was employed on special judicial commissions, his proceedings under which he was commanded, in 12 and 13 Edward II., to carry into the Exchequer to be estreated.

In the following year, on October 16, 1320, he was constituted a justice of the Common Pleas; and the fines levied before him continue till the octave of Michaelmas, 27 Edward III., 1353; and yet Dugdale introduces him into his list of justices of the King's Bench from 17 Edward II., 1323–4, till the end of that reign. As the authority quoted for this is only a liberate, no doubt ordering the payment of a salary, we should have supposed that Dugdale had mistaken the words 'justiciarius domini regis,' by which title the judges of both benches were then often called, as designating that he was a justice of the King's Bench, but that we find that John de Stonore, on May 3, 1324, in the same seventeenth year, was again constituted a judge of the Common Pleas, the patent containing no special words of explanation. As none of the commissions upon which he was placed, and none of his summonses to parliament about this period, in the slightest degree distinguish the court to which he belonged, we are unable to account for his re-appointment to the Court of Common Pleas, except by supposing that, though there is no record of it, he was for a short time removed from that court, and was replaced at the above date. However this may have been, there is no doubt that John de Stonore continued from that time a judge of the Common Pleas till the end of the reign, for we find his name to a fine in Trinity Term in 1326 (*Orig.* 94), and that he was re-appointed by Edward III. a few days after he was proclaimed king.

On February 22, 1329, 3 Edward III., he was made chief baron of the Exchequer, and on September 3 in the same year was further advanced to be chief justice of the Common Pleas, superseding William de Herle, who, however, was restored two years afterwards, on March 2, 1331; and John de Stonore, on April 1, was placed in the second seat in the court. From this he seems to have been removed, on July 16, 1333, by Geoffrey le Scrope; but on July 7 in the following year, on the resignation of William de Herle, Stonore was reinstated as chief justice.

On the king's return from Tournay, at the end of the year 1340, both he and several other judges, for some alleged misconduct, the particulars of which have not transpired, were removed from their places and imprisoned (*Barnes's Edw. III.* 273), and Roger Hillary was constituted his successor on January 8, 1341. No record remains of the investigation that followed, nor does Stonore's name occur for the next sixteen months; but we may presume that the charges against him were not very heavy, or that they were not substantiated, inasmuch as he was restored to his place of chief justice of the Common Pleas on May 9, 1342, and remained undisturbed in it till 1354, when he died, leaving large possessions in nine counties, to which his son, also named John, succeeded.

STOPINDON, JOHN, received the appointment of archdeacon of Colchester on May 19, 1433, 11 Henry VI., as one of the masters in Chancery, in which character we find him mentioned in the previous year, and as keeper of the Hanaper in this. (*Rymer*, x. 523.) He was appointed master of the Rolls on November 13, 1438. In his patent on that occasion special reference is made to his services to the last two kings in France and Normandy, the nature of which is not recorded, but may be inferred from his being employed in December 1440 as one of the commissioners to conclude a treaty of alliance with the ambassadors of the Archbishop of Cologne. He became archdeacon of Dorset on July 19, 1440, and died between March and May 1447. (*Le Neve*, 196, 281; *Acts Privy Council*, v. 126.)

STOUFORD, JOHN DE (sometimes spelled Stonford), is said by Prince, in his 'Worthies of Devon,' to have been born at Stowford, in the parish of West Down, about 1290. A John de Stoford was a manucaptor in 1307 for a burgess returned to parliament for Plympton (*Parl. Writs*, ii. 5), in the neighbourhood of his native place. A John de Stoford was one of the custodes of the 'terra maritima' of Devon in 14 Edward III. (*N. Fœdera*, ii. 1112); and in the same year a John de Stovord was made one of the king's serjeants-at-law. The first of these was probably the father of the judge; and in the two latter, with little doubt, we have the judge himself.

He was raised to the bench of the Common Pleas on April 23, 1342, where he remained till November 10, 1345, when he was placed for about a month in the office of chief baron of the Exchequer, being superseded on December 8 by Robert de Sadington. This was no doubt a temporary arrangement for the accommodation of the latter, who had lately been removed from the office of chancellor, as John de Stouford certainly resumed his place in the Common Pleas, fines acknowledged before him from that time till Midsummer 1372, 33 Edward III., being still extant. (*Dugdale's Orig.* 45.) There is no evidence of his living after the latter date, and his death is stated to have occurred at his house at Stouford, his remains being buried in the church of West Down. There are several entries of grants made by him for pious uses, and he is reputed to have built the bridge over the Taw, near Barnstaple, besides another between that town and Pilton, in consequence of finding a poor woman and her child drowned in the neighbourhood.

He married Joan, a coheir of Tracy of Wollocombe, a name assumed by the family in the reign of George I.

STOWE, WILLIAM DE, whose name first appears as a witness to the release executed to King Edward III. in 1327 by the widow of Aylmer, late Earl of Pembroke (*N. Fœdera*, ii. 698), was made a baron of the Exchequer on January 20, 1341, 14 Edward III. He continued in that court till the twentieth year, when we find him recorded among the judges from whom loans were required (*Rot. Parl.* ii. 453), but he is omitted in the list of those for whom in the following year robes were ordered. (*Abb. Rot. Orig.* ii. 192.)

We know not whether he is the same William de Stow who is mentioned in connection with the abbey of St. Edmund's Bury in 9 Edward III. (*N. Fœdera*, ii. 924); but he was parson of the church of Sabrithesworth, and it does not seem improbable that his removal from the Exchequer was occasioned by a complaint made against him under that description in the parliament of Hilary, 21 Edward III., for maintenance and menaces against the petitioners. (*Rot. Parl.* ii. 179.) He was still alive in the twenty-sixth year, when he endowed that church with a house in the parish. (*Abb. Rot. Orig.* ii. 224.)

STRANGE, GUY LE, was the son of Guy le Strange (*Extraneus, L'Estrange*), the first of the family so called, who is believed to have been a younger son of the Duke de Bretagne in the latter part of the Conqueror's reign.

To Guy the son King Henry II. gave the lordships of Weston and Alvithele in Shropshire, and appointed him sheriff of that county at two periods. It was in this character that he acted in 20 Henry II., 1174, as justice itinerant for setting the assize or tallage on the king's demesnes there. (*Madox*, i. 124.)

He died between 6 Richard I., 1194, and 1 John, 1199, leaving a son, named Ralph, and three daughters, who, upon their brother's death without issue, became heirs of the property. (*Dugdale's Baron.* i. 663.)

STRANGE, ROGER LE. Roger le Strange was a grandson of John le Strange, the brother of the above Guy le Strange. His father was also named John, who, by his wife Amicia, left four sons, of whom this Roger was the youngest.

His brother Hamon granted to him the manor of Ellesmere, to which Henry III. added several others, with the sheriffalty of Yorkshire, which he held during the last two years of that reign and the first two of Edward I. In the latter of these he was proceeded against for divers extortions he had committed while he was bailiff of the honor of Pec in Derbyshire. He does not appear to have been again employed till 8 Edward I., when he was appointed steward of the king's household with Hugh Fitz-Otho. In 11 Edward I. he became justice of the forests south of the Trent, and it is in that character that he is introduced into Dugdale's list of justices itinerant in 1292. (*Cal. Rot. Pat.* 48, 50; *Abb. Placit.* 187.) He was summoned to parliament in 1295, 1296, and 1297, in the last of which years, 25 Edward I., he surrendered the office of justice of the forest, being 'adeo impotens' that he could not conveniently perform its duties. (*Year Book*, pt. i. 39.) In 1303 he obtained a licence for a market and fair at his manor of Chesworthine in Shropshire, and died in 5 Edward II. (*Abb. Rot. Orig.* i. 182), without leaving issue by his wife, Matilda, widow of Roger de Moubray.

From his brothers, John and Robert, sprang the baronies of Strange of Knockyn and Strange of Brackmere, both of which have been a long time in abeyance among daughters. (*Nicolas's Synopsis.*)

STRANGE, JOHN, was the son and heir of John Strange, of Fleet Street. He was for some time a pupil of Mr. Salkeld, of Brooke Street, Holborn, the attorney in whose chambers Lord Hardwicke had before had a seat, and was called to the bar by the Middle Temple in 1718. He acted as junior counsel for the crown in 1722 and for several years after, and in 1725 he was engaged for the defence in the impeachment of the Earl of Macclesfield, the result of which, notwithstanding the able advocacy of himself and his colleagues, was so disastrous to his noble client.

His Reports, which were not published till after his death, were commenced in Trinity Term 1729. He was appointed king's counsel in February 1736, when he was called to the bench of his inn, and elected autumn reader in the following year. In the previous Hilary Term he became solicitor-general, and was elected member for West Looe, commencing his senatorial career by a long speech against the provost and city of Edinburgh arising out of the murder of Captain Porteous. In November 1739 he was elected recorder of London, and in the next year he received the honour of knighthood.

To the surprise of Westminster Hall, he resigned his two offices in December 1742, and in his Reports (p. 1176) thus accounts for his retirement:—

'Memorandum.—Having received a considerable addition to my fortune, and some degree of ease and retirement being judged proper for my health, I this term resigned my offices of solicitor-general, king's counsel, and recorder of the city of London, and left off my practice at the House of Lords, Council Table, Delegates, and all the courts in Westminster Hall except the King's Bench, and there also at the afternoon sittings. His majesty, when at a private audience I took my leave of him, expressed himself with the greatest goodness towards me, and honoured me with his patent to take place for life next to his attorney-general. Anno ætatis meæ 47.'

The only occasion on which he appears not to have persisted in his resolution to confine his practice to the Court of King's Bench was in assisting at the trials in 1746 at St. Margaret's Hill, Southwark, and in the House of Lords, of the prisoners implicated in the then late rebellion.

His last promotion was on January 11, 1750, when he was selected to supply the vacancy in the office of master of the Rolls. After enjoying it for about four years, he died on May 18, 1754, and was buried in the Rolls Chapel. He continued in parliament till his death, representing Totnes since 1741. Five years after his decease his son published his Reports in all the four courts, extending from 1729 to 1748, which were considered of so much value as to require three subsequent editions. He enjoyed the esteem and friendship of Lord Hardwicke; and the Duke of Newcastle on his death speaks of him as 'one whom he honoured and loved extreamly for his many excellent publick qualities and most amiable private ones.' He adds, 'I scarce know any man with whom I had so little acquaintance that I should more regret.'

He married Susan, daughter and coheir of Edward Strong, Esq., of Greenwich, by whom he had two sons and seven daughters. His eldest son, John, became British resident at Venice, and was a very distinguished antiquary and naturalist. (*State Trials*, xvi.–xviii.; *Parl. Hist.* x. 275; *Strange*, 1068, 1133, 1176; *Harris's Hardwicke*, iii. 11; *Notes and Queries*, 3rd S. i. 353.)

STRANGEWAYS, JAMES, was of a Yorkshire family, and one of the lords of Whorlton in that county. In 2 Henry IV. he was sent up to London with letters to the council from Sir Henry Percy, who called him his 'bien bon ame amie.' He took the degree of serjeant-at-law on February 3, 1411; and in 1415 he was appointed by Henry V. one of his serjeants. On February 6, 1426, 4 Henry VI., he was raised to the bench of the Common Pleas, from which time fines were levied before him till Michaelmas, 21 Henry VI., soon after which he probably died.

His son Sir James was speaker of the House of Commons in the first parliament of Edward IV. (*Acts Privy Council*, i. 151.)

STRATFORD, JOHN DE (ARCHBISHOP OF CANTERBURY), was born at Stratford-on-Avon in Warwickshire, where he had property. (*Cal. Inquis.* p. m. ii. 46.) That his parents were in easy circumstances may be inferred from the fact that he was educated at Merton College, Oxford, in which university he took the degree of Doctor of Laws. He is believed to have been the nephew of Ralph Hatton de Stratford, Bishop of London.

That he occupied some official position as early as the year 1317, 10 Edward II., there can be little doubt, as he was summoned among certain judges and other legal persons to advise with the council on various important subjects. In like manner he was summoned to parliament in the four following years; and, from the place in which his name occurs, it would seem that he was either an officer of the Exchequer, or, perhaps, a clerk in the Chancery. (*Parl. Writs*, ii. p. ii. 1471.)

On September 13, 1319, he was admitted to the archdeaconry of Lincoln (*Le Neve*, 156); and in December 1321 he was sent on a mission to the pope on the affairs of Scotland. Archbishop Hubert Walter appointed him dean or chief judge of his Court of Arches, in which office he exhibited, not less in his knowledge of law than in the adjudication of the cases before him, the quickest discernment and the most consummate prudence. From 1321 to 1323 he was engaged in frequent embassies to the papal court at Avignon; and being there on the death of his colleague, Reginald de Asser, Bishop of Winchester, on April 12 (*N. Fœdera*, ii. 462–515) in the latter year, he succeeded, notwithstanding the king's urgent applications in favour of Robert de Baldock, in obtaining a bull rom Pope John XXII., dated June 20, 1323, conferring upon him the vacant bishopric.

The king's anger was excessive. He remonstrated with the pope, issued directions to the bailiffs of the different ports to arrest any messengers coming into England with letters on the subject, and expressed the bitterest rancour against the new-made prelate, calling him, in one of his missives, 'pseudo nuntium' and 'adversarium nostrum,' and dismissing him from his ambassadorial functions in terms of indignation. On his arrival in England proceedings were immediately commenced against him in the Court of King's Bench, which were removed to the parliament summoned for February 1324; in them he was addressed merely by his name, without the episcopal title, an omission which he, in his answers, was most careful always to supply. No further record of the process appears; but, by the intercession of the pope, Stratford was at last reluctantly recognised, and had his temporalities restored by a patent dated June 28, 1324. (*Ibid.* 526–557.) It seems, however, that this was purchased by the bishop's bond to pay the king 10,000*l.*, 8000*l.* of which was to be void on the death of the king or the bishop. (*Parl. Writs*, ii. p. ii. 258.) No part even of the 2000*l.* was claimed during that reign; for from that time he enjoyed the full confidence of the king, by whom he was employed in his negotiations with the court of France, and to whom he faithfully adhered when others had deserted the royal cause. After Edward's retirement he joined in the election of the prince as custos of the kingdom. On October 26, 1326, and on November 6, he was constituted *locum tenens* of the treasurer, and remained so for a short time. It is some credit to Queen Isabella that she thus showed her respect for the bishop's fidelity to her husband, and that she then employed him in prosecuting the treaty with France, although she insisted on the payment of 1000*l.* of his bond. It was not, however, till her removal from power, and the assumption of the kingly office by her son, Edward III., that the bishop was called to a prominent position in the royal councils. He was then constituted chancellor on November 28, 1330, 4 Edward III., and immediately was released from all arrears of his old obligation. (*Rot. Parl.* ii. 60.) He accompanied the king to France in the following April, both of them, according to Barnes, assuming the disguise of merchants, in performance of a certain vow; and in the next November he was sent abroad on a mission relative to the affairs of the duchy of Acquitaine, from which he returned in time to open the parliament at Westminster on March 12, 1332.

He was translated to the archbishopric of Canterbury November 3, 1333; and on September 28, 1334, he resigned the Great Seal, which was given to Richard de Bury, Bishop of Durham, who held it only till June 6, 1335. It was then restored to Stratford, and retained by him for nearly two years—viz., till March 24, 1337—his brother, Robert de Stratford, Bishop of Chichester, being appointed his successor. During the whole of this time he was continually engaged in embassies to France and other powers, and was actively employed in similar duties during the three next years, and in presiding over the council while the king was absent. (*N. Fœdera*, ii. 883–1115.)

On April 28, 1340, 14 Edward III., he was a third time constituted chancellor; but on June 20 following, on account of his increasing infirmities, he resigned the Seal to the king, which was thereupon again entrusted to his brother, Bishop Robert.

From the commencement of his first chancellorship till his final retirement from the office the archbishop had been the chief counsellor of the king; and even now, on Edward's proceeding to France, he was.

left as president of his council. But the French wars had emptied the Exchequer; the king's arms were unsuccessful before Tournay, and his allies were pressing in their demands for money, which was not forthcoming. Irritated by his forlorn condition, he listened to the intimations of his courtiers that his officers were unfaithful and treacherous; and coming suddenly to England, on November 30, 1340, he removed the chancellor, confined some of the judges, and hastily sent for the archbishop. The primate, however, thought it prudent to escape to Canterbury, and to refuse to answer except before his peers. Edward issued a declaration full of accusations, to which the archbishop replied, justifying his conduct, and successfully refuting the charges. The wordy war continued till the parliament met in April, when, though the prelate went submissively into the Exchequer to hear the information that had been filed against him, he was for some time refused admittance into the hall, but was at last allowed to take his seat. The Lords supported his appeal to their jurisdiction, and the question was referred to a committee, who reported in his favour. By the intercession of both houses, however, the business was stifled; and the archbishop having humbled himself, and the king having pardoned him, the proceedings were annulled in the next parliament in Easter 1343, as contrary to reason and truth. (*Ibid*. ii. 1141-1154.)

In July 1345 he was appointed the head of the council left as advisers of the king's son Lionel, to whom the custody of the kingdom had been entrusted, and a similar confidence reposed in him in the following year (*Ibid*. iii. 50, 85) is the last record of importance in his career. He died at Mayfield in Sussex on August 23, 1348, and was buried in Canterbury Cathedral.

His liberality to his church, his charity to the poor, his humble and pleasing manners, and his natural sense and general learning are acknowledged by all his biographers. That his reputation was high as an able politician, a loyal counsellor, and a man of deep legal knowledge for the time, is evidenced not more by the number of years during which he was engaged in high employments than by firmness in meeting his temporary disgraces, and the alacrity with which his talents were again put in requisition. He is said to have crossed the Channel thirty-two times in the public service. (*Godwin*, 106-224; *Barnes's Edw. III*. 43-216; *State Trials*, i. 57.)

STRATFORD, ROBERT DE (BISHOP OF CHICHESTER), brother of John, was also born at Stratford-on-Avon, and was parson of the church there. It is probable that he, like his brother, was educated at Oxford, as he afterwards became chancellor of that university, and distinguished himself by his firmness and prudence in settling the violent differences that had arisen between the northern and southern scholars as to the election of proctors.

The first time his name occurs is on April 1, 1331, 5 Edward III., in the first chancellorship of his brother, who, being then about to accompany the king to France, sent the Great Seal to his house in Southwark, in charge of Robert, under the seal of the master of the Rolls, after which they both continued to seal with it till the chancellor's return on April 20. In the same year he was made chancellor of the Exchequer. (*Cal. Rot. Pat*. 112.) The Seal was again left in the hands of these two on November 21 following, and on June 23, 1332, Robert de Stratford was alone appointed by his brother to receive it, and to do the business appertaining to the office. During the time it now remained in his possession he was called the chancellor's *locum tenens*, and he was one of the three commissioners named to open the parliament in the following December. (*N. Fœdera*, ii. 848.) He was a third time entrusted by his brother with the Seal on April 6, 1334, to be kept by him under the seals of two of the clerks of the Chancery.

His brother's first chancellorship terminated on September 28 following, on which occasion Robert is for the first time called archdeacon of Canterbury. He was also a canon in St. Paul's and Lincoln Cathedrals. When his brother the archbishop was made chancellor a second time on June 6, 1335, the Seal was again given to Robert as *locum tenens*, and it is probable that he continued to act in that capacity till March 24, 1337, when, on his brother's resignation, he was himself constituted chancellor. In the following September he was raised to the bishopric of Chichester, and on July 6, 1338, he was exonerated from the chancellorship, but accepted the appointment a second time on June 20, 1340. He accompanied the king to France in September, and was with him before Tournay. When he quitted the camp he left enemies behind him, who whispered in the king's ear that his disappointment in receiving supplies was attributable to his ministers at home. The king was too easily persuaded, and, making a hurried journey, arrived at the Tower of London in the middle of the night on November 30, and the next morning not only took the Great Seal away from the bishop, but threatened him with imprisonment, being only prevented from carrying his intentions into execution by the Clementine prohibition against such an indignity on ecclesiastics of that rank.

The bishop does not appear to have been included in the subsequent proceedings against his brother; but if he were, he no doubt participated in the pardon, for in May 1343 he was sent on a mission to the pope, and was left one of the council when Prince Lionel was appointed custos of the kingdom in July 1345. (*N. Fœdera*, ii. 1223, iii. 50.)

He survived his brother nearly fourteen years, and died at Aldingburne on April 9, 1362, whence his body was removed to his own cathedral for burial.

He was a prelate of great resolution and courage, and, notwithstanding the king's charges against him, seems to have been uncorrupt and faithful. He is mentioned as a considerable benefactor both to the place of his birth and the city of his cathedral. (*Godwin*, 507; *Barnes's Edw. III.* 213.)

STRATTON, ADAM DE, was a clerk in the Exchequer, 49 Henry III., when the office of weigher of the Exchequer (ponderator de Scaccario) was vested in him. He was still called clerk in 56 Henry III., and in the first year of the reign of Edward I. he was discharged, in virtue of his clerkship, from a suit before another jurisdiction. In the same year he was deputed by the Countess of Albemarle to act in her office in the Exchequer of Receipt, and in 4 Edward I. that lady granted to him the manor of Sevenhampton, with the hamlets of Worth, Stratton, and Crikelade, together with the chamberlainship of the Exchequer, to hold of the king and his heirs, to him and his heirs, doing the duties of chamberlain as she and her ancestors had done. (*Madox*, ii. 23, 264, 296–8, 308.) Two years afterwards the offices he held were taken into the king's hands 'ex certa causa.' (*Ibid.* ii. 5.) At this time he seems to have been in some difficulties, for in the same year he was charged with destroying a charter of liberties granted by the Countess of Albemarle (for whom he appears generally to have acted) to the abbey of Quarr, in the Isle of Wight, of which he was convicted in the following year, and was committed to prison. He, however, was restored to the offices he held. In 16 Edward I. he lent the Earl of Surrey 300*l.* upon mortgage of the manor of Gnoston, with a condition that if the money was not repaid in four years the manor should be Adam's for ever. (*Abb. Placit.* 196, 280.)

When King Edward, in 1289, discovered and punished several of the judges and others for corruption, Adam de Stratton was most deeply involved. What was the precise cause of his disgrace is nowhere clearly stated: corruption is charged by one, and felony by another. The latter is expressly mentioned in several records, but its nature is not described. It must, however, have been some serious crime, for not only was he dismissed from the office of chamberlain on January 17, 1290, and from the moiety of that of usher of the Exchequer, which, it seems, belonged to him (*Ibid.* 223, 283; *Madox*, ii. 299, 300), but his person was imprisoned, and the whole of his property forfeited, besides the imposition of a fine. The amount of this fine has been magnified to the sum of 35,000 marks; but by a record dated June 12, 1290, it appears that it was only 500 marks, on the payment of which he was released from prison, and his transgression pardoned. The property seized by the king at the time of his arrest, which all became forfeited, was no doubt considered as forming part of the fine, and that, independently of the manors, may be estimated at the value of 26,000*l.*, according to his petition to the parliament held at the following Michaelmas for restitution of some part of it—a petition which appears to have been refused, notwithstanding the previous pardon. (*Rot. Parl.* i. 57.) The word 'felo' is attached to his name in the escheats of 22 and 33 Edward I. (*Cal. Inq. et Esch.* i. 121, 201.)

Dugdale calls him a baron of the Exchequer at the time of this disgrace, and Weever, Chauncy, and other authors, even style him chief baron. It seems, however, that there is no sufficient ground for presuming that he held either of these titles. The office of chief baron, *eo nomine*, did not then exist, and the authority quoted by Dugdale for calling him a baron is by no means satisfactory. He cites Leland's 'Collectanea,' but that work contains two contradictory passages. In the one quoted by is certainly called 'baro de Scaccario,' but in the other he is, in relation to the same event, merely designated 'clericus Thesaurarii' (*Leland's Coll.* i. 356, 443), neither of which was his actual title, but both sufficiently near to account for the error of the monastic annalists from whom they are extracted; as, being chamberlain, he would sometimes sit with the barons, and might in a certain degree be called a clerk of the Treasury.

STREET, THOMAS, was born in 1625 in the city of Worcester, where his family had for a long time held a considerable position, one of them having represented it in parliament in the reign of Queen Elizabeth, and several of them having ranked among its bailiffs and mayors. He held for some years the office of town clerk to the corporation, and was in such esteem with his fellow-citizens that he was returned by them to the four successive parliaments of 1659, 1660, 1661, and 1679. He was also sub-secretary to the dean and chapter of Worcester from 1661 to 1687, and from 1663 was one of their 'consiliarii.'

He was partly educated at Oxford, but, in consequence of the death of his father, George Street, in 1643, he left the university without taking a degree, being called home to manage the paternal estate. A petition against his return to Protector Richard's parliament was presented, charging him with having borne arms for the king and with being a common swearer, and also that he was chosen by the profane rabble and cavaliers. In the Committee of Privileges, where Mr. Finch, afterwards Lord Nottingham, defended him, evidence was given of his siding with the royalists in 1645, of his being taken prisoner by the parliament army, and being exchanged. This was met by a denial that he ever used a sword against the parliament, that his capture was accidental, and that he refused the exchange; and the charge of swearing dwindled down to his having used the words 'by my faith and troth.' The report was repeatedly adjourned till the dissolution, the house evidently scouting the complaint, as the offence of a youth not of age, which had been passed over unnoticed for twelve or thirteen years. (*Burton's Diary*, iii. 70, 253, 425, iv. 244.)

He was called to the bar by the Inner Temple on November 24, 1653, and rose to the position of bencher in 1669. His practice till the Restoration seems to have been confined to the country. In July 1660 he obtained a grant of the office of receiver of the fines under the statutes concerning sewers. (*Cal. St. Papers* [1660], 144.) In February 1677 he was appointed a judge of assize for the counties of Glamorgan, Brecon, and Radnor, and in the next Michaelmas Term he was honoured with the coif. From this he was promoted on October 25 in the following year to be king's serjeant, but he does not appear to have had any employment in the courts of Westminster. On April 23, 1681, being then the chief justice on his Glamorgan Circuit, he was constituted a baron of the Exchequer and knighted; and in the same year at Derby assizes he condemned George Busby for high treason, as a Romish priest, but reprieved him. In 1683 he was in the commission for the trials at the Old Bailey of those who were charged with being concerned in the Rye House Plot, but did little more than give his opinion with the rest of the judges against the validity of Lord Russell's challenge of a juror for not having a freehold. His patent as baron was revoked on October 29, 1684, upon his being removed into the Court of Common Pleas, where on King Charles's death in the following February he was continued by King James. In the next year the great question was agitated in the Court of King's Bench, in the case of Godden v. Sir Edward Hales, whether the king could legally dispense with the oaths of allegiance and supremacy required by the Test Act, the king claiming to do so by his royal prerogative, and having granted an office to the defendant, a Roman Catholic, with a patent of dispensation. Chief Justice Herbert, though decidedly in favour of the prerogative, thought proper to obtain the opinions of the twelve judges on the point, and afterwards stated that all of them concurred with him, except Judge Street. (*T. Raymond*, 431; *State Trials*, viii. ix. xi.) Luttrell soon after this event (i. 382) says, 'There is a discourse as if Judge Street were turned out, and that Mr. Serjeant Wild is ordered to go the circuit.'

As the decision was of course most unpopular in the country, the dissenting judge was looked up to at the time with great admiration, and his courage and honesty were lauded by writers for more than a century afterwards. But within the last few years it has been the fashion to assume that this dissent from his brethren was given collusively, and prompted by the court, with the view of inducing the public to believe that the judgment of the bench was entirely independent, and not influenced in any degree by royal dictation. This suggestion is founded on the facts that Street was the only judge not dismissed by James, and that he was not re-appointed at the Revolution, with a passage in Lord Clarendon's Diary (ii. 236) explaining the reason why his lordship did not present him to King William to be that Lord Coote, in reporting to his majesty the judge's 'true character,' had described him as 'a very ill man.' No particulars are stated upon which Lord Coote founded this condemnation, and it is remarkable that he gives the judge credit for 'not joining in the judgment for the dispensing power,' without hinting a doubt of its sincerity. It seems more than probable that his lordship's prejudice arose from some family quarrel, he himself adding that the judge had married one of his relations. Lord Clarendon on the contrary declares that he 'had long known the judge, and that he took him to be a very honest man,' and no other recorded incident of his life seems to justify a different conclusion. It is curious that the writers who impute collusion are all whigs. Sir James Mackintosh first ' suggests the painful suspicion;' Lord Macaulay reiterates it more emphatically; and Lord Campbell, without a scintilla of additional evidence, asserts it as a positive fact; each of them forgetting that in the total change of the judges at the Revolution it was not likely that one should be excepted who was a tory in principle, and notoriously a friend to the excluded family. Without supposing therefore that Sir Thomas Street was better than James's other judges, there seems no probability, and certainly there is no proof, of his being guilty of the baseness which these authors have attributed to him. From the absence of the slightest hint of such an imputation when the judges were questioned on the subject by the parliament of 1689, a strong inference may be drawn that it has no foundation.

At the Revolution he retired to his native city, where he died on March 8, 1696, and was buried in the cloisters of its cathedral. It is some evidence that collusion in giving his opinion against the dispensing power was not suspected by his family, or his neighbours, or his contemporaries, that on the handsome monument erected to his memory the fact is prominently and encomiastically recorded.

He married Penelope, daughter of Sir Rowland Berkeley, of Cotheridge in Worcestershire, his colleague in the parliament of 1661. By this lady, who it seems was a relation of Lord Coote, he left an only daughter, but the name still survives in descendants of the judge's brother. (*Nash, Chambers, Granger, and Green; Luttrell,* i. 386.)

STRINGER, THOMAS, whose father was of the parish of St. Sepulchre in London, was educated at Peterhouse, Cambridge, where he took his two degrees in arts. He was called to the bar at Gray's Inn in July 1652, and became an ancient in May 1667. To what family of Stringer he belonged is uncertain, but probably to that settled at Sharleston in Yorkshire, as he was returned member for the not far distant borough of Clitheroe in part of the second parliament of Charles II., and in those of March and October 1679 and of 1681, in none of which did he take any prominent part. The date or occasion of his knighthood has not been ascertained, but he is described with the title when summoned to take the degree of the coif in July 1677. In 1679 he was promoted to be one of the king's serjeants, and he was employed in the prosecution of the presumed murderers of Sir Edmondbury Godfrey and the trials connected with the pretended plot. In April 1687 he was discharged from being king's serjeant. In the following October his eldest son married the daughter of Lord Chancellor Jeffreys, which no doubt was one of the causes which led to Sir Thomas's promotion in October 1688 to be a judge of the King's Bench, a position which he did not enjoy for many months, as he was not re-appointed by King William. He possessed the manor of Durance in Enfield, and died in September 1689. (*State Trials,* vii. 162, 261, viii. 504; *Luttrell,* i. 402, 417, 470, 587.)

He does not appear to have been connected with another Thomas Stringer who flourished at this time as secretary of Lord Chancellor Shaftesbury.

STRODE, JOHN DE LE, was among the justices itinerant appointed in 52 Henry III., 1268, to visit Somersetshire and Dorsetshire, besides eleven other counties; but little more can be said of him than that he was of a family holding large estates in them, which descended from Warinus de la Strode, a companion of the Conqueror.

STUART, JOHN, is the senior of the three present vice-chancellors. He is a Scotchman by birth, being the second son of Dugald Stuart, Esq., of Ballychelish in the parish of Appin in Argyleshire. He was born in 1793, and, entering Lincoln's Inn, he attained the degree of a barrister in 1819. He practised in the Court of Chancery for twenty years before he was made a queen's counsel, in 1839, and held that dignity for thirteen years more with a very considerable lead in the court. For the last six of those years he was a member of parliament, representing Newark for the whole time, except the last two months, when he was returned for Bury St. Edmunds.

He was appointed vice-chancellor on September 14, 1852, in the first ministry of Lord Derby, and has presided in his court ever since.

In 1813 he married the daughter of Duncan Stewart, Esq.

STUTEVILLE, ROBERT DE. A Norman noble of this name, surnamed Grandeboef, or Fronteboef, after the death of the two Williams, joined the fortunes of Robert, the eldest son of the Conqueror, against his younger brother Henry, and, being captured at the disastrous battle of Tenchebray, in 1106, shared his prince's fate, and was imprisoned for life. His son Robert de Stuteville was one of the valiant northern barons who distinguished themselves in the battle of the Standard, fought against the Scots in August 1138.

Robert de Stuteville was employed in 16 and 17 Henry II., 1170-1, as justice itinerant in the counties of Cumberland and Northumberland. (*Madox,* i. 144, 146.) He was then likewise sheriff of Yorkshire, an office which he retained for a few years afterwards. In 1175 he had an allowance for the sums he had expended for the knights and sergeants, horse and foot, which he had with him in the king's service in the war (*Ibid.* 370, 702, ii. 157, 200), having in the previous year, assisted Ranulph de Glanville at the battle near Alnwick, where the Scottish army was routed, and William, their king, taken prisoner.

Dugdale attributes these facts to Robert the son, and even carries him down to 23 Henry II., 1177, as a witness to the arbitrament between the Kings of Castile and Navarre. He makes him the father of another Robert, his successor, of whom he

T T

relates no events, but that he gave certain lands to the monks of Rievaulx, and that he married twice. Now, seeing that the first Robert was imprisoned for life in 1106; that the battle in which the next Robert distinguished himself was in 1138, when he may be supposed to have been between forty and fifty years of age; that the third battle was in 1174, when, if it were the same person, he must have been between eighty and ninety, it seems not improbable that Dugdale has confounded the incidents of two lives. This is rendered more likely from his omission of all dates with regard to the third Robert, and from the fact that he places William, the third Robert's successor, in the prominent situation of governor of Topclive Castle in Yorkshire, so early as 20 Henry II., 1174, a date previous to the assigned termination of the second Robert's career. For these reasons it seems more correct to make the justice itinerant the third, and not the second baron.

The second baron married Erneburga, and, besides the third Robert, had another son, named Osmund. The third Robert married two wives: by the first, Helewise, he had one son, the next-mentioned William, and two daughters; by the second, Sibilla, sister of Philip de Valoines, he had one son, named Eustace. One or other of these two Roberts, and I think the last, founded two monasteries for nuns, one at Rossedale, the other at Keldholme, in Yorkshire, besides making several rich benefactions to Rievaulx Abbey, and to the monks of St. Mary's in York. (*Dugdale's Baron*. i. 455.)

STUTEVILLE, WILLIAM DE, the son and successor of the above Robert de Stuteville, was in 1174, 20 Henry II., made governor of Topclive Castle in Yorkshire, and three years afterwards governor of Roxburgh Castle in Scotland.

In 1 Richard I. he was among the justices itinerant in Yorkshire (*Pipe Roll*, 34), and in the next year he was sheriff of Northumberland. Although during the king's absence he seems to have sided with Prince John, he joined King Richard after his return from captivity in his expedition to Normandy, and was appointed one of the commissioners to determine the controversy between the Archbishop of York and the canons of his church, and also one of the custodes of that county over the archbishop, then sheriff. (*Madox*, i. 33.)

On the accession of John, that king rewarded his former adherence to him with many favours, not, of course, forgetting the imposition of a considerable fine in the first instance. He made him sheriff of Yorkshire, Northumberland, Cumberland, and Westmoreland, gave him the custody of all the castles therein, and granted him charters for fairs and markets on several of his manors. William also obtained a grant of the lordships of Knaresborough and Boroughbridge, with a variety of other privileges and advantages, among which he no doubt considered the honour of entertaining his sovereign on one of his progresses at his house at Cotingham in Yorkshire. Royal favours in those times, however, were seldom granted without a pecuniary equivalent, and we accordingly find on the rolls large fines imposed, or rather, perhaps, considerable payments made, for some of these honours. (*Rot. de Oblatis*, 55, 68, 109; *Rot. Chart*. 12-107.)

He died in 5 John, leaving by his wife Berta, the niece of Ranulph de Glanville, the chief justiciary, two sons, Robert and Nicholas, for the wardship of whom the Archbishop of Canterbury paid no less a sum than four thousand marks. (*Rot. de Liberate*, 48.) The elder of these died the following year without issue, and the younger in 17 Henry III., leaving only daughters. None of the collaterals being subsequently summoned to parliament, the family ceased to be barons of the realm. (*Baronage*, i. 455.)

SUDBURY, SIMON DE (ARCHBISHOP OF CANTERBURY), whose family name was Thebaud, or Tibbald, was the son of Nigel and Sarah Thebaud, who resided at Sudbury in Suffolk at the time of his birth. Being intended for the clerical profession, he assumed the name of his native place, although these substitutions were gradually becoming uncommon. While yet a young man he was sent abroad, where he distinguished himself in several foreign schools, and took the degree of Doctor of the Canon Law in France. He was received with favour by Pope Innocent VI., who appointed him one of his chaplains and auditor of his palace, an office of considerable responsibility, by which he is designated in a mandate of King Edward III. on July 7, 1358. (*N. Fœdera*, iii. 402.) By the pope's influence he was made chancellor of Salisbury in 1360, and Bishop of London in the following year. During the fourteen years that he held this see his services were frequently required by the king in the arrangement of truces and treaties of peace; and these duties he continued to perform for the rest of the reign after he became Archbishop of Canterbury, his elevation to the primacy occurring on May 26, 1375.

On July 4, 1379, 3 Richard II., the Great Seal was placed in his hands as chancellor. He had held the office less than two years, when the populace rose in many parts of England, instigated in the first instance by the seditious harangues of a discontented Kentish priest, named John Ball, who preached the common absurdity of a community of goods, 'for the which folysshe wordes he had ben thre tymes in the bysshop of Canterburie's prison.' (*Froissart*, i. 640.) The indignation of the people was further excited by the insolent misconduct of one of the collectors of the capitation tax in the same county, who, professing to doubt the age of a young girl, made an indecent attempt to ascertain it. Her father, called Wat the Tyler, from his trade, took summary vengeance for the insult by knocking out the brains of the perpetrator; and his neighbours, joining this to other grievances, as well fancied as real, collected together for the purpose of redressing them, and placed Wat Tyler at their head. Similar risings taking place in other parts of the country, he soon found himself the leader of a rabble of above 60,000 men. Joining John Ball, and another man called Jack Straw, in the command, he led his followers towards London; and having, in his way thither, stopped at Canterbury, they dismantled the palace of the archbishop, against whom it was natural that Ball should entertain hostile feelings as the cause of his former imprisonment, and to whom, as the king's chancellor and minister, the people would not fail to attribute all the evils of which they complained. They at last reached Blackheath; and on their arrival there, on June 12, 1381, they sent Sir John Newton, the governor of Rochester Castle, whom they had forced to accompany them, to the king, then in the Tower of London, to represent how ill-governed the kingdom had been, 'and specially by the archebysshop of Caunterberie, his chaunceller, wherof they wolde have accompt;' and to desire that he himself would come and hear their complaints. The knight took back the royal promise that he would speak to them; and we can imagine the distress and difficulty of his counsellors, what course they should advise their royal master to adopt. It may be presumed that they considered the removal of an unpopular minister would most effectually tend to assuage the fury of the populace; and we accordingly find that the archbishop on that day resigned the Great Seal into the king's hands, the record saying that he did so 'for certain causes.'

The king, on the next day, though he proceeded down the river, was not allowed to land; whereupon the irritated concourse entered London, and early on the 14th appeared before the Tower, and demanded access to the king. He promised to meet them at Mile End, whither the greatest part of the assembly flocked. The leaders, however, not satisfied, remained with a large body of their followers; and when the king had passed out of the gates and issued on his way, they burst into the Tower, and, seizing the archbishop, and Robert de Hales, the master of the Knights of St. John, who, being treasurer, was peculiarly obnoxious to them, they dragged them to the common place of execution on Tower Hill, and there barbarously murdered them. The archbishop, after quietly remonstrating, and giving absolution to his murderers, calmly submitted to his fate; and with such carelessness and inhumanity was the deed performed, that it was not till after eight strokes of the sword that his head was severed from his body. The head, after being paraded through the city, was suspended on London Bridge, and the body was left untouched till the next day, when they both were removed for interment to Canterbury, where they lie in the south part of the altar of St. Dunstan. Wat Tyler met his reward, and his followers were dispersed through the intrepidity of King Richard, from whose conduct on this occasion his subjects nourished hopes which were doomed to be sadly disappointed.

As in most scenes of violent commotion the innocent suffer, so it was in this case. The character of the archbishop, as represented by the historians, was such as to make him least liable to popular hatred. He was of a liberal, free, and generous spirit, admired for his wonderful parts, for his wisdom, his learning, and his eloquence, and revered for the piety of his life, the charity he dispensed, and the merciful consideration he universally exhibited.

While Bishop of London he was a munificent benefactor to his native town, and during the short period that he held the archbishopric of Canterbury he expended large sums on the cathedral. (*Godwin*, 117; *Barnes*, 872.)

SUDLEY, RALPH DE, was of a noble English family, older than the Conquest, whose chief seat was at Sudley in Gloucestershire. (*Baronage*, i. 42.) In 24 Henry III., 1240, he was the second named of the justices before whom a fine was acknowledged at York; after which date there is no further mention of him. He was succeeded by his son Bartholomew, whose grandson John died in 1367, leaving two daughters, between the descendants of whom the barony remains in abeyance. (*Nicolas's Synopsis*.)

SUFFOLK, EARL OF. *See* M. DE LA POLE.

SUGDEN, EDWARD BURTENSHAW (LORD ST. LEONARD'S). This erudite jurist may boast of having raised himself by his own industry and merits from an inferior rank in the estimation of the world to the highest grade in the law, and to an honoured place among the peers of the realm. Lord St. Leonard's and Lord Tenterden are splendid instances of the excellence of the British constitution, which, regardless of birth or position, freely admits the most deserving to a competition for the honours it has to dispense. Richard Sugden the father of the chancellor followed the same business in London, though on a larger scale, that John Abbott the father of the chief justice practised in Canterbury; and each may well feel pride in reflecting on his origin.

He was born in 1781, and was placed as a member of Lincoln's Inn, by which society he was called to the bar in 1807. For ten years afterwards he practised as a conveyancing counsel, and soon became the most distinguished follower of that branch of the science. His early success was promoted by his publication of a 'Practical Treatise on the Law of Vendors and Purchasers of Estates' (written before he was twenty-one), two editions of which were exhausted before his call to the bar. This was followed in 1808 by his 'Practical Treatise on Powers.' Then came his 'Series of Letters to a Man of Property on buying, selling, &c., Estates,' of which he issued fifty years afterwards a seventh edition under the new title of 'A Handy Book on Property Law.' In 1811 he published a most masterly edition of 'Gilbert's Law of Uses and Trusts.' By the excellence of these and other works, all written in the clearest and most vigorous style, and combining legal research with practical ability, for which frequent editions were called, and always issued with valuable additions and improvements, he established such a name that few felt their titles good unless they were submitted to his revision. The natural consequence was that he gained a larger income than any competitor, but at the same time was so overloaded with abstracts to inspect and deeds to settle that at length he felt it necessary to withdraw from that laborious pursuit and confine himself to court practice.

He went in 1817 into the Court of Chancery, but there he did not obtain much relief, for briefs came in as abstracts had formerly, and he soon had as many litigant parties to plead for as he before had purchasers to advise. He received a silk gown in 1822, and in June 1829, just a year before the death of George IV., he succeeded Sir Nicolas Tindal as solicitor-general, and received the order of knighthood.

This office he resigned when the whigs came into power in November 1830, and remained out of office for more than four years; but during that time he lost little from the exclusion, as he had the undisputed lead in the Court of Chancery. When in December 1834 the conservatives regained the ascendency, Sir Edward Sugden was at once selected to fill the highest office in Ireland, being appointed lord chancellor of that country. The short tenure of the conservative power obliged him to resign in April 1835, but such judicial capacity did he exhibit that on the exclusion of the whig government in September 1841 he was, with the approbation of all parties, replaced in his former position at the head of the High Court of Irish Chancery. Up to this time he was an active member of parliament, sitting successively for Weymouth and Melcombe Regis, St. Mawes, and ultimately for Ripon.

He retained his seat on the Irish bench with the highest reputation for nearly four years, and it was with sincere regret that the practitioners in his court saw him depart on another change of ministry in July 1846. He had then above five years more of comparative idleness, till his political friends again resuming power availed themselves of the opportunity of showing their estimation of his brilliant abilities and useful services, by raising him to the highest office in the law, lord high chancellor of Great Britain, to which he was appointed on February 27, 1852, being created the day after a peer of England by the title of Baron St. Leonard's of Slaugham in Sussex. The inconvenient system of changing the lord chancellor with the ministry obliged him to resign at the end of ten months, on December 28 in the same year. Exceeding at that time the age of seventy years, he has refused office on the several accessions of the conservatives to power; but in his place in parliament and in the judicial committee of the privy council he has continued to afford his valuable assistance. Among minor honours, he was nominated high steward of Kingston-on-Thames and a deputy-lieutenant for Sussex, and in 1833 received the degree of LL.D. from the university of Cambridge.

As he is still living, it would be indelicate to enter into any other incidents of his life, and presumptuous to attempt any criticism of his powers; but no one will refuse to endorse the opinion that in all questions of the law of real property the name of Sugden will be perpetually quoted as an infallible authority.

By his marriage with the daughter of Mr. John Knapp he has several children.

SULYARD, JOHN, of Wetherden in Suffolk, was the son of John Sulyard, Esq., and Alice the daughter of Sir John Barington. He studied the law at Lincoln's Inn, where the name of Sulyard (probably his father) appears as reader in 1465, and again in 1470. In 1477 John Sulyard (probably the son) appears again as reader, and in that year received the degree of the coif. (*Dugdale's Orig.* 249, 257.)

In May 1483, during the short reign of Edward V., he was united with Chief Justice Bryan to go the Home Circuit (9 *Report Pub. Rec.*, *App.* ii. 1), serjeants being then, as well as now, joined in the commission. In the second year of the reign of Richard III., October 22, 1484, he was raised to the office of justice of the King's Bench, and, with the other judges, was re-appointed on the accession of Henry VII. in the following year.

That king named him, on November 10, 1487, as one of the commissioners to execute the office of steward at the coronation of Queen Elizabeth (*Rymer*, xii. 328), a ceremony which he did not survive above four months. He died on March 18, 1488, and was buried in Wetherden Church. (*Probate of his Will.*)

He had two wives. His first was Anne, daughter and heir of — Hungate; and his second was Anne, daughter and coheir of John Andrewes, of Baylam in Suffolk. By both marriages he had several children. Sir William Sulyard, who was a person of great repute in the law and one of the governors of Lincoln's Inn in 23 Henry VIII., was his grandson.

SUMERI, ROGER DE, was the grandson of John de Sumeri, who acquired the barony of Dudley in Worcestershire, and the son and ultimately the heir of Ralph. In 17 Henry III. his estates were seized because he came not to be bound with the belt of knighthood, and he was compelled to fine for their restitution. (*Excerpt. e Rot. Fin. Introd.* xvii.) He married Nichola, third sister and coheir of Hugh de Albini, Earl of Arundel, on the partition of whose inheritance, in 28 Henry III., he had the manor of Barewe in Leicestershire assigned for the chief seat.

In 45 Henry III., 1261, he was selected as a justice itinerant for Cambridge and Huntingdon.

He was a loyal and a valiant knight, and fought under the king at the battle of Lewes, sharing in his defeat and his subsequent imprisonment. He was afterwards one of those appointed to carry into execution the dictum of Kenilworth. He died in 1272, and was buried at the priory of Dudley. By his first wife he had four daughters; but marrying, secondly, Amabilia, the daughter of Robert de Chaucomb, and widow of Gilbert de Segrave, he left by her two sons and a daughter. The eldest son, Roger, succeeded, and the family is now represented in the House of Lords, partly through females, by the earldom of Dudley. (*Baronage*, i. 513; *Nicolas's Synopsis.*)

SURREY, EARL OF. *See* J. and W. DE WARRENNE.

SUTHILL, JOHN (ABBOT OF HYDE), was one of the justices itinerant in Dorsetshire in 7 Richard I., 1195-6. (*Madox*, i. 502.) He was elected to the abbey situated near Winchester in 1181. In 1185 he went to Rome to bring the pall for Baldwin, the new Archbishop of Canterbury. Browne Willis (19) states that he died in 1222, 6 Henry III. (*Dugdale's Monast.* ii. 431.)

SUTTON, ELIAS DE, whose father, of the same name, died in 1262, became a judge of the King's Bench in 13 Edward I., 1285, and he is further mentioned in that character after Easter, 15 Edward I. He died in 1289. (*Cal. Inq.* p. m. i. 21; *Abb. Rot. Orig.* i. 276, 278.)

SUTTON, THOMAS MANNERS (LORD MANNERS), was the grandson of John Manners, third Duke of Rutland, and the son of Lord George Manners, his grace's third son, who assumed the name of Sutton when he succeeded to the estate of his mother's father, Lord Lexington. Lord George, by his first wife, Diana, daughter of Thomas Chaplin, of Blankney in Lincolnshire, Esq., had a family of seven sons and six daughters. The fourth of these sons became Archbishop of Canterbury, and was the father of Charles Manners Sutton, who after presiding over the House of Commons from 1817 to 1834 was created Viscount Canterbury.

Lord George's fifth son, Thomas, the subject of the present sketch, was born on February 24, 1756. From the Charterhouse he went to Emmanuel College, Cambridge, and distinguished himself by being placed as fifth wrangler in 1777. He was called to the bar by Lincoln's Inn in November 1780. Well read in the law, he obtained a considerable practice in the Court of Chancery, and received the honour of a silk gown in 1800, being at the same time appointed solicitor-general to the Prince of Wales. In that character he brought before the parliament of 1802, to which he was returned member for the family borough of Newark, the claims of his royal highness to the revenue of the duchy of Cornwall, and urged them with so much grace and talent that he not only excited the eulogy of both Mr. Pitt and Mr. Fox, but was promoted by Mr. Addington, then prime minister, in the following May, to the office of solicitor-general to the king, being knighted on the occasion. He executed the duty which soon after devolved upon him, of replying to the evidence brought forward by Colonel Despard on a charge of high treason, with great temperance and ability. He assisted also in the trial of M. Peltier for a libel on Napoleon Bonaparte during the short peace with France, the speedy conclusion of which saved the defendant from being called up for judgment. (*Parl. Hist.* xxxvi. 332, 406, 1202; *State Trials*, xxvii. 469, 530.)

He was appointed a baron of the Exchequer on February 4, 1805, when he resigned the recordership of Grantham, which he had held for some years.

He only sat as an English judge for two years, when, on the dissolution of the short-lived ministry of 'All the Talents,' he was selected as lord chancellor of Ireland in April 1807, having been on the 20th of that month called up to the House of Peers by the title of Baron Manners of Foston in

Lincolnshire. He presided there during the remainder of the reign of George III. and until the eighth year of George IV., when in November 1827, being then in his seventy-second year, he resigned the Seal, having for more than twenty years exercised the important functions of his high office with universal approbation. His decisions as an equity judge were held in high estimation; and so little jealousy had he of criticism that he refused an application for an attachment against an attorney for publishing some proceedings in his court, expressing his opinion that the publicity given to law proceedings not only prevented unjust sentences, but answered many other salutary purposes.

He lived nearly fifteen years after his retirement, and occasionally joined in the debates in the House of Peers. At the age of eighty-six he died at his house in Brook Street, on May 31, 1842. By his first wife, Anne, the daughter of Sir John Copley, Bart., of Sprotborough, he left no issue; but by his second wife, Jane, daughter of Lord Caher and sister of the Earl of Glengall, he left an only son, the father of the present peer.

SWEREFORD, ALEXANDER DE, is described by Madox as a 'most excellent man, whose memory is yet held in high esteem among antiquaries.' He took his name from a parish so called in the county of Oxford, of which he was first the vicar, and afterwards the rector. He was a clerk in the Exchequer, and was appointed domestic chaplain by William de Cornhill, Bishop of Coventry, who had himself been an officer of that branch of the court. In February, 17 John, he had letters of conduct to go abroad with the bishop, and in the following April the troubled state of the country rendered it necessary for him to apply for them for the purpose of travelling throughout England on the bishop's affairs. About 1219 he was made archdeacon of Salop or Shrewsbury, and on January 15, 1231, is mentioned as treasurer of St. Paul's, having been previously a canon in that cathedral. 18

On July 6, 1234, Henry III., he was assigned to take his place in the Exchequer ' tanquam baro,' and attested writs in connection with that office as late as October 1245; and dying on November 14, 1246, was buried at St. Cedda's altar in St. Paul's, where he founded a chantry. He gave all the lands and rents he had in Hertfordshire to St. Bartholomew's Hospital.

He is chiefly celebrated as the compiler of the Red Book of the Exchequer, in which he collected out of the Great Rolls of the Pipe the memorials concerning the scutages assessed in the reigns of Henry II., Richard I., John, and the first fifteen years of that of Henry III., with many other curious particulars relative to the officers and practice of the department of the revenue in the King's Court, and in which he preserved the valuable work of Richard Fitz-Nigel, Bishop of London, called 'Dialogus de Scaccario.' (*Madox*, i. 624, 677, ii. 54, 335; *Chauncy's Hertfordshire*, 237; *Dugdale's Orig.* 21; *Rot. Pat.* 17 *John*, 166, 176.)

SYDENHAM, RICHARD, belonged to the county of Somerset, where his father, Roger de Sydenham, was possessed of Combe, in the parish of Monksilver. (*Cal. Inq.* p. m. ii. 306.) He was educated as a lawyer, and was raised to the bench as a judge of the Court of Common Pleas, on the impeachment of four of its members in the parliament of February 1388, 11 Richard II.; and the fines levied before him extend to the octaves of Trinity 1396, 19 Richard II. (*Dugdale's Orig.* 46.) This was no doubt the period of his death; for his name does not occur afterwards, and his successor was appointed in the following July.

He married Joan, daughter and coheir of Robert Delnigrige, of Bromfield, and was father of two sons, Henry and Simon, the latter of whom became Bishop of Chichester. One of the descendants of Henry, the eldest, in 1641 received a patent of baronetcy, which became extinct in 1739.

T

TABLIR, RALPH, appears only as a justice itinerant in 3 Henry III., 1219, in the home counties. In some of the fines levied during that iter he is called Ralph Tabbett.

TALBOT, CHARLES (LORD TALBOT), traced his descent from illustrious ancestors, ennobled almost from the time of the Conquest. The branch to which he directly belonged was that of Sir Gilbert Talbot, the third son of John, second Earl of Shrewsbury, who flourished in the reign of Henry VIII. In lineal succession from Sir Gilbert came William Talbot, Bishop successively of Oxford (1699), of Salisbury (1715), and of Durham (1722), who, by his second wife, Catherine, daughter of — King, an alderman of London, was the father of a large family of sons and daughters. His eldest son was the future lord chancellor, who was born in the year 1684, and was sent in 1701 to complete his education at Oriel College, Oxford. He was elected fellow of All Souls' College, and purposed to devote himself to the clerical profession. But by the recommendation of Lord Chancellor Cowper he was induced reluctantly to forego this intention, and to enter the legal arena, as more calculated to exhibit and turn to useful account the extraordinary talents with which he had been gifted.

He accordingly entered the Inner Temple in June 1707, and was called to the bar in September 1711. His abilities were soon recognised, and before many years he had acquired the leading practice in the equity courts. He was appointed in May 1717 solicitor-general to the Prince of Wales, and in April 1726 he was promoted to the same office in the service of the king. In that year he was elected bencher, treasurer, and Lent reader to his original inn of court, the Inner Temple; and also bencher, treasurer, and master of the library to Lincoln's Inn, to which society he had been also admitted in 1718, for the purpose of occupying chambers there. He became a member for Tregony in 1719; and in 1722 and 1727 he was returned for Durham, of which his father had then been made bishop.

That king continued him in his office of solicitor-general, and he and the attorney-general, Sir Philip Yorke, exercised an almost absolute supremacy in the practice of the Court of Chancery, remedying, it is said, even when engaged on opposite sides, the somnolency of Lord Chancellor King, by settling the minutes in the causes with justice to both parties. Mr. Talbot's professional income at this time must have been very large; but he was unworthily taxed by the munificent extravagance of his father, being obliged on two several occasions to pay the debts which the bishop had incurred in excess of his splendid revenue.

So meagre are the accounts of forensic or parliamentary eloquence at this time that few examples remain of that which Mr. Talbot displayed either as an advocate or a senator, and those only of an official character. But there can be no doubt, not only of his general reputation as an orator, but of the esteem and respect in which he was held both as a lawyer and as a man, since his elevation to the highest judicial dignity in the state met with universal approbation. That occurred on the resignation of Lord King, when the Great Seal was delivered to him as lord chancellor on November 29, 1733, a few days after which he was ennobled with the title of Baron Talbot of Hensol in Glamorganshire, an estate formerly belonging to the celebrated Welsh judge David Jenkins, which he had acquired by his marriage in 1711 with the judge's descendant, Cecil, daughter and heir of Charles Matthews, Esq., of Castle Mynach in that county. His promotion was celebrated at the Inner Temple by a splendid entertainment, noted as the last of the ancient revels, in the performance of which the inns of court were wont to take so much pride.

No man ever occupied the high position he had attained with more unmixed admiration; nor did the death of any great judicial dignitary ever cause so much general lamentation. Living too short a time to excite the jealousy of his colleagues in the ministry, or to become obnoxious to the opposition, he presided long enough in his court to prove himself a most efficient and impartial judge. His patience in listening to arguments, his discrimination in sifting facts, his readiness in applying precedents, and the reasons upon which he founded his judgments, made his decrees acceptable to the legal community, and prevented murmurs even among the unsuccessful litigants. The purity of his life, his unblemished integrity, his humanity to the distressed, his liberality to all, his gentleness of manners, his urbanity, cheerfulness, and wit, gained him so many friends, and were so universally recognised, that he not only escaped the vituperation of political writers during his life, but both parties after his death vied with each other, both in prose and verse, in unqualified encomiums on his character.

A story is told of him, that after he had promised a valuable living to a friend of Sir Robert Walpole, the curate of the late incumbent called upon him with a petition from the parishioners, testifying to his merits and his poverty, and entreating his lordship to use his influence with the new rector to continue him in the curacy. After some little conversation with him and finding that his stipend was only 50l. a year, his lordship kindly promised not only to comply with the request, but also to do what he could to get the salary raised. When the rector-expectant came to thank him for his promise, his lordship mentioned the curate's petition, and begged it might be granted. 'I should be happy to oblige your lordship,' replied the clergyman, 'but I have promised my curacy to a particular friend.' 'Promised your curacy! what, sir, before the living is yours?' 'Yes, my lord.' 'Then, sir,' exclaimed the chancellor, with warmth, 'I will afford you an admirable opportunity of dismissing your friend; I will dispose of the living elsewhere;' and, without suffering a reply, dismissed him. On the curate's waiting upon him to know the result of his application, he told him that he was sorry to say that he could not get him the curacy; but on the poor man bowing and offering to retire, the chancellor stopped him and said, 'Though I cannot give you the curacy, I can give you the living, and yours it is; so you may write to your family and tell them that, although you applied only for the curacy, your merit and your modesty have obtained for you the living.' (*Law and Lawyers*, ii. 147.)

His short but illustrious career was terminated on February 14, 1737, by an attack of inflammation on the lungs. His remains were interred in the church of Barrington in Gloucestershire, where his residence was situated.

By his lady he left five sons. His successor, William, was created Earl Talbot in 1761, but in 1782 the earldom became extinct, but was two years afterwards granted to his cousin, John Talbot, by whose descendant it is still borne, together with the earldom of Shrewsbury, to which the father of the present peer succeeded in 1856. (*Welsby's Judges*, 263; *Birch's Lives*, 148; *Collins's Peerage*, v. 234.)

TALEBOT, GILBERT (Talbot), was the son of Richard Talebot, lord of Linton in Herefordshire, by Alina, his wife, who was the daughter of Alan Basset, of Wycombe, and widow of Drogo de Montacute. In 44 Henry III., 1260, he was made governor of the castles of Grosmont, Skenfrith, and Blancminster, which, with that of Monmouth, he was ordered to fortify against the disturbances of the Welsh. In the next year he was appointed one of the justices itinerant for Herefordshire and five other counties.

He married Guenthlian, the daughter and eventually the heir of Rhese ap Griffith, Prince of Wales, whose arms he thenceforward adopted instead of his own. By her he had a son, Richard, who succeeded him at his death in 2 Edward I., 1274, one of whose descendants in 1384 became, by his marriage with the heiress, Baron Strange. His son, John Talbot, acquired the barony of Furnival by marriage in 1409, and was created Earl of Shrewsbury in 1442. These titles, after falling twice into abeyance, ultimately devolved in 1856 on the father of the present Earl Talbot. (*Baronage*, i. 325.)

TALFOURD, THOMAS NOON. That a devotion to literature, and the possession of a poetic genius, are not necessarily incompatible with abstruser studies, nor absolute impediments to professional success, is exemplified in the career of Sir Thomas Noon Talfourd, who from the beginning to the end of his life united to the labours of the law the more agreeable avocations of an essayist, a poet, and a dramatist. The union of these apparently opposite studies did not prevent him from obtaining a considerable mastery of both; nor did the general reputation of this double occupation induce the legal world to suppose that he would neglect or fail in his exertions for them, because he employed himself occasionally in lighter pursuits. It is not, perhaps, too much to say that he owed his success and his promotion as much to his literary as to his legal character; and it is not improbable that in future he will be remembered more as the author of 'Ion' and as the friend and biographer of Charles Lamb, than as one of the judges of Westminster Hall.

He was the son of Edward Talfourd, a brewer at Reading, not in very prosperous circumstances, and of a daughter of the Rev. Thomas Noon, an independent minister there. He was born at Reading on January 26, 1795. His education commenced at the dissenters' school at Mill Hill, and proceeded at the grammar school at Reading, then holding a high character under the guidance of the celebrated Dr. Valpy. At the latter were strengthened and confirmed those poetic and dramatic inclinations which he had shown from his earliest youth, and he always attributed his future more matured efforts to the classical taste which he imbibed from his accomplished preceptor.

After gaining many of the prizes and other distinctions of the school, stern necessity obliged him to seek the means of subsistence in London. There, to support himself, he obtained employment as a newspaper reporter, and as a regular contributor to periodical publications. At the same time he sought instruction in the intricacies of law from the eminent special pleader Mr. Joseph Chitty.

His novitiate being completed, he was called to the bar by the Middle Temple on February 9, 1821. He attended the Oxford Circuit, where for some time he was engaged in reporting the assize business for the 'Times,' and obtained great credit for the impartial manner in which he detailed the exertions of his colleagues, and for the modest avoidance of his own name when he happened to be engaged. Thus gaining the respect of his associates, his genial qualities soon made him a general favourite; and the observance of his industry in reporting, and the competent knowledge which it indicated, brought him a gradual increase of business. To these recommendations was added a powerful and attractive style of oratory, which greatly availed him when taking a leading part, and at the end of twelve years the position he had secured justified him in applying for the distinction of a silk gown. He took the degree of a serjeant in 1833; and when the Court of Common Pleas was soon after opened to all barristers he received a patent of precedence which gave him rank in all the courts. He had two years before been selected as deputy recorder of the town of Banbury.

From this time he proceeded with distinguished success, and eventually became the acknowledged head of his circuit. In the metropolis also he shared with the eminent counsel who then graced the courts the conduct of the more important conflicts that engaged them, never sacrificing the interests of his clients to a love of display, and being as successful in their management and gaining as many verdicts as the most popular of his competitors. Two events occurring in the year 1835 tended greatly to extend his fame—his entrance into parliament as the representative of his native town, and the appearance of his tragedy of 'Ion' on the stage. In the former he soon became conspicuous, not only for his oratorical powers, by which lawyers do not generally make themselves acceptable to the house, but for two great measures which he advocated with extraordinary zeal and effect—one securing to the mother the right to have access to her children as long as her character is unstained; and the other securing to the author an extended period during which he or his family may enjoy the fruits of his labours. To the next parliament of 1841 Mr. Serjeant Talfourd was not returned, but in that of 1847 he resumed his seat for Reading till his elevation to the bench. His dramatic efforts during this interval did not meet with the brilliant success that attended the production of 'Ion.' They consisted of 'The Athenian Captive' and 'The Massacre of Glencoe,' which were both acted, and 'The Castilian,' which was privately circulated. His other publications were numerous, among the most important of which were 'Vacation Rambles,' a 'Life of Charles Lamb,' and an 'Essay on the Greek Drama,' contributed to a cyclopædia.

In July 1849 he was made a judge of the Common Pleas, when he received the accustomed honour of knighthood. The periodical press was loud in the expression of the universal feeling of pleasure which the appointment occasioned, and during the five years that he administered justice on the bench he did not disappoint the general expectation. Though not what is called a black-letter lawyer, his great good sense and extreme desire to do justice, his vigorous intellect and his practical experience, his personal amiability and urbanity towards all, made him a most satisfactory judge. His career was closed by an awful termination. While delivering his charge to the grand jury at Stafford on March 13, 1854, and recommending in emphatic terms a closer connection between the rich and the poor, he was, in the middle of an effective passage, suddenly struck with apoplexy, and ere a few moments had elapsed had gone to his great account.

He married in 1821 the daughter of Mr. John Towell Rutt, a merchant of London, and she brought to him a numerous family.

TAMETONE, WILLIAM DE, was a man of some importance in Yorkshire. In 4 Henry III. he was commissioned with Walter Mauclerk and others to enquire by twelve men into the state of the castle of Pickering in that county, after the peace between the king and Prince Louis; and there are two instances in which he was one of those before whom an assize of last presentation, and one of novel disseisin, were directed to be heard. In the general appointment of justices itinerant in 10 Henry III., 1226, he was selected for Northumberland. (*Rot. Claus.* i. 436, ii. 138, 151.)

TANFIELD, LAURENCE, was the son of Francis Tanfield, of Gayton in Northamptonshire. He became reader at the Inner Temple in Lent 1595. (*Dugdale's Orig.* 166.) He had long before acquired professional fame, for the Reports introduce his name as an advocate as early as 1579. In Easter 1603 he received the degree of the coif. He was member of the first parliament of King James's reign, and on January 13, 1606, he was constituted one of the judges of the King's Bench. He did not long remain in that position, being advanced on June 25, 1607, to the office of chief baron of the Exchequer, over which court he presided with much credit for integrity, independence, and learning during the remainder of his life. In the public acts of his time in which he was engaged—viz., in the case of the post-nati, the proceedings against the Countess of Shrewsbury for contempt, the trial of the Countess of Somerset for the murder of Sir Thomas Overbury, and the prosecution of Mr. Wraynham for slandering Lord Chancellor Bacon—no record is preserved of the part he took, except with regard to the latter, in which the judgment he pronounced is distinct and impressive. (*State Trials*, ii. 96, 609, 770, 952, 1076.)

That he was a favourite with his contemporaries may be inferred from the name of his residence in the Temple, theretofore called Bradshaw's Rents, being changed to Tanfield Court in compliment to him. (*Dugdale's Orig.* 146.) He survived King James about a month, and dying on April 30, 1625, was buried under a costly monument in Burford Church, Oxfordshire, where he had purchased the Priory with the manor of Great Tew and other lands. By his wife, Elizabeth Evans, of Loddington in Northamptonshire, he left an only daughter, Elizabeth, who married Sir Henry Carey of Aldenham, first Viscount Falkland; and Burford Priory afterwards became the property of Sir William Lenthall, who married another Elizabeth Evans of Loddington. (*Clarendon's Life*, i. 42; *Athen. Oxon.* iii. 604; *Notes and Queries*, 2nd S. x. 209.)

TANK, WILLIAM, was constituted chief baron of the Exchequer on February 3, 1374, 48 Edward III. He is mentioned as an advocate in the Year Books from the twentieth year. During the short period that he presided in the court he acted as a judge of assize, and there are two instances of grants to him of the custody of lands pending the minority of the heir, both of which being in Sussex, it is not improbable that he was settled in that county. He was succeeded as chief baron on November 12, 1375. (*N. Fœdera*, iii. 997; *Abb. Rot. Orig.* ii. 331, 336.)

TAUNTON, WILLIAM ELIAS, whose father, of the same name as himself, was clerk of the peace for the county and town-clerk of the city of Oxford, and had received the honour of knighthood, and whose mother was Frances, daughter of Stephen Grosvenor, Esq., sub-treasurer of Christ Church, was the eldest of a large family. He was born in 1773, and was educated first at Westminster and then at Christ Church, where he distinguished himself by gaining the chancellor's prize in 1793 for the best English essay, the subject being 'Popularity.' In the next year he entered Lincoln's Inn, and applied himself zealously to the study of the law, in which, when he was called to the bar in Easter Term 1799, he was deeply grounded. He joined the Oxford Circuit, uniting with it, according to the practice of the time, that of the district of South Wales. He soon acquired the reputation of a black-letter lawyer, and to great legal knowledge he added considerable abilities as a speaker. His style of eloquence was considered rather ponderous, but occasionally he burst into vigorous thought and beauty, and in language pure and terse exhibited the vast extent of his acquirements.

In 1805 he was elected deputy recorder of Oxford to Mr. Charles Abbot, afterwards Lord Colchester, upon whose resignation he succeeded as recorder. He also became one of the Commissioners of Bankrupts, and in 1822 received a silk gown as king's counsel. When, eight years after, the addition of another judge was required in each court, he was selected on November 18, 1830, to take the place in the King's Bench, and proved himself a most accomplished judge. His judgments were remarkable for originality of thought and felicity of expression, proceeding from a thoroughly independent mind. His judicial career, however, was a very limited one; in five years it was terminated by his sudden death, on January 11, 1835, at his house in Russell Square.

In 1814 he married Maria, daughter of Henry William Atkinson, Esq., provost of the Company of Moneyers, Royal Mint, by whom he left two sons and three daughters.

TAYLOR, JOHN, is supposed by Anthony Wood (*Fasti Oxon.* i. 62) to have had a tailor for his father, and to have been born in a poor cottage at Barton in the parish of Tatinhill in Staffordshire. He was one of three produced at a birth, who, being presented as a curiosity to the king while hunting in that county, were by the royal command all carefully educated. Whatever was his origin, he did credit to his instructors by becoming an eminent canonist of his day.

It would appear, from Wood's description of him as 'a doctor of decrees and of the sacred canons *beyond the seas*,' that he took his degree in a foreign university; and this seems likely from his being incorporated at Cambridge in 1520, and at Oxford in May 1522. He was ordained sub-deacon in 1503, being then rector of the parish of Bishop's Hatfield in the diocese of Lincoln, and afterwards received several other benefices. In August 1504 he was united with Dr. John Yonge and others in negotiating the treaty of commerce with Philip Duke of Burgundy, and in the first year of Henry VIII., 1509, he was made clerk of the parliament, and immediately afterwards was appointed master in Chancery. In June 1513 he accompanied the king in his invasion of France, witnessing the battle of Spurs, &c.; and his interesting diary of the events of the expedition, in Latin, is now in the State Paper Office. In 1514 he was chosen prolocutor of the convocation, having just previously been collated to the archdeaconry of Derby, which was followed in the next year by that of Buckingham.

At this time he was an attendant on the court, and was sent to greet the Venetian embassy at Deptford, on its arrival in May 1515. The answer which he made by the king's command to the ambassador's Latin oration on his introduction is preserved among the Cotton MSS. in the British Museum (Nero, b. vii. fo. 12).

In 1525 he was again engaged in diplomatic duties, and in 1526 he was sent to France with the ostensible object of congratulating Francis on his release from captivity, but in reality to induce his majesty to violate the treaty he had just concluded with the emperor. Dr. Taylor's success in this negotiation received the reward not unusually conferred for such services. On June 26, 1527, he was appointed master of the Rolls, and was soon after sent with several others to invest the French king with the order of the Garter. He was also named as one of the commissioners to try the validity of King Henry's marriage with Queen Catherine, the duty of examining the witnesses devolving upon him. After being seated at the Rolls for above seven years, he delivered up his patent to be cancelled on October 6, 1534, in order that the king might invest his favourite, Cromwell, with the place. His death followed very soon after, a successor in the archdeaconry being collated before the end of the year. (*Le Neve*, 135, 168; *Rymer*, xiii. 105, xiv. 106; *State Trials*, i. 312; *Lingard*, vi. 86; *Cal. State Papers* [1615–18].)

TENTERDEN, LORD. *See* C. ABBOTT.

THESIGER, FREDERICK (LORD CHELMSFORD), whose family is of German origin, is the grandson of a native of Dresden in Saxony, who, on coming into England, was introduced to the Marquis of Rockingham, and was employed as his lordship's confidential amanuensis or secretary. One among his children was Sir Frederick Thesiger, who distinguished himself in the navy under Lord Nelson, and took that gallant admiral's celebrated flag of truce on shore at Copenhagen in 1801. Another was Charles Thesiger, who went with Admiral Bentinck, when governor of St. Vincent, as secretary, and became successively comptroller and collector of customs in the island, the latter office being in those days highly lucrative. Besides which he obtained a grant of land there from the crown. He had seven children, of whom Frederick the future chancellor was the youngest.

Frederick was born in London on April 15, 1794, and received the early part of his education at the school of the eminent Grecian Dr. Charles Burney, of Greenwich. But his inclinations turning towards the sea, he left the Grecian, and entered into a naval academy at Gosport, kept by another Dr. Burney, equally eminent in producing good officers as his namesake in producing good scholars. After a year's preparation, he, like his great predecessor Lord Chancellor Erskine, commenced his active life as a midshipman, joining in 1807 the Cambrian frigate, commanded by the Hon. Charles Paget, and being present in that year at the second bombardment of Copenhagen, as his uncle had been at the first. Soon afterwards, when by the death of his last surviving brother he became the heir of his father's West India estate, his life was considered too valuable to be risked in the naval service, and to his great regret his name was removed from the Navy List. After two years spent at an indifferent private school, he went at seventeen to St. Vincent, as he had been heard to say, 'to make his father's acquaintance.' There, after due consideration, it was determined that the young man should qualify himself for the bar of St. Vincent, and for that purpose should enter one of the inns of court in England, and on his return should with his practice as a barrister unite the superintendence of the property.

The latter part of this plan was soon after defeated, by the eruption of a volcano of the Souffriere mountain, at the foot of which the estate was situate. This event, which happened on April 30, 1812, totally annihilated the whole property, burying it under a mass of stones and ashes; but, though it diminished the young man's prospects, it did not change his legal destination.

Returning to England, he entered into the society of Gray's Inn on November 5, 1813. With the purposed object of eventually joining the West Indian bar, his preparation was devoted to every branch of the law, and the knowledge that he thus acquired was of eminent use in his future career. He went first to a conveyancer, then to an equity draughtsman, and finished his course by becoming a pupil of Mr. Godfrey Sykes, the eminent special pleader. To that gentleman's remonstrances young Thesiger owes his establishment at the English bar. His master thought so well of his pupil that he said it was a 'shame' to go back to the West Indies without trying his fortune in this country. Not having the slightest connection with any one likely to contribute to his advancement, he hesitated, but, though hopeless of success, decided as his kind instructor wished him.

He was called to the bar on November 18, 1818, and travelled the Home Circuit, joining the Surrey sessions. In the latter he was fortunate in getting into early business, and in two or three years became leader. By the purchase of the place of one of the four counsel of the Palace Court, instituted in the reign of Charles II. for the trial of causes of small amount within twelve miles of the Palace of Westminster, which sat on every Friday throughout the year, he acquired those habits of business, and that experience in conducting causes, that few counsel have an opportunity of gaining so early in the superior courts.

One of the cases on the circuit in which he highly distinguished himself was as counsel for Hunt, an accessory with Thurtell in the murder of Mr. Weare, tried in January 1824; but the case in which he obtained the greatest *éclat* while in a stuff gown, and to which he mainly attributed his future advance, was an ejectment against his client the lord of a manor, tried at Chelmsford in 1832, as to the right to some unenclosed strips of land by the side of the highway, in which, after three trials, he succeeded in establishing his client's title. Mr. Thesiger afterwards chose his own title of Lord Chelmsford in memory of this triumph. During this time he was obtaining very considerable employment in Westminster Hall, and evidently commanding the ear of the judges. The author of these pages was himself present on two occasions when Chief Justice Abbott highly complimented him to the jury on his management of cases which he had been called upon to lead in the absence of his senior.

In 1834 he was made king's counsel, and for the next ten years he remained the leader of his circuit.

In 1840 he entered into the political arena as member for Woodstock; and on April 15, 1844, he was, after twenty-six years of continued labour, selected by Sir Robert Peel's government to be the solicitor-general, in the place of Sir William Follett, who became attorney-general. With this eminent man and extraordinary advocate, who was as remarkable for his legal acquirements and his effective eloquence as for the charm of his manner and the music of his voice, Mr. Thesiger (who was knighted soon after his promotion) would have been delighted to act as a subordinate. But the health of his leader, broken down by too intense exertions in his profession, soon after obliged him to quit England, and to leave the solicitor-general, quite a novice in the duties of his own office, to encounter the work of both. This he successfully performed for above ten months, and it is pleasing to record the generous and ready assistance he received from his old political opponent Sir Thomas Wilde, who voluntarily offered and kindly gave the aid of his experience, when he saw the difficult position in which Sir Frederick was placed. On Sir William Follett's death, Sir Frederick was appointed attorney-general, on June 29, 1845, and retained the office till July 3, 1846, when he retired with the ministry of Sir Robert Peel, on the occasion of the repeal of the corn laws.

Two days after his resignation Lord Chief Justice Tindal died, and thus Sir Frederick lost the succession to the vacant seat, which would have fallen to him as of course had the death occurred a few days before. It was naturally given by the new ministry to their attorney-general, Sir Thomas Wilde. That ministry remained in power for nearly six years, during which Sir Frederick resumed his former leading position at the bar without office. When they were in turn defeated, Sir Frederick was restored to his previous office on February 27, 1852, but only held it till December 28 in that year, his party being again obliged to retire, and then again he returned into the ranks as a private barrister, for the next six years employed in all the great cases which occupied the attention of the public.

Among the '*causes célèbres*' in which he was engaged during the last decade of his forensic career was the famous attempt of a Miss Smith to charge the Earl of Ferrers with breach of promise of marriage, in which Sir Frederick's speech in defence of the earl, exposing the fraud and forgery by which the charge was supported, was considered so eloquent and effective that one of his most distinguished colleagues, since a chief justice, is said to have declared to him that he would rather have made that speech than any he had ever heard at the bar. Another remarkable case in which Sir Frederick was equally successful was in exposing a man who pretended to be the son of Sir Hugh Smyth, and to be entitled to vast estates in Gloucestershire and other counties. There the benefit of the electric telegraph was fully exemplified, as well as the advantage of the publication of legal proceedings, for in the interval between the two days of trial a full confirmation of the plaintiff's villainy was communicated to the defendant's counsel, and the perjured claimant, instead of gaining possession of the coveted estates, ended his life in prison.

Sir Frederick was not only ingenious and eloquent in the conduct of his cases; he enlivened them also with his witty repartees. Of these it is difficult to give specimens, because they applied mostly to local circumstances, or were conveyed in professional diction. One, however, may be recorded as an apt example. He was opposed by a learned serjeant, who in his examination of his witnesses was very irregular in putting leading questions. Sir Frederick, remonstrating, appealed to the judge, on which the learned serjeant said, 'I have a right to *deal* with my witnesses as I please.' 'Yes,' said Sir Frederick, 'he may *deal*, my lord, but he must not *lead*.'

In his parliamentary career he was a firm supporter of the conservative party. In 1844 he exchanged Woodstock for Abingdon, and in 1852 he was returned for Stamford, for which he sat till he was raised to the peerage. His friendship with Sir Robert Peel continued till the death of that distinguished statesman, by whose side he was seated when he made his last speech. Sir Frederick, on some occasions after the repeal of the corn laws, found himself obliged to oppose Sir Robert when giving support to some of the measures of the whig ministry, and joined what is called the Protectionist party, from which the Peelites became after the death of their leader more and more widely separated.

On Lord Derby coming into office for the second time, Sir Frederick was raised from the rank of a barrister to the head of the law. The Great Seal was delivered to him as lord chancellor on February 26, 1858, and on the next day he was called to the House of Lords as Baron Chelmsford. His qualifications for and his merits in the performance of the duties of that high office I have bound myself not to notice. He held it for only sixteen months, and resigned it on June 18, 1859, on the break-up of Lord Derby's ministry. For the next seven years he kept his habits of business in full practice by devoting himself most assiduously to the hearing of appeals in the House of Lords and the privy council.

At the end of that time Lord Derby again came into power, and replaced Lord Chelmsford in his former position as lord chancellor on July 6, 1866; but on the resignation of the prime minister, Mr. Disraeli, his successor, for political reasons, removed Lord Chelmsford, who gave up the Great Seal on February 29, 1868, to Lord Cairns, who was himself obliged to retire with the conservative party before the end of the year. True to his party, Lord Chelmsford still pursues the same course and performs the same duties as devotedly as in his former recess from office.

Among the congratulations which he received on his first promotion, the address of the Incorporated Law Society, whose standing counsel he had been for the last thirteen years, must have given him peculiar pleasure, as proving that the esteem in which he was held was not confined to his brethren of the bar, but was extended over both branches of the profession. It contained the following passage: 'The council, and they believe the profession at large, rejoice to perceive in the elevation of your lordship to the highest official dignity in the power of the crown to bestow, the appropriate termination of a long and distinguished career, in which—unaided by the accidents of fortune—brilliant abilities, united to unwearied industry, unsullied honour and spotless integrity, the firm, fearless, and dignified maintenance of the rights, the honour, and the independence of the profession, joined to a courtesy which never failed, and which knew no distinction of rank or station, have at length achieved their just and fitting reward.' To this affectionate testimonial Lord Chelmsford returned a most graceful and feeling reply.

In 1822 he married the daughter of William Tinling, Esq., and niece of Major Peirson, who lost his life in defending the island of Jersey. Of his issue by her he has seven surviving children, four sons and three daughters. The eldest son is a colonel in the army, and distinguished himself at Sebastopol and in India, where he is now adjutant-general; and one of his daughters is the widow of Major-General Sir John Eardley Wilmot Inglis, K.C.B., celebrated for his gallant defence of the Residence at Lucknow, who died from the consequences of his exertions there.

THIRNING, WILLIAM, was of a family probably settled at Thirning in Huntingdonshire, as he is mentioned in a grant of certain land, houses, and rents of the manor of Hemingford Grey in that county to the prior and convent of Harwolde. (*Cal. Inq.* p. m. iii. 218.)

His name first appears in the Year Books in 44 Edward III., 1370; but it was not till April 11, 1388, 11 Richard II., that he was appointed a judge of the Common Pleas. Within eight years he was raised to the chief seat in that court, on January 15, 1396, 19 Richard II. (*Cal. Rot. Pat.* 216, 229.)

Hitherto he seems to have confined himself to the performance of his judicial functions, with no other variation than arose from acting as a trier of petitions in parliament. But he was soon called upon to take part in the political scenes which then agitated the country. When King Richard had resumed his royal power, and had contrived in his twenty-first year to summon a parliament ready to do his bidding, the legality of the attainder of the judges ten years before was discussed by both houses, and the legal and judicial officers were called upon to state what they thought of the answers of their predecessors for which they had been condemned. Chief Justice Thirning replied, somewhat evasively, that 'the declaration of treason not yet declared belonged to the parliament, but that had he been a lord of parliament, if he had been asked, he should have answered in the same manner.' (*Rot. Parl.* iii. 358.) All the proceedings of the eleventh year were thereupon of course repealed, and the surviving sufferers recalled from banishment.

Recollecting that these enactments of 21 Richard II. were all annulled within two years in the first parliament of Henry IV., it seems somewhat extraordinary that Sir William Thirning (for he was then a knight), after giving such an opinion, should have been selected as one of the commissioners to receive Richard's resignation of the crown, and should have been put forward so prominently as the spokesman of the parliament in pronouncing his deposition. But Henry was a politic prince, and probably deemed it wiser to overlook what might be considered as an act of political necessity than to make enemies of the lawyers. He no doubt also thought that it would give a judicial weight to the solemn proceeding if it was conducted under the auspices of the oldest and most respected judge upon the bench. Thirning also may be supposed to have undertaken the office, not from any strong dissatisfaction with Richard's government, nor any positive approval of Henry's title, but because a change having already been made inevitable by Henry's proceedings, he considered it his duty so to act that such change should be effected as peaceably as possible.

Thirning accordingly, with his coadjutors, attended on Richard in the Tower on September 29, 1399, and there received his renunciation of the throne. On the next day it was presented to the parliament, which thought fit, in addition, to allege thirty-three articles of misgovernment against him, and to depute seven commissioners, of whom Thirning was one, to pronounce a sentence of deposition. This being done, the same commissioners were directed, as procurators of the people, to communicate the proceedings to the fallen king, and to resign and give back to him the homage and fealty of his former subjects. The delicate duty fell upon Sir William Thirning, who spoke in the name of them all; and it is but just to say that he confined himself to the words of the sentence, not aggravating it by any harsher language than that in which it was expressed. (*Rot. Parl.* iii. 416–24.)

His last duty in that parliament was to pronounce its sentence on the lords who had appealed the Duke of Gloucester and his friends in 21 Richard II.; and in the following parliament the objects for which it was called were declared in a speech delivered by him. (*Ibid.* 451, 454.) After this his name does not appear in any political transactions, but his judgments are regularly recorded throughout the reign in numerous reports in the Year Books.

On the accession of Henry V. he received his new patent on May 2, 1413; but he must have died very shortly afterwards, for his widow Joan brought an action of debt in the next Trinity Term (*Y. B.* p. 6), and his successor, Sir Richard Norton, was appointed chief justice in his place on June 26, 1413.

THOMAS was elected abbot of Winchcumb in Gloucestershire in 1220, and was at the head of the commission issued in May 1226, 10 Henry III., to the justices itinerant for Worcestershire, according to a then common practice of placing an ecclesiastic in that position. He died on October 3, 1232. (*Browne Willis.*)

THOMSON, ALEXANDER, was born in 1744. Practising in the courts of equity, he was promoted on May 11, 1782, to a mastership in Chancery, and continued to act in that character for nearly four years, when on January 4, 1786, he became accountant-general of that court. In another year he was raised to the bench, being sworn a baron of the Exchequer on February 9, 1787, and knighted. After remaining in that seat for twenty-seven years, he was appointed the head of his court in Hilary Vacation 1814, a position which he fully merited by his legal knowledge and the excellence of his judicial decisions. He presided for little more than three years, and died at Bath at the age of seventy-three on April 15, 1817, being then by many years the father of the bench.

His reputation as a lawyer and as a judge was of the highest order, his acquirements in scholastic literature were very great, and his disposition as a man was eminently social and kind. To his deep learning and comprehensive understanding was united a great love of jocularity. The jokers of Westminster Hall nicknamed him 'The Staymaker,' from a habit he had of checking witnesses who were going too fast. (1 *Term Rep.* 551; 5 *Taunton,* 415; 1 *Moore,* 98.)

THOMSON, WILLIAM, whose life presents both an uncommon succession of offices and an extraordinary combination of them, was first recorder of London, and then solicitor-general—a legitimate advance; next, on being dismissed from the latter, he accepted the insignificant office of cursitor baron of the Exchequer, and, lastly, he was raised to the bench of that court as an actual judicial baron. But what was most remarkable was that he retained the place of city recorder after his appointment to his three other posts, and held it till his death—a plurality which was either forced upon him by the general impression of his superior abilities, of which there is no evidence, or was the effect of a greediness of gain, which blinded him to the impropriety of filling positions in some measure incompatible with each other, and certainly with respect to his last promotion differing greatly in their dignity and degree.

He was the second son of a barrister and bencher of the Middle Temple of the same names, and, with his elder brother Stephen, was admitted into that society in 1688, but not called to the bar till 1698. In 1708 he was returned to parliament as member for Orford in Suffolk; and to him the whig party entrusted the enforcement of the third charge in their suicidal impeachment of Dr. Sacheverell. He performed this duty with sufficient point, and so satisfactorily to the promoters of the prosecution that he was employed as junior counsel in the proceedings against the rioters, whom the popular disgust had inflamed to the commission of unjustifiable outrages. The consequence was that he lost his seat in the new parliament of 1710; but in the following parliament of February 1714, called within a few months before the death of Queen Anne, he was elected for Ipswich, which he continued to represent till he was raised to the bench; and on March 3 of that year he was chosen recorder of the city of London, but so nearly were parties divided that it was only by the casting vote of the lord mayor that he succeeded. In this character it was his fortune to read the addresses of congratulation to both George I. and George II. On the former occasion probably he was knighted, as he is designated with the title shortly after, when acting as one of the managers on the trial of the Earl of Wintoun for the part taken by him in the rebellion of 1715. (*State Trials*, xv. 157–869.)

In February 1717 he succeeded as solicitor-general; but by his jealous and grasping disposition he lost it in three years, and was expelled from the office with disgrace. In the numerous charters of incorporation granted to the joint-stock companies by which the public were then tempted and tricked, the Attorney-General Lechmere had benefited by the fees more largely than himself. Sir William, envious of his colleague's advantages, had the folly to denounce him as guilty of corruption before the committee appointed to enquire into all those companies, alleging that he had not only pocketed large bribes, but had permitted public biddings for charters at his chambers as at an auction. Lechmere of course could not allow such an imputation to remain upon him; a searching investigation was made into its truth, and the result was a unanimous vote that the charges were malicious, false, scandalous, and utterly groundless. For this disgraceful slander Sir William was dismissed on March 17, 1720. Sir William, in no ways abashed, still kept his seat in parliament and his place as recorder, and in 1724 so far recovered his position as to obtain the grant of an annuity of 1200*l.*, and a patent of precedence in all courts after the attorney and solicitor general. (*Townsend's Ho. of Com.* i. 451.)

Not yet content, he accepted on June 27, 1726, the inferior place of cursitor baron of the Exchequer, and occupied it for the remainder of the reign of George I., and for two years in that of George II., still acting as recorder by himself or his deputies, Serjeants Raby and Urling. On November 27, 1729, he was, by a very unusual step, advanced from the executive office of cursitor baron to that of a judicial baron, having been on the previous day made a serjeant for the purpose, and his present patent differing from the former by designating his new appointment as that of baron 'of the coife.' Even with this honourable office of one of the twelve judges of England, he would not deprive himself of the profits of the inconsistent place of recorder; but, after sitting in the Exchequer for nearly ten years, he died in the possession of both, on October 27, 1739, at Bath. (*Gent. Mag.* ix. 554.) By his will he left a ring to all the aldermen of London, and his portrait to the corporation. He married Julia, daughter of Sir Christopher Conyers, of Horden in Durham, and widow of Sir William Blackett, of Wallington in Northumberland, Bart.

THORESBY, JOHN DE, or **THURSBY** (ARCHBISHOP OF YORK), was born at a manor of that name in Wensleydale in Yorkshire, which had been long in the family, and was the second son of Hugh de Thoresby, who was lord of it in 9 Edward II. (*Parl. Writs*, ii. p. ii. 410.) He greatly distinguished himself while at Oxford by his attainments in the study of divinity, taking a high degree in both laws. So early as 1 Edward III. he was the last named in a mission to the pope to procure the canonisation of Thomas Duke of Lancaster. At that time he probably was a clerk in the Chancery, where he continued to act for several years; and having in 10 Edward III. been served in open court with a monition to appear before the pope on some appeal, the papal messengers were straightway committed to prison as guilty of a contempt, and were only released by the intercession of Queen Philippa. (*Prynne on 4th Inst.* 16.) This, however, did not prevent his being again sent to the pope, four years afterwards, to obtain a dispensation for the proposed marriage between Hugh le Despencer and the daughter of the Earl of Salisbury.

In the following year, on February 21, 1341, he received the appointment of master of the Rolls; and during the illness and at the death of Chancellor Parning, in 1343, he did the duties of the Seal, and, with two of the clerks of the Chancery, held it till Robert de Sadington was invested with the office.

He continued master of the Rolls certainly as late as May 20, 1345, being about that time made keeper of the privy seal. (*N. Fœdera*, ii. 897, 1119, iii. 39, 53.)

In the previous year he obtained a canonry in Lincoln Cathedral, and again visited the papal court as one of the king's ambassadors, performing the same duty in France in 1346. (*Ibid.* iii. 25, 54, 92.)

On September 3, 1347, he was consecrated Bishop of St. David's; and on June 16, 1349, he was appointed chancellor. On the 4th of the following November he was translated to the bishopric of Worcester, and was raised to the archbishopric of York on October 22, 1352. He was left one of the custodes of the kingdom when King Edward renewed his invasion of France in 1355 (*Ibid.* 305); but on his sovereign's return after the battle of Poictiers in the ensuing year, his advancing age prompted him to apply for liberty to retire from the chancellorship, which he had held with credit and honour longer than any other chancellor of this reign, though for little more than seven years in all, during four of which he had been archbishop. He was accordingly, 'benevole et gratanter,' exonerated from his duties on November 27, 1356.

His political duties during the seventeen remaining years of his life were confined to conducting various treaties with the Scottish king; but for the most part he devoted himself to his episcopal functions, and to the renovation of his cathedral. He laid the first stone of the new choir on July 29, 1362; and, besides exciting the nobles and clergy of his province to aid his endeavours, he expended large sums in carrying on that splendid work, and also in restoring and ornamenting the chapel of St. Mary, where his remains were afterwards deposited. The question of precedence between the two archbishops, which had for many years occasioned unseemly contests, was settled by agreement between him and Archbishop Islip; and Pope Innocent IV., in his confirmation of the arrangement, introduced the nice distinction of primate of England, and primate of *all* England. He is said by some to have been created a cardinal by Pope Urban V., but his name does not appear in the most authentic lists, nor is he ever so called in the English records.

He died at his manor of Thorpe on November 6, 1373, having been engaged in the public service for nearly forty-eight years of Edward's reign, with a character honourably described as 'contentionum et litium hostis, et pacis et concordiæ amicus.' Besides several other religious works, he wrote a commentary in the English tongue on the Lord's Prayer, the Decalogue, and the Articles of Faith, for the use of the people of his province. That on the Ten Commandments is printed by Thoresby in the appendix to his 'Vicaria Leodensis.' (*Godwin*, 464, 581, 687; *Drake's Eboracum*, 434.)

THORNTON, GILBERT DE, or DE TORENTON, is mentioned as the king's attorney from 8 to 14 Edward I., 1280-6; but it is uncertain whether this office was similar to that of the attorney-general of the present day, or anything more than a special appointment to act on the part of the king in a particular proceeding. There were evidently at these times two or three so acting in different counties under the designation of 'narratores pro rege.' (*Abb. Placit.* 274.)

On the disgrace of Ralph de Hengham he was constituted chief justice of the King's Bench, 1289, with a salary of 40*l.* per annum; and there is evidence of his acting as late as August 1295 (*Rot. Parl.* i. 134), soon after which Roger le Brabazon was raised to the same post. But whether the vacancy occurred by Gilbert de Thornton's death or resignation does not appear; and there is no trace of his private history, except the fact that a messuage and two carucates of land at Caburn in Lincolnshire were conveyed to him in 17 Edward I. by John Priorell. (*Abb. Placit.* 218.)

During his presidency of the court he composed a Compendium of the Law, which was in the nature of an abridgment of Bracton's work, but which has never been printed. The manuscript, which Selden found in Lord Burleigh's library, states that Gilbert de Thornton 'tempore illo scientiâ, bonitate, et mansuetudine, floruit eleganter.' (*Legal Bibliog.* 336; *Dugdale's Orig.* 57.)

THORPE, ROBERT DE, was appointed a judge of the Common Pleas when Edward I., in 1289, punished nearly all the judges for corrupt practices in their office; and the fines levied before him commence on the octaves of the Purification, 18 Edward I., 1290, and continue for no more than a year. (*Dugdale's Orig.* 44.) He probably died shortly after, as his name does not again occur. His wife was named Aveline. (*Rot. Parl.* i. 18, 31, 33, 198.)

THORPE, JOHN DE, the son of Robert de Thorpe and Maud his wife, of a considerable family, possessing Rolands, Combes, Uphall, and other manors in Norfolk and Suffolk, was returned as knight of the shire for Norfolk in 33 Edward I., and acted in the same year as assessor and collector of the aid to the king in that county. (*Parl. Writs*, i. 863.) In 35 Edward I., 1307, he held the second place among the justices of trailbaston then appointed for those two counties. (*Rot. Parl.* i. 218, 301.) He 'and his companions' are mentioned as justices in Norfolk in 8 Edward II., and various judicial duties were assigned to him up to the seventeenth year. In 13 Edward II. he was made sheriff of the county. (*Parl. Writs*, ii. 1503-5; *Abb. Rot. Orig.* i. 252, 278.)

He married Alice Mortimer: and at his death, on May 16, 1324, 17 Edward II., his son Robert succeeded him, but does not appear to have been summoned as a baron. (*Cal. Inq. p. m.* i. 310; *Rot. Parl.* i. 169, 419, 420; *Blomefield's Norfolk*, i. 137, 611, &c.)

THORPE, ROBERT DE, who was a justice itinerant into Derbyshire in 4 Edward III., 1330, was clearly a different person from the chief justice and chancellor in a later period of the reign; but the Thorpes were so numerous that it would be merely guesswork to attempt to fix the family to which he belonged. He may have been the son of John and Alicia de Thorpe, of Creek in Norfolk, and Combes in Suffolk; and if so, he died in the same year he acted as justice itinerant, and was succeeded by his son John. (*Cal. Inq. p. m.* i. 310, ii. 20, 139.)

THORPE, ROBERT DE, of Thorpe, near Norwich, was educated at Cambridge, in which university he laid the foundation of the divinity schools, with the chapel over them, in 1356, and was afterwards master of Pembroke College. He commenced his career as an advocate as early as 14 Edward III., 1340, attaining the rank of king's serjeant in 1345. Coke calls him 'a man of singular judgment in the laws of this realm.' He was appointed one of the justices to try felonies in the county of Oxford in 1355, and was frequently employed as a justice of assize, but held no seat on the judicial bench at Westminster until he was appointed chief justice of the Common Pleas, on June 27, 1356, 30 Edward III. Nine years afterwards he had an extended grant of 40*l.* a year to support the dignity of knighthood which the king had conferred upon him; and he continued to preside in that court for nearly fifteen years. So high a character did he acquire that when the Commons petitioned the king that none but laymen should be placed in the higher offices of the state, he was deemed the fittest man to supersede William of Wykeham, Bishop of Winchester, as chancellor; and the Great Seal was accordingly delivered to him on March 26, 1371.

He enjoyed this dignity little more than a year, his death occurring on June 29, 1372.

He married Margaret, the daughter of William Deyncourt, but left no children. (*Abb. Rot. Orig.* ii. 337; *Cal. Inq.* p. m. 322; *Master's C.C.C. Cambridge,* 28.)

THORPE, WILLIAM DE, appears in the Year Books as an advocate as early as 7 Edward III. In 15 Edward III., 1341, he was made one of the king's serjeants, and is called the king's attorney in the following year. In that year, on April 23, 1342, he was raised to the bench. The words used are 'unus justiciariorum ad placita in Banco.' (*Cal. Rot. Pat.* 142.) Dugdale thereupon inserts him among the justices of the Common Pleas; but, as he does not mention any fines levied before him, and introduces his name as a justice of the King's Bench in the nineteenth year, on the authority of the Liberate Roll, without mentioning the date of his removal from the Common Pleas, it may be doubtful whether his first appointment was not to the King's Bench, especially as he became the chief of it on November 26, 1346. In that character he opened the parliaments of the two following years. (*Rot. Parl.* ii. 164, 200.)

Towards the end of 1350 charges were made against him of malversation in his office; and the king issued his writ, on November 3, to five commissioners to have him before them, and to do justice according to his demerits. They immediately proceeded on their commission, when he confessed that he had received bribes from Richard de Salteby, of 10*l.*; from Hildebrand Bereswerd, of 20*l.*; from Gilbert Haliland, of 40*l.*; from Thomas de Derby, of St. Bartholomew, of 20*l.*; and from Robert de Dalderby, of 10*l.*; all of whom had been indicted before him at Lincoln; and that he had therefore caused the writ of exigent against them to be stayed; whereupon he was committed prisoner to the Tower of London, and all his lands and goods were ordered to be seized into the king's hands, until the royal will and pleasure should be known.

With this legal and reasonable judgment, however, the king was not satisfied; and accordingly issued another writ on November 19, commanding the same parties immediately to pronounce judgment that he should be degraded and hanged. This was accordingly done, and thereupon, on the same day, the king, by writ of privy seal, signified that he 'gave and forgave him his life,' but ordered his body to be remitted to prison. The record and process were afterwards laid before the parliament, which confirmed the judgment. (*N. Fœdera,* iii. 208; *Rot. Parl.* ii. 227.) Coke says (3 *Inst.* 145) that Sir William Thorpe was pardoned and restored to all his lands, 'as by the record appeareth;' but the record, as published, only says that the execution of the judgment of hanging was pardoned to him, and that he was remitted to prison to await the king's favour. The remainder of the judgment, 'that all his land and goods should be forfeited to the king,' is left unnoticed, and consequently unpardoned; and by entries on the records of that year (*Abb. Rot. Orig.* ii. 211, 212), it appears that the sheriffs of Lincoln and other counties were directed to take his lands, &c., into the king's hands, as convicted of certain crimes; and that four of his horses, 'cum sellis, frenis, et garconibus, were seized by one of the sheriffs of London.

In the following year, however, he received the king's pardon, with the restoration of part of his lands—viz., the manor of Changton in Sussex. (*Cal. Rot. Pat.* 160.) He was not restored to his office of chief justice; but after an interval of eighteen months he was made second baron of the Exchequer, on May 24, 1352, unless the William de Thorpe who then received that appointment was a different person. In the absence of any evidence to the contrary, there is good reason to believe that he was the same person; the more especially as there are instances, ten years before, of the king's reinstating judges against whom charges had been made, and as it was extremely improbable that a person, of whom no previous notice exists of his being connected with the court, should be at once raised to the office of second baron, above the other occupants of that bench.

From a passage in the 'Liber Assisarum' of 28 Edward III. (p. 145), where Thorpe is said to have been 'then made chief justice,' it might be inferred that he was restored to his former place; but attention to the context clearly proves that the expression merely means that he was made chief justice in the commission of assizes in Sussex, in the place of H. Green, who had been sent on some other service; as we should now say, the senior judge of assize.

Whether the baron of the Exchequer were the same or a different person, he was present among the judges in the parliament of 28 and 29 Edward III. (*Rot. Parl.* ii. 254, 267), but not later.

Within a few years three William de Thorpes are mentioned—in Nottingham, Northampton, and Sussex (*N. Fœdera*, 221, 457, 464); but we cannot satisfactorily identify either with the judge.

THORPE, THOMAS, of what family is uncertain, was an officer of the Exchequer in 20 Henry VI., 1442, when he was commissioned to receive the 'great good' which the king expected would accrue from the general pardon he had granted to his subjects, and to apply it to the defence of Calais. (*Acts Privy Council*, v. 186.) Dugdale does not introduce him among the barons of the Exchequer till November 1458; but he had clearly then held the office between five and six years; and we have a curious exhibition of the mode of his obtaining it in a petition to the parliament of 33 Henry VI., 1455. (*Rot. Parl.* v. 342.)

Thorpe was remembrancer of the Exchequer when the Earl of Worcester was appointed treasurer in April 1452. That nobleman, who was a partisan of the Duke of York, immediately turned Thorpe out of the office, and gave it to Richard Forde, the clerk of the Pipe. Thorpe was not a man to submit, and therefore obtained letters patent for his restoration from the king, who no doubt listened readily to the complaint of his own adherent against the encroachment of one whom he looked upon as little less than a rebel. Thorpe accordingly retook possession of the place, and would not give it up, as the petition with simplicity avers, 'onlesse thenne he myght bene preferred to be third baron of the seid Eschequier.' The dismissed remembrancer thereupon negotiated with William Fallan, then the third baron, whom he induced to resign by giving him a bond undertaking to pay him forty marks yearly for his life or till otherwise provided for.

The king of course made no difficulty in giving Thorpe his patent, and the date of his appointment may be fixed in the early part of 1453. There is little doubt that he held it when he was elected speaker of the House of Commons on March 8 of that year (*Rot. Parl.* v. 227); and it is certain that he did so in the following June, for his wife, who died on the 23rd of that month, is described on her tombstone in St. John Zachary's, in London, as 'Joanna, the wife of Thomas Thorp, one of the barons of the Exchequer, and speaker of the parliament.' (*Weever*, 391.)

The parliament was prorogued on July 2, and Baron Thorpe was present at no less than five meetings of the king's council in that and the following months. (*Acts*, 152–331.) It was probably during those sittings that he was directed to seize 'certeine harnesse and other habiliments of warre' which the Duke of York had collected at the Bishop of Durham's. For this act the duke brought an action against him in the Court of Exchequer, 'for somuche that the same Thomas was oon of the court,' and obtained a verdict against him for 1000*l.* damages and 10*l.* costs. On this judgment he was cast into the Fleet Prison, and remained in custody when the parliament reassembled on February 14, 1454.

The Commons then claimed their ancient privileges, and that in accordance with them their speaker should be liberated. But the duke, by his counsel, stating the fact of the seizure of the goods—omitting, however, to mention what those goods were,—the Lords referred the question of the speaker's liberation to the judges. These learned persons, although they stated that they ought not to answer it, for the justices had never been used to determine the privileges of the high court of parliament—adding, with humorous evasion, 'for it is so high and mighty in his nature that it may make lawe, and that that is lawe it may make no lawe, and the determination and knowledge of that privilege belongeth to the lordes of the parliament and not to the justices,'— yet honestly concluded by declaring that if any member were arrested except for treason or felony, or for surety of the peace, or for a condemnation had before the parliament, 'it is used that all such persons be released of such arrests and make an attorney so that they may have their freedom and liberty, freely to intend upon the parliament.' Fortescue was then the chief justice, but he merely spoke as the organ of his brethren.

The first part of this answer is precisely of the same character as that which the judges gave seven years afterwards, when they were called upon for their opinion on the claim of the Duke of York to the crown. They then stated that they had to determine such matters as came before them in the law between party and party, and that the matter in question was so high and above the law that it passed their learning, and that it pertained to the lords of the king's blood and the appanage of his land to meddle in such matters. (*Rot. Parl.* v. 239, 376.) In both cases it is evident that their answers were dictated by their fears and not by their conviction; and in the former it is curious that, while they disclaim the right to judge, they do actually determine the case before them by stating the custom which had been hitherto recognised.

The Lords, notwithstanding the opinion so explicitly given, decided in direct opposition to it, and, no doubt influenced by the Duke of York, who was upon the eve of being appointed protector, adjudged that Thorpe should still remain in prison, 'the privilege of parliament, or that the same Thomas was the speaker of the parliament, notwithstanding;' and they charged the Commons to proceed to a new election. The Commons quietly submitted to this iniquitous encroachment on a privilege founded on the justest principle—the freedom of their own members.

The king recovered before the end of the year, when no doubt Thorpe was restored to liberty, since he received his salary as a baron on April 16, 1455. (*Devon's Issue Roll*, 479.) He was also present at the first battle of St. Albans, on May 22 following, and he is said to have 'fled and left his harness behind him cowardly.' (*Archæol.* xv. 526.) We must recollect, however, that the encounter was rather a surprise than a battle, and that many others joined in the flight. In the parliament that met in July he was charged, with the Duke of Somerset and William Joseph, with suppressing two letters sent by the Duke of York and the Earls of Warwick and Salisbury to the chancellor and the king the day before the battle, whereby the bloody conflict was occasioned; and though the king was compelled to accept the excuses then made by the duke and the earls, and to approve them as true and faithful liegemen, he refused his assent to two bills aimed against Thorpe—the one to deprive him of all offices, and to condemn him to an imprisonment of twelve years and a fine of 1000*l*.; and the other to restore all the officers of the Exchequer who had been removed except Thorpe. (*Rot. Parl.* v. 280, 333, 339.)

That Thorpe was replaced in his seat there can be no doubt, as he was advanced to be second baron on November 30, 1458; and he soon after received a grant of the reversion of the office of chancellor of the Exchequer on the death of Thomas Witham, which was excepted in the act of resumption passed in the parliament of November, 38 Henry VI. (*Ibid.* 366.) His prosperity, however, was not to last long. The Earl of Warwick's invasion forced the king again into the field. The faithful baron was by his side and shared his fate in the battle of Northampton on July 10, 1460. He was at first confined in Newgate and then in the Marshalsea; and on February 17, 1461, the very day on which the queen gained the second battle of St. Albans he was beheaded in Haringey Park in Middlesex. (*Ibid.* vi. 294.)

In his continued persecution by the Yorkists we not only see the inveteracy to which party spirit was then carried, but an evidence also that the baron was endowed with talents and courage which they felt it their interest to subdue; and we cannot but admire a man whose devotion and loyalty prompted him to quit a peaceful occupation to fight by his sovereign's side and to suffer in his cause. His history also affords a proof that a baron of the Exchequer was not then considered in the same light as the judges of the other courts, inasmuch as he was eligible to be a member of parliament. His son Roger was another victim of the same party. (*Ibid.*)

THORPE, FRANCIS (descended from the Yorkshire family of Thorpe, of Thorpe in Holderness), was the eldest son of Roger Thorpe of Birdshall, by Elizabeth, daughter of William Danyell of Beswick. (*Harl. MSS.* 1437, 205, 503; 1394, 122.) He was born in 1595, and being admitted a member of Gray's Inn, where his father had studied before him, he was, on May 11, 1621, called to the bar, and became reader in 1641. He held the post of recorder of Beverley from 1623 till he was raised to the bench in 1649, and was one of the witnesses examined against the Earl of Strafford, who had taken offence against him in Yorkshire for moving for prohibitions. (*Rushworth*, iv. 116.) He obtained a seat in the Long Parliament in September 1645 for the borough of Richmond, and was made a serjeant on October 12, 1648, when the vacancies in the law were filled up. (*Parl. Hist.* ii. 625.) After the king was beheaded (for the trial of whom Thorpe was named a commissioner, but never attended) (*State Trials*, iv. 1051), he was raised to a seat in the Exchequer on June 1, 1649, being no doubt selected on account of the 'good service' done by him in the last Northern Circuit, on which, as was common with the serjeants, he rode as judge of assize. (*Whitelocke*, 405, 409.) In an elaborate charge to the grand jury at York (afterwards printed) he endeavoured to justify the murder of the king, and to vindicate the parliament in their proceedings, raking up all the invidious and scandalous invectives against kings and monarchy which the most celebrated republicans up to his time had ever written. (*Drake's York*, 171.) He was therefore again sent on that circuit for the summer assize, and was presented with 200*l*. for his zeal in the former. (*Com. Journals*, vi. 144.) He fully confirmed the opinion which the ruling powers had formed of him by his condemnation of Lieut.-Colonel Morrice at York, though his conduct at the trial was more merciful than that of Judge Puleston. (*State Trials*, iv. 1249.)

In the parliament called by Cromwell in

September 1654, and dissolved in the following January, Thorpe, though a judge, was returned for Beverley. He became disgusted with the protector's proceedings, and, excusing himself from trying the prisoners in the north as contrary to his conscience, he and Judge Newdigate, who had the same scruples, received their writs of ease on May 3, 1655. His disgrace at court made him so popular in his native county that in the next parliament, in 1656, he was elected for the West Riding; but not obtaining the council's, or rather Cromwell's, certificate of approbation, he and above ninety others were excluded from its sittings. They thereupon published a spirited remonstrance, so violent in its language that it is surprising that the powers which had stirred up this resistance took no means to punish it. (*Godwin*, iv. 181; *Whitelocke*, 625, 653.) He afterwards took his seat, and several of his speeches are reported in Burton's Diary.

Thorpe was not returned to Protector Richard's parliament in January 1659, but when the Long Parliament was restored he took his seat as a member. On January 17, 1660, he was replaced on the bench as a baron of Exchequer (*Ibid.* 693), and was appointed to go the Northern Circuit. His judicial career was of course closed by the return of Charles II.

In 'The Mystery of the Good Old Cause' he is described as a bitter enemy to his prince, and as 'receiver of the money in Yorkshire, charged by some of the country for detaining 25,000*l.*' (*Parl. Hist.* iii. 1608.) This charge was probably alluded to when a motion was made that his name should be excepted from the bill of indemnity, which was seconded by Prynne, 'who mentioned one Thorpe, a judge in Edward the II.nd's time, who for taking bribes and other misdemeanors was punished, and therefore desired that this Judge Thorpe might also suffer the same.' He had a narrow escape, but several members speaking in his behalf, he was acquitted. (*Ibid.* v. 75.)

He married the daughter of — Oglethorpe, widow of — Denton, but it does not appear that he left any children.

THORPE, SIMON DE. *See* S. DE TROP.

THURKILBY, ROGER DE, of whose lineage and early life history is silent, first appears in 24 Henry III., 1240, as one of the four justices itinerant appointed for the southern district. Less than two years afterwards fines were levied before him, and so continued to be till just before his death —viz., from Michaelmas 1241 to Michaelmas 1259. (*Dugdale's Orig.* 43.)

In the circuits from 1245 to 1256 he was invariably placed at the head of the commission for the counties he visited, except when a bishop or abbot was joined to them; but it does not appear that he was as yet the chief justice of either court. On October 3, 1258, he was the first named of the three who were assigned 'ad tenendum Bancum Regis' at Westminster, until the king more fully regulated that bench; and on December 29, 1258, he had a grant of one hundred marks, as 'residens ad Bancum:' but whether the bench alluded to was the Bancum Regis, to which he was appointed the previous year, or the Common Bench or Common Pleas, seems doubtful. It is difficult to decide, also, what position he held in the court; but, considering that the salary of Henry de Bathonia was 100*l.*, and his only one hundred marks, it would seem that he occupied the second place. Nevertheless, there are some royal letters and commissions among the public records apparently addressed to him as the head (5 *Report Pub. Rec.*, App. ii. 63, 64), and an anonymous writer, in mentioning his sudden death in the following year, describes him as 'Justiciarii Angliæ gerens officium.' (*Leland's Collect.* i. 245.) He is represented as being second to none in his knowledge of the laws, and with the higher credit of opposing, though vainly, the iniquitous introduction of the non-obstante clause in the royal writs. (*Prynne on Coke's* 4 *Inst.* 132; *Rapin*, iii. 101.)

THURLAND, EDWARD, was descended from the ancient family of Thurland of Thurland Castle in Nottinghamshire. He was son of Edward Thurland, who, by his marriage with Elizabeth, daughter and one of the coheirs of Richard Elyot of Reigate, became a resident in that town, and was 'vice comes,' or undersheriff, of Surrey in 1623. (*Harl. MSS.* 1433, p. 40; *Addit. MSS.* 12,478, p. 2; 4963, p. 40.) He was born there in 1606, and was called to the bar by the Inner Temple on October 2, 1634. He was returned member for his native town to the short parliament that met in April 1640; but, luckily perhaps for him, was not re-elected for that which was summoned in the following November, so notorious in the annals of the kingdom. That he had made good use of his time, and was a proficient in the law, is shown by his being made steward of the manor of Reigate, his charge to the jury of which in August 1644 is preserved in Manning and Bray's 'Surrey' (i. 295). His intimacy with Jeremy Taylor and John Evelyn is a sufficient evidence of his pious and exemplary life, the correspondence between them exhibiting the friendly and confidential terms in which they lived, and the latter entrusting him with the stewardship of his courts. He composed a work on prayer, which he sent to Evelyn, who strongly recommended its publication; but it does not appear whether it was ever issued from the press.

In the Healing Parliament of 1660 he was again chosen representative for Reigate, and also in 1661; but he did not take an active part in either. (*Evelyn*, ii. 302, 410, iv. 5, &c.)

Soon after the Restoration he was elected recorder of both Reigate and Guildford, and was selected by James Duke of York as his solicitor, being thereupon knighted. In 1662 he became autumn reader of his inn of court, having been called to the bench of that society on November 24, 1652. From this time his name appears very frequently in the Reports, till he was elevated to the bench on January 24, 1673, when he was appointed a baron of the Exchequer. After sitting six years he arrived at that age when his growing infirmities warned him to prepare in quiet for meeting his last moments. He therefore tendered his resignation, and received his discharge on April 29, 1679. (*T. Jones's Rep.* 34; *Raleigh Redivivus*, 80.) He retired to his mansion at Reigate, where he died on December 19, 1682, aged seventy-six.

By his wife, Elizabeth, daughter of — Wright of Buckland in Surrey, he left an only son, Edward, also brought up to the law, who died five years after his father, without issue. A nephew, another Edward, who died in 1731, is described on his monument at Reigate as 'ultimus antiquæ stirpis masculus.' (*Harl. MSS.* 1480, p 37; *Manning and Bray's Surrey*, i. 325, ii. 498.)

THURLOW, EDWARD (LORD THURLOW), has been as much praised and as much abused as any man who ever held the Great Seal, and for his different qualities equally deserved both the approbation and censure he received. To a coarseness, partly natural and partly assumed, to a presumptuous haughtiness of demeanour, to a pretended disregard for the opinion of mankind, and to gross looseness of morals, were added undoubted talents, courage under difficulties, love of literature, and natural good-nature. With an affected singularity, he refused to enlighten an enquirer who asked him whether he was connected with the family of Secretary Thurloe, by saying that he could claim no relationship with Thurloe the statesman, being only descended from Thurlow the carrier. In Suckling's 'History of Suffolk' (ii. 33), however, the family is traced as possessing an estate at Burnham Ulph in Norfolk from the reign of Henry VIII., which was sold just before the chancellor's birth. His father was the Rev. Thomas Thurlow, rector of Ashfield in Suffolk, and afterwards of Stratton St. Mary's in Norfolk. His mother was Elizabeth, daughter of Robert Smith, Esq., of the former place, and he was the eldest of three sons. The second son was successively advanced in the Church during his brother's chancellorship to the deanery of Rochester and the bishoprics of Lincoln and Durham. The third son was a merchant at Norwich, of which city he eventually became an alderman and mayor.

Edward Thurlow was born at Ashfield about 1732. From his early childhood he showed a contumacious spirit and an overbearing disposition, which he displayed not only at home, at Scarning School, and at the King's School at Canterbury, but also at Caius College, Cambridge; and numerous stories are told of his insolence and insubordination. But there was always some humour mixed with his escapades, and amidst his irregularities he did not neglect his studies, but succeeded in laying up no inconsiderable store of classical learning. His career at Cambridge began in October 1748, and was terminated in 1751, by what was not far short of expulsion; for having been punished for one of his breaches of discipline by an imposition to translate a paper of the 'Spectator' into Greek, instead of taking it up, as was his duty, to the dean who inflicted the penalty, he left it with the tutor; and on being called before the authorities of the college to explain his conduct, he made the matter worse by coolly saying that he had done so from no motive of disrespect to the dean, but simply from a compassionate wish not to puzzle him. Rustication being too small and expulsion too great a retribution for this insult, Thurlow was recommended to withdraw his name from the books, a hint which he was obliged to take. Before this dean, who is an elective and temporary officer of the college, he had been frequently summoned to appear for various offences, and having answered on one occasion with some disrespect, was sharply asked 'whether he knew that he was talking to the dean.' Thurlow of course answered, 'Yes, Mr. Dean,' and ever after when they met addressed him as 'Mr. Dean,' and so frequently reiterated the title that the dean felt himself insulted by the banter. If this story be true, there is a graceful pendant to it, for on the impudent youth becoming chancellor he sent for his old enemy, and on his entering the room addressed him as usual. 'How d'ye do, Mr. Dean?' 'My lord,' replied the other sullenly, 'I am not now a dean, and do not deserve the title.' 'But you are a dean,' said his lordship, giving him a paper of nomination; 'and so convinced am I that you will do honour to the appointment that I am sorry any part of my conduct should have given offence to so good a man.' (*Law and Lawyers*, i. 94; *Notes and Queries*, 2nd S. iii. 283.)

It has been said that Thurlow was at first articled to an attorney, but there is no other authority for this statement than that he attended for some time the office of Mr. Chapman, a solicitor, with William

Cowper the poet. This was a practice then, and it is now frequently adopted by young students for the bar, to give them an insight into the practical working of the profession. Having been entered at the Inner Temple, though he had the character of being an idle and dissipated man during his novitiate, it is abundantly clear that he employed a sufficient portion of his time in laying a solid foundation for those legal acquirements of which his subsequent career proved him to be master.

He was called to the bar in November 1754, and went the Home Circuit. He obtained great credit in one of his earliest causes, Luke Robinson v. The Earl of Winchilsea, for the courage with which he resented the accustomed rudeness and arrogance of Sir Fletcher Norton, the opposing counsel. As Sir Fletcher was hated by the profession, this castigation made Thurlow popular among the attorneys, and procured him some briefs. His business, however, was still so small in amount that he excited considerable surprise by accepting a silk gown in Hilary Term 1762, when he had been little more than seven years at the bar. The occasion of his promotion is variously stated, in various improbable stories; but the most natural inducement operating upon Thurlow to seek and to accept a promotion accompanied with so much risk, was that confidence he had in his own powers, which future events proved was not misplaced. He was at the same time elected a bencher of his inn of court.

In proceeding on his ambitious career he took his seat in parliament for Tamworth at the general election of 1768, during the sittings of which he was obliged to undergo two re-elections—one in March 1770, when he was made solicitor-general on the accession of Lord North's ministry; and the other in January 1771, when he succeeded as attorney-general. He represented the same place till he was raised to the peerage. During the whole time he was in the House of Commons he gave an unflinching support to the ministry, and by the boldness of his assertions and the audacity of his language, more than by the force of his reasoning, he was considered Lord North's ablest coadjutor. On the questions relative to the administration of criminal justice and the law of libel, which then agitated the public mind, he was a strenuous advocate for leaving things as they were, and treated contemptuously those by whom alterations were pressed; and in all the debates relative to America he asserted the right of England to tax it, and stigmatised those who resisted as traitors and rebels.

In his official capacity as solicitor-general he assisted in the conduct of the several prosecutions of John Almon, H. S. Woodfall, and John Miller for publishing Junius's letter to the king, and as attorney-general he prosecuted John Horne Tooke for a seditious libel. In all of these he appears to have confined himself strictly to his duty as advocate for the crown, and to have argued the cases according to the interpretation of the law as it then existed, though in the last he had to submit to the pertinacious vituperation of the defendant. He also conducted the extraordinary prosecution of the Duchess of Kingston for bigamy.

On Lord Bathurst's resignation in 1778 he was appointed lord chancellor on June 3, being at the same time ennobled by the title of Baron Thurlow of Ashfield in Suffolk. He lived at that time in Great Ormond Street. He held the Seal for twelve years, except a short interval of seven months during which it was put into commission.

He maintained in the House of Lords the same energy, not to say effrontery, which he had exhibited in the House of Commons. He perpetually was rising in his place, speaking on every subject, and treating the arguments of the other peers with coarse sarcasm and indignity, as if he were the schoolmaster of a set of boys, instead of the speaker of an august assembly. By this course he not only was considered a bore by all his brother peers, but excited the indignation of those who were the objects of his attacks. All inclination, however, to call his conduct in question was subdued within a year after his entrance into the house by an incident which is related by Mr. Butler in his 'Reminiscences,' though no notice is taken of it in the 'Parliamentary History.' The Duke of Grafton, stung by something he had said, most unadvisedly reproached him for his plebeian extraction and his recent admission into the peerage. 'His lordship,' says Mr. Butler, 'rose from the woolsack, and advanced slowly to the place from which the chancellor generally addresses the house; then, fixing on the duke a look of lowering indignation, "I am amazed," he said, in a level tone of voice, "at the attack which the noble duke has made upon me. Yes, my lords," considerably raising his voice, 'I am amazed at his grace's speech. The noble duke cannot look before him, behind him, or on either side of him, without seeing some noble peer who owes his seat in this house to his successful exertions in the profession to which I belong. Does he not feel that it as honourable to owe to these as to being the accident of an accident? To all these noble lords the language of the noble duke is as applicable and as insulting as it is to myself. But I don't fear to stand single and alone. No one venerates the peerage more than I do;

but, my lords, I must say that the peerage solicited me, not I the peerage. Nay, more—I can say, and will say, that, as a peer of parliament—as speaker of this right honourable house—as keeper of the Great Seal—as guardian of his majesty's conscience—as lord high chancellor of England—nay, even in that character alone in which the noble duke would think it an affront to be considered—but which character none can deny me—as a MAN—I am at this moment as respectable, I beg leave to add I am at this time as much respected, as the proudest peer I now look down upon." The effect of this speech,' Mr. Butler adds, 'both within the walls of parliament and out of them, was prodigious. It gave Lord Thurlow an ascendency in the house which no chancellor had ever possessed; it invested him in public opinion with a character of independency and honour.'

Having thus silenced his opponents, the frequency of his own speeches was not diminished, though perhaps they were more cautious and less vituperative. During the remainder of Lord North's ministry he was a hearty and effective justifier of all his measures, and when at last the administration was driven from the field in March 1782 it was expected that he would retire with his colleagues. But to the surprise of every one he still kept the Seal. The king, in whose presence alone he dropped his bearish demeanour, forbad the mention of any other chancellor. The consequence of submitting to such an intrusion among men who and whose opinions had been the perpetual subject of his abuse was soon felt. Before the session was concluded in which the new ministers had taken office Lord Thurlow had openly but ineffectually opposed two measures introduced by them. Towards the close of that session the Marquis of Rockingham died, and, notwithstanding the division between the surviving members of the administration, Lord Thurlow still retained the Seal under Lord Shelburne, till that nobleman was expelled by the Coalition Ministry, when it was placed in the hands of three commissioner on April 9, 1783. In less than nine months that administration was excluded in its turn, and that ministry was commenced under Mr. Pitt which defied all opposition for nearly eighteen years. Lord Thurlow, who claimed the title, and was generally looked upon as the king's friend, and who had been all along the private adviser of his majesty and the chief instigator of the successful opposition to Fox's India Bill in the House of Lords, of course resumed his place, and continued to preside for the second time in Chancery for more than nine years—from December 23, 1783, to June 15, 1792. The ascendency which Mr. Pitt obtained and preserved in the royal counsels during the whole of this time excited the jealousy of the chancellor, who, conceiving that he had a stronger hold on the king's confidence and regard, made various attempts, at first guardedly, but at last openly, to destroy the influence of the premier. Mr. Pitt, who was well aware that Lord Thurlow, during the agitation of the regency question on the insanity of the king in 1788, had been privately negotiating with the prince's friends, soon felt that he had not only a lukewarm, intractable, and inefficient, but a treacherous counsellor in his cabinet; but for a time submitted to the infliction rather than distress the king by an exposure. George III. and the public in general, who were ignorant of Thurlow's private dealings with the opposition, believed in the solemn professions of affection and gratitude that he made as soon as the king's recovery put an end to 'the hopes of the whigs. But on his attempting the same course he had pursued towards the Rockingham administration by openly opposing some measures of the government, and charging them with attacking the prerogative, Mr. Pitt found it absolutely necessary to bring the question to an issue. He therefore represented to the king that it was impossible that he could conduct the affairs of the kingdom if Lord Thurlow continued chancellor. George III., who probably had gained an insight into the true state of affairs, at once sacrificed the chancellor, and removed him from his office on June 15, 1792. As a mark of royal favour, however, Lord Thurlow, having no children, received a new patent of peerage, with a remainder to his brothers and their male issue. This dismissal excited the indignation of the excluded lord, but no complaints or regrets in any other quarter. The whigs were especially aware of his hypocrisy; and Burke, a few days after one of Lord Thurlow's lachrymose effusions of affection for king, declared that 'the iron tears which flowed down Pluto's cheeks rather resembled the dismal bubbling of the Styx than the gentle murmuring streams of Aganippe.'

Lord Thurlow lived fourteen years after his retirement from office, but never gained his former ascendency. The inconsistency of his political conduct prevented his being received into intimate relations with whig or tory, or rather with Foxites or Pittites; and, though he occasionally spoke in the House of Lords, and at one time sided with the opposition, he at length fell into the class of those who are called independent members. He was a great sufferer from the gout, and as his age advanced his increasing infirmities obliged him frequently to betake himself to the Bath waters. He died at Brighton on September 12, 1806, and was buried at the Temple Church in London.

With great natural abilities, with a considerable knowledge of law, and with undoubted rhetorical powers, he could scarcely be considered in any other light than as a political chancellor; and having failed in that character, his reputation as a judge does not at the present day stand very high. Though some of his judgments exhibit great learning and research, their excellence was attributed to the care and erudition of that eminent lawyer Mr. Hargrave, whose able assistance the chancellor notoriously used. The roughness with which he treated those who practised in his court tended no doubt to deprive him of such credit as he deserved; for it cannot be supposed that a private prompter could always be at hand to advise him in the daily calls for his decisions. Mr. Butler, a great contemporary authority, speaks of his decrees as 'strongly marked by depth of legal knowledge and force of expression, and by the overwhelming power with which he propounded the results;' but he adds that 'they were often involved in obscurity, and sometimes reason was rather silenced than convinced.' This last characteristic may be also given of his orations in parliament. The effect of his speeches was greatly enhanced by this authoritative bearing and the terrors of his countenance, which, by its dark complexion, its stern and rugged features, and his bushy eyebrows, made him, as Mr. Fox said, 'look wiser than any man ever was.'

That the retention of power and the acquisition of wealth influenced him on two occasions to desert his party will ever be a blot on his character. On the other hand, though not affecting to be a good churchman, the disposition of his clerical patronage has not been complained of; and there are many instances of his encouragement of the men of art and literature of the time, and of his great liberality towards them in his peculiar rough way. Among those who enjoyed his patronage were Shepherd, Potter, Horsley and Johnson, Hayley, Romney and Crabbe. The affection with which the amiable poet Cowper regarded him goes far to prove that he was not so great a bear as he tried to make the world believe, and many anecdotes told of him show the natural kindness of his heart.

He was never married; but his title devolved, under his second patent, on his nephew, the son of the Bishop of Durham, who with his own poems published some translations from Homer and other classics into verse, by which the chancellor had amused his retirement.' (*Lives by Roscoe, Burke, and Lord Campbell.*)

TINDAL, NICOLAS CONYNGHAM, could trace his relationship to two distinguished men, the Rev. Dr. Matthew Tindal, and the Rev. Nicholas Tindal, who both made themselves names in the literary world by the works they produced, to the latter of whom he was great-grandson. His father was Robert Tindal, an attorney-at-law living at Coval Hall, near Chelmsford, who by his wife Sarah, only daughter of John Pocock of Greenwich Hospital, had three sons, of whom he was the eldest. By various intermarriages of the family the chief justice might claim connection and descent from many legal celebrities, as well as from other eminent men; among them are the following judges: John Hall, Lewis Fortescue, and Roger Manwood.

Nicolas Conyngham Tindal was born at Coval Hall on December 12, 1776. The first part of his education he received at a school at Chelmsford, from whence he was removed in 1795 to Trinity College, Cambridge. His career at the university was most creditable, terminating with the honourable place of eighth wrangler on taking his bachelor's degree in 1799, to which was added the distinction of obtaining the senior chancellor's medal. He proceeded M.A. in 1802, and was elected fellow of his college. Having entered Lincoln's Inn, he became a pupil of Mr. (afterwards Judge) Richardson, and soon after commenced the practice of a special pleader. In this branch he exhibited an extraordinary capacity, and acquired such a character that business flowed in upon him to a considerable extent. He was so successful that in 1809 he felt himself able not only to be called to the bar, but to give up his fellowship by entering into the marriage state. His bride was Merelina, youngest daughter of Thomas Symonds, Esq., captain in the royal navy, and sister of Admiral Sir William Symonds, C.B., surveyor of the navy.

He selected the Northern Circuit, where, and in Westminster Hall, the reputation he had already gained below the bar in no long time secured him a sufficiency of employment. His chambers were resorted to by many pupils, among whom were Lords Brougham and Wensleydale. His knowledge of law and his reasoning talent soon had abundant exercise in the most difficult questions submitted to him; and though not gifted with great rhetorical powers, he was remarkable for the logical skill with which he argued them. Among the important cases entrusted to him was that of Ashford against Thornton (*Barnewall and Alderson*, 405), which was an appeal of murder, when on the part of the appellee he claimed the wager of battle, and succeeded by his recondite argument on this most abstruse law in saving his client. The discussion arising from this case had the happy effect of producing an enactment (stat. 59 Geo. III. c. 46) abolishing the oppressive proceeding of appeal for murder, treason, or felony, and the absurd method of proving innocence by a trial by battle. He was selected in 1820, by the recommendation of his former pupil Lord Brougham, as one of the counsel for Queen Caroline, in the conduct of whose defence, his learning, caution, and sagacity were of most material assistance.

Though he shared in the popularity that attended the queen's advisers on her temporary triumph, he did not lose the interest felt for him by the prime minister, Lord Liverpool, who indeed had endeavoured, but had been too late, to retain him for the crown. That nobleman took an early opportunity of appointing him, though he had not yet had the precedence of a silk gown, solicitor-general on September 20, 1826, when he received the usual honour of knighthood.

Sir Nicolas had already entered the political arena two years before as member for Wigton, which in 1826 he exchanged for Harwich; but in the following year he vacated that seat to become a candidate for the representation of his university, and having succeeded, he continued its member till he was raised to the bench. In parliament he exhibited all those solid qualities for which as a barrister he was distinguished, never pushing himself forward in party contests, but always assisting the debates by his legal and historical acquirements.

He held the office of solicitor-general from September 1826 to June 1829, during which time there were two vacancies in the post of attorney-general. The first was occasioned by the retirement of Sir Charles Wetherell in 1827, on his opposition to the Roman Catholic claims, when Sir Nicolas with characteristic modesty gave way to Sir James Scarlett; and the other was when Sir Charles Wetherell resumed his place under the administration of the Duke of Wellington in 1828. In the next year, however, he received his reward in being appointed chief justice of the Common Pleas; and from June 9, 1829, he presided over the court for seventeen years, with that grave urbanity, calm dignity, and invariable good temper which completely repressed the indecent ebullitions which had too often been exhibited; and with that legal erudition and sound exposition of the principles on which his decisions were founded which commanded the approval and acquiescence of both his learned and unlearned auditory.

In the ordinary and vulgar sense of popularity he was certainly not a popular judge, for he sided with no party, and professed none of the opinions which attract the million. But no judge was ever looked up to or respected more than he was. There was an indescribable something about his manner that induced not merely the agreement but the perfect confidence, that engaged not merely the admiration but the affection of those with whom he associated or conversed, while his courteous and amiable affability invited friendship, the habitual gravity of his deportment prevented undue familiarity, and few could approach him without feeling a sort of filial respect and regard. Yet beneath this exterior he greatly enjoyed a joke, and many examples of a quiet dry wit are related of him. His professional jokes were the best. One of the learned serjeants coming too late for dinner at Serjeants' Inn Hall found no place left for him. While waiting for a seat, 'How now,' said the chief justice, 'what's the matter, brother? You look like an outstanding term that's unsatisfied.' Of another serjeant he was asked whether he thought him a *sound* lawyer. 'Well, sir,' said he, 'you raise a doubtful point, whether *roaring* is unsoundness.' When another stormy leader was addressing a jury in the civil court at Buckingham, he spoke so loud that the chief justice, who was delivering his charge in the criminal court, enquired what that noise was. On being informed that Serjeant —— was opening a case, 'Very well,' said he, 'since Brother —— is *opening*, I must *shut up*,' and immediately ordered the doors between the two courts to be closed. The following, though not strictly professional, will perhaps be deemed quite as good. When Lady Rolle, on her husband's death, refused to let the hounds go out, a learned serjeant asked the chief justice whether there would be any harm if they were allowed to do so with a piece of crape round their necks. 'I can hardly think,' said Sir Nicolas, 'that even the crape is necessary; it ought surely to have been sufficient that they were in *full cry*.'

His useful life was terminated on July 6, 1846, after a short illness, leaving three sons and one daughter.

TIRWHIT, ROBERT, whose family (now called Tyrwhitt) is a very ancient one, long seated at Kettleby in the county of Lincoln, was the son of Sir William Tirwhit of that place by the daughter and heir of — Groval, and is mentioned as an advocate in Richard Bellew's Reports in the reign of Richard II. He was made one of the king's serjeants in the first year of the following reign, and he is among those serjeants who in the fourth year were called on for loans to enable the king to resist the Welsh and the Scotch, with 100*l*. set against his name. (*Acts Privy Council*, i. 203.)

In 9 Henry IV., 1409, he was raised to the bench. Dugdale, by mistaking the reading of the Liberate Roll, places him in the Common Pleas; but that this is an error may be seen in the first place by a letter from the king to the chancellor, dated May 9, 1409, in which he names a serjeant to supply the place of Robert Tirwhit, who he says is made one of the justices 'de *nostre* Bank.' (*Rymer*, viii. 584.) It is positively shown also in the patents above referred to, and in the Year Books of Easter, 12 Henry IV., and Michaelmas, 13 Henry IV.

A petition to parliament presented in the latter year, in which he is distinctly called a justice of the 'Bank le roy,' contains a curious illustration of the manners of the times, and shows somewhat of a violent disposition on the part of our judge. It appears that a suit had been instituted by him relative to the right of common of pasture, turbary, and estovers at Wraweby, to which the tenants of Lord William de Roos's manor of Melton Roos laid claim; that the decision of the question had been referred to Chief Justice Gascoigne, who had appointed the parties to meet on the spot with their evidences on a certain day, which in the record is called a 'loveday;' and that instead of coming as agreed with a limited number of friends according to this decree, Tirwhit had assembled five hundred men 'armed and errayed ageyn the pees, to lygge in awayte for the same Lord de Roos, and there hym to harme and dishonure.' On the reading of this petition the dismayed judge was obliged to humble himself before the king, and, acknowledging that 'he ne hath noght born hym as he sholde have doon,' to offer to submit himself to the ordinance of any two lords the Lord of Roos would name of his kin. The matter by the king's desire was submitted to the Archbishop of Canterbury, and Lord de Grey the chamberlain, who awarded that the question of right of common should be decided by Chief Justice Gascoigne in the manner he had before prescribed; and that as to the offence complained of, Robert Tirwhit should send two tuns of Gascony wine to Melton Roos, and at a time appointed by Lord de Roos should 'brynge to the same place two fatte oxen, and twelf fatte shepe, to be dispended on a dyner to hem that there schal be,' and should then attend with 'all the knightes, and esquiers, and yomen that had ledynge of men on his partie atte forsaid loveday,' and should there rehearse a speech of apology, which is fully set forth, and concludes with these words: 'Zet, for as myche I am a justice, that more than a comun man scholde have had me more discretly and peesfully, I knowe wele that I have failled and offende yow, my Lord the Roos, whereof I beseke yow of grace and mercy, and offre you v c. mark to ben paied at youre will.' This tempting offer, however, the Lord of Roos is to refuse, and 'nothing take of the forsayd Robert but the forsayd wyn, oxen, and shepe, for the dyner of them that been there present;' and then he is to forgive the humiliated Robert and all his party. (*Rot. Parl.* iii. 649.)

Tirwhit does not seem to have suffered from this disgrace, for we find him regularly pursuing his duties through the whole of the reign of Henry V., and up to February 1428, 6 Henry VI., when his death is noted in an order of council. (*Acts Privy Council*, iii. 283.)

His wife was a daughter of — Kelke, of Kelke in Yorkshire, by whom he left a son, Sir William, almost all of whose descendants were of knightly degree. One of them, Sir Philip, was among the first who were honoured by James I., in 1611, with the dignity of baronet. That title became extinct in 1760; but a second baronetcy was conferred in 1808 on another descendant, which still survives. (*Wotton*, i. 178.)

TOCLIFFE, RICHARD (BISHOP OF WINCHESTER), called by some Richard More, and by others Richard of Ilchester, was, according to Ralph de Diceto, born at Soc in the diocese of Bath. Brought up to the clerical profession, he at an early period of his life obtained an inferior situation in the King's Court, where it was his duty to make copies of all the summonses issued from it, and to write the writs and the entries on the rolls. In this office he showed so much diligence and care, and his ability and industry were so prominent, that he was gradually advanced, until at last a place was assigned to him in the Exchequer on the right hand of the chief justicier, in order that he might be next to the treasurer, assist in the accounts, and carefully superintend the writer of the roll. (*Dial. de Scacc.*; *Madox*, ii. 362.) Thus he was regularly present in the court at its sittings, and at length, assisting in its deliberations, became one of the justiciers. Under this character he is named with several others as sitting in the Exchequer in 11 and 12 Henry II., 1165-6. He is then called archdeacon of Poictiers, to which preferment he had been advanced. That the position he held in the Curia Regis was a very high one is evident from his always being named first in the pleas of the several counties in which he acted as a justice itinerant, from 14 Henry II. until the 20th year of that reign, 1174. The roll of 23 Henry II. also mentions pleas before him under the name of Richard, archdeacon of Poictiers (*Madox*, i. 4, 123, 129, 143-9), but it has reference to arrears due on pleas of former years. On October 6, 1174, 20 Henry II., he was consecrated Bishop of Winchester. Of this see, as well as that of Lincoln and also of the abbey of Glastonbury, he had been the custos while they were in the king's hands.

In 1176 he was appointed chief justiciary of Normandy, and on the retirement of Richard de Luci in 1179, the same high office in England was entrusted to him jointly with the Bishops of Ely and Norwich, and they were respectively placed at the head of three of the four circuits into which England was then divided by the council of Windsor. (*Dugdale's Orig.* 20.) Ranulph de Glanville succeeded them in the following year, in consequence, as some state, of a remonstrance from the pope disapproving of ecclesiastics being so employed. That he acted, however, after this in the judicial business of the court is evident from his name appearing as one of the justiciers before whom fines were levied in 28 Henry II., 1182. (*Hunter's Preface.*)

To his see he gave the manors of Hamm and Groel, and after presiding over it above fourteen years, he died in December 1188, and was buried in his cathedral. (*Godwin*, 216; *Lord Lyttelton*, ii. 416, 434, iii. 138.)

TOMLINS, RICHARD, was the son and heir of Edward Tomlins, of Todinton in the county of Gloucester, and was admitted at the Inner Temple in May 1606, after which no more is recorded of him till he was assigned as counsel to assist Bastwick and Burton in their complaint of the cruel sentence pronounced against them in the Star Chamber. (*State Trials*, iii. 701, 709.) He was not long in being rewarded for his exertions. In consequence of the illness of Baron Trevor, the only judge of the Court of Exchequer who adhered to the parliament, and Cursitor Baron Leeke having joined the other barons at Oxford, a difficulty arose in September 1645 as to who was to receive the customary presentation of the sheriffs of London, and to attend the other ceremonies usually performed on the 30th of that month. The Lords, therefore, on the day previous recommended Mr. Christopher Vernon as Leeke's successor; but upon sending to the Commons for their concurrence, they unanimously substituted the name of Richard Tomlins, who was thereupon sworn into the place of cursitor baron quamdiu bene gesserit. He was resworn on the death of the king, and kept his place through all the succeeding changes, his name being recorded in the Exchequer Books of Hilary Term 1653-4, on the assumption of the protectorate by Oliver Cromwell, and of Michaelmas Term 1658, on the succession of Protector Richard. (*Lords' Journals*, vii. 606; *Commons*, iv. 292; *Whitelocke*, 174, 175, 383.)

He must have been a garrulous humorist, to judge from a speech printed as having been addressed by him to the sheriffs of London in 1659, on their coming to the Exchequer to be sworn. Its absurdity is too great to be supposed to be a faithful transcript of his words; but it is doubtless a true representation of his style and manner, taken by some auditor who was amused with the address, and who describes him as 'Baron Tomlinson.' He was then, as he says, a very old man, and he either died or was displaced at the Restoration, when Thomas Leeke, who was cursitor baron before him, resumed his office.

TORELL, WILLIAM, held some office in the court so early as 4 Henry II., 1158. (*Pipe Rolls*, 144.) His name occurs in fines of 28 Henry II., 1182, as one of the persons before whom they were acknowledged in the Curia Regis at Westminster. (*Hunter's Preface.*) He is not, however, named on any other occasion with a judicial character. It may be possible, therefore, that he was not a justicier, as in this early period of the adoption of fines it is not unlikely that the officer who filled up the instrument may have thought it necessary to insert the names of all who were present, whether attending judicially or officially.

His position was certainly a prominent one, since the sheriffalty of the two counties of Gloucester and Hereford was entrusted to him in 29 and 30 Henry II.

Yeovil and Odecumb in Somersetshire belonged to him, and by the Great Roll of 1 Richard I. it appears that he died about that time. (*Pipe Rolls*, 147, &c.)

TORNOURA, ADAM DE, was one of four justices itinerant who, in 3 Richard I., 1191-2, imposed a fine of forty shillings on the hundred of Edelmeton (Edmonton) for a murder, and for not appearing on the first summons. (*Madox*, i. 544.)

TOTINGTON, SAMSON DE (ABBOT OF ST. EDMUND'S BURY), though introduced neither by Dugdale nor Madox into their lists of justices itinerant, is expressly stated to have filled that office by Jocelíne de Brakelonda, who was his chaplain, and may be called his biographer. The precise date is not mentioned, but in the arrangement of the chronicle the fact occurs between 1182 and 1187. In the 'Monasticon' it is asserted that he was made one of the king's justiciaries in 6 Richard I., but no authority is cited, nor is there any other evidence of the fact.

Samson de Totington was so called from a place of that name in the hundred of Weyland in Norfolk, of which he was a native. He became a monk in the abbey of St. Edmunds in 1166, and in process of time was appointed master of the novices, and afterwards sub-sacrist. At the death of Abbot Hugo the king adopted a curious mode of electing his successor, the result of which was the appointment of Samson. The wisdom of the choice was soon apparent. By his prudence and energy the affairs of the convent were extricated in a short time from the disorder into which the weakness and indolence of his predecessor had plunged them.

He repaired the dilapidated buildings, visited his manors, and cleared off the debt which pressed on the revenue. He repressed the irregularities of the monks, successfully resisted the encroachments of the knights and townspeople, stood up in every way for the rights of his house, whether against prince or peer, and yet found favour in the sight of his sovereign. In a short time after his election the pope appointed him a judge '*de causis cognoscendis*,' and not long afterwards he was constituted by the king one of the justices itinerant. Jocelin dwells with pride on the admiration which his judicial powers excited, and relates that one of the suitors cursed his court, where, he complained, neither gold nor silver would avail to confound his adversary. Osbert Fitz-Hervey (himself a judge) said, 'That abbot is a shrewd fellow; if he go on as he begins, he will cut out every lawyer of us.'

In 1188 he was desirous of joining those who had assumed the cross, but King Henry found him so useful in the kingdom that he would not permit his departure. The fall of Jerusalem afflicted him so heavily that he put on hair garments and abstained from flesh during the rest of his life. In the year 1190 he procured the banishment of the Jews from St. Edmund's Bury.

During King Richard's absence he supported the royal authority against Prince John, and when Richard was detained in Germany he offered to go in search of him, and actually, when his prison was discovered, went to him with rich gifts.

He obtained many privileges for his house from Popes Lucius III., Urban III., and Clement III., and illustrated his rule by founding the hospital of Babwell, or St. Saviour's, repurchasing from the crown the manor of Mildenhall for a thousand marks, and building the schools of St. Edmund's Bury. Little is mentioned of his proceedings in the reign of King John, except that he received that monarch at the abbey soon after his coronation, and again in 1203. His death occurred on December 30, 1211. (*Chron. Jocel. de Brakelonda*, [Camden Soc.]; *Dugdale's Monast.* iii. 104.)

TOUTHEBY, GILBERT DE, was an advocate of considerable eminence. His name frequently appears in the Year Books during the reign of Edward II., and in the first two years of Edward III., often abbreviated 'Toud.' In 9 Edward II. he was employed in prosecuting and defending the king's suits, being at that time a king's serjeant-at-law. The next year he was summoned among the legal assistants to parliament; and so continued to be during the remainder of the reign. He is first mentioned in a judicial capacity as one of the justices appointed in Lincolnshire in March 1318, and most of his future commissions were in that county. It is evident that these occasional employments as a judge did not prevent his pursuing his profession as an advocate; for we not only find him engaged in cases as a serjeant-at-law in 14 Edward II., but on the accession of Edward III. his stipend for prosecuting and defending the king's causes was renewed to him. He certainly acted as a justice of assize under the latter king; but there is no mention of him later than the third year. (*Rot. Parl.* i. 352, 370, 433, ii. 402; *Parl Writs*, ii. p. ii. 1518.)

TOWNSHEND, ROGER, whose family was established at Rainham in Norfolk so early as the reign of the first Henry, was the only son of John Townshend of that place, by Joan, daughter and heir of Sir Robert Lunsford, of Rumford in Essex, and of Battle in Sussex. He studied the law at Lincoln's Inn, and was elected a governor in 1 Edward IV., 1461, and reader in 1468 and in 1474. His name occurs in the Year Books from Hilary 1465; and in 1472, the year after the final exclusion of Henry VI. from the throne, he represented the borough of Calne in parliament; but, notwithstanding his eminence as a lawyer, he was not called to the degree of the coif till October 1477. In the last week of the short reign of Edward V., June 1483, he was appointed one of the king's serjeants. (*Rymer*, xii. 186.) His patent was of course renewed in the following week by Richard III., by whom he was made a judge of the Common Pleas about January 1484. Although he was thus evidently patronised by the usurper, it was the policy of Henry VII., on his accession, to make no changes in the administration of justice, so that he was not only retained on the bench, but received the order of knighthood previous to the coronation.

According to Dugdale (*Orig.* 47), the last fine acknowledged before him is dated at Midsummer 1493, and the genealogists have generally placed his death in that year (probably on that account); but the Year Books contain ample evidence that he continued to sit in the court for every subsequent year till Michaelmas 1500, after which his name disappears.

He married Anne, daughter and coheir of Sir William de Brewse, of Wenham Hall in Suffolk; and their lineal descendants are now represented in the House of Lords by the Marquis Townshend and Viscount Sydney.

TRACY, HENRY DE, possessed the barony of Barnstaple in Devonshire, including Tavistock and various other manors, succeeding to it on the death of his father, Oliver de Tracy, in 12 John.

In 17 Henry III., 1232, he was placed at the head of the justices itinerant into Cornwall, no doubt as a resident nobleman only, as no other instance occurs of his appointment to that office. An assize of novel disseisin, &c., was, however, directed to be taken before him in Devonshire in 41 Henry III. (*Excerpt. e Rot. Fin.* ii. 253); and in 45 Henry III. his name appears among the barons of the Exchequer. (*Madox*, ii. 319.) In the former year he was made governor of the castle of Exeter. He died at a good old age, about 2 Edward I., 1273. (*Baronage*, i. 622; *Rot. Pat. John*, 101; *Rot. Claus.* i. 137, 283, 405.)

TRACY, ROBERT, was the eldest son of Robert, second Viscount Tracy in Ireland (descended from the above Henry de Tracy), by his second wife, Dorothy, daughter of Thomas Cocks, Esq., of Castleditch in Herefordshire. He was born in 1655, and was called to the bar by the Middle Temple in 1680.

In July 1699 King William made him a judge of the King's Bench in Ireland, but soon translated him, on November 14, 1700, from that country to be a baron of the Exchequer in England. In less than two years he had a second removal to the Common Pleas, in Trinity Term 1702, soon after the accession of Queen Anne. Here he remained for four-and-twenty years, during which period he was selected both by that queen and by George I. to be one of the commissioners of the Great Seal on vacancies in the office of lord chancellor—viz., from September 14 to October 19, 1710; and the second from April 15 to May 12, 1718. He resigned his place on the bench on October 26, 1726, on the plea of ill health, but he lived nine years afterwards in the enjoyment of a pension of 1500*l.* a year. He died on September 11, 1735, aged eighty, at his seat at Coscomb in the parish of Didbrooke, Gloucestershire.

He is described as 'a complete gentleman and a good lawyer, of a clear head and honest heart, and as delivering his opinion with that genteel affability and integrity that even those who lost a cause were charmed with his behaviour.' This character, as it was written at the time of his death, may be regarded, with some allowance for its affected phraseology, as substantially true, especially when the Duke of Wharton in one of his satires declares that he will be constant to his mistress until the time

When Tracy's generous soul shall swell with pride.

(*Smyth's Law Off. Ireland*, 100; *Lord Raymond*, 605, 769, 1420; *Luttrell*, iv. 707, v. 184, vi. 633.)

He married Anne, daughter of William Dowdeswell, of Pool Court in Worcestershire, and had, besides two daughters, three sons—Robert, Richard, and William. An alleged descendant of the latter claimed the title of Viscount Tracy in 1843; but the House of Lords, after various hearings, which extended to 1849, were not satisfied with the evidence in support of his claim.

TRAVERS, JOHN, was of a Lancashire family, and member for that county in 33 Edward I. Under Edward II. he was frequently employed in it as commissioner of array, assessor of the aids, and custos of the lands forfeited by Thomas Earl of Lancaster. In 2 Edward III. he was engaged with the seneschal of Gascony and the constable of Bordeaux in treating with certain German princes; and on March 2, 1329, he was a judge of the Common Pleas. He is mentioned in the Year Book of the reign as late as Michaelmas 1333. About that time he was appointed constable of Bordeaux, and died within four years after. (*Parl. Writs*, i. 868, ii. p. ii. 1520, *Cal. Rot. Pat.* 103, 105, 118; *Dugdale's Orig.* 45, 143, 271.)

TREBY, GEORGE, was the son of Peter Treby, a respectable gentleman of Plympton in Devonshire, by his wife Joan, daughter of John Snellings, of Chaddlewood, Esq. He was born in 1644, was placed at Exeter College, Oxford, in 1661, and was entered of the Middle Temple. Having been called to the bar in 1671, he was soon regarded as a rising man, and was chosen as representative for his native town in both the parliaments of 1679, in the latter of which he acted as chairman of the committee of secrecy relative to the Popish Plot, and was selected as one of the managers to conduct the impeachment of Lord Stafford as a participator in it. In December 1680 he was elected recorder of London, was knighted, and was also made a bencher of his inn. When the city charters were attacked by the quo warranto two years afterwards, he stood up boldly and ably in their defence, and of course was removed from his place when judgment was given against them, to make way for the court favourite, Sir Thomas Jenner. (*State Trials*, vii. 1308, viii. 1099.) He sat in the last parliament of Charles II., which, meeting at Oxford, was allowed to continue its deliberations for no more than a week in March 1681; and from the single parliament called by James II. he was excluded.

Refusing to give countenance to that king's claim to dispense with the penal laws, he declined to plead for the plaintiff in the sham action brought by Sir Edward Hale's coachman against his master, and was naturally, both for his legal ability and his known liberality, selected as one of the counsel to defend the seven bishops. When the king, alarmed by the threatened approach of the

Prince of Orange, deemed it prudent to restore the city's charters, Sir George was requested to resume his office of recorder, but for two months declined to do so, until on the prince's arrival he was induced to consent. He took his seat on December 10, 1688, and four days after delivered an address of congratulation to the prince, which was the subject of general admiration. (*Luttrell*, i. 380, 446.) To the Convention Parliament in the following month he was returned by his old constituency of Plympton.

In the early discussions of that parliament he took a leading part in proposing, and in the conference with the Peers in supporting, the resolution declaring the abdication of the king. On some symptoms of mutiny in the army, he advised the house not to waste their time in discussions, but at once to oppose force with force. When Sir Henry Pollexfen was appointed attorney-general in February 1689, Treby was made solicitor, but succeeded to the former post in May. The town of Plympton returned him again to William's second parliament of March 1690; and he was still a member of it when he was constituted on May 3, 1692, lord chief justice of the Common Pleas. At this time he resigned the recordership of London, which he had, contrary to the usual practice, continued to hold notwithstanding his official position; and he was complimented by the common council with a present of one hundred guineas. (*Ibid.* 506, 522; *Parl. Hist.* iv. 40, &c.) In 1700 he held the Great Seal with his two brother chiefs from May 5 to 21, and seven months afterwards his career was terminated by his death on December 13, at his house in Kensington Gravel Pits. He was buried in the Temple Church. (*Luttrell*, iv. 446; *Lord Raymond*, 566, 627.)

His excellence as a lawyer is universally admitted; and his various arguments on the question of monopolies, in defence of the city charters, and in the bankers' case (in which he differed from his colleagues), sufficiently attest the extent of his learning. His high character as a judge, besides being lauded by Evelyn (iii. 386), receives the best confirmation from the following lines in an ode on his death (*State Poems*, iv. 365):—

Great without pride, and without wrinkles wise,
Obliging without art, and just without disguise,
Wise in his counsels, humble in discourse,
Good without noise, and pleasant without force,
Easy of access, willing to bestow,
Regarded virtue, and forgot his foe.

He wrote the annotations in the margin of Dyer's Reports, and was the author of several occasional pamphlets.

His first wife was Dorothy Westcott; his second, Dorothy, daughter of Ralph Grange, Esq., of the Temple; and his third, Mrs. Brindley, who brought him a fortune of 10,000*l*. His eldest son by his first wife became secretary at war, and his grandson master of the household to George II. and a lord of the Treasury. The family still survives, and resides at Plympton House, built by the chief justice's son. (*Athen. Oxon.* iv. 499; *Noble's Granger*, ii. 166; *Luttrell*, iii. 11.)

TREMAYLE, THOMAS, was descended from a family seated at Sand, in Sidbury in Devonshire. He was a member of the Middle Temple, and the Year Book dates his appearance in court from Easter, 12 Edward IV., 1472; he took the degree of the coif in Trinity Term 1478, and was made king's serjeant in November 1481. During the short reign of Edward V. he was united with Judge William Jenney in the commission of assize on the Oxford Circuit. His promotion as a justice of the King's Bench took place on July 16, 1488, 3 Henry VII.; and there is evidence, in Keilwey's Reports, of his acting as late as Hilary Term 1507. (*Risdon's Devon*, 34; 9 *Report Pub. Rec.*, App. ii. 2.)

TRESILIAN, ROBERT, was in all probability a Cornishman. He possessed several manors and extensive lands there (*Cal. Inq.* p. m. iii. 106), and was an advocate at the assizes of the county in 43 Edward III., 1369. (*Liber Assisarum*, 278, 279.) He was educated at Oxford, and was elected fellow of Exeter College about the year 1354.

He appears to have been a king's serjeant in the first year of Richard II., at the end of which, May 6, 1378, he was constituted a justice of the Court of King's Bench, where he sat as the only puisne judge for four years.

He was promoted to the office of chief justice on June 22, 1381, a week after the murder of John de Cavendish, and the first duty to which he was called was the punishment of the insurgents. Some of the worst were those who had risen in Hertfordshire, and forcibly compelled the abbot of St. Alban's to grant them various immunities. To that town he accompanied the king, and the mode of trial he adopted was somewhat novel. He forced one jury of twelve to present the ringleaders, according to a list previously prepared; a second jury was next empanelled, who confirmed the finding of the first; and then the same course was adopted with a third jury. No witnesses appear to have been examined, but every party charged was condemned on the personal knowledge of these thirty-six men. (*Newcome's St. Albans*, 263.) The executions here and in other counties are described as being most numerous, and Tresilian's cruelty as having had no parallel till the campaign of Judge Jeffreys three centuries afterwards. Knighton, a contemporary chronicler, states that whoever was accused before him, whether guilty or innocent, was sure to be condemned; and other writers have extended the number of the sufferers to fifteen hundred. (*Lingard,* iv. 182; *Rapin,* iv. 25.)

The excited state of the country might perhaps justify some stringent proceedings; but both he and others, engaged in putting down the rebellion, seem to have been conscious that they had greatly exceeded any warrantable licence; inasmuch as, in the parliament of the following November, an act of pardon and indemnity was deemed expedient for those who had acted 'without due process of the law.'

No complaint appears to have been made against his judicial conduct in civil matters, but in his political career he was not so fortunate. Instead of using the influence of his position to check the royal extravagance and folly, he became, by countenancing whatever was agreeable to the king, a favourite at court, and a partisan of Robert de Vere, Duke of Ireland. The effect of this misplaced confidence was soon visible in the disordered state of the revenue, and the adoption of unpopular taxes to supply its deficiencies. Not only did the people murmur, but the houses of parliament found it necessary to put a stop to the maladministration of de Vere and his associates.

One of these, the Chancellor de la Pole, was impeached in the first instance, and his conviction was followed by a statute placing the management of the state and the control of the revenue in the hands of eleven permanent commissioners, at the head of whom were the king's uncles, the Dukes of York and Gloucester. Although this commission was solemnly confirmed by the king's letters patent, dated November 19, 1386, the parliament was no sooner dissolved than de Vere and the rest of the king's friends, representing to him his dependent state, urged him to take active measures to release himself from the thraldom in which the obnoxious ordinance had placed him. The king's chief advisers, besides de Vere and Tresilian, were Alexander Neville, Archbishop of York; Michael de la Pole, the late chancellor; and Sir Nicholas Brambre, an alderman of London. After endeavouring in vain to tamper with the sheriffs of the several counties to insure the election of subservient members for the next parliament, they summoned all the judges to a council at Nottingham on August 25, 1387, and by violent threats compelled them to attach their signatures to a series of questions and answers, which had been already prepared by Chief Justice Tresilian, the purport of which was to declare the 'new statute, ordinance, and commission to be derogatory to the royalty and prerogative of the king;' that all the persons concerned in procuring and making it were traitors, and ought to be punished with death; and that the judgment against Michael de la Pole was erroneous and revocable.

So awkwardly, however, had they concerted their plans that the whole plot came speedily to the knowledge of the lords commissioners, who forthwith appealed the archbishop, de Vere, de la Pole, Tresilian, and Brambre of high treason. This occurred on November 17, 1387, when the king promised to summon a parliament in the following February, that justice might be done. During the interval the archbishop, de Vere, and de la Pole found safety in flight; not, however, without some futile attempts on the part of de Vere to resist the commissioners by force of arms. Tresilian also in the first instance fled, and might have escaped but for his own infatuation. His place as chief justice was filled up on January 31, 1388, by the appointment of Walter de Clopton; and on February 3, the parliament having met, the five lords who acted as appellants—viz., the Duke of Gloucester, and the Earls of Arundel, Nottingham, Derby, and Warwick—delivered in no less than thirty-nine articles of impeachment, charging the accused with encroaching to themselves royal power by enslaving the king and blemishing his prerogative, and detailing various acts in proof of their guilt. Not the least prominent among these was the constraint they had put upon the justices to set their hands to the answers to the unconstitutional questions which had been propounded to them, and their endeavours by virtue thereof to get the lords and others, who had agreed to make the ordinance in the last parliament, attainted as traitors. All of the appellees, except Brambre, who was in custody, were pronounced guilty for default of appearance; and the duke, the earl, and Tresilian were sentenced to the death of traitors, and to forfeit their property to the king, the archbishop's temporalities being also taken into the king's hands. (*Rot. Parl.* iii. 229-237.)

Nicholas Brambre was next brought forward to undergo his trial, and while it was proceeding Tresilian was taken and brought before the parliament. The circumstances of his capture are related with some slight variations. The king had joined the Duke of Ireland at Bristol, and being desirous of knowing what proceedings were contemplated by his uncles at Westminster, Tresilian had volunteered to undertake the perilous journey. He reached London without discovery, and taking up his lodging in an alehouse, or, according to another account, at an apothecary's, opposite the palace gate, he had ensconced himself in a window so that he could observe every one who passed. His disguise, however, though sufficient to mislead ordinary observers, could not deceive a squire of the Duke of Gloucester's who had been often in his company. Thinking that he recognised the chief justice, he went in and had an interview which satisfied him that he was not mistaken, although Tresilian represented himself as a farmer on Sir John Holland's estate in Kent, come up to town in order to obtain redress for some wrongs done to him by the men of the Archbishop of Canterbury. The squire, pretending to believe him, went directly to the duke, his master, by whose orders he returned with a sufficient guard, and brought the unfortunate judge before the council. His fate was not long delayed, for, after a short colloquy with the duke, he was asked what he had to say why execution should not be done according to the judgment pronounced; and becoming as one struck dumb, so that he could not answer, he was led away to undergo his sentence. Froissart (ii. 285) says he was beheaded, and after hanged upon a gibbet; but the Parliament Roll states that he was taken to the Tower, and thence drawn through the city, and hanged at Tyburn. (*Holinshed*, ii. 794.) His body was buried in the church of the Grey Friars.

These events, it is agreed by all, occurred on February 19, 1388; and the attainder against him and the others was confirmed in the same parliament. Although all these proceedings were reversed by the parliament of 21 Richard II., when the king regained his power in the state, they were again revived and confirmed on the accession of Henry IV.

The confiscation of Tresilian's property was not delayed for an instant. No less than eleven manors in Cornwall are mentioned as belonging to him, besides other extensive possessions in that county and in Oxfordshire. (*Cal. Inq.* p. m. iii. 106, 120.)

By his wife, Emeline, the daughter of William Hiwishe, of Stowford in Devonshire, he left one son, named John; and a daughter, who married John Hauley, of Dartmouth.

TREVAIGNON, JOHN DE, was of a Cornish family, the descendants of which still flourish in that county. His name appears in the reign of Edward II. as an advocate; and in 4 Edward III. he had the degree of the coif, and was afterwards one of the king's serjeants. On September 24, 1334, 8 Edward III., he was constituted a judge of the Common Pleas, and probably died within the next year, as no fines were acknowledged before him subsequent to Michaelmas Term, 9 Edward III.

TREVETT, THOMAS, was the father of Nicholas Trevet, the author of numerous works, one of which, entitled 'Annales sex Regum Angliæ, qui a comitibus Andegavensibus originem traxerunt,' has been published (1845) by the English Historical Society. The editor, in his preface (p. v.), says that 'the judge, according to Leland, was descended from a family of some note in Norfolk; a statement which is confirmed by a descent preserved in Sir Richard St. George's Heraldic Collections; though the documents from which this has been compiled refer exclusively to certain lands in the county of Somerset.' Thomas Trevet was appointed, in 49 Edward III., to assess the tallage on the 'Villam de Shaftonia,' in Dorsetshire. (*Madox*, i. 742.) He acted as a justice itinerant for that and the neighbouring counties from 52 to 55 Henry III.

In August 1272, 56 Henry III., the priory and cathedral of Norwich having been maliciously burnt by the citizens, he was sent there, according to the statement of his son in the 'Annales' (279), to try the malefactors. He calls his father 'justiciarium militem quendam, Thomam Treveth dictum, qui et justiciarius itineris fuerat de corona.' The first clause of the description seems to warrant the idea that he was something more than a justice itinerant. He died in 11 Edward I. (*Abb. Rot. Orig.* i. 36, 37.) His son became a Dominican friar, and is stated to have been prior of their monastery in London, and to have died in 1328. (*Preface*, vii.; *Hutchins's Dorsetsh.* ii. 441.)

TREVOR, THOMAS, was the youngest of five sons of John Trevor, Esq., of Trevallyn in Denbighshire, of an ancient and noble Welsh family, by Mary, daughter of Sir George Bruges of London, and was born July 6, 1586. He was admitted a member of the Inner Temple, and became reader there in autumn 1620. He was soon after knighted, and made solicitor to Prince Charles, who, when he ascended the throne, called him to the degree of the coif, and nominated him one of his serjeants on April 8, 1625. On the 12th of the following month he was advanced to a seat of the Exchequer. (*Rymer*, xviii. 637.)

Nothing is told of him for the first ten years of his judicial life, except that at the Bury assizes, trying a cause about wintering of cattle, and thinking the charge immoderate, he said, 'Why, friend, this is most unreasonable; I wonder thou art not ashamed, for I myself have known a beast wintered one whole summer for a noble.' 'That was *a bull*, my lord, I believe,' retorted the man, to the infinite amusement of the auditory. (*Anecdotes and Traditions* [Camden Soc.], 79.)

But more serious matters soon occupied him. The imposition of ship-money was attempted, and Baron Trevor united with the rest of the judges in 1636 in subscribing a joint opinion in favour of its legality, which he afterwards supported in a most foolish inconclusive speech in the case of

Hampden. (*State Trials*, iii. 1152.) On the meeting of the Long Parliament in 1640 proceedings were commenced against him and five of the other judges, who were eventually impeached for the judgment they had delivered. Trevor was sentenced to imprisonment and a fine of 6000*l*., but upon payment he was discharged and permitted to resume his duties. In 1643 the king had issued proclamations to adjourn the term from Westminster to Oxford; but, as these had been hitherto fruitless, 'for want of the necessary legal form of having the writs read in court,' the judges at Oxford could not proceed to business there till that formality had been observed. The parliament, having then assumed the sovereign power, had published orders to the contrary; yet the king, thinking that the judges remaining in London would obey him rather than the parliament, sent messengers in Michaelmas Term with directions to deliver them the writs. There were only three judges then sitting in London—Justice Bacon in the King's Bench, Justice Reeve in the Common Pleas, and Baron Trevor in the Exchequer. The two latter were served, but immediately ordered the apprehension of the messengers, who, being tried by a council of war, were condemned as spies, and one of them was actually executed as an example. The fears that then influenced Trevor seem to have been dispersed by the tragic termination of the king's life. On February 8, 1649, he was one of the six judges who boldly refused to accept the new commission offered them by the then ruling powers. (*Clarendon*, iv. 287, 342; *Whitelocke*, 47, 76, 378.)

He lived nearly eight years after his retirement, and dying on December 21, 1656, was buried at Lemington-Hastang in Warwickshire, the manor of which belonged to him.

He was twice married—first to Prudence, daughter of Henry Butler, Esq.; and secondly to Frances, daughter and heir of Daniel Blennerhasset, Esq., of Norfolk. An only son he had by the former, named Thomas, was created a baronet in 1641, but the title became extinct in 1676. (*Stow's London*, 875; *Wotton's Baronet.* iii. 143.)

TREVOR, JOHN, may claim a descent from an elder branch of the old Welsh family from which the above Thomas Trevor sprung, his ancestor being seated at Brynkynalt in Denbighshire at his death in 1494. He was second but eldest surviving son of John Trevor of that place, by Mary, daughter of John Jeffreys, of Helon in the same county, the aunt of the Judge Jeffreys of infamous memory. At the time of his admission to the Inner Temple, in November 1654, his father is described of Ross-Trevor in Ireland, whither he had probably retired in reduced circumstances, if Roger North's statement (218) be true, that the son 'was bred a sort of clerk in the chambers of old Arthur Trevor, an eminent and worthy professor of the law in the Inner Temple.' 'A gentleman,' he adds, 'that observed a strange-looking boy in his clerk's seat (for no person ever had a worse sort of squint than he had), asked who that gentleman was: "A kinsman of mine," said Arthur Trevor, "that I have allowed to sit here to learn the knavish part of the law."' That he was bettered by the instruction may be doubted; but that he became an able proficient there is evidence in the reputation he gained of being the best judge in all gambling transactions, of the tricks and intricacies of which he had personal experience.

He was called to the bar in May 1661, became treasurer of his inn in 1674, and reader in 1675. He was knighted in 1671, and there is no doubt that he was indebted to his cousin, George Jeffreys, for some of his future preferments. In the parliament of March 1679 he was elected for Beeralston, which returned him again for that called in October of the same year. In the Oxford parliament of March 1681 he represented his native county of Denbigh; and Sir John Bramston (208) records that he was the only man who spoke in favour of Jeffreys when the complaint against him as recorder of London was discussed in the house.

On the accession of James II., his cousin, who was then chief justice, had an opportunity of showing his gratitude. Trevor having obtained a seat in that king's only parliament for the town of Denbigh, Jeffreys, in opposition to Lord Keeper North, succeeded in recommending him to be the speaker. So inefficient was he in the requirements of the office that he was even obliged to read from a paper the few formal words in which he announced to the house the king's approbation, and was guilty of some other irregularities that were inexcusable in one who had had so long a senatorial experience. He showed more boldness and self-possession on the occasion of presenting the revenue bill on May 30, when he assured the king that the Commons entirely relied on his majesty's sacred word to support and defend the religion of the Church of England. Of this reminder of the royal promise the king took not the slightest notice, nor apparently any offence, as on the 20th of the following October he promoted Sir John to the office of master of the Rolls, then vacant. (*Bramston*, 197, 207; *Parl. Hist.* iv. 1359.)

This elevation occurred at the period when his relative and patron had returned from his bloody campaign and been rewarded with the Great Seal. The Court of Chancery was then presided over by two judges of kindred spirit, and it might be a question which of the two exceeded the other in want of principle, or in the use of coarse vituperation. Yet they both deserve praise in the exercise of their judicial functions, and the decrees they pronounced in private causes were able and just. A sort of rivalry, however, soon rose up between them. Jeffreys sometimes reversed his coadjutor's decrees and adopted other irritating measures against him. Trevor, who could on occasion imitate not unsuccessfully the objurgatory style of his patron, now feeling himself no longer a dependent, assumed a dictatorial manner, found fault with the chancellor's proceedings, and very early after his appointment told him that if he pursued Alderman Cornish to execution, it would be no better than murder. Indeed, Roger North tells us, 'like a true gamester, he fell to the good work of supplanting his patron and friend, and had certainly done it if King James's affairs had stood right much longer, for he was advanced so far with him as to vilify and scold with him publicly at Whitehall.'

He was not admitted to the privy council till July 6, 1688; and on August 24 he was sent for in a hurry from 'the Wells' to be present at that meeting when the king resolved to have another parliament. He was again present in October, when proof was given of the genuineness of the birth of the Prince of Wales; and after the king's first escape he was one of the faithful councillors who attended at his levee on his return from Rochester. (*Bramston*, 311; *State Trials*, xii. 123.)

At the Revolution he, with all the other judges, lost his place. But he managed by his open professions of adherence to the extreme doctrines of the Church of England to keep up some degree of popularity with that party which was gradually superseding the ministers, who, though they had been chiefly instrumental in effecting the great change in the government of the kingdom, soon disgusted the king by assuming so great a control over him. To the Convention Parliament he did not venture to offer himself; but the borough of Beeralston returned him again on a vacancy. Before the end of the year he entered into the debates as boldly as if he had never been connected with King James's court. In the next parliament of March 1690 he was returned for Yarmouth, and was selected by the minister Carmarthen to be the speaker of it, as the most fit instrument in the practice, too openly encouraged and too long continued, of buying off those members who opposed the government. (*Burnet*, iv. 74.)

A very graphic description of him is given by Lord Macaulay (iii. 547).

Being 'a bold and dexterous man,' Trevor soon after had a renewal of his legal honours. On January 13 he was replaced in his old position as master of the Rolls; and on May 14 he was made one of the lords commissioners of the Great Seal, an office which he enjoyed for nearly three years, till the nomination of Somers as lord keeper on March 23, 1693. Not satisfied with all these honours and the emoluments that flowed from them, Trevor with unblushing rapacity participated largely in the corruption that then too universally prevailed. In the investigation instituted by the parliament it was found that he had, among other bribes suspected but not proved, received a present from the city of London for getting the orphans' bill passed, which had several times before been brought into the house without success. He was condemned to sit for six hours hearing himself abused, and at last was obliged to put the question and to declare himself guilty of 'a high crime and misdemeanour.' A new speaker was immediately appointed, and he was expelled the house on March 16, 1695, having only a fortnight before attended in all state the queen's funeral in Westminster Abbey. (*Parl. Hist.* v. 901–10; *Bramston*, 386.) No further punishment being awarded, the wits remarked 'that justice was blind, but bribery only squinted.' He never afterwards offered himself as a member; but so little was he abashed by his expulsion that soon after, on meeting Archbishop Tillotson, he muttered loud enough to be heard, 'I hate a fanatic in lawn sleeves.' The archbishop answered, 'And I hate a knave in any sleeves.'

This disgrace did not deprive him of the mastership of the Rolls, that office having been conferred upon him for life. Though Lord Raymond (p. 566) names him as joined with the three chiefs as commissioner of the Great Seal on the dismissal of Lord Somers in 1700, the 'Crown Office Minute-book' (p. 141) proves that the appointment was to the three chiefs alone, his commission being solely to hear causes till a new lord keeper was appointed. He continued master of the Rolls for twenty-two years after his expulsion, possessing so high a reputation as a lawyer that he was frequently appealed to as authority in doubtful points by Lord Chancellor Harcourt, but with the character of being dead to every sense of shame, and of treating the counsel who attended his court with coarse and unfeeling brutality. So rough were his public reproaches to a nephew of his that it is said the sensitive young barrister sunk under them and never recovered. The only honour he received in the reign of Queen Anne was that of constable of Flint

Castle in 1705, in the place of his father-in-law, Sir Roger Mostyn. He died on May 20, 1717, at his house in Clement's Lane, and was buried in the Rolls Chapel. (*Luttrell*, iv. 641, v. 540.)

The avarice for which he was notorious was not redeemed, as it often is, by occasional fits of generosity. Various stories are told of his meanness. One of them is that on a relation calling upon him while he was drinking his wine, he exclaimed to the servant, 'You rascal, you have brought my cousin Roderick Lloyd, Esq., prothonotary of North Wales, marshal to Baron Price, and so forth, up my back stairs. Take him down again immediately, and bring him up my front stairs.' During the operation the bottle was removed, and Sir John saved his wine. (*Yorke's Royal Tribes of Wales*, 109.)

He married Jane, the daughter of Sir Roger Mostyn, Bart., and the widow of Roger Puliston, of Emeral in Flintshire, and had by her four sons and a daughter, who by her marriage with Michael Hill, of Hillsborough in Ireland, was the mother of Arthur, first Viscount Dungannon, who, succeeding to his grandfather's estates, took the name of Trevor. Anne, the daughter of Arthur, was the mother of the great Duke of Wellington. (*Townsend's Ho. of Commons*, ii. 53; *Woolrych's Judge Jeffreys*.)

TREVOR, THOMAS (LORD TREVOR), was the grandson of Sir John Trevor, of Trevallyn in Flintshire, an elder brother of the above Sir Thomas Trevor. His father, also Sir John, became secretary of state to Charles II. and died in 1672, leaving by his wife, Ruth, a daughter of the celebrated John Hampden, four sons, of whom this Thomas was the second. Born about 1659, he entered the Inner Temple in 1672 (just before the death of his father, who had been a bencher of the inn), and was called to the bar on November 28, 1680. So early did he distinguish himself in the courts that he was elected a bencher in 1689, and was elevated to the post of solicitor-general on May 3, 1692, and thereupon knighted. He refused the attorney-generalship in 1693, but on June 8, 1695, accepted the office. (*Luttrell*, iii. 68; *Lord Raymond*, 57.)

During the six years that he filled that responsible place he had to conduct the trials of the persons implicated in the Assassination Plot, in all of which he acted with a fairness and candour that formed a remarkable contrast to the criminal proceedings in the late reigns. In the progress of those trials the act of parliament (St. 7 Will. III. c. 3) for regulating trials for treason, which gave to the prisoners so charged the privilege of having counsel, came into operation, and Sir Thomas met the multiplied objections that were consequently urged by the defending advocates with temper, ability, and learning. On the removal of Lord Somers in May 1700 he declined the offer to be made lord keeper; but on June 28, 1701, he accepted the more permanent place of chief justice of the Common Pleas. He was member of one parliament only, that of 1695, in which he represented Plympton, and according to Speaker Onslow he divided against Sir John Fenwick's attainder, although he was an officer of the government. (*State Trials*, vols. xii. xiii.; *Luttrell*, iv. 645; *Burnet*, iv. 234.)

On the accession of Queen Anne he was re-appointed chief justice, and presided in the Court of Common Pleas during the whole of her reign. In the short interval between the chancellorships of Lords Cowper and Harcourt, from September 26 to October 19, 1710, he was entrusted with the Great Seal as first commissioner; and on December 31, 1711, he was called to the peerage by the title of Baron Trevor of Bromham in Bedfordshire, being one of the twelve peers whom Queen Anne by an unusual exercise of her prerogative created at once, to secure a majority for the proposed peace in the House of Lords. He was the first chief justice of the Common Pleas who was ennobled while holding that office. Though commencing his professional career as a whig, and being united in office with Somers, he gradually joined the tory party, and attached himself to it while Queen Anne reigned. He is thus described in the account of the judges of the different courts given by Lord Cowper to George I. on his accession:—

'The first [the chief justice] is an able man, but made one of the twelve lords, wch the late ministry procur'd to be created at once (in such haste, y^t few, if any, of their patents had any preamble, or reasons of their creation), only to support *their peace*, wch the House of Lords, they found, would not without that addition. From that time, at least, he went violently into all the measures of that ministry, and was much trusted by them; and when they divided, a little before the queen's death, he sided wth Ld Bolingbr.; and for so doing, 'tis credibly said, was to have been made l^d president. Many of ye lords think his being a peer an obj^n to his being a judge; because, by ye constitution, ye judges ought to be *assistants* to the House of Lords, wch they can't be, if a *part* of that body. Ther is but one example known of the like; wch is that of Ld Jefferys, ch. just. of the King's Bench, and after chancellor to K. Ja. ye 2nd. 'Tis natural to think, ye other judges stomach ye distinction, while he is among them: and tis said y^t ye suitors dislike ye difference they find in his behaviour to them since he had this distinction. He is grown very wealthy. If it be thought fit to remove him, Sr Peter King, record^r of the City of London, I should humbly propose as fit to succeed him.' (*Lord Campbell's Chanc.* iv. 349.)

Upon the hint thus given Lord Trevor was removed on October 14, 1714. As his appointment was 'quamdiu se bene gesserit,' he said he would have tried the question as to the king's power to eject him if Chief Justice Holt had not, by taking out a new commission when Queen Anne came to the throne, decided that in his opinion his former commission had expired on the demise of the crown. (*Lord Raymond*, 1318; *Burnet*, v. 12 n.) Lord Trevor lived sixteen years afterwards, and, changing his party again, became in 1726 lord privy seal, and in the next year was one of the lords justices during the last absence of George I. He retained the privy seal under George II., by whom he was raised, on May 8, 1730, to the high office of lord president of the council, an honour which he did not enjoy for more than six weeks, as he died on the 19th of the next month at his seat at Bromham, where he was buried under a monument with an elegant Latin inscription.

He was generally admitted to have been an able and upright judge, though Chief Justice Holt is said to have disparaged his law. But the facility with which he deserted one party to side with the other, and returned again to the party he had left, could not but be detrimental to his character. Yet Speaker Onslow says (*Burnet*, iv. 344, n.), 'He was the only man almost that I ever knew that changed his party as he had done, that preserved so. general an esteem with all parties as he did. When he came back to the whigs he was made lord privy seal and afterwards president of the council, and had much joy in both. He liked being at court, and was much there after he had these offices, but was very awkward in it, by having been the most reserved, grave, and austere judge I ever saw in Westminster Hall.' Lord Hervey (i. 114) describes him as being 'by principle (if he had any principle) a Jacobite. However, from interest and policy he became, like his brother convert and brother lawyer Lord Harcourt, as zealous a servant to the Hanover family as any of those who had never been otherwise; for as these two men were too knowing in their trade to swerve from the established principles of their profession, they acted like most lawyers, who generally look on princes like other clients, and without any regard to right or wrong—the equity or injustice of the cause—think themselves obliged to maintain whoever fees them last and pays them best.'

This is a very prejudiced portrait and a most unfair judgment of lawyers. Trevor, like most sensible men, did not approve of the extreme views of either party, and, seeing the impossibility of restoring the exiled family, and that any attempt to do so would inevitably be accompanied by all the horrors of a civil war, wisely lent his aid in supporting the Hanoverian princes in the peaceful possession of the throne to which they had been called.

He married twice. By his first wife, Elizabeth, daughter and coheir of John Searle, Esq., of Finchley, he had two sons and three daughters; and by his second wife, Anne, daughter of Robert Weldon, Esq., and widow of Sir Robert Bernard, Bart., he had three sons. The fourth of these five sons became Bishop of Durham in 1752, and the three elder brothers held the title of Lord Trevor successively. The last of them, Robert, fourth Lord Trevor, adopted the name of Hampden in 1754, in compliance with the will of his relative John Hampden, and in 1776 was advanced to the dignity of Viscount Hampden, both titles becoming extinct in 1824. (*Collins's Peerage*, vi. 302; *Nicolas's Synopsis*; *Luttrell*, v. 421, 468.)

TRIKINGHAM, LAMBERT DE, whose legal and judicial life extended from the reign of Edward I. to that of Edward III., belonged to a family so called from a place of that name in Lincolnshire; and Alexander de Trikingham, who acted in the assessments of that county in the early part of the reign of Edward I., was probably the judge's father. (*Parl. Writs*, i. 871, ii. 1324.)

The first mention of Lambert occurs in 27 Edward I., 1299, as a justice itinerant into Kent. In the next year he was raised to the bench at Westminster as a justice of the Common Pleas, and the fines levied before him continued till Midsummer 1816, 9 Edward II. On August 6 in the latter year he was removed to the King's Bench, where he remained exactly four years, retiring from that court on August 6, 1320, and being immediately made a baron of the Exchequer. We do not find him acting as a baron, nor summoned to parliament among the judges, later than the seventeenth year of that reign, and it is most probable that he left the bench about that time, as a new baron was named at the close of the year, apparently in his place. He still, however, was employed as a justice itinerant, and he is placed next to the chief justice in the commission into Northamptonshire as late as 1329, 3 Edward III. (*Dugdale's Orig.* 44; *Rot. Parl.* 161-380.)

In 1317 he received the mastership of Sherbourn Hospital in Durham. (*Surtees' Durham*, i. 138.)

TROP, or THORPE, SIMON DE, took his name from the place in Northamptonshire, which was in those times as often spelled Thorpe as Trop. His father, Ralph, met with a violent death in 5 Henry III., and three persons were charged with being concerned in it. One of them, being a clergyman, was delivered over to ecclesiastical jurisdiction, where he purged himself of the accusation. (*Rot. Claus.* i. 454, 464, 486, 611.) Simon, there can be very little doubt, was brought up to the law, for he was appointed no less than four times, from 1252 to 1256, to act as a justice itinerant, not in his own county alone, but in several others.

He died in January 1259, 43 Henry III., leaving, by his wife, Maria, sister and coheir of Robert de Salceto, a son named Ralph, who did homage for his lands in Northamptonshire. (*Excerpt. e Rot. Fin.* i. 296, ii. 293.)

TRUMPINGTON, WILLIAM DE, so called from a place of that name in Cambridgeshire, forfeited his lands by joining the barons against King John. On his submission at the beginning of the next reign they were restored to him, after which he made his loyalty sufficiently apparent to be appointed in 3 Henry III. one of the justices itinerant into his own county and the neighbouring shires. (*Rot. Pat.* 176; *Rot. Claus.* i. 272, 273, 326.)

TRURO, LORD. *See* T. WILDE.

TRUSSEL, WILLIAM, seems to have belonged to a Warwickshire family, as there was a suit relative to property in that county in which he was concerned in 26 Henry III. He was constituted a justicier, Dugdale says of the Common Pleas, on September 3, 1252, and fines were acknowledged before him till November 1254 (*Dugdale's Orig.* 43), in which year he went as one of the justices itinerant into the counties of Gloucester and Stafford. That he continued to act as a judge till September 1257 is evidenced by the payments made for assizes before him recorded in the Rot. de Finibus (ii. 162–262). He and his wife claimed the advowson of the church of Sharneford in Staffordshire against the prior of Kirkeby, who in 53 Henry III. substantiated his right of possession. (*Abb. Placit.* 178.)

TRUSSEL, WILLIAM, is usually described by historians as a justiciary, but he certainly was not a judge of either of the courts of Westminster, nor a regular justice of assize. His judicial functions seem to have been confined to the special trials with which his name is connected. He was apparently descended from the above William Trussel, and was second son of William Trussel, of Cublesdone (Kibblesdone) in Staffordshire, and of other manors in Northamptonshire, by Maud, daughter and heir of Warin de Manwarin.

After his father's death he was returned member for the county of Northampton in 12 Edward II., and is named among the knights of that county and the county of Stafford in the seventeenth year, 1324. In the interim he had been in arms against the government, and was with the Earl of Lancaster in the defeat at Boroughbridge. He was there taken prisoner, and appears to have been in custody on July 20, 1322, but a writ for his pursuit and capture on August 2 proves that he had made his escape. In the next year he was at the head of those who ravaged the estates of the Despencers. (*Parl. Writs*, ii. p. ii. 1528.) Joining the queen in France, he accompanied her on her landing in England in September 1326, and was present at the fall of Bristol and the seizure of the elder Despencer. Some writers say that the aged earl was executed without hearing or trial, while others state that he was accused before Sir William de Trussel, but there are no remains of any regular proceedings against him. The younger Despencer, on his capture, was arraigned before Trussel in an equally informal manner, his speech, in pronouncing the horrible sentence, seeming to have been the only indictment. That speech recapitulated all the popular charges against the prisoner and his father, and, after minutely particularising the punishment awarded, concluded by dismissing the fallen favourite with coarse vituperation. Trussel is neither before nor after described as a judge, and the actor in so summary a process, which has the appearance of martial law, is scarcely entitled to be so designated.

Although there is no record that Trussel was returned as a knight or burgess to the parliament that assembled at Westminster on January 7, 1327, there is no doubt that he was present in some character, as he was appointed procurator for the whole parliament, and deputed to proceed, with certain prelates and peers, to Kenilworth Castle, where the king was confined, and to pronounce the renunciation of their homage and fealty to him.

This formality completed, Edward III. was proclaimed, and Trussel received the reward of his devotion by being immediately constituted the king's escheator south of Trent. He was, however, removed from this office in the following year, having made himself an enemy in Roger de Mortimer, the queen's favourite, on whose death he was reinstated in the fourth year. In 7 Edward III. some change took place in the office, and he had a grant of certain lands in the Isle of Anglesey, of which he was soon after made sheriff, and constable of the castle of Beaumaris. From the ninth to the fourteenth year we find him again king's escheator, sometimes on one and sometimes on the other side of the

Trent. (*Abb. Rot. Orig.* ii. 4–14, 42–71, 78, 82, 103–136.)

After this time it is difficult to trace distinctly whether the entries apply to his son William or to him; but it seems most probable that it was the son who was the admiral of the fleet in 13 and 16 Edward III., and who is stated by Dugdale (*Baronage*, ii. 143) to have been summoned as a baron to parliament in the latter year. If so, however, it is difficult to understand how 'Monsr. William Trussel' answers as the representative of the Commons—that is to say, their speaker—in the parliament held at Westminster in May, 17 Edward III. (*Rot. Parl.* ii. 136); but the question is of little importance, because it is allowed that neither he nor any one of his posterity was ever afterwards summoned as a baron.

TUNSTALL, CUTHBERT (BISHOP OF DURHAM), was grandson of Sir Thomas Tunstall of Thurland Castle in Lancashire, whose two sons, Richard and Thomas, have each at different times been described as the father of Cuthbert; but the evidence adduced by Surtees (*Durham*, i. lxvi.) tends strongly to fix the parentage on Thomas. His birth is said to have been illegitimate; and a curious story told by George Holland in the genealogical table of his family, compiled in 1563, may be supposed to give some grounds not only for this belief, but also for the report that Richard, and not Thomas, was his father. He says, 'Cuthbert Tunstall, late Bishop of Durham, in his youth near two years was brought up in my great-grandfather Sir Thomas Holland's kitchen unknown, 'till being known, he was sent home to Sir Richard Tunstall his father, and so kept at school, *as he himself declared in manner the same to me.*' (*Blomefield's Norfolk*, i. 232.)

He was born in 1474 or 1475, at Hatchford in Richmondshire, and was entered at Balliol College in Oxford in 1491, but, on account of the plague then raging there, was removed to the sister university as a member of King's Hall, now part of Trinity College. He then completed his studies at the university of Padua, where he took the degree of Doctor of Laws, and on his return to England entered into holy orders, being only sub-deacon in 1508.

At this date he received the rectory of Stanhope in Durham, which was followed by that of Harrow-on-the-Hill in Middlesex, by prebends in the churches of Lincoln and York, and by the appointment of vicar-general from Archbishop Warham. Introduced by that prelate to King Henry, the talents and learning for which he had been recommended were soon employed in diplomatic services. In October 1515 he was sent as ambassador to negotiate a treaty of peace with the Archduke Charles (*Rymer*, xiii. 537), his success in which no doubt led to his nomination on May 12 in the following year to the office of master of the Rolls. In 1519 he was made archdeacon of Chester, and soon afterwards was engaged with Sir Thomas More in settling the provisions under the commercial treaty with Charles, now emperor. While at Brussels on this embassy his friendship commenced with Erasmus, in whose house he lodged. In May 1521 he became dean of Salisbury, and was elected Bishop of London in January 1522, soon after which he resigned the mastership of the Rolls.

Surtees says that just previous to this he was made keeper of the Great Seal; and Parry in his 'Parliaments and Councils' mentions him as chancellor at the parliament of April 1523. But both authors are manifestly mistaken, for Cardinal Wolsey was then in the plenitude of his power. Tunstall was, however, appointed keeper of the privy seal on July 12, 1523; and in November he had the grant of a pardon for the escape from his custody as bishop of John Tompson, an attainted clergyman. (*Ibid.* xiv. 1, 10.)

Before his next advance in the Church he rendered further service in various embassies—soliciting the release of Francis I. when a prisoner after the battle of Pavia, accompanying Cardinal Wolsey in his ostentatious visit to that monarch in 1527, and concluding, with Sir Thomas More in 1529, the treaty of Cambray. On March 25, 1530, he received restitution of the temporalities of Durham, to which see he had been translated on the resignation of Cardinal Wolsey. (*Le Neve*.)

In the changes which Henry VIII. subsequently introduced, Bishop Tunstall displayed some weakness and irresolution; and on the king's assumption of the title of supreme head of the English Church, he 'hesitated, argued, and submitted.' By thus temporising he preserved the personal favour of the king, who made him president of the North, and appointed him one of the executors of his will, with a legacy of 300*l.* (*Testam. Vetust.* 41.)

Under the reign of Edward VI., when Protestantism was more strictly enforced, though in parliament he protested against the changes in religion, yet when they were adopted he obeyed the law.

He would have continued safe in his quiet retirement, but that Dudley the new Duke of Northumberland had a craving for his episcopal possessions. A false charge was accordingly concocted against him, on which a bill for his attainder was introduced into parliament; but, though it passed the House of Lords, the Commons were not satisfied, and would not sanction it. The persecuted bishop was not allowed thus to escape. A commission was issued to the duke's own creatures, who deprived him of his bishopric, and sent him to the Tower on August 14, 1552.

Mary, immediately on her accession, released him from prison, and restored him to his see. He assisted at her coronation and at her marriage (*Q. Jane and Q. Mary* [Camden Soc.], 31,142), but kept aloof from the cruel persecutions that disgraced her reign. Though named in several commissions, he devoted himself to his pastoral duties; and by his lenity and toleration his diocese enjoyed an uninterrupted peace, in happy contrast with the rest of the kingdom. He discouraged too severe an investigation into men's opinions, saying to his chancellor, when desirous of examining a preacher supposed to entertain heretical opinions, 'Hitherto we have had a good report among our neighbours: I pray you bring not this man's blood upon my head.'

When Elizabeth, whose godfather he had been, ascended the throne, he was near eighty-four years old—an age not likely to give up preconceived opinions, nor to be swayed by worldly considerations. The queen, influenced by the moderation he had exhibited, regarded him at first with favour, and employed him in the consecration of several bishops; but at length, on his persisting in his refusal to take the oath of supremacy, she was compelled after a year's trial to deprive him. Instead, however, of sending the aged man to prison, she committed him in July 1559 to the custody of Archbishop Parker, in whom he found a kind and considerate host for the few remaining months of his life. He survived till November 18, and was buried in the chancel of Lambeth Church, at the expense of the archbishop.

In addition to his professional works, he published a treatise on arithmetic, 'De Arte Supputandi,' in 1522, the year of his elevation to the episcopal bench. (*Godwin; Surtees; Brit. Biog.*)

TURNER, GEORGE JAMES, was one of those modest and retiring persons who owe their prosperity to no extraordinary incident in their lives, nor to any political or extraneous interest, but simply to their honest efforts to do their duty in that state of life to which it has pleased God to call them. Little therefore can be recorded to render his biography interesting, beyond the important lesson that a steady reliance on Providence will bless all human exertions, when accompanied by integrity of purpose and persistent and intellectual industry. He was one of a large family, and was born in 1798 at Great Yarmouth, where his father, the Rev. Richard Turner, B.D., was for thirty years the minister.

His education was commenced at the Charterhouse (where he became a governor), and finished at Pembroke College, Cambridge, of which his uncle, Dr. Joseph Turner, dean of Norwich, was then master, by obtaining the distinction of a wrangler's place in 1819, and soon after being elected to a fellowship there. He had previously entered the society of Lincoln's Inn, and was called to the bar in July 1821, first preparing himself by becoming a pupil to Mr. Pepys (afterwards Lord Cottenham). Attaching himself to the Court of Chancery, he worked diligently and successfully for nineteen years as a junior, when in 1840 he was honoured with a silk gown. During the next eleven years his energies were brought more into play as well in his legitimate court of the Rolls, and in cases of appeal, as in the House of Lords and in the judicial committee of the privy council. In the latter he had particularly distinguished himself by his elaborate and triumphant argument for the Rev. Mr. Gorham, the appellant against a decision of the Bishop of Exeter.

From 1847 to 1851 he sat in the House of Commons as member for the city of Coventry. So conspicuous were his legal attainments, and so peculiarly qualified was he allowed to be for a judicial position, that on April 2, 1851, he was selected as one of the vice-chancellors, and was then knighted, and placed on the privy council. Two years afterwards, when Lord Cranworth became lord chancellor, Sir George was promoted to his place of lord justice of the Court of Appeal in Chancery, on January 10, 1853, as the colleague of Sir James Lewis Knight-Bruce. By their united administration of justice, in the necessarily difficult cases they had to decide, so much satisfaction was given, both to the suitors and to the bar, that when a change took place by the removal of one of them the deepest regret was felt by all. This regret was doubled by the death of both within eight months of each other, his colleague dying in November 1866, and he following on July 9, 1867.

By his marriage with Louisa, one of the daughters of Edward Jones, Esq., of Brackley in Northamptonshire, Sir George had a family of six sons and three daughters. One of his sons was made Bishop of Grafton and Armidale, in Australia, in February 1869.

TURNHAM, STEPHEN DE, who is called by different writers Stephen of Tours, or de Turonis, de Turnham, or de Mazzai, was the younger son of Robert de Turnham, who founded the priory of Cumbwell in Kent. He was seneschal of Anjou in the latter part of the reign of Henry II., with whom he was a great favourite, and over whom he exercised considerable influence. He assisted that king in his last fatal wars, and was with him at Mans when it was besieged by Philip of France; and intending to destroy the suburbs by fire, the flames unfortunately extended to the city itself, and obliged Henry to fly.

On Henry's death, he was taken by King Richard, and loaded with chains; nor was he released until he had delivered up all the castles and treasures which the late king had entrusted to him, nor, as Richard of Devizes asserts, without the payment of an enormous fine. He was, however, soon restored to favour, and, accompanying Richard on his expedition to Jerusalem, was, with Richard de Camville, entrusted with the government of Cyprus, and afterwards is enumerated among those noted 'for their high valiance' in the holy war. In 1193 he was appointed to conduct Queen Berengaria into Poictou, and after the king's return he was employed in the Curia Regis as one of the justiciers. His name appears on several fines levied there in the last two years of Richard's reign, and as acting as a justice itinerant in the counties of Essex, Hertford, and Surrey. During the first four years of John's reign also he was engaged in the same duties. (*Madox*, i. 565, 733-7, 743.)

He then appears to have retired from active employment, inasmuch as in 5 John he fined one thousand marks to be discharged from all accounts, fines, &c. (*Rot. Pat.* 41.) That this was intended to be a favourable close of his account, and that he still enjoyed the confidence of his sovereign, appears from the close of the entry, whereby the king excuses him three hundred marks, and orders that out of the residue he should be allowed one mark a day for the custody of the king's niece, the sister of the unfortunate Prince Arthur.

In 7 John he received several payments of one mark each for the use of the queen (*Rot. de Præstito*, 273-4), and in 11 John a gift from the king of one hundred marks. (*Rot. Misæ*, 154.) The Rotuli Misæ of the latter year and of 14 John contain entries of frequent payments to messengers to and from Winchester conveying the correspondence between the king and him, and in 14 John he was commanded not to allow any one to see the king's son Henry without special order. (*Rot. Claus.* 121, 123.)

His property was considerably increased by his marriage with Edelin, the daughter and one of the heirs of Ranulph de Broc. He held one of the estates so acquired by the service of 'Ostiarius Cameræ Regis,' and by another which he held in wardship he was marshal of the king's household.

He died in 16 John, in which year his widow paid sixty marks and a palfrey for liberty to marry with whom she pleased, and his lands were divided among his five daughters. (*Ibid.* i. 168; *Excerpt. e Rot. Fin.* i. 25; *R. de Wendover*, ii. 459, iii. 1; *Ric. Devizes*, 6, 7; *Holinshed*, ii. 202, 222, 232; *Manning and Bray's Surrey*, i. 15, 83.)

TURNOR, CHRISTOPHER, was the eldest son of Christopher Turnor, Esq., of Milton-Erneys in Bedfordshire, by Helen, daughter of Thomas Sarn, Esq., of Printon, Hertfordshire. He was born on December 6, 1607, and was educated at Emmanuel College, Cambridge, to which in after life he contributed a liberal donation towards rebuilding its chapel. He took the degrees of B.A. and M.A. in 1630 and 1633, and, having been admitted a student at the Middle Temple, was called to the bar in November 1633, and became bencher in 1654. His name does not frequently appear in the Reports, and he is not mentioned as taking any prominent part in the troubles. But that he had a fair legal reputation is manifest from his being selected at the Restoration as third baron of the Exchequer on July 7, 1660. He was thereupon knighted. On his first circuit he refused to try three persons indicted for murder in Gloucestershire, for the very sufficient reason that the body had not been found. His successor on that circuit at the next assize, Sir Robert Hyde, not influenced by the same consideration, condemned and hanged the prisoners, whose innocence was some years afterwards established by the reappearance of the man supposed to have been murdered.

A gossiping letter preserved in the State Paper Office (*Cal.* [1660], 539), dated in March 1661, relates that 'Judges Atkins and Turner, who went on the Midland Circuit, are taken ill, the latter struck blind and deaf.' It adds that 'it is thought a judgment for their severe conduct to poor honest men.' As no other record of the severity of the two judges appears, we may hope that it existed only in the writer's imagination. The visitation on Sir Christopher, if at all true, was only temporary, for he continued to perform the duties of his office during fourteen subsequent years. His death occurred in 1675, and his remains were deposited at Milton-Erneys.

By his wife, Joice, sister of Sir William Warwick, secretary of the Treasury, he left several children, the descendants of whom still flourish at Stoke-Rochford in Lincolnshire. (*Gent. Mag.* lii. 69; 1 *Siderfin*, 3; *State Trials*, xiv. 1318.)

TURNOUR, EDWARD, was of a family which is said to be derived from a Norman who was one of the rewarded warriors of William the Conqueror, and whose descendants were long seated at Haverhill in Suffolk, where Edward Turnour his grandfather resided, and was a bencher of the Middle Temple in the time of James I. Arthur, the judge's father, was a serjeant in the next reign, and was seated at Little Paringdon in Essex. By his wife, Ann, daughter of John Jermy, of Gunton in Norfolk, he had several children, the eldest being the future chief baron, who was born in 1617 in Threadneedle Street, at the house of his uncle Sir Thomas Moulson, lord mayor of London. Educated first under Dr. Goodwin, author of the 'Antiquities of Rome,' at the free school at Abingdon, and next at Queen's College, Oxford, he was on October 30, 1633, admitted to the Middle Temple; and being called to the bar on June 19, 1640, became bencher on June 29, 1660, and afterwards treasurer. He was elected steward of Hertford in 1648. (*Athen. Oxon.* 1060.)

He represented Essex in Cromwell's second and third parliaments, and in that of 1658, called by the Protector Richard; but that he was but a moderate republican, and veered at last to the side of monarchy, is apparent from his being returned member for the same county to the Convention Parliament of April 1660, and from his being knighted immediately on the Restoration; and that he was well reputed as a lawyer may be concluded from his being engaged as counsel for the king in the trials of the regicides, particularly in those of Harrison and Cook, and from his being made solicitor, and afterwards attorney, to the Duke of York. Being again returned to the parliament of May 1661, as member for Hertford, he was elected speaker (*Manning's Speakers*, 354); and his speeches on this and subsequent occasions, though not without some touch of eloquence, are remarkable for their excessive adulation and their amusing reference to sacred and profane history. (*State Trials*, v. 1015, 1103; *Parl. Hist.* vols. iii. iv.; *Burton*, iv. 431.)

In December 1663 he had a grant of 2000*l.* as a free gift, and another of 5000*l.* in July 1664. This parliament lasted for nearly eighteen years, during which there were no less than four speakers—Sir Edward Turnour for twelve years, Sir Job Charlton for little more than twelve days, Sir Edward Seymour for five years, and Sir Robert Sawyer for the remaining months. The speakers at that time were always attended by the mace, even during the adjournment of the house, and, being lawyers, forbore to practise. In 1668, the king having adjourned the parliament for a longer time than usual (they did not meet for eighteen months), Sir Edward was naturally anxious to be freed from that formality and interference with his professional pursuits; but on his application to be released from it the Commons declared that he ought to be attended by the mace as in time of shorter adjournments. But having on May 11, 1670, during a six months' adjournment of the ninth session, received the appointment of solicitor-general to the king, it must be presumed that the above vote did not forbid his practising. When the parliament met in October he resumed the chair, but, according to Roger North (p. 52), he had lost much of his former credit and authority in consequence of having received a small present, in other words a bribe, from the East India Company.

The session was terminated by a prorogation in April 1671; and on the 23rd of the next month Sir Edward was removed from the chair of the House of Commons to the seat of chief baron of the Exchequer, an elevation somewhat extraordinary for a man suffering under such an imputation. No complaint, however, has been made of his presidency, which lasted only four years. He died while on circuit at Bedford on March 4, 1676, and was buried in the chancel of Little Paringdon Church.

He seems to have been prouder of his oratory than his law, for his publications were confined to his speeches. Of his two wives, the first was Sarah, daughter and heir of Gerard Cole, alderman of London; the second, Mary, daughter and heir of Henry Ewer, of South Mimms, Middlesex. By the first he had several children, the eldest of whom was Sir Edward, M.P. for Orford in Suffolk, whose daughter Sarah was the grandmother of Edward Garth, who, succeeding to the estates, assumed the name of Turnour, and was in 1761 created baron, and in 1765 Earl of Winterton in Ireland. (*Manning and Bray's Surrey*, ii. 7; *Biog. Peerage*, iv. 85.)

TURRI, JORDAN DE, was an officer of the Exchequer in 1 Richard I., the Great Roll of that year recording that the sheriffs of London and Middlesex accounted for certain expenditure, 'per visum Jordani de Turri et per testimonium Willelmi de S. Mariæ Ecclesiæ.' (*Madox*, i. 370.) In 4 John, 1202, he was among the justiciers at Westminster before whom fines were levied, present, perhaps, only as an officer. He died about 6 John, in which year certain houses he held in London were ordered to be given to Hugh de Wells. (*Rot. Claus.* i. 18, 35.)

TURRI, NICHOLAS DE, was a justicier as early as 35 Henry III., 1251, payments being made from March in that year for assizes to be held before him. These continue uninterruptedly till May 1270, 54 Henry III. (*Excerpt. e Rot. Fin.* ii. 100–513.) Dugdale, however, does not mention him till 44 Henry III., 1260, and then only as a justice itinerant. In the iters of 46 and 47 Henry III. he stands at the head of all the commissions on which he is named. In the former of these years Dugdale introduces him among the justices of the Common Pleas, with a grant of 40*l.* a year; and the only fine he notices as having been acknowledged before him is in 48 Henry III. In 51 Henry III., 1267, a writ directing the removal of a process from his court to the Exchequer is addressed 'Nicholao de Turri et sociis suis justiciariis' (*Madox*, i. 236), which would seem to imply that he was then at the head of the court. He died most probably in 1270, when he ceased to act; and if so, he would then have sat on the bench between nineteen and twenty years. From an entry among the pleas of Michaelmas, 51-52 Henry III., relative to a messuage and some land at Gretelington in Wiltshire, it appears that Nicholas de Turri was parson of the church of All Saints in that place. (*Abb. Placit.* 165.)

TURTON, JOHN, was the grandson of John Turton, of West Bromwich in Staffordshire, of whose two sons, John and William, the former was the ancestor of Sir Thomas Turton, created a baronet in 1796 (now extinct); and the latter was the father of the judge by his wife, Eleanor, daughter of Thomas Fownes.

He was born at Alrewas, his father's residence in the same county, and, becoming in 1669 a member of Gray's Inn, was called to the bar in 1673. At the general election for the last parliament of Charles II., in 1681, his name is contained in a double return for the town of Tamworth; but as the dissolution occurred before it had sat a week, the claims of the candidates were never decided. History is silent as to Turton's conduct during James's reign; but that he was a friend to the Revolution, and distinguished among his legal brethren, is apparent from his being selected as a baron of the Exchequer on May 4, 1689, and knighted. He sat in that court for seven years, when he was transferred on July 1, 1696, to the King's Bench. There he continued during the remainder of William's reign, and was re-appointed on the accession of Queen Anne in March 1702. On June 4 following, however, he received a message from the lord keeper that he might forbear to sit on the next day, the first day of Trinity Term, her majesty designing to give him his quietus, and he accordingly received his supersedeas on the 9th. This removal no doubt was caused by the prevalence of tory politics, which then ran to great extremes. It became the fashion to decry all King William's acts, and even in an address to the throne the victories of the Duke of Marlborough were spoken of as signally 'retrieving' the ancient honour and glory of the English nation. That Sir John Turton felt himself aggrieved may be well supposed, and the sentiments of his family on the subject were expressed by his grandson in a memorial presented to George I. in 1721, stating that the judge 'fell the first sacrifice to the rage and malice of the enemies of that glorious prince [King William] at the very beginning of the succeeding reign, and that his disgrace was occasioned by his honest and firm adherence to the Revolution interest.'

He survived his discharge for six years, and died suddenly on March 12, 1708. His wife was Anne, daughter of Samuel More, of More and Linley in Staffordshire. His portrait is in Gray's Inn. (*Erdewick's Staffordsh.* 234; *Luttrell,* v. 181, vi. 278; 2 *Lord Raymond,* 768; *State Trials,* xiii. 451, 485, xiv. 221, 228.)

TURVILL, MAURICE DE, was in the service of King John, by whom in 1215 he was sent with three associates to the earls, barons, and others of the county of Hants, to convey the royal commands and to explain the affairs of the kingdom. In the same year he and William de Faleise were custodes of the castle of Winchester. (*Rot. Pat.* 128, 136.) His only appearance in a judicial capacity was in 1219, as one of the justices itinerant into Wilts, Hants, Berks, and Oxford. He held the office of one of the three coroners of the county of Gloucester, all of whom were superseded, 'propter debilitatem,' in 1225, when the sheriff was ordered to cause three others to be elected in their stead. (*Rot. Claus.* ii. 25.)

TUTTEBURY, THOMAS, was of a Derbyshire family, and is first mentioned in 1 Henry IV. with the designation of clerk, as keeper of the king's wardrobe, in which character he received two sums of 66*l.* 13*s.* 4*d.* and 13*l.* 6*s.* 8*d.* 'for the costs and charges incurred for the carriage of the body of Richard, late King of England, from Pountfreyt Castle to London.' On June 27, 1401, he was rewarded for this service by being constituted second baron of the Exchequer. In May 1402 we find him sending a messenger to the king announcing 'the capture of a certain ship sent to Scotland to victual those parts.' Beyond July 1403, when he received payments on account of his former office, among which is the sum of 253*l.* 9*s.* for fish, no entry concerning him is published. (*Devon's Issue Roll,* 275-294; *Cal. Rot. Pat.* 244.)

TWISDEN, THOMAS. The family of Twysden is one of the most ancient in the county of Kent, and can be traced from the reign of Edward I., when it possessed a manor of that name in the parish of Sandhurst. In the reign of Henry VIII., William Twysden, by his marriage with Elizabeth, one of the daughters and coheirs of Thomas Roydon, came into possession of Roydon Hall in East Peckham, thence the chief seat of the family. This William was the grandfather of Sir William Twysden, the first baronet, who by his marriage with Anne, daughter of Sir Moyle Finch, of Eastwell, Bart., had five sons, through the eldest of whom, Sir

Roger Twysden, renowned as much for his antiquarian and constitutional learning as for his loyal and exemplary life, the title has descended to the present time. (*Wotton's Baronet.* i. 211; *Hasted*, v. 96.) This Thomas was Sir William's second son, and on establishing a new family altered the usual spelling of his name from Twysden to Twisden, in order to distinguish the two branches. (*Ex inf. of the late Rev. Lambert B. Larking.*)

He was born at Roydon Hall on January 8, 1602, and became a fellow commoner of Emmanuel College, Cambridge, to the rebuilding of the chapel of which he afterwards was a liberal contributor. Being admitted a member of the Inner Temple in 1618, he was called to the bar in 1625. He was not raised to the bench of the society till November 5, 1646, but long before that time he was in full employment as an advocate, his name appearing in the Reports of Croke, Styles, Aleyn, &c. After the death of Charles I., Siderfin mentions him frequently; and it is evident he acquired much eminence in his profession, as Cromwell, in Hilary Term 1654, called him to the degree of serjeant, a dignity which he says he accepted 'animo reluctante.' In the next year Cony's case arose. This gentleman had been illegally imprisoned for refusing to pay certain customs imposed without any authority but the protector's dictum. He either brought an action for false imprisonment, or sued out his Habeas Corpus (for the accounts differ), and he employed Serjeants Twisden, Maynard, and Wadham Wyndham as his counsel. Their advocacy was so effective that they were tyrannically silenced by being sent to the Tower, from which they did not get release till they petitioned the protector. (*Ludlow*, 223; *Clarendon*, vii. 296; *Harris's Lives*, iii. 446.)

Twisden, like the rest of his family, was a staunch loyalist; and that his wife shared in his feelings is apparent from a letter addressed to her by Charles II. in 1650, in which, after stating that he has assurance of her readiness to perform his desires, he gives her directions as to the delivery of 'the George and Seals,' according to her 'brother's promise' to 'his blessed father.' This lady, whom Mr. Twisden married in 1639, was Jane, daughter of John Tomlinson, Esq., of Whitby in Yorkshire; and the brother alluded to was Matthew Tomlinson, a colonel in the parliamentary army, under whose charge Charles I. was placed during the time of his trial, and on the day of his execution. Unlike others about the king, he treated him with kindness and civility. This considerate conduct was gratefully acknowledged by his majesty in his last moments, when he presented the colonel with his gold toothpick and case as a remembrance, and entrusted him with the George and Seals to be transmitted to his son. Though Tomlinson was afterwards one of Cromwell's peers, and a commissioner for the management of Irish affairs, he reaped at the Restoration 'the effect and fruit' of his generous treatment of the fallen monarch by being called as a witness on the trial of the regicides, instead of being arraigned as an accomplice in their guilt. (*Evelyn*, v. 183; *Whitelocke*, 666, 693; *State Trials*, v. 1178.)

The serjeant continued the practice of his profession through all the subsequent changes, and it may well be supposed that the king's return was gladly welcomed by him. Laying down the dignity which had been forced upon him by the usurper, he was legitimately invested with the coif a few days after; and on July 22, 1660, he was sworn in as one of the judges of the King's Bench, and knighted. He retained the office for the remainder of his life, but ceased to exercise its functions in October 1678, more than four years before his death, the king, in consideration of his great age, or, as Noble says (*Cromwell*, i. 438), from being too virtuous for the place he held, then excusing him from further attendance in court.

Though on the commission for the trial of the regicides, he took little part in it, the principal conduct being left to the lord chief baron, Sir Orlando Bridgeman; and in the trials of the Fifth Monarchy men and Sir Harry Vane in the King's Bench, he is only mentioned as speaking on points of law. He was one of the judges in the harsh proceedings against George Fox and other Quakers for not taking the oath of obedience, and seems to have been somewhat puzzled to answer the arguments of the zealous disputants. (*State Trials*, vi. 74, 156, 206, 634.)

Roger North (*Examen*, 56) gives an amusing account of an accident which befell the judge in Hilary Term 1673:—

'His lordship (Lord Shaftesbury) had an early fancy, or rather freak, the first day of the term (when all the officers of the law, king's counsel and judges, used to wait upon the Great Seal to Westminster Hall) to make this procession on horseback, as in old time the way was when coaches were not so rife. And accordingly the judges were spoken to to get horses, as they and all the rest did by borrowing or hiring, and so equipped themselves with black foot-cloaths in the best manner they could: and diverse of the nobility, as usual, in compliment and honour to a new lord chancellor, attended also in their equipments. Upon notice in town of this cavalcade, all the show company took their places at windows and balconies, with the foot guard in the streets, to partake of the fine sight, and being once settled for the march, it moved, as the design was, statelily along. But when they came to straights and interruptions, for want of gravity in the beasts, or too much in the riders, there happened some curvetting which made no little disorder. Judge Twisden, to his great affright, and the consternation of his grave brethren, was laid along in the dirt, but all at length arrived safe, without loss of life or limb in the service. This accident was enough to divert the like frolic for the future, and the very next term after they fell to their coaches as before.'

The author speaks of this as the revival of an ancient custom; but it is one which could not have been long left off, for in October 1660, only thirteen years before, Pepys (i. 116) says, 'In my way I met the lord chancellor and all the judges riding on horseback and going to Westminster Hall, it being the first day of the term.' And Aubrey (ii. 386) fixes the date of its discontinuance at the death of Sir Robert Hyde in 1665.

Sir Thomas's health began to fail him in the year 1677, and in October of the next year he received his quietus in the honourable manner before related, being allowed to retain the title of judge with a pension of 500*l*. a year during the continuance of his life. He enjoyed the reputation of being a sound lawyer and an upright judge, though withal somewhat passionate, so that the contemporary reporters, in recording his judgments, begin, 'Twisden, *in furore*, observed,' &c. (*Lord Campbell's Ch. Justices*, i. 559.) Having purchased Bradburn, a seat in East Malling in Kent, at a very early period, the king in June 1666 conferred on him a baronetcy of that place. There he died on January 2, 1683, and was buried under a monument in the church of that parish. He was the father of eleven children, five sons and six daughters; but the baronetcy, after being enjoyed by seven of his descendants, became extinct in 1841.

TYRRELL, THOMAS, was one of the military lawyers of the Commonwealth. He was the third son of Sir Edward Tyrrell, of Thornton in Buckinghamshire, a knight of very ancient family (descended from that Sir Walter who shot William II. in the New Forest), by his second wife, Margaret, daughter of Thomas Aston of Aston in Cheshire, and relict of Thomas Egerton of Walgreve. Sir Edward, by his first wife, Mary, daughter of Benedict Lee, Esq., of Huncote, Bucks, had a son also named Edward, who obtained a baronetcy in 1627, which became extinct in 1749.

Thomas was born about the year 1594, and began his legal career at the Inner Temple, where he was called to the bar on November 13, 1621. His military career began in May 1642, when he accepted the office of deputy lieutenant of his native county under Lord Paget, having Hampden and Whitelocke among his colleagues. He soon after received a commission as colonel in the parliament army, but nothing is recorded of his prowess, except that in a quarrel that arose in Westminster Hall between him and Sir William Andrews, in April 1645, he 'behaved himself discreetly,' and was called into the house and thanked 'for his carriage therein.' Pleased perhaps with the flattering expressions addressed to him, he became desirous of entering the parliament as a member, but did not succeed. During the next thirteen eventful years history makes no mention of him, though probably he resumed his practice at the bar; but at the end of them he was returned to Protector Richard's parliament of January 1659, as member for Aylesbury. In that short session the colonel took an active part in all questions connected with the law, and sat as chairman of the Committee of Grievances and Courts of Justice. On the dissolution of the parliament, and the consequent expiration of Richard's power, the Long Parliament met again; and soon after its revival, dismissing the late commissioners of the Great Seal because they were members of the house, they committed its custody to Tyrrell in conjunction with Bradshaw and Fountaine on June 4 for a period of five months.

On the 13th he was called to the bench of his inn of court, being designated 'Thomas Lord Tyrrell,' and on the 16th the parliament made him a serjeant-at-law. The three commissioners held the Seal till November 1, when the army having again prevented the house from meeting, and nominated a committee of safety, it was transferred to Whitelocke as sole keeper. When the Long Parliament was again permitted to sit, Tyrrell was restored on January 18, 1660, with Fountaine one of his former colleagues and Sir Thomas Widdrington. The Convention Parliament, soon after summoned (to which Tyrrell was returned as member for his county), caused Charles II. to be proclaimed on May 7, and at the same time named the Earl of Manchester, the speaker of the House of Lords, as another commissioner of the Seal, which was retained by all four till it was ordered to be defaced just before the return of the king. When that event took place Tyrrell was considered to have acted with so much discretion that he was confirmed in his degree of the coif, and on July 27 was advanced to the bench as a justice of the Common Pleas, and knighted.

King Charles in 1663 granted him in fee the estate of Castlethorpe in Bucks, where he died on March 8, 1671-2, at the age of

78, and in the church of which he was buried under a stately monument with his effigy in robes and coif. He married thrice, but the names of two of his wives only are known, the first and the third—viz., a daughter of — Saunders, of Buckinghamshire; and Bridget, one of the daughters of Sir Richard Harrington, of Ridlington, Rutland, Bart., who was also the father-in-law of his colleague John Fountaine. By his first wife he had, besides daughters, two sons, Thomas and Peter, the latter of whom married a daughter of Carew Raleigh, eldest surviving son of Sir Walter Raleigh, and was created a baronet during his father's life in 1665, but the title became extinct in 1714. (*Lipscombe's Bucks*, iv. 89; *Wotton's Baronet.* ii. 77; *Whitelocke*, 55, 144, 167, 680–700; *Burton's Diary*, iv. 1, 126, &c.; 1 *Siderfin*, 3.)

U

ULECOT, JOHN DE, was probably a younger branch of the same family as the undermentioned Philip de Ulecot, and from the employments which he is recorded to have held seems to have been a retainer of the court. He was sub-sheriff of Northamptonshire in 6 John, and of Cambridge and Huntingdon for four years from 5 Henry III. The only time he acted as a justice itinerant was in 14 Henry III., 1229, when he was appointed for Sussex and Rutland. Ten years afterwards he and Everard de Trumpington, probably as the king's escheators, were commanded to extend the lands of John, late Earl of Chester and Huntingdon, beyond the county of Chester, and cause the same to be divided among the heirs of the earl. (*Madox*, i. 226; *Excerpt. e Rot. Fin.* i. 318.)

ULECOT, PHILIP DE, was a northern knight of great power and possessions, and was fined 100*l.* and a complete horse in the first year of King John's reign for his marriage with Johanna, the sister of the wife of Sewel Fitz-Henry, part of which fine was subsequently remitted. (*Rot. de Oblatis*, 5; *Rot. de Liberat.* 25.) In 5 John he was appointed constable of Chinon in Touraine (*Rot. Pat.* 40); and it would appear that he was taken in battle, as the king gave him two hundred marks for his redemption (*Rot. Claus.* i. 62); a very large sum in those times, and showing by the demand his value as a knight, and by the payment the extent of the royal favour. In this he gradually advanced, and in 14 John was invested with the office of forester of Northumberland, with a grant of several manors. (*Rot. Chart.* 190). To these was added the sheriffalty of that county, in conjunction with the Earl Warren and the archdeacon of Durham, who, with him, were also appointed custodes of the bishopric of Durham during its vacancy. (*Rot. Pat.* 93, 94; *Rot. de Fin.* 476, &c.) The sheriffalty he then held alone for the remainder of this and the first four years of the reign of Henry III. In 1216, King John having constituted him and Hugo de Baliol governors of all the country to the north of the Tees, they stoutly defended the castles committed to their charge from the attacks made upon them by the King of Scots in behalf of Louis of France. (*R. de Wendover*, iii. 430, 433.)

Soon after the accession of Henry III. some quarrel seems to have occurred between him and Roger Bertram, for they were both summoned to appear before the council, and shortly afterwards the sheriff of Nottingham was commanded to seize his lands if he did not give up the castle of Midford to Roger, according to the king's frequent commands. His favour was soon restored, for in the very next month the manor of Corbrig was assigned for his support while in the king's service (*Rot. Claus.* i. 336, 357, 360), which was followed by various other grants. In 3 Henry III. he was one of the justices itinerant in the three northern counties, and in the next year he received the appointment of seneschal of Poictou and Gascony; and for his conveyance thither the barons of Hastings were ordered to provide three good ships. In this service he died, and the king, in a mandate dated November 2, 1220, 5 Henry III., announcing his death to the sheriff of Northumberland, calls him 'dominus tuus,' showing that he still continued governor of the northern district. (*Ibid.* 430, 433, 449, 466, ii. 20; *Excerpt. e Rot. Fin.* i. 56.)

UPSALE, GEOFFREY DE, of a Yorkshire family, was among the justices itinerant for pleas of the forest only in the northern counties in 54 Henry III., 1270; but he never appears to have been engaged in general judicial duties. (*Excerpt. e Rot. Fin.* ii. 419.)

URSWYKE, THOMAS, named probably from the parish of Urswick in Lancashire, was common serjeant of the city of London, from which he was raised to the office of recorder in 1455. In that character he was one of those named in the commission to try treasons at Guildhall in July 1460, when Sir Thomas Brown was convicted. (*Rot. Parl.* vi. 19.) In the following year, after the queen had gained the second battle of St. Albans, and was advancing to

London, the mob prevented the lord mayor from sending her a supply of provisions, and deputed Urswyke, with the Duchess of Bedford and some bishops, to make his excuses, and to give her majesty hopes of being received into the city as soon as the people were appeased. (*Rapin*, iv. 505.) The recorder willingly announced the stoppage of the supplies, but no doubt did not participate in the encouragement held out. A strong partisan of the Yorkist faction, he knew its power within the walls, and rejoiced to see the Earl of March enter them shortly after, and mount the throne as Edward IV.

In the first parliament of the new king he was returned as the representative of the city; and again in 1467, when he was one of the members selected to investigate the silver coinage. (*Rot. Parl.* v. 634.) He still held the recordership when Henry VI. re-assumed the crown; but, retaining his loyalty to Edward IV., he showed his devotion to that prince by admitting him through a postern gate into the city before the battle of Barnet, when the slightest impediment might have given time for Warwick's army to arrive, and thus have brought about a different consummation. King Henry and the Archbishop of York were at the Bishop of London's palace, and had ridden through the streets to urge 'the peple to be trew unto hym;' to which the chronicler adds, 'Nevere the latter, Urswyke, recordere of Londone, and diverce aldermen, such that hade reule of the cyte, commaundede alle the peple that were in harnes, kepynge the cite and Kynge Herry, every manne to goo home to dynere; and in dyner tyme Kynge Edwarde was late in, and so went forthe to the Bisshoppes of Londone palece, and ther toke Kynge Herry and the Archebisschoppe of Yorke, and put theme in warde, the Thursday next before Ester-day.' (*Warkworth Chron.* 15, 21.) In the middle of May the recorder, 'being well armed in a strong jacke,' did good service in repelling the forces of the bastard Fauconbridge which in their attempt upon London had assaulted Aldgate. (*Holinshed*, iii. 323.)

Urswyke was immediately knighted; and soon after Edward had re-established himself on the throne he received a more substantial reward by being made chief baron of the Exchequer on May 22, 1471, the very day of Henry's death in the Tower, when he resigned the recordership.

Although, filling the office of recorder, he must have been brought up as a lawyer, it is evident that he held no eminent rank in his profession, as his name never once occurs in the Year Books before he was advanced to the bench. Even then he does not seem to have taken a prominent part in the judgments in the Exchequer Chamber there recorded, being only mentioned in four terms, in the fifteenth and sixteenth years, during his continuance in office.

He presided over the Court of Exchequer eight years, and died in the commencement of 1479. By the inquisition taken on his death (*Cal.* iv. 397), it appears that he was possessed of the manors of Markes and Doneres in Essex, and other property in the county.

V

VALOINES, THEOBALD DE, is called by Le Neve (189) archdeacon of Essex in 1218; but he is not so designated in October 1223, 7 Henry III., when he was commanded to give possession of the bishopric of Carlisle (of which he was custos) to Walter Mauclerk, the newly-elected bishop. In 1225, however, he is so described, when he was constituted justice itinerant in the county of York. Le Neve adds that he is also mentioned as archdeacon in 1228. (*Rot. Claus.* i. 573, ii. 8, 77.)

VAUGHAN, JOHN, whose family is traced by Cambrian genealogists as high as the founder of one of the noble tribes of Wales, and whose property of Trowscoed in Cardiganshire is stated by them to have been in possession of his forefathers for ten generations, was the eldest son of Edward Vaughan and Letitia his wife, the daughter of John Stedman, of Strata Florida in the same county, and was born at Trowscoed in 1603. He was educated at the King's School at Worcester, and Christ Church, Oxford, and went in 1621 to the Inner Temple. So many of the same names appear in the books of that society that it is difficult to give the precise date of his call to the bar. A. Wood (iii. 1025) states that he for some time devoted himself to the study of poetry and mathematics (a curious combination), until by his intimacy with the learned Selden he was led to apply himself to the law with so much zeal and industry that he soon established the character which he afterwards maintained. He also associated with Edward Hyde, the future chancellor, who (*Life*, i. 37), though giving him credit for his superior attainments, describes him as magisterial and supercilious in his humour, and proud and insolent in his behaviour. But as the chancellor at the close of his career believed that he had some reason to complain of

Vaughan's ingratitude, the harshness of the picture might require a little softening, were it not that he is painted in the same colours by others of his contemporaries. (*Pepys*, ii. 408.) Though Hyde says 'he looked to those parts of the law which disposed him to least reverence to the crown and most to popular authority,' he proved his disgust at the violent measures taken by the Long Parliament, to which he was returned as member for the town of Cardigan, by retiring from the scene at the very commencement of them. That assembly, therefore, treated him as a malignant, disabled him from sitting, and gave his library to John Glynn, then recorder and afterwards chief justice. He withdrew at the same time from the practice of his profession, and spent the twenty years that elapsed before the Restoration in his own county, unharmed by the different rulers in the interval. The Mr. Vaughan named by Whitelocke (177, 361) among other members as prisoners to whom on December 12, 1648, 'liberty was given upon their paroles,' was either Charles or Edward Vaughan, two of the victims of Pride's Purge.

In 1654 he acted as one of Selden's executors, and shared in the bequest of his estate with Sir Matthew Hale and Rowland Jewkes. They preserved his valuable collection of books, amounting to 8000 volumes, by presenting it to the Bodleian Library, where it was deposited in a noble room, now generally known by the name of the Selden End.

In the Convention Parliament of 1660 Vaughan was returned for Cardiganshire, and again sat for the same county in the first parliament called by Charles II. In the former he does not appear to have taken any part in the debates; but in the latter he is noticed by Burnet (i. 225) and Pepys (ii. 111, 125, 416) as taking a prominent part in opposition to the court, and is spoken of by the latter as 'the great speaker.' In 1667 the proceedings against the Earl of Clarendon took place, and were pressed with so much vehemence by Vaughan that, considering his alleged intimacy with that nobleman in early life, and his subsequent professions of friendship and respect for him, it is somewhat difficult to account for his conduct. (*Parl. Hist.* iv. 373, &c.) The bill for Clarendon's banishment passed in December 1667, and in the following May Vaughan was raised to the judicial bench, by being appointed chief justice of the Common Pleas, on May 23, 1668, and knighted. He proved himself worthy of his promotion by the learning, discrimination, and judgment which he displayed during the period of his presidency. That did not extend beyond six years and a half, and was terminated by his death, which took place suddenly at his chambers in Serjeants' Inn on December 10, 1674. His remains lie in the Temple Church, where there is a marble to his memory.

He has the credit of having put an end to the iniquitous practice of fining and imprisoning juries for not giving such verdicts as the court approved, by the famous judgment, concurred in by all the judges, which he delivered in the case of Bushell, who being imprisoned with the rest of his fellows, for acquitting Penn and Mead contrary to the opinion of the mayor and recorder at the Old Bailey sessions, had brought his Habeas Corpus. He was rather overbearing in his language, and treated the ignorance of others with too much contempt. Even his colleagues on the bench did not escape. It is told of him that on the hearing of a cause in which ecclesiastical points arose, and the canon law being cited, two of the judges interrupted the argument, owning they had no skill in that law, and priding themselves on that account. On which the chief justice, lifting up his hands towards heaven, exclaimed, 'Good God ! what sin have I committed that I should sit on this bench between two judges who boast in open court of their ignorance of the canon law ?' (*Vaughan's Reports*, 135 ; *Law and Lawyers*, ii. 204.) To the evidence of his high character which the friendship of Selden gives may be added the unwilling testimony of Lord Clarendon, who describes him as 'in truth a man of great parts in nature, and very well adorned by arts and books.' Evelyn (ii. 293) calls him 'a very wise and learned person ;' Harris (v. 301) speaks of 'his honesty and courage ;' and his legal learning is proved by his Reports on the special cases argued while he was chief justice, which were published by his son Edward three years after his death.

He married Jane, daughter of John Stedman of Kilconnin. His eldest son Edward was the father of John Vaughan, who in 1695 was raised to the Irish peerage by the title of Baron of Fethers and Viscount Lisburne, titles to which the earldom of Lisburne was added in 1776.

VAUGHAN, JOHN, was of a different lineage, as well as of a different character, from his above namesake. He was a native of the county of Leicester, and the second of five sons of Dr. James Vaughan, a physician at Leicester, and of Hester, daughter of John Smalley, alderman of that borough, and granddaughter of Sir Richard Halford, the fifth baronet of that name. Three of the judge's brothers became eminent in their respective professions: the eldest, Henry, was the distinguished court physician in the reigns of the three last sovereigns, being honoured with a baronetcy in 1809, and assuming the name and arms of

Halford in 1814, on succeeding to the Halford estates; the third son, Peter, rose to be dean of Chester; and the fourth son, Sir Charles Richard, was employed as our envoy extraordinary to the United States.

John was born in 1768, and was educated at Westminster School, from which he entered at once into the study of the law at Lincoln's Inn, and was called to the bar in Trinity Term 1791. He chose the Midland Circuit, and by his agreeable manners and good connection speedily succeeded. His advance was rapid: first he was elected recorder of his native place, Leicester, and in 1799 he took the degree of serjeant-at-law. During the next twenty-eight years he had an immense business, which he owed less to his legal acquirements than to his fluency of speech and the energy and pertinacity which he always displayed for his clients. In fact, he was not deeply learned in the science, and knew little of the law of real property. But he was industrious and painstaking, and, though his manner was somewhat boisterous, his addresses to the jury were humorous and effective.

For his subsequent advances, in 1814 as solicitor and in 1816 as attorney general to Queen Charlotte, in the same year as king's serjeant, and lastly, on February 24, 1827, as a baron of the Exchequer, he was no doubt greatly indebted to the influence of his brother, the royal physician; and when he received the latter appointment the bar joke was, that no one had a better title to it, as he was a judge *by prescription*. After sitting in the Exchequer for seven years, he exchanged on April 29, 1834, with Sir Edward Alderson into the Common Pleas, and was at the same time honoured with a seat in the privy council. In his new court he remained till his sudden death in September 1839, of a heart complaint. As a judge he was much respected for his kind and gentlemanly demeanour, and, though not pretending to any superior legal knowledge, his good sense, patience, impartiality, and care enabled him to perform his judicial functions very satisfactorily.

He was married twice. His first wife was Augusta, daughter of Henry Beauchamp, twelfth Lord St. John of Bletsoe; and his second was Louisa, daughter of Sir Charles William Rouse Broughton, Bart., and widow of St. Andrew, thirteenth Lord St. John.

VAUX, ROBERT DE, or **DE VALLIBUS**, was the son of Hubert de Vaux, to whom Ranulph de Meschines granted the barony of Gillesland in Cumberland, and of Græcia his wife. (*Baronage*, i. 525.) In 19 Henry II., 1173, he was governor of the castle of Carlisle; and when William, King of Scots, in 1174, laid siege to it, he made so brave a defence that the king was obliged to turn the siege into a blockade. Pressed for provisions, Robert de Vaux agreed to surrender, if he was not relieved by Michaelmas; but before that period the Scottish king was, by the gallantry of Ranulph de Glanville, defeated and taken prisoner before Alnwick. (*Lord Lyttelton*, iii. 134.) He also held the sheriffalty of that county from 21 to 30 Henry II., and during some of those years he acted as one of the justices itinerant for the northern counties, having been selected for that duty when the council of Northampton made the judicial division of the kingdom in 1176. (*Madox*, i. 130–136.)

There is an entry on the Pipe Roll of 1 Richard I. (137) of a fine of one hundred marks which he incurred for allowing certain prisoners to escape out of his custody, and for permitting, during his sheriffalty, the currency of the old coin after it had been prohibited.

He married Ada, the daughter and heir of William de Engaine, and afterwards had a second wife, named Alice. He founded the priory of Lanercost in Cumberland (*Monast.* vi. 228), and gave the church of Helton to the canons of Carlisle. His death occurred just before or just after the accession of King John, leaving two sons, Robert and Ranulph, who in turn succeeded him.

VAUX, OLIVER DE, was descended from Robert, a younger brother of Hubert, the father of the above Robert de Vaux. This branch of the family was settled in Norfolk, where they founded the priory of Pentney. Oliver was the second of seven sons of Robert de Vaux, and, on the death of his elder brother without issue, succeeded to the estate. (*Baronage*, i. 526.) In 9 John is a curious entry, authorising the constable of Winchester Castle to permit Jordan de Bianney, a knight whom he had in custody, to go out of his prison twice a day or more, 'ad eskermiandum,' so that he retained Oliver de Vaux in his place till his return, when Oliver might be discharged. A caution, however, is given to the constable, as he loves his goods and his body, to keep Jordan safe. (*Rot. Claus.* i. 88.) In 12 John he accompanied the king to Ireland (*Rot. de Præstit.* 182, 200, 226); but afterwards joining the barons in their hostile measures against him, all his possessions were seized and distributed among the adherents to the royal cause. Early in 2 Henry III. he obtained their restoration; and in 10 Henry III. his name appears at the head of those selected to assess the quinzime for Norfolk and Suffolk. (*Rot. Claus.* i. 235, 252, 374, ii. 146.) He was appointed to act as a justice itinerant in two of the commissions in 1234.

The date of his death is not recorded, but he lived beyond 1245, when he is mentioned in the Pipe Roll. By his wife, Petronilla, the widow of Henry de Mara and also of

William de Longchamp, he left several sons. The succession of this barony devolved on the eldest, on the death of whose two sons, William and the under-mentioned John, without male issue, it fell into abeyance. Oliver's fourth son, Roger de Vaux, however, was the lineal ancestor of Nicholas Vaux, who was created Baron Vaux of Harrowden, by Henry VIII, in 1523. This title fell into abeyance in 1662, which was terminated in 1838 in favour of George Mostyn, the present peer.

VAUX, JOHN DE, was one of the justices itinerant appointed in 6 Edward I., 1278, to visit the northern counties, and also up to the fourteenth year in various other counties. (*Rat. Parl.* i. 29, 218; *Madox,* i. 531.) As he takes precedence on all these occasions of three who were regular justices, he was no doubt selected as a principal baron of the district to head the commission.

He was the grandson of the above Oliver de Vaux. His father, Robert, died either in the lifetime of Oliver or soon afterwards, leaving several sons. William, the eldest, died without children in 1253, when this John succeeded. In 49 Henry III., after the battle of Evesham, his fidelity to his sovereign procured him the sheriffalty of Norfolk and Suffolk, and a grant of certain houses 'prope Garther' in London. (*Cal. Rot. Pat.* 39.) Under Edward I., besides the duties which he performed as a justice itinerant, he was, in the eleventh year of that reign, appointed steward of Aquitaine. He died in 1288, leaving by Sibilla, his wife, two daughters. (*Baronage,* i. 526.)

VAVASOUR, WILLIAM LE, is inserted by Dugdale as a justice itinerant in 34 Henry II., 1188; and in the roll of the previous year he appears with two others as setting the assize in the counties of Lincoln and York. (*Madox,* i. 635, 713.)

In 1 Richard I. (*Pipe Roll,* 139) his pleas are recorded in the northern counties. During the vacancy of the archbishopric of York he was one of the custodes of its rents and manors. (*Madox,* i. 309.)

His own property was at Haslewood in that county. His father was Mauger le Vavasour, who gave some property to the monks of Sallcey; and his son Robert was the grandfather of the next-mentioned William le Vavasour.

VAVASOUR, WILLIAM LE, was the great-grandson of the above William le Vavasour, and the son of John le Vavasour of Haselwood. He served his king in the expedition into Gascony and in his wars in Scotland, and his prowess is pithily described by the poetical historian of the siege of Carlaverock (8, 113) in 1300 in these lines:—

E de celle mesme part
Fu Guillemis li Vavasours
Ki darmes nest muet ne sours.

In 33 and 34 Edward I. he was appointed one of the justices of trailbaston for several northern counties. (*N. Fœdera,* i. 970; *Rot. Parl.* i. 186, 218; *Parl. Writs,* i. 407.) He was summoned to parliament from 27 Edward I. to 6 Edward II., the year in which he died. (*Cal. Inq.* p. m. i. 249.)

He had three sons by his wife, Nichola, the daughter of Sir Stephen Wallis of Newton, neither of whom, nor their descendants, were summoned to parliament; but there are now two baronets derived from the same stock. (*Baronage,* ii. 119.)

VAVASOUR, JOHN, was the son of John Vavasour of Haselwood, by Isabel, daughter and coheir of Thomas de la Haye, lord of Spaldington, who brought that lordship to the family. (*Proc. Soc. Antiq.* iv. 79.) He is described as a member of the Inner Temple when he was called serjeant in 18 Edward IV. (*Y. B.* 10.) His first employment in court that is recorded in the Year Books is in Trinity Term 1467; and having been invested with the coif as above in 1478, he was in the last fortnight of the reign of Edward V. appointed one of the king's serjeants, his patent for which was renewed both by Richard III. and Henry VII.

In the first year of Henry's reign it happened that Miles Metcalfe, the recorder of York, died, when, in opposition to the king's recommendation of Thomas Middelton, and to the Earl of Northumberland's in favour of Richard Greene, the corporation thought fit to exercise their privilege of naming their own officer, and accordingly their election fell on Mr. Serjeant Vavasour. This disregard to the king's wishes did not prevent him from visiting that city in April 1486, when he was welcomed in a speech by the newly-made recorder, who in the following year had a further opportunity of ingratiating himself with the monarch, by being the bearer of important despatches from the corporation with regard to the junction of the Earl of Lincoln in Lambert Simnel's rebellion. He soon after received the honour of knighthood, and it was not long before his loyalty, or his talent, was rewarded with a seat on the bench. On August 14, 1490, he was constituted a justice of the Common Pleas. (*Gent. Mag.* May and November 1851; *Proc. Archæol. Inst. at York.*)

From a memorial dated in 20 Henry VII., it is much to be feared that he was one of those who were influenced by the infamous Sir Richard Empson to pervert the course of justice in a lawsuit which the latter had instigated against Sir Robert Plumpton. (*Corresp.* cxvii.)

The last fine levied before him was in Michaelmas 1506, soon after which the date of his death may be fixed. (*Dugdale's Orig.* 47.)

VENTRIS, PEYTON, was of a family foreign in its origin, but traced in England for at least three centuries, when it became divided into two branches, established respectively in the counties of Bedford and Cambridge, to the latter of which the judge belonged. One of his ancestors represented the borough of Cambridge in the reign of Philip and Mary, and was its mayor in that of Elizabeth. He and his descendants possessed considerable property in the county, and were connected in marriage with the Evelyns, the Brewes, the Holts, and other distinguished families. Edward Ventris, the senator's great-grandson, inherited from his father the manor of Granhams in Great Shelford, and the rectory of Stow Quy in that county, together with other estates in Suffolk and Essex. He was a barrister of Gray's Inn, and died in 1649 at the age of thirty, leaving by his wife, Mary, daughter of Sir John Brewe, of Wenham Hall in Suffolk, four children, the eldest survivor of whom was the future judge, then under four years old.

Peyton Ventris was born in November 1645 at Wenham, the seat of his maternal grandfather, and, having entered the society of the Middle Temple, was called to the bar on June 2, 1667. That he was a diligent student, and a competent master of the intricacies of his profession, he gave early proof by commencing in 1668 his reports of cases adjudged in the King's Bench and Common Pleas. These he continued during the rest of the reign of Charles II., and in part of that of James II.; and in the reign of William and Mary he recorded those in his own court as long as he sat there as judge. They were first published after his death, and in the customary allowance of the publication all the judges expressed their 'knowledge of the great learning and judgment of the author.' The editor also refers to his eminence in the profession and his great worth, and the high reputation of the work is evidenced by the demand of no less than four editions in thirty years.

As a constitutional lawyer he could not but be disgusted with the recent encroachments of the crown, nor fail to rejoice at the prospect of the beneficial change which the arrival of the Prince of Orange opened. He represented Ipswich in the Convention Parliament, but sat there only four months, being appointed a judge of the Common Pleas on May 4, 1689, and knighted in the following October. The honourable estimation in which his character is regarded, although he graced the bench for less than two years, is the best proof of the excellence and efficiency with which he performed the responsible duties of his office. His phraseology on the bench was rather familiar. On a question whether a devisee in fee could disclaim the estate devised, he said that ' a man cannot have an estate put into him in spite of his teeth.'

He died on April 6, 1691, at Ipswich, and was buried in the church of St. Nicholas there. By his wife, Margaret, daughter and coheir of Henry Whiting, Esq., of Coggeshall in Essex, he left several children, one of whom held the post of master of the King's Bench. Some members of the original stock still survive, and to the kind information of the Rev. Edward Ventris, incumbent of Stow Quy, the present representative of both branches of the family, who possesses the original portrait of the judge by Riley, I owe many of the particulars here recorded. (*Luttrell*, i. 529, 598, ii. 205; *Parl. Hist.* v. 29.)

VERDUN, BERTRAM DE, was a powerful baron, who signalised himself both in a civil and military capacity, acting as a judge and counsellor under Henry II., and doing his devoir as a soldier under his lion-hearted successor, Richard.

His grandfather, of the same name, was of French extraction, probably coming over with the Conqueror, as in his time he was possessed of Farnham-Royal in Buckinghamshire, which he held by the service of providing a glove, on the day of the king's coronation, for his right hand, and of supporting his right arm while he held the royal sceptre. This service is now attached to the lord of the manor of Worksop in Nottinghamshire, that estate having been granted by letters patent of King Henry VIII., dated November 26, 1541, to Francis Earl of Shrewsbury, then the proprietor of Farnham-Royal, in exchange for the latter, and upon the same tenure.

Bertram's father was Norman de Verdun, who possessed Lutterworth in Leicestershire, and his mother Luceline, the daughter of Geoffrey de Clinton, chamberlain to Henry I.

Bertram de Verdun held his principal seat in Staffordshire in 1166, and was sheriff or fermer of the counties of Warwick and Leicester from the 15th to the 30th years of the reign of Henry II.

In 1175, 21 Henry II., and the three following years, he was regularly present as a baron in the judicial proceedings of the Curia Regis; and from the 22nd to the 26th of the reign, and probably later, he acted as a justice itinerant in eight counties. (*Madox*, i. 94-137.) There are some entries of his pleas on the Pipe Roll of Richard I. (164), but they are clearly arrears of former years.

These and other employments show, not only that he enjoyed the confidence of his sovereign, but also that his talents were of a superior order. The remainder of his career was devoted to his attendance on King Richard in his expedition to the Holy

Land, whither he accompanied him in the second year of his reign. In the agreement between the Kings of England and Sicily he was one of the sureties for its due performance on the part of Richard, who committed Acre, on its being taken, to his custody. Two years afterwards, in 1192, he died at Joppa, and was buried at Acre.

His religious benefactions were numerous. He was twice married. His first wife was Maud, daughter of Robert de Ferrers, Earl of Derby, by whom he had no issue. By his second wife, Rohese, he had two sons, Thomas and Nicholas, who in turn succeeded him. Rohese, the only daughter of the latter, married Theobald le Butiller, and was the mother of the next-mentioned John de Verdun. (*Dugdale's Baron.* i. 471; *Monast.* v. 660.)

VERDUN, JOHN DE, was the son of Theobald le Butiller, and his wife Rohese de Verdun, the daughter and sole heir of Nicholas de Verdun, and the granddaughter of the above Bertram de Verdun. Being heir of the barony and of the large possessions attached to it, she retained her surname, which continued to be borne by her descendants. John was among the twelve who were appointed at the parliament of Oxford in 1258 to treat for the whole community on the common business, and as a baron-marcher was in 1260 called upon to resist the incursions of the Welsh. In the same year he was constituted one of the justices itinerant for Shropshire, Staffordshire, and the neighbouring counties. He stood on the part of the king in the subsequent troubles, and was employed in pursuing such of the rebellious barons as held out after the battle of Evesham. In 54 Henry III. he took the cross with Prince Edward, and the next year went to the Holy Land. He died on October 21, 1274, 3 Edward I., leaving Alianore, his second wife, surviving. His first wife was Margerie, the daughter of Gilbert de Lacy, and heir to her grandfather, Walter de Lacy. (*Excerpt. e Rot. Fin.* i. 446.) By her he had a son, Theobald, who succeeded him and was summoned to parliament; on the death of whose son, also Theobald, the barony fell into abeyance among his four daughters. (*Baronage*, i. 473.)

VERDUN, WALTER DE, was probably a junior branch of the noble family noticed above. He was in King John's service in the eleventh and twelfth years of his reign, accompanying him to Ireland in the latter. (*Rot. Misæ*, 123; *Rot. de Præstit.* 193, &c.) In 16 John he and Robert de Courtenay were sent into Shropshire for the defence of that county, and the custody of the castle of Bridgenorth was committed to them. (*Rot. Pat.* 136.) In 1 Henry III. he held the office of one of the escheators of Lincolnshire; in the next year he seems to have had the custody of the Tower of London; and in 3 Henry III. was sheriff of Essex and Hertfordshire. In that year also a fine was levied before him and his associates, justices itinerant, at Westminster; and he again was selected to perform the same duties in 9 Henry III. for the county of Oxford. Between the two last dates his services were required in a diplomatic capacity, he being sent to Rome in 4 Henry III., and in the next year to Poictou. (*Rot. Claus.* i. 158, 313, 320, 384, 433, 477, 525.) His death occurred in 1229, in March of which year his son Ralph was admitted to the seisin of his land at Blokesham in Oxfordshire, on the payment of a relief of a hundred shillings. (*Excerpt. e Rot. Fin.* i. 182.)

VERE, ALBERIC DE, was the son of a Norman baron of the same name, who accompanied King William on his conquest of England, and who received for his reward Kensington and other lordships; and of Beatrice, daughter of Henry, castellan of Bourbourg, and niece and heir of Manasses Count of Ghisnes.

The priory of Colne in Essex was founded by them in 1111. (*Monasticon*, iv. 99, 100.)

The first mention that occurs of Alberic Junior, as he was called, is in a charter of King Henry, granting power to the prior of Christchurch, or the Holy Trinity, in Aldgate, London, to enclose a way near the church, addressed 'To Richard, Bishop of London, and Albericus de Vere, sheriff, and all his barons and lieges of London.' (*Ibid.* vi. 155.) Stow also mentions that Henry sent 'his sheriffs, to wit, Aubrey de Vere, and Roger, nephew to Hubert,' to invest that priory with the soke of the English Knighten Guilde, in pursuance of his charter addressed to the same bishop, and witnessed by Queen Adelisa. This, therefore, must have been between 1121, when Adelisa was married, and 1127, when Bishop Richard died. The office of sheriff or portgrave of London corresponded with that of the present mayor, but was in those times one of considerable dignity, and held by persons of high rank.

Both Dugdale and Spelman introduce him into their lists of chief justiciaries of England, but there does not appear sufficient authority for so designating him. That he acted judicially with the other barons in the Curia Regis there can be no doubt, and that he shared highly in the confidence of the king there is as little question. But that he never filled the highest judicial office, the above and other documents that remain afford strong presumptive evidence.

In the ancient Exchequer Roll of 31 Henry I. (1130) he appears to have had, in conjunction with Richard Basset, the control over eleven counties as sheriff or fermer, but Richard Basset's name invariably stands first. That this was an office of at least as much trouble as honour appears from the fact that he fined, in the same year, to be relieved from the burden in Essex and Hertfordshire. The preceding entry, that he was charged with 550*l*. and four war-horses for the escape of a prisoner, shows, perhaps, the cause of his retirement.

In 1134 King Henry granted to him and his heirs the office of his magistra cameraria (great chamberlain) of all England, in which character he was present at the general council held the first year of Stephen; and when that king, in the fourth year of his reign, was summoned to a council by the Bishop of Winchester, to answer for having seized the old Bishop of Salisbury, and his nephew Alexander, Bishop of Lincoln, and confiscated their property, he sent Alberic de Vere to defend him, as one experienced in those matters. This, however, required more of policy than law, and his attendance in the Curia Regis would sufficiently instruct him in the latter. The selection, however, by no means proves him to have been chief justiciary at the time, and William of Malmesbury's designation of him as 'Albericus *quidam* de Ver,' homo causarum varietatibus exercitatus,' and as 'causidicus Albericus,' certainly bears no appearance that he was so.

He was killed in London on the ides of May 1140, probably in performing some of his duties as portgrave of the city. A query is raised by Spelman whether there were not two Alberics, one the earl and the other the portgrave; but he suggests no adequate reason for the doubt.

He married Adeliza, the daughter of Roger de Yvery, who came over with William the Conqueror, and whose son Roger was chief butler to William II.

Alberic, their eldest son (the third of that name), was created Earl of Oxford in 1155. The ninth earl was advanced to the titles of Marquis of Dublin and Duke of Ireland, but forfeited his honours. The earldom was granted to his uncle; and on the death of the twentieth earl, without issue, in 1702, the title became extinct; but the office of great chamberlain had, by the death of the eighteenth earl, without issue, passed with his aunt Mary to the family of Bertie Baron Willoughby de Eresby, afterwards Earls of Lindsey and Dukes of Ancaster, whose representative, the present Baron Willoughby de Eresby, is now great chamberlain of England. (*Stow's London*, 116; *Morant's Essex*, ii. 292; *Madox*, i. 13, 56, 164, 327, 458; *Baronage*, i. 188; *Leland*, i. 129.)

VERE, WILLIAM DE (BISHOP OF HEREFORD), was a son of Alberic de Vere, the third of that name, Earl of Oxford. In 23 Henry II., 1177, he was engaged with Walter de Gant in building the church at Waltham, and they had 40*l*. allowed to them towards the expenses. (*Madox*, i. 226.) He was raised to the bishopric of Hereford on August 10, 1186, and presided there for thirteen years.

His pleas as a justice itinerant in the counties of Buckingham and Bedford, Lincoln and Derby, appear on the Pipe Roll of 1 Richard I., 1189 (32, 58, 156); but they seem to refer to a former year. He acted in the same capacity in 7 Richard I., imposing fines in Staffordshire and assessing tallages in Gloucestershire. (*Madox*, i. 546, 703.) In the latter year, also, fines were levied before him as a justicier. He died on December 24, 1199, and was buried in his own cathedral. (*Godwin*, 484.)

VERE, ROBERT DE (THE THIRD EARL OF OXFORD), was grandson of the above Alberic de Vere, and the son of Alberic the first earl, by Lucia his wife, who became first prioress of Heningham in Essex, founded by her husband. After the death of his brother Alberic the second earl he joined the rebellious barons, for which he was not only excommunicated (*R. de Wendover*, iii. 297, 355), but had his lands seized into the king's hands in May 1215. In the following June, however, they were restored to him; but before the end of the year he again fell off from his allegiance, and again was in negotiation for a return to favour, which does not appear to have been completed at King John's death. But soon after the accession of Henry III. this was accomplished, and the whole of his possessions were once more put into his hands. (*Rot. Claus.* i. 115–337; *Rot. Pat.* 171, 172.)

Dugdale introduces him as a justicier in 4 Henry III., 1220, on the authority of fines acknowledged before him from the Easter of that year to the same festival in the following. As none of these fines are stated to have been levied at Westminster, and as there is no evidence of his having on any other occasion acted in the King's Court, there may be some reason to doubt whether he was more than a justice itinerant before whom fines were frequently levied on the circuits. He was certainly at the head of the itinerant justices sent in the following year into Hertfordshire (*Rot. Claus.* i. 444, 473), and not improbably had previously acted in a similar commission, at the head of which noblemen were frequently placed. Still it is to be remembered that from the death of his father in 1194, till that of his brother in 1214, he held the position of a younger son, and may therefore have adopted the profession of the law as an honourable means of support, and been eventually advanced to a seat on the bench.

He died in October in 1221, leaving a son Hugh, a minor, by his wife, Margaret de Bolebec. (*Excerpt. e Rot. Fin.* i. 74, 101, 435.)

VERNEY, JOHN, was the youngest son of George fourth Lord Willoughby de Broke, by Margaret, daughter and heir of Sir John Heath, of Brasted in Kent, the son of Sir Robert, the persecuted judge in the reign of Charles I. He studied the law at the Middle Temple, where he was called to the bar in 1721. He represented Downton in the last parliament of George I. and in the first of George II., and while a member of the former he was made a judge of South Wales. George II. selected him to be one of his counsel, and in 1729 appointed him attorney-general to Queen Caroline. His next promotion was in December 1733 as chief justice of Chester; and he was appointed master of the Rolls on October 9, 1738. After enjoying this comfortable judicial seat not quite three years, he died on August 5, 1741.

He married Abigail, only daughter of Edward Harley of Eyewood in Herefordshire, and sister of the first Earl of Oxford; and by her he left a son, John Peyto Verney, who, upon the death of his uncles without issue, became sixth Lord Willoughby de Broke. (*Collins's Peerage*, iv. 71, vi. 701.)

VERNON, WILLIAM DE, was a knight of the county of Lancaster, and was at the head of a body of archers in 5 John. (*Rot. de Liberat.* 78.) A few years afterwards he was imprisoned for some offence, and paid a fine of twenty marks for his release. (*Rot. de Fin.* 416; *Rot. Claus.* i. 99.) He accompanied the king to Ireland in 12 John (*Rot. de Præstit.* 218), and was attached to the service of William Earl Ferrers, under whom he held various lands in Nottingham and Derby. He had also other possessions in Berkshire, Oxfordshire, Buckinghamshire, Staffordshire, and Lancashire. (*Rot. Claus.* i. 206-631.) It was probably in respect to the latter that he was appointed in 3 Henry III., 1219, one of the justices itinerant for the northern counties (*Rymer*, i. 154), an office which he afterwards exercised in 1225 in Nottingham and Derby. In 11 Henry III. he was excused the scutage on his property in those counties. (*Rot. Claus.* ii. 77, 204.)

VERNON, GEORGE, was descended from the noble and ancient family of Vernon in Normandy, which established itself in this country at the Conquest. He was the son of Sir Thomas Vernon, of Haslington in Cheshire, and his wife, Dorothy, the daughter of William Egerton, Esq., of Betley. Becoming a member of the Inner Temple, he was called to the bar in 1603, and was elected reader in 1621. On July 4, 1627, he was raised to the degree of the coif, an honour which Judge Whitelocke states that he paid for—*dedit aurum*. In four months, no doubt as part of the bargain, he was made a baron of the Exchequer, his patent being dated November 13. After remaining in that court three years and a half, he was removed to the Common Pleas on May 8, 1631. (*Rymer*, xix. 348.) In the great case of ship-money in 1637 he abstained from stating his reasons on account of his want of health, but delivered his opinion, not only in favour of the charge, but also asserting that a statute derogatory from the prerogative did not bind the king, and that the king might dispense with any law in cases of necessity. (*State Trials*, iii. 1125.) For these ultra sentiments he escaped the retribution which in the parliament of 1640 visited those of his colleagues who pronounced a similar judgment, by his death, which occurred on December 16, 1639, at his chambers in Serjeants' Inn, Chancery Lane. He was buried in the Temple Church. Croke (*Car.* 565), his brother judge, describes him as being 'a man of great reading in the statute and common law, and of extraordinary memory,' but says nothing of his integrity or independence.

His first wife was Jane, daughter of Sir George Corbett, of Morton Corbett in Shropshire. By her he had an only daughter and heir, Muriel. Of his second wife nothing is known, except that she produced no issue.

VERULAM, LORD. *See* F. BACON.

VESCY, WILLIAM DE, was a descendant of Yvo de Vesci, who came over with the Conqueror, and was rewarded by receiving in marriage the heiress of the lordships of Alnwick in Northumberland, and Malton in Yorkshire. He was second son of William de Vesci, and of Agnes, one of the daughters of William de Ferrers, Earl of Derby. His elder brother dying without children in 1289, he succeeded to the barony. (*Baronage*, i. 90.)

Having begun his career as a younger son, he had pursued the profession of the law, and was advanced to the office of justice of the forests beyond Trent, receiving his appointment in 1285 (*Abb. Rot. Orig.* i. 50, 90); and in the following year he was at the head of the justices itinerant for pleas of the forest in Nottinghamshire and Lancashire. He retained his place till 1289, when he was appointed governor of Scarborough Castle; and in the following year he was constituted chief justice of Ireland. Three years afterwards, while in the execution of his duties, he was charged by John Fitz-Thomas with confederating against the king. The Rolls of Parliament contain a curious account of the proceedings taken by him against the accuser for defamation; of the duel that was awarded; of the summons to appear before the king at Westminster, when De Vesci came fully armed, but Fitz-

Thomas kept away; and of the ultimate annulling of the process in 23 Edward I., on account of some irregularity. (*Rot. Parl.* i. 127, 132; *Abb. Placit.* 234.) It does not appear that any further proceeding took place, but it is evident that the charge was not believed, as he was in the same year summoned to parliament, was employed in the wars of Gascony in that and the following year, and; had grants showing the favour of his sovereign.

On the death of Margaret, Queen of Scotland, in 1290, he became one of the competitors for that crown, in right of Margaret, daughter of William the Lion, and sister of Alexander, King of Scotland, whom his ancestor Eustace de Vesci had married. From the immediate dismissal of this claim, and those of other daughters of William the Lion, a doubt has arisen as to their legitimacy, the pretensions of Baliol and Bruce being founded on a title which, but on that presumption, would have been posterior. (*Tytler's Scotland*, i. 90.)

He died on July 19, 1297, at his manor of Malton. His wife was Isabel, daughter of Adam de Periton, and widow of Robert de Welles. By her he had a son John, who died before him.

VETERI PONTE, ROBERT DE, whose ancestor of the same name (Vieuxpont, or Vipont) flourished in the reign of the Conqueror (*Baronage*, i. 347), held an office in the treasury at the beginning of the reign of King John, and probably at the end of that of Richard I. The Rotulus Cancellarius of 3 John makes him account for several ferms in Northamptonshire and Nottinghamshire for the 9 and 10 Richard I. In 2 John the necessaries for the queen and her company, at Marlborough, were ordered to be provided 'per testimonium Roberti de Veteri Ponte.' Similar entries are recorded in 3 and 5 John. (*Rot. de Liberat.* 7, 15; *Rot. Cancell.* 306.) From this time the rolls contain numerous orders to him to pay money from the treasury, showing his connection with that department. They evidence also his continual attendance on the king, and that prisoners taken in the French war were in his custody. (*Rot. Pat.* 9-23.)

That his services were at this time highly appreciated by his royal master, ample proof is given by the grant he received, in 4 John, of the castles of Appleby and Burgh, with the barony of the former, including divers manors and castles, among which was Brougham Castle. To these was added the sheriffwick of the county of Westmoreland (*Ibid.* 25, 27), which remained in his family long after the male branch of it became extinct. In 5 John the castle of Bowes in Richmondshire was committed to him, and was delivered to his nephew Eudo to keep (*Rot. de Liberat.* 63); and various other evidences are recorded of the favour which he then enjoyed. In that year, also, the bailiwick of Caen in Normandy was committed to his charge, as that of Rouen had been in the previous year. In the following year he was appointed constable of Nottingham Castle, with the sheriffalty of that county and of Derby, in which he continued till 11 John. (*Ibid.* 26, 33, 46.)

Up to this period he does not appear to have acted in a judicial capacity; but in 8 John, Mr. Hunter introduces him into his list of justiciers before whom fines were acknowledged. It is not improbable that he performed this duty in one of his journeys with the king, who frequently was himself present on these occasions. This, however, was the sole year in John's reign in which he is so noticed. During the remainder of it he was actively engaged in many responsible and important trusts.

In 9 John he had the custody of the bishopric of Durham, and had a patent of approval and confirmation of the sale he had made of the woods, and the terms on which he had let the lands, of the Archbishop of York. (*Ibid.* 76, 81.) From 12 to 17 John he held the sheriffalty of Devonshire, and from 12 to 15 John that of Wiltshire. He accompanied the king to Ireland and Wales in 12 John (*Rot. Misæ*, 141-231), and adhered to him both during the interdict and in his subsequent wars against the barons. The king's son, Richard, was committed to his charge, to be taken to his father (*Rot. Pat.* 104); and in 17 John he was entrusted with the custody of the castles of Carlisle and Durham, together with the county of Cumberland, and all the manors on the Tyne and the Tees (*Ibid.* 152, 163), and, with Brian de Insula and Geoffrey de Luci, was appointed the king's lieutenant of all the castles and other royal possessions in Yorkshire.

The first notice under the reign of Henry III. is a grant to him of the manor of Hardingesthorn in Northamptonshire, which belonged to his brother Yvo, who had joined the insurgent barons (*Rot. Claus.* i. 299); a grant probably made with a view to its ulterior restoration to his brother. He was among the loyal barons at the siege of the castle of Montsorel, and assisted in the relief of Lincoln, receiving in reward the forfeited possessions of several of the rebels. In 3 Henry III. he was made sheriff of Cumberland; and was also selected as one of the justices itinerant in the counties of York and Northumberland; and again performed the same duty in 10 Henry III. in Yorkshire. Dugdale adds that fines were levied before him in the following year. Roger de Wendover states that he was one of the barons who continued to plunder after the termination of the war with Louis of France; and that, after some resistance, he was obliged in 1224 to deliver up to the king the castles he had in his custody. The above appointments, however, as justice itinerant, with several instances of favours and employments conferred upon him about the same time, manifest no great animosity on the part of the government. Thus, in 7 Henry III., 1222, five bucks and fifteen does were given to him from the forest of Olive for his park at Isenden; two years afterwards, his debts to the king were respited from February to Michaelmas; and in the ensuing May, the quinzime of Westmoreland and of the bishopric of Carlisle was directed to be collected under his conduct. (*Ibid.* 518, ii. 15, 75.)

He died in 12 Henry III., previous to March 2, 1228, leaving his wife surviving, who was Idonea, the daughter of John de Builly, lord of Tickhill. By her he had a son named John, who died leaving a son Robert, on whose death, without male issue, in 49 Henry III., at the battle of Evesham, his possessions, though seized by the king, were regranted to his two daughters, one of whom, Isabel, married Roger de Clifford, a justice itinerant before noticed, ancestor of the present Baroness de Clifford, and of Lord Clifford of Chudleigh. (*Baronage*, i. 347; *R. de Wendover*, iii. 237, 301, 353, iv. 15, 19, 34, 93.)

VEYM, RICHARD DE, was appointed, in 9 Henry III., 1225, to act as a justice itinerant in Gloucestershire, where his property was situate. During the troubles at the end of King's John reign his land had been given to Robert de Vernay; but it may be presumed it was afterwards restored to him, as he was selected in 10 Henry III. as one of those who were to assess and collect the quinzime of the county. (*Rot. Claus.* i. 262, ii. 64, 76, 147.)

W

WADHAM, JOHN, whose family took its name from the place of its residence in the parish of Knowston, near South Molton, in Devonshire, was the son of Sir John Wadham, knight, and was educated as a lawyer. His name appears among the advocates in R. Bellewe's Reports, and he was eventually made one of the king's serjeants. His appointment as a justice of the Court of Common Pleas is not recorded, but it probably took place in 11 Richard II., at the time when the court was almost cleared by the impeachment of all the judges except Sir William de Skipwith. The fines levied before him commence in 12 Richard II., 1388, and continue till 1397 (*Dugdale's Orig.* 46); and as beyond that year he was not summoned to parliament, he probably was then removed, or resigned. He lived till 1411 (*Cal. Inq.* p. m. iii. 338), and it is said of him 'that being free of speech, he mingled it well with discretion; so that he never touched any man, how mean soever, out of order, either for sport or spight; but with alacrity of spirit and soundness of understanding, menaged all his proceedings.'

His descendants continued in lineal succession till Nicholas, who, with his wife Dorothy, the daughter of Sir William Petre, secretary of state to Queen Elizabeth, founded the college at Oxford which bears his name. (*Collins's Peerage*, vii. 273; *Prince*.)

WAKERING, JOHN (BISHOP OF NORWICH), so called from a village of that name in Essex, was certainly one of the masters, or clerks of the higher grade, in Chancery in 19 Richard II., 1395, when he acted as receiver of the petitions to parliament. (*Rot. Parl.* iii. 337.) He probably held the office for some time before, as he was instituted to the valuable living of St. Benet Sherehog in the city of London in 1389. He was advanced on March 2, 1405, to the mastership of the Rolls, which he enjoyed for more than ten years. During this period he twice held the Great Seal as keeper, in 11 and 12 Henry IV., in the absence of the chancellor.

He became archdeacon of Canterbury in 1405, and canon of Wells in 1409. On June 3, 1415, he exchanged the office of master of the Rolls for that of keeper of the privy seal (*Kal. Exch.* ii. 130-2), and in the following year was elected Bishop of Norwich.

When the Council of Constance was held in 1417, to settle the contention between the three claimants of the papal chair, the bishop was one of the six ecclesiastics who were selected to attend on the part of England, and he is said to have gained the applause of the assembly by his learning and wisdom. One of the candidates resigned, the two others were formally deposed from their assumed authority, and the election fell on Martin V.

On the accession of Henry VI. he was named as one of the special council of assistance to the protectors; but his services in the third year of that reign were terminated by his death at his manor of Thorpe on April 9, 1425. He was buried in his cathedral.

He is spoken of as having been a person of extraordinary merit, pious, bountiful, and affable, and governing his see with prudence and moderation. (*Godwin*, 438; *Blomefield's Norwich*, i. 528; *Hasted*, xii. 581; *Rot. Parl.* iv. 175, 201.)

WALCOT, THOMAS, derived his descent from Llewelyn with the Golden Chain, lord of Yale in Denbighland, one of whose descendants married the heir of Sir John Walcot, of Walcot in Shropshire, and thereupon assumed the name with the extensive estates. He was the second surviving son of Humphrey Walcot, who was sheriff of the county in 1631, and suffered considerably by his adherence to the royal cause, by Anne, daughter of Thomas Dockwra, of Poderich in Hertfordshire.

Born in 1629, and admitted to the Middle Temple, he was called to the bar in 1653, became a bencher in 1671, and Lent reader in 1677. He was elected recorder of Bewdley in 1671, and in 1679 was summoned to take the degree of the coif. In the parliament of October 1679, dissolved in January 1681, he was elected member for Ludlow, and in the same year he received the honour of knighthood. On October 22, 1683, he was constituted a judge of the King's Bench by Charles II., but retained his seat there for less than two years, dying in the Trinity vacation which followed King James's accession. When the sentence pronounced by that court in June 1684 against Sir Thomas Armstrong, on his attainder by outlawry, was taken up by parliament in January 1689, it appeared that Mr. Justice Walcot had died intestate, and had not left an estate sufficient to pay his debts. In the only other public trials in which his name appears, those of Rosewell and Titus Oates, he made no remark indicative of either his character or his talents.

He married Mary, daughter of Sir Adam Littleton, of Stoke Melbury in Shropshire, Bart., and by her had several children. He was seated at Bitterly Court in that county, which, by various intermarriages, has become the property of the senior branch of the family, the Walcot estate having been sold in 1764 to Lord Clive. (*Pedigree of the Family; Nash's Worcester*, ii. 279; *State Trials*, x. 119, 151, 1198; *2 Shower*, 434.)

WALDHULL, SIMON DE, probably meaning Wahull, is introduced by Dugdale as a justicier in 12 John, 1210, on the authority of a fine levied before him. But Mr. Hunter omits him in the list he has given, and certainly his name does not appear on any of the fines in those counties which have been hitherto published.

There was a barony of Wahull in Bedfordshire, the lord of which at this time was John de Wahull, of whom this Simon may have been a younger brother. (*Baronage*, i. 503.)

WALDRIC appears as chancellor to the concord between the abbot of Fescamp and Philip de Braiosa made at Salisbury on January 13, 1103–4; and there are four other documents of this reign in the 'Monasticon,' attested by him in the same character, which, though bearing no date, must have been executed about this time. (*Monast.* i. 164, vi. 1083, 1106, 1273.)

In 1106 a charter occurs, granted to the church of Tewkesbury, one of the signatures to which, immediately following the king's, is that 'Walteri, Cancellarii;' and the same signature is added to another charter granted to the priory of Thetford, which is dated at Ramsey, *in transitu regis*, on February 14. (*Ibid.* ii. 66, v. 149.) The year is not mentioned, but it probably was signed when the king went to Normandy, in the same year. No author notices such a chancellor as Walter, and the name only occurs on these two occasions. It may fairly be presumed, therefore, that they are merely errors, either of the scribe or the printer, in substituting them for Waldric.

In the preceding notice of Galdric, the chancellor under William II., it is suggested that he may be the same as this Waldric; and an account is given of his taking Duke Robert at the battle of Tenchebrai, and being rewarded with the bishopric of Laon. It will be observed that all the above-mentioned instruments were executed before that battle, which was fought on September 28, 1106, and that the last of them was probably dated before embarking on the expedition against Duke Robert.

That the name neither of Waldric nor of Galdric occurs at any subsequent date, and that Ranulph soon after appears as chancellor, if affording no positive confirmation, at least offers no contradiction to the suggestion.

WALEDENE, HUMFREY DE, was an officer in the Exchequer long before he became a baron of that court. In 19 Edward I. the manor of Horsington was committed to him, during the minority of the heir, at a rent of 50*l*. a year. In 28 Edward I. he was appointed to perambulate the forests of Somerset, Dorset, and Devon. In 30 Edward I. the bishopric of Worcester was committed to him during its vacancy, and four years afterwards the archbishopric of Canterbury. (*Abb. Rot. Orig.* i. 66, 119, 150; *Parl. Writs*, i. 398.)

He was appointed a baron of the Exchequer on October 19, 1306, 34 Edward I.; but he only retained his office till the following July, when the reign terminated. (*Madox*, ii. 46–325.)

Although he was not one of the barons sworn in on the accession of Edward II., there is nothing to show that he was disgraced. On the contrary, he is found among the justices of Oyer and Terminer, in the fourth and eighth years of that reign, for Essex and Hertford. In 13 Edward II. he had an extensive grant of the stewardship of various royal castles and manors in eleven counties—among which was the park of Windsor,—and of the auditorship of their accounts. He is mentioned also as steward to the Earl of Hertford, and seems to have been appointed, at his desire, one of the justices to take an assize in which he was interested. (*Abb. Rot. Orig.* i. 252, 276; *Rot. Parl.* i. 398.)

He was restored to his place on the Exchequer bench on June 18, 1324, 17 Edward II.; but, though he acted during the remainder of the reign, it does not appear that he sat as a baron under Edward III. He died in the fifth year of that king, leaving an infant heir, who became escheator of Essex and Hertford in 23 Edward III. (*Abb. Rot. Orig.* 50–203; *Cal. Inq.* p. m. ii. 37.)

WALEIS, WILLIAM LE, was one of the justices itinerant for Dorsetshire in 9 Henry III., 1225, and in the next year was appointed to assess and collect the quinzime in that county.

WALERAND, ROBERT, was a favourite of Henry III., and frequently employed in his service, particularly in the Welsh wars. The rolls contain frequent proofs of the confidence reposed in him, and of the favour he enjoyed. In 30 Henry III., 1246, he had the custody of the lands and castles of William Mareschall, late Earl of Pembroke, and in the next year those of John de Munchanes. In 34 Henry III., 1250, the castles of Carmarthen and Cardigan, with the lands of Meilgon Fitz-Meilgon, were committed to his charge at the small annual rent of forty marks; and three years afterwards he paid a fine of forty shillings of gold for the marriage of Beatrice, the daughter of Robert de Brus. (*Excerpt. e Rot. Fin.* i. 458, ii. 14, 87, 158.)

From June 1251 there can be little doubt that he was a regular justicier, many entries occurring on the Rotulus de Finibus of payments made for assizes to be taken before him. These continue, with slight interruption, till August 1258. (*Ibid.* ii. 107–286.)

He is described as the king's seneschal in 36 Henry III. (*Ibid.* ii. 358) and the following years; and it probably arose from his attending the court as seneschal that in 46 Henry III., 1262, the Great Seal was temporarily put into his and Imbert de Munster's hands during the chancellorship of Walter de Merton.

The Earl of Leicester's ravages in 1263 were specially directed against him as one of the king's chief favourites; but after Henry regained his authority he resumed his former position, and received some compensation for his losses. From April 1268 till August 1271, the frequent entries of assizes to be held before him prove that he was restored to his place on the bench. (*Ibid.* iii. 441, 468–546; *Abb. Placit.* 182.)

He died about Edward I., and was found possessed of sixteen manors, and extensive possessions in eight counties. (*Cal. Inq.* p. m. i. 48.)

WALKINGHAM, ALAN DE, whose family had considerable possessions in Yorkshire, was probably the son of John de Walkingham, whose widow, Agnes, paid for an assize in that county in 1267. (*Excerpt. e Rot. Fin.* ii. 434.) He pursued the legal profession, and was appointed in 8 Edward I., 1280, one of the justices to take assizes in different counties. In the next year he acted as the king's advocate, or local attorney-general, in the pleas before the justices itinerant in Yorkshire, and in 10 Edward I. was added to the commission of justices itinerant in Cornwall. He died in 12 Edward I. (*Cal. Inq.* p. m. i. 34, 128; *Madox*, ii. 112.)

WALLOP, RICHARD, belonged to the Hampshire family which was ennobled by George I. with the earldom of Portsmouth. His branch was settled at Bugbroke in Northamptonshire, and his father, Richard, was resident in that place. He was called to the bar by the Middle Temple in February 1646, and was elected a bencher in 1666. Though not mentioned by the reporters till 1661, his future success in his profession may be estimated by the numerous state trials in which he was engaged; and his political tendencies are apparent from his being generally retained against the government during the reigns of Charles II. and James II. In 1680 he was leading counsel for Lord Stafford, one of the five Popish lords. In 1681 he was selected as counsel for the Duke of York on the indictment for recusancy, and was assigned to argue points of law in defence of Edward Fitzharris, and of Stephen Colledge. In 1682 he assisted in defending the city of London against the quo warranto, and was engaged as counsel for the Earl of Danby. He was peculiarly obnoxious to Chief Justice Jeffreys, who took every opportunity of browbeating him. When Wallop, on the trial of Bradford and Speke in 1684 for asserting that the Earl of Essex was murdered in the Tower, persisted in asking some question of the witness, which the chief justice disapproved, his lordship exclaimed, 'Nay, Mr. Wallop, be as angry as you will, you shall not hector the court out of their understandings;' and upon Wallop's saying, 'I refer myself to all that hear me, if I attempted such a thing as to hector the court,' he was checked thus intemperately by the judge: 'Refer yourself to all that hear you! refer yourself to the court. It is a reflection on the government, I tell you the question is, and you sha'n't do any such thing while I sit here by the grace of God, if I can help it;' and again, 'Pray behave yourself as you ought, Mr. Wallop; you must not think to huff and swagger here.' On the trial in the same year of Thomas Rosewell for high treason the chief justice took another opportunity of showing his prejudice against the unfortunate counsel. Seeing him in court, he asked him what business he had there, and on his saying that he only came from curiosity to hear the trial, Jeffreys declared that it should not proceed while he remained. Wallop, however, had the pleasure afterwards of moving successfully in arrest of the judgment. Another instance of this judge's brutality towards Mr. Wallop occurred shortly after, when he was counsel for Richard Baxter. 'Mr. Wallop,' said Jeffreys, 'I observe you are in all these dirty causes; and were it not for you gentlemen of the long robe, who should have more wit and honesty to support and hold up these factious knaves by the chin, we should not be at the pass we are at.' Mr. Wallop mildly answered, 'My lord, I humbly conceive that the passages accused are natural deductions from the text.' Upon which the infuriated chief cried out, 'You humbly conceive! and I humbly conceive; swear him, swear him.' Wallop attempted to proceed, but Jeffreys stopped his advocacy by saying, 'Sometimes you humbly conceive, and sometimes you are very positive; you talk of your skill in Church history, and of your understanding Latin and English; I think I understand something of them as well as you; but in short I must tell you that if you do not your duty better, I shall teach it you.' (*State Trials*, vols. vii.–xi.; *Luttrell*, i. 69, 195, 297; *Woolrych's Jeffreys*, 145.)

These attacks upon him originated probably from some personal antipathy, as every other judge treated him and his arguments with respect. They continued during the whole of the coarse chief justice's presidency of the court, and were regarded with the greater disgust from the object of them being an old man approaching his seventieth year.

After ten or eleven years more of hard forensic duty, he obtained a retirement from his labours in the snug office of cursitor baron of the Exchequer, to which he was appointed on March 16, 1696. Not long was his enjoyment of it, Narcissus Luttrell (iv. 32, 267) recording that 'old Mr. Wallop, cursitor baron,' died on August 22, 1697.

WALMESLEY, THOMAS, of an honourable family settled at Sholley in Lancashire, was the eldest son of Thomas Walmesley, by his wife, Margaret, daughter of — Livesay. He was born about 1537, and commenced his legal studies either at Barnard's Inn or Staple Inn, for each claims him as having been a student, before he was entered at Lincoln's Inn. He was called to the bar by the latter society on June 15, 1567; and being elected one of the governors in 1575, he became reader in 1578, and again in 1580. On the last occasion he had just received his summons to take the degree of the coif, which he accordingly assumed on October 18. (*Dugdale's Orig.* 253, 261; *Holinshed*, iv. 432.) Chief Justice Dyer having named the barristers whom he had selected to receive that honour, Mr. Justice Francis Wyndham wrote to Lord Burleigh, suggesting that two in the list might be spared 'in respect of suspicion of their religion.' These were Mr. Maryot, of the Inner Temple, and Walmesley; and the judge's representations, though failing in regard to the latter, seem to have been successful against the former. (*Manning's Serv. ad legem.*)

He was constituted a judge of the Common Pleas on May 10, 1589. On King James's accession he was re-appointed and knighted, and was one of the 'Thomases' alluded to by Lord Ellesmere as differing both in the House of Lords and the Exchequer Chamber from the majority of the judges on the question of the post nati. (*State Trials*, ii. 576, 669.)

His account of presents received and expenses incurred on some of his circuits, a very curious record, has been preserved among the Petre Papers. By this document it appears that he went the Western Circuit with Mr. Justice Fenner for five consecutive years, from autumn 1596 to spring 1601. At each place of holding the assize it was the custom for the mayor and the sheriff to present some article of consumption, varying according to their means or liberality. The eatables consisted of 'half a bucke,' 'one mutten,' 'one veale,' lambs, capons, quayles, conyes, turkies, herneshawes, chickings, ducks, gulles, samons, lobsters, gurnetts, soales, haddocks, and, among numerous pies and pasties, 'one redd deare pie.' Of drinkables there were wine (without naming the sort) and several 'hoggesheades of beare.' The noblemen and gentry of the county also sent similar contributions of bucks, muttons, &c.; besides which these additional articles are recorded: 'One kidd,' pigeons, a pecock, pewetts, 'two peeces of turbett,' 'one isle of sturgeon,' 'artychocks and peases,' and 'xii suites' (sweets?). The sheriff of Devon seems to have been a most munificent caterer, for, besides presenting half a buck and two hogsheads of beer, he provided the judges with an excellent supper during the whole time they were at Exeter.

The 'Rewardes' paid by the judges for these presents, varying from 5s. down to 6d., amounted to 6l. 15s. Besides what they thus received, they had themselves to furnish a plentiful supply of food, so that their joint expenses of one circuit amounted to 47l. 18s. 10d. To Judge Walmesley's half of this, 23*l*. 19*s*. 5*d*., are added his private charges, for horse-meat, &c., servants, and 20*d*. at each place 'to the poore,' amounting to 23*l*. 2*s*. 5*d*., making the whole circuit cost him 47*l*. 1*s*. 10*d*. (*Ex. inf. of Wm. Durrant Cooper, Esq., F.S.A.*)

He retained his seat above twenty-three years, and died on November 26, 1612, aged seventy-five. He was buried at Blackburn in Lancashire, where his magnificent monument was demolished by the parliamentary soldiers in 1642. The epitaph on it commenced with the following quaint lines (*Lansdowne MSS.* No. 973, fo. 88):—

Tombs have their period, monuments decay,
And rust and age wear Epitaphs away.
But neither rust nor age nor time shall wear
Judge Walmesley's name that lies entombed here,
Who never did for favour nor for awe
Of great men's frowns quit or forsake the lawe.
His inside was his outside, he never sought
To make fair showes of what he never thought.

He had the repute of having amassed considerable wealth by great rapacity in his practice of the law; but no evidence is given of the charge. He became possessed of the estate of Dunkenhalgh, in the parish of Whalley, near Blackburn, on which he built a fine mansion. By his wife, Anne, the rich heiress of Robert Shuttleworth, Esq., of Hackinge in the same county, he left an only son, whose male descendants failed at the beginning of the last century, and the large property passed into the families of Lord Petre and Lord Stourton, who were the first and second husbands of the last possessor's sister and heir. (*Shuttleworth Accounts*, Chetham Soc. 1856.)

WALSH, JOHN, called sometimes WELSH, was the only son of another John Walsh, of Cathanger, in the parish of Fivehead, Somersetshire, by Jane, daughter of Sir Edward Broke. He became a reader at the Middle Temple in 1555, having been previously mentioned as a barrister in Plowden's Reports. He was of those summoned in the last month of Mary's reign to take the degree of the coif in the following Easter, when by a new writ from Queen Elizabeth they were admitted on April 19, 1559. His next step was to the bench of the Common Pleas, of which he was constituted a judge on February 10, 1563, and had fines acknowledged before him as late as February 1572. (*Dugdale's Orig.* 48, 217.) In that year he died, and was buried in the parish church of Fivehead.

He left an only daughter, who married Sir Edward Seymour, the eldest son of the first Duke of Somerset by his first wife, who was excluded from the title till the failure of the issue of the duke's second wife. This failure occurred in 1740, when a descendant of Sir Edward's succeeded to the dukedom, which now remains in his, the elder family. (*Collinson's Somerset*, i. 42.)

WALSHE, THOMAS, like many of the other barons, began his career as an officer in the Exchequer. He was clerk of estreats in 1516, and was made treasurer's remembrancer in April 1523, and was promoted to a seat on the bench of that court as fourth baron on April 27, 1536. It appears by an order of the privy council in June 1541 that he was then engaged as a commissioner in Ireland on some of the king's business, and that he was directed to return to England to make his report. (*Acts Privy Council*, vii. 201.) He continued baron till August 6, 1542, when his place was filled up.

WALSINGHAM, LORD. See W. DE GREY.

WALSINGHAM, RICHARD DE, was a knight residing in Norfolk, his family being so called from the town of that name. He was returned for the county to the parliaments of 28, 29, and 33 Edward I.; and it was probably on that account that he was placed in the latter year among the five justices of trailbaston appointed for Norfolk and Suffolk, and was re-nominated in the new commissions of 1307.

He was summoned among the justices to parliament in the first year of Edward II., and during the remainder of his life was occasionally employed in judicial business. He still continued to represent Norfolk in parliament up to 7 Edward II., and is last mentioned in 12 Edward II. In the following year his executors were directed to bring in the proceedings before him. (*Parl. Writs*, i. 892, ii. 1574; *Rot. Parl.* i. 218.)

His wife, whose name was Anastasia, was buried in the Black Friars at Thetford. (*Weever*, 828.)

WALTER, HUBERT (ARCHBISHOP OF CANTERBURY), born at West Dereham in Norfolk, was one of the sons of Hervey Walter, whose barony was in that county. His mother was Maud, the daughter of Theobald de Valoines, and the sister of Berta, the wife of Ranulph de Glanville, the great justiciary. Brought up under that celebrated man to the two learned professions of the church and the law, his advance in both, under such instruction and with such patronage, could not be doubtful.

So early as 31 Henry II., 1185, his name appears among the barons and justiciers before whom fines were levied in the Curia Regis. Soon afterwards he was raised to the deanery of York. Even at this early period of his career he gave evidence of his piety and his gratitude by founding a monastery for Præmonstratensian monks at his native place, for the souls of his father and mother, and of his patron Ranulph de Glanville and his wife.

Immediately after the coronation of Richard I. he was elected to the see of Salisbury, and in the following year he accompanied that monarch on the crusade, and, with Archbishop Baldwin and his uncle Ranulph de Glanville, was placed in command of the forces before Acre. He alone of the three survived the campaign, and by his spirit and wisdom was of the greatest service to the army during Richard's illness, being mainly instrumental in procuring the truce with Saladin when the King of France had deserted the cause. Before his return to England he had the satisfaction of visiting Jerusalem.

The king was so deeply impressed with his talents and prudent counsel that when he heard of the sudden death of Reginald Fitz-Josceline, Archbishop of Canterbury, he took every means, even before his own release from prison, to procure Hubert's appointment to the vacant primacy. His election having taken place on May 30, 1193, the new archbishop exerted himself in collecting the ransom for the release of his sovereign. In September 1193 he was raised to the office of chief justiciary, and his power was afterwards greatly increased by his being appointed legate of the apostolic see.

On Richard's return he was high in his confidence, officiated at his second coronation in April 1194, and continued for four years to perform the duties of his office with firmness and moderation. By his advice weights and measures were regulated, and other laws against fraud were ordained. The possessor of power, however, is certain to have enemies, and he must be fortunate indeed who, in its exercise, commits no act which is obnoxious to censure. The archbishop was charged with neglecting his ecclesiastical duties, and with having violated the right of sanctuary in directing the execution of William Fitz-Osbert, a factious demagogue, who had taken refuge in the church of St. Mary-le-Bow. These and other representations to his disadvantage were urged upon Pope Innocent by the monks of Canterbury, who, however, are stated by Roger de Wendover to have been instigated by the fear lest a magnificent church which the archbishop was erecting at Lambeth should occasion the removal of the archiepiscopal seat from their city. Nevertheless, their application was successful; the new church was ordered to be demolished, and the king, under the threat of an interdict, was compelled to part with his chief justiciary on the shallow pretence that it was not lawful for bishops to be engaged in secular affairs. Hubert's resignation was reluctantly accepted in July 1198, 9 Richard I.

Although he had been a faithful servant to Richard, his absence in the Holy Land had prevented him from coming into collision with the king's brother, John. That prince then, on Richard's death, knowing the respect with which he was regarded, deputed him and William Mareschall, Earl of Pembroke, to receive the fealty of the English barons. How the archbishop was induced to set aside the more legitimate claims of Prince Arthur does not appear; but, as no improper motive is imputed to him, it may be presumed that he had not obtained an insight into John's real character, and that he considered the safety of the kingdom in its then unsettled state would be risked in the weak hands of a youthful sovereign. He placed the crown on John's head on May 27, 1199, being Ascension-day, and either on that day or immediately after was constituted his chancellor. There is a charter given under his hand as chancellor, dated on June 6, being ten days after that solemnity. (*Rymer*, i. 75.) His acceptance of this post did not escape remark as a proof of his cupidity. It was sneeringly observed to him that 'Heretofore chancellors have been created archbishops, but no archbishop before you has vouchsafed to become chancellor.' The fact, however, merely proves that the office of chancellor was then advancing in importance, and was rapidly treading on the heels of that of chief justiciary, which in a few years, in reference to all political power, it entirely superseded. In October 1201 he again crowned King John, with his second wife, Queen Isabella, at Westminster, and soon afterwards repeated the ceremony at Canterbury.

He continued to perform all the duties of the office of chancellor, if not to enjoy the favour of his sovereign, during the remainder of his life. (*Madox*, i. 57.) He died at Tenham on July 13, 1205, and was buried in Canterbury Cathedral.

Few persons who have filled such high offices have passed through their career with so little blame. Commencing his life under the eye of his illustrious uncle, he acquired that knowledge and laid the foundation for that experience and discretion which gained him the confidence of three kings of very opposite characters, without degrading himself by any low arts or undue subserviency. His private worth is evidenced by the friendship of Archbishop Baldwin, who entrusted him with the execution of his will; his resolution and high spirit were shown by his accompanying King Richard in his dangerous enterprise in the Holy Land; his loyalty and gratitude by his energetic efforts to release him from captivity; his wisdom by his administration of the government, and the useful laws he introduced; and if, from his secular employments, he neglected some of his ecclesiastical duties, those of hospitality and charity were not forgotten. Besides the monastery at Dereham, he founded another at Wolverhampton, enriched the revenues of his see, ornamented it with many buildings, and procured for it some valuable privileges. He presented also the living of Halegart to the church of Canterbury, devoting its revenues to the support of the library there, and obtained from King John the liberty of a mint for coining money in the city of Canterbury. (*Dugdale's Orig.* 8.)

He was the brother of the next-mentioned Theobald Walter. (*Godwin*, 83, 342; *Atkyns's Gloucestersh.* 9; *Weever*, 218; *Hasted*, xii. 346; *R. de Wendover*, iii. 30–183; *Lingard*, &c.)

WALTER, THEOBALD, was one of the four brothers of the above Hubert Walter. King Richard granted him the lordship of Preston in Lancashire, with the whole wapentake and forest of Amundernesse; and he became sheriff of that county in 5 Richard I., and so continued till 1 John. In 9 Richard I., 1197-8, he was one of the justices itinerant to set the tallage in Colchester. (*Madox*, i. 733.)

In 5 John he paid a fine of two palfreys for licence to go to Ireland, where he held the office of chief butler, and where he possessed large property. He founded two abbeys in that kingdom, that of Wotheny in Limerick, and that of Nenagh in Tipperary, besides the monastery of Arkelo. In England, also, he founded an abbey at Cockersand in Lancashire, for canons regular of the order of St. Augustin.

He died in 9 John, and his widow, Maud, the daughter of Robert le Vavasour (*Rot. Pat.* 74), a few years afterwards married Fulke Fitz-Warren. His son, Theobald, assumed the name of Boteler, from his office, and was the progenitor of the noble family of that name, the head of which is the present Marquis of Ormond. (*Dugdale's Baron.* i. 633; *Nicolas.*)

WALTER, JOHN, was the son of Edmund Walter, of Ludlow in Shropshire, an eminent counsel in the reign of Queen Elizabeth, and chief justice of South Wales. The family was an offshoot of that of the above Hubert and Theobald. His mother was Mary, the daughter of Thomas Hackluit, Esq., of Eyton in Herefordshire. He was born in 1563, and, after completing his education at Brazenose College, Oxford, was admitted a member of the Inner Temple, and in 1590 was called to the bar, and became reader there in 1607. Previously to this time he had sufficient reputation as a barrister to be employed with Serjeant Altham and Mr. Stevens, before the council and the judges, in defence of the rights and privileges of the Court of Exchequer, and as counsel before the Peers in defending the king's title to alnage. (*Issue of Exch.* 32, 64.) He was also counsellor for the university of Oxford, and received from it on July 1, 1613, the degree of M.A. In the same year he was selected as attorney-general to Prince Charles, and was knighted on May 18, 1619. He still held this place, when on a brief being sent to him against Sir Edward Coke, then prosecuted by the court, he had the courage to decline it, saying, 'Let my tongue cleave to the roof of my mouth when I open it against Sir Edward Coke.' (*Brit. Biog.* iv. 179.) This generous conduct, forming such a contrast with Bacon's on a similar occasion, did not prevent his advancement. Immediately on Charles's coming to the crown he appointed Sir John Walter one of his serjeants, and a month after he raised him to the chief seat in the Exchequer, on May 12, 1625. (*Rymer*, xviii. 638.)

The new chief baron, however, did not answer the king's expectations. He was too independent and too honest to suit the royal will. For some cause or other, which is not precisely described, the king was dissatisfied with his conduct, and would have discharged him, had he submitted to be thus thrown aside. But he alleged that by his patent he held his office 'quamdiu se bene gesserit,' and he refused to retire without a *scire facias* to show 'whether he did bene se gerere, or not;' a course which the king did not think proper to adopt, but was obliged to be contented with forbidding him to sit in court. Before this event had taken place—viz., on February 14, 1628-9—he and the other barons had given the somewhat equivocating answer to the House of Commons for refusing to deliver back the goods seized for tonnage and poundage. (*Parl. Hist.* ii. 472.) But the immediate cause of his disgrace was said to be that he disagreed with the rest of the judges as to the legality of proceeding criminally against a member of parliament for acts done in the house. (*Whitelocke*, 16.) Sir W. Jones (*Reports*, 228) says he received his prohibition to sit in court in the beginning of Michaelmas Term 1630, and that he forbore till he died. The interval between the two events was but short, for his decease took place on November 18, at his house in the Savoy. He was buried in the church of Wolvercote, near Oxford, where there is a splendid monument to him and his two wives. (*Fasti Oxon.* i. 355.)

His contemporary Judge Croke (*Car.* 203) describes him as 'a profoundly learned man, and of great integrity and courage;' and Fuller (*Worthies*, ii. 260) joins his testimony to the same effect, adding that he 'was most passionate as Sir John, most patient as Judge Walter;' and that such was his gravity that once when Judge

Denham said to him, 'My lord, you are not merry,' he answered, 'Merry enough for a judge.' In the year after his elevation he obtained a curious licence for himself and his wife, and any four friends invited to his table, to eat meat on the prohibited days, on payment of 13s. 4d. per annum to the parish where he resided. (*Rymer*, xviii. 309.)

His first wife was Margaret, daughter of William Offley, Esq., an eminent London merchant; his second was Anne, daughter of William Wytham, Esq., of Leastone in Yorkshire, and relict of Sir Thomas Bigges, of Lenchwike in the county of Worcester, baronet. By the latter he left no issue, but by the former he had four sons and four daughters. His eldest son was created a baronet in 1641, but the title became extinct in 1731.

WALTHAM, JOHN DE (BISHOP OF SALISBURY), was born at Waltham, near Grimsby, in Lincolnshire, in the church of which his father and mother were buried, with the following monumental inscription (*Archæol. Journ.* vii. 389):—

Hic jacent Johes et Margareta ux' ei quond'm pater et mater
Joh'is Walth'm nup' Sar' Ep'i quoy' aiab3 p'piciet' deus. ame'.

It is not known whether he was a clerk of the Chancery before he received his patent as keeper of the Rolls from Richard II., on September 8, 1381. He held the place for more than five years, during which, on the allegation that it was incumbent upon him to visit his archdeaconry, he obtained a patent enabling him, as often as he should absent himself for that or any other reasonable cause, to depute any person, whom the chancellor should consider sufficient, to exercise his office in his absence, the power of such deputy to cease after his return.

It appears, from a petition of the Commons in the reign of Henry V. (*Rot. Parl.* iv. 84), that he extended the jurisdiction of the Court of Chancery by the introduction of the writ of subpœna; a form of proceeding of which they complained, but which, the king refusing to discontinue it, has survived to the present time.

On the discharge of the chancellor, Richard le Scrope, from July 11 to September 10, 1382, he was one of the persons to whom the custody of the Great Seal was entrusted till the appointment of a new chancellor. In 1386 he twice performed the same duties: on one occasion, from February 9 to March 28, two clerks of the Chancery were associated with him; but on the other, from April 23 to May 14, he acted alone.

After the death of his predecessor, William de Burstall, he became keeper of the House of Converts, a benefice which was ever after appended to the office of master of the Rolls. He resigned both on October 24, 1386, and was then appointed keeper of the privy seal. (*Rot. Parl.* iii. 229.)

In the meantime his ecclesiastical preferments were numerous. He became successively canon of York, archdeacon of Richmond, master of Sherburn Hospital, Durham, and sub-dean of York, and had not long resigned the mastership of the Rolls before he was elected Bishop of Salisbury, the papal provision being dated April 3, 1388. (*Rymer*, vii. 369, 416; *Surtees' Durham*, i. 138; *Le Neve*, 258, 325.) He was called upon to serve the responsible office of treasurer in 1391, 14 Richard II., and he retained it till his death, about September 17, 1395.

The favour with which he was regarded by his sovereign, testified by the various dignities he received, was more strongly evidenced at his death, when the king, notwithstanding the murmurs of many objectors, caused his remains to be interred in the royal chapel of Westminster Abbey, where they now lie near the monument of Edward I.

He was one of the bishops who resisted the right of Archbishop Courteneye to visit his diocese, but was soon frightened into submission; for within two days after sentence of excommunication was pronounced against him he underwent the visitation. (*Godwin*, 348.)

WALTHAM, WILLIAM DE, was doubtless in some way related to the above, but how does not clearly appear. He became keeper of the Hanaper about 18 Richard II., 1394, and had, with the master of the Rolls, the temporary custody of the Great Seal on October 1. He granted a messuage and a shop in St. Martin's-le-Grand, London, to the abbot and convent of Croyland, in 21 Richard II., after which date we find no further mention of his name. (*Cal. Inq. p. m.* iii. 219.)

WALTHAM, ROGER. There was a Roger de Waltham who was keeper of the wardrobe in the latter part of the reign of Edward II. (*Rot. Parl.* ii. 383, 463), and it seems not improbable that this person was not only the progenitor of both the above, but also of this Roger Waltham, the baron of the Exchequer.

Of the latter, as of those of his coadjutors on that bench, scarcely any memorials can be found. All that is known of him is that he was appointed a baron in 1418, 6 Henry V. (*Cal. Rot. Pat.* 267); but we have not the date of his resignation or his death. He was not, however, re-appointed by Henry VI., so that he could not have held his place more than four years.

WARBURTON, PETER, descended, indirectly, from the ancient Cheshire family of Warburton and Arley, was the son of

Thomas Warburton (an illegitimate son of John Warburton of Northwich in that county), and Anne, the daughter of Richard Maisterson of Winnington. (*Family Pedigree.*)

He was born at Northwich, and began his legal studies at Staple Inn (where his arms are in the south window of the hall), finishing them at Lincoln's Inn. By the latter he was called to the bar in 1572, became one of the governors in 1581, and was elected Lent reader in 1584. (*Dugdale's Orig.* 253, 261.) He was then, and for some time after, resident in a mansion called the Black Hall, Watergate Street, Chester, formerly the house of the Grey Friars; and in this year he was recommended by Henry Earl of Derby to the mayor of Chester, to be an alderman of that city. (*Harl. MSS.* 2173.) Though it is evident, from the large purchases he made in the county, that he had a considerable practice as a barrister, it was probably chiefly in the provinces, for his name does not occur in the Reports of Westminster till 1589, four years before he took the degree of the coif, on November 29, 1593. In September 1593 he was appointed vice-chamberlain of Chester, and in November 1599 he appears as one of the commissioners 'de schismate supprimendo.' (*Peck's Desid. Cur.* b. v. 1; *Egerton Papers*, 192; *Rymer*, 386.)

His elevation to the bench at Westminster soon followed, his patent as a judge of the Common Pleas being dated November 24, 1600. King James renewed it on his accession, and knighted him. In none of the state trials at which he was present does he seem to have taken a prominent part, and no record remains of his argument in the great case of the post nati. Chamberlain, the letter-writer, records that in October 1616 he was in disgrace at court for hanging a Scotch falconer of the king, contrary to express commands. (*Cal. State Papers* [1611–18], 398.) He died on September 7, 1621, at Grafton Hall in Cheshire, a stately building erected by him on a manor he purchased after he became a judge. He was buried in the church of Tilston, the parish in which the manor is situate. (*Ormerod's Cheshire.*)

He was thrice married. His first wife was Margaret, daughter and sole heir of George Barlow, of Dronfield-Woodhouse in Derbyshire; his second was Elizabeth, daughter and coheir of Sir Thomas Butler, of Bewsey in Lancashire; and his third was Alice, daughter and coheir of Sir Peter Warburton, of Arley Hall. By the first only he had issue. His son John died in infancy, and his only surviving daughter, Elizabeth, inherited all his rich possessions. By her marriage with Sir Thomas Stanley, of Wever and Alderley, she is the ancestress of the present Lord Stanley of Alderley.

WARBURTON, PETER, was a direct descendant from the same family as the above. It originated from one of five brothers who came over with the Conqueror, and who were all largely rewarded. The township of Warburton in Cheshire was acquired by a younger son, one of whose descendants, Peter, first assumed its name in the reign of Edward II., and it has been since borne by his posterity. The seat of Arley Hall in the same county was built in the time of Henry VII., and thenceforward became the residence of the family.

The second Peter Warburton, in legal biography, was the grandson of Peter the purchaser of Hefferston Grange, who was the third son of Sir Peter Warburton, of Arley, knight. He was born in 1588, and acquired the rudiments of the law in Staple Inn, of which he was a member in 1618, probably completing his studies at Lincoln's Inn, where several of his family had previously been educated.

The first account of him is that he was appointed by the Long Parliament in March 1647 one of the judges in Wales, and that John Bradshaw and he were joined together on the Chester Circuit. His next advance was on June 1, 1649, when he was raised to the bench at Westminster as justice of the Common Pleas (*Whitelocke*, 240, 405, 407), in which character he was one of the commissioners for the trial of John Lilburn in October following, but he does not seem to have taken any active part in it. At a later period, apparently about June 1655, he was removed to the Upper Bench, but the date is not precisely given. He is mentioned as sitting in that court in Style's and Siderfin's Reports, and on the trial in 1657 of Miles Sindercome for attempting to murder the protector. (*State Trials*, iv. 1269, v. 841.) His name does not appear in Siderfin's Reports after Easter Term 1659, and, though he did not die till February 26, 1666, his name is not among the judges who were named by the Rump Parliament in January 1660, nor among the serjeants re-made by Charles II. He was buried at Fetcham in Surrey. (*Ormerod's Cheshire*, ii. 93; *Family inf.*; *Nichols's Lit. Anecdotes*, v. 529.)

WARD, WILLIAM, was an officer of the Exchequer, and in 1 Henry V., 1413, was appointed to audit the accounts of the receivers, &c., of the duchy of Cornwall. (*Devon's Issue Roll*, 333.) In the first year of the following reign he was constituted king's remembrancer; and on May 26, 1426, 4 Henry VI., he became a baron of that court (*Cal. Rot. Pat.* 269, 273); but how long he retained his seat on the bench does not appear.

WARD, EDWARD, is described by Noble (*Granger*, ii. 181) as a native of Northamptonshire; and Luttrell (iv. 277) says that in 1697 he purchased an estate in that county of 2000*l*. a year. He was called to the bar by the Inner Temple in 1670, and soon got into good practice. The tendency of his political opinions may be inferred from his being engaged by Lord Russell to argue points of law on his trial in 1683. He had married in 1676 Elizabeth, the third daughter of Mr. Thomas Papillon, of Acrise in Kent, a merchant of London, who was afterwards a candidate for the office of sheriff of that city in the famous contest that took place in 1683. He brought an action against Sir William Pritchard, the lord mayor, for a false return, and the lord mayor in his turn brought an action against Mr. Papillon for a malicious arrest. Mr. Ward was one of the counsel employed to defend his father-in-law, and being obnoxious to Sir George Jeffreys, before whom it was tried, not only on account of his politics, but of his known connection with the defendant, the chief justice took the opportunity of attempting to browbeat him. While making a very temperate statement, and endeavouring to show that there was probable cause for the arrest, Jeffreys rudely interrupted him, telling him that he did not understand the question at all, but that he launched out in an ocean of discourse that was wholly wide of the mark, and desired him not 'to make excursions *ad captandum populum*, for he would suffer none of his enamels nor his garnitures.' On Mr. Ward's attempting to explain, Jeffreys repeated his remarks so insultingly that the people hissed. This of course made the chief justice more irate, but at length he was obliged to succumb, silenced by the respectful firmness of Mr. Ward, and by a confirmatory sentence from Serjeant Maynard. (*State Trials*, ix. 589, x. 336; *Topog. and Geneal.* iii. 35, 511.)

In 1687 Ward was elected a bencher of his inn, and at the Revolution he modestly declined a judgeship that was offered to him. But on March 30, 1693, he accepted the office of attorney-general; and on June 8, 1695, he was appointed chief baron of the Exchequer, and knighted. In this office he remained during King William's life, and nearly all the reign of Queen Anne. For a brief interval of three weeks in May 1700 he held the Great Seal as one of the commissioners. (*Clarendon's Diary*, ii. 273; *Luttrell*, i. 522; 1 *Lord Raymond*, 57, 566.)

He seems to have been an honest and intelligent judge, with sufficient legal knowledge and discretion; but his name is not distinguished by any prominence of character. He died at his house in Essex Street on July 16, 1714, a fortnight before his royal mistress, and was buried at Stoke Doyle in the county of Rutland. By his wife he had twelve children. Two of his sons became lawyers of considerable eminence, and the family is now represented by G. Ward Hunt, Esq., the descendant of Jane, the chief baron's eldest daughter, and member for North Northamptonshire. (*Ex inf. T. Papillon, Esq., of Crowhurst.*)

WARE, RICHARD DE, who was elected abbot of Westminster, December 15, 1258, was placed at the head of the commission of justices itinerant into the three northern counties in 6 Edward I., 1278; and in that year he was sent on an embassy to John Duke of Brabant, to negotiate a marriage between that prince's eldest son and Margaret, the king's daughter. His name does not appear on any future iter.

He presided nearly twenty-five years, during which he procured many immunities for the abbey, and adorned it with the mosaic pavement before the high altar, the rich materials of which he brought from Rome. Besides the employments above mentioned, he was engaged in 1261 in an embassy to France, and in 1281 was treasurer of the Exchequer, in which office he died on December 2, 1283, this epitaph being placed over his tomb:—

Abbas Richardus de Ware, qui requiescat
Hic, portat lapides, quos huc portavit ab Urbe.

(*Monasticon*, i. 273; *Madox*, ii. 37.)

WARENNE, WILLIAM DE (EARL WARENNE and EARL OF SURREY). The Norman family of Warenne was ennobled long before the conquest of England, bearing the name of St. Martin before the earldom of Warenne was conferred upon them. William de Warenne was distantly related to the Conqueror, his aunt Gunnora having been that prince's great-grandmother. This connection was further cemented by his subsequent marriage with Gundreda, one of the daughters of King William and Matilda. An attempt has lately been made to prove that she was the daughter of Matilda by a former marriage with Gerbodo, an avoué of St. Bertin, at St. Omer (*Archæol. Journ.* iii. 1, 26); but the hypothesis is fully and satisfactorily overturned by an able paper in the 'Archæologia' (xxxii. 108).

He was entrusted with a command at the battle of Hastings, and greatly contributed to its successful result. In reward, the lavish Conqueror conferred upon him lordships and lands in almost every part of the kingdom, his share of the spoil amounting to 298 manors. He built castles at Reigate in Surrey, Castle Acre in Norfolk, Conisburgh in Yorkshire, and Lewes in Sussex, at the latter of which he fixed his residence.

When the king left England in 1073 he and Richard Fitz-Gilbert were appointed chief justiciaries of the kingdom. Their government was principally distinguished by overcoming the rebellion raised by the Earls of Hereford and Norfolk; but they disgraced their victory by cruelly ordering the right feet of their prisoners to be amputated—a barbarous practice for which they had the example of the king in some of his Norman wars.

On the death of the Conqueror, William de Warenne assisted his second son, William, to mount the throne, and was in such favour with that monarch that he was created Earl of Surrey at his coronation. He did not long survive this honour, dying in the following June. The two earldoms devolved on his eldest son William, whose son, William, dying in 1148 without male issue, that of Surrey passed with his daughter Isabel to her husband, Hameline Plantagenet, and ultimately, through sisters, first to the Fitz-Alans, and afterwards to the Howards, Dukes of Norfolk, in which title it is now merged. (*Baronage*, i. 73; *Horsfield's Lewes*, i. 116; *Turner*, *Lingard*, &c.)

WARENNE, REGINALD DE, was grandson of the above William, and was one of the sons of the second William, who succeeded to both earldoms, by his wife Elizabeth, daughter of Hugh the Great, Earl of Vermandois, and widow of Robert Earl of Mellent.

He was appointed by the convention between King Stephen and Henry Duke of Normandy to have the custody of the castles of Bellencumbre and Mortimer in Normandy. Under Henry II. he became an attendant at the court, and his name appears as the first of the witnesses to a concord at the Exchequer soon after Richard de Luci was made chief justiciary. (*Madox*, i. 215.) He naturally took the part of the king in the contest with Becket; but his devotion to the cause was somewhat too violent, if it be true that he threatened to cut off the archbishop's head when he landed in England. But although he joined Gervase de Cornhill, the sheriff of Kent, in appearing on the shore of Sandwich on that occasion, the intervention of John of Oxford prevented any mischief.

From the 14th to the 23rd Henry II., 1168–1177, he was regularly employed as a justice itinerant, his pleas appearing in twenty-one counties. (*Ibid.* i. 123–149.) He was also sheriff of Sussex for seven years, ending 23 Henry II.

By his marriage with Alice, the daughter and heir of Robert de Wirmgay, in Norfolk, he became possessed of that barony. He died before 31 Henry II., leaving a son, the next-mentioned William. (*Dugdale's Baron.* i. 83; *Lord Lyttelton*, i. 542, ii. 583.)

WARENNE, WILLIAM DE, the son of the above Reginald de Warenne, like his father, pursued the profession of the law, and in 5 Richard I., 1193–4, was a justice itinerant in the counties of Essex and Hertford. (*Madox*, ii. 20.) From 7 Richard to 1 John, 1195–1200, his name frequently appears among the justiciers of the Curia Regis at Westminster, before whom fines were levied. (*Hunter's Preface.*)

In the next year he was appointed justice of the Jews, and the rolls contain various mandates to him and his fellows in that capacity till the ninth year of that reign, 1207–8. His death must have occurred shortly afterwards, as in 11 John his daughter Beatrice fined in three thousand one hundred marks, to be paid in four years, for having his lands. (*Madox*, i. 490.) He founded the priory of Wirmgay, and gave sixty acres of land to the canons of Southwark.

She was the daughter of his first wife, Beatrice, and at the time of his death was the widow of Doun Bardolf, and afterwards became the wife of Hubert de Burgh, Earl of Kent.

By his second wife, Milicent, widow of Richard Muntfichet, he left no family. (*Baronage*, i. 83; *Monast.* vi. 591.)

WARENNE, JOHN DE, or PLANTAGENET (EARL WARREN and EARL OF SURREY), was the grandson of the third Earl William, who left a daughter Isabel, whose son, named William, succeeded to the earldoms and married Maud, sister and one of the coheirs of Anselm Mareschall, Earl of Pembroke, and widow of Hugh Bigot, Earl in Norfolk. They were the parents of this Earl John.

At the time of his father's death, in 1240, he was a minor (*Excerpt. e Rot. Fin.* i. 338, 447), but attained his full age before 1248, when he sat with the rest of the earls in the parliament held in London.

The only time he acted as a justice itinerant was in 1260, when he headed the commission into Somersetshire, Dorsetshire, and Devonshire.

In the contests between the king and the barons he sided with his sovereign, but is stated to have fled from the battle of Lewes. He redeemed his character, however, at Evesham, where the barons were defeated. During the rest of this reign little worthy of note is recorded of him, except the violent attack he made in Westminster Hall on Alan de Zouche and his son, occasioned by some contest between them relative to the title to certain land, in which he killed the former and wounded the latter, and for which he was compelled to make satisfaction, and was fined ten thousand marks, part of which he was afterwards pardoned in the next reign.

He lived during thirty-two years under King Edward, and signalised himself on various occasions against the Welsh and Scotch, by the latter of whom, after several successful campaigns, he was eventually defeated in 25 Edward I.; but peace between the two countries was declared the next year. Not only was he a loyal supporter of his sovereign's rights, but a bold assertor of his own. When he was asked by the judges, under the recent statute enacted at Gloucester, called Quo Warranto, by what title he held his lands, he drew his sword, and said, 'This is my warranty! My ancestors coming into this land with William the Bastard did obtain their lands by the sword, and by it I am resolved to defend them.' Another time, when questioned as to the authority under which he claimed free warren in Wurth and other lands in Sussex, he pleaded that all his ancestors had adhered to the Kings of England; that when Normandy was lost, where they were earls, they also lost their lands there, because they would not join the King of France against King John; that in compensation they had grants of other lands in England, with the privilege of free warren over them, in regard of their surname de Warenne; and his plea was allowed.

So highly were his services valued by the king that on his death on September 27, 1304, 32 Edward I., a royal precept was directed to the bishops and abbots to recommend prayers for his soul, and indulgences were granted to those who joined in them. He was buried in the abbey of Lewes.

He married Alice, daughter of Hugh le Brun, Earl of March, by Isabel, the widow of King John, and consequently half-sister to Henry III. By her he had, besides two daughters, a son, William, who died in his father's lifetime, leaving a son, named John, who succeeded to the title. On John's death, without issue, in 1347, his sister Alice, the wife of Edmund Earl of Arundel, became his heir, and the title still survives in her descendant, the present Duke of Norfolk.

(*Baronage*, i. 73-81; *Nicolas*.)

WARHAM, WILLIAM (ARCHBISHOP OF CANTERBURY), was born at Walsanger in the parish of Okely in Hampshire, the residence of his father, Robert Warham, whose family had been long seated there. His education was commenced at William of Wykeham's school at Winchester, and continued at New College, Oxford, of which he became fellow in 1475. He took the degree of doctor in both laws, and left his academical retirement to enter into a more active career in 1488, having previously been admitted into holy orders, and received from his college the living of Horewood Magna, in the diocese of Lincoln.

Entering as an advocate in the Court of Arches, he distinguished himself in such a manner as to be selected by Henry VII., in July 1493, to go on an embassy with Sir Edward Poynings to the court of Archduke Philip, the real object of the mission being to obtain the surrender of Perkin Warbeck, who had taken refuge in Flanders. Although they failed in their negotiation, it is evident that the king was not dissatisfied with Warham's conduct, since he was advanced on the 13th of the following February to the mastership of the Rolls, an office which he held for eight years. During this period he was frequently engaged in diplomatic services, and in his clerical character was instituted to the living of Barley in Hertfordshire in 1495, and preferred, on April 28 in the next year, from the precentorship of Wells, to which he had been appointed on November 2, 1493, to the archdeaconry of Huntingdon.

He was elected to the see of London in October 1501, and resigned the office of master of the Rolls on February 1, 1502. On August 11 he was appointed keeper of the Great Seal, and was raised to the primacy in November 1503. In January 1504 the king changed his title of keeper for the more dignified one of lord chancellor of England, which he retained during the rest of the reign, taking a prominent part in the administration of the kingdom. (*Rymer*, xii. 544, 655, 668, xiii. 13, 21, 27, 90.)

In 1506 the archbishop was elected chancellor of his university, and his presidency only terminated with his life, a period of twenty-six years, during which he showed his love for his alma mater by many benefactions, in return for which he was regarded with a feeling approaching to veneration.

Standing high as Warham did in the favour of the father, he was naturally retained in his elevated post of chancellor when Henry VIII. succeeded to the throne; but it was not long ere he lost the ascendency which he had hitherto possessed in royal councils. Wolsey, with no higher office than that of almoner, was gradually acquiring an influence over the king's mind, which enabled him at length to attain the highest position in the state; and Henry, not well pleased perhaps with the early scruples which the archbishop had raised against his proposed marriage with Catherine of Arragon, was probably aware that, though in his character of primate he performed the ceremony, he did not heartily approve it. He continued, however, to hold the Great Seal for the first six years and a half of the reign, although his palpably decreasing power and the purposed indignities offered to him by the new favourite, especially since the acquisition of the archbishopric of York and the cardinalship, had several times induced him to tender his resignation. Having been obliged to remonstrate with Wolsey for causing his cross to be carried before him in the province of Canterbury, contrary to established practice, the wily cardinal seemingly submitted, but forthwith took steps to obtain from the pope the appointment of legate *à latere*, which would give him a better claim to the disputed right. This at once decided Warham, who two months after, on December 22, 1515, retired from his office of chancellor, which was immediately given to his rival. The pride and insolence of the cardinal were exhibited against the archbishop on many subsequent occasions, and he even went so far as to take offence at his subscribing himself 'your Brother of Canterbury.' Warham bore these insults with calmness while they affected himself alone, although during Wolsey's power his ecclesiastical dignity was reduced to a mere shadow; but when his clergy were interfered with and his archiepiscopal authority invaded, by the erection of a legatine court and the arbitrary judgments pronounced there, Warham made a representation to the king, who, declaring his ignorance, charged him to convey to the cardinal the royal pleasure that these things should be amended. However annoying such a command must have been when delivered by such a messenger, it was followed by a still more bitter reprimand from the king himself, which compelled the ambitious priest to exercise greater caution.

On Wolsey's disgrace in 1529, some writers say that Warham declined the offer of his former office of lord chancellor, while others assert that the king had determined that no churchman should hold the Great Seal. Indeed, the archbishop must have been then too old to desire such an addition to his responsibilities in times so dangerous. Attached as he was to the ancient system, and a supporter of the papal authority, he must have looked with an anxious eye on the king's proceedings; and it may be readily conceived how grating it must have been to his feelings when he was compelled in convocation to pass a grant with a preamble acknowledging the king 'to be the protector and, under God, the only supreme head of the Church and clergy of England.' His subsequent private protest against any statute that derogated from the authority of the pope shows how fortunate it was for him that the king's supremacy was not recognised by parliament till after his death. That event occurred on August 23, 1532, at St. Stephen's, near Canterbury, in the house of his relative, Archdeacon Warham. His remains were deposited in a chapel built by himself near the martyrdom in his cathedral.

His liberality during his life was evidenced by his poverty at his death, when, though he had filled the profitable office of chancellor for thirteen years, and had enjoyed the primacy for twenty-eight, he left barely sufficient to satisfy his creditors. On the approach of his decease he is said to have asked his steward how much money remained in his hands, and, on being told that he had but thirty pounds, to have cheerfully answered 'that was enough to last till he got to heaven.'

His zeal for the Church made him too great a persecutor of those who differed from him to leave his character quite free from blame. To the same cause is to be attributed his unavailing prohibition of Tyndal's Bible; and his tendency to superstition may be seen in his too easy credence in the pretended miracles of Elizabeth Barton, the Holy Maid of Kent. But, notwithstanding these drawbacks, it is impossible not to admire a man who in other respects passed through his public career with so much credit, and who, as an ecclesiastic, has so many claims on our respect.

The principal descriptions of the private life of the archbishop are derived from Erasmus (*Epist.* 138; *Ecclesiastes*), of whom he was one of the earliest English patrons, contributing towards his expenses when he came to England in 1509, and supporting him wholly here in the following year. (*Athen. Oxon.* ii. 738; *Godwin*, 133, 190; *Le Neve; Rapin; Lingard*, &c.)

WARINE (PRIOR OF LOCHES). The only mention made of 'Magister Guarinus,' prior of Loches in Touraine, is that his authentication appears to a royal charter to the monastery of Bonport, dated at Bellum Castrum de Rupe, on February 28, 1198, 9 Richard I., with the words 'tunc agentis vicem Cancellarii' added to his name. (*Monast.* vi. 1110; *Neustria Pia.* 897.) He probably died soon after, as Peter de Rupibus is called prior of Loches in a charter dated July 30, 1199, 1 John. (*Rot. Chart.* 10, 34.)

WARLEE, INGELARD DE, was of the clerical profession, and was procurator for the archdeacon of Worcester in the parliament of 35 Edward I. (*Rot. Parl.* i. 190, 341.) Sir T. D. Hardy has introduced him as keeper of the Great Seal on May 11, 1310, 3 Edward II., because on the resignation of the chancellor on that day the king delivered it to him to be kept in the wardrobe. He was then keeper of that department, in which, during any vacancy, the Seal was ordinarily deposited merely for safe custody. It so remained, on this occasion, only till the next day, when it was delivered to certain clerks of the Chancery, to perform the duties, and afterwards re-deposited there. Ingelard de Warlee continued keeper of the wardrobe till the eighth year of that reign. In 10 Edward II., on December 29, 1316, he was appointed a baron of the Exchequer, and he so continued till his death, which occurred in June 1318. There is an entry in the wardrobe accounts, that 'two pieces of Lucca cloth' were laid upon his body, buried in the church of St. Martin's-le-Grand. (*Archæologia*, xxvi. 340.)

WARNEVILLE, RALPH DE. Roger de Wendover (ii. 370) states that Ralph de Warneville, sacrist of Rouen and treasurer of York, was constituted chancellor of England in the year 1173; and Matthew

Paris repeats the account in the same words; but neither of them says whom he succeeded in the office, nor how long he retained it. Le Neve (319) inserts him among the treasurers of York on the authority of a similar passage in Matthew of Westminster, and places Richard Pudsey next in the list, on whom he says the treasurership was conferred by the king in 1189. Ralph de Diceto (567) is the only author who makes any addition to this announcement. He describes Ralph de Warneville as not altering in his advancement the simple course of living which he had adopted in his private life, and adds that he committed his duties in the Curia Regis to Walter de Constantiis, a canon of Rouen.

There are two charters in the 'Monasticon' (vi. 1067, 1106) bearing his attestation as chancellor, both dated at 'Juliam Bonam' (Lillebonne), but with nothing to indicate the year in which they were granted. It seems clear that he held the seals till the appointment of Geoffrey Plantagenet, the king's illegitimate son, in 1181. He afterwards became Archbishop of Lisieux. (*Robert de Monte.*)

WARWICK, EARL OF. *See* J. DE PLESSITIS.

WATH, MICHAEL DE, was of a Yorkshire family, and in 16 Edward II., 1322, was a surety for one of the adherents of the Earl of Lancaster. He is then described as 'clericus,' and two years afterwards is named in a commission to assist the Archbishop of York in removing foreign priests in the East Riding of that county. In June 1332, 6 Edward III., he was one of the tallagers there (*N. Fœdera*, ii. 574, 840), and was probably a clerk in the Chancery, which was often held at York; for he received the appointment of master of the Rolls on January 20, 1334, and was sworn in at the abbey of St. Mary at York.

He held this office little more than three years, surrendering it on April 28, 1337. It is remarkable that during that time he never held the Great Seal as the substitute of the chancellor, as was then the custom with masters of the Rolls. But he was subsequently appointed to that duty in conjunction with two associates, at the end of the year 1339; and several entries prove that he continued to act as one of the clerks of the Chancery in 1338 and 1340. (*Rot. Parl.* ii. 112.)

In the latter year he was one of the sufferers on the king's angry return from France, and, with some of his brother officers, was cast into prison for maladministration in his department. John de Stratford, Archbishop of Canterbury, remonstrating against his imprisonment as a clergyman, procured his release; but he does not again appear in connection with the Chancery, though he is named as one of the commissioners to enquire as to some complaints of the inhabitants of Frismerk in Yorkshire as late as 1347. (*Angl. Sac.* i. 20; *Barnes's Edward III.* 212, 217; *Rot. Parl.* ii. 187.)

WATSAND, ALAN DE, is called by Matthew Paris 'clericus regis.' He was raised to the bench about 1246, 30 Henry III., and sat there till his death in November or December 1257, up to which former month there are entries of payments for writs of assize to be taken before him. His name is often written Wassand. (*Dugdale's Orig.* 43; *Excerpt. e Rot. Fin.* ii. 6-219; *Abb. Placit.* 126.)

WATSON, WILLIAM HENRY, was born at Bamborough in 1796, and when only fifteen years old became a soldier, being the son of Captain John Watson of the 76th foot, upon whose early death the Duke of York gave his son a commission in the 1st royal dragoons in 1811. Raised the next year to a lieutenancy, he exchanged into the 6th dragoons, and shared in the glories of the Peninsular war, and in the crowning victory of Waterloo. His march into Paris with the allied army very shortly preceded his retirement from the service, as the peace which followed promised no active occupation.

He then determined to adopt the legal profession, and, entering Lincoln's Inn in 1817, he pursued the study so diligently that he soon made himself competent to commence business as a special pleader. He continued in this laborious branch of practice for a great number of years with continually increasing success, till at last in 1832 he felt it necessary both for his health and the prospect of advancement to be called to the bar. During the interval he published two books, one 'On Arbitration' in 1825, and the other on 'The Office and Duties of Sheriff' in 1827, the excellence and usefulness of which have been proved by their being frequently reprinted. Both on the Northern Circuit, which he joined, and in London, his previous reputation secured to him full employment, which increased so much that in 1843 he felt justified in accepting a silk gown. As a leader he was most successful by his hearty and forcible style of address; and by his friendly disposition and cordial *bonhomie* he was most popular among his companions on the circuit.

In the meantime he had entered parliament in 1841, and sat for Kinsale till 1847, and afterwards in 1854 for Hull, and continued its member till he was raised to the bench. That event did not occur till November 1856, when he was constituted a baron of the Exchequer. His judicial career was not of long duration. On the spring circuit of 1860 he had opened the commission at Welshpool on March 12, and had just concluded his charge to the grand jury, when he was seized with apoplexy, and very shortly after breathed his last.

He married first a sister of Sir William Armstrong, the inventor of the new artillery; and secondly Mary, the daughter of Anthony Capron, Esq. (who afterwards took the name of Hollist), of Lodsworth, near Petworth, in Sussex.

WAUTON, JOHN DE, by his marriage with Alice, the sister and heir of Odo de Dammartin, became possessed of lands in the counties of Surrey, Norfolk, and Suffolk. By a mandate in 1 Henry III. for the restoration of his estates, it would appear that he had been an adherent to the barons in the last years of King John, and so had lost them. His name ought scarcely to be included in the list of justices itinerant; for although, in 9 Henry III., 1225, he was one of those at first appointed for Surrey, another was put in his place, as he was not able to be present. He died about September 1230. (*Rot. Claus.* i. 324, ii. 37, 76, 83; *Excerpt. e Rot. Fin.* i. 202, 227, 256.)

WAUTON, SIMON DE (BISHOP OF NORWICH), was born at Wauton, or Walton Deyville, in Warwickshire. He was brought up to the clerical profession, to which, according to the fashion of the times, he united the study of the law. In 7 John he was the king's clerk or chaplain, and had a grant of the church of St. Andrew in Hastings, and in the two following years received letters of presentation to the churches of Slapton and Colered. (*Rot. Pat.* 61, 68, 75.)

In 30 Henry III., 1246, he was justice itinerant into the northern counties, and performed the same duty again in 1249 and 1250 in other parts of England. He was raised to the judicial bench in 1247, the Fine Rolls containing entries of payments for assizes to be taken before him of that date, which are regularly continued till May 1257, just before he was elected to the bishopric of Norwich; and he received the acknowledgment of fines till about the same period. (*Excerpt. e Rot. Fin.* ii. passim; *Abb. Placit.* 127, 132, 143; *Dugdale's Orig.* 43.)

In his circuits of 1253 and 1255 he stood at the head of his commissions, except that an abbot was placed for ornament before him in the last. On April 13, 1257, Robert de Briwes was ordered to be associated with Simon de Wauton, 'et sociis suis, justiciariis de Banco,' from which it may be conjectured that he was then at the head of the court. In the following August he was confirmed Bishop of Norwich, after which he does not appear to have acted on the legal bench. He presided over that see till his death, on January 2, 1265, and obtained the pope's permission to retain all his ecclesiastical preferments *in commendam*

for four years. (*Godwin*, 431; *Weever*, 700; *Le Neve*, 209.)

WAYNFLETE, WILLIAM (BISHOP OF WINCHESTER), took his name from the market town in Lincolnshire so called, where he was born. His father was Richard Patten of that place, and his mother was Margery, the daughter of Sir William Brereton, possessing considerable property in Cheshire, who held the post of governor of Caen in Normandy, and greatly distinguished himself in the wars with France. That he bore the name of Barbour also appears from a formal declaration made by Juliana Churchstile, that she was the heir of the bishop, being 'sole daughter of Robert Patten, brother and heir of Richard Patten, otherwise called Barbour of Waynflete, father of the bishop.' It will also be presently seen that the bishop himself at first used the name of Barbour.

Richard Patten, besides his two sons William and John (who became dean of Chichester), is said to have had a third, named Richard, who settled at Boslow in Derbyshire, and was the progenitor of the respectable line of the Patten family, which, removing into Lancashire, is now represented by John Wilson-Patten, Esq., of Bank Hall, one of the representatives of that county in parliament. According to his pedigree, the family is as old as the Conquest, was settled in Essex in 1119, removed to Waynflete in Lincolnshire in the reign of Edward III., and the prelate's father was the third in succession of those who lived there. But Dr. Chandler gives several reasons for doubting whether this Richard was a brother of William and John. William went to Wykeham's school at Winchester, and thence proceeded to Oxford, but to what college there is uncertain.

In April 1420 *William Barbor* is recorded in the Lincoln Registry as one of the unbeneficed acolytes; and in January of the following year, 1420-1, it is stated that '*William Barbor* became a subdeacon by the style of *William Waynflete* of Spalding.' In the following March he was ordained deacon by the latter name, and in January 1426 presbyter, on the title of the house of Spalding.

It was not long before he attracted the notice of Robert Fitz-Hugh, then archdeacon of Northampton, in the same diocese, and afterwards Bishop of London; for when that learned divine was appointed to go on a mission to Rome, ' William Waynflete in legibus bacallarius' was one of those designed to accompany him; and his letter of protection, which was to last for one year, was dated July 15, 1429. (*Acts Privy Council*, iii. 347.) In the same year his talents and acquirements, and the excellence of his character, gained him the appointment of master of Wykeham's school at Winchester, the scene of his early education. Several ecclesiastical preferments have been appropriated to him about this time, but there is considerable doubt whether he held any of them, as the name of Waynflete was not of uncommon occurrence, and some with his Christian name are clearly shown to have been different persons. It is certain, however, that Cardinal Beaufort conferred upon him the mastership and chantry of the hospital of St. Mary Magdalen, about a mile from Winchester. He was in possession in 1438, and continued to enjoy it till he himself was raised to the see.

When Waynflete had filled the office of master of Winchester School for about eleven years, and had acquired a high reputation for the diligence, judgment, and success with which he had performed his duties, King Henry, who had begun to found Eton College on the same model, paid a visit to Winchester for the purpose of personally inspecting the system. So satisfied was he with his examination that he resolved to give the mastership of his new school to Waynflete, who accordingly removed there in 1442 with five of the fellows and thirty-five of the scholars of Winchester to commence the seminary. On December 21, 1443, he was promoted to be provost of Eton.

The king regarded him with such especial favour that on the very day of his uncle Cardinal Beaufort's death, on April 11, 1447, he wrote to the church at Winchester to proceed immediately to a new election, with an urgent recommendation of his 'right trusty and well-beloved clerc and concelloure, Maister William Waynflete,' for their bishop; and on the same day he granted Waynflete the custody of the temporalities of the see. The pope's confirmation was given without delay, and the king himself honoured the new prelate's enthronisation with his presence on August 30, 1448.

In the contentions which then agitated England the bishop had a difficult course to steer; but while his devotion to his sovereign, to whom he was bound by the ties of loyalty and gratitude, was always firmly exhibited when his counsels were called for, in allaying the storms created by the insurrection of Jack Cade, the loss of the French acquisitions, and the first rising of Richard Duke of York, his mildness and prudent conduct secured him from that inveterate enmity which followed others who took so decided a part. Even after the first battle of St. Albans in 1455, and the assumption of power by the duke, apparently confirmed as it was by the growing imbecility of the king, the bishop remained unmolested; and when, on the king's recovery, the energetic conduct of the queen had for a time restored the royal ascendency, he was selected for the then onerous post of chancellor in the place of Bourchier, Archbishop of Canterbury, whose ministry was deemed of too timeserving a character. The Great Seal was placed in his hands on October 11, 1456, and he held it for nearly four years—a disastrous period, during which, though he at first effected a temporary accommodation between the contending parties, the country was distracted with the horrors of civil war, and it was soon evident that the contest could not be terminated but by the absolute ruin of one or the other. Disheartened at last by the reverses of the field, in perpetual anxiety by the doubtful event of each successive conflict, probably feeling that his services were misapplied in so bloody a controversy, and perhaps dissenting from the violent measures of his party, he resolved to retire. Accordingly on July 7, 1460, three days before the battle of Northampton, so fatal to the Lancastrians, he surrendered the Seal of the kingdom in the king's tent on the field. The same day a full pardon was granted to him for all offences which he might have previously committed; and the pious king, though defeated and a prisoner, cleared him from any imputation of disloyalty or lukewarmness in an affecting letter which he wrote to the pope in the following November, bearing 'ample testimony to the bishop's innocence, his meritorious services, and unblemished reputation.'

During this anxious period his friend Sir John Fastolf died, leaving him one of his executors. The 'Paston Correspondence' (i. 102) contains his instructions as to the execution of the will, which show that he was a man of business, and of a pious and liberal mind.

That King Edward duly appreciated the merits of Bishop Waynflete, and did not treat him with any harshness in consequence of his attachment to the fallen Henry, appears from the bishop's being appointed a trier of petitions in the first parliament of that reign (*Rot. Parl.* v. 461), and from the just decision made by the king in that parliament against the claims which had been raised by some of the bishop's tenants in Hampshire. These acts were followed by others of an equally generous character, till at last, in the eighth year of the reign, February 1, 1469, a full pardon was granted to him, with an introduction declaring his manifest good deserts, and that the king had admitted him into his special favour. Whatever part the bishop took in the following year, when King Henry was for a while restored, of which we have no clear account, it was overlooked by Edward on regaining the throne, and a new pardon released the bishop from any fears he might have entertained. During the remainder of Edward's reign, though he received frequent tokens of the king's goodwill towards him, he continued to enjoy the regard of the Lancastrian party, owing both to the mild virtues of his character, and the absence of intemperance on the one side and of servility on the other.

Shortly after the usurpation of Richard III., and before the murder of the princes in the Tower, Bishop Waynflete was obliged to assist in the reception of the king at Oxford, where the royal condescension and generosity seem to have made a favourable impression. It may be presumed, however, that the bishop, although the college which he founded was benefited by some royal grants, was no friend to the character of the usurper, and that he rejoiced greatly at the triumph of the Lancastrians in the accession of their representative. Henry VII. at once showed his regard to the prelate by confirming all the gifts which had been conferred on his college.

Of that college, where, after an interval of more than three centuries, his memory still survives and his virtues still are celebrated, it would be out of place to attempt more than a short account. So early was Waynflete impressed with the low state of learning at the universities, that he had no sooner been invested with the mitre than he commenced his exertions to improve the condition of indigent students. He obtained a royal licence on May 6, 1448, to found a hall at Oxford for the study of divinity and philosophy; and he lost no time in procuring adequate premises within the city, including Bostar Hall and Hare Hall, which he united under the name of St. Mary Magdalen Hall, of which the first president received possession on August 29 in the same year. Besides this officer, the foundation was to consist of fifty poor scholars, graduates, with a power to augment or diminish their numbers, and they had the right to use a common seal. The means of the hall were afterwards considerably increased by several royal and private benefactions. With these the bishop was about to enlarge the site of his establishment, when he obtained the king's consent on July 18, 1456, to convert the hall into a college. For this purpose he purchased the hospital of St. John the Baptist, without the eastern gate of the city, where the college is now situate. Its conversion and the erection of the new buildings were long retarded by the public distractions; but when tranquillity was restored he proceeded diligently in his work, receiving numerous donations of valuable endowments, which were made from the respect in which he was held, and the high admiration which his pious efforts awakened.

The edifice is one of the principal ornaments of the university, and is a lasting memorial of the taste as well as the munificence of the founder, who spared no expense in its erection. He lived to see the whole completed, and to find that the statutes he had prepared for its regulation practically answered the purposes he contemplated.

With the same desire of encouraging learning and piety in his native town, he erected there a school and chapel of handsome construction, which he also dedicated to St. Mary Magdalen, with a liberal endowment to the master.

The last scene of the venerable prelate's useful life was now approaching, and he piously prepared for its termination. His will was dated April 27, and he died on August 11, 1486, of a disease which, after a life of uninterrupted health, suddenly attacked him. He was buried at Winchester in a magnificent mausoleum which he had provided in his lifetime. It is difficult to speak too highly of his character, as there is scarcely a virtue which has not been attributed to him. (*Dr. Chandler's Life of the Bishop.*)

WEDDERBURN, ALEXANDER (LORD LOUGHBOROUGH, EARL OF ROSSLYN), is another example of a political chancellor, who, although he was gifted with great talents, and possessed many accomplishments and undoubted eloquence, failed to gain the respect of either party in the state, because he was 'everything by turns,' and his own interests and advancement seemed to prompt his various tergiversations. According to the common custom when a peerage is conferred, the descent of Alexander Wedderburn is traced from a family that held lands in the county of Berwick at the time of the Conquest. Then follow a succession of individuals noticed in various ways in Scottish history, till we arrive at his father, Peter Lord Chesterhall, eminent in the law, and advanced by that title in 1755 to be one of the senators of the college of justice, who married Janet, the daughter of Colonel Ogilvie.

He was born at Edinburgh on February 13, 1733, and commenced his education at a school at Dalkeith, finishing it at the university of Edinburgh, through which he passed with great distinction. He naturally selected the law as his profession, and applied himself so successfully to the study of civil law and municipal jurisprudence that he was admitted a member of the faculty of advocates in June 1754, being then only twenty-one. Before he took this step he had shown a strong inclination to the English bar by entering himself at the Inner Temple on May 8, 1753, and keeping his terms there. He was, however, persuaded to try his fortune at the Scottish bar, as his father's present position at it, and still more his elevation in 1755 to the Scottish bench, seemed to promise prosperous results. The early death of the new lord in the next year would have dissipated those hopes, had not the young man attained a certain eminence among his colleagues by his association with the literati of his country, and by his connection with the general assembly of the Church of Scotland. He had been long on intimate terms with Robertson, Adam Smith, and particularly with David Hume, whom he had lately successfully defended against an attack upon him in the general assembly. In that arena, too, he soon after strenuously opposed a censure upon Home for his tragedy of 'Douglas,' and upon all persons, lay and clerical, who attended the theatre. He had been a prominent member of the Poker Club, and of its successor the Select Society, formed for the discussion of questions of history, law, and ethics. In that society he had the honour of presiding on its first meeting in May 1754, numbering among his associates, besides the four eminent men just named, Hugh Blair, Sir David Dalrymple, Drs. Alexander Munro and John Hope, and other persons famous in the law and the Church. He had taken a leading part in projecting the first 'Edinburgh Review,' to which he was during its short existence both editor and contributor. With the prestige arising from all these causes, Wedderburn still continued at the Scottish bar till about a year after his father's death, when his connection with it was wholly terminated by an incident in the court, originating in a premeditated insult to Mr. Lockhart, then the dean of faculty, or chief of the advocates.

Lockhart was so notorious for treating the junior advocates with rudeness and insult that four of them agreed together that the first who was the subject of his vituperation should publicly resent it. The chance fell upon Wedderburn, whom in an argument he called a 'presumptuous boy;' and Wedderburn in his reply was not wanting in the attack that had been planned. Among other passages, he said, 'I do not say that the learned dean is capable of *reasoning*, but if *tears* would have answered his purpose, I am sure tears would not have been wanting.' On Lockhart's look of vengeance, he unwarrantably added, 'I care little, my lords, for what may be said or done by a man who has been disgraced in his person and dishonoured in his bed,' alluding to some circumstances in the dean's private life. The lord president very properly stopped him, and said that 'this was language unbecoming an advocate and a gentleman,' on which the irate junior exclaimed that 'his lordship had said that as a judge which he could not justify as a gentleman.' The indignant court at once called upon him to retract and apologise, on pain of deprivation, when Wedderburn deliberately took off his gown, and, laying it on the bar, said, 'My lords, I neither retract nor apologise, but I will save you the trouble of deprivation; there is my gown, and I will never wear it more:—virtute me involvo.' Then, bowing to the judges, he quitted the court.

He immediately left Scotland, to which he never returned, and was called to the English bar four months afterwards, on November 25, 1757. During the first months after his arrival in London he applied himself, under the instruction of the elder Sheridan and Macklin, to the study of English pronunciation, with such effect that the peculiarities of the Scottish accent were almost entirely eradicated. Through this theatrical connection he obtained the early business he had; but among his Scotch friends was the Earl of Bute, who had belonged to the 'Select Society' in Edinburgh, and under his patronage he became member of the burghs of Ayr, &c., in the first parliament of George III. In allusion to his histrionic alliances and senatorial efforts, Churchill introduced him into the 'Rosciad,' in a most severe passage, inserted in 1763, showing that even at that early period those unfortunate characteristics were visible which were attributed to him throughout his career.

Becoming a member of a club of literary natives of Scotland which met at the British coffee-house in Cockspur Street, to which many Englishmen were soon admitted, his success was gradually forwarded by the influence of his associates. But still his business was so small that lawyers were astonished at his boldness in accepting a silk gown soon after his patron Lord Bute became prime minister. He received a patent of precedence in Hilary Term 1763. He now selected the Northern Circuit, from which its leader Sir Fletcher Norton had just retired, and in London attached himself to the Court of Chancery, where, and in the House of Lords upon Scotch appeals, he achieved great success. He was remarkable for the clearness of his statements and for the subtilty of his arguments, and he particularly shone in the great Douglas cause, his speech in which was universally admired.

In the House of Commons, to which he was returned to the new parliament of 1768 as member for Richmond, he displayed similar efficiency. After Lord Bute's retirement, Wedderburn, from being one of the 'king's friends,' assumed the character of a 'patriot,' strenuously defending Wilkes, and taking the part of the Americans. For his conduct with regard to the former he felt himself in March 1769 obliged to vacate his seat for Richmond, which had been given to him as a tory, but was returned as a whig in the following January for Bishop's Castle in Shropshire. This seat he owed to the gratitude of Lord Clive for his eloquent and earnest defence of him, which his lordship further exhibited by a munificent present of a mansion at Mitcham. His secession from the court party was hailed by the oppositionists with a complimentary dinner, and his subsequent efforts on that side were rewarded by the freedom of the city of London and the plaudits of Lord Chatham. Wedderburn continued his patriotic exhibitions during the first year of Lord North's ministry, personally pitting himself against that nobleman, and exposing with great eloquence and power all his measures. Towards the end, however, of that year he was evidently laying himself out for a junction with the minister; and to the infinite disgust of all, but to the surprise of few, on the meeting of parliament on January 25, 1771, he was gazetted as solicitor-general, bound to support all he had so recently and earnestly resisted. Well might Junius say of him, 'As for Wedderburn, there is something about him which even treachery cannot trust.' Yet, notwithstanding this decided opinion and various similar expressions by this extraordinary writer with regard to Wedderburn, there were some who attributed to him the authorship of Junius's Letters, a notion which could have no foundation except in the elegance and force of his style, and which no one who investigates the subject can possibly support. Braving the sneers of the opposition bench, he soon, by his admirable tact and insinuating eloquence, recovered his ascendency in the house.

In 1774 he pronounced the tremendous invective against Franklin before the privy council, which increased the exasperation of the Americans, and assisted in stirring up the civil war, in the progress of which he gave the most unflinching support to the ministers, with undaunted front defending them from the attacks of the opposition. Upon that speech and its consequences the following lines were produced :—

Sarcastic Sawney, full of spite and hate,
On modest Franklin pour'd his venal prate ;
The calm philosopher, without reply
Withdrew—and gave his country liberty.

But he could not yet make himself happy in his position. He fancied that his services were insufficiently appreciated, and that he was neglected by Lord North; yet when he was offered the chief barony of the Exchequer at the end of 1777, he refused it unless it was accompanied by 'a place in the legislature,' and talked of taking an 'opportunity of extricating' himself from office. As ministers had some experience of his dexterity in shifting the scene, means were taken to quiet his impatience, and in the following June he became attorney-general. He occupied this post for just two years, and on June 14, 1780, his longing for promotion and peerage was gratified by the appointment of chief justice of the Common Pleas and by being created Baron Loughborough.

During the whole period of his holding office he had been a most zealous and effective supporter of the ministerial measures, charming the house by his sarcasm and his wit, as well as leading it by the force and eloquence of his advocacy. Professionally he continued to distinguish himself by his industry and management. His speech on the prosecution of the Duchess of Kingston is an admired specimen of his forensic excellence, remarkable for clear and close argument and lucid arrangement. In his last act as attorney-general he has the credit of being the first to put an effectual stop to the No Popery riots, by the advice he gave to the privy council that the military might act without regard to the Riot Act.

His first public appearance after his appointment was to preside in the next month at the trials of the rioters, when his charge to the grand jury, while it displayed his usual eloquence, is blamed as being more like the inflammatory address of an advocate than the calm direction of a judge. During the twelve years that he held the office he preserved its dignity and acquired a well-deserved reputation for his impartial administration of justice, as well as for his patience and courtesy to those who practised under or came before him. But he had not much credit as a lawyer, and his decisions are not greatly regarded. Not content with the arena of Westminster Hall and the circuits, he acted as chairman of the quarter sessions in Yorkshire, where he had property; and it is said that the Court of King's Bench maliciously rejoiced when it had occasion to overturn his decisions.

But his aspirations had a higher aim than the presidency of his court. He looked with longing to the chancellor's seat, but despaired of it while Lord Thurlow was patronised by the king. Though he supported Lord North during the tottering remainder of his ministry, it was principally by his silent vote, and when Lord Rockingham came in he could not expect to be advanced. But under Lord Shelburne's administration he renewed his intrigues, and when by the aid of his exertions in parliament that ministry was forced to resign, he hoped that the coalition which followed, and which he had the credit of advising, would give him his expected reward. He was, however, disappointed; the Seal was put in commission, and he was obliged to content himself with being the first commissioner, a post which he filled during the short existence of that unpopular administration, from April 9 to December 13, 1783. When the coalitionists were indignantly dismissed, Lord Loughborough exerted himself strenuously in aid of the factious proceedings in the lower house, till, by the dissolution of the parliament, Mr. Pitt was firmly established as prime minister. He had now become a whig and a Foxite, and was considered the leader of the party in the House of Lords. For the next five years nothing occurred to give him hopes of a chance, but with the illness of the king in 1788 his prospects brightened in the view of the regency. His first most unwise and unconstitutional advice to the Prince of Wales was that the government should at once be assumed by him as of right; but his royal highness was most fortunately influenced by more moderate counsels, and the bill was allowed to proceed, Lord Loughborough and his party vainly endeavouring to mitigate its more objectionable restrictions. On the discovery of Lord Thurlow's double-dealing, the transfer of the Great Seal seemed secure, when the king's sudden recovery reduced the whigs and their politic adherent to their former unpromising position. Lord Loughborough continued from this time to act steadily with the whig party, and even so late as February 1792 supported Lord Porchester's motion censuring Mr. Pitt and his colleagues for their conduct with regard to Russia. (*Parl. Hist.* xxvii. 896.) On Lord Thurlow's dismissal from his office in the following June, and the Seal being put again in commission, his lordship's hopes began to revive; and advantage being taken of a breach in the whig ranks, in consequence of Mr. Fox's opinions and conduct in reference to the French Revolution, negotiations were opened by the ministers which resulted in his joining the seceders and accepting the bauble he had so long ardently desired. He became lord chancellor on January 28, 1793, and kept his seat till April 14, 1801, a month after the termination of Mr. Pitt's first administration.

He was now once more called upon necessarily to advocate many measures which he had before opposed; but, being joined by some others of the alarmist party, he boldly performed the task, notwithstanding the vituperation of the Foxites. He stimulated the national excitement caused by the affairs in France; supported, if he did not originate, the stringent laws that were enacted; and advised those prosecutions for constructive treason against Hardy, Horne Tooke, and others, which were so ignominiously defeated. During the eight years of his chancellorship he kept outwardly on good terms with Mr. Pitt; but towards the end of them he privately intrigued for that minister's dismissal. Although he had formerly professed himself a warm friend to Catholic Emancipation, he now secretly and artfully encouraged the scruples which the king entertained with regard to the coronation oath, hoping that he should thus certainly secure himself in the possession of his office in the event of a change. The change took place; but to Lord Loughborough's infinite chagrin and disappointment he was himself superseded. The king was too well aware of his previous intrigues to have any confidence in him, and was glad to have the opportunity of availing himself of the services of Lord Eldon, as an adviser whom he esteemed to be both zealous and honest.

The tenacity to office of the discarded chancellor was indecently exhibited after his dismissal by his attending unsummoned the meetings of the cabinet, until Mr. Addington was obliged to give him a formal notice that his presence was not required. His hope of restoration appeared from his constant presence at court, from his taking a house in the neighbourhood of Windsor in order to enjoy frequent access to his majesty, and also from following the royal movements to Weymouth. But it all availed him nothing; the king, though courteous and kind to his fallen minister, never really respected him; and when, after four years of these fruitless attempts, death terminated his career, the king's real opinion of him is said to have been expressed by a very strong exclamation. Lord Loughborough was the first chancellor who benefited by the act passed in 1799, by which that officer became entitled to an annuity of 4000*l*. His lordship was also solaced by an advance in the peerage, being created Earl of Rosslyn, with a special remainder to the heirs male of his sister, the widow of Sir Henry Erskine, in whose favour he had already received in 1795 a new patent of the barony of Loughborough.

Whatever opinions may be formed of his political conduct, his judicial career was free from objection. Though not regarded as very deep or learned in his profession, nor having the credit of introducing any improvements in the practice of the court, he had considerable reputation as an equity judge. His decrees were well considered, and were seldom overturned; they were always delivered in forcible and elegant language, and were remarkable for the perspicuity of the argument by which they were enforced. He used his ecclesiastical patronage with discrimination and kindness. Once when he pronounced a judgment in the House of Lords, which reduced a virtuous clergyman from affluence to penury, he immediately walked to the bar, and, addressing the unfortunate man, said, 'As a judge I have decided against you: your virtues are not unknown to me: may I beg your acceptance of this presentation to a vacant living which I happen fortunately to have at my disposal?' It was worth 600*l.* a year. (*B. Montagu's Bacon*, xvi. cclii. note e.)

His bearing towards the bar was courteous and gentlemanlike; and to those members of it who assisted the profession by their learning, but who failed of success in practice, he was a kind and liberal patron. To the suitors he was a favourite judge, for, while they admired the patience with which he heard their cases, and the clearness of statement by which he proved that he understood all the circumstances, he generally contrived, when he had to decide against any suitor, to say something to soften his disappointment and to soothe his feelings. His only contribution to legal literature was a 'Treatise on English Prisons,' containing many useful suggestions for their improvement, which he published in the year he became chancellor.

Though his lordship's public career cannot be regarded with more honour or respect by the present generation than it was by his contemporaries, yet in his private life there was much to extenuate his failings. In his family he was amiable and affectionate; to his friends, and he had many, he was constant and true; and to his opponents, who varied with his political changes, he bore no malice. He was munificent in his charities at the French Revolution. He gave De Barretin, the ex-chancellor, a house to live in, and allowed him 600*l.* a year till the peace of Amiens. He loved literature and the society of literary men, encouraging and assisting those who needed help. He procured the pensions that Dr. Johnson and Shenstone enjoyed; he recommended Gibbon to the place he held under government, and Maurice to a post in the British Museum; and he overcame the objection made by the benchers of Lincoln's Inn to allow Sir James Mackintosh to deliver his lectures in their hall. In all his manners and actions he was a complete contrast to Thurlow, who, though hating his rival, was candid enough, on hearing of his death, to allow that 'he was a gentleman.'

The earl died suddenly at his house at Baylis, between Slough and Salt Hill, on January 2, 1805. His remains were deposited in the crypt of St. Paul's. Though married twice, he left no issue. His first wife was Betty Ann, daughter and heir of John Dawson, of Morley in Yorkshire. His second wife was Charlotte, daughter of William, first Viscount Courtenay. His titles and estates devolved upon his nephew, Sir James St. Clair Erskine, Bart., by whose grandson they are now enjoyed. (*Lives by Townsend, Lord Campbell*, &c.)

WELLEFORD, GEOFFREY DE, was a clerk of the Chancery in 35 Edward I. (*Parl. Writs*, i. 191.) When Walter Reginald, Bishop of Worcester, went to the king at Berwick, on December 12, 1310, 4 Edward II., the Great Seal was committed to Adam de Osgodby, the keeper of the Rolls, to be kept under the seals of Robert de Bardelby and Geoffrey de Welleford. They retained it till the chancellor's return, a week afterwards. He appears again, under similar circumstances, on December 1, 1319. The last record of his acting as a clerk of the Chancery is on May 20, 1321, when he was present at the delivery of the Seal.

Of his private history little that is certain remains, and it is doubtful whether he was connected with the family of the under-mentioned Ralph de Welleford. He had a grant, in 6 Edward II., of a messuage in the parish of St. Dunstan's, near the New Temple, at an annual rent of forty shillings. (*Abb. Rot. Orig.* i. 193.)

WELLEFORD, RALPH DE, in 9 Richard and 1 John, was among the justiciers before whom fines were levied (*Hunter's Preface*); and in 3 John he was one of the justicier itinerant into Gloucestershire. (*Rot. Cancell.* 42.)

He seems to have got into disgrace about 6 John, as he then paid ten marks and a Norway hawk for having seisin of his lands, of which he had been disseised by the king's precept, for taking away the corn 'de terra Veile,' which was reserved for the king. Geoffrey Fitz-Peter, Earl of Essex, also, in the same year, became his surety for another hawk, in which he was fined for taking the corn of Dorsington contrary to the king's prohibition. Both these entries are in Warwickshire, where he had some land at Sturton; and he is mentioned as one of the pledges for the fine which Alicia Countess of Warwick agreed to pay for her widowhood, to the extent of 200*l.*, with a further responsibility, in conjunction with Reginald Basset, for 27*l.* and ten palfreys. (*Rot. de Finibus*, 220, 259, 276-7; *Abb. Placit.* 100.)

WELLES, WILLIAM DE, held either part or the whole of a knight's fee in Grimsby in Lincolnshire, of the honor of Richmond. He was one of the adherents of the barons at the end of John's reign, and still continued so at the commencement of that of Henry III., for his land was then given to Fulco de Oyri. Soon afterwards, however, it was restored to him on returning to obedience; and in 5 Henry III. he was employed as one of the escheators of his county. He was next appointed a justice itinerant there in 9 Henry III. (*Rot. Claus.* i. 309–471, ii. 77; *Rot. de Fin.* 588), after which his name is not mentioned till his death in June 1261, 45 Henry III., when his son and heir Thomas (by his wife Emma) did homage for the lands he held of the king. (*Excerpt. e Rot. Fin.* ii. 353.) His descendants were summoned to parliament from 1299 till 1503, when the barony fell into abeyance. (*Baronage,* ii. 10; *Nicolas's Synopsis.*)

WELLS, HUGH DE (BISHOP OF LINCOLN), so called from the place of his birth, was a brother of the next-mentioned Josceline de Wells. He is sometimes corruptly called Wallis. The Rot. de Oblatis of 1 John shows that he held an office in the Camera Regis, as it records several payments made to him there. In the next year he and Hugh de Bobi were appointed custodes of the see of Lincoln, then vacant. (*Rot. Chart.* 99, 154.) His abilities soon attracted such notice that in 5 John he was sent into Normandy on the king's service, a good and secure ship being ordered for the voyage. (*Rot. de Liberat.* 71, 81.) In this mandate he is styled 'clericus noster,' so that he was then one of the king's chaplains; and in April of the same year, 1204, he was preferred to the dignity of archdeacon of Wells. Several other benefices were afterwards conferred upon him, and grants were made to him of the manors of Ceddra and Axebrige in Somersetshire, and of the custody of the lands and heirs of Geoffrey de Evercrez and Richard Cotel. (*Le Neve; Rot. Chart.* 127.) Ultimately, on December 12, 1209, he was elevated to the see of Lincoln. At this point he lost the royal favour, by disobeying the king's commands to obtain confirmation from the Archbishop of Rouen. Instead of doing this, he proceeded to Langton, Archbishop of Canterbury, and received that rite from him, whereupon the king seized the temporalities of the bishopric, and detained them for five years. Roger de Wendover adds to this that he was at that time chancellor, and that the king immediately removed him from his office, and delivered the Great Seal to Walter de Grey. This relation, however, is altogether erroneous, because Walter de Grey had purchased the chancellorship in October 1205, held it at this very time, and continued to hold it, with one short interval, till July 1214. Matthew Paris, following Roger de Wendover, also calls him chancellor when he was raised to the episcopal bench; and Dugdale, Philipot, and Spelman all unite in giving him that title. Dugdale quotes as his authority a charter of 6 John; but there is no charter which so distinguishes him. There are, indeed, many charters of that year which are subscribed 'Data per manum Hugh de Welln. archid. Wellens.;' but this merely shows that he was the official instrument for the chancellor of the time; and three or four others were employed in similar duty at the same period. On the roll there are several charters that were so signed by him and John de Brancestre jointly, as early as 2 John; and his separate authentication of charters appears under two successive chancellors, Archbishop Hubert and Walter de Grey, from July, 5 John, 1203, till April, 10 John, 1209. This long period of nearly five years, during which he was in constant official attendance on the court, accounts for the mistake of the historians; but the antiquary ought to have known that no one record ever describes him as chancellor. Sir T. D. Hardy introduces him as keeper of the Seal under the two above-named chancellors; but he seems rather, as others also who performed the same duty, to have been an officer of the Treasury of the Exchequer, where the Seal was usually deposited, or a clerk of the Chancery, to whom the formal duty of affixing it on these occasions was delegated.

It is worthy of remark that in 6 John he was one of the justiciers at Worcester before whom fines were levied, described by his ecclesiastical title only, which would not have been the case had he been either chancellor or vice-chancellor. So also in 9 and 11 John, in the latter of which years he is styled 'Lincolniæ Electus.'

To avoid the king's fury, the bishop had fled from England, but returned with his brethren after the removal of the interdict. Disgusted with the tyranny of the king, he joined with the barons who resisted it; and, as his reward, was in his turn excommunicated by the pope, who now supported the monarch whom he had forgiven. He could only obtain absolution by a fine of one thousand marks to the pontiff, and a bribe of one hundred to the legate. He had the gratification of being present on the glorious day of Runnymede, as Wendover slyly adds '*quasi* ex parte regis.'

After the accession of Henry III. he was at the head of the justices itinerant for the counties of Lincoln, Nottingham, and Derby, in 1219 and 1226. In 1225 he was employed in an embassy to France in conjunction with the Bishop of London.

Having held the bishopric for nearly a quarter of a century, he died on February 7, 1234. Roger de Wendover calls him 'omnium virorum religiosorum inimicus,' meaning only that he was ' an enemy to all monks.' The hospital which he and his brother, Bishop Josceline, built at Wells, and his legacy of five thousand marks for pious uses, prove that the words do not admit of a more general application. He was buried in his own cathedral. (*Godwin,*

288; *R. de Wendover*, iii. 228-302, iv. 324; *Trivetus*, 181.)

WELLS, JOSCELINE DE (BISHOP OF BATH AND WELLS), brother of the above Hugh de Wells, was born and educated at Wells, from which place, as was common among the clergy, he took his name, and was a canon of the church there. By a liberate (97) of 5 John, 1203-4, it appears that he had been one of the custodes of the bishopric of Lincoln during its vacancy, from which it may be inferred that he held some office in the Exchequer or the Camera Regis. His name is also recorded among the justiciers before whom fines were levied at Westminster, and also in the country when the king was present. Sir T. D. Hardy introduces him at this time as keeper of the Great Seal, on the authority of a charter of 6 John given under his hand; but it may be questioned whether this fact is of itself sufficient evidence to warrant such a presumption, as others were performing the same duty at the same time, and as neither in the charter nor in the contempory fines is he distinguished by that designation. His name appears in the same manner to numerous other charters between February and September 1205, during the greatest part of which period Hubert, Archbishop of Canterbury, was chancellor, for whom, as an officer of the Chancery or the Exchequer, he probably took his turn of duty in affixing the Seal.

About this period he had various benefices conferred upon him (*Rot. Chart.* 119, 142, 161); and on May 28, 1206, he was consecrated Bishop of Bath and Wells, or rather Bishop of Bath and Glastonbury, for it was not till his time that the contest with the monks of Glastonbury was terminated, and the union of Bath and Wells permanently established. He, with the other bishops, was compelled to absent himself from England during the five years which the interdict lasted, but on its removal he returned to his see. For the remainder of John's reign he attached himself to his sovereign, and was present at the signature of Magna Charta. Under Henry III. he continued to enjoy the royal favour. His signature to many documents shows his regular attendance on the court, and his name appears at the head of the justices itinerant for the counties of Cornwall, Somerset, Devonshire, and Dorset, in the third year of that reign. (*Rot. Claus.* i. 387.)

He presided over his see for thirty-seven years, during which he not only united with his brother, Hugh, Bishop of Lincoln, in founding the hospital of St. John in his native place, but rebuilt the beautiful cathedral there, and made several liberal endowments to his church. He died on November 9, 1242, and was buried in the choir of his cathedral under a tomb he had erected during his life, which was ornamented with a flat brazen figure of himself, being one of the earliest recorded instances of that species of memorial in England. (*Godwin*, 371; *Archæol. Journal*, i. 199.)

WELLS, SIMON DE. *See* S. FITZ-ROBERT.

WELSON, WILLIAM (BISHOP OF THETFORD), is known also by the names of Galsagus and De Bellofago, with their varieties of Beaufo and Belfagus. He was of a noble house, and was chaplain to William I. He held the chancellorship probably between 1083-1085, after Maurice. There is a charter (*Monast*. iii. 216) confirming the grant of Yvo Tailboys of the manor of Spalding to St. Nicholas of Angiers, to which the attestation of 'William the Chancellor' is appended, which must have been dated after 1080, as another of the witnesses is William, Bishop of Durham, who was not elected till November in that year. At Christmas 1085 he received the bishopric of Thetford, and he was one of the most munificent benefactors of the see, by enriching it with many of the manors and other lands which he received from the royal bounty.

He died about 1091, leaving his family very rich. One of his sons was Richard de Bellofago, archdeacon of Norwich in 1107, and another, Ralph de Bellofago, sheriff of Norfolk and Suffolk in the reign of Henry I. (*Godwin*, 426; *Blomefield's Norwich*, ii. 465, 531, 638.)

WENSLEYDALE, LORD. *See* J. PARKE.

WESTBURY, LORD. *See* R. BETHELL.

WESTBURY, WILLIAM (named probably from Westbury in Wiltshire, as he endowed a chantry there with lands in that place, and possessed the manors of Bores and Lady Court and other property in that county), was one of those who refused a serjeant's coif, and was called before the parliament and compelled to take it in 1417. (*Rot. Parl.* iv. 107.) For ten years previous to this he had been a practiser in the courts, and in another ten years he was raised to the bench. He was placed in the Court of King's Bench on February 6, 1426, 4 Henry VI., and in the same year had a licence to take recognitions wherever he might be. (*Cal. Rot. Pat.* 273.)

In consequence of riots in Norwich and Norfolk in 21 Henry VI., Sir John Fortescue the chief justice and he were sent there to try the delinquents. They made their report to the council on March 13, 1443, and in the following May Westbury received 10*l.* for his services. (*Acts Privy Council*, v. 247, 268.) He continued on the bench certainly till the twenty-third year of the reign, but did not die till 28 Henry VI., when he is described as

'William Westbury, senior.' The William Westbury who succeeded Bishop Waynflete in 1448 was probably his son. (*Cal. Inq.* p. m. iv. 241, 303; *Cal. Rot. Pat.* 291.)

WESTBY, BARTHOLOMEW, was a member of the Middle Temple, for the complimentary address to the three members of that house who were called serjeants in 19 Henry VII. was delivered by him. Three years before, on May 12, 1501, he had been raised to the bench of the Exchequer as second baron, and he received a new patent on the accession of Henry VIII. In the third year of that reign he and Sir Robert Southwell were appointed general surveyors and approvers of the king's manors, &c. In 1514 he was made one of the 'almess' knights of Windsor, but did not on that account vacate his seat in the Exchequer, no new second baron being named till 1521. (*Dugdale's Orig.* 113; *Ashmole's Order of the Garter,* 95.)

WESTCOTE, JOHN DE, was located in Sussex, where he had property in the township of Leominster, and obtained a licence that the abbot of Battle might grant him the manor of Anstigh for the term of his life. He was an advocate in the courts, and his name occurs in the Year Books in the early part of the reign of Edward II. In the fourth year he was not only one of the three justices of assize appointed for Essex and Hertford, and the four neighbouring counties, but was also in a commission in Hampshire and Wiltshire. He is not named in any judicial employment later than 8 Edward II., and his death occurred between that date and June in the thirteenth year, when his executors were commanded to bring all proceedings before him into the Exchequer. (*Abb. Rot. Orig.* i. 198; *Parl. Writs,* ii. p. ii. 1601; *Rot. Parl.* i. 300.)

WESTMINSTER, EDWARD DE, the son of Odo the goldsmith, having in 24 Henry III., 1240, purchased the office of fusor, or melter, of the Exchequer, for twelve marks of silver which he paid to Odo, son of John, who was proceeding to the Holy Land, soon established his character so well that in 30 Henry III. he and the abbot of Westminster were appointed treasurers of a new Exchequer the king had founded for the receipt of moneys for the fabric of the church at Westminster, or, as they are called in another record, custodes of the operations there. (*Madox,* ii. 3, 310; *Excerpt. e Rot. Fin.* i. 449.) In 1248 Madox introduces him among the barons sitting at the Exchequer, and in the same year the seal of the office of chancellor of the Exchequer was placed in his custody. In 37 Henry III. he and Philip Luvel were directed by the king to remove all his gold and silver and jewels from Westminster and the New Temple to the Tower of London, but to leave the regalia at Westminster; and two years afterwards the same two had the city of London placed in their hands on occasion of a transgression of the assize, connected no doubt with the city's refusal to be tallaged. So late as 48 Henry III. he is described as a baron of the Exchequer in the attestation of a charter; but he was dead before 51 Henry III., when his son Odo had possession of his office of fusor, and received permission to appoint a deputy for two years, while he pursued his studies. (*Madox,* i. 270, 712; ii. 52, 248, 265, 310, 318, 319.)

WESTON, RICHARD, whose genealogy is traced as high as Rainaldus de Balliole, in Normandy, lord of Weston, Berton, Broton, and Newton, in Staffordshire, in the reign of the Conqueror, was the second son of John Weston, of Lichfield, who was fourth son of John Weston, of Rugeley, by Cecilia, sister of Ralph Nevil, Earl of Westmoreland. This grandfather is elsewhere described as William Weston, of Prested Hall in Essex, and of London, mercer. Having been entered of the Middle Temple, he arrived at the rank of reader in autumn 1554. His name appears occasionally in Dyer's Reports as an advocate during the reign of Queen Mary, who on November 20, 1557, made him her solicitor-general. From this office Queen Elizabeth called him to the degree of the coif by a special patent on January 24, 1559, and appointed him one of her serjeants on the 13th of the next month. This was followed by his promotion to the bench on October 16 as a judge of the Common Pleas, where he sat for nearly thirteen years (*Dugdale's Orig.* 48, 215), dying on July 6, 1572, in possession of Sprenes, in Roxwell, and other considerable property in Essex.

His brother, Dr. Robert Weston, dean of Wells, was dean of the Arches, and was raised in 1567 to the chancellorship of Ireland, which he enjoyed till his death in May 1573.

The judge was thrice married. His first wife was Wiburga, daughter of Thomas Catesby, of Seaton in Northamptonshire, and widow of Richard Jenour, of Dunmow in Essex; his second was Margaret, the daughter of Eustace Burneby; and his third was Elizabeth, daughter of Thomas Lovel, of Astwell in Northamptonshire, the latter having had two previous husbands (as he had two previous wives), namely, Anthony Cave and John Newdigate. His son Hieronymus, by his first wife, was the father of Sir Richard Weston, who was made chancellor of the Exchequer by James I., and was created by Charles I. Lord Weston of Neyland in 1628, from which he was advanced to the earldom of Portland in 1633, filling the office of lord high treasurer till his death. These titles expired in 1688 by the death of the fourth earl without issue. (*Erdeswick's Staffordsh.* 136; *Morant's Essex,* i. 136; *Nichols's Leicestersh.* 370; *Collins's Peerage,* iv. 401.)

WESTON, JAMES, was the nephew of the above Richard Weston, being the third son of James Weston of Lichfield (the judge's brother), who died in 1589. His mother, Margeria, daughter of Humfrey Lowe of Lichfield, died in 1587. He was then very young; but three years after his father's death he was entered of the Inner Temple, where, having been called to the bar in 1600, he attained the post of reader in autumn 1618. He was summoned to take the degree of serjeant on March 19, 1631, evidently for the purpose of being made a baron of the Exchequer, to which office he was appointed on the 16th of the following May (*Rymer,* xix. 256, 348), and knighted. His career as a judge was of very short duration, for in the vacation between Michaelmas 1633 and Hilary 1634 he died in his chamber in the Inner Temple, being described by Croke (*Car.* 339) as a 'wise and learned man, and of courage.'

By his wife, Maria, daughter of William Weston, Esq., of Kent, he had an only daughter. (*Erdeswick's Staffordsh.* 136.)

WESTON, RICHARD, of the same family as both the above, was the son of Ralph Weston of Rugeley.

Like his relative, he pursued his legal studies in the Inner Temple, where he was elected reader in 1629. On May 25, 1632, he became a judge on the Welsh Circuit; and on Sir James Weston's death he was appointed, no doubt by the interest of Lord Weston, to succeed him as baron of the Exchequer, his patent being dated April 30, 1634. (*Rymer,* xix. 433, 528, 607.) He thereupon received the honour of knighthood. In his argument in favour of ship-money, which was delivered four years after, though it evinced some learning, was more technical than conclusive. (*State Trials,* iii. 1065.) He was consequently one of the six judges who were impeached by the Long Parliament in 1641, and though he was not brought to trial, he was, by a vote of the Commons on October 24, 1645, disabled from being a judge 'as though he was dead.' (*Whitelocke,* 47, 181.)

He lived till March 18, 1651, leaving by his wife, Katherine, a son, Sir Richard, who joined the army of Charles I., and was slain in the Isle of Man. (*Erdeswick's Staffordsh.* 136.)

WESTON, RICHARD, of no known connection with the above, entered at Corpus Christi College, Cambridge, in 1639, but took no degree. He is described in his admission to Gray's Inn in 1642 as the son and heir apparent of Edward Weston of Hackney, and having been called to the bar in 1649, he arrived at the post of reader in 1676. His arguments in court are reported by Sir T. Raymond from the year 1662, but it was not till 1677 that he attained the degree of the coif. He was made king's serjeant in 1678, and thereupon knighted; and on February 7, 1680, he was raised to the bench of the Exchequer.

In the summer assizes after his appointment he had occasion to show his energy and independence as a judge by publicly checking the insolent forwardness of Sir George Jeffreys, at Kingston, in browbeating, as his manner was, the other side in their examination of witnesses. On being told by the judge, after some words had passed between them, to hold his tongue, Jeffreys declared he was not treated as a counsellor, being curbed in the management of his brief. 'Ha!' returned the baron, 'since the king has thrust his favours upon you in making you chief justice of Chester, you think to run down everybody; if you think yourself aggrieved, make your complaint; here's nobody cares for it.' (*Woolrych's Jeffreys,* 65.) This rebuff shows plainly how well the bench and the bar understood Jeffreys' character. It is not improbable that the malice it engendered in Jeffreys' mind was the real cause of the complaint made against Baron Weston in the next parliament. In December the Commons voted an impeachment against him upon the extraordinary accusation that certain expressions used by him in his charge to the grand jury at Kingston on the same circuit were in derogation of the rights and privileges of parliament. He had inveighed against Calvin and Zuinglius and their disciples for their fanatical and restless spirit, and had said that 'now they were amusing us with fears, and nothing would serve them but a parliament;' adding, 'for my part I know no representative of the nation but the king: all power centres in him. It is true, he does intrust it with his ministers, but he is the sole representative; and, i'faith, he has wisdom enough to intrust it no more in these men who have given us such late examples of their wisdom and faithfulness.' The dissolution of the parliament, however, took place before the impeachment was brought in, and the baron died before the next parliament had proceeded to business. As a high prerogative man, he was, according to Roger North (*Examen,* 566), hated bitterly by the opposition, and was of course a great favourite with that writer, who relates of him that, while the other judges looked grave and solemn at this terrible sound of an impeachment, he was as gay and debonair as at a wedding, and was only sorry that he had not an opportunity of talking in the House of Commons, to have had his full scope of arguing his own case. Even Burnet (i. 485) speaks well of his courage in granting an Habeas Corpus to Sheridan, who had been committed by the House of Commons. His judicial career was a very short one, as he died on March 23, 1681, at his house in Chancery Lane.

Roger North gives some insight into his personal character. He describes him 'a learned man, not only in the common law, but in the civil and imperial law, as also in history and humanity in general; and would often in his charges shine with his learning and wit.'

He married Frances, second daughter of Sir George Marwood, of Little Bushby, Bart.

WESTWODE, ROGER, was made second baron of the Exchequer on March 1, 1403, 4 Henry IV.; and he was re-appointed at the commencement of the two next reigns. No other fact is known of him.

WEYLAND, THOMAS DE, was a younger son of the next-mentioned William de Weyland, who possessed large estates in the county of Norfolk. His mother was Marsilia, who afterwards married John Brandon. (*Spelman's Reliq.* 140.) He had attained sufficient eminence in 56 Henry III., 1272, to be associated with Roger de Seyton as a justice itinerant into the counties of Essex and Hertford. He was constituted a judge of the Court of Common Pleas as early as Michaelmas, 2 Edward I., some fines having been levied before him at that date. From this he was promoted to be chief justice of the same court in 6 Edward I., 1278; and fines continued to be levied before him till 17 Edward I., 1280 (*Dugdale's Orig.* 44; *Madox*, ii. 66), at the close of which year charges were made against him and the rest of the judges of bribery and corruption in their office. All of them were convicted, except two, and were subjected to large fines. Against Thomas de Weyland, however, a more heinous crime was imputed—that of instigating his servants to commit murder, and then screening them from punishment. After his apprehension he escaped from custody, and, disguising himself, obtained admission as a novice among the friars minors at St. Edmund's Bury. On the discovery of his retreat, the sanctuary was respected for the forty days allowed by the law, after which the introduction of provisions into the convent was prohibited. The friars, not inclined to submit to starvation, soon retired; and the fallen judge, finding himself deserted, was compelled to deliver himself up to the ministers of justice, and was conveyed to the Tower. The king's council gave him the option to stand his trial, to be imprisoned for life, or to abjure the realm. To the latter he was entitled by virtue of his sanctuary, and he chose it. The ceremony consisted of his walking barefoot and bareheaded, with a crucifix in his hand, from his prison to the sea-side, and being placed in the vessel provided for his transportation. All his property, both real and personal, stated to have been of the value of 100,000 marks, was forfeited to the crown. (*Lingard*, iii.; *Abb. Rot. Orig.* i. 61–4.) His wife, Margery de Morse, had a grant of her clothes and jewels, and also of 60*l.* out of his lands.

From entries on the Parliament Rolls, it may be inferred that he transferred to the abbot of St. Edmund's Bury two of his manors as a consideration for the asylum he sought there, and that several others of his manors were saved from the general wreck, by means of his wife and children being co-feoffees of them with him. (*Rot. Parl.* i. 48, 51, 66.)

No account of his future career is given, nor is the date of his death mentioned. He left three children, Thomas, Richard, and Alienor; and the family is now represented by John Weyland, Esq., of Woodrising in Norfolk.

WEYLAND, WILLIAM DE, was the son of Herbert de Weyland, and Beatrix his wife. From September 1261, 45 Henry III., he was escheator south of Trent, and there is one instance of a mandate addressed to him in that character on April 24, 1265. In 1272 his name is inserted in the commission directed to the justices itinerant to the county of Leicester; and, inasmuch as the roll of that year contains an entry of a payment made in September for an assize to be held before him for another county (Suffolk), there is very little doubt that he was then appointed a justicier at Westminster; the more especially as he was certainly a judge of the Common Pleas in the first year of Edward I., his name then appearing on the acknowledgment of a fine. There is no subsequent mention of him as a judge. By his wife, Marsilia, he left three sons, Richard, Nicholas, and the above-mentioned Thomas. (*Excerpt. e Rot. Fin.* 360–485, 580; *Dugdale's Orig.* 44.)

WHIDDON, JOHN, whose family was long established at Chagford in Devonshire, was the eldest son of John Whiddon of that place by a daughter of — Rugg. His school of law was the Inner Temple, where he was elected reader in 1528 and 1536, three years after which he filled the office of treasurer. He was nominated as a serjeant at the close of Henry VIII.'s reign, but the death of that monarch occurring before he was instituted, the solemnity took place under a new writ, in the first week after that event. On Mary's succession to the throne he was one of the first judges she appointed, his patent as a judge of the Queen's Bench being dated October 4, 1553; and he received the honour of knighthood on January 27, 1555.)

He is noticed as introducing the new practice of riding to Westminster Hall on a horse or gelding, instead of a mule as was the previous custom. (*Dugdale's Orig.* 38, 118, 164, 170; *Machyn*, 342.) In April 1557, when Thomas Stafford, having surprised and taken Scarborough Castle, was defeated by the Earl of Westmoreland, Judge Whiddon was sent down to try the prisoners, and is said to have been clothed with the commission of a general, giving him authority to raise forces to quell any insurrection that might happen; and he is even stated to have sat on the bench in armour on that occasion, from the apprehensions then entertained of a rising.

His patent was renewed on Queen Elizabeth's accession, and during nearly eighteen years of her reign he continued to exercise his judicial duties. His death occurred on January 27, 1575, at Chagford, where he was buried. He married twice. By his first wife, Anne, daughter of Sir William Hollis, he had one daughter; by his second, Elizabeth, daughter and heir of William Shilston, he had a large family of six sons and seven daughters, whose posterity long flourished in his native place. (*Prince's Worthies*.)

WHITCHESTER, ROGER DE, so named from that place in Northumberland, was probably the son of Robert de Whitchester, who was sheriff of that county in 5 and 6 Henry III. He was raised to the bench at least as early as October 9, 1252, 36 Henry III., that being the date of the first entry of payments made for assizes to be held before him. These entries continue till August 1258, 42 Henry III.; and he went the circuit from 1254 to 1257. Dugdale describes him as a canon of St. Paul's. (*Excerpt. e Rot. Fin.* ii. 141–286; *Dugdale's Orig.* 21, 43.)

WHITELOCKE, JAMES, was the youngest of twin sons of Richard Whitelocke, who belonged to an ancient family seated at the Beeches, near Oakingham, Berkshire, but, being a younger son, became a merchant in London, and died at Bordeaux. His mother was Joan, the daughter of John Colte, of Little Munden, Herts, and widow of a London merchant named Brockhurst, and, being early left a widow, brought up her children carefully, and sent James, who was born on November 23, 1570, to Merchant Taylors' School, whence he was elected a scholar of St. John's College, Oxford, in 1588, and eventually became a fellow. He took the degree of Bachelor of Civil Law in 1594, and held his fellowship till June 1598, residing principally at the university. During the same period, however, he kept his terms at the Middle Temple (having previously spent a year of preparation at New Inn), and was called to the bar in 1600. Not only did his college appoint him steward of their lands, but he soon obtained an honourable and profitable practice; and, going the Oxford Circuit, he was elected recorder of Woodstock in 1606, for which borough he was returned member in 1609. In the same year he was made steward and counsel of Eton College, and in 1610 of Westminster College also. In parliament he supported the argument that the king had not the power to set impositions on merchants' goods without the assent of parliament, whereat the king took great offence, of which he soon after felt the consequence. On May 18, 1613, he was summoned before the council and committed to the Fleet, and kept in confinement till June 13. He himself states that the cause of his commitment was that, in a cause between the College of Westminster and the Bishop of London, he had been taunted and checked by the lord chancellor (Ellesmere), who in another cause, between two members of the College of Arms, when Whitelocke had occasion to argue in opposition to the power of the Earl Marshal's Court to hear and decide it, inveighed against him in open court, and threatened to certify to the king that he had spoken against the royal prerogative. The privy council books, however, found the complaint wholly on an opinion Whitelocke had given to Sir Robert Mansell against the validity of a royal commission relating to the navy.

His 'simply giving a private opinion as a barrister,' as the charge is thus represented, is almost too incredible even for those arbitrary times. From the whole tenor of the Attorney-General Bacon's speech (and weak enough it was) it would rather appear that Whitelocke had urged in court an elaborate argument, contending that some commission which the king had issued was not strictly according to law—an argument which any counsel might assuredly use, whether by private opinion or in open court, without blame, if he did it in a decent and unobtrusive manner. Whitelocke made his submission and was discharged from custody, the king taking 'special and good liking' of the sentence from Tacitus with which he concluded his submission: 'Tibi summum rerum imperium Dii dederunt, nobis obedientiæ gloria relicta est.' His son, in a speech to the Long Parliament, publicly and without contradiction attributed his father's imprisonment to 'what he said and did in a former parliament.' (*Bacon's Works* [Montagu], vii. 381; *State Trials*, ii. 705.)

That this incident had no injurious effect on his character is evidenced by the fact that in the short parliament that met in April 1614, to be dissolved in June, he was not only returned for Woodstock, but for Corfe Castle also. In this short session he was one of those appointed to conduct the conference with the Lords concerning impositions; and immediately after the dissolution this most ridiculous farce was enacted. All the conductors were called before the council and made to deliver up the arguments they had prepared for the discussion, to be burnt. This was done, not only in the presence of the council, but of the king himself, whom Whitelocke says he saw 'throughe an open place in the hangings about the bignes of the palm of ons hand.' The court cloud still hovered over him, and prevented him from being elected recorder in 1618; but in autumn 1619 he was chosen reader in the Middle Temple, and took for his subject the Statute 21 Henry VIII. c. 13, his reading upon which is now preserved in MS. in the Ashmolean Museum at Oxford. He again represented Woodstock in James's third parliament, in 1621.

In the meantime his political offences had been atoned for or overlooked. On June 18, 1620, he was called serjeant, and on October 29 he was knighted and made chief justice of Chester. He was appointed a judge of the King's Bench on October 18, 1624, a few months before King James's death.

His patent was renewed by Charles, and, as junior judge, he had in the first year to adjourn Michaelmas Term to Reading on account of the plague then raging in London. The state of that city, and the terror of those who approached it, are depicted by his son (*Mem.* 2) in his description of the judge going from his house in Buckinghamshire, and arriving early the next morning at Hyde Park Corner, ' where he and his retinue dined on the ground, with such meat and drink as they brought in the coach with them, and afterwards he drove fast through the streets, which were empty of people and overgrown with grass, to Westminster Hall, where the officers were ready, and the judge and his company went strait to the King's Bench, adjourned the court, returned to his coach, and drove away presently out of town.' He retained his place till his death; and in the seven years that intervened the two great cases of Habeas Corpus came before the court. For the first judgment, which was against those who refused to contribute to the loan, he and the other judges gave their reasons to the Lords in the next parliament (*State Trials*, iii. 161), which led to the Petition of Right. On the second, when the court refused to discharge the members imprisoned for their conduct in the previous parliament, without sureties for their good behaviour, and afterwards, upon their refusing to plead, fined and imprisoned them, the judges were called to account by the Long Parliament. On a motion that reparation should be made out of their estates, Judge Whitelocke, who had been long dead, on the representation of his son, confirmed by several other members, that he was of the same opinion with Judge Croke, was excused from censure. (*Whitelocke*, 39.)

Judge Whitelocke died on June 22, 1632, at his house at Fawley in Bucks, and was buried there under a stately monument erected by his son. Though an advocate for the rights of the people, he was a conscientious supporter of the king's prerogative. King Charles said of him 'that he was a stout, wise, and learned man, and one who knew what belongs to uphold magistrates and magistracy in their dignity,' and even designed him for the place of lord chief baron. All authorities allow him to have been an able lawyer and a deeply learned man. Of his skill in the Latin tongue he gave a remarkable proof when sitting as judge of assize at Oxford. Some foreigners of distinction coming into court while he was addressing the grand jury, 'he repeated the heads of his charge to them in good and elegant Latin, and thereby informed the strangers,' his son adds, ' of the ability of our judges, and the course of our proceedings in law and justice.' (*Whitelocke*, 11, 17.) He was an excellent genealogist, and was not only deeply versed in Jewish history, but conversant with that of his own country, being one of the early members of the Society of Antiquaries in the reign of Elizabeth, to which he contributed papers on the 'Antiquity of Heralds,' of 'Places for the Students of the Law,' and of 'Lawful Combats in England.'

His wife was Elizabeth, eldest daughter of Edward Bulstrode, of Bulstrode in Upton, Esq., and Cecilia, daughter of Sir John Croke, of Chilton, so that he was closely connected with both the Judges Croke. Besides two daughters, he had only one surviving son, the next-mentioned Bulstrode Whitelocke.

He kept a record of the principal events of his career, under the title of 'Liber Famelicus,' now published by the Camden Society, under the excellent editorship of the late John Bruce, Esq., F.S.A., to which I am indebted for many of the above facts.

WHITELOCKE, BULSTRODE, was the only son of the above Sir James Whitelocke, and was born on August 6, 1605, in Fleet Street, at the house of the eminent lawyer Sir George Croke, the uncle of his mother, and was christened with his mother's maiden name, she being Elizabeth, daughter of Edward Bulstrode, Esq., and sister of the reporter. He received his early education at Merchant Taylors' School, and was entered in 1620 as a gentleman commoner at St. John's College, Oxford. From Dr.

(afterwards Archbishop) Laud, the then president, who was the intimate friend of his father, he received much kindness and attention. Soon after Laud's promotion to the see of St. David's he left the university without taking a degree, and, having been admitted as a student at the Middle Temple, he was called to the bar in Michaelmas Term 1626. At Christmas 1628 he was chosen Master of the Revels by his brother Templars, and was becomingly proud on receiving a frolicsome fee, and a prophecy of future greatness, from Attorney-General Noy, when he attended that officer on a matter arising out of these Christmas revels; and on the four inns of court joining together in 1633 in performing a masque before the king and queen, he was united with Mr. Edward Hyde (afterwards Earl of Clarendon) to act for the Middle Temple in the committee of preparation. This probably was the commencement of the intimacy which the earl records as existing between him and Whitelocke, of whom he always speaks with kindness; and to the reminiscences of that friendship Whitelocke was not improbably indebted for the impunity he experienced on the restoration of Charles II. The inclination of both of them at that time was to the popular party, each desiring to give what assistance he could to remove the grievances that pressed hard upon the people.

Whitelocke's first public display in politics was at the quarter sessions at Oxford in 1635, when in his charge to the grand jury he ventured some allusions to the power of the temporal courts over ecclesiastical matters, which had begun to be questioned. He was engaged by the country gentlemen to defend their forest liberties and privileges, which were attacked; and he was advised with in the defence which Hampden so nobly maintained against ship-money. These evidences of his opinions resulted in his being returned as member for Marlow to the Long Parliament in November 1640. In one of the earliest debates he took occasion to make a spirited defence of his father, who was charged as being one of the judges who had refused to bail Selden and his fellow-prisoners, and succeeded in exonerating his father's memory from the imputation. He was chosen chairman of the committee appointed to prepare the impeachment and arrange the evidence against the Earl of Strafford, and at the trial had the charge of the last seven articles. The unfortunate earl gave Whitelocke the credit of having used him like a gentleman; and Whitelocke seems evidently impressed, if not with the earl's innocence, with his eloquent defence and his whole conduct before his accusers and judges. (*State Trials*, iii. 14, 38.) In the debate on the militia Whitelocke made a compromising speech; but on the passing of the bill he accepted the deputy lieutenancy of two counties, Buckingham and Oxford; and in the great question of taking up arms he argued forcibly against commencing a civil war, but concluded by voting for its adoption. Actively engaged in his county for the parliament, and commanding a 'gallant company of his neighbours,' he experienced the usual consequences. When the royal troops marched towards London, his house at Fawley Court became the quarters of a regiment of horse, who in the spirit of destruction despoiled it of all that was valuable. He was with the army opposed to the king at Brentford in November, and in the January following was one of the commissioners appointed to treat with his majesty for peace at Oxford.

This negotiation failing, Whitelocke in the next year repeated his endeavours, in a speech recommending a renewal of pacific overtures, which was followed in November 1644 by a second commission to Oxford, partly English and partly Scotch, authorised merely to take certain propositions of the parliament and to obtain the king's answer, but not to treat with him concerning them. Whitelocke details an interesting conversation which the king had privately with him and Mr. Holles at a complimentary visit they paid to the Earl of Lindsey, in which they were gratified with the royal acknowledgment of the sincerity of their wish to put an end to the unhappy dissensions. The propositions were such that the king could not with honour accede to them; but by his answer he suggested that persons should be named on both sides to discuss the various subjects and conclude a treaty. It was arranged that this conference should take place at Uxbridge, where the commissioners, of whom Whitelocke was one, accordingly met on January 29, 1645; but the same fate attended it. After quarrelling with obstinacy on both sides, upon subjects of Church government and the settlement of the militia, the treaty was broken off on February 22.

During the intervals between these several negotiations Whitelocke had the courage to refuse to serve on the committee appointed to manage the charges against his early instructor and friend Archbishop Laud, and the house had the grace to admit his excuse. He was a member of the Assembly of Divines, and both there and in parliament he spoke against the opinion that the government of the Church by presbyteries was *Jure Divino*. In 1644 he was made attorney of the duchy of Lancaster by the parliament; and in the next month he and Serjeant Maynard were placed in the awkward position of being called upon by the Lord General Essex and the Scots to advise whether Cromwell, of whom they began to be jealous, could be proceeded against as an incendiary. The counsel given by the two lawyers was such that the charge was deferred; and Cromwell, to whom this incident was soon reported, was of course pleased with the two advisers, and set himself to work to countercheck his enemies. This he effectually accomplished by the Self-Denying Ordinance, which resulted in the resignation of Essex. Whitelocke made a strong speech against the ordinance, but in the end, as his manner was, voted for it.

In April 1645 he was appointed governor of Henley-on-Thames and of the fort of Phillis Court, with a garrison of 300 foot and a troop of horse; and in July he and Mr. Holles had to defend themselves against a violent attempt of the independent party to fix a treasonable charge upon them for their communication with the king at Oxford. They succeeded, however, in obtaining a full acquittal by the house, with a permission to prosecute their accuser, Lord Savile. On the termination of the civil war Whitelocke resumed his forensic duties, and was so successful that on the circuit he was retained in almost every cause. Nor was his practice confined to the common law courts, but extended to the Chancery, the House of Lords, and also the Court of Wards till it was abolished in the beginning of 1646. To the suppression of that court he gave his aid in parliament, and was otherwise serviceable in that assembly, being commonly named on all committees on foreign affairs. In May 1647 he advised and spoke against disbanding the army, though the party to which he was attached had proposed the measure. This of course disposed Cromwell more strongly in his favour, and saved him from being included in the attack made by General Fairfax and the officers against eleven of his colleagues, and from the consequences to which it led.

To his high standing in his profession, to his industrious labours in parliament, and perhaps more than all to the favour of the general, and to the opinion which Cromwell had formed of his accommodating disposition, he owed his elevation to the important position to which he was next raised. On March 15, 1648, the two houses concurred in appointing him to be one of the four commissioners of the Great Seal for one year; and in October he was named by the parliament a serjeant-at-law and king's serjeant. The latter appointments were, however, deferred in order that as lord commissioner he might swear in the other new serjeants. This he did on the 18th of the next month, having three days before sworn in Chief Baron Wilde. His speeches on both these occasions, which he has preserved in his Memorials, are long and laborious dissertations on the antiquity of the two courts and the dignity and duties of the officers. He was evidently fond of these antiquarian displays, for he reports two others in 1649—one on the appointment of new judges; and the other addressed to the House of Commons on a motion to exclude lawyers from parliament; and a third, still more elaborate, in 1650, historically vindicating the laws of England, in support of the act which directed all legal proceedings to be in the English tongue.

The commissioners were soon interrupted in their judicial proceedings at Westminster by Pride's Purge, when, in order to avoid the tumult, they were obliged to sit in the Middle Temple Hall. This was followed by various conferences which Cromwell had with Whitelocke and his brother commissioner Widdrington, with the pretended object of settling the kingdom; while at the same time he was making active preparations in the House of Commons for bringing the king to trial. The two commissioners determined to refuse their countenance to the measure, and, on being sent for, escaped together to Whitelocke's house in the country, till the Commons had passed the ordinance for the trial without the concurrence of the Lords. They then returned to their duties, and shortly afterwards they obeyed an ordinance, made by the same mutilated authority, to adjourn Hilary Term, that it might not interfere with the solemnity of the trial.

The bloody deed accomplished, the functions of the four commissioners ceased. The House of Lords was next abolished, and Whitelocke, though he spoke against it, drew up the ordinance for the purpose. Whitelocke justified his accepting the Great Seal under the new government by a speech in which, acknowledging the parliament as the only existing authority, he maintained the absolute necessity that the place should be filled, in order that 'right and justice' should be done to men. He was therefore sworn in, with L'Isle and Keeble for his colleagues. He accepted a seat in the Council of State also, and was appointed high steward and keeper of Greenwich Park, an office which he exchanged for that of constable of Windsor Castle and keeper of the forest. He also was made high steward and recorder of Oxford, and keeper of the library and medals at St. James's.

Cromwell was named lord general in June 1650; and in September in that and the following year he won two great victories, the first over the Scots at Dunbar, and the second over the king's army at Worcester. On the latter occasion Whitelocke was one of the four members deputed by the house to convey its congratulations, and was rewarded by Cromwell with a horse and two prisoners, to whom Whitelocke immediately gave their liberty, and passed them home to Scotland. After this defeat of the royalists, Cromwell began to feel his way, how far he was likely to succeed in attaining absolute authority, the object of his present aspirations. To this end he called a conference to consider the settlement of the kingdom. The general opinion was in favour of a mixture of monarchical government, which accorded with Cromwell's wishes; but when, on the question in whom the power should be placed, Whitelocke and others suggested one of the sons of the late king, the meeting was dissolved, with no other result than a discovery of the inclinations of those who composed it. Some months afterwards (in November 1652) Cromwell again broached the subject, and in a curious conversation sounded Whitelocke as to his assuming the title of king; and pressed for his opinion as to the best means to obviate the existing difficulties and dangers. The recommendation he received from Whitelocke—that he should apply to Charles, and, by a private treaty for his restoration, in which the rights and liberties of the people should be maintained, and proper limitations placed on the monarchical power, secure to the nation all they had been fighting for, and to himself, his family, and friends, not only impunity for the past, but riches and honours as his reward—he professed to be worthy of consideration; and they parted. From this time Whitelocke says Cromwell altered his carriage towards him, and ceased to advise with him intimately. The general had before been displeased with Whitelocke for his 'non-compliance with his pleasure in some things, and particularly in some Chancery causes,' and was suspected of an attempt to get him out of the way, by appointing him chief commissioner in Ireland, which he refused.

Whitelocke's opposition to the dissolution of the parliament confirmed Cromwell's distrust in him, but did not prevent the violent dismissal of that assembly in April 1653. In June, Cromwell, who now assumed the whole power, called a sort of council of 120 persons, afterwards nicknamed the Barebone's Parliament. To this assembly Whitelocke was not summoned, and by an early vote the Court of Chancery was ordered to be taken away. The ordinance was however suspended before completion, and never came into operation, so that the existing commissioners still preserved some influence in the state. The plans which Cromwell had formed he was aware were obnoxious to Whitelocke, whom therefore he was desirous of sending out of the way, in order that no obstacle might be raised to the attainment of his ulterior designs. This could only be safely effected by an appointment to some honourable trust which would temporarily exile Whitelocke from England. The pseudo parliament accordingly, by Cromwell's dictation, named him ambassador to the Queen of Sweden, an office which, however distasteful on many accounts, Whitelocke deemed it prudent not to refuse, conscious of the power of the general, and doubtful of the consequences of resistance. (*Burton's Diary*, i.) He sailed on November 6, 1653, and began his voyage gracefully, by releasing a Dutch vessel which he took, with all her cargo, to the poor skipper, who would have been ruined by their detention and loss. He was absent from England till the 30th of the following June, and succeeded in effecting a treaty of amity with Queen Christina, the last public act that she transacted before her abdication. Both by her and Prince Charles Gustavus, who succeeded her, Whitelocke was treated with the greatest distinction and respect. He was honoured with her order of Amarantha, and on all occasions was admitted to private and familiar conferences. In his voyage out, as well on his return, he kept a daily journal, which is most interesting in reference to the description of the country through which he passed, his manner of travelling, and the detail of his receptions, the progress of his negotiations, the conversations which he had with the queen and her ministers, particularly the Chancellor Oxenstiern, and his tenaciousness with the latter as to all forms of ceremony, lest the honour and dignity of the Commonwealth should be compromised. This Journal is more minute as to personal matters than his Memorials, and, bating a rather copious sprinkling of vanity and ostentation, impresses the reader with a good opinion of his piety and judgment in the ordering of his household, and his abilities in diplomacy. This Journal was not published till near a century after the author's death.

During Whitelocke's eight months' absence the little parliament had resigned its power into the hands of Cromwell, who was immediately inaugurated protector of the three kingdoms. A new commission for the custody of the Great Seal was issued in April 1654, in which Whitelocke (though absent) was the first named, with his old associate Widdrington and his later one L'Isle. On his return to England he gave an account of his embassy to Cromwell and his council. Consenting to act under the new government, he was sworn into his office on July 14, and was soon after made one of the commissioners of the Exchequer. Such was his popularity at that time that in the parliament which was summoned by Cromwell he was elected by three several constituencies, the county of Bucks, the town of Bedford, and the city of Oxford, while his son James was returned for the latter county. The parliament was opened on September 4 in great state, when Whitelocke carried the purse before the protector, and two days after he made a second recital of his negotiation in Sweden to the assembly, and not only received public thanks from the speaker, but also a vote of 2000*l*. for his services. This sum was not however paid to him till the vote was renewed in February 1657. Cromwell dissolved this parliament on December 31, as not sufficiently compliant with his views. Looking with jealousy upon Whitelocke, whose ascendency in the house he thought too great, and whose inclinations against his government he suspected, he soon found an opportunity of removing him from office. He caused an ordinance to be made by the council for new regulations of the Court of Chancery, which were so objectionable both in matter and form that Whitelocke and his colleague Widdrington declined to adopt them. They were accordingly deprived of the Seal on June 6, 1655.

Being thus dismissed from the office which he had held for above six years, he resumed for a short time his practice at the bar; but in the next month he was made commissioner of the Treasury, with the same salary he had lost. He was subsequently appointed on the committee for trade, and also one of the commissioners to negotiate with the Swedish ambassador, with whom a treaty was concluded on July 17, 1656. In the next parliament, which met in the following September, he was again chosen for the county of Bucks; and upon the illness of Sir Thomas Widdrington, the speaker, he was elected to supply his place till his recovery, three weeks after. The important question of the settlement of the nation soon after engaged the house, and, considering the sentiments professed by Whitelocke, it is surprising that he was named chairman of the committee appointed to confer with Cromwell on the subject, and still more so that he should endeavour to induce the protector to take the title of king, and urge arguments against his pretended scruples. The army having remonstrated, Cromwell refused the monarchical title, but accepted a new instrument of government confirming to him the title of lord protector, and empowering him to declare his successor, and to nominate seventy members of the 'other house,' that being the modest name under which an intended House of Lords was designated. A solemn inauguration followed in June 1657, in which Whitelocke took a prominent part, and new commissions were issued for all the offices of state. Dissatisfied with politics, Whitelocke soon after sought for the provostship of Eton, then vacant, but was disappointed in his application. He was however consoled by being created one of the lords of Cromwell's 'other house,' in preparation for the meeting of parliament in January 1658. The jealousy of the Commons of that 'other house' caused a dissolution in the course of a fortnight, and no doubt had its effect in disinclining Whitelocke to accept the title of viscount, with which Oliver wished in the following August to distinguish him. Cromwell's death took place on the 3rd of the next month, and his son Richard was proclaimed his successor.

Whitelocke was confirmed in his place in the Treasury by the new protector (4 *Report Pub. Rec., App.* 198), who on January 22, 1659, replaced him in his former position as first commissioner of the Great Seal, which he retained for less than four months. At the termination of Richard's short reign, and the restoration of the Long Parliament, he was again deprived of it on May 14, and of course lost also his shortlived peerage, resuming his seat in the House of Commons. He was however placed on the Council of State and voted its president; and when the subsequent dispute with the army occurred, and the Long Parliament was a second time dismissed, he was nominated one of the Committee of Safety, which, after some hesitation, he was induced to undertake. One of the first acts of that committee was to appoint Whitelocke sole keeper of the Great Seal on November 1; and on the 5th he received a commission to raise a new regiment of horse to oppose General Monk, who had declared himself in favour of the discarded parliament. When that parliament was again restored, at the end of December, Whitelocke, apprehensive of his being sent to the Tower for acting on the Committee of Safety, concealed himself in the country, leaving the Great Seal with his wife to be delivered to the speaker. He remained in retirement till the final dissolution of that parliament by its own act on March 16, 1660, nor did he venture to offer himself as a candidate for the Convention that succeeded it. He does not again mention himself in his Memorials of the time, which terminate with Charles's solemn entry into London on May 29.

Great indeed must have been Whitelocke's perplexity in the various changes of the last year; and the conduct he pursued demonstrates by too conclusive evidence his utter want of principle. The Protector Richard's entrusted keeper of the Seal, he became a member of the Council of State of the party that dethroned him; and when that party was in turn dismissed by the army he again changed sides, and acted in the Committee of Safety and as keeper of the Seal; and, to crown all, though the professed object throughout the various changes was the settlement of the Commonwealth 'without a king,' yet he proposed to General Fleetwood to go over to Charles and offer him the crown; not from any loyal feeling, but merely, as he himself acknowledged, to forestall Monk in his supposed intentions, and to secure impunity for the past.

It is not surprising, therefore, that many who had seen him acting in high stations in every revolution since the king's death, always adhering to the side that was uppermost, should have deemed him a person so obnoxious as to be properly excepted from the act of pardon and oblivion passed at the Restoration. But, though his enemies were bitter, his friends were strong and numerous. His undoubted merits and ability pleaded for him, and particularly his moderation when in power stood him in great stead; and consideration for his numerous family united with the rest to preserve him, with some difficulty and by a small majority, from the ruin that threatened him. He no doubt owed much to his old friend Hyde, now lord chancellor, who accounts for Whitelocke's fluctuating conduct by the weakness of his character. In his domestic relations he was kind, amiable, and good-humoured, and was evidently much beloved by his family; as a lawyer, if not deep, he was well read and intelligent; his practice at the bar was consequently very extensive, and his decisions on the bench were uncomplained of; as a scholar the learned Selden's frequent letters to him would be sufficient, without other evidences from his speeches and writings, to prove him erudite in historical and classical literature; and the manner in which he performed the duties of the various employments in which he was engaged shows that, with whatever motive he entered on them, he exerted himself strenuously to effect their object. His real deficiency was the want of moral courage, and his great weakness was vanity. The sentiments of mankind with regard to him are a mixture of affection and contempt, acquitting him of all the harsh feelings attributed to the leading opponents of the monarchy, but convicting him of aiding, by his respectability, in their success. His character is ably summed up by Clarendon, who says 'he bowed his knees to Baal, and so swerved from his allegiance, but with less rancour and malice than other men; he never led, but followed; and was rather carried away with the torrent than swam with the stream; and failed through those infirmities, which less than a general defection and a prosperous rebellion could never have discovered.'

He is said to have had an interview with the king, when the merry monarch good-humouredly told him to go into the country, and not to trouble himself with state affairs, but to take care of his wife and sixteen children. He could not expect any better encouragement, and he wisely followed the advice. He lived fifteen years after the Restoration, and dying in his retirement at Chilton Park in Wiltshire, on January 28, 1676, he was buried at Fawley in Bucks, where his family property was situate.

He was thrice married. His first wife was Rebecca, daughter of Thomas Bennet, Esq., an alderman of London; his second was Frances, daughter of Lord Willoughby of Parham; and his third, a widow named Wilson, the daughter of — Carleton, Esq., who survived him. He had children by each, but none of his male descendants remain. (*Whitelocke's Memorials, and his Embassy to Sweden*, ed. Henry Reeve; *Lord Clarendon's Life*, &c.)

WHITTINGTON, THOMAS, of the ancient family of that name long seated at Pauntley in Gloucestershire, was grand-nephew of Sir Richard Whittington, the famous lord mayor of London, and son of Sir Guy Whittington, who was high sheriff of the county in 1428 and 1434. He himself filled the same office in 1475; but beyond his appointment as second baron of the Exchequer, on February 3, 1481, 20 Edward IV., the published records of the law are wholly silent about him. He was not, however, removed from his place under Edward V.; but immediately on the accession of Richard III. Brian Roucliffe was constituted second baron in his place, the patent being dated June 26, 1483, the second day of that usurper's reign. He lived several years afterwards, his will being dated in 1490.

By his marriage with Margaret, daughter and heir of John Edwards, 'famosus apprenticius in lege peritus,' he became possessed of the manor of Rodmarton in Gloucestershire, and other large estates, which devolved on his only daughter, Maud, who married William Wye, of Leppiet in that county. (*Ex inf. of the Rev. Samuel Lysons.*)

WICHINGHAM, WILLIAM DE, of Wichingham in Norfolk, was probably the son of William de Wichingham, M.P. for Norwich in the reign of Edward II. He is first mentioned as an advocate in 21 Edward III. at the assizes, but not till seven years after in the court at Westminster, he having in the meantime been employed as a justice to fix the wages of labourers in his native county. His name appears as a justice of assize from 34 Edward III., and two years afterwards he was created a king's serjeant. His elevation to the bench as a justice of the Common Pleas took place on October 29, 1365, 39 Edward III.; and he continued to act in that court till the end of the reign, but was not re-appointed on the accession of Richard II. Spelman (*Icenia*, 151) calls him 'clarissimus nominis illius jurisconsultus.' (*Rot. Parl.* ii. 455, iii. 4; *Dugdale's Orig.* 43.)

WICHINTON, HENRY DE, is inserted by Dugdale as a justicier before whom a fine was levied at Westminster in 9 Richard, 1197–8; but Mr. Hunter's list notices his name as occurring only in the first three years of the reign of John.

In 8 Richard I. he was discharged from the sum of sixty marks which he had fined for the custody and marriage of the daughter of Philip de Niewebote, the king having granted the same to Ralph de Gernemue. (*Madox,* i. 202, 323.)

WICHINTON, WILLIAM DE, or WYTHINTUNE, for the name is spelled both ways, was no doubt selected as an itinerant justice in the counties of Cambridge and Huntingdon in 9 Henry III., 1225, in consequence of his being at that time seneschal or steward of the great abbey of Ramsey. In the next year he was one of those appointed to assess and collect the quinzime for those counties. His property lay in Northamptonshire, and was seized into the king's hands at the latter end of John's reign, but restored to him soon after the accession of his successor. (*Rot. Claus.* i. 250, 320, ii. 77, 146.)

WIDDRINGTON, THOMAS, belonged to a junior branch of the ancient and loyal family of Widdrington, of Widdrington in Northumberland, one of whom was the gallant squire renowned in the ballad of 'Chevy Chase.' Thomas was the eldest son of Lewis Widdrington, of Desbourne Grange in Norfolk, and, after spending some time at both universities, was admitted a member of Gray's Inn in 1618, where he became a barrister and bencher, and was elected reader in 1641. (*Athen. Oxon.* iii. 661.)

He was recorder of Berwick, and addressed King Charles in a loyal speech when passing through that town on June 2, 1633, in his progress to Scotland, concluding with the affectionate wish 'that the throne of King Charles, the great and wise son of our British Solomon, may be that of King David, the father of Solomon, established before the Lord for ever.' Being elected in 1638 to the more important office of recorder of York, he had to perform the same duty on the king's arrival in that city on March 30, 1639, when his oration exceeded the former in fulsome adulation. How lamentable to contrast these ardent speeches with the different language soon to be common, and with the recorder's future career! He was rewarded with the honour of knighthood. (*Rushworth,* i. 179, ii. 887; *Drake's York,* 368.)

In 1640 he was elected member for Berwick, and soon distinguished himself as a zealous Presbyterian by taking a prominent part in the violent proceedings of the times.

He prepared the impeachment of Bishop Wren, and introduced it into the House of Lords with an intemperate and abusive speech (*Parl. Hist.* ii. 861, 886), the result of which was the bishop's imprisonment in the Tower for eighteen years. He was one of the commissioners sent by the parliament to the army in June 1647, to know what would satisfy them; and, turning to the independent party, he received the appointment of a commissioner of the Great Seal on March 15, 1648 (*Whitelocke,* 252, 293, 295), for which he was probably indebted as much to his connection with the general Lord Fairfax, whose sister he had married, as to his abilities in his profession. In October following he was called to the degree of the coif, and by the parliament declared king's serjeant. He and Whitelocke, the other commissioner of the Seal, were so determined against having anything to do with the trial of the king that they both retired to Whitelocke's house in the country to 'avoid the business.' (*Ibid.* 342, 349, 360–365.)

When the tragedy was over, Sir Thomas, though named as commissioner by the new government, declined to serve; and the Commons had so much respect for his scruples as not only to excuse him, but to order that he should practise within the bar, and have a quarter's wages more than were due to him. He, however, was made serjeant for the Commonwealth on June 9, 1650, and became member of the Council of State in February 1651; he was present at the meeting at the speaker's house in the following December when Cromwell discussed with those present what was fit to be done for a settlement of the nation after the battle of Worcester. Widdrington on that occasion advocated a mixed monarchical government as the most suitable, and in answer to the objection that the late king's eldest son had been in arms against them, and his second son was their enemy, suggested that the third son, the Duke of Gloucester, was still among them, and was too young to be infected with the principles of their enemies. This hint was not relished by Cromwell, who soon broke up the conference. Nor had Widdrington's resistance to his proposal in April 1653 to put a period to the parliament any better effect, for the day after the general violently turned the members out of doors by his own authority. Notwithstanding this opposition, Widdrington was reinstated in his former place of commissioner of the Great Seal on April 5, 1654, soon after Cromwell became protector. In July he was elected member for the city of York in Cromwell's second parliament, and in August he was placed on the commission for the Treasury, for which he had an additional 1000*l.* a year. He did not enjoy his office much above a year, for Cromwell and his council having made 'an ordinance for the better regulating and limiting the jurisdiction of the High Court of Chancery,' which Whitelocke and Widdrington considered injurious to the public, and illegal in itself, both of them refused to put it into execution, and were consequently dismissed on June 6, 1665. (*Ibid.* 378–597, 621–627.) Cromwell in discharging them expressed no displeasure at their scruples; and before the end of the year Widdrington was appointed chancellor for the county palatine of Durham, with a salary of 50*l.* a year. (5 *Report Pub. Rec., App.* ii. 253.)

In the new parliament of September 1656 Widdrington was returned both for the city of York and for Northumberland. His residence being at Chisburn Grange in that county, he elected to sit for it, and, having received the council's approval, was allowed to enter the house, and was chosen speaker. The first business that devolved upon him was the reception of the spirited remonstrance of those members who had been excluded for want of the council's certificate of approbation. (*Parl. Hist.* iii. 1484–6.)

It became his duty in March to present 'The humble Petition and Advice' to the protector, calling upon him to take the title of king, which he introduced in a speech showing the antiquity of the title, and the present convenience and necessity of its being assumed, very ingeniously but somewhat fancifully illustrated. When this was declined, and a new constitution established, Sir Thomas administered to Cromwell the new oath as lord protector, prefacing it by delivering to him the robe of purple, the Bible, the sceptre, and the sword, with a pithy comment on each. (*Burton's Diary*, i. 397, ii. 513.) The parliament was dissolved on February 4, 1658, principally because the Commons wasted their time in debating the title to be given to the 'other house;' and Widdrington, whose arbitrary conduct as speaker had been frequently complained of by the members, was rewarded with the vacant office of lord chief baron of the Exchequer on June 26. (*Siderfin*, 106.) The death of Cromwell, which occurred on September 3, made no difference in his position, the Protector Richard re-appointing him; but before Richard was deposed, Serjeant Wilde petitioned the parliament to be reinstated in his former place of lord chief baron. (*Burton*, iv. 390, 468.) The serjeant's application was not at that time successful; but when the Long Parliament reassumed the government, Widdrington, having been appointed one of the Council of State, was transferred on January 17, 1660, from the Court of Exchequer to be principal commissioner of the Great Seal (*Whitelocke*, 693), in which place he continued till the return of the king.

In the Healing or Convention Parliament of April 1660 Sir Thomas was elected for two places, Berwick and York, and sat for the latter. On the restoration of Charles II. he had the benefit of the Act of Indemnity, and was the first named of the re-appointed serjeants on June 1. (*Siderfin*, 3.) A few days after he boldly opposed a proviso, moved by Colonel Jones and Mr. Prynne, compelling all officers during the protectorate to refund their salaries, saying that if he was included in it he had much better have been excluded from the act. The clause was rejected. In December he was confirmed in his previous appointment of chancellor of Durham, and in May 1661 he was again returned for Berwick. He resigned the recordership of York in 1662, and dying on May 13, 1664, was buried in the chancel of St. Giles's-in-the-Fields, with a handsome monument to his memory. Though evidently an accomplished man, and well versed in his own profession, there is much in his career to prove the truth of what was said of his character, that it had 'more of the willow than the oak.'

He married Frances, daughter of Ferdinand Lord Fairfax of Cameron, the father of the parliamentary general, and had by her four surviving daughters.

He left behind him a 'A Description or Survey of the City of York.'

WIGHENHOLT, JOHN DE, was appointed in 15 John constable of the castle of Wallingford, he being then sheriff of Berkshire. (*Rot. Pat.* 109.) He held both till the end of that reign, and during part of the next, and in 17 John was presented to the church of Stokes in the diocese of Lincoln, and became one of the royal chaplains. In 3 Henry III., 1219, he was a justice itinerant in the counties of Wilts, Hants, Oxford, and Berks (*Ibid.* 166), being probably named as connected with the latter county, and because it was usual to add a clerical associate. In 11 Henry III. a mandate was addressed to him as a justice of the forests. (*Rot. Claus.* ii. 215.)

WIGHTMAN, WILLIAM, was born in 1785 in Dumfriesshire, where his family had been long established.

After entering University College, Oxford, he was elected to a Michell fellowship at Queen's College, and took his degree of M.A. Becoming then a student in Lincoln's Inn, he practised for some years as a special pleader before he was called to the bar. On taking that step in 1821, the reputation he had already acquired insured him at an early period a very considerable business. His character for solid legal learning may be estimated by his being employed for ten or twelve years as the assistant of the attorney-generals of the day, in the office of junior counsel of the Treasury, a post familiarly designated as that officer's 'devil,' and requiring a qualification which eminently belonged to him—that of the most unerring accuracy and precision. This also led to his appointment as one of the commissioners for enquiring into the practice and proceedings of the common law courts in 1830, and in 1833 in another commission for digesting the criminal law.

With such antecedents his ultimate promotion was certain. It took place in February 1841, when he was constituted a judge of the Queen's Bench, and was thereupon knighted. The selection was more than justified: during the period of nearly three-and-twenty years in which he sat in that court, notwithstanding his exalted position, and the high estimation in which he must have been conscious that he was held, he never lost that innate modesty for which from the first he was distinguished. To his profound knowledge of the law he added those judicial qualities of patience in listening, discrimination in judging, and clearness in explaining, which are so essential and becoming on the bench.

His labours and his life were suddenly terminated at York on December 10, 1863, by an attack of apoplexy, while attending the Northern Circuit, being the third judge who has during the reign closed his career while in the exercise of his duties at the assizes, the two others being Mr. Justice Talfourd and Mr. Baron Watson.

He married in 1819 the daughter of James Baird, Esq., of Lasswade, near Edinburgh.

It is with pride and pleasure that I am permitted to append to this slight memoir a letter from one of Sir William Wightman's former fellow-labourers on the bench. The elegant and affectionate style of the writer will be recognised by many of my readers, who cannot fail to remark that in the amiable character and the judicial excellence which he justly attributes to his friend he has unconsciously delineated his own:—

'July 25, 1864.

'MY DEAR SIR,—I have delayed the fulfilment of my promise to you respecting my late colleague and friend Mr. Justice Wightman longer than I intended—in great measure because the considering it with a view to its fulfilment has convinced me that it was somewhat rashly made. Much, indeed, might be said respecting him by one competent to the task, and of an interesting character both to lawyers and to general readers; but it might be hardly suitable to the plan of your work; and his professional career, though one of uninterrupted success, and, for the part of it during which he was a judge, of eminent utility to the public, was not an eventful one: it was a stream flowing on to its close with increasing volume, but without breaks, without falls, without overflows.

'He and I were not on the same circuit, when at the bar; but we sate in the same row in court, and I had sufficient opportunity to form a high opinion of his great legal knowledge and practical ability, both as a special pleader and advocate. It so happened that we were engaged on the same side in the prosecutions which grew out of the Bristol Riots, and were conducted under a special commission; and also in the informations against the mayor and aldermen of Bristol which followed. Gradually there grew up between us a good deal of friendly feeling and familiar intercourse. He was a most agreeable companion. I do not think that he could be said, at the time I speak of, to have done his intellect full justice in the way of literary cultivation. It might be owing to his genuine modesty and very undemonstrative character; he certainly, however, did not show at that time much of general reading or scholarship in his talk; but he was full of information and anecdote, and a rich vein of humour ran through all his conversation—humour, as indeed it commonly is, quite untranslatable, which no narrative can give an adequate idea of, and removed the farther from common appreciation, but the more racy to professional hearers, from its very commonly clothing itself in quaint professional diction. I was raised to the bench some years before him; and when I went upon the Northern Circuit as judge, I found him nearly, if not quite, the first junior and engaged in nearly every important case. To this position he clung, seemingly having no desire for the distinction of a silk gown, and certainly very averse to that which ambitious juniors are said sometimes to covet—the being called on to lead a cause owing to the unexpected absence of his leader. He desired no such opportunities of distinction. I remember in vain putting on him all the pressure fairly in my power upon an occasion at Liverpool when we were dividing the causes, and trying them at the same time in two courts. I wished him to lead a cause, but he resolutely declined. No one doubted that in the majority of causes he would have led with exquisite judgment, or that he would have exercised a powerful influence over a jury. With this disposition and these unquestioned qualifications, he did not covet promotion, and remained with a stuff gown on his back, until, in the spring of 1841, Mr. Justice Littledale resigned, and he was, with the universal approbation of the profession, called by Lord Chancellor Cottenham to fill his place. Few men, perhaps, at that time would have been reckoned equal to the retiring judge in the knowledge of the common law; but Wightman was a successful student in the same school, and he brought with him a greater knowledge of mankind and habits of a more prompt decision. The duties which he now entered on he continued to discharge to the last day of his life; and it is not merely the exaggeration of a friend to say that he did so with ever-increasing satisfaction to the public. As at the bar, so on the bench, he was never a volunteer of labour which it was not his duty to undertake, nor covetous of any occasional distinction; but he shrank from no labour which the discharge of his duty called on him to undertake; and whenever circumstances compelled him to be prominent, he was found to fill the post with ease and dignity of manner, as well as simplicity. He had, of course, often to prepare written judgments for himself, and not seldom for the court: he did this with great care, in a clear style, and with a very lucid arrangement. Generally, indeed almost universally, he commenced with a statement of what he considered to be the facts, that, as he said, it might at all events appear on what he decided; he arranged his authorities, or stated his principles of decision, and then drew the conclusion. I have always considered them as models of that class of composition; and his reasoning faculty was so sound, that he did not often miss a logical conclusion; to use a professional expression, he was eminently "a safe judge." He never exceeded in length; indeed, it might have been well if one so competent had on some occasions travelled wider afield, and illustrated his decision of the matter in hand by analogies, of which his learning would have furnished him with apt and striking instances. He served with three chief justices in succession, and I believe there was no one of them who did not feel and gratefully acknowledge the value of his effective assistance—always zealously and never ostentatiously rendered.

'When he sat alone at Nisi Prius, or in the trial of criminal cases, it was in a good sense a great judicial display—always careful as to his appearance and dress, dignified without the slightest ostentation, very courteous, yet very firm, quiet, saying little, but that little very pointedly, in the course of the cause, very attentive, and losing nothing; disposing of points as they arose, shortly, and with ease and distinctness; presenting the question, and the circumstances as they bore on it, to the jury with the greatest precision, and inevitably making them feel entire confidence in his impartiality. The man who had a good cause, or the innocent prisoner, rejoiced that he had him for the judge; while he against whom the verdict passed, felt at least the satisfaction that no favourable point had been overlooked or undervalued, nothing adverse exaggerated or unduly pressed. Yet, with all this mastery over the position, what we call anxious cases—cases of great length or complication, or those which might end in capital punishment—did make him very anxious; and to those who were near him on such occasions there were sometimes—outbreaks they can hardly be called, but slight outpourings of querulousness, free from ill-temper, and at which no one was more ready to smile than himself when the cause had passed away.

'I saw him for the last time, I think, on November 29, 1863, when he called on me, just before he started on that circuit from which he was never to return. He had walked a considerable distance from his own house in Eaton Place; and he was about to walk home, making other visits by the way. He had then nearly completed his eightieth year; yet he looked fresh and firm, walked uprightly, saw and heard perfectly, and was in the full vigour of his mental faculties. As we parted, I reminded him of the last winter circuit at York, on which we had been together, and how we had then both agreed that that should be our last. He only smiled, and we parted without a foreboding on either side. He found at York a heavy calendar, and from the beginning it seemed to oppress him more than was usually the case. We are apt, after an event of importance has happened, to recollect slight circumstances and casual expressions which, if nothing had happened, we should have forgotten or thought quite immaterial. It is remembered now that the chaplain had omitted to mention him in the bidding prayer before his assize sermon. "There was no one in the minster," said he after the service, "who more needed the prayers of the people than the judge who has this list of prisoners to dispose of."

'On the last day of his life he was in court early, and tried a complicated case, which lasted the whole day: it was one which excited much interest in the county, and the hall was crowded. He felt oppressed; but this did not appear to the audience, who listened with admiration to a masterly summing up of the long evidence—with admiration not unmixed with wonder to see such vigour of intellect and clearness of recollection, supported by such activity of the bodily faculties, at such an advanced age. But it was the bright burning of the taper before its sinking into darkness. He returned to his lodgings, where, happily for himself and for her, Miss Wightman was waiting for him. The father and the child passed the evening quietly together. He complained a little of his work overcoming him, and spoke cheerfully of resignation and rambling on the Continent. He talked much and with overflowing affection of the different members of his family. So the evening passed, and he retired to his room. There was just enough in his tone and manner to excite a little uneasiness, and it is said that Miss Wightman made an excuse some time after to tap at his door and enquire how he was. He answered cheerfully, but he never rose from his bed: the old man's strength, it should seem, had been too severely tried, and he sank on the following day.

'It may well be supposed how awfully and sadly the news broke on the crowded city of York. That a man at his time of life should pass away without note of warning might seem not extraordinary; but it is remarkable that, old as he was, nothing in his appearance or manner called up associations with the approach of death. Even to his nearest friends and relations the event came with the shock of surprise; and here the bar, the jury, the witnesses, the crowd of interested spectators, had seen him last, and but the day before, on the judgment-seat, administering justice with the vigour and clearness of a man in the prime of life—with the wisdom and consideration, but without a shadow of the weakness of old age. It may be truly said that the feeling of surprise was not greater or more universal than that of regret. Not in the first moment, but after time allowed for consideration, which only added substance to the feeling, a meeting was held, and it was resolved to place a window in the minster in commemoration of his public services, his private virtues, and the sorrow of his friends and the public for the loss they had sustained.

'I am not writing my friend's eulogy, nor attempting to describe at full his character; nor must I venture to lift up the veil, which must remain drawn before the long happinesses and sacred sorrows of domestic life, though it shuts out from respectful and loving admiration the best parts, it may be, of a good man's character. It is enough to say that he left a widow who has to be thankful for nearly half a century of unbroken harmony and happiness, and four daughters and numerous grandchildren, the objects of his constant affection and care. Life must to them be changed indeed; but it may safely be hoped that she and they will all be supported under their great affliction by His hand, who has ordained it for them.

'I am afraid I have been led to do what, at the outset, I prepared you for my carefully avoiding; and perhaps I have written what should have no place in your book: but you will consider over how many years of friendly and intimate intercourse my memory wanders, and that he who can look back so far can hardly have escaped the infirmity to which length of days is most liable.

'I sometimes think, with regret, that had he timely spared the unusual strength which was vouchsafed to him, and retired some few years since to labours less exhausting than those of the common law bench, he might now be among us, conferring happiness on his family, and real benefits on the public. But such regrets are as unwise as they are unavailing. He lived happy in the course he pursued, and he died as I think he would have wished to die—his loins girded, his harness on his back, in the faithful and conscientious discharge of his duty.

'I remain, my dear Sir,
'Yours, &c.'

WIGRAM, JAMES, was of Irish extraction. His father was Irish; his paternal grandfather, John Wigram of Wexford; and his paternal grandmother, Mary, daughter of Robert Clifford of Wexford, were also Irish. His father, Sir Robert Wigram, was born at Wexford, and, settling in England, became one of the most eminent of its merchants. In 1805 he was honoured with a baronetcy, which is now possessed by his grandson, whose father, the second baronet, assumed the name of Fitzwygram. Sir Robert Wigram married two wives, and was the parent of twenty-three children, of whom Sir James, the vice-chancellor, was his third son by his second wife, Eleanor, daughter of John Watts, Esq., of Southampton. He was born at his father's seat, Walthamstow House, Essex, on November 5, 1793. Feeling that the seven years he spent at a private school had been wasted, he had the courage, at the age of sixteen, to follow the advice of the Rev. Thomas Bourdillion, of Fen Stanton, with whom he was then placed as pupil, and to begin his education again from the beginning. This he did so successfully that at Cambridge (where he began his residence at Trinity College in 1811, under the private tutorship of the Rev. Charles Webb le Bas, subsequently principal of the East India College, Haileybury) he became fifth wrangler in 1815, and in autumn 1817 gained a fellowship at Trinity, taking his degree of B.A. in 1815, and that of M.A. in 1818. In December 1818 he married Anne, daughter of Richard Arkwright, Esq., of Willersley in Derbyshire, and granddaughter of Sir Richard Arkwright, and in the following year he was called to the bar by the society of Lincoln's Inn. Attaching himself to the Court of Chancery, he practised there with such success that in 1834 he was made one of the king's counsel, having in 1831 published a treatise entitled 'An Examination of the Rules of Law respecting the

Admission of Extrinsic Evidence in aid of the Interpretation of Wills,' which has already gone through four editions. This treatise was followed in 1836 by another, entitled 'Points in the Law of Discovery,' which is equally useful and highly esteemed. These publications led to a very interesting correspondence with some of the American judges, among whom was Dr. Story, the celebrated author of the well-known Commentaries.

While enjoying a distinguished lead in the courts of equity, he entered parliament as member for Leominster in June 1841, but had little opportunity of exhibiting any senatorial talent, for within four months he received the reward of his forensic labours, and vacated his seat upon being raised to the bench. On October 28 of that year, on the passing of an act of parliament (5 Vict. c. 5, s. 19) authorising the appointment of two new judges of the Court of Chancery, to be called vice-chancellors, Mr. J. L. Knight-Bruce and Mr. James Wigram were selected from the equity bar to fill those offices. They were both knighted in January following, and sworn in as members of the privy council. Sir James Wigram presided over his court for nine years, his decrees being remarkable for the lucid exposition of the legal principles involved in the cases on which he had to adjudicate. They were the subject of general approbation, and were highly extolled by those most competent to form a judgment. As reported by Mr. Thomas Hare, all of them have the special advantage of having been seen and approved by the judge before publication.

In consequence of ill-health, which resulted in total loss of sight, Sir James felt himself compelled to resign his post in Trinity Vacation 1850. Serenely patient under his affliction, he lived many years afterwards, and died on July 29, 1866. For many of the facts in this sketch I am indebted to the courteous liberality of Sir James Wigram.

WILDE, JOHN, descended from a family that resided at Holt in the county of Denbigh about the reign of Henry IV., was the son of George Wilde, of Droitwich in Worcestershire, a serjeant-at-law in the reign of James I., and of Frances, daughter of Sir Edmund Hudleston, of Sawston in Cambridgeshire. He was educated at Balliol College, Oxford, where he took the degree of B.A. in 1607, and of M.A. in 1610. Following his father's profession, he entered the Inner Temple, where he was elected reader in 1631. (*Fasti Oxon.* i. 321, 338; *Dugdale's Orig.* 168.) A member of Charles's second parliament in 1626, he took part in the debate against the Duke of Buckingham, arguing from Bracton that common fame was a sufficient ground for accusation. (*Parl. Hist.* ii. 53.) In 1636 he was called to the degree of serjeant. (*Rymer*, xx. 22.)

In the Long Parliament he was member for Worcestershire, and was a prominent actor in its proceedings. He was chairman of the committee appointed to prepare the impeachment against the thirteen bishops concerned in making the new canons, which, on August 3, 1641, he presented to the House of Lords. In December he presided over a committee of enquiry as to a plot to bring in the army to overawe the parliament; and in January 1642 he reported a conference with the Lords as to the attorney-general (Sir Edward Herbert) having impeached the five members, and conducted the impeachment against that officer which the Commons ordered. (*Parl. Hist.* ii. 895, 1039, 1121.) In the same year he subscribed two horses and their maintenance for the defence of the parliament (*Notes and Queries*, 1st S. xii. 338); and in February 1643 he was recommended as chief baron of the Exchequer in the unsuccessful propositions made by the Commons to the king. (*Clarendon*, iii. 407.)

The parliament having ordered a new Great Seal in place of that which had been carried to the king by Lord Lyttelton, principally on the arguments of Mr. Serjeant Wilde, showing its necessity, resolved to entrust it to six commissioners, two lords and four commoners, and on November 10, 1643, the serjeant was elected as one of the latter. By successive votes these commissioners, notwithstanding the Self-Denying Ordinance, retained the custody of the Seal for three years, when on October 30, 1646, they surrendered it to the speakers of the two houses. During this time Serjeant Wilde still kept his seat in the Commons, and was one of the managers on their part in the impeachment of Archbishop Laud, whose trial commenced on March 12, 1644. His speeches against the primate were more conspicuous for political and religious rancour than for argument or good taste. When Mr. Herne, the archbishop's counsel, argued that none of the charges amounted to treason, the serjeant said it had not been alleged that they did so, 'but we do say that all the bishop's misdemeanours put together do, by way of accumulation, make many grand treasons.' Herne immediately replied, 'I crave your mercy, good Mr. Serjeant; I never understood before this time that two hundred black rabbits would make a black horse.' The trial was superseded, as in the Earl of Strafford's case, by a bill of attainder, under which the archbishop suffered on January 10, 1644-5. Wilde was elected recorder of Worcester in July 1646. (*Journals*; *Whitelocke*, 77, 218; *State Trials*, iv. 351-598.)

After the Seal was taken from the serjeant, he was several times employed as judge of assize, and does not seem to have been very scrupulous in his proceedings. He is accused at one time of hanging Captain John Burley at Winchester for causing a drum to be beaten for God and King Charles at Newport in the Isle of Wight, in order to rescue his captive sovereign; and at another, of directing the grand jury to ignore the bill of indictment preferred against Major Edmund Rolph for intending to murder the king. The Commons voted their thanks to him for his great and good service done to the parliament in that circuit, and Anthony Wood (*Fasti*, i. 336) states that he received 1000*l.* for each of these transactions, adding that it 'was all one to him whether he hung or hung not, so he got the beloved pelf.'

On October 12, 1648, the parliament took upon them to fill the vacancies on the judicial bench, and appointed Serjeant Wilde to be chief baron of the Exchequer, who was sworn into office on November 16. He still retained his position when the king was beheaded, took the new oaths, and was placed on the Council of State. (*Whitelocke*, 343–381.) When Cromwell assumed the protectorate in December 1653, he did not, for some unrecorded reason, continue Wilde as chief baron, but appointed William Steele. (*Hardres' Reports.*) There is a letter from Wilde, dated July 12, 1654, complaining that after all his services he is removed, addressed to Whitelocke (*Swedish Emb.* ii. 461) on his return from the Swedish embassy, who says that it was 'a usual reward in such times for the best services,' and adds that he moved the protector on Wilde's behalf, 'but to no effect, the protector having a dislike to the serjeant, but the ground thereof I could not learn.'

Wilde remained out of employment during the rest of Cromwell's life, but was elected member for Droitwich in Protector Richard's parliament of 1558–9. He there presented a petition from himself, praying a restoration to his former office, and for payment of the arrears of 1300*l.* due to him for his salary. The former was refused, but the latter was granted. (*Burton's Diary*, iv. 390.)

On the return of the Long Parliament Serjeant Wilde resumed his place as a member, and on January 17, 1659–60, was restored to his judicial seat by the same power that had first appointed him. (*Whitelocke*, 693.) Short, however, was his enjoyment of it. The return of the king in May, and the immediate nomination of Sir Orlando Bridgeman as lord chief baron, terminated the serjeant's legal career. In consequence of his having assisted the Lords in several committees of the Convention Parliament, he escaped further question, and, absolved by the Act of Indemnity, he retired to his house at Hampstead. There he died about 1669, and was buried at Wherwill in Hampshire, the seat of Charles Lord de la Warr, the husband of his only daughter and heir, Anne. (*Collins's Peerage*, i. 287, ii. 166, v. 24.) His wife was Anne, daughter of Sir Thomas Harries, of Tonge Castle, serjeant-at-law and baronet.

Whitelocke describes him as 'learned in his profession, but of more reading than depth of judgment,' and as executing his place 'with diligence and justice;' but the testimony of his other contemporaries is strongly against him. Clarendon calls him 'an infamous judge;' and Archbishop Laud, in the account of his trial, says, 'I had a character given me before of this gentleman which I will forbear to express, but in this speech of his, and his future proceedings with me, I found it exactly true;' and Anthony Wood's opinion of him has been already stated. Burton also speaks of his tiresome speeches.

WILDE, WILLIAM, born about 1611, was the son of William Wilde, of Clifford's Inn, London, and was called to the bar by the Inner Temple in 1637, became a bencher in 1652, and was elected recorder of London on November 3, 1659. That he was considered one of the moderate party may be presumed from his being returned as member for that city to the Convention Parliament that met in April 1660, from his being knighted immediately on the king's return, from his being called to the degree of serjeant at the second call after the Restoration, and from his being further dignified with a baronetcy on September 13 in the same year. As recorder he was of course named on the commission for the trial of the regicides. On November 10 in the following year he was made one of the king's serjeants, which position, with that of recorder, he enjoyed until April 16, 1668, when he resigned the latter office on being appointed a judge of the Common Pleas. In that court he remained nearly five years, and then on January 22, 1673, was removed to the King's Bench, where he sat as judge above six years more. (1 *Siderfin*, 4; *Parl. Hist.* iv. 4; *T. Raymond*, 217; *T. Jones*, 43.)

On April 29, 1679, his patent was revoked at the same time as those of three other judges—viz., Vere Bertie, Thurland, and Bramston. Burnet (i. 450) says that Sir William Wilde, 'a worthy and ancient judge,' was turned out for his plain freedom in telling Bedlow, one of the witnesses of the Popish Plot, that 'he was a perjured man, and ought to come no more into court, but go home and repent.' In the preceding February, Green, Berry, and Hill were tried for the murder of Sir Edmundbury Godfrey; and on April 16 Nathaniel Reading was tried for tampering with the king's evidence; the conviction on both trials being founded materially upon the evidence of Bedlow. Justice Wilde took an active part in each, pronouncing sentence of death in the former, and saying that the conviction of the latter was 'a very good verdict.' So that his discovery of Bedlow's false swearing and his use of the expressions recorded by Burnet must have happened between April 16 and 26. (*State Trials*, vii. 222, 261.) He survived his dismissal only seven months, dying on November 23, 1679. He was buried in the Temple Church.

He appears to have been well grounded in the law, and an honest and considerate judge. Sir Henry Yelverton's Reports were published by him in French in 1661, when he was king's serjeant, and in English in 1674, when he was judge. His residence when recorder was in Great St. Bartholomew's Close, and afterwards at Lewisham, Kent, until he purchased the manor of Goldston, or Goldstanton, in Ash in the same county.

He married three wives. The name of the first is not recorded; that of the second was Jane, daughter of Felix Wilson, of Hanwell in Middlesex; and the third was Frances, daughter of John Berecroft, of Chard in Somersetshire. He had a son by each of the two latter, but both dying without male issue, the baronetcy became extinct. (*Add. MSS.* 5507, 65*; *Hasted*, i. 503, xi. 196.)

WILDE, JAMES PLAISTED (LORD PENZANCE), is the fourth son of Edward Archer Wilde, Esq., an eminent attorney and solicitor in London, for which city and the county of Middlesex he served the office of sheriff in 1828. His father was the brother of the late Lord Truro, who for some time was engaged in that branch of the legal profession.

He was born in 1816, and after his preliminary education at Winchester School proceeded to Trinity College, Cambridge, where he took his degrees of B.A. in 1838 and M.A. in 1842. With so much legal blood in his veins he was naturally devoted to the same profession, and, having been entered of the society of Lincoln's Inn, was called to the bar in 1839. He attached himself to the Northern Circuit, and in the next year was appointed junior counsel to the Excise and Customs. Soon distinguishing himself by his deep knowledge of mercantile and maritime law, he rapidly advanced in professional reputation; in 1855 he obtained an acknowledged lead as queen's counsel, and in 1859 he was made counsel to the duchy of Lancaster.

He was appointed a baron of the Exchequer on April 13, 1860, and was thereupon knighted; and had not sat in that court more than three years and four months before the lamented death of that excellent judge Sir Cresswell Cresswell occasioned a vacancy in the Court of Probate and Divorce. It speaks highly of the judicial ability which Sir James Wilde had exhibited that he should have been called upon to undertake the responsible and delicate duties attached to the office of chief judge of the new court. He was appointed to it on August 26, 1863, and so satisfactory has been his performance of its duties that it is the universal wish, both of the bar and the public, that he may long be able to undergo the heavy and incessant labour that devolves upon him. He was honoured with a seat in the privy council; and on April 6, 1869, he was called up to the House of Peers by the title of Lord Penzance.

He has shown that he is not merely a careful administrator of the law, but also an able analyst of its principles. In an excellent address delivered by him as president of the department of jurisprudence and amendment of the law, in a late meeting of the Social Science Congress at York, he gave a rapid account of our original social institutions, of the gradual formation of the laws that regulated them, of the various additions that the advances of civilisation necessitated, and of the evils that arose from the complication occasioned by the admixture of the new enactments with the old, which, though obsolete, remained unrepealed. He pictured the consequent difficulties felt by the judges, which compelled them frequently, in order to do justice, to become legislators instead of interpreters; and in pointing out that the cases they decided were so numerous, and the decisions they pronounced were often so conflicting, the learned lecturer declared that he could see no remedy but in a Digest, bringing together the broad principles on which the common law reposes, and which tacitly guide the decisions of our courts.

He married Lady Mary Bouverie, the youngest daughter of William, third Earl of Radnor.

WILDE, THOMAS (LORD TRURO). The career of Thomas Wilde affords a most uncommon instance of the rise from the lowest to the highest step in the law, passing through the different grades of attorney, barrister, serjeant, king's serjeant, solicitor and attorney general, chief justice, and lord chancellor.

He was born on July 7, 1782, in Warwick Square, and was the second son of Mr. Thomas Wilde, an attorney-at-law, by his wife, Margaret Anne Knight, whose two other sons were brought up in the same profession; the elder becoming a barrister and ultimately chief justice at the Cape of Good

Hope; and the younger, Edward Archer Wilde, holding a high rank as an attorney in London, the father of the above James Plaisted Wilde, Lord Penzance.

Thomas Wilde received his education at St. Paul's School, and in after life showed how much he appreciated the advantages he had derived from that establishment, by presenting to it 1000*l.*, the interest of which he directed to be annually expended in prizes to the best scholars. He was admitted as an attorney in 1805, and continued to practise with great success in that department for nearly twelve years. In 1813 he married Mary, daughter of William Willman, Esq., and widow of William Devaynes, Esq., the banker. At this time, dissatisfied with the limited sphere in which he acted, and conscious that his powers were adapted to a more extended range, he entered the Inner Temple, and was called to the bar on February 7, 1817, being then in his thirty-fifth year.

Overcoming all the obstacles in the way of one who, as it were, intrudes himself into a higher branch of his profession, he almost instantly acquired a considerable proportion of business. He is said to have conquered an impediment in his speech, which prevented him from uttering certain words, by forming a list of synonymes, and substituting them whenever the words occurred which he could not pronounce. This perseverance was his peculiar characteristic, and exemplified itself so remarkably in every cause in which he was engaged that he won general confidence. His firmness and independence secured the attention of the judges; and the character he had thus acquired, with his reputation for the power of precise arrangement and for extraordinary industry, no doubt caused him to be selected, in 1820, when he had been only three years at the bar, as assistant counsel in the defence of Queen Caroline, who was so pleased with his exertions on her behalf that she appointed him one of her executors. This naturally raised Mr. Wilde in professional estimation, and his business increased so greatly that he felt warranted in accepting the degree of the coif when offered to him, in Easter 1824, by Lord Eldon, although as a whig he was opposed to that nobleman's political principles. In 1827 he had a further advance in being made king's serjeant. He attained so prominent a lead in the Common Pleas that in a short time there was scarcely a single cause tried in that court in which he was not engaged on one side or the other. Fortunate were those litigants who secured his services, for indefatigable were his exertions for their success; and his were not the perfunctory consultations too commonly granted for a short half-hour, but real discussions into the points to be argued, and the evidence to be given in their support. Lord Tenterden is said to have described him as having 'industry enough to succeed without talent, and talent enough to succeed without industry.'

Not satisfied with his forensic triumphs, he sought parliamentary distinction; and in May 1831, after many previous struggles, he secured his seat for Newark-on-Trent, a borough which he continued to represent through the subsequent parliaments till 1841, when he was returned for Worcester. In the senate he took the liberal side of politics, and was remarkable more for the clearness of his statements and closeness of his arguments than for the fascination of his eloquence. His steady support of the whig party, and his commanding position at the bar, naturally recommended him to the government for employment, and on February 9, 1840, he was consequently made solicitor-general and knighted.

In the following June he lost his wife, after a union of twenty-seven years; and having remained a widower for five years, he married Augusta Emma D'Este, the daughter of the Duke of Sussex and Lady Augusta Murray, whose legitimacy he had previously endeavoured to establish before the House of Lords.

In June 1841, for the two months during which the administration of Lord Melbourne was doomed to last, he filled the office of attorney-general, of course retiring from it with the minister. For the five following years he remained out of office, but on the restoration of the whig party under Lord John Russell in July 1846, he was replaced as attorney-general, to be again removed in three or four days, on being promoted to the office of lord chief justice of the Common Pleas on the 7th of that month, a vacancy in that court having been occasioned by the death of Sir Nicolas Tindal only the day before.

When he had presided in the Common Pleas for four years, he was constituted lord chancellor of Great Britain, receiving the Great Seal on July 15, 1850, together with a patent of peerage, by which he was created Baron Truro of Bowes in Middlesex. This high dignity he held for nineteen months only, the prime minister, Lord John Russell, being compelled to retire in February 1852, when Lord Truro was necessarily superseded.

It must not have been the least gratifying circumstance attending his elevation to receive an affectionate address of congratulation from nearly five hundred members of that branch of the profession to which he had originally belonged, expressive of their strong appreciation of his honourable conduct through life, of his zealous and indefatigable exertions as an advocate, and of the unvarying courtesy they had experienced at his hands. This address was accompanied by a request that his lordship should sit for his portrait, to be placed in the hall of the Incorporated Law Society, where it now ornaments the walls, and reminds the young student that by personal industry and exertion he may raise himself to the same honours.

During the short period in which Lord Truro held the Seal he was deeply engaged in promoting various important law reforms. He appointed a commission to enquire as to the pleading and practice of his court, and assisted Lord St. Leonards, who succeeded him in his office, in carrying into effect the most important regulations in the report. He established a system of paying the fees of the court by means of stamps, and greatly reduced their amount. He effected that most important change in the constitution of the court, by the appointment of the Court of Appeal, which at once remedied the great evil of delay so long complained of, and relieved the chancellor of one of the most oppressive parts of his duties. His exertions were not limited to reforming the Court of Chancery; they were extended also to the common law courts, with regard to which he originated many important changes, which have been greatly beneficial to the suitors, in preventing delay and reducing expense. Both as chief justice and chancellor he showed the most untiring patience, and the judgments he pronounced have been considered by the profession to be highly satisfactory. It is no small proof of their value that only one was appealed from, though many of them were reversals of decisions of the vice-chancellors, and that one was affirmed.

His courtesy and kindness were not confined to his professional clients nor to his political partisans, but were distinctive marks of his general character. He exhibited a pleasing proof of his generous feeling when Sir Frederick Thesiger became solicitor-general in 1844, and before he had acquired any experience in his office had the additional duties of the attorney-general thrown upon him by the illness and consequent absence of Sir William Follett. Though Sir Frederick was of the adverse party in politics, and a coolness had existed between them from their having been opposed to each other in the contest for Newark, Sir Thomas Wilde, as soon as he saw the difficulty of Sir Frederick's position, most liberally offered and gave every assistance and advice in his power as to the professional, apart from the political, duties of the office.

Lord Truro survived his retirement for nearly four years, during two of which he suffered much from a painful illness, which terminated in his death on November 11, 1855, at his house in Eaton Square. He was buried in the mausoleum erected by Sir Augustus D'Este, at the church of St. Lawrence, Ramsgate.

By his wife he had issue two sons and a daughter, who is married to her cousin Charles Norris Wilde, Esq., the brother of Lord Penzance.

Lady Truro, soon after his lordship's death, gracefully offered the whole of his law books to the library of the House of Lords, and must have felt amply repaid for her generous gift by the encomiums that were uttered by every leading peer when accepting it, on the legal attainments and judicial excellence of her husband, and on his honourable exertions for the public and the disinterestedness that characterised him.

WILFORD, GERVASE DE, belonged to a family who possessed the manors of Clifton and Wilford in Nottinghamshire, one branch of which used the name of Clifton, and the other that of Wilford. He was of the latter, and, having been remembrancer (*Hospitallers in England*, 284), was made baron of the Exchequer on January 20, 1341, 14 Edward III. He was instituted to the living of Barnack in Northamptonshire, and in 18 Edward III. he assigned various lands in Norfolk to the prior and convent of Shouldham in the latter county.

He became chief baron on April 7, 1350, and presided in the court till 1361. The entry on the roll states that he was exonerated, being broken down by age. In 1359 he obtained the Bishop of Lincoln's licence 'alere et fovere pueros sub virga magistri, in lectura, cantu, et grammatica facultate, ad augmentum cultus divini in sua parochia, et eosdem informare, clericis post pestem diminutis.' (*Thoresby's Notts*, i. 105; *Cal. Inq.* p. m. ii. 119; *Cal. Rot. Pat.* 138, 159, 174, 222; *Ellis's Letters, &c.*, 325.)

WILLES, JOHN, was of one of the most ancient families in Warwickshire. They were settled at Newbold Comyn in that county, in the church of which is a memorial of one of them in stained glass dated 1577. He was the son of the Rev. Dr. John Willes, rector of Bishop's Ickington and canon of Lichfield, by Anne, daughter of Sir William Walker, mayor of Oxford; and his brother Edward became in 1743 Bishop of Bath and Wells. (*Berry's Genealogies, Berks.*)

He was born on November 29, 1685, and received his education at Lichfield grammar school, and Trinity College, Oxford. Entering Lincoln's Inn, he was called to the bar in June 1713. He then went the Oxford Circuit, and arrived at the dignity of king's counsel in 1719. In his early life he was much more noted for hilarity and licentiousness than for learning and

3 B

ability, though he was by no means deficient in the latter. He sought advancement by entering into the career of politics under the patronage of Sir Robert Walpole, and in the parliament that met in October 1722 he procured a seat for Launceston. In May 1726 he was appointed second judge on the Chester Circuit; and thereupon vacating his seat for Launceston, he was not re-elected; but a vacancy soon after occurring in Weymouth, he was returned for that borough. In the parliament of 1728 he represented West Looe; and before its close he was obliged to undergo two re-elections, one on his being promoted to the chief justiceship of Chester in February 1729, and the other on being appointed attorney-general in January 1734. He was again returned for West Looe to the new parliament of 1735, and sat for it till he was advanced to the bench. His speech against the repeal of the Septennial Act in 1734 is the only recorded specimen of his senatorial eloquence, and appears to deserve the praise it elicited.

He was knighted as attorney-general, and filled that office exactly three years when in January 1737 he was appointed lord chief justice of the Common Pleas. Over that court he presided for nearly five-and-twenty years, during the whole of which period he was hankering after the Great Seal, which, when it was at last within his grasp, he lost by his own folly. He was in perpetual expectation that the chancellorship of Lord Hardwicke would be terminated by a change of ministry, and took such measures as he thought would secure him the succession. During the rebellion of 1745 he endeavoured to organise a regiment of volunteers among the lawyers, for the defence of the king's person, of which he was to be the colonel; but if we may believe a satirical song of the time, he never got his commission; and the danger being ended, his majesty declined their services. The poet slyly concludes with this couplet (*Ex inf. W. Durrant Cooper, Esq., F.S.A.*):—

If you ask why a judge should attempt the command,
I'll tell you—To take the Great Seal sword in hand.

When at last Lord Hardwicke did resign, Sir John was designed to take his place; but some objection being made by George II. to give him the sole power, he was obliged to content himself with being the first of three commissioners to whom the Great Seal was entrusted. They held it for seven months, from November 19, 1756, to June 30, 1757, when the Duke of Newcastle's and Mr. Pitt's administration commenced. Sir John was then offered the chancellorship, which he was willing enough to accept, but stipulated that a peerage should be added. This was refused, and he, thinking to obtain his terms by standing out, made this a condition *sine quâ non*. (*Harris's Lord Hardwicke*, iii. 139.) Great then was his confusion and indignation on finding that the ministers had taken him at his word, and appointed the attorney-general, Sir Robert Henley, lord keeper. He lived four years afterwards, and died at the advanced age of seventy-six on December 15, 1761. He was buried in the family vault at Bishop's Ickington.

That in the exercise of his judicial functions, both as chief justice and first commissioner, he showed great learning and ability, the reports of his decisions prove; but out of court he was ambitious and intriguing, joining the different factions as he thought they would promote his views. He had a great enmity against Lord Hardwicke, whom he looked upon as his rival, and as impeding the royal favour; and his lordship had little respect for him, on account of his questionable morality, and his indiscreet involvements. Horace Walpole (*Memoirs*, i. 77), who was inclined to be one of his admirers, tells a story which shows that even when chief justice he still pursued his old propensitities. 'A grave person came to reprove the scandal he gave, and to tell him that the world talked of one of his maidservants being with child. Willes said, "What is that to me?" The monitor answered, "Oh! but they say it is by your lordship." "And what is that to you?" was the reply.'

He married Margaret, daughter and co-heir of — Brewster, Esq., of Worcester, and had by her four sons and four daughters.

WILLES, EDWARD, was the second son of the above, and was called to the bar at Lincoln's Inn in February 1726. He is often confounded with his namesake who was lord chief baron of the Irish Exchequer from 1757 to 1766, and who died in 1768. He acquired the rank of king's counsel in 1756; and in 1766, five years after his father's death, he was made solicitor-general. On the death of Lord Bowes, chancellor of Ireland, in 1767, attempts were made to confer that appointment upon him; but he was obliged to content himself with a seat in the King's Bench, to which he was promoted on January 27, 1768. Soon after the questions relative to Mr. Wilkes came before the court, exciting the public to an intense degree. The judges were unanimous in their opinion on the various points raised in his favour, and, though they were then charged with corrupt bias, calmer times have confirmed their judgment. In the dean of St. Asaph's case Mr. Justice Willes dissented from the other judges, and his declaration that juries had the right to give a general verdict was one of the causes which led to the passing of Mr. Fox's libel act.

Mr. Justice Willes did not accept the usual honour of knighthood. He outlived all his first colleagues except Lord Mansfield, and after nineteen years of judicial life, unmarked by any other peculiar characteristics than a certain flippancy of manner and a neglect of costume, he died on January 14, 1787, and was buried at Burnham in Berkshire. By his wife, Anne, daughter of the Rev. Edward Taylor, of Sutton, Wilts, he left three sons. (4 *Burrow*, 2143; 1 *Term Reports*, 551; *State Trials*, xix. 1091, 1123, xxi. 1040.)

WILLES, JAMES SHAW, is one of the present judges of the Court of Common Pleas. He belongs to an Irish family of English extraction. His grandfather and father, both named James, were resident at Cork, the former as a merchant, and the latter as a physician. His mother was Elizabeth Aldworth, daughter of John Shaw, Esq., mayor of Cork in 1792. He was born in Cork on February 13, 1814, and finished his education at Trinity College, Dublin, where he took his degree of B.A. in 1836, and was called to the bar at the Inner Temple on June 12, 1840. He edited Smith's 'Leading Cases' in conjunction with Mr. Justice Keating in 1847, another edition of which was published by them in 1856, and in 1850 he was selected as a common law commissioner. His practice was principally in the Court of Exchequer, where he filled the post of tubman from 1851 till his elevation to the bench on July 3, 1855, as a judge of the Court of Common Pleas, when he was knighted. A pregnant proof of the estimation which he commands as a lawyer is afforded by his being placed on the Indian law commission in 1861, and on the English and Irish law commission in 1862.

Devoting his body as well as his mind to the service of the country, and considering that 'the post of honour is the private station,' he has served in the ranks of the Inns of Court Volunteer Corps since its formation in 1859. In 1860 the degree of LL.D. was conferred upon him by his alma mater, 'stipendiis condonatis.'

He married Helen, daughter of Thomas Jennings, Esq., of Cork.

WILLIAM, ARCHDEACON OF HEREFORD from 1200 to 1221, was one of the justiciers present with the king at Bristol in 10 John, 1208, when fines were acknowledged before him, but I find no other record of his performance of judicial duties. He had a grant of that portion of the church of Ledbury which Henry Banastre held. Le Neve (118) thinks his name was Fitz-Walter. (*Rot. Chart.* 80.)

WILLIAM, ARCHDEACON OF TOTNESS, occurs with that dignity as one of the justiciers present in the Curia Regis at Westminster before whom a fine was levied in 1189. He is not mentioned as archdeacon of Totness in Le Neve's list.

WILLIAM, DAVID, seems to have been a native of Wales. Among the accounts of the keepers of the House of Converts, now remaining in the records of the kingdom, his commence in 2 Henry VII., and refer to his appointment on February 22, 1487, that office being then always held in conjunction with the mastership of the Rolls. He held the first place among the receivers of petitions in the parliaments that met in 1487 and 1488, but in that of 1491 he was absent. (*Rot. Parl.* xii. 385, 409.) It is not unlikely that this was occasioned by an illness which terminated in his death before May 5, 1492, the date of the patent of John Blyth, his successor.

WILLIAMS, DAVID. It was not till the reign of Henry VIII. that the Welsh began to abandon the practice of changing their names at each generation. The son had previously assumed the Christian name of his father, uniting it to his own Christian name by the word 'ap' (signifying 'son of'), in the same manner that the word 'Fitz' was used by the English in earlier times before surnames were generally introduced among them. Thus this judge was originally called David ap William, his father's name being William ap Ychan, and it was not till he removed into England that he adopted the simpler appellation of David Williams.

The father, descended, it is said, from Bleddin ap Maenyrch, lord of Brecknock in 1091, was a substantial yeoman, whose property was situate in the parish of Ystradvelte in Brecknock. By his wife, Margaret, daughter of Rhys Griffith Bevan, Melin, he had three sons, the youngest of whom, this David, born about 1550, went to seek his fortune in England. Entering himself at the Middle Temple, he was called to the bar in 1576, and arrived at the post of reader in 1590. This honour was repeated in Lent 1594, as a customary compliment on his taking the degree of the coif, according to his writ of summons dated in the previous November. (*Dugdale's Orig.* 218.) It may be presumed, from his name not occurring in any of the Reports till after he became a serjeant, that his practice was principally in the provinces. That it was considerable may be inferred from his being appointed recorder of Brecon in 1587, and also from his acquisition of many manors and lands at Bampton in Oxfordshire; at Guernevet, near the Hay, in his native county; and at Kingston-Bagpuze in Berkshire, where he principally resided, and to the church of which he gave a new bell-tower.

The estimation in which his professional abilities were held appears from his being mentioned by Lord Burleigh as a proper person to fill a vacancy on the Exchequer bench; and when King James, soon after his accession, determined to add a fifth judge to each of the two superior courts, Lord Chief Justice Popham, in a letter to Lord Ellesmere, dated January 28, 1603–4, recommended four serjeants, Danyell, Williams, Tanfyld, and Altham, for the king to make choice of two. The first two were selected, and Williams received his patent as a judge of the King's Bench on February 4, and was thereupon knighted. In 1608 he coincided with the majority of the judges in the decision pronounced in the case of the post nati (*State Trials*, ii. 576), but his argument is not reported. Among the 'Egerton Papers' (388, 447) is a letter from Archbishop Abbot to Lord Ellesmere, dated January 22, 1611–12, in which, speaking of the condemnation of Legat and Wightman for imputed heresy, he says, 'Mr. Justice Williams was with mee the other day, who maketh no doubt but that the lawe is cleare to burne them. Hee told me also of his utter dislike of all the Lord Coke his courses,' who seems to have been of a contrary opinion.

He died exactly a year after the date of this letter. In his will, which was executed a week before his death, is contained the following curious legacy, which shows the friendly terms on which he lived with his brethren on the bench : 'And whereas it hath been heretofore agreed between my good and kind brother Warburton and myself that the survivor of us twayne should have the other's best scarlet robes, now I do will that my said good brother Warburton shall have the choice of either of my scarlet robes, and he to take that shall best like him, praying him that as he hath been a good and kind brother unto me, so he will be a good and kind friend to my children.' He likewise gives to the lord chancellor (Ellesmere) a great gilt standing cup with a cover, in token of his love and affection, and begs him to be overseer of his will. A tablet in old Kingston church records that his bowels were interred there, but his body was removed for burial to the church of St. John the Evangelist at Brecon, where there is a sumptuous monument to his memory, presenting his effigy in judicial habiliments. The inscription by himself states that out of nine sons and two daughters only four sons and two daughters remained, and concludes with these lines :—

Nuper eram judex, nunc judicis ahte tribunal
Subsistens paveo; judicor ipse modo.

These children were all by his first wife, Margaret, a daughter of John Games, of Aberbran in the county of Brecon, Esq., by a daughter of Sir William Vaughan, of Porthaml. His second wife was Dorothy, daughter and coheiress of Oliver Wellsborn, of East Hanney, Berks, Esq., and widow of John Latton, of Kingston in that county, Esq., by whom he had no children. Henry, the eldest of Sir David's surviving sons, received in 1644 the dignity of baronet. He was described of Guernevet, where he entertained King Charles when he was a fugitive after the battle of Naseby. The title became extinct in 1798.

WILLIAMS, JOHN (BISHOP OF LINCOLN and ARCHBISHOP OF YORK), was the youngest of five sons of Edmund Williams, Esq., a gentleman of an ancient Welsh family, by Mary, the daughter of Owen Wynne, Esq., and was born at Aberconway in Carnarvonshire, the residence of his father, on March 25, 1582. From the grammar school of Ruthin he was removed in 1598 to St. John's College, Cambridge. There he pursued his studies so diligently, taking it is said but three hours' sleep out of the twenty-four, and acquired such commendation for his proficency, that when he commenced bachelor of arts in 1603 he was immediately elected fellow of his college. His degree of master he took in 1605, and about the same time was admitted into clerical orders. He soon after was called to preach before the king at Royston, and was so much admired for his learning and eloquence that Lord Chancellor Ellesmere in 1611 appointed him one of his chaplains. In the next year he became proctor to the university, and, though he performed its duties with general applause, he incurred the enmity of the vice-chancellor, Dr. Gouch, by the activity and earnestness he displayed in the elections of the headship of St. John's and the chancellorship of the university, both of which became vacant in his year of office. (*Royal Tribes of Wales*, 149, 153.) At its termination he resumed his position as chaplain, and sat in the convocation of 1613 as one of the archdeacons of Wales. The livings of Walgrave and Grafton-Underwood in Northamptonshire were soon presented to him, to which were added a residentiaryship in Lincoln Cathedral, and a choral place in those of Peterborough, Hereford, and St. David's. Increasing in favour, he was treated with the greatest confidence by the lord chancellor, who frequently discussed with him the causes before the court, entrusted him during his illness with various messages on state affairs to the king, and, just previous to his death in 1616, presented him with his manuscript collections for the regulation of parliament and the council board, and the different courts over which he presided, as 'tools to work with,' a legacy of which

Williams soon learned the value. Bacon offered to retain him in his service, but he declined the honour, and was forthwith sworn one of the royal chaplains. In 1617 he disputed in the schools for his doctor's degree, on the occasion of the Archbishop of Spalatro's visit to the university. In September 1619 he was presented with the deanery of Salisbury. In his personal attendance on the king, from being at first conversed with for his learning and his wit, he came by degrees to be consulted for the wisdom of his counsel. He ingratiated himself with Buckingham by forwarding the favourite's marriage with Lady Katherine Manners, and converting her from the Romish faith. Thus favoured, he was advanced on July 12, 1620, to the deanery of Westminster; and when the parliament that met in the following January began to cry out against the oppressions of the people, and to proceed against Sir Giles Mompesson and other offenders, Buckingham, who feared that he himself might be hit, and the king, who knew not where the bolt might fly, appealed for advice to the dean. He gave them this counsel: 'Swim with the tide, and you cannot be drowned. . . . Throw the cormorants overboard in the storm. . . . Cast all monopolies and patents of griping projections into the Dead Sea after them. . . . Damn all these by one proclamation, that the world may see that the king, who is the pilot that sits at the helm, is ready to play the pump to eject such filth as grew noysome to the nostrils of his people.' Acting on this advice, the storm passed over with only one other victim, Lord Chancellor Bacon.

Hacket, with regard to this event, exhibits a somewhat suspicious reserve, stating merely the fact of Bacon's downfall, and the dean's surprise at his own elevation. There seems, however, to be no sufficient ground for charging Williams with assisting in the chancellor's disgrace, and still less with advising the king and Buckingham to prevent him from defending himself. Any defence was hopeless, and Williams's recommendation not to dissolve the parliament for the purpose of stopping the proceedings appears to have been as honestly as it was wisely offered. Ben Jonson (*Gifford*, viii. 452), whose partiality for Bacon is evident more than once in his works, both in prose and verse, would scarcely have addressed a complimental epigram to Williams on his removal from the Seal, had he been suspected of any underhand or unfriendly dealing towards Bacon.

The Seal for the next two months was placed in the hands of commissioners, and, according to Hacket, the dean was consulted as to the different candidates for the office, and was himself selected by the king and Buckingham in preference to all of them without any application on his own behalf. The latter fact is confirmed by the record itself, which, in stating his appointment on July 10, 1621, as lord keeper, adds, 'præter suam expectationem.' In the previous month he had been sworn of the privy council, and designated for the bishopric of Lincoln. His consecration was delayed by the unfortunate occurrence which happened to Archbishop Abbot in accidentally killing a man while aiming at a buck; and at last, in consideration of the lord keeper's scruples, that ceremony was performed by four bishops on November 11. Being allowed to retain his deanery, his canonry in Lincoln Cathedral, and his living of Walgrave, he was fairly subject to the remark made of him, 'that he was a perfect diocese in himself, being at the same time bishop, dean, prebendary, and parson.' He took his seat in the Court of Chancery on October 9, the first day of Michaelmas Term, no ecclesiastic having presided there since Archbishop Heath in the reign of Queen Mary.

In the performance of his legal functions he supplied his want of knowledge of the rules of the court by obtaining the frequent assistance of two of the judges. His industry was extraordinary, leaving him scarcely any leisure, and, though he was in the habit of checking any unnecessary argument, he became soon a general favourite with the bar. At first some of the advocates endeavoured to take advantage of his inexperience, and one of them, to puzzle him, 'trouled out a motion crammed like a granado with obsolete words, coins of far-fetched antiquity, which had long been disused.' The lord keeper, nothing baffled, answered him 'in a cluster of most crabbed notions, picked out of metaphysics and logic, as categorematical and syncategorematical, and a deal of such drumming stuff,' so that the motioner was foiled at his own weapon, and well laughed at by the court.

In the Star Chamber he was ever merciful in his judgments, and where they were heavy for the sake of example, he interceded with the king to lighten the penalty. He would not only with soft words turn away wrath, but would often venture on a facetious jest to pacify the royal displeasure. By his leniency he incurred by turns the suspicions of the antagonistic religious parties, at one time being stigmatised as a favourer of Roman Catholics, and at another as one of the Puritans. The former charge may be answered by his opposition to the erection of titular Popish prelates in the kingdom, and the latter by his addition of four scholars to Westminster College, with a liberal endowment to St.

John's College, Cambridge, and two fellowships to be chosen out of them, with four rich benefices for their ultimate provision.

In the parliaments over which he presided his speeches were marked with ingenuity and wit, the customary flattery to the king not being altogether omitted, but more delicately administered.

But the brightness of his fortune began to be obscured. The fickleness of Buckingham, and his jealousy of the reliance shown by the king on the lord keeper's judgment, with probably, too, his displeasure at Williams's occasional insubjection to his will, were soon exhibited in his attempts to sink the man whom he had aided to raise. His favour had been transferred to Bishop Laud, and, taking pretended offence at some of the lord keeper's proceedings, and indignant at some expressions of confidence which the king had used, all the cunning of the duke was exerted to hasten Williams's ruin. It was ineffectual, however, during the life of King James, who, appreciating his keeper's loyalty and prudence, and admiring his learning and wit, acted steadily as his friend, and preserved him in his office to the end of his reign. But some of the ill effects of the want of the favourite's countenance could not fail to be experienced. As soon as it was perceived that Buckingham's eye began to look frowningly on the lord keeper, disappointed suitors were ready to complain of his decrees, and accusations accumulated against him in both houses of parliament. He triumphed over them all. The Commons dismissed seven-and-thirty in one day, and the Lords punished one with the pillory for slander. (*Parl. Hist.* i. 1399.) King James died in March 1625, and Williams preached his funeral sermon, drawing a parallel between him and Solomon.

Though King Charles retained Williams as lord keeper, the latter soon felt the instability of his position. Buckingham was more than ever resolved to effect his ruin, and endeavoured to induce Chief Justice Hobart to complain of his unfitness for his place on account of his ignorance and inability. The honest judge, though tempted with the promise of the post on Williams's removal, answered, 'My lord, somewhat might have been said at first, but he should do the lord keeper great wrong that said so now.' Buckingham was not easily thwarted. The king was already prejudiced against Williams, and the grave advice which he gave to his majesty and the favourite not to quarrel with the parliament completed his disfavour. The Seal was taken from him on the 25th of October 1625, and placed in the hands of Sir Thomas Coventry.

There was a kind of reconciliation with Buckingham just before his assassination in 1628; but Bishop Laud, whom Williams had formerly befriended, then became his bitter enemy, under the supposition that he was a promoter of the Petition of Right, and, what was considered worse, an encourager of the Puritans. Continuing thus in disgrace at court, vexatious complaints were made against him, all of which failed in their object until 1637, when his enemies succeeded in procuring a conviction in the Star Chamber for a pretended offence committed nine or ten years before, in having revealed the king's secrets, and on a false accusation of tampering with the witnesses, for which he was sentenced to pay a fine of 10,000*l*., to be imprisoned, and to be suspended from his ecclesiastical functions.

This sentence was executed with the greatest rigour. His property was wantonly despoiled under pretence of raising his fine, his person was incarcerated for three years and a half, and his desire to offer submission was met by the demand of such degrading and ruinous terms that he felt compelled to reject them. He only procured his liberation at last by presenting a petition to the House of Lords in November 1640, detailing his grievances and demanding his writ. On his discharge he forgot his personal complaints in the distress of the state, and boldly stood up for his order and the monarchy. His conduct, of course, pleased as much as it surprised the king, who not only erased all memorial of the proceedings against him, but admitted him to his favour, took counsel of him in the difficulties that surrounded the throne, and on December 4, 1641, translated him to the archbishopric of York.

The cry against the bishops at that time ran high, and twelve of them, of whom the archbishop was at the head, were soon after his translation committed to the Tower under a ludicrous accusation of high treason for presenting a petition to the Peers, complaining that the mob prevented their access to the house, and declaring that whatsoever was done there during their forced absence was invalid and of none effect. The act excluding the bishops from parliament having passed during their confinement, the prosecution dropped, and the archbishop and his colleagues were released, after being detained for eighteen weeks, in the course of which Williams was reconciled to Archbishop Laud, then an inmate of the same prison.

Retiring to his diocese, the archbishop was soon obliged hurriedly to leave his castle of Cawood, in consequence of the advance of Sir John Hotham's son against it; and after having supplied the king with what aid in men and money he could, he fled to his native country, where he exerted himself to defend the royal cause. After fortifying Conway Castle at his own expense, he attended the king at Oxford, where he is said to have cautioned his majesty particularly against Cromwell, and to have urged his being either won by great promises or cut off by stratagem. His subsequent advice to the king to submit to the parliament on terms not being relished, he returned to Conway Castle, in the government of which he was superseded the year after by Sir John Owen, under a commission from Prince Rupert. Those who had deposited their money and jewels there were refused restitution, and the archbishop's appeal to the king on their and his own behalf was slighted; so that when Colonel Milton, with an overpowering force, came into the country on the part of the parliament, they represented their case to the colonel, and, upon his promise to restore to them their property, agreed to assist him in obtaining possession. In doing this they were aided by the archbishop, whose conduct on the occasion subjected him to the imputation of having deserted the king and assisted the rebels. He defended himself by asserting that, as the king's cause in Wales was past hope, he was justified in obtaining the restoration of the property of his friends, and in making the best terms he could for his countrymen's immunities.

'From the fidelity of the king he never,' says Bishop Hacket, 'went back an inch,' and when the last scene of the tragedy was over, he deeply mourned his royal master's death in solitary retirement; his cheerfulness forsook him, and he seldom spoke. He survived the king little more than a year, and died on his birthday, March 25, 1650, at Glodded, in the parish of Eglwysrose, Carnarvonshire, the house of his kinswoman Lady Mostyn. His body was removed for burial to the church of Llandegai, where his nephew and heir, Sir Griffith Williams, erected a monument to him, to which his former chaplain, Bishop Hacket, supplied the inscription.

It is difficult to form a just estimate of the character of any individual who lived in the times during which Archbishop Williams flourished. 'Men's passions were so strong, their prejudices so great, and their animosity against opposite opinions so violent, that acts in themselves indifferent were frequently misinterpreted, and what was lauded by one party was abused by the other. Clarendon and Heylin, enemies of the archbishop, look with a jaundiced eye on his whole career; and Bishop Hacket, his chaplain and friend, and Wilson the historian, give perhaps too partial a colouring to everything he did; so that entire reliance is not to be placed on either. The weight of evidence, however, clearly preponderates in his favour, though it must be allowed that, as a counsellor of state, he was too much of a temporiser, and no excuse can justify the casuistry with which he recommended Charles to consent to Strafford's death. But he was honest and sincere, and generally wise, in the advice which he offered; and to the monarchs whom he served he was faithful and true.

In person he was dignified and comely; in manner affable and kind; and though in temper he was warm, as most Welshmen are, yet his anger was quickly mollified; and, notwithstanding the oppressions which he suffered, he showed no wish for revenge. He was laborious in the performance of his duties, both political and clerical, and refined in the choice of his relaxations, music, in which he was a proficient, being his delight. His learning was undoubted; and his eloquence, according to the fashion of the times, was superior to that of most of his contemporaries, his allusions and illustrations being more apt and ingenious, and his wit more lively and delicately pointed. He was profusely hospitable in his household, and liberal to learned poverty, and the sums which he expended in repairing Westminster Abbey, and in building the library at St. John's College, Cambridge, and the chapel at that of Lincoln, in Oxford, witness his generous munificence.

His works were principally on clerical subjects, but that which excited the most observation was entitled 'The Holy Table, Name, and Thing,' published in opposition to the innovations introduced by Archbishop Laud. (*Lives by Bishop Hacket and A. Philips; Clarendon; and Heylin's Reformation* [Robertson].)

WILLIAMS, EDWARD VAUGHAN, who in 1865 retired from the bench, having served for nearly nineteen years as one of the judges of the Common Pleas, during the whole of which time he fully maintained the high reputation he had previously earned by his useful and learned publications, was a lawyer from his birth, his father, John Williams, Esq., being the serjeant in the reign of George III. who added valuable notes to an edition of Chief Justice Saunders's Reports. Though of Welsh extraction, he was born in London, and was educated at Westminster School.

He was called to the bar by the society of Lincoln's Inn on June 17, 1823, and naturally chose the South Wales and Chester Circuit. In the very next year he commenced his career as an author by publishing an edition of Saunders's Reports, enriching it, in conjunction with the late Mr. Justice Patteson, with admirable notes to his father's edition, bringing the history of the law down to the date of the work. For the twenty-three years that he remained at the bar he varied his forensic occupations by issuing from the press several other works, among which were a 'Treatise on the Law of Executors,' in 1832, which is in high estimation; and an edition of Burn's 'Justice,' in 1836, in conjunction with Mr. Serjeant D'Oyley.

He served an apprenticeship to the judicial office as recorder of Kidwelly, the corporation of which on his resignation expressed their high estimation of him for his 'undeniable integrity as a citizen, and his well-deserved reputation as a profound lawyer.' He was raised to the bench of the Common Pleas in October 1846, from which failing health obliged him to retire at the end of Hilary Term 1865, when he was sworn of the privy council.

He married Jane Margaret, a daughter of the Rev. Walter Bagot, of Pype Hall in Staffordshire.

WILLIAMS, JOHN, in whom we had another example of the union of law and literature, and an additional proof that the deepest scholastic attainments are not incompatible with professional success, was of Welsh extraction, being descended from an ancient family in Merionethshire, but was born at Bunbury in Cheshire, of which his father was vicar, as well as holding a living in the former county. He was born in January 1777, and imbibed his classical tastes at the grammar school of Manchester, from whence proceeding to the university of Cambridge, he gained a scholarship at Trinity College at the age of eighteen. In his progress he won many prizes, and, graduating as B.A. in 1798, he succeeded in obtaining a fellowship after a strenuous competition.

His legal school was the Middle Temple, where he took his degree of barrister in 1804. On the Northern Circuit and at the Manchester and Chester sessions he made his first attempts, where, though his progress was slow, his merits were so great, and his reputation for accuracy, ingenuity, and boldness became so well established, that in 1820 he was selected to assist Mr. Brougham and Mr. Denman in the defence of Queen Caroline, in the course of which he fully confirmed the character he had obtained. This naturally made him a marked man; but, though it increased his professional employment, it delayed his acquisition of professional rank. This, however, may perhaps be accounted for by his attacks upon Lord Chancellor Eldon in the House of Commons, of which he had been elected a member for Lincoln in 1823. No sooner had parliament met than Mr. Williams commenced that series of motions upon the delays in Chancery which ultimately, after some years, led to a commission of enquiry and the introduction of bills for reforming the proceedings in that court. These motions exhibited undoubtedly too much acerbity, and seemed to be dictated as much by personal as they certainly were by political feelings against Lord Eldon. In 1827 he attained a silk gown; and on the accession of William IV. he was appointed, first solicitor, and then attorney general, to Queen Adelaide, and on February 28, 1834, was advanced to the bench as a baron of the Exchequer. In the following term, however, changing places with Mr. Justice Parke, he took his seat in the Court of King's Bench, having received the accustomed honour of knighthood.

During the whole of this period he never deserted his classical favourites, contributing several articles on the Greek Orators to the 'Edinburgh Review,' and translating some of their best orations. He was also an adept in the turn of a Greek epigram, and Lord Tenterden speaks of several that he had written when queen's solicitor, speaking of him as 'an admirable scholar.' He afterwards published a collection under the title of 'Nugæ Metricæ.'

He remained on the bench for a little less than thirteen years, when he died on September 14, 1846, at his seat, Livermore Park, near Bury St. Edmund's. At his outset in the judge's office he was ignorant of the minor details of practice, and many curious anecdotes are told of his perplexing counsel and attorney by refusing to grant orders of course, which involved some absurd and since disused fiction of law. He soon overcame this difficulty, and became an excellent judge. With much eccentricity of manner, and a strong and decided way of expressing his opinions, he was a great favourite both with his brethren and the bar, from the cordiality and kindness of his nature. To the last he would spout Horace and Demosthenes by the hour if he could obtain an audience; and there was nothing so annoyed him as to hear counsel perpetrate a false quantity.

He married Harriet Catherine, the daughter of Davies Davenport, Esq., of Capesthorne Hall, Macclesfield, for many years M.P. for Cheshire. (*Law Mag.* Feb. 1847.)

WILLOUGHBY, THOMAS, was the fourth son of Sir Christopher Willoughby, whose grandfather was the second son of William, the fifth Baron Willoughby de Eresby, and whose eldest son, William, the judge's brother, succeeded to that title in 1508, as seventh baron, on failure of the senior branch. Thomas, as was common with younger brothers, was destined to the law; and preparing himself for his forensic career in Lincoln's Inn (of which he was admitted a member on July 16, 1502), he was nominated reader in 1517. In 1521 he became a serjeant-at-law, and in 1530 was constituted king's serjeant. While holding that dignity he and John Baldwin were made knights in 1534, being the first serjeant who had then ever accepted that distinction.

He was raised to the bench as a judge of the Common Pleas on October 9, 1537, and dying on September 29, 1545, lies buried in the church of Chidingstone, Kent.

By his marriage with Bridget, or, as some call her, Catherine, daughter and coheir of Chief Justice Sir Robert Read, he acquired the estate of Bore Place, in Chidingstone, which devolved on his son Robert, whose descendant Francis was made a baronet in 1677, and his successor, Thomas, was in 1712 created Lord Middleton of Middleton, Warwick, a title which still survives.

WILMOT, JOHN EARDLEY, the antiquity of whose family extends beyond the Conquest, was the son of Robert Wilmot, of Ormaston in Derbyshire, by Ursula, one of the daughters and coheiresses of Sir Samuel Marow, of Berkswell in Warwickshire, Bart.; and the brother of Robert Wilmot, who became secretary of the lord lieutenant of Ireland, and was rewarded with the baronetcy of Ormaston in 1772.

He was born on August 16, 1709, at Derby, in the free school of which town he received his first instruction. He was then placed under the Rev. Mr. Hunter of Lichfield, where he numbered Samuel Johnson and David Garrick among his schoolfellows, and where no less than four of his contemporary judges were educated. He next was removed to Westminster School, and afterwards to Trinity Hall, Cambridge. His great ambition was to become a fellow of that society, and to devote himself to the Church; but, in obedience to his father's wish, he adopted the profession of the law, and in December 1728 was entered at the Inner Temple.

He was called to the bar in June 1732, and for many years confined himself principally to country practice, with occasional attendance on the London courts, and in the House of Commons on contested elections. In the latter arena Horace Walpole (*Memoirs of Geo. II.* ii. 107) tells us that 'he was an admired pleader,' but being reprimanded on the contested election for Wareham with great haughtiness by Pitt, who told him he had brought thither the pertness of his profession, and being prohibited by the speaker from making a reply, he flung down his brief in a passion, and never would return to plead there any more.' The same lively author describes him as 'a man of great vivacity of parts, and loving hunting and wine, and not his profession.' Though his merits were so conspicuous as to gain the esteem of Sir Dudley Ryder and Lord Hardwicke, yet public life was so distasteful to him that he not only declined the offer of a silk gown, but resolved on retiring entirely to his native county, and in 1754 made a farewell speech in the Court of Exchequer. He was not long however allowed to enjoy his repose. In the next year, persuaded by his friends and the demands of an increasing family, he was sworn in as a judge of the King's Bench on February 11, 1755, and knighted.

Nothing can show more clearly the high estimation in which he was held than his being appointed on the resignation of Lord Hardwicke, although the junior judge upon the bench, one of the three commissioners to whom the Great Seal was entrusted on November 19, 1756, and who held it for upwards of seven months, till June 30, 1757. So ably did he perform his duties in the office that it was confidently reported that he was likely to be appointed lord keeper. On hearing this rumour he expressed his repugnance to his brother in these words: 'The acting junior in the commission is a spectre I started at; but the sustaining the office alone I must and will refuse at all events. I will not give up the peace of my mind to any earthly consideration whatever. . . . Bread and water are nectar and ambrosia, when contrasted with the supremacy of a court of justice.' While engaged as lord commissioner he still went the circuit, and in the spring assizes of 1757 he had a narrow escape of his life by the falling of a stack of chimneys through the roof of the court at Worcester. Several persons were killed by the accident, but the judge, though his clerk who was sitting under him was one of the victims, escaped without injury.

By an epitaph which he composed for himself it is evident that he contemplated his retirement from Westminster Hall after a service of ten years; and when that period had expired he endeavoured to obtain a removal to the quiet post of chief justice of Chester. The negotiations however failed; but ere another year had passed his hopes of retirement were to be severely tested. The elevation of Lord Camden to the chancellorship made a vacancy in the office of chief justice of the Common Pleas, and the government without hesitation offered Sir Eardley the place, feeling that, from his learning, his judgment, and his character, he was the only fit and proper person to fill that station. Though he endeavoured to divert the offer, and had actually written a letter declining it, yet at the earnest persuasions of his friends he was at last induced reluctantly to give way; and he was sworn lord chief justice of the Common Pleas on August 21, 1766. The appointment was universally approved, and was especially satisfactory to the legal world, which both admired and respected his talents and urbanity.

The publication of No. 45 of the 'North

Briton' occurred during his judicial career, and his conduct in regard to it fully exemplified his impartiality. On the part of the crown, as a judge of the King's Bench, in pronouncing judgment against John Williams, the publisher, he unhesitatingly stigmatised the libel as most scandalous and seditious, most malignant and dangerous to the state; and as chief justice of the Common Pleas, on the appeal to the House of Lords, he delivered in a learned speech the unanimous opinion of his colleagues and himself in confirmation of the judgment and sentence pronounced against Mr. Wilkes, the author of the libel. (*State Trials*, xix. 1127.) On the other hand, on the part of the people, his summing up in the action brought by Wilkes against Lord Halifax is a bold exposure of the illegality of general warrants, with the expression of his opinion that the plaintiff was entitled to liberal damages for the injury he had suffered by that issued in his case.

The Great Seal was pressed upon him on the resignation of Lord Chancellor Camden, and again on the death of the Hon. Charles Yorke, and also during the subsequent commission; but he showed the sincerity of his wish for privacy by refusing the proffered honour, and took advantage of the last opportunity to tender his resignation of the office which he held. His retirement took place on January 24, 1771; and, notwithstanding his repugnance to a pension, the king insisted that he should receive one of 2400*l*. a year as a mark of approbation for his exemplary services. In return for this liberal allowance, he thought it his duty to assist in hearing appeals to the privy council, till his increasing infirmities obliged him wholly to retire in 1782. He lived for ten years more, and dying on February 5, 1792, at the age of eighty-two, he was buried in Berkswell Church in Warwickshire.

The 'Opinions and Judgments' of Sir Eardley, and an affectionate memoir of his life, were published by his son, and both contain ample evidence to prove that the judge was not only an erudite lawyer, but a good man; that he was devoted to his duties as an advocate, a judge, and a Christian; that his merit solely raised him to the places which his modesty and diffidence would have declined; and that in the private relations of life—as a friend, a husband, and a father—he acquired the love and veneration of all around him.

By his marriage with Sarah, the daughter of Thomas Rivett, Esq., of Derby, he had issue three sons and two daughters. The second son, who was the author of the memoir, became a master in Chancery, and was the father of Sir John Eardley Wilmot, who received a baronetcy (of Berkswell) in 1831, being the third baronetcy in the family.

WILSON, JOHN, is regarded as one of the worthies of Winandermere. He was born on August 6, 1741, at the Howe in Applethwaite, where his father, whose Christian name he bore, resided. He matriculated at Peterhouse, Cambridge; and while an undergraduate in 1760 he distinguished himself by a very able reply to an attack which Dr. Powell, master of St. John's, had made upon the 'Miscellanea Analytica' of Dr. Waring, the Lucasian Professor of Mathematics. (*Nicholls's Lit. Anecd.* ii. 717.) In 1761 he was senior wrangler, and then became a private tutor, one of his pupils being Dr. Paley. He took his legal degree at the Inner Temple in January 1763, and soon, by his talents and industry, gained a considerable practice. Attending the Northern Circuit, Dunning thought so much of him that he employed him to answer many of his cases, and several of the opinions signed by Dunning were really the opinions of Mr. Wilson, who soon became a leader himself; and to his encouragement, and that of Sir James Mansfield, is to be attributed the continuance in Westminster Hall of that great luminary of the law John Scott, Earl of Eldon, who, not succeeding so rapidly as he expected, had determined in 1780 to retire to the country, when Mr. Wilson, earnestly advising him to give up the idea, generously offered to insure him 400*l*. the next year. (*Twiss's Eldon*, i. 123.)

Mr. Wilson, keeping entirely aloof from politics, never sought a seat in parliament; and for his professional merit alone was recommended by Lord Thurlow, with whom he had had no previous acquaintance, to fill a vacant seat in the Common Pleas, to which he was appointed on November 7, 1786, receiving the honour of knighthood. He was so highly respected as a judge, and performed his duties with so much patience and discrimination, that he was, on the retirement of Lord Chancellor Thurlow, appointed one of the commissioners of the Great Seal, from June 15, 1792, to January 28, 1793. Before the end of that year he was seized with paralysis, and died on October 18, 1793, at Kendal, where, on his tomb, is an inscription from the pen of Bishop Watson, eloquently descriptive of his merits as a lawyer, his uprightness as a judge, and his worth as a man. In 1783 he became a fellow of the Royal Society. He married the daughter of Mr. Serjeant Adair, and left a small infant family. (*H. Blackstone*, 211; *Gent. Mag.* lxii. 965, lxiv. 1051.)

WILTON, RICHARD DE, was sheriff of Wiltshire from 10 to 27 Henry II. In the 19th year of that reign, 1173, he set the assize as one of the justices itinerant in Devonshire, and in the following year in his own county. (*Madox*, i. 123, 701.)

WILTON, LAURENCE DE, was an ecclesiastic, and one of the justices itinerant in

3 Henry III., 1219, for Cumberland, Westmoreland, and Lancashire. (*Rymer*, i. 154.) The only previous notice of him is in 7 John, when he obtained, on a fine of two palfreys, the king's charter, confirming to him a certain Stone House in Cunning Street, York, which Robert de Stuteville had granted to him and his heirs at the annual rent of a pair of gilt spurs. (*Rot. Chart.* 163.)

WILTON, WILLIAM DE, had fines levied before him in Trinity 1247, 31 Henry III., and the two following years. In 1248, 1248, and 1250 he acted as a justice itinerant, as his brethren did (*Dugdale's Orig.* 43), but from that date till August 1253 his name does not occur. During the latter and the two next years there are several entries of payments for writs of assize to be taken before him; and then there is another omission of his name for three successive years more. These payments are resumed in July 1259 (*Abb. Placit.* 134); and in the next two years he appears among the justices itinerant, in the last of which, 1261, he is placed at the head of three of the commissions.

On December 11, 1261, he had a grant of 100*l.* per annum to support him 'in officio justiciariæ,' being the allowance then made to those who held the chief place. Whether the court over which he presided was the King's Bench or the Common Pleas does not distinctly appear, but there seem sufficient grounds to show he was then chief justice of the King's Bench. That at first he belonged to the Common Pleas has been presumed from fines having been acknowledged before him. But, as none were so acknowledged after 33 Henry III., he was in all likelihood, on his restoration to office (for that he was twice removed there is reason to conjecture), placed in the King's Bench, and continued there till he was raised to the head of it. Writs of assize to be taken before him were granted up to November 1263, 48 Henry III. (*Excerpt. e Rot. Fin.* ii. 407.)

While some of the judges of this period were evidently members of the ecclesiastical body, others did not consider military service inconsistent with their judicial character. According to a manuscript preserved in Leland's 'Collections' (i. 175), William de Wilton was killed at the battle of Lewes, on May 14, 1264, fighting on the side of his royal master.

He and his wife, Roesa, had a charter for a market in an unnamed place in Kent in 1256. (*Excerpt. e Rot. Fin.* ii. 245.)

WILUGHBY, PHILIP DE (whose name is variously spelled), was appointed a baron of the Exchequer before Michaelmas, 3 Edward I., 1275, when he is mentioned as being present with that title. He soon after received the custody of one of the four keys of the royal treasury, his annual fee in the former capacity being forty marks, and in the latter 10*l.* He was raised to the office of chancellor of the Exchequer about 1283, and filled it till his death in 1305, a period of twenty-two years. During this time he frequently acted as locum tenens of the treasurer, and seems to have been so indefatigable in his attention to the duties of his office that in 30 Edward I. the king, taking into consideration the length of his service, gave him a licence to attend at the Exchequer when it suited his leisure and convenience. (*Madox*, ii. 54, 96, &c., 320–325; *Abb. Placit.* 281.)

Like most of the officers of the court, he was of the clerical profession, and first obtained as his reward a canonry of St. Paul's, from which he was advanced in June 1288 to the deanery of Lincoln. (*Le Neve*, 145.) At his death he was possessed of the manor of Byflete in Kent, and lands in Notts and Middlesex. (*Cal. Inq.* p. m. i. 196.)

WILUGHBY, RICHARD DE, the original surname of whose family was Bugge, which was changed to Wilughby from their lordship of that name in Nottinghamshire, was the son of Richard de Wilughby, who purchased the manors of Wollaton in the same county, and Risley in Derbyshire. In 17 Edward II. he was substituted for his father as the representative in parliament for his native county, and was about the same time appointed chief justice of the Common Pleas in Ireland. (*Parl. Writs*, ii. p. ii. 1616; *Cal. Rot. Pat.* 78, 94, 97.)

On the accession of Edward III. he was removed from this position, and it would appear that he resumed his practice at the English bar, as he is mentioned in the Year Book as an advocate in the first year. On March 6, 1328, in the second year, however, he was placed on the bench of the Common Pleas in England, and was further advanced on September 2, 1329, to be the second justice of that court. On December 15, 1330, he was removed into the Court of King's Bench; and when Geoffrey le Scrope, the chief justice, went abroad with the king, Wilughby occupied the chief seat during his absence, at different times from 1332 till Geoffrey le Scrope ultimately resigned in the middle of 1338. From this time there is no doubt that Wilughby presided in the court until he was displaced on July 24, 1340, and on the 9th of October following he was restored to the Common Pleas.

Stephen Birchington (*Angl. Sac.* i. 21) says that he was one of the judges who were arrested by the king on his hasty return to England at the end of November 1340, for some alleged misconduct; and it is to be remarked that neither in the Book of Assizes, nor in the Rolls of Parliament, nor in any other document, does his name appear as a judge till the seventeenth year.

He then certainly had a new patent (*Cal. Rot. Pat.* 146), and from that date fines were levied before him till Trinity, 31 Edward III. (*Dugdale's Orig.* 45), when, as the Year Book does not record any of his judgments of a later date, he probably retired from the bench, though he lived for five years afterwards.

It is related of him that about Christmas 1331, which was before he was chief justice, he was attacked on his way to Grantham by one Richard Fulville, and forcibly taken into a wood, where a gang of lawless men, large bodies of whom then infested the country, compelled him to pay a ransom for his life of ninety marks. (*Barnes's Edw. III.* 62.) This violence, however disagreeable to its object, had the happy effect of causing measures to be taken to put a stop to these combinations.

He died in 36 Edward III., possessed of extensive estates in the counties of Nottingham, Derby, and Lincoln, &c., besides a great house situate in 'le Baly' in London. (*Cal. Inq.* p. m. ii. 256.)

He married three wives—1, Isabel, daughter of Sir Roger Mortein; 2, Joanna; and 3, Isabella—and had several children. Two of his descendants, Sir Henry Willoughby of Risley, and Sir William Willoughby of Selston, were created baronets, the former in 1611, and the latter in 1660; but both titles became extinct on their deaths.

WIMER is called 'the Chaplain' in every place where his name occurs, no doubt as filling that office in the king's court. He held the sheriffalty of Norfolk and Suffolk for seventeen years and a half, commencing 16 Henry II., 1170. He is mentioned in the Chronicle of Joceline de Brakelonda (19) as being present as sheriff at the inauguration of Samson to the abbacy of St. Edmund's in 1182. In the 1st year of Richard I. (*Pipe Roll*, 44) he paid a fine of two hundred marks for his quittance from that sheriffalty, and from all complaints against him and his serjeants during the time he had held it; offered probably by the sheriff as an easy discharge of long-continued accounts, and received by the king as a convenient addition to his funds for the crusade.

His name occurs once only as a justice itinerant in 1173, when he and three others assessed the tallage on the king's demesnes in Essex and Hertfordshire. He also accounted for the abbey of Hulme, then vacant and in the king's hands. (*Madox*, i. 308, 701.)

Possibly he may be the same with *Winemerus*, mentioned in Le Neve (153, 161) as subdean of Lincoln in 1185, and archdeacon of Northampton in 1195.

WINCH, HUMFREY, of Everton in the county of Bedford, was born about 1545, and was called to the bar at Lincoln's Inn in 1581, became a bencher there in 1596, and reader in 1598. He must have acquired some character as a lawyer, for he sat in the last three of Elizabeth's parliaments for the town of Bedford, and was invested with the degree of the coif in Trinity Term 1606, for the purpose of taking upon him the office of chief baron of the Exchequer in Ireland, to which he was appointed on November 8. He was then knighted, and two years afterwards he succeeded Sir James Ley as lord chief justice of the King's Bench in that country, with a salary of 300*l.* a year. He only retained that appointment from December 8, 1608, till November 7, 1611 (*Smyth's Law Off. Ireland*, 88, 140), during which his character for 'quickness, industry, and dispatch' is recommended for imitation by Bacon, in his speech to Sir William Jones, on taking the same place. (*Bacon's Works* [Montagu], vii. 2, 64.) Sir Humfrey was immediately translated into England, and constituted a judge of the Common Pleas, where he sat for the next fifteen years. In August 1613 he was sent into Ireland with three other commissioners to examine into the complaints of the people. (*Pell Records*, 169.) Three years after he fell deservedly into some disgrace, in consequence of condemning and executing, at the summer assizes at Leicester, no less than nine women as witches, on the evidence of a boy, who pretended that he had been bewitched and tormented by them. The king, on a visit to the town a month after the trial, personally examining the boy, discovered and exposed the imposture, but too late to save the unfortunate victims of this absurd superstition. (*Leicester Records, MSS.*)

He died suddenly while robing to go into court on February 4, 1625, and was buried in the cloisters of Pembroke Hall, Cambridge. His reports of 'Choice Cases' in his own court were published in 1657; and Croke (*Jac.* 700), his colleague on the bench, calls him a 'learned and religious judge.'

By his wife, Cecily, daughter of Richard Onslow, Esq., recorder of London and speaker of the House of Commons, he left, besides other issue, a son named Onslow Winch, who was sheriff of Bedfordshire in 1633; but his male representatives terminated with Humfrey Winch, of Hawnes in that county, who was created a baronet in 1660, and died without male issue in 1703. (*Wotton's Baronet.* iv. 475.)

WINCHESTEDE, JOHN DE, stands the last of six justices itinerant before whom a fine was levied at Westminster in 3 Henry III., 1219, but no further mention of him occurs in any of the records of that period.

WINCHESTER, EARL OF. *See* S. DE QUINCY.

WINCHESTER, MARQUIS OF. *See* W. PAULET.

WINGHAM, HENRY DE (BISHOP OF LONDON), was born at Wingham in Kent, from which he took his name. He was probably brought up in one of the offices of the Exchequer, since 200*l*. was entrusted to him in 26 Henry III. to be expended in the king's service, and he was assigned in 30 Henry III., 1245, in conjunction with John de Grey, the justice of Chester, to assess the tallage for that city. (*Pell Records*, iii. 25; *Madox*, i. 735.) He was then one of the king's escheators (*Excerpt. e Rot. Fin.* i. 458–464, ii. 4–36), and, besides being appointed chamberlain of Gascony, was employed in two embassies into France. The patent, dated July 2, 1253, 37 Henry III., 'De provisione facta ad gubernationem regni,' when the king left the government in the hands of his queen during his absence, is signed 'per manus H. de Wengham,' showing, probably, that he was then connected with the Chancery. On January 5, 1255, the Great Seal was delivered into his custody; but the title of chancellor does not appear to have accompanied it. (*Madox*, i. 68, 69.) In 1257 he was collated to the chancellorship of Exeter, and soon afterwards was advanced to the valuable deanery of St. Martin's. He was one of the twelve selected on the part of the king when the Mad Parliament of Oxford, in June 1258, appointed twenty-four barons to draw up provisions for the government of the kingdom; and was continued in his office on swearing not to put the Seal to any writ which had not the approbation of the council as well as of the king.

Soon after this, on the flight of the king's half-brother, Ethelmar, who had been elected Bishop of Winchester, the monks of that church chose Henry de Wingham for their bishop; but he, being unwilling to mix in their dissensions, and doubtful perhaps of King Henry's real approbation, declined the proffered mitre, alleging his insufficiency. This, however, did not prevent his acceptance of the bishopric of London, to which he was shortly afterwards appointed, and consecrated on February 15, 1260. On October 18 he retired from the Chancery, and the king's approval of his conduct was shown by the permission he received to retain his deaneries and all his other ecclesiastical preferments, consisting of ten valuable prebends and rectories.

This discreet and circumspect courtier died on July 13, 1262, and was buried in his own cathedral. (*Godwin*, 182, 221; *Le Neve*, 88, 177; *Weever*, 359; *Brady's Engl.* i. 625-635, *App.* 188, 199; *Rapin*, iii. 133.)

WISEBEC, REGINALD DE, so called probably from having been born at Wisbeach, was among the clergy named as justices itinerant at the council held at Windsor in 25 Henry II., when the kingdom was divided into four parts for judicial circuits. He was one of the king's chaplains, and no doubt was selected on that account. He does not appear to have acted in any subsequent year.

WITEFELD, ROBERT DE, was a justicier appointed by the same great council held in 25 Henry II., 1179. His presence in the Curia Regis when fines were taken is also noticed in the 30th, 33rd, and 35th Henry II. (*Hunter's Preface.*)

In 1 Richard I. he was associated with other judges to aid the chief justiciaries in the government of the kingdom during his absence (*Madox*, i. 34), and his name appears as witness to a final concord in 3 Richard I. (*Introd. to Rot. Cur. Regis*, cvii.)

There are two notices of his pleas among those of the reign of King John, one in the first year, and the other without date; but they apparently refer to the previous reign. (*Abb. Placit.* 25, 69.)

He was sheriff of the county of Gloucester in the 29th and 30th Henry II.

WODEHOUSE, ROBERT DE, was the son of Sir Bertram de Wodehouse, a Norfolk knight of great possessions, who is thus described in a rhyming pedigree of the family. He

Attended that brave king, Edward the First,
Into the north, when he the Scots disperst,
Slew twenty thousand, Edinborough shook,
Dunbar and Barwick, where they homage took.

His mother was Muriel, daughter and heir of Hamo, lord of Felton; and his eldest brother, Sir William, was the ancestor of the present Baron Wodehouse of Kimberly, Norfolk.

Being brought up to the Church, he became chaplain to Edward II., from whom he received the office of escheator. (*Abb. Rot. Orig.* i. 174-194.) On July 24, 1318, 12 Edward II., he was constituted a baron of the Exchequer, and was summoned to parliament among the judges as late as November 1322, 16 Edward II., when he probably resigned or was removed, as about this time he became keeper of the king's wardrobe, an office which he held at the end of that reign, and at the commencement of the next. (*Rot. Parl.* ii. 388.)

In 1 Edward III. he was presented to the archdeaconry of Richmond, and on April 16, 1329, was replaced on the Exchequer bench as second baron; but again resigned his seat on September 16, when he was made chancellor of the Exchequer, by which title he had a grant to him in the next year of the manor of Ashele, with the bailiwick of the forests of Bere in Hampshire. (*Abb. Rot. Orig.* ii. 43, 127.) On March 10, 1339, he was promoted to the office of treasurer of the Exchequer, but seems only to have continued in it till the following December.

He probably died in January 1346, 19

Edward III., as his will was proved on the 3rd of the following February, wherein he ordered his body to be buried in the choir of the Augustine monks at Stamford. (*Le Neve*, 325.)

WODESTOKE, JAMES DE, of Holshute in Hampshire, was member for the county of Berks in 1336. He wore the judicial ermine for a very short period, his patent, as a judge of the Common Pleas, being dated on February 4, 1340, 14 Edward III., and his death occurring either at the end of that or the beginning of the next year. From the eighth year of that reign his name occurs in several commissions for the trial of offences, gradually rising from the lowest to the highest step in them. His place of birth may be presumed from his name, and from his being employed in 9 Edward III. to raise money for the king in Oxfordshire. At his death he was in possession of the manor of Brunes Norton in that county, and of that of Holshute and Appleton in Berkshire. (*Dugdale's Orig.* 45; *Cal. Inq. p. m.* ii. 99; *Rot. Parl.* ii. 78, 449; *Abb. Rot. Orig.* ii. 99; *N. Fœdera*, ii. 875, 897.)

WOGAN, JOHN, was a referee, in conjunction with Hugo de Cressingham, of the dispute between the queen and William de Valence and his wife, the result of which was stated to the parliament of 18 Edward I. At the same parliament Hugo de Cressingham complained against him that he entered the queen's court at Haverford, and impeded the proceedings, to which Wogan answered that he did so only to prevent one of the tenants from doing fealty to the queen for a tenement he held of William de Valence; and the case was referred for enquiry, but the decision does not appear. (*Rot. Parl.* i. 31, 33.) In 20 Edward I., 1292, he was one of the justices itinerant assigned for the four northern counties; and was appointed chief justice of Ireland on October 18, 1295 (*Cal. Rot. Pat.*), continuing to hold that important post for the remainder of that, and for the first twelve years of the next reign, when Roger de Mortimer was put in his place.

During the whole of this period he is occasionally mentioned in parliament, but does not appear to have acted judicially in England in the reign of Edward II.; for though he was named as a justice itinerant into Kent on May 13, 1313, 6 Edward II., he was removed from the commission ten days afterwards, on account of other business requiring his attention, and another was substituted for him. (*Parl. Writs*, i. 910, ii. 1631.)

WOLLAVESTON, or WOLLAVINTON, HENRY DE, is mentioned under the former name as a justice itinerant, in 52 Henry III., 1268, into eleven counties; and again, under the latter name, in 1272, into Essex. (*Rot. Claus.* i. 459.) From May 1269 there are entries of payments made for assizes to be held before him, in each year, till May 1272, which raises a question whether he may not be considered as a regular justicier. There are parishes of the name of Woolavington both in Somersetshire and Sussex, from which the latter name might have been derived; but if the former is the correct one, it was probably taken from the manor of Wollaston in Staffordshire, where a family so designated was seated at this period.

WOLLORE, DAVID DE, named from the town of Wollore in Northumberland, is little known before he became master of the Rolls. The only previous notice we have met with is that he was sent to attend the parliament which King Edward Baliol summoned in Scotland in 8 Edward III., that his mission occupied eighteen days, and that he was allowed three shillings a day for his expenses. (*N. Fœdera*, ii. 875, 897.) There is no evidence to show that he was a clerk in the Chancery, nor does the date of his appointment as master of the Rolls appear. He is first mentioned in that office on July 2, 1346, 20 Edward III. (*Ibid.* iii. 85.)

He continued in that office about five-and-twenty years, during which time he frequently had the custody of the Great Seal—in 1349, 1351, and 1353. He was receiver of petitions in the parliaments from 36 to 43 Edward III. (*Rot. Parl.* ii. 268–299.)

In his clerical character he was a canon of St. Paul's and rector of Bishop's Wearmouth, his successor in which was inducted in 1370, the year of his death. (*Surtees' Durham*, i. 231.)

WOLSELEY, RALPH, belonged to one of the most ancient families in Staffordshire, whose principal estate was called Wlselia. He was the son of Thomas de Wolseley, by Margery, daughter of William Brocton, of Longdon in the same county. Brought up in the Exchequer, he received a grant of the office of victualler to the town of Calais. This he surrendered in December 1466, and on the 29th of September following he was raised to the bench of the Exchequer as a fourth baron. In the same year a grant he had received of all the wood and underwood called Hopwashay in Staffordshire was excepted out of the act of resumption then passed. (*Rot. Parl.* v. 602, 615.)

He was superseded as baron on June 14, 1470, 10 Edward IV., but was re-appointed on March 8, 1478, 18 Edward IV., and retained his place on the accessions of Edward V. and Richard III. He died in the early part of the second year of the latter reign.

He was twice married. By his first wife, who was a daughter of Lord Mountjoy, he had no issue. By his second, Margaret, daughter of Sir Robert Aston, of Heywood, knight, he left a son, John, in whose posterity two baronetcies now flourish—one created in 1628, and the other in 1744. (*Wotton's Baronet.* ii. 133.)

WOLSEY, THOMAS (ARCHBISHOP OF YORK and CARDINAL). The events of no man's life have been so frequently recorded as those of Cardinal Wolsey. No history of this country, nor indeed of any other European state during the period in which he flourished, can avoid the introduction of his name, or omit the scenes in which he acted; and numerous have been the separate biographies which have described his career. The picturesque memoirs by his faithful gentleman usher George Cavendish, ably illustrated as they have been by Dr. Wordsworth and Mr. Singer; the pithy 'Observations' of David Lloyd in his 'State Worthies;' the fearful folio of Dr. Fiddes, rendered valuable by his 'Collections' of original documents; the earliest literary effort of John Galt; the various articles in biographical dictionaries; the interesting summary by Anthony Wood: the able 'Life' in the Library of Useful Knowledge; and, lastly, the elegant and excellent contribution to Lardner's Cabinet Cyclopædia, render it almost a work of supererogation to repeat the oft-told tale. The following slight sketch is formed principally from the materials which these authors have supplied.

Thomas Wolsey was born at Ipswich in March 1471. The Christian names of his parents were Robert and Joan; and the surname is spelled Wuley in the father's will, and so did the cardinal himself spell it as late as August 1508, if a bull of Pope Julius II. of that date, confirming a dispensation granted to him by Pope Alexander VI. in 1501, in both of which he is so called, may be taken as authority. But in letters of his preserved in the State Paper Office his signature is 'Thomas Wulcy,' which name is also used in a petition from one of his relatives. Some error therefore must have crept into the former documents, which is not unlikely in the careless writing of the day; and the letter e, by an easy mistake in reading or transcribing, may have been substituted for c. The letters are so subscribed as late as September 1513, a few months after which he became Bishop of Lincoln, when he signed with his spiritual title. He altered it in 1509, when he became almoner to the king. (*Rymer*, xii. 783, xiii. 217, 267; *Fiddes, Coll.* i.)

Tradition states that his father was a butcher; and the popular voice and satirical song of the time make the tale probable. Some of his biographers have given no credit to the story; but it may certainly be inferred, from the absence of all mention, and apparently the careful concealment, of his employment, that, if not a butcher, he followed some other obscure trade, of which his son in his pride did not delight to speak. His first biographer, George Cavendish, who had been his gentleman usher, describes him as 'an honest poor man's son;' and the father, in his will, refrains from introducing any designation of his calling.

This will was proved on October 11, 1496, having been made eleven days previously. In it he gives to his son, who was then twenty-five years old, ten marks, 'if he be a priest' within a year after his death, as a salary for singing for him and his friends for the space of a year; 'but if he be not a priest, then another honest priest' was to have the ten marks for the same service. He then devises all his lands, &c., in the parishes of St. Nicholas, in Ipswich, and in St. Stoke, to his wife, the extent and value of which may be fairly presumed not to be larger in amount than would be sufficient for her maintenance, as he makes no provision whatever for his son. Cavendish, therefore, is probably correct in stating that he was maintained 'by means of his good friends' at the university of Oxford, to which he was sent at a very early age.

There the first proof he gave of his capacity—as it was perhaps the first incentive to his ambition—was the attainment of the degree of bachelor of arts at the early age of fifteen; and in after times he used to pride himself in having been called the boy bachelor. Such an early proficiency soon placed him as a fellow of Magdalen College, and shortly afterwards raised him to the mastership of the grammar school attached to that foundation. He was bursar of the college in 1498, when the great tower was finished that goes by his name. There is an idle story of his having misapplied the college funds towards its erection; but it is supported by no authority.

He could not have availed himself of the conditional legacy, for he was not admitted into orders till nearly four years after his father's death. In October 1500 he was instituted to the living of Lymington in Somersetshire, on the presentation of the Marquis of Dorset, not only in grateful acknowledgment of his pains and success in the education of that nobleman's three sons, who had been put under his charge at Magdalen School, but in admiration of the agreeable manners and conversational talent which he displayed when he accompanied his three noble pupils to their father's mansion in the previous Christmas. As if it were in anticipation of his future preferments, he immediately applied for and obtained a dispensation from the pope (that already referred to of 1501) for holding more benefices than one, and for non-residence on any. 'The honesty of his life and manners, and his other laudable merits of probity and virtue,' which are assigned in the bull as motives for granting it, together with the presentation of the living itself, afford a sufficient refutation of the traditionary scandal about the misapplication of the college funds.

Wolsey is represented as a very handsome man at this time, though afterwards he had a blemish in his right eye, so disfiguring him that in his portraits he is always represented in profile. He was also rather more free and easy in his manners and habits than modern ideas of what a clergyman should be warrant. An event is stated to have occurred soon after he took up his residence at Lymington, which, though the particulars may be embellished, is undoubtedly true in the main. Though attended with unpleasant consequences at the moment, it was perhaps a fortunate incident for him, as it taught him to be more circumspect in his public conduct for the future. It is said that, going with some boon companions to a fair in the vicinity, he got into a drunken row, and that thereupon Sir Amyas Paulet, a neighbouring justice, to whom probably he had not paid sufficient deference, set him in the stocks. This was an insult to his position as a priest which it must be allowed no pretence could justify; but it would have been more dignified in him to forget it when he had overcome the disgrace, and filled the high post of lord chancellor. Instead of doing so, he sent for the inconsiderate knight, and, after giving him a sharp reprimand, dismissed him from his presence with an injunction not to leave London without licence. In no very enviable state of suspense, he remained in the Middle Temple for four or five years, till at last, thinking that the best mode of appeasing the cardinal's displeasure was to flatter his vanity, he rebuilt the gate-house there, and embellished it with Wolsey's arms and ecclesiastical badges — an offering which had the desired effect. The disgrace inflicted on Wolsey of course obliged him to retire from his parish, but he did not resign the preferment till 1509. (*Fasti Oxon.* i. 28.)

In the interval between this retirement and his resignation he became chaplain to Henry Dene, Archbishop of Canterbury, when he was for a short time lord keeper of the Great Seal; and subsequently, on the archbishop's death in February 1503, he proceeded to Calais as chaplain to Sir John Nanphant, the treasurer there. Sir John was a man stricken with age, and was glad to avail himself of the assistance of his chaplain in performing the duties attached to his place; and it is not unlikely that Wolsey by his assiduity in these transactions acquired his first insight into state affairs. By the interest of Sir John, who was soon after compelled by his infirmities to return to England, he obtained the appointment of one of the king's chaplains—his first step on the ladder of preferment. In this capacity he succeeded in ingratiating himself with Bishop Fox and Sir Thomas Lovel—the former holding the office of lord privy seal, and the latter being treasurer of the household. His tact and cleverness, joined to his courtly manners and a commanding address, induced them to recommend him to Henry VII. to be employed on a delicate mission which that king was desirous of sending to the Emperor Maximilian in Flanders, with reference to his projected marriage with Margaret Duchess of Savoy, the emperor's daughter. The king, in a personal interview with Wolsey, having satisfied himself of the singular capacity of the new diplomatist, at once gave him his instructions, and so extraordinary was the expedition Wolsey used on the occasion that he presented himself at the English court four days afterwards. The king, on seeing him, angrily rebuked him for delaying his departure so long; great therefore was his majesty's surprise when Wolsey delivered to him the emperor's letters in reply, and soon was added the royal admiration of his envoy's acuteness in supplying a defect in his credentials which had not been discovered till after he was gone.

The deanery of Lincoln soon becoming vacant, the grateful king was enabled to present it to his active servant on February 2, 1509, about two months before his reign was terminated by his death. To this dignity two prebends in the same church were afterwards added, he having been previously instituted to the rectory of Redgrave in Suffolk, and the livings of Lyde in Kent, and St. Bride's, London.

On the accession of Henry VIII., Wolsey had completed his thirty-eighth year. The recent activity he had displayed was not likely to be overlooked; and his clerical position giving him ready access at the court, he soon recommended himself to his new sovereign by his wit and gaiety, which he managed so to temper with discretion as not to outrage his ecclesiastical character, nor yet to conceal those more solid qualities which he must have been conscious of possessing. Henry was not long in availing himself of his services, appointing him one of his council, and on November 8, 1509, granting him the office of almoner. (*Rymer*, xiii. 267.) Thus placed in intimate communication with the king, he gradually relieved the youthful monarch of most of his political labours; and thus, an acknowledged favourite, he not only received the usual royal compensations for his assiduity, but, according to Cavendish, 'presents, gifts, and rewards came in so plentifully that he lacked nothing that might either please his fantasy or enrich his coffers.'

Professional preferment naturally followed. First the rectory of Torrington in Devonshire was given to him, and then a canonry of Windsor; he was next made registrar of the order of the Garter, and dean of Hereford; and on resigning the latter, he received in February 1513 the deanery of York, holding each with his former preferment as dean of Lincoln; in addition to which he was collated in the following July to the precentorship of St. Paul's.

When King Henry undertook the expedition against France in June 1513, Wolsey not only accompanied him, but had the sole direction of the supplies and provision for the royal army. He was present at the taking of Terouenne and Tournay, and was rewarded with the bishopric of the latter. He derived, however, very little profit from this piece of preferment, a French competitor, who had been previously elected, intercepting the revenues. But he was soon compensated by an English see, being raised in February 1514 to the episcopal bench as Bishop of Lincoln. He rapidly rose to the highest position he held in the Church, for within six months he was translated to the archbishopric of York; and on September 7 in the following year he received the cardinal's hat from Pope Leo X., with the title of St. Cecilia, which was quickly succeeded by a commission from the pontiff as legate à latere.

Although the only ostensible office in the king's court hitherto held by Wolsey was that of the royal almoner, he had for some time been the principal adviser and mover in all affairs of state. That he was considered as having the greatest influence with his royal master is evidenced by the flatteries he received from foreign princes, and the applications for his intercession from eminent personages who sought the king's favour. The dignities granted to him by the Roman pontiff were manifestly prompted by the wish to conciliate King Henry; the confidential letters he received from Queen Catherine herself so early as 1513, and his correspondence with the king's sister, the Princess Mary, in reference to her two marriages with King Louis XII. of France, and Charles Brandon Duke of Suffolk, show how highly his assistance was estimated; and the annuity of 10,000 ducats granted to him by the Duke of Milan incontestably exhibits the ascendency which was attributed to him. That his influence was not overrated may be judged from the quick succession of ecclesiastical preferments that were heaped upon him, and more particularly by the familiar and confidential style of the letters addressed to him by the king. In July 1515 the Venetian ambassador says of him, 'He really seems to have the management of the whole of this kingdom,' and in the next year calls him 'ipse rex,' and 'rex et autor omnium.' (*Ellis's Letters*, 1st S. i. 78–89; *Fiddes's Coll.* 14, 15, c. ; *Four Years at the Court of Henry VIII.* 110, 155, 160.)

That such a rapid advance in the short period of ten years from the comparatively humble position of a court chaplain to the elevated ranks of cardinal and legate in the Church, and chief minister of the kingdom, should have made an ordinary man 'inebriated with prosperity,' as Archbishop Warham described him, would cause no wonder; but that it should produce such an effect upon a person possessing the superior endowments and firmness of character that distinguished Wolsey may well excite surprise. And yet it is manifest from his whole history that not merely the charge of vanity, but also that of an insatiable appetite for the accumulation of riches, had some foundation. Of the latter we have proof in his holding two deaneries and various prebends and livings at the same time ; in the rewards, which would now be called bribes, acknowledged by his friendly biographer to have been taken by him in his office; and in the pension which he accepted from a foreign power. Of the former there are too many childish examples—in the state he observed in his household, in his assumption of the cross of York within the prohibited province of Canterbury, and in the anxiety he evinced to give a greater degree of consequence to the mission sent by the pope with the cardinal's hat, by staying the journey of the messengers till he could procure a retinue which he considered more suitable to his high estate.

Wolsey was not yet satisfied. There was still another dignity to which he aspired. The lord chancellor had for a long series of years, previous to the present reign, been looked up to as the head of the council, and as the prime minister. Wolsey accordingly thought his power would be incomplete without the possession of the Great Seal. Archbishop Warham had held it for thirteen years; and, though Wolsey had for some time deprived him of the real power of the chancellorship, there can be no doubt that his great aim was to supersede the modest primate in the title also. The indignities with which he treated the archbishop have so much the appearance of an attempt to enforce his resignation that Wolsey's resistance, when the resignation at last took place, can only be regarded as a mere pretence.

The entry on the rolls of Wolsey's

appointment as lord chancellor, which is dated on December 22, 1515, affords an instance of his fondness for vain display, and of his desire to depreciate others. Instead of the simple manner in which former transfers of the Great Seal were generally made, he has caused all his titles to be written at length, even that of 'Primate of England,' while Archbishop Warham is described in the same instrument in the most curt manner, and is docked of his title of 'Primate of all England.' The same ostentation is visible in all the numerous documents which are contained in Rymer's 'Fœdera.' Even, to gratify this love of show, the simple bag in which the Great Seal was deposited, which for centuries before had been composed of linen or of leather, and which, when delivered to him, was 'a bag of white leather,' was transformed to a magnificent purse, something like that which is now carried before the chancellor, being described as 'a bag or purse of crimson velvet, ornamented with the arms and emblems of England.' The present practice also of bearing a silver gilt mace before the chancellor is supposed to have originated with him.

The description given by Cavendish (in Wordsworth, i. 486) of his daily processions to Westminster Hall, besides showing the studied formality of his household, affords another specimen of his love of ostentatious display.

For the manner in which he exercised the jurisdiction of the Chancery during the fourteen years he presided in it his reputation stands high. Nowithstanding the perpetual and varied demands on his time, and the importance of his political duties, his attendance on the court was regular and punctual, and, whatever opinion may be formed by different writers of his character as a statesman, his decrees as chancellor are acknowledged to have been equitable and just.

Holinshed says (iii. 615) that, being tired of hearing so many causes himself, Wolsey, by the king's commission, erected four 'under-courts to hear complaints;' and Lord Campbell, in his recent work, has at once designated these as 'four new courts of equity.' For this there exists no authority whatever. The only other court in which causes in Chancery were heard was that of the master of the Rolls, and that was by no means newly introduced by Wolsey, the ancient records proving that bills in Chancery were addressed to and suits heard by the master of the Rolls separately, as now, so early as the reign of Henry VI. The only proof of Wolsey requiring assistance in the court of equity is a commission from the king, issued shortly before the close of his career—only four months, in fact, previous to his removal—when the perplexities of the divorce case, the trial of which was then proceeding, were added to his other anxieties. This patent was dated on June 11, 1529, and it authorised the master of the Rolls, three of the judges, six of the masters in Chancery, and ten other persons, to hear all causes in Chancery, not less than four being present, of whom two were to be of the first-named ten. (*Rymer*, xiv. 299.)

The other courts referred to by Holinshed were probably the Star Chamber, in which he usually presided, the legantine courts, which he held under the pope's authority, and other minor courts connected with the various offices he held.

The powers granted him by the pontiff were most extensive, and the manner in which he used them was the subject of universal complaint. Had he confined himself to the enforcement of a more strict discipline and morality among the clergy, which at that time was sufficiently lax, he might have expected and despised the enmity of those whose actions were subjected to his censure; but he is charged with employing under him a judge of bad character, who took bribes to stifle exposure, with arrogating an authority in reference to wills and administrations which was beyond his commission, and, what was far worse in the estimation of the bishops and nobles, with encroaching on their general patronage. When these arbitrary proceedings came to the king's ear, Archbishop Warham was ordered to admonish him—an infliction we may suppose not very grateful to the proud cardinal,—and the king himself afterwards found it necessary to administer a rebuke.

The account given of him by Sebastian Giustinian, ambassador from the Seigniory of Venice from 1515 to 1519, describes him as subject to violent fits of bad temper. He would sometimes keep the ambassador waiting for an audience for three hours, though he admitted others. Nor was this indignity peculiar to the representative of a powerful state, for such Venice then was; even the pope's nuncio did not escape his indecent violence. When irritated, he would keep gnawing with his teeth on a little cane which it was his custom to carry in his hand, and the ambassador declares himself unable to convey an idea of his rabid and insolent language during these paroxysms, but he adds that he sometimes had the good sense to retire to his bed when these mad fits of rage came upon him, and not to see any one.

Notwithstanding these failings, which were of course kept out of the royal sight, the favour with which Wolsey had been regarded by the king before he became chancellor continued to increase after he was possessed of the Great Seal. The most unbounded reliance was placed on his judgment, and no transaction in the state of the slightest importance was decided without his advice and concurrence. The multitudinous series of documents in the thirteenth and fourteenth volumes of Rymer's 'Fœdera' give some idea of the variety and extent of his labours, and plainly prove the consideration in which he was held, not only in this country, but by all the foreign potentates of the age. The estimation of the importance of his services was not merely expressed in letters of complimental flattery, which were numerous and fulsome, but in the more substantial form of pensions from the different contending powers in Europe, from the pope, from Castile, from the emperor, and from France. So large a space did he fill, so great an influence did he exercise in all the events of the time, that a detail of the political occurrences of his life would comprehend the history of the civilised world during the period of his unbounded power. For his successive negotiations with the Emperor of Germany and the King of France, and the motives that dictated his changeable policy with regard to those two great antagonists,—for the splendour of his embassies to both powers, and the extraordinary consideration with which he was treated by each,—for a description of the Field of the Cloth of Gold, arranged under his sole direction, and of the alternate meetings of King Henry with these princes, —and for the varied transactions with the minor governments of Europe, reference must be made to those historical works where they have been gracefully and philosophically treated.

The income of Wolsey must have been enormous in amount, and is said to have even exceeded the royal revenue. Besides the proceeds of the archbishopric, of the Chancery, and of the legantine commission, the various pensions he received from foreign crowns, and the profits derived from numerous grants of lands and offices, he secured to himself the abbacy of St. Alban's, and was allowed to hold the bishopric of Bath and Wells *in commendam* in 1518. This he afterwards resigned for that of Durham in 1522, which in 1529 he again changed for the still more valuable see of Winchester. His expenditure was on a proportionate scale. The Venetian ambassador says, 'He always has a sideboard of plate worth 25,000 ducats, wherever he may be, and his silver is estimated at 150,000 ducats. In his own chamber there is always a cupboard with vessels to the amount of 30,000 ducats, this being customary with the English nobility.' Cavendish delights in detailing the state and magnificence of his household, the number and rank of his attendants, the sumptuousness of his banquets, and the glories of his masques. Nobles were proud, or professed to be proud, to wait on him, and their sons were sent to be educated in his palace. Such universal homage made him forget his original littleness, and prompted him to yet higher aspirations. The popedom was the object at which he now aimed; and twice did it seem within his grasp, supported as he was by the hearty wishes of his own sovereign, and by the apparently as hearty promises of the emperor. But on both occasions was he doomed to disappointment—in 1522 by the election of Adrian VI., and two years afterwards by that of Clement VII. According to the report of the Venetian ambassador four years before, one would have supposed that he might well have been satisfied with his actual position; for he is described as 'in very great repute, seven times more so than if he were pope,' and as ruling both the king and the kingdom. He relates that on his first arrival the cardinal used to say to him, 'His majesty will do so-and-so;' that subsequently by degrees he went forgetting himself, and commenced saying, 'We shall do so-and-so;' but at last he reached such a pitch that he says, 'I shall do so-and-so.'

In the deference paid to one thus invested with almost absolute authority, it is difficult to distinguish between flattery and truth. It is impossible, however, not to see that the respect shown to Wolsey by both the universities, in submitting their statutes to his correction and amendment, was dictated as much by a sincere appreciation of his wisdom as by a consideration of his power; and, besides other evidences before adverted to, the ascendency he acquired over such a man as Henry VIII., enabling him to resist so long the machinations of those who were disgusted with his pride and jealous of his greatness, could not have been attained without the possession of mental powers and personal qualities which would warrant the expression of unsuspected admiration. That he was too fond of adulation was one of his foibles, and that he was jealous of any attempt to turn him into ridicule, or to derogate from his high reputation, was a natural consequence. This feeling he exhibited by imprisoning Serjeant Roe, the author of a masque performed by the students of Gray's Inn, in the allegory of which he discovered, and not perhaps without some cause, an attack upon himself and his government. His anger does not seem to have been long in appeasing, and the punishments he inflicted on other occasions were in no instance accompanied by personal cruelty. The only charge to the contrary is the trial and death of the Duke of Buckingham; but, in the total absence during the cardinal's ministry of any other evidence of a sanguinary disposition, that execution may, with greater justice and probability, be attributed to the jealous suspicions of the king, and the imprudent bearing of the duke.

He preserved the reputation of a scholar which he had attained in the commencement of his career. He encouraged learning and learned men. He was long the correspondent of Erasmus, and in the university where he was educated he established and endowed various lectures, and otherwise promoted classical studies, which were peculiarly obnoxious to the bigotry of the times. As a more lasting record of his fame, he founded two colleges, one at Oxford and the other at Ipswich—the latter being a sort of nursery to the other—thereby imitating the two similar establishments, by William of Wykeham, of New College and Winchester. To the college at Oxford, for the erection of which several priories and smaller houses were dissolved, was given the name of 'Cardinal College,' which, on Wolsey's fall, the king, to deprive him of the merit of the establishment, refounded under the name of King's College. A few years afterwards, however, when the episcopal see was translated to Oxford, its name was again changed to its present designation, Christ Church; Ipswich fell with its founder.

The fall of Wolsey was as sudden as his elevation. The efforts of his enemies proved unavailing until the resentment of Anne Boleyn at his supposed opposition to her advance was added to the scale. Her charms formed the weight that pulled him down; their power suggested the first doubt in the king's mind, whether real or pretended, as to the legality of his union with Queen Catherine. Wolsey could not but see the difficulties that surrounded the question, nor overlook the political dangers which it involved; but knowing, as he did, the wilfulness of his royal master, he was obliged to qualify his real sentiments. The consequence was that he wavered in his proceedings, appearing now to encourage enquiry, and now to delay the decision, so that he made both the queen and the intended usurper of her bed equally doubtful of his sincerity. The enmity of the latter was the most dangerous, and was finally effective. The pretended trial before him and Cardinal Campeggio was scarcely over before Wolsey found that his power was slipping away; and although in his last audience with the king at Grafton on September 19, 1529, the friendly manner in which he was treated gave him hopes that the royal displeasure was abated, within a little month those hopes were entirely dissipated.

On the first day of Michaelmas Term legal proceedings were commenced against him, on the absurd charge of having, by the exercise of his legantine powers under the pope's bull, transgressed an old statute of the reign of Richard II. Although two days afterwards he received the royal authority to appoint two attorneys to appear for him, under which he selected John Scuse and Christopher Jenney, the future judge (*Rymer*, xiv. 348, 350), and although he had a complete defence to the indictment, in the royal licence confirming the authority under which he acted, he at once saw, in this revival of an obsolete statute, which had been violated in numberless previous instances with impunity, a preconcerted determination to effect his ruin. Feeling, therefore, the inutility of resistance, and hoping to mitigate the royal displeasure by submission, he not only allowed the judgment to go against him, but gave up all he had to the king. The Great Seal, which he surrendered on October 17, was almost immediately placed in the hands of Sir Thomas More, who, after a few years, fell also a victim to the cruelty of his capricious master.

Wolsey was commanded to retire to Esher, an unfurnished house belonging to his bishopric of Winchester; and, though kind messages from the king had been presented to him, both in his way thither and afterwards, and letters had been even issued on November 18 taking him under the royal protection, he soon found that his trials were not terminated. In the parliament then sitting a bill of impeachment was introduced by his enemies, consisting of forty-four mostly frivolous articles. It was dated on December 1, and was signed by Sir Thomas More, the new chancellor, and by fourteen peers and two judges; but how far it was approved by the king may be questioned, since Cromwell, who had been in Wolsey's service, and was either then or soon after admitted into that of Henry, was allowed to oppose its adoption in the House of Commons. There his zealous and eloquent advocacy of his old master's cause was so effective that the bill was rejected, a course upon which neither Cromwell nor the Commons would have ventured without some assurance of his new master's approbation.

There are many proofs that, notwithstanding the efforts of his enemies, the king retained much affection for his fallen minister. He sent his own physician, Dr. Butts, to Esher, when the cardinal was ill; he permitted him, when convalescent, to remove to a more commodious and healthy residence at Richmond; and eventually, on February 12, 1530, he granted to him a free pardon in the fullest terms. In consideration however of these favours, the whole of Wolsey's personal property was sacrificed, except 6374*l*. 3*s*. 9½*d*., which he received back in money and goods as a donation from the king. The revenues of the bishopric of Winchester and the abbacy of St. Alban's were given up, except an annuity of 1000 marks from the former; and from the archbishopric of York, which alone he was permitted to retain, he was compelled, by an illegal grant to the king, to dismember York Place, which had been the London residence of his predecessors for three centuries. When urged to do this by Judge Shelley, after a long resistance he at length consented, but said, 'I say unto you in this case, although you and other of your profession perceive by the orders of the lawe, that the king may lawfully doe the thing which ye require of me; how say you, Mr. Shelley, may I doe it with conscience, to give that away which is none of mine, from me and my successors?' He was obliged to submit; and the king, having obtained possession of this magnificent palace, changed its name to Whitehall.

In the following April, Wolsey was required to go to his diocese; but even this command was accompanied by proofs of the king's consideration for him, in royal letters warmly recommending him to the attention of the Northern nobility. There he spent six months, and so ingratiated himself with all ranks by his piety, courtesy, and hospitality that when he was taken from his palace at Cawood on a charge of high treason he was accompanied by the tears and the blessings of the people.

His increasing popularity in the North excited his enemies at court by the fear that he would in time re-establish his former ascendency, and they took their steps accordingly. He had never visited his cathedral, and by the custom of the place he could not do so without being installed as its archbishop. Preparations were therefore made for the ceremony, when, three days before it was to take place, he was arrested by the Earl of Northumberland on November 4, 1530. The charges then made against him have not been recorded, and it is difficult to imagine what they could be, after the general pardon he had received from the king. He was allowed to travel towards London by easy journeys, which, indeed, the state of his health rendered necessary. At Sheffield he was entertained by the Earl of Shrewsbury, with whom he remained a fortnight, at the end of which a violent dysentery had reduced his strength so much that on his arrival on the 26th at the monastery of Leicester he was so conscious of his approaching end that he said to the abbot, 'Father abbot, I am come to lay my bones among you.' There he died on the morning of the 29th, closing his life with the well-known and deeply suggestive address to Sir William Kingston, the governor of the Tower:

'I do assure you, I have often kneeled before the king, sometimes for three hours together, to persuade him from his will and appetite, but could not prevail. And, Master Kingston, had I but served my God as diligently as I have served my king, He would not have given me over in my grey hairs. But this is the just reward that I must receive for my diligent pains and study, not regarding my service to God, but only to my prince.'

He was buried in the abbey with decent solemnity, but no monument covered his remains.

It is remarkable that the king's divorce from Queen Catherine, and his marriage with Anne Boleyn, the cause of Wolsey's fall, were not completed till two years and a half after his death.

Altogether, Wolsey was certainly the most extraordinary man that, as favourite or minister, ever ruled the destinies of this kingdom. By his own abilities he raised himself from a humble origin to a position of respectability and character in the university; by his patient wisdom he counteracted an early disgrace; and by his assiduity and willingness to assist those whom he served, he attained the stepping-stone from which he was to spring almost at once to his topmost height. The first matter with which he was entrusted so fully manifested his activity and political dexterity that he secured the approbation not only of an aged and wise monarch, but also of a young and ambitious prince. Over the latter, almost from the moment of his accession, Wolsey acquired such an influence as to set all other favourites, and almost all other counsellors, aside, and to engross, solely and singly, the whole government of the realm. During his sway, which extended over nearly twenty years, there are no such instances of cruelty, or of oppression, or even of caprice on his part, as too often disgraced the career of powerful favourites in former reigns; the interior of the kingdom was peaceful, its commerce flourishing, and its wars triumphant; it assumed a higher rank in the scale of nations than it had before attained, and its aid and alliance was sought by popes, emperors, and kings. To conclude with the summary of the historian Lingard: 'The best eulogy on his character is to be found in the contrast between the conduct of Henry before and after the cardinal's fall. As long as Wolsey continued in favour, the royal passions were confined within certain bounds; the moment his influence was extinguished, they burst through every restraint, and by their caprice and violence alarmed his subjects and astonished the other nations of Europe.'

Yet, notwithstanding these undoubted claims to our admiration, there is something about Wolsey's character that precludes the possibility of regarding it with entire respect. There was too much of statecraft in his policy, too great an absence of straightforward dealing, and too little regard for the sacred obligation of an oath in the treaties he negotiated. His personal vanity and pompous assumption, his greediness in accumulating wealth, his delight in the obsequiousness of those around him, the arrogance of his demeanour and his fondness for parade and ostentatious display, all exhibit a littleness of mind which it is very distasteful to contemplate. He was too proud in his prosperity, too abject when misfortune overtook him. During his long career there is a total absence of any striking personal incident or noble act on which we can delight to dwell, all the transactions in which he was engaged seeming to be tinged with an attempt to glorify and benefit himself. Even his magnificent erection of Hampton Court Palace, and the foundation of his two colleges at Oxford and Ipswich, are disfigured by marks of vainglory and a disregard to the property of others.

It is a remark of Bacon, that 'prosperity doth best discover vice, and adversity doth best discover virtue.' The truth of this apophthegm is exemplified in Wolsey's career. If his faults and frailties clouded the day of his success, his excellences shone the more brightly in the evening of his downfall. The only part of his life in which an undivided interest can be felt for him are the six months of his exile in the North. His whole conduct in those his last days was so exemplary that he becomes the object of our commiseration, and we cannot but exclaim with our poet—

Nothing in his life
Became him like the leaving it.

WOOD, THOMAS, is said (*Lyson's Cheshire*, 501) to have built Hall o' Wood, in Balterley, which, though now occupied as a farmhouse, was the seat of the family for many generations.

His appearance in court as an advocate is first noticed in the Year Book of Trinity Term 1477, and he was included in the first call of serjeants by Henry VII. in 1485. He received a patent as king's serjeant on June 3, 1488, and was elevated to the bench as a judge of the Common Pleas on November 24, 1495. After sitting in that court for about five years, he was advanced to its head on October 28, 1500, and presided there till his death, which occurred in 1502. (*Keilwey's Reports*, 46.)

He married a daughter of Sir Thomas de la More, and Sir Henry Wood of Lowdham Hall in Suffolk is stated by H. Phillips to have been his descendant in 1684. (*Grandeur of the Law* [1684].)

WOOD, GEORGE, was a native of Roystone, near Barnsley, in Yorkshire, his father residing as the clergyman there. He was born in 1740, and, being intended for the junior branch of the legal profession, was articled to Mr. West, an attorney at Cawthorne. He was so assiduous in his studies, and showed so much ability during his articles, that at the end of them his master urged him to try his fortune at the bar. This advice he fortunately took, and, entering the Middle Temple, he commenced as a special pleader on his own account. He soon got into full practice, and established such a reputation that pupils flocked to him. Among them he gave the initiatory instructions to Mr. Law, afterwards Lord Ellenborough, in 1773, to Mr., afterwards Lord Erskine, in 1779, and to Mr. Abbott, afterwards Lord Tenterden, in 1787, besides many others of the most eminent lawyers of the day. So great was his celebrity as a master of the science that when he was called to the bar he was engaged on the part of the crown in all the state prosecutions commencing in December 1792. He joined the Northern Circuit, and was as successful in his practice in the country as he was in Westminster Hall.

On one occasion he was the cause of a special pleading joke from the bench. He had bought a horse with a warranty that it was 'a good roadster, and free from vice;' but when he attempted to leave the stables nothing could induce the horse to move. On hearing this evidence at the trial, Lord Mansfield gravely exclaimed, 'Who would have thought that Mr. Wood's horse would have *demurred*, when he ought to have *gone to the country?*' This excellent joke, in the changes of the art of pleading, may possibly soon become unintelligible.

A character so distinguished for legal erudition was not likely to be long neglected by those whose duty it was to supply the vacancies on the bench. Mr. Wood accordingly received his promotion as a baron of the Exchequer in April 1807, and was knighted. He performed his judicial functions for nearly sixteen years, with great advantage to the community, and with all the credit to himself which was anticipated from his previous career. In February 1823 he resigned his seat, and lived little more than a year afterwards. His death occurred on July 7, 1824, at his house in Bedford Square, and he was buried in the Temple Church.

He printed for private circulation some valuable 'Observations on Tithes and Tithe Laws,' discussing the subject with great shrewdness and ability. This treatise was afterwards published, and the principle he recommended for the arrangement of the charge was partially adopted in the bill for the commutation of tithes. (*State Trials*, xxii.–xxix.; *Law and Lawyers*, i. 29, 142; *Gent. Mag.* Aug. 1824, p. 177.)

WOOD, WILLIAM PAGE (LORD HATHERLEY), the present Lord Chancellor of England, is descended from a branch of ancient family of some note in the counties of Cornwall and Devon, called by the names of Att-wood and Wood. (*Gilbert's Cornwall*, ii. 332.) One of his immediate ancestors acted as squire at the funeral of Catherine Countess of Devon, sister of Edward IV.; but the family gradually becoming reduced in circumstances, his grandfather, who carried on the business of a serge manufacturer, was incapable of making any provision for a numerous progeny. The eldest of his children, Matthew Wood, by his persevering industry and commercial integrity as a hop-merchant in Falcon Square, London, restored the fortunes of the house, first becoming a common councilman and then an alderman of the city of London. Extremely popular, from the liberal opinions he entertained, he was returned member for the city in 1815, and retained that honourable post, through nine successive parliaments, to the end of his life—a period of 28 years. In the same year he was elected lord mayor, and in the next year, such was the activity and intelligence he displayed that he had the honour, which for centuries had been unknown, of being elected a second time. Uniformly liberal in politics, he was vehemently opposed to the Corn Laws and to the Test and Corporation Acts, and a firm advocate for Catholic emancipation and parliamentary reform; and before his death he had the satisfaction of seeing both the latter effected, and all the former repealed. He took a most prominent part in support of Queen Caroline on the accession of George IV., and was created in December 1837 a baronet by Queen Victoria. It was owing to his recommendation to the Duke of Kent, for whom he acted as trustee, that the duke returned to England from Brussels, in order that his eldest child might be born a Briton. He married Maria, daughter of John Page, of Woodbridge in Suffolk, surgeon, and upon his death in 1843 he left five surviving children—two daughters, both married; and three sons, the eldest of whom, Sir John Page Wood, the present baronet, is rector of St. Peter's, Cornhill, and vicar of Creping in Essex; the youngest, Western Wood, Esq., died recently as representative of the city of London; and the second is the subject of the present memoir. Sir Matthew's brother, Benjamin Wood, Esq., successfully contested a seat in parliament for the borough of Southwark with the late Mr. Walter, proprietor of the 'Times,' and represented that borough till his death.

William Page Wood was born on November 29, 1801, and was named after his uncle William Woods Page, to whom is to be attributed the early taste he acquired for literature. Spending his infancy at his grandmother's at Woodbridge, he received the rudiments of his education at the free grammar school of that town. After staying there for a year, he went to Dr. Lindsay's at Bow for three years. In 1812 he was removed to Winchester College, where, under the able instruction of Dr. Gabell and Dr. Williams, head master and second master of the school, he acquired, besides the complete mastery of the usual branches of learning, that clearness and precision of statement which is his peculiar characteristic. In May 1818, being then a prefect, he was engaged in the rebellion which was organised against the master, and which was not suppressed without the aid of the military. When taken, he refused an escape from expulsion, to which the other prefects were subjected, which was offered him on account of the favour which he had acquired with the master by the general regularity of his conduct, and his success in gaining the prize in every class through which he had passed. The lord chancellor must look back to this period of his life, notwithstanding its unfortunate termination, with peculiar pleasure, not only for the learning and experience he acquired, but still more for the lasting friendship which he formed at school with Dr. Hook, the present dean of Chichester, who, besides the excellence of his literary compositions, is deservedly renowned for his untiring energy and extraordinary success in his former incumbencies of Coventry and Leeds. To his appointment to the latter parish the lord chancellor had the delight of being accidentally, or rather providentially, instrumental; and it is worthy of record that during each of the twenty-three years of his ministry there he procured the erection of a church, a school, and a parsonage; and so effective was his influence with the inhabitants that he was able to levy 10,000*l*. a year among them. The calamity which lately befell Chichester Cathedral has now made a new demand on his exertions, which have been equally successful. With this remarkable man the lord chancellor united in forming among their schoolfellows an order of Shakspeare and Milton knighthood, they being of course the first members. Their reading was not confined to those authors, but extended to all the Elizabethan classics, the study of which was much encouraged by Dr. Gabell.

During the vacations the lord chancellor obtained his first experience of law by accompanying his father the alderman to the Old Bailey sessions, and took an early disgust at the proceedings there, especially at the wholesale sentences of death then pronounced against prisoners, few of whom were intended to suffer the extremity of the law. In accompanying his father to the House of Commons also he had the advantage of hearing all the principal parliamentary orators; and during the two years of his father's mayoralties his mind was further opened by association with the great men of all parties, who were entertained at the Mansion House; and in a short visit to Paris at the conclusion of the mayoralty he was admitted, whilst yet a boy, into the highest French society. Such intercourse formed an important part in young Wood's education, and he naturally imbibed his father's political sentiments, then entertained by a comparatively small but increasing class, which subjected him to much ridicule among his church-and-state contemporaries at Winchester.

After leaving Winchester College he spent the next two years at Geneva, profiting greatly under the excellent lecturers of that university, among whom was the eloquent and learned Rossi, who was afterwards murdered when minister to Pope Pius IX. From his instruction young Wood acquired a knowledge of the Roman law; and from the association with Genevan society, and that of the variety of foreigners of all nations who flocked there, he gained such an acquaintance with their several languages as gave him great advantages in his future intercourse with the world. He passed his first year's examination with great credit, but unfortunately was prevented taking his degree in the second year, by being obliged, by direction of his father a fortnight before the examination took place, to come to England in the suite of Queen Caroline. Being then in his nineteenth year, he was naturally much employed in the previous negotiations, and deeply interested in the subsequent progress, of the lamentable proceedings against her; accompanying from June till October the persons sent to Italy to collect evidence on her behalf, and occasionally acting as translator of the necessary documents, and as interpreter on the examination of the various witnesses. The result upon his mind, from their testimony, from his own observation, and from the esteem with which many Italian families of the highest respectability regarded her, was that she was wholly innocent of the charge brought against her, and guilty of nothing beyond imprudence.

In October 1820 he joined his brother at Trinity College, Cambridge, where he obtained a scholarship on his first trial, and was always in the first class at the examinations. In the second year he gained one of the declamation prizes, the question being 'Whether the Revolution or the Restoration had conferred the greater benefit on our country,' he arguing in favour of the former. Notwithstanding the rank he had earned in his college by his attainments, yet, owing to a serious illness, occasioned by too laborious an application to his studies, he failed in obtaining a higher place in the list of honours, in January 1824, than that of twenty-fourth wrangler. In October of that year, however, he stood for a fellowship in his college, and succeeded in obtaining it, though nearly rejected by the veto of the master and one fellow, in consequence of the supposed radicalism of his prize declamation. The threatened veto was, however, withdrawn, and as a Cambridge University commissioner he has since assisted in abolishing this power on the part of the master. In the previous Trinity Term he had been entered at Lincoln's Inn, having already placed himself under the late Master Roupell for instructions in equity drawing. During his Cambridge career he prominently assisted in his father's energetic measures on behalf of the Spanish and Italian refugees, then flocking to this country in extreme destitution, by which a subscription of above 100,000l. was collected for their support.

While studying for the bar he placed himself as a pupil under that great master of the law of real property, John Tyrrell, Esq., when that branch of learning was in a transition state between the mass of verbiage that had disgraced the conveyances of land, and the more simple forms which were then in a gradual course of adoption. By Mr. Tyrrell's careful mode of instruction and indefatigable attention to his young pupils, Mr. Wood acquired that deep insight into English law which he exhibits on the bench. Our student's labours in this period were relaxed by another visit to Italy, where he was introduced to that extraordinary linguist Cardinal Mezzofanti, and by associating with many celebrities of the time, among whom were Irving, Carlyle, Procter (Barry Cornwall), and Coleridge. Most of these he met at the house of Basil Montagú, for whose edition of Bacon's Works he translated the 'Novum Organum,' which has been since separately printed, and is described in the late Oxford edition as the best rendering of that wonderful work, and is now used in that university. Just before his call to the bar, after the battle of Navarino, he wrote a long letter, which was first published in the 'Times' and afterwards in the 'Pamphleteer,' recommending an alliance between France and England for the purpose of strengthening Turkey against Russia; in consequence of which he was offered by the then editor of that influential paper full employment if he would undertake to write for the press. Mr. Wood, however, feeling that it would interfere with his professional prospects, declined the flattering proposal.

Mr. Wood was called to the bar on November 27, 1827, and established himself in the same chambers with a learned and intellectual barrister, William Lowndes, Esq., afterwards a judge of the local court at Liverpool. He was soon well employed as an equity draftsman and conveyancer, and when engaged in court experienced the different but characteristic treatment of the two principal judges, being visited by one of the usual rebuffs of Sir John Leach, and being encouraged by the natural courtesy of Lord Lyndhurst. On the introduction in the next year of the railway system he was fortunate in obtaining a large share in the new business then brought before the committees of the Houses of Commons and Lords, as either the supporter or opposer of the various speculations to which it gave rise. In January 1830 he married Charlotte, the only daughter of Major Edward Moor, F.R.S., of Great Bealings, near Woodbridge, the author of the 'Hindoo Pantheon,' and of various other works on interesting Indian subjects. In 1834 he was himself elected a fellow of the Royal Society, and has since served as a member of the council and as a vice-president of the society. Although largely engaged in parliamentary practice, he did not neglect his business in Chancery, and both fully employed him. In the year 1841, however, the increased labour and demand on his time consequent on the appointment of two additional vice-chancellors compelled him to confine himself to one or the other practice. He wisely selected the latter, though then infinitely less profitable; and, attaching himself to Vice-Chancellor Wigram's court, found his account by the encouragement he received in a great accession of business. About this time the long litigation relative to the will of Mr. James Wood of Gloucester was terminated, by which Sir Matthew Wood's right to a very large portion of the testator's estate was fully established, and his son's prospects materially benefited. In February 1845 he was appointed queen's counsel, and in 1847 was returned to parliament as member for the city of Oxford, which he continued to represent till his elevation to the bench. In parliament he took a very prominent part, advocating the admissibility of Jew members on taking a modified oath, and introducing bills to allow the testimony of scrupulous persons to be received on such declarations as would bind their own consciences, but under the usual penalties for perjury. He was a friend to reform in the representation, and even to vote by ballot; but, though advocating these liberal views, he avowed himself a firm supporter of the Church establishment, and resisted the motions for the abolition of church-rates and for legalising marriages with a deceased wife's sister.

In May 1849 he accepted the office of vice-chancellor of the county palatine of Lancaster, offered to him by Lord Campbell, then the chancellor of the duchy, on condition that a bill should be passed for the reform of the court there, which from its antiquated proceedings was then nearly useless; and he had the satisfaction of obtaining the desired enactment, by which the jurisdiction has been since rendered highly effective.

On March 28, 1851, Mr. Wood was selected by Lord John Russell for the office of solicitor-general, and was soon afterwards knighted. He was then appointed one of the commissioners for reforming the Court of Chancery, the result of whose labours was that the master's offices were abolished, and the expense and delay of the proceedings materially diminished. This and other improvements, proposed while Lord John Russell was prime minister, were so much approved by the succeeding government that they were at once adopted and passed the legislature. The act for the appointment of the lord justices of appeal was passed while Sir William Page Wood was solicitor-general, and Lord Chancellor Truro then offered Sir William the post of vice-chancellor, which at the request of Lord John Russell he declined. In 1851 the university of Oxford conferred on him the honorary degree of D.C.L. He of course retired from office on the resignation of Lord John in February 1852, when Lord Derby succeeded and remained minister till December. The government being then surrendered to Lord Aberdeen, and Sir George Turner being soon after constituted one of the lords justices, the vacant vice-chancellorship was offered to Sir William Page Wood, who was appointed on January 10, 1853.

Both before and after his elevation his services were put into active requisition on numerous commissions connected both with the Church and the law, which involved him in perpetual labour. But he felt himself repaid by the knowledge of the benefits produced by the legislature's adoption of many of the recommendations contained in their reports. He was selected by Lord Chancellor Cranworth to act with Lord Wensleydale and Sir Lawrence Peel as arbitrators between her majesty and the King of Hanover with reference to certain crown jewels claimed by that king. A decided and conscientious Churchman, he has actively assisted the exertions of several societies for the promotion of Church objects and the instruction of the people. In his own district, that of St. Margaret's and St. John's, Westminster, where, when he first knew it, there were only two churches, a dilapidated chapel of ease, and five clergymen, with little more than two hundred children at school, there are now ten churches, twenty-six clergy, and more than ten times the original number of schools. To this amendment Sir William Page Wood greatly contributed by his personal activity and extensive influence; and he had the satisfaction of materially aiding in the establishment in his district of the only free library under Mr. Ewart's act in the metropolis, the benefit of which is proved by its being visited by 3000 persons every month, and by 4000 books being lent for reading during the same time. In 1867 he published 'The Continuity of Scripture,' a most valuable work, which has passed through several editions. On March 5, 1868, he was promoted to the office of lord justice of the Court of Appeal in Chancery, when his colleague Lord Justice Selwyn, though previously appointed, gracefully gave up to him the seniority, in deference to his long services and greater experience. But ere that year had ended he was called upon to vacate this high position, in order to fill one of more elevated rank. On Mr. Gladstone's appointment as prime minister, Sir William Page Wood was selected as lord chancellor on December 9, 1868, and was called up to the House of Peers by the title of Lord Hatherley, in both which characters he now retains that deserved estimation which he had attained in all his previous judicial career.

Of the manner in which he has exercised his judicial functions for the seventeen years during which he has presided in his different courts, it would be unbecoming to say more than that while he was vice-chancellor litigants were generally desirous of having their causes set down in his paper. He is in the habit of pronouncing his judgments *ore tenus*, not from prepared notes, and, notwithstanding the discourteous and somewhat indecorous reflections made upon the practice by Lord Chancellor Campbell, he still continues it, satisfied with revising his judgments before they are printed by the regular reporters of his court, and justifying himself by the consciousness that so much writing is injurious to his health, and by the conviction that the delay the preparation of them would occasion would be much more detrimental to the suitor than could be compensated by any supposed clearness in the composition.

WOTTON, WILLIAM, was probably of Norfolk extraction, as in 1510 he was placed on the commission of the peace for that county, and on that for gaol delivery for the city of Norwich. (*Cal. St. Papers* [1509-14], 191-198.) He was admitted a member of Lincoln's Inn in July 1493, and appointed to read there in autumn 1508, 23 Henry VII., his name appearing among the governors of the house as late as 1527. He was appointed second baron of the Exchequer on July 10, 1521, and in November 1523 he acted as collector of the anticipation of the subsidy assessed on the judges and barons, his own property being valued at 200*l*. (3 *Report Pub. Rec.*, App. ii. 63.)

WRAY, CHRISTOPHER. Various are the accounts of the lineage of Sir Christopher Wray, but three of them agree that he was born at Bedale in Yorkshire. (*Fuller's Worthies*, ii. 506; *Wotton's Baronet*. i. 242; *Plowden's Reports*, 342.) As to his parentage, the tales are so different and contradictory that it would be absurd to judge which of them is the most probable one; enough is shown from all of them to indicate the humble state of the family, till the chief justice by his honourable exertions raised it from obscurity.

The unquestioned part of the story is that he was a student at Buckingham College, Cambridge, which, during his residence, was refounded as Magdalen College, to which he was afterwards a great benefactor; and that he removed thence to Lincoln's Inn, where he was called to the bar on February 2, 1550. He attained the rank of reader in 1562, and again in 1567, when, according to Plowden, he dwelt at Glentworth in Lincolnshire, as a compliment then frequently paid when a member was called serjeant, to which degree he was admitted in Easter Term, and was further honoured by being appointed queen's serjeant on June 18. (*Dugdale's Orig.* 253.) That he was a favourite with his brethren at the bar appears from the following order in Chancery in the suit 'Brind *v.* Hyldrache,' on April 27, 1562: 'Forasmuch as it is informed that, because the matter in question toucheth Mr. Wray, of Lincoln's Inn, the plaintiff cannot get any to be of counsel with him, therefore Mr. Bell and Mr. Manwood are appointed by this court to be of counsel with the said plaintiff.' His eminence in the profession is evinced by his being returned as member for Boroughbridge, or Grimsby, or Ludgershall, in all the parliaments during Mary's reign, as well as in those of Elizabeth up to the thirteenth year, when he was chosen speaker of that which assembled on April 2, 1571. His speech to the queen on the occasion is remarkable for nothing but its length; its delivery is said to have occupied two hours. This parliament was dissolved in less than two months, and was the last in which Wray had a seat. (*Parl. Hist.* i. 728, 772.)

On May 14, 1572, he was promoted to the bench, not, as stated by Dugdale, as a judge of the Common Pleas, but as a judge of the Queen's Bench, a special commission, preserved in the 'Bagade Secretis,' and dated the same day as his patent, distinctly calling him 'another justice of the Queen's Bench.' (4 *Report Pub. Rec., App.* ii. 270.)

He was raised to the head of the Queen's Bench on November 8, 1574; and he presided there, being then knighted, above sixteen years, with a character which Sir Edward Coke (3 *Reports*, 26) sums up by describing him as 'a most reverend judge, of profound and judicial knowledge, accompanied with a ready and singular capacity, grave and sensible elocution, and continual and admirable patience.' A letter of his to the Bishop of Chester, relative to an application from the prelate and the Earl of Derby to dissolve a prohibition to the ecclesiastical commissioners granted by the Court of Queen's Bench, affords a proof of the manliness and independence of his character. (*Peck's Desid. Cur.* b. iii. 35.)

His judgments in the Queen's Bench are reported by Dyer, Plowden, and Coke; and the 'State Trials' contain some over which he presided. Whatever may be thought of the criminal judicature of the period, it must be acknowledged that Chief Justice Wray not only abstained from all intemperance and partiality, but exhibited great calmness and forbearance. He was present during the proceedings against the Scottish queen, but does not appear to have taken any part in them; and in the farcical arraignment of Secretary Davison in the Star Chamber for sending down the warrant for Mary's execution, the chief justice (in consequence of the illness of Lord Chancellor Bromley) presided in the temporary character of lord privy seal. It is ludicrous to note how on this latter occasion all the commissioners in turn began by praising the secretary's intent, but finished by punishing him for his act; a chorus which was wound up by the chief justice's well-known distinction, 'Surely I think you meant well, and it was *bonum*, but not *bene*.' (*State Trials*, i. 1049-1239.)

He performed his duties so much to Queen Elizabeth's satisfaction that she granted to him the profits of the coinage till he had built his noble house at Glentworth; and he retained her favour till his death, which occurred on May 7, 1592. He was buried in the chancel of Glentworth Church, under a magnificent monument, on which he is represented in his robes.

He was as exemplary in his private as in his judicial life; and he appears to have been fond of putting his rules of conduct into pithy forms. He is said by David Lloyd (*State Worthies*, 580), who wrote in the next century, to have been 'choice in five particulars: 1, his friend, which was always wise and equal; 2, his wife; 3, his book; 4, his secrets; 5, his expression and garb. By four things he would say an estate was kept: 1, by understanding it; 2, by spending not till it comes; 3, by keeping old servants; and 4, by a quarterly audit. He was mindful of what is past, observant of things present, and provident of things to come.' By his will, in which his servants and the poor are charitably remembered, besides giving directions for the maintenance by his heirs for ever of six poor persons in the almshouse at Glentworth, he orders that they shall have their dinner every Sunday at Glentworth Hall, and in case of default he authorises the dean and chapter of Lincoln to distrain upon the land.

By his wife, Anne, daughter of Nicholas Girlington, of Normanby, Yorkshire, Esq., he had a son, William, who was created a baronet in 1612, as was his grandson in 1660, but both the titles have become extinct. (*Wotton's Baronet.* i. 242-249.)

WRIGHT, ROBERT, was the son of Jermyn Wright, settled at Wangford in Suffolk, by his wife, Anne, daughter of Richard Bachcroft, of Bexwell. He was educated first at the free school of Thetford, and then at Peterhouse, Cambridge, where he took the degrees of B.A. in 1658, and of M.A. in 1661. Previously to his admission to the Inner Temple he had been included in the list of those who were qualified to be made knights of the intended order of the Royal Oak, with an estate in Norfolk of the value of 1000*l.* a year. (*Blomefield's Norfolk*, i. 368; *Wotton's Baronet.* iv. 372.)

Roger North informs us in his life of Lord Keeper Guilford (p. 247) that Wright went the Norfolk Circuit, and that by his marriage with Susan, one of the daughters of Bishop Wren, he was 'set in credit in the country... Of a comely person, airy and flourishing in his habits and manner of living,' he for some time commanded a greater share of business than his companion Mr. North, but 'was so poor a lawyer that he could not give an opinion on a written case, but used to bring his cases to his friend Mr. North, who wrote the opinion on a paper, which Wright copied and signed as if it were his own.' This practice he continued even when Mr. North was in London, and put off his clients upon pretence of taking more consideration. His deficiency could not be long concealed; and, not getting much by the law, he 'by favour was made treasurer of the chest at Chatham, and by his voluptuous unthinking course of life' became embarrassed to so considerable a degree that his friend North, from whom he had occasionally borrowed money, paid off his other debts and took a mortgage of his estate for 1500*l.* The author adds the disgraceful fact that some years afterwards he obtained of Sir Walter Plummer 500*l.* more upon an original mortgage of the same estate, and made an affidavit that it was clear from all incumbrances.

In the meantime his name appears as representing King's Lynn on a vacancy during the second parliament of Charles II. In 1678 he was appointed counsel for the university, and in August 1679 was elected deputy recorder of the town of Cambridge. Having contracted a close friendship with Sir George Jeffreys, he had been in the Easter preceding raised to the coif and knighted, and was further promoted to be king's serjeant on May 17, 1680. In the next year he was made chief justice of Glamorgan, and on October 30, 1684, was appointed a baron of the Exchequer. (*T. Raymond*, 431.) Roger North relates that Wright, being on the brink of ruin, applied to Jeffreys (then chief justice) to rescue him by getting him made a judge. On the king suggesting his name, Lord Keeper North answered that 'he knew him but too well, and was satisfied that he was the most unfit man to be made a judge.' It was therefore for some time delayed, but upon being again pressed the lord keeper detailed what he knew of him—that he was a dunce, and no lawyer, of no truth or honesty, guilty of perjury, and not worth a groat, having spent all his estate in debauched living. Having thus done his duty, the lord keeper left the decision to the king, who, urged by Jeffreys, at last gave way, and sent his warrant for the appointment.

He was elected recorder of Cambridge on February 10, 1685, four days after the accession of James II., who not only renewed his patent as judge, but selected him to accompany his patron Jeffreys on the bloody western assize, and on October 11, immediately after his return therefrom, removed him to the King's Bench. Eighteen months afterwards he was further promoted to the chief justiceship of the Common Pleas, on April 16, 1687. This office he held only five days, during which the case of the deserter came before the Court of King's Bench, when Chief Justice Herbert, having given an opinion adverse to the king's claim to exercise martial law in time of peace, was removed to the Common Pleas to make way for Sir Robert Wright, as more willing to forward the king's designs. He was therefore appointed chief justice of the King's Bench on April 21, and the first proof of his servility was to grant the order for hanging the poor soldier, which his predecessor was dismissed for refusing. The next was in fining the Earl of Devonshire, who had always distinguished himself by his opposition to the court, for an assault on Colonel Culpepper in the king's presence-chamber, in the exorbitant sum of 30,000*l.*, and committing him to prison till it was paid, the chief justice saying that the offence was 'next door to pulling the king out of his throne.' Next he was one of the ecclesiastical commissioners, and was sent down with Bishop Cartwright and Baron Jenner on the famous visitation of Magdalen College, Oxford, when the president and all the fellows except three Papists were expelled. (*Athen. Oxon.* iv. 505; *State Trials*, ix. 1354, xii. 26.) From his being selected as a member of that commission, from his saying to one of the fellows, 'Your Oxford law is no better than your Oxford divinity,' and from King James granting him dispensation from taking the oaths and subscribing the test, it would seem not improbable that he had been, or was willing to be, converted to the religion of the court. In the following June he presided at the trial of the seven bishops, when, though he so far accommodated himself to the king's anxiety to condemn them as to declare their petition to be a libel, he was at the same time so evidently awed by the general voice in their favour as to conduct the proceedings with great apparent decency and impartiality. (*Bramston's Autob.* 283; *State Trials*, xii. 42.)

Within six months from this time, when the king deserted the throne, the chief justice, conscious of his danger, retired to some place of concealment. The character he bore among his contemporaries may be judged from the following lines in a lampoon of the time:—

Farewell Brent, farewell William,
Farewell Wright, worse than Tresilian;
Farewell chancellor, farewell mace,
Farewell prince, farewell race.

His retreat was discovered on January 15, 1689, by Sir William Waller, who took him before Sir John Chapman, the lord mayor, by whom he was committed to Newgate on a charge 'that hee, being one of the judges of the Court of King's Bench, hee had endeavoured the subversion of the established government by alloweing of a power to dispence with the laws; and that hee was one of the commissioners for ecclesiastical affairs.' (*Jesse's Court of England*, iv. 419; *Bramston*, 346.) He was brought before the House of Lords on May 6, in relation to the case of the Earl of Devonshire, when, though the committing of the earl was declared a manifest breach of privilege, and the fine of 30,000*l.* to be excessive and exorbitant, no further proceedings appear to have been taken against the judges. On the 18th of the same month Sir Robert died in Newgate of a fever, and thus escaped being excepted from the Act of Indemnity. In the debate on June 18 it was resolved that he should be excepted, though dead; but in the act itself, which was not passed till May 1690, his name was omitted, though that of Lord Chancellor Jeffreys, also deceased, was retained. (*State Trials*, ix. 1367; *Parl. Hist.* v. 339.)

He was thrice married. His first wife was Dorothy Moor, of Wiggenhall St. Germans; his second was Susan, daughter of Matthew Wren, Bishop of Ely; and his third was Elizabeth, daughter of Chief Justice Scroggs, by the two latter of whom he had several children.

WRIGHT, NATHAN, was the son of Dr. Ezekiel Wright, rector of Thurcaston in Leicestershire, and Dorothy, sister and co-heir of Sir John Onebye. Two baronetcies granted to the elder branches of the family are now extinct.

He was born in 1653, and was educated at Emmanuel College, Cambridge, but took no degree, and becoming a student at the Inner Temple, was called to the bar on November 29, 1677; but more than a year before had married Elizabeth, daughter of George Ashby, of Quenby, who had been sheriff of Leicestershire. In 1679 he was enabled to purchase the estate of the Earl of Stamford at Broughton Astley (*Nichols's Leicester*), and thus obtained such an influence in his native county that he was chosen recorder of Leicester in 1680. He held the office (with a short interval when the town was deprived of its charter) till he was made lord keeper. On his resignation he presented to the corporation what was long after known as 'the loving cup of Leicester,' which was sacrificed under the Municipal Corporation Act of 1835, but preserved by a private gentleman and exhibited to the Society of Antiquaries in 1851. (*Proceedings*, ii. 147.)

In the trial of the seven bishops in 1688 Mr. Wright was engaged for the prosecution, and Luttrell then calls him 'Young Mr. Wright.' He was the junior counsel, and only opened the proceedings, taking no other part in the discussion. In 1692 he was called to the degree of the coif, and in January 1697 he was made king's serjeant, and knighted. Luttrell states that he received these honours for his learned arguments in the House of Lords in support of the bill of attainder against Sir John Fenwick; and Speaker Onslow in his notes on Burnet says that he managed the business so well as to raise his character very much at the time. Unfortunately his speech is not reported in the 'State Trials,' but that collection contains those made by him as counsel for the crown against the Earl of Warwick for murder, against Mr. Duncombe for falsely indorsing Exchequer bills, and against Mary Butler for forging a bond for 40,000*l*.; and also when employed in 1700 for the Duke of Norfolk in support of the bill for dissolving his marriage. Luttrell also frequently notices his legal engagements. (*Luttrell*, i. 446, iv. 164; *Burnet*, v. 219; *State Trials*, xiii. 954, &c.)

When King William in 1700 took the tory party into power and dismissed Lord Chancellor Somers on April 17, he must have been somewhat surprised at the difficulty he found in filling the vacant office. The two chief justices and other great lawyers of the time declined to accept the Seal. Easter Term was then about to commence, and the business of the Chancery could not be interrupted without great inconvenience. The Seal was therefore temporarily placed on May 5 in the hands of the chiefs of the three other courts, together with the master of the Rolls, and in the meantime negotiations were going on, which were at last ended by Sir Nathan Wright accepting the responsible office of lord keeper on May 21. In the next parliament he presided on the trial and pronounced the acquittal of his predecessor, and at the end of the session he was appointed one of the lords justices during the king's absence abroad. A new parliament met in December 1701, but before the termination of its first session the king died on March 8, 1702. Queen Anne confirmed the tories in the ministry, retaining the lord keeper. The only subsequent proceedings connected with his name of any importance are his acting on a commission for the union with Scotland, which owing to the difficulties raised by the Scots was not at that time successful, and his returning the thanks of the House of Lords to the Duke of Marlborough on the close of the campaign of 1704, which was signalised by the battle of Blenheim. (1 *Lord Raymond*, 567; *Parl. Hist.* v. 1313, vi. 27, 374.)

In the following year, the whigs having regained their ascendency, Sir Nathan, who had failed to acquire the respect of either party, was obliged to retire. Though he was a good common lawyer, he was accounted a weak and inefficient keeper; but still there was no complaint of his decisions in equity. Burnet, with no friendly feeling towards him, though he says that money did everything with the lord keeper, who was sordidly covetous, yet acknowledges that he never heard him charged with bribery in his court. A story is told of a watchmaker, a day or two before the hearing of a suit in which he was a party, sending a very fine timepiece to the lord keeper, who returned it with a message, 'That he had no doubt of the goodness of the piece, but it had one motion in it too much for him.' Burnet alludes to a 'foul rumour' of livings being set up for sale by the officers under him; and Speaker Onslow adds in a note that in Baron Bury's book of accounts it appeared that the baron had given the lord keeper 1000*l*. for making him a judge. Whatever truth there may be in this scandal, there is no doubt that he became extremely rich, that he obtained a valuable office for his son, and bestowed the best livings on his poor relations. He survived his removal from the Seal for sixteen years, and died on August 4, 1721, at Cancot Hall in Warwickshire. His remains were removed to a manor he had purchased at Gothurst, near Newport Pagnell, in the church of which there is a monument with his effigy in white marble. His wife was Elizabeth, daughter of George Ashby, by whom he left several children. One of his sons was clerk of the crown, another was recorder of Leicester, and a third was a clergyman, and married a granddaughter of the Marquis of Winchester. (*Burnet*, v. 139, 218; *Maxby's Secret Service*, 41; *Noble's Granger*, i. 35; *Evelyn*, iii. 382.)

WRIGHT, MARTIN, is believed to have been of a Hampshire family, his possessions and his purchases being principally in that county. He was born on March 24, 1691, and was the younger brother of Thomas Wright, Esq., whose daughter Elizabeth married Sir John Guise, of Highnam, Bart. He received his legal education at the Inner Temple, and was called to the bar in June 1718.

His publication in 1730, 'An Introduction to the Law of Tenures,' which went through many editions, no doubt assisted his elevation to the bench of the Exchequer in November 1739, and his removal to the Court of King's Bench on November 28, 1740. He was not knighted till November 23, 1745, when he went up with the judges' address on the rebellion; and after being nearly sixteen years on the bench he resigned his seat on February 1, 1755. He lived more than twelve years after, and died at Fulham on September 26, 1767, leaving by his wife, Elizabeth, daughter and coheir of Hugh Willoughby, Esq., M.D., of Barton Stacey in Hampshire, two sons and two daughters, who all died without issue. The youngest son, an eccentric character, on his decease in 1814, at the age of eighty-seven, bequeathed his estates, amounting to 3000*l*. a year, to Lady Frances Wilson, the wife of Sir Henry Wilson of Chelsea Park, with whom he was totally unacquainted, but had seen and admired her at the opera nearly twenty years before, when she was Lady Frances Bruce. (*Strange*, 1148; *Gent. Mag.* vols. ix. x. xv. xxxvii. lxxxiv.)

WRIOTHESLEY, THOMAS (LORD WRIOTHESLEY, EARL OF SOUTHAMPTON), belonged to a family of heralds. His grandfather Sir John, first noticed as Faucon herald, was advanced successively in the reign of Edward IV. to the offices of Norroy and Garter king at arms. Both the sons of Sir John were brought up to the same study—the elder, Thomas, becoming Garter; and the younger, William, being York herald, and the father of the chancellor, by his wife Agnes Drayton. He was born at Garter Court in Barbican, and educated at St. John's College or Trinity Hall, Cambridge. (*Fuller's Worthies*, ii. 70; *Athen. Cantab.* i. 98.) In 1529 he appears in the position of clerk to the cofferer of the household (*Trevelyan Papers*, 160), and in 1530 he obtained the place of clerk to the Signet under Henry VIII.; and it was probably in the latter character that he accompanied Mr. Brereton, one of the gentlemen of the privy chamber, on a message from the king to Wolsey at Southwell, when Cavendish intimates that they were not friends to the cardinal and disdainfully accepted his reward. According to Dugdale, he was entered at Gray's Inn in 1534; but he does not appear to have taken any office in that society, nor does his name occur in any law report. In 1537, however, he was appointed coroner and attorney in the Court of Common Pleas, and in 1538 he was placed in the responsible post of one of the king's secretaries, and knighted. Attached to the principles of the old religion, he had already secretly favoured those who were devoted to it, by changing the rigours with which the Friars Observants were pursued, into banishment from our shores. Yet he so accommodated himself to the king's caprices that he was employed on several important missions, one of which was the negotiation of a treaty of marriage between Henry and Christiana Duchess of Milan, the second daughter of the king of Denmark, in which he failed. (*Kennet's Hist.* ii. 214.) He was afterwards one of the special council assigned to receive the declaration of Anne of Cleves, by which she abandoned her matrimonial rights. (*Kal. Exch.* i., *Introd.* cii.)

In 1540 he was made constable of Southampton Castle, and two years afterwards of that of Porchester; and to these honourable appointments was added the profitable one of chamberlain of the Exchequer. In 1545 he acted as one of the commissioners for managing the treaty of league with the Emperor Charles, and on January 1, 1544, was raised to the peerage by the title of Baron Wriothelsey of Tichfield in Hants, the monastery of which had been granted to him. The sickness of Lord Audley quickly following, the Great Seal was placed in Wriothesley's hands on April 22 as keeper, a title which was changed on May 3 to that of lord chancellor, on Audley's death. Before the end of the year he was installed a knight of the Garter.

The change from Lord Chancellor Audley to Lord Chancellor Wriothesley was a fatal one to many of those who were proselytes to the new religious tenets. The king having publicly exhibited his own sentiments, by passing the act of the Six Articles, Wriothesley, always a secret supporter of these extreme doctrines, now pursued to extremity those who impugned them. His zeal even attempted to prejudice the king against his new wife, Catherine Parr, whose attachment to the reformed opinions he dreaded as dangerous to himself, and whose imprudence in disputing on the subject with her opinionative husband gave him too easy a handle. Had it not been for her ready wit, she would perhaps have followed her predecessors to the scaffold; but by an artful submission, she foiled her malicious foe, who, having prepared articles against her, when he came to take her into custody, instead of receiving his intended victim, was met by reproaches from her pacified lord. (*Kennet*, ii. 263.) Connected with this was the charge against Anne Askew, for the purpose of obtaining from whom matter to implicate the queen, Wriothesley is (perhaps wrongfully) accused of having himself applied the torture, when the common executioner appeared to compassionate the sufferer. (*Lingard*, vi. 353.) By the will of Henry VIII., Lord Wriothesley (with a legacy of 500*l*.) was made one of the sixteen executors of it, and ' councillors of the privy council with our son Edward, both in his private and public affairs.' (*Testam. Vetust.* 41.) Immediately after the accession of Edward VI. the Earl of Hertford, the king's uncle, was appointed protector of the realm and guardian of the king's person, notwithstanding the warm opposition of Wriothesley, who contended that under the will all the executors were invested with equal power. His resistance was the more earnest because Hertford was a known supporter of the new doctrines; but he was quieted by being elevated within three weeks of the king's death to the earldom of Southampton, and by having an additional income granted to him for the support of his new dignity. This title had not been long extinct; and it is curious that the late earl, the great naval commander, left Wriothesley by his will the best of his gilt cups. (*Ibid.* 708.) At the same time the Earl of Hertford became Duke of Somerset.

The majority of the council of regency were reformers. Wriothesley was imperious and dogmatical, and so troublesome in his intercourse with his brethren that every endeavour might be expected to put an end to his power. By his own inadvertence he soon gave them an opportunity. On February 18 he put the Great Seal to a commission empowering the master of the Rolls and three masters in Chancery to hear causes and pronounce decrees in his absence. Although this was a mere renewal of a commission issued to the same parties for the same purpose in 1544, it was immediately seized hold of as an illegal act, inasmuch as he had no licence for it, either from the king or the regency, while for the former he had the late king's authority. The judges, who were formally appealed to, gave this as their decision, and that the offence was punishable with the loss of office and fine and imprisonment at the king's pleasure. The council hastened to act on this opinion, and, after an ineffectual resistance, Wriothesley was obliged on March 6, 1547, to give up the Seal to Lord St. John, and to remain a prisoner in his house in Ely Place till June 29, when he was discharged on entering into a bond to pay any fine the king might impose upon him.

Though thus deprived of his office, he was not excluded from the council; but, cautioned by what had passed, and intimidated by the severity with which Somerset enforced his absolute sway, he was obliged to submit to those active measures, so repugnant to his known sentiments, by which the Reformation was advanced. The protector's turn of unpopularity at length arrived, and Wriothesley, as might be expected, joined the Earl of Warwick in the proceedings which hastened Somerset's ruin. The satisfaction of his revenge, however, was unaccompanied by any restoration of his own power; for Warwick as well as Somerset looked with suspicion on his intriguing spirit, and passed him over in the distribution of office. Wriothesley withdrew from the court a disappointed man, and within a few months his vexation at the slight thus put upon him produced the illness which terminated in his death. That event occurred on July 30, 1550, at his house in Holborn, then called Lincoln Place, but afterwards from him Southampton House. He was buried in St. Andrew's Church, but his body was removed thence to a chapel in the parish church of Tichfield, where a sumptuous monument still exists.

Few persons who have held a prominent position in the state have had so little said to their credit as Wriothesley, Earl of Southampton. He seems to have been looked upon as haughty towards his inferiors, and slavishly subservient to those who were above him. When advanced to high office, his conceited opinion of his own superiority made him treat with disdain those who differed from him, and this disposition operated with peculiar force against those who advocated the reformed doctrines. His severity and cruelty towards them, even if they could be ascribed to the dictates of his conscience, necessarily raised a prejudice against him in all moderate minds; and not having the wisdom to modify his views where he must have seen that his party was powerless, the majority of the council risked no loss of popularity by silencing so intractable a member of their body. Though devotedly attached to the Romish religion, he showed no scruples in sharing the plunder arising from its destruction, and not only enriched himself with grants from King Henry, but even accepted others from the council that was planning his disgrace.

By his wife, Jane, the heiress of William Cheney, of Cheshamboys, Bucks, he had one son and five daughters. His titles were held after him by three succeeding generations, when they all became extinct, together with the earldom of Chichester, which the fourth Earl of Southampton had acquired by a special remainder on the death of that nobleman in 1667 with no other issue than Rachel his daughter and heiress, whose name has been handed down to us as the devoted wife of the illustrious but unfornate William Lord Russell, and as the author of letters which still continue to delight all virtuous minds. (*Baronage*, ii. 383; *Hayward; Rapin; Lingard.*)

WROTHAM, WILLIAM DE, was the grandson of Geoffrey de Wrotham, of Radenville, near Wrotham, in Kent, who had been a domestic servant of several Archbishops of Canterbury, and whose son William, by his wife, Maud de Cornhill, was the father of the judge. (*Collinson's Somerset*, iii. 63.) As both Williams, father and son, held similar offices, some of the following entries may apply to the elder, for the name frequently occurs in the Curia Regis. In 10 Richard I., and in 8 and 10 John, fines were acknowledged before him at Westminster; and there are entries on the rolls showing that he acted as a justicier in some of the intervening years.

His career was an active one, and he filled many offices of responsibility and trust. He was for a long period custos of the stannaries of Devonshire and Cornwall, his accounts for the issues of the mines there appearing on the rolls from 10 Richard I., 1199, to 14 John, 1213. (*Rot. Cancel.* 28; *Madox*, ii. 132.) In the early part of John's reign he was evidently in great favour, both with his sovereign and the people, for he had grants of Newenton and Lintemore, with other privileges from the king (*Rot. Chart.* 29); and the inhabitants of Dorset and Somerset paid a fine of 100*l.* for his appointment as forester for those counties. In the same year he was constituted sheriff of Devonshire, and four years afterwards he appears as one of the collectors of the quinzime of merchandise (*Madox*, i. 771.) He is mentioned in 5 John as one of the canons of Wells, and in the following he was raised to the archdeaconry of Taunton, and was soon after further gratified with presentations to the churches of Wardon in Shepey, and of East Malling in Kent. (*Rot. Chart.* 183; *Rot. Pat.* 59, 66; *Le Neve*, 46.)

By an entry on the Fine Roll of 9 John (412), it appears that he paid 2300 marks for the king's favour, 'benevolentiam regis.' Were it not for the continued marks of honour and grants of personal advantage that distinguished him at this time, and that the other rolls of that and the previous year show that there was no interruption of the royal confidence, this fine might be considered as proving that he had incurred the king's displeasure. It was probably, however, no more than a donum presented to the king at the time of his father's death, as much with hopes of future benefit as in acknowledgment of past favours.

In 11 and 12 John he was warden of the seaports, and in that character he is ordered, as late as 16 John, to provide a ship to William de Percy, on the king's service. (*Rot. de Fin.* 547.) The Rotulus Misæ of 11 John, and that de Præstito of 14 John, show that he was with the king in those years; and in 15 John he had an additional ecclesiastical benefice, in the grant of a prebend in the church of Hastings. He is mentioned by Roger de Wendover (iii. 237) as one of the king's advisers during the time of the interdict. In the wars at the end of the reign he quitted the country, whether in consequence of his having joined the barons or on his own affairs does not appear; but in 17 John letters were granted to him, permitting him to come to England and return in safety. (*Rot. Pat.* 106, 180.)

His death occurred in 2 Henry III. (*Rot. Claus.* i. 352-3.)

Le Neve says he was archdeacon of Canterbury in 1206; and there is certainly an entry on the Close Rolls (70), dated May 19 in that year, in which he is called 'W. de Wrotham, Arch.Cant.;' but, inasmuch as he is on no other occasion so styled, and as five days afterwards he is designated by his title of archdeacon of Taunton, it is probable that the word 'Cant.' is a misreading, or an error of the transcriber for 'Tant.,' the usual abbreviation for Taunton.

WYKEHAM, WILLIAM OF (BISHOP OF WINCHESTER). The name of William of Wykeham is held in such universal reverence, and the interest felt in every particular of his life is extended over so many classes of society, whether as admirers of his works or partakers of his bounty, that we cannot wonder at the more than ordinary degree of diligence which has been exercised in seeking out and recording everything that can illustrate his history. The results exhibit an active mind never unoccupied; an energy subdued by no difficulties; foresight in the contrivance, caution in the development, and an union of judgment and taste in the execution of his works; an absence of all arrogance throughout his rapid advance in clerical honours; and that discreet exercise of political power which enabled him to hold the first place in the royal counsels without incurring the jealousy of the people. Few men have lived whose career has displayed such continued exertions for the public good, and none have left so many examples of practical wisdom and well-applied munificence.

He was born at Wykeham in Hampshire between July and September 1324, 18 Edward II.; and, notwithstanding some doubts which had been expressed on the subject, the evidence that has been collected supports the presumption that the name of his birthplace, by which he is known, was not that of his family.

His father and mother, according to that evidence, were John and Sybil Longe, who were of good reputation and character, but not sufficiently prosperous in their circumstances to be able to advance the education of their son. His mother was of gentle extraction, being the daughter of William Bowade, whose wife was the daughter of William and Amicia Stratton, of Stratton, near Selborne. They and his sister were buried in the church of Suthwyk Priory, not far from Wykeham. (*Archæol. Journ.* iii. 221.)

Tradition says that Nicholas de Uvedale, lord of the manor of Wykeham, and governor of Winchester Castle, was the benefactor who sent him to school at Winchester; and it is recorded that he afterwards acted as the governor's secretary. There is no evidence whatever of his having studied at either university, although some writers have stated that he was at Oxford for nearly six years. The presumption is strongly in opposition to this assertion; but whatever he lost of scholastic knowledge by the want of that advantage was more than compensated by the zeal and industry with which he pursued the sciences which were more practically useful, in the acquisition of which he evinced so much mastery, and in their application so much taste, that he was soon, by the recommendation of his first patron, distinguished by the notice of William de Edington, Bishop of Winchester, who, finding his personal merits equalled the talents he exhibited, employed him in his service, and availed himself of his architectural talents in the improvements he projected at Winchester.

As Bishop Edington had not possession of his see till February 1346, 20 Edward III., Wykeham was then little more than twenty-one years of age. There is a record of a beneficial grant to him, in 1350, of the custody of the manor of Rokeford, in his native county, at a small annual rent, until the heir of Sir William Bottreaux attained his majority (*Abb. Rot. Orig.* ii. 209), which he probably owed to the intercession of his patron the bishop.

There is no record of his actual employment for the next six years, except that he was attorney for the bishop in 1352, in taking possession of certain lands; but it is suggested that he probably assisted in the erection of the great tower at Windsor Castle, called the Tabula Rotunda, about which the king was then engaged. His merits must have been prominently displayed at an early period, as on May 10, 1356, he had advanced so far as to be placed in the responsible position of clerk of all the king's works in his manors of Henle and Yestampsted. There is a curious entry on August 20 in that year of an allowance to him of 2l. 10s. for the keep of the king's eight dogs at Windsor for nine weeks, taking for each dog three-farthings a day, and twopence a day for a boy to keep them. (*Pell Records*, iii. 163.) In the following October he was appointed surveyor of the works at the castle and in the park of Windsor, with power to press artificers and provide materials and carriages, and with the then liberal payment of two shillings a day besides extra allowances. In the next year the sale of all the beasts in Windsor Park was committed to him and two other persons (*Ibid.* 244); and in 1354 he had another royal patent, constituting him chief custos and supervisor of the castles of Windsor and Ledes, and of the manors and parks belonging to them. During this period he projected and accomplished those splendid works at Windsor Castle which at this day give celebrity to his name. Queenborough Castle, erected under his direction between 1361 and 1367, showed his extraordinary skill and abilities as an architect, but no longer exists as an example of them.

This, however, is not the place to enlarge on his architectural excellences, although to them, and his readiness in executing the king's magnificent projects, he no doubt primarily owed his future fortunes. But we know too much of Edward's character to suppose that these alone would have been sufficient; and it is evident that Wykeham must have exhibited other qualifications of greater weight to have suggested his employment in the important offices, both lay and ecclesiastical, which he was called upon to fill.

It seems probable that Bishop Edington induced him to take the clerical tonsure; for he is called 'clericus' as early as 1352, and in 1359 the king describes him as 'clericum suum,' showing he was then one of the royal chaplains. He was not ordained priest till June 12, 1362. Before this he had received in succession, from the king's presentation, the rectory of Pulham in Norfolk in 1357; the prebend of Flixton, in Lichfield Cathedral, in 1359; and in the next year the deanery of St. Martin's-le-Grand in London. The latter he retained for three years, during which he gave the first proof of his liberality by rebuilding the cloisters of the chapter-house and the body of the church. (*Monasticon*, vi. 1323.) In 1363 he became archdeacon of Northampton, which he exchanged for that of Lincoln, and according to Le Neve (156, 162, 167) was also archdeacon of Buckingham. In addition to these benefices he received several other prebends and livings, the list of which is contained in the certificate delivered in October 1366, by virtue of the pope's bull requiring a return of all pluralities. The value of the whole is stated to have amounted to the gross sum of 873*l*. 6*s*. 8*d*., an enormous provision in those days, even on the assumption, suggested by Dr. Lowth, that he held high offices in the state, and was designed for the earliest vacancy on the episcopal bench. But it is truly said that he only received the revenues of the Church with one hand to expend them in her service with the other.

During this period he had been appointed, in 1361, custos of the forests south of the Trent, in conjunction with Peter Attewode (*Abb. Rot. Orig.* ii. 263); and on April 2, 1364, he is described as holding the office of keeper of the privy seal. (*Pell Records*, iii. 182.) Although the pope addresses him in the following June as the king's secretary, he did not fill that position till two years afterwards, holding it with the privy seal, which he retained till he was appointed chancellor. In 1365 he was one of the commissioners to treat of the ransom of the King of Scotland, and the prolongation of the truce with that country; and, besides many records of his presence in the king's council, his influence with his royal master is evidenced by the expression of Froissart, that at this time 'everything was done by him, and nothing was done without him.' In his letters of pardon in 1 Richard II. he is described as being at that period 'clericus privati sigilli, et capitalis secreti consilii, ac gubernator magni consilii.' (*Rot. Parl.* iii. 388.)

The death of Bishop Edington on October 7, 1366, enabled King Edward to gratify his wishes by rewarding Wykeham with the vacant see of Winchester. Before his consecration, which did not take place till October 10, 1367, he was constituted chancellor in the place of Simon Langham, Archbishop of Canterbury. The date of his appointment does not appear; but on September 16 he is so called in a grant of free warren to Archbishop Islip.

He held this high dignity for three years and a half. During his administration King Edward resumed the title of King of France, which he had dropped for nine years, and renewed the war with some disadvantage. The chancellor's speeches on opening the parliament were distinguished by the omission of quotations from Scripture, which his predecessors had been in the habit of introducing into their addresses, and by his confining them in a judicious and business-like manner to a clear statement of the emergencies of the state, and a lucid exposition of the object of their assembling. His removal from the office arose from the necessity the king felt of giving way to the repeated representations of the Lords and Commons that the affairs of the kingdom were prejudiced by the government being always in the hands of the Church; and he accordingly made room for a lay chancellor, Sir Robert de Thorpe, by resigning on March 24, 1371.

He still, however, retained the confidence of his sovereign, and faithfully sided with him in his declining years, when the Duke of Lancaster and Alice Perrers were taking advantage of his weakness, and assuming the government of the kingdom. When the Prince of Wales, then in a desperate state of health, made a strong effort in the 'good parliament' of 1376 to break this party, the bishop was one of the council then appointed to advise the king, and on the prince's death in June, Richard his son was declared Prince of Wales.

No sooner was the parliament dismissed than the duke and his adherents resumed their power, and vented on the bishop part of their resentment. They exhibited against him seven charges of crimes alleged to have been committed during his administration, on which they relied so little as to offer no proof in their support, but added an eighth, as to cancelling a roll, and reducing a fine from 80*l*. to 40*l*. in favour of John Grey, of Retherfeld. Upon this trifling charge his temporalities were adjudged, on November 17, to be seized into the king's hands, and he was forbidden to come within twenty miles of the court. The further proceeding thereon had been adjourned till January 20, 1377, but it was never brought to a hearing, although the Duke of Lancaster, in the parliament of that month, procured his exception from the general pardon then granted to all offenders on occasion of the jubilee of the king's reign. From this parliament the bishop had been excluded; but the convocation, to which he had been summoned as usual by the mandate of the Archbishop of Canterbury, made strong representations to the king of the injuries which the bishop had unjustly suffered. The duke induced the king, instead of complying with the clergy's petition, to grant the temporalities of the bishopric to the Prince of Wales; but the people were so little satisfied with these proceedings that they attacked the duke's palace and insulted his person, refusing to desist unless he would suffer the bishop to be brought to his answer, and be judged according to law. The effect of this was the restoration of the temporalities on June 18, for which, however, a contribution to a considerable amount in ships and men, towards the defence of the kingdom, was demanded from him. The total extent of his disgrace, therefore, did not exceed seven months.

Three days afterwards King Edward died, and one of the earliest acts of the new reign was to pronounce the bishop's pardon in the fullest and most extensive terms, declaring him wholly innocent and guiltless of all the matters alleged against him, and remitting the burdens to which he had been subjected (*Rymer*, vii. 163), a proceeding which was ratified and confirmed by the petition of the Commons in the next parliament.

The confidence of the parliament in the bishop's integrity was still further evinced, in 1380, by his being appointed one of the commissioners to enquire into the abuses of the late and the present reigns, and afterwards to investigate the causes of the great insurrections which had recently disturbed the kingdom. Indeed, his influence with both the Lords and the Commons is apparent by their frequent recurrence to him on points of difficulty, availing themselves of his wisdom and experience, and giving to his advice that weight and authority which in such times could have been only secured by the complete reliance they had on his honesty and prudence.

Although avoiding as much as possible any unnecessary interference in state affairs, such was his reputation that in the subsequent contests occasioned by the extravagance and weakness of the king, the bishop was always one of the persons appointed by the popular party to check the royal prerogative and control the government expenditure. Yet no proof can be stronger that, in the exercise of these duties, his conduct was tempered with mildness and moderation, than the fact that when King Richard, claiming the rights of his majority, took the government into his own hands, and discharged the officers who had been imposed upon him, he compelled the bishop, much against his inclination, to accept the office of chancellor, and he accordingly received the Great Seal for a second time on May 4, 1389.

His first step was to quiet the apprehensions which naturally arose in the people's minds on the hazardous course the king had taken. He obtained a confirmation of all the pardons granted for the late disturbances, and a suspension of the pressing subsidies that had been imposed. He announced to the parliament the king's desire to preserve peace, to secure to every rank the enjoyment of its privileges, to cause all evils to be redressed, and justice and right to be administered as well to the poor as to the rich; and he acted with so much caution and forbearance that the Commons, on his resigning the Seal into the king's hands, expressed their approbation of his fidelity and good conduct, upon which he immediately resumed his functions.

During the two years and a half that he retained the Great Seal he had the happiness to restore the public tranquillity so effectually that the parliament thanked the king for his good government; and could he have been induced to remain in office, it is probable that his wise counsels might have checked the king's intemperance, and prevented the fatal consequences that followed. He finally gave up the Seal on September 27, 1391, and never appeared prominently in any subsequent political transaction of the reign. He seems to have been still treated with respect by the king, although the party with whom he had acted incurred the royal vengeance; but as a payment for this escape from the reaction by which his friends were sacrificed, a loan of 1000*l*. was extorted from him, which he was not in a condition safely to refuse.

Richard II. resigned his crown on September 30, 1399, and Wykeham, being then very far advanced in years, seems no further to have interfered in public affairs. His coming infirmities had warned him to procure a bull from the pope, enabling him to appoint one or more coadjutors to perform the duties of his diocese when he found himself incapable, and of this he occasionally availed himself during the last two years of his life. Still, however, he continued to transact business till within four days of his death, which occurred at South Waltham on September 27, 1404, when he had attained the full age of eighty years. He was buried in the splendid oratory in the cathedral, which he had erected in the very place where he had been accustomed to perform his daily devotions in his youth.

He had presided over the see of Winchester for thirty-seven years, and, notwithstanding his almost constant employment in the public service, he had been unremitting in his attention to his episcopal duties, and in preserving the rights of his church. He lost no time in putting all the episcopal buildings into substantial repair, expending therein above 20,000 marks. He corrected the abuses of the various religious houses in his diocese, and introduced a complete reform in the hospital of St.

Cross. The other houses subject to his visitation submitted to his authority, and suppressed the irregularities which he discovered.

But the great and noble object of his life was to found an institution for the education of youth, with the intent of supplying the deficiency in the priesthood occasioned by the recent plagues, which were said to have swept away nine parts out of ten of the clergy. The earlier years of his prelacy were occupied in a careful formation of his plans, and, having fully arranged them, he proceeded to take measures to secure their execution. He determined to erect two colleges—one at Winchester, the place of his own education, for elementary learning; and the other at Oxford, for the completion of the studies and for the provision of the scholars. He commenced the first in 1373 by establishing a temporary school at Winchester for such poor scholars as he chose to send there; and he prepared for the last, not only by making a similar arrangement at Oxford by forming a society there under a warden, and lodging them in various parts of the city, but by gradually making such purchases as would eventually put him in possession of the site which he had resolved on, so that from the very outset he was devoting his income to this wise and charitable purpose, and raising a supply of occupants for his Oxford College when it was finished.

The erection of the latter was his first care. The foundation stone of New College, or more properly of St. Mary College of Winchester, in Oxford, was laid on March 5, 1380, and the building was finished for occupation on April 14, 1386. The society consisted of a warden and seventy poor scholars, whose studies were specially regulated by statutes, on the preparation of which he bestowed the greatest attention and care. These were amended by him at various subsequent periods, the last of which was in 1400, and, as then enlarged, they still remain in force. On the completion of this building he began that at Winchester, on the very spot where he had received his own education. The first stone of St. Mary College there was laid on March 26, 1387, and full possession was taken on March 28, 1393. It afforded instruction to seventy poor scholars, and was governed by a warden, with ten fellows, and other officers and masters. The statutes were formed in accordance with those at Oxford, and received similar corrections from his hand.

His laws were found so practically useful that they were adopted by Henry Chicheley, Archbishop of Canterbury, one of his own scholars, in the foundation of All Souls' College at Oxford, and afterwards by King Henry VI. in the colleges of Eton and Cambridge. The bishop himself had the gratification not only of witnessing the full success and good effects of both his establishments, but of selecting from those who were educated in them men of learning and character to assist him in his business, and to be rewarded with the preferments in his gift.

No sooner had he finished his two colleges, which he most liberally endowed, than he undertook the reparation of his own cathedral, great part of which, being in a very decayed state, he soon found it necessary to rebuild. This he did in a truly magnificent manner, thus occupying the remaining ten years of his life. His works there are most lucidly detailed by Professors Willis and Cockerell in the 'Proceedings of the Archæological Institute at Winchester, 1845.'

His will is a most extraordinary document, and shows that he preserved to the last that precision and considerate prearrangement for which he was so remarkable. It is of very great length, and the legacies bequeathed by it are numerous and liberal. No person, high or low, who had a claim on his respect or gratitude, or who was attached to his colleges, is omitted, all his connections and his servants are remembered, his piety and devotion are exemplified by various bequests for prayers on his behalf, and due care is taken that charity to the poor shall not be forgotten. In this disposition of his property he was merely carrying on the daily practice of his life. During its whole continuance he seems to have employed his riches in aiding his tenants, advancing his friends, relieving the needy, and in a large and munificent hospitality, besides assisting in the repair of churches, highways, and bridges.

It seems astonishing that there could ever be two opinions as to the meaning of William of Wykeham's motto, assumed no doubt soon after the commencement of his prosperity—

Manners makyth man.

It is difficult to suppose that any one could seriously believe that a person of his character intended to intimate that man's worldly interests are best forwarded by elegant behaviour and general politeness, or that he could possibly be so absurd as to hold himself up as an example of the truth of the sentiment. Without raising the question whether the advocates of this interpretation can produce a single instance in which the writers of the age have used the word 'manners' in the sense they ascribe to it, it may be fairly asked—looking at the obscurity of his origin (which he could not hope, and which there is no evidence that he wished, to conceal) and to the active industry and practical employment of his earlier years, and considering the sacredness of his profession, and the frequent and ostentatious use of this motto in his educational colleges—whether it is not palpable that it was his intention, by its adoption, to inculcate the principle that man's success and estimation, even in this world, depended not on his birth, or his fortune, or his talents, but on his conduct and moral worth. (*Life by Dr. Lowth*.)

WYMBURN, WALTER DE, is called in 46 Henry III., 1261, the king's clerk, but whether civil or ecclesiastic is uncertain. He had then a grant of the king's year and a day on some land which had been escheated. (*Excerpt. e Rot. Fin.* ii. 363.) In 4 Edward I., 1276, he was appointed a judge of the King's Bench, and we find him acting in the same character as late as October 1288. Spelman (*Gloss.* 342) erroneously states that during the tenth and thirteenth years of the reign he was chief justice.

WYMUNDHAM, THOMAS DE, was ordered to be paid thirty shillings, for writing thirty pair of statutes, 'triginta paria statutorum,' to be sent to all the justices in eyre and sheriffs throughout the realm, and also four shillings and sixpence for the parchment on which they were written. (*4 Report Pub. Rec., App.* ii. 152.) In 42 Henry III., 1258, he is inserted in Madox's list of barons of the Exchequer, and Dugdale mentions his appointment as treasurer of the Exchequer in the same year. In 50 Henry III. he was addressed by that title, and the king granted to him the first wardship that should fall in worth 50*l*. a year, together with the marriage of the heir, unless he should first provide him with some dignity, prebend, or benefice of the annual value of 200 marks. In less than two years he accordingly received the precentorship of Lichfield, being first so called in a record of 52 Henry III. This is the last year in which he is described as treasurer, but according to Le Neve (128) he was alive in 1275, 3 Edward I. (*5 Report Pub. Rec., App.* ii. 63; *Madox*, ii. 42, 48, 52, 186, 307, 319.)

WYNDHAM, FRANCIS, belonged to a branch of an ancient family which took its surname from the town so called in Norfolk, and which have been distinguished from the reign of Edward II. both in the council and the field. Sir Thomas, of Felbrigge and Crounthorpe, the grandfather of the judge, was vice-admiral to Henry VIII.; and Sir Edmund, his father, while sheriff of Norfolk in 2 Edward VI., was active in suppressing Ket's insurrection. His mother was Susan, daughter of Sir Roger Townsend, of Raynham.

After an education at Cambridge he prosecuted his legal studies at Lincoln's Inn, and, becoming a bencher there in 1569, was appointed a reader in 1572, in which year he represented the county of Norfolk. He was elected recorder of Norwich in 1576, and in Michaelmas Term of the following year was called to the degree of the coif. The precise date of his becoming a judge of the Common Pleas is not stated, but the first fine acknowledged before him as a judge is dated in October 1579. (*Dugdale's Orig.* 48, 253.)

He is mentioned as one of the judges in the commission for hearing causes in Chancery in the interval between November 1591 and May 1592.

His death occurred at his house at Norwich in July 1592. Over his remains, in the church of St. Peter's Mancroft in that city, was erected a stately monument, on which he is represented in his judge's robes, and in the Gold-hall of that city there is a picture of him as recorder.

By his wife, a daughter of Sir Nicholas Bacon, the lord keeper, he left no issue. (*Blomefield's Norwich*, i. 359, ii. 221; *4 Report. Pub. Rec., App.* i. 272, 273.)

WYNDHAM, HUGH. Sir John Wyndham, the uncle of the above Francis Wyndham, was not only the progenitor of this and the next-named judge, but also of three baronetcies, all of which are now extinct.

Hugh Wyndham was the sixth son of Sir John, of Orchard-Wyndham in Somersetshire, and of Felbrigge in Norfolk, knight, by Joan, the daughter of Sir Henry Portman. He was born about 1603, and received his legal education at Lincoln's Inn, where he was called to the bar on June 16, 1629. Though his practice as an advocate is not recorded, he had acquired in 1654 sufficient reputation as a lawyer to be dignified with the coif, and to be sent as a temporary judge on the Northern Spring Circuit, and afterwards to be raised to the bench of the Common Pleas by Cromwell, notwithstanding his objection to act under the protector's commission. Whitelocke states that he was appointed on May 30, 1654, and was re-appointed on November 27, 1658, on the accession of Richard Cromwell to the protectorship. In July 1659 and in January 1660 Whitelocke again records his appointment, the former being at the resumption of the Long Parliament, and the latter after the dissolution of the committee of safety and the rearrangement of the courts in consequence of the resignation of Chief Justice Glynne. (*Whitelocke*, 591, 675, 681, 693; *Burton*, ii. 340, 438.)

The restoration of Charles of course put an end to Wyndham's judicial functions; but he was immediately confirmed in his degree of serjeant-at-law. In this character he resumed his practice, until eighteen months after the death of his younger brother, the next-noticed Judge Wadham Wyndham, when, on June 20, 1670, he was promoted to the bench as baron of the Exchequer, and received the customary honour of knighthood. On January 22, 1673, he was removed to the Common Pleas. In neither court did he particularly distinguish himself, not interfering much in those trials arising out of the Popish Plot in which he was among the presiding judges. He died at Norwich while engaged on the circuit on July 27, 1684, in his eighty-second year, having sat on the bench, during the Commonwealth and since the Restoration, for twenty years. His monument at Silton in Dorsetshire records the names of his three wives—viz., Jane, daughter of Sir Thomas Woodhouse, of Kimberley, Norfolk, Bart.; Elizabeth, daughter of Sir William Minn, of Woodcott, Surrey, and widow of Sir Henry Berkeley, of Wimondham, Leicestershire, Bart.; and Katherine, daughter of Thomas Fleming, of North Stoneham, Hants, and widow of Sir Edward Hooper, of Boveridge, Dorsetshire. By the first of these only he left issue. (1 *Siderfin*, 3, 465; *Hutchins's Dorset*, ii. 145, 324.)

WYNDHAM, WADHAM, the younger brother of the above, received his baptismal name from his grandmother, Florence, daughter of John Wadham, Esq., of Merrifield in Somersetshire, descended from the before-mentioned judge of the Common Pleas of that name in the reign of Richard II. He was, like his brother, a member of Lincoln's Inn, and was called to the bar on May 17, 1636. His name appears in several law reports during the time of the Commonwealth, and he was one of the advocates who were imprisoned for pleading the cause of Cony, as related in the life of Judge Twisden, and who, like him, could not procure his release until he had petitioned the protector. Not receiving the coif under Cromwell's government, he was selected as one of the fourteen who were summoned to be serjeants a month after the Restoration, having been previously called upon to consult with the judges at Serjeants' Inn, Fleet Street, with respect to the proceedings against the regicides, he being one of the counsel engaged in the prosecution. (1 *Siderfin*, 4; *Kelyng*, 7; *State Trials*, v. 1023.)

At the end of these trials he was, on November 24, 1660, promoted to be a judge of the King's Bench, in which court he sat for eight years. During the whole of that time, according to the evidence of his contemporaries, he maintained a high character for learning and impartiality. Siderfin (393) says of him that he was of 'great discretion, especially in his calm and sedate temper upon the bench;' that he was 'in all respects well qualified for the place;' and that he held it for several years 'to the great satisfaction of those at the bar and others.' Sir Thomas Raymond (174) calls him a good and prudent man; and Sir John Hawles, solicitor-general in the reign of William III., speaks of him as the 'second best judge which sat in Westminster Hall since the king's restoration.' (*State Trials*, ix. 1003.)

He died on December 24, 1668, at which time he was seated at Norrington in Wiltshire. By his wife, Barbara, daughter of Sir George Clarke, of Watford, Northamptonshire, he left a large family, whose descendants still flourish in various counties and promise a long continuance of the name. Thomas, one of his grandsons, was, like him, a distinguished lawyer, and being made, first, chief justice of the Common Pleas in Ireland, and then lord chancellor there, was raised to the peerage of that kingdom, by the title of Baron Wyndham of Finglass, in 1731, but, leaving no children at his death in 1745, the title became extinct.

WYNFORD, LORD. *See* W. D. BEST.

WYNTON, ELIAS DE. The error which Dugdale has committed in introducing him as a baron of the English, instead of the Irish, Exchequer, is explained under the name of Richard de Saham.

WYTHENS, FRANCIS, was of a family originally settled in Cheshire, but, migrating to the south, one of them, Robert Wythens, became an alderman of London. His eldest son, Sir William, was sheriff of Kent in 1610, and dying in 1630, his residence at Southend in the parish of Eltham was in the possession of this judge at the time of his death in 1704; but whether he inherited it as the son, or grandson, or nephew of Sir William is uncertain. (*Hasted*, i. 204, 478.)

The earliest notice of him is as high steward of the Franchise Court of Westminster, and as a successful candidate for that city in October 1679, but the opening of parliament was deferred by seven prorogations to October in the following year, when his return was disputed by Sir William Waller and Sir William Pulteney. In the interval, numerous petitions having been presented to the king praying for the meeting of parliament, which were met by counter-addresses expressing abhorrence of the practices of the petitioners as interfering with the king's prerogative, Wythens took an active part in getting up the latter, and on presenting one from the grand inquest of the city of Westminster he received the honour of knighthood on April 18, 1680. As soon as the parliament met in October, Sir Francis, as a member, was the first who was charged with the fact as an offence against the rights of the people; and upon evidence taken and his own confession he was ordered to be expelled the house, and to receive his sentence on his knees at the bar. The speaker accordingly addressed him in these terms: 'You, being a lawyer, have offended against your own profession;

you have offended against yourself, your own right, your own liberty, as an Englishman. This is not only a crime against the living, but a crime against those unborn. You are dismembered from this body.' This castigation must have been doubly painful to the recipient, inasmuch as only a few days after the committee on the petition against his return reported that he was not duly elected. (*Luttrell,* i. 41; *Commons' Journals.*)

Soon after his election for Westminster he was engaged as counsel to defend Thomas Knox on an indictment against him and John Lane for a conspiracy to defame the notorious witnesses to the Popish Plot, Titus Oates and William Bedlowe, when, though his client was not acquitted, he was let off with a more merciful judgment than Chief Justice Scroggs was accustomed to pronounce. Sir Francis also assisted in the prosecution of Henry Carr for a libel in publishing 'The Weekly Packet of Advice from Rome,' exposing some of the tricks of Popery. The chief justice was called to account by the parliament for his conduct on both of these trials, and was removed from his office. Under his successor, Sir Francis was employed by the crown in the cases of Edward Fitzharris, the Earl of Shaftesbury, and Count 'Coningsmark (*State Trials,* vii. 801, 1125, viii. 269, 1125, ix. 15), and on all these occasions he acted the part, if not of an able, of an intelligent advocate.

He was made a judge of the King's Bench on April 23, 1683, and concurred in the following term in the judgment against the charter of the city of London. In the other prosecutions during the life of King Charles in which he acted as one of the judges, though there is nothing harsh or violent in his observations or his language towards the parties on their trials, he was evidently, as Roger North describes him, so weak and timid a man that he had not the courage to differ from his more resolute chiefs. Consequently he assented to all the iniquitous judgments that disgraced that period, and incurred a larger share of odium than the other judges, from his being, according to the form of the court, the mouthpiece which pronounced most of the sentences. Evelyn (iii. 104) is indignant that Sir Francis was at a city wedding on December 5, 1683, when he and Chief Justice Jeffreys danced with the bride and were exceeding merry, spending 'the rest of the afternoon till eleven at night in drinking healths, taking tobacco, and talking beneath the gravity of judges who had a day or two before condemned Mr. Algernon Sidney.' But, instead of 'a day or two,' the trial had taken place a fortnight before this time, and it is most probable that Evelyn's disgust at the verdict influenced his opinion as to the private conduct of the judges.

Without approving the prevalent levity of the time, we must think it rather hard upon judges to expect that they should assume a solemn aspect because they had presided at a capital conviction a fortnight before.

On Charles's death, in February 1685, Sir Francis received a new patent, and in the following November was elected recorder of Kingston-on-Thames. He accompanied Chief Justice Jeffreys in his bloody campaign after the Duke of Monmouth's rebellion, and continued for two years to exercise his judicial functions with his accustomed pliancy, till a sudden boldness, or a prophetic policy, prompted him to unite with Chief Justice Herbert in denying that the king could exercise martial law in time of peace without an act of parliament. The consequence was his immediate discharge from his office on April 21, 1687, the punishment usually inflicted by King James on the slightest non-compliance with his will. Shower reports (ii. 498) that on the next day he came to Westminster Hall and practised as a serjeant, which seems to evidence his reliance on the popularity of his decision.

As this sole instance of his insubordination was too great to be overlooked by James, so it was too little to plead in his favour in the next reign, for he was one of the thirty-one persons who were excepted out of the Act of Indemnity. Before this bill was passed there had been various debates in the House of Commons (*Parl. Hist.* v. 338) relating to trials in which Judge Wythens had been concerned as one of the judges, and many of the judgments and decisions had been declared arbitrary and illegal; but the principal matter urged against him was his concurrence in the opinion in favour of the king's dispensing power. Beyond the insertion of his name in the act, it does not appear that he was visited with any penalty, except removal from the recordership of Kingston. He survived his discharge till 1704, when he died at his family seat at Eltham, and was buried in the church there on May 12.

Sir Francis married Elizabeth, sister of Sir Thomas Taylor, of Parkhouse, Bart., who, if the account given by Mrs. Manley in the 'New Atalantis' (ii. 257) is to be credited, though clever and witty, brought no comfort to her husband, and acquired for herself a very bad reputation. That she involved him in expenses for the purpose of putting him in prison appears from an action brought against him in 1693 for extravagant outlay in dresses, &c., which he was obliged to pay. After his death she married Sir Thomas Colepeper, of Aylesford, Bart. (*Wotton's Baronet.* i. 218; *Skinner,* 348.)

WYTHER, WILLIAM, seems to have been

merely a justice itinerant for pleas of the forest in Lancashire in 15 Edward I., 1287. The only legal or judicial character in which he afterwards appears is as the last named of four commissioners appointed in 35 Edward I. to hear and determine a cause in North Wales between the Earl of Arundel and others. (*Rot. Parl.* i. 206.)

WYVILLE, JOHN DE, is placed by Dugdale among the barons of the Exchequer in 37 Henry III., 1253; but he perhaps sat there as one of the justices of the Jews, in which character he is named by Madox (ii. 318) among the barons two years previously. He was constituted a justice (of the Common Pleas according to Dugdale) on February 1, 1256, from which time till February 1263 he was present at the acknowledgment of fines. In an undated letter he begs the king to excuse him from the office of justice of Oyer and Terminer on account of his bodily infirmity and poverty; but he acted on the iters in 40, 44, and 47 Henry III. (*Dugdale's Orig.* 43; *Excerpt. e Rot. Fin.* ii. 280–391; 5 *Report Pub. Rec.*, App. ii. 75.)

His death may be fixed about the latter year. His property was in Hampshire. If the baronetcy of Wyville in Yorkshire (extinct in 1774) was derived from his lineage, the family still survives at Burton Constable, tracing its descent from Humphrey de Wyvill, of Slingsby Castle, who came over with the Conqueror.

Y

YATES, JOSEPH, descended from an old county family of Lancashire. His grandfather and father, both named Joseph Yates, resided at Stanley House in that county, in which the former was a magistrate, and the latter high sheriff in 1728. In 1730 he became possessed, under the will of a relation, of the estate of Peel Hall, near Manchester, with its large beds of coal, involving so great an expenditure that his means were eventually reduced, and his affairs seriously embarrassed. By his marriage with Ellen, daughter of William Maghull of Maghull, he had two sons, the younger of whom was the future judge.

Joseph Yates was born in 1722, and from the grammar school of Manchester he went to Queen's College, Oxford, where he could not have continued, owing to his father's difficulties, had it not been for the timely assistance of his relative Mr. Serjeant Bootle, who generously stepped forward and enabled him to finish his course at the university, and to pursue his legal studies. For this purpose he entered Staple Inn, on the south window of the hall of which society his arms may still be seen. From Staple Inn he removed to the Inner Temple, and practised as a special pleader from Michaelmas 1748 till July 1753, when he was called to the bar. Here he rapidly rose in reputation, and acquired a practice so large that his fee-book records a profit of 2313*l.* in one year. He had general retainers for the corporation of Liverpool, for Greenwich Hospital, and for the East India Company, and was employed by the crown in the militia riots of 1758, and in the proceedings against John Wilkes in 1763. But the only legal rank which he received before his elevation to the bench was that of king's counsel for the duchy of Lancaster in June 1761. His labours required frequent and intense application, and when it became burthensome he was in the habit of relieving himself by reading a few pages in Dean Swift's works, which always sent him back cheerfully to his studies. On some extraordinary success in 1760 he was presented with a silver vase, now preserved in the family, bearing the following inscription :—' Jurisconsulto perito, Josepho Yates, ob auxilium insigne legum cognitoribus præstitum, Grati Clientes D.D.D.'

So remarkable were his legal attainments that when he had been little more than ten years at the bar he was offered a judgeship of the King's Bench, which with considerable reluctance he was prevailed on to accept on January 23, 1764, when he received the customary honour of knighthood. In February 1765 the chancellorship of Durham was added. He ventured sometimes to differ from his noble chief, Lord Mansfield, who chafed so much under any opposition of opinion that Sir Joseph, to avoid his lordship's covert sarcasms, determined to take the first opportunity to leave his court. This resolution is the subject of strong observation in Junius's first letter to Lord Mansfield. On the resignation of Mr. Justice Clive in February 1770 he induced Sir William Blackstone, for whom the place was designed, to exchange it for the King's Bench. He thus obtained his removal to the Common Pleas on February 16, 1770, preferring the quiet of a junior seat in that court to the unseemly contests in which his continuance in the senior place in the King's Bench seemed likely to involve him. Not long did he enjoy the benefit he anticipated. Within four months his mortal career was terminated. He died on June 7, 1770, of a neglected cold falling on his chest, and was buried at Cheam in Surrey, where he had a house. (*Blackstone's Reports*, 450, 681, 714.)

He was universally acknowledged to be a most able and learned judge; and the points on which he differed from Lord Mansfield were subsequently recognised as good law, and confirmed by the House of Lords. Of his inflexible integrity a story was circulated, that he returned a letter brought to him from the king unopened, the minister having already tampered with him in vain previous to some trials involving the rights of the crown. Though the precise details of this transaction are not known, there seems too good reason to believe that the fact occurred, as it was publicly stated in parliament by Alderman Townshend soon after the judge's death, and, though repeated by another speaker, remained uncontradicted by any member of the administration. (*Parl. Hist.* xvi. 1228, 1295.) It tells well however for Lord North, that soon after the death of Sir Joseph he called on Lady Yates, and, after saying much that was most gratifying to her and complimentary to the deceased, delicately enquired into her circumstances. The visit concluded by his saying that 'the widow of so great a man ought not to be left with so small a provision,' and, regretting that the funds at his disposal would not admit of his offering more, asked whether a pension of 200*l.* a year would be worth her acceptance—a graceful act in the government, and a flattering testimony of the estimation in which he was held by a court whose temptations he had the virtue and the courage to resist. Another, less delicate, but more significant, proof of his general reputation appeared at the time in the following lines:—

> Hadst thou but ta'en each other judge,
> Grim Death, to Pluto's gates,
> Thou might'st have done 't without a grudge,
> Hadst thou but left us Yates.

In his private life he was most amiable and considerate. He commenced his career under great pecuniary difficulties, and considerable feebleness of constitution, but from the time of his leaving college he was able by his industry to contribute largely to his father's comfort, and the advancement of his brother's children. One of his weaknesses was a great attention to his dress, by which he acquired the character of being 'a fine gentleman,' and was the subject of some ludicrous stories.

At his father's decease he succeeded to the estate of Peel Hall; and at his own he left one son and one daughter, by his wife, Elizabeth, daughter and coheir of Charles Baldwyn of Munslow in Shropshire, a lady of very ancient Scotch descent.

YATTINDEN, NICHOLAS DE, had writs of assize addressed to him from September 1270, to August 1271, 54 and 55 Henry III.; and in the next year a record of a trial before him 'et sociis suis' occurs, in which he is called 'justic. domini regis.' In 36 Henry III. he was pardoned 55*s.* 2½*d.* out of the issues of the lands of Stephen de Hampton, the custody of which he had till the heir was of age; and in 53 Henry III. the castle and forest of Windsor with other manors were placed in his charge. He married Aliva, the widow of Henry de Bathonia, and died in 1 Edward I. possessed of considerable property in Berkshire and Norfolk. (*Excerpt. e Rot. Fin.* ii. 141, 522–546; *Abb. Placit.* 183; *Blomefield's Norfolk*, i. 185; *Cal. Inq.* p. m. i. 48, 51.)

YELVERTON, WILLIAM, belonged to an ancient family established in the reign of Edward II. in Norfolk, but apparently previously settled in Dorsetshire. He was the son of John Yelverton, of Rackheath in the former county, recorder of Norwich in 1403, by his second wife, Elizabeth, daughter and heir of John Read, of Rougham, and widow of Robert Clere, of Stokesby. He is stated to have been a reader in Gray's Inn, and was called to the degree of serjeant-at-law in Michaelmas, 18 Henry VI., 1439. In 1427 he was one of the justices of the peace in Norwich; and he held the office of recorder of that city from 1433 to 1450.

In the parliament of 14 Henry VI. he was returned as member for Yarmouth; but after his attainment of the coif it does not appear that he was again elected.

He was appointed a judge of the King's Bench some time in 1443, 21 Henry VI. (*Cal. Rot. Pat.* 285), and sat there till the deposition of that monarch. Edward IV. not only continued him in his place, but created him a knight of the Bath previous to the coronation.

It seems probable, indeed, that soon after Edward's accession he was suspected of some implication in the late king's affairs, as we are told by one of the Paston letters (i. 131, 150, 172) that a privy seal had come to him requiring his presence at court, and that he refused to go; and in a subsequent letter we hear that he and Jenney 'are like for to be greatly punished, for because they came not to the king.' He however must have succeeded in excusing himself, since he still remained on the bench when Henry VI. was replaced on the throne. Although that luckless king included him in the new patents appointing the judges on October 9, 1470, Yelverton appears to have again fallen under suspicion, as Sir John Paston, on November 15, desires his brother to tell him 'that he may not appear of a while in no wise,' and promises to send him word when he may. (*Ibid.* ii. 57.) The Year Book, however, proves that he acted as a judge of the King's Bench during some part of the short restoration.

Whether he died or not in that brief interval is uncertain; but on the return of Edward IV. his name was omitted from the list of the King's Bench judges then appointed, and no subsequent mention of him occurs. Weever (821) gives the inscription on his monument at Rougham, but unfortunately the date of his death is omitted. On it he is described 'quondam Justic. dom. Regis de suo Banco,' which would seem to imply that he was not so at the time of his death.

The brave and slandered knight Sir John Fastolf was Sir William Yelverton's early patron and lasting friend till his death. There is a letter from Sir William to him, praying his interference with the king, the lord chancellor, and other lords, in case any attempt to injure the judge should be made by certain parties in opposition to him, 'that no credence be given to mine hurt in mine absence.' He was one of Fastolf's executors in 1459, and was engaged in the violent controversy which arose out of the will. Another letter records the curious and scarcely credible fact that in one of the proceedings he 'came down from the bench and plete the matter.' (*Paston*, i. 12, 149.)

During the progress of the controversy he is described as 'the cursed Norfolk justice;' but as this is the expression of an antagonist, it decides little as to his character. That seems to have been remarkable for its energy; and mention is made of the 'thank he had of the king (Edward, in 1462), at Cambridge, for cause he declared so well the charge of extortion done by sheriffs and other officers, &c., for the which declaration the king took him by the hand, and said he cowde him great thanks, and prayed him so to do in this country (Norfolk).' An earlier letter shows that he was tainted with the superstitious credulity of the time. Speaking of Our Lady's house at Walsingham, he says, 'for truly if I be drawn to any worship or welfare, and discharge of my enemies' danger, I ascribe it unto Our Lady.' (*Ibid.* 10, 151.)

He married Agnes, daughter of Sir Oliver le Gross, of Crostwick, Norfolk, and apparently widow of John Rands, and was the progenitor of the two next-named judges. (*Blomefield's Norwich*, i. 125-156.)

YELVERTON, CHRISTOPHER, was the son of William, who came in direct descent from the above Sir William Yelverton, with four generations between them, enjoying the same property in Norfolk, and pursuing the same profession. He held the office of reader in Gray's Inn in 1535 and 1542, and it was probably he whose name appears in the debates in the parliaments of 1571 and 1572. (*Parl. Hist.* i. 747, 762, 779.) He died in 1585, leaving, by his marriage with Anne, daughter and heir of Sir Henry Fermor, of East Barsham in Norfolk, a large family. Henry, his eldest son, succeeded to the estates, and was father to Sir William, who obtained a baronetcy (of Rougham) in 1620, which expired in 1649.

Christopher was the third son, who, entering himself in 1552 at Gray's Inn, relieved his legal studies there by an occasional offering to the Muses. When 'Jocasta,' a tragedy translated from Euripides by George Gascoigne and Francis Kynwelmersh, was performed there in 1566, the epilogue was supplied by Yelverton (*Athen. Oxon.* i. 436), and he assisted in other devices and shows of the society. He became reader in 1574, and again in 1583, and in 1589 he was called to the degree of the coif, and made queen's serjeant in 1598. (*Dugdale's Orig.* 295, 298.)

In the parliament of October 1597 he was elected speaker. His disabling speech on that occasion gives a description of his person and position; and the prayer which, according to the custom of those times, he composed and read to the house every morning, has much devotional beauty. In this parliament, which was dissolved in the following February, it is observable that the queen 'refused or quashed forty-eight several bills which had passed both houses.' (*Parl. Hist.* i. 897, 905.) His conduct in the house was so satisfactory that his promotion to be queen's serjeant took place three months after the dissolution. In this character he opened the indictments against the Earl of Essex and the other conspirators in 1600, but the principal duty of urging the evidence fell on Coke and Fleming, the attorney and solicitor general. (*State Trials*, i. 1336, 1419.)

Lord Burleigh thought very highly of him, and on February 2, 1602, he was nominated a judge of the King's Bench. On the accession of James I. in the following year his patent was renewed, and he received the honour of knighthood. It fell to his lot to pronounce sentence of death upon Robert Creighton, Lord Sanquire, for procuring the murder of Robert Turner, a fencing master, who had by mischance struck out his eye while playing with the foils. (*Ibid.* ii. 752.)

Sir Christopher died in November 1612, at Easton-Mauduit, an estate he had purchased in Northamptonshire, which has remained the seat of his family up to the present time. About two years before his decease, Robert Cecil, Earl of Salisbury, gave this character of him to his son Henry: 'He is a gentleman, a learned man, and a lawyer; one that will deliver his mind with perspicuous reason and great comeliness.' (*Archæologia*, xv. 52.)

His wife, Margaret, daughter of Thomas Catesby, of Ecton and Whiston in Northamptonshire, Esq., brought him two sons and four daughters. One of his two sons was the next-noticed Henry.

YELVERTON, HENRY, was the eldest son of the above, by his wife, Margaret, daughter of Thomas Catesby, Esq., and was born, as some say, at his father's seat at Easton-Mauduit in Northamptonshire, or, as others assert, at Islington, near London, on June 29, 1566. He was educated in the university of Oxford, but Anthony Wood does not state at what college, and then became a member of Gray's Inn, where his ancestors had pursued their legal studies. Having been in due course called to the bar, he was appointed reader in 1607. (*Dugdale's Orig.* 296.) But long before that time he had been elected recorder of Northampton.

To the first parliament of James I. he was returned as member for Northampton, and as a representative of the people he took an independent, but not a factious, part. He supported the subsidy, but advocated its gradual instead of its immediate payment, and in all questions brought before the house he freely expressed his real opinions, without considering whether they were acceptable to either party, and without weighing over-nicely the expressions with which he urged them. But he was popular as an advocate, and consequently had professional enemies jealous of his fame. His plain dealing and the freedom of his language were accordingly misrepresented at court, and phrases were singled out of his speeches to prove that he hated the Scotch, and had no respect for the king. These reports gradually made their way to James's ear, and Yelverton found after some time that he was looked upon with a suspicious and unfriendly eye, not only by his sovereign, but by the Scotch nobles around him. George Hume, Earl of Dunbar, the lord treasurer of Scotland, took offence, when a question arose in parliament as to the confirmation of certain land granted to the earl on the confines of Scotland, contiguous to Lord Hume's land on the confines of England, at Yelverton's using the cumulative words '*humus super humum*,' conceiving they were intended as a personal reflection. The king also felt himself grievously offended because one of Yelverton's arguments for the naturalisation of Lord Kinloss was that he was not all Scot, but half English; and he was 'much enraged' that on another occasion Yelverton had said 'that he would weigh the king's reasons as he did his coin.' It was natural, therefore, that a man all whose intentions were loyal should be desirous of understanding and explaining the charges made against him; and Yelverton took the straightforward course of seeking an interview both with the earl and the king. This he effected through the means of the Lady Arabella and the lord chancellor of Scotland, the Earl of Dunfermline, and he gives a very interesting and curious account of his interviews, in which he was successful in satisfying both. He stated that, so far from opposing the union, he refused the employment when assigned to argue the case of the post nati on the part contrary to his majesty's desire. The whole transaction of the reconciliation is very creditable to all the parties. The grounds of complaint are openly avowed, and the ingenious justification generously admitted. No unfair compromise of principle is demanded or promised, and on a subsequent visit to Robert Cecil, the lord treasurer, that nobleman says that he shall assure himself that Yelverton, to please the king, will not speak against his conscience. (*Archæologia*, xv. 27–52.) The argument attributed to him in the 'State Trials' (vol. ii. p. 478) against the impositions of the crown on merchandise, and not published till 1641, eleven years after his death, was really the speech of James Whitelocke, afterwards a judge. (*Notes and Queries*, 2nd S. ix. 383, x. 39; *Parl. Debates in* 1610, 85, 103.)

Yelverton had to wait nearly four years before he reaped any fruits of his reconciliation with the king. His father, the judge, died in 1612, and on October 29, 1613, he was made solicitor-general, and knighted. In little more than two years his patron the Earl of Somerset was indicted for the murder of Sir Thomas Overbury; but Sir Henry, though this was a state prosecution and he held an office under the crown, is said to have declined to appear against his patron, and he is not recorded as having taken any part in the trial. Bacon, who was the attorney-general at the time, must have felt this courageous refusal as a reflection on his own conduct with regard to the Earl of Essex, especially as it was not visited by any evil consequences, such as he had pretended to fear. Yelverton had always acted a friendly part towards Bacon. When the House of Commons showed some hesitation in allowing the attorney-general to sit as a member, Yelverton came to the rescue and Bacon was admitted; and when Bacon had become lord keeper, and had got into temporary disgrace both with the king and Buckingham for his interference in respect to the marriage of Sir John Villiers with Sir Edward Coke's daughter, Yelverton, who had succeeded as attorney-general on March 7, 1617, wrote him a letter of excellent advice how to act under the circumstances. But whether Bacon was offended at Sir Henry for not following his example in pleading against the Earl of Somerset, or for his presumption in offering counsel to his superior, or more probably because he wished to ingratiate himself with Buckingham, he frequently speaks injuriously of Yelverton in his correspondence with that nobleman. (*Bacon's Works* [Montagu], xii. 263–5, 331, 387.) Yelverton was no favourite with the duke, who was prejudiced against him from his connection with Somerset, from his being suspected of implication in Bacon's interference in regard to the marriage, and particularly from his declared independence of the duke's protection. Judge Whitelocke (*Liber Famelicus*, 55) gives a curious account, which he had from Yelverton's own mouth, of the 'manner of his coming to the place' of attorney-general. Though pressed by the courtiers to apply to Buckingham, who 'was agent to another, and did crosse him,' he refused to 'deal with him about it nor speak to him,' but protested 'he would leave it to the king, who he knew had judgment enough to chuse his own servants.' At last Buckingham sent to him to bring his warrant, and expostulated with him that he had not used his help, telling him that he looked not for any recompense, though Sir James Ley had offered 10,000*l*. for the place. Yelverton protested to Whitelocke 'that he neither gave to the erl, or to any other subject in the kingdom, one farthing to cum to the place, . . . but when the businesse was done, he went privately to the king, and told him he did acknowledge how like a good master and worthye prince he had dealte with him; and although there was never mention, speech, or expectation of anything to be had for his having of this place, but he came to it freely, yet out of his duty he wolde give him 4000*l*. reddy money. The king,' proceeds the relation, 'tooke him in his armes, thanked him, and commended him muche for it, and told him he had need of it, for it must serve even to buy him dishes.'

One of the first public duties Yelverton was called upon to perform was to pray an order of the court for execution of Sir Walter Raleigh, on the judgment pronounced against him fifteen years before; and the language in which he did it forms a strong contrast with that adopted by Sir Edward Coke on his trial. (*State Trials*, ii. 33.)

He held his office for three years, supported by the favour of the king; but Buckingham, whom he further displeased by his opposition to some of the illegal patents which were afterwards the subject of enquiry, was resolved to remove him. An opportunity was at last found. A new charter had been granted to the city of London, into which the attorney-general was charged with having introduced certain clauses not comprehended in the king's warrant. Yelverton's submission not being considered satisfactory by the council, they recommended that he should be sequestered and proceeded against in the Star Chamber. He was accordingly superseded on June 27, 1620, and the proceedings in the Star Chamber commenced, in which Yelverton cleared himself of any corruption, but acknowledged himself guilty through ignorance; and Bacon making a jesuitical speech against him, and Coke pressing him hard, he was sentenced to imprisonment during pleasure, and to a fine of 4000*l*. Bacon's letters, and his expression 'how I stirred the court I leave it to others to speak,' show his mean endeavours to aid Buckingham's inveteracy. (*Bacon's Works*, xii. 266, 446–9.) Yelverton was committed to the Tower, and while there the parliament by which Bacon was condemned met. In the course of their investigations into the grievances of patents the Commons implicated Yelverton, who, in his answer to the Lords, cleared himself from the charge, boldly asserting his innocence, and attributing his present imprisonment to the course which he had taken in the Patent of Inns. The king thereupon took the matter up, and, though in his speech he acquitted Sir Henry, who he acknowledged disliked and resisted the proceedings intended against the innkeepers, yet, because in his defence he had inferred that 'all the punishment upon him was for his good service done to his majesty,' he called upon the Lords, 'who are able to do him justice, to punish Sir Henry Yelverton for his slander.' Yelverton, on being afterwards brought up again, made this inference more clear, by directly charging Buckingham with being 'ready, upon every occasion, to hew him down,' and with threatening that he 'should not hold his place a month if he did not conform himself in better manner to the Patent of Inns,' and by roundly asserting 'that he suffered unjustly by his lordship's means.' This was naturally deemed an aggravation of his offence, and on May 16, 1621, he was sentenced to be imprisoned, and to pay 10,000 marks to the king, and 5000 to Buckingham, who immediately remitted his part of the fine, and the prince and the Lords agreed to move his majesty to mitigate the other. (*Parl. Hist.* i. 1232–5, 1243–8, 1255–9.)

He did not long continue a captive in the Tower. It is related that Buckingham came to him there in disguise, and from the result of the interview (the very improbable details of which Sir Anthony Weldon (*Court of James*, 157) professes to give), he made his peace, and procured his immediate release. He resumed his practice at the bar in the following Michaelmas Term, when his name appears in Croke's Reports, and for the remaining four years of the reign.

That the reconciliation was complete is apparent from the fact that, within six weeks after King Charles came to the crown, Buckingham procured for him a seat on the bench of the Common Pleas, not to supply any vacancy, but in addition to the court as a fifth judge. He received his patent on May 10, 1625; and, according to Bishop Hacket (ii. 19), there were rumours of his being made lord keeper by the removal of Lord Coventry, which was only prevented by the assassination of the duke, within eighteen months of which Sir Henry's own career was closed by his death on January 24, 1630, at his house in Aldersgate Street. His remains were removed for interment in the church of Easton-Mauduit, where a monument is placed with recumbent effigies of himself and his lady.

He was much respected and admired by his contemporaries for his eloquence, his courage, his integrity, and his learning. His reputation as a lawyer was very great, and was not diminished by the subsequent publication, by Sir W. Wylde, of his 'Reports of Special Cases.' Cecil Earl of Salisbury, at an early period of his career, gave this testimony of him to his face: 'Indeed, I must say your father's education of you, that have made you so lively resemble himself, for you have good elocution and sound reason, whereby the apprehension of them that hear you is made more active, and so hath your father, which is a great merit in the professors of the law.' (*Archæologia*, xv. 51.)

He married Margaret, daughter of Robert Beale, Esq., clerk of the council to Queen Elizabeth, who had the unpleasant duty of reading the warrant for the execution of Mary Queen of Scots at the scaffold on which she suffered. He left several children, the eldest of whom, Christopher, was created a baronet in 1641, and was succeeded in the title by his son, Sir Henry, who married Susan, in her own right Baroness Grey de Ruthyn. This title (after the extinction in 1799 of two others subsequently granted) survived, and has been since borne by many generations, and is now in abeyance. (*Athen. Oxon.* ii. 476; *Collins's Peerage*, vi. 624.)

YONGE, THOMAS, several of whose ancestors were merchants of Bristol, in such high estimation as to be elected representatives of that city from the reign of Edward III., was the son of Thomas Yonge, who was mayor of Bristol in 12 Henry IV. The maiden name of his mother, Joan, is not known. He was the elder of two brothers, the younger of whom, John, was member for London in 33 Henry VI., lord mayor in 4 Edward IV., and knighted in 11 Edward IV.

He was a member of the Middle Temple, and represented his native city in seven parliaments from the thirteenth year of the reign of Henry VI. In that of the thirty-third year he moved that, as Henry was without children, the Duke of York should be declared heir presumptive to the crown. The time, however, had not arrived for the duke's partisans to speak out; and the indiscreet member, for this premature exhibition of his zeal, was straightway committed to the Tower. (*Lingard*, v. 141.) His party having shortly afterwards gained the ascendency, he petitioned the parliament for damages on account of his imprisonment, which he laid at one thousand marks; and the king was compelled to assent to the prayer, referring it to the lords of his council to provide what should be thought convenient and reasonable. (*Rot. Parl.* v. 337.)

His attendance in parliament did not prevent his practising at the bar, and the Year Book records his name from 27 Henry VI. The accession of Edward IV. insured him legal honours, and accordingly he was summoned to take the degree of the coif on November 7, 1463, and was appointed one of the king's serjeants on the very next day. On the first opportunity he was raised to the bench, being constituted a judge of the Common Pleas about November 1467. The first fine levied before him was in the following February. (*Dugdale's Orig.* 46.)

Notwithstanding his known attachment to the Yorkists, he was not removed from his seat when Henry VI. was restored to the throne in October 1470, the advisers of that unfortunate monarch probably deeming it politic to make as little change as possible in the administration of the law. But when Edward IV. returned, at the end of six months, Yonge was superseded, or at least was not re-appointed. That this was more the result of his own choice than of any displeasure felt against him by the king may be presumed from the fact that in the act of resumption, passed two years afterwards, the grant of an annual tun of wine which had been made to him for his life in 9 Edward IV. was excepted from its operation. (*Rot. Parl.* vi. 82.)

He however resumed the judicial ermine in 15 Edward IV., being constituted a judge, not of his old court, but of the King's Bench, on April 29, 1475. He died in the following year, 1476, and was buried in Christ Church, London. (*Stow's London* [Thoms], 120.) By his wife, Joan, he left several sons, one of whom is believed to have been the under-mentioned John Yonge. One of the descendants of the judge's eldest son, Thomas, was in 1661 honoured with a baronetcy, which became extinct in 1810.

YONGE, JOHN, whom Fuller in his 'Worthies' has mistaken for a John Young who was made Bishop of Callipoli in Thrace in 1517, a year after this John Yonge's death, is believed to have been one of the sons of the above Thomas Yonge, and to have been born at Rye, receiving his education first at Wykeham's college at Winchester, and then at New College, Oxford. He graduated as doctor in both laws, and practised as an advocate in the ecclesiastical courts, taking, as was then usual, holy orders also. In March 1502 he was presented to the church of St. Stephen, Walbrook; in March 1504 to that of St. Mary le Bow; and in July 1513 to that of Cherfield in the archdeaconry of Huntingdon, the latter of which was given to him by Cardinal Wolsey, whom he succeeded on May 17, 1514, as dean of York, when he resigned his other preferments.

The first mention of him in connection with politics is on May 16, 1503, as a witness to the enrolment of the bull relating to the chapel of Windsor. In August he was at the head of the commissioners to negotiate a mercantile treaty with Philip Duke of Burgundy; and in May 1505 he was employed to treat for the marriage of the king with Margaret Duchess of Savoy (*Rymer*, xiii. 61, 105, 128), an object which was subsequently relinquished. Yonge's exertions were not overlooked, the office of master of the Rolls being given to him on January 22, 1508, 23 Henry VII.

On the accession of Henry VIII. Dr. Yonge's appointment was renewed; and his diplomatic services were afterwards occasionally demanded. (*Lingard*, vi. 9.) He retained the mastership of the Rolls till his death, which happened on April 25, 1516, two years after he had become dean of York. On his monument in the Rolls Chapel, the work of Pietro Torregiano, a very eminent Florentine, he is represented in a scarlet robe with a four-cornered cap.

Besides the favour of Wolsey, he has the credit of having been the friend of Dean Colet and the patron of Erasmus. (*Athen. Oxon.* ii. 727; *Dugdale's Orig.* 335.)

YORK, WILLIAM OF (BISHOP OF SALISBURY), was brought up as an ecclesiastic and a lawyer, and in 1226, 10 Henry III., was granted 10*l.* for his expenses on an iter into Lincolnshire. (*Rot. Claus.* ii. 119.) His name occurs as justice itinerant in Cumberland and the liberties of the bishopric of Durham, in 11 and 12 Henry III. (*Ibid.* 213), about which time he was probably appointed one of the regular justiciers at Westminster. Fines were levied before him from 1231 to 1239. (*Dugdale's Orig.* 43.) On July 6, 1234, on the nomination of three judges of the Common Pleas, they were directed to be admitted by Robert de Lexinton and William of York, who were most likely the two senior judges, and perhaps presided in the two branches of the court. This receives some confirmation from the fact that the former was placed at the head of the justices assigned for the northern counties, and the latter at the head of those for the southern counties, who were sent throughout England in 1240, under the pretence of redressing grievances and easing the people, but with the real object of collecting money for the royal treasury by means of fines and confiscations. About this time he was made provost of Beverley, was subsequently rector of Eton and of Gatton, and in December 1246 was elected Bishop of Salisbury. His elevation to the episcopal bench does not appear to have removed him from his judicial duties, as in 35 Henry III. he stands at the head of a commission to hear the pleas of the city of London, which were wont to be decided before the justices itinerant. Matthew Paris mentions him as most learned in the laws, and a great favourite with the king.

He died on January 31, 1256, and was buried in his own cathedral. (*Godwin*, 344; *Le Neve*, 257; *Excerpt. e Rot. Fin.* i. 292, 431; *Abb. Placit.* 106–120.)

YORKE, PHILIP (EARL OF HARDWICKE). The character of this great man and distinguished judge has had scanty justice done to it by his biographers. Living when party spirit ran extravagantly high, it is not surprising that the estimate formed of it by the opposing factions should be as wide apart as their political opinions; but even his greatest vituperators, while criticising, and perhaps condemning, his proceedings as a statesman, are forced to acknowledge his transcendent abilities as a magistrate. It is, however, curious to see two of his opponents differ widely in their remarks. Lord Chesterfield says that Lord Hardwicke 'was never in the least suspected of any kind of corruption;' that 'he was an agreeable eloquent speaker in parliament;' and that 'he was a cheerful instructive companion, humane in his nature, decent in his manners, and unstained by any vice (except avarice).' Horace Walpole, to whom he was a subject of personal aversion, on the contrary insinuates the reverse of all this, speaking of 'the extent of his baseness,' and asserting that 'in the House of Lords he was laughed at, in the cabinet despised,' thus carrying his inveteracy to so absurd a degree that no reliance can be placed on anything that he relates. The best memoir is the one in Mr. Welsby's collection; but both that and Lord Campbell's give too much weight to the 'sketch' published by Mr. Cooksey in 1791, and to the gossiping and malicious stories contained in the letter introduced in the sketch from an anonymous correspondent, who vents the most virulent abuse, and even commits the gross extravagance of charging Lord Hardwicke with causing his nephew to be sent on a fatal expedition, in order that by his death he might succeed to his property—in short, accusing him of a conspiracy to murder. Lord Campbell, though of the same party and approving his political principles, and of the same profession and cognisant of the veneration with which his memory is regarded by its members, seems to grudge the encomiums he is obliged to bestow, attenuating them by so many qualifications that the reader cannot but regret that his lordship did not recollect his own remark, that 'historians and biographers make sad mistakes when they begin to assign motives—which however they often do as peremptorily as if they lived in familiar confidence with those whose actions they narrate.' A subsequent Life has been published by Mr. George Harris in three volumes, which is written in so lengthy and uninteresting a style, and interlarded with so much extraneous matter and so many insignificant details, that it has not met with the favour to which it would have otherwise been entitled, for the valuable materials and authentic documents which the author has had an opportunity of furnishing.

Simon Yorke, the grandfather of Lord Hardwicke (descended, according to the inscription on his grave in St. James's Church, Dover, from the ancient family of Yorke long settled in North Wiltshire), left his native county at the time of the Great Rebellion, and established himself as a merchant at Dover. By the council books of that corporation it appears that at the Restoration he was *restored* to the office of common councilman. At his death in 1682 he left several sons, one of whom, Philip, pursued the profession of the law with great success in the same town, where he filled the office of town clerk, and occupied one of the handsomest houses, the antique beauty and great extent of which are remembered by some of its present inhabitants. This Philip married Elizabeth, daughter and heir of Richard Gibbon of Dover, and widow of her cousin Edward Gibbon of Westcliffe, near that town, whose namesake and descendant became illustrious in literature as the historian of the 'Decline and Fall of the Roman Empire.' Of the numerous family he had by her only three survived him—one son, the subject of the present sketch, and two daughters. That his death did not occur till June 1721 is a pregnant refutation of the report that he was distressed in his circumstances and died in despair, inasmuch as his son had long before that date gained an eminent position at the bar, had for the seven previous years been a member of parliament, and for more than a year had held the prominent and profitable post of solicitor-general. This report originated, as far as I can trace (for no allusion is made to the alleged indigence of the father by any of the son's contemporaries), in the anonymous letter before mentioned, which Mr. Cooksey thought fit to publish, although containing a variety of frivolous details not tending, as the writer candidly professes, 'to flatter his lordship's memory.' The tale, without any better authority, has been subsequently repeated; and Lord Campbell perpetually harps upon the penury under which the chancellor commenced his career. Its improbability is apparent from the fact that several estates belonging to the father have remained in the family till the present generation; and it is contrary to all likelihood that a prosperous son who inscribed a tablet in St. James's Church, Dover (still existing), to the memory of his parents at the death of his mother in 1727, concluding with the expressive line

Quos amor in vitâ conjunxit, non ipsa mors divisit,

would suffer poverty to overtake them during their lives.

Philip Yorke the son was born at Dover on December 1, 1690, and received his education at a school of considerable reputation at Bethnal Green, kept by Mr. Samuel Morland, a man of great classical attainments. He continued there till Christmas 1706, having by his diligence, his talents, and general behaviour earned the affection of his master, who for some years afterwards kept up a Latin correspondence with him. Two of Mr. Morland's letters are preserved. The first is dated in February 1706-7, written soon after Yorke left the school, in which the proud tutor not only predicts his pupil's future celebrity, but declares that he reputes *that* the happiest day of his life on which he was entrusted with his education. The other is dated October 1708, and addressed to his pupil at Mr. Salkeld's in Brooke Street, Holborn, to whom his father had sent him for his elementary legal studies. Mr. Salkeld was not, as some biographers have stated, the learned serjeant of that name (a natural mistake, as he was then in full practice, and lived for several years after, and as his well-known Reports were first published under the care of Lord Hardwicke); but he was the serjeant's brother, and an eminent attorney, who must have held a high rank among his brethren, since in his office Viscount Jocelyn, lord chancellor of Ireland, Sir Thomas Parker, lord chief baron, and Sir John Strange, master of the Rolls, besides Lord Hardwicke, the most eminent of all, were at different times seated as pupils.

That Mr. Salkeld was Mr. Yorke's London agent, or that he received the son as his 'gratis clerk,' there is no other authority than the gossip of Mr. Cooksey's anonymous correspondent. The improbability, if not the falsehood, of both stories is evident from the fact that Mr. Yorke, two months before his son left school, commissioned a relative in London to find an eminent attorney with whom to place his son, which would have been quite unnecessary had he had any previous connection with Mr. Salkeld; and in the same letter, so far from alluding to his supposed poverty, or intimating a wish to avoid the expense, he desires his friend 'to learn the termes on which he may be disposed of.' Neither does it appear at all, though generally asserted, that the son was intended for his father's branch of the profession; but, on the contrary, the expression used by his father in the above letter is that he is 'desirous to place him with an eminent attorney in the Common Pleas *for three years*, that by the practis of the lawe he may be better qualified for the study of it.' This term was not a sufficient service then, any more than it is now, to enable a clerk to be admitted an attorney, and the father's expression seems clearly to show his inclination to bring his son up to the bar. Jeremy Bentham also, in a letter to Mr. Cooksey (54, 72), states expressly that the father, '*intending him for the bar*, very judiciously placed him with Mr. Salkeld' (*Harris*, i. 27, 29); and that he did so intend is confirmed by the fact that before the young student had been two years with Mr. Salkeld he was, on November 29, 1708, actually admitted a member of the Middle Temple.

The anecdote told of Mrs. Salkeld sending him on family errands, and to fetch in little necessaries from the markets, and of the ingenious mode he took for putting a stop to the practice by charging Mr. Salkeld with coach-hire for the carriage, has little bearing on the question. Besides the recollection that youth was not so tenacious and dignified as in the present age, it proves nothing more than that the lady took too great advantage of the extreme good-nature for which the young pupil was no doubt then as famous as he was in after life.

Soon after his admission he left Mr. Salkeld's, and took chambers in Pump Court in the Temple, where he not only pursued with assiduity his legal studies, attending the courts and noting cases, but employed his leisure hours in polite literature and philosophical enquiries. There he composed, there is little reason to doubt, though it has been disputed, the letter which appeared in the 'Spectator' of April 28, 1712, under the signature Philip Homebred, ridiculing the common practice of sending unfledged youth on foreign travel; the only literary, not legal, performance on which he ever ventured. About this time he was introduced to Lord Macclesfield, lord chief justice of the King's Bench, either (for the narrations vary) by Mr. Salkeld, or Mr. George Parker, the chief justice's son, or by Mr. Thomas Parker, the chief justice's nephew. The latter was a clerk in Mr. Salkeld's office, but probably not at the same time, as he was five years Yorke's junior; so that if he was the introducer, it would appear that Yorke frequented Mr. Salkeld's office after his admission to the Middle Temple, and also was a brother-student with Parker in that society. Whatever was the object of the introduction, it led to an intimacy most beneficial to the young man when he went to the bar. It turned out, however, very injurious to the peer, as, it is asserted, the favour he showed to Yorke in the Court of Chancery excited the jealousy of some of his seniors so much that it gave additional inveteracy to the earl's prosecution.

Yorke was called to the bar on May 6, 1715, and almost immediately obtained considerable employment. That for this success he was partly indebted to his legal connection, and partly to the influence of his patron, there can be no doubt; but neither would have availed him had he not shown himself competent to improve the opportunities thus put in his way. His superiority of talent was soon recognised, and that it procured him a large accession of business is proved by the anecdote related in the memoir of Sir Littleton Powys. Other and better testimonies of the estimation in which he was regarded are to be found in the two following facts. Before he had been four years at the bar he was sent down by the government to supply a vacancy in the borough of Lewes, and was returned its member on May 2, 1719. And, secondly, his marriage later in the same month with Margaret, the daughter of Mr. Charles Cocks of Worcester, by the sister of Lord Somers, and the young widow of Mr. William Lygon of Maddresfield. This lady he had met at her uncle's, Sir Joseph Jekyll, whose strong recommendation of him and his future prospects overcame the objections of the father to a suitor who had no present means of making a settlement.

He kept up constant intercourse with his family and friends at Dover, and was appointed recorder or steward of that corporation. Nothing appears in this intercourse that gives the slightest insinuation of the imputed penury of his father. The correspondence to which Mr. Harris has had access contains the strongest proofs of Yorke's affection for both his parents, and of his kindness to his sister, and liberality to her and her unfortunate husband, whose indigence was caused by his dissipation and misconduct. It also affords ample evidence that throughout Yorke's career in life he never deserted the friends of his youth, but did what he could to advance them; thus manifestly showing the malice of Mr. Cooksey's anonymous correspondent in inventing tales of a contrary tendency, which it is to be regretted have been too easily repeated by Lord Campbell, without sufficient enquiry into their truth. His father lived to see the first fruits of his son's success, and died in June 1721, fifteen months after his first promotion.

That promotion took place in less than two years after his marriage, when he was appointed solicitor-general on March 22, 1720, being knighted, and soon after becoming bencher, treasurer, and reader of his inn. On January 31, 1724, he succeeded to the office of attorney-general, and thus within nine years after his call to the bar, and before he had attained thirty-four years of age, he had outstripped all his colleagues and become the leader in Westminster Hall. If he had been a scion of nobility, or surrounded with the highest connections, it would be idle to suppose that he could have attained this eminence by means of mere patronage.

He filled this office for above ten years, four under George I. and six under George II., and his excellence both as an advocate and as a public prosecutor was acknowledged as well by his political opponents as his friends. The first is evidenced by the frequent recurrence of his name in the Reports of the time, and by the anxiety expressed in many private letters from parties desirous of his aid. The last is proved by his speeches, remarkable at the same time for their humanity and temperance and for their force and effect, and is unmistakably confirmed by the applause of both sides of the House of Commons on an accidental allusion by him to his conduct while in office. A magistrate against whom he was engaged as counsel thought proper to challenge him, and was obliged to ask his pardon in open court in order to prevent a criminal information. (*Gent. Mag.* i. 29.) His general success is manifested by his being enabled to purchase in 1725 the manor and estate of Hardwicke in Gloucestershire, which cost him about 24,000*l.*

He continued in parliament from his first election for Lewes in 1719 till he was promoted to the upper house in 1733, being returned for Seaford in the two intervening parliaments of 1720 and 1727. Each of these seats he owed to the patronage of the Duke of Newcastle, who from the first saw his merit, and to the last never deserted him. With whatever disregard the character of his grace may be treated, he cannot be refused the credit of discrimination in this early recognition of the talents of a young man who became one of the most efficient supports of his administration. Sir Philip's reported speeches as a commoner exhibit that power of argument and lucid arrangement for which he was always remarkable, and fully justify the respect and deference which were paid to his opinion in the house. To this feeling on the part of his senatorial colleagues may be attributed his being excused from taking any part in the impeachment of the Earl of Macclesfield, on account of the close friendship that existed between them. That he took no more steps in the earl's behalf than by speeches in his place in parliament has been unjustly made the ground of animadversion, without a suggestion of what more he could have done, and without considering that, being a member of the House of Commons, he could not take a professional part in the defence of one whom that house had chosen to prosecute. It is rather laughable that, more than a century after the earl's death, he should be pitied for the desertion of a friend—of which he himself was never conscious—with whom he kept up a cordial intercourse from the time of his trial to his death, and to whom in his last letter he describes himself as his 'most *affectionate* and most faithful humble servant.' (*Harris*, i. 179, 222.)

In 1727 he published anonymously a work, which has been erroneously fathered on Sir Joseph Jekyll, entitled 'A Discourse on the Judicial Authority belonging to the Master of the Rolls in the High Court of Chancery.' It was apparently in answer to 'The History of the Chancery,' published the year before by Mr. Samuel Burroughs, whom Lord Chancellor King rewarded with a mastership in Chancery. Sir Philip's book evinced great learning and research, and on being answered by Burroughs, with the assistance of Warburton, afterwards Bishop of Gloucester, in a work called 'The Legal Judicature in Chancery Stated,' was republished in a second edition with a preface containing an elaborate reply to all the opposing arguments. (*Ibid.* 195.)

Lord Chief Justice Raymond died on March 19, 1733, and his place in the Court of King's Bench remained vacant for nearly eight months, although Sir Philip Yorke was regarded as the only competent successor, and although the Duke of Somerset was assured by the Duke of Newcastle that it was at his own choice to succeed. (*Ibid.* 130.) It is not unlikely that there was some prudent hesitation on his own part to leave the profitable position of attorney-general, for he says to the Duke of Somerset, 'I am doubtful how suitable the office of chief justice of the King's Bench may be to my circumstances at this time of life, and with a numerous family.' Some time probably elapsed in overcoming that hesitation, and the rest may be well accounted for in arranging the means of doing so. It was at last effected by increasing the salary of 2000*l.* to 4000*l.* a year, which Sir Philip insisted should not be for himself alone, but for his successors also. He was also to be raised to the peerage. He was accordingly appointed chief justice on October 31, 1733, and created Lord Hardwicke on November 23.

Much credit cannot be placed on the statement made by some that he aimed at the Seals, but gave way to his friend the Solicitor-General Talbot; and still less to the assertion, made by others, that they were actually offered to him and declined. In 1734 he was elected recorder of Gloucester, and continued to hold the office till his death, when he was succeeded in it by his son Charles Yorke.

During the three years and a half that he presided over the King's Bench he more than satisfied the expectations of those who had formed the most favourable opinion of him. His legal knowledge, his habitual caution, his firmness and discrimination, gave weight to his decisions, and excited unquestioned admiration from even those to whom they were adverse. In the House of Lords also he shone with equal brilliancy. In the speeches he delivered there was so much solidity, argument, and eloquence that his brother peers welcomed him as an accomplished colleague. With this superiority both as a judge and a senator, his advance to a higher dignity could not but be anticipated. The opportunity soon occurred. Lord Talbot died after a short and brilliant career; and on the very day of the event the Great Seal was pressed upon Lord Hardwicke. He hesitated to accept the precarious honour, and to give up a permanent position, to the duties of which he was accustomed, and in which he had the opportunity of providing for his family by the expected falling in of a valuable office. This difficulty being soon overcome by giving him an equivalent in a grant in reversion to his eldest son of a tellership of the Exchequer, he undertook the office and was constituted lord chancellor on February 21, 1737.

For the next four months Lord Hardwicke held both the offices of lord chancellor and lord chief justice, and occasionally sat in the King's Bench till June 8, when the appointment of Sir William Lee to the latter court took place.

He retained the Great Seal for nearly twenty years of his life, and rendered his name illustrious both as a statesman and a judge. The acts and policy of the government, for which as a member of it he was responsible, and which he moderated by his prudent counsel and supported by his powerful eloquence, belong more to the history of the country than to the biography of the man. But under Sir Robert Walpole's ministry, and those that succeeded it, he still maintained his influence, accommodating the personal disputes and feuds in the cabinet, and looked up to with respect and deference by all parties in the senate. He seems to have excited the animosity of no one except Horace Walpole, who, for some cause or other, takes every opportunity to vilify him by putting false constructions on his actions and false colouring to his opinions. For his character as a judge, whether estimated by his decisions, or by the arguments by which he supported them, or by the principles on which they were founded, or, to take a lower standard, by the unadorned eloquence in which they were delivered, we have only to refer to the satisfaction they gave to his contemporaries, to the deference with which they are still always quoted, and to the veneration with which his very name is regarded, even at this distance of time, by the ablest practisers of the law.

Lord Hardwicke's entrance into the chancellorship was anything but auspicious. He at once was made to experience the disagreeables of office, by being forced to enter into the personal disputes of the royal family. He was commanded by the king on the very day of his appointment to carry an unwelcome message to the Prince of Wales, the sting of which however he managed to make less poignant; and in the future progress of the quarrel, harsh on one side, and foolish and insolent on the other, he exerted himself as much as possible to effect a reconciliation.

In the frequent absences of the king from England, Lord Hardwicke was always left as one of the lords justices; and with the Duke of Newcastle and his brother, after Sir Robert Walpole's resignation, had the principal management of the affairs of the kingdom. During one of these intervals commenced the Rebellion of 1745, which was treated at first with apathy and indifference, and as of trifling moment, till the success of the Young Pretender at Preston Pans and his march into England roused the country from its lethargy, and led to the retreat of the rebel army and its subsequent defeat at Culloden. In the trials of the lords engaged in the conspiracy Lord Hardwicke acted as lord high steward, conducting them with dignity and firmness; and, though some writers have considered his address to Lord Lovat as unnecessarily harsh and personal, it should not be forgotten that the occurrence of a second rebellion soon after that of 1715 required a more solemn and circumstantial exposition of its enormity, while the vile character and disgraceful conduct of the titled criminal justified any severity of remark.

In July 1749 he was unanimously elected high steward of the university of Cambridge, an honour for which he had reason to be proud, conferred as it was on one who, without the claim of an academical education, had acquired the reputation of high classical attainments, in addition to the eminent intellectual powers with which he was endowed. After having several times declined an advance in the peerage, though pressed upon him by ministers, he was at last induced to accept it, and on April 2, 1754, was created Earl of Hardwicke and Viscount Royston, dignities which were universally recognised as fitting rewards for his long and valuable services. For two years and seven months after this elevation he continued to execute the duties of his high office, and to be one of the most active and efficient advisers in the administration. But when the Duke of Newcastle was forced to succumb to the opposition and give way to the Duke of Devonshire as first lord of the Treasury, Lord Hardwicke took the opportunity to retire with his friend, and, notwithstanding all the efforts of the new ministry to retain him, on November 19, 1756, resigned the Great Seal, after holding it, according to his own computation, 'nineteen years, eight months, and sixteen days.' Only two previous holders of the Seal, whether as keeper or chancellor, had exceeded this length of service—Sir Nicholas Bacon, who was keeper for twenty years; and Sir Thomas Egerton, Lord Ellesmere, who retained the Seal as keeper and chancellor twenty years and ten months; and only one subsequent lord chancellor, John Lord Eldon, whose occupation of office extended to twenty-four years, ten months, and twenty-four days, with an interval of about a year.

On the return of the Duke of Newcastle to power and his junction with Mr. Pitt in the following June, Lord Hardwicke again refused the Great Seal, but aided the ministerial counsels in the cabinet; and it is a curious circumstance that he prepared all the speeches from the throne till the year 1762, as he had previously done while in office. On Lord Bute's accession to the ministry, Lord Hardwicke, though offered the privy seal, retired altogether into private life. His health began to decline in October 1763, and, gradually sinking, he died on March 6, 1764, at his house in Grosvenor Square, in the seventy-fourth year of his age. He was buried in the church of Wimpole in Cambridgeshire, where he had purchased in 1740 the large estate of the Earl of Oxford, the mansion on which he had greatly improved. A handsome monument to him and his lady by Scheemakers adorns the church.

Lord Chesterfield, his opponent in politics, acknowledges that he was 'unstained by any vice (except avarice),' but brings no proof to sustain the exception; neither do we find anything in his career that substantiates it. That he was careful of his gains, and neither profuse nor wasteful in his expenditure, are rather proofs of his prudence as a man who has first to establish himself in the world, and next to support the prominent position to which he was called at an early period. That he kept up the dignity of the various stations which he filled, that he showed no penuriousness in the education of his seven children, that he was liberal in his charities, and, above all, that he declined the offer made to him of a pension on his retirement, leave a very contrary impression.

It is not too much to say that the reputation gained and deserved by Lord Hardwicke as a lawyer and a judge was not exceeded by any previous holder of the Great Seal, and has never been equalled, except perhaps in one instance, by any of his successors. The justice of his decisions no one has ventured to impugn; all have been satisfied with the equitable principles they established, and have admired the reasoning by which he supported them. That only three of those pronounced in the course of nearly twenty years were the subject of appeal, and that none of them were reversed either during or after the termination of his chancellorship, must, notwithstanding the depreciating remarks of Lord Campbell, be regarded at the present time as a substantial proof of the excellence of his decrees, as it was in his own time acknowledged by the President Montesquieu to be ' un éloge au dessus de toute la flatterie.' (*Harris*, ii. 398.) One of his contemporaries who practised under him and became the ablest common law judge that ever sat upon the bench, Lord Mansfield, said that 'when his lordship pronounced his decrees, Wisdom herself might be supposed to speak.' Even Horace Walpole, whose personal antipathy is apparent in all he writes of him, does not deny his claims in this respect; and the depreciating characteristics which he malignantly seeks to attach to him need no other refutation than the contradictions which the writer himself unconsciously produces.

Every contemporary account shows how great was the influence he exercised both in the House of Commons and in the House of Lords. His ascendency in the cabinet is manifest by the deference paid to his opinion by Sir Robert Walpole and the Duke of Newcastle, and by the respect and affection with which he was regarded by his sovereign. Some critics have objected to him that he was not a law reformer, seeming to consider that it is incumbent on every lord chancellor to distinguish his season of power by some legislative alteration in the existing laws; while at the same time they complain of the onerous multiplicity and the absorbing nature of his various avocations. Lord Hardwicke probably thought that he was better employed and doing more essential good to his country by establishing that system of equitable jurisprudence of which he has the renown of being the framer, than in attempting to remove some slight defects which might incumber the proceedings. His justification has been made apparent by the many abortive attempts at amelioration that have recently seen the light. But though he abstained from interfering in these minor grievances, he devoted his attention as a legislator to those of more importance. By him was the bill for abolishing the feudal powers and the separate jurisdiction in Scotland framed. He succeeded in passing an act for the naturalisation of the Jews, with a view to remove civil disabilities on account of faith, which, however, popular prejudice induced parliament to repeal in the following year. And he put an end to the miseries to which every English family was liable by introducing the act for the prevention of clandestine marriages—a measure for which all parents (ay, and all youths, masculine and feminine) have reason to bless his name.

The beauty of his person, the urbanity of his manners, and the peculiar sweetness of his voice enhanced the admiration which could not fail to be excited by his excellence as a judge. His popularity among those who practised under him could not be exceeded, and few would deny the truth of the expression of one of them, that when he quitted his high station 'he left a name that will be mentioned with honour as long as Westminster Hall lasts.' (*Wynne's Serjeant-at-Law*, 103.) The unfortunate poet Richard Savage, in his 'character' of Judge Page, thus alludes to him:—

Were all, like Yorke, of delicate address,
Strength to discern, and sweetness to express,
Learn'd, just, polite, born ev'ry heart to gain,
Like Cummins mild, like Fortescue humane,
All-eloquent of truth, divinely known,
So deep, so clear, all Science is his own.

The Countess of Hardwicke, after a happy union of forty-two years, died before her husband, leaving five sons and two daughters. The eldest son, Philip, succeeded his father and died without male issue, but by his marriage with Lady Jemima Campbell, granddaughter of Henry Grey, first Duke of Kent, was the father of two daughters, who by special limitations became successively Baronesses Lucas and Countesses De Grey, titles which are now united with the earldom of Ripon.

The chancellor's second son, the next-mentioned Charles, was the father of the third Earl of Hardwicke, and his descendants still inherit that title.

The third son, Joseph, was in 1788 raised to the barony of Dover, which at his death in 1792 became extinct.

The fourth son, John, was clerk of the crown, F.R.S., and M.P. for Reigate; and the fifth son, James, enjoyed in succession the bishoprics of St. David's, Gloucester, and Ely.

Elizabeth, the elder of the chancellor's daughters, married Admiral Lord Anson; and Margaret, the younger daughter, married Sir Gilbert Heathcote, Bart.; but both died childless. (*Cooksey's Sketch; and Lives by Mr. George Harris, and in Welsby's Collection, and in Lord Campbell's Chancellors*, &c.)

YORKE, CHARLES, was the second son of the above Philip Earl of Hardwicke. He was born in January 1722, while his father was solicitor-general. At about ten years of age he was sent to a private school at Hackney, from which in 1739 he was removed to Corpus Christi College, Cambridge. At both he was an earnest and successful student, and at the latter he gave early proofs of his classical attainments and his refined taste by his contributions to the 'Athenian Letters,' printed for private use in 1741. His father, destining him for his own profession, had entered him at the Middle Temple in December 1735, but upon his taking his degree he was transferred to Lincoln's Inn at the end of 1742, and assiduously availed himself of his father's experience by listening to his decisions in court, and hearing their explanations in private, as well as by a diligent study of the ordinary books of legal instruction. In the beginning of 1745, while yet a student, he issued an anonymous publication, entitled 'Considerations on the Law of Forfeiture,' in support of his father's bill to attaint the Pretender, then daily expected to land, in which he so ably illustrated the constitutional argument by classical allusions that the treatise was greatly admired and went through several editions. The author was called to the bar of Lincoln's Inn on February 1, 1745-6.

The son of a chancellor, with a capacity to improve the advantage, was not likely to be long unemployed, and consequently we find him pleading successfully in the very next year before the House of Lords, and receiving the praise of his father, who, as his brother says, 'is not flippant in his commendations.' He became his father's pursebearer, and was made one of the clerks of the crown in Chancery. In 1747 he was returned for the family borough of Reigate, which he continued to represent in all the subsequent parliaments till that of 1768, when he was elected for the university of Cambridge. In the Parliamentary Reports there are few specimens of his speeches, but contemporary letters and records prove that he took a prominent part in the debates. Amid all his legal and senatorial avocations he found time for intellectual relaxations, and for the enjoyment of friendly intercourse. He kept up a constant correspondence with the President Montesquieu, and with Bishops Warburton and Hurd, for both of whom he exerted his interest.

In 1751 he was appointed counsel to the East India Company, and in the next year he narrowly escaped being burnt to death. His chambers in Lincoln's Inn were directly over Mr. Wilbraham's, which caught fire, and Mr. Yorke had barely time to run down stairs almost naked, and take refuge with an opposite neighbour. His whole property was destroyed, including his books and manuscripts, and, what was of more importance, the valuable collection of state papers left by his great-uncle Lord Somers, which had been deposited with him for examination, and of which only a very small part was saved. Lord Hardwicke became extremely anxious about him in this visitation, as he knew that 'his spirits were not of the best and firmest kind,' and wished to do something to encourage him by some permanent provision. An attempt was accordingly made to obtain for him the appointment of solicitor-general, which was not however successful; but he was nominated soon after solicitor-general to the Prince of Wales, with a patent of precedence. On Lord Hardwicke's resignation of the Great Seal in November 1756, the king promoted him to the solicitorship, as a mark of his approbation of his father's services. Mr. Yorke had at this time so large a practice and so high a reputation that the appointment caused no surprise or jealousy among his brethren. After a few months a new ministry was formed by the junction of the Duke of Newcastle with Mr. Pitt, in which Lord Hardwicke, though without office, had great power; who in January 1762 saw his son invested with the attorney-generalship.

On the formation of the Bute ministry in the following May, the new attorney-general began to feel his position uncomfortable, and wrote seriously to his father of his intention, if he resigned his office, of retiring altogether from the bar. Although his father was at least in latent opposition to Lord Bute's administration, Charles Yorke remained attorney-general during its continuance, and at its termination he advised the prosecution of the famous No. 45 of the 'North Briton,' published on April 23, 1763; but he had nothing to do with the general warrant on which its firebrand author John Wilkes was arrested. In the subsequent ministry of George Grenville he defended the king's messengers in the actions brought against them for acting under it; but in subsequent debates he acknowledged the illegality of such warrants. In August 1763 an attempt was made to form a new administration on a whig basis, and the king had apparently a satisfactory interview with Mr. Pitt; but a sudden and unaccountable stop was put to the negotiation. On the 3rd of November following this failure Mr. Yorke thought proper to resign his office; and in the debate that soon after took place in the House of Commons he maintained his opinion against that of Chief Justice Pratt. On his quitting office he attended the court on the outside bar in his stuff gown, although when appointed solicitor-general to the Prince of Wales in 1754 he had received a patent of precedence, deeming probably that that patent was rendered void by his resignation. His brethren of the bar however paid him the compliment of giving him the privilege of precedence and pre-audience over them. He was chosen recorder of Gloucester in 1764 in the room of his father, who had died in March.

On the subsequent death of Sir Thomas Clarke the post of master of the Rolls was offered to him and refused; but he accepted a patent of precedence next after the attorney-general. In the miserable ministerial differences that followed, which resulted in the Marquis of Rockingham becoming prime minister, Mr. Yorke was induced again to accept the office of attorney-general in July 1765, upon the king's promise that he should have the Great Seal in less than a twelvemonth. When, however, in the following year by another intrigue the ministry was again changed, and Mr. Pitt (now created Earl of Chatham) obliged the king to make Lord Camden chancellor, Mr. Yorke again threw up his office, but kept his lead at the bar with the same success that had ever attended him. The Earl of Chatham soon retiring, the Duke of Grafton became the head of the ministry, against whose measures a strong opposition was formed, in which the Earl of Hardwicke was one of the most zealous; and Mr. Yorke, though taking no very active share, was of course united in the same ranks with his brother. Lord Camden, though chancellor, at length felt obliged to give utterance to his condemnation of the policy of his colleagues, and was accordingly deprived of his office in January 1770. The Duke of Grafton knew not where to look for a successor, the tenure of his power being so frail that none of his own party, if any were competent, would accept the precarious honour; and among his political antagonists he could not expect to find one who would not spurn the temptation. The attempt was made on Mr. Yorke, then the most popular lawyer among them, and he had given the duke an absolute refusal. This he had reiterated to the king, but in an evil hour he was induced to have a second interview with his majesty, when, by flattery, by pressing entreaties, and even by threats, he was so overborne as at last unwillingly to consent, without making any stipulations for his personal benefit. This occurred on January 17, 1770.

His brother was, as he says, 'astounded,' and the opposition were loud in their disapproval; but all observations were soon silenced by the public being overwhelmed by the announcement three days after of his sudden death. It is not to be wondered at that under such circumstances a report should have arisen that he died by his own hand, that it should be circulated with minute details in various publications, and even that it should still be believed by many, though no proof was ever produced that it had any substantial foundation. The evidence on the contrary seems to be —that no inquest was holden by the coroner; that persons were immediately after the death admitted to view the body; that Horace Walpole (no friend to the family), in a private letter written at the time, states that the death was caused by a high fever and the bursting of a blood-vessel; and that on a recent revival of the report the surviving members of the family gave it a distinct and positive contradiction. (*Morn. Chron.* May 12, June 6, 1828.) The subject is too delicate for discussion, which would lead to no useful result. It is enough to say that the melancholy event, however it occurred, was to be attributed to the vexation caused by his friends' disapprobation, and to his anxiety how to meet the confusion of the times. The patent conferring upon him the title of Lord Morden, which had been prepared, but had not passed the Great Seal, was after his death pressed upon but declined by his widow.

Such was the termination of the aspirations of Charles Yorke. To be the second chancellor of his family was a natural ambition. It was an office to which his undoubted talents, his extensive practice, and the high positions he had held in the profession entitled him to aim; moreover, in which he would have had the universal suffrage of the bar; and which the favour and even the absolute promise of his sovereign warranted him in expecting. But, of a reserved habit, fickle and irresolute, jealous of honour, yet sensitive of the slightest blame, he fell upon times when it was difficult to define the shades of party, and almost impossible to pursue an entirely independent and unexceptionable course. Twice had he accepted and twice resigned the office of attorney-general, and each acceptance and resignation seemed to be dictated more by personal than political impulses; and at last, partly by flattery and partly by fear, he was induced to permit the great object of his hopes to be thrust into his unwilling hands, not only against his settled and expressed convictions, but at a time when he was sure to be assailed with the deepest rage of his recent associates, and to risk the more dreaded coldness of his family and friends.

His first wife was Catherine, daughter and heir of William Freeman, Esquire, of Aspeden Hall, Herts. His second wife was Agneta, one of the daughters and co-heirs of Henry Johnson, of Great Berkhamstead. By each he had issue. Philip, his son by his first wife, became third Earl of Hardwicke by the death of his uncle without issue in 1790, and was himself succeeded in the title in 1834 by his nephew, the present peer.

Z

ZOUCHE, ALAN DE, was the son of Roger de Zouche, of Ashby in Leicestershire, and of North Moulton in Devonshire, who was grandson of the Earl of Brittany. (*Baronage*, i. 688.) In 34 Henry III. the custody of all the king's lands in Cheshire and North Wales was granted to him. This Dugdale notices in his 'Baronage,' but makes no mention there of his being a justice of the King's Bench, although he has so introduced him into his 'Chronica Series,' from a patent of the same date, adding the words 'et ejus ampla potestas,' implying apparently that he was chief of that court. The two quotations are no doubt taken from the same grant which included in his office of custos of Chester the power also of acting as king's justice there (*Abb. Placit.* 142), to which the latter words refer. It may be questioned, therefore, whether he was one of the justices at Westminster, as his name is not otherwise mentioned among them. In 41 Henry III. he was appointed justiciary of Ireland. (*Cal. Rot. Pat.* 28; 4 *Report Pub. Rec., App.* ii. 145.) He acted as a justice itinerant in the counties of Huntingdon, Buckingham, and Northampton in 47 Henry III., being one of the years in which he was sheriff of the latter county, an office which he held from 45 to 50 Henry III. (*Fuller.*) In the former of these years, 1261, he was constituted justice of all the king's forests south of Trent (*Excerpt. e Rot. Fin.* ii. 369, 404, 409), and in 47 Henry III. was seneschal to the king. (*Cal. Rot. Pat.* 32, 34.)

After the battle of Evesham he was one of the persons nominated to carry into execution the dictum of Kenilworth, and on June 25, 1267, was appointed constable of the Tower of London (*Ibid.* 40), in which latter character, no doubt, it was that Stow calls him custos of that city. Maitland inserts him in his List of Mayors both in 1267 and 1268, and both these authors allude to the site of his house in Lime Street.

His death arose from a broil touching some title to land with John Earl Warren, who assaulted him and his son Roger in Westminster Hall, and grievously wounded both. Some accounts say that Alan was slain on the spot, and others that he did not die till two years from that time. It is certain, however, that his death occurred before October 20, 1270, 54 Henry III., his son Roger doing homage for the lands of his father, 'lately deceased.' Earl Warren was compelled to make satisfaction before he was pardoned for his offence in that year, and a fine of ten thousand marks was imposed upon him. (*Baronage*, i. 78, 688; *Excerpt. e Rot. Fin.* ii. 525.)

He married Helena, one of the daughters and heirs of Roger de Quincy, Earl of Winchester. Roger, his son, succeeded, but the barony failed in the male line in 1314, and is now in abeyance. (*Nicolas's Synopsis*.) Besides the above-mentioned Roger, they had a younger son named Eudo, who, by his marriage with Milisent, widow of Roger de Montalt, and one of the sisters and coheirs of George de Cantilupe, baron of Bergavenny, became lord of Haringworth and many other manors, and was apparently the father of the next-mentioned William de Zouche.

ZOUCHE DE HARINGWORTH, WILLIAM DE. In the early part of the reign of Edward III. three eminent individuals named William de Zouche flourished, one being of Ashby, and the other two of Haringworth. Of the two latter, one held the barony, and the other was of the clerical profession, archdeacon of Exeter in 1330, dean of York in 1336, Archbishop of York in 1342, and died in 1352. There are two reasons which seem to prove that the justice itinerant into Derbyshire in 4 Edward III., 1330, was the baron and not the priest. Had it been the latter, he would probably have been described by his clerical title and dignity; and the only other commission of justices itinerant issued during that year was headed, as we conceive this to have been, by a nobleman.

If this be the case, William de Zouche was the grandson of the above Alan de Zouche, through his younger son, Eudo.

The manor of Haringworth in Northamptonshire, with other extensive property, came into William's possession at the death of his mother, Milisent, one of the sisters and coheirs of George de Cantilupe, baron of Bergavenny, in 27 Edward I. Under Edward II. he distinguished himself as an adherent of the Earl of Lancaster, and ultimately assisted in the deposition of that unfortunate monarch. He died on March 12, 1352.

He married Maude, the daughter of John Lord Lovel of Tichmersh, and the barony continued in the male line till 1625, when it fell into abeyance till 1815. It was then terminated in favour of Sir Cecil Bishopp, who died in 1828, leaving only two daughters. The consequent abeyance was terminated in 1829 in favour of the elder, the wife of the Hon. Robert Curzon, the mother of the present baron. (*Parl. Writs*, ii. 1650; *Baronage*, i. 690; *Nicolas's Synopsis*.)

ADDENDA.

ADDENDA.

BACON, JAMES, was a member of Gray's Inn, and was called to the bar on May 16, 1827. He received silk in 1846. He was made one of the Commissioners of Bankruptcy, and on the establishment of the new court he was appointed chief judge. On July 2, 1870, he was elevated to the post of vice-chancellor in the place of Sir William Milbourne James, still, however, retaining his place of chief judge.

GIFFARD, SIR GEORGE MARKHAM, died July 13, 1870, after only a short illness, having filled the post of lord justice of appeal a little more than eighteen months. He was considered one of the most able judges on the Equity bench. The remarks of Lord Justice James on his taking his seat in court on July 15, which are annexed, show the estimation in which he was held by his brethren: 'I cannot proceed to the business of the day without saying a few words on the sad event which cast its black shadow over this court. During the short period in which I have been in this seat it has been my misfortune not to have sat by the side of my lamented colleague, but it has been my happiness to have known him well, intimately and as a friend, from the very commencement of his professional life, and for many years we sat side by side in the court of Vice-Chancellor Wood. He at the very outset obtained an amount of business under which a mind of less strength might well have failed. But he applied himself to it with an industry which never to the end flagged. His acute intellect, sound judgment, and unsurpassed knowledge of legal principles made him the safest of advisers to the numerous clients who sought his counsel. What his powers as an advocate were those only know and can tell who, like myself, were frequently engaged against him and found how formidable an opponent he was. But he was not only a great lawyer and a great advocate; he was every inch an English gentleman. When, after many years of successful practice, he was elevated to the bench as vice-chancellor, and afterwards promoted to the office of lord justice, his elevation and promotion were received by his brethren with one unanimous acclaim, and the whole profession recognised in his appointments the just rewards of pure professional merits, honours and distinctions most worthily won and honourably bestowed. We all hoped that he had a long period of useful life before him, and that in this court and the judicial committee of the privy council the suitors, the profession, and the public would for many years have had the benefit of the great judicial qualities which had already made him as eminent as a judge as he had been distinguished as a counsel. But it has seemed otherwise good to the Almighty Disposer of our lives. The loss to me, who had hoped to have sat by him, is very great; it is scarcely less great to you who have practised before him. I know and feel that this tribute to his memory, which has come from the bottom of my heart, finds an answering echo in yours. May we in our respective careers be the better for thinking of what he was in them before us.'

MELLISH, GEORGE, appointed lord justice of appeal in the place of the late Sir G. M. Giffard, was a student of the Inner Temple, and was called to the bar on June 9, 1848. After practising successfully for thirteen years in the common law courts, and on the Northern Circuit as a junior, he took silk in 1861, when his reputation increased rapidly, and of late years he has rarely been left out of any cause in which any deep point of law was involved. He was appointed lord justice on August 4, 1870, with general satisfaction, though he had principally practised at common law, and shortly afterwards was knighted and made a member of the privy council.

POLLOCK, SIR FREDERICK, late chief baron of the Exchequer, died on August 23, 1870, in his eighty-eighth year. He had retired from the bench four years, but retained to the last the vigour of his intellect.

www.ingramcontent.com/pod-product-compliance
Lightning Source LLC
Chambersburg PA
CBHW031152020526
44117CB00042B/227